CHI2013
CHANGING PERSPECTIVES

CONFERENCE PROCEEDINGS

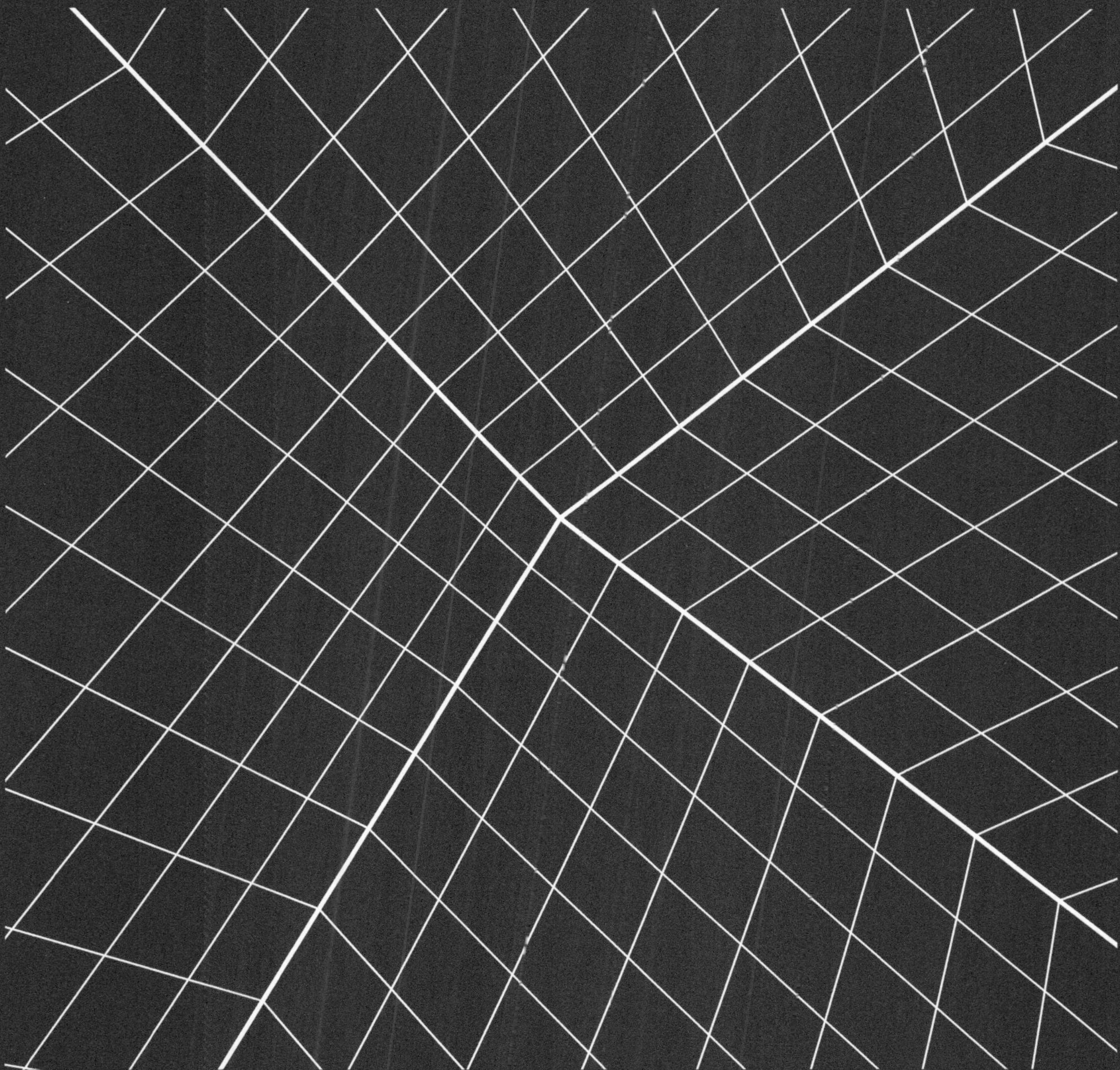

The 31st Annual CHI Conference on Human Factors in Computing Systems
27 APRIL - 2 MAY 2013 • PARIS • FRANCE

Association for Computing Machinery

SIGCHI

EDITORS:
Susanne Bødker, *Papers Co-Chair*
Steven Brewster, *Papers Co-Chair*
Patrick Baudisch, *Technical Program Co-Chair*
Michel Beaudouin-Lafon, *Technical Program Co-Chair*
Wendy E. Mackay, *General Conference Chair*

Association for
Computing Machinery

Advancing Computing as a Science & Profession

The Association for Computing Machinery
2 Penn Plaza, Suite 701
New York, New York 10121-0701

ISBN: 978-1-4503-1899-0 (Digital)

ISBN: 978-1-4503-2447-2 (Print)

Additional copies may be ordered prepaid from:

ACM Order Department
PO Box 30777
New York, NY 10087-0777, USA

Phone: 1-800-342-6626 (USA and Canada)
+1-212-626-0500 (Global)
Fax: +1-212-944-1318
E-mail: acmhelp@acm.org
Hours of Operation: 8:30 am – 4:30 pm ET

Printed in the USA

Bienvenue and Welcome to CHI 2013 in Paris, France!

CHI 2013 is located in the Palais des Congrès in central Paris, a few blocks from the Arc de Triomphe. Often described as the most beautiful city in the world, Paris is home to world-class museums, excellent food and breath-taking architecture, just steps away or a short ride on the metro.

CHI is the premier international conference on human-computer interaction, offering a central forum for sharing innovative interactive technologies that shape people's lives. CHI gathers a multidisciplinary community from around the world: our great strength is our ability to bring together students and experts, researchers and practitioners, scientists, designers and engineers, drawing from their diverse perspectives to create new visions of human-computer interaction.

This year's theme, changing perspectives, is symbolized by the Louvre's elegant pyramid. Its transparency reveals the technical, modern structure within, as it reflects the classic architecture surrounding it, changing color and texture in the shifting Paris light. Our eminent keynote speakers offer similarly contrasting perspectives, from design, engineering and the social sciences. We open with Paola Antonelli, Senior Curator and Architecture & Design Director for Research & Development at MOMA in New York and we close with Bruno Latour, author of Science in Action and head of Paris's Médialab at Sciences Po.

Vint Cerf, President of ACM and fondly referred to as the 'father of the internet', will give a joint keynote on May 2 with ACM's First European Computing Research Congress (ECRC), organized in collaboration with CHI 2013. On that day, participants may attend each other's sessions and discover new perspectives on computing and interaction.

CHI 2013 includes two days of focused workshops and four days of technical content, including CHI's prestigious technical program, with 16 parallel sessions of rigorously reviewed research Papers, engaging Panels, Case Studies and SIGs, an extensive Course program and invited talks from SIGCHI's award winners: George Robertson, Jacob Nielsen, and Sara Czaja. This year, RepliCHI joins the Honorable Mention and Best Paper awards, to recognize excellence in the research process. We also host student research, design, and game competitions, provocative alt.chi presentations and last-minute Birds-of-a-Feather sessions for discussing current topics.

Interactivity showcases the best of interactive technology, both advances in research and artistic explorations, and we highlight over 300 Works-In-Progress posters. Evening events include the CHI 2013 reception, Sponsors and University events, local performances, the job fair and the Video Showcase.

We received a record number of submissions (over 3500) and accepted over 1000 that will appear in the ACM Digital Library. To help you navigate through this immense program, we introduce Video Previews, 30" clips that describe each event in the main program. Before the conference, browse through them on the CHI 2013 website. At the conference, get an overview of the upcoming session on the large Interactive Schedule displays and add your favorites to your Mobile App. Or, browse the videos, papers and extended abstracts on the CHI 2013 flash drive.

After the conference, create a video montage to share with colleagues at home or link to them from ACM's YouTube channel or the Digital Library.

We are deeply indebted to the vast number of volunteers, without whom CHI 2013 would not be possible, including over 2000 reviewers, over 200 senior members of the program committee, over 50 venue chairs on the CHI 2013 conference committee and, of course, the student volunteers. We thank you all!

We are excited by the opportunity to host CHI 2013 and wish you a productive and enjoyable stay in Paris!

Wendy E. Mackay
INRIA
CHI 2013 General Conference Chair

Patrick Baudisch
Hasso Plattner Institute
CHI 2013 Technical Program Co-Chair

Michel Beaudouin-Lafon
Université Paris-Sud
CHI 2013 Technical Program Co-Chair

From ACM SIGCHI's President and Vice President for Conferences

SIGCHI is proud to sponsor the premier annual conference in the field of human-computer interaction. We are extremely grateful to the CHI 2013 Conference Chair Wendy Mackay, to Technical Program Chairs Patrick Baudisch and Michel Beaudouin-Lafon, and to their wonderful crew, who succeeded to build an impressive program and experience.

CHI 2013 turns back to Europe, and, for the first time, resides in Paris with its vibrant French HCI community, 31 years after the first conference, on Human Factors in Computer Systems, in Gaithersburg, MD, on March 15-17, 1982. The second and third conferences were a year and a half apart, and from then on CHI, as the conference has been called since 1983, has been an annual event with the official name: "ACM Conference on Human Factors in Computing Systems".

That first conference drew over 900 attendees, and since then CHI has continued to grow and broaden its range of topics and contributing disciplines: the founding psychologists and software engineers began to meet new visions from ethnography, sociology, communication sciences and arts, among others. Relevant industries, as well as research institutes and academia, showed an increasing - and often long-lasting - interest and involvement (through volunteers and through sponsorship for conference expenses).

CHI is an ideal forum for people to meet formally as well as informally, to exchange knowledge and views, to share experiences, and to learn. The CHI conference brings together professionals from research and practice; people from industry, academia, and from government; long-term veterans of HCI, young professionals and students; all in an environment designed to encourage interaction. We invite you to actively participate in that interaction: introduce yourself to people, interact with presenters and speakers, renew old friendships and make new ones.

CHI is organized on behalf of ACM's Special Interest Group on Computer-Human Interaction (SIGCHI), an international community of professionals who share an interest in the many diverse facets of HCI. SIGCHI is committed both to advancing the field of HCI, to facilitate exchange of information within the SIGCHI community, and to support students to enter the domain.

The CHI conference is arguably the single most visible activity of SIGCHI, but we also sponsor and support a wide range of specialized conferences and workshops in areas ranging from interactive systems design to user interface technology to computer-supported cooperative work to "intelligent" user interfaces. Visit the SIGCHI website at **http://www.sigchi.org** to find our conference schedule, listing upcoming as well as past conferences.

SIGCHI and ACM produce some of the most respected publications in the field. All members receive interactions, a highly-acclaimed magazine covering the broad field of HCI and user interface design. ACM Transactions on Computer-Human Interactions (ToCHI), now in its 20st year, is our flagship journal - a quarterly publication with the top-quality archival research aimed at researchers and those translating research into practice.

SIGCHI is truly an international organization, with over 30 local chapters and 3 student chapters in 23 countries on 5 continents. We encourage all SIGCHI members to join their local chapter - or if there isn't one in your area, we would love to help you create one. And don't forget virtual communities! SIGCHI hosts dozens of electronic mailing lists on topics ranging from HCI and the Web, to HCI educations, to public policy and beyond. Those lists range from dozens of subscribers to thousands, and are an excellent way to keep up with the field and with friends and colleagues.

Finally, on behalf of ACM SGICHI, we again want to thank the conference committee and all of the hundreds of volunteers who make this conference possible. Their work makes this a rewarding experience for all of us.

Gerrit C. van der Veer
SIGCHI President

John "Scooter" Morris
SIGCHI Vice-President for Conferences

About SIGCHI

CHI 2013 is sponsored by ACM's Special Interest Group on Computer-Human Interaction (ACM SIGCHI). ACM, the Association for Computing Machinery, is an educational and scientific society uniting the world's computing educators, researchers, and professionals to inspire dialogue, share resources, and address the field's challenges. ACM strengthens the profession's collective voice through strong leadership, promotion of the highest standards, and recognition of technical excellence. ACM supports the professional growth of its members by providing opportunities for life-long learning, career development, and professional networking. ACM offers its more than 100,000 worldwide members cutting edge technical information through world class journals and magazines, dynamic special interest groups, and globally recognized conferences.

Visit **www.acm.org** for more information about the ACM.

SIGCHI is the premier international society for professionals, academics, and students who are interested in human-computer interaction (HCI). We provide a forum for the discussion of all aspects of HCI through our conferences, including our flagship CHI conference, publications, web sites, email discussion groups, and other services. We advance education in HCI through courses, workshops, and outreach, and we promote informal access to a wide range of individuals and organizations involved in HCI. Members can be involved in HCI-related activities with others in their region through local SIGCHI chapters. Come to the SIGCHI Town Hall meeting on Wednesday, May 1, at 12:40 in Meeting Room 241, or visit **www.sigchi.org** to learn more about SIGCHI.

ACM, the Association for Computing Machinery **http://www.acm.org/**, is an educational and scientific society uniting the world's computing educators, researchers and professionals to inspire dialogue, share resources and address the field's challenges. ACM strengthens the profession's collective voice through strong leadership, promotion of the highest standards, and recognition of technical excellence. ACM supports the professional growth of its members by providing opportunities for life-long learning, career development, and professional networking. ACM offers its 100,000 members cutting-edge technical information through world class journals and magazines, dynamic special interest groups and globally recognized conferences.

Welcome to CHI 2013!

The CHI Papers and Notes program is continuing to grow along with many of our sister conferences. We are pleased that CHI is still the leading venue for research in human-computer interaction.

CHI 2013 continued the use of subcommittees to manage the review process. Authors selected the subcommittee they believed was best qualified to review their work: For clarity, we retained the same committee identifiers as last year. Due to the continuing growth in submissions, we split several subcommittees into more manageable sizes. We are pleased with the subcommittee process: By dividing the work, each paper received much more careful discussion than would otherwise have been possible.

This year we had 1963 total submissions, including 1347 papers and 617 notes, representing a 24% growth over last year. We accepted 392 submissions (20%): 316 papers and 76 notes.

The CHI review process demands a tremendous amount of work from all areas of the human-computer interaction community. As co-chairs of the process, we are amazed at the ability of the community to organize itself to accomplish this task. We would like to thank the 2680 individual reviewers for their careful consideration of these papers. We also deeply appreciate the huge amount of time donated to this process by the 211-member program committee, who paid their own way to attend the face-to-face program committee meeting, an event larger than the average ACM conference.

We are proud of the work of the CHI 2013 program committee and hope that you enjoy these papers and notes, which represent the best research in human-computer interaction.

Stephen Brewster, *Glasgow University*
Susanne Bødker, *University of Aarhus*
CHI 2013 Papers & Notes Chairs

Table of Contents

Session 15: Crowdsourcing: People Power

Session Chair: Tapan Parikh
(University of California, Berkeley, USA)

Session 16: Multitouch and Gesture

Session Chair: James Fogarty
(University of Washington, USA)

Session 19: Gaze

Session Chair: Lyn Bartram
(Simon Fraser University, Canada)

Session 20: Technologies for Life 1

Session Chair: Jeffrey Bigham
(University of Rochester, USA)

Session 22: Evaluation Methods 1

Session Chair: Anthony Jameson
(German Research Center for Artificial Intelligence (DFKI), Germany)

Session 24: Co-Design with Users

Session Chair: Andrea Parker
(Northeastern University, USA)

Session 26: Language and Translation

Session Chair: Gahgene Gweon
(KAIST, Korea)

Session 27: Brain Sensing and Analysis

Session Chair: Petra Isenberg
(INRIA, France)

Session 30: Crowdwork and Online Communities

Session Chair: Krzysztof Gajos
(Harvard University, USA)

Session 31: Keyboards and Hotkeys

Session Chair: Mark Dunlop
(University of Strathclyde, UK)

Session 32: Flexible Displays

Session Chair: Edward Lank
(University of Waterloo, Canada)

Session 34: Smart Tools, Smart Work

Session Chair: Steven Dow
(Carnegie Mellon University, USA)

Session 36: Creating and Authoring

Session Chair: Andrew Ko
(University of Washington, USA)

Session 38: Exploring Games

Session Chair: Lennart Nacke
(University of Ontario Institute of Technology, Canada)

Session 50: Interacting Around Devices

Session Chair: Géry Casiez
(LIFL & INRIA Lille, University of Lille, France)

Session 52: Design for the Home

Session Chair: Nadir Weibel
(University of California, San Diego, USA)

Session 54: Social Creativity

Session Chair: Gary Hsieh
(Michigan State University, USA)

Session 58: Design for Classrooms 2

Session Chair: Judy Kay
(University of Sydney, Australia)

Session 59: Reflecting on Phones

Session Chair: Joonhwan Lee
(Seoul National University, Republic of Korea)

Session 63: Technologies for Life 2

Session Chair: Predrag Klasnja *(University of Michigan, USA)*

Session 64: Gesture Studies

Session Chair: Yang Li
(Google Research, USA)

Session 65: Manipulating Video

Session Chair: Steven Feiner
(Columbia University, USA)

Session 67: Sustainable Energy

Session Chair: John Zimmerman *(Carnegie Mellon University, USA)*

Session 69: Impairment and Rehabilitation

Session Chair: Karyn Moffatt *(McGill University, Canada)*

Session 107: Studying Digital Artifacts

Session Chair: Siân Lindley
(Microsoft Research, UK)

Session 109: Ethics in HCI

Session Chair: Michael Massimi
(Microsoft Research Cambridge, UK)

Session 110: Embodied Interaction 2

Session Chair: Lian Loke
(The University of Sydney, Australia)

Session 114: Design Research

Session Chair: Daniela Busse
(Samsung R&D Research Center, USA)

Session 115: Developing the World

Session Chair: Jon Froehlich
(University of Maryland, USA)

Session 116: Collaborative Creation

Session Chair: Xianghua Ding
(Fudan University, China)

Session 118: Aesthetics and the Web

Session Chair: Effie Law
(University of Leicester, UK)

Session 120: Evaluation Methods 2

Session Chair: Manfred Tscheligi
(University of Salzburg, Austria)

Session 122: Design for the Blind

Session Chair: Shaun Kane
(University of Maryland, Baltimore County, USA)

Session 125: Mobile Interaction

Session Chair: Scott Hudson
(Carnegie Mellon University, USA)

Session 125: Performing Interaction

Session Chair: Leah Findlater
(University of Maryland, USA)

Session 129: Engagement

Session Chair: Eva Hornecker
(Bauhaus Universität Weimar, Germany)

Session 130: Knowledge Management

Session Chair: Volker Wulf
(University of Siegen, Germany)

Session 131: Touch Interaction

Session Chair: Emmanuel Pietriga
(INRIA, Orsay, France & INRIA Chile, France)

Session 174: Design for Children

Session 175: Evaluation Methods 3

Session 178: Visual Perception

Session 179: Searching and Finding

Session 180: Mobile Gestures

Session 182: Design for Developers
Session Chair: Steven Drucker
(Microsoft Research, USA)

Session 184: Perception and Awareness
Session Chair: Joanna McGrenere
(University of British Columbia, Canada)

Session 185: Spatial Interfaces
Session Chair: Daniel Wigdor
(University of Toronto, Canada)

Session 187: Autism
Session Chair: Bilge Mutlu
(University of Wisconsin, Madison, USA)

Session 205: Design Strategies

Session Chair: Mark Selby
(The University of Nottingham, UK)

Session 208: Tensions in Social Media

Session Chair: Valentina Nisi
(University of Madeira, Portugal)

CHI 2013 Conference Organization

Conference Chair
Wendy Mackay, *INRIA, France*

Technical Program

Technical Program Chairs
Patrick Baudisch, *Hasso Plattner Institute, Germany*
Michel Beaudouin-Lafon, *Université Paris-Sud, France*

Technical Program Chair Assistant
Dominik Schmidt, *Hasso Plattner Institute, Germany*

Papers and Notes
Stephen Brewster, *University of Glasgow, UK*
Susanne Bødker, *Aarhus University, Denmark*

Panels
Jofish Kaye, *Yahoo! Labs, USA*
Gillian Hayes, *University of California, Irvine, USA*

Case Studies
Jonathan Arnowitz, *Google, USA*
Michael Arent, *SAP, USA*
Dirk-Jan Hoets, *Flipside, The Netherlands*

Courses
Gregorio Convertino, *Xerox Research Centre Europe, France*
Wiliam Hudson, *Syntagm Ltd, UK*

Interactivity
Floyd Muller, *RMIT University, Australia*
Steve Benford, *University of Nottingham, UK*
Danielle Wilde, *RMIT University, Australia*
Atau Tanaka, *Goldsmiths College, UK*

Video Showcase
Jeffrey Bardzell, *Indiana University, Boomington, USA*
Nicolas Roussel, *INRIA, France*

SIGs
Kaisa Väänänen-Vainio-Mattila, *Tampere University of Technology, Finland*
Albrecht Schmidt, *University of Stuttgart, Germany*

Doctoral Consortium
Marti Hearst, *University of California, Berkeley, USA*

Mobile Apps

Workshops
Ido Guy, *IBM Research, Israel*
Nadir Weibel, *University of California, San Diego, USA*

Works in Progress
Henriette Cramer, *Yahoo! Labs, USA*
Jakob Bardram, *IT University of Copenhagen, Denmark*
Christian Holz, *Hasso Plattner Institute, Germany*
Dan Vogel, *University of Waterloo, Canada*

Student Design Competition
Thecla Schiphorst, *Simon Fraser University, Canada*
Carola Zwick, *Weissensee Art Academy Berlin, Germany*

Student Research Competition
Shaowen Bardzell, *Indiana University, Boomington, USA*
Celine Latulipe, *UNC Charlotte, USA*

Student Game Competition
Seth Cooper, *University of Washington, USA*
Heather Desurvire, *User Behavioristics Research, Inc., USA*
Magy Seif El-Nasr, *Northeastern University, USA*
Katherine Isbister, *NYU Poly, USA*
Regina Bernhaupt, *Université Paul Sabatier, France*

alt.chi
Amanda Williams, *Wyld Collective Ltd, Canada*
Daniela Rosner, *University of Washington, USA*

TOCHI papers
Jeffrey Nichols, *IBM Research, USA*

Best of CHI Awards
Scott Hudson, *Carnegie Mellon University, USA*

RepliCHI
Max Wilson, *University of Nottingham, UK*

Industry days
Elizabeth Dykstra-Erickson, *Nuance Communications, Inc., USA*
Evan Gerber, *Fidelity Investments, USA*
Scott Weiss, *Misys, UK*
Jonathan Arnowitz, *Google, USA*

Communities

Communities Chairs
Bo Begole, *Samsung Information Systems, USA*
Kristina Höök, *KTH, Sweden*

Design Community
Patrick Olivier, *Newcastle University, UK*
Ellen Yi-Luen Do, *Georgia Tech, USA*

Engineering Community
Fabio Paterno, *CNR-ISTI, Italy*
Philippe Palanque, *Université Paul Sabatier, France*

Management Community
Janice Rohn, *Experian, USA*
Carola Fellenz Thompson, *zSpace, USA*

Child Computer Interaction Community
Janet Read, *University of Central Lancashire, UK*
Juan Pablo Hourcade, *University of Iowa, USA*

Sustainability Community
Lisa P. Nathan, *University of British Columbia, Canada*
Samuel Mann, *Otago Polytechnic, New Zealand*

Health Community
Karen Cheng, *University of California, Irvine, USA*
Kelly Caine, *Clemson University, USA*

Arts Community
David England, *Liverpool John Moores University, UK*
Jill fantauzzacoffin, *Georgia Tech, USA*

User Exp. & Usability Community
Virpi Roto, *Aalto University, Finland*
Arnold Lund, *GE Global Research, USA*

Entertainment and Games Community
Regina Bernhaupt, *ruwido, Austria*
Katherine Isbister, *NYU Poly, USA*

Operations

Student Volunteer Coordinators
Bobby Beaton, *Virginia Tech, USA*
Lindsay Reynolds, *Cornell University, USA*

Technology Liaison
Scooter Morris, *University of California, San Francisco, USA*

Technical Liaison
Sara Drenner, *BI Worldwide*

Data
Max von Kleek, *MIT, USA*

Graphic Design
Jeremy Boy, *INRIA, France*
Lora Oehlberg, *INRIA, France*
Dario Rodighiero, *Sciences Po, France*

Webmaster
Cary-Anne Olsen, *University of Texas, Austin, USA*
Caris Hurd, *University of Texas, Austin, USA*
Vicky McArthur, *York University, Canada*

Social Media
Cliff Lampe, *University of Michigan, USA*
Katie Panciera, *Facebook, USA*

Video previews
Gene Golovchinsky, *FX Palo Alto Laboratory, Inc., USA*
Gonzalo Ramos, *Microsoft, USA*

Proceedings
Michael Ekstrand, *University of Minnesota, USA*
Stéphane Conversy, *ENAC, France*

Proceedings
Robert J. Teather, *York University, Canada*

Proceedings
Robert J. Teather, *York University, Canada*
Stephen Oney, *Carnegie Mellon University, USA*
Jason Wiese, *Carnegie Mellon University, USA*
Eiji Hayashi, *Carnegie Mellon University, USA*

Interactive Schedule
Arvind Satyanarayan, *Stanford University, USA*
Daniel Strazzulla, *INRIA, France*
Clemens Klokmose, *Aarhus University, Denmark*

Community-sourcing and Scheduling
Steven Dow, *Carnegie Mellon University, USA*
Paul André, *Carnegie Mellon University, USA*
Lydia Chilton, *University of Washington, USA*
Juho Kim, *MIT, USA*
Rob Miller, *MIT, USA*
Haoqi Zhang, *Northwestern & MIT, USA*

Posters
James Eagan, *Telecom ParisTech, France*

Publicity
Molly Mackinlay, *Stanford University, USA*

PC Meeting Liaison
Eric Lecolinet, *Telecom ParisTech, France*

CHI Women's Breakfast
Allison Druin, *University of Maryland, USA*

Sponsors and Exhibits
Carol Klyver, *Foundations of Excellence*

Reviewing Software
James Stewart, *Precision Conference, Canada*

Conference Logistics
Janeé Pelletier, *Conference & Logistics, USA*
Allison Perrelli, *Conference & Logistics, USA*

Local Logistics
François Tapissier, *Dakini, France*

Registration
Yvonne Lopez, *Executive Events, Inc., USA*
Jill Skuba, *Executive Events, Inc., USA*

CMC Liaison
John "Scooter" Morris, *University of California, San Francisco, USA*

ACM Staff Liaison
Ashley Cozzi, *ACM, USA*

CHI 2013 Sponsors, Supporters, Contributors, & Friends

acm Association for Computing Machinery

SIGCHI

CHI Hero & Champion Sponsors

JCDecaux

Bloomberg

DAUPHINE UNIVERSITÉ PARIS

Google

ebay™ PayPal™

Inria INVENTORS FOR THE DIGITAL WORLD

Microsoft

TELECOM ParisTech

CHI Contributing Sponsors

AUTODESK

digiteo Research in science and technology of information

facebook

îledeFrance

NOKIA

YAHOO!

Friends of CHI

(Return to Top)

gano Graphics, Animation and New Media

IBM

GE

The Many Faces of Facebook: Experiencing Social Media as Performance, Exhibition, and Personal Archive

Xuan Zhao, Niloufar Salehi, Sasha Naranjit, Sara Alwaalan, Stephen Voida, Dan Cosley
Information Science, Cornell University
301 College Ave., Ithaca, NY, 14850
{xz298, ns685, shn22, sa782, svoida, drc44}@cornell.edu

ABSTRACT
The growing use of social media means that an increasing amount of people's lives are visible online. We draw from Goffman's theatrical metaphor and Hogan's exhibition approach to explore how people manage their personal collection of social media data over time. We conducted a qualitative study of 13 participants to reveal their day-to-day decision-making about producing and curating digital traces on Facebook. Their goals and strategies showed that people experience the Facebook platform as consisting of three different functional regions: a *performance region* for managing recent data and impression management, an *exhibition region* for longer term presentation of self-image, and a *personal region* for archiving meaningful facets of life. Further, users' need for presenting and archiving data in these three regions is mediated by temporality. These findings trigger a discussion of how to design social media that support these dynamic and sometimes conflicting needs.

Author Keywords
Reminiscing; personal archives; curation; identity; exhibition

ACM Classification Keywords
H.5.m. **[Information interfaces and presentation (e.g., HCI)]:** Miscellaneous.

INTRODUCTION
Hundreds of millions of users are generating digital traces of their daily lives in social media. Social media serve many purposes, the most salient of which relate to their original functions of communication and social connectedness. Research around these platforms has focused on issues that arise in the context of social interaction, such as how these systems support identity presentation [5, 16] and how they help people build social capital [6]. These studies generally conceptualize social media as a platform for context-specific, selective "performance," following Goffman's theatrical "front stage/back stage" metaphor for impression management and the enactment of social roles [7].

A more recent metaphor extends Goffman, arguing that social media's reviewability and searchability lend social media the feeling of an art exhibition in a museum [11]. In this metaphor, performances leave behind digital traces that act as digital artifacts of the performance, and the accumulation and collection of these artifacts causes these spaces to take on the character of a long-term identity "exhibition," rather than that of an ephemeral performance.

The value of these exhibitions is not limited to others. Much of the content that people create in social media has personal meaning [4], and the emerging personal value of content in these media has been explored in recent studies [15, 25, 29]. Thus, despite these systems' focus on social purposes, it is fair to say that "*today there is an increasing desire to use online social media as a way for archiving life experiences and reflecting on identities*" [9, p15].

These shifts and emerging goals triggered us to rethink the nature of social platforms, the curation of data that they afford, and the ways that individual users conceptualize and experience social media and the data they create in them.

Both the archive and the exhibition metaphors point to the importance of the past in social media. However, except for recent work around reminiscing [29], reflection [33], and digital possessions [27], there has been little study of how people make decisions about their past content. Likewise, little is known about how the performance, exhibition, and archiving perspectives coexist. As we move into a world where one's digital traces express more of who we are, it is important to learn and design around not only how and why people produce digital traces, but also how and why they take care of this data, and how the relationship between users and their data might change over time.

To address these questions, we conducted a study of 13 active, long-term Facebook users about their day-to-day experience of creating and managing Facebook data. Their responses indicate a complex, dynamic relationship between people and their data, in which the combination of concerns and goals that people have and the tools the platform provides fall into three broad "regions" that roughly align with the perspectives described above: a *performance region*, an *exhibition region*, and a *personal region*. By "region" here, we mean a set of goals, concerns, contexts, and corresponding system features.

As we shall argue, these three regions have both spatial and temporal aspects, with both elements of the interface and elements that depend on the recency of content and duration

CHI'13, April 27 – May 2, 2013, Paris, France.

of goals helping to define them. We identify the implications of these regions in social media systems, particularly in the tensions and opposing needs people experience as they manage their Facebook data. Finally, we discuss how thinking about these regions and the ways current platforms support them suggest metaphors that might drive designs that better support all three regions together.

RELATED WORK

"The Moving Finger writes; and, having writ,
Moves on: nor all thy Piety nor Wit
Shall lure it back to cancel half a Line,
Nor all thy Tears wash out a Word of it."
—Omar Khayyam
translated by Edward Fitzgerald

We explore the complexity of social media from two perspectives: as a space that extends in time and as a space that serves both public and personal purposes.

An Identity Platform that Extends in Time

Goffman's notion of selective self-presentation [7] is widely used in studies that examine how people interact with each other in online spaces, for example, work that focuses on impression management [1, 3] and privacy management [32, 34]. In his dramaturgical approach, Goffman conceptualizes the "front stage" as where a performance is given in presence of an audience. People often need to selectively present themselves in order to meet social expectations and cultural values. In comparison, the "back stage" is a place where only the performer exists, without the audience and where other aspects of personal identity might be revealed.

This metaphor maps well onto salient elements of social media. It matches well with the fact that behaviors in social media are socially embedded and observed, activating concerns about others' expectations. The metaphor also emphasizes present action: "*The Moving Finger writes; and having writ, moves on.*" Most social media systems emphasize the present, featuring recent content and burying the past both to support goals such as awareness of friends [13] and to draw repeat visitors with fresh content [26].

The past, however, does not have to be buried, as illustrated by Facebook's own Timeline interface (Figure 1). Timeline explicitly organizes a person's content around a linear timeline that supports browsing far into the past, including links directly to activity that happened years ago. This makes the past much more salient than in pre-Timeline versions of the interface, where past status updates and wall posts were available, but required tedious paging through a list; and past photos were available, but organized in albums rather than as a temporal stream.

Hogan's exhibition metaphor calls attention to these past data [11]. He conceptualizes social media as a storehouse, where users submit their personal data, and the system acts as an invisible curator who manages, redistributes, and selectively displays content for audiences who have access to the user's data. Systems provide users with limited control:

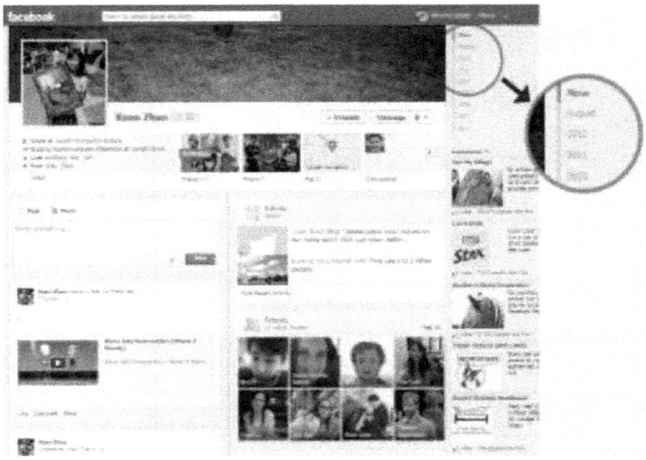

Figure 1: Facebook's Timeline interface and the time links (see inset) that provide rapid access to past content.

"*nor all thy Piety nor Wit shall lure it back to cancel half a Line*" resonates with the feeling that many people have when trying to manage privacy settings. Hogan emphasizes that "performance" is closely associated with a specific "time-space-identity-locus", but that once the data associated with a performance are recorded, they become artifacts that others will view at different times and contexts. Therefore, social media data are used more for asynchronous exhibitions than synchronous performances.

Most current research either studies users' activity and motivations for using social media as a snapshot in time [13, 22] or their collective usage patterns over time [8, 17]. Hogan's approach emphasizes the need to think about the relationship between *individuals* and their data over time. Given the persistence of social media data, it becomes interesting to consider how notions of performance and exhibition manifest on the same platform. In particular, there is an uneasy relationship between people and their past data when the data becomes detached from their original context. For example, Wang et al.'s descriptive taxonomy towards Facebook regret behaviors [35] begs a deeper discussion of *why* people regret, and take explicit management efforts such as deleting, detagging, and unfriending.

An Identity Platform for the Self

Both the performance and exhibition perspectives frame social media behavior from an outward-facing, public perspective. This framing is natural given the social nature of these media, but the emerging practice of using social media for personal archiving [9] leads us to consider whether the self has also become an important audience. One conceptualization of these data is the notion of "digital possessions" that carry and display meaningful events, places, and people for both the self and others to view [21, 27].

A second line of work explores how social media data traces can mediate and support reflection processes. These traces appear in many media: e-mail [10], text chat [36], and social media including Flickr, Picasa, last.fm, twitter, Blogger, and Facebook [29]. On balance, this work has focused on individual sensemaking and use, although there has been some attention to supporting relationships and family using both digital traces and physical possessions [30, 31] and studying how people use digital content to think about and enact their friendships [33] and romantic relationships [37]. Information generated and owned by others can play an important role in this meaning-making process [33], although issues around third-party ownership can make the management and curation of these data difficult [27].

This research suggests that digital traces left in social media contain great potential for stimulating and supporting self-reflection and reminiscing activities. Both the intentional use of social media as a "life logging" tool and the potential usefulness of digital traces for memory and reflection highlight the importance of understanding how people balance the public functions and personal value of social media. For instance, the unwritten rule limiting public displays of affection in Facebook might prevent people from recording as much about relationships as they would like, while changes in a relationship might cause content previously important for public affirmation to become instead a source of pain [37]: "*Nor all thy Tears wash out a Word of it.*"

STUDY DESIGN

Our study aims to explore how practices of online presentation, exhibition, and archiving are intertwined; how needs for different activities contrast or align with each other; and how designs might help to balance, support, and enrich these practices. We approach this problem by investigating how and why people manage their Facebook data. We seek to provide a deep understanding of how aforementioned theories manifest in the interaction between users and their own data, to identify how these perspectives are relevant to social media systems, and to discuss implications for designing systems that support these practices.

Research Context and Data Collection

On December 22, 2011, Facebook launched Timeline. As described earlier, this user interface makes past data more salient for both the user and members of their social network, highlighting a number of the issues in which we are interested related both to temporality and the tension between public and personal goals. Now a standard part of the interface, Timeline was originally opt-in and adoption was slow, allowing us to sample a set of users as they began to use the interface and grapple with these issues.

We conducted our study in May and June of 2012, around six months after the new interface was launched. To try to improve the diversity of our sample, we used Facebook advertising to recruit participants. The ad was targeted at Facebook users living in our local community (a small city in the northeastern United States) to facilitate bringing participants to our lab for an interview. We also targeted people who had used Facebook for several years and had generated a significant amount of social media content. Participants were compensated with $15 in cash.

A total of 13 people (9 female, 4 male; 8 White/Caucasian, 2 Asian, 2 Hispanic/Latino, 1 American Indian/Alaskan Native; aged 18 to 43, $M = 22$) with an average of 4.3 years of Facebook activity completed the study. Participants first completed a pre-survey with questions about their Facebook use and demographics. Seven of our participants had already installed Timeline at the time of the study, while the others were instructed to adopt it after completing the pre-survey to capture their initial reactions to the interface.

Each participant then completed a daily online diary for two weeks about aspects of Facebook use related to data creation, curation, and sensemaking around digital traces—questions derived from the theoretical perspectives above. We asked them to record whether they had updated or changed their profiles by adding a new post, changing privacy settings, and so on; whether they had reviewed their own or others' past content; and whether they had managed past content of any sort. The daily diary allowed us to record actions and reactions close to when they happened and provided us with examples to reference during interviews. We reminded participants about the diary via daily e-mails.

After two weeks, participants came to our lab for a one-hour interview. We asked them to log in to their Facebook account and to review their profiles during the interview, both to reflect on their experience and to enrich their responses. We asked general questions about their overall Facebook usage and privacy attitudes, in order to encourage them to reflect on the kind of management behaviors in which they engage. We specifically asked about their Facebook activity from a temporal perspective, such as how they felt about their past content and how they valued it, in order to understand what Facebook data means to them, as well as if, when, and why they take explicit action to manage it. Other questions included how and why they view others' past content and their attitude toward Timeline after having used it. We also encouraged them to talk about offline archiving experiences such as journaling and their experience with other social tools (such as Flickr and Twitter) and to compare these experiences with their use of Facebook.

Data Analysis

To develop a holistic understanding of participants' use of Facebook, we included data from both diary entries and interviews in our analysis. We conducted a collaborative, inductive analysis process.

In the first analytic phase, four researchers met together face-to-face and used open coding to develop a set of primary categories and, subsequently, subcategories to help organize our initial insights. Our primary categories included themes such as real-time decision-making of Facebook activities (resonant with Goffman [7]), management behaviors (resonant with Hogan [11]), browsing behaviors, and general use of Facebook. Through continued, iterative analysis, we identified subcategories of these themes, for example, within "management behaviors" we identified descriptions of behaviors, motivations for managing, and strategies for managing. By the end of this first phase of analysis, we had established a high-level agreement upon and common ground for organizing, discussing, and interpreting the data. In phase two, we used TAMS Analyzer to map all interviewees' statements onto our categories and subcategories. Each of the four researchers independently reviewed half of the transcripts, such that all data were examined by two researchers[1]. The goal of this categorization phase was to sort the data so that we could easily review related data together in the third phase of our analysis. In the third analytic phase, we conducted a series of face-to-face meetings in which we used concept charting [19] to expand on and refine our understanding of the interrelationships among the themes that we had previously identified. In this phase of the analysis, we further unpacked our data to arrive at two main themes. The first is the idea that although Facebook is a single platform, it provides multiple regions of activity including performance, exhibition and personal regions. The second is the key role of temporality in how transitions between and tensions among these regions occur.

Below, we present these themes using representative quotes from participants and discuss how future designs might better account for the multiple regions of Facebook by providing appropriate curation tools and metaphors.

ONE PLATFORM, MULTIPLE REGIONS

Our data provide strong evidence that people do, in fact, experience Facebook from the analytical perspectives identified earlier, around the performance and exhibition regions ("public regions") and the personal region. In this section, we explore the shape of these regions, as well as the tensions and opposing needs people experience as they manage their Facebook profiles across multiple regions.

Performance Region: Creating Content

Consistent with Goffman [7], the *performance region* is where users make decisions about creating and managing content for current self-presentation needs. The content is usually targeted to, or associated with contexts and audiences relevant to the moment.

> *(There is) a video posted by my girlfriend that was related to a phone conversation we were having.* (P2)

> *I updated my status to show team support for a big meet.* (P18)

Decisions made in the performance region also include who people decide to be friends with, with context influencing their behaviors as well, making "friending" another sort of performance act.

> *[I friended him] because he was at camp with me so after camp I guess I just got friend requests from people there or friended people who were there ...* (P16)

> *[I friended them] just to be friendly. Like, it's just kind of rude [not responding] if someone is friending you ... If I really dislike somebody, I won't accept it. But if they're a nice person and maybe have something interesting to say, I'll—I'll accept it.* (P9)

Constraints in the performance region change over time, and participants leverage features such as profile pictures to customize their self-presentation for specific situations:

> *I changed my timeline cover, because the soccer game Barcelona vs. Chelsea is coming up soon and I want to show my support to Barcelona.* (P2)

The fact that both the old Facebook profile page and the new Timeline interface prioritize content based on recency ensures that context-relevant performance is positioned for maximum exposure, both in the flow of updates on one's profile page and in others' news feeds. In general, the performance region is closely associated with a time-space locus that focuses on current activity and current goals:

> *Yeah. I mean overall I'd say I am [conscious about how my page appeared to other people]. But I think it more so applies to like my current content.* (P6)

Exhibition Region: Managing Content

Due to the persistence of social media data, content initially bounded by a specific time-space locus gradually goes into the *exhibition region*, modeled after Hogan [11]. For the most part, this region focuses on past data and longer-term needs around constructing identity. However, while Hogan's discussion of exhibition focuses on the system's role in data curation [11], our results show that users, too, wish to play an active role in curating data in this region.

Participants were not always concerned about the past, but when they were, they encountered decision-making challenges regarding the changing contexts and the appropriateness of the content on their profiles. These challenges sometime resulted in an explicit competition between the performance and the exhibition region that drove management behaviors. We define management here as a conscious behavior for evaluating personal profiles or tweaking one's public presentation in social media over time.

The concept of management hints at a conscious effort, consistent with how previous literature defines personal information management as a practice that involves maintaining, organizing, retrieving, and redistributing personal information for task-related purposes [14]. It was common for people to express concerns about past data that was emotional, hard to interpret, inappropriate for their self image, or irrelevant to themself or others.

Managing emotional content. Emotional or self-expressive content was frequently mentioned as the content needing

[1] We do not report inter-coder reliability; as argued by Armstrong et al. [1], reliability measures are most useful when the coding breakdown is the primary output of analysis. When the codes are a first step toward further interpretation, measures like kappa give little information about the quality of the analysis.

the most attention. At the time of performance, this content might have been quite useful: *"I was so frustrated at the time, posting a status about it was a slight relief from the situation"* (P6), but it became undesirable, or subject to misinterpretation, out of context: *"Because I thought my status may have come off as a bit whiney or condescending..."* (P6). This finding is consistent with prior work that looks at tactics for self-presentation in face-to-face situations [18] and experiences of regret in social media [35].

One aspect of context that came up often as a trigger for managing emotional content was how others might interpret a given post:

> *I was in a certain mood right then and I posted something ... I went back and read it I realized that people probably wouldn't take it sarcastically. That's so hard about communicating online, is people can't tell ... your emotion behind stuff.* (P12)

Managing overall self-image. When people take a critical eye towards their Facebook profiles, they are usually concerned about whether the content still promotes or adds to their overall self-image. Over half of participants mentioned that they have deleted content that is related to a specific event or a specific conversation but does not have value for long-term exhibition of the self:

> *I would delete it, yes, like after the event happens it's like really useless. It doesn't add onto my life or my timeline. I try to keep it clean.* (P2)

These concerns would also trigger based on participants' desire to control how much they revealed about themselves:

> *I'm an organized person and like things to be more concise and ... I want to limit how much I'm showing people about my life at a time.* (P10)

About one-third of participants also mentioned their concern towards old content, which seemed to be appropriate, "cool," or "funny" at the moment but became undesirable as people's values changed over time:

> *I had an [photo] album in ... 2007 ... I thought it was cool...and two years later I was looking at it and it embarrassed me so much that I deleted some of the pictures.* (P3)

Managing relevance. For most participants, it was important to keep data on their profile relevant, both in the sense of content and temporal relevance. More than half of the participants actively manage recent content *"...just to kind of keep it relevant"* (P7) to their current life. People would delete bits of information about having read articles, or listening to music, even if *"it's not hurting anything. It's just kinda cluttering what's there"* (P12).

Most participants also recognized that recent content was most likely to get attention from others, leading management activities to focus on recent content:

> *[I manage] just the most recent stuff because I assume that most people don't have the time or patience or desire to go back further than that.* (P5)

Managing friends. Besides content that expires in time, people also treat the relationship of being a Facebook friend as a dynamic concept. They frequently adjust their friend list to make sure that people who have access to their profiles are appropriate audiences for their long-term exhibition. In particular, they were sometimes motivated to control others' access to their information:

> *Sometimes I would friend people for like a specific purpose like I'm working with them on a project ... but like afterwards do I need to have them see all my information all the time.* (P6)

The other major reason for removing friendships was relationship change:

> *After a really horrible suite/living situation with now ex-friends, I did end up deleting, blocking, and changing the privacy settings on my Facebook because I felt that they could find out things about my day, my schedule, my emotions, by reading my Facebook if we remained friends and I wanted nothing to do with them anymore.* (P11)

Friend list management corresponds closely with Hogan's observation that once a performance becomes recorded, the content submitter (user) may have little control over how their content will be consumed by others who have access to the exhibition. The ability to delete friends seems to be one common strategy that people use for transitioning content into the exhibition region.

Personal Region: Curating Content for the Long-Term

When participants responded to our questions about how and why they manage their profiles, exhibiting their image to the public was not the only concern. Almost all participants noted that Facebook has significant *personal* value, serving as a "personal locker" on the Internet that archives their personal and social memories.

We define the *personal region* as the place where users perceive or manage their Facebook data around a perceived personal value such as reminiscing and reflecting, as opposed to traditionally rendered public values such as self-presentation to others. This region is also focused on the past, and on features that promote archival storage:

> *Because I don't keep everything on e-mail or on my computer or written down someplace. So a lot of times Facebook is the way that I remember stuff ... And I like to go back and see how ... my silly friends and I were back in the day.* (P12)

Whether or not they frequently use Facebook as a reminiscing tool, participants found this archival space to be reassuring: *"I mean I actually like having the past stuff, not that I frequently look at it but if I ever do want to reminisce something ... it's cool that it's there"* (P3).

On balance, most participants preferred to have a record of "everything" happening on Facebook, negative or positive, even in the case of difficult relationship endings:

> *I'm not friends with a lot of people that I was friends with years ago. And sometimes it ended really badly ... but sometimes I get nostalgic, I go back and I smile and I remember and it makes me feel really warm sort of like comforting to know that stuff happened and reflect upon it.* (P5)

Decisions about whether to archive or access specific content, however, might change over time:

> *So like at least for me, I'm now best friends with my previous boyfriend, so there would be no reason to delete these pictures. I think though I remember at the time untagging myself in pictures and then ended up retagging myself ... I was angry when we broke up ... but then I went back and retagged some of them because I liked the picture.* (P6)

Tensions Between Public and Personal Regions

The fact that Facebook is designed primarily to support social and public activity raises tensions between the public and personal regions. People do struggle to balance what is desirable for public display and what they want to keep for personal archival, sometimes facing the *"ongoing tug of war"* (P5) to sacrifice one or the other:

> *I look weird in that picture ... Oh my goodness. I don't like it at all but I don't know if I would delete it because I like having that memory.* (P6)

Photos are seen as being especially valuable in the personal region. However, photos also have a significant public component as well, since people are often tagged in one another's photos. People who value this collection or are used to claiming the ownership of photos in this way face more of a psychological burden when they don't think that the photo is publicly desirable:

> *I've had people post photos of me and be like wow this is a bad photo. But I mean ... if I untagged all the photos that were bad I would have no photos at all.* (P7)

However, untagging yourself from a photo removes your access to it, and, as with deleting content, can lead to regret:

> *I tend to delete, untag myself off of a lot of pictures, and sometimes I think it's a mistake because then afterwards when I want to look back I'm not going to have that much to look back on ... But, anyway, I still like to just keep the things I think are relevant (on Facebook) even though it's probably a mistake.* (P2)

One way that people deal with this tension in ways that minimize regret is by using Timeline features that provide more control over the exhibition region. The most frequently used such feature is "hiding" content, which prevents it from appearing on the Timeline but leaves it accessible from elsewhere, such as albums:

> *I rarely un-tag photos that I don't like of myself but I'll hide it from my timeline, it's like I don't need that to be like the first thing anyone sees when they're on my page. But I do like to keep them just because like most of them are nice memories.* (P6)

Leaving tagged pictures "awaiting approval" of the tag is another way to keep photos without exhibiting them:

> *I leave it in the approval section, like where you have to click yes or no ... I don't delete it because it's kind of nice to remember the stupid, funny nights ...* (P4)

The personal region seems to be more tolerant than public regions, in that most people prefer to have a record of all that's happening on Facebook—negative, positive or informative—versus the need to be vigilantly selective about content visible to the public. However, this raises important questions around how Facebook might better support the personal region, since content normally must first pass through the public performance region unless people take special care to use non-default privacy controls.

TEMPORAL TRANSITIONS BETWEEN REGIONS

This brings us to our second major theme, which highlights the important role that temporality plays in mediating among these regions, one reason that we define regions as having both a spatial and temporal component.

Between Performance and Exhibition Regions

As content moves from performance to exhibition regions, people are faced with the need to re-evaluate and re-select content. Temporal relevance serves not only as one important factor that people consider when managing their profiles, but also as an important boundary for separating performance and exhibition regions. Participants tended to perceive their "recent" content (in contrast to their "former" content) as providing a more accurate representation of self, reflecting who they are right now and what they're up to. As specific performances "expire" in time, needs for managing content, such as deleting, might arise.

Participants commonly talked of content that was *relevant*, *recent*, *current*, and *past*, highlighting the importance of temporality. In general, they tied the notion of recent content to the front page of their profiles; however, they had widely varying perceptions of what counted as "recent." Some participants perceived recent content as being comprised of a day's worth of content, while others felt it might include up to a month or a year. The closest commonality we found was that there was broad agreement that recent content would help people catch up on one's life, and tended to represent current aspects of the self well:

> *I think when I look at my page it's like ... Like wow, this is what Katherine's been up to lately, like okay*

> *like that's what she looks like, pretty background ... she got into [university name].* (P10)

The notion that current Facebook content represents the self well is closely tied to the notion that the "big events" in their lives are documented on Facebook, such that an audience can easily catch up with a person's present state:

> *I mean, obviously, there's more to my life than just what you see on the Facebook, but as far as like big events happening, like getting into [university] and like running that race and ... Those are just some big things that have been happening ...* (P10)

Big events also served to make the transitions between performance and exhibition regions salient, when people faced meaningful life events or turning points. For example, relationship changes, *"applying for a job"* (P2), and graduation were all commonly mentioned as triggers:

> *Then we got into a really bad spat and then, like, it was just getting, like, kind of nasty about it. So, like, I just took them [friends] off Facebook.* (P4)

> *It usually depends on sort of what jobs I'm looking for or what internships and it's whether that's like changing the profile picture to be more professional or just having it be like slightly more casual.* (P1)

Other than that, Facebook content management tasks were a more sporadic activity that people undertook when they *"have a lot of time to kill"* (P5).

Between Public and Personal Regions

Temporality also plays an important role in mediating between the public and personal regions. We found that as social media data "expires" from the public's attention, it also gradually transitions into a personal space where it is mostly seen as an archive of meaningful memories.

Part of this idea of content expiration comes from a perceived norm that public attention only focuses on recent content. Participants predominantly felt that if they are not viewing the past content of others, then no one else is viewing their past content, either: *"most people don't have the time or patience or desire to go back further"* (P5). When personal content exceeds its "shelf life," it crosses over into an awkward state that users perceive as "implicitly private." People expressed discomfort when others accessed their old data: *"I think it's weird when people comment on my old stuff because you can sort of tell that they're digging"* (P1). Participants also felt that they were invading others' privacy when accessing old data, even for short definitions of "old":

> *It would be weird, like if I came down and I like ... even like to a week ago it would be weird if I like now commented.* (P6)

> *Because it means that you're like digging through their profile and sometimes that's ... I don't know, I mean, because it's like referred to as creeping on someone—in a nice way—but if I go through old photos I usually wouldn't comment on them.* (P7)

Although the archive is not necessarily seen as appropriate for others, it has value to the self:

> *I think it's good to have [an archive], if not for someone else, for myself. Because I don't keep everything on e-mail or on my computer or written down someplace. So a lot of times, Facebook is the way that I remember stuff ... I want to be able to go back ... I do like that.* (P12)

Timeline Creates and Alleviates Temporal Tensions

Timeline also provides a nice case in point about how interfaces can interact with these temporal tensions. As shown in Figure 1, the interface provides a kind of temporal data segmentation. Content generated around years and months are gathered and arranged within sections of one's Timeline, and access points are provided on the front page.

This design both creates and alleviates tensions among different functional regions. On one hand, the easy access to old data led many participants to engage in significant management of their Facebook content because the sudden availability of older content blurred the lines between performance and exhibition: *"When I first got Timeline, it was showing me like all the stuff from the past. I hid things that I was like, people don't need to know about that"* (P5). However, other participants felt that attaching timestamps to data helped to resolve the "temporal context collapse" between performance and exhibition regions:

> *Timeline does kind of embrace your history ... maybe it's the ambiguity [of the old profile] that makes me want to just delete it just to have the current and relevant stuff ... But I guess with Timeline it's like—oh, okay—you see these pictures, but they are from 2008.* (P10)

DESIGNING FOR THE MANY FACES OF FACEBOOK

These tensions highlight the uneasy coexistence of these multiple regions in a single platform. Facebook supports some goals (mostly social) and some curation strategies well, but its support for user curation and the personal region are not strong and often run afoul of users' needs.

Here, we discuss the sometimes-uneasy relationship between the system and users curating together, along with the need for better designs and more effective metaphors for supporting dynamic needs and multiple regions emerging from the same "overloaded" platform.

Who Curates, and How?

Hogan's discussion of past data emphasizes the role of the system as content curator [11]. Our study points to a more complex story, including the user's role in curation and the various strategies that the system and its users engage in, alone and collaboratively, to manage performance, exhibition, and personal archiving. Some decisions, such as the format of Timeline or the algorithms used to filter content, are executed by the system unilaterally. Users also have some unilateral choices, particularly around the decision about whether or not to post content in the first place.

After the creation of content, users' ability to curate their data and exert control over how they will be exhibited is both empowered and limited by system features, such as the ability to delete content, to create sharing and privacy policies, to manage friend lists, and so on. In observing users' active role in curating their content, we found that some system features effectively supported their curation needs. For example, hiding content and delaying approval of tags were both used to accomplish high-level goals around controlling the exhibition of data.

At other times, however, the tools don't align with people's needs or mental models. For example, although Facebook provides privacy settings that support personal use, it provides no obvious personal spaces for private reflection and meaning making around this personal content:

> *I notice I have a few things that are private only to me but like they're not separate in any way. They're not like special, "oh, these are only for me ...".* (P10)

Lack of visibility about how the system curator works can also confuse people [12], resulting in distrust and defensive behaviors. One example of users trying, but failing, to embrace system curation tools is in the use of privacy settings. All participants in our study used Facebook's privacy settings, such as only allowing friends to view their profiles. However, there is confusion about how effective these controls actually are, resulting in people relying on—but not always fully trusting—the system:

> *We were young enough when it (Facebook) went public that we saw kind of a year or two before us getting really scrutinized heavily by future employers and I know there's all sorts of workarounds on Facebook that they can use to hack in and see your stuff so I don't really trust Facebook's privacy settings.* (P1)

Likewise, although one-third of participants actively used the ability to hide Timeline content to manage tensions between public and personal regions, a similar number didn't understand how this mechanism might support their use of this hidden data because the interface didn't make clear what would happen or how to access it:

> *So, in terms of hiding things (from Timeline), like, for me, if I hid it, it's gone because ... I don't know ... I don't even know how I would get that back ... So hiding and deleting is kinda the same thing.* (P6)

Another problem arises when curation is too costly. Consistent with previous work [20], audience segmentation is seen as being useful for managing information inflow, but is too hard to use to control one's own sharing:

> *If I could wave a wand and just say only my writer friends, then that would be ... I might do that, but it's just such a ... it would be such a pain to sort everybody and to think about that every time.* (P9)

Finally, goals for curating personal data feel awkward in the social context of Facebook. Though in principle it supports self-archiving through its privacy settings, this feels unnatural in the current platform:

> *I notice when I created my most recent album that it was ... only visible to me and I was like, well, if it was only visible to me, why would I put it on Facebook because I would just keep it on my computer.* (P7)

These aspects of features, models, cost, and norms around curation highlight the need to think about how system curation decisions and tools affect users' behavior and norms. When we step back and think about Facebook's curation policies, the most salient is based on temporality. Facebook, like most other social media platforms, arranges content around the time that it is created, resulting in recent content being prioritized while earlier content flows backwards into one's online identity exhibition. On that note, even though no participants explicitly commented about it, we wonder to what extent this taken-for-granted system curation policy has shaped users' perceptions, such as perceiving the Facebook norm as "going forward," and their behaviors, such as how they tend to manage temporally adjacent content in Timeline. This possibility raises interesting issues about the role of personal data on a public platform, and has important design implications for future interfaces.

Metaphors Matter

Our findings about different functional regions of social media, and the corresponding metaphors of performance, exhibition, and personal locker, lead us to revisit how we should design social media as an identity platform for both context-specific performance and long-term exhibition, for both others and self.

One can argue that Facebook actually does well compared to many other social media. It serves performance well through the newsfeed and exhibition fairly well through Timeline, and also provides some features for personal spaces, such as the privacy option "visible for me". Many other interfaces focus only on one region: Twitter and Google Buzz, for instance, provide functionality mainly supporting performance; Pinterest is largely about exhibition; and Flickr and Path are largely tools for archiving. All of these could, in principle, serve multiple goals: in Flickr, people can perform for those who follow their photo stream, and exhibit to at least some extent through the album mechanism. Likewise, Pinterest could, in principle, support collections of past data for both personal sensemaking and exhibition to others, although its normal use as an exhibit of one's tastes and desires is so strong that it may be hard for these other uses to gain footing.

There are arguments to be made for the use of separate platforms for separate purposes and for not trying to be "all things to all people." But, in practice, people do use social media for multiple purposes, and designs should respect that. Inviting people to upload their personal histories to Timeline may align with Mark Zuckerberg's beliefs in the value of "radical transparency." But the Timeline metaphor and its affordances that favor public exhibition are a bad match for most people's goals in archiving personal data. Careful attention to how people might wish to use the data that social media increasingly capture will lead to designs that better serve people's needs and respect their wishes.

One way to mitigate these tensions and improve social media platforms' ability to support multiple regions is to think about how system curation could become "smarter" or "more considerate" when managing one's digital traces. The way temporality mediates content between public and personal regions raises the possibility of designing a "two-sided" system, where content that falls out of the public attention will be automatically moved into a private space designed for personal archival. Instead of being implicitly private, these data would become explicitly personal. There is much value in systems that forget after a while, and even in systems that help us in our own forgetting [23]. However, our users' re-visitation of old content and regret around decisions to delete it suggest that actual deletion of data is not to be taken lightly.

Another, more extended metaphor, is inspired by work from Miller et al. on the relationship between people's identity and personally owned artifacts [24]. We wonder if drawing on people's practices for displaying physical artifacts around their houses might be a useful tool for thinking about social media design, somewhat like Odom et al.'s exploration of how people manage virtual processions relative to the ways that they arrange physical space [28].

If we conceptualize one's Facebook data as a collection of artifacts displayed in one's house, physical places where people traditionally display artifacts could have strong connotations for supporting the multiple regions. Pictures on the wall might function to display one's long-term identity exhibition, not unlike the way that one's basic information on Facebook is always explicitly displayed and easy to access. Grouped pictures in frames might serve to organize specific facets of people's identity or highlight meaningful groups of friends or family. Stickers or drawings on the refrigerator might represent items that are temporarily important but are replaced or augmented with new content over time, not unlike how one's profile photos and cover photos are currently used. Pictures put on the bedroom table might have significant personal meanings that only trusted others can access, somewhat like "implicitly private" Facebook content. A diary locked in a drawer might be strictly personal and private, such as the personal archival space that some of our participants expressed interest in having as a part of the platform. Then, the system might provide tools that help people move, arrange, and tell stories about data among these display spaces.

Note that we are not arguing that Facebook should be, literally, a house or a neighborhood or some other physical space, although systems like Second Life and LambdaMOO have had some success using these metaphors literally. We are, however, proposing that metaphors that call attention to the multiplicity of regions, transitions, and curation needs of social media users might have real value above and beyond the relatively simple, time-based metaphors that are commonly used in social media systems.

CONCLUSION

Our study applied both Goffman's [7] theatrical and Hogan's [11] exhibition metaphor for examining the actions that users take for managing social media data over time. Our analysis highlighted spatial and temporal tensions brought on by the persistence of data, extending previous literature on self-presentation, which mainly focuses on the decision-making process in the moment. The need for creating digital content for performance purposes might contradict one's intended long-term image as time goes by, as both goals and audiences change. It is also important to note the sense of expiration for digital content on social media, that is, that recent content plays a role as the focus of attention for purposeful self-presentation, and digital content created in the past becomes "invisible" as new content accumulates.

As an extension to Hogan's exhibition approach, we also found that as social media data expire from public attention, they not only move to an exhibition region that affords presenting one's long-term image, but also gradually become part of a personal region, where social media data functions as a personal archive and repository for meaningful memories. Past interaction data has been commonly described as "implicitly private," where people feel strange accessing others' pasts and don't expect an audience for their own.

We also discovered an implicit negotiation between users and the system in terms of how personal data on social media platform should be "exhibited". Emphasizing users' role in curating their digital traces both extends the concept of curation in Hogan's theoretical model and allows us to rethink appropriate design metaphors for social media that nicely support users' needs and expectations.

Popular social media systems, such as Facebook, naturally afford the accumulation of user data over time. We hope that our findings about social media being a combination of different functional regions and our proposals of alternative metaphors for conceptualizing social media might inspire future designs to better accommodate the many functions, values, and faces of people using social media.

ACKNOWLEDGMENTS

This work was supported by NSF grant IIS 0845351.

REFERENCES

1. Armstrong, D., Gosling, J., Weinman, J., & Marteau, T. The place of inter-rater reliability in qualitative re-

search: An empirical study. *Sociology* (1997), 31, 597-606.
2. boyd, d. Friendster and publicly articulated social networking. *Proc. CHI* (2004), 1279–1282.
3. boyd, d. Why youth (heart) social network sites: The role of networked publics in teenage social life. In D. Buckingham (Ed.), *Youth, Identity, and Digital Media*. MIT Press, Cambridge, MA, 2007, 119–142.
4. Cosley, D., Sosik, V.S., Schultz, J., Peesapati, S.T., & Lee, S. Experiences with designing tools for everyday reminiscing. *HCI 27*, 1–2 (2012), 175–198.
5. Ellison, N., Heino, R., & Gibbs, J. Managing impressions online: Self-presentation processes in the online dating environment. *JCMC 11*, 2 (2006), Article 2.
6. Ellison, N., Steinfield, C., & Lampe, C. Connection strategies: Social capital implications of Facebook-enabled communication practices. *New Media & Society 13*, 6 (2011), 873–892.
7. Goffman, E. *The presentation of self in everyday life*. Anchor: New York, 1959.
8. Golder, S., Wilkinson, D., & Huberman, B. Rhythms of social interaction: Messaging within a massive online network. *Proc. C&T* (2007), 41–66.
9. Greengard, S. Digitally possessed. *Communications of the ACM 55*, 5 (2012), 14–16.
10. Hangal, S., Lam, M., & Heer, J. MUSE: Reviving memories using email archives. *Proc. UIST* (2011), 75–84.
11. Hogan, B. The presentation of self in the age of social media: Distinguishing performances and exhibitions online. *Bulletin of Science, Technology & Society 30*, 6 (2010), 377–386.
12. Hull, G., Lipford, H.R., & Latulipe, C. Contextual gaps: Privacy issues on Facebook. *Ethics and Information Technology 13*, 4 (2011), 289–302.
13. Joinson, A.N. Looking at, looking up or keeping up with people?: Motives and use of Facebook. *Proc. CHI* (2008), 1027–1036.
14. Jones, W. *Keeping found things found: The study and practice of personal information management*. Morgan Kaufmann, Boston, 2008.
15. Kamal, N., & Fels, S. Online social networks for personal informatics to promote positive health behavior. *Proc. WSM* (2010), 47–52.
16. Krämer, N.C., & Winter, S. Impression management 2.0. The relationship of self-esteem, extraversion, self-efficacy, and self-presentation within social networking sites. *J. Media Psychology 20*, 3 (2008), 106–116.
17. Lampe, C., Ellison, N.B., & Steinfield, C. Changes in Use and Perception of Facebook. *Proc. CSCW* (2008), 721–730.
18. Leary, M.R. *Self Presentation – Impression Management and Interpersonal Behaviour*. Westview, Boulder, CO, USA, 1996.
19. Lofland, J., Lofland, L. *Analyzing social settings: A guide to qualitative observation and analysis*. Wadsworth, Belmont, CA, 1994.
20. Madejski, M., Johnson, M.L., & Bellovin, S.M. The failure of online social network privacy settings. *Columbia Research Report CUCS-010-11*, 2011.
21. Marshall, C.C., & Shipman, F.M. Social media ownership: Using twitter as a window onto current attitudes and beliefs. *Proc. CHI* (2011), 1081–1090.
22. Marwick, A.E., & boyd, d. I tweet honestly, I tweet passionately: Twitter users, context collapse, and the imagined audience. *New Media & Society 13*, 1 (2011), 114–133.
23. Mayer-Schonberger, V. *The Virtue of Forgetting in the Digital Age*. Princeton University Press, 2009.
24. Miller, D., Jackson, P., Thrift, N., Holbrook, B., & Rowlands, M. *Shopping, place and identity*. Routledge, London, 1998.
25. Munson, S., Lauterbach, D., Newman, M., & Resnick, P. Happier Together: Integrating a Wellness Application Into a Social Network Site. *Proc. Persuasive* (2010), 27–39.
26. Nielsen, J. *Web usability*. New Riders, New York, 2000.
27. Odom, W., Sellen, A., Harper, R., & Thereska, E. Lost in translation: Understanding the possession of digital things in the Cloud. *Proc. CHI* (2012), 781–790.
28. Odom, W., Zimmerman, J., & Forlizzi, J. Teenagers and their virtual possessions: Design opportunities and issues. *Proc. CHI* (2011), 1491–1500.
29. Peesapati, S.T., Schwanda, V., Schultz, J., Lepage, M., Jeong, S., & Cosley, D. Pensieve: Supporting everyday reminiscence. *Proc. CHI* (2010), 2027–2036.
30. Petrelli, D., Whittaker, S., & Brockmeier, J. AutoTopography: What can physical mementos tell us about digital memories? *Proc. CHI* (2008), 53–62.
31. Petrelli, D., & Whittaker, S. Family memories in the home: Contrasting physical and digital mementos. *Personal and Ubiquitous Computing 14*, 2 (2010), 153–169.
32. Robinson, L. The cyberself: The self-ing project goes online, symbolic interaction in the digital age. *New Media & Society 9*, 1 (2007), 93–110.
33. Sosik, V.S., Zhao, X., & Cosley, D. See friendship, sort of: How conversation and digital traces might support reflection on friendships. *Proc. CSCW* (2012), 1145–1154.
34. Tufekci, Z. Grooming, gossip, Facebook and MySpace. *Information, Comm. & Society 11*, 4 (2008), 544–564.
35. Wang, Y., Norcie, G., Komanduri, S., Acquisti, A., Leon, P.G., & Cranor, L.F. "I regretted the minute I pressed share": A qualitative study of regrets on Facebook. *Proc. SOUPS* (2011), Article 10.
36. Zhao, O.J., Ng, T., & Cosley, D. No forests without trees: Particulars and patterns in visualizing personal communication. *Proc. iConference* (2012), 25–32.
37. Zhao, X., Sosik, V.S., & Cosley, D. It's complicated: How romantic partners use Facebook. *Proc. CHI* (2012), 771–780.

Favors from Facebook Friends: Unpacking Dimensions of Social Capital

Yumi Jung, Rebecca Gray
Michigan State University
409 Comm Arts Building
East Lansing, MI 48224
[jungyum1, grayreb2]@msu.edu

Cliff Lampe, Nicole B. Ellison
University of Michigan
105 S. State St
Ann Arbor MI, 48109
[cacl, enicole]@umich.edu

ABSTRACT
Past research has demonstrated a link between perceptions of social capital and use of the popular social network site, Facebook. Williams' Internet Social Capital Scales, based on Putnam's formulation, tap into sub-dimensions of social capital that have not been broadly used yet may enlighten our understanding of the different ways in which connecting with others online can facilitate access to resources embedded within our social relationships. In this study, we segment Williams' Internet Social Capital Scales into various sub-dimensions using factor analysis and explicate the distinct facets of social capital through a lab experiment in which Facebook users (N=98) request a small favor from their Facebook network. We find that some sub-dimensions play a significant role in getting favors from Facebook friends while bonding and bridging social capital do not significantly predict responses to favor requests.

Author Keywords
Social capital; Favor asking; Facebook network

ACM Classification Keywords
H.5.3. Information interfaces and presentation (e.g., HCI): Group and Organization Interfaces.

INTRODUCTION
Social media tools can support how people build, maintain, and benefit from social relationships. In CHI and related fields, one way these relational benefits have been measured is through the construct of social capital [5, 14, 19]. Social capital is a conceptual framework that considers the resources held by those in one's social network and which are available to an individual [3, 8, 22]. Researchers have argued that social network sites (SNSs) such as Facebook reduce the transaction costs of maintaining a larger (and potentially more diverse) social network, enable individuals to engage in relationship maintenance activities with their connections, and facilitate the extraction of resources from the network [9, 11, 15].

One important characteristic of social capital is its ability to be converted into other kinds of benefits such as educational and health outcomes [23]. Previous social capital literature has explored social capital as related to hierarchical social status such as income, social class, or performance (e.g., academic or job performance). However, there are many everyday life situations that can also be framed as outcomes of social capital, such as getting small favors from friends and acquaintances. In this study, we create an opportunity for participants to request help from their network in a way that renders these offers of assistance visible – and thus measurable – in an attempt to capture one outcome of social capital in everyday life.

Another contribution of this study stems from our efforts to break down the social capital variable to its simplest components or sub-dimensions. Most of the work examining the role of social media and social capital has focused on the use of perceptual measures, primarily the Internet Social Capital Scales (ISCS) developed by Dmitri Williams [33]. The questions used in surveys have often collapsed social capital into two major dimensions, which may be missing more fine-grained nuances of the overall concept. Since Putnam [22] integrated several lines of research in his popular book *Bowling Alone*, researchers have focused on bridging social capital, a type of social capital which often results from distant ties within a network, and bonding social capital, which is associated with closer relationships. Although Williams' [33] survey scales, based on Putnam's work, are often used, his discussion of the sub-dimensions of social capital has not been broadly utilized. We believe they provide a thoughtful approach to studying the different ways our social relationships provide resources, and thus explore them here.

In this paper, we examine an artificially induced instance of social capital conversion – a task in which people asked their Facebook Friends for a favor – in order to document its relationship to social capital measures. In exploring this relationship, we show how social capital, which has typically been measured as two main dimensions, actually contains multiple facets. We identify distinct facets of social capital through a factor analysis and show that considering these multiple facets may help scholars better understand the way in which online behaviors mediate access to social resources embedded in one's social network, thus enabling them to design social computing systems that capitalize on these social capital dynamics.

LITERATURE REVIEW

Social capital describes the benefits individuals can access through their social network; these benefits can include emotional support, material support, and novel information [3, 8, 16, 22]. Thus, the constitution of one's social network is directly related to one's level of perceived social capital. The relationship between perceived social capital and activities with one's online social network have been examined in many social media studies [5, 6, 14, 26, 31].

Putnam [22] identified different components of social capital – bridging and bonding social capital – that describe resources that can be mobilized from different types of social network connections or relationships. As previously mentioned, bonding social capital is related to strong ties, like a connection between similar kinds of people such as family and close friends, and is associated with access to meaningful social and emotional support. Bridging social capital is associated with interactions with weak ties, such as casual friends and acquaintances [32]. Weak ties are more likely to be bridging ties, connecting dispersed clusters, and are more likely to represent access to the novel, diverse perspectives and information [20, 22] that are hallmarks of bridging social capital.

One example of social capital in action is getting help or information from someone in one's social network when in need. Asking questions is a way of seeking information on SNSs [15, 18], and SNS users can request favors from their online social network by broadcasting requests via status updates. As described above, previous research has found a positive relationship between social capital and SNS use. Most of these studies have examined *perceptions* of social capital, as opposed to actual instances of resource exchange. This is due in large part to the difficulty of translating social capital dynamics to an experimental, artificial situation. This study examines an actual instance of social resource mobilization to examine the effects of social capital more empirically.

Stefanone et al. [25] explored this question by conducting an empirical study about users getting help from their Facebook networks. The study measured perceived bridging and bonding social capital using Williams' online social capital measures [33] to look at the relationship between social capital and support from Facebook friends in the form of help on class-related tasks. In the study, there was no significant relationship between either form of perceived social capital and getting support from their online social networks [25]. Possible reasons for the lack of significant relationships between social capital and receipt of support from Facebook Friends include the closeness of these Friends with the participants (participants were instructed to ask both closest and weakest ties for help). These individuals may or may not represent their larger networks. For instance, social capital support (measured here as a response to a request for help) from mid-range ties in one's network was not assessed.

The insignificant relationship might also be due to the fact that sub-dimensions of social capital were not considered. We believe that unpacking the bonding and bridging dimensions of social capital to consider other instrumental aspects of the concept, in order to see what specific factors affect the responsiveness of one's network when asking favors, represents a useful approach to this issue.

In past research on the measurement of social capital, Williams [33] created a measure of online social capital by merging different dimensions of social networks based on Putnam's [13, 22] conceptual criteria for social capital. Williams' Internet Social Capital Scales consists of two ten-item scales (bonding and bridging) that encompass multiple dimensions of the concepts. Williams' bridging social capital measure consists of four different conceptual dimensions: *outward looking, contact with a broad range of people, a view of oneself as part of broader group,* and *diffuse reciprocity with a broader community* [13, 33]. His bonding social capital measure consists of another four dimensions: *emotional support, access to scarce or limited resources, ability to mobilize solidarity,* and *out-group antagonism* [33]. Because each sub-dimension has a different conceptual orientation, different dimensions might have different effects on certain outcomes. For example, although all the three sub-dimensions of bonding social capital are related to a higher level of closeness, *social resources for emotional support* and *access to limited resources* might be different. In the same way, there is a possibility that *emotional support* affects getting favors while the *ability to mobilize solidarity*, a different dimension of bonding social capital, does not.

Most social media studies of social capital employ the simpler bridging and bonding scales and typically do not acknowledge or make use of the sub-dimensional measures. Ferlander [12] pointed out that "although social capital is seen as a multidimensional concept, most empirical studies rely on one-dimensional measures" ([12], p.119). Although Williams developed the sub-dimensions of the bonding and bridging social capital scales conceptually, he only statistically distinguished between the two factors of bridging and bonding social capital; he did not statistically confirm the groupings of the sub-dimensions.

To tease apart and assess the different dimensions of these forms of social capital in relationship to an empirical social capital outcome (performing a favor), this study employs both ways of measuring social capital, using the bonding and bridging measures as well as the sub-dimensions of bonding and bridging social capital as separate variables. Specifically, this study looks at the relationship between perceived social capital and getting responses to a favor request, as well as the relationship between each sub-dimension of social capital and the number of responses.

H1: Bridging and bonding social capital will be positively associated with the number of responses to a favor request on Facebook.

RQ1: How do different dimensions of social capital relate to the number of responses to a favor request on Facebook?

Facebook-specific Variables

Actual Friends

Early work on the relationship between social capital and Facebook use employed a measure of Facebook use that aggregated the number of total Friends on the site, time on the site, and six attitudinal measures. This aggregate measure, Facebook Intensity (FBI), was positively predictive of both bonding and bridging social capital perceptions among a sample of college undergraduates [27]. Later work employed a different measure and examined both the number of "total Facebook Friends" and the number of "actual" Facebook Friends; "actual" friends assessed users' perceptions of how many of their total connections on the site could be considered actual friends, or more meaningful ties [11]. This work found that the number of "actual" friends on Facebook was predictive of perceived bridging social capital, whereas "total" friends was not. As we expect perceptions of bridging social capital to be positively related to the number of responses individuals receive to their favor request, we similarly expect "actual" friends to be a significant positive predictor of the number of responses received. Thus, we predict:

H2: Participants with more actual Facebook friends will receive more favor responses from their Facebook network.

Relational maintenance and reciprocity on Facebook

Reciprocity is a key facet of social capital. The expectation of reciprocity is an inherent component of building social capital, although expectations can be violated [21]. One way in which social capital is maintained is through social grooming activities and other relationship maintenance behaviors that signal attention to one's network. Facebook is an effective context for performing these kinds of social interaction because it enables individuals to engage in social grooming with a larger network than might otherwise be possible [9]. Ellison et al. [11] test the role of a variable labeled "Signals of Relational Investment (SRI)," which captures the propensity to perform Facebook-enabled reciprocal relational maintenance behaviors, such as answering a question posed to one's network or writing "Happy Birthday" on a Friend's Wall. The performance of these signals of relational investment positively predicted bridging social capital in other work [11], thus we expect:

H3: Participants' propensity to perform signals of relational investment will be positively related to the number of responses to a favor request.

Question-Asking and Favor Requests on Facebook

Beyond the number of Friends to whom one is connected online and the relational maintenance behaviors one reports performing, we wonder what effect previous experience asking help of one's network may have on the reception of later favor requests. Although no extant research has looked at how the frequency with which one asks questions or favors of her network impacts the success of subsequent requests, we believe the routine or frequent performance of these behaviors may lead to more fruitful outcomes for favor-askers. It may be that frequently asking questions of one's network leads to greater overall visibility in the News Feed according to the algorithm used by Facebook to prioritize posts [2]; thus, more frequent posters may be more likely to receive responses when posting a request for a favor on the site. Another possibility is that frequently asking questions may give individuals experience that makes them more effective question-askers over time. This experience may translate to the realm of getting help with favors and thus lead to more success (a higher number of responses). Thus, we ask:

RQ2: Does the frequency of asking for help on Facebook impact the number of responses one receives to a favor request on the site?

Rhetorical features of online requests and network responsiveness

Although network structure, closeness with others, and other behaviors on Facebook may serve as meaningful predictors of the extent to which Friends will respond to an online favor, past research suggests that the actual *way* in which one asks for help may impact the responses one receives from his or her network. Burke, Joyce, Kim, Anand and Kraut [4] examined rhetorical properties of messages posted on Usenet, finding that actual requests were more likely to receive responses than were non-requests. More recently Teevan, Morris, and Panovich [29] explored the effects of various question characteristics on response quality, quantity, and speed within Friend networks on Facebook. When information-seekers targeted specific audiences in their requests, kept questions brief, and utilized question marks, the Facebook users obtained faster, higher-quality responses [29].

In the present study, in which participants were asked to request a small online favor of their Facebook friends, we similarly expect that particular characteristics of the favor request may be more or less instrumental in eliciting responses. Thus we explore the relationship between the number of strategies that participants use and the number of responses participants receive from their network.

H4: Participants who use more strategies are more likely to get a higher level of responses from their Facebook networks.

Finally, we are interested in both identifying the types of rhetorical strategies that participants use and determining which of these strategies are most effective at gaining responses from one's network.

RQ3: What types of strategies are most effective for getting a higher level of responses from Facebook networks?

METHOD

Data collection

Data presented in this paper were collected as part of a larger research study of SNS-enabled information-seeking. Non-faculty staff at a large, public Midwestern university were invited in October-November 2011 and February-March 2011 to complete an online survey about their use of online communication tools, which explored many aspects of (and attitudes toward) Facebook use, question-asking in SNS settings, and dimensions of social capital. Of the 3150 staff members invited to take the survey, 666 participated (21% response rate), and 106 of the survey respondents were recruited to participate in a lab study, based on self-reports of performing question-asking behavior on Facebook. All participants received a minimum of $10 in Amazon.com credit but had the opportunity to receive up to $15 (described below).

During the lab session, participants were asked to post a status update asking their Facebook Friends to do them the "favor" of filling out a brief questionnaire, provided in a hyperlink. In order to incentivize participants, prior to posting the survey/favor request in a status update, participants were informed that for each of the first 10 responses they received, they would receive an additional $0.50 on their Amazon card (amounting to an additional incentive of up to but not exceeding $5). Participants were able to write whatever they chose to encourage their Friends to click on the link and complete the survey and were also given a copy of the survey for reference. Our rationale for choosing a short questionnaire to serve as the "favor" was that – unlike a question, which may require specific knowledge to answer – any Facebook Friend could perform the favor task.

Variable	Mean (*SD*)
Actual friends	102 (105)
Frequency of asking help	2.88 (.73)
Signals of Relational Investment (SRI)	4.09 (.50)
N of strategies	3.08 (1.17)
Bridging Social Capital	3.77 (.49)
Bonding Social Capital	3.68 (.56)
New variables from bridging social capital	
Outward-looking	3.98(.48)
Broader group	3.80(.63)
New people	3.41(.95)
New variables from bonding social capital	
Individual benefit	3.86 (.50)
Collective action (More sacrifice)	3.52 (.66)

Table 1: Sample characteristics

The favor questionnaire was comprised of 9 items, including questions about the connection between the responder and the participant (e.g., relational closeness, relationship type), expectations of reciprocity, Facebook use, and education level. One of the items also asked the favor respondents to fill in the name of the person that asked them to complete the questionnaire. This allowed us to link the data from the favor survey to the participant data in the main survey. Note that filling out the questionnaire was low effort and was likely to take only a few moments of the favor doers' time, although we did ask them to add a Facebook application before accessing the online questionnaire to help link the data.

A total of 98 lab participants completed this task, posting the request and survey link on Facebook. Participants were 73.2% female, an average of 42.7 years old, and 85% had obtained a Bachelor's degree or higher.

Measures

Facebook use.

Actual friends is a 1-item measure created by Ellison et al. [10] which asks: "Approximately how many of your TOTAL Facebook friends do you consider actual friends?" Participants had an average of 102 (SD = 105) actual Facebook Friends. Table 1 shows average and mean values of each variable.

Frequency of asking for help was measured with two items: "How often do you use Facebook to (1) ask questions of your Facebook friends? (2) ask your Facebook friends for favors?" Each item was asked with a 5-point scale (1 = Never, 2 = Rarely, 3 = Sometimes, 4 = Often, 5 = Very often). The items were averaged and inter-item correlation for the two is .56. Using the inter-item correlation is recommended when a variable has two items, and 0.5 is considered a good value [30].

Signals of Relational Investment (SRI) This 5-item scale (alpha = .78, M = 4.09, SD = 0.50) has been used in previous work, and it measures the extent to which participants report signaling attention to specific Facebook Friends in their network. The items capture users' perceptions of the extent to which they respond to Friends' posts and reach out to offer support. One of the items also probes how likely participants are to post "Happy Birthday" on their Friends' Walls, which represents another method of signaling that one is paying attention to specific Friends. Example items include "When I see someone asking a question on Facebook that I know the answer to, I try to respond" and "When I see someone asking for advice on Facebook, I try to respond."

Social capital

The Facebook social capital measure was adapted from Williams' [33] Internet Social Capital Scales. The wording of each item was adjusted to the Facebook context, and both bonding and bridging social capital were assessed.

Factors		Items	Factor loading	Alpha
Bridging social capital				
Outward-looking	1	Interacting with people in my Facebook network makes me interested in things that happen outside of my town.	.709	.74
	2	Interacting with people in my Facebook network makes me want to try new things.	.721	
	3	Interacting with people in my Facebook network makes me interested in what people unlike me are thinking.	.566	
	4	Talking with people in my Facebook network makes me curious about other places in the world.	.524	
Broader group	5	Interacting with people in my Facebook network makes me feel like part of a larger community.	.869	.79
	6	Interacting with people in my Facebook network makes me feel connected to the bigger picture.	.888	
	7	Interacting with people in my Facebook network reminds me that everyone in the world is connected.	.633	
	8	I am willing to spend time to support general Facebook community activities.	.457	
Meeting new people	9	Interacting with people in my Facebook network gives me new people to talk to.	.965	.69 (inter-item correlation)
	10	Through my Facebook network, I come in contact with new people all the time.	.721	
Bonding social capital				
Individual benefit	1	There are several people in my Facebook network I trust to help solve my problems.	.633	.76
	2	There is someone in my Facebook network I can turn to for advice about making very important decisions.	.829	
	3	There is no one in my Facebook network that I feel comfortable talking to about intimate personal problems.	(Not included)	
	4	When I feel lonely, there are several people in my Facebook network I can talk to.	.561	
	5	If I needed an emergency loan of $500, I know someone in my Facebook network I can turn to.	.621	
	7	The people I interact with in my Facebook network would be good job references for me.	.561	
Collective action (More sacrifice)	6	The people I interact with in my Facebook network would put their reputation on the line for me.	.888	.76
	8	The people I interact with in my Facebook network would share their last dollar with me.	.858	
	9	I do not know people in my Facebook network well enough to get them to do anything important.	.413	
	10	The people I interact with in my Facebook network would help me fight an injustice.	.523	

Table 2 Sub-dimension variables from bridging and bonding social capital

Bridging social capital (alpha = .81 M=3.77, SD = .49) is a 10-item scale that captures the extent to which participants feel they have access to new information and diverse perspectives within their Facebook social network. Example items include: "Interacting with people in my Facebook network makes me want to try new things" and "Interacting with people in my Facebook network makes me feel connected to the bigger picture."

Bonding social capital (alpha = .78 M=3.68, SD = .56) is a 10-item scale that taps into perceptions of access to significant social and emotional support within their Facebook networks. Example items include: "When I feel lonely, there are several people in my Facebook network I can talk to," and "The people I interact with in my Facebook network would share their last dollar with me."

Sub-dimensions of social capital

To construct the bonding social capital measure, Williams [33] initially created 24-items representing five sub-dimensions: emotional support, access to limited resources, ability to mobilize solidarity, out-group antagonism, and homogeneity. He created 22 items for bridging social capital from four sub-dimensions: outward-looking, interaction with new people, part of a broader group, and diffuse reciprocity. Williams reduced both bridging and bonding to ten items each through exploratory factor analysis. Thus each scale for bonding and bridging social capital collapses these different conceptual sub-dimensions. Through this reduction process, all items from *ability to mobilize solidarity*, *homogeneity*, and *diffuse reciprocity* were excluded, so bonding and bridging social capital had three factors respectively.

In order to confirm sub-factors of the two-scale, 20-item measurement, we performed confirmatory factor analysis (CFA) based on the conceptual dimensions. CFA was conducted using AMOS 20.0 to examine the construct validity of a three factor-solution extracted from the original bridging and bonding social capital scales. The model fit was assessed by Chi-Square, CFI (comparative fit index) and RMSEA (root mean square error of approximation). The Chi-Square value is the basic measure for checking overall model fit, and CFI evaluates the model by comparing the chi-square value to the chi-square of the null model. CFI is customized for a small sample size [28]. The RMSEA is a supplementary statistic of chi-square to assess model fit. The CFA model's fit is acceptable when ratio of χ^2 to *df* is less than 3.00, comparative fit index (CFI) is .95 or higher, and root mean square error of approximation (RMSEA) is between .06 and .08 [33].

Sub-dimensions of bridging social capital

The three-factor model showed a good fit with the data, χ^2 (32) = 46.16, χ^2/df=1.44, CFI= .95, and RMSEA = .068. Cronbach's alphas for sub-scales were .74 (outward-looking) and .79 (broader group) respectively. The third variable (meeting new people) consisted of two items and its inter-item correlation was .69.

Sub-dimensions of bonding social capital

The CFA model fit was not adequate with the three-factor model. The CFA modification indices in the present study suggested controlling correlations among item numbers 1, 2, 4, 5, and 7, and the modification suggested a two-factor model rather than three factors. See Table 2 for items in the two factors.

Modification is one of the functions in AMOS to suggest a better model fit. One item (No. 3 in the table) measuring emotional support was excluded because it had a very low factor loading value and reduced the reliability of the scale. The two-factor model showed a good fit with the data, χ^2(26) = 35.220, χ^2/df=1.35, CFI= .97, and RMSEA = .058. Cronbach's alphas for sub-scale were .76 (individual benefit) and .76 (collective action) respectively. After completing the CFA tests, we averaged items in each factor.

Among the three new variables from bridging social capital, the participants had an average scores in *outward-looking* of 3.98 (*SD* = .48), *broader group* of 3.80 (*SD* = .63), and *new people* of 3.41 (*SD* = .95). Regarding the two variables from bonding social capital, the participants had, on average, an *individual benefit* score of 3.86 (*SD* = .50) and a *collective action* score of 3.52 (*SD* = .66).

Rhetorical strategies to elicit responses

Content analysis was used to analyze the posts the favor-doers broadcasted to their network during the lab session. One of the authors made a first pass through the favor-asking posts and made a list of recurring rhetorical strategies utilized by participants to elicit responses from their network. The research team finalized six types of strategies through multiple iterations. Two members of the research team coded all of the posts using the categories. The two coders were allowed to assign multiple strategies to each post. Besides the rhetorical strategy coding, the aggregate number of strategies per post was counted to create a new variable, "number of strategies," for regression analysis. Cohen's Kappa was calculated for each strategy and the total number of strategies. The Kappa for all categories was 1.0. Table 3 contains the categories and status update examples.

Strategy categories	Example	Number of posts & percent utilizing strategy
Thanks in advance*	"Thank you for helping me"	52 (53.1%)
Signal of brevity*	"Take a couple of minutes and do so!"	43 (43.9%)
Research study/science*	"I'm participating in a research study that is examining..."	27 (27.6%)
University mention*	"I'm in the process of going through a survey for the C Dept at [university]"	21 (21.4%)
Spam disclaimer*	"This isn't a spam"	81 (82.7%)
Money incentive mentioned*	"I will get $.50 in an Amazon cash (which is like Gold!!) for everyone of you complete the survey"	79 (80.6%)

*Yes = 1

Table 3: Favor-asking strategy categories

RESULTS

Effects on the number of responses

The dependent variable of this study was the total number of responses to the favor-asking posting. This is count data without negative numbers. Poisson regression was invented for analyzing count data. The assumption of distribution for Poisson regression is that the mean value should be close to the variance. But the present data contains evidence of overdispersion, which means variance is much higher than the mean value (*M* = 3.4, variance=12.5), so negative binomial analysis is a more appropriate choice.

We examined the correlation matrix for multicollinearity in Table 4. In this sample, no correlations above the value of *r* > .8 were identified. The variance inflation factors (VIFs) were below the critical value of 10 (highest VIF = 1.63), indicating no serious biasing effect. The tolerance statistic for all variables have values greater than 0.1 [34]. We therefore concluded that there was no significant threat to the validity of the regression analysis.

Table 5 shows the results from the negative binomial regression including both the original bridging and bonding social capital measures (model 1) and the sub-dimensions of social capital (model 2) as independent variables separately. Average marginal effect estimations are shown in Table 5. Model 1 includes the original Williams social capital measures, and the model is statistically significant (p = 0.035) with a Pseudo R^2 of 0.031. Model 2 includes the sub-dimensions of social capital as separate independent variables. The model is statistically significant (p = 0.045), with a Pseudo R^2 of 0.018.

Model 1						
Variables	1	2	3	4	5	6
1 Actual friends	-					
2 F of asking help	.375**	-				
3 SRI	.387**	.250**	-			
4 N of strategies	.004	-.101	.204*	-		
5 Bridging SC	.213*	.334**	.504**	.138	-	
6 Bonding SC	.238*	.195*	.259**	.128	.213*	-

Model 2									
Variables	1	2	3	4	5	6	7	8	9
1 Actual friends	-								
2 F of asking help	.375**	-							
3 SRI	.387**	.250**	-						
4 N of strategies	.004	-.101	.204*	-					
5 Outward looking	.129	.254**	.334**	.185	-				
6 Broader group	.214*	.278**	.443**	.168	.399**	-			
7 New people	.127	.218*	.351**	-.067	.382**	.284**	-		
8 Individual benefit	.164	.108	.184	.097	.147	.076	.046	-	
9 Collective action	.241*	.195*	.307**	.116	.196*	.350**	.052	.479**	-

Table 4. Correlation matrices

In model 1, neither bridging nor bonding social capital has a significant effect on the number of responses, in effect failing to support *H1* which predicted a positive association between perceptions of bridging and bonding social capital and the number of responses to a favor request. In Model 2, the sub-dimensions *meeting new people* of bridging social capital and *individual benefit* of bonding social capital have significant relationships with *the number of responses*. The results show that sub-dimensions of social capital affect the number of responses to the favor differently. Some sub-dimensions have no significant impact on the response rate, providing insight into *RQ1*, which asked "*how do different dimensions of social capital relate to the number of responses to a favor request?*" A one-unit increase in *individual benefit* leads to a 1.68 unit increase in a *number of responses* (β=1.68, p<0.05). *New people* had a marginal negative effect, so a one-unit increase in *new people* leads to a .90 unit decrease in a *number of responses* (β=-.90, p=0.05).

Independent Variable	Model1 *Average Marginal Effect (SD)*	Model2 *Average Marginal Effect (SD)*
Actual FB friends	-.00 (.00)	-.00 (.00)
F of asking help	1.87* (.91)	1.78* (.86)
SRI	1.23 (1.14)	1.36 (1.15)
N of strategy	.96* (.46)	1.02* (.46)
Bridging Social Capital	-1.97 (1.35)	
Bonding Social Capital	.77 (.92)	
New variables from bridging social capital		
Outward-looking		-1.27 (1.13)
Broader group		.50 (.86)
New people		-.90' (.52)
New variables from bonding social capital		
Individual benefit		1.68* (.86)
Collective action		-1.07 (.78)
Constant	3.61 (.49)	3.63 (.48)
Log-likelihood value	-211.67	-208.46
Pseudo R^2	0.031*	0.018*
Likelihood Ratio	13.54	19.97
P-value	0.035*	0.045*

* P< 0.001, '***' ; P< 0.01, '**' ; P<0.05, '*'; p<0.10, '''

* Coefficients are from a marginal effect analysis of the negative binomial regression.

Table 5: Negative binomial regression predicting number of responses (N=98)

In both models, the effects of the *number of actual friends* and *SRI* are not significant, so *H2* and *H3* , which predicted a positive relationship between *number of actual friends* and the *number of favor responses* and between *SRI* and the *number of favor responses* respectively, are not supported.

The frequency of asking for help (*RQ2*) has a significant, positive effect on the number of responses in both models. A one-unit increase in the *frequency of asking for help* leads to a 1.87 unit increase in the *number of responses* on average (β = 1.87, p = 0.5) in model 1. In model 2, a one-unit increase in *frequency of asking for help* leads to 1.78 unit increase in the *number of responses* (β=1.78, p<0.05).

H4, which predicted a positive relationship between the *number of rhetorical strategies utilized* and the *number of responses* to a favor request, was supported. A one-unit increase in the *number of strategies* leads to a .96 unit increase in the *number of responses* on average (β=.96, p= 0.5) in model 1. In Model 2, a one-unit increase in the *number of rhetorical strategies* leads to a 1.02 unit increase in the *number of responses* (β=1.02, p<0.05).

Types of rhetorical strategies to elicit favors

Partial correlation was assessed to investigate *RQ3*, the relationship between types of strategies utilized and the number of responses received. Because the total number of responses is expected to relate to the total number of possible favor-doers, we controlled for *total Facebook friends*. Since the dataset has many zero responses (N=22; those who did not get any responses), the number of responses was recoded to a dummy variable to look at difference between zero-response group and non-zero response group (N=76; those with one or more respondent).

Strategy (Yes=1)	N of responses	Zero vs. non-zero responses (Zero=0)
Thanks in advance	.02	-.08
Signal of brevity	.02	-.13
Research study/science	.18	.05
University mention	.25*	.15
Spam disclaimer	.07	-.06
Money incentive mentioned	.13	.24*
Total N of strategies used	.28*	.06

Table 6: Partial correlation between strategies and continuous and binary coding of responses.

As shown in Table 6, the total number of rhetorical strategies utilized and, specifically, the mention of the university at which the study occurred, were positively correlated to the number of response. This could be because referencing a specific sub-cluster helps to reduce the cost for that network in deciding whether they should respond or not. This is similar to the "uniqueness" dimension that has been shown to be effective in reducing social loafing [17]. For zero vs. non-zero comparison, the money incentive mention strategy is related to the non-zero group. This result implies that each strategy has a different rate of responses, and the rhetorical strategies that are associated with eliciting at least a single response are not the same as those associated with eliciting *more* responses.

DISCUSSION

Social capital is a useful framework for explicating the value of our social networks, and consequently the value of the socio-technical tools, such as Facebook, that enable us to better maintain these connections. We see two main ways in which this study has expanded our understanding of the intersection of social capital and social computing systems. First, because social capital comprises a vast set of communication practices, resources, and structures within a social network [7], this study captures a specific outcome of social capital that is available to all members of one's network: getting a small favor from a Facebook Friend. We asked our participants to request a favor that anyone in their network could provide and then used the number of responses as an outcome of social capital. Second, we examine a common framework for understanding different types of social capital, bridging and bonding, and extend those concepts to include more nuances of that framework. We used Williams' [33] survey items which tap into individuals' perceptions of bridging and bonding social capital, but also examine the sub-dimensions of the Williams' [33] measures as potentially important predictors of relational outcomes and online behavior.

First, we examined the relationship between perceived social capital and the number of responses to a favor request using both measures of social capital: the original bridging and bonding scales, as well as the sub-dimensions of social capital developed through factor analysis guided by the conceptual distinctions articulated in Williams work. The relationship between favors and social capital was insignificant when using the standard bridging and bonding scales, so *H1* was not supported. However, we found an interesting answer to *RQ1*, which asked "*how do different dimensions of social capital relate to the number of responses to a favor request?* We found a significant relationship between the number of responses and one "revised" sub-dimension (*individual benefit*) of bonding social capital when we examined the more granular sub-dimension measures.

Given the cross-sectional nature of these data, we don't have empirical evidence that clearly illustrates why these differences might be occurring. Based on Burt's [7] work on the importance of communication behaviors in generating social capital, it could be that users who perceive higher levels of the *individual benefit* sub-dimension of bonding social capital are more likely to interact with their networks in ways that are able to generate more responses to favors. The type of favor requested may be another factor to consider. Filling out the survey is a simple task or favor that anyone can perform, as opposed to a task requiring more time, effort, expertise, or other resources.

Among the sub-dimensions of bridging social capital, there was a significant relationship between *meeting new people* and the number of favor-doers, but this was a negative association. Those who were more likely to perceive Facebook as an ideal place to interact with new people received fewer responses to their favor requests, perhaps because they were more likely to use the site as a way to interact with new and different kinds of people but not as a place to build up stores of reciprocal interactions with the same individuals over time.

The number of actual Facebook Friends and signals of relational investment (SRI) were not significantly related to the number of responses received, such that *H2* and *H3* were not supported. This was unexpected given previous work identifying a link between these variables and perceived social capital, and points to the importance of employing other measures. Because the favor required little time investment, expertise, or familiarity with the favor requestor and thus could be completed by anyone in one's Facebook network, it may be that "actual" friends were not important for this instance, although we would expect that SRI and actual friends might be associated with other kinds of informational or emotional support – instances in which more intimate knowledge of the support requestor is necessary to respond.

We also found that participants who reported a higher level of frequency of asking for help from their Facebook Friends were more likely to get a higher number of responses from their Facebook networks (*RQ2*). Asking questions and favors of one's network may be a way to utilize the "social lubrication" components of the site by engaging in interaction with one's network. Additionally, individuals who frequently ask for help from their Facebook networks may be more skilled at framing their requests in ways that elicit more responses. Future research should explore these potential explanations using other methods.

Implications for Practice

We have shown that different types of perceptions of social capital can lead to different outcomes in terms of using a site like Facebook to ask for favors. Work in this area can help practitioners understand how they might construct tools that allow for relationship maintenance in such a way as to evoke the different aspects of social capital explicated here. For example, designers interested in supporting *individual benefit* effects for their users might provide tools that make instances of exchanged favors between other users more visible, or that help emphasize requests for help over other types of messages in the system.

Limitations

As with any work based on Facebook interactions, specific features of the system may influence our results. Because Facebook's Edge Rank algorithm selects which content appears in Friends' News Feeds, we do not know how many people saw the requests posted by our participants [2]. The reasons why some requests were more successful than others were most likely affected by the variables we measure here, but also may have influenced by their visibility in the News Feed of our participants' networks. As with other work similar to this, we are looking at relationships between variables, and do not have evidence of causal relationships. Additionally, those Friends who did see the favor requests may have been deterred from completing the survey because after clicking the link to the survey, they were directed to a Facebook application page that required them to "allow" or "deny" the application to download some basic data about them before continuing to the survey. We believe that this extra step may have reduced the number of responses received to the favor requests – albeit across all participants – as these applications are often associated with privacy risks to users [1]. Future research utilizing a similar design should forego the use of a Facebook application.

The task we chose, asking members of the network to fill out a survey, likely carries dependencies that would be different had another task been used. Capturing instances of social capital conversion in action has been a challenge for researchers in this area, and given the likely effects of the form of the favors that mark social capital conversion, more work needs to be done in this area.

CONCLUSION

Social capital is a way of framing positive outcomes from engagement with a social network, including contexts in which one's social network is mediated by information and communication technologies. Past scholarship on social network sites has articulated how the affordances of these socio-technical systems can shape the generation and expression of social capital [24]. Sub-dimensions of social capital allow for a better matching between technical and social affordances. In this paper, we've shown that social capital is multi-dimensional, and that different aspects of this concept may be associated with different types of outcomes in socio-technical systems. Social capital has proven to be a useful concept in understanding how technologies support relationships, and we are hopeful that expanding our understanding of this concept will lead to future insights regarding the design, deployment, and effects of socio- technical systems such as Facebook.

ACKNOWLEDGMENTS

This material is based upon work supported by the National Science Foundation under Grant No. 0916019. Jessica Vitak and Brandon Brooks assisted with data collection.

REFERENCES

1. Besmer, A., Lipford, H.R., Shehab, M. and Cheek, G. Social applications: exploring a more secure framework *Proceedings of the 5th Symposium on Usable Privacy and Security*, ACM, Mountain View, California, 2009, 1-10.
2. Bosworth, A. News feed is a robot *Facebook Blog*, 2007.
3. Bourdieu, P. The forms of capital. in Richardson, J.G. ed. *Handbook of theory and research for the sociology of education* Greenwood, New York, 1986, 241-258.
4. Burke, M., Joyce, E., Kim, T., Anand, V. and Kraut, R. Introductions and requests: Rhetorical strategies that elicit response in online communities. *Third International Conference on Communities and Technologies.*, 2007.
5. Burke, M., Kraut, R. and Marlow, C., Social capital on Facebook: Differentiating uses and users. in *CHI*, (Vancouver, BC, Canada, 2011), New York: ACM.
6. Burke, M., Marlow, C. and Lento, T., Social network activity and social well-being. in *28th International Conference on Human Factors in Computing Systems*, (Atlanta, 2010), New York: ACM.
7. Burt, R.S. *Neighbor networks: Competitive advantage local and personal.* . Oxford University Press, Oxford, 2009.
8. Coleman, J.S. Social capital in the creation of human capital. *The American Journal of Sociology*, *94*. 95-120.
9. Donath, J.S. Signals in social supernets. *Journal of Computer-Mediated Communication*, *13*. 231-251.
10. Ellison, N., Steinfield, C. and Lampe, C. Connection Strategies: Social capital implications of Facebook-enabled communication practices. *New Media & Society*.
11. Ellison, N., Vitak, J., Gray, R., Lampe, C. and Brooks, B. Cultivating Social Resources on Facebook: Signals of

Relational Investment and their Role in Social Capital Processes *iCS-OII 2011 "A Decade in Internet Time" Symposium.* , Oxford, UK, 2011.

12. Ferlander, S. The importance of different forms of social capital for health. *Acta Sociologica, 50* (2). 115-128.

13. Kobayashi, T. Bridging social capital in online communities: Heterogeneity and social tolerance of online game players in Japan. *Human Communication Research, 36* (4). 546-569.

14. Lampe, C., Ellison, N. and Steinfield, C., A familiar face(book): profile elements as signals in an online social network. in *ACM CHI 2007 Conference on Human Factors in Computing Systems* (2007), New York: ACM, 435-444.

15. Lampe, C., Vitak, J., Gray, R. and Ellison, N., Perceptions of Facebook's Value as an Information Source in *30th International Conference on Human Factors in Computing Systems (CHI)*, (Austin, TX, 2012), ACM Press.

16. Lin, N., Cook, K.S. and Burt, R.S. *Social capital : theory and research.* Aldine de Gruyter, New York, 2001.

17. Ling, K., Beenen, G., Ludford, P., Wang, X., Chang, K., Li, X., Cosley, D., Frankowski, D., Terveen, L., Rashid, A.M., Resnick, P. and Kraut, R. Using social psychology to motivate contributions to online communities. *Journal of Computer-Mediated Communication, 10* (4).

18. Morris, M.R., Teevan, J. and Panovich, K., What do people ask their social networks, and why? A survey study of status message Q&A behavior. in *Proceedings of the 28th international conference on Human factors in computing systems*, (Atlanta, Georgia, USA, 2010), ACM.

19. Panciera, K., Priedhorsky, R., Erickson, T. and Terveen, L. Lurking? cyclopaths?: a quantitative lifecycle analysis of user behavior in a geowiki *Proceedings of the 28th international conference on Human factors in computing systems*, ACM, Atlanta, Georgia, USA, 2010.

20. Papacharissi, Z. and Mendelson, A. Toward a new(er) sociability: Uses, gratifications and social capital on Facebook. in Papathanassopoulos, S. ed. *Media perspectives for the 21st century*, Routledge, New Tork, 2011, 212-230.

21. Portes, A. Social capital: Its origins and applications in modern sociology. *Annual Review of Sociology, 22.* 1-24.

22. Putnam, R. *Bowling alone: The collapse and revival of American community.* Simon & Schuster, New York, 2000.

23. Resnick, P. Beyond bowling together: Socio-technical capital. in Carroll, J. ed. *HCI in the new millennium*, Addison-Wesley, New York, NY, 2001, 647-672.

24. Smock, A.D., Ellison, N.B., Lampe, C. and Wohn, D.Y. Facebook as a toolkit: A uses and gratification approach to unbundling feature use. *Computers in Human Behavior, 27* (6). 2322-2329.

25. Stefanone, M.A., Kwon, K.H. and Lackaff, D. Exploring the relationship between perceptions of social capital and enacted support online. *Journal of Computer-Mediated Communication.*

26. Steinfield, C., DiMicco, J.M., Ellison, N.B. and Lampe, C., Bowling online: Social networking and social capital within the organization. in *Fourth International Conference on Communities and Technologies*, (2009), New York: ACM, 245-254.

27. Steinfield, C., Ellison, N.B. and Lampe, C. Social capital, self-esteem, and use of online social network sites: A longitudinal analysis. *Journal of Applied Developmental Psychology, 29.* 434-445.

28. Tabachnick, B.G. and Fidell, L.S. *Using Multivariate Statistics.* Allyn and Bacon, New York, 2007.

29. Teevan, J., Morris, M.R. and Panovich, K. Factors Affecting Response Quantity, Quality, and Speed for Questions asked via Social Network Status Messages. *ICWSM*, 2011.

30. Trochim, W. *The research methods knowledge base.* Cornell University Press, New York, 2001.

31. Valenzuela, S., Park, N. and Kee, K. Is there social capital in a social network site?: Facebook use and college students' life satisfaction, trust, and participation. *Journal of Computer-Mediated Communication, 14.* 875-901.

32. Williams, D. The impact of time online: Social capital and cyberbalkanization. *CyberPsychology & Behavior, 10* (3). 398-406.

33. Williams, D. On and off the 'Net: Scales for social capital in an online era. *Journal of Computer-Mediated Communication, 11.* 593-628.

34. Yang, Z.L., and Peterson, R.T. Customer Perceived Value, Satisfaction, and Loyalty: The Role of Switching Costs, *Psychology and Marketing, 21*(10). 799-822.

Quantifying the Invisible Audience in Social Networks

Michael S. Bernstein[1,2], Eytan Bakshy[2], Moira Burke[2], Brian Karrer[2]

Stanford University HCI Group[1]
Computer Science Department
msb@cs.stanford.edu

Facebook Data Science[2]
Menlo Park, CA
{ebakshy, mburke, karrerb}@fb.com

ABSTRACT

When you share content in an online social network, who is listening? Users have scarce information about who actually sees their content, making their audience seem invisible and difficult to estimate. However, understanding this invisible audience can impact both science and design, since perceived audiences influence content production and self-presentation online. In this paper, we combine survey and large-scale log data to examine how well users' perceptions of their audience match their actual audience on Facebook. We find that social media users consistently underestimate their audience size for their posts, guessing that their audience is just 27% of its true size. Qualitative coding of survey responses reveals folk theories that attempt to reverse-engineer audience size using feedback and friend count, though none of these approaches are particularly accurate. We analyze audience logs for 222,000 Facebook users' posts over the course of one month and find that publicly visible signals — friend count, likes, and comments — vary widely and do not strongly indicate the audience of a single post. Despite the variation, users typically reach 61% of their friends each month. Together, our results begin to reveal the invisible undercurrents of audience attention and behavior in online social networks.

Author Keywords

Social networks; audience; information distribution

ACM Classification Keywords

H.5.3 Group and Organization Interfaces: Web-based interaction

General Terms

Design; Human Factors.

INTRODUCTION

Posting to a social network site is like speaking to an audience from behind a curtain. The audience remains invisible to the user: while the invitation list is known, the final attendance is not. Feedback such as comments and likes is the only glimpse that users get of their audience. That audience varies from day to day: friends may not log in to the site, may not see the content, or may not reply. While established media producers can estimate their audience through surveys, television ratings and web analytics, social network sites typically do not share audience information. This design decision has privacy benefits such as plausible deniability, but it also means that users may not accurately estimate their invisible audience when they post content.

Correct or not, these audience estimates are central to media behavior: perceptions of our audience deeply impact what we say and how we say it. We act in ways that guide the impression our audience develops of us [17], and we manage the boundaries of when to engage with that audience [2]. Social media users create a mental model of their imagined audience, then use that model to guide their activities on the site [26, 37]. However, with no way to know if that mental model is accurate, users might speak to a larger or smaller audience than they expect.

This paper investigates users' perceptions of their invisible audience, and the inherent uncertainty in audience size as a limit for users' estimation abilities. We survey active Facebook users and ask them to estimate their audience size, then compare their estimates to their actual audience size using server logs. We examine the folk theories that users have developed to guide these estimates, including approaches that reverse-engineer viewership from friend count and feedback.

We then quantify the uncertainty in audience size by investigating actual audience information for 220,000 Facebook users. We examine whether there are reasonable heuristics that users could adopt for estimating audience size for a specific post, for example friend count or feedback, or whether the variance is too high for users to use those signals reliably. We then test the same heuristics for estimating audience size over a one-month period.

While previous work has focused on highly visible audience signals such as retweets [5, 31], this work allows us to examine the invisible undercurrents of attention in social media use. By comparing these patterns to users' perceptions, we can then identify discrepancies between users' mental models and system behavior. Both the patterns and the discrepancies are core to social network behavior, but they are not well understood. Improving our understanding will allow us to design this medium in a way that encourages participation and supports informed decisions around privacy and publicity.

We begin by surveying related work in social media audiences, publicity, and predicting information diffusion. We then perform a survey of active Facebook users and compare their estimates of audience size to logged data. We then de-

CHI 2013, April 27–May 2, 2013, Paris, France.

scribe the inherent unpredictability of audience size on Facebook, both for single posts and over the course of a month.

RELATED WORK

Social media users develop expectations of their audience composition that impact their on-site activity. Designing social translucence into audience information thus becomes a core challenge for social media [16, 15]. In response, speakers tune their content to their intended audience [12]. On Facebook and in blogs, people think that peers and close online friends are the core audience for their posts, rather than weaker ties [24, 37]. Sharing volume and self-disclosure on Facebook are also correlated with audience size [10, 39]. However, as the audience grows, that audience may come from multiple spheres of the user's life. Users adjust their projected identity based on who might be listening [17, 26] or speak to the lowest common denominator so that all groups can enjoy it [20]. Social media users are thus quite cognizant of their audience when they author profiles [8, 14], and accurately convey their personality to audiences through those profiles [18].

Our notion of the invisible audience is tied to the imagined audience in social media [26]. The imagined audience usually references the types of groups in the audience — whether friends from work, college, or elsewhere are listening. In this paper, we focus not on the composition of the audience but on its size. Both elements play important roles in how we adapt our behaviors to the audience.

Cues can be helpful when estimating aspects of a social network, but there are few such cues available today. For example, to estimate the size of a social network, it can be helpful to base the estimate on the number of people spoken to recently [21] or to focus on specific subpopulations and relationships such as diabetics or coworkers [27]. However, it can be difficult to estimate how many people within the network will actually see or appreciate a piece of content. Public signals such as reshares [31] and unsubscriptions [22] give users feedback about the quality of their content, but users often consume content and make judgments without taking any publicly visible action [3, 13]. In addition, there are consistent patterns in online communities that might bias estimates: for example, the prevalence of lurkers who do not provide feedback or contribute [29] and a typical pattern of focusing interactions on a small number of people in the network [4].

Questions of audience in social media often reduce to questions of privacy. Users must balance an interest in sharing with a need to keep some parts of their life private [2, 30]. However, early studies on social network sites found no relationship between disclosure and privacy concerns [1, 33, 39]. Instead, people tended to want others to discover their profiles [39], and filled out the basic information in their profile relatively completely [23]. However, young adults are increasingly, and proactively, taking an active role in managing their privacy settings [34].

Design decisions with respect to audience visibility can influence users' interactions with their audience [9]. For example, Chat Circles allows members of a chat room to modify their audience by moving their avatar closer or further from other participants [38]. Visualizations can also support socially translucent interactions by making the members of the audience more salient [25, 11] or displaying whether an intended audience member has already seen similar content [7]. BlackBerry Messenger, Apple iMessage, and Facebook Messenger all provide indicators that the recipient has opened a message, and online dating sites OkCupid and Match.com reveal who has viewed your profile. Few studies have addressed users' reactions to this explicit audience indicator [32], though some users of the social networking site Friendster expressed concerns that they were uncomfortable with this level of social transparency and would consequently not view as many profiles [28].

Our work pushes the literature forward in important respects: we augment previous research with quantitative metrics, we focus on contexts where the intended audience is friends and not the entire Internet, and we empirically demonstrate that audience size is difficult to infer from feedback. We also contribute empirical evidence for the wide variance in audience size, something not previously possible for blogs or tweets, because we can track consumption across the entire medium.

METHOD AND DATA

To study audiences in social media, we use a combination of survey and Facebook log data. Most Facebook content is consumed through the News Feed (or *feed*), a ranked list of friends' recent posts and actions. When a user shares new content — such as a status update, photo, link, or check-in — Facebook distributes it to their friends' feeds. The feed algorithmically ranks content from potentially hundreds of friends based on a number of optimization criteria, including the estimated likelihood that the viewer will interact with the content. Because of this and differences in friends' login frequencies, not all friends will see a user's activity.

Audience Logs

We logged audience information for all *posts* (status updates and link shares) over the span of June 2012 from a random sample of approximately 220,000 US Facebook users who share with friends-only privacy. We also logged cumulative audience size over the course of the entire month. To determine audience size, we used client-side instrumentation that logs an event when a feed item remains in the active viewport for at least 900 milliseconds. Our measure of audience size thus ensures that the post appeared to the user for a nontrivial length of time, long enough to filter out quick scrolling and other false positives. However, being in the audience does not guarantee that a user actually attends to a post: according to eyetracking studies, users remember 69% of posts that they see [13]. So, while there may be some margin of difference between audience size and *engaged* audience size, we believe that this margin is relatively small. Furthermore, we note that univariate correlations are unaffected by linear transformations, so the correlations between estimated and actual audience are the same regardless of whether a correction is applied to the data.

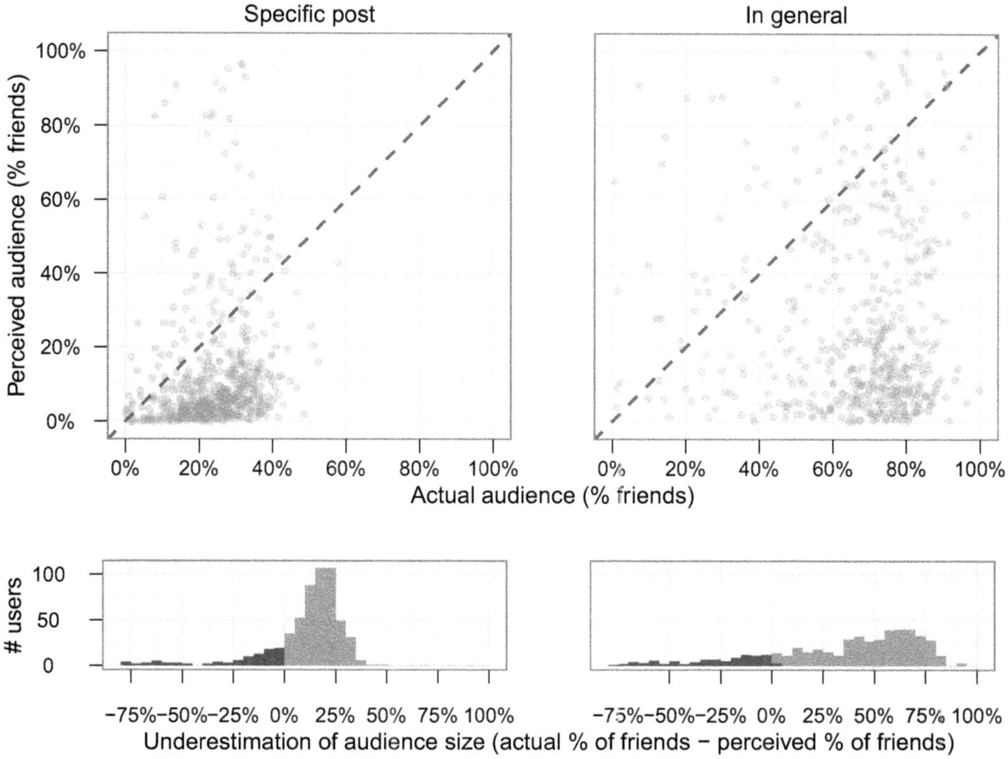

Figure 1: Comparisons of participants' estimated and actual audience sizes, as percentages of their friend count. Most participants underestimated their audience size. The top row displays each estimate vs. its true value; the bottom row displays this data as error magnitudes. Left column: The specific survey, where participants were shown one of their posts, comparing estimated audience to the true audience for that post. Right column: The general survey, where participants estimated their audience size "in general," comparing estimated audience to the number of friends who saw a post from that user during the month.

Our logging resulted in roughly 150 million distinct (source, viewer) pairs from roughly 30 million distinct viewers. All data was analyzed in aggregate to maintain user privacy. The number of *distinct friends providing feedback*, given in terms of likes and comments, was also logged for each post.

In our analysis, we did robustness checks by subsetting our data, e.g., active vs. less active users, and users with different network sizes. We saw identical patterns each time, so we report the results for our full dataset.

Survey

To compare actual audience to perceived audience, we surveyed active Facebook users about their perceived audience. Participants might estimate their audiences differently when they anchor on a specific instance than when they consider their general audience, so we prepared two independent surveys: *general* and *specific* audience estimation. In the general survey, participants answered the question, *"How many people do you think usually see the content you share on Facebook?"* In the specific survey, participants clicked on a page that redirected them to their most recent post, provided that post was at least 48 hours old. Specific survey participants then answered the question, *"How many people do you think saw it?"* In both surveys, participants then shared how they came up with that number. Finally, participants shared their desired audience size on a 5-point scale ranging from "Far fewer people" to "Far more people".

We advertised the survey to English-speaking users in our random sample who had been on Facebook for at least 90 days, had logged into Facebook in the past 30 days, and who had shared at least one piece of content (e.g., status update, photo, or link) in the last 90 days. The general audience survey had 542 respondents, and the specific audience survey had 589. Sixty-one percent of respondents were female, with a mean age of 32.8 ($sd = 14.7$), and a median friend count of 335 ($mean = 457$, $sd = 465$).

PERCEIVED AUDIENCE SIZE

In this section, we investigate how users' perceptions of their audience map onto reality. This investigation has three main components. First, we quantify how accurate users are at estimating the audience size for their posts. Second, we perform a content analysis on users' self-reported folk theories for audience estimation. Third, we explore users' satisfaction with their audience size.

Audience size: perception vs. reality

We compared participants' estimated audience sizes to the actual audience size for their posts. Participants underestimated their audiences. Figure 1 plots actual audience size against perceived audience size for the two surveys. Accurate guesses lie along the diagonal line, where the actual audience is equal to the perceived audience. The cluster of points near the x-axis indicates that the majority of participants significantly underestimated their audience.

For participants considering a specific post in the past (Figure 1, left column), the median perceived audience size was 20 friends ($mean = 60$, $sd = 163$); the median actual audience was 78 friends ($mean = 99$, $sd = 84$). Transformed into percentages of network size, the median post reached 24% of a user's friends ($mean = 24\%$, $sd = 10\%$), but the median participant estimated that it only reached 6% ($mean = 17\%$, $sd = 31\%$). In fact, most participants guessed that no more than fifty friends saw the content, regardless of how many people actually saw it. We note that this data is skewed and long-tailed, as is common with many internet phenomena: as such, we rely on medians rather than means as our core summary statistic.

We quantify the $relative\ error$ as $1 - \frac{perceived\ audience\ size}{actual\ audience\ size}$. The median relative error is 0.73, meaning the median estimate was just 27% of the actual audience size. In other words, the median participants underestimated their actual audience size by a factor of four.

Participants in the general survey also underestimated their audiences (Figure 1, right column). The median perceived audience size in the general survey was 50 ($mean = 137$, $sd = 236$), while the median actual audience (number of friends who saw any post the user produced in the previous month) was 180 ($mean = 283$, $sd = 302$). The median relative error was 0.68, indicating that participants underestimated their general audience by roughly a factor of three.

Figure 1 (bottom row) shows the distribution of errors in both surveys. In both cases, participants tended to underestimate their audiences, and there was greater variance in the general version of the survey.

Not surprisingly, estimates of audience size "in general" were significantly larger than those for a specific post in the past ($mean = 137$ vs. 60, $p < 0.001$). As disjoint sets of friends may see different pieces of content, it makes sense that in a month, more people would see a given user's content than would see any single post she made. Survey participants correctly accounted for this.

To further quantify this relationship, we can fit a linear model to measure the correlation between estimated and actual audience size. The model does not explain much variance at all: $R^2 = 0.04, p < .001$.

Folk theories of audience

What heuristics are guiding users' estimates, and why are users underestimating so much? To answer these questions, we investigated the theories that participants reported when estimating their audience size. We performed a content analysis on the survey responses for how participants came up with their estimates. The authors inductively coded a subset of the responses to generate categories, then iterated on the coding scheme until arriving at sufficient agreement (Fleiss's Kappa = 0.72).

Theory	Prevalence
Guess	23%
Based on likes and comments	21%
Portion of total friend count	15%
How many friends might log in	9%
Who they regularly see on the site	5%
Number of close friends and family	3%
Who might be interested in the topic	2%
Based on privacy settings	2%
Another explanation given	8%

Table 1: The relative prevalence of folk theories for estimating audience size. Participants most often used heuristics based on the amount of feedback they get on their posts or their number of friends.

The categories and their relative popularities across both surveys appear in Table 1. Nearly one-quarter of participants said they had no idea and simply guessed. The magnitude of this number indicates how little understanding users have of their audience size. The most popular strategy (other than guessing) was based on feedback: the number of likes and comments on a post. Participants explained, *"I figured about half of the people who see it will 'like' it, or comment on it,"* or *"number of people who liked it x4."*

Others made a rough guess at how many people might log in to Facebook: e.g., *"I'm guessing one hundred of my frieds [sic] actually read facebook daily"* and *"not a lot of people stay up late at night."* Many respondents based their estimates on a fixed fraction of their friend count: *"figure maybe a third of my friends saw it."* Others assumed that the people they typically see in their own feeds or chat with regularly are also the audience for their posts: *"Judging by the number of people that regularly share with me"*, *"I assume the number of people who see me are the same people that show up on my news feed."* Finally, some respondents mentioned their close friends or family, or friends who would be interested in the topic of the post: *"I'm sure a lot of people have blocked me because of all the political memes I've been putting up lately,"*, *"Friends that are involved with paintball would catch a glimpse of me mentioning MAO."* A small number mentioned their privacy settings: *"Based on the privacy and sharing rules I have set-up, I would imagine it's close to that number."* Particularly savvy users transferred knowledge from other domains, like *"based on the FB page of a business that i'm admin on."*

We compared the audience estimation accuracy of each group. Despite the variety of theories of audience size, no theory performed better than users who responded "guess".

Perceptions of audience size and satisfaction

Though users have limited insight into their own audience size, their perceptions may play a strong role in their satisfaction with their posts' reach. In this section, we investigate survey participants' responses to the question, *"How many people do you wish saw this piece of content?"*

Table 2 reports summary statistics for our survey results. Only 3% of participants wanted a smaller audience than they

Desired audience	Count	Median perceived audience	Median actual audience
Far fewer people	6	1%	8%
Fewer people	9	19%	28%
About the same	295	9%	26%
More people	145	5%	23%
Far more people	125	5%	22%

Table 2: Summary statistics for survey participants who desired smaller, the same, or larger audiences. Perceived and actual audiences shown as a percentage of friend count.

thought they had, while slightly less than half (270) wanted a larger audience and another half (295) were satisfied with their audience size. The fifteen individuals who wanted smaller audiences had large variance in their responses: those who wanted "far fewer people" had the smallest perceived audience (1%) and those who wanted "fewer people" had the largest perceived audience (19%).

Given the small number of people who wanted smaller audiences, we combined the two groups that desired larger audiences and ended up with two comparison groups: those who were satisfied with their audience size (N=295), and those who wanted a larger audience (N=270). Those who desired the same audience size typically estimated that 9% of their friends would see a post ($mean = 20\%, SD = 32\%$), while those who wanted "more people" or "far more people" typically estimated 5% of their friends (combined $mean = 12\%, SD = 28\%$). A nonparametric Wilcoxon rank-sum test comparing these means is significant ($W = 47179, p < .001$), indicating that those who wanted to reach a larger audience estimated that their reach was smaller.

UNCERTAINTY IN ACTUAL AUDIENCE SIZE

The survey results suggest that people do a poor job of estimating the size of the invisible audience in social networks. Is this inaccuracy inevitable? Is audience size too uncertain to estimate accurately?

In this section, we investigate sources of uncertainty when estimating the invisible audience, broadening our view from survey users to our entire dataset of over 220,000 users. We investigate the audience for individual posts in our dataset, then the cumulative audience size for each user over a month. We demonstrate that there is a great deal of variability in audience size, and that audience size is difficult to infer using visible signals. These results suggest that audience size can be quite unpredictable and that users simply do not receive enough feedback to predict their audience size well.

Audience per post

Each time a Facebook user creates a new post, there is a new audience. This section investigates the variance in actual audience sizes for individual posts. We consider how well we can predict a new post's audience using the visible folk theory signals such as fraction of friends and feedback.

Relationship between friend count and audience size

A user's total friend count is the upper limit on their audience size. Is friend count strongly related to audience size?

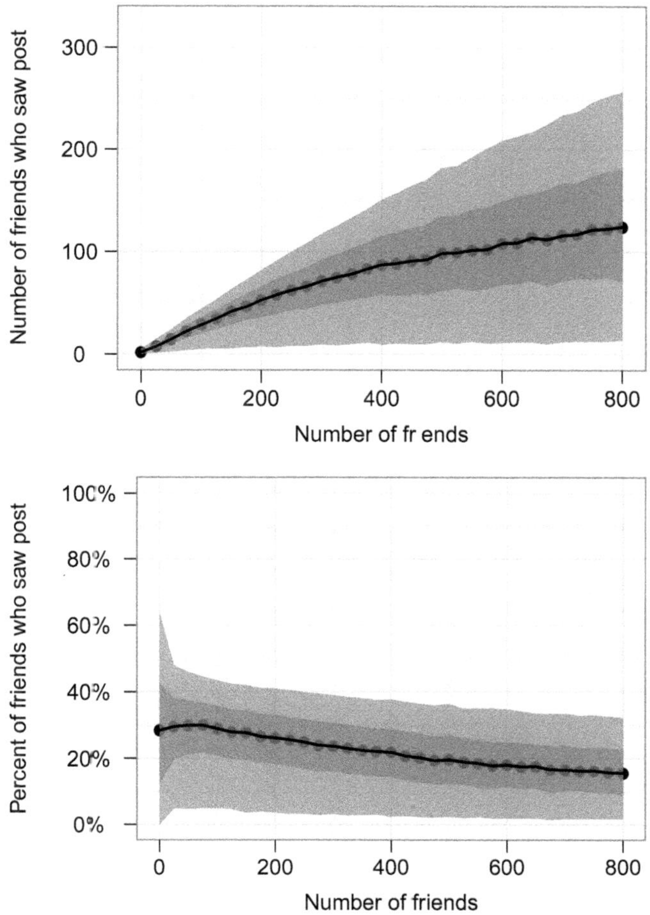

Figure 2: Users with the same number of friends have highly variable audience sizes. Panels show the distribution of the number of friends (top) and fraction of friends (bottom) who saw a post as a function of friend count. The line and bands indicate the median, interquartile range, and 90% region.

Across all posts in our sample, the mean and median fraction of friends that see a post among users is 34% and 35%, respectively. However, this quantity is highly variable. As Figure 2 demonstrates, the interquartile range for the fraction of friends that see a post is approximately 20%, and the 90th percentile range can be as large as 84% (12–96% of the friend count). While the fraction of friends who see a post remains relatively stable, it is important to note that if we consider a user with a fixed number of friends, the actual number of friends who see the post is quite variable. Figure 3 illustrates this relationship: the standard deviation in the audience size increases with the number of friends. As a result, post produced by a user with many friends has more variability in the audience size than one produced by a user with few friends.

Audience size grows most rapidly as a function of number of friends for users with fewer than 200 friends, then tapers off for users with more friends (Figure 2, top). Likewise, the fraction of friends who see a user's post is greatest when users have fewer friends (Figure 2, bottom). This result might be explained by the fact that users with many friends are likely to

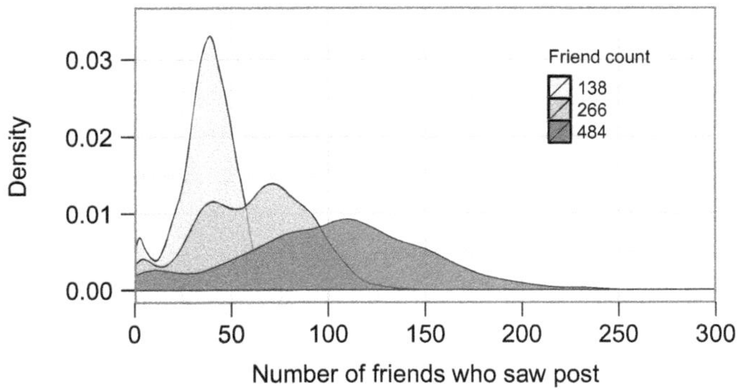

Figure 3: The distribution of audience sizes for users at the 25th, 50th and 75th percentile of friend count within our sample, corresponding to 138, 266, and 484 friends.

have friends who also have large networks [36]; in a system with limited attention, highly connected users may have less opportunity to see all of their friends' content.

To quantify this uncertainty, we can fit a linear model to predict the fraction of friends viewing a post using the number of friends as input. This model explains relatively little variance ($R^2 = .12, p < .001$). The mean absolute error of the model is .08, meaning that the average actual audience is 8% of friends away from the prediction.

Informativeness of feedback

Feedback is the main mechanism that users have to understand their audience's reaction to a post. It was also one of the most popular folk theories in our survey. Does feedback actually help users understand their audience size?

Figure 4 reports the median audience sizes for posts, depending on the amount of feedback they get from friends liking and commenting on the post. Audience size grows rapidly as posts gather more feedback, though this growth slows when a post has feedback from five unique friends. Posts with no likes and no comments had an especially large variance in audience size: the median audience was 28.9% of the user's friends, but the 90% range was from 1.9% to 55.2% of the user's friends. So, while users may be disappointed in posts that receive no feedback, the lack of feedback says little about the number of people it has reached.

Like with friend count, we can fit a linear model that uses feedback indicators such as unique commenters and unique likers to predict the fraction of friends that see a post. This model also explains very little variance ($R^2 = .13, p < .001$). Like the previous model, its mean absolute error is 8%, so the average prediction is off by 8% from the actual percentage of friends who saw the post. These results are nearly identical to those for the linear predictor based on friend count.

Joint model

Neither friend count nor feedback individually are very accurate predictors of audience size. However, they may be contributing data that is jointly informative. We fit a linear model using all three predictors from before — friend count, unique commenters, unique likers — to predict the fraction of friends in the audience. This model explained around twice as much variance (*adj.* $R^2 = .27, p < .001$), but this is still not a highly predictive model. The mean absolute error for this model was 7% of the friend network.

So, even using all three signals that users can view, it is difficult to predict actual audience size.

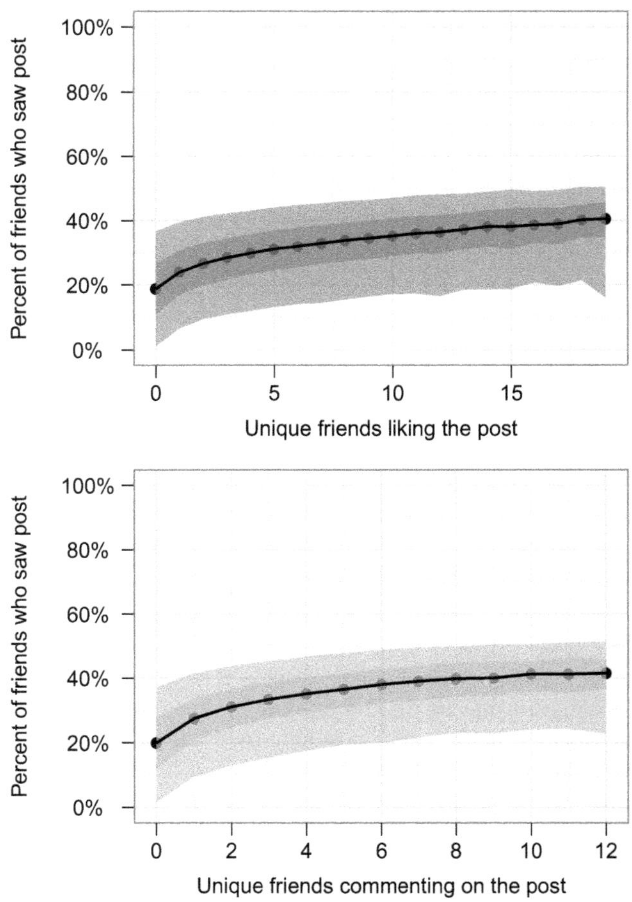

Figure 4: The number of unique friends leaving likes (top) and comments (bottom) is positively associated with audience size, but has large variance.

Cumulative audience

Audience size estimates for the general survey were significantly higher than those specific to a single post. Likewise, users evolve their understanding over extended periods of time. To capture these longer-term processes, we analyzed *cumulative audience*: the total number of distinct friends who saw or interacted with each user's content over the span of an entire month. Three quarters of the users in our sample produced more than one piece of content during the month, and half the users in our sample produced five or more pieces of content.

Relationship with friend count

Cumulative audiences are much larger than those for a single post. The median size of a user's cumulative audience is

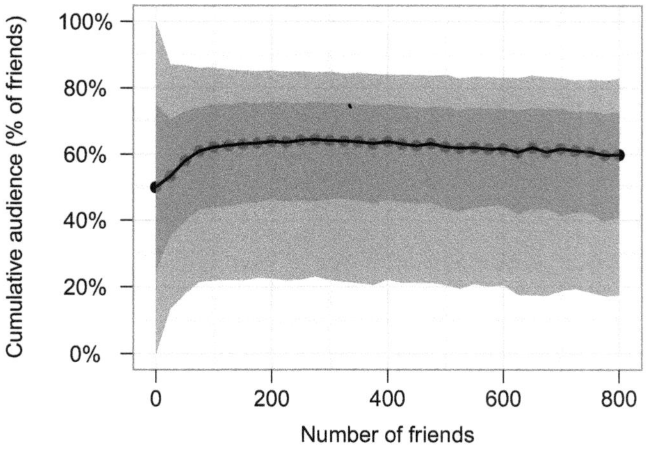

Figure 5: Roughly 60% of users' friends see at least one item they share each month. Cumulative audience size is aggregated over all content produced by a user over 28 days.

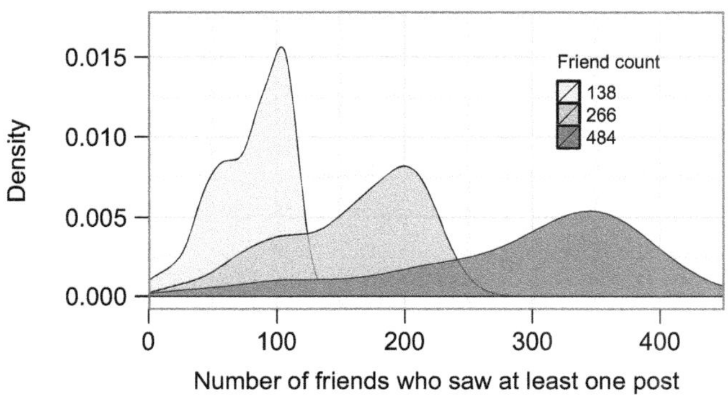

Figure 6: The distribution of cumulative audience sizes across all content produced over one month for users at the 25th, 50th and 75th percentile of friend count in our sample (138, 266, and 484 friends).

61% of that user's friends, compared to 35% for a single post. The relationship between friend count and monthly cumulative audience as a fraction of friend count appears in Figure 5. Again, this relationship can be quite variable: the interquartile range is 31% and the 90% range is 65%. The more friends the user has, the larger the variation (Figure 6).

Informativeness of feedback

If users develop a sense of their invisible audience over time by observing the number of friends who provide feedback, how much can they learn about their audience size? Figure 7 shows the fraction of friends that consitute a user's cumulative audience over the span of one month, given a certain number of unique friends who have provided feedback. For example, approximately 60% of a typical (median) user's friends will see at least one of their posts in a month, given that exactly two distinct friends commented on their posts. While some minimal amount of feedback is indicative of wider distribution, users who have greater than 10 friends who like their posts, or 5 friends that comment, all have fairly

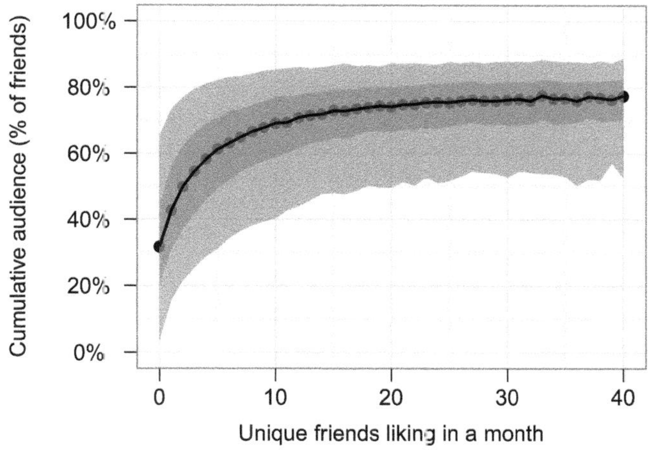

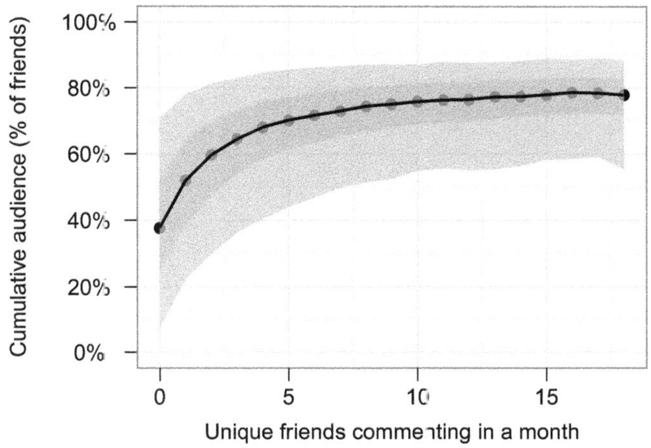

Figure 7: The distribution of the fraction of friends who had seen at least one post by a user as a function of the number of distinct users who had liked (top) or commented on (bottom) at least one piece of the user's content during a one month period. Horizontal axis extends to the 95th percentile of likes and comments for users in our sample.

large audiences. Furthermore, only a small fraction of users' audiences provide feedback over the month: 95% of the users in our sample have 40 or fewer friends who like their posts, and 18 friends who comment on their posts.

Joint model

Though the cumulative audience is much larger than the audience for single posts, it exhibits no less variance. We trained a linear model to predict audience size, using the same predictors as with previous models (friend count, number of unique commenters, number of unique likers) and one new predictor: the number of stories the user produced that month. The model explains no more variance than the joint model for individual posts ($R^2 = .25, p < .001$).

DISCUSSION

Our analysis indicates that social media users underestimate how many friends they reach by a factor of four. Many users who want larger audiences already have much larger audiences than they think. However, the actual audience cannot be predicted in any straightforward way by the user from visible cues such as likes, comments, or friend count.

The core result from this analysis is that there is a fundamental mismatch between the sizes of the perceived audience and the actual audience in social network sites. This mismatch may be impacting users' behavior, ranging from the type of content they post, how often they post, and their motivations to share content. The mismatch also reflects the state of social media as a *socially translucent* rather than *socially transparent* system [15, 16]. Social media must balance the benefits of complete information with appropriate social cues, privacy and plausible deniability. Alternately, it must allow users to do so themselves via practices such as butler lies [19].

The mismatch between estimated and actual audience size highlights an inconsistency: approximately half of our participants wanted to reach larger audiences, but they already had much larger audiences than they estimated. One interpretation would suggest that if these users saw their actual audience size, they would be satisfied. Or, these users might instead anchor on this new number and still want a larger audience.

Reasons for the audience mismatch

Why do people underestimate their audience size in social media? One possible explanation is that, in order to reduce cognitive dissonance, users may lower their estimates for posts that receive few likes or comments. A necessary consequence of users *underestimating* their audience is that they must be *overestimating* the probability that each audience member will choose to like or comment on the post. For these posts without feedback, it might be more comfortable to believe that nobody saw it than to believe that many saw it but nobody liked it. Our data lend some support for this belief: users estimated smaller audiences when we showed them a specific recent post than when they considered their posts in general, and we found the same results when we piloted a separate survey that focused users on a specific post they might create in the future.

Several of the folk theories suggest that users are influenced by whom they have interacted with recently. So, some underestimation may also be due to reliance on the *availability heuristic*, which suggests that prominent examples will impact peoples' estimates [35]. If true, the underestimation might be due to the fact that many social systems have more viewers than contributors [29]. Specifically, users might base their estimates on whom they *see* on Facebook, not accounting for those who might be reading but not responding.

Finally, users' estimates may be affected by the ranking and filtering Facebook performs on the News Feed. Other social network sites have different filter designs: Twitter shows content in an unfiltered reverse-chronological order, while Google+ gives users a slider to choose how much content to filter from each circle. One might hypothesize that not filtering users' feeds (e.g., Twitter) might increase diversity and thus increase audience size. However, we believe that filtering plays a more minor role in audience size: algorithmic feed filters might prefer content from strong ties, but the many weak ties in social networks have a large collective influence on users' feed consumption and sharing practices [6].

Limitations

Our study methodology carries several important limitations. Some concerns are associated with the limits of log data. First, techniques for estimating whether a user saw a post have a precision-recall tradeoff: depending on how the instrument is tuned, it might miss legitimate views or count spurious events as views. However, the instrument would need to be overestimating audience size by a factor of four for our conclusions to be threatened, and we believe that this is unlikely. Second, just because a user saw a status update, we cannot be certain that they focused their attention on it or would remember it [13]. Our survey attempted to be clear that we were interested in how many people *saw* the content, but some participants may have blurred the distinction. Finally, we focused on one month of data; changes to site features or norm evolution may impact audiences over longer periods.

Our survey methodology has limitations as well. To validate the instrument, we tested different formulations of the audience estimation question. Variations included comparing "saw the content" to "read the content", as well as different wordings asking for raw numbers, percentages, and Likert-style radio button responses. The results were similar for all formulations. However, it is possible that some participants still filtered out users who they think might not have paid attention to the content. In addition, the survey format did not go into depth on participants' perceptions: interviews could further explore this phenomenon.

Our methods introduce sampling bias. Our log data selects for active users, in particular those who produce content. The survey also selects for users who produce content, those who log in to Facebook, and those who care enough about Facebook to participate in a survey advertised at the top of the News Feed. One known bias is that active users can have larger friend counts than the typical Facebook population.

Design implications

This research raises the question of whether showing actual audience information might benefit social media. This design might come in many flavors: highlighting close friends who saw the post, showing a count but no names or faces, or (in the extreme) showing a complete list of every person who saw the post. Some Facebook groups now display how many group members have seen each post, while sites such as OkCupid show who has browsed your profile. Adding audience information could certainly address the current mismatch between perceived and actual audience size.

Our results do not paint a clear picture as to whether audience information would be a good addition. Some measure of social translucence and plausible deniability seems helpful: audience members might not want to admit they saw each piece of content, and sharers might be disappointed to know that many people saw the post but nobody commented or "Liked" it. Underestimating the audience might also be a comfortable equilibrium for some users who feel more comfortable speaking to a relatively small group and would not post if they knew that they were performing in front of a large audience. On the other hand, many users expressed a desire for a larger audience, and demonstrating that they do in fact have a large audience might make them more excited to participate.

Pragmatically, this work suggests that social media systems might do well to let their users know that they are impacting their audience. Because so many members of the audience provide no feedback, there may be other ways to emphasize that users have an engaged audience. This might involve emphasizing cumulative feedback (e.g., 400 friends saw their content last month), showing relative audience sizes for posts without sharing raw numbers, or encouraging alternate modes of feedback [3].

CONCLUSION

We have demonstrated that users' perceptions of their audience size in social media do not match reality. By combining survey and log analysis, we quantified the difference between users' estimated audience and their actual reach. Users underestimate their audience on specific posts by a factor of four, and their audience in general by a factor of three. Half of users want to reach larger audiences, but they are already reaching much larger audiences than they think. Log analysis of updates from 220,000 Facebook users suggests that feedback, friend count, and past audience size are all highly variable predictors of audience size, so it would be difficult for a user to predict their audience size reliably. Put simply, users do not receive enough feedback to be aware of their audience size. However, Facebook users do manage to reach 35% of their friends with each post and 61% of their friends over the course of a month.

Where previous work focuses on publicly visible signals such as reshares and diffusion processes, this research suggests that traditionally invisible behavioral signals may be just as important to understanding social media. Future work will further elaborate these ideas. For example, audience composition is an important element of media performance [26], and we do not yet know whether users accurately estimate which individuals are likely to see a post. We can also isolate the causal impact of estimated audience size on behavior, for example whether differences in perceived audience size cause users to share more or less. Finally, these results suggest that there are deeper biases and heuristics active when users estimate quantities about social networks, and these biases warrant deeper investigation.

ACKNOWLEDGMENTS

We would like to thank our survey participants for their insight and time. In addition, we thank Cameron Marlow, Dan Rubinstein, Sriya Santhanam and the Facebook Data Science Team for valuable feedback.

REFERENCES

1. A. Acquisti and R. Gross. Imagined communities: Awareness, information sharing, and privacy on the facebook. In *Privacy enhancing technologies*, pages 36–58. Springer, 2006.
2. I. Altman. *The Environment and Social Behavior: Privacy, Personal Space, Territory, and Crowding.* ERIC, 1975.
3. P. André, M. Bernstein, and K. Luther. Who gives a tweet?: evaluating microblog content value. In *Proc. CSCW 2012*, 2012.
4. L. Backstrom, E. Bakshy, J. Kleinberg, T. Lento, and I. Rosenn. Center of attention: How facebook users allocate attention across friends. In *Proc. ICWSM 2011*, 2011.
5. E. Bakshy, J. Hofman, W. Mason, and D. Watts. Everyone's an influencer: quantifying influence on twitter. In *Proc. WSDM 2011*, 2011.
6. E. Bakshy, I. Rosenn, C. Marlow, and L. Adamic. The role of social networks in information diffusion. In *Proceedings of the 21st international conference on World Wide Web*, WWW '12, 2012.
7. M. Bernstein, A. Marcus, D. Karger, and R. Miller. Enhancing directed content sharing on the web. In *Proc. CHI 2010*, 2010.
8. d. boyd. Friends, friendsters, and myspace top 8: Writing community into being on social network sites. *First Monday*, 11(12), 2006.
9. d. boyd. Social network sites: Public, private, or what? *Knowledge Tree*, 13(1):1–7, 2007.
10. M. Burke, C. Marlow, and T. Lento. Feed me: motivating newcomer contribution in social network sites. In *Proc. CHI 2009*, 2009.
11. K. Caine, L. Kisselburgh, and L. Lareau. Audience visualization influences disclosures in online social networks. In *Ext. Abst. CHI 2011*, 2011.
12. H. Clark and G. Murphy. Audience design in meaning and reference. *Advances in psychology*, 9:287–299, 1982.
13. S. Counts and K. Fisher. Taking it all in? visual attention in microblog consumption. *Proc. ICWSM 2011*, 2011.
14. N. Ellison et al. Social network sites: Definition, history, and scholarship. *Journal of Computer-Mediated Communication*, 13(1):210–230, 2007.
15. T. Erickson and W. Kellogg. Social translucence: an approach to designing systems that support social processes. *ACM TOCHI*, 7(1):59–83, 2000.
16. E. Gilbert. Designing social translucence over social networks. In *Proc. CHI 2012*, 2012.
17. E. Goffman. The presentation of self in everyday life. *Garden City, NY*, 1959.
18. S. Gosling, S. Gaddis, S. Vazire, et al. Personality impressions based on facebook profiles. In *Proc. ICWSM 2007*, 2007.

19. J. Hancock, J. Birnholtz, N. Bazarova, J. Guillory, J. Perlin, and B. Amos. Butler lies: awareness, deception and design. In *Proc. CHI 2009*, 2009.

20. B. Hogan. The presentation of self in the age of social media: distinguishing performances and exhibitions online. *Bulletin of Science, Technology & Society*, 30(6):377–386, 2010.

21. P. Killworth, E. Johnsen, H. Bernard, G. Ann Shelley, and C. McCarty. Estimating the size of personal networks. *Social Networks*, 12(4):289–312, 1990.

22. H. Kwak, H. Chun, and S. Moon. Fragile online relationship: a first look at unfollow dynamics in twitter. In *Proc. CHI 2011*, 2011.

23. C. Lampe, N. Ellison, and C. Steinfield. A familiar face (book): profile elements as signals in an online social network. In *Proc. CHI 2007*, 2007.

24. C. Lampe, N. Ellison, and C. Steinfield. Changes in use and perception of facebook. In *Proc. CSCW 2008*, 2008.

25. E. Lieberman and R. Miller. Facemail: showing faces of recipients to prevent misdirected email. In *Proc. SOUPS 2007*, 2007.

26. A. Marwick et al. I tweet honestly, i tweet passionately: Twitter users, context collapse, and the imagined audience. *New Media & Society*, 13(1):114–133, 2011.

27. C. McCarty, P. Killworth, H. Bernard, E. Johnsen, and G. Shelley. Comparing two methods for estimating network size. *Human Organization*, 60(1):28–39, 2001.

28. R. Metz. Friendster outs voyeurs. *Wired*, 2005.

29. B. Nonnecke and J. Preece. Lurker demographics: Counting the silent. In *Proc. CHI 2000*, 2000.

30. L. Palen and P. Dourish. Unpacking privacy for a networked world. In *Proc. CHI 2003*, 2003.

31. B. Suh, L. Hong, P. Pirolli, and E. Chi. Want to be retweeted? large scale analytics on factors impacting retweet in twitter network. In *Proc. SocialCom 2010*, 2010.

32. J. Y. Tsai, P. Kelley, P. Drielsma, L. F. Cranor, J. Hong, and N. Sadeh. Who's viewed you?: the impact of feedback in a mobile location-sharing application. In *Proc. CHI 2009*, 2009.

33. Z. Tufekci. Can you see me now? audience and disclosure regulation in online social network sites. *Bulletin of Science, Technology & Society*, 28(1):20–36, 2008.

34. Z. Tufekci. Facebook, youth and privacy in networked publics. In *Proc. ICWSM 2012*, 2012.

35. A. Tversky and D. Kahneman. Availability: A heuristic for judging frequency and probability. *Cognitive psychology*, 5(2):207–232, 1973.

36. J. Ugander, B. Karrer, L. Backstrom, and C. Marlow. The anatomy of the facebook social graph. *CoRR*, abs/1111.4503, 2011.

37. F. Viégas. Bloggers' expectations of privacy and accountability: An initial survey. *Journal of Computer-Mediated Communication*, 10(3), 2005.

38. F. Viégas and J. Donath. Chat circles. In *Proc. CHI 1999*, 1999.

39. A. Young and A. Quan-Haase. Information revelation and internet privacy concerns on social network sites: a case study of facebook. In *Proc. C&T 2009*, 2009.

Gender, Topic, and Audience Response: An Analysis of User-Generated Content on Facebook

Yi-Chia Wang
Language Technologies Institute
Carnegie Mellon University
yichiaw@cmu.edu

Moira Burke
Facebook
mburke@fb.com

Robert Kraut
Human-Computer Interaction Institute
Carnegie Mellon University
robert.kraut@cmu.edu

ABSTRACT
Although both men and women communicate frequently on Facebook, we know little about what they talk about, whether their topics differ and how their network responds. Using Latent Dirichlet Allocation (LDA), we identify topics from more than half a million Facebook status updates and determine which topics are more likely to receive feedback, such as likes and comments. Women tend to share more personal topics (e.g., family matters), while men discuss more public ones (e.g., politics and sports). Generally, women receive more feedback than men, but "male" topics (those more often posted by men) receive more feedback, especially when posted by women.

Author Keywords
Social networking sites; Facebook; computer-mediated communication; gender; topics; natural language analysis

ACM Classification Keywords
H.5.3 [Information Interfaces and Presentation]: Group and Organization Interfaces - Web-based interaction.

INTRODUCTION
The majority of Internet users participate in social networking sites (SNS) such as Facebook and Twitter, sharing personal stories, political views, and what they had for lunch [9]. Although users generate a large volume of text on SNS every day, we know little about this content and how user characteristics influence what they talk about. In this paper, we examine whether male and female Facebook users talk about different topics, and how their audiences respond.

There are longstanding differences in how men and women communicate [2, 14]. As early as 1922, researchers eavesdropping on conversations in the streets documented that women's conversations centered on people and relationships, while men's centered on work and money [2]. Though social roles and technology have changed, differences in how men and women speak persist. Computer-mediated communication (CMC) may remove many visual and temporal cues between writer and reader, but writers "give off" gender signals [7], both in discourse style—women are more supportive, use more emoticons, write shorter posts, and use less profanity—and in topic, with women writing about personal issues and men more likely to write about matters external to their lives [10, 11].

Most research on gender differences in CMC has been limited to adults. However, gender socialization starts in childhood, and identity formation is a major developmental challenge for teenagers. Therefore we expect that gender differences in language will not be the same among teens and adults. In the present work, we apply an automated, large-scale approach to examine topic differences between the sexes, including separate analyses of teens and adults, and aim to answer the following research question:

RQ1.How are gender differences in topics expressed among adults and teens on Facebook?

Next, we examine how audiences respond to these different topics. When users broadcast content on SNS, their friends and followers may leave feedback, such as @replies or "favorites" on Twitter, or comments and "likes" on Facebook. Previous research has shown that this kind of feedback has positive consequences for the users who receive it and for the site as a whole. For example, on Facebook, users who receive feedback perceive they have more social support [5] and share more content in the future [6]. How does the poster's language elicit responses? In newsgroups, a message's rhetorical strategy, language complexity, and word choice all influence whether others reply [1]. Polite posts receive more responses in technical groups, while rude ones spur more responses in political groups [4]. However, we know less about how topic is related to feedback. The popular press describes "annoying Facebookers" like the "The Let-Me-Tell-You-Every-Detail-of-My-Day Bore" and "The Sympathy-Baiter" [8]. Do the data support these stereotypes? Do audiences reward certain topics with positive feedback?

RQ2.Which topics are associated with greater audience responsiveness?

This paper consists of two parts. In order to understand what people talk about on SNS, we first applied machine learning to discover topics that characterize status updates on Facebook. We then examined topic differences between men and women, and the impact of topics on audience responsiveness.

CHI 2013, April 27–May 2, 2013, Paris, France.

METHOD

Data Collection

Facebook users share many kinds of content, including photos, links, location check-ins, private messages, songs played, and responses to the prompt, "What's on your mind?" The latter are known as status updates, and are the focus of the present work because they are text-based, directed at more than one friend, and have the potential to receive comments and likes, potential metrics of quality.

We randomly sampled one million English status updates posted by U.S. Facebook users in June 2012 from Facebook's server logs. For each status update, we analyzed metadata including post time, number of viewers, and number of comments and likes within three days of posting. We also collected demographic information about the poster, including gender, age, friend count, and days since the poster registered. The data processing procedures described below were validated by analyzing the authors' own status updates. All posts in the dataset were analyzed automatically and in aggregate on Facebook's servers according to Facebook's data use policy; models were then built from counts of topic terms, such as those in Table 1.

Text Processing and Topic Modeling

To identify the topics common in Facebook users' status updates, we applied Latent Dirichlet Allocation (LDA), a statistical generative method often used to discover hidden topics in documents and the words associated with each topic [3]. It analyzes large amounts of unlabeled documents by clustering words that frequently co-occur.

We went through several steps to pre-process and clean the data before constructing topic models. Our experience suggests that this pre-processing results in far superior topic models than those from raw data. Status updates were tokenized with the OpenNLP toolkit [12], stemmed with the Porter stemmer [13], and lowercased. We removed punctuations and replaced URLs, email addresses, and numbers with tags. Updates were then represented as an unordered set of unigrams (single words) and bigrams (word pairs).

Across all terms in the one million status updates, 71% of unigrams only appeared once, and 500 unigrams accounted for 55% of all text. For example, 10% of updates contained "love," the most frequent unigram. Because high frequencies terms like "love" co-occur with so many different terms they are not very useful in topic modeling. Similarly, very low frequency terms are not useful because they do not co-occur often enough with other terms. Therefore, we pruned high and low frequency unigrams and bigrams (those that occurred in more than 0.5% or less than 0.01% of the updates) to reduce noise and vocabulary size. In addition, we excluded 500 unigrams from a stoplist (e.g. "the" and "in"); bigrams were excluded if both words were stopwords. After pruning, approximately 50% of the status updates had fewer than eight unigrams or bigrams; these documents were too short for successful model training.

To identify topics, we built LDA topic models from the remaining 521,636 status updates, treating each as a document.

Topic	Sample Vocabulary
Sleep	last night, this morning, wake up, sleep, bed
Food	lunch, cook, coffee, beer, chicken, cake, ice cream
Clothing	shop, line, wear, store, cloth, dress, to put, bag
House	door, my house, cat, street, box, window, floor
Work	back to, to work, just got, decide, at work
Weather/travel	road, weather, cold, city, air, town, fly, storm
Family fun	great day, time with, kid, swim, cousin, evening
Girlfriend/boyfriend	best friend, a girl, red, boyfriend, my favorite
Birthday	I love, love you, my baby, happy birthday, bday
Father's Day	happy father, father day, children, my dad
Sports	beat, fan, ball, la, hello, king, ring, play, Miami
Politics	country, nation, American, president, vote, law
Love	my heart, gave, strong, love me, fill, in love, joy
Thankfulness	thank you, visit, my family, appreciate, thank god
Anticipation	wait for, celebrate, can't wait, until, camp, yay
Asking for support/prayers	my friend, worry about, help me, right now, continue, pray for, support, and family, I ask
Medical	drop, doctor, hospital, test, shot, blood, stress
Memorial	I miss, memory, everyday, peace, grandma, rip
Negativity about people	say, people who, judge, waste, some people, piss
Complaining	I hate, I guess, talk to, a lot, tried of, hate when
Deep thoughts	idea, success, human, create, sign, goal, universe
Christianity	the lord, faith, shall, church, christ, god is, spirit
Religious imagery	die, a man, star, death, born, angel, earth, the sun
Slang	wen, luv, bt, gud, tht, shock, knw, mi, coz, jst, plz
Swearing	if u, I wanna, when u, fake, fucking, fuck up, u know, a fuck, dumb, wanna go, dick, a bitch, shit

Table 1. Samples of vocabulary in LDA topic dictionaries

One of LDA's disadvantages is that there is no standard method for deciding model parameters. Typically researchers examine the output of different models and decide which one is more interpretable, which is the approach we took. We were able to interpret an LDA model with 50 latent topics better than models with 10, 30, 60, or 100 topics. We then generated dictionaries to represent each topic from the 500 terms most strongly associated with that topic. Two experts familiar with SNS content manually labeled each dictionary (e.g. *Food*). We also excluded were topics that judges could not interpret. Because the status updates were from a single month's text, several topics were clearly capturing popular short-term memes from that month and were excluded from analysis because of their limited generalizability. This left 25 topics. These topics with their top terms are shown in Table 1.

After constructing dictionaries to represent the 25 topics, we defined a status update as containing one of these topics if it contained at least three unigrams or bigrams from the corresponding dictionary. For example, the post: *"Weekend plans include camping, rafting, and total domination of the mud obstacle course. West Virginia, consider yourself warned."* would map to the *Weather/travel* topic because it contains the terms *raft*, *west*, *virginia*, and *warn*. By this definition, 50% of status updates had two topics. This dictionary-based approach can be applied quickly at scale.

RESULTS AND DISCUSSION

Topics of Status Updates

Figure 1(a) shows the percentage of status updates containing each of the 25 topics. This pattern suggests Facebook users frequently disclosed personal information (e.g. *Thankfulness*, *Asking for support*), talked about holidays and family events (*Father's day*, *Birthday*, *Family fun*), and waxed philosophical (*Deep thoughts*, *Christianity*). Although some topic representing details of daily life were common (*Work, Sleep*), most daily-life topics were less common (*House, Food*).

To understand how gender and age influence the topics people use on Facebook, we recalculated topic popularity–the percent of status updates containing each topic—separately for men, women, boys and girls. Fig 1(b) presents the differences in topic popularity for women and men aged 25 and older, ordered by overall topic popularity. Women's posts are disproportionately about relationships and personal details (*Father's Day, Family fun, Birthday, Anticipation*), while men are more likely to write about sports and abstract concepts, like *Politics, Deep thoughts*, and *Christianity* ($p < 0.001$ for each difference). Despite the differences in format and audience on SNS, this finding is consistent with previous work on gender differences in face-to-face communication and blogs.

Teens, on the other hand, were more homogeneous across genders. Figure 1(c) presents differences in topic popularity between teen girls and boys aged 13 to 17. In contrast to the adults shown in Fig 1(b), teens had fewer gender differences. For example, *Complaining, Girlfriend/Boyfriend*, and *Slang* were the most popular topics for both teen girls and boys. One possible explanation for the topic similarity among teens is that both genders are going through a common set of life stages, including defining relationships with romantic partners and peer groups. High school may be a common source of complaining and negativity. Teens use more slang, and so some of their similarity is stylistic, though their slang may be about semantically different topics. However, some patterns seen in adults are evident in teens, as well; teen girls are less likely to talk about sports, and boys are less likely to talk about family events.

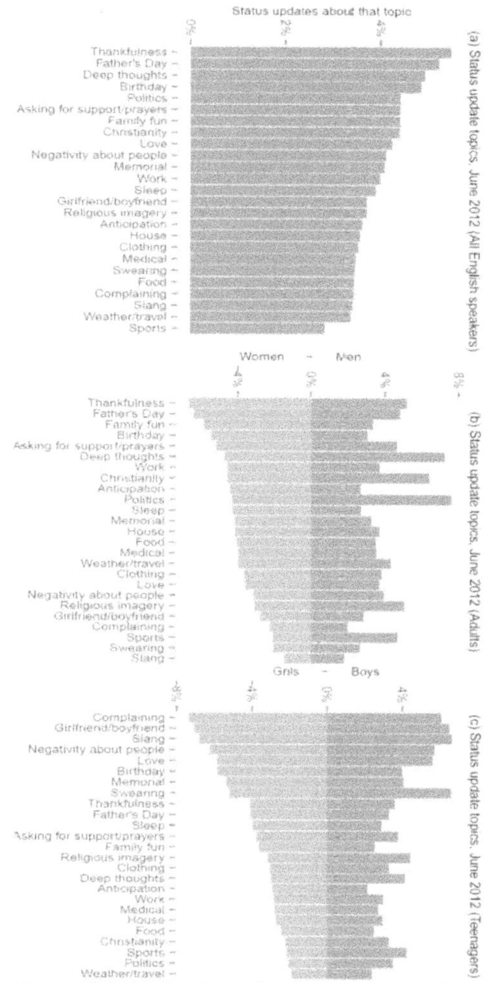

Figure 1. Distribution of status update topics

Gender, Topics and Audience Responsiveness

To determine whether certain topics generated more feedback and whether gender moderates that effect, we built a linear model of responsiveness, with the status update as the unit of analysis.

Audience responsiveness is the dependent variable, operationalized as the number of comments a status update received within three days of its post date. Because the distribution of responses was highly skewed, we used the logged number of comments, base 10, after adding a value of 1. Results are qualitatively similar using "likes" rather than comments, with some exceptions discussed below.

Each **topic** is a binary independent variable with one (1) indicating that a status update contained the topic or a zero otherwise (0). Because topic choice is not independent of the author's gender and age, we control for these features in the model as well as other variables known to be associated with responsiveness. For example, users with more friends tend to receive more responses, as do updates posted on weekdays. We also control for other demographics, including days since posters joined Facebook, their friend count and the average number of comments per post the posters received the prior week, a rough measure of the posters' popularity or interestingness. By controlling for these variables, we can make claims about the content of an update rather than about the poster. We also controlled for whether the post appeared on a weekday (1) or not (0), the number of times the update was seen, and the length of the update.

Table 2 presents results from the regression predicting responses. The intercept indicates a message with all variables at their means and all binary variables set to zero (in this case, an average-length update written by a woman on the weekend) would receive $(10^{.311})$-1 or 1.04 comments. Betas represent the effect on comments from a one-unit increase in continuous independent variables, or a binary variable having a value of 1. To make the results more interpretable, we include the estimated number of comments an update will receive. For example, Table 2 shows that males received .02 fewer comments than females. Older posters received more comments, as do longer posts and those on weekdays. The number of comments posters previously received was highly predictive, suggesting that users who had written posts that elicited many responses in the past continue to write evocative content, or that audiences that tend to be responsive one week continue to be responsive the next. Posts that receive more views receive more comments, a cyclical relationship related to the site's algorithmic ranking of content, such that posts that receive comments are more likely to be shown to more people, resulting in even more comments. After controlling for the number of times a post was viewed, poster friend count is negatively correlated with comments.

Topics are listed in order of comments received, with *Medical* posts receiving the most feedback and *Christianity* receiving the least. All topics shown in Figure 1 were included in the regression, but only those with absolute beta values greater than 0.025 and statistically significant at the $p < 0.001$ level are included in Table 2. An otherwise average post *Asking for support or prayers* received 1.17 comments, while an average post about *Sleep* received only 0.83 comments (30% fewer). While the results were qualitatively similar when likes rather than comments was the dependent variable, there are some exceptions: negatively-valenced topics, such as *Medical*, re associated with fewer likes. Abstract topics, like *Love* and *Christianity*, get more likes but fewer comments, possibly because audiences don't know how to respond to but still want to show support.

To identify whether gender moderates the relationship between topic and responsiveness, we calculated a *maleness score* for each topic, the ratio of the percent of status updates written by men containing that topic to the percent of status updates written by women containing that topic. By separately normalizing by the number of updates posted by men and women, this score accounts for women posting twice as many updates as men. The maleness score for a post is the average maleness score for all of the post's topics. The interaction in Table 2 between the poster's gender and the post's maleness score shows that although men generally receive fewer comments than women, "male" topics generally receive more comments, and the effect is slightly greater for female posters.

CONCLUSION

This study demonstrates gender differences in the topics of status updates on SNS. Adult women are more likely to write about personal topics, while men are more likely to write about philosophical topics. For teens, the gender differences are muted. Although men get fewer comments than women, "masculine" topics receive more comments. One interpretation is that women are more likely to attract attention when subtly defying gender expectations.

One limitation of this work is that LDA automatically generates "topics" from words that frequently co-occur, but this may not capture "topics" in a deeper linguistic sense, as might be captured by human judges manually annotating a smaller corpus. Furthermore, LDA does not distinguish between style (e.g., *Slang*) and substance (*Medical*) "topics." However, the method can be applied at scale and the resulting topics are meaningful, as seen in Table 1. This work also does not consider audience composition; men and women may *respond* differently to topics. More generalizable topics may be generated from a longer data collection period than one month.

Our findings have several implications. They show that certain topics evoke more feedback (e.g. *Asking for support*), while others elicit less (e.g. *Sleep*). To promote interaction, ranking algorithms could promote topics that viewers are more likely to respond to. Furthermore, the correlation between topic and feedback suggests that assisting individuals with content construction might improve their experiences on SNS.

		Comments received [1]		
		Beta	Std. Err.	Est. # of Comments
Controls	(Intercept)	0.311 ***	0.001	1.04
	Male	-0.006 ***	0.001	1.02
	Age (years) [3]	0.030 ***	0.001	1.19
	Days since registration [3]	0.010 ***	0.001	1.09
	Friend count [2]	-0.048 ***	0.001	0.83
	Comments per prev. post [2]	0.066 ***	0.001	1.38
	IsWeekday	0.045 ***	0.001	1.27
	Post views [2]	0.134 ***	0.001	1.78
	Post length (words) [2]	0.025 ***	0.001	1.17
Topics	Medical	0.084 ***	0.002	1.48
	Swearing	0.028 ***	0.002	1.18
	House	0.028 ***	0.002	1.18
	Asking for support/prayers	0.026 ***	0.002	1.17
	Deep thoughts	-0.031 ***	0.002	0.90
	Family fun	-0.032 ***	0.002	0.90
	Religious imagery	-0.042 ***	0.002	0.86
	Love	-0.047 ***	0.002	0.83
	Sleep	-0.047 ***	0.002	0.83
	Christianity	-0.069 ***	0.002	0.75
	Maleness score of post [3]	0.006 ***	0.001	1.07
	Male * Maleness score	-0.003 **	0.001	1.03

1: Logged (base 10) 2: Logged (base 10), standardized, centered
3: standardized and centered. *p<0.05, **p<0.01, ***p<0.001

Table 2. Linear regression predicting comments on Facebook status updates based on topic.

REFERENCES

1. Arguello, J., Butler, B., Joyce, E., Kraut, R., Ling, K. S., & Wang, X. (2006). Talk to me: foundations for successful individual-group interactions in online communities. In *CHI 2006*, 959-968.
2. Bischoping, K. (1993). Gender differences in conversation topics, 1922-1990. *Sex Roles*, 28, 1-18.
3. Blei, David M., Ng, Andrew Y., & Jordan, Michael I. (2003). Latent Dirichlet allocation. *Journal of Machine Learning Research*, *3*(Jan), 993-1022.
4. Burke, M. and Kraut, R. (2008). Mind your Ps and Qs: The impact of politeness and rudeness in online communities. In *CSCW 2008*, 281-284.
5. Burke, M., Kraut, R., & Marlow, C. (2011). Social capital on Facebook: Differentiating uses and users. In *CHI 2011*, 571-580.
6. Burke, M., Marlow, C., and Lento, T. (2009). Feed me: Motivating newcomer contribution in social network sites. In *CHI 2009*, 945-954.
7. Goffman, E. (1959). *The presentation of self in everyday life*. Garden City, NY.
8. Griggs, B. (2008). The 12 most annoying types of Facebooker. *CNN*. Retrieved September 18, 2012, from http://edition.cnn.com/2009/TECH/08/20/annoying.facebook.updaters/
9. Hampton, K. N., Sessions, L., & Her, E. J. (2011). Core networks, social isolation, and new media: How Internet and mobile phone use is related to network size and diversity. *Information, Communication & Society*, *14*(1).
10. Herring, S.C. (2000). Gender differences in CMC: Findings and implications. *Computer Professionals for Social Responsibility Journal*, Winter.
11. Herring, S. C., & Paolillo, J. C. (2006). Gender and genre variation in weblogs. *Journal of Sociolinguistics*, *10*(4), 439-459.
12. OpenSource. (2010). OpenNLP: http://opennlp.apache.org.
13. PorterStemmer: http://tartarus.org/martin/PorterStemmer.
14. Tannen, D. (1990). *You just don't understand: Women and men in conversation*. Ballantine, NY: Morrow.

Using Contextual Integrity to Examine Interpersonal Information Boundary on Social Network Sites

Pan Shi
The Pennsylvania State University
University Park, PA 16802
pzs125@ist.psu.edu

Heng Xu
The Pennsylvania State University
University Park, PA 16802
hxu@ist.psu.edu

Yunan Chen
University of California,
Irvine, CA 92697
yunanc@ics.uci.edu

ABSTRACT
Although privacy problems in Social Network Sites (SNS) have become more salient than ever in recent years, interpersonal privacy issues remain relatively understudied. This study aims to generate insights in understanding users' interpersonal privacy concerns by expounding interpersonal information boundaries in SNS. Through a case analysis of Friendship Pages on Facebook, this paper identifies users' interpersonal privacy concerns that are rooted from informational norms outlined in the theory of contextual integrity, as well as the tensions that occur within and cross these informational norms. This paper concludes with a discussion of design implications and future research.

Keywords
Interpersonal privacy issues; Social network sites (SNS); Privacy boundary; Facebook; Friendship Pages.

ACM Classification Keywords
K.4.1 [Public Policy Issues]: Privacy; H.1.2 [User/Machine Systems]: Human factors.

INTRODUCTION
Social Network Sites (SNS) are platforms that provide users with various features to facilitate social connectivity, active content sharing, and relationship development. Over 800 million users are currently active on Facebook and are constantly generating contents that may not only disclose their own information but also reveal the identities of their friends (e.g., tagging a friend in a status update or photo or place checked-in). Such highly interactive nature of interpersonal communication and data exchange impels us to think about privacy as a communal matter. This is because a user's identity can be easily exposed by contents generated or tagged by his or her friends, and vice versa. Therefore, users' personal information could be easily leaked through their friends' information sharing and cross-referencing actions on SNS [10]. The need for interpersonal privacy management arises due to the inability to monitor friends (i.e., co-owners of shared information) and their behaviors on SNS.

A growing body of privacy research in HCI has studied the *behavioral* and *technological* mechanisms for users to enact interpersonal privacy practices for co-managing shared contents [e.g., 3, 7, 14]. For example, Lampinen et al. [7] identify *behavioral* means to collectively manage users' shared information, *e.g.*, negotiating "rules of thumb" or asking for approval before disclosing content from those involved. In terms of *technological* mechanisms, privacy researchers have proposed technical tools associated with interpersonal privacy management [e.g., 6, 13].

Although research has touched interpersonal privacy issues in terms of *how* users react and *what* their privacy practices (via behavioral and technological mechanisms) could be, Barkhuus [2] notes that few studies in HCI have explored *why* users reacted the way they behaved. According to Barkhuus [2], research that addresses *why* is increasingly important because it is rare to see studies that collect in-situ data from implemented real systems. To respond to such compelling call for "contextually-grounded research that explores privacy issues in the wild" [2, p.8], we aim to examine the underlying contextually grounded reasons or triggers for users' interpersonal privacy concerns in SNS. Specifically, we obtained data from users' comments posted on Facebook's official blog[1] to study interpersonal privacy issues mediated through the use of a particular feature – Friendship Pages on Facebook.

CONTEXTUAL INTEGRITY
The theory of *contextual integrity* is particularly useful to understand privacy expectations and the norms of information transmission in a given context [8]. Nissenbaum [8] suggests that information ought to be distributed and protected according to norms governing distinct social contexts. Four key parameters are proposed to conceptualize context-relative information norms [8]: *contexts* are the situations in which the information flows occur; *actors* including senders of information, recipients

[1] Facebook Blog serves not only as a public platform for introducing new features and announcing significant events, but also enables users to discuss and give feedbacks towards these announcements. Prior to the data collection, we carefully reviewed and agreed to Facebook's Terms: http://www.facebook.com/apps/site_scraping_tos.php

of information, and information subject (whom the information is about); *attributes* are defined as the types of information in the information flow; *transmission principles* are the constraints to the information flow from one party to another in a given context.

In this paper, we base our argument on the theory of contextual integrity [8] because it ties the notion of privacy to *"norms of specific contexts, demanding that information gathering and dissemination be appropriate to that context and obey the governing norms of distribution within it*" (p.101). According to Nissenbaum [8], what people really care about when they complain and protest that privacy has been violated is not the act of sharing information itself, but the inappropriate handling of shared information.

RESEARCH CONTEXT AND METHOD

In Oct 2010, Facebook introduced the Friendship Page, which aggregated two friends' social interactions including their wall posts, common tagged photos, comments they share, things they both like, events they attended together, and mutual friend lists (see Figure 1). We chose this feature as a crucible to study users' interpersonal privacy concerns because we believe that it is a representative artifact which can reveal dynamism inherent in users' interpersonal interactions and information sharing.

We conducted a qualitative analysis of user comments posted on Facebook's official blog in response to its release of Friendship Pages [1]. We believe that analyzing user comments posted on Facebook's blog allowed us to not only get data from real users but also explore the contextually grounded reasons explaining users' interpersonal privacy concerns and reactions mediated through their actual use of Friendship Pages. We downloaded a total of 1463 comments users made on the topic of Friendship Pages between Oct 28th, 2010 to Jan 14th, 2011 [1] using an API provided by Facebook. To ensure the reliability of our findings, two researchers independently reviewed these comments and extracted privacy related comments for in-depth coding. For the initial round of data analysis, an open coding approach was adopted to identify new concepts arisen from the data. We then used an iterative coding process of collapsing our first round of codes into conceptually distinct themes.

FINDINGS

Our results describe users' interpersonal privacy concerns that can be aligned with the key parameters outlined in the theory of contextual integrity. Our findings indicate that violations or changes of *contexts*, *actors*, *attributes* and *transmission principles* in context-relative information norms could result in users' interpersonal privacy concerns.

Contexts

According to Nissenbaum [8], the parameter of *contexts* in contextual integrity refers to the circumstances in which information flows are situated. In our dataset, it seemed clear that before the introduction of Friendship Pages, the contextual norms of information flows were in place regarding whom users expected to view their interpersonal information.

Figure 1. Illustration of a Friendship Page on Facebook

This communally understood information boundary was blurred after the introduction of Friendship Pages. For example, users indicated their concerns on potential misperceptions of information flows: "*...the extraction and condensation [of information] can cast the comments and posts in a different light from what I intended.*" Further, some users worried about potential negative consequences of using this feature and thus complained: "*Thank you facebook ... for the dawning of a new era where a new boyfriend and girlfriend will haunt the 'relationships' of their exes and their new partner's exes.*"

These user comments illustrate Nissenbaum's sense that appropriating information from one situation and introducing it in another can be perceived as a privacy violation by users. Such violation of social appropriateness is rooted from the problem which Boyle and Greenberg [4] called *decontexualization* of interpersonal interactions. In the case of Friendship Pages, when examining a short segment of a conversation between two friends, viewers often have to invent contextual information for appropriate interpretation. The inability to obtain the contexts in which conversations and interactions took place could lead to misinterpretation or even wilful distortion of the relationship information displayed on Friendship Pages, which may raise a user's concern about one's own image and privacy pertaining to interactions with others.

Transmission Principles

According to Nissenbaum [8], the violation of transmission principles often happens when new practices entail a change in the process of information transmission, or when shared information travels beyond the desired boundary. In our case of Friendship Pages, users pointed out that this new feature interrupted their expected flow of personal information: "*Suddenly all of my interaction with a specific person is subject to scrutiny by uninvited guests, all on one convenient page.*" Although most users were aware of the fact that the visibility of information shown on Friendship Pages would be determined by their own privacy settings, they still expressed their worries about the information aggregation practice employed by Friendship Pages: "*I understand that all of this is visible anyway, but putting it all in one place is too much, especially since you can view two other people, and not just your own relationships...*"

Interestingly, although the Friendship Page did not reveal any new information, its new activity of chronicling the history of social interactions between two friends widely triggered users' privacy concerns. This is because the new practice of combining information could entail changes in the information flow. As Solove notes: "a difference in quantity becomes a difference in quality—it enhances the risk of the harms of disclosure" [12, p.537]. Aggregating interpersonal information on a single and accessible page could result in synergies that can potentially reveal more details about a person and his or her social ties in new and unexpected ways.

Actors and Attributes

Among all parameters outlined in the theory of contextual integrity, *actors*' roles are among those most influential factors that can directly affect people's perceptions over whether privacy has been violated or properly respected [8]. In the case of launching Friendship Page, making friendship information visible to those who were not involved in that interaction raised users' concerns on unwanted recipients of Friendship Page (i.e., inappropriate actors), which may violate users' privacy expectations. For example, one user commented: "*If it was just a relationship between ME AND MY FRIEND I would be totally stcked. I do not like that I can see relationships between other friends. Nor do I like that they can see relationships between me and other friends all in one place like that. Please fix this.*"

According to Nissenbaum [8], the parameter of *attributes* in contextual integrity circumscribes how different types of information should be revealed or shared in a particular context. It has been found in prior research that individuals hold different sensitivity levels for different types of information [11]. Our results showed that users' comfort levels for having different types of information to be displayed on their Friendship Pages were very different. For example, some users expressed their specific concerns on displaying common events and photos: "*How can I disable this [feature] so people are NOT able to research which events I attended together with another friend or which photos we're jointly tagged in?*"

In addition, our findings suggest that failing to maintain the *temporal boundary* of interpersonal privacy could lead to the breach of context-relative information norms. According to Palen and Dourish [9], temporal boundaries are associated with possible tensions between *actions* on revealed information and *interpretations* of revealed information along the timeline. In the case of Friendship Page, threats to temporal boundaries are due to the persistence of data to which the access can be made in the future. For example, one user complained: "*There is no way of deleting two year old posts on ex's wall. I do not like being reminded of this sh**.*" Thus, future accessibility to disclosed information creates tension in boundary management of interpersonal privacy by prompting concerns on undesired use and interpretation after the initial disclosure.

DISCUSSION AND CONCLUSION

The case of Friendship Page indicates that violations or changes of *contexts, actors, attributes* and *transmission principles* in context-relative information norms could result in users' interpersonal privacy concerns. Besides voicing their explicit concerns on privacy, users directly expressed their emotional reactions by describing the feature as: *creepy, scary, disgusting*, or *invasive*. Some rational users asked for more privacy enhancing features such as an opt-out option or a turn-off button.

Nevertheless, without having control over their Friendship Pages, many users expressed their intentions to leave Facebook, deactivate accounts, delete profiles, and use less frequently. For example, one user complained: *"...i have begun deleting my photos online, and have untagged myself and all of my friends."*

This work demonstrates the theoretical contribution of the contextual integrity of privacy to the understanding of tensions or conflicts that a user faces when creating contents that may connect with others' identities. The question of *how* this understanding can be turned into powerful but flexible designs of privacy enhancing features is still a challenge. We argue that it is crucial to align the design of privacy enhancing features with users' privacy needs and information access in *context*. Towards this end, future research should consider the approach of *Privacy by ReDesign* [5]. This approach suggests that it is not always possible to design appropriate privacy enhancing features from the outset; instead, the design should be based on an understanding of the actual system-in-use embedded in a user's daily behaviors.

In conclusion, this qualitative study of users' comments on the launch of Friendship Page on Facebook provides preliminary insights in understanding users' interpersonal privacy concerns. Our work sheds light on future research to investigate the problem of interpersonal privacy that lies beneath social and technical specifications of interpersonal information disclosure and privacy management. We are continuing this research from two perspectives: *measurement* and *design*. First, privacy measurement has focused more on emphasizing informational privacy concerns at the individual level [11] and is less effective at capturing interpersonal and interactional privacy concerns. We are in the process of extending and validating the components of interpersonal and interactional privacy concerns through a large-scale survey. Second, this work has straightforward and practical significance for re-designing existing privacy enhancing features or privacy settings on Facebook. The interpersonal and interactional dynamics we identified in this work should be embedded in context-relative information norms, as they reveal the ways in which existing privacy features could be designed to align with users' understandings and behaviors in *context*.

ACKNOWLEDGMENTS

The authors are very grateful to the AC and anonymous reviewers for their constructive comments on an earlier version of this manuscript. The authors gratefully acknowledge the financial support of the U.S. National Science Foundation under grant CNS-0953749. Any opinions, conclusions or recommendations expressed in this material are those of the authors and do not necessarily reflect the views of the National Science Foundation.

REFERENCES

1. Telling the Story of Friendships. *Facebook Blog* (2010), online available at: http://blog.facebook.com/blog.php?post=443390892130
2. Barkhuus, L. The mismeasurement of privacy: using contextual integrity to reconsider privacy in HCI. *Proc. CHI 2012*, ACM (2012), 367-376.
3. Besmer, A. and Lipford, H. Moving Beyond Untagging: Photo Privacy in a Tagged World. *Proc. CHI 2010*, ACM (2010), 1563-1572.
4. Boyle, M. and Greenberg, S. The language of privacy: learning from video media space analysis and design. *ACM Transactions on Computer-Human Interaction, 12*, 2 (2005), 328-370.
5. Cavoukian, A. and Prosch, M. *Privacy by ReDesign: Building a Better Legacy*. 2011.
6. Kolter, J., Kernchen, T. and Pernul, G. Collaborative Privacy Management. *Computers & Security, 29*, 5 (2010), 580-591.
7. Lampinen, A., Lehtinen, V., Lehmuskallio, A. and Tamminen, S. We're in it Together: Interpersonal Management of Disclosure in Social Network Services. *Proc. CHI 2011*, ACM (2011), 3217-3226.
8. Nissenbaum, H. *Privacy in Context: Technology, Policy, and the Integrity of Social Life*. Stanford Law Books, 2010.
9. Palen, L. and Dourish, P. Unpacking "privacy" for a networked world. *Proc. CHI 2003*, ACM Press (2003), 129-136.
10. Pesce, J. P., Casas, D. L., Rauber, G. and Almeida, V. Privacy Attacks in Social Media Using Photo Tagging Networks: A Case Study with Facebook. *Workshop on Privacy and Security in Online Social Media*, ACM (2012), Article 4.
11. Smith, H. J., Dinev, T. and Xu, H. Information Privacy Research: An Interdisciplinary Review. *MIS Quarterly, 35*, 4 (2011), 989-1015.
12. Solove, D., J. A Taxonomy of Privacy. *University of Pennsylvania Law Review, 154*, 3 (2006), 477-560.
13. Squicciarini, C. A., Xu, H. and Zhang, X. CoPE: Enabling Collaborative Privacy Management in Online Social Networks. *Journal of the American Society for Information Science and Technology 62*, 3 (2011), 521-534.
14. Wisniewski, P., Lipford, H. and Wilson, D. Fighting for my space: Coping mechanisms for SNS boundary regulation. *Proc. CHI 2012*, ACM (2012), 609-618.

Older Adults as Digital Content Producers

Jenny Waycott[1] Frank Vetere[1] Sonja Pedell[2] Lars Kulik[1] Elizabeth Ozanne[3] Alan Gruner[4] John Downs[1]

[1] Department of Computing and Information Systems, The University of Melbourne, Australia, [jwaycott, f.vetere, lkulik, jpdowns]@unimelb.edu.au

[2] Faculty of Design, Swinburne University of Technology, Australia, spedell@swin.edu.au

[3] Department of Social Work, The University of Melbourne, Australia, eao@unimelb.edu.au

[4] Benetas Aged Care Services, Melbourne, Australia, agruner@benetas.com.au

ABSTRACT

Older adults are normally characterized as consumers, rather than producers, of digital content. Current research concerning the design of technologies for older adults typically focuses on providing access to digital resources. Access is important, but is often insufficient, especially when establishing new social relationships. This paper investigates the nature and role of digital content that has been created by older adults, for the purpose of forging new relationships. We present a unique field study in which seven older adults (aged 71-92 years), who did not know each other, used a prototype iPad application (*Enmesh*) to create and share photographs and messages. The findings demonstrate that older adults, even those in the "oldest old" age group, embraced opportunities to express themselves creatively through digital content production. We show that self-expression and social engagement with peers can be realized when socio-technical systems are suitably designed to allow older adults to create and share their own digital content.

Author Keywords

Older Adults; User-Generated Content; Social Connection

ACM Classification Keywords

H.5.m. Information interfaces and presentation (e.g., HCI): Miscellaneous.

INTRODUCTION

User-generated content has been the subject of much research and discourse in recent years. Most of this research has focused on young people, with older adults either overlooked or characterized as consumers, rather than active producers of content [1]. Even social technologies designed specifically for older adults often prioritize functions that allow users to easily *access* content produced by others, rather than to create and share their own digital media [e.g., 4, 6, 28].

CHI'13, April 27 – May 2, 2013, Paris, France.

In this paper we demonstrate that creating and sharing personally meaningful digital content helps older adults build connections with their peers. Research into older adults' communication preferences suggests a need for social technologies that enable older people to express their individuality and to actively engage in reciprocal communications with others [14, 21]. While there has been some development in this area, with new tools encouraging older adults to share information with remote family members [e.g., 15], there has been little research exploring digital content production as a means for older adults to build new connections with their peers. Concerns about social isolation among older people, particularly for those who live independently with diminishing social networks and few opportunities to meet others, makes this an important area for research and development [6].

Our research contributes to a growing body of literature concerned with the design of technologies for older users. Much of this literature has focused on engaging older adults in participatory design [16, 30], evaluating older users' interactions with different interfaces [10, 26], or understanding older adults' attitudes towards new technologies [1, 13]. In this paper, we focus on older adults as content producers. This research builds on earlier work that developed a photo-sharing application to support grandparent and grandchild communications [29]. Here, we extend that work and introduce a new application for the iPad, *Enmesh*, that aims to support older adults build new connections within small peer communities.

We begin with a review of the relevant literature that has trialed social technologies for older adults and examined older adults' experiences and attitudes towards digital content production. We then describe the Enmesh application and present the results of a field study in which a small group of older adults, mostly aged in their 80s and 90s, used Enmesh to create and share digital photographs and messages. The findings demonstrate that digital content production provides older adults with opportunities to engage with others and share stories about their lives in personal and creative ways.

SOCIAL TECHNOLOGIES FOR OLDER ADULTS

There is a growing interest in the design of social technologies for older users. This is motivated, in part, by an underlying aim to address the needs of an ageing population, including helping to alleviate older people's experience of social isolation [4, 6, 8]. Much of the work in this field focuses on the use of technologies *to strengthen existing social connections*. For example, older adults who are housebound or living in nursing homes have been provided with digital photo frames so that family members can send photographs and messages to their relatives [4, 28]. However, older adults who are socially isolated may not have family and friends to communicate with. It is therefore important to also consider how technologies can be best used *to help older adults forge new social connections*.

One recent development in this field is found in the *Building Bridges* project [6]. Researchers developed and trialed a communication device used to build connections within a group of older adults who did not know each other. The design prioritized methods of communication that were familiar to older users, such as the telephone. Participants were given the opportunity to listen to audio content that was broadcast simultaneously on all participants' devices. They were then able to join group telephone conversations to discuss the broadcasts. The device included a facility to create and send text messages and, according to a post-trial survey, this was the most popular feature. However, users were frustrated by the space allowed for their messages (160 characters) and were limited by privacy restrictions. Feedback suggested participants would have welcomed the opportunity to share personal information and to meet each other in person to build rapport with others.

Another example is the *Photostroller* for use by residents in an aged care home [7]. The Photostroller is a movable device, configured to display photographs streamed from the *Flickr* website in response to pre-programmed keywords. Although used in a nursing home environment where participants were co-located, one of the underlying aims of the device was to build social connections between strangers. An ethnographic study of the nursing home setting revealed that residents had vastly different personal histories and limited shared interests, rarely engaging with each other during their daily activities. A trial of the Photostroller revealed that it was successful in building connections: nursing home residents often viewed the content together, responding to the photographs with stories about their own life histories.

These are good examples of technologies that help older adults build new social connections. However they tend to prioritize consumption, rather than production of content. Even the Building Bridges project, which did provide the opportunity for users to create and send messages, aimed primarily to build connections through the shared experience of listening to audio broadcasts and talking on the telephone. The text messaging feature was popular, but was primarily used to arrange telephone conversations. The participants expressed a desire to share personal information in order to build connections with the others. This finding suggests a need for further work to examine the role of content creation and sharing in helping older adults to build new social connections.

A growing body of research suggests that producing and sharing digital content can provide older adults with important opportunities to express themselves and communicate with others in creative and meaningful ways. We discuss this body of work below.

OLDER ADULTS AS CONTENT PRODUCERS

While older adults are not usually perceived as creators of digital content, they are becoming increasingly active online [3]. There are numerous online discussion groups that cater for older people. Content analyses of these communities have revealed they provide an intellectual and creative outlet for many users [20]. A qualitative study by Burmeister [2] also found that online communities provide an important forum for older adults to share information about common life experiences (e.g., retirement, bereavement, health difficulties), helping to create a mutually supportive community. The older people interviewed in Burmeister's study valued the feeling of belonging that they got from contributing to the online community. They viewed this as similar in nature to a neighborhood community.

Karahasanovic and colleagues [12] focused on an existing neighborhood community in an ethnographic study that aimed to explore how older adults could potentially engage in the co-creation of online content. The authors found that digital content production could provide important opportunities for this group of participants, who participated in "collective memory" storytelling about their neighborhood and demonstrated a desire to express themselves through user-generated content.

A case study of a video blogger by a man in his 80s clearly demonstrates the opportunities for sharing and reflecting on life experiences that can arise when older adults produce and share content [11]. Harley and Fitzpatrick analyzed eight YouTube clips posted by Peter Oakley (*Geriatric 1927*). Peter's video blogs described his experiences in World War II, his family life, career, and lifelong interest in motorbikes. Producing and sharing content appeared to enhance Peter's social connectedness, providing an opportunity for him to engage with a global intergenerational audience. The viewers, who ranged in age from 14 to 56 years, were supportive, sometimes asking questions of Peter or encouraging him to tell more about particular aspects of his life.

While Harley and Fitzpatrick's research provided an interesting profile of an older adult who successfully produced and published content openly on the Web, it is unlikely that Peter is typical of other older technology users. Studies have shown that older adults tend to view social media as youth-oriented spaces, used for frivolous and self-promoting activities [e.g., 1, 13, 32]. Bloch and Bruce observed an apparent disconnect from online participation among older adults. Their interviewees, aged 62 to 84, described using the Internet for consuming information (e.g., reading newspapers, accessing health information), but not for producing content. They argued that limited online participation puts older adults at risk of disengagement from "democratic life", suggesting a need for research "to understand better what is involved in making online activity [for older users] go from passive consumption to active participation" [1, p. 6].

Researchers have also demonstrated that older adults may be reluctant to share content publicly online [8, 32]. For instance, Gibson and colleagues presented various social networking sites to groups of older people and conducted focus group discussions to gauge participants' perceptions of the sites. They found their participants were resistant to using online social networking; they were concerned about exposure and preferred to maintain privacy [8].

If older adults are to become digital content producers as well as consumers, then, it is necessary to provide tools enabling them to easily create and share content in nonthreatening and supportive environments. One such environment is within the family. There has been much research and development in recent years examining the use of technologies by older adults to share information with younger family members [23, 25, 29]. For example, the *Wayve* device was trialed in the homes of an older couple, their adult children, and their grandchildren [15]. The device was used to display and send photographs, text messages, handwritten notes and drawings. The findings demonstrated that the grandfather, in particular, embraced the opportunity to produce content to share with his family. Many of the messages he sent to his grandchildren were creative and playful, a finding that aligns well with earlier research demonstrating how technology can mediate playful interactions between grandparents and grandchildren [29].

One of the key features of Wayve was that the sent messages and photographs were displayed prominently on the device, promoting serendipitous engagement with the content as users walked past the display. The display also appeared to fuel participants' creative efforts. That is, knowing their contributions would be viewed by significant others inspired a creative approach to content production. Other researchers have also noted the importance of prominent displays for encouraging and shaping content production [17, 22].

The studies reviewed here demonstrate that social engagement is possible when older adults produce and share content in two contexts. Firstly, older adults have used technologies to produce content for familiar audiences (in the context of family communications). Secondly, there are studies of older adults who produce content for a wider audience (mostly strangers) via publicly available forums. However, as noted above, research has shown that some older adults may be reluctant to share information publicly online. Existing research has yet to examine the role of user-generated digital content for enabling older adults to create new relationships. In this paper we examine how new social connections can be forged when older adults create images and text messages to share with each other, using a specially designed touch tablet application.

ENMESH: ENGAGEMENT THROUGH MEDIA SHARING

Our prototype iPad application, Enmesh (ENgagement through MEdia SHaring), was designed for use by older adults to create and share photographs and messages. The choice of the iPad was based, in part, on the fact that older adults tend to find touch-screen interfaces more accessible than other input devices such as a mouse or keyboard [18]. The iPad provides Internet connectivity and has an inbuilt camera and keyboard, making it ideal as a vehicle for both capturing and exchanging photographs and messages.

Enmesh features a unique interactive display (Figure 1). The photographs and messages float down the iPad screen in a cascading motion. The appearance of items is controlled by a semi-random algorithm that displays recent items more frequently and older items less often.

Figure 1. The Enmesh display

Figure 2. Interfaces for taking photographs and writing messages

All those connected to the Enmesh network can see the same configuration of photographs and messages as they move down their individual iPad screens. People can move objects around the screen, reduce or enlarge them, and temporarily remove them from the display by "flicking" them to the side with a swiping motion. Importantly, these movements are visible to all other users viewing the display. When a person touches a photograph or message, a label appears on its border saying "touched by [user's name]". By making these interactions visible to other users, we hoped to build a sense of social presence within the user community. The display is controlled by a central server. If two users try to move a photograph at the same time, the server will use the most recent information. As a result, only one user can effectively manipulate an object on the display at a time.

Users can create and send photographs and messages by tapping on a "+" symbol at the bottom of the screen. A dialogue box then provides the option of taking a photograph, writing a message, or both (Figure 2). When a photograph or message has been recorded, users can press "send" to upload the content to the shared display.

FIELD STUDY

Enmesh was trialed with a group of seven older adults, aged between 71 and 92, who lived in their own homes. They were all clients of a local aged care provider and received regular visits from a care manager. None of the participants knew each other prior to the study. They were selected to participate because they had been identified by their care managers as being, or at risk of being, socially isolated. Two care managers also took part in the trial, using Enmesh to view the content their clients had shared, and to share their own photographs and messages.

Participants

Seven older adults participated in our study. Some details about the participants are provided below, with pseudonyms used to identify each participant:

Betty (88) lives alone, with no children or surviving siblings. She has no computer, but admires her friends' use of the Internet.

Charlotte (77) lives with her disabled daughter and has several health problems. She has never used a computer.

Donald (85) lives alone. His daughter and grandchildren live overseas. His daughter bought him a new computer primarily for Skype, but he finds it hard to use.

Emma (89) lives with her 95-year old husband. They have some family living nearby. Emma has a computer but rarely uses it.

John (92) is a widower who lives alone. His family visits occasionally. He uses an old computer for email.

Lynne (71) lives alone and regularly visits her 94-year old husband in residential care. She has a computer and uses it for emails and information access via the Internet.

Sophie (92) lives alone and has no children. She regularly visits her sister and spends time with nieces and nephews. Sophie has never used a computer or keyboard before.

Procedure

The trial took place over three months. Each participant was provided with an iPad. At the start of the trial, a researcher visited participants to show them how to use Enmesh. For the first two weeks, participants used Enmesh to share photographs and messages with their care managers only.

After two weeks participants had the opportunity to meet each other at a social event. From this point, all participants were connected to each other, with the display showing everyone's messages and photographs. A second social event was held after six weeks and a third at the end of the trial. These gatherings gave participants the opportunity to build rapport through face-to-face contact, and also helped to build participants' confidence and engage them in the research and evaluation process [31].

Data Collection and Analysis

Interviews

The participants (older adults) were interviewed three times: at the start, middle, and end of the trial. One participant withdrew due to health problems and was only interviewed once. Care managers were interviewed at the end of the study, although their responses are not reported here. In this paper we are interested in the motivations and outcomes of user-generated digital content for older adults. We therefore focus on comments made by older adults during the final interviews.

The interviews followed a semi-structured format, asking participants to reflect on their experiences of taking part in the study and using the Enmesh application. Key themes were identified through a thematic analysis. Here we focus on comments that reveal participants' reflections on their experiences of creating and sharing content.

Enmesh content

The research data also consisted of photographs and messages that participants sent to the shared display. These were recorded on a server and reviewed and examined for key themes. Since the focus of this paper is on older adults creating and sharing digital content to build peer connections, digital content created by care managers was excluded from the analysis. The analysis focused on identifying common themes that emerged in the content that participants shared. These themes were: 1) domestic spaces, 2) objects and artwork, 3) interests and hobbies, and 4) daily activities. Each of these is examined below, followed by a discussion of the social interactions that occurred during the study.

FINDINGS

Here we present the findings in two sections. First, we describe the content that participants produced, beginning with an overview of the number of objects sent, followed by a discussion of the key themes. We then describe the social interactions that occurred during the study, as revealed by the messages exchanged and the comments participants made during interviews.

Content Produced

Participants produced 231 photographs and messages over ten weeks. Table 1 shows the number of items sent by each participant. Most photographs were complemented by a caption. John adopted a "leader" role [24], sending nearly as many items as all the other participants combined. Thus many items discussed in the findings are from John. Nevertheless other participants remained engaged and provided a critical role as audience.

Domestic spaces

Many of the photographs showed details of participants' domestic spaces, such as exterior views of or from the home, interior rooms and spaces, decorations and objects, and photos of the garden. This is not unexpected, given that participants spent a lot of time at home. What is noteworthy is that many of these photographs described aspects of participants' daily lives and domestic spaces

Participant	Text only	Photographs with text caption	Photographs without text caption	Total sent items
Charlotte	2	9	0	11
Donald	1	8	4	13
Betty	8	3	5	16
Lynne*	9	5	2	16
Sophie	4	4	11	19
Emma	15	28	4	47
John	52	56	1	109
Total	91	113	27	231

Table 1. Number of photos & messages sent by participants (* Lynne participated for four weeks only)

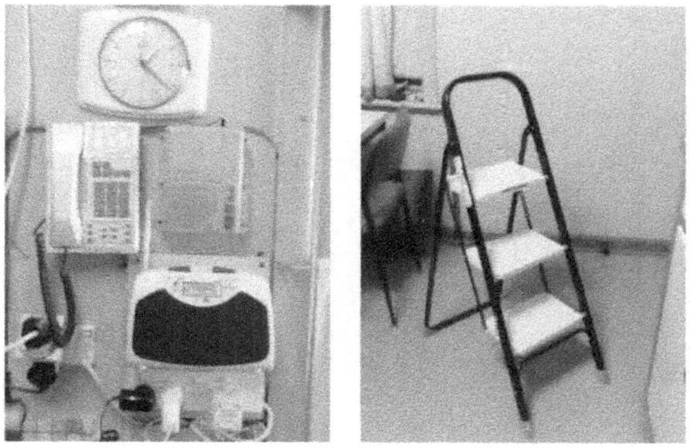

Figure 3. John's photographs of his (a) "NASA rocket control centre" and (b) "household elevator"

that were important to them. For example, Donald shared a photograph of his refrigerator with the caption, *"My own birthday present"*. John shared numerous photographs illustrating his domestic surroundings, and these were often accompanied by captions that reflected on the limitations of old age. A photograph of the exterior of his home was captioned, *"my prison for most of the time,"* while he described his motorized scooter as *"freedom machine when on parole"*. A poignant example was the photograph of his empty garage (*"Had a car once but don't drive any longer – too old"* [John]).

These brief messages reveal a combination of lighthearted and somber reflections on ageing. John also frequently used humor to describe his domestic surroundings. He shared an image showing a radio in his kitchen set up for emergency calls: *"My kitchen is starting to look like a NASA rocket control centre, wires everywhere."* A photograph of a stepladder in his home was labeled *"The household elevator. Forbidden territory for me according to my carers, but what do I do when I need to get to a high shelf? Hire a forklift?"* (Figure 3).

Objects and artwork

Participants also shared photographs of household objects and artworks. These objects were often associated with personal memories and familial histories. Donald, for instance, shared photographs of ornaments, with the caption *"The Holland collection,"* and a photograph of a framed painting hanging on his wall that depicted a Dutch windmill. During the interview, Donald explained these were important to him because he had grown up in Holland. The windmill and ornaments represented *"the place where we used to live,"* reminding him of his childhood and his brothers who had all passed away.

Similarly Betty shared images of a framed Parisian print, with the caption *"gay Paris"*. During the interview it transpired that Betty had been an avid traveler. She had visited Europe many times and the artwork on her wall was a cherished memento from this part of her life.

Figure 4. Sophie's photograph of three sisters

Artwork and objects in the home often had special meaning because they were associated with loved ones. John shared a photograph of a tapestry on his wall: *"My late wife's handiwork – about 22000 stitches"*. Many photographs showed framed portraits of family members, on display in the home. Sophie shared an image of two adjacent portraits of herself with her two sisters, both as young girls and as older women (Figure 4). This photograph, although not captioned, was very popular with the other participants. In the interviews, participants noted that they enjoyed trying to match the people in the two pictures.

Photographs of sentimental objects and artwork enabled participants to create and share aspects of their history in a simple and visual way. Other photographs showed objects relevant to current activities. For example, John shared a photograph of a head-mounted light, explaining:

"Something that is very necessary for me when reading fine print or doing close work. Must have it because my vision is much impaired with macular degeneration. Just another old age disability that I have to put up with, but I seem to manage adequately though in spite of it." [John]

This example illustrates the personal meaning attached to the objects that participants chose to photograph and share. John associated this object with old age, but also with maintaining his ability to undertake productive work.

Figure 5. (a) Bowling room, and (b) Workshop

Interests and Hobbies

Participants shared photographs and information that expressed their personal interests and hobbies. Emma, for instance, shared a photograph of a dedicated *"bowling room"* in her home, while John shared a photograph of a building in his garden with the caption: *"Workshop – my lifeline for many years."* (Figure 5)

Sophie and Charlotte shared photographs of their garden, sometimes naming the flowers or providing a story about the plant: *"My beautiful tree from a seed from Ambon a prison of war camp"* [Sophie]. Emma shared several photographs and messages that described birdlife. She captured an image of a computer screen showing two birds and described their significance with this caption:

"These two birds we had as pets when our children were young. The galah is pale - grey above and pink below. The corella is a white cockatoo with very small crest. They were great birds." [Emma]

John provided some insight into his life as an engineer and hobbyist, sharing photographs of machinery and objects he had used or built. He shared a photograph of a drafting table which he described in a message to Emma:

"I built it myself some time ago with a view to doing some contract drafting work after I retired but it never came to anything. However it has been a big help with all my hobby work since and I have used it a lot." [John]

John also created a series of photographs showing the different steps of a repair job he was undertaking on a lawn mower. Each photograph was titled "Mr. Fixit" and included a brief caption describing the project.

Daily activities

Participants sometimes shared photographs and messages that described their daily activities, such as meal preparations, visits from grandchildren, and other aspects of domestic life. For instance, Lynne shared a message saying *"Today theme is food in fridge and what's for tea"*. This was followed by a photograph of a plate of prawns. Some weeks later, Betty posted this comment:

"I saw some mention of prawns which reminds me oh horrors I have some in the fridge. And I think they may be a little Weary! Must go and check!" [Betty]

Later she added: *"Soo my poor prawns are now languishing in the rubbish bin! Never to be enjoyed by anyone. Ah well such is the fate of the poor prawn!"*

For some participants, health concerns were central to their daily activities. Lynne, for example, documented one day with a series of photographs and messages that began with the message: *"A diabolical day. Xrays show broken vertebrae. Sorry no pics except bed in turmoil."*

This was followed by a photograph of her unmade bed, with the caption, *"Bed after struggle to climb out."* A later message said she did not feel like eating that night,

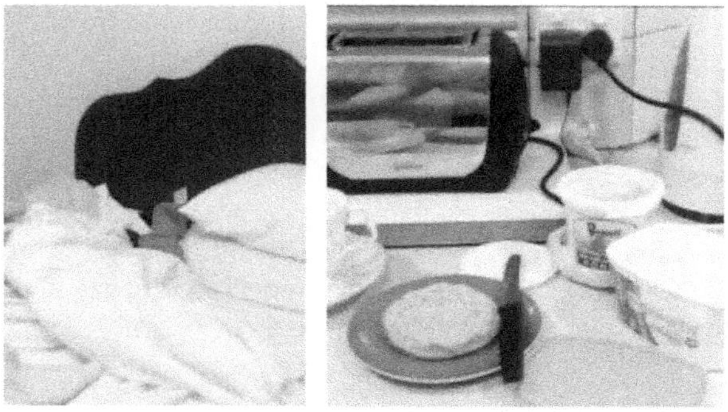

Figure 6. Photographs illustrating Lynne's "diabolical day"

but this was soon followed by a photograph of a simple meal of tea and toast, with the caption *"Hunger pangs set in after all!"* (Figure 6). The day ended with a photograph of her preparations for bed, *"Back warmers, pain killer and walking stick ready for bed."*

Social Interactions

Participants did not, at first, actively respond to each others' posts. Over time, however, social activity increased and people referred more often and with longer responses to each other's messages. Participants established conventions to effectively communicate when their messages – which could all be seen by everyone in the group – were directed at particular people. A shared language developed for group communications (*"hello fellow iPadders"*), while participant names were used for messages directed to individuals (*"Hi John, greetings from Sophie"*).

Sometimes participants asked questions to prompt a response from their audience. For example, Sophie shared a photograph of her garden with the caption: *"Friends – how do you like my tree?"*

Participants found the onscreen keyboard difficult to use and messages often contained mistakes. Interestingly, this led to exchanges between participants, such as John's teasing comment to Emma:

"Interesting messages Emma!! First a letter "A" then "R". Miss out on something? Not to worry though, my typing is way off too. Don't see too well that's why." [John]

In another example, John asked Emma to clarify the meaning of a photograph, which she had mistakenly captioned *"koo"*. A lively exchange developed and after some discussion, Emma was finally able to explain the photograph:

"Have just found the koo which you mentioned it was supposed to read Viking tree made by my granddaughter as a school project. I sure mucked that one up." [Emma]

The interactive shared display also prompted participant interactions. When participants noticed others moving items, they often created a message to initiate contact, e.g., *"John, I can see you are having fun moving the pictures"* [Donald] and *"Hello Emma ! see you moving pics around. How are you tonight?"* [John].

Many of the messages to the group contained comments or questions about the technology (e.g., *"How do you move the cursor"* [Lynne]). These questions and their responses served two purposes: they contributed to an evaluation of the technology, enabling the researchers to identify difficulties participants were experiencing, and they fostered the development of a shared sense of purpose within the group.

This shared purpose helped to create a sense of community. The development of community became evident at a social event held for all clients of the aged care provider. Managers from the organization were interviewed at the end of the study and they noted the social cohesion between the study participants:

"It created friendships - I don't know if you heard about our Christmas party last week. They got together that little group – that little group knew each other. They supported each other. One in particular took the others under the wing and looked after them for a couple of hours." [Aged care manager]

In addition, the three social events held as part of the study were particularly important for building rapport. After meeting each other face-to-face, participants felt as though they were sharing information with friends, rather than strangers. As Sophie said, *"they became a person where otherwise it was only a face"*.

Nevertheless, sharing information with a group of people who were effectively strangers at the start of the study did present some challenges. Both John and Emma – the most prolific content producers – commented on these challenges during the interviews.

For John, the content shared by others sometimes had insufficient information to capture his interest:

"I noticed that a lot of the messages were not directed to anyone ... It was 'this is a house across the road' and nobody would react to it and I found this was a bit of a miss, because I thought if someone puts something on it should be a bit described." [John]

Conversely, he was disappointed that his own efforts to engage interest from others were sometimes unsuccessful:

"I took a photo of my back fence and said 'you can see the TAFE [building] in the background' and I thought people would [comment on] it... If I put on something that is of interest to me I would hope someone else would comment or it would strike someone with a similar interest, but it has not happened." [John]

Emma, too, tried to imagine what people would be interested in, and this influenced her choices about content to share. Concern about the interests of the audience sometimes limited her content creation:

"I started sending messages without a photo, because I ran out of things around the home. You look to find something that is interesting – to some people at least not to you anyway." [Emma]

This concern also limited Betty's contributions, who said she *"didn't write many messages"* because she *"couldn't think of anything original to say."* [Betty]

Like John, Emma found there were times when her efforts to engage interest fell short, although she also acknowledged that people may have enjoyed her photos but not responded to them:

"I tried to put on things that people might be interested in. Of course I am a bowler so I put on a photo of the bowling room, nobody responded to that so obviously there was no bowler [in the group]. Lots of people were interested in the birds. Lots of people might be interested but might not write a response back." [Emma]

This observation is supported by interview comments made by other participants, suggesting they enjoyed viewing the shared content and felt a sense of connection within the community. Donald, for instance, called the iPad his *"friend"* and described the Enmesh display as *"an illustrated book by many authors."* Although he did not contribute as actively as others, he saw himself as a co-author of the display and felt part of the community.

DISCUSSION: CONTENT PRODUCTION FOR SELF-EXPRESSION AND SOCIAL ENGAGEMENT

The examples presented above demonstrate opportunities for self-expression and social engagement that emerge when older adults create and share photographs and messages. Some of our participants were clearly more active content producers than others and for them the benefits appeared more pronounced. Aged 92, John was one of our oldest participants as well as the most prolific. He shared photographs with captions that richly described his life, reflecting on both his past experiences and his current activities and lifestyle. The content John created suggests there may be important opportunities for digital technologies to enable those in the "oldest old" age group to express themselves in new creative ways. This age group is frequently overlooked in studies that aim to design technologies for older users [12]. Studies that do focus on the oldest old tend to emphasize consumption, rather than production, of content [e.g., 7].

The analysis of content sent to the Enmesh display reveals a wide range of topics. Participants did not shy away from sharing some of their bad days, but they mostly tried to find positive aspects in their daily life, often using humor to describe their experiences. By sharing information about their daily activities and surroundings, participants provided others with a "window" into their world. This enabled them to build rapport and find common interests. Similar findings have been found in Computer-Supported Cooperative Work (CSCW) literature, suggesting that sharing photographs and information about personal events can help to build rapport among distributed workers [e.g., 27]. Studies of photo-sharing in other contexts have also found that photographs are valuable for building connections between strangers [e.g., 17, 19].

Interestingly, our participants were not overly concerned about privacy, which contrasts with other research on older adults and social networking [8, 32]. Enmesh was designed specifically for use by older adults within a closed social network where participants got to know each other through face-to-face meetings. This may have contributed to trust in the system and a belief that participants' privacy was being respected. The shared display also helped to create a sense of community. Participants could observe each other interacting with the display, sometimes commenting on those interactions with messages directed to that person. These greetings provided a form of lightweight communication. They were used to announce to the other person "I can see you," much as a wave to a neighbor would communicate in a face-to-face context. In this way, our study supports earlier research that has shown how presence and awareness can be forged through computer-mediated communication within distributed groups [5, 9].

Our findings suggest two important considerations for enhancing older adults' experience of producing content. Firstly, technologies for content creation should provide *opportunities for self-expression and creativity*. The core function of Enmesh was to enable participants to create and share photographs and messages. This combination of imagery and text communication enabled participants to describe and share personal objects and spaces that communicated details of their histories and everyday lives. Through this medium, participants were able to express themselves in creative and meaningful ways.

Additionally, photographs and text communication provide powerful tools for supporting storytelling and reminiscence. In some cases narratives emerged from the combination of messages and photographs sent to the display, such as Lynne's description of her "diabolical day" and John's "Mr. Fixit" photographs. This was an interesting use of Enmesh that we had not anticipated. Enmesh was appropriated by some participants for supporting digital storytelling, which demonstrating a desire by older adults to engage in creative content production.

A second important consideration is *how* the content will be *displayed and shared* with others. For content production to be a rewarding and engaging activity, it needs to reach an interested and responsive audience. The audience plays an important role in defining any content production activity, as illustrated by Harley and Fitzpatrick's case study of "Geriatric 1927" [11]. We found that considerations of audience were important in shaping the content participants chose to create and share.

Considerations of audience were mediated by the shared display. As noted above, the shared display fostered a sense of presence among users. The display of content influences users' understandings of, and interactions with, their audience [15, 17, 22]. In our field study, the users were both the creators and the audience of the content produced and this affected the way they approached the content creation activity. Participants tried to imagine what others would be interested in seeing and this was guided, in part, by considerations of their own preferences for the content they viewed on the display.

Successful participant interactions occurred during the study, particularly in the messages participants exchanged in response to each other's photographs. Some participants also noted, however, that engaging with a relatively unfamiliar audience involved some "hits" and "misses." It was challenging to share content with peers who were initially strangers. This was moderated to some extent by the three social gatherings held during the study. While these events have not been discussed in depth here, we acknowledge that they were a crucial part of building social connections between participants. This can be contrasted with findings from the Building Bridges project [6], which did not provide opportunities for participants to meet in person. One of the key findings from that study is that participants felt it would have been easier to build rapport if they had met face-to-face.

Our study involved trialing a socio-technical system, encompassing the technology, the social events and the care organization. This research contributes to broader work that aims to support older adults who choose to "age in place" or live at home for longer. Aged care providers that offer community-based care help to make this possible. Given the central role the care organization played in our participants' lives, involving care managers in the study helped ensure participants felt comfortable contributing to the project and using Enmesh [31]. Future work is needed to explore how similar technologies could be used when face-to-face contact is not possible, or when care providers are unable to actively contribute.

CONCLUSION

In this paper we have presented findings from a field study in which a small group of older adults created photographs and messages for a shared display. Our field study was unique in a number of ways. Firstly, the Enmesh application provided opportunities for older adults to *create and share* digital content. Secondly, most of our participants were aged over 85 and are therefore considered to be in the "oldest old" age group. It is rare for people in this age group to be thought of as producers, as well as consumers, of digital content. Thirdly, participants did not know each other prior to the study. Research into the design of social technologies for older adults has typically focused on strengthening *existing* social and family connections. Our findings demonstrate that creating and sharing content provides opportunities for older adults to build *new social connections* within a small peer community. We found that participants were willing to share personal information in this forum, building a sense of community within the group. Participants demonstrated a capacity to create meaningful content for the Enmesh display. Some participants in particular appeared to thrive on the opportunity to express themselves creatively using this communication tool. In this way, our study demonstrates that digital content production can provide important opportunities for older adults for social engagement and self-expression.

ACKNOWLEDGMENTS

This work was supported by IBES (Institute for a Broadband-Enabled Society), Benetas, and the Australian Research Council (LP120100022). We thank the participants and care managers who participated in the project. This research was approved by the University of Melbourne's Human Research Ethics Committee.

REFERENCES

1. Bloch, N. and Bruce, B. C. Older adults and the new public sphere. In *Proc. iConference 2011* (2011), 1-7.
2. Burmeister, O. K. What seniors value about online community. *Community Informatics, 8,* 1 (2012).
3. Crawshaw, K. and Hendy, S. *Older Victorians online: A community survey exploring the usage patterns of older Victorians online*, 2012.
4. David, J., Benjamin, W., Baecker, R., Gromala, D. and Birnholtz, J. Living with pain, staying in touch: Exploring the communication needs of older adults with chronic pain. In *Ext. Abstracts CHI 2011,* ACM (2011), 1219-1224.
5. Dourish, P. and Bellotti, V. Awareness and coordination in shared workspaces. In *Proc. CSCW '92,* ACM Press (1992), 107-114.
6. Garattini, C., Wherton, J. and Prendergast, D. Linking the lonely: an exploration of a communication technology designed to support social interaction among older adults. *Univ. Acc. in the Inf. Soc., 11,* 2 (2012), 211-222.
7. Gaver, W., Boucher, A., Bowers, J , Blythe, M., Jarvis, N., Cameron, D., Kerridge, T., Wilkie, A., Philliips, R. and Wright, P. The Photostroller: Supporting diverse care home residents in engaging with the world. In *Proc. CHI '11,* ACM Press (2011), 1757-1766.
8. Gibson, L., Moncur, W., Forbes, P., Arnott, J., Martin, C. and Bhachu, A. S. Designing social networking

sites for older adults. In *Proc. BCS '10,* British Computer Society (2010), 186-194.

9. Gutwin, C., Roseman, M. and Greenberg, S. A usability study of awareness widgets in a shared workspace groupware system. In *Proc. CSCW '96,* ACM Press (1996), 258-267.
10. Hanson, V. L. Influencing technology adoption by older adults. *Interacting with Computers, 22,* 6 (2010), 502-509.
11. Harley, D. and Fitzpatrick, G. YouTube and intergenerational communication: the case of Geriatric1927. *Univ. Acc. in the Inf. Soc., 8,* 1 (2009), 5-20.
12. Karahasanovic, A., Brandtzaeg, P. B., Heim, J., Luders, M., Vermeir, L., Pierson, J., Lievens, B., Vanattenhoven, J. and Jans, G. Co-creation and user-generated content - elderly people's user requirements. *Computers in Human Behaviour, 25,* 3 (2009), 655-678.
13. Lehtinen, V., Nasanen, J. and Sarvas, R. "A little silly and empty-headed" - Older adults' understandings of social networking sites. In *Proc. British HCI Conf.,* British Computer Society (2009), 45-54.
14. Lindley, S. E., Harper, R. and Sellen, A. Designing for elders: Exploring the complexity of relationships in later life. In Proc. *British HCI Conf.,* British Computer Society (2008), 77-86.
15. Lindley, S. E. Shades of lightweight: supporting cross-generational communication through home messaging. *Univ. Acc. in the Inf. Soc., 11,* 1 (2012), 31-43.
16. Lindsay, S., Jackson, D., Schofield, G. and Olivier, P. Engaging older people using participatory design. In *Proc. CHI '12,* ACM Press (2012), 1199-1208.
17. Lindtner, S., Chen, J., Hayes, G. R. and Dourish, P. Towards a framework of publics: Re-encountering media sharing and its user. *ACM Trans. Comput.-Hum. Interact., 18,* 2 (2011), 5.1-5.23.
18. McLaughlin, A. C., Rogers, W. A. and Fisk, A. D. Using direct and indirect input devices: Attention demands and age-related differences. *ACM Trans. Comput.-Hum. Interact., 16,* 1 (2009), 2.
19. Miller, A. D. and Edwards, W. K. Give and take: A study of consumer photo-sharing culture and practice. In *Proc. CHI '07,* ACM Press (2007), 347-356.
20. Nimrod, G. The fun culture in seniors' online communities. *The Gerontologist, 51,* 2 (2011), 226-237.
21. Pedell, S., Vetere, F., Kulik, L., Ozanne, E. and Gruner, A. Social isolation of older people: the role of domestic technologies. In *Proc. OzCHI '10,* ACM Press (2010), 167-170.
22. Perry, M. and Rachovides, D. Entertaining Situated *Messaging at Home. Comput. Supported Coop. Work,* 16, 1-2 (2007), 99-128.
23. Plaisant, C., Clamage, A., Hutchinson, H. B., Bederson, B. B. and Druin, A. Shared family calendars: Promoting symmetry and accessibility. *ACM Trans. Comput.-Hum. Interact., 13,* 3 (2006), 313-346.
24. Preece, J. and Shneiderman, B. The reader-to-leader framework: Motivating technology-mediated social participation. *AIS Trans. on Hum.-Comput. Interact., 1,* 1 (2009), 13-32.
25. Rodriguez, M. D., Gonzalez, V. M., Favela, J. and Santana, P. C. Home-based communication system for older adults and their remote family. *Computers in Human Behaviour, 25,* 3 (2009), 609-618.
26. Stößel, C., Wandke, H. and Blessing, L. Gestural interfaces for elderly users: Help or hindrance?, In *Gesture in Embodied Communication and Human-Computer Interaction.* Springer, (2010), 269-280.
27. Thom-Santelli, J. and Millen, D. R. Learning by seeing: Photo viewing in the workplace. In *Proc. CHI '09,* ACM Press (2009), 2081-2090.
28. van Dijk, B., Dadlani, P., van Halteren, A. and Biemans, M. Life changes, connection stays: Photo sharing and social connectedness for people with special needs. In *Proc. ECCE,* ACM Press (2010), 135-142.
29. Vetere, F., Davis, H., Gibbs, M. and Howard, S. The Magic Box and Collage: Responding to the challenge of distributed intergenerational play. *Int. J. Hum.-Comput. Stud., 67,* 2 (2009), 165-178.
30. Vines, J., Blythe, M., Lindsay, S., Dunphy, P., Monk, A. and Olivier, P. Questionable concepts: Critique as a resource for designing with eighty somethings. In *Proc. CHI '12,* ACM Press (2012), 1169-1178.
31. Waycott, J., Pedell, S., Vetere, F., Ozanne, E., Kulik, L., Gruner, A. and Downs, J. Actively engaging older adults in the development and evaluation of tablet technology. In *Proc. OzCHI '12,* ACM Press (2012), 643-652.
32. Xie, B., Watkins, I., Golbeck, J. and Huang, M. Understanding and Changing Older Adults' Perceptions and Learning of Social Media. *Educational Gerontology, 38,* 4 (2012), 282-296.

Health Vlogger-Viewer Interaction in Chronic Illness Management

Leslie S. Liu[1], Jina Huh[1], Tina Neogi[2], Kori Inkpen[4], and Wanda Pratt[1,3]

[1]Biomedical and Health Informatics, [2]Department of Family Medicine, [3]The Information School
University of Washington
{lsliu, jinahuh, tneogi, wpratt}@uw.edu

[4]Microsoft Research
One Microsoft Way
Redmond, WA USA
kori@microsoft.com

ABSTRACT
Health video blogs (vlogs) allow individuals with chronic illnesses to share their stories, experiences, and knowledge with the general public. Furthermore, health vlogs help in creating a connection between the vlogger and the viewers. In this work, we present a qualitative study examining the various methods that health vloggers use to establish a connection with their viewers. We found that vloggers used genres to express specific messages to their viewers while using the uniqueness of video to establish a deeper connection with their viewers. Health vloggers also explicitly sought interaction with their viewers. Based on these results, we present design implications to help facilitate and build sustainable communities for vloggers.

Author Keywords
Health vlogs; YouTube; video blogging; chronic illness management; communication; patient-centered.

ACM Classification Keywords
J.3. Life and Medical Sciences (Medical information systems)

General Terms
Human Factors.

INTRODUCTION
Lily's first video on her YouTube channel showed her joking about wearing a *"beautiful [neck] brace"* due to lesions on her spine because of her breast cancer. Sixty-three videos and 10 months later, the last video uploaded showed a solemn man, Lily's husband. *"This update is long and coming. I apologize for its tardiness...Lily passed last Saturday. She lost the battle."* As he paused and continued to speak about the messages (*"don't take labels, be yourself, make a difference in the world"*) his wife wanted to remind her viewers, he became emotional and apologized, *"Forgive me, this is a little hard."* Although it had only been 7 days since his wife had passed away, Lily's husband still felt the need to update his wife's viewers, treating them as if they actually knew her and were friends. It is clear that Lily felt a strong connection with those who watched her videos (her videos had a total of 11,806 views). Many people like Lily opt to share their story with the public through social networking websites and blogs. Over the years traditional text-based blogs have evolved to support various presentation forms—art blogs, photoblogs, sketch blogs, audio blogs, and video blogs (vlogs in short).

Vlogs have been widely used for e-learning [39], citizen journalism [23], product marketing [17], and daily interaction with family and friends [22]. Another emerging area is health vlogs, in which individuals with health conditions share their stories with others. Sharing personal experiences with others has been proven to be helpful for peer-support, especially for those who have chronic illness [3]. The connection between the vlogger and the viewers is critical in health vlogs as past literature has shown that social support or connections with others work as self-therapy [36]. Despite the apparent advantages in further developing health vlogs, few studies have explored ways to improve patients' connections with others in health vlogs.

In this paper, we present our study on chronic illness patients' use of health vlogs on YouTube. We examined how health vloggers attempt to connect with viewers and identified different genres of health vlogs. We then discuss the affordances that video provides as a blogging tool, and the challenges vloggers' face in practice. Finally, we discuss implications for the design of health vlogging tools.

RELATED WORK
Video sharing sites such as YouTube, Vimeo, and DailyMotion are affordable, accessible media production sites where amateur video producers can share their messages with a worldwide audience. People use vlogs for various purposes, ranging from daily personal diaries to informal music learning [42] to health communication [8].

Studies have shown that vlogs are useful in a wide variety of domains. For example, rural Brazilian communities adopted vlogs to empower citizen journalism and build self-sustainable telecommunication centers [9]. The D/deaf community also uses vlogging as an alternative medium for rich communication [15]. Raun discussed vlogs as a Do-It-Yourself (DIY) Therapy [30], where vlogs have become an arena for "truth telling" as seen in self-help groups and political gatherings [41] and "confession," a mode of governance [10]. Vlogs often carry the forms of personal speaking to invisible listeners, and conducting such an activity can help the speaker feel better [24].

Some studies have investigated the use of vlogs in the domain of health. Molyneaux and O'Donnell [26] found that participants reported high levels of interest in watching user-generated video as a source of awareness and learning around health information. The Kaiser Family Foundation also uses vlogs to target young people about the impact of HIV. The young people get to hear first-hand how HIV has affected people their age and how they can prevent or test for HIV [16]. While Chou *et al.* [6] looked at cancer vlogs on YouTube to understand what made a cancer narrative effective, many of these studies do not examine the connection between the vlogger and the audience.

Blogging

Sundar *et al.* [35] discussed how seminal work around virtual worlds [40] and blogging and identities [27] bleeds over to help understand the motivations and benefits of health blogs. Nardi *et al.* [27] discussed five general motivations for blogging: autobiographical narratives, commentary, catharsis, muse, and community forum. Bloggers telling the story of their lives for catharsis can be particularly important for people dealing with a mental illness because telling one's life story "can renew a sense of meaning and possibility" [33].

Similar to vlogs, relatively few studies have examined health blogs as an independent genre. Miller and Pole [25] showed that half of 951 health blogs published between 2007 and 2008 were written by health professionals, one third by patients, and a few by unpaid caregivers. Previous research has shown that cancer patients benefit emotionally by sharing their experience with other patients through blogs [7]. Many bloggers also explored multiple identities through blogging.

It is unclear how much the results around blogs apply to health blogs on other diseases not necessarily dominated by emotional problems (*e.g.*, diabetes), highly stigmatized (*e.g.*, HIV), or often terminal (*e.g.*, cancer). Although much of what we know about blogs and virtual worlds will carry over to health vlogs, the video medium affords high personal information disclosure and suggests new kinds of phenomena around health vlogging. Though Ressler *et al.* [32] found that blogging about chronic pain and illness helped patients feel less of an isolation because of the online connection, Nardi *et al.* [28] found that bloggers were not interested in "holding any but a minimal conversation" between their readers. However, this may hold differently for health vlogs due to the affordances of video. Furthermore, few studies have explicitly examined design issues around health vlogging tools.

Presenter and Audience

Goffman suggests the concept of presentation of self [13]. If we consider vloggers to be similar to an actor on a stage, and a vlogger's viewers as their audience, the goal of the presentation is acceptance from the audience. Essentially, if the actor has succeeded in the presentation, the audience will see the actor as the actor intended. This idea of self-expression and self-representation is one of the affordances that vlogs offer. However, there has been little work in examining the interaction between the vlogger and the viewers and the affordances that vlogs allow.

Social Support and Self-Therapy

According to Thoits, social support is defined as a social "fund" that people draw from when handling stressors [37]. Social support can include help in material aid, behavioral assistance, intimate interaction, feedback, and positive social interaction [1]. Many studies have shown the importance of social support for anyone [2]. However, with chronic illnesses, the feelings of isolation can be exacerbated [5], and thus social support becomes essential.

Giving support to others has been shown to help the patients themselves as well; helping others creates a type of self-therapy. One study looked at elderly patients and found that those who gave informal assistance to others reported enhanced feelings of personal control [19]. Similarly, another study suggested that women who were abused saw the ability to provide help to others as proof of their own recovery [14]. Schwartz and Sendor suggested that peer supporters (those who provided support to people with the same disease) were able to reframe their disease experience, resulting in an enhanced perception of quality of life [34].

A few video resources for social support are available to the public[1,2]. Although these examples are considered health videos, they are curated by an organization, and in some cases, use actors rather than the patients. Instead, we were interested in understanding health videos that patients generated and maintained, particularly to explore self-therapy or to help others.

Building on existing work, we examine how health vloggers attempt to build a viewer connection as a form of self-therapy and social support. We also examine remaining challenges and suggest potential design features.

METHODS

Data Collection

To examine health vloggers who post a series of health vlogs, rather than a one-time vlog, we studied health vlogs on three chronic diseases that require self-management activities over time: HIV (human immunodeficiency virus), diabetes, and cancer, though cancer is not always a chronic

[1] http://www.healthtalkonline.org/

[2] http://www.nytimes.com/interactive/2009/09/10/health/Patient_Voices.html

	HIV	Diabetes	Cancer
Sex	12M	9M/3F	8M/4F
Age (Min/Max)	27 (21/51)	33 (15/75)	38 (25/49)
Videos per person (Min/Max)	46.5 (2/150)	14 (2/1027)	23 (6/197)
Views per person (Min/Max)	14,808 (258/341788)	5,441.5 (570/313235)	14,808 (258/341788)
Subscribers (Min/Max)	232.5 (1/1457)	21 (4/405)	22.5 (1/505)

Table 1. Descriptive data for each category of vloggers. Values are the Median (Min/Max) per person.

disease. We chose these three diseases because they have a high prevalence in the world for us to be able to collect a reasonable amount of data, differ in ways in which self-management strategies are formed and maintained, and have different levels of social stigma.

We considered all forms of diabetes, and we did not distinguish cancer types. Because YouTube did not have a specific health category, we utilized YouTube's search mechanism by using the keywords "<disease name> blog" to get the search results. We received 2500, 2090, and 12900 search results for diabetes, HIV, and cancer, respectively. We narrowed down the list to a set of vloggers who we considered health vloggers using the following inclusion criteria: (1) The vlog title contained words directly related to diabetes, HIV, or cancer. Examples include "blood sugar" for diabetes, and "chemotherapy" for cancer; (2) Either verbally in the video or written in the caption, the vlogger confirmed that he/she was diagnosed with the illness; (3) The vlogger was the diagnosed patient him/herself and not an institution or organization. We chose these criteria because many videos uploaded by an institution are professionally edited, but we were more interested in looking at amateur vloggers.

We reached data saturation after 36 vloggers (the first 12 vloggers for each disease). For each vlogger, we analyzed their first and last health vlog posted (72 vlogs total). Certain characteristics of the vloggers (*e.g.*, all HIV vloggers were homosexual males) were a result of the selection process. Table 1 shows more information on each disease vlog group. We changed names of the vloggers throughout the paper.

Analysis
Each of three coders separately analyzed 6 videos for each disease, resulting in 18 videos of 9 unique users in total to develop descriptive codes as a group. The resulting descriptive codes focused on the following attributes: basic information about the vlog (title, post date, vlog length, caption), demographical information about the author, medical information about the author (disease timeline, emotional stage), visual information (video editing, scripted, location), and other information that describes the different styles of authors' performance and attitude, as well as the way stories are presented (attitude, message of the video, intended audience, purpose).

Next, we used open coding to analyze 18 more videos each, for a total of 54 in this round (72 in total, including the 18 to develop coding). We iteratively developed our coding schemes by continuously revising the coding scheme as a group, merging them, and then generating subsets of codes as we found common and contrasting themes. Through our analysis, we identified relevant themes that emerged from both the descriptive codes and the open coding schemes. The three coders then came together to perform an affinity diagram analysis.

RESULTS
In this section, we describe how vloggers used vlogs as a medium to connect with their viewers as a form of self-therapy while helping others. We first discuss different genres that vloggers devised to convey specialized messages to the viewers. We then discuss how video affords richer viewer connection than text-based media. Lastly, we discuss various methods that vloggers used to explicitly interact with viewers.

Health Vlogging Genres
Vloggers produced different genres of vlogs, depending on the stage they were in, their illness trajectory, the chronic illness they were suffering from, and their purpose for vlogging. The different genres, discussed below, reflected the messages vloggers wanted to convey and how they wanted to present their messages to the viewers.

Teaching
In teaching vlogs, vloggers attempt to educate viewers with information about their illness and management strategies. Vloggers typically created teaching vlogs with content highlighting their own knowledge and experience. Teaching vlogs allowed vloggers to cast themselves as an expert to viewers in what they do.

More of the diabetes vlogs in our study were for the purpose of teaching (42%), compared to vlogs for the other illnesses—HIV (13%) and cancer (17%). For diabetes management, self-education is critical. Because diabetes is a chronic illness that can be managed through diet and personal lifestyle, many diabetes vloggers offered suggestions to viewers. Examples included eating certain types of food, such as cinnamon (DIB12a) or a particular brand of pasta (DIB8b), or advocating for a lifestyle change, such as a vegan lifestyle (DIB9a). Thus, one would expect that many diabetes vloggers would attempt to teach strategies and solutions that others could use.

In teaching videos, vloggers shared information on characterizing their illness and strategies to manage the illness. For example, Anthony wanted to distinguish between Type 1 and Type 2 diabetes, by giving an overview of the differences:

"When people talk about diabetes, they're almost always thinking that it's diabetes Type 2... For me, I'm Type 1 so... we just don't produce insulin...But for Type 2 diabetics, they could have complete insulin resistance, so that's a whole other thing." (Anthony, DIB5b)

We observed frequent "show-and-tell" behavior throughout the teaching videos, which is difficult to convey through text-based blogs. For example, vloggers demonstrated how a device worked, how to cook low-carb meals (DIB4a, DIB7a), or how to replace gauze on open wounds (CAN12a). One diabetes vlogger explained that he had a heart monitoring device and said, *"I have electrodes attached to my chest"* (DIB4b) before showing how the heart monitor device worked. John showed how he got blood tests done (HIV4a). Vloggers also used hand descriptions to show the size of a swollen testicle using their index finger and thumb (CAN6a) or where and how long in length the stitches were (CAN4b).

Vloggers also used a mixture of video recordings, still images, and hand drawings to present informational material. As shown in Figure 1, Sue created a scenario and rendered it on a still image, which was then inserted into her vlog as teaching material (DIB1b). Similarly, Figure 2 shows another vlogger explaining how uterine cancer affects pregnancy by drawing a diagram on paper (CAN7a).

Personal Journals

One of the most common genres of videos was a *personal journal.* In this genre, vloggers gave updates on their current emotional and physical status or experiences during major stages in their illness trajectories. According to Raun, by sharing such day-to-day changes, vloggers can create a sense of connection with others and reflect upon themselves, working as a therapeutic activity [30].

Many vloggers included current updates to their treatment and shared their thoughts and feelings, akin to a written diary. Some vloggers explicitly mentioned that the goal of their vlog was to serve like a journal (CAN1a, CAN8a). Other vloggers not only gave updates on their disease, but also on their personal lives. In one case, Andy, a diabetes vlogger explained that his video was to update his viewers about the results of his daughter's diabetes test as negative (DIB10b). Other vloggers updated their medication practices. Nick updated his viewers about his experience with a new medication:

"Today's the first day I took the medication, and it's Complera....I'm very nauseous...pain in my chest...stomach is a little hurting." (Nick, HIV8a)

Sharing such day-to-day experience provides viewers with information about the medication while also building personal connections with consistent followers.

HIV vloggers, compared to other vloggers, tended to be more reflective, sharing their revelations and acceptance of having HIV. Matthew reflected on why he might have

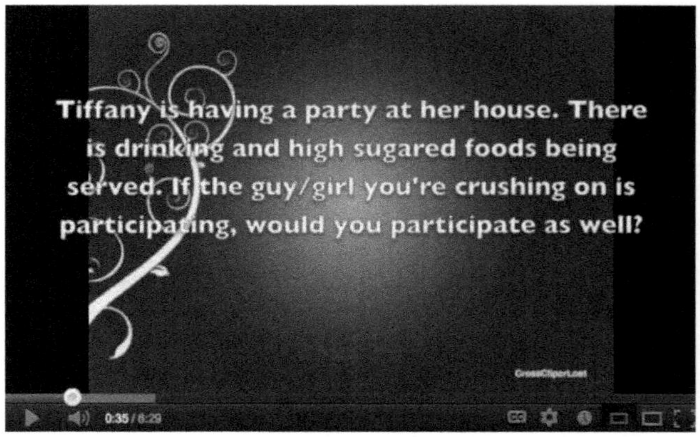

Figure 1. A scenario created by a health vlogger was to teach viewers everyday strategies for diabetes management.

Figure 2. A drawing by a cancer vlogger showed and explained how uterine cancer could affect pregnancy.

contracted HIV: *"I love people more than myself – that's probably one of the reasons I got HIV"* (Matthew, HIV1a).

In one case, Blake stated that he was struggling with accepting HIV in his life. He also said that he felt that everyone was constantly judging him, even strangers. Finally, he came to an epiphany on living with HIV and shared it with the viewers:

"[HIV] was owning me. It was taking over...I was so tired of it wearing me down. And I say 'was' because I had this epiphany. I was just like...don't let it own me, own it. How do I do that? Hmm. Personalize it maybe? Own it. Meaning, it's yours. HIV—the Human Immunodeficiency Virus or BIV—the Blake Immunodeficiency Virus. That's when it hit me; I don't have HIV. I have BIV! Own it, bitch!" (Blake, HIV10b)

Viewers for Blake's video commented that it inspired them greatly, thanking him. Steven, another HIV vlogger, began reading a letter he wrote to HIV:

"I can only blame me, not you, for coming into my life. Since our relationship began, I focused on what I lost, and neglected to see what you've actually given me – my life..." (Steven, HIV6b)

Through this letter, Steven was able to share how he integrated HIV as part of his life with his viewers. His interesting approach on speaking directly to HIV, as if it were a person, triggered thanks from the viewers, and many agreed with his thoughts.

Many *personal journals* used a stylistic format of a *talking head*, only featuring the author and their head. This style follows the idea of virtual social proxemics [29] and other work that has shown that the size of the image often affects the interaction of a videoconference [11]. Yet, unlike remote videoconferencing, vlogs are one-sided. Vloggers are not able to get immediate feedback from their audience.

Vloggers discussed how they were feeling, current updates, or past experiences using this style. Many would also share past experiences with the audience. In one example, an HIV vlogger explained his initial experience after his diagnosis, *"There were times in my life I got really involved in drinking, and I just wanted to forget about life. I wanted it to end"* (HIV1b).

Often, vloggers would also take the opportunity to plead for viewers to take action. In the case of HIV, Dan begged viewers to get tested if they hadn't already and to be safe and protected. He repeatedly said, *"It's not worth your life…yes, I'll live to a ripe old age, but how long will I live? I don't know"* (HIV7a). A cancer vlogger shared her past experience before getting diagnosed with uterine cancer, explaining some of the symptoms that showed up. She urged viewers that if they were experiencing any of these symptoms to *"please go see a doctor to make sure you're fine and that this is not happening to you"* (CAN7a). From these pleas, vloggers are able to show their concern and care for viewers, thus potentially increasing the connection between the vlogger and the viewers.

Self-Documentaries

Vlogs have the ability to capture situated, in-the-moment information that traditional text blogs cannot. Vloggers took advantage of this capability and allowed their viewers a glimpse into their highly situated experiences.

For instance, Sean, audio-recorded a confirmed diagnosis with his doctor, providing subtitles against a black screen. Although the viewers could not see the video of what was happening, the audio, together with the subtitles, intensified the delivery of what happened inside the clinic.

Beyond clinics, vloggers took the camera with them as they participated in various events. Jen had her husband film her during a triathlon (CAN3b). Another vlogger filmed his time at an AIDS conference (HIV9b). One vlogger brought his camera with him as he finished a military-like 5K run (HIV12b). Bringing the camera and allowing the viewers to get a peek into their lives, regardless of whether the content was directly related to the illness or not, allows moments of connectedness between the vlogger and the viewers.

Video Compilations

Vloggers also used creative ways to inspire and encourage their viewers by compiling video portraits of people sending positive messages. Although they were patients, the vloggers in these genres were not the main information givers of the vlogs, but rather, information gatherers.

Video compilations helped create a sense of community with those who are going through the same illness. For example, one diabetes vlogger uploaded a video that simply contained messages from people who attended a diabetes conference, saying their name, how long they have had diabetes, and *"you can do this!"* or *"I'm Type Awesome!"* (DIB3a) As written in the caption of the vlog, the purpose of this vlog was to give support to those struggling with living with diabetes.

In another vlog, Nicole started off by dancing and then explained that her friend's daughter who had Type 1 diabetes was about to get glasses, but was worried that people might make fun of her for wearing glasses and an insulin pump. Nicole said to the camera, *"So this video is for her, and I have a few friends that want to help me…c'mon guys!"* (DIB3b) and showed a slideshow of both photos and video clips of more than 50 people who were wearing both insulin pumps and glasses.

Some vloggers brought their viewers back into their vlogs for further inspiration for others. For example, Sean compiled videos sent from other viewers into a series. He introduced the series by saying,

> *"Several people have emailed me because the blog has touched people in so many different ways, so I'm providing an opportunity for people to tell their stories… how they became positive."* (Sean, HIV5b).

Here, the vlogger actively engaged his viewers through his vlogs, which in turn connected him with his viewers.

The Affordances of Video

Vlogs allow a form of presentation that traditional text blogs do not allow. Vloggers used cameras to film themselves talking, show their cats, capture real-time moments, use animations, demonstrate how to do things, or make picture slide shows. This high level of customization enabled vloggers to take control of their vlogs' presentation and content, which is a means for self-expression [38]. In the following, we discuss several affordances of video, including *non-verbal cues, other actors*, and *context filming* as ways vloggers took control of their vlog presentation.

Nonverbal Cues: Connection and Building Rapport

Nonverbal cues are typically visual cues without words. We observed our vloggers trying to build personal connections and rapport with viewers through their nonverbal cues, such as pausing, crying, or giving facial expressions.

Subtle but powerful pauses in speaking can create a range of emotions that vloggers and viewers can share. Jen, who wanted to express how much compassion she had for another cancer survivor's video, looked directly into the camera and paused for ten seconds, occasionally sniffing to hold back tears and said *"I feel closer to you now that I know your family history"* (CAN3a_0). Similarly, Felicia, another breast cancer survivor continuously suppressed her tears as she shared her update:

> *"As much as I don't want to deal with that, I understand that I have to because it is part of my journey. <pauses and sniffs, sighs> But um, I'm really, really grateful <sniffs, looks down, pauses> that the surgery was a success <clears the throat>. I'm really grateful that I am cancer free."* (Felicia, CAN4b)

Blake wanted to share his emotional state at the time of diagnosis as HIV positive with his viewers (HIV10a). He paused, glanced, gave emotional expressions, and eventually sobbed (Figure 3), which helped create a personal connection that would have been hard to do with traditional text-blogs.

The vloggers also used humorous expressions to build rapport with the viewers. John wanted to show how regular blood work for HIV patients is done. He asked the nurse to explain the purpose of blood work, blood containers, and then the needle, to which he changed the camera angle to show his face humorously frowning (HIV4a). Eric, a cancer vlogger, adjusted his webcam while making a silly face at the camera (CAN2a).

Most importantly, for highly stigmatized diseases such as HIV, disclosing one's face, name, and family history in front of a worldwide audience can be quite intimidating. Yet, the vloggers used this disclosure to create intense and personal connections with the viewers.

Other Actors

Another unique component we saw from vlogs was incorporating more than one actor in the scene. These actors included significant others (CAN3b, HIV7b), pets (CAN2b, CAN3a), or health care providers (CAN6b) who provided further context about the vloggers and their situation.

Other actors participated in vlogs to send messages for the vloggers when the vlogger was not available (CAN1b, CAN3b), broadcasted events in the moment as vloggers participated in those events (CAN3b, HIV4a), or became the ambiance of the video that added meaning to the message being delivered to the viewers (HIV7b, DIB7b).

For instance, the goal of Dan's vlog was to deliver a teaching message on what to do after having unprotected sex with someone who is HIV positive. In this video, Dan's partner, who is HIV negative, was sitting beside him. The caption of the video says:

> *"If you think you may have been exposed to HIV or a condom has broken or if you are having unprotected sex, please watch this as this video was done by my partner who is HIV negative and I thank him for his courage...he is amazing"* (Dan, HIV7b)

Figure 3. Blake (HIV10a) wiped away tears as he shared his experience about being newly diagnosed with HIV.

Having an HIV negative person disclose their face with an HIV positive partner can be a highly stigmatized activity. This strengthened Dan's delivered message of safe sex.

In Sean's video, his doctor was present, though only through voice. As a form of self-documentary, Sean captured the moment of being diagnosed, shocked by his doctor's words that Sean had a large viral load (HIV5a).

> Doctor: *"It's a positive viral load...you expected that."*
> Sean: *"I did?"*
> Doctor: *"So...your viral load right is like, a 5,517,000."*
> Sean: *"5 million? Oh my god. Wow, okay. I was hoping for, like, 12."* (Sean, HIV5a)

The next scene shows Sean's concerned face outside the hospital, telling the camera that he is now flying home to tell his parents about the diagnosis. In the vlogs, Sean showed himself as being nervous but trying hard to stay calm and positive.

Using the voice exchange with his physician in the video, the emotional progress, and externalization of his inside voices, Sean was able to capture his fear, anger, sadness, and surprise in that moment.

Context-Filming

Videos have a great ability to capture "in-the-moment" without needing to describe them in text. The most frequent background in vlogs was the vloggers' rooms, especially the back wall behind the vloggers' talking head. In this case, viewers would then focus on the message being delivered by the vlogger. However, once vloggers began to push the boundaries of where the vlog was filmed as well what their appearance was, richer context began to add onto the vlogs. Furthermore, they began adding rich context to augment and intensify their messages to viewers.

For instance, Ted filmed his first vlog at home in his room, but his last video titled, "My HIV Life 'Obstacles'", showed himself in front of a red brick wall. He explained that the red bricks were a symbol of strength because they stayed the same throughout any obstacle: *"I wanted to intentionally film in front of the red brick wall, so that we all get over obstacles for a reason and to stay strong." (Ted, HIV3b)*

Background transitions in vlogs also helped vloggers effectively convey context. Paul started his cancer vlog by describing his synovial sarcoma and history with the hospital waiting room as his background. As he progressed through the hospital visit, the backgrounds changed from the waiting room to the hospital room, where he was getting his chemotherapy, and then back home. During this transition, he walked through his medical history, current status, and remaining treatments to be done. In the vlog, he gave small show-and-tells, for instance, explaining specifics of how the warm blanket around his arm allowed for easier IV insertion and then showing his arm with the IV inserted (Figure 4). Such show-and-tells, tied with a hospital setting as a background, was Paul's choice to deliver his context more effectively to his viewers, as he noted, *"Once they call me in, I'm just going to go over the different things that they do in the chemo room"* (Paul, CAN9a).

Vloggers also captured their vulnerable appearance to inspire others and to help them learn. Ely, a brain tumor patient, filmed himself in a vulnerable state, while lying in a hospital bed with a nasal cannula and wires around him. He then stated, *"I wanted to take my experience as a photo journalist to help people learn from my tragedy"* (CAN11a). Similarly, Tom presented himself as vulnerable and not willing to live, filming himself in bed 7 days after his diagnosis of HIV. He repeatedly stated, *"I refuse to participate in this world"* (HIV2a). In contrast, a year after the initial vlog, he posted a photo slideshow as part of his HIV vlog series, where he was standing in front of the White House holding up a picket saying, *"I am HIV+"* along with pictures of him and many supporters smiling.

One of critical elements in peer patient support is sharing emotional experience situated in context [20]. Through health vlogs, vloggers brought an intense personal connection to the viewers, through nonverbal cues and enriched context of major illness events using other actors and background context. Accordingly, health vlogs are particularly useful for peer patient support. At the same time, not only peer patients but any individual interested in the health problem, such as undiagnosed patients or care providers, could learn about the disease from health vlogs more thoroughly than through traditional text-based blogs.

Requesting Viewer Interaction

In contrast to the implicit methods for vloggers to establish viewer connection that we just described, in this section we describe explicit methods used to request viewer interaction and build a connection with viewers.

Vloggers also sought viewer interaction by verbally responding to comments or certain groups of viewers. In one example, Roger used his vlog to address his reaction to a certain group of his viewers:

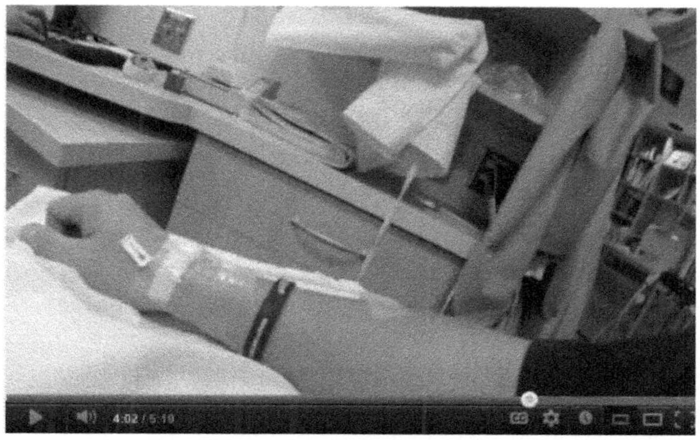

Figure 4. : Paul (CAN9) showed viewers what his IV insertion looked like.

> *"All of you HIV denialists that keep hitting me up and keep leaving comments on my channel...stating that I am misinformed, informing me how HIV is nothing but some kind of scam that was cooked up by the government and Illuminati...I appreciate what you guys are doing, but I will frankly have to say, carry that bullshit to someone else's page...I don't want to hear that..."* (Roger, HIV11b)

Other vloggers solicited viewers' interactions by requesting comments or questions. Anthony ended his video with the following message to explicitly request interaction: *"If you have any comments or questions, go ahead and shoot it back to me, and I'd be more than happy to answer that"* (Anthony, DIB5a).

Another vlogger encouraged his viewers to help guide the direction of future videos by saying, *"If you see this, comment on it. I'll try to add more as I go on"* (CAN5a). Others asked the viewers to correct them if they gave out incorrect information, using the viewers as gatekeepers. For example, Anthony said, *"Questions, comments, you want to call me out on something? Maybe I got something wrong? Maybe I got lots of things wrong"* (DIB5b).

These types of interaction requests were fairly common for many of the vloggers, but some tried to engage their viewers in a unique way to spark further interaction. Carl, a diabetes vlogger uploaded a vlog about a prize giveaway:

> *"Just leave a comment on this post that includes the words 'Bacon Wrap My Pump', and you can be one of six lucky winners of this sweet bacon skin for your Medtronic insulin pump!"* (Carl, DIB6b)

Some vloggers provided a way for viewers to communicate by providing external links such as to their Facebook, Twitter, email, website, and even a phone number. Steven, for instance, wrote his phone number and email address on a piece of paper and showed it to the camera, telling the viewers to contact him if they need help (HIV6a).

DISCUSSION

Our results show that health vloggers use a variety of implicit and explicit ways to create a connection with their viewers. Below, we discuss how the vlogger-viewer connection is critical for two main motivations in health vlogging: self-therapy and helping others.

Self-Therapy

Many vloggers stated that they created vlogs for their own benefits. Some mentioned that vlogging was something their psychiatrist recommended, while others just hoped that it would help them in some way. Nonetheless, the self-therapeutic aspect of health vlogs was not confined to helping oneself. As vloggers mentioned in their vlogs, having the added benefit of helping others while helping themselves gave vlogging a greater purpose than a means to indulge in narcissism [12]. Although there was usually no validation that their vlogs had helped anyone, knowing that there was the potential helped many vloggers.

Particularly for the vloggers with diabetes or HIV where the illnesses were dependent on self-management strategies, creating vlogs helped hold the vloggers accountable for their actions. If vloggers stated a plan of action or even suggested their viewers to act upon a plan, vloggers would then be expected to follow suit.

Helping Others: Dealing with the Invisible Audience

Many vloggers also stated in their vlogs and captions that their main purpose was to help others by inspiring them and teaching them with the expertise they gained over many years. In our findings, we discussed altruistic motivations playing into teaching and personal journal vlogs. Many explained that they wanted to share their experiences with those who were recently diagnosed or were struggling with their illness because vloggers did not receive the right kinds of help when they needed them.

However, the interpretation of "helping others" varied. In personal journal vlogs, some vloggers believed that speaking freely to the camera about what was on their mind would be helpful to others. As shown in the teaching vlogs, others took an educational route by including tangible strategies and solutions that could be useful to viewers.

Although vloggers explicitly mentioned helping others as one reason for creating vlogs, we did not find much evidence that they received confirmation from their viewers saying that it was helpful, unless viewers contacted vloggers through comments or private messages. This notion of an *invisible audience*, where vloggers do not have any knowledge of their viewers, was observed throughout many of the vlogs. For example, Dan, an HIV vlogger said:

> *"[If] one person listens, and one person doesn't catch this chronic illness...I'll never meet you–whoever you are–then, I'll sleep better tonight."* (Dan, HIV7a)

For vloggers, simply believing that they helped others gave them a sense of peace, perhaps, serving as self-therapy too.

At the same time, as we discussed in *requesting viewer interaction*, some vloggers attempted to gain explicit feedback from their viewers. The attempt to explicitly connect with viewers may have been vloggers' struggle to grasp their invisible audience into companions, whom vloggers can consider as partners of social support.

DESIGN IMPLICATIONS

Health vloggers experienced challenges in their attempts to interact with their viewers. Below, we walk through those challenges and discuss design implications.

Allowing Personalized Presentation and Message Delivery

Health vloggers used nonverbal cues to enable intense personal connection with their viewers and used various genres to convey their messages more effectively. Current vlogging systems underexplore using vloggers' nonverbal cues as information resources or giving vloggers the ability to tailor presentation and deliver of vlogs. Health vlogging systems have the potential to use new signal processing techniques to record metadata about the frequency and quality of nonverbal cues (*e.g.*, [4]). Machine learning techniques could be used to determine metadata features automatically. Using this metadata, systems could inform vloggers about their use of nonverbal cues and their potential impact on viewers' interpretation of the vlog. Systems could also suggest vlogs based on this metadata to viewers who are looking for intense personal connection more so than informational content. However, with current technologies, searching for content and style is much easier to do in text than in video. This search challenge indicates an important gap that requires further research.

Currently, the quality of presentation depends on the vloggers' technical knowledge and software. Health vlogging systems can provide users with templates to help users create various genres and style of presentation. For instance, for vloggers who want to teach disease management strategies, the wizard can provide templates to use images, pointers, and screen shots. The wizard can also provide ideas for presenting and delivering messages using examples from other vloggers. Health vlogging systems can also support the creation of vlogs through mobile devices, letting users create and upload videos in the moment.

Supporting Distinct Disease Characteristics

About social stigma. Because of YouTube's open and public nature as well as the identifying characteristics of video and audio, vloggers must be willing to make a public disclosure. HIV vloggers in our study intentionally disclosed their diagnosis to the worldwide audience as a tool to overcome social stigma. However, all the HIV vloggers we studied were homosexual males, implying that the stigmatization of the disease still prevents some from vlogging about their disease thereby limiting the amount of self-therapy they can receive by using this helpful media.

Health vlogging systems could allow vloggers to customize the level of disclosure. YouTube currently offers an option called Xtranormal Movie Maker[3] which allows the vlogger to "set up [a] scene, type in [a] script, and animate it instantly." This feature lets the vlogger share their story and experience without having to fully disclose their face, voice or name. Yet, we did not observe any of the vloggers in our study using this feature. Furthermore, the system allows vloggers to generate a "mask" to hide facial features or to upload only voice with photo slideshows or even blank screen with titles. Systems could further utilize this feature to allow vloggers to restrict personal information and encourage those who are wary to share their experiences.

About differing content. Vloggers used different genres depending on the stage of the disease and emotional state., In turn, these genres created different kinds of interaction. Diabetes vlogs used graphic tools to present workable self-care strategies, whereas vloggers attempting to inspire the newly diagnosed used nonverbal cues, such as crying or sharing raw footage of the time of the diagnosis.

Providing additional information or resources to viewers is not something that is as well supported by current vlogging systems. YouTube allows the vlogger to write a description below the video, but information can sometimes get lost if there is too much of it. To address this problem, health vlogging systems could create a sidebar by the vlog where vloggers can add information at specific timestamps. The information could be about chapters in their teaching messages, stages of illness trajectory, their personal history, resources they might have mentioned, or points of nonverbal cues that viewers can use either to skim what the vlog is about or to "fast-forward" to the moment of their interest. This feature provides more related content to the viewer. It also allows the viewer to search for or scan and choose what segments of the video they are interested in, instead of having to watch the entire video.

Providing Sustainable Viewer Connections

In online communities, members have sustained relationships and reciprocity in sharing experiences and information. However, we saw little of such vlogger-viewer interaction happening in YouTube. The only viewer interaction mechanisms that YouTube support are commenting and voting features. Because the current organization allows for vloggers to interact with a general audience, vloggers can be attacked by harsh comments [21]. This also does not promote long-term connections with viewers. Health vlogging systems should be able to facilitate sustained viewer engagement and community. A variety of modalities could help accomplish this goal. Integrating asynchronous video-based communication systems, such as VideoPal [18], into health vlogging systems could help sustain viewer connection and generate a sense of community. Viewers could leave comments inside particular segments of the vlog. Viewers could also utilize video as a way to communicate back to the vlogger. Systems can record information about participants in these comments to profile users, which then can be used to suggest viewers and vloggers into vlogs or topic based communities within the health vlogging tools. The system can further support local meet ups, virtual gatherings, and suggestions of advocacy and fundraising events.

[3] http://www.youtube.com/create_detail/Xtranormal

CONCLUSION

Health vlogs allow individuals with chronic illnesses to share their experience, knowledge, and stories with others. Connections among patients, such as those between vloggers and their viewers, have shown to be a form of social support and are self-therapeutic for health vloggers. However, little has been done in trying to sustain and strengthen health vloggers' connections with their viewers.

We presented the results of a qualitative study to understand how health vloggers attempt to connect with their viewers as a form of self-therapy and social support. Our results show that health vloggers use the uniqueness of video as a way to create rich and strong connections. Vloggers also use specific genres and other explicit methods to communicate personalized messages and connect with their viewers. Based on the results of our study, we presented design implications to improve and provide more sustainable viewer connections. By supporting and encouraging the vlogger-viewer connection, new technologies can enable health vloggers to help others while helping themselves.

ACKNOWLEDGMENTS

This work was supported in part by the NIH NLM training grant (2T15LM007442). We also thank the iMed research group, Gillian Hayes, Norman Makoto Su, and Patrick Shih for their valuable feedback on previous drafts.

REFERENCES

1. Barrera, M., Ainlay, S. The Structure of Social Support: A Conceptual and Empirical Analysis. Journal of Community Psychology, 133-143. 1983.
2. Biemans, M., van Dijk, B., Dadlani, P., van Halteren, A. Let's Stay in Touch: Sharing Photos for Restoring Social Connectedness between Rehabilitants, Friends, and Family. In Proc. SICACCESS'09, 179-186.
3. Brubaker, J., Lustig, C., Hayes, G.R. PatientsLikeMe: Empowerment and Representation in a Patient-Centered Social Network. CSCW'10; Workshop on Research in Healthcare: Past, Present, and Future.
4. Byun, B., Awasthi, A., Chou, P.A., Kapoor, A., Lee, B., Czerwinski, M. Honest Signals in Video Conferencing. In Proc. ICME'11, 1-6.
5. Charmaz, K. Loss of Self: A Fundamental Form of Suffering in the Chronically Ill. Journal of Sociology of Health and Illness, 168-195. 1983.
6. Chou, W.S., Hunt, Y., Folkers, A., Auguston, E. Cancer Survivorship in the Age of YouTube and Social Media: A Narrative Analysis. Journal of Medical Internet Research. 2011.

7. Chung, D.S., Kim, S. Blogging Activity Among Cancer Patients and Their Companions: Uses, Gratifications, and Predictors of Outcomes. JASIST, 297-306. 2008.
8. Fernandez-Luque, L., Elahi, N., Grajales III, F.J. An Analysis of Personal Medical Information Disclosed in YouTube Videos Created by Patients with Multiple Sclerosis. Studies in Health Technology Information, 292-296. 2009.
9. Figueiredo, M.A., Prado, P., Camara, M.A., Alburquerque, A.M. Empowering Rural Citizen Journalism via Web 2.0 Technologies. In Proc. C&T'09, 77-84.
10. Foucault, M. The History of Sexuality, Vol. 1: An Introduction. Éditions Gallimard. 1978.
11. Grayson, D., Coventry, L. The Effects of Visual Proxemic Information in Video Mediated Communication. SIGCHI Bulletin, 30-39. 1998.
12. Griffith, M., Papacharissi, Z. Looking for You: An Analysis of Video Blogs. First Monday. 2010.
13. Goffman, E. The Presentation of Self in Everyday Life. Anchor. 1959.
14. Henderson, A. Abused Women and Peer-Provided Social Support: The Nature and Dynamics of Reciprocity in a Crisis Setting. Issues in Mental Health Nursing, 117-128. 1995.
15. Hibbard, E.S., Fels, D.I. The Vlogging Phenomena: A Deaf Perspective. In Proc. ASSETS'11, 59-66.
16. Hoff, T., Mishel, M., Rowe, I. Using New Media to Make HIV Personal: A Partnership of MTV and the Kaiser Family Foundation. Cases in Public Health Communication & Marketing '08, 190-197.
17. Hoffman, D.L, Fodor, M. Can You Measure the ROI of Your Social Media marketing? MIT Sloan Management Review, 41-49. 2010.
18. Inkpen, K., Du, H., Roseway, A., Hoff, A., Johns, P. Video Kids: Augmenting Close Friendships with Asynchronous Video Conversations in VideoPal. In Proc. CHI'12, 2387-2396.
19. Krause, N., Herzog, A.R., Baker, E. Providing Support to Others and Well-being in Later Life. Journal of Gerontology, 300-311. 1992.
20. Kurtz, L.F. Self-Help and Support Groups: A Handbook for Practitioners. Sage. 1997.
21. Lange, P.G. Commenting on comments: Investigating responses to antagonism on YouTube. Conference of the Society for Applied Anthropology '07, 1-26.
22. Lange, P.G. Publicly Private and Privately Public: Social Networking on YouTube. Journal of CMC, 361-380. 2008.
23. Markham, T. Hunched Over Their Laptops: Phenomenological Perspectives on Citizen Journalism. Presented at MeCCSA'10.
24. Matthews, N. Confessions to a New Public: Video Nation Shorts. Media Culture Society, 435-449. 2007.
25. Miller, E.A., Pole, A. Diagnosis Blog: Checking Up on Health Blogs in the Blogosphere. American Journal of Public Health, 1514-1519. 2010.
26. Molyneaux, H., O'Donnell, S. Patient Portals 2.0: The Potential for Online Video. In Proc. COACH'09, 1-15.
27. Nardi, B.A., Schiano, D.J., Gumbrecht, M., Swartz, L. Why We Blog. Communications of ACM '04, 41-46.
28. Nardi, B.A., Schiano, D.J., Gumbrecht, M. Blogging as Social Activity, or, Would You Let 900 Million People Read Your Diary? In Proc. CSCW'04, 222-231.
29. Olson, G.M., Olson, J.S. Distance Matters. HCI, 139-178. 2000.
30. Raun, T. DIY Therapy: Exploring Affective Aspects of Trans Video Blogs on YouTube. Palgrave Macmillian. 2012.
31. Renov, M., Suderburg, E. Resolutions: Contemporary Video Practices. University of Minneapolis Press. 1996.
32. Ressler, P.K., Bradshaw, Y.S., Gualtieri, L., Chui, K.K.H. Communicating the Experience of Chronic Pain and Illness Through Blogging. Journal of Medical Internet Research. 2012.
33. Ridgeway, P. Restorying Psychiatric Disability: Learning from First Person Recovery Narratives. Psychiatric Rehabilitation Journal, 335-343. 2001.
34. Schwartz, C.E., Sendor, R.M. Helping Others Helps Oneself: Response Shift Effects in Peer Support. Social Science & Medicine, 1563-1575. 1999.
35. Sundar, S.S., Edwards, H.H., Hu, Y., Stavrositu, C. Blogging for Better Health: Putting the "Public" Back in Public Health. Routledge. 2006.
36. Tan, L. Psychotherapy 2.0: MySpace Blogging as Self-Therapy. AJP, 143-163. 2008.
37. Thoits, P.A. Stress, Coping, and Social Support Processes: Where Are We? What Next? Journal of Health and Social Behavior, 53-79. 1995.
38. Tremayne, M. Blogging, Citizenship, and the Future of Media. Routledge. 2006.
39. Trier, J. "Cool" Engagements With YouTube: Part 1. Journal of Adolescent & Adult Literacy, 408-412. 2007.
40. Turkle, S. Looking Toward Cyberspace: Beyond Grounded Sociology. Contemporary Sociology, 643-648. 1999.
41. Valverde, M. Experience and Truth-Telling in a Post-Humanist World: A Foucauldian Contribution to Feminist Ethical Relations. University of Illinois Press. 2004.
42. Waldron, J. YouTube, Fanvids, Forums, Vlogs and Blogs: Informal Music Learning in a Convergent On- and Offline Music Community.International Journal of Music Education, 1-16. 2012.

Accessible Online Content Creation By End Users

Katie Kuksenok, Michael Brooks
University Of Washington
Seattle, WA 98105
kuksenok@cs.washington.edu, mjbrooks@uw.edu

Jennifer Mankoff
Carnegie Mellon University
5000 Forbes Ave, Pittsburgh, PA 15206
jmankoff@cs.cmu.edu

ABSTRACT
Like most online content, user-generated content (UGC) poses accessibility barriers to users with disabilities. However, the accessibility difficulties pervasive in UGC warrant discussion and analysis distinct from other kinds of online content. Content authors, community culture, and the authoring tool itself all affect UGC accessibility. The choices, resources available, and strategies in use to ensure accessibility are different than for other types of online content. We contribute case studies of two UGC communities with accessible content: Wikipedia, where authors focus on access to visual materials and navigation, and an online health support forum where users moderate the cognitive accessibility of posts. Our data demonstrate real world moderation strategies and illuminate factors affecting success, such as community culture. We conclude with recommended strategies for creating a culture of accessibility around UGC.

Author Keywords: Accessibility, User-generated content

ACM Classification Keywords: H.1.2 **[User/Machine Systems]:** Human factors, Human Information Processing

INTRODUCTION
The ease with which end users can generate content is a defining feature of the World Wide Web. The ease of authoring HTML initially encouraged end user content creation. As more complex web technologies like CSS and Ajax have become ubiquitous, content editors provided by social media sites such as blogs and wikis have made it even easier to create content. Although the diversity and amount of user-generated content is increasing, much of it suffers from accessibility problems.

Web accessibility has been a rich research area for decades, including identification of accessibility problems (*e.g.*, [1] [2]), accessibility metrics [3], automatic improvement of website accessibility through content extraction [4] and crowd-sourcing [5], and both server and client side content modification (*e.g.*, [6]). This work has tended to focus on content producers who have the resources to generate their own HTML/CSS and/or run studies of web accessibility. In contrast, end users generating content must deal with third party tools (such as WordPress.com or forum sites), and end users consuming content are dependent on both third party tool creators and end user content creators for accessible content. Studies of end-user content generation tools (*e.g.*, [7], [8]) point to the need for accessible authoring tools (*e.g.*, [8], [9]) but much of the work in this area has focused on the end user experience rather than the author experience.

Our contribution to this literature is a qualitative study of end user moderation of accessibility based on online data drawn from two existing communities. Our analysis, based on data drawn from Wikipedia's *Accessibility* project and from an online health forum, LymeSpace (a pseudonym), demonstrates the existence of a variety of mediation strategies that arise when authors are asked to make content more accessible. Our findings demonstrate that good authoring tools alone cannot ensure accessibility. The culture of a website and the training and personal circumstances of the author producing content impacts the accessibility of the content created. For example, users who have difficulty accessing content may have an intrinsic incentive to produce accessible content.

We demonstrate that accessible end user content creation requires structural support that goes beyond rules in the existing World Wide Web consortium (W3C) accessible content creation guidelines [10]. These needs include better tools, organizational support, support for author advocacy for other authors or readers, and support for the fluid way in which accessibility may be defined across different communities.

Next, we present a literature survey highlighting what is known about the accessibility issues and solutions currently being used across four main types of UGC: Wikis, Blogs, Forums and Social Networks. Following that we present our two case studies (Wikipedia and LymeSpace). We end with implications for design, proposing goals for UGC platform developers that focus on creating tools that can support a culture of producing accessible content.

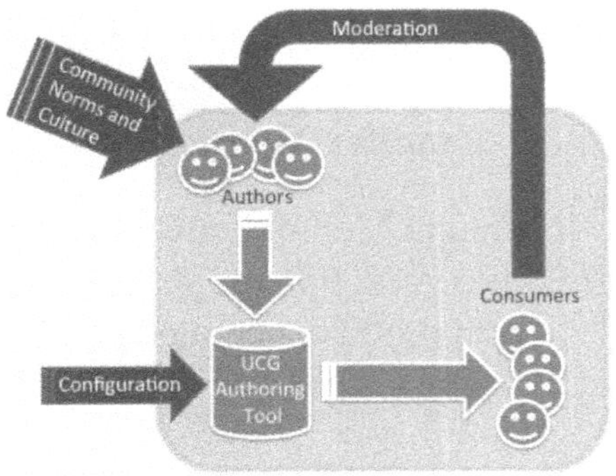

Figure 1: Content is generated by end users (*authors*) using a UCG authoring tool (such as a wiki or blog) and read by end users (*consumers*) who may also be authors. Existing guidelines focus primarily on the UCG authoring tool, and most studies of this domain focus on the consumer experience. Our studies of authors show that additional factors, such as moderation strategies and community norms and culture, can affect the accessibility of content.

AUTHORING ACCESSIBLE UGC

Breakdowns in accessibility involve three primary factors: UGC authoring tools, content *authors*, and content *consumers* (who may also be authors). Figure 1 summarizes these (in red). As our studies show, factors such as community norms and culture may also influence the accessibility of content. However the focus of existing literature and guidelines has primarily been on the consumer experience and the features of authoring tools.

Authoring tools that support accessible content are of broad interest, evidenced by the existence of the W3C's authoring tool accessibility guidelines (www.w3.org/TR/ATAG10/). These guidelines focus on both authoring tool accessibility and how authoring tools can support the production of accessible content. They emphasize the need to guide users in creating accessible content, assist authors in checking for accessibility problems, and promote accessibility features.

For example, developers of a wiki or a blog may hide the underlying HTML from a user with a simplified markup language or a WYSWYG editor. As a result the user may never see whether an image has an ALT attribute—a piece of metadata optionally associated with images in webpages, and used by screen readers. Additionally, structural elements of a site, like the navigation bar, are often pre-specified. The placement or existence of accessibility features may be completely outside of the control of the author of the content itself. For example, skip links, which allow users of screen readers to skip over navigation and reach the content of a page, are typically in the navigation area of a page, which UGC authors do not control. Authoring software may allow content authors to make use of headings appropriately, caption images using the ALT attribute, or edit the raw HTML. However, even then, authors may not be comfortable doing so, or may not know how to use these options to improve content accessibility.

Existing research has focused on the accessibility of specific types of UGC (*e.g.*, Wikis [8] and Facebook [11]). We summarize existing work in the context of four popular types of end user generated content: Wikis, blogs, discussion forums, and social network sites.

Wikis

Wikis, which range from personal places such as a Google Sites home page to vast public websites such as Wikipedia, are comprised entirely of content generated by users through iterative edits over time. The variation in wiki software is huge. Taras *et al.* [8] separate accessibility concerns into content viewing; content authoring (including accessibility of authoring tools and their capacity to support the production of accessible content); and actions that are specific to Wikis such as comparing versions of content, navigating recent changes, and so on. They point to the benefits of *group authoring* in helping to build accessibility "step by step."

Valtolina *et al.* describe a wiki, VisualPedia, designed to be accessible to content consumers [12]. It provides features such as image simplification, and was designed to meet as many accessibility guidelines as possible. Taras *et al.* propose a set of goals for Wiki accessibility that focus accessibility as the "conjunction of web authoring and viewing" [8]. An explicit focus on accessibility of authoring – and the capacity to support authoring of accessible content is an important goal that few have focused on.

Blogs

Blogs typically have only one or a few authors, and posts are usually organized chronologically and may be read over an RSS reader, by email, or on the website itself. Some blog sites also double as wikis of a sort.

The American Foundation for the Blind (AFB) studied two popular blogging platforms and 4 popular blogs [9]. Their survey identified accessibility issues in blog creation, most prominently inaccessible CAPTCHAs that affected account creation. Once an account is created, authors can create blog posts fairly easily. However, in the case of more structured, complex content, such as tables, authors typically must edit HTML directly to add table captions, and documentation for this is not consistently available.

Reading a blog presents far fewer problems than authoring a blog. However getting a sense of a blog can be difficult due to the large amount of content found on many blogs, and the AFB recommends allowing readers to receive content through alternative means (such as email) [9].

Discussion Forums

A discussion forum facilitates threaded discussions between members. Interestingly, although we found studies of forum content generated by individuals with disabilities (*e.g.* [13] [14] [15]), we found none that address the question of content accessibility. Rather, these studies contrast online forums with offline support groups in terms of accessibility (online forums win here). Perhaps the accessibility of end user generated content is not an issue, because of the relative simplicity of websites such as forums and blogs in comparison to shopping sites, email sites, and so on. Or perhaps accessibility is seen as an inherent property of the site and is therefore not a topic of discussion for end users. However, in our case study, some forum users are concerned about accessible content generation, and forum software may present barriers to creating accessible content.

Social Network Sites

Social network sites refer to sites that allow a user to create a profile and share it with others. Most also support a variety of other activities (often based around sharing information with others). In a survey of visually impaired users, Leahy *et al.* [7] found that the accessibility of social websites was a major challenge for 80% of their participants. Some of the major accessibility challenges include lack of descriptions of non-textual content (a major issue for 65% of visually impaired respondents); misuse of tables (62%); badly designed online forms (70%); use of an inaccessible CAPTCHA for sign up (95%) and difficulty controlling video/audio players (63%) [7].

End users may not think about social network participation as authoring in the same way that blog or wiki authors do. As a result, *indirect* support for accessibility is important. For example, simplified mobile versions of online platforms may implicitly address accessibility problems. In a study comparing Facebook and Facebook Mobile, blind participants using the mobile interface with a screen reader had higher completion rates and shorter completion times on sample tasks [11]. Despite possible accessibility advantages of mobile UIs, Wentz *et al.* urge application developers not to rely on separate "accessible" and "inaccessible" interfaces as a solution [11]. Separate UIs provide distinct functionality, and the accessible version may not be kept up to date. An Application Programming Interface (API) can also support accessibility. For example, using Twitter's API an independent developer can replicate Twitter in an accessible fashion (*e.g.,* easychirp.com) [16]. The intentional minimalism of Twitter's features and an accepted diversity of wrappers for Twitter facilitate this.

Survey Conclusions

End user content generation tools are neither accessible to authors nor do they easily facilitate the production of accessible UGC. To meet basic accessibility guidelines, authors may have to edit HTML directly, which is overly burdensome for most authors. Despite the difficulty of authoring accessible UGC, consumers may still be able to read UGC by leveraging existing alternative interfaces such as email updates from blogs and mobile interfaces to social network sites, or by using a third party interface that builds on an API that encapsulates key features of a site, as in the case of Twitter. However, these work-around solutions raise questions about a dual standard for access, and do not address many of the key recommendations in the W3C's guidelines for authoring accessible UGC.

Thus, accessibility must be addressed during content authorship. However, improved authoring tools is not sufficient. Accessibility can be hard for non-expert UGC authors to evaluate [2]. Like usability, it is best achieved using an iterative process, involving multiple people. This may require additional time and effort from authors who may or may not value accessibility. As a result, community norms and expectations, although not a focus of the work we surveyed, are likely to play a critical role in real world attempts to create accessible UGC.

The studies presented next show how community culture may encourage or discourage accessible content creation. To explore this issue we turn to examples where end users themselves encourage accessible content creation. We call this process *accessibility moderation*. Although end-user moderation of accessibility may be unusual, studying it can provide valuable insights into what it takes to generate accessible UGC. The next two sections explore two exemplary communities of practice we uncovered.

CASE STUDY ONE: WIKIPEDIA

Wikipedia, an online encyclopedia written by volunteer authors, has a complex social structure and mechanisms for coordination among editors [17]. All Wikipedia pages have a *Talk* page where discussions relevant to the content of that page take place. Our analysis focused on *Talk* pages that included discussions of accessibility issues. We will refer to the specific author of a page as the *author* or (A#), other editors involved in accessibility discussions as *moderator* (M#), and content consumers as *readers.*

Wikipedia has a formal channel for handling accessibility problems. The *AccessibilityDispute* template can be added to a content page by any moderator when they believe that there is an accessibility problem with a page. This adds a message at the top of the content page declaring that "this article's accessibility is in question." The specific problems are discussed on the content's associated *Talk* page, where moderators or authors can work out a resolution for the problem. Wikipedia also has an *Accessibility* Project, where meta issues about how to handle accessibility are discussed, and individuals can post accessibility-related questions.

In addition to content itself, authors can create templates, which function as a sort of intermediary between authors and the authoring tool. These templates are at times themselves the subject of accessibility discussions.

Wikipedia Method

We used a snowball sample to collect data for our analysis of Wikipedia, starting with the *AccessibilityDispute* template page and the *Accessibility* project and talk pages. These three pages are central to the work being done around accessibility on Wikipedia. Wikipedia's *WhatLinksHere* feature lists all of the links to a page. Using

WhatLinksHere, we downloaded the text from 68 pages linking to the *AccessibilityDispute* template and 50 pages linking to the *Accessibility* project and talk pages as of September 2012. After removing duplicates and pages whose content was not accessibility related, we were left with 29 pages in our final sample. Some had a single paragraph of text relating to accessibility, others had many pages of text containing many different accessibility discussions. Across all 29 pages, we identified 179 accessibility discussions involving 82 contributors. Of these, ten contributors currently have their name listed on the main Accessibility project page (these ten participated in 33% of the discussions, and are referenced as moderators M1-M10 when quoted). The remaining participants are referred to as authors A11-A82 when quoted.

The data was coded by the third author. Through open coding, we generated 69 codes, which were then grouped into 22 categories using selective coding. Based on these categories, we identified central themes such as the importance of authority. We present our data using representative quotes, modified to preserve anonymity.

Wikipedia Case Study Results

Wikipedia's Accessibility project, run by 32 moderators, centralizes efforts to make Wikipedia more accessible. The scope of accessibility problems as defined by the project is based on the WCAG 2.0 guidelines, aiming for level AA compliance. Although accessibility in Wikipedia is defined according to accepted national standards, we will show that the definition of accessibility was still disputed.

In practice, most problems discussed in our data set had either to do with visual elements (9 discussions about color, font size, animations, ALT tags, *etc.*); tables (5 discussions); or internationalization (2 discussions).

We identified several roles assumed by moderators within the Accessibility project. When moderating *content accessibility,* a moderator provides advice, guidance, or critique relating to an author's content. When moderating *Wikipedia accessibility*, the moderator is influencing meta-issues such as Wikipedia policy. Guideline design and tool configuration were also issues of concern for moderators.

Moderation Styles and Outcomes

A moderator officially initiates moderation of content by adding an *AccessibilityDispute* template to a page. However, other kinds of moderation are also common, such as educating authors (by restating or explaining guidelines; encouraging authors to download a screen reader for testing; or linking to articles on accessibility); and directly editing content. Sometimes an accessibility dispute arises without moderation and is then brought to the attention of the *Accessibility* project *via* a post to a project page.

Even moderators who were already oriented toward accessibility issues struggled to accomplish it ("didn't realise this accessibility stuff would be so difficult" [M15]). As a result, moderators or authors sometimes requested experts to step in and help with a discussion. For example:

> "Could an expert explain why it is important not to skip heading levels at [link to discussion]....I feel I cannot do it justice" [A11].

> "After [another author reverted my change] I was wondering if you could provide advice about placement [of visual element] because I could not find helpful information." [A15]

More experienced moderators can provide evidence and authority to support an author's position and help make a change successful.

The Role of Authority. Moderators tended to have more authority than other authors, but their background also affected their authority. For example, one moderator pointed out that "since [a person with a disability] began to help with improving accessibility, he has been listened to more than all of us" [M10]. M10 actively encouraged other users with disabilities to participate in moderation.

Authority is important for moderators, because sometimes authors did not want to comply with moderator requests. Although moderators sometimes idealized the process ("It isn't that hard to make sure a page is accessible - just use conventional formatting and heading standards" [M2]), in eight discussions, moderators and authors spent significant time on tensions between accessibility goals and other editing goals. For example, authors/moderators worried that accessibility would require them to remove valued moving images; increase markup (in violation of another Wikipedia policy); and change page titles (affecting google search results). Additionally, some authors simply disagreed with or reverted changes made by moderators.

Tools as Moderators. Moderators occasionally discussed editing intermediate representations and tools through the provision of CSS, templates, Flash plugins, and so on. Thus, discussions turned at times to the need for bots (automated software scripts) that could fix some accessibility errors, the use of CSS to provide unified templates solving problems for many authors at once, and other technical fixes that are relatively sophisticated compared to what one might find in other UGC settings.

Moderating Wikipedia Accessibility

Wikipedia moderators were concerned not only with the accessibility of specific content pages, but also with fostering a culture of accessibility across Wikipedia, making Wikipedia more accessible to disabled authors.

Creating Appropriate Structures for Accessibility. Some moderators advocated the adoption of a Universal Access policy, an issue that lies at the intersection between the goals of the *Accessibility* project and structural aspects of Wikipedia that influence authorship. Between 2007 and 2011, these moderators discussed and drafted a proposal to the WikiMedia foundation to modify the Manual of Style. The Manual of Style currently has an entire page on accessibility, an apparent outcome of these efforts. They also discussed marking articles as accessible, but the idea was discarded because, "It would be as if people went and marked templates as 'This is an article with a Neutral POV' and 'This is an article that is well referenced' [A31, discussing with M5]. Finally, moderators discussed creating a "Cleanup Template for accessibility" by [M3] that would be available on Wikipedia:Template messages/Cleanup. Currently, the AccessibilityDispute template discussed earlier is used.

Defining Accessibility. The creation of accessibility guidelines was itself a topic of discussion. A combination of changing standards (such as the impact of the introduction of W3C's accessibility guidelines 2.0) and a wish to support a variety of impairments led to dispute over what exactly should go in guidelines. For example, M16 comments that "[M10]'s view is that providing ALT tags is all you can do.... I would prefer to [ask for more] because without a mouse some people can't access the alt text." There was no agreement on how accessibility is to be verified, aside from several mentions of using tools such as a screen reader to find problems or check solutions.

Moderator as Advocate. Moderators also discussed participating in advocacy on behalf of specific disabled authors. Some of this was moderator initiated. For example, moderators heard about and discussed advocating for a blind user who could not create an account because of an inaccessible CAPTCHA, and a user with a disability affecting their participation style who was asked to stop editing pages. Moderators were also concerned by a hostile environment created by unfriendly discussions on a talk page. Sometimes authors asked moderators to help. For example, A81 posted on a moderator's *Talk* page: "I feel hounded by some administrators because of my [disability]" [A81]. However, moderators were concerned that not everyone would speak up to them, and discussed pro-actively addressing situations. This raises questions of autonomy from a disability studies perspective [2]. Moderators seemed to understand this and commented on the difficulty of advocating for other authors:

> I could be [an author advocate] but what exactly would I say? "Don't ban this person, they have [disability]."? That might not work. [M1]

> No, how about "Hi, this user has identified herself as being [disease], which is probably why [this problem arose]. Before we ban her ... she seems to have her heart in the right place and has a lot to offer our community. Obviously, this would not apply to users who are violent or angry..." [M4]

Discussions of moderator-initiated author advocacy in the data lacked any reference to whether it had actually been done successfully or whether authors would want this.

Summary

In Wikipedia, moderation of accessibility occurs along formal channels with respect to content, as well as through informal channels and advocacy efforts. Our findings illustrate the importance of subtle issues such as moderator authority, automation, and structural support for accessibility. Advocacy, though not directly involved in accessible content generation, contributes to a culture of accessibility, an important prerequisite for successful moderation.

CASE STUDY TWO: HEALTH FORUM

Our second case study focuses on a very different domain: A discussion forum, LymeSpace (pseudonym), used by individuals with Lyme disease. LymeSpace is one of the most established and high volume social support sites for individuals with Lyme disease. It includes a large and diverse set of patients and caregivers, a subset of whom have a cognitive impairment. Thus, this group of people is motivated to consider the needs of individuals with cognitive impairments when creating content, but authors may not all have a cognitive impairment themselves. LymeSpace had a total of over 70,000 threads with 600,000 replies and about 8,500 users at the time of our analysis. A small population of users post frequently and respond to many new user posts.

We selected LymeSpace because its users actively moderate content to improve cognitive accessibility. Lyme disease is the most common vector-born disease in the United States today [18] and may cause a complex set of persistent physical and neurological symptoms [19]. One in particular, typically referred to as "brain fog" by patients, led participants in our study to modify how they wrote forum posts. Brain fog describes cognitive impairments that may encompass: fatigue; short-term memory impairment; poor concentration; difficulties in formulating ideas; difficulties in word finding; difficulties in judgment; and difficulties in naming objects [19]. Additional issues found in our case study that affected the use of online content include: easy distraction when faced with visuals ranging from animated advertisements to bold text; difficulty remembering the start of a long passage by the end of the same passage; and getting lost among multiple pages of content. Cognitive impairments can be extremely heterogeneous, and can affect web accessibility [20].

LymeSpace Qualitative Method

We collected all of the posts made on LymeSpace over the period from 2001 through 2009 (almost 150,000 posts and 67,000 threads). Using this data, we conducted an initial, exploratory qualitative study, where we discovered several types of end-user moderation. Examples of such moderation, as well as some responses to it, demonstrate the diversity and culture around accessibility moderation in this forum. Additionally, we analysed the incidence and effect of one particular kind of moderation we found across 300 discussion threads using automatically extracted quantitative metrics.

For the qualitative portion of our analysis, we randomly selected six forum members from this data set. We specifically sampled from forum members who produced few (1 to 5) or many (6 or more) posts which led to further discussion (which we operationalized as any post having at least one response). Once the six forum members were selected, we randomly selected a maximum of 50 threads started by each of them. We then opportunistically added any moderators who participated in these threads to our user set, and added further examples of moderation from each moderator we identified. Finally, we removed discussions from the qualitative data set that had not been moderated. At the end, our data set had 97 discussions, involving three different moderators.

For the analysis of this data, two authors independantly read all of the data, and grouped the data into two sets of categories: styles of moderation and moderation outcomes. Within these top level categories, sub-categories were identified in a bottom-up fashion. Both authors discussed the resulting sub-categories until they were in agreement.

For the quantitative portion of our analysis, we automatically identified 300 threads where an author had been moderated (asked to make a post more accessible) by matching against several key phrases present in one prolific moderator's moderating posts (*eg,* "please break up your wordy sentences into one sentence paragraphs"). In each case, after one or more posts, the moderator requested that content be made more accessible, following which 240 of the 300 authors responded and 60 did not. Next, we randomly selected 300 other threads. This selection procedure was weighted by thread size, in number of posts, so longer threads were more likely to be selected. Thus, our final sample contained 240 threads where the author *responded to moderation*, 60 where the author *did not respond to moderation,* and 300 *random* threads.

For the analysis of this data, we used easily calculated metrics that corresponded to specific accessibility issues defined by the community as important through moderating posts. Our focus was on metrics that would be easily visible to content consumers including the number of characters per block (paragraph), and the frequency with which all caps, punctuation, and bold text were used. For clarity, we reiterate the metrics with precise formulations when we present the results of this analysis.

Moderation Approaches and Outcomes

Accessibility in LymeSpace was defined in terms of the cognitive impairments experienced by its members. The community defined the meaning of accessibility through its moderation posts, and we used their definition in our analysis. To them, accessibility meant addressing the impact of brain fog, using: (1) short paragraphs to avoid big blocks of text; (2) double-spacing between paragraphs to provide more visual space around blocks of text; and (3) generally making text simpler and easier to read.

LymeSpace has a less formal, more varied, set of strategies for managing accessibility than Wikipedia. As summarized in Table 1, two of the three moderators in our data set were

Table 1: Summary of moderators we analyzed and their moderation styles

Name	Style	Comments
M1	Educational; Positive Re-enforcement; Reformatting	Power user and moderator
M2	Educational	Casual user; Less than 50 posts total
M3	Reformatting; Teaching by example	Casual user; Taught by example (reposted other' posts with correct formatting)

primarily content consumers with no particular authority or role beyond contributor in the forum. The third, M1, was a p ower user who responded to almost every new user on the forum and cared deeply about setting community standards for accessibility. We explore these moderators' different styles of moderation and users' responses to moderation.

Styles of Moderation

Moderators employed several strategies when intervening to moderate the accessibility of content. M1 sometimes used a post containing guidelines to educate new posters about the standards of the community, including guidelines for accessible content. Interestingly, the guidelines themselves were not always accessible. For example, M1 sometimes used ALL CAPS for emphasis, a violation of her own guidelines.

M1 also used positive reinforcement to encourage compliance. For example, one of her welcome posts mentioned that she liked how the original poster visually separated text into individual thoughts and made it simple.

Non-power-users also engaged in moderation. An example is this post by M2, who had less than 50 posts overall:

> I wasn't able to read your entire post.
>
> Maybe you could go back and break up your paragraphs so they are easier to read? [M2]

As opposed to the sanctioned guidelines provided by power users like M1, these posts were more casual and reactive in nature.

Moderation was not always explicit. For example, M3 reformatted an inaccessible post and reposted it "with added ••• at a couple points for emphasis" [M3]. M3's approach of reformatting and reposting content represents a more direct form of help than M1's critiques and advice.

M3 also wrote posts that referred to her own experiences with Lyme disease in support of M1's guidelines. For example, in one post M3 included a medical text that M1 had reformatted in an earlier thread. M3 gave credit to M1 for making the text easier to read. Although this was not a moderating post, it helped to reinforce the ethics of the community with regard to cognitive accessibility.

Responses to Moderation

Moderation met with varying success among the posts that we examined. In the best case, we observed *uptake*, where a poster adapted her style after receiving a moderating prompt of some kind. For example, the first thread that A2 started began with a fifteen hundred word text. Three different moderators responded (two were educational, a third was a reformatted version of the original post). A2 then indicated approval by replacing the original post body with the reformatted version.

In another example, A1's posts included ellipses, double punctuation, and rogue capitalization. After M1 suggested adherence to the posting guidelines, A1's posting habits improved. Most notably, she had split up her thoughts visually into smaller blocks of text. For example, a portion of her later post read:

> Thanks everyone for your help. I know my sx are lyme and ms symptoms. Hopefully being that I've had two Normal MRI's it isn't MS.
>
> I ordered my Igenex test yesterday.
>
> Do most people not test positive on reg WB? Like I said I only had Reactive bands at IGG 31,41 on Quest. [A1]

In some cases, a poster may explicitly respond to moderation. For example, in response to moderation A3 edited a post to be more accessible and wrote:

> I apologize for my original post. I thought it was just me... losing my place and reading the same lines over and over...I'm still learning...hope this is better [A3]

Sometimes, users responded negatively to moderation. For example, A5 was a new member who tended to write one paragraph posts without capitalization, and with non-standard punctuation (*i.e.,* an excess of ellipses). A5 posted three times on LymeSpace. M1 responded to one of A5's posts by welcoming her, without a moderating section to the post, and directed her to check her private messages for the response. A5 continued to request information with increasing desperation in 10 more posts, including one similar to her initial question, which M1 believed she had answered. Eventually, A5 commented on M1's moderation:

> ...please be more supportive. Thanks. [A5].

Not all attempts at moderation succeed. Users may be unsure how to interpret the welcome message and advice about posting guidelines, or how to create a post that is likely to get an answer. This may be further confounded by the overall stress associated with, possibly, having just received a difficult diagnosis. We cannot know why a user does not respond to moderation. However, when the only response to a plea for help is a request to increase accessibility, this might drive a user away from the site.

Influence of the Authoring Tool on Post Accessibility

LymeSpace suffers from usability problems. Methods for posting new threads and retrieving private messages are unintuitive. As a result, some posts asking users to edit their message or change formatting include detailed and lengthy instructions. For example, A6 provides a method for using Firefox scripting to disable bolding. Without his script, quoted text is displayed in bold, which is inaccessible for readers and goes against group guidelines.

LymeSpace authors can edit their posts after they are posted. For example, if another reader points out that a post is difficult to read, some posters may edit that original post. However when something is reposted by a moderator, the original poster loses control over her own potentially sensitive content, as no user without special administrative privileges can delete or edit another user's post.

Summary

To summarize, our qualitative data indicates that cognitive accessibility on LymeSpace is something that even casual users take seriously. Authors may respond positively and at times even apologetically to requests to improve their posting habits. Even occassional posters re-inforce these goals, perhaps in part because they themselves benefit when authors post more accessible text. However, a limitation of our analysis is the small number of authors and moderators that we studied. The next section addresses this by using quantitative methods to explore community norms acrosss 600 separate threads.

Incidence and Effect of Moderation

To further explore moderation incidence and its impact on author behavior, we used 600 threads (240 moderated by M1 with further responses, 60 moderated by M1 without response, and 300 random threads not moderated by M1). We calculated metrics that characterized accessibility based on the types of changes found in our qualitative data and the specific changes asked for in M1's moderating post:

Characters per block: Number of alphanumeric or punctuation characters, in each visually distinct block (defined as piece of text two or more newlines away from each adjacent piece of text).

Capitalization: Percent capitalized characters per block

Punctuation: Percent punctuation characters per block

Bold: Percent characters per block enclosed in bold tags

For authors who responded to moderation, we calculated separate mean scores for their posts before and after moderation. For authors who did not respond, and in randomly selected threads, we calculated a single score. We had two hypotheses, based on our qualitative data:

H1—Moderation improves compliance. *Each metric would decrease from before to after moderation.*

H2—Random posts are in between. *Random posts would score worse (higher) on each metric than post-moderation content. Random posts would score better on each metric than pre-moderation content.*

Because the distributions for each measure were not normal, we used non-parametric tests in our analysis. A

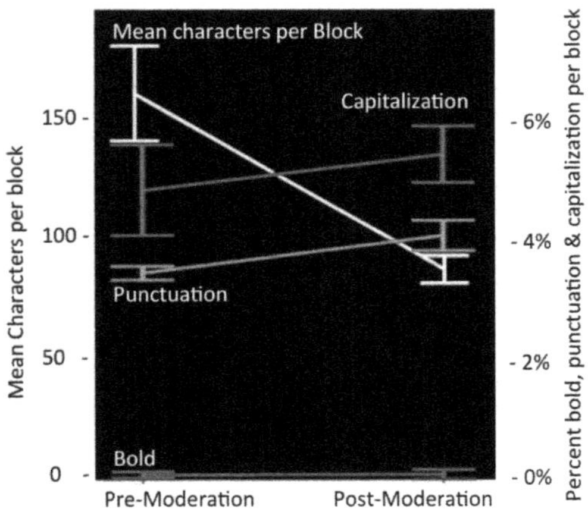

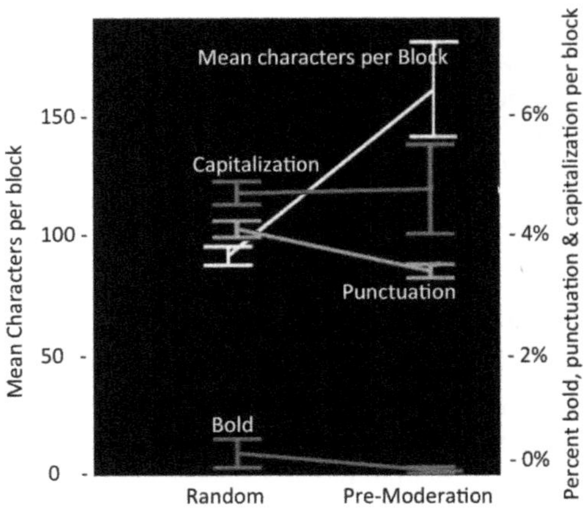

Figure 3: (LEFT) Mean characters per block were twice as high prior to moderation as after moderation (white line). Other lines: Percentage of characters that are bold did not change, but punctuation and capitalization increased. **(RIGHT)** Mean characters per block in randomly selected, unmoderated posts (representing the group norm) is half that of posts about to be moderated. Other lines: Percentage of characters that are bold and punctuation is slightly higher in random posts than posts that are about to be moderated. Percentage capitaized characters is about equal.

Wilcoxon Signed Ranks test was used to compare matched pairs of measurements (before and after moderatio n). This test was done over the 300 moderated samples, of which 240 had *before* and *after* measures, and 60 only had *before* measures. For comparing random threads to moderated threads, a Mann-Whitney U test was used. We corrected for multiple comparisons using the Bonferroni method.

Moderation improves compliance, but not in the way we expected. As expected, responses to moderation modified their characters per block, reducing characters per block to half that of posts about to be moderated (white line, Fig. 2 left; $Z=-7.797$, $p<0.001$). Randomly selected threads also had almost half as many characters per block as posts that were about to be moderated (white line, Fig. 2 right; $Z=-7.797$, $p<0.001$). In other words, after moderation, authors conformed to the group norm, as represented by the random threads. For characters per block, *H1—Moderation improves compliance* is supported, but *H2—Random posts are in between* is rejected.

This effect is reversed for punctuation: The group norm is to have more punctuation than found in threads just prior to moderation. The use of bolded characters was less salient (though the random posts used bold significantly more than the pre-moderatino posts). Capitalization increased slightly as a result of moderation.

Thus, *H1—Moderation improves compliance* is strongly supported for characters per block, and the opposite effect (though smaller) is seen for punctuation and capitalization. Although ellipses and all-caps are a problem, unpunctuated run-ons may potentially be a worse or more common one. Also, M1 was seen to use all caps to signpost lengthy posts, and this behavior may be emulated by modarated authors, even though it is not explicitly requested. *H2—Random posts are in between* is rejected, but this seems to be because group norms are *better* than we expected. If random posts are *already* compliant with accessible content goals this could mean that most unmoderated posts are not moderated *because they do not need moderation.*

This analysis is limited in its focus on a single moderator. Our qualitative findings show that there are many other kinds of moderation, such as teaching by example, that were not addressed in this analysis. In future work, we would like to explore their impact as well.

DISCUSSION AND IMPLICATIONS FOR DESIGN

The case studies presented focus on two very different situations. In the first case, we explored a very large and established Wiki (Wikipedia) with a complex management structure and many authors that work together to create content for a larger audience. Moderators made use of accepted standards drawn from W3C guidelines, and operated within a variety of structural and cultural forces in their attempts to improve accessiblity.

In the second case, we explored a small community forum with minimal management structure, creating content pimarily for themselves. Accessibility was defined by the community based on the typical cognitive impairments experienced by its members.

Despite the differences in these communities, both include end users who are motivated to make content more accessible, yet limited by the tools available to them. In both cases, we can see that standard definitions of accessiblity do not suffice; the meaning and practice of accessible content creation is negotiated. Technology could support this practice in several ways:

Support for accessibility should be proactive: Existing literature as well as our case study indicate that barriers to accessible content persist despite the best of intentions, so the software itself should do what it can to automatically meet accessibility guidelines. As we saw in Wikipedia accessibility moderation practices, many problems may be addressed by automated, technical solutions that can often be articulated by some of the end-users involved. Although the templates and bots used on Wikipedia are helpful, we believe that more could be achieved by explicitly engaging users in the process. For example, Burke *et al.* created a tool that helps users to compose posts more likely to receive a response by suggesting modifications before the post was finalized [21]. Our quantitative analysis of LymeSpace suggests that a similar tool could be created to help authors improve the accessibility of their text before it is posted. A similar approach could also be used to prompt users for *alt* text, table descriptions, appropriate use of headers, readable text, and so on.

The definition of accessibility should be negotiable: The accessibility issues that matter to end users may vary with each community and may include specific issues not covered by more generic accessibility guidelines [10]. As we saw in the Wikipedia study, although moderators leveraged existing standards, even these standards were not static. Furthermore, accomodations for some disabilities (such as cognitive impairments) are not well defined in standard guidelines. Despite this, as on LymeSpace, participants knew what would address their specific needs. Clear and easy control over parameters that relate to accessibility, such as formatting properties, including the use of bold for quoted text, could help to support accessibility. Additionally, UGC-driven websites would benefit from allowing users to have a formal channel for discussion of accessibility concerns, such as a designated thread on a forum, or the talk page we saw on Wikipedia. Although many users may not know how to adjust the presentation of information to make it more accessible, bringing such options to the forefront and enabling active collaboration could make moderation more effective.

UGC platforms should leverage varying expertise and ability: The diversity of experience and motivation of end users presents an opportunity for UGC sites. The lengths to which users will go to achieve accessibility is impressive. In our study, this included switching browsers; writing scripts and tutorials to fix browsers; and writing new Wikipedia Templates. Developing custom code to share with other users or a custom interface using a platform's API represents an extreme case of the negotiated standards mentioned above. UGC platforms could scaffold this sort of involvement more explicitly by adding API support, providing access to CSS, and enabling the creation of forms to intermediate between authors and UGC plaftorms.

Allow users to take on a diversity of roles: Wikis and blogs, which may have multiple authors, can leverage the varying motivation and expertise of groups of authors to achieve greater accessibility than would be possible by any one author alone. UGC platforms can encourage readers to flag problematic content, and authors to indicate their areas of expertise for fixing problems. This can allow matching authors with problems, or provide data that could be used in the long run to automate the detection or correction of inaccessible content. Support for emergent standards, such as in LymeSpace, and emergent roles, such as the advocacy role in Wikipedia, is also important. This could help sites customize their definition of accessibility to match that of the community of users being supported.

Connect formal channels with informal practice: A formal channel for discussing accessibility problems and solutions exists in Wikipedia, but not LymeSpace. The informal moderation on LymeSpace was epehmeral and decentralized, but nevertheless effective in setting group norms. The changes that are called for in more formalized channels on Wikipedia talk pages are more persistent, but arguably less integrated into authoring culture. Strategies such as involving authors with disabilities in the discussion and educating authors when they first begin to produce content, are important complements to formal channels.

CONCLUSIONS AND FUTURE WORK

User generated content is an important, growing source of information online. Unlike most other web content, UGC authors and consumers often overlap, and typically have little web design or accessibility experience. We cannot expect end users to become experts in accessibility, make use of complex authoring tools, or investigate the accessibility of their content. Instead, a combination of automated and active support for accessibilty can enable end users to meet accessibility goals, as they define them.

Basic standards of documentation and usability are not met by many UGC platforms. It is not enough for UGC platforms to document the importance of accessible content creation. Such documentation exists, yet the literature demonstrates that it does not result in accessible content (*e.g.*, [7], [9]). Users are unlikely to seek and read documentation without better support and incentives. Providing direct support in the authoring interface for accessibility is also not enough. Support must at a minimum be useable (*i.e.* not require authors to directly edit the HTML of their content) and discoverable (*i.e.* define or explain of terms such as "Alternative Text" on image dialogues). Authoring tools for some of today's most popular sites fail to meet this standard.

However documentation and usability of UGC creation tools are unlikely to be enough. If UGC is to be truly accessible, we also need to develop a better understanding of the role of culture and authorship abilities in the process of content creation. This suggests additional opportunities for UGC tools to amplify the accessibility of UGC that have not been discussed in the literature.

We have presented two case studies of UGC communities with a culture of self-moderating accessibility. We investigated Wikipedia, which deals with the full range of accessibility issues but focuses on access to visual information and navigation. We also studied LymeSpace, whose members cope with cognitive impairments. In both cases, we showed how a small group of people marshaled accessible content and educated authors. We explored issues such as authority, the definition of accessibility, uptake or rejection of moderation. Wikipedia moderators became engaged in advocacy as well as moderation, demonstrating the need to support a variety of roles. Accessibility on both sites was influenced not only by decisions of posters but also by community culture, the site design, usability issues, and technology constraints.

Further work should examine the full range of UGC platforms, including not only blogs, wikis, social network sites, and discussion forums, but also data collection and sharing platforms (such as FourSquare), content management systems, and email programs. These communities reflect the sustained effort of individuals with a common goal. UGC platforms should channel this effort constructively toward the important goal of making content accessible to a broad audience.

ACKNOWLEDGMENTS

Funding was provided by NSF GRFP (first author), NSF IIS-0916459 and Google.

REFERENCES

1. Ivory, M. Y., Mankoff, J. & Le, A. (2003) Using automated tools to improve web site usage by users with diverse ability. *Info. Tech. & Society*, 3(1):195-236
2. Mankoff, J., Fait, H., & Tran, T. (2005) Is your web page accessible? A comparative study of methods for assessing web page accessibility for the blind. In *CHI*, 41-50.
3. Vigo, M. & Brajnik, G. (2011)Automatic web accessibility metrics: where we are and where we can go. *Interacting with Computers*, 23(2):137-155.
4. Gupta, S., Kaiser, G., Neistadt, D., & Grimm, P. (2003) DOM-based content extraction of HTML documents. In *WWW*, 207-214.
5. Takagi, H., Kawenaka, S., Kobayashi, M., Itoh, T., & Asakawa, C. (2008) Social accessibility: Achieving accessibility through collaborative metadata authoring. In *ASSETS*, 193-200.
6. Fairweather, P. G., Hanson, V. L., Detweiler, S. R., and Schwerdtfeger, R. S. (2002) From assistive technology to a Web accessibility service. In *ASSETS*, 4-8.
7. Leahy, D. & Broin, U. Ó. (2009) Social networking sites and equal opportunity: The impact of accessibility. In *22nd Bled eConference: eEnablement: Facilitating an Open, Effective and Representative eSociety*, 41.
8. Taras, C., Siemoneit, O., Weißer, N., Rotard, M., & Ertl, T. (2008) Improving the accessibility of Wikis: A basic analytical framework. In *ICCHP*, 430-437.
9. American Foundation for the Blind. *Is blogging accessible to people with vision loss?* Archived by WebCite® at http://www.webcitation.org/67PvGjdh6.
10. Chrisholm, W., Vanderheiden, G., & Jacobs, I. (1999) *W3C Web Content Accessibility Guidelines 1.0.*
11. Wentz, B. & Lazar, J. (2011) Are separate interfaces inherently unequal? An evaluation with blind users of the usability of two interfaces for a social networking platform. In the *2011 iConference*, 91-97.
12. Mesiti, M., Ribaudo, M., Valtolina, S., Barricelli, B. R., Boccacci, P., & Dini, S. (2011) Collaborative environments: Accessibility and usablity for users with special needs. In Pardede, Eric, ed., *Community-built Databases: Research and Development*. Springer.
13. Braithwaite, D. O., Waldron, V. R., and Finn, J. (2009) Communication of social support in computer-mediated groups for people with disabilities. *Health Communication*, 11(2):123-151.
14. Maloney-Krichmar, D. and Preece, J. (2005) A multilevel analysis of sociability, usability, and community dynamics in an online health community. *TOCHI*, 12(2):201-232.
15. Finn, J. An exploration of helping processes in an online self-help group focusing on issues of disability. *Health Soc. Work*, 24, 3 (1999), 220-231.
16. Ellis, K. & Kent, M. (2010) Community accessibility: Tweeters take responsibility for an accessible Web 2.0. *Fast Capitalism*, 7(1) http://www.uta.edu/huma/agger/fastcapitalism/7_1/elliskent7_1.html.
17. Kittur, A. & Kraut, R. E. (2008) Harnessing the wisdom of crowds in Wikipedia: Quality through coordination. In *CSCW*, 37-46.
18. Weintraub, P. (2008). *Cure unknown: Inside the Lyme epidemic.* NY: St. Martin's Press.
19. Cairns, V. & Godwin, J. (2005) Post-Lyme borreliosis syndrome: A meta-analysis of reported symptoms. *International J. of Epidemiology*, 34(6):1340-1345.
20. WEBAIM (Web Accessibility in Mind). *Cognitive Disabilities: Introduction.* 1999-2012.
21. Burke, M., Joyce, E, Kim, T., Anand, V., & Kraut, R. E. (2007) Introductions and requests: Rhetorical strategies that elicit response in online communities. In *Intern. Conf. on Communities & Technologies*, 21-40.

Augmented Endurance: Controlling Fatigue while Handling Objects by Affecting Weight Perception using Augmented Reality

Yuki Ban[1], Takuji Narumi[1], Tatsuya Fujii[1], Sho Sakurai[2], Jun Imura[1], Tomohiro Tanikawa[1], and Michitaka Hirose[1]
[1]Information Science and Technology,
[2]Graduate School of Engineering,
the University of Tokyo,
7-3-1 Hongo, Bunkyo-ku Tokyo, Japan
{ban, narumi, fujii, sho, imura, tani, hirose}@cyber.t.u-tokyo.ac.jp

ABSTRACT
The main contribution of this paper is to develop a method for alleviating fatigue during handling medium-weight objects and augmenting our endurance by affecting our weight perception with augmented reality technology. To assist people to lift medium-weight objects without a complex structure or various costs, we focus on the phenomenon that our weight perception during handling objects is affected by visual properties. Our hypothesis is that this illusionary effect in weight perception can be applied to reduce fatigue while handling medium-weight objects without mechatronics-based physical assistance.

In this paper, we propose an augmented reality system that changes the brightness value of an object in order to reduce fatigue while handling the object. We conducted two fundamental experiments to investigate the effectiveness of the proposed system. Our results suggested that the system eliminates the need to use excess energy for handling objects and reduces fatigue during the handling task.

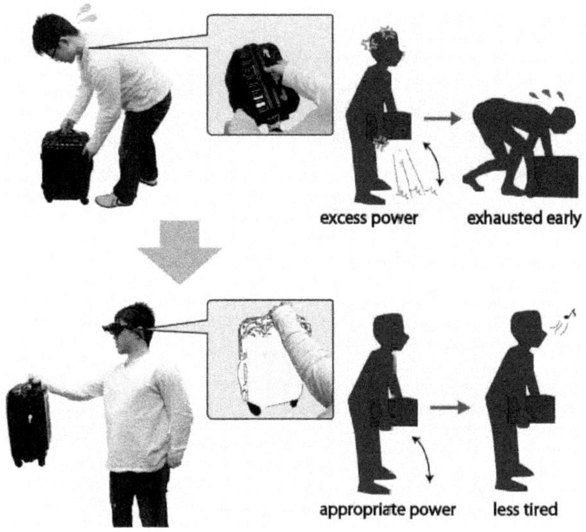

Figure 1. Augmenting endurance by affecting weight perception with augmented reality.

Author Keywords
Cross-modal Interaction; Augmented Reality; Weight Perception; Assistance for Physical Work

ACM Classification Keywords
H.5.1 Information Interfaces and Presentation (e.g. HCI): Multimedia Information Systems - Artificial, augmented, and virtual realities

INTRODUCTION
There is a great demand for an assistance system to make physical work easier. In our daily life, there are numerous situations where we need help lifting or handling medium-weight objects, such as when housecleaning, shopping, or working. Recently several assistance systems have been developed for helping individuals while handling heavy objects. There are two major classes of existing systems to assist our physical work: "Stand-alone types" and "Wearable types." Examples of the former are heavy machinery, handling robots, or remote control robots (e.g. RI-MAN(Robot Interacting with Human) [21] and Robot for Interactive Body Assistance [20]). Examples of latter type are powered exoskeletons, (e.g. Hybrid Assistive Limb [13] and Human Universal Load Carrier). They help users handle heavy objects and reduce the fatigue of the users by generating a physical force mainly with motors [25].

These physical assistance systems using mechatronics for heavy lifting require complex structures and are costly. The costs include not only the development costs but also time and effort to wear and maintain these systems. Because of the complexity and costs, most of these systems were designed for special purposes, such as military operations and caring for the elderly or the injured. These systems mainly focus on assisting with physically exhausting tasks that are impossible to complete with only human power. On the other hand, there are few systems which help us to handle medium or light weight objects during daily tasks.

Meanwhile, in the study of presenting multi-sensory information, the phenomenon referred to as "cross-modality [27]" comes under the spotlight in these days. This phenomenon indicates that perception through one sensory modality is changed by stimuli that are simultaneously received through other senses because our senses are highly interconnected. A psychological study on the sense of weight revealed that our weight perception is affected by the visual properties of objects. Among these, the most well-known phenomenon is the "Charpentier illusion". "Charpentier illusion" is a weight illusion that reveals people underestimate the weight of a larger object when compared to a smaller object of the same mass [7].

Based on this knowledge, we hypothesize that this illusionary effect in weight perception can be applied to reduce fatigue during handling of medium-weight objects without the use of complex mechanical structures. An assistance system that reduces fatigue from physical work based on the effect will be able to affect our weight perception and fatigue only with visual stimuli. This kind of system will be enough simple and convenient to apply for daily tasks. Therefore, we propose an augmented reality system that changes the brightness value of an object for reducing fatigue while handling the object (Figure 1). The first reason for choosing the brightness is that it induces a learning effect less than size-weight illusion with our paradigm [12]. The second reason is that the brightness value affects the weight estimation of an object more powerfully than other visual properties, hue and saturation [8].

In this paper, we first discuss results from previous conventional studies on the influence of visual properties on haptics and weight perception, and next we describe the proposed system. Finally, we report the result of two fundamental experiments to investigate the effectiveness of the proposed system. One experiment is for confirming the ability of our proposed method to modify an identified weight of objects and reduce fatigue by quantitative evaluation with a myoelectric sensor and subjective assessment with a questionnaire. Another is for measuring how much fatigue the proposed system can reduce by comparing the performance of repeated tasks under different conditions. By doing so, we have tried to reveal the implicit effect of augmented reality on our behavior and realize a method to utilize it for human interfaces. Finally, we discuss the validity and effectiveness of the proposed system through the results of the experiments.

VISUAL PROPERTIES THAT AFFECT THE HAPTIC SENSATION AND WEIGHT PERCEPTION

Perception is traditionally regarded as a modular function. It has long been thought that different sensory modalities operate independently of each other. However, recent behavioral and brain imaging studies are changing this view by suggesting that cross-modal interactions have an important role in our perception [27]. Indeed, many psychophysical studies have shown that haptic perception and weight perception are influenced by visual stimuli.

Haptic illusions which combine the presentation of forces with manipulated visual stimuli, have a long history, dating back to the Charpentier illusion (size-weight illusion) [7], which showed that subjects estimated the weights of objects with equal mass, based on their apparent visual size. In his work, it was revealed that subjects perceived an object to be lighter when it appeared larger in their vision. This illusion explained our inherent weight estimation and feedforward adaptation to use the appropriate force for handling objects. Humans expect that larger objects are heavier than smaller ones from their experience. Therefore, smaller objects feel heavier than their expected weight. Kim et al. examined the effect of this illusion in the virtual reality space, and they revealed that subjects also got size-weight illusion with computer graphics images [14].

In other words, our weight expectations are based on knowledge and past experience. There is a top-down component of weight perception that is based on experience with not only material densities but also specific objects such as the material weight illusion [11, 6] and golf-ball illusion [10]. These illusions are quite robust since they result from our previous experiences. On the other hand, it is suggested that the size-weight illusion diminishes gradually during the static phase of the lift, where weight-related information is available via sensory feedback, and will disappear [12]. Some other illusions affected by the weight perception have been revealed. Proffitt et al. revealed that people judge hills to be steeper when wearing a heavy backpack [4]. They argued that these overestimates are actually misperceptions by the weight perception. In addition, Durgin et al. revealed that the effect of backpacks on slope judgments was due to the intuitions that the climbing hills is harder when we're carrying a heavy bag rather than to an effect of pyhsiological changes on conscious perception [9].

Pseudo-haptics [16] is also one of the most famous illusions associated with cross-modal interactions. Pseudo-haptics, which is an illusional phenomenon triggered by this characteristics of our senses, was first introduced by Lécuyer. Lécuyer et al. had subjects push their thumbs against a piston, which in turn pushed against an isometric Spaceball device. Simultaneously, subjects were visually presented with a compressed virtual spring. Even though the Spaceball device was not compressed, the virtual spring influenced the subjects' perception of stiffness [18]. It has also been revealed that we can modify such things as the perception of texture [17], shape of objects [3], and the identified placement of edges [2]. There is great potential to use these phenomena for generating haptic sensations using only visual feedback, without the need for applying any physical devices.

Similarly, other visual properties such as the color of objects affect our weight perception. For example, Alexander et al. suggested that weights are estimated to be heavier as the saturation of an object increases [1]. Moreover, the brightness value of an object ' s surface influences people ' s estimation of the object ' s weight. The brightness value affects the weight estimation of an object more powerfully than hue and saturation [8]. Decreasing the level of brightness leads to an increase in the estimated weight. This kind of illusion occurs not only in chromatic colors but also in achromatic colors. Thus, dark gray objects seem heavier than light gray objects. Humans intuitively control their output power based on the estimation of an object ' s weight when they lift the object. Walker concluded that people perceive darker objects to be lighter than brighter objects when they actually lifting the objects, while darker objects are estimated to be heavier than brighter objects [31]. This is thought to be due to the feedforward adaptation based on incorrect estimations, which allows us produce excess muscular power implicitly. In fact, Birren claimed that simply changing black boxes to white boxes reduced the fatigue of workers in a factory [5].

In our hypothesis, augmented reality technology can reduce fatigue during handling objects by changing its visual characteristics which induces these effects. We consider that we may assist with physical work and reduce fatigue using augmented reality, which can change the size, movement and color of objects. In our present study, we decided to choose the brightness value as the visual property that we can control using augmented reality.

CONTROLLING WEIGHT PERCEPTION AND FATIGUE WHILE HANDLING OBJECTS BY CHANGING THEIR BRIGHTNESS USING AUGMENTED REALITY

As described above, humans intuitively control their output power at the unconscious level, and the perception of weight can be modified not only by haptic stimuli but also by visual stimuli. However, there is a tradeoff between the degree of produced muscular power and the degree of fatigue during physical work.

Therefore, it is expected that humans will be easily exhausted while excessively working their muscles when handling objects, although they do not actually need such high power (the lower in Figure 1). On the other hand, if humans could output the correct power without thinking and effort, it is expected that humans will be able to do physical work with minimal fatigue since they would not need to use excess energy (the upper in Figure 1).

Augmented reality has recently undergone significant growth in several fields. It has great potential for enhancing and modifying our perception of real life experience. This is accomplished by presenting computer-generated virtual sensations in a semantic context with real environmental elements. Sensory feedback with Augmented Reality has the power to modify our behavior on an unconscious level. For example, we developed an "Augmented Perception of Satiety" system which modifies a subject's perception of satiety and eating behavior by changing the apparent size of food while keeping the feeling of holding it using augmented reality, and controls nutritional intake [22].

In the above example, "Augmented Perception of Satiety" system realized the "implicit interaction" which modify subject's perception of satiety at the unconscious level by changing visual stimuli using Augmented Reality. In this paper, we also aim to realize the "implicit interaction" which modify the perception of weight and fatigue using Augmented Reality.

In the studies on perception of weight, some systems using augmented reality were also developed, such as the system which generates a size-weight illusion [15] and the system which modifies an identified barycentric position of objects by superimposing the virtual bag whose shape is different from the real one onto the real bag [24]. Based on these studies, it is conceivable that augmented reality can also modify our weight perception and control our fatigue by affecting our produced muscular power implicitly. By doing so, we consider that we can reduce fatigue while handling objects without the use of any physical devices.

Therefore, we propose an augmented reality system that modifies an identified weight of objects by changing a visual property to reduce weariness while handling the object. We then made a prototype system to confirm the possibility and the effectiveness of the proposed system. As described in the previous chapter, we focused on the brightness value of objects as the visual property which we controlled based on the results of previous research.

Prototype System

We constructed a prototype system that changes the brightness of objects that subjects were handling. In this system, a user wore only a Head Mounded Display (HMD) with a camera that realized video see-through. Using the captured image taken by this web camera, the system composed the image in which the brightness values of objects were changed by image processing and presented this composed image via the HMD. This system was composed with devices described bellow.

- HMD: VUZIX Wrap920AR(Resolution:640 480, Field of view: 31-degree)
- Web camera: Logicool HD Pro Webcam C920
- PC: Panasonic Let's Note CF-SX1(CPU: Core i5-2540M(2.60GHz))

Figure2 shows the captured image and the image composed by our system. First, the system extracted an area of the object that was being held from captured image. Next, we decreased saturation value of the pixel in the extracted area to zero, and change the brightness value as shown in the Figure2. The reason why we decreased the saturation value of the target object to zero is that De Camp et al. revealed that the effect of the brightness value on an object ' s weight estimation is more powerful with achromatic objects than with chromatic objects [8]. For example, when we change the color of the object to white (i.e. enhancing the brightness), the range of the brightness of the object are converted from [0,255] to [192,255] ([α, β] means the value of range from α to β). Using this method, we can modify the brightness value without loss of asperity, texture, or shading of an object's surface. The imaging speed of this process was 25 frame per seconds with this prototype system.

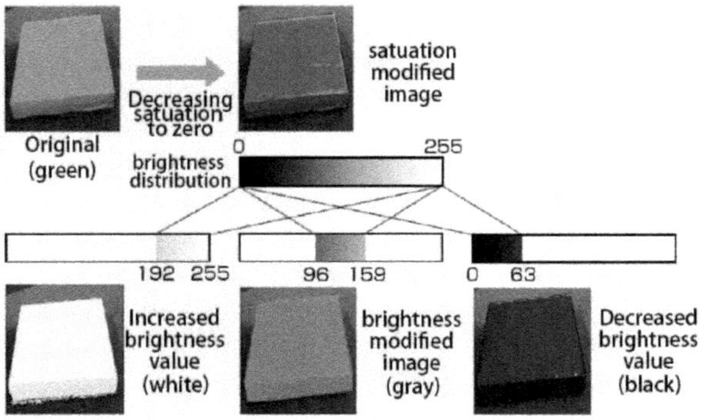

Figure 2. Top: white(increase brightness value), Middle: green(original), Bottom: black(decrease brightness value) (when changing to white: V_{new}=V_{old}/4 + 192, when changing to black: V_{new}=V_{old}/4)

REDUCING FATIGUE DURING HANDLING OBJECTS BY CHANGING APPARENT BRIGHTNESS OF OBJECTS

First of all, in designing the proposed augmented reality system which reduces fatigue while handling objects, we conducted an experiment to investigate how our produced muscular power and subjective fatigue during lifting a target object would change by changing the apparent brightness of the object with our prototype system. Subjects were asked to do tasks in which they move objects up and down, and we measured their cumulative fatigue during these tasks. To provide accurate assessment, we evaluated both objective and subjective fatigue in this experiment [23]. Subjects were not made aware of the true purpose of the experiment to avoid bias that may have affected the accurate assessment of our system.

We used the HMD system which can control the brightness of the target objects as described above. In this experiment, the system detected the area of handled object with only a color image captured by a web camera. We set the color of a target object which the subject handle to green and the system extracted an area of the object from the captured image based on HSV color.

Setup of the Experimental System

The experiment used a within-subjects design. We designed a testing booth with gray wall in front of the subjects using gray cloth as shown in Figure 3 to prevent subjects from watching something other than the experimental environment during the session. There was a table with a gray table cloth in the booth. There were five green colored boxes and a stand was set on the table. Each box was 180 [mm] wide, 260 [mm] long and 27 [mm] high (Figure 4). The weight of each box was 680 [g]. These boxes were the target objects for changing the apparent brightness that were to be handled by the subjects. The size and the weight of the boxes were determined by reference to the size and the weight of what is often handle in daily life. The stand was 235 [mm] wide, 320 [mm], long and 120 [mm] high and fixed to the table. The subject sat down in a chair in front of the table during the experiment.

During the experiment, subjects did two types of tasks, a fatigue task and a measuring fatigue task.

The fatigue task caused fatigue in subjects through physical work with our augmented reality system. During the fatigue task, subjects were instructed to lift up and put five boxes on the center stand, and lift up and pull down all of them on the table five times (Figure 5). Subjects looked at the boxes, the color of which was changed by our system through the HMD (Figure 5). During each fatigue task session, subjects were presented with one of three boxes colored by our augmented reality system: Black (the brightness value is 0-63), Gray (the brightness value is 96-158) and White (the brightness value is 192-255). Moreover subjects were instructed to use only one of two hands, which was designated by an experimenter during a single fatigue task session. Thus, there were six conditions in the fatigue task: Black-Right hand condition, Black-Left hand condition, Gray-Right hand condition, Gray-Left hand condition, White-Right hand condition and White-Left hand condition. The integrated power spectrum density (IPSD) measured by an electromyograph was indicative of the muscle power which subjects produced in this experiment [30], and the product of this IPSD and the time to accomplish the tasks (IPSD $\times$ time) was defined as a volume of work during the fatigue task.

The measuring fatigue task is for evaluating both subjective and objective fatigue. First, subjects were asked questions regarding their fatigue subjectively during the measuring fatigue task session. We used visual analogue scale (VAS) ratings [19]. Subjects rated the fatigue that they felt on an analogue scale in this testing method. Subjects answered the question "How exhausted are you now?" by rating fatigue on a 100 [mm] line anchored by "not exhausted at all" on the left and "extremely exhausted" on the right.

In addition, we evaluated the muscle fatigue by measuring the change of the muscle potential as an objective fatigue. Generally, mean power frequency (MEPF) and median power frequency (MDPF) decrease when a muscle is exhausted [29, 26]. These values are used as the standards of evaluating muscle fatigue [28]. The spectral shift is concerned with conduction velocity of action potential along the muscle fibers. These values are used as the standards of evaluating muscle fatigue. We regard this muscle fatigue as objective fatigue. For comparing these values to evaluate the fatigue, the muscle potential should be measured in the same posture with the same load. Therefore, subjects were instructed to hold a dumbbell with their back and elbows against the backrest, keeping their forearms horizontal and looking at the dumbbell, as shown in Figure 6 without the HMD and keep the their body still for five seconds during the measuring fatigue task. The weight of the dumbbell was 2.5 [kg].The difference of the MEPF and MDPF between before and after the fatigue task means the fatigue that is accumulated during the task in each condition. Therefore the measuring fatigue task was performed before and after each fatigue task session without any exception.We used Fast Fourier Transform for the frequency analysis.

Seven men in their twenties participated in this experiment. All of them were healthy and right-handed.

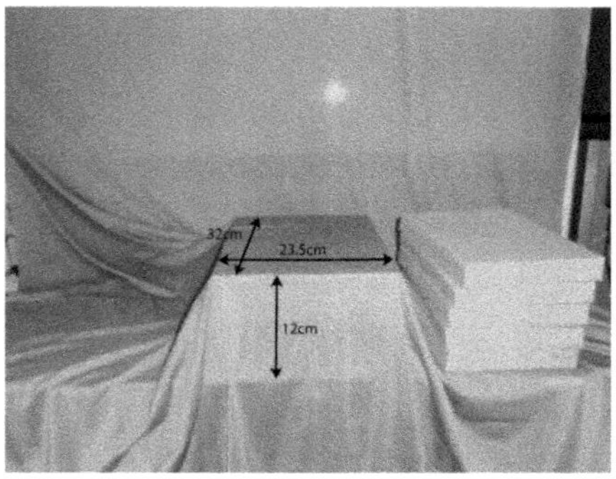

Figure 3. The booth covered with gray cloths.

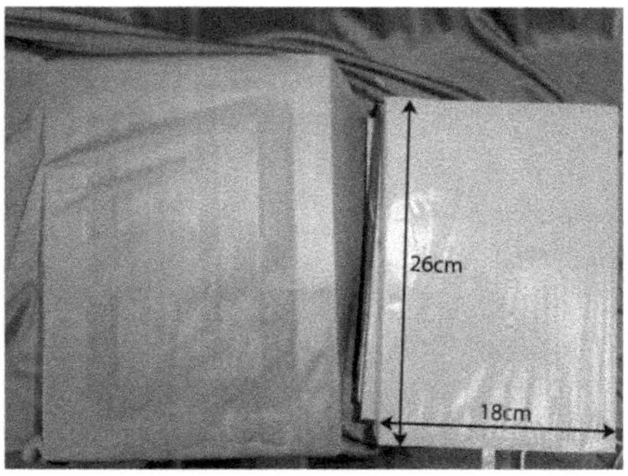

Figure 4. Target objects which subjects handled.

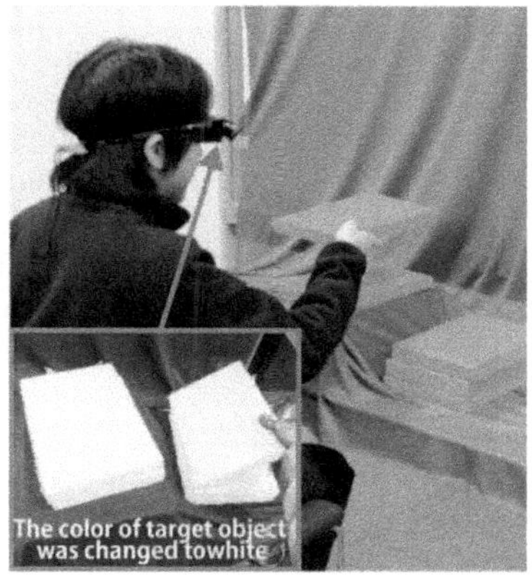

Figure 5. A subject during the fatigue task.

Procedure

At first, subjects fixed sensors to the biceps of both arms with tape. We use a Polymate II (TEAC corp.) as a wireless electromyograph to quantify the objective fatigue (Figure 6). We then confirmed whether the sensors sent data correctly. If not, the locations of the sensors were changed appropriately. These sensors were kept fixed to the subjects until the experiment ended.

Next, the subjects were instructed to do the first measuring fatigue task by left or right hand. Then, subjects were set up with the HMD and were instructed to repeat fatigue tasks. This task was performed with the arm designated by the experimenter. The subjects did the tasks alternately with left arm and right arm. The number of subjects who started with the left arm and those who started with right arm were balanced. The fatigue tasks were conducted in the following order.

First, the task with gray condition was conducted as a reference. Then subjects performed the fatigue task with the black condition four times and the fatigue task with the white condition four times in the order indicated by the experimenter. The subjects did the tasks with one hand (left or right) alternately with the black condition and white condition. The number of subjects who started with black and those who started with white were balanced in order to eliminate the order effect. After that, the task with gray was conducted. For example, two subjects do the task in (Gray-Left, Black-Right, White-Left, White-Right, Black-Left, Black-Right, White-Left, White-Right, Black-Left, Gray-Right). And other two subjects do the task in (Gray-Right, Black-Left, Black-Right, Wight-Left, Wight-Right, Black-Left, Black-Right, White-Left, White-Right, Gray-Left) and so on. Because too many task trials imposes an enormous drain on subjects, we mainly collected data on the white and black condition tasks, and reduced the number of trails for the gray condition task, which was expected to have results that were intermediate between the black and white conditions. In addition, to avoid giving excess fatigue to subjects, subjects had a break for two minutes between each trial and they had a break for ten minutes every five trials.

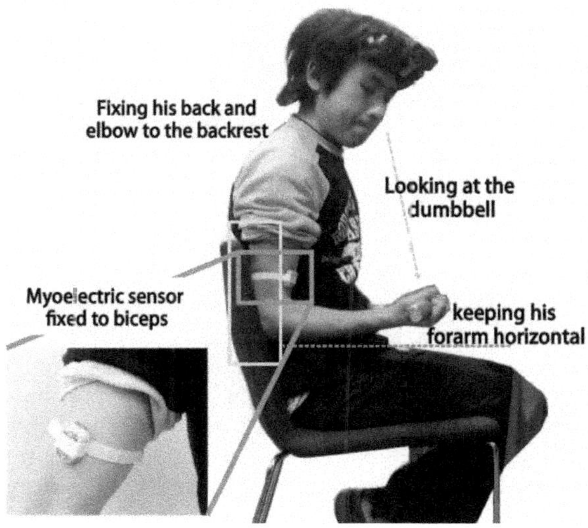

Figure 6. The posture during measuring muscle fatigue.

Result and Discussion

This experiment used a within-subjects design. First, Figure 7 shows the increase in subjective fatigue measured by using visual analog scale ratings, and Figure 8 shows the decrease in MEPF and MDPF through the fatigue task in each color condition. The former shows how subjects feel fatigue subjectively and the latter shows how muscles were exhausted when we presented one of three color changed by our augmented reality system. The result of a Kruskal Wallis test revealed a significant effect of color (VAS: $[\chi^2(2) = 12.34, p < 0.01]$, MEPF: $[\chi^2(2) = 10.56, p < 0.01]$, MDPF: $[\chi^2(2) = 9.77, p < 0.01]$). Then, we used a Wilcoxon signed-rank tests with Steel-Dwass correction and the result showed a significant difference in each index between the white versus black condition ($p < 0.01$).

These results show that the effect of an object's brightness on our weight perception revealed by psychological studies is also provoked when we modify the color of an object virtually using augmented reality. Furthermore, these results mean that the muscle fatigue accumulated in the fatigue task is significantly decreased when we enhanced the brightness of objects. These results quantitatively suggest that our system actually control not only the subjective fatigue but also the objective muscle fatigue.

While, MEPF and MDPF can be used not as absolute indices which shows the degree of reduced fatigue but as relative indices which shows the difference between conditions. The relationship between the degree of the decrease of MEPF and MDPF and the degree of fatigue (or represented workload) is linear within particular range, but it is non-linear out of the range. The range changes depending on the size (diameter) of the muscle fibers. The size differs depending on individual. This is because we cannot convert the average of the decrease of the MEPF and MDPF to absolute value which indicates the degree of reduced fatigue. Instead, we did the experiment to quantify the reduced fatigue with the number of repetitions that subjects can perform in the next section.

Second, Figure 9 shows IPSD which indicates the muscle power which subjects produced, the time to accomplish the tasks and the amount of work (IPSD $\times$ time) during the fatigue task session. These data are normalized with the results of gray condition tasks. We used a repeated measures ANOVA for IPSD and this test revealed a significant difference in the effect of color for each index (IPSD: $[F(2,12) = 4.92,\ p < 0.05]$, time: $[F(2,12) = 7.38,\ p < 0.05]$, work: $[F(2,12) = 12.36,\ p < 0.05]$). Then, we used a repeated measures ANOVA and Wilcoxon signed-rank test with Bonferroni-Holm correction. This test revealed a significant difference between the white versus black condition for IPSD and the amount of work ($p < 0.05$). On the other hand, there is a no significant effect on time. These results show that subjects produce stronger force in the black condition than in the white condition, and that the system suppresses the surplus power unconsciously without decreasing of the task performance.

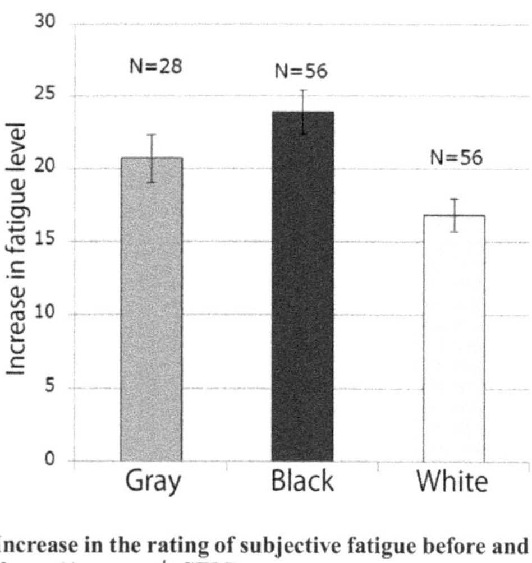

Figure 7. Increase in the rating of subjective fatigue before and after the fatigue task. (Average $\pm$ SEM)

We found that our method, which changes brightness value of target objects with augmented reality technology, could control users' fatigue both objectively and subjectively and that it is possible to improve the energy effectiveness by enhancing brightness value of target objects.

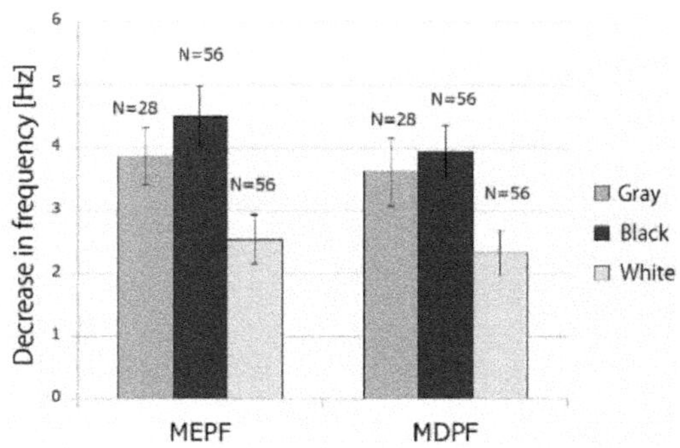

Figure 8. Decrease in objective muscle fatigue before and after the fatigue task. (Average $\pm$ SEM)

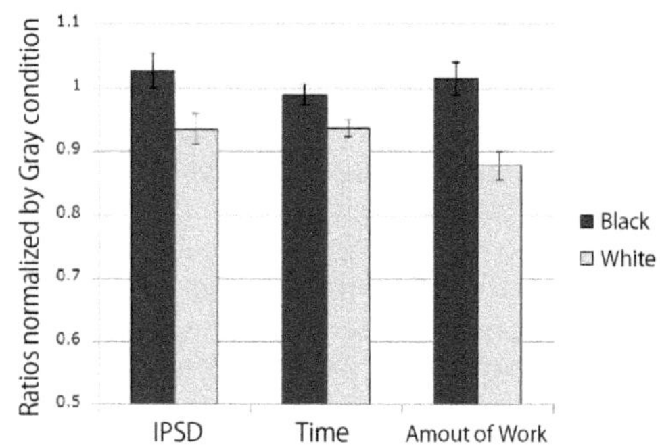

Figure 9. IPSD, Task time and Works during the fatigue task. (Average $\pm$ SEM)

MEASURING THE REDUCTION OF FATIGUE WHILE HANDLING OBJECTS BY CHANGING THE BRIGHTNESS VALUE

From the result of the experiment in the previous chapter, we revealed that our proposed method, changing the brightness value of an object has the potential to reduce the fatigue while handling objects. Therefore, we conducted another experiment to show the effectiveness of the proposed augmented reality system by investigating how much the system reduces fatigue and how long it extends the ability to work with the same degree of fatigue. The purpose of this experiment is to quantify the effectiveness of our system by comparing the number of accomplished repetition tasks by enhancing and reducing the brightness of the lifted object.

Setup for the Experiment

This experiment also used a within-subjects design. In this experiment, subjects wore the HMD and watched the composed image in which the brightness value of a target object was changed, as in the experiment described in the previous section. To evaluate how much fatigue our method is able to reduce, we asked subjects to perform the repetitive task and then counted the number of accomplished tasks. Subjects continued a biceps curl with a dumbbell as long as they were able to do in strict form and at a tempo of 20 times per minute. The weight of the dumbbell that was used in this experiment was 5.0 [kg]. During the experiment, subjects sat in a chair and fixed their backs and the elbow of the arm that was in use to the backrest of a chair. Subjects were instructed to lift the dumbbell from their thighs to a fishing line located

360 [mm] above the seat of the chair. Subjects were also instructed to lift up the dumbbell until their wrists touched the fishing line and to lift down it until its bar touched their thighs (Figure 10).

Sixteen men and one woman in their twenties participated in this experiment. There were 1 left- and 15 right-handed subjects.

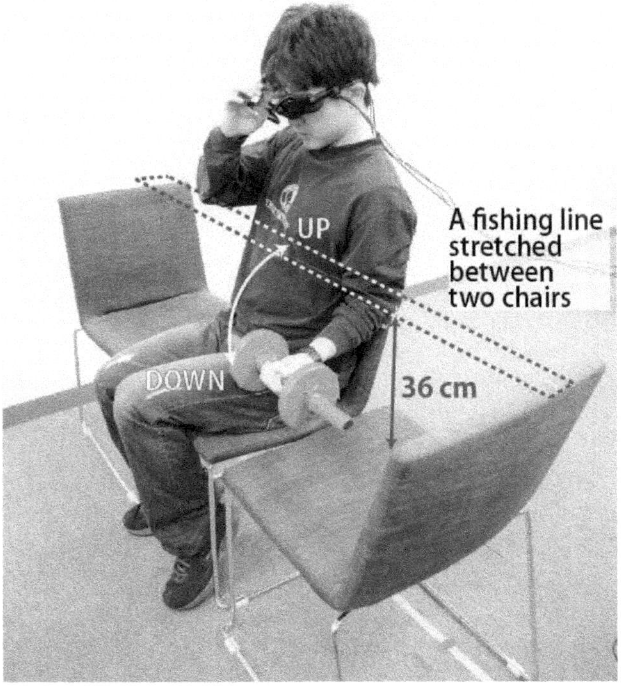

Figure 10. Setup for the repetition task.

Procedure

We conducted this experiment over two days for each subject. A subject did two trials each for the left and right hands per day. Each subject did four trials in different conditions (white or black color, left or right hand). Subjects were asked to keep their activity level as similar as possible on the day before each testing session, and they were asked to refrain from strenuous exercise before the experiment. Subjects measured their own grasping power of each hand by a grip dynamometer immediately before each testing session. This measurement was to select suitable subjects with sufficient grasping power and to confirm that their fatigue level was similar to that of the previous experimental day. If their conditions and fatigue levels differed from that of the day prior to the previous testing session, we postponed the testing session for at least one day.

The first portion of the experiment required subjects to sit down in the chair and to conduct practice trials by lifting the dumbbell five times with each hand. Next, subjects took a break for two minutes, and were fitted with the HMD. They were instructed to lift the dumbbell as many times as possible at a predetermined tempo.

Figure 11. The result of changing color of the dumbbell.

We instructed the subjects to watch the dumbbell through the HMD and to avoid putting the dumbbell on their thighs for rest during a trial. After our signal to start, subjects began a trial at their timing with one hand, keeping pace with a metronome rhythm of 40 beats per minute. The trial ended if subjects could not continue the biceps curl or could not keep pace with the tempo. We compared the number of repetitions between the condition with the superimposed black color (bottom left in Figure 11) and the condition with the superimposed white color (bottom right in Figure 11). After the first trial, subjects were allowed to rest for two minutes, and they did the second trial with their other hand.

On the second day, an experimenter confirmed that there is no problem with their condition. If there was no problem, the second experiment was conducted like the one on the first day using the other conditions. For example, if right-white and left-black were used on the first day, right-black and left-white were used on the second day.

Result and Discussion

The average gripping power of subjects who participated in this experiment is 37.8 $\pm$ 1.8 kg (average and standard error of the mean). The number of repetitions in each experimental condition was as follows: black superimposed condition: 28.1 $\pm$ 2.6; white superimposed condition: 31.7 $\pm$ 2.6. We used the Student's paired t-test between the repetitions of each subject in the white and black conditions. There was a significant difference between the averages of repetitions (p

< 0.05). This result shows the rates of the number of repetitions under the black superimposed conditions to that of under the white superimposed conditions are 17.9 ± 4.1 %.

These results indicated that subjects' fatigue accumulated in the task could be reduced significantly when the brightness of objects they lifted is heightened, identical to the results of the experiment in the previous chapter. Moreover, these results also suggested that our proposed method improves the endurance capacity of subjects by approximately 18 %. However the effect of 18 % improvement of the endurance capacity is the difference between in black and white conditions made by our system, not between real and augmented reality environments. It is estimated that our proposed system produces an effect as this experimental result when the low brightness value of objects is used; however, if the original brightness value of a target objects is high, the effect of our proposed method will be a low effect. It is also estimated that this system is able to modify the perception of weight and controlling fatigue for the same object as the situation demands. For example, it can be possible that this system is applied to the rehabilitation or the training, by controlling the muscle fatigue without changing actual physical load and putting the precise controlled load for different purposes and degrees.

CONCLUSION

In this paper, we aimed to realize a method for alleviating fatigue during handling medium-weight objects by affecting our weight perception with augmented reality technology. To confirm the possibility and to evaluate the effectiveness of this proposed system, we designed a experimental system which changes the brightness value of a target object, and conducted two experiments.

Using this system, we confirmed whether it is possible to alleviate fatigue while moving medium-weight objects with augmented reality technology. The result suggested that it is possible to modify the fatigue with the proposed system, and the system reduces fatigue during the handling task by eliminating the need to use excess energy for handling objects. With this experiment, we also revealed that the proposed system reduce both subjective and objective fatigue.

Moreover, we evaluated the effectiveness of the proposed system. As a result of increasing the brightness of objects, the number of repetitions that subjects can perform is increased by 18 % ,as compared with a result of decreasing the brightness of objects. This result indicates that using augmented reality technology it can be possible to control fatigue practically without complex mechanical equipment.

In the experiments of this paper, this system can only change the brightness of objects whose color is green because of using only a RGB image. However, this method can be expanded with various objects and arbitrary backgrounds by using a depth map or by employing a different object-recognition paradigm such as natural feature point based recognition. Moreover future research should seek other cross-modal effects between the perception of vision and haptics such as size-weight illusion, although in this paper we only used the cross-modal effect between the perception of weight and the brightness of objects. We will focus on and measure the effectiveness of other visual features besides the brightness value that can reduce the perception of weight and fatigue. It seems that the size, the displacement and the speed are comprised in visual features that have the potential to reduce the perception of weight and fatigue.

Based on these measurements, we will reveal the most effective combination to reduce fatigue. Then using this combination, we aim to realize a more effective system which has the potential to control the perception of weight and, in turn, reduce fatigue with augmented reality techniques.

We believe that we can build a practical system that alleviates fatigue for various situations by combining illusions based on weight perception and processing methods. We will be able to realize a system that can help people with daily tasks involving the handling of medium- or light-weight objects.

REFERENCES

1. Alexander, K., and Shansky, M. Influence of hue, value, and chroma on the perceived heaviness of colors. *Attention, Perception, & Psychophysics 19*, 1 (1976), 72–74.
2. Ban, Y., Kajinami, T., Narumi, T., Tanikawa, T., and Hirose, M. Modifying an identified angle of edged shapes using pseudo-haptic effect. *Haptics: Perception, Devices, Mobility, and Communication* (2012), 25–36.
3. Ban, Y., Kajinami, T., Narumi, T., Tanikawa, T., and Hirose, M. Modifying an identified curved surface shape using pseudo-haptic effect. *The 2012 IEEE Haptics Symposium (HAPTICS2012)* (2012), 211 – 216.
4. Bhalla, M., and Proffitt, D. Visual–motor recalibration in geographical slant perception. *Journal of Experimental Psychology: Human Perception and Performance; Journal of Experimental Psychology: Human Perception and Performance 25*, 4 (1999), 1076.
5. Birren, F. *Color Psychology and Color Therapy: A Factual Study of the Influence of Color on Human Life*. Kessinger Publishing, 2006.
6. Buckingham, G., Ranger, N., and Goodale, M. The material–weight illusion induced by expectations alone. *Attention, Perception, & Psychophysics 73*, 1 (2011), 36–41.
7. Charpentier, A. Experimental study of some aspects of weight perception. *Arch Physiol Norm Pathol 3* (1891), 122–135.
8. De Camp, J. The influence of color on apparent weight. a preliminary study. *Journal of experimental psychology 2*, 5 (1917), 347.
9. Durgin, F., Baird, J., Greenburg, M., Russell, R., Shaughnessy, K., and Waymouth, S. Who is being deceived? the experimental demands of wearing a backpack. *Psychonomic Bulletin & Review 16*, 5 (2009), 964–969.

10. Ellis, R., and Lederman, S. The golf-ball illusion: evidence for top-down processing in weight perception. *PERCEPTION-LONDON- 27* (1998), 193–202.

11. Ellis, R., and Lederman, S. The material-weight illusion revisited. *Attention, Perception, & Psychophysics 61*, 8 (1999), 1564–1576.

12. Gordon, A., Forssberg, H., Johansson, R., and Westling, G. Visual size cues in the programming of manipulative forces during precision grip. *Experimental Brain Research 83*, 3 (1991), 477–482.

13. Hayashi, T., Kawamoto, H., and Sankai, Y. Control method of robot suit hal working as operator's muscle using biological and dynamical information. *Intelligent Robots and Systems, 2005.(IROS 2005). 2005 IEEE/RSJ International Conference on* (2005), 3063–3068.

14. Kim, J., Hong, S., Koike, Y., and Sato, M. and makoto sato: How the humans respond to the 'size-weight illusion' in virtual environments. *The Eighth International Conference on Virtual Systems and Multi Media (VSMM2002)* (2002), 300–309.

15. Kim, J., Hong, S., Sato, M., and Koike, Y. Examination of the size-weight illusion by utilizing the spidar. *Transactions of the Virtual Reality Society of Japan 7*, 3 (2002), 347–354.

16. Lécuyer, A. Simulating haptic feedback using vision: A survey of research and applications of pseudo-haptic feedback. *Presence: Teleoperators and Virtual Environments 18*, 1 (2009), 39–53.

17. Lécuyer, A., Burkhardt, J. M., and Etienne, L. Simulating haptic feedback using vision: A survey of research and applications of pseudo-haptic feedback. In *Proceedings of the SIGCHI conference on Human factors in computing systems*, no. 1 in CHI '04 (2004), 239 – 246.

18. Lecuyer, A., Coquillart, S., Kheddar, A., Richard, P., and Coiffet, P. Pseudo-haptic feedback: Can isometric input devices simulate force feedback? In *IEEE Virtual Reality* (2000), 83–90.

19. Lee, K., Hicks, G., and Nino-Murcia, G. Validity and reliability of a scale to assess fatigue,. *Psychiatry Research 36* (1991), 291–298.

20. Mukai, T., Hirano, S., Nakashima, H., Kato, Y., Sakaida, Y., Guo, S., and Hosoe, S. Development of a nursing-care assistant robot riba that can lift a human in its arms. In *Intelligent Robots and Systems (IROS), 2010 IEEE/RSJ International Conference on*, IEEE (2010), 5996–6001.

21. Mukai, T., Onishi, M., Odashima, T., Hirano, S., and Luo, Z. Development of the tactile sensor system of a human-interactive robot " ri-man ". *Robotics, IEEE Transactions on 24*, 2 (2008), 505–512.

22. Narumi, T., Ban, Y., Kajinami, T., Tanikawa, T., and Hirose, M. Augmented perception of satiety: controlling food consumption by changing apparent size of food with augmented reality. In *Proceedings of the 2012 ACM annual conference on Human Factors in Computing Systems*, CHI '12 (2012), 109 – 118.

23. Öberg, T., Sandsj, L., and Kadefors, R. Subjective and objective evaluation of shoulder muscle fatigue. *Ergonomics 37*, 8 (1994), 1323–1333.

24. Omosako, H., Kimura, A., Shibata, F., and Tamura, H. Shape-cog illusion: Psychophysical influence on center-of-gravity perception by mixed-reality visual stimulation. In *Virtual Reality Workshops (VR), 2012 IEEE* (march 2012), 65 –66.

25. Rosen, J., Brand, M., Fuchs, M., and Arcan, M. A myosignal-based powered exoskeleton system. *Systems, Man and Cybernetics, Part A: Systems and Humans, IEEE Transactions on 31*, 3 (2001), 210–222.

26. Roy, S. H., and DeLuca, C. J. Evolving characteristics of the median frequency of the emg signal. *Computer-Aided EZectromyography and Expert Systems, edited by J. E. Desmedt. New York: Elsevier* (1989), 206–221.

27. S, S., and L, S. Sensory modalities are not separate modalities: plasticity and interactions. *Current opinion in neurobiology 11* (2001), 500 – 509.

28. Sadoyama, T., and Miyano, H. Frequency analysis of surface emg to evaluation of muscle fatigue. *European Journal Of Applied Physiology And Occupational Physiology 47*, 3 (1981), 239–246.

29. Stulen, F. B., and Luca, C. J. D. Frequency parameters of the myoelectric signal as a measure of muscle conduction velocity. *IEEE Transactions on Biomedical Engineering* (1981), 515–523.

30. Viitasalo, J. H. T., and Komi, P. V. Signal characteristics of emg during fatigue. *European Journal of Applied Physiology and Occupational Physiology 37* (1977), 111–121.

31. Walker, P., Francis, B., and Walker, L. The brightness-weight illusion: Darker objects look heavier but feel lighter. *Experimental psychology 57*, 6 (2010), 462.

In Search of Learning: Facilitating Data Analysis in Educational Games

Erik Harpstead, Brad A. Myers, and Vincent Aleven
Human-Computer Interaction Institute
Carnegie Mellon University
Pittsburgh, PA 15213
{eharpste,bam,aleven}@cs.cmu.edu

ABSTRACT
The field of Educational Games has seen many calls for added rigor. One avenue for improving the rigor of the field is developing more generalizable methods for measuring student learning within games. Throughout the process of development, what is relevant to measure and assess may change as a game evolves into a finished product. The field needs an approach for game developers and researchers to be able to prototype and experiment with different measures that can stand up to rigorous scrutiny, as well as provide insight into possible new directions for development. We demonstrate a toolkit and analysis tools that capture and analyze students' performance within open educational games. The system records relevant events during play, which can be used for analysis of player learning by designers. The tools support replaying student sessions within the original game's environment, which allows researchers and developers to explore possible explanations for student behavior. Using this system, we were able to facilitate a number of analyses of student learning in an open educational game developed by a team of our collaborators as well as gain greater insight into student learning with the game and where to focus as we iterate.

Author Keywords
Educational Games, Analysis of Learning, Toolkits, Logging.

ACM Classification Keywords
H.5.2 User Interfaces: Evaluation/methodology;
K.3.1 Computer Uses in Education: Computer-assisted instruction (CAI); K.8.0 Personal Computing: Games.

INTRODUCTION
Video games have become a compelling medium for instruction. Games possess many potential benefits for education including their ability to motivate students as well as provide them with authentic environments to practice new skills with minimal personal risk. This has led education researchers to begin to establish a field of educational games studies [9,10]. Despite this glowing potential of games for education, many researchers demand that more rigor be applied to the methods of proving educational effectiveness within games [10,21]. One of the challenges in meeting this demand for rigor is a lack of generalizable methods for measuring learning within educational games. While many methods have been proposed [8,14,18,19], it remains difficult for game developers to know which method of measurement to use and how to integrate particular method into their games during the process of iterative development. Additionally, because games often incorporate novel student activities for which there are no well-established existing measurement methods, the measures often need to be developed along with the game, also in an iterative fashion. These challenges are compounded if a researcher or developer wants to apply multiple methods of measuring learning to their game, as each method may require a slightly different perspective of the player's behavior. To address these challenges, we have developed a toolkit for capturing and analyzing student behavior within open educational games that can support the application of multiple methods of measurement and can also be used to address questions beyond whether learning is observed from the game. This approach was developed as part of a larger collaborative effort between game designers and researchers to develop a collection of educational games to teach basic physics concepts to young children, the first of which is RumbleBlocks [5] (see Figure 1).

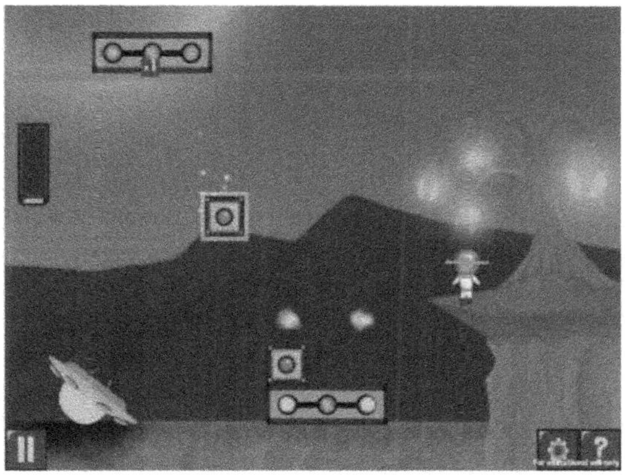

Figure 1. RumbleBlocks is a game where players must construct a tower high enough to reach the alien while also covering all of the blue energy balls.

The contributions of this paper are:

- A novel approach to recording and analyzing students' performance in educational games, which uses introspection of the properties of re-created game states to facilitate analyses of player learning in the game. This approach can be used both as a formative analysis during iterative development to improve the game, and after the game is deployed to evaluate the students' learning.
- A toolkit, implemented in C# and Unity (unity3d.com/), which supports this approach, and has been used to record and analyze logs for 174 children playing the RumbleBlocks game. This toolkit can be used to answer many different questions posed by researchers and educators about the children's learning and performance.
- A collection of measures for the RumbleBlocks game derived from re-created game states which other researchers have demonstrated successfully measure learning of physics principles in 5-8 year olds.

RumbleBlocks

RumbleBlocks (Figure 1) is an educational game designed to teach basic structural stability and balance concepts to children in kindergarten through grade 3 (5-8 years old). Its main focus is on three basic principles of stability: objects with wider bases are more stable, objects that are symmetrical are more stable, and objects with lower centers of mass are more stable. These principles are derived from goals outlined in the National Research Council's Framework for New Science Educational Standards [7] and other science education curricula for the target age group.

The game follows a sci-fi narrative where the player is helping a group of aliens who are stranded across four planets when their mother ship is damaged. Each level consists of an alien stuck on a cliff with their deactivated space ship lying on the ground. The player must use blocks to construct a tower that is tall enough to reach the alien on the cliff. Additionally, they must make sure that their tower covers a series of blue "energy balls" so that the spaceship can have enough power to take off. Once the player is confident about their tower, they can place the spaceship on top, which triggers an earthquake. If, after the earthquake ends, the tower is still standing and the spaceship is still on top of it, then the player progresses to the next level. If the tower or spaceship falls, then the player has to start over from the beginning of the level.

Each set of levels in RumbleBlocks is designed to focus on a different principle of stability. The targeting of different principles is accomplished mainly though level design. The energy balls can be used to both scaffold and limit the students' solution to a level, forcing them to prioritize one principle over another. However, even with this scaffold design, there are an unknown number of possible valid solutions to any given level because the earthquake mechanic relies on the dynamics of a real-time physics engine to evaluate the student's structure. That is, even though the level designer may intend for a particular tower design to be the solution, other designs may also work (see Figure 2).

RumbleBlocks is built within the Unity game engine. Unity is a popular game engine and development environment that is designed to allow game developers to rapidly prototype and iterate on game ideas by providing a suite of tools that automate many common game development tasks. One of these tools is the built-in physics engine, NVidia's PhysX engine, used to simulate realistic rigid body physics. This allows developers to create an accurate physical environment with much less effort. RumbleBlocks takes advantage of this feature to simulate the interactions of the blocks and the spaceship within the game. This means that the spaceship and blocks will respond to gravity and collisions as if they were real objects.

RumbleBlocks falls into a class of games that Spring and Pellegrino referred to as *open games* [19]. Open games are characterized by having a set of overarching rules that gov-

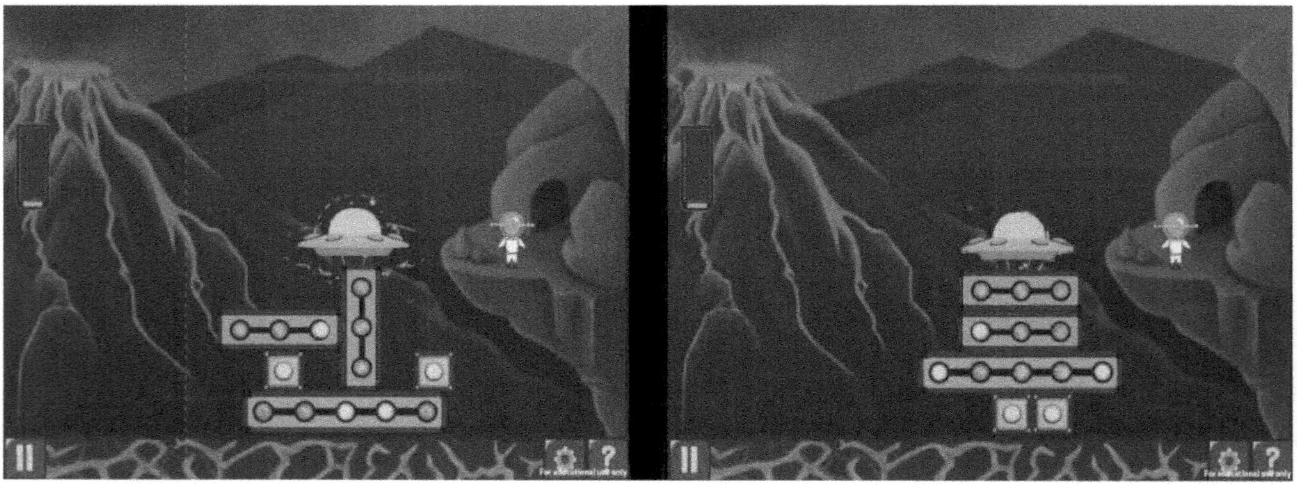

Figure 2. Two example solutions to a level in RumbleBlocks. Both solutions were successful, but knowing only that, it is hard to tell which principles each student understands.

ern the interactions of the game's elements, as well as a non-restrictive structure that allows players to explore multiple paths to a solution. These elements make open games attractive from an educational perspective because they allow students to gain lots of practice in an authentic setting that carries few substantive consequences for failure, all tenants of Gee's principles of learning in games [9]. This authentic setting, however, can make it difficult for designers to know whether or not a student's behavior demonstrates understanding of a specific piece of target knowledge. For an illustration of this issue in RumbleBlocks, refer to Figure 2. In this example, the level is designed to target the principle of structures with a low center of mass are more stable. Both student answers were successful after the earthquake and passed the level, but it is not readily clear how well either student has grasped the target principle. The tower on the right represents the answer envisioned by the level designer; however, the tower on the left actually has a lower center of mass.

Measuring Learning in Games

Educational games are ultimately judged by their capacity to show transferable learning outside of the game environment. Given how important evidence of learning is, it benefits educational game developers and researchers to have methods for measuring student learning from gameplay. The only way to truly claim that a game results in student learning is to conduct controlled lab or classroom experiments where students' improvement in understanding can be measured external tests. These kinds of evaluations, at least in their most rigorous form, are best saved for the end of the development cycle due to their cost in time and labor. The truly ideal situation is to develop measures for learning that can be evaluated within the game. While these measures also require grounding through controlled studies that measure out-of-game transfer of learning, it can be helpful to develop and iterate on them along with the game. Once validated, in-game measures allow the game to serve as an assessment in itself, opening up avenues for large scale data collection such as those used by Stamper *et al.* and Anderson *et al.* [2,20].

A number of methods for measuring within-game learning from student play exist in the literature. One simple method is to measure how many levels a player passed, or, relatedly, recording the last level the student completed. The benefit of this approach is that it is very straightforward and relatively easy to implement. Delacruz, Chung, and Baker used a measure of last level beaten when they found validity evidence for a game to be used as a standalone assessment of student math ability [8]. A single level success metric was also used by Andersen *et al.* [2] in a study of the effects of different tutorial styles on gameplay learning, i.e. how well a player was learning to play a game. This approach works well when the mechanics of gameplay are well-aligned to the target content being taught, and in the case of Andersen *et al.* they are the same thing. However, it cannot always be assumed *a priori* that gameplay and target knowledge are well aligned. An example of poor alignment came up during the early stages of developing RumbleBlocks. During playtests it was found that some students' towers were falling against the alien's cliff, which prevented them from truly falling over, and allowed players to succeed at levels they maybe should not have. This had the effect of providing players with inconsistent feedback on their constructions. If a player who uses a poor strategy passes a level that they should not have, they will never be required to reflect on the faults in their design, and thus will miss out on an important learning opportunity. To address this problem, the game designers moved the cliff farther from the construction area in an attempt to bring the game's feedback into better alignment with its educational goals.

A further limitation of using success per level as an indicator of learning is that it is very coarse-grained. This approach might work well when the learning task within each level is relatively straightforward, and does not involve a wide range of knowledge components, so that it is straightforward to attribute failure on a level to specific missing or incorrect piece of knowledge. However, games do not always have that characteristic. In fact, one reason why games are attractive for purposes of learning and assessment is that they can present learners with tasks that are more complex than those typically found in classrooms or paper-and-pencil tests.

A number of more complex methods also exist in the realm of measuring learning in games. One such method is the use of Evidence Centered Design (ECD) [16]. ECD relies on three major components: a competency model, an evidence model, and a task model. The competency model describes the target knowledge for the system. The evidence model analyzes a student's interactions with a system based on a researcher-defined rubric for scoring. The evidence model also expresses a relationship between the competency model and the observed scores. Finally, the task model provides a framework for describing the tasks a learner performs within the system. One of the benefits of ECD is that it does not require direct instrumentation into a game; however, this comes at the expense of having to analyze video recordings of player performance. Shute and colleagues have applied the ECD process successfully to existing commercial games [18].

Another complex method, drawn from work on intelligent tutoring systems, is Bayesian Knowledge Tracing (BKT) [6]. BKT tries to infer a student's knowledge state for a set of knowledge components based on their performance. It does this by assigning every action in a system to different knowledge components that can be correctly or incorrectly performed. It then takes the sequence of correct and incorrect student actions and runs them through a Bayesian Network to determine the probability that the student understands each knowledge component based on the observed pattern. Manske and Conati have used similar Bayesian network analysis to measure student learning within an educational mathematics game [14].

A further method from the intelligent tutoring literature is the use of empirical learning curves to plot the performance of students [15]. This method assigns student actions as correct or incorrect in terms of a particular piece of target knowledge, similar to BKT. It then plots the error rate of each knowledge component on each successive opportunity to apply the knowledge component. If a student is learning the content (i.e., the targeted knowledge component) being measured then the learning curve will follow the shape of a power curve, following the "power law of practice" [17]. Formulating student performance this way allows for comparison between systems based on the slopes of their respective curves. Baker and colleagues have applied learning curve analysis as a way of measuring the increase in fluency of players' ability to judge divisors of numbers in an educational math game [3].

Each of these methods requires a different formulation of data, a different perspective of student performance, and a different grain size of examination. When looking at raw performance within a game, such as the rate at which the student passes levels, or how many levels they manage to beat, the analysis is concerned with the results of an entire level, whereas BKT requires information about individual student knowledge components, and ECD and learning curve analysis can work at multiple levels. Data for one method is not generally compatible with another without translation, forcing designers to choose a particular direction. Our approach is designed to enable all of these kinds of analyses to be done on the log data.

Questions beyond Learning

While evidence of learning is the primary goal when looking at educational games, it is not the only question that can be asked about a game. Many other questions can arise over the course of development. Here is a brief list of questions that were raised by researchers during the development of RumbleBlocks:

- Are the goals of the game actually rewarding the kinds of behaviors we want to be encouraging? Does success in the game (e.g., a tower that withstands an earthquake) align well with educational objectives?
- Can we measure the "difficulty" of levels? Does the difficulty of the levels progress in an appropriate way?
- How many different solutions are there to each level? Are there solutions to levels that we did not intend?
- What measures correlate with the "fun" of levels?

Answering these questions can affect the interpretation of learning measures as well as provide implications for redesigning gameplay mechanics. Furthermore, we have found that the researchers and educators on the team continually come up with new questions they would like to answer about the game. When selecting methods to measure learning, it would be helpful if they could also address some of these kinds of questions, and could facilitate answering new questions on the existing dataset from previous players.

OUR APPROACH

To this end, we have developed our approach as a way of exploring multiple questions from the same set of player data. The system we developed had to be capable of answering learning-related questions as well as facilitating exploration of other possible questions. Our approach has two major components in it: a toolkit for logging player actions within the game, and an architecture for a Replay Analysis Engine that rebuilds and annotates a player's session. Currently the system is implemented within the Unity game engine, but it is not conceptually restricted to this environment.[1]

Play log analysis is a common practice of game user research with many pre-existing examples in the field [1,12]. Our approach differs from prior approaches by examining a student's play session as a live instantiation of the game state within a running game engine. This allows analysis to consider a much deeper picture of a student's performance, which can be analyzed from multiple perspectives, and provides access to more contextual properties of game objects than a designer may have thought to measure initially. One of the hallmarks of our design is the ability to adapt new analysis onto existing data, freeing education researchers from having to rerun large classroom studies while experimenting with new measurement or analysis techniques.

Logging System

The logging system uses an adaptation of the PSLC DataShop XML format, which is a commonly used format for describing student interactions with intelligent tutoring systems [13]. The primary motivation behind the design of the logs in our system is to be descriptive and to defer assessment to the analysis stage, whereas the original DataShop format records both the action the student took and the assessment of the tutor system as a single transaction.

Logs of student behavior are captured at the level of a basic action, defined as the smallest unit of meaningful action that a player can exert on the game world. These actions are meant to be contextualized to the game world, i.e. picking up or dropping an object, rather than the raw input of the player, i.e. mouse down at position (x, y). The reason for recording the smallest possible actions is to allow for analysis at various grain sizes by capturing data at the finest grain size. Additionally, it is easy for the game implementer

[1] The library for logging actions can be found at https://github.com/eharpste/Unity-Logger and the implementation of the replay system for RumbleBlocks is available upon request from the authors.

to see where logging calls need to be inserted into the game code because the basic actions make up the base mechanics of the game.

In addition to basic actions, logs also carry contextual information, such as the beginnings and ends of sessions and levels and whether levels were beaten or not. This information can also carry the initial conditions of the level, which might be relevant to analysis. Capturing this information facilitates coarse grain analyses dealing with whole level performance. This information can also be used to focus fine grain analysis on particular levels.

A log of a single action is described using the Selection-Action-Input paradigm borrowed from DataShop [13]. In a log, the Selection is defined as the entity the player is acting on, in most cases the name of the entity, or some other unique identifier. The Action is what the player is doing to the entity, a text description of the type of action. The Input is a parameter to the action being performed. The meaning of the Input field is contextual to the type of action, and is not always meaningful, such as in the case of button presses which use "-1" for Input as a standard convention. In the case of RumbleBlocks, the Inputs of block-related actions correspond to the position, rotation, and velocity of the block being acted on, the origin position when picking up blocks and the resultant position when releasing them.

There is also capacity to log actions that are not performed directly by the player through the same mechanism, which we refer to as engine actions. In RumbleBlocks, engine actions are used to record when the system activates the earthquake mechanism, and when the blue energy balls are covered and uncovered.

The novel aspect of our logging system is that each action is also paired with a description of the state of the game just before the action took place; this appears in the logs as a separate entry that is paired with the action by a unique transaction ID. This allows analyses to consider each action within the context in which it took place, and know the initial conditions of an action that may take time to broadly affect the game environment. The logging system also uses the state just before the action to account for actions that might remove an entity. The contents of a state are defined by the game developer and should contain only objects that are deemed relevant to ensure accurate replay. There is also capacity for simpler actions to not have accompanying states, such as pressing a "Level Start" GUI Button. In RumbleBlocks, the state describes the position, rotation, and velocity of the spaceship and all of the blocks currently on the field. The position of the cliff and blue energy balls are not needed in the state descriptions because they are immutable and instead are logged as initial conditions.

It should be noted that the actions being captured are not necessarily the set of actions that are deemed relevant by a method of analysis. ECD, for example, may consider a set of actions irrelevant to measuring a particular piece of learning. The recorded actions are the set of actions that are relevant to gameplay. This stance is in keeping with the motivation to make logs descriptive of what is happening in the game. Using purely descriptive logs allows researchers to revisit old data in light of new findings or new analysis methods without having to run additional expensive field or classroom studies.

The logging library was written in C# and is designed to be straightforward to use. For each player action and special event such as level start and end, the implementer adds a call to a function that takes as parameters the Selection, Action, and Input of the action. (For convenience, there are also simpler versions of this call that leverage the standard properties that all Unity game objects have.) In order to log the state, the implementer keeps up-to-date a global list of all relevant game entities, and the logger automatically logs the relevant properties. For convenience, the implementer can alternatively attach a script to these objects using Unity's interactive builder at design-time rather than adding them to the list programmatically.

The highly descriptive nature of the logs can make them somewhat large. The entire RumbleBlocks dataset we discuss here, contains logs from two sessions of play (approx. 20 minutes per session) by 174 children, and is roughly 850MB in size. The system is primarily designed to log to a webserver: however, when running classroom studies, we have found that the volume of logs can become intractable for some school networks and so a locally logged version is also available.

Replay and Analysis Engine

A novel aspect of our system is that the analyses of student performance are evaluated using an active replay of the student's game session in the running engine rather than on the raw logs themselves. This replay process happens within the second main component of the approach, which we call the Replay Analysis Engine (RAE). This tool is also implemented in C# for the Unity engine. The log replay system reads in a student log and reconstructs the student's play session action-by-action. For each action, the RAE first constructs the state in which the action took place and then enacts the student action to let the Unity game engine calculate the consequences of that action. For example, if the action is to let go of a block, then the RAE will use the game engine to calculate where the block ends up after it finishes falling.

The RAE makes use of Unity's "prefab" architecture. A *prefab* is a Unity construct that serves as a master copy of a complex game object to allow for easy instantiation and duplication. Using this system allows the analysis designer to ensure that the game objects on which they run their analysis behave exactly the same as the ones the player experienced. This, in turn, ensures that any analysis is a valid reproduction of student performance in the game.

The RAE has a few different options for determining when to stop the simulation and run the analyses. By default, the logged state is re-instantiated and simulation is stopped immediately. Another option (and the primary one used in RumbleBlocks analysis) is that once the state is re-instantiated, the simulation is run until all the objects in the interface have stopped moving. Once this happens, the simulation is stopped and the analyses are run. There is also an option to run the simulation for a defined amount of game time, which can also be accelerated without loss of accuracy.

The RAE supports two different ways to analyze the logs. The first way is through an API that allows access to the states created by student actions. The analysis implementer can write C# code which leverages this library to generate metrics. This is useful when the analyzer needs to access specific properties of the objects. For example, in RumbleBlocks we were interested in the properties of structures students built, such as their centers of mass. We used our API to examine the instantiated version of blocks to find which ones were part of a connected tower, which then allowed us to average their centers of mass to create a center of mass for the structure as a whole. Without the ability to access the collider information or rigid body properties of game objects in the live engine we would not have been able to do this.

Implementing an analysis using the RAE API resembles creating a new level for the game. The analysis developer first creates a skeleton level containing any entities that are common to all levels of the game and an entity provided by the library that runs the actual replay. The developer must also include any prefabs of objects that may appear in a state message. The RAE provides a set of routines to iterate through the actions in a student log, and to inspect the elements of a current action state. It also provides routines for accessing the success and failure of each level in the log so the analysis designer can easily have access to whatever properties of the performance they want to analyze.

The second way of using the RAE is by running student logs through predefined analyses. This process generates spreadsheets of data that can be used for statistical analysis. We have used the API provided by the RAE to develop a set of common measures to filter logs based on their properties, such as outputting only specific levels or users. Access to these common filtering operations is provided through onscreen menus while the RAE is running to control which data are recorded in the spreadsheets.

The benefit of the RAE approach is the ability to create a set of potential measures and analyses and iterate on them separately from the development of the game itself. Since the analysis system contains all common level elements, it is agnostic to level design and to some changes in mechanical design. One slight limitation is that it requires the game developers to maintain old copies of prefabs within the game files so that future analysis of old data will remain consistent. There are situations where one might want to break this rule, to explore if the responses to previous players' actions may have had different results if a particular rule was changed.

USE IN ANALYSIS FOR RUMBLEBLOCKS

We used our toolkit with RumbleBlocks as part of a formative analysis of the game's design, so we and other members of our team of collaborators were able to perform a wide range of analyses. The data we discuss here were gathered as part of a classroom study in two Pittsburgh area public schools, with subjects taken from kindergarten to third grade classrooms (roughly 5 to 8 year-olds). This study was meant to both check the progress of the game design and attempt to ground, for the first time, measures of learning within the game against external (i.e., out-of-game) assessments of the educational objectives of the game.

For the purposes of this study, two sets of levels were selected to be used as in-game pre- and post-tests counterbalanced across students. These levels were chosen out of the collection of regular building levels but altered to have their blue energy balls removed, in addition to removing the ability to allow students to retry on a failed attempt. These special levels were placed after a short collection of tutorial levels, which explained the mechanics of the game. The intention of this design was to allow us to get a sense of the kinds of structures students would build before they had a large amount of experience with the game, and after they had a chance to practice building. In addition to these in-game evaluations, players also took out-of-game paper and pencil tests, developed by our colleagues, before and after playing the game. These tests contained items relating to stability and construction, based on our three principles of base width, low center of mass, and symmetry. We only touch on a subset of these learning analyses here, since the full results will appear elsewhere.

Learning Analysis

Our team was interested in exploring many questions, such as those listed above about RumbleBlocks but chief among them was whether or not we could say there was evidence of within-game learning related to the game's educational objectives (i.e., understanding and application of the three principles of stability). We measured a slight, yet significant, increase in performance from pretest to posttest on the out-of-game measures ($p < .05$); however, we were also interested in whether learning could be measured in the game, using data provided by our system. In looking at the difference in raw performance, i.e., the pass rate of the in-game pre-test and post-test levels, there is a small, yet significant, improvement in the passing rate ($p < .001$). This improvement however could potentially be attributable to simply learning the game mechanics (although that explanation would not account for the increase in performance measured on the out-of-game pre-test and post-test).

Figure 3. Illustrations of measurements used in Rumble-Blocks evaluation. The length of the red line is the base width, the length of the blue line is the height of the center of mass and the size of the green angle measures symmetry.

To explore this issue further, we wanted to see if, within the game, there were performance gains in terms of the specific principles. We are interested in this measurement as a way of getting a clearer picture of *exactly what students were learning* and not just that they were getting better at passing levels. This would mean that from pre to post, students would build towers that showed a better awareness that (1) a structure with a wide base is more stable, (2) a structure with a lower center of mass is more stable, and (3) a structure that is symmetrical is more stable. To find out whether they did, we instrumented the replay system to calculate a variety of metrics based on the final state of each level that a student played. These metrics were: the width of the tower's base, the position of the tower's center of mass relative to the ground, and a measure of symmetry defined as the angle formed by a ray from the center of the base to the center of mass and the ground (illustrated in Figure 3). These measures were then compared to values calculated across

Measure	Mean (SE)		T-Statistic
	Pretest	Posttest	
Width of Base	0.60 (.01)	0.64 (.01)	-2.767**
Symmetry Angle	5.98 (.34)	5.20 (.27)	1.9783*
Center of Mass	1.61 (.02)	1.63 (.02)	-0.663

Table 1. Pre and posttest means and significance values for metrics. Note for the width of base measure, a higher value is more desirable, whereas for the symmetry angle and center of mass measures, a lower value is more desirable.
* $p < .05$, ** $p < .01$

all other players for that same level in order to create a relative score for each player. In the case of base width, this score is relative to the maximum observed width for that level; for center of mass position, the score is relative to the lowest observed position for that level; and for symmetry a score is calculated relative to 90 degrees which would represent perfect symmetry. When comparing the average relativized pre and post scores, we saw a significant improvement, with a one-tailed t-test, for the wide base and symmetry principles (see Table 1), meaning that at the end of playing the game, students were beginning to design towers that had wider bases and more symmetrical layouts. However, we did not see any significant difference in terms of center of mass position, meaning that students did not seem to attempt to lower the center of mass of their structures. This result would suggest that the game is currently not successfully teaching the center of mass principle. A recommendation to the game designers from this finding would be to explore ways of making the center of mass of a tower more salient to the player so that they might be able to account for it when creating their solution to a level.

Gameplay Alignment Analysis

Another interesting question that we explored was how well the game was aligned to its educational objectives. Many researchers have pointed to the importance of alignment of game goals to instructional goals [15,18,22]. The basic question is: does the game properly incentivize the behavioral patterns that we want to foster? Additionally, in the case of RumbleBlocks, we wanted to know if levels that were designed to target a particular piece of knowledge (i.e., one of the three principles of stability) actually succeeded in doing so. Answering this question during a formative evaluation can have implications for level design and even on the design of a game's core mechanics if there are alignment problems. We instrumented a new set of metrics in addition to the ones used in the learning analysis described above, including what we call the "stability metric." From the standpoint of realistic earthquake physics, the stability metric is the amount of energy that would be required to overturn a tower about its weakest foot, and so a high value in this metric would represent a stronger design.

In using these metrics for analyzing alignment, we wanted to explore how well metrics that should indicate a well-constructed tower actually corresponded to students passing a given level. To do this, we created 3 groups by collecting together the levels that target each of the three principles, and then we performed logistic regressions using each of the metrics of the players' towers to predict success on a level. The results of the regression analyses can be found in Table 2. When looking at the level-relevant metrics for base width, center of mass height, symmetry, and the stability metric, we found a significant predictive relationship between them and success on level, which is what would be expected, however the direction of the relationship for the center of mass metric was in the wrong direction. This

Group	Coefficient	Estimate	Standard Error	Z-Statistic
Levels targeting the Wide Base Principle	Width of Base	0.26227	0.05667	4.628***
	Center of Mass	-0.13203	0.122101	-1.091
	Symmetry Angle	-0.03086	0.01041	-2.965**
	Energy Required	-0.28414	0.12115	-2.345*
Levels targeting the Low Center of Mass Principle	Width of Base	0.036602	0.026918	1.360
	Center of Mass	0.783418	0.107301	7.301***
	Symmetry Angle	-0.003038	0.005309	-.0572
	Energy Required	-0.061895	0.114265	-0.542
Levels targeting the Symmetry Principle	Width of Base	0.066311	0.028741	2.230*
	Center of Mass	0.167317	0.073404	2.279*
	Symmetry Angle	0.022834	0.008717	2.620**
	Energy Required	0.389674	0.107243	3.634***

Table 2. The results of logistic regression predicting level success based on metrics within groups of levels targeting a specific principle. Note for the width of base measure, a higher value is more desirable, whereas for the symmetry angle and center of mass measures, a lower value is more desirable.
$* p < .05$, $** p < .01$, $*** p < .001$

would mean that, counter to what the target principles suggest, students that build with higher relative centers of mass are more likely to succeed on the levels that target the center of mass principle. One possible explanation for this comes from the level designs for the center of mass levels. In an attempt to have the center of mass levels isolate the center of mass principle from the highly related wide base principle, the level designers created a few levels where the intended solution had a very narrow base. This has the effect of actually raising the center of mass for successful structures and possibly introducing confounds. The results of this alignment analysis as well as the learning analysis suggest that the design of these levels should be revisited.

Solution Space Analysis

An ongoing initiative in our research group is to attempt to answer the question of how many unique solutions students have created for each level. While every level was designed around a particular envisioned solution, there is no requirement that players use it. Understanding the solutions that students actually created can lead to many further analyses, such as finding solutions we did not intend that might bypass the learning goals of the game, or exploring relationships between particular solution patterns and better performance on transfer measures, or analyses of how challenge, fun, and levels having multiple solutions are related.

A novel way to approach counting unique solutions is to employ expectation maximization clustering along metrics that describe student solutions with cross validation to determine an optimal number of clusters that describes the set of all solutions to a given level, with each cluster representing a unique solution. We have been exploring the use of the metrics derived from our previous analysis as features to feed into the clustering algorithm. This is somewhat problematic as the raw metrics, like center of mass location and width of base, cannot render true equality between two states in the game as quite different structures could have similarly located centers of mass or bases of the same width. Our initial analysis attempts that used clustering on our existing metrics were promising but not readily satisfying. This led us to brainstorming a larger collection of features to build into the RAE that could be beneficial in clustering student solutions together. Among these new metrics are measures of the towers' extents, such as total height and maximum width, as well as measures to capture the position of the spaceship relative to the student's tower. It is our hope that this initiative will render a tractable set of student solutions out of the large set that we currently have in log data. Once a smaller set has been determined, they could be used diagnostically to make inferences as to how a student might perform on transfer tests based on which designs they used.

Another possible way of attacking the question of how many student answers there are is to use plan recognition. This method would require us to decide on a grammar or set of production rules that we can apply in the RAE to annotate the log. Once a collection of higher-order actions is gathered, students can be grouped by the plans they demonstrate. This is a promising direction for analysis and remains part of our ongoing work.

Further Analyses

Going forward, our team will be exploring other analyses through the data afforded by our approach. One of these is to explore more fine-grained analysis by applying BKT as a way of corroborating our coarse grained measures. This would require that we identify knowledge components present within RumbleBlocks that can be mapped to particular actions. Experimenting with different mappings is a time intensive task, but it is made easier by already having a way of formalizing the actions a student can take within the game and having a dataset to test models with.

Another open question that we will tackle is whether or not the difficulty in the game increases in a reasonable manner. One way of measuring problem difficulty is by looking at the amount of time and number of actions it takes to beat different levels. If certain levels seem to take inordinate amounts of time to beat then this might indicate that the level is too difficult. This method, however, cannot properly factor out learning of game mechanics or physics content without randomizing the level order, which is hard to do in a game with a narrative context such as RumbleBlocks. Another way of exploring difficulty is to look at how many times players have to backtrack when trying to find a successful answer (i.e., build a successful tower). This can be accomplished by defining patterns of actions that are indicative of backtracking, such as placing a block back into the inventory or deconstructing a structure and throwing blocks to the side. Levels with a high degree of backtracking could also indicate levels that are more challenging.

A final question that will be explored arises from our game design partners in asking if there is evidence of the game being fun or not. This might be measured by looking at how long players played and how often they returned to the game. This data is readily available from the logs we currently possess; however, since our formative evaluation was conducted in a classroom setting, this data is confounded by the fact that players were a captive audience. Another way we might approach this question is by looking at the rate at which players experiment with the game's mechanics as a measure of playfulness; the cluster analyses and plan recognition initiatives could help with this by looking at the diversity of solutions within a student's actions.

DISCUSSION

So far our approach has facilitated many different analyses that have benefited our educational game development project. We were able to explore course grain learning analysis on a principle level, and found that RumbleBlocks appears to be teaching players to address the wide base and symmetry principles when building simple structures. We were also able to examine the alignment of gameplay to our stated content goals, and found that the alignment is fine for two of the three targeted principles, but that there are potential issues with the alignment of levels targeting low center of mass, which may help explain the results of our learning analysis. Finally, we have also used our technique to begin to map the solution space of RumbleBlocks, giving us a better understanding of what kinds of student answers we are seeing. Each of these findings can help provide feedback for further refining the game.

Each of the analyses we have explored so far requires a slightly different perspective on the performance of players. The learning analysis asked questions about our players by looking at their final solutions to levels. The alignment analysis was concerned with the design of the game itself and used student solutions as a corpus for analysis. Mapping solution space and measuring fine grained progress required a representation of the steps students took throughout the game. Without the benefit of our replay analysis engine exploring each of these questions would have necessitated a different expensive classroom study, and a different characterization of student performance.

As our team continues to move forward and develop new games we will also continue to evolve the system. Currently the implementation of the toolkit is restricted to the Unity environment and many aspects of the log replay system rely heavily on Unity-specific constructs, such as the prefab architecture. There is no reason that the approach could not be implemented in other environments, however. At its core, the approach requires that the entities in the game can be recreated dynamically without loss of accuracy. Given that dynamically creating large numbers of similar game objects is a common requirement for games, many existing engines contain such capabilities.

However, this approach is certainly not applicable to all game types. Our work so far, and into the foreseeable future, is focused on single-player physics games, which do not have to deal with issues such as the interactions of multiple players or the open three dimensional movements of player avatars, such as those present in multi-user virtual environments like River City or Quest Atlantis [4,11]. Applying our process to these kinds of environments would demand more data aggregation on the logging side to avoid information overload from logging every player's minute movements. An alternative might be to only log when players enter and leave certain areas rather than the individual movement commands. This would end up yielding data similar to the "heat map" analysis already commonly used in game user research [1].

As we begin to publish our games online, we are also interested in exploring the capacity to make them adaptive to learners' needs. One of the benefits of our architecture that readily serves this goal is the fact that the analysis measures are built in the exact same environment as the game itself. This means that once we are satisfied by the reliability of a particular measure, it can be easily moved into the live game to serve as an on-line assessment. When the measure reveals that students are struggling, we could then try to serve them levels adaptively to focus their learning.

CONCLUSION

Open educational games have proven to be difficult to analyze. We have developed an approach for looking at student performances in open educational games that facilitates multiple kinds of analysis through log reinterpretation, and we implemented this approach in a toolkit and set of analysis tools for Unity in C#. Using a more traditional logging approach, this kind of analysis would have required multiple expensive classroom studies to gather data as new questions and measures were envisioned by our team. Additionally, analysis at the level of individual principles would not have been possible using only success on levels as a metric.

The toolkit is available to others to extend and apply to their own games. It is our hope that others will embrace the methodology for recording players' behavior in games as a way of exploring multiple measures of learning. Having consistent measurement and analysis techniques will help bolster the methodological rigor of the field of educational game design.

ACKNOWLEDGMENTS

We would like to thank development team of Rumble-Blocks as well as our collaborators on the ENGAGE Project. This work was supported in part by the DARPA ENGAGE research program under ONR Contract Number N00014-12-C-0284 and by a Graduate Training Grant awarded to Carnegie Mellon University by the Department of Education # R305B090023.

REFERENCES

1. Ambinder, M. Valve's Approach to Playtesting: The Application of Empiricism. *Presented at GDC 2009*, (2009).
2. Andersen, E., Rourke, E.O., Liu, Y., et al. The Impact of Tutorials on Games of Varying Complexity. *Proc. CHI 2012*, (2012), 59–68.
3. Baker, R.S.J. d, Habgood, J.M.P., Ainsworth, S.E., and Corbett, A.T. Modeling the Acquisition of Fluent Skill in Educational Action Games. In *User Modeling 2007*. 2007, 17–26.
4. Barab, S., Thomas, M., Dodge, T., Carteaux, R., and Tuzun, H. Making Learning Fun: Quest Atlantis, a Game without Guns. *Educational Technology Research and Development 53*, 1 (2005), 86–107.
5. Christel, M.G., Stevens, S.M., Maher, B.S., et al. RumbleBlocks: Teaching Science Concepts to Young Children through a Unity Game. *Proc. CGames 2012*, (2012), 162–166.
6. Corbett, A.T. and Anderson, J.R. Knowledge tracing: Modeling the acquisition of procedural knowledge. *User Modelling and User-Adapted Interaction 4*, 4 (1995), 253–278.
7. Council, N.R. *A Framework for K-12 Science Education: Practices, Crosscutting Concepts, and Core Ideas*. The National Academies Press, 2012.
8. Delacruz, G.C., Chung, G.K.W.K., and Baker, E.L. *Validity Evidence for Games as Assessment Environments (CRESST Report 773)*. Los Angeles, CA, 2010.
9. Gee, J.P. *What video games have to teach us about learning and literacy*. Palgrave Macmillan, New York, 2003.
10. Honey, M.A. and Hilton, M. *Learning Science Through Computer Games and Simulations*. National Academic Press, Washington, D.C., 2011.
11. Ketelhut, D.J. The Impact of Student Self-efficacy on Scientific Inquiry Skills: An Exploratory Investigation in River City, a Multi-user Virtual Environment. *Journal of Science Education and Technology 16*, 1 (2006), 99–111.
12. Kim, J.H., Gunn, D. V, Schuh, E., Phillips, B.C., Pagulayan, R.J., and Wixon, D. Tracking Real-Time User Experience (TRUE): A comprehensive instrumentation solution for complex systems. *Proc. CHI 2008*, (2008), 443–451.
13. Koedinger, K.R., Baker, R.S.J. d, Cunningham, K., Skogsholm, A., Leber, B., and Stamper, J. A Data Repository for the EDM community: The PSLC DataShop. In C. Romero, S. Ventura, M. Pechenizkiy and R.S.J. d. Baker, eds., *Handbook of Educational Data Mining*. 2010, 43–55.
14. Manske, M. and Conati, C. Modelling Learning in an Educational Game. In C.-K. Looi, M. Gord, B. Bredeweg and J. Breuker, eds., *Artificial Intelligence in Education: Supporting Learning through Intelligent and Socially Informed Technology*. IOS Press, Amsterdam, Netherlands, 2005, 411–418.
15. Martin, B., Koedinger, K.R., Mitrovic, A., and Mathan, S. On Using Learning Curves to Evaluate ITS. *Proc. AIED 2005*, (2005), 419–426.
16. Mislevy, R.J., Steinberg, L.S., and Almond, R.G. On the Structure of Educational Assessments. *Measurement: Interdisciplinary Research and Perspectives 1*, 1 (2003), 3–62.
17. Newell, A. and Rosenbloom, P.S. Mechanisms of skill acquisition and the law of practice. In J.R. Anderson, ed., *Cognitive skills and their acquisition*. Lawrence Erlbaum Associates, Hillsdale, NJ, 1981, 1–56.
18. Shute, V.J. Stealth Assessment in Computer-Based Games to Support Learning. In S. Tobias and J.D. Fletcher, eds., *Computer Games and Instruction*. Information Age Publishers, Charlotte, NC, 2011, 503–524.
19. Spring, F. and Pellegrino, J.W. The Challenge of Assessing Learning in Open Games : HORTUS as a Case Study. *Proc. GLS 2011*, (2011), 200–208.
20. Stamper, J.C., Lomas, D., Ching, D., Ritter, S., Koedinger, K.R., and Steinhart, J. The Rise of the Super Experiment. *Proc. EDM 2012*, (2012).
21. Young, M.F., Slota, S., Cutter, A.B., et al. Our Princess Is in Another Castle: A Review of Trends in Serious Gaming for Education. *Review of Educational Research 82*, 1 (2012), 61–89.

Optimizing Challenge in an Educational Game Using Large-Scale Design Experiments

Derek Lomas[1], Kishan Patel[2], Jodi L Forlizzi[1], Kenneth R Koedinger[1]

[1] Human Computer Interaction Institute
Carnegie Mellon University
5000 Forbes Ave, Pittsburgh, PA 15212
dereklomas@cs.cmu.edu
917-544-4171

[2] Dhirubhai Ambani Institute of Information and Communication Technology (DAIICT)
Gandhinagar, Gujarat, India 382007
kishan@playpowerlabs.com
91-972-433-2824

ABSTRACT
Online games can serve as research instruments to explore the effects of game design elements on motivation and learning. In our research, we manipulated the design of an online math game to investigate the effect of challenge on player motivation and learning. To test the "Inverted-U Hypothesis", which predicts that maximum game engagement will occur with moderate challenge, we produced two large-scale (10K and 70K subjects), multi-factor (2x3 and 2x9x8x4x25) online experiments. We found that, in almost all cases, subjects were more engaged and played longer when the game was easier, which seems to contradict the generality of the Inverted-U Hypothesis. Troublingly, we also found that the most engaging design conditions produced the slowest rates of learning. Based on our findings, we describe several design implications that may increase challenge-seeking in games, such as providing feedforward about the anticipated degree of challenge.

Author Keywords
Games; Education; Crowdsourcing; Design

ACM Classification Keywords
H.5.m. Information interfaces and presentation (e.g., HCI): Miscellaneous.

General Terms
Human Factors; Design; Measurement.

INTRODUCTION
In previous periods of educational game development there were few studies regarding the effectiveness of games [6, 14]. However, contemporary games have the benefit of networked data collection and large online audiences. As a result, contemporary educational games permit large-scale online experiments investigating the effects of game design factors on both motivation and learning.

Measuring the effects of design elements (such as time limits, animations, or reward settings) on motivation can be relatively straightforward. In an experimental design with random assignment, if one version of a game results in a greater duration of voluntary play, it may be described as more intrinsically motivating or more engaging. For instance, Tom Malone's early game research [11] involved the progressive removal of design elements from games and measuring differences in the average amount of time children spent on the different game versions.

Recently, Andersen *et al.* [2] demonstrated that online games can be an excellent laboratory for investigating motivation and its measurable outcome, player engagement. They quantified player engagement as the total time spent playing a game and as the number of game levels attempted. Then, the researchers randomly assigned thousands of game players to a series of A/B tests varying different design elements. They found, for instance, that music had no significant effect on engagement, celebratory animations had some positive effect, and the presence of "bonus coins" (an optional challenge) had a strong negative effect on engagement. This last finding was surprising, as the longstanding belief was that bonus challenges would be appealing to players (and make them play longer). Their study demonstrates how online experiments can be used to empirically test common hypotheses regarding the effects of design on motivation.

CHALLENGE SEEKING IN GAMES
One interesting aspect of games is that their challenge is a motivating force [12,18,20]. In everyday life, people might be expected to minimize challenge—unless, of course, the challenge leads to greater rewards. While software design portrays "ease of use" as an essential quality, game design is based on the idea that players seek challenge.

How do games promote this challenge-seeking behavior? And why would anyone seek a challenge? In many cases, greater challenges lead to greater rewards, both tangible and intangible. For instance, one may chose a challenging activity if success in that activity leads to a greater status,(as in a sporting match). Status is a key motivational element in games and also in educational environments (e.g., scores, grades and teacher reports). Because status and challenge will often correlate, we question whether challenge alone would be motivating.

Why would someone engage in a more challenging activity, if a less challenging activity leads to a perfectly equal reward? Several theorists have suggested that completing challenging tasks brings greater internal rewards than completing easy tasks [7,9]. For instance, children will smile more after completing longer, more difficult word-scramble puzzles [7]. This pleasure is believed to arise from one's enhanced sense of self-efficacy or the sense of competence [4] that comes from the accomplishment.

Under this explanation, it is the *successful completion* of a challenging task that is more satisfying—not the act of *doing* something challenging. Still, a significant body of evidence indicates that, if given a choice, people will *choose* moderately difficult activities over activities that are very easy or very hard [7,17,1]. Moreover, there is evidence that people enjoy *doing* activities with moderate levels of challenge, not just completing them or choosing them. For instance, using Experience Sampling Methods to interrupt individuals' daily activities, Mihaly Csikszentmihalyi [1] found that people report high levels of enjoyment during challenging tasks; he characterized this enjoyment as a conscious phenomenon called "flow." The construct of flow and "flow states" have been widely adopted in theories of game enjoyment [20,12 ,21,18].

Recently, Abuhamdeh and Csikszentmihalyi sought to experimentally test the idea that optimal enjoyment occurs during moderately challenging activities [1]. They describe the idea in terms of an inverted-U: "...the notion that we most enjoy optimally challenging activities that are not too easy or too difficult implies a curvilinear, inverted U-shaped relation between difficulty and enjoyment, so that increases in difficulty should lead to increases in enjoyment up to an optimal level (i.e., the apex of the curve), after which further increases in difficulty lead to decreases in enjoyment."

To explore this "Inverted-U Hypothesis", Abuhamdeh and Csikszentmihalyi conducted a large-scale observational study of online chess players [1]. They quantified the challenge of each game as the numeric difference between the international chess ranking of two players. Enjoyment was measured through a survey taken by players immediately after each game. Their results showed that the greatest enjoyment occurred when players faced an opponent with a higher chess rating, but not too much higher. This provided strong evidence to support the Inverted-U Hypothesis.

Notably, the authors identified another factor governing the enjoyment of individual games: regardless of the difference in chess ranking or who won, players reported feeling greatest enjoyment while playing "close games." A closer game is one that ends with a smaller difference between the point value of the pieces taken by each player. Therefore, when the difference in points was minimal, and the outcome was most uncertain, players reported that the game was most enjoyable. This finding supports previous theory and evidence [3,18,12] about the motivating nature of uncertain outcomes.

Applying the Inverted-U Hypothesis to Online Games
The Inverted-U Hypothesis seems appropriate for predicting the effect of challenge on player motivation in videogames. Indeed, many game design guides [5,18,20] and psychological theories [1,3,4,8,17,13,20,21] suggest that optimal engagement will occur at a moderate level of difficulty. However, there is little guidance about precisely how difficult a game should be.

In our research, we use large-scale experimentation to test the Inverted-U Hypothesis in an educational game context. We seek to determine whether there is a particular degree of challenge that optimizes player engagement. To identify the optimal level of challenge, we randomly assigned players to different design configurations and modeled the effect of the varying challenge on player motivation. The Inverted-U Hypothesis predicts that engagement will be highest at a moderate level of challenge, neither too hard nor too easy (Figure 1). In these studies, we operationalized challenge as the probability of success [3,17] and motivation as the duration of voluntary game engagement [2,12].

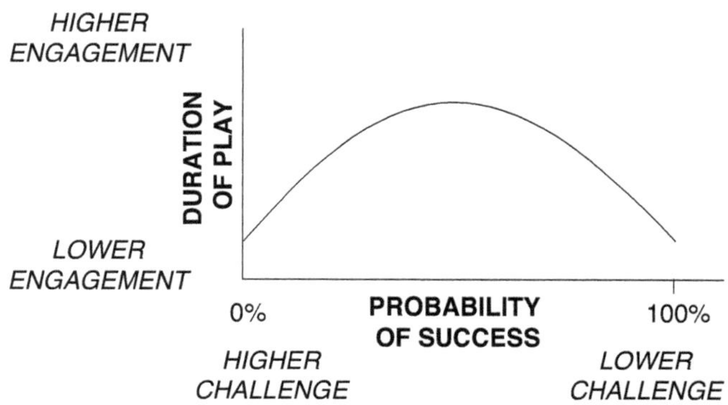

Figure 1: The "Inverted-U Hypothesis" suggests that optimal engagement (measured as duration of voluntary play) will occur at a single intermediate level of game challenge (measured as probability of success). Factors that increase or decrease challenge from this level should reduce engagement.

ONLINE EXPERIMENT 1

To document the relationship between difficulty and engagement, we used *Battleship Numberline*, an online Flash game where players attempt to explode target ships and submarines by estimating numbers on a number line. Classroom experiments have shown that the game produces significant improvements in number line estimation accuracy after only 20 minutes of game play [11].

On the basis of the Inverted-U Hypothesis, we anticipated that a manipulation of the difficulty of the game from very easy to very hard would produce an inverted U-shaped effect on engagement. To manipulate difficulty in the game, we varied two different design factors: target type and target size.

Target Type
The target type can be either a visible ship or a hidden submarine. With the visible ship (see Figure 2), a battleship is visible on the number line and players need to type a

number that approximates its location. With the hidden submarine target, players are instead presented with a number indicating the location of the hidden submarine; the player then needs to click on the location of the number line that they believe corresponds to the number provided. Both the task of locating a given number on a number line and the task of naming a given location on number line are educationally relevant practice activities that may vary in their challenge.

Target Size

A larger target is easier to hit; estimates can be less accurate and still be successful. Therefore, the target size can be described in terms of "error tolerance", where a higher error tolerance indicates a larger target (Figure 2).

Take the case of a player estimating the location of a submarine that is "spotted at 20" on a number line from 0-100. If the player clicks on the number line location corresponding to 29, their estimate would have a 9% error—and an accuracy of 91%. If the target were larger, 20% of the length of the number line (an error tolerance of 10%), the estimation attempt would be successful. However, if the target were smaller (10% of the line or 5% error tolerance), the estimation attempt would miss the submarine. As a result, increasing or decreasing the size of the ship greatly affects the challenge of the game.

Figure 2: The left image shows the game's original ship that is 10% of the number line (5% error tolerance). The ship on the right is 40% of the line (20% error tolerance), which seemed simply too easy.

Game Design

Players are either presented with a visible ship or a number indicating the location of a hidden submarine. Once the player has typed in their estimate (in ship mode) or clicked on an estimated location (in submarine mode), a bomb falls at that location on the number line. If the bomb hits the target, there is a satisfying explosion and a gold star is released, incrementing the player's star count in the scoreboard. If the player misses, the bomb splashes in the water and corrective feedback is displayed along with the accuracy of their estimate. A running tally of the player's average accuracy is displayed in one corner of the screen and a count of the number of stars collected on the other. There is no final "winning" or "losing" state in the game—instead, players can continue to play as long as they wish. Additionally, there are no leaderboards or other mechanisms that allow players to directly compare status.

Experimental Design

To explore the effect of challenge on engagement, we constructed a 2x3 between-subjects experiment involving target size (error tolerance of 3%, 5% and 10%) and target type (ship or submarine). The experiment took place among players who had chosen to estimate whole numbers. In all conditions the players received the same 20 whole number estimation items (between 0-100) in random order; at the end of this set, the items would be repeated in another random order. Players had the option of dropping out at any time but the total number of trials was capped at 80 trials. The time limit for the ship condition was 15 seconds and 10 seconds for the sub condition.

Measuring Challenge and Engagement

Our operationalized measure of challenge was the estimated success rate of each game configuration, where success rate is measured as the percent of successful estimates divided by the total number of estimates. Engagement was measured as the average duration of play in each condition, either as the total trials played (number of estimates attempted) or the total time played (sum of reaction times across estimates).

Participants

Battleship Numberline was made available on the *GameUp* platform on Brainpop.com, which is a popular site for classroom teachers in grades 4-8. The vast majority of play occurred during school hours, with large drop offs during weekends and holidays. However, subjects were completely anonymous and were not tracked over time. As a result, the unit of experimental manipulation was on a game session, rather than a subject. A game session began when players clicked on one of the game choices (fractions, decimals or whole number estimation) and ended when players exited or made no further actions after a time-out. Each game session represented a unique experimental assignment and a single player could receive multiple versions of the game by exiting and starting over. While allowing the same individual to participate in multiple experimental assignments may appear to distort our data, the purpose of the experiment was to measure implicit user preference. Therefore, choosing to disengage from one condition and start another only enhances our measure of engagement.

Approximately 1,000 game sessions were played per day, ranging from 200 per day over school holidays to 10,000 per day when the game was "featured" by BrainPop. This scale made it possible to run a broad number of experiments simultaneously from the same subject pool. The data presented here is from one such experiment, which was conducted between 12/16/2011 to 3/8/2012 and involved 10,478 game sessions.

RESULTS

Target Size

As expected, bigger targets made the game significantly easier: the largest targets had an average success rate of 63% (sd=34%) while the smallest targets had a success rate of 29% (sd=25%). The larger and easier-to-hit targets were also significantly more engaging, resulting in 34% more estimates and 18% more time spent than the smaller and more difficult-to-hit targets (See Table 1).

While players take significantly less time to estimate the larger targets ($p<0.001$), there was no significant difference between the accuracy of their estimates ($p=0.34$). In other words, the larger targets did not appear to make players more careless in their estimates.

Targ. Size	N	Total Trials	Total Time	Accur-acy	Success Rate	React Time
3%	3462	12.6 (13.1)	60.9 (54.1)	78.8% (26.5)	29.2% (25.2)	6.8 (5.8)
5%	3479	14.6 (14.4)	66.5 (55.5)	79.5% (26.0)	43.3% (30.3)	6.6 (5.6)
10%	3537	17.0 (15.8)	71.6 (55.4)	79.6% (25.6)	62.8% (34.1)	6.3 (5.6)

Table 1. Main Effects of Target Size (with standard deviation). 3% is a smaller target than 10% and more difficult to hit. All differences are significant at $p<0.001$, except Accuracy, p=.36

Target Type

The main effects from the design factor *target type* (Table 2) are contradictory, depending on how engagement was measured: the submarine target was significantly more engaging based on the number of trials (p<0.001) but the ship target was significantly more engaging based on the amount of time (p<0.001). As the ship target asks players to type an estimate on the keyboard, each trial takes more time than the click required for the submarine target. Still, given this contradiction, it is unclear which condition can be said to be more engaging/motivating.

Targ. Type	N	Total Trials	Total Time	Accur-acy	Success Rate	React Time
Sub	5596	17.0 (16.2)	60.3 (53.8)	84.8% (15.5)	44.6% (32.1)	4.1 (2.5)
Ship	4882	12.2 (12.0)	73.3 (56.0)	73.0% (33.3)	45.9% (34.2)	9.3 (6.9)

Table 2. Main Effects of Target Type (with standard deviation). Sub involves clicking a location to estimate a number, while Ship involves typing a number to estimate a location. All differences are significant at p<0.001, except Success Rate, p=.05. The difference in N between subs and ships results from players quitting before completing one trial.

Combined Scale for Measuring Engagement

The amount of "time spent" and "challenges attempted" are useful measures of engagement [2], though they can sometimes contradict one another, as above. To resolve this contradiction, using a common psychometric practice, we created a combined measure that consists of the log transformation of the number of trials times the number of seconds of play (sum of reaction time). Though this combined measure of engagement has the limitation of making it more difficult to compare the units of engagement, it allows us to compare all design factors along a single scale. Notably, the scale balances the weight of both measures through a correlation with log(time) and log(trials) of .95 and .96, respectively. This measure corroborates that target size has a highly significant effect on engagement, but suggests that there is no significant effect of target type on engagement (p=0.57).

Challenge as a Latent Variable

To explicitly test the hypothesis that challenge has an inverted-U shaped relationship with engagement, we need a quantitative measure of challenge. Therefore, we used the average success rate of each of the six possible design configurations: the lower the observed success rate for a given level design, the greater the challenge it posed. This is similar to previous research that uses observed probability of success as a measure of challenge [3,9,17].

Figure 3 plots the relationship of challenge to engagement. In contrast to the Inverted-U hypothesis, our results show a linear relationship between difficulty and engagement (the quadratic fit was not significant, $p=0.8$). In short, the easier the game, the longer people played.

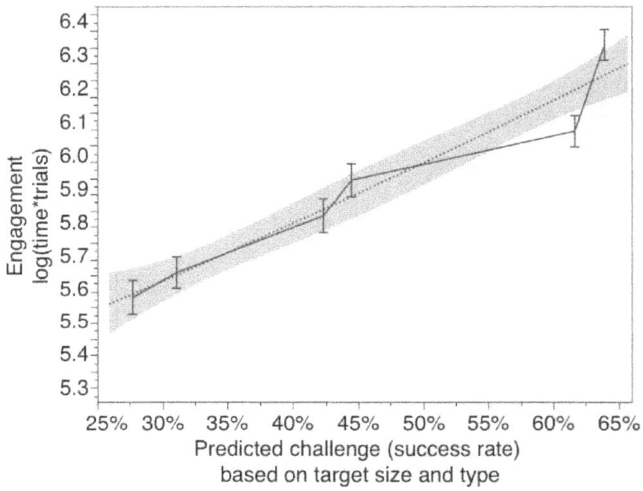

Figure 3: Relationship of challenge (predicted success rate) and engagement. Quadratic line of fit shown as dotted line with surrounding confidence of fit. The line graph plots the specific average engagement at each level of difficulty with error bars representing one standard error.

Discussion

In contrast with the Inverted-U Hypothesis, experiment 1 showed that challenge had a linear effect on engagement—the less challenging, the longer people played. However, it is possible that the game was not made easy enough, given that the average success rate of the easiest conditions were still <70%; therefore, it is possible that we only measured the left side of the Inverted U.

ONLINE EXPERIMENT 2: SUPER EXPERIMENT

To further explore the Inverted-U Hypothesis, we developed a larger experimental design that involved additional game design factors, including time limits, item sets and item sequences. Additionally, as the challenge of a game is likely relative to a player's ability (i.e., players with a higher ability will have a higher probability of success), we included an in-game pretest to formally assess player ability prior to the experiment, as a covariate.

Target Size and Target Type
We significantly expanded the range of the target size as a percentage of the number line, including the following nine sizes: 4%, 6%, 8%, 10%, 16%, 20%, 24%, 30%, and 40%. We hypothesized that the very large ship sizes would prove trivially easy to players, resulting in an inverted U-shaped curve. We maintained the two different types of targets from experiment 1 (Ship and Submarine).

Time Limit
While the time limit in Experiment 1 was consistently 10 seconds (and 15 seconds for ship targets), we tested 8 different time limits: 2, 3, 4, 5, 8, 10, 15 and 30 seconds (ship targets included an additional 5 seconds). We hypothesized that very large time limits would further reduce the challenge of the game and allow us to detect declining engagement with increased success on the right side of the Inverted-U.

Item Sets
While Experiment 1 gave all players the same set of estimation items, Experiment 2 randomly assigned players to a broad range of item sets. An item set consists of the specific target numbers that are to be estimated over the course of a level. The item sets were constructed to vary in difficulty by using data from previous experiments to create bins of items with high and low success rates [19]. Item sets also varied in the number of items presented and the endpoints of the number line. Players were randomly assigned to an item set within the estimation domain of their choice. There were 8 whole number sets, 7 decimal sets and 10 fraction sets for a total of 25 different item sets.

Item Sequencing
In Experiment 1, all items were presented in random order. In Experiment 2, we also tested three additional sequencing algorithms. Naïve0 repeats incorrect items immediately (on the next turn), while Naïve1 and Naïve2 repeats incorrect items after a delay of 1 or 2 turns, respectively.

Experimental Design
The combination of the above design factors with an ability covariate (high or low pretest score), results in a 2x2x9x8x4x25 between-subjects experiment with 28,800 possible unique configurations. Our analysis focuses on the main effects and 2-way interactions of these factors.

In-Game Pretest
After players chose to play Fractions, Decimals or Whole Numbers, they received an in-game pretest consisting of four estimation items. To construct this pretest, we used previously collected online data [19] and applied Item Response Theory methods to select items that effectively discriminated between players of different abilities and also maintained high reliability with overall performance in the game. The pretests were reasonably successful, despite having only four items, achieving a .46 correlation with the hit rate in the experiment and reliability score (Cronbach's alpha) of .62. If a player's pretest accuracy was above the median, they were labeled "high ability"; else they were labeled as "low ability."

Participants
This experimental dataset consists of game log data from 69,642 play sessions of *Battleship Numberline* that were collected from March 25, 2012 to May 4, 2012 from Brainpop's *GameUp* platform. These were players who completed the 4-item pretest described above, which occurred prior to the randomization event.

RESULTS
In an ANCOVA, all five factors (target type, target size, time limit, item sets, and item sequencing) and the pretest score had a significant main effect on the game's challenge and engagement (all p's < 0.0001).

Target Type
Like study 1, we found that the submarine target was significantly more engaging (p<0.001) and less challenging (p<0.001) than the ship target. Differences in engagement between target types were greatest among low-ability players (first column in Figure 4).

Target Size
Surprisingly, the extremely large targets did not lead to less engagement than moderately sized targets (second column in Figure 4). As in study 1, the larger the target was, the greater the success rate and the greater the engagement.

Time Limit
Time limit had a significant effect on player performance and engagement (third column in Figure 4). Longer time limits increased both success and engagement. The impact was greatest for the shorter time limits such that the shortest time limits were the most disengaging of any design factor.

Item Sequencing
The manipulation of item sequencing showed a significant effect on player success rates, but a minimal effect on player engagement. Naïve0 repeated unsuccessful items immediately after their first presentation, which had the effect of significantly increasing player success relative to random sequencing, for both high and low-ability players (p<0.001). Despite the improved success rate, Naïve0 had a minimal effect on engagement. Only low-ability players found Naïve0 more engaging than random presentation. (p=0.024). This result shows that improving performance may not always increase engagement, particularly when the improved performance results from repetition.

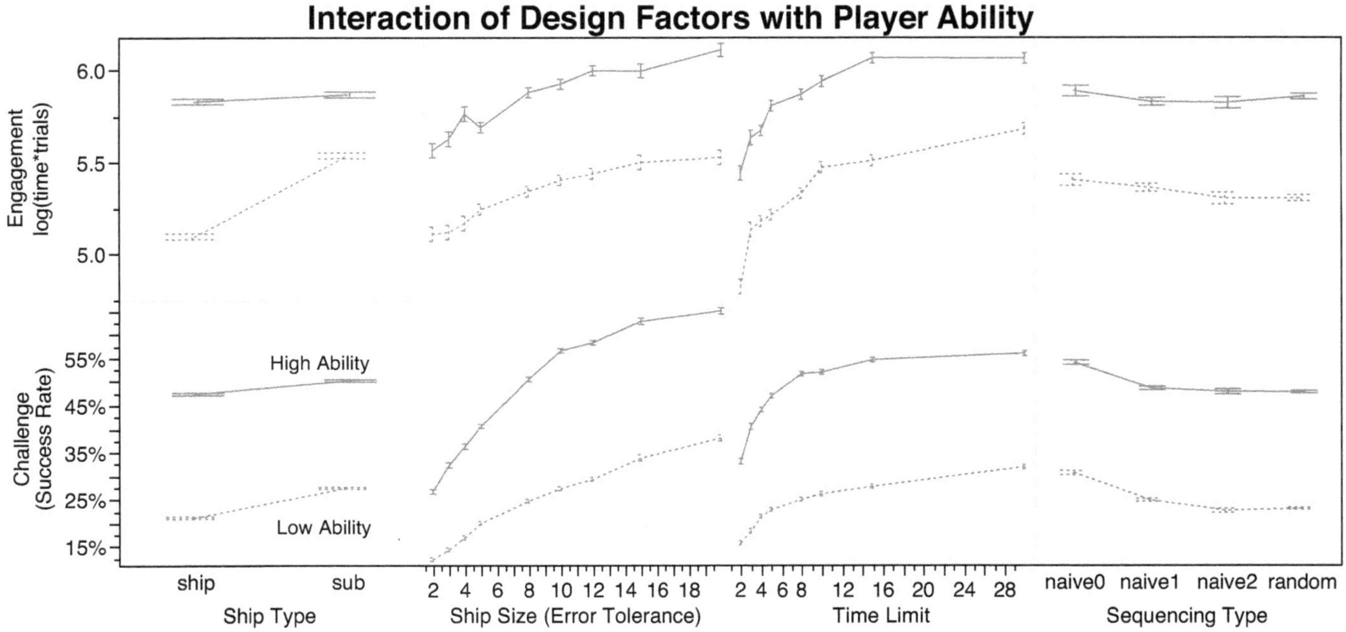

Figure 4: The effect of four design factors and player ability on challenge and engagement. The dotted lines are players with pretest scores below the median, while solid lines are players with pretest scores above the median. All four factors influence success rate and, in all cases, greater success is associated with greater engagement. Error bars show standard error of the mean.

Item Sets

As suggested by the analysis of Item Sequencing, we found that increasing the total number of items presented to a player (decreasing repetition) had the effect of improving player engagement. Additionally, we found that increasing the challenge of item sets decreases player engagement.

Item sets are the set of unique estimation items presented to players in a level. The analysis reported here focuses on a subset of fraction item sets (Figure 5). Based on previous data collection, we created an "Easy" set of 15 fractions, a "Hard" set of 15 fractions, and an "All Items" set that included easy, medium and hard items (45 total). We also deployed a set of 6 "Benchmark" fractions (1/2, 1/4, 2/4, 3/4, 1/3, 2/3). Finally, this analysis included only high ability students, as low ability students were not as sensitive to the differences between these item sets.

In the first and second columns of Figure 5, we control the number of items but vary the challenge. This shows that the easier (more successful) item set produced greater engagement. However, the third column seems to contradict this evidence, as the more difficult item set ("All Items") achieves greater engagement. This could be evidence to support the Inverted-U hypothesis, as the moderately difficult level achieved more engagement than the easy or difficult levels. However, our comparison of the third and fourth columns refutes this interpretation. Here, the difficulty (success rate) was controlled while the number of items was varied. Looking back to columns two and three, this suggests that the greater engagement of "All" results from having a greater number of items in the level.

We hypothesize that increasing the number of items increases engagement by increasing the diversity/novelty of the overall gameplay experience. This has support from at least one model of game entertainment [22], which postulates that diversity is one of the major factors accounting for the fun of games.

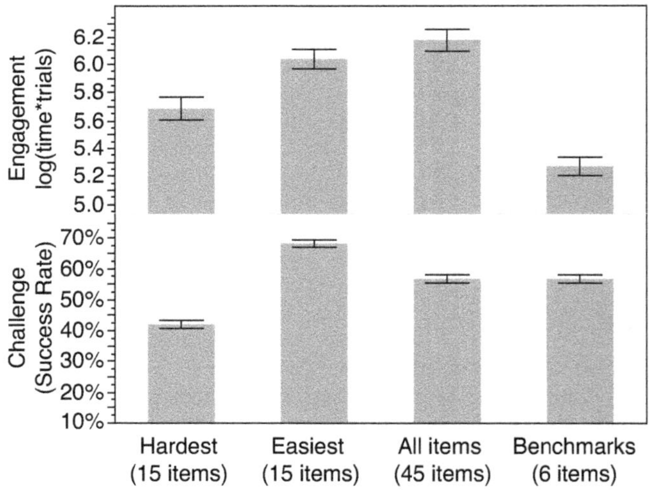

Figure 5: The relationship of challenge to engagement in item sets. When controlling the number of items (from Hardest to Easiest), easier items are more engaging. When the challenge is controlled (from All Items to Benchmarks), having more unique items is more engaging.

Challenge as a Latent Variable

Following our approach in study 1, we estimated the challenge of each level configuration, where challenge was defined as the predicted success rate of a level (lower challenge has higher success rates). The estimates produced by this model were used to plot the main effect of challenge, as a latent variable, on overall player engagement (Figure 6).

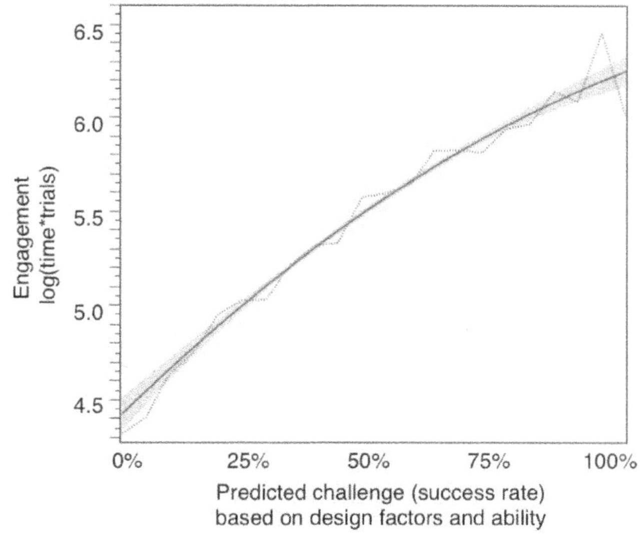

Figure 6: Plotting the effects of challenge (predicted success rate) on player engagement. Graph shows quadratic line of fit and a smoothed mean (dotted line). This shows that as the predicted success rate increases (and challenge decreases), players are likely to play for longer. In contrast to the Inverted-U Hypothesis, low levels of challenge (high success rates) never appear to negatively affect player engagement.

Success rate was predicted based on a multiple linear regression model, which included main effects of all our design factors (target size, target type, time limit, item sets and item sequencing) and the 2-way interactions between all the above design factors. To improve validity, this model was weighted by the number of trials played by each player. This produced a model with R^2=.34. As a player's ability (high/low) was expected to impact the predicted success rate of a level, we expanded our model by adding this factor and its interactions with the design factors. This improved the fit substantially, R^2=.46.

This model of challenge (predicted success rate), which involved all design factors and player ability, was used to produce the x-axis values in Figure 6. This graph illustrates the estimated engagement across the range of estimated challenge. As such, it shows that players are motivated to play for longer as the game gets easier. While the effect of game challenge is slightly curvilinear, it is not U-shaped – the model does not predict a point where low challenge reduces player motivation. Taken together, this evidence suggests that we may want to reject the generality of the Inverted-U Hypothesis.

Analysis of Learning Curves

What's wrong with making the game very easy? One hypothesis is that low levels of challenge could reduce the rate of learning. To address this question, we operationally defined learning as improvement over time, or specifically, improvement in estimation error over the log of practice opportunities (*log of opportunities* is typically the x-axis in plots of learning curves, [15]), where error was measured as the absolute value of the estimated number minus the actual number, divided by the length of the number line [16].

To address the question of whether players with large targets learned at a different rate than players with small targets, we plotted and compared their learning curves. To do so, we analyzed a subset of data that tracked each player's entire sequence of estimation attempts. This subset consisted of 1392 players who were assigned to random sequencing and who played over 30 trials in the decimal domain. We only analyzed learning in their first 30 trials to prevent player attrition from significantly affecting the measurement of learning curves. To achieve greater power, we binned the 9 different target sizes into large, medium and small targets.

Our analysis shows that larger targets result in a slower rate of learning, as compared to smaller targets; i.e.. target size has a significant interaction with the rate of learning (p=0.02). Therefore, while the largest targets were optimal for engagement, they do not appear to be optimal for learning.

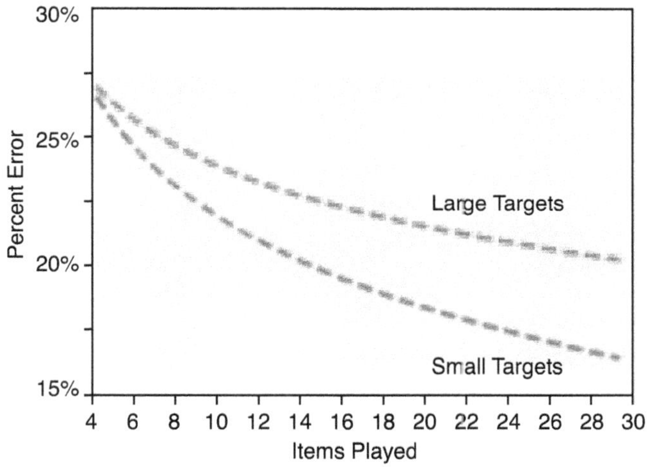

Figure 7: Learning curves show players' learning (reduction in error) over 30 items. The model suggests that larger and easier targets produce a slower rate of learning in comparison to the smaller and more challenging targets.

Limitations

There are several limitations to our approach. For instance, one could argue that there is a different *kind* of learning occurring when estimating large and small targets, making this a comparison of apples and oranges. Secondly, our claims are only meaningful for players who played for >30 trials—and this may represent a particular subset of the population that does not generalize more broadly. Finally, the high rates of attrition in online experiments make this comparison subject to critique. For example, we found that low ability students had a significantly steeper learning curve (p=0.002) than high ability students; if there were a greater proportion of low ability students in the small and medium conditions, this might suggest that the effect occurred as result of selective attrition. In this case, however, the proportion of low-ability students differed across conditions by only 2 percentage points—a difference too small to account for our reported effect. The above critiques notwithstanding, our preliminary evidence suggests that the easiest targets, which were optimal for engagement, were not optimal for learning.

DISCUSSION

In two experiments, we systematically manipulated the design space of an online learning game to determine the optimal level of challenge for supporting maximum engagement. In contrast to the Inverted-U hypothesis, which predicts that a moderate level of challenge should lead to maximum engagement, we found that the easier the game, the longer people played. This is a surprising finding, given the substantial amount of theory [4,9,8,11,20] and evidence [1,3,7,17] that suggests that moderate levels of challenge will lead to greater motivation.

It is possible that, despite our efforts, we never made the game easy enough. The Inverted-U hypothesis could still stand if the theoretically optimal success rate is very high (>90%)—in that case, we may not have observed the negative effects of decreasing challenge because we lacked sufficient data in this area of very high performance. In many video games, for instance, the vast majority of user actions are rewarded, with only an occasional setback.

Still, past researchers predicted and observed much lower optimal success rates. For instance, Atkinson [3] predicted that motivation would be greatest when the uncertainty of success is highest (i.e., a 50% probability of success). Shapira [16] predicted that the optimal success rate would be even more difficult, from 25-40% probability success depending upon individual differences. Furthermore, Csikszentmihalyi's online chess study [1] found that chess players reported greatest enjoyment when their probability of success was approximately 20% (i.e., facing opponents with a chess rating 262 points greater than their own).

Differences Between the Studies

If online chess players find a 20% success rate most enjoyable, why might our game produce greatest engagement with far less objective challenge? There are many differences between the present study and the online chess study that may account for this difference.

Random Assignment: While we randomly assigned players to a particular game configuration, participants in the online chess study freely chose their opponents. *Feedforward:* While the chess players were given information about their game's challenge (i.e., the ranking of their opponent) prior to playing, our players were not given information indicating the amount of difficulty they were encountering. *Status Opportunities*: While the chess players could improve their chess ranking by beating more advanced players, our game provided no opportunity to improve one's status. *Measure of Challenge*: Their study measured challenge using self-report and the difference of chess rankings between players. The difference in chess rankings corresponds to a probability of success (e.g., players with identical rankings have a 50% probability of success). Our study quantified challenge not as the probability of successfully winning a game, but of the probability of hitting individual targets. *Measure of Enjoyment/ Motivation*: Their study modeled the effect of challenge on self-reported enjoyment while our study modeled the effect of challenge on engagement (the duration of play). Engagement may or may not correspond to enjoyment. *Population Characteristics*: Their players were older than our players and their players likely had greater expertise in chess than our players had expertise in *Battleship Numberline*.

Theoretical Hypotheses and Design Implications

Given these broad differences between the studies, we now propose four concrete hypotheses that can add explanatory value and suggest implications for design.

Effectance Motivation Hypothesis

Our players were clearly motivated by success—the more successful they were, the more motivation they had to keep playing. The idea that success will increase motivation is predicted by the Effectance Motivation hypothesis [8]. A key implication of this hypothesis is that increasing player success rates is likely to increase player motivation. While one might accomplish this by making the targets even larger, the player might attribute their success to the game, rather than to their own achievement. Therefore, we predict that increasing success will have a greater effect on engagement if it results from a mechanism that players can attribute to their own competence. For instance, the game could improve performance by increasing in-game learning (which is, after all, the goal!). This improved learning could occur through explicit in-game instruction (e.g., a tutorial) or by providing more informative feedback (such as labeling each prior attempt, as in the constructive feedback described in Malone [12]).

Expertise Hypothesis

There is ample evidence that some groups of people demonstrate strong "challenge-seeking" behaviors (e.g., rock climbers, chess players, and video gamers). Perhaps challenge-seeking only tends to occur after individuals have acquired some significant level of expertise. Therefore, perhaps we did not observe the inverted-U because the players of our online game likely had little prior experience. This hypothesis predicts that player expertise will interact with the effect of challenge on player engagement, producing an inverted-U for players with high expertise, but not for low expertise players (who would be expected to prefer very low levels of challenge One implication for design from the Expertise Hypothesis is to make the first level of the game as easy as possible, and introducing greater challenges only after some degree of expertise has been attained.

Feedforward Hypothesis

Models of achievement motivation predict that people will attribute more value to success when the task is more challenging [1,8,9]. However, players did not have any information about the challenge of their particular game configuration (other than observations of their own performance). This is a key difference from the online chess study, where players knew their opponent's international chess ranking.

Therefore, an implication for design is to provide feedforward to players about the challenge of the task they are playing. This may allow players to more appropriately value their success and failure in the face of challenge.

Close Game Hypothesis

Abuhamdeh and Csikszentmihalyi's hypothesis [1] about "close games" may help explain our results. They hypothesize that a player's motivation will increase during close games, when there is high uncertainty about winning or losing. However, this kind of uncertainty does not occur in *Battleship Numberline*, as the game does not indicate to players whether they have won or lost (players can continue to play for as long as they like). Without winning or losing, there can be no close games. Additionally, close games only occur when the challenge of the game is closely matched to the player's ability. In other words, players with greater ability may find challenging games more engaging when the challenge increases their uncertainty about winning or losing.

The Close Game Hypothesis predicts that a clear win/lose state should make challenge motivating when the winning/losing criterion is closely matched to player's ability. As the performance criterion approaches a player's performance capacity (and when the outcome is most uncertain), the player is predicted to experience greatest motivation.

CONCLUSION

Our research investigated the effects of various game design factors on challenge, motivation and learning. While we hypothesized that moderate levels of challenge would maximize engagement (the inverted-U hypothesis) we instead observed that the easier the game, the longer people played. This is a surprising finding that prompts new research questions. For instance, given that the most engaging conditions were not the most optimal for learning, we can investigate methods for jointly optimizing learning and engagement. From a design perspective, we can investigate game design patterns that support challenge-seeking behavior, as players in more challenging conditions may benefit from a faster pace of learning.

This study contributes one approach to harnessing the crowd to optimize game designs. We used a large-scale factorial experiment and thousands of online users to identify which configuration of game design factors best supported player engagement; the same approach can be used to identify the optimal designs for supporting player learning.

Limitations

One limitation of our study was that it was susceptible to self-selection effects: it was relatively common for players to abandon games and start again, where they would be placed in a new experimental condition. This suggests that players may have deliberately exited a less preferred condition to find a more preferred condition. Though this self-selection was not intended, since the main goal of our study was to measure how design factors affected player motivation, it seems unlikely to alter our main results.

Still, online game experiments are highly limited by the fact that the data collected are from anonymous and remote subjects. This means that researchers have a very limited capacity to gain qualitative insight into *why* subjects are responding the way that they do. This suggests the importance of triangulating findings between online experiments and laboratory or field studies [20]. For instance, we may discover that "duration of play" does not, ultimately, sufficiently correlate with player enjoyment.

Our operational definition of challenge is also subject to critique. We defined the challenge of a particular level configuration as the inverse of its predicted success rate. Success rate has been used as a measure of challenge in previous research [3,17,7,8,9] and it is similar to the notion of a difference in chess ranking in [1] (since this difference corresponds to a probability of success). Still, there is evidence that *perceived challenge* is a greater predictor of enjoyment [7,1] than objective challenge. This may reflect the fact that the objective measure of challenge does not adequately capture the feeling of effortfulness that is associated with the perception of challenge.

Future Work

Perhaps increasing objective challenge (lowering probability of success) is simply not desirable to many game players. Interestingly, challenge is often correlated with increased gameplay diversity; a feature that we found to be a highly engaging. As increased gameplay diversity can outweigh the negative effects of challenge (as was the case in the "all items" level), it will be important to carefully separate these two variables in future research.

Future work should also address the validity of the operational definitions of challenge and engagement. The promise of online game research relies on valid metrics obtained in the context of anonymous gameplay. For instance, is the maximization of motivation/engagement, measured as voluntary time on task, appropriate as a data-driven game design goal? This question is particularly important for applied research goals, which seek to maximize outcome measures like engagement or learning. Future applied research may also investigate more efficient experimental designs, to minimize the cost of experimentation to designers and game players.

Very large numbers of voluntary participants gives online game research the potential to significantly expand theories of human learning and motivation. The implications for design in our discussion (in-game tutorials, feedforward about challenge, easy first levels and winning/losing states) are very standard design patterns that are widely used in games. However, by framing these game design elements as embodiments of a specific theoretical hypothesis, we can use them to test or extend theories of motivation. Therefore, it may be fruitful to systematically explore well-known game design patterns in order to generate additional hypotheses.

ACKNOWLEDGMENTS

Game Programming: Nirmal Patel and Nikhil Poonwala. Game Animation: Jeremy Galante. Statistical Support: Jonathan Steinhart. For conceptual inspiration, much thanks to Prof. Sharon Carver, Prof. Robert Siegler, Prof. Mike Cole, Prof. Mike Levine, "The Shark Game" and the playpower.org community. For advising the experimental design and analysis, much thanks to Prof. Joel Greenhouse, Prof. Trent Gaugner and Prof. Brian Junker. Thanks to Dixie Ching, Beau Dabbs, Burr Settles and Turadg Aleahmad for reading preliminary drafts. Thanks to the members of PIER and SERG for helpful feedback! Game R&D supported by funding from the National STEM Game Competition Prize, Marvell's Educational Application Grand Challenge, and the Next Generation Learning Challenge (MFDC). Graduate funding from IES Program for Interdisciplinary Education Research (PIER) and DARPA. Data analyses were conducted in the highly recommended statistical package JMP 10. Special thanks to BrainPop.com for supporting educational research!

REFERENCES

1. Abuhamdeh, S. and Csikszentmihalyi, M. The Importance of Challenge for the Enjoyment of Intrinsically Motivated, Goal-Directed Activities. *Personality and Social Psychology Bulletin 38*, 3 (2012), 317–330.
2. Andersen, E., Liu, Y., Snider, R., Szeto, R., and Popovic, Z. Placing a value on aesthetics in online casual games. *CHI 2011, May 7–12, 2011, Vancouver, Canada* (2011).
3. Atkinson, J. Towards Experimental Analysis of Human Motivation in Terms of Motives, Expectances, and incentives. In J. Atkinson, ed., *Motives in fantasy, action and society*. Van Nostrand, Princeton, NJ, (1958) 288–305.
4. Deci, E. L., & Ryan, R. M. (2000). The "what" and "why" of goal pursuits: Human needs and the self-determination of behavior. *Psychological Inquiry, 4,* 227–268.
5. Gee, J.P. What video games have to teach us about learning and literacy. *Computers in Entertainment*, 1 (2003), 20.
6. Hays, R. *The effectiveness of instructional games: A literature review and discussion*. 2005. Technical report 2005-004, Naval Air Warfare Center Training Systems Division, Orlando, FL.
7. Harter, S. Pleasure derived from challenge and the effects of receiving grades on children's difficulty level choices. *Child Development 49*, 3 (1978), 788–799.
8. Harter, S. Effectance Motivation Reconsidered: Towards a developmental model. *Human Development; Human Development*, (1978), 34–64.
9. Heckhausen, H. Achievement motivation and its constructs: A cognitive model. *Motivation and emotion 1*, 4 (1977), 283–329.
10. Heffernan, N. and Koedinger, K.R. A developmental model of algebra symbolization: the results of a difficulty factors assessment. *Proc. Twentieth Annual Conference of the cognitive science society*, (1998), 484-489.
11. Lomas D., Ching D., Stampfer, E., Sandoval, M., Koedinger, K. Battleship Numberline: A Digital Game for Improving Estimation Accuracy on Fraction Number Lines. *Conference of the American Education Research Association (2012)*
12. Malone, T. Toward a theory of intrinsically motivating instruction. *Cognitive Science 5*, 4 (1981), 333-369.
13. Malone, T.W. What Makes Things Fun to Learn? Heuristics for Designing Instructional Computer Games. 1980, ACM.
14. Randel, J., Morris, B., Wetzel, C., and Whitehill, B. The effectiveness of games for educational purposes: a review of recent research. *Simulation & Gaming 23*, 3 (1992), 261–276.
15. Ritter, F. and Schooler, L. The Learning Curve. *International Encyclopedia of the Social and Behavioral Sciences*, 2001, 8602–8605.
16. Rittle-Johnson, B., Siegler, R.S., and Alibali, M.W. Developing Conceptual Understanding and Procedural Skill in Mathematics: An Iterative Process. *Journal of Educational Psychology* 93, 2 (2001), 346–362.
17. Shapira, Z. Task choice and assigned goals as determinants of task motivation and performance. *Org. Behavior & Human Dec. Proc.* 44, 2 (1989), 141–165.
18. Schell, J. *The Art of Game Design.* Morgan Kaufmann (2008)
19. Stamper, J., Lomas, D., Ching, D., Ritter, S., Koedinger, K., and Steinhart, J. The Rise of the Super Experiment. *Educational Data Mining*, (2012), 196–200.
20. Sweetser, P. and Wyeth, P. GameFlow: a model for evaluating player enjoyment in games. *Computers in Entertainment (CIE) 3*, 3 (2005), 1–24.
21. Yannakakis, G.N., Denmark, S., and Hallam, J. Towards optimizing entertainment in computer games. (2007), 933-971

From Competition to Metacognition: Designing Diverse, Sustainable Educational Games

Stephen R. Foster
UC San Diego
9500 Gilman Dr. # 0404
La Jolla, CA 92093-0404
srfoster@cs.ucsd.edu

Sarah Esper
UC San Diego
9500 Gilman Dr. # 0404
La Jolla, CA 92093-0404
sesper@cs.ucsd.edu

William G. Griswold
UC San Diego
9500 Gilman Dr. # 0404
La Jolla, CA 92093-0404
wgg@cs.ucsd.edu

ABSTRACT
We investigate the unique educational benefits of 1-on-1 competitive games, arguing that such games can be just as easy to design as single-player educational games, while yielding a more diverse and sustainable learning experience. We present a study of chess and *StarCraft II* in order to inform the design of similar educational games and their communities. We discuss a competitive game we designed to teach Java programming. We evaluate the game by discussing its user study.

Our main contributions are 1) an argument that the use of 1-on-1 competition can solve two existing problems inherent to single-player games, 2) an analysis of the features that make competitive games effective learning environments, and 3) an early but encouraging description of the emergent learning environment one can expect from designing an educational game with these features.

Author Keywords
Education; Games

ACM Classification Keywords
K.3.1 [Computer Uses in Education]: Collaborative learning

General Terms
Human Factors; Design

INTRODUCTION
A classic and previously criticized [6] exemplar of first-wave educational games is the 1990s version of *Math Blaster*, which sought to teach the academic subject of arithmetic through repetitive drilling. The game serves up arithmetic problems, seeking to make the process fun by conspicuously interleaving these drills with much more engaging (non-academic) gameplay. Such games have been criticised as "chocolate-covered broccoli" [23, 6].

In recognition that such educational games may not be living up to the genre's full potential, designers have more recently advanced the aesthetic principle of "seamlessly interweaving" academic subject matter with gameplay [24, 20]. One exemplar of an "interwoven" educational game is, *Zombie Division* [18, 19], which seeks to teach division by placing players into a virtual environment with zombies (who have numbers on their chests) and weapons (which also have numbers). Students must employ the weapon whose number divides into the zombie's number in order to defeat the zombie. Similarly, the recent game *Refraction* [36] seeks to teach fractions by giving players problems that can be solved by splitting (and thus dividing) beams of light in order to power spaceships. In both of these games, the academic content is tightly woven with gameplay, making the games quite engaging.

While the aesthetic trend away from "chocolate broccoli" style games does make games more enjoyable, we take the position that there are at least two critical concerns which have not been adequately addressed by the "seamless interweaving" trend, and which are economically difficult to address in single-player games at all:

Diversity. Not only are first-wave, "chocolate broccoli" games not fun (compared to other games), but they exhibit a narrow pedagogical scope. Arithmetic, for example, is only a small part of what mathematics education is all about. For that matter, solving out-of-context arithmetic problems is only a small part of what *arithmetic* education is all about. Interestingly, second-wave educational games such as *Zombie Division* and *Refraction* – in seeking to "seamlessly interweave" rather than to sugar-coat – have further decreased pedagogical diversity by only teaching division.

Sustainability. On a related note, the system of educational interactions between the player and the game must inevitably collapse when the player successfully covers the material – e.g. acquires the knack for working simple arithmetic problems, or can easily defeat all of the zombies and solve all the refraction problems. Even if the player keeps playing, the educational experience has come to an end.

We now examine the games of chess and *StarCraft II*, which neatly solve the diversity and sustainability problems within their admittedly non-academic domains. Each game is surrounded by a large and growing body of (diverse) theory; and each game has shown incredible staying power (sustainability).

Their diversity yields an incredible amount of replay value

(sustainability): every time one plays, the game takes a different path through an astronomically large possibility space. Being pitted against fellow creative human beings, in a tremendously complex domain, makes for a diverse range of playing styles, strategies, and in-game experiences. This is in stark qualitative contrast with single-player games, in which the level of diversity is constrained by what can be designed upfront. Whereas the educational content of single-player games can eventually be depleted, the games of chess and *StarCraft II* have proven to be quite self-sustaining. We observe that this is because every competitor is implicitly incentivised to be a content producer as a byproduct of competitive play. In essence, each competitor crafts an experience for the other player – a kind of collaborative co-productivity in the midst of what is generally thought of as competition.

As we will demonstrate in the final section, the insights gained from studying chess and *StarCraft II* can be used to design personalized, authentic [5, 12] learning environments with high diversity and sustainability. We show this by discussing an environment centered around a 1-on-1 competitive game for teaching Java programming. The game's strategy revolves around crafting magic spells written in the Java language, and countering such spells crafted by other players.

RELATED WORK

Learning Theory

We are investigating the learning environments that arise from community interactions centered around 1-on-1 competitive games. From this perspective, the intellectual lineage of our approach can be said to begin with Vygotskian learning theory [37], which places great import upon the social contexts of learning – both for the purposes of understanding learning and for designing new learning environments.

There are several ideas from the learning sciences that have guided our analysis of competitive learning environments:

Metacognition

As this paper unfolds, we will take a particular interest in metacognition – the activity of reflecting on one's own learning process. Metacognition has been widely recognized by the research community as a critical factor in optimizing both the depth of learning [39, 30], as well as the ability to transfer learned knowledge to new contexts [29, 13]. Indeed, one of the key arguments in the Research Council report *How People Learn* was that learning, teaching, and the construction of learning environments can all be improved by taking into account the importance of metacognition and explicitly promoting it [4].

Self-theory

Related to metacognition is the notion of self-theory – the beliefs a learner possesses regarding his or her own ability to learn. As famously claimed by Carol Dweck, there exist at least two distinct outlooks or "mindsets" toward learning – a growth-mindset and a fixed-mindset [11]. A growth-mindset is one in which an individual believes she can improve, which correlates with high levels of resilience to failure and ultimately with high levels of success. A fixed-mindset, by contrast, is characterized by the belief that one's intelligence or skill is a fixed quantity, which tends to have a detrimental effect on one's acquisition of skills. The importance of these mindsets has been studied quite extensively in academic disciplines such as computer science [33, 25].

Feedback

It has been observed that effective metacognition can be enabled by effective feedback [29, 13]. High quality feedback that is timely and formative (rather than summative) can expose the innerworkings of a learner's process to that learner, which can in turn facilitate self-reflection [4]. It has also been observed that video games make effective learning tools precisely because they give constant and immediate feedback to the player [16]. Such feedback allows for effective metacognition through accurate self-modeling of one's own strengths and weaknesses [28].

Dweck has argued that certain types of feedback can be beneficial in relation to positive self-theory as well. Feedback that reinforces a fixed-mindset (e.g. "You're so smart!") should be supplanted by feedback that reinforces a growth-mindset (e.g. "You've worked really hard!").

Because of the importance of feedback in both metacognition and self-theory and because good video games have such effective feedback mechanisms, it becomes evident why even so-called "non-educational" games have been identified as effective learning tools [15]. We will see that 1-on-1 competition offers unique benefits in terms of feedback. In particular, 1-on-1 competition is a feedback mechanism that scales particularly well in the face of high diversity and sustainability.

CHESS AND STARCRAFT II

Why these games?

Diversity and Sustainability

We examine chess and *StarCraft II* because both games have exhibited extraordinary staying power (sustainability) and because both games have become surrounded by a rich body of theory to help players navigate diverse, in-game possibility spaces. Hence, they have established themselves as model domains for sustainability and diversity.

StarCraft is a real-time strategy game (RTS) which was released in 1998. Players assume control of a futuristic army and struggle for military dominance. Owing partly to the release of the game's expansion pack (*Brood War*), the *StarCraft* franchise quickly became a worldwide sensation – unofficially dubbed the "national sport" of South Korea. The site http://sc2ranks.com suggests that there are more than 4 million competitive players. Today, compared to other two-player competitive video games, *StarCraft II* consistently boasts the most tournaments, the most players across the globe, and the most spectators, making it one of the crown jewels of the growing phenomena known as "e-sports". The popularity of the world's number one strategy game has attracted researchers in sociology, anthropology, cognitive science, and artificial intelligence [7, 22, 21, 27]. Although it has been speculated that the game of *StarCraft II* and its community may have strong educational benefits [3], we give the first-ever analysis of *StarCraft II* as a learning environment.

Effective Learning Tools in Spite of Diversity and Sustainability

Both games have produced players that the learning sciences research community would consider "experts" in their field. Indeed, chess has long been considered a drosophila for studying human expertise [10, 26, 17], in order to draw conclusions about more socially relevant domains such as academic or professional expertise. This is because the domain complexity of chess and *StarCraft* begins to approximate the diversity and depth found in many academic fields. These games require incredible skill, precision, focus, and acquired knowledge. It has been estimated that grandmaster chess players make decisions based on knowledge of more than 50,000 familiar chess patterns [34].

Not surprisingly, the games take years to master. Yet in spite of this, both games have consistently proven to promote sufficient motivation for players to invest the required "time on task" (for chess this can be from 50,000 to 100,000 hours [35]). Furthermore, throughout this lengthy journey from novice to expert, the mechanism of 1-on-1 competition (against one's peers) serves as a valuable feedback mechanism. One's statistical likelihood of winning games against players of a given strength is a strong indicator of the degree to which one has internalized the necessary theory and skills.

The robustness of this feedback mechanism in the face of such a diverse domain and sustained play is, we think, quite elegant and worth studying. It is very difficult to imagine a single-player game that could sustain 50,000 hours of diverse play, while providing valuable feedback to anyone from novice to world-class expert.

A Natural Research/Design Agenda

For those wishing to design educational games that exhibit similar sustainability and which serve to teach something similarly diverse (such as an academic subject), one path is to:

- Analyse how chess and *StarCraft II* promote diversity and sustainability.
- Analyse what makes chess and *StarCraft II* such effective learning tools in spite of domain diversity.
- Design a similar game that interweaves academic content without sacrificing the above qualities.

We begin now with an investigation of the first two points regarding qualities of chess and *StarCraft II*. We finish the paper by taking a stab at the third point.

Investigating chess and StarCraft II

One of the authors has been an active member of the chess and *StarCraft* communities for more than 10 years. The following analysis is based on a deep insider perspective, bolstered where appropriate by empirical research. For the gathering of empirical data, our methodology was the same for both chess and *StarCraft II*. We conducted a series of surveys on the relevant subreddits, first surveying 350 members of the *StarCraft II* community, and following up by surveying 40 members of the chess community (largely as a "sanity check" for the generalizability of the *StarCraft II* results). Although not this paper's main contributions, many of the empirical results following from these surveys are novel contributions in themselves and can serve to inform future anthropological investigations of the *StarCraft II* community.

Our investigation was motivated by an interest in the following research questions:

- What is the nature of diversity and sustainability in these gaming domains, and what are the takeaways for game designers?
- What is the nature of 1-on-1 competitive feedback in relation to the above, and does such feedback effectively facilitate metacognition, positive self-theory, and domain knowledge acquisition for members of the community?

Designing for Diversity: Balance is Key

In spite of the relative simplicity of chess's mechanics, its possibility space is combinatorially large. As such, a significant body of theory has been generated to serve as a guide through the space of possibilities. Within the body of theory, numerous open questions remain: Is it superior to occupy the center with pawns (the "classical" school of thought) or to control the center from a distance (the "hypermodern" school of thought)? Is it better for the first player to open by moving the King's Pawn or the Queen's Pawn? Does the Pirc Defence lead to a stronger position than the Modern Defence? Is the sacrifice of a pawn for an attack justified in the Queen's Gambit? To this day, such questions remain a matter of taste – largely aesthetic in nature. Differences of opinion exist in all echelons of chess expertise.

As it turns out, the body of theory surrounding *StarCraft II* exhibits a similar balance between differing ideologies. Of the three races[1], it remains an open question as to which is "best", with winning statistics being roughly equal for all three races (which is due, in large part, to Blizzard's rebalancing efforts – see below). Furthermore, when playing a single race, a variety of ideological approaches are available to players, with new ones being discovered and popularized constantly.

For example, consider a player who is playing as the "Terran" race (the human race). She has numerous decisions to make in the opening few minutes of the game. She knows she must build a Barracks in order to train infantry soldiers. She can even build more than one Barracks in order to train soldiers faster. Doing so comes with an opportunity cost, however, because each Barracks requires expending in-game resources. Building an early second Barracks makes other options impossible – for example, a player cannot build a Factory as quickly. Because Factories are used to produce tanks, building two Barracks while one's opponent builds a Barracks and a Factory, might lead to a scenario wherein one has lots of early infantry, whereas one's opponent has fewer infantry but also has a tank.

[1] Instead of assuming command over one of two symmetric armies (white or black), a *StarCraft II* player can choose from one of three asymmetric "races" – each with their own unique soldiers, their own overall strengths and weaknesses.

There are also numerous other reorderings to the sequence of decisions one can make in the early minutes of the game. Many of these courses of action have been given names: e.g. the One-Rax Fast-Expand (building a single Barracks and expanding one's base immediately after); the One-One-One (building one Barracks, one Factory, and one Starport in rapid succession); etc. The point, however, is that a large number of these so-called "build orders" are viable. Having a surplus of infantry and no tanks against an opponent who does have tanks is hardly an immediate death sentence for either player. Players must struggle to position their chosen units where they will be most effective, choosing engagements carefully, and continuing to make decisions that reenforce one's strengths and repair one's weaknesses as the game unfolds. Having an army with a different composition from the opposing army gives the struggle an asymmetric nature – with each player employing a different style. Diverse gameplay is an immediate outgrowth of the coexistence of various, equally viable approaches to the game.

Designing for Balance. Blizzard's approach to encouraging balance in *StarCraft II* is to carefully monitor data acquired from all games of *StarCraft II* played online. Blizzard periodically "rebalances" the game by releasing patches that tweak the relative value of certain units in the game – i.e. increasing the cost of a particular soldier, or decreasing the power or range of certain attacks, etc. This alters the competitive advantage of some races over others and some styles of play over others. By enforcing balance within the game, diverse gameplay is maintained.

In the final section of this paper, we show how we designed our own competitive possibility space – in which players craft offensive and defensive magic spells by writing Java code. Our user study was conducted over a long period of time precisely to determine whether the resulting body of theory that arose around the game exhibited features of balance between various approaches to the game. We recommend a similar empirical investigation to other designers interested in crafting educational games within the 1-on-1 gaming paradigm.

Assessment and Feedback through Competition

Having mentioned prior work on the importance of feedback, we now consider feedback from a game designer's perspective. In a single-player game, the burden of assessing the player's performance and providing feedback must be carried by the environment. This means that, in turn, the burden of designing assessment mechanisms and feedback mechanisms falls to the designer. In a game like *Math Blaster*, positive feedback is given when the player successfully solves math problems. Similarly, *Zombie Division*, players successfully kill zombies when they choose the weapon with the correct divisor. The diversity of content in single-player educational games is, therefore, partially constrained by what kinds of player activities can be checked and reported upon during runtime.

By comparison, the feedback mechanism in 1-on-1 competition is provided not by an algorithm, but by one's opponents. If a player consistently wins against a particular opponent, this is a strong indicator that the winner has a superior, more expert-level grasp of the game's body of theory[2]. The crowd-sourced nature of feedback in 1-on-1 competitive games has unique drawbacks and benefits that should be understood by designers.

Drawbacks. Winning (or losing) a competitive game is a form of feedback. From a learning sciences perspective, the main drawback of such feedback is that a win/loss result is a purely digital, 1-bit judgement over a very complex cognitive task. A player does not necessarily know if she won because her king-side pawnstorm was a good idea; or because the opponent failed to make a timely counter-punch in the center; or because she elected to exchange her light-squared bishop to double the opponent's pawns; etc. Likewise, in *StarCraft* it is not always immediately clear what factors of good play, bad play, and/or randomness most contributed to the outcome. Thus, it is not always clear what weaknesses or misconceptions a learner must target for future training.

Benefits. Ascertaining the "truth" of a win/loss result can require significant analysis. Although this can be a drawback, it is this very drawback that shapes some of the practices that surround these games. It is generally accepted etiquette at chess tournaments, for example, for opponents to leave the tournament hall in the wake of a finished chess game and to discuss it privately with each other – a procedure known as the "post-mortem". Moreover, players of all levels study their own games, sometimes with the help of peers, stronger players, or computerized analysis to identify their own weaknesses. This is just as critical in *StarCraft II*, where (in contrast to chess) one does not have perfect information about what the opponent is doing during the game. Because one cannot see the opposing army except when it is near one's own units, it is quite common, especially for novice players, for an onslaught to "come out of nowhere", taking a player by surprise and leading to defeat. Examining the game's replay (wherein all troop movements are revealed) is necessary in order to determine how such a *blitzkrieg* was possible, and to prevent it from happening in the future. The act of analysing one's own games and the games of others in order to make sense of win/loss result is a powerful form of metacognition, which can be extremely beneficial. We examine metacognition and the relevant metacognitive practices of the community in more detail momentarily.

Another benefit is that the aggregate of 1-bit feedback results, over time, begins to paint a more meaningful picture of one's playing strength. This has been mathematically formalized with the so-called Elo rating system, which assigns to players a numerical value called a "rating". The Elo rating system is a statistical model that undergirds the selective matchmaking algorithms used at chess tournaments and on chess servers to automatically pair up opponents who have similar ratings[3]. Today, the same or similar statistical models have been applied to a variety of competitive games – from Go, to soccer, to baseball. A player's rating relative to other players in

[2]This is true because it is essentially a tautology: The game's body of theory is precisely the knowledge that, when mastered, leads to more consistent victories.

[3]If two players have the same rating, they each have a 50% chance of winning.

the community is a very accurate indication of that player's strength. The more a player plays, the more statistically reliable the rating becomes.

Although Blizzard does not make its exact matchmaking algorithm public, it does seek to match players of similar skill, thus increasing the probability that each game is a challenge for both players. And although Blizzard does not reveal to players their exact numerical rating, Blizzard does categorize players into "leagues" (Bronze, Silver, Gold, Platinum, Diamond, Master, and Grandmaster) and does rank players within these leagues. Just as chess players ratings can increase and decrease over time (due to iterated wins and losses), a *StarCraft II* player can be promoted and demoted to different leagues as a result of changes to one's hidden rating. The result is that players can chart their improvements over time, allowing them to obtain a general picture of how effective their training regimens have been. We expound upon the nature of these training regimens momentarily.

Finally, another benefit is that 1-on-1 competition is a feedback mechanism that scales well in the face of domain complexity. This is because the feedback mechanism does not hinge upon a designer's ability to embed algorithmic feedback into the game environment. Designers need only construct an environment that can algorithmically detect when a game is won or lost. As we have alluded to, the body of theory surrounding both games is large, growing, and difficult to master. The road to domain expertise is a long one. Yet chess players were able to acquire meaningful, accurate performance feedback in the midst of these complexities long before Deep Blue came along and made automated performance feedback a reality. Likewise, even with the "Deep Blue" of *StarCraft II* still far off, obtaining accurate feedback over the full range of one's *StarCraft II* playing abilities is easy, due to the crowd-sourced nature of competitive feedback from one's approximate peers. Thus, 1-on-1 competition is a tool that designers can potentially leverage when automated feedback is difficult or impossible to implement.

Training Regimens

With a complex domain requiring mastery and a 1-bit feedback mechanism at one's disposal, we wanted to investigate how players undertake the journey from novice to expert. Given the popularity of video games, it is no surprise that our surveys found that chess and *StarCraft II* players spend a considerable amount of time playing their game of choice. What has thus far *not* been observed in research literature, however, is that players also spend a significant amount of time on supplemental training.

Chess players engaged in 8.3 hours of practice on average per week, with about 20% of this devoted to supplemental training (working chess puzzles, reading chess books, watching chess online, or analysing chess games). Likewise, *StarCraft II* players reported spending on average 11.6 hours per week practicing *StarCraft II*, with about 27% of this time devoted to supplemental training – e.g. sparring with team mates, watching live streams, watching web shows about *StarCraft II* strategy, analysing the games of strong players, or taking lessons.

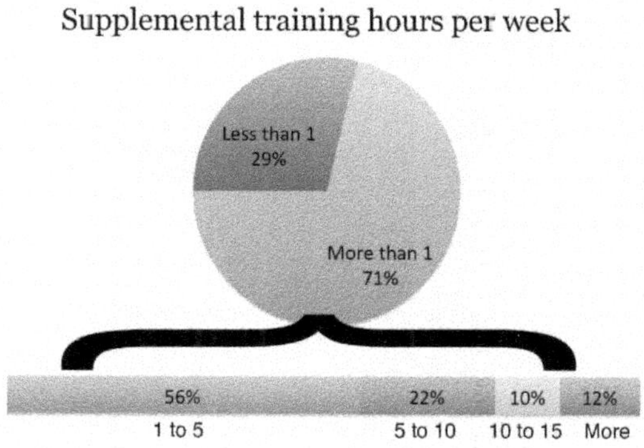

Figure 1. Results of a survey investigating *StarCraft II* players' training habits – *aside* from merely playing *StarCraft II*.

Figure 1 summarizes the average hours spent on supplemental training (over and beyond just playing *StarCraft II*).

Not only are these empirical results novel, but we think they may come as a surprise to some members of the research community. In our experience, video game researchers seem to realize that gamers *play* a lot – but not that gamers invest a considerable amount of time *training*. Chess and *StarCraft II* players realize that "all play and no work" is not the key to success.

Metacognition: Analysing Games

A large component of the training regimens observed in the previous section involves the performance of metacognitive acts – e.g analysing one's games after the fact. We also consider analysing the games of others (e.g. grandmasters) to be an important metacognitive act: when doing so, a player cannot help but perceive the grandmaster's game through the lens of her current level of understanding, noticing decisions made by the other player which are the same or different from the ones she would have made in the same situation. An awareness of the surprising features of a stronger player's game is actually an awareness of one's own potential shortcomings; and an awareness of the features which seem "obvious" is actually an awareness of one's own strengths.

We surveyed the community to investigate the perceived importance of analysing games – either one's own games or the games of others. 82% of chess players and 71% *StarCraft II* players we surveyed said that they spent the majority of their supplemental training time engaged in such activities – for example: analysing their own games, studying grandmaster replays, watching web shows about replays, or watching games being streamed live. Indeed, Figures 2 and 3 summarize players' perceptions regarding whether one can reach high levels of play *without* engaging in some kind of metacognitive activity – over and beyond simply playing games. Members of both communities clearly consider metacognitive activities to be highly beneficial (or necessary) for reaching upper performance echelons.

The site chessgames.com makes over 650,000 chess game records available over the internet. Chess games played in

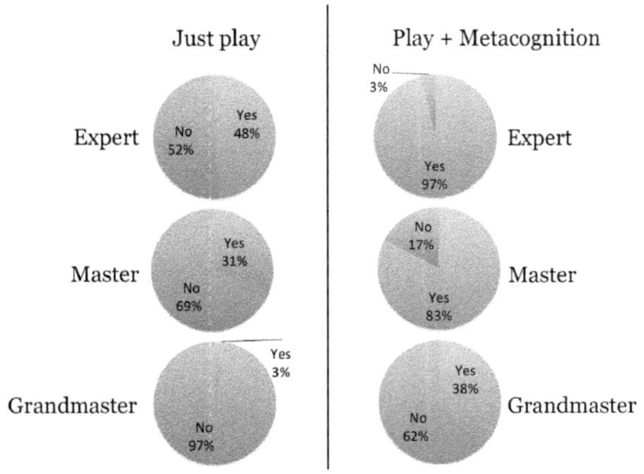

Figure 2. Results of a survey investigating chess players' perceptions of how proficient one can get with and without the benefit of metacognitive activities. For example: 48% of those surveyed believed that the level of Expert could be achieved by *only* playing chess

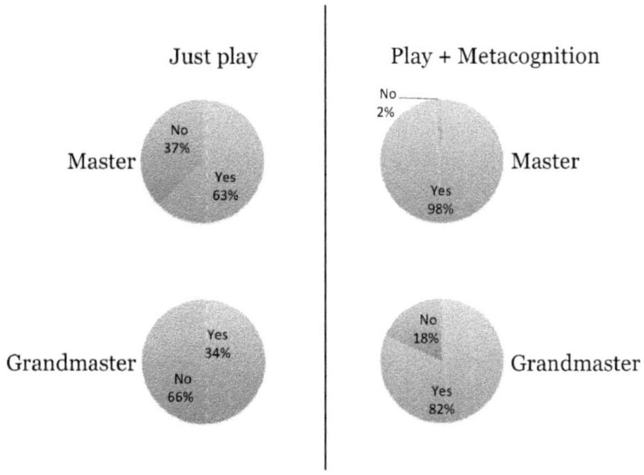

Figure 3. Results of a survey investigating *StarCraft II* players' perceptions of how proficient one can get with and without the benefit of metacognitive activities. For example: 34% of those surveyed believed that the level of Grandmaster could be achieved by *only* playing *StarCraft II*.

most major tournaments become part of the public domain, thus adding to the instructional content available to the community. Weaker players routinely study these games in order to sharpen their own skills.

StarCraft II games are recorded automatically and can be streamed live via screen capture. Like records of chess games, *StarCraft II* replays serve a vital community function. The site gamereplays.org contains 65,000 uploaded replays. Games by top players are routinely downloaded more than 5,000 times within just days of being posted. It is not uncommon for replays of championship matches by world-class players to be downloaded more than 10,000 times [14]. A popular web-show *Day 9 Daily* (viewed live by thousands) centers around high-level commentary of replays. And thousands of people tune in online to watch players of various strengths stream their games live [22]. This phenomenon is a sustainable practice of the community largely because strong players enjoy playing, and because many weaker players want to play like strong players. (Moreover, popular players can be further incentivised by sites like Twitch.tv, which apportion a cut of their advertising revenue to streamers.)

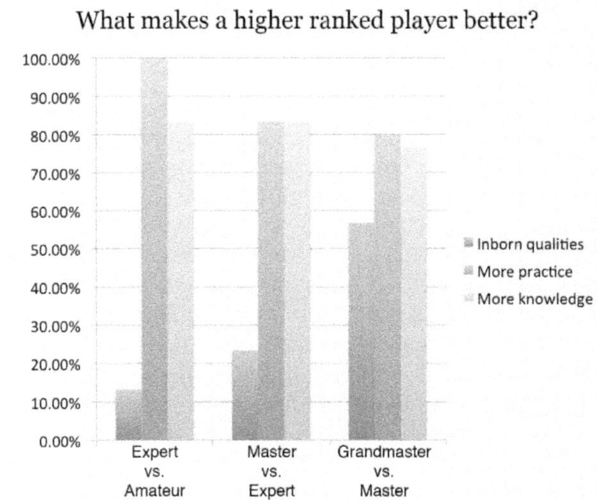

Figure 4. Results of a survey investigating chess players' perceptions of what makes a higher ranked player better than those in a slightly lower-ranked category. For example: 100% of those surveyed believed that experts are better than amateurs due (in part) to having practiced more.

Positive Self-Theory

The road from novice to expert in chess or *StarCraft II* is fraught with continual failure. And by design, failure is a daily occurrence: players are automatically matched with other players who have a similar rating, meaning that, even for good players, losses are as common as wins. One could imagine that this aggregate of losses could begin to instill negative self-theory.

We surveyed the community to investigate this potential drawback. In particular, we asked the gaming communities a series of questions about why certain players perform better than others. Following in Dweck's theoretical framework, we were mainly interested in whether players believed that a predisposition to certain cognitive skills was inborn (which would indicate a fixed-mindset) or whether these skills could be improved (which would indicate a growth-mindset) – or some combination of these. Figure 4 summarizes our findings for chess. As can be seen from Figure 5, the trend with regard to *StarCraft II* is very similar.

In both communities, players believed that, at all levels of play, a combination of 1) a greater amount of practice and 2) more previously acquired knowledge were the primary causes of better performance. In-born talent was viewed as a possible deciding factor only at the highest echelons of skill. Since the average player (and 100% of those surveyed) are not members of these echelons, it is safe to say that the average player views her own skill or lack thereof as a non-fixed, changeable, "growable" quantity. This mindset is especially pronounced in the *StarCraft II* community. Only 5% of the community believes that inborn qualities have a bearing on amateur-level competition. And since masters and grandmasters comprise only the top 2% of all *StarCraft II* players [2],

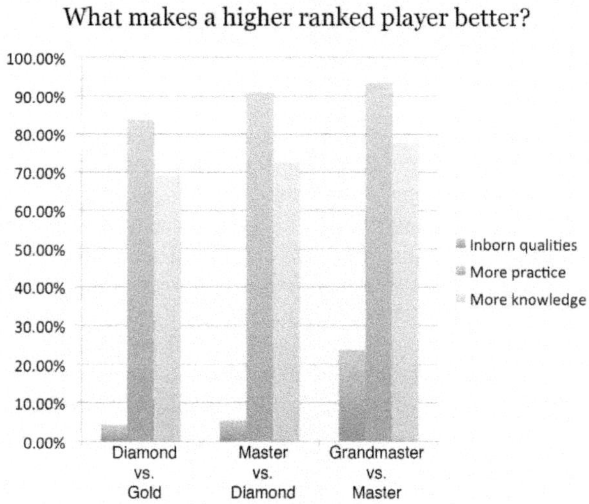

Figure 5. Results of a survey investigating SC2 players' perceptions of what makes a higher ranked player better than those in a slightly lower-ranked category. For example: about 25% of those surveyed believed that Grandmasters are better than Masters due (in part) to inborn advantages.

amateur-level competition is the bulk of the iceberg in a community of millions.

However, we must be cautious about drawing the conclusion that 1-on-1 competition somehow *instills* a positive self-theory. We can only conclude that those who elect to join and remain members of these communities *have* a positive self-theory. Naturally, we could not survey players who may have played for a while, become discouraged, and quit forever. It is possible that these games may attract or retain players who are more disposed to having a positive self-theory in the first place.

THEORY INTO PRACTICE

Overview

The salient features of the design, implementation, and evaluation of our game – *CompetitiveSourcery* – flow directly from the insights gleaned from studying the 1-on-1 competitive games of chess and *StarCraft II*.

- *A large possibility space.* Players can write arbitrary Java code in order to craft magic spells to spawn and control various in-game 3D objects within a simulated-analog 3D world.
- *Competitive Feedback.* Spells are designed to slay or entrap opponents. Players compete in iterated 1-on-1 competitions, pitting their spells against the spells of other players.
- *A long-term study.* We studied the dynamics of our game in the long term in order to determine whether the resulting body of theory (if any) which arose around the game exhibited the kind of balance that correlates with diversity in chess and *StarCraft II*.
- *A small group of users.* We did our study on a small group of users in order to debunk the potential misconception that a diverse body of theory is only possible when a community of millions is exploring the possibility space.

Design and Implementation

To implement *CompetitiveSourcery*, we leveraged the pre-existing *CodeSpells* platform [8] – a single player, non-competitive game. Although the game is for novices, it has an extensible underlying framework allowing us to implement networked multi-player support that *CodeSpells* lacks and to build a new 1-on-1 competitive game around the notion of "dueling wizards". The interface features an in-game IDE through which spells can be written. It also features a powerful spell-crafting Java API for manipulating the 3D environment around the spell-caster.

The rules of *CompetitiveSourcery* are relatively simple. One player assumes the role of the red wizard, and the other the role of the blue wizard. Both wizards appear in an outdoor arena, where they attempt to eliminate each other. Competition in *CompetitiveSourcery* revolves around attempting to cause collisions between one's opponent and wooden boxes of one's own color. Each such collision reduces the health of the wizard in question. The first player to lose all of her health loses the game. Since red boxes will not damage the red wizard (and blue boxes will not damage the blue wizard), one's boxes may be assembled into structures such as towers and platforms which are hostile to the opponent but safe to oneself. Importantly, boxes may only be created and moved via code crafted at runtime inside the game's IDE.

There was one other critical aspect of our study which was not explicitly designed into the game: the subjects in our user study understood that they were members of a three-person intramural team that would represent their department in an upcoming *CompetitiveSourcery* tournament[4]. Partly inspired by recent investigations of team practice environments [9], we felt that engendering a team mindset would help contextualize all inter-subject competition as friendly collaboration. Games of *CompetitiveSourcery* played between subjects were, on the one hand competitive (with an objective winner and a loser), but on the other hand were contextualized as making the team stronger. This allowed us to preclude the various negative emotions that can be associated with 1-on-1 competition.

Evaluation

We were mainly interested in whether the game of *CompetitiveSourcery* would turn out to be nuanced enough to inspire a body of theory to arise around it. If so, we wanted to know whether the body of theory exhibited features of balance (e.g. multiple viable approaches to the game) and, thus, whether gameplay was likely to be sustainable and diverse. And above all, we wanted to know if the process of discovering and learning the game's body of theory would have pedagogical merit for intermediate programmers.

[4]This tournament is still three months away at the time of this writing.

We chose to do an in-depth study with three users over the course of two months. These users were all intermediate programmers with fewer than 2 years of undergraduate instruction. The users gathered together three or more times per week for two hours at a time to play *CompetitiveSourcery*. Over all, this totalled to almost 150 man-hours of time devoted to playing and/or to metacognitive activities thereupon. The content of these two-hour sessions was not dictated by the researchers and was left to the discretion of the three-person team.

We observed these sessions and took detailed field notes, regardless of what team-related activities the subjects chose to engage in: e.g. playing games of *CompetitiveSourcery*, discussing strategies, debugging each other's code, or updating the team wiki.

Diversity and Sustainability

The first week of the study saw the rise and fall of a crude strategy which initially appeared to be unstoppable: Players would write an infinite loop that spawned a new box at some arbitrary location L on every iteration. Because this resulted in a multitude of boxes being spawned on top of each other within a short period of time, the game's built-in physics engine would cause the boxes to fly away from the origin point L in non-deterministic directions as if they had collided at a high speed. This strategy was named the "Bomb" and prevailed for about two days – bringing consistent victory to whomever employed it. The Bomb strategy's high level of efficacy virtually forced both players to mutually employ the *same* strategy, at which point the gameplay was characterized by each player trying to avoid the other player's bombs while casting bomb spells of their own. In this case, winners were generally determined by who could best outmaneuver the opponent. Also, many games ended in a draw – with both players having spawned more boxes than the game's imposed limit (about 100).

At first, we were worried that a tipping point had been reached and that players would no longer be encouraged to write new Java programs. However, in short order, one of the subjects discovered that she could write a spell to pick up and carry a box by making a loop that would continually set the location of the box relative to the position of her avatar. In this way, she could carry the box directly to her opponent in order to inflict damage. This was dubbed the "Battering Ram" and immediately made the Bomb obsolete – owing to the fact that the Battering Ram was much more precise and did not suffer from the 100-box limit.

Gameplay then began to take on a fencing-esque character – with players trying to maneuver in such a way that they could tag their opponent with their battering ram without being tagged in turn. However, the strategic arms race escalated further with the introduction of the first viable *defensive* strategy: One of the subjects discovered that he could write a spell to levitate a crate of his own color and move it along his avatar's forward vector – the utility being that (if he was standing on the box), he could fly. While flying, he could inflict damage on his opponent by using the Bomb strategy, flying overhead and spawning crates at his own location, causing them to bombard his opponent from above. This was dubbed the "Fokker"[5]. Using the Fokker, a player could easily defend against the earth-bound Battering Ram, countering it effectively from the skies.

Two counter-strategies arose next: the Fokker Battering Ram (a combination of the Battering Ram and the Fokker), and the Gun. The Gun was a spell that would spawn a box at the avatar's location and launch it forward, creating a dangerous projectile. The Gun was first employed as a ground-based anti-aircraft strategy to shoot down players employing the Fokker. However, it was later combined with the Fokker to create the Fokker Gun strategy, which (along with the Fokker Battering Ram) could be used to do air-to-air combat against someone employing any of the aforementioned Fokker-based strategies.

This was less than one month into the study, and the pool of viable strategies was quickly growing. This divergence, in and of itself, had a noticeable effect on the characteristics of strategies that came later: Because it was impossible to know beforehand what strategy one's opponent would employ, the best strategies were the ones that were most flexible in the face of uncertainty. Players would, for example, open the game by flying (i.e. the Fokker), but would delay the dropping of bombs until the opponent had committed to a ground-based or aerial counter strategy. In the case of a ground-based counter strategy, the traditional Fokker (i.e. with bombs) appeared was quite effective. In the case of an aerial counter strategy, the Fokker Gun or the Fokker Battering Ram was better suited for air-to-air combat. In short, the growing pool of strategies necessitated that new strategies be more complex to cope with the growing uncertainty.

In the interest of length, we cannot go into detail about every strategy developed during the course of the study. The team wiki page describes over 30 distinct strategies, some requiring the user to correctly write and execute three or more distinct spells in-game and to accurately adapt to what the opponent is doing.

All in all, we were pleased to see a divergence of effective strategies – rather than a convergence toward a single dominant strategy. We are pleased to report that, to date, after 150 man hours have been spent in search of a dominant winning strategy, no such strategy has surfaced.

Furthermore, the arms race continues to this day. At this time, our subjects are developing a style of play based on teleportation – where the player teleports from place to place in an attempt to confuse the enemy. Other promising strategies have intriguing architectural characteristics: the building of walls, bridges, stairwells, ceilings, and moving platforms.

Pedagogical Merit

Having shown that the set of viable strategies exhibits signs of increasing diversity, it is still worth asking how diverse the academic skills being sharpened through *CompetitiveSourcery* are. If it should happen that some of the

[5]An allusion to a World War I German aircraft – one of the earliest examples of a plane that could fly while dispatching machine gun fire.

strongest strategies involve Java programs that can be written without loops or branches, for example, then the pedagogical benefits could be jeopardized due to insufficient content coverage.

Coding Constructs. We can report, though, that even the most basic of spells written during our study tended to draw from the entire bag of first-year programming constructs: if-statements, loops, boolean expressions, arrays, etc. And the more powerful spells almost always tended to be the more flexible ones – i.e. the ones with more control structures. Also, each individual spell is structured as a Java class, which introduces a need for object oriented programming, particularly in cases when two or more spells must work together – which became common as strategies became complex.

Software Engineering. At an even higher level: The software engineering concept of "modularity" arose quite naturally after less than one month of the study. Our subjects realized that using many small spells to execute a complex strategy was more flexible than using a single monolithic spell. For example, the spell to fly – one of the two spells involved in the basic Fokker – was kept separate from the spell to bombard the opponent from above, because this allowed the basic Fokker to be easily switched to the Fokker Gun or the Fokker Battering Ram as necessary.

Furthermore, because the space of known strategies was in constant flux, the subjects had to understand, evaluate, and design against ever-shifting requirements – a skill set that (in our experience) can help software engineers keep pace in the modern tech industry climate. They had to maintain their code and its documentation when innovative new counter strategies were discovered. Refactoring and software maintainance were common activities.

Human Factors. Subjects were also forced to wrestle with tough HCI challenges – e.g. figuring out how to make powerful strategies more straightforward to execute in-game. For example, one subject discovered that she could write spells that would stall (in a loop) until she pressed the spacebar to make her avatar jump. Thus, after casting more than one of these "delayed spells" in a safe location, she could activate all spells at once with a single button press at an opportune moment. This was much easier than casting one spell after another during the heat of battle.

The aforementioned breadth of academic content is worth comparing to traditional single-player educational games – where the range of academic material is limited to narrow domains in which algorithmic feedback can be provided (e.g. arithmetic or simple division). By contrast, our subjects were exposed to academic diversity spanning from first-year programming skills all the way to fourth-year skills and beyond.

The team practice environment bears more resemblance to that of a startup company than a college classroom – which, from a learning sciences standpoint, is a positive quality. Students are known to learn better when concepts are encountered in a meaningful context, rather than as disembodied abstractions [1]. Many researchers have also called for a greater level of authenticity in education – where learning environments are crafted to reflect the "authentic" [5, 12] activities of the relevant "community of practice" [38]. We believe the team practice environment centered around *CompetitiveSourcery* qualifies as "thickly authentic" [31, 32], capturing an unabstracted mix of the hard and soft skills that real computer scientists use every day.

Metacognition

The team of subjects tended to follow each game by doing a post-mortem, in which the subjects were frequently observed saying things like, "I lost because I need to write that spell faster next time. I couldn't remember it well enough." or "I messed up the loop, so the spell didn't work. That was silly." These are compelling examples of how the feedback provided by lost games serves to highlight weaknesses in the player's coding abilities. In the wake of these post-mortems, subjects proceeded to strengthen these self-identified weaknesses through further drilling and practice.

We also observed a different sort of discussion during the post-mortems – e.g. "I don't think strategy X is working well against strategy Y. What if I were to tweak X by doing Z?" From a pedagogical perspective, these responses to losing a game are undeniably encouraging. They are instances of creative problem-solving, and they routinely emerged as a result of the win-loss feedback provided by competing with one's team members. Many of the novel Java spells implemented by the team were devised in this way – as changes to existing code, prompted by a new understanding of the requirements arising from the analysis of a competitive result.

During analysis, subjects spent a considerable amount of time discussing and deriving new creative strategies. Indeed, as much time was spent on these activities as on playing the game itself. As mentioned previously, bouts of creativity tended to occur when reflecting on why some strategy did not perform as well as expected. These metacognitive acts no doubt have pedagogical benefits as well – sharpening the so-called "soft" skills of being able to talk intelligently about code and to solve problems collaboratively.

Key Differences and Future Work

The main difference observed between the lab and our "in the wild" studies was that our subjects were generating a body of theory from scratch, whereas chess players and *StarCraft II* players tend to leverage an existing body of theory. This is to be expected, and we anticipate that this will change as the size of the body of theory and the size of the community grows. As this happens, we plan to analyse any pedagogically relevant changes that the learning environment may undergo.

In three months, we are hosting the first *CompetitiveSourcery* tournament. By encouraging intramural and interscholastic competition at both the high school and college levels, we hope to expand the *CompetitiveSourcery* community and to study the emergent educational properties of a medium-to-large-scale educational ecosystem.

CONCLUSION

We have argued that two aesthetic principles *diversity* and *sustainability* have yet to be addressed in recent trends in educational game design. To help contribute a solution, we turn to existing 1-on-1 competitive games that appear to have these qualities. We present an analysis of these games in order to inform the design of competitive educational games. We use insights gained from this analysis to design and evaluate *CompetitiveSourcery*, a gaming environment for educating intermediate Java programmers. The results of our long term study indicate that our environment is both sustainable and diverse, inspiring high levels of content coverage, engagement, and metacognition.

ACKNOWLEDGMENTS

This work is supported by two NSF Graduate Fellowships and a Google Research Grant.

REFERENCES

1. Barab, S. A., and Plucker, J. A. Smart people or smart contexts? cognition, ability, and talent development in an age of situated approaches to knowing and learning. *Educational Psychologist 37* (2002), 165–182.
2. http://us.battle.net/sc2/en/blog/2053471, August 2012.
3. Bauman, E. B. *Game-Based Teaching and Simulation in Nursing and Health Care*. Springer, 2012.
4. Bransford, J. D., on Developments in the Science of Learning., N. R. C. E.-U. C., on Learning Research, N. R. C. E.-U. C., and Practice., E. *How people learn : brain, mind, experience, and school*, 2 ed. National Academy Press, Sept. 2000.
5. Brown, J., Collins, A., and Duguid, P. Situated cognition and the culture of learning. *Educational Researcher 18*, 1 (1989), 32.
6. Bruckman, A. Can educational be fun? In *presented at the Game Developers Conference '99, San Jose, CA.* (1999).
7. Cheung, G., and Huang, J. Starcraft from the stands: understanding the game spectator. In *Proceedings of the 2011 annual conference on Human factors in computing systems*, CHI '11, ACM (New York, NY, USA, 2011), 763–772.
8. codespells.blogspot.com, August 2012.
9. Dabbish, L., Kraut, R., and Patton, J. Communication and commitment in an online game team. In *Proceedings of the 2012 ACM annual conference on Human Factors in Computing Systems*, CHI '12, ACM (New York, NY, USA, 2012), 879–888.
10. degroot, A. D. *Thought and Choice in Chess*. Mouton, The Hague, The Netherlands, 1965.
11. Dweck, C. *Mindset: The New Psychology of Success*. Ballantine Books, 2007.
12. Falkner, K., and Palmer, E. Developing authentic problem solving skills in introductory computing classes. *SIGCSE Bull. 41*, 1 (Mar. 2009), 4–8.
13. Fisher, R. Thinking about thinking: Developing metacognition in children. *Early Child Development and Care 141* (Feb 1998), 1–15.
14. http://gamereplays.org, August 2012.
15. Gee, J. P. What would a state of the art instructional video game look like. *Innovate Journal of online education 1*, 6 (2005).
16. Gee, J. P., and Shaffer, D. Looking where the light is bad: Video games and the future of assessment. *EDge* (2010).
17. Gobet, F., and Charness, N. Expertise in chess. In *Chess and games. Cambridge handbook on expertise and expert performance*, F. Gobet and N. Charness, Eds. Cambridge University Press, Cambridge, Massachusetts, USA, 2006, 523–538.
18. Habgood, M. J., and Ainsworth, S. E. Motivating children to learn effectively: Exploring the value of intrinsic integration in educational games. *Journal of the Learning Sciences*, 1 (2011).
19. Habgood, M. P. J., Ainsworth, S. E., and Benford, S. Endogenous fantasy and learning in digital games. *Simulation and Gaming 36*, 4 (2005), 483–498.
20. Isbister, K., Flanagan, M., and Hash, C. Designing games for learning: insights from conversations with designers. In *Proceedings of the 28th international conference on Human factors in computing systems*, CHI '10, ACM (New York, NY, USA, 2010), 2041–2044.
21. Joshua M. Lewis, Patrick Trinh, D. K. A corpus analysis of strategy video game play in starcraft: Brood war. In *Proceedings of the 33rd Annual Conference of the Cognitive Science Society*, T. S. L. Carlson, C. Hlscher, Ed. (2011), 687–692.
22. Kaytoue, M., Silva, A., Cerf, L., Meira, Jr., W., and Raïssi, C. Watch me playing, i am a professional: a first study on video game live streaming. In *Proceedings of the 21st international conference companion on World Wide Web*, WWW '12 Companion, ACM (New York, NY, USA, 2012), 1181–1188.
23. Linehan, C., Kirman, B., Lawson, S., and Chan, G. Practical, appropriate, empirically-validated guidelines for designing educational games. In *Proceedings of the 2011 annual conference on Human factors in computing systems*, CHI '11, ACM (New York, NY, USA, 2011), 1979–1988.
24. Malone, T. W. Toward a theory of intrinsically motivating instruction. *Cognitive Science 5*, 4 (1981), 333 – 369.
25. Murphy, L., and Thomas, L. Dangers of a fixed mindset: implications of self-theories research for computer science education. In *Proceedings of the 13th annual conference on Innovation and technology in computer science education*, ITiCSE '08, ACM (New York, NY, USA, 2008), 271–275.
26. Reingold, E. M., Charness, N., Pomplun, M., and Stampe, D. M. Visual span in expert chess players: Evidence from eye movements. *Psychological Science 12* (2001), 48–55.
27. Robertson, G., and Watson, I. Case-based learning by observation: preliminary work. In *Proceedings of The 8th Australasian Conference on Interactive Entertainment: Playing the System*, IE '12, ACM (New York, NY, USA, 2012), 24:1–24:1.
28. Sadler, D. R. Beyond feedback: developing student capability in complex appraisal. *Assessment and Evaluation in Higher Education 35*, 5 (2010), 535–550.
29. Scardamalia, M., Bereiter, C., and Steinbach, R. Teachability of reflective processes in written composition. *Cognitive Science 8*, 2 (1984), 173–190.
30. Schoenfeld, A. H., and Mathematical Association of America, Washington, D. *Problem Solving in the Mathematics Curriculum. A Report, Recommendations, and an Annotated Bibliography. MAA Notes, Number 1 [microform] / Alan H. Schoenfeld*. Distributed by ERIC Clearinghouse, [Washington, D.C.] :, 1983.
31. Shaffer, D. W. Pedagogical praxis: The professions as models for post-industrial education. *Teachers College Record 106* (2004), 1401–1421.
32. Shaffer, D. W. Epistemic games. *Journal of Online Education* (2005).
33. Simon, B., Hanks, B., Murphy, L., Fitzgerald, S., McCauley, R., Thomas, L., and Zander, C. Saying isn't necessarily believing: influencing self-theories in computing. In *Proceedings of the Fourth international Workshop on Computing Education Research*, ICER '08, ACM (New York, NY, USA, 2008), 173–184.
34. Simon, H. A., and Chase, W. G. Perception in chess. *Cognitive Psychology 1* (1973), 33–81.
35. Simon, H. A., and Chase, W. G. Skill in chess. *American Scientist 61* (1973), 394–403.
36. Smith, A. M., Andersen, E., Mateas, M., and Popović, Z. A case study of expressively constrainable level design automation tools for a puzzle game. In *Proceedings of the International Conference on the Foundations of Digital Games*, FDG '12, ACM (New York, NY, USA, 2012), 156–163.
37. Vygotskii, L. S., and Cole, M. *Mind in society : the development of higher psychological processes / L. S. Vygotsky ; edited by Michael Cole ... [et al.]*. Harvard University Press, Cambridge :, 1978.
38. Wenger, E. *Communities of Practice: Learning, Meaning, and Identity (Learning in Doing: Social, Cognitive and Computational Perspectives)*, 1 ed. Cambridge University Press, Sept. 1999.
39. White, B. Y., and Frederiksen, J. R. Inquiry, Modeling, and Metacognition: Making Science Accessible to All Students. *Cognition and Instruction 16*, 1 (1998).

Why Interactive Learning Environments Can Have It All: Resolving Design Conflicts Between Competing Goals

Martina A. Rau
Carnegie Mellon Univ.
5000 Forbes Ave
Pittsburgh, PA 15213
marau@cs.cmu.edu

Vincent Aleven
Carnegie Mellon Univ.
5000 Forbes Ave
Pittsburgh, PA 15213
aleven@cs.cmu.edu

Nikol Rummel
Ruhr- Univ. Bochum
44780 Bochum, Germany
nikol.rummel@rub.de

Stacie Rohrbach
Carnegie Mellon Univ.
5000 Forbes Ave
Pittsburgh, PA 15213
stacie@cmu.edu

ABSTRACT

Designing interactive learning environments (ILEs; e.g., intelligent tutoring systems, educational games, etc.) is a challenging interdisciplinary process that needs to satisfy multiple stakeholders. ILEs need to function in real educational settings (e.g., schools) in which a number of goals interact. Several instructional design methodologies exist to help developers address these goals. However, they often lead to conflicting recommendations. Due to the lack of an established methodology to resolve such conflicts, developers of ILEs have to rely on ad-hoc solutions. We present a principled methodology to resolve such conflicts. We build on a well-established design process for creating Cognitive Tutors, a highly effective type of ILE. We extend this process by integrating methods from multiple disciplines to resolve design conflicts. We illustrate our methodology's effectiveness by describing the iterative development of the Fractions Tutor, which has proven to be effective in classroom studies with 3,000 4th-6th graders.

Author Keywords

Design conflicts; instructional design; interactive learning environments; Cognitive Tutors.

ACM Classification Keywords

K.3.1 [Computers and Education]: Computer Uses in Education – Computer-assisted instruction

H.5.2 [Information Interfaces and Presentation]: User Interfaces - User-centered design

INTRODUCTION

To design interactive learning environments (ILEs), instructional designers identify stakeholder goals and address them within the constraints of the given educational context. Often, stakeholder goals can readily be identified as they are in part dictated by state requirements (e.g., performance on standardized tests) and the context (e.g., the necessity for classroom management). In addressing these goals, developers can draw on many frameworks which guide the design of ILEs to identify and address stakeholders' goals while matching resource limitations [1-7].

But in reality, it is inevitable that different stakeholders have different goals, that there are significant resource limitations, and that design goals (even if they were agreed upon by all stakeholders) need to be traded off against each other. Unfortunately, existing design frameworks for ILEs do not address how to resolve such design conflicts. This may in part be due to the fact that different types of design frameworks are relevant to the development of ILEs: some frameworks focus on user-centered design [1-2, 4], others incorporate learning science [3] and educational psychology research [5-7]. However, these different types of frameworks rarely reference one another. For this reason, developers often have to rely on ad-hoc methods to resolve conflicts that arise in the interdisciplinary field of ILEs. For instance, a math teacher who wants to help students learn deeply may provide complex real-world problems [3]. Yet, [7] suggest to practice part-tasks: discrete tasks that are necessary for the completion of complex problems (e.g., practicing math facts). At the same time, students find complex problems interesting, but the teacher might worry that their learning is jeopardized because the problems do not provide just-in-time feedback [7].

It crucial that we pay attention to the conflicting goals that inevitably occur in complex educational settings. If we fail to address stakeholders' competing goals, our ILE will never be as successful as it can be: students may dislike the ILE because it is either boring or too challenging, or teachers – who might well believe it will help their students learn deeply – fail to use the ILE within the constraints of their day-to-day job which requires them to prepare students for standardized tests and manage a class of students. However, if we succeed in integrating stakeholders' needs within the constraints of their contexts into the design of our ILE, the dissemination of our product will hugely benefit.

Nevertheless, to integrate competing goals and constraints, developers of ILEs typically have to rely on ad-hoc approaches to resolve design conflicts. What is needed is a principled methodology that developers can apply to resolve such conflicts. The goal of the present paper is to describe a new approach to resolving conflict that arise between multiple goals and constraints in educational settings.

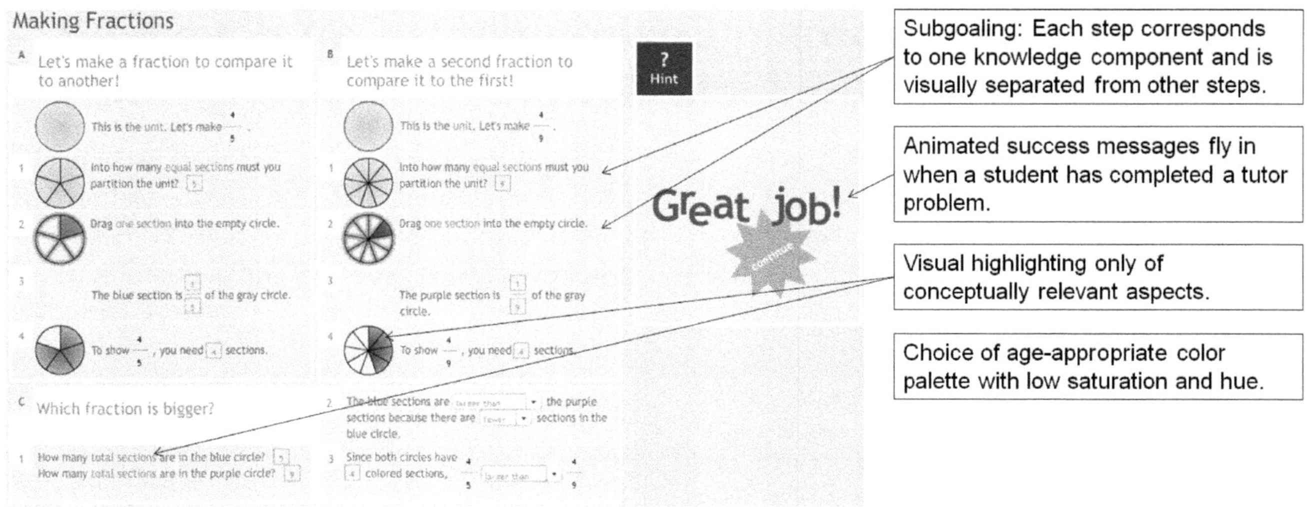

Figure 1. Example problem in the Fractions Tutor that employs the subgoaling strategy.

We illustrate our multi-method approach by describing our research within a particularly successful ILE: Cognitive Tutors. Cognitive Tutors are grounded in cognitive theory and artificial intelligence. They pose rich problem-solving tasks to students and provide individualized support at any point during the problem-solving process. At the heart of the Cognitive Tutors lies a cognitive model of students' problem-solving steps. The model is used to provide individualized support for students during the learning process [8-10]. Cognitive Tutors have been shown to lead to significant learning gains in a variety of studies [8-12]. They are currently being used in close to 3,000 U.S. schools. Cognitive Tutors are particularly suitable for describing our approach to resolving design conflicts as their development follows a well-described design process that integrates design recommendations originating from a number of fields, including HCI, learning science, and education [13]. We extend this process by providing a new approach for resolving conflicting design recommendations and constraints. In particular, our methodology combines focus groups and affinity diagramming to develop a goal hierarchy, parametric experiments, and cross-iteration studies. The novelty of our approach lies in a principled combination of methods that originate in a variety of disciplines, including from HCI, learning sciences, education, and ILE design.

We illustrate the success of our methodology using the Fractions Tutor as example (see Figure 1) – a successful Cognitive Tutor that has gone through several iterations of classroom experiments and lab studies with over 3,000 students. The Fractions Tutor has been shown to significantly enhance students' learning. In a recent classroom study with a total of 599 4th- and 5th-graders [14], after 10 hours of instruction with the Fractions Tutor, students improved significantly with a medium effect size of $d = .40$ at the posttest ($p < .01$). When we administered a delayed posttest a week later, we found that students retained these learning gains with an effect size of $d = .60$ ($p < .01$).

The success of the Fractions Tutor, like that of other Cognitive Tutors [15-17], has been shaped by incorporating stakeholder goals into the design process. In doing so, we employed a principle-based approach which we believe is not unique to the domain of fractions or Cognitive Tutors in particular, but that can inform design decisions made during the development of a wide range of ILEs.

COGNITIVE TUTOR DESIGN PROCESS

Before we present our novel approach to resolving conflicts in designing ILEs, we review the development process for Cognitive Tutors [5, 8-9]. This process comprises a set of iterative, non-linear stages.

Stage 1: Stakeholder and Problem Identification

The first step in Cognitive Tutor design is to identify the educational problem to be addressed as well as stakeholders and their objectives. To accomplish this goal, one may interview students, teachers and curriculum developers, review education literature, national and state standards.

The development of the Fractions Tutor was motivated by the fact that students struggle with fractions as early as elementary school [18-19]. Fractions are considered an important educational goal in and of itself, and an important prerequisite for later algebra learning [18]. Interviews with teachers confirmed the need for an effective ILE that can help students overcome their difficulties with fractions.

Stage 2: Identifying Assessment and Practice Problems

Based on the educational problem, designers should identify a set of assessment tasks (i.e., tasks learners should be able to solve after having worked with the ILE). Assessment tasks should guide the selection of practice problems (i.e., problems students should solve as part of the ILE). A search of the education literature will yield a set of domain-specific target problems both for assessment and for practice. In addition, developers and teachers should brainstorm about novel problems for assessment and practice.

The outcome of stage 2 is a set of domain-specific assessment tasks and practice problems.

Stage 3: Cognitive Task Analysis

The goal of stage 3 is to understand student learning and student thinking in the domain. In doing so, we identify the knowledge and strategies the ILE should cover, using cognitive task analysis techniques [21]. Cognitive task analysis seeks to identify the knowledge components (i.e., units of knowledge) that students need to acquire to perform well on assessment and practice problems. Cognitive task analysis is based on think-alouds and observations of student learners (novices) or proficient student (experts), or based on a theory of what knowledge learners need to acquire. Think-alouds and observations are often combined with difficulty factors assessment [22] – a method to identify features of tasks that reliably change the difficulty of the task.

Several iterations between stages 2 and 3 are recommended. After each iteration, developers should update the collection of assessment and practice problems based on insights gained from cognitive task analysis and difficulty factors assessments. They should review the problems in focus groups or in interviews with teachers, while also discussing problem sequences within the ILE. Observations of teacher-student tutoring can help guide the instructional design, by providing insights into successful instructional strategies.

The outcome of stage 3 is a set of knowledge components and of practice problems that address all knowledge components in order of ascending difficulty.

Stage 4: Cognitive Modeling and Tutor Development

Stage 4 aims at developing the Cognitive Tutor. As part of this stage, developers will create the Cognitive Tutor interface, a cognitive model of student problem solving that will serve as a basis for individualized support, and a curriculum that contains a collection of problem types and that span across a variety of topics within the given domain.

Typically, stage 4 includes several cycles of rapid, low-fidelity prototyping and high-fidelity prototyping. These rounds of testing are usually conducted in the laboratory with a small number of students from the target population. Between each round of testing, the materials are updated based on the findings and issues identified. To develop the Fractions Tutor, we used the Cognitive Tutor Authoring Tools (CTAT, [23]), which allows for rapid prototyping and fast implementation of iterative design changes. We recommend including teachers in the development process. Involving teachers will not only improve the quality of the ILE – it will also benefit the dissemination of the final product and is likely to reveal further stakeholder goals.

The outcome of stage 4 is a set of working Cognitive Tutor problems ready for further testing.

Stage 5: Pilot studies and parametric studies

The goal of stage 5 is to formally evaluate and iteratively improve the ILE. A set of methods are available during this phase. First, pilot testing in the laboratory is useful to get in-depth insights with students solving practice problems while thinking aloud, which can help identify gaps in their knowledge that the ILE does not yet address. Second, testing the ILE in classrooms is indispensible. We can gather a variety of data from these classroom studies. Students' learning gains should be assessed based on pretests and posttests that integrate the target problems identified during earlier stages, including both standardized test items and transfer items that assess students' ability to apply their knowledge to novel task types. Informal observational data of students' interactions with the ILE in classrooms, interviews and focus groups with teachers as well as surveys with students and with teachers will yield valuable insights into usability issues and reveal crucial aspects of the stakeholders' goals. Log data gathered while students use the ILE provides a useful basis for identifying issues in usability and difficulty level of particular steps within the ILE.

Since fractions instruction typically uses a variety of graphical representations (e.g., circles, rectangles, and number lines) [18-20, 24], the Fractions Tutor includes multiple interactive graphical representations. To inform our design choices in integrating these graphical representations, we conducted a series of parametric studies in classrooms. As a consequence of these studies, the Fractions Tutor uses graphical representations in the following manner:

- The Fractions Tutor switches frequently between different graphical representations, as opposed to providing several practice problems with one graphical representation before moving on to another graphical representation.
- The Fractions Tutor provides support for relating graphical representations (e.g., circles) to symbolic representations (e.g., ½) in the form of menu-based self-explanation prompts.
- The Fractions Tutor provides support for relating different graphical representations (e.g., circles and number lines) that requires students to become active in making these relations, rather than having the ILE provide these connections automatically.

The outcome of stage 5 is a set of updated stakeholder goals, as well as an updated and iteratively improved ILE that is ready for classroom dissemination.

Stage 6: Classroom Use and Evaluation

After several iterations with the ILE, it is time to evaluate the system. Randomized field trials are the method of choice during this phase. A large number of classrooms should be randomly assigned to using the ILE or to work with another commonly used type of ILE, or a curriculum without an associated ILE. The success of the ILE should not only be evaluated based on students' performance on pretests and posttests. Observations in randomly selected classrooms, interviews with randomly selected teachers and student or teacher surveys will identify problem-solving behaviors and learning processes. Further, the analysis of student log data during problem solving can help detect issues with specific problem-solving steps, for example by identifying steps on which students make many errors.

IDENTIFYING STAKEHOLDER GOALS AND INSTRUCTIONAL DESIGN PRINCIPLES

We now describe our novel contributions to the design processes just described. We formulate a hierarchy of stakeholder goals. Then, we identify the instructional design recommendations to address these goals and identify conflicts between instructional design recommendations. Finally, we present three approaches to resolving these conflicts.

Forming a Goal Hierarchy

Across the stages and iterations of ILE development, one must not lose sight of stakeholder goals. We recommend conducting focus groups and interviews with teachers and students as part of each stage. Further, we suggest creating a goal hierarchy to identify and resolve goal conflicts.

To develop a goal hierarchy, we use affinity diagrams, a common HCI technique [25]: we write each goal on a sticky note and then work bottom-up to organize them into a hierarchy. Once all notes are collected in groups, we name the group. We then identify a set of instructional design recommendations that can help us achieve each goal.

Identifying Goals and Design Recommendations

Table 1 provides an overview of the goals and instructional design recommendations we identified for the Fractions Tutor. We identified the overarching goal to support students' robust learning of fractions (G1). Based on these interviews and based on the review of of educational standards [18-20], we identified teachers' goals to promote students' learning of robust knowledge about fractions which can transfer to new problem types and that lasts over time (G1). Based on the education standards and mathematics literature, we formulated domain-specific goals to promote conceptual understanding of fractions as parts of a whole, as proportions, and as measurements. Both the mathematics education literature and the learning sciences literatures suggest that instruction should employ graphical representations to illustrate these different interpretations of fractions (id1) [18-20,24]. Furthermore, education standards describe the need for students to learn multiple strategies to solve fractions problems (id2) [18-20]. For instance, students should be able to compare fractions with like numerators or like denominators by reasoning about the relative size of fractions, and using benchmarks and equivalent fractions. To enhance learning of a variety of strategies, the education literature suggests practicing different strategies to solve the same problem [26] and to discuss why they lead to the same [27]. Further, students should be exposed to a variety of problem types [28], which should enhance their ability to transfer their knowledge to novel problem formats (id3). To further enhance robust learning, the learning sciences result literature recommends using complex realistic problems with cover stories (id4) [29], to introduce encourage abstraction (id5) [28], to illustrate the structural components

Goals	Instructional Design Principles	Conflicts
G1: Robust domain knowledge that lasts and transfers to new problems types	G1: use variety of graphics (id1), use a variety of problem formats (id2), practice variety of strategies (id3), use cover stories (id4), introduce abstract terms (id5), subgoaling, (id6), use lean design that highlights only conceptually relevant aspects (id7), use complex holistic problems (id8)	C1 (within G1): provide complex, holistic problems (id8) vs. use subgoaling (id6)
G2: Performance on standardized tests	G2: solve problems that are structurally similar to the target problems (id9), provide opportunities for extended practice to master one strategy (id10)	C2a (with G1): practice with a variety of problem formats (id2) vs. practice with problem formats that are structurally similar to the target problems (id9) C2b (with G1): practice a variety of strategies (id3) vs. rote practice of one strategy that is most likely to always lead to the correct answer (id10)
G3: Ease of classroom management	G3: engaging, usable system (id12), gather information about students' performance (id13), self-paced learning and individualization (id15)	C3 (with G1): provide complex real-world problems with cover stories (id4) vs. provide an engaging, easy-to-use system (id12)
G4: Tasks that invoke self-efficacy	G4: employ concrete language that students can understand intuitively (id11)	C4: use abstract language that applies to a variety of situations (id6) vs. use of intuitive language that uses concrete examples (id11)
G5: Fun, interest, entertainment	G5: game-like colorful and flashy elements (id14)	C5: include game-like, colorful elements whose main purpose is to visually appeal young students (id14) vs. lean designs that use colorful highlighting to emphasize conceptually relevant aspects (id7)

Table 1. Goals and Instructional Design Principles.

of a problem-solving procedure using subgoaling (id6) [30]. Subgoaling is a procedure that aims at communicating the goal structure of a problem by breaking it into clear substeps, thereby "making thinking visible." Instructional design principles suggest to use color only sparingly, and to highlight only conceptually relevant aspects of the problem (id7) [6].

Our focus groups, surveys, and interviews with teachers revealed a further important goal: to help students perform well on standardized tests (G2). To address this goal, one might suggest to provide opportunities for practice on problems that are structurally similar to the target assessment problems (id9) [31], and to master one strategy that will lead to the correct answer (id10) - to the extent one can predict the kinds of items that appear on such tests.

Our classroom observations demonstrated teachers' needs for classroom management while using the Fractions Tutor (G3), including the ability to focus on students who struggle with the content, monitoring students' progress, and a quiet classroom of students who concentrate on their work. For instance, when asked what they like about using ILEs, teachers reported: "I like using it because it is so interactive for the students. They stay very involved," or "The programs that I use with my students are interactive, colorful, and can hold their attention." To address teachers' goal for classroom management, we used focus groups with teachers to identify possible obstacles that our system created within the classroom. We discovered that any aspect that makes the ILE difficult to use for students results in teachers helping students out with usability issues rather than helping with the content. An ILE that is easy to use and that includes easy math problems (see G4) would thus help achieve this goal (id12). Furthermore, teachers expressed their interest in a system that would gather real-time information about individual students' performance on the practice problems, so that they could more easily identify struggling students and help them out (id13).

Furthermore, teachers' concerns about the difficulty of practice problems, in particular of complex real-world problems, revealed their goal of using a low level of difficulty (G4). Think-alouds and interviews with students further demonstrated that students value easy tasks that invoke feelings of self-efficacy; i.e., tasks that make them feel like they can do math. To make problems easier for students, instructional materials should employ concrete language that students can understand intuitively (id11).

Finally, surveys with students demonstrated their goal to have fun and to be entertained (G5). This need might best be achieved focusing on age-appropriate design elements resembling games with colorful and flashy elements (id14). Also, complex real-world problems might address students' need for interesting practice problems (see id4).

Forming a Hierarchy of Stakeholder Goals

Next, we create a hierarchy of the goal categories we identified. In doing so, focus groups with the stakeholders can help inform the ranking of goals. In our case, an important question regarded the relative importance of the goal to promote robust learning (G1) and the goal to help students perform well on standardized tests (G2). As mentioned, these goals do not always result in competing design recommendations: The purpose of standardized tests is to assess students' robust learning. Practicing with only one format of questions may be detrimental to students' performance on the test if the test contains questions other than the ones that were anticipated. Since our interviews and focus groups with teachers demonstrated that they cared deeply about students' deep learning, we felt that the stakeholders' goals were best represented by ranking the goal to promote students' robust learning (G1) higher than the goal to do well on standardized tests (G2).

<table>
<tr><th>Goal</th><th>Effects</th><th>Impact</th></tr>
<tr><td rowspan="2">G3: Classroom management</td><td>Information about which students are struggling allows teachers to help them out, and increases these students' learning (+ learn)</td><td rowspan="2">1 + 1
= 2</td></tr>
<tr><td>A quiet classroom allows students to concentrate better and will help them learn (+ learn)</td></tr>
<tr><td rowspan="4">G4: Self-efficacy</td><td>Easy problems increase students' enjoyment (+ G5: fun)</td><td rowspan="4">0.5(-1 + 1 + 1 – 1) + 1 – 1 + 0.5(1+1)
= 0.5</td></tr>
<tr><td>Easy, but somewhat challenging problems enhance students' learning (+ learn)</td></tr>
<tr><td>Too easy problems do not require deep processing of the content and do not help students learn (- learn)</td></tr>
<tr><td>Students have less trouble with easy problems, which positively affect classroom management (+ G3: management)</td></tr>
<tr><td rowspan="4">G5: Fun</td><td>Distracting elements are known to impede learning (- learn)</td><td rowspan="4">-1 + 1 + 1 – 1
= 0</td></tr>
<tr><td>Fun software is more motivating, which might enhance learning (+ learn</td></tr>
<tr><td>Fun software may help classroom management if it motivates students to work on the task (+ learn)</td></tr>
<tr><td>Fun software might impede classroom management if it decreases students' concentration (- learn)</td></tr>
</table>

Table 2. Impact Factors of Stakeholder Goals.

Understanding the context of our ILE can also crucially inform our goal hierarchy. In schools, teachers and superintendents are the ones who decide to acquire and use educational software. Performance on standardized tests is one highly important metric on which teachers are evaluated. In other words, the ability to promote performance on standardized tests is a prerequisite for the dissemination of ILEs. We therefore consider performance on standardized tests (G2) as highly important.

For the goals on which we cannot find consensus in focus groups (i.e., G3-5), we again use affinity diagrams to identify classes of goals based on the effect they have on students' learning and on the dissemination of the ILE. In doing so, a brainstorming session with experts (who have good knowledge of the relevant literatures) about the effects of common interventions to meet the goals can help create the goal hierarchy. We then regroup the generated items to create a diagram for the effects. The resulting categories are provided in italics in the list below. We then computed the impact of each goal. To do so, we assigned a value of 1 to each positive effect (e.g., the intervention will promote learning) and a value of -1 to each negative effect (e.g., the intervention will harm students learning). To account for effects of one goal on another related goal (e.g., if one of the effects of G4, providing easy tasks is to enhance G5, having fun), included the effects of the second goal (e.g., + fun = -1 + 1 + 1 - 1) while discounting them by 0.5 (since they constitute an indirect effect). Table 2 provides an overview of the effects we identified for each goal and of their impact factor. We note that the calculus in Table 2 can be used as a guideline: more crucial than the actual impact factors is the consideration of the specific effects of achieving goals and the interactions among multiple goals.

Based on these impact factors we update the goal hierarchy: after robust learning (G1) and performance on standardized tests (G2), classroom management (G3) is the next-most important goal, followed by easy tasks (G4), and fun (G5).

Conflicts between design recommendations

We will now turn to mapping out the conflicts that arise from competing goals and from the resulting instructional design recommendations described in the previous section. To identify these conflicts, we recommend to conduct focus groups with learning sciences experts who have in-depth knowledge of the empirical research on the various design recommendations. Table 1 summarizes the conflicts we identified based on this method for the Fractions Tutor.

A number of conflicts arise between the various instructional design recommendations that address the goal to promote the learning of robust domain knowledge (G1), and with teachers' requirements to enhance students' performance on standardized assessments (G2). The need to perform well on standardized assessments does not always dictate approaches that compete with deep learning – but when such conflicts do arise, they are not trivial, and being aware of them is crucial. One such *conflict C2a* exists between the goal to promote the learning of robust domain knowledge (G1) through practice with a variety of problem formats (id2) and the goal to enhance students' performance on standardized tests (G2) through practice with problem formats that are structurally similar to the target problems (i.e., standardized test items, to the extent they are known, id9). Another *conflict C2b* exists between the recommendation promote robust learning (G1) to practice a variety of different strategies (id3), and to enhance students' performance on standardized tests (G2) through practice of one strategy that is most likely to always lead to the correct answer (id10).

Conflicts also arise between design recommendations that address the same goal. One such *conflict C1* exists within the goal to promote robust learning (G1) by providing holistic and complex problems (id8) or by using subgoaling to break the problem up into small steps (id4).

Further conflicts can arise from constraints within schools and students' abilities. For example, before the background of students' poor reading ability, *conflict C3* occurs between the goal to promote robust learning (G1) by providing complex real-world problems with cover stories (id4) and teachers' needs to facilitate classroom management (G3) by providing an easy-to-use system (id12): In our own classroom studies, we found that teachers were busy helping students understand problem statements which were lengthy due to the realistic cover stories the tutoring system provided.

Finally, conflicts arise between design recommendations on how to promote robust learning (G1) and students' emotional and cognitive needs. One such *conflict C4* results from promoting robust learning (G1) through the use of abstract language that applies to a variety of situations (id6) and students' need for easy problems (G4) through the use of intuitive language that uses concrete examples (id11). Another *conflict C5* exists between students' preference for flashy designs recommend the inclusion of game-like elements whose main purpose is to visually appeal to young students (id14), and the use of lean designs so as to not distract the user from the learning task, and that use colorful highlighting only sparingly to emphasize conceptually relevant aspects (id7).

RESOLVING CONFLICTS

In the following, we provide a principled process to address the conflicts we identified. In doing so, we describe three approaches: (1) resolve conflicts based on the goal hierarchy where possible, (2) conduct parametric experiments, and (3) conduct cross-iteration studies. Although we present these three approaches as a sequence, they complement each other. Crucial to the success of the conflict resolution is the careful evaluation of design solutions based on lab studies and classroom evaluations. In this sense, conflict resolution is most likely to occur as part of stage 5 in the Cognitive Tutor design process described above.

Resolving Conflicts Based on the Goal Hierarchy

First, we use the goal hierarchy to resolve some of the conflicts we previously identified. Conflict C2a exists between the goal to promote robust learning (G1) and the goal to promote performance on standardized tests (G2) (i.e., practice with a variety of problem formats (id2) versus practice with problem formats that are structurally similar to the target problems (id9)). Both goals are important, but we prioritize the goal to promote robust learning (G1). We thus recommend to practice with a variety of formats (id2), rather than to practice with only the problem format that is structurally equivalent to the test format (id9). However, practice items that structurally correspond to the test format should also be included in the variety of practice items.

A similar conflict C2b exists between the goal to promote robust learning (G1) and to promote performance on standardized tests (G2) (practice a variety of different strategies (id3) versus practice of one strategy that is most likely to always lead to the correct answer (id10)). Here again, we recommend giving larger weight to robust learning (G1) and practice of a variety of strategies (id3) than to practicing only one strategy (id10). However, even while practicing a variety of strategies, we can prioritize one strategy, especially when using mastery learning within Cognitive Tutors. Mastery learning employs a Bayesian decision process to decide whether students should continue solving problems to practice the target problem-solving strategy, based on the probability that the student has learned that knowledge [13]. This process can be used to ensure that all students master at least one strategy while also being exposed to multiple strategies.

Another conflict C5 is between robust learning (G1) and students' goal to have fun (G5) (i.e., inclusion of game-like, colorful elements whose main purpose is to visually appeal young students (id14) versus lean designs that use colorful highlighting to emphasize conceptually relevant aspects (id7)). Given that our goal hierarchy places the highest priority on supporting robust learning (G1), whereas the whereas the goal to have fun (G6) has lowest priority, it is clear that we should prioritize on employing color-based highlighting only conceptually relevant aspects. However, we can do so in a way that is visually appealing to students of our target age group. Further, we can integrate flashy and exciting elements where (or when) they do not distract, for instance, at the end of a practice problem.

Figure 1 illustrates several key aspects of the solution we chose for the Fractions Tutor. First, our choice in color reflects the finding that students in grades 4 and 5 have a preference for less intense colors with lower saturation and hue, compared to younger students [32-33]. We also made sure the colors we selected are gender neutral [33]. Second, in the service of using color to emphasize only conceptually relevant aspects, we use orange to highlight key words in each problem step. Finally, Figures 1 and 2 show a success message that we display at the end of a problem. The message contains a short movie clip that flies in.

Across different problems, we provide a variety of different success messages. Data from a survey that 429 students filled out after working with the Fractions Tutor shows that students found it visually appealing. To the question whether they liked the layout and color choice of the interface, 61% of students responded "Yes, a lot!", 28% responded "I don't care," and only 12% responded "No, not at all!" The difference between these response options was statistically significant, χ^2 (2, N = 429) = 236.86, $p < .001$.

Parametric Experiments to Resolve Conflicts

Conflicts that cannot be resolved based on the goal hierarchy require more careful inspection. We recommend conducting parametric experiments using multiple metrics to address important remaining conflicts. These studies can be carried out as part of stage 5 in the design process described earlier. We addressed conflict C1 between holistic problems and subgoaling as part of a parametric experiment.

As mentioned, the subgoaling strategy (illustrated in Figure 1) breaks up problems into their substeps, in order to communicate the problem's goal structure [29]. However, our surveys show that students tend to dislike multi-step problems. In a survey following an early classroom study in which 311 students worked with the Fractions Tutor, a student commented, for instance: "A suggestions i would make is stop the repeating and give more fun stuff because i heard from people even me not to be mean but most of it ws boring sorry." Another student said: "in my opinion that there were too many questions in one problem!!"

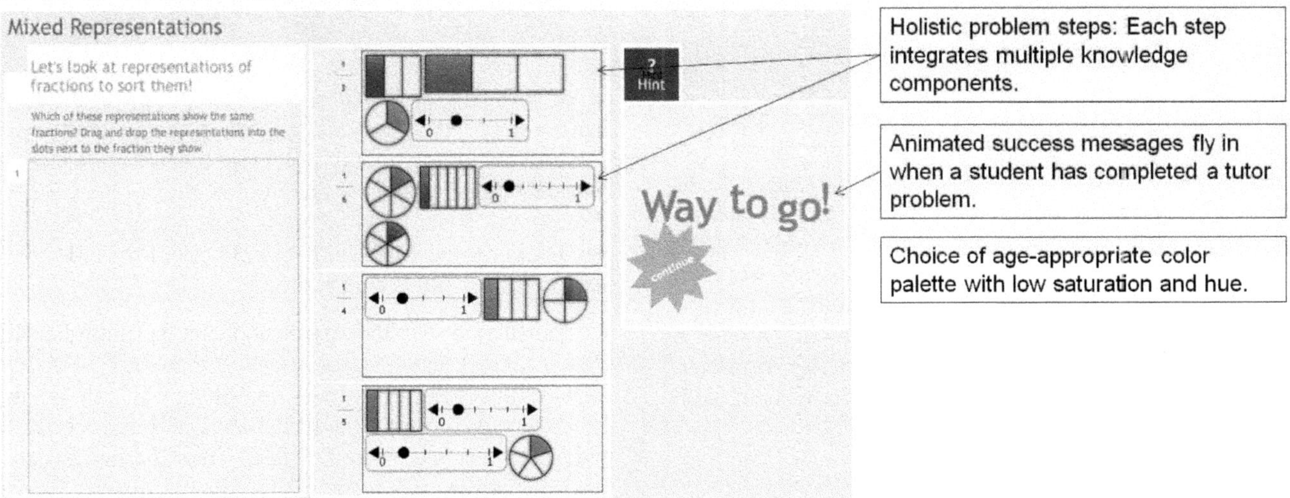

Figure 2. Example Problem in the Fractions Tutor that Employs a Holistic Approach.

Having many steps within a problem seems to overwhelm students. For example, a student reported: "I think there was too many questions." To address this issue, we decided to investigate whether we can enhance students' learning by decreasing the grain-size at which we support their problem solving. In an experimental study that we conducted with 599 students, we investigated the impact of the proportion of tutor problems with subgoaling to those with holistic problems on students' learning and on their enjoyment of the Fractions Tutor. Specifically, we compared versions of the Fractions Tutor in which 100%, 75%, or 50% of practice problems employed the subgoaling strategy (AllSubgoal vs. 75Subgoal vs. 50Subgoal).

Students first took a pretest, then worked with the Fractions Tutor for a total of 10 hours, then took an immediate posttest. One week after the immediate posttest, students took a delayed posttest. The tests comprised test items that assessed students' learning of the content covered in the Fractions Tutor, and their ability to transfer that knowledge to new task types. All tests were equivalent (i.e., they contained the same type of test items, but not identical test items). Students who completed all tests, and who completed their work on the tutoring system were included in the analysis, yielding a total of $N = 428$. The number of students who were excluded from the analysis did not differ between conditions, χ^2 (6, N = 169) = 4.34, $p > .10$. A repeated measures ANCOVA with pretest as covariate, immediate posttest, and delayed posttest as dependent mea sures and condition as independent factor showed a marginally statistically significant main effect for condition, $F(2, 424) = 2.74$, $p = .06$. Figure 3 depicts students' scores on the immediate posttest by condition. Post-hoc comparisons showed that students who worked with the AllSubgoal or the 75Subgoal versions of the Fractions Tutor significantly outperformed students who worked with the 50Subgoal version (*ps* < .05). There were no statistically significant differences between the AllSubgoal version and the 75Subgoal version ($p = .13$). Results from our survey showed that while 53% of the students reported that they liked the tutor problems with subgoaling, 77% of the students reported that they liked the tutor problems without subgoaling.

Taken together, results from the parametric experiment demonstrate that by including some holistic problems, we could improve students' enjoyment while working with the Fractions Tutor without harming their learning gains. Holistic problems may be more engaging as they resemble real-life tasks which are complex in nature [7]. Further, we identified what proportion of problems can use a holistic approach without harming students' learning: 50% of holistic problems impedes students' learning, as Figure 3 illustrates. However, 25% of problems can take a holistic approach, without hampering learning.

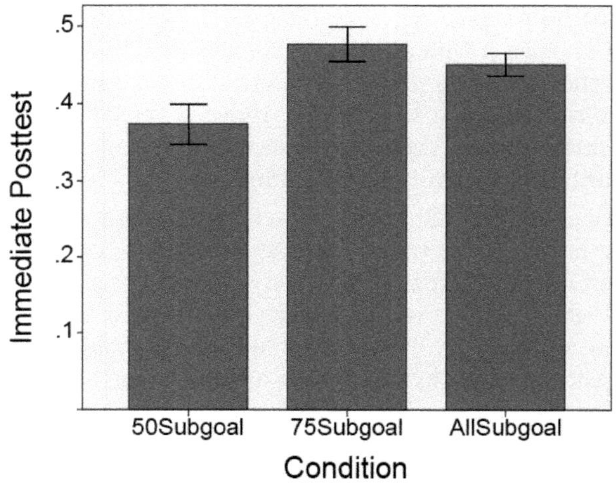

Figure 3. Students' posttest scores by condition.

Cross-Iteration Studies to Resolve Conflicts

Unfortunately, it is not possible to conduct a controlled experiment for every design decision. In this case, we recommend that developers conduct cross-iteration studies. We addressed conflict C3 between the goal to promote robust learning (G1) by providing complex real-world problems with cover stories (id4) and the goal to facilitate classroom management (G3) by providing an easy-to-use system (id12) based on the effects of the design decision across several iterations of the Fractions Tutor.

Initially, we resolved conflict C3 based on our goal hierarchy, which prioritizes robust learning. However, when employing a version of the Fractions Tutor that included cover stories in classrooms, we faced challenging issues. Students complained about having to read a lot, and teachers expressed their concern about being able to use the ILE in their classrooms without extra help. Several teachers suggested including an audio function, so that students could listen to the problem statement via headphones. However, since many schools lack the necessary equipment (i.e., headphones), we discarded that idea. Instead, we decided to exclude cover stories from the Fractions Tutor. However, in a subsequent classroom study, our classroom observations demonstrated that students had trouble making sense of the rather abstract problems in the tutor. An anonymous survey with 331 students revealed that students thought the problems were too hard and that they were not fun. One student commented, for instance: "I don't like how the problem didn't give clear, vivid questions. It confused the way I was taught." Several students commented on the ILE being boring, for instance: "it was good but it got boring at times."

We thus included introductory problems that introduced the graphical representations used in the Fractions Tutor based on realistic cover stories (e.g., describing circle diagrams in the context of pizza). Our next round of classroom testing with a new version of the Fractions Tutor did not reveal any persisting issues with reading levels or the abstract language our system uses. An anonymous survey with 429 students revealed generally positive comments. One student responded, for example: "fractions tutor is a really good learning program.the reason i like it was because it wasnt too hard and wasnt too easy. it was just right for me.also i learn alot just from this." Many students reported that they had fun with the tutor, for example: "i like about it is fun it makes people smart it was a lot fun."

These cross-iteration changes to the Fractions Tutor illustrate that in cases where design choice based on the goal hierarchy proves to be impractical, several iterations may be necessary to find a balance between the disadvantage of the desired design choice, and alternative solutions. By carefully monitoring the effect of each design choice, we believe that the combination of cover stories in introductory problems and less reading-intensive, abstract problems is an effective and practical solution for the young population the Fractions Tutor is designed for.

CONCLUSION

This paper presents a principled, multi-method approach to resolving the conflicts that inevitably arise between competing design goals in complex educational settings. We provide empirical evidence that our approach lead to the development of a successful ILE which not only significantly improves students' learning, but which both students and teachers find easy and enjoyable to use.

Although at times, design decisions are situational, highly contextualized and occur under the pressure of deadlines and therefore are bound to be (to some extent) arbitrary, our approach addresses the common scenario in which developers of ILEs need to rely on ad-hoc methods to resolve conflicts between conflicting goals of multiple stakeholders. We combine focus groups and affinity diagramming to develop a goal hierarchy, parametric experiments, and cross-iteration studies, thereby extending existing instructional design processes by integrating methods from multiple disciplines. Specifically, we use a goal hierarchy to resolve conflicts, in combination with parametric experiments and cross-iteration studies.

Although we developed and evaluated our approach within the context of a Cognitive Tutor, a specific type of ILE that is widely used across 3,000 schools in the United States, we are confident that our approach will generalize to other types of ILEs. For instance, MIT's edX system, an open-source learning technology, which makes course materials at the college level accessible online, faces unique design challenges due to the learners' contexts and goals: they may be students from around the world using the system for exam preparation, or teachers who access the system in order to fulfill their continued education requirement. Conflicts might exist between the users' goal to relate the learning content to specific contexts, such as for an engineering project (if the user is a college student majoring in engineering), or for a high-school classroom (if the user is a teacher). Addressing these goals is difficult because tailoring the content to these different interest groups would result in having highly specific content that is not at the same time relevant to all interest groups. Yet, MIT has an interest in the edX system being widely used across different groups of users. In applying our approach to create a goal hierarchy for different types of users, in conducting parametric experiments and cross-iteration studies, trade-offs such as the one just described can be explicitly identified and addressed.

The scenario with edX illustrates that the approach we describe in this paper might serve as a framework to stimulate future research on ILE development, not only to improve specific ILEs, but also to evaluate and further extend the presented approach. Only with a well-researched and principled approach to incorporating multiple (and, as described, often conflicting) stakeholders' goals can we have it all: popular, usable, and effective ILEs.

ACKNOWLEDGMENTS

This work is supported by the National Science Foundation, REESE-21851-1-1121307. We thank Ken Koedinger, Mitchell Nathan, Kathy Cramer, Peg Smith, Jay Raspat, Michael Ringenberg, Brian Junker, Howard Seltman, Cassandra Studer, the students, teachers, and principals, the CTAT and the Datashop teams.

REFERENCES

1. Soloway, E., Jackson, S. L., Klein, J., Quintana, C., Reed, J., Spitulnik, J., Stratford, S. J., Studer, S., Eng, J. and Scala, N. *Learning theory in practice: Case studies of learner-centered design.* In *Proc. CHI '96,* ACM Press, (1996).
2. Design-based research collective. An emerging paradigm for educational inquiry. *Educational Researcher, 32*, 1 (2003), 5-8.
3. Bereiter, C. and Scardamalia, M. Learning to work creatively with knowledge. In E. de Corte (Ed.), *Powerful learning environment*, (2003).
4. Jackson, S., Krajcik, J. S. and Soloway, E. The design of guided learner-adaptable scaffolding in interactive learning environments. In *Proc. CHI '98,* ACM Press, (1998).
5. Koedinger, K. R. *Toward evidence for instructional design principles: Examples from Cognitive Tutor Math 6.* In *Proc. PME/NA XXXII* (2002).
6. Mayer, R. E. The promise of multimedia learning: Using the same instructional design methods across different media. *Learning and Instruction*, 13, 2 (2003), 125-139.
7. van Merrienboer, J. J. G., Clark, R. E. and de Croock, M. B. M Blueprints for complex learning: The 4C/ID-model. *Educational Technology Research and Development*, 50, 2 (2002), 39-64.
8. Koedinger, K. and Corbett, A. *Cognitive Tutors: Technology bringing learning science to the classroom.* Cambridge University Press, 2006.
9. Corbett, A. and Anderson, J. Locus of feedback control in computer-based tutoring: Impact on learning rate, achievement and attitudes. In *Proc CHI 2001,* ACM Press, (2001).

10. Corbett, A. and Trask, H. Instructional interventions in computer-based tutoring: Differential impact on learning time and accuracy. In *Proc CHI 2000,* ACM Press, (2000).

11. Corbett, A. T., Koedinger, K. and Hadley, W. S. *Cognitive tutors: From the research classroom to all classrooms.* Lawrence Erlbaum Associates, 2001.

12. VanLehn, K. The relative effectiveness of human tutoring, intelligent tutoring systems and other tutoring systems. *Educational Psychologist, 46*, 4 (2011), 197-221.

13. Corbett, A., Koedinger, K. R. and Anderson, J. R. *Intelligent tutoring systems*. Elsevier Science Publishers, 1997.

14. Rau, M. A., Aleven, V., Rummel, N., Rohrbach, S. Sense Making Alone Doesn't Do It: Fluency Matters Too! ITS Support for Robust Learning with Multiple Representations. In *Proc ITS 2012,* Springer, (2012).

15. Ogan, A., Aleven, V. and Jones, C. Pause, predict, and ponder: Use of narrative videos to improve cultural discussion and learning. In *Proc CHI 2008,* ACM Press, (2008).

16. Corbett, A., Kauffman, L., MacLaren, B., Wagner, A. and Jones, E. A cognitive tutor for genetics problem solving: Learning gains and student modeling. *Journal of Educational Computing Research*, *42*, 2 (2010), 219-239.

17. Ritter, S., Anderson, J. R., Koedinger, K. R. and Corbett, A. T. Cognitive Tutor: Applied research in mathematics education. *Psychonomic Bulletin & Review*, *14*, 2 (2007), 249-255.

18. Siegler, R. S., Carpenter, T., Fennell, F., Geary, D., Lewis, J., Okamoto, Y., Thompson, L. and Wray, J. *Developing effective fractions instruction: A practice guide*. U.S. Department of Education, 2010.

19. NMAP. *Foundations for Success: Report of the National Mathematics Advisory Board Panel*. U.S. Government Printing Office, 2008.

20. NCTM *Principles and Standards for School Mathematics*. National Council of Teachers of Mathematics, 2000.

21. Schraagen, J. M., Chipman, S. F. and Shalin, V. L. *Cognitive Task Analysis*. Erlbaum Associates, 2000.

22. Baker, R. S. J. d., Corbett, A. T. and Koedinger, K. R. The difficulty factors approach to the design of lessons in intelligent tutor curricula. *International Journal of Artificial Intelligence in Education*, *17*, 4 (2007), 341-369.

23. Aleven, V., McLaren, B. M., Sewall, J., & Koedinger, K. R. Example-tracing tutors: A new paradigm for intelligent tutoring systems. *International Journal of Artificial Intelligence in Education, 19*, 2, (2009), 105-154.

24. Charalambous, C. Y. and Pitta-Pantazi, D. Drawing on a Theoretical Model to Study Students' Understandings of Fractions. *Educational Studies in Mathematics*, *64*, 3 (2007), 293-316.

25. Beyer, H., & Holtzblatt, K. *Contextual Design: Defining Customer-Centered Systems*. Morgan Kaufmann, 1998.

26. Große, C. S. and Renkl, A. Effects of multiple solution methods in mathematics learning. *Learning and Instruction*, *16* (2006), 122-138.

27. Yang, D.-C. and Reys, R. E. One fraction problem, many solution paths. *Mathematics Teaching in the Middle School*, *7*, 3 (2001), 164-166.

28. Reed, J. A structure-mapping model for word problems. *Journal of Experimental Psychology: Learning, Memory, and Cognition*, *13* (1987), 124-139.

29. Thußbas, C. Beeinflussen Cover Stories mathematischer Texaufgaben analogen Transfer in der Mathematik? *Zeitschrift für Experimentelle Psychologie*, *48*, 4 (2001), 272-289.

30. Catrambone, R. and Holyoak, K. J. Learning and subgoals and methods for solving probability problems. *Memory & Cognition*, *18* (1998), 593-603.

31. Thorndike, E. L. *The psychology of arithmetic*. Macmillan, 1922.

32. Pett, D. and Wilson, T. Color research and its application to the design of instructional materials. *Educational Technology Research and Development*, *44*, 3 (1996), 19-35.

33. Jakobsdottir, S., Krey, C. L. and Sales, G. C. Computer graphics: Preferences by gender in grades 2, 4, and 6. *Journal of Educational Research*, *88*, 2 (1994), 91-100.

Electric Materialities and Interactive Technology

James Pierce, Eric Paulos
Human-Computer Interaction Institute, Carnegie Mellon
5000 Forbes Avenue, Pittsburgh, PA, USA
jjpierce@cs.cmu.edu

ABSTRACT

This paper offers new theoretical and design insights into interactive technology. By initially considering electric technology broadly, our work informs how HCI approaches a range of specific interactive or digital things and materials. Theoretically, we contribute a rigorous analysis of electric technology using the experiential lens of phenomenology. A major result is to characterize electric technology by three forms of materiality: the electric object, its electric materiality, and electric power. In terms of design, we present and analyze novel interactive form prototypes. Our theoretical contributions offer new insight into design artifacts, just as our novel design artifacts help reveal new theoretical insight.

Author Keywords

Design theory; interaction design; electricity

ACM Classification Keywords

H.5.m

INTRODUCTION

HCI is concerned with a wide array of technologies, ranging from common electrical appliances to the latest electronic hardware and software. These technologies have been described as digital materials [31], interactive materials "without qualities" [20], computational composites [32] and generally as design materials [10,28]. Indicative of these works is a recent and substantial interest in HCI with understanding technology through a focus on "materiality". Concerns with interactive materials [e.g.,1,11,12,18,19,27,28] have been referred to as a "material move" [7] or "material turn" [29] in interaction design. A related cluster of work has investigated the material qualities of old and new technologies to inform HCI research, often focusing on differences between high-tech and traditional things [e.g.,8,30]. Instead of focusing on design materials, these works emphasize the materiality of technological things as they are used and incorporated into everyday contexts and practices. Outside of HCI, fields as diverse as new media studies, critical theory, philosophy and anthropology have looked at technologies from digital media [e.g.,21] to artifacts in general [e.g.,13,16]. However we note a lack of such theory that focuses on the materiality of interactive technologies and in a way that speaks to particular concerns of HCI.

However one might end up characterizing the technologies that HCI is primarily concerned with, there is a distinct element that precedes and underlies all such technologies: electricity. In order to advance theoretical understandings of the materiality of technological things, and the possibilities and limits of technology as a material in design, we begin with the basic notion of *electric technology*. One important theoretical result of our work is to characterize electric technology in terms of three forms of materiality: an *electric object*, its *electric materiality*, and *electric power*. To arrive at such new theoretical framings we draw on phenomenology, a form of inquiry that investigates subjective experience. The other main component of our approach involves "research through design" [e.g.,2,9,34]. In addition to analyzing *ordinary* electric technologies, we present and discuss new design prototypes that focus on an *uncommon* technology: bodily-powered electric technology.

While environmental sustainability has occupied a central position in prior energy and materiality research in HCI [e.g., 1,27]—including in our own work—here we largely sideline sustainability discussions. This move allows us to rigorously investigate electric technology independent of any one particular issue. However, concerns with sustainability and emerging energy systems [25] form an implicit backdrop for this work and an explicit point of engagement for future applications and extensions.

The contribution of this paper is threefold. First we develop new theoretical understandings of electric technology. Second, we concretely demonstrate how these understandings can inform design-oriented research. Third, we demonstrate how designing and building technology can "talk back" and inform theory. Following a discussion of methodology, the paper has 4 sections that correspond to (1) theoretical description, (2) design exploration, (3) design spaces/strategies and (4) general discussion.

METHODOLOGY

Our approach involves doing both design and phenomenology. There three main reasons we have combined phenomenology and design. First, phenomenology helps us articulate and make sense of our

Figure 1. Form studies in bodily-generated LED illumination: (Left to right) Tap LED, Crank LED, Spin LED and Drop LED. The interactions of tapping a surface, cranking a wheel, spinning a flywheel and dropping a weight generate electric power that illuminates an LED. (Note: Each prototype depicted is functional; a selective black and white filter has been applied to the images for emphasis.)

design work. This includes particular designs as well as more general design spaces. While theory can be useful for inspiring and generating design—as we have found—it is its value in articulating and making sense of design artifacts that we propose as potentially more applicable and valuable for the HCI community. As others have argued [e.g., 2,9,34], we believe design research can stand on its own without relying on theory from other fields. Nonetheless, we find that such theory can play a vital role by articulating new insight about design outcomes and processes [c.f. 1,4,6,10,11,12,20,26,27,32]. One idea this suggests to us is a type of annotated portfolio [2,9] with *phenomenological annotations* or other theoretically-informed annotations.

Second, we find a general lack of theory that helps us make sense of both our own design work and the design of electric technology in general. Specifically we identify a lack of detailed phenomenological accounts of electric technology with a focus on materiality [c.f. 10,16,26]. Consequently we found a need to generate theory by building on prior work outside of HCI. More generally we believe HCI theory should seek to identify and address such theoretical gaps in research originating outside of our field.

Finally, our design work helps us advance our phenomenological inquiry. Designing and building novel electric things has highlighted gaps in our analysis and surfaced new theoretical insight. More generally, we believe that the exemplars created by design-oriented research can be used in *building theory*—regardless of whether the designers intended to inform theory or whether theory informed their design.

Approaching electric technology phenomenologically

Phenomenology has been described as a "style of thinking which concentrates an intense examination on experience in its multifaceted, complex and essential forms" [15, p. 17]. Phenomenology has appeared across several areas of HCI research [e.g., 3,5,10,26,35], and coincides with the so-called "third wave" HCI shift toward "experience". Our inquiry will begin with a *phenomenological description* of experiential features of ordinary electric technology (ordinary in the sense of familiar and common to everyday practices). The phenomenological style adopted here is based closely on the work of Don Ihde [15,16,17] and in turn the foundational works of Edmund Husserl [14] and Martin Heidegger [13]. Our style of analysis is aligned with what Ihde describes as a Husserlian-style phenomenology of *presence* [15]. (Although our work also reflects a concern with *praxis* and the "background" of experience, following Heidegger as well as Ihde, again, in this regard.) A fundamental aspect of this approach is to "attend to the phenomena of experience as they appear" [17, p. 34]. This excludes attending to *explanations* of phenomena, including both scientific and everyday explanations. A related rule is to *describe rather than explain* the phenomena.

A phenomenology of electric technology is faced from the outset with a dilemma regarding electricity as both a scientific and everyday explanation. Initially we "put out of play" or *bracket*, in Husserlian terms, electricity as a concept. As we will see, things commonly identified as "electric" exhibit forms of *activeness*. Further, we come to encounter a *source* that enables this activeness, which we ordinarily refer to as "power" or "electricity". These phenomena, which appear within experience, are taken as more primary than explanations of electricity.

Another key feature of the approach is a *variational method* for investigating phenomena, first introduced by Husserl. This involves obtaining many *variations*, or examples, of phenomena to arrive at *invariant,* or *essential,* features of experience. A mathematician by training, Husserl favored the use of fantasy or *imaginative variations.* Ihde's approach favors the use of *perceptual variations*. The use of perceptual variations leads to an empirical phenomenology in the sense that it is grounded in actual observed and hence *fulfillable experience* [15]. Stylistically we use the written form "One can _____" to indicate an experience that has actually occurred for the authors. For example, "One can make these words appear on the computer screen."

Design Form Explorations / Designed Variations

In the later sections of the paper we present prototypes that focus on bodily-powered electric generation (e.g., Figure 1). These have been refined and carefully selected from a much larger set of concepts and forms we have constructed with varying degrees of fidelity. The main goal of our prototypes is to explore specific interactive forms separated from specific applications, uses or practices [c.f. 3,11,19], rather than addressing more holistic concerns such as user needs and desires. Here we do not formally present the prototypes to others. While user studies are often considered the norm in HCI, a range of prior works have argued and demonstrated other methods of analyzing and reflecting on designs [e.g.,1,3,10,11,12,22, 27].

Here we present a phenomenologically-informed analysis of our prototypes. There are several reasons why have chosen this type of analysis. The primary purpose of our prototypes is to explore, identify and illustrate possibilities that we are able to confirm based on our own experiences. We do not make strong empirical claims about aspects such as routine use, appropriation, usefulness or desirability. We will be mainly concerned with understanding basic perceptual and interactive elements of bodily-powered electric technology. In this way, our work is similar to prior explorations of interactive design materials that do not rely on traditional user studies [e.g.,1,3,10,11].

While our analysis is based on our actual experience, it is not a strict phenomenology. Further, our use of *designed variations* straddle the space between perceptual variations and imaginative variations. Stylistically, we indicate analysis that is partly imaginative by putting it in the form "One may ___". For example, one may be able to read this paper on a bodily-powered display..." (although neither of the authors has actually done so).

ORDINARY ELECTRIC TECHNOLOGY & EXPERIENCE

In this first part of our inquiry we analyze everyday experience of electric technologies yielding a set of thematic features. Our analysis in the present section will serve as a foundation for identifying, understanding and intentionally amplifying differences between ordinary and bodily-powered technologies.

Electric Objects, Materialities and Sources of Power

Let us begin by taking account of the electric things that surround us. Within our ordinary experience (although only within the last century) electricity and electric technology have become familiar notions. As I walk into a room or down the street I can readily identify a diverse range of everyday material objects as "electric"—the laptop computer, the radio, the ceiling fan, the streetlight, and so on. What is it that distinguishes these from other objects?

The laptop, the radio, the ceiling fan and the streetlight are, to begin with, objects. These objects present themselves to as stable material objects and as useful, usable everyday things. However, these objects are each distinguished in that they become *activated* or *enlivened.* The radio sounds, the ceiling fan moves around, the streetlight illuminates and the laptop presents a multiplicity of moving and moveable media forms (music, video, text, voice, etc.). When these objects become activated, they present and make available material forms that were not previously present and available. When they are *deactivated* they hold the possibility of making these forms present and available.

The materialities they make available are in each case *active*: the ceiling fan moves, the light glows, the radio sounds and the laptop changes its imagery. However, this active materiality can exhibit different "distances" from the electric object. When looking at the spinning ceiling fan, one can see the fan's materiality that was once stationary as now active and moving. One can experience it as *activated materiality.* With a lamp, one can experience the illumination as *emanating from* the object. The illumination of the lamp can also be experienced as being *apart from* one's direct experience of the lamp—for example, when using its light to read.

The *activeness* of this materiality has a distinct temporality. The ceiling fan begins to spin when the wall switch is flipped and comes to a stop when it is switched off. The radio can similarly be controlled. The electronic music player can further be paused and later resumed. Even hallway safety lighting that is "always on" in the apartment building at some point ceases to be active—during a power outage, or when the bulb burns out. And even the momentary activeness of the television remote control has a distinct temporality both in its constant readiness to control the television and in its instantaneity of switching.

The activeness of this materiality is furthermore highly *controllable.* I can control the activeness of many everyday things around me. Those that are not directly within one's immediate control can still be experienced as capable of being controlled (e.g., the city streetlights have been programmed by "the city"). In each case, these forms can be *activated* and *deactivated.* And they can be reactivated again and again. One need only flip a switch to re-illuminate the light or make the fan spin at a regular, consistent speed.

There is a diverse range of *activated forms*: the mechanical movements of the ceiling fan, the sounds of the radio, the moving and illuminated imagery of the computer screen. (Although some are apparently absent: One does not activate smells or tastes in the same way.) There are also degrees and varieties of activeness. For example, a laptop may be actively downloading a file but without giving signs of activity. One can also identify or predict forms of activeness based on familiar forms. For example, one recognizes the activate-able display screen, even when it is inactive. One recognizes any object with a power cord or battery as activate-able.

It is this activeness that allows electric things to be used. It is only when active that one can utilize the illumination of the electric lamp, the moving and moveable graphic elements on the computer screen, and the cool breeze of the fan. However, this active materiality and usability can become *unavailable.* This occasionally yet familiarly occurs when one is unable to find a power outlet or a battery "dies". In this situation, the object can be encountered as unable to be activated. This inability to be activated can be attributed to a lack of power. It is in this way that electricity as electricity is typically encountered—as a source of power, as a thing that activates. *It is here, in its absence, that one most directly encounter* ***electricity as an entity****; and it is because of this entity one knows the radio, the laptop, the streetlight, and the ceiling fan as electric things.*

To summarize, we have identified several important ways in which electric technology can be experienced: the electric object, the electrified object, the electric materiality the object, the de-electrified object, the unable-to-be-electrified object, and the source that electrifies. More succinctly, it useful to characterize electric technology in terms of three forms of materiality:

(1) An **electric object** (a stable, physical object)
(2) The plural **electric materiality** of that object
(3) The sources that electrify (**electric power**)

In the remainder if this section we discuss additional thematic features of ordinary electric technology.

Outlets and Batteries: Tethering and Replenishing

The availability of ordinary electric materiality depends on connecting to a source of electric power. There are two basic ways this occurs. The first is through the power cord, power plug and power outlet (a connection to a larger system: a power grid). We refer to this as *tethering*, since it requires that an electric object be tied to a particular source. Electric objects are ordinarily tethered through a flexible cord or an inflexible fixture (e.g., a street light, ceiling fan). The second way of connecting to a power source is with a *battery*. An electric object can be tethered to a stand-alone battery, but typically it has an integrated battery. Batteries allow electric technologies to be electrified while *untethered.* However, a battery must periodically be *replenished* by tethering it, or else replacing it.

Tethering and replenishing are general and familiar features of ordinary experience. They are easily taken-for-granted, yet they have some important implications. Tethering and replenishing imply that an ordinary electric technology must, at least on occasion, be physically connected to something other than itself—either a power outlet (and a larger power grid) or a new battery (and a larger manufacturing system). This has two notable effects.

First, tethering and replenishing shape the temporal and spatial contexts in which electric materiality can be activated. Put another way, they give definition to *electrifiable space*. If a device is tethered, electrifiable space is limited to within proximity of a power outlet. If a device can be battery-powered, then this substantially expands electrifiable space. However, a battery-powered device must still periodically be tethered or replaced. The expanded electrifiable space that batteries create can disappear; it has temporal limits. The possibility of a device "dying" consequently can shape one's interactions with it.

Second, tethering and replenishing are two important ways in which electric things are distinguished from non-electric things. Plugging in to an electric power outlet and replacing batteries are clearly unique to electric things. But more significantly this form of dependency separates electric technology and electric materiality from many other everyday things. Books, bicycles, knives, reading glasses, tables and host of other everyday things can be used without the same type of routine dependency (although we omit a lengthier analysis more firmly locating differences in this form of dependency). This suggests that electric things that do not require tethering or replacing batteries may exist in ways more similar to traditional and other non-electric things, such as books and manual tools [c.f. 8,30]. Indeed, tethering and replenishing are not invariant, or essential, aspects of electric technology and electric materiality. While ordinary electric technologies are tethered or battery powered, it is technologically possible to activate electric technology by other sources, such as the sun; the human body (e.g., motion, blood sugar); ambient sound, heat, vibration; and wireless power technologies.

Electric Power as External to Self, Object and Context

While electricity tends to fall into the background of everyday experience, it nonetheless does routinely albeit infrequently present itself. Pierce and Paulos note several ways in which electricity can be become present [26]. While the notion of "external power" is commonly used in engineering, here we phenomenologically locate two ways in which the "externality" of electricity can be encountered: (1) as external to oneself and electric objects and (2) as external to the context of use and immediate environment.

Ordinary electric power can be experienced as external to oneself, to the electric object, and one's interaction with this object. One typically cannot generate a source of power to activate electric materiality. This is unlike the ways in which one can make a ball active by throwing it, or make a bicycle active by riding it, thus setting or keeping it in motion with one's body. One cannot transfer his or her bodily power to an electric object in order to electrify (activate) it. One also cannot *store-up* power as with the mechanical wristwatch that is wound. The appearance of ordinary power as external to oneself and to the object is not directly evident during use. But this externality does become evident when one is without an outlet or the battery "dies". In this situation one finds that he or she cannot power the device oneself.

Ordinary electric power can also be experienced as external to one's immediate environment and the context of use. A source of power typically cannot be located or generated within the room or building that one occupies. Often one further cannot see the technologies that generate power (an exception would be seeing a power plant in the distance). Again, this is not typically apparent when using an electrified object. However, when there is a power outage, then one can experience this externality. One can realize the source of power is not "here" but rather comes from "away".

However, these "externalities" are also not invariant features of electric technology. For example, the source of power for solar-powered calculators is typically not experienced as originating outside of the immediate environment. Rather, a source of power can be experienced as originating from the sunlight or from electric lighting in the room. If a source of power is encountered for a "self-winding" quartz electronic watch, this source may be experienced as originating "within" the device and the interaction between one's body and the watch. These examples suggest how one's relationship to the electric object, electric materiality and electric power can change depending on where a source of power is variously located or attributed. For example, solar-powered calculators and quartz watches may be seen as "perpetually activate-able" devices, since they do not require tethering or conscious replenishing. As such, an electric object that is less reliant on "external power" may exist more similarly to traditional technologies such as book, bicycles, and furniture.

Electric-Interactions

In this final section of our descriptive analysis of ordinary electric technology we focus on forms of interaction. We identify 4 basic types of electric-interaction: *plugging-in*, *switching-on*, *staying-on* and *directing-about*.

Staying-on

Typically, the activeness of electric objects can *stay on*. For example, the electric light stays illuminated. Someone may turn it off, or the bulb may fail, or it may lose power during a power outage, but typically it reliably and consistently stays illuminated. It remains active. The radio also remains active, although its sound varies, expectedly, over time. One can *step back* and *step away* from the radio and the electric lamp while each continues to be active. One can recognize a general form of staying-on with many electric things: the light is "on", the phone is "on", the laptop is "on". One can also note particular staying-ons: the laptop screen, the word processor, the text I am composing.

The mobile phone also stays on although it may not give signs of an active presence. One treats his or her mobile phone as active and recognizes it as "being on", yet it gives no signs of activity. It is not illuminated, sounding or vibrating, or even noticeably emitting heat. Yet it may suddenly become active and begin to illuminate, sound and vibrate when receiving a call. This staying-on is not a continuing to be perceivably active but rather a working in the background. This can be understood as an *inactive activeness*. More generally this is an example of a *background relation*, a "present absence" of technology [16]. We have thus identified two types of staying-on: staying-on as a continuing to be perceptually active and staying-on as continuing to be inactively active, in the background. We also noted a *general staying-on* and *particular staying-ons*.

Directing-about

The activeness of electric objects can variously be *directed-about*. For example, one can alter the illumination of a lamp by dimming or brightening it. Similarly one can adjust the radio volume or the speed of the ceiling fan. One can direct-about the activeness of the electric materiality. One can also, in the present moment, direct-about future activity. The alarm clock can be set to become active at a certain time. It is this form of directing-about that Hallnäs and Redström point toward when they write: "What characterises computational technology as a design material, then, are the temporal structures that are generated when programs are executed." [11, p.106].

One can also direct-about inactive activeness. One can put a mobile phone in a "silent mode" by pressing a physical button on the side of the object yet without activating an electric materiality that one can directly perceive. However, such interactions are uncommon. The careful use of feedback (often through LEDs) is employed in most interactive technologies specifically to avoid confusion that may arise when activating an inactive activeness.

The *directing* in the directing-about can originate from several sources: *I* can direct-about (I turn on light), *others* can direct-about (someone calls me and makes my phone ring, someone has programmed the street lights to go on at a certain time), *the device* can direct itself (the robotic vacuum acts on its own, the ATM makes requests, my alarm clock wakes me up), and *the environment* or *other things* can direct-about (my laptop screen automatically dims when the ambient light changes, the smoke detector is activated by smoke from the oven, a wireless router causes my laptop to try to connect). This source of direction is *multistable* with respect to use, context, and culture in the sense discussed by Ihde [16]. The ringing of the phone can be constituted as a person calling me, as my leaving the phone on (*I* forgot to turn it off), as a non-human other calling me (an automated voice message), or as the device itself ringing (*it* is bothering me). In passing, we note that the source of directing is related to perceptions of agency among human and non-human things (e.g., [33]).

Switching-on and plugging-in

There are many different ways of directing-about (adjusting brightness, transmitting data wirelessly, setting an alarm to sound in the future). Two basic and ubiquitous modes of directing-about are *switching-on* and *switching-off*. Many everyday electric technologies have a general mode of being switched-on and switched-off. Specific forms or degrees of being switched-on and -off also occur (e.g., powering off a laptop versus putting it in a low-power state so one can quickly activate it). When switching something off one can make it *stay-off*. Two other ubiquitous forms of interaction are connecting and disconnecting from a source of power. By plugging in the electric lamp one enables the possibilities for switching-on, staying-on, and directing-about; by unplugging it one can prevent these possibilities.

General implications and future analysis

Based on our analysis of electric-interactions we highlight two general points. First, staying-on is a familiar yet crucial aspect of most ordinary electric-interactions. A steady and consistent staying-on is the condition of possibility for many forms of directing-about. In passing, we note that instances of each of Ihde's 4 general human-technology relations [16] are often dependent on staying-on if the technology is electric. For example, if the technology does not continue to stay-on, then one cannot create holes *through* one's use the electric drill (an embodiment relation), read an article *with* the computer screen (a hermeneutic relation), relate *to* the otherness of the alarm clock upon waking (an alterity relation) or possess the feeling of security that one's alarm clock will sound at certain time (a background relation). As we will see, a host of interaction design challenges—as well as opportunities—emerge when electric technologies do not utilize external power from tethering or batteries. With bodily-powered technologies, for example, the forms of staying-on change drastically.

Second, directing-about/staying-on is precisely the juncture in our analysis where we begin to characterize interactions that are distinctly "electronic", "digital", "computational" and "interactive". Directing-about and staying-on are future points of departure for investigating various forms of electric-interaction and electric materialities. For example, future extensions of our analysis could investigate how "control", "transitions" and "states" in "computational composites" [31] emerge phenomenologically as forms of directing-about and staying-on. Similarly, future work could look at the various directing-abouts and staying-ons of accelerometers, RFID and wireless sensor networks as a design material [31].

Transition: From Ordinary to Uncommon Technologies

While our analysis may be valuable for explaining current interactions with electric technology, or as a foundation for critiquing technology, in the remainder of this paper we will focus on its value in expanding, refining, articulating and generally helping to make sense of a design space. Our approach will be to locate and intentionally amplify differences between ordinary and less common technologies. While such differences are evident across a range of new and emerging technologies, here we focus on bodily-powered electric technologies. In part, this is because it represents extreme variations, thus surfacing additional insight into ordinary technology. Bodily-powered generation also suggest interesting albeit relatively limited applications—from useful to provocative [e.g.,1,24,25,34].

BODILY-POWERED ELECTRIC TECHNOLOGY

Ordinary electric technologies are electrified via the plug and the outlet or the battery. However, electric technologies need not only be powered in this way. In the following sections we focus on one alternative: bodily-powered electric technology. Commonplace examples are rare, though two examples are hand-crank flashlights and dynamo powered bicycle lights. Generally we describe bodily-powered electric technology as consisting of: (1) A *bodily-powered electric object,* which involves an integrated mechanism for electrifying the device. (2) The object's *bodily-generated electric materiality.* (3) The *bodily-generated electric power* that electrifies the object, generated through an interaction between one's body and the power-generating mechanism.

Here we focus specifically on bodily-powered generation—as bodily-kinetic-generation—rather than human-powered electric technology more generally (thus excluding electric generation from human sound, heat, and metabolic energy) [24]. Importantly, we additionally focus on technologies that do not allow bodily-generated electric power to be *stored-up* using a battery or capacitor. Pierce and Paulos have previously introduced human-powered microgeneration [24], yet do not carefully articulate a distinction between directly powering and storing-up energy. Villar and Hodges notion of "interaction powered" electronics more clearly locates this distinction [34]. We further note there is a range of interesting variations in between, such as short-term mechanical storage with a flywheel or electric capacitors. We will look at such possibilities in the next section. Prior to this we extend our previous discussion by outlining three general ways in which bodily-powered technology differ from ordinary, externally powered technology. These will serve as themes of departure for our design studies.

1. Never without power (yet never externally powered). A bodily-powered electric technology can be activated without being tethered or without a battery. As such, it can *be* an electric object without possessing a power plug or a space to connect a battery (i.e., without possessing the possibilities for externally powering). It can also be mobile yet not "die" like a battery powered device in the sense that there is a source of power available via one's interaction it.

2. Power originating within the context of interaction. If the source of power is generated only via one's interaction with the technology and experienced as such, then one does not experience the power as external to the immediate context of use as can be the case with ordinary electric technology. Instead, one can experience this power as something able to be personally generated or created.

3. Demanding/inviting bodily exertion and involvement. If one must exert oneself bodily in order to power the technology, than one is not able to switch-on in order for the technology to stay-on as with ordinary electric technologies. Switching-on, staying-on and directing-about are instead directly dependent on bodily exertion.

INTERACTIVE FORM STUDIES IN BODILY-GENERATION

We now begin our move from phenomenologically describing current electric technology toward designing new technologies, interactions and experiences. We begin with 4 form studies in hand-generated electroluminescence.

Hand-generated LED-illumination

We focus on 4 form prototypes, each of which involves a single electrifiable element: a light-emitting diode (LED). Our functional form prototypes do not use batteries or capacitors to store-up power. Instead bodily-generated electricity is either directly materialized as light or else is momentarily stored up mechanically using a flywheel or the potential energy of a mass. The operation of each form prototype will become more apparent throughout our discussions, but we introduce each with a short description (see Figure 1, p. 2). **Tap LED** involves a piezo element to generate a momentary illumination via a tapping or pressing/depressing interaction (depending on the polarity). **Crank LED** involves a DC gear motor (100:1 ratio) to illuminate via a cranking or turning interaction. **Spin LED** involves a DC gear motor (30:1 ratio) to illuminate by spinning a disc, which acts as a flywheel. **Drop LED** involves a DC gear motor (100:1) connected to a pulley around which a string around which a hook is wound. Placing a weight on the hook causes the pulley to rotate and illuminate the LED. Each form prototype is constructed for easy disassembly into basic electrical/electronic components, power transmission components and housing/mounting components. This "transparency" highlights the lack of batteries, capacitors and power cords.

We present a focused selection of observations emerging from our form study exploration below.

Each form study object mediates different forms of LED-illumination. Differences in temporal forms of illumination are especially pronounced. The Drop LED materializes a sustained glow with a temporality defined by the length of the cord and the weight attached to it. The distance from the weight to the ground also creates a defined limit on the duration of the "drop glow". However, one can intervene with the falling weight by stopping it with one's hand, or pulling on the cord directly. When one spins the disc of the Spin LED, one generates a brightness that fades in concert with the slowing of the wheel. However, there is a pronounced speed at which the illumination suddenly ceases. One may also repeatability spin to generate a sustained glow. The Crank LED allows greater variation in the spatial and temporal form of illumination, allowing for continuous illumination at my discretion. Yet slight variations in brightness can be difficult to negate. A continuous glow is impossible with the Tap LED; a *blink* or *series of blinks* are the only fulfillable forms.

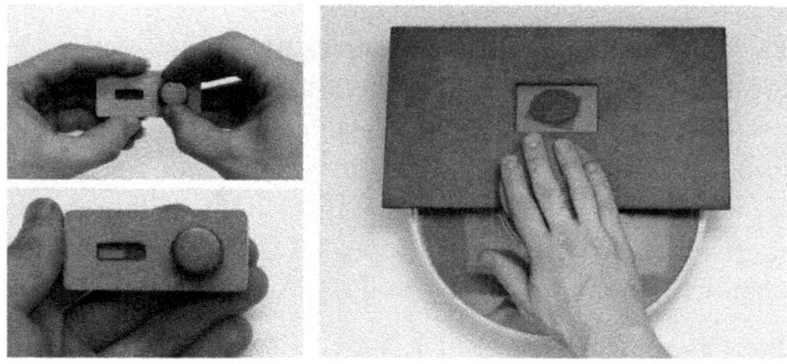

Figure 2. Form studies in bodily-generated displays. Turning the dial /motor (left) adjusts the e-paper display bar. Pushing (right) drives a screw mechanism that spins a flywheel, activating an OLED display.

Generalizing from these observations, we see that certain forms tend to emerge owing to the ways in which the form of generation mediates or affords certain forms of interaction. Some forms are facilitated and encouraged (e.g., a sustained glow from Dropping; a short, fading glow from Spinning), while other—possibly expected—forms are difficult or impossible to materialize (e.g., a sustained glow by Tapping, a rapid succession of blinks by Dropping).

There is a direct relationship between the form of electric generation in terms of my bodily involvement and the form of LED-illumination one generates, though this relationship varies across the form studies. In order for the Crank LED to become illuminated one must crank. One must exert oneself bodily, and moreover one must continue exerting myself in a way that is proportional to the illumination that is generated. Consider now the Drop LED. Again, one must exert oneself bodily in order to illuminate this object. In this case, one places a weight on the hook (and tugs on it) in order to set in motion to fall, generating a sustained and consistent glow. One may now stand back and watch the electrified object glow without one's direct involvement. However, one can still see, feel and hear the steady and continuous spinning of the gear motor and descending of the weight. After a short time, the weight reaches its limit and the LED ceases to glow. Finally, consider the Tap LED. The tapping or pressing motions that illuminate the LED are similar to the familiar and ubiquitous button-press interaction. However, in contrast to the button on a battery powered flashlight, tapping or pressing creates only a momentary illumination—a *blink*. There is no possibility here for a continuous, sustained glow.

Our form studies help us to see how and in what particular ways some forms of bodily-generation are better matched to certain forms of LED-illumination (and activation more generally) than to others. Tap, for example, is not well suited for a continual activation. Drop, on the other hand, is well suited for a sustained activation in which one may *step away*, yet is not well matched to a momentary activation.

Each form study object "stays-on" differently. With the Crank LED, the illumination does not persist without one's direct bodily involvement. One must generate and sustain its illumination. With the Tap LED, illumination also requires one's direct bodily involvement, but there is no possibility of generating a sustained, uninterrupted glow. With the Drop LED, the LED may stay illuminated but only for duration of time defined by the length of the cord and the distance to the ground. Repeated illumination is further dependent on one re-raising and re-dropping the weight.

The Crank LED, Spin LED and Drop LED suggest a continuum of staying-on in terms of my bodily exertion and involvement. The Crank LED requires direct exertion to *constantly maintain* its activeness; the Spin LED allows one to exert and then *step back* while the LED continues to be illuminated; and the Drop LED allows one to further *step away* from the active LED. An LED light that uses a battery or outlet for power allows for an even more prolonged staying-on independent of my bodily involvement. The extreme ideal case in the trajectory is the Perpetually-Illuminated LED (similarly as impossible as the coveted perpetual motion machine).

A Look at Bodily-powered Electric Visual Displays

We now briefly extend our explorations in LED illumination to more complicated electric displays. Here we consider two types of low-power display technologies: OLED and electronic paper (e-paper). Based on our prototypes discussed previously, it should be easier to now imagine variations such as a Drop OLED Display, Spin LCD Display and Tap E-Paper Display. We present two additional form prototypes, which introduce two new forms of generation: **Push-to-spin OLED Display** and **Turn E-Paper Display.** (See Figure 2 for a description of each). In contrast to our previous prototypes, these two form studies do not actually generate power to activate the displays. However, they do require an amount of bodily exertion comparable to the power requirements for each display. We restrict our discussion to two important areas.

Display stability

The temporal stability of the OLED-activated imagery is dependent on its continually being electrified. In contrast, the e-paper displays used in our prototypes do not require electrical power in order to remain visually stable. Electronic paper may thus have a "staying-on" that may not be experienced as an active staying-on. The directing-about that occurs is a momentary switching. Thus, momentary interactions such as Tap, Press, and Turn may activate a change in the display. In contrast, a bodily-powered OLED display must be continually powered to continue displaying. E-paper is a very unique electric technology owing to its display stability, relative to ordinary electric displays.

Display involvement

A primary function of visual electronic displays is to be seen and read. Reading a bodily powered display, however, requires bodily exertion to activate the display (e.g., Tapping, Dropping, Cranking). Consider three general ways this may be experienced. (1) Activating the display may be experienced as *effortful*. For example, pushing the OLED display may be tiring and distract one from my viewing imagery being displayed. (2) Activating the display may be experienced as *effortless*. For example, turning the knob on the Turn E-Paper Display may be experienced similar to many common everyday interactions with various electric switches and dials. One may forget, or never even realize, that one's bodily exertion is actively powering the directing-about of the display. (3) Activating the display may be experienced as *engaging*. The Push-to-Spin Display may be initially experienced as a fun surprise. If it is not experienced as effortful, the demand for bodily exertion may encourage one to engage with the video, rather than walking away. (The distinction between engagement and effort owes to Verbeek [33]. Here we introduce "effortless" as an additional form of involvement.)

BODILY-GENERATION DESIGN SPACES/STRATEGIES

We now expand outward to reflect on our forms studies in relation to general structural differences between ordinary and bodily-powered electric technologies. We present three design spaces for bodily-powered technology.

Expanding Electrifiable Space

Bodily-powered electric technologies may *enable new and less common contexts for electric-interactions to occur, for electric materialities to be activated, and for electric technologies to "live"*. An important implication of bodily-powered technology is the potential for activation independent from the power grid and other sources "external" to the interaction between a human body and the technology. While power grids and batteries have created expansive electrifiable space, consider several ways of further expanding: Bodily-powered technology may (1) *live apart from the grid* (e.g., a bodily-powered display is left at a remote location such as campsite or mountain summit to communicate with future visitors), (2) *live for when the grid is unavailable* (e.g., a hand-crank flashlight is kept in the automobile for emergencies), (3) *live "off the grid" within the grid* (e.g., an activist/artist places an electric intervention in a public urban space where it can be continually electrified without utilizing municipal power infrastructure), and (4) *live to fill in pockets of space not electrified by the grid* (e.g., a paper map at a bus stop is replaced with a hand-powered interactive e-paper map). Bodily-powered technology may also (5) *live more similarly alongside non-electric things*. For example, digital photos of high sentimental value might be uploaded to a hand-powered photo locket, which is kept in a wooden box alongside paper letters, film photographs and other sentimental possessions. Decades later the photo locket may be removed and the images immediately materialized without having to locate an outlet or battery. In this sense, the hand-powered digital photo locket may live more similarly alongside the paper letters and photographs—spatially and temporally.

Engaging through Bodily Involvement

Bodily-powered electric technologies may *mediate new and less common forms of interaction through and with them*. If not experienced as effortful, they may be experienced as distinctly engaging. Bodily-powered technology is particularly interesting to explore in the context of "third-wave" HCI concerns such as slowness and reflection [e.g., 12,23]; intimacy, playful engagement, and provocation [e.g.,1]; and provenance, durability and heirloom qualities [23,30]. For example, consider the Crank Video prototype (Figure 3), one of several prototypes in a series we are currently developing around the theme of hand-captured and hand-instantiated digital media devices. Cranking in one direction allows for the recording of a digital video while cranking in the opposing direction plays back the video. The necessity for direct bodily involvement may, for example, help mediate a slower, more reflective capturing and viewing of video. Designed to connote sentimentality, the Crank Video prototype may mediate more engaging interactions through the act of hand-generating the displaying and capturing of video.

Forging Relationships to Electric Technology

Bodily-powered electric technologies may *mediate new and less common relationships to electric technology itself (including the electric object, its electric materialities, and the source of power)*. For example, consider again the Crank Video (Figure 3). One may relate to this electric object as more durable since it can be activated independent of outlets or batteries. One may also relate to the device as unique and special, as standing apart from ordinary battery/outlet powered things. Similarly, the bodily-powered aspects of the device may also affect one's relationship to the digital media (both the active video and its inactive electric storage). For example, one may relate to the video as special owing to the way it is generated.

SUMMARY OF DESIGN INSIGHTS AND IMPLICATIONS

Our form prototypes concretely highlight a range of interesting and useful forms of bodily-generation including Tap, Crank, Spin, Drop, Push-to-Spin and Turn. We further presented display stability and display involvement as two important considerations. E-paper was highlighted as a unique electric technology owing to its display stability (a no-power "staying-on") and activation (a low-power directing-about that is possible with momentary interactions such as Tap, Press and Turn.) Effortful, effortless and engaging surfaced as three important types of involvement especially pertinent to electric displays, but also more generally to the intrinsic exertion characteristic of all bodily-powered electric technology. We then articulated three design spaces/strategies: bodily-generation may be used to expand electrified space, engage through bodily involvement, and forging new relationships to electric technology. The Crank Video was offered as an example of a hand-captured and hand-instantiated digital media device related to a number of "third wave HCI" themes. As this example suggests, *it is the "limitations" of bodily-powered electric technologies—relative to ordinary ones—whose exploitation and amplification afford the greatest design possibilities.*

Figure 3. Crank Video. Video is captured and displayed by turning a finger-crank power generator.

DISCUSSION, CONCLUSIONS AND FUTURE WORK

In closing we reflect on our work and present two key areas for future extensions and applications.

Other technologies / specific research areas. Bodily-generation is an interesting yet relatively limited area in terms of its potential to replace current, everyday electric things. While its "limitations" can be positive features (e.g., it can be exploited as a unique and special type of technology), there are many other applicable, relevant and timely technologies to consider. One prominent example is solar power. While we have not conducted in-depth phenomenological analysis or form studies for photovoltaic generation, our work offers insight. For example, mobile devices that passively harvest solar power might be experienced as electric things that "never die" or "won't die". These suggest different relationships to the object (e.g., possibly more lasting and durable) as well as new attributions of agency (consider domestic robots that do not require tethering or batteries). While our discussions have been relatively agnostic to specific research agendas, we note that our work may be of particular value to a variety of application domains (e.g., electronic music) and broader issues (e.g., environmental sustainability).

Advancing HCI theory/reflection. Our work is of particular relevance to research concerned with both understanding the materiality of useful, everyday technologies, and the possibilities and limitations of electric technologies as design materials. A specific research question that we here emphasize has to do with locating similarities and differences among technologies [e.g.,8,30,32]. Phenomenologically, we propose two differences to account for. The first is ordinary or typical differences. A clear example of an ordinary difference is that electric things have batteries and power cords, whereas non-electric things do not. However, as we have noted, this is not an invariant or essential difference. Hence, a second category is "essential" differences. Locating and explaining essential differences—which in practice involve *approximations* thereof—can help us grapple with questions such as why e-books are different than paper bound books. In terms of design, such differences can indicate essential limits of technology. For example, our work suggests dimensions in which electronic text can *never be like* paper books (the electric materiality is unstable and active relative to ink on paper; it has an "impermanence" owing to its possibilities for being directing-about and deactivated; paper books are not dependent on sources of electric power).

We also argue that research through design can (and does) create exemplars that may be useful in locating important similarities and differences among technologies. For example, consider the well-cited Power Aware Cord, which visualizes the electricity flowing through it [1]. Our Crank LED and the Power Aware Cord both "visualize" the electricity being used, but represent key differences. For example, the "amount" of power is primarily *seen and read with* The Power Aware cord, whereas it is unavoidably *felt and embodied through* the Crank LED. And together, these examples suggest that usable electricity, in contrast to wood fuel or gasoline, is essentially imperceptible to "naked", non-technologically-mediated human perception [16]; electricity cannot stand apart, on its own, as *an object*.

Based on this discussion, we close with two considerations. First, HCI theory can benefit from taking into account and explaining uncommon and extreme design variations. Second, research through design should perhaps be allowed even more freedom to create novel, interesting, even radical exemplars that do not strictly require validation in terms of usefulness and desirability to "users".

ACKNOWLEDGMENTS
Financial support for this work was provided in part by National Science Foundation Grant #IIS- 1018340.

REFERENCES
1. Backlund et al. 2006. Static! The aesthetics of energy in everyday things. Proc. DRS Conf.
2. Bowers, J. 2012. The logic of annotated portfolios: communicating the value of 'research through design'. Proc. DIS '12.
3. Djajadiningrat, T., Wensveen, S., Frens, J. & Overbeeke, K. 2004. Tangible products: redressing the balance between appearance and action. Pers. Ubiq. Comp.,(8)5.
4. Dourish, P. 2001. *Where the action is*. MIT Press.
5. Fallman, D. 2011. The new good: exploring the potential of philosophy of technology to contribute to human-computer interaction. Proc. CHI '11.
6. Fallman, D. 2003. Design-oriented human-computer interaction. Proc. CHI '03.
7. Fernaeus & Sundström. 2012. The material move: how materials matter in interaction design research. DIS '12.
8. Fernaeus, Y., Jonsson, M. & Tholander, J. 2012. Revisiting the jacquard loom: threads of history and current patterns in HCI. Proc. CHI '12.
9. Gaver, W. 2012. What should we expect from research through design? Proc. CHI '12.
10. Hallnäs, L. and Redström, J. 2002. From use to presence: on the expressions and aesthetics of everyday computational things. *Trans. CHI,* 9(2):106-124.
11. Hallnäs, L. & Redström, J. 2002. Abstract information appliances: methodological exercises in conceptual design of computational things. Proc. DIS '02.
12. Hallnäs, L. & Redström, J. 2001. Slow Technology; Designing for Reflection. In: Personal and Ubiquitous Computing, Vol. 5, No. 3, 2001, pp. 201-212.
13. Heidegger, M. 1962. *Being and time*, trans. J. Macquarrie and E. Robinson. Blackwell.
14. Husserl, E. 1962. *Ideas*: *General introduction to pure phenomenology*. trans, Boyce Gibson. Collier.
15. Ihde, D. 2007, 1976. *Listening and voice: Phenomenologies of sound*. State Univ. of NY.
16. Ihde, D. 1990. *Technology and the lifeworld*. Indiana Univ.
17. Ihde, D. 1986. *Experimental phenomenology: An introduction*. State Univ. of NY.
18. Jung, H. & Stolterman, E. 2010. Material probe: exploring materiality of digital artifacts. Proc. TEI '10.
19. Lim, Y-K., Lee, S-U. & Lee, K-Y. 2009. Interactivity attributes: a new way of thinking and describing interactivity. Proc. CHI '09.
20. Löwgren, J. & Stolterman, E. 2004. Thoughtful interaction design. MIT Press.
21. Manovich, L. 2001. The language of new media. MIT.
22. Neustaedter, C. & Sengers, P. 2012. Autobiographical design in HCI research: designing and learning through use-it-yourself. Proc. DIS '12.
23. Odom, W., Selby, M., Sellen, A., Kirk, D., Banks, R. & Regan, T. 2012. Photobox: on the design of a slow technology. Proc. DIS '12.
24. Pierce, J. & Paulos, E. 2012. Designing with human-power and interactive microgeneration. Proc. DIS '12.
25. Pierce, J. & Paulos, E. 2012. Beyond energy monitors: interaction and emerging energy systems. Proc. CHI '12.
26. Pierce, J. & Paulos, E.. 2011. A phenomenology of human-electricity relations. Proc. CHI '11.
27. Pierce, J. & Paulos, E. 2010. Materializing energy. Proc DIS '10.
28. Redström, J. 2005. On technology as material in design. In A.-M. Willis, ed., Design Philosophy Papers,p.31–42.
29. Robles, E. & Wiberg, M. 2010. Texturing the "material turn" in interaction design. Proc. TEI '10.
30. Rosner, D. K. & Taylor, A.S. 2011. Antiquarian Answers: Book Restoration as a Resource for Design. Proc. CHI '11.
31. Sundström, Taylor, Grufberg, Wirström, Belenguer, & Lundén, M. 2011. Inspirational bits: towards a shared understanding of the digital material. Proc. CHI '11.
32. Vallgårda, A. & Redström, J. 2007. Computational composites. Proc. CHI '07.
33. Verbeek, P-P. 2004. *What things do*. MIT Press.
34. Villar & Hodges. 2010. The Peppermill: The peppermill: a human-powered user interface device. Proc. TEI '10
35. Winograd, T. & Flores, F. 1986. *Understanding computers and cognition: a new foundation for design*.

A Conversation Between Trees: What Data Feels Like In The Forest

Rachel Jacobs[1], Steve Benford[1], Mark Selby[1], Mike Golembewski[1], Dominic Price[1], Gabriella Giannachi[2]

[1]Mixed Reality Laboratory & Horizon
University of Nottingham
Nottingham, UK
{firstname.lastname}@nottingham.ac.uk

[2]Centre for Intermedia
University of Exeter
Exeter, UK
G.Giannachi@exeter.ac.uk

ABSTRACT
A study of an interactive artwork shows how artists engaged the public with scientific climate change data. The artwork visualised live environmental data collected from remote trees, alongside both historical and forecast global CO_2 data. Visitors also took part in a mobile sensing experience in a nearby forest. Our study draws on the perspectives of the artists, visitors and a climate scientist to reveal how the work was designed and experienced. We show that the artists adopted a distinct approach that fostered an emotional engagement with data rather than an informative or persuasive one. We chart the performative strategies they used to achieve this including sensory engagement with data, a temporal structure that balanced liveness with slowness, and the juxtaposition of different treatments of the data to enable interpretation and dialogue.

Author Keywords
Environmentally engaged art; sustainability; climate; slowness; liveness; sensory; embodied; performance

ACM Classification Keywords
H.5.2 [Information Interfaces And Presentation]: User Interfaces - Interaction styles

INTRODUCTION
Climate change is now a major topic of public concern and discussion. It is also a deeply challenging and politically charged issue, raising heated debate over whether it is happening, why it might be happening, and what we might do about it. Part of the problem is that the global and long-term nature of climate change data defies easy or immediate comprehension. Thus, while some parties furiously discuss the veracity and meaning of scientific data, there is a risk of the wider public becoming disenfranchised, unwilling or unable to engage with the underlying data, and therefore increasingly distanced from the debate [20].

From an HCI perspective, a recent survey of the burgeoning field of sustainable HCI identified a variety of research 'genres' including persuasive technologies, sustainable interaction design, and citizen science, with each embodying different issues and underlying approaches [5]. Of particular relevance here is the potential of 'ecologically engaged art' to open up, stimulate and frame public debate around sustainability [4]; by engaging the public in emotional experiences on a human scale, artists may open up new opportunities for analysis and debate [10].

Against this broad backdrop, we study the distinctive role played by a particular group of artists in engaging the public with climate change data. We present the design and study of our touring artwork called *A Conversation Between Trees* that juxtaposed different sources of scientific data in a novel and unusual manner. Our study contributes to HCI's knowledge of artistic approaches to sustainable HCI in three ways. First, we focus on how this group of artists interpreted and presented scientific data as part of an artwork. Second, we present a detailed account of the design of this artwork from the ground up as well as how it was experienced by the public as it toured. Third, we draw on three different perspectives within the study, those of the artists, the public, but also of a climate scientist.

We begin with a brief overview of related work, followed by a general overview of *A Conversation Between Trees* before turning to our study and findings. These subsequently inform a discussion of the general role of artists in engaging the public with scientific data, relating the strategies observed within the work to ongoing concerns and discussions in HCI.

RELATED WORK
A growing community of 'environmentally engaged artists' is working with environmental data as a tool or medium to trigger conceptualizations of the environment in response to socio-political issues around climate and environmental change [1, 3, 10]. This work is unfolding alongside a growing interest in data visualisation within contemporary design and broader new media practices, responding to the increasing availability of public data and cheap mobile sensing devices. Artists have for some time explored how to visualise and interpret environmental and locative data

through playful, visual and sensory interactive experiences, while at the same time, interaction designers have been developing 'eco-visualisations' to help communicate environmental concerns such as energy usage [13]. Holmes has extended the term 'eco-visualisation' to artists focusing on 'good environmental stewardship', laying the groundwork for a discussion of activism and the value of alternative interpretations of environmental data within an interdisciplinary context, and specifically within HCI [12].

Contemporary artists such as Sacks [10], Polli [1], Jeremijenko [4] (to name but a few) have sought new approaches to environmentally engaged art that focus on a more conceptual 'syntheses of science, action and art' [25]. Giannachi suggests that these new approaches embrace an aesthetic that is 'experienced by audiences as traces and footprint representations', bringing together scientific perspectives, critical theory and artistic intervention. [10]

Within this context, Bunting [3] argues for a clearer perspective on our expectations of the role of artists in terms of what she calls the 'environmental crisis'. In discussing a series of exhibitions that focus specifically on climate change she suggests that artists are creating opportunities for a powerful thematic narrative around climate change, but questions whether it is the role of artists to inform the public about science. Bindi, in her essay about the work of the environmental artist Polli, suggests that artists' distinctive interpretations of scientific data can create new ways to communicate science. Looking back at the history of hybrid artworks that span science and art, she reflects that current artworks dealing with climate can offer new interpretations of the assumptions of scientific data, opening up a perspective that looks to the 'community and the future' [1].

Our study extends this body of work by revealing in detail how artists can provoke a powerful emotional engagement with data. We document an approach that can be broadly termed as performative, drawing on sensory engagement, a distinctive temporal structure that balances slowness and liveness, and the deliberate juxtaposition of contrasting clearly related elements, in order to invite the public into interpretation and dialogue. We also reveal how in following this approach artists have to walk a line between the artistic and scientific treatment of data.

THE ARTWORK – A CONVERSATION BETWEEN TREES

The artwork *A Conversation Between Trees (ACBT)* was created by the artists Active Ingredient in collaboration with a Senior Climate Change Scientist from the UK Met Office Hadley Centre and researchers at the University of Nottingham. It was first inspired by a visit to the Atlantic Forest around Rio de Janeiro, Brazil as part of a larger arts and schools exchange project and subsequently developed during a series of artist residencies in Brazil and the UK. *ACBT* toured to three public arts centres that were located in different UK forests. Further information, including documentary video, can be found at: http://hello-tree.com.

The overall intent of the work is to establish a live connection – or conversation – between a distant tree in the Atlantic forest and a local tree at each venue in the UK. This involves arranging three key elements within an overall exhibition:

- Environmental sensor data is captured and streamed live from each tree, to be visualized on two large displays that face each other across the gallery.
- Juxtaposed between these visualizations is located the 'climate machine', an unusual device that visualizes recorded and predicted global CO_2 levels by slowly burning circular graphs onto large circular disks of recycled paper. These are subsequently hung up and displayed in the gallery space.
- Visitors can also elect to experience a walk in the local UK forest during which they enact being a sensor, using a mobile phone to capture and visualize images of the forest and answering questions about their sensation of being in the forest.

The resulting experience is therefore a complex juxtaposition of different locations (gallery, local forest and remote forest), datasets (live environmental data and official scientific CO_2 data), and technologies (sensors, phones, projections and climate machine) that comes together as one coherent artwork. We now describe each of the major elements of the artwork in further detail.

Figure 1: The two visualisations in a gallery with the climate machine between them.

The instrumented trees and visualisations

In order to capture live environmental data from the chosen trees the team developed a bespoke Arduino sensor hub connected to an Android Nexus One phone via USB. This equipment is housed in a robust and waterproof wooden casing ready for mounting in a tree. Once a minute this sensor kit takes a photograph looking up into the tree and simultaneously measures local temperature, humidity, decibel and CO_2 levels, all of which are transmitted via 3G to a server in the UK. The data from each tree is then pulled into an animated 3D visualisation. Each visualisation responds dynamically to the light and colour content of the images captured by the mobile phone camera, and the temperature, humidity, decibels and CO_2 levels captured by the sensors. Each change in the data triggers a change in the image, causing it to blur, move, change hue, colour and shape in response to the dynamic environment around the tree. The aim is to create visual representations of the changes in the environment around the tree to suggest the sensation of standing under it (e.g. the image becoming blurry and watery as humidity increases around the tree).

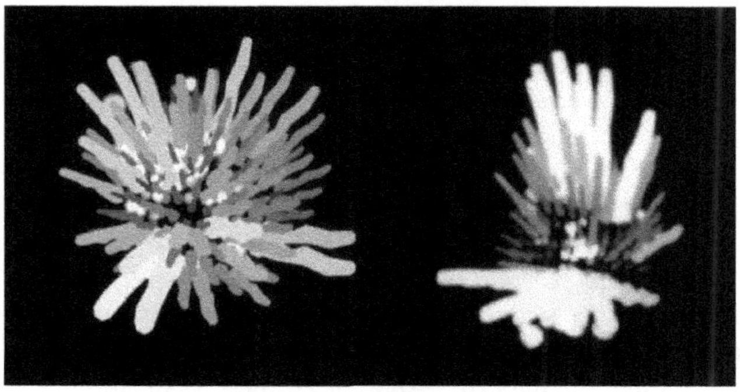

Figure 2: Visualisations of a Mango tree in the Atlantic Forest, Brazil (left) and Ash tree in the UK (right).

The climate machine

In the centre of the gallery space, placed between the two projections, the Climate Machine slowly visualizes annual changes in global CO_2 levels according to a freely available scientific dataset that was recommended by the climate change scientist who advised on the project.

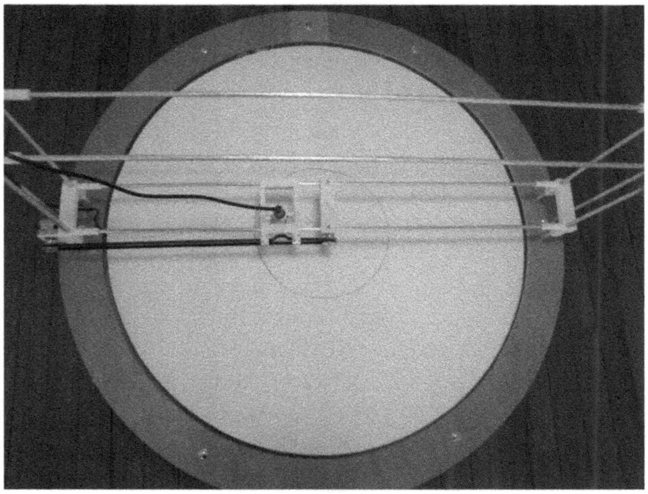

Figure 3: the Climate Machine

The Mauna Loa dataset [15] is a long series of monthly average CO_2 readings recorded at the Mauna Loa observatory in Hawaii dating back to 1959. While there are monthly fluctuations in these readings, the underlying trend is one of an increase in recorded levels over this long period that is taken by many as scientific evidence that human generated increases in CO_2 are contributing to climate change. A turntable rotates with a stack of paper on it, while a drawing arm that holds a heating element (a soldering iron) moves in and out; each paper disc represents a single year of CO_2 readings. The further from its centre the paper is scorched, the higher the amount of carbon dioxide measured or predicted at that time. This produces a roughly circular track burned into the paper that conveys the level(s) of CO_2 measured or predicted that particular year. Thus, a drawing of data from 1959 shows a very small circle close to the centre of the paper, while one from 2010 is close to the outside edge. The machine moves very slowly so as to scorch the paper effectively. Our artists orchestrate this process, layering the paper discs on the machine, pressing the button to start the machine, and removing the discs.

Figure 4: Burning the IPCC data onto a paper disc

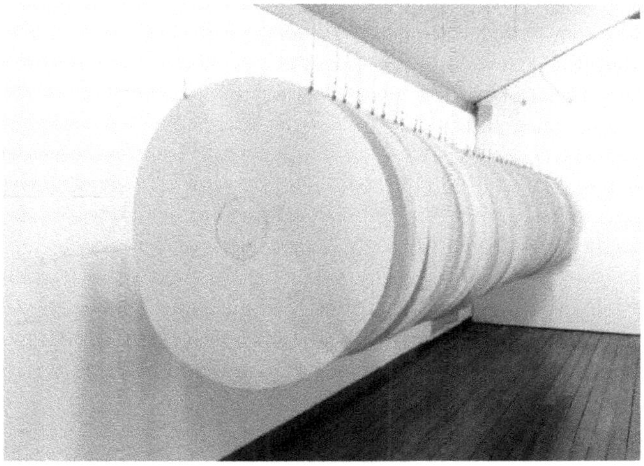

Figure 5: Hanging discs representing a data series

They also label the discs, marking them with the year and yearly average CO_2 level in ppm (parts per million) before hanging each paper disc in the gallery. This results in a lengthy time-based 'performance of data'. At the end of two weeks of performance a full set of annual CO_2 data from 1959 to 2050 fills the space. This complete set of heat drawings, looking to both past and future, continued to be exhibited in the gallery as a representation of the scale of change in CO_2 levels.

The forest walk

The third component of the exhibition involves visitors heading out into the local forest with a borrowed mobile phone. As they walk, this phone automatically captures images of the forest once every ten seconds (displaying a visible count down so that the visitor can chose to deliberately focus the camera on particular scenes should they wish). These photographs are then transformed into a visualisation on the phone screen using the same algorithms as for the two visualisations back in the gallery, driven by data that is relayed from the sensors in the nearby (local) tree. The raw data also appears in the corner of the screen. Visitors can interact with this visualization using the touch screen, zooming in and out to discover for themselves how the light, colour and data from each photograph map to the resulting visualisation.

Figure 6: the mobile app visualising an image taken by the phone camera and sensor data from a tree in the forest

Visitors also listen to a soundtrack (using earphones) that consists of a dialogue between two of the artists who narrate a journey through the forest from their artists' perspectives. Finally, visitors are periodically invited to perform the role of being a sensor by estimating current levels of humidity, light, sound, and air quality on a scale of 1-10 and entering these values along with three words that describe how they feel. This data is recorded and uploaded to an online server.

OUR APPROACH TO THE STUDY

As HCI's interest in artistic and cultural uses of computers continues to grow, so the question of how to study them increasingly comes to the fore [22]. The aim of this particular study was to understand how *ACBT* engaged people with climate data. In order to achieve this we triangulated three distinct perspectives: those of the artists who created the work, the visitors who experienced it, and also the climate scientist who advised on the project.

The artists' perspective: We first captured the artists' rationale for the work. This involved our lead artist/researcher documenting the design of the work herself, especially the intentions behind the design, both at general and detailed levels. This included three interviews with the artist team: the designer of the climate machine; the developer of the visualisations and mobile application; and the collaborating artist in Brazil. The artist/researcher also wrote a rationale of the exhibition in advance of studying the audience engagement with the work, so as to avoid as far as possible reconstructing the artists' rationale after hearing from the audience.

The visitor's perspective: We captured the audience perspective through semi-structured interviews that took place immediately after the experience. We conducted 20 semi-structured interviews. Feedback questionnaires were also made available to all visitors as is common practice with public exhibitions and we gathered 37 of these. We opted for an interview rather than a primarily observational approach in order to highlight visitors' feelings about the work and to avoid interfering with the experience. It should also be noted that not all of the interviewees fully viewed all the elements that constituted the entire artwork. The interviews, backed up by records of giving out phones, suggest that the majority experienced the visualizations and climate machine in the gallery, but that just under half chose to undertake the forest walk.

The climate scientist's perspective: We engaged a professional climate scientist from the UK's national meteorological centre to advise on the project, including recommending datasets for us to use. This scientist also visited the exhibition and was subsequently interviewed in order to capture their perspective of the work and their view of the role of the artists' engagements with climate change.

Before presenting our findings, we briefly clarify two points concerning the nature and presentation of our data.

First, it is important to acknowledge from the outset that our data reflects the views of people who engaged with the work in a serious way, that is who spent considerable time on one or more of its three elements and were willing to be interviewed afterwards. We note that a good many visitors who entered the gallery did not engage with the work. There may have been many reasons for this including lack of time and competing motivations for visiting the forests such as a family walk or cycle in the woods. Some undoubtedly found the work to be initially difficult to comprehend or generally not to their taste. This is common with contemporary artworks, particularly when presented in venues that are not 'contemporary art galleries'. It was not feasible to capture data to indicate how many people chose not to engage. One member of the audience who did not engage with the work agreed to be interviewed, describing their reason for disengagement: *"as soon as I walked in, it just, I couldn't see the reasoning behind it, it did nothing for me visually ... I couldn't see what it was all about"*

Second, our primary researcher was also one of the core artists in the team. This raised practical challenges of gathering data while simultaneously working onsite as an artist. It also raised the further issue of needing to carefully separate artist and researcher voices at different points in the research process so as to deal with questions of validity and potential bias. This position reflects the approach of 'designing from within' in which artists simultaneously engage in the performance and study of interactive artworks

[23]. In our case, given that the term 'artists' defines a group of collaborators (and not solely one artist/researcher), we have chosen to talk about the artists' perspective in the third person when presenting our data so as to maintain a clear separation between the roles of artist and researcher (even though this may sometimes feel a little artificial).

FINDINGS

In analyzing our data, we were keen to explore the distinctive role played by our artists in engaging the public with climate change data: what did they set out to do, how was this made manifest in their design, how was it experienced by visitors, and what were the challenges and tensions between the different perspectives involved in the work? This led us to identify four key themes that appear to be critical to the work and that frame the presentation of our findings in what follows:

- How the artists adopted a distinctive perspective or 'voice' when *engaging audiences with climate data*;
- How they *embedded data into an embodied experience*;
- How they *performed data* as a way of conveying the long timescales involved;
- How they juxtaposed different elements so as to enable *multiple interpretations and dialogue.*

Engaging audiences with climate data

We begin by considering the different experiences and uses of the data within the artwork from the perspective of the 'distinctive voice' of our artists, meaning how the artists framed their relationship to climate change science and how this was understood by visitors.

The artists talked of aiming for a distinct approach to conceptualizing climate change data that was separate from that of scientists, stating that it was not their intention to express an overt interpretation of the data, but rather to subtly engage the public in reflection and dialogue, without attempting to tell them what to do or what to think. This idea was evident from the very start in the title of the work as well as in its description on the website as *"a playful conversation about forest environments, building public understanding of climate science."* As artists, rather than scientists, they were aware of being on their own trajectory of learning about climate change and interpreting data and wanted to inspire visitors to do the same.

Interviews with visitors revealed that many experienced a strong emotional reaction to the artists' portrayal of scientific data, often using words such as *'scary'*, *'shocking'*, *'emotional'* and *'depressing'*. For example: *"It's not good for nature is it? What man's done to it really... slowly and surely, scary really."*

Visitors noted how the subtlety of the visualizations and the climate machine helped them understand and engage with climate data in ways that they had not previously been able to through mainstream media or scientific education and/or information sources: *"I think you were trying to make visual some scientific data that's usually inaccessible to normal people... I look at figures and graphs and things and I just have a shutdown."*

Other visitors emphasized the importance of provoking curiosity without directly trying to nudge behavioral change: *"I don't think you've touched on how our behavior might affect climate change and I think in a way that's quite a good thing because people don't necessarily come and engage in these type of exhibitions and then be kind of guilted into changing behavior."*

Rather, visitors were clear about the importance of enabling people to make their own interpretations of climate data: *"In some ways the artist is trying to make people who come to see it make their own judgment, make their own interpretation of what they see"*

In turn, the climate scientist was clear that collaborating with artists introduced a distinct sensitivity with the potential to compliment a scientific perspective: *"In climate science especially it's quite important engaging with the public, interacting, not necessarily to trigger action ... in a sense I want to be sure it is understood and is useful to the wider possible communication and in that sense having a connection or an interaction with artists I think can help with that process ... scientists should not have (and largely don't have) a political agenda. Still some of their conclusions are politically relevant."*

In particular, he appreciated the focus on encouraging the public to 'observe' the data, rather than delivering a fixed narrative: *"I think people like the fact that it wasn't the usual narrative around climate change, doom and so on, it was, its observation. Put to you in way that we think is interesting, but basically observation."*

Embedded and embodied experience

Having seen that the artists adopted a distinctive voice in *ACBT*, we now begin to consider how this was made manifest in the various details of its design. One of the key ways of expressing this artistic voice was through the distinctive aesthetics embedded in each component of the artwork, and in particular how the climate change data was embedded into the experience by being embodied in various material and sensory forms.

The artists described in particular how the visualisations were inspired by their sensory experience of walking in forests in both the UK and Brazil, further influenced by the patterns they found in nature and their own sensations of standing under the canopy of trees: *"What the data was and where it was from, you know often it had creative influences in the sense that you know we were thinking about things like pollen spores and forests and woods and trees and branches and leaves and all those sorts of things, and simple ways to visualise things like temperature."*

Our interviews revealed how visitors responded strongly to the distinctive aesthetic of the artwork. This was sometimes revealed as an immediate and basic response to the visual aesthetics, in terms of the visualizations: *"I didn't know what they represented in terms of you look for meaning in shape and colour and I couldn't work that out without some external explanation, but even though, if I hadn't of had that I would have found them quite beautiful to look at"*

Others picked up on how this also extended beyond the images to the embedded design of the technology of the Climate Machine: *"It's visualising through the scorch mark on the paper the data that is fed through ... I think sometimes if things are a bit too slick they tend to alienate people but it's got a nice handmade hand assembled quality to it, and you know it rotates and scorches, a circular pattern in the circular paper, there's something really... quite kind of a fundamental image that circular form, is kind of, understand it quite intuitively."*

Key to these embedded experiences were several metaphors that ran throughout the artwork. The artists described how The Climate Machine was intended to make metaphorical connections between wood, burning, trees, paper and carbon dioxide, revealing layers of meaning embedded in the data and demanding questions of the viewer that pure statistics might not do on their own. They drew attention to the visual metaphor of burning the circular graphs as being 'tree rings' and the set of hanging paper discs as a sliced 'tree trunk'. They referred to the general circular motif that was repeated throughout the artwork as being an organic shape linking to nature and natural forms [24]. The deliberate burning of data and damaging of paper was a further important reference to climate change as the artist who designed the machine noted: *"You've got this dataset that goes back 60 years or whatever and then physicalising in a way that is meaningful I think is really interesting. So you know the stuff with the paper and kind of accumulation and like the way it marks the paper, the damage of it and then the kind of record of all these bits of paper.... This creates a tangible and sensory metaphor (it smelt of burning) for climate change and the increase in CO_2 in the earth's atmosphere."*

Visitors referred back to these visual and conceptual metaphors in their interviews suggesting, that they had a level of universality or ability to connect with a wide variety of visitors. Descriptions of the Climate Machine often expressed these metaphors such as *"the tree ringer"*, *"like a seismograph of trees"* and *" it's like a giant etch-a-sketch of trees."*

The smell of the burning as well as the visual metaphor connected the data to universally understood temporal representation of changes in carbon dioxide enabled the visitors to embody the experience of this data. The climate change scientist also expressed excitement about how the artists' conceptualizations could engage the non-scientific public with climate data in new ways: *"The fact that you made the CO_2 trend from Mauna Loa so evident in something people can relate to, I think was really exciting. I mean some of the comment of the people who came to the Haldon Hill (forest) exhibition about the fact that you know the dataset suddenly made sense to them, you know really, interesting to hear, because for me an x, y plot or some numbers are as exciting as your very nice plot but I thought totally acknowledge that for other people it can be totally different."*

We have already considered the tangibility of The Climate Machine and the sensory nature of burning data onto physical paper, even extending to its smell. However, it was in the design of the forest walk that this commitment to a sensory aesthetic was perhaps most evident. The artists described how the mobile phone experience was intended to enable visitors to re-enact and 'humanise' their experience of the sensors in the trees. For them, the mobile phone became a device to mediate a sensory experience of the forest in which visitors would directly embody and enact the sensor technology, moving through the environment and regularly sampling images, light levels, sound, temperature, humidity and air quality while also commenting on their feelings. The regular and enforced timing of taking photographs once every ten seconds placed visitors in a position of being part of an automated sensing system

Some visitors described how this experience pushed them into a new form of sensory engagement with the forest, 'tuning in' and focusing on details that they might normally have missed: *"I could hear the sounds more and I could see the some of the forest like really clearly, and really it was almost like a I walked into the forest just kind of a bit shut off really, and in 2D and I walked back in 3D, it was like Avatar. I was walking back, it was quite bonkers, I could see some of the leaves, I just really noticed how amazing the forest was... I had shamefully been tuned out."*

However, visitors also reported that this aspect of the experience could sometimes interfere with their interactions with one another when participating in groups, a finding that has been reported in previous studies of museum interactions [21], suggesting that this approach to embodied sensory engagement may work best when visitors are alone and are able to inwardly reflect on the sensations of the forest revealed through the devices.

Performing data

One of the most challenging aspects of engaging with climate change data is to appreciate the long timescales that are involved. The artists' response to this was to give the work a distinctive temporal structure, one that involved a 'performance of data' that combined slowness with liveness in an attempt to encourage visitors to relate their immediate experience of a forest to data series that had been gathered or projected over many decades.

Slowness

The artwork was intended to evolve over time to reflect the incremental nature of change in the datasets and engage visitors in a slow reflection. This slowness was most striking in the overall performance of burning the discs of data that unfolded over several weeks. However, the artists described how slowness was also deliberately incorporated into The Climate Machine that took twenty-five minutes to scorch each paper disc with data, and also into the projected visualisations that slowly rotated and changed in response to data that was captured from the trees once a minute. The forest walk also had an unusual temporal rhythm with photographs being captured every ten seconds.

Many visitors were observed sitting on benches placed in the gallery, watching the live visualizations and the machine whilst engaging in discussions about CO_2, deforestation and climate change. One stayed as long as eighty minutes. Several visitors indicated that the slow movement of The Climate Machine and slow changes over time of the dynamic visualisations opened up these opportunities for reflection noting a sense of the data representing changes in global CO_2 over the past, present and future in both the visualizations and The Climate Machine: *"... it allows you to condense time and see what's happening in the real world within a shorter space, that you could actually see what was, the change in CO_2 across years or either past or future."*

Visitors were also observed searching through the hanging circular sheets for their birth year in order to establish a personal sense of the scale of climate change in relation to their own lifespan. Some also related the slow movement of the visualisations back to their wider experiences of nature: *"... kind of slow abstract compositions that are, they're kind of slowly spiraling or slowly turning, they're made up of spokes of different colours ... what I was really intrigued by is the fact that they look a bit like spores or kind of natural forms not in a kind of lens based realistic way but they refer to more forms that you would find in nature."*

The scientist observed that a key part of understanding the challenge of human perception of climate change is to find ways to engage with slow processes: *"Understanding how we behave or how we cope with slow processes is a very interesting question because it is the centre of the problem as well, so how should we shut down our emotional fear, response and let intervene another process that is based on something else, or develop an emotional response to something that is completely on a different time scale and it is interesting because strangely enough this is happening also on the, how do we deal with risk or how have we dealt with risk over the course of our existence as a species."*

However, this unusual temporal structure also raised significant challenges for the artists. First, slowness demands an unusually high level of commitment from visitors; several minutes are needed to see changes in the projected visualizations, tens of minutes to see a cycle of operation of The Climate Machine, and the best part of an hour to engage in the forest walk. Consequently, it was felt to be important that there were several different elements to the work, each requiring a different commitment of time from visitors. This flexible structure enabled visitors to engage at their own pace according to available time.

Liveness

In contrast to slowness, the artists also emphasized how it was vital that the work should make a live connection between two remote forests in order to support a localized and viscerally real experience. This aspect of the work was appreciated by many visitors: *"I think I will go away today with that feeling that I haven't just been to Haldon today, I've experienced another forest, a very long way away. You know and the great similarities as well as the differences, and I am going away thinking why? I feel like it's brought up a lot of questions, all this."*

However, our study also revealed significant challenges in maintaining this crucial sense of liveness when working with 'scientific' data in an artistic context. Specifically, there were times when the artists needed to make decisions over whether to prioritize public experience of the artwork or strict accuracy of the data. For example, there were occasional problems with the mobile sensors in the trees or dropouts in network connectivity with the result that live sensor data became temporarily unavailable. At these times, the artists decided to replay prerecorded data as if it were live in order to maintain the experience of liveness, although at the expense of strict accuracy. Our artists recognized the tension between maintaining liveness versus accuracy, but on balance felt that, in this case, the occasional use of recorded data was sufficiently 'real' and their presentation of it sufficiently ambiguous, to justify a degree of artistic license, certainly when the alternative was not to show any data at all. In short, it was felt appropriate to emotionally engage new visitors rather than adhering to the data being strictly live (in the sense of 'right now').

The climate change scientist also reflected on this tension by questioning the artists' decisions: *"From my personal view its absolutely fundamental the data is live, it would actually alter my perception very significantly because while I do understand the reasons... it can be some sort of augmented or distorted reality, you take reality, you change it according to a metric, but it's an artistic metric somehow, but its related to reality... if you break that then what's the point."* However, he also recognized a tension between the value of provoking an immediate 'gut' reaction versus a desire for rational consideration of complex data, revealing the key challenge of working with scientific data in such an artwork: *"...it's a problem that is beyond human scale we do not perceive it, so you reach it only through rational thinking, you see the data you make your judgment and then you plan your response based on your thinking"* and *"... feeling doesn't quite help, because it's not, you shouldn't base your response to your gut feeling."*

This tension between accuracy and experience also extended to the choice of data to be used. At one point during development the climate scientist had suggested working with a richer multi-dimensional dataset, although in the end it was a joint decision to opt for the simpler data: *"I would say from a scientific point of view it was quite an easy dataset, it was a monodimensional time series while in general climate data tend to be fairly complex, so I think it was central but out of many possible datasets we decided to go for relatively simple one and maybe because of that it was possible to build a nice interface."*

Finally on this theme, the sense of liveness was also enhanced by the artists' presence in the exhibition, especially the performance of burning and hanging the disks. The artists reported that they were required to improvise continuously throughout the exhibition in order to create an experience of liveness; they made choices about how they expressed these issues to the audience, whether to reveal the tensions between engagement in the live experience and maintaining the authenticity of the data or to create a 'smoke and mirrors' effect to ensure the public's 'suspension of disbelief' in the artwork [18].

Multiple Interpretations and Dialogue

Up to now, we have explored how individual elements of the artwork were designed to convey a distinctive artistic voice. However, there is considerably more to the matter than this. A notable feature of ACBT is its complexity, assembling a variety of contrasting elements into an overall experience. This juxtaposition of often contrasting parts was a key part of the artists' strategy to provoke interpretation and dialogue. Our study reveals how visitors specifically made sense of the conceptualisations of the data within each element of the artwork, but also how the overall composition of the work and possibilities for dialogue with the artists when they were present supported this.

Perhaps the most striking feature of *A Conversation Between Trees* is the way in which visitors were invited to assemble their own experience and hence interpretation of scientific climate data. One the one hand, the juxtaposition of different elements within one artwork (the visualisations, the machine and hanging sheets and the mobile experience), live and historical datasets, involves deliberately creating contrasts between each of the elements. On the other hand commonalities between these elements encourage visitors to make comparisons, between them, further encouraged by various interrelated metaphors and themes. Thus the visualisations and phone experience draw on the same sensors and employ common visual techniques.

Moreover, the gaps between the elements provided opportunities for dialogue between visitors, with the artists when present to perform the work, or with gallery assistants fulfilling one of the core intentions of the work – to facilitate conversation: *"When I first looked at them I could see that they represented something of the trees and I think you'd have to stand there and see the data and maybe you'd sort of get an idea of what's going on but some explanation was really good, 'cos that really brought it to life."*

Some visitors appreciated being able to assemble their own experience: *"Well firstly I just thought it was something like a pattern someone created on a camera, but when you look on the bottom right hand corner it is a picture of trees... it's almost like when someone hasn't got their glasses on and everything's blurred and you realise that your actually looking at trees in a different form."*

A member of the gallery staff noted how some visitors reinterpreted the work, creating a dialogue between them: *"A group of young boys pretended to do a presentation of the data in front of their parents, saying what they had found out, pointing at the projection while the parents sat on the bench."*

Within this general arrangement, each element stood alone and visitors were not required to encounter them in a particular order. This provided flexibility as to how deeply they engaged, with each visitor or group of visitors constructing their own journey through the work

The climate change scientist reflected on the juxtaposition of the different datasets and how they weren't necessarily datasets he would have put together: *"The comparison I thought as you say was very emotional at the same time I would not really have tried to put the two on the same sort of axis. So these are the historical observations and these are the observations that you see here, which have huge fluctuation because they are CO_2 but if you do a long term average you realise that actually these value is not too dissimilar to the one you get from Mauna Loa."*

DISCUSSION

In discussing our findings and revisiting related work we now reflect on two broader questions: what role did these artists play in engaging the public with climate change data and what strategies did they adopt to foster this engagement? In each case, we relate our answers to the growing discourse concerning sustainable HCI.

The role of the artists

The intention of participatory sensing, citizen science and sustainable HCI research is often to inform the public of what data means and/or persuade them to change their behavior [2]. However, DiSalvo and colleagues have argued that 'ecologically engaged art' often aims to stimulate environmental debate rather than directly informing or persuading [4]. They have proposed that, historically, such artworks have tried to bridge the artificial division between culture and nature, engaging the public with environmental concerns, while also engaging the political as part of art practice. Their paper ends with a rallying cry for a deeper understanding of the relationships between ecologically engaged art and sustainable HCI, including a more nuanced treatment of arts and humanities perspectives.

Our paper can be seen as a response to this call, providing a detailed account of how a group of artists set out to engage the public through unusual treatments of climate change data. In its broadest terms, our study has shown how artists can play a powerful and distinctive role in engaging people with climate change data, and by extension perhaps more generally with the debate around climate change and sustainability. In this case, the artistic voice is not about presenting canonical interpretations of data, or about informing, or even about persuasion. Nor is it about activism. Rather, we have documented how our artists worked with scientific data recommended by a climate scientist, questioning it through different presentations but without adopting an explicit scientific or political position (as might be the case with more activist artworks [6]). The artists therefore positioned themselves as questioning the data more than knowing what it meant, with the intention of encouraging public visitors to do the same

So what then *is* the role of *ACBT* in engaging the public with climate change data? Our study shows that it is fundamentally about enabling visitors to observe the data for themselves and through this to provoke an *emotional* response. *ACBT* is about making people feel strongly about the data, sufficiently so that they may wish to reflect on it afterwards or to discuss it with others. It also reaches out to an audience that might not normally engage with scientific data when presented in more traditional ways. However, our study also revealed that working with scientific data can be challenging for artists. We saw how they had to walk a line between the need to create an emotionally compelling experience for visitors and scientific authenticity. This can be seen in their choice of data – a relatively simple dataset instead of a complex multidimensional dataset – and their response to occasional technical failures – keeping the experience running by replaying recorded data as if live.

Creating an emotional response is an important part of reaching a wide audience and a first step towards enabling people to clarify their perspective on the data and the wider issues. Giannachi argues that a change in perspective needs to occur before you can change behavior [10]. Bunting [3] also suggests that it is not a lack of available information on climate change that creates distance and misunderstandings, but rather an issue of how people can respond to the information that is available.

How artists provoke engagement and interpretation

So how can artists set about creating this powerful emotional engagement with data? What specific strategies did our artists invoke and how does this speak to HCI? Our study has shown that three broad strategies were combined

First was to encourage a sensory engagement with data. McCarthy and Wright have identified the 'sensory' as being one of the four key threads of user experience [16], a view that was clearly reflected in the artists' conception of *ACBT*. By giving the data material form and by requiring visitors to take on the role of a sensor when walking through the forest, our artists were creating a deeply embodied experience of the data [7] contrasting strongly with more conventional disembodied visualizations that suggest a rational but more detached engagement.

Second, was to bring a unique temporality to engagement with the climate data. Temporality – including both slowness and liveness – has previously emerged as an issue in the HCI literature. Di Salvo *et al* noted temporality as a key concern of many ecologically engaged artworks [4], while there is a growing general in interest in both slowness [17] and liveness [14] in HCI. Hallnas *et al* [11] suggest one of the opportunities that slow technology can provide is the ability to enable reflection. Friedman *et al* discuss [9] how the challenges of slow datasets and multi-lifespan design can require different approaches to designing information systems. *ACBT* reflects these ideas in its strategies for designing interpretations of climate data. Despite the inherent tensions in the artists' strategies the study shows that a more human scale perspective was made possible by shifting focus away from veridical representation towards more emotional and personal engagements with the data. Key to the temporal structure is that the data is 'performed'. Not only does the painstaking nature of this slow performance direct attention to the temporal character of the data, but it also demands an extended engagement from the viewer, which is important to engaging their emotions.

The third strategy is the juxtaposition of different elements that present contrasting datasets – live, recorded and predicted – in various different ways. Our study noted that visitors particularly appreciated being given space and time to arrive at their own responses and interpretations. This resonates with previous research such as the *Shape* project that created a museum experience where visitors explored locations around an ancient castle that were juxtaposed with interactive installations inside [8]. However, *ACBT* is distinct in that it quite deliberately contrasts the different elements of the live visualizations from the climate machine, while the forest walk involves a very different experience again. And yet, these elements are linked through common designs and metaphors. We suggest that it is this arrangement of multiple elements that makes the design of *ACBT* open to multiple interpretations, the importance of which has previously been discussed by Sengers and Gaver [19]. In turn, it is the interstitial gaps between these elements that provide the space for dialogue among visitors or with artists and gallery staff.

CONCLUSION

There has been a growing focus on the role of environmentally engaged artworks in relation to sustainable HCI, especially how they may facilitate new forms of public engagement with sustainability issues. Our contribution here has involved focusing specifically on the strategies that a group of artists used to engage with scientific climate change data; and by triangulating between the perspectives of the artists, visitors and a climate change scientist, to understand how these worked.

We have seen how the artists engaged the public with data on an emotional level, trying to make them feel something rather than trying to inform or persuade. We have also seen how they tried to engage them at a human-scale, making data that unfolds over very long timescales meaningful to them in the here and now. This distinctive artistic voice was realized through three broad strategies:

- Embodying scientific data in various material ways so as to provide a rich sensory and aesthetic experience;
- Adopting a performative temporal structure that combined both slowness with liveness;
- Juxtaposing multiple, contrasting and yet related, elements so as to invite comparisons while opening up spaces between them for interpretation and dialogue.

However, we also saw that delivering an emotional engagement while remaining 'true' to the authenticity of the scientific data is not a simple matter, requiring the artists to walk a line between artistic license and strict accuracy. Despite such challenges, our study has revealed that environmentally engaged artworks do have a distinctive and powerful role to play in relation to climate change and sustainability; one that HCI needs to understand as it continues to move into this territory, and one from which it might ultimately learn about how to bring an emotional treatment to many other forms of data.

ACKNOWLEDGMENTS

We thank the partners, funders and audiences involved in *A Conversation Between Trees*, and especially Dr Carlo Buontempo from the UK Met office. We gratefully acknowledge support from the Horizon Doctoral Training Centre (EP/G037574/1) and EPSRC Dream Fellowship award (Steve Benford, EP/J005215/1).

REFERENCES

1. Bindi G., Man at the Centre of the Climate, *Parco Arte Vivente*, Centro de Arte Contemporanea Torino, 2011
2. Brynjarsdóttir H., Håkansson M., Pierce J., Baumer E., DiSalvo C., Sengers P., Sustainably Unpersuaded: How Persuasion Narrows Our Vision of Sustainability, *CHI '12*, May 5–10, Austin, Texas, USA, ACM, 2012
3. Bunting M., Art and Climate An Essay: does the art stop when the persuasion starts?, *RSA Arts and Ecology Magazine*, RSA, 2008 (accessed 11/09/12)
4. DiSalvo, C., Boehner, K., Knouf, N. and Sengers, P., Nourishing the Ground for Sustainable HCI: considerations from ecologically engaged art, *CHI '09*, 385-394, ACM, 2009
5. DiSalvo, C. Sengers, P., Brynjarsdóttir, H. Mapping the Landscape of Sustainable HCI, *CHI '10*. ACM, 2010
6. Dourish P., HCI and Environmental Sustainability: The Politics of Design and the Design of Politics, *DIS 2010*, August 16-20, Aarhus Denmark, ACM, 2010
7. Dourish, P., *Where The Action Is: The Foundations of Embodied Design*, MIT Press, 2004
8. Fraser, M., Stanton, D., Ng, M., Benford, S., O'Malley, C., Bowers, J., Taxen, G., Ferris, K., Hindmarsh, J., Assembling History: achieving coherent experiences with diverse technologies, *ECSCW'03*, 179-198, Kluwer, 2003
9. Friedman B., Nathan L., Multi-lifespan Information System Design: a research initiative for the HCI community, *CHI '10*, Atlanta, Georgia, ACM, 2010
10. Giannachi, G., Representing, Performing and Mitigating Climate Change in Contemporary Art Practice, *Leonardo*, 45: 2, 124-131, 2012
11. Hallnas L., Redstrom J., Slow Technology – Designing for Reflection, *Journal of Personal and Ubiquitous Computing*, 5 (3), Springer-Verlag, August 2001
12. Holmes T. G., Eco-visualization: combining art and technology to reduce energy consumption, *6th ACM Conference on Creativity & Cognition*, ACM, 2007
13. Holmquist, L. E., Skog, T., Informative Art: information visualization in everyday environments, *Proc GRAPHITE '03*, 229-235, ACM, 2003.
14. Hook J., Schofield G., Taylor R., Bartindale T., McCarthy J., Wright P., Exploring HCI's Relationship with Liveness, *CHI '04 EA*, 2771-2774 ACM, 2012
15. IPCC http://www.ipcc-data.org/ 13. Mauna Loa Series, Trends in CO_2 www.esrl.noaa.gov/gmd/ccgg/trends/
16. McCarthy J., Wright, P., *Technology as Experience*, MIT Press, 2007
17. Odom W., Banks R., Durrant, A., Kirk, D., Slow Technology: Critical Reflections and Future Directions, *DIS '12*, June 11-15, 2012, Newcastle, UK, ACM, 2012
18. Pfister, M., Halliday, J., *The Theory and Analysis of Drama*, Cambridge University Press, 1988
19. Sengers, P., Gaver, W., Staying open to interpretation: engaging multiple meanings in design and evaluation, *DIS '06*, 99-108, ACM, 2006
20. Spence A., Poortinga W., Butler C., Pidgeon N., Perceptions of Climate Change and Willingness to Save Energy Related to Flood Experience, *Nature Climate Change*, Volume 1, Macmillan, 2011
21. Szymanski, M., Aoki, P., Grinter, R., Hurst, A., Thornton, J., Woodruff, A., Sotto Voce: Facilitating Social Learning in a Historic House, *JCSCW*, 17, 1 5-34, Klumer, 2008
22. Paulos E., *HCI Cannot Be Used To Evaluate Art*, Human-Computer Interaction Institute, 2007
23. Taylor, R., Schofield, G., Shearer, J., Wallace, J., Wright, P., Boulanger, P., Olivier, P., Designing from within: Humanaquarium, *CHI '11*, 1855-1864, 2011
24. Tuan, Y., *Space and place: the perspective of experience*, University of Minnesota Press, 1977
25. Wilson S., *Information Arts: Intersections of Art, Science, and Technology*, MIT Press/Leonardo Books 2002

Unlimited Editions: Three Approaches to the Dissemination and Display of Digital Art

Mark Blythe, Jo Briggs
School of Design
Northumbria University, UK
{mark.blythe, jo.briggs}@northumbria.ac.uk

Jonathan Hook, Peter Wright, Patrick Olivier
Culture Lab
Newcastle University, UK
{j.d.hook, p.c.wright, p.l.olivier}@ncl.ac.uk

ABSTRACT

The paper reflects on three approaches to the dissemination and display of digital art. "s[edition]" is a novel, web-based service that offers limited editions of "digital prints". Analysis of user comments suggests that the metaphor of a "limited digital edition" raises issues and to some extent is resisted. The second approach is the Flickr Brushes Gallery, where digital painters post images and comment on one another's work. Analysis of comment boards indicates that the shared art and comments are a form of gift exchange. Finally, the paper discusses a field study in which artists exhibited their work as it develops over time in digital frames and also in an immersive digital projection room. Analysis of field notes and interviews indicate that the digital frame approach was unsuccessful because of aesthetic and environmental concerns. The immersive projection suggested that more experiential approaches may be more interesting. It is argued that there is an inherent resistance in digital media to previous models of art commoditization. None of the approaches discussed here resolve the dilemma but rather indicate the scope and complexity of the issues.

Author Keywords

Interaction design; ethnography; art; digital culture.

ACM Classification Keywords

H.5.m. Information interfaces and presentation (e.g., HCI): Miscellaneous.

INTRODUCTION

Digital technology has transformed all aspects of the creative industries: music, film, and art. It has never been easier to record a song, make a movie or paint a picture. Although digital tools mean that art is easier to make it is harder for artists to earn a living. The ease with which digital files can be copied and shared presents profound challenges for the creative industries. There has been a well-documented crisis in the music industry for something like twenty years. Statistics are produced almost annually to show how much revenue is being lost because of file sharing [e.g. 6]. Successive attempts to ban file sharing sites like Napster, Kazaa and most recently the Pirate Bay have all failed to curb the practice. Although individual outlets may be temporarily disabled like heads of the hydra new ones quickly reappear. Streaming sites such as Spotify are generating healthy profits but very little of this goes to the artists. Zoe Keating recently made her earnings from Spotify public claiming that she was paid just £179.90 for 72,800 plays [5]. According to PPL, a music licensing company 90% of musicians earn less than £15,000 a year and 90% of song-writers and composers earn less than £5000 (ibid). It is increasingly difficult for any kind of artist (novelist, actor, director, film maker or musician) to make a living wage from their work [18]. A third of visual and applied artists earn less than £5000 a year from their work. A recent survey of artists found that 57% earned less than a quarter of their annual income from their art (ibid).

This paper explores alternative models for the dissemination of digital content and takes art as a context. When artworks are created digitally the notion of an "original" and a "limited print run" begin to break down. The British artist David Hockney has received much attention for drawings he has made both on the iPhone and iPad. These images have been both produced and disseminated digitally, leading critics to ask what or where the "original" image might be [2]. In this context the notion of a digital original is at best a paradox and at worst a contradiction in terms [12, also see 8]. This may not be an issue for established artists such as Hockney but for many new and aspiring digital artists it presents serious challenges. The question addressed in this paper then is how can artists add value to digital work.

The paper reflects on three approaches. The first is s[edition] a new online service offering "limited edition" digital copies of work by very well established artists [30]. The second is the Brushes Gallery, a users' group on Flickr [15] which archives and exhibits images created by its members using the Brushes mobile painting app [14]. Finally, findings from a field study where artists were invited to show their work in digital frames and in an immersive digital environment is reported. It is argued that there are complex issues inherent in all of the approaches in terms of developing sustainable models of income generation for artists.

METHOD

A qualitative content analysis of user comments was conducted for the two online studies, s[edition] and the Flickr Brushes Gallery. Comments were assigned a category and counted to give an overall sense of the shape of the data [28]. User comments for both s[edition] and the Flickr Brushes Gallery are quoted, as posted online, complete with spelling and grammar mistakes, text speak and profanity, as translating them would risk distortion. For the field study, interviews with artists and visitors to the gallery were recorded and transcribed. Detailed field notes of observations were also made on site. A thematic analysis was conducted on the transcripts, where data was summarized in open-ended codes and grouped together into key themes [4, 16]. Each of the three case studies is followed by a reflective summary, drawing on wider literature.

s[edition]

"s[edition]" launched in November 2011 and described itself as a "revolutionary new way to collect art". An onsite video introduction explains: "*Originals by well known artists, works that would normally command astronomical prices, can be had here for as little as six Euros*". The artists' work is offered in digital format only for viewing on smart phones, tablets or TVs. Users sign up to an account and are given a "vault" where they can go to view the artwork that they have purchased. Work in the vault is shown without the copyright watermark, which runs across the centre of the publically accessible images on the site. The buyer is also sent a "certificate of authenticity" which is "signed" by the artist or at least, includes an image of the artist's signature. Still images are available as jpegs to download when purchased but video files can only be viewed online in the vault. Buyers must agree to certain terms and conditions including never printing out the jpeg of the image or the certificate of authenticity. Figure 1 shows the three best selling digital prints with the presale watermark.

Figure 1: From left: Elmgreen and Dragset "Powerless Structures"©, Damian Hirst "Xylosidase"© and Wim Wenders "Lounge Painting 1"©. Copyright retained by each artist. Reproduced on license to and with the permission of [s]edition.

At the time of writing there are eighteen artists whose works are sold on the site. There are discussion boards below each work where members can post comments. All site comments were gathered in September 2012 (last checked on the 12th). A qualitative content analysis [28] was conducted on the seventy top selling pieces.

Prices of the digital prints range from £5 to £1000. The majority (43) are less than £20. A further thirty one are priced between £20 and £125. There are only two items that are more expensive than this. One is a video called "For Heaven's Sake" by Damien Hirst. This shows a rotating baby's skull covered in diamonds and this is priced at £500. Another called "Prada Marfa" by Elmgreen and Dragset, is an image of a Prada shop in the desert priced at £1000. The more expensive works are released in smaller "editions". Hirst's video is in an edition of 500, Elmgreen and Dragset's Prada image is limited to an edition of 1000. The other artworks are in limited editions of 1500–2000, 5000 or 10,000. The site notes that once editions have sold out then collectors will be permitted to resell their editions in the s[edition] marketplace. At the time of writing the most collected item had 77% of its edition still remaining. The next most collected item (the Hirst print in the centre of Figure 1) had 96% of its edition remaining.

The number of "collectors" varies greatly. Forty-two of the artworks have between 1 and 50 collectors. Just two works have sold more than 300. One, "Xylosidase", a spot painting by Damien Hirst (the centre image in Figure 1) had 415 collectors at the time of writing. The most collected piece was "Powerless Structures" (the first image in Figure 1) by Elmgreen and Dragset, which had by far the highest number of collectors at 1172.

The number of comments posted did not reflect the number of collectors. Some of the comments indicated that site moderators were deleting more critical remarks and in total there were just 129 comments. There were never as many comments as there were collectors and 32 of the 70 images had no comments at all. Table 1 summarizes the coding of the comments.

Category	Number	Percentage
Art Appreciation	106	54.9
Idea Appreciation	26	13.5
Skepticism	21	10.9
Questions	11	5.7
Thanks to s[edition]	9	4.7
Other	7	3.6
Interpretation	7	3.6
Debate	6	3.1

Table 1: s[edition] website members' comments on artworks

Secondary codes indicated where comments could be assigned to more than one category; the table shows only the primary code that summarized the main point of the comment.

Art Appreciation

By far the most frequent kind of response was appreciation of the artwork. Often this appreciation was limited to very brief phrases such as "*love it*". Some were more detailed e.g. "*This is probably the most beautiful thing I've seen in a long time*". Some of these appreciative comments took the form of a direct address to the artist, for example "*Shepherd you can do no wrong*" to the artist Shepherd Fairey. More often the appreciation was a one word comment "*wow*" or "*magic*" or "*like*☺". A large number used the word "love". This was sometimes in the form of a sentence e.g. "*I LOVE THIS*" or the phrase and a smiley face "*love this*☺" or enthusiastic repetitions with symbols: "*jajajajajajajaja I* ♥ *you*". Three of these comments were expressions of desire for possession e.g. "*want it*".

The majority of the appreciation comments then were brief statements of approbation and liking often drawing on web-based conventions of abbreviation such as smiley faces and symbols. However there were a small number of more detailed statements of appreciation. For instance, a Wim Wenders photograph received this comment: "*I like the same but slightly different cars and cropped voyeuristic letterbox framing*" (Henry Estorffe Founder, Designer HED). Similarly: "*I am mesmerized by Bill Viola's video installations and sound "environments". I said, MESMERIZED.*" (Timmy Colman). It is not possible to leave anonymous comments and many of the names and accompanying details were quite specific lending the comments an additional weight or sense of authority.

Interpretation

A small number of the comments offered an interpretation of the work. For instance this analysis of Noble and Webster's "Forever", a video of that word spelled out in flashing light bulbs: "*The cheap, Vegas-style lighting in combination with the word "forever" is what I love about this piece. "Forever" isn't a word that one would normally associate with glam. Energy for this type of lighting doesn't last forever, and "nothing lasts forever". Your first thought is that it's a romantic piece, then there are all these levels to consider [...] In the end, it's still a romantic image*" (Laurel O Conner, University of Windsor). This level of art criticism is unusual in the comments but other briefer interpretations indicate a similar familiarity with critical discourse. For instance Noble and Webster's "Puny Under Nourished Kid", a video of a neon sculpture of a child with words like "void" across the forehead is described in one comment as "*conceptual body language*" (Jill Ellen Shulze). This kind of interpretation is similar to the onsite PR write ups about the work which follow the rhetoric of much contemporary art criticism, where work is described as "asking questions" about this or "challenging" that [23].

Thanks to s[edition]

Also related to appreciation were the comments which offered thanks to the s[edition] team. These were mainly confined to the comments in response to "Powerless Structures" (the first image in Figure 1). Some of these comments make reference to a particular event: "*I was there this morning. THANK YOU*". (Cleyenne Lazzarotto Miotto, Central St. Martins College of Art and Design). Most of these comments were made on the 23rd of February, which was the date that 5000 free limited editions of the Powerless Structure video were given away to celebrate the artists' unveiling of the piece on the empty fourth plinth at Trafalgar Square. There is a tradition that the fourth plinth in Trafalgar Square remains empty and guest artists have for many years shown temporary exhibits there. The artists made Powerless Structures in association with s[edition] and launched it as a virtual work so that the plinth remained empty except for an augmented reality image available when a phone with the Aurasma app was pointed at the space [20]. It seems likely then that the thanks come from some of the individuals who received free copies.

Idea Appreciation

After art appreciation, the next most frequent comments were related to the idea of the website itself, in the main these comments praised it for innovation. For instance shinyart writes "*Transforming flat screens into "canvases" for video art. Now that's an initiative we can support"*. A later comment from the same user restates the idea and notes that they are "committed" to it. Such comments were from those involved in technology and arts businesses. Alex Morrison the Managing Director at Cogapp writes "*s[edition] digital art market. This is a really extraordinary idea. How wonderful!"* Similarly Keiko Noah, listed as the owner of Mouche gallery writes" "*This is wild, new, fresh, so coming into our lives! Limited Edition Digitals.*" Lo Ba of Oxford Royale Academy notes "*it is a so new concept. it going to revolutionnate art! you are inspirators for tomorrow artists!"* Most of the comments praising the idea were made by people affiliated with art related institutions or businesses.

Broadly supportive comments sometimes also contained doubt: "*now electronic art... trying to wrap my head around 'owning' but not 'having'. I like the concept and yet find myself very uncomfortable with the intangible (pretty sure this is how we wake up old*)." (Kristen Corning Bedford, Seattle, Washington). Critical reflection on the notion of owning but not having was taken much further in directly skeptical and dismissive comments as outlined in the next section.

Skepticism

More than a tenth of the comments were skeptical and critical of the idea. This criticism is perhaps best expressed by George Nada who does not disclose where he works but does list himself as "58 years old" above the following terse comment: "*£50 for a jpeg! GREAT DEAL*!" Elsewhere, Jessica Greenman of the University of Bristol notes "*This leaves me in no doubt about the power of stupidity*". Similarly an Associate Professor at Penn State Harrisburg asks "*Are you people on drugs?*" One of these comments notes that it is an interesting new idea but adds "*interesting to see if there will be enough crazy people*" (Signe Rirdance). Several comments though broadly supportive, are critical of pricing. A Tracey Emin print is described as a "*great idea, bit pricey though*". Similarly a Shepherd Fairey print attracts this comment: "*for the price, seems to me only hipsters will be buying this.*" Other criticisms were of particular artists and pieces.

There was a long and detailed accusation of plagiarism leveled against Shepherd Fairey's "Peace Guard". Petra Lichtenecker alleges the work is a: "*copy of the costume/image of a Japanese guitarrist from the 90s: Mana of Malice Mizer. [...] That's not only unoriginal, it's downright plagiarism.*" The member goes on to link to source material and challenge the webmasters: "*gonna delete this comment again like last time?*" Shepherd Fairey is best known for the Obama "Hope" picture, which also caused controversy when the original Associated Press (AP) photograph was discovered. Fairey was recently fined $25,000, given 300 hours of community service and two years probation in a criminal contempt case after he pleaded guilty to destroying documents and fabricating evidence in his court battle with AP [7]. The copyright sign immediately below his s[edition] limited prints takes on an ironic significance in this context.

The use of source material is a complex issue for graphic designers and artists alike. The point at which a source becomes new work is debatable. But the relatively rigid terms of copyright on the s[edition] site itself provokes this response: "*Shepherd Fairey, I was one of your biggest supporters back in the day. You have lost all credibility with me joining this site and selling movies of your work. Ten years ago you would have laughed at this stupid idea.*" (Chris Rockwell Breshears). Such critiques indicate central issues with the metaphor at the heart of the site. This metaphor equates a limited print edition with a limited digital edition glossing over the inherent reproducibility of the digital.

Other comments were questions about the site, several wanted to know what the size of the piece was and attracted puzzled responses such as "*not sure I understood your question correctly, but the Vault version of this image is at 3000x3000 pixels.*" (Konstantin K, The University of Edinburgh). There was also some debate about e.g. the merits of the artist Yoko Ono. A small number of the comments could not be coded because resources were not available to translate them and two because they were ambiguous e.g. beneath Hirst's £500 video called "For Heaven's Sake" someone had written: "*for heaven's sake*" which could be read equally as praise or blame.

REFLECTION ON S[EDITION]

Though s[edition] is undoubtedly innovative its approach is largely based on old production models of paper printmaking. Older models exploit the "Veblen effect", where value is perceived in an object because the price is high and availability is scarce [25]. Although the prices in s[edition] are undoubtedly high the images are not scarce. Removing a digital watermark on an image and capturing a video are relatively simple procedures. The certificate of authenticity aims at providing the kind of connection with an artist that a signature on a paper print might evoke, but that signature is also just another digital image.

"s[edition]" is curated by people, "cultural intermediaries" in Bourdieu's [10] sense of the "taste makers" or "gate keepers" who arbitrate the taste of the bourgeoisie. But this is not a venue for new or aspiring artist: all of the contributors are well established. It may be that the concentration on established artists lends the concept credibility. The institutions with which the users are identified indicate they are highly educated people with affiliations very often to higher education or technology.

Although the comments are moderated and sometimes made by cultural intermediaries who are broadly supportive of the initiative there nevertheless remain issues with the notion of the limited digital edition, or, "having and not owning". A recent initiative by [s]edition includes a "buy for free" offer, whereby new members to the site are given an introductory $10 voucher with which they may "purchase" a print. This "buy without buying" scheme perhaps indicates the difficulty of the notion of owning but not having.

Slavoj Ž ižek [34] has argued that there is a crisis in IP generally because digital technology itself tends towards communal ownership. The following section then considers an alternative economic and cultural model: an online gallery that is based on freely displaying art in an open community.

BRUSHES GALLERY IPAD / IPHONE ART

Brushes is an iPad and iPhone app that allows the user to "paint" using a range of predefined marks which can be controlled for size, density and hue. Users can also see a "playback" of their work, an animation of the sequence of marks made building up to the final image. This can be can played on the iPad itself or exported and converted to a movie file. Still images can be sent directly from the iPad to email accounts or to the online photosharing library Flickr. The Flickr Brushes Gallery is included in this study as an example of how digitisation has fostered mass-engagement in not only the creative production but also the display and dissemination of digital art. The group had at the time of writing 4008 members. The "group pool" of images contained 41,458 items.

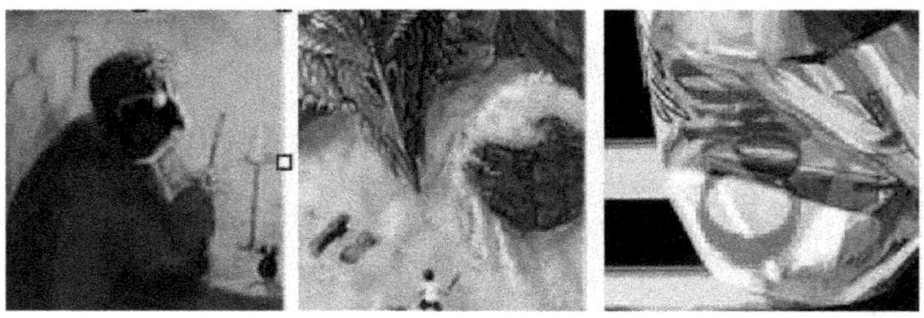

Figure 2: Top 3 Brushes Gallery returns for art, by, from left: Matthew Watkins, Luis Peso (9monos), suzi54241. Reproduced with the permission of the artists©.

A search was performed within the group on the word "art" which produced 8726 results that were then sorted by the Flickr "interesting" category. This is a proprietary algorithm so its operation is not known but it seems to weight a combination of views, comments and favorites to rank the order in which search returns are displayed. The search results were last checked on the 14th of September 2012. A sample of the most popular images were selected in order to compare the kinds of comments generated here and in s[edition]. Seventy were chosen to match the number available in s[edition].

Most of the images (60 of the 70) had between 300 and 1300 views. Others had more, ranging up to 3329 views. The top 70 was dominated by a relatively small number of contributors. There were just 15 artists within the top 70 returns. Those with the most images in the group were: Suzi54241 with 20 images; Lumilyon with 11; and Matthew Watkins with 10. Eight of the artists had between two and six images each. Four had just one image each. Most of the images (57) had between 11 and 40 comments. There was no direct correlation between the number of views and the number of comments. In total there were 2127 comments. Again, a qualitative content analysis [28] was performed on the comments. Table 2 shows the most frequent types of comment made.

Comment	Number	Percentage
Appreciation	1412	66.4
Thanks	373	17.5
"Seen in" Tags	238	11.2
Subject	20	0.9
Tutorial	19	0.9
Story	14	0.7
Questions	13	0.6
Links	11	0.5
Personal	10	0.5
Explanation	9	0.4
Invitation	8	0.4

Table 2: Flickr Brushes Gallery Comments

Secondary codes were used where comments could be coded under more than one category; Table 2 shows the primary code that summarized the main point of the comment.

There is a degree of similarity with the s[edition] comments in that the majority of comments express appreciation of the work. However it is important to note that the fifteen artists themselves made many of the comments, as they regularly show support for one another's work.

Art Appreciation

There were no negative comments at all perhaps because Flickr allows comment moderation by the author of the content that is commented on. As with the s[edition] appreciative comments these were often very brief exclamations such as "*WOW!*" and "*amazing!*" Several of the comments proclaim the work as a "*masterpiece*" and the artist a "*genius*". For example "*Wow!!!!! Great mood!!!! It's magical and can smell the wood in there!! Amazing masterpiece!!!!!*" The responses from the artists indicate that the accolades of genius are not meant or received altogether seriously.

A very small number of the appreciative comments referenced other artists or art history. For example "*I can see a bit of my admired Turner there...am I wrong?*" But this kind of appreciation was unusual. More often comments would be personal reflections, e.g. "*It brings me back to my childhood.*" Certain subjects would provoke appreciative comments which focused not only on the artwork but also the subject. Susi54241's work, for example, often features food or drink and this occasionally provoked comments about feeling hungry. One subject provoked more comments than any other and that was a portrait of Steve Jobs by MiaBia DC. This elicited a number of "*RIP*"s as well as tributes to the greatness of the man and the sadness of the loss. Similar non-art related comments referenced the short stories that accompanied one of the artist's work.

There were no instances of art criticism or interpretation sometimes invoked in the s[edition] comments. This absence will be returned to in the second reflection.

Thanks

Perhaps the most striking difference between the comments here and those on s[edition] is thanks by the artists themselves. Often the thanks would include mutual appreciation, for example "*Great thanks my friends ! Both love your works ;)*". There is evident pleasure in the exchanges "*Huge thanks my friends, for your feedback and compliments!*" This on occasion became slightly flirtatious, e.g. "*Oh Luis, I love a man who shivers...... and is so good with kind words! Thank you.*" Susi54241, one of the most prolific and popular artists returned in the search is also one of the most generous commenters on other people's work. Susi54241 reflects here on the value of the support: "*I'm very lucky. And I'm even luckier to have such a supportive team of artists around. How cool is that. AND have you all noticed how much better we're getting, especially from our first posts?*" There is then personal support but also technical and practical support as evidenced in the questions and explanations.

This generous praise and gratitude perhaps indicates that the principal economy here is gift exchange. Gift exchange has previously been identified as an important motivation amongst teenagers sending one another texts and in other social networking contexts [19, 32, 33]. The "gifts" here are in the form of social-relational transactions, rather than being purely about or driven by money. This kind of exchange has been referred to as a "renaissance of the commons" [17]. This will also be returned to.

Questions and Explanations

It is clear that the artists here follow one another's work and notice when something technically new has been accomplished. Although this is the Brushes group the artists use this app in conjunction with other apps such as

Autodesk's Mobile Sketchbook, here referred to as SB: "*first brushes and then SB? Why? What you find in SB that you are not in brushes? Not problem with definition exporting through ipod gallery? Skin colors extracted from a photo or selected with color editor? Wow, I want to learn from you.*" Susi54242 responds with a 499 word account of her process which details the use of particular apps and tools. Another of her posts is titled "tutorial" and provides examples and illustrations of her process. This has over 2000 views though the number of comments remains small and they are from the usual friends or community of practice.

The standard of photorealism which Luis Peso achieves in "The Dancer" leads one user to ask what kind of lens he used to take the shot. Peso responds: "*I would say immediately, but I did not use any lens, just my finger and a stylus with Brushes on iPad (it's a painting) but I highly appreciate your comment!! ;)*". Peso also posts a link to YouTube [29] where a movie of its creation can be viewed. A number of responses to questions and comments point to such links. These are to other media e.g. a news interview where an artist was featured.

Seen it Tags, Invitations and Personal Comments

"Seen it Tags" refer to automated messages that are posted from other groups. This allows users to "like" the work without sending their own message. Invitations referred to such groups asking particular artists to join them. Often membership seemed to boost viewing figures. Finally there were a small number of personal comments such as exchanges of happy birthday and responses to a question one contributor asked about whether to become an artist or a scientist.

REFLECTION ON BRUSHES GALLERY

The Brushes Gallery provides an online venue where hobbyists and practicing artists can meet [13], share techniques, compliment and encourage one another. It has been argued that the explosion in social media has effectively turned the gaze of what Guy Debord described as a society in thrall to mass media spectacle [26]. Michon et al claim: "the individual has become the spectacle and data its currency" where the only measure of success is peer recognition. It is interesting to note that, in stark contrast to the total disclosure of identity in s[edition] users here do not for the most part identify themselves except through screen-names. Just three of the fifteen artists work under anything remotely resembling a real name. Most of the artists have assigned their works as rights protected or "some rights protected". But the use of anonymous nametags suggests that financial returns are not the main concern for these artists. The economy appears to be one of gift exchange where the images facilitate sociality and the formation of a group identity.

The myriad of digital resources spanning open-source and commercial proprietary tools have enabled mass participation in activities which involve the generation and display of artefacts and identities online. These digital cultural practices are not exclusive to "cultivated" or educated individuals. As Bourdieu has noted (in relation to the popularity of hobbyist "camera clubs") [11] wider socio-cultural groups are enabled to explore more aesthetic interests. While the Brushes Gallery artists present their work on the World Wide Web, prospectively exposing their work to scrutiny and critical feedback, they also exert some level of "reputation management" by controlling total personal identity disclosure by using screen names.

Cultural intermediaries such as curators and collectors have long been criticized as expressing and promoting little more than class taste [10]. In the Brushes Gallery group, networks of users and search algorithms occupy a curatorial role but it is not organized in a hierarchy of cultural legitimation as with traditional galleries. This may appear then, to be a communal artistic utopia but it is important to remember that space here must in effect be rented from Flickr which is now owned by Yahoo. The identity of artist may be easier to adopt but harder to sustain. To paraphrase Andy Warhol, in the future everyone will be an artist for fifteen minutes.

The intangibility of files was a concern in some s[edition] comments and Flickr artists such as BueJayWay make the work tangible by making large prints when they attempt to sell it [13]. Studies of file sharing amongst music fans have suggested that making digital content more tangible might be a means of adding value [e.g. 1, 21]. The final section of the paper then considers a field study where artists were encouraged to display digital work in the tangible form of interactive digital frames in a physical gallery and later in a four wall projection room.

DIGITAL ORIGINALS EXHIBITION

The final study was a piece of "in the wild" field work which was inspired by the Brushes "replay" function. We exhibited off the shelf prototypes in an art gallery in order to examine audience responses to notions of digital authenticity and originality. An artwork called "Layered Landscapes" was developed with Mike, a local digital artist [9]. Mike produces his work by making initial sketches on paper and then scanning these into Photoshop before adding layers of line and colour to build up a final piece. He then makes high quality "giclee" prints of the work which he sells in local shops and art galleries. Working with the project team, Mike outputted separate image files of each Photoshop layer (see Figure 3) and these were loaded onto digital frames. This showed how the work built up in the manner of a Brushes animation to reveal the process and development of the work. Following the notion of "Autobiographical Design" [31] the first author lived with this "layered landscape" for several months before the exhibition [9].

For this study, seven off-the-shelf digital frames were purchased and preloaded with content. Cheaper frames were loaded with image sequences from a single picture,

Figure 3. Images from a Layered Landscape© presented in digital frames. Copyright the artist.

more expensive frames were loaded with multiple images of up to five sea and cityscapes, with each image constituting around 20 individual layers.

Two of the digital frames featured images from one other local artist, Jim, who had been loaned an iPad as part of the project. Jim was of interest to the team as he worked entirely in traditional media but had made some forty abstract iPad paintings using the Brushes and ArtRage apps. Selections of still images were shown in two frames, and additionally, Brushes movies showing the creation of the images were shown on an iMac. The exhibition was held in the print section of a gallery in the north of England for a period of three days from the 25th August 2012 (Figure 4).

Figure 4: Digital Originals Exhibit: Layered Landscapes©.

Fields notes were made by two researchers throughout the exhibition. Discussions and interviews were transcribed for thematic analysis [4]. Categories of codes were developed to summarise the data and organized into themes (ibid).

RESPONSES TO THE EXHIBITION

Discussions in the art gallery with the artists, gallerists and public, centered around *resources* in terms of time and the environment, the art *market* in terms of copyright and authenticity, and *aesthetics* in terms of sensuality and experience.

Resources: time and environment

One of the artists, Jim, had been highly skeptical about selling work in a digital frame. Although he had produced over forty digital paintings on the iPad he pointed out that he had spent years mastering oil paint and only months with the new digital media. Yet he was pleased with the work he had produced and agreed to show it in the exhibition.

The exhibition ran over a public holiday which coincided with a major local racing event. Although many tourists passed the shop very few came in. There were around 30 visitors on Saturday, fewer than 20 on Sunday. On Monday there was a drinks reception event where the artists invited friends and colleagues and around 50 visitors attended.

Most of the visitors over the first two days spent no more than four minutes walking around the sales area of the gallery where the digital frames were displayed. They would typically circle the room at walking pace looking at giclee prints on the walls as they went, sometimes pausing to look more closely at a particular wall hanging but usually for no more than a few seconds. They would usually end in the far right hand side corner and spend most time looking at postcards, which were the cheapest items in the gallery. Some would linger over the racks of giclee prints before leaving. Very few people looked at the work in the digital frames at all. Although the layered landscapes were conceived as changing slowly the frames were set at a maximum speed of every three seconds to highlight the changes. However most visitors did not notice that the images changed because they did not look at them for longer than three seconds. At night the frames stood out against the dark street and some passers by were observed to pause to see the changes. Doormen outside a nightclub on the other side of the street crossed the road to look more closely. But in the day it was not obvious that there was anything to look at and most passed by.

During the day glare from the window meant that the images did not show up well. The frames were moved to the back of the gallery and this improved visibility but no sales were made. Indeed there was only one sale during the whole of the three days. This was of a giclee print of the image in the window poster (see Figure 4) and the couple who bought it did not notice the digital frames.

One visitor was shown what was happening and she immediately responded very positively: "*Oh I see. Oooh I seee! Oh! Right! "I think that's quite amazing actually.*" But it was clear that most people did not notice or were not interested. Rather than unduly influence reactions the researchers refrained from explaining or pointing out the frames at all. The speed of the visitors did not surprise one local artist, William who visited Jim on the third day: "*That's the problem you've got with all visual media. [...] Artists know this. Mike knows it, I know it. [...] People do not spend very long, they don't, they scan, they walk away. [...] We do it. I go to the National Gallery. I know what I want to see.*" He argued that every aspect of our environment, the streets we walk down, the screens we work on, are saturated with visual media. The environment was also discussed in relation to energy consumption as well as visual overload. The gallery staff were particularly concerned about the environmental impact of viewing pictures through a machine rather than on paper or canvas. This concern was echoed in a number of discussions with artists and visitors.

Market: copyright and authenticity

Jim was not optimistic about sales; he had asked several people if they would buy work in a digital frame and received a flat "no". Mike was more optimistic and insisted on raising all of the prices on the first day. The two most expensive frames were loaded with five layered landscapes each. One was a set of coastal landscapes and the other was a set of places within the city. Each could be observed in various states of completion cycling through the layers so there were approximately fifty to sixty image files in each. Mike suggested £395 because he would sell single giclee prints for £80 each. Smaller cheaper digital frames which retailed at £20 each were loaded with a single image sequence and Mike suggested £80 for these.

Visitors generally agreed that they were very expensive items. The artists maintained that they were cheap even though none of them sold. There were cheaper versions of Jim's Brushes movies available at £2 each. Jim was happy to sell files in this way but Mike did not want to sell the files directly because people could "*do what they wanted*" with them. He was in effect selling the files on the SD cards in the frames but this did not worry him so much because it was not explicit. By contrast, William, the artist friend, was deeply concerned about the possibility that someone would take the SD card out and copy the work. He suggested sealing the SD cards in so that it was impossible to remove without damaging the frame. Jim objected that if the frame broke then the customer would lose the work but William thought that this would be fair enough: "*You can't have the thing removable and lose you're integrity. [...] They're buying that as a thing and at unit price — hundred and twenty pounds, it's a bargain. If it's got twelve images on it and that's an artefact in their home that's a bargain. That's how I see it. If it busts it busts.*" William returned to the idea of integrity many times and his notion of this was closely related to forms of copyright.

William discussed two forms of revenue for artists: royalties and sales. He had recently been approached by a publisher who supplied prints to architects. He had turned them down because "*the print prices were pennies*". Although there was a possible income it was tiny. Jim asked: "*What if ten thousand people had nicked* [stolen] *my stuff? I'd be quite chuffed*". William replied "*I wouldn't*" and maintained: "*Software can be seen as the new panacea: it isn't. [...] Aesthetics haven't changed since time immemorial.*" The topics of copyright, technology and aesthetics were fluid and slipped easily from one to the other.

Aesthetics: tangibility and experience

Ewan is a painter working in the urban realist tradition whose work is sold in international markets from a major London gallery. He has mentored both William and Jim and is the most successful of the local artists and his opinion is respected. Ewan also visited on the third day and for him Jim's Brushes movies playing on the iMac were very successful. The Brushes movies held his attention and he stood watching them for fifteen to twenty minutes. He also responded positively to Jim's still iPad paintings in the digital frames and noted that they were recognizably Jim's although he usually worked in oil paint. He was more critical of Mike's work, because of the use of recognizable Photoshop filters.

The frames themselves attracted some very negative aesthetic judgments from Ewan and many others. One of the larger and more expensive frames was mounted in a walnut veneer. This was described by the gallerist as "*horrendous*". Another visitor said that he didn't like digital frames because they were "*a fad*" and thought that the cheaper ones displaying single works looked like "*a sat nav in a Jaguar*". Several visitors compared some of the frames to TVs. One of Mike's friends said he preferred to see a still image on a wall and sequences in a book. A minority thought they were "*great*" and preferred the incomplete stages of the pictures with colour and white line. This was however a small minority of visitors.

Despite the lack of sales Jim was influenced by Ewan's reaction and considered the event a success. Ewan suggested projecting Jim's work on a large scale and this led to a further intervention at a university facility equipped with a four-wall immersive projection environment called the 3sixty room. Experimenting in this environment the artists found a space for digital painting that they found aesthetically and experientially satisfying (Figure 5).

Figure 5: The artists painting on walls in the four wall projection "3sixty" room.

The 3sixty room at York University provides an immersive environment in which it is possible to project images and film onto all four walls from floor to ceiling. An iPad was connected to project live images on to one wall and Jim's previous iPad paintings were displayed on the three others. Jim and William gasped when they first saw the work appear and were clearly delighted. Jim immediately began to paint, throwing light up the wall as he brushed his fingers over the tablet. The spectacle was powerful and the researcher remarked that it was like standing inside one of Jim's paintings. William, who had been consistently skeptical about becoming involved in the project admitted "*I came here to sneer, but I'm a convert.*" Both artists immediately expressed interest in creating an exhibition of digital work in the 3sixty room. This was for the artists and researcher a far more direct experience of the work. This was not a jpeg or mpeg but immersion in the work where the art was the only light source in the room.

Unlike the metaphor of the digital limited edition in s[edition] or the more tangible digital frames this was experiential [27] in the sense that it was time limited and confined to a particular space.

REFLECTION ON THE FIELD STUDY

In a study of amateur multimedia production [3] Bardzell pointed out that the identifiable use of presets in software such as fades and transitions sometimes signified the work of an amateur. Ewan was similarly critical of the content of Mike's work for the use of pre-set filters. But the use of off the shelf frames also perhaps signaled amateurism. More successful was the experimentation in the 3sixty room which indicated the potential of more experiential approaches.

The development of VHS technology was seen by many as the beginning of the end for cinema. Yet cinema endures because it offers a particular kind of experience not available in other forms: the group consumption of media on a very large screen. Similarly, live music continues to provide a source of income for musicians because it offers a unique experience not available in other formats. The 3sixty room enchanted and excited the artists and it is possible that such environments may offer opportunities for art making and viewing. Although environments such as the 3sixty room are not widely available it is not unique and it seems likely that screens in home environments are likely to enlarge until they occupy whole walls. It is possible to imagine then, services like Spotify for art, where users rent or subscribe to work, or bodies of work, and form relationships with particular artists or studios. Like the social exchanges observed in the Brushes Gallery, experiential approaches to digital art may be a route to value different to models like s[edition] which attempt to replicate older forms such as the limited edition.

DISCUSSION

This paper has considered three potential approaches to the dissemination and display of art, and reflected on how each model upsets traditional economic and cultural models. The first, s[edition], is largely conceptual and attempts to reproduce previous forms of commercially-viable limited editions. But the comparison of a digital edition to older forms of limited print editions is strained and resisted. The second, a Brushes Gallery group on Flickr, operates through forms of gift exchange. These are of clear social value but profits accrue to the owners of the aggregating site Yahoo, from whom the artists effectively rent space. The third approach attempted to embed digital content in tangible formats through utilization of digital frames. The intervention was crude and reliant on off the shelf technologies but nevertheless provoked enough responses from artists and visitors to indicate issues with this approach in terms of a negative environmental impact as well as poor aesthetic effects. The gallery exhibit led to further experimentation with immersive projection environments that perhaps suggest the potential value of experiential approaches.

Each of the approaches discussed are responses to the resistance of digital material to standard models of commoditization in the art market. Digital artwork presents difficulties for models of value based on scarcity because any digital file is infinitely reproducible. The digital also presents challenges to theories of value in terms of labour as digital methods makes the production of images faster and easier.

As noted in the introduction, many of the issues discussed here also affect the music industry. In a recent polemical book Joran Lanier argues that career options in the music industry are now very narrow [24]. He claims that the "giant musical act" dominates having become successful in the pre-digital era. He acknowledges new roles for aggregator websites that collect the music of thousands of others and also new opportunities for different forms of vanity career but these offer him little hope. There are parallels to Lanier's analysis of the music industry and the approaches to art considered here: s[edition] features work by "giant" artists primarily known for non-digital work; the Brushes Gallery is an aggregator site collating the work of thousands of artists and the artists could be seen as enjoying a form of vanity career. Approaches to making the digital more tangible did not generate sales. The reasons for this may be multiple but this initial investigation suggests that experiential approaches may be more promising.

The issue of how artists are to make any kind of living from their work may seem trivial. We are used to the notion of artists starving in garrets and new technology has not really changed this. However the art market is increasingly polarized. A small elite of art superstars makes obscene amounts of money in an unregulated market [23]. The function of the work of art is now to hang on a wall and become more valuable [22]. A society where only a tiny elite can make a living in this way is culturally diminished and impoverished.

CONCLUSION

This paper has reported findings from three related studies of digital art. Each of these focused on the ways in which artists might address the contradictions inherent in the creation of digital media. "s[edition]" offers users a metaphor where access to a digital file is equated with the ownership of a limited edition paper print. This is conceptually difficult entailing the idea of "owning but not having" as one user put it. The Brushes Gallery offers users a valuable social experience and operates as a form of gift exchange. However, the main beneficiary of this model is the aggregating site. The field study explored the strategy of making digital files more tangible by making layers of images available in digital frame. This was largely unsuccessful due to aesthetic and environmental issues but it suggested further possibilities for experience based approaches. It is not clear that any of approaches discussed will enable artists to make a living in the digital age and it may be that future manifestations offer combinations of these strategies. Although it is too early to dismiss entirely any of the approaches there are clearly issues with models that simply attempt to reproduce pre-digital models.

REFERENCES

1. Alonso, M.B. and Keyson, D.V. (2005) Music Cube: Making Digital Music Tangible. *CHI '05*, ACM Press (2005), 1176–179.
2. Appleyard, B. David Hockney Interview, *Sunday Times* 30 Jan 2011, available: http://www.bryanappleyard.com/david-hockney-interview/
3. Bardzell, J. Creativity in Amateur Multimedia: popular culture, critical theory and HCI. *Human Technology 3.* 1 (2007) 12–33.
4. Braun, V.A. and Clarke,V. Using thematic analysis in psychology. *Qualitative research in psychology*, 3 (77), (2006), 77–101.
5. *BBC*. Streaming Revenues Up 40% globally in 2012. http://www.bbc.co.uk/news/entertainment-arts-19270362 (2012).
6. *BBC*. A Glimpse At Piracy in the UK and Beyond. http://www.bbc.co.uk/news/technology-19599526. (2012).
7. *BBC*. Obama "Hope" artist Shephard Fairey fined. http://www.bbc.co.uk/news/world-us-canada-19522210 (2012).
8. Benjamin, W. The Work of Art in the Age of Mechanical Reproduction. In: *Illuminations*. Fontana, London, (1992 paperback ed.), 211–235.
9. Blythe, M., Briggs, J., Olivier, P. and Hook, J. Digital Originals: Reproduction as a Space for Design. *NordiCHI '12*, ACM (2012), 1–10.
10. Bourdieu, P. (1986). *Distinction: a social critique of the judgement of taste.* Routledge and Kegan Paul, London.
11. Bourdieu, P. (1990). *Photography: A middle-brow art.* Polity Press, Cambridge.
12. Briggs, J. and Blythe, M. 2012. No Oil Painting: Digital Originals and Slow Prints. In: Slow Technology: Critical Reflection and Future Directions, *DIS '12.*
13. Briggs, J. and Blythe, M. Post Anxiety Art: Economies and cultures of digital painting. In *Post Digital Art, Proc of the 3rd Computer Art Congress*, Paris (2012) 161–168.
14. *Brushes App* http://www.brushesapp.com/
15. *Brushes Gallery* http://www.flickr.com/groups/brushes/
16. Charmaz, K. (2006). *Constructing Grounded Theory.* Sage, London.
17. Clippenger, J. H. and Bollier, D. (2005). A Renaissance of the Commons: How the New Sciences and Internet are Framing a New Global Identity and Order. In: R. A. Ghosh (ed.) *CODE: Collaborative Ownership and the Digital Economy*. MIT, Cambridge MA, 259–286.
18. Day, E. (2012). Can You Make Any Kind of Living As an Artist? *The Guardian*. 2012. http://www.guardian.co.uk/culture/2012/jul/29/artists-day-job-feature.
19. Faraj, S. and Johnson, S.L. (2011). Network exchange patterns in online communities. *Organization Science*, 22(6), 1464–1480.
20. *Gadgetspeak* 5000 Free, Limited Edition Artworks to celebrate Trafalgar Square Sculpture Unveiling. 23 February 2012.
21. Gallardo, D. and Jordà, S. Tangible jukebox: back to palpable music. *TEI '10*. ACM (2010), 199–202.
22. Hughes, R. (1990). *The Shock of the New: Art and the Century of Change*. Thames and Hudson, London.
23. Hughes, R. (2008). *The Mona Lisa Curse*. Director Chang M. Oxford Film and Television.
24. Lanier, J. (2010). *You Are Not A Gadget: A Manifest.* Allen Lane. Penguin Group, London.
25. Lidwell, W. and Holden, K., (2003). *Universal Principles of Design*. Rockport Publishers Inc., MA USA.
26. Michon, A., Flazinski, C. and Chalubert, C. On the Separation Between the Aesthetic and the Functional and how the Digital will Steal Form. In *Post Digital Art, Proc of the 3rd Computer Art Congress*, Paris (2012).
27. McCarthy, J. and Wright, P. (2004) *Technology as Experience*. MIT Press, MA USA.
28. Mayring, P. (2004) Qualitative Content Analysis. In U. Flick, E. von Kardoff, and I. Steinke (eds), *A Companion to Qualitative Research.* Sage, London.
29. Peso, L. (2011). *The Dancer* retrieved from: http://www.youtube.com/watch?v=okhhY-sTe0k&feature=youtube_gdata_player
30. *s[edition]* http://www.seditionart.com
31. Sengers, P., Boehner, K., David, S. and Kaye, J., Reflective Design. *CC 2005* ACM Press (2005) 49–58.
32. Skågeby, J. (2010). Gift-giving as a conceptual framework: framing social behavior in online networks. *Journal of Information Technology*, 25(2), 170–177.
33. Taylor, A. and Harper, R. (2003). The Gift of the Gab?: A Design Oriented Sociology of Young People's Use of Mobiles. *Computer. Supported Cooperative Work* 12, 3 (2003), 267–296.
34. Žižek, S. (2008). *Living in the End Times*. Verso, London.

'See Me, Feel Me, Touch Me, Hear Me': Trajectories and Interpretation in a Sculpture Garden

Lesley Fosh[1], Steve Benford[2], Stuart Reeves[2], Boriana Koleva[2], Patrick Brundell[2]
University of Nottingham
Nottingham, UK
[1]psxlf@nottingham.ac.uk, [2][firstname.lastname]@nottingham.ac.uk

ABSTRACT
We apply the HCI concept of trajectories to the design of a sculpture trail. We crafted a trajectory through each sculpture, combining textual and audio instructions to drive directed viewing, movement and touching while listening to accompanying music. We designed key transitions along the way to oscillate between moments of social interaction and isolated personal engagement, and to deliver official interpretation only after visitors had been given the opportunity to make their own. We describe how visitors generally followed our trajectory, engaging with sculptures and making interpretations that sometimes challenged the received interpretation. We relate our findings to discussions of sense-making and design for multiple interpretations, concluding that curators and designers may benefit from considering ‚trajectories of interpretation'.

Author Keywords
Galleries; museums; trajectories; interpretation; art; sculpture; collaboration; audio; instructions.

ACM Classification Keywords
H.5.m. Information interfaces and presentation (e.g., HCI).

INTRODUCTION
A ‚Holy Grail' for galleries and museums is to create a deep personal engagement with exhibits that leads visitors into making interpretations. This is challenging for a combination of deeply-rooted reasons. First, many public visitors are not able to easily make interpretations, lacking either specific knowledge or a general training in how to interpret art works or historical artefacts. Indeed, this is one reason why cultural institutions suggest interpretations through labels, catalogues and interactive technologies. Second, visitors may find it difficult to instantaneously switch into a mode of deep engagement with an exhibit. While films and books are able to engage a viewer or reader over considerable time, a museum exhibit has only a few seconds in which to attract attention and frame engagement. Finally, even when visitors do engage, numerous distractions may interfere, notably the presence of other visitors and the demands of group members.

Perhaps unsurprisingly then, galleries and museums have proved fertile ground for HCI research. Much of this has focussed on the design of new interactive technologies including mobile guides, especially those exploiting location-based services [1, 2] and augmented reality [23], tangible and tabletop technologies [12], and also more unusual bespoke interactive artworks [8, 14]. There have also been numerous studies of visitor behaviour in both HCI and museum studies, covering issues such as dwell times [20], categorising visitor behaviour [21] and collaborative interaction [13, 14, 24]. In spite of this extensive body of work, the fundamental challenge remains – it is notoriously difficult to create a deep engagement between visitors and exhibits.

In this paper we explore whether a recent idea to emerge from HCI – that of ‚trajectories' – might offer a solution. The notion of ‚interactive trajectories' emerged from studies of collaborative behaviour in galleries and museums in which visitors' interactions were seen to shape those of subsequent visitors. These studies inspired a series of trajectory-related concepts including principles for the design of spectator interfaces [17], chaining public displays [15], and a general framework for designing extended cultural experiences in terms of canonical, participant and historic trajectories [4, 5]. To date, these concepts have been used to compare existing experiences or to analyse data from studies [10], with a focus on interactive performances [3]. They have not, as yet, been proactively applied to the design of new experiences, reflecting a wider challenge for HCI of putting theory into practice [18].

In response, we describe an attempt to directly apply the concept of trajectories to the design of a visiting experience from the outset. The experience in this case is visiting a sculpture garden. We describe how we designed a global trajectory through the garden, as well as detailed local interactional trajectories through each sculpture, weaving together instructions, music and interpretation in an attempt to frame moments of deep personal engagement. We describe how pairs of visitors experienced this trajectory, very often following it, but not without some interesting tensions. We conclude by affirming how existing trajectory concepts were helpful in designing the visiting experience, describing our own contributions to the theory, and introduce the broader idea of designing ‚trajectories through interpretation'.

DESIGN OF THE SCULPTURE GARDEN EXPERIENCE

The setting for our experience is Rufford Abbey, a historic country house whose extensive grounds include the sculpture garden that is the focus of our design. It attracts a wide population of visitors, from elderly couples to family and school groups, and from those interested in art, to those who have come to enjoy the countryside. The sculpture garden is home to over 25 works that have been collected and commissioned over a 30 year period. These vary in form, structure and materials (stone, metals, ceramic, etc.). The sculptures are arranged along a path with relatively little additional interpretation; three are accompanied by a plaque giving the name of the sculpture, the artist, and a short thematic description, while the remainder stand unadorned. This provided us with a ‚blank canvas' against which to explore how to enhance engagement and interpretation. While no formal observations studies were carried out into how visitors experienced the sculpture garden without our intervention, our initial observations were that visitors tended to walk around in groups, sometimes stopped to look at sculptures, but did not on the whole engage very deeply or for very long, touch sculptures or otherwise engage physically with them.

Our overall process was to commission a sound designer and a performance poet to help us compose an extended visiting experience. The sound designer chose a specific piece of music for each of the nine sculptures we had selected from the garden. The performance artist then designed a series of performative interactions to match each sculpture and music track, encouraging visitors to engage by standing or moving in certain ways, adopting unusual viewpoints, or touching the sculptures. The net result was an unusual experience in which visitors were invited to engage with a series of sculptures alongside other artists' responses to – or interpretations of – them. The experience was designed to be used by groups of visitors who are visiting the sculpture garden together, interacting with both the sculptures and each other. The whole experience evolved over several months of iterative design and testing.

Our approach was to work with the idea of trajectories from the very outset, broadly following the framework of concepts set out in [4, 5]. To quickly recap these: cultural user experiences may extend over multiple and hybrid spaces, timescales, roles and interfaces and can be expressed using three types of trajectory. The designer's plan for the experience is expressed by one or more *canonical trajectories* which pass through key *transitions* including *beginnings*, *endings*, *role and interface transitions*, *access to physical resources*, *episodes*, and *seams* in the underlying infrastructure. *Participant trajectories* express what each participant actually does and the designer needs to consider how these may *diverge* and *reconverge* with canonical trajectories, but also how they *interleave* through *encounters*, moments of *isolation* and *pacing*. Finally, *historic trajectories* provide opportunities to reflect on and recount experiences. We now consider how these various concepts informed our design.

Designing the canonical trajectory

We first set about designing our *canonical trajectory* through the experience. This involved thinking at two levels of scale: establishing a global trajectory through the garden based on a sequence of *episodes* involving individual sculptures, and designing local trajectories that would enhance engagement with each individual sculpture. At the global level, a visitor can choose to experience up to nine sculptures, presented as a list on a smartphone interface. We arranged the list to reflect the order in which the sculptures would naturally be encountered when following the highly visible path that runs through the garden. We anticipated that visitors would most likely follow this existing canonical trajectory, though they were free to diverge and visit the sculptures in any order they wished. Key to our design was the structure of local trajectories into and through each sculpture. We divided these into five stages – approach, engage, experience, disengage and reflect – as shown in Figure 1, with each requiring us to consider key *transitions*.

Approach

The approach phase describes the journey from choosing a 4sculpture, finding it in the garden, to standing in front of it. This is supported by a series of textual instructions delivered on the smartphone. The initial list gives the name of each sculpture along with two words that suggest the kind of experience that is to follow, so as to provide a gentle framing. We used the set of words: "contemplate", "look", "imagine", "interact", "pretend", "touch", "move", "pose" and "think". On selecting a sculpture the visitor learns its title, the sculptor's name, the material, a one sentence history, and also a clue as to where to find it.

We considered the key transition of *seams*, gaps and inaccuracies in the underlying infrastructure of positioning and communications systems. Early testing revealed that the seams in GPS would cause glitches in the experience. However, we also realised that visitors should be able to find the sculptures for themselves from just an image and a clue given their distinctive form, the constrained nature of the garden and the visible path. We therefore dropped GPS (or indeed any other automated positioning service) in favour of simply showing visitors an image of the sculpture and asking them to manually confirm when they had found it. The approach therefore ends when the visitor stands in front of a chosen sculpture and presses *"I am here"*.

Engage

They now enter the engage phase that aims to prepare them for a deep and personal engagement with the sculpture. The first step involves a further key transition, that of *putting on an interface*. The visitor is given the text instruction: *"when you are ready to start the experience, put on your headphones and press OK"*. The donning of headphones is intended to signal a shift of focus, isolating the visitor from the outside world. They now hear a series of audio instructions that have been written and recorded by our performance poet and that ask the visitor to undertake a particular action while at the sculpture.

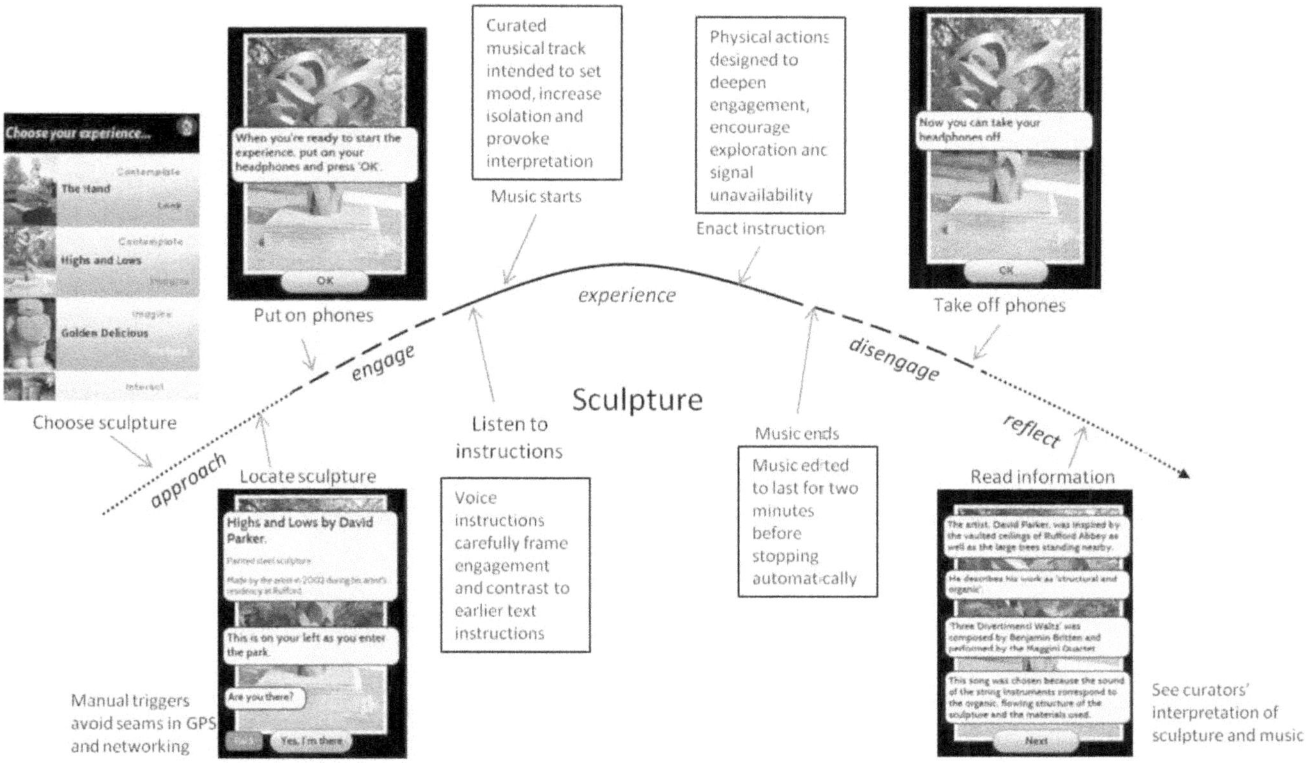

Figure 1. Design of the local trajectory through each sculpture

Sculpture			Musical accompaniment	Physical action
1	The Hand		*Music For a Found Harmonium* by Penguin Cafe Orchestra	*There are words written on this sculpture. How many will you read today? What story do they tell you?*
2	Highs and Lows		*Three Divertimenti Waltz* by Benjamin Britten	*Rest your eyes on the bottom of this metallic structure. Now let your mind weave in and out of the passages, along and in between the branches. Where do you end up?*
3	Golden Delicious		*Noah's Ark* by CocoRosie	*This man has brought you an apple. Why don't you take it and put it in your pocket? Or maybe you would like to eat it?*
4	Two Vessels		*Sonata V* by John Cage	*Take your hands and move them down the pillar to feel the texture. How did it get like that?*
5	Young Girl	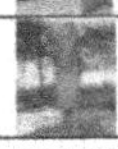	*Girl* by PJ Harvey	*Why don't you take a closer look at this girl? Who is she? What does she look like?*
6	Chimney Stacks and Iron Bridge Archway	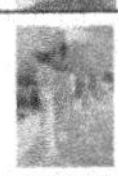	*Allegro Maestoso (Water Music Suite 2)* by George Frideric Handel	*Is anyone around? Why don't you hold your head high and march through the arches? There are many different paths, but which one will you choose?*
7	Fruit Gatherers		*Heartbeat Drum Song* by Robbie Robertson and the Red Road Ensemble	*Choose a place in the group and stand there, still as a statue. Who are the others in your group? What is your story?*
8	The Shrine at Nemi		*Dovehouse Pavan* by Alfonso Ferrabusco	*Diana might be watching you, but climb up the steps and peer into the tiny temple. What do you see?*
9	Pine Cube	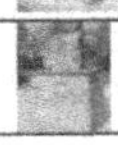	*Mentiras* by John Zorn	*Why don't you take a seat? If you close your eyes, count to ten and then open them, have the shapes moved?*

Table 1. Musical accompaniment and instruction chosen for each sculpture

These instructions were designed to encourage the visitor to *access the physical resource* of the sculpture in a distinctive way, adopting specific viewpoints, moving in particular ways, and reaching out and touching. A key part of this transition involved presenting the instructions as audio in order to disengage the visitor from the screen, reengage them with our poet's performative voice, and enable them to gracefully fade into the subsequent music. The audio track began with an opening introduction designed to set the tone for subsequent instructions: *"Hello, my name is Francesca Beard. I'm a poet, and I'll be your guide on this tour of the sculpture garden ..."*

Experience

The experience stage begins as the voice fades out and the selected music track fades in. At this point, we expect the visitor to carry out the suggested action. Table 1 summarises the musical accompaniment and action chosen for each sculpture (numbered 1-9 in the order they would be encountered along the path), while the following paragraphs outline the rationale behind these choices.

Physical actions

We designed a range of actions so as to sustain novelty and surprise at each new episode of interaction. It was important that each action was meaningful in the context of its particular sculpture, encouraging an unusual but relevant form of engagement. For example, the sculpture *Pine Cube* is surrounded by benches, so it seemed natural to ask people to sit here, while *Two Vessels* had an interesting texture that begged to be touched. Some sculptures did not suggest such obvious physical interactions, leading us to suggest more figurative instructions that stimulated the imagination. Thus, instructions might ask visitors to look closely at particular parts of a sculpture, answer questions, imagine stories, or undertake physical actions such as sitting, standing or climbing, marching or stroking.

Drawing on our performance poet's experience of leading improvisation workshops, we decided that the wording of the instructions should be gently persuasive rather than prescriptive, using opening phrases such as *"Why don't you..."* rather than simply telling the visitor what to do. We expanded upon the basic instruction to set the mood for the engagement and to encourage the visitor to reflect. For example, at *The Hand*, the instruction reads, *"There are words written on this sculpture. How many will you read today? What story do they tell you?"* The frequent use of „you' was intended to personally engage the visitor.

Music

The selection of music was designed to reflect the actions at a sculpture while gently reinforcing its themes and materials. Our sound artist listed keywords for each sculpture, drew up a shortlist of songs, and then listened to these while viewing the sculpture in situ. Tracks that worked especially well were those that evoked a strong mood or mirrored visual form. The final selection ranges across genres, mixing pop and classical. Almost all tracks were instrumental, and the few vocals that were present were very much in the background, as it was felt that lyrics would distract the visitor from the sculpture. By way of example, the steel sculpture *The Hand* was assessed by studying the sculpture and reading background information, revealing the key themes of communication, inclusivity and positivity with respect to disabled children. *Music for a Found Harmonium* by Penguin Café Orchestra was chosen as its rhythm, tempo and simple structure were deemed to match the sculpture's busy form while the upbeat melody fitted with its themes.

Disengage

Each musical accompaniment was edited to play for up to one and a half minutes before fading out, at which point we anticipated that the visitor would disengage. We had discussed enabling the visitor to control the timing of the track for themselves, ending it when ready or even allowing the full track to play on. However, we eventually decided against any design features that would invite the visitor to look at or interact with the smartphone while engaged with the sculpture. Fading the music before its normal end might also leave a sense of something being unfinished, a hanging question that invites closure. The visitor is then asked to remove the headphones, a key transition in reengaging with the surrounding world.

Reflect

Building on the concept of the *historic trajectory*, a key feature of our design was the idea to give the official interpretation of a sculpture only after encountering it. Our intention was to invite visitors to make their own interpretations (encouraged by the physical actions and the music) before explaining ours. We extracted key material about each sculpture from the official visitor centre website and combined those with information about the musical accompaniment (including why it has been selected) to produce a single screen of official interpretation that was presented to the visitor shortly after they had been asked to remove the headphones and that they could digest while walking away from the sculpture.

Interleaving trajectories

The trajectories conceptual framework emphasizes the importance of considering how different participants' trajectories may overlap and the need to explicitly design in moments of *isolation* as well as *encounter*. In response, the above trajectory was designed to consciously switch the visitor from being engaged with their partner while moving between sculptures, to being „isolated' from them when experiencing a sculpture. The use of text instructions during the approach and reflect stage allows for talking, while additional information during the reflect stage was intended to stimulate discussion. In contrast, donning headphones was intended to isolate visitors from social interaction while at the sculpture, and the relatively unusual physical actions were designed to signal to others that the visitor was engaged in a special activity and so should not be interrupted. The problems of using headphones in group visiting have been discussed in previous literature, and novel solutions have been proposed such as group members being able to eavesdrop on others' audio guides [2]. Our solution here is to employ them to create and mark a key transition between isolation and encounter. Our aim was not to make the visit any less (or indeed more) social, but rather to achieve a more balanced and productive separation between moments of contemplative reflection and of rich discussion between partners.

STUDYING THE SCULPTURE GARDEN EXPERIENCE

While we have described the *intended* trajectory through the experience, we now consider how visitors *actually* experienced it, and how it shaped their experience.

We studied our experience being used at the sculpture garden over a period of two weeks. The application was uploaded onto two Apple iPhone 3GS smartphones that were given out to (mostly) pairs of visitors. Overall, 29 people took part in the study, 26 in pairs and 3 lone visitors who were enthusiastic to try the technology while their partners preferred to experience the sculptures in the traditional way. Of these 29, 17 were female; 12 were male; 4 were aged 16 – 25; 12 were aged 26 – 40; and 13 were older than 40. 17 visitors were recruited by being approached at the site while a further 12 were recruited beforehand through a network of people interested in interactive cultural experiences.

Once recruited, visitors were asked to sign a consent form, given a mobile device each and a set of over-ear headphones, before being introduced to the system, including how to operate the touch-screen and use the volume controls. Visitors were then told to commence their visit when they were ready, using the guide. They were informed that while only a subset of sculptures had content loaded onto the guide they were free to explore the entire set of sculptures. Visitors spent between 20 minutes and an hour on the experience.

We used video to record visitors' interactions from a distance, capturing an overview of their physical actions but without interfering with the experience. When visitors had finished touring the sculpture garden they were interviewed in pairs. The interview followed a semi-structured format, covering their experience of the instructions; physical actions; musical accompaniments; the information they received; and their interactions with partners. They were also asked how their experience of using the system compared to their usual visiting habits and were given opportunities to offer views on topics of their own choosing.

In the following, we report our findings under three themes: Did visitors follow our trajectory? How did they engage with individual sculptures? And how did this lead them into making interpretations?

Following the trajectory

In general, the technology worked very reliably and visitors quickly picked up how to use it and understood what they were supposed to be doing. Figure 2 provides a summary overview of the extent to which visitors followed our trajectory and engaged with the sculptures. Each row represents an individual visitor (with pairings highlighted), while each column represents a given sculpture (numbered as in Table 1). Each cell is coloured with an estimation (from reviewing the videos) of the extent to which this visitor followed the instructions at this sculpture. Red shows when they did not appear to follow the instructions at all, standing at a distance, looking away or making no attempt to act in the prescribed way. Orange represents partially following the instruction, clearly making an attempt, but one that was hesitant, for example only briefly touching a sculpture. Yellow shows cases of closely following an instruction over an extended time, for example completing a prescribed sequence of movements or continuing to touch for the duration of the music. Grey-shaded cells show where a visitor missed out this sculpture altogether; asterisks show sculptures that were visited out of sequence (i.e. not in the canonical order); and musical notes show where the music was replayed.

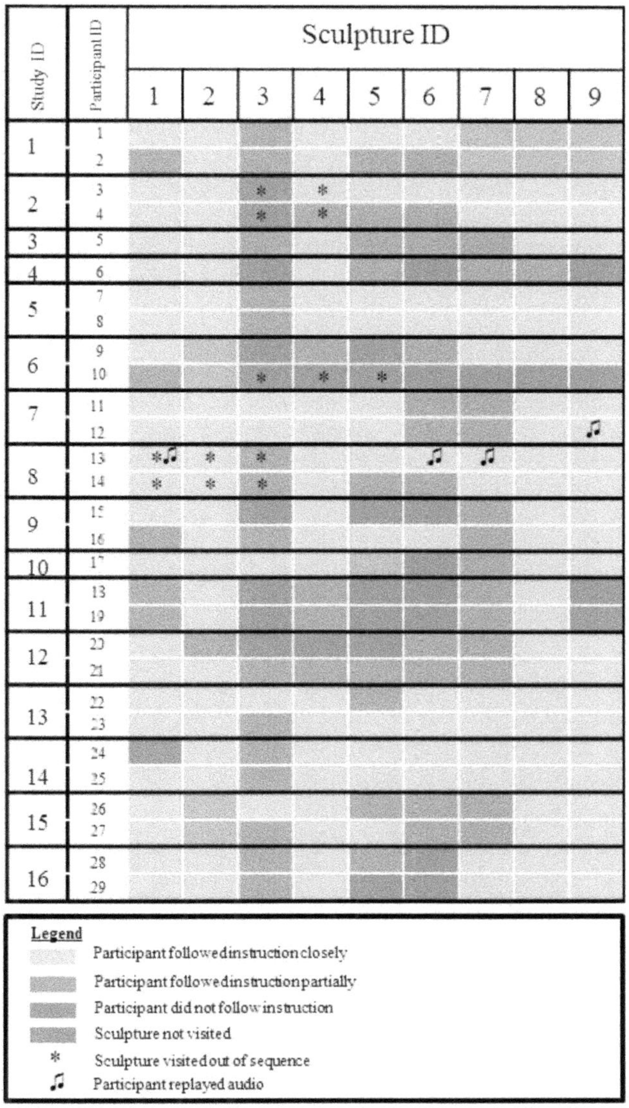

Figure 2. Table showing visitor behaviour at sculptures

Our table reveals that the large majority of visitors followed the global trajectory, completing all nine sculptures, and mostly in the canonical order (only one pair stopped before the end, two pairs missed out the second sculpture, and the occasional reversals of order in the middle of sequence). We see just a few examples of repeating the music; this always involved just one partner in a pair and was carried out immediately. In two cases the action was also repeated, once when one play of the music was not enough to fully complete the action (*Chimney Stacks*) and once to repeat the action from a different viewpoint (*Fruit Gatherers*).

There is also evidence that many people followed our local trajectories through sculptures. It was the case *in all of the examples* that visitors listened through to the end of the music before disengaging. Moreover the rough coding of physical actions in the table suggests that people very often attempted to carry out the instructions to some degree, and appeared to closely follow them more than half of the time. Sculpture 3 (*Golden Delicious*) was perhaps the most problematic in terms of visible engagement, and it is notable that this calls on the imagination by demanding an impossible physical action.

Pairs mostly stayed together throughout the visit, attending to the same sculptures at the same time and walking together between sculptures. They often attempted to coordinate putting on their headphones and triggering the audio instructions and music, usually when they had arrived at a sculpture, but sometimes as they approached. We did not see any visitors deliberately starting the audio separately, for example, taking turns. Pairs also tended to wait for each other to finish before moving on to the next sculpture. Pair 6 was the only one to separate during the experience (visiting different statues) and they varied greatly in their responses. Pair 11 was unusual in that they were the only couple who discussed and shared the decision about how to respond before physically engaging. A small number of visitors kept their headphones on throughout the experience, which caused uncertainty for their partners.

In short, the initial impression from video observations is that visitors followed our trajectories to a first approximation. The next question is what did this involve in detail, specifically how did the trajectory shape their engagement with the sculptures?

Engaging with sculptures

We now consider how our trajectory led visitors to engage with the sculptures: how they performed the physical actions, and how they coordinated this as pairs.

Performing physical actions

We noted above that visitors most often made an attempt to follow the instructions for physical action. However, the fine details of what this meant and how they felt about it varied considerably. For example, at *Fruit Gatherers*, visitors were asked to *"Find a place in the group and stand there, still as a statue"*. Responses ranged from standing still *near* the sculpture for only a few seconds, to standing visibly still *among* the figures for the duration of the music.

Instructions that directed visitors' attention to detailed features and information were very often followed, for example at *The Hand* (*"There are words written on this sculpture. How many will you read today?"*) and at *The Shrine at Nemi* (*"Climb the steps and peer into this tiny temple"*). At these sculptures, visitors tended to begin the audio while standing back from the sculpture, on the path. Upon hearing the instruction, they would begin moving to see the parts of the sculpture that had been pointed out. For example, having approached *The Hand* and positioned themselves in front of it, the two visitors in Figure 3 hear the instruction and then physically move around the sculpture to read the text written around its sides. This level of compliance at *The Hand* was seen by 23 of the 29 participants, as shown in Figure 2.

Instructions that required a slightly higher level of physical engagement, such as touching a sculpture or adopting a pose, were often followed. Upon hearing an instruction, most visitors did not hesitate before carrying it out and remained physically engaged throughout the music. For example, at *Two Vessels* (*"Take your hands and move them down the pillar to feel the texture"*) visitors would typically hear the instruction, approach the sculpture to begin feeling it, and remain at the sculpture, touching it and looking at it, until the music had faded. This level of compliance at *Two Vessels* was displayed by 22 out of the 29 visitors (as shown in Figure 2). Most visitors welcomed being given license to touch the sculptures: *"I especially liked ones where it was like ‚touch it', because I always want to touch sculptures and I'm never sure if you're really meant to"*. Indeed, we observed that once instructed to touch one sculpture, visitors became more tactile with subsequent sculptures. However, some remained nervous at breaking what is seen as a taboo behaviour: *"I'm very conscious of walking through art when you're not allowed to touch ... the very first one it said ‚what does it feel like?' and I just thought, I can't touch it, surely?"*

Figure 3. Reading the text at *The Hand*

Instructions demanding theatrical rather than tactile engagement, for example marching through the arches of *Chimney Stacks*, invoked greater reluctance. Having been asked, *"Is anyone around? Why don't you hold your head high and march through the arches?"* some visitors stood back to listen (Figure 4), while others hesitated before carrying out the action, and many performed it half-heartedly as if to minimise their visibility. In fact, 8 out of the 29 visitors at *Chimney Stacks* made no attempt to follow the instruction, and 11 followed it only partially. When asked in the interviews how they felt about carrying out these more performative actions, visitors admitted to feeling "silly" or "self-conscious" about doing them. As one commented: *"I did not march with my head high, because I was conscious there were people around who were already looking at us thinking what on earth are they doing?"* That said, a minority embraced being asked to perform this sort of action and did so in a flamboyant way.

Finally, other instructions were challenging because they demanded impossible actions, for example "*This man has brought you an apple. Why don't you take it and put it in your pocket? Or maybe you would like to eat it?*" at *Golden Delicious* couldn't be followed literally. Most visitors were not able to interpret it as a clear instruction for action and remained stood still in front of it. However, a few (only 5 out of 29) made attempts to touch or grab the apple.

Figure 4. Standing back from *Chimney Stacks*

Coordinating engagement

The large majority of conversations took place while moving between sculptures or after the audio had finished and headphones had been removed at a sculpture. For the most part, visitors did not try to talk to or otherwise interrupt one another once the headphones were on and the audio was underway, apart from the occasional short exclamation (e.g., *"It's warm"* on touching *Two Vessels*) which largely passed unacknowledged. In a few exceptional cases, visitors moved their headphones off of one ear to hear a partner's comments, while there were occasional periods where pairs communicated intensively, for example taking a series of photographs of one another. However, such behavior was atypical, and for the most part visitors seem to mutually respect their isolated engagement.

There were, however, many examples of tacit coordination in synchronizing engagement with sculptures. We noted earlier that pairs generally tried to begin their engagement together. However, the two devices were not technically synchronised and so there was often a few seconds delay between them. We often observed a quick exchange of glances and smiles between pairs to confirm that they had heard the instructions before both had followed them.

Figure 5. Exchanging glances while engaging

Physical contention for the sculptures was usually not a problem as the garden was relatively quiet, but there were a few problematic cases where limited physical access meant that one partner had to wait for the other, for example at *The Shrine at Nemi* where visitors are invited to climb the steps and look through a small aperture. *Chimney Stacks* provided another example of coordinating actions, with cases of one partner following the other, sometimes copying their actions in solidarity, but with at least one case of one partner marching ahead and the second following with reluctance. Local coordination was also evident when one partner would wait nearby while the other replayed a music track before both moved on together, as we see in Figure 6 where one partner takes photos while the other repeats her experience at *Chimney Stacks*.

Figure 6. One partner waits while the other replays the music

Making an interpretation

This shaping of engagement with sculptures could often lead to a deeper understanding. Our interviews showed that an important part of this was how the physical actions led to distinctive ways of viewing them. At *Pine Cube*, one visitor found after closing and opening their eyes: *"you can actually see the shapes, and then it like reframes itself, things like that*", while at *The Shrine at Nemi* a visitor described discovering further detail: "*I went up the stairs and looked through the thing after she said because I wouldn't have known that was there otherwise"*. Furthermore, visitors found this led to a deeper understanding: *"because you were being prompted to look at certain things ... possibly helps you to understand what the artist was trying to achieve and the mood they were trying to set, and, you know, the cultural or ethical reasons they made the art. So yeah, I guess from that point of view, it defined what you needed to look at a bit more."*

Interviews also revealed the significant role of the music in interpretation. Visitors mostly judged the music choices on whether they „worked' or not, meaning whether they could make a connection between the music and the sculpture. One of the ways music was deemed to work for visitors was by setting a general emotional tone for engaging with the sculpture. A slow, dragging guitar piece (*Girl* by PJ Harvey) was selected to accompany the sculpture *Young Girl*, with the intention of creating an eerie mood to accompany the headless sculpture. Visitors picked up on this mood, with one even reporting feeling apprehensive before approaching the sculpture: *"I didn't like the one for the statue without the head, because that made me not want to go near it."* More positive emotional reactions were reported at Golden Delicious: *"It kind of cheered me up... I was kind of looking at him and then the music and the app encouraged me to like, engage with it and feel jolly, and get into a cheeky mood and it, it was quite uplifting. The music definitely influenced that one."*

Others looked to make specific meaningful connections. The sculpture *Fruit Gatherers* abstractly depicted a group of Native American women carrying fruit on their heads. The traditional Native American music chosen for this sculpture enabled one visitor to focus on it: *"It did make you look at it and realise what it was, and picture the ladies actually there, actually putting the fruit on their heads."*

Ultimately, it was the performing of physical actions, as seen by most visitors, and the effects of the music, which the interview data suggests prompted visitors to engage intellectually or emotionally with the sculpture, that suggested that visitors were experiencing deep engagement and which fostered interpretation: *"What you were being asked to look at and contemplate, and after you'd done that for a little second then obviously your mind drifts because of the music, but, that was a nice experience because it allowed you to think about it in your own way as well, rather than just the way you're being told."*

This notion of ‚not being told' seems to have been especially important, and had been directly embedded in our trajectory in that interpretive information was only provided at the visitor's completion of the trajectory. The majority of visitors appreciated learning the official interpretation after engaging with the sculpture rather than before: *"I think you need to look at it first. And then have the information. Because if you have the information up front it colours how you look at a sculpture."*

As a result, visitors' interpretations were not always in agreement with our own. Some criticized our musical interpretation of the sculptures. The choice of the experimental jazz piece, *Mentiras* by John Zorn, to accompany the sculpture *Pine Cube* was criticized by several people: *"I thought that the last Pine Cube, the music for me was completely alien to what we were looking at. I couldn't understand... I know it was explained but it didn't feel right for me."* Another criticized our musical choice for *The Shrine at Nemi*: *"I didn't think that, since it was a sculpture about Roman things, and the music was about from Italy, they were totally different eras, they didn't seem to quite, it didn't add anything."* There were also disagreements with our visual interpretation of the statues: *"At the start it told you to look up into the tree, and that twisty metal sculpture. It hadn't registered that that was what it was trying to do because it didn't, it was a sculpture that was enclosing, it didn't open out like a tree does to the sky."* It seems then, that our trajectory did help visitors reach *their own* interpretations, importantly, ones that were not always in agreement with the ‚official' view derived from the visitor centre's website.

DISCUSSION

We now discuss the implications of our work. Practically, how trajectories shaped the design of our experience, what new contributions we have made to the theory, and how these can be used in designing cultural visiting experiences. Theoretically, how might we relate trajectories to wider notions of engagement and interpretation within HCI?

Using trajectories to design visiting experiences

Our experience shows that it can be productive to apply the idea of trajectories to the design of mainstream cultural visiting experiences. Several innovations in our design can be traced back to key concepts from the framework. At the heart of our design is a *canonical trajectory* that follows the existing path through the sculpture garden, passing into and through each sculpture. This led us to consider how the journey might unfold through key phases of approach, engage, experience, disengage and reflect. It was especially productive to consider key *transitions* along this trajectory:

- considering *interface and role transitions* led us to consider the moment of putting on and taking off headphones as being critical to a visitor's engagement with a sculpture. Consequently, we made a sharp distinction between using text and image instructions during the approach and reflect stage versus audio instructions during the experience phase;
- considering *access to physical resources* led us to design a series of distinctive physical actions at each sculpture that would shape how visitors view and engage with them through posing and touching;
- considering *seams* led us to reject the use of location-based content in favour of the manual triggering of interactions by visitors themselves.

Another key aspect of trajectories is considering how each participant trajectory might *diverge* from the canonical trajectory, and how it might be *orchestrated* so as to subsequently *reconverge*. In response, we allowed visitors to choose the order of the sculptures, self-orchestrating their experience to fit with local conditions such as the presence of other visitors. Conversely, we decided to take firm control of the local trajectory at each sculpture, including choosing exactly how long the accompanying music would last. The framework also encouraged us to consider how visitors' trajectories might interleave, leading us to design a trajectory that deliberately oscillates between moments of social encounter and isolated personal engagement. Key to our design was the use of instructions that told the visitor how to traverse the global trajectory into each local trajectory, how to experience sculpture within the local trajectory, while preventing the need for any live orchestration. Previous research on instructions has identified four aspects of compliance with instructions: locational, sequential, comportmental and relational [22], however in our experience we separated the locational and sequential aspects, delivered as text, and the comportmental and relational aspects, which were presented as audio. Finally, the concept of *historic trajectories* inspired us to reconsider at what point visitors should receive ‚official' information, inspiring the idea that this should be delivered as they walk away.

Extending the trajectories framework

In addition to using existing concepts of the trajectories framework, we found it necessary to extend the framework in a number of ways unique to our design. First, we structured the canonical trajectory at each sculpture into five stages – approach, engage, experience, disengage and reflect. By splitting the trajectory into these stages we were able to judge where best to place interface transitions and switches in media modality in relation to the visitor's experience. We also found it useful to break down the previous idea of multi-scale trajectories into clearly defined global and local trajectories. By designing trajectories on these two levels we were able to separate out the flexibility required in the order in which visitors experienced sculptures with the carefully thought out local trajectory that would enhance engagement at each sculpture.

Our study suggests that pairs of visitors mostly followed the local trajectories, often leading to a deep engagement with and consequent interpretation of sculptures. We saw a strong tendency for visitors to experience the sculptures together (rather than splitting up to visit different sculptures) which led to various tensions in following the trajectory. The most evident of these was the desire to synchronise the beginning of each engagement with a sculpture, for which there was no technical support. However, engaging in the same physical actions at the same time resulted in some contention for key viewpoints (relating to the seam of *access to physical resources*). Some visitors wanted to repeat the experience at a sculpture, while their partner did not and had to wait for them. This suggests a deeper consideration of the *pacing* of local trajectories at each exhibit.

Finally, we recognise that in designing an experience for pairs of adult visitors at a sculpture garden, we have chosen a relatively easy setting for this initial work. We anticipate further challenges in adapting our trajectory to other more crowded settings or to larger groups, which will heighten the challenges of local pacing and interruptions. Busy museums and galleries will involve greater contention for exhibits, noise and other distractions, as well as the presence of strangers. In addition, it will be important to design accessible trajectories that support varying abilities, an important concern for many cultural institutions.

Trajectories through interpretation

Our final contribution to the theory of trajectories is the broader idea of designing *trajectories through interpretation.* A fundamental goal of galleries and museums is to engage visitors with exhibits in order to foster interpretation. Interpretation has also been an important topic within HCI, initially in terms of cognitive approaches to interpreting the workings of interfaces, but more recently widening out to consider more cultural interpretations of interfaces and their content. There is a sense in which our experience combines multiple interpretations from the sound artist, the performance poet and us ‚curators', but the openness of our design lies in when interpretations are made and given. Our trajectory organises this by first leading visitors into a relatively open situation in which they are presented with deliberately juxtaposed materials – sculptures and music – but without being given an explanation as to how they relate. This ambiguity [11] asks a question – inviting them to make an interpretation in order to resolve the experience. However, a novel twist is that we subsequently offer our ‚received' interpretation, but only after they may have reached their own. Thus, we move between being open to multiple interpretations at some moments while suggesting specific interpretations at others. In short we establish a *trajectory through interpretation*, establishing mood, engaging the senses and the imagination, openly inviting sense making, before then revealing our own interpretation.

Of particular relevance here is a body of work that emphasizes the importance of embodied experience [9] and the roles of interpretation and reflection in making sense of sensory experiences [16]. In our case, the embodied and multi-sensory nature of our visitors' experience, adopting unusual viewpoints, touching sculptures and listening to music, appear to have been important in stimulating their imaginations and inviting them to resolve relationships, most notably between the sculpture and accompanying music. A key aspect of our trajectory is that it frames the experience in a way that gives visitors license to engage in unusual ways, for example touching sculptures. This may involve taking them out of their comfort zone or requiring them to act in unusual ways in a public setting, reflecting recent discussions of the deliberate use of discomfort, including the idea that discomfort can arise through the visibility of one's actions, and that moments of discomfort should be embedded into a trajectory [6]. Others have called for interfaces that are open to multiple interpretations rather than focussing on a single received interpretation.

We suggest that trajectories through interpretation, moving back and forth between openness and closure and through multiple interpretations, may be suitable for many cultural experiences, especially ones that involve a didactic element such as museums and exhibitions. Thus we suggest ways in which we might create richer trajectories of interpretation.

In relation to [11], we could open up the space for interpretation by exposing different visitors in a group to different and contrasting experiences at each exhibit, for example different musical accompaniments or instructions. This relates to the much discussed idea of personalisation and how we can create personalised visiting experiences that adapt to individual's interests or visiting styles [25]. Our final proposal takes us back to the concept of the historic trajectory, which suggests that participants should be provided with opportunities and resources to tell their own stories from an experience. While our experience invited visitors to reflect between sculptures, we did not support them in reflecting on the whole experience afterwards or on creating their own accounts of the experience, nor did we follow up the study with further interviews to investigate how interpretations had developed over time. This is currently a popular idea with many museums and galleries who are keen to reflect the visitor's own voice. Carefully designed historic trajectories may allow visitors' interpretations to form another layer in the multiple interpretations that surround cultural experiences, along with those of artists, historians, and curators.

FINAL WORD

We have described a conscious attempt to apply trajectories to the design of a cultural visiting experience. Our experience suggests that thinking in terms of trajectories has purchase for engaging people with exhibits in new ways and provoking interpretation. Whereas discussions of trajectories to date have tended to focus on the structural aspects of experiences, we suggest that it may also be beneficial to also think about ‚trajectories through interpretation' in which visitors' own interpretations are mixed with canonical ones, and are fed back into the experience through historical ones.

ACKNOWLEDGEMENTS

Lesley Fosh is supported by the Horizon Doctoral Training Centre at the University of Nottingham (RCUK Grant No. EP/G037574/1). This work was also supported by the CHESS project (*http://chessexperience.eu*), which is co-funded by the European Commission (Grant No. 270198), and also by EPSRC Dream Fellowship award EP/J005215/1.

REFERENCES

1. Abowd, A., Atkeson, C., Hong, J., Long, S., Kooper, R., Pinkerton, M., „Cyberguide: a mobile context-aware tour guide', Wireless *Networks, 3(5)* Kluwer (1997) 421-433.
2. Aoki, P., Grinter, R., Hurst, A., Szymanski, M., Thornton, J., Woodruff, A., Sotto voce: exploring the interplay of conversation and mobile audio spaces, *CHI 2002*, ACM (2002) 431-438.
3. Benford, S., Crabtree, A., Flintham, M., Greenhalgh, C., Koleva, B., Adams, M., Tandavanitj, N., Row Farr, J., Giannachi, G., and Lindt, I., Creating the spectacle: Designing interactional trajectories through spectator interfaces. *ACM Trans. Comput.-Hum. Interact.* 18, 3, Article 11 (August 2011), 28 pages.
4. Benford, S., Giannachi, T., Koleva, B., Rodden, T., From Interaction to Trajectories: designing coherent journeys through user experiences, *CHI 2009*, ACM (2009), 709-718.
5. Benford, S., Giannachi, G. *Performing Mixed Reality*, MIT Press, 2011.
6. Benford, S., Greenhalgh, C., Giannachi, G., Walker, B., Marshall, J, Rodden, T., Uncomfortable interactions, *CHI 2012*, ACM (2012), 2005-2014.
7. Brignull, H. & Rogers, Y., Enticing people to Interact with Large Public Displays in Public Spaces, *Interact*, IOS Press, (2003), 17-24.
8. Costello, B., Muller, L., Amitani, S., Edmonds, E., „Understanding the Experience of Interactive Art: Iamascope in Beta_space', *Proc. 2nd Australasian Conference on Interactive entertainment*, Sydney (2005), 49-56
9. Dourish, P., *Where the action is: the foundations of embodied interaction*, MIT Press, 2006
10. Flintham, M., Reeves, S. et al., Flypad: Designing Trajectories in a Large-Scale Permanent Augmented Reality Installation. *ECSCW 2011*, (2011) 233-252.
11. Gaver, W., Beaver, J., Benford, S., Ambiguity as a resource for design, *CHI 2003*, ACM (2003), 233-240.
12. Geller, T., Interactive Tabletop Exhibits in Museums and Galleries, *IEEE Computer Graphics and Applications*, 26 (5) IEEE Press (2006), 6-11.
13. Grinter, R.E., Aoki, P.M., Szymanski, M.H., Thornton, J.D., Woodruff, A., & Hurst, A., Revisiting the visit: understanding how technology can shape the museum visit, *CSCW 2002*, ACM (2002) 146-155.
14. Hindmarsh, J., Heath, C., vom Lehn, D., Cleverly, J., Creating assemblies: aboard the Ghost Ship, *CSCW 2002*, ACM (2002), 156-165.
15. Koppel, M., Bailly, G., Müller, J., Walter, R., Chained displays: configurations of public displays can be used to influence actor-, audience-, and passer-by behavior, *CHI 2012*, ACM (2012) 317-326.
16. McCarthy J., Wright, P., *Technology as Experience*, MIT Press, 2007.
17. Reeves, S., *Designing Interfaces in Public Settings*, Springer, 2011.
18. Rogers, Y., *HCI Theory: Classical, Modern and Contemporary*, Morgan & Claypool, 2012.
19. Sengers, P., Gaver, B. Staying open to interpretation: engaging multiple meanings in design and evaluation. *Proc DIS 2006*, ACM (2006), 99-108.
20. Serrell, B., Paying attention: The duration and allocation of visitor's time in museum exhibitions. *Curator: The Museum Journal*, 40(2), (1997) 108-113.
21. Sparacino, F. The museum wearable: real-time sensor-driven understanding of visitors' interests for personalized visually-augmented museum experiences. *Proceedings of Museums and the Web* (2002), 17-20.
22. Tolmie, P., Benford, S., Flintham, M., Adams, M., Tandavantij, N., Row-farr, J., & Giannachi, G., "Act Natural": Instructions , Compliance and Accountability in Ambulatory Experiences. *CHI 2012*, ACM (2012) 1519-1528.
23. Vlahakis, V., Karigiannis, J., et al., „ARCHEOGUIDE: First results of an Augmented Reality, Mobile Computing System in Cultural Heritage Sites', *Proc. VAST 2001*, ACM (2001), 131 - 140.
24. vom Lehn, D., Heath, C., & Hindmarsh, J., Exhibiting interaction: Conduct and collaboration in museums and galleries. *Symbolic Interaction 24(2)*, (2001), 189–216.
25. Zimmermann, A. & Lorenz, A., LISTEN: a user adaptive audio-augmented museum guide. *User Model User-Adap Inter* (2008) 18:389–416.

Pointing at 3D Target Projections with One-Eyed and Stereo Cursors

Robert J. Teather, Wolfgang Stuerzlinger
York University
Toronto, Ontario, Canada
{rteather, wolfgang}@cse.yorku.ca

ABSTRACT
We present a study of cursors for selecting 2D-projected 3D targets. We compared a stereo- and mono-rendered (one-eyed) cursor using two mouse-based and two remote pointing techniques in a 3D Fitts' law pointing experiment. The first experiment used targets at fixed depths. Results indicate that one-eyed cursors only improve screen-plane pointing techniques, and that constant target depth does not influence pointing throughput. A second experiment included pointing between targets at varying depths and used only "screen-plane" pointing techniques. Our results suggest that in the absence of stereo cue conflicts, screen-space projections of Fitts' law parameters (target size and distance) yield constant throughput despite target depth differences and produce better models of performance.

Author Keywords
3D pointing; cursors; selection; Fitts' law.

ACM Classification Keywords
H.5.1 [Information Interfaces and Presentation]: Multimedia Information Systems – virtual reality. H.5.2 [Information Interfaces and Presentation]: User Interfaces – input devices, interaction styles.

INTRODUCTION
Pointing at three-dimensional objects to select them is a fundamental task in 3D user interfaces and is analogous to 2D pointing in graphical user interfaces. However, 3D selection is complicated by a number of issues not found in 2D systems. First, 3D graphics systems use perspective; much like reality, far objects appear smaller, which may influence pointing task difficulty. Second, many graphics systems, including some games and virtual reality, use stereo display. This introduces stereo cue conflicts, and issues such as cursor diplopia (double-vision). Third, there is no universally accepted 3D pointing technique or device, unlike the 2D domain where the mouse is commonly used.

We investigate the interplay between pointing device, technique, and stereo cursors when selecting perspective-scaled 3D targets. Since a primary goal of our research is to develop better methods to directly compare 2D and 3D pointing, we include both mouse and remote pointing in our studies. Both devices are used with both a screen-plane (2D) pointing technique and a depth-cursor (3D) pointing technique. Although the mouse works with many desktop 3D systems [18], it is impractical in immersive VR systems, and 3D trackers are still frequently used (see e.g., [5, 10, 21]). We "bridge the gap" between these types of systems by comparing both classes of device.

A mouse cursor with ray-casting affords selection of 3D objects via their screen-space projections. However, projections of far objects are smaller due to perspective, and such objects may be harder to hit with the mouse or remote pointing. Therefore, we consider the effect of perspective due to target depth. In our first experiment, target depth is constant between targets. Our second study uses varying target depth. We propose to model the effect of perspective with extensions to the 2D formulation of Fitts' law [3] and the ISO 9241-9 standard [7], rather than extending these toward 3D models. We argue that this is more appropriate in such "2.5D" or projected pointing tasks.

Extending our previous work [20], we investigate stereo cursors, primarily at which the depth the *cursor* should be displayed. Simply displaying a stereo cursor in the screen plane yields stereo cue conflicts and cause diplopia when trying to select objects at different depths. In contrast, a one-eyed (mono) cursor, first suggested by Ware *et al.* [23], eliminates stereo cue conflicts by displaying the cursor only to the dominant eye. It is thus also immune to diplopia.

Our contributions are:

- A comparison of one-eyed and stereo cursors, extending Ware [23] with a more robust experimental paradigm. We show that one-eyed cursors improve performance with screen cursors, but hinder ray-based techniques.
- A novel screen-plane ray technique that outperforms standard ray-casting and may be more adaptable to immersive VR/AR systems than mouse pointing.
- Evidence that 2D projected Fitts' law parameters are more appropriate than 3D extensions when using screen-plane techniques.
- Evidence that consistent target depth does not affect performance with screen-plane cursors

RELATED WORK
Ray-based pointing techniques work with either 2DOF (degrees-of-freedom) input devices, like the mouse, or

3/6DOF ones, such as 3D trackers. There is much interest in these techniques in both 2D [8, 14, 22] and 3D [5, 9, 10, 17, 24] user interface research. Ray-based techniques test a virtual line originating at the input device for object intersections. Ray techniques are often used with large displays [8] and collaborative systems [14]. A drawback of ray techniques is the relative difficulty in selecting remote objects [9]. Far objects take up proportionally less screen space due to perspective. However, in a static scene, far targets also appear closer together. Thus, according to Fitts' law [3], pointing at objects at the same visual depth from the viewer projected onto a screen should be unaffected by object depth, since both width and distance parameters scale by the same factor. This does not hold if targets are presented at different depths.

Ware and Lowther [23] report that a "one-eyed" cursor outperforms a stereo cursor in 3D selection tasks with a 3DOF tracker. The stereo cursor required matching the position in all three dimensions. Their one-eyed cursor ignored tracker depth and moved the mono-rendered cursor in the screen plane, effectively pointing at object screen projections. Thus, there are large differences between these two techniques and their study did not account for differences in degrees-of-freedom or input device. Our study expands on this by comparing cursor rendering style across both 2 and 3DOF techniques.

Jota et al. [8] investigated eye and device-centric rays and found that device-centric rays are better for pointing, while eye rays are better for tracing/steering. They used only targets at the screen plane. In contrast, we use targets displayed at varying depths in stereo. Argelaguet et al. [1] also looked at similar ray techniques. Their RCE technique maps tracker rotation to the orientation of a ray originating at the user's eye. RCE was significantly faster than standard ray-casting, especially for (partially) occluded targets.

Fitts' Law and Pointing

Fitts' law [3] is an empirical model of the tradeoff between speed and accuracy in pointing tasks. The model is $MT = a+b\times\log_2(D/W+1)$. MT is movement time, D is target distance, and W is target size, while a and b are empirically derived via linear regression. Fitts' law implies that the smaller and farther a target, the more difficult it is to hit it accurately. The log term is known as the index of difficulty (ID) and indicates overall pointing task difficulty. The law is associated with a measure of performance known as throughput. Two variations on this are commonly used: one given as $TP = 1/b$, and the other given as $TP = ID_{avg}/MT_{avg}$. A discussion of the merits of both options is omitted for space reasons, but can be found elsewhere [16, 25].

An international standard [7] recommends a post-experiment adjustment for accuracy to fix the error rate to 4% by re-sizing targets to their "effective" size (W_e). This "normalized" accuracy enables computation of (effective) throughput, a measure that incorporates both speed and accuracy. Here $TP = \log_2(D_e/W_e+1)/MT$, where D_e is the average of the measured movement distances. The effective width, W_e, is computed by projecting the cursor onto the task axis (the line between subsequent targets) and multiplying the standard deviation of the distances by 4.1333. We previously suggested [19] using the distance between the selection ray and the target as a more accurate representation of the effective width W_e, as the actual 3D cursor position may be arbitrarily far away on near misses.

The main advantage of effective measures is that throughput variability for the same condition tends to be lower [16]. Consequently, results of pointing studies are more consistent and comparable. This helps account for the speed-accuracy tradeoff, i.e., optimizing for speed typically hurts accuracy, and vice versa. Throughput scores are largely insensitive to this tradeoff [12].

Although Fitts' law was developed originally for one-dimensional motions, it works extremely well for 2D motions and is commonly employed in the evaluation of pointing device performance [11]. Straightforward extensions to 3D pointing generally focus on improving the correlation between MT and ID. Note however that adding *any* extra free parameter in a regression analysis will always improve the correlation [15]. Thus, it is not always clear if extra factors improve models' predictive capabilities appropriately.

For example, Murata and Iwase [13] used a 3D tracked device to evaluate pointing tasks on a vertically oriented 2D plane. This was not a true 3D task, as it did not involve hitting targets at varying depths. They derived a model for ID incorporating the angle to the target, and report a higher correlation between MT and their ID model. Grossman *et al.* [4] investigated pointing at tri-variate 3D targets, i.e., targets varying in height, width and depth. Their model considered the direction of movement as a vector through the target. Yet, they used only targets positioned on a single "ground plane" parallel to the floor, effectively a 2D task. They experimentally validated their model using a volumetric display and a tracked input device. Volumetric displays provide more complete depth cues than stereo systems. Moreover, they used a 3D cursor, rather than screen-plane cursors as in our study.

The model presented by Kopper et al. [9] favors the use of "angular" width and distance parameters to model remote pointing. Effectively, this results in targets closer to the user being easier to hit (effectively larger), due to increased ray precision near the ray origin. While the model was validated for 2D target selection tasks on large screen displays, it theoretically will also work for ray-based selection in virtual environments. Our proposed model is similar, in that targets are effectively resized based on the degree of perspective scaling they are subject to.

POINTING TECHNIQUES

While our current work is largely focused on cursor properties, we also consider the effect of the input device, as the two are not independent. Thus, we use two different cursor modes with each device. The first uses a screen plane cursor and the second a sliding cursor [19]. Our first study included all four combinations depicted in Figure 1.

The first mouse technique, which we refer to as MC (mouse cursor), (Figure 1a) displays a cursor in the screen plane and uses the eye-cursor ray for selection. This represents typical 3D selection techniques with the mouse. The sliding mouse cursor, or MS (mouse slide), (Figure 1b) instead displays the cursor where the (same) selection ray intersects the *scene*. Thus, the cursor slides across the geometry. Our novel "ray-screen" technique, RS, (Figure 1c) displays a screen cursor where the device ray intersects the screen, but does not use this ray for selection. Instead, the ray from the eye through this cursor is used for selection. This effectively affords selection of object projections via a user-controlled cursor on the screen, similar to mouse pointing. This is different from Argelaguet et al. [1], who used solely input device rotation to control the cursor. While RS is somewhat similar to zoomable interfaces, it also affords off-axis pointing and uses an implicit zoom control (as a function of perspective scaling). The final technique, RC, (Figure 1d) is traditional ray casting: a device-centric ray that requires users to point the device directly at the 3D target position, which is a form of sliding cursor.

SCREEN PLANE POINTING & PERSPECTIVE SCALING

We hypothesize that selecting targets presented at the same depth yields constant performance. Here *ID*, which depends on *D* and W, is unaffected by target depth as both parameters are scaled by the same factor due to perspective. Perspective scaling of targets is depicted in Figure 2. The same scaling applies to distances as well. Consequently, we expect that screen-plane pointing techniques, such as mouse and ray-screen, are not affected by target depth, assuming a one-eyed cursor is used to avoid diplopia. This does not apply to targets presented at different depths nor when head-tracking is used since both affect how targets project to the screen. In a head-tracked system, ID would constantly change for screen-plane conditions as each head motion could affect the target size and distance. In both cases, the *D* and *W* parameters scale by different factors, and *ID* will subsequently change from what was presented. For small head movements or targets that are far away this change may be insignificant, though.

METHODOLOGY

Here we describe the two user studies we performed to investigate the effect of cursors, devices, and target depth on performance. The first study looks only at cursors and devices for motions between targets at equal depths. The second study investigates a subset of the conditions on motions between targets at different depths.

USER STUDY 1

This study establishes a baseline for essentially 2D target selection of 3D target projections. Consequently, targets were presented at a consistent depth, i.e., in each circle of

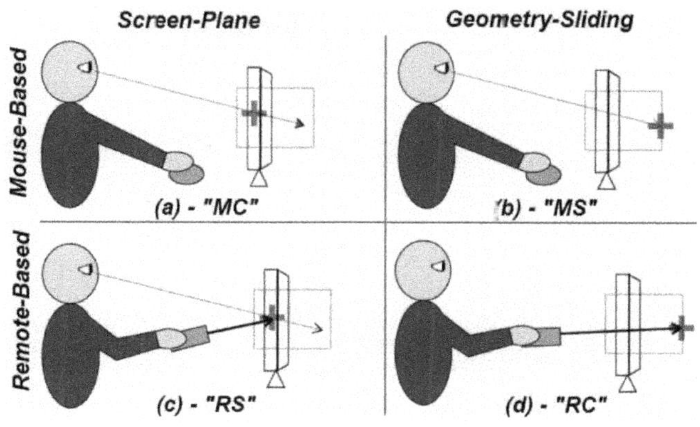

Figure 1. The four 3D pointing techniques used in the first study. Our second study used only the screen plane techniques on the left of the figure: mouse cursor and ray-screen.

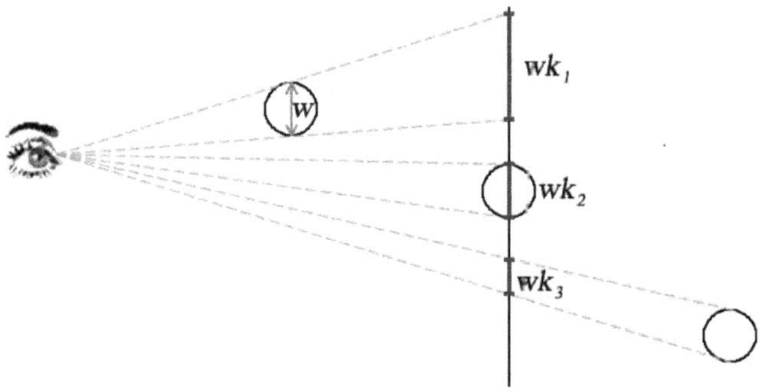

Figure 2. Three targets (circles) positioned at three distinct depths relative to the eye are all of size *w*. They project to different sizes (wk_1, wk_2, and wk_3), nonlinearly depending on distance, onto the display surface, depicted as the black line. The same argument applies to target distance.

11 targets, all targets were at the same visual depth from the viewer. All trials in a circle used the same depth. However, depth was varied *between circles* to determine if performance was constant, despite target depth.

Participants

We recruited sixteen paid participants (mean age 23.1 years, *SD* 6.1), all undergraduate students at our university. Eight were female. All use the mouse with their right hand and have normal stereo viewing capability. Six participants had previously used 3D input devices in pointing studies.

Apparatus

We used a 3 GHz PC with Windows XP, an Nvidia *Quadro 4400*, and a 24" 120 Hz stereo LCD. The participant sat approximately 65 cm away from the display on a fixed chair. Although the system supports head-tracking, this was disabled to avoid the potential confounds discussed above. Instead, the user sat in a fixed chair. The stereo LCD was synchronized via an RF hub with NVidia *3DVision Pro* shutter glasses. Five NaturalPoint *Optitrack S250e* cameras were used for 3D tracking. The tracked remote pointing device was calibrated to 0.7 mm RMS. End-to-end system latency was about 65 ms. No smoothing was used, as noise was already very low and the latency cost of additional

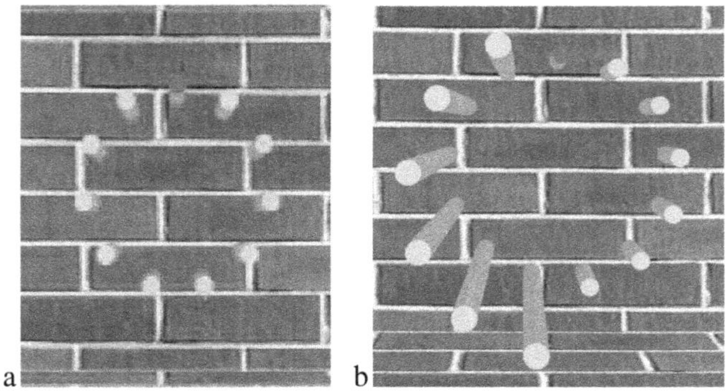

Figure 3 (a). User Study 1 setup: the scene depicting a target circle at –20 cm depth. (b) User Study 2 setup: The scene depicting targets at varying depths. Targets on the right side of the circle are at a depth of –20 cm, while targets on the right are presented at a depth of +8 cm relative to the screen.

filtering may outweigh the benefits [18]. Mouse acceleration was disabled, and gain was set to one level lower than default, for a constant gain of 0.75 [2]. Although low gain levels may increase clutching and impact performance, we rarely observed this in our study.

The 3D scene was a 30 cm deep box matching the display size, see Figure 3a. We used textures and cylinders to facilitate spatial perception of the 3D scene. Target spheres were placed on top of cylinders arranged in a circle. The active target was highlighted in blue. Targets highlighted red when intersected by the cursor. Selection was indicated by pressing a button on the device. The cursor was always displayed as a small 3D crosshair, either at the screen plane or in the 3D scene, depending on the current condition. The center point of the 3D crosshair had to be inside the target sphere for successful selection; otherwise, the software recorded a miss. In one-eyed mode, the cursor was displayed only to the viewer's dominant eye. In ray mode, the 3D device ray was also displayed to improve feedback. Stereo display was active in all conditions, regardless of cursor style. Target size, distance, and depth were constant within target circles, but varied between circles. Target depth was measured relative to the screen surface; negative depth indicates a target behind the screen.

Procedure

Participants were first instructed on the task. To partially compensate for their lack of familiarity with remote pointing, participants were asked to perform 10–20 practice trials with the ray techniques, until they felt comfortable. Participants were instructed to select the blue highlighted target as quickly and accurately as possible. The general experimental paradigm followed that of ISO 9241-9 [7]. Target order started with the "top-most" target (highlighted in Figure 3) and always went across the circle.

Design

This study used a 2x4x4 within-subjects design. The independent variables were cursor style (one-eyed, stereo), technique (MC, MS, RS, RC), and target depth (+8, 0, –8, –20 cm). The dependent variables were movement time (ms), error rate (percentage of targets missed), and throughput (bits per second). There were 10 trials recorded per target circle. Each target circle represented a different index of difficulty, combinations of 3 distances and 2 sizes. Target distances were 7, 15, and 19 cm, while sizes were 0.9 or 1.5 cm. This yields six distinct *IDs* ranging from 2.5 to 4.5 bits, representing a typical range of pointing task difficulty. Each participant completed a total of 1920 trials, for a total of 30720 recorded trials overall.

Results & Discussion

Data were normally distributed according to a Shapiro-Wilks test at the 5% level. Results were analyzed using repeated measures ANOVA and Tukey-Kramer multiple comparisons at the 5% significance level (with Bonferonni correction). Statistical results are reported in Table 1.

Movement time

Overall there was a significant main effect of technique on time. Movement times are shown in Figure 4. Both mouse techniques were significantly faster than the remote pointing ones. Ray-screen was significantly faster than ray-casting. On average, the one-eyed cursor (μ = 1321 ms, σ = 554 ms) increased movement time compared to the stereo one (μ = 1211 ms, σ = 839 ms). However, there are strong interaction effects with technique, as ray-casting was far worse with the one-eyed cursor.

Effect		Movement Time		Error Rate		Throughput	
	d.f.	*F*	*p*	*F*	*p*	*F*	*p*
(T)ech	3, 15	62.7	***	13.5	***	103.1	***
(C)ursor	1, 15	16.9	**	3.4	.08	0.26	ns
(D)epth	3, 15	7.4	**	6.1	*	18.1	***
T×C	3, 45	46.7	***	8.7	**	52.0	***
T×D	9, 45	11.7	***	2.0	*	7.7	***
C×D	3, 45	13.4	***	2.9	*	5.3	**
T×C×D	9, 135	4.3	***	0.97	ns	4.9	***

Table 1. User Study 1 statistical report. Significant effects are marked * for p <. 05, ** *for* p < .001 and * for p < .0001.**

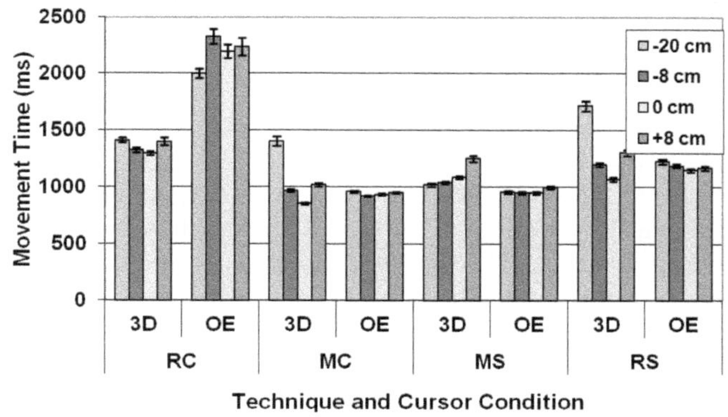

Figure 4. Movement time for each condition. One-eyed cursor conditions are represented with "OE", stereo cursor conditions with "3D". Error bars show ±1 standard error.

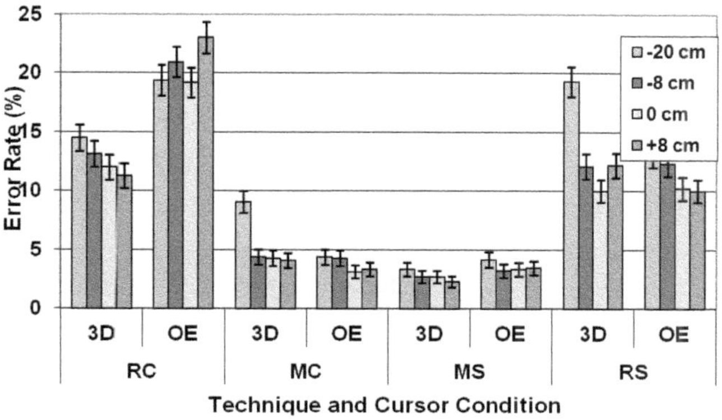

Figure 5. Error rates for each condition. Error bars show ±1 standard error

There was a significant two-way interaction between cursor style and technique. Ray-casting with the one-eyed cursor was significantly worse than all other conditions. The other conditions all *benefitted* from the one-eyed cursor. A significant three-way interaction effect between technique, cursor style, and target depth reveals that the screen-plane conditions (mouse and ray-screen) with the stereo cursor performed significantly worse at the -20 cm depth.

Error Rate

Error rate is the percentage of trials where the participant missed the target. There was a significant main effect of technique on error rate, see Table 1 and Figure 5 for error rates. Both mouse techniques had significantly lower error rates than both remote techniques, around 4%, consistent with 2D pointing experiments. A significant interaction between technique and cursor style revealed that the one-eyed cursor increased error rates with the RC technique.

Throughput

(Effective) throughput was computed as described earlier. There was a significant main effect of technique on throughput, see Table 1 and Figure 6. A Tukey-Kramer test revealed three groups: both mouse conditions were close to 4 bits per second and consistent with 2D pointing, followed by RS at around 3 bps, and finally RC at 2.5 bps. Cursor style alone did not affect throughput. However, there was a significant interaction effect between technique, cursor style, and target depth. Throughput fell dramatically for targets at -20 cm depth with the stereo cursor for both the mouse and ray-screen conditions. The one-eyed cursor hindered the RC technique, which was the worst condition overall, regardless of target depth.

Modeling

Fitts' law can also be used as a predictive model, by regressing movement time on index of difficulty. We performed this analysis for each technique for both the stereo and one-eyed cursor, as presented in Figure 7 and Figure 8. The predictive quality of the model (as expressed by the R^2 values) is very high. However, it is worth noting that the one-eyed cursor consistently improved R^2 values. The one-eyed mouse cursor conditions both show $R^2 \approx 0.97$, indicating almost perfect prediction for both the

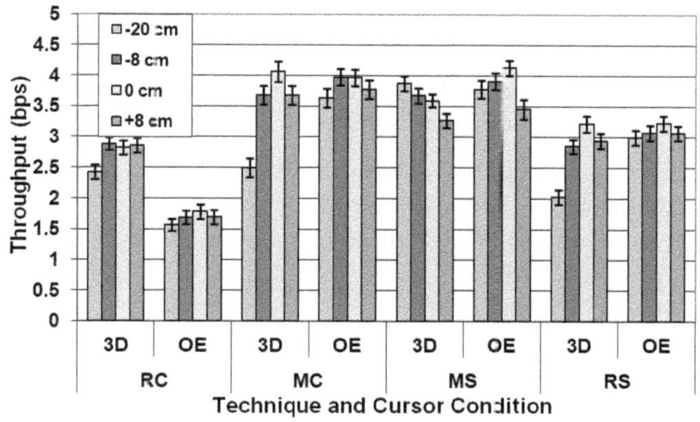

Figure 6. Throughput for each condition. Error bars show ±1 standard error. Higher throughput is better.

MC and MS conditions. The stereo cursor degrades the correlation, especially for the MC and RS techniques, likely due to the more pronounced stereo conflicts on deeper targets. The sliding cursor is affected much less, likely because cursor and target depths are the same most of the time. Overall, this illustrates that the predictive capabilities of Fitts' law are unaffected by target depth for 3D pointing techniques that use 2DOF input and a 2D cursor visualization.

Discussion

Consistent with previous results [23], the one-eyed cursor improved performance, but only for certain pointing techniques. Only the mouse, mouse-slide, and ray-screen

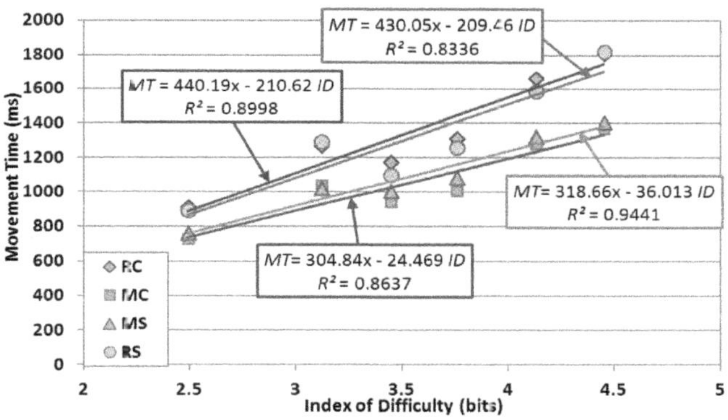

Figure 7. Fitts' law models for stereo cursor conditions.

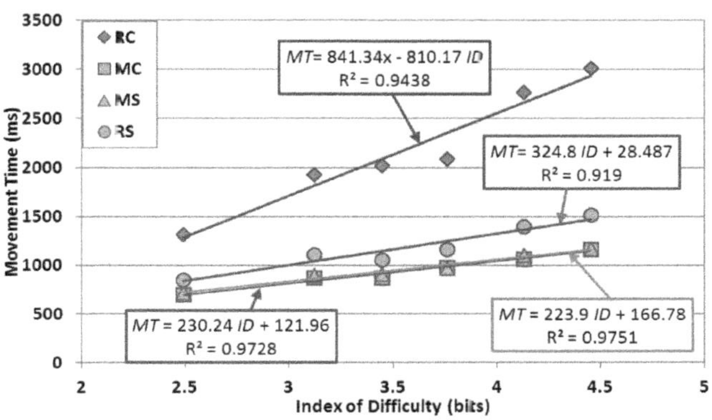

Figure 8. Fitts' law models for one-eyed cursor conditions.

conditions benefitted, while ray-casting performed worse with the one-eyed cursor. Our results also quantify the benefits of the one-eyed cursor in a more robust experimental paradigm compared to the original [23].

The one-eyed cursor improved performance with mouse-based techniques by reducing the impact of target depth in these conditions. The depth effect is most noticeable in the screen-plane stereo cursor conditions. In particular, throughput peaked at 0 cm depth (i.e., at the screen surface) and fell for targets at different depths. The +8 cm and −8 cm depths show similar throughput, but the −20 cm condition shows a dramatic degradation of performance. This is likely due to diplopia. The one-eyed cursor does not suffer from this problem, as it eliminates cursor depth cues altogether, and is thus immune to diplopia. See Figure 6.

Movement time for the mouse slide technique using the stereo cursor was significantly faster for deeper targets compared to closer ones. This seems to be related to participants sliding the cursor up the sides of the target cylinder instead of relying on it "popping" to the front. We previously observed this suboptimal behavior when using sliding cursor techniques [18]. The one-eyed cursor *eliminated* this problem, and participants reported that they could not tell the difference between that condition and the one-eyed mouse (screen) condition. The movement times for these conditions are nearly identical independent of depth, and are not significantly different ($F_{1,15} = 0.23$, ns).

Our results reveal also the differences between pointing techniques. The mouse techniques performed best, but the new ray-screen technique was competitive and significantly outperformed standard ray-casting. We thus recommend this style of image plane technique over classical ray-casting for VR systems and games alike. This is similar to Argelaguet's results [1], but does not agree with Jota's work [8]. Our study used a stereo desktop VR system, while Jota used a large non-stereo display system. This difference may account for the discrepancy and our results may thus not generalize to large displays. The multiple interaction effects indicate that most techniques work best with a one-eyed cursor, while some require a stereo cursor. Similarly, some techniques perform best for deeper targets, while others perform best for close targets.

Finally, the one-eyed mouse cursor afforded throughput similar to a standard 2D mouse cursor. This was fairly consistent for both one-eyed mouse conditions. The one-eyed ray-screen condition was also unaffected by target depth. The movement times confirm that performance is unaffected by the perspective scaling of a scene with targets displayed *at the same depth* when using screen-plane techniques. The following study expands our investigation by looking at pointing for targets *at different depths.*

USER STUDY 2

In this study, target depth varied between subsequent targets. As a result, perspective distortion affected the projection of the targets. The objective of this study was to empirically measure and model the effect of perspective. To keep the size of the study manageable, we included only the best-performing mouse and ray techniques from the first study, i.e., the mouse cursor and ray-screen conditions.

Participants

Twelve participants (mean age 29.4 years, *SD* 5.7) took part in the study. Nine were male, and all were right-handed.

Apparatus

The hardware setup was identical to that used in Study 1. However, the software was modified such that target depth varied from target to target. Each target circle was arranged such that every *other* target was at a different depth. This ensured that every subsequent target selection required moving either from a deep target to a near target, or vice versa. This can be seen in Figure 3b. Correspondingly, data were later split into "up" and "down" motions to analyze each separately. This design is one of the few options for accurately analyzing 3D movements with the ISO standard, which requires uninterrupted "circles" of targets.

Procedure

While the apparatus was modified, the procedure was identical to that of the previous study.

Design

The study used a 2×2×3×3 within-subjects design. The first two independent variables were cursor style (one-eyed, stereo) and technique (MC, RS). The remaining independent variables were all nine possible combinations of the three target depths (+8, 0, −20 cm). The dependent variables were movement time (ms), error rate (percentage of targets missed), and throughput (bits per second). There were 12 trials recorded per target circle. Each target circle represented a different index of difficulty, combinations of 3 distances and 2 sizes. Target distances, more precisely the distances between cylinders, were 7, 15, and 19 cm apart, while target sizes were 0.9 or 1.5 cm in diameter. This yielded six distinct *IDs* ranging from 2.5 to 4.5 bits, when computed according to the conventional formulation of Fitts' law (discussed further below). Thus each participant completed a total of 2592 recorded trials, for a total of 31104 trials overall.

Results & Discussion

Approximately 8% of all trials were dropped as outliers. Trials were considered outliers if their movement times were more than three standard deviations from the grand mean time. After outlier removal, the data were normally distributed according to a Shapiro-Wilks test at the 5% level. Results were analyzed using repeated measures ANOVA and Tukey-Kramer multiple comparisons at the 5% significance level (with Bonferonni correction). We separated the data for each "round" of trials with different target depths into two sets: upwards and downwards movements and treated these two separately from then on, including the calculation of standard deviations.

Effect		Movement Time		Error Rate		Throughput	
	d.f.	*F*	*p*	*F*	*p*	*F*	*p*
(T)ech	1, 11	16.7	*	37.0	***	9.3	*
(C)ursor	1, 11	3.1	.11	8.8	*	1.2	.30
(D)epth	8, 11	16.9	***	17.3	***	9.4	***
T×C	1, 11	1.1	.32	3.1	.11	0.03	ns
T×D	8, 88	3.8	***	6.9	***	1.1	.39
C×D	1, 88	11.7	***	4.2	***	10.3	***
T×C×D	8, 431	1.5	.19	2.5	*	1.8	.08

Table 2. Statistical results for User Study 2. Significant effects are marked * for $p <. 05$, ** *for* $p < .001$ and * for $p < .0001$. Depth represents all combinations of target depths.**

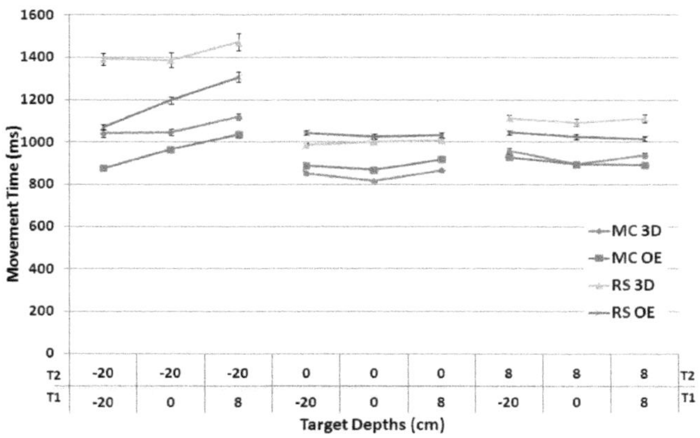

Figure 9. Movement time by depth combination, cursor mode, and input technique for study 2. Error bars show ±1 standard error. T1 and T2 are the start and end depths of each trial.

Movement time

Movement times are shown in Figure 9 and statistical values are shown in Table 2. Technique had a significant main effect on movement time, while cursor style did not. However, depth combination did have a significant effect, suggesting that it was a greater source of variability. Significant interactions between technique and depth suggest that ray-screen is more strongly affected by increasing movement *into* the scene. This is likely because these targets are perspective-scaled to appear smaller while target distance stays (mostly) constant, and the ray technique is subject to greater input device noise. An interaction between depth and cursor style suggests that stereo cursor performance falls with deep targets, regardless if the target depths are the same (e.g., the –20 to –20 condition) or not. The slowest conditions overall were ray-screen with stereo cursor and motions involving –20 cm deep targets. Movement *out* of the scene or in front of the screen had relatively little impact on performance, regardless of technique or cursor style, see Figure 8. The fastest condition was the ray-screen/stereo cursor condition at the screen surface, i.e., when all targets were at 0 cm.

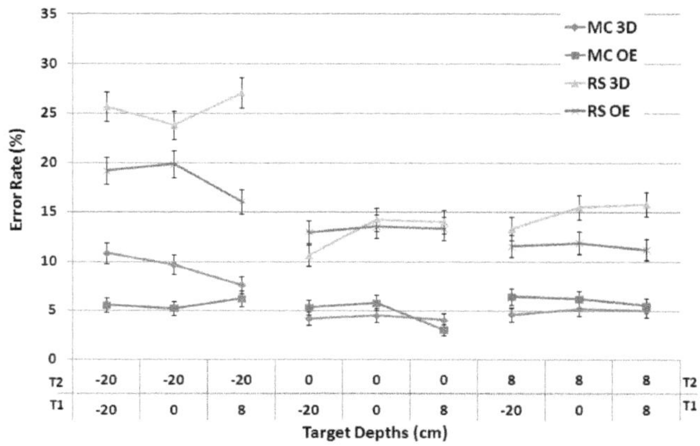

Figure 10. Error rates by technique, cursor style, and depth combination. Error bars show ±1 standard error. T1 and T2 are the start and end depths of each trial.

Error Rate

Error rate is the average percentage of trials where participants missed the target for a given condition. Statistical results for error results can be found in Table 2. Error rates are summarized for each condition in Figure 10. Every investigated condition had a significant main effect on error rate. The error rate for the one-eyed mouse cursor is around 5.5%, slightly higher than in the previous study.

For the RS technique the average error rate is much higher than for the mouse, between 10% and 25%. This is highlighted by the significant interaction effect between the technique, depth, and cursor conditions. While the ray-screen condition is significantly worse than the mouse cursor, it is unsurprisingly far worse with a stereo cursor when pointing at deep targets. This can be seen in Figure 10 for any target depth ending at a –20 cm target. On the other hand, the mouse cursor error rate is essentially constant with the one-eyed cursor, regardless of the depth of the start or end target. This is further evidence that this condition is unaffected by target depth.

"Euclidean" Throughput

Initially, we computed throughput as in the previous study and also in our previous work [19], by using the 3D distances between the target and the closest point of the ray from the eye through the cursor position at the "click". Yet, this artificially inflates throughput scores for movements with greater depth differences. In Figure 11 this manifests as a "dip" in the middle, with inexplicably higher throughput scores for greater depth differences. One can see a similar "dip" in some conditions in Figure 12 in previous work [19], especially for ray-casting.

Screen-projected Throughput

To avoid this inflation, we argue that for pointing techniques that require effectively only 2D input, such as mouse cursor, ray-screen, and to a large degree ray-casting, performance should be evaluated in the screen plane. This motivates the development of a new screen-projected throughput score, which first projects the pointing task onto the screen plane.

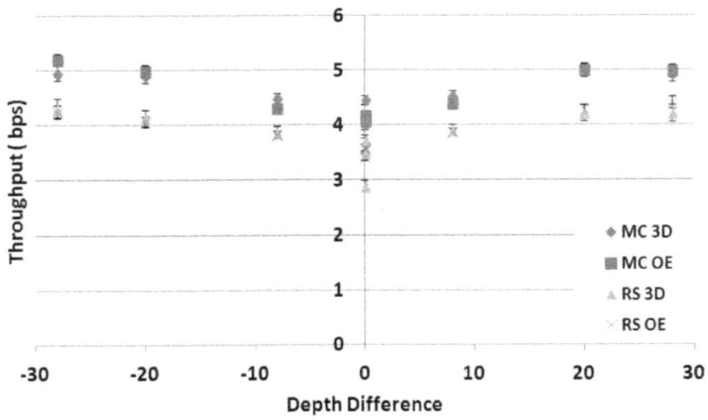

Figure 11. "Euclidean" throughput, illustrating the artificial inflation of throughput scores for movements with greater depth differences.

For this, we first project target and cursor positions to the screen plane, depending on target depth. Effective width is then computed using the standard deviation of the *2D* distances from the projected target to the projected cursor instead of 3D distances. For simplicity, we ignore the (small) effect of perspective onto the shape of the target spheres. Effective distance is computed as the 2D distance between the two projected clicks for each trial. Throughput is then computed normally from these values. The statistical results for screen-projected throughput are shown in Table 2 and mean throughput scores can be found in Figure 12.

Technique had a significant main effect on the new screen-projected throughput while cursor style did not. The combination of start and end target depth did have a significant effect as well. Overall, the mouse cursor affords significantly higher throughput than the ray-screen technique. There is a significant interaction effect between cursor style and target depth combination. Pointing at deeper targets is significantly worse with the stereo cursor than with the one-eyed cursor. The end target depth of the current trial (T2) seems to matter most here. For example, throughput is fairly consistent for all –20 cm deep targets, irrespective of the depth of the start target depth (T1).

Discussion

Screen plane throughput was not affected by depth with either technique (MC OE, or RS OE). To reiterate the results of the Tukey-Kramer post-hoc test, target depth does not significantly affect the mouse ($F_{6,101} = 0.96$, ns), nor ray-screen ($F_{6,101} = .85$, ns). In the absence of diplopia this suggests that perspective scaling of targets due to depth does not affect pointing performance. This makes sense and supports our argument that screen-projected throughput is an appropriate measure for such tasks. Similar to how throughput behaves for changing distances and sizes in 2D and considering the properties of the pointing techniques when used with a one-eyed cursor, throughput *should* remain constant regardless of target depth. Note that head position may affect this. But we did not consider this in our studies, also because participants did not move their heads much during the experiment.

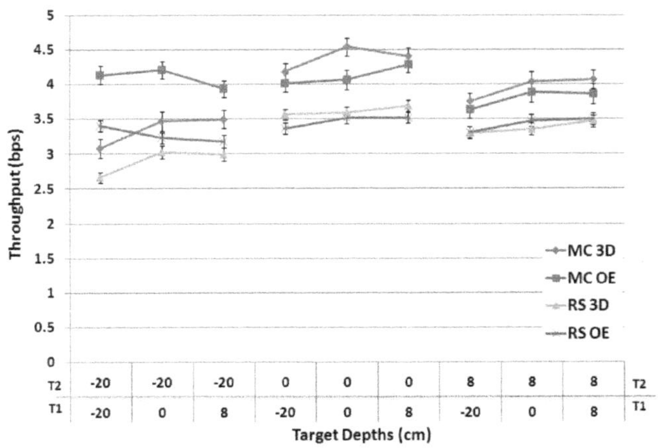

Figure 12. Screen-projected throughput by technique, cursor style, and depth combination. Error bars show ±1 standard error. T1 and T2 are the start and end depths of each trial.

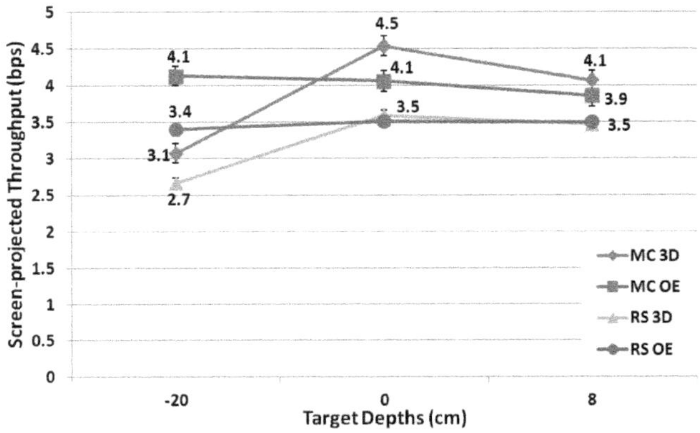

Figure 13. Screen-projected throughput by pointing technique and cursor style for each combination of same-depth targets. Error bars show ±1 standard error.

Perspective Scaling of Same-Depth Targets

We hypothesized that selecting targets subject to the same perspective scaling should yield constant performance when using screen-plane techniques. Hence, if all targets in a circle are at the same depth, then throughput should not change regardless of depth. To verify this, we analyzed this effect in user study 2 for the same-depth conditions, i.e., [–20 to –20], [0 to 0], and [+8 to +8 cm]. Figure 13 depicts the mean screen-projected throughput for each condition.

Figure 13 illustrates that performance for both techniques was mostly constant with the one-eyed cursor. There is at most 5% variation in throughput for the mouse and only 1% for ray-screen. Neither are significant (mouse, $F_{2,33} = 0.3$, ns; ray-screen, $F_{2,33} = 0.16$, ns). While this does not conclusively prove that depth has no effect, it indicates that we cannot reject the null hypothesis – that there is no difference due to depth – and we conclude that this is currently the best explanation for our data. Performance was much more variable with the stereo cursor for both pointing techniques. Due to the stereo cue conflicts present in these cases, this is not unexpected. In particular, the -20 cm depth condition was strongly affected by diplopia, as in our first user study.

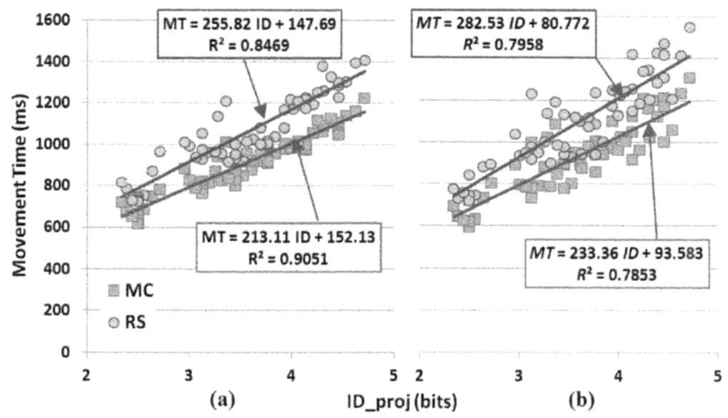

Figure 14. Regression models for the one-eyed (a) and stereo cursor conditions (b) using *ID_proj*, i.e., screen-projected ID. These models include all target depth combinations.

Depth Diff. (cm)	Target Depths (cm)	Mouse, One Eyed Cursor			Ray-Screen, One-Eyed Cursor		
		Intercept (*a*)	Slope (*b*)	R^2	Intercept (*a*)	Slope (*b*)	R^2
-28	8, -20	254.5	198.3	.8554	435.7	199.9	.8113
-20	0, -20	253.5	189.9	.9066	188.2	257.9	.8059
-8	8, 0	77.2	230.8	.9826	52.6	268.5	.9355
0	-20, -20	166.8	198.8	.9551	154.5	252.8	.8781
0	0, 0	111.4	211.3	.9962	119.7	251.0	.9042
0	8, 8	10.3	246.59	.9826	18.4	279.4	.9601
+8	0, 8	54.7	240.3	.9886	-15.4	296.2	.9309
+20	-20, 0	185.0	204.8	.9685	208.5	242.6	.9236
+28	-20, 8	277.9	191.8	.9585	312.7	214.9	.9074

Table 3. Regression models between projected ID and movement time for the one-eyed cursor conditions for each distinct depth difference. Target depths indicate the starting and ending depth of a pointing task.

Modeling

We produced models for each condition using screen-projected target size and distances. We do not incorporate any additional parameters, as screen-projected ID should be sufficient to explain the effect of perspective scaling. Figure 14 presents the aggregate models for each pointing technique, using both one-eyed (Figure 14a) and stereo (Figure 14b) cursor styles.

The models fit slightly worse than one would expect of Fitts' law. This may be due to the time required to re-adjust the eyes to different depths in presence of accommodation-vergence conflicts [6]. Therefore, we performed separate regression analyses for each target depth combination. These models are summarized in Table 3. As expected [6], participants required more time to adjust for greater depth differences. This is visible both as higher intercepts and worse predictive qualities, R^2. The models fit well for near-screen conditions, where depth cue conflicts are weakest.

We did not include regression analyses for the stereo cursor conditions, as the effect of diplopia is too strong to produce reasonable models. Moreover, we are unaware of a model to predict the additional time required to acquire a target in the presence of both diplopia and the aforementioned accommodation-vergence conflict. We intend to investigate this further in future work.

OVERALL DISCUSSION

We did not directly compare our models to others (e.g., [4, 9, 13]) for several reasons. First, our task is essentially 2D, as it involves pointing at 2D projections of targets on the screen plane. Murata's model [13] may be applicable, but we feel their addition of a free parameter is not well justified. There several differences between our task and those used by Grossman [4] or Kopper [9]. In contrast to Grossman's work, we did not use a position-controlled 3D cursor and trivariate targets. Consequently, Kopper's work is a better comparison point. However, a primary objective of our work was a direct comparison of mouse and ray techniques. Kopper's model focused exclusively on remote pointing, and thus likely does not apply to the mouse. Hence, a direct comparison of models between devices is not feasible. Additionally, they used neither stereo display nor varying target depths. Thus their results are not subject to the stereo cue issues we observed. Although we found somewhat lower correlations, our mouse model matches or exceeds their model's predictive capabilities for ray-casting for individual depth conditions.

Implications for Designers

Our results show that 3D user interface designers should be wary of using stereo cursors for selecting targets displayed away from the screen. Interestingly, both studies seem to indicate that stereo cursors offer slightly better performance for targets near the display surface. However, screen-based stereo cursors hurt performance when targets presented away from the screen. This is likely due to diplopia and/or the accommodation-vergence conflict. Our second study suggests that it is the intended target depth that matters most, rather than the actual depth difference.

This also suggests that developers of stereo 3D games should avoid screen-plane stereo cursors. Unfortunately, they are currently common practice in games. Overall, both studies indicate that the advantages of stereo cursors are minimal. But, in general, their usage can significantly *hinder* user performance in 3D pointing. Thus, we recommend that developers consider including a one-eyed cursor option. This leaves the decision of whether to use a stereo cursor to the user, and permits them to avoid performance degradation in stereo display systems.

Finally, there is now interest in the development of stereo touchscreen interfaces [21]. Such interfaces suffer the same problems when interacting with stereo targets far from the screen. Much like a stereo mouse cursor, a finger on a stereo touchscreen is also subject to diplopia! Our work indicates how much of an impact this effect may have.

CONCLUSION

We conducted two studies to investigate stereo cursor properties and the effect of perspective on target selection. Our results quantify the benefits of the one-eyed cursor in a more well-refined experimental paradigm compared to previous work [23] and suggest that the one-eyed cursor is not universally beneficial. We also provide evidence that consistent target depth does not affect pointing performance. Our second study identified that varying target depth affects performance, but this can be (at least partly) accounted for by using screen-plane projections of targets. Overall, mouse-based techniques tended to perform best. But our new "ray-screen" selection technique also outperforms traditional ray-casting! Consequently, we suggest adaptation of this new technique for immersive 3D systems that use remote pointing devices.

Future Work

To investigate the effect of perspective in isolation, we plan to reproduce our study using only mono display. While our current "screen-projected" model fits the data well, is does not account for stereo conflicts. Thus, we are also planning to incorporate a new term into the model to account for the cost of stereo cue conflicts during depth movements.

Acknowledgements

Thanks to the anonymous reviewers for their helpful suggestions to improve the final paper. Thanks to Andriy Pavlovych for proof-reading the final version.

REFERENCES

1. Argelaguet, F. and Andujar, C., Efficient 3D pointing selection in cluttered virtual environments, *IEEE Computer Graphics and Applications, 29*, 2009, 34-43.
2. Casiez, G. and Roussel, N., No more bricolage!: methods and tools to characterize, replicate and compare pointing transfer functions, *ACM UIST 2011*, 603-614.
3. Fitts, P. M., The information capacity of the human motor system in controlling the amplitude of movement, *Journal of Experimental Psychology*, *47*, 1954, 381-391.
4. Grossman, T. and Balakrishnan, R., Pointing at trivariate targets in 3D environments, *ACM CHI 2004*, 447-454.
5. Grossman, T. and Balakrishnan, R., The design and evaluation of selection techniques for 3D volumetric displays, *ACM UIST* 2006, 3-12.
6. Hoffman, D. M., Girshick, A. R., Akeley, K., and Banks, M. S., Vergence-accommodation conflicts hinder visual performance and cause visual fatigue, *Journal of Vision*, *8(3)*, 2008, 1-30.
7. ISO 9241-9, Ergonomic requirements for office work with visual display terminals (VDTs) - Part 9: Requirements for non-keyboard input devices. International Organization for Standardization, 2000.
8. Jota, R., Nacenta, M. A., Jorge, J. A., Carpendale, S., and Greenberg, S., A comparison of ray pointing techniques for very large displays, *Graphics Interface 2010*, 269-276.
9. Kopper, R., Bowman, D. A., Silva, M. G., and McMahan, R. P., A human motor behavior model for distal pointing tasks, *International Journal of Human-Computer Studies*, *68*, 2010, 603-615.
10. Kunert, A., Kulik, A., Lux, C., and Fröhlich, B., Facilitating system control in ray-based interaction tasks, *ACM VRST 2009*, 183-186.
11. MacKenzie, I. S., Fitts' law as a research and design tool in human-computer interaction, *Human-Computer Interaction*, *7*, 1992, 91-139.
12. MacKenzie, I. S. and Isokoski, P., Fitts' throughput and the speed-accuracy tradeoff, *ACM CHI 2008*, 1633-1636.
13. Murata, A. and Iwase, H., Extending Fitts' law to a three-dimensional pointing task, *Human Movement Science*, *20*, 2001, 791-805.
14. Oh, J.-Y. and Stuerzlinger, W., Laser pointers as collaborative pointing devices, *Graphics Interface 2002*, 315-320.
15. Pagano, R. R., *Understanding statistics in the behavioural sciences*. Wadsworth Publishing, 2006.
16. Soukoreff, R. W. and MacKenzie, I. S., Towards a standard for pointing device evaluation, perspectives on 27 years of Fitts' law research in HCI, *International Journal of Human-Computer Studies 61*, 2004, 751-789.
17. Steinicke, F., Ropinski, T., and Hinrichs, K., Object selection in virtual environments using an improved virtual pointer metaphor, *Computer Vision and Graphics*, vol. 32, *Computational Imaging and Vision*, Springer Netherlands, 2006, 320-326.
18. Teather, R. J., Pavlovych, A., Stuerzlinger, W., and MacKenzie, I. S., Effects of tracking technology, latency, and spatial jitter on object movement, *IEEE 3DUI Symposium 2009*, 43-50.
19. Teather, R. J. and Stuerzlinger, W., Pointing at 3D targets in a stereo head-tracked virtual environment, *IEEE 3DUI Symposium 2011*, 87-94.
20. Teather, R. J. and Stuerzlinger, W., Cursors for 3D Pointing, in *3DCHI Workshop*, 2012.
21. Valkov, D., Steinicke, F., Bruder, G., and Hinrichs, K., 2d touching of 3d stereoscopic objects, ACM CHI 2011, 1353-1362.
22. Wang, G., McGuffin, M. J., Berard, F., and Cooperstock, J. R., Pop-up depth views for improving 3D target acquisition, *Graphics Interface 2011*, 41-48.
23. Ware, C. and Lowther, K., Selection using a one-eyed cursor in a fish tank VR environment, *ACM Transactions on Computer-Human Interaction*, *4*, 1997, 309-322.
24. Wingrave, C. A., Tintner, R., Walker, B. N., Bowman, D. A., and Hodges, L. F., Exploring individual differences in raybased selection; strategies and traits, *IEEE VR 2005*, 163-170.
25. Zhai, S., Characterizing computer input with Fitts' law parameters—the information and non-information aspects of pointing, *International Journal of Human-Computer Studies*, *61*, 2004, 791-809.

Creating and Analyzing Stereoscopic 3D Graphical User Interfaces in Digital Games

Jonas Schild[1], Liane Bölicke[1], Joseph J. LaViola Jr.[2], Maic Masuch[1]

[1]University of Duisburg-Essen
Entertainment Computing Group
Forsthausweg 2, 47057 Duisburg, Germany
jonas.schild@uni-due.de

[2]University of Central Florida
Department of EECS
4000 Central Florida Blvd. Orlando, FL 32816
jjl@eecs.ucf.edu

ABSTRACT

Creating graphical user interfaces (GUI) for stereoscopic 3D (S3D) games is a difficult choice between visual comfort and effect. We present a S3D Game GUI Design Space and a list of S3D-specific attributes that emphasizes integrating visually comfortable interfaces into the game world, story and S3D view. To showcase our approach, we created two GUI concepts and evaluated them with 32 users. Our results show quality improvements for a combination of bottom position and visual attachment for a menu. In a referencing interface, placing the reference near to the target depth significantly improved perceived quality, game integration, and increased presence. These results confirm the need to create S3D GUIs with perceptual constraints in mind, demonstrating the potential to extend the user experience. Additionally, our design space offers a formal and flexible way to create new effects in S3D GUIs.

Author Keywords

Stereoscopic 3D; game; graphical user interface; design space; depth; user experience; presence; visual 3D quality.

ACM Classification Keywords

H.5.m. Information interfaces and presentation (e.g., HCI): Miscellaneous. H.5.2 User Interfaces (D.2.2, H.1.2, I.3.6)

INTRODUCTION

Many of today's digital games can be played with S3D vision. However, only a few games are explicitly designed with stereoscopic vision in mind, offering the same content with added perceived depth. Thus, common GUI patterns like a global menu bar or labels referencing specific 3D objects somehow appear on top of deep spatial impressions of the game world. The added depth suddenly changes how we perceive these GUIs. For example, they might suddenly appear too distant from an underlying object. Given the expected growth of S3D content in the coming years due to next generation video game consoles and the arrival of autostereoscopic displays, we lack a formal approach of creating interesting and comfortable GUIs in these games.

CHI 2013, April 27–May 2, 2013, Paris, France.

Figure 1: S3D image pair of our evaluation game prop. (use parallel free view for S3D impression)

The aim of this paper is to support creating new and comfortable game GUIs (e.g., menus and icons) in S3D games. We first analyze benefits, challenges and perceptual requirements of S3D GUIs. This analysis led to our proposal of a S3D Game GUI Design Space and specific S3D interface patterns that relate to spatial and diegetic integration of game UI elements in stereo games. We subsequently showcase using the design space to develop two S3D game GUI concepts. A user study explores their impact on user experience within the context of several metrics including perceived 3D image and game GUI quality, game integration, presence, and simulator sickness. The final section discusses transfer of this impact back into the design space and its applicability in S3D GUI creation.

RELATED WORK

Benefits of Stereoscopic 3D

Playing S3D games is often preferred over non-stereoscopic versions [22]. S3D provides additional information about spatial location, size, shape, or orientation of 3D objects [7]. In medical telepathology settings, S3D offers superior image quality with regard to resolution, color and surface structures [8]. Performance in visual information processing can be increased up to ten times [27]. An actual performance benefit in video games was not found in general, only in isolated 3D manipulation tasks [13]. Virtual scenes [11], video clips [9] and games [22] experienced in S3D induce an increased perceived presence and immersion [18]. Images appear more natural in S3D [18] and gamers tend to interact more directly with them [22]. An S3D scene draws more attention towards details requiring more time to explore it [10].

Challenges and Disadvantages of S3D

S3D benefits can only be expected if the stereoscopic vision is not accompanied by distortions (e.g., contradicting depth cues, ghosting/cross-talk, exaggerated disparity) [29].

Another important issue is the accommodation convergence conflict: the accommodation is fixed to the distance of the screen plane while the convergence varies with the fixated parallax; the two cues are separated, causing an unnatural viewing experience. To solve this issue, the parallax should remain within a so-called comfortable viewing range (CVR) [24]. Bad S3D can cause a negative experience due to visual discomfort [15] associated with symptoms of visual fatigue (e.g., eye strain, headache) [6]. Even watching high quality S3D can induce simulator sickness [19].

Existing Findings concerning S3D Game Interfaces

Based on psychophysiological findings, previous work proposes recommendations for GUI design: A head-up-display (HUD) should be positioned at screen depth or close-by, using depth and transparency. Some elements can be raised slightly to add visual interest [21]. A previous analysis of game GUIs for designing visual elements in 3DTV recommends reducing the amount of graphical information by showing explicit information, (e.g., current round in a racing game), only when the value is updated [23]. The authors further recommend to integrate information implicitly into the scene (e.g., by showing ammunition on the weapon model as in Dead Space), also noted by Mahoney et al. [16]. Referencing objects (e.g., the cross-hair) should be positioned in depth; a laser pointer helps to travel between foreground depths of the weapon to the target object in distant depths [23] as people perform better with a spatial pointing tool than just with a cursor; as viewing the tool helps to assess spatial configuration [25]. It is further proposed to position elements in depth near to the referenced object without being occluded by closer objects, as achieved in Portal 2 [23]. Aside from these findings, we found no formal user evaluation that supports these effects. Given the complex perceptual requirements, a concise design framework could support designers creating and experimenting with game GUI elements in S3D.

APPROACHING S3D GAME INTERFACE CREATION

We start our approach towards developing such a design framework by looking at game GUIs with the special characteristics of S3D vision in mind. The goal is to provide a comprehensive tool that helps designing GUI elements in S3D games, considering their functional purpose, and possible parameters specific to S3D games. A game interface enables the player to communicate with the game and to exchange information in bi-directional ways [20]. Providing feedback and control are the two main goals. We focus on the specialties of graphical S3D feedback. Visual feedback communicates current status of the game (e.g., health, score) or describes concepts within the game [1].

Integration into Story and the Game World

We also take secondary goals into account, namely immersion and atmosphere, which can be combined as presence describing the experience of the game as one's own experience [28]. Hence, the fictional level of the game and the impact of the GUI on the immersive experience is a first main concern towards creating S3D game GUIs.

The other central aspect of stereoscopy is of course the added sense for space and depth. As described, depth positioning implicates a comprehensive set of opportunities and challenges, weighing effect against visual comfort. We thus consider the optimal spatial integration of visual UI elements as our second goal.

In many games, the GUI is designed as an abstract layer, partly occluding the game scene with text or icons, sometimes even parts of the screen are reserved for menus. These elements are clearly separated from the game content itself. By shifting those elements in depth into the game world, to reduce the range of parallaxes in favor of visual comfort, the GUI elements may become part of the game world itself, possibly interfering with the immersion or even appearing to be part of the fictional experience. So how can we arrange GUI elements in 3D space and what does this mean for the fictional level of the game?

In their analysis of visual UI elements in S3D games as an inspiration for 3DTV content, Schild and Masuch group elements into explicit, implicit, and referencing information visualization in games [23]. Explicit elements are common GUI elements giving information on an abstract layer aside. Implicit elements are elements containing functional information through their design within the game world (e.g., the weapon model shows the currently selected weapon). Being part of the game world, these implicit items should be spatially integrated. Referencing elements are part of the HUD but reference objects inside the world.

This categorization describes a gradient between spatial and fictional integration. We further explore this topic using the concept of diegesis. In video games, diegesis comprises the narrative game world, its characters, objects and actions [5] which can be called intra-diegetic. Status icons or menu bars are not part of the game world itself, a game character does not know about them. Those items are extra-diegetic. Considering the spatial position in S3D games, it would be intuitive to position extra-diegetic items on the screen layer, on top of the deeper game world. However, they can still be positioned in the same depths of the game world as well. Also intra-diegetic items can reflect narrative content on an abstract but diegetic meta-level which could not be visualized as an explicit object inside the game world (e.g., making the border of the screen flash bloody red when the main character is hit in a first person shooter). A suitable design space that reflect both the diegetic and the spatial characteristic was proposed by Fagerholt and Lorentzon [4].

Fixing Interfaces to the World and the View

One additional design aspect in S3D games is how interface elements are displayed in the view and how this changes when the view changes within the world. Kim et al. analyzed 3D menus in a head-mounted display. They divided menus into three configurations: world fixed, object-fixed, and view-fixed menus [12]. This concept helps us to identify upcoming challenges and possible solutions.

A view-fixed GUI element stays at a fixed position and orientation within the view of the player (e.g., a head-up display). It may visually interfere with the game world. This could be solved by using a shine-through effect. The parallax can be adjusted to show the world securely behind the screen layer, positioning all view-fixed GUI elements at screen depth. Still, visual design and alignment of the GUI on screen may have a unique impact on usability in S3D. A *world-fixed* menu has a static world position (e.g., the player has to walk to a certain position within the virtual world to control the menu). An object-fixed menu would move with its referenced world object. We combine world-fixed and object-fixed elements into a single world-fixed category with specific issues: How is a reference between a world-fixed GUI and an object visualized (e.g., a spatial line may help changing between depth planes)? Where around the object should the GUI be positioned, what happens if the element is occluded?

Shell-Interface (SI) Describes the start and configuration of the game, e.g., main menu, settings, save and load, often separated from the game on an extra screen.	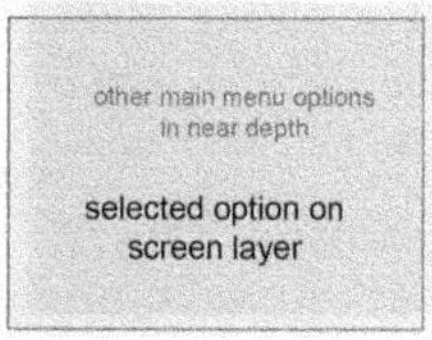 **SI1**: selected/deselected options on different layers (Just Cause 2)	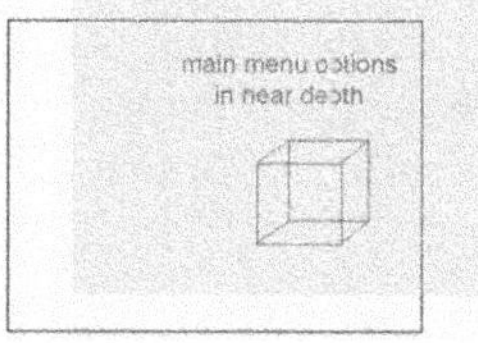 **SI2**: distribute different options on different layers (Blur)	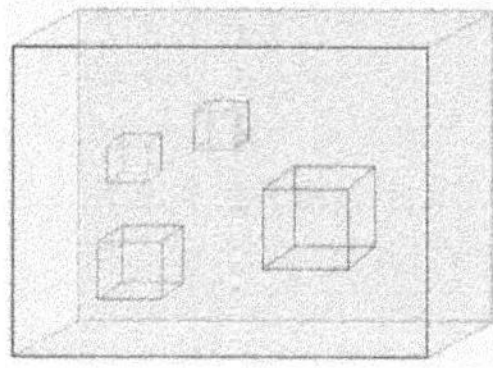 **SI3**: menu as scattered 3D objects in 3D space (Metro 2033)
Global Control Interface (GCI) Can provide global status information (e.g., inventory, next task, current position on a map, health status) and menu functionality (e.g., select army, mode switches).	 **GCI1**: opaque elements at screen depth, fixed to the screen border (Civilization 5)	 **GCI2**: transparent or diegetic 3D objects at near depth (mobile phone in GTA4)	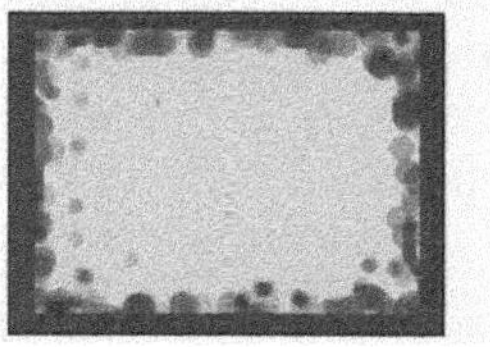 **GCI3**: semi-transparent meta-diegetic effects in periphery of view (Far Cry 2)
Referencing Interface (RI) Augments the world with additional explicit information on specific world objects shown through text or an icon.	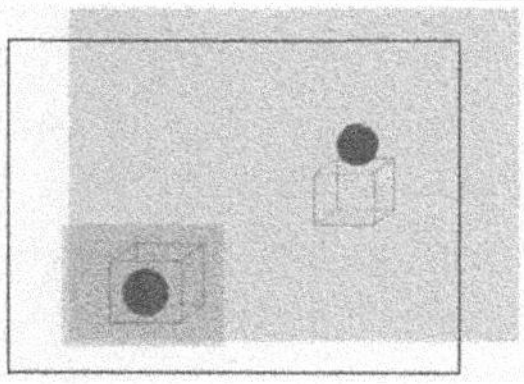 **RI1**: icon or text in front of object or above an object at object depth (Portal 2, Blur).	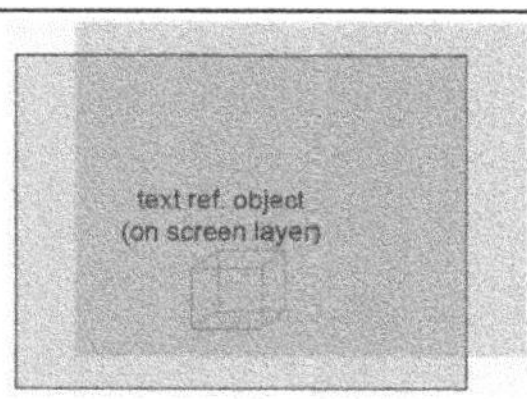 **RI2**: icon or text at screen layer referencing an object in depth (Far Cry 2, Fifa Soccer 2011)	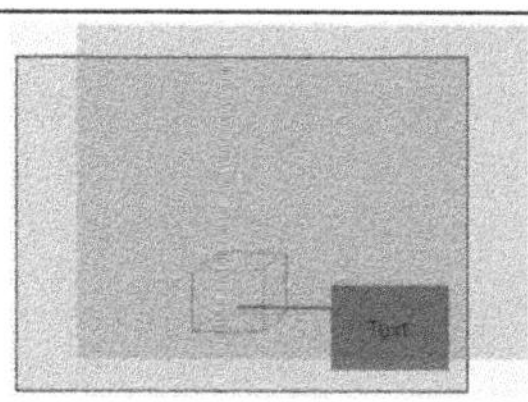 **RI3**: text at screen layer connected with a line to the 2D positon of depth object (Batman: AA.)
Cross-hair Interface (CI) Describes direction of shooting, is a direct spatial reference of the foreground weapon (fixed to the view) towards the target object (fixed to the game world).	 **CI1**: cross-hair is semi-transparent at close depth (Avatar)	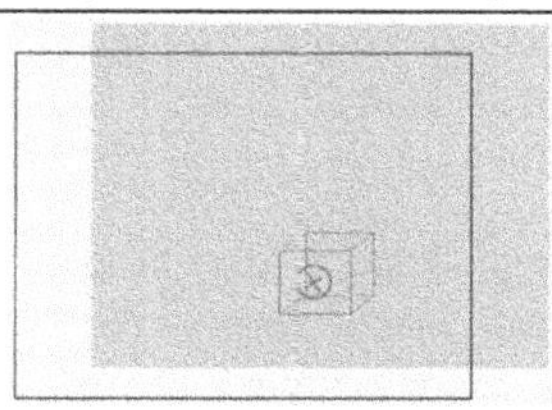 **CI2**: cross-hair has dynamic depth positon, limited by the target object (Crysis 2, Just Cause 2)	 **CI3**: diagetic weapon model at screen depth simulated gun sight (Far Cry 2)
Text Interface (TI) Textual elements provide dialogues, in-game status information, e.g., current speed, or player instructions.	 **TI1**: Text on screen layer	 **TI2**: Text on semi-transparent object at screen layer (Portal 2)	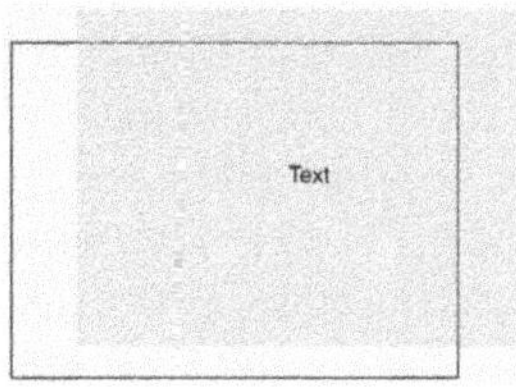 **TI3**: 2D/3D Text at close depth (Blur)

Table 1. Overview of game UI classifications and possible S3D versions.

A Design Space for Stereoscopic 3D Game GUIs

Based on the previous assumptions, we propose to combine the two models: we exchange the yes/no decision on world-integration [4] with a classification of view-fixed vs. world-fixed elements, similar to Kim et al. [12]. This enforces the focus onto the view which is a key aspect in S3D vision.

Some interface items might even contain properties of both view and world (e.g., position next to a world object but orientation with the view). The same might be true for the intra-/extra-diegetic classification, when game characters directly address the player (e.g., asking to press a certain button during a tutorial). This concept is known as "Breaking the fourth wall", used in more than 200 games[1]. We hence choose seamless dimensions instead of a sharp classification.

The proposed space is a two-fold S3D game GUI design grid covering the categories view-fixed and world-fixed on the horizontal axis and extra-diegetic vs. intra-diegetic on the vertical axis (see Figure 2). The grid helps to decide the spatial and fictional integration of GUI elements, giving each element a 2D position in the grid. This step supports designing a UI element either in resemblance with, or in contrast to the diegetic and spatial design of the game.

Classification of Game Interfaces

As a next step, we describe five typical design patterns commonly used in visual game interfaces: shell interfaces, global control interfaces, referencing interfaces, cross-hair interfaces, and text interfaces. According to what we found in playing existing S3D games, adding depth in S3D vision to these patterns occurs in various ways. Table 1 describes and visualizes exemplary variations for each category

Design Properties of Stereoscopic 3D Game Interfaces

Based on the analysis of related work and many existing games, we extracted a list of properties which might help in crafting UI elements particularly in S3D games. This list is by no means complete as creativity should always try to extend its boundaries. It provides a selected set of design decisions weighing S3D effect against comfort with a certain impact on the spatial and diegetic experience.

Peripheral position: Centered elements are often expected to relate to the world (PeP1). Most elements in the periphery are extra-diegetic control or status displays (e.g., a score value) (PeP2). Diegetic graphical elements in the periphery of the view can implicitly inform about the game status (e.g., blood splatters at low player health) (PeP3).

Vertical position: Elements in the foreground or fixed in the view should be positioned at the bottom (VPo1). Elements in the background/world are expected in an upper part of the view (VPo2). The more diegetic, the more physically correct (in terms of the game physics) it must behave.

Spatial design: World-fixed/diegetic objects should contain the spatial property and thus scale of parallaxes of the scene (SpD2). Extra-diegetic/view-fixed objects should still be embodied (not flat) but at other spatial scales (SpD1).

Depth motion: Dynamic depth motion creates a space around objects which might better fit into the world (DMo2) than being fixed to the view. Here, static design may be better (DMo1).

Attachment: Floating GUIs appear especially abstract and unnatural in stereo. This can be avoided by attaching elements to a surface or to the screen frame which fits view-fixed objects (PhA1). Objects in the world should be physically attached to (PhA2).

Amount of parallax: Objects on the screen layer provide best readability which fits abstract non-diegetic information (AoP1). Spatially positioned near to the screen border, they can be related to the view. A fair amount of parallaxes better references the world (AoP2). Extreme parallaxes cause discomfort and may break diegesis (AoP3).

Sign of parallax: Pop-out effects have to occur without edge violation which at best fits to static view objects. Only few world-objects can use this effect (SoP1). The deeper behind the screen layer an object is, the more it seems belonging to the world (SoP2).

Blur: Abstract, non-diegetic objects should provide visual clarity (Blu1). Blur has a natural quality, which fits better to diegetic GUI objects in the world (Blu2).

Opacity: Occlusion occurs both in the view and in the world. Semi-transparency or a shine-through effect can be used to keep a GUI in the view (Opa1). Interpenetration decreases the diegetic character of an element and seems unnatural. Occlusion feels natural in the world (Opa2).

Reference: Object-specific references often refer to both the view and the world (Ref1), especially the extra-diegetic ones. Highlights marking selections of world objects should be well integrated into the world (Ref2). Global references, describing a game status should only be in the world, when they are diegetic (Ref3), or else fixed with the view (Ref4).

Grouping: As with depth-motion, view-fixed objects should be grouped per depth layer, to avoid creating new spaces which interfere with the world-space (Gro1). Scattering is more natural, fitting to world-fixed elements (Gro2).

Fitting S3D Properties and Interfaces to the Design Space

In Figure 2a, we inserted the aforementioned attributes into our design space, as to how we expect their impact on diegetic/spatial interaction. Likewise, we put all the GUI variants from Table 1 into the same space in Figure 2b. By comparing the two figures, we can easily consider nearby or distant attributes and reflect on creating alternative versions and their effects on user experience. We evaluate this approach in the next section.

1 http://www.giantbomb.com/breaking-the-fourth-wall/92-138/

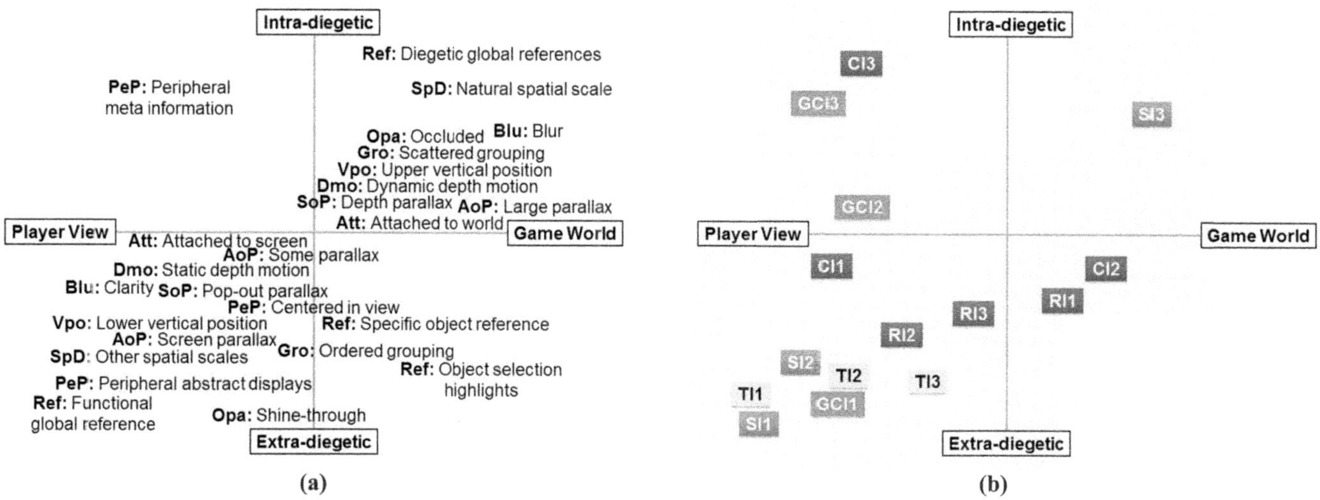

Figure 2. The S3D design grid with (a) various characteristics of the aforementioned S3D design attributes; (b) the same grid showing the aforementioned game GUI classifications. By looking up the 2D position for a certain GUI, important S3D-related design decisions can be extracted.

S3D GUI DESIGN CASE STUDY

The main purpose of our study is to evaluate perceived quality and spatial/diegetic integration of variants created using our S3D GUI design space. There are two general approaches. First, we can check nearby properties, and evaluate their impact on the perceived quality. Is it really important to address these properties as recommended based on psychophysiological findings? A second option is to try shifting an interface towards a different experience. We can address multiple characteristics of a design attribute and evaluate varying versions of our interface. In our case, we will try to increase the perceived spatial integration into the game world. We hypothesize that:

1. Integrating S3D design attributes in the design of game interfaces increases the perceived S3D quality.
2. Varying game interfaces according to S3D specific characteristics affects the perceived spatial experience.

We tasked 32 participants in a simulated gaming situation to rate short S3D video sequences showing different variants of two GUIs in a fictional S3D game scenario.

Method

Prototype Game Setting

To provide a both immersive and controllable game setting, our game prototype consists of a diegetic introduction and video mock-ups: To let users experience a natural game-like situation, we provided the users with a document featuring an introduction to the game situation, an overview map and icon descriptions, along with a background story that puts the test cases into diegetic context:

Short version: *"Yesterday, inspector B. Nocular reached Paris after a long and stressful journey. For a long time he had tried to disclose the secret of the inventor of stereoscopic 3D. One hint has reached him, where a French optician had built the first stereoscopic apparatus in 1850. This information led Mr. Nocular on a sticky afternoon to the old attic of 21 Rue de l'Odéon. The roof is crowded with old furniture, rummages and a lot of boxes. The inspector brought a tool box with useful equipment with one to collect new information about the stereoscope."*

We evaluated visual effects using video mock-ups of the game scene. Non-interactive videos have been successfully used to evaluate interactive interfaces for more than twenty years. They "produce extremely quickly multiple videos which have only one variable changing from the base-line"[2]. As Buxton notes, a video can provide "a real sense of experiencing what this would be like" [3].

The game scene was implemented using Autodesk 3ds Max based on a free 3D model. The model was selected for a balanced arrangement between foreground and background as well as for a depth budget of 10 m at maximum with scattered objects in many depth layers. The avatar (Mr. Nocular) moves in first person view along a predefined animation path through the attic. The parallaxes of the model range from 0 mm to 29 mm (positive). To watch the scene in comfortable S3D, two cameras separated by 63 mm (average inter-ocular distance), were integrated with the additional script "StereoCam Modifier" [17]. Each scene was rendered into a S3D video showing 1680x1050 pixels at 30 fps with a length of 10 seconds. The videos were displayed on a 22" LCD screen at 120 Hz natively running the video resolution in the Stereoscopic Player (3dtv.at) using Nvidia 3D Vision driver and shutter glasses.

Test Cases

Of this scene, we selected two sets which each focus on different design attributes and GUI category: (1) the vertical position and attachment characteristic of a global control interface and (2) the choice of depth layer for a referencing icon interface.

(a) GCI	Attached (At)		Floating (Fl)	
Top (To)	ToAt	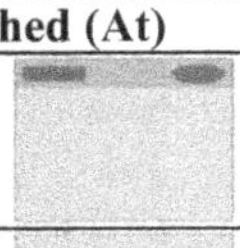	ToFl	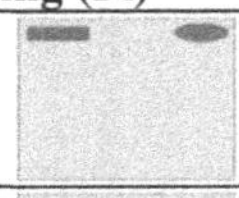
Bottom (Bo)	BoAt	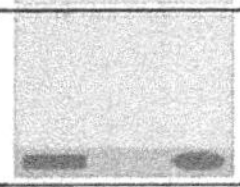	BoFl	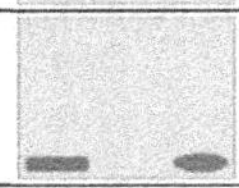

(b) RI	In front (Fr)		Above (Ab)	
Distant depth (Dd)	DdFr	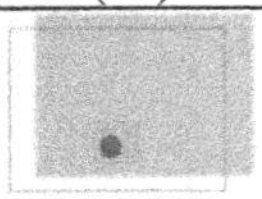	DdAb	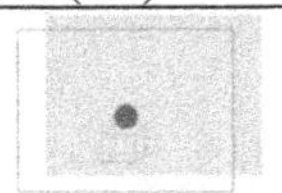
Near depth (Nd)	NdFr		-	
Screen depth (Sd)	SdFr	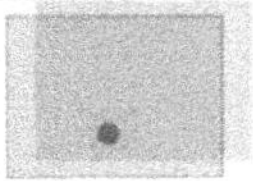	-	

Table 2: Variants (a) of the global control interface (GCI) test case and (b) of the referencing interfaces (RI) test case.

The first set of test cases integrates a status bar as a *global control interface* (containing, a score value, a toolkit and a map) as used in many games (GCI1 in our classification). Regarding our design grid, related attributes include choosing a *lower vertical position*, *screen parallax*, using *other spatial scales*, and *attaching objects to the edge* to avoid floating in stereo. We address the impact on user experience by varying two of these attributes: vertical position and attachment characteristic. Does being used to seeing nearer objects in the lower field of view actually have an influence? Do floating objects really cause issues in S3D? For the two variables we created four different test variants (see Table 2a).

The second set of test cases examines *referencing interfaces* which provide abstract information in reference to a part of the game world (cf. RI1). In monoscopic viewing, showing an icon in front of an object is a clear reference indicator. In S3D the chosen depth layer might influence the perceived reference. The four variants of the referencing interface show an icon indicating a point of interest for a certain object using a similar 2D position. Looking up RI1 in our design grid, we find it next to the specific object reference and near to *some parallax*. *Large parallax* and *screen parallax* are further apart, ranging more towards the view or the world. Respectively we vary the depth position of the icon from screen level, between object and screen, and near to the object at a distant layer. We test the latter variant in two sub-variants: above or directly in front of the reference object (see Table 2b). The icon consists of a blue world-fixed spatial model with the same spatial scale as the scene. It has a black exclamation mark texture and is displayed in relation to a chest in the background of the scene or alternatively in the left corner above a cradle at a similar depth layer (eight variants at four different depth positions).

a) 3D Image Quality		b) GUI Quality	
ImQ	Image Quality	PiD	Position in Depth
Sha	Sharpness	VPo	Vertical Position
Nat	Naturalness	Des	Design
ViC	Viewing Comfort	ExC	Expressive Clarity
DeE	Depth Experience	Rea	Readability
c) Game Integration		**d) Simulator Sickness SSQ**	
SpI	Spatial Integration	Nau	Nausea
GwI	Game-world Integr.	Ocu	Oculomotor
StI	Story Integration	Diso	Disorientation
Int	Potent. Interactivity	Tot	Total SSQ
e) Spatial Presence Questionnaire MEC-SPQ			
AA	Attention Allocation		
SSM	Spatial Simulation Model		
SP:SL	Spatial Presence: Spatial Location		
SP:PA	Spatial Presence: Possible Actions		
HCI	Higher Cognitive Involvement		
SoD	Suspension of Disbelief		

Table 3: The set of metrics used in our study with acronyms.

Participants

The sample comprised 32 participants (16 female), mostly students of our university (n=30). The age varied between 20 and 34 years, with a median of 24 years. The participants were offered free fruits, candy and beverages during the test sessions. They received "study points" they need to earn in their courses. The evaluation was approved by our ethics board. All participants were informed about the aim and procedure of the study and had to sign an agreement including a list of possibly occurring symptoms. All participants successfully passed a prior S3D vision test. Over 80% of the sample reported prior experience with S3D cinema movies, 40.6% of the participants about 4-9 times and another 21.9% of the sample more than 10 times. Previous experience for 1-3 times with S3D-TV is reported by about 32% and with S3D games by about 25% of the sample group. General game experience was reported by 28 subjects (87%) with an average game time per week of 1-5 hours (n=16) up to more than 30 hours (n=1).

Metrics

Our set of metrics consists of a combination of adapted image quality metrics and standardized questionnaires (see Table 3). Our *3D Image Quality* metric includes five dimensions (see Table 3a), based on an extended 2D image quality metric (ITU-R Rec. BT. 500) (cf. Lambooij et al. [14]). The analysis of the quality of the game GUI (*GUI-Quality*) was also divided into five dimensions (see Table 3b). All these factors were rated on a continuous scale ranging from "bad" to "excellent". Additionally, the perceived *Game Integration* of the game GUIs was measured with four more items (see Table 3c). Possible dizziness or other subjective disorders were measured using the *Simulator Sickness* Questionnaire (SSQ) [26], (see

(a) GCI[1]		BoAt>ToAt	BoAt>BoFl	BoAt>ToFl	ToAt>Bofl	ToAt>ToFl	BoFl>ToFl	ANOVA
GUI-Quality (cf. Table 3b)	VPo	p<.01, *d*=1.36		p<.01, *d*=1.62	p<.01, *d*=1.28		p<.01, *d*=.1.55	F(2.163, 67.062)=30.658, p<.01*
	PiD			p<.05, *d*=.71				F(3, 93)=5.101, p<.01
	Des			p<.05, *d*=.61				F(2.338, 72.483)=4.061, p<.05*
	Rea			p<.05, *d*=.68		p<.05, *d*=.56		F(3, 93)=5.360, p<.01
(b) RI[2]		**DdAb>DdFr**	**DdAb>NdFr**	**DdAb>SdFr**	**DdFr>NdFr**	**DdFr>SdFr**	**NdFr>SdFr**	**ANOVA**
3D-Quality (cf. Table 3a)	ImQ			p<.05, *d*=. 46				F(1.531, 47.450)=5.202, p<.05*
	Sha					p<.05, *d*=.58		F(1.906, 59.099)=4.951, p<.05*
	Nat		p<.05, *d*=. 76	p<.01, *d*=.95		p<.05, *d*=.64		F(2.491, 77.219)=7.781, p<.01*
	ViC		p<.01, *d*=.63	p<.01, *d*=1.15		p<.01, *d*=.88	p<.05, *d*=.59	F(2.325, 72.076)=16.351, p<.01*
	DeE			p<.01, *d*=1.03	p<.05, *d*=.75	p<.01, *d*=1.04		F(2.239, 69.413)=11.825, p<.01*
GUI-Quality (cf. Table 3b)	VPo	p<.05, *d*=.87	p<.01, *d*=.86	p<.01, *d*=1.21				F(2.515, 77.969)=8.734, p<.01*
	PiD		p<.01, *d*=1.68	p<.01, *d*=2.71	p<.01, *d*=1.16	p<.01, *d*=2.09	p<.01, *d*=.72	F(3, 93)=49.855, p<.01
	Des		p<.05, *d*=.6	p<.01, *d*=.86				F(3, 93)=6.059, p<.01
	ExC		p<.01, *d*=.93	p<.01, *d*=1.11		p<.01, *d*=.5		F(2.37, 73.455)=10.261, p<.01*
	Rea							F(2.110, 65.423)=4.535, p<.05*
Game Integration (cf. Table 3c)	Spl		p<.01, *d*=.93	p<.01, *d*=1.6		p<.01, *d*=1.04	p<.01, *d*=.64	F(1.984, 61.504)=15.148, p<.01*
	Gwl		p<.05, *d*=.6	p<.01, *d*=1.08		p<.01, *d*=.8	p<.05, *d*=.51	F(3, 93)=12.237, p<.01
	Stl		p<.01, *d*=.7	p<.01, *d*=.973	p<.01, *d*=.54	p<.01, *d*=.82		F(2.369, 73.449)=15.424, p<.01*
	Int				p<.05, *d*=.74	p<.01, *d*=1.17		F(2.098, 65.027)=8.509, p<.01*
MEC-SPQ (cf. Table 3e)	SP:SL			p<.01, *d*=.8		p<.05, *d*=.77		F(2.330, 72.230)=14.022, p<.01*
	SP:PA			p<.01, *d*=1.1		p<.01, *d*=.99		F(2.013, 62.413)=8.576, p<.01*
	HCI					p<.05, *d*=.66		F(2.140, 66.352)=3,07, p=.05*
	SoD			p<.05, *d*=.46		p<.01, *d*=.5		F(3, 93)=3.681, p<.05

[1]cf. Table 2a, [2]cf. Table 2b, * Significance using „Greenhouse-Geisser"-correction; *d* = Cohen's *d* effect size..

Table 4. Pairwise comparisons of significant differences (a) for the Global Control Interface and (b) the Referencing Interface

Table 3d).It contains three dimensions, measured through 16 items on a 4-level Likert scale (ranging from "no symptoms" to "severe symptoms"). The three dimensions are combined in a Total SSQ metric. *Spatial Presence* was measured by the short version of the MEC Spatial Presence Questionnaire (MEC-SPQ) [28]. It includes six dimensions (see Table 3e), each assessed using four items.

Procedure

The study was conducted in a testing lab on campus. Test material, metrics, hardware, lighting conditions and viewing distance remained identical. Two computers were used to display test videos and questionnaires separately. The participants could switch computers by turning their chair. We collected demographic and SSQ pre-condition data and started with an entry video of the attic scene (30 seconds long, repeated for 2-3 times). After the introduction the investigator took a back seat without watching the displays. Each participant then viewed 8 test sequences, four sequences with the GCI and four sequences with the RI in one of both variants (reference to chest or cradle) in randomized order. Each video sequence included three repetitions (10 seconds each), separated by a black image (3 seconds). After each sequence, the screen remained black and the questionnaire (S3D quality metrics and MEC-SPQ) was presented at the other computer. The participants could then start the next sequence. The post-SSQ was measured to detect physiological discomfort. Finally the investigator thanked for the participation and handed the gratification. A whole session took about 80 minutes per participant.

Results

The results are analyzed using repeated-measures analysis of variance (ANOVA) with Bonferroni post-hoc-correction for pair-wise analysis. In case of a positive Mauchly-Test the Greenhouse-Geisser correction is used. For the sake of clarity, we divide the rating/likert scales into three equal parts, calling mean values "low/negative" (0 to 30 for the rating; 0 to 1.33 for likert), "average/medium" (30.1-60; 1,34-2.66), or "high/positive" (60.1-90; 2.67 to 3).

Global Control Interface (GCI)

The *3D Image Quality* analysis of the GCI shows no significant differences between the mean values of the four variants for all five metrics. They all range positively. The game *GUI-Quality* was judged more differently. Most dimensions are positive except for average means in both top position menu configurations (ToFl, ToAt) in Vertical Position and for ToFl in Position in Depth. Bottom placement and attachment (BoAt) always gains the highest mean score, while ToFl shows always the lowest mean. These differences are significant in VPo, PiD, Design, and Readability. The largest effect is in VPo: For both settings of attachment, the bottom vertical position is significantly preferred (BoAt>ToAt; BoFl>ToFl). The attached versions gain higher means across all items than the according floating versions with identical vertical positions, but none

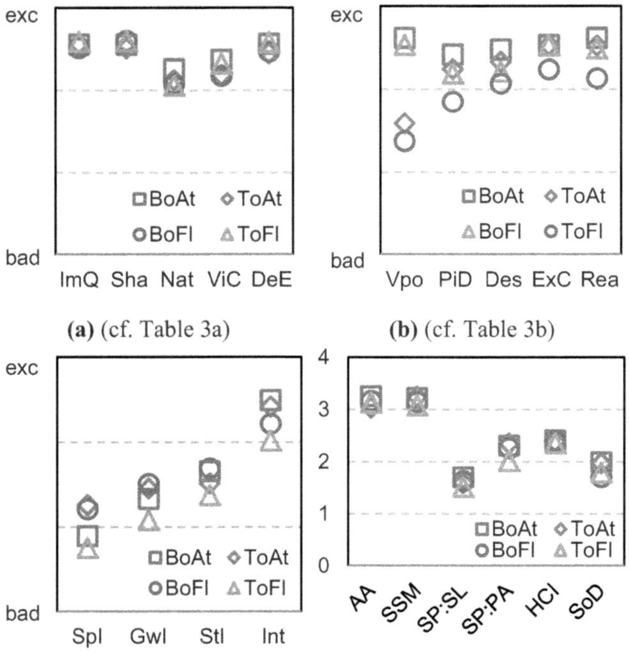

(a) (cf. Table 3a) (b) (cf. Table 3b) (c) (cf. Table 3c) (d) (cf. Table 3e)

Figure 3. GCI results in (a) 3D Image Quality, (b) GUI Quality, (c) Game Integration and (d) Presence.

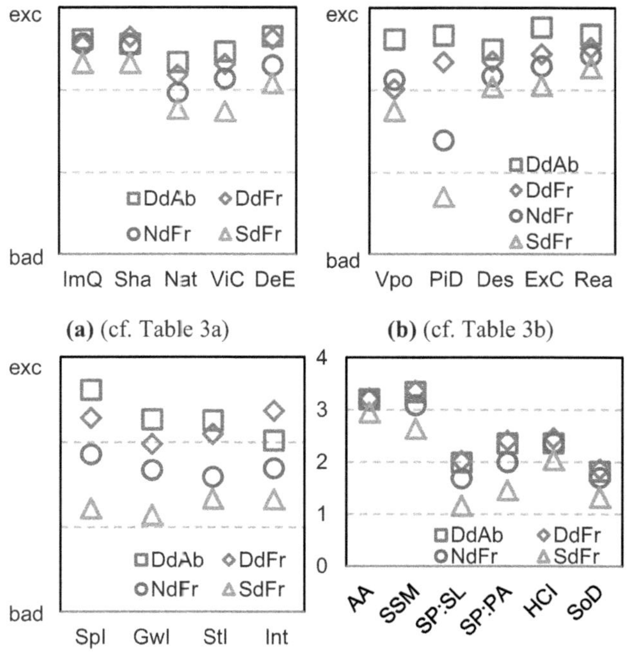

(a) (cf. Table 3a) (b) (cf. Table 3b) (c) (cf. Table 3c) (d) (cf. Table 3e)

Figure 4. RI results in (a) 3D Image Quality, (b) GUI Quality, (c) Game Integration and (d) Presence.

of these differences are significant except one: Rea is significantly yet slightly higher for ToAt than for ToFl.

The results for the *Game Integration* items resulted in low to average means for Spatial Integration, average values for Game-world and Story Integration. All mean values for potential Interactivity are positive. The ANOVA shows a significant impact of the design variants in Spl and Int, but we found no pairwise significant effects. *Presence* results generally show high means for AA, SSM, average means for SPPA and HCI, and low means for SPSL and SoD. We found no significant impact on presence by the different variants, except for a trend in SPPA (BoAt > ToFl).

Referencing Interface (RI)

In contrast to the GCI, the analysis of the *3D Image Quality* of the RI shows interesting effects for the variants. Positioning the icon at screen depth (SdFr) constantly provides the lowest mean values across all dimensions. The highest mean scores are delivered by the icon position directly above the related object at distant depth (DdAb), except for Sharpness with a preference for the presentation in front of the object at distant depth (DdFr). Generally, all means are positive except for a rather average Nat at SdFr and NdFr and average ViC at SdFr. The pairwise comparison shows significant differences between one or both distant depth conditions (DdAb, DdFr) and SdFr (sometimes even with NrFr), indicating improvements for all *3D Image Quality* metrics at the more distant depth.

As to the *GUI-Quality*, DdAb again scored the highest means and SdFr the lowest across all items. All other values are positive except the following: SdFr is rated especially low in Position in Depth and average in Vertical Position, NdFr gets an average mean rating in PiD. Both Distant depth conditions (DdAb, DdFr) are rated significantly more positively for PiD than the other two depth conditions (NdFr, SdFr) and even the NdFr is rated better than SdFr. Means of DdAb are significantly higher than all other conditions in VPo, even than DdFr, and higher than SdFr and NdFr in Design and Expressive Clarity.

Likewise for the *Game Integration* ratings, DdAb scores the highest means for DdAb in all dimensions, except for DdFr is highest in Interactivity. SdFr always receives the lowest means. DdAb and DdFr are rated positively across all dimensions, except DdFr is average in Game-world Integration. All integration means for SdFr and NdFr are average. This difference is reflected significantly in the post-test: Both Dd conditions significantly outperform SdFr and partly NdFr in Spatial Integration, Story Integration, and Gwl. Even NdFr is significantly rated higher than SdFr in Spl and Gwl. DdFr is rated significantly more potentially interactive than SdFr and NdFr.

In contrast to the GCI, the RI variants influence the perceived *Spatial Presence*: We found highest mean values for DdFr and lowest for SdFr, but little absolute difference between DdFr, DdAb and NdFr. In general, we found high means for AA, mostly high SSM (except SdFr), and average means in SP:PA, SP:SL, HCI and SoD, except for SdFr, which received low means in SPSL and SoD. These differences were significant between the Distant depth conditions and SdFr in SP:SL, SP:PA, and SoD. For HCI we only found a significant effect with DdFr to SdFr. AA and SSM show no significant differences.

SSQ and other findings

Regarding *Simulator Sickness*, we found higher post-values in Ocu, Diso, Total, but not in Nau. However, based on a Wilcoxon-signed-rank test, none of these differences were significant. Looking at the genders separately, we found both strong and significant effects only with females in Diso (Z=1.981, p<.05), Ocu (t_{15}=-2.328, p<.05) and Total SSQ (t_{15}=-2.229, p<.05). As to the different versions of the RI videos, four referencing a chest and four referencing a cradle, we found no significant differences in any metrics.

DISCUSSION

Our study revealed interesting impact from varying visual effects on user experience using the test cases.

Global Control Interface

With the view-fixed status bar at the bottom or the top, either attached to the edge using a semi-transparent bar, or floating freely, we found a significant impact of the vertical position as a design aspect in S3D GUIs, directly affecting how the quality of the GUI is judged. The other dimensions are only influenced by vertical position in combination with the semi-transparent background versus the floating version. No significant decrease was found by just putting a menu to the top position with an unchanged attachment condition. All mean values for attached variants are higher than their floating counterparts, but not significantly, except for one: Visual attachment improved readability over Floating only in the top position conditions. Therefore both vertical position and visual attachment may significantly influence perceived quality of a foreground GUI object, but at best in a certain combination of the two. In our case, designing a menu bar at the bottom with a semi-transparent background to provide attachment to the screen was clearly preferred over floating objects at a top position.

Referencing Interface

The analysis of the RI with the spatial icon, positioned in depth to relate to a world object, brought more comprehensive results. Overall, the distant depth conditions clearly outperform the screen depth conditions across all tests. Choosing a depth plane next to the world object significantly improved *3D Image Quality* including Visual Comfort and Naturalness, and *GUI-Quality*, with preferred Vertical and Depth position, and gains in perceived Design, and Expressive Clarity. The Distant depth position also increased how integrated the GUI feels with the game space and the story, helping to perceive it more as part of the game world. Our participants noted a higher potential of Interactivity. These effects are further constituted in higher presence results in Self Location and Possible Actions.

Besides the problematic Screen depth, placing the icon at Near depth brought some improvement but was still outperformed by Distant depth condition in many tests and felt less natural. Within the two Distant depth conditions, the Above condition scored higher mean scores, except for presence. Of these differences, only Vertical Position in the *GUI-Quality* test was significant, though.

Based on these results, moving a referencing interface into the depth of the target object and placing it slightly above is highly recommended. It can improve visual and interactive quality and adds to the spatial and diegetic integration into the game world. However, such a design can cause occlusion problems, when the icon is referencing an occluded object. In our case, the cradle and so the icon were partially occluded during the video by foreground balks. This had no effect our results. It would be interesting to examine perceived quality and game world integration when showing the icon shining through occluding balks.

Reflections on the S3D Game GUI Design Space

We created our test cases using the proposed design grid which lets designers put GUI attributes in relation to the view or game space and to the game story or an abstract layer. Both our test cases report an impact on quality by different characteristics of S3D-relevant attributes (e.g., Vertical Position, visual attachment, or Position in Depth). This confirms our first hypothesis. Only for the second test scenario, we found an impact on *Game Integration*. As a result, the different Distant depth-variants would be positioned more to the upper right on the grid in comparison to RI1, describing the added spatial and diegetic integration. This repositioning also fits to the direction of the near and distant parallax attributes. This result not only confirms our second hypothesis but shows that we can vary the design towards more distant S3D attributes, increasing the experience of world integration and presence, one of the few known improvements in S3D games. Likewise, in case of the first test case, we chose to vary attributes quite near to the GUI pattern within the design space—and found no impact on world integration.

CONCLUSIONS

We have proposed a S3D Game GUI Design Space that emphasizes the spatial and diegetic integration of GUI elements within the game world. We used the design space to create a global control interface, a menu, with varying vertical position and visual attachment, and a referencing icon interface exploring the choice of depth layer.

As posed in our hypotheses, the created variants affected UX differently: We found strong quality improvements for a combined use of bottom position and visual attachment for the foreground menu. In a referencing interface, putting the reference near to the depth of the object significantly improved perceived quality, spatial and diegetic integration, and increased presence. The impact on spatial and diegetic integration can even be mapped back into the design space.

This shows how visual S3D interface design and perceptual constraints can influence user experience. It further demonstrates applicability of the S3D Game GUI Design Space. As a first formal yet flexible creation tool, it is intended to support others in creating novel S3D Game GUI designs and evaluations with their games and genres. Such future creations and analyses will eventually lead to even more generally valid findings for designing S3D GUIs.

REFERENCES

1. Adams, E. *Fundamentals of Game Design (2nd Edition)*. New Riders Press.
2. Benyon, D., Turner, P., and Turner, S. *Designing Interactive Systems: People, Activities, Contexts, Technologies*. Addison Wesley, 2005.
3. Buxton, W. *Sketching User Experiences: Getting the Design Right and the Right Design*. Morgan Kaufmann, 2007.
4. Fagerholt, E. and Lorentzon, M. Beyond the HUD User Interfaces for Increased Player Immersion in FPS Games. 2009.
5. Galloway, A.R. *Gaming: Essays On Algorithmic Culture*. Univ Of Minnesota Press, 2006.
6. Hoffman, D., Girshick, A., Akeley, K., and Banks, M.S. Vergence–accommodation conflicts hinder visual performance and cause visual fatigue. *Journal of Vision 8*, 3 (2008), 1–30.
7. Hubona, G.S., Wheeler, P.N., Shirah, G.W., and Brandt, M. The relative contributions of stereo, lighting, and background scenes in promoting 3D depth visualization. *ACM Transactions on Computer-Human Interaction 6*, 3 (1999), 214–242.
8. Hutarew, G., Moser, K., and Dietze, O. Comparison of an auto-stereoscopic display and polarized stereoscopic projection for macroscopic pathology. *Journal of telemedicine and telecare 10*, 4 (2004), 206–13.
9. Häkkinen, J., Kawai, T., Takatalo, J., Leisti, T., Radun, J., and Hirsaho, A. Measuring Stereoscopic Image Quality Experience with Interpretation Based Quality Methodology. *System 6808*, January (2008), 27–31.
10. Häkkinen, J., Kawai, T., Takatalo, J., Mitsuya, R., and Nyman, G. What do people look at when they watch stereoscopic movies? *Displays 7524*, (2010).
11. IJsselsteijn, W., Ridder, H. de, Freeman, J., Avons, S.E.E., and Bouwhuis, D. Effects of Stereoscopic Presentation, Image Motion, and Screen Size on Subjective and Objective Corroborative Measures of Presence. *Presence: Teleoperators & Virtual Environments 10*, 3 (2001), 298–311.
12. Kim, N., Kim, G.J., Park, C., Lee, I., and Lim, S.H. Multimodal Menu Presentation and Selection in Immersive Virtual Environments. *Science And Technology*, (2000), 1–8.
13. Kulshreshth, A., Schild, J., and LaViola, J.J. Evaluating user performance in 3D stereo and motion enabled video games. *Proceedings of the International Conference on the Foundations of Digital Games - FDG '12*, ACM Press (2012), 33.
14. Lambooij, M., IJsselsteijn, W., Bouwhuis, D.G., and Heynderickx, I. Evaluation of Stereoscopic Images: Beyond 2D Quality. *IEEE Transactions on Broadcasting 57*, 2 (2011), 432–444.
15. Lambooij, M.T.M., IJsselsteijn, W.A., and Heynderickx, I. Visual discomfort in stereoscopic displays: a review. *Proceedings of SPIE 6490*, May 2010 (2007), 64900I–64900I-13.
16. Mahoney, N., Oikonomou, A., and Wilson, D. Stereoscopic 3D in video games: A review of current design practices and challenges. *2011 16th International Conference on Computer Games (CGAMES)*, IEEE (2011), 148–155.
17. Marcoux, L. AREA Autodesk. *Stereoscopy in 3ds Max with StereoCam Modifier*, 2009. http://area.autodesk.com/blogs/louis/stereoscopy_in_3ds_max_with_stereocam_modifier/.
18. Meesters, L.M.J., IJsselsteijn, W. a., and Seuntiens, P.J.H. A Survey of Perceptual Evaluations and Requirements of Three-Dimensional TV. *IEEE Transactions on Circuits and Systems for Video Technology 14*, 3 (2004), 381–391.
19. Obrist, M., Wurhofer, D., Förster, F., et al. Perceived 3DTV Viewing in the Public : Insights from a Three-Day Field Evaluation Study. *Human Factors*, (2011), 167–176.
20. Saunders, K. and Novak, J. *Game Dev. Essentials Game Interface Design*. Cengage Learning, 2006.
21. Schertenleib, S. (SCCE). *Optimization for Making Stereoscopic 3D Games on PlayStation*. 2011.
22. Schild, J., LaViola, J., and Masuch, M. Understanding User Experience in Stereoscopic 3D Games. *Proceedings of the 2012 ACM annual conference on Human Factors in Computing Systems – CHI '12*, ACM (2012), 89-99.
23. Schild, J. and Masuch, M. Designing Stereoscopic Information Visualization for 3D-TV: What can we learn from S3D Gaming ? *Proc of SPIE Vol. 8288: Stereoscopic displays and applications XXIII*, (2012).
24. Shibata, T., Kim, J., Hoffman, D.M., and Banks, M.S. The zone of comfort: Predicting visual discomfort with stereo displays. *Journal of vision 11*, 8 (2011), 1–29.
25. Stuerzlinger, W. and Wingrave, C. The Value of Constraints for 3D User Interfaces. In *Virtual Realities: Dagstuhl Seminar 2008*. Springer, 2011, 203–224.
26. Taylor, P., Kennedy, R.S., Lane, N.E., Berbaum, K.S., and Lilienthal, M.G. Simulator Sickness Questionnaire : An Enhanced Method for Quantifying Simulator Sickness Simulator Sickness Questionnaire : An Enhanced Method for Quantifying Simulator Sickness. *International Journal*, 912873516 (2010).
27. Ware, C. and Mitchell, P. Reevaluating stereo and motion cues for visualizing graphs in three dimensions. *Proceedings of the 2nd symposium on Applied perception in graphics and visualization - APGV '05*, ACM Press (2005), 51.
28. Wirth, W., Schramm, H., Böcking, S., et al. Entwicklung und Validierung eines Fragebogens zur Entstehung von räumlichem Präsenzerleben. Halem, 2008, 70–95.
29. You, J., Jiang, G., Xing, L., and Perkis, A. Quality of Visual Experience for 3D Presentation – Stereoscopic Image. In M. Mrak, M. Grgic and M. Kunt, eds., *High-Quality Visual Experience*. Springer Berlin Heidelberg, Berlin, Heidelberg, 2010, 51–77.

BeThere: 3D Mobile Collaboration with Spatial Input

Rajinder S. Sodhi, Brett R. Jones, David Forsyth, Brian P. Bailey
University of Illinois at Urbana-Champaign
Department of Computer Science
{rsodhi2, brjones2, bpbailey, daf}@illinois.edu

Guiliano Maciocci
Qualcomm Research Cambridge
Cambridge, UK
gmaciocc@qualcomm.com

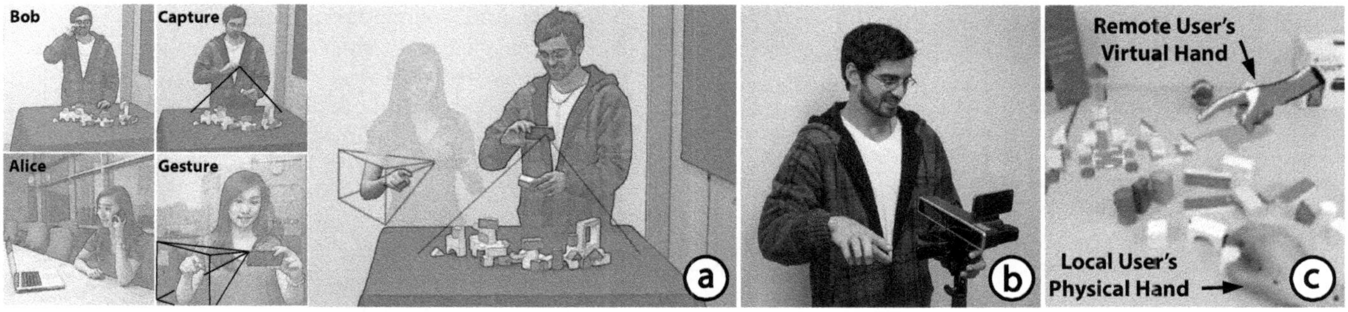

Figure 1. The (a) *BeThere* concept - a self contained mobile smartphone with integrated depth sensors. Bob is in need of help constructing a wooden block model and decides to capture and share a 3D representation of his local environment with remote user Alice. With Alice's mobile device, she can perform spatial and gestural interactions that can be seen by Bob. In (b), a user is shown holding our proof of concept system that simulates a mobile smartphone of the future and (c) shows what a user like Bob sees in their mobile device. Here, remote user Alice is controlling a 3D virtual hand in a shared representation of the environment in order to show where local user Bob should place the physical blocks.

ABSTRACT
We present *BeThere*, a proof-of-concept system designed to explore 3D input for mobile collaborative interactions. With *BeThere*, we explore 3D gestures and spatial input which allow remote users to perform a variety of virtual interactions in a local user's physical environment. Our system is completely self-contained and uses depth sensors to track the location of a user's fingers, as well as to capture the 3D shape of objects in front of the sensor. We illustrate the unique capabilities of our system through a series of interactions that allow users to control and manipulate 3D virtual content. We also provide qualitative feedback from a preliminary user study which confirmed that users can complete a shared collaborative task using our system.

ACM Classification Keywords
H.5.2 [Information interfaces and presentation]: User Interfaces. - Graphical user interfaces.

Author Keywords
Around Device Interaction; Collaboration; Depth Sensors, Augmented Reality

INTRODUCTION
Close physical proximity easily enables communication with one another, yet we spend a large amount of our time apart. Our mobile phones play an important role in how and when we communicate, yet they limit our interactions to verbal or video modalities. For example, imagine receiving a call from a family member asking to help fix malfunctioning hardware on a computer. Using words alone can be challenging and while video can help, deictic words such as "this", "here", and "there" could be more meaningful if we had a way to interact *in* the environment.

Low-cost commercial depth sensors allow us to capture the real-time shape and appearance of physical objects. Depth sensors integrated into today's communication devices could help realize the expansive possibilities of 3D mobile, remote collaboration and make the environment a core part of the communication.

Previous work in Virtual Reality has shown intriguing interactions for supporting 3D remote collaboration, but require users to wear head-worn displays or body worn markers [1]. With Augmented Reality (AR), users with mobile devices can overlay 3D virtual content on top of the real world. However, users are typically required to instrument physical objects with tracking markers and interactions are largely limited to touching the screen [8].

In this paper, we present *BeThere*, a proof-of-concept system that simulates mobile communication devices with multiple integrated depth sensors (Figures 1, 2). Our system is built for two users: the **local user** who has a physical object or environment to share and the **remote user** who would like to perform 3D interactions in the shared environment. The

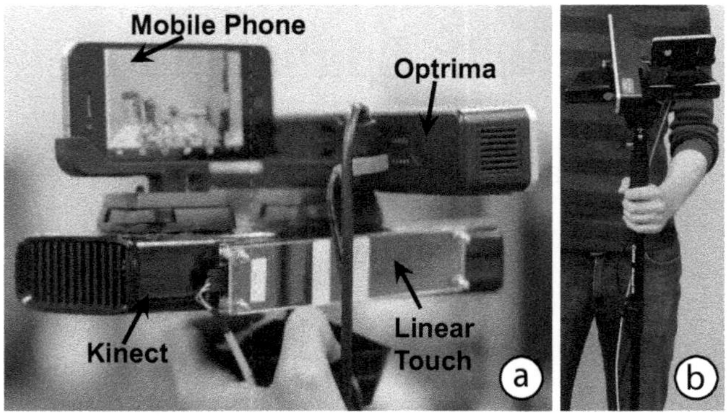

Figure 2. Our prototype *BeThere* system (a) is composed of a standard mobile smartphone, a front facing Kinect to capture the environment, a side facing Optrima short range sensor to sense spatial input and a touch strip for clutching. The hardware (b) is instrumented on a monopod to provide additional support for our users.

remote user may have expertise related to the object or environment, or simply needs the environment to be part of the communication. For example, an expert computer technician (remote user) can help a customer (local user) fix hardware issues. Or, a child with a lego set (local user) can ask a parent, away from home (remote user), to help find the right place for a lego piece. Finally, a remote user can drive an animated character around a physical desk belonging to their friend (local user) to create an interactive AR gaming experience.

The *BeThere* system has a number of advantages. First, our prototype system enables a user to easily capture and share a 3D representation of their physical environment with a remote user. Second, 3D spatial input enables a user to perform interactions that map naturally to interactions we perform everyday in the real world (e.g., pointing our hand toward a physical object). Third, we allow each user to have their own unique viewpoint of the shared 3D environment independent of what each user sees.

With *BeThere*, we explore the feasibility of creating future mobile devices with depth sensors and their utility for mobile communication. We present the following contributions: (1) the first proof-of-concept system composed of a side facing and front facing depth sensor (designed to simulate 3D interactions with mobile devices) (2) spatial input techniques for driving 3D interactions, including a unique point-pinch technique; (3) a qualitative user study which confirmed that users can perform a complex shared collaborative task together using our system.

RELATED WORK

Our work relates to video-mediated communication, augmented reality, free space interactions and touch input techniques related to 3D object manipulation.

Video Mediated Collaboration

A large body of work has been conducted to understand how to make video communication more effective (e.g., [9, 37]). For example, a number of tele-conferencing systems use gaze-tracking techniques to coordinate the views for large group conversations [11]. These approaches also include telepointing style methods to guide video based gestural interactions [14]. Previous work (e.g, [31, 29]) has also explored how to automatically control the perspective of a remote user by using multiple cameras or detecting salient features of the scene. In contrast to video based approaches, *BeThere* enables 3D interaction (e.g., 3D pointing) on a mobile device and enables distributed users to share a 3D representation of the space.

3D Virtual and Augmented Spaces

Merging physical and virtual environments has been an active research topic in the AR and VR communities. Previous work has focused on rendering realistic representations of humans with the intent of accurately mimicking non-verbal cues such as head pose, gaze direction, body posture and facial expressions [4]. The emergence of mobile AR systems have enabled remote users to aid local users in performing complex maintenance style tasks [8]. For example, AR based tele-pointers are known to be better than verbal communication alone for remote help [1]. Stafford et al. used a 3D virtual hand representation in collaborative AR tasks based on GPS tracking [36]. Maimone et al. created a system that enabled real-time 3D capture of room-sized scenes which could be viewed through a tiled-display with the correct perspective view [26]. In contrast to these system, *BeThere* uses precise finger tracking and overcomes the constraint of carefully placed markers in the environment.

Recent work by Gauglitz has demonstrated the feasibility of enabling remote collaboration with mobile devices without the need for instrumenting the environment[10]. While the system supported 2D persistent annotations with promising results, the system concentrates on intrinsically 2D tasks (e.g., place markers on a flat simulation of an aircraft panel). In contrast, *BeThere*'s goal is to provide users with 3D spatial cues for inherent 3D collaborative tasks.

In contrast to a number of previous approaches aimed at using projector-camera systems for 3D collaboration [32, 25, 35, 39], curved displays [2], and wearable devices [12], our intentions are to develop 3D collaborative interactions that can be implemented in handheld mobile devices.

Enabling Mobile Free Space Input

An active area of research investigates the use of free space input on mobile devices [6, 22]. Previous work has focused on exploring off-screen coarse grained gestures for input. For example, Imaginary Interfaces explored 2D interactions such as free-space sketching and pointing without the use of a mobile display [13]. We leverage design principles from previous work to support depth based spatial input specifically for mobile collaborative 3D interactions.

A number of sensing modalities including magnetometers and infrared markers have been used in previous work to track fingers or hands for Around Device Interaction [18, 34]. While these approaches allow the user to perform unconstrained free-form movements, users must wear an input ring on each finger to interact with the device. The emergence of low cost depth sensors have enabled others to explore a new

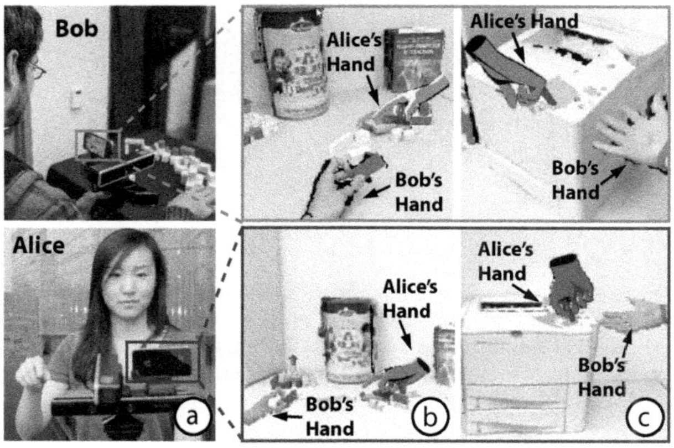

Figure 3. In (a), local user Bob has access to the physical environment which he captures and shares with remote user Alice. In (b), we show a shared repair task, where Alice manipulates a virtual 3D hand to show Bob how to fix the printer.

Figure 4. If remote user Alice is pointing at an object while Bob is looking away, then Bob has missed the interaction. Here, a user turns on a visual aid to see what the other user currently sees. This aid allows a user to ensure that an interaction (e.g., pointing) is seen by the other user.

class of interactions in a mobile setting [17]. The SideSight project explored detecting interaction to the side of a mobile device using a low resolution mobile depth sensor [5]. Similarly, PalmSpace used a time-of-flight sensor attached to a mobile smartphone [23]. However, previous work has been largely limited to coarse-grained gestures without exploring how free space input can be used for 3D mobile collaboration.

Manipulating Virtual Objects with Touch

One challenge in communicating in a shared virtual space is the need for manipulating 3D objects. Previous research has shown how 2D multi-touch input can be extended for 3D virtual object manipulation [16, 33, 27]. Others have shown improvements for 2D mouse input performance over 3D free space input [3], but far less has been done to compare 2D mobile touch input to 3D free space interactions. Jones et al. explored more complex 3D mobile spatial input to allow users to perform simultaneous panning and zooming tasks[21]. A direct comparison between mobile touch and 3D spatial input was made with results showing equivalent task completion times for a search task. While many of the 3D interactions of *BeThere* can complement touch input (e.g., [38]), we explore the use of intuitive 3D mobile free space input that naturally maps to interactions we perform everyday (e.g., pointing).

BETHERE DESIGN

BeThere is a mobile smartphone configuration (Figure 2) equipped with a front-facing depth sensor and side facing short range depth sensor that is designed to allow two users to perform 3D mobile collaboration. To use *BeThere*, a user follows three steps: (1) capture and share a 3D representation of the physical environment, (2) navigate the 3D shared environment and (3) perform 3D spatial and gestural input in the shared environment. Here, we describe the three steps, the hardware configuration and finger tracking algorithms used to support the experience as well as limitations of the design.

Capturing the Real World

Our system allows the local user to capture a real-time 3D model of the scene. This is made possible by using KinectFusion, which allows a user holding a standard Kinect depth sensor to move within any indoor space to capture the 3D geometry of the scene [20]. KinectFusion continuously combines new depth maps of the scene generated by the Kinect to create a persistent 3D model of the environment. Furthermore, the approach allows for 6 degrees-of-freedom (DOF) tracking of the Kinect camera's pose (Figure 5). For a full explanation of the algorithms and techniques used to implement KinectFusion, interested readers can see [20] for details.

Once the environment is scanned, the *BeThere* system extracts a 3D mesh of the local user's environment. Then realtime depth map of the local user's space is merged with the extracted background mesh to display foreground objects in the scene. Additionally, we extract the normals associated with the surface geometry, as well as the position and orientation data, for tracking the local and remote user in their physical environments. In a future implementation of *BeThere*, we envision that users would be able to carrey their mobile device around the environment and seamlessly share the environment by "calling" a remote user. However, currently we facilitate this step by scanning the environment, and then manually establish a shared connection between our two devices.

Remote Viewpoint

To provide accurate 3D views to the remote user of the local user's physical scene, *BeThere* must track the position and orientation of the remote user's depth sensor and generate a viewpoint for the remote user that is independent of the what the local user sees.

Tracking the Remote User

In *BeThere*, the remote user can move their mobile device to create their own independent view of the physical environment. Closely related to traditional Augmented Reality interactions where users can navigate a 3D scene with device motion [7], a remote user's natural 6 DOF movements map

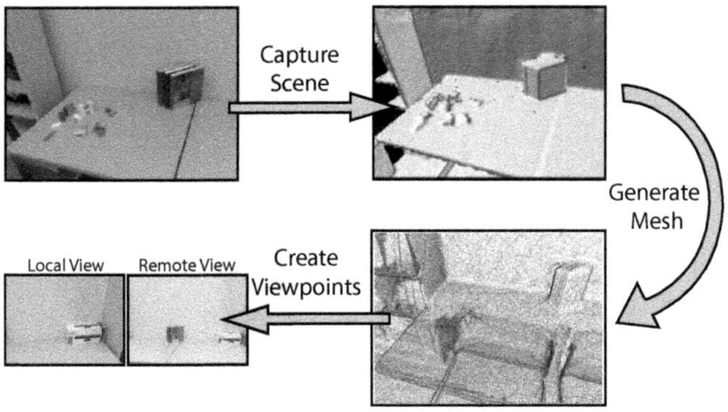

Figure 5. For two users to collaborate with each other, the local user must first capture a 3D representation of the scene. We use KinectFusion to allow the local user to capture and generate a 3D mesh which can be shared with the remote user. The system allows for independent viewpoints by creating a virtual 3D depth sensor for the remote user without requiring physical presence.

to movements in the local user's physical environment. For example, the remote user can walk around their own physical environment to navigate the local user's environment. A remote user can zoom into a physical object in the local user's space by moving the *BeThere* prototype in the forward facing direction, or see around a 3D object by moving their device to the right or left. To detect the relative position of the remote user, we once again use KinectFusion but only rely on it's ability to provide 3D position and orientation of the Kinect [20].

Creating the Remote View
To allow the remote user to see into the local user's real world, we compute a projection of the 3D data of the physical environment. This creates a virtual image as seen by the remote user in the local user's physical world. To generate the virtual image, each point in the 3D world is transformed from the local user's coordinate system into world coordinates using the local user's extrinsic parameters. This 3D world point is then transformed into the virtual camera coordinates of the remote user by extracting the position and orientation of the remote user's depth camera in their physical space. Each (x, y) position in the remote user's virtual image contains a depth value that allows them to perform real time depth scene queries of the local user's environment. Using this approach, there are no limits to the number of virtual views we can create. This allows remote interactions to include more than just two users; we leave this exploration to future work.

Performing Spatial Input
Here we outline our design decisions for why we use a side facing depth sensor to support spatial input. In addition, we describe the core *pointing* spatial technique which uses a touch sensor for clutching. While this technique requires users to coordinate spatial input between their hands (e.g., spatial input with dominant and clutch with non-dominant hand), later in the paper, we further describe a new spatial input technique that requires only a single hand for input.

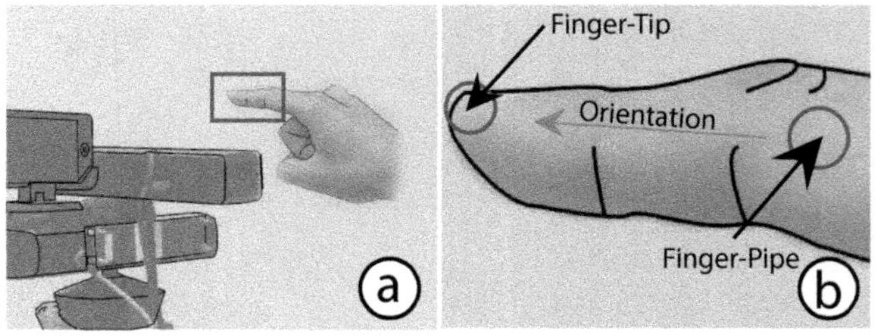

Figure 6. In (a), a simple pointing technique allows a user to provide 3D input to drive an interaction. In (b), a zoomed in view shows how our system simultaneously supports finding the position (finger-tip) and orientation (direction from the beginning of the finger to the finger-tip) of the finger.

Interaction Volume
Jones et. al. found that 3D interactions around a mobile phone most comfortably occur directly to the side of the device [21], approximately 10cm away from the side facing depth sensor. As such, we use a side facing short range depth sensor to allow users to perform depth-based input with fingers next to the mobile display. The *BeThere* system also uses simple visualization techniques that describe how close the user is to the extents of the tracking volume. When the user approaches the extents of the interaction volume, a simple 3D arrow and tracking lost notifications are used to help guide a remote user back to the optimal interaction region.

In addition, spatial interactions are scaled to allow users to cover large distances with small movements. This allows the user to perform smaller movements while staying close to mobile device. Through initial pilot studies, an optimal gain setting was chosen that most comfortably allowed users to cover a sufficiently large distance in the shared environment, while providing enough control to point to small objects.

Pointing
We leverage a simple 3D pointing gesture that allows remote users to map 3D movements on the side of the device to 3D movements in the local user's physical environment (Figure 6). An important aspect of our technique is that our system can extract both the 3D position and orientation of the remote user's fingers. To activate the *pointing* technique, the user presses and holds (with their non-dominant hand's thumb) the touch sensor located on the prototype and moves their gesturing finger in a free-form manner. The advantage of this bi-manual interaction is that users can perform free form input with their dominant hand while using their non-dominant hand to control when the system accepts input. To inactivate the technique, the user releases their non-dominant hand from the touch sensor.

Finger Tracking
The *BeThere* software framework uses a depth-based approach for *ad-hoc* finger tracking. Our finger tracking implementation requires no calibration or training and can resolve the X, Y and Z position of fingers as well as 2 DOF orientation (pitch and yaw). The finger tracking extends Hackenberg et al.'s depth-based approach which looks at extracting finger tip and finger pipe features from a depth map [15]. The Bresenham circle radius is determined for each pixel in the depth

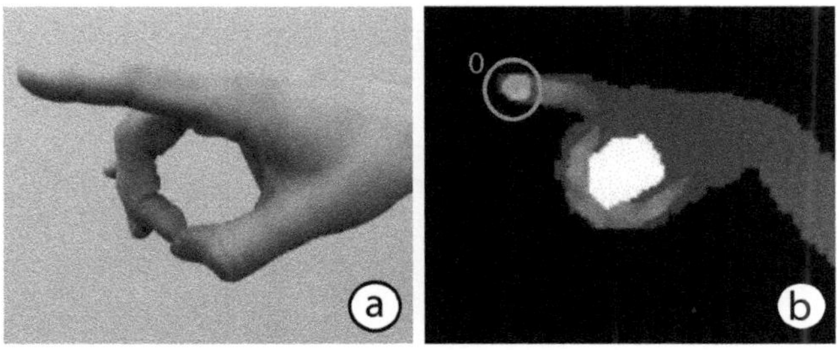

Figure 7. The *BeThere* system can (a) detect finger tip positions as well as the finger's orientations. The centroid of the finger-pipe and finger-tip position are used to determine the direction the user is pointing. In (b), our system looks for the largest connected component inside the hand to determine if a pinch gesture was performed.

map by first projecting a pixel and it's neighboring values into the image to determine their relative distance. The arcs of the Bresenham circle are used to analyze objects in the scene for their pipe and tip like features. Pipe and tip feature maps are extracted and correlated to determine finger locations. Additionally, 2 DOF orientation is extracted for each detected finger by using the centroid of the pipe to the finger tip.

BeThere Hardware

BeThere consists of a number of off the shelf components including a single mobile smartphone (an iPhone 4), a forward facing Kinect depth sensor, a side facing Optrima DS311 short range depth sensor and a PC with an Nvidia GTX 5700 graphics card. The side facing depth sensor is mounted on top of the forward facing depth sensor. The Soft Kinetic sensor's depth-range allows users to place their hand within 10cm of the sensor to reliably detect depth and has a resolution of 160x120. All of the components are configured on top of a monopod that users can optionally extend to the ground plane for support.

In our implementation, we created two devices connected to two computers. This greatly simplified the development of our prototype and allowed us to perform a controlled lab study. To transfer data to the mobile device, we use the *SplashTop* mobile remote desktop client to stream images over the network.

Limitations of Our Design

One limitation of the *BeThere* prototype was that the open source version of KinectFusion used did not include support for foreground object modeling. As a result, our prototype merged the foreground objects in the depth map with the background mesh extracted from KinectFusion. This means that when the local user moves their camera away from any foreground object, the remote user is no longer able to see the shared objects. While we do not feel that this appreciably affected the interactions and results, we included an extra visual aid to allow users to visualize each others view in the shared environment (see Figure 4).

Another limitation is that the depth sensors are heavy enough to make the prototype difficult to hold in one hand. To support the additional weight and provide users with enough mobility, we used a monopod. As depth sensors continue to decrease in size, a true mobile scenario could soon be feasible. We leave this updated prototype to future work.

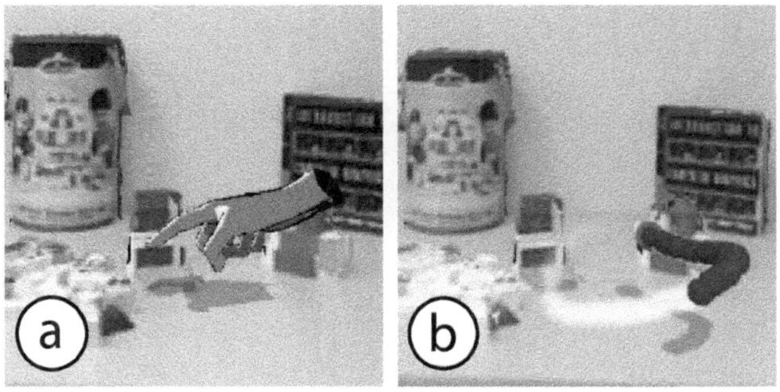

Figure 8. Here we show different awareness cues for directing attention. A remote user can choose to (a) control a virtual 3D hand that matches the movement of their physical hand or (b) perform 3D annotations of the environment. These virtual proxies also help to differentiate between the local's users hand and the remote user's virtual interactions in the shared environment.

AWARENESS CUES

BeThere supports two awareness cues for directing a user's attention. The virtual 3D objects used to represent the awareness cues were pre-selected and placed in the shared environment. Labels were placed along the touch strip to help users remember where to activate a particular feature (e.g., helping hand, annotations). All 3D models were purchased on the web.

Helping Hand

The *helping hand* is a 3D virtual proxy representation of a user's physical hand that can be manipulated using the *pointing* spatial technique (see Figure 8a). A user can activate the 3D virtual hand on the surface by pressing the touch sensor and *pointing* on the side of the mobile device. When the user changes the position and orientation of their finger, the virtual model changes to match the orientation of the finger (see Figure 9). For example, a remote user can perform circular pointing motions to direct a local user's attention at a region in the physical space or spatially gesture at how an object should be oriented in the physical environment.

3D Annotations

The *3D Annotations* cue allows users to perform a *pointing* interaction that leaves a motion trail in the 3D shared environment (see Figure 8b). The motion trail follows the path of a user's finger movement and can be left in the 3D shared environment to annotate objects of interest. This added information can be used to show how a 3D object should be moved in the shared 3D environment.

USER STUDY

We conducted a user study to test if users could perform a collaborative task using one example interaction of our system. Specifically, we wanted to test if users could use the system to accomplish a remote help task with a simple *pointing* technique. Our goal was to show whether mobile spatial input can be used successfully in the context of mobile collaboration.

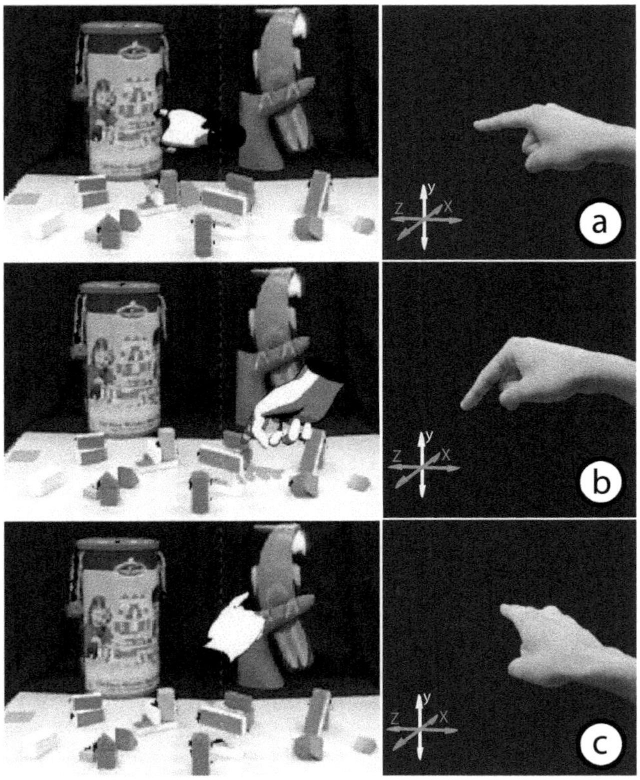

Figure 9. A user can control both the position and orientation of the virtual hand by using a pointing technique. In (a) a user is pointing their finger to the left, (b) pointing to the finger downward, and (c) pointing the finger to the right oriented up.

We were primarily interested in user responses to the feel of the interaction, the language used to communicate to each other, potential use cases as well as to identify opportunities for improvement.

Participants

We recruited 8 participants comprised of 4 groups from our local area (1 female), ranging in age from 18 to 29, with a mean of 24. The study took approximately 45 minutes and included a gratuity.

Task

To test the capabilities of the *BeThere* system, we use a similar Lego building task as Rajin et al. in which a remote user is asked to aid a local user in constructing a model out of wooden blocks [31]. We chose wooden blocks due to their reasonably complex shapes (a typical set contains 150 pieces) and their abilities to be sufficiently recognized given the spatial resolution of our depth sensor.

One member of the group, user A, was told to build a model and subsequently told to remove three blocks that were required to complete the construction. The unfinished model was then given to user B. User A and user B were then separated with a divider. User A then acted as the remote user helping user B complete the construction. This entire process served to simulate a local user requiring the aid of a remote user to complete a series of steps in a complex procedure. When the incomplete construction was laid out on the local user's table, a mix of multi-colored blocks were laid around the incomplete construction to make the task sufficiently complex, i.e., users should not be able to say, "take the blue block in the bottom right." The process was repeated to allow both user A and B to play the part of the remote user.

Procedure

Each user in a group was given 15 minutes to construct their respective wooden models and to choose which three block pieces to remove from their models. Users took no more than ten minutes to construct their models.

After the wooden models were created, each user was given a ten minute training period to get accustomed to controlling the virtual 3D hand as well as to move the *BeThere* hardware around their environments. A standard desk was chosen as the supporting surface. To ensure that mistakes could be adequately communicated with one another (e.g. picking up the wrong block among two neighboring blocks of the same color), we allowed users to verbally communicate as they would when making a normal phone call. A divider was set up in our lab space to prevent users from seeing one another.

We used a LiliPad external monitor mounted with a resolution of (800 x 480) and a 5in. display size in place of a mobile phone to remove the affects of any latency created from streaming images to the mobile phone. An experimenter recorded observations during the task and kept detailed contemporary notes of conversations and follow-up interviews with participants.

User Experience

Figure 10 shows example constructions generated by our users. All users of the study were able to use our prototype to successfully complete the experiment. Users took no more than ten minutes to complete the task. This suggests that *BeThere* is a viable and useful approach to 3D mobile communication.

Typical constructions would contain several layers of blocks and users would perform complex visual and verbal tasks to help a local user finish the construction. For example, one user workflow included moving the virtual hand to the top of a wooden model while asking a local user to, "remove **this** white block," revealing an opening inside the construction. The remote user would then say, "take **this** red cylinder and put it inside **this** opening." The dialogue relied on the use of a virtual 3D hand and the word "this" to direct the local user to an exact position in the physical space. The sequence of instructions would contain pauses (5-10 sec) between steps to allow the local user to complete an instruction. While the remote user would try to rely on the color of the blocks to help the local user, the task included a variety of colored blocks of different shapes and sizes to make the task sufficiently complex.

Additionally, users would move the virtual hand in various configurations to visually communicate the orientation of a block. For example, one user would move the virtual hand to

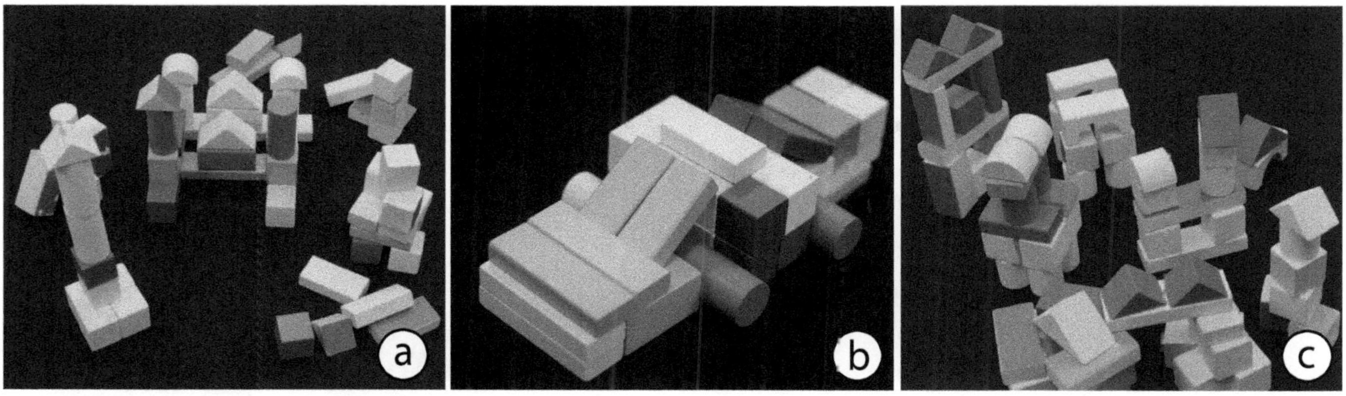

Figure 10. Here we show example construction results of our user study which demonstrate that remote users could help a local user construct objects of complex geometrical structure. The dialogue between users involved the use of words like "look at this block" to indicate that a local user should direct their attention to a specific location on the construction. This dialogue provides evidence that our virtual 3D hand was integral during the task.

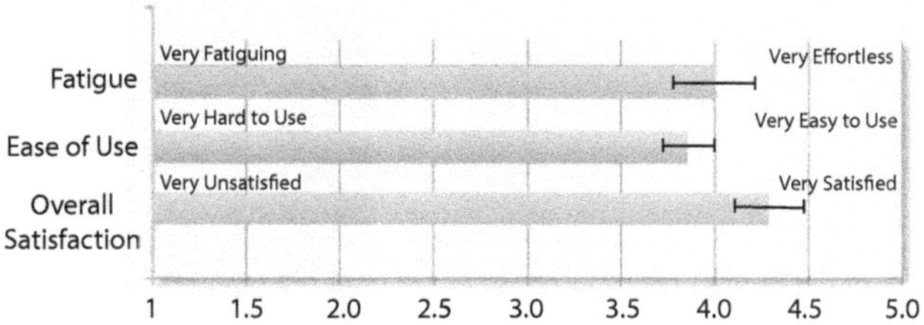

Figure 11. The chart shows user feedback where 5=very effortless, very easy to use, and very satisfied, suggesting that users found the system easy to use and were satisfied overall with the experience. Importantly, our users had no problems with regard to fatigue in completing the task. In post-task interviews, all users commented that they would find a system like *BeThere* to be useful in their mobile devices.

a point on the table and subsequently move the virtual hand side to side to indicate that a block should be laid horizontally on the table. Users performed this interaction on several occasions for objects that required specific orientations.

Figure 11 shows results reported through questionnaires regarding ease of use (mean=3.856, std=0.378), fatigue (mean=4.0, std=0.577) and overall satisfaction (mean=4.285, std=0.487). Among all deictic references, the words "this" and "here" were used most frequently. These results suggest that users generally found the task easy and effortless to perform on our prototype. In post task interviews, all of our users also commented that they would find features of *BeThere* to be useful in their mobile devices. When asked about experiences interacting with the helping hand, users responded that it was intuitive to see a virtual hand orient itself with their own physical hand movements. Some of our users even commented that the features of our system would be particularly useful in a heads up display system like Project Google Glass.

Advantages and Limitations

Users were asked for ways in which the system might be practically useful to them. Many of our users mentioned being able to help with problems dealing with hardware. Specifically, users mentioned, "pointing at buttons," or "fixing computers." As one user mentioned, "When speaking with my parents, they recently got WiFi and I couldn't really tell them how to plug in the cable. They didn't really understand what a port is." In one case, a user mentioned that he could even see using the 3D hand to play a "chinese checkers game."

Users also commented on the general ease of use of changing views. However, users occasionally remarked about the limitations of Kinect sensor's spatial resolution. While we use a fully textured KinectFusion generated mesh for the supporting surfaces and background, the *BeThere* system relies on the point cloud generated from the depth sensor of the local user to generate 3D foreground objects. This means that while a remote user's views could be independent from the local user, they could only stray so far away from the local user's viewpoint. This problem is inherent in any single 3D depth sensor configuration as seen in previous work [2]. Even with this limitation, remote users were still able to provide complex instructions to complete a construction with 3D mobile spatial interactions. As one user mentioned, "it was useful for peeking around objects." Another user mentioned, "it's good to be able to see a different perspective because the other party may not be seeing things right."

The largest bottleneck for users was the interaction volume. As described earlier, a visual 3D arrow was used to help guide users back to the optimal sensing region on the side of the device. However, users were not receptive to the cue and would leave the tracking volume temporarily losing the ability to control the virtual hand. After a few instances of exiting the tracking volume however, users started to understand the optimal placement of the hand given the sensor position and orientation. One explanation for this is that users' intuition to point naturally requires a large interaction volume. This result supports findings in previous mobile free space work [21] and suggests that hardware designers should support large field of views to enable users to naturally perform spatial input.

BEYOND POINTING

In addition to pointing, we developed a variety of spatial input techniques to explore other applications that can benefit from 3D mobile interaction. We outline these techniques as well as show their utility by creating mappings to two example application scenarios (see Figure 12).

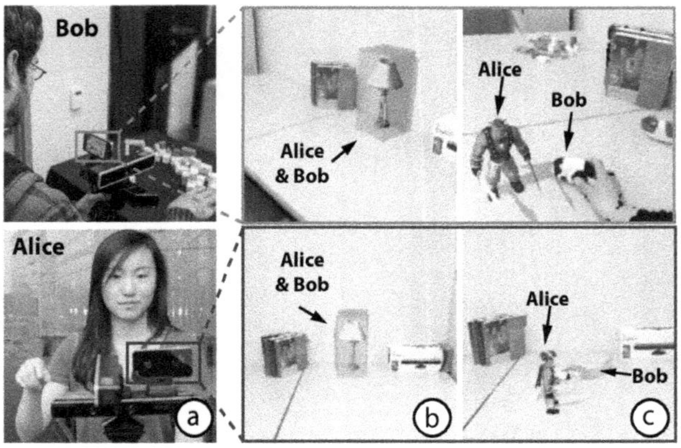

Figure 12. In (a) we show local user Bob and remote user Alice interacting with each other in two application scenarios: In (b), remote user Alice and Bob are discussing the decor of their environment and are using a virtual lamp model which can be manipulated by both users. In (c), local user Bob is playing an Augmented Reality game with Alice. Here Alice is using gestures supported by the *BeThere* prototype to move an Ogre character in Bob's environment.

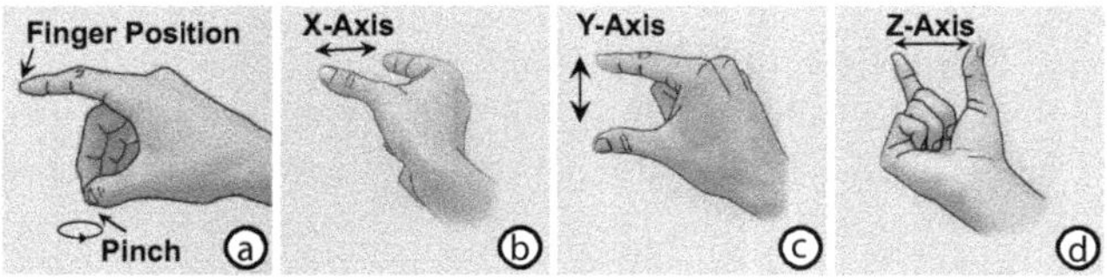

Figure 13. In (a) we show our pinch-point technique, where users can perform a pinch gesture to simultaneously clutch and provide input with a single finger. In (b)-(d), we use a multi finger gesture along three canonical orientations to support interactions that require the distance between the index finger and thumb for input.

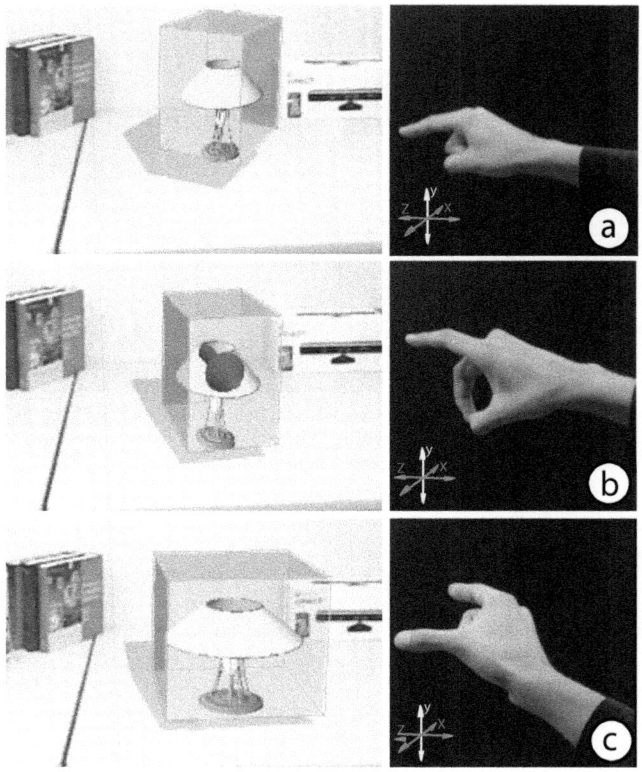

Figure 14. Users can transform a virtual model in a discussion of possible decorations on top of a physical desk. Here, we show two users manipulating (a) position of a virtual 3D lamp by using a simple *pointing* technique, the (b) orientation by using the *pinch-point* technique and the (c) scale by using the *two-finger span* technique.

Home Decoration

BeThere allows virtual 3D models to be quickly and imprecisely manipulated in the local user's physical environment. Imagine a local user is browsing the web and wants advice on a lamp to buy to decorate a desk. The local user shares a 3D representation of the desk with a remote user and places a virtual 3D lamp that both users can manipulate (see Figure 12b). To make the environment a part of the communication, we created a number of spatial input techniques to allow a user to manipulate virtual 3D objects, such as the lamp in Figure 14. Users can change the position, scale, orientation and the underlying structure of the virtual 3D model.

Position, Rotation, Scale

Users can change the position of 3D virtual object by simply using a *pointing* technique used to control a virtual 3D hand proxy. While there isn't a direct mapping that's akin to controlling a 3D hand, a user can easily position an object by tapping the touch strip and moving their finger around the side of the device.

To support rotating 3D objects, we developed a unique *pinch-point* gesture. With the *pinch-point*, users can both simultaneously clutch and perform spatial input with one hand (in contrast to bi-manual interaction [28]). To use the *pinch-point* technique to rotate the lamp (see Figure 13a), users place a single extended finger to the side of the device. Users can activate the system for input by performing a pinch gesture, where their non-extended fingers and thumb touch together. The initial position of the finger is used as a reference point to move the virtual hand relative to its current position. Thus, the initial state of the *pinch-point* technique does determine the orientation of the virtual proxy but not the position.

When the rotation is activated, a 3D arrow extends from the lamp's forward facing direction to match the movement of the user's finger (see Figure 14b). This interaction technique requires that users orient their pinched fingers in such a way that the sensor can see the connected component generated by the pinch (see Figure 7) [40].

To change the scale, we use a *two finger span* spatial technique which allows users to manipulate the size of a 3D virtual object by using the distance between the index and thumb positions for input. *BeThere* supports the *two finger span* along the X, Y and Z axis (see Figure 13(b)-(d)). To activate this technique for input, the remote user positions their index finger and thumb to the side of the device and presses the touch strip. For example, if a user wants to increase the height of a virtual 3D lamp, the user first uses the *two finger span* technique oriented on global Y-Axis. The user then presses the touch sensor to activate the spatial input. Increasing the distance between the finger and thumb scales the object in the y-axis. Releasing the sensor inactivates the technique.

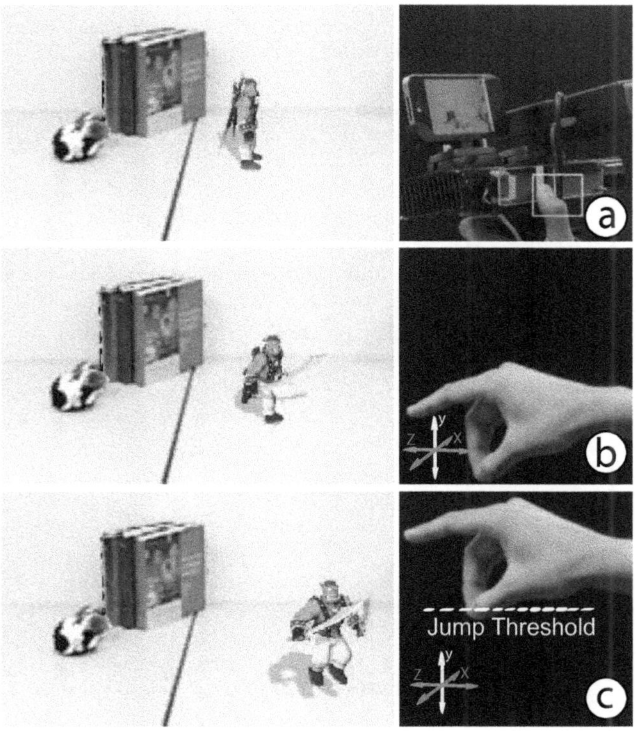

Figure 15. *BeThere* can be adapted to allow for a variety of mappings from spatial input to 3D character control. For example, we adapted the system to map (a) finger movement running and (b) finger lift to jumping. In (c), the remote user uses the touch sensor to activate the Ogre's swords. Touching the sensor again swings the ogre's swords.

Exploded View

Users can also break apart a 3D virtual model into its subcomponents to see the underlying spatial relationships between parts [24]. This allows users to quickly view and discuss components of the model (e.g., the lamp shade or stand). To start the exploded view, a user moves the model to the desired location with a *pointing* technique and performs a *pinch-point* spatial technique. A simple exploded view model can be generated by having users move their finger away from the initial pinch start position.

Augmented Reality Game

BeThere can also support a variety of mappings that allow spatial input to control non-rigid 3D models, such as an animated Ogre with swords. Imagine a child who wants to play a pretend fighting game on a friend's physical desk. A variety of mappings can be used that allow a child to control a 3D virtual character like an Ogre (see Figure 15) to fight the local user's physical toy.

To first move the virtual character, the user performs a *pinch-point* technique similar to the technique used in the home decoration scenario. When the user's finger moves away from the initial pinch start position, the virtual character follows the direction of the user's finger. When the user moves their finger up, the character jumps into the air before falling back to the table top, simulating the natural physics of the environment. Once the 3D character falls back to the physical surface, the user can tap the touch sensor to engage the character's swords. The user can tap the touch sensor again to swing the swords while simultaneously moving the virtual character around the environment with the *pinch-point*, combining both touch and spatial input.

DISCUSSION AND FUTURE WORK

With *BeThere*, we take a step towards allowing users to make the environment a fundamental part of the communication process. Our goals were to provide remote users with a feeling of being physically present in the environment. While we are encouraged by our exploration, there are many challenges that lie ahead to achieve this goal.

We allowed users to move the device to change views and gesture at the same time and found that users were able to perform a combination of small movements and gesture simultaneously. However, it may not be easy for all (or even most) users to move the device over larger distances and gesture effectively at the same time. While very high tracking and rendering techniques likely help, this is most likely an issue of coordinate movement. Users could find it difficult to coordinate locomotion, device movement, and gesture. For example, it is hard to keep control gestures inside the sensing volume when you take a virtual character like our Ogre on a tour around a room. One might deal with this by showing summary views of the whole space; incorporating other mappings from the device to the room; or dynamically revise the scaling of spatial input relative to physical movements.

We did not deeply investigate the value of constraining the virtual environment to implement physically realistic aspects of the world. For example, one might insist that virtual objects not penetrate real surfaces (e.g, a virtual hand should not be able to move through a table). Techniques for implementing such physics are available, and it is interesting to speculate that incorporating them might enrich the interaction.

We focused on pointing, because making deictic references meaningful seems to have very high potential impact. Pointing is relatively easy to transduce. One could speculate that incorporating much richer kinematic representations of the hand (e.g., [30]) could produce other interesting interactions. One could also simulate mobile stereo views and evaluate the benefit of 3D cues in mobile scenarios [19].

One concern that does not seem to have manifested itself is fatigue. The user study shows no evidence the task is fatiguing in the short term, and users worked on fairly complex models. This may be because the device can be placed so the pointing techniques we use are easy to make. The uses we suggest involve quite short interactions (pointing out a cable socket, for example), but long tasks (e.g, tearing down an engine) with a system like ours might produce a great deal of fatigue. We feel that the short interactions offer enough value to justify building our system.

Future mobile devices may turn out not to have depth sensors, but we think this is unlikely. First, it seems clear now that such sensors could offer real value. Second, while active sensors impact device power budgets, passive stereo-based sensing is becoming practical and well understood methods exist for how to map stereo algorithms to specialized hardware. Therefore, it is possible that every day mobile devices will have depth sensors that can be carried in our pocket.

CONCLUSION

We described *BeThere*, a novel system that demonstrates the feasibility of bringing spatial 3D interactions to mobile communication devices by exploring remote help tasks, interior design and new gaming experiences. We described a range of spatial interaction techniques that can be performed on the side of a mobile device. These elementary interactions were composed to allow users to perform higher order interactions such as the ability to control a 3D hand proxy and to perform natural and intuitive gestures like pointing at objects. Results from our user study indicate that users could perform a shared collaborative task using our system. The main contribution of this work is demonstrating the feasibility of remote 3D collaboration with our mobile devices when combined with a shared 3D representation of our physical environment. We hope that *BeThere* has provided a glimpse into the rich interaction possibilities of future mobile devices.

REFERENCES

1. Bauer, M., and Kortuem, G. Where Are You Pointing At ? A Study of Remote Collaboration in a Wearable Videoconference System. In *Wearable Computers*. (1999), 151–161.
2. Benko, H., Jota, R., Wilson, A. D., and Inesc-id, V. MirageTable : Freehand Interaction on a Projected Augmented Reality Tabletop. In *Proc. of CHI* (2012), 199–208.
3. Bérard, F., Ip, J., Benovoy, M., El-Shimy, D., Blum, J., and Cooperstock, J. Did minority report get it wrong? superiority of the mouse over 3d input devices in a 3d placement task. In *Proc. of INTERACT* (2009), 400–414.
4. Billinghurst, M., Cheok, A., Kato, H., and Prince, S. Real World Teleconferencing. In *Proc. of CHI* (1999), 194–195.
5. Butler, A., and Izadi, S. SideSight: multi-touch interaction around small devices. In *Proc. of UIST* (2008), 3–6.
6. Ens, B., Ahlström, D., Cockburn, A., and Irani, P. Characterizing user performance with assisted direct off-screen pointing. In *Proc. of MobileHCI* (2011), 485–494.
7. Fitzmaurice, G. W., Zhai, S., and Chignell, M. H. Virtual reality for palmtop computers. In *Trans. on Info. Sys.*, vol. 11 (1993), 197–218.
8. Friedrich, D. W. ARVIKA: Augmented Reality for Development, Production and Service. In *Proc. of ISMAR* (2002), 1–2.
9. Fussell, S., Setlock, L., Yang, J., Ou, J., and Mauer, E. Gestures Over Video Streams to Support Remote Collaboration on Physical Tasks. In *Hum.-Comput. Interact. 19* (Sept. 2004), 273–309.
10. Gauglitz, S., Lee, C., Turk, M., and Hollerer, T. Integrating the Physical Environment into Mobile Remote Collaboration. In *Proc. of Mobile HCI* (2012), 241–250.
11. Gergle, D., and Clark, A. T. See What I m Saying ? Using Dyadic Mobile Eye Tracking to Study Collaborative Reference. In *Proc. CSCW* (2011), 435–444.
12. Gurevich, P., Lanir, J., Cohen, B., and Stone, R. TeleAdvisor: a versatile augmented reality tool for remote assistance. In *Proc. of CHI* (2012), 619–622.
13. Gustafson, S., and Bierwirth, D. Imaginary interfaces: spatial interaction with empty hands and without visual feedback. In *Proc. of UIST* (2010), 3–12.
14. Gutwin, C., and Penner, R. Improving interpretation of remote gestures with telepointer traces. *Proc. of CSCW* (2002), 49.
15. Hackenberg, G. Lightweight Palm and Finger Tracking for Real-Time 3D Gesture Control. *Building*, March 2010 (2011), 19–26.
16. Hancock, M., ten Cate, T., and Carpendale, S. Sticky tools: full 6dof force-based interaction for multi-touch tables. In *Proc. of ITS*, ITS '09 (2009), 133–140.
17. Harrison, C., Benko, H., Wilson, A. D., and Way, O. M. OmniTouch : Wearable multitouch interaction everywhere. In *Proc. UIST* (2011), 441–450.
18. Harrison, C., and Hudson, S. Abracadabra: wireless, high-precision, and unpowered finger input for very small mobile devices. In *Proc. UIST* (2009), 121–124.
19. Hilliges, O., Kim, D., Izadi, S., Weiss, M., and Wilson, A. Holodesk: direct 3d interactions with a situated see-through display. In *Proc. of CHI* (2012), 2421–2430.
20. Izadi, S. KinectFusion : Real-time 3D Reconstruction and Interaction Using a Moving Depth Camera. In *Proc. of UIST* (2011), 559–568.
21. Jones, B., Sodhi, R., Bailey, B., Maciocci, G., and Forsyth, D. Depth-based Around Device Interaction for Multiscale Navigation. In *Proc. MobileHCI* (2012), 83–92.
22. Kratz, S., and Rohs, M. HoverFlow : Expanding the Design Space of Around-Device Interaction. In *MobileHCI* (2009), 1–8.
23. Kratz, S., and Rohs, M. PalmSpace : Continuous Around-Device Gestures vs . Multitouch for 3D Rotation Tasks on Mobile Devices Categories and Subject Descriptors Interaction on Mobile Devices. In *Proc. of AVI* (2012), 181–188.
24. Li, W., Agrawala, M., Curless, B., and Salesin, D. Automated Generation of Interactive 3D Exploded View Diagrams. In *Proc. of SIGGRAPH* (2008), 101–107.
25. Lincoln, P., Welch, G., Nashel, A., Ilie, A., State, A., and Fuchs, H. Animatronic Shader Lamps Avatars. In *Proc. of ISMAR*, Ieee (Oct. 2009), 27–33.
26. Maimone, A. A First Look at a Telepresence System with Room-Sized Real-Time 3D Capture. In *Proc. ICAT* (2011), 4–9.
27. Martinet, A., Casiez, G., and Grisoni, L. Integrality and separability of multitouch interaction techniques in 3d manipulation tasks. *Trans. on Vis. and CG 18*, 3 (Mar. 2012), 369–380.
28. Nancel, M., Wagner, J., Pietriga, E., Chapuis, O., Mackay, W., Orsay, F., and Orsay, F. Mid-air Pan-and-Zoom on Wall-sized Displays. In *Proc of CHI*, no. May (2011), 177–186.
29. Neill, J. O., Castellani, S., Roulland, F., and Hairon, N. From Ethnographic Study to Mixed Reality : A Remote Collaborative Troubleshooting System. *Proc. of CSCW* (2011), 225–234.
30. Oikonomidis, I., Kyriazis, N., and Argyros, A. Efficient model-based 3D tracking of hand articulations using Kinect. *Proc of the BMVC* (2011), 101.1–101.11.
31. Ranjan, A., Birnholtz, J. P., and Balakrishnan, R. Dynamic Shared Visual Spaces : Experimenting with Automatic Camera Control in a Remote Repair Task. In *Proc. of CHI* (2007), 1177–1186.
32. Raskar, R., Welch, G., Cutts, M., Lake, A., Stesin, L., and Fuchs, H. The office of the future. In *Proc. SIGGRAPH* (1998), 179–188.
33. Reisman, J. L., Davidson, P. L., and Han, J. Y. A screen-space formulation for 2d and 3d direct manipulation. In *Proc. of UIST*, UIST '09 (2009), 69–78.
34. Ring, M.-t. F., Ashbrook, D., Baudisch, P., White, S., Str, P.-d.-h., and Potsdam, D. Nenya : Subtle and Eyes-Free Mobile Input with a. In *Proc. CHI* (2011), 2043—-2046.
35. Sakong, K. Supporting telepresence by visual and physical cues in distributed 3D collaborative design environments. In *Proc. CHI* (2006), 1283–1288.
36. Stafford, A. Piekarski, W., and Thomas, B. Implementation of god-like interaction techniques. In *Proc. of ISMAR (2006)* (2006), 165–172.
37. Tang, J., and Minneman, S. VideoDraw: A Video Interface for Collaborative Drawing. In *ACM Trans. Inf. Syst. 9* (1991), 170–184.
38. Wigdor, D., Forlines, C., Baudisch, P., Barnwell, J., and Shen, C. Lucid touch: a see-through mobile device. In *Proc. of UIST*, ACM (2007), 269–278.
39. Wilson, A., and Robbins, D. Playtogether: Playing games across multiple interactive tabletops. In *Proc. of IUI* (2006).
40. Wilson, A. D. Robust Computer Vision-Based Detection of Pinching for One and Two-Handed Gesture Input. In *Proc of UIST* (2006), 255–258.

SpaceTop: Integrating 2D and Spatial 3D Interactions in a See-through Desktop Environment

Jinha Lee[1,2] **Alex Olwal**[1] **Hiroshi Ishii**[1] **Cati Boulanger**[2]

MIT Media Laboratory[1]
75 Amherst St. Cambridge, MA, USA

Microsoft Applied Sciences Group[2]
1 Microsoft Way Redmond WA, USA

{jinhalee, olwal, ishii}@media.mit.edu, catib@microsoft.com

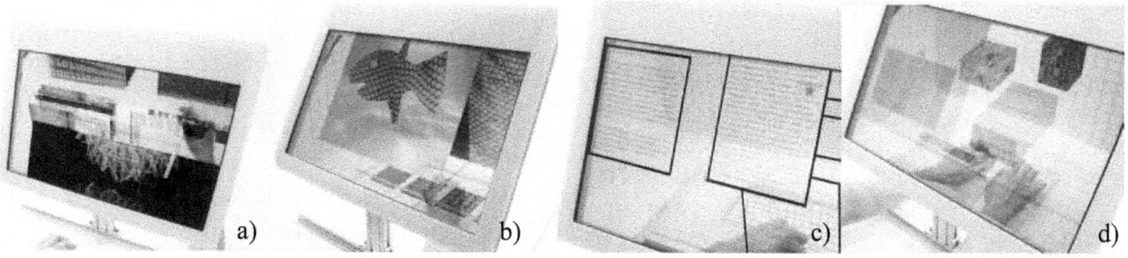

Figure 1. SpaceTop affords a) 3D direct spatial interaction, b) 2D direct touch, c) 2D indirect interaction, and d) typing. It aims to meld seams between these modalities by accommodating them in the same unified space and enabling fast switching between them.

ABSTRACT

SpaceTop is a concept that fuses 2D and spatial 3D interactions in a single desktop workspace. It extends the traditional desktop interface with interaction technology and visualization techniques that enable seamless transitions between 2D and 3D manipulations. SpaceTop allows users to type, click, draw in 2D, and directly manipulate interface elements that float in the 3D space above the keyboard. It makes it possible to easily switch from one modality to another, or to simultaneously use two modalities with different hands. We introduce hardware and software configurations for co-locating these various interaction modalities in a unified workspace using depth cameras and a transparent display. We describe new interaction and visualization techniques that allow users to interact with 2D elements floating in 3D space and present the results from a preliminary user study that indicates the benefit of such hybrid workspaces.

Author Keywords:

3D UI; Augmented Reality; Desktop Management

ACM Classification Keywords

H.5.m. Information interfaces and presentation (e.g., HCI)

General Terms

Human Factors; Design; Measurement.

INTRODUCTION

Desktop computing today is primarily composed of 2D graphical user interfaces (GUI) based on a 2D screen with input through a mouse or a touchscreen. While GUIs have many advantages, they can constrain the user due to the limited screen space and interaction bandwidth, and there exists situations where users can benefit from more expressive spatial interactions. For instance, switching between overlapping windows on a 2D screen adds more cognitive load than arranging a stack of physical papers in 3D space [7]. While there has been advances in sensing and display technologies, 3D spatial interfaces have not been widely employed in everyday computing. Despite advantages from spatial memory and increased expressiveness, potential issues related to precision and fatigue make 3D desktop computing challenging.

We present SpaceTop, an experimental prototype that brings 3D spatial interaction space to desktop computing environments. We address the previously mentioned challenges in three interdependent ways. First, SpaceTop accommodates both conventional and 3D spatial interactions in the same space. Second, we enable users to switch between 3D I/O and conventional 2D input, or even use them simultaneously with both hands. Finally, we present new interaction and visualization techniques to allow users to interact with 2D elements floating in 3D space. These techniques aim to address issues and confusion that arise from shifting between interactions of different styles and dimensions.

RELATED WORK

Previous work has explored 2.5D and 3D representations to better support spatial memory in desktop environments [1, 7]. Augmented Reality systems exploit the cognitive benefits of co-locating 3D visualizations with direct input in a real environment, using optical combiners [8, 6, 5]. This makes it possible to enable unencumbered 3D input to directly interact with situated 3D graphics in mid-air [5, 9]. SpaceTop extends these concepts with an emphasis on streamlining the switching between input modalities in a

CHI 2013, April 27–May 2, 2013, Paris, France.

unified I/O space, and the combination of such 3D spatial interaction with other conventional input modalities, to enable new interaction techniques.

Other related research explores the transitions between 2D and 3D I/O by combining multi-touch with 3D direct interaction [3], or through 2D manipulation of 3D stereoscopic images [4], with an emphasis on collaborative interaction with 3D data, such as CAD models. Our work focuses on how daily tasks, such as document editing or task management, can be better designed with 3D spatial interactions in existing desktop environments.

SPACETOP IMPLEMENTATION

At first glance, SpaceTop looks similar to a conventional desktop computer, except the transparent screen with keyboard/mouse behind it. Users place their hands behind the screen to scroll on the bottom surface, or type on the keyboard. Through the transparent screen, users can view graphical interface elements appearing to float, not only on the screen plane, but also in the 3D space behind it or on the bottom surface. The users can lift their hands off the bottom surface to grab and move floating windows or virtual objects using "pinch" gestures.

We accommodate 3D direct interaction, 2D touch and typing, with an optically transparent LCD screen and two depth cameras (Figure 2) in a 50×25×25 cm^3 volume.

Display: Prototype LCD with per-pixel transparency

We use a display prototype by Samsung, designed to show graphics without backlights in contact with its transparent LCD. The 22" transparent LCD displays 1680×1050 pixels images at 60 Hz with 20% light transmission. It provides maximum transparency for white pixels, and full opaqueness for black pixels. We use the unique per-pixel transparency to control the opacity of graphical elements, allowing us to design UIs that do not suffer from the limitations of half-silver mirror setups, where pixels are always partially transparent. We ensure that all graphical elements include clearly visible opaque parts, and use additional lights for the physical space behind the screen, to improve the visibility of the user's hands and keyboard.

Head and hand tracking with depth cameras

One depth camera (Microsoft Kinect) faces the user and tracks the head to enable motion parallax. This allows the user to view graphics correctly registered on top of the 3D interaction space wherein the hands are placed. Another depth camera points down towards the interaction space and detects position and pinch-gestures of the user's hands [11].

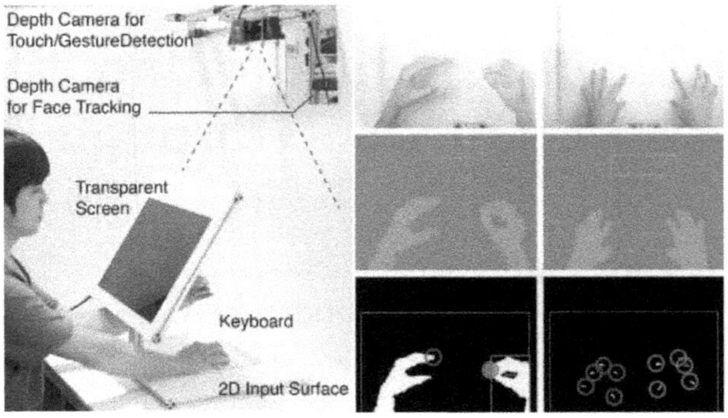

Figure 2. SpaceTop hardware configuration (left). Hand tracking and pinch detection (right).

The setup also detects if the user's hands are touching the 2D input plane based on the technique described in [10].

INTERACTION AND VISUALIZATION

2D in 3D: Stack Interaction

In SpaceTop, graphical UI elements are displayed on the screen or in the 3D space behind it. In our scenarios, details or 2D views of 3D elements are shown on the foreground plane (coinciding with the physical screen). While objects can take various forms in 3D space, we chose to focus on window interaction and 2D content placed in 3D space, such that the system can be used for existing desktop tasks. Another advantage of the window form factor in 3D is that it saves space when documents are stacked. It can, however, become challenging to select a particular window from the dense stack.

We designed various behaviors of stacks and windows to ease retrieval in stacks, as illustrated in Figures 3a–f. Users can *drag-and-drop* a window from one stack to another, to cluster it. As the user *hovers* his finger inside a stack, the layer closest to the user's finger gets enlarged and more opaque. When the user pinches on the stack twice, the dense stack *expands* to facilitate selection. The surface area below the stack is used for 2D gestures, such as scrolling. Users can, for example, *scroll* on the bottom surface of the stack to change the order of the documents in the stack.

We designed a *Grid and Cursor* system to simplify the organization of items in 3D. It provides windows and stacks with passive reference cues, which help guide the user's hands. The cursor is represented as two orthogonal lines parallel to the ground plane that intersect at the user's finger tips. These lines penetrate the grid box that represents the interaction volume, illustrated in Figure 3a.

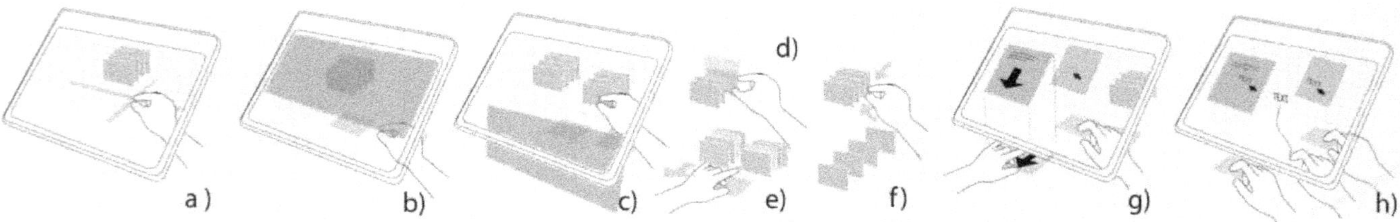

Figure 3. a) 3D grid and cursor. b), c) Sliding door. d) Highlighting. e) Scroll to change the order of windows. f) Expansion of a stack. g) Shadow Touchpad. h) Inter-shadow translation.

Figure 4. Users can spatially manage windows in 3D space, and leverage spatial memory to retrieve tasks.

Modeless Interaction

Our guiding principle for designing high-level interfaces and visualizations is to create a seamless and modeless workflow. Experiments have shown that when users shift from one interaction mode to another, they have to be visually guided with care, such that the user can mentally accommodate the new interaction model. Particularly, smooth transition between 2D and 3D views, and between indirect and direct interactions are challenging, since each of them is built on largely different mental models of I/O.

Sliding Door: Entering the Virtual 3D space

In the 2D interaction mode, the user can type or use a mouse or touchpad to interact with SpaceTop, as in any conventional 2D system. When the user lifts her hands, the foreground window slides up or fades out to reveal the 3D space behind the main window. When the hands touch the bottom surface again, the foreground window slides down again, allowing users to return to 2D-mapped input. The sliding door metaphor can help users smoothly shift focus from the "main" 2D document to "background" contents floating behind (See Figures 3b-c).

Shadow Touchpad: One Touchpad per window

Touchpad interaction with 2D windows floating in 3D space introduces interesting challenges. Especially when working with more than one window, it is not straightforward how to move a cursor from one window to another. Indirect mapping between the touchpad and the window can conflict with the direct mapping that each window is forming with the 3D space. To address this issue, we propose a novel concept called Shadow touchpad, which emulates a 2D touchpad below each of the tilted 2D documents floating in 3D space. When a window is pulled up, a *shadow* is projected onto the bottom surface, whose area functions as a touchpad that allows the user to interact with that window. When multiple screens are displayed, each of them has its own shadow touchpad area.

Inter-shadow translation of 2D element

Users can move 2D objects (e.g., text and icons) from one window to another by dragging the object between the corresponding shadow areas. The object will be visualized as a floating 3D object during the transition between the two shadow touchpads, similarly to the balloon selection technique [28], as shown in Figure 5.

Task Management Scenario

Effective management of multiple tasks has been a central challenge in everyday desktop computing. In SpaceTop, the background tasks occupy a fixed position in the 3D space

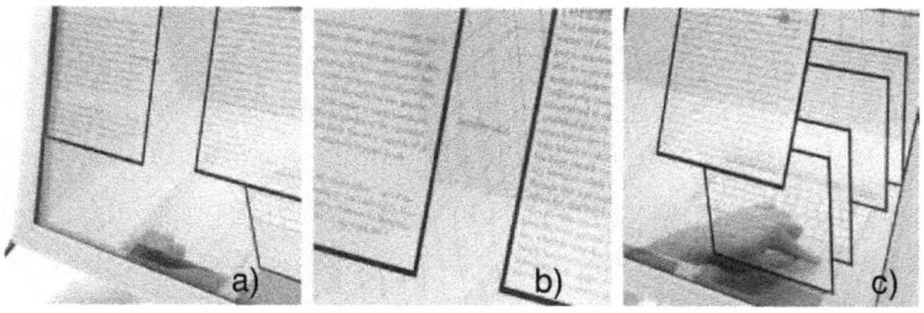

Figure 5. a) Selecting a piece of text and dragging it out of the source document. b) Text appears to be floating in open space while being moved from one document to another. c) The text appears again in the destination document.

behind the main task, allowing users to rely on their spatial memory to retrieve them. This spatial persistence mitigates some of the cognitive load associated with conventional task management systems. Sliding door or stack interaction can be directly applied to categorize, remember, and retrieve tasks (Figure 4).

Bimanual, Multi-fidelity Interaction

Interesting interactions arise when each hand is interacting in different styles and fidelities. The following applications demonstrate the potential of such bimanual, multi-fidelity interaction.

Document Editing Scenario

When composing a document, the user often needs to copy portions from other documents, such as, previous drafts or outside sources. SpaceTop allows the user to use the dominant hand to scroll through a main document, while simultaneously using the other hand to quickly flip through a pile of other documents, visualized in 3D space, to find a relevant piece of text. The user can then drag that piece of text into the main document through the more precise touchpad interaction. In this way, SpaceTop allows users to quickly switch back-and-forth between low-bandwidth , high-precision interactions (copying lines) and high-bandwidth, low-precision interactions (rifling through documents), or use them simultaneously.

3D Modeling Scenario

While 3D spatial interactions provide means for the user to materialize their design through spatial expression, much of the interaction in CAD require precise manipulation and is controlled in 2D. SpaceTop allows for natural transitions between these interaction modes. The user can start prototyping a model with free-form manipulation. Once fine control is required, the user can select a surface of the 3D model and pull up an editing console to the foreground

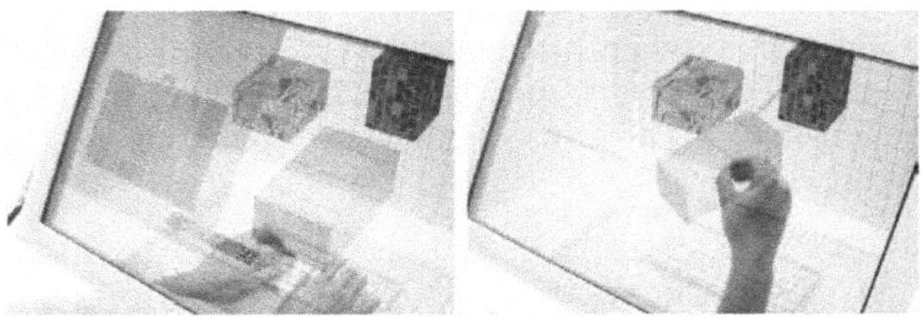

Figure 6. Modeling Applications. The user can pull up a face to the foreground windows, edit it on the 2D screen, and manipulate in 3D space.

of the screen. The user can then precisely modify dimensions by dragging a side, typing a number, or choose material properties by touching a 2D palette on the ground.

PRELIMINARY USER EVALUATION

Ten participants (age 19–29, 2 female) were recruited from a university mailing list, none of whom had previous experience with 3D user interfaces. They were able to familiarize themselves with the system until they performed each action comfortably (3–6 min). The total experiment time for participants was between 70-80 min.

Switching between indirect 2D vs. direct 3D interaction

12 partially overlapping colored windows (red, green, blue, or yellow), containing a shape (triangle, square or star), were shown. Participants were given tasks, such as "grab the yellow square and point to its corners", or "trace the outline of the blue triangle". They performed four different, randomized tasks for three spatial window configurations, for a total of 12 trials for each of two blocks. The *SpaceTop block* used spatial window placement with head-tracking and participants used a combination of gesture, mouse and keyboard interaction, for constant switching between typing, 2D selection and 3D interaction. In the *baseline block*, windows were shown in the display's 2D plane and only mouse and keyboard interaction was available.

Questionnaire responses (5-point Likert scale) indicate that the SpaceTop interactions were easy-to-learn (3.9). Participants did however find it slower (3.2 vs 4.2) and less accurate (3.2 vs 4.6) than the baseline. Users' comments include "after I repeated this task three times (with the same arrangement), my arm starts moving towards the target even before I see it", "switching to another window is as simple as grabbing another book on my (physical) desk". Another user commented that the physical setup constrains his arm's movement which makes him exhausted easier.

Text editing: Search and copy/paste

Participants skimmed the contents of six different document pages placed in the 3D environment. They were then asked to find a specific word and pick-and-drop it into the document on the foreground screen (see Figure 5).

Six participants commented that it felt compelling to be able to quickly rifle through a pile of documents with one hand while another hand is interacting with the main active task. One user commented: "it feels like I have a desktop computer and a physical book next to it". "This feels like a natural role division of right/left hand in the physical world". Three users reported that they had a hard time switching their mental models from 2D indirect mapping (touchpad) to 3D direct mapping (spatial interaction), which occurs when the user tries to drag a word out of a shadow.

DISCUSSION

Users' comments suggest that fast switching and bi-manual interaction provide compelling experiences, and that they can benefit from spatial memory (task 1). We also gained some insights for future improvements. A few users also commented that they might perform better with a stereoscopic display, in addition to the aid of the grid and cursor. Although previous work indicates that stereoscopy has limited benefit over monoscopic display with motion parallax [5], we plan to also explore a stereoscopic version of SpaceTop. We think that the visual representation could be better designed to provide users with clearer guidance. While the current configuration allows us to rapidly prototype and explore interactions, we plan to improve ergonomics and general usability with careful design of the physical setup.

CONCLUSIONS AND FUTURE WORK

SpaceTop is a concept that accommodates 3D and conventional 2D (indirect/direct) interactions in a single workspace. We designed interaction and visualization techniques for melding the seams between different interaction modalities and integrating them into modeless workflows. Our application scenarios showcase the power of such integrated workflows with fast switching between interactions of multiple fidelities and bimanual interactions. We believe that SpaceTop is the beginning of an exploration of a larger field of spatial desktop computing interactions and that our design principles can be applied to a variety of current and future technologies. We hope that this exploration offers guidelines for future interaction designers, allowing better insight into the evolution of the everyday desktop experience.

ACKNOWLEDGMENTS

We would like to thank Akimitsu Hogge and John Weiss for assistance in implementation, and Steven Bathiche, Vivek Pradeev, Otmar Hilliges, Andy Wilson, Hrvoje Benko, Pranav Mistry, and Microsoft Applied Sciences for valuable discussions.

REFERENCES

1. Agarawala, A., and Balakrishnan, R., 2006. Keepin' it real: pushing the desktop metaphor with physics, piles and the pen. CHI '06, 1283–1292.
2. Benko, H., and Feiner, S. 2006. Balloon selection: A multi-finger technique for accurate low-fatigue 3d selections. 3D UI '06, 79–86.
3. Benko, H., Ishak, E., and Feiner, S. 2005. Cross-dimensional gestural interaction techniques for hybrid immersive environments. VR ' 05, 209–216.
4. Hachet, M., Bossavit, B., Cohé, A., and Rivière, J., 2011. Toucheo: multitouch and stereo combined in a seamless workspace. UIST '11, 587–592.
5. Hilliges, O., Kim, D., Izadi, S., Weiss, M., and Wilson, A. 2012. HoloDesk: direct 3d interactions with a situated see-through display. CHI '12, 1283–1292.
6. Olwal, A., Lindfors, C., Gustafsson, J., Kjellberg, T., and Mattsson, L. 2005. ASTOR: An autostereoscopic optical see-through augmented reality system. ISMAR '05, 24–27.
7. Robertson, G., Czerwinski, M., Larson, K., Robbins, D., Thiel, D., and Dantzich, M. 1998. Data mountain: using spatial memory for document management. UIST '98, 153–162.
8. Schmandt, C. 1983. Spatial input/display correspondence in a stereoscopic computer graphic work station. SIGGRAPH '83, 253–261.
9. Treskunov, A., Kim, S. W., Marti, S. 2011. Range Camera for Simple behind Display Interaction. IAPR MVA '11, 160–163.
10. Wilson, A. Using a depth camera as a touch sensor. ITS '10, 69–72.
11. Wilson, A. 2006. Robust computer vision-based detection of pinching for one and two-handed gesture input. UIST '06, 255–258.

3D Object Position using Automatic Viewpoint Transitions

Michaël Ortega
Laboratoire d'Informatique de Grenoble
Université Grenoble I / CNRS
385, rue de la Bibliotheque, B.P. 53 F-38041 Grenoble cedex 9, France
michael.ortega@imag.fr

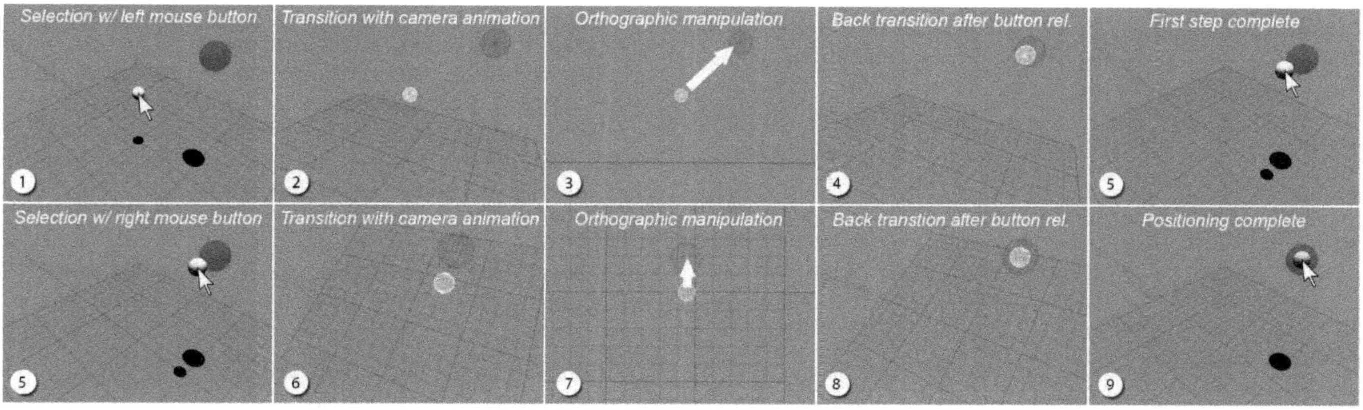

Figure 1. Steps with IUCA. 1: Selection of the object with the left mouse button down;1 to 3: Animation of the camera parameters (extrinsic and intrinsic); 3: Manipulation of the object to reach the target, then button release; 3 to 5: Reverse animation; 5: Second selection of the same object with right mouse button down; 5 to 7: Second animated transition; 7: Manipulation of the sphere then mouse release; 7 to 9: Reverse animation.

ABSTRACT

This paper presents IUCA (Interaction Using Camera Animations), a new interaction technique for 3D objects manipulation. IUCA allows efficient interaction in a full-resolution perspective view by integrating transients animated transitions to orthographic views *into* the manipulation task. This provides an interaction in context, with precise object positioning and alignment. An evaluation of the technique shows that, compared to the classical configurations, IUCA allows to reduce pointing time by 14% on average. Testing with professional 3D designers and novice users indicate that IUCA is easy to use and to learn; and that users feel comfortable with it.

Author Keywords

3D interaction; Four-views configuration; 3D modeling; 3D pointing; Fitts' law

ACM Classification Keywords

H5.2 Information interfaces and presentation: User Interfaces - Graphical user interfaces

INTRODUCTION

3D designers need perspective and orthographic views to complete precise objects manipulation. In the perspective view (PV), the scene is rendered using a center of projection (the position of the virtual camera). Objects in the distance appear smaller than objects close by. This provides depth perception, and contributes to the realism and the perception of relative 3D positions. This view is mainly used for context. In contrast, orthographic views (OV) uses projection lines which are orthogonal to the projection plane. The point-of-view is then free from parallax and also from depth effects. This allows precise positioning and easier alignment of 3D objects.

The current approach, called the "four-views configuration" (4VC) [8], includes these two projection methods. 4VC displays 4 different views of the scene at the same time, allowing manipulation in each of them. It is composed by three OVs (usually front, top and left views) and one PV. However, it presents the following limitations:

- Reduced display and manipulation space. Workspaces are reduced to the currently selected view. This forces the designer to compensate by frequently adapting the zoom factor of each view.

- Cognitive overload. The use of multiple views increases the load on the users' working memory and requires additional cognitive efforts for comparison and context switching [12, 4] (the effort increases with heterogeneous representations: solid and wireframe).

- Selection difficulty. The selection of a non-lighted wireframe object in the OVs present a high index of difficulty (in terms of Fitts' Law). Moreover, lines of different objects frequently align, resulting in occlusion.

4VC is often used by novices. Because of its workspace issues, more expert users prefer another configuration called here the "Switch View Configuration" (SVC). SVC only offers one view at a time in full-screen resolution, and allows switching between views with keyboard shortcuts. SVC, however, only copes with the first of the three issues introduced above.

We design, implement and evaluate IUCA (Interaction Using Camera Animations), a new technique to fluently switch between views during manipulation. IUCA alleviates these previous limitations by providing: (1) a main PV for context overview in full-screen resolution; (2) easier objects selection in PV before switching to other views; (3) semi-automatic selection of the OVs for manipulation; (4) animated view transitions integrated *into* the manipulation task (see Figure 1). We report on a user study with novice users, and on a presentation of IUCA to 3D designers. The results of the study show that IUCA improves performance compared to SVC and 4VC. Post-study interviews revealed that users, especially professionals, feel comfortable using IUCA.

RELATED WORK

Many studies have been proposed for improving 3D manipulation in a single PV, and a description of most of them can be found in Bowman et al. [2]. These studies mainly aim at suppressing the need of orthographic projections, and focus on providing accurate manipulation in context (all in the PV). However, 3D designers still need orthographic projections that are free from parallax and depth cues, and that better support precise manipulation, object alignments and quick size comparison.

A first step in integrating OV advantages in the PV was presented by Herndon et al. [7] with the "Interactive shadows" technique. The technique allows user to manipulate 3D objects in a PV via their projected shadows on a floor plane and on two walls. The technique, however, can not entirely replace OVs for precise manipulations because it is sensitive to degenerated configurations, when manipulation axes are orthogonal to the viewport projection plan for instance. Moreover, designers of complex scenes do not want to systematically use floor planes or wall planes. The technique has been adapted by Ayatsuka et al. [1] for augmented reality environment, but with the same limitations.

Recently, two studies [5, 10] introduced the use of animated transitions between views, building on the results of Robertson et al. [11]: animated transitions assist in preserving the spatial relationships between views; they shifts some of the user's cognitive load to the human perceptual system, therefore reducing the cognitive overload and overall interaction time. Grossman et al. [5] introduced a technique for constructing 3D curves by drawing a series of 2D curves with the 2D tape drawing technique. In this configuration, working in an OV is essential for precise manipulation of the points defining the curve. Designers also have to frequently switch to PVs to get a global view. The authors chose to animate the transitions between the views, and demonstrated the benefits. However, in contrast with IUCA, animations are not integrated into the manipulation task: designers have to do an extra action for switching, which is time consuming. The same limitation is present in the "ViewCube" technique proposed by Khan et al. [10]: an orientation indicator of the view can be manipulated for fluently changing the view. Moreover, object selection is done in OVs, a high difficulty task as discussed above.

In all these studies, the viewpoint is changed before and after the object manipulation. IUCA introduces a viewpoint switch *during* the object manipulation. IUCA exhibits several benefits that will be detailed in the following paragraphs: 1) selection is easier because it is always performed in the PV; 2) animations maintain the context and help users orient themselves; 3) user performance is improved; and 4) users mainly prefer IUCA because they perceive the 3 previous benefits that improve the comfort in manipulation.

IUCA

IUCA consists of integrating transient animated transitions between views "into" the manipulation task. It is composed of 4 steps:

1. Selection of both the object and the OV. Selecting an object, in the PV, with left or right mouse click selects a group of possible OVs: respectively vertical (including front, left or right views) or horizontal (including top or bottom views). The system then automatically choose one view in the selected group. The selected view is the one which projection plan is the *most parallel* to the current camera's projection plan.
2. Animated transition. Camera parameters are animated for a transition from the current perspective projection to the selected orthographic one. This is done in two steps. First, extrinsic parameters are animated: the direction of the camera is modified to become orthogonal to the selected plan, its position is modified to have the selected object in the middle of the screen at the same distance than before the selection (see Figure 2). Secondly, intrinsic parameters are animated to achieve a parallel projection (see Figure 3). We conducted informal studies that revealed that these two steps are better performed one after the other in this order to offer comprehensible transitions.
3. Object Manipulation in OV. After the animation, the camera keeps the orthographic projection until the manipulation is done (i.e. until the mouse button is released).
4. Animated back transition. Once the manipulation is done, the camera is animated back to its original PV (i.e. original intrinsic and extrinsic parameters).

In our implementation of IUCA, left or right mouse click respectively select the vertical or horizontal OV group. This could be done with a keyboard shortcuts depending on the 3D designers convenience.

The mouse cursor disappears during the manipulation, and comes back after the return animation. This is critical for the pointing movements as the cursor always reappear at the position of the selected object (see Figure 1). The user can

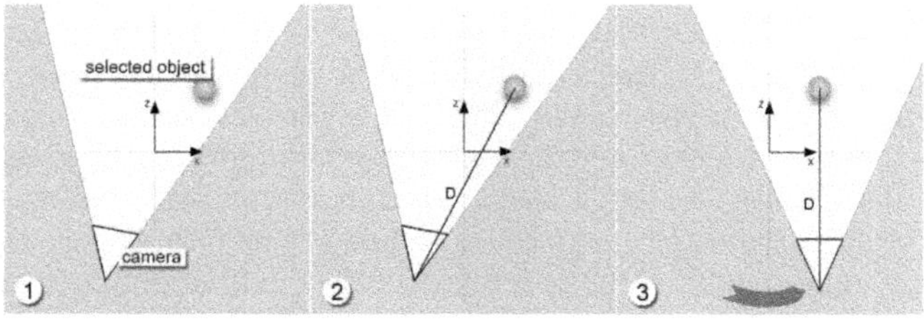

Figure 2. Extrinsic animation. The distance D between the camera and the object is preserved. The camera rotates until becoming aligned with the chosen orthographic projection plane, and having the selected object in the centre.

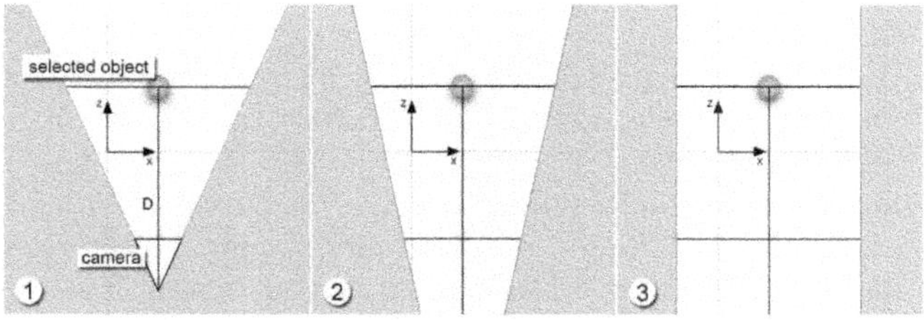

Figure 3. Intrinsic animation. The orthographic proj. surface is defined by the intersection of the camera's clipping volume with the plane defined by the object position and X and Y. Object ratio on screen is kept.

then concatenate the manipulations of a same object, with few mouse movements.

EVALUATION

We conducted a study to evaluate IUCA for object positioning in a 3D environment, in terms of pointing time, usability and user comfort. The study involves the most frequent task in 3D design: translating an object from its initial position to another position. Most of 3D designers need high precision in positioning (3D architectural design for instance), and this cannot be done in a single PV. We compared IUCA to the standard 4VC and SVC techniques. For the quantitative results (pointing time), the proposed task is not ecological: the 3D environment is minimized in order to avoid any bias. Professionals used IUCA in an ecological way, with an Autodesk Maya Plugin, in order to provide more realistic qualitative results.

In the quantitative part, participants had to perform successive 3D pointing tasks. They selected a small sphere with a fixed radius, and brought it into another sphere. Movement time (*MT*) was measured from the participant's click on a start button, until the last mouse button release. Transition animations had the same duration for each task with the first animation at 0.5 s. and the return animation at 0.2 s. These durations seems comfortable.

The difficulty of the task was computed using the adaptation of the Fitts' law proposed by Kabbash et al. for area cursors [9], and adapted for volumes as Hancock et al. did [6].

$$ID = \log_2(\frac{D}{2 * (Rt - Rs)} + 1) \qquad (1)$$

4 difficulties were presented: 3, 5, 6 and 7. Difficulties are obtained by changing the target size and the distance between the target and the small sphere in 3D. Considering *Rs*: the radius of the small sphere, *Rt*: the target radius, and *D*: distance between both spheres in 3D, the difficulty *ID* is obtained by the formula (1). For each configuration, 80 tasks were computed and each difficulty is equally and randomly presented. Participants had to complete all the tasks of a configuration before changing to another. A training session of 8 trials (2 trials per difficulty) was performed before each configuration. In each configuration, the 4 difficulties were equally and randomly presented, and the randomness was different for each user. The configurations were counterbalanced for each subject using a latin square ordering.

For the qualitative evaluation, we collected participant's opinions with a questionnaire regarding comfort, perceived performances, possible tiring and disturbing effects. We used a Brooke System Usability Scale (*SUS* [3]) to compute a quantitative estimation on the usability of IUCA. We wanted to know if IUCA is usable, and we estimated that 4VC and SVC are, just because they are used of lot.

Participants 15 regular computer user (with ages in the range [25, 35]) participated in the experiment. They were all member of the laboratory and had no 3D modeling experience. We enrolled novice users in 3D modeling to avoid biases on previous 4VC and SVC experience.

Apparatus The experiment was run on a 30" screen with a resolution of 2560x1600 pixels. Participants were in a desktop configuration mode. They sat in front of the screen during the experiment. The only interaction devices were a classical 2D mouse with two buttons, and a keyboard. The questionnaire was filled after the experiment.

RESULTS

Movement Time Figure 4 shows the average *MT* for each configuration and for each *ID*. In all configurations, the average *MT* increases with the difficulty, as suggested by Fitts' law. For each difficulty IUCA is faster than 4VC and SVC. A repeated measures ANOVA shows that the configuration has a statistically significant effect ($F_{1,585} = 226.8$, $p < .0001$), and this is also true for each participant. On average, IUCA is 16.6% faster than the 4VC, and 13.8% faster than SVC. Moreover, thanks to constant animation times (1.4sec for each *MT*) IUCA does not only improve task accomplishment time, but also depth perception and then the perception of relative positioning of 3D objects.

Error Rate For the three configurations, error rate increased with *ID*. This confirms Fitts' law again. The 3 configuration had similar error rate, and a Chi^2 test did not reveal any significant difference.

Novice Opinions The Brooke SUS provided a numerical evaluation of the usability of IUCA. The global mean rate is $3.69/4.0$ (= 92%). IUCA was thus assessed as "easy to learn and easy to use". Most of the participants seemed comfortable using it. However, half of participants judged that the system was, or could be, perturbing and tiring *at the beginning*. We discuss this problem in the next section.

Professional Opinions 4 professionals, aged between 20 to 42 years old, tested the Autodesk Maya plugin of IUCA. They were recruited from 4 different companies providing various services around 3D modeling: architecture, 3D models, an-

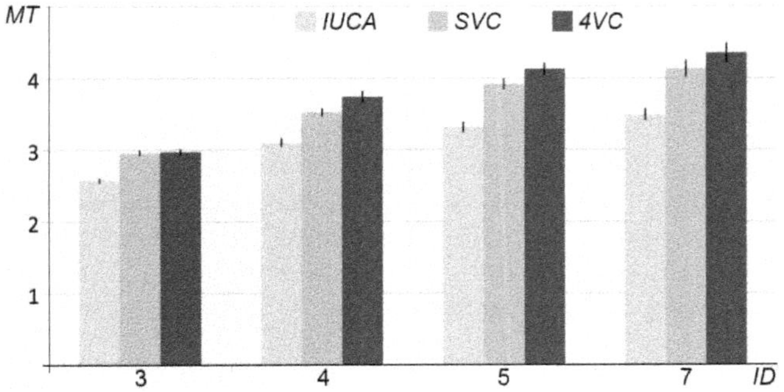

Figure 4. Average Movement Time (*MT*) for each *ID*. For each configuration, *MT* increases as *ID* increases, but in IUCA *MT* is always significantly lower ($p < .0001$). IUCA is 17% average faster than 4VC, and 14% average faster than SVC. (Error Bars: +/- 1SE)

imation, design, ... Two of them used 3DSmax Autodesk Software, and the two others used Blender (open-source and freeware). All were familiar with 4VC and SVC. After some time provided to understand, manipulate and integrate IUCA, the 4 participants filled the Brooke SUS: the global mean rate was 3.62/4.0 (=91%). IUCA appears usable, useful, easy to learn and not tiring. When asked about their opinions, professionals expressed that they "easily recover their previous habits" (P4), and "have a real feeling of winning time" (P2). P1 "would like to use it every day for modeling". P3 needed more time than others for understanding the technique (this is discussed in the next section), but after 10min he started to model a complex scene and also expressed an interest on using IUCA every day.

LIMITATIONS AND FUTURE WORK

The evaluation provides encouraging results on the benefits and potential of IUCA. However, some limitations exist, and professionals have noticed it when using IUCA in "real-world" tasks. The first one is related to repetitive tasks. An example is the adjustment of the position of several points in a 2D curve. Manipulating each point, one by one, implies many successive animations while the user would rather like to switch once to the appropriate OV at the beginning, and switch back at the end. The current version of IUCA does not allow staying on an OV for a while. Some solutions based on a pseudo-mode, like holding a mouse button, will be investigated.

Another limitation is that multiple selection are not possible. A solution could be the inspired by WIMP interaction: with a click in the background and a mouse drag to select many objects with an elastic box. Then, a click on one of the selected object launches IUCA, and the selection is considered as one object. This will be studied with the Maya plugin.

The unpredictability of the maximum translation distance in OVs is also a limitation. For instance, when the moving object reaches the border of the OV, the user has to release the mouse, to change the camera parameters in the PV, and to re-launch IUCA for finishing the task. A first solution could be "automatic camera translations" when an object reaches the border of the OV. But this requires further studies.

Finally, some users were perturbed by IUCA *at the beginning*, i.e. before they well understood and anticipated animations. Indeed, when the pointing task starts, camera animation implies target movements. The 2D projections of the direction between the starting position and the target are different before and after the animation (as visible in Figure 1-5 and Figure 1-7), and could be totally opposed. During the training phase, some users started their pointing movement in the "before animation" direction, and had to correct it. But after a training time, all users managed to anticipate. This learning effect will be studied by observing the evolution of the cursor movements during training.

CONCLUSION

IUCA improved user performance by integrating transient animated transitions into the manipulation task. The technique proposes an optimal use of the screen resolution, better performances in pointing time than classical configurations, and easier objects selection. We will now focus on the areas of improvement proposed in the previous section, and we will investigate orientation tasks.

ACKNOWLEDGMENT

Thanks to Laurence Nigay, Renaud Blanch and François Bérard (LIG) for their fruitful reviews, and to Nadine Mandran (LIG) for helping with the statistics. This work was supported in part by a BQR grant from Grenoble-INP (INTUACTIVE project).

REFERENCES

1. Ayatsuka, Y., Matsuoka, S., and Rekimoto, J. *Penumbrae for 3D interactions*. in Proc. of UIST (1996), pp. 165 - 166.
2. Bowman, D. A., Kruijff, E., LaViola, J. J., and Poupyrev, I. *3D User Interfaces: Theory and Practice*. Addison-Wesley Professional (2005).
3. Brooke, J. *SUS: a quick and dirty usability scale*. In P. W. Jordan, B. Thomas, B. A. Weerdmeester, and A. L. McClelland. Usability Evaluation in Industry. London: Taylor and Francis (1996).
4. Cockburn, A., Karlson, A., and Bederson, B. B. *A review of overview+detail, zooming, and focus+context interfaces*. in Journal of ACM Computing Surveys (2009), pp. 2:1 - 2:31.
5. Grossman, T., Balakrishnan, R., Kurtenbach, G., Fitzmaurice, G., Khan, A., and Buxton, B. *Creating principal 3D curves with digital tape drawing*. in Proc. of CHI (2002), pp. 121 - 128.
6. Hancock, M., Carpendale, S., and Cockburn, A. *Shallow-Depth 3D Interaction: Design and Evaluation of One-, Two- and Three-Touch Techniques*. in Proc. of CHI (2007), pp. 1147 - 1156.
7. Herndon, K. P., Zeleznik, R. C., Robbins, D. C., Conner, D., Snibbe, S. S., and van Dam, A. *Interactive shadows*. in Proc. of UIST (1992), pp. 1 - 6.
8. Johnson, T. E. *Sketchpad III: a computer program for drawing in three dimensions*. in Proc. of AFIPS (1963), pp. 347–353.
9. Kabbash, P., and Buxton, W. A. S. *The "prince" technique: Fitts' law and selection using area cursors*. in Proc, of CHI (1995), pp. 273 - 279.
10. Khan, A., Mordatch, I., Fitzmaurice, G., Matejka, J., and Kurtenbach, G. *ViewCube: a 3D orientation indicator and controller*. in Proc. of I3D (2008), pp. 17 - 25.
11. Robertson, G. G., Mackinlay, J. D., and Card, S. K. *Cone Trees: animated 3D visualizations of hierarchical information*. in Proc. of CHI (1991), pp. 189 - 194.
12. Wang Baldonado, M. Q., Woodruff, A., and Kuchinsky, A. *Guidelines for using multiple views in information visualization*. in Proc. of AVI (2000), pp. 110 - 119.

Form Digitization in BPO: From Outsourcing to Crowdsourcing?

Jacki O'Neill[1] **Shourya Roy**[2] **Antonietta Grasso**[1] **David Martin**[1]
[1] Xerox Research Centre Europe
6 Chemin de Maupertuis
Meylan, 38240, France
[name.surname]@xrce.xerox.com
[2]Xerox Research Centre India
Bangalore, India
shourya.roy@xerox.com

ABSTRACT
This paper describes an ethnographic study of an outsourced business process – the digitization of healthcare forms. The aim of the study was to understand how the work is currently organized, with an eye to uncovering the research challenges which need to be addressed if that work is to be crowdsourced. The findings are organised under four emergent themes: Workplace Ecology, Data Entry Skills and Knowledge, Achieving Targets and Collaborative Working. For each theme a description of how the work is undertaken in the outsourcer's Indian office locations is given, followed by the implications for crowdsourcing that work. This research is a first step in understanding how crowdsourcing might be applied to BPO activities. The paper examines features specific to form digitization – extreme distribution and form decomposition – and lightly touches on the crowdsourcing of BPO work more generally.

Author Keywords
Crowdsourcing; Ethnography; Business Process; Outsourcing.

ACM Classification Keywords
J.4 [Social and behavioral sciences] Sociology; H.5.3 [Group and Organization Interfaces]: Collaborative computing.

General Terms
Human Factors; Design.

INTRODUCTION
When the Web moved from a publishing platform to a collaborative one, a new set of possibilities for distributed and collaborative working arose. Web 2.0 has made possible a scale of collaboration that was not conceivable before. We use the term collaboration in a loose manner: many individuals can contribute small parts to create some greater whole without necessarily having to work together or coordinate overtly. Crowdsourcing – basically where task outsourcing is delegated to a largely unknown Internet audience – is emerging as a major example of such collaboration.

Crowdsourcing is the *act of taking a task traditionally performed by an employee or contractor, and outsourcing it to an undefined, generally large group of anonymous people, in the form of an open call*[1]. Over the last few years crowdsourcing has been becoming increasingly popular due to factors such as the proliferation of Internet access and mobile devices in emerging nations like India, and increasing numbers of people opting for alternate modes of employment [11]. Amazon Mechanical Turk (AMT) is probably the best known crowdsourcing micro-task platform where a group of individuals or organizations (*requesters*) post small tasks in large volumes to be taken up by individuals (*workers*) for execution. After execution, the workers post back their results for evaluation and get paid on acceptance by the requester. Examples of such tasks range from digitization of scanned documents, translation of text, to transcription of audio files and so on. AMT has thousands of such tasks of small granularity which often can be executed in seconds and minutes, with payments usually in the order of a few cents.

In the business world questions are being raised about whether crowdsourcing could be a replacement for outsourcing, and a number of small scale start-ups seem to be quite convinced about the business potential. CrowdEngineering, Microtask, CrowdFlower, ClickWorker, LiveOPs, GetSatisfaction, DSTTechnologies, are a few representative ones. Whilst some companies employ task-specialized crowds, others make use of general micro-task platforms such as AMT to execute tasks which companies used to previously outsource.

Business Process Outsourcing (BPO) started gaining critical mass nearly two decades ago when companies from USA and Europe started migrating 'non-core' business processes like administration and customer care to the new BPO specialists primarily as a means of cost saving. This was followed closely by 'off-shoring' where the work was moved to countries with lower labour costs, such as India. Technology innovation was crucial in this radically different delivery model where work origin and workers

[1] http://en.wikipedia.org/wiki/Crowdsourcing

were geographically separated. For tasks like digitization of insurance claim forms, the offshore delivery models have been extremely successful in spite of critical data privacy and security concerns. BPO companies send work to thousands of workers in global service delivery centers, proving that the security and privacy concerns (along with geopolitical risks) can be successfully mitigated. As part of the ongoing pursuit of cost savings, new labour markets such as crowdsourcing come under scrutiny as possible alternatives to the existing work organization. Crowdsourcing offers several advantages over outsourcing:

- It can be more cost effective, even when employers are operating at the minimum wage level, because there is a large reduction in infrastructure costs, as employers are no longer required to host workers themselves – thus saving on building, security and technology costs.
- Crowdsourcing can bring together diverse groups of people, from all over the world. It could tap into the labour pool of people who, for whatever reason, are unable or unwilling to work full-time in an office environment, but who could put in some (extra) hours a week. The *flexibility* offered by Crowdsourcing coupled with *global reach* can lead to accessing better qualified workers, leading to higher quality output. Related to this, crowdsourcing offers interesting possibilities for Corporate Social Responsibility (CSR), in particular providing jobs where needed (e.g. in rural India) to populations who currently have limited work opportunities and could benefit from even small amounts of extra income. This requires both technological infrastructure and education and in India, for example, the Government is pursuing an aggressive program to deploy broadband to rural areas. The rise of rural BPO's [12] attests to the number of literate, educated workers in these areas.
- Crowdsourcing offers greater possibilities for on-demand labour, with easier ramping up and down of workforces, although this depends partly on task learning and expertise requirements. There is a possibility for easier 24/7 labour as workers self-select, either preferring non-office hours e.g. choosing to work 4-6am or coming from different time zones. This is important, since the requirement to work shifts is a major driver of attrition.

Despite these advantages, there remain a number of challenges to be overcome before crowdsourcing can be viewed as a viable alternative to outsourcing. Fundamental research questions pertaining to branches of computing such as HCI, analytics and machine learning, as well as social science, economics and so on need to be solved. Challenges include managing data security, quality assurance and the extreme work distribution often involved in crowdsourcing.

This paper contributes to the research into whether crowdsourcing is an appropriate next step for outsourcing, by examining one specific area of BPO work – healthcare form digitization. We undertook an in-depth ethnographic field study of the work involved in digitizing healthcare forms, as done today in outsourced operations. Our goal was to understand what challenges – social, technical and organizational – need to be overcome and in what ways the work might need to be reordered if it were to be completed by a crowdsourced labour force, whilst at the same time meeting key business constraints. This research was undertaken as part of a larger project which aims to understand the applicability of crowdsourcing to various types of BPO work and to produce technology innovation in this domain. Our approach differs from that of much of the ongoing research in the crowdsourcing domain, which tends to focus on experimental studies of AMT use. We start by understanding the organization of the work as it is currently achieved by one labor force, as a way of revealing the challenges which might arise if distributed to an alternate workforce. This approach was chosen in part because the business constraints of timeliness of completion – TurnAround Time (TAT) - and the strict quality criteria outlined in the Service Level Agreement (SLA) impose additional levels of complexity. We also believe that starting with the work, as done now, brings a fresh perspective to crowdsourcing research.

In the rest of this paper, we outline relevant related research (Section 2). Then, in Section 3, we describe how the work is currently organised to achieve TAT and quality at minimum cost, and highlight some of the issues that need to be taken into account if the work is to be undertaken through crowdsourcing. In the following section 4, we present our findings from the ethnographic field study and their implications for the crowdsourcing of that work. The findings are organised around four themes which emerged from the data: Workplace Ecology, Data Entry Skills and Knowledge, Achieving Targets and Collaborative Working. In Section 5, we discuss the import of these findings for BPO work in general and form digitization in particular, especially around extreme distribution and form decomposition. We sum up with a short conclusion (Section 6). At this point we raise more questions than we answer, but we believe this is still of value to the HCI community given their growing interest in crowdsourcing. If we are to design robust crowdsourcing systems for BPO work, then we believe that an understanding of that work can inspire innovative design to remodel that work for the crowdsourcing environment as well as make us aware of the challenges and risks.

RELATED WORK

Much of the research so far has consisted of experimental studies using AMT to investigate various aspects of the crowdsourcing of micro-tasks. Whilst they rarely include common BPO tasks, much can be learned from these studies. Early research focused on the wisdom of the crowd, in particular demonstrating that the crowd could produce results of equivalent value to those produced by experts. For example, [10] carried out experiments on AMT comparing crowd and expert ratings of Wikipedia articles to understand how the crowd would perform in different circumstances. They observed low correlation between the two groups which was primarily owing to large number of malicious users gaming the system. They found that it was important to have multiple ways of detecting suspicious responses and that honest completion of tasks should not require significantly more effort than deliberately giving bad answers. In Soylent [4], the authors described an AMT based interface for shortening, proofreading and general editing of documents. They demonstrated that good performance could come from putting such work out to the crowd – with good quality summaries produced. They introduced the notion of *crowd programming* i.e. that by designing tasks in certain ways the crowd could be 'programmed' to perform well. For example, they described a crowd programming pattern known as Find-Fix-Verify where complex crowd intelligence tasks were split "into a series of generation and review stages that use independent agreement and voting to produce reliable results". They also described two extremes of crowd worker – neither of which produced the best results: the *Eager Beaver*, who put in almost too much effort, shortening the text so much that meaning was lost versus the *Lazy Turker* who might only change one or two words.

Getting the best out of the crowd

Another set of papers have explored various mechanisms for getting the best out of the crowd by manipulating parameters such as task design, pay, difficulty and interest of work. For example [9] manipulated a number of factors such as effort required to complete a task, incentive and so on. They found that higher pay increases completion rate, time spent on the task and quality, but that qualified workers are less affected by pay. In contrast another paper [15] found that pay did not increase quality, although it did increase throughput. [5] Focused on experiments used to build theoretical models to predict how people would respond to different price/task scenarios and also how to tune them dynamically to account for individual biases. These models accounted for "(1) how workers decide whether or not to participate in a crowdsourcing project and (2) how workers decide the amount to produce". One finding was that wage per job was not the sole motivator, but that workers also focused on their ability to reach salient targets, e.g. whether there was enough work in this category for them to earn some target amount. [2] Examined incentives and reputation (of the crowd worker) in a competitive software development portal, where challenges are set and prizes awarded to winning solutions. Not surprisingly the prize amount was a strong determinant of individual performance, however they also found that reputation has significant economic value i.e. workers would take jobs which are likely to improve their reputation ratings. Workers also considered the specificities of individual jobs and how they relate to their personal skill set, rather than being swayed by task design factors such as the length of the requirements document.

Other papers examine how quality can be determined, for example, by using multiple workers on the same task [1]. The underlying principle being, if two or more people independently agree on an output it can be considered correct. This is known as "output agreement" or "independent agreement" and works well for tasks like image tagging, where giving a true answer exists. Where there is no single response, e.g. translation, another mechanism, Tournament Selection (typically used in Genetic Algorithms to select the best individual from a population of individuals), has been applied [21]. In this scenario, one group of people generates a set of plausible answers (population) which subsequently undergo multiple rounds of pair-wise selection steps by other groups of people where the winner moves to the next round (crossover). It was found that after three or four rounds the best answer is found.

A problematic issue, particularly for business process crowdsourcing, is that for work currently crowdsourced not only does completion time vary but some tasks never get completed [6] and there is a tail where some tasks need an inordinate amount of time for completion [7]. In the latter paper it was also found that there is no stable average completion time of tasks posted on AMT. Clearly these findings pose potential problems for tasks where timeliness of completion is crucial.

Other research examines crowd collaboration. [18] Looked at translation and story writing and found that collaboration enabled higher quality output and encouraged learning, as users could, for example, ask for the meaning of words while translating. They coined the term Social Crowdsourcing to describe this. Another study demonstrated how difficult semantic tasks could be completed by an iterative crowdsourcing process i.e. one where each worker builds on the output of the previous worker [19]. Whilst this is not direct collaboration, the output might be considered to be collaborative, and most importantly they showed great success in addressing tasks which were too difficult for a single person. E.g. the transcribing of almost illegible documents (such as doctors prescriptions) were near perfect after around five iterations.

Crowdsourcing for BPO

Some research has focused on the BPO environment. For example, in the call centre environment, [22] described how orchestration of resources and control of processes with respect to time, delivery and quality are key requirements for enterprise crowdsourcing. They proposed a concept of customer calls being redirected (as calls or transcribed messages) to be resolved by online communities. This resonates well with our domain. Whilst we are not looking at call centres with their extreme responsiveness requirements, the ability to complete processes rapidly to high quality standards will be crucial.

A key player exploring crowdsourcing for BPO is IBM, who have been experimenting with different types of crowdsourcing in their business. In one paper [23] they used crowdsourcing for IT optimization using a tool called PeopleCloud. PeopleCloud is a platform which a) enables the enterprise to access an online scalable workforce, and b) provides an interface to those services required for carrying out the crowdsourcing tasks. It enables different roles to be defined including Requestor (define a problem), Business Owner (approves tasks and provides rewards), Service Providers (execute tasks, essentially crowd), Collaborator (team formation, providing inputs). Using this platform they created an up-to-date data repository for around 4,500 business applications using user input. Previously the data repository had been very out of date since it was maintained by overstretched systems administrators. The crowd results considerably improved the situation at little cost and to the benefit of all. The paper is interesting as it presents a business crowdsourcing application where the contributors are 'paid' in points not money, but they can perform the tasks at little cost to themselves (being as they are regular users of the business applications and have the information to hand), with a consequent benefit to themselves and others. This differs from the work in the second paper from IBM [8], which is much closer to our business domain. The authors advocate the idea that outsourced service delivery centres will become Virtual Service Delivery Centers (VSDC), where currently outsourced processes will be carried out through a mixture of automation and crowd processes. The role of these centres then will be to pass the parts of the process which can be automated to the relevant automation service, and for the rest to mediate between the business and the crowd. Overall they would be in charge of guaranteeing availability, quality, anonymity, privacy and security. They describe a novel way to enable an OCR correction task to be crowdsourced and raise a number of issues of relevance to our domain, such as: 1) Quality control and pay - by introducing known errors into the data, worker quality can be judged and pay scales determined; 2) Security issues are addressed through extreme task decomposition; 3) Workforce availability to achieve TAT - since the task is very low skilled people can be pulled into the workforce and trained up rapidly to maintain a large pool of employees. Unfortunately the authors did not give any figures or examples of how this worked in practice, given that this was a short paper; 4) Quality assurance for SLA is handled using the skill level determined by the worker assessment mechanism described in 1) above to determine whether the same data will go to 1, 2 or 3 employees and the results matched. This research is the closest to our application domain and is a first step at addressing some of the major domain issues. In this paper however we take a wider focus. Rather than considering just one aspect of the task itself (in our case digitisation of *handwritten* forms not suitable for OCR), we look at the wider context of the work, i.e. including social and learning aspects and the work that is done to ensure the forms are processed according to business requirements.

Finally, other less task specific work focuses on features essential for crowdsourcing of BPO work, such as scheduling. [17] Describes a scheduling and monitoring mechanism that can monitor the capabilities of the crowd, trigger agreement violations, and deploy counteractions to compensate service quality degradation. The idea is to provide a means for organising the mixture of skills and availabilities of the crowd so they will act in a way that will fit with the customer's business needs, in particular their SLA's and time and quality measures. They include the idea of 'distinguished' crowd members becoming responsible points of reference. These members mediate the crowd, settle disagreements, organize activities, schedule tasks, and monitor behaviour.

METHOD AND FIELD SITE

Although crowdsourcing seems to offer the potential to revolutionise some types of outsourcing, this is not unproblematic technically or organisationally. In an effort to understand what it would take to crowdsource a particular form of BPO work – relatively low-skilled data entry work – we embarked on an in-depth field study of that work as it is undertaken now in an outsourced environment. The aim being to uncover the opportunities and challenges that would be faced if this work were to be crowdsourced and indeed at a more fundemental level to see whether this work would be crowdsourceable.

We followed the HCI and CSCW tradition in which ethnomethodological ethnographies have long been used to understand the application domain and inform design thinking [3]. By understanding the work as it is undertaken now and given a particular technology scenario, in this case crowdsourcing, we can begin to map out what is required to undertake that work in this new setting, as has previously done with, for example, mobile payments [13].

The work setting under investigation was a BPO operation involved in the digitisation of healthcare forms for US insurance companies. This is basically data processing work with a heavy human element. Forms arrive in dedicated mail rooms from all over the US. They are scanned and where possible undergo OCR. The scanned forms and OCR output are routed to various offshore centres in India, Mexico, and Ghana. In these centres a series of human and systems steps are undertaken to ensure that the correct information is transferred from the scanned form to the electronic database within various time limits.

This field study was carried out at two Indian locations: Bangalore and Kochi between March and August 2011, with approximately 5 working weeks spent in the field. The ethnographic study primarily consisted of observation of the entire offshore workflow handled in India for three different clients, supported by in situ interviewing of the people involved. The offshore human data processing workflow consists of a number of sequential steps. The following are undertaken for all clients 1) **data entry** – both full-key (where forms are not suitable for OCR e.g. handwritten forms, they must be keyed into the database from scratch by hand) and partial-key (the system detects possible errors in OCR which need to be checked by a human); 2) **verification**, through double key i.e. the agents enter the information anew, but receive prompts if their entries are different from those of the prior agent; 3) **review**, where agents check specific fields as suggested by a rules engine – this includes potential keying errors plus pre-defined checks e.g. if the claimed amount is greater than $5,000. In addition, extra functions may be performed according to client need such as **look-up** of healthcare providers in a client directory; **reject review**, ensuring that forms which are rejected (i.e. where one of the agents has said they cannot be keyed because they do not meet some pre-set criteria) have been rejected for a legitimate reason; and **splits**, where a form which has been rejected for containing e.g. two patient names is divided into two claims, one for each patient, and sent back to the agents for data entry.

There are a number of other activities which are carried out outside of the workflow to ensure the smooth running of the business, that customer requirements are met and that the workflow activities run smoothly. This articulation [20] and management work includes 1) quality audits and six sigma projects to improve particular quality problems; 2) supervision and management, including shift organisation, reporting and floor-walking (i.e., on floor supervision, which will be discussed in more detail later); 3) production control – a specific function for monitoring the flow of forms (known as claims) through the all the various workflow steps, both onshore and offshore, and troubleshooting when problems occur.

A fundamental difference between this type of work when it comes to crowdsourcing and other BPO work that has already been attempted is the ongoing nature of the work, which is regulated by tight time and quality requirements, of which we will discuss more later. In this paper we concentrate on what it would mean to crowdsource the data entry steps for non-OCR forms. This is considered low skill data entry work, but as we will show it already poses considerable challenges for crowdsourcing.

FIELDWORK FINDINGS AND THEIR IMPLICATIONS FOR CROWDSOURCING

In this section we will describe some of the key findings about how the work is carried out now and discuss what this means for crowdsourcing. The findings are organised around four themes which emerged from the data: Workplace Ecology, Data Entry Skills and Knowledge, Achieving Targets and Collaborative Working. Before we move to these themes, however, we found that there are a number of enablers for crowdsourcing already present in the way that the work has been organized as outsourced labour.

Outsourcing to Crowdsourcing; Facilitators

A number of advantages, as far as crowdsourcing is concerned, come from studying an already outsourced process:

1) The process is already distributed: any of the sequential steps of the workflow can be done by any capable team of agents at any site.

2) The process is managed semi-automatically by a powerful Workflow Tool (WT) and a group of employees known as Production Control. Together they manage distribution between sites and agents, given upcoming deadlines, agent skill sets and volume.

3) There is little interdependence between each of the sequential steps: it is not necessary to know who did the prior step or who will do the next step, there is no need to discuss what was done previously and what will be done next when processing any particular claim. Any quality implications, e.g. data entry errors uncovered in subsequent steps, are handled outside of the processing workflow in a separate quality process.

4) The work is carried out on specifically designed applications, which allow agents access only to the current form they are processing and to enter (or check) data for that form. Other activities are not allowed and access to client systems is not given.

In terms of technology, the agent sees the scanned image of the form on the top of the screen and a database form on the bottom of the screen. The database may be prefilled or empty, depending on OCR and the stage of the workflow. For the standard forms, the field of the form (on both the scanned copy and the database system) to which the agent must attend next is highlighted enabling the agent to move quickly through the form.

In effect then one might think that the challenges of distribution have been solved and to a large extent this is true in the sequential steps of the workflow through which each claim passes which is controlled by the workflow tool. However, much of the work to make the workflow work is carried out locally. That notwithstanding the very fact that the process has already been outsourced and is widely distributed across teams and countries gives us a head start when thinking of crowdsourcing but is not sufficient.

Workplace ecology

The outsourcers' offices in both Bangalore and Kochi are located on several floors across a couple of multi-story office blocks in two technical parks. Data entry operations are configured by client. That is, employees work on data entry for single clients; client groupings are located as separate functional units within these floors. Either by seating area, indicated by banners, or in separated-off access-controlled offices. Personnel need a security pass, or to register as a visitor, to enter the tech park itself and then to enter the outsourcers' general offices, which are manned by security guards. For many clients, particularly those with independently secured office spaces, there are lockers outside where staff have to leave their bags and phones during the shift. Typically no paper or pens are allowed in the office areas. Agents usually work shifts, with each shift having at least one team leader present. By being collocated with their teams, team leads can monitor the activity on the floor. They spend a large amount of their time walking around the floor, answering queries from the agents and keeping an eye on their activity. In addition staff occupying other roles such as quality and management generally have either offices or desks within the unit. They do not work shifts however they often time their office hours to overlap at least partially with their client's (US) office hours. On each floor there is a break area with free coffee and water, and tables and chairs. In both sites the tech parks have a number of shops, restaurants and banks. Production control is located elsewhere: mostly in the USA, but for one group of clients they are on another floor in the Bangalore offices. Each production control group handles the workflows for a number of client operations.

Since health care forms contain personal information of the clients' customers, including social security numbers, name and address details, the security of the data is governed by US laws, in particular HIPPA compliance, which strictly controls who may access the data and protects against unauthorized distribution and use. These laws are there to ensure that no customer data can fall into the wrong hands and this is the main reason why mobile phones, pens and paper are not allowed in the office. Data security is a key concern of the clients and therefore of the outsourcer. So the systems and workflows have been designed to ensure maximum security. For many of the clients, the agents access the data through iGELs (a type of thin client) rather than PC's. iGELs have no USB or other data retrieval ports and do not store any information. Data is not stored locally; rather it is stored in the US and pulled in batches to the agents' computers as they are ready to process it. Any software modifications are done through the US. In addition to this technical enforcement of data security, data is also secured through the physical set-up (restricted access to offices) and social means (supervisors enforce the rules so agents cannot copy any of the data). Agents are also trained in HIPPA compliance when they join the company and have refresher training regularly.

Implications for crowdsourcing

In summary, data security is currently enforced through physical (office space), social (supervision and training) and technical (iGels, batching, etc.) means. The main implication for crowdsourcing comes from the distribution of the workers from controlled office environments into their own homes or unsecured Internet cafes and their lack of a contractual relationship with the company. The control the outsourcer can exercise over the people doing the work is necessarily reduced. In effect then, security can no longer be enforced by physical and social means and solutions to HIPPA compliance etc. will have to be wholly technical.

Data entry skills and knowledge

Agents have a decent level of education (graduate or undergraduate), good English language skills and good typing speed. The data entry work is known as 'key what you see' and is considered low skilled work; nonetheless the learning curve of an average new entrant is around seven weeks to meet speed and quality expectations. This is because in reality data entry is not simply 'key what you see,' rather the agents must interpret what they see according to an extensive rule set. To illustrate, the most straightforward data entry task is the HCFA form: a standard form for claiming insurance on medical procedures undertaken. The name field of this form has around 13 rules for how the name should be entered i.e. which is the first name, surname, middle name and credentials. This is just one of 33 fields. The outsourcer processes a number of different forms and other documents for each client, thus agents need to learn how the various rules apply for all the different form types. In addition, task complexity is *situational*. It differs *between form types* e.g. HCFAs are relatively standard, whereas Correspondence is by its nature non-standard. Data entry for Correspondence is only 4 fields (name, social security number, etc.) compared to 33 fields for HCFA forms, however each item of Correspondence can take considerably more time to complete as the information may be anywhere or nowhere on the form: identifying that information is *not* present often takes longer than finding and entering that information where it is present (because of the need to double or triple check). In addition, for some types of jobs, agents have to first check that the information matches between different pages of the scanned image, before doing a data entry step, e.g. Explanation of Benefits (EOB) jobs. Whilst data entry is rapid, checking is slower. At this point we should mention the pay structure for the agents. Agents are paid on the basis of performance (Performance Related Pay (PRP)) – that is, they are paid per keystroke or per form (depending on the job type) with quality taken into account. Thus their work speed is of immediate concern to them.

As well as complexity differing between form types, in predictable ways, complexity also differs *within form types* i.e. across individual claims. Thus handwriting and poorly printed forms can be difficult to read. Just like learning the rules, handwriting deciphering is a learned skill. Even the newest agent was better at deciphering handwriting than the fieldworker and the team and quality leads could often decode text that the fieldworker thought unrecognisable. Another type of within form complexity is where forms need to be rejected for some reason – that is they do not fit the criteria for data entry so the agents cannot enter them into the database. This may be because of poor scanning (alignment, too faint, etc.) or because they do not comply to the rules e.g. containing information about more than one patient or health care provider. Reject decisions take time because they also require double checking and agents are accountable for their rejections i.e. wrongly rejected forms will bring the supervisor's attention. Finally, non-standard means non-standard, so a piece of correspondence may have a cover sheet with all the information required for data entry on it, or the information may not be found in the document at all. Within form complexity can only determined on a document by document basis and would not be easy to predict in advance.

Implications for crowdsourcing

Certainly it would be good to develop techniques to accommodate the learning curve, starting the workers on just one form type, or splitting the form into sections so that agents only need to learn the rules for one particular section. Such specialization is commonly thought to be an essential element of crowdsourcing [8] and indeed recent research has taken this concept a step further by introducing the notion of *Hyperspecialization* [14]. We could also imagine techniques for making the rules more easily available for agents *in situ*. However, when crowdsourcing just as within the office, it is clearly beneficial to both employer and worker for speed and quality to have *experienced agents*. Thus we may want to think of crowd models that encourage agents to specialise and become skilled.

Secondly, the fieldwork raises the question of how incentives can be determined given the *situational complexity of the work*. Currently different pay scales are determined on the basis of form type, but agents have social and organisational pressures on them to encourage them to complete the batches they pull e.g. supervisors will hold them accountable for rejecting batches (discussed below). In the crowdsourcing situation, what is to stop agents from rejecting difficult work? Assuming this will happen we need models which spot and deal with such instances whether these are incentive schemes - although incentive schemes may not work on their own - or hybrid models of in-house and crowd workers.

Achieving targets

The SLA is the contractual agreement between the outsourcer and the client specifying what will be achieved. In the case of healthcare data entry two components are key - the TurnAround Time (TAT) and quality - and penalties are often in place if either is not met to agreed levels. Different job types for different clients have different TATs i.e. time from receipt of form to claim being processed. Targets include a) daily cut off times, by which all forms of a certain type must be completed, or b) all forms must be out of the system within some time limit based on when they came into the system (typically 24 hours, but it can be as low as 2-4 hours). Quality levels also vary between clients and forms.

Performance Related Pay (PRP) is a strong motivating factor, however pay alone is not enough to ensure the SLA is achieved. Team and quality leads put in extra work to make the agents *accountable* for their performance. For example, during a shift the team lead will call people up and talk to them about their performance. To illustrate, for one client the data entry of medical records, must be completed by 8am IST. A key concern then of the 6am shift is completing all remaining medical records before the deadline. The team leaders communicate the pressures of the queue to the agents – 'agents key fast' 'everyone on medical records please' 'key fast but accurately'. In addition after the deadline for finishing medical records has past the team leader calls up 3-4 agents at a time and talks to them (rather publically) about their performance. For example, "Krishna, you only did 16 medical records in an hour and a half. What was that about?" "Ok the target of 50 is not attainable but I would expect you to be doing at least 30. You need to improve." Thus the agents are called upon to account for their performance; similarly if they have made particular errors. In addition, it shows how management work to *make the targets achievable* for their team – rather than telling someone only doing 16 medical records they should be doing 50 which might seem unachievable and therefore be demotivating, they set a more realistic target. Thus the team lead is still showing the agent that they need to improve, but giving them something easier to aim for. Agents are similarly made accountable for their performance when they reject batches of forms. Team leads monitor which batches are being rejected and will ask agents why they rejected a particular batch and if a batch is rejected a couple of times will assign it to someone whom they will tell they must complete it. In this way there a balance is achieved between the agent's desire to do easy work quickly and the requirement to get all the work in the workflow completed in a timely manner.

Currently training includes information on the whole workflow so agents know how their work fits into the wider process. This is done to improve quality, as agents are made aware of which fields are checked and which are not in later stages of the process. It is also a good general principle, for enabling workers to make the workflow work in the best way [16].

Implications for crowdsourcing

The current model of work is a *push model*, with a) the work being assigned dynamically (by the workflow tool and production control) according to agents skill set, i.e. what forms and what tasks they have been trained on, and queue; and b) various social (and financial) pressures.

In contrast the model of work in crowdsourcing is a *pull model*; work is self-selected by the agents and they will not have the same accountability for completing tasks as the contracted workers. Any crowdsourcing system needs to be designed to ensure that the work is completed in a timely manner to good quality, for which coordination of the workflow will be key. We may also want to consider whether communication about the pressures of the queue would be motivating for workers in the crowd or not and whether incentive schemes linked to the urgency of the work would be effective.

Collaborative working

Explicit collaboration has been designed out of the *workflow* - claims progress through workflow steps from agent to agent and even country to country automatically as each prior step is completed. However, work is *collaborative at the claim level*. That is, the routine troubles encountered in data entry are solved with colleagues or floorwalkers and it is not uncommon to see a group of two or three people around a screen discussing an issue. Typical issues that arise are deciphering handwriting or determining which rule applies in this particular circumstance. Since forms are filled in by people all sorts of phenomena may be seen, e.g. arrows showing a name has been entered the 'wrong way round', crossings out and reentries, clarifications written on the form and so on. Not all of these are described in the rule set, which is updated as 'typical incidences' arise. A large part of a team lead's job is floor-walking to answer such queries. However, there is typically just one team lead and many agents so team leads are not always immediately available when needed. Since time is money for the agents and any time not entering data is money not earned, they may turn to their colleagues when the team lead is not available. Some teams encourage this, with newcomers sat by experienced neighbours (thus promoting *collaborative learning*), others discourage it. A fairly typical rule of thumb however is that where the issue is deciphering handwriting, agents will typically ask their neighbour first, only turning to the team lead if needed. For questions of rules the team lead is the first port of call, with fellow agents only being asked when the team lead is busy and typically it will nonetheless be followed up with the team lead. Such troubles rarely take long to solve, in the order of seconds rather than minutes, and it is undoubted that this collaboration improves both speed and quality of data entry.

Implications for crowdsourcing

We might want to think about enabling collaborative set-ups amongst crowd members, enabling them to help one another, or to have sub-crowds with particular skills, such as handwriting deciphering to which data fragments might be sent, although this implies more complex workflow management. Although there is a general assumption that crowdsourcing is supervision free, is there value in considering pull models of 'supervision' and feedback loops to enable on the job learning?

DISCUSSION

In the previous section we have described in some detail how the work is organised now to achieve TAT and quality at minimum cost and highlighted some of the issues that need to be taken into account if the work is to be undertaken through crowdsourcing. We hope that understanding the detail of how such seemingly simple work is carried out now, is already a useful contribution to the research on crowdsourcing of business process activities. The variety of issues it raises are not completely new in themselves, with security issues, collaboration and specialization, and the desire to have an experienced crowd (as seen with the various reputation systems), being covered elsewhere as reported in the related work section. In contrast, some of the issues are rarely discussed, such as how to manage situationally determined complexity (i.e. diversity of seemingly similar tasks), support for learning in the crowd and the impact of reduced accountability. However, even for the issues touched on elsewhere our study gives grounded examples from real work processes, bringing out the subtlety of their connotations, not found elsewhere and crucially grounded in a study of real work processes. Before we turn to the connotations of this research for the crowdsourcing of form digitisation, namely extreme distribution and form decomposition, we want to briefly discuss how the findings relate to the crowdsourcing of BPO work more generally.

Implications for BPO work more generally

The core change for BPO work more generally is the lack of contractual relations between the work provider and the worker and closely related to this the reduction in accountability of workers. This is likely to have different impacts depending on the type of work being crowdsourced. For example, in this case a major impact is on data security, which can no longer be ensured through contractual and supervisory means. However, the implications are more generic; crowdsourcing involves a pull model of work, where workers self-select what they will and will not do, the employer has much less control over them. In the employer-employee relation there are myriad ways in which employees are made socially accountable. In most crowdsourcing models these mixed social and financial incentives/motivators are replaced almost solely with monetary ones, even though it is clear that money is not considered an adequate motivator on its own for the in-office workers and there is no reason to suspect that money will be the only motivator for crowdworkers (see for e.g. [4]). Worse is that these financial incentives tend to be at lower levels of pay per item/hour than received by office workers! Of course, in reality social aspects will remain part of the work; given a fair working environment, workers will continue to do their best and take pride in their work. Also for this work, as with much crowdsourced work, reputation (of worker) will be a crucial factor in determining who the work can be selected by, at what price, etc. Along with financial incentives, such social factors need to be understood and fairly applied.

It is also important to remember that the seemingly standard work of form digitization is not unique in having 'hidden' complexities. Currently managed by a variety of routine techniques in house, such features become important when the work is put out to potentially untrained workforces, such as the crowd. To deal with this it is important to understand in advance the detail of the work and then we can envisage the use of hybrid workforces and the development of methods for on-the-job learning even for crowdworkers.

Extreme distribution and form decomposition

Turning now to form digitization specifically we need to take into account how extreme distribution can be managed. Although the work is already distributed between sites, countries and agents, crowdsourcing will necessitate a further distribution – to individuals at individual sites (homes, internet cafes…) and quite likely of the data itself. That is, whereas forms are currently distributed as a whole to individual agents to work on them (for data entry, but also for data correction, where the forms have been through OCR) it is likely that only segments of each form would be sent to any one agent in the crowdsourcing model. This serves two purposes; 1) specialization e.g. reducing the number of rules to be learned and hopefully increasing throughput, and 2) to address issues of data security and HIPPA compliance by removing problematic context from presented data elements. An important question therefore becomes, will decomposition and further distribution disrupt the coherency of the work? The work of data entry itself does not typically fall into a class of work where collocation plays a major role in facilitating the work because of, for example, the requirement for people to troubleshoot vexing problems [19] or the strong interrelation of different work sections [16]. For this type of data entry there is no need to know who did the step before you or who will do the step after you or where they will be even if the outsourcer does train workers on how their work fits into the larger workflow. This should make the work easier to distribute; it is only cooperative in a limited way and not interdependent at the same sort of level as for example call centre and back office work – which is often distributed to very negative effect. However, by further decomposing and distributing the work a number of things are potentially lost:

- **Learning from peers.** In this case, how to apply the right rules for this instance, plus potentially learning the rules in the first place.
- **Interpreting challenging data**, in this case, handwriting. Both of these stem from the further distribution of workers and could impact on output quality and worker's learning and progression.
- **Supervision and motivation**, especially given the new model of employment inherent in crowdsourcing
- **Team feeling and social interaction**, although it might be hoped that this is mitigated by the self-selection of the crowd i.e. in an ideal world those who would thrive in an office environment can work in that way, whilst those who prefer to work in isolation can choose to work in the crowd. One could also imagine crowd working models where workers are based out of internet centres – where social interaction and team feeling comes not from employer-based groups but rather from crowd working groups.
- **Relative ease of scheduling**. Scheduling will become even more complex, since different parts of the forms are interdependent and some tasks (such as rejects) can require viewing the whole form. In addition to workflow management, ensuring there are enough people to complete the work in a timely manner to the required levels of quality is also a potential concern [9, 19]. Are we just to assume that the necessary people in the crowd will always be there to do the work when needed? This is rather big leap of faith and for the crowdsourcing of key business process activities needs to be proven.
- **The question of context.** To what extent is the knowledge that the data entry is for healthcare insurance important? Is it important that a data element is understood in relation to other elements in the form? There are clearly intra-document dependencies that relate to form validity but it is an open question as to whether these can all be handled at a technical level.
- **Transparency of workflow** might be negatively impacted by form splitting, as it becomes harder to know where your work fits in the wider workflow and consequently what you need to take particular care about. This might, but in this case not necessarily, impact on quality. To understand this better one might want to experiment with different set ups to enable lightweight transparency and measure its effect.

CONCLUSION

Crowdsourcing is an emerging paradigm for very large scale distribution of knowledge work. While it is being leveraged extensively for data collection, digitization of text and localization of content, its application in on-going business processes has thus far been limited. In particular, there has been little work towards attempting to answer if crowdsourcing will be the next evolution of outsourcing. In this paper, we presented results from an ethnographic field study of form digitization with the objective of understanding challenges to crowdsourcing this activity. We identified four key issues which we described in detail, and articulated corresponding crowdsourcing implications. We believe that these are key issues for business process crowdsourcing and present interesting technical and organization challenges. In doing this we hope this helps frame an agenda for other researchers in this area.

REFERENCES

[1] Ahn, L.V., and Dabbish, L. 2004. Labeling images with a computer game. In Proceedings of the SIGCHI conference on Human factors in computing systems (CHI '04). ACM, New York, NY, USA, 319-326

[2] Archak, N. 2010. Money, glory and cheap talk: analyzing strategic behavior of contestants in simultaneous crowdsourcing contests on TopCoder.com. *Proceedings of the 19th international conference on World wide web* (WWW '10). ACM, New York, NY, USA, 21-30

[3] Bentley, R., Hughes, J. A., Randall, D., Rodden, T., Sawyer, P., Shapiro, D., and Sommerville, I. 1992. Ethnographically informed systems design for air traffic control. In *Proc. CSCW'92*. (1992), 123-129.

[4] Bernstein, M.S., Littl, G., Miller, R.C., Hartmann,B. Ackerman, M. S., Karger, D. R., Crowell,D. and Panovich, K. 2010. Soylent: a word processor with a crowd inside. In Proceedings of the 23nd annual ACM symposium on User interface software and technology (UIST '10). ACM, New York, NY, USA, 313-322.

[5] Horton, J. J. and Chilton, L. B. 2010. The labor economics of paid crowdsourcing. In *Proceedings of the 11th ACM conference on Electronic commerce* (EC '10). ACM, New York, NY, USA, 209-218.

[6] Huang,E. Zhang,H. Parkes,D.C., Gajos,K.Z. and Chen, Y .2010. Toward automatic task design: a progress report. In Proceedings of the ACM SIGKDD Workshop on Human Computation (HCOMP '10). ACM, New York, NY, USA, 77-85.

[7] Ipeirotis, P. G. 2009. Blog post Your estimated waiting time: Infinite!. Available at http://www.behind-the-enemy-lines.com/2009/02/your-estimated-completion-time-infinite.html. Last Accessed on 19th Nov, 2011

[8] Karnin, E. D., Walach, E. and Drory, T. 2010. Crowdsourcing in the document processing practice. *Proceedings of the 10th international conference on Current trends in web engineering* (ICWE'10). Springer-Verlag, Berlin, Heidelberg, 408-411.

[9] Kazai, G. 2010. An Exploration of the Influence that Task Parameters have on the Performance of Crowds. In CrowdConf 2010, San Francisco, USA.

[10] Kittur,A., Chi, E. H., and Suh, B. 2008. Crowdsourcing user studies with Mechanical Turk. In Proceeding of the twenty-sixth annual SIGCHI conference on Human factors in computing systems (CHI '08). ACM, New York, NY, USA, 453-456

[11] Knowledge@Wharton. 2011. From Freelancers to Telecommuters: Succeeding in the New World of SolitaryWork. Published in Knowledge@Wharton. June 29, 2011. Available at http://knowledge.wharton.upenn.edu/article.cfm?articleid=2806. Last Accessed on 19th Nov, 2011.

[12] Knowledge@Wharton. 2010. It Takes a Village: The Rise of Rural BPO. Published in Knowledge@Wharton. February 11, 2010. Available at http://knowledge.wharton.upenn.edu/india/article.cfm?articleid=4450. Last Accessed on 19th Nov, 2011.

[13] Kumar, D., Martin, D., and O'Neill, J. 2011. The times they are a-changin': mobile payments in india. In proceedings of *CHI 2011*, 7-12th May, Vancouver, Canada.

[14] Malone, T. W., R. J. Laubacher and T. Johns. 2011. The age of hyperspecialization. Harvard Business Rev. 89(7/8): 56-65.

[15] Mason, W. and Watts, D.J.2009. Financial Incentives and the "Performance of Crowds". In Proceedings of the ACM SIGKDD Workshop on Human Computation (HCOMP '09). ACM, Paris, France.

[16] O'Neill, J., Martin, D., Colombino, C., and Grasso, A. 2011. When a little knowledge isn't a dangerous thing. *CHI 2011*.

[17] Psaier, H., Skopik, F., Schall, D. and Dustdar, S. 2011. Resource and Agreement Management in Dynamic Crowdcomputing Environments. In *Proceedings of the 2011 IEEE 15th International Enterprise Distributed Object Computing Conference* (EDOC '11). IEEE Computer Society, Washington, DC, USA, 193-202

[18] Rzeszotarski, J .2011. Worker Collaboration in Crowdsourcing Markets. ACM SIGCHI 2011 Workshop on Crowdsourcing and Human Computation.

[19] Sachs, P. 1995. Transforming Work: Collaboration, Learning and Design. *Communications of the ACM* 38 (9). 36-44.

[20] Schmidt, K., and Bannon, L. 1992: 'Taking CSCW Seriously: Supporting Articulation Work', *Journal of CSCW*, vol. 1, 1992, no. 1-2, pp. 7-40

[21] Sun, Y., Roy, S., and Little, G. 2011. Beyond Independent Agreement: A Tournament Selection Approach for Quality Assurance of Human Computation Tasks. AAAI Workshops, North America, Aug. 2011. Available at: http://www.aaai.org/ocs/index.php/WS/AAAIW11/paper/view/3904. Date accessed: 19 Nov. 2011.

[22] Vecchia, G.L. and Cisternino, A.. 2010. Collaborative workforce, business process crowdsourcing as an alternative of BPO. In Proceedings of the 10th international conference on Current trends in web engineering (ICWE'10), Florian Daniel and Federico Michele Facca (Eds.). Springer-Verlag, Berlin, Heidelberg, 425-430

[23] Vukovic, M. Lopez, M., and Laredo, J. (2010). PeopleCloud for the Globally Integrated Enterprise. In Lecture Notes in Computer Science (6275), Service-Oriented Computing. ICSOC/ServiceWave 2009 Workshops. 109-114.

Crowdsourcing Performance Evaluations of User Interfaces

Steven Komarov, Katharina Reinecke, Krzysztof Z. Gajos
Intelligent Interactive Systems Group
Harvard School of Engineering and Applied Sciences
33 Oxford St., Cambridge, MA 02138, USA
{komarov, reinecke, kgajos}@seas.harvard.edu

ABSTRACT

Online labor markets, such as Amazon's Mechanical Turk (MTurk), provide an attractive platform for conducting human subjects experiments because the relative ease of recruitment, low cost, and a diverse pool of potential participants enable larger-scale experimentation and faster experimental revision cycle compared to lab-based settings. However, because the experimenter gives up the direct control over the participants' environments and behavior, concerns about the quality of the data collected in online settings are pervasive. In this paper, we investigate the feasibility of conducting online performance evaluations of user interfaces with anonymous, unsupervised, paid participants recruited via MTurk. We implemented three performance experiments to re-evaluate three previously well-studied user interface designs. We conducted each experiment both in lab and online with participants recruited via MTurk. The analysis of our results did not yield any evidence of significant or substantial differences in the data collected in the two settings: All statistically significant differences detected in lab were also present on MTurk and the effect sizes were similar. In addition, there were no significant differences between the two settings in the raw task completion times, error rates, consistency, or the rates of utilization of the novel interaction mechanisms introduced in the experiments. These results suggest that MTurk may be a productive setting for conducting performance evaluations of user interfaces providing a complementary approach to existing methodologies.

Author Keywords

Crowdsourcing; Mechanical Turk; User Interface Evaluation

ACM Classification Keywords

H.5.2. Information Interfaces and Presentation (e.g. HCI): User Interfaces-Evaluation/Methodology

INTRODUCTION

Online labor markets, such as Amazon's Mechanical Turk (MTurk), have emerged as an attractive platform for human subjects research. Researchers are drawn to MTurk because the relative ease of recruitment affords larger-scale experimentation (in terms of the number of conditions tested and the number of participants per condition), a faster experimental revision cycle, and potentially greater diversity of participants compared to what is typical for lab-based experiments in an academic setting [15, 24].

The downside of such remote experimentation is that the researchers give up the direct supervision of the participants' behavior and the control over the participants' environments. In lab-based settings, the direct contact with the experimenter motivates participants to perform as instructed and allows the experimenter to detect and correct any behaviors that might compromise the validity of the data. Because remote participants may lack the motivation to focus on the task, or may be more exposed to distraction than lab-based participants, concerns about the quality of the data collected in such settings are pervasive [11, 19, 23, 26].

A variety of interventions and filtering methods have been explored to either motivate participants to perform as instructed or to assess the reliability of the data once it has been collected. Such methods have been developed for experiments that measure visual perception [8, 12, 3], decision making [20, 27, 14], and subjective judgement [11, 19, 21].

Missing from the literature and practice are methods for remotely conducting performance-based evaluations of user interface innovations — such as evaluations of novel input methods, interaction techniques, or adaptive interfaces — where accurate measurements of task completion times are the primary measure of interest. Such experiments may be difficult to conduct in unsupervised settings for several reasons. First, poor data quality may be hard to detect: For example, while major outliers caused by a participant taking a phone call in the middle of the experiment are easy to spot, problems such as a systematically slow performance due to a participant watching TV while completing the experimental tasks may not be as easily identifiable. Second, the most popular quality control mechanisms used in paid crowdsourcing, such as gold standard tasks [1, 18], verifiable tasks [11], or checking for output agreement [13, 17], do not have obvious equivalents in this setting.

In this paper, we investigate the feasibility of conducting remote performance evaluations of user interfaces with anonymous, unsupervised, paid participants recruited via MTurk. We implemented three performance experiments to

CHI 2013, April 27–May 2, 2013, Paris, France.

re-evaluate three previously well-studied designs: the Bubble Cursor [7], the Split Menus [25], and the Split Interfaces [5]. We conducted each experiment both in lab with participants recruited from the local community and online with participants recruited via MTurk. We focused our investigation on three questions: (1) Would the data collected in the two settings demonstrate the presence of the same statistically significant differences? (2) If so, would the effect sizes be comparable across the two settings? (3) Would the absolute values of the measurements obtained in the two settings be similar?

The analysis of our results did not yield any evidence of significant or substantial differences in the data collected in the two settings. All statistically significant differences detected between experiment conditions in lab were also present on MTurk and the effect sizes were very similar. In addition, there were no significant differences in the raw task completion times, error rates, consistency, or the rates of utilization of the novel interaction mechanisms introduced in the experiments.

These results suggest that MTurk may be a productive setting for conducting performance evaluations of user interfaces.

In summary, in this paper we make the following contributions:

1. We present results of three experiments conducted on MTurk and in lab. By showing that the results are closely matched, we build a case for the feasibility of MTurk as a tool for user interface research.
2. We synthesize a number of practical considerations that had substantial impact on the quality of the data we collected. These considerations included mechanisms for ensuring instruction comprehension, accounting for age- and device-related differences in performance, techniques for robust outlier detection, and implementation challenges.

PRIOR RESEARCH

In behavioral economics, there is mounting evidence that MTurk participants perform just like lab-based participants. Replications of a number of classic experiments including those related to judgement and decision-making [20], public goods [27], and others [9, 22], have all shown no differences between results collected on MTurk and those collected in lab.

Similarly, Heer and Bostock [8] presented compelling evidence that experiments related to graphical perception can be reliably conducted on MTurk. However, their work also identified several potential pitfalls for experimenters. For example, variations in hardware and software had significant impact on the results — keeping careful records of these factors and controlling for them in the analysis overcame the problem. Also, many participants demonstrated signs of not having understood the instructions, presumably because they hurried through that part of the experiment. Qualification tasks, which required Turkers to demonstrate proficiency with a concept or skill, proved to be an adequate mechanism for enforcing instruction comprehension. Novel research has already been published in graphics and information visualization based primarily on data collected on MTurk [3, 12].

In contrast, survey-based research and research collecting simple subjective judgements have been less successful in leveraging MTurk. A number of researchers reported problems with persistently low-quality data or outright malicious participant behavior [11, 19, 26]. These results are frequently attributed to two properties of surveys and similar instruments: the truthfulness of responses is hard to verify, and the effort required to provide truthful and accurate responses is substantially higher than just selecting random responses. This attracts "spammers," who often find that they can earn the payoff easily with little chance of being caught.

To mitigate the data quality problems on MTurk, researchers have investigated several classes of approaches. Gold standard tasks [1, 18], instructional manipulation check [19], the Bayesian Truth Serum [21], or certain behavioral measures [23] have all been used to detect low quality data and unreliable participants. Excluding such data from analysis can substantially improve the reliability and the statistical power of the subsequent analyses [19]. An ideal solution, however, would prevent low quality data from being collected in the first place. Data quality can be improved, for example, if participants are forced to see the question for a certain "waiting period" [10]. However, attempts to manipulate participants' intrinsic motivation have been generally unsuccessful in improving quality of the work [2, 26]. Financial incentives generally help with faster recruitment and may incentivize participants to do more work, but generally do not impact the quality of the work either [16, 26] (though there is some evidence that quality-related financial bonuses or punishments may help [26]).

So far, we are not aware of any systematic evaluation of MTurk as a platform for performance-based evaluations of user interface technologies. There are good reasons to believe that such tasks will fare well on MTurk: Turkers' incentives to finish the task as quickly as possible align with the goals of the experimenters. However, the unsupervised and uncontrolled nature of the participants' environments leaves open the possibility that social and environmental distractions will introduce unacceptable variance or a systematic bias into the data.

EXPERIMENTS

We begin by investigating whether experiments comparing user performance on two or more user interface variants yield the same results both in lab and on MTurk. Specifically, we ask two questions. First, are the conclusions of the statistical comparisons of the primary performance measures (task completion times and error rates) between experimental conditions the same in both lab and MTurk settings? Second, are the effect sizes comparable?

Methodology

To answer these questions, we conducted — both in lab and on MTurk — three experiments evaluating three previously investigated user interface designs. These designs were the *Bubble Cursor* [7], the *Split Menus* [25], and the *Split Interfaces* [6]. These experiments are illustrative of the types of evaluations that are the focus of this paper: the experimental tasks are largely mechanical (i.e., target acquisition with a mouse pointer) as opposed to cognitively demanding (e.g., solving a problem, generating a creative artifact). Also, each of the three experiments we chose required a different level of attention from the participants. The baseline condition in the Bubble Cursor experiment was comprised entirely of simple pointing tasks requiring minimal cognitive engagement. In contrast, Split Menus and Split Interfaces are adaptive techniques that operate by copying useful functionality to a more convenient location. To reap the performance benefits afforded by these adaptive mechanisms, the user has to consciously monitor the adaptive part of the user interface to determine if a useful adaptation has taken place. In prior studies, participants reported that scanning for useful adaptations required conscious effort and most participants missed useful adaptations at least part of the time [5, 6]. Because concerns about online participants' lack of attentiveness are common [19, 20], we included the Split Menus and the Split Interfaces as probes of the differences in cognitive engagement between lab- and MTurk-based participants.

We implemented all three experiments for web-based delivery. We used the same software and the same instructions in both the lab and MTurk settings. For lab experiments, we recruited between 10 and 14 subjects each. These numbers were similar to those used in the original studies and were sufficient to demonstrate the main significant differences. For experiments conducted on MTurk we recruited approximately 100 participants for each experiment taking advantage of the ease of recruitment and the negligible marginal effort required to include additional participants.

Lastly, we sought to establish a clear criterion for identifying and excluding extreme outliers. A common approach in HCI research is to exclude results that are more than two standard deviations from the mean. This approach is not robust in the presence of very extreme outliers that are different from the rest of the data by orders of magnitude because such outliers introduce large errors to the estimates of the mean and the standard deviation. Unfortunately, such outliers, while rare in general, can be expected on MTurk and did, indeed, occur in our data. For example, one participant spent over 2 minutes on a trivial target selection task that he accomplished previously in 1.5 seconds — presumably the participant got distracted by an external event in the middle of the experiment.

To guard against such extreme outliers, we chose an outlier removal procedure that relies on a more robust statistic, the inter-quartile range (IQR), which is defined as the difference between the third and first quartiles. With this procedure, an extreme outlier is one that is more than $3 \times IQR$ higher than the third quartile, or one that is more than $3 \times IQR$ lower than the first quartile [4]. For normally distributed data, this procedure would remove less than 0.00023% of the data compared to 4.6% removed by the more typical mean $\pm$ 2 standard deviations approach. Thus, it targets the most extreme outliers without reducing legitimate diversity of the data.

We performed outlier detection based on two measurements: log-transformed per-participant mean selection time and log-transformed per-participant maximum selection time. A participant was removed from analysis if he or she was flagged as an outlier according to either measurement.

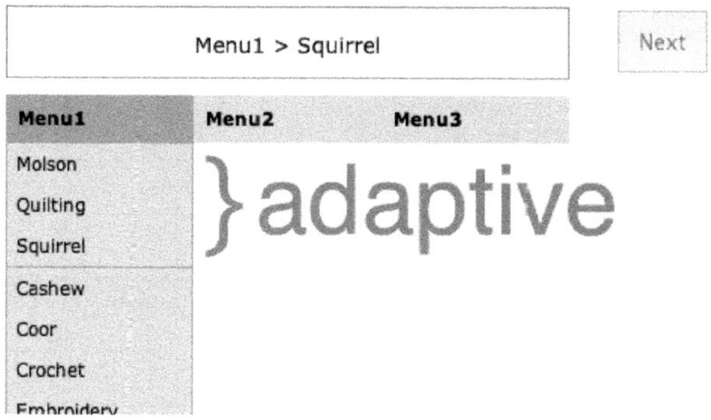

Figure 1: Split Menus. The three most recently selected items are copied in the adaptive top part of the menu.

This proved to be both a robust and an acceptably conservative approach. While 30% exclusion rates are typical for MTurk, and some researchers discarded data from up to half of their participants [8], our procedure resulted in the exclusion of between 0% and 6% of MTurk participants in our three experiments.

Experiment 1: Adaptive Split Menus

In Split Menus, a small number of menu items that are predicted to be immediately useful to the user are copied[1] to a clearly designated adaptive area at the top of the menu (Figure 1). The items copied to the adaptive area represent the system's best prediction for the user's next selection. The choice of a predictive algorithm varies across implementations, but the use of the the most recently used (MRU) and the most frequently used (MFU) algorithms is common.

Whether the Split Menus improve performance depends on the accuracy of the predictive algorithm and on the willingness of the user to pay attention to the adaptive portion of the menu.

Tasks and Procedures

In our experiment we used a menu with three categories (Menu1, Menu2, Menu3) each containing 16 items, ordered alphabetically. The adaptive portion at the top of each category contained the three most recently used items, which were initialized randomly at the beginning of each block. For each category we generated a random sequence of 60 selections, constrained such that for 79% of the selections the goal item was in the adaptive portion. The three sequences of 60 selections were then randomly shuffled to obtain the final a sequence of 180 selections.

As the control condition, we used a typical static menu design, which differed from the split menu only in the lack of an adaptive portion at the top. At the beginning of the

[1] In the original design [25] items were *moved* rather than copied, but in all modern implementations of this concept items are copied.

Experiment	Participants				Task completion time (ms)				Errors			
Split Menus	Setting	rem	out	kept		Static	Split	ANOVA		Static	Split	Wilcoxon Signed-Rank
	Lab	0	0	14		1400	1280	F(1,13)=5.8, p=0.032		2.43	1.71	z=−0.14, p=0.887
	MTurk	6	1	89		1375	1252	F(1,88)=56, p<0.0001		2.45	2.22	z=−0.95, p=0.343
Split Interface	Setting	rem	out	kept		Low	High	ANOVA		Low	High	Wilcoxon Signed-Rank
	Lab	0	1	9		1784	1548	F(1,8)=42, p<0.0001		4	2.56	z=−1.38, p=0.169
	MTurk	6	0	86		2112	1774	F(1,85)=285, p<0.0001		3.87	3.55	z=−1.99, p=0.046
Bubble Cursor	Setting	rem	out	kept	point	b1	b3	ANOVA	point	b1	b3	Friedman
	Lab	0	1	12	1119	1122	909	F(2,22)=65, p<0.0001	7.58	2.33	1.08	$\chi^2(2)=17$, p<0.0001
	MTurk	9	6	108	1417	1410	1205	F(2,214)=110, p<0.0001	8.34	3.4	1.77	$\chi^2(2)=108$, p<0.0001

Table 1: All experiments: main effects. The "rem" column shows the number of participants removed due to a self-reported faulty device or medical condition. The "out" column shows the number of participants removed as extreme outliers.

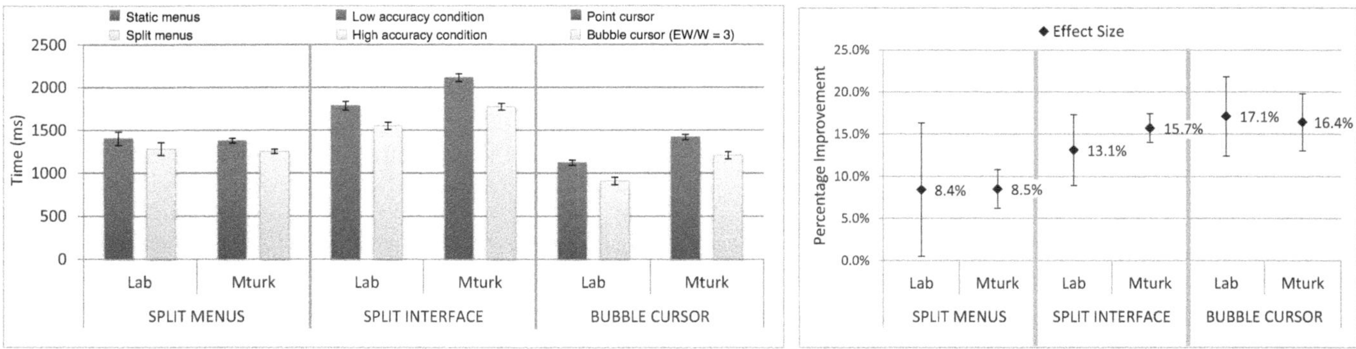

(a) Mean selection times. Error bars represent SEM.

(b) Effect sizes. Error bars represent 95% CI.

Figure 2: Task completion times and effect sizes in all three experiments.

experiment, each participant completed a 30 selection split-menu practice block. Next, they performed four experimental blocks: two 90-selection split-menu blocks and two 90-selection static-menu blocks, alternating (the selection of the starting condition was counterbalanced across participants). At the beginning of each trial, participants had to click the "Next" button for the prompt to display the next target item. The experimental UI is shown in Figure 1.

Design and Analysis

We used a within subjects design with one factor (the menu design) with two levels (static or split). We analyzed two measures: trial completion time (measured from clicking on the category header to the correct item selection within the category), and number of errors per block. We recorded an error if a participant clicked on an incorrect item in a menu or clicked on an incorrect category label. However, the latter proved unnecessary as practically all errors were item errors. We log-transformed the timing data to account for the skewed distributions found in such data. We analyzed the timing data using repeated measures ANOVA and we used the Wilcoxon signed-rank test for the error analysis.

Participants

We recruited 14 participants (10 male, 4 female) aged 18–35 (M=26) from our university to participate in the lab version of the study. We recruited 96 MTurk participants (US-based, 95% approval rate, minimum of 500 completed HITs, 49 male, 47 female) aged 18–65 (M=30) for the online variant of the study.

Results

Adjustments of Data

There were 6 participants on MTurk who reported having a medical condition or a faulty hardware device that might have interfered with their work, and we discarded their data without further inspection. Among the remaining 90 participants, 1 was classified as an extreme outlier and was removed from analysis. In lab, there were no extreme outliers.

Main Effects

The results are summarized in Table 1 and are visualized in Figure 2(a). In both settings (lab and MTurk) we observed the main effect of the menu type (split vs. static) on task completion time. In both settings, participants were significantly faster with the adaptive split menus than with the static baseline design. All participants committed fewer errors in the split condition, however the differences were not significant.

There were no substantial or significant differences in the magnitude of the effect size between the two settings (Figure 2(b)).

Experiment 2: Adaptive Split Interface

Split Interfaces are a generalization of Split Menus. In Split Interfaces, the items predicted to be most immediately useful to the user are copied to specially designated part of the user interface [5]. Therefore, just as in Split Menus, when the system correctly places the desired item in the adaptive part of the interface the user has the choice to either use the adaptive copy or to access the item at its usual location in the static part of the interface.

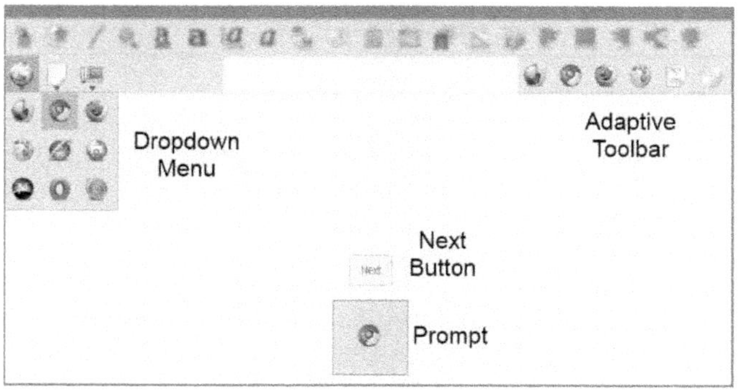

Figure 3: Split Interface. The 6 most recently used items (2 per category) are copied to the adaptive toolbar.

We reproduced an experiment, which demonstrated the impact of the accuracy of the predictive algorithm on users' performance [6]. That is, the experiment compared two otherwise identical variants of a Split Interface (illustrated in Figure 3), which differed only in their behavior: in one condition the desired item was present in the adaptive part of the interface with a 50% probability and in the other with a 70% probability.

In our experiment, the adaptive part of the interface was placed at the opposite side of the screen from the static part of the interface used during the experiment. Therefore, to take advantage of the adaptation, users had to consciously direct their gaze to the adaptive part of the interface.

Tasks and Procedures

We used a design with three categories of items for users to select: browsers, file types, and computer devices. Each category had 9 items arranged in a 3-by-3 square-grid formation. Each category was represented as a button on a toolbar. Clicking this button opened up a drop down menu containing all the items in that category. The adaptive toolbar contained the two most recently selected items per category for a total of six items. At the beginning of each trial, a copy of the target item, used as the prompt, was displayed in the middle of the screen. Also located there was a "Next" button used to proceed to the next selection. Thus, the typical selection trial consisted of clicking the "Next" button, looking at the prompt to learn the appearance of the target, and selecting the target from either the adaptive toolbar or from the drop down menu.

Each participant started with a practice block of 10 selections in which they had to use the adaptive toolbar at least once or otherwise were asked to repeat the block. This ensured that the participants understood the purpose of the adaptive toolbar. Next, they completed a second practice block consisting of 60 selections across all three categories such that in 60% of the selections the adaptive toolbar had a copy of the target. During this second practice block and in the main experiment, the use of the adaptive toolbar was left entirely to each participant's discretion. The main experiment consisted of two blocks with 60 selections each. One of the blocks had predictive accuracy of 70% of containing the target item (high accuracy condition) and the other had predictive accuracy of 50% (low accuracy condition). The ordering of high and low accuracy conditions were counter-balanced across participants. The same selection sequences were used across all participants.

Design and Analysis

We used a within-subjects design with one factor (the prediction accuracy) with two levels (low=50% and high=70%). We measured two variables: trial completion time (measured from clicking on the "Next" button to the selection of the target in either the regular menu or in the adaptive toolbar), and number of errors per block. There were two types of errors: when the participant selected a wrong category and when the participant selected a wrong item. We used the sum of the two in the analysis. We log-transformed the timing data to account for skewed distributions found in such data. Timing data were analyzed with a repeated measures ANOVA. Errors were analyzed with the Wilcoxon signed-rank test.

Participants

For the lab study we recruited 10 students from our university (6 male, 4 female) aged 21–34 (M=26.5). From MTurk we recruited 92 participants(US-based, 95% approval rate, minimum of 500 HITs, 54 male, 38 female) aged 18–63 (M=27).

Results

Adjustments of Data

There were 6 participant on MTurk whose data was discarded because they reported a medical condition or an unreliable pointing device that might have affected their performance. There were no extreme outliers on MTurk. In lab one participant was removed as an extreme outlier, because he was substantially slower than the rest of the participants for a reason we could not determine.

Main Effects

As before, the results are summarized in Table 1 and visualized in Figure 2(a). We observed a significant main effect of the predictive accuracy on task completion time both in lab and on MTurk. In both settings participants were faster in the high accuracy condition, and there was no evidence of a substantial difference in effect size (Figure 2(b)). In addition, participants in both settings made fewer errors in the high accuracy condition. On MTurk the difference was significant, while in lab it was not (Table 1).

Experiment 3: Bubble Cursor

The Bubble Cursor [7] is a pointing enhancement where the size of the cursor's hot spot changes dynamically to always overlap the closest target. The Bubble Cursor will completely contain the closest target (Figure 4(b)), unless this would cause it to intersect the second closest target. In that case, the size of the cursor is reduced and the primary target is decorated with an outline as shown in Figure 4(c). The Bubble Cursor takes advantage of the sparsity of the targets to increase their effective sizes. The more sparsely the targets are distributed, the greater the potential benefits conferred by this design compared to the traditional point cursor. We reproduced a study comparing the Bubble Cursor (at two different target density settings) to the point cursor.

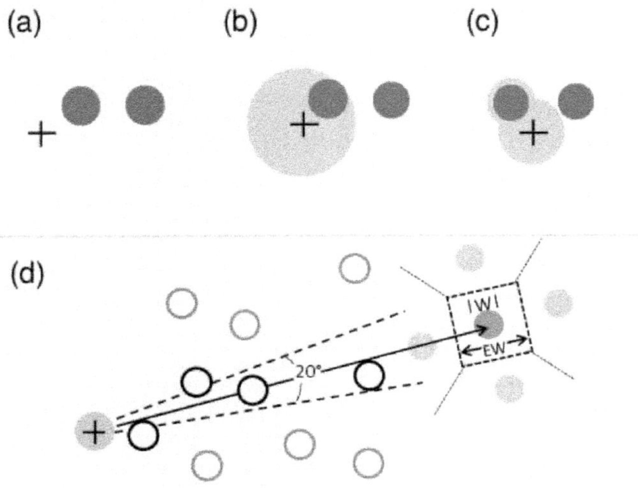

Figure 4: Point and Bubble Cursors. (a) Point (crosshair) cursor. (b) and (c) The size of the hotspot of the bubble cursor changes dynamically to intersect with the closest target while avoiding any other target. (d) The *effective width (EW)* of the target can be manipulated by changing the proximity of the closest four distracter targets (shown in yellow) to the goal target (shown in green). This figure based on [7].

Tasks and Procedures

There were five independent variables in the original Bubble Cursor experiment. Cursor type $CT = \{Point, Bubble\}$; amplitude A (i.e., the distance to the target); target width W; the ration of effective width to width EW/W, where effective width is the width of the target W plus all surrounding pixels that are closer to it than to any other target (as illustrated in Figure 4(d)); and distracter density D, which, as also illustrated in Figure 4(d), is the density of the targets in the 20 degree slice between the starting point and the target.

In our replication of the experiment, we varied only the cursor type CT and the EW/W ratio, while fixing the other variables: W=12px, D=0.5, A=Uniform(200px,400px).

Each participant completed a practice block (CT=Bubble, EW/W=3) consisting of 30 target selections. Participants were required to use the "bubble" capability of the Bubble Cursor at least once during the practice block (i.e., they had to acquire a target such that the center of the cursor was outside the target, but the target was captured by the "bubble") or else they were forced to repeat the practice block. This ensured that all participants understood the special capability of the Bubble Cursor. In all other blocks, the use of the "bubble" mechanism was used to each participant's discretion.

The practice was followed by three 80-selection blocks ordered randomly for each participant: (baseline condition with CT=Point), (CT=Bubble, EW/W=3), and (CT=Bubble, EW/W = 1.33). For convenience, we will refer to these conditions as $point$, $b3$, $b1$, respectively. As in the original version of the experiment, the target was rendered as green disc, the distracters as grey discs, and the bubble cursor as a semi-transparent grey disc. Both the active target and the distracters were filled with red when the cursor captured them.

Design and Analysis

We used a within subjects design with one factor (cursor type) with three levels (point, b1, b3). We measured two variables: trial completion time (measured from clicking on the previous target to clicking on the current target), and the number of errors per block (errors were defined as clicks that did not capture the target). We log-transformed the timing data to account for the skewed distributions found in such data. We analyzed the timing data using repeated measures ANOVA. For the error data, we used the Friedman test.

Results

Participants

We recruited 13 participants from our university (10 male, 3 female) aged 21–53 (M=25), and 123 MTurk participants (US-based, 95% approval rate, minimum of 500 HITs), (65 male, 58 female) aged 18–68 (M=27.5).

Adjustments of Data

There were 9 MTurk participants who reported having a medical condition or an unreliable input device that might have interfered with their work, and we discarded their data without further inspection. From the remaining 114 participants 6 were excluded from the analysis as extreme outliers. In lab, one participant was excluded because he mistakenly used a touchpad instead of the provided mouse.

Main Effects

As before, the results are summarized in Table 1 and visualized in Figure 2(a). We observed the main effect of cursor type on task completion time in both the lab setting and on MTurk, and the pairwise comparison (Bonferroni adjusted) showed significant difference ($p < 0.0001$) between $point$ and $b3$, and $b1$ and $b3$ for both lab and MTurk participants (Figure 2(a)). In neither setting was the difference between $point$ and $b1$ significant. There was no significant difference in effect size between lab and MTurk (Figure 2(b)). All participants committed the most errors in the $point$ condition, and the fewest in the $b3$ condition. The effect of cursor type on error rate was significant in both the lab and the MTurk settings.

COMPARISON OF LAB VS. MTURK RESULTS

The results in the previous section suggest that the *relative* differences between experimental conditions are the same whether measured in lab or remotely with participants recruited via MTurk. In this section, we address the question of whether there are systematic differences in the *absolute* magnitudes of the measurements collected in lab and on MTurk. Is either population systematically faster, more accurate, or more consistent? We compare the populations of the lab and MTurk participants in terms of speed, error rates, consistency, and utilization of the novel interactive mechanism presented in each experiment. We also characterize the demographics of the two populations. Finally, we investigate the reproducibility of the MTurk-based results.

Methodology

To compare the lab and MTurk populations, we captured the following measures:

- **Mean task completion times.**
- **Consistency.** We used the per-participant standard deviation in task completion times as a measure of how consistently they performed throughout the experiment.
- **Error rates.**
- **Utilization of the novel interactive mechanisms.** Each of our experiments included a novel interaction mechanism (adaptive area at the top of the Split Menus, adaptive toolbar in the Split Interface, and the ability to acquire the target without placing the pointer directly over it in Bubble Cursor). In all experiments, the use of these novel interaction mechanisms was designed to improve performance, but was optional and required a small amount of cognitive effort to use. We define utilization as the fraction of times when the user used the novel interaction mechanisms when one was available.
- **Fraction of extreme outliers.** This measure captures the fraction of participants who were excluded from analysis because they were classified as extreme outliers.

As before, we log-transformed the timing data before analysis. We used ANOVA to analyze timing, consistency, and utilization data. We used the (between-subjects) Wilcoxon rank-sum test to analyze error data.

The Bubble Cursor experiment posed additional challenges for the analysis, because computer performance had a significant effect on participant performance. The experiment was implemented using the HTML5 canvas element, whose performance depends on browser type, browser version, operating system, graphic acceleration, and CPU speed. Aware of these differences, we implemented an automatic performance check: Turkers whose browsers did not appear capable of redrawing the canvas in 30 ms or less were not allowed to proceed with the experiment. We determined this threshold as the slowest drawing speed at which the performance of Bubble Cursor appeared smooth and did not register any perceptible lag. For reference, the computer used in the lab study performed at 6 ms per frame (MSPF). The automatic performance check provided only an estimate of actual performance so we also logged the actual drawing performance during the experiment. In reality, the Turkers' computers performed in the range of 4 to 50 MSPF. Contrary to our expectations, even such short drawing times had a significant impact on performance: drawing time was positively correlated with selection time ($r = 0.267, n = 324, p < 0.0001$) and negatively correlated with errors ($r = -0.121, n = 324, p = 0.029$).

To account for different distributions of the background variables related to the participants' demographics and environment we used two redundant, parallel methods of analysis, both of which led to the same conclusions. In the first method, we included gender, input device, computer performance (bubble cursor only), and age as factors or covariates in the general linear model associated with the ANOVA. The advantage of this approach is that it leveraged all available data, but as a linear regression model it made two assumptions: (1) participant performance was linear with age and computer performance and (2) gender and device had a constant additive effect. In our second method we removed the need of the first assumption by matching the data in terms of age and computer performance using cutoff values. Results from both methods are shown in Table 2, in which all reported means (except for errors) are least-squares adjusted means computed based on the estimated parameters of the linear regression.

Results

Table 2 summarizes the results from this analysis.

Split Menu

Both analyses indicated that Turkers were slightly faster than lab participants, had lower individual standard deviations, had higher utilization rate, but made more errors. However, the differences were not significant. These differences were also relatively small: the differences in task completion times between the two populations were 3.5% in the analysis that included all data and 2.8% in the analysis with matched data. In comparison, the performance differences between the two experimental conditions (the static menus and the Split Menus) were larger than 8.4% (Figure 2(b) in the previous section).

Split Interface

In both analyses, Turkers were slower than lab participants, had higher standard deviations, made more errors, and had lower utilization rates. As before, the differences were not significant. The differences in task completion times between the two populations were 5.9% in the analysis that included all data and 6.3% in the analysis with matched data. In comparison, the performance differences between the two experimental conditions (as reported in previous section) were larger than 13.1%.

Bubble Cursor

In both analyses, Turkers were slower, had higher individual standard deviations, made more errors, and had lower utilization rates, but none of the differences were significant. The differences in task completion times between the two populations were 3.0% in the analysis that included all data and 4.9% in the analysis with matched data. In comparison, the performance differences between the two experimental conditions (as reported in previous section) were larger than 16.4%.

			Task completion time		Individual St. D.		Utilization		Errors					
			Mean	Significance	Mean	Significance	Mean	Significance	Mean	Sig.	Mean	Sig.	Mean	Sig.
split menus									Split		Static			
	all age	Lab	*1373*	F(1,200)=0.931,	*643*	F(1,200)=0.002,	*0.811*	F(1,98)=1.839,	1.71	z=0.571	2.43	z=0.737		
		MTurk	*1327*	p=0.336	*640*	p=0.963	*0.875*	p=0.178	2.22	p=0.568	2.45	p=0.461		
	age<35	Lab	1310	F(1,133)=0.057,	629	F(1,133)=0.401,	0.841	F(1,65)=0.033,	1.85	z=0.838	2.62	z=0.904		
		MTurk	1274	p=0.450	599	p=0.527	0.863	p=0.857	2.63	p=0.402	2.75	p=0.366		
split interface									High		Low			
	all age	Lab	*1846*	F(1,184)=2.129,	*791*	F(1,184)=2.231,	*0.959*	F(1,90)=0.731,	2.56	z=0.064	4	z=-0.781		
		MTurk	*1955*	p=0.146	*971*	p=0.137	*0.912*	p=0.382	3.55	p=0.949	3.87	p=0.435		
	age<40	Lab	1788	F(1,149)=2.179,	771	F(1,149)=0.902,	0.959	F(1,67)=0.857,	2.56	z=0.307	4	z=0.639		
		MTurk	1901	p=0.142	966	p=0.344	0.899	p=0.358	2.96	p=0.759	4.04	p=0.523		
bubble cursor									point		b1		b3	
	all age	Lab	*1331*	F(1,352)=0.728,	*257*	F(1,352)=2.878	*0.413*	F(1,233)=1.927,	7.58	z=0.201	2.33	z=0.036	1.08	z=0.251
	all mspf	MTurk	*1371*	p=0.394	*318*	p=0.091	*0.347*	p=0.166	8.34	p=0.841	3.4	p=0.971	1.77	p=0.802
	age<35	Lab	1171	F(1,77)=1.957,	195	F(1,77)=3.598,	0.418	F(1,42)=3.347,	8.44	z=0.222	1.78	z=0.78	1.22	z=0.805
	mspf<8	MTurk	1228	p=0.166	271	p=0.062	0.319	p=0.074	9.99	p=0.824	3.81	p=0.436	2.11	p=0.421

Table 2: Task completion times, individual standard deviations, utilization, and number of errors in all experiments. Except for errors, all reported values are least-squares means adjusted for device and gender. Values in *italics* are additionally adjusted for age and computer performance. None of the differences are statistically significant.

All experiments combined

We repeated the ANOVA analyses using the combined data from all experiments. The advantage of combining the data from all experiments is the increase in power of the test, making it possible to show statistically significant results for even smaller differences. However, despite the increased power, we did not observe a significant effect of setting on speed ($F(1,353) = 1.607, p = 0.206$), consistency ($F(1,353) = 1.509, p = 0.22$), or utilization ($F(1,353) = 2.037, p = 0.154$).

Outliers

In total, after the removal of participants with self-reported medical conditions or technical difficulties, 7 out of 290 (2.4%) Turkers and 1 out of 36 (2.8%) lab participants were classified as extreme outliers and excluded from the analysis across the three experiments.

Reproducibility

We run all the previously reported MTurk experiments on weekdays in the evenings at 7pm EDT (4pm PDT). The make up of the Turker population is known to change over time. To investigate if it would have impact on the reproducibility of the results, we rerun the Split Interface experiment on a weekday morning at 11am EDT (8am PDT). There were, indeed, substantial differences between the populations that participated in the two instances of the experiment: the morning population was 74% female, with median age of 43, and with 63% of the participants using a mouse and 27% using a touchpad. In contrast, the evening population was only 57% female, with median age of 32, and with 86% of the participants using a mouse and 14% using a touchpad. These differences had substantial impact on the average performance, but these performance differences became negligible and non-significant once age and device were introduced as factors into the analyses.

Demographics

Across the three experiments, we analyzed data from 283 MTurk participants (US-based, 95% approval rate, minimum of 500 HITs) aged 18–68, M=28. For the lab studies we analyzed data from 35 participants aged 18–53, M=26. Table 3 summarizes the demographics of the two populations. In lab, the age group 45–65 was underrepresented.

DISCUSSION

In all three experiments we have conducted, the data collected in lab and the data collected remotely with the participants recruited via MTurk both resulted in the same conclusions of the statistical comparisons and showed very similar effect sizes. We also did not observe any significant differences in the absolute measurements of task completion times, error rates, consistency of performance, or the rates of utilization of novel interface mechanisms between the lab and MTurk populations. Further, the results of the Split Menus and Split Interface experiments show that the Turkers did as well as lab-based participants on tasks where efficient operation of the user interface required some amount of cognitive engagement. We also found MTurk to be reliable in that when we repeated the same experiment at two different times of the day, we got nearly identical results after correcting for different age and input device distributions. We also detected very few outliers in our data: only 7 out of 290 participants (or 2.4%) had to be removed from the analysis across the three experiments. This is in contrast to other researchers who ended up discarding up to half of their MTurk-based data [8].

Although we designed our experiments as within-subjects comparisons, the close match in the absolute values of the measurements between the lab-based and online populations, as well as the lack of significant differences when the same measurements were repeated multiple times online, suggest that between-subjects designs could also be conducted robustly on MTurk.

		MTurk				Lab			
		Bubble	SplitIface	SplitMenu	**Overall**	**Overall**	SplitMenu	SplitIface	Bubble
Age	mean	30.9	31.7	32.2	**31.6**	**27.4**	26.1	26.4	29.6
	st.d.	11.13	12.39	9.67	**11.01**	**7.31**	5.68	4.84	9.99
	median	26.5	27	30	**28**	**26**	26	27	24
	range	[18,68]	[18,63]	[18,65]	**[18,68]**	**[18,53]**	[18,35]	[21,34]	[21,53]
	age>40	20	16	16	**52**	**2**	0	0	2
Gender	male:female	57:51	51:35	45:44	**153:130**	**24:11**	10:4	5:4	9:3
Device	mouse:tpad	78:30	59:27	62:27	**199:84**	**30:5**	9:5	9:0	12:0

Table 3: Demographics and pointing device of the final sample of participants, after excluding those classified as extreme outliers and those who reported a medical condition or a faulty device.

These positive results can be explained by the fact that participants were naturally motivated to complete tasks as quickly as possible, which aligned with the goals of the experiments. However, we cannot discount the possible effects of the novelty factor: a number of the MTurk participants commented spontaneously that our experiments were more enjoyable than typical tasks available on MTurk.

Our results suggest that remote performance evaluations of user interfaces can usefully be conducted with participants recruited via MTurk. However, because it is a novel methodology that hasn't been broadly validated, a small-scale lab-based validation may be a prudent choice for any new experiment.

Practical Considerations

Throughout this research, a number of practical considerations emerged that proved to be important for successful remote experimentation with Turkers. Although a number of these considerations have already been mentioned in earlier sections, we synthesize them all below.

- **Ensuring instruction comprehension.** During our preliminary studies, we saw ample evidence that a fraction of the Turkers did not understand the novel capabilities afforded by the user interface mechanisms we were testing. For example, some participants always brought the center of the Bubble Cursor over the target, while others never took advantage of the adaptive toolbar in Split Interfaces. To ensure that all participants understood what each interface afforded, we required that the participants used the novel capability of the UI being tested at least once during the practice block. If they didn't, they were shown the instructions again and were forced to repeat the practice block. We made it clear to participants that they were free to use their own judgement whether to take advantage of the novel UI capabilities during the actual experimental blocks. The comparable utilization rates between lab- and MTurk-based populations suggest that these interventions were effective.
- **Accounting for age- and input device–related differences.** Both age and the input device impact performance on input tasks such as pointing and text entry. While controlling for the diversity of age and input devices was not an issue for demonstrating within-subjects effects, between-subjects comparisons may not be reliable unless these factors are accounted for either when allocating participants to conditions or during the analysis. Because the make up of the MTurk work force changes on an hour-by-hour basis, running all conditions simultaneously is a common design choice that further contributes to the reliability of the results.
- **Robust outlier detection.** Some of the outliers we observed were more than an order of magnitude different from the typical performance. Such extreme outliers substantially impact the estimates of mean and standard deviation. Thus, the popular method of excluding values more than 2 standard deviations away from the mean may not be reliable. Instead, we have used a method based on the inter-quartile ranges, which is much more robust to very extreme outliers [4].
- **Implementation issues.** Some experiments, like the Bubble Cursor evaluation presented in this paper, will be sensitive to the hardware and software performance on the participants' computers. We both included automatic checks for detecting slow performing hardware/software configurations and we logged the actual time taken to render critical interface updates. Further, different participants will have different network connectivity. Standard techniques, such as preloading media, helped ensure that network performance was not a factor during the actual experiments.
- **Encouraging honest reporting of problems.** Twenty-one Turkers who completed our experiments reported having either a disability or a technical difficulty that might have impacted their performance during the experiment. We encouraged honest reporting of such problems by assuring participants that it would not affect their eligibility to receive compensation for participating in the study. While we didn't analyze the data from these participants, it is conceivable that not including them in the analysis contributed positively to the overall high quality of the data and the low outlier rates.

CONCLUSION

We have performed three distinct experiments both in a controlled laboratory setting and remotely with unsupervised online participants recruited via Amazon's Mechanical Turk (MTurk). The analysis of our results did not yield any evidence of significant or substantial differences in the data collected in the two settings: All statistically significant results detected in lab were also observed on MTurk, the effect sizes were similar, and there were no significant differences in the raw task completion times, error rates, measures of performance consistency, or the rates of utilization of the novel interface mechanisms introduced in each experiment. Repeated measurements performed on MTurk at different times of the day showed changes in the demographics of the MTurk population, but yielded similar results after correcting for different age and input device distributions observed at different times.

These results provide evidence that MTurk can be a useful platform for conducting experiments that require participants to perform largely mechanical user interface tasks and where the primary measures of interest are task completion times and error rates.

We have also highlighted a number of practical challenges — and our solutions to them — related to instruction comprehension, accounting for age- and device-related differences in performance, techniques for robust outlier detection, as well as the effects of software, hardware, and network performance on participants' experience.

Compared to lab-based methods, conducting online experiments with participants recruited through micro task labor markets such as Amazon's Mechanical Turk can enable larger-scale experimentation, access to a more diverse subject pool, and a faster experimental revision cycle. Although this is a novel methodology that has not been broadly validated, we believe it can provide a valuable complement to the existing approaches.

ONLINE APPENDIX

To enable others to validate and extend our results, the data set and more information about the design of our experiments can be found at http://iis.seas.harvard.edu/resources/.

ACKNOWLEDGEMENTS

Steven Komarov was supported by the National Science Foundation under fellowship number DGE-1144152. Katharina Reinecke was supported by the Swiss National Science Foundation under fellowship number PBZHP2-135922. We thank Mike Terry and the CHI reviewers for helpful feedback on earlier versions of this manuscript.

REFERENCES

1. Callison-Burch, C. Fast, cheap, and creative: evaluating translation quality using amazon's mechanical turk. In *Proceedings of the 2009 Conference on Empirical Methods in Natural Language Processing: Volume 1 - Volume 1*, EMNLP '09, Association for Computational Linguistics (Stroudsburg, PA, USA, 2009), 286–295.
2. Chandler, D., and Kapelner, A. Breaking monotony with meaning: Motivation in crowdsourcing markets. Working Paper, May 2010.
3. Cole, F., Sanik, K., DeCarlo, D., Finkelstein, A., Funkhouser, T., Rusinkiewicz, S., and Singh, M. How well do line drawings depict shape? *SIGGRAPH '09: SIGGRAPH 2009 papers* (July 2009).
4. Devore, J. *Probability and Statistics for Engineering and the Sciences*, seventh ed. Thomson Higher Education, 2008.
5. Gajos, K. Z., Czerwinski, M., Tan, D. S., and Weld, D. S. Exploring the design space for adaptive graphical user interfaces. In *AVI '06: Proceedings of the working conference on Advanced visual interfaces*, ACM Press (New York, NY, USA, 2006), 201–208.
6. Gajos, K. Z., Everitt, K., Tan, D. S., Czerwinski, M., and Weld, D. S. Predictability and accuracy in adaptive user interfaces. In *CHI '08: Proceeding of the twenty-sixth annual SIGCHI conference on Human factors in computing systems*, ACM (New York, NY, USA, 2008), 1271–1274.
7. Grossman, T., and Balakrishnan, R. The bubble cursor: enhancing target acquisition by dynamic resizing of the cursor's activation area. In *Proceedings of the SIGCHI conference on Human factors in computing systems*, CHI '05, ACM (New York, NY, USA, 2005), 281–290.
8. Heer, J., and Bostock, M. Crowdsourcing graphical perception: using mechanical turk to assess visualization design. In *Proceedings of the 28th international conference on Human factors in computing systems*, CHI '10, ACM (New York, NY, USA, 2010), 203–212.
9. Horton, J. J., Rand, D. G., and Zeckhauser, R. J. The online laboratory: Conducting experiments in a real labor market. *Experimental Economics* (2011).
10. Kapelner, A., and Chandler, D. Preventing Satisficing in Online Surveys: A "Kapcha" to Ensure Higher Quality Data. In *CrowdConf* (2010).
11. Kittur, A., Chi, E. H., and Suh, B. Crowdsourcing user studies with mechanical turk. In *Proceeding of the twenty-sixth annual SIGCHI conference on Human factors in computing systems*, CHI '08, ACM (New York, NY, USA, 2008), 453–456.
12. Kong, N., Heer, J., and Agrawala, M. Perceptual Guidelines for Creating Rectangular Treemaps. *Visualization and Computer Graphics, IEEE Transactions on 16*, 6 (2010), 990–998.
13. Little, G., Chilton, L., Goldman, M., and Miller, R. Turkit: human computation algorithms on mechanical turk. In *Proceedings of the 23nd annual ACM symposium on User interface software and technology*, ACM (2010), 57–66.
14. Mao, A., Chen, Y., Gajos, K., Parkes, D., Procaccia, A., and Zhang, H. Turkserver: Enabling synchronous and longitudinal online experiments. In *Proceedings of HCOMP'12* (2012).
15. Mason, W., and Suri, S. Conducting behavioral research on amazon's mechanical turk. *Behavior Research Methods* (2010), 1–23.
16. Mason, W., and Watts, D. Financial incentives and the "performance of crowds". *HCOMP '09: Proceedings of the ACM SIGKDD Workshop on Human Computation* (June 2009).
17. Noronha, J., Hysen, E., Zhang, H., and Gajos, K. Z. Platemate: Crowdsourcing nutrition analysis from food photographs. In *Proceedings of UIST'11* (2011).
18. Oleson, D., Sorokin, A., Laughlin, G., Hester, V., Le, J., and Biewald, L. Programmatic gold: Targeted and scalable quality assurance in crowdsourcing. In *Proceedings of HCOMP'11* (2011).
19. Oppenheimer, D., Meyvis, T., and Davidenko, N. Instructional manipulation checks: Detecting satisficing to increase statistical power. *Journal of Experimental Social Psychology 45*, 4 (2009), 867–872.
20. Paolacci, G., Chandler, J., and Ipeirotis, P. Running experiments on amazon mechanical turk. *Judgment and Decision Making 5*, 5 (2010), 411–419.
21. Prelec, D. A Bayesian Truth Serum for Subjective Data. *Science 306*, 5695 (Oct. 2004), 462–466.
22. Rand, D. G. The promise of Mechanical Turk: How online labor markets can help theorists run behavioral experiments. *Journal of theoretical biology* (2012).
23. Rzeszotarski, J. M., and Kittur, A. Instrumenting the crowd: Using implicit behavioral measures to predict task performance. In *Proceedings of the 24th annual ACM symposium on User interface software and technology*, UIST '11, ACM (New York, NY, USA, 2011).
24. Schmidt, L. Crowdsourcing for human subjects research. In *CrowdConf* (2010).
25. Sears, A., and Shneiderman, B. Split menus: effectively using selection frequency to organize menus. *ACM Trans. Comput.-Hum. Interact. 1*, 1 (1994), 27–51.
26. Shaw, A. D., Horton, J. J., and Chen, D. L. Designing incentives for inexpert human raters. In *Proceedings of the ACM 2011 conference on Computer supported cooperative work*, CSCW '11, ACM (New York, NY, USA, 2011), 275–284.
27. Suri, S., and Watts, D. Cooperation and contagion in networked public goods experiments. *Arxiv preprint arXiv10081276* (2010).

A Multi-Site Field Study of Crowdsourced Contextual Help: Usage and Perspectives of End Users and Software Teams

Parmit K. Chilana[1], Andrew J. Ko[1], Jacob O. Wobbrock[1], Tovi Grossman[2]
[1]The Information School | DUB Group
University of Washington
Seattle, WA 98195 USA
{pchilana, ajko, wobbrock}@uw.edu
[2]Autodesk Research
210 King St. E
Toronto, ON Canada M5A 1J7
tovi.grossman@autodesk.com

ABSTRACT
We present a multi-site field study to evaluate LemonAid, a crowdsourced contextual help approach that allows users to retrieve relevant questions and answers by making selections within the interface. We deployed LemonAid on 4 different web sites used by thousands of users and collected data over several weeks, gathering over 1,200 usage logs, 168 exit surveys, and 36 one-on-one interviews. Our results indicate that over 70% of users found LemonAid to be helpful, intuitive, and desirable for reuse. Software teams found LemonAid easy to integrate with their sites and found the analytics data aggregated by LemonAid a novel way of learning about users' popular questions. Our work provides the first holistic picture of the adoption and use of a crowdsourced contextual help system and offers several insights into the social and organizational dimensions of implementing such help systems for real-world applications.

Author Keywords
contextual help; crowdsourced help; field studies; field deployments; help systems; software support;

ACM Classification Keywords
H.5.2 [**Information interfaces and presentation**]: User Interfaces. *Graphical user interfaces.*

INTRODUCTION
Most software help is simply not helpful. One-on-one technical support is time-consuming, frustrating, and rarely puts users in touch with the experts who have answers [18]. Documentation, tutorials, and tooltips rarely provide the task-specific help that people need [19,29,31] because software designers cannot anticipate at design time the full range of *how*, *why*, *what*, and *where am I* questions that people ask [31]. Even crowdsourced solutions such as technical support discussion forums require users to browse lengthy, scattered, and often irrelevant conversations in search for even one helpful reply [22,32]. Worse yet, many users do not find these discussions at all, as the search queries that users write often omit the key application terminology necessary for retrieving relevant help [11].

To address these problems of discoverability, recent approaches have explored integrating crowdsourced help within the application's user interface (UI). For example, the *CHIC* framework [34] for Eclipse adds links from each UI control to a wiki where users can author help. *TurboTax* help [37] and *IP-QAT* [24] display help discussions relevant to the current view in a sidebar within the application. The *LemonAid* help system [8] lets users retrieve Q&A at an even finer granularity by selecting a label, widget, link, image or another UI element relevant to a given help need.

Although these *crowdsourced contextual help* systems are quite promising, many questions remain about their effectiveness at providing help during real tasks. For example, while IP-QAT's initial evaluation [24] showed that it was more useful and easier to use than a basic discussion board, the study involved only one instrumented application and was carried out with paid volunteers who were *required* to contribute 3 items per day. LemonAid's initial evaluation [8] showed that LemonAid could retrieve relevant help in the top 2 results for over half of help seeking scenarios, but this finding was based only a simulated community of users and pre-defined tasks. As social systems often interact with the social and organizational contexts in which they are implemented [14], it is difficult to know if and when these lab study results apply to real users and their real situations and tasks [20,28].

To understand how crowdsourced contextual help is perceived in real settings and to increase the ecological validity of LemonAid's design [8], we partnered with multiple software teams to deploy and evaluate LemonAid in the field. After extending the original LemonAid prototype with community Q&A, answer notification, and back-end analytics features, we deployed it on a set of four diverse sites for periods ranging from 7 to 15 weeks, reaching user populations of 150 to over 40,000 users in size. From over 1,200 logs, 168 exit surveys, and 36 interviews with end users, we report on end users' perspectives on LemonAid's helpfulness, usability, and desirability for reuse, and how it compared to alternative forms of help seeking. We also present software teams' perspectives on issues related to LemonAid's adoption and integration and the utility of LemonAid's analytics data.

The result of these deployments is the first holistic picture of the adoption and use of a crowdsourced contextual help system, contributing:

- Extensions to LemonAid's crowdsourced contextual help [8] that support participation by end users and software teams, moderation of help activity, and improved discoverability of help content;
- Empirical findings that highlight the unique strengths of crowdsourced contextual help and selection-based help in particular, but also tradeoffs in integrating help into an application user interface;
- Results that illustrate the factors affecting software teams' adoption of a crowdsourced contextual help tool and teams' perceptions of the value of crowdsourced contextual help analytics data;
- Insights into the process of developing and integrating help systems into existing applications, and how help systems fit into larger social and organizational contexts.

RELATED WORK

Field Evaluations of Help Systems

Although "in-the-wild" field studies are increasingly common in HCI [4], field studies of software help have been rare. Although not directly in the domain of software help, Ackerman's [1] evaluation of *AnswerGarden,* a question-answering tool, comes closest to our study design. The study used multiple data collection procedures including questionnaires, usage data, and interviews and the findings provided rich insights into whether augmenting organizational memory was possible, and also contributed a number of lessons for designing organizational memory systems. Brandt et al. [3] evaluated their *Blueprint* tool for programmers and followed-up with a 3-month deployment at a large company, collecting usage data and interviews. The field study component helped them gain valuable insights into how participants integrated Blueprint into their everyday programming workflow. Although not a field evaluation, the study of IPQAT is one of the first to evaluate crowdsourced contextual help with users [24]. While the study ran for 2 weeks and there were 36 participants, all of these participants were using the same application and most of them were already users of product discussion forums. Furthermore, these participants were required to contribute 3 items per day and received additional monetary incentives to contribute more. In contrast to these works, our field study investigates the use of crowdsourced contextual help by hundreds of users for their real tasks across multiple sites.

Help Seeking Behavior

Early studies of help seeking showed that when people experience breakdowns in using software, they begin a process of trial-and-error to find a resolution [5]. Carroll calls this the "paradox of the active user" [5], because even though it would be more efficient for the user to get help, the user opts to tackle the task on her own first [27]. In particular, users of early systems were known to avoid printed manuals [29,30] because such manuals were difficult to follow and were usually plagued with system-specific vocabulary [11]. The advent of searchable, online help documentation offered an improvement, but the static nature of the help content remained to be a problem [12]. Recently, online forums have become a new platform for help, with millions of users seeking help, and a smaller but still large population of people asking and answering questions [22,32]. Although forums offer a rich repository of application-specific help, they are often not easily navigable or searchable [32]. While crowdsourced contextual help approaches can bring more relevant help to users within the user interface, our study sheds light on several social, organizational, and technical factors that have to be aligned to deliver such help.

Software Support Field Studies

Another body of work evaluates software product support from the perspective of software teams. Many of these studies have focused on organizational, procedural, and management problems in the provision of support [18,26] and knowledge and management of support issue repositories [10,15,16]. Other efforts have focused on diagnosis and web-based one-on-one support practices [6]. A large body of work has also investigated peer-to-peer help in open source software (OSS) communities, where users can directly communicate with one another and with developers about support issues and bugs [21,22,32]. Still, we know little about how organizations integrate new provisions for help and support or how they may use data from these systems to inform design. To our knowledge, we are the first to contribute insights into how teams adopt a new crowdsourced contextual help tool and how teams perceive the value of the analytics data it generates.

EXTENDING LEMONAID FOR FIELD DEPLOYMENT

The key idea behind LemonAid [8] is that users enter a semi-transparent help mode overlaid onto the application's user interface and find help by selecting a label or image they believe is relevant to their problem (as seen in Figure 1.1). Upon a selection, LemonAid retrieves questions and answers related to the selection (Figure 1.2) based on an algorithm that retrieves help based on the text, tag type, and location of the selection within the user interface (described in detail in [8]). Users can then select a retrieved question to view its answers and indicate their helpfulness, or if they do not find a relevant question, they can submit one. Support staff and other users can then answer them. Users can also use keywords to search through existing questions, allowing LemonAid to behave like a site-specific Q&A search.

The prototype described in [8] included only a retrieval algorithm and a selection user interface. For deployment, we added several critical features:

Improving discovery of existing help content. One of our design goals was to facilitate users' navigation of the existing help content upon entry into the help mode. To facilitate this, LemonAid adds yellow question marks next to elements that have at least one question attached (Figure 1.1). These

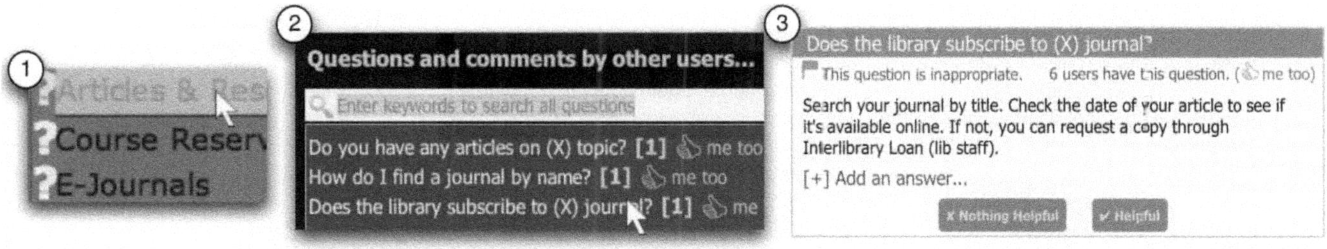

Figure 1. Main components of the LemonAid interface in the help mode: (1) a user selects an on-screen label or image highlighted in yellow; (2) the user's selection triggers the retrieval of relevant questions; (3) the user can click on a question to see the answer(s) for that question and indicate whether the answer was helpful or not helpful.

questions marks are dynamically generated as soon as a user enters the help mode based on the selections of previously asked questions. To help users remember which UI elements they have already viewed, the system modifies the color of the visited question marks.

Encouraging user participation. Another goal was to encourage users to contribute questions and answers. When users add a new question in LemonAid, they can provide their email address and be notified of new answers without having to return to the site. LemonAid also allows users to report potential spam and offer "me too" votes on questions (Figure 1.2). When users view answers, they also contribute data on whether the answer was helpful or not helpful in order to dismiss the answer window (Figure 1.3).

Moderating help content. Many of the software teams that we approached were concerned about users' ability to deface their site with unwanted content. Therefore, we added basic a moderation feature, allowing support staff to receive e-mail notifications of new questions and answers so that they can both approve content, answer new questions, and improve user-contributed answers. The moderators also get notified when a user flags a post as inappropriate.

Analytics dashboard for monitoring help activity. We added a web-based administrator "dashboard" that shows an aggregate view of users' activities in LemonAid, specific to the host deployment site. Moderators can get a real-time snapshot of the elements where users are looking for help. They can also see rankings of popular questions based on views and votes, and the helpfulness of answers.

Implementation and setup: To set up LemonAid for each site, we needed: (1) a whitelist of the UI literals where Q&A would be attached in the interface, to prevent users from selecting privacy-sensitive content; and, (2) access to the team's source to include the LemonAid functionality on the site. We hosted all of the Q&A data, logs, and scripts related to LemonAid on our own servers. For (1), the previous version of LemonAid [8] offered a mechanism for extracting UI literals from the source code; teams desired more control over what part of the interface would actually become selectable on the screen, so we created a plug-in that would help us interactively choose selectable labels and images on specific pages. For (2), software developers only had to embed a link to the main LemonAid JavaScript file in their source code (as is required to use tools such as *Google Analytics*, for example). One team decided to embed this link at the root level so that LemonAid would appear on all pages in the site; the other three teams placed LemonAid on their home page and selectively on other frequently accessed pages.

We also created a client-side browser plug-in that allowed us to test LemonAid on any site. Except for mobile devices, we were able to support LemonAid on most major browsers and platforms (although we did have problems with LemonAid on Internet Explorer versions 8.0 and lower for two of the deployments). We also had to resolve some minor JavaScript namespace conflicts on sites that used different versions of common JavaScript libraries, such as *jQuery*. The plug-in allowed us to sort out most of the compatibility issues independently of the host software teams, before deployment.

METHOD

Field Deployment Sites

The context for all of our deployment sites was a large university and its various software teams developing web applications to support teaching and research. To recruit field deployment sites, we met with software developers and site administrators across campus. Prior to making a commitment, the teams had a chance to see LemonAid demos, learn details about the field study, and discuss time and effort that they would be willing to commit. Six teams were enthusiastic about participating; the first site served as a pilot deployment and one of the remaining five had to leave the study due to conflicting schedules. The pilot site was a local intranet used by about 20 staff and students for internal project management. The pilot site allowed us to assess the usability of the interface, uncover implementation issues that had to be addressed for larger cross-platform deployments, and collect pilot data for improving our set-up and logging. We describe the four web sites augmented with LemonAid in Table 1.

Before making LemonAid live, we asked each software team to seed the help database with FAQs or other help content relevant to each page. In two cases, additional staff and the first author were also involved in seeding the help content.

Mixed-Method Data Collection

We treated each deployment as an individual case [36], but used the same data collection procedure for each site. We used a mixed-method approach to better capture the plurality of experiences and perspectives of users [13,36]. We collected data from three sources: (1) usage logs, (2)

Site	Description	User Population
LIBRARY	Provided access to a wide range of print and electronic resources available within the university library system and on web. One of the largest academic library systems in the US with millions of cataloged books, journals, and other materials.	Over **40,000** university students, faculty, and staff, visiting scholars, and the general public.
DEPT	A large academic department site that offered information about courses, upcoming events, admission, faculty, collaboration opportunities, and research facilities.	Over **900** undergraduate and graduate students, faculty, staff, prospective students, and the public.
EDC	An electronic data capture (EDC) system used for collecting data from clinical trials in an electronic format. Offered features for data entry, creating reports, analyzing data, exporting data, and sharing data with multiple users.	Over **500** staff personnel within the medical school and affiliated research center (restricted access).
RDB	A records database management system for storing and organizing data needed to maintain internal records of staff researchers. Used periodically by staff to review and update personal information, publications, grants, and to collaborate.	Over **150** staff and researchers in a unit within School of Medicine (restricted access).

Table 1. Summary of the four deployment sites.

surveys, and, (3) interviews. The data collection occurred during the spring and summer of 2012.

Usage Log Data

We instrumented LemonAid to gather a time-stamped log including: entry into help mode, exit from help mode (by clicking on the exit help button or leaving the current page), selections of elements on the screen, selections of questions, helpfulness of answers viewed, votes on questions, flags used to mark questions as spam, content of submitted questions and/or answers, content of search keywords, and lists of users subscribed to receive answers to questions. LemonAid gathered all of the foregoing data anonymously, meaning that we could not ascribe activity in the help mode to individual users, only users in aggregate.

Exit Survey

When users exited the help mode for the first time (detected by LemonAid's browser cookie), they were presented with a brief exit survey. Users had the option of being included in a $50 gift card drawing as an incentive to participate and could win additional prizes if they wanted to participate in a follow-up interview. Survey responses and identities of the respondents were not linked.

The survey asked users three questions about their experience, each scored on a 7-point Likert scale, ranging from "strongly disagree" to "strongly agree." These questions were: (1) "I found something helpful;" (2) "I would use this help feature again," and (3) "the help feature was intuitive." We also asked users closed demographic questions about their role (e.g., staff, student, faculty, etc.), their frequency of website use (ranging from daily, few times a week, few times during the quarter, or few times a year), and preferred method of getting help for web applications ("using the site's help", "searching online", "asking someone", "calling a support line", or "trying on my own"). We required users to provide a response for each of these questions to maintain consistency in the responses.

One-on-One Interviews with Users and Software Teams

Using the list of survey respondents who wished to be interviewed (~56% of all respondents), we recruited interviewees from each deployment site. We conducted all interviews on campus, except four were on the phone.

The interviews were semi-structured and lasted around 30 minutes on average. Our goal was to understand users' help seeking behavior in the context of modern help tools and how users saw LemonAid fit in with these tools. Interviewees had access to LemonAid during the interview to facilitate recall. We also probed into interviewees' perceptions of LemonAid's usability and usefulness, particularly compared to other help formats. We also probed into aspects of LemonAid that the interviewees believed were confusing or could be improved.

Near the end of each deployment period, we also interviewed the software team members involved in the deployments. We began the interviews by probing into teams' perspectives on the experience of integrating LemonAid compared to other forms of help. We also asked interviewees to describe how they currently managed user feedback and whether the feedback was used to inform design decisions. We also showed them usage data captured by LemonAid's Administrative Dashboard and asked them to explore and comment on the utility of the aggregated data, if any. These interviews lasted about 45 minutes.

Analysis

To assess how LemonAid was used in practice and whether LemonAid was helpful, usable, and desirable for reuse, we used the concept of data triangulation [17] and looked for convergence in the logs, survey data, and interview data. We began the analysis by parsing the usage logs to get an overview of usage patterns and help activity in LemonAid (the main variables are shown in Table 2). For the survey responses, we investigated associations between our key outcome variables and user demographics.

To analyze the qualitative data, we audiotaped and transcribed each interview, then organizing, coding, and analyzing with qualitative data analysis software. In the first pass, we coded for data related to questions about LemonAid's usage, and end users' perceptions of utility and usability. In the next pass, we examined interviewees' descriptions of help seeking strategies using an inductive analysis approach [25,35]. This inductive analysis approach was useful for seeing patterns in the data and in identifying recurring themes across the different deployments. A similar inductive approach was also used for analyzing interviews with software team members.

LEMONAID USAGE AND USERS

The first set of results we present concern who used LemonAid and what they did with it, based on the usage data and demographic survey responses.

	LIBRARY	DEPT	EDC	RDB
Length of deployment	15 weeks	6 weeks	8 weeks	8 weeks
# of help sessions	972	185	65	40
# of element selections	2057	509	141	91
# of answer views	562	194	61	36
% of viewed answers marked as helpful	77.7%	71.0%	75.1%	69.2%
# of new questions posted	16	7	3	5
# of answer views on new questions	121	27	30	13
% of answers to new questions marked helpful	74.3%	55.6%	67.7%	57.1%
# of search queries	43	23	4	4

Table 2. Summary of usage activity across the 4 LemonAid deployments.

Role	LIBRARY (n=121)	DEPT (n=33)	EDC (n=9)	RDB (n=5)
Grad Student	40.0%	29.0%	--	--
Undergrad	39.1%	35.5%	--	--
Staff	8.2%	16.1%	100%	100%
Faculty	6.6%	3.2%		
Other	8.0%	12.9%	--	--

Table 3. Distribution of survey respondents' roles. EDC and RDB were restricted access sites accessed only by staff.

LemonAid Usage Activity

To describe the usage activity in LemonAid, we use an individual *help session* as the unit of analysis since we were unable to track individual users. We define a help session as an episode consisting of all the activities that occurred when a user entered the help mode and pressed exit or left the page. In our analysis, we ignored all of the help sessions where entry into the help mode was immediately followed by an exit out of the help mode or the current page. About 20% of the logs followed this pattern.

LemonAid's deployments across the four different sites resulted in over 1,200 help sessions. Table 2 summarizes this activity for each deployment site. Since the LIBRARY site was the longest deployment and had the largest user base, it yielded the highest usage of LemonAid (972 help sessions). The LIBRARY logs showed that 16 new questions were added during the deployment, constituting about 1.6% of the total help sessions. We also found that no end users answered a question; library staff answered all new questions. We did find that the 16 new questions asked by users received 121 views, accounting for about 21.5% of all question views and 74.3% of the corresponding answers were marked as helpful. Prior work has shown that this level of activity is typical of what occurs in technical forums [21,22,24] and more broadly on the Internet (e.g., "*the 1% rule*" [2]) where most users are consumers of online content rather than contributors.

Demographics of Survey and Interview Participants

We received 168 responses to exit surveys across the different deployments (with the highest number of responses from the LIBRARY site (n=121, response rate=12%), followed by the DEPT (n=33, response rate=18%), EDC (n=9, response rate=12%), and RDB (n=5, response rate=13%). A breakdown of the survey respondents based on their role is shown in Table 3. Note that the EDC and RDB sites required authentication and had respondents who were exclusively staff members at the university or an affiliated institution. The LIBRARY and the DEPT sites were largely public sites (with only some features requiring authentication) and garnered responses more broadly from the university's graduate and undergraduate students, staff, faculty, and external visitors.

We interviewed 36 users across the four deployments, with the majority of interviewees being users of the LIBRARY site (18), followed by DEPT (8), EDC (6), and RDB (4). Our interviewees represented a similar proportion of roles as the survey respondents, with graduate students and staff constituting the majority. Table 4 shows the breakdown of the interviewees based on their role. The graduate and undergraduate students came from a range of departments including Psychology, Drama, Communications, Biostatistics, Political Science, Computer Science, Information Science, among others. The staff were primarily from the School of Medicine and affiliated clinical research centers.

Grad Student	31.4%
Staff	25.7%
Undergrad	22.9%
Admin Staff	17.1%
Faculty	2.9%

Table 4. Interviewee roles.

Our survey data for the LIBRARY site showed that the majority of respondents were regular site users, with 70% reporting visiting site the daily or few times a week (Figure 2a). To get a sense of how users normally found help on web sites, we asked respondents to indicate their preferred method of finding help. For the LIBRARY deployment, users' preferred form of help (Figure 2b) differed significantly (Pearson $\chi^2_{(4,N=121)}$=36.15, p<.0001), with "trying on my own" and "using the site help" accounting for most responses (35.5% and 28.9%, respectively).

END USERS' PERSPECTIVES ON LEMONAID

We present our main findings about end users' perceptions of LemonAid by combining quantitative analyses from logs and surveys and qualitative findings from interviews.

Helpfulness of LemonAid

To assess the helpfulness of LemonAid, we sought convergence in our three sources of data: (1) helpfulness of Q&A selections captured during actual use (Figure 1.3); (2) data collected from an exit survey which explicitly asked whether users found something helpful; and, (3) interview data that shed light on why or why not something was helpful.

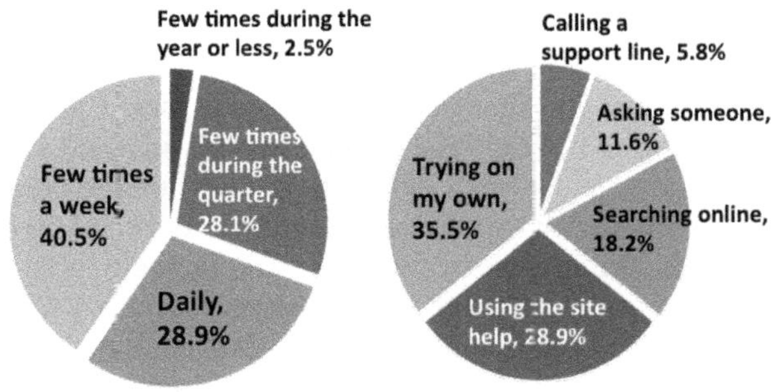

Figure 2. (a) Frequency of site use among LIBRARY users; (b) Preferred method of help seeking among LIBRARY users.

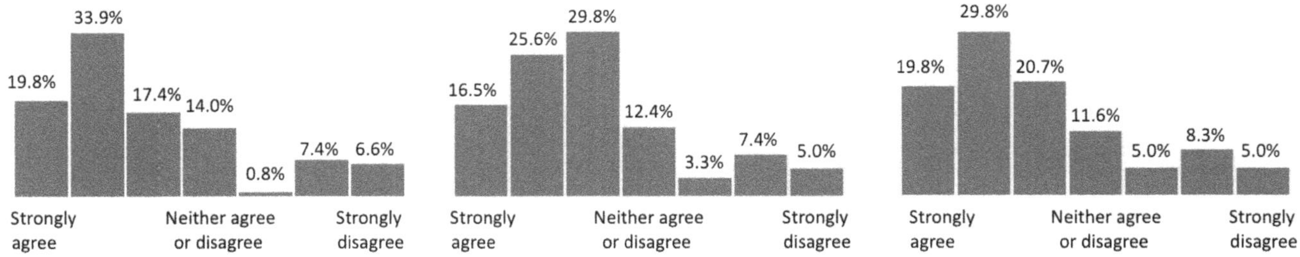

(a) "I found something helpful" **(b)** "I found the help feature to be intuitive" **(c)** "I would use the help feature again"

Figure 3. Distribution of LIBRARY users' survey responses.

Across all four deployment logs, we found that users selected "helpful" for over 73.2% of the viewed answers (LIBRARY=77.7%, DEPT=71.0%, EDC=75.1%, RDB=69.2%, Table 2). There is some noise in this log data—some of our interviewees indicated that they were simply browsing questions and not looking for help on a particular topic, but were forced to assess the helpfulness of the answer set anyway. Still, our exit survey data largely corroborates the log data: 70.6% of respondents on average indicated having found something helpful during the use of LemonAid (LIBRARY=71.1%, DEPT=65.6%, EDC=77.8%, RDB= 80.0%). The distribution of the survey responses from the LIBRARY site is shown in Figure 3a. A majority of users felt LemonAid was helpful (Pearson $\chi^2_{(6,N=121)}$=60.25, p<.0001). Only 14.9% of respondents disagreed at some level that LemonAid was helpful, whereas 71.1% agreed at some level.

We also analyzed whether certain types of users were more likely to find LemonAid helpful. For the LIBRARY data, we found that respondents' frequency of site use was correlated significantly and negatively with whether they felt LemonAid was helpful (Spearman ρ=-.23, N=121, p<.01), meaning users who indicated visiting the site more frequently were less likely to find something helpful through LemonAid. Our interview data corroborates this finding as the more frequent users indicated that they were already familiar with the site's main features and many of the existing help questions were "too basic" for them. In contrast, the interviews consistently revealed that new or less frequent site users found LemonAid to be helpful for learning about unfamiliar parts of the interface:

Well, what I liked about it is that...you might find a question that you didn't even know you had, so I like that...I was just hovering and looking at stuff and somebody asked a question about audio books, and it reminded me, "oh yeah, I need to get an audio book." So I like that about it, so I think it's good in that when you don't have a specific question or you are just looking at what other people are asking, then it's really helpful. (p5)

We analyzed the relationship between users' preferred method for finding help and helpfulness of LemonAid for the LIBRARY data (shown in Table 5). Although this association was not significant (Spearman ρ=.06, N=121, p=.54), we did learn from the interviews that users who normally preferred to find help using the site's existing help through FAQs or documentation found LemonAid's contextual Q&A approach to be more helpful. Although Table 5 shows that users who normally preferred to find help by asking someone were less likely to find LemonAid helpful, this accounted for only about 12% of users overall who asked someone for help (Figure 2b). Many of our interviewees felt that there was often a social cost to asking someone for help. LemonAid, in contrast, allowed users to learn from other people's experiences without having to bother anyone or lose face:

I think that students nowadays like to help themselves a lot more. In terms of figuring out a website, it can be kind of embarrassing to not know how to get around a website. So I think the nice thing about this [LemonAid] is that it's 24/7 and it doesn't require that stepping out of what maybe your comfort zone, you know. If English is your second language, or you're really new...and you're nervous walking up to the librarian at the library, or someone's just not available when you want a question answered, I think it [LemonAid] can be a real positive experience...(p16)

Still, many of our interviewees noted that in-person explanations were richer and allowed opportunity for instant back-and-forth than textual, asynchronous Q&A. Some interviewees also revealed that even if they did not ask others for help, they were sometimes on the *other* side answering technical questions for less tech-savvy family members or friends. In these cases, the interviewees felt that hands-on help was the most preferred form of help (regardless of the available alternatives that improved help retrieval):

They really just want somebody to do it for them. They really don't want to learn, it they just want it done so they'd rather just call someone and have it talked through or done for them even though there's a help function that'll explain it step by step... [p19]

Perhaps more visual, interactive, and synchronous forms of Q&A in future versions of LemonAid could make the content appear more "hands on" and be more helpful for such users.

Usability of LemonAid

Survey responses across *all* deployments indicated that on average 72.5% of users agreed to some extent that the LemonAid help feature was intuitive (LIBRARY=71.9%, DEPT=68.8%, EDC=75.0%, RDB=100.0%). The distribution of the responses from the library deployment is shown in Figure 3b. Users expressed significant agreement as to

	Agree	Neither Agree/Disagree	Disagree
Asking someone	64.3%	14.3%	21.4%
Calling a support line	85.7%	0.0%	14.3%
Searching online	77.3%	4.5%	18.2%
Trying on my own	58.1%	23.3%	18.6%
Using the site help	82.9%	11.4%	5.7%

Table 5. Cross tabulation of LIBRARY users' responses to "preferred method of help" vs. "*I found something helpful*"

LemonAid's intuitiveness (Pearson $\chi^2_{(6,N=121)}$=44.74, p<.0001), with a majority of respondents indicating that they felt LemonAid was intuitive (71.9%).

Our interviews also revealed that most users found the help interface to be easy to understand even though it was their first time using this crowdsourced contextual help tool. One consistent theme was that users appreciated having direct access to help content without having to visit a separate interface, unlike most other help tools:

I liked the visual overlay. I think for a second I thought, "Whoa!" I'm not searching through a separate site to get to the help screen like [default help] where a different window pops up and you scroll through topics...I think that [LemonAid] is extremely intuitive. Having the help topics spread out by the areas in which I would need them as opposed to having a separate window open... (p6)

This finding is consistent with other studies that show that switching modes between an application and help often causes users to forget why help was requested in the first place and it takes them longer to return to their task [9]. Users also liked that they could simply turn off the help mode when finished with their help-seeking task and could return back to the application. But, some users mentioned that if they were working on a complex, multi-step task, going back and forth in the help mode could be distracting and having keyboard short-cuts perhaps would be useful.

Potential Reuse of LemonAid

As our survey and interviews primarily probed the first use of LemonAid, we also wanted to know if users were likely to use it again. Our survey results (Figure 3c) showed that 72.3% of respondents indicated they would use LemonAid again (Pearson $\chi^2_{(6,N=121)}$=44.74, p<.0001): (LIBRARY=70.3%, DEPT=81.3%, EDC=66.7%, RDB=100.0%). Whether users found LemonAid helpful correlated significantly and positively with whether they felt they would reuse LemonAid again (Spearman ρ=.63, N=121, p<.001).

These results are a strong contrast to prior work that has shown that users are frustrated with help systems and fear clicking on help [29]. In fact, about two-thirds of our interviewees said that they would like to see LemonAid even on other sites and desktop applications. For example, one interviewee recounted frustration with a site and its internal help tools she used recently, wishing that she could instead access help via LemonAid on that site:

You search [on the site] and it gives you three very different things. The only two hits have nothing to do with what I want. If there was a LemonAid type help for each section it would help... I could type in the keywords into LemonAid and see how many other administrators across campus have the same question or other questions...that would be helpful! (p21)

Utility of LemonAid Compared to Other Forms of Help

In addition to getting insights about LemonAid's usage, our interviews also focused on understanding how LemonAid compared with modern help tools such as built-in help, FAQs, online searching, and discussion forums.

LemonAid Provides More Relevant Help Content

The majority of interviewees expressed frustration in using current forms of software help. Although a third of the users said they consulted built-in help, the vast majority of users completely avoided consulting help because they feared seeing "long pages of text." Although this behavior has been known for years [29], countless applications still offer only textual built-in help. Users also felt that the built-in help content was often outdated, even though more updated content and tips were available through online channels:

Sometimes it feels that they [tech support] don't go through and update...even if they do set up 5 standard categories, it feels like they're not looking at other message boards to see the huge need for this other thing...they're not adapting and updating that (p23)

In contrast, users felt that the help content in LemonAid was more current and relevant since it could be added and edited at any point and could represent a wide range of actual problems rather than those anticipated by software designers. Furthermore, several users mentioned that the questions and answers in LemonAid were easier to understand than official built-in FAQs that often used a lot of system-specific jargon and were presented in a long list:

FAQ's are a pain because, first of all, they don't use the same language that a normal user would most of the time but rather an internal jargon. I tried LemonAid and I could relate to the questions if I was a student or whoever. This pushes the popular questions out. An FAQ is more like an artificial taxonomy giving a lot of useless information. (p29)

LemonAid Reduces the Burden on Choosing Keywords

Although about 30% of our interviewees said they prefer to search when seeking help, they identified a number of problems with keyword-based searching. One common reason that users were not able to find relevant content was due to the mismatch between how users described their questions versus how other users or system designers may have answered the same questions (the classic "vocabulary problem" [11]). The issue of choosing relevant keywords was particularly acute for non-Native English speakers.

As seen in Table 2, only a small percentage of users ended up using the built-in LemonAid search feature (e.g., there were 43 search queries in the LIBRARY deployment or about 4.4% of all help sessions). Although it is possible that some users may not have noticed this feature, many interviewees pointed out that LemonAid reduced the need to search altogether because they could find relevant questions and answers by clicking around in the interface:

When you're looking at something in the forums, you have to know what it's called...people can call it different things. With the kind of thing you're talking about, you have to know the terms then you may not find what you're looking for...With this [LemonAid], you're like, 'Oh, I don't know what's happening here!', click the Help button, click on what's confusing you and you don't have to worry about inputting any terms, or what it's called; I like that.. (p9)

This supports the key premise behind LemonAid's selection-based retrieval of relevant results, that users will be more able to choose relevant keywords and terms in the UI than to come up with keywords themselves to find help [8].

LemonAid Facilitates In-Context Social Learning

Another recurring theme in our interviews was that users appreciated the social aspects of retrieving help through LemonAid—for example, being able to browse through other users' questions, answers, and votes:

It's sometimes nice to hear what other people's experience is. Sometimes it can be kind of validating. If I'm confused about something, it's nice to know that other people have been similarly confused. (p6)

Users also felt that the discovery of new information or tips through LemonAid was valuable because the content came from other users or staff and not a predefined document. For example, one user of the LIBRARY site explained:

I think [LemonAid] may save time if you are doing research or something like that so you have the ability to get input from other sources very quickly at your fingertips. To me, it's almost like a gold mine in that sense because it leads me into a direction that I may have not been able to get just going through traditional methods. (p14)

Despite the advantages of social learning, some users also raised concerns about the authority and quality of answers posted on forums (and in LemonAid in the future):

You never know the technical level of people in the forum. So sometimes, there's great help...other times, there are people who barely figure out how to turn the thing on, and they're looking for very basic help on the topic, and it's very difficult to differentiate until you just read sometimes pages of content... (p3)

Another user described the frustration of wading through repetitive questions and comments on forums:

...you have to sort through a lot of stuff to get there [answer in a fourm]...and there's repetition, so part of that depends on how well the forum is moderated and how well it's cleaned up so that repetitive answers or answers that are just slightly different but still the same aren't just clogging up the numbers of response... [p11]

Although few users contributed questions and answers in our deployments, it is possible that problems that impede social learning on forums could affect LemonAid as well. However, as some users pointed out, because users invoked LemonAid from within the application rather than from a separate forum, people were perhaps more cautious about posting content because the help seemed "official," as it was overlaid on the application itself. LemonAid perhaps also succeeds in limiting the number of repetitive "I have the same question" comments because users tended to find relevant questions and could express the same sentiment by clicking on *me-too*, rather than posting a new redundant question. In fact, none of the new 16 questions posted on the LIBRARY site were duplicate questions and users voted "me-too" 63 times.

SOFTWARE TEAMS' PERSPECTIVES ON LEMONAID

In addition to understanding end users' perspectives on LemonAid, we also wanted to gauge the reactions of the teams who deployed LemonAid. For each of the deployments, we interviewed the lead developer who handled the integration of LemonAid, and for the LIBRARY and DEPT deployments, we also interviewed one site administrator and two support staff (7 people in total).

Motivation for Integrating LemonAid

Although every software team that we worked with had different motivations for integrating LemonAid, a common theme was that with small teams, it was difficult to offer one-on-one support. Although the sites already offered some forms of built-in help, their developers felt that LemonAid could improve the discoverability of existing help, especially at locations in the interface where users were more likely to need it. Another motivation was curiosity about what kind of questions users would *want* to know answers to.

A more practical motivation was that the developers did not have to change the underlying code of their website:

What was appealing [about LemonAid] was that it was an overlay on top of it [the site] and since you're not requiring me to write any code, I think that's what sold it to me, I didn't have to write any code. It's really easy to do...(T02)

Deploying and Moderating LemonAid

Two teams were initially concerned about the possibility of spam, especially since the tool did not require a login. Despite the initial concerns, we found that spam was not a major issue during the deployments—only 5 questions were marked as spam across the four deployments over several weeks. Upon inspection, we found that 4 of these 5 questions were originally put in by staff and were not actually spam; 1 other question was an incomplete sentence that was marked by a staff member to flag it for removal.

Similar to the concerns of end users, administrators were also concerned about maintaining the quality and accuracy of answers. Furthermore, administrators also had concerns about the "public defacing" that was possible with LemonAid's content overlaid on the site:

[Help through LemonAid] is more on the site...and I really like that. The only thing is that...the information needs to be 100% correct and the people who are able to put in answers to the questions need to really make [sure] that it is [correct], you know, because of liability and lawsuits. (T05)

Another administrator mentioned that he once had to intervene in a discussion on a user mailing list when he sensed that users' answers were projecting incorrect information. He would consider his job in administering LemonAid to be no different:

It definitely takes the load off of the administrators to have users helping each other, right? But you do have to monitor and make sure that they are giving the correct information. I've already seen a few occasions where I had to clarify something on an email [in a mailing list] that some user sent out. (T03)

Utility of LemonAid Analytics Data

Teams had few formal methods for learning about users after deployment. The common theme was gathering basic usage analytics data through services such as Google Analytics. Although teams collected support questions through emails or phone calls, there was no systematic process that teams used to inform designs based on this data. This is consistent with studies that show the disconnect between software support and usability engineering [7].

After asking teams about these existing practices, we showed them the LemonAid data for their site in the form of a basic dashboard, like the one found in web-based analytics tools. Most of the interviewees felt that they were not able to obtain this type of data from anywhere else and LemonAid would be a useful way to augment existing usage-based analytics services. For example, one software developer pointed out that unlike LemonAid, data from tools such as Google Analytics did not reveal users' intentions in terms of why users were clicking on certain areas or spending more time on a particular page:

I think a harder thing to get at in regular analytics is what people actually struggle with...you can get the stuff that they like, you know the stuff that's popular or works well...but stuff that people are confused about, you don't get through regular analytics...and this LemonAid is useful because it's not just about numbers...it's showing the actual questions that people have...and phrased in a way that they [users] would post these questions, in their language...(T04)

Another administrator was particularly excited to see data about what users considered to be relevant questions based on where they clicked and what they voted on:

I think from the useful perspective, just seeing what questions people have on what elements and what are being asked. Because that kind of informs us where we might have some problems, lack of understanding, or where we can do some PR. And that's a lot of where we need some help...how do we make [the site] more accessible? (T07)

Although some team members were enthusiastic about using this data to argue for design and content changes, they also felt that it would be most useful over a longer period of deployment and with greater user participation.

DISCUSSION

The primary goal of this field study was to investigate how users perceive the usability, helpfulness, and reuse value of crowdsourced contextual help in real tasks. Although we found that LemonAid was helpful, intuitive, and desirable for reuse for over 70% of end users across all the deployment sites, our findings point to several social aspects of generating and maintaining help content that should be addressed in the design of crowdsourced contextual help systems.

The majority of concerns raised by end users were about the timeliness, quality, and authority of answers in the long run. As mentioned in our results, frequent site users were less likely to find LemonAid to be helpful than new users. The frequent users often had more advanced questions but were not sure if and when their questions would be answered and who would be providing the answers. Even though staff moderators were ready to promptly answer users' questions as they emerged, the availability and role of moderators in the help interaction could perhaps be conveyed more clearly to users in the interface.

In the current set of deployments, the host teams were able to devote staff time and resources to monitor the questions and provide answers. It may be that to sustain the same level of quality in answers, a long-term commitment from the host teams would be necessary. Since many modern organizations have already opted to create peer-to-peer support forums [22,33], perhaps engaging with users through crowdsourced contextual help will be a natural extension. In particular, the teams felt that investing in one-to-many support is more efficient and provides greater cost-savings in the long run compared to supporting users one-on-one.

Still, in many cases, the true value of crowdsourced help may be from users helping each other, particularly when staff moderators are not the power users of the application. Future work in crowdsourced contextual help should explore strategies for encouraging the contributions of these power users, reducing the burden on staff while maintaining the authority and quality of answers. For example, the badges, awards and leaderboards that help make sites such as *Stack Overflow* successful [23] might translate well to crowdsourced contextual help systems.

Although the web offers a plethora of resources for software help, as seen in our results, about two-thirds of users still preferred to find help by (1) trying on their own, or, (2) using the site's help. This finding suggests that users overall are reluctant to leave the interface when seeking help. Our results further suggest that the majority of users who benefit from modern forms of help (e.g., searching, forums) are more likely to be tech-savvy users. Users who are less tech-savvy are more likely to need help, but they are also less likely to search for help on the web or on forums. Thus, we believe that there is potential in further understanding users' software help-seeking behavior in different contexts and in exploring strategies for delivering more relevant help in the context of the users' tasks. LemonAid and other crowdsourced contextual help systems offer only one step in this direction.

Study Limitations

Our study has several limitations that should be taken into account when interpreting our findings. First, the field study method inherently lacks the control and precision that could be attained in a controlled setting [36]. There is also a sampling bias given that all of our participants had some level of university education and our deployment sites were all hosted within one U.S. university. Some of the initial usage at each site was possibly influenced by a novelty effect as announcements were sent out to users to advertise the feature. Administrators for each site did point out, however, that the number of LemonAid-based help sessions overall were similar to the number of help requests they receive on average. The way the interview data was collected and coded affects its interpretation and there may be alternative explanations.

CONCLUSION

Our field study of LemonAid contributes the first field evaluation of crowdsourced contextual help, showing that LemonAid and similar help systems have a strong potential to both simplify how users find software help, but also provide novel data to software designers about an applications' usability and utility. This study shows that, while difficult, field evaluations can be quite valuable in demonstrating not only that an innovation is valuable, but why it is valuable in the context of social and organizational factors.

ACKNOWLEDGEMENTS

We thank Bryan Dosono, Neeraja Duriseti, Padma Vaithyam, and Diana Djiang for their help with the deployments. We also thank all of the software teams that integrated LemonAid and cooperated with us during the field study. This material is based in part upon work supported by a Facebook PhD Fellowship, Google Research, and the National Science Foundation under Grant Numbers CCF-0952733 and CCF-1153625.

REFERENCES

1. Ackerman, M.S. Augmenting organizational memory: a field study of answer garden. *ACM Trans. Inf. Syst. 16*, 3 (1998), 203–224.
2. Arthur, C. What is the 1% rule? *The Guardian*, 2006.
3. Brandt, J., Dontcheva, M., Weskamp, M., and Klemmer, S.R. Example-centric programming: integrating web search into the development environment. *ACM CHI* (2010), 513–522.
4. Brown, B., Reeves, S., and Sherwood, S. Into the wild: challenges and opportunities for field trial methods. *ACM CHI* (2011), 1657–1666.
5. Carroll, J.M. and Rosson, M.B. *Paradox of the active user.* The MIT Press, 1987.
6. Chilana, P.K., Grossman, T., and Fitzmaurice, G. Modern software product support processes and the usage of multimedia formats. *ACM CHI* (2011), 3093–3102.
7. Chilana, P.K., Ko, A.J., Wobbrock, J.O., Grossman, T., and Fitzmaurice, G. Post-deployment usability: a survey of current practices. *ACM CHI* (2011), 2243–2246.
8. Chilana, P.K., Ko, A.J., and Wobbrock, J.O. LemonAid: selection-based crowdsourced contextual help for web applications. *ACM CHI* (2012), 1549–1558.
9. Clark, I.A. Software simulation as a tool for usable product design. *IBM Systems Journal 20*, 3 (1981), 272–293.
10. Das, A. Knowledge and productivity in technical support work. *Management Science 49*, 4 (2003), 416–431.
11. Furnas, G.W., Landauer, T.K., Gomez, L.M., and Dumais, S.T. The vocabulary problem in human-system communication. *CACM 30,* 11 (1987), 964–971.
12. Goodall, S.D. Online help: a part of documentation. *ACM SIGDOC* (1992), 169–174.
13. Greene, J.C. and Caracelli, V.J. Defining and describing the paradigm issue in mixed-method evaluation. *New Directions for Evaluation 1997*, 74 (1997), 5–17.
14. Grudin, J. Why CSCW applications fail: problems in the design and evaluationof organizational interfaces. *ACM CSCW* (1988), 85–93.
15. Halverson, C.A., Erickson, T., and Ackerman, M.S. Behind the help desk: evolution of a knowledge management system in a large organization. *ACM CSCW* (2004), 304–313.
16. Jiang, W., Hu, C., Pasupathy, S., Kanevsky, A., Li, Z., and Zhou, Y. Understanding customer problem troubleshooting from storage system logs. *USENIX* (2009), 43–56.
17. Jick, T.D. Mixing qualitative and quantitative methods: Triangulation in action. *Admin Sci Quat 24*, 4 (1979), 602–11.
18. Kajko-Mattsson, M. Problems within front-end support. *J Software Maintenance & Evolution 16*, 4-5 (2004), 309–29.
19. Kearsley, G. *Online help systems: design and implementation*. Ablex Publishing Corp., 1988.
20. Klein, H.K. and Myers, M.D. A set of principles for conducting and evaluating interpretive field studies in information systems. *MIS Q. 23*, 1 (1999), 67–93.
21. Ko, A.J. and Chilana, P.K. How power users help and hinder open bug reporting. *ACM CHI* (2010), 1665–1674.
22. Lakhani, K.R. and Von Hippel, E. How open source software works:"free" user-to-user assistance. *Research policy 32*, 6 (2003), 923–943.
23. Mamykina, L., Manoim, B., Mittal, M., Hripcsak, G., and Hartmann, B. Design lessons from the fastest q&a site in the west. *ACM CHI* (2011), 2857–2866.
24. Matejka, J., Grossman, T., and Fitzmaurice, G. IP-QAT: In-product questions, answers, & tips. *ACM UIST* (2011), 175-84.
25. Miles, M.B. and Huberman, A.M. *Qualitative Data Analysis: An Expanded Sourcebook*. Sage Pub, 1994.
26. Negash, S., Ryan, T., and Igbaria, M. Quality and effectiveness in web-based customer support systems. *Information & Management 40*, 8 (2003), 757–768.
27. Novick, D.G., Elizalde, E., and Bean, N. Toward a more accurate view of when and how people seek help with computer applications. *ACM SIGDOC* (2007), 95–102.
28. Olsen Jr, Dan R. Evaluating user interface systems research. *ACM UIST* (2007), 251-258.
29. Rettig, M. Nobody reads documentation. *Commun. ACM 34*, 7 (1991), 19–24.
30. Rieman, J. A field study of exploratory learning strategies. *ACM Trans. Comput.-Hum. Interact. 3*, 3 (1996), 189–218.
31. Sellen, A. and Nicol, A. Building user-centered on-line help. *Human-computer interaction*, Morgan Kaufmann (1995), 718–723.
32. Singh, V. and Twidale, M.B. The confusion of crowds: non-dyadic help interactions. *ACM CSCW* (2008), 699–702.
33. Steehouder, M.F. Beyond technical documentation: users helping each other. *IEEE IPCC* (2002), 489– 499.
34. Stevens, G. and Wiedenhöfer, T. CHIC - a pluggable solution for community help in context. *ACM NordiCHI* (2006), 212-21.
35. Strauss, A. and Corbin, J. *Basics of Qualitative Research: Techniques and Procedures for Developing Grounded Theory*. Sage Publications Inc, 1998.
36. Yin, R.K. The case study method as a tool for doing evaluation. *Current Sociology 40*, 1 (1992), 121–137.
37. TurboTax Support. http://turbotax.intuit.com/support/.

A Pilot Study of Using Crowds in the Classroom

Steven Dow
HCI Institute
Carnegie Mellon University
spdow@cs.cmu.edu

Elizabeth Gerber
Segal Institute of Design
Northwestern University
egerber@northwestern.edu

Audris Wong
Department of Economics
Carnegie Mellon University
audriswong@cmu.edu

ABSTRACT
Industry relies on higher education to prepare students for careers in innovation. Fulfilling this obligation is especially difficult in classroom settings, which often lack authentic interaction with the outside world. Online crowdsourcing has the potential to change this. Our research explores if and how online crowds can support student learning in the classroom. We explore how scalable, diverse, immediate (and often ambiguous and conflicting) input from online crowds affects student learning and motivation for project-based innovation work. In a pilot study with three classrooms, we explore interactions with the crowd at four key stages of the innovation process: needfinding, ideating, testing, and pitching. Students reported that online crowds helped them quickly and inexpensively identify needs and uncover issues with early-stage prototypes, although they favored face-to-face interactions for more contextual feedback. We share early evidence and discuss implications for creating a socio-technical infrastructure to more effectively use crowdsourcing in education.

Author Keywords
Crowdsourcing, innovation, education, feedback.

ACM Classification Keywords
H.5.3 [Group and Organization Interfaces]: Crowdsourcing

INTRODUCTION
Educating students about innovation practices can be difficult in classroom settings, where students typically lack interaction with the real world. To facilitate a more authentic environment, many institutes have integrated interdisciplinary project-based learning approaches into their formal curricula [10,11,24]. While this approach effectively teaches teamwork and open-ended problem solving, students typically only receive formative feedback from a few instructors, peers, or target users. There exists a need for instructional methods and technologies that engage authentic users' opinions and realistic market forces. *Can online crowds fulfill this need?*

The modern Web allows anyone to leverage the scale, diversity, and immediacy of online crowds. Everyday, people can pose complex problems to the crowd [41], hire a consultant to build a prototype [42], create a competition to design a logo for a new venture [43,44], test two different versions of a website [18,31,45], raise funds from thousands of online donors [46], or promote an idea through social networks [47] or online advertising [48].

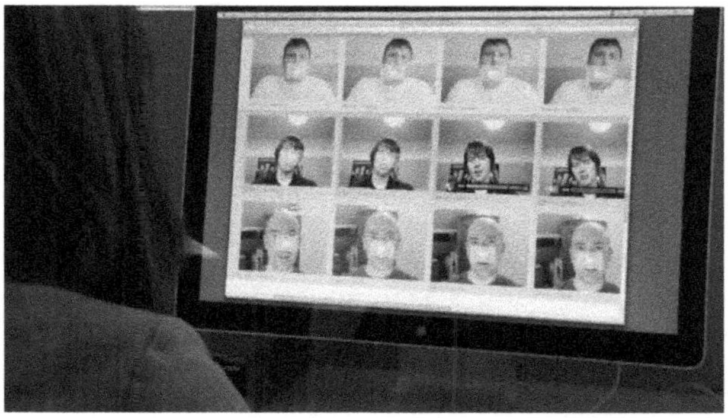

Figure 1: Student getting feedback from potential consumers on a crowdsourcing platform, MindSwarms.com

These emerging crowd technologies are changing how people innovate. As a motivating example, two friends with an idea but few connections to capital used Facebook to get feedback on their novel coffee invention and then raised $306,944 in 34 days on a crowdfunding platform to manufacture and fulfill orders for their product [49]. In the process of using these crowd-based technologies, they learned how to develop an innovative coffee product, how to communicate the idea, and how to manage customers' feedback — key tasks associated with innovation [12]. Eight months after launching their product, they were invited to the White House to be recognized as one of top 100 companies run by young innovators [49]. This case study illustrates the potential of crowd-based technology to support innovation learning. While many businesses have embraced crowd-based technologies [50], human computer interaction (HCI) and education researchers have yet to explore the efficacy of such techniques for innovation education.

Crowd-based technologies have the potential to transform innovation education by providing a link between the public and traditional, isolated classrooms. Our proposed approach builds on the "Learning by Design" framework where learners take on design challenges, learn principles through participation, and get feedback through regular and public interaction [20]. Further, following on Shaffer and Resnick's "thick" view of authenticity, we hypothesize that crowd-based technology makes learning more personally meaningful to the learner and connects educational activities with real-world outcomes [30]. Such an approach models an innovation process with real beneficiaries and benefactors and provides assessments that align instructor feedback with feedback from external parties — building on theories of cognitive apprenticeship [6].

While online crowds have the potential to shape innovation education, these resources also present a risk to students. Online crowds can be inconsistent and undereducated [17]. Online crowds may misunderstand the context for innovation and lack concern for the innovation goals and/or the learners' goals [22].

To better understand the benefits and risks of employing crowd-based methods in innovation education, we conducted a pilot study integrating the crowd into classroom settings at two universities. We explored the use of crowds on four key stages of the innovation process: *needfinding* to identity real world opportunities, *ideating* to generate novel and useful solutions to a problem, *testing* prototypes through feedback from potential consumers and users, and *pitching* novel solutions to obtain early-stage funding. Within these stages of innovation, we developed pedagogical interventions aimed to leverage different crowd-based technology (see Table 1).

In this paper, we begin by describing the limitations of contemporary approaches to innovation education and the potential benefits and risks of introducing online crowds into the classroom. We provide detailed descriptions of the interventions for the pilot course and share student reflections as captured from essays, blog entries, and a summative open-ended questionnaire. Our data suggest that while students valued the crowd as a source of cognitive stimuli during the early stages of the innovation process, they struggled with the noise and uncertainty of crowd data – preferring the clarity and richness of interacting with people face-to-face as the innovation process progressed. Further, students expressed anxiety about asking the crowd, particularly friends and family, for financial resources to crowdfund their project work. We conclude the paper with a discussion of implications for creating a socio-technical infrastructure to more effectively use crowdsourcing platforms in innovation education.

APPROACHES TO INNOVATION EDUCATION

In a climate of international competition and economic uncertainty, there is an increasing need for strong innovators: individuals who can understand real problems, creatively generate solutions, build and test prototypes, and pitch and carry them forward to implementation [12]. To meet this need, innovation education has evolved to accommodate student needs through business case studies and project-based learning. Further, industry-sponsored internships and extracurricular initiatives help extend innovation education beyond the classroom [38].

Business Case Studies

In the early twentieth century, the Harvard Business School introduced case studies to provide students with historical descriptions of actual business situations [51]. Case studies fulfilled a need that textbooks failed to provide: authentic information about an organization's products, competition, financial structure, and other factors that affect business decision-making. Students read the case studies and think through strategies the firm could employ moving forward. Through interactive discussions, students debate opposing views and begin to recognize the underlying learning objectives [51]. Many business schools have replicated and transformed this approach to bring real-world situations into the classroom.

Innovation Stage	Goal of Innovation Stage	Crowd-based technology
Needfinding	Identity real-world opportunities	Special-interest blogs, Twitter, and Facebook
Ideating	Generate novel and useful solutions to a problem	Amazon Mechanical Turk
Testing	Elicit feedback on prototypes from potential consumers and users	MindSwarms and Amazon Mechanical Turk
Pitching	Obtain early-stage funding	IndieGoGo and Kickstarter

Table 1: Our crowd-enhanced curriculum for innovation education explored a range of crowd platforms across four stages of innovation.

Project-Based Learning

Beyond reading and discussion, universities increasingly integrate project-based courses into their formal curricula to give students hands-on experience seeking opportunities, taking risks, and pushing ideas into reality [21]. In these classes, student teams typically partner with an industry client to solve real-world problems and receive mentoring by expert coaches from industry. While instructors simplify the innovation process, they aim to give students an authentic experience within classroom constraints. For example, projects conclude by pitching a new product or venture to an external review board or competing in a simulated market [11]. Instructors use these final presentations and competitions as well as self-evaluation and peer-assessments to assign grades to students [7,11].

Project-based classes are often taught by a single discipline, such as business [28] or engineering [10], or taught by an interdisciplinary team of instructors from these disciplines [11]. Students typically take innovation project-based classes taught as a first year cornerstone class, a senior year capstone class [10], or as an elective graduate course. Class sizes range from 16 at Northwestern University to 300 at Boston University [11]. Students find these project-based approaches to innovation education an improvement over traditional lecture-based and content-centered classes because they experience the challenges and excitement of innovation first hand [4].

While most project-based courses involve interaction in a physical classroom, a number of institutions are exploring online project-based learning. Students interact online with professors and industry leaders, and learn about innovation from experts throughout the world [52,53]. While project-based learning and online learning experiences extend learning beyond the temporal and spatial boundaries of higher education, students demand even more real-world experiences [38].

Real World Experience

In response, many educational institutions support situated learning through industry-sponsored summer internships. Further, students are choosing to work together outside of class time on real-world projects through extracurricular activities such as robotics competitions [54], solar car teams [55], "hackathons" [56], and design studios [13]. Such student-driven initiatives emphasize the co-creation of knowledge by students, peer mentors, professionals, and faculty in a non-evaluative environment over an extended timeframe. The challenges are often complex societal challenges and demand regular testing and feedback from communities of practice [13]. Not only are such initiatives popular among students, researchers have shown they positively impact students confidence and skills related to innovation, such as applying technology to business needs [27]. This paper explores how educators may utilize online crowds to bring in more of these real-world interactions.

USING CROWDS IN THE CLASSROOM

Crowdsourcing allows someone to recruit a large group of people online to perform work towards a common goal [15]. Crowds have been tapped for numerous creative activities, such as submitting visual designs for contests [43], sketching creative combinations [40], and creating animated movies and cartoons [57].

Several properties of online crowds give it potential to use as an intervention in the classroom. It is relatively easy to hire a large crowd and to get results in a short amount of time [2]. Crowds are also relatively inexpensive to hire, especially on platforms like Amazon Mechanical Turk, where the majority of tasks pay less than one US dollar [16]. Online crowds can be diverse with people of different genders, races, nationality, languages, education, skills, and so on [29]. These crowd properties lend themselves to different aspects of innovation, such as providing inspiration through generation of sample designs [36] or feedback on existing ideas [39], where innovators seek many diverse perspectives at a low cost.

The same properties of crowds that inspire potential for innovation may also present risks. Workers on Amazon Mechanical Turk are notoriously inconsistent and often try to cut corners [14,17]. Simple efforts in task design, such as making the work more meaningful [5], inserting gold standard questions [17], priming workers with visual stimuli [22], and providing workers feedback [9] can improve work quality. Despite these approaches, information produced by crowds can often be noisy, ambiguous, and contradictory. Pedagogical interventions that use online crowds have the prospect of adding uncertainty to an already inexact innovation process.

METHOD

We conducted a pilot study to examine if and how crowds can support innovation in the classroom.

Study Context and Participants

Fifty students (28 male, 22 female) participated in our study. The students were enrolled in one of three human centered innovation classes offered by Carnegie Mellon University and Northwestern University. The first class was an elective masters' level class taking place at Carnegie Mellon University from January to May in 2012. The second class was a required masters' level class, while the third class was an elective undergraduate level class. The second and third classes took place at Northwestern University from April to June in 2012.

Master's students had zero to eight years of professional experience and were seeking advanced training to take leadership roles in industry. The undergraduate students were juniors and seniors and had limited professional experience. Participants' focus of study included engineering, design, psychology, education, and business.

In these classes, the students worked in 3-4 member project teams to solve real world problems ranging from helping senior citizens receive accurate and speedy prescription refills at pharmacies to promoting more accessible voting. The primary aim of the class was to provide opportunities for students to develop skills they will need for professional practice in design, engineering, and business and to adopt the habits of mind required for leadership and human-centered innovation.

Pedagogical Interventions

Like the project-based innovation classes we described above, our students engaged in traditional activities related to needfinding, ideating, testing, and pitching. They observed users in context during the needfinding stage, brainstormed ideas with their team during the ideating phase, created paper prototypes and tested them with users face-to-face, and they pitched their ideas (in verbal and written format) to a live audience during mid-term and final presentations. However, to supplement each stage, we introduced the crowd-based activities described below. For each innovation stage, we describe the learning objectives, the potential for online crowds to enhance student learning, and details about crowd-based pedagogical activities.

Needfinding

Innovation students should learn how to identify and understand real opportunities to make an impact [11]. Following a needs-driven process, students learn how to engage in contextual inquiry observing consumers and their behavior in the context of their lives [3,24]. Students seek to understand diverse stakeholder perspectives, investigate all possible causes of a problem, and begin to empathize with the potential beneficiaries. From this needfinding process, students extract out key facts and constraints, and form opportunity statements that set the stage for ideating novel solutions.

During this stage, online crowds have the potential to help students gain a deeper understanding of needs and to stay motivated throughout their project. Social media, where crowds share intimate thoughts and concerns online, can help students tap into diverse and personal perspectives. Casting a wider net can help students avoid bias and premature solution generation. It could also have motivational benefits if students can better understand the scale and the extent of the need they are addressing.

In our courses, the needfinding intervention began with a 20-minute lecture on social media analysis. Students read case studies of how professionals collect and analyze social media to determine the needs of their users and what demands exist for certain solutions. As a take home assignment, students were asked to conduct three in-person interviews and to harvest at least fifty comments or blog entries from one or more online forums that talk about the problem space. During class, students shared and collaboratively analyzed their preliminary findings with students from other teams and later delivered a short presentation of their social media data analysis and the key opportunities areas in class.

Ideating

Student innovators must learn to generate or produce solutions that are both novel and useful [32]. To support creative problem solving, students typically learn techniques for group brainstorming where people generate a large quantity of solutions to a given problem [26]. Quantity increases the likelihood that one will be successfully implemented [34].

Online crowds have the potential to significantly increase the number of valid ideas on the table, but only if the crowd understands the problem space and contextual constraints. The diverse demographics of crowds can produce an abundance of ideas that either confirm or expand students' thinking and give them more paths forward.

In our courses, the ideation intervention began two weeks after the first intervention with a 20-minute lecture on different brainstorming and synthesis techniques [19,26] and the operational details of using Mechanical Turk (getting an account, paying, designing a task, etc). First, students were asked to generate at least 50 ideas on their own. Then, student teams were asked to recruit 40 crowd workers to generate at least 5 ideas each with the goal of seeding 200 or more ideas for their problem space. Students used one or more synthesis techniques and narrowed the idea space down to about six possible solutions that could be prototyped in the next phase of the project. During an in-class critique, students described their ideation process and presented the top three to six of their most promising ideas from both the crowd and their own brainstorming session.

Figure 2: Screenshot of one student teams' alternative designs for A-B testing on Amazon's Mechanical Turk.

Testing

While many people have creative ideas, testing a concrete manifestation of an idea helps student innovators yield rich feedback from users, peers, and experts [23]. Prototypes help people construct new knowledge through hands-on experimentation [35]. When creating prototypes, students reason about uncertainty, make estimates, and choose among alternatives [10].

At this stage, online crowds have the potential to generate formative feedback that can help students shape specific design solutions. Students potentially find value in the rapid turnaround and the authenticity of getting input from an audience outside of instructors and classroom peers.

For this stage of innovation, we attempted two different interventions for obtaining feedback from crowds: online "speed dating" [8] and A-B testing [18]. Course lectures covered storyboarding, "speed dating", wireframing, Web analytics, and A-B testing. At CMU, students sketched storyboards for six of their proposed solutions and then gathered feedback online using a service called MindSwarms[1], where consumers record one-minute long responses to questions [58]. Each of the team's six storyboards yielded twenty-eight video clips. The following week, students presented their findings about how people reacted to their ideas and provided rationale for which idea(s) they were going to develop into a prototype.

The courses at CMU and Northwestern University both offered a unit on A-B testing. Students created two different solutions to compare (see Figure 2). CMU students created working Web prototypes; NU students created wireframes. Students hosted their solutions online, installed Google Analytics to collect usage data, and prepared an online questionnaire to gather qualitative feedback. Student teams were asked to solicit feedback and usage data from at least thirty workers on Mechanical Turk. Students shared the results of their A-B testing during in-class presentations.

Pitching

In innovation education, students learn to clearly and succinctly state the problem and promote their proposed solution [25]. Students learn basic communication concepts including audience, genre, and purpose [24]; they also

[1] MindSwarms typically charges a professional fee, but provided limited access to students for free to support this research.

practice communicating with clients and peers using text, graphics, charts, and oral presentations. Instructors increasingly require students to use basic video editing in programs such as iMovie to present their concept to a panel of "experts" at the end of the semester.

At this stage, online crowds have the potential to serve as an "authentic" audience to judge the efficacy of student solutions. This authenticity can encourage students to continually refine their pitch to connect with diverse audiences. Moreover, it can give students an opportunity to vet solutions that may have real market potential.

In our courses, the pitch project followed two weeks after the prior intervention. Lectures covered crowdfunding, early-stage funding, and the basic components of a crowdfunding campaign. For their main assignment, student teams created an IndieGoGo or Kickstarter crowdfunding campaign. Students wrote a script, sketched a storyboard for a video, and then produced a video no longer than three minutes. To promote their campaign, students wrote a project description for the crowdfunding platform, designed a reward structure for their funders, and created shorter versions of their project description appropriate for different social media (ex. Facebook, Twitter, etc). Student teams gave final presentations of their crowdfunding pitch in class. Northwestern students did not have time to launch their campaigns due to their shorter ten-week term. The Carnegie Mellon students launched and promoted their crowdfunding campaigns for four weeks and shared their campaign results in the final presentation.

In all, the total in-class time devoted to these four crowd-based interventions was approximately four hours out of a possible 40-60 hours of instruction.

Data Collection

Throughout the term, the main co-authors (who also served as course instructors) collected observations of students' attitudes and actions related to the pedagogical interventions. We collected written reflections after each intervention and the "raw input" provided by the crowd. At the conclusion of the course, all students completed a thirty-minute online survey in Qualtrics [59] asking them to reflect on each of the four crowd-based interventions. Survey responses were anonymous with a response rate of 100%. The survey primarily investigated these questions:

- How did students react to crowd-enhanced interventions in the innovation process?
- Does interacting with the crowd throughout the innovation process influence the products and services they create, and if so, how?

Data Analysis

We employed selective coding and analysis to understand the experience of crowd-based interventions [33]. First, we read through all of the responses, flagging each instance where students described their experience with a particular intervention. We did not have a categorization scheme a priori since we did not know how students' would react to crowd-based interventions. After identifying instances of experiences, we clustered them into conceptual categories. At this stage of the research, we were interested in capturing students' overall perceptions of crowd work and how these may have evolved throughout the course. The data is primarily qualitative and we report the quotes in the original form as provided by the students.

FINDINGS

Our findings cover the courses from both Carnegie Mellon (CMU) and Northwestern (NU). We report initial findings according to four stages of the innovation process: need-finding, ideating, testing, and pitching. In each stage, we identify opportunities and challenges with the goal of better understanding how we engage the crowd in innovation education.

Needfinding: Social Media Help Uncover Diverse Needs

Our evidence suggests the crowd can support innovation education by helping students to identify and scope real world opportunities. Engaging with the crowd is particularly useful at the beginning of the innovation process when students have limited domain expertise and need a broad understanding of the problem space. On average, students consulted twenty-three different web sources and collected data from about fifty perspectives. A graduate student described social media as a *"stepping off point"* for the project and useful for *"researching the scope of possible ideas."* A graduate student in engineering remarked, that the social media analysis was particularly *"useful when we [were] less familiar with pain points in the field."* Another student described the social media analysis as *"very cool,"* because it provided a compelling way to quickly survey an unfamiliar domain using a familiar medium.

Many students perceived the social media analysis as more efficient than other qualitative research methods. One student compared the efficiency of social media analysis to the often time-consuming process of arranging and conducting qualitative interviews with stakeholders:

"...it would have taken us a lot longer to conduct the same amount of research and to structure our project."

While efficient and inexpensive, students identified limitations of the social media analysis. Although many opinions are captured in social media, some populations of interest share less. Students struggled to conduct a social media analysis for crowds with low web visibility. An undergraduate design student remarked:

"I don't think social media helped at all since it was a project based on helping [a specific] community and there isn't much social media on [this particular community]".

Because of the lack of existing social media on his chosen topic, the student created a Facebook page asking his friends to comment on their personal experience with the problem he was tackling. Within 24 hours, the page had over 100 "friends" who had contributed comments about their experience. In class, he expressed surprise and satisfaction that so many people had thoughts to share, but had no outlet for doing so.

Once the social media data was collected, the students categorized the remarks according to behaviors, feelings, and thoughts. Due to the abundance and richness of the data, many students requested more time to analyze the data. One student complained that she did *"not have enough time"* to fully analyze the rich data she had collected. Another student reiterated her concern that she was both learning a new data collection technique (social media mining) as well as an analysis technique.

"The instruction was not clear to those who do not have an HCI background."

In addition to more time spent in analysis, students also wanted to better understand the history and case studies of using social media in the innovation process. One student offered a particular suggestion.

"I would have liked to have had more time learning how the designers of those services used such tools."

While students found social media useful during the early stages of the understanding process, the usefulness of social media mining declined as students narrowed their project scope and better understood their problem domain. As one student explained,

"It seemed to just confirm information that we had already known."

After the initial excitement of understanding stakeholders using social media, students admitted to preferring the richness of contextual inquiry. A student noted: *"Talking to people in context was far more interesting."*

The evidence suggests that social media analysis provides a rapid research tool for understanding a problem space in very early stages; however, contextual inquiry remains critical and preferable for revealing deeper insights.

Ideating: Crowds Produce a Large Quantity of Ideas

Our findings suggest that Mechanical Turk was helpful for generating a large number of ideas for the problems the students identified during the needfinding process. However, students were disappointed in the quality.

On average, teams generated 74 unique solutions on their own. Teams then paid an average of 28 MTurk workers $0.25 to generate 5 ideas each, yielding a total of about 140 ideas per group, and roughly 75% of ideas were unique. An undergraduate student described the pleasure and usefulness of generating ideas with the crowd: *"I really liked building up this massive number of ideas."*

Not only was ideating with the crowd fun and helpful for generating a large number of ideas, students found the ideation process liberating. A master's student described her experience. *"We got to let loose and create more crazy ideas, which was enjoyable."*

However, ideation requires not only generating a large number of novel ideas but also generating useful ideas. Students expressed disappointment with the crowd's ability to generate useful ideas. One master's student explained:

"The quality of the responses was too low and I don't think even one of the Turker's ideas made it into our final 10."

In addition to the low quality, students found the responses to be redundant to other respondents in the crowd. One undergraduate student reported: *"MTurk ideas are largely overlapping with each other."*

Should the quality of ideas improve, students felt that individuals in the crowd should be identified and credited for their contribution. A student generating ideas for her project reported her concern:

"I don't know if it's valid to just use the idea from Turkers without giving them any credit."

We found students were motivated to work with the crowd to generate a large quantity of ideas, however they expected the same quality that might result from working with an established team member who understands the context and is incentivized to generate high quality ideas. With overly high expectations, students may lean on the crowd for ideas, rather than simply using the ideas as a springboard towards a more refined concept. This can be particularly problematic for students new to working with the crowd and learning the innovation process.

Testing: Crowds Helped Shape Student Concepts

Our data suggest that online crowds can support classroom innovation by providing students with feedback on prototypes. Students praised the speed and diverse points of view, but also commented on the lack of interactivity from the particular crowd tools used for this intervention. At CMU, where students got video-based feedback on early-stage storyboards from participants at MindSwarms, one student praised the speed of the crowd feedback:

"I can't think of other better ways to get a lot of user input very quickly."

The students found the crowd to represent of a "broad" set of target users. A student working on a redesign of a service commented:

"[MindSwarms] was great tool that helps designers connect with potential target people easily."

Another student explained the usefulness of crowd feedback as obtaining *"different opinions from each other."* As expected, students used the feedback to inform the next steps of their project. A student explained: *"[It] helped direct and improve our design of prototype."*

Although many students described the feedback from MindSwarms as "better" than the feedback received through Mechanical Turk, students were more suspicious of the veracity of the feedback. A student described her concern:

"I have the nagging feeling that the people were too positive and were just trying to guess which answer we wanted in order to make us happy."

Another downside to the particular crowdsourcing platforms selected for prototyping and testing was that neither enabled back and forth interaction with the crowd. A master's student explained:

"I think [MindSwarms] is better than MTurk, but still, I'm not sure if that's a good way to do evaluation because we cannot instruct people about the correct way to understand our ideas."

Similarly, another student reported:

"We can't really interact with [the crowd]... [I] have follow up questions... to figure out what they think and want."

Unlike testing concepts with close friends or family, testing with the crowd prevented students from clarifying their concepts when collecting feedback or reconnecting with users at later stages in the testing.

The usefulness of the feedback may have also been affected by the student's ability to express their ideas in different media. Students who struggled to communicate their ideas found it intimidating to test ideas with the crowd. One student explained the relationship between his technical drawing skills and his enjoyment with the testing phase.

"I did not enjoy this [stage] much mainly because I'm not very good at getting my ideas across through drawings. This is something I need to work on."

At both CMU and NU, students conducted A-B testing and recruited participants from MTurk. While students again reported enjoying learning about A-B testing and specific crowd-based platforms, several students suggested that they were not quite ready for this level of A-B testing.

"I felt that the amount of time available and the fidelity of the prototype does not provide a strong case for A-B tests or web analytics. It could have been better to test the usability of the interface using techniques like think-alouds with less number of users. I feel that would have given us more insights compared to log analysis and A-B testing."

A student reiterated the point that A-B testing is perhaps best reserved for higher fidelity prototypes.

"I think the A-B test and Web analytics would be more useful for a complete system, or prototype with several screens. A think aloud test could have been more useful."

Students seemed to prefer communicating with people who could give them rich feedback. One student disliked talking with users entirely and would have preferred receiving feedback from peers during class time: *"I preferred the small feedback sessions with smaller groups."*

Another student reiterated her enthusiasm, reporting:

"I love learning from my classmates, hearing about their ideas, and receiving feedback from them!"

Overall, students benefited from their interactions with online crowds, but they wanted richer, more interactive communication. This suggests that online crowds may serve best as a supplement to face-to-face techniques for helping students get feedback on innovation concepts.

Pitching: Crowds Demand Accountability

Our data suggest that while students found preparing pitches for a crowdfunding campaign useful, launching and running an actual campaign was challenging due to the added responsibilities and pressure of delivering a product or service after the class ended.

Students began by researching the requirements for either the IndieGoGo or Kickstarter crowdfunding platforms and then opened an account. Next, they wrote a pitch to identify and direct their appeal to a target audience. Students also storyboarded scripts, and recorded and edited 1-3 minute video using simple video editing software such as iMovie. This activity caused them to consider the potential differences between users (those who use) and financial backers (those who provide financial resources) and motivations for backing a project.

Whether they launched their campaign (CMU students) or not (NU students), all students prepared budgets for executing their campaign. Budgets ranged from $1,310 to $14,000. The CMU students who actually launched their campaigns raised an average of $391, approximately 22% of the combined funding goal. No groups met their funding goal, but one raised as much as $870 (64% of their goal).

Overall, students appreciated what they learned by going through the steps of creating a pitch, as one student said:

I enjoyed this project because this skill of pitching an idea will be need[ed]...in my future work.

Another student reiterated the real-world nature of the activity and the confidence it fostered.

"It gave me the feeling that I could plan and execute a decent crowdfunding campaign for real when I needed money for a venture."

Students learned about the repetitive nature of pitching and the necessity of asking again and again. One student commented: *"I learned crowdfunding is tedious."*

While students found crowdfunding novel, they were uncomfortable asking people in their network for financial support, despite evidence that campaigns typically first gain momentum through close ties [60]. A student described her concern for asking for money when she felt she could not provide a valuable reward for investing.

"I think the experience of conducting a [crowdfunding] campaign is interesting... [but] I am concerned about the fund raising, especially from close friends and family. It feels that asking for a hundred dollar gift from your friend [is not fair], when we have [nothing] to return to them."

Another student reiterated this concern about the motivations required to run a successful crowdfunding campaign.

"The main problem with the crowdfunding piece of the class was that few students, as far as I could tell, actually wanted to raise the money. Most students in the class have other plans and weren't planning to continue working on their idea. Crowdfunding is great if you are passionate about an idea and really driven to make it happen, but the context of a course project didn't quite fit that."

While the instructors explicitly told students they would not be graded on how much funding they raise, many students expressed disappointment when they did not reach their funding goal and they realized the majority of fundraising came from friends and family. A student explained:

"As most of our funding is from the friends or family. I felt sad [about] this result."

Students discounted the financial backing as positive feedback because most of the funding came from friends and family.

"Next time [the class should] just ask for and collect money from strangers so it's a real way to test whether or not you have a good pitch of your project, not anything else."

Most students would prefer not to rely on friends and family at all. But as one student explained, he could envision asking for support if his intentions were true.

"To me it wouldn't be awkward at all just to ask my family or friends to do things if I decided to do it for real. I think the most awkward point, to me, is that in my pitch video I talked about 'we see this problem and we'd like to do this', but in our minds, we already know that this is just going to be a prototype that cannot be put in the real world. So that made me feel really weird about asking my friends and family, because they say 'so is it going to be a real thing?' and when I say 'no' then 'why should I donate?'"

A handful of students did not consider pitching as a critical skill for innovators, and consequently, they were hesitant to participate in crowdfunding. *"I don't understand how it relates to creativity in any real manner."*

Overall, students valued the experience of preparing materials for a crowdfunding campaign. However, launching the actual campaign proved challenging to students who did not have ideas they actually wanted to pursue. Consequently, they resented the responsibilities and expectations required for actual implementation.

Overall Student Impressions

Students enjoyed using contemporary tools, referring to them as "novel" and "cool." As one student remarked:

"Being exposed to sites like Kickstarter ...learning about tools out there to get feedback, [and] talking to more people ... was interesting."

Students were also attracted to the idea of interacting with people beyond the walls of their classroom. As one student described:

"I've learned in this project how great it can be to connect people and share ideas."

Further, the inexpensive and targeted interaction appealed to students who were strapped for cash and time.

DISCUSSION

Increasingly, students, industry, and the academy demand educational experiences that bridge to real-world situations. Online crowds provide one potential solution. This solution ties deeply into two ongoing trends. 1) Many students increasingly turn to the crowd to find information and to connect through social networks; our solution embraces these behaviors in an educational setting. 2) To have a successful career in HCI or innovation, students will need to be prepared to learn skills such as crowdsourcing, data mining, and online experimentation.

The research reveals many advantages and challenges of engaging online crowds in the classroom. In the early stages of the innovation process, crowds helped uncover diverse needs for students. As the process progressed into the ideating and testing stages, students valued the relative ease of obtaining a large quantity of feedback from online crowds, but were often disappointed with the low quality due to the lack of context. In general, students were positive about creating crowdfunding campaigns, however launching the actual campaign proved challenging to students who did not have ideas they actually wanted to pursue. These outcomes supported our focus on teaching students how to gather, analyze, and take action based on data from online crowds. As instructors, we are more concerned that students learn new methods (process outcomes), rather than produce novel innovations (product outcomes).

While online crowds elevated the amount of information and the authenticity of their projects, we use the emerging key challenges to propose three guiding design principles for future crowd-enhanced courses: 1) set expectations, 2) enable deeper interactions, and 3) handle uncertainty.

Set Expectations

When integrating the crowd into the classroom, instructors should set expectations appropriately. For needfinding and ideating, crowds seem to be most useful for stimulating cognition, not supplanting it. Instructors can introduce crowd-enhanced activities alongside other HCI creativity support tools such as Idea expander [37] and Momentum [1], which display images to facilitate team ideation. While such tools are generally helpful, in some cases, they can be distracting or provide too much stimuli when focused attention is needed. Like professional innovators, students need to learn when more or less stimulation is needed.

Enable Deeper Interactions

Crowd-based interactions are designed for resource exchange, be it financial or information. While engaging with the crowd lowers the cost and speed of this exchange, it potentially increases the quantity of resources available to the student, and indirectly, the responsibility required by the student to appropriately manage the resources. When launching their crowdfunding campaigns at CMU, many students asked for financial resources they did not desire or intend to follow through with. We suggest concluding the class with a completed, but un-launched campaign so that students do not need to have interactions for which they cannot follow through. If funding is a component, instructors need to teach students how to get funding from people other than friends and family.

Handle Uncertainty

Students need instruction on how to manage uncertainty, inherent in both working with the crowd and conducting an innovation process. Upon entering higher education, few students have had to competently deal with uncertainty. Rather they are accustomed to instructors and parents handling this for them. To mitigate some of these risks and to ensure that students learn, our crowd-enhanced classes kept conventional course mechanisms in place. Instructors gave detailed input on student projects at every stage. Students also provided peer-to-peer feedback during in-class critiques. Further, instructors shepherded student teams by scaffolding students on how to interact with crowds, providing tutorials on how to sort and analyze feedback, and advising teams on how to discern valuable crowd insights from noise.

FUTURE WORK

Given the initial appeal and success of these interventions, it is reasonable to assume that online crowd can supplement innovation education. Yet more study is needed to understand the mechanisms and refine the instructional methods around crowds. Based on what we learned in this pilot study, we intend to examine the qualities of crowd-based platforms that best support relevant and high-quality feedback for project based course activities. This focus will allow us to conduct comparative studies on characteristics of crowd-based platforms that we believe will impact the feedback including: (a) expertise in domain, (b) channel of communication (synchronous vs. asynchronous; text vs. video) (c) motivation to give feedback (intrinsic vs. extrinsic), and (d) relationship to the students (anonymous vs. identifiable; one-time vs. multiple interactions).

Moreover, we will create and disseminate new instructional materials to support crowd-enhanced learning that teachers can adopt in their own settings. We will develop lectures and in-class activities for students to practice collecting and analyzing data with the support of the instructor as well as a database of case studies for instructors to demonstrate the how crowds inform professional practice. A long-term goal is to understand how the instructor's role will change as new methods for engaging external audiences become available and valuable for students.

CONCLUSION

Higher education is criticized for being out of touch and therefore inadequately preparing students for the real world. The Internet offers unprecedented opportunities to break down the barriers between higher education and the real world. We have asked if and how the classroom can be enhanced through interactions with the crowd. Answering this question through a pilot study of a crowd-enhanced curriculum has revealed new opportunities and challenges for using such systems in a learning environment.

ACKNOWLEDGEMENTS

We thank our students for their participation, and MindSwarms for educational access to their service. This work is funded through NSF Grant IIS-1217096.

REFERENCES

1. Bao, P., Gerber, E., Gergle, D., and Hoffman, D. Momentum: getting and staying on topic during a brainstorm. *Proc of conf on Human factors in computing systems*, ACM (2010), 1233–1236.
2. Bernstein, M.S., Brandt, J., Miller, R.C., and Karger, D.R. Crowds in two seconds: enabling realtime crowd-powered interfaces. *Proc ACM symposium on User interface software and technology*, ACM (2011), 33–42.
3. Beyer, H. *Contextual Design: Defining Customer-Centered Systems*. Morgan Kaufmann, 1997.
4. Blumenfeld, P., Soloway, E., Marx, R., Krajcik, J., Guzdial, M., and Palincsar, A. Motivating Project-Based Learning: Sustaining the Doing, Supporting the Learning. *Educational Psychologist 26*, 3 (1991), 369–398.
5. Chandler, D. and Kapelner, A. Breaking monotony with meaning: Motivation in crowdsourcing markets. *University of Chicago mimeo*, (2010).
6. Collins, A., Brown, J., & Holum, A. Cognitive Apprenticeship: Making Thinking Visible. American Educator, 6-46.
7. Cynthia J Atman, D.K. Characterizing design learning: A mixed-methods study of engineering designers' use of language. (2008).
8. Davidoff, S., Lee, M.K., Dey, A.K., and Zimmerman, J. Rapidly Exploring Application Design Through Speed Dating. *Proceedings of Ubicomp*, (2007).
9. Dow, S.P., Kulkarni, A., Klemmer, S.R., and Hartmann, B. Shepherding the Crowd Yields Better Work. In *Proc of Computer Supported Cooperative Work*, (2012).
10. Dym, C.L., Agogino, A.M., Frey, D.D., and Leifer, L.J. Engineering Design Thinking, Teaching, and Learning. *Journal of Engineering Education 94*, (2005), 103–120.

11. Fixson, S.K. Teaching Innovation through Interdisciplinary Courses and Programmes in Product Design and Development: An Analysis at 16 US Schools. *Creativity and Innovation Management 18*, 3 (2009), 199–208.
12. George, J.M. 9 Creativity in Organizations. *The Academy of Management Annals 1*, 1 (2007), 439–477.
13. Gerber, E., Olson, J.M., and Komarek, R. Extracurricular Design-Based Learning. *International Journal of Engineering Education 28*, 2 (2012).
14. Heer, J. and Bostock, M. Crowdsourcing graphical perception: using mechanical turk to assess visualization design. *Proceedings of the intl conference on Human Factors in Computing Systems*, ACM (2010), 203–212.
15. Howe, J. *Crowdsourcing: Why the Power of the Crowd Is Driving the Future of Business*. Crown Business, 2008.
16. Ipeirotis, P.G. Analyzing the Amazon Mechanical Turk marketplace. *XRDS: Crossroads, The ACM Magazine for Students 17*, 2010, 16–21.
17. Kittur, A., Chi, E.H., and Suh, B. Crowdsourcing user studies with Mechanical Turk. *Proc of conference on Human factors in computing systems*, (2008), 453.
18. Kohavi, R., Henne, R.M., and Sommerfield, D. Practical guide to controlled experiments on the web: listen to your customers not to the hippo. *Proc of ACM intl conf on Knowledge discovery and data mining* (2007), 959–967.
19. Kolko, J. Abductive Thinking and Sensemaking: The Drivers of Design Synthesis. *Design Issues 26*, 1 (2011), 15–28.
20. Kolodner, J., Hmelo, C.E., and Narayanan, N.H. Learning by Design[TM] from Theory to Practice. *In Proc of Intl Conference of the Learning Sciences*, (1998), 16–22.
21. Kuratko, D.F. The Emergence of Entrepreneurship Education: Development, Trends, and Challenges. *Entrepreneurship Theory and Practice 29*, 5 (2005), 577–598.
22. Lewis, S., Dontcheva, M., and Gerber, E. Affective computational priming and creativity. *Proc of the conf on Human factors in computing systems*, ACM (2011), 735–744.
23. Lewitt, T. Creativity Is Not Enough. *Harvard Business Review*, 2002.
24. Mckenna, A.F., Colgate, J.E., Carr, S.H., and Olson, G.B. IDEA: Formalizing the Foundation for an Engineering Design Education. *International Journal of Engineering Education 22*, 3 (2006), 671–678.
25. Miron, E., Erez, M., and Naveh, E. Do personal characteristics and cultural values that promote innovation, quality, and efficiency compete or complement each other? *Journal of Organizational Behavior 25*, 2 (2004), 175–199.
26. Osborn, A.F. *Applied Imagination: Principles and Procedures of Creative Problem Solving*. Charles Scribner's Sons, 1963.
27. Peterman, N.E. and Kennedy, J. Enterprise Education: Influencing Students' Perceptions of Entrepreneurship. *Entrepreneurship Theory and Practice 28*, 2 (2003), 129–144.
28. Plaschka, G. and Welsch, H. Emerging Structures in Entrepreneurship Education: Curricular Designs and Strategies. *SSRN eLibrary*, (1990).
29. Ross, J., Irani, L., Silberman, M.S., Zaldivar, A., and Tomlinson, B. Who are the crowdworkers? *In extended abstracts on Human Factors in Computing Systems*, (2010).
30. Shaffer, D.W. and Resnick, M. "Thick" authenticity: new media and authentic learning. *J. Interact. Learn. Res. 10*, 2 (1999), 195–215.
31. Siroker, D. How Obama Raised $60 Million by Running a Simple Experiment. 2010. http://blog.optimizely.com/how-obama-raised-60-million-by-running-an-exp.
32. Sternberg, R.J. *Handbook of Creativity*. Cambridge University Press, 1998.
33. Strauss, A.C. and Corbin, J.M. *Grounded Theory in Practice*. Sage Publications, Inc, 1997.
34. Terwiesch, C. and Ulrich, K. *Innovation Tournaments: Creating and Selecting Exceptional Opportunities*. Harvard Business Press, 2009.
35. Thomke, S.H. *Experimentation Matters: Unlocking the Potential of New Technologies for Innovation*. Harvard Business Press, 2003.
36. Tidbell, B., Mulder, I., and Stappers, P.J. Online Design Contests: A Network of Inspiration for Designers. (2011).
37. Wang, H.-C., Cosley, D., and Fussell, S.R. Idea expander: supporting group brainstorming with conversationally triggered visual thinking stimuli. *Proc of ACM conf on Computer Supported Cooperative Work*, (2010), 103–106.
38. Westerberg, C. and Wickersham, C. Internships Have Value, Whether or Not Students Are Paid. *The Chronicle of Higher Education*, 2011.
39. Xu, A. and Bailey, B.P. A crowdsourcing model for receiving design critique. *In extended abstracts on Human Factors in Computing Systems*, ACM (2011), 1183–1188.
40. Yu, L. and Nickerson, J.V. Cooks or cobblers?: crowd creativity through combination. *Proc of ACM conf on Human Factors in Computing Systems*, (2011), 1393–1402.
41. Innocentive. www.innocentive.com.
42. oDesk. https://www.odesk.com.
43. 99designs: http://99designs.com/.
44. Crowdspring. www.crowdspring.com.
45. Optimizely. www.optimizely.com.
46. Indiegogo. www.indiegogo.com.
47. Facebook. www.facebook.com.
48. Google Ad Words. https://adwords.google.com.
49. Coffee Joulies on Kickstarter. http://www.kickstarter.com/projects/705847536/coffee-joulies-your-coffee-just-right.
50. Open Innovation. www.openinnovation.net.
51. Case Study. http://en.wikipedia.org/wiki/Case_study.
52. Coursera. www.coursera.org.
53. Stanford Technology Ventures. http://stvp.stanford.edu/.
54. FIRST Robotics Competition. www.pittsburghfirst.org/.
55. Solar Car Teams. http://en.wikipedia.org/wiki/List_of_solar_car_teams.
56. Tartan Hacks. www.tartanhacks.com.
57. Newgrounds. http://www.newgrounds.com/.
58. MindSwarms. www.mindswarms.com.
59. Qualtrics. www.qualtrics.com.
60. IndieGoGo blog. http://www.indiegogo.com/blog/.

Flexpad: Highly Flexible Bending Interactions for Projected Handheld Displays

Jürgen Steimle
MIT Media Lab
Cambridge, MA
steimle@media.mit.edu

Andreas Jordt
Christian-Albrechts-Universität
Kiel, Germany
jordt@mip.informatik.uni-kiel.de

Pattie Maes
MIT Media Lab
Cambridge, MA
pattie@media.mit.edu

ABSTRACT
Flexpad is an interactive system that combines a depth camera and a projector to transform sheets of plain paper or foam into flexible, highly deformable, and spatially aware handheld displays. We present a novel approach for tracking deformed surfaces from depth images in real time. It captures deformations in high detail, is very robust to occlusions created by the user's hands and fingers, and does not require any kind of markers or visible texture. As a result, the display is considerably more deformable than in previous work on flexible handheld displays, enabling novel applications that leverage the high expressiveness of detailed deformation. We illustrate these unique capabilities through three application examples: curved cross-cuts in volumetric images, deforming virtual paper characters, and slicing through time in videos. Results from two user studies show that our system is capable of detecting complex deformations and that users are able to perform them quickly and precisely.

Author Keywords
Flexible display; handheld display; tracking; projection; depth camera; deformation; bending; volumetric data.

ACM Classification Keywords
H5.2. User interfaces: Graphical user interfaces (GUI), Input devices and strategies, Interaction styles.

INTRODUCTION
Projecting visual interfaces onto movable real-world objects has been an ongoing area of research, e.g. [3, 15, 28, 35, 11]. By closely integrating physical and digital information spaces, they leverage people's intuitive understanding of how to manipulate real-world objects for interaction with computer systems. Based on inexpensive depth sensors, a stream of recent research presented elegant tracking-projection approaches for transforming real-world objects into displays, without requiring any instrumentation of these objects [37, 11]. None of these approaches, however, interpret the deformation of flexible objects.

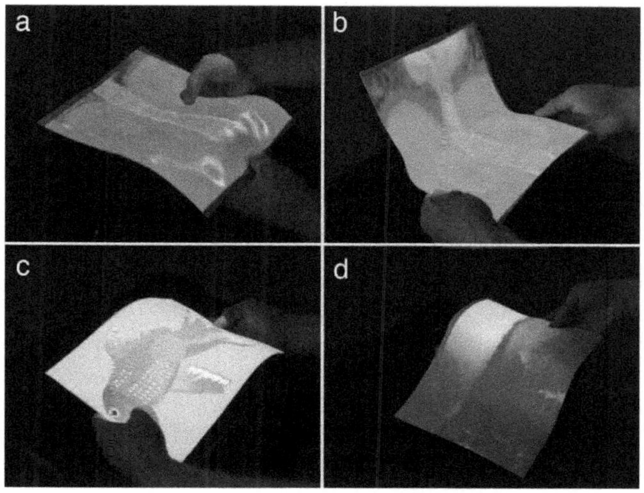

Figure 1: Application examples of Flexpad: Curved cross-cuts in volumetric images (a, b); animation of characters (c); slicing through time in videos (d)

Flexible deformation can expand the potential of projected interfaces. Deformation of everyday objects allows for a surprisingly rich set of interaction possibilities, involving many degrees of freedom, yet with very intuitive interaction: people bend pages in books, squeeze balls, model clay, and fold origami, to cite only a few examples. Adding deformation as another degree of freedom to handheld displays has great potential to add to the richness and expressiveness of interaction.

We present Flexpad, a system that supports highly flexible bending interactions for projected handheld displays. A Kinect depth camera and a projector form a camera-projection unit that lets people use blank sheets of paper, foam or acrylic of different sizes and shapes as flexible displays. Flexpad has two main technical contributions: first, we contribute an algorithm for capturing even complex deformations in high detail and in real time. It does not require any instrumentation of the deformable handheld material. Hence, unlike in previous work that requires markers, visible texture, or embedded electronics [15, 22, 12, 35, 18, 19], virtually any sheet at hand can be used as a deformable projection surface for interactive applications. Second, we contribute a novel robust method for detecting hands and fingers with a Kinect camera using optical analysis of the surface material. This is crucial for robust capturing of deformable surfaces in realistic conditions, where the user occludes significant parts of the surface while deforming it. Since the solution is inexpensive, requiring only standard hardware components, it can be envisioned that deformable handheld displays become widespread and common.

The highly flexible handheld display creates unique novel application possibilities. Prior work on *immobile* flexible displays has shown the effectiveness of highly detailed deformations, e.g. for the purposes of 2.5D modeling and multi-dimensional navigation [30, 7]. Yet, the existing inventory of interactions with flexible *handheld* displays [32, 23, 20, 18] is restricted to only low detail deformations, mostly due to the very limited flexibility of the displays and limited resolution of deformation capturing. Flexpad significantly extends the existing inventory by adding highly flexible and multi-dimensional deformations.

We present three application examples that each leverage rich and expressive, highly flexible deformations. The first application supports exploration and analysis of volumetric data sets (Fig. 1 a, b). We show how highly flexible displays support intuitive and effective exploration of the volumetric data set by allowing the user to easily define curved cross-sections, to get an overview, and to compare contents. The second application enables children to deform and animate 2D characters (Fig 1 c). A third application shows how detailed deformation can be used for slicing through time in videos (Fig. 1 d). These applications demonstrate the utility of Flexpad and introduce transferrable ideas for future handheld devices that use active flexible displays.

To evaluate the feasibility of our approach, both with respect to technology and human factors, we conducted two evaluation studies. They show that the tracking provides accurate results even for complex deformations and confirm that people can perform them fast and precisely.

The remainder of this paper is structured as follows. After reviewing related work, we present the concept and implementation of Flexpad. This is followed by an overview of applications. Finally, we present the results of two evaluation studies and conclude with an outlook on future work.

RELATED WORK

Deformation Capturing

Our work relates to a body of research that realizes handheld displays using optical capturing of the projection surface and spatially aligned projection, either with a static or a handheld projector, e.g. [3, 15, 24, 28, 35, 11, 18].

Many methods exist for capturing the pose and deformation of a mobile projection surface – information required for accurate texture mapping. Existing methods include passive or active markers, stereo cameras, structured light, time of flight, analysis of visible texture via features [36], color distances [6] or optical flow [14] as well as analysis of the object's contour [8]. The commercial availability of inexpensive depth cameras has recently stimulated a lot of research that produces a detailed geometrical model of a real-world scene for enabling novel forms of HCI. LightSpace [37] uses several depth cameras and projectors to augment walls and tables for touch and gesture-based interaction with projected interfaces. KinectFusion [16] automatically creates a very detailed model of a static scene, enabling physics-based interactions on and above surfaces and objects. Omnitouch [11] uses a depth sensor to support multi-touch input on projected interfaces on virtually any non-instrumented surface. However, none of these approaches model real-time deformation of objects. Very recent work [13, 5] uses proxy particles to model deformable objects, allowing for a range of physics-based interactions that are based on collision and friction forces. However, tracking particles over a sequence of frames requires optical flow, which is not possible with untextured surfaces. Other work [17] captures deformable surfaces from Kinect depth data, but the approach does not support capturing detailed deformations in real time, which is critical for interactive applications. We present an approach that is capable of capturing the pose and detailed deformation of a deformable surface from depth data in real-time, to support very fine-grained interactions and natural deformations. Due to a novel detection of hands and fingers, our approach is very robust to occlusions, which is crucial when users deform objects in natural settings.

Flexible Display Interfaces

Our research is also influenced by existing work on deformation-based handheld interfaces. Here, two streams of work can be distinguished:

First, prior work proposed using a deformable tape or sheet as an *external input device*, to control GUI applications by deformation. Output is given on a separate, inflexible display. An early and influential work is ShapeTape [2] that allows users to create and modify 3D models by bending a tape that is augmented by a deformation sensor. Other applications use a deformable sheet for controlling windows on the computer desktop [10] and for AR purposes [26].

A second type of research, more directly related to our work, studies *deformation of handheld displays*. Prior work has investigated interactions with interfaces of flexible smart phones and e-readers [32, 23, 19, 18, 1, 20] and for volumetric datasets [22]. Most of this work uses projection or simulates flexible displays with existing inflexible displays; PaperPhone [23] and Kinetic [20] use an active flexible display. Lee et al. [25] elicited user-defined gestures for flexible displays. A recent study [21] examined how device stiffness and the extent of deformation influenced deformation precision. While no pronounced influence was identified, users preferred softer rather than rigid materials.

This stream of work represents an important step towards fully flexible displays, yet existing work is limited by quite restricted deformability. It supports only slight bending and captures only simple deformations, which ultimately limits the expressiveness of deformation to mostly one-dimensional interactions. We contribute novel interactions that extend the inventory of interactions by leveraging more flexible deformations.

FLEXPAD OVERVIEW

Flexpad enables users to interact with highly flexible projected displays in interactive real-time applications. The setup consists of a Kinect camera, a projector, and a sheet of paper, foam or acrylic that is used as projection surface.

Our current setup is illustrated in Fig. 2. A Kinect camera and a full HD projector (ViewSonic Pro 8200) are mounted to the ceiling above the user, next to each other, and are calibrated to define one coordinate space. The setup creates an interaction volume of approximately 110 x 55 x 43 cm within which users can freely move, rotate, and deform the projection surface. The average resolution of the projection is 54 dpi. The user can either be seated at a table or standing. The table surface is located at a distance of 160 cm from the camera and the projector. Our implementation uses a standard desktop PC with an Intel i7 processor, 8 GB RAM, and an AMD Radeon HD 6800 graphics engine. While we currently use a fixed setup, the Kinect camera could be shoulder-worn with a mobile projector attached to it, as presented in [11], allowing for mobile or nomadic use.

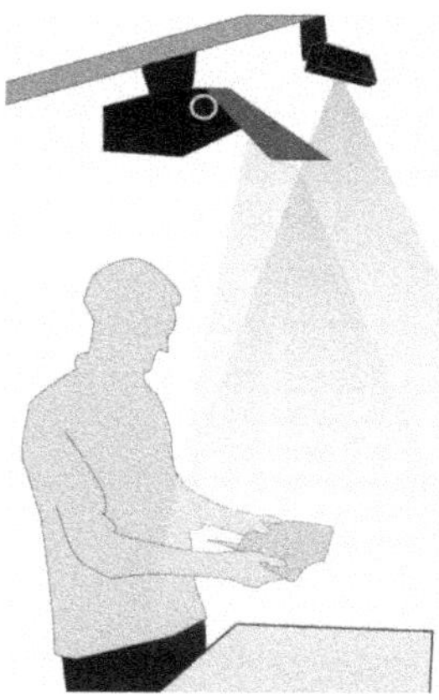

Fig. 2: Physical setup

The key contribution of Flexpad is in its approach for markerless capture of a high-resolution 3D model of a deformable surface, including its pose and deformation (see section about the model below). The system is further capable of grabbing 2D image contents from any window in Microsoft Windows and projecting it correctly warped onto the deformable display. Alternatively, it can use 3D volume data as input for the projection. The detailed model of deformation enables novel applications that make use of varied deformations of the display. We will present some example applications below.

Flexible display materials

Sheets of many different sizes and materials can be used as passive displays, including standard office paper. In our experiments, we used letter-sized sheets of two materials that have demonstrated good haptic characteristics:

The *fully flexible display* is 2 mm thick white foam (Darice Foamies crafting foam). It allows the user to change between different deformations very easily and quickly. The bending stiffness index S_b^* of this material was identified as 1.12 Nm^7/kg^3, which is comparable to the stiffness of 160g/m^2 paper. ($S_b^* = S_b/w^3$ is the bending stiffness normalized w.r.t. the sheet's basis weight w in kg/m^2 [27].) The display's weight is 12 grams.

The *shape-retaining display* retains its deformation even when the user is not holding it. It consists of 2 mm thick white foam with Amalog 1/16" armature wire attached to its backside. It allows for more detailed modeling of the deformation, for easy modifications, as well as for easy holding. To characterize its deformability, we measured the minimal force required to permanently deform the material. We affixed the sheet at one side; a torque as small as 0.1Nm is enough to permanently deform the material, which shows that the material is very easy to deform. The sheets' weight is 25g.

FLEXPAD IMPLEMENTATION

Existing image based tracking algorithms of deformable surfaces [36, 6, 14] rely on visible features. In this section, we present an approach that requires only image data from a Kinect depth sensor. This allows for tracking an entirely blank (or arbitrarily textured) deformable projection surface in high detail. Moreover, since the depth sensor operates in the infrared spectrum, it does not interfere with the visible projection, no matter what content is projected.

A challenge of depth data is that it does not provide reliable image cues on local movement, which renders traditional tracking methods useless. The solution to this problem is a more global, model-based approach: We introduce a parameterized, deformable object model that is fit into the depth image data by a semi-global search algorithm, accounting for occlusion by the user's hands and fingers.

In the following, we explain 1) the removal of hands and fingers from the input data, 2) the global deformation model and 3) how a global optimization method is used to fit the deformation model to the input data in real time.

Optical Surface Material Analysis for Hand and Finger Detection

While the user is interacting with the display, hands and fingers partially occlude the surface in the depth image. For a robust deformation tracking, it is important to classify these image pixels as not belonging to the deformable surface, so the model is not fit into wrong depth values. The proposed tracking method is able to handle missing data, so the solution lies in removing those occluded parts from the input images in a preprocessing step.

Due to the low resolution of the Kinect depth sensor it is difficult to perform a shape-based classification of fingers and hands at larger distances. In particular, when the finger or the flat hand is touching the surface, the resolution is insufficient to differentiate it reliably from the underlying surface. Existing approaches use heuristics that work reliably as long as the back of the hand is kept at some distance above the surface [11]. These restrictions do not hold in our more general case, where people use their hands and fingers right *on* the surface for deforming it.

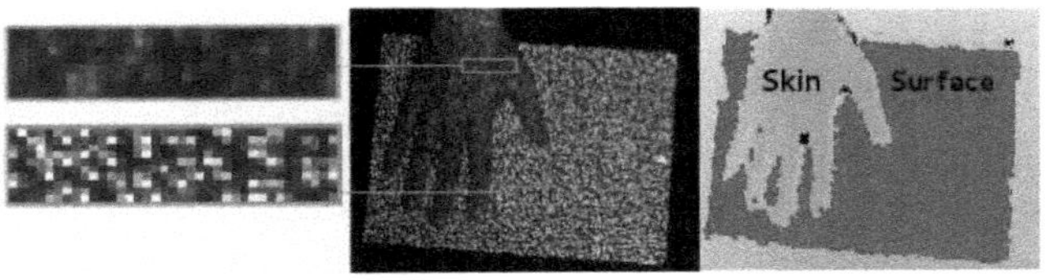

Figure 3: Detection of skin by analyzing the point pattern in the Kinect infrared image. Center: Input. Right: Classification

We introduce *optical surface material analysis* as a novel method of distinguishing between skin and the projection surface using the Kinect sensor. It is based on the observation that different materials have different reflectivity and translucency properties. Some materials, e.g. skin, have translucency properties leading to subsurface scattering of light. This property causes the point pattern, which is projected by the Kinect, to blur. This reduces the image gradients in the raw infrared image, which is given by the Freenect driver (see Fig. 3). The display surface, made out of paper, cardboard, foam or any other material with highly diffuse reflection, varies from skin in reflectivity as well as translucency; so low peak values or low gradient values provide a stable scheme to classify non-display areas.

The projector inside the Kinect has a constant intensity and the infrared camera has a constant shutter time and aperture. Hence, the brightness of the point pattern is constant for constant material properties and object distances and angles. As a consequence, the surface reflectivity of an object with diffuse material can be determined by looking at the local point brightness. However, because the brightness in the infrared image decreases with increasing distance, the local gradients and peak values have to be regarded with respect to the depth value of the corresponding pixel in the depth image. Pixels that cannot be associated to a dot of the pattern are not classified directly, but receive the same classification as the surrounding pixels by iterative filtering. Results from an evaluation, reported below, show that this classification scheme works reliably at distances up to 1.50 m from the camera.

Modeling the Deformable Surface

Without local movement cues in the image, such as feature movement or optical flow, and with incomplete depth data, it is important to formulate very precisely what the tracking method should find in the image, i.e. to define a deformation model. We present a model that is generic enough to approximate a wide variety of deformations, including complex ones, while still being efficient to calculate.

The model is based on a rectangular 25 x 25 vertex plane at the size of the actual display surface. Using 25 vertices per dimension proved to provide stable tracking results while keeping the computational costs small. We then define a set of 8 basic deformations, 4 diagonal and 4 axis-aligned bends, each deforming half the surface plane (Fig. 4 upper left). It is important to note that all of these basic deformations are *combined* by using weighted factors, such that the model supports complex curvatures.

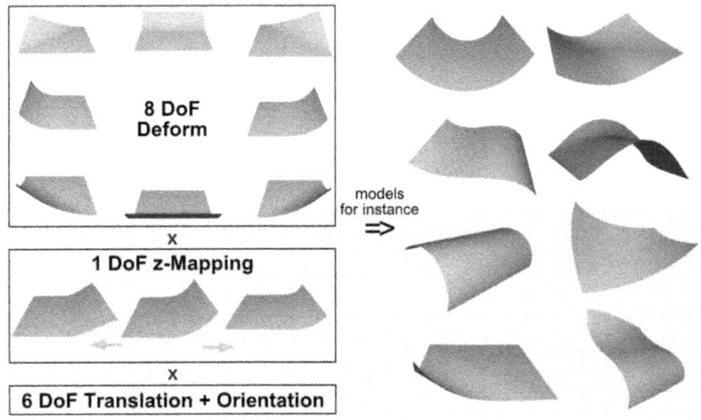

Figure 4: Dimensions of the deformation model (left) and examples of deformations it can express (right).

A drawback of this model is that it lacks the ability to shift the starting point of a deformation, e.g. for distinguishing between a smaller and a larger dog-ear. To add this ability to the deformation model while keeping it computationally efficient and robust through low dimensionality, an additional mapping function for the z components of the vertex position is applied after the deformed vertex positions are calculated. The mapping can change from a square-like function, via the identity function to a square root-like function. This parameterized function is applied to every z-component of each surface vertex to change the shape of the deformation. This largely increases the set of deformations in the model by only adding one additional deformation parameter.

In summary, as shown in Fig. 4, the deformation model is a 15 dimensional vector, containing the angles of the 8 basic deformations, the z mapping parameter as well as 6 variables for the degrees of freedom that are required for the affine 3D transformations. Figure 4 (right) gives some examples of the complex deformations the model supports.

Real-time Calculation

Given this deformation model, the overall tracking goal can be defined as finding the parameters of the model that describe an object that, when synthesized as a depth image, matches the input depth image best. Such approaches are known as Analysis by Synthesis (AbS) or direct tracking methods [17]. The advantage of such methods is the ability to work completely without information on feature movement or optical flow. Such evaluation allows for formulating the tracking as an optimization problem, turning the tracking task into a mathematically well-defined objective of finding the parameter vector that produces the most suitable deformation.

To determine the deformation parameters, the AbS approach synthesizes the depth measurements of the 25x25 pixels to which the model vertices would be projected and compares the vertex-camera distance to the real input depth image. Thereby, areas that were identified as skin by the occlusion handling step are ignored. The average difference over all vertices provides an error value that examines the

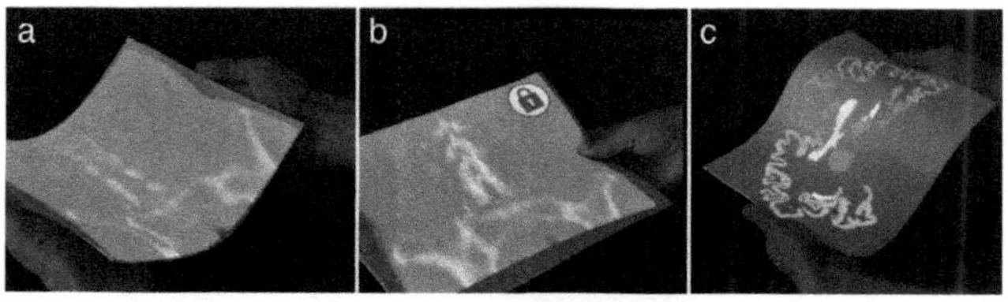

Figure 5: Exploring curved cross-sections (a), flattening the view (b), comparing contents across layers (c)

quality of the parameter guess to model the deformed object in the image. Due to the uneven measurements and the noise in the Kinect image, this error function contains many local minima, making it intractable for common local least squares optimization. Hence, we apply the CMA-ES optimization scheme [29] to find an approximation of the optimum since CMA-ES combines two important properties: it is a global optimization algorithm, which allows for coping with large numbers of local minima, and it applies a smart distribution scheme minimizing the necessary number of function evaluations to find the optimum.

The optimization process is initialized at the first frame with a vertex set describing a planar surface of the display size and shape, placed at the center in the depth image. In the beginning of each following frame, the optimization is initialized with the optimization result of the preceding frame. This allows for initially finding the sheet not only at this position, but also at different locations and orientation within the instrumented volume. Should the depth error of the optimization result rise above a given limit, it is most likely that the tracking failed, e.g. because the user has removed the deformable sheet from the camera's viewport. In this case, the initialization step is automatically executed again, until the depth error falls below this limit.

To further increase the performance, our approach leverages the fact that the user cannot make high precision deformations while moving the object quickly, but only when the object is held steadily or slowly moved. The number of iterative optimization steps per frame is automatically adjusted by the pose difference of the preceding frames. During large movements, the number of iterations is reduced (on our hardware, 50 iterations yield 25 fps). During very slow movements, the number is increased, smoothly reducing the frame rate (200 iterations yield 8 fps), allowing for the highest possible accuracy of deformation capturing.

Limitations

Our approach allows for robust real-time tracking of a large variety of deformations with a variety of deformable surfaces. However, due to the real-time constraint and restrictions of the depth sensor, several limitations apply. Obviously, it is only possible to track deformations that can be observed directly by the Kinect camera. Folding, which occludes large parts of an object, as well as very steep bending angles that occlude parts of the object to the camera cannot be handled by the presented system. For the cost of installing and calibrating additional Kinect sensors and projectors, this limitation can be overcome. Moreover, the presented deformation model makes a trade-off between tracking stability and the set of detectable deformations. Hence, very sharp bends, in particular folds, and stretchable materials cannot be reliably captured.

APPLICATION EXAMPLES

Flexpad supports many application and interaction possibilities. Its unique strength is the high flexibility of the display and the detailed capturing of its deformation. A direct 1:1 mapping between the deformed physical shape and virtual model space enables novel applications with expressive interactions that were not possible with rigid or slightly flexible handheld displays. It is worth emphasizing that all proposed interactions also transfer to future active displays.

Exploring and Analyzing Volumetric Datasets

Analysis of volumetric images and datasets is important in many fields, such as medicine (CT and MRI scans), geology and earth sciences (atmospheric and submarine datasets). Prior research has shown that curved cross-sections are required for analyzing important medical phenomena [31]. We contribute interactions that significantly go beyond existing work on visualization of volumetric datasets, which support only planar cross-cuts [35], only very restricted curvatures [22] or make curvature very hard to control [31].

Our application maps the volumetric dataset to a 3D volume in physical space and lets the user slice through that volume with the display. By deforming the highly flexible display, the user can easily create *non-planar cross-sections* to analyze a large variety of curved structures that would not be visible on planar or only slightly deformed cross-sections. Figures 1 and 5 illustrate several examples: the spine (Fig. 1a) and the pelvis (Fig. 5a). For detailed analysis of a cross-section, the user can *lock the view* by pressing a foot button. When locked, the display can be moved and deformed without affecting the visualization (Fig. 5b). For instance, this allows for *flattening the view* and easy measurement of distances that were on a curve in the original view. It also allows for handing the view over to a colleague. It is worth noting that this application is not only helpful for medical experts, but also supports non-experts who are interested in exploring the inner workings of the human body in an intuitive way. In addition to following a layer, deformation also proves powerful in supporting *curved cuts across layers*. Consider the example of a reservoir engineer exploring the best locations for a new well in an oil field. The engineer can select the desired curvature of the well (nowadays many wells are curved) by bending the display and then skim through the entire volume.

Deformation also supports *better orientation and overview* in the dataset. For instance, one part of the display remains at a visually salient feature while the user curves the other part to explore the surrounding area in the dataset (Fig. 1b). Furthermore, deformation of the highly flexible display provides an intuitive way of *comparing data across layers*. By deforming the display into a wave bend, the user sepa-

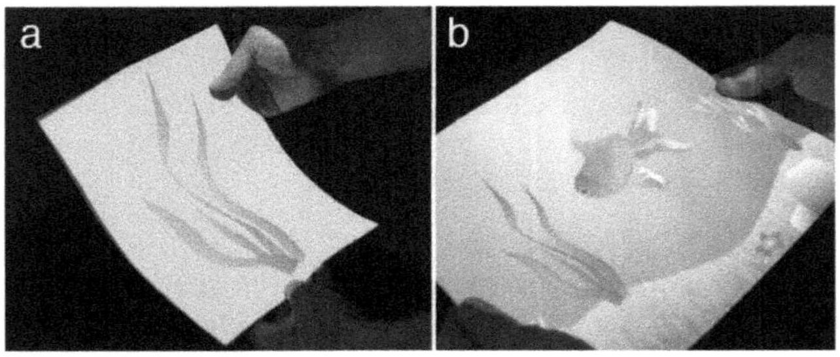

Figure 6: Animating virtual paper characters

rates the display into two slices that are located at different depth levels (Fig 5c). By varying the bend, the user can smoothly select the distance between both slices.

Our proposed interactions can be easily integrated with functionality for cross-cuts of volumetric datasets that have been presented in prior work, such as additional views on external displays [35], panning and zooming, or saving of 2D snapshots for subsequent analysis and presentation.

Animating Virtual Paper Characters

To demonstrate the wide applicability of highly deformable handheld displays, we next present an application for children that leverages deformation as a simple and intuitive means for animating paper characters in an interactive picture. By deforming the display and moving it in space (Fig. 1c and 6a), the creature becomes animated. High-resolution deformation allows very individualized and varied animation patterns. Once animated, the creature is released into the virtual world of the animated picture (Fig. 6 b). For example, fish may move with different speeds and move their fins. A sea star may lift some of its tentacles. A sea worm may creep on the ground. A flatfish may meander with sophisticated wave-form movements and seaweed may slowly bend in the water.

Such rich deformation capabilities can be easily combined with concepts from previous research on animating paper cut-outs [4] that address skeleton animation, eye movement, and scene lighting. Also 3D models could get animated by incorporating as-rigid-as-possible deformation [33]. It is worth noting that our concept can be readily deployed with standard hardware.

Slicing through Time in Videos

A third application of Flexpad enables people to create slices through time in videos, inspired by the ingenious Khronos projector [7]. In contrast to Khronos, which required a very bulky, several cubic meters big, immobile setup with a fixed screen, Flexpad brings similar functionality to virtually any sheet of paper. The user can load a video from YouTube, which is automatically mapped to a virtual volume, whereby time is mapped to the z dimension. By moving and deforming the display within this volume, the user creates ever new combinations of different moments in time that open up new artistic perspectives on the video. Figure 7 depicts an example, in which a tree is "moved" in time to glow in the sunset. However, this functionality is best illustrated in the video that accompanies this paper.

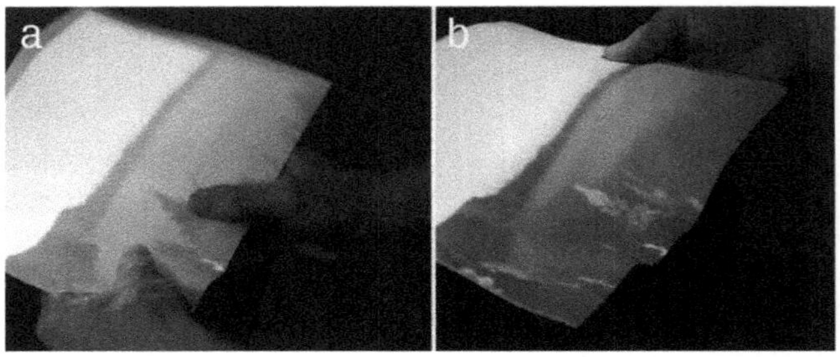

Figure 7: Slicing through time in a video by deformation

In contrast to the fixed display of Khronos, the flexible handheld display allows for defining a curvature, i.e. a time gradient, and then move this gradient to different areas within one frame or across frames. Moreover, the handheld display allows for selecting any frame of the video to start with deforming, whereas deformations in Khronos always start at the topmost frame, going in only one direction. This allows for novel, expressive interactions with videos.

EVALUATION

To evaluate the feasibility of the Flexpad approach, we conducted two evaluations, examining both system performance and the users' ability of precise interaction with highly deformable displays.

Tracking Performance

To evaluate the precision of tracking in a natural real-time scenario, we recruited 10 volunteer participants (5f, 5m, median age 26). Their task was to use the slicing-through-time application and freely create interesting renderings by deforming the display. This application is particularly well suited for a technical evaluation of the system, for the unstructured nature of the interface stimulates users to deform the display in highly varied, complex ways. We recorded the raw video stream from the Kinect camera while the user performed the task, overall 35 minutes of footage. We used this data as an input for our algorithm, calculating the RMS error in each frame from the distance between the model surface to the corresponding depth image values. The average RMS error over all 20,217 frames is 6.47 mm (SD 3.33 mm). This shows that the tracking performs very adequately even in challenging realistic tasks.

To test the abilities of the tracking method in a more distinct way, we additionally picked a set of 8 deformations, ranging from simple bends to complex deformations. Each deformation was recorded 20 times at 90 and 150 cm distance to the Kinect camera. Figure 8 shows the deformations and the average RMS error for each deformation. In addition, we evaluated the preprocessing step, which removes hands and fingers from the input data, in an informal study. The Kinect data of hands from 10 users (aged 25 to 54) occluding three different display materials (paper, card board, plastic) was recorded. Analysis showed that

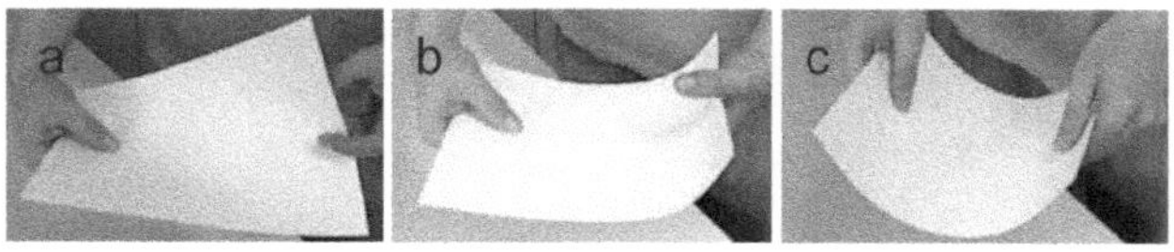

RMS90: **2.10 mm** (1.1) RMS90: **1.91 mm** (1.2) RMS90: **2.67 mm** (1.6)
RMS150: **2.64 mm** (1.3) RMS150: **3.07 mm** (1.7) RMS150: **6.1 mm** (4.2)

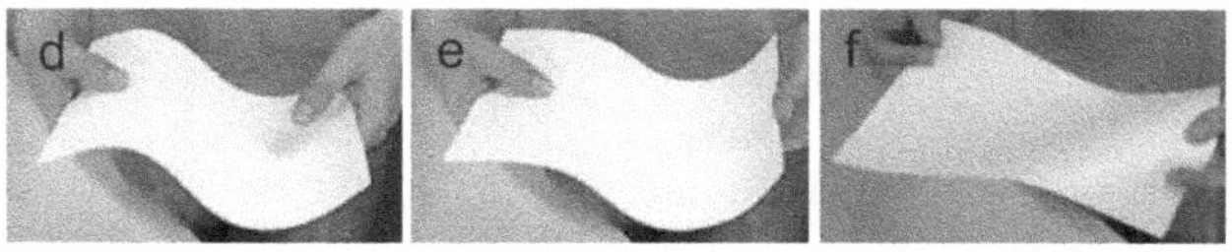

RMS90: **4.58 mm** (1.9) RMS90: **4.82 mm** (2.2) RMS90: **4.93 mm** (2.1)
RMS150: **5.45 mm** (2.7) RMS150: **5.15 mm** (2.5) RMS150: **6.38 mm** (3.8)

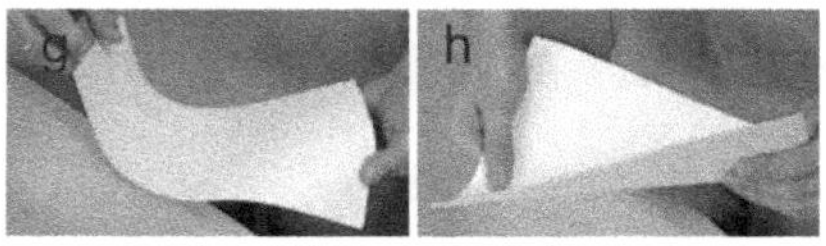

RMS90: **5.39 mm** (2.2) RMS90: **2.41 mm** (1.2)
RMS150: **7.03 mm** (4.1) RMS150: **4.56 mm** (2.3)

Figure 8: Average RMS error of a set of representative deformations (at 90 cm and 150 cm distance between Kinect and the object; the standard deviation is given in brackets).

independently of skin color, the preprocessing step correctly removed over 99% of the skin pixels without the need to adjust the thresholds for reflection or translucency. Figure 9 shows data from six users and the classification results.

User Performance of Deformation

For the feasibility of the Flexpad approach, it is essential that users are able to perform deformations with the display with ease and sufficiently high precision. To evaluate these human factors, we conducted a controlled experiment with users. Our aim was to evaluate how fast and precise users are able to perform deformations and to examine the influence of flexible vs. shape-retaining display materials. Our hypothesis was that the task completion time increases with the complexity of the deformation and the level of precision required. Moreover, we hypothesized that the shape-retaining material would increase task completion times. We aimed at quantifying this influence. As such, our study adds to an emerging body of experiments on the manipulation of paper-like displays, including target acquisition performance in 3D space with rigid paper displays [34] and performance of deforming slightly flexible displays [21].

We recruited 10 volunteer participants (5f, 5m, all right-handed, median age 26). The two participants who performed the task fastest were offered a $10 gift card. The experiment consisted of a series of trials that required the participant to deform the display surface as quickly as possible to match a given target shape within a specific precision level (see below). A perspective rendering of the target shape was displayed before each trial. During the trial, a real-time visualization on the display guided the participant on how to deform it to match the shape; to match the shape, all red areas had to turn green (Fig. 10). The trial was solved when the target shape was held during 250ms. The completion time for each trial was measured. After each trial, the participant had to rate the perceived difficulty on a five-point Likert scale.

Figure 10: Interactive visualization during a trial

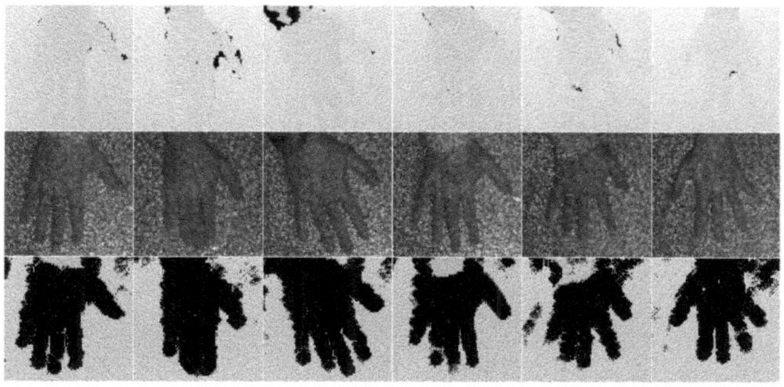

Figure 9: Classification of skin. Top: depth input. Center: infrared input. Bottom: depth image after classification with skin parts removed.

We selected five deformation classes: two one-sided deformations, which are oriented with the corner (Fig. 8a) and oriented with the edge (Fig. 8b), and three two-sided ones: center (Fig 8c), symmetric wave (Fig. 8d) and asymmetric wave (Fig. 8e). Each of these classes contains not only the basic deformation, but all variations of it, on all four sides of the display, and each also flipped vertically. This set of deformations was informed by the deformations made in our application examples, and for reasons of feasibility of this study, focused on deformations along one dimension in landscape format. From each deformation class, we randomly selected 2 deformations for each participant.

Each deformation had to be performed with two precision levels: +/- 8 degrees and +/- 6 degrees. In a pre-study with 5 participants, we identified these precision levels as challenging, but still feasible, whereas a level of +/- 4 degrees turned out not to be reliably reachable. The sequence of trials was randomized. To compare influences of the display material, participants performed the tasks with the fully flexible and with the shape-retaining display, as described in the system overview section. The order was counterbalanced. In summary, the within-subject, multi-factorial experimental design was as follows:

5 deformation classes x 2 instances per class x 2 precision levels x 2 materials x 10 participants = 400 trials

Before the experiment, participants could practice the tasks with both materials until they felt fully confident. After the experiment, participants freely explored a medical dataset in the volumetric application as well as the slicing-through-time application. This was followed by a semi-structured interview. Each session lasted approximately 1 hour.

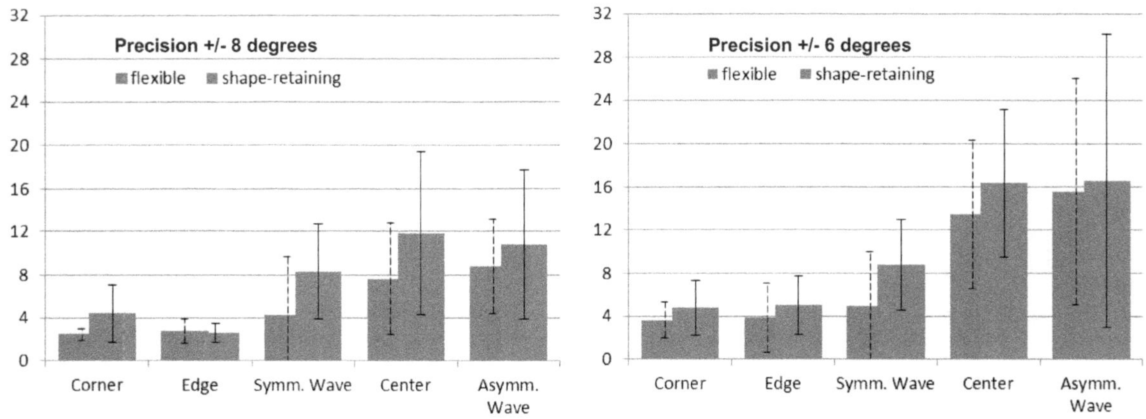

Figure 11: Average trial completion time in seconds. Error bars show the standard deviation.

Results

Figure 11 (left) depicts the average trial completion times for the five basic deformations and both materials for the lower precision level. With the fully flexible material, times range between 2.4 and 8.8 seconds; with the shape-retaining material, values range from 2.6 to 10.8 seconds. Figure 11 (right) depicts those values for the higher precision level. In this case, times range between 3.6 and 15.6 as well as 4.8 and 16.5 seconds, for the two materials, respectively. The rather high standard deviations reflect different levels of manual dexterity of users.

We first performed a multifactorial repeated measures ANOVA with all factors, including rotation and vertical flip of the deformations. We found no significant effect of rotation and vertical flip; therefore, in the following analyses, we group the trials into the five basic deformations, regardless of their rotation and vertical flip.

To identify systematic dependencies, we performed a r-ANOVA with the factors deformation, precision level, and material. Significant main effects were found for deformation ($F_{(4,36)} = 16.13$; $p < 0.001$), precision level ($F_{(1,9)} = 13.17$; $p = 0.005$) and material ($F_{(1,9)} = 8.86$; $p = 0.016$). As expected, more complex deformations, a higher precision level, and the shape-retaining material resulted in higher task performance time. On average, completion time of trials that were performed with the shape-retaining material was 33% longer than of trials with the fully flexible material. When the higher precision level was required, completion time of trials was 46% longer than of trials performed at the lower precision level.

To further analyze differences between the five deformation classes, we conducted post-hoc tests with Bonferroni-adjusted alpha-levels of .01. Results showed highly significant differences between: edge and center (mean difference = 8.77; $p = .004$), edge and asymmetric wave (MD = 9.36; $p = .006$); corner and center (MD = 8.53; $p = .001$), as well as corner and asymmetric wave (MD = 9.12; $p = .004$). This shows a distinctive difference between deformations requiring bending only one versus both sides. The symmetric wave deformation does not differ statistically from both groups due to a highly material-dependent behavior, which is visible in Fig. 11.

Simple (edge or corner) deformations had an average task completion time of 3.67 seconds (SD = 1.72). Even the most difficult deformations, in high precision level, resulted in an average task performance time of 15.6 seconds (SD = 9.54). The average rating of all trials was 2.06 (SD = 0.88). Analyzed separately for all combinations of deformation, precision level and material, the average ratings range from 1.2 to 3.1, i.e. from very easy to medium. Perceived difficulty and completion times of the trials showed a very high bivariate correlation (Pearson's $r = .75$, $p < .001$). Therefore, our following analyses are based on the completion times, but transfer to the difficulty of the task.

We identified one exception to the general finding that the deformations were performed without difficulties: the asymmetric wave deformation in the higher precision level, performed with the shape-retaining material. While average time is in line with those of the other complex deformation, the standard deviation is much higher, as can be seen in Fig. 11 (rightmost column). Statistical testing using Grubbs' Test for outliers showed that this SD is indeed an outlier ($G = 2.68$, $p = .005$.) This high SD shows that some participants were able to perform this deformation rather quickly, whereas other participants could only perform it reliably within a disproportionately long time.

As presented above, and in accordance with our hypothesis, the ANOVA found a significant effect of material. Because of the advantages of the shape-retaining material for complex deformations that were stated above, we will now analyze this effect in more detail for double-sided deformations (symmetric wave, center, and asymmetric wave).

The penalty on completion time in the lower precision level that is due to the shape-retaining material averages out at 95% with symmetric wave, 56% with center and 24% with asymmetric wave. For the higher precision level, the penalties introduced by the shape-retaining material are 77%,

21%, and 6%, for the three deformations respectively. Most notably, the penalty introduced by the shape-retaining *decreases* with increasing difficulty of the deformation and increasing level of precision. This relationship is illustrated by significant medium-sized negative correlations between the difficulty of the deformation (symmetric wave, center, asymmetric wave) and the penalty on completion time, separated for precision level (lower precision level: $r = -.38$, $p = .018$; higher precision level: $r = -.39$, $p = .016$). A similar result was obtained when difficulty of the deformation and level of precision combined were correlated with the penalty on completion time ($r = -.39$, $p = .001$).

DISCUSSION AND CONCLUSIONS

Summary of study findings

The results of the controlled experiment show that users are capable of using highly flexible displays with ease. Users can make various single and dual deformations with both materials quickly and easily, even with a high precision level of +/- 6 degrees. The single exception is the asymmetric dual deformation, which, under high precision level, some participants had difficulties performing reliably with the shape-retaining material. Therefore, we suggest for this deformation a lower bound of +/- 8 degrees as the maximum precision if time is an issue in the application.

The results further showed that use of a shape-retaining material has only a modest average influence on task performance. While the fully flexible material is better suited for applications with only simple deformations, the shape-retaining material is well suited for use in applications with complex deformations. Notably, the time penalty introduced by the shape-retaining material decreases with increasing complexity of the deformation and the level of precision required. For the most complex deformation, it induces a temporal penalty of only 6 %, while it allows for easily holding deformations over time, for easily modifying them, and for modeling curvatures that involve more than two deformations. These quantitative findings are underpinned by qualitative observations. In the interviews, many participants commented that they preferred the fully flexible material for the task of the controlled experiment, whereas they preferred the shape-retaining material for analyzing curved phenomena in the medical dataset. For instance, P3 commented: *"The flexible one is easier to do the first assignment. But this one [the shape-retaining material] is easier to keep. It is more reliable. I can hold it even with just one hand. And I know that I gonna have what I want. It's way easier."* P4 stated: *"The less flexible material allows me to freeze a structure. (...) I don't have to bother with holding the shape."* P7 commented: *"I prefer the sensation of the flexible material, but the other one gives me more precision."* In future work, we plan to perform a qualitative analysis of our video recordings to analyze which deformations participants spontaneously made with both materials.

Results from the technical evaluation show that our tracking approach performs with high accuracy to support all of the proposed applications. Even in a technically very challenging task that encouraged participants to make very complex arbitrary deformations, the average error was below 7 mm. These values can be further decreased in a mobile setup, where the Kinect camera is closer to the projection surface. Then, the average RMS error for many of the deformations is close to the random noise of the Kinect sensor.

Touch input on deformable displays

A logical extension of Flexpad is touch input. With respect to this question, future work should address several challenges. Technically, this involves developing solutions for Kinect sensors to detect touch input reliably on real-time deformable surfaces. On a conceptual level and building on Dijkstra et al.'s recent work [9], this also involves an understanding of where users hold the display and where they deform it. This is required to identify areas that are reachable for touch input and to inform techniques that differentiate between touches stemming from desired touch input and false positives that result from the user touching the display while deforming it. An informal analysis from our study data showed that users made single deformations almost exclusively by touching the display close to the edges and on its backside. This also held true for dual deformations with the fully flexible display material. This suggests that touches in the center area of the display can be reliably interpreted as desired touch input. In contrast, the participants touched all over the display for dual deformations with the shape-retaining material. A simple spatial differentiation is not sufficient in this case; more advanced techniques need to be developed, for instance based on the shape of the touch point or on the normal force involved.

Active flexible displays

While this work focuses on projected displays, all of our application examples transfer to future active flexible displays. Currently available prototypes are still very limited in their flexibility, so that they cannot be used to realize our concepts. Given the rapid advancements in display technology, this is very likely to change in the future.

Smart materials: programmable stiffness and stretchability

Future work should investigate smart materials for flexible displays. As discussed above, both fully flexible and shape-retaining displays have unique capabilities. A material that can programmatically switch between both of these states would combine all these advantages. Moreover, future work should examine handheld displays that, in addition to being deformable, are stretchable. This will further increase the expressiveness of interactions with flexible displays.

ACKNOWLEDGMENTS

We gratefully acknowledge Reinhard Koch, James D. Hollan and Simon Olberding for helpful discussions and feedback on earlier versions of this paper. We thank Clemens Winkler and Cassandra Xia for help with the video. The time lapse video used in one application was provided by courtesy of Dan Heller. This work has partially been funded by the Cluster of Excellence Multimodal Computing and Interaction within the German Federal Excellence Initiative.

REFERENCES

1. Alexander, J., Lucero, A. and Subramanian, S. Tilt displays: designing display surfaces with multi-axis tilting and actuation. In *Proc. MobileHCI'12*, ACM Press, 2012.
2. Balakrishnan, R., Fitzmaurice, G., Kurtenbach, G. and Singh K. Exploring interactive curve and surface manipulation using a bend and twist sensitive input strip. In Proc. I3D '99, 1999.
3. Bandyopadhyay, D., Raskar, R. and Fuchs, H. Dynamic shader lamps: Painting on movable objects. In Intl. Symp. Augmented Reality, 2001.
4. Barnes C., Jacobs D., Sanders, J. and Goldman B. D., Rusinkiewicz, S., Finkelstein A. and Agrawala, M. Video puppetry: a performative interface for cutout animation. In *Proc. SIGGRAPH Asia'08*, ACM Press, 2008.
5. Benko, H, Jota R., and Wilson, A. MirageTable: freehand interaction on a projected augmented reality tabletop. In *Proc. CHI '12,* ACM Press, 2012.
6. Cagniart, C., Boyer E., and Ilic, S. Probabilistic deformable surface tracking from multiple videos. In *Proc. ECCV'10.*
7. Cassinelli, A and Ishikawa, M. Khronos projector. In *Proc. SIGGRAPH'05,* ACM Press, 2005.
8. Chen, Y., Rui, Y., and Huang, T.S. Multicue HMM-UKF for real-time contour tracking. *IEEE Transactions on Pattern Analysis and Machine Intelligence.* 2006.
9. Dijkstra, R., Perez, C., and Vertegaal, R. Evaluating effects of structural holds on pointing and dragging performance with flexible displays. In *Proc. CHI '11,* ACM Press, 2011.
10. Gallant, T. D., Seniuk, G.A., and Vertegaal, R. Towards more paper-like input: flexible input devices for foldable interaction styles. In *Proc. UIST '08,* ACM Press, 2008.
11. Harrison, C., Benko, H., and Wilson, A.D. OmniTouch: wearable multitouch interaction everywhere. In *Proc. UIST '11,* ACM Press, 2011.
12. Herkenrath, G., Karrer, T., and Borchers, J. Twend: twisting and bending as new interaction gesture in mobile devices. In *Proc. CHI '08 Extended Abstracts,* ACM Press, 2008.
13. Hilliges, O., Kim, D., Izadi, S., Weiss, M., and Wilson, A. HoloDesk: direct 3d interactions with a situated see-through display. In *Proc. CHI '12,* ACM Press, 2012.
14. Hilsmann, A., Schneider, D. C., and Eisert, P. Realistic cloth augmentation in single view video under occlusions. *Comput. Graph.*, 2010.
15. Holman, D., Vertegaal, R., Altosaar, M., Troje, N., and Johns D. Paper windows: interaction techniques for digital paper. In *Proc. CHI '05,* ACM Press, 2005.
16. Izadi, S., Kim, D., Hilliges, O., Molyneaux, D., Newcombe, R., Kohli, P., Shotton, J., Hodges, S., Freeman, D., Davison, A., and Fitzgibbon, A. KinectFusion: real-time 3d reconstruction and interaction using a moving depth camera. In *Proc. UIST '11,* ACM Press, 2011.
17. Jordt, A and Koch, R. Direct model-based tracking of 3d object deformations in depth and color video. *Intl. J. Computer Vision*, 2012.
18. Khalilbeigi, M., Lissermann, R., Kleine, W., and Steimle J. FoldMe: interacting with double-sided foldable displays. In *Proc. TEI '12,* ACM Press, 2012.
19. Khalilbeigi, M., Lissermann, R., Mühlhäuser, M., and Steimle, J. Xpaaand: Interaction techniques for rollable displays. In Proc. *CHI '11,* ACM Press, 2011.
20. Kildal, J., Paasovaara, S., and Aaltonen, V. Kinetic device: designing interactions with a deformable mobile interface. In *Proc. CHI 2012 Extended Abstracts,* ACM Press, 2012.
21. Kildal, J. and Wilson, G. Feeling it: the roles of stiffness, deformation range and feedback in the control of deformable UI. In *Proc. ICMI'12,* 2012
22. Konieczny, J., Shimizu, C., Gary Meyer, and D'nardo Colucci. A handheld flexible display system. In *Proc. IEEE Visualization 2005*, IEEE Press, 2005.
23. Lahey, B., Girouard, A., Burleson, W., and Vertegaal, R. PaperPhone: understanding the use of bend gestures in mobile devices with flexible electronic paper displays. In *Proc. CHI '11,* ACM Press, 2011.
24. Lee J. C., Hudson, S. E., and Tse, E. Foldable interactive displays. In *Proc. UIST '08,* ACM Press, 2008.
25. Lee, S. S., Kim, B., Jin, B., Choi, E., Kim, B., Jia, X., Kim, D., and Lee, K. P. How users manipulate deformable displays as input devices. In *Proc. CHI '10,* ACM Press, 2010.
26. Looser, J., Grasset, R., and Billinghurst, M. A 3D flexible and tangible magic lens in augmented reality. In *Proc. ISMAR '07*
27. Mark, R., Borch, J., Habeger, C., and Lyne, B. *Handbook of Physical Testing of Paper Vol. 1.* CRC Press, 2001.
28. Mistry, P., Maes, P., and Chang, L. WUW - wear ur world: a wearable gestural interface. In *Proc. CHI '09 EA,* 2009.
29. Ostermeier, A. and Hansen, N. An evolution strategy with coordinate system invariant adaptation of arbitrary normal mutation distributions within the concept of mutative strategy parameter control. In *Proc. Genetic and Evolutionary Comp. Conf.*, 1999.
30. Piper, B., Ratti, C., and Ishii, H. Illuminating clay: a 3-d tangible interface for landscape analysis. In *Proc. CHI'02*, 2002.
31. Saroul, L., Gerlach, S., and Hersch, R. D. Exploring curved anatomic structures with surface sections. In *Proc. IEEE Visualization,* 2003.
32. Schwesig, C., Poupyrev, I., and Mori, E. Gummi: a bendable computer. In *Proc. CHI '04,* ACM Press, 2004.
33. Sorkine, O. and Alexa, M. As-rigid-as-possible surface modeling. In *Proc. Eurographics*, 2007.
34. Spindler, M., Martsch, M., and Dachselt, R. Going beyond the surface: studying multi-layer interaction above the tabletop. In *Proc. CHI'12,* ACM Press, 2012.
35. Spindler, M., Stellmach, S., and Dachselt, R. PaperLens: advanced magic lens interaction above the tabletop. In *Proc. ITS'09,* ACM Press, 2009.
36. Varol, A., Salzmann, M., Tola, E., and Fua, P. Template-free monocular reconstruction of deformable surfaces. In *Proc. Computer Vision,* 2009.
37. Wilson, A. D. and Benko, H. Combining multiple depth cameras and projectors for interactions on, above and between surfaces. In *Proc. UIST '10,* ACM Press, 2010.

A Multi-touch Interface for Fast Architectural Sketching and Massing

Qian Sun* Juncong Lin† Chi-Wing Fu* Sawako Kaijima‡ Ying He*
*Nanyang Technological University †Xiamen University ‡Singapore University of Technology and Design

ABSTRACT
Architectural sketching and massing are used by designers to analyze and explore the design space of buildings. This paper describes a novel multi-touch interface for fast architectural sketching and massing of tall buildings. It incorporates a family of multi-touch gestures, enabling one to quickly sketch the 2D contour of a base floor plan and extrude it to model a building with multi-floor structures. Further, it provides a set of gestures to users: select and edit a range of floors; scale contours of a building; copy, paste, and rotate a building, i.e., create a twisted structure; edit profile curves of a building's profile; and collapse and remove a selected range of floors. The multi-touch system also allows users to apply textures or geometric façades to the building, and to compare different designs side-by-side. To guide the design process, we interacted with a domain expert, a practicing architect. The final interface was evaluated by architects and students in an architecture department, and the results demonstrated that the system allows rapid conceptual design and massing of novel multi-story building structures.

Author Keywords
Building design; multi-touch; sketching; massing

ACM Classification Keywords
H.5.2 Information Interfaces and Presentation: User interfaces

INTRODUCTION
Building design involves complex considerations and requires designers to explore a vast problem space. Such complexity challenges our perceptual capabilities, demands multiple rounds of trial and error, and the decomposition of the problems into numerous smaller parts. This is a rather time-consuming process and the exploration is usually limited by time and budget.

Sketching and massing are two fundamental design techniques widely used in the early stages of building design [10, 1]: *sketching* is a common design method used for generating ideas and exploring options with pen and paper, while *massing* is a design process normally used for understanding the overall shape and size of a building in relation to its surrounding environment, incorporating approximate volumetric information. During the early stages of design, architects explore multiple scenarios to clarify their design ideas and to arrive at a coherent building solution. Sketching and massing are not merely presentation devices, but are also effective approaches to enhancing the designers' spatial cognition process [22]. Hence, the functionality and the quality of design methods such as sketching and massing can significantly improve the design development process.

In the early design stages, a fast feedback loop between design actions and visualization helps architects to develop their design, and facilitates communication among design teams and clients. Although there are many off-the-shelf commercial software products for 3D modeling, e.g., Maya, 3Ds Max, AutoCAD, etc., most of them can be exceedingly complex, and are targeted mainly at general 3D modeling tasks and highly-experienced/well-trained users, e.g., artists, engineers, designers, etc. Conversely, fast prototyping tools such as Google SketchUp are easy to learn and intuitive for both experts and novice users, allowing one to quickly mock up prototype 3D structures. However, existing prototyping tools still focus mostly on general 3D shapes.

This paper is a result of collaborative work with a domain expert who is an architect. We develop a novel, multi-touch interface design for supporting the early stages of building design, aiming to combine aspects of sketching and massing to aid the design process. In particular, we focus on the design of tall buildings due to the scale and complexity involved in such design. We note the trend in tall buildings to have more elaborate silhouettes due to the enhanced capabilities of modern construction techniques (see Figure 1). We propose a family

Figure 1: *Buildings with progressively-varying and twisted structures:* Burj Al Arab *in Dubai,* Taipei 101 *in Taipei,* Turning Torso *in Sweden, and* The Shard *in London (left to right).*

CHI 2013, April 27–May 2, 2013, Paris, France.

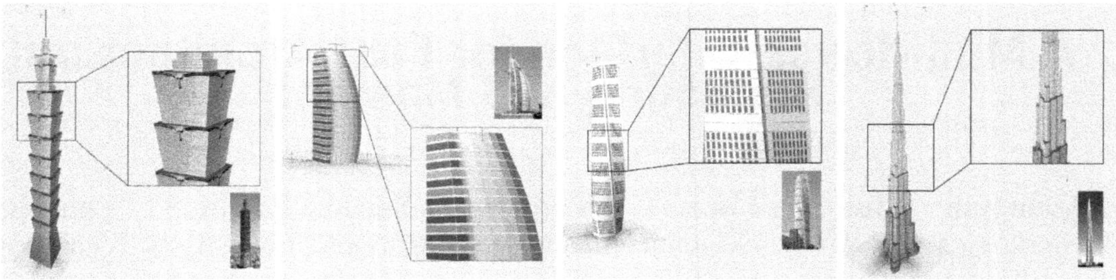

(a) Taipei 101 (183s) (b) Burj Al Arab (67s) (c) Turning torso (86s) (d) Burj Khalifa (273s)

Figure 2: *An architect constructed prototypic models of famous buildings using our multi-touch interface. The time taken to create these 3D building prototypes is shown below each model.*

of multi-touch gestures that permit the user to start by sketching and editing the 2D contour of the base floor, and then to extend that contour to create a 3D building model with fairly complex geometric features in a matter of minutes (see Figure 2). Simple drag-and-drop texturing can further enrich the model's appearance. In addition to 3D modeling, our interface computes and provides assorted architectural parameters for the building design, e.g., its dimensions, façade area, and volume, thereby providing useful hints for guiding the design process.

Compared to the conventional keyboard-mouse interface, our interface incorporates *hand-oriented actions* such as sketching, slicing, curving, and twisting, which allow one to quickly define the geometry and manipulate its volume (massing). Moreover, we also develop a number of novel interface tools for fast geometric modeling (such as symmetry snapping and easy texturing of image and façade geometry) on the building model, along with various editing operations. Thus, our interface can contribute to the conceptual phase of contemporary building design, where building designers and architects can apply it to do quick mockups, try alternative ideas, and get fast feedback to support major design decisions. Moreover, our proposed interface can serve as a rapid 3D modeling tool for creating content in digital media and games, which require buildings with good-looking shapes and appearance rather than a high level of detail. Such rapid 3D building prototyping is not easily achievable with conventional multi-touch 3D modeling interfaces, existing 3D sketching tools, or general 3D modeling software.

To the best of our knowledge, this is the first work to explore and develop multi-touch interactions for rapid creation and editing of tall buildings with non-trivial geometry. Here we summarize our technical contributions:

- We propose a novel multi-touch design interface, facilitating rapid creation of non-trivial contemporary buildings through step-by-step editing of floors, structures, and appearance. Our interface is not limited to modeling 3D buildings; it can be adapted to other types of 3D models with repeated geometric features, rotational/planar symmetry, or curved profiles.
- We propose an effective symmetry snapping method, allowing us to keep the local symmetry when editing 2D floor layouts with multi-touch. This is especially useful with imprecise finger interaction, and can be applied to editing 2D patterns and 3D models with symmetry.
- Following suggestions by experienced architects, we propose a set of novel multi-touch gestures; some are particularly useful for massing, e.g., multi-touch twisting for progressively-varying floor structures, cropping for quick editing and testing of building designs (to meet the sunlight regulations prohibiting casting shadows over neighboring buildings), etc.

RELATED WORK

The ability to collect user input simultaneously from multiple fingers can greatly enrich our interaction. Igarashi et al. [14] proposed scenarios for how multi-touch can be used to manipulate and deform complex 2D shapes. Moscovich and Hughes [18] devised the multi-finger cursor technique, offering smoother interaction with graphical displays. Benko et al. [5] developed a new technique to use multi-touch to improve precision when selecting small targets on a touch screen. Bau et al. [4] enhanced touch interfaces by a new tactile method that used the electro vibration principle to control the electrostatic friction between the finger and surface.

Recently, a number of research works have focused on studying the use of multi-touch to manipulate 3D content. Grossman et al. [11] presented a family of multi-touch gestures to manipulate 3D wireframe objects over a spherical volumetric display. Later, Hancock et al. [12, 13] proposed a multi-touch concept called *Sticky Fingers* to grab and manipulate 3D objects on a tabletop. Reisman et al. [20] formulated a screen-space method, allowing users to directly rotate-scale-translate 3D objects with three or more contact points. Kim et al. [15] designed multi-touch interactions on an iPhone/iPod Touch to control walking in a 3D virtual environment. Chang et al. [6] presented an interesting origami modeling interface by proposing a family of specially-designed multi-touch gestures. Fu et al. [9] proposed multi-touch gestures for controlling navigation in a large-scale astrophysical simulation shown on a wall display. Cohé et al. [8] adopted the use of 3D transformation widgets to transform 3D objects with multi-touch. Kin et al. [16] proposed multi-touch gestures for positioning, arranging, and scaling 3D objects in virtual organic environments, while Chiu et al. [7] explored document folding actions and proposed practical multi-touch gestures for various manipulation scenarios. Compared to the above work, which mainly focuses on the manipulation of 3D contents/views or navigation in virtual space, we aim to create a fast architectural sketching and massing tool for designing tall buildings. Our interface offers a rich set of novel multi-

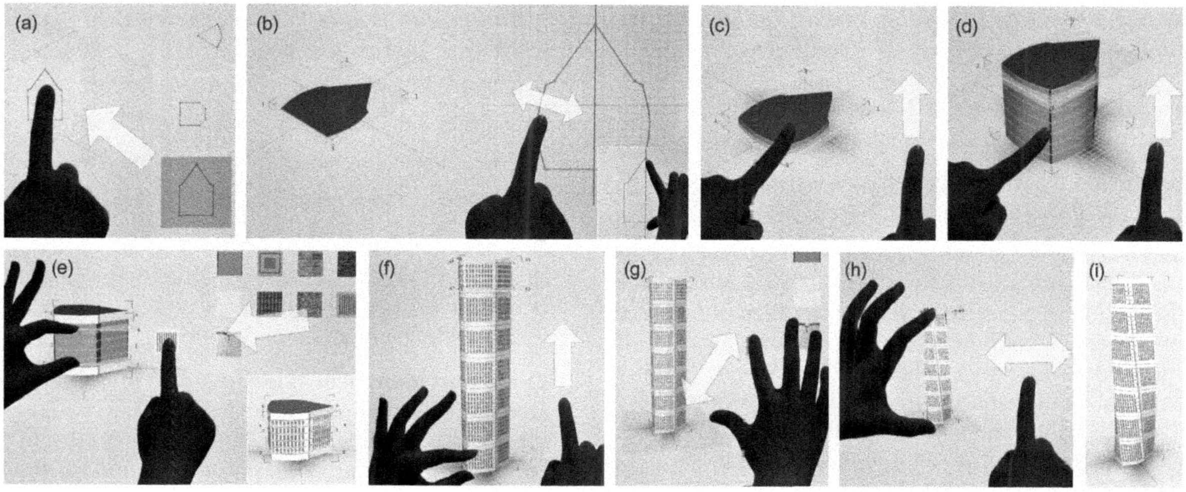

Figure 3: *System overview. Here we show our design pipeline with the* Turning Torso *building. The user starts by creating a 2D floor plan, which can either be selected from the tabbed panel (see (a)) or sketched by the user. After that, the user can freely edit the 2D floor contour using the 2D floor plan editor by manipulating the control points on the 2D contour. Our system provides multi-touch gestures and a novel grid&symmetry snapping mechanism for users to edit the 2D floor contour (see (b)). The inset for the two-finger anchor gesture specifies the symmetry axis. Later, the user employs one finger to select the floor plan and create the first ground-level floor (see (c)). After that, the user can create multiple floors by duplicating the ground floor (see (d)). Then, the user can apply an image texture to the selected floors by a simple drag-and-drop (see (e)). Our interface also allows the user to easily copy and paste selected floors to extend the building levels (see (f)), and zoom out using a two-finger pinch (see (g)). Finally, the user can select the whole building and use a one-finger horizontal drag to twist the building structure (see (h)) to produce the final result (see (i)).*

touch gestures dedicated to efficiently designing a non-trivial geometry (sketching) and manipulating its volume (massing) in a matter of minutes, which has great potential for the conceptual phase of contemporary building design.

MozArt [21] is a multi-modal interface that supports speech and gesture input to Google SketchUp. Unlike MozArt, our interface does not rely on voice input, and supports a much wider range of modeling functions, allowing the users to make non-trivial shapes. TreeSketch [17] is a system for modeling complex, natural-looking trees using Palubicki et al.'s algorithm [19]. Taking advantages of a multi-touch tablet, the user can directly grow a tree structure by using a few sketches to intuitively specify the direction of the trunk and branches. All the other controls, such as changing parameters as the tree grows, interleaving controlled and autonomous growth, and editing generated forms, are still based on the conventional interface with menus, dialogs, buttons, and scrollbar. In contrast, users of our system can make a complete 3D building by multi-touch gestures alone. Bae et al. [2] presented ILoveSketch, a pen-gesture-based 3D curve sketching system, which enables professional designers to efficiently create conceptual 3D curve models. Later, they improved the sketching system by incorporating many new interactions [3]. Unlike their pen-based gesture design concept, our system offers a rich set of direct finger gestures, and allows rapid design of non-trivial modern buildings. In addition, the output of our system can be directly imported into general modeling software such as Autodesk and 3Ds Max.

OVERVIEW

This section introduces our multi-touch user interface, and then presents its usage scenario.

User Interface. Our multi-touch interface consists of a main working window and a floating-tabbed panel. These are shown on the left and right sides of Figure 4(b), respectively. The main window has three buttons on the left, allowing the user to undo/redo a sequence of operations, enable/disable control point snapping when editing a 2D floor plan, and bring out different designs for comparison. Note that the current GUI layout is mainly for right-handed users, but we may re-arrange the floating tabbed panel to the left and adapt the interface for left-handed users.

The main working window shows a perspective view of the current 3D building design. See again Figure 4(b). In this window, the user can perform basic multi-touch manipulations to control the camera view as well as apply various multi-touch gestures to edit and decorate the design. The floating-tabbed panel consists of a number of windows: 1) a

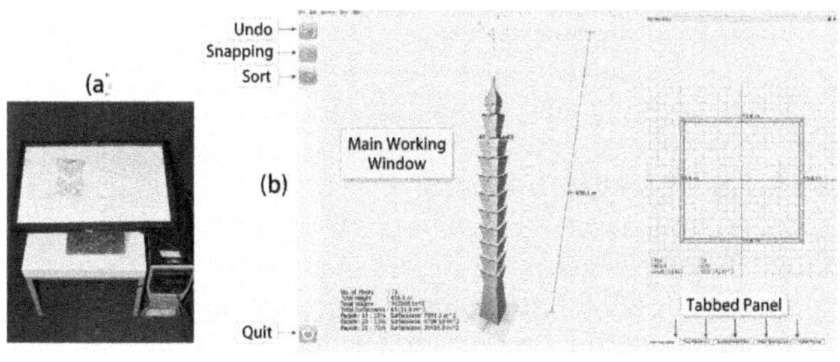

Figure 4: *(a) Our multi-touch display system; (b) Our GUI interface consists of a main working window (left) that presents the building design in 3D and a floating tabbed panel (right) that offers a 2D floor plan editor, a building profile editor, and various resource libraries.*

floor plan editor (see Figure 4(b)) for one to view and edit the 2D contour of the selected floor, 2) a building profile editor for editing the profile curve, and 3) resource libraries for one to retrieve and apply pre-defined floor plans, walls, window images, and geometric façades by simple drag-and-drop.

Usage Scenario. There are three major stages to mock up a 3D building design, as illustrated in Figure 3(a)-(i):

1. **Initial Design.** First, we begin by constructing the 2D contour of the ground level floor. The user can either pick an existing floor plan from the related resource library (see (a)) and/or sketch&edit his/her own contour using the 2D floor plan editor (see (b)). Then, the user drops the floor plan into the main working window, creates a single floor (see (c)), adjusts its height, and then duplicates it to create many other floors and form an initial design (see (d)).
2. **Structure Editing.** After that, we enter the structure editing stage, where the user edits the building structure by various multi-touch gestures. Here, the user applies various multi-touch gestures (e.g., copying (see (f)), scaling (see (g)), twisting (see (h&i)), and slicing, etc) to edit the entire building or a range of selected floors. Various building parameters including the façade area and volume are recomputed and presented interactively to guide the design.
3. **Appearance Enhancement.** Lastly, the user decorates a building design by dragging and dropping image textures or geometric façades (see (e)) from the library resources.

Note that we group the interactive operations into these three stages to facilitate our understanding of design strategy, but in practice, one can perform them in any order as long as the operation being performed is appropriate to the current condition of the building design. For example, we can drag-and-drop image texture (see Figure 3(e)) onto the initial ground floor before the structure editing stage. As shown in Figure 3, a user can rapidly create a 3D building design with non-trivial geometry in a matter of minutes. However, such a task could be very tedious and time consuming, even when performed by experienced users with general 3D modeling software.

Besides the above major stages, the user can also record multiple building designs and compare them side by side visually in the main working window with their key architectural parameters. Moreover, the user can load a surrounding environment, put the current building design into it, and examine its relation to the surroundings. These features, as suggested also by an architect, allow one to clarify the design and to arrive at a more coherent building solution.

DESIGN CONSIDERATIONS

Our system is implemented on a 3M M2256PW (22") multi-touch display system (see Figure 4(a)). We tilted the display to a near horizontal orientation, which allowed the users' elbows to rest on the display border during the interaction. In the following, we present the interface design considerations that guide and direct our user interaction design:

1) Sufficient modeling capability. The interface should provide sufficient modeling capability for one to design contemporary buildings, so that we can create different forms of structures and shapes that can be found in various existing buildings, see Figure 1, e.g.,

- Curved profiles, see *Burj Al Arab*, Dubai;
- Disrupted floor plans, see *Taipei 101*, Taiwan;
- Twisted structures, see *Turning Torso*, Sweden;
- Symmetric floor plans, see *Burj Al Arab*, Dubai;
- Slanted sides, see *The Shard*, London.

Regarding this, we surveyed a wide range of contemporary buildings and examined their shapes and structures before formulating the interaction design.

2) Fast architectural sketching and massing. The interface should support the rapid design of tall buildings. Regarding this, we identified three major stages needed in the overall building prototyping process: *initial building*, *structure editing*, and *appearance enhancement*, as well as assorted modeling and editing operations. The interface also allows the user to compare all the designs side by side and put a design into the target surrounding environment, so that the user can easily identify both the merits and defects, and make further improvements if necessary. Besides the editing capability, the interface also shows the key building parameters, such as dimensions, façade area, and volume, to help guide the design.

3) Easy-to-learn gestures. As a fast prototyping interface, the gestures should also be easy to learn, so that users can quickly understand the interface and perform the necessary operations to rapidly develop and evolve their designs. Regarding this, we organize relevant interactions by their types and operational stages to facilitate a consistent sequence of interaction. As users usually prefer a small number of gestures, it is highly desirable to re-use the gestures (especially the standard ones) in different scenarios without ambiguity. Furthermore, the most frequently used gestures should be designed to be simple to perform.

4) Taking advantage of direct manipulation. Structure editing is usually the most critical and challenging part of the whole design process. To enable the users to focus on this task, we provide them with a direct-manipulation interface, where all structure editing operations, e.g., viewpoint navigation, floor selecting, and façade editing, can be done with multi-touch gestures. By this, the users can fully focus their attention on the main working window.

MULTI-TOUCH GESTURES

This section presents our interaction design and the related implementation. Our design includes four sets of multi-touch gestures organized as follows:

1) Initial Building

In the process of prototyping a building, our approach is to first create an initial 3D building design and then further refine it by editing its 3D structure (next stage: *structure editing*) and enhancing its appearance (another stage: *appearance enhancement*). To sketch an initial design, we basically need to create a floor plan and then extrude it to form an initial building. In summary, we propose the following operations relevant to this stage:

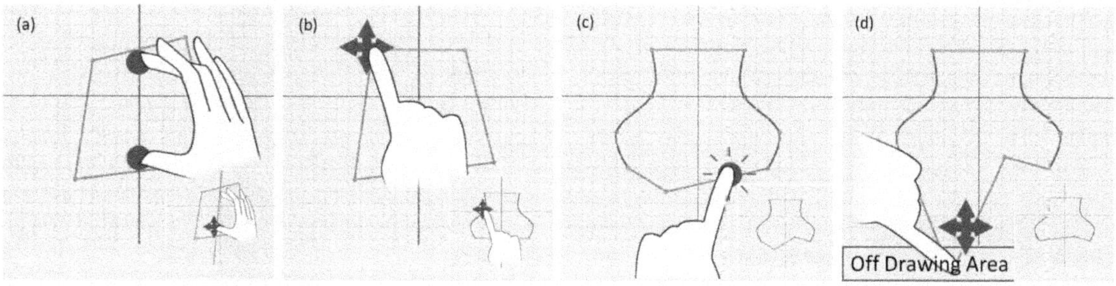

Figure 5: *Multi-touch gestures for editing 2D floor plan contour. (a) Two fingers to specify the axis for symmetry snapping; while we hold the fingers on screen, we can still move them to adjust the symmetry axis (see the inset); (b) We can freely move a control point with a finger and it could snap to a mirror location of a point on the other side of the symmetry axis; see the inset for making a symmetric shape; (c) To add a control point, we can double-tap on a line/curve segment. The inset shows the result; (d) To remove a control point, we can drag it off the drawing area.*

i) Sketching and editing a floor plan. In our system, a floor plan is represented by a 2D floor plan contour, or simply a floor contour, which is a closed curve made up of polylines and spline curve segments (we use interpolatory splines). Hence, we can create non-trivial shapes for floor plans, see Figure 3. In detail, the user can pick a built-in floor plan from the library resource, or sketch a closed curve as a floor contour by free-style sketching using the floor plan editor. With the editor, the user can directly use fingers to manipulate the control points on the floor contour to adjust the contour shape, see Figure 3(b). Furthermore, double-tapping on a line segment can create a new control point for refining the contour shape, see Figure 5(c); double-tapping on an existing control point can toggle its status between straight and curved; while dragging a control point off the drawing area can remove it, see Figure 5(d). Lastly, the user can also store an edited 2D floor plan in the library resource as a future asset.

ii) Grid snapping. To improve precision in editing the floor contours, our interface provides a grid snapping function that allows the user to precisely snap and put a control point on grid points. This function is enabled by default but can be toggled by the snapping button on the left hand side of the interface, see Figure 4(b).

iii) Symmetry snapping. Like most everyday objects, contemporary buildings usually contain strong symmetric structures. To improve the editing efficiency, we allow users to preserve the symmetry (local or non-local) of floor plans during the multi-touch interaction by our novel multi-touch technique: *symmetry snapping*. The user can start with a *two-finger anchor gesture* on the display - holding two fingers on the floor plan editor for two seconds to create a straight line, see the inset in Figure 5(a). Once a symmetrical line is formed, the user can fine-tune its position (possibly snapping its control points to the grid also) by moving the two fingers on the screen. After that, symmetry snapping is enabled with the constructed line serving as the symmetry axis:

- When the user manipulates a control point, he/she can move it close to the mirror image position of points on the other side of the axis. After releasing his/her finger, our interface snaps the control point to a mirror image position.
- Furthermore, once two points are snapped together, the two points are said to be bound, and can be moved together to maintain local symmetry, see Figure 5(b). If one wants to break this symmetry, one just needs to use another finger to hold one of the two points and move the other. This is a novel and efficient technique for creating and editing symmetric patterns in multi-touch manipulation - a process that usually involves imprecise finger movements.

Lastly, to ensure consistency in successive symmetry snapping, our interface remembers all symmetry axes created so far per floor plan. Thus, if a new axis is found to be close to a previous axis, our interface will snap it to the previous axis. Finally, dragging the symmetry axis out of the main working window can take it out and disable symmetry snapping.

iv) Initial building from a floor plan. Once an edited floor plan is ready in the floor plan editor or we find a desired floor plan in the library resource, we can drag and drop the floor plan to the main working window with a single finger. After that, we can use one finger to touch and select a floor plan, and then use another finger to drag up to control the height of this initial ground floor. The floor height will be used for every single floor in the entire building design unless the user rescales some floor heights later. After we have created the first floor, we can touch the resulting floor to select it and then apply the copy gesture (to be described later) to duplicate this floor to form all other floors above it, see detail in the next subsection. Finally, an initial building can be readily modified by the structure editing operations in the next stage.

2) Structure Editing

Our interface provides a family of multi-touch gestures, allowing one to quickly edit and mock up a design that mimics a contemporary building structure, see previous section. In short, one can first select a range of floors (or a particular floor) to be edited, and then perform the relevant gestures to modify the structure/geometry/appearance of the selected range of floors. Typically, the user of this approach will first employ the fingers of one hand to make the selection, and will then use the fingers of the other hand to do the editing. If no floors are selected, the editing applies to the entire building.

i) Floor selector. Whenever the user puts a finger on the building, a floor selector is created for the associated floor being touched, and is presented as a semi-transparent yellow thin-plate tagged with a floor number, see Figure 3 (b,c&d).

Now, the user can use his/her finger to drag the selector up/down to choose a particular floor. To select a range of floors, he/she can use two fingers to touch two different floor levels. In this way, a pair of floor selectors can be created simultaneously with all floors in-between (inclusively) selected, see Figure 3(e). Once a floor selector is created and shown, we can still touch it and drag it to a different floor level on the building. To de-select the floor(s), the user can simply tap on a screen region outside the building. If there are no selected floors, the entire building is considered to be selected and the user edits will be applied to the entire building. Using this selection mechanism, the user can hold down the floor selection, allowing us to disambiguate the reuse of drag and pinch for object manipulation in the same window.

ii) Copy floors. To facilitate the modeling of tall buildings, we offer a simple gesture to copy blocks of floors. After selecting a single floor(or a range of floors) and holding down the selection, one can apply a one-finger vertical drag up to copy the selected floor(s) above the selected floors. The number of copies is proportional to the vertical distance between the initial and end touch points. Since the 3D building design can change interactively with the finger drag, the user can observe the visual changes in the prototyping design and adjust the number of copies interactively from the visual feedback, see Figure 3 (b&c) for copying a single floor and Figure 3(f) and Figure 6 for copying a range of floors.

iii) Removing floors. As well as creating more floors, one can also remove the selected floors by a one-finger vertical drag-down gesture, which is a reversed version of copying floors, see Figure 6(b).

iv) Rescaling floor height. Since rescaling floor height is a rather infrequent action, we assign a more complicated gesture for it: a two-finger vertical pinch open gesture. By repeating this two-finger pinch open gesture, one can continue to increase the height of the selected floor(s); reversing it (after a slight pinch open) with a pinch close can decrease the floor height.

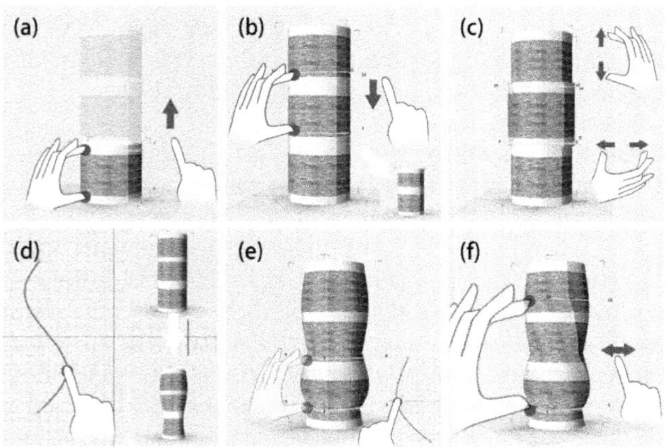

Figure 6: *Multi-touch gestures for structure editing: (a) copying floors; (b) removing floors; (c) scaling floors (heights or contours); (d) editing the building profile for the entire building; (e) editing the building profile locally on selected floors; and (f) twisting.*

v) Scaling floor plan. In addition, one can uniformly scale the contours of a range of floors simultaneously to quickly try out different shapes on the building design. This can be done by a simple two-finger horizontal pinch on the screen after selecting one or more floor(s), see Figure 6(c). Note that to allow a more comfortable execution of this gesture and prevent possible strain to the wrist, we do not require the two-finger gesture to be performed horizontally to the display. As long as the pinch angle is 45° degrees or below on the display, we regard it as a horizontal pinch.

vi) Twisting. Modern structural engineering allows the construction of complicated buildings with creative profiles. One of these is the twisted structure, see again the Turning-Torso building in Figure 1. To create a design with twisted appearance, one can first select a range of floors (at least two floors), and then use a one-finger horizontal drag to control the amount of twisting, see Figure 6(f).

In our implementation, we first compute the total twisting angle relative to the finger drag displacement, and divide it by $n-1$ to obtain the twisting angle between successive floors, where n is the total number of selected floors. Like the copy gesture, one can again interactively perform this gesture to observe the results while moving one's finger(s). Lastly, since buildings normally cannot be twisted to a large angle due to structural constraints, we employ six degrees as the upper limit of the twisting angle between successive floors.

vii) Editing profile curve. Another interesting feature of contemporary buildings is the curved profile shape, such as the Burj Al Arab Hotel (see again Figure 1). We can use the building profile editor in the tabbed panel to edit a profile curve to control the amount of scaling on the selected range of floors, see Figure 6(d)-(e). As shown in the building profile editor view, such a profile curve is constrained, and must start from the top and end at the bottom, corresponding to the top most and bottom most floors currently selected. The user can interactively manipulate the control points in ways similar to those used in the floor plan editor, and can observe the visual changes on the building design as his/her fingers move.

viii) Cropping the façade. Lastly, our interface also offers a handy editing tool for producing a slanted side, as in the modern building *The Shard.* As illustrated in Figure 7, the user can tap four fingers on any region outside the region in the main window to enable cropping. Then he/she can sketch a freeform curve on the building silhouette and cut out a portion of the building. Note that apart from artistic concerns, a number of real building designs have to be modified by such a cropping to allow sufficient sunlight to reach surrounding buildings in accordance with some building construction reg-

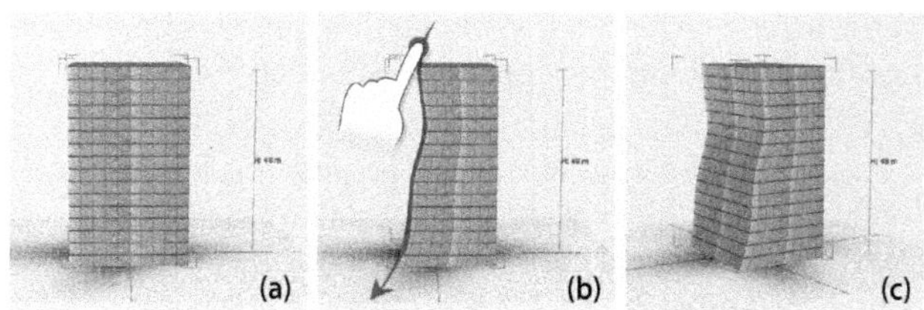

Figure 7: *Cropping the façade.*

ulations. This interface feature allows us to quickly modify the building and observe its relation to the surroundings.

3) Appearance Enhancement

With the aforementioned gestures, the user can quickly make a building design with non-trivial geometry. However, the design lacks surface details, such as its façade. Our interface provides libraries of image textures and geometric façades for the user to quickly drag and drop to apply to the building.

The more complicated operation here is in fact the underlying implementation behind the user interaction. To map an image texture onto the building, our interface first computes the u and v texture coordinates for each vertex, where the v coordinate is simply interpolated along the height of a floor, whereas the u parameter can be found by an arc-length parameterization of each floor contour. Regarding a geometric façade, which is in fact a 3D geometric texture (e.g., windows), our interface can compute a volumetric space with the w texture coordinate in addition to u and v, where w is defined along the local normal direction on the building surface. In this way, we can appropriately map and attach a 3D geometry texture by deforming each geometric façade and fit them one by one onto the building surface like a 3D image.

4) Camera View

Camera view controls offer basic but essential operations for users to see their designs from different views. However, instead of allowing unrestricted control as in general 3D modeling software, we constrain the camera view to center only on locations along the building's central vertical axis from the ground to its tip. As a sketching and massing interface, this control is sufficient and brings greater efficiency since our view always focuses on the design without taking off.

In summary, our interface has the following camera-view gestures, see also Figure 8:

- First, we can rotate using a one-finger drag (left): the horizontal component of the drag rotates the building about its central vertical axis while the vertical component of the drag updates the camera's elevation angle, whose range is restricted from 0 (i.e., the camera cannot go below the ground) to 90 degrees (i.e., the camera cannot tilt beyond the building top);
- Second, a two-finger drag (middle) can move the view up and down by translating the view center (look-at) along the central vertical axis of the building;
- Last, users can also zoom in/out using a standard two-finger pinch (right), or double-tap to quickly zoom out (reset) to see the entire building design.

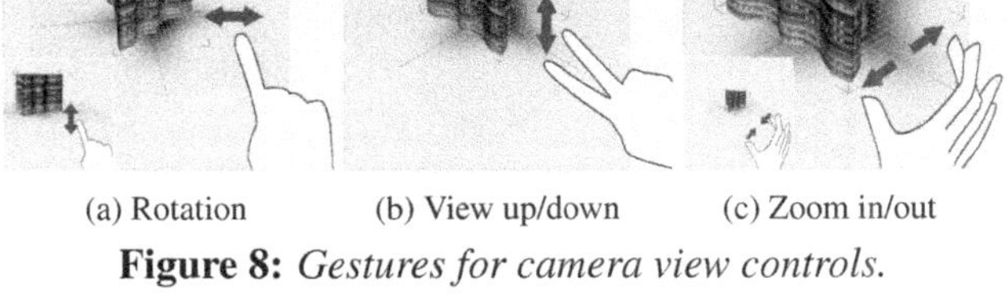

(a) Rotation (b) View up/down (c) Zoom in/out

Figure 8: *Gestures for camera view controls.*

5) Design Coherency

In the building design process, one may have come up with various designs with (slightly) different variations. With our interface, the user can touch any screen region outside the building with three fingers. Then all existing designs can be displayed for comparison. Similar to the camera view control for a single building, the user can explore *all* buildings simultaneously. To delete a model, the user can simply drag it out. Furthermore, the user can touch the Sort button to re-order all the buildings according to a selected architectural parameter such as the façade area. After identifying the model that requires further editing, the user can double-tap it and put it into the normal editing mode. This comparison feature is desirable to allow the users to clarify their design ideas and to arrive at a coherent building solution, see Figure 9.

Figure 9: *Side-by-side comparison of designs is desirable for users to clarify their design ideas and to arrive at a coherent building solution. To delete a design, one can simply drag-and-drop it (a); the view can be updated (b).*

IMPLEMENTATION AND RESULTS

Our multi-touch building prototyping interface was built on a Dell workstation T3500 with a 2.67GHz Xeon CPU, 12GB memory, and a GeForce GTX295 (1792MB) graphics card, as well as a 3M M2256PW (22") multi-touch display system, see Figure 4(a). The software is written in C++ and Qt4.7.

With our multi-touch interface, users can quickly design 2D floor plans with non-trivial shapes, as well as 3D buildings with non-trivial appearance by twisting, profiling, cropping, and local non-uniform scaling. Figure 2 shows a collection of building models that mimic famous contemporary buildings around the world. All these models can be constructed in a matter of minutes by a 3D modeling artist, who only needs some pictures of each building, see Figure 2.

EXPERT REVIEW

We invited three architects to evaluate our multi-touch interface: two with 10+ years experience and one with three years experience. All were very familiar with multi-touch devices, such as the iPad, iPhone, etc. The purpose of this expert review was to evaluate our interface from the architects' perspective, e.g., could our system meet their requirements? Was our interface easy-to-use? Did the architects enjoy using our interface and did they want to use it in their case studies?

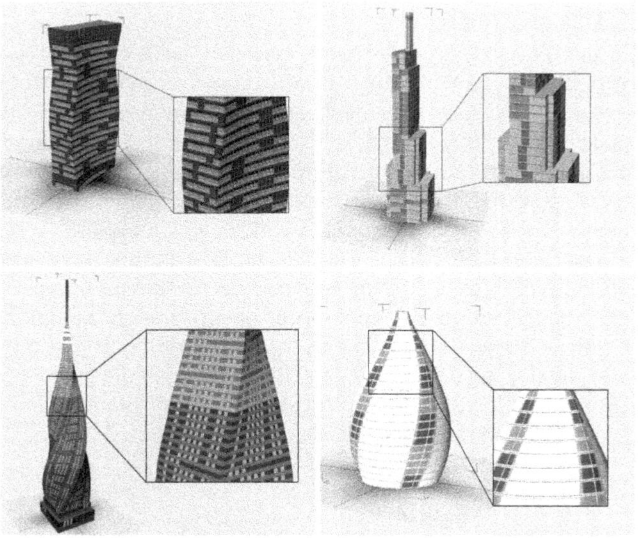

Figure 10: *Some results from the architects who participated in the expert review. All models were made in a few minutes.*

The architects first watched a 5-minute video tutorial that demonstrated the interaction gestures for 3D navigation, initial modeling, structure editing, appearance enhancement, and design comparison. The tutorial also contained step-by-step instructions for constructing the Turning Torso building. Next, they were provided with a gesture table, and were given 10 minutes to practice all the gestures. Then, each of them had 30 minutes to freely make building designs with our tool. All the participants were impressed by our multi-touch interface, and made various non-trivial designs, some of which are shown in Figure 10. Lastly, each participant was asked to complete a questionnaire and rate our interface on a scale from 1 to 5, see results in Figure 11.

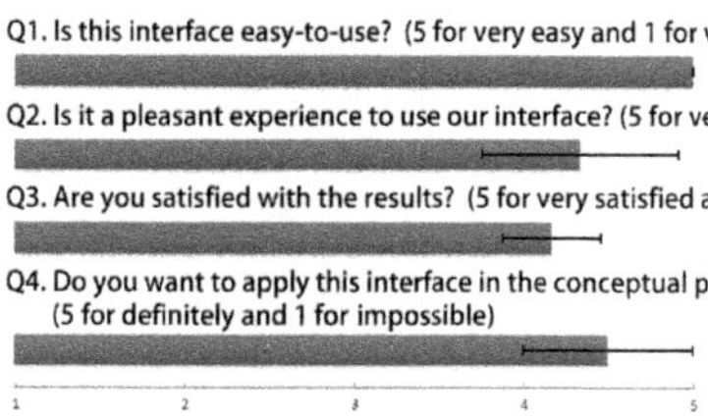

Figure 11: *Questionnaire in the expert review.*

Some gestures in our interface are also common in other multi-touch applications, e.g., the two-finger pinch for camera zoom in/out, and the one finger drag to change view (see Figure 8(a) and (c)). To reduce the user's learning curve, we also extend the usage of these gestures to other scenarios. For example, during the structure editing, when a range of floors is selected, a two-finger pinch vertically (resp. horizontally) scales the floor plan (resp. height), see Figure 6(c)).

The architects also commented that our gesture set was easy to use. We observed that after the 15-minute training period (watching the video tutorial and practicing for 10 minutes), all the architects had been able to learn the gestures well. Furthermore, the gestures were also easy to recall, as evidenced by the fact that the architects seldom needed to look at the gesture table during the building design stage. Our system also recorded the frequency of each gesture when the architects performed them during the design stage. Statistics show that the most frequently used gestures were camera rotation (26%), floor selection (25%), editing 2D floor plan (17%), and applying the texture (12%). The least frequently used gestures were floor duplication (1%), floor scaling (3%), and initial building from the ground floor plan (3%).

All the participants agreed that our interface was easy to use, and was efficient for designing buildings. They were also satisfied with the results produced by our interface. In addition, they were very pleased with the capability of our interface to allow the entire building to be made just with the fingers, without any other form of input. They also appreciated that all the frequently used editing and navigation operations could be done completely by gestures, and that there were very few buttons for undoing, sorting and snapping. They could use drag-and-drop texturing to flexibly apply texture to a range of floors or to the entire building, which was very effective for improving the appearance. Such a texturing procedure is often tedious with conventional 3D modeling tools. Moreover, our multi-hand gestures, such as twisting, scaling, and duplication, were very powerful for 3D editing, and they had not found their equal in any other multi-touch applications. However, they also pointed out several limitations of our current prototype system. The interface was limited to designing a *single* tall building, thus, it could not be used for the Petronas Twin Towers in Kuala Lumpur or a group of buildings. Moreover, the interface could not support the design of *freeform* structures, such as the Milan Trade Fair Complex.

USER STUDY

To quantitatively evaluate the performance of our interface, we compared our interface with Google Sketchup, a popular general-purpose 3D prototyping tool. Furthermore, we installed a multi-touch plug-in[1] on Google Sketchup, so that users could perform simple multi-touch gestures, such as pinching. We recruited twenty participants, 10 males and 10 females aged from 18 to 26. All were undergraduate or postgraduate students in a university architecture department.

[1]Sketchup MultiTouch project by Sharma, Solyga, and Bintahir: `http://code.google.com/p/sketchupmultitouch/`

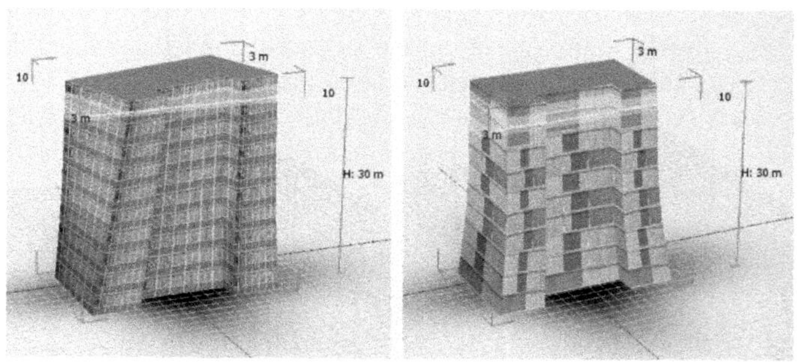

(a) Experiment #1 (b) Experiment #2

Figure 12: *User study. We designed two experiments for buildings with non-trivial geometry to compare the efficiency of our multi-touch interface against Multi-touch Google Sketchup in terms of fast building prototyping.*

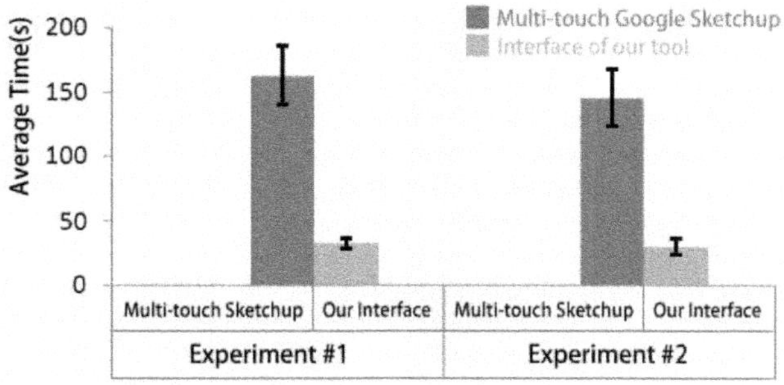

Figure 13: *User study results. The vertical axis shows the average time taken for the participants to complete each experiment. The black vertical line on each bar is the standard deviation. Time was measured in seconds.*

We designed two experiments to compare our interface with multi-touch Google Sketchup. The first experiment was to create a 10-storey building with a concave floor contour and curved/twisted profile (see Figure 12(a)). Each participant had to first perform the initial modeling gestures to create a 2D floor contour and then extrude the floor plan to make a 3D building. Next, the participant had to non-uniformly scale only the building profile for the top levels, edit the related profile curve, and then twist it. Finally, the participant had to attach image textures to improve the appearance. The second experiment was to further improve the appearance of a building (produced from the first experiment) by applying image textures to it (see Figure 12(b)). There were three façade textures available to the participants, and we also provided a table that specified the texture to be applied to each floor.

At the beginning of the user study, we introduced our *multi-touch* tool and tutored each participant in the same way as we did in the expert review process. After being given the figures that show the buildings in experiments #1 and #2, each participant was asked to complete the buildings, and our interface recorded the time taken by each of them. After that, we introduced multi-touch Google Sketchup to the participants. As a general purpose 3D modeling tool, Google Sketchup has many buttons, thus posing extra difficulty for beginner users. Though the plug-in enables participants to use Google Sketchup with simple multi-touch gestures, modeling operations such as extruding a face can only be done by first tapping a button. To reduce the learning curve for the participants and thus allow a fairer comparison, we discussed which buttons were necessary for the participants in order to complete the experiments. To assist the participants to tap these buttons, we reset the screen resolution to enlarge the buttons. The participants were given 15 minutes to familiarize themselves with these functionalities. Finally, they were asked to repeat the experiments with multi-touch Google Sketchup.

As shown in Figure 13, the average times taken to complete the two experiments with our multi-touch interface were 33 and 30 seconds, respectively, whereas the times taken with multi-touch Google Sketchup were 163 and 146 seconds, respectively. To analyze the user study data, we conducted a paired t-test with the null hypothesis H0: the mean values of the task completion time using the two interfaces are equal. We used a significance level of 0.005, given H0 is true. The resultant t values for experiments one and two were 27.6 and 26.2, respectively. Both values were larger than the critical value, i.e., 2.86, (with a degree of freedom DOF=19) obtained from the t-test table; hence, we could reject H0, and showed that our interface can help users to complete the tasks faster.

Multi-touch Google Sketchup is slower than our interface for the following reasons. First, although users can use basic multi-touch gestures in Google Sketchup, they have to frequently tap various buttons to perform the different modeling operations needed to complete the tasks; this is not only tedious but also distracting to the users. Second, our drag-and-drop texturing function allows the users to quickly apply textures to a selected range of floors (or the entire building). Although multi-touch Google Sketchup also allows users to apply textures to selected faces (i.e., windows in a floor), such selection is done on polygon levels (rather than semantic levels on the buildings); an approach, which is typically tedious and prone to error.

CONCLUSION

This paper proposes a novel multi-touch interface comprising a rich set of direct finger gestures to facilitate rapid prototyping of modern building structures. Using our interface, users can quickly mock up, in a matter of minutes, reasonably complex building structures that can be found in many renowned modern buildings around the world.

In our approach, we divide the prototyping process into three stages, and devise effective multi-touch gestures dedicated to relevant modeling and editing needs in different working stages. Among them, our work contributes particularly to a number of novel modeling and editing techniques, including symmetry snapping for constrained multi-touch 2D editing, interface design for efficient multi-touch modeling of buildings, as well as a collection of effective gestures for quick refinement of building designs, e.g., copy and collapse, non-uniform deformation, profile curve editing, and twisting. These interaction gestures are not only efficient and relatively easy to learn and use, but also have great potential for supporting more general 2D/3D modeling and editing in other application scenarios. Finally, we developed a working system, and also evaluated its effectiveness with a number of users. The expert review justified that our interface has the potential for use in the conceptual phase of contemporary building design.

Generalization. Existing multi-touch techniques to interact with 3D contents focus mainly on 3D navigation, 3D object manipulation, physical simulation, and virtual scene design. However, our work advances the multi-touch interaction technology with a comprehensive and novel set of 3D modeling and editing gestures. With this, we can enhance the capability of multi-touch for designing 2D shapes as well as 3D models with non-trivial structures involving twisting, profiling, and local non-uniform scaling. It is worth noting that the proposed multi-touch interface is not limited to designing 3D buildings. In addition, it can be used for other types of geometric designs: 1) for 3D models with repeated geometric features, e.g., bookshelves, cabinets, etc., see Figure 14(a)(b),

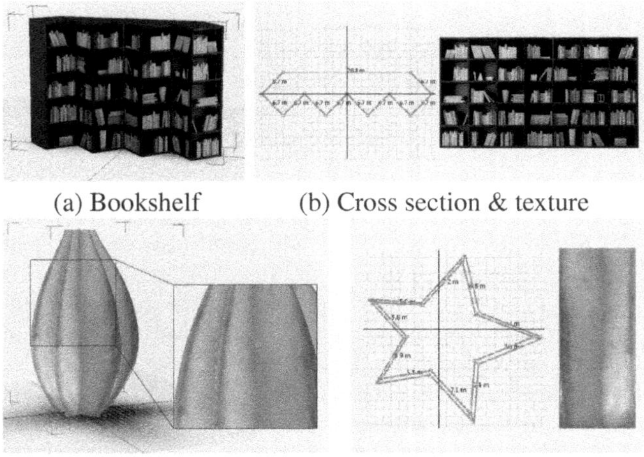

(a) Bookshelf (b) Cross section & texture

(c) Star fruit (d) Cross section & texture

Figure 14: *Our interface can be used with other types of 3D design, where the 3D models have repeated geometric features, planar/rotational symmetry, or curved profile.*

which shows a bookshelf created with our interface; we first sketched the cross-section of the bookshelf using the 2D floor plan editor, and then adjusted the number of levels by the floor select/extruding feature in our tool; and 2) for 3D models with progressively varying and symmetric cross-sections, e.g., vases, bottles, bowls, etc. See the star fruit 3D model shown in Figure 14(c)(d). It can be quickly made with our interface in just two minutes.

Acknowledgment. We would like to thank the reviewers for their various helpful comments, and the architects and students (from SUTD and NUS, Singapore) who participated in our expert review and user study. Photos shown in Figure 1 are from Flickr, courtesy of photographers James Cridland, My Hourglass, NASA Videographer, and failing_angel (left to right). This project is supported in part by NRF2008IDM-IDM004-006 and the MOE Tier-1 Grant (RG 29/11).

REFERENCES

1. Akin, O., and Moustapha, H. *Strategic use of representation in architectural massing*. Elsevier, 2003.
2. Bae, S.-H., Balakrishnan, R., and Singh, K. ILoveSketch: as-natural-as-possible sketching system for creating 3D curve models. In *ACM UIST '08* (2008), 151–160.
3. Bae, S.-H., Balakrishnan, R., and Singh, K. EverybodyLovesSketch: 3D sketching for a broader audience. In *ACM UIST '09* (2009), 59–68.
4. Bau, O., Poupyrev, I., Israr, A., and Harrison, C. TeslaTouch: Electrovibration for touch surfaces. In *ACM UIST '10* (2010), 283–292.
5. Benko, H., Wilson, A. D., and Baudisch, P. Precise selection techniques for multi-touch screens. In *ACM CHI '06* (2006), 1263–1272.
6. Chang, S. H.-H., Stuart, L., Plimmer, B., and Wünsche, B. Origami simulator: A multi-touch experience. In *ACM CHI Extended Abstracts* (2009), 3889–3894.
7. Chiu, P., Liao, C., and Chen, F. Multi-touch document folding: Gesture models, fold directions and symmetries. In *ACM CHI '11* (2011), 1591–1600.
8. Cohé, A., Décle, F., and Hachet, M. tBox: A 3D transformation widget designed for touch-screens. In *ACM CHI '11* (2011), 3005–3008.
9. Fu, C.-W., Goh, W.-B., and Ng, J. A. Multi-touch techniques for exploring large-scale 3D astrophysical simulations. In *ACM CHI '10* (2010), 2213–2222.
10. Gänshirt, C. *Tools for Ideas: An Introduction to Architectural Design*. Birkhäuser GmbH, 2007.
11. Grossman, T., Wigdor, D., and Balakrishnan, R. Multi-finger gestural interaction with 3D volumetric displays. In *ACM UIST '04* (2004), 61–70.
12. Hancock, M., Carpendale, S., and Cockburn, A. Shallow-depth 3D interaction: Design and evaluation of one-, two- and three-touch techniques. In *ACM CHI '07* (2007), 1147–1156.
13. Hancock, M., ten Cate, T., and Carpendale, S. Sticky tools: full 6DOF force-based interaction for multi-touch tables. In *ITS '09* (2009), 133–140.
14. Igarashi, T., Moscovich, T., and Hughes, J. F. As-rigid-as-possible shape manipulation. *ACM TOG 24*, 3 (2005), 1134–1141.
15. Kim, J.-S., Gracanin, D., Matkovic, K., and Quek, F. iPhone/iPod touch as input devices for navigation in immersive virtual environments. In *IEEE VR '09* (2009), 261–262.
16. Kin, K., Miller, T., Bollensdorff, B., DeRose, T., Hartmann, B., and Agrawala, M. Eden: A professional multitouch tool for constructing virtual organic environments. In *ACM CHI '11* (2011), 1343–1352.
17. Longay, S., Runions, A., Boudon, F., and Prusinkiewicz, P. TreeSketch: interactive procedural modeling of trees on a tablet. In *SBIM '12* (2012), 107–120.
18. Moscovich, T., and Hughes, J. F. Multi-finger cursor techniques. In *Graphics Interface '06* (2006), 1–7.
19. Palubicki, W., Horel, K., Longay, S., Runions, A., Lane, B., Měch, R., and Prusinkiewicz, P. Self-organizing tree models for image synthesis. *ACM Trans. Graph. 28*, 3 (2009), 58:1–58:10.
20. Reisman, J. L., Davidson, P. L., and Han, J. Y. A screen-space formulation for 2D and 3D direct manipulation. In *ACM UIST '09* (2009), 69–78.
21. Sharma, A., Madhvanath, S., Shekhawat, A., and Billinghurst, M. MozArt: a multimodal interface for conceptual 3D modeling. In *ICMI '11* (2011), 307–310.
22. Tversky, B. *The Cambridge Handbook of Visuospatial Thinking*. Cambridge University Press, 2005, ch. Functional Significance of Visuospatial Representations.

Gesture Studio: Authoring Multi-Touch Interactions through Demonstration and Declaration

Hao Lü*
Computer Science and Engineering
DUB Group, University of Washington
Seattle, WA 98195
hlv@cs.washington.edu

Yang Li
Google Research
1600 Amphitheatre Parkway
Mountain View, CA 94043
yangli@acm.org

ABSTRACT
The prevalence of multi-touch devices opens the space for rich interactions. However, the complexity for creating multi-touch interactions hinders this potential. In this paper, we present Gesture Studio, a tool for creating multi-touch interaction behaviors by combining the strength of two distinct but complementary approaches: programming by demonstration and declaration. We employ an intuitive video-editing metaphor for developers to demonstrate touch gestures, compose complicated behaviors, test these behaviors in the tool and export them as source code that can be integrated into the developers' project.

Author Keywords
Multi-touch gestures; programming by demonstration; declaration; probabilistic reasoning; state machines.

ACM Classification Keywords
H.5.2 [User Interfaces]: Input devices and strategies, Prototyping.

INTRODUCTION
Multi-touch interaction, enabled by many modern touch-sensitive devices [1,2,6,15], has fundamentally shifted how a user interacts with computing devices. Unlike pointing-and clicking via a mouse—a typical behavior of graphical user interfaces, multi-touch interaction allows a user to directly manipulate the interface simultaneously with multiple fingers, which often leads to an intuitive, expressive and dynamic user interface [4].

However, in the meantime, the richness and intuitiveness of multi-touch interaction often comes at the cost of posing a great challenge for developers to construct these behaviors. The touch state transitions from multiple fingers and their simultaneous movements result in a convoluted event model such that it is difficult for developers to program, test and iterate on these behaviors [14]. To address this challenge, we seek high-level tools that allow developers to

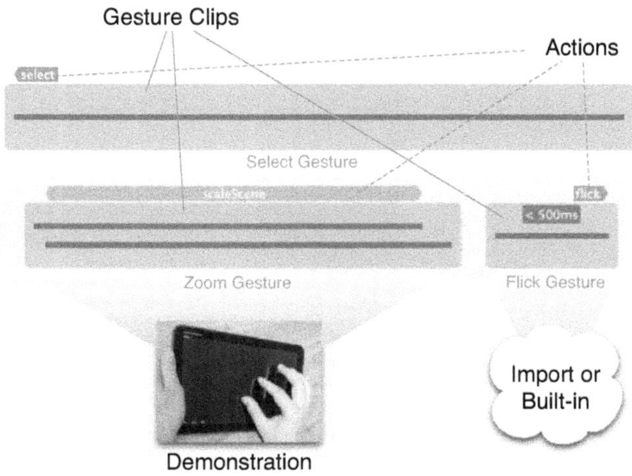

Figure 1. Gesture Studio allows a developer to create multi-touch interaction behaviors by demonstration and declaration via a video-editing metaphor. A designer here combines three gestures, each visualized as a clip, and attach actions to them, to form a compound behavior. A basic gesture can be either demonstrated, imported from other projects, or built-in.

easily create multi-touch interaction behaviors.

Historically, there are two distinctive approaches for empowering developers to create complex interaction behaviors: programming by *declaration* and *demonstration* [3,10]. A declaration-based approach intends to hide programming details by allowing a developer to describe interaction behaviors via a high-level specification language. Previously, several tools have been developed for creating multi-touch gestures using declaration [7,8,9,18]. In particular, Proton [8,9] allows developers to program multi-touch gestures using regular expressions of basic finger actions (i.e., up, down and move). A declaration-based approach can be effective as it allows a developer to directly inform the system an intended behavior. However, it can become slow and inefficient to use when a behavior is difficult to describe, such as geometric changes of finger movements, or when an interaction behavior becomes complicated.

CHI 2013, April 27–May 2, 2013, Paris, France.

* This work was conducted during an internship with Google Research.

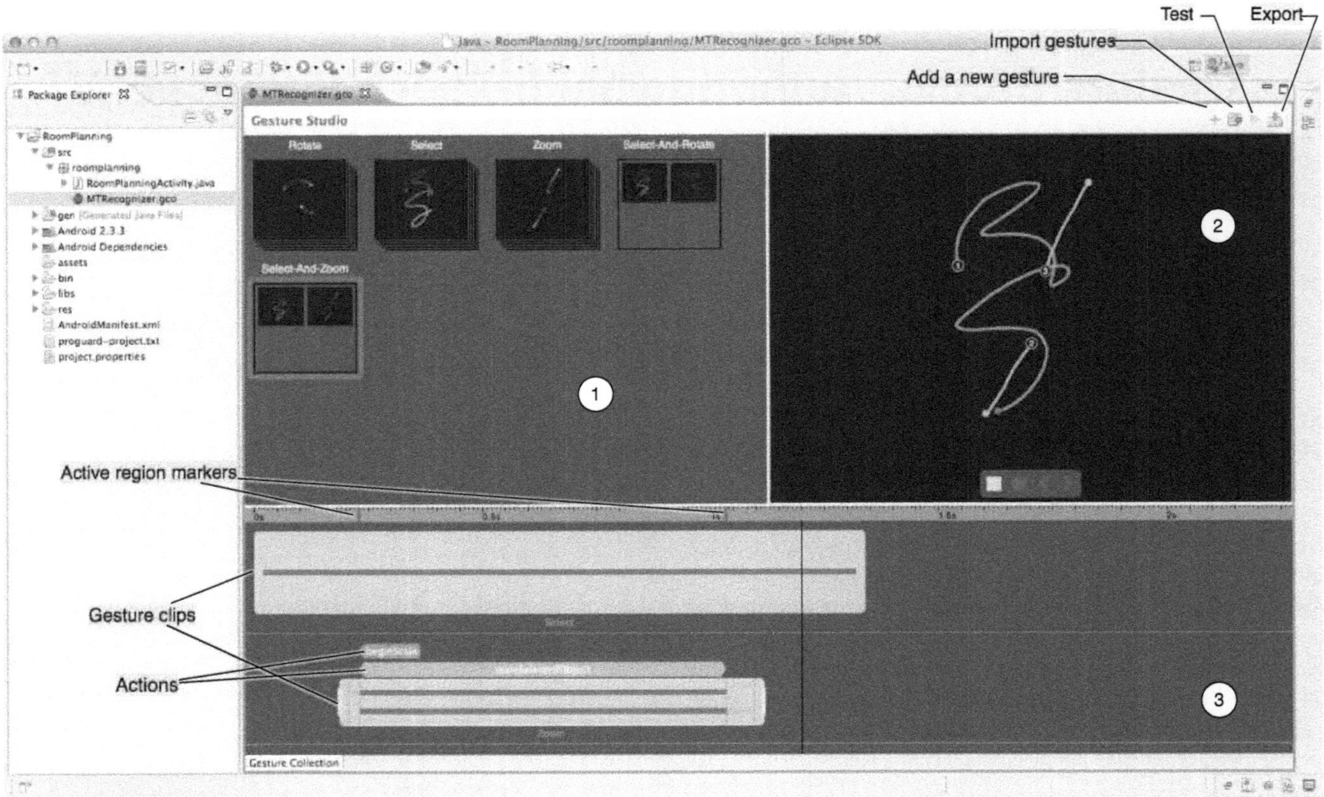

Figure 2: The main UI of Gesture Studio is designed based on a video-editing metaphor and consists of three panels: 1) Gesture Bin, which lists all the gestures in the project, 2) Gesture Player, for the developer to record a demonstration and replays a created gesture, and 3) Timeline, which allows the developer to revise a demonstration and compose compound behaviors.

In contrast to declaration, programming by demonstration (PBD) is aimed at enabling developers to create a target interaction behaviors by example [13,17]. Previously, Gesture Coder [14] allows developers to program multi-touch gestures by directly demonstrating them on a touch-sensitive device. It learns from the demonstrated examples and generates source code that developers can directly use in their own applications to handle these gestures. Although its ease of creating primitive multi-touch gestures is promising, such an approach is limited in describing high-level behaviors. For example, in a multi-touch drawing pad, a user might need to use one finger to pan or affix the canvas and the second finger to draw on top of it. This compound behavior involves two individual gestures, each invokes a different action (panning or drawing), and one is conditioned on the other in that drawing can only happen after the panning finger is in place. These high-level behaviors are difficult to learn from the limited examples given by the developer.

In this paper, we present Gesture Studio that combines the strengths of both programming by demonstration and declaration (see Figure 1). It allows a developer to demonstrate individual gestures in a way that is similar to Gesture Coder. However, it also allows a developer to explicitly inform the system—by declaration—high-level behaviors such as drawing has to happen after panning already takes place in an intuitive manner.

Gesture Studio unifies both demonstration and declaration in a single tool through a novel, video-editing metaphor (see Figure 2). In Gesture Studio, a developer can *demonstrate* a gesture (analogous to recording a video clip), *revise* the demonstration (analogous to cutting a clip), *compose high-level, compound behaviors* by assembling demonstrated gestures on a timeline (analogous to composing a video), and *attach callback actions* (analogous to mixing audio). Gesture Studio treats each gesture in the way that is similar to a video clip, which can be replayed and composed.

Each gesture comes with a timeline, a central component in our interface, where a developer can revise a demonstrated gesture, assemble individual gestures, specify properties such as time constraints (difficult to learn from examples), and attach event callbacks. Developers can test these gestures in the tool and export source code that handles these multi-touch behaviors to integrate with their own application.

The paper offers three important contributions:

- a novel UI that is based on the video-editing metaphor that integrates both programming by demonstration and declaration for authoring multi-touch behaviors;
- a set of methods for creating complex, high-level touch behaviors based on a timeline metaphor, including flexible transition, sequential and parallel composition;

- a set of algorithms for learning touch motion recognizers and probabilistic event models from both demonstrated and composed touch behaviors.

In the rest of the paper, we first discuss how a developer would use Gesture Studio to create rich touch-based interaction behaviors. We then discuss the type of touch behaviors we address. Third, we elaborate on our algorithms for learning a probabilistic event model and touch motion recognizers from the examples given by the developer. Next, we report on a user study on Gesture Studio and a discussion about the limitation and future work. Finally, we give a survey of related work and conclude the paper.

GESTURE STUDIO: AN EXAMPLE

To describe how a developer can create multi-touch interactions using Gesture Studio, assume a developer, Ann, wants to implement a multi-touch application that allows a user to design a room layout, by moving and resizing objects in the scene with finger. The application should allow the user to 1) select and move an individual object with one finger, 2) zoom the entire scene with two-finger pinching, 3) rotate the scene with two-finger rotating, 4) resize a object with one-finger selecting the object and two-other-finger pinching, and 5) rotate a object with one-finger selecting the object and two-other-finger rotating. Panning and zooming should be mutually exclusive; that is, only one can be active at a time, to avoid unintended changes to the scene or object being manipulated.

Our description here is based on the current implementation of Gesture Studio that is based on the Android platform and its standard development environment Eclipse. However, our general approach is applicable to any programming environment and platform that supports multi-touch input.

Instead of implementing these interaction behaviors manually by writing code, Ann opens the Gesture Studio environment in her Eclipse project. Gesture Studio runs as a plugin in Eclipse and is embedded as part of the Eclipse interface (see Figure 2). The Gesture Studio interface consists of three major components. The Gesture Bin at the top left contains a collection of gestures, which can be demonstrated, imported from other projects or built-in. The Gesture Player at the top right displays the finger events and motion trajectories of a gesture when it is being recorded or replayed. The Timeline at the bottom presents basic temporal information of a selected gesture, and relationships (such as parallel and sequential) between multiple gestures that are involved in a compound behavior. With Gesture Studio, Ann can transfer her knowledge in video editing to creating interaction behaviors.

Demonstrating Gestures on a Multi-Touch Device

Ann first connects a multi-touch tablet to her laptop where she develops the application, via a USB cable. In the background, Gesture Studio launches a touch sampling application on the connected device remotely and establishes a socket connection with it. The touch sampling application, running on the tablet device, will capture touch events and send them to Gesture Studio.

To add an example of multi-touch gestures, Ann clicks on the Add button in the Gesture Studio toolbar (see Figure 2). This adds a new gesture to the Gesture Bin. Ann then gives the gesture a name, Rotate, by clicking and typing on its default name. To demonstrate what a Rotate gesture is, Ann clicks on the Record button in the Gesture Player view, and performs a two-finger rotation gesture on the connected tablet's touchscreen.

As Ann performs the gesture, the Gesture Player visualizes finger landing and lifting as well as finger motion trajectories that Ann produces on the tablet in real time (see Figure 2). The traces allow Ann to verify if the gesture has been performed correctly. Once the demonstration is finished (by clicking on the Stop Recoding button or after a timeout), the demonstrated example is added to the current gesture—Rotate in our case. Meanwhile, the Gesture Player returns to the playback mode such that Ann can replay the recorded example.

A developer can demonstrate multiple examples for a gesture, and navigate between examples by clicking on the Previous and Next buttons. In the Gesture Bin, a gesture that has multiple examples is visualized as a stack of clips (see Figure 2). To continue on Ann's project, she adds examples for three gestures: one-finger Select (and Move), two-finger Zoom and two-finger Rotate.

Revising a Demonstration by Specifying Active Region

When a gesture example is selected, its touch sequence is visualized in the Timeline view as a *clip*, i.e., a rounded gray-colored rectangle. Each finger involved in the gesture example is visualized as a horizontal blue line in the clip. The start of the line corresponds to when the finger touches down and the end denotes when the finger lifts up.

A gesture example often involves multiple changes in the number of fingers on the touchscreen. Each of such changes is visualized as a vertical line in the clip, and these vertical lines divide the clip into multiple *segments*. For example, for a two-finger Zoom gesture, the number of fingers in a demonstration will transit from 0 to 1 and to 2, and then decrease to 1, and finally return to 0. It is often a design choice of the developer to determine which segment of the sequence matters to a target gesture. The developer might want to include the 0 and 1-finger segments such that a user has to lift all his fingers when finishes the gesture, before starting next gesture, or exclude the 0-finger segments so that a user can, for example, switch to Move without having to lift his finger—returning to 0 finger.

Gesture Studio allows a developer to specify the segments of the finger sequence—from a demonstrated example—that matters to a target gesture, using *active regions*. When the developer clicks on a gesture clip, its active region is marked by two vertical bars on the timeline ruler (see Figure 2). These two markers denote the beginning and end of the active region. By default, Gesture Studio automatically infers the active region by selecting segments that have significant time duration, e.g., in Ann's case, only the 2-finger segment of the Rotate example is included. The developer can change the default active region of an example by dragging these two markers to another change point on the timeline.

Composing Compound Interaction Behaviors

With the three basic gestures that Ann has demonstrated, Ann can create the compound behaviors, 4) and 5), defined at the beginning of the section, by composition. Similar to creating a basic gesture, Ann clicks on the Add button in the Gesture Studio toolbar to create a gesture named Select-and-Rotate in the Gesture Bin.

Instead of using demonstration, Ann composes these target behaviors, by reusing the basic gestures that she has demonstrated earlier. To do so, she drags the Select gesture from the Gesture Bin and drops it into the first track of the Timeline view, then drags the Rotate gesture into the second track. She then moves and resizes the Select and Rotate clips in the Timeline view so that the Select clip begins before the Rotate clip starts and lasts at least when the Rotate clip ends. This graphically declares the temporal constraints that an object can be rotated by two fingers only when it is already selected and remains so by another finger. Similarly, Ann creates Select-and-Zoom.

In addition to a *parallel composition* that we just demonstrated, which involves multiple parallel tracks on the timeline, a developer can also specify a *sequential composition*, i.e., one gesture can only happen after another gesture has finished. To do so, the developer adds two or more gestures into the same track.

Attaching Callback Actions on the Timeline

Gesture Studio allows a developer to not only create gesture input but also specify callback actions that should be invoked when a gesture event takes place—an indispensable part of an interaction behavior.

In Gesture Studio, a callback action is an object that can be attached to a segment in a clip on the timeline. A developer can choose to attach one or more callbacks to the beginning of the segment, the end of it, or for the entire duration of the segment (e.g., constantly zooming the scene as the fingers pin). The developer can also give the callback action a descriptive name such as *scaleSelectedObject* or *zoomScene*. A callback action can also be attached for a timeout event since the beginning or the end of a segment. A callback action is shown as an attachment on top of the corresponding segment in the timeline view.

Testing the Generated Recognizer Anytime

Once these target behaviors are demonstrated and composed, Ann wants to find out if Gesture Studio can handle these gestures correctly. She begins this process by clicking on the Test Run button in the Gesture Studio's toolbar; this brings up the Test window. Similar to demonstrating an example, the Test window visualizes finger movements as Ann performs these multi-touch behaviors on the connected tablet.

As Ann tests different gestures, the Test window displays test results in real time in its Console, including the type, state, and probability distribution of all the target gesture types. The Console also shows if a callback action is invoked if one is attached. Ann can correct a misinterpreted behavior by adding more examples to a demonstrated gesture or revising a composition. Once satisfied with the testing results, she clicks on the Export button from the Gesture Studio toolbar. This exports the source code for handling these target touch behaviors to Ann's project.

BASIC AND COMPOUND MULTI-TOUCH GESTURES

To design appropriate support for creating multi-touch gestures, we look into the characteristics of these interaction behaviors. As we have demonstrated in our running example, many rich touch behaviors are often built on top of a set of basic gestures. By applying certain constraints (such as temporal relationships) to a combination of basic gestures, a compound gesture enables new behaviors and can invoke different application semantics.

Previous work does not make the distinction between compound and basic gestures. Using a single approach, either demonstration or declaration, to address the entire range of touch gesture behaviors is extremely difficult and inappropriate. The challenge is essentially rooted in different characteristics of user input that these two types of gesture behaviors are aimed to capture.

A basic gesture such as pinching is often to perform a coherent motion with a group of fingers. It is concerned with primitive events such as finger landing or lifting, and fine movements such as two fingers moving apart. Specifying a basic gesture based on these low-level, noisy events can be tedious, unintuitive and intractable to manage. In contrast, a demonstration-based approach can efficiently capture these gestures by learning from examples due to the large amount of training samples generated by repetitive movements of such a gesture.

Compared with basic gestures, a compound gesture such as Select-and-Rotate employs high-level constraints such as temporal relationships between basic gestures. For example, the order of execution of each basic gesture in the compound gesture is crical for correctly performing a target behavior. These high-level constraints often appear succinct to the developer, and it is more efficient to directly describe them instead of demonstrating them.

As a result, in Gesture Studio, we employ a combination of approaches to address basic and compound gestures and to integrate them to form rich interaction behaviors. We use a demonstration-based approach to create basic gestures and a declaration-based approach to compose compound ones.

To help us design effective algorithms for handling these gesture behaviors, we intend to understand input characteristics that each of these gestures should capture. One important question is if we should track the order of different fingers in action. For a basic gesture, the order of which finger lands or lifts is often irrelevant as long as a designated number of fingers are in action. Covering all the possible finger orders is not only unnecessary, but more importantly can result in extremely complex specifications that can be error-prone [8,9] or inefficient inference models [14] that are sensitive to specific finger orders. For example, in a five-finger-pinch gesture, the number of different sequences that the five fingers can lift up are 5x4x3x2x1 = 60. In contrast, in a compound gesture, a different finger (often from a different hand) might be used to perform a different basic gesture. As the order of execution of each basic gesture in the composite matters, it is important to capture the order of finger groups in action, although within each group—a basic gesture, the finger order becomes less important.

ALGORITHMS

In this section, we describe our algorithms for realizing Gesture Studio's demonstration and declaration. In particular, we elaborate on how we derive a probabilistic state machine from the developer's examples and compositions via the timeline, and how we parameterize a learned probabilistic state machine for addressing finger ordering and mapping at runtime—for inference.

Probabilistic Event Models for Multi-Touch Behaviors

A multi-touch interaction behavior essentially takes a sequence of user touch events—the input—and invokes a set of user intended actions—the output. The central topic in handling multi-touch behaviors is to find an appropriate interpretation of touch event sequences that matches the user's expectation. Unfortunately, such a process is often non-deterministic, i.e., a touch event sequence might have multiple possible interpretations thus multiple application actions to invoke. For example, when two fingers touch down, both zooming and rotating are possible.

A typical approach for modeling event sequences is a Deterministic Finite State Machine (D-FSM) that has been extensively used in modeling interaction behaviors for graphical user interfaces. In D-FSM, at any time, there is only one active state (the current state) and one possible transition (interpretation) given an event and the current state. When a state becomes active or inactive, the actions associated with the state (an action can also be associated with a transition in a typical FSM) are invoked. However, D-FSM is ineffective to capture sequences that might have multiple interpretations, as the above example. When D-FSM is used for capturing ambiguous event sequences [14], it often requires more states and complicated transitions that are difficult to maintain and computationally expensive.

In contrast, a probabilistic Finite State Machine is able to effectively model an ambiguous event sequence by allowing multiple active states and multiple transitions to be fired at a time thus multiple actions are possible. Previous research [5,20] has explored using such a model to address ambiguity in user interaction. In Gesture Studio, our inference model is also based on a probabilistic FSM (or a probabilistic event model). We here describe how we use such a model to recognize multi-touch behaviors and how we parameterize such a model at runtime to address finger mappings—a unique challenge raised by parallel composition of a compound gesture and fluid transitions between gestures.

Given a probabilistic state machine, we want to calculate a probabilistic distribution over next possible states, S_{n+1}, given a sequence of touch events, e_i (the i_{th} event in the sequence), as the follow:

$$P(S_{n+1}|e_{1:n+1}) = P(S_{n+1}|e_{n+1}, e_{1:n}) \quad (1)$$

In our state machine, a state represents an interpretation for a set of fingers on the touch surface, which includes the gesture being performed as well as the current stage (segment) of the gesture, and how these fingers are assigned if multiple basic gestures are involved in the gesture. To simplify our state machine—reduce the number of states needed, we treat the finger assignment as an attribute of the state, which is determined only at the inference time. In other words, our state machine is parameterized at the inference time with various finger assignments.

A touch event can be *finger-down* (when a finger lands), *finger-up* (when a finger lifts) and *finger-move* (when one or more fingers moves on the screen). As touch events come in sequentially, we reformulate Equation 1 by leveraging the probabilistic distribution over the current states, S_n, to allow incremental inference at runtime. We acquire:

$$\sum_{s_n} P(S_{n+1}|e_{1:n+1}s_n)P(s_n|e_{1:n}) = \sum_{s_n} P(S_{n+1}|e_{n+1}s_n)P(s_n|e_{1:n}) \quad (2)$$

Equation 2 leverages the fact that S_{n-1} only relies on its previous state S_n and the touch event at step $n+1$, e_{n+1}.

In a touch event sequence, a finger-move event can often have different interpretations for user operation. For example, for a two-finger movement event, based on how much the distance between the two fingers has varied, it is often uncertain to determine if the movement is to perform a pinching or rotating operation. Thus, we introduce another type of random variable, o_i, into our deduction to accommodate such uncertainty.

$$\sum_{s_n}\left[P(s_n|e_{1:n})\sum_{o_{n+1}}P(o_{n+1}|e_{n+1})P(S_{n+1}|o_{n+1},s_n)\right] \quad (3)$$

o_i denotes a single user operation inferred from the touch event at step i. A user operation, o_i, can be finger-down, finger-up or a gesture-specific user operation (based on finger movements)—learned from demonstrated examples, e.g., pinch. In particular, when e_i is a finger-down or up event, $o_i = e_i$.

We can rewrite $P(S_{n+1}|o_{n+1},s_n)$ using a state machine convention.

$$\sum_{s_n}P(s_n|e_{1:n})\sum_{o_{n+1}}P(o_{n+1}|e_{n+1})P(s_n\xrightarrow{o_{n+1}}s_{n+1}) \quad (4)$$

Notice that Equation 4 is recursive in that $P(s_n|e_{1:n})$ can be calculated in a similar way. As each touch event is observed, we can incrementally update the probabilistic distribution of possible states in the state machine. To use Equation 4, there are essentially two types of quantities that we need to calculate: $P(o_{n+1}|e_{n+1})$ and $P(s_n\xrightarrow{o_{n+1}}s_{n+1})$. In the next section, we will describe how to learn these probabilistic distributions from demonstrated examples and timeline compositions.

Learning the Probabilistic State Machine

The previous section defines our inference model—a probabilistic state machine—that handles multi-touch gesture behaviors. In this section, we describe how we automatically learn such a model from demonstrated examples and timeline compositions.

As we recall, our inference model needs to compute two quantities upon each touch event occurs (see Equation 4): $P(o_{n+1}|e_{n+1})$ is concerned with recognizing user operations from a finger-move event, while $P(s_n\xrightarrow{o_{n+1}}s_{n+1})$ relies on the state machine transitions.

The rest of the section is concerned with $P(s_n\xrightarrow{o_{n+1}}s_{n+1})$, for which we describe how we 1) learn the state machines for basic gestures from the demonstrated examples, 2) create state machines for compound gestures by aggregating those of basic gestures based on the products of multiple state machines, and finally 3) derive a global state machine by unifying identical states and capturing possible transitions across different gestures.

Learning a State Machine for a Basic Gesture

We first discuss how to construct a state machine from a demonstrated gesture. A demonstrated gesture can be divided into a sequence of segments by the number of fingers involved at different times. A segment may involve finger-move events that are either intended by the user for performing repetitive operations of the gesture (e.g., continuously zooming) or accidental (e.g., for a two-finger gesture, the first landed finger might have moved slightly before the second finger lands). As we described previously, Gesture Studio automatically eliminates segments that might have accidental movements from the gesture's active region. The developer can revise this by editing the active region inferred by the system.

We then create a chain of states based on the segments in a gesture example. For a segment within the active region, we name its corresponding state using the name of its gesture and its order in the active region, e.g., Pinch/0, DoubleTap/2.

For the segments outside of the active region, we name their states in such a way that is independent of the gesture that the segment resides in. We name a state IDLE-BEFORE$_N$ (IB$_N$) if it is before the active region, where N is the number of fingers, and IDLE-AFTER$_N$ (IA$_N$) if it is after the active region. For example, the initial state before any finger touches down is IB$_0$. IDLE means these states are not associated with any gestures, and represents when no gestures are recognized.

For example, Figure 3a shows the clip of a basic gesture two-finger-rotate. There is only one segment in the active region, marked by the two blue bars on the time scale. The clip results in a state machine that includes a state corresponding to the segment in the active region, Rotate/0. Rotate/0 is preceded by IB$_0$ and IB$_1$ for the segments before the active region, and followed by IA$_1$ and IA$_0$ for those after the active region. Finally, we added transitions triggered by finger events such as finger-up (+) and finger-down (-) between these states.

Learning a State Machine for a Compound Gesture

The state machine for a compound gesture is aggregated from the state machine of each of its basic gestures via a two-step process. We first generate a state machine for each track of the compound gesture, by combining the state machines of each basic gesture on the track (from sequential composition). We then acquire the state machine for the entire compound gesture by assembling the state machine generated for each of its tracks (due to parallel composition).

In the first step, we connect the state machines of adjacent gestures on each timeline track, by merging the idle states between their active regions. In the second step, we construct a state machine using the product of all the state machines from the first step, from which we remove the states and transitions that violate the temporal constraints reflected on the timeline (see Figure 3b).

The temporal constraints are inferred from the order of the gesture clips in the timeline view. For example, when gesture clip A starts earlier than gesture clip B in the

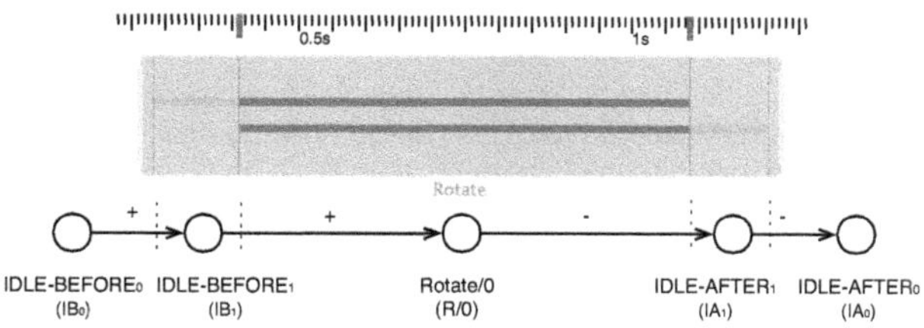

(a) Creating a state machine from a gesture clip. Each segment of the clip is mapped to a state.

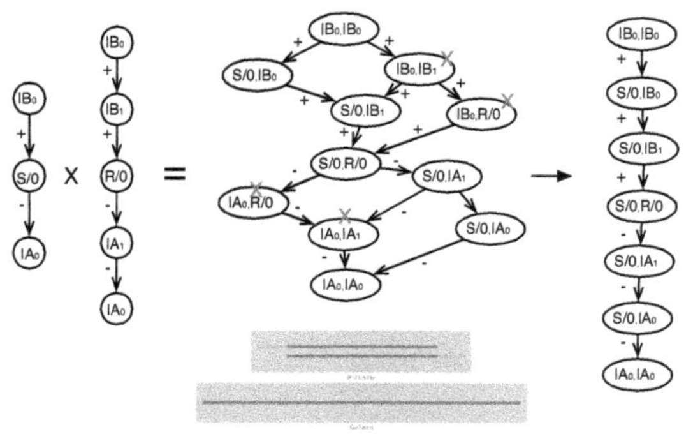

(b) For parallel composition, combining state machines of basic gestures to form a compound behavior by using their product and removing states that violate the timeline temporal constraints.

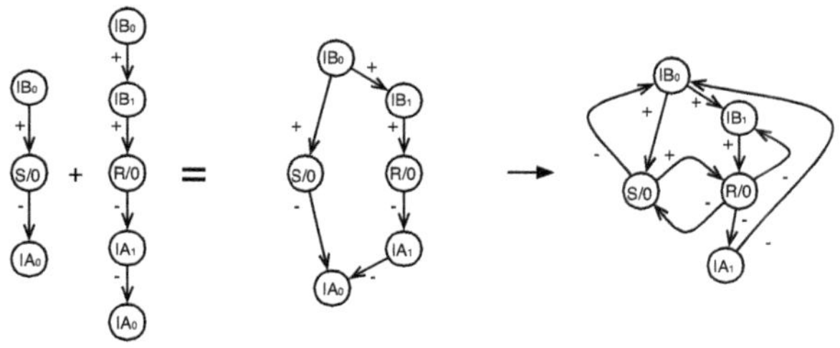

(c) Creating a global state machine by stitching state machines of individual gestures using their idle and transitional states.

Figure 3: Learning state machines from demonstrated examples and composed compound gestures.

timeline view, it imposes a temporal constraint that gesture A needs to reach its active region before any touch event for gesture B occurs.

Constructing a Global State Machine for Inference

Through previous steps, we have acquired a state machine for each gesture, basic or compound, in the target set that the developer is concerned with. Finally, we combine the state machine of each of these gestures to form a single global state machine, by merging identical idle states (see Figure 3c) and adding transitions across different gestures between their *transitional* states to enable fluid transitions between gestures.

There are two types of transitional states. The *beginning states* of a gesture—before or when the gesture begins—can be entered from other gestures and the *ending states*—after or when the gesture ends—can transition to other gestures. We can identify these states and establish transitions from an ending state to a beginning one based on the following rules.

The states that precede and correspond to the beginning of the active region are identified as beginning states. Similarly, the states that follow and correspond to the end of the active region are ending states. For a compound gesture, its active region is the union of the active regions of all the involved gestures on the timeline. An ending state can transition from a beginning state if the difference of the number of fingers they use is one and the transition is assigned a finger-down event if the number of fingers decreases or a finger-up event if increases (see the rightmost figure in Figure 3c). Finally, since actions and time constraints are specific to a segment of a basic gesture, we attach them to the corresponding state of the segment in the state machine.

Recognizing User Operation

In the last section, we described how we learned the event-transition quantity from data. In this section, we discuss the other quantity of our interest, $P(o_{n+1}|e_{n+1})$, i.e., how we recognize user operations from a finger-move event. A user operation is a gesture-specific interpretation of a finger-move event, e.g., a pinch or rotate, which is demonstrated in examples.

Prior work [14] uses decision trees trained from the demonstrated examples. However, not only that it can be expensive (i.e., train and keep a decision tree for each possible set of competing movement patterns), but more importantly, it cannot be directly applied here. For example, in a two-track compound state, $P((o^1_{n-1}, o^2_{n+1})|(e^1_{n+1}, e^2_{n+1}))$, we do not directly have the training data for the compound movements. To address these issues, in Gesture Studio, we use likelihood probability to approximate the posterior probability.

$$P(o_{n+1}|e_{n+1}) = \alpha P(e_{n+1}|o_{n+1})P(o_{n+1}) \propto P(e_{n+1}|o_{n+1}) \quad (5)$$

We can also compute estimation for compound states, for example for a two-track compound state,

$$P((o^1_{n+1}, o^2_{n+1})|(e^1_{n+1}, e^2_{n+1})) \propto P((e^1_{n+1}, e^2_{n+1})|(o^1_{n+1}, o^2_{n+1})) \quad (6)$$

and from the independence between tracks, we have,

$$P((e^1_{n+1}, e^2_{n+1})|(o^1_{n+1}, o^2_{n+1})) = P(e^1_{n+1}|o^1_{n+1})P(e^2_{n+1}|o^2_{n+1}) \quad (7)$$

To learn the likelihood probability distribution from the demonstrated examples, we first compute a set of continuous features that characterize the movement of e_{n+1} relative to its preceding events in a predefined spatial window: $\{dx, dy, dr, da\}$, which correspond to the moved distance of the centroid of the fingers along X-axis and Y-axis, the average moved distance of the fingers along the

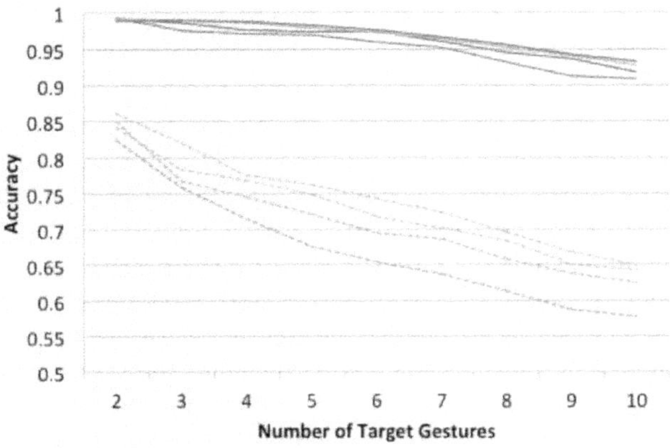

Figure 4: The performance of Gesture Studio's motion recognizer (GS), denoted as solid lines, versus that of Gesture Coder's (GC), denoted as dashed lines. Each recognizer was tested under different learning difficulty, by varying the number of examples for training from 1 to 4 and the number of targets to predict from 2 to 10.

radius direction around the centroid, and the average moved distance of the fingers along the circular direction around the centroid. Each of these features share the same domain, i.e., [-*w*, *w*], where w is the window size. We then discretize these continuous features into three bins, -1, 0, and 1, which correspond to [-w, -w/3), [-w/3, w/3], and (w/3, w] respectively, and use the occurrence frequency of the feature tuple in the training data as the likelihood of a given sample. By leveraging the repetitive nature of multi-touch move events [14], we can treat each finger-move event i.i.d such that more samples become available for training.

To evaluate the performance of our touch operation (motion) recognizer, we compare it with the decision tree motion classifier used in Gesture Coder. We used the same gesture data set as the previous experiment, which was collected from a café study setting [14]. We excluded five gestures from the evaluation: 1-Finger-Hold and 1-Finger-Hold-Then-Move, 1-Finger-Tap, 1-Finger-DoubleTap, and 1-Finger-Trippled-Tap, which are not related to motion trajectories. For the remaining ten gestures, we followed the same procedure as the previous experiment [14]. As shown in Figure 4, our likelihood-based motion classification method significantly outperformed the previous approach.

INTEGRATION AND API

To integrate the inference model we acquired in the previous section into the developer's project, a developer lets Gesture Studio export the learned probabilistic state machine as source code. The developer can invoke application-specific actions in the callbacks that she has attached to a gesture segment in the Gesture Studio. A callback is named based on the name of the callback action

```
recognizer = new MTRecognizer(this);

recognizer.addSelectAndZoomGesturePinchListener(
  new SelectAndZoomGestureListener() {
    @Override
    public void scaleSelectedObject(GestureEvent event) {
      if (event.rank == 1) {
        // zoom
        return GestureEvent.ENGAGE;
      }
      return super.scaleSelectedObject(event);
    }});
```

Figure 5: An example code snippet for listening to the callback from the generated multi-touch model.

that is given by the developer at the composition time, e.g., *scaleSelectedObject* (see Figure 2). The developer then adds the code for rotating an object in the callback (see Figure 5). Gesture Studio creates a gesture listener class for each gesture, and within each gesture listener class, the developer-specified callbacks are added as methods.

A callback function passes a single parameter to developers, the *GestureEvent* object, from which developers can access the touch data related to the segment that the callback is registered to. A set of commonly used parameters, such as changes on X and Y axes, rotation angles, and scaling factors, are also provided in the event object. Developers can easily apply these parameter values to performing application-specific actions. The *GestureEvent* object also consists of the probabilities of the current states, as well as their ranks in the possible states. Developers can use this information as a suggestion on when they can take action as seen in Figure 5.

Instead of passively waiting for the system to invoke a callback, a callback function can also signal the system in terms of how future events should be dispatched. A callback function can return one of the four possible values: CONTINUE, STOP, REMOVE_SELF, and ENGAGE. When CONTINUE is returned, the system will continue firing other callbacks in the dispatching list determined by the current probabilistic distribution. When STOP is returned, the system will stop firing other callbacks in the list. When REMOVE_SELF is returned, the system will no longer fire this callback. When ENGAGE is returned, the system will only fire this callback in the future.

PRELIMINARY EVALUATION

To gain an initial understanding of how developers would react to such a tool, we conducted a user study on Gesture Studio. In particular, we intend to investigate 1) if developers can understand the new features such as the timeline and active region and use them to create compound gestures and fluid gesture transitions, and 2) if developers can analyze and handle gesture probabilities during integration.

We recruited 7 developers (all males, aged from 20 to 40 with a mean age of 30). 6 of them were familiar with Java Eclipse IDE and Android programming. None of the participants considered themselves experienced in programming multi-touch gestures even though one participant attended the original user study of Gesture Coder. Three participants never programmed any touch interaction.

Study Setup

We asked each participant to implement a simple drawing application with Gesture Studio. The drawing application requires 4 gesture behaviors: one-finger move to pan the canvas, two-finger pinch to zoom the canvas, two-finger rotate to rotate the canvas, and one-finger-hold-and-one-finger-draw to draw on the canvas. These gesture behaviors mimic the manipulation of a paper in the physical world. We expect participants to use composition to create the one-finger-hold-and-one-finger-draw gesture. To focus the study on the questions that we intended to investigate, we created the skeleton code for the application and provided the participants with necessary methods to draw, pan, zoom and rotate the canvas, and left the part for creating touch interactions for the participants to finish.

We first gave the participant a quick tutorial on Gesture Studio. We introduced them to all the features that they might need to use to complete the tasks by demonstrating several simple examples. We then let the participant implement the four target gestures for the drawing application in 45 minutes. After the main task, we asked the participant to create fluid transition between the draw, pan, zoom, and rotate gestures that he has just implemented.

Observations & Initial Feedback

6 out of 7 participants finished their tasks using Gesture Studio within 45 minutes. The participant who was unfamiliar with Java and Eclipse failed the task. He was able to finish the pan and hold-and-draw gestures though.

We asked the participants to answer a post-study questionnaire about the usefulness and usability of Gesture Studio using a 5-point Likert scale (1: Strongly Disagree and 5: Strongly Agree)[1]. Overall, the participants thought Gesture Studio was useful (5 Strongly Agreed and 2 Agreed) and easy to understand (3 Strongly Agreed, 3 Agreed and 1 Neutral). In particular, the participants all found timeline visuals useful (5 Strongly Agreed and 2 Agreed). All participants were able to easily understand combining gestures on the timeline and 5 of them were able to use active regions to create fluid transition.

These initial observations indicated that developers appreciated the intuitiveness and usability of Gesture Studio. The participant who had attended the original user study of Gesture Coder thought that Gesture Studio is a significant advance beyond Gesture Coder. He commented:

> *"Creating very complex gestures is exactly as easy as creating easy gestures. The learning curve becomes flat. It is very intuitive to use, and can be picked up in a few minutes."*

Although the participants thought our API for dealing with probabilistic results easy to understand (2 Strongly Agreed, 3 Agreed and 2 Neutral), they asked why they had to handle probabilities in the API themselves, instead of letting the system handle them. It seems that developers still tend to think deterministically and do not appreciate the flexibility for being able to access this information.

Another interesting observation was that 5 out of 7 participants attempted to create the hold-and-draw gesture by demonstration, instead of composing the gesture on the timeline—what we had expected. Because demonstration alone, inherited from Gesture Coder, is insufficient for creating this gesture, they all switched to using timeline composition. When we asked the participants why they chose demonstration instead of composition initially, a common response was that "why should I?" This implies that it is unclear to developers what can be achieved with demonstration and what cannot, and developers tend to try out a simpler approach such as demonstration first.

RELATED WORK

It is an important topic to create tools that allow developers to easily create interaction behaviors. To lower the floor and raise the ceiling [16], there have been two typical approaches. Programming By Demonstration [13,16,21] is to learn a set of target interaction behaviors from examples provided by the developer. In particular, Gesture Coder [14] allows developers to program multi-touch gestures by directly demonstrating them on a touch-sensitive device. In contrast, a declaration-based approach often provides a high-level language or visual representation to specify target behaviors [7,8,9,18]. Recently, Proton [8,9] allows developers to create multi-touch gestures by specifying regular expressions in a graphical editor. In contrast, Gesture Studio employs both approaches to address basic gestures, those concerning with raw touch event sequences, and compound gesture, those concerning with temporal constraints among basic gestures.

Gesture Studio significantly went beyond Gesture Coder [14] by allowing developers to modify a demonstrated example (using the active region) and to create compound gestures that involve multiple basic gestures under temporal constraints. It also incorporates the design of output actions in the process, which gives developers more fine-grained control over where to attach callbacks and offers a holistic view of creating multi-touch behaviors—concerning both input and output.

---

[1] Note that these Likert-scale results are not meant to be compared with findings of previous tools such as Gesture Coder, because the tasks used in the study are different. In particular, gestures such as one-finger-hold-and-one-finger-draw cannot be easily created in Gesture Coder—using a pure demonstration-based approach.

Gesture Studio uses a video-editing metaphor to streamline the process of creating multi-touch behaviors. In particular, UI operations such as recording and replaying have been extensively used in prior PBD work for capturing user examples [11,21]. Gesture Studio enable these UI features in a coherent way that is analogous to a video-editing environment, which allows developers to transfer their video-editing experience to creating interaction behaviors. Traditionally, timelines are often used for describing temporal constraints in designing interaction behaviors [3,12]. Gesture Studio uses timeline visualization for revising a demonstrated example and composing compound gestures. The timeline intuitively supports the two types of compositions, sequential and parallel, as well as the specification of the active region.

Our inference model is based on probabilistic state machines. Pioneer work by Hudson and Newell [5] has applied such kind of state machine in capturing uncertainty in user interfaces. Recently, Schwarz et al. derived a general framework for handling ambiguous user input [19,20]. We designed a probabilistic state machine that captures intrinsic properties of basic and compound gestures. More importantly, we contributed a learning process to automatically create such a state machine from examples and high-level timeline specifications.

CONCLUSION & FUTURE WORK

We presented Gesture Studio, a novel tool for creating multi-touch interaction behaviors by combining programming by demonstration and declaration approaches. Via an intuitive video-editing metaphor, it supports several important steps for creating multi-touch behaviors, including demonstrating gesture examples, revising demonstrated examples, and composing compound gestures that involve multiple gestures under certain temporal constraints. We also contributed a novel computational model for inferring touch behaviors as well as a set of algorithms for automatically constructing such a model from gesture examples and timeline compositions. A performance experiment showed that our touch motion recognizer—an important component in the inference model—significantly outperformed the previous work. The initial feedback from a user study with seven programmers indicated that Gesture Studio is intuitive to understand and easy to use.

REFERENCES

1. Apple iPad. http://www.apple.com/ipad/.
2. Google Nexus. http://www.google.com/nexus/.
3. Hartmann, B., Abdulla, L., Mittal, M., and Klemmer, S.R. Authoring sensor-based interactions by demonstration with direct manipulation and pattern recognition. *Proc. CHI 2007*, ACM Press (2007), 145–154.
4. Hinrichs, U. and Carpendale, S. Gestures in the wild: studying multi-touch gesture sequences on interactive tabletop exhibits. *Proc. CHI 2011*, ACM Press (2011), 3023–3032.
5. Hudson, S.E. and Newell, G.L. Probabilistic state machines: dialog management for inputs with uncertainty. *Proc. UIST 1992*, ACM Press (1992), 199–208.
6. iPhone 4. http://en.wikipedia.org/wiki/IPhone_4.
7. Khandkar, S.H. and Maurer, F. A language to define multi-touch interactions. *Proc. ITS 2010*, ACM Press (2010), 269–270.
8. Kin, K., Hartmann, B., DeRose, T., and Agrawala, M. Proton: Multitouch Gestures as Regular Expressions. *Proc. CHI 2012*, ACM Press (2012).
9. Kin, K., Hartmann, B., DeRose, T., and Agrawala, M. Proton++: a customizable declarative multitouch framework. *Proc. UIST 2012*, ACM Press (2012), 477–486.
10. Lau, T. Programming by Demonstration : a Machine Learning Approach. Ph.D. Dissertation. University of Washington, Seattle, WA, USA. 2001.
11. Leshed, G., Haber, E.M., Matthews, T., and Lau, T. CoScripter: automating & sharing how-to knowledge in the enterprise. *Proc. CHI 2008*, ACM Press (2008), 1719–1728.
12. Li, Y., Cao, X., Everitt, K., Dixon, M., and Landay, J.A. FrameWire: a tool for automatically extracting interaction logic from paper prototyping tests. *Proc. CHI 2010*, ACM Press (2010), 503–512.
13. Lieberman, H., E. *Your Wish Is My Command: Programming by Example*. Morgan Kaufmann, San Francisco, CA, USA, 2001.
14. Lü, H. and Li, Y. Gesture coder: a tool for programming multi-touch gestures by demonstration. *Proc. CHI 2012*, ACM Press (2012), 2875–2884.
15. Motorola Xoom. http://developer.motorola.com/products/xoom/.
16. Myers, B.A. *Creating user interfaces by demonstration*. Academic Press, 1988.
17. Rubine, D. Specifying gestures by example. *ACM SIGGRAPH Computer Graphics 25*, 4 (1991), 329–337.
18. Scholliers, C., Hoste, L., Signer, B., and De Meuter, W. Midas: a declarative multi-touch interaction framework. *Proc. TEI 2011*, ACM Press (2011), 49–56.
19. Schwarz, J., Hudson, S., Mankoff, J., and Wilson, A.D. A framework for robust and flexible handling of inputs with uncertainty. *Proc. UIST 2010*, ACM Press (2010), 47–56.
20. Schwarz, J., Mankoff, J., and Hudson, S. Monte carlo methods for managing interactive state, action and feedback under uncertainty. *Proc. UIST 2011*, ACM Press (2011), 235–244.
21. Cypher, A., ed. *Watch What I Do: Programming by Demonstration*. MIT Press, 1993.

EventHurdle: Supporting Designers' Exploratory Interaction Prototyping with Gesture-Based Sensors

Ju-Whan Kim, Tek-Jin Nam
CIDR lab, Department of Industrial Design, KAIST
291 Daehak-ro, Yuseong-gu, Daejeon, 305-701, Republic of Korea
juwhan.k@gmail.com, tjnam@kaist.ac.kr

ABSTRACT
Prototyping of gestural interactions in the early phase of design is one of the most challenging tasks for designers without advanced programming skills. Relating users' input from gesture-based sensor values requires a great deal of effort on the designer's part and disturbs their reflective and creative thinking. To deal with this problem, we present EventHurdle, a visual gesture authoring tool to support designers' explorative prototyping. It supports remote gestures from a camera, handheld gestures with physical sensors, and touch gestures by utilizing touch screens. EventHurdle allows designers to visually define and modify gestures through interaction workspace and graphical markup language with hurdles. Because the created gestures can be integrated into a prototype as programming code and automatically recognized, designers do not need to pay attention in sensor-related implementation. Two user studies and a recognition test are reported to discuss the acceptance and implications of explorative prototyping tools for designers.

Author Keywords
Gesture-Based Interaction; Exploratory Prototyping; Visual Programming

ACM Classification Keywords
H.5.2. User Interfaces - Prototyping

General Terms
Design

INTRODUCTION
Fluent prototyping is essential for interaction designers to externalize ideas and to realize hidden design problems in the early design process. As prototypes stimulate reflections, designers take advantage of them in framing, refining, and discovering possibilities [10,13,22,30]. The uncertainty and incompleteness of prototyping allow designers to discover a different aspect of design problems and provides inspiration [5]. To make full use of the benefits, rapidity and iteration of prototyping are indispensable.

In recent times, gesture-related sensors for capturing users' spatial movement or position are frequently used in interactive prototypes. In order to facilitate prototyping by designers, both hardware and software prototyping tools have been introduced, such as Arduino [3], Phidgets [13], Exemplar [14], and d.tools [15]. In spite of researchers' ongoing efforts, designers still face difficulties in prototyping interactive products with gesture-based sensors. This is due to the necessity of comprehensive technical understanding for carrying out a series of tasks. For example, connecting various types of sensors requires an understanding of sensor characteristics and electronic knowledge. Identifying features from raw sensor value and classifying users' input demand machine learning knowledge. Additionally, textual programming is needed for integrating gesture interactions with a prototype.

Assistance from engineers is an absolute necessity for a designer lacking such technical knowledge. The process, however, demands considerable time and communicational overhead. Even a designer with engineering or programming expertise often spends too much time and effort on technical implementation instead of for creative design thinking.

Programming-by-Demonstration (PBD) is a typical approach to implementation of gesture interactions for non-experts [7,14,25]. Building program logic "under the hood," PBD has the advantage of programming without thinking about algorithms and raw sensor values. However, reflection from data may be cut off by lack of understanding of raw data and features, while gesture ideas are constrained within existing interactions. Considering the advantages of reflection from data and designers' knowledge sets, a new gesture authoring scheme is necessary.

To fulfill this need, we present EventHurdle, a visual gesture event authoring tool for designers without advanced programming skills. It is a software application that helps users graphically define gestural sensor input, such as gestures on touch pads and a pattern of physical or vision sensor values that trigger an interaction flow. It has three key features: (1) the interaction workspace visualizes various types of sensors in a unified way so that designers can interpret physical gestures as two-dimensional movement in space; (2) graphical markup language with hurdles offers an intuitive and extensible definition scheme for gestures; and (3) the automated code generation process enables designers to easily and rapidly integrate gestures in prototypes. The generated code automatically connects to the appropriate sensors and dispatches events when created gestures are performed.

The rest of this paper is organized as follows: we first present the design directions of EventHurdle as a sketch tool, and then we outline EventHurdle, describing its key features in detail and illustrating usage scenarios with three prototype examples. We then report the results of two user studies and a recognition test to evaluate the tool's usability and utility. We discuss some potential possibilities of EventHurdle. Lastly, we present related work in the HCI and design domain, followed by the conclusion.

EVENTHURDLE

Design Directions

Our design direction is based on the idea that exploratory design tools should support rapid, inexpensive and unfinished prototyping. This perspective is in line with Buxton's notion of sketches [5] as follows.

Exploratory prototyping should be fast and timely. Low cost of prototyping in terms of time and price is a prerequisite for iterative and rich idea exploration. In addition, its timing and agility are necessary for designers to "stay in flow" [6] of design thinking. Buxton similarly points out the attributes that make sketches more productive and generative: *quick, timely, inexpensive, disposable,* and *plentiful.*

Expression should be abstract and unfinished. Lim et al. [22] and Gaver [11] assert that the incompleteness and ambiguity of prototypes can lead to development of new design alternatives and stimulate idea generation. Bellamy [4] takes a similar view, mentioning that a lack of refinement keeps the design space open and free to change as needed. Related sketch properties by Buxton include *clear vocabulary, distinct gesture, minimal detail, appropriate degree of refinement, ambiguity* and *suggestion and exploration rather than confirmation.*

Exploratory prototyping tools should utilize the strength of visual language. Gestural interactions can be described as spatial movements or postures of the human body. It is natural and intuitive when gestures are dealt with in visual space instead of with sensor values. On the other hand, the human brain is highly specialized for processing optical data. As such, visually presented information may be significantly richer than numbers and text because it can be promptly understood. As designers are particularly specialized in visualization and interpretation of information [31], it would be beneficial for them to visually manipulate numeric quality.

Outline of EvnetHurdle

Considering three design directions, we developed EventHurdle (Figure 1.C), a prototyping aid that provides an integrated gesture authoring environment with hurdle-based markup language. It automatically generates a set of gesture recognition programming code, allowing designers to quickly integrate and test gestures in prototypes.

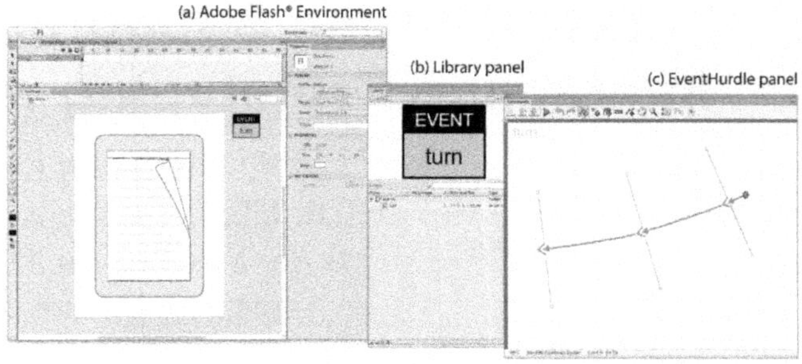

Figure 1. Development environment of EventHurdle. As an extension plugin for Adobe Flash (a), EventHurdle (c) provides an intuitive and easy gesture authoring environment. Hurdle event recognizers are automatically generated and stored in the Library panel (b), and they become active when dragged-and-dropped onto the Flash canvas window (a).

EventHurdle is an extension software for Adobe Flash, which is one of the most popular platforms for design prototyping in education and practice. EventHurdle employs various sensors to support three different gesture types: remote gestures, handheld gestures, and touch gestures.

EventHurdle has three key features: (1) it uses a conceptual *interaction workspace* that necessary sensor data is visually projected on; (2) it allows versatile and easy gesture definition by using *visual markup language with hurdles*; and (3) it generates a set of programming code, called *hurdle event recognizers*, to be used in prototypes. Hurdle event recognizers can be easily applied and automatically connected to gesture-based sensors and trigger events.

Interaction Workspace

To handle gesture-based sensors, we designed a two-dimensional *interaction workspace* in which sensor information is visually projected. The interaction workspace is a conceptual two-dimensional plane that shows relevant sensor information and allows designers to directly compose gesture movement over the sensor layer. Instead of displaying every digit of sensor values in text or in a timeline graph, the two-dimensional representation helps designers easily relate virtual trajectory with physical gestures. Also, designers who are practiced in existing CAD tools with canvas-style workspaces will be able to easily grasp the interaction workspace.

Reported values from gesture-based sensors are projected as a point of two-dimensional coordinates in real time, and their trail of the final two seconds (50 frames) remains in the space. The *sensor trajectory* helps designers to follow the sensor value changes, to catch its movement speed (longer trajectory indicates faster movement), and to easily memorize the gesture movement as a curved shape.

Available sensors are Phidget 3-axis accelerometers, general Phidget analogue sensors that can be connected to the Phidget I/O interface board series, USB cameras, any pointing devices (including touch screen and mouse), and any other data sources that can be handled by the Flash internal script language.

The X-Y coordinate of the sensor point is determined by a sensor combination of two among the given sensors. Sensor values from general Phidget analogue sensors connected to Phidget I/O boards are projected between 0 and 500. Two acceleration values of three-axis accelerometers are first multiplied by 100 (1G = 100), then projected onto the space after being filtered by exponential noise reduction. Vision sensor values can also be easily connected. EventHurdle receives 320 x 240 x 24 fps video from a USB camera and tracks changing blobs. The motion vector of the center point of the changing blobs is projected onto the interaction workspace after being filtered by an exponential noise filter. Inputs from pointing devices such as a touch screen or mouse do not require point mapping; instead, designers can compose gesture patterns at a 1:1 scale and test them directly on EventHurdle. In addition, advanced users may directly manipulate sensor points or use other sensors since EventHurdle supports custom sensor trajectory control through programming.

To support an easy-to-use authoring interface, designers can insert horizontal and vertical guides into the interaction workspace, which are movable afterwards. Designers use the guide system to gain a sense of scale and a conceptual area partition. In addition, visual markup elements can be snapped to guides.

Visual Markup Language

Designers can visually compose gestural interactions by drawing graphical markup language components over the sensor trajectory layer in the interaction workspace. In providing an intuitive authoring process for designers, we applied the Stylator scheme [32]. The Stylator scheme classifies and recognizes a stroke trajectory by testing the intersection with predefined line segments. In EventHurdle, designers can create the directional line segments, called *hurdles*, by drawing them in the space. The *path* component defines the sequential order between hurdles that the sensor trajectory should pass.

Figure 2 shows a simple usage scenario of authoring gestural movement, illustrating how hurdles and path schemes are defined in EventHurdle. First, hurdle 1 and hurdle 2 are created (Figure 2.a). The star shape in the center represents a starting point. Next, the starting point is linked with a path (Figure 2.b). This operation is to define the first hurdle that the sensor trajectory should cross over. Another path connecting hurdle 1 to hurdle 2 is then drawn (Figure 2.c). The final gesture design here defines a specific pattern of sensor trajectories that cross hurdle 1 from left to right and change its direction to the left until reaching hurdle 2.

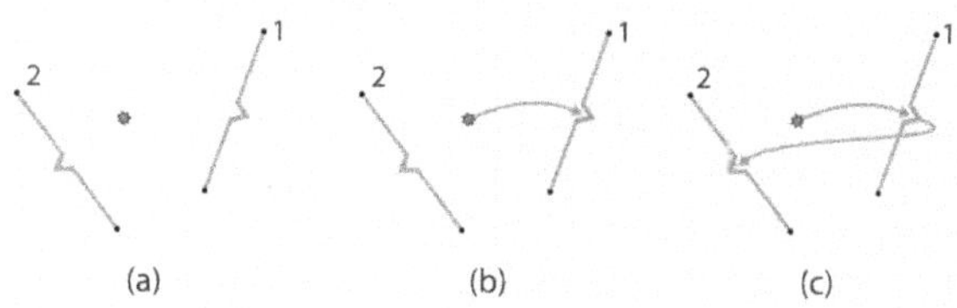

Figure 2. Making paths from starting point to hurdles.

Users can input the period of crossing time for each hurdle from 0 to infinite in milliseconds. The timing parameter enables users to filter out or differentiate gestures that have the same trajectory but different movement speeds. Combining two-dimensional position and timing information affords a variety of potential features, such as speed of gesture, halt, and movement acceleration.

While many pattern recognition schemes support linear data patterns, EventHurdle distinguishes itself from other schemes by providing flexible configuration of hurdles with paths. Figure 3 displays diverse hurdle configuration examples. For example, the top-middle configuration in Figure 3 (a→b) is stricter than the top-left configuration (a) with its additional interim hurdle. Also, the fact that it is a two-step gesture makes it more interactive since the appropriate sensor trajectory will trigger two events. The top-right configuration (a or b) has the same gesture definition as (a), but it can distinguish sensor trajectories that have different vertical displacements. EventHurdle's markup language can define repetitively circulating patterns, such as the last configuration (rep(a→b→c→d)), which cannot be defined by other one-stroke-based pattern learning algorithms. Another application of hurdle use is a *false hurdle*. Designers can avoid unwanted trajectory path by putting false hurdles on the way.

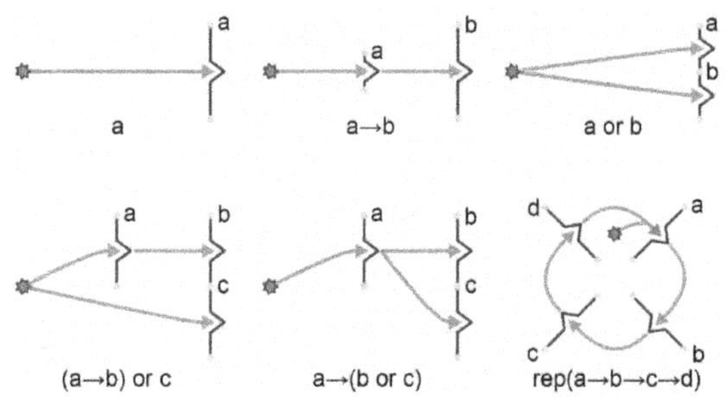

Figure 3. Hurdle configurations: gestures with one hurdle, serial and parallel compositions, combination of serial/parallel connections, and recursive composition.

In order to overcome the limitations of authoring three or higher dimensional gestures, we have introduced a linkage of hurdles in different workspaces. Instead of employing a cumbersome three-dimensional authoring interface, this approach maintains simplicity of use. Gestures that involve three or more sensors (e.g., three axes of an accelerometer) can be composed by separating sensors into two dimensions. Two hurdles of different workspaces can be connected through a time-wise relationship. EventHurdle offers an *AND* and *AFTER* relationship. AND relation dispatches an event when two sensor trajectories cross designated hurdles simultaneously (less than 500 ms interval by default). AFTER relation defines the consecutive crossing of the hurdles. In Flash programming, users are able to use easy-to-understand event names, for example, "hurdle1_and_ hurdle2" or "hurdleA_after_hurdleB." Event linking allows users to handle three-dimensional gestures or multi-touch gestures.

The benefit of using visual markup language is easy and versatile gesture modification: once a hurdle is placed in the space, users can graphically manipulate its location, angle, and length. By adjusting the lengths of hurdles, designers have the freedom to define strict or flexible conditions for a specific gesture movement.

Automated Gesture Recognition in Prototyping

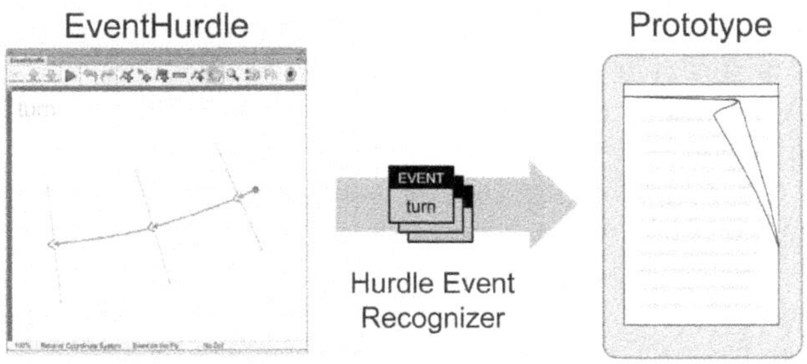

Figure 4. EventHurdle, Hurdle Event Recognizers, and prototypes

EventHurdle provides an easy and simple way to apply authored gesture to prototypes. It automatically produces ActionScript programming code for Adobe Flash, which is one of the most popular prototyping platforms for designers. EventHurdle can execute Flash macro script language (JSFL) command that creates a visual object (a symbol) with programming code into a Flash prototype. The created symbol, called a *hurdle event recognizer* (Figure 4), becomes active when it is inserted into a prototype. The embedment process described above is completed in three steps: first clicking the export button, then inputting the name of gesture, and finally dragging-and-dropping the hurdle event recognizer onto the Flash canvas.

The hurdle event recognizers minimize users' textual coding tasks. Its script includes connection to necessary sensors, sensor data receiver, and Flash event dispatcher for hurdle events. Hurdle event recognizers execute all processes automatically. Thus, there is no longer a need for any programming task related to sensors.

Multiple hurdle event recognizers can be applied to one prototype. Each hurdle event recognizer independently connects and tracks sensor data and respectively dispatches gesture events. The completely automated and independently enclosed programming code ensures that designers stay in flow and focus on design thinking.

After testing a prototype, designers can quickly come back to EventHurdle and continue their design cycle: experience-and-revise. XML-formatted gesture authoring information is registered in a hurdle event recognizer including sensor types, guides, hurdles, paths, and its assigned events. One simple drag-and-drop action enables users to select a hurdle event recognizer to be edited. This user-friendly interface enables a quick gesture design modification process and shortens the time to iterate the experience-and-revise cycle in a flow-like way.

Implementation

A line segment intersection test is carried out for every frame to recognize hurdle crossing by sensor trajectories: a line segment between the current position of a two-dimensional sensor point and the position of the last frame ($P_{n-1}P_n$) and the candidate hurdles (H_aH_b).

Hurdle event recognizers determine hurdles of interest based on a state machine. In the initial state, only hurdles that are connected to starting points (Figure 2) are checked with the line segment intersection test. When a candidate hurdle satisfies the test, the state is changed and connected hurdles become candidates. If it times out (5 s) or no hurdle follows the last hurdle, then the state resets to the initial state in order to track the next gestures repeatedly.

Input sources from pointing devices are treated in a different way. One reason is that starting and ending gesture movements are reported by mouse click down and up, unlike other physical sensors. Single point touch gesture is also treated as a pointing device. Hurdle event recognizers for pointing devices become active when a mouse button is down and inactive when it is up. The state machine does not revert to the initial state to prevent repetitive event dispatching in a single stroke; instead, the state machine is initialized with a mouse button down event. EventHurdle provides a manual option for location sensitivity, whether the gesture movement is location-sensitive or location-invariant. In the location-invariant mode, each cursor position of a mouse button down event becomes a new origin point; therefore, only the route and scale matter. This option allows defined location-insensitive gestures such as web page panning as well as location-sensitive gestures such as dragging a certain object on the screen.

We did not include orientation invariance and scale invariance. This is because the more technical options there are available to users, the more they become distracted from design thinking. Designers have a tendency to ignore thinking of new ideas while they work on technical details. Furthermore, the main purpose of idea exploration through prototyping is to gain explorative use experience and reflections rather than accuracy of gesture recognition, which can be gained with such options.

APPLICATION SCENARIOS

To illustrate how designers can define gesture interactions using EventHurdle, we use three hypothetical gesture design tasks. For the three tasks, let us imagine a designer who wants to implement gesture-based interactions on a mobile phone.

Designing Handheld Motion Gestures

First, she creates a physical mock-up with laser-cut acrylic sheets to experience the feeling of grip and weight. A Phidget 3-axis accelerometer is attached to it (Figure 5). The designer plugs the USB connector into her laptop computer and runs EventHurdle with Flash CS. She opens the sensor configuration dialog box and assigns the Z-axis acceleration value to the X coordinate and the X-axis value to the Y coordinate in EventHurdle.

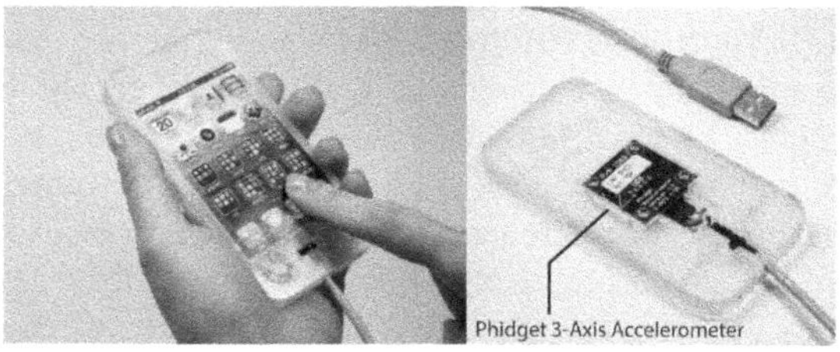

Figure 5. Study mock-up: Laser-cut acrylic sheets are stacked, and a Phidget 3-axis accelerometer is attached.

She takes a look at the sensor trajectory of acceleration values on the screens while performing picking-up motions several times. (Figure 6 bottom left shows the real trajectories collected by 10 different users in green lines.) She sees that the sensor trajectory has apparent visual patterns in the interaction workspace. First, the sensor trajectories start from area A in Figure 6 (bottom left) and move toward area B. Area A is the spatial distribution of Z-Y acceleration values when the prototype is horizontally placed on a desk. She also understands that area B is the distribution of the sensor values when the prototype goes close to her ear. On the other hand, she discovers that the sensor trajectory is distributed in area C when the prototype is placed upside-down. The designer starts hurdle designs as shown in Figure 6 (bottom right) and tests it several times. She exports the hurdle event recognizer and completes her prototype. The usage scenario of the prototype is as follows:

Ringtone rings and the caller's information appears. As soon as a user picks up the phone and moves it towards her ear (A→B), the call begins. Alternatively, the call is denied when she flips the phone over (A→C).

Looking back on her usage flow, the designer repeatedly observed sensor trajectories and realized that the angle against gravity determines the sensor's position in the interaction workspace. She also saw that the sensor trajectories vary depending on detail movement diversity; for example, use of the left or right hand shows different trajectories, and switching the holding hand during the motion shows a zigzagging sensor trajectory. She intended

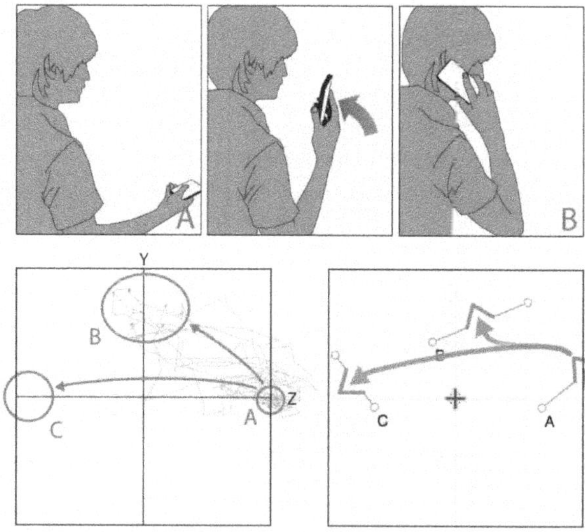

Figure 6. Phone picking-up gesture, sensor trajectories in interaction workspace, and gesture design.

to focus on trajectories that go outwards from area A and in toward area B regardless of their movement in the middle. She also "discovered" area C, which represents upside-down placement during the observation phase, and took advantage of graphical markup language to branch the gesture motion definition.

The next task given to her is to design more physical handheld gestures for mobile phones. She designs four more gesture motions: Flipping, Putting-in-a-Pocket, Shaking, and Tapping-on-a-Palm. Flipping is a gestural action of flipping the phone and putting it on a desk. Putting-in-a-Pocket is a motion of inserting the phone in a trouser pocket. Shaking is a motion of flourishing the phone from left to right twice. Tapping-on-a-palm is a motion of two sequential gentle hits on a palm with the phone. Figure 7 shows illustrations of gesture paths and their hurdles.

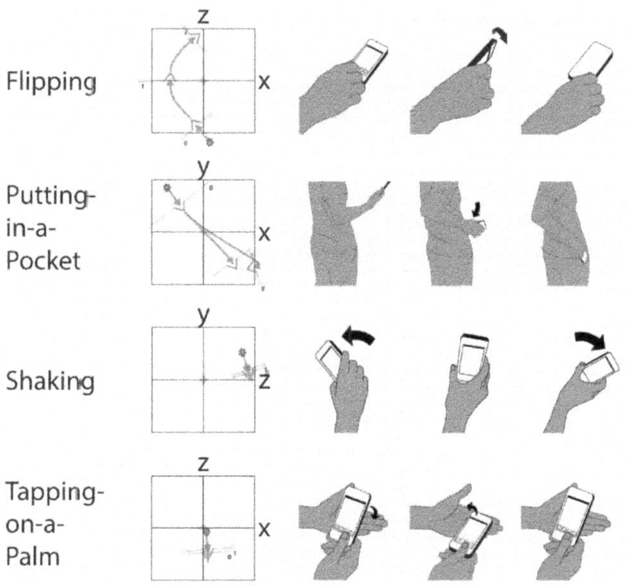

Figure 7. Handheld gesture designs for mobile devices.

Designing Remote Gestures

The next example task is to prototype a camera-attached device supporting remote gesture recognition. The designer wants to test a hand swipe gesture 50 cm above the cellular phone. To build the physical properties of the prototype, she attaches a USB-connected camera to the previous acrylic mock-up and puts it on the desk (Figure 8).

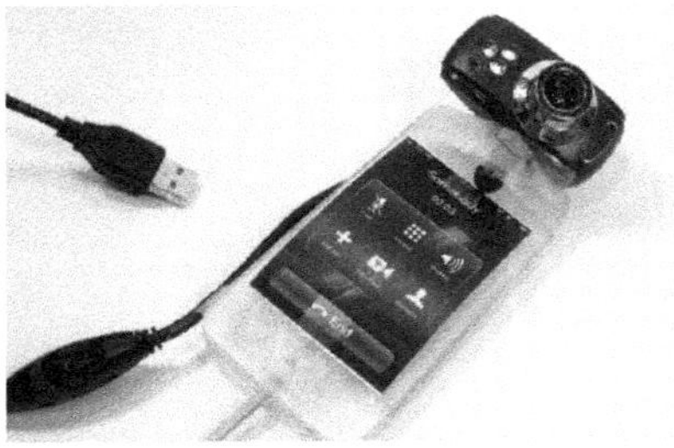

Figure 8. A prototype for testing remote gestures.

She sets the camera motion as the input source for EventHurdle. Similar to the previous example, she explores the interaction workspace by observing the sensor trajectory. She realizes that hand waving has apparent sensor trajectories. She designs a gesture of hand waving from left to right with two hurdles. She tests and modifies the designed gesture several times and exports the hurdle event recognizer when it appears to be stable. She applies the gesture to the prototype.

Since motion vectors from the camera provide limited video information, the functionality of remote gestures seemed restricted. However, on the other hand, she might discover an unexpected sensor trajectory, try to replicate the previous motions physically, and develop her own original idea. This usage scenario resembles unexpected discoveries made during brainstorming with idea sketches.

Designing On-Screen Gestures

The last design project is to test an eBook application interface on a tablet PC. Let us assume she tests with a 7-inch touch-screen monitor. A mouse is selected as the input source because the touchscreen translates touch input to a mouse click. She defines an on-screen swipe gesture motion as depicted in Figure 9.

She creates an empty Flash document with the monitor size 600×1024 pixels, and a hurdle event recognizer named "turn" (Figure 9 left). The event recognizer is inserted in the Flash prototype. She produces a series of animation images (Figure 9 right).

```
1    stop();
2    addEventListener( "turn", handler );
3    function handler ( e:* ){
4        if( e.index == "A") gotoAndStop( 2 );
5        if( e.index == "B") gotoAndStop( 3 );
6        if( e.index == "C") gotoAndPlay( 4 );
7    }
```

The above programming code is inserted. Line 1 commands the default image to be displayed until an event is called.

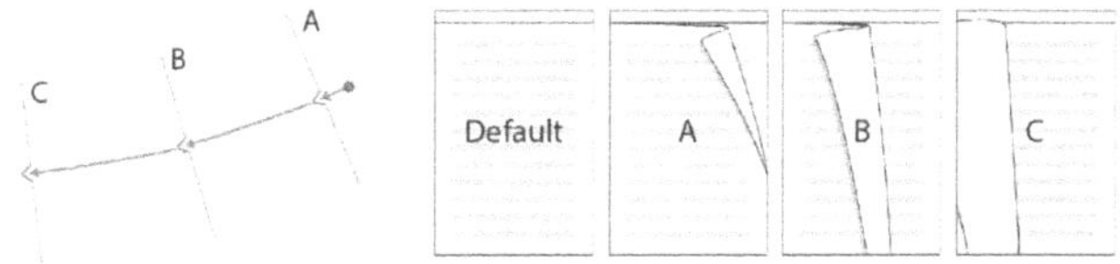

Figure 9. An eBook flipping gesture design and its corresponding states.

Line 2 defines hurdle event "turn" as to be handled by "handler." The "handler" takes *e* parameter that contains *event index*. According to *e.index,* lines 4 to 6 determine which image is to be shown on the screen.

Using the graphical markup language of EventHurdle, she is able to develop a three-step animation effect with real-time gesture input.

EVALUATION AND REFINEMENT

To examine its use threshold and acceptance by young designers, EventHurdle was tested in a design class environment. Experiments with professional designers and graduate design researchers were conducted to evaluate its usefulness in design exploration as well as to assess its usability. Lastly, its reliability as a prototyping tool was evaluated by the testing recognition rate.

Establishing Threshold with a First-Class Deployment

To test the ease of use of our tool, we conducted the first use test in a class environment. Participants consisted of 19 students (18 from industrial design and 1 from engineering). Most of them had some general design education, and they reported themselves as below average in prototyping using Adobe Flash (μ=2.26 on the 5-point Likert scale). In groups of three, participants were asked to prototype one open-ended design idea in a week. They received a three-hour tool training session.

Five gesture-based prototypes were successfully created. For example, a touch screen-based movie player application for tablet PC that used four shape gesture commands (Figure 10) was implemented. Another prototype was a camera-based body motion game in which a player holds a color marker in her hand and has to follow a given path without being caught by a villain.

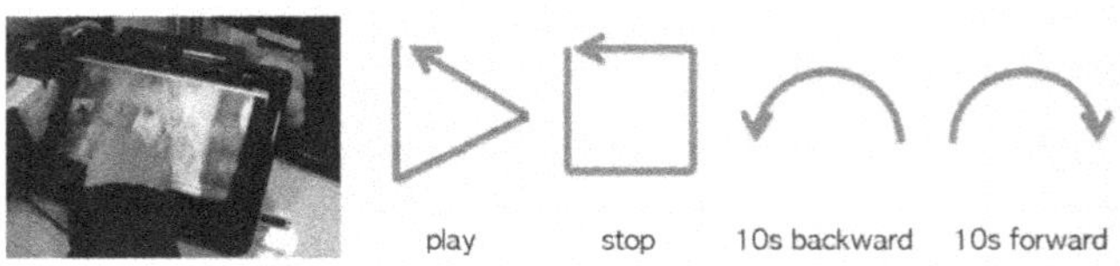

Figure10. A gesture player developed by students.

Strengths

Participants highly valued EventHurdle as it supports advanced programming of gesture recognition, which is a difficult task for them. One participant reported, "*Instead of using only keyboard or mouse input, EventHurdle allows me to attempt using gestures in prototypes.*" Another participant noted, "*It was good that I didn't have to deal with programming and I could focus more on gesture itself.*"

They easily understood the concept of hurdles and paths. Another participant said, "*Logic is tailored for designers.*" Every group was able to master EventHurdle in one week. Participants reacted positively to the use of the hurdle event recognizer instead of textual library importing.

In a post-test survey, participants gave EventHurdle high marks for shortening the time required to build prototypes (μ=3.83 on the 5-point Likert scale), shortening the time to test prototypes (μ=3.83), helping them to test more ideas (μ=3.67), and ease-of-understanding (μ=3.61).

Weaknesses and Improvement

Although participants understood the concept of interaction workspace and hurdles well, its usability seemed unsatisfactory to designers. Since the previous version of EventHurdle did not offer undo and redo functions, participants could not drastically modify the gesture definitions. Additionally, other participants suggested that textual programming in using external sensors should be reduced further.

To help designers stay in flow, the interface was revised to meet designers' needs. We benchmarked existing CAD tools that most designers use every day, undo and redo functions were added, and the interface for loading and exporting hurdle event recognizers was simplified. We also added a recognition test mode for checking hurdle gestures before they are exported to prototypes.

Evaluating Usability by Professional Designers

We conducted two group workshop sessions to re-evaluate the improved usability and to receive open feedback from a wider audience. The study participants consisted of 5 graduate design students and 4 professional UX/UI designers with at least three years of experience in practice developing mobile user interfaces or interactive system interface. They participated in a 60-minutes tutorial session and a 60-minutes prototyping session. Participants were required to create working gesture-based interactions for a video chat application for mobile phones. USB-connected cameras and common video chat GUI were given to participants.

In total, 19 camera-based remote gestures were successfully implemented. Prototypes included a drawing gesture of a heart to send a heart icon, a drawing gesture of a repeated circle to magnify the central video area, and a rotation gesture to rotate the other user's video.

Strengths

Participants reported that the usability does not distract the flow of thinking, and that the undo and redo functions enable designers to change gestures without any delay. They also liked the recognition test mode, which was updated after the initial study. They used the test mode to examine recognition accuracy so that they could quickly test and improve it in authoring mode. One participant mentioned, "*The guide system and its smart snapping function satisfy designers.*"

In the group discussion following the session, participants gave feedback on whether EventHurdle allows idea evolution through repetitive test-and-revision process. One professional UI designer answered, "*The gesture design started with very simple gestures and gradually became complex and elaborate.*"

The study also confirmed the usefulness of the tool in practical use. A mobile UX designer involved in a smartphone manufacturing company said that the current mobile UX design process lacks prototyping in the early design phase. Designers had to rely on imagination and inference until engineers tested it. The participants had a consensus on the needs of such a tool and they agreed that EventHurdle would be the first to surpass their minimum expectations.

Weaknesses and Improvement

Although EventHurdle supports gradual idea development, participants responded that it was less supportive in inspiring radical new ideas. One participant recommended an online gesture library that suggests relevant gestures for more inspiration.

Some participants pointed out that initial exploration of the interaction workspace seemed unnecessary for very simple gestures such as swipe; they wanted Programming-By-Demonstration style hurdle suggestions at the beginning.

EventHurdle was revised to automatically connect Phidgets sensors and USB cameras without textual programming. The interface with camera-based gesture authoring adopted the plug-and-play style without any technical configuration.

Examining Recognition Rate

A recognition test was carried out to examine robustness, in which the five motion gestures introduced in the previous section (Flipping, Picking-Up, Putting-in-a-Pocket, Shaking, and Tapping-on-a-Palm) were tested.

Twenty student participants (F=14, M=6) were asked to perform each motion 10 times and we collected three-axis acceleration data of each motion. EventHurdle was used to compose each motion. Each gesture design took 2 to 4 hurdles and was modified a couple of times (the final hurdle designs are illustrated in Figures 6 and 7). The correct recognition rate for 200 right motions and the false recognition rate for 800 different motions were tested.

Result

The success rate was 90.9% and the error rate was 2.53% on average (Figure 11). The four hurdle event recognizers besides the Shaking gesture exceeded 95%. The false recognition rate was at most 5.63%, in which the Picking-up hurdle event recognizer misrecognized the gesture as the Tapping-on-palm and Shaking motions.

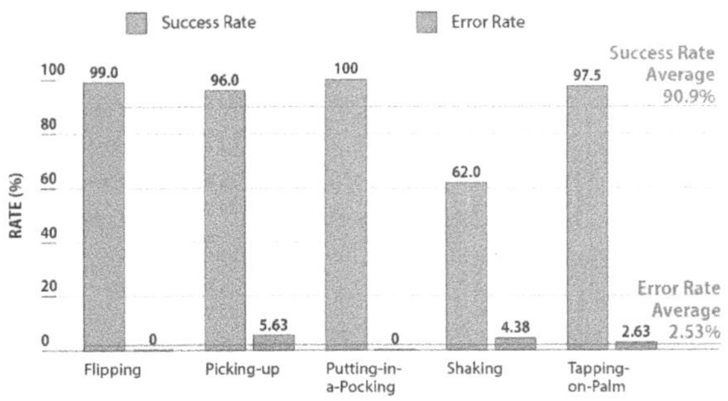

Figure 11. Recognition test result.

The success rate of recognizing the Shaking gesture was 62.0% because only two hurdles could not cover its trajectory distributions. The sensor trajectories of Shaking motions were widely spread because each participant performed the shaking gesture motion with different wrist angles and amplitudes of snaps. Its recognition rate can be improved by adding more hurdles for distributed sensor trajectories. This result proves EventHurdle's reliability in designing and testing gesture motions. Despite the fact that recorded gestures are the control samples, simultaneous gesture recognition is stable for testing its use experience with prototypes.

DISCUSSION

In this section, we discuss the benefits of the hurdle metaphor compared to machine learning and the potential usefulness in exploring the gesture-experience relationship as well as the limitations of EventHurdle.

Free Feature Definition

The hurdle metaphor provides freedom in feature definition to users. Selection of gesture features is very important in gesture design since the feature or authoring tool defines the characteristics of the gesture set. For example, the speed of the gesture is important for Exemplar [14], which uses Dynamic Time Warping (DTW) for gesture recognition and is disregarded for $1 Recognizer [37], which samples a fixed number of points with equidistant intervals from a stroke. Gesture Coder [25] and Proton [18] are relatively strong at zooming, panning, and swipe gestures, since they take account of finger configurations (e.g. the sequence of multi finger touch event) and are less supportive in global geometry. Understandability is also important considering that not every designer is familiar with machine learning. Given a demonstration gesture, a hurdle metaphor can

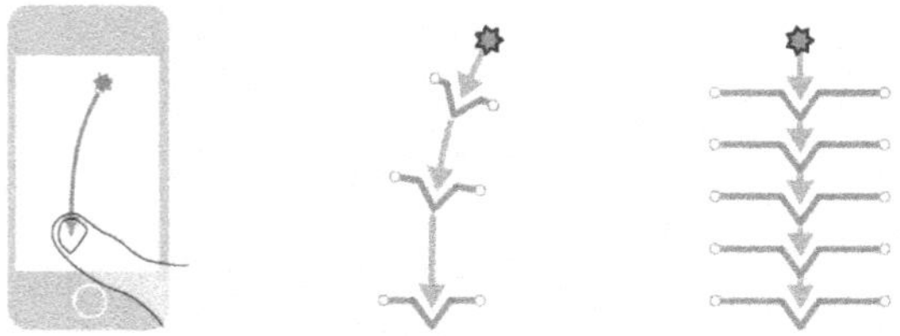

Figure 12. Feature definition for global geometry and for vertical displacement.

clearly define its gesture feature (Figure 12). Combining hurdles also allows users to set necessary thresholds for specific parts of gesture design while most algorithms impose the same weight of tolerance.

EventHurdle benefits designers as it allows them to explore gesture interaction ideas. This is possible because the hurdle metaphor provides more freedom in defining features and understandability compared to existing machine learning algorithms. However, limitations exist, for example, finger configuration of touch gesture, scale invariant geometry, and using sophisticated gesture information other than kinematics, i.e. position in interaction workspace and timing.

Gesture-Affection Relationship

EventHurdle has potential use in affectively-aware design applications. As recent research shows, gestures contain rich emotional information [9,19]. Emotion-related gesture properties can be dealt with through custom hurdle combinations. For example, hurdles can separately define gestures that have different lengths and/or speeds, which are closely related to users' affective mental state. We expect that EventHurdle will assist designers in examining the gesture-experience relationship.

Limitations

Several improvements need to be made to EventHurdle. EventHurdle is capable of a limited range of gesture properties in terms of emotion, and we plan to handle diverse gesture characteristics such as jerkiness, pressure, and shape in the future. Authoring of multi-point gesture will also be supported in the future. Meanwhile, many designers requested EventHurdle for different platforms such as Android, HTML, processing, and Max/Msp. Finally, the hurdle-based authoring scheme has limitations in defining sophisticated sensor trajectories such as handwriting. In the future, EventHurdle may support diverse definition methods besides hurdles.

RELATED WORK

Related work falls into three core areas: (1) general prototyping aid tools for designers and artists; (2) recognizing sensor inputs of intended interaction; and (3) visual programming that inspired this research.

Prototyping Aid Research

To implement prototypes of interactive attributes, designers must build application logic that makes prototypes appropriately react to users' inputs. Many research works are based on statechart-based application logic. DENIM [23], d.tools [15], and STCtools [26] are proposed. This approach provides an intuitive logic implementation process with graphical user interface. Adobe Flash, Processing [27], and Max/Msp have often served as logic development platforms because they support the easy use of multimedia data such as images, sounds, and videos. EventHurdle succeeds in the benefit of the Flash platform. Arduino [3], BOXES [16], Caldar toolkit [21], iStuff [1,2], Phidgets [13], Teleo Kit, and VoodooIO [33] allow fast and simple use of physical sensors for novice developers, which has enabled many design projects today. EventHurdle utilizes Phidget sensors to provide ease-of-connecting. Yet, relating raw sensor values to users' gestures remains to be solved.

Relating Sensor Value and Users' Action

There has been much research focused on understanding users' inputs or contexts from raw sensor data. CAPpella [8], Exemplar [14], and Gesture Coder [25] are representative research works in the HCI community. CAPpella and Gesture Coder support different user populations with different respective needs and expectations. CAPpella is a Programming-by-Demonstration-based context aware tool in indoor environments for end-users. Gesture Coder is a touch screen-based gesture interface design tool for tablet PC applications developers. In contrast, EventHurdle integrates sensor connection, authoring, and prototyping for designing various types of gestures. Exemplar is a PBD-based sensor pattern authoring tool for designers. Though Exemplar and EventHurdle have similar research purposes, they are functionally very different. While Exemplar dispatches one single event at the end of gestures, EventHurdle can trigger as many events as designers want by inserting hurdles at any necessary point of gesture movement. The interaction workspace of EventHurdle clearly shows the phase difference of two sensors, whereas Exemplar independently processes each sensor. For example, sensor value trajectories of clockwise and counterclockwise rotation gestures of a two-axis joystick may look similar in the Exemplar interface: two sine curves. However, EventHurdle displays them clearly as points that rotate in different directions.

The Wizard of Oz method [12,20] could be another alternative to address this issue. Its strengths are ease of implementation and manlike recognition performance. However, it requires one or more pre-instructed operators and a lab environment with monitoring equipment. This may obstruct quick authoring-and-testing cycles and distract from design thinking.

Many technical research outcomes support a technical background for recognizing gestures. Representative methods include Dynamic Time Warping [34], Hidden Markov Model, uWave [24], Rubine [29], and $1 Recognizer [37]. These algorithms support sophisticated and reliable results, but it is hard for designers to understand what is going on in the background. Also, textual programming of those algorithms requires significant amount of skills, time, and costs for designers. Meanwhile, research on critical region or path-based recognition has been conducted, such as EdgeWrite [35,36] and the Stylator scheme [32]. Although path-based recognition is limited in recognizing sophisticated sensor trajectories such as handwriting, this approach is employed in EventHurdle for its visual intuitiveness.

Visual Programming

This research was also inspired by visual programming languages. Scratch [28] and Lego Mindstorms NXT [17] offer a flowchart-style visual logic programming scheme. Max/MSP, Apple Quartz Composer, and Grasshopper are examples of another category of visual language that offers graphical dataflow programming environments. Visual programming has clear benefits over textual programming: (1) visual representation of programming elements causes visual affordance; (2) it is free from grammatical errors; (3) programming flow or dataflow is visually apparent and understandable; and (4) in many cases, it displays real-time dataflow directly in the programming environment. These benefits make visual programming easy to learn and visually intuitive. However, they still require algorithmic knowledge to build sophisticated application logic.

CONCLUSION

This paper presents EventHurdle, a visual gesture authoring tool for designers that supports connecting gesture-based sensors, visually intuitive gesture definitions, and easy prototyping without programming expertise.

EventHurdle expands the technical breadth of prototyping of designers through automated code generation. EventHurdle offers an integrated development environment to deal with remote gestures, handheld gestures, and touch gestures from connecting sensors in creation of prototypes. Various types of gesture-based sensors are easily controlled by simple and unified sensor trajectory visualization in 2D space. Intuitive and rapid gesture authoring with graphical markup language encourages rich and fast realizations for idea exploration. EventHurdle offers design alternatives through the exploration of interaction workspace with gesture-based sensors. Lastly, its designer-tailored interface makes it easy to use and learn.

EventHurdle is expected to offer active design exploration by prototyping gesture-based interactions in both education and practice. Furthermore, delivering prototypes as communication media, EventHurdle can facilitate precise, concrete, and rich communications between a design team and other professionals such as engineers and marketers.

ACKNOWLEDGEMENT

This research was supported by the SW Computing R&D Program of KEIT(2012,10041313, UX-oriented Mobile SW Platform) funded by the Ministry of Knowledge Economy, Republic of Korea.

REFERENCE

1. Ballagas, R., Memon, F., Reiners, R., and Borchers, J. iStuff mobile: rapidly prototyping new mobile phone interfaces for ubiquitous computing. *Proc. CHI 2007*, 1107–1116.
2. Ballagas, R., Ringel, M., Stone, M., and Borchers, J. iStuff: a physical user interface toolkit for ubiquitous computing environments. *Proc. CHI 2003*, 537-544.
3. Banzi, M. *Getting Started with Arduino*. Make, 2011.

4. Bellamy, R., Desmond, M., Martino, J., et al. Sketching tools for ideation (NIER track). *Proc. ICSE 2011*, 808–811.
5. Buxton, B. *Sketching user experiences : getting the design right and the right design.* Elsevier/Morgan Kaufmann, Amsterdam; Boston, 2007.
6. Csikszentmihalyi, M. *Flow*. Harper Perennial Modern Classics, 2008.
7. Cypher, A. and Halbert, D.C. *Watch What I Do.* The MIT Press, 1993.
8. Dey, A.K., Hamid, R., Beckmann, C., Li, I., and Hsu, D. a CAPpella: programming by demonstration of context-aware applications. *Proc. CHI 2004,* 33-40.
9. Gao, Y., Bianchi-Berthouze, N., and Meng, H. UCL Discovery - What does touch tell us about emotions in touchscreen-based gameplay? *ACM Transactions on Computer-Human Interaction (2012).*
10. Gaver, W. Making spaces: how design workbooks work. *Proc. CHI 2011*, 1551-1560.
11. Gaver, W., Beaver, J., and Benford, S. Ambiguity as a resource for design. *Proc. CHI 2003*, 233-240.
12. Gould, J.D., Conti, J., and Hovanyecz, T. Composing letters with a simulated listening typewriter. *Communications of the ACM 26*, 4 (1983).
13. Greenberg, S. and Fitchett, C. Phidgets: Easy Development of Physical Interfaces through Physical Widgets. *Proc. UIST 2001*, 209–218.
14. Hartmann, B., Abdulla, L., Mittal, M., and Klemmer, S.R. Authoring sensor-based interactions by demonstration with direct manipulation and pattern recognition. *Proc. CHI 2007*, 146–154.
15. Hartmann, B., Klemmer, S.R., Bernstein, M., et al. Reflective physical prototyping through integrated design, test, and analysis. *Proc. UIST 2006*, 299–308.
16. Hudson, S.E. and Mankoff, J. Rapid Construction of Functioning Physical Interfaces from Cardboard, Thumbtacks, Tin Foil and Masking Tape. *Proc. UIST 2006*, 289–297.
17. Kelly, J.F. *Lego Mindstorms Nxt 2.0.* Springer, 2009.
18. Kin, K., Hartmann, B., DeRose, T., and Agrawala, M. Proton: Multitouch Gestures as Regular Expressions. *Proc. CHI 2012*, 2885-2894.
19. Kleinsmith, A. and Bianchi-Berthouze, N. Affective Body Expression Perception and Recognition: A Survey. *IEEE Trans Affective Computing,* (2012).
20. Klemmer, S.R., Sinha, A.K., Chen, J., Landay, J.A., Aboobaker, N., and Wang, A. Suede: a Wizard of Oz prototyping tool for speech user interfaces. *Proc. UIST 2000*, 1–10.
21. Lee, J.C., Avrahami, D., Hudson, S.E., Forlizzi, J., Dietz, P.H., and Leigh, D. The Calder Toolkit: Wired and Wireless Components for Rapidly Prototyping Interactive Devices. *Proc. DIS 2004*, 167–175.
22. Lim, Y.K., Stolterman, E., and Tenenberg, J. The anatomy of prototypes: Prototypes as filters, prototypes as manifestations of design ideas. *ACM Transactions on Computer-Human Interaction 15*, 2 (2008).
23. Lin, J., Newman, M.W., Hong, J.I., and Landay, J.A. DENIM: finding a tighter fit between tools and practice for Web site design. *Proc. CHI 2000*, 510–517.
24. Liu, J., Zhong, L., Wickramasuriya, J., and Vasudevan, V. uWave: Accelerometer-based personalized gesture recognition and its applications. *Pervasive and Mobile Computing 5*, (2009), 657–675.
25. Lü, H. and Li, Y. Gesture coder: a tool for programming multi-touch gestures by demonstration. *Proc. CHI 2012*, 2875–2884.
26. Nam, T.J. Sketch-based rapid prototyping platform for hardware-software integrated interactive products. *Extended abstracts of CHI 2005*, 1689-1692.
27. Reas, C. and Fry, B. *Processing*. The MIT Press, 2007.
28. Resnick, M., Maloney, J., and Monroy-Hernández, A. Scratch: programming for all. *Communications of the ACM 52*, (2009), 60–67.
29. Rubine, D. Specifying Gestures by Example. *Proc. SIGGRAPH 1991*, 329-337.
30. Schön, D.A. *The reflective practitioner.* Ashgate Pub Co, 1995.
31. Suwa, M. and Tversky, B. External Representations Contribute to the Dynamic Construction of Ideas. *Proc. DIAGRAM 2002*, 341-343.
32. Teitelman, W. Real Time Recognition of Hand-Drawn Characters. *Proc. AFIPS 1964*, 559-575.
33. Villar, N., Gilleade, K.M., Ramdunyellis, D., and Gellersen, H. The VoodooIO gaming kit. *Computers in Entertainment 5*, 3 (2007), 7.
34. Vintsyuk, T.K. Speech discrimination by dynamic programming. *Kibernetika* 4, (1968), 81-88
35. Wobbrock, J.O. and Myers, B. Trackball text entry for people with motor impairments. *Proc. CHI 2006*, 479-488.
36. Wobbrock, J.O., Myers, B.A., and Kembel, J.A. EdgeWrite: A Stylus-Based Text Entry Method Designed for High Accuracy and Stability of Motion. *Proc. UIST 2003*, 61-70.
37. Wobbrock, J.O., Wilson, A.D., and Li, Y. Gestures without libraries, toolkits or training: a $1 recognizer for user interface prototypes. *Proc. UIST 2007*, 159-168.

Small, Medium, or Large? Estimating the User-Perceived Scale of Stroke Gestures

Radu-Daniel Vatavu[1], Géry Casiez[2] and Laurent Grisoni[2]
[1]University Stefan cel Mare of Suceava, Romania
[2]LIFL & Inria Lille, University of Lille, France
vatavu@eed.usv.ro, gery.casiez@lifl.fr, laurent.grisoni@lifl.fr

ABSTRACT
We show that large consensus exists among users in the way they articulate stroke gestures at various scales (i.e., *small*, *medium*, and *large*), and formulate a simple rule that estimates the user-intended scale of input gestures with 87% accuracy. Our estimator can enhance current gestural interfaces by leveraging scale as a natural parameter for gesture input, reflective of user perception (i.e., no training required). Gesture scale can simplify gesture set design, improve gesture-to-function mappings, and reduce the need for users to learn and for recognizers to discriminate unnecessary symbols.

Author Keywords
Gesture recognition; gesture scale; gesture size; Bayes' rule; gesture articulation; pen gestures; human factors.

ACM Classification Keywords
H.5.2 Information Interfaces and Presentation: User Interfaces

General Terms
Human Factors; Design; Measurement.

INTRODUCTION
Stroke gestures are commonly employed as shortcuts to invoke commands on touch-sensitive devices for which keyboard shortcuts are either not available, or demand substantially more cognitive effort [3]. Once the gesture has been recognized [14,16,19], the command is fired away. However, some commands need parameters to be specified (e.g., "go to page *26*" or "change font to *bigger* size"). One option is to enter such parameters after the gesture has been articulated [14], or to employ mode specifiers that set the meaning of the command in a particular context (e.g., placing two or more fingers on the multitouch surface can affect object position, rotation, and scale). Another option is to map geometric or kinematic features of the articulation profile to parameter values, such as pen pressure for selecting menu items [13], or descriptors of oscillatory movements to control zoom and pan levels [9]. Simple geometric features have also been used to inform gesture design, such as stroke direction for marking menus [6] and stroke orientation for Unistrokes[1].

[1]The 26 letters of the Unistrokes alphabet use 5 basic strokes that come in 4 orientations and 2 directions, see http://www.yorku.ca/mack/hci3-f14.gif.

CHI 2013, April 27–May 2, 2013, Paris, France.

We investigate the use of gesture scale to enter discrete parameters for a command. Our goal is to enrich the expressibility of gesture input, without increasing the physical or cognitive load of gesture articulation or the complexity of the recognizer. We are motivated by the ability of people to write at different sizes [5] without affecting the form of the produced symbols [12]. In addition, gestures drawn at different scales are perceived by users as dissimilar [8], and, therefore, can have different meanings in an application. In turn, exploiting gesture scale opens many opportunities to enhance today's gestural interfaces. For example, a small "S" saves a file, while a large "S" could invoke "Save as". For e-books, the scale of forward and backward flicks can specify the number of pages to go back or forward. However, despite such simple and intuitive ways to map scale with command parameters, gesture scale has not been exploited yet in user interfaces. This can be explained by today's lack of understanding on the relationship between user-intended scale (e.g., small or large) and the actual size of produced strokes (e.g., in pixels), which can vary across users and input surfaces.

We show that large consensus exists among users articulating stroke gestures at various scales, which legitimates the search for an estimator of user-intended gesture scale. Using Bayes' classification technique, we derive a simple, training-free estimation rule that can be directly implemented in today's gestural interfaces with just three lines of code. We report 87% accuracy for user-independent and device-independent tests.

EXPERIMENT
We designed an experiment to determine whether a relationship exists between the intended scale at which users produce gestures (i.e., *small*, *medium*, and *large*) and actual gesture size (e.g., in pixels or cm). We are interested in whether the size of gestures produced for a given scale label is consistent across users, and whether user perception of gesture scale is influenced by the size of the available input area.

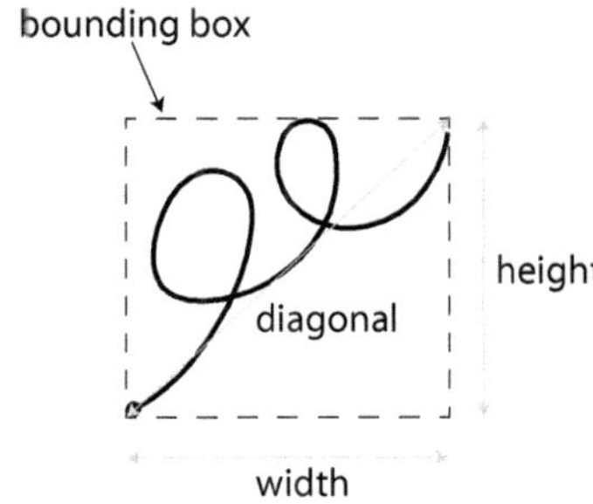

Figure 1. Gesture size evaluated as the area of its bounding box.

Scale labels and size measurements for gestures
We make distinction between the *scale* of a gesture and its *size*. Whereas we understand by *scale* a linguistic label denoting amplitude at a subjective level (e.g., small gesture), *size* is the result of an objective measurement on the produced gesture shape (e.g., 125 pixels wide). Following Niels et al. [11] and Stößel et al. [15], we employ three scale labels (*small*, *medium*, and *large*), which are in relation to Mandler's three classes of the psychological perception of space [10]. Following previous work [1,2], we measure gesture *size* as the area of the gesture bounding box (see Figure 1).

Apparatus & Participants
Gestures were entered on a 12.1" Wacom Cintiq 12WX display with 1280 × 800 pixels (124 DPI). The display was positioned horizontally to approximate a physical pen and paper context. Forty unpaid participants with ages between 19 to 24 years old, all right-handed, were recruited for the experiment. None of them had previous experience with pen gesture input.

Task
The task consisted in entering gestures at various scales, as guided by a software application that controlled the experiment. Gestures were entered inside a square input area centered on screen. The application displayed a text message before each trial indicating the gesture to articulate and the requested scale (e.g., "draw a small rectangle" or "draw a large circle"), without displaying any visual feedback of gesture shape. A trial ended once the pen was lifted. Participants were instructed to enter gestures at their regular speed and at the size they best felt it matched the instructions (e.g., "draw a large circle"). No additional indication was provided for gesture scale other than the one in the text message. A practice session preceded the experiment in order for participants to become accustomed with the stylus and the interactive display. The session consisted in gesture drawings in Microsoft® Paint under the supervision of the experimenter. No scale indication was provided during this phase.

Design
A mixed-subjects design was used. The independent variables were the size of the input area in which participants entered gestures (INPUT-AREA-SIZE), the scale at which participants were instructed to produce gestures (SCALE), and the gesture type (GESTURE). INPUT-AREA-SIZE was administrated as a between-subjects factor while SCALE and GESTURE were administrated as within-subjects factors.

INPUT-AREA-SIZE was evaluated with five levels: 4 × 4, 6 × 6, 8 × 8, 10 × 10, and 12 × 12 cm^2. These values were chosen to cover the input areas available on current mobile phones (e.g., the iPhone 4S[2] has a display of 7.5 × 5.0 cm^2), and get close to the maximum size of the largest tablets (e.g., the iPad[3] has a display of 19.8 × 14.7 cm^2). SCALE was evaluated with three levels: *small*, *medium*, and *large* [11,15]. GESTURE was evaluated with four levels: rectangle, diamond, circle, and triangle. We preferred gestures with clear meaning to participants, considering they were indicated as text during the experiment (e.g., "draw a small rectangle").

Participants were divided into five equal groups corresponding to each value of INPUT-AREA-SIZE to prevent learning effects from one input size to another. Each combination of GESTURE and SIZE was repeated for five times and randomly presented to participants. The experiment took around five minutes per participant. In summary, the experimental design was: 5 INPUT-AREA-SIZE × 8 participants × 4 GESTURE × 3 SCALE × 5 repetitions = 2,400 total trials.

RESULTS
The dependent variable was the area of the gesture bounding box (SIZE), reported in cm^2. Repeated measures ANOVA[4] showed a significant main effect of repetition on SIZE ($F_{1.7,60.3}$=21.4, $p<0.001$). Post-hoc tests showed significant differences ($p<0.001$) between the first repetition (17.2 cm^2) and the subsequent ones (20.3 cm^2). The first repetition was therefore removed from subsequent analysis. We also found a significant main effect of GESTURE on SIZE ($F_{2.3,79.7}$=6.1, p=0.002), and post-hoc tests revealed significant differences ($p<0.004$) between the triangle (19.0 cm^2) and all the other gestures (20.7 cm^2). It is important to note that no interaction was found between GESTURE and the other factors.

We found a significant main effect of SCALE on SIZE ($F_{1.1,33.9}$=175.1, $p<0.001$), as well as a significant SCALE × INPUT-AREA-SIZE interaction ($F_{4.3,33.9}$=15.0, $p<0.001$). Post-hoc analysis revealed significant differences ($p<0.05$) between the three SCALE levels for each INPUT-AREA-SIZE. This shows that participants' executions and their perception of scale were indeed influenced by the size of the available input area. On average, medium gestures were 4.3 times larger than small ones, and large gestures were 3.0 times larger than medium ones. Figure 2 shows gesture sizes for each INPUT-AREA-SIZE and SCALE, with a monotonic trend clearly identifiable. Regression analysis revealed power functions with the highest fit ($R^2 > 0.90$): $\text{SIZE} = a \times \text{INPUT-AREA-SIZE}^b$, with $a \in \{0.91, 3.73, 10.03\}$ and $b \in \{1.14, 1.18, 1.26\}$ for {*small*, *medium*, and *large*} gestures.

ESTIMATING GESTURE SCALE FROM MEASURED SIZE
In the following, we are interested in devising an automatic procedure that would reliably estimate the user-intended scale of input gestures by analyzing gesture measured size. As gesture size was found to be affected by the size of the input area, we normalize SIZE by INPUT-AREA-SIZE, and refer to the outcome as the SIZE-RATIO of gesture g:

$$\text{SIZE-RATIO}(g) = \frac{\text{SIZE}(g)}{\text{area of INPUT-AREA-SIZE}} \quad (1)$$

Results showed a mean of 0.05 (SD=0.03) for small, 0.21 (SD=0.10) for medium, and 0.61 (SD=0.20) for large gestures. Figure 3 shows the distribution of SIZE-RATIO for the 2,400 samples from our data set, together with normal distributions overimposed for each gesture SCALE.

Our estimation problem can now be rephrased in terms of classification theory as finding a mapping between the normalized values of gesture size, SIZE-RATIO, and the three

[2] http://www.apple.com/iphone/specs.html

[3] http://www.apple.com/ipad/specs/

[4] ANOVA was run using SPSS and the GLM command with Greenhouse-Geisser correction. Post-hoc analyses used Bonferroni correction.

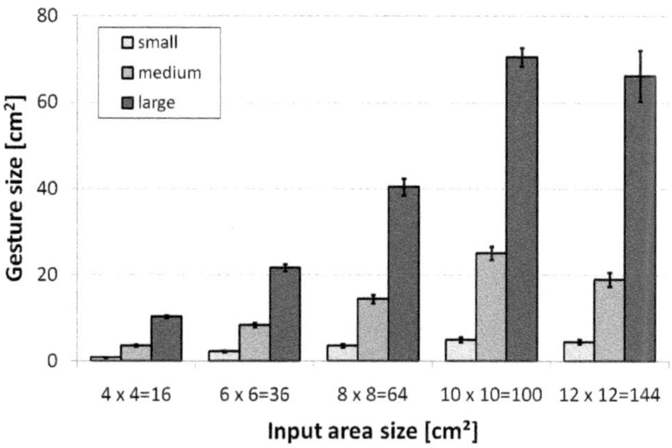

Figure 2. Gesture size vs. input area size. Error bars show 95% CI.

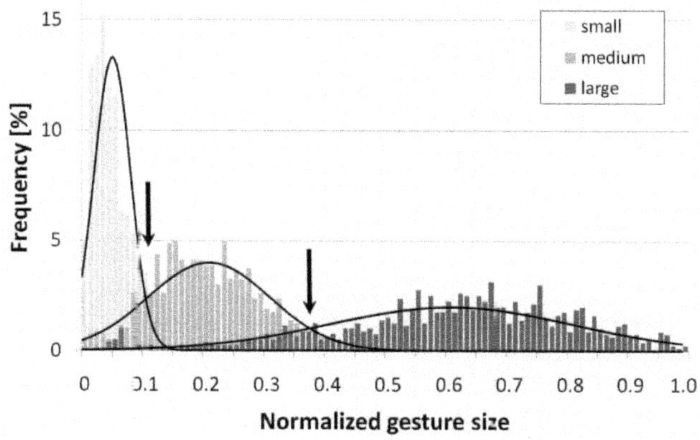

Figure 3. Frequency distribution of SIZE-RATIO. Normal curves are shown overimposed for each gesture SCALE (see mean and SD values in the text). Arrows indicate thresholds 0.1 and 0.4 as class separators.

SCALE classes. When class distributions can be easily approximated with known functions (as is our case with normal curves, see Figure 3), Bayes' rule is the preferred classifier choice as it minimizes classification error [18](p. 7). Bayes' rule uses class-conditional density probabilities (i.e., the probability for a randomly chosen gesture g to belong to class SCALE, denoted $p(g|\text{SCALE})$), together with the *a priori* probability of each class (i.e., how likely it is to observe a gesture class, denoted $p(\text{SCALE})$), in order to compute the *a posteriori* probabilities for g to belong to each class. In the end, Bayes' rule assigns gesture g to class SCALE for which the a posteriori probability $p(\text{SCALE}|g)$ is maximized:

$$\arg\max_{\text{SCALE}} \{p(\text{SCALE}|g)\} = \arg\max_{\text{SCALE}} \{p(g|\text{SCALE})\cdot p(\text{SCALE})\} \quad (2)$$

with SCALE $\in$ {small, medium, large}.

As informed by the shape of the distributions illustrated in Figure 3, we estimate the unknown class-conditional density probabilities $p(g|\text{SCALE})$ with normal models[5]:

$$p(g|\text{SCALE}) = \frac{1}{\sigma_{\text{SCALE}}\sqrt{2\pi}} \cdot exp\left\{-\frac{(\text{SIZE-RATIO}(g)-\mu_{\text{SCALE}})^2}{2\sigma^2_{\text{SCALE}}}\right\} \quad (3)$$

for which means (μ_{SCALE}) and standard deviations (σ_{SCALE}) were reported above. The a priori probabilities are estimated in practice as the ratio of samples falling into each class, for which we choose the equal chance option: $p(\text{SCALE}) = 1/3$.

Estimation accuracy

We evaluated the accuracy of the Bayes' classifier using the standard leave-one-out cross-validation technique that has the desirable property of being almost unbiased [18] (p. 255). Data from a single participant was used for testing while the classifier was trained employing data from the remaining participants. Training consisted in computing the means (μ_{SCALE}) and standard deviations (σ_{SCALE}) for the normal distribution of each class. We repeated this procedure for each participant and averaged recognition rates. In total, we report results from 40 (testing participants) $\times$ 60 (executions per participant) = 2,400 classification tests. User-independent accuracy was 87.3% which confirms the high level of consensus between participants' articulations of gesture scale.

[5]Estimating unknown density probabilities with normal models represents a frequent option in practice due to the simple form of normals, even when the model fit is not perfect [18] (p. 34-35).

We also evaluated the generalization power of the classifier across different screen sizes (i.e., not only user-independent, but also input area-independent testing). This time, data from a single INPUT-AREA-SIZE was used for testing and the classifier was trained with the remaining input areas. The testing procedure was repeated for each value of INPUT-AREA-SIZE and recognition rates were averaged. We report results from 5 (input areas) $\times$ 480 (executions) = 2,400 classification tests. Input area-independent estimation accuracy was 86.9%.

A simple estimation rule

Bayes' rule reports the class corresponding to the maximum probability for a given value of SIZE-RATIO, which points to the normal curve being "on top" in Figure 3. This observation can be used to derive a much simple classification rule in which thresholds serve as class separators, while preserving the principle of maximum a posteriori probability. The intersections of the three normal distributions are approximatively given by values 0.1 and 0.4. We therefore introduce the following rule to estimate the user-intended scale of gesture g:

$$\text{SCALE}(g) = \begin{cases} small & \text{if SIZE-RATIO}(g) \leq 0.1 \\ medium & \text{if SIZE-RATIO}(g) \in (0.1, 0.4] \\ large & \text{otherwise} \end{cases} \quad (4)$$

The simplified rule achieved 87.2% accuracy on the same data set and same leave-one-out user-independent testing methodology. A Wilcoxon signed-rank test showed no significant difference between the accuracy of Bayes' classifier and that of the simplified rule ($Z_{(N=40)}$=−0.269, n.s.). Input area-independent testing also revealed 87.2% accuracy, not significantly different from that reported by Bayes' classifier.

The accuracy of this simple, easy-to-implement, and training-free rule is comparable to that delivered by today's common gesture recognizers, $1 and Protractor[6] [7,19]. Although both recognizers report 99% accuracy with user-dependent training, this value drops to 91% for user-independent tests [16] (p. 275). Our rule achieves a comparable 87% accuracy, is training-free, user- and device-independent, and can be used in conjunction with any gesture recognizer.

[6]$1 and Protractor are scale-invariant, but scale normalization can be easily disabled for $1, which could potentially report both gesture type and scale.

DISCUSSION

We illustrate interactive scenarios for scale gestures and note interesting directions for future work.

Illustrative scenarios. Gesture scale can be exploited in many applications with semantically-close commands. For example, a small flick can turn one page at a time, a medium flick five pages, while a large flick goes to the next chapter. The same principle can be used to browse images, fast-forward a movie, or browse contacts in the address list. In a video game, a small gesture can fire a single shot and a large gesture several. The gesture set can be reduced by reusing the same symbol with different meanings at different scales: small "S" saves the current document, medium "S" the project, and large "S" the entire solution; small "R" replies to the first contact, large "R" replies to everyone for an email client. Text input can reuse the same symbols for lower and upper case letters: small "A" and medium "A" can output different cases, without the need for users and recognizers to memorize two different symbols (i.e., "a" and "A"). This idea is similar to [4], which used pressure to enter mixed-case text (small pressure for lower case, large pressure for upper case), but extends it to devices with no pressure-sensing features.

Upper bounds for gesture size. We note the interesting observation that the size of gestures entered for the 12×12 cm^2 area was smaller than for 10×10 cm^2 (Figure 2). Although significant, this difference could suggest that the notions of small, medium, and large could remain roughly the same starting from some area size (e.g., $\geq 10 \times 10$ cm^2).

Articulation differences. Large gestures were produced at significantly higher speeds (11.2 cm/sec) than medium (8.9 cm/sec) and small (5.9 cm/sec) gestures, ($\chi^2(2) = 156.380$, $p < .001$). This result was expected due to findings from motor control theory showing dependency between writing speed and path length (i.e., homotetic behavior in the time domain for learned motor sequences [17]). In turn, this advocates large gestures as practical shortcuts, as people compensate the extra path length with increased articulation speed.

Simultaneous use of different devices. Our scale estimation rule is device-independent, but frequent transitions between devices with different form factors could affect the size of articulated gestures, as an effect of short-term muscle memory. However, we hypothesize the effect is negligible due to handwriting adaptation with input area size [12]. Future work will investigate the existence of such cross-device effects.

User training. Our rule is user-independent and training-free, which inevitably affects estimation accuracy (87%). User training will likely increase accuracy and we suggest this option for practitioners, should they absolutely need the extra accuracy for their specific gesture sets.

More/less scale levels. We considered three scales only as they are reflective of the perception of psychological space [10] and were used by gesture works before [11,15]. A partial, 2-level rule could discriminate between *small* and *large* gestures only. A second, shorter experiment[7] revealed a threshold value of 0.14 for these two scales, confirming eq. 4. However, the labels of a 4-level scale may not be that easy to find. Such investigations are left as future work. For now, we deliver a simple rule (eq. 4) of immediate practical importance. We align our work in the tradition of simple techniques with high potential impact, such as the 2-level pressure text input of Brewster and Hughes [4] or the 4-level pressure marks of Ramos and Balakrishnan [13].

[7]The 2-level experiment design: 8 participants $\times$ 4 gestures $\times$ 2 scales $\times$ 5 repetitions = 320 executions for an input area of 8×8 cm^2.

CONCLUSION

We presented a simple rule that estimates the user-intended scale of stroke gestures with 87% accuracy. Our estimator works with any gesture recognizer, is training-free, user- and device-independent, and can be immediately integrated into existing gestural interfaces with just three lines of code. We hope this simple rule will be useful for practitioners prototyping gestural interfaces to leverage scale as a naturally-articulated gesture parameter, reduce the size of application gesture sets, and reduce learning requirements for users.

REFERENCES

1. Andersen, T. H., and Zhai, S. Writing with music: Exploring the use of auditory feedback in gesture interfaces. *ACM Trans. Appl. Percept. 7*, 3 (June 2008), 17:1–17:24.
2. Appert, C., and Bau, O. Scale detection for a priori gesture recognition. In *CHI'10*, ACM (2010), 879–882.
3. Appert, C., and Zhai, S. Using strokes as command shortcuts: cognitive benefits and toolkit support. In *CHI '09*, ACM (2009), 2289–2298.
4. Brewster, S. A., and Hughes, M. Pressure-based text entry for mobile devices. In *MobileHCI'09*, ACM (2009).
5. Galen, G. P. V., and Weber, J. F. On-line size control in handwriting demonstrates the continuous nature of motor programs. *Acta Psychologica 100*, 12 (1998), 195–216.
6. Kurtenbach, G., and Buxton, W. User learning and performance with marking menus. In *CHI'94*, ACM (1994), 258–264.
7. Li, Y. Protractor: a fast and accurate gesture recognizer. In *CHI '10*, ACM (2010), 2169–2172.
8. Long, Jr., A. C., Landay, J. A., Rowe, L. A., and Michiels, J. Visual similarity of pen gestures. In *CHI'00*, ACM (2000), 360–367.
9. Malacria, S., Lecolinet, E., and Guiard, Y. Clutch-free panning and integrated pan-zoom control on touch-sensitive surfaces: the cyclostar approach. In *CHI '10*, ACM (2010), 2615–2624.
10. Mandler, J. Representation. In *Handbook of child psychology*, P. Mussen, Ed., 4th ed. New York: John Wiley & Sons, 1983, 420–494.
11. Niels, R., Willems, D., and Vuurpijl, L. The nicicon collection of handwritten icons. In *ICFHR'08* (2008), 296–301.
12. Phillips, J. G., Ogeil, R. P., and Best, C. Motor constancy and the upsizing of handwriting. *Hum. Mov. Sci. 28*, 5 (2009), 578–587.
13. Ramos, G. A., and Balakrishnan, R. Pressure marks. In *CHI '07*, ACM (2007), 1375–1384.
14. Rubine, D. H. *The automatic recognition of gestures*. PhD thesis, Pittsburgh, PA, USA, 1992. UMI Order No. GAX92-16029.
15. Stößel, C., Wandke, H., and Blessing, L. Gestural interfaces for elderly users: help or hindrance? In *GW'09*, Springer-Verlag (2010), 269–280.
16. Vatavu, R.-D., Anthony, L., and Wobbrock, J. O. Gestures as point clouds: a $p recognizer for user interface prototypes. In *ICMI '12*, ACM (2012), 273–280.
17. Viviani, P., and Terzuolo, C. 32 space-time invariance in learned motor skills. In *Tutorials in Motor Behavior*, vol. 1. 1980, 525–533.
18. Webb, A. *Statistical Pattern Recognition, 2nd Edition*. John Wiley & Sons Ltd., West Sussex, England, 2003.
19. Wobbrock, J. O., Wilson, A. D., and Li, Y. Gestures without libraries, toolkits or training: a $1 recognizer for user interface prototypes. In *UIST'07*, ACM (2007), 159–168.

Indirect Shear Force Estimation for Multi-Point Shear Force Operations

Seongkook Heo, Geehyuk Lee
Department of Computer Science, KAIST
Daejeon, 305-701, South Korea
seongkook@kaist.ac.kr, geehyuk@gmail.com

ABSTRACT
The possibility of using shear forces is being explored recently as a method to enrich touch screen interaction. However, most of the related studies are restricted to the case of single-point shear forces, possibly owing to the difficulty of independently sensing shear forces at multiple touch points. In this paper, we propose indirect methods to estimate shear forces using the movement of contact areas. These methods enable multi-point shear force estimation, where the estimation is done for each finger independently. We show the feasibility of these methods through an informal user study with a demo application utilizing these methods.

Author Keywords
Shear force, multi-touch, force sensing, touch screen

ACM Classification Keywords
H.5.2. Information interfaces and presentation (e.g., HCI): User Interfaces – Input devices and strategies

INTRODUCTION
A display with force vector detection capability was presented by Herot and Weinzapfel [6] in 1978 and also by Minsky [11] in 1984. With increased interest in touch screen interaction, the possibility of using force vectors has been revisited to increase the input dimensions of touch screen interaction. Heo and Lee [4] presented the concept of Force Gestures, which use normal and shear forces to enrich touch gestures. Harrison and Hudson [3] presented use scenarios that can be enabled, only if shear forces are used. Lee et al. [10] conducted an experiment to study the performance of using shear forces on a touch screen. However, the touch screen prototypes used in these previous studies were capable of sensing shear force at a single location only. Therefore, the use of multiple shear forces, such as pinching with shear forces, has not yet been studied.

Multi-touch input operations, such as pinching or rotating, are now commonly available on most smartphones and tablet computers. These multi-touch operations may be further extended and enriched when a sensing method for shear forces at multiple points becomes possible. In order to detect shear forces at multiple touch locations, we could use a camera-based method that can detect local shear forces [9]. Further, as introduced by Holz and Baudisch [8], fingerprint sensors can be used to accurately measure finger deformations to estimate shear forces for each finger. However, camera-based methods and fingerprint sensor methods are not feasible for touch screen mobile devices, as they require space for a camera or are difficult to integrate with a display.

For multiple touch locations, we propose a method to estimate shear forces applied on the touch screen, instead of directly measuring shear forces. When a finger applies shear force on a screen, the fingertip is deformed because of the friction between the fingertip and the surface. Because of the deformation of the fingertip, the center of the contact area shifts slightly toward the direction of the shear force. In order to use this shift to estimate the shear force, one has to be able to discern whether the shift is due to the deformation of the fingertip or due to an actual finger movement. In this paper, we describe two different solutions to this problem.

RELATED WORK
Various properties of touch, such as the force, velocity, and size of contact, are used to augment touch interfaces. One commonly studied feature is the normal force applied to the screen. Normal force is one of the key pieces of information that a tablet stylus provides; therefore, a majority of studies on normal force are based on a stylus interface [13, 14]. For a finger-based touch screen, Miyaki and Rekimoto [12] attached a force-sensitive resistor on the back of a mobile device and used vertical force for continuous zooming and scrolling. Rosenberg and Perlin [16] introduced a touch device capable of detecting vertical forces on multiple locations. Another method uses the velocity of a finger tap using an accelerometer embedded in the device. Hinckley and Song [7] presented scenarios that became possible only by combining touch and motion. Heo and Lee [5] explored possibilities of distinguishing between a gentle tap and a strong tap. The use of contact area sizes [1] was also studied. Roudaut et al. [17] showed that a touch movement caused by a finger roll can be recognized and used for additional touch gestures. Recently, using shear force [3, 4, 10] is being studied actively, because it augments touch inputs by using two dimensions, while other features, such

as the velocity or the strength force, augment touch inputs by using only one dimension.

MULTI-POINT SHEAR FORCE ESTIMATION

In order to avoid slipping, normal force must be applied to the screen at the same time as shear force. When we apply shear force and normal force on a screen at the same time, the bottom of the fingertip does not move due to friction, and the fingertip is deformed instead. The result is that the center of the contact area shifts slightly, as shown in Figure 1. This shift is roughly proportional to the applied shear force. A capacitive touch screen determines only the center of a contact area, and, therefore, it reports such a shift as a touch movement. (For the rest of this document, we will use "a touch movement" to specifically refer to a touch movement reported by a touch screen.)

Using the direction and the amplitude of a touch movement, we can estimate the direction and amount of the shear force applied by a finger. Because a touch movement for each finger is independently measured and reported by the touch screen, it is possible to estimate shear forces at multiple locations.

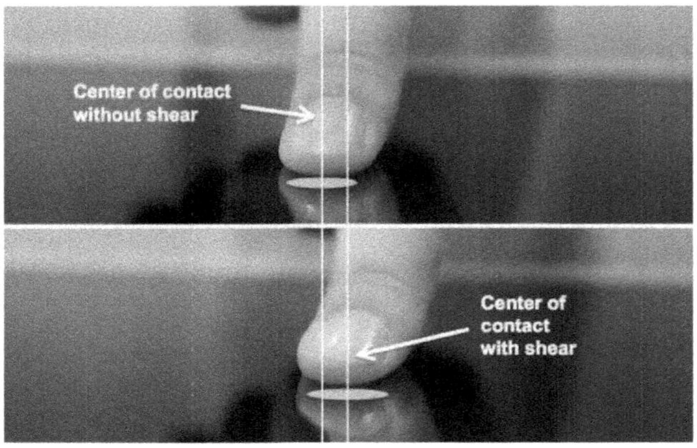

Figure 1. The shift of the center of a finger contact area: (top) before and (bottom) after applying a shear force.

Detection of a Shear Force Event

In order to use a touch movement to estimate shear force, we should be able to discriminate between a shear force event and a slide event. In this paper, we consider two methods for this discrimination.

The first method, which we call the *Force method*, measures normal force, using force-sensitive resistors (FSRs) under the screen. This method works because normal force is necessary when applying shear force; however, it requires additional force sensors under the touch screen. On the other hand, adding sensors under the screen is easier than adding sensors around the screen in order to sense shear forces, as in the cases of [4, 10]. In addition, some mobile phones in the market already come with FSRs under the touch screen [15].

The second method, which we call the *Area method*, uses contact area information from a touch screen to indirectly estimate the normal force. Using a contact area to infer the normal force [2] or to enable an alternative input [1] has already been studied. However, estimating normal force this way is not very reliable, because the size of the contact area is not only dependent on an applied force, but also on the pose and the location of the finger, as described in FatThumb [1]. Despite its inaccuracy, this method is a possible option, because detection of a shear force event does not require the estimation of the normal force to be very accurate. In addition, this method may be a more attractive option than the Force method, because this method does not require additional sensors.

Both methods have their advantages and disadvantages. In the Force method, more accurate pressure sensing is possible; therefore, discrimination of a shear force event will be more reliable. However, detecting pressed states independently at multiple locations is not easy, even with an array of force sensors under a touch screen. In the Area method, the main advantage is that it does not require any additional sensors and it can be applied to the current touch screens in the market. Another important advantage is that normal forces can be independently estimated at multiple touch locations. However, as previously mentioned, discriminating a shear force event from a slide event is relatively unreliable.

Algorithm Details

The shear force estimation algorithms of the two methods are almost the same. The only difference is in identifying a shear force event.

In the Force method, the algorithm performs a calibration at the moment the finger comes into contact with the screen. This is done to offset the effect of gravity, which changes as the orientation of the device changes. When the force applied by the finger on the touch screen exceeds a predefined threshold, the system transitions to the Pressed state (see Figure 2). In the Area method, a gravity calibration step is not necessary, and a contact area is used to determine when to transition to the Pressed state.

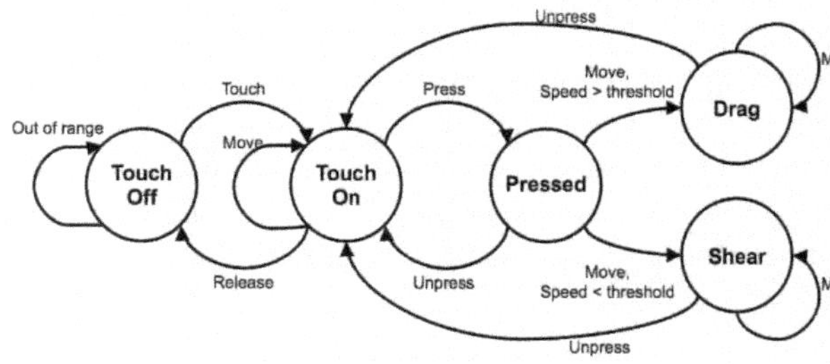

Figure 2. State transition diagram

We assumed that a finger could not slip in the Pressed state due to friction, and that a touch movement in this state could be used to estimate a shear force vector. In a pilot test, however, we observed that participants could make a slide operation even in the Pressed state. Because a shear force (Shear) operation and a forceful slide (Drag) operation have clearly different intentions, we needed to distinguish between these two inputs. The problem was that the touch movement is similar in both cases. One of the data features that turned out to be useful for distinguishing these two cases was the speed of the touch movement. When a touch movement is faster than a certain threshold (approx. 200 mm/s), the movement is regarded as the start of a Drag operation, and a transition to the Drag state is triggered. Otherwise, it is regarded as the start of a Shear operation, and a transition to the Shear state is triggered. The algorithm records the touch location upon transition to the Shear state and uses it as the origin of the shear force vector. While in the Shear state, the value of the shear force vector changes as the touch location changes. Because Drag is not a common touch operation and it is not easy to slide fingers while applying pressure [4], we decided to use Drag operations for four directional gestures only. In addition, a slow Drag cannot be detected and is recognized as a Shear operation.

When two fingers are touching the screen, the state of each touch is determined independently in the Area method. In the Force method, however, two fingers share the same state, because it is difficult to separately determine the normal forces applied by the two fingers.

In a pilot test, we observed that a finger slides slowly on the touch screen during a Shear operation. This sliding invalidates the origin of the shear force vector, which was set upon transition to the Shear state. Therefore, it was necessary to update the origin continuously while a finger touch is in Shear state. In the final algorithm, the update of the origin is done by a simple low-pass filter of the shear force vector; that is, the origin moves in the direction of the vector by 1% of its magnitude every 0.03 ms.

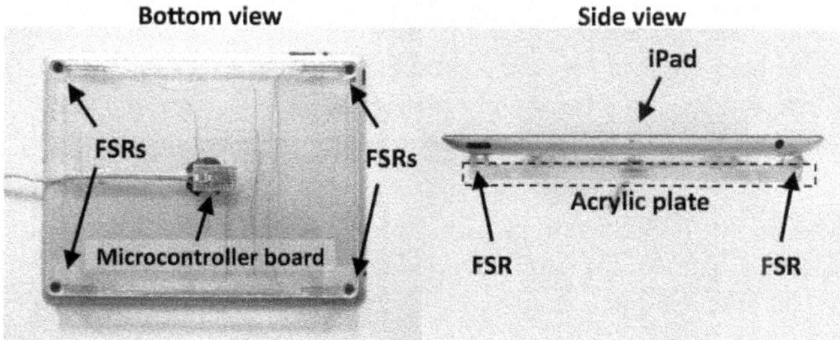

Figure 3. Bottom view and side view of the prototype

PROTOTYPE IMPLEMENTATION

We implemented a prototype to test the feasibility of the proposed methods. The main part of the prototype is a third generation iPad, which detects and handles touch events and performs required calculations. Under the iPad is a sensing plate, which is a 7 mm thick acrylic plate with four FSRs (with a sensing range of 0.2 N to 10 N). A Teensy board with an ATMEGA32 microcontroller performs 10-bit analog-digital conversions and transfers sensor data to the iPad. Normal force is calculated by summing up the sensor values from the four FSRs. Figure 3 shows the bottom view and the side view of the prototype. The acrylic plate can be omitted when sensors can be placed directly under the screen glass.

A DESIGN EXAMPLE: BUG HUNTER

In order to show the feasibility of the two proposed methods, we implemented a simple computer game called Bug Hunter. The goal of the game is to kill all ants, while ignoring other bugs such as snails and caterpillars. In the game, traditional touch screen operations such as Slide and Pinch are used to pan across and to zoom in/out of the game field. Instead of a weapon, shear force operations are used for attack. The shear force gestures used in the game are shown in Figure 4. Users can swing a light saber by using a Shear operation, create a valley by using a Shear Pinch operation, dig a hole to trap bugs by using a Shear Spread operation, and call for air support by using a Drag operation.

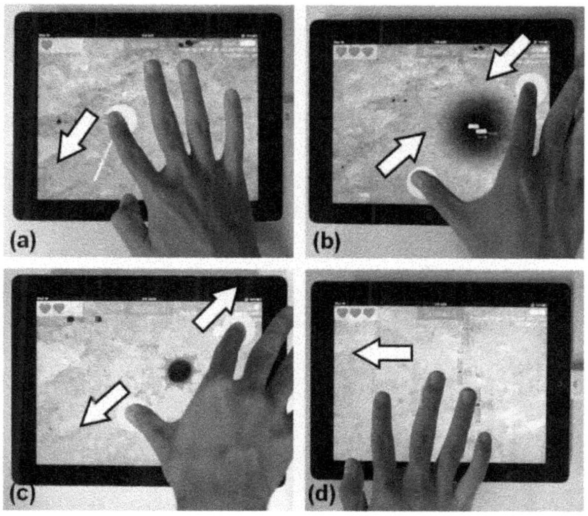

Figure 4. Shear force operations used in Bug Hunter: (a) Shear (b) Shear Pinch (c) Shear Spread (d) Drag

We recruited eight participants (three females and five males, mean age = 20.6) for an informal evaluation session. After a short demonstration, we allowed the participants to play the game once with the Force method and another time with the Area method. In the demonstration, we clearly explained the difference between the two methods. To eliminate ordering effects, four participants played with the Area method first, and the other four played with the Force method first. We asked them to speak freely when they encounter any inconvenience or have a problem. We recorded their comments and observed them while they were playing the game. After the experiment, participants were asked to answer 5-point Likert scale questions about intuitiveness, ease of learning, fatigue, ease of use, level of enjoyment, and conflicts between touch operations. They were also asked to choose a preferred method and to describe the reason for their preference.

In the results, all participants answered that there was a significant difference in usability between the two methods. All but one participant answered that they preferred the Force method, because there were less conflicts between Push and other operations. In the questionnaire, participants gave higher ratings to the Force method than to the Area method in all questions, especially in "easy to use" and "less conflict." Most errors were made when a user tried to perform a Shear operation with the Area method, which often misidentified Shear operations as Slide operations. These errors were more frequent with upward shear force operations, where the finger is slightly lifted and the contact area is smaller. Some participants commented that the Area method could be acceptable after a period of familiarization; however, the Force method would still be preferable.

DISCUSSION

Figure 5 shows the extended design space of touch screen operations that will be made possible by using multiple shear forces. The columns of the table are the different types of operations: Slide operations, Shear operations, and composite operations, which are combinations of different types of operations, including Drag operations. The rows are the numbers of contact fingers. There are two different two-finger cases: Cooperative and Independent. Cooperative indicates that the movements of two fingers are cooperative like pinch or rotate operations. Independent indicates that the movement of one finger is not related to the movement of the other.

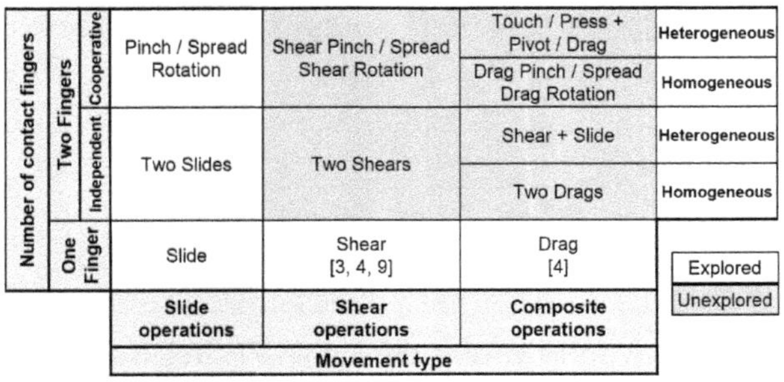

Figure 5. The extended design space of touch screen operations made possible by using multiple shear forces.

In Figure 5, the first column has been the subject of extensive research [18]. In the second and third columns, however, only the one-finger case is getting research focus and only recently [3, 4, 10]. The remaining cases marked in gray have not yet been explored systematically, possibly due to the lack of a hardware platform or technique to support multi-point shear force sensing. More complex touch screen interactions will become possible when this unexplored space can be fully utilized.

In the Bug Hunter example, we mapped Shear operations to new application-specific interactions only in order to emphasize new possibilities. Shear operations can be used to enable more general functions, such as rate-controlled panning or zooming.

CONCLUSION

We designed two methods to indirectly estimate shear forces at multiple points, and we showed their feasibility by implementing a hardware prototype and a demo application that utilizes multi-point shear force operations. In the example game application, we demonstrated a few novel interaction techniques using multi-point shear forces. We also presented a summary of new design space that will be enabled by multi-point shear force sensing methods.

ACKNOWLEDGEMENTS

This work was supported by the IT R&D program of MKE/KEIT [10039161].

REFERENCES

1. Boring, S., Ledo, D., Chen, X., Marquardt, N., Tang, A., Greenberg, S. The Fat Thumb: Using the Thumb's Contact Size for Single-Handed Mobile Interaction. *MobileHCI '12*.
2. Davidson, P.L., Han, J.Y. Extending 2D object arrangement with pressure-sensitive layering cues. *UIST '08*.
3. Harrison, C., Hudson, S. Using Shear as a Supplemental Two-Dimensional Input Channel for Rich Touchscreen Interaction. *CHI '12*.
4. Heo, S., Lee, G. Force gestures: augmenting touch screen gestures with normal and tangential forces. *UIST '11*.
5. Heo, S., Lee, G. Forcetap: extending the input vocabulary of mobile touch screens by adding tap gestures. *MobileHCI '11*.
6. Herot, C., Weinzapfel, G. One-point touch input of vector information for computer displays. *SIGGRAPH '78*.
7. Hinckley, K., Song, H. Sensor synaesthesia: touch in motion, and motion in touch. *CHI '11*.
8. Holz, C., Baudisch, P. The generalized and perceived input point model and how to double touch accuracy by extracting fingerprints. *CHI '10*.
9. Kamiyama, K., Vlack K., Mizota, T., Kajimoto, H., Kawakami N., Tachi S. Vision-based sensor for real-time measuring of surface traction fields. *Computer Graphics and Applications* 25, 1, IEEE (2005), pp.68–75.
10. Lee, B., Lee, H., Lim, S., Lee, H., Han, S., Park, J. Evaluation of human tangential force input performance. *CHI '12*.
11. Minsky, M. Manipulating simulated objects with real-world gestures using a force and position sensitive screen. In *Proc. 11th annual conference on Computer graphics and interactive techniques*, 1984, pp.195–203.
12. Miyaki, T., Rekimoto, J. GraspZoom: zooming and scrolling control model for single-handed mobile interaction. *MobileHCI '09*.
13. Ramos, G., Boulos, M., Balakrishnan, R. Pressure widgets. *CHI '04*.
14. Ramos, G., Balakrishnan, R. Pressure marks. *CHI '07*.
15. Research In Motion^{TM}, SurePress^{TM} Technology http://us.blackberry.com/specifications/communication/surepress-touch-screen.html
16. Rosenberg, I., Perlin, K. The UnMousePad: an interpolating multi-touch force-sensing input pad. *SIGGRAPH '09*.
17. Roudaut, A., Lecolinet, E., Guiard, Y. MicroRolls: expanding touch-screen input vocabulary by distinguishing rolls vs. slides of the thumb. *CHI '09*.
18. Westerman, W., Hand tracking, finger identification, and chordic manipulation on a multi-touch surface. University of Delaware, 1999.

Still Looking: Investigating Seamless Gaze-supported Selection, Positioning, and Manipulation of Distant Targets

Sophie Stellmach and Raimund Dachselt
Interactive Media Lab
Technische Universität Dresden
Dresden, Germany
{stellmach, dachselt}@acm.org

ABSTRACT
We investigate how to seamlessly bridge the gap between users and distant displays for basic interaction tasks, such as object selection and manipulation. For this, we take advantage of very fast and implicit, yet imprecise gaze- and head-directed input in combination with ubiquitous smartphones for additional manual touch control. We have carefully elaborated two novel and consistent sets of gaze-supported interaction techniques based on touch-enhanced gaze pointers and local magnification lenses. These conflict-free sets allow for fluently selecting and positioning distant targets. Both sets were evaluated in a user study with 16 participants. Overall, users were fastest with a touch-enhanced gaze pointer for selecting and positioning an object after some training. While the positive user feedback for both sets suggests that our proposed gaze- and head-directed interaction techniques are suitable for a convenient and fluent selection and manipulation of distant targets, further improvements are necessary for more precise cursor control.

Author Keywords
Eye tracking; gaze interaction; visual attention; mobile touch input; distant displays; selection; positioning

ACM Classification Keywords
H.5.2 Information interfaces and presentation: User Interfaces: Input devices and strategies

General Terms
Design, Human Factors

INTRODUCTION
In our daily lives, we are surrounded by a growing diversity of display setups, for example, multiple screens at work, large-sized TV sets at home or wall-sized information displays. Regardless of the particular display configuration, fundamental interaction tasks include the selection, positioning, and manipulation of displayed content. One interesting way for seamlessly interacting with such diverse displays is a multimodal combination of a user's gaze as an implicit and coarse pointing modality and ubiquitous smartphones for more explicit and manual fine adjustments [16, 17].

The ongoing developments in mobile eye tracking systems will soon allow for pervasive and unobtrusive gaze interaction in everyday contexts [7]. As frequently pointed out, a user's gaze may serve as a beneficial pointing modality (e.g., [4, 16, 20]). It is fast, it requires low effort, and it is very implicit as a person's eye gaze reaches a target prior to a manual pointer [4]. On the downside, several challenges have to be considered for convenient gaze-based interaction that are summarized in the following:

Inaccuracy: Based on the physiological nature of our eyes and the limitation of eye tracking systems, gaze data is inherently inaccurate. While coarse gaze pointing is practical for selecting large graphical items or roughly indicating a user's region of interest, several approaches for overcoming inherent eye tracking inaccuracies exist [16]. This includes local magnifications of small items or multimodal combinations to enhance pointing precision [16, 23]. Several works investigate gaze-based object selection (e.g., [2, 16]). However, further investigations are required about the fluent execution of a series of interaction tasks.

Double role: If our eye gaze is used for interaction, it assumes a double role for visual observation and control. As a result, we have to carefully consider the nature of interaction tasks for convenient and non-distracting gaze-based controls. As an alternative to gaze input, a user's head direction can be used to roughly indicate a user's region of interest and to resolve this double role (e.g., [11]). However, head-directed pointing is less implicit and requires higher physical effort.

Midas Touch: Since our gaze is an *always-on device* [10], mechanism have to be provided to prevent users to unintentionally issue an action. This can be accomplished by gaze dwelling at a certain location, which however impedes fast and continuous interaction. Alternatively, this issue can be addressed by a multimodal combination of implicit gaze input with explicit manual controls to confirm a user's intention.

In this paper, we investigate how a user's gaze or more roughly head direction may aid in *selecting*, *positioning*, and *manipulating* (e.g., rotating or scaling) an item of interest. On the one hand, we take advantage of fast and implicit gaze input for coarse pointing. On the other hand, we use local target expansions and manual touch input for precise and reliable gaze-supported pointing. For this, we utilize ubiquitous smartphones as flexible and popular interactive multi-touch

CHI'13, April 27–May 2, 2013, Paris, France.

devices. We contribute two practical and consistent sets of gaze-supported interaction techniques (see [16, 17] for an introduction to this style of interaction) that allow for fluent *coarse and fine* object *selection and positioning* of distant targets. The elaborated sets have been evaluated in a user study with 16 participants to help us assess the benefits and limitations of the proposed multimodal techniques. Both sets were very positively assessed by participants, although further improvements are required for more fine-grained object selection and positioning.

The remaining paper is structured as follows: First, we give a brief overview of *Related Work* about mobile multi-touch devices and multimodal gaze-based techniques for selecting and manipulating distant targets. Subsequently, we describe several *Design Considerations* that we took into account for the development of our gaze-supported interaction techniques. In the subsequent section, we specify the two sets of gaze-supported interaction techniques that we have developed and report on their evaluation in the *User Study* section. The paper concludes with a *Discussion* of results and future work.

RELATED WORK

A comprehensive body of work about multimodal interaction with distant displays exists (e.g., [3, 5, 15, 16, 19]). With respect to our intended input combination, we concentrate on the use of mobile multi-touch interfaces and multimodal gaze input for interacting from a distance in the following.

Distant Interaction with Mobile Multi-touch Interfaces

Nancel et al. [15] compare different input modalities for pan-and-zoom operations in a large high-resolution multi-display environment. They show that simple linear touch gestures on a mobile multi-touch device are faster and more reliable compared to freehand gestures. Keefe et al. [12] also use a mobile multi-touch interface in a similar display context for selecting, querying, and visually exploring data visualizations. They highlight the advantage to quickly and accurately select items from various positions, which is vital for observing details. For performing selections they propose an extended gesture set mainly based on flicking touch gestures on the handheld device. Han et al. [9] use multiple handhelds (one in each hand) for remote interaction with large vertical displays. For target selection and translation they use one-handed controls; for rotation and scaling two-handed input, e.g., two-handed pinch gesture (in the air).

Boring et al. [6] present Touch Projector, which enables users to select and position content shown on a distant display through touch input on live video on a smartphone. While this works well for large target sizes on the mobile screen, errors occur due to hand jitter and imprecise touch input, which both hinder fine precision tasks. To provide more stability, Boring et al. [6] propose a combination of zooming in on a target and freezing the video. With respect to gaze-based input, in [16] we propose a similar approach for our so-called semi-fixed gaze-directed local zoom lens that works in combination with a handheld smartphone to interact with distant displays. The lens does not move while the user looks within the magnified region (frozen lens). The user can zoom in further by simply sliding upwards on the mobile touch screen to perform more fine-grained selections.

All these works demonstrate the high flexibility for using mobile multi-touch devices to interact with distant displays. However, investigations about a fluent transition between selecting, positioning, and manipulating targets with respect to a user's visual attention are lacking.

Gaze-supported Selection and Manipulation

Already in the early 1980's, Bolt has envisioned how we could benefit from eye gaze as an additional input modality for fast and natural interactions [5] with large distant displays. Since then, several works have investigated how to facilitate the interaction with distant displays by integrating gaze data with additional modalities, such as keyboard controls (e.g., [13, 14, 20]), mouse input [8, 23], hand gestures (e.g., [22]), or touch input (e.g., [16, 17, 18, 21]). Most of these works investigate how to speed up the selection of graphical items at a distant display. One prominent idea for this is to warp the cursor to the vicinity of the user's point-of-regard and to make manual fine adjustments (by moving the mouse) from there [23]. This idea has been advanced to better indicate when the cursor is supposed to follow the user's gaze using a touch-sensitive mouse [8] and a mobile touch screen [16].

In this context, in previous work we have investigated a combination of gaze and touch input for distant object selection and data exploration [16, 17]. While these investigations do not take a broader interaction process into account (e.g., from selecting, positioning, and manipulating a target), they provide interesting insights and a good foundation for the design of more advanced gaze-supported interaction. Turner et al. [18] also investigate a combination of gaze and touch input for target selection *and* positioning. They distinguish between distinctly selecting and positioning a target (*Eye Cut & Paste*) and seamlessly combining both (*Eye Drag & Drop*). For the latter, a user looks at a target, begins touching a multi-touch surface, looks at a desired destination and releases the touch. Turner et al. do not evaluate the proposed techniques or discuss how these could be applied for the selection of small or closely positioned targets.

Instead of using gaze as a direct pointing modality, Kaiser et al. [11] use a user's head direction to indicate the (approximate) region of interest. This is used in combination with multimodal controls, including speech and finger tracking to allow for decreasing the ambiguity for object selection in a virtual 3D scene. Argelaguet & Andujar [1] also propose combining pointing rays from a user's eyes and hand to select items in cluttered virtual environments more efficiently.

In a nutshell, while several works have dealt with gaze/head input as pointing modality, only little work has investigated how to use it for a fluent combination of interaction tasks.

DESIGN CONSIDERATIONS

In the following, we present key design issues that we have taken into account for our gaze-supported interaction techniques. Some of these considerations are based on our prior work on gaze-supported interaction with distant displays [16, 17]. In addition, although not considering gaze input, Bezerianos & Balakrishnan [3] describe several design goals for object selection and manipulation in distant locations. This includes, e.g., consistency and minimized physical movement. In the scope of this paper, we focus on single users to build a solid foundation for multimodal gaze-supported interaction before targeting multi-user or collaborative applications.

Interaction Tasks: The intended gaze-supported interaction techniques shall allow for selecting, positioning and manipulating graphical objects shown at a distant display. For this, we aim for convenient selection of large and small or closely positioned objects (i.e., *coarse* vs. *fine* selection). In addition, we distinguish between *coarse* and *fine* target positioning (also see [19]). While roughly moving an item is sufficient to make room for other objects, more precise input is required for exact graphical layouts. Finally, while we mainly focus on object selection and positioning in the scope of this paper, we take additional interaction tasks into account. For this, we consider basic manipulation tasks, such as scaling and rotating a selected target.

Input Combination: On the one hand, we benefit from gaze for direct, fast and coarse pointing. On the other hand, the interaction with a smartphone serves for indirect and more fine-grained input. With this, we follow up on the promising principle *"gaze suggests and touch confirms"* [16].

Eyes-free Interaction: A user's main visual attention should remain at the distant display and not the mobile screen. Thus, it is vital that the smartphone can be controlled without having to look at it. This means, for example, that simple touch events and relative touch gestures should be favored over additional virtual buttons.

Low Effort: The more frequent an action has to be performed, the easier and quicker the interaction should be. For example, to confirm a selection, a tap on the touch screen should be preferred over a complex multi-touch gesture.

Consistency and Seamlessness: A consistent and seamless combination of interaction techniques supports users in performing tasks in an effective and fluent way. This becomes especially vital when taking a longer chain of interaction tasks into account (e.g., selection, positioning, and manipulation). In addition, we need to consider that in some cases users may only want to select a target, but may not want to immediately reposition it. Thus, we distinguish between a *distinct* and *seamless* combination of selection and positioning.

DESIGN OF INTERACTION TECHNIQUES

For the design of gaze-supported interaction techniques, we follow two parallel lines of development differing in how to overcome eye tracking inaccuracies: (1) a touch-enhanced gaze pointer and (2) a gaze-directed zoom lens. With this, we build on our promising gaze-supported target acquisition techniques that we have proposed in [16], which also use a combination of gaze and touch input. However, we extend these investigations by addressing how to fluently select *and* position differently sized objects (from a distance) considering a user's gaze/head direction. For this, we have elaborated two conflict-free sets of interaction techniques combining gaze/head and touch input. We discuss benefits and limitations of gaze- and head-directed input for object selection and for directly controlling a target (for repositioning). As a minor aspect, we also consider how manipulation tasks, such as object scaling and rotation, can be seamlessly integrated. In the following, we first introduce the basic principles of the *touch-enhanced gaze pointer* and *gaze-directed zoom lens* and then describe how the specified interaction tasks can be performed with them.

Touch-enhanced Gaze Pointer

One way to address inaccurate gaze data is to allow for manual fine adjustments of the coarse gaze cursor [8, 16, 23]. Zhai et al. [23] introduce the *Manual And Gaze Input Cascaded* (MAGIC) pointing technique to speed up object selections: The cursor is warped to the vicinity of a currently looked at target and can be repositioned via mouse or touchpad controls. Based on this, our *MAGIC touch* technique [16] focuses on object selections using a combination of gaze data and touch input from a handheld smartphone. To extend on this, we propose an advanced *touch-enhanced gaze pointer* (**TouchGP**) that is applicable for gaze-supported object selection *and* positioning. For this, a user's gaze information serves for roughly indicating an area of interest (*coarse* selection and positioning) and the touch input for more precise adjustments (*fine-grained* selection and positioning). While the cursor movement for the original *MAGIC touch* is limited to a certain boundary around the current gaze point, we lift this restriction to provide higher flexibility. If the user touches the mobile display, the cursor on the distant screen stops following the user's gaze and instead follows the relative touch movement on the mobile display. For this, the initial touch position serves as a reference location from which movements can be performed in all directions. The mapping of touch movements to the movement of the distant cursor can be adapted to different levels of precision. For example, a touch movement of 50 pixels on the mobile display could be mapped to only 5 pixels for very precise cursor positioning.

Gaze-directed Zoom Lens

A common approach for overcoming inherent eye tracking inaccuracies is the use of local magnification lenses to increase apparent target sizes [2, 16]. While an *eye-slaved* zoom lens, a lens that immediately follows a user's gaze, is beneficial for easy gaze-based target selections, it is also more visually distracting and error-prone as the lens is always moving according to the *imprecise* gaze cursor [2, 16]. A *semi-fixed* zoom lens [16], that gradually starts moving towards user's current point-of-regard when looking outside the lens' boundary, provides a higher stability. However, users have mentioned that it is distracting to have to look away from the actual object-of-interest to move the lens.

We propose a hybrid type which we call *Gaze-directed Zoom Lens* that takes advantage of the quickness of the *eye-slaved* zoom lens and the higher stability of the *semi-fixed* one. For this, we distinguish a three-zone design for the zoom lens (also see Figure 1), for which we assume that the cursor is directly mapped to the current gaze position (i.e., gaze-directed

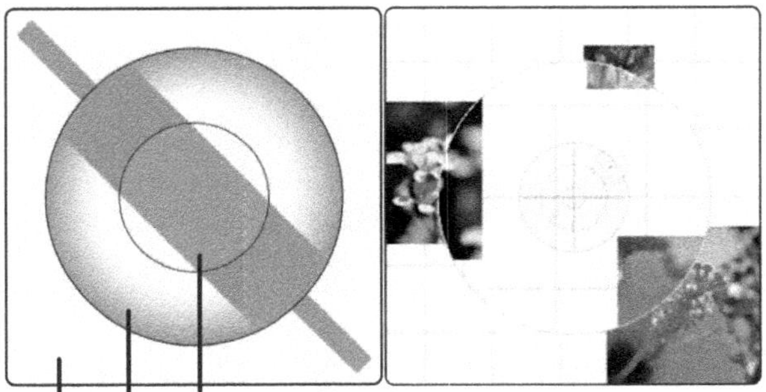

Figure 1. The enhanced semi-fixed zoom lens follows a three-zone design (left). The right image is an actual screenshot from our prototype. The size and magnification level can be adapted via touch controls. An additional crosshair is displayed if a target has been selected (as shown in the right image).

cursor): (1) *Inner zone* – While looking within this zone (i.e., moving the gaze-directed cursor in this region), the lens is not moving. (2) *Active rim* – The further a user looks away from the inner zone towards the outer zone, the faster the lens will follow the user's gaze (*semi-fixed lens behavior*: relative gradient-based lens positioning). (3) *Outer zone* – If a user looks outside the lens, the lens center will be immediately set to the current gaze position (*eye-slaved lens behavior*: absolute lens positioning).

In contrast to the semi-fixed zoom lens, users do not need to look outside the lens to move it and can still benefit from an increased stability if looking close to the lens center. For our prototype, the radius of the *Inner zone* is always half the size of the *Active rim*. Thus, if increasing the *Active rim*/lens size, the *Inner zone* automatically adapts in size as well. The lens can be controlled more smoothly and precisely with a larger *Active rim* as the gradient-based speed values are distributed across a larger region (cf. Figure 1, left). The lens size can be adapted using a horizontal sliding gesture, the zoom level using a vertical one (also see next section and see Figure 2). Finally, the lens is always on and thus no additional input is required for activation. However, the lens is designed in a subtle way to limit visually distracting the user.

Pre-Study: From Gaze- to Head-directed Zoom Lens

We conducted a preliminary interview with three participants to get first insights about the suitability of the gaze-directed zoom lens for selecting and positioning objects. While participants mentioned that the lens has potential for easing gaze-based selections, it was described as awkward and even impractical for positioning a target. This was due to the circumstance that it was very difficult to position an object, while having to look away from it to move the lens. Sometimes a user merely wanted to check whether an object was aligned correctly at all sides and would then accidentally reposition it. This leads back to a challenge of the double role of our eye gaze for convenient gaze-based interaction. Nevertheless, local magnification lenses that are based on a user's visual attention are promising as frequently pointed out [2, 13, 16]. As a conclusion, we decided to refrain from using gaze input to steer the lens, but instead take a user's head direction into account to still take advantage of the rough estimation of a user's visual field. Thus, a user can move the lens by turning his/her head towards a region of interest without any gaze input. In the remaining paper, we refer to this as *Head-directed Zoom Lens* (**HdLens**) instead of *Gaze-directed Zoom Lens*.

Multimodal Gaze-supported Interaction Techniques

We elaborated a set of interaction techniques for **TouchGP** and for **HdLens** that allow for fluently transitioning between roughly and precisely selecting and positioning objects displayed at a distant screen. As a minor aspect, we also consider how manipulation tasks, such as scaling and rotating a target, can be seamlessly appended. For these techniques we assume a single user standing or sitting in front of a large (distant) screen and holding a smartphone in his/her hand. We distinguish two main approaches: The *seamless* combination of selecting and positioning a target (i.e., drag-and-drop) and the dissociation of them in *distinct* phases. This means that a user can first select a target, then explore the displayed content further (e.g., to select additional targets), and finally position the selected items. However, in the context of this paper, we will focus on single targets for now. An overview of the elaborated interaction techniques is illustrated in Figure 2. In the following, these two approaches (*distinct* vs. *seamless*) for object selection and positioning are described in more detail for both **TouchGP** and **HdLens**.

Distinct Selection

For both **TouchGP** and **HdLens**, large targets can be simply selected (*coarse selection*) by looking/turning towards them and briefly tapping the touch screen (single tap). To select small items (*fine selection*), the techniques differ for **TouchGP** and **HdLens**. For **TouchGP**, the user looks at the intended target and slides the finger on the smartphone for finer cursor positioning. For this, the cursor stops following a user's gaze once he/she touches the mobile screen. For **HdLens**, small targets can be selected by increasing the lens' magnification level using a simple upwards sliding gesture on the mobile screen (downwards to zoom out). Once an object is selected, a crosshair is displayed at the center of the lens as a positioning aid (also see Figure 1, right).

Distinct Positioning

After an object has been selected, the user can directly position it to the current gaze location (*coarse positioning*) by briefly tapping the touch screen twice (double tap). To position it more precisely (*fine positioning*), techniques differ for **TouchGP** and **HdLens** again: For **TouchGP**, if a user touches the mobile screen, a preview of the currently selected target is shown at the gaze location and the (distant) cursor stops following the user's gaze. From this location, the object can be manually repositioned more precisely via touch input (slide gesture). For fine positioning with **HdLens**, first the lens can be further zoomed in with an upward touch sliding gesture. To not distract the user while looking around, a preview only appears after touching the mobile screen for a longer time (hold). The target is then attached to the lens center, as this provides a higher stability and control compared to the imprecise head-directed cursor. The lens and attached

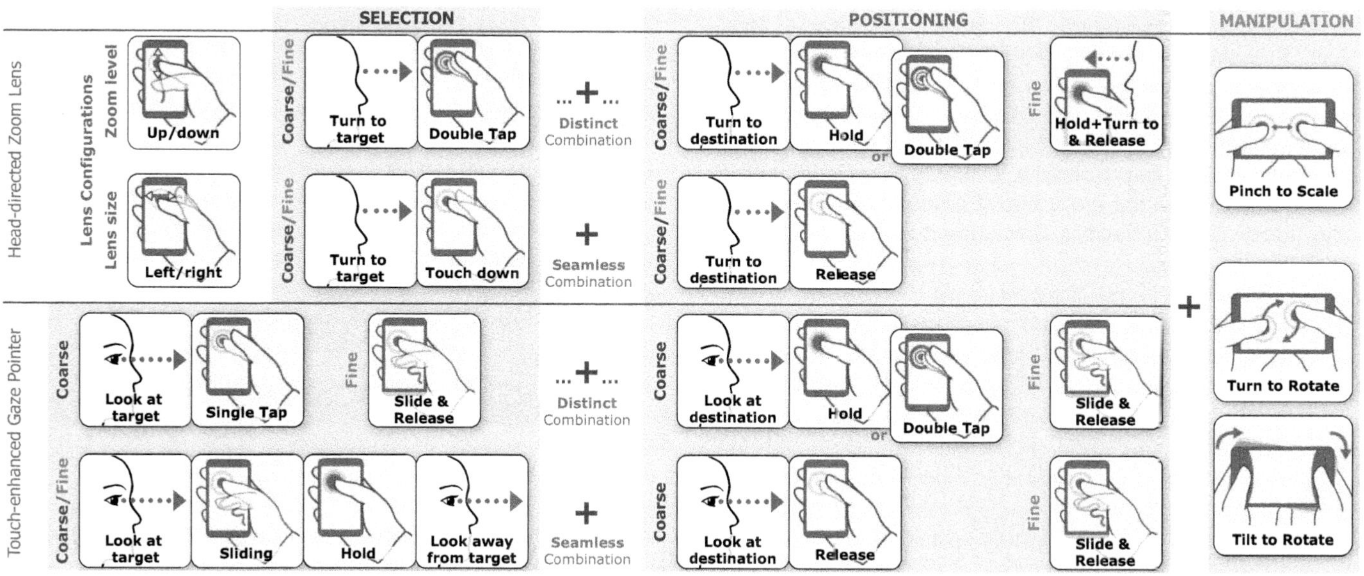

Figure 2. Overview of our proposed gaze-/head-supported interaction techniques for selecting, positioning, and manipulating an object.

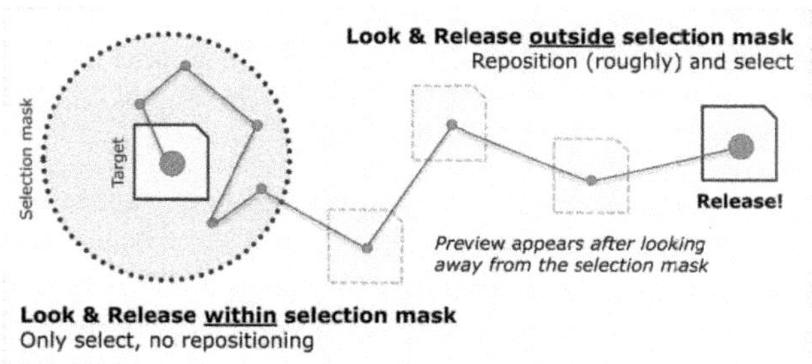

Figure 3. Example of gaze-/head-directed drag-and-drop.

object can be positioned more precisely by moving the head-directed cursor into the *Active rim* or *Outer zone* of the lens (cf. Figure 1, left). Once the user releases the mobile touch screen, the preview disappears, and the object is set to the current lens center. Alternatively, a user can reposition the lens via head-directed input first (without touching the mobile device) and then perform a double tap to warp the object directly to the lens center.

Seamless Selection & Positioning

In the following, we describe how users can *seamlessly* select and position an object using **TouchGP** and **HdLens**. For this, we propose a gaze-/head-directed drag-and-drop approach that is illustrated in Figure 3. The user can simply look at a target and begin touching the mobile screen to mark it for selection (*coarse selection*). For more *precise selections*, the cursor can be repositioned by either moving the finger on the touch screen (**TouchGP**) or performing a vertical slide gesture to zoom in further (**HdLens**). As soon as the mobile screen is touched, the cursor stops following the user's gaze and a *selection mask* is displayed, as illustrated in Figure 3. If releasing the touch while still looking within the boundaries of this selection mask, the marked target is selected but not repositioned. This prevents unintentionally moving an object due to jittery eye movements. If the user looks beyond the selection mask's boundaries and still holds on to the touch screen, a smooth transition from target selection to positioning is achieved (*drag-and-drop*). After crossing the selection mask's boundary, a preview appears and starts following the user's gaze. In case of **HdLens**, a crosshair and a preview of the marked target is displayed at the lens center. The user can simply release the touch for *coarse object positioning* or can continue touching the device for more precise object positioning. As before, *fine positioning* is either achieved moving the finger on the mobile screen (**TouchGP**) or performing a vertical sliding gesture to zoom in further (**HdLens**).

Manipulation Mode

As previously pointed out, we also considered how additional interaction tasks, such as scaling and rotating an object, could be seamlessly combined with the proposed sets of interaction techniques. For simple target manipulations, we wanted to reuse some low-effort touch gestures, such as a one-finger sliding gesture. For this, it is however necessary to distinguish different interaction modes, in our case a *selection & positioning* and a *manipulation* mode. In the manipulation mode, the user can position, rotate, and scale an already selected item. To reach the manipulation mode, we aimed for a quick and reliable mode change that does not require the user to look at the smartphone. Considering common multi-touch manipulation techniques, such as pinch-to-zoom (i.e., moving two fingers together/apart to zoom in/out), we decided that the user can simply flip the smartphone to landscape mode and hold the device in two hands to allow for a *two-thumbs* interaction (see Figure 2, lower right). The shape of the cursor at the distant display will change to provide immediate feedback about the mode change (which again supports eyes-free interaction with the handheld device).

A two-thumbs pinch gesture is used to scale a selected target. To rotate it, the user can perform a two-thumbs turn-to-rotate gesture (i.e., the touch points move into the same clockwise or counterclockwise direction – see Figure 2, right). Alternatively, the user can also tilt the smartphone to rotate an object. For this, the user has to hold the smartphone parallel to the distant screen and can mimic the current orientation of the target. Then, the user needs to touch two active regions at the left and right side of the mobile screen to indicate that the target should start imitating the smartphone's orientation. Thus, this follows the metaphor of holding a large picture at the sides with both hands and rotating it to align it.

USER STUDY

To further investigate the elaborated sets of interaction techniques for **TouchGP** and **HdLens**, we conducted a user study (within-subjects design). Since a seamless combination of gaze-supported object selection and positioning has not been investigated before, we were particularly interested in finding out more about the practicality and suitability of the proposed techniques for these interaction tasks. For this, we varied target sizes and respective destination areas to investigate how the individual techniques would be suited for fine and coarse object selection and positioning. Our main interest was to receive valuable user feedback (both qualitative and quantitative) to gain further insights into gaze-supported interaction. Thus, in this study, we did not aim at beating a given baseline, but instead wanted to find out how people cope with the developed techniques for achieving a given task.

Apparatus. For gathering gaze data we used a head-mounted ViewPoint PC-60[1] eye tracker from Arrington Research. It allows for tracking both eyes (binocular) with an accuracy of about 0.25°-1.0° visual angle, however, without the compensation of head shifts. To track a user's head movements, we used a ceiling-mounted visual tracking system, the OptiTrack V100:R2 IR setup[2], with six cameras at 50 Hz with a 640x480 pixel resolution. For this, IR markers have been attached to the head-mounted eye tracker frame. The gathered gaze/head data was stabilized [16]. For the smartphone interaction, we used a Samsung Galaxy SIII GT-I9300[3] deploying Android 4.0.4. It has a 4.8" display with a resolution of 1280x720. For moving the distant cursor via touch input, we used a 1:1 mapping. Thus, if the touch point moves 50 pixels on the smartphone screen, the distant cursor will also move 50 pixels. Data from the ViewPoint system, OptiTrack server, and smartphone were sent via TCP/IP and an adapted VRPN interface to the application computer, which runs Microsoft's XNA Game Studio 4.0 (based on C#) for the creation of our virtual test environment. Finally, the distant screen projection was 1.5 m wide and 2.5 m high. Participants were seated about 2.2 m away from the screen. An overview of the setup used in this user study is shown in Figure 4.

Participants. Sixteen volunteers (8 male, 8 female) participated in our user study ranging in age from 22 to 33 (Mean (M) = 27.6). None of the participants wore glasses, as we encountered problems with the deployed eye tracker due to reflections. If necessary, participants used contact lenses to correct their vision. All participants indicated that they use computers on a daily basis. Nine participants have used eye trackers before, but only once or twice. Twelve participants own a smartphone and five a multi-touch tablet.

[1]http://www.arringtonresearch.com/scene.html

[2]http://www.naturalpoint.com/optitrack/products/v100-r2/

[3]http://www.samsung.com/global/galaxys3/specifications.html

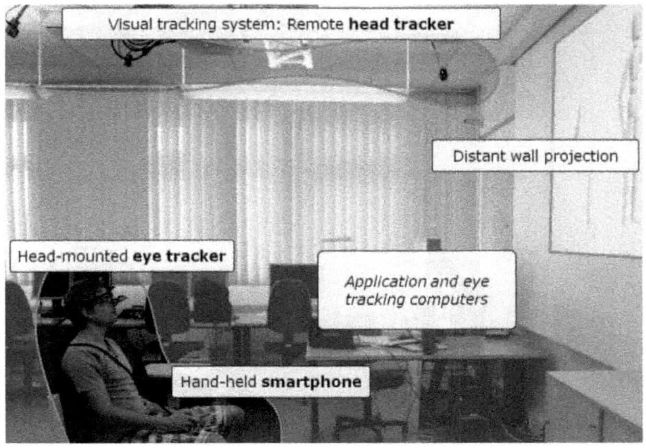

Figure 4. Overview of the hardware setup in the user study.

Procedure. After welcoming participants, a demographic questionnaire was handed out. Participants were seated in front of the projection screen and were instructed to sit fairly still, but without physically restricting their movement. We counter-balanced the order in which the input conditions (**TouchGP** and **HdLens**) were tested.

For **HdLens**, the OptiTrack system has been calibrated beforehand to ensure that the markers that have been attached to the eye tracker frame could be properly tracked. After participants put on the head-mounted gear, we asked them to sit in a comfortable position and to look at the center of the distant screen. This head position and orientation were taken as a reference to account for different user heights. For **TouchGP** we additionally performed a 16-point eye tracker calibration.

After ensuring that the tracking of gaze and head data worked as anticipated, we followed the same procedure for each technique. One input condition (i.e., **TouchGP** or **HdLens**) was tested at a time. First, we explained the interaction principles for **TouchGP/HdLens**. Participants could directly get acquainted with them in a demo application as long as they felt necessary. While this training phase usually did not take longer than 5-10 minutes, we noticed that in particular those users with little experience with smartphones took considerably longer to get used to the indirect touch interaction, as they usually performed rather coarse touch movements which led to cursor overshooting beyond a targeted location. The demo application showed parts of a 3D model that had to be assembled (see Figure 4, right). After the training phase, we proceeded with *Task One* and *Task Two* (cf. Figure 5) that are described in the following.

In *Task One*, we wanted to investigate the suitability of our techniques for *fine & coarse selection & positioning*. For this, a single target had to be selected and positioned as fast as possible. One target at a time appeared at a random screen corner but always with the same distance to the screen center. Targets always had to be positioned in or towards the opposite diagonal corner. Target sizes and corresponding destination sizes were varied (see Figure 5 for an overview). Target sizes

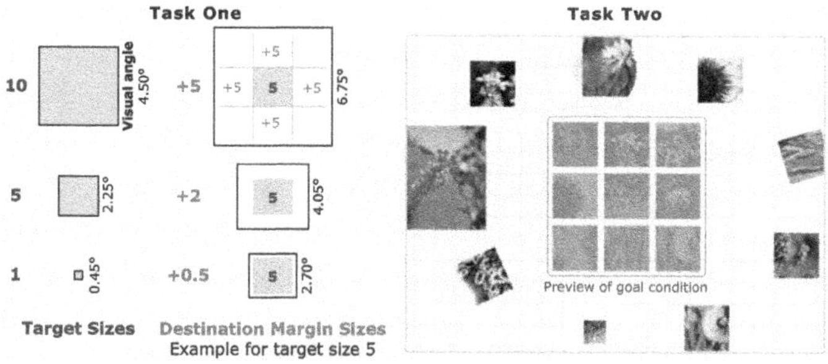

Figure 5. Overview of the two main task scenarios. In *Task One*, target and destination sizes are varied to investigate the suitability of TouchGP and HdLens for fine and coarse selection and positioning. *Task Two* is an open task in which users were asked to select, position, scale, and rotate nine images. For this, the entire set of techniques for TouchGP or HdLens had to be used in concert.

differed from 10 (large) to 5 and 1 (small) based on an internal unit. With respect to our particular setup, the sizes ranged from 4.5° (size 10) to 0.45° (size 1) of visual angle. The size of the destination area was the sum of the current target size plus an additional margin to distinguish between coarse and fine object positioning (see Figure 5 for an example for target size 5). These destination margins ranged from +5 (large), +2 to +0.5 (small). Finally, to add some variation to the tasks, we used two different distances between target and destination. At the beginning of each run, participants had to look at the center of the screen and touch the mobile device to confirm readiness (a circle displayed at the screen's center turned green if looking at it to give a better feedback). This was meant to improve comparability between the task completion times. The described procedure for *Task One* was carried out twice, leading to 36 tasks to complete: three target sizes x three destination margin sizes x two distances x two runs.

In *Task Two*, we added an informal part (no logging of task completion times) in which we wanted to let users freely *play around* with the entire set of techniques for **TouchGP** and **HdLens** to select, position, and manipulate several objects after each other. Here, we wanted to investigate how users would assess the usability of the different selection and positioning techniques in concert. After describing the manipulation techniques to the users, they had to move, scale and/or rotate nine images to match nine preview images shown at the center of the screen (cf. Figure 5, right).

Measures. Since we focused on substantial user feedback about the developed interaction techniques, we handed out several questionnaires at different stages during the study: an initial demographic, two intermediate, and a final questionnaire. The intermediate and final questionnaires contained both quantitative and qualitative questions. All quantitative questions were based on 5-point Likert scales from 1 - *Strongly disagree* to 5 - *Strongly agree*.

The intermediate questionnaire consisted of four parts and was handed out after completing both *Task One* and *Task Two* with a given set of techniques. In the first two parts, users had to rate eight general usability statements for *object selection* (IQ1) and also for *object positioning* (IQ2) (see Figure 7). In the third part (IQ3), we asked individual questions about

	1st run	2nd run
TouchGP	$F_T(2,45)=3.38$, **$p<.05$** $F_D(2,45)=3.55$, $p=.06$	$F_T(2,45)=19.65$, **$p<.001$** $F_D(2,45)=6.86$, **$p<.05$**
HdLens	$F_T(2,45)=5.03$, **$p<.05$** $F_D(2,45)=2.71$, $p=.08$	$F_T(2,45)=9.92$, **$p<.001$** $F_D(2,45)=7.85$, **$p=.001$**

Table 1. Overview of the influence of target sizes (T) and destination sizes (D) based on the overall task completion times for a respective input condition within a run. Significant results are printed in bold.

particular aspects of **TouchGP** (10 questions) and **HdLens** (14 questions). Finally, participants were asked for qualitative feedback about what they particularly liked and disliked about **TouchGP/HdLens** (IQ4).

In the *final questionnaire*, we asked six questions about how users liked the manipulation techniques (e g., the type of scaling and rotation). In addition, we asked participants for a final assessment of and for concluding comments about **TouchGP** and **HdLens**. On average, each participant took about 120 minutes for the described procedure.

RESULTS

For the evaluation of **TouchGP** and **HdLens**, we were particularly interested in user feedback about their assessed usability, usefulness and possible improvements. However, we start the evaluation by briefly assessing the basic practicality of the techniques for coarse and fine object selection and positioning. For this, we evaluate logged data for the time it took users to successfully select and position a target. Please note that only *Task One* was time-measured and that this task was executed twice (run 1 and 2) for each input condition. To investigate statistically significant differences in the logged data, we used a repeated-measures ANOVA (Greenhouse-Geisser corrected) with post-hoc sample t-tests (Bonferroni corrected).

Task Completion Times

An overview of the average times it took users to *select* an appointed target and *position* it within a designated destination area (for *Task One*) is listed in Figure 6. First, we consider how the individual input conditions, **TouchGP** and **HdLens**, are suited for coarse and fine object selection based on varied target sizes. Subsequently, we address their suitability for coarse and fine object positioning based on varied destination margin sizes.

Target Sizes. Although all users were able to select even small targets (size 1) with both input conditions, users needed significantly longer than for larger targets (see Table 1 for statistical results). No significant differences exist for targets of size 5 and 10. Users could select targets significantly faster with **TouchGP** than with **HdLens** for both runs ($F(3,135)=25.11$, $p<.05$). While participants could significantly improve their performance with **TouchGP** between the two runs ($p<.05$), no significant learning improvements exist for **HdLens** in this respect.

Destination Sizes. Users were able to position all given targets in the designated destination areas. However, users were slower with both input conditions for precise target positioning (i.e., destination margin size = +0.5) than for

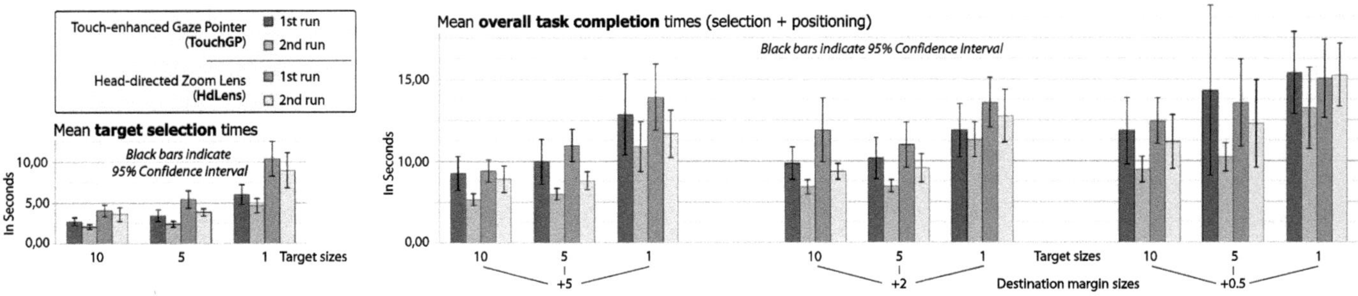

Figure 6. Mean selection and overall task completion times (selection+positioning) across varied target and destination margin sizes for *Task One*.

coarse positioning (significantly in the second run, see Table 1 for statistical results). For **HdLens**, the performance decrease from margin size +5 to +0.5 was even highly significant (p<.001). Finally, task completion times significantly differed across the techniques and associated runs (F(3,360)=14.68, p<.001). Users could significantly improve their performance from the first to the second run for both input conditions (both p<.05). In addition, users were significantly faster with **TouchGP** (second run) compared to **HdLens** (in both runs (p<.001)).

General Usability Ratings

In the first part of the intermediate questionnaires, we asked participants to rate several statements on the usability of **TouchGP** and **HdLens** for object selection (IQ1) and positioning (IQ2). An overview of the gathered user ratings is shown in Figure 7. The ratings for **TouchGP** and **HdLens** do not differ significantly. Interestingly, although users were able to perform tasks significantly faster with **TouchGP** (see previous section), the perceived *speed* at which actions could be performed was assessed lower than for **HdLens**. Some participants explained that they actually had the feeling that they could be faster with **TouchGP**, but that fine adjustments (both for selection and positioning) were difficult with it due to difficulties with the indirect touch input. In this line, the *accuracy* with which actions could be performed was not perceived as satisfactory, whereby users found that they could be more precise with **HdLens**. Both **TouchGP** and **HdLens** were assessed as *easy to learn*, however, with a bit more effort for using them for target positioning. Concerning the *ease of use*, both **TouchGP** and **HdLens** were assessed highly suitable for coarse selection and positioning. All in all, users found the techniques *intuitive* and suitable for achieving tasks as anticipated (*task-driven use*). In the *overall user rating*, **TouchGP** received similar and even slightly better ratings than **HdLens** (but not significantly).

User Feedback

In the following, we report and discuss the remaining quantitative (IQ3) and qualitative (IQ4) user feedback from the intermediate questionnaires and the feedback from the final questionnaire. For IQ3, participants had to rate how they liked particular aspects of **TouchGP** and **HdLens** based on 5-Point-Likert scales.

Touch-enhanced Gaze Pointer

All in all, users liked **TouchGP** (M=4.19, SD=0.81) and the particular combination of touch and gaze input (M=4.60, SD=0.61). In fact, fourteen participants explicitly mentioned that they enjoyed to roughly position the distant cursor via gaze (M=4.56, SD=0.61) and to precisely position it via touch (M=4.88, SD=0.33). However, the interaction was not found particularly convenient (M=3.56, SD=0.93), as many users explained that they found the touch input too imprecise and tiring for precise selection and positioning (M=3.00, SD=1.00). Users liked the seamless *drag-and-drop* combination for **TouchGP** (M=4.00, SD=0.87). Finally, users liked to double tap (M=3.88, SD=0.99) or hold on to the touch screen (M=3.81, SD=1.07) to position a target. However, they usually preferred performing a sliding gesture to warp the target to the current gaze position and immediately make fine adjustments from there (M=4.38, SD=0.98). In *Task Two* (cf. Figure 5), it became apparent that deselecting a target is not well handled with **TouchGP**, since the sliding gesture is assigned both for fine-grained selection as well as positioning. Thus, with the intention in mind to select a new target while another object has already been selected, users would accidentally reposition the still selected target by performing a sliding gesture.

Head-directed Zoom Lens

Users highly appreciated **HdLens** (M=4.38, SD=0.48). Four participants emphasized that they found it very intuitive to use, especially with respect to the seamless combination of selection and positioning (i.e., drag-and-drop) (M=4.44, SD=0.61). User liked the double tap for quick object positioning (M=4.31, SD=0.98). Users appreciated the three-zone lens design with the inactive inner zone (M=4.69, SD=0.68), the continuous gradient-based lens control (M=4.75, SD=0.43), and the absolute positioning if quickly turning away from the current lens position (M=4.80, SD=0.40). Five people particularly pointed out that they found it very useful that the lens did not move while the cursor was within the inner lens region. Participants also positively assessed that the lens already moved while looking within the magnified region (as in contrast to the semi-fixed zoom lens as proposed in [16]) (M=4.50, SD=0.71). While participants liked the vertical sliding gesture to adapt the magnification level (M=4.38, SD=0.70), the horizontal sliding gesture for changing the lens size was less appreciated (M=4.00, SD=0.71). This is probably due to the fact that many participants rather tried to achieve a task without

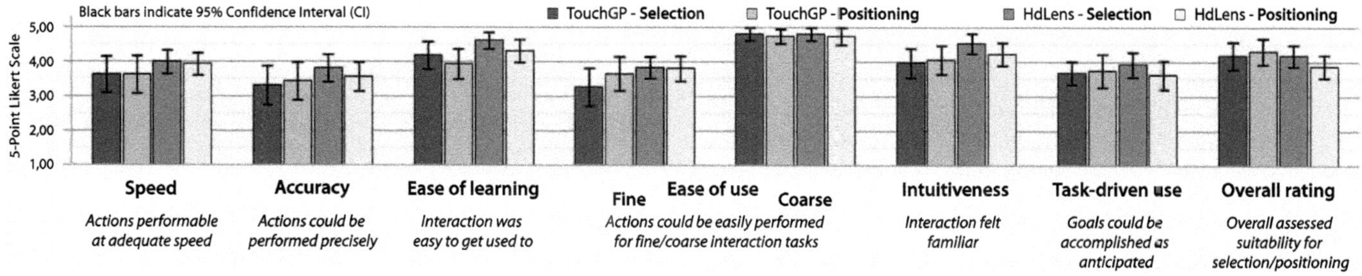

Figure 7. Overview of quantitative user feedback from the intermediate questionnaires IQ1 and IQ2 (with 5 – Strongly agree to 1 – Strongly disagree).

altering the lens size and thus did not assess this feature as important as zooming in, which was vital for selecting tiny targets. In this respect, nine participants particularly mentioned that they appreciated the possibility to adapt lens parameters, especially the magnification level. The provided visual feedback, i.e., target previews, target highlighting, and the crosshair at the lens center were appreciated (M=4.25, SD=1.03). However, additional auditory feedback to confirm a selection was desired (three participants). Three participants also mentioned that the head-directed cursor and crosshair should be more *eye-catching*, as they sometimes had difficulty to immediately detect it. All in all, the head-directed interaction was often described as less distracting, but also as more explicit and straining in the long run compared to **TouchGP** (five participants). Four people particularly mentioned that they preferred steering the lens via their head instead of their gaze, because it gave them more control.

Manipulation. Users did not find the mode change (i.e., turning the smartphone to the side) particularly convenient (M=3.25, SD=1.30). Four participants asked for either integrating all interaction tasks into one single mode or to use an alternative mode switch that would allow for an even quicker mode change. Furthermore, while participants liked the pinch gesture for scaling a target (M=4.44, SD=0.61), they preferred the tilt-to-rotation technique (M=3.94, SD=0.90) over the turn-to-rotate touch gesture (M=3.50, SD=1.17).

DISCUSSION

The positive user feedback suggests that our proposed gaze- and head-directed interaction techniques are suitable for a convenient and fluent selection and positioning of distant targets. Both **TouchGP** and **HdLens** were assessed as intuitive and easy to use in particular for *coarse* object selection and positioning. Users were in general faster with **TouchGP** for which they preferred to look at a destination and slide the finger on the touch screen to precisely position a target. Nevertheless, several participants found that head-directed input with **HdLens** provided a higher feeling of control, as it was less overwhelming than the interaction via eye gaze. However, it was also described as less implicit and more straining in the long run (higher fatigue). In addition, participants appraised the three-zone lens design and well-chosen function mappings (e.g., speed of lens movement). Finally, our gaze-supported drag-and-drop approach for seamlessly selecting and positioning targets was highly appreciated.

While the positive user feedback affirms that our careful design of gaze-supported object selection and positioning is feasible, several improvements are possible. For more precise cursor movements, a more appropriate mapping of touch input to the relative movement of the distant cursor has to be chosen for **TouchGP**. This would allow users to perform coarser touch movements on the smartphone for only slightly moving the distant cursor/target. Further improvements for **TouchGP** include a better way to deselect objects. One simple solution would be to make the respective interaction mode dependent on the current gaze position. Thus, if a user looked at a new target and performed a sliding gesture, the selection mode would be active. Instead if a user looked at a void spot on the screen, the positioning mode would be considered. However, this would pose a problem for overlapping images. As an alternative, an additional control at the back of the device could be used as a mode switch, especially since the remaining four fingers holding the smartphone have no other task so far than to stabilize the device in the user's hand. For **HdLens**, object positioning was found cumbersome at times due to the unusual indirect object positioning as users had to turn their heads to move the lens/the currently selected item. However, this is also closely related to the problem that precise lens movements were sometimes difficult to achieve. For more precise cursor/lens movements with **HdLens**, a smoother distribution of speed values in the *Active lens rim* could help.

The combination of gaze-/head-directed input with a smartphone may benefit diverse user contexts, for example, for the interaction with large-sized or multiple display setups at home or in offices. Virtual objects could be quickly selected and moved across different screens and devices simply by looking at them and touching the smartphone. Another interesting application context is also the integration of the presented techniques with modern gaming consoles and large-sized TV screens for more immersive game experiences.

Further work includes how to integrate additional interaction tasks while still maintaining a fluent interaction. For this, additional investigations are required to find out to what extent we can take advantage of simple manual input that users would naturally prefer without actually having to look at a handheld device (eyes-free). Finally, further studies have to determine how **TouchGP** and **HdLens** would compete against other techniques for interacting with distant displays (e.g., as presented by Nancel et al. [15], for example, in terms of speed, error rate, and comfort.

CONCLUSION

In summary, we have presented two novel sets of multimodal gaze-/head-supported interaction techniques that allow for seamlessly interacting with distant displays. For this, we take advantage of a user's gaze-/head-directed input as a coarse and fast pointing modality and a handheld touch screen from a ubiquitous smartphone for fine-grained input. The sets are based on two basic principles to overcome inaccurate gaze/head pointing: (1) additional manual touch control and (2) local magnifications. With these sets, users can fluently select a small or large target, position it to a desired location, and rotate and scale it. This means that our techniques support both *fine and coarse* target *selection and positioning*. Furthermore, we support both *distinct*, subsequent interactions and a *seamless combination* of target selection and positioning. Both multimodal interaction sets were evaluated in a user study with 16 participants. We received very positive feedback for both sets, which encourages further investigations into how to extend and improve these techniques. Overall, users were fastest with a touch-enhanced gaze pointer after some training. After all, both sets demonstrated a high potential for a practical, low-effort and fluent interaction with distant displays using gaze/head and touch input. However, further improvements are required especially for more precise object selection and positioning.

ACKNOWLEDGMENTS

This research is supported by the German National Merit Foundation.

REFERENCES

1. Argelaguet, F., and Andujar, C. Efficient 3D pointing selection in cluttered virtual environments. *Computer Graphics and Appl., IEEE 29*, 6 (11 2009), 34–43.
2. Ashmore, M., Duchowski, A. T., and Shoemaker, G. Efficient eye pointing with a fisheye lens. In *Proc. of GI '05* (2005), 203–210.
3. Bezerianos, A., and Balakrishnan, R. The vacuum: Facilitating the manipulation of distant objects. In *Proc. of CHI '05*, ACM (2005), 361–370.
4. Bieg, H.-J., Chuang, L. L., Fleming, R. W., Reiterer, H., and Bülthoff, H. H. Eye and pointer coordination in search and selection tasks. In *Proc. of ETRA'10*, ACM (2010), 89–92.
5. Bolt, R. A. Gaze-orchestrated dynamic windows. In *Proc. of SIGGRAPH '81*, ACM (1981), 109–119.
6. Boring, S., Baur, D., Butz, A., Gustafson, S., and Baudisch, P. Touch projector: mobile interaction through video. In *Proc. of CHI '10*, ACM (2010), 2287–2296.
7. Bulling, A., and Gellersen, H. Toward mobile eye-based human-computer interaction. *IEEE Pervasive Computing 9* (2010), 8–12.
8. Drewes, H., and Schmidt, A. The MAGIC touch: Combining MAGIC-pointing with a touch-sensitive mouse. In *Proc. of INTERACT'09*, Springer-Verlag (2009), 415–428.
9. Han, S., Lee, H., Park, J., Chang, W., and Kim, C. Remote interaction for 3D manipulation. In *Proc. of CHI EA '10*, ACM (2010), 4225–4230.
10. Jacob, R. J. K. What you look at is what you get: eye movement-based interaction techniques. In *Proc. of CHI '90*, ACM (1990), 11–18.
11. Kaiser, E., Olwal, A., McGee, D., Benko, H., Corradini, A., Li, X., Cohen, P., and Feiner, S. Mutual disambiguation of 3D multimodal interaction in augmented and virtual reality. In *Proc. of ICMI '03*, ACM (2003), 12–19.
12. Keefe, D. F., Gupta, A., Feldman, D., Carlis, J. V., Krehbiel Keefe, S., and Griffin, T. J. Scaling up multi-touch selection and querying: Interfaces and applications for combining mobile multi-touch input with large-scale visualization displays. *Int. J. Hum.-Comput. Stud. 70*, 10 (Oct. 2012), 703–713.
13. Kumar, M., Paepcke, A., and Winograd, T. EyePoint: practical pointing and selection using gaze and keyboard. In *Proc. of CHI '07*, ACM (2007), 421–430.
14. Monden, A., Matsumoto, K., and Yamato, M. Evaluation of gaze-added target selection methods suitable for general GUIs. *Int. J. Comput. Appl. Technol. 24* (June 2005), 17–24.
15. Nancel, M., Wagner, J., Pietriga, E., Chapuis, O., and Mackay, W. Mid-air pan-and-zoom on wall-sized displays. In *Proc. of CHI '11*, ACM (2011), 177–186.
16. Stellmach, S., and Dachselt, R. Look & touch: gaze-supported target acquisition. In *Proc. of CHI '12*, ACM (2012), 2981–2990.
17. Stellmach, S., Stober, S., Nürnberger, A., and Dachselt, R. Designing gaze-supported multimodal interactions for the exploration of large image collections. In *Proc. of NGCA'11*, ACM (2011), 1–8.
18. Turner, J., Bulling, A., and Gellersen, H. Combining gaze with manual interaction to extend physical reach. In *Proc. of PETMEI '11*, ACM (2011), 33–36.
19. Vogel, D., and Balakrishnan, R. Distant freehand pointing and clicking on very large, high resolution displays. In *Proc. of UIST'05*, ACM (2005), 33–42.
20. Ware, C., and Mikaelian, H. H. An evaluation of an eye tracker as a device for computer input. In *Proc. of CHI'87*, ACM (1987), 183–188.
21. Yamamoto, M., Komeda, M., Nagamatsu, T., and Watanabe, T. Development of eye-tracking tabletop interface for media art works. In *Proc. of ITS '10*, ITS '10, ACM (2010), 295–296.
22. Yoo, B., Han, J.-J., Choi, C., Yi, K., Suh, S., Park, D., and Kim, C. 3D user interface combining gaze and hand gestures for large-scale display. In *Proc. of CHI EA'10*, ACM (2010), 3709–3714.
23. Zhai, S., Morimoto, C., and Ihde, S. Manual and gaze input cascaded (MAGIC) pointing. In *Proc. of CHI'99*, ACM (1999), 246–253.

Individual User Characteristics and Information Visualization: Connecting the Dots through Eye Tracking

Dereck Toker, Cristina Conati, Ben Steichen, Giuseppe Carenini
Department of Computer Science
University of British Columbia, Vancouver, Canada
{dtoker, conati, steichen, carenini}@cs.ubc.ca

ABSTRACT

There is increasing evidence that users' characteristics such as cognitive abilities and personality have an impact on the effectiveness of information visualization techniques. This paper investigates the relationship between such characteristics and fine-grained user attention patterns. In particular, we present results from an eye tracking user study involving bar graphs and radar graphs, showing that a user's cognitive abilities such as perceptual speed and verbal working memory have a significant impact on gaze behavior, both in general and in relation to task difficulty and visualization type. These results are discussed in view of our long-term goal of designing information visualisation systems that can dynamically adapt to individual user characteristics.

Author Keywords

User Characteristics, Information Visualization, Eye Tracking, Adaptive Information Visualization.

ACM Classification Keywords

H.5.m. Information interfaces and presentation (e.g., HCI): Miscellaneous.

General Terms

User Studies; Human Factors; Design; Measurement.

INTRODUCTION

Information visualization (Infovis for short) aims to assist users in exploring, managing, and understanding the ever-growing amount of digital information. While visualizations have gained increasingly in terms of general usage and usability, they have traditionally followed a one-size-fits-all model, typically ignoring user differences. However, recent research has shown that individual differences can indeed have a significant impact on task effectiveness and user satisfaction during Infovis usage. For example, personality traits have been found to impact a user's performance with different Infovis designs [31, 15]. Velez et al. [30] found that a user's abilities for spatial reasoning (e.g., spatial orientation) were correlated with visualization comprehension. Similarly, Conati & Maclaren [3] and Toker et al. [28] found that cognitive abilities such as perceptual speed, visual/verbal working memory and expertise can impact user performance or subjective preference with a given visualization.

These studies indicate that it is important to investigate the possibility of user-adaptive information visualization systems, namely, Infovis that can dynamically adapt to individual differences. User-adaptive interaction has been shown to be effective in a variety of applications such as web search, desktop assistance, and e-learning [18], but it is largely unexplored in information visualization. Notable exceptions are [13, 14], which monitor a user's interaction data to detect and adapt to suboptimal usage patterns. In contrast, our research goal is to investigate how to detect and adapt to longer-term user cognitive abilities, which have been shown to be relevant for effective information visualization processing.

While Conati & Maclaren [3] investigated the impact of these cognitive abilities on overall user performance with different visualizations, the research presented in this paper aims to gain a more fine-grained understanding of the impact that these cognitive abilities have on visualization processing. One of the most informative (and sometimes the only available) sources of real-time information on visualization processing is a user's gaze data, because visual scanning and elaboration are fundamental components of working with a visualization (they are in fact the only components for non-interactive visualizations). Therefore, in this paper we aim to determine if and how features in user gaze behavior are impacted by different user characteristics. In particular, we aim to answer the following questions:

1) Do individual user characteristics influence a user's gaze behavior in a way that is detectable by state of the art eye tracking?

2) If yes, (a) which gaze features are influenced by which user characteristics? (b) Is the effect modulated by task context (e.g., task difficulty), and visualization type (e.g., bar vs. radar graph)?

Answering these questions can provide a better understanding of how specific user characteristics influence the processing of both information visualizations in general, as well as different visualization types (e.g., bar graphs), and individual visualization components (e.g., a graph's legend). Moreover, these answers can help drive the design of user-adaptive visualizations. In particular, by finding that user characteristics influence a user's gaze behavior in a way that is detectable via eye tracking, we can consider exploring eye tracking as a source of real-time information to provide adaptive interventions targeting these characteristics. For instance, if an Infovis system could detect from gaze data that the current user has low perceptual speed (an element that, as we will see later in the paper, may negatively impact the user's interaction with a visualization), it could then generate interventions to facilitate visualization processing, e.g., through highlighting or by explanatory material.

In exploring these research questions, this paper makes the following contributions. First, we present a statistical analysis using Mixed Models [8] to investigate how a user's gaze behavior relates to user characteristics, task difficulty, and visualization type. We argue that a Mixed Model analysis is the most suitable statistical model to leverage at best the generally noisy eye tracking data. Secondly, we present a novel definition of task difficulty, derived through applying Principal Component Analysis to a selection of both objective and subjective performance measures. Thirdly, the results from the analysis show that user characteristics indeed have a significant influence on user gaze behavior, and that this influence is detectable through a variety of eye tracking metrics. We discuss these results in detail, as well as how they can inform the design of user-adaptive information visualizations.

RELATED WORK

The use of eye tracking has long been established in Psychology as a means for analyzing user attention patterns in information processing tasks [20]. Research in this field has also investigated the impact of individual user differences on reading and search tasks [23].

Researchers in human-computer interaction and information visualization have also started to use eye tracking technology to investigate trends and differences in user attention patterns and cognitive/decision processing. This research has typically focused on either identifying differences in gaze patterns for different visualizations [12], task types [17, 26], and activities within a task [4], or on explaining differences in user accuracy between alternative visualization interfaces [22]. While these studies provide valuable insights on how different tasks and/or activities affect a user's gaze behaviors, they have traditionally ignored individual differences among study participants.

Recent research however, has shown that user differences can have a significant impact on a user's performance during Infovis tasks. For example, Ziemkiewicz et al. [31] and Green and Fisher [15], looked at the influence of personality traits, showing that locus of control impacts performance across different visualizations. Cognitive measures such as perceptual speed and visual memory have been shown to influence a user's ability to complete a task effectively [3, 30]. These results were extended in a recent study [28] showing that perceptual speed and visual/verbal working memory influence not only task performance, but also a user's subjective preference for two different visualizations. While each of these studies clearly indicate that user differences should be considered in Infovis, they do not explain why or how these differences impact visualization processing, nor do they examine how this impact could be detected in real time. In this paper, we address these issues by providing a detailed analysis of how a set of user characteristics (including three cognitive measures and visualization expertise) influences a variety of eye gaze features during visualization processing.

To the best of our knowledge, there is no established comprehensive theory connecting eye gaze patterns and individual user traits that could guide our investigation of gaze patterns during visualization processing. Previous work has empirically identified relationships between eye gaze and individual user differences in attention-related tasks [21] (e.g., measuring a user's susceptibility to distraction), which is not directly relevant to our focus. Our research adds to this body of empirical work by providing detailed evidence of how individual differences affect a user's gaze patterns during Infovis usage. The closest to our research is work by Tai et al. [26] and Tang et al. [27], who focused on a single, domain-specific user trait (task-domain expertise), showing that domain experts and novices display different gaze behaviors. The scope of our work is broader, since we investigate a comprehensive array of user characteristics including cognitive abilities and *visualization expertise*, (i.e., expertise on specific visualizations). These characteristics are domain-independent, thus our results are more general across different Infovis tasks. Furthermore, we perform a detailed analysis of gaze data in order to link different characteristics to standard Infovis components (e.g., legends).

One approach to analyze eye tracking data is to apply data mining techniques, such as Hidden Markov Models [4], Scan-Path clustering [11], or specifically defined unsupervised algorithms [5, 16]. While data mining methods can quickly identify clusters of similar attention patterns during visualization tasks, the results they return are often difficult to interpret, since unsupervised algorithms are typically applied as black-boxes. By contrast, although traditional human-guided statistical analyses can be more time-consuming, its findings tend to be more transparent and easier to interpret. Our paper presents such a human-guided analysis of how user gaze behavior relates to user, task, and visualization characteristics. In particular, the paper provides fine-grained insights on how a set of user characteristics interact with different visualization types, components, and task difficulty to impact gaze patterns.

USER STUDY

In this section, we describe the study that we conducted to investigate the relationship among user characteristics, task difficulty and gaze patterns while using different visualizations. As case studies, we considered two basic visualization techniques: bar graphs (Figure 1, top) and radar graphs (Figure 1, bottom). Bar graphs were chosen because they are one of the most popular and effective visualization techniques. We chose radar graphs because, although they are often considered inferior to bar graphs on common information seeking tasks [7], they are widely used for multivariate data. Furthermore, there are indications that radar graphs may be just as effective as bar graphs for more complex tasks [28].

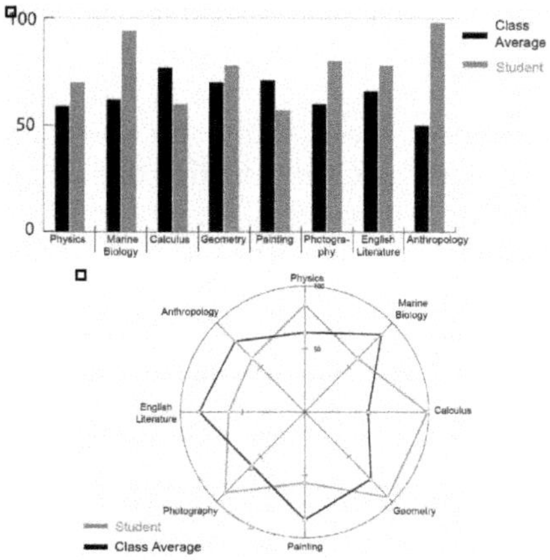

Figure 1. Sample bar (top) and radar graph (bottom)

User characteristics explored in the study

The user characteristics that we investigate in this study consist of two measures of prior *visualization expertise*, one for each of the two visualizations, as well as three cognitive abilities: *perceptual speed* (a measure of speed when performing perceptual tasks), *verbal working memory* (*verbal WM* - a measure of storage and manipulation capacity of verbal information), and *visual working memory* (*visual WM* - a measure of storage and manipulation capacity of visual and spatial information). Visualization expertise was chosen because we hypothesized that users with different levels of expertise might exhibit different gaze behaviors. For our study, participants self-reported their expertise by expressing their agreement with the statement "I am an expert in using radar(bar) graphs," on a Likert-scale from 1 to 5. Perceptual speed and visual WM were selected because they were among the perceptual abilities explored by Velez et al. [30], as well as among the set that Conati and Maclaren [3] found to impact user performance with radar graphs and a Multiscale Dimension Visualizer (MDV). We chose verbal WM because we hypothesized that it may affect performance in processing textual components of a visualization (e.g., labels/ legends).

Experiment tasks

Participants were asked to perform a set of tasks related to evaluating student performance in eight different courses. This task domain was chosen because it did not require any specific background knowledge, thus domain expertise was not a factor in our study. The tasks were based on a set of low-level analysis tasks that Amar et al. [1] identified as largely capturing people's activities with visualizations. The tasks were chosen so that each of our two target visualizations would be suitable to support them. A first battery of tasks involved 10 questions comparing the performance of one student with the class average for eight courses, e.g., *"In how many courses is Maria below the class average?"*. A second battery of tasks involved 4 questions comparing the performances of two different students with respect to the class average, e.g., *"Find the courses in which Andrea is below the class average and Diana is above it"*.

Procedure

Thirty-five subjects (18 female), ranging in age from 19 to 35, participated in the experiment. Participants were recruited via advertising at our university, with the aim of collecting a heterogeneous pool of participants with suitable variability in the target characteristics. Ten participants were CS students, while the rest came from a variety of backgrounds, including microbiology, economics, classical archaeology, and film production. The experiment was a within-subjects study, designed and pilot-tested to fit in a single session lasting at most one hour. Participants began by completing tests for the three cognitive measures: a computer-based OSPAN test for verbal WM [29] (lasting between 7 and 12 minutes), a computer-based test for visual WM [10] (10 minutes long), and a paper-based P-3 test for perceptual speed [6] (3 minutes long). The experiment was conducted on a Pentium 4, 3.2GHz, with 2GB of RAM and a Tobii T120 eye tracker as the main display. Tobii T120 is a remote eye tracker embedded in a 17" display, providing unobtrusive eye tracking. After undergoing a calibration phase for the eye tracker, each participant performed the 14 tasks described in the previous section twice, once with each of the two target visualizations. The presentation order with respect to visualization type was fully counterbalanced across subjects. Each task consisted of presenting the participant with a radar/bar graph displaying the relevant data, along with a textual question. Participants would then select their answer from a set of available options, and click OK to advance to the next task. Before seeing the next task, participants were shown a screen asking them to rate their confidence in their answer on a Likert scale from 1 to 5. The experimental software was fully automated and coded in Python.

DATA ANALYSIS

Independent Measures

The independent measures for our study consisted of the collected cognitive abilities and expertise measures (continuous), visualization type (categorical: bar vs. radar), and task difficulty (continuous - values described in the next section). Table 1 presents summary statistics on the user characteristics data collected from the study. The rather large variances for most measures indicate that we succeeded in collecting a diverse pool of participants. We also verified our results with other studies involving the same tests and found similar results from other populations.

Measure	N	Min	Max	Mean	Std. Dev
Percep. Speed	35	54.00	96.00	85.70	11.64
Visual WM	35	0.3	5.4	2.72	1.36
Verbal WM	35	2	6	4.58	1.10
Bar Expert	35	2	5	4.15	0.87
Radar Expert	35	1	5	2.12	1.22

Table 1. User characteristics collected from our study

Task difficulty

Defining tasks as being easy or difficult a priori is challenging, since difficulty depends upon user expertise and perceptual abilities, which were varied on purpose in our study. We therefore defined task difficulty a posteriori, based on four different measures (two objective and two subjective) aggregated using a principal component analysis [8]. Because there was a ceiling effect on task correctness, our first objective measure of task difficulty is *task completion time* (assuming that, in general, more time is needed for more difficult tasks). However, longer completion times may also simply be an indication of a task being longer while not necessarily being more difficult. Therefore our second objective measure of difficulty is the *standard deviation of completion time* for each task, across all users. A high value of this metric indicates a high variability among users' completion times, an indicator that the task may be difficult or confusing for some users.

Our two chosen subjective measures of task difficulty are based on the users' reported confidence of their performance, which was elicited after each task. The first subjective measure is the *average confidence* reported by users on each task. Intuitively, less difficult tasks would have higher values for this average. However, we also want to take into account that some users may tend to be more confident overall than other users. Therefore, our second subjective measure is the *average deviation of confidence* for each task across all users and is computed as follows. For each user, we look at their average confidence across their tasks. Then, for each task, we compute the *deviation of confidence* as the difference between the user's reported confidence for that task and the user's average confidence across tasks. Finally, for each task, we average the deviation of confidence across all users. This average indicates for which tasks users were giving confidence ratings that were above or below their typical input.

In order to combine the four variables above, we performed a *Principal Component Analysis (PCA)*. PCA is a form of dimension reduction that allows one to identify and combine groups of inter-related variables into components more suitable for data analysis [8]. A PCA on our four measures of task difficulty resulted in one output component. Bartlett's test of sphericity ($x^2 = 73.35$, $df = 6$, $p < .001$) indicated that the principal component analysis was appropriate. Kaiser's sampling adequacy was 0.55 and all variables showed a communality > 0.52 which was above the acceptable limit of 0.5[1] [8]. The component we generated had an eigenvalue over Kaiser's criterion of 1 and explained 62.22% of the variance. In sum, we use the output component generated by this PCA (i.e., dimensional reduction) as the measure of task difficulty that we will investigate in our analysis.

Dependent Measures: Eye Tracking Features

Eye tracking measures

An eye tracker captures gaze information in terms of *fixations* (i.e., maintaining gaze at one point on the screen) and *saccades* (i.e., a quick movement of gaze from one fixation point to another), which can then be analyzed to derive a viewer's attention patterns. In this paper, we use a large set of basic eye tracking features described by Goldberg and Helfman [11] as the building blocks for comprehensive gaze processing. These features are built by calculating a variety of statistics upon the basic eye tracking measures that are described in Table 2.

Measure	Description
Fixation rate	Rate of eye fixations per millisecond
Number of Fixations	Number of eye fixations detected during an interval of interest
Fixation Duration	Time duration of an individual fixation
Saccade Length	Distance between the two fixations delimiting the saccade (d in Figure 2)
Relative Saccade Angles	The angle between the two consecutive saccades (angle y in Figure 2)
Absolute Saccade Angles	The angle between a saccade and the horizontal (angle x in Figure 2)

Table 2. Description of basic eye tracking measures

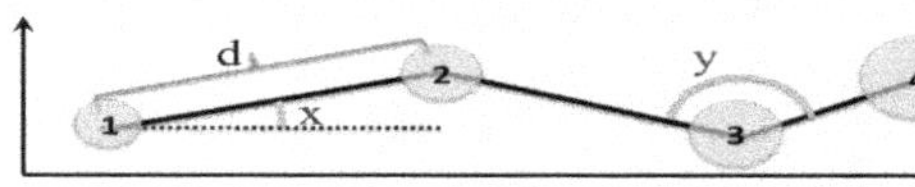

Figure 2. Saccade based eye measures

Among the measures described in Table 2, fixation rate, number of fixations, and fixation duration are widely used. In addition, we included saccade length, relative saccade angle, and absolute saccade angle, as suggested by Goldberg and Helfman [11], because these measures are useful to summarize trends in user attention patterns within a specific interaction window (e.g., if the user's gaze seems to follow a planned sequence as opposed to being scattered).

The gaze features for our analysis are obtained by computing statistics such as sum, average, and standard deviation over the measures shown in Table 2, at two levels of granularity. At the *Task Level*, features are computed over each task as a whole (Table 3). At the *AOI level,*

[1] All subsequent PCA results reported meet the required criteria, and for simplicity we only report the value of Bartlett's test.

features are computed based on gaze activity within a specific region of the screen, or *Area Of Interest* (Table 4), including transitions between pairs of defined AOIs (five in our analysis, as described in the next section). To limit our analysis to a reasonable number of features, at the AOI level, we opted to calculate only proportionate features and did not include features related to path angles (note that each AOI feature increases complexity by a factor of 5). In total, we included 49 different features in our analysis (14 Task-level and 35 AOI-level), computed by processing raw data from the Tobii using customized Python scripts[2].

Total Fixation rate
Total Number of Fixations
Sum, Mean and Std. Dev. of Fixation Durations
Sum, Mean and Std. Dev. of Saccade Lengths
Sum, Mean and Std. Dev. of Relative Saccade Angles
Sum, Mean and Std. Dev. of Absolute Saccade Angles

Table 3. Task-level eye tracking features

Proportion of Fixation Durations
Proportion of Total Number of Fixations
Number of Transitions from this AOI to each other AOI (5 separate measures for each AOI)

Table 4. AOI-level eye tracking features

Areas of interest (AOI)

A total of five AOIs were defined for each of the two visualizations. These regions were selected in order to capture the distinctive and typical components of these two information visualizations. Figure 3 and 4 show how these AOIs map onto bar graph and radar graph visualizations.

- *High Area:* covers the upper half of the data elements of each visualization. This area is the graphical portion of an Infovis that contains the relevant data values. On the bar graph, it corresponds to a rectangle over the top half of the vertical bars (see Figure 3); for the radar graph, it corresponds to the combined area of the 8 trapezoidal regions covering the data points (see Figure 4).
- *Low Area:* covers the lower half of the data elements for each visualization.
- *Labels Area:* covers all the data labels in each graph.
- *Question Text Area:* covers the text describing the task to be performed.
- *Legend Area:* covers the legend showing the mapping between each student and the color of the visualization elements that represent her performance.

The selection of these five AOIs is the result of a trade-off between having detailed information on user attention by measuring very specific areas that are salient for task execution, versus keeping the number of AOIs manageable for data interpretation and analysis. Because each added AOI increases transition analysis by n^2, we opted to include fewer AOIs (e.g., we don't have an AOI for each bar in the bar graph or radial element in the radar graph), while still capturing distinctive areas that can be considered general components of many Infovis.

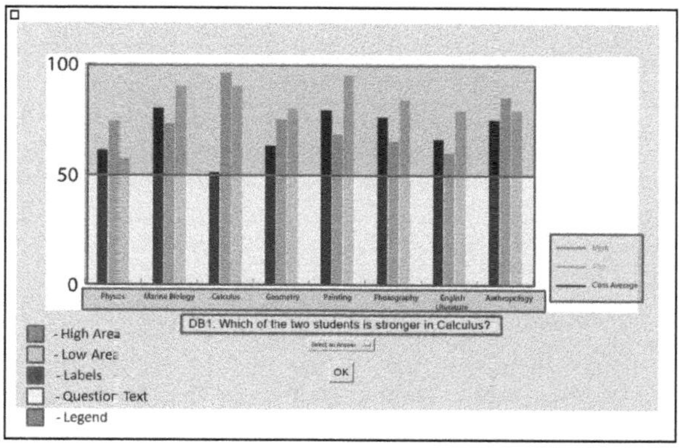

Figure 3. The five AOI regions defined over Bar Graph

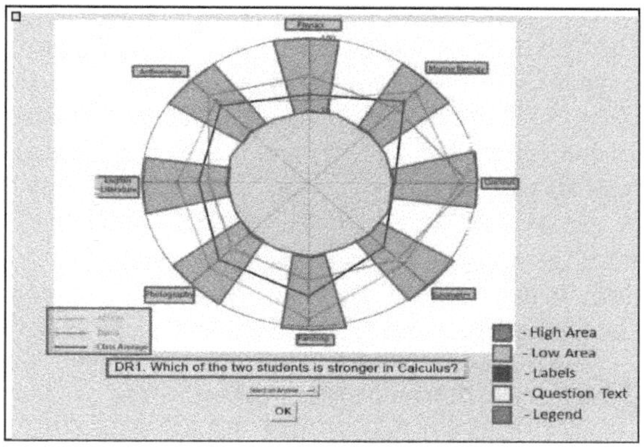

Figure 4. Five AOI regions defined over Radar Graph

Feature Reduction: Principal Component Analysis

To account for correlations among measures, we used three PCAs on our initial set of 49 gaze features. We grouped the gaze features into three non-overlapping families according to how the measures were intuitively related, namely (i) task-level features (e.g., *fixation rate*); (ii) AOI proportionate features (e.g., *proportion of fixation durations* in each AOI); and (iii) AOI transitions (e.g., *number of transitions* from one AOI to another). One PCA was performed on each of these three families, which allows us to discuss results in terms of high-level related gaze components rather than many low-level features.

The task level family consisted of 14 gaze features. Five components were generated[3] using PCA (x^2 = 15434.49, df = 91, $p < .001$), explaining 86.69% of the variance. Table 5 shows the breakdown of the original 14 features into the five components. Note that, for most components, it is quite easy to identify intuitive commonalities among its features, as reflected in the components' names (e.g., all

[2] These scripts are part of EMDAT (Eye Movement Data Analysis Toolkit), an open-source toolkit developed by our group.

[3] The number of components generated is always determined by using the Catell scree test, or if this test results in an ambiguous scree plot, we then use Kaiser's criterion to select only components with eigenvalues greater than 1 [8].

features of the first component are based on sums, all features in the second component relate to fixation measures, etc.). The same is true for the components resulting from PCA on the other two families of features.

Component Name	Task-Level Measures
Sum Measures	*num. fixations, sum rel. path angles, sum abs. path angles, sum path distance, sum fixation duration*
Fixation Measures	*mean fixation duration, std. dev. fixation duration, fixation rate***
Path Distance	*mean path distance, std. dev. path distance*
Std.Dev. Path Angles	*mean rel. path angles, std. dev. rel. path angles, std. dev. abs. path angles*
Mean Abs. Path	*mean abs. path angles*

Table 5. Generated components for the Task-Level Family
****fixation-rate is the only measure that inversely correlates with the other members of its component**

The AOI proportionate family consisted of 10 gaze features. Five components (see Table 6) were produced from the PCA (x^2= 5706.32, df = 300, p < .001) and explained 97.13% of the variance. The AOI transitions family consisted of 25 features and the PCA generated four components (see Table 7), (x^2 = 8506.86, df = 45, p < .001), which explained 45.24% of the variance. Note that PCA proved to be especially useful for reducing the many AOI transition features to a small set of meaningful components, each including features mostly related to a specific AOI.

Component Name	AOI Proportionate Measures
Low prop.	*low prop. num. fixations, low prop. time*
Label prop.	*labels prop. num. fixations, labels prop. time*
Legend prop.	*legend prop. num. fixations, legend prop. time*
Text prop.	*text prop. num. fixations, text prop. time*
High prop.	*high prop. num. fixations, high prop. time*

Table 6. The components for AOI Proportionate Measures

Component Name	AOI Transition Measures
Legend Transitions	*legend to legend, legend to high, high to legend, text to legend, legend to text, legend to low, text to text, low to legend, legend to labels, labels to legend*
Low Transitions	*high to low, low to high, text to low, low to low, low to text*
Label Transitions	*labels to labels, labels to low, low to labels, text to labels, labels to text*
High Transitions	*high to labels, labels to high, high to text, high to high, text to high*

Table 7. Components for the AOI Transitions Family

Mixed Model Analysis

Since the study data involved repeated measures (e.g., each subject performed the same task type with each of the two different visualizations), a suitable means for analysis is a *Mixed Model* [8]. Mixed models can handle both repeated measures as well as the mix of categorical and continuous independent measures that we consider. An alternative model commonly used for repeated-measures analysis is a General Linear Model Repeated Measures analysis (GLM for short) [8]. GLM, however, is less suitable than a Mixed Model for eye tracking analysis, because it is less resilient to missing data. This issue is due to the fact that GLM requires data to be in wide format, where all repeated measures (trials) for each participant are listed in one data entry row. When there is an invalid trial, GLM is forced to discard the entire data for that participant. This can be costly in an experiment with several invalid trials, as is often the case when using unobtrusive eye trackers that do not constrain subjects' movements. By contrast, a Mixed Model uses data in long format, listing each trial as a different data entry, and discarded invalid trials do not interfere with valid ones. Thus, a Mixed Model analysis is able to leverage at best potentially noisy eye tracking data.

For each of our three families of gaze features (i.e., task level, AOI Proportionate, and AOI transition) we ran a mixed model over each of the generated PCA components within that family[4]. Each mixed model was a 2 (visualization type) by 2 (visualization order) model, with the user characteristics and task difficulty as the model's covariates. We report statistical significance at the .05 level. Effect sizes of our results are reported small for r = 0.1, medium for r = 0.3, and large as r = 0.5 [9]. In the next section, we report the most salient results of the analysis. When going over the results involving directionality, the reader should keep in mind that our dependent measures are PCA components, each consisting of a single value that represents a much larger collection of underlying measures. Each component is generated by (i) calculating the weighted values of its underlying members; (ii) aggregating and scaling these values into one number typically ranging from -1 to +1. If an underlying member is positively correlated to its corresponding component the directionality will be the same, otherwise it will be opposite.

RESULTS

In this section, we present results that provide answers to our original research questions: do individual user characteristics influence a user's eye gaze behavior in a way that is detectable by state of the art eye trackers? If so, which gaze features are influenced by which particular user characteristics, and is the effect modulated by task difficulty and visualization type? The analysis results are discussed per user characteristic.

Perceptual Speed - Main Effects

We found main effects of perceptual speed on three PCA components (see Table 8).

One main effect was at the task level (first row in Table 8), showing that high perceptual speed users had lower values

[4] Mixed Models are univariate analyses (ANCOVA), thus do not support having more than one dependent measure per model. We adjusted our models for family-wise error by applying the Bonferroni adjustment to each family of results, according to the number of components within that family.

of *Fixation Measures* than low perceptual speed users. An analysis of the underlying members of this component shows that users with high perceptual speed had a higher fixation-rate than low perceptual speed users, indicating that they were able to scan the screen more quickly. They also had lower average and standard deviation of fixation durations, i.e. shorter and more consistently timed fixations. These combined findings closely match the definition of perceptual speed, and are interesting because they show that individual differences for this cognitive ability may be captured via eye tracking measures that are not related to information on specific elements of the visualization.

Family	Component	F-Ratio	Effect Size	Sig. Value
Task level	Fixation Measures	F(1,27) = 8.9	r = 0.37	p = 0.03
AOI	Legend Proportion	F(1,21) = 25.2	r = 0.21	p < 0.001
	Legend Transitions	F(1,26) = 10.25	r = 0.16	p = 0.016

Table 8. Main effects of perceptual speed

The other two main effects of perceptual speed are at the AOI level (see Table 8), showing that this cognitive ability also affects eye gaze measures relating to specific visualizations elements. The main effects are on the two components *Legend Proportion* and *Legend Transitions*: low perceptual speed users spent more of their time in the legend AOI and transitioned to it more often than high perceptual speed users. This result indicates that users with low perceptual speed took more time to process/store legend-related information and looked at the legend more frequently (possibly because they tended to forget the contained information).

Perceptual Speed - Interactions

We found significant interactions of perceptual speed with both task difficulty and visualization type.

Family	Component	F-Ratio	Effect Size	Sig. Value
AOI	Legend Transitions	F(1,686)=6.85	r = 0.10	p < 0.05
	Label Transitions	F(1,676)=7.97	r = 0.11	p = 0.02

Table 9. Interaction effects for perceptual speed and task difficulty.

Interactions with Task difficulty. There are significant interactions of task difficulty and perceptual speed on both the *Legend Transitions* and *Label Transitions* components (see Table 9). For *Legend Transitions,* all users generate more legend-related transitions with difficult tasks than with easy tasks (see Figure 5), likely due to the fact that an increased difficulty increases cognitive load and causes users to forget some of the information in the legend. This effect, however, is higher for low perceptual speed users.

For *Label Transitions* (Figure 6), all users show more label-related transitions for easy tasks, but the difference is much higher for low perceptual speed users. This effect is not as intuitive as the one found on *Legend Transitions*, but, irrespective of what causes users to have more label-related transitions for easy tasks, it seems to affect low perceptual speed users the most.

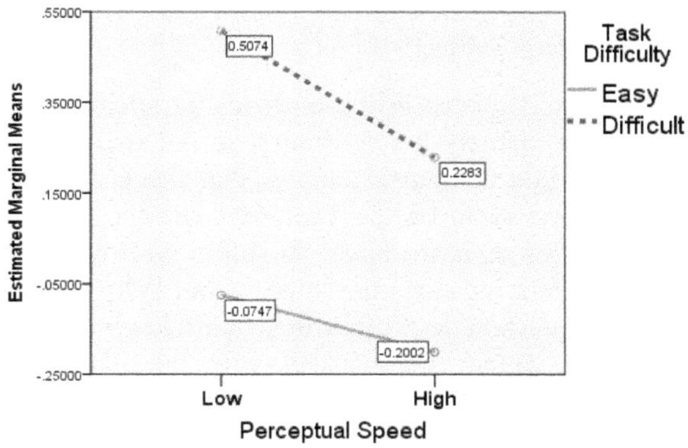

Figure 5. Interaction between perceptual speed and task difficulty on *AOI Legend Transitions*

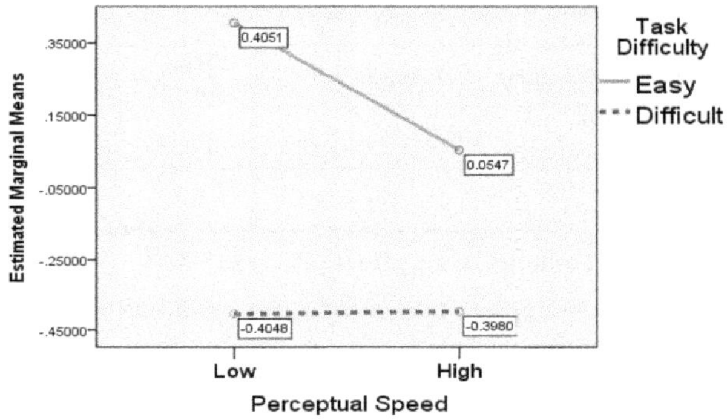

Figure 6. Interaction between perceptual speed and task difficulty on *AOI Label Transitions*

Interactions with visualization type. There was a significant interaction effect between perceptual speed and visualization type in terms of the *High AOI Transitions* component (F(1,680)=22.2, r=0.18, p < 0.001) (see Fig. 7).

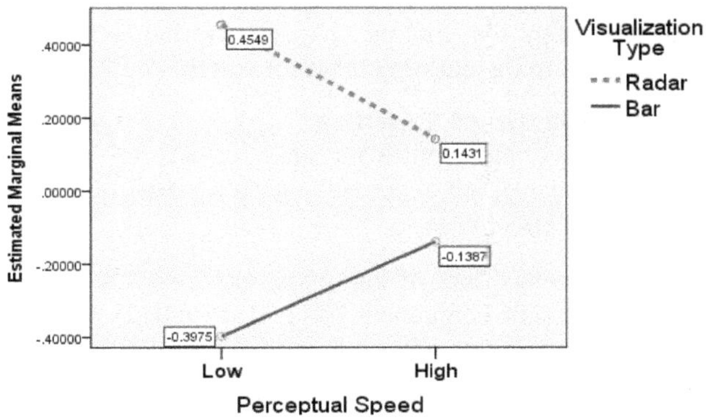

Figure 7. Interaction between perceptual speed and visualization type for *High AOI Transitions*

All users showed more High AOI related transitions with the radar graph than with the bar graph, but the difference is much higher for low perceptual speed users. Given that the High AOI is the graphical portion of an Infovis that contains the relevant data values, this effect indicates that low perceptual speed users are more affected by different ways of visualizing data.

Verbal WM - Main Effects

There are two main effects of verbal WM: one on the *Text Proportion* component and one on *Standard Deviation of Path Angles* (see Table 10).

Text Proportion relates to the most textual element in our visualizations, namely the question text. An analysis of the members of this component shows that the proportionate amount of time spent on the Text AOI and the number of fixations in this area are lower for users with high verbal WM. This effect indicates that high verbal WM users refer to the task question less often than their low verbal WM counterparts, which is consistent with the definition of verbal WM as a measure of storage and manipulation capacity of verbal information. This result is interesting because it shows that differences in users' verbal WM can be directly captured by eye tracking features related to the primary textual elements of a visualization.

Family	Component	F-Ratio	Effect Size	Sig. Value
AOI	Text Proportion	$F(1,28) = 7.24$	$r = 0.36$	$p = 0.04$
Task Level	Std.Dev. Path Angles	$F(1,25) = 8.06$	$r = 0.32$	$P < 0.05$

Table 10. Main effects of verbal WM

Std. Dev. Path Angles: this component essentially captures the consistency of a user's gaze patterns during a visualization task, because it is built upon features related to measuring the deviation of angles between subsequent saccades. Users with low verbal WM had higher values for *Std. Dev. Path Angles* than users with high verbal WM. When these values are higher, it indicates that a user is frequently looking across different areas of the screen, rather than following more planned or consistent path directions. Therefore, the finding that users with low verbal WM had higher values for *Std. Dev. Path Angles* is consistent with the finding that low verbal WM users referred back to the question text more often.

Bar and Radar Graph Expertise

There are two non-significant main effects of both bar graph and radar graph expertise, which we discuss because of their large effect sizes.

There is a main effect of bar graph expertise on the *AOI Label Proportion* component, ($F(1,21) = 6.042$, $r = 0.80$, $p = 0.1$), showing that users with high bar expertise spent a greater proportion of their time looking at labels compared to non-experts. Similarly, there is a main effect of radar graph expertise on the *AOI Legend Proportion* component ($F(1,21) = 5.732$, $r = 0.78$, $p = 0.129$), with radar experts spending less time looking at the legend when compared to non-experts. The discrepancy between strong effect sizes for these two expertise-related measures and the lack of statistical significance is likely due to limited statistical power. The power for the effect of bar graph expertise on the *AOI Label* is 0.67, and the power for the effect of radar graph expertise on *AOI Legend* is 0.64. A commonly recommended value of power is 0.8 [8], and we would have to add 17% (or 6) more users to reach this value.

It may seem surprising that we did not find stronger influences of visualization expertise on gaze patterns. This result, however, is consistent with findings in [28], which showed that bar and radar graph expertise may only have significant effects on user visualization preference, but not on performance. These findings suggest that there might not be easily detectable differences in the visualization processing behaviors of experts and novices, as defined by our self-rated measures of expertise.

Visual WM

We found no effects worth reporting for visual WM. This lack of findings may be due to the fact that the study tasks were relatively easy and that the visualizations were static in nature. It is thus likely that users did not require to reach their maximum visual memory capacity, especially since they could easily get an overview of the whole graph in a single look. Moreover, individual tasks were independent of each other, thus users were not required to store any successive visual information (one of the functions affected by visual WM).

SUMMARY OF FINDINGS & DISCUSSION

The goal of our study was to investigate 1) If user characteristics impact gaze patterns during visualization processing, and if the impact can be detected though eye tracking; 2) Which gaze measures are influenced by which user characteristics, as well as if/how the influence is mediated by task difficulty and visualization type. In this paper, we chose to focus on the five characteristics listed in Table 11 and, as shown in this table, we found a number of effects (either statistically significant or with large effect sizes) on various gaze measures.

Perceptual speed is the cognitive measure with the highest number of effects. This finding provides encouraging evidence that this cognitive ability could be reliably detected in real time using gaze information. This result is particularly important for our long-term goal of designing user-adaptive visualizations, especially in light of previous studies, which showed that low perceptual speed can negatively affect task performance, in terms of both accuracy [3] as well as task completion time [28]. We have shown that perceptual speed influences AOI-specific gaze measures relating to the Legend, Labels and High AOIs. These findings suggest that adaptive interventions could be particularly useful if they support the access and/or processing of such AOIs for low perceptual speed users. In addition, the interaction effects we found for perceptual speed suggest that task difficulty and visualization type should be taken into account, if known, when providing adaptive interventions. For instance, we found that low perceptual speed users tended to access a visualization legend more than high perceptual speed users, suggesting that they should be specifically supported in terms of legend processing. However, we also found that this effect is exacerbated in the presence of difficult tasks. Thus, while it may not be worthwhile disrupting a low speed user with a legend-related intervention for tasks known to be easy, it may be important to do so as task difficulty increases.

User Characteristic	Eye tracking measure component
Perceptual Speed	*Fixation Measures* (main effect) *Legend Proportion* (main effect) *Legend Transitions* (main & interaction effect) *Label Transitions* (interaction effect) *High AOI Transitions* (interaction effect)
Verbal WM	*Std. Dev. Path Angles* (main effect) *Text Proportion* (main effect)
Bar Expertise	*Label Proportion* (p> 0.05, but large effect size)
Radar Expertise	*Legend* (p> 0.05, but large effect size)
Visual WM	*None*

Table 11. Overall Results

The results on *verbal WM* indicate, intuitively, that this cognitive ability affects eye tracking features related to the main textual element of a visualization, and thus may be detectable in real time by tracking these features. In our experiment, the textual element was the question text, but in other settings this could be the visualization caption or the portion of text in which the visualization is embedded (e.g., a verbal description of the displayed data). In terms of adaptation, it is plausible that users with low verbal WM may benefit if textual elements of a visualization were given more emphasis than the purely graphical elements. However, because we do not have information on whether verbal WM affects performance during Infovis processing, it remains a topic for future research to investigate if and how adaptive interventions would impact visualization effectiveness for users with different levels of verbal WM.

We discussed two non-significant main effects of the expertise-related user characteristics because of their large effect sizes. *Bar expertise* had a large effect on label access, while *radar expertise* had a large effect on legend access. These results may indicate that non-experts could benefit from adaptive interventions that guide them to access these elements in a way that is more similar to experts. However, we need to run further studies with more reliable, objective measures of expertise (the ones used in this study were self-reported) before we can make a more informed decision on how to provide adaptive support for novice users.

In summary, we have identified a set of user abilities that have a strong impact on gaze measures related to specific AOIs of a visualization, and discussed how adaptive interventions driven by these abilities and targeting such AOIs may improve a user's experience with a given visualization. While our study has only investigated two simple visualization techniques, several results may be generalized to a wider array of visualization designs, since they involve AOIs that are common to most types of visualizations (such as a graph's labels or legend). In fact, the majority of our results are effects that are actually independent of visualization design. Similarly, while the study has focused on an artificial data set involving student grades (in order to eliminate domain expertise as a study factor), the actual tasks were derived from an established set of general, low-level analysis tasks for information visualization [1]. Lastly, while this work has focused on an analysis for the purpose of adaptive information visualization, similar user studies could be performed in other areas of HCI (e.g., desktop interfaces), to determine whether the influence of individual user differences on gaze features can also be detected in those scenarios.

CONCLUSION AND FUTURE WORK

We presented research aimed at investigating the relationship between a set of user cognitive and expertise measures, task difficulty, and user attention patterns when using different visualization techniques. Our analysis reveals that some of the tested user characteristics do have a significant influence on user gaze behavior, and that this influence is detectable through a variety of eye tracking metrics. Based on these findings, we provided general suggestions for adaptive visualization design in relation to components that are common to most types of visualizations, for example suggesting that low perceptual speed users may need support in processing legends. Our results may therefore be of interest when designing systems for specific user groups that are known to have high/low cognitive abilities (e.g., older adults and people with autism are known to have lower values for perceptual speed).

We see the analysis presented here as a first step towards understanding the complex relationships between user traits, visualizations, and gaze patterns. However, additional studies are necessary to investigate these relationships at the level of more basic Infovis properties such as color, size, and shape. Similarly, studies should be run to investigate these relationships in more complex visualizations such as time series, networks, as well as interactive visualizations. Along these lines, we are currently applying the experimental design described in this paper to investigate the impact of user traits on different versions of a complex interactive visualization involving multiple, aligned bar charts [2] for preference elicitation. Because of the added complexity, we expect the impact of user characteristics, task difficulty, and visualization type to be even more pronounced than in the current study. The next step of our research is to show that the relevant user characteristics can be detected in real-time to drive adaptive interventions benefiting users with those characteristics. We are currently investigating a variety of machine learning techniques to perform this real-time inference task, and we already have encouraging results [25]. Lastly, we are in the process of running a user study to test different ways of providing adaptive interventions, both in general, and in relation to individual user differences.

REFERENCES

1. Amar, R.A., Eagan J., & Stasko, J.T. Low-Level Components of Analytic Activity in Information Visualization. In 16th IEEE Vis. Conf., (2005), 15-21.
2. Bautista, J., & Carenini, G. An integrated task-based framework for the design and evaluation of visualizations to support preferential choice. Proc. of the conf. on Adv. Vis. Interf. (AVI '06), (2006), 217-224.
3. Conati, C., & Maclaren, H. Exploring the Role of Individual Differences in Information Visualization. In Proc. of the working conf. on Adv. visual interfaces (AVI '08). ACM, New York, NY, USA, (2008), 199-20.
4. Courtemanche, F., Aïmeur, E., Dufresne, A., Najjar, M., & Eboa, F.H.M. Activity recognition using eye-gaze movements and traditional interactions. In Proceedings of In-teracting with Computers, (2011), 202-213.
5. Eivazi, S., Bednarik, R. Predicting Problem-Solving Behavior and Performance Levels from Visual Attention Data. In the proceedings of 2nd Workshop on Eye Gaze in Intelligent Human Machine Interaction at IUI 2011, (2011), 9-16.
6. Ekstrom, R., French, J., Harman, H. and Dermen, D, Manual from Kit of Factor-References Cognitive Tests. Educational Testing Service, Princeton, NJ, (1976).
7. Few, S. Keep Radar Graphs Below the Radar - Far Below: Information Management Magazine, (2005), 48.
8. Field, A. Discovering Statistics Using SPSS, Third Edition. Sage Publications, London, (2009).
9. Field & Hole, How to Design and Report Experiments. Sage Publications, (2003).
10. Fukuda, K., & Vogel, E.K. Human variation in overriding attentional capture. Journal of Neuroscience, (2009), 8726-8733.
11. Goldberg, J.H., & Helfman, J.I. Comparing Information Graphics: A Critical Look at Eye Tracking, BELIV '10, (2010), 182-195.
12. Goldberg, J.H., & Helfman, J.I. Eye tracking for visualization evaluation: Reading values on linear versus radial graphs. Inf. Vis. 10(3), (2011), 182-195.
13. Gotz D., & Wen, Z.. Behavior-Driven Visualization Recommendation. Int. Conf. on Intelligent User Interfaces, (2009), 315-324.
14. Grawemeyer, B. Evaluation of ERST – an external representation selection tutor. In Proc. of the 4th int. conf. on Diagram. Repr. and Inference, (2006), 154-167.
15. Green, T.M., & Fisher, B. Impact of personality factors on interface interaction and development of user profiles: Next steps in the Personal Equation of Interaction. Inf. Visualization, 11(2), (2012), 1-17.
16. Grindinger, T., Duchowski, A., & Sawyer, M. Group-wise similarity and classification of aggregate scanpaths. In Proceedings of the 2010 Symposium on Eye-Tracking Research 38, (2010), 101-104.
17. Iqbal, S.T., & Bailey, B.P. Using eye gaze patterns to identify user tasks. In: The Grace Hopper Celebration of Women in Computing, (2004).
18. Jameson, A. (2008). Adaptive Interfaces and Agents. The human-computer interaction handbook: Fundamentals, evolving technologies and emerging applications (2nd ed.), pp. 433–458.
19. Jarodzka, H., Scheiter, K., Gerjets, P., & Van Gog, T. In the eyes of the beholder: How experts and novices interpret dynamic stimuli. Learning and Instruction. 20, (2010), 146-154.
20. Keith, R. Eye movements and cognitive processes in reading, visual search, and scene perception. Eye Movement Research Mechanisms, Processes, and Applications. North-Holland Press, (1995).
21. Kruschke, J. K., Kappenman, E. S., & Hetrick, W. P. Eye gaze and individual differences consistent with learned attention in associative blocking and highlighting. Journal of Experimental Psychology: Learning, Memory, and Cognition, 31, (2005), 830–845.
22. Plumlee, M.D., & Ware, C. Zooming versus multiple window interfaces: Cognitive costs of visual comparisons. ACM Trans. Comput.-Hum. Interact, 13, 2, (2006), 179-209.
23. Rayner, K. Eye movements in reading and information processing: 20 years of research. Psychological Bulletin 124, (1998), 372-422.
24. Simola, J., Salojarvi, J., & Kojo, I. Using hidden Markov model to uncover processing states from eye movements in information search tasks. Cognitive Systems Research. 9, (2008), 237-251.
25. Steichen, B., Carenini, G., & Conati, C. User-Adaptive Information Visualization - Using eye gaze data to infer visualization tasks and user cognitive abilities. Int. Conf. on Intelligent User Interfaces, (2013), (to appear).
26. Tai, R.H., Loehr, J.F., & Brigham, F.J. An Exploration of the Use of Eye-Gaze Tracking to Study Problem-Solving on Standardized Science Assessments. International Journal of Research & Method in Education 29, 2, (2006), 185-208.
27. Tang, H., Topczewski, J.J., Topczewski, A.M. & Pienta, N.J. Permutation test for groups of scanpaths using normalized Levenshtein distances and application in NMR questions. In Proc. of the Symposium on Eye Tracking Research and Applications, (2012), 169-172.
28. Toker, D., Conati, C., Carenini, G., & Haraty, M. Towards Adaptive Information Visualization: On the Influence of User Characteristics. In Proc. of the 19th international conference on user modeling, adaptation, and personalization, UMAP, (2012), 274-285.
29. Turner, M. L., & Engle, R.W. Is working memory capacity task dependent? Journal of Memory and Language, 28(2), (1989), 127-154.
30. Velez, M.C., Silver, D., & Tremaine, M. Understanding visualization through spatial ability differences. Proceedings of Visualization, (2005), 511-518.
31. Ziemkiewicz, C., et al. How Locus of Control Influences Compatibility with Visualization Style. Proc. IEEE VAST, (2011), 81-90.

EyeContext: Recognition of High-level Contextual Cues from Human Visual Behaviour

Andreas Bulling
Max Planck Institute for Informatics
Saarbrücken, Germany
andreas.bulling@acm.org

Christian Weichel
Lancaster University
Lancaster, United Kingdom
c.weichel@lancaster.ac.uk

Hans Gellersen
Lancaster University
Lancaster, United Kingdom
hwg@comp.lancs.ac.uk

ABSTRACT
In this work we present *EyeContext*, a system to infer high-level contextual cues from human visual behaviour. We conducted a user study to record eye movements of four participants over a full day of their daily life, totalling 42.5 hours of eye movement data. Participants were asked to self-annotate four non-mutually exclusive cues: *social* (interacting with somebody vs. no interaction), *cognitive* (concentrated work vs. leisure), *physical* (physically active vs. not active), and *spatial* (inside vs. outside a building). We evaluate a proof-of-concept EyeContext system that combines encoding of eye movements into strings and a spectrum string kernel support vector machine (SVM) classifier. Our results demonstrate the large information content available in long-term human visual behaviour and opens up new venues for research on eye-based behavioural monitoring and life logging.

Author Keywords
Context Recognition; Eye Movement Analysis; Visual Behaviour; Electrooculography (EOG)

ACM Classification Keywords
H.5.m Information Interfaces and Presentation (e.g., HCI): Miscellaneous; I.5.4 Pattern Recognition: Applications — *Signal processing*

INTRODUCTION
Practically everything we do in our lives involves our eyes, and the way we move our eyes is linked to our goals and tasks. This makes the eyes a particularly rich source of information: one that, as we will show in this work, can provide basic cues on very different aspects of what we do, at any point in time. Figure 1 illustrates our idea: to provide a system that is able to produce diverse inferences, about social, cognitive, physical and spatial aspects, all from eye movement as single source of information.

Our contribution is two-fold. First, we introduce the *EyeContext* system for cue inference from eye movement. The system takes continuous eye movement as input, and produces a vector of cues as output. The cues are binary descriptors of daily life situations at any given time. In our proof-of-concept system, the cues describe whether or not we: socially interact; concentrate on a mental task; engage in physical activity; are inside or outside. At the core of our system, we introduce a novel method for inferring such cues from eye movement. We encode eye movement as string of symbols that represent movements in different directions. Patterns of successive movements thus become represented by words of different lengths, which we use as basis for our binary classification problems. The underlying hypothesis is that we find different patterns for when we interact or not; are inside or outside; etc. We use a string kernel support vector machine (SVM) for classification, inspired by their original use in bioinformatics for efficient large-scale protein sequence classification [7].

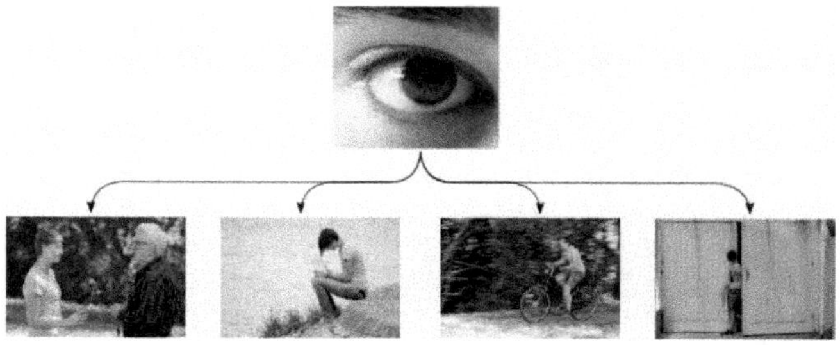

Figure 1. The *EyeContext* system infers contextual cues about different aspects of what we do, by analysing eye movement patterns over time (from left to right): *social* (interacting with somebody vs. no interaction), *cognitive* (concentrated work vs. leisure), *physical* (physically active vs. not active), and *spatial* (inside vs. outside a building).

Our second contribution is an evaluation of the system for which we collected eye movements of four participants over a typical daily life from morning to evening. Participants self-annotated the four cues of interest as our ground truth reference. Using person-dependent training, we assessed the recognition performance for each of our cues. The results validate the EyeContext system but moreover provide evidence that eye movement holds contextual information about very diverse aspects of our daily life. Each individual cue, for example whether we are engaging in physical activity, might be approached with other means (e.g. body motion [2]), while eye movement can provide cues ranging from social to cognitive to physical and spatial.

THE EYECONTEXT SYSTEM
The EyeContext system takes continuous eye movement signals as its input. In this work, we used electrooculography

CHI 2013, April 27–May 2, 2013, Paris, France.

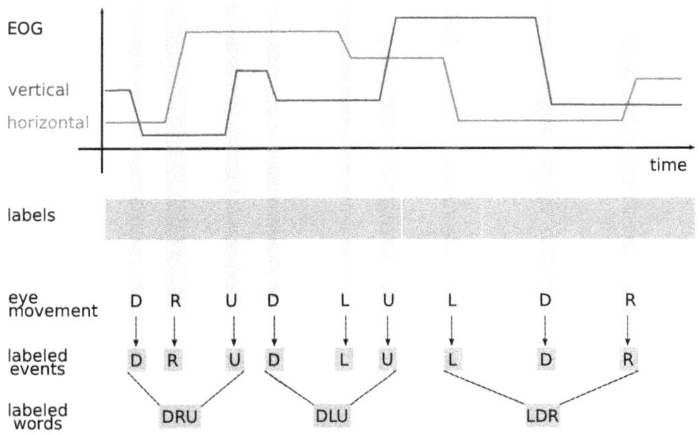

Figure 2. For classification using a spectrum string kernel SVM, saccades are first detected in the vertical and horizontal EOG signal. Saccades are encoded into characters and combined into a string of eye movements. The resulting string is split up into non-overlapping words of fixed length s (here $s = 3$), each labelled using majority voting.

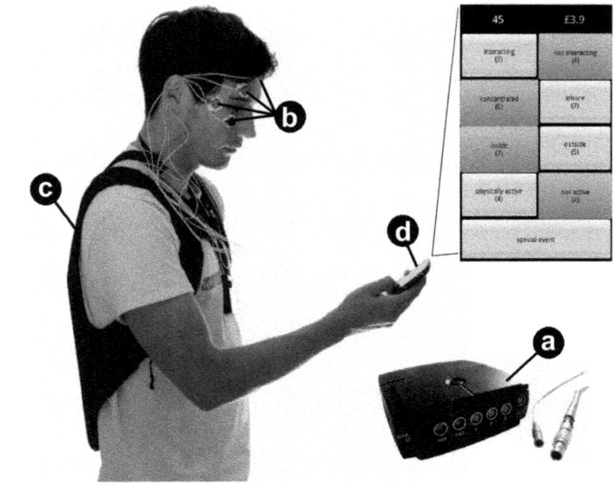

Figure 3. Experimental equipment used for data collection consisting of the Mobi (a), five EOG electrodes (b), a laptop for data recording (c), as well as a smartphone for self-annotation (d).

(EOG) signals but EyeContext is independent of the specific measurement technique and works as well on eye movement signals recorded using a video-based eye tracker. The system processes these signals offline, detects and encodes saccades, models saccadic behaviour using machine learning, and generates continuous context labels using this model as its output.

The system removes noise from the recorded eye movement signals using a median filter as well as baseline drift using a wavelet packets approach. The system then detects and removes blinks using the *Continuous Wavelet Transform – Blink Detection* algorithm and saccades using the *Continuous Wavelet Transform – Saccade Detection* (CWT-SD) algorithm [4]. Briefly, CWT-SD detects saccades by thresholding on the continuous 1-D wavelet coefficient vector computed from the processed eye movement signals.

Detected saccades are encoded into eye movements using an alphabet $\mathcal{A}$ of eight distinct characters based on the saccades' direction. For example, a saccade to the left is encoded as "L" while a saccade to the diagonal right is encoded as "B". These characters are merged into a single string that represents the sequence of consecutive eye movements for each participant. For classification, EyeContext splits this string into words S_i of fixed length s using majority voting for words that cover several ground truth labels (see Figure 2). These words are used as input to a spectrum string kernel SVM classifier.

A spectrum string kernel $K(S_i, S_j)$ of power k is defined as

$$\begin{aligned} K(S_i, S_j) &= \langle \Phi(S_i, k), \Phi(S_j, k) \rangle \\ \Phi(S_i, k) &= \left[\phi_{a_1}(S_i) \; \dots \; \phi_{a_{|\mathcal{A}|^k}}(S_i) \right]^T \end{aligned}$$

Intuitively, $\phi_a(S_i)$ counts the position-independent occurrences of all contiguous eye movement patterns $a \in \mathcal{A}^k$ of length k (also called k-mers or k-grams) contained in S_i. The set of all k-mers is also called the k-spectrum of a string with each k-mer representing one dimension of the feature space (for details see [7]). The two main parameters of a spectrum string kernel are the word length s, i.e. the length of each input string to the SVM, and the power k of the kernel, i.e. the length of the eye movement patterns.

STUDY

We designed a user study to answer the fundamental question of whether analysing human visual behaviour can be used to automatically recognise four high-level contextual cues. The example cues that we explore in this work are:

1. Social cues: Social (face to face) interactions with another person versus no interaction.
2. Cognitive cues: Concentrated work, such as reading, versus leisure, which includes all forms of passive consumption (e.g. watching a video) or non-goal driven activities (e.g. a night out with friends).
3. Physical cues: Physically active, such as walking, versus resting, such as standing or sitting.
4. Spatial cues: Being inside or outside, e.g. a building, a car, or a train.

Apparatus

We used EOG to be able to record continuously for more than 12 hours. For EOG data recording we used a Mobi system by Twente Medical Systems International. The Mobi was worn by the participants and transmitted data sampled at 2 kHz over Bluetooth to a laptop carried in a shoulder bag. EOG signals were picked up using five Ag/AgCl wet electrodes. Pairs of electrodes were attached to the outer edge of the left and right eye, above the right eyebrow and below the right eye, and an additional reference electrode was placed on the forehead. Ground truth annotation was performed using a custom software running on an Android smartphone (see Figure 3).

Procedure

For data collection we recruited four full-time researchers from the lab. Their typical work day is characterised by lots of work with only little leisure. Specifically, their everyday life includes commuting to the university, working concentrated

	P1	P2	P3	P4	Total
concentrated	454	341	268	374	1,437
leisure	268	286	354	210	1,118
inside	698	600	525	521	2,344
outside	24	28	97	63	211
social interaction	116	215	238	299	868
no interaction	606	413	384	285	1,688
physically active	114	76	278	99	566
resting	608	551	345	485	1,989

Table 1. Overview of the recorded dataset. The table shows the amount of data labelled for each contextual cue in minutes.

at the desk, interacting with colleagues throughout the day, occasionally leaving the building, e.g. for lunch, and commuting back home in the evening. We asked them to self-annotate such non-mutually exclusive transitions as accurately as possible, while still retaining their daily routine. In an initial physical meeting in the lab participants were introduced to the recording system and shown how to attach the electrodes and start the recording. Participants were instructed to start the recording at home in the morning and stop it in the evening.

Data Analysis

All parameters of the signal processing and saccade detection algorithms were fixed to values common to all participants. We considered four individual binary classification problems, one for each contextual cue. As class distributions were considerably skewed (see Table 1), similar to [1], we used a discrete HMM model to oversample the smaller class until both classes were of the same size. The predictions returned by the string kernel SVM were compared to the annotated ground truth using a person-dependent evaluation scheme: the dataset for each participant was split using 70% for training and 30% for testing. Classification was only performed on the test set. During classification the values of k and s were optimised with respect to recognition accuracy. This evaluation was run five times (5-fold cross-validation) and the following performance measures averaged. Precision was calculated as $\frac{TP}{TP+FP}$, recall (true positive rate) as $\frac{TP}{TP+FN}$, and false positive rate (FPR) as $\frac{FP}{FP+TN}$, where TP, FP, TN and FN represent true positive, false positive, true negative and false negative counts, respectively.

RESULTS

We were able to record a dataset of more than 42.5 hours of eye movement data (see Table 1). The dataset comprises nearly 24 hours of concentrated work (18.5 hours of leisure), 39 hours were spent inside (3.5 hours outside), 14.5 hours of social interactions (28 hours of no interaction), as well as 9.3 hours of physically active periods (33.2 hours of resting).

Figure 4 plots the recognition performance for each contextual cue and participant, as well as the means over all participants. The best mean result is for recognising social interactions for which the system performed well for all participants (85.3% precision, 98.0% recall on average). The worst result is for recognising physical activities (75.3% precision, 74.4% recall) with a notably lower recall than for the cognitive cue (73.2% precision, 83.1% recall) and the spatial cue (74.0% precision, 85.0% recall). These results show that while the system has similar performance in correctly recognising actual activity, cognitive and spatial cue instances, it has a harder time in spotting all activity instances. Figure 4 also indicates tendencies of particular participants to perform consistently worse than others. Table 2 confirms this finding. The highest performance is achieved for P4 (84.0% precision, 86.0% recall, 15.8% FPR), while the worst result is for P3 (66.3% precision, 79.8% recall, 38.4% FPR). On closer inspection of the raw EOG data, it turned out that the signal quality for P3 was much worse compared to the other participants and saccades could not be robustly detected. Dry skin or poor electrode placement are the most likely culprits.

	P1	P2	P3	P4	mean
precision	81.4%	75.5%	*66.3%*	**84.0%**	76.8%
recall	**88.6%**	87.4%	*79.8%*	86.0%	85.5%
FPR	19.8%	27.7%	*38.4%*	**15.8%**	25.4%

Table 2. Precision, recall and false positive rate (FPR) for each participant averaged over all four contextual cue as well as the mean over all participants. Best results are indicated in bold; worst results in italic.

DISCUSSION

Our EyeContext system demonstrates a novel way in which eye movements can be embraced for human-computer interaction. At the human-computer interface, eye movements were previously studied mostly for explicit control or specific diagnostics. Recent related work demonstrated automated recognition of particular activities, such as reading and writing, from eye movements [3, 4]. The current work differs fundamentally, as it demonstrates the feasibility of inferring contextual cues that are not limited to particular activities but broadly descriptive of our situation at any point in time.

Previous works on eye-based activity recognition used a computationally complex feature-based recognition approach. In contrast, the proof-of-concept system described in this work focuses on eye movement patterns that are first encoded and then classified using a string spectrum kernel method. This approach is computationally simple – as it does not require to extract a large number of low-level eye movement features – and it also implements the assumption that high-level contextual cues are characterised by differences in repetitive visual behaviours. It will be interesting to see how this approach compares to other methods geared to processing large amounts of sequences of symbols, such as networks of motifs [9].

Limited recording time and bulky equipment still prevent current video-based eye trackers from being used for long-term recordings in daily life. We thus opted to use EOG, which is light-weight and can be implemented as a low-power wearable system. It is important to note that neither the eye movement encoding and recognition approach, nor EyeContext in general are limited to the specific measurement technique used in this work. The system can also be used with other

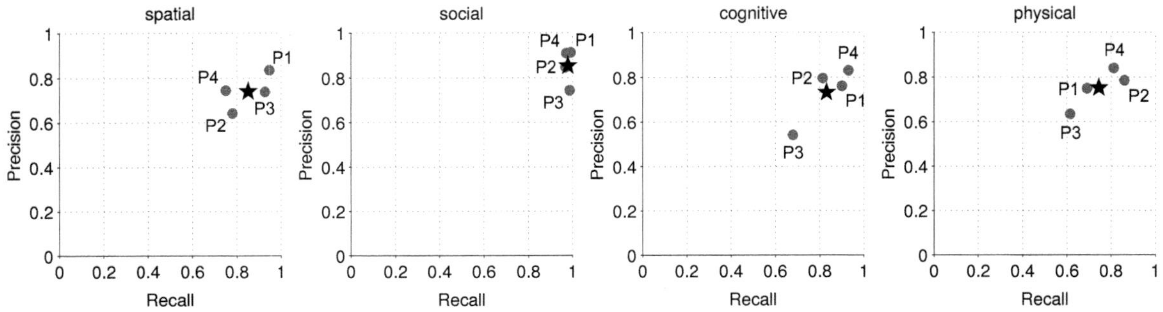

Figure 4. Overall best performance in terms of precision and recall for each cue and participant. Black stars mark the mean performance.

portable and ambient eye trackers and we strongly believe that even totally unobtrusive tracking will become feasible.

As any dataset, the one we presented here has limitations in terms of the number of days and participants that we recorded. Although larger variability is always desirable, it has to be stressed that there was a high degree of variability of activities within each class. For example, every instance of a conversation recorded by a user will have varied considerably, as it occurs in different daily life situations. The class distributions within the dataset were considerably skewed (unbalanced) for three of the four contextual cues (see Table 1). It is deliberate that we did not constrain the participants in any way (e.g. by scripting their entire working day) but opted for a data collection that is as imbalanced as the real world is.

The contextual cues investigated in this work are only exemplary but potentially useful for a number of applications. For example, logging one's life in digital form has a long held fascination and research has shown that recordings in everyday life can support memory, sharing, and behaviour analysis [8, 10, 5]. While capture technology is well explored [6], automatic annotation and filtering of long-term life logging data is still a significant challenge. Recognition of when a person is physically active or indoor/outdoor is promising for filtering because it is less narrow than annotation of specific activities and useful for breaking down the search space. Recognition of social cues may allow caregivers to automatically measure how socially active elderly or people with autism spectrum disorders are. Information on cognitive load may provide valuable insights into cognitive abilities relevant for medical or behaviour monitoring. EyeContext, however, is not restricted to these cues or the specific experimental settings investigated here but can be extended to other cues and everyday situations by using additional binary classifiers.

CONCLUSION

In this work we described EyeContext, a system that infers high-level contextual cues about different aspects of our daily life by analysing visual behaviour over time. Based on a proof-of-concept implementation and four long-term eye movement datasets we showed that we could robustly recognise four example binary cues. While previous work demonstrated the rich information content available in low-level eye movement characteristics, these results show that additional and equally valuable information is contained in the general eye movement patterns that we perform throughout a day.

REFERENCES

1. Beigi, M., Zell, A. Synthetic protein sequence oversampling method for classification and remote homology detection in imbalanced protein data. *Proc. of the 1st Int. Conf. on Bioinformatics Research and Development* (2007), 263–277.
2. Blum, M., Pentland, A., Tröster, G. InSense: Interest-Based Life Logging. *IEEE Multimedia 13*, 4 (2006), 40–48.
3. Bulling, A., Ward, J. A., Gellersen, H. Multimodal Recognition of Reading Activity in Transit Using Body-Worn Sensors. *ACM Trans. on Applied Perception 9*, 1 (2012), 2:1–2:21.
4. Bulling, A., Ward, J. A., Gellersen, H., Tröster, G. Eye Movement Analysis for Activity Recognition Using Electrooculography. *IEEE Trans. on Pattern Analysis and Machine Intelligence 33*, 4 (2011), 741–753.
5. Doherty, A. R., Caprani, N., O Conaire, C., Kalnikaite, V., Gurrin, C., O'Connor, N. E., Smeaton, A. F. Passively recognising human activities through lifelogging. *Computers in Human Behavior 27* (2011), 1948–1958.
6. Hodges, S., Williams, L., Berry, E., Izadi, S., Srinivasan, J., Butler, A., Smyth, G., Kapur, N., Wood, K. Sensecam: a retrospective memory aid. *Proc. of the 8th Int. Conf. on Ubiquitous Computing* (2006), 177–193.
7. Leslie, C., Eskin, E., Noble, W. S. The spectrum kernel: a string kernel for SVM protein classification. *Proc. of the Pacific Symp. on Biocomputing* (2002), 564–575.
8. Sellen, A. J., Fogg, A., Aitken, M., Hodges, S., Rother, C., Wood, K. Do life-logging technologies support memory for the past?: an experimental study using sensecam. *Proc. of the SIGCHI Conf. on Human Factors in Computing Systems* (2007), 81–90.
9. Sinatra, R., Condorelli, D., Latora, V. Networks of motifs from sequences of symbols. *Physical Review Letters 105*, 17 (2010), 178702.
10. Truong, K. N., Hayes, G. R. Ubiquitous computing for capture and access. *Foundations and Trends in Human-Computer Interaction 2*, 2 (2009), 95–171.

A Preliminary Investigation of Human Adaptations for Various Virtual Eyes in Video See-Through HMDs

Joong Ho Lee, Sei-Young Kim, Hae Cheol Yoon,
Bo Kyung Huh, Ji Hyung Park
Human Centered Interaction & Robotics Research Center,
Korea Institute of Science and Technology
Hwarangno 14-gil 5, Seongbuk-gu, Seoul 136-791, Republic of Korea
{022756, 022859, yhchahaha, t12456, jhpark}@kist.re.kr , 82-2-958-5632

ABSTRACT
A video see-through head mounted display (HMD) has a different viewing point than does the real eye, resulting in visual displacement (VD). VD deteriorates visuomotor performance due to sensory conflict. Previous work has investigated this deterioration and human adaptation by comparing fixed VD and real eye conditions. In this study we go a step further to investigate whether any differences in visuomotor and adaptation trends exist across 16 distinct VD conditions. The performance tasks studied were of two types: foot placement and finger touch. In contrast to our initial prediction, the results showed equal task performance levels and adaptation within about 5 minutes regardless of VD conditions. We found that human adaptation covered a variety of VDs — up to 55 mm in the *X, Y* direction; up to 125mm in the *Z* direction; and up to 140mm of interocular distance (IOD). In addition, we found that partial adaptation gave participants the interesting experience of a sense of body structure distortion for a few minutes.

Author Keywords
video see-through; HMD; immersive reality; adaptation; visual displacement; visuomotor; task performance.

ACM Classification Keywords
H.5.1. Information interfaces and presentation (e.g., HCI): Multimedia Information Systems.

General Terms
Human Factors; Design; Measurement.

INTRODUCTION
What would happen if one's eyes were in front of one's face? Video see-through HMDs raise this problem. A demand is emerging for a portable display that supports fully immersive information services. To meet the needs posed by that trend, it is essential to supply HMDs having a wearable design and offering high levels of immersion.

CHI 2013, April 27–May 02 2013, Paris, France

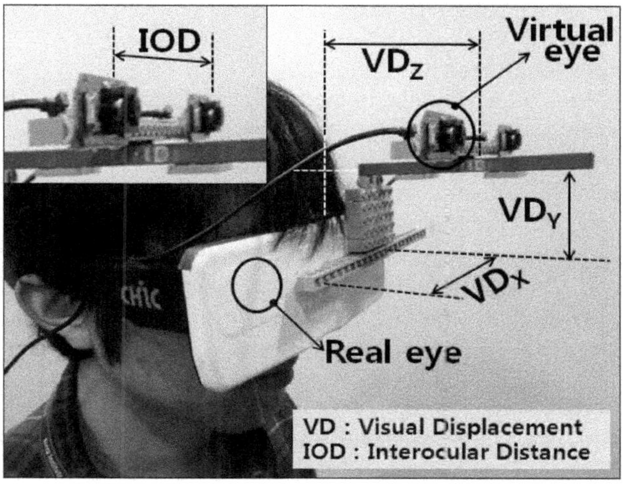

Figure 1. Our developing video see-through HMD provides various VD setups, including X, Y, and Z directional VD and IOD. Human task performance and adaptation were investigated under 16 VD conditions.

See-through HMDs have been studied [10] with those purposes in mind. In video see-through HMDs, the conversion of one's perspective into video clips through digital photography offers an advantage in allowing your real view to be naturally mixed with virtual information in real time. However, in comparison to optical see-through, video see-through indirectly displays the real world so that sensory conflict due to visual displacement (VD) is unavoidable, given that VD is induced by a mismatch between the position of the real eye and the location of the cameras (i.e., virtual eyes), as shown in Figure 1. The VD has been found to induce feelings of discomfort and dizziness and to decrease visuomotor performance [3, 11]. However, Biocca and Rolland [2] showed that human adaptation rearranges these sensory conflicts in a short period of time. A prism adaptation study similarly found that the adaptation process is affected by coordination between the visual system and the motor system when participants wear prisms [7]. Such studies have indicated the presence of adaptation aftereffects once prisms are removed. However, there has thus far been no comparison of various levels of HMD VD. We progressively investigate adaptation trends and performance variance across 16 VD conditions. We firstly expected that adaptation and task performance patterns would emerge with increased VD. Task performance was measured in two ways: foot placement, which requires human balance, and finger touch.

Foot placement task

Foot placement has been used to test balance associated with postural behavior [8]. The study of prism adaptation related to walking and stepping tasks has shown typical visuomotor mismatch adaptation and aftereffects [1]. Morton and Bastian demonstrated prism adaptation associated with whole body movement during a walking task [9]. Along the same lines, we studied foot placement adaptation among VDs, including IODs.

Finger touch task

It is well known that the finger touch task is associated with adaptation to limb visuomotor coordination and demands more accuracy than does the foot task [5]. We investigated human performance in touching an exact point on a touch screen. Li [6] described how participants learned motor coordination when undertaking an open-loop (i.e., lacking visual feedback) pointing task wearing prism goggles. In our study, participants were asked to recognize foot and finger positions during a closed-loop process task.

METHOD

We designed 16 combinations of test conditions with 5 factors as shown in Table 1: test order, IOD, and transforming of the cameras in the *X* (right to left), *Y* (upward), and *Z* directions (in front, the minimum possible distance from the real eye for our prototype was 70 mm). This study employed the "Taguchi method," which uses an orthogonal array to minimize the number of tests [12]. Traditionally, to investigate all test conditions, a 4(test order) X 4(IOD) X 4(VDx) X 4(VDy) X 4(VDz) experiments necessitates 1024 tests. However, the orthogonal array allows us to use only 16 sets of test conditions and still effectively represent all combinations based on its unique characteristic of equally and independently separating the effects of each factor on the others.

No. of test Condition	Test order	IOD (mm)	X (mm)	Y (mm)	Z (mm)
1	1	65	0	0	70
2	2	65	25	25	95
3	3	65	40	40	110
4	4	65	55	55	125
5	1	90	25	40	125
6	2	90	0	55	110
7	3	90	55	0	95
8	4	90	40	25	70
9	1	115	40	55	95
10	2	115	55	40	70
11	3	115	0	25	125
12	4	115	25	0	110
13	1	140	55	25	110
14	2	140	40	0	125
15	3	140	25	55	70
16	4	140	0	40	95

Table 1. Experimental test conditions

Participants

Twelve participants undertook this test (age, 28.5 (5.9); 9 men, 3 women). Ten were right handed, all had normal vision, and all had an inter-pupillary distance of 64~66mm. There were no self-reported abnormalities of balance or motion sickness susceptibility. Three participants had had a great deal of experience with 3D or HMD, 6 had had some experience and 3 had had little. All participants gave their informed consent prior to testing and responded to a preliminary questionnaire. We followed Declaration of Helsinki ethical standards and obtained IRB approval.

Apparatus and measures

Video see-through HMD: We developed a video see-through HMD with 2 individual 30mm, 30 fps screens in front of the eyes. This HMD had 2 parallel cameras offering a straightforward install not requiring toe-in setup, and which do not generate vertical parallaxes under conditions of up to 140mm of IOD. During the test, participants had no difficulty with convergence because the HMD provided about 40 cm of convergence distance at 140mm of IOD. The HMD had a 640×480 display resolution and an FOV of 48° in the horizontal and 18° in the vertical.

Foot placement performance measures: To measure foot placement performance, participants were asked to step onto a 150mm-high box placed in front of them and to step down every 5 seconds to a target on the ground indicated by foot markers. A step was counted as a failure when the participant's foot landed 30mm outside the markers. This failure criterion was determined to yield 80 ~ 90% of accuracy on average after adaptation, corresponding to the findings of Rolland and Biocca [2] and Martin [7]. During the test, an experimenter counted the number of successes for each trial and informed participants of each instance. This test was composed of 20 trials.

Finger touch performance measures: Participants were asked to touch a 20mm-diameter red blob that appeared on a monitor screen (285 mm×165 mm) within a given amount of time: The blob appeared for 5 seconds before moving to another position. This task was repeated 20 times for each participant. During the task, a program counted the success of the trial and informed participants in each instance. The distance from the chair to the monitor was 60cm.

Test procedure

After filling out preliminary questionnaires, participants were divided into 4 groups of 3 each. For example, Group 1 performed test conditions 1-2-3-4 in order, and Group 2 performed conditions 5-6-7-8, as shown in Table 1. Before the main test, we made preliminary observations and inquired concerning difficulties participants experienced in controlling their bodies while wearing the video see-through HMD. In the main test, participants performed the foot placement task for 20 trials and the finger touch task for 20 trials in sequence as shown in Figure 2. Paricipants completed a total of 80 trials for each task because each participant repeated each task 4 times.

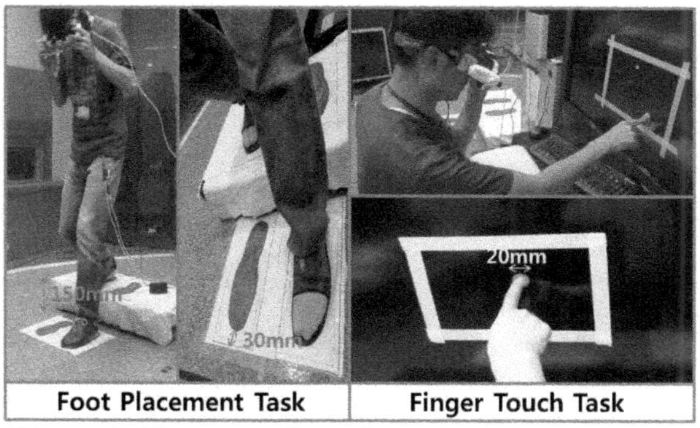

Figure 2. Human task performance measurements consisted of foot placement and finger touch tasks.

RESULTS

We examined whether 4 levels of VD and IOD influenced human task performance variation. However, we found no significant differences, as shown in Figure 3. These results imply that human adaptation occurred for a variety of VDs, up to 55 mm in the *X* and *Y* direction, up to 125mm in the *Z* direction, and up to 140mm of interocular distance (IOD). For example, even with a 55mm disparity in virtual eye position in the *X* direction, participants could rapidly modify their visuomotor performance to suit the new viewing point (by about 78%) as compared to about 76% in the 0mm condition. We investigated these correlations via a T-test (SPSS 18.0), and found no relationship between each VD and IOD and task performance (P>0.05).

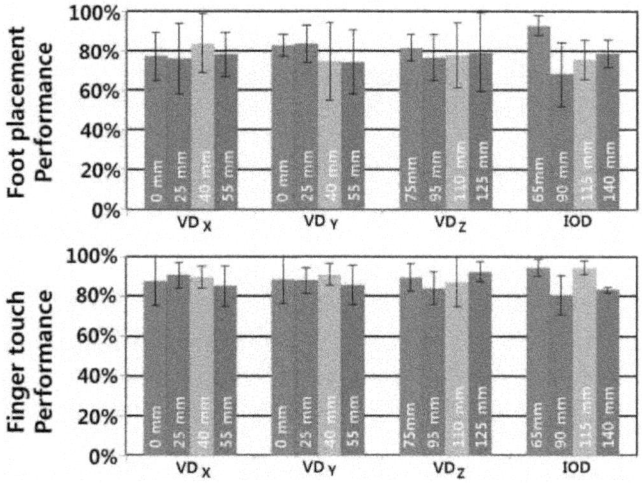

Figure 3. Human task performance under various levels of VD and IOD.

We also analyzed the correlation among test time, task performance and task type. Figure 4 (covering the entire test period) and Figure 5 (covering each test session) show the average of all tasks to illustrate overall adaptation trends. In the foot task, a significant adaptation pattern (r=0.844, P<0.01) emerged, while the pattern was not as significant for the finger task (r=0.762, P<0.1). After 5 minutes of engaging in the foot task, participants performed correctly around 80% of the time, 60% higher than the initial state.

Most participants remarked that the foot task was harder than the finger task due to the difficulty of balancing one's entire body. A few participants staggered when trying to control their body movements in the beginning. However, by the end of the test, almost all participants showed 90% accuracy in performance on both the foot and finger tasks.

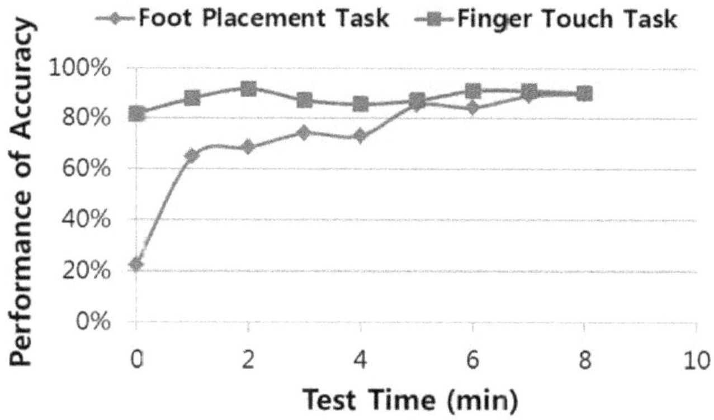

Figure 4. Overall adaptation effects

Figure 5 shows the short adaptation period for each test session. Each participant repeated the task 4 times under various test conditions. Obvious adaptation trends also emerged in the foot task (r=0.586, P<0.01) while only vague adaptation trends emerged for the finger task.

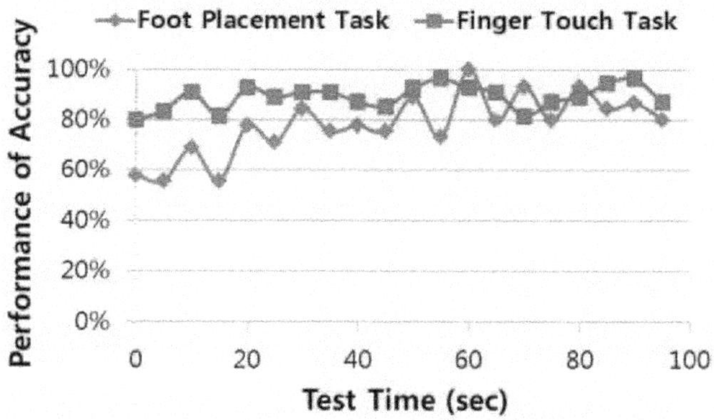

Figure 5. Adaptation effects per test session

DISCUSSION

Adaptation to VD: In the first 10 minutes of a test process, participants tended to rapidly adapt to the new visual sense regardless of the degree and style of VD. Consequently we are cautiously optimistic about the possibility of using a video see-through HMD with wide VDs in practical applications. Our results would help video see-through HMD designers determine a rough range for workable camera positions. A certain amount of deviation in camera position does not seriously deteriorate task performance thanks to the human capacity for visual adaptation. However, VD may pose long-term safety or health risks; we hope to assess that possibility in a subsequent study.

Viewing distance: We considered that viewing distance could have influenced the difficulty of the task types. In the foot placement task, participants stepped down and onto the target over a longer distance as compared to that required for the finger touch task. This difference may have given rise to the difference in adaptation patterns. In the case of the finger task, a more precise task would likely have shown a more distinct adaptation pattern; we will consider this likelihood in designing future tests.

Partial body adaptation: Harris [4] found the presence of an illusion of limbs during visuomotor coordination for a finger-pointing task while participants were wearing a wedge prism. We found the same phenomenon when using the video see-through HMD. During the test, partial body adaptation gave participants a feeling of body structure distortion, including a sense of linkage between their left arm and their chest, and their head being on their right shoulder. This phenomenon was most distinct with the VDx. About 50% of participants mentioned this experience, which occurred as they shifted their attention to a new body part. Even though one may adapt the left hand, one's right hand can remain unadapted, resulting in poor cognition of body structure consistency. For example, when one first looks at an unadapted arm, it appears in an unexpected position, and one then tries to adjust for the perceived positions of the adapted and unadapted arm by reconstructing a sense of linkage. During that time, partial body adaptation occurs. In fact, after the foot test, all participants were asked to remove the HMD for several minutes. During this period, unexpected adaptation to the real view could have occurred. We predict that if participants were to continue to wear the HMD as they changed from the foot task to the finger task, more would have reported this phenomenon more intensely.

CONCLUSION

We suggest that there were no significant differences in task performance using a video see-through HMD despite variations amounting to dozens of millimeters in VD and IOD conditions. This result supports allowance of a wide range of HMD camera positions. In line with the results of previous studies, we found adaptation patterns for the foot and finger tasks with more distinct adaptations emerging in the foot placement task. The foot task was much more influenced by VDs, but the human capacity for adaptation allowed participants to recover successfully from any sensory conflicts in both tasks in a short time.

FUTURE WORK

We are designing the next test procedure to employ a wider VD range, of up to 500mm. We are also considering assessing additional VD factors, such as visual angle and video streaming speed. We also intend to conduct an in-depth investigation of long-term adaptation. A longer period wearing the HMD during normal daily activities should yield interesting results. We will also undertake studies in the future to assess safety and health risks associated with VD and HMD use.

ACKNOWLEDGMENTS

This work was supported by the Global Frontier R&D Program on <Human-centered Interaction for Coexistence> funded by the National Research Foundation of Korea grant funded by the Korean Government (MEST) (NRF-M1AXA003-2012M3A6A3055691)

REFERENCES

1. Alexander, M. S., Foldin, B. W., and Marigold, D. S. Prism adaptation and generalization during visually guided locomotor tasks. *J Neurophysiology, 106*(2011), 860–871.
2. Biocca, F. A., Rolland, J. P. Virtual eyes can rearrange your body: Adaptation to virtual displacement in see-through, Head-Mounted Displays. *Presence, 7*(1998), 262–277.
3. Cobb, S.V.G. Measurement of postural stability before and after immersion in a virtual environment. *Applied Ergonomics, 30*(1999), 47–57.
4. Harris, C., S. Adaptation to displaced vision: Visual, motor, or proprioceptive change? *Science, 140*(1963), 812–813
5. Hoffmann, E. R. A comparison of hand and foot movement times. *Ergonomics, 34*(1991), 397–406.
6. Li, A. Experiencing visuo-motor plasticity by prism adaptation in a classroom setting. *The Journal of Undergraduate Neuroscience Education* (JUNE).
7. Martin, T. A., J. G. Keating, H. P. Goodkin, A. J. Bastian, W. T. Thach. Throwing while looking through prisms. I. Focal olivocerebellar lesions impair adaptation. *Brain, 119*(1996a), 1183–1198. II. Specificity and storage of multiple gaze-throw calibrations. *Brain, 119*(1996b), 1199–1211.
8. McIlroy, W. E., Maki, B. E. Preferred placement of the feet during quiet stance: Development of a standardized foot placement for balance testing. *Clinical Biomechanics, 12*(1997), 66–70.
9. Morton, S. M., and Bastian, A. J., Prism adaptation during walking generalizes to reaching and requires the cerebellum. *Journal of Neurophysiology, 92*(2004), 2497–2509.
10. Rolland, J. P., Fuchs, H. Optical versus video see-through Head-Mounted Displays in medical visualization. *Presence, 9*(2000), 287–309.
11. Stanney, K. M., Kennedy, R. S., Drexler, J. M., Harm, D. L. Motion sickness and proprioceptive aftereffects following virtual environment exposure. *Applied Ergonomics, 30*(1999), 27–38.
12. Taguchi, G. Introduction to quality engineering: Designing quality into products and processes. Asian Productivity Organization, Tokyo: The Organization, 1986.

'Digital Motherhood': How Does Technology Support New Mothers?

Lorna Gibson and Vicki L. Hanson
School of Computing
University of Dundee, Dundee, DD1 4HN, UK
{lgibson, vlh}@computing.dundee.ac.uk
+44 (0)1382 385050

ABSTRACT
New mothers can experience social exclusion, particularly during the early weeks when infants are solely dependent on their mothers. We used ethnographic methods to investigate whether technology plays a role in supporting new mothers. Our research identified two core themes: (1) the need to improve confidence as a mother; and (2) the need to be more than 'just' a mother. We reflect on these findings both in terms of those interested in designing applications and services for motherhood and also the wider CHI community.

Author Keywords
Motherhood; new mothers; social support; ethnography

ACM Classification Keywords
H.1.1 [**Models and Principles**]: User/Machine Systems – *human factors*. H.4.3 [**Information systems applications**]: Communications applications; K.4.2 [**Computing Milieux**]: Computers and Society

General Terms
Human Factors, Design

INTRODUCTION
With approximately 131.4 million births every year worldwide (4.3 million in the US and 780 thousand in the UK) new mothers represent a significant number of individuals [9]. For these new mothers, the change in lifestyle and the recovery period forces a physical isolation that can cause social isolation. This exclusion is particularly prevalent in the first few weeks, but may extend throughout the first year and sometimes beyond.

Becoming a parent can be one of the most stressful experiences in a person's life [16]. Mothers in particular are faced with physical tiredness (associated with recovery from the birth, lack of sleep and the constant demands associated with motherhood) and mental tiredness (associated with uncertainty and constant learning) [2]. These issues can contribute to parenting stress, relationship strain and in some cases to postnatal depression. Further difficulties are encountered if the infant or mother experiences health complications following the birth. In this situation, the mother can experience distress and a sense of disempowerment through the loss of the maternal role and prolonged physical separation from her infant [10].

Access to social support and interactions for new parents has been linked to better maternal health, relationship satisfaction, child development outcomes, and parent-child interactions [19]. It also increases parent confidence and reduces emotional and physical stress [2]. Research suggests that new mothers often seek support most from other new mothers with similar backgrounds [2]. Attendance at antenatal (prenatal) classes (a common precursor to birth but not mandatory) is one place where friendships and the corresponding social support can develop [25]. For those who do not attend an antenatal class, or find that they have nothing in common with those they meet at classes, the weeks following childbirth can be particularly isolating.

However, even those with a wide social network can find the first few weeks isolating. The reasons for this are varied. For example, recent research shows that despite the availability of online networks (such as *Netmums* in the UK [22]) and more immediate support in the family and community, many mothers feel socially isolated, especially those aged between 35 and 44 [27]. Demographic changes over the last 20 years have shown more and more women having children later in life. Often, these older mothers have established careers prior to giving birth and, consequently, much of their social contact takes place within the work setting. Other factors that can lead to isolation for new mothers include changes in society, such as geographic mobility and family separation that have affected the social support available through family and friends.

The potential for technology to provide interaction, information and support is immense. Through the use of technology, new mums could retain social connections and forge new (relevant) connections for their new status (motherhood) in life.

The power of social connectedness and interactions for new mums is profound [19]. Not only does it significantly impact their maternal wellbeing, but also that of the child, particularly better parent-child interactions leading to children who are confident and secure exploring their world and surroundings. While social connectedness has real benefits for the mother, child and the surrounding family, social isolation can have profoundly negative consequences. The changes in hormones and the overwhelming responsibility felt for another can put new mums at risk from postnatal depression. While many mums will experience the 'baby blues' (a common but short-lived state during the perinatal period), approximately 1 in 10 mums in the UK will experience postnatal depression during the first year [20]. Furthermore, many of those experiencing postnatal depression find it difficult to get support or admit they need it [8]. Maternal postnatal depression has been linked to short and long-term negative effects for the child's behaviour, emotional and social wellbeing [e.g. 1, 12].

Technologies such as social networking sites, tablet PCs and smart phones have the potential to provide new mothers with ad hoc social interaction and support. This research set out to identify where technology and motherhood meet and how technology might be used to support new mothers. This research had the goal of understanding the intersection between motherhood and technology and providing a stimulus to others within the CHI community to design to support the needs of new mothers.

RELATED WORK

Within the Human-Computer Interaction (HCI) community, there has been some research interest in issues surrounding motherhood [such as 13, 28] including a Motherhood and HCI workshop planned for CHI 2013.

Other fields (such as nursing, midwifery, child health, social and cultural geography) have also researched the relationship between motherhood and technology. There is a body of work looking at the online information seeking behaviour of parents, with specific work relevant for new mothers such as searching for information relating to pregnancy and childbirth [15] and relating to their newborn child [5].

Considering mothers as a whole, it is reported that the Internet serves the needs of mothers better than any other form of media, particularly in relation to relaxation with 48% saying that their time online is often the most peaceful part of their day [3]. The survey fails to drill down for a reason but perhaps it is most relaxing because going online coincides with an infant nap and an opportunity to sit down. Nevertheless, the Internet does provide a variety of benefits for mothers: it is convenient, always available, there are a range of audiences and no appointment is necessary in order to seek advice [17]. It can also provide support for groups whose access is restricted, such as mothers living in geographically remote areas [17]. There is, however, disagreement within the literature over the importance of support and information provided from the Internet with some reporting it as the most important source support and information [17] while others report it has nominal importance [27].

In response to social isolation in new mothers and the increased use of the Internet to provide informational and emotional support, a variety of online resources aimed at pregnancy and parenthood have emerged. Much is made about the potential of online services such as social networking sites in providing social connectedness and social support, with studies looking at specific web sites which offer features that allow social support to be exchanged online [26, 17].

Evidence suggests that use of these sites contributed to a high general *perception* of support (our emphasis) [26], a greater sense of empowerment [27] and seemed to rival the support traditionally found in neighbour communities [4].

Blogging has also been investigated within the context of motherhood, finding that blogging is a reasonably popular phenomenon among new mothers [18, 14]. In their study of 157 mothers McDaniel et al. found 61% authored their own blog. They suggested that frequency of blogging positively predicted feelings of connection to extended family and friends.

Recently, the smart phone was identified as the device that 'helps mums get through the day' [3]. It is seen as a lifeline with which you can communicate, share, find information and take a break. It is reported that in the US 54% of mothers own a smartphone [24] which is similar to the UK which reports over 50% of mothers own a smart phone [3]. Related research also shows that mothers are more active in their use of smart phones for social networking (50%) than the general population (37%) or females overall (39%) [23]. While these statistics look at mothers as a whole population, new mothers are generally younger and potentially more tech savvy so it is not inappropriate to suggest that these numbers may be larger for new mothers.

In the current research, we ask the question "How does technology affect new mums' experience of motherhood?" Ethnography allowed us to capture a cultural snapshot on tech-savvy mums approach to early motherhood.

METHODOLOGY

Experimental context

A critical ethnographic approach was used for the study. The work was based within a small geographical area of the UK. Given the proximity to a large university, the population sampled would be characterized as relatively affluent and well educated.

Contact with new mothers was facilitated by the researcher being a relatively new mother herself, thus making it easier to gain acceptance and access to the cultural knowledge within this specific community. Research participants were recruited solely from five parent and child groups. They were community based groups so attendance varied from regular attenders to those who came and tried it but did not return. One group attracted a lot of ad hoc attendance through the advertisement of a 'special guest' each month (for example, a health visitor[1], a paediatric nurse talking about meningitis, a psychologist talking about play and infants development) who could complete a short talk. It is sometimes difficult to attend a new group so the researcher did not approach newcomers with a consent form on their first visit. However, there were five occasions where the participants (someone new to the group) shared stories relevant to the research that the researcher approached the participant at the end and asked if they would be willing to consent to the researcher noting their story. All consented. Only two out of the five attended the groups subsequently having expressed an indifference or time constraint to attending the groups again.

A rapport developed between the participants and the researcher based on the shared experience of pregnancy, childbirth and motherhood. This helped build a relaxed and informal atmosphere. The relationship built between the researcher and the mothers was transparent; the researcher explained she was interested in their experiences of motherhood and anywhere technology featured and hoped learning about their experiences would exercise her 'baby' brain. From the participants' point of view, any interest the researcher showed in discussions was made palatable by their empathy about still using her brain (many of them were also engaged in activities to 'use their brain' such as open university courses, foreign language learning or new hobbies). The researcher was constantly aware of her dual role (both as a researcher and also as a member of the community being studied). As a researcher, every attempt was made to try to remain neutral, but the emotive nature of the subject and the personal interest in it causes the researcher to admit that full neutrality was difficult. In response, the voice of the participants (using extensive quotes) strongly features in the results section [6].

Unusually, in this research the researcher attended each group with her child. On the positive side this was (1) a practical option as the research took place while the researcher was on maternity leave, (2) it added a sense of authenticity to the research interest, (3) facilitated a connection to the group, and (4) provided focal points for discussion to help establish good relationships. On the negative side, the children could be distracting and when the children provided an interruption that required the adults' attention the information being shared was suddenly stopped, providing an overview of the facts but without the richness of the previous storytelling.

[1] A health visitor is an NHS nurse who makes regular visits to check on the health of new mothers and their babies.

Various methodological workarounds seemed to help ensure good data was being gathered. These were attending during feeds or nap time (particularly easy in the early months) and nappy (diaper) breaks in the bathroom provided opportunities for interim notes to be taken. Finally, the research came to a natural end both when there was a period where no new data was gathered but also when the increased mobility of the researcher's child precluded quality data gathering.

Participants

The study was conducted from 2011 to 2012 over a period of 8 months. Permission was granted for the study by the School of Computing Ethics Committee; the mothers participated through Informed Consent. The study was in two parts: firstly a series of ethnographic observations and secondly a small group of ethnographic interviews.

Ethnographic observations [N=42; M=29.3 years old; SD=3.6 years] took place in five parent and child groups in Central Scotland. All mothers had been working up until the arrival of their infant apart from two mothers who were made redundant shortly before they found out they were pregnant. The purpose of the groups was to provide a place for parents to bring their babies to meet new people and find support. Two of the groups were based in a rural community, two groups were based in a small city and one group was based in a suburb of the city. The groups were based in moderate to high socio-economic areas. All women had an infant under 1 year old [N=43; M=23.8 weeks; SD=9 weeks]. It should be emphasized that the discussions of technology always emerged from the participants and the primary researcher did not lead the discussions in anyway. As such there were many observation sessions where technology never came up.

The observations and conversations were complemented by six in-depth personal interviews with new mothers [N=6; M=30.5 years old; SD=4 years] who had a baby within the last 12 months. Informal efforts were made to recruit participants that would represent the diversity of the population, based on education (2 university education, 2 college education and 2 high school education), work status (3 planning to return to work, 1 not planning to return, 1 unsure whether to return and 1 currently unemployed), and geographical area (3 from the city and 3 from rural town near the city). The efforts were informal as they required the participant to agree to participate, find a mutually suitable time and not have to cancel due to infant or maternal illness. Interviews were rearranged multiple times with two original participants requiring to be replaced.

Each interview lasted approximately one hour. We presented the findings (concepts) from the preliminary analysis (see below) and asked the participants to discuss and elaborate whether this is something they have experienced. The aim of the interviews was to explore and contextualize the primary findings. The interviews took the form of informal conversations and were conducted in neutral locations such as local coffee shop. Infants were present during interviews.

Data analysis

The ethnographical data consisted of observations of in-situ group conversations and individual conversations while looking after or playing with the infants. Data recording relied on written field notes made immediately after each group meeting. Data was anonymised by assigning each mother with an unique ID starting with *Mum A* (using a different letter in the alphabet for each participant and then double letters after 26 participants) up until *Mum PP*.

The ethnographical data was analyzed by using the constant comparison technique of the Grounded Theory approach for qualitative analysis [11]. The data was read and open-coded to produce an initial code list, which was re-worked until the analysis reached theoretical saturation with respect to the amount of information. At the same time, relationships were established between the categories identified in the open coding through axial coding. The data was then selectively coded in terms of core and subcategories from the initial and axial list. Preliminary data was analyzed at 4 months to gain a better picture of what had been gathered and to identify emerging issues on which to focus.

Full analysis (as described above) was repeated on all the data collected after 8 months of observations/conversations and in-depth person interviews.

FINDINGS

There were two core categories that emerged from the analysis, which will be used to tell the story of new mothers and technology:

- Improving confidence as a mother: seeking advice; breaking into the 'new' community; technology for parenting.
- More than 'just' a mother: identity preservation; connecting to the world outside their bubble.

Improving confidence as a mother

Seeking advice

Mothers in this study used the Internet to source information on parenting, developmental stages, feeding and health concerns.

I might go as far as saying my search engine is my best friend. I certainly use it as my first port of call when I have a niggle, concern or question. Maybe I use Google too readily and should start listening to my instinct but well, to be honest, I like the confirmation or reassurance it provides. [Mum FF]

It is perhaps unsurprising that the mothers reported using the Internet as a tool to find information to answer their questions and concerns. There is an abundance of web sites available presenting information relevant for motherhood. While there was no mention of checking the credibility of the information they found, many of the mothers did highlight the appropriateness for them to check multiple sources in order to determine a consensus. So in a sense they were doing an informal consistency check.

I check a few web sites, just to make sure that everyone is saying more or less the same thing. Once or twice the first page I looked at was alarming (worst case scenario type thing) but the rest of the sites helped balance this out a bit more. [Mum X]

Many of the mothers reported that they felt many of their questions in the early days could be perceived as 'silly' and searching the Internet provided them with a less embarrassing place to ask 'silly' questions.

I google for answers all the time – particularly when I think I should know the answer. I don't really want the health visitor or my sister or even my new friends to think I am a bad mum because I don't know the answer to simple things. [Mum F]

The potential for the Internet to provide a safe place to ask embarrassing questions is a powerful form of support (if used with the proper judgment on the credibility of the information sourced) for new mothers. We can therefore extend the similar finding by Madge and O'Connor [17] (on one specific web site) to include the Internet in a wider context.

Web sites with forum features such as *Netmums* in the UK [22] were specifically discussed as they ranked highly in most of the search results. Mothers reported that they often could find the answer to their question without having to ask the question themselves. This is specific to web sites whose discussions are open and therefore the output from forum discussions become part of collective knowledge available. Consequently, they get their answer instantly and deal with it straight away.

As I say to my husband all the time "If in doubt, google it". I have yet to ask Google something it can't help me with which is brilliant. I deal with the problem before I could even get the health visitor on the phone. [Mum L]

I have picked up loads of tips on forums just by having a wee nosy about. I don't like to write anything – probably because I haven't got anything to contribute but I like to have a nosy. [Mum CC]

Other mothers reported that when they looked for advice on situations they were struggling with such as reflux or sleep deprivation, it was reassuring to find that others were in similar situations.

I battled with Amy's reflux – she was such an unhappy and unsettled baby we rarely left the house until she was about 5 months old. One day I searched the web for more information on reflux (beyond what the doctors had told me) I came into a discussion on reflux on a web site and was thrilled (oops did I just say that – sounds mean doesn't it) to find others were having a horrible time too. [Mum C]

At first when I went out and about, I saw nothing but mums who had got it all together and were 'natural' mothers. Thank goodness, I read comments on one of the baby web sites about someone who felt terrible that she still felt overwhelmed one month in. And then when I saw all the responses she had from people feeling the same way, I felt so relieved. I wasn't alone, I wasn't a crap mother, I was just normal. [Mum F]

Madge and O'Connor also found that new mothers gained reassurance and strength from realizing that others had the same hurdles to overcome [17] and Brady & Guerin found the power of shared experiences in contributing to feelings of normalcy [4]. Access to the Internet and consequently a variety of web services provides the opportunity for new mothers gain strength from these shared experiences.

While forums were popular, many mothers complained that forums were only truly usable on a PC or laptop. As will be discussed later in this paper, smart phones provided mothers with quick and easy access to the Internet. Mothers in this study reported the frustration and difficulties encountered trying to use forums on a smart phone.

Social networking sites, in particular Facebook, seem to fill a gap for online help (possibly made easier by the standard installation of the Facebook app on most smart phones). While data is not currently available for UK use, recent evidence for the US suggests 72% of American mothers use Facebook [24] with 50% actively participating in social media access platforms via mobile devices [23].

The web chat forums are fab but they are too finicky to work using my iPhone. I don't have time to switch the laptop on and look for answers. And, you know, I tend to want to get help at 3 o'clock in the morning so I use my phone as it is there beside my bed. So I use Facebook, you have to wait for people to respond, rather than view what has gone before but even with that it is still way easier. [Mum LL]

Mothers from this study used Facebook to ask questions and receive responses from their online social circle. They found this very easy to do as it was integrated into a medium they already used, and accessed frequently. In addition, unlike some of the web sites they tried to access using their smart phones, Facebook did not require additional log on credentials. Previous research has shown that social networking sites were not significant sources of advice and support for parents [27]. Our participants perceived a benefit of using Facebook and suggested that it was for support and advice but this could be a side effect of an increased sense of empowerment experienced by the mother using Facebook [27].

Breaking into the 'new' community

There is a perception with the mothers in this study that the (non-commercial) social and supportive groups suitable for parents and babies are a hidden community. They reported that it was both difficult to discover and to access the parent community.

When I first had James I had an idea that there was this secret world out there where local mums met up for cake and coffee but I had no idea how to find where AND how to get invited. I began to think that things would only improve when he went to school. It wasn't nice thinking about 5 long years with no real mummy pals. [Mum A]

I had the support of one other mum, we palled about together, but even then we felt we were missing out and not in the loop. [Mum A]

The mothers all knew the importance of 'getting out and about' both for maternal health and perspective but also in order to meet other parents to share their experience with. However, they all stressed how difficult it was when they had not been invited to join a group.

It is not what you know it is who you know! Another mum (who I met at the doctors) pointed me in the direction of my local baby group. I went along and never looked back [Mum BB]

The key problem emphasized by almost every mother in this study was how difficult it was to find community groups they could attend. For mothers who had previously been in employment and used the Internet extensively, they were frustrated that a basic Internet search failed to provide any results for community groups meeting within their local area. Most of the mother and baby groups that were advertised were structured classes than were run as businesses. It is not surprising that commercial baby groups would advertise online to potentially increase revenue. However, while these groups are great, as these classes require a more substantial payment they have a fixed structure and tend to provide less opportunity for developing social connections or provide social support. Community groups tend to be unstructured and as such provide plenty of opportunity to develop friendships with other mothers. Due to the nature of many community groups, particularly those organized and run by volunteers (who are also busy looking after young children), is that often the skills, time and understanding are not available to seek out ways to advertise online.

I never knew about the local baby groups until my eldest was 3 and went to the local playgroup. It was then that I got to know mums from the village and found out about all the activities close to home. Up until that point we travel to the local city to attend activities that were advertised online through Netmums and never met anyone from my area. [Mum J]

In some places, information is provided (in leaflet form) from health visitors who visit new mothers shortly after they come home with their infant but it is often unclear which groups welcome babies, for example groups with the word toddler in the name. This was a source of frustration with the mothers interviewed as it is most crucial to establish a social network of mums when they are babies.

Once membership with these groups had been established many mothers pointed out that internal groups formed such as Facebook groups or text/email groups (where a single message was sent out to all on the text or email list) to facilitate additional 'meet ups'.

A bunch of us local mummies made a private group on Facebook for chatting, sharing and planning get togethers. It is much easier to use that than texting out to mums because everyone can see the responses. [Mum EE]

Parenting by technology

There were a few examples where new mothers had taken conventional technology and used it for their own unique purpose. While research suggests blogging is not an unusual practice for a mother [18], one particular mother used blogging as a buffer to the external interest and sometimes intrusion she encountered.

I made a blog for my son and it will sound odd to say this but it was for a bit of self-preservation. I have 3 siblings and so does my husband, add in the grandparents, one set of great grandparents, the odd auntie and close friends – we had to field a lot of calls. Plus we were the first out of the family and our social circle to have kids so I guess there was a bit of novelty too. Before he was born, because I was 2 weeks overdue, we were inundated with calls (every day). Don't get me wrong it was great that they cared but so much of our time was spent telling the same thing to each person. I made a blog which we updated regularly (daily at first) with what he weighed, if he had been out and about etc. I think it worked people tended to call less but when they did they seemed to know how things were going and were happy. [Mum X]

Other more conventional blogging strategies are discussed later, for example for self-expression.

Other mothers used technology in a specific and unique fashion. For example, one mother used an online Google document to note timings of feeds, naps and nappy changes while she was learning to understand her infant and develop a schedule. While another used Twitter for the same purpose and her husband made a software application that aggregated the tweets into a summary of the day.

Interestingly these mothers were using their smart phone (specifically apps on their phones) to do these activities. In our study, mothers with smart phones accounted for 88% of participants. This is much higher than the national average, which shows just over 50% of mothers owning a smart phone [3]. Only 12% in our study mentioned having downloaded an app designed specifically for parents despite the plethora available. Perhaps this is because discovery of these apps was largely driven by helpful family members, in particular the father and not the mother herself.

I used a small notebook at first to track feeds, nappy changes and naps. It helped me get to know my son and work out what he needed when. My husband downloaded an app to my phone which did all this for me. Rather than writing, I can press buttons for each activity. It is quick and easy and it even suggests why he might be crying. I don't use it as much as I did but it really helped us get in sync. [Mum H]

My husband put an app on my phone to track feeding. You know just the basic how long (using a timer) and from what side but it was really pretty rubbish. I loved the idea but it had to stay open to work and I wanted to go check Facebook or read the news. If I did that it didn't save that feed. [Mum EE]

More than 'just' a mother

Identity Preservation

Many of the mothers spoke about ways in which their identities changed following the arrival of their child (and tied up with leaving the workplace irrespective of whether this was a temporary or permanent move). Certainly, they were aware that during the peri-natal period the world did seem to revolve around the child and their role as the mother of that child. There was a strong feeling and need by most mothers that they needed to preserve their identity as a person in their own right.

There was a number of ways that mothers used to preserve their own identity. Firstly, using social networking sites such as Facebook provided them with a place to post and share *their* thoughts (emphasis on their as it was stressed that they wanted to share based on what made them unique such as interests they had or a quirky sense of humour and NOT a baby diary with daily photos of the infant). This purpose is very different from the baby storytelling in other studies [14].

I love posting snippets to Facebook and then checking later for likes and comments. I particularly like exchanging banter with some of my close friends. It's a bit of a giggle. [Mum K]

Another form of identity preservation discussed was blogging, in particular for self-expression or as a form of therapy. Only 3 (7%) mothers in our sample reported blogging: one mentioned earlier used it to buffer external attention; and the other two used it to share some of their experiences of their journey into motherhood. This is vastly different from other studies which found 61% of mothers in their sample [18].

My blog is more or less my journey with baby brain. I seem to keep forgetting things or getting myself into a pickle and rather than worry about it, I thought I would write it down and have a good laugh at myself. [Mum Y]

In our study, while the topic was motherhood, these blogs were still all about attempts to preserve their identity because they were mainly focused on their journey and not about the child.

I have a blog – feels a bit naughty but it is so therapeutic for me. I studied English at University so I would call it a 'stream of consciousness' but basically I just empty my head every evening of all my thoughts, worries and feelings. I have no idea if anyone reads it and to be fair I don't really care. I write under a different name so no one I know would know it was me. But I leave it public for the sole purpose that it might help some poor mum out there who is feeling just as daunted and overwhelmed by me half the time. [Mum AA]

When blogging came up in conversation, many of the mothers found the basic concept difficult to understand and why their fellow mothers would blog. However, hearing the examples from other mothers they could better see the purpose but still were not convinced that it would be something that they would spend their time on.

Connecting to the world outside their bubble

All mothers reported that in the early days there was a disconnection from what they termed as 'the outside world' or 'the world outside my bubble'. This covered contact with their social circle, awareness of current affairs and knowledge of day and date. The mothers who had been in employment prior to having a child reported one of the biggest adjustments (after having a whole new person to care for) was the change in their social circle. Specifically, that they did not appreciate how much of their social network consisted of people they worked with or other people who worked. They found this particularly problematic as it made it much harder to communicate with their social network particularly at times when they most needed it, for example when they were home alone during the day they did not want to disturb someone while they were at work.

When I worked my pet peeve was people who would email instead of picking up the phone [for social communication]. It wasn't until I was at home with my daughter did I truly understand both the potential of email and probably why some people use it so much. With email I can send it at 3am in the morning where a phone call wouldn't cut it. I can also start and stop an email (because I am distracted by a crying child etc) in a way that stopping and starting a telephone call would be irritating. It is nice to be able to email work friends from time to time to maintain some form of contact. I also email friends trying to arrange coffee etc. [Mum S]

Often, this feeling of disconnection from their existing social network can lead to feelings of isolation, particularly where people in their immediate social network do not have children. Technologies that allowed asynchronous communication such as Facebook and to a lesser extent email were thought to be a benefit for maintaining some social contact with their existing social network.

I liked Facebook before but what I realized as a mum is how fab it is. I can get in touch with someone when I am free. And they can read or respond to it when they are free. It never occurred to me until I became a mummy how huge that would be. [Mum P]

In addition, just the passive use of social networking sites allowed them to browse what others were doing and consequently they reported that they felt less lonely knowing they had some grown up contact (even though this was completely passive). This is not dissimilar to the benefits from 'lurking' on forums [4].

[About Facebook] I didn't have to actually make an effort to message people if I didn't feel up to it but I could log in and see that other people were still living their lives. [Mum C]

The desire for social interactions by new mothers can be particularly potent. For example, it can encourage technology adoption where there has been previous strong resistance.

I felt funny about joining Facebook before I had my son. I wasn't really sure of the point of it and I wasn't keen to share too much stuff with lots of people. In fact I took many opportunities to declare what a nonsense I thought it was. But other mums were using it to arrange meeting up so I thought I should join and not miss out. I certainly have my finger on the pulse more now knowing what things I can go to. [Mum Z]

The use of social networking sites such as Facebook seemed to be a popular way to maintain some form of awareness of the world outside their front door.

I just wanted to know that there was other things happening out there (in the real world, outside the bubble I was living in). I wanted something in my life that was for me and was more than just being a mother. Facebook was great for this – I didn't have to actually make an effort to message people if I didn't feel up to it but I could log in and see that other people were still living their lives. [Mum C]

Beyond contact with their social network, mothers felt a strong need for exoteric awareness and to be able to connect to the world around them. One common example was the need to know about current affairs.

I wanted to feel I could contribute to an adult conversation, if I ever got the chance and have just two minutes not being a mummy. I wanted to say to my husband "isn't is terrible what happened in X?". Although I can't even think of an example to give you here. I just wanted to say hey I know what is happening in the world at the moment. [Mum S]

Overwhelming, mothers cited their ownership of mobile phones, specifically smart phones, as one of the best tools for a modern mother. Smart phones provided them with instant access to the Internet, email, social networking and much more. The power of smart phones to provide social inclusion to mothers was apparent very early in the data gathering. In fact, many of the new mothers interviewed talked about their smart phones as 'life-lines' not too dissimilar to previous findings [3]. Rather than a tool typically used for communication, connection and some entertainment, they were using it to increase their emotional and maternal wellbeing.

Michael needed a wee feed boost about 5am every morning so I would use that time to play with my phone. I loved later in the morning when my husband woke up that I could tell him news items that he didn't already know about. I felt a bit smug if I am honest in the 'look at me my fingers on the pulse' sort of way. [Mum F]

The potential to connect to the world in the middle of the night by using a smart phone was felt to be a life-line for many of the mothers.

My phone is great. I set the screen to be dim so that when I have those middle of the night feeds I can check the news and have a crafty wee game of Sudoku. Somehow that makes being up in the middle of the night feel less traumatic [Mum F]

I can't believe how much I enjoy the night feeds knowing I have something to do other than sit quietly in the dark and try not fall asleep holding the baby. [Mum O]

It also allowed them to gain some control over activities they were responsible for and feel more productive.

I confess to shopping online at midnight either food shopping or an order to Amazon for birthdays that were coming up. I would do it while I would do Hazel's dream feed and I had such a sense of satisfaction at knowing I had been a productive person. [Mum P]

Many suggested that they would not have utilized these online services as much if they had to go to their desktop computer or laptop and wait for it to load up. Interestingly, a small amount of mothers reported the ownership of a tablet PC (sometimes bought as a present or a treat around the time of childbirth) but the feeling was that they were not a useful as they hope they would be.

I got a iPad as a present just before the birth of my daughter. I was used to having online access for most of the day through my job so I thought this would be the perfect solution once the baby was here. What I hadn't appreciated was as a mum I would have to learn to do everything one handed as I would be cradling her, feeding her, entertaining her etc. The iPad doesn't really work for that but my 2 year old HTC is brilliant. I can hold it in one hand easily and can use my thumb to load apps and scroll etc. [Mum Y]

Smart phones also provided new mothers with access to apps undiscovered before the arrival of their infant, such as apps to promote inclusion for the parent who is out at work.

I managed to put something called What'sApp on my phone and it means I can send free picture messages to my husband when he is out at work. That way he doesn't miss out on some of the funny things that happen to Maree. [Mum F]

DISCUSSION

It has been suggested that technology which supports social inclusion could have real impact on new mothers [19]. Due to their age, new mothers tend not to have problems with access to the technology. However, circumstances (specifically their infant) provide restrictions to that access. Mobile devices offer an opportunity for new mothers to regain access without relocating to a PC and offer the potential for access while caring for their child. They offer particular opportunities during the middle of the night, potentially providing new mothers an activity to help them stay awake while feeding or an opportunity to unwind after settling a fractious infant.

This research set out to understand whether technology affects new mothers, and, if so, how it affects them. In doing so, we identified two key themes: improving confidence as a mother and being more than 'just' a mother. Mostly the findings centred around the access to and provision of support, typically informational, emotional and companionship. This is hardly surprising. However, it is the role of technology in reclaiming their identity and their place/connection within the world that was more surprising.

These two themes provide designers some direction on ways to support new mothers. By considering the motivations of the user group, rather than the process of motherhood (pregnancy, childbirth, postnatal care of the infant), there is a potential for engaging this community. The themes speak to the role of the technology in the lives of users – themes that have the potential to motivate other socially excluded groups of people.

Previous work has suggested a lack of research focused on how parents use the Internet on the whole during their journey into parenthood [7]. The present research makes some steps in this direction by looking at where technology and motherhood intersect. This research focuses on motherhood not to discount the impact that parenthood has on the father, but mainly because within current UK society mothers are still largely the primary carer and consequently they were the demographic available at the groups we attended. To our knowledge the level of detail obtained from the present ethnographic work has not been previously reported.

The themes identified in this study are not dissimilar to the findings in other studies [25, 2]. What is novel in this study is the identification of where technology features within these themes. While other studies have looked at technology and motherhood they have concentrated on the use of one specific web site [17, 26, 4] or a specific type of activity such as Blogging [18, 14]. This study attempted to build a wider overview of where technology and motherhood intersect.

The data does need to be viewed within the context it was gathered. Specifically, the sample was predominately white women with good education levels living within the UK. No attempts are made to determine whether the results will generalize to other populations, particularly as some cultures experience motherhood in different ways, for example the prevalence of alloparenting[2] in come cultures.

Understanding the use of technologies by mothers and indeed, the experiences they encounter could help and enhance development for future mothers and influence health professional's approach and support provision. The documented benefits of social inclusion for new mothers suggests that better and appropriate technologies for new mothers can provide real impact.

There are also commercial implications to understanding this demographic as demonstrated by Mothercare [21] (a large commercial group who sell mother and baby products both online and in store) who adopted a unique marketing campaign during the first half of 2012. Using Facebook they posted a discount offer for a popular product only available for a few hours in the early hours of the morning thus tapping into a captive audience but also making those up at that time feel valued.

Mothercare does this thing where offer specific products at reduced rate (advertised via Facebook) where the advert goes out at say 2am and the offer ends at 7am. I love that they do this – it is a great nod to those mums suffering by being up in the night but also makes you feel part of a secret and special group. [Mum BB]

This has been a smart move by Mothercare who seemed to experience a lot of good will from the participants in our study who had seen these offers. With the economic downturn, they have made a strategic move to be viewed as a company that truly cares about mothers by understanding that they are often up during the night.

CONCLUSION

Motherhood is constantly reconstructed in response to changes in society [17] and on some levels motherhood today is vastly different from previous generations. The availability and pervasiveness of technology today has the potential to further reconstruct a person's approach to motherhood.

We note the relevance of the current findings to many current topics in HCI research. For example, there are immediate implications for digital engagement. Many of the mums reported they found technology to be a powerful ally. This was manifested by technology supports that allowed them to increase their confidence in mothering through seeking information and reassurance on their choices or concerns, that allowed them to assert their position as 'more than a mother,' and that allowed them to take part in some self-directed therapy either through blogging or social networking sites. In addition, we uncovered motivations for technology use where there was previous resistance. Specifically, some new mums reported connections motivated them to use Facebook, which previously they had resisted.

We also note the relevance of the current findings for digital identity research. Technology played a key part in helping mums maintain both a sense of their (old) self as well as forge out a new identity.

Our findings also provide new evidence about social networking sites as community builders. The new mums in our study were kept up-to-date, had a means of contacting other mums, and could invite others to do something together. Furthermore, community groups could use Facebook as a communication tool where a traditional web presence was impossible (due to lack of skills or funding).

Future work is needed to more fully understand the role of technology in the emotional and physical wellbeing of new mothers. The present work, however, paves the way for understanding key roles of such support.

[2] Form of parenting where members of extended family or individuals from the community take an active role on a day-to-day basis.

ACKNOWLEDGMENTS

The authors thank the participants who helped with this research. The authors acknowledge support from RCUK Digital Economy Research Hub EP/G066019/1 "SIDE: Social Inclusion through the Digital Economy" and a Royal Society Wolfson Merit Research Award to the second author.

REFERENCES

1. Avan, B., Richter, L.M., Ramchandani, P.G., Norris, S.A., and Stein, A. Maternal postnatal depress and children's growth and behaviour during the early years of life: exploring the interaction between physical and mental health. *Archives of Disease in Childhood*, 95, (2010), 690-695.
2. Barclay, L., Everitt, L., Rogan, F., Shmied, V., and Wyllie, A. "Becoming a mother" – an analysis of women's experience of early motherhood. *Journal of Advanced Nursing,* 25, (1997), 719-728.
3. BabyCenter. BabyCentre's "2011 21st Century Mum Report". 22 September 2011. URL: http://www.investegate.co.uk/article.aspx?id=20110922 11000571560. Last accessed on 3rd September 2012.
4. Brady, E., and Guerin, S. "Not the Romantic, All Happy, Coochy Coo Experience": A Qualitative Analysis of Interactions on an Irish Parenting Web Site. *Family Relations: Interdisciplinary Journal of Applied Family Studies*, (2010) 15, 14-27.

5. Bernhardt, J.M., and Felter, E.M. Online Pediatric Information Seeking Among Mothers of Young Children: Results From a Qualitative Study Using Focus Groups. *Journal of Medical Internet Research* (2004) 6,1.

6. Borning, A. and Muller, M. Next Steps for Value Sensitive Design. *Proc. CHI 2012*, ACM Press (2012), 1125-1134.

7. Daneback, K., and Plantin, L. Research on Parenthood and the Internet: Themes and Trends. *Journal of Psychosocial Research on Cyberspace (Cyberpsychology),* (2008), 2(2), article 2.

8. Dennis, C., and Chung-Lee, L. Postpartum Depression Help-Seeking Barriers and Maternal Treatment Preferences: A Qualitative Systematic Review. *Birth*, (2006), 33(4), 323-331.

9. Ecology – Ecology Global Network. Birth and Death Data. URL: http://www.ecology.com/birth-death-rates/. Last accessed 30th December 2012.

10. Furman, L., and O'Riordan, M. How do mothers feel about their very low birth weight infants? Development of a new measure. *Infant Mental Health Journal 27*(2), (2006), 152-172.

11. Glaser, B.G., and Strauss, A.L. *The discovery of grounded theory: strategies for qualitative research.* Aldine Transaction, New Jersey (2006).

12. Halligan, S.L., Murray, L., Martins, C., and Cooper, P.J. Maternal depression and psychiatric outcomes in adolescent offsprint: A 13-year longitudinal study. *Journal of Affective Disorders 97* (2007), 145-154.

13. Hui, M., Ly, C., and Neustaedter, C. MammiBelli: Sharing Baby Activity Levels Between Expectant Mothers and Their Intimate Social Groups. *Proc. EA CHI 2012*, ACM Press (2012), 1649-1654.

14. Jomhari, N., Gonzalez, V.M., and Kurniawan, S.H. See the Apple of My Eye: Baby Storytelling in Social Space. Proc. *BCS HCI People and Computers XXIII*, (2009), 238-243.

15. Larsson, M. A descriptive study of the use of the Internet by women seeking pregnancy-related information. *Midwifery*, 25 (2009), 14-20.

16. Leigh, B., and Milgrom, J. Risk factors for antenatal depression, postnatal depression and parenting stress. *BMC Psychiatry*, (2008) 8, 24.

17. Madge, C., & O'Connor, H. Parenting gone wired: empowerment of new mothers on the internet? *Social & Cultural Geography*, (2006) 7:02, 199-220.

18. McDaniel, B.T., Coyne, S.M., and Holmes, E.K. New Mothers and Media Use: Associations Between Blogging, Social Networking, and Maternal Well-Being. *Maternal and Child Health Journal*, (2012), 16(7), 1509-17.

19. Meadows, S. The association between perceptions of social support and maternal mental health: A cumulative perspective. *Journal of Family Issues*, (2011), 32, 181-208.

20. MIND. URL: http://www.mind.org.uk. Last accessed on 30th December 2012.

21. Mothercare. URL: http://www.mothercare.com. Last accessed on 30th December 2012.

22. Netmums. URL: http://www.netmums.com. Last accessed on 3rd September 2012

23. Nielsenwire. Infographic: Getting to know (and Like) the Social Mum. URL: http://blog.nielsen.com/nielsenwire/online_mobile/getting-to-know-and-like-the-social-mom/ Oct 25th 2011. Last accessed 30th December 2012.

24. Nielsenwire. Infographic: The Digital Lives of American Moms. URL:http:// http://blog.nielsen.com/nielsenwire/online_mobile/digital-lives-of-american-moms/ May 11, 2012. Last accessed 3rd September 2012.

25. Nolan, M.L., Mason, V., Snow, S., Messenger, W., Catling, J., and Upton, P. Making Friends at Antenatal Classes: A Qualitative Exploration of Friendship Across the Transition to Motherhood. *The Journal of Perinatal Education*, (2012), 21(3), 178-185.

26. Sarkadi, A., and Bremberg, S. Socially unbiased parenting support on the Internet: a cross-sectional study of users of a large Swedish parenting website. *Child: Care, Health and Development* (2004) 31, 1, 43-52.

27. Social Issues Research Centre. *Changing Face of Motherhood.* (2011).

28. Thomas, J.O., Rankin, Y.A., Tuta, M., and Mibuari, E. Supporting Greater Access to Pre- and Post-natal information and Services for Women in Rural Kenya. *Proc. CHI 2011*, ACM Press (2011), 2353-2358.

Age-Related Performance Issues for PIN and Face-Based Authentication Systems

James Nicholson
PaCT Lab
Northumbria University
Newcastle, UK
james.nicholson@unn.ac.uk

Lynne Coventry
PaCT Lab
Northumbria University
Newcastle, UK
lynne.coventry@unn.ac.uk

Pam Briggs
PaCT Lab
Northumbria University
Newcastle, UK
p.briggs@unn.ac.uk

ABSTRACT
Graphical authentication systems typically claim to be more usable than PIN or password-based systems, but these claims often follow limited, single-stage paradigm testing on a young, student population. We present a more demanding test paradigm in which multiple codes are learned and tested over a three-week period. We use this paradigm with two user populations, comparing the performance of younger and older adults. We first establish baseline performance in a study in which populations of younger and older adults learn PIN codes and we follow this with a second study in which younger and older adults use two face-based *graphical authentication systems employing* young faces vs. old faces as code components. As expected, older adults show relatively poor performance when compared to younger adults, irrespective of the authentication material, but this age-related deficit can be markedly reduced by the introduction of age-appropriate faces. We conclude firstly that this paradigm provides a good basis for the future evaluation of memory-based authentication systems and secondly that age-appropriate face-based authentication is viable in the security marketplace.

Author Keywords
Graphical codes; usable security; authentication; older adults

ACM Classification Keywords
K.6.5 Management of Computing and Information Systems: Security and Protection.

General Terms
Human Factors; Security.

INTRODUCTION
User authentication is a requirement for secure environments that provide access to confidential information or offer personalised services. The most common authentication systems are knowledge-based and typically rely upon the users ability to commit a password or PIN to memory. Problems arise because the user typically needs to generate passwords and PINs for multiple accounts. The memory load becomes onerous, with the result that poor authentication practices prevail. Users duplicate passwords, choose family names or keep stronger codes written down in a drawer or wallet [1,20,23]. Authentication can be challenging to all users, but is particularly problematic for older adults who show a notable decline in memory capacity past the age of fifty (e.g. [10,11,32]).

Graphical authentication (GA) systems have been developed as a potential solution to the usability problems posed by PIN and password systems. In a typical recognition-based GA system, the user is presented with a set of images, a subset of which form that user's authentication code. To log in the user must successfully respond to a series of challenges in which they must select their target image from a set of distractors or decoys. One well-known example of such a system is Passfaces [39], in which the authentication codes comprise a set of faces that the user must recognise from a grid of distractor faces.

There have been a number of evaluations of GA systems in the research literature, but these evaluations are often conducted with sets of relatively young users, who could arguably represent the most able population in terms of memory performance. In addition, usability testing has often been conducted in single laboratory sessions, sometimes but not always involving the requirement to learn multiple codes. This is important, as one of the key memory demands in this space is the requirement to remember which code is associated with which account and interference effects are rife.

In this paper, we have three objectives: Firstly, we wish to introduce a robust test paradigm for new, purportedly 'usable' authentication systems. To this end we introduce a test procedure in which users learn multiple codes in two batches and are repeatedly tested (weekly) on these codes over a period of three weeks. Secondly, we wish to explore the extent to which GA can provide an inclusive solution for older as well as younger adults. Finally, we wish to make design recommendations that are realistic in their technical demands and could legitimately be rolled out to a large population.

CHI 2013, April 27–May 2, 2013, Paris, France.

BACKGROUND RESEARCH

Passwords and PINs are generally assumed to be more difficult to remember than recognition-based GA codes because they rely on the more cognitively demanding process of recall as opposed to recognition [24]. GA systems typically ask users to *recognise* a set of target stimuli when they are set within a context of multiple distractors, although some utilise a click-based approach where users are required to recreate the selection of specific location-based points within a single or series of images, one example being PassPoints [8,42].

Recognition-based GA systems usually employ pictorial stimuli, including photographs [13] or digital art [15], playing to another known aspect of human cognition: a picture superiority effect in which concepts are more likely to be remembered if they are presented as pictures rather than as words [30]. In this paper we are particularly interested in those GA systems, like Passfaces, that use *faces* as stimuli, taking advantage of humans' innate ability to effectively recognise large numbers of known faces [7,35]. For a comprehensive review of GA systems see [5].

In user testing, GA systems have been found to be more memorable than password or PIN based systems in a variety of different studies (e.g. [13,15]). However, usability testing in this field suffers from a number of methodological weaknesses: Firstly, only a few of the published studies have presented a rigorous challenge to the user, for example by including the requirement to learn *multiple* GA codes and reproduce these codes over longer time periods (e.g. [8,19,27]). Secondly, user evaluations in this field have relied rather heavily on university students and so often fail to reflect the needs of older users. Finally, tasks are relatively simple and so ceiling effects are common and these can mask differences between systems.

Those studies that have explored the cognitive demands of using more than one graphical system typically show that the advantages of using GA codes may be short-lived as performance dropped off over time, although it is worth noting that users' performance with graphical systems in several published studies was *at worst* equal to their performance with text passwords [8,19,27]. In the study by Chiasson et al., 65 participants were required to remember either 6 textual or 6 graphical user-generated click-based code conditions [8]. During the first trial, participants in the graphical condition were more likely to remember their code than those in the password condition, following only a short 30 second delay (99% recall versus 88%). About two weeks later, 70% could recall their textual password and only 57% could recall their click-based code but this difference was not statistically significant.

Moncur and LePlâtre looked at the memorability of 5 system-generated codes in a study in which 172 university participants were assigned to one of 5 conditions: 4 digit PIN code; graphical code (photograph of an object); graphical code + colour; graphical code + mnemonic; graphical code + colour + mnemonic [27]. Participants were required to return twice, each time after a 2-week delay. The researchers had an extreme problem with drop out, with 64% of participants not returning and they suggested that drop out for the PIN condition was greatest because it was the most difficult task. The initial success rate for the 5 PIN condition was approximately 10% while it was over 50% for graphical codes. However, after the first two-week period all success rates dropped to approximately 10%.

Face-based graphical authentication

In recent years, a number of face-based authentication systems have been proposed, the most widely reported being Passfaces a commercial systems developed by RealUser. Brostoff and Sasse conducted an evaluation of the Passfaces system in a field study that found that participants using Passfaces experienced approximately 95% login success rate compared to 85% for alphanumeric password users, despite accessing the system less frequently [6]. Other evaluations conducted by Valentine discovered that users had low expectations that they would remember Passfaces codes over a long period of time [39,40], citing, amongst other things, the difficulties they would experience in trying to write down their codes. However, Valentine found that users' short-term memory (99.98% accuracy) and long-term memory (84% accuracy) for Passfaces was significantly better than for conventional passwords. It should be noted that in the three studies reported above users were required to only remember one Passfaces code. Interestingly users were allowed to personalise their code, by selecting the faces presented on the subsequent system, Such personalisation can lead to security breaches, as reported by Davis et al. [12].

These face-based systems offer an interesting domain for authentication with older adults because they do well in a recognition task provided that faces are drawn from an appropriate age group (e.g. [2,3,21,35,37]). It makes sense to assume that a face-based GA system may work well with older adults, provided that they are presented with age appropriate faces.

In this study we explore for the first time the performance of older and younger adults on a GA system that uses different types of face stimuli (young and old faces), in a new evaluation paradigm in which multiple authentication codes are learned over several weeks. We would predict that older adults are likely to perform less well than younger adults at memory-based authentication but that this deficit could be overcome with the use of age appropriate faces. Further, we also seek to understand baseline performance for this paradigm and for these user groups (both older and younger adults) with a PIN-based authentication system. We therefore present a first study in which older and younger adults learned PINs for different notional 'accounts' and measured the memorability for these over a three-week period, before taking the same paradigm and exploring performance on face-based systems. We have chosen a system-generated PIN study as baseline as it is one of the most common forms of knowledge-based authentication and PINs are thought to disadvantage older users [36] but there is relatively little good empirical evidence that compares older and younger adults available in the research literature.

STUDY 1: PIN AUTHENTICATION

Experimental Design

Participants were recruited into two groups of young adults and two groups of older adults. Participants in each age group were randomly assigned to a high or low cognitive load condition and were tested over a three-week period. In the *low load* condition participants acquired a set of two PINs in week 1 (labelled SET 1 for analysis purposes) which were tested during weeks 1, 2 and 3 and they then acquired two more PINs in week 2 (labelled SET 2) which were tested during weeks 2 and 3. In the *high load* condition three PINs were allocated in week 1 (SET 1) and three more in week 2 (SET 2). The dependent measure was the number of successful authentications (maximum of five per account) made in each session.

Analysis of SET 1 PINs took the form of a 2 (old vs. young) x 2 (high load vs. low load) x 3 (time of testing: week 1 vs. 2 vs. 3) ANOVA. Analysis of SET 2 PINs was via a 2 (old vs. young) x 2 (high load vs. low load) x 2 (time of testing: week 2 vs. 3) ANOVA. For this and for the subsequent faces study, time taken to complete the attempts was also measured, however there was never any sign of a speed accuracy trade-off and so the accuracy data alone is presented here. Note that design decisions about loading and delay were made following a pilot trial to ensure floor and ceiling effects would be avoided and that the final design was subject to ethical approval by Northumbria University Life Sciences Research Ethics Committee.

Participants

Thirty-six adults were recruited from the area of Newcastle upon Tyne, UK. Participants were either younger adults aged 18-30 (n = 18, 12 female; mean = 20 years; SD = 3.07 years) or older adults aged 65-75 (n = 18, 14 female; mean = 70 years; SD = 3.83 years). Younger participants were recruited using the university's online recruitment system where the study was publicised and received course credit. Older participants were recruited using our own participant database and various regional charities and were financially compensated for travel expenses to and from the university.

Participants were not screened for gender, cognitive ability or educational attainment. However, research shows that neither education nor gender have an effect on memory for numbers [41], and that education does not predict difficulty in remembering PINs [36]. Screening for cognitive ability was ruled out because the known cognitive decline in older adults [11] would lead to a skewed matched selection of younger adults.

Materials

A simple computer-based PIN system was designed that consisted of an initial image depicting the account followed by text instructing the participant to enter their PIN. The system would display on the screen whether the code was correct or incorrect after entering the four-digit PIN code on the number pad. No feedback was given as to individual digits selected, only on the code as a whole. The system recorded all the digits inputted as well as the time taken to input each digit. In this paper we will only report the accuracy data. Participants were given a randomly generated PIN code along with an account name for each of four (low load) or six (high load) accounts. The six accounts used were alarm (1929), credit card (8360), debit card (2040), library (3126), telephone (9984) and television (5088).

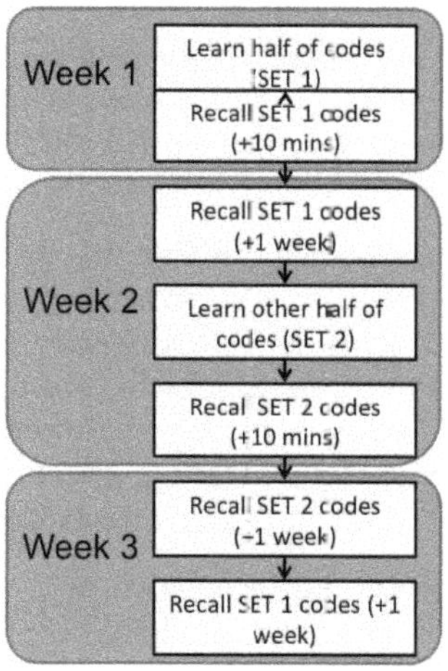

Figure 1: Overview of procedure over the three weeks

Procedure

The study had three phases: enrolment, distraction and authentication. During the enrolment phase, participants learned each PIN code and associated it with a particular account. They were then given the opportunity to practice by entering the code for a particular account 5 times. If they entered it incorrectly 3 times they were shown the code again. Then followed a distraction phase: a ten-minute discussion with the investigator, focussing on their experiences of current authentication systems. Authentication then followed. Participants were required to enter their PIN for each account five times – a realistic number of attempts before dictionary attacks become a serious threat in a real-world scenario. After each attempt they were told if they had entered the PIN correctly, but at no time were then reminded of the correct code.

During week 1, participants were randomly assigned to the high or low load condition and were randomly assigned half of their codes (SET 1) passing through the enrolment, distractor and authentication phase. During week 2 participants learned SET 2 codes, with distractor following and were then asked to authenticate on both SET 1 and SET 2. During week 3 participants were asked to authenticate again on SET 1 and SET 2 (order counterbalanced). See Figure 1 for an overview. Note that the one-week delay allows a measurement of long-term retention before a significant decrement in memory affects older adults [33] and also reflects a common interval used in authentication studies (e.g. [13,15]).

Results and Discussion

The number of successful attempts to recall the codes was analysed using two 3-way Analyses of Variances (ANOVAs), with the three variables remaining stable: age, cognitive load, and time. One ANOVA was conducted for SET 1 data (with authentication data from weeks 1, 2 and 3) and a separate ANOVA conducted for SET 2 data (with authentication data from weeks 2 and 3).

For SET 1, a main effect of age was found ($F(1,32)=4.759$, $p<.05$), with younger participants (mean: 3.96) performing significantly better than the older participants (mean: 2.61). No further main effects or interactions were found.

For SET 2, a main effect of age was also found ($F(1,32)=6.150$, $p<.05$) where younger participants (mean: 3.88) performed significantly better than the older participants (mean: 2.51). There was also a main effect of time ($F(1,32)=5.681$, $p<.05$) where participants performed significantly better in week 2 (mean: 3.48) than week 3 (mean: 2.91). No interaction effects were found.

Taken together, then, these data provide empirical evidence for the commonly held belief that multiple PINs provide a memory challenge and that this challenge is particularly onerous for older adults. Based on the mean successful attempts, older adults risk losing access to their accounts when traditional 'three-strikes' systems are in place. Note, too, the poorest authentication performance took place when older adults were trying to remember those PINs acquired relatively late in the process (i.e. SET 2 PINs) following a week's delay between learning and test.

STUDY 2: A COMPARISON OF FACE-BASED SYSTEMS

Experimental Design

As before, participants were recruited into two groups of young adults and two groups of older adults. Participants in each age group were randomly assigned to a young face or old face condition and were again tested over a three week period, learning three system-generated account codes during week 1 (SET 1) and week 2 (SET 2). Note that this was then the equivalent of the 'high load' condition in the earlier study. The dependent measure was the number of successful authentications (maximum of five per account) made in each session. Analysis of SET 1 took the form of a 2 (old vs. young) x 2 (old face vs. young face) x 3 (time of testing: week 1 vs. 2 vs. 3) ANOVA. Analysis of SET 2 was via a 2 (old vs. young) x 2 (old face vs. young face) x 2 (time of testing: week 2 vs. 3) ANOVA.

Participants

Participants were screened for adequate vision and prosopagnosia (a face recognition deficit). Seventy-two participants were recruited in total. 36 younger participants (12 female) were recruited from the student population in the university. The mean age for those allocated to the younger faces group was 19 (SD: 1.61) and for those allocated to older faces, the mean age was 20 (SD: 0.86). Younger participants were recruited using an online participation pool maintained by the university and were given participation credits for taking part.

36 older participants took part (12 female). The mean age of those allocated to the younger faces group was 70 (SD: 3.60) and for the older faces group the mean age was 71 (SD: 3.68). These participants were recruited using the lab's participant database and through regional advertising. All older participants were financially compensated for travel expenses to and from the university.

Materials

As in Study 1, six fictional 'accounts' were created and each was paired with four-item authentication codes of either four younger or four older faces. Four-item codes are common practice in GA systems and are thought to be comparable to 4-digit PINs in terms of theoretical security. A prototype face-based graphical authentication system was built to evaluate the two experimental configurations. Initially the system displayed instructions for participants, followed by four challenge grids that were displayed for each code containing an image from the participants code and 8 distractor images (see examples in Figures 2 and 3). After all four selections were made, the system informed participants whether the code was correct or not.

Grid Composition

As faces were being gathered from different sources, all faces were converted to grey scale to avoid any confound effects: all faces should carry the same chance of being selected and no one face should stand out due to other selection criteria (e.g. hair colour). Face recognition literature typically uses black & white stimuli and there is no evidence to suggest an associated recognition deficit.

Old faces were obtained from a number of online databases as no one source could supply a sufficient number of suitable images. The final *old face* pool consisted of 80 male faces from the Max Planck Institute [18], University of Aberdeen, and Utrecht University. Note that no young faces were used from the Max Planck Institute.

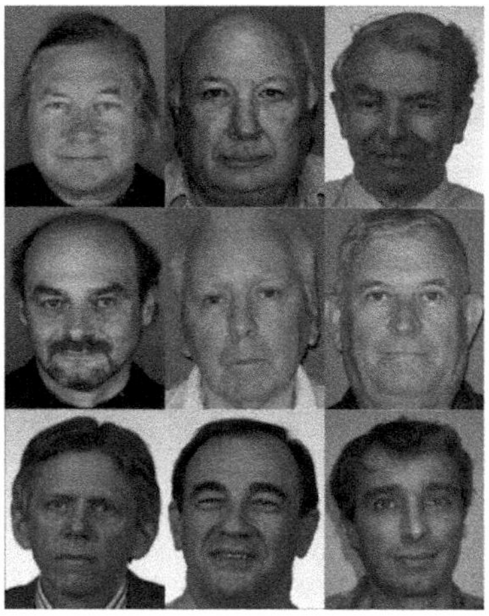

Figure 2: Sample grid for old faces.

Young faces were obtained with permission from a pool held by Newcastle University. The face pool consisted of 280 young males from which 80 were chosen at random.

Figure 3: Sample grid for young faces.

From each pool of 80 faces, 24 unique target young and 24 unique target old faces were selected randomly from the bank using a random number generator. There were no faces that appeared in more than one code to minimise potential code-binding problems [29]. Each of the target faces was assigned 12 decoy faces that would appear on the challenge grids. The decoys were initially assigned randomly from the remaining faces but then examined to ensure similarity of the decoys with the target. Some decoy images were present in more than one grid across codes. The grids were constructed to be visually similar to protect against possible observation attacks (see Figures 2 and 3). Previous research by Dunphy et al. demonstrated that participants were able to guess a face code based on a description more easily if the grids were constructed randomly than if they were constructed to be visually or verbally similar [17].

Procedure

The procedure for this study matched that of the 'high-load' condition in the previous PIN study. The one difference was the addition of a familiarisation phase during the enrolment stage This was thought to be a necessary difference as enforcing a strategy for learning numbers can be detrimental [14] but research has shown that older adults benefit from strategies when learning other items [28]. During the familiarisation phase all participants were given the account name and the 4 target faces that formed the code for that account. They were shown each face individually and asked to engage in an elaboration process that encouraged the user to think more about the face i.e. to think of answers for seven questions about this face: What is this person's name? How old is [name]? Does [name] remind you of anyone you know? Does [name] look like a friendly person? What is [name]'s occupation? Where does [name] live? What can you tell me about [name]'s family?

Results and Discussion

A 3-way ANOVA with repeated measures on one factor (time of testing) and the independent factors of participant age and face age was carried out on both SET 1 and SET 2 with the dependent variable being the number of successful authentication attempts (max = 5).

For the first set of faces learned (SET 1), a main effect of participant age was found ($F(1,68)=17.154$, $p< .001$) with younger participants (mean: 4.84) achieving more successful attempts than older participants (mean: 3.91). A main effect of time was also present ($F(2,67)=8.059$, $p=.001$) with pairwise comparisons showing a significant difference in accuracy between week 1 (mean: 4.60) and week 2 (mean: 4.30), and week 1 and week 3 (mean: 4.16), but no difference in accuracy between week 2 and week 3 (see Figure 4). There was no main effect of face-age.

A significant interaction effect was found between participant age and time ($F(2, 67)=8.783$, $p<.001$) where no significant difference was found for the younger group in accuracy between weeks 1 (mean: 4.82), 2 (mean: 4.84), and 3 (mean: 4.84) ($F(2,107)=0.031$, $p>.05$) while a significant difference was found for the older group in accuracy where older participants were significantly more accurate in week 1 (mean: 4.40) when compared with week 3 (mean: 3.50) (see Figure 4). No further interactions were found.

For the second set of codes, a main effect of participant age was found ($F(1,68)=1092.447$, $p< 001$) with younger participants achieving more successful attempts (mean: 4.71) than older participants (mean: 3.60). A main effect of time was also present ($F(1,68)=14.216$, $p<.001$) with participants achieving more successful attempts in the second week (4.38) compared to the third week (3.92).

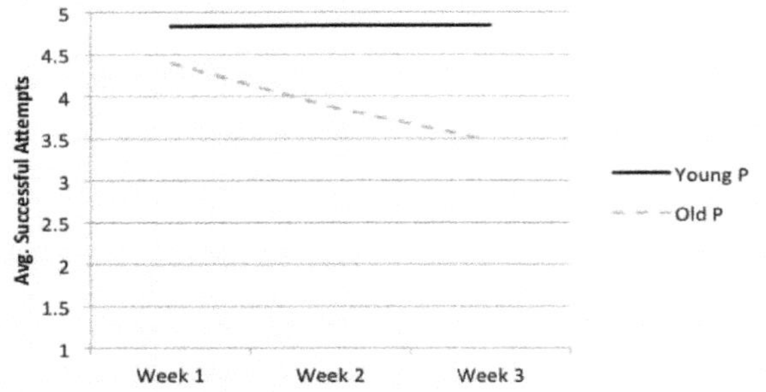

Figure 4: Interaction between Week and Participant Age for the first set of faces learned (SET 1).

An interaction effect was found for SET 2 between participant age and face age (F(1,68)=12.642, p=.021) where the younger group showed no significant difference in accuracy between the young faces and the old faces (t(70)=1.749, p>.05) while the older group were significantly more accurate with the old faces (mean: 4.05) than the young faces (mean; 3.14: t(70)=2.455, p<.05) (see Figure 5).

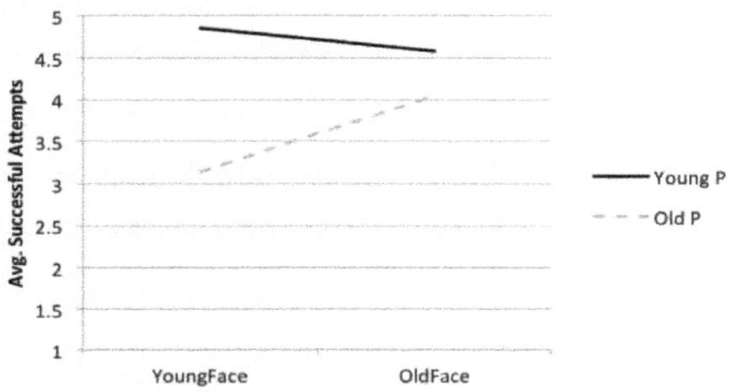

Figure 5: Interaction between Participant Age and Face Age for the second set of faces (SET 2).

There was a 3-way interaction between participant age, face age and time (F(1,68)=4.146, p=.046: see Figure 6) where the same-age face advantage was seen at its strongest in week 3. Independent samples t-tests showed that young adults experienced no face-age effect – i.e. by week 3, there was no significant difference between their recall of old vs. young faces (t(34)=1.484, p>.05). The same could not be said of older adults – who showed a clear recognition advantage for older faces by week 3 (t(34)=2.237, p<.05).

This is an interesting finding for those involved in the design of face-based GA systems, as it suggests that the use of older faces would produce significant benefits for an older population without creating undue problems for younger users, although we should be cautious here: it is possible that our results are demonstrating a ceiling effect for younger users and there may still be some mileage in considering age-appropriate faces as optimal stimuli. We discuss this later, following a comparison, below of relevant PIN and face data from this study.

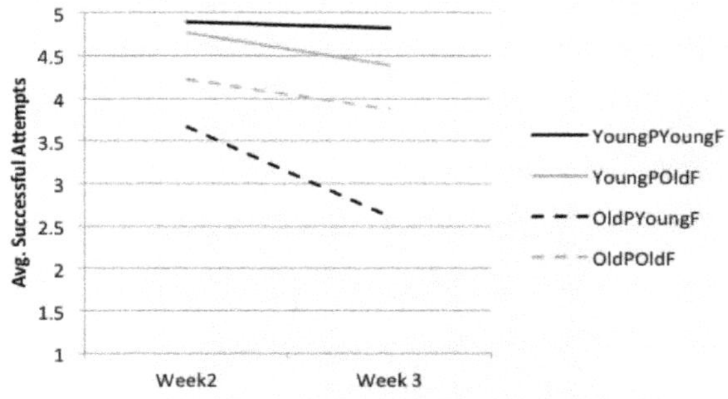

Figure 6: Three-way interaction between Participant Age, Face Age and Time of testing (SET 2).

STUDY 1 AND STUDY 2 COMPARED

In Study 1 we presented an empirical comparison of younger adults and older adults tasked with recalling multiple PIN codes over the course of three weeks. The results demonstrated that older adults were disadvantaged when compared with younger adults and their overall accuracy was below an acceptable level. These results did not come as a complete surprise due to previous self-report evidence suggesting older adults struggled remembering their PIN codes (e.g. [36]), but nonetheless is the first empirical study to demonstrate the extent of the problem. In study 2, we presented two face-based system which compared the performance of the younger and older adults on authentication systems that comprised young faces or old faces.

Our findings suggest that a face-based GA system can be useful for older adults provided age appropriate faces are used as stimuli. However it would be useful to understand the relative performance of our two age groups on PIN vs. face systems and so we conducted a secondary analysis, comparing PINs with the most inclusive of the two face systems we tested – i.e. that based on older faces.

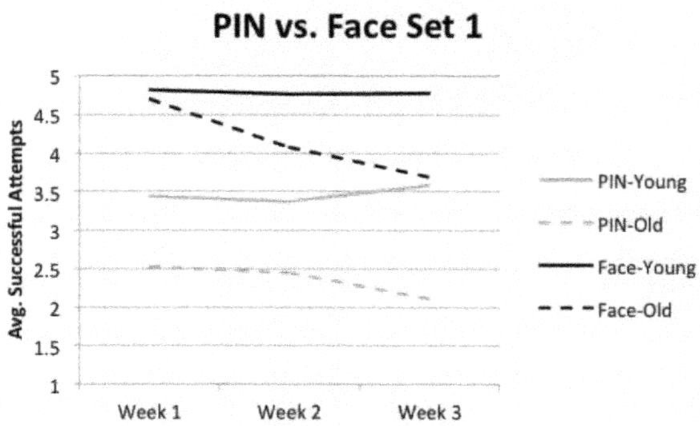

Figure 6: Accuracy of younger and older participants with PIN and Faces (SET 1).

A 3-way mixed ANOVA was carried out on a subset of the data from Studies 1 and 2. Firstly we used the high-load condition from Study 1, as participants in that condition were asked to learn six account codes, the same as in Study 2. Then we selected the old face condition as a point of comparison as this design was shown to be most effective for older adults. Both studies used a common research methodology, however we acknowledge that secondary analyses across separately conducted studies can result in increased type 1 error and so we have utilised a stricter Alpha level of 0.01 in our analysis.

For SET 1, we found a main effect of age ($F(1,50)=5.518$, $p<.001$) where the younger group (mean: 4.13) was significantly more accurate than the older group (mean: 3.26). A main effect of system was also found ($F(1,50)=17.625$, $p<.001$) where participants were more accurate with Faces (mean: 4.47) than with PIN (mean: 2.91). No interaction effects were found.

For SET 2, we found a main effect of age ($F(1,50)=19.535$, $p<.001$) where the younger group (mean: 4.42) was significantly more accurate than the older group (mean: 3.00). A main effect of system was also found ($F(1,50)=13.690$, $p=.001$) where participants were more accurate with Faces (mean: 4.31) than with PIN (mean: 3.12). A main effect of time was also present ($F(1,50)=15.271$, $p<.001$) showing that participants were significantly less accurate during week 3 (mean: 3.42) than during week 2 (mean: 4.01).

An interaction was found between age and system ($F(1,50)=7.721$, $p>.01$) where the difference in accuracy between the two systems was not significant for the younger group (PIN: 4.28, Faces: 4.57) ($t(52)=1.027$, $p>.01$) while the older group were significantly less accurate with PIN (mean: 1.96) when compared with Faces (mean: 4.05) ($t(52)=4.987$, $p<.001$). In Figures 6 and 7 we plot these results, allowing a visual comparison between performance on the PIN vs. older-face system with younger and older adults.

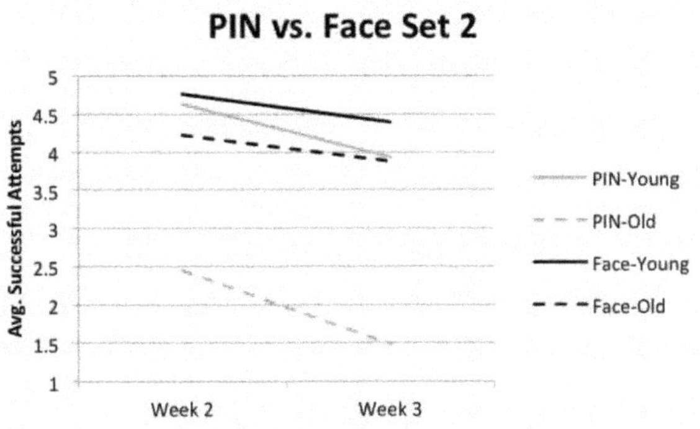

Figure 7: Accuracy of younger and older participants with PIN and Faces (SET 2).

If we look firstly at SET1 (Figure 6) performance, the older adult disadvantage shows up clearly, as does the performance advantage for the face-based GA system – present for both younger and older adults. If we look at SET 2 (Figure 7) data we can see that the initial PIN problems experienced by the older adults have been exacerbated with the addition of a second set of PIN codes, such that their accuracy levels by week 3 are very poor. In contrast, older adults performance with the second set of face codes seems more robust.

GENERAL DISCUSSION

Age is an important issue for designers of authentication systems and in this paper we have provided data on the ways in which specific authentication stimuli can differentially affect performance in younger and older adults. This is a key issue, as the proportion of older adults in the general population is rising and older adults have become the fastest-growing group of Internet users [22]. It is therefore important to consider this population in the design of future, more inclusive authentication systems. We recognise that the total elimination of an age-related performance decrement for authentication will be difficult, given the well-known decline of long-term memory with age [11], but our intention is to explore ways in which we can ameliorate this problem.

Specifically, in this paper we have shown that a face-based GA system using old faces was associated with a significant improvement in older adults' authentication performance. Further, we showed that we could achieve this improvement without unduly penalising performance in the younger adults. Our first conclusion, then, is that the existing Passfaces' database of young faces does not provide an optimal, fully inclusive authentication solution.

In exploring the design space for face-based authentication, we are studying only the tip of the iceberg. In this study we took advantage of a known same-age effect in face recognition [37]. However, it should be noted that the impact of the same-age effect on authentication may be greater than that reported here as the majority of our participants were females and yet the faces in our system were males. Own-gender effects also exist for females where they are better able to recognise female faces over male faces – an effect not present for males [25] and so it is arguable that the best form of inclusive design would either be based on female faces, or would include a gender-matched set of stimuli. This opens up the question of how realistic it may be to employ personalised design in face-based GA involving authentication stimuli that are matched on gender, age or ethnicity

Personalised Authentication

Let us consider an authentication design solution where face-based stimuli are tailored to the specific characteristics of the user. This would arguably be the most appropriate solution if our sole concern is to improve performance across the largest possible user base but we need to consider whether it is also a more secure solution and also consider whether it is realistic as a design aim.

The characteristics of a personalised face-based system would rely on three key user characteristics: the user's age, the user's ethnicity, and the user's gender. In this paper we have focused on an own-age effect that seems to be effective in an authentication context and that is backed up by a vast psychology literature [37]. This literature is also in agreement that people are better able to recognise faces from their own ethnic origin than from other ethnicities [26] and that females are better able to recognise female faces than male faces, suggesting a limited same-gender effect [25]. Note, however, the absence of a recognised same-gender similar effect for males, suggesting that only females would benefit from gender-specific face assignment.

Security

How would such personalised systems impact on the security of an authentication system? By assigning users faces based on personal characteristics that they are particularly sensitive to, there is an argument that the system would be more, rather than less secure, as discrepancies between the face images would be notable and highly salient to that class of user, but not particularly salient to other potential attackers. This would be akin to assigning a mechanic an image of a car engine and having that user select the correct engine from a grid consisting of nine car engines. While the mechanic will be able to differentiate between the nine engines, an untrained user (e.g. a doctor) will not necessarily notice the subtle differences [9]. From a security standpoint, then, a personalised system may disadvantage untrained attackers who would be less likely to pick up on key cues in the stimulus array. Such a personalised system would have the advantage of maximising image discriminability for the individual while maximising perceived image similarity for the general population. Certainly there is an important security issue in ensuring that images in a GA grid are sufficiently similar – Dunphy et al. have shown that visually similar grids are much less vulnerable to description attacks [17].

Are such personalised systems realistic as an inclusive design aim? We believe they are provided that the stimuli are system-generated. This is important for two reasons: firstly it creates a much more tractable design problem in which the system needs to know relatively little about the user in order to generate an appropriate set of GA codes. Secondly, system-generated grids are actually more secure. The literature has many examples of the problems that can follow user-selection of GA codes. For example, example, 90% of black males would chose a black face as part of their security code, which is obviously a problem if the array offers mixed ethnicity. Further, the same author found that the worst 10% of the codes generated by men were available to potential attackers in only two guesses [12]. Users' preferences have been shown to be affected by gender, race and attractiveness, but all of these could be controlled in a system-generated array.

Note that a similar user-generated effect has also been found in click-based graphical authentication schemes. PassPoints has vulnerabilities that arise from structural aspects of visual perception – i.e. users may be strongly attracted to certain "hotspots" within an image which are predictable. Thus the entire system is rendered vulnerable to security attacks [16,31,34]. Security studies are starting to use volunteers via Mechanical Turk in their studies in order to learn more about these common behaviours [38] and one could imagine a scenario where such volunteers inadvertently help criminals by identifying hotpots, faces or images most likely to be selected as user codes.

It is possible, of course, that user privacy concerns may be greater for personalised systems, where the authentication codes themselves could reflect sensitive race, gender or age information about the user. However, we should note that the use of authentication codes in public spaces (such as with an ATM) can lead to observation attacks where both codes and user attributes can be acquired directly.

While user selection may be preferable for memory, it does not solve memory problems such as associating the code with the item to be accessed and may be too big a security cost. For security, system generated codes are required to assure the optimum entropy of a system and we must understand how to maximise the memorability of such codes. With the personalisation of codes, it may be possible to improve security without sacrificing usability

The evaluation paradigm

In this study a new evaluation paradigm was developed that allowed us to explore the effects of age (young vs. old), system (old faces vs. young faces), time (week 1 vs. week 2) and cognitive load (high vs. low) for more than one set of learned codes and with testing taking place over several weeks. This paradigm can be applied to other usable security studies with the purpose of evaluating the effect of multiple codes and we would recommend it, as some of the strongest effects that we observed were absent with the first set of authentication codes learned, but only became manifest once users had to learn a second set – an effect that can be attributed to proactive interference [4] where early learning can have a negative impact upon the subsequent learning of similar material.

Looking at the history of testing new systems, at first new authentication systems were tested only using a single code [6,13,15,39,40]. These studies suggested extraordinary performance gains over existing systems, yet they did not address the major problem affecting current systems – multiple codes. More recently, multiple systems have been tested to provide a more realistic measure of performance [8,19,27]. However, very different methodologies have been used to test both single and multiple codes, making it difficult to compare results across studies. Additionally, many of those recent studies that have employed multiple codes have lacked ecological validity in the way the codes have been assigned.

Participants have been given or have chosen all codes during the same session, while we have split the acquisition of codes to multiple sessions, representing the progressive real-world way users gradually acquire codes to their different accounts.

As we have noted, one advantage of using the paradigm presented here lies in the separation of different code sets in analysis, where it yields short-term and long-term performance data for both 'old' and 'new' codes. This is useful for understanding where the performance decrement is most prominent. Hence, rather than reporting an age effect with a system, we are able to determine where exactly the problem is occurring and relate this more closely to our understanding of the cognitive attributes of a particular user population.

Design Guidelines and Conclusions

In addition to informing more realistic and comparative evaluations of graphical authentication codes, our results have direct implications for the design of graphical authentication systems. To maximise usability of graphical authentications systems and to achieve a balanced approach to security the following guidelines should be considered:

- Use independent non-overlapping codes to remove the association deficit problem (i.e. [29]), although it may only be possible if a central organisation distributes the images;
- Personalise images to maximise memorability (e.g. age, gender and race appropriate faces) as suggested by psychology literature (e.g. [37]) and demonstrated here with age-appropriate faces;
- Use elaboration techniques when learning the graphical image (i.e. ask questions about the image) similar to [6,39];
- Use system generated images to maximise entropy and reduce guessing as previously suggested by [12];
- Employ similar images to reduce guessing and giving away (i.e. [17]).

In this paper we have presented a face-based GA system that gives superior performance for both younger and older adults when compared to a PIN system when the requirement to learn multiple codes was tested over a three-week period. Further, we have shown an effect of the face stimuli themselves, such that older face stimuli would be the better selection for a more inclusive design as they were associated with much more successful authentication performance in older adults. We argue that age-appropriate faces could be a useful development in this design space, but suggest other ways in which personalised design could be used to maximise performance across the entire user population.

REFERENCES

1. Adams, A. and Sasse, M.A. Users are not the enemy. *Communications of the ACM 42*, 12 (1999), 40–46.
2. Anastasi, J.S. and Rhodes, M.G. Evidence for an own-age bias in face recognition. *North American Journal of Psychology 8*, 2 (2006), 237–252.
3. Anastasi, J.S. and Rhodes, M.G. An own-age bias in face recognition for children and older adults. *Psychonomic Bulletin & Review 12*, 6 (2005), 1043–1047.
4. Baddeley, A. and Scott, D. Short term forgetting in the absence of proactive interference. *The Quarterly Journal of Experimental Psychology 23*, 3 (1971), 275–283.
5. Biddle, R., Chiasson, S., and Oorschot, P. Van. Graphical passwords: Learning from the first twelve years. *ACM Computing Surveys (CSUR) 44*, 4 (2012), 1–43.
6. Brostoff, S. and Sasse, M. Are Passfaces more usable than passwords? A field trial investigation. *In Proc. of HCI*, (2000), 405–424.
7. Bruce, V., Burton, M., and Dench, N. What's distinctive about a distinctive face? *The Quarterly Journal of Experimental Psychology Section A 47*, 1 (1994), 119–141.
8. Chiasson, S., Forget, A., Stobert, E., Oorschot, P.C. Van, and Biddle, R. Multiple Password Interference in Text and Click-Based Graphical Passwords. *In Proc. of CCS*, (2009), 500–511.
9. Clancy, S.M. and Hoyer, W.J. Age and skill in visual search. *Developmental Psychology 30*, 4 (1994), 545–552.
10. Craik, F. and Jennings, J. Human Memory. In *The Handbook of Aging and Cognition*. 1992, 51–110.
11. Craik, F. and Bialystok, E. Cognition through the lifespan: mechanisms of change. *Trends in Cognitive Sciences 10*, 3 (2006), 131–138.
12. Davis, D., Monrose, F., and Reiter, M. On user choice in graphical password schemes. *In Proc. of the 13th conference on USENIX Security Symposium-Volume 13*, USENIX Association Berkeley, CA, USA (2004), 11.
13. De Angeli, A., Coutts, M., Coventry, L., Johnson, G., Cameron, D., and Fischer, M. VIP: a visual approach to user authentication. *In Proc. of the WCAVI*, (2002), 316–323.
14. Derwinger, A., Stigsdotter Neely, A., MacDonald, S., and Bäckman, L. Forgetting numbers in old age: strategy and learning speed matter. *Gerontology 51*, 4 (2005), 277–84.
15. Dhamija, R. and Perrig, A. Deja vu: A user study using images for authentication. *In Proc. USENIX Security Symposium*, (2000), 45–48.

16. Dirik, A.E., Memon, N., and Birget, J.-C. Modeling user choice in the PassPoints graphical password scheme. *In Proc. SOUPS*, (2007), 20–28.

17. Dunphy, P., Nicholson, J., and Olivier, P.L. Securing Passfaces for Description. *In Proc. SOUPS*, (2008), 24–35.

18. Ebner, N.C., Riediger, M., and Lindenberger, U. FACES--a database of facial expressions in young, middle-aged, and older women and men: development and validation. *Behavior Research Methods 42*, 1 (2010), 351–62.

19. Everitt, K.M., Bragin, T., Fogarty, J., and Kohno, T. A comprehensive study of frequency, interference, and training of multiple graphical passwords. *In Proc. of CHI*, ACM New York, NY, USA (2009), 889–898.

20. Feldmeier, D. and Karn, P. Unix password security-ten years later. *In Proc. of CRYPTO*, (1990), 1–20.

21. Ferris, S.H., Crook, T., Clark, E., McCarthy, M., and Rae, D. Facial recognition memory deficits in normal aging and senile dementia. *Journal of Gerontology 35*, 5 (1980), 707–14.

22. Hart, T., Chaparro, B., and Halcomb, C. Evaluating websites for older adults: adherence to 'senior-friendly' guidelines and end-user performance. *Behaviour & Information Technology 27*, 3 (2008), 191–199.

23. Ives, B., Walsh, K.R., and Schneider, H. The domino effect of password reuse. *Communications of the ACM 47*, 4 (2004), 75–78.

24. Kausler, D.H., Salthouse, T., and Saults, J.S. Temporal memory over the adult lifespan. *The American Journal of Psychology 101*, 2 (1988), 207–215.

25. Lovén, J., Herlitz, A., and Rehnman, J. Women's own-gender bias in face recognition memory. *Experimental Psychology 58*, 4 (2011), 333–340.

26. Meissner, C. a. and Brigham, J.C. Thirty years of investigating the own-race bias in memory for faces: A meta-analytic review. *Psychology, Public Policy, and Law 7*, 1 (2001), 3–35.

27. Moncur, W. and LePlâtre, G. Pictures at the ATM - Exploring the usability of multiple graphical passwords. *In Proc. of CHI*, (2007), 887–894.

28. Naveh-Benjamin, M., Brav, T.K., and Levy, O. The associative memory deficit of older adults: the role of strategy utilization. *Psychology and Aging 22*, 1 (2007), 202–208.

29. Naveh-Benjamin, M., Hussain, Z., Guez, J., and Bar-On, M. Adult age differences in episodic memory: further support for an associative-deficit hypothesis. *Journal of Experimental Psychology: Learning, Memory, and Cognition 29*, 5 (2003), 826–837.

30. Nelson, D., Reed, V., and Walling, J. Pictorial superiority effect. *Journal of Experimental Psychology: Human Learning and Memory 2*, 5 (1976), 523–528.

31. Oorschot, P.C. van, Salehi-Abari, A., and Thorpe, J. Purely Automated Attacks on PassPoints-Style Graphical Passwords. *IEEE Transactions on Information Forensics and Security 5*, 3 (2010), 393–405.

32. Park, D., Puglisi, J., and Smith, A. Memory for pictures: Does an age-related decline exist? *Journal of Psychology and Aging 1*, 1 (1986), 11–17.

33. Park, D., Royal, D., Dudley, W., and Morrell, R. Forgetting of Pictures Over a Long Retention Interval. *Psychology and Aging 3*, 1 (1988), 94–95.

34. Peach, S., Vorster, J., and Heerden, R. Van. *Heuristic attacks against graphical password generators.* 2010.

35. Pike, G., Kemp, R., and Brace, N. The psychology of human face recognition. *IEE Colloquium on Visual Biometrics*, (2000), 11–17.

36. Rasmussen, M. and Rudmin, F.W. The coming PIN code epidemic: A survey study of memory of numeric security codes. *Electronic Journal of Applied Psychology 6*, 2 (2010), 5–9v.

37. Rhodes, M.G. and Anastasi, J.S. The own-age bias in face recognition: a meta-analytic and theoretical review. *Psychological Bulletin 138*, 1 (2012), 146–74.

38. Thorpe, J. and Oorschot, P. van. Human-seeded attacks and exploiting hot-spots in graphical passwords. *16th USENIX Security Symposium*, (2007), 103–118.

39. Valentine, T. *An evaluation of the Passface personal authentication system.* (Technical Report). London: Goldsmiths College University of London, (1998).

40. Valentine, T. *Memory for Passfaces after a long delay.* (Technical Report). London: Goldsmiths College University of London, (1999).

41. West, R.L., Crook, T.H., and Barron, K.L. Everyday memory performance across the life span: effects of age and noncognitive individual differences. *Psychology and aging 7*, 1 (1992), 72–82.

42. Wiedenbeck, S., Waters, J., Birget, J.-C., Brodskiy, A., and Memon, N. PassPoints: Design and longitudinal evaluation of a graphical password system. *International Journal of Human-Computer Studies 63*, 1-2 (2005), 102–127.

The Presentation of Health-Related Search Results and Its Impact on Negative Emotional Outcomes

Carolyn Lauckner, Gary Hsieh
Communication Arts and Sciences
Michigan State University
laplan13,garyh @msu.edu

ABSTRACT
Searching for health information online has become increasingly common, yet few studies have examined potential negative emotional effects of online health information search. We present results from an experiment manipulating the presentation of search results for common symptoms, which shows that the frequency and placement of serious illness mentions within results can influence perceptions of symptom severity and susceptibility of having the serious illness, respectively. The increase in severity and susceptibility can then lead to higher levels of negative emotional outcomes experienced–including feeling overwhelmed and frightened. Interestingly, health literacy can help reduce perceived symptom severity, and high online health experience actually increases the likelihood that individuals use a frequency-based heuristic. Technological implications and directions for future research are discussed.

Author Keywords
Online health information; negative effects; health literacy

ACM Classification Keywords
H.3.3. Information Search and Retrieval: (search process).

General Terms
Experimentation; Human Factors

INTRODUCTION
Health-related websites generate a significant amount of Internet traffic; Google [14] recently reported that, among the top 1000 websites worldwide, general health-related sites (e.g., nih.gov, webmd.com, medicinenet.com) together have an estimated 117.8 million unique monthly visitors. Separately, WebMD [31] has reported that they receive 111.8 million unique monthly visitors. These statistics corroborate with those found by Pew Internet stating that 80% of Internet users look online for health information, and that it is the third most popular online activity, after checking email and using a search engine [12]. Research has found that 66% of individuals looking for health information begin at a search engine [13], and one analysis of search logs found that about 250 thousand users (about one quarter of the total sample) engaged in a health-related search during an 11-month period [33]. Together, these findings suggest the importance of these tools in determining the content viewed by users.

Viewing online health information has been shown to be helpful for individuals in a variety of ways. Aside from the obvious benefit of providing knowledge, research has found online health information seeking to be associated with feeling more comfortable with information received from a health professional [20, 37], suggesting that it can serve a warranting purpose. Online health content has also had positive effects on medication adherence [24] and ability to make informed healthcare decisions [25]. Among caregivers, it has assisted with problem solving, coping, and communication with health professionals [17].

Yet, while there are clear benefits associated with online health information seeking, can there also be negative consequences of this behavior? A study of cancer patients found that one third felt more confused after reading online cancer information, and nearly one quarter felt more nervous, anxious, or upset [16]. In the general population, health-related Internet use has been found to be associated with increases in depression [4]. This is particularly an issue with college students—the subject population of our study—as about 44% felt confused the last time they searched for health information, 26% felt frustrated, 19% felt overwhelmed, and 15% felt frightened [5].

Due to the important implications associated with health issues and individuals' subsequent emotional involvement, it is not surprising that these effects occur, but it is unclear what makes them more likely to happen. Some research has suggested that the use of search engines may exacerbate these effects through the provision of potentially harmful information [30] or individuals' treating them as diagnostic devices to find medical causes for their symptoms [33]. Additionally, one study found that results from a web search, compared to general online content, give more weight to serious illnesses when individuals search for common symptoms. For example, when they performed a basic web crawl of 40 million pages listed in the Open Directory Project for the term "muscle twitches," the probability of ALS (Lou Gehrig's Disease) being associated with the symptom was 0.07. In contrast, when they did a web search using Microsoft's *Live Search* engine, the probability of ALS appearing among the results was 0.5 [33]. Clearly, search engine results are not a representative sampling of the wider population of content online.

To inform this study, the authors examined search results obtained for the common medical symptoms used in this experiment: headaches, abdominal pain, muscle twitches, and chest pain. Overall, there were several instances of serious illnesses being associated with the symptoms; heart attacks, for example, were mentioned in all of the first ten search results for chest pain. Additionally, appendicitis was mentioned in eight of ten results from an "abdominal pain" search. The frequency of these occurrences suggests that appendicitis is common, but only about 7% of Americans will get appendicitis in their lifetime [15]. Altogether, this brief analysis suggests that consumers are exposed to many instances in which serious illnesses are linked to common symptoms that often have benign causes. This could likely distort perceptions of the threat presented by the symptoms.

Therefore, this study examined how viewing online search results related to symptoms may affect perceptions and outcomes. Specifically, an experiment manipulated the presentation of results mentioning serious illnesses related to the symptoms and assessed effects on perceived symptom severity and susceptibility of experiencing the serious illness. In turn, the relationship of these perceptions to negative emotional outcomes was determined. Overall, the goal was to examine how simple changes in presentation, while keeping informational content consistent, changed outcomes. We found that manipulating the frequency and placement of search results that mention serious illnesses had effects on perceived severity and susceptibility, which both had effects on individuals feeling frightened and overwhelmed. Thus, even if basic information is kept consistent, the presentation of results can have significant effects on perceptions and emotional outcomes.

This paper offers multiple contributions. First, it demonstrates empirically that viewing severe health conditions in search results can indeed influence our negative emotions, such as fear. While this concern associated with using search engines has been speculated, it has never been experimentally demonstrated, to the authors' knowledge. Second, this paper extends research findings related to judgment heuristics and biases to the realm of health information seeking, and highlights the effects of placement and frequency on our perceived severity and susceptibility of severe conditions. Lastly, the findings suggest strategies for search engine developers and users that may help to avoid negative emotional outcomes.

SEARCH ENGINES AND HEURISTIC ASSESSMENTS

Although search engines are common and useful tools for finding health information, they are far from perfect sources. For example, a content analysis of search engine results related to complementary/alternative medicine found that links on the first page were most often commercial, led to pages containing content that could lead to physical harm, and were frequently trying to sell products [30]. Such results demonstrate that many of the highest-ranked pages may not come from unbiased, knowledgeable sources. In addition, search engine results can lead to negative effects by providing information that is inappropriate to the individual users' situation. Research studying "cyberchondria" has found that almost nine out of ten individuals have had experiences in which a web search for basic symptoms led to a review of information on serious illnesses, called an "escalation." In an observation of search logs, about 5% of online searches (about 600 occurrences) for health symptoms escalated into searches for more serious conditions—for example, people who began by searching for a headache eventually searched for brain tumor information [33]. The likelihood of a person having a brain tumor related to a headache is very low, so such an escalation is inappropriate to the situation.

Escalation has been found to occur more often when users see a serious explanation for their symptom before a benign explanation on a web page [34]. This suggests that people may be using cognitive shortcuts, or heuristics, when making judgments about online health information. This heuristic-based browsing has also been empirically demonstrated among women searching for menopausal information online [27]. Although such heuristics can be helpful in sorting through large amounts of information, they can also lead to biases or errors in judgment [28].

Anchoring and Availability Heuristics

In this paper we explore two types of heuristics that may play a role in evaluating results from health searches—*anchoring* and *availability*.

When individuals are operating under the anchoring heuristic, they make estimates of likelihood or probability by starting from an initial value and making subsequent adjustments until they decide on a final estimate. Often, the adjustments people make are inadequate, thus making their estimates biased toward the initial value [28]. In other words, individuals tend to stick with their first impressions, which is easier than thoroughly analyzing each new piece of information uncovered [23]. A study by Peters, Slovic, Hibbard, and Tusler [21, 33] found that different anchors (low vs. high) influenced individual's death estimates; for example, telling participants that 400 people die of appendicitis each year vs. 40,000 people dying of kidney disease led to lower death estimates for other conditions. Such studies suggest that this anchoring effect does indeed hold in the health realm. For this study, it is predicted that, if individuals first see a result mentioning a serious condition, they will form an initial impression that the symptom is severe, which will lead to a bias in their overall opinions of severity:

H1a: The placement of results discussing serious health conditions will have an effect on perceived symptom severity, such that when serious conditions are mentioned at the top of the results list, individuals will have higher perceptions of symptom severity.

Additionally, this study seeks to examine the role of online health information in bringing about negative emotional outcomes, as previous research has demonstrated can occur. It is suggested that, the more severe an individual perceives a symptom to be, the more threatening the symptom will be, which is a key premise of the extended parallel process model [35]. Because of a high level of threat, individuals will experience negative emotional outcomes (including feeling frightened and overwhelmed). The following hypothesis captures this prediction:

H1b: Perceptions of symptom severity will be positively related to reported negative emotional outcomes.

When individuals are operating under the availability heuristic, they are making judgments of the frequency, probability, or likelihood of an event based on how easy it is to recall instances or occurrences. The easier it is to think of examples of an event, the higher the perceived likelihood of the event occurring [28]. Researchers have discussed the role that this heuristic may play in medical decision-making. For example, Redelmeier [23] argues that, when doctors determine diagnoses, it is much more convenient (and often more appropriate) to make judgments based on one's past experiences with a given health condition than it is to memorize probabilities or epidemiological statistics. Among non-medical professionals, media mentions of cancer have been found to increase individuals' perceptions of risk and their subsequent cancer screenings [6, 11]. In these cases, it is likely that, because individuals heard about cancer more often and were thus able to think of more examples of diagnoses, their estimated likelihood of diagnosis increased.

Our hypothesis draws upon this availability heuristic, suggesting that the frequency of serious illness mentions within search results will provide more examples that a user can bring to mind, which will in turn affect their perceived likelihood of experiencing that serious illness. Specifically, it is predicted that the more often a serious illness associated with a given symptom is mentioned in the search results, the higher individuals' perceived susceptibility of experiencing the illness will be. This hypothesis is presented as follows:

H2a: The frequency of results discussing serious health conditions will have an effect on perceived susceptibility, such that serious conditions discussed frequently will lead to higher perceptions of susceptibility toward those conditions.

Because a higher level of susceptibility toward a serious condition is likely to heighten perceptions of threat, it is also predicted that higher susceptibility will lead to more negative emotional outcomes [35]:

H2b: Perceived susceptibility of the serious health condition will be positively related to reported negative emotional outcomes.

In addition to heuristics, other personal factors may play a role in how people interpret search results. Two of these factors, health literacy and online health experience, were of special interest to this study and will be discussed in the following section.

Factors Impacting the Effects of Online Information Seeking

Conflicting results have been found about the role of online health information seeking experience on individuals' responses to online health information. Research has demonstrated that individuals who have a better understanding of online health information are more likely to use the Internet, over a doctor, as their primary source [18]. Additionally, individuals who have engaged in frequent health searches are less likely to judge search results for health topics as relevant to their initial queries, suggesting that they may be more critical of the results retrieved [19]. To explore the role of online health experience on individuals' responses to health-related search results, the following research question is posed:

RQ1: Does the extent of experience with online health information moderate the relationships between placement and severity and frequency and susceptibility?

Another quality that has been shown to have an effect on individuals' responses to health information is their overall health literacy, which has been defined as "a constellation of skills, including the ability to perform basic reading and numerical tasks required to function in the health care environment" [20]. Low health literacy has been linked to greater levels of distress [26], lower self-efficacy for screening behaviors, lower information seeking [29], lower knowledge regarding cancer, and more negative attitudes toward screening [8]. Given these effects, it seems likely that health literacy may have an impact on the way that people interpret health information from search engines, which is why the following research question was posed:

RQ2: Does health literacy moderate the relationships between placement and severity and frequency and susceptibility?

To test these hypotheses and research questions, a within-subjects experimental design was employed that explored individuals' perceptions of and reactions to search results about various symptoms. The details of this method are described in the following section.

METHOD

We conducted a 2x2 within-subjects experiment, in which we manipulated the presentation of health-related search results for four different symptoms: abdominal pain, chest pain, muscle twitches, and headaches. Manipulations changed the frequency (frequent vs. sparse) and placement (top vs. bottom) of serious illness mentions within the results list in order to study differential effects on outcomes.

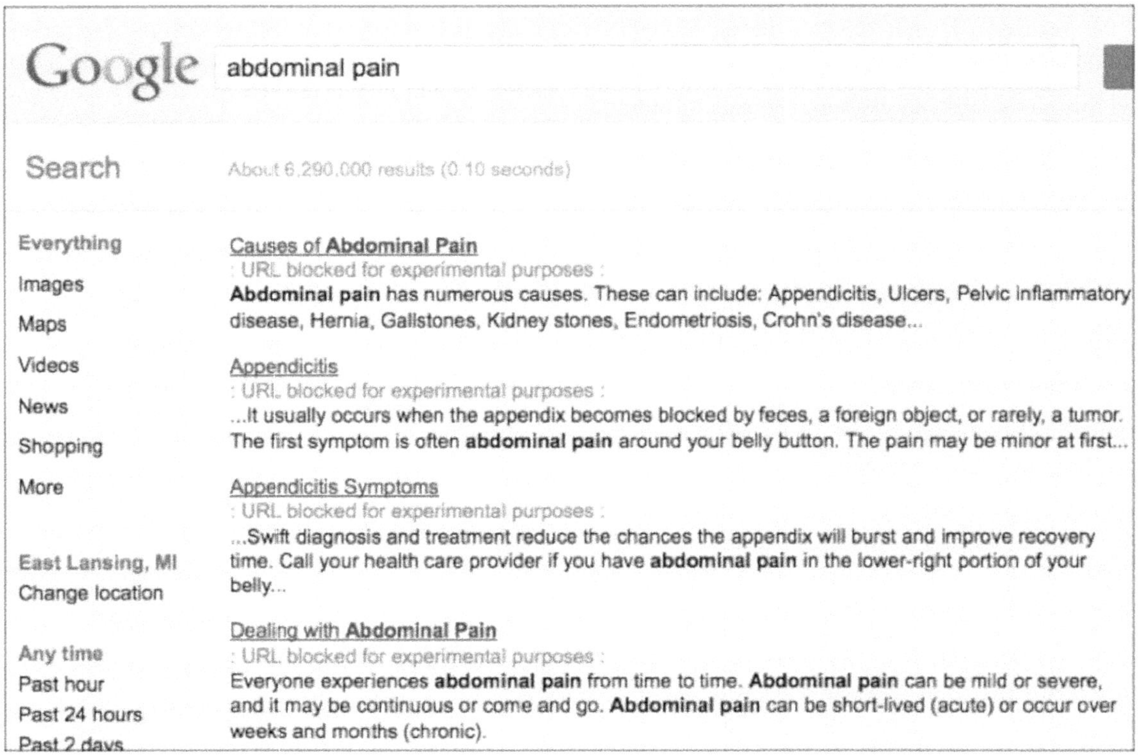

Figure 1. Example search results page

Recruitment and Participants

Participants were recruited from undergraduate communication courses at a large Midwestern university. In exchange for their participation, respondents were given course credit. 310 participants were recruited, but the final sample (N=274) contained only those who completed the entire experiment. The average age of respondents was 20, and 48.4% of respondents were female.

College students frequently engage in online health information seeking; studies have found that about 75% of students have viewed health information online [10, 12]. Additionally, studies have shown that college students are susceptible to negative emotions arising from health information seeking [5]. These reactions, combined with the well-documented anxiety, depression, and stress experienced by college students [3], suggest that viewing online health information could exacerbate negative psychological states in an already-fragile population. Thus, they are an interesting population to study in this context.

Study Setup

Participants completed the study online. They were instructed to place themselves in the mindset of someone experiencing a symptom (headaches, chest pain, muscle twitches, and abdominal pain) who was looking for information as to the potential cause. Importantly, the majority of participants had, at some point, experienced each of the four symptoms of concern to this study: 89.7% had experienced a headache, 77.2% had experienced abdominal pain, 77.6% had experienced muscle twitches, and 65.4% had experienced chest pain. This suggests that they were likely able to place themselves in the correct mindset and adds to the validity of this experimental set-up. Participants were then presented with a search results page for the symptom. The results page looked exactly like a Google search with 10 links, but links to anything other than the results were disabled (see Figure 1). Additionally, though it was hosted on a non-Google domain, the results page was placed in a JavaScript frame within the survey that prevented participants from seeing the URL, thus maintaining some realism. Participants were encouraged to click on the search results and read the information carefully to diagnose their symptoms.

The search results and linked pages were created for the study. Content was paraphrased from trusted websites (e.g., nih.gov, mayoclinic.org). Additionally, the design of these pages was kept simple to avoid design effects, but varied slightly from page to page in order to preserve some realism. Figure 2 shows an example of one of these pages.

Study Manipulations

Each symptom scenario was randomly paired with one of our 2 x 2 conditions—varying the frequency and the placement of the results mentioning serious illnesses in its title or short description (see Figure 3). Each symptom was consistently associated with one serious illness or condition: chest pain with a heart attack, abdominal pain with appendicitis, muscle twitches with ALS (Lou Gehrig's disease), and headaches with brain tumors.

Importantly, the actual content of the linked pages was kept the same across conditions. For example, every page

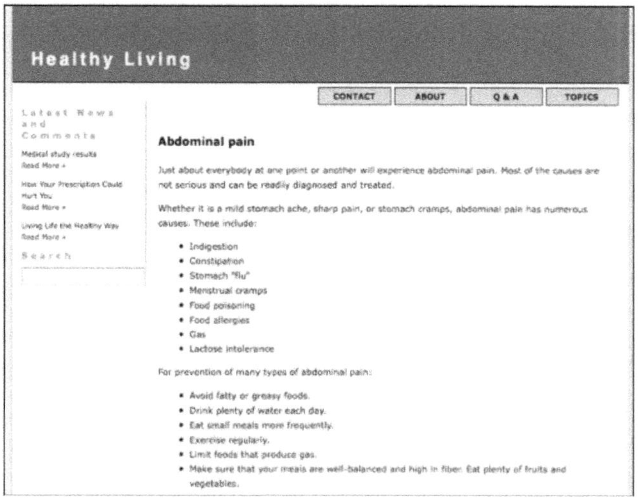

Figure 2. Example health content page

mentioning brain tumors said that they were rare, but some conditions presented such pages more often or at different places in the results list. Thus, if readers made judgments based solely on the information they read, they should arrive at the same conclusions regardless of condition.

Measures

After each symptom scenario, respondents were asked to what extent viewing the health information made them feel overwhelmed or frightened (7-point Likert scale from "not at all" to "very much"). These questions, chosen to ensure high face validity, have been used by in previous research [5, 13]. Additionally, participants were asked about their perceptions of severity and susceptibility using 6 items based on the Risk Behavior Diagnosis scale [36], listed in Table 1. The severity scale had high reliability (Cronbach's alpha=0.93), and the average of the three items was calculated to form a composite variable. The third item in the susceptibility scale was dropped due to poor reliability, which resulted in a scale with good reliability (Cronbach's alpha=0.76). These items were averaged to create a composite variable.

After all the conditions were viewed, respondents were asked about their history of viewing online health information (see Table 1), their health status, how often they experienced each of the four symptoms, and their demographic information. Last, their health literacy was assessed using the Newest Vital Sign (NVS) [22], a six-item tool (5 yes/no, 1 open-ended) that has been shown to have good reliability and validity [32]. The open- ended item in the NVS was dropped for this study to simplify analysis, and a composite health literacy score was created by adding up the number of correct answers (maximum score=5).

Variable Measured	Survey Items (7-pt Likert scale: from "not at all" to "very much")
Severity	[Symptom] is a serious symptom
	[Symptom] is harmful
	[Symptom] is a severe threat
Susceptibility	If I have [symptom], I am at risk for having [serious condition]
	It is likely that I have [serious condition] if I experience [symptom]
	[Symptom] is nothing to worry about. (reverse coded)
Online Health Experience	How often do you view health information online?

Table 1. Example survey questions

		Serious Illness Frequency	
		Sparse (3/10)	*Frequent (7/10)*
Serious Illness Placement	*End of search results*	Condition 1: 3 serious illness mentions, placed in the last 3 results on the page	Condition 2: 7 serious illness mentions, placed in the last 7 results on the page
	Beginning of search results	Condition 3: 3 serious illness mentions, placed in the first 3 results on the page	Condition 4: 7 serious illness mentions, placed in the first 7 results on the page

Figure 3. Explication of Study Conditions

Data Analysis

To analyze these data, mixed-model Analysis of Covariance (ANCOVA) was used. Before running any tests, variables that had non-normal distributions (i.e., susceptibility, frightened, and overwhelmed) were transformed by computing their square root values in order to correct for skewness. In all analyses, participant was treated as a random effect to account for potential correlation between responses due to the within-subjects design. The effects of anchoring and availability on severity and susceptibility (H1a and H2a) were tested with three predictors: placement and frequency, which were both binary variables reflecting the different manipulations, and their interaction. All of these variables were included in analyses to account for the non-independent nature of frequency and placement, which were both present in each condition.

These composite measures of susceptibility and severity were also used as predictors in the tests of H1b and H2b, testing their effects on potential negative outcomes (i.e.., frightened, overwhelmed). Similarly, participant was treated as a random effect due to repeated measures.

To test RQ1, the following predictors were used: frequency, placement, the interaction between frequency and placement, and experience with online health information (a binary variable, as a result of a median split). Additionally, the interaction between placement and online health experience was added to test effects on severity, and the interaction between frequency and online health experience was added to test effects on susceptibility. RQ2 was tested in the same manner, except a binary variable for health literacy was used (also as a result of a median split) instead of online health experience.

To explore the causal chain of the effects of placement and frequency on negative emotions, a path analysis, a statistical method of structural equation modeling, was used. The AMOS 20.0 program was employed to obtain maximum-likelihood estimates of the model parameters, and the model was edited until reasonable model fit was obtained. In these analyses, frequency and placement were treated as exogenous variables, while susceptibility, severity, and the two negative outcomes were endogenous variables. Additionally, two control variables, individual subjective health rating (ranging from "poor" to "excellent") and the order in which participants saw each condition, were added in as exogenous variables. Goodness-of-fit index (GFI) was used to assess model fit.

RESULTS

To assess the level of participation and adherence to the study directions, logs of participants' actions were collected. Overall, participants clicked on an average of 14 links (35% of all possible links) and spent an average of 101 seconds on each link. Though these data show that the participants typically did not view every line of text in the study, they do show a reasonable level of engagement.

Hypothesis 1: Placement, Severity, and Outcomes

H1a predicted that placement of results discussing serious illnesses would have an effect on perceived severity. Our analysis supported this hypothesis, as there was a significant effect of placement on perceived severity, $F(1, 813) = 20.94$, $p < .001$. Means are displayed in Table 2. H1b predicted that perceived severity would be associated with negative outcomes. Results also supported this hypothesis. Perceived severity was positively associated with feeling frightened ($F(1, 1059.08) = 201.62$, $p < .001$) and overwhelmed ($F(1, 1000.12)=47.68$, $p < .001$).

Hypothesis 2: Frequency, Susceptibility, and Outcomes

H2a predicted that frequency of results mentioning a serious illness would have an effect on perceived susceptibility. Our analysis supported this hypothesis, as frequency had a significant effect on susceptibility, $F(1, 813)=5.50$, $p = .02$. Means are displayed in Table 2. H2b predicted that perceived susceptibility would be positively related to negative outcomes. Overall, this hypothesis was supported. Perceived susceptibility was positively related to feeling frightened ($F(1, 1084.89) = 94.45$, $p < .001$) and overwhelmed ($F(1, 1036.55) = 23.08$, $p < .001$).

	Susceptibility Mean (SE)
Frequency	
Low	3.17(.06)
High	3.32 (.06)
Health Literacy	
Low	3.44 (.08)
High	3.16 (.05)
	Severity Mean (SE)
Placement	
Last	3.66 (.06)
First	4.00 (.07)
Health Literacy	
Low	4.05 (.08)
High	3.73 (.05)

Table 2. Means and Standard Errors

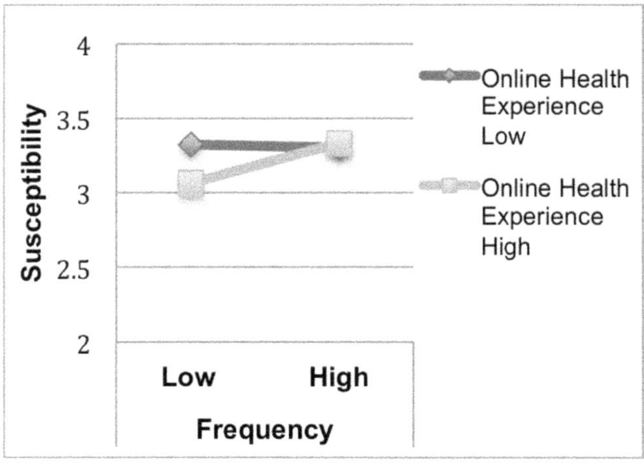

Figure 4. Moderating effect of online health experience

RQ1: Online Health Experience as a Moderator

RQ1 explored the moderating effects of online health experience on the relationships between placement and severity and between frequency and susceptibility. Online health experience did not have a statistically significant effect on severity, and the interaction between placement and online health experience was not significant. In the relationship between frequency and susceptibility, experience with online health information did not have a significant main effect on susceptibility. However, the interaction between frequency and online health experience was significant, $F(1, 813) = 4.39$, $p < .04$. For those with low experience in viewing online health information, frequency of serious illness mentions had little to no effect. Among those with high online health experience, however, frequency had an effect in the predicted direction: the more serious illness mentions, the higher the perceived susceptibility. This relationship is illustrated in Figure 4.

RQ2: Health Literacy as a Moderator

RQ2 explored the moderating effect of health literacy on the relationship between placement and severity and frequency and susceptibility. Health literacy had a statistically significant effect on severity, $F(1, 270) = 6.01$, $p < .02$. The interaction between placement and health literacy was not significant, however. Health literacy did not have a statistically significant effect on susceptibility, nor was the interaction between frequency and health literacy significant. Means are displayed in Table 2.

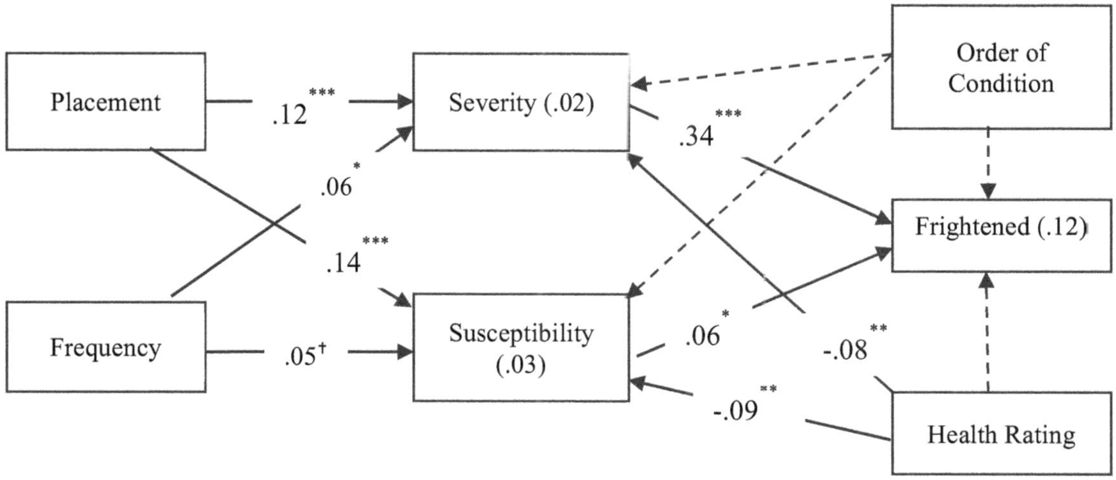

Note: Only significant coefficients are presented. All the coefficients are standardized. R^2 for each endogenous variable is reported in the parentheses. † < .10, *p < .05, ** p < .01, *** p <.001

Figure 5. Exploratory Path Analysis: Standardized Coefficients and Multiple Correlations

Exploratory Analysis: Path Model

Up to this point, we have shown that frequency and placement can affect severity and susceptibility and that severity and susceptibility correlate with negative emotions. In order to further examine the causal chain from frequency and placement to negative emotions, as well as to address the small *F* values associated with several variables (e.g., frequency), multiple iterations of a path model were tested. The model presented here has an acceptable fit, with GFI=0.90 (Figure 5). Overall, this model explained 12% of the variance in individuals' levels of fright. Results showed that frequency has a small, weakly-significant effect on both severity and susceptibility. Comparatively, placement had much stronger effects on both severity and susceptibility. An individual's subjective health rating had a significant negative effect on both susceptibility and severity, but not on their level of fright. The order in which an individual saw a given condition was not found to be significantly associated with any of the variables.

DISCUSSION

Heuristic-Based Browsing and its Effects

This study examined the effects that the presentation of search results for medical symptoms has on individuals' perceptions and their reactions. Results indicated that, even when informational content is kept consistent, the frequency and placement of serious illness mentions on a search results page can have an effect on perceived susceptibility and severity. Additionally, perceived severity and susceptibility were positively associated with feeling frightened and overwhelmed after viewing the search results.

The hypothesized mechanisms behind these negative responses are anchoring and availability heuristics, and the results lend support to research that has found that users rely on heuristic processing when viewing search results [27]. Users are not attending to the content enough to make judgments based on the information alone. Instead, they are relying on cues provided in the link titles and page text. This is concerning, as our pre-study analyses of Google's search results, as well as previous research [33], have shown that serious illnesses are over-represented within search results, especially those found on the first page. Based on the findings of this study, one could extrapolate that individuals viewing *actual* search results for their own symptoms are forming perceptions of symptom severity and susceptibility of having a serious illness that are more inflated than the actual incidence rates would suggest. These perceptual effects alone are significant, as they demonstrate the potential cognitive inaccuracies resulting from viewing search results. This could lead to persisting beliefs about the associated symptoms that may resurface every time they are encountered by the individual. These perceptions of severity and susceptibility, as we found in our study, would then likely lead to negative emotions for these individuals. This is in line with previous research on threat, which is composed of perceived severity and susceptibility and has been shown to lead to fear arousal [35].

It is important to note that the statistical results showed relatively small effects, but this is likely the result of the subtle nature of the experimental manipulations. Overall, placement of serious illness mentions accounted for 12% of the variance in severity and 14% of the variance in susceptibility. Considering the increasing frequency with which individuals search for online health information, even just 12% of variance explained translates to large groups of individuals. Additionally, although negative outcomes were present to a certain degree in this study, respondents did not report strong feelings in response to the search results. In general, respondents were not highly frightened (*M*=3.16, *SD*=1.71) or overwhelmed (*M*=3.38, *SD*=1.72). It is likely that this was also a product of the experimental design, as individuals were simply asked to place themselves in the mindset of someone who had experienced the symptom at hand. Low involvement and relevance may have led to the weak reactions. However, observation studies using participants with high involvement in the health topic have found that such users still use heuristic processing [27]. Thus, it is likely that the findings from this study would be replicated in such populations and individuals would experience even stronger negative emotions due to the real-life implications of the content they encounter. Our findings highlight the need for additional research examining negative emotional outcomes stemming from online health information behaviors.

Investigating the Causal Chain

Our path analysis revealed that, after controlling for an individual's health status and the order in which they saw the various conditions, the tested variables explained about 12% of the variance in levels of fright. Additionally, the path analysis showed that the placement of serious illness mentions had a much stronger effect than frequency. A potential explanation is that study participants mainly looked at links above the fold of the results page. This is consistent with the logs from this study, which showed that individuals clicked on approximately four links per condition—which is about how many were visible above the fold. Thus, the effects of frequency were limited because, by not attending to all the links, the manipulations were not fully apparent. However, the placement manipulations of serious illnesses were always visible, even if they did not look at all the links on the page. This interpretation is in line with previous research, which has found that users focus much more attention on the first few links in a search results page than on links further down the list [7]. Overall, these results demonstrate that placement of serious illness mentions within search results is a much more important factor when it comes to influencing individual perceptions.

Effects of Health Literacy and Online Health Experience

Another interesting finding of this research is the interaction between experience with online health information and frequency of serious illness mentions. When serious illnesses were mentioned sparingly, individuals with high levels of online health experience had lower perceptions of susceptibility than when mentions were frequent. This suggests that they were more sensitive to the cues we manipulated within the results. The reasons why this occurred are unclear, particularly because we anticipated that individuals with more experience would be *less* susceptible to the experimental manipulations, simply due to more exposure to online health content. It may be the case that these individuals have had to develop tactics over time for sorting through the immense amount of health information online. In other words, they have grown to rely on heuristic cues as a means of saving time during their browsing sessions.

Interestingly, individuals with low levels of online health experience had virtually the same scores on perceived susceptibility across conditions. The mean scores show that, on average, individuals with low experience had higher scores of perceived susceptibility (M=3.32, SD=1.40) than individuals with high levels of experience (M=3.20, SD=1.40). Perhaps individuals with low online health experience are simply alarmed by *any* mention of serious illnesses, as they are not accustomed to the presence of such content in relation to seemingly innocuous symptoms. Conversely, individuals with more experience in online health may have trained themselves to be more skeptical of online content. Further research should explore the mechanisms by which experienced vs. inexperienced online health users form perceptions of online content, as this could help to target websites toward specific users.

Although health literacy did not have a moderating effect, it did have a significant and negative relationship to severity. Regardless of condition, individuals with low health literacy had higher perceptions of symptom severity. As previous research has demonstrated that low health literacy is associated with lower knowledge [8] and information seeking [29] regarding health issues, it may be the case that these individuals did not have contextual knowledge regarding the likelihood of serious illnesses being related to common symptoms. Thus, overall, their perceptions of the severity of a given symptom may have been inflated. Conversely, individuals with high health literacy likely had an increased ability to assess likelihood based on the information they read, as well as more general knowledge regarding the health issues at hand. This, in turn, helped them to see past the heuristic cues and "correct" for potentially inflated perceptions of the likelihood of the serious illnesses occurring. Such findings highlight the importance of educating individuals to develop their health literacy skills so that they may better interpret health information both online and offline.

Technological Implications

These findings have important implications for the presentation of health-related search results. Developers of search engines may, in the future, develop algorithms to determine when users are searching for health information, and tailor the results page to help educate the users about search results. For example, a simple warning could be placed alongside the results telling users to read content carefully and contact a health provider with any concerns. Or, Google could direct users to their custom search engine for health topics, which searches only the 50 most reliable websites to ensure that search results are trustworthy [1]. This may not mitigate all negative effects, but can help to avoid users encountering results that inaccurately portray risk information.

Interestingly, since this study was conducted, Google has started providing "related searches" at the top of the results page for some health symptoms. For example, Figure 6 shows the related searches for one of the symptoms used in this study, muscle twitches. Many muscle twitches are benign, and can be caused by diet deficiencies, caffeine, stress, or exercise [9]—however, this is not reflected in

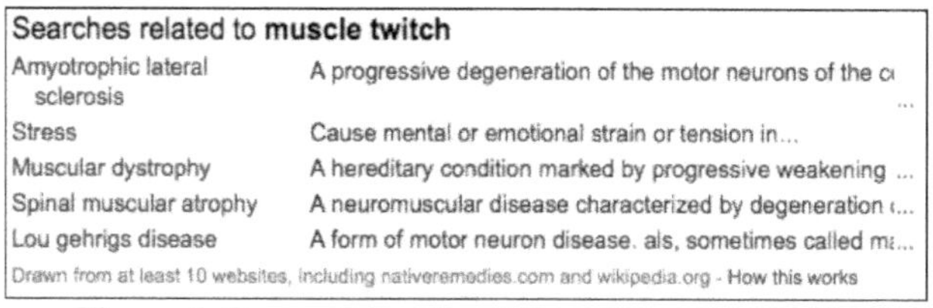

Searches related to **muscle twitch**	
Amyotrophic lateral sclerosis	A progressive degeneration of the motor neurons of the c ...
Stress	Cause mental or emotional strain or tension in...
Muscular dystrophy	A hereditary condition marked by progressive weakening ...
Spinal muscular atrophy	A neuromuscular disease characterized by degeneration ...
Lou gehrigs disease	A form of motor neuron disease. als, sometimes called m...

Drawn from at least 10 websites, including nativeremedies.com and wikipedia.org - How this works

Figure 6. Current display of Google search results

these related searches. These suggest that twitches are associated with serious conditions, including ALS (Lou Gehrig's disease) and muscular dystrophy. Based on our results, because these are placed at the top of the page, this may lead to more negative effects among users. Thus, this strategy may need to be re-considered if optimal outcomes are to be achieved and negative reactions are to be avoided.

Some website developers have sought to accommodate individuals with low health literacy levels when developing content [2], which, based on our study, could help mitigate some negative emotional outcomes. In addition, search engines may consider including educational support in interpreting the search results page in order to offset some of the more popular judgment heuristics, such as availability and anchoring. However, health information search is a complex process and our findings have highlighted the need for additional research to better improve existing search engines to support our various health-related needs.

LIMITATIONS AND GENERALIZABILITY

The use of the college student population for this study raises concerns of generalizability because young people tend to have fewer health problems than older populations. This was especially apparent as related to the symptom of chest pain, which only around 60% of the participants had actually experienced. Research with more diverse individuals is needed for studying this topic and will help to better reflect the experiences of the average online health information seeker.. Additionally, while our experimental approach allowed us to specifically test the effects of placement and frequency, it did come at the cost of realism. Future studies should build on this research to confirm our findings in less controlled but more realistic field settings and with different population groups. It is important, however, to consider the ethical implications of such research: manipulating information related to symptoms in order to induce specific emotional effects is potentially problematic if individuals are actually experiencing the symptom. For example, if a person with a headache reads that it may be a sign of a brain tumor, they may experience significant emotional trauma or distress. Future studies should consider the consequences of such research and seek creative ways of examining this phenomenon without causing harm to participants. Last, the measures used to assess emotions were simplistic, with only one question included for each emotion. This was done in order to reduce participant burnout and to increase face validity, but it may have limited the robustness of our analysis. The measures of severity and susceptibility were validated, however, and represent significant results in and of themselves.

CONCLUSION

This experimental research has demonstrated that the presentation of search results related to health symptoms can affect individuals' impressions. This study has furthered research in this area by not only examining negative effects, which are often overlooked in research, but by also examining specific features of search results that can affect perceptions. The presence of serious illnesses at the beginning of a search results page for a common symptom, as well as a high frequency of serious illness mentions, can lead to increased perceptions of threat. In turn, this leads to negative emotional responses. In many cases, these perceptions are inflated and the reactions are unfounded if one considers the actual incidence rates of serious conditions. This study, and future research, can help to eliminate factors that cause fear and other negative outcomes when they are inappropriate, with the ultimate goal of making online health information viewing as helpful as possible.

REFERENCES

1. Google Custom Search: Health Search Engine. http://www.google.com/cse/home?cx=010964806533120826279:7vbttpkazxm
2. Bastian, H. Health literacy and patient information: Developing the methodology for a national evidence-based health website. *Patient Education and Counseling*, *73*, 3 (2008), 551-556.
3. Bayram, N. and Bilgel, N. The prevalence and socio-demographic correlations of depression, anxiety and stress among a group of university students. *Social Psychictry and Psychiatric Epidemiology*, *43*, 8 (2008), 667-672.
4. Bessiere, K., Pressman, S., Kiesler, S. and Kraut, R. Effects of internet use on health and depression: a longitudinal study. *Journal of Medical Internet Research*, *12*, 1 (2010).
5. Buhi, E. R., Daley, E. M., Fuhrmann, H. J. and Smith, S. A. An observational study of how young people search for online sexual health information. *Journal of American College Health*, *58*, 2 (2009), 101-111.
6. Cram, P., Fendrick, A. M., Inadomi, J., Cowen, M. E., Carpenter, D. and Vijan, S. The impact of a celebrity promotional campaign on the use of colon cancer screening: the Katie Couric effect. *Archives of Internal Medicine*, *163*, 13 (2003), 1601.
7. Cutrell, E. and Guan, Z. What are you looking for?: an eye-tracking study of information usage in web search. In *Proc., CHI 2002*, ACM (2007), 407-416.
8. Dolan, N. C., Ferreira, M. R., Davis, T. C., Fitzgibbon, M. L., Rademaker, A., Liu, D., Schmitt, B. P., Gorby, N., Wolf, M. and Bennett, C. L. Colcrectal cancer screening knowledge, attitudes, and beliefs among veterans: Does literacy make a difference? *Journal of Clinical Oncology*, *22*, 13 (2004), 2617-2622

9. Dugdale, D. C. Muscle twitching. http://www.nlm.nih.gov/medlineplus/ency/article/003296.htm.
10. Escoffery, C., Miner, K. R., Adame, D. D., Butler, S., McCormick, L. and Mendell, E. Internet Use for Health Information Among College Students. *Journal of American College Health*, *53*, 4 (2005), 183-188.
11. Fiandt, K., Pullen, C. and Walker, S. Actual and perceived risk for chronic illness in rural older women. *Clinical excellence for nurse practitioners: the international journal of NPACE*, *3*, 2 (1999), 105.
12. Fox, S. Health topics. http://www.pewinternet.org/Reports/2011/HealthTopics.aspx
13. Fox, S. Online health search 2006. http://www.pewinternet.org/Reports/2006/Online-Health-Search-2006.aspx
14. The 1000 most-visited sites on the web. http://www.google.com/adplanner/static/top1000/#.
15. Hardin, D. M. Acute appendicitis: Review and update. *American Family Physician*, *60*, 7 (1999), 2027-2034.
16. Helft, P. R., Eckles, R. E., Johnson-Calley, C. S. and Daugherty, C. K. Use of the Internet to obtain cancer information among cancer patients at an urban county hospital. *Journal of Clinical Oncology*, *23*, 22 (2005), 4954-4962
17. Kinnane, N. and Milne, D. The role of the Internet in supporting and informing carers of people with cancer: a literature review. *Supportive Care in Cancer*, *18*, 9 (2010), 1123-1136.
18. Knapp, C., Madden, V., Marcu, M., Wang, H., Curtis, C., Sloyer, P. and Shenkman, E. Information seeking behaviors of parents whose children have life-threatening illnesses. *Pediatric Blood & Cancer*, *56*, 5 (2011), 805-811.
19. Lopes, C. T. and Ribeiro, C. Context effect on query formulation and subjective relevance in health searches. In *Proc. IIiX 2010*, ACM Press (2010), 205-214.
20. Parker, R. M., Williams, M. V., Weiss, B. D., Baker, D. W., Davis, T. C., Doak, C. C., Doak, L. G., Hein, K., Meade, C. D. and Nurss, J. Health literacy-Report of the Council on Scientific Affairs. *Journal of the American medical association*, *281*, 6 (1999), 552-557.
21. Peters, E., Slovic, P., Hibbard, J. H. and Tusler, M. Why worry? Worry, risk perceptions, and willingness to act to reduce medical errors. *Health Psychology*, *25*, 2 (2006), 144.
22. The Newest Vital Sign: A health literacy assessment tool. http://www.pfizerhealthliteracy.com/asset/pdf/NVS_Eng/files/nvs_flipbook_english_final.pdf
23. Redelmeier, D. A. The cognitive psychology of missed diagnoses. *Annals of internal medicine*, *142*, 2 (2005), 115-120.
24. Samal, L., Saha, S., Chander, G., Korthuis, P. T., Sharma, R. K., Sharp, V., Cohn, J., Moore, R. D. and Beach, M. C. Internet health information seeking behavior and antiretroviral adherence in persons living with HIV/AIDS. *AIDS Patient Care and STDs*, *25*, 7 (2011), 445-449.
25. Seckin, G. Cyber patients surfing the medical web: Computer-mediated medical knowledge and perceived benefits. *Computers in Human Behavior*, *26*, 6 (2010), 1694-1700.
26. Sharp, L. K., Zurawski, J. M., Roland, P. Y., O'Toole, C. and Hines, J. Health literacy, cervical cancer risk factors, and distress in low-income African-American women seeking colposcopy. *Ethnicity and Disease*, *12*, 4 (2002), 541-546.
27. Sillence, E., Briggs, P., Harris, P. R. and Fishwick, L. How do patients evaluate and make use of online health information? *Social Science &; Medicine*, *64*, 9 (2007), 1853-1862.
28. Tversky, A. and Kahneman, D. Judgment under uncertainty: Heuristics and biases. *Science*, *185*, 4157 (1974), 1124-1131.
29. von Wagner, C., Semmler, C., Good, A. and Wardle, J. Health literacy and self-efficacy for participating in colorectal cancer screening: The role of information processing. *Patient Education and Counseling*, *75*, 3 (2009), 352-357.
30. Walji, M., Sagaram, S., Sagaram, D., Meric-Bernstam, F., Johnson, C., Mirza, Q. N. and Bernstam, V. E. Efficacy of quality criteria to identify potentially harmful information: A cross-sectional survey of complementary and alternative medicine web sites. *Journal of Medical Internet Research*, *6*, 2 (2004), e21
31. WebMD announces fourth quarter and year end financial results. http://investor.shareholder.com/wbmd/releasedetail.cfm?ReleaseID=651179&CompanyID=WBMD
32. Weiss, B. D., Mays, M. Z., Martz, W., Castro, K. M., DeWalt, D. A., Pignone, M. P., Mockbee, J. and Hale, F. A. Quick assessment of literacy in primary care: The Newest Vital Sign. *The Annals of Family Medicine*, *3*, 6 (2005), 514-522.
33. White, R. W. and Horvitz, E. Cyberchondria: studies of the escalation of medical concerns in web search. *ACM Transactions on Information Systems (TOIS)*, *27*, 4 (2009), 23.
34. White, R. W. and Horvitz, E. Predicting escalations of medical queries based on web page structure and content. In *Proc. SIGIR 2010*, ACM Press (2010), 769-770.
35. Witte, K. Fear control and danger control: A test of the extended parallel process model (EPPM). *Communications Monographs*, *61*, 2 (1994), 113-134.
36. Witte, K., Meyer, G. and Martell, D. *Effective health risk messages: A step-by-step guide*. Sage Publications, Inc, 2001.
37. Ybarra, M. and Suman, M. Reasons, assessments and actions taken: Sex and age differences in uses of Internet health information. *Health Education Research*, *23*, 3 (2008), 512-521.

Age-Related Differences in Performance with Touchscreens Compared to Traditional Mouse Input

Leah Findlater[1], Jon E. Froehlich[2], Kays Fattal[1], Jacob O. Wobbrock[3], Tanya Dastyar[2]

[1] College of Information Studies | HCIL, University of Maryland, College Park, MD

[2] Dept. of Computer Science | HCIL, University of Maryland, College Park, MD

[3] The Information School | DUB, University of Washington, Seattle, WA

{leahkf@umd.edu, jonf@cs.umd.edu, kfattal@umd.edu, wobbrock@uw.edu, tdastyar@gmail.com}

ABSTRACT

Despite the apparent popularity of touchscreens for older adults, little is known about the psychomotor performance of these devices. We compared performance between older adults and younger adults on four desktop and touchscreen tasks: pointing, dragging, crossing and steering. On the touchscreen, we also examined pinch-to-zoom. Our results show that while older adults were significantly slower than younger adults in general, the touchscreen reduced this performance gap relative to the desktop and mouse. Indeed, the touchscreen resulted in a significant movement time reduction of 35% over the mouse for older adults, compared to only 16% for younger adults. Error rates also decreased.

Author Keywords

Older adults; input; touchscreens; accessibility.

ACM Classification Keywords

H.5.2 [Information interfaces and presentation]: User interfaces - *input devices & strategies*.

INTRODUCTION

The potential of touchscreen devices for older adults has been explored in research applications from health information [12] to social networking [9]. Their universal ease and intuitiveness has also been lauded by abundant anecdotes and media attention. Despite this apparent popularity, little is known about the psychomotor performance benefits of touchscreens for older adults, especially in comparison to younger adults and traditional computing setups (*e.g.*, mouse and desktop). Put simply, *do* touchscreens reduce the performance gap between younger and older adults as compared to desktop computers?

Although limited, previous work suggests that touchscreens may be especially beneficial for older adults: Schneider *et al.* [14] showed that a touchscreen reduced the performance difference between adults aged 60-75 and a middle-aged group (40-59) compared to mouse input. For a dragging task, however, Wood *et al.* [19] found that a touchscreen was slower and *more* difficult than the mouse for older adults. These mixed findings suggest a need for more comprehensive examinations of touchscreens versus traditional desktop input. While we acknowledge that motor performance is only one aspect of usability, it is the fundamental basis for all interactions and thus has significant influence over a device's overall ease-of-use.

We report on a study with 20 older and 20 younger adults, comparing mouse and touchscreen performance across four tasks: *pointing*, *dragging*, *crossing*, and *steering*. On the touchscreen, we also evaluate *pinch-to-zoom*. Our results show that, while older adults were significantly slower than younger adults in general, the touchscreen reduced this performance gap relative to the desktop and mouse. Indeed, the touchscreen resulted in a significant movement time reduction of 35% over the mouse for the older adults, compared to only 16% for the younger adults. Error rates also decreased. Steering, which was particularly problematic for older adults on the desktop, achieved the greatest improvement. Finally, touchscreen dragging was relatively slow, extending previous work [3] to older adults.

RELATED WORK

Few studies have evaluated touchscreen input performance for older adults beyond pointing and dragging. Rogers *et al.* [13] found that older adults were slower than younger adults for pointing and sliding (scrolling) tasks on a touchscreen, and that small button sizes were particularly problematic for the older adults. Piper *et al.* [12] showed that older adults can complete a range of touchscreen gestures with little difficulty, although no detailed performance comparison was provided. Stößel *et al.* [17] compared older *vs.* younger adults' abilities to draw a large set of gestures, finding that the older adults were slower but not more error-prone than younger adults. Finally, Kobayashi *et al.* [8] studied older adults' abilities to point, drag, and pinch/zoom on a touchscreen, but neither a younger control group nor an alternative input device was included. Even combined, these studies do not offer a systematic and complete understanding of age-related differences across a range of touchscreen interactions.

With a traditional mouse, older adults consistently perform less well than younger adults (*e.g.*, [1, 2, 7, 16, 18]). Chaparro *et al.* [1] showed that older adults were slower for pointing and dragging tasks with a trackball and a mouse. Movement analyses show that older adults have a higher noise-to-force ratio [18] and do not travel as far in their primary movement or reach the same peak velocity as

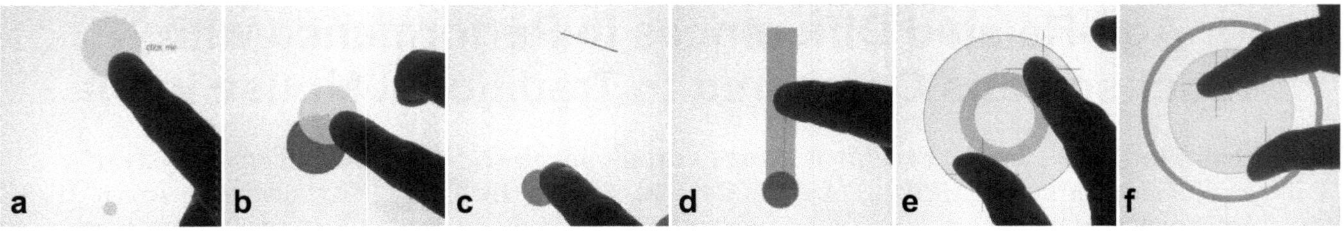

Figure 1. The six tasks: (a) *pointing* to a circle (next target is also shown in light gray); (b) *dragging* one circle and dropping it on another; (c) from a start circle, *crossing* over a target line; (d) from a start circle, *steering* through a rectangle; (e) *zooming out* and (f) *zooming in* using two touch points to resize a circle to fit within a gray ring. Only tasks (a)-(d) were completed on the desktop.

younger adults [7]. Older adults also have more difficulty clicking and double-clicking than younger adults [16]. For the general population, mouse versus touchscreen interaction has received more attention, *e.g.*, examining target size [15], bimanual tasks [4], and dragging [3]. The lattermost paper highlights the surprisingly small amount of comparative work on touchscreens beyond pointing.

STUDY METHOD

Participants

We recruited 20 adults aged 19–51 ($M = 27.7$, $SD = 8.9$) and 20 adults aged 61–86 ($M = 74.3$, $SD = 6.6$). The younger and older groups contained 8 and 14 females, respectively. All but four participants reported daily computer use, while 12 younger and 9 older adults reported daily touchscreen use. Very few (1 younger; 3 older) had never or almost never used touchscreen devices. Three participants were left-handed and 2 were ambidextrous.

Apparatus

The experimental testbed was built in JavaScript, HTML5 and PHP. It ran on Apple iPad 3's in the Safari browser and Apple laptops (Mac OS X 10.7) in the Chrome browser. The laptops were connected to identical external monitors set to a resolution of 1152×870 and to Logitech M310 optical mice with identical mouse gain settings. Chrome was put in full-screen mode before the desktop tasks began. For the touchscreen, the iPad lay flat on the table.

Care was taken to ensure the iPad and desktop setups were equivalent. Pointing, dragging, crossing, and steering were implemented based on the ISO 9241-9 circle 2-D Fitts' law task [6]. Figure 1 shows the touchscreen tasks; Table 1 shows distances to target, that is *amplitudes* (A), and target *widths* (W). For pointing, dragging, crossing and steering, A was 344 px based on the size of the iPad (1024×768 px). The minimum target width for the touchscreen had to be much larger than for the desktop: 9.2 mm (48 px), which was based on our own pilot studies and previous literature [11]. Since A was held constant across devices, W's of 64 and 96 resulted in the same Fitts' law *index of difficulty* (*ID*) regardless of device. *ID* is the ratio between distance to a target and the target's width, which determines how "difficult" the target is to acquire: $ID = \log_2(A/W+1)$. Thus, trials with the same *ID* should be equivalently difficult across devices, allowing us to isolate the effect of the input device itself (mouse *vs.* touchscreen). Zooming was implemented for touchscreen only and required two touch points to resize a circle to fit within a ring. The A parameter was the difference between the original circle's radius and the ring's radius, while W, the width of the ring, varied.

Task	A (px)	W (px)	
		Desktop	*Touchscreen*
Pointing, steering, crossing, dragging	344	16, 32, **64**, **96**	48, **64**, **96**, 128
Zooming out and in	128	not tested	16, 32, 64, 96

Table 1. Tested amplitudes (*A*) and target widths (*W*). Widths representing overlapping *ID*s between the devices are in bold.

Procedure

The procedure fit in a single session: one hour for younger adults and up to two hours for older adults. Participants first completed a background survey, which included previous technology experience. Participants then used the touchscreen and desktop presented in counterbalanced order, with the four tasks (pointing, dragging, crossing, steering) in randomized order within each device. Since the zooming tasks were secondary, they appeared (randomized) at the end of the touchscreen phase of the study.

For each task, instructions were presented on screen in text and video form. Then, a set of 8 practice trials was given, with the option to repeat the set once before starting the test trials in earnest. Target sizes were presented in random order, with 10 test trials per size. Spatial outliers were automatically redone by appending them to the end of the current set of trials. Based on prior work [10], outliers occurred when: (i) the movement was less than half the distance of A, or (ii) the end of the trial (*e.g.*, mouse click) occurred more than twice the target width W from the ideal endpoint (*e.g.*, target center). Finally, subjective task difficulty ratings were collected using 7-point Likert scales.

Movement time calculations per trial were specific to each task. *Pointing*: last click or touch up of previous trial to last click or touch up of this trial. *Dragging* and *Zooming*: time from initiating the movement (mouse button or touch down) to ending it (mouse button or touch up). For *Steering* and *Crossing*, the mouse cursor or finger needed to first come to rest in a circular "start" area, at which point timing started; end of timing occurred when the cursor or finger crossed over or near (in the case of an error) the target line for crossing, or end of the column for steering (Figure 1c, d).

Design and Analysis

In total, 16,000 trials were completed: 40 participants ×10 trials × 4 target widths × 10 tasks. Trials flagged as spatial outliers accounted for 1.2% of all trials. Our main analysis compared the devices for trials with equivalent *IDs*, where *W* was 64 or 96 pixels. We selected *only* these trials for each input device and ran a 3-way repeated measures ANOVA with movement time as the dependent variable: *Group* (2 levels; between-subjects) × *Device* (2 levels; within-subjects) × *Task* (4 levels; within-subjects). For zooming, we ran a 2-way ANOVA with movement time as the dependent variable: *Group* (2 levels; within-subjects) × *Task* (2 levels; within-subjects). Since error rate and Likert scale data often violate the normality assumption of ANOVA, we ran non-parametric Friedman tests to compare tasks within each device (touchscreen *vs.* desktop) and participant group. *Post hoc* pairwise comparisons for ANOVAs and Friedman tests, the latter using Wilcoxon signed ranks tests, were protected against Type I error using a Holm's sequential Bonferroni adjustment [5]. For the ANOVAs, we tested sphericity using Mauchly's test and used a Greenhouse-Geisser adjustment when the Mauchly's test was significant; this adjustment can result in fractional degrees of freedom. One younger participant was removed because her trial completion times were on average over 4 standard deviations away from the mean for that group.

RESULTS

We focus on comparing the mouse and touchscreen for the subset of trials with overlapping indexes of difficulty.

Movement Time

Movement time results are shown in Figure 2. All main and interaction effects were significant. As expected, older adults were slower than younger adults, completing trials on average in 1.34 seconds versus 0.72 seconds (main effect of *Group*: $F_{1,37} = 42.23$, $p < .001$, $\eta^2 = .53$). A main effect of *Device* also showed that the desktop was significantly slower than the touchscreen ($F_{1,37} = 44.46$, $p < .001$, $\eta^2 = .55$). Finally, a main effect of *Task* revealed the tasks impacted movement time differently ($F_{3,111} = 33.29, p < .001, \eta^2 = .47$).

Our main hypothesis was that the touchscreen would be relatively easier compared to the desktop for older adults than for younger adults. The devices did have a differential effect on the participant groups: a *Group* × *Device* interaction was significant ($F_{1,37} = 16.87$, $p < .001$, $\eta^2 = .31$). Older adults' movement time decreased by 35% when moving from desktop trials ($M = 1.62$ seconds) to touchscreen trials ($M = 1.06$ seconds); *post hoc* pairwise comparisons revealed this was a significant improvement ($p < .001$). For the younger adults, an improvement of 16% from the desktop to the touchscreen (0.79 to 0.66 seconds) was only a trend ($p = .082$).

While older adults improved more than younger adults from the desktop to the touchscreen, the degree of change was different for some tasks more than others (*Group* × *Device* × *Task* interaction: $F_{1.62,59.88} = 6.91$, $p = .004$, $\eta^2 = .16$). For older adults, *post hoc* pairwise comparisons revealed that crossing and pointing were the

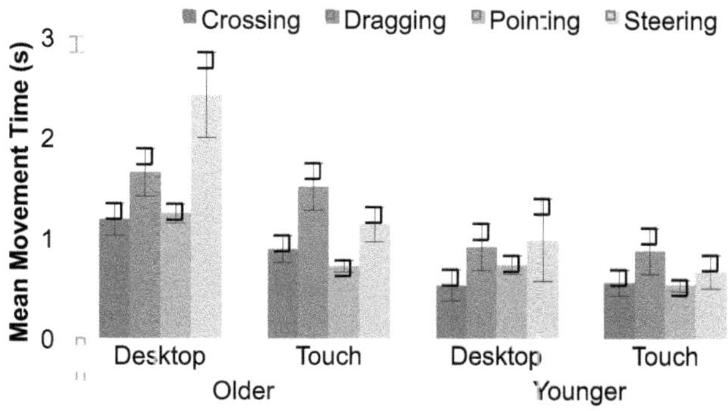

Figure 2. Mean movement time per trial for Desktop and Touch devices. While older adults were generally slower than younger adults, steering on the desktop was particularly slow. (*N* = 39; error bars show 95% confidence intervals.)

fastest tasks on the desktop, followed by dragging, with steering the slowest. As can be seen in Figure 2, however, the relative movement times for each task were different for the touchscreen. On the touchscreen, older adults were slowest with *dragging*, followed by steering. Crossing and pointing were fastest and not significantly different from each other. For younger adults, the only significant differences were dragging *vs.* crossing on the desktop and dragging *vs.* pointing and crossing on the touchscreen. Reported *post hoc* pairwise comparisons: $p < .05$.

The remaining significant interaction effects on movement time were *Task* × *Group* ($F_{2.36,87.20} = 7.64$, $p < .001$, $\eta^2 = .17$) and *Device* × *Task* ($F_{1.17,59.89} = 20.83$, $p < .001$, $\eta^2 = .26$). We did not conduct *post hoc* pairwise comparisons on these interaction effects because they did not contain both of our primary factors of interest (*Group* and *Device*).

Error Rate

Error rates were higher for the desktop than for the touchscreen for both groups. For older adults, error rates were on average 4.18% ($SD = 4.71\%$) for the desktop versus 0.75% ($SD = 1.02\%$) for the touchscreen. Younger adults made 2.89% errors on average on the desktop ($SD = 2.36\%$), compared to 0.26% ($SD = 0.67\%$) on the touchscreen. The difference between desktop and touchscreen was significant with both participant groups using a Wilcoxon signed rank test (older: $Z = -3.42$, $p = .001$; younger: $Z = -3.35$, $p = .001$). When comparing the error rates of older versus younger adults, no significant differences were found with Mann-Whitney U tests for either the desktop or the touchscreen.

Subjective Difficulty

Figure 3 shows perceived difficulty ratings. While we analyzed performance only for only a subset of trials (those with overlapping IDs) subjective difficulty ratings were collected based on *all* trials. It is thus not fair to compare subjective ratings between the touchscreen and desktop because the desktop had higher overall IDs. Instead, we examine ratings within each group and input device. The touchscreen tasks were all perceived to be relatively easy for participants in both groups, with an average rating of 1.62 ($SD = 0.97$) on a scale from 1 (easy) to 7 (difficult).

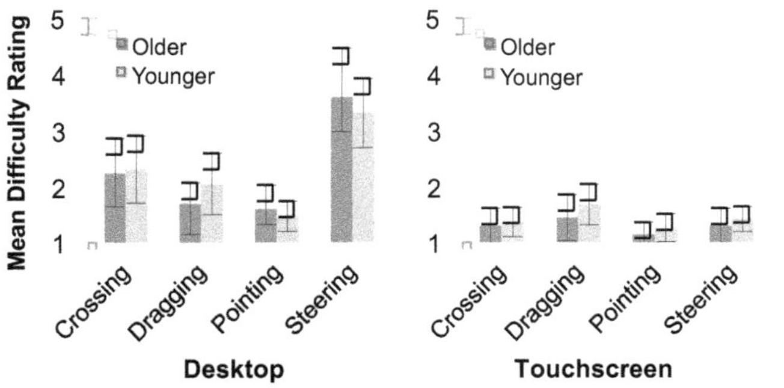

Figure 3. Perceived difficulty ratings: 1 (easy) to 7 (difficult). Desktop steering was deemed particularly difficult. (N = 39; error bars show 95% confidence intervals.)

No significant effects of task on subjective difficulty rating were found for the touchscreen. For the desktop, however, some tasks were perceived to be more difficult than others, with significant main effects of *Task* on perceived difficulty for both older ($\chi^2_{(3,N=20)} = 30.93$, $p < .001$) and younger ($\chi^2_{(3,N=19)} = 28.74$, $p < .001$) adults. Steering was hardest for the older adults, followed by dragging; no difference was found between pointing and crossing. For the younger adults, steering was more difficult than pointing and crossing. Reported *post hoc* pairwise comparisons: $p < .05$.

Zooming Out and In (Pinch-to-zoom)

For our secondary analysis on zooming, older adults were again slower than younger adults: on average 1.88 seconds per trial versus 1.13 seconds (main effect of *Group*: $F_{1,36} = 32.11$, $p < .001$, $\eta^2 = .47$). Counter to Kobayashi *et al.* [8], zooming out was slower than zooming in (main effect of *Task*: $F_{1,36} = 11.76$, $p = .002$, $\eta^2 = .25$); however, Kobayashi *et al.* did not report a significance level for this comparison. No significant interaction effect was found between *Group* and *Task*. Finally, error rates were uniformly low. Older adults made on average 1.58% ($SD = 2.92$) errors for zooming out and 2.00% ($SD = 4.97$) for zooming in. On average younger adults made 0.26% ($SD = 1.14$%) errors for zooming out and no errors for zooming in.

CONCLUSION

This study showed that the touchscreen did reduce the performance gap between older and younger adults compared to a traditional desktop setup. Across dragging, pointing, steering and crossing, older adults' movement times decreased by 35% when moving from the desktop to the touchscreen; younger adults only saw a 16% reduction. Interestingly, while the steering task was most difficult on the desktop, the dragging task was slowest on the touchscreen. This finding expands on previous work showing a similar tradeoff between pointing and dragging for younger adults [3]. Future work is needed to uncover whether the negative impact of the touchscreen on dragging performance has to do with occlusion by the finger, or perhaps extra friction as users press hard to keep "hold" of the dragging target. Finally, while motor performance is only one component of overall usability, it is a fundamental and critical base for all interactions. Our findings strengthen the case that touchscreens are easy to use for older adults.

ACKNOWLEDGMENTS

Thank you Brenna McNally and Carol Fuentevilla. This research was funded by a Google Faculty Research Award.

REFERENCES

1. Chaparro, A., Bohan, M., Fernandez, J., Choi, S. D., Kattel, B. (1999). The impact of age on computer input device use: Psychophysical and physiological measures. *Int'l J. of Industrial Ergonomics*, 24, 503–513.
2. Charness, N., Holley, P., Feddon, J., Jastrzembski, T. (2004). Light pen use and practice minimize age and hand performance differences in pointing tasks. *Human Factors*, 46(3), 373-384.
3. Cockburn, A., Ahlström, D., Gutwin, C. (2012). Understanding performance in touch selections: Tap, drag and radial pointing drag with finger, stylus and mouse. *IJHCS*, 70(3), 218–233.
4. Forlines, C., Wigdor, D., Shen, C., Balakrishnan, R. (2007). Direct-touch vs. mouse input for tabletop displays. *Proc. CHI '07*, 647–656.
5. Holm, S. (1979). A simple sequentially rejective multiple test procedure. *Scandinavian Journal of Statistics*, 6(2), 65–70.
6. International Organization for Standardization. (2002). Ergonomic requirements for office work with visual display terminals (VDTs)—Requirements for non-keyboard input devices. Ref. No. ISO 9241-9:2000(E).
7. Ketcham, C.J., Seidler, R.D., Van Gemmert, A.W.A., Stelmach, G.E. (2002). Age-related kinematic differences as influenced by task difficulty, target size, and movement amplitude. *Journal of Gerontology*, 57(1), 54–64.
8. Kobayashi, M., Hiyama, A., Miura, T., Asakawa, C., Hirose, M., Ifukube, T. (2011). Elderly user evaluation of mobile touchscreen interactions. *Proc. IFIP Interact 2011*, 83–99.
9. Leonardi, C., Albertini, A., Pianesi, F., Zancanaro, M. (2010). An exploratory study of a touch-based gestural interface for elderly. *Proc. NordiCHI '10*, 845–850.
10. MacKenzie, I.S. and Isokoski, P. (2008). Fitts' throughput and the speed-accuracy tradeoff. *Proc. CHI '08*, 1633-1636.
11. Parhi, P., Karlson, A. K., Bederson, B. B. (2006). Target size study for one-handed thumb use on small touchscreen devices. *Proc. MobileHCI '06*, 203–210.
12. Piper, A. M., Campbell, R., Hollan, J. D. (2010). Exploring the accessibility and appeal of surface computing for older adult health care support. *Proc. CHI 2010*, 907–916.
13. Rogers, W. A., Fisk, A. D., McLaughlin, A. C., & Pak, R. (2005). Touch a screen or turn a knob: Choosing the best device for the job. *Human Factors*, 47(2), 271-288.
14. Schneider, N., Wilkes, J., Grandt, M., Schlick, C. M. (2008). Investigation of input devices for the age-differentiated design of human-computer interaction. *Proc. HFES*, 52, 144–148.
15. Sears, A., Shneiderman, B. (1991). High precision touchscreens: design strategies and comparisons with a mouse. *International J. of Man-Machine Studies*, 34(4), 593–613.
16. Smith, M. W., Sharit, J., Czaja, S. J. (1999). Aging, motor control, and the performance of computer mouse tasks. *Human Factors*, 41(3), 389–396.
17. Stößel, C., Blessing, L. (2010). Mobile Device Interaction Gestures for Older users. *Proc. NordiCHI 2010*, 793–796.
18. Walker, N., Philbin, D.A., Fisk, A.D. (1997). Age-related differences in movement control: adjusting submovement structure to optimize performance. *J. of Gerontology*, 52B(1), 40–52.
19. Wood, E., Willoughby, T., Rushing, A., Bechtel, L., & Gilbert, J. (2005). Use of computer input devices by older adults. *Journal of Applied Gerontology*, 24(5), 419–438.

Access Lens: A Gesture-Based Screen Reader for Real-World Documents

Shaun K. Kane, Brian Frey
Department of Information Systems
UMBC
Baltimore, MD 21250 USA
{skane, frey1}@umbc.edu

Jacob O. Wobbrock
Information School | DUB Group
University of Washington
Seattle, WA 98195 USA
wobbrock@uw.edu

ABSTRACT
Gesture-based touch screen user interfaces, when designed to be accessible to blind users, can be an effective mode of interaction for those users. However, current accessible touch screen interaction techniques suffer from one serious limitation: they are only usable on devices that have been explicitly designed to support them. *Access Lens* is a new interaction method that uses computer vision-based gesture tracking to enable blind people to use accessible gestures on paper documents and other physical objects, such as product packages, device screens, and home appliances. This paper describes the development of Access Lens hardware and software, the iterative design of Access Lens in collaboration with blind computer users, and opportunities for future development.

Author Keywords: Accessibility; blindness; gestures; computer vision; augmented reality.

ACM Classification Keywords: H.5.2 [Information Interfaces and Presentation]: User Interfaces - Input devices and strategies.

INTRODUCTION
Until recently, many mainstream touch screen applications were inaccessible to blind people. However, in the past several years, a number of research projects (*e.g.,* [4]) have demonstrated that, by combining audio or tactile output with accessible gestures, blind people can effectively use touch screen interfaces, even if they are unable to see the screen. The creators of mainstream touch screen devices have incorporated some of these accessible gestures into their products, and many devices now provide accessible gestures for blind users.

Although touch screen accessibility has improved in recent years, many touch screen devices are still inaccessible. Furthermore, accessible gestures themselves suffer from a fundamental limitation: they are only usable on devices and applications that have been explicitly designed to support them. For example, a blind smartphone user may use accessible gestures to interact with her favorite apps, but will be unable to use those gestures to read her paper mail or read a campus map.

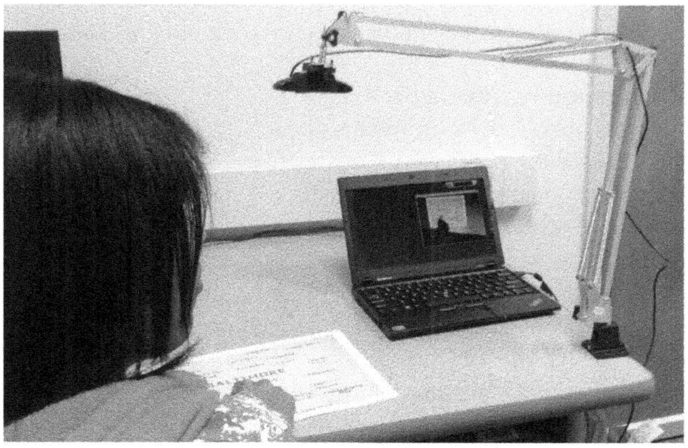

Figure 1. A blind person uses Access Lens to read a paper map using gestures. Access Lens recognizes the labels on the map and reads them as the user touches them with her finger.

To explore the potential of applying accessible gestures to the physical documents, we introduce Access Lens (Fig. 1), a system that allows blind users *to apply accessible gestures to real-world objects,* including paper documents. Access Lens (AL) uses a camera and computer vision to identify and recognize text in the environment, and tracks the user's hands in space, describing objects in the environment using synthesized speech. As a result, AL enables users to explore otherwise inaccessible objects using accessible gestures.

In this paper, we describe the design of Access Lens, including its computer vision and gesture tracking techniques. We also describe a formative study in which 5 blind computer users tested the prototype, and discuss opportunities for future development of the AL platform.

RELATED WORK
Reading Aids for Blind People
Prior projects such as the KNFB Reader Mobile[1] have used optical character recognition (OCR) to capture an image of

[1] http://www.knfbreader.com

a document and read it out using synthesized speech. However, AL provides the additional feature of exploring documents using gestures, which makes it ideal for exploring complex documents and spatial data. VizWiz [1] allows blind people to ask questions about their surroundings by taking a photograph and dictating a query, which is answered by a remote human worker. VizWiz provides limited support for searching for objects by moving the camera through space, but does not currently support gesture control, and relies upon remote human workers for feedback. AL uses automated recognition techniques, and can be used offline and in other situations in which the user does not wish to involve human workers.

Augmented Workspaces
AL was inspired by prior augmented workspaces such as the DigitalDesk [11] and Bonfire [3]. These projects used computer vision to track a user's hand gestures over a surface, enabling them to interact with virtual information in an otherwise uninstrumented environment. However, these systems focused primarily on visual interaction for sighted users. In contrast, AL is designed to enable blind users to explore objects using gestures. EyeRing [8] is a finger mounted camera that can be used to provide blind people with information about text or objects in their environment. AL has a similar goal, but uses a very different form factor (a mounted camera *vs.* a finger-worn camera), and leverages this form factor to support gestural exploration and spatial guidance.

DESIGN OF ACCESS LENS
The AL system comprises: (1) camera hardware mounted in the user's workspace; (2) computer vision software for recognizing text and tracking gestures. AL was developed through iterative testing with blind computer users.

Hardware
The AL prototype comprises a Logitech C910 webcam mounted on a lamp arm, connected to an Apple MacBook Air laptop with a dual-core 2.13 GHz processor and 4GB RAM (Fig. 1). However, AL's camera could be attached to any desktop or laptop PC. One benefit of a desk-mounted configuration is that the user does not need to aim the camera, which can be difficult for blind people [12].

Software
AL's primary functions are: scanning text in documents and other objects, and enabling the user to explore text using hand gestures and speech commands. AL was implemented using Python 2.7 on a laptop using Windows 7. AL uses OpenCV [2] for core computer vision algorithms, and Microsoft's .NET speech libraries for spoken commands.

When launched, AL captures an image of the user's workspace, and uses background subtraction [9] to identify new objects placed in the workspace. When the user wishes to scan an object, he or she places the object within the workspace and presses a predefined *Scan* key on the computer keyboard. AL locates the largest foreground object and attempts to scan its text. As AL is primarily intended to scan paper documents, and because the camera may be placed at an oblique angle relative to the scanned object, AL attempts to identify the corners of a rectangular object and de-skew that object using a homographic transform [10]. The user is notified if a rectangle cannot be found, such as when a document is partially outside the camera's view, or if a non-rectangular object is scanned.

When an object has been detected, AL identifies likely text regions [13] and passes them to an OCR engine.[2] Recognized text may be optionally checked against a dictionary file, and corrected by finding a match with the minimum string distance [6]. Once the text has been recognized, the user's hand is identified by combining the foreground/background model with a color-based skin detector [7]. AL assumes that the user is pointing with a single finger (as in Fig. 2), and identifies the fingertip as the point on the hand furthest from the user's body location.

Interaction Modes
AL provides several methods for reading document text using hand gestures and speech commands. In its most basic mode, known as *direct touch mode*, AL tracks the user's fingertip and speaks the text closest to it (Fig. 2). Direct touch mode enables blind users to read previously inaccessible documents simply by touching them. Furthermore, because text is read as the user touches it, the user may also learn the document's spatial layout.

While direct touch mode provides the ability to read previously inaccessible documents, exploring a document using direct touch and audio can be difficult, especially when trying to locate a specific item. To improve browsing efficiency, AL offers two supplementary navigation features: *edge menus* and *voice commands.*

Edge menus: To enable faster browsing of scanned objects, AL provides a virtual *edge menu overlay* inspired by Access Overlays [5]. When edge menus are activated, AL adds a column of virtual buttons along the right edge of the current object (*e.g.,* at the right edge of the scanned page). This menu lists all recognized text fragments in alphabetical order. Touching a button on the edge reads the name of that item. Dwelling on a menu item causes AL to provide *guided speech directions* to the item's actual location (*e.g.,* "Down, down, left, ..."), as in Access Overlays [5]. Figure 2 shows an edge menu along the right edge of the page.

Voice commands: AL's voice commands are activated by pressing a key on the laptop keyboard. Saying *"list"* causes AL to read all on-screen items. Saying *"find <item>"* provides guided speech directions to the named item. Voice commands may also be used to scan a new document or to toggle edge menus.

[2] ABBYY FineReader (www.abbyy.com)

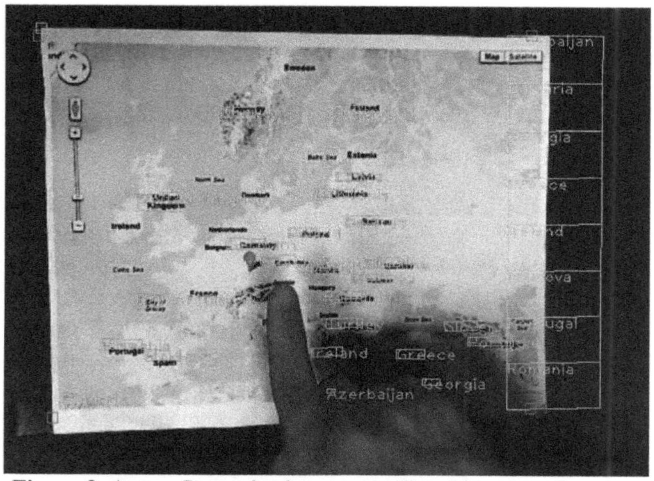

Figure 2. Access Lens viewing a map. Touching near the map labels speaks their names. An *edge menu* along the right edge of the page shows a sorted index of on-screen items.

While AL is focused on reading text, it also supports a *color identification mode.* When this mode is active, AL names the color closest to the user's finger. This mode can be used to scan documents, clothing, and other objects.

FORMATIVE EVALUATION OF ACCESS LENS

As AL offers a fundamentally new user interface for blind people, we were initially unsure whether users would even be able to use it. We tested early prototypes of AL with 5 blind computer users (3 female, average age 34.8). Data from these sessions was used to refine parameters for the underlying algorithms. Pilot participants were enthusiastic about AL, and suggested new uses for the system, such as color identification, which we added to the final prototype.

We then conducted a formative evaluation of AL with 5 blind users (3 female, average age 33.8). All participants were regular computer users; 2 used a screen reader exclusively, while 3 used both a screen reader and a screen magnifier. All participants had previously used a touch screen-based device, and 4 owned such a device. Three participants had participated in the pilot tests of AL. The goals of the evaluation were: 1) to collect participants' feedback about the AL; 2) to compare AL's interaction modes; 3) to compare AL across document types; and 4) to identify potential usability and reliability challenges.

Each participant used AL for one 60-minute session. Each participant received a 10-minute introduction to AL and each method of interaction (direct touch, edge menus, voice commands, and color identification), using a US state map. Participants then used AL to freely explore 3 documents for approximately 10 minutes each: a *diagram* of the human body, a *map* of Europe (Fig. 2), and a *table* containing political poll results. Participants tested *color identification mode* for approximately 5 minutes using these documents and an image of a US state flag. A member of the research team was present throughout the activity to place the documents in the workspace, to observe the participant, and to answer any questions about the task or about the document being explored. Following the session, participants provided verbal feedback about their experiences, and rated each interaction method and document type on a 7-point Likert scale (Table 1).

Observations from the Formative Evaluation

Overall usefulness: Overall, participants were very enthusiastic about AL. When asked to rate the overall usefulness of AL on a 7-point Likert scale, participants gave AL a median rating of 6, and all but one rated it 6 or higher. Participants expressed interest in using AL to read maps, charts, bus schedules, bills, sheet music, magazines, medical documents, and clothing.

Interaction modes: Participants provided ratings for each interaction mode on a 7-point Likert scale (Table 1, left). Participants rated all modes positively, but rated direct touch most highly. Given that participants were novices, it is possible that the more advanced features would be rated more highly after participants gained more experience. One participant, who was extremely technically savvy, praised the idea of the virtual edge menu as "kind of brilliant."

Document types: Participants also rated AL's usefulness for various document types (Table 1, right). Participants enjoyed the diagram and map tasks, but were less positive about using AL to navigate a table. During the study, participants sometimes had difficulty following the rows and columns of the table with their fingers. Several participants suggested adding a "table mode" that would provide feedback about the table structure and support traversing the table with gestures.

Interaction mode	Mdn. Rating	Document type	Rating
Direct touch	7	Diagram	5
Edge menus	6	Map	6
Voice commands	5	Table	4
Color recognition	7		

Table 1. Likert-scale responses (1=worst, 7=best): 1) preferred interaction mode; 2) best documents to use with Access Lens.

Usability and reliability challenges: All participants in the lab study were able to use AL to complete the tasks. However, participants did encounter some usability problems. Some participants had difficulty keeping track of the camera's view. Often, participants inadvertently moved the document as they were reading, causing AL to report text at incorrect locations. This problem could be addressed by securing the document to the surface, or by re-scanning the document. Participants also confused the gesture tracker by placing both hands on the document, or by holding their hands at an angle. AL's gesture tracker expected users to clearly extend the pointer finger, as in Figure 2. As a result, AL sometimes tracked the side of the participant's hand, rather than the finger. During the study, we reminded participants to extend their fingertip, although a more robust finger-tracking algorithm could also solve this issue.

A second question raised by this study is the degree to which AL is ready for real-world deployment. We found that AL's vision system performed reliably under varying indoor lighting conditions, but that camera settings sometimes required manual adjustment to ensure proper gesture tracking, which could present challenges when deployed to blind users in the wild. OCR generally took between 30 seconds and 1 minute. OCR accuracy varied greatly with lighting, camera settings, and camera position, but was typically well above 50%, even correctly recognizing proper names and numbers. However, these results are likely bound to our chosen lab setting, and results from the wild may differ significantly. Our planned field study, described below, will provide more information about the robustness of AL's vision system in the wild.

FUTURE WORK

The present work demonstrates the usability of AL in a lab setting. However, we intend to improve AL by adding new features and by increasing its robustness to real-world environmental conditions. One persistent challenge is the inevitable presence of OCR errors. To address this problem, we developed a crowdsourced OCR module based on QuikTurkIt [1]. Crowd OCR is currently slower than automated OCR, taking 2-3 minutes per page,[3] but is more accurate, especially when image quality is low. As there are performance, privacy, and cost tradeoffs between recognizers, we are developing an interface that will allow the user to select their preferred recognizer, and fall back to a secondary recognizer if the primary recognizer fails.

We also intend to conduct an extended field evaluation of AL. While AL performed well in the lab, field study participants will likely encounter environmental conditions that will negatively affect performance. Improving performance in these contexts may require better camera calibration algorithms, especially since blind participants may not be able to manually calibrate the camera themselves. This field study will help us to identify which types of objects users are most interested in scanning, which may allow us to optimize our recognition algorithms.

While we believe that AL provides valuable accessibility support in its current form, there is much potential in alternative form factors for AL, especially mobile form factors. We have constructed a wearable hardware prototype in the form of a pendant camera combined with an ultra-mobile PC. However, creating a reliable mobile version of AL will require further improvements to camera calibration and OCR. Furthermore, mobile AL will require a way to detect movement of the camera or scanned object, and to recalibrate the locations of the scanned text.

Finally, we are interested in extending AL to recognize additional content beyond text and color. Future versions could identify images or glyphs printed on maps, signs, or other artifacts. We have also experimented with using AL to read computer displays and non-accessible touch screens, and will further explore this use case in the future.

[3] Recognition time can likely be reduced via improved crowd algorithms.

CONCLUSION

While the rapid adoption of touch screen-based devices first seemed to be a threat to accessibility for blind users, the development of accessible gestures has helped to ensure that such devices remain accessible. Access Lens leverages advancements in accessible gestures to create a new form of assistive technology. While much of the previous research on accessible gestures has focused on providing access to specific technologies, our study shows that accessible gestures can also provide access to the physical world.

REFERENCES

1. Bigham, J.P., Jayant, C., Ji, H., Little, G., Miller, A., Miller, R.C., Miller, R., Tararowicz, A. White, B., White, S., and Yeh, T. VizWiz: nearly real-time answers to visual questions. *Proc. UIST '10,* (2010), 333–342.
2. Bradski, G. The OpenCV library. *Doctor Dobbs Journal 25*, 11 (2000), 120–126.
3. Kane, S.K., Avrahami, D., Wobbrock, J.O., Harrison, B., Rea, A.D., Philipose, M., and LaMarca, A. Bonfire: a nomadic system for hybrid laptop-tabletop interaction. *Proc. UIST '09,* (2009), 129–138.
4. Kane, S.K., Bigham, J.P., and Wobbrock, J.O. Slide Rule: making mobile touch screens accessible to blind people using multi-touch interaction techniques. *Proc. ASSETS '08,* (2008), 73–80.
5. Kane, S.K., Morris, M.R., Perkins, A.Z., Wigdor, D., Ladner, R.E., and Wobbrock, J.O. Access Overlays: improving non-visual access to large touch screens for blind users. *Proc. UIST '11, (2011),* 273–280.
6. Levenshtein, V.I. Binary codes capable of correcting spurious insertions and deletions of ones. *Problems of Information Transmission 1*, 1 (1965), 8–17.
7. Mahmoud, T.M. A new fast skin color detection technique. *WEAST 43*, (2008), 501–505.
8. Nanayakkara, S., Shilkrot, R., and Maes, P. EyeRing: a finger-worn assistant. *Proc. CHI EA '12, (2012),* 1961–1966.
9. Stauffer, C. and Grimson, W.E.L. Adaptive background mixture models for real-time tracking. *Proc. CVPR '00*, 252–258.
10. Sukthankar, R., Stockton, R.G., and Mullin, M.D. Smarter presentations: exploiting homography in camera-projector systems. *Proc. ICCV '01*, 247–253.
11. Wellner, P. Interacting with paper on the DigitalDesk. *Communications of the ACM 36*, 7 (1993), 87–96.
12. White, S., Ji, H., and Bigham, J.P. EasySnap: real-time audio feedback for blind photography. *Proc. UIST '10*, (2010), 409–410.
13. Wong, E.K. and Chen, M. A new robust algorithm for video text extraction. *Pattern Recognition 36*, 6 (2003), 1397–1406.

LEMtool - Measuring Emotions in Visual Interfaces

Gijs Huisman
University of Twente, Human Media Interaction Group
gijs.huisman@utwente.nl

Marco van Hout
SusaGroup
marco.vanhout@susagroup.com

Betsy van Dijk
University of Twente, Human Media Interaction Group
e.m.a.g.vandijk@utwente.nl

Thea van der Geest
University of Twente, Media, Communication & Organisation
t.m.vandergeest@utwente.nl

Dirk Heylen
University of Twente, Human Media Interaction Group
d.k.j.heylen@utwente.nl

ABSTRACT
In this paper the development process and validation of the LEMtool (Layered Emotion Measurement tool) are described. The LEMtool consists of eight images that display a cartoon figure expressing four positive and four negative emotions using facial expressions and body postures. The instrument can be used during interaction with a visual interface, such as a website, and allows participants to select elements of the interface that elicit a certain emotion. The images of the cartoon figure were submitted to a validation study, in which participants rated the recognizability of the images as specific emotions. All images were found to be recognizable above chance level. In another study, the LEMtool was used to assess visual appeal judgements of a number of web pages. The LEMtool ratings were supported by visual appeal ratings of web pages both for very brief (50 milliseconds) and for long (free-viewing) stimulus exposures. Furthermore, the instrument provided insight into the elements of the web pages that elicited the emotional responses.

Author Keywords
LEMtool; emotion; user experience; visual appeal; web pages.

ACM Classification Keywords
H.5.2. User Interfaces: Evaluation/methodology.

INTRODUCTION
Emotions play a vital role in our everyday lives. Everything from our most basic perceptions [50] to our deepest, most heartfelt love [37] is influenced by affective processes. This is not only true for encounters in the 'real world', but also extends to our experiences with digital technology [32]. In the past three decades human-computer interaction (HCI) research has started to adopt a more holistic view of the experience of computer interaction, recognizing non-instrumental elements such as fun (see for instance [5]). This field of investigation has been referred to as User eXperience (UX), and is principally concerned with studying emotional responses to HCI [18, 19, 25, 29].

In HCI, emotions can have a broad range of effects on, for instance, the shaping of the interaction, the communication about the interaction, as well as the evaluation of the object of interaction [14, 18]. Consequently, measuring emotions in interaction with a broad range of interactive products [17] and interfaces [24] has been a primary concern of UX researchers. The methods used for such investigations are often validated emotion measurement instruments from the field of experimental psychology (see for instance [18, 28, 40]). A downside of these methods is that they are not always well suited for the highly interactive nature of digital media. Most methods are applied post-hoc, providing a measurement of the overall experience. Consider for instance websites, where users can quickly navigate between different pages through hyperlinks. In such a case a post-hoc measurement would only provide insight into the cumulative experience of all the pages. The range of emotional responses that people experience in relation to individual pages, or elements of individual pages, would be lost. Therefore, the investigation of emotions in UX research would benefit from methods specifically geared towards highly interactive contexts, such as interaction with websites. The development process and initial validation of such an instrument is reported in this paper.

RELATED WORK
Visual interfaces such as websites, mobile, and desktop operating systems, can elicit emotions in a number of ways. Hassenzahl [16] proposes that an individual's experience with technology depends on the perceived pragmatic and hedonic qualities of the product. Pragmatic quality resembles the notion of usability (e.g. ease of use), while hedonic quality refers to pleasure of use. Pragmatic quality is in essence a

"hygiene factor" [18] that will not produce positive emotions in itself, but can result in strong negative emotions when, for example, usability breaks down. Unresponsive controls for instance, can cause negative affective responses in the user [36]. Similarly, an overly complex and unclear ordering of visual elements of an interface can lead to heightened arousal and less positive evaluations of that interface [28, 40, 47]. Hedonic quality on the other hand can be a source of positive affect. An oft studied element of hedonic quality, visual appeal, influences the user's experience early on in perception [26, 27, 41], in the form of a rapid affective judgement ([30, 50] see also [27]). Furthermore, a good visual design has the potential to negate existing usability problems, resulting in more favorable evaluations of the interface [39, 42]. The initial affective reaction to the visual appeal of an interface can have a priming effect [51], and influence later evaluations of that interface [7]. The impact of visual appeal is thus not limited to the initial perception.

Measuring emotions

The measurement of emotions typically involves methods that measure a single component of emotion. These components include activation of the autonomous nervous system, motor expressions, behavioral tendencies, and subjective feelings [38].

Psychophysiological measurements

Psychophysiological measurements are often used to obtain continuous measurements of emotions during interaction with an interface. Scheier et al. [36] used galvanic skin response (GSR), and blood volume pulse (BVP) to measure activation of the autonomous nervous system as an indication of emotional arousal resulting from a frustrating game. Ward and Marsden [47] used similar measurements of emotional arousal (i.e. GSR, BVP, and heart rate) to detect usability problems occurring during interaction with a website. Physiological responses to usability issues were also studied by Thüring and Mahlke [40] who, next to GSR as a measure of arousal, employed facial electromyography (EMG) to measure minute changes in electrical activity of two facial muscles as a measure of emotional valence (i.e. positive/negative judgements). Similarly, Hazlett and Benedek [20] measured the desirability of certain software functions, using facial EMG as a measure of emotional valence. An issue with using psychophysiological measurements to measure emotions that occur during interaction with a visual interface is that it is often difficult to find which element of the interface is responsible for the emotional reaction. The autonomous nervous system may be activated by non-emotional events, such as increases in concentration, which could confound measurements of emotion [48]. Furthermore, measurements of changes in physiology are an indirect measurement of emotions, thus a delay between the measurement and the actual emotion is to be expected [43]. This is especially problematic when considering the highly interactive nature of most visual interfaces, for instance while rapidly going back and forth between two web pages, or opening and closing programs in an operating system.

Self-report

The most common method used to ascertain someones affective state is self-report measurements [2, 33]. This is partly due to the complexities of psychophysiological measurements. Malhke and Minge [28], for instance, found ratings of valence and arousal using the Self Assessment Manikin (SAM) [1] to corroborate physiological measurements during interaction with a mobile phone interface. Deng and Poole [7] successfully used self-report measurements of valence and arousal to measure emotional responses to different web page designs. A strength of emotional self-report is that it is easy to apply and interpret. Downsides are that it is a subjective measure, sensitive to bias, as well as subject to priming effects of forced-choice questionnaires [15, 37]. Unlike physiological measurements, which are continuous, emotional self-report is mostly used as a post-hoc measurement. Feldman-Barrett [13] argues that the time that passes between the stimulus and the reported emotion may negatively influence the accuracy of the measurement. The longer the time between the stimulus presentation and the self-report of emotion, the more the respondent will rely on memory to report his or her subjective feelings [13, 33]. In addition, as most self-report methods are verbal measurements, they are difficult to apply cross-culturally, as well as difficult to use with less literate populations (e.g. children) [1, 8]. Furthermore, emotions are difficult to verbalize, thus responding to one's emotional state with verbal labels requires considerable cognitive involvement which may influence the response [8, 49].

Non-verbal self-report

In an attempt to improve on verbal self-report methods, researchers have developed non-verbal self-report methods to measure the subjective feeling component of emotion. One of the most well-known is SAM [1], which is based on an abstract cartoon figure that conveys emotional valence, arousal and dominance. Each of these dimensions is represented by five different visualized states on a horizontal 9-point scale. While the dominance dimension is often unused because it lacks discriminative power, SAM has proven successful in measuring the valence and arousal dimensions [1], which are considered the underlying dimensions of all emotions [35]. Desmet [8] took a different approach with the development of PrEmo (Product Emotion), an instrument to measure emotional responses to products. PrEmo consists of fourteen animations of a cartoon character that expresses specific emotions through facial, bodily, and vocal expressions. After being exposed to a product, people indicate, for each animation, how strongly the depicted emotion was felt. PrEmo is based on the notion that people can accurately identify discrete emotions from bodily signals such as facial expressions [10] and body language [46]. Recognition of the PrEmo animations in western cultures (i.e. Finland, the Netherlands, and the United States) ranges from 63 to 100 percent [8]. PrEmo has been applied in studies into automobile designs [8] and mobile phone designs [9]. Similarly, the Pictorial Mood Reporting Instrument (PMRI) [45] uses three sets of cartoon figures (i.e. male, female, and genderless) that express one neutral mood and eight specific moods taken from the circumplex model of affect [34]. The initial validation study showed that the PMRI images were recognized with an accuracy between 38 and 94 percent. A considerably lower recognition accuracy was obtained for positive moods compared to negative ones. PMRI is envisioned as a communication tool to share moods between users, as well as a general tool to measure moods. In comparison to emotions, moods are more diffuse affective states that are relatively long in duration, are less intense, and often do not have specific elicitors [37]. This distinction is important in that the PMRI would seem particularly well suited to measure someone's general affective state (i.e. mood) at a point in time, but would be less suitable to measure emotional responses to specific elicitors such as products or interfaces.

Evaluation methods that are strongly related to non-verbal emotional self-report scales, are found in pain assessment scales for children [6, 21, 22]. For example the Faces Pain Scale-Revised [21] uses six facial expressions in a horizontal orientation with the endpoints representing "no pain" and "very much pain". The instrument has been proven to be a highly reliable method of pain assessment for children [22]. Comparable in design to the Faces Pain Scale-Revised, but different in application area, is the Smileyometer. This instrument also consists of a scale of five abstract facial expressions, and is used to measure children's experience with technology [31]. Though not specifically aimed at measuring emotions, these types of scales do provide valuable insights into how pictorial representations might be used instead of words in self-report measurements, especially measurements taken from children.

Figure 1. The eight images of the LEMtool.

THE DESIGN OF THE LEMTOOL

As was outlined in the previous section there are a number of ways to measure emotions. However, each of the methods described has its downsides. For in-process measurements, psychophysiological signals can be used, but these measures can be difficult to apply and interpret [48]. Verbal self-report methods might be easier to interpret, but add the difficulty of having to translate words for different languages, as well as adding cognitive load [8, 49]. Therefore, non-verbal self-report measures of emotion provide a viable alternative to verbal self-report measures. However, considering the measurement of emotions during interaction with a visual interface, a number of things stand out in regard to existing non-verbal self-report methods. First, methods either use continuous scales of the underlying dimensions of emotion (SAM [1]), scales of emotion related concepts (pain assessment [21]) or scales for reporting experience with technology [31]. Second, the only method that measures specific emotions uses an animated cartoon figure (PrEmo [8]), while the only method that uses still images of discrete affective states is geared towards measuring moods instead of emotions (PMRI [45]). Finally, no method is specifically aimed at measuring emotions during interaction with visual interfaces.

The LEMtool (Layered Emotion Measurement tool) [23] was developed with the requirements that it should be easily deployable during interaction with a visual interface (i.e. measurements in-process), that it should be comprehensible (i.e. not too demanding for the participant), and that it should have the possibility to be used cross-culturally. Similarly to PrEmo [8], the idea behind the LEMtool was to measure a finer granularity of discrete emotions rather than general emotional states. However, PrEmo uses animations, which take time to play in their entirety. This would severely disrupt the interaction with a visual interface, making the use of animations unsuitable for deployment during interaction. For these reasons it was decided that the development of a new set of visualizations was necessary.

Selecting and visualizing emotions

The LEMtool consists of a cartoon figure that expresses eight discrete emotions using facial expressions and body postures. The instrument consists of four positive and four negative emotions (see Figure 1). The emotions were selected from a study into the emotional impact of web pages, in which emotion terms from the circumplex model of affect [34] were divided into eight octants along the valence and arousal dimensions [4]. Emotion words that represented states with a neutral valence were not considered, as these words might denote non-emotional states (see also [37]). In the selection of the eight emotion words from the remaining six octants, the possibilities for visualizing each emotion term was considered. Findings from studies into facial expressions [10], as well as the emotions that were visualized in PrEmo [8] were taken into account here. Furthermore, the concept of emotion families was considered [11]. This concept states that although there are numerous emotion terms, each term may belong to a group of related affective states. For instance, dissatisfaction would belong to the same emotion family as anger and rage, but represent a less intense emotional state. It is suggested here that dissatisfaction might be a more relevant emotion than anger or rage in the context in which the LEMtool will be employed (i.e. evaluations of visual interfaces)[2]. That is not to say these more intense emotions cannot be elicited during such interactions, just that respondents using the LEMtool are more likely to experience dissatisfaction with an interface than to be enraged by it.

The design of the LEMtool is based on the notion that people can identify specific facial and bodily expressions of emotion [10, 12, 46], especially when such expressions are caricatured (i.e. undone of any elements distracting from the expression) [3]. The LEMtool images were created in collaboration with a professional cartoonist, who was provided with general guidelines about the composition of the facial expressions and body postures. The LEMtool was designed as an interactive instrument deployed during interaction with a visual interface, allowing participants to indicate responses in-process. The way the LEMtool is used during interaction with a web page, is depicted in Figure 2.

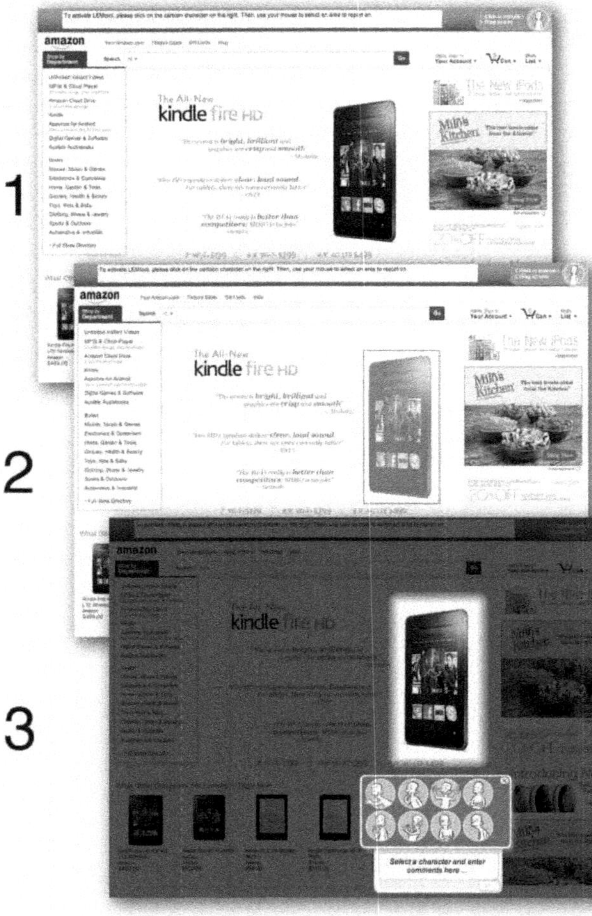

Figure 2. The steps required to indicate an emotion for a certain area of a visual interface, in this case a web page. Step 1: activate the LEMtool. Step 2: select an area of the website. Step 3: indicate an emotion.

VALIDATION OF THE LEMTOOL IMAGES

A validation study was conducted in order to assess the recognizability of the LEMtool images. Using a number of different response formats, participants were asked to indicate which emotions they thought the LEMtool images were displaying.

Pilot study

Prior to the validation study, a pilot study was conducted. The goal of the pilot study was to obtain a baseline for the recognizability of the LEMtool images.

Image	Target label percentage
Joy	83.9
Desire	83.9
Fascination	81.7
Satisfaction	80.6
Sadness	80.6
Disgust	96.8
Boredom	100
Dissatisfaction	87.1

Table 1. Recognition accuracy of the LEMtool images in the pilot study. All images were recognized at above chance level (i.e. 50%, $p < .001$).

Participants

Participants were Master's students at the Technical University of Delft enrolled in a course on product experience. In total 38 male and 55 female students participated (N = 93). Age ranged from 21 to 31 (M = 23.4, SD = 1.9).

Apparatus

Participants were presented with two sheets of A4 paper stapled together. The LEMtool images were printed in black-and-white with a size of 5 by 5 centimeters. The eight emotion terms corresponding to the images were presented in English next to each image.

Procedure

The procedure was explained to the entire group by the lecturer. Participants were asked to select either one or more of the eight given emotion terms, or add a word of their own, that according to them, would best describe the emotion expressed by the LEMtool image. This last option was added to reduce response bias as a result of the forced-choice format [15]. Finally the participants were instructed to indicate their gender, age and first language. Participants were specifically told that they were not allowed to talk to each other. The entire procedure took no more than five minutes.

Results

Table 1 lists the percentages of participants who selected the target label for each LEMtool image. Only selection of the target label was considered a correct response. Responses containing selection of more than one label, or responses consisting of an added label were considered an incorrectly selected label. Binomial tests were computed for the proportion of participants who selected each emotion label for a given target label. Chance was set to 50% for each emotion. This chance level was based on Ekman's [10] considerations on how some facial expressions might be most likely confused with similar expressions. Here the chance level reflects a choice between two emotions that may be expected to be confused based on their morphology (i.e. joy-satisfaction, desire-fascination, sadness-boredom, and disgust-dissatisfaction). Note that the chosen chance level is more stringent than that typically suggested for forced-choice facial expression recognition tasks (see [15]). Table 1 shows that all of the LEMtool images were recognized as the emotions they were intended to display at above chance level ($p < .001$). These results are comparable to, and in some cases

Image	Rating for target label (5-point scale)	Std. Deviation
Joy	4.9	0.3
Desire	4.8	0.6
Fascination	4.4	0.9
Satisfaction	4.9	0.6
Sadness	4.7	0.6
Disgust	4.6	0.8
Boredom	4.9	0.4
Dissatisfaction	4.7	0.7

Table 2. Average ratings for target emotion label in the first task of the validation study. All target emotion labels were rated significantly higher than all other labels ($p < .001$).

Image	Target label percentage
Joy	95.1
Desire	89.0
Fascination	89.0
Satisfaction	91.5
Sadness	89.0
Disgust	86.6
Boredom	100
Dissatisfaction	93.9

Table 3. Recognition accuracy of the LEMtool images in the second task of the validation study. All images were recognized at above chance level (i.e. 50%, $p < .001$).

exceed, recognition accuracies obtained in studies into basic facial expressions [10], as well as results from studies using similar visualizations of emotions [8, 45]. This indicates that the LEMtool images were relatively accurately recognized as the emotions they were intended to display. Based on these findings, it was decided not to make any changes to the images at this point.

Validation study

The validation study was carried out to assess possible confusions between images, using a broader sample of participants, and different response formats as compared to the pilot study.

Participants

A notice of the study was posted on the student website of the University of Twente, and on a design and emotion related website. In total 46 male and 36 female participants took part in the study (N = 82). Participants' ages ranged from 18 to 59 (M = 30.0, SD = 10.2).

Apparatus

The study was conducted using a purpose-built website. The website was compliant with the most popular browser standards (i.e. Microsoft Internet Explorer, Mozilla Firefox, Opera) presenting the contents of the study consistently across browsers. The LEMtool images were 200 by 200 pixels in size and displayed in an orange circle (see Figure 1).

Procedure

Participants were first presented with an introductory text detailing the goal of the study and outlining the general procedure. In the first task, participants were presented with a list of the eight emotion terms and for each of the eight subsequently presented LEMtool images were asked to rate, on a five-point scale, the terms that they thought were most prominently present in the presented image. The scale ranged from 1 ("This emotion is not present") to 5 ("This emotion is strongly present"). Intermittent response options were not labeled. The order of the eight emotion terms, as well as the order in which the images were presented, was randomized for each participant. In the second task, participants were asked for each of the eight subsequently presented images, to select one of eight emotion terms that they felt best described the emotion expressed in the image. The response option "none of these terms" was added to reduce response bias. Again, the order of the eight emotion terms, as well as the order in which the images were presented, was randomized for each participant. All texts in both tasks were presented in Dutch.

Results

Table 2 lists the average rating given to the target label for each LEMtool image. For all images, a one-sample *t*-test was performed, comparing the average rating for each target label with the average rating of all other labels. For all images the target label was rated as significantly higher ($p < .001$) than all other labels. This indicates little confusion between the emotions depicted in the LEMtool images. Additionally, the low standard deviations in Table 2 indicate consensus among participants about the most appropriate label. Table 3 lists the percentages of participants who selected the target label for each LEMtool image. Only selection of the target label was considered a correct response. Identical to the pilot study, chance level was set to 50%. Binomial tests were computed for the proportion of participants who selected each emotion label for a given target label. Table 3 shows that all of the LEMtool images were recognized as the emotions they were intended to display at above chance level ($p < .001$). Again, these results are highly comparable to previous research [8, 10, 45].

Conclusions

Findings from the validation study show that participants were relatively successful in decoding the emotions intended by the LEMtool images. Similarly high recognition accuracy was obtained using a number of different response formats, limiting the possibility that findings are an artifact of the response format (see also [15]). The fact that the recognition accuracy of the images is comparable to, and in some cases exceeds, that of existing instruments such as PrEmo [8] and PMRI [45] is encouraging, and shows the potential of using the LEMtool images to measure emotional responses. As a first application of the LEMtool a study was designed to see if the instrument could be used successfully to indicate emotional responses to visual stimuli.

CASE STUDY: VISUAL APPEAL

Visual appeal is an important element of the hedonic quality of an interface [18]. Research suggests that judgements of visual appeal are in essence emotional judgements that occur rapidly, and can bias later judgements of visual appeal [27].

Therefore it is important for the LEMtool to be able to measure responses to the visual appeal of interfaces. A study was conducted to assess whether the LEMtool could be used to measure emotional responses to the visual appeal of web pages. As a first application of the LEMtool to measure visual appeal of web pages, the focus was on visual appeal as a general concept. The accent of the case study was therefore on measuring the difference between high and low visual appeal web pages. Both brief (50 ms) and long (free-viewing) exposure times were used. Additionally, the case study served as a first evaluation of the way the LEMtool was envisioned to be used, namely by having participants indicate positive and negative emotions on different areas of a number of web pages.

Manipulation check

Two independent web designers created a high and a low visual appeal version of the same web page. The designers were only provided with guidelines aimed at keeping the type, organization, and presentation of information, as well as the content and perceived functionality of the web page, consistent. No specific instructions were given to the designers regarding manipulations of visual appeal. The manipulations of visual appeal relied on the expertise of the designers. The 24 web pages covered three topics, namely: Einstein, a holiday island, and medical information about headaches [44].

In an online survey, promoted through social media (i.e. Twitter, Facebook), a total of 31 participants rated the visual appeal of the 24 web pages. Similar to [41] a ten-point rating scale (1 = very unappealing, 10 = very appealing) was used. Each web page screenshot was displayed for 500 ms, in a resolution of 1024x768 pixels, without visible browser elements. All texts were presented in Dutch.

A paired-samples *t*-test was performed, comparing the visual appeal ratings for high visual appeal and low visual appeal web pages. Overall, high visual appeal web pages received a mean rating of 5.39 (SD = 1.34) while low visual appeal web pages received a mean rating of 3.08 (SD = 1.15). This difference was significant ($t(30) = 14.4$, $p < .001$). From this result it was concluded that the web pages did indeed differ on visual appeal, and were therefore suitable for use in the main study.

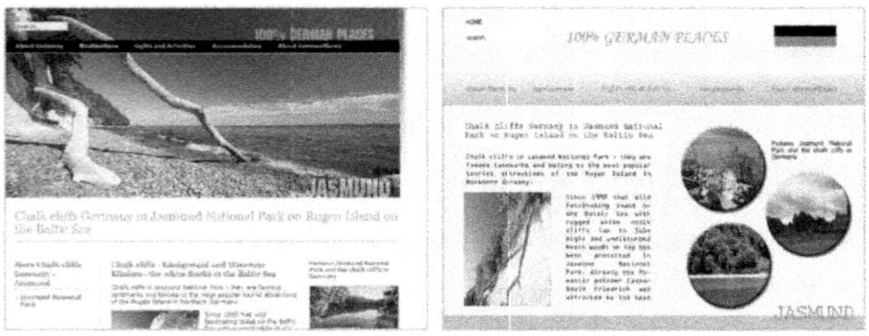

Figure 3. Example of a holiday island high visual appeal web page (left) and a holiday island low visual appeal web page (right) used in the study.

Visual appeal study

Participants

In total 43 (13 male, 30 female) individuals participated in the study. Twenty-four of these participants were first and second year psychology and communication science students who received course credits for participation. The remainder of the participants were approached by the researcher and asked to volunteer in the study. Participants age ranged from 18 to 31 (M = 22.4, SD = 3.19). Participants with color blindness were excluded.

Apparatus

The study consisted of two separate phases. In the 50 ms phase, stimuli were presented using E-Prime 2.0 displayed on a 17 inch Samsung SyncMaster 750s CRT monitor (Samsung Electronics, Seoul, South Korea). The monitor was set to a screen resolution of 1024x768 pixels at 60 Hz. Brightness was set to 85 and contrast to 100 with color temperature set to 9300 °K. Participants used a standard computer keyboard to indicate their responses. In the free-viewing phase, stimuli were presented using a purpose built online environment running in Firefox 3.6.3, displayed on an HP Compaq LE1711 17 inch LCD monitor (Hewlett-Packard, Palo Alto, California). The monitors native resolution of 1280x1024 pixels at 60 Hz was used. The monitor was set to a brightness level of 90 and contrast to 80 with color temperature set to 6500 °K.

Procedure

Participants were given a written explanation of the procedures. After informed consent was obtained, participants took place behind the CRT monitor and followed the instructions on the screen. First, five test web page screenshots (e.g. amazon.com, cnn.com) were shown for 50 ms each, to allow participants to get used to the short exposure time. Participants pressed the space bar to present the next web page, and used the keys 1-0 on the keyboard to indicate a response from 1 (visually unappealing) to 10 (visually appealing). After participants gave a response the eight LEMtool images appeared. Each image corresponded to a numbered key (1 to 8) on the keyboard. By pressing a single key corresponding to a single LEMtool image, participants indicated the emotion that the web page elicited in them. Participants could use the 0-key to indicate that the web page did not elicit any emotion. Once the participants had rated all five test web pages, a selection of twelve web pages (6 high and 6 low visual appeal) was subsequently presented in random order to the participants. The procedure was identical to that of the test pages. After rating all web pages in the 50 ms phase, participants moved on to the free-viewing phase. Instructions for the use of the LEMtool (see Figure 2) were given in the online environment used to present the stimuli. Participants were again presented with the same five test web pages displayed in random order. Each web page would stay on the screen until participants pressed a key 1 to 0 representing a rating of 1 (visually unappealing) to 10 (visually appealing). After giving a visual appeal rating, the LEMtool would appear in the top-right corner of the screen and participants had to select areas of the web page using the computer mouse, and attach a LEMtool image to that area. Participants could give as many LEMtool indications as they liked, but were instructed to only rate elements that were related to the visual appeal of the web page. They were told that reading texts on the web pages was not required.

	Visual Appeal ratings grouping				
LEMtool image	N	1	2	3	4
Joy	14	7.50	-	-	-
Desire	36	7.67	-	-	-
Fascination	108	-	6.19	-	-
Satisfaction	63	-	6.08	-	-
Sadness	70	-	-	4.39	-
Boredom	106	-	-	3.70	-
No emotion	18	-	-	4.00	-
Disgust	78	-	-	-	2.35
Dissatisfaction	23	-	-	-	2.30

Table 4. Tukey's HSD for average visual appeal ratings per LEMtool indication in the 50 ms phase. All groups differ from each other at p <.001

Once participants had rated the five test web pages, the twelve stimulus web pages (6 high and 6 low visual appeal, for each participant different from those in the 50 ms phase) were displayed in random order. The exact same procedure as with the test web pages was followed. The second phase was concluded after participants had rated all 12 web pages using the 10-point rating scale and LEMtool and had indicated their age, gender, and native language. All texts in both phases were presented in Dutch.

Results

First a paired-samples t-test was calculated for the average visual appeal ratings given to high visual appeal and low visual appeal web pages with a 50 ms exposure time. Overall, high visual appeal web pages were rated with a 5.61 (SD = .82) while low visual appeal web pages were rated with a 3.85 (SD = 1.12). This difference was significant ($t(42) = 11.47$, $p < .001$). An identical analysis was conducted for the free-viewing phase, during which high visual appeal web pages were rated with a 5.93 (SD = 0.99) and low visual appeal web pages with a 3.47 (SD = 1.04). Again, this difference was significant ($t(41) = 16.34$, $p < .001$). In addition, a significant correlation was found between ratings in the 50 ms and free-viewing conditions (r = .88, $p < .001$). These results match findings by Lindgaard et al. [27] showing that the visual appeal of web pages can be judged in 50 ms, and that this judgement does not change substantially after longer exposure.

To determine whether the LEMtool would show a similar difference between high and low visual appeal web pages, for both the 50 ms and free-viewing phases, a cross-tabulation for visual appeal (two rows, high and low visual appeal) and LEMtool image (nine columns for the 50 ms phase, and eight columns for the free-viewing phase) was constructed. A Chi-square test of independence was performed to assess significance. For both the 50 ms phase ($\chi^2 = 89.56$, $df = 8$, $p < .001$) and the free-viewing phase ($\chi^2 = 251.01$, $df = 7$, $p < .001$) the difference between high and low visual appeal web pages was significant. Thus, for both brief and extended exposure times, the LEMtool differentiated between high and low visual appeal web pages.

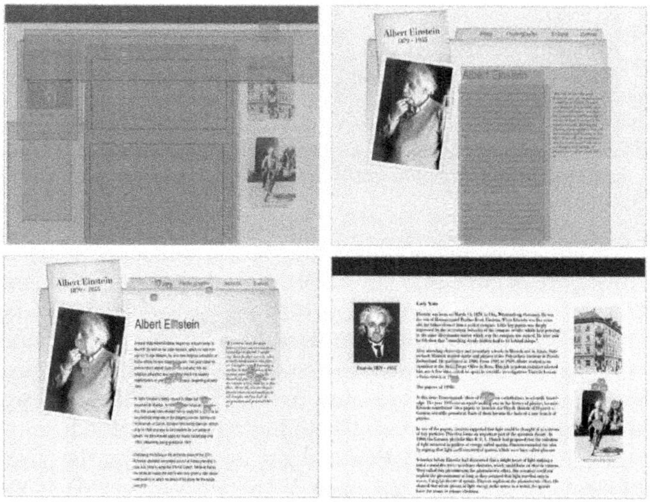

Figure 4. Two high visual appeal web pages about Einstein (Einstein - early years on the left, and Einstein - Albert Einstein on the right) used in the case study. The top two pages show a visualization for the LEMtool boredom emotion. The grey areas were selected by participants indicating boredom. The bottom two pages show a visualization for the LEMtool fascination emotion. The dots indicate the centre of a selection area indicated by participants.

To assess the relation between the visual appeal ratings and the LEMtool indications more in-depth, a one-way ANOVA with LEMtool indications (9 levels) as the independent variable and visual appeal ratings as the dependent variable, was computed ($F(8) = 113.68$, $p < .001$). A post-hoc Tukey's HSD revealed that certain LEMtool images were related to different visual appeal judgements (see Table 4). These findings indicate that the LEMtool images covered a range of emotional responses related to visual appeal. Moreover, the LEMtool images that display positive emotions were related to higher visual appeal ratings, while LEMtool images displaying negative emotions were related to lower visual appeal ratings.

To illustrate how the LEMtool can provide more detailed information about individual web pages, Figure 4 depicts two data visualization methods for two similar looking high visual appeal web pages from the same topic (i.e. Einstein). Note that this is only an example of a method for treating LEMtool data. A more comprehensive analysis of LEMtool indications for elements of all the web pages would be beyond the scope of this paper. Table 5 shows the cross-tabulation for both pages. What can be observed from both the visual data, as well as the table, is that, while both web pages are high visual appeal web pages, the composition of LEMtool emotions attached to each page differs. This was most apparent for the most selected emotions for each page (i.e. fascination, satisfaction, and boredom). The visualizations at the top of Figure 4 show that the "early years" page on the left elicited boredom in participants, more than the "Albert Einstein" page on the right did. For both pages, boredom was mainly indicated for the central text area, but considerably more so for the early years page. In addition, for the early years page the image of Einstein was also indicated as boring, which was not the case for the image on the Albert

Web page	Joy	Desire	Fascination	Satisfaction	Sadness	Boredom	Disgust	Dissatisfaction	Total
Einstein - Early Years	3	0	13	16	4	17	2	2	57
Einstein - Albert Einstein	1	4	22	23	3	3	3	0	59
Total	4	4	35	39	7	20	5	2	116

Table 5. Cross-tabulation for the LEMtool emotions indicated for two high visual appeal Einstein web pages. A Chi-square test of independence shows the web pages differ significantly on the LEMtool emotions (χ^2 = 20.69, df = 7, p <.01)

Einstein page. Furthermore, the visualizations at the bottom of Figure 4 show that the Albert Einstein page elicited more fascination in the participants than the early years page. For both web pages, the images, as well as the main text elicited fascination, but this was more so for the Albert Einstein page. Additionally, the header and quoted text in the right web page elicited fascination. The differing LEMtool indications for the web pages in Figure 4 are supported by the visual appeal ratings for each page. The early years page was rated at 5.14 (SD = 1.68) overall, while the Albert Einstein page was rated at 6.67 (SD = 1.32) overall. This difference was significant ($t(40) = -3.27$, p <.01). As indicated by the cross-tabulation (Table 5) the LEMtool revealed a similar difference between both pages. Moreover, as shown by the visualizations in Figure 4, the LEMtool provides additional insight into why these web pages differ on visual appeal. This difference mainly stems from differing LEMtool indications for boredom, fascination and satisfaction (Table 5). The Albert Einstein page was rated as more satisfying, fascinating and less boring than the early years page.

Conclusions

The goal of the case study was to demonstrate that the LEMtool can be used to differentiate between high and low visual appeal web pages. Furthermore, the case study served as a first evaluation of the way the LEMtool was envisioned to be used (see Figure 2). First of all, the case study demonstrated that participants were able to use the LEMtool to select specific areas of a web page and indicate their emotional response. While a test session was required for participants to familiarize themselves with the way the LEMtool is used, all participants were capable of indicating their responses without issues. Second, the case study supports findings by Lindgaard et al. [27] by showing that the visual appeal of a web page can be judged accurately after participants have seen the web page for only 50 ms. Moreover, this judgement remained consistent for visual appeal ratings after longer stimulus exposure. The results from the case study showed that the LEMtool revealed a similar differentiation between high and low visual appeal web pages for both the 50 ms phase and the free-viewing phase. Moreover, findings showed that the LEMtool images relate to a range of visual appeal judgements. The LEMtool emotions Joy and Desire were related to high visual appeal judgements, Fascination and Satisfaction to moderately high judgements, Sadness and Boredom to moderately low judgements, and Disgust and Dissatisfaction to low visual appeal judgements. The alternative explanation that these findings represent confusion between the images is unlikely, because little confusion was found between the LEMtool images in the validation study (see Table 2). Thus, these findings indicate that the positive LEMtool emotions are related to positive visual appeal judgements and that the negative LEMtool emotions are related to negative visual appeal judgements. Third, results from the free-viewing phase of the case study, in which participants used the LEMtool to select areas of web pages that elicited a certain emotion, illustrated how the LEMtool can provide additional insights. Analysis of two high visual appeal web pages showed that the LEMtool could aid in revealing which elements of a web page are mainly responsible for the outcome of a certain visual appeal judgement.

CONCLUSIONS AND DISCUSSION

In this paper the development process and initial validation of the LEMtool were outlined. A validation study revealed that the recognition accuracy of the images was comparable to, and in some cases exceeded, recognition ratings found in other research into non-verbal self-report of emotions [8, 45]. In a case study on visual appeal judgements, results obtained with the LEMtool were supported by findings from visual appeal ratings. Using an interactive version of the LEMtool, participants were able to select areas of web pages to indicate their emotional responses. Results revealed that the LEMtool could provide additional insights into which elements of the web pages were most prominent in forming the visual appeal judgements.

A number of limitations of the current research deserve mentioning. First, the validation study was carried out for one culture only. While the current validation study offers a good starting point for validating the LEMtool images, additional studies are required to further assess the validity of the images across different cultures. Second, while the use of screenshots in the case study allowed for better experimental control in studying the relation between visual appeal judgements and the LEMtool, emotions resulting from usability issues during interaction with a visual interface were not studied. However, considering the vital role visual appeal plays in the perception of and interaction with visual interfaces [26, 27, 39, 42], it can be argued that studying the LEMtool's capabilities to measure visual appeal judgements is crucial for the validation of the instrument. Finally, one could argue that in the free-viewing phase of the case study participants not only rated the web pages on visual appeal, but were also influenced by texts and images. However, the use of complete web pages instead of, for instance, abstract mock-ups without texts and images, makes the study more ecologically valid. Moreover, visual appeal ratings between the 50 ms phase and the free-viewing phase of the study, were highly comparable. Considering that it is unlikely that participants in the 50 ms phase reported on anything other than a first visual impression [27], it would seem that participants were actually able to focus on rating visual appeal in the free-viewing phase.

Taking these limitations into account, the investigation presented in this paper provides a good starting point for the further development of the LEMtool. Our aim is to provide a useful tool for designers in different stages of the design process of a visual interface. Early on in the design process, the LEMtool could be used to compare different prototype designs, in a similar fashion to the example in the case study. This could provide valuable insights into different design decisions. Furthermore, the LEMtool could provide insights during interactions with a visual interface. Here, the changing emotional responses of users can be studied over time, and, based on the reported emotions, interventions can be made during different stages of the interaction. For example, if a user indicates dissatisfaction at a certain point during a search task, such indications could be used to actively prompt users with information they might be looking for. Finally, we hope to further develop the LEMtool as a general research tool for measuring emotional responses during interaction with a visual interface.

ACKNOWLEDGEMENTS

This publication was supported by the Dutch national program COMMIT, and SusaGroup.

REFERENCES

1. Bradley, M. M., and Lang, P. J. Measuring emotion: The self-assessment manikin and the semantic differential. *Journal of Behavior Therapy and Experimental Psychiatry 25*, 1 (1994), 49 – 59.

2. Brave, S., and Nass, C. Emotion in human-computer interaction. In *Handbook of Human-Computer Interaction*, J. Jacko and A. Sears, Eds., Lawrence Erlbaum Associates. (2008), 77–92.

3. Calder, A. J., Rowland, D., Young, A. W., Nimmo-Smith, I., Keane, J., and Perrett, D. I. Caricaturing facial expressions. *Cognition 76*, 2 (2000), 105 – 146.

4. Capota, K., van Hout, M., and van der Geest, T. Measuring the emotional impact of websites: a study on combining a dimensional and discrete emotion approach in measuring visual appeal of university websites. In *Proceedings of DPPI '07*, ACM (2007), 135–147.

5. Carroll, J. M., and Thomas, J. M. Fun. *SIGCHI Bulletin 19*, 3 (1988), 21–24.

6. Chambers, C., Giesbrechta, K., Craiga, K., Bennett, S., and Huntsman, E. A comparison of faces scales for the measurement of pediatric pain: children's and parents ratings. *Pain 83*, 1 (1999), 25–35.

7. Deng, L., and Poole, M. S. Affect in web interfaces: a study of the impacts of web page visual complexity and order. *MIS Quarterly 34*, 4 (2010), 711–730.

8. Desmet, P. *Designing Emotions*. Unpublished doctoral thesis. Delft University of Technology, Delft, The Netherlands, 2002.

9. Desmet, P., Porcelijn, R., and Van Dijk, M. HOW to design WOW Introducing a layered-emotional approach. In *Proceedings of DPPI'05*, J. Jacko and A. Sears, Eds. (2005), 71–89.

10. Ekman, P. Strong evidence for universals in facial expressions: A reply to Russell's mistaken critique. *Psychological Bulletin 115*, 2 (1994), 268 – 287.

11. Ekman, P. Basic emotions. In *Handbook of Cognition and Emotion*, T. Dalgleish and M. Power, Eds. John Wiley & Sons Ltd., 1999, 45–60.

12. Ekman, P., and Friesen, W. V. Constants across cultures in the face and emotion. *Journal of Personality and Social Psychology 17*, 2 (1971), 124 – 129.

13. Feldman-Barrett, L. Feelings or words? Understanding the content in self-report ratings of experienced emotion. *Journal of Personality and Social Psychology 87*, 2 (2004), 266 – 281.

14. Forlizzi, J., and Battarbee, K. Understanding experience in interactive systems. In *Proceedings of DIS '04*, ACM Press (2004), 261–268.

15. Frank, M. G., and Stennett, J. The forced-choice paradigm and the perception of facial expressions of emotion. *Journal of Personality and Social Psychology 80*, 1 (2001), 75 – 85.

16. Hassenzahl, M. The Thing and I: Understanding the Relationship Between User and Product. In *Funology*, M. Blythe, K. Overbeeke, A. Monk, and P. Wright, Eds., vol. 3 of *Human-Computer Interaction Series*, Springer Netherlands (2005), 31–42.

17. Hassenzahl, M. User experience (ux): towards an experiential perspective on product quality. In *Proceedings of IHM '08*, ACM Press (2008), 11–15.

18. Hassenzahl, M., Diefenbach, S., and Gritz, A. Needs, affect, and interactive products facets of user experience. *Interacting with Computers 22*, 5 (2010), 353 – 362.

19. Hassenzahl, M., and Tractinsky, N. User experience-a research agenda. *Behaviour & Information Technology 25*, 2 (2006), 91–97.

20. Hazlett, R. L., and Benedek, J. Measuring emotional valence to understand the user's experience of software. *International Journal of Human-Computer Studies 65*, 4 (2007), 306 – 314.

21. Hicks, C. L., von Baeyer, C. L., Spafford, P. A., van Korlaar, I., and Goodenough, B. The faces pain scale revised: toward a common metric in pediatric pain measurement. *Pain 93*, 2 (2001), 173 – 183.

22. Huguet, A., Stinson, J. N., and McGrath, P. J. Measurement of self-reported pain intensity in children and adolescents. *Journal of Psychosomatic Research 68*, 4 (2010), 329 – 336.

23. Huisman, G., and Van Hout, M. The development of a graphical emotion measurement instrument using caricatured expressions: the LEMtool. In *Emotion in HCI-designing for people: proceedings of the 2008 international workshop*, C. Peter, E. Crane, M. Fabri, H. Agius, and L. Axelrod, Eds., Fraunhofer (2010), 5–7.

24. Kim, J., Lee, J., and Choi, D. Designing emotionally evocative homepages: an empirical study of the quantitative relations between design factors and emotional dimensions. *International Journal of Human-Computer Studies 59*, 6 (2003), 899 – 940.

25. Law, E. L.-C., Roto, V., Hassenzahl, M., Vermeeren, A. P., and Kort, J. Understanding, scoping and defining user experience: a survey approach. In *Proceedings of CHI '09*, ACM Press (2009), 719–728.

26. Lindgaard, G., Dudek, C., Sen, D., Sumegi, L., and Noonan, P. An exploration of relations between visual appeal, trustworthiness and perceived usability of homepages. *ACM Transactions on Computer-Human Interaction 18*, 1 (2011), 1–30.

27. Lindgaard, G., Fernandes, G., Dudek, C., and Brown, J. Attention web designers: You have 50 milliseconds to make a good first impression! *Behaviour & Information Technology 25*, 2 (2006), 115–126.

28. Mahlke, S., and Minge, M. Consideration of multiple components of emotions in human-technology interaction. In *Affect and Emotion in Human-Computer Interaction*, C. Peter and R. Beale, Eds., vol. 4868 of *Lecture Notes in Computer Science*, Springer Berlin Heidelberg (2008), 51–62.

29. McCarthy, J., and Wright, P. *Technology as Experience*. MIT Press, 2004.

30. Norman, D. *Emotional design: Why we love (or hate) everyday things*. Basic Books, 2004.

31. Read, J. Validating the fun toolkit: an instrument for measuring childrens opinions of technology. *Cognition, Technology & Work 10* (2008), 119–128.

32. Reeves, B., and Nass, C. *The Media Equation: How People Treat Computers, Television and New Media Like Real People and Places*. CSLI Publications, 2002.

33. Robinson, M. D., and Clore, G. L. Belief and feeling: Evidence for an accessibility model of emotional self-report. *Psychological Bulletin 128*, 6 (2002), 934 – 960.

34. Russell, J. A. A circumplex model of affect. *Journal of Personality and Social Psychology 39*, 6 (1980), 1161 – 1178.

35. Russell, J. A. Emotion, core affect, and psychological construction. *Cognition & Emotion 23*, 7 (2009), 1259–1283.

36. Scheirer, J., Fernandez, R., Klein, J., and Picard, R. W. Frustrating the user on purpose: a step toward building an affective computer. *Interacting with Computers 14*, 2 (2002), 93–118.

37. Scherer, K. R. What are emotions? And how can they be measured? *Social Science Information 44*, 4 (2005), 695–729.

38. Scherer, K. R. The dynamic architecture of emotion: Evidence for the component process model. *Cognition & Emotion 23*, 7 (2009), 1307–1351.

39. Sonderegger, A., and Sauer, J. The influence of design aesthetics in usability testing: Effects on user performance and perceived usability. *Applied Ergonomics 41*, 3 (2010), 403–410.

40. Thüring, M., and Mahlke, S. Usability, aesthetics and emotions in human-technology interaction. *International Journal of Psychology 42*, 4 (2007), 253–264.

41. Tractinsky, N., Cokhavi, A., Kirschenbaum, M., and Sharfi, T. Evaluating the consistency of immediate aesthetic perceptions of web pages. *International Journal of Human-Computer Studies 64*, 11 (2006), 1071–1083.

42. Tractinsky, N., Katz, A., and Ikar, D. What is beautiful is usable. *Interacting with Computers 13*, 2 (2000), 127–145.

43. Van den Broek, E., Janssen, J., Westerink, J., and Healey, J. Prerequisites for affective signal processing (ASP). In *Proceedings of Biosignals '11*, Springer (2009), 426–433.

44. Van Dongelen, R. *What is beautiful is good and usable*. Unpublished master thesis. University of Twente, Enschede, The Netherlands, 2008.

45. Vastenburg, M., Romero Herrera, N., Van Bel, D., and Desmet, P. PMRI: development of a pictorial mood reporting instrument. In *Proceedings of CHI '11*, ACM (2011), 2155–2160.

46. Wallbott, H. G. Bodily expression of emotion. *European Journal of Social Psychology 28*, 6 (1998), 879–896.

47. Ward, R., and Marsden, P. Physiological responses to different web page designs. *International Journal of Human-Computer Studies 59*, 12 (2003), 199 – 212.

48. Ward, R., and Marsden, P. Affective computing: problems, reactions and intentions. *Interacting with Computers 16*, 4 (2004), 707 – 713.

49. Wiles, J. A., and Cornwell, T. B. A review of methods utilized in measuring affect, feelings, and emotion in advertising. *Current Issues and Research in Advertising 13*, 1-2 (1991), 241–275.

50. Zajonc, R. B. Feeling and thinking: Preferences need no inferences. *American Psychologist 35*, 2 (1980), 151 – 175.

51. Zhou, H., and Fu, X. Understanding, measuring, and designing user experience: The causal relationship between the aesthetic quality of products and user affect. In *Human-Computer Interaction. Interaction Design and Usability*, J. Jacko, Ed., vol. 4550 of *Lecture Notes in Computer Science*, Springer (2007), 340–349.

Exploring Personality-Targeted UI Design in Online Social Participation Systems

Oded Nov
Polytechnic Institute of New York University
onov@poly.edu

Ofer Arazy
University of Alberta
ofer.arazy@ualberta.ca

Claudia López
University of Pittsburgh
cal95@pitt.edu

Peter Brusilovsky
University of Pittsburgh
peterb@pitt.edu

ABSTRACT
We present a theoretical foundation and empirical findings demonstrating the effectiveness of personality-targeted design. Much like a medical treatment applied to a person based on his specific genetic profile, we argue that theory-driven, personality-targeted UI design can be more effective than design applied to the entire population. The empirical exploration focused on two settings, two populations and two personality traits: Study 1 shows that users' extroversion level moderates the relationship between the UI cue of audience size and users' contribution. Study 2 demonstrates that the effectiveness of social anchors in encouraging online contributions depends on users' level of emotional stability. Taken together, the findings demonstrate the potential and robustness of the interactionist approach to UI design. The findings contribute to the HCI community, and in particular to designers of social systems, by providing guidelines to targeted design that can increase online participation.

Author Keywords
Theory-driven design; user interface; personality; extroversion; emotional stability; audience size; anchoring.

ACM Classification Keywords
H.5.m. Information interfaces and presentation (e.g., HCI): Miscellaneous.

INTRODUCTION
Understanding how psychology can inform the design of social technologies has been the subject of extant HCI research in recent years [13, 22, 44, 47]. While the design of web-based applications to support social participation has been largely based on intuition, trial and error [43, 62], researchers of social participation in online settings have been trying to develop theories that will guide practice. To date, much of the HCI research in the area has focused on the general user population, overlooking personality differences. In these design-based studies, controlled experiments are used to test the effect of UI design features on user behavior, building on psychology theories to inform design choices [13, 22, 47]. This approach enables researchers to draw conclusions about design effectiveness. However, to date, studies based on this approach did not take into account differences in users' fundamental idiosyncratic attributes, such as their personalities or motivations; in other words, to follow a medical metaphor, this is equivalent to testing the effectiveness of a medical treatment by providing it to all patients, regardless of their specific genetic make-up.

CHI 2013, April 27–May 2, 2013, Paris, France.

We argue that an understanding of personality differences is essential for designing HCI for online participation, as different personalities are expected to respond differently to design cues. Drawing on the interactionist tradition in psychology research [17, 67], whereby situation and personality interact to determine people's behavior, we combine controlled experiments, design manipulations, surveys, and system data, to test the effectiveness of design features that target participants' idiosyncratic personal attributes. The Psychology literature is divided on the extent to which personality traits are viewed as stable and could predict behavior. While the "personality" approach focuses on individual differences as the primary predictor of behavior, the "situation" approach emphasizes on the characteristics of the situation where behavior takes place. The interactionist approach tries to bridge these opposing views and highlights the joint contribution of personality and situation factors to explaining human behavior [17, 35]. As such, this perspective incorporates a broader range of explanations and allows researchers to test the effect of one set of variables while controlling for the other. The interactionist perspective has been applied in a variety of contexts to explain behaviors such as individuals' creativity [70] and reactions to organizational change [59].

RELATED WORK
Our approach to applying the interactionist perspective to the problem of online participation is inspired by the literature on individual differences, technology use and online engagement. Studies in that field showed how participants' personal attributes, such as motivations or personality traits, are correlated with technology use [49, 51, 55] and online contribution [25, 57].

Relevant to our research is the literature on personalization (e.g., [10, 23, 48]). Work in that area often develops a user model based on users' task-specific interactions (e.g. movie views by the user in a movie recommender system). In the present paper, on the other hand, we classify users based on pre-existing categories informed by psychology research (personality traits, in this case). In other words, while personalization often involves defining user personas based on task-specific prior activities, we define user profiles based on more fundamental user attributes that transcend specific settings.

In recent years, there is an attempt to explore personality differences within the context of HCI. For example, several studies have explored the interaction between users' personality and persuasive messages they receive. For example, [41] investigated the interaction between the trait of "persuadability" and health-related persuasive messages on people's participation in health-related activity; and [40] studied how the interaction between personality and influence strategies affects online purchase intentions. [34] took these ideas to the design of health-promoting mobile applications, and studied the effects of the interaction between personality and persuasive strategies on people's usage intentions. While such studies had the ultimate goal of informing design, they did not directly test the effects of UI design manipulations.

In the related field of adaptive UI, there has been prior experimental work on the interaction between personality traits and UI design features [30, 53]. The primary objective of these studies has been to reduce users' cognitive load and make their interaction with the computer more efficient. The differences in goals between such studies and ours (reduce cognitive load vs. influence online participation), make them different in terms of the applicable design manipulations.

Building on these prior works, the goal of the present paper is to investigate the interaction between personality and design features on online participation.

THE PROPOSED APPROACH

Applying the interactionist approach to HCI design, we address the following general research question: can differences in users' idiosyncratic personal attributes explain the effects of design interventions on users' online participation? Using the medical metaphor mentioned above, the proposed approach is analogous to testing the effectiveness of a medical treatment being applied to individuals based on their specific genetic profile, rather than the same treatment applied to the entire population. While the proposed approach is applicable in a variety of design settings, we use as the setting of this research two social recommender systems, following the approach of MovieLens [25, 47], a social movie recommender system used as an online, live laboratory setting for researchers to test the effect of design on user behavior.

In a recent study [56], we reported a preliminary exploration of the interactionist approach, following the experimental design outlined in Table 1, in which we showed how users' conscientiousness levels determine their response to a particular design intervention (manipulating an indicator presenting the number of past contributors in an online setting). In the present study we explore new design contexts. We describe two studies in which we examine how the interaction between personality traits (extroversion in Study 1 and emotional stability in Study 2) and design interventions (experimental manipulation of perceived audience size and social anchoring in studies 1 and 2 respectively) affect user participation.

	Experimental manipulations	
Personal Attributes	*Design intervention: low level*	*Design intervention: high level*
Low level of personal attribute	Outcome for: low attribute level X low intervention	Outcome for: low attribute level X high intervention
High level of personal attribute	Outcome for: high attribute level X low intervention	Outcome for: high attribute level X high intervention
	Experimental Outcomes	

Table 1. Experimental design: attributes X interventions.

This paper makes several contributions to HCI research. Study 1 helps explain the inconclusive evidence concerning users' response to UI indicator of group (or "audience") size, and shows that users' extroversion/introversion moderates the relationship between the UI manipulation and users' online participation. Study 2 expands the limited HCI literature on social anchoring. It demonstrates the effectiveness of UI indicators that serve as anchors in encouraging online contributions depends on users' level of emotional stability. Taking the results of these two studies together, we demonstrate the potential and robustness of the interactionist approach to UI design in different settings. We show that for different combinations of personality traits and design manipulation, users' personal idiosyncratic attributes play a significant role in determining the extent to which UI design manipulation encourage contribution in online social systems. Finally, our study contributes to HCI practitioners, and in particular to designers of recommender systems, by providing guidelines to targeted design that can increase online contributions.

In the sections that follow, we present two studies - the first focuses on the moderating effect of extroversion on the relationship between perceived audience size and online participation, and the second investigates the differential effects of social anchoring on online helping behavior, moderated by emotional stability. In each study we present the relevant literature, develop hypotheses about the factors affecting user behavior, test the hypotheses in an experimental setting, and discuss the findings briefly. We then conclude the paper with a broader discussion of the results, the interactionist approach to UI design, and the implications for theory and practice.

STUDY 1: EXTROVERSION AND AUDIENCE SIZE

A large body of research on social technologies has been concerned with identifying effective ways to encourage contribution of public goods, such as users' knowledge in online settings [6, 7, 9]. A prominent avenue of research involved the analysis of the relationship between audience size and individuals' contribution levels [5, 7, 71]. However, research in this area offer inconsistent perspectives: for example, a study of Facebook newcomers [7] found a positive relation between perceived audience size and contribution levels, and [71] found that a reduction in the Chinese Wikipedia audience size (as a result of the blocking of Wikipedia in mainland China) led to a decrease in contributions among those users who were not blocked, suggesting a positive relation between contribution and audience size. Such empirical findings, however, stand in contrast with extant research on private provision of public goods, which suggests that the incentive to contribute is inversely related to group size due to free riding [71]. In many social technologies and online contribution settings (e.g., Wikipedia, yelp, open source software) a potential audience size is similar to the group size, since all readers can contribute and vice versa.

We offer a new perspective on such conflicting evidence, which allows for examining the response to UI indicators of audience size by different types of users. A fundamental factor that distinguishes individuals from one another is personality - the dispositions and interpersonal strategies that explain people's behavior, and the unique and relatively stable patterns of behaviors, shown by individuals [72]. A personality trait highly relevant to understanding users' response to the potential audience for their contribution is extroversion. Extroversion represents sociability, cheerfulness, and optimism, such that extroverts seek out new opportunities and excitement [51] and are sensitive to positive or pleasure cues in their social environment [12]. Introverts, on the other hand, are reserved and distant toward other people [32].

Extroversion has been associated with different patterns of Internet use [58]. Introverts were found to be more likely to prefer online to offline communication [16] and to spend more time on chat rooms than extroverts [4]. Introverts also reported that they can express themselves better in an online context than offline [3]. Introverts' preference for online communication can be explained by the "online disinhibition effect" theory [58]. This theory [66] states that some aspects of online communication may lead to less restrained communication and greater self-disclosure online. Among these characteristics, the dissociative anonymity, invisibility and asynchronicity aspects of online communication can make it more appealing to introverts. Being anonymous, remaining invisible to others, being unable to see others' physical communicational cues, and having time to think about what will be posted can help introverts to feel more comfortable online. On the other hand, other studies have found that extroverts were more likely than introverts to use the Internet to maintain their relationships with friends and family, to meet new people online and to frequent chat rooms [42]. Extroverts were also more likely to use social networking sites for maintaining relationships, entertainment and information expression [45]. An argument that can explain such results is that social networking sites are built around the user's preexisting offline social network [58]. This can make the factors that lead to the online disinhibition effect (e.g. anonymity) less salient, thus favoring extroverts rather than introverts.

In the present study we test the hypothesis that extroverts will respond to a UI design feature indicating audience size in a different way than introverts. In other words, we hypothesize that users' extroversion level will moderate the relationship between perceived audience size and the likelihood they will participate in an online social setting.

We expect that a small audience size will be associated with lower contribution among extroverts and higher contribution among introverts. The reasoning behind this hypothesis is as follows: extroverts tend to be sociable, assertive, talkative and active, whereas introverts are shy and reserved [31]. Extroverts also tend to seek rewards, with little attention to the potential of negative consequences of such pursuit, whereas introverts are more oriented toward avoiding punishment than toward gaining rewards [32]. A large audience size may represent the potential benefit of making the contributor look knowledgeable and helpful among a large user population (or online "audience"), but also increases the potential for *evaluation apprehension* [15], whereby the presence of others leads people to refrain from expressing their views in social settings (e.g., classroom, meetings), because they are uncertain about how their views will be received [26]. Introverts, who seek to minimize the risks associated with their behavior, are expected to exhibit greater evaluation apprehension when the perceived audience size is larger (which increases the likelihood that the views they express will be received negatively by someone in the audience), and consequently, will tend to contribute less. Extroverts, on the other hand, will tend to play up the potential benefits of reaching a larger audience who may appreciate their contribution, and will therefore be more likely to participate when a larger audience is present. Furthermore, extroverts - who tend to be sociable and relish the company of others - are likely to be encouraged by the prospect of interacting with a large audience, whereas shy and reserved introverts may be intimidated by this prospect. We acknowledge that an alternative hypothesis might be that anonymity and identifiability in online communication can change group members' behavior. The Social Identity model of Deindividuation Effects [60, 61] and the online disinhibition effect theory have been used to explain how anonymity and identifiability in online communication can affect the group members differently than in offline communication and encourage participation among users – such as introverts – who might be more inhibited in offline settings. The specific setting of our study, however, makes the latter hypothesis less applicable, given that all users come from the same graduate school, and therefore the perception of complete anonymity may be hard to maintain.

Study 1: Methodology

The experimental setting for testing the hypothesis in the present study was CourseAgent [21], a community-based study planning system for graduate students in the School of Information Sciences (iSchool) at the University of Pittsburgh. CourseAgent allows students to plan their studies and evaluate courses that they have taken, reflecting workload and relevance to personal career goals. The system serves as a source of knowledge about the suitability of graduate courses given specific career goals. Currently, the system has over 100 active users.

During the experiment period, the CourseAgent landing page (see Figure 1) invited participants to answer a short questionnaire which included personality items. Participants were surveyed only once during this period, and the response was measured dichotomously as providing – or not – at least one course evaluation. Self-report surveys are commonly used in social science research to identify personal attributes, and have been used extensively in HCI and CSCW studies [51, 65]. The two extroversion trait questionnaire items used a 7-point Likert scale and were taken from the Ten Item Personality Instrument [31], a short version of the Big Five instrument which has been validated and tested numerous times in prior studies.

The experimental manipulation included changing the UI indicators for audience size. A highly noticeable banner on the top of every interface of CourseAgent showed the number of visitors during the prior month. These numbers were manipulated to include two conditions – of small and large audience – applied in random. For the small-audience condition, the value assigned to the number of visitors was between 7 and 10 (values in this range applied randomly). For the large-audience condition, the number of visitors was 100 (ranging between 90-110). Figure 1 shows a screenshot of the large audience size condition. In summary, users were assigned to one of the four experimental conditions described in Table 1.

Manipulation check: The low and high values of audience size (of roughly 10 and 100 respectively) were established after a pilot test conducted by using Amazon Mechanical Turk. In that experiment, participants were directed to a webpage describing a simple scenario.

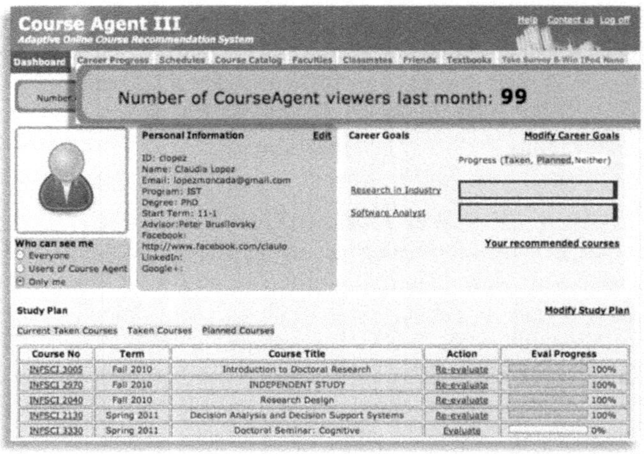

Figure 1. Audience size manipulation: large audience size.

According to this scenario, the participant heard about a web site that provides movie recommendations based on users' ratings; when visiting the website, the participant finds out that its number of viewers last month was X (where X is manipulated by the researchers and is randomly assigned either the low or high audience size values). Having seen this, the participant in the pilot study is asked to what extent they agree with a statements that the movie reviews website has a large audience. Responses ranged between 1 (strongly disagree) to 7 (strongly agree) using a Likert scale. The mean responses of the populations' of the two experimental conditions were compared. 161 people took part in this pilot study. The low audience size indicator received the average score of 4.13 out of 7, and the high audience size indicator received the average score of 4.94. A t-test was used to compare the means, and difference between them was found to be significant ($p<0.001$). The results supported the assumption that the two anchors represent large and small audience size.

Study 1: Data analysis

We first distinguished between extroverts and introverts by performing a median split, such that respondents whose extroversion score was above the sample median were classified as high-extroversion and those below the median as low-extroversion respondents. Cronbach's alpha of the extroversion responses was 0.77, representing satisfactory reliability. The independent variables in the analysis included extroversion (high = 1, low = 0), perceived audience size (high = 1, low = 0), and the interaction between them. We were interested in understanding how the independent variables affect the likelihood that a user will decide to contribute. Therefore, the outcome variable was contribution, defined as providing at least one evaluation (Evaluated = 1, Not evaluated = 0). In order to examine the effects of personality and design, as well as their interaction, and due to the dichotomous outcome variable, we used a factorial logistic regression in the statistical analysis.

Study 1: Results and discussion

Overall, 53 people participated in this study, of which 31 (58.5%) were women. The average age was 28.3 (stdev=7.1). On average, participants contributed 1.9 evaluations and 43.4% of them contributed at least one evaluation. A between-subject comparison showed that contribution was characterized by power-law distribution. Examining the effect of the audience size alone, revealed no significant difference in contribution rate: 44.0% of those in the large audience condition and 42.9% of those in the large audience condition provided at least one evaluation. In other words, on average, audience size did not lead to more participation. However, as expected, a closer look at the participation rates of the sub-populations, considering both the external manipulation and the users' extroversion level, revealed a more intricate relationship (see Figure 2).

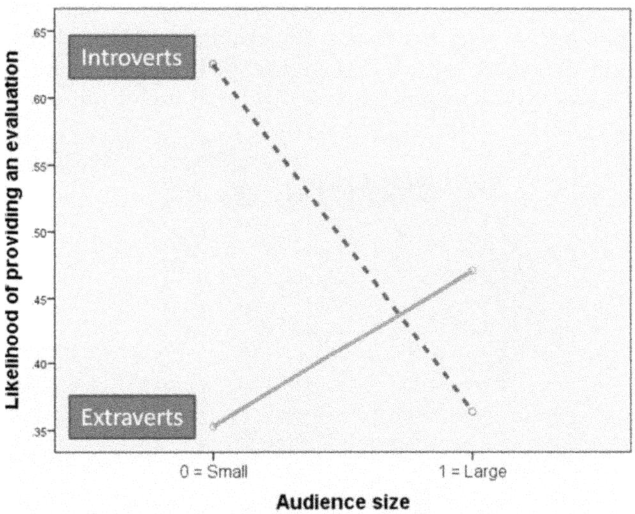

Figure 2. The differential effects of audience size: audience size and contribution are related positively among extroverts and negatively among introverts.

The results of the logistic regression showed that the main effects of the independent variables were not statistically significant (B=-.59, Wald=.58, p=.45 for extroversion and B=-1.50, Wald=2.52, p=.11 for audience size). Examining the focus of our analysis, the interaction between audience size and extroversion level and its effect on contribution, was found to be significant, in the expected direction (B=2.68, Wald=4.73, p<.05).

The findings support the hypothesis that the interaction between extroversion and audience size is such that perceived large audience size is associated with increased contribution among extroverts and decreased contribution among introverts, whereas perceived low audience size will be associated with increased contribution by introverts and decreased contribution by introverts (see Figure 2).

The results call into question the effectiveness of a common practice in the design of social technologies, and highlight the potential effectiveness of a more nuanced person-situation interactionist approach: providing cues that emphasize the potential for a large audience size may be an effective way to increase participation among extroverts, but should be avoided when users are more introvert. Future work is needed in order to identify other personal attributes - such as social orientation or community commitment - that may interact with perceived audience size. As a practical matter, surveying new users about their personality traits as part of their joining process could provide a minimally intrusive way to learn about users' personal attributes. With such information, social systems' designers can develop adaptive user experience, which include theory-driven design cues based the idiosyncratic personal attributes of users.

STUDY 2: EMOTIONAL STABILITY AND SOCIAL ANCHORING

Human judgment tends to be influenced by *anchoring*: when asked to make a quantitative judgment, people are often influenced by externally presented information when such information is available to them [52]. Anchoring is seen as one of three basic heuristics in intuitive judgment [39]. Extant psychology research demonstrates the cognitive effects of anchoring: experimental manipulation of the initial values, or anchors, leads to estimates that are biased toward the anchor [18, 28]. As a result, studies of the effects of anchoring on human behavior were carried out in a variety of disciplines, including finance [36], law [33] and marketing [1]. Some of the psychological mechanisms underlying anchoring are confirmatory hypothesis testing, numeric or magnitude priming, and insufficient adjustment. Recent studies took a broader view of anchoring and adopted an attitudes and persuasion perspective, focusing on the social context in which anchors arise [69]. We use the term *social anchoring* to refer to an anchoring effect where the social context, and in particular the anchor's source, elicit processes of persuasion and social influence and affect judgment [19].

Generally speaking, HCI research on the effects on anchoring has been relatively scarce [2], with the notable exception of [11], who found that when users of a movie recommender system were asked to re-rate movies while (experimentally manipulated) "predicted" rating were presented to them, they tended to change their rating toward the "prediction" anchor. More recently, [2] showed that users' ratings can be influenced by a recommender system's (experimentally manipulated) anchors, and that the effects of anchoring can be separated from the effects of the system's perceived reliability. We build on this prior work and extend it to explore whether some people are more sensitive to anchoring than others.

The interaction between personality traits and anchoring has been the subject of recent research. For example, it was shown that individuals who are high in the openness-to-experience personality trait were significantly more influenced by anchoring cues relative to participants low in this trait [52], and [20] found that those high on agreeableness and conscientiousness but low on extroversion were more susceptible to anchoring. In contrast, [27] found no significant interaction between anchoring cues and the personality traits of openness-to-experience. Our focus is on the personality trait of emotional stability, sometimes known as the opposite of neuroticism [54, 68], which we take to be highly relevant for the anchoring context: people characterized by high emotional stability tend to be secure and self-assured [12], whereas those who are low in emotional stability (i.e. high in neuroticism) tend to be insecure and self-doubting and experience the world as distressing [14]. We argue that emotional stability has the potential to explain user behavior in the presence of anchoring: since individuals who are high in emotional stability tend to be more secure and self-assured, we expect that they will be less susceptible to the influence of social anchoring cues. Individuals who are high on neuroticism, on the other hand, tend to have an external control of reinforcement [37, 38]. Internal versus external control (i.e. 'locus of control') refers to the degree to which people believe events in their life and rewards they receive are the result of their own behavior or outside of their control [63, 64]. Hence, because those high in neuroticism tend to be externally focused, we expect them to be more susceptible to the influence of others, and in particular to be more influenced by anchors representing the opinions of others. In sum, we hypothesize that the effect of social anchoring cues on users' rating will be weaker among high- emotional stability participants compared to low- emotional stability participants.

Study 2: Methodology

We tested our hypothesis using a simulated online recommender system called PetLink which we developed as an experimental platform. PetLink is presented as a research project in need of feedback from users: its landing page invites participants to answer a very short personality questionnaire, and a simulated recommender system returns a picture of a pet that purports to present the "best match" for the participant's personality (see Figures 3-5).

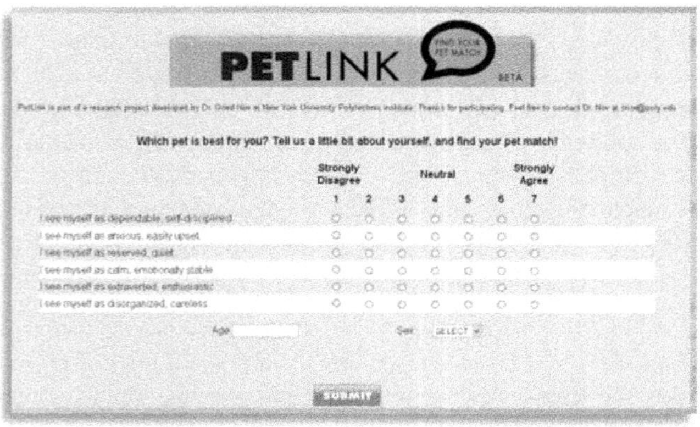

Figure 3. PetLink landing page screenshot.

The PetLink environment facilitates the implementation of a 2X2 factorial experimental design illustrated in Table 1, consisting of: (1) measurement of personal attributes (through a short questionnaire), (2) design intervention, and (3) opportunities for users to rate the accuracy of the recommendation and provide feedback. As such, PetLink serves as an experimental platform through which we can address research questions on the interactions between personal attributes, design choices, and user behavior.

Participants in the study were recruited via Amazon Mechanical Turk. They received $0.05 and took part in the study only once. Participants were led to believe that PetLink is part of an academic research project involving the development of a technique to match respondents' personality traits and the pet that would suit them most. This was communicated to participants in a recruitment announcement, and on the PetLink site itself.

The PetLink landing page (see Figure 3) invited participants to answer a short personality questionnaire. The two emotional stability questionnaire items used a 7-point Likert scale and were adapted from the Ten Item Personality Instrument [31], a short version of the Big Five instrument.

Figure 4. PetLink image page screenshot.

After filling out the short questionnaire respondents were presented with their purported "best match" (see Figure 4): an image of an animal based on the responses to the survey questions, such that each combination of responses was associated with a specific pet image. Unbeknown to the respondents, the system consistently, but arbitrarily, paired certain images with certain personality profiles, with no attempt to match images to personalities. At this stage, respondents were requested to rate the quality of the match on a five-star scale (see Figure 4). In line with the experimental design presented in Table 1, a median split was performed such that respondents with an emotional stability score above the sample median were classified as high-emotional stability participants, and those below the median as low- emotional stability.

The experimental manipulation consisted of high and low social anchor level: In addition to the image, respondents were also presented with information about the average rating for the particular pet image presented to them (along the lines of UI design common on popular recommender systems such as Amazon or Netflix). The "Average Rating" value (see Figure 5), representing the social anchor, was experimentally manipulated and randomly assigned either high level (4.5 stars) or low level (1 star).

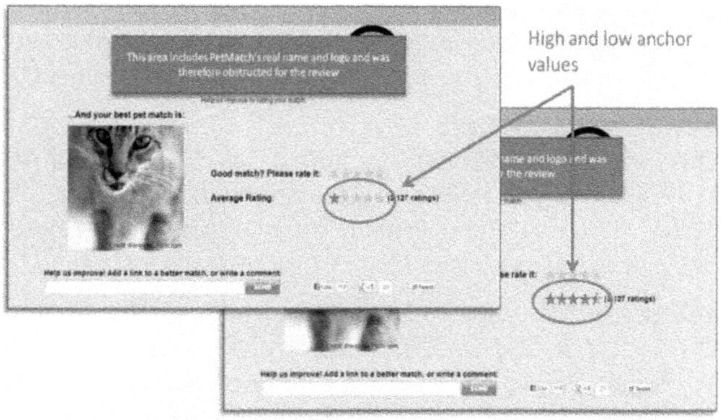

Figure 5. Experimental manipulation: two anchor values.

In summary, at this stage all users were assigned to one of the four experimental conditions described in Table 1, and following a between-subjects study design, their responses were compared.

Study 2: Data analysis

Overall, 375 people participated in this study, of which 47.2% were women. The average age was 28.7 (stdev=9.9). 249 participants (66.4%) provided rating. Cronbach's alpha of the emotional stability responses was 0.74, representing satisfactory reliability. To test our hypothesis that anchoring is less effective among people with high emotional stability, we ran a regression with the independent variables of emotional stability (high emotional stability = 1, low emotional stability = 0), perceived social anchor (high = 1, low = 0), and the interaction between them. The outcome variable was the average rating (ranging between 1-5 stars) provided by the participants.

Study 2: Results and discussion

The average rating among participants in all experimental conditions was 3.04. Consistent with prior studies, ratings were biased toward the anchors, with mean rating = 3.36 among high-anchor participants and 2.71 and among low anchor participants. The results of the regression revealed an insignificant main effect of emotional stability (p=.6) and a significant effect of perceived social anchor (p<.01). As expected, both the regression and an ANOVA revealed that the interaction between the independent variables was significant (p<.05), thus supporting our hypothesis: on average, all participants were susceptible to anchoring (i.e., provided higher rating when shown the high social anchor), however, the effect of anchoring on high emotional stability participants was weaker than its effect on low emotional stability (neurotic) participants (see Figure 6).

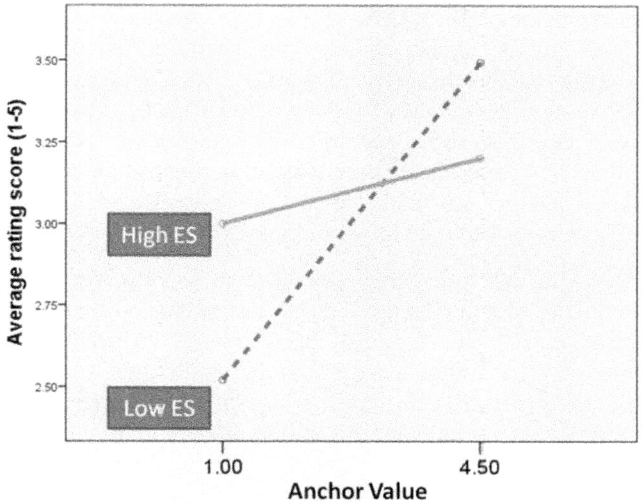

Figure 6. The differential effect of social anchoring: high Emotional Stability participants are less susceptible to social anchoring than low Emotional Stability participants.

The results highlight the potential effectiveness of the personality targeted interactionist approach: anchoring may be a universal phenomenon, but its magnitude is highly person-specific. From an interaction design perspective, using anchors as a way to influence behavior is more effective among some users, and further work is needed to identify other personal attributes that may influence the effect of anchoring. Another related open question concerns the identification of other UI design interventions that may interact with the Emotional Stability personality trait.

OVERALL DISCUSSION AND CONCLUSIONS

In the two studies described here, we tested the effectiveness of personality-targeted design approach as a way to influence participants and increase their participation. Specifically, by focusing on audience size and social anchoring cues, we sought to examine relatively popular HCI design practices (namely, displaying others' behavior, including others' rating and the number of others' prior visits), in order to (1) demonstrate how insights from psychology research can be used in novel ways in an HCI context to improve the effectiveness of social technologies, and (2) use HCI design as a large-scale experimental tool through which to contribute to psychology research.

The UI design cues we tested were shown to have a differential effect on participants with different levels of the extroversion and emotional stability, supporting our hypotheses and illustrating the potential value of personality-targeted design.

While specific design implications were discussed for each study separately, a more general implication from the findings is that we cannot necessarily expect indicators of community's activity (such as audience size, or others' rating) to equally affect all participants . Instead, a more nuanced, targeted approach to UI design is needed. This is made particularly evident in the case of Study 1, where displaying the number of other users' past visits led to effects in opposite directions (see Figure 2). These effects cancel each other out when not considering the personal attributes of users. In other words, certain design intervention may seem ineffective, whereas a closer look at the interaction between these intervention and the users' attributes will reveal effective ways to encourage contribution.

More broadly, our proposed approach to targeted design highlights the need to tailor design features to personality or other idiosyncratic personal characteristics, such that front-end and back-end design features will cater to users' particular personal attributes. In recent years, a number of studies have investigated the effects of users' personal traits on UI design. Studies on persuasion strategies have shown how personality determines people's reaction to persuasive messages [40] and have suggested that this approach is applicable to the design of system interfaces [34]. Studies on adaptive UI have demonstrated that personality-based design can reduce users' cognitive load [30, 53]. Our studies build on and extend such prior work, showing that personality-targeted design can enhance online participation.

Another implication of our results is the need to explore systems that can automatically adapt their features to users' personal attributes. In the area of e-learning, where survey-based assessment of learner individual traits is common, research on adaptation to individual traits has already become popular [24]. To reduce users' burden of answering long personality questionnaire, designers may survey new users as part of their joining the system, or make it part of a game-like activity (such as PetLink).

Recent research opens interesting prospects for unobtrusive adaptation to user personal traits. Since the survey approach used in the present study may be less appropriate in other kinds of interactive systems, there are less intrusive methods for automatically detecting aspects of users' personality. Such methods may include a measurement of invariable traits and dispositions (e.g., by creating a user profile), or even capturing users' transient preferences and attitudes such that the UI is not only personalized across users but also tailored to a users' particular attitude at particular points in time. Recent research has demonstrated the feasibility of recognizing user traits in "rich" multi-modal and dialog interfaces [30, 46, 50], and in Web and mobile phone interfaces [8, 29].

A limitation of the studies presented here stems from their experimental design: by exploring one design intervention and one personal attribute at a time, we limit the scope of the findings. Future work may address this by examining simultaneously a larger number of interventions and personal attributes. Another limitation is the measurement of personal attributes at a single point in time.

Future research may also involve the differential effects of a larger set of design interventions in a wider range of contexts, including mobile and haptic interfaces. It may also consider a wider range of personal attributes, beyond personality traits, such as motivations and context-specific attitudes. The present study demonstrates the utility of considering such factors, simultaneously, in the design of social technologies.

ACKNOWLEDGMENTS

This work was partially supported by NSF Award IIS 1149745, by the Fulbright Program and by CONICYT, Chile. We thank Erez Heiman for site design, and Durga Bhavani and Manasa Ranjitha Alla for research assistance.

REFERENCES

1. Adaval, R. and Wyer Jr, R. S., "Conscious and Nonconscious Comparisons with Price Anchors," *Journal of Marketing Research,* 48, 355-365, 2011.
2. Adomavicius, G., Bockstedt, J., Curley, S., and Zhang, J., "Recommender systems, consumer preferences, and anchoring effects," *Proc. RecSys Workshop on Human Decision Making in Recommender Systems*, 2011.
3. Amichai-Hamburger, Y., Wainapel, G., and Fox, S., ""On the Internet no one knows I'm an introvert"," *CyberPsychology & Behavior,* 5, 125-128, 2002.
4. Anolli, L., Villani, D., and Riva, G., "Personality of people using Chat," *CyberPsychology & Behavior,* 8, 89-95, 2005.
5. Antin, J. and Cheshire, C., "Readers are not free-riders: reading as a form of participation on wikipedia," *Proc. ACM conference on Computer Supported Cooperative Work*, Savannah, GA, 2010.
6. Antin, J., Cheshire, C., and Nov, O., "Technology-mediated contributions: editing behaviors among new wikipedians," *Proc. ACM conference on Computer Supported Cooperative Work (CSCW)*, Seatttle, WA, 2012.
7. Burke, M., Marlow, C., and Lento, T., "Feed me: motivating newcomer contribution in social network sites," *Proc. 27th international Conference on Human Factors in Computing Systems* 2009.
8. Chittaranjan, G., Blom, J., and Gatica-Perez, D., "Mining large-scale smartphone data for personality studies," *Personal and Ubiquitous Computing,* 1-18, 2012.
9. Choi, B., Alexander, K., Kraut, R. E., and Levine, J. M., "Socialization tactics in wikipedia and their effects," *Proc. 2010 ACM conference on Computer Supported Cooperative Work (CSCW)*, 2010.
10. Chu, W. and Park, S.-T., "Personalized recommendation on dynamic content using predictive bilinear models," Proc. 18th International Conference on the World Wide Web (WWW), Madrid, Spain, 2009.
11. Cosley, D., Lam, S. K., Albert, I., Konstan, J. A., and Riedl, J., "Is seeing believing?: how recommender system interfaces affect users' opinions," *Proc. SIGCHI conference on Human factors in computing systems*, Ft. Lauderdale, FL, 2003.
12. Costa, P. and McCrae, R., "NEO Personality Inventory–Revised (NEO-PI-R) and NEO Five-Factor Inventory

(NEO-FFI) Professional Manual," *Odessa, FL: Psychological Assessment Resources,* 1992.
13. Dabbish, L. and Kraut, R., "Awareness displays and social motivation for coordinating communication," *Information Systems Research,* 19, 221-238, 2008.
14. Diefendorff, J. and Richard, E., "Antecedents and consequences of emotional display rule perceptions," *Journal of Applied Psychology,* 88, 284, 2003.
15. Diehl, M. and Stroebe, W., "Productivity loss in brainstorming groups," *Journal of Personality and Social Psychology,* 53, 497-509, 1987.
16. Ebeling-Witte, S., Frank, M., and Lester, D., "Shyness, Internet use, and personality," *CyberPsychology & Behavior,* 10, 713-716, 2007.
17. Endler, N. and Parker, J., "Interactionism revisited," *European Journal of Personality,* 6, 177-198, 1992.
18. Englich, B., Mussweiler, T., and Strack, F., "Playing dice with criminal sentences," *Personality and Social Psychology Bulletin,* 32, 188-200, 2006.
19. Epley, N. and Gilovich, T., "Anchoring unbound," *Journal of Consumer Psychology,* 20, 20-24, 2010.
20. Eroglu, C. and Croxton, K. L., "Biases in judgmental adjustments of statistical forecasts," *International Journal of Forecasting,* 26, 116-133, 2010.
21. Farzan, R. and Brusilovsky, P., "Encouraging user participation in a course recommender system: An impact on user behavior," *Computers in Human Behavior,* 27, 276-284, 2011.
22. Farzan, R., Dabbish, L., Kraut, R., and Postmes, T., "Increasing commitment to online communities by designing for social presence," *ACM 2011 Conference on Computer Supported Cooperative Work (CSCW),* Hangzhou, China, 2011.
23. Felfernig, A., Mandl, M., Tiihonen, J., Schubert, M., and Leitner, G., "Personalized user interfaces for product configuration," *Proc. 15th International Conference on Intelligent User Interfaces*, Hong Kong, China, 2010.
24. Ford, N. and Chen, S., "Individual differences, hypermedia navigation, and learning," *Journal of educational multimedia and hypermedia,* 9, 281-311, 2000.
25. Fugelstad, P., Dwyer, P., Filson Moses, J., Kim, J., Mannino, C. A., Terveen, L., and Snyder, M., "What makes users rate (share, tag, edit...)?: predicting patterns of participation in online communities," *Proc. ACM 2012 conference on Computer Supported Cooperative Work*, 2012.
26. Furnham, A. and Yazdanpanahi, T., "Personality differences and group versus individual brainstorming," *Personality and Individual Differences,* 19, 73-80, 1995.
27. Furnham, A., Boo, H. C., and McClelland, A., "Individual differences and the susceptibility to the influence of anchoring cues," *Journal of Individual Differences,* 33, 89, 2012.
28. Galinsky, A. and Mussweiler, T., "First offers as anchors," *Journal of Personality and Social psychology,* 81, 657, 2001.
29. Golbeck, J., Robles, C., Edmondson, M., and Turner, K., "Predicting personality from twitter," *IEEE International Conference on Privacy, security, risk and trust (PASSAT)*, 2011.
30. Goren-Bar, D., Graziola, I., Pianesi, F., and Zancanaro, M., "The influence of personality factors on visitor attitudes towards adaptivity dimensions for mobile museum guides," *User Modeling and User-Adapted Interaction,* 16, 31-62, 2006.
31. Gosling, S., Rentfrow, P., and Swann, W., "A very brief measure of the Big-Five personality domains," *Journal of Research in Personality,* 37, 504-528, 2003.
32. Graziano, W. G., Feldesman, A. B., and Rahe, D. F., "Extroversion, social cognition, and the salience of aversiveness in social encounters," *Journal of Personality and Social psychology,* 49, 971, 1985.
33. Guthrie, C., Rachlinski, J., and Wistrich, A., "Blinking on the bench," *Cornell Law Review,* 93, 1, 2007.
34. Halko, S. and Kientz, J., "Personality and persuasive technology: An exploratory study on health-promoting mobile applications," *Persuasive technology,* 6137, 150-161, 2010.
35. Hough, L. and Furnham, A., "Use of personality variables in work settings," *Handbook of psychology,* 2003.
36. Johnson, J. E. V., Schnytzer, A., and Liu, S., "To what extent do investors in a financial market anchor their judgments excessively?," *Journal of Behavioral Decision Making,* 22, 410-434, 2009.
37. Judge, T., "Core self-evaluations and work success," *Current Directions in Psychological Science,* 18, 58-62, 2009.
38. Judge, T., Erez, A., Bono, J., and Thoresen, C., "Are measures of self-esteem, neuroticism, locus of control, and generalized self-efficacy indicators of a common core construct?," *Journal of personality and social psychology,* 83, 693-710, 2002.
39. Kahneman, D., Slovic, P., and Tversky, A., *Judgment under uncertainty: Heuristics and biases*: Cambridge University Press, 1982.
40. Kaptein, M. and Eckles, D., "Heterogeneity in the effects of online persuasion," *Journal of Interactive Marketing,* 26, 176-188, 2012.
41. Kaptein, M., Lacroix, J., and Saini, P., "Individual differences in persuadability in the health promotion domain," *Persuasive technology,* 6137, 94-105, 2010.
42. Kraut, R., Kiesler, S., Boneva, B., Cummings, J., Helgeson, V., and Crawford, A., "Internet Paradox Revisited," *Journal of Social Issues,* 58, 49-74, 2002.
43. Kraut, R., Maher, M. L., Olson, J., Malone, T. W., Pirolli, P., and Thomas, J. C., "Scientific Foundations: A Case for Technology-Mediated Social-Participation Theory," *IEEE Computer,* 43, 22-28, 2010.

44. Kraut, R. E. and Resnick, P., *Evidence-based social design*: MIT Press, 2011.
45. Langstedt, E., "An Examination of the Five Factor Model Personality Traits as Predictors of Online Social Network Use," University of Connecticut, 2011.
46. Lepri, B., Mana, N., Cappelletti, A., Pianesi, F., and Zancanaro, M., "Modeling the personality of participants during group interactions," *User Modeling, Adaptation, and Personalization,* 114-125, 2009.
47. Ling, K., Beenen, G., Ludford, P., Wang, X., Chang, K., Li, X., Cosley, D., Frankowski, D., Terveen, L., and Rashid, A., "Using Social Psychology to Motivate Contributions to Online Communities," *Journal of Computer-Mediated Communication,* 10, 2005.
48. Liu, J., Dolan, P., and Pedersen, E., "Personalized news recommendation based on click behavior," *Proc. 15th International Conference on Intelligent User Interfaces*, Hong Kong, China, 2010.
49. Ludford, P. and Terveen, L., "Does an individual's Myers-Briggs type indicator preference influence task-oriented technology use?," *Proc. International Conference on Human-Computer Interaction*, 2003.
50. Mairesse, F., Walker, M., Mehl, M., and Moore, R., "Using linguistic cues for the automatic recognition of personality in conversation and text," *Journal of Artificial Intelligence Research,* 30, 457-500, 2007.
51. McElroy, J., Hendrickson, A., Townsend, A., and DeMarie, S., "Dispositional factors in internet use," *MIS Quarterly,* 31, 809-820, 2007.
52. McElroy, T. and Dowd, K., "Susceptibility to anchoring effects," *Judgment and Decision Making,* 2, 48-53, 2007.
53. McGrenere, J., Baecker, R., and Booth, K., "An evaluation of a multiple interface design solution for bloated software," *Proc. SIGCHI conference on Human factors in computing systems*, 2002.
54. Mobbs, D., Hagan, C., Azim, E., Menon, V., and Reiss, A., "Personality predicts activity in reward and emotional regions associated with humor," *PNAS,* 102, 16502, 2005.
55. Nov, O. and Ye, C., "Users' personality and perceived ease of use of digital libraries: The case for resistance to change," *Journal of the American Society for Information Science and Technology,* 59, 845-851, 2008.
56. Nov, O. and Arazy, O., "Personality-Targeted Design: Theory, Experimental Procedure, and Preliminary Results," *Proc. ACM Conference on Computer Supported Cooperative Work (CSCW 2013)* San Antonio, TX, 2013.
57. Nov, O., Naaman, M., and Ye, C., "What drives content tagging: the case of photos on Flickr," *Proc. 26th annual SIGCHI Conference on Human Factors in Computing Systems* 2008.
58. Orchard, L. J. and Fullwood, C., "Current Perspectives on Personality and Internet Use," *Soc. Sci. Comput. Rev.,* 28, 155-169, 2010.
59. Oreg, S., "Personality, context, and resistance to organizational change," *European Journal of Work and Organizational Psychology,* 15, 73-101, 2006.
60. Postmes, T., Spears, R., and Lea, M., "Breaching or Building Social Boundaries?: SIDE-Effects of Computer-Mediated Communication," *Communication Research,* 25, 689-715, December 1, 1998 1998.
61. Postmes, T., Spears, R., Sakhel, K., and de Groot, D., "Social Influence in Computer-Mediated Communication," *Personality and Social Psychology Bulletin,* 27, 1243-1254, 2001.
62. Preece, J. and Shneiderman, B., "The Reader-to-Leader Framework," *AIS Transactions on Human-Computer Interaction,* 1, 13-32, 2009.
63. Rotter, J. B., "Some problems and misconceptions related to the construct of internal versus external control of reinforcement," *Journal of consulting and clinical psychology,* 43, 56-67, 1975.
64. Rotter, J. B., "Internal versus external control of reinforcement: A case history of a variable," *American psychologist,* 45, 489-493, 1990.
65. Seay, A. and Kraut, R., "Project massive: self-regulation and problematic use of online gaming," *Proc. SIGCHI conference on human factors in computing systems*, 2007.
66. Suler, J., "The online disinhibition effect.," *CyberPsychology & Behavior,* 7, 312-326, 2004.
67. Swann, W. B. and Seyle, C., "Personality psychology's comeback and its emerging symbiosis with social psychology," *Personality and Social Psychology Bulletin,* 31, 155-165, 2005.
68. Vittersų, J., "Personality traits and subjective well-being:: emotional stability, not extroversion, is probably the important predictor," *Personality and Individual Differences,* 31, 903-914, 2001.
69. Wegener, D., Petty, R., Blankenship, K., and Detweiler-Bedell, B., "Elaboration and numerical anchoring," *Journal of Consumer Psychology,* 20, 5-16, 2010.
70. Woodman, R. and Schoenfeldt, L., "An Interactionist Model of Creative Behavior," *The Journal of Creative Behavior,* 24, 279-290, 1990.
71. Zhang, X. and Zhu, F., "Group size and incentives to contribute," *The American economic review,* 101, 1601-1615, 2011.
72. Zweig, D. and Webster, J., "What are we measuring? An examination of the relationships between the big-five personality traits, goal orientation, and performance intentions," *Personality and Individual Differences,* 36, 1693-1708, 2004.

Using Crowdsourcing to Support Pro-Environmental Community Activism

Elaine Massung, David Coyle, Kirsten Cater, Marc Jay, Chris Preist
Department of Computer Science,
University of Bristol,
Bristol, BS8 1UB, UK
{elaine.massung, david.coyle, kc6678, chris.preist}@bristol.ac.uk, marc.jay@bristolalumni.org.uk

ABSTRACT
Community activist groups typically rely on core groups of highly motivated members. In this paper we consider how crowdsourcing strategies can be used to supplement the activities of pro-environmental community activists, thus increasing the scalability of their campaigns. We focus on mobile data collection applications and strategies that can be used to engage casual participants in pro-environmental data collection. We report the results of a study that used both quantitative and qualitative methods to investigate the impact of different motivational factors and strategies, including both intrinsic and extrinsic motivators. The study compared and provides empirical evidence for the effectiveness of two extrinsic motivation strategies, pointification – a subset of gamification – and financial incentives. Prior environmental interest is also assessed as an intrinsic motivation factor. In contrast to previous HCI research on pro-environmental technology, much of which has focused on individual behavior change, this paper offers new insights and recommendations on the design of systems that target groups and communities.

Author Keywords
Community activism; sustainability; participatory urbanism, crowdsourcing; gamification; motivation

ACM Classification Keywords
H.5.m. Information interfaces and presentation (e.g., HCI): Miscellaneous.

INTRODUCTION
Community activist groups, including pro-environmental groups, are typically driven by a core group of highly motivated individuals. These people are often willing to dedicate a great deal of time and effort to help bring about desired changes within their community. While they may derive intrinsic personal satisfaction from their activities, and enjoy the benefits of participation in a group, there is often no expectation of, or need for, other extrinsic rewards, e.g. financial remuneration.

The research in this paper was undertaken in collaboration with a pro-environmental community activist group called Close the Door (CTD). This group aims to reduce energy waste by encouraging shop owners to keep their doors closed during cold weather. In spite of winning national environmental advocacy awards and having dedicated core members, the CTD campaign faces challenges that are common to many community activist groups. In particular, they have found that to achieve scalable and sustainable change, it is not sufficient to rely purely on their core members. Activist groups also need to develop effective strategies for drawing on support from casual volunteers. One particular challenge for CTD is to maintain their database of shops and monitor the behavior of shop owners on an ongoing basis. In this paper we evaluate different strategies through which computer-supported citizen science and crowdsourcing techniques [6, 7, 36] can be brought to bear to help in addressing this challenge. We focus on developing mobile applications (apps) that allow members of the public to undertake lightweight environmental data collection. The aim is to increase the scalability of activist groups like CTD by collecting data on a much larger scale than otherwise possible and freeing core members to focus on high impact advocacy activities.

Members of the public are unlikely to be as motivated as community activists and overcoming public apathy is often difficult for pro-environmental movements. The question thus arises: what design strategies can we apply to motivate people to engage in pro-environmental data collection? The key contributions of this paper are to implement a set of mobile data collection apps and then provide both qualitative and quantitative evidence for the effectiveness of the different motivational strategies that are applied in the apps. Overall we developed three apps. The first used "pointification", a subset of gamification that uses game mechanics such as points, badges, and leaderboards to encourage engagement and competition [11, 27, 38]. The second offered participants financial incentives to carry out data collection tasks [29]. The final app did not use any explicit motivational strategies and acted as a control.

We conducted a study in with each app was used by 16 participants for two weeks. Results show that pointification increased performance, though not to a statistically significant level. However, financial rewards led to a significant increase in the amount of data collected. Surprisingly, interest in environmental issues and existing

CHI 2013, April 27–May 2, 2013, Paris, France.

tendencies towards pro-environmental behavior did not correlate with greater data collection. Qualitative data, collected through semi-structured interviews, allowed us to investigate such issues in greater details. For example we found that the factors that encourage people to initially take part in a community activism project can differ from those that maintain interest. Also, although *motivational factors* impact a person's use of an app, motivation is complex and is only half the battle. Designers must also consider the *enabling factors* that influence casual volunteers' use of crowdsourcing apps.

The research presented in this paper extends HCI research on pro-environmental technologies in several key ways. Prior research in this area has largely focused on systems targeting individual behavior change [13, 17, 21]. This paper provides new insights on systems targeting groups and communities rather than individuals. It provides both quantitative and qualitative evidence on the effectiveness of different motivational and enabling strategies. By drawing on this evidence we provide recommendations to guide the design of crowdsourcing applications that support pro-environmental community activism.

RELATED WORK

This paper builds on prior research on pro-environmental behavior change, citizen science and participatory urbanism, and motivational techniques for crowdsourced data. We will begin by considering the pro-environmental literature that has influenced our research.

Pro-Environmental Behavior Change

Prior HCI research on technology-supported environmental behavior change has been dominated by systems targeting individual behavior change [13, 17]. Such systems are often driven by rational choice models, which assume that individual behavior is driven by self-interest. For example, rational economic models assume that – given access to the relevant information – people behave in such a way as to maximize rewards and minimize costs (although costs and rewards need not be purely financial), thus adopting behaviors that are advantageous [17, 21]. An alternative approach to behavior change, which has received less attention in pro-environmental HCI research, focuses on communities rather than individuals. Theories such as the norm-activation model hypothesize that individual behavior is strongly shaped by community norms and everyday practices [17]. Rather than focusing on individual reward, such approaches recognize the benefits of collective and coordinated actions. These approaches are beginning to be applied to pro-environmental behavior [28, 33], and some studies, such as [30], have shown that these norms can more positively affect behavior than traditional pro-environmental messages or messages highlighting money saving opportunities.

The CTD campaign, and apps described in this paper, aim to take advantage of both individual (rational choice) and community (norm-activation) strategies.

Citizen Science and Participatory Urbanism

With the increasing ubiquity of smart phone technology, mobile data collection through crowdsourcing is increasing. It has been used in citizen science to collect data in support of scientific research, including monitoring the spread of invasive plants through the What's Invasive app [18] and monitoring animal population distributions through the reporting of roadkill [5]. It has also been used in participatory urbanism, by municipal authorities seeking to engage people in monitoring and improving their urban environments. Examples include monitoring noise pollution [26] and repairing potholes and streetlights [24]. The boundary between these two genres blurs in applications such as water quality [23] and air quality [31] monitoring, where the data both increases scientific understanding and can also contribute to local management policies. Our work can be viewed as a form of participatory urbanism, but rather than supporting the efforts of municipal authorities it instead supports the efforts of community activists. As such, it adopts a similar position to the work of Kuznetsov et al. [25], who engage local citizens with their concerns around air quality with portable sensing equipment.

Motivating and Engaging Contributors

In common with all crowdsourcing approaches, Citizen Science and Participatory Urbanism face key challenges in engaging contributors – namely how to recruit them, and how to get them to make an active ongoing contribution. In a review of crowdsourcing literature, Doan et al. [14] categorize common approaches, including (amongst others) coercion, payment, intrinsic enjoyment and competition. In citizen science literature, Kim et al. [23] report the use of incentives, competition, entertainment and education to support ongoing engagement. However, neither compared or analyzed the effect of these different types of approaches to assess their effectiveness on recruitment or contribution. Rotman et al. [32] explored the motivation of volunteers in projects making a scientific contribution and found a complex network of factors at play, with initial scientific interest and curiosity moving towards a desire for attribution and acknowledgment over time.

Focusing on motivation, the factors that motivate individuals can be viewed as either intrinsic or extrinsic. People who are intrinsically motivated are willing to do an activity "for its inherent satisfactions rather than for some separable consequence" [10]; examples of intrinsic motivators include interest, curiosity, competence, and enjoyment [21]. Within the context of sustainability, De Young [9] posits that behavior that is intrinsically motivated is more effective for self-sustaining individual behavioral change. In community activist campaigns such as CTD, core members are likely to have a high degree of intrinsic motivation. Extrinsic motivation is carrying out an activity "to attain some separable outcome", such as material incentives or social reinforcement [10, 21].

"Gamification" is an approach that has rapidly gained prominence as a motivational technique. Deterding et al.

define it as "using game design elements in non-gaming contexts" [11]. Elements can include point scoring, leaderboards, goal setting, questing, and artifact collecting. Gaming techniques have been applied in the domain of eco-feedback technology. A series of games concentrating on creating awareness of household energy in adolescents were trialed through the use of smart meters and mobile phone applications [2, 19], and participants often compared the changing ambient display of UbiGreen to gaming levels [16]. However, these applications focused on the behavior of an individual, with the ultimate goal of awareness or behavior change by system users, rather than data collection. Providing participants with small financial rewards in return for carrying out basic tasks such as image identification has also been successfully employing as a way of attracting and motivating participants, e.g. Amazon's Mechanical Turk [29]. This approach has been found to increase the amount of effort expended [32]; however, it has also been suggested that financial rewards may reduce intrinsic motivation [10].

The study in this paper provides the first systematic analysis of the effectiveness of two forms of extrinsic motivation on environmental data collection performance: a financial pay-for-results scheme, and a virtual reward scheme, which uses points, badges and a leaderboard. We also analyze the effect of intrinsic motivation by examining if a positive disposition towards environmental behaviors affects performance. Furthermore, through a qualitative study, we examine the interrelationships between different motivators and the other factors affecting the motivation and performance of people using the CTD app.

THE CLOSE THE DOOR CAMPAIGN

On UK high streets it is common to see shop doors propped open to encourage potential customers to step over the threshold. However, during cold weather these open doors allow heat to escape. A detailed study of typical 150m^2 UK high street shops found that keeping doors closed can reduce emissions and energy from heating by 30-50% [3]. The CTD campaign was established in response to this finding. Since its inception in 2007 it has grown to include chapters in nine UK and two international cities, and it was named Best Campaign by UK Climate Week 2012.

Considered purely in terms of energy costs, closing doors is a rational choice for shop owners. However owners fear that they will lose customers if they close their doors whilst other shop doors remain open. This is a classic "I will if you will" environmental problem [34]. The CTD campaign attempts to combat this problem by sending volunteers to shopping streets to record whether shops have their doors open or closed. Owners or managers are then approached to determine if they want to join the campaign – i.e. keep their doors closed when heating or air-conditioning systems are running. Shops that join the campaign are listed on the CTD website and Facebook page, and are given a door sticker to publicize their membership. To incentivize participation by shops, the CTD team also runs a public information campaign. Members of the public are given information about the environmental benefits of closed doors and encouraged to support shops carrying a CTD logo. The message to the public is: *"If a shop will not Close the Door: don't shop there, go elsewhere."* By targeting both shop owners and their customers, the campaign aims to make closed doors the accepted norm. Ultimately this new norm benefits both shop owners and the environment.

DESIGN OF THE CLOSE THE DOOR APPS

Through conversations with members of the CTD campaign, we found that the time spent recruiting and retaining shop owners is critical to their success. However, in order for this advocacy to work, members need to collect data about shops in the local area. This is time and labor intensive and must be undertaken on an ongoing basis to check that shops continue to follow the Close the Door policy. It has placed great strain on the core members of the campaign. Working in collaboration with campaigners, we therefore decided to develop mobile apps that allow casual participants to record shop doors via a smartphone. If people use our apps on a regular basis it would allow the CTD campaign to scale up their data collection and would also free campaigners to focus on advocacy activities.

Rather than evaluating a single data collection app, we chose to design three iPhone apps. Each app applied a different strategy to encourage users to collect data. By comparing the effectiveness of these apps we aimed to provide evidence of the effectiveness of different motivational strategies that can be applied to engage casual participants to collect pro-environmental data. In designing the apps, we deliberately sought to keep things simple. Rather than exploring a wide range of functionality and overlapping motivational strategies, our aim was to compare and provide strong evidence on the relative effectiveness of particular strategies.

Our apps are designed to allow people to collect data while they go about their daily routines. Each app is built around a core design that uses the map and GPS functionality on an iPhone. As people move around a city they can open a map that shows an overlay of shops in their vicinity (Figure 1a). People can click on shops – represented by door symbols – and record whether the shop door is open (red) or closed (green), Figure 1b. The initial shop database was populated using the CTD campaign's existing list of shops. If a shop was not in the existing database a user could add it manually. A traffic light system was employed to signal a shop's status: a consistently opened door would appear as red, an occasionally open door as yellow, and a consistently closed door as green (Figure 1a). Participants also had the option to report any problems, such as duplications, incorrect shop names, or to record if a store was permanently closed, allowing the database to be kept up to date. The statuses of shops were updated in real time to reflect participants' ongoing ratings.

(a) (b) (c) (d)

Figure 1. Screenshots from left to right: (a) the map view shop doors, (b) the submission screen, (c) badges, collected and available, (d) the financial leaderboard with points and financial tally.

Across all our apps, two approaches were used to promote **data quality** and help to avoid cheating. Firstly, a system of independent verification by a second user was used to validate new shops. Thus, new shops only appeared on our maps when validated by two independent users. Secondly, participants were only able to add new shops or to record doors within 200 yards of their present location and could only rate a shop once each day.

Our first app acted as a **Control**. It used the full functionality described above. Participants using this app were asked to record as many shop doors as possible and could also add new shops to the database.

The second app – the **Virtual** reward app – again used the full functionality described above, but also incorporated pointification techniques. Participants earned points and badges for their contributions. They received 2 points for rating a shop already in the database and 15 points for adding a new shop (but only after it was independently verified by a second participant). Participants could also earn up to 15 badges (gold stars) worth 15 points each. Badges were earned for activities such as using the app for five days in a row or for rating a shop on the weekend. Participants could keep track of their point score and badges and get information on how to earn new badges through a status screen (Figure 1c). The Virtual app also included a leaderboard. This showed people their position and point score relative to other Virtual app users. The Virtual app therefore augmented the Control app with extrinsic rewards (points and badges) and a source of extrinsic motivation for the participants: the desire to achieve a high score and a high position on the leaderboard. The leaderboard listed usernames rather than real names.

The **Financial** app was an adapted version of the Virtual one. It also had a leaderboard, but in this case participants received a financial reward based on their points score and position on the leaderboard (see experimental procedure for reward values). The leaderboard showed a real-time tally of the amount of money each participant would earn based on this running point total (Figure 1d). Participants also earned money for each badge achieved. The Financial app therefore augmented the Virtual app with another source of extrinsic reward and motivation: a payment related to their relative performance in collecting data.

Participants

Participants were recruited through a mixture of sources: a university bulletin board, an online classified service, and local environmental sustainability groups. Participants were told they could earn gift vouchers for taking part in a study that would involve using an iPhone application and was undertaken in collaboration with the CTD environmental campaign. Overall we recruited 48 participants: 60% female, aged 17-59, with a mean age of 27 (SD = 10.4).

Experimental procedure

Our participants were randomly assigned to three groups – Control, Virtual and Financial – with 16 participants per group. In all cases, participants were asked to record data on as many shop doors as possible while going about their everyday routines for a period of 2 weeks. The Control group were advised that they would receive a £50 voucher in return for participation. The Virtual group were also advised that they would receive a £50 voucher for participating in the study, but in addition that virtual points, badges and a leaderboard would be available to track their individual performance. The Financial group were told that what they earned (in vouchers) would depend on how much they used the app relative to other participants. They were told they would receive £2 per badge earned, plus a share of a fixed pot based on their relative performance on the leaderboard. The size of the pot was set so that the total amount available to the participants was equivalent to £50 per head, i.e. equivalent to the total payment to other groups, but shared based on badges earned and relative performance on the leaderboard.

All the participants completed a preliminary online questionnaire to assess their attitude to environmental sustainability. Questions were adapted from Diekmann and Preisendörfer's study regarding environmental behavior discrepancies [12], and covered both attitudes and

Figure 2. A map showing some areas of the city mapped by participants.

	Shops Added	Total Points	Total Badges
Control	221	3158	92
Virtual	274	4492	90
Financial	618	13112	165

Table 1. The total doors recorded, new shops added, points and badges earned by each group.[1]

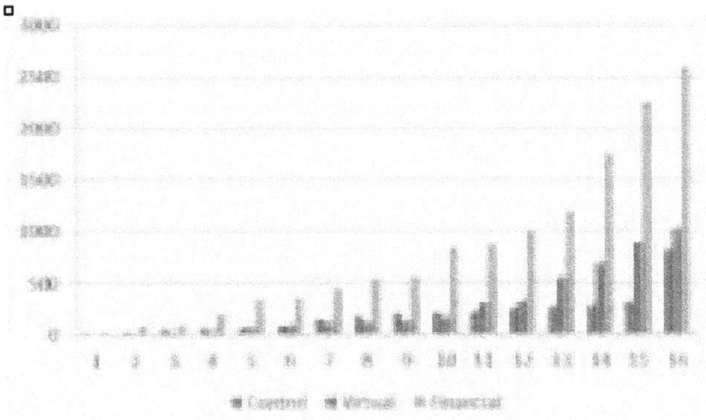

Figure 3. Points scored by the 16 participants in each group.

frequency of pro-environmental behaviors, e.g. recycling and energy/water conservation. The question took the form of a five-point Likert scale. Past studies in environmental psychology have shown that an individual's general environmental attitude is not a guaranteed predictor of whether they will behave in a pro-environmental way [22, 35]. For that reason, we calculated an environmental disposition score for each participant by summing their responses to the behavior questions only. This provides a measure of their intrinsic motivation to engage in environmental activities. The app was then distributed through Apple's TestFlight software, which relied on the participants to actively install the relevant CTD app on their iPhone, mimicking real-life deployment. The study then ran for two weeks. The participants' usage of the app itself was recorded through the software, providing a breakdown of points and badges earned, and measurements such as the number of retailers manually added by each participant and the amount of time the app was used. The Control app kept track of the points and badges that the participants would have earned from their behavior to allow for comparison between the three groups, but this information was not revealed to participants. At the end of the two-week test period, a follow-up survey was sent to all participants to obtain an overview of their opinions on the app. Finally, based on total points, two high, two mid-range, and two low scorers from each group were selected for a semi-structured interview. This delved into further detail about app usage and motivational factors. Ethical permission was granted by the University of Bristol Ethics Committee.

QUANTITATIVE RESULTS AND ANALYSIS

Overall, the three apps proved very successful in allowing us to map and monitor shops. Over the two-week period, participants made 6674 individual recordings and added 1113 new shops to the CTD database. As illustrated in Figure 2, this resulted in a detailed mapping of key shopping streets in the city center. Table 1 shows the total points scored by participants, together with the number of new shops added and badges earned. As can be seen, the Financial group achieved the highest points totals, with the Virtual group second and the Control group third.

Data quality was very high across all experimental conditions. Using Google maps and local knowledge, we checked a random 10% of all added shops (including unverified ones) across the three groups. All but one was found to be accurate. The remaining one was unverifiable, not necessarily wrong.

Figure 3 plots the points earned by participants in each group. The behaviors within each group do not follow a normal distribution, so the non-parametric Kruskal-Wallis Test was carried out to test for differences between the groups. This showed a significant difference across both points earned and shops added to the database: (Points: $\chi^2(2, n = 48) = 9.79, p = 0.007$; Shops added: $\chi^2(2, n = 48) = 21.48, p = 0.001$). We then conducted post-hoc Mann-Whitney U Tests, with Bonferroni correction, to further assess the differences:

Control / Virtual

Points: $U = 125.0, z = -0.11, p = 0.91, r = 0.016$

Shops added: $U = 122.5, z = -0.22, p = 0.83, r = 0.032$

Control / Financial

Points: $U = 49.0, z = -2.98, p = 0.003, r = 0.43$

Shops added: $U = 18.5, z = -4.16, p = 0.001, r = 0.60$

Virtual / Financial

Points: $U = 64.5, z = -2.40, p = 0.017, r = 0.35$

Shops added: $U = 30.0, z = -3.72, p = 0.001, r = 0.54$

The points collected and shops added by participants in the Financial group were significantly greater than those in the Control and Virtual groups. There was no significant

[1] Note that the "shops added" totals include those that were not independently verified by a second participant within the 2 weeks, and so did not score points.

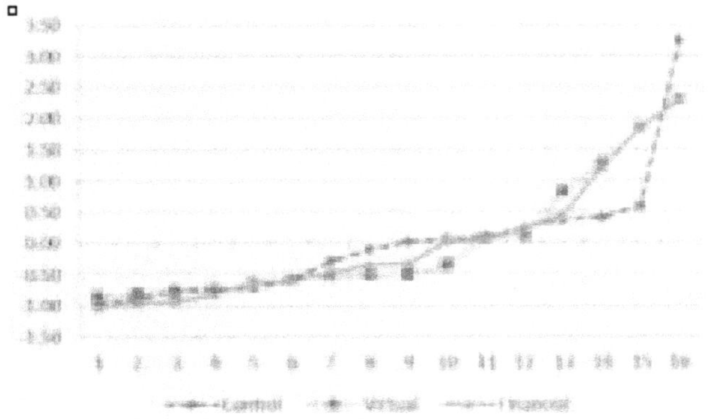

Figure 4. Z-scores for the 16 participants in each group.

difference between the Control and Virtual groups. The effect size (*r*) between the Financial group and the Control and Virtual groups ranges from medium to very large.

Though there is no significant difference in performance of participants of the Virtual and Control groups, visual inspection of Figure 3 suggests a different distribution of performance in these groups. The higher scorers in the Virtual group outperformed the Control, but the lower performers were comparable or lower than their Control equivalent. This is reinforced by the observation that, although the mean point score in the Virtual group (281) is greater than that of the Control (197), the median of the Virtual (112.5) is less than that of the Control (197). To investigate this further we plotted the Z-scores of all participants to test the relative comparative performance of individuals in each group (Figure 4). Results show that that the Virtual and Financial groups followed a roughly similar trajectory, with the top three or four participants outperforming the others. The Control group, with the exception of the highest scoring participant, follows a flatter trajectory showing a more even spread of behavior. The highest-scoring participant from the Control group earned a score over three standard deviations from the mean and, per the extreme studentized deviate method, her result can be considered an outlier (critical value of $Z = 2.58$, $p < 0.05$). Overall the Z-scores suggest that competition, both in the Virtual and Financial groups, motivated the higher performers, but may have demotivated some of the middle performers. This issue was investigated further our semi-structured interviews.

It appears that the option of collecting badges did not have a significant effect on participants' behavior. In fact, the Virtual group earned two fewer overall than the Control, despite the Control group being unaware of what they were earning. Furthermore, it was predicted that a majority of the Financial participants would earn the full set of 15 badges, worth £30.00 in online vouchers. However, only 25% did so. The interviews helped elucidate the badge discrepancy; many participants reported being unaware of how to earn the badges despite prior instruction: *"I wasn't really aware of when you would get a badge. I think you could press them to find out what you needed to get but I didn't go in that far, I just saw that the badge wasn't highlighted."* As a result, the motivating effect of deliberately earning a virtual badge could not be adequately assessed.

Effect of Existing Environmental Tendencies

In addition to testing extrinsic motivational factors, our study was also designed to examine whether pre-existing environmental tendencies would function as an intrinsic motivator and influence app usage. We therefore performed a correlation analysis within each group comparing participants' environmental disposition scores, from the initial questionnaire, and their point scores. The results showed no significant correlation: Control $r = 0.16$; Virtual $r = -0.30$; Financial $r = 0.18$. This is in line with previous studies [1]. Again, this finding is explored further in our qualitative study.

QUALITATIVE RESULTS AND ANALYSIS

The results and analysis presented in this section are derived from the follow-up survey completed by all participants, and from semi-structured interviews with 18 participants, six from each group. The interviews were audio recorded and transcribed. We then undertook a thematic analysis [4]. The following sections address the key themes that emerged.

The Usability of the Apps

A vast majority of the participants felt that the app was intuitive and easy-to-use. For example: *"It was easy to use, only two taps on the screen were needed to report the status of a shop door."* Some participants expressed frustration at the GPS receiver not accurately locating their position. This occasionally prevented them for rating a shop. Overall, however, it is unlikely that basic usability issues impacted on the results of our study.

Motivators and Enablers

In considering the design of systems to target individual behavior change, Fogg emphasizes the importance of both motivation and ability [15]. A similar trend emerged in our thematic analysis. However rather than the term ability, we use the more holistic term "enablers" to address the joint impact of app functionality and contextual factors (e.g. lifestyle) on app usage. Alongside motivational factors, enablers proved critical to participants' engagement.

Motivator: Performance-Related Financial Incentives

As presented above, the Financial group gathered a significantly greater quantity of data/points, confirming that an extrinsic financial incentive tied to contribution served to motivate users far more than either the extrinsic motivation of leaderboard position or intrinsic motivation to contribute to an environmental activity. However, the qualitative data suggested that this came with a cost. Participants in both the Control and Virtual groups reported 100% agreement, when asked in the follow-up survey, whether they would be willing, without financial compensation, to continue using an app like CTD to help a community organization on an ongoing basis. This decreased to 75% of those within the Financial group, corroborating Deci's hypothesis [10] that intrinsic motivation, such as helping a charity, is reduced when performance is explicitly linked to financial rewards.

Motivator: Competition

Quantitative results suggested that the participants near the top of the Virtual and Financial leaderboards were actively competing for the top position, and that this competitive aspect can provide extrinsic motivation to maintain engagement with the app. The interviews backed this up, with some high scoring participants reporting feeling encouraged by competition, and indicating they were willing to use the app more than they would have otherwise: *"The competition was an extra element that I wasn't expecting with the app ... I would check it* [the leaderboard] *even if I knew I wasn't going to go out that day to see if people were coming up near me, and if they were then I'd be like, 'Right I've got to get on with it'."* Conversely, distant competition, for participants who were hundreds or thousands of points behind, had the opposite effect and served as a very clear demotivator. One low-scoring participant described this, stating: *"I gave up as I felt as though there was never a chance to catch the leaders. When I saw that someone had stacked up hundreds of pounds all my motivation dissipated. Games rely on positive feedback for the player to want to continue. This de-motivated me massively so for me the game failed."*

Several of the participants interviewed adopted "self-gamification" strategies, in which they set goals or challenged themselves to record more than previously. Two high-scoring participants in particular exhibiting a tendency to self-gamify: *"I think being kind of competitive with myself, like 'Today I'll do a few more than I did yesterday, maybe I'll walk up that street because I've not been up there before so I don't know what's up there'."* This trend has also been found in previous research on eco-feedback technologies, such as smart meters, which are not explicitly gamified [37]. Whilst this issue was not specifically addressed by the app designs used in this study, it would be interesting to investigate how designs that encourage self-gamification can be used to motivate participants who find head-to-head competition to be demotivational.

Motivator: Community Norms

As well as a source of potential competition, leaderboards can also provide feedback regarding the behavior of the community, and may therefore result in "norm activation" in participants, another source of extrinsic motivation. We have some evidence of this occurring. For example, activity on the leaderboard acted as a motivational trigger for a participant who initially delayed using the app: *"I think it* [seeing people with points] *probably did make me go, 'Oh, okay, people have got started I should probably make sure that I make an effort to do it when I go out'. Yes, that probably did give me a bit of a kick."*

Despite the anonymous leaderboard, some participants also expressed a desire for what we can call "acceptable mediocrity", i.e. not a desire to be the best through competition, but to show that they had put some effort into using the app. For example, a participant felt the leaderboard *"was an indication obviously on how much other people were using it and I wanted to make sure I was sort of in the middle or top half rather than the bottom end."* Overall, the simple pressure or desire to be seen as an active member of the community, by having an acceptable presence on the leaderboard, regardless of score, appeared to affect app usage: *"It made me feel bad because I realized that people had used it more than I had ... I felt guilty that I hadn't started using it so then I used it."* It is interesting to observe that this occurred even though the leaderboard in our study was anonymous and participants were not known to each other.

Motivator: Environmental Interest

As shown in quantitative results section, environmental tendencies were not a guarantee of engagement or app use. The qualitative responses supported this, showing that both high and low-scoring participants were equally likely to describe pro-environmental tendencies (e.g. another low-scoring participant: *"I notice doors being open and closed, and I make sure when I leave a shop I try and close it, although some shops are like, 'No, you can't close the door.'"*) Furthermore, one participant informed us they had previously volunteered for the CTD campaign, yet was a low-scoring member of the Virtual group. However, the topic of the app cannot be dismissed in its entirety as it can serve as a threshold motivator, encouraging people to engage initially. Regardless of their final score, the idea that an easy-to-use mobile app allows a participant to make a small contribution of time and effort to support an environmental cause was cited by several participants as a positive element, and given as a reason for signing up in the first place. e.g.: *"Definitely the whole environment thing, that definitely motivated me because I like to think of myself as the kind of person, I might not be destined for greatness but I can have a part to play, a little role that helps do something great, helps to make a change, and all I have to do is use an iPhone app."*

Enabler: Lifestyle

Interviews suggest that participants' lifestyles played a significant role in this use of the app. For some, their lifestyles acted as an enabler to active participation, while others' lifestyles reduced their opportunities for data collection. A common factor shared by the highest scoring participants from each group was that they were not in regular employment during the testing period, and therefore could use the CTD app as and when they saw fit. For example, the high-performing outlier in the Control group was on maternity leave: "... *when I'm out with her she tends to sleep when I'm walking and it gives me something to do so I walked out of my way a lot of the time just to make sure I would catch as many shops as I could on the way."* In contrast, one low-scoring participant reported using the app only when walking to or from work, or while on breaks: *"Well, most of the time I use it because I work on a retail estate so I used it when I was on my break, up and down because all the shops are within meters of each other."* Another expressed enthusiasm about the CTD app in terms of its purpose to reduce energy waste, but admitted: *"I didn't have that many opportunities ... to go out to different places to have a look ... to go out to the different shops to try it".*

Overall these responses reveal that while people may be intrinsically motivated in terms of supporting a cause, at the same time they can be "disabled" by the lack of opportunities to actually use the app. Given this, organizations needing data collection on a compressed timescale may wish to seek out participants who are time rich, even if they do not seem to be part of a target motivational group.

Enabler: Technology

The use of smartphones to collect data cannot be overlooked as a possible threshold motivator to initially attract participants. Several participants mentioned that our recruitment advertisement specifically asking for iPhone users attracted their attention: *"My partner works in IT anyway so I've got a soft spot for new bits and pieces and obviously I'm a bit of a MAC fan so it went together."*

As previously mentioned, technology did serve as a disabler on occasions where the GPS receiver was not accurate, and prevented participants from recording data. Some participants also expressed concerns that the app used their mobile data connection and might cause them to exceed their monthly data allowance. Allowing the data to be stored and uploaded at a later time would avoid this problem, but it could also affect the pointified elements if the real-time nature of the leaderboard was influenced. Further research is needed to determine whether this delay would have an impact on app engagement.

Enabler: Weather

Wasting heating energy by leaving doors open in cold weather is the very *raison d'être* of the CTD campaign. However, the changing weather itself came up in the interviews as affecting a participant's ability to conduct the task. Good weather acted as an enabler, encouraging people to spend more time outside and around the city. However, there is also evidence that some participants avoided using the app if they felt a shop was justified in leaving a door open on an unusually warm day during the trial.

Cold and wet weather acted as a disabler. This was due to one of four reasons: (1) the participant decided not to go out because of the weather; (2) the participant used a car or public transport instead of walking, precluding use of the app; (3) the participant did not want to get the phone wet; and (4) participants went out but were in a hurry due to the weather, so did not use the app. This reliance on weather must be taken into account if an environmental data collection app is to be successful. For example, a mobile app designed to record blocked drainage in the streets during severe wet weather is unlikely to be used frequently enough to be useful, as the necessity of recording in the rain is unappealing to participants.

Behavior and Awareness

The CTD app was developed to investigate how a mobile app could be used to scale up the activities of a pro-environmental community activist group. It did not seek to alter behavior or raise the participants' awareness of an environmental issue. Nonetheless, there is evidence in the interviews that it did have some affect. One-third of the 18 interviewees reported reading the CTD website as a direct result of taking part in the study. These were spread among groups, but tended to be those who had a stronger environmental disposition in the initial questionnaire. Furthermore, two participants claimed to have even changed their shopping habits to favor shops with doors closed: *"Using the app made me much more aware of my surroundings as I walk around the city. It has made me consider the environmental impact of choices I make when shopping. I also find I am more inclined to visit a business whose door is closed!"*

Whether this is a lasting, or even genuine, change is unknown. However it does highlight another potential use of such data collection apps: as a way of drawing attention to the issue in a wider population and attracting more permanent volunteers to the organization. Those who enjoy the app or have an interest in the subject may be willing to get further involved and take on additional responsibilities.

RECOMMENDATIONS

Based on the quantitative and qualitative results presented in the previous sections, we can make recommendations to researchers and organizations, such as CTD, wishing to exploit the potential of digital data collection.

1. *Seek those whose lifestyle is likely to enable them to participate.*
2. *Use passion for a cause as a threshold motivator, but do not assume it acts as an engagement motivator.*

The people in our study who were mobile but not "goal directed" in their mobility made the greatest contributions – the parent walking with a pram being our archetypal example. Hence a good recruitment strategy for CTD would be to target online discussion boards for new parents, who are likely to have a lifestyle that would allow ongoing contribution, and use an environmental message as a threshold motivator to attract those with compatible intrinsic motivation to volunteer. This is likely to be more effective than recruitment through an environmental forum, which may initially yield many enthusiastic volunteers who are motivated to cross the threshold to participation but then do little or no data recording due to lifestyles incompatible with ongoing contribution.

3. *Make competition available, but easy to ignore.*

It is clear that close competition among leaders is productive, but also clear that it demotivates those not in the leading group. Applications such as foursquare provide multiple and customizable leaderboards, allowing a participant to choose who they compete with. Some have weekly resets, ensuring that an existing player cannot build up a long-term, unassailable lead. Additionally, we could envisage the use of 'adaptive leaderboards' to provide competition when it is likely to be motivating. This would consist of a set of leaderboards (e.g. day, week, etc.) by default in the background, a given board only moving to the foreground for a participant able to engage in close competition on it. Alternative approaches to doing this, and assessments of effectiveness, are areas for further research.

4. *Provide information regarding 'community norms' in a way which motivates desired behavior.*

A number of interviewees were motivated by "doing their bit" as opposed to being top. Based on this, it is perhaps as important to "normify" an app as it is to "gamify" it. For example, providing the average amount of data collected by participants may encourage some to try to meet this figure, even if they cannot compete with the leader. Recent research in the area of domestic energy reduction has also provided evidence to support this approach [30, 33].

5. *Use financial motivation carefully.*

It is clear from the quantitative data that a "pay for results" approach is a powerful motivator and resulted in more data being collected. However our interviews also suggested that it decreased participants' willingness to use the app in the future, with only 75% of Financial group participants expressing willingness in comparison with 100% of other participants. Hence this short-term gain may be offset by a longer-term loss of engagement. For that reason, it may be a better use of financial resources to adopt an approach combining a small payment as a threshold motivator [8] and funding prizes and rewards linked to both gamified and normified achievements. Exploring the size, quantity and structure of alternative reward mechanisms and their impact on behavior is a fruitful area for future research.

CONCLUSIONS AND FUTURE WORK

In this paper, through quantitative and qualitative approaches, we have assessed the impact of different motivating factors and design strategies on the performance of subjects collecting data for the CTD pro-environmental campaign. In our trials a pay-per-results financial reward mechanism resulted in significantly increased data collection, though there is also evidence to suggest it may reduce long-term intrinsic motivation to participate in such activities. We also found that pointification increased performance, though not to a statistically significant level. Our analysis suggested that this was because close competition acted as an effective motivator of those who were high ranking, resulting in their increased performance relative to the Control group. However, this effect was to some extent offset by reduced performance of lower ranking participants because of the demotivating effect of distant competition. We also identified that a leaderboard can have the effect of inducing social norms to encourage performance. Finally, we showed that intrinsic motivation to carry out environmental actions was not correlated with performance, identifying qualitative evidence that an appropriate lifestyle had a bigger impact. Based on our findings, we made recommendations for organizations wishing to design and use mobile apps to support community activism. Note that, though our trial participants were paid, all but the last of these recommendations apply equally to organizations recruiting unpaid volunteers.

As this paper is amongst the first to use both quantitative and qualitative techniques to explore motivators and enablers for pro-environmental data collection, there remain many topics for further research in addition to those addressed here. Firstly, our trial was not long enough to explore how participants' behavior changes over time, so valuable work could be conducted to examine motivation over a longer time period and what can be done to support continued engagement. Secondly, our participants were *a priori* unknown to each other and remained anonymous on our leaderboards. As a result, we have not explored the motivating effect of competing with one's own social group, something that foursquare provides as an option. Nor have we explored the effect of allowing teams of participants to compete together – something that the FoldIt citizen science game [20] has used to good effect. Also, we have not investigated the effects of gamification approaches beyond simple pointification. In particular, we believe the intrinsic pleasure of carrying out an enjoyable activity for its own sake is an important motivator, which our work has (consciously) not explored, due to our focus on simplicity in the app design. Our qualitative results suggest that "self gamification" – allowing participants to set themselves challenges and compete against their prior performance – may act as a strong motivator for some participants. Each of these areas warrants further exploration.

Finally, and perhaps most importantly, research is needed on effective design strategies to "close the loop" between casual volunteers and the "targets" of the community activist campaigns – in our case shop owners. This could have several positive effects. Firstly, by providing feedback to the participants on the ongoing effectiveness of the CTD campaign, such as newly signed-up shops or a measure of ongoing carbon emissions saved, intrinsic motivation may be increased as volunteers may gain a greater sense of contributing to a project with real impact. Secondly, by providing data on local shops that keep doors shut, users could search for shops that support the CTD campaign and place pressure on retailers to change their behavior. Finally, by providing data to the retail community, such as maps of local areas highlighting those shops who do maintain a doors-closed policy, retailers can see the spread of a community norm which is both environmentally and economically beneficial, potentially resulting in an increased speed of uptake of the norm. Through ongoing research on these issues, digital technology may further contribute to the spread of pro-environmental behavior.

ACKNOWLEDGEMENTS
We would like to thank Sue Pollard and Phil Holtam from the Bristol-branch of the Close the Door campaign, Darren Hall from Bristol Green Capital, and the participants of the study. This work was part funded by UK Research Council Digital Economy grant number EP/1000151/1.

REFERENCES

1. Bamberg, B. How does environmental concern influence specific environmentally related behaviors? *J. Environmental Psychology 23* (2003), 21-32.
2. Bang, M., Gustafsson, A. & Katzeff, C. Promoting new patterns in household energy consumption with pervasive learning games. Persuasive 2007, 55-63.
3. Basarir, M. & Overend, M. Interim Report on the Energy Appraisal of Retail Units: Assessing the effect of open doors on energy consumption and thermal comfort. University of Cambridge (2010). CUED/D-STRUCT/TR232.
4. Braun, V. & Clarke, V. Using thematic analysis in psychology. *Qual Research in Psych 3*, 2 (2006), 77-101.
5. California Roadkill Observation System, Annual Report (2011): wildlifecrossing.net/california. Road Ecology Center & Information Center for the Environment at UC Davis.
6. Cohn, J.P. Citizen Science: Can Volunteers Do Real Research? *BioScience 58*, 3 (2008), 192-97.
7. Cooper, S., Khatib, F., Treuille, A., Barbero, J., Lee, J., Beenen, M., Leaver-Fay, A., Baker, D. & Popović, Z. Predicting protein structures with a multiplayer online game. *Nature 466* (2010), 756-760.
8. Crowston, K. & Prestopnik, N.R. Motivation and data quality in a citizen science game: A design science evaluation. International Conference on System Sciences 2013, in print.
9. De Young, R. Changing behavior and making it stick: the conceptualization and management of conservation behaviour. *Environment and Behavior 25*, 3 (1993), 485-505.
10. Deci, E.L. Effects of externally mediated rewards on intrinsic motivation. *Journal of Personality and Social Psychology 18*, 1 (1971), 105-115.
11. Deterding, S., Sicart, M., Nacke, L., O'Hara, K. & Dixon, D. Gamification. using game-design elements in non-gaming contexts. ACM CHI EA 2011, 2425-2428.
12. Diekmann, A. & Preisendörfer, P. Environmental Behavior: Discrepancies between aspirations and reality. *Rationality and Society 10* (1998), 79-102.
13. DiSalvo, C., Sengers, P. & Brynjarsdóttir, H. Mapping the landscape of sustainable HCI. ACM CHI 2010, 1975-1984.
14. Doan, A., Ramakrishnan, R. & Halevy, A.Y. Crowdsourcing systems on the World-Wide Web. *Communications of the ACM 54*, 4 (2011), 86-96.
15. Fogg, B.J. A Behavior Model for Persuasive Design. Persuasive 2009.
16. Froehlich, J., Dillahunt, T., Klasnja, P., Mankoff, J., Consolvo, S., Harrison, B. & Landay, J.A. UbiGreen: investigating a mobile tool for tracking and supporting green transportation habits. ACM CHI 2009, 1043-1052.
17. Froehlich, J., Findlater, L. & Landay, J. The design of eco-feedback technology. ACM CHI 2010, 1999-2008.
18. Graham, E.A., Henderson, S. & Schloss, A. Using Mobile Phones to Engage Citizen Scientists in Research. *Eos Trans. AGU 92*, 38 (2011), 313-15.
19. Gustafsson, A., Bang, M. & Svahn, M. Power explorer: a casual game style for encouraging long term behavior change among teenagers. ACE 2009, 182-189.
20. Hand, E. Volunteer army catches interstellar dust grains. *Nature 466* (2010), 685-687.
21. He, H.A., Greenberg, S. & Huang, E.M. One size does not fit all: applying the transtheoretical model to energy feedback technology design. ACM CHI 2010, 927-936.
22. Hines, J.M., Hungerford, H.R. & Tomera, A.N. Analysis and synthesis of research on environmental behavior. A meta-analysis. *Journal of Environmental Education 18* (1987), 1-8.
23. Kim, S., Robson, C., Zimmerman, T., Pierce, J. & Haber, E.M. Creek watch: pairing usefulness and usability for successful citizen science. ACM CHI 2011, 2125-2134.
24. King, S.F. & Brown, P. Fix my street or else: using the internet to voice local public service concerns. Conference on Theory and Practice of Electronic Governance 2007, 72-80.
25. Kuznetsov, S., Davis, G., Cheung, J. & Paulos, E. Ceci n'est pas une pipe bombe: authoring urban landscapes with air quality sensors. ACM CHI 2011, 2375-2384.
26. Maisonneuve, N., Stevens, M., Neilssen, M., Hanappe, P. & Steels, L. Citizen noise pollution monitoring. International Conference on Digital Government Research 2009, 96-103.
27. Malone, T. Heuristics for designing enjoyable user interfaces: Lessons from computer games. ACM CHI 1982, 63-68.
28. Mankoff, J., Matthews, D., Fussell, R. & Johnson, M. Leveraging social networks to motivate individuals to reduce their ecological footprints. HICSS 2007, 87-96.
29. Mason, W. & Watts, D. Financial incentives and the "performance of crowds". SIGKDD Explorations 11, 2 (2008), 100-108.
30. Nolan, J., Schultz, P., Cialdini, R., Goldstein, N. & Griskevicius, V. Normative social influence is underdetected. *Personality and Social Psych Bulletin 34* (2008), 913-23.
31. Paulos, E., Honicky, R.J. & Hooker, B. Citizen Science: Enabling Participatory Urbanism. In *Handbook of Research on Urban Informatics: The Practice and Promise of the Real-time City*, M. Foth, editor (2009).
32. Rotman, D., Preece, J., Hammock, J., Procita, K., Hansen, D., Parr, C., Lewis, D. & Jacobs, D. Dynamic changes in motivation in collaborative citizen-science projects. ACM CSCW 2012, 217-226.
33. Studley, M., Chambers, S., Rettie, R. & Burchell, K. Gathering and presenting social feedback to change domestic electricity consumption. Workshop on Persuasion, Influence, Nudge & Coercion Through Mobile Devices 2011.
34. Sustainable Consumption Roundtable, "I will if you will": towards sustainable consumption. 2006, Sustainable Development Commission & National Consumer Council.
35. Wiegel, R.H. Environmental attitudes and the prediction of a behavior, in *Environmental Psychology*, N.R. Feimer and E.S. Geller, editors (1983), 257-287.
36. Wiggins, A. & Crowston, K. From Conservation to Crowdsourcing: A Typology of Citizen Science. International Conference on System Sciences 2011, 1-10.
37. Woodruff, A., Hasbrouck, J. & Augustin, S. A bright green perspective on sustainable choices. ACM CHI 2008, 313-22.
38. Zichermann, G. & Cunningham, C. Gamification by Design: Implementing Game Mechanics in Web and Mobile Apps. Sebastopol, CA: O'Reilly Media (2011).

Designing and Theorizing Co-Located Interactions

Thomas Reitmaier
Dept. of Computer Science
University of Cape Town
treitmaier@gmail.com

Pierre Benz *
Dept. of Computer Science
University of Cape Town
benz.pierre@gmail.com

Gary Marsden
Dept. of Computer Science
University of Cape Town
gaz@cs.uct.ac.za

* Note: Benz is joint-first author with Reitmaier. Please abbreviate citation to Reitmaier & Benz *et al.*

ABSTRACT
This paper gives an interwoven account of the theoretical and practical work we undertook in pursuit of designing co-located interactions. We show how we sensitized ourselves to theory from diverse intellectual disciplines, to develop an analytical lens to better think about co-located interactions. By critiquing current systems and their conceptual foundations, and further interrelating theories particularly in regard to performative aspects of identity and communication, we develop a more nuanced way of thinking about co-located interactions. Drawing on our sensitivities, we show how we generated and are exploring, through the process of design, a set of co-located interactions that are situated within our social ecologies, and contend that our upfront theoretical work enabled us to identify and explore this space in the first place. This highlights the importance of problem framing, especially for projects adopting design methodologies.

Author Keywords
co-located interaction; co-presence; design research; theory

ACM Classification Keywords
H.5.m. Information interfaces and presentation (e.g., HCI): Miscellaneous.

INTRODUCTION
Communication is about humanness. It is what we do, who we are, and what makes us into a society. Because communication is so central to our being we take to new media and communication channels, as they give us new or different means of doing what we love to do: expressing ourselves and telling our stories. But not all views of communication are equal; Harper critiques a pervasive vision of the communicating human, which many researchers within CHI and ubicomp have adopted – the one that emphasizes the mechanics of human communication and can "overlook the humans who are doing the communicating" [13,p.49]. Here, communication acts are thought of as messages that are transferred through a medium — be it face-to-face or on a phone — from one person to another. To be sure, this model has proven generative potential, but the deeper problem, as Harper alerts us, is that "the vision used to orient design is of a world that is not the same as the one real people populate" [13, p.240]. Instead, we need to figure "communication between people [as] a performance that ties people together (or throws them apart) in various ways" [13, p.247]. Seeing communication as a performance highlights that it is not just about *what* we say, but *how*, and *where* we say it. These different characterizations of communication, as messages and performances respectively, help us understand why research agendas tend to focus on communication with absent others, and now provoke us to think about how to design for more meaningful co-located interactions.

In fact, an intrinsic assumption around most research in mobile design is that the devices we use most commonly – mobile phones – are *tele*phones, implying interaction at a distance. But research also shows that people wish to interact with their handsets when co-located [14]. This is especially true in regions with high network costs, such as Africa, where many users own a handset, but cannot afford to send a text, let alone share multimedia data [24]. To address these issues, some of our earlier work looked to create an image sharing system, where a user may broadcast an image from their handset over WiFi or Bluetooth to other users within signal range. Results showed that the system was well received [21], leading us to ask two key questions:

What else would people want to do when they are together? Rather than building endless prototypes, we look to theories of proxemics and social interaction to inform our ideas.

How do we support mobile co-located interactions? Whilst it is possible to imagine many types of digitally supported proxemic interaction, is it possible to build a platform on current hardware that would allow us to explore that space?

It is within the context of those questions that we undertook the work presented here. To advance this goal we first show how we *sensitized* ourselves to theories on proxemics, context, identity, and embodiment to obtain a more nuanced understanding of performative aspects of communication and co-located interactions. We explain how we used these theories as a critical lens to examine and *critique* current systems that support co-located interactions. But far from just critiquing, we also show how we applied and refined this lens to *generate* and map out a new set of co-located interactions on mobile devices. We then explain how we integrated insights, sensitivities, and critical stances, derived from theory, to *explore* these through the process of design, culminating in the design of two probes that express and explore key concepts. We present these aspects of our work in four sections, *sensitizing*, *critiquing*, *integrating* & *generating*, and *exploring*. In choosing this structure, we depart from conventional practice, where related work, usually discussing theory and related systems, is presented as an upfront baseline that is often bracketed out from 'actual' research. Here we show how theory, related systems and even our own previous work were central *throughout*: a constant, yet productive, site of struggle. Our theoretical understandings, drawn from a variety of different intellectual disciplines, emerged as we engaged with them at the different stages of our research. So beyond generating and exploring co-located interactions, it is this story that we tell.

SENSITIZING

Focusing on performance-based aspects places the importance of communication at the heart of the human condition, and destabilizes the assumption that the message of a communication act is somehow more important than how it is bound to context, time, and identity. This broader view opens up a path for research that looks at how co-located people might want to produce and engage with the media stored on their phones. Here, we turn to theory to sensitize ourselves to profound concepts such as *context, time,* and *identity* to understand how we might design for more meaningful co-located interactions, as well as how we shouldn't.

Understanding co-located practices

Two major conceptual lenses used to describe and analyze co-located situations and interactions are Adam Kendon's *F-formations* and Edward Hall's *proxemics*.

Kendon calls the space used in the course of an activity a transactional segment [19, p.3]. So, the transactional segment for a person watching TV incorporates the cone-like space between the couch and the TV. In co-located situations the transactional segments of the people involved typically overlap. A common space is established in which a common activity, for instance looking at a photo or having a conversation, can take place. In analyzing the spaces formed in the course of co-located interactions, Kendon noticed how people "orient and space themselves in relation to one another directly reflects how they may be involved with one another" [19, p.3] In Kendon's terms, cooperative spatial arrangements sustained over time are called *formations*. And formations with a shared transactional space are called *F-formations* (Figure 1). These consist of three segments: the *o-space*, or inner 'sharing-space', the *p-space*, which provides placement of the participant's bodies, and the *r-space*, which serves as the separator between the activity of the interaction and the outside world.

The power of *F-formations* lies in their simplicity; they are widely applied as a conceptual lens to analyze interactions between people. This can be done quickly and does not require knowledge of the nature of the interaction taking place within the F-formation. Using F-formations we can

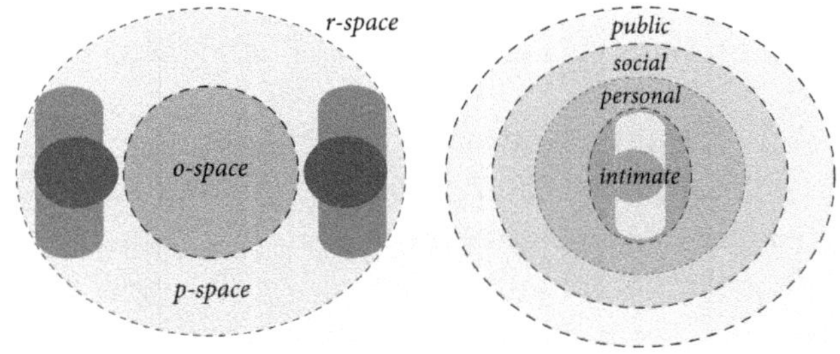

Figure 1. Kendon's *F-formations* & Hall's *proxemic zones*.

learn about a space, by analyzing where people are and aren't interacting. For instance, if you overlook a public space from above you can see all kinds of different F-formations being formed and dissolving again and, over time, gain an appreciation its interactional properties.

Another major work in this area is Hall's theory of *proxemics* [12]. Hall has coined the term proxemics for people's use and perception – through eyes, ears, nose, and skin – of space. Many of Hall's observations focus on how *fixed-feature spaces* (e.g. architecture) interact with *semifixed-feature spaces* (e.g. furniture), and how this affects people, and how they interact with one another. While our experience of space certainly depends on the interplay of fixed- and semifixed-feature spaces, for Hall the most significant category of spatial experience is a mostly unstated, informal space: the distances maintained in encounters with others. He proposes that a person does not end at his or her skin, but is surrounded by a series of expanding and contracting fields: a space, whose size and properties vary on account of culture (more generally) and personal relationships. These can be classified into four, discrete proxemic zones of Figure 1: *intimate*, *personal*, *social*, and *public*. While many of his observations seem commonsense, they relate to a behavior – our use and perception of interpersonal space – that largely lies outside of our awareness; we take it for granted. Hall uncovers these through his descriptions of causes and effects, highlighting how these are interpreted. For instance, people who are angry will move in close to make their point, just as people who are amorous will move in close to express affection. And it's not just touch, but also sensing the heat of another person that combine as we feel intimacy. But the very same sensations (touch & heat) can make you feel claustrophobic in a packed train, so we keep our muscles taught to maintain *our* space.

Researchers who have grounded their work in Hall's proxemic theory and terminology [e.g, 11] acknowledge, as we also suspected in our readings, that Hall's theory is at best suggestive to design and that "we just don't understand the HCI of proxemics" [11, p.50]. But we can find inspiration in Hall's approach that *reflexively* integrates observations. Harper advocates for a similarly reflexive approach to understand everyday actions, such as a son brewing his mother a cup of tea to be ready for her when she gets home. We don't need theories to explain the significance of such acts: "we [need] to use the expertise about the world that we [gain] by living *in* that world" [13, p. 194].

Understanding boundaries of people & time

If we only focus on certain aspects of communication, such significances can easily be lost. Much research to date has focused on mediating the 'bodily mechanics' of communication through computers, such as capturing and conveying gestures or glances [13]. While, bodily mechanics are important, focusing solely on them creates boundary around individuals. Hutchins argues to soften such boundaries and advocates that "the proper unit of analysis is [...] not bounded by the skin or the skull. It includes the socio-material environment of the person" [16, p. 292]. Similar arguments apply to time. Experience, as Hutchins notes in a later article, "is not only multi-modal, but also multitemporal or temporally extended in the sense that it is shaped both by memories of the past (on a variety of time scales ranging from milliseconds to years) and by anticipation of the future (over a similar set of time scales) [17, p.432]. We integrate our memories of the past, experience of the present, and anticipation of the future when we engage with others [34] and with artifacts of our world [17]. Rigid boundaries of time or bodies cut through lines of interaction and obscure relevant phenomena, such as the significance of a cup of tea brewed in anticipation of mother's arrival.

Understanding identity

If we soften boundaries of bodies and time, then important implications follow for identity that contrast with most, if not all, ontologies in computer science. These start with an instance or individual – an anatomical, self-referential unit – and associate a unique identity to it, to discriminate one instance from another. They further group instances together to form sets, classes, collections, etc. based on common attributes. To be sure, this is a powerful model, but it is also one that views identity rigidly. While identity is something unique to us, it also "implies a relationship with a broader collective or social group of some kind" [3, p.1]. In softening borders, the question then becomes how does identity interact with the broader collective over time? Buckingham argues against rigid views because: "who I am (or who I think I am) varies according to who I am with, the social situations in which I find myself, and the motivations I may have at the time" [3, p. 1]. In discussing different disciplinary orientations towards identity, he alerts us that identity is not something we *posses*, or something we *are,* but is something we *do*. It is something that comes into being in dialogue between self and other.

One of the more prominent theorists on identity is Erwin Goffman, who sees identity as something that is performed [10]. Goffman approached identity through the metaphor of theater to describe how individuals use their physical and social surroundings to present themselves to the world and, in turn, how the 'world' interprets their 'performance'. He noted that the relationship between the performer and the audience is one of *impression management*; through their (inter)actions performers project themselves, whether intentionally or unintentionally, to an audience that interprets their (inter)actions. So both parties are involved in negotiating a 'performance'. Goffman also classified two types of performance *'regions'* that a performer has access to and is used to maintain their impressions, namely the *front-stage* and the *back-stage*. The front stage is an attempt by the performer to give the appearance that their performance is their de facto standard. Clothing, posture, speech, gesture, and expressions, can also affect performances. In turn, the backstage is the region where the performer can openly contradict front-stage performances, drop their front and "step out of character" [10. p. 70]. While Goffman is not without critics [3], he, like Hall, was a perceptive observer of social interactions. He elevated the world of social interactions from the obscurity of plain sight, by giving us a vocabulary to talk about and observe it.

Understanding context

The discussions so far show that co-located interactions, like communication acts in general, are highly contextual. But as Dourish alerts us, it is a context of a particular nature [7]. Especially face-to-face, context is an interactional, dynamic, occasional property that arises from activity. This characterization departs from how we usually delineate context, as something that is stable and can be measured and encoded without reference to the activity at hand. Within any dialogue what is and what isn't contextually relevant cannot be established a-priori; a comment can trigger a memory and lead the dialogue down a different path. So something that wasn't contextually relevant before, now is. In fact, negotiating context is a very *ordinary* achievement [7]; we do it almost automatically often without noticing. This interactional view of context suggests inquiries and designs that focus not on how to re-present context, but rather on flexibly accommodating changing contexts.

Harper argues that to sensitize ourselves to the performative nature of communication acts, then we must see these along three dimensions: "the how of the act itself (the bodily skills involved), the who of the act (where one needs to be alert to the intentions of the actor themselves and how the undertaking of some act conveys a sense of identity or self for that person and to the audience or recipient of the act), and third, the where of the act (the location of its performance)" [15, p.245]. Or, in short, context, communication, and identity are enmeshed in *performance*.

Understanding photographic (co-located) practices

To show how this enmeshing works in practice, we identified (mobile) photography as a salient practice in which the theories we have discussed take hold in a way that also relates them to (digital) media. Photos usually depict unique, memorable, happy, events and rarely the routine, sad, or ordinary [28]. In a sense they re-present an idealized self [10]. Photos with family or friends contribute to a sense of belonging and of self. Related practices of photo viewing and sharing re-produce and mediate deeply rooted social practices such as gift giving [25] and storytelling [36].

Kindberg et al examined how 34 people in the US and UK use their camera phone, their intentions at the time of capture, and subsequent usage patterns [20]. The authors distinguish these intentions along two dimensions: *affective-functional;* and *social-individual*, where social use is further broken down into *co-located viewing* and *absent sending/viewing*. Their study shows affective photos outnumbering functional, and social outnumbering individual photos. Most image sharing happened in the moment and on the phone's screen, and rarely via Bluetooth or MMS. Results also show that post hoc sharing didn't happen nearly as often, because "the time and effort one must put into sending these 'gifts' [is] difficult to achieve in the moment" [20]. Some participants simply 'hadn't gotten around to it yet,' forgot or lost the impulse to share. When post hoc sharing did happen, it often involved storytelling.

Chalfen further analyzes how people communicate and tell stories with photos [4]. He contends that photographers are reluctant to create self-containing visual narratives. The narrative remains in the head of the photographer: "a picture may be 'worth a 1000 words' ... [but] pictures don't literally 'say' anything—people do the talking" [4, p.70]. This does not mean that photos always need to be accompanied by a narrative especially if shared with close-knit, yet absent friends [20]. But it does illustrate why post hoc, co-located sharing is a practice of enduring importance [36]. Photos, especially those we cherish, re-present memories, usually of "moments of positively valued change, marked by parties, official recognition, or public celebration" [4, p. 96]. In this sense, photos link to identity, group belonging, and presentation of self. The stories we tell around photos do more than contextualize a photo but also contribute to our biographical 'narratives' – the stories that explain ourselves to ourselves [3]. Face-to-face sharing lets people adapt their presentation of photos, and with it their presentation of self, to their social surroundings. Such face-to-face sharing is a "dynamic, improvisational construction of a contingent situated interaction between story-teller and audience" [36, p.1073]. This explains why applications, explicitly designed for *tele*communication of photos [e.g. 27] still find their use in co-located situations.

CRITIQUING

In the last section we looked at co-located practices and developed a performative lens of co-located interactions by sensitizing ourselves to concepts of identity, context, and time. This lens destabilizes simpler, yet prevalent, views of interacting humans. Here, we show how we applied and refined our sensitivities by critiquing related work through this lens. We identify two examples of related work that are representative of how co-located or proxemic interactions are commonly conceptualized. We intend for discussions to be productive, a chance for us to contextualize and interrelate what we learned and to identify opportunities for design. But we also recognize that criticism, an embraced part of more mature design disciplines, can be perceived as negative and unhelpful, so to set the tone for a constructive discourse, we start by critiquing our own previous work.

Mobile Digital Stories

In our previous work we designed a mobile digital storytelling system to suit the needs and functions of rural African communities. Informed by ethnography and technology experiments involving storytelling, we implemented a design workshop to involve users in a rural community in South Africa's Eastern Cape in the design of a mobile digital storytelling system. Using this method, we created a mobile digital storytelling prototype to suit the needs of rural users. Details of our design process and the resulting prototype, that can flexibly accommodate different digital storytelling techniques, have been published elsewhere [30]. For our critique we focus on how we field-tested the prototype in a rural community in Kenya. During this formative evaluation, we didn't consider *performative* aspects of story*telling* and focused instead on how people *created* stories – how they took photos, recorded audio, and stitched them together into digital stories – on our prototype. While we also gained more diverse experiences and recorded these in our field notes and pictures, our unit of analysis during storytelling activities was centered largely on the prototype and the person interacting with it. It was only after sensitizing ourselves to theories of distributed cognition [16] and situated action [34] that we understood the lines of interaction that were being cut. People did not merely create, nor tell, digital stories, they *performed* them. One storyteller paid little attention to the prototype when recording her story and instead looked deep into our eyes. Users tailored performances to specific (co-located) audiences; they engaged within their physical and with their social surroundings, often in co-located and collaborative creativity. While we were able to reflect on our activities with more appropriate analytical lenses, we only begun to understand the meanings users created well after the fact [29]. This illustrates how narrow disciplinary orientations obscure important aspects of co-located interactions on mobile devices/applications, especially how these are constituted in and inseparable from physical and social contexts of use.

Mobiphos

Mobiphos is a novel interface that supports photo capture and automatic co-located, synchronous sharing within a predefined group [5]. Reading that paper, we suspected that privacy would be a major issue; but to our and the researchers surprise it was not. Because photo-capture is automatically linked to co-located sharing, the consequences of people's actions are apparent – all members of the group will be able to see all the photos you take. So, people adapted their photo taking behavior to take this into account. Users created meanings by matching the possibilities of the technology to their ongoing goals, on the fly; instead of worrying about privacy they adapted their photo taking behaviors and at different times collaborated or took mischievous and funny photos for other to see.

While Mobiphos can provide an enchanting experience, it works better for certain genres of photography, such as tourist photography [4]. This is also the scenario in which Mobiphos was deployed. Likewise, the tourist is an established social role [10], that carries with it conventions and norms that also relate to photo taking, for instance that photos tend to be of places and objects. The design and deployment of Mobiphos also sets an explicit timescale that is limited to the duration of the co-located 'camera recreation.' What happens before? What happens after? How do groups form? How do people leave or join in later? What happens to the photos and how is privacy negotiated then?

Proxemic Interactions

Greenberg et. al recognize the importance of spatial relationship in proposing and formulating an admittedly speculative vision of ubicomp, namely *proxemic interactions*: "just as people expect increasing engagement and intimacy as they approach others, so should they naturally expect increasing connectivity and interaction possibilities as they bring their devices in close proximity to one another and to other things in the ecology" [11, p.44]. Proxemic interactions are triggered by sensing relationships between people and digital as well as non-digital objects. These relationships are characterized and measured along five dimensions: *distance*, *orientation*, *movement*, *identity*, and *location*. In developing different scenarios and applications, they show how Hall's proxemic zones (see Figure 1) [12] can: "regulate implicit and explicit interaction; trigger such interactions by continuous movement or by movement of people and devices in and out of discrete proxemic regions [Hall's zones]; mediate simultaneous interaction of multiple people; and interpret and exploit people's directed attention to other people and objects" [1, p.121]. The researchers have implemented a number of prototypes, making use of 'fine-grained knowledge' of these dimensions by tracking them through a motion capture system. Most prototypes are rule-based. The proxemic presenter augments traditional presentation tools, and shows presenter notes when the person presenting turns towards the display. The proxemic media player pauses when a person starts to read a book. It can interpret pointing gestures to allow users to select different media items, and displays the movie title when another person enters the room. These applications are intuitively appealing, and show that Greenberg et al. are correct that devices should react to proxemics. But we are concerned that such information is encoded in a representational view of context [7]. Likewise, Goffman teaches us that people behave differently in relation to different contexts. We are concerned that such proxemic interactions are operationalized along too ridged and narrow a definition of identity that "uniquely describes the entity" [11, p.44]. What might proxemic or co-located interactions look like, that are built upon a performative account of identity and an interactional understanding of context? And what would they look like, not in the conference or living room of the future, but on the presently ubiquitous mobile phone.

INTEGRATING & GENERATING

The theories we considered so far have largely been formulated prior to or independent of a device that is shaping the communication landscape around us: the mobile phone. In this section we revisit the theory we outlined earlier to integrate and relate these to how people (might want to) engage with each other and their mobile devices when co-located. In the process, we generate new design spaces and suggest underexplored phenomena and avenues for research.

A key aspect of our performative lens is Goffman's theory on the presentation of self. It has been widely applied to analyzing how we present ourselves on social media outlets, such as Facebook and MySpace, where we write ourselves into being [2], using text, but also media. In everyday co-located interactions, however, our bodies, not our profiles, are the focal point of that performance. We use gesture, speech, and facial expressions; augment them with clothing styles, in order to project who we are [10]. Combining these perspectives, leads us to question what role media plays in our co-located 'performances'? To do so, we first need to understand how media links to performative aspects of identity? Perhaps a better way of understanding identity is when we are stripped of it. In *Asylums,* Goffman describes how this can happen when mental patients are institutionalized [9]. Names are replaced by numbers; our clothing with a uniform; our hair gets shaved off; our pockets are emptied; and the small paraphernalia that we carry on our person – wallet, often containing pictures, briefcase, purse, handbag, book, etc. – are also removed. These items form a person's *'identity kit'*, crucial items for the management of a personal front [9]. For some, the mobile phone, as a physical object, is an intimate part of their identity kit: the brand, the color, and how it is accessorized. But the mobile is more than a physical device; it is a repository of information and histories [22]. So beyond physical devices, how do mobiles figure into our identity kits? What does the stuff on the device – the playlists, gallery, call and SMS log, etc – say about us? What role do these personal repositories play in how we present ourselves face-to-face?

To answers these questions we revisit Goffman's concepts of impression management through front and backstage regions. Looking at mobile phones and the applications we use on them, we might say that they are *front stage* devices, as they provide "insights into our tastes, our style of consumption, and perhaps our allegiance to certain groups" [22,p. 96]. But we might also say the mobile is a *back stage* device, as it has "evolved into a significant repository of personal information" [22, p.97], often containing sensitive information which might, to use Goffman's terminology, contradict the performer's front. But it isn't a purely back stage device either, as we draw upon this repository on applications, like Facebook, Flickr, messaging, and email, to present aspects of ourselves to the people we communicate with, enabling and sustaining a *front stage* performance. This dual characterization of the device also explains, why when co-located, people are reluctant to let go of their mobiles, opting instead to show a photo to their friends while holding onto the device. We argue that a better way of figuring the mobile is as a *back stage* device that interfaces with the *front stage*, both asynchronously using Facebook and Email or synchronously when co-located.

One of the main implications of a device that functions in both *front* and *back stage* regions, like the mobile, is that maintaining the device in co-located situations can be problematic. Consider the example of displaying photos from the phone's gallery to a co-located friend. Since photos are usually displayed chronologically, the act of going through one's photos together could easily become uncomfortable, if the presenter accidentally shows a photo that, although chronologically next, shows the presenter in an entirely different context. Or it can lead to overload, with the presenter having to manage the presentation, as well as the performance, resulting in the presenter 'breaking their performance' to ensure that only correct images are shown. We identify a need for mobile devices and applications to accommodate both *front* and *back stage* management, especially when used in relation to co-located contexts.

We must also consider what happens in the situation itself. The act of coming together, the essence of co-located interactions, is not a virtual activity but a physical one; we do it in relation to our bodies. As such, we revisit Kendon's *F-formations,* as they explain how groups form and are maintained during interactions. Our aim is not to replicate physical formations, but to find *inspiration* in them. Beyond physical characteristics of group formations, we are inspired by Kendon's descriptions of how groups form and change over time. Consider if you want to join a group of chatting people. By moving towards the group you make a bid for entry. But the often circular arrangement of groups creates a boundary, forcing you to wait along its periphery. The group must accept your bid and does so by *making space* for you. Groups do this almost automatically and fluidly by changing their placing, posture, formation, and perhaps even their conversation topic. We find inspiration in the fluid and visible dynamic of this practice. If our mobile devices could reflect this 'coming together' of people and devices, what are suitable gestures for forming or bidding entry into such a group? Once established, how would mobiles adapt and reconfigure themselves to reflect such a coming together? What are suitable interface metaphors and interactions? Without disrupting the fluid dynamic of co-located interactions, how might mobile applications augment such encounters? How are such encounters sustained? How do they change? Do they live on after dissolving?

When thinking about co-located interactions, it is easy to see these as isolated events. But the bonds between people remain intact, as they move between periods of absence and presence – rhythms that punctuate life. Or as Suchman reminds us, interactivity, or engaged participation with others, does not just require a *presence*, but also an *autobiography*, and a *projected future* [34]. Far from isolated events, we look forward to our get-togethers. To be sure, some get-togethers are spontaneous, but rarely completely unexpectedly as a substantial degree of ordinariness characterizes our lives [7]. During get-togethers, we use our mobiles to share a past experience, a piece of our autobiography so to speak [36]. So why can't we use our mobiles to project into the future and support such practices? Can a system be designed for people to draw upon the media they produce and consume while being mindful of absent others, but rather than sharing in the moment or forgetting altogether [20], project into the future? That is, to anticipate future presence and the joy of sharing photos face-to-face might bring, where intersubjectivity is richer [15], and where we can co-orient [26] towards and make sense of the media together?

EXPLORING

All of these questions provoke us to think about what meaningful co-located interactions on mobile devices might look like. We identify two, to a degree interrelated, design spaces that highlight different aspects of our discussions so far. As they are shaped by our performative lens, they share many characteristics – how they approach issues of identity and context; and how they interweave with existing practices – but differ along a few dimensions that we outline next.

The first, which we call *Share Face2Face,* assumes that the natural co-located sharing pattern is not necessarily a pattern of sending files, but a pattern of co-consumption and co-orientation. Within this class the natural sharing gesture is *show-and-tell*, in which a small group of people co-orient themselves towards the mobile's screen to look at a photo or listen to a song, together. *Share Face2Face* does not see these events as isolated, but as something that people might look forward to. As such it has a softened boundary of time, and will explore how to enhance these encounters, by allowing people to draw upon the media that they produce and consume while apart and being mindful of others at a different time and place; and then to bring this act of mindfulness into a co-located situation, at a later time or in a different place. This extended timeframe renders *Share Face2Face* into a design space that is more deliberate, slow, and curatorial; that leaves room for pausing and pondering; and allows people to anticipate and look forward to future presence. It is not about sharing across distance in the right-here-and-now, but sometime in the future, when the time is right, when we re-connect face-to-face.

Our second interpretation challenges the pervasive cloud-computing paradigm. People take to the cloud because services, such as Facebook, Flickr, Soundcloud, allow them to discover and share media and engage with it socially. Much ink has been spent on performative aspects of social media use and the difficulties of portraying oneself in front of a largely imagined audience while retaining privacy. But in co-located situations the audience is very real and it does not require us to imagine a context in which someone might view media we make available. As a consequence, some of the issues surrounding privacy could be offloaded into the real world, or negotiated on-the-fly by more closely matching media we might want to, or want others to, engage with to the situation at hand. We envision *Cloudlets* to be hyper-localized, ad-hoc instantiations of the cloud that are more or less independent of cloud infrastructure, but nevertheless provide similar services and opportunities for both virtual and physical engagements surrounding media. As an underlying infrastructure *Cloudlets* can make applications aware of, and provide opportunities for engaging with, nearby people and devices. Such co-located engagements surrounding media happen in real-time, affording rich ways to interact with our data when co-located. For instance, music-playing applications can allow friends to broadcast selected songs and albums to one another, virtually merging collections, highlighting similar tastes, or providing ways to discover new music. Calendars applications could show past or future common events and match free time for co-located people to schedule future get-togethers. In short, just like Cloud services annotate our data with semantics, *Cloudlets* aims to make our mobiles more aware of, and provide opportunities for engaging with, co-located people.

If we look at these design spaces closely, how they interweave with social practices, how they are informed by a theoretical scaffolding of a variety of intellectual disciplines, we see a wicked problem; our formulation of the situation is an integral part to addressing it [8]. As such, it warrants a research through design (RtD) approach [38]. While crossing disciplinary boundaries during our ongoing theoretical ponderings are an invaluable resources that help us to observe, talk, and think about co-located interactions, in choosing a RtD approach we should also remain true to *our* disciplinary orientations, namely interaction design and computer science. In crossing boundaries, it is easy to become dismissive of our own skill set, which in comparison to the perspectives and insights that *others* bring to the situation appear unremarkable and ordinary. As reflective and reflexive design researchers, we embrace the unique perspectives and skill sets that we bring to the situation and recognize how we generate knowledge. As interaction designers, we have developed a deep understanding of what software, interfaces, and sensors can and cannot do. These understandings and skill-sets color our interpretations of theories. We agree with Gaver when he says, "the practice of making is a route to discovery" [8, p.942]. Thus, the prototype [35] presents a chance to express, and through the process of prototyping, further our understandings of these co-located interaction spaces. We experiment with technological *possibilities* – new arrangements of people, contexts, and technologies – to build the *right* thing [37], to change and possibly disrupt behavior [31] and see what reality could become [23]. We design and implement prototypes to understand and explore these spaces in the lab and through unfolding activities of co-operative design-in-use [35]. In the following discussion, we call prototypes that have been designed and deployed in this fashion *probes*. We chose a probing approach because the possibilities afforded by current technologies don't support co-located interaction in a way that resonates with our earlier discussions. By building probes, left strategically incomplete and flexible, we engage with the more synthetic aspects of design, that "allows for a richer more situated understanding" [8, p.942] – not just in theory, but in practice by presenting users with real usage contexts [18]. In the following two sections we introduce these probes and how they express our understandings of design spaces we identified above.

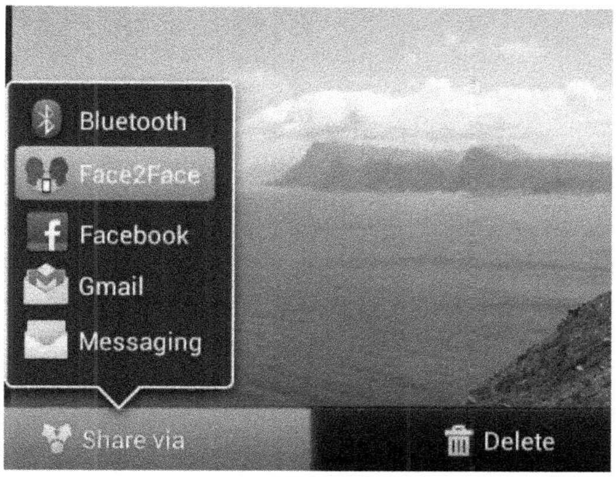

Figure 2. The *Share Face2Face* probe.

Share Face2Face

In looking for pragmatic design solutions [24] – ones that don't require adding infrastructure – we explored ways to convey our operative image of *Share Face2Face* on existing camera phones. Researchers studying camera phones have identified that the impulse to share is strongest in the moment [20]. Looking at how media is shared, posted, or 'Bluetoothed' on current devices we identified that all camera phones have built in sharing mechanisms. In most cases, these can be accessed from the contextual menu of a particular media item, revealing a list of sharing options: Bluetooth, Email, Facebook, or Messaging. To encapsulate our operative image, we wanted to present a similar option to users called *Face2Face* and created a suitable icon (see Figure 2). To keep our probe simple and interpretatively flexible [33], we created a dummy application on an Android phone that hooks into the Android's built in sharing mechanism. As a consequence, the Share Face2Face probe was displayed next to media sharing technologies such as Email, Bluetooth, and Facebook, which we hoped would make users reflect on how they currently share media [32]. If indeed a piece of media needs to be shared in the right-here-and-now, or if sharing it face-to-face later on might bring about a different experience, for instance by seeing the reaction of a friend's face when they look at a photo or listening to a song together. While we intend to use this probe on a larger scale, to first test out its feasibility we first went around the university campus during lunchtime to informally interview about 10 students.

We first showed them the concept, which we accessed through phone's contextual share menu from an image we took earlier. The *Share Face2Face* concept immediately caught the imagination of the students we interviewed. They talked about how face-to-face sharing of a photo is different experience from Facebook: "*facial expressions say more than likes.*" But when queried about how they might like to use such an application, their answers were characterized by *vagueness*. In their view such an application would be useful in general, but we only elicited a few specific scenarios, such as showing a botanist friend a picture of a flower a student saw on a recent hike. Reflecting on these results we realized that we failed to consider how the probe only takes on *specific* meanings in relation to *specific* images, evoking *specific* feelings. Clicking on the Face2Face sharing option can be seen as lodging an intent to share this media item face-to-face. This reminded us of Suchman's theory of *Plans & Situated Action* – commonly misinterpreted as a theory of only situated action, neglecting the important imaginary and discursive practice of planning [34]. It is through planning that we project into the future and imagine how things might be. Such sharing *intents* – or plans – are an important resource within the situated action or practice of face-to-face image sharing. This suggests a discourse exploring the relationship between plans and situated action; how do these sharing intents relate to, and might be useful within, face-to-face encounters; how might they change with time? To explore this relationship within the *Share Face2Face* design space, we subsequently expanded our initial probe with a diary functionality to let users create text and voice notes that link to the specific media items that they intend to share face-to-face. This will allow us to explore more specific scenarios and intents to help us further understand this design space.

Cloudlets

In order to investigate whether *Cloudlets* are a suitable means for engaging with media in co-located situations, we needed to test whether current mobile phones actually support such an infrastructure, before we could tackle some of the more interesting questions that surround *Cloudlets*. So, we prototyped an ad-hoc infrastructure that allows three devices to interconnect via Bluetooth in a seamless manner. To render this infrastructure visible to users, we developed two probes. The first probe was a messaging application that broadcasts a message to each connected device as it is being typed; and the second probe was a photo-displaying application, which displayed selected photos from connected devices in a vertical list of photo-streams, designed to be similar to most mobile photo-sharing applications, such as Flickr. The probes were designed to demonstrate the real-time nature of the content being shared and were not feature-filled applications. This was done to supplement an experimental session, as we were unsure how participants would approach the technology or what features it would require. As such, the aim of the experiment was to stimulate discussion with the users and investigate whether they could understand and envision other applications that make use of this underlying infrastructure.

With the probes in place, we then performed an experiment to test if our more theoretical ponderings did indeed have practical relevance, as well as to identify whether the basic concept behind *Cloudlets* – people and their devices coming together to create a localized cloud – is something that resonates with users. Empathizing with the participants, we did not explicitly engage with the more theoretical concepts surrounding identity and performance. Because, taken out of context, Goffman's characterisation of *front* and *back-stage* can be misunderstood to imply that the *back-stage* is somehow more honest and the *front-stage* somehow less.

The experiment included a total of ten participants, which were split in two groups of five. The participants' ages ranged from 18 – 22 years and contained a total of three groups of friends and four strangers. This format was chosen to target an age group comfortable with mobile sharing and to understand the application features needed due to both friend and stranger relations. To get participants talking, we first discussed their current practices of sharing media in co-located situations. Most of them used cloud-based services, such as BBM, WhatsApp, and Facebook, or displayed the mobile phone screen to others in a show-and-tell gesture. When questioned about Bluetooth, they mentioned that it was too slow and clumsy to use, reverting instead to cloud services or show-and-tell gestures. They did note that they would only hand their mobile device to another if it was a small gathering of people or if they knew the person very well; but even then it was assumed that the 'shared' would only view the content and not do anything else with the device. We followed this with an introduction and demonstration of the probes. We encouraged participants to interact with the applications and asked questions pertaining to the probes. The probes caught the imagination of the participants; they envisioned several co-located scenarios surrounding media, such as photo-sharing, lecture-material broadcasting and mobile music-streaming. They were also surprised to learn that the probes used only Bluetooth; a technology that they never imagined could function in the manner demonstrated. This was encouraging, as it not only demonstrated that participants could envision novel uses for *Cloudlets*, but also exemplified that participants want richer co-located sharing experiences surrounding media than currently possible.

We then questioned participants about applications classes, such as co-located photo-sharing or an overlapping group calendar. In relating their everyday experiences to these classes, participants saw their usefulness and could imagine using them, but quickly raised issues relating to privacy and identity management: who has control over who sees what; how they gain access to it; how they limit or specify what they are sharing and with or to whom; what others do with the content; who owns the content; how do they enable and disable this technology; how do you specify who can connect to your device; etc. These concerns were amplified when the participants were asked to collaboratively sketch out two applications, a calendar and a photo-sharing application, that used Cloudlet infrastructure. Overall, participants wanted more control over content and sharing granularity. The experiment indicates that *Cloudlets* resonated with participants; they find the possibilities for richer co-located sharing exciting, and our theoretical ponderings on privacy and identity management are of central importance.

FUTURE WORK

Moving forward, we are interrogating the scenarios proposed by users, and unpacking the subtle distinction between what is given (implying giving ownership) and what can only to be viewed while co-located. Beyond static read/write distinctions within file-management, this suggests a more refined, social conception around permissions and how acts or gestures might operationalize these. After all, co-located interactions surrounding media render these into social objects. Comments on group formation are leading us to consider more dynamic privacy models around groups, as well as more appropriate interface metaphors, allowing users to better negotiate privacy and identity management. We are developing these through further experiments around refined probes, to further situate and conceptualize *Cloudlets* and how they might be utilized in practice.

In fact, the functionality we see emerging in Cloudlet applications could well be based on set theory. In essence people bringing together data in co-located situations want to find the intersection, union and difference of such data: we might want to find songs we have in common (intersection) or dates when we are all free (difference). By adding set theory based operators to our Cloudlet applications, we can explore new forms of co-located interaction. So we postulate that it is not just social theory, but something as abstract as set theory, that can be used as a lens to understand and generate new forms of co-located interaction.

CONCLUSION

Co-located or any type of social interactions are characterized by their ordinariness [7]; we take them for granted. These interactions are enmeshed with unwritten rules, feelings, expectations, anxieties, and experiences [10,12]. So, we drew upon theory to develop analytical lenses and sensitize ourselves to key practices, sometimes rendering these visible to us in the first place. We have characterized this approach as a constant, yet productive site of struggle that depends on one pervasively misunderstood activity: *reading* [6]. When we speak of reading we see it as an act of habitation rather than consumption. Just like a renter furnishing her apartment with objects, acts, and memories, by continually engaging with (or reading) theoretical texts at different stages of our research, we have made these texts our own. We used analytical lenses derived and refined through reading to understand and critique approaches and conceptual foundations of related work including our own. These understandings showed us that we needed a better way to think about co-located interactions on mobile devices. By interrelating theories we uncovered that such interactions are situated primarily in a *social* ecology with devices, not in a device ecology with people. Our dialogic engagement with theory allowed us to develop such grounding principles. We have identify two design spaces *Cloudlets* and *Share Face2Face*, and have begun to explore them through the process of design, which so far has differed from more traditional user-centered design (UCD) processes.

In his widely cited paper on context, Dourish notes that if we are to sensitize ourselves to different disciplinary orientations on profound concepts such as context, identity, and communication, this not only implies "a change to the ways in which we go about designing technologies, but also a change to the technologies that we design" [7]. This is more than a change in process, because the results of a PD or UCD process can still be stable, static, and closed [7]. It was after all "a circular move of writing a cognitivist rationality onto machines and then claiming their status as models for the humans" [34, p.259] – a view that is not only prevalent in academic but also in everyday discourses. While we firmly believe in the philosophies of PD and UCD, in practice we have so far not adhered to them. Although we are currently transitioning into more traditional UCD cycles, the discussions presented thus far characterize a different, first step that doesn't fit into UCD. We call it *trying to understand.* In our account, we have articulated – sometimes explicitly and other times deliberately implicitly – this *theory on design* [38] in the process of uncovering implications for the design of co-located interactions. If we, as the CHI community, take design seriously, this should happen in parallel. We aren't saying that every project should engage with theory in such a manner, but it was the right approach within this project, and is an emerging trend in HCI [31]. We also believe that it is an approach that could benefit other projects that latch onto more tacit aspects of our everyday lives. This is why we report and interrelate them here, because *theory on design* makes more sense in relation to *specific* design problems [8]. To develop research through design as a methodology and to hold ourselves accountable to the decisions we, while struggling with, nevertheless made, we respond to Zimmerman et al.'s call to action by documenting the *whole* process, showing "how theories from other disciplines were integrated" and beginning with the crucial first step: *problem framing* [38, p.316]. But further than theory on design, we hope that our discussions, interpretations of theory in relation to co-located interactions, probes, and technology experiments surrounding the probes, will serve as placeholders that open a new and fruitful design space: the space of co-located interactions that fit primarily into our social ecologies and not just our device ecologies. We hope that others will join us to explore (and theorize) this space.

ACKNOWLEDGEMENTS

We thank participants for their time and efforts, Yvonne Rogers for helping us develop our understandings of theory, and reviewers for their insightful discussions.

REFERENCES

1. Ballendat, T., Marquardt, N., & Greenberg, S. Proxemic Interaction. *ACM Intl. Conf. on Interactive Tabletops and Surfaces – ITS'10*, ACM (2010), 121–130.
2. boyd, d. Why Youth (Heart) Social Networking Sites. In D. Buckingham, ed., *Youth, Identity, and Digital Media.* MIT Press, Cambridge, MA, 2008, 119–142
3. Buckingham, D. Introducing Identity. In D. Buckingham, ed., *Youth, Identity, and Digital Media.* MIT Press, Cambridge, MA, 2008, 1–22.
4. Chalfen, R. *Snapshot: Versions of Life.* University of Wisconsin Press, Madison, WI, 1987.
5. Clawson, J., Voida, A., Patel, N., et al. Mobiphos: A Collocated–Synchronous Mobile Photo Sharing Application. *MobileHCI '08*, ACM (2008), 187–195.
6. de Certeau, M. *The Practice of Everyday Life.* University of California Press, Berkeley, CA, 1984.
7. Dourish, P. What we talk about when we talk about context. *Pers. and Ubi. Computing 8*, 1 (2004), 19–30.
8. Gaver, W. What should we expect from research through design? *CHI '12*, ACM (2012), 937–946.
9. Goffman, E. *Asylums.* Anchor Books, New York, 1959.
10. Goffman, E. *The Presentation of Self in Everyday Life.* Anchor Books, New York, 1959.
11. Greenberg, S., Marquardt, N., Ballendat, T., Diaz-Marino, R., Wang, M. Proxemic Interactions *interactions 18*, 1 (2011), 42–50.
12. Hall, E.T. *The Hidden Dimension.* Anchor Books, New York, 1966.
13. Harper, R. *Texture: Human Expression in the Age of Communications Overload.* MIT Press, Cambridge, MA, 2010.
14. Harper, R., Regan, T., Mosawi, K.A., & Rouncefield, M. Trafficking: Design for the Viral Exchange of TV Content on Mobile Phones. *MobileHCI'07*, ACM (2007), 249–256.
15. Hollan, J. and Stornetta, S. Beyond Being There. *CHI '92*, ACM (1992), 119–125.
16. Hutchins, E. *Cognition in the Wild.* MIT Press, Cambridge, MA, 1995.
17. Hutchins, E. Enaction, Imagination, and Insight. In J. Stewart, O. Gapenne & E.A. Di Paolo, eds., *Enaction: Towards a New Paradigm for Cognitive Science.* MIT Press, Cambridge, MA, 2010, 425–450.
18. Kangas, E. and Kinnunen, T. Applying user-centered design to mobile application development. *Communications of the ACM 48*, 7 (2005), 55–59.
19. Kendon, A. Spacing and Orientation in Co-present Interaction. In A. Esposito, N. et al. eds., *Development of Multimodal Interfaces: Active Listening and Synchrony.* Springer, Berlin, 2010, 1–15.
20. Kindberg, T. Spasojevic, M. Fleck, R. & Sellen, A. The Ubiquitous Camera: An In-Depth Study of Camera Phone Use. *Pervasive Computing 4*, 2 (2005), 42–50.
21. Kun, L. & Marsden, G. Co-present photo sharing on mobile devices. *MobileHCI'07*, ACM (2007), 277–284.
22. Ling, R. *New Tech, New Ties: How Mobile Communication is Reshaping Social Cohesion.* MIT Press, Cambridge, MA, 2008.
23. Löwgren, J. & Stolterman, E. *Thoughtful Interaction Design.* MIT Press, Cambridge, MA, 2004.
24. Marsden, G., Maunder, A., & Parker, M. People are people, but technology is not technology. *Philosophical transactions. Series A, Mathematical, physical, and engineering sciences 366*, 1881 (2008), 795–804.
25. Mauss, M. The Gift: The Form and Reason for Exchange in Archaic Societies. Routledge, London 2011.
26. McLeod, J., & Chaffee, S. Interpersonal approaches to communication research. *American Behavioral Scientist*, 16, (1973), 469-499
27. Naaman, M., Nair, R. & Kaplun, V. Photos on the Go. *CHI '08*, ACM (2008), 1739–1748.
28. Shove, E., Watson, M., Hand, M., and Ingram, J. *The Design of Everyday Life.* Berg, Oxford, UK, 2007.
29. Reitmaier T. 'She looked deep into our eyes': reflections on cross-cultural practice. *Knowledge Management for Development Journal 7*, 3 (2011), 327–339.
30. Reitmaier, T., Bidwell, N.J., and Marsden, G. Situating digital storytelling within African communities. *Int. J of Human-Computer Studies 69*, 10 (2011), 658–668.
31. Rogers, Y. *HCI Theory: Classical, Modern, and Contemporary.* Morgan Claypool, 2012.
32. Sengers, P., Boehner, K. et al. Reflective design. *Proc. Critical computing – CC'05*, ACM (2005), 49–58.
33. Sengers, P. & Gaver, B. Staying open to interpretation. *DIS '06*, ACM (2006), 99–108.
34. Suchman, L. *Human-Machine Reconfigurations: Plans and Situated Actions.* Cambridge Univ. Pr., NY, 2007.
35. Suchman, L., Trigg, R., and Blomberg, J. Working artefacts: ethnomethods of the prototype. *The British journal of sociology 53*, 2 (2002), 163–179.
36. Van House, N.A. Collocated photo sharing, storytelling, and the performance of self. *Int. Journal of Human-Computer Studies 67*, 12 (2009), 1073–1086.
37. Zimmerman, J., Forlizzi, J., and Evenson, S. Research through design as a method for interaction design research in HCI. *CHI '07*, ACM (2007), 493–502.
38. Zimmerman, J., Stolterman, E., and Forlizzi, J. An Analysis and Critique of Research through Design. *DIS'10*, ACM (2010), 310-319.

Scenario-Based Interactive UI Design

Koki Kusano **Momoko Nakatani** **Takehiko Ohno**
NTT Service Evolution Laboratories
1-1 Hikari-no-oka, Yokosuka-Shi, Kanagawa, 239-0847 Japan
{kusano.kouki, nakatani.momoko, ohno.takehiko}@lab.ntt.co.jp

ABSTRACT
Clearly picturing user behavior is one of the key requirements when designing successful interactive software. However, covering all possible user behaviors with one UI is a complex challenge. The Scenario-based Interactive UI Design tool is designed to support the characterization of user behavior based on scenarios and then using the information in UI design. Scenarios make it easy to understand and share user behavior even if we have little design knowledge. However, they have two big weaknesses; 1) integrating several scenarios in one UI is difficult, even if we can create appropriate scenarios, 2) maintaining the links between scenarios and the UI is a heavy task in iterative design. Our tool solves the above problems through its hierarchical scenario structure and visualized overview of scenarios. It enhances the designer's skill in writing scenarios and designing UIs smoothly and easily.

Author Keywords
User interface design; Scenario; Design tool; Traceability

ACM Classification Keywords
H5.2 [Information interfaces and presentation]: User Interfaces. - Graphical user interfaces.

INTRODUCTION
A good understanding of user behavior is essential when designing interactive software that must provide high usability and user experience. Scenarios, which describe how people accomplish tasks, are a popular design tool; they are one way of making the user image concrete and extracting user requirements in Scenario-Based Design (SBD) [1]. In the human-computer interaction field, scenarios are also utilized by designers when designing UIs [2]. Scenarios that are written in a natural language are comprehensible even if the writer has insufficient experience in considering user-computer interaction. Hence, scenarios help a designer to facilitate agreement and consistency with stakeholders (ex. developers, clients).

However, managing scenarios becomes more difficult as the number and complexity of scenarios increases [3]. Therefore, scenarios should offer an overview of their contents by using some form of graphical representation to assist in the understanding of user behavior [4]. This is a critical requirement if the designer has to find common points and trade-offs among the scenarios and integrate all points into one UI [3]. In addition, updating the links between scenarios and UI is very tough when the design is iterated [5]. When a designer revises a UI based on the results of usability testing, he/she has to refer to not only the UI but also the original scenarios at the same time; this process should be iterated to reach the required quality. This difficulty renders scenarios less useful.

Therefore, designers must be able to overview, understand and manage scenarios easily and smoothly when designing a UI. Unfortunately, no tool well supports this requirement, and efficiency strongly depends on the designer's skill. In this paper, we solve these problems with the Scenario-based Interactive UI Design Tool (see Figure 1): we especially focus on 1) managing scenarios and 2) visualizing the relationships among multiple scenarios. First, our tool supports the designer to reorder the sentences in each scenario to more clearly express the hierarchical structure of the scenario. In addition, a designer can attach a tag that expresses a target user requirement to any sentence. Second, the tool automatically visualizes the scenario structure (overview) by using the tags. The designer can directly alter the UI via the overview. The overview provides easy understanding by focusing on the key common points and conflicts among the scenarios. In addition, the tool maintains the links among sentences, tags, visualization and UI. The above features allow a designer to write and manage scenarios and design a UI easily and smoothly in an iterated design process.

RELATED WORK
Most SBD methods iterate the following four steps: 1.field study, 2.create user image and scenarios, 3.design UI, 4.evaluate UI.

First, the field specialist observes target-users conducting interviews that reveal their actions in the target situation. Second, the designer creates a concrete user image and writes scenarios as needed based on the field data. Each scenario contains one user goal, situation, and behaviors to achieve the goal. Scenarios don't contain UI-components or functions to avoid the technology constraint trap. Next, the designer extracts user-requirements and functions, and then details the scenarios that contain UI-components. Third, the

CHI 2013, April 27–May 2, 2013, Paris, France.

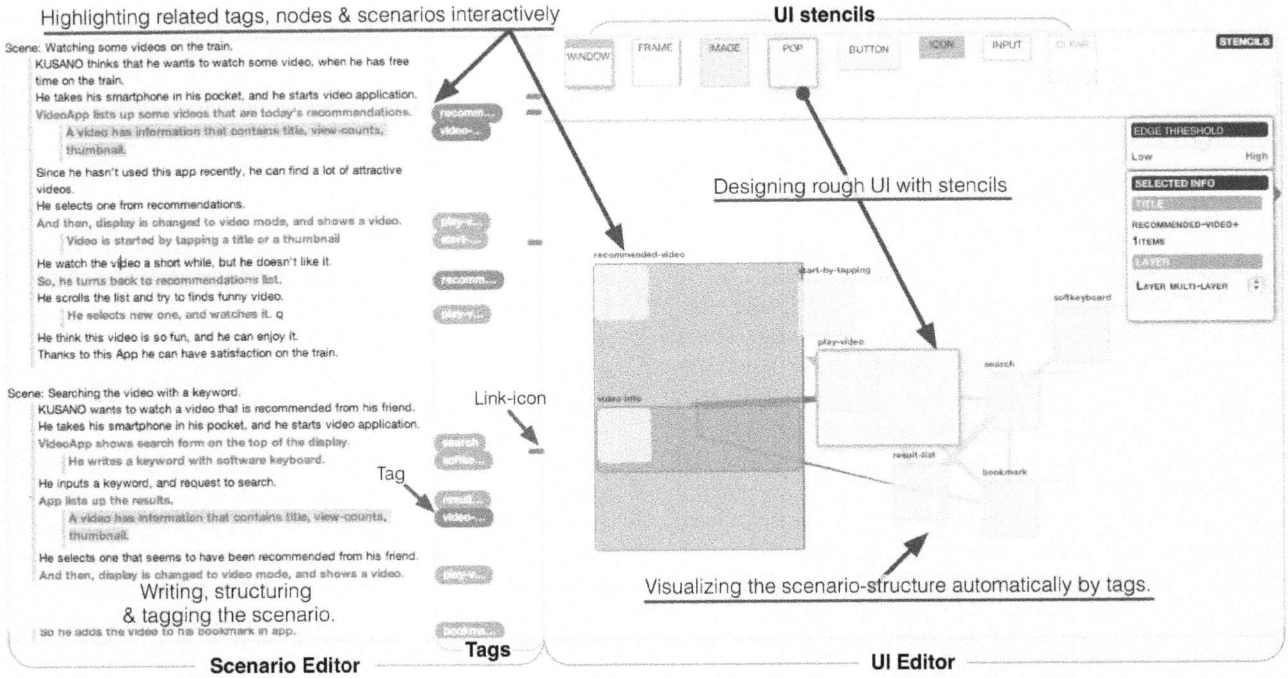

Figure 1: Scenario-Based Interactive UI Design Tool

designer designs the UI based on the scenarios. This process should be iterated with the scenario detailing step because the designer can realize which UI-components or functions are needed by observing the UI. Fourth, the designer evaluates the UI through usability testing and then revises the UI based on the test-results.

The process between step-two and step-three contains a problem; it is difficult to understand and manage scenarios and UI. Candidate solutions include structured-scenarios [6] or graphics and flow-charts [4]. These proposals certainly help the designer to understand the user requirements, however, they fail to support the management of the links among scenarios, requirements, and UI.

The task of maintaining traceability between requirements and program-codes has been well studied [7]. The model-driven UI automatic generation approach has been studied for many years [8]. This approach makes it easier to manage traceability. However, the model is difficult to understand without special knowledge. This characteristic is not suitable for designing UIs since there are various stakeholders who don't have specialist knowledge as regards UI design. In the field of SBD, to maintain the links between requirements and scenarios for software development, scenario-browser [9] or agile development process with scenario [10] has been proposed. However, they have not focused on managing the links among scenarios, user requirements and UI.

Finally, various prototyping tools have been proposed to design and evaluate UIs efficiently, and some of them have been utilized in real projects [11]. Prototyping tools obviously support the designer by allowing the design appearance of the UI to be more rapidly settled. However, current prototyping tools are unable to integrate all scenario information into one UI.

SCENARIO BASED INTERACTIVE UI DESIGN TOOL

The scenario based Interactive UI design tool provides support for scenario management and UI design based on scenarios. Furthermore, it offers traceability between scenarios and UI such that a designer can efficiently iterate the UI design-evaluation process. Figure 1 shows the GUI of the proposed tool; a browser-based application developed in HTML5 and JavaScript. Its key parts are the Scenario Editor and UI Editor. The designer is able to smoothly switch between them depending on the situation.

Support of Scenario Management.

The Scenario Editor has three steps for creating and managing scenarios: 1.Writing a scenario, 2.Structuring the scenario and 3.Tagging the scenario.

First, the designer writes, like a novel, a scenario that contains user behavior when using the software (ex. background, motivation, goal, steps).

Second, the designer creates hierarchies of sentences based on sentence detail. This operation is similar to the use of the outline-view. For the example shown in Figure 1 left, the first hierarchy layer holds scene titles. The second layer holds user behavior with no reference to UI expressions. The third layer holds concrete UI expressions. The hierarchy clearly shows the details of each sentence (does it contain UI components or not). Traditional SBD separately writes scenarios with and without UI components. The drawback of traditional scenarios is they make it hard to maintain the links because the two types of scenarios are written separately. On the other hand, our tool uses hierarchy to integrate them. However, we feel that users need to understand the adjustment rules that will yield the proper hierarchy. Thus, our tool shows tooltips as guides for hierarchy adjustment. For example, if there are UI-component expressions (ex. window, button, icon) in the second layer, the tooltip recommends moving them to the third layer.

Third, the designer extracts tags, text labels, from the scenarios. The designer selects a sentence that contains requirements that impact UI design and manually creates a tag for the sentence. A floating tag box is used to input tags as shown Figure 2. The designer can quickly reuse registered tags since this box support incremental tag search. The tool automatically maintains each tag and links between the sentence and the tag.

Support of Designing UI

The UI Editor automatically visualizes the relationships of sentences by the tags (see Figure 1 right); this helps the designer to overview the scenarios and create a rough UI. The relationship is visualized as a graph that uses nodes (translucent square with dashed border) as tags and edges (line) as the relationships between tags, which is based on the tag position in the scenario hierarchy. The visualized-node positions are calculated by the spring-model. Node-size increases with frequency of usage in the scenario. Edge-width is calculated from the distance between tags in the scenario structure (sentences on same layer and next/previous sentences have strong ties). An edge is automatically created if tag distance is under a distance threshold (edge-threshold).

Graphs are very effective for overviewing relationships. In particular, using a graph to visualize the scenario structure helps the designer to visually consider groups of requirements and possible conflicts. For example, a node that has many edges is visually obvious and logically important in the graph because this node (tag) is related to many scenarios and can be the cause of user confusion. The current prototype focuses on several tens of nodes, and the default edge threshold is optimum for up to ten scenarios and tens of nodes. Hence, it provides only plain interaction (no zooming and filtering) with the graph. However, users can manually adjust the threshold for the number of nodes by slider operation; the graph is automatically updated.

The designer can create UI-components directly on the graph by selecting a stencil (see Figure 1 top) and dropping it on a node; nodes can be moved and layouts created. Figure 1 right shows the middle part of the UI design process (intermediate between graph and UI). It shows that our tool can maintain the links among scenarios, tags, graphs and UI. This feature shortens the design time. Even if the designer sets a UI-component to a node, both the visualized data and the UI-component can be easily

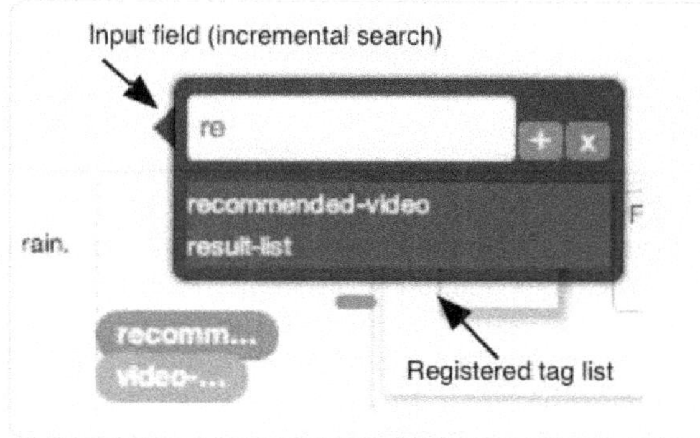

Figure 2: Floating Tag Box

recognized due to the overlaying of visualized data. The designer easily turns off the graph with single click. Incidentally, the current prototype does not focus the creation of a click-through prototype. This functionality can be added, however, it is well supported by various prototyping tools.

Provides Traceability among Scenarios, Tags and UI

Our tool always maintains the data of scenarios, scenario-structures, tags, UI-components and the links created by the designer. Because of this, it allows scenario construction to become a environment in which to envisage the design at a rough scale and then detailing that design by re-linking design choices back to earlier versions.

Figure 1 shows the linkage between highlighted nodes, tags, and scenarios. Highlighted nodes and edges have different color and tone. The designer understands quickly the number of tags used and their source sentences, since the scenario editor shows link-icons (see Figure 1). If the designer clicks a link-icon, the scenario editor immediately shows the linked sentence and the tag in question. For example, after setting a UI-component on each node and laying the nodes out, if the designer selects a scenario to better understand the links between the scenario and its UI-components, our tool automatically highlights only those UI-components related to the sentence in question. In addition, our tool warns users when they delete a sentence that has a tag; the node that was linked to the deleted sentence changes its color.

The above features offer high traceability and interactivity between scenario writing and UI designing. They encourage the designer to concentrate on imagining user behavior and designing the UI. Additionally, this feature strongly supports iterative-design, since it allows quick reference to data related to the issue. In iterative-design, the designer has to repeatedly evaluate the UI, find an issue and fix it. This means that the designer should refer to not only the UI, but also the related data of scenarios and tags. It is obviously a heavy task without our tool.

Furthermore, the designer must create test scenarios for usability testing. First, the designer decides which part of the UI should be evaluated; he/she can quickly refer to the related scenarios and choose to create an abstract scenario or a concrete scenario depending on the evaluation objective. This feature strongly supports iterative design.

USER STUDY

We conducted a preliminary user study to get user feedback. Three participants who were unfamiliar with SBD used a prototype of our tool. We requested them to design one UI suitable for two situations; Scene 1, user uses a smartphone application to browse a movie website, and Scene 2, user wants to search and watch a movie recommended by a friend via a smartphone application. We mainly observed design activities related to writing, structuring, and tagging scenarios and designing a rough UI.

The participants commented that writing and structuring the two scenarios was useful for clarifying user behavior and for finding vague points. This result confirms the effectiveness of the hierarchy structure. However, they also commented that it was difficult to set appropriate hierarchies at first. One solution is to show scenario samples or tutorials.

Furthermore, they noted the benefit of the graph-based form of visualization. They could understand quickly which tags were key and which were related tags. Our proposed visualization and interaction method is simple, but we could confirm its effectiveness for understanding relationships between tags. Note that this benefit strengthens with scenario size. Thus, we plan to extend visualization by adding some of the interaction techniques proposed in the research field of visualization that will enhance its scaling performance and conduct further experiments to confirm this strength.

In the UI design stage, when the participants identified some shortfall in the UI, they could quickly and easily trace and revise the related sentences and tags. This means that the participants performed the iterated design process, while smoothly tracing the data relationships identified by highlighted sentences, tags and UI components. On the other hand, when participants wanted to detail the UI, a new sentence had to be created to anchor the new UI-component. This seems to be somewhat inefficient. This case study revealed that implementing an annotating-function that does not involve the addition of sentences would further enhance the iterative process. The above results show that this tool is effective for managing scenarios and designing UIs.

CONCLUSION

We have presented the Scenario-based Interactive UI Design tool; it supports designers in structuring scenarios and maintains the links among scenarios, tags, and UI. We also have shown that it enables designers to concentrate on design-tasks and allows the iterative design process to be conducted smoothly and efficiently by providing highly effective support. A user study gathered positive feedback from all participants. In the future, we will conduct examine bigger scenarios to more fully evaluate the effectiveness of interactivity and traceability among scenarios, tags and UI. We also plan to put our tool into commercial use (in-house) to observe the resulting design activities for a detailed evaluation of its practicality.

REFERENCES

1. Carroll, J. M. *Making Use: Scenario-Based Design of Human-Computer Interactions.* The MIT Press, 2000.
2. Cooper, A., Reimann, R., and Cronin, D. *About face 3: the essentials of interaction design.* John Wiley & Sons, Inc., New York, NY, USA, 2007.
3. Hertzum, M. Making use of scenarios: A field study of conceptual design. *International Journal of Human-Computer Studies 58* (2003), 215–239.
4. Gough, P. A., Fodemski, F. T., Higgins, S. A., and Ray, S. J. Scenarios-an industrial case study and hypermedia enhancements. *In Proceedings of the Second IEEE International Symposium on Requirements Engineering*, IEEE Computer Society (1995), 10–17.
5. Nielsen, J. Iterative user-interface design. Computer 26, 11 (1993), 32–41.
6. Yanagida, K., Ueda, Y., Go, K., Takahashi, K., Hayakawa, S., and Yamazaki, K. Structured Scenario-Based design method. In Human Centered Design, vol. 5619 of *Lecture Notes in Computer Science*. Springer Berlin / Heidelberg (2009), 374–380.
7. Winkler, S., and von Pilgrim, J. A survey of traceability in requirements engineering and model-driven development. *Software and Systems Modeling 9* (2010), 529–565.
8. Sousa, K., Mendonca, H., Vanderdonckt, J., Rogier, E., and Vandermeulen, J. User interface derivation from business processes: a model-driven approach for organizational engineering. *In Proceedings of the 2008 ACM symposium on Applied computing*, ACM (2008), 553–560.
9. Rosson, M. B., and Carroll, J. M. Integrating task and software development for object-oriented applications. *In Proceedings of the SIGCHI conference on Human factors in computing systems*, ACM Press/Addison-Wesley Publishing Co. (1995), 377–384.
10. Obendorf, H., and Finck, M. Scenario-Based usability engineering techniques in agile development processes. *In CHI '08 extended abstracts on Human factors in computing systems*, ACM (2008), 2159–2166.
11. Tang, L., Yu, Z., Zhou, X., Wang, H., and Becker, C. Supporting rapid design and evaluation of pervasive applications: challenges and solutions. *Personal Ubiquitous Comput. 15, 3* (2011), 253–269.

Regularly Visited Patches in Human Mobility

Yan Qu
placenous.com
yan.qu@acm.org

Jun Zhang
Pitney Bowes Inc.
Jun.zhang@pb.com

ABSTRACT
In this paper, we propose a new analytic unit for human mobility analysis – the patch. We developed a process to identify Regularly Visited Patches (RVP) and a set of metrics to characterize and measure their spatial patterns. Using a large dataset of Foursquare check-ins as a test bed, we show that RVP analysis reveals fundamental patterns of human mobility and will lead to promising research with strong implications for businesses.

Author Keywords
Human Mobility; Regularly Visited Patches; OPTICS.

ACM Classification Keywords
H.1.2 [User/Machine Systems]: Human information processing

INTRODUCTION
Understanding human mobility becomes increasingly important with the rapid adoption of smart phones and blossoming of location-based services. Research based on mobile location data has found high regularities in human mobility [2] and identified important places in people's life [5].

In previous human mobility analyses, the geographic point, as captured in a location history, was the analytic unit of choice. In this work, we propose a paradigm shift to an analytic unit with a higher degree of granularity: the patch. The word "patch" refers to an area different from its surroundings from a certain perspective. It was originally used in animal foraging theories for areas containing intensive activities, and was later introduced into HCI research [7]. Patches exist in geographic environments (e.g. retail agglomeration, administrative district), in people's daily activities (e.g. home area, office area), and in human's cognitive map (e.g. a safe neighborhood, an expensive shopping area), which are all factors heavily influence human's location-based behavior. Therefore patch-level mobility analysis is natural and meaningful. It may reveal mobility patterns that a point level analysis fails to catch.

We focused our study on Regularly Visited Patches (RVPs), defined as a spatial area people routinely visit in their daily life. Real life experience suggests that such patches exist. For instance, people visit multiple stores in a shopping area for grocery and other needs. Or we frequent different lunch places on the blocks next to our office. RVPs are shaped by an individual's personal, social, and economic behavior, and restricted by underlying structures like roads, neighborhoods, and the location of retail stores. Understanding the morphology of RVPs and the factors that shape them is critical to understanding human mobility and has significant implications for businesses.

The paper is organized as follows: first, we briefly review related work; second, we illustrate the process of identifying RVPs using one person's data; then we describe metrics to characterize RVPs and test RVP analysis on a large Foursquare dataset. We conclude the paper with a discussion of the importance and implications of RVP analysis.

RELATED WORK
Studies have found high degree of spatial and temporal regularity in human mobility [4]. Specifically, people frequently return to a few locations such as where they live and work [4][5]. This school of research used Call Detail Records (CDR) – data containing where and when people made phone calls, provided by mobile companies. The recorded locations in CDR are that of the cell phone towers instead of callers' actual positions. Therefore each location point represents an area around a cell phone tower. Thus, although these analyses use point-level methods, they can be considered as implicit patch-level analyses and their results reveal certain regularities at this level. However, these cell towers are positioned by mobile carriers to maximize the coverage. The spatial distribution and granularity of these implicit patches is very different from behavior-based patches we looked at.

Our work examined patch-level regularity using high precision GPS-based location data. This data is precise to the degree of several meters and can reveal detailed location information (e.g. a retail store). Cheng et al. [2] conducted point-level analysis on millions of Foursquare check-in data and found periodic patterns in check-ins and return probability. They also explored the geographic, social, and economic factors that influence mobility. Cranshaw et al. [3] clustered all check-ins in a city and generated neighborhood-like areas. Their analysis of population dynamics revealed that different groups of people prefer different neighborhoods. The patch-level pattern that emerged from the aggregated population data further motivated us to explore the patch-level patterns in individual mobility.

IDENTIFYING REGULAR VISITED PATCHES

Given a person's location history, we can identify RVPs by looking for areas where visits clustered over a long period of time. We expected a wide variety of shapes, sizes, densities, and distributions for RVPs due to different environmental factors, life styles, and personal preferences. For example, a person living in Manhattan may have small and dense RVPs close to home and subway stations, while a person living on a ranch in Montana may have large but less dense RVPs distributed across several towns. To explore the morphology of RVPs, we needed tools to cluster location data without presuming its character. After reviewing spatial analysis methods, we chose OPTICS [1] because it can identify clusters varying in shape, size, and density, and does not require presetting global parameters such as the number of clusters and cutting thresholds.

The OPTICS is a density-based clustering algorithm that orders points based on their closeness to each other to identify spatial structures. Intuitively speaking, OPTICS tries to map points from a higher dimensional space to a 1-D space while maintaining distance relationships. Two parameters are required to set a very loose density upper cap for all clusters. Given an area with radius ε, there must be at least *MinPts* data points in it. In our work, we set ε = 10km and *Minpts* = 10. Therefore, at least 10 check-ins in a neighborhood with a radius of 10km were needed to form a cluster. Any RVP structure denser than this cap will be extracted by the algorithm. A "Reachability" value is also calculated for each point, roughly indicating the distance (in kilometers) of a data point to its left neighbor.

As an example, we used OPTICS to identify RVPs for an active Foursquare user who gave us 6 months of check-in data and his home location. Figure 1 is the Reachability plot. The x-axis shows the 1,288 check-ins in order. The y-axis is the Reachability value of each check-in point. A valley in the Reachability plot corresponds to a set of check-ins that are close to each other, which is a patch in the geographic map (Figure 2). The wider a valley is, the more check-ins in the patch; The deeper the valley is, the denser the patch is; The higher the edge of a valley is, the further the patch is from others. Small valleys inside a bigger valley are sub-patches inside a larger patch. Therefore, the Reachability plot provides an overview of a hierarchical structure with patches of different sizes, densities, and intra distances.

If the check-ins in a patch occur over a relativel long period of time (e.g. 30 days), then the patch is a RVP. On Figure 1, we marked several valleys (numbered 1-7) corresponding to RVPs marked in Figure 2. Notice that valleys 1, 2, and 3 are inside a larger valley showing a hierarchical RVP structure. The unmarked valleys with high edges and the black area on the right are small RVPs or isolated check-ins. We added a red curve on the plot to show the distance from each check-in to the person's home. In extreme cases, a RVP contains multiple check-ins at a single location point, such as RVP 3 which has multiple check-ins at that person's home (distance to home = 0). In a brief interview with the user, he told us that all the identified RVPs are meaningful. RVP 3 is his home, RVP 1 and 2 are places he often visits near his home (e.g. his gym), RVP 5 is close to his office (e.g. places he eats lunch), while RVP 4, 6, and 7 are regular shopping and eating areas. Therefore, the OPTICS algorithm successfully identified RVPs showing not only spatial but also semantic segmentations.

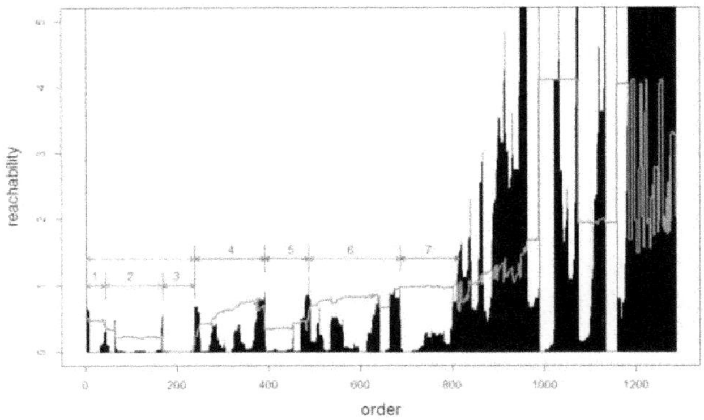

Figure 1. Reachability Plot

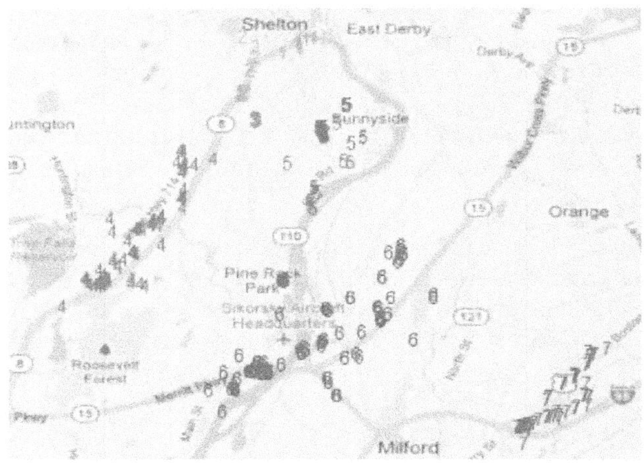

Figure 2. Regularly Visited Patches resulted from OPTICS

To automatically detect hierarchical structures in the Reachability plot, we used a cluster extraction algorithm mentioned in [1], which detects the steep slopes on both sides of each valley. We customized this algorithm to identify valleys that were big and deep enough, and regularly visited. For each valley, we required:

- *The check-in number* >= 10, so it was visited with relatively high frequency.
- *Time duration* > 30 days, so it was visited over a long period of time.
- *R_bottom* < min(*R_edge* * 0.1, (*R_edge* – 0.1km)) *R_bottom* is the Reachability value at the valley bottom. *R_edge* is the Reachability value at the lower edge. So the valleys have to be relatively deep, which means a much shorter inner-patch distance than intra-patch distance.

RVP ANALYSIS ON LARGE MOBILITY DATA

The Dataset and Data Screening

Our dataset was drawn from six months of Foursquare check-ins from Nov. 2011 to May 2012. It was collected using a similar method described in [2] by mining Foursquare-Twitter linked accounts. It contains 15,424,555 check-ins from 407,968 unique users. Compared to mobile phone logs, this user generated data is much sparser and regarded as less reliable because of varying motivations for using the service [6]. However, it provides a large dataset with fine grained spatial information that is otherwise not available. The data is a good test-bed to help us explore mobility patterns as long as we keep its limitations in mind when interpreting the results. For our analysis, we needed data from active users, so we screened all users based on their number of check-ins and length of activity. We also removed a user's duplicate check-ins at a single location at the same day to avoid disproportionally emphasizing those locations. Our final screening criteria were:

- *Number of check-ins* > 180 (approximately an average of one check-in per day during a 6 month period)
- *Active time period* > 60 days (last active day – first active day > 60 days)
- "Home" in a person's profile is in US, so we can augment the data with US census information.

The screening process left us with 9,029 active users with 2,749,008 check-ins.

General RVP Analysis

Running the OPTICS algorithms on this dataset, we found a total of 128,845 RVPs, 64,490 of which were leaf RVPs and could not be divided into smaller RVPs. We focused exclusively on these leaf RVPs and call them RVPs in the rest of the paper. Among the 2,749,008 check-ins in our dataset, 1,853,134 of them (67.4%) were in RVPs, indicating that RVPs capture a large portion of people's location-based activities and there is high patch-level regularity.

A set of metrics characterizing the morphology RVPs was developed, which is shown in Table 1.

#RVP	Number of RVPs a person has.
#Chkin	Number of check-ins a RVP has.
RVP_Rg	Radius of gyration of a RVP. An indicator of the spatial size of the RVP. More details below.
R_edge	Reachability value at the valley edge in the Reachability plot. An indicator of the intra-distance among RVPs
Person_Rg	Radius of gyration of all RVPs a person has. Calculated using the mass centers of the person's RVPs, weighted by the #Chkin of each RVP. An indicator of a person's range of mobility.

Table 1. Metrics characterizing RVPs

RVP_Rg is defined as follows:

$$RVP\_R_g = \sqrt{\frac{1}{n}\sum_{i=1}^{n} dis(l_i - l_{RVPcm})^2}$$

Where l_i is the location of the ith check-in in a RVP. l_{RVPcm} is the location of the center of mass of a RVP. $dis(l_i - l_{RVPcm})$ is the distance between the two locations. n is the number of check-ins in a RVP.

Table 2 shows the statistics of all the RVP metrics listed in Table 1, allowing us to draw a rough picture of their morphology. In the median case, a person has 6 RVPs. Each RVP contains about 21 check-ins. Its radius of gyration (RVP-Rg) is about 0.37km. It is about 1.08km from its neighbor RVPs. The person_Rg is about 9.6km. All the metrics have long tailed distributions, meaning that there exists a small portion of RVPs that are much larger, or sparser, or further away from others. Compared to previous studies using low resolution CDR data, where a single cell tower covers about 3 km^2 on average [4], our analysis using GPS-based locations can capture mobility patterns at a more precise scale. In our data set, a large portion of RVPs are smaller than the cell tower patches, which means they would be lost in the coarse resolution of CDR based analysis.

	Min	Median	Mean	Max
#RVP	1	6	6.97	44
#Chkin	10	21	28	579
RVP_Rg (km)	0	0.37	1.01	10.0
R_edge (km)	0.1	1.08	2.78	10
Person_Rg (km)	0	9.64	73.89	3809

Table 2. Stats of RVP metrics

RVPs in Different Social and Temporal Context

To understand how RVPs vary by environmental context, we compared RVPs from areas of different settlement contexts and Weekday vs. Weekend.

RVPs in Different Settlement Contexts

We chose two groups of people with most of their activities in a very different settlement context. One group was from Urban areas (House hold per mile^2 > 1000) and the other was from Rural areas (House hold per mile^2 < 200). To reduce the influence of check-in numbers on the RVP patterns, only people with less than 300 check-ins were selected. The screening resulted in 1,081 people in the Urban group and 268 people in the Rural group.

The result shows that RVPs from the Rural group are more sparsely located in larger areas than the Urban group. The Rural group has a much higher median of *Person-Rg* than Urban populations (12.1km versus 6.8km), indicating a significantly larger range of mobility. Figure 4 shows the histogram of *Person_Rg* for the two populations in the range of [0,50]. Meanwhile, the Rural group has a larger *R_edge* than the Urban group (median: 0.97 vs. 1.52. KS test, D=0.14, p<0.001), indicating a longer distance between RVPs.

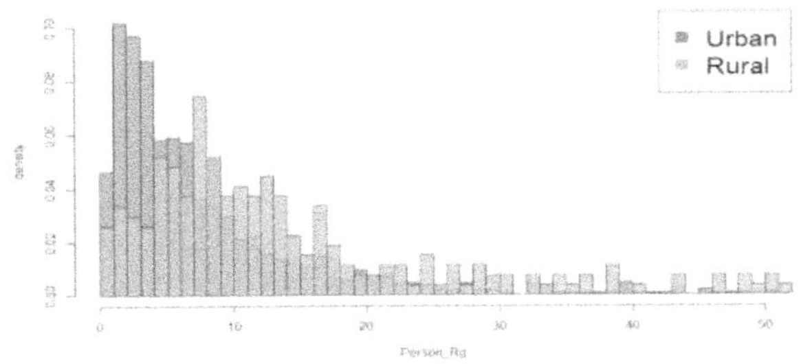

Figure 4. Histogram of of *Person_Rg* for (Urban vs. Rural)

Furthermore, although the total number of check-ins was similar (median: urban 220, rural 221), the Rural group had significantly more check-ins in their RVPs (median 161) than Urban group (median 143). This implies that rural populations have more regularity in their mobility patterns than urban populations. The Rural group had more RVPs per person *(#RVP*, median, rural 7 vs. urban 5; KS test, D = 0.21, P<0.001), while the number of check-ins per RVP were almost the same *(#Chkin*, median, rural 21 vs. urban 22). The spatial size of the RVPs were larger for the Rural group (*RVP_Rg*, median, rural 0.47 vs. urban 0.40; KS test, D=0.08, p<0.001), thus their RVPs had lower densities.

In summary, the RVP analysis on these two groups indicate that people living in rural areas have a longer travel distance for their regular activities, forming larger size but less dense patches that are sparsely distributed. This reveals the impact of different settlement contexts on human mobility that point level analyses may not catch.

RVPS during Weekends and Weekdays

We ran separate RVP analyses on Weekend and Weekday check-ins. There were 734,219 Weekend check-ins and 2,014,789 Weekday check-ins in our dataset, 65% and 70% of them were in RVPs respectively. Weekends had fewer check-ins, and they formed fewer RVPs than Weekdays. In the median case, a person has 2 Weekend RVPs and 5 Weekday RVPs. The total number of check-ins within each RVP was comparable: 20 for Weekend RVPs and 21 for Weekdays RVPs.

Interestingly, the Weekend RVPs are closer to a person's most frequent check-in location and are of larger spatial size and more sparsely distributed than Weekday RVPs. We calculated the distance from the most frequently checked-in location to the center of mass of a person's Weekend and Weekday RVPs and found that Weekend RVPs are of shorter distance (median:4.57) than the Weekday RVPs (median: 6.57) (KS test, D = 0.16, p<0.001). The median *RVP_Rg* of Weekend and Weekday RVPS are 1.32 and 0.40 respectively (KS test, D=0.32, p<0.001), indicating that the Weekend RVPs are much larger in spatial size. The median of *R_edge* of Weekend RVPs and Weekday RVPs are 3.40 and 1.21, respectively (KS test, D = 0.30, p<0.001), indicating much larger intra distances among Weekend RVPs.

In summary, RVPs were larger but looser on the weekend and smaller and more compact during the week. The difference is likely due to the different types of activities conducted in weekend and weekdays.

CONCLUSION & DISCUSSION

We believe that patches are a fundamental unit of spatial structure in human mobility and demand further study as an aspect of location-based behavior. As an example of patch-level analysis, RVPs demonstrates a novel yet basic ways of describing and characterizing mobility patterns omitted in point-level analysis. These included whether location-based activities cluster in space, the size and density of these clusters, and how clusters are distributed over space. Although more systematic examination is needed, it is very likely that different spatial patches serve different purposes in people's life (e.g. shopping area vs. working area), thus the spatial pattern may reflect intrinsic structures in social-geographic environment or in human behavior. Further exploration in this direction may lead to a new set of theories and models of location-based behavior, such as models of people's activities centers based on RVPs or patch-based shopping reference models. This line of study also has direct business implications, such as a mobile advertising network that can automatically bundle and send coupons from several stores within a RVP in a batch instead of send individual store coupons separately.

REFERENCES

1. Ankerst, M., Breunig, M. M., Kriegel, H.-P. & Sander, J. OPTICS: ordering points to identify the clustering structure. *In Proc. SIGMOD Rec.* 28, 49–60, 1999.
2. Cheng, Z., Caverlee, J., Lee, K. & Sui, D. Z. Exploring millions of footprints in location sharing services. *In Proc. AAAI ICWSM* 2011.
3. Cranshaw, J., Schwartz, R., Hong, J. I., & Sadeh, N. The livehoods project: Utilizing social media to understand the dynamics of a city. *In Proc. ICWSM* 2012.
4. González, M. C., Hidalgo, C. A. & Barabási, A.-L. Understanding individual human mobility patterns. *Nature* 458, 238–238, 2009.
5. Isaacman, S., Becker, R., Cáceres, R., Kobourov, S., Martonosi, M., Rowland, J., Varshavsky, A. Identifying important places in people's lives from cellular network data. *Pervasive Computing*, 133-151, 2011
6. Lindqvist, J., Cranshaw, J., Wiese, J., Hong, J. & Zimmerman, J. I'm the mayor of my house: examining why people use foursquare - a social-driven location sharing application. *In Proc. CHI* 2011, 2409–2418.
7. Pirolli, P.L. *Information foraging theory: Adaptive interaction with information.* Vol. 2. Oxford University Press, USA, 2007.

Large-Scale Participation: A Case Study of a Participatory Approach to Developing a New Public Library

Peter Dalsgaard
Participatory IT Centre
Department of Aesthetics and Communication
Aarhus University, Denmark
dalsgaard@cavi.au.dk

Eva Eriksson
Division of Interaction Design,
Department of Applied Information Technology,
Chalmers University of Technology, Sweden
eva.eriksson@chalmers.se

ABSTRACT
In this paper, we present a case study of a participatory project that focuses on interaction in large-scale design, namely, the development of the new Urban Mediaspace Aarhus. This project, which has been under way for ten years, embodies a series of issues that arise when participatory design approaches are applied to large-scale, IT-oriented projects. At the same time, it highlights the issues public knowledge institutions face, when interactive technologies challenge their fundamental roles and practices; by extension, this case offers examples of how these challenges may be explored and addressed through IT-based participatory initiatives. We present a range of such activities carried out during the past ten years, and present the main lessons from the project, based on interviews with three key stakeholders. These lessons focus on how to make participation work in practice, how to align different paradigms of inquiry and practice in a project of this scale, and how to capture and anchor the insights from participatory events to inform the ongoing design process.

Author Keywords
Participatory Design; Interaction Design; Large-Scale Projects; Design Methods; Citizen Involvement

ACM Classification Keywords
H.5.2. Information interfaces and presentation: User Interfaces – Theory and Methods, User-Centered Design

INTRODUCTION AND BACKGROUND
Architect Christopher Alexander once said that perhaps the most difficult thing about big public buildings is the fact that the design and building processes really have to be remarkable, and that people must be the core of the building, that inspiration comes from the deep feeling of the users [1]. In our research, we have worked for a number of years at the intersection of interaction design and the built environment, exploring the potential of methods and techniques from participatory design in this field. This includes research in large-scale projects, which are typically characterized by one or more of the following factors: long time spans, large or diverse groups of users, and result in products and systems that are complex or extensive in scope. In the case reported on in this paper, all of the above factors were in play - a decade long project addressing a large and diverse group of stakeholders and users, resulting in a multi-use media library. While Alexander's proposition that people should be at the core of the development process resonates with the widespread adoption of user-centered design approaches, user involvement in large-scale projects is far from common today. There are few indications of change, such as Sanders participatory prototyping of the physical environment in the development of a new hospital [19]. Although researchers such as Shapiro [21] have prompted the interaction design community to change and engage in the development of large-scale systems, the fact remains that participatory design projects have a history of being small-scale and stand-alone, as found by Oostveen and van den Besselaar [17], and Simonsen and Hertzum [20]. Our response is to offer a case study that resonates with the theme of design at CHI, in that it explores how participatory activities, scaffolded by interactive systems, can play a major part in the development of large-scale projects.

The case in question concerns the development of a new public library, called The Urban Mediaspace Aarhus. The construction of the new library represents a significant investment of the municipality's resources, and is intended to be an icon for the city. Traditionally, projects of this nature have been developed "top-down", and in many cases, without much emphasis on participation. A prime example of this is the Bibliothèque Nationale in Paris, which was reportedly developed without consulting librarians [16], and which imposes a hierarchical system of access to the media it houses [9]. In many ways, The Urban Mediaspace Aarhus case is a counterexample to such approaches, in that it is permeated by a participatory agenda. Our involvement in the project initially focused on using participatory design approaches to develop interactive installations for the future library, but over the course of time we came to realize that the overarching project of developing the new library is of interest to the wider CHI community, because it represents a pioneering attempt to situate participation and user involvement, often scaffolded by interactive technologies, as the central drivers of a large-scale project.

In this paper, we present a study of how participatory approaches and user involvement activities have been employed in The Urban Mediaspace Aarhus project. The key issues we address in the paper are *how and why participatory approaches and the values of user involvement have been incorporated into the project*, *how participatory activities have been carried out*, *how the knowledge and insights from these activities have informed the project*, and *outcomes of the participatory approach in practice*.

The contribution of this paper is two-fold: First, we offer a detailed study of a large-scale participatory project. As outlined, projects of this scale are rarely explored in our field, and we hope that this work will inspire further studies of user involvement and the use of participatory approaches on a larger scale. Secondly, we present key lessons from adopting the participatory approach, on based on interviews with three key stakeholders in the project. While these lessons spring from this specific project, we believe that they may inform practitioners who engage in large-scale projects akin to The Urban Mediaspace Aarhus case.

The paper is structured as three main sections. First, we offer a detailed description of The Urban Mediaspace Aarhus case, including an overview of the many participatory activities that have been parts of the project. We then outline five key lessons from adopting a participatory approach based on interviews with key stakeholders and project participants. This is followed by a discussion in which we develop a series of design considerations for large-scale participatory projects.

CASE: THE URBAN MEDIASPACE AARHUS

The case described in this paper is called The Urban Mediaspace Aarhus project, and is a large-scale project where a new area of Aarhus and a new public building are under development (see Figure 1). Aarhus is the second largest city in Denmark, with about 300,000 inhabitants, and the the country's principal harbor. This new urban area is a 23,000 m^2 harbor site, which will be transformed from shipping to park space, involving a large-scale restructuring of piers, transport routes, rerouting of trams, and so on. The building will cover about 28,000 m^2, and will house the city's new public library, citizen services, private businesses, and a large automated parking cellar for 1000 cars. This project cost about EUR200 million, and is the largest development project in the history of the municipality. Grand ambitions surround this project, including that it will house the largest automatic car park in Europe, be the most accessible building in Europe, a landmark, and a sustainable icon. The project was ratified in 2001, and will run until 2015.

The project organization is quite complex, but in broad terms, the principal developer is the municipality of Aarhus, as this is a public project. The project board consists of representatives of a large foundation that sponsors the project, as well as the mayor and the city council members. There is also a general steering committee in charge of the entire project, and a sub-committee responsible for the construction. A strategy group consisting of local institutions and organizations contributes to the process on a strategic level, and an idea group contributes to technologies, architecture, communication, and library development. The project management is responsible for the planning, development, and coordination of the project, and refers to the steering committee and the sub-committee.

Figure 1. Rendering of The Urban Mediaspace Aarhus.

The project is not only a large-scale building project, it is also a project using participatory design inspiration for developing the city, the identities of the organization and institution, new services, roles, and use, while developing and building up the new residential and urban area.

Research Approach and Author Involvement

This paper describes a case study, and as such it comes with a series of inherent strengths and weaknesses, when compared to other types of contributions. We will focus on presenting an overview of the project, and outlining the different types of user involvement activities in some detail. From these, we will select a subset of issues within the project that may be of particular interest to the CHI community. While our engagement in this project represents a unique opportunity to study a large-scale participatory project, we must stress that, as per the notion of "wicked problems", first explored by Rittel and Webber [18], and subsequently by many others in the field of interaction design, a case study of this nature presents opportunities which cannot be replicated, and once an event has unfolded, it cannot be undone. Therefore, we do not present specific conclusions regarding best practices for large-scale public projects; rather, we present a series of design considerations regarding topics that have proved to be central to the user involvement in The Urban Mediaspace Aarhus case. In discussing the benefits and drawbacks of case studies in research, Flyvbjerg states that "... the case study is a necessary and sufficient method for certain important research tasks in the social sciences" [10, p 241]. Among other things, Flyvbjerg argues that case studies are important because they offer what Kuhn [14] has described as *exemplars*, that is, instances or cases that embody salient traits of the field. As pointed out in the introduction, there are very few exemplars when it comes to large-scale user involvement projects, and we hope to demonstrate that The Urban Mediaspace Aarhus serves as an exemplar in this field.

The authors, together with several research colleagues, have been involved in developing directions for interactive services for The Urban Mediaspace Aarhus since 2004, and have been connected with the project in several ways during this time [5, 6, 7, 8, 13, 15]. The research group did not participate in the initial planning process of the project, but has been active in various projects that had The Urban Mediaspace Aarhus project in mind. Coming from interaction design, we have actively participated in design research projects where interactive prototypes have been developed, implemented, and tested at full scale. These projects have been developed in cooperation with various libraries, companies, and individual users as active contributors. We have also moderated participatory design workshops concerning the development of The Urban Mediaspace Aarhus project, primarily with a focus on the integration of interactive technologies in the building. The past year has seen more active participation on almost all levels of the development of The Urban Mediaspace Aarhus project. Thus, our knowledge of the project and the process stem from various sources: first, from the extensive web-based documentation of the project available to the public [24]; secondly, from various research projects, with hands-on experience and learning; thirdly, from meetings, workshops, and interviews with project leaders, architects, users, partners, and so on.

User Involvement and Participation as Cornerstones of The Urban Mediaspace Aarhus Project

The Urban Mediaspace Aarhus project is not a participatory design project in the traditional sense, due, for instance, to the size, political frameworks, and execution structure, but is instead a project based on participatory design values and techniques. There is a political vision of establishing Aarhus as a city of knowledge, highly sensitive to changes to institutions such as the library, which are posed by emerging digital technology. Participation and user involvement have been official driving forces behind the project since 2005. When referring to "users" in this paper, it indicates both library employees and the public.

The Urban Mediaspace Aarhus project aims to provide a unique place for cooperation, with many current and future collaborating partners [24]. During winter 2005-2006, a wide range of experts, collaborating partners, networks, and library staff were invited to participate in the development of a series of core values for The Urban Mediaspace Aarhus project. The seven core values are: *The citizen as key factor*, *Lifelong learning and community*, *Diversity, cooperation, and networks*, *Culture and experiences*, *Bridging citizens, technology, and knowledge*, *A flexible and professional organization*, and finally, *A sustainable icon for Aarhus*.

Subsequently, these core values were matched with the citizens' values through City Voices, a citizen involvement initiative [22]. Its purpose was to gather the voices of citizens regarding the core values they find important for The Urban Mediaspace Aarhus Project. A physical, interactive table was developed, that featured built-in audio scenarios related to different places in the city, and included the option of recording one's comment. Everybody had the opportunity to record messages on the table, and thus express their opinions. In extension of this, ten focus group interviews were completed around the table, and the physical installations were complemented with a website. The citizens' comments were analyzed and incorporated into the results, in the seven core values of The Urban Mediaspace Aarhus, and in the program for the architectural competition, where participation was an important part of the agenda. The brief for the competition even stated that the proposals would be judged on the basis of how these values, combined with methods for user participation, were addressed by the architectural process

To further establish user participation as a cornerstone of the project, and to brand the project, in 2007 the main library in Aarhus initiated a project called Unleash the users, aimed at trying out methods of user involvement and user participation [23]. Through cooperation with external partners with varied experience of user involvement, the project resulted in several publications describing methods and examples of user involvement [23]. The goal of the project was threefold: to try out a model for user driven innovation, where the users are active participants, to make the library more attractive for the user, and finally, to develop models for cooperation between libraries and users, which might be used by other libraries, and inform The Urban Mediaspace Aarhus project. The project results concluded that user involvement is important in the development process, for five different reasons. These are: to test services, to develop new products in cooperation with the users, to show that you are an open minded organization, to foster greater loyalty to the library among the users, and to establish a kind of democracy within the library system. The methodology developed in this project has been incorporated into the library organization, and guided the development process of The Urban Mediaspace Aarhus project.

Project Overview and Time Frame

The approximately forty different participatory design inspired projects that have informed The Urban Mediaspace Aarhus project may be divided into two groups. The first group consists of the projects leading to the architectural competition program, up to 2007. The second group of projects led to the specific construction, following the architectural competition, as is shown in figure 2. The participatory design inspired activities changed in character and scale over the course of the entire project. In some activities, a large number of the library employees and the general public were active participants and co-designers; in other activities, for instance, when discussing accessibility issues in the new building, specific user groups such as disabled guests participated, to contribute to both interior and exterior design decisions, as well as to discuss software and integrated technologies. A detailed account of all these activities exceeds the scope of this paper; however, several have been described in previous publications, and we will refer to these for further details. An overview of selected projects, divided into two different phases, before and after the architectural competition, follows.

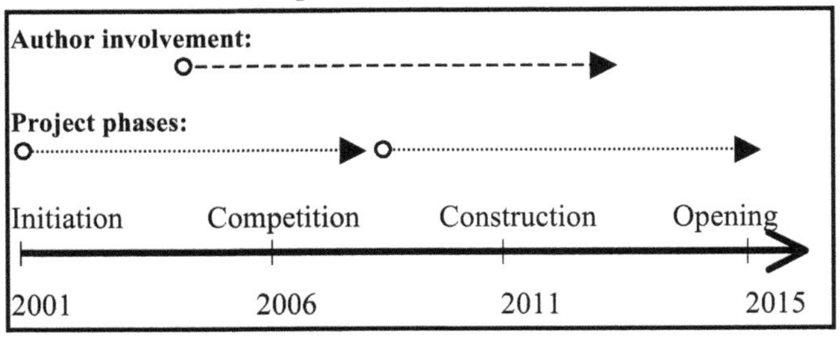

Figure 2. Timeline of the project, from initiation to opening.

The First Phase: 2001-2008

During the first years, several new initiatives were launched involving cooperation with both researchers and new partners, and also playing with the possibilities of new resources, for instance IT.

One project initiated during this phase was the Interactive Children's Library [8], see Figure 3. The project presented a new way of thinking about libraries, with a playful approach to pervasive technologies within the physical space. The Interactive Children's Library project vision of developing prototypes of new IT services and physical installations embedded in the challenging physical spaces of the library, supported and promoted an interest in children's play and learning activities. The project generated new knowledge by infusing design thinking into The Urban Mediaspace Aarhus project, in extension of a huge number of new design concepts, and developed two computational prototypes, StorySurfer and BibPhone. StorySurfer is a 5×3.6 meter spatial book browsing installation for children [7], and the BibPhone enables children to annotate physical material such as books with digital recordings [15].

The design process was significantly driven by research and informed by users. The project was the first step toward involving researchers in development projects, and inspired subsequent cooperation. The project has had a great influence in the children's library community, but also more generally, by introducing creative and playful ways of experimenting, providing means and materials for realizing projected scenarios at public libraries [2].

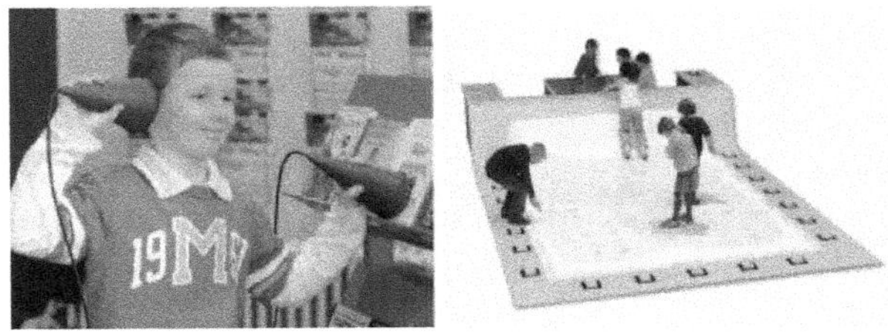

Figure 3. BibPhone and StorySurfer in use.

Through the experiences gained from these new types of constellations, materials, methods, and projects, the overall attitude shifted to a more experimental mode. A three year project, Transformation Lab, was initiated, which effectively changed the library space several times [25]. Transformation lab recognizes the current digital revolution and sees the library as an interactive interface for accessing both digital and physical resources. The Transformation Lab project explores the interaction between user, space, and material. Several experiments were staged in the adaptable foyer of the main library, from open jam sessions to interactive installations, such as the iFloor, an interactive question and answer floor surface that supports and stimulates community participation and interaction among collocated people at a municipal library, through shared interaction [13]. Library employees were involved as designers of new settings and services, just as users were invited not only as visitors and testers, but as designers. The Transformation Lab project revealed that flexible adaptable spaces are necessary, open events are well received, the physical library needs to be augmented with interactive technology, networking is critical, and finally, users need to more visible roles in the library [25].

Inspired by the possibilities disclosed by the experiments at the library, the development of ideas for the new building and process started to take form. The framework for the architectural competition was established, as were the previously mentioned core values guiding the entire process. This period was highly colored by the need to gather data from the employees and visitors, develop values, and find inspiration. Methods such as Traffic analysis and Focus group meetings were employed, and the visitors and employees were very involved at various levels, and new networks and co-operation were developed. The level of participation intensified during this period, when both employees and visitors were invited as designers. For instance, children's design labs were set up, to design the library of the future [24], user involvement methods were tried out in the previously described project, "Unleash the users" [23], IT artifacts, such as the previously mentioned "The City's voices" were developed to gather data in new ways, about visitors' use of the library and the city [22], and for six weeks employees worked to develop activities and ideas.

During 2008, the project competition was finally launched, tenders were negotiated, and several public information meetings were held [24]. Further development of services and activities took place while the process of developing strategies for involving users, and methods for how to open the organization was in focus [23].

The Second Phase: 2009-2015

During 2009-2010, the winner of the competition was selected, and the development of the architecture and services could start to take form. Also, the project and process could be designed, and enterprise tenders negotiated. The user involvement took shape in dialogue and critique sessions, vox pop interviews, and in co-design projects aimed at designing new services such as those seen in Digital Trendspotting [24], the results of which were published in a book of future concepts.

New projects were restarted, as a result of the new library prioritizing children and families as user groups, and in order to test new roles for the librarians. Families at Play in the library is a two year project involving public libraries from three different Danish cities, and two research centers [6]. The project investigates shared play culture through innovative new services and family activities at the library, with a focus on play, and also how new play concepts, consisting of different types of installations, services, and settings, support families playing together at public libraries. Examples of relevant concepts are a time music machine, an interactive treasure hunt, a pirate world, a nostalgic playroom, and the interactive installation, U.F.O.scope [6]. U.F.O.scope seeks to stimulate families' desire to explore the unknown together, while also discovering the physical library and its different types of resources, such as text, video, audio, and images, see Fig 4.

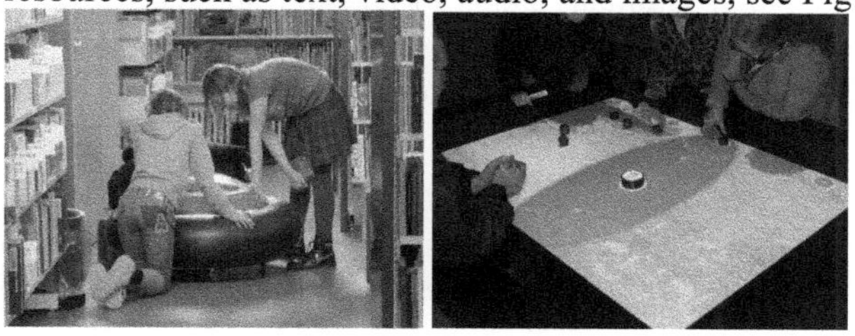

Figure 4. U.F.O.scope and the Interactive treasure hunt in use.

Simultaneously, experiments with new partners and networks take place to take the library "out of the box", and new tools for user involvement developed, such as Mobile probes [24]. Mobile Probes was an exploratory project with the purpose of digitizing the Cultural Probes method on a mobile platform, and test the concept in a number of companies and institutions. Aarhus Main Library participated as a test company, implementing the projects Families at Play in the Library and Tweens, as test cases [24]. As a Mobile Probes case, Families at Play in the Library worked with the concept development of the previously mentioned treasure hunt. Technically, the treasure hunt revolves around an interactive table in the lobby of the main library. User involvement via Mobile Probes ensures the relevance of the service to the target group, and qualifies the history/framework, as well as the actual activities of the treasure hunt. In the Tweens case, Mobile Probes has also been used to gather input and inspiration for developing library services for tweens, in the current library as well as for the "tweens lounge" that is being planned for the new library. By asking questions and giving assignments to a group of twelve- and thirteen-year-olds, the library investigated what tweens are focused on, with respect to the services the library already provides, or could establish for them. Focus is on space, media, and culture, as well as forms of learning.

In the final phases of The Urban Medispace project, until the project's completion in 2015, there will be continuous experimentation and refining. This is when the main project will be designed and executed. Users will be involved in the design of details such as the building's name, accessibility for the handicapped and new services, roles, and activities in the new library. A second round of Transformation Lab has been initiated, with the purpose to iteratively develop and test new services, networks, interior, methods, skills, and roles, before the move to the new building. The employees will be included in new ways, for instance, by staging experiments involving their own roles, and where they will co-design their workplace. So far, this has contributed to new, creative physical set-ups, as well as improved flexibility and movement among the employees, and even a break with traditional titles and work tasks. There is also more emphasis on analyzing digital needs and digital support of communication in physical spaces, where employees, members of the public, and partners are active design participants. In this phase, the emphasis is also on raising awareness of the project and on creating new partnerships.

KEY LESSONS FROM CENTRAL PROJECT PARTICIPANTS AND STAKEHOLDERS

It should be clear at this point that the number and types of participatory activities in The Urban Mediaspace Aarhus project are extensive. As a consequence, a large number of lessons from, and experiences of how participatory approaches to large-scale projects work in practice are embedded in the project organization. Some of these lessons have been articulated in reports and official documents, others have been manifested in the project in the form of competition proposals and building blueprints, for example, while other lessons remain tacit among project participants and stakeholders.

In addition to our aforementioned involvement in the project (outlined in the section, *Research approach and the authors' involvement*), we have carried out a series of interviews with key project participants and stakeholders, in order to establish an overview of these lessons. These encompass three structured interviews with 1) the principal architect, 2) the main project manager for The Urban Mediaspace Aarhus project, 3) the library consultant in charge of the participatory activities related to library services, and also a series of informal interviews with library staff. For the formal interviews, we developed comprehensive interview guidelines to ensure that we obtained different perspectives on central issues such as the main problems/challenges of adopting a participatory approach, the role of participation in the project, how participatory activities have been carried out, and how the results have affected the ongoing process. We then codified and analyzed the interviewees' responses. As part of this analysis, we identified five key themes related to large-scale participatory efforts, namely, aligning different paradigms of practice and inquiry, making participation work, capturing and anchoring insights from participatory activities, key challenges and key benefits of the participatory approach. While we also interviewed a number of users and participants over the course of our involvement in the project, we have chosen to focus on these three principal stakeholders, not because we believe that they hold all the answers, but because they have had to orchestrate many of the user involvement events, and made decisions regarding how insights from these events might inform the ongoing project.

Aligning Different Paradigms of Practice and Inquiry

The extent and prominence of participation in The Urban Mediaspace Aarhus project was new to all partners involved. Even The Urban Mediaspace Aarhus project management team, which was initially responsible for the participatory framing, was, by their own account, venturing into unknown territory. The principal architects first encountered the participatory agenda during the competition phase, during which they developed the preliminary proposals for the building, and while they had encountered requests for participation in previous projects, the complexity and the extent to which participation was integrated into the process was unlike that of any previous project. By their accounts, the traditional approach in architectural practice is to work with user involvement in the projecting phase, not in the programming phase, as was the case here.

Involving users in the programming phase is demanding, as it affects more aspects of the project. This was compounded by the scale, complexity, and integration into large-scale urban transformation inherent in The Urban Mediaspace Aarhus project. In their interviews, The Urban Mediaspace Aarhus project manager, the library services consultant, and the principal architect emphasized the challenge of approaching the process from different traditions and finding a common ground. While there is a need for clear division of labor, the project partners must also develop a shared language. The difference in paradigms of practice and inquiry come to light in various phases, for instance, in a joint workshop on dynamic and interactive building services, in which the different partners collaborated on developing concepts for the building. The library services consultant states that this drew attention to "the difficulties in communicating with partners who speak a different language and have a somewhat different agenda or a different set of ideals – all groups want to deliver the best possible product, but they have different conceptions of what that means. The architects may focus on the building in itself as experience, while the library sees the content and activities as experience." (Interview: library consultant).

All parties stress the need for mutual understanding and that, in a large-scale participatory project, it is not enough for practitioners such as architects learn about use practices; for the project to succeed, it is also crucial for librarians, for example, to learn about architectural practices. This latter insight seems particularly interesting from a participatory design perspective, since it echoes discussions on designers "going native" vs. users becoming aspiring designers through a project.

Capture and Anchor Insight from Participatory Activities

One of the main issues that The Urban Mediaspace Aarhus project manager, the principal architect, and the library services consultant raise during the interviews was a clear need for an improved and more structured way of capturing insights emerging from participatory activities. As stated by the library consultant: "Insights are scattered across a myriad of documents, much resides as tacit knowledge with people in the project... and much of what has been discovered is integrated into aspects of the process." The project manager mentions that one example of knowledge from participatory events being integrated into the process may be seen in how the seven values developed during the initial project phase subsequently became parts of the architectural program, which in turn will be manifested in the final building. Similarly, the principal architect considers the different milestone subprojects to be condensations of insights.

All partners expressed a desire to look elsewhere for best practice examples. While library representatives went on field trips to examine other new library projects, and hosted international conferences on the future of libraries, they did not uncover such best practice models. First, this indicates the need for the development of new process models and routines that can support the ongoing capture of insights from participatory events; secondly, this underscores the fact that large-scale participatory projects such as Urban Medispace Aarhus are indeed embracing new areas of participation.

Making Participation Work

The participatory activities in The Urban Mediaspace Aarhus project have been two-fold. Involving the public comprised the first phase, in which issues such as navigation, finding media, arrival areas, areas for children and infants, and so forth, were discussed. The second phase involved library employees. There have been about 20 user groups, with responsible key representatives, and there have been both individual and joint discussions. While all involved partners state that orchestrating these participatory efforts and bringing the information from them into the ongoing process has been complicated and challenging, they presented us with insights into how they have made participation work in practice.

First, both the principal architect and project manager note that deadlines and deliverables help to make the participation process concrete, as they give direction and purpose. The project manager employs the terms "qualitative time", that is, experienced time, and "last responsible minute", that is, deadlines associated with roles and responsibilities, as parts of the strategy for making the project present and relevant to those involved, by always having constructive milestones and associated deadlines in the near future, even if the project has a very long timeline.

Secondly, the principal architect emphasizes that in order to make participation work, it is important to hold collaborative, working workshops with a constructive purpose, in a language that all the involved parties understand: "It is important to recognize the difference between the parties, for example, the library people prefer words, while the architects are much more visual." Examples of establishing a shared language include the use of collaborative sketching, discussions around models, and the use of reference images in discussions, in order to concretely address spatial issues of the building process.

Thirdly, the library services consultant emphasized that although the project is so expansive that it may be difficult to classify it as a participatory design project in the traditional sense of the word, the use of participatory design methods and techniques, such as cultural and mobile probes, mock-up sessions, and collaborative prototyping may generate very concrete insights into the project. Finally, all partners emphasized that the single most important factor in making participation work was the project's committed and engaged leadership, when it comes to the participatory agenda, and on the levels of concrete project and library management, and the local politicians, who are ultimately the decision-makers behind the project.

Key Challenges of the Participatory Approach

According to all the partners involved, undoubtedly the biggest challenge of adopting a participatory approach in a large-scale project is that it demands a lot of time and resources. This is compounded by the fact that, in many ways, Urban Mediaspace Aarhus is a pioneering project and the involved partners must continuously develop new methods and techniques that match the participatory agenda. Indeed, part of the challenge is to develop the skills to carry out participatory events, as stated by the library services consultant: "It takes a special skill set to conduct participatory events, and you have to develop these skills in the project organization. It is also important to establish knowledge about what you can use participatory input for." (Interview: library services consultant).

According to the project manager, another challenge in a project of this scale is to understand the decision-making structure. The library services consultant expresses similar concerns regarding the inherently political nature of the project, and the need to find a fit between political decision structures and participatory events. For the principal architect, some of the main concerns in this vein have been that with so many participatory events at work it is difficult to know when different participating groups have finished their contributions, and how their outcome might affect the process, and force changes to aspects they considered complete. The architect states that: "For designers, it is hard to constantly run into compromises... User involvement can both clarify and obscure and the latter may be avoided by having an overview and a focus on clear architectural principles." (Interview: principal architect).

A third major challenge, according to the library services consultant, is analyzing all the data and input from the participatory events, and making these insights inform the rest of the process. She states that: "Sometimes, the step between information and decision is lacking." (Interview: library services consultant). Analyzing and clarifying the connections between data, analysis, and decisions, and communicating this to the parties involved is something which, in her opinion, could have a bigger focus. A fourth challenge is to engage potential future users and stakeholders in the project, first because of the long timeline of the project and its distant goal, secondly because the project is of such a scale that individual input may seem trivial. As touched on previously, this was a challenge that the involved partners continuously had to address by segmenting the project into smaller parts with specific deliverables, and by working with what project manager denotes "qualitative time".

Key Benefits of the Participatory Approach

While the participatory approach has taxed resources, all project partners agree that that it has been worth it, and each identified a number of benefits during the interviews, pertaining to both the project as a whole, and to their specific areas of practice. One aspect that all partners agreed is a major benefit was that the approach provides a sense of ownership and responsibility among participants, a sense that everyone has been a part of the creative process, not just the designers and decision makers. From the architects' perspective, engaging in the project brought about a change in perspective: "first of all it is a change of attitude, from 'we'll ask the users but we are the experts' toward an appreciative understanding of user insights and inputs." (Interview: principal architect). Participation is also an increasingly important parameter in many architectural projects, so architects will need to further develop skills in this area, and being a partner in The Urban Mediaspace Aarhus project hones these skills. Furthermore, the principal architect stressed that the dialogue that appears in participatory activities can really move things forward when it is focused on concrete and specific issues related to the building, and that the building has gained much in terms of quality and depth from focused user participation.

From the perspective of the project manager, the key benefit of using a participatory approach is that it provided "ongoing qualification of vision, idea, and product. In some cases, you learn something new that makes the project better and leads to changes, but even if you thought you knew, you get backing and qualified understanding of why something was a good idea." (Interview: The Urban Mediaspace Aarhus project manager). The project manager also emphasized the importance of empowerment and influence among future users, librarians, and the public, as is a primary benefit. This is echoed by the library services consultant, who stated that "Many great ideas and concepts would never have emerged without participatory activities." (Interview: library services consultant). She further stated that while the explicit, overarching argument for using participatory design is to develop something that fits user needs, it also provided political leverage: "It gives you backing for arguments, for instance when presenting proposals, because you can show that they are grounded in more than designers' ideas." (Interview: library consultant).

DISCUSSION AND DESIGN CONSIDERATIONS

Are there limits to how user involvement and participatory approaches can inform large-scale projects? There are a number of differences between traditional design cases and The Urban Mediaspace Aarhus project. These are mainly the scale, the time frame, and the diversity of users. The wide range of services provided by The Urban Mediaspace Aarhus also increases its complexity.

In a CHI context, an important consideration is how the participatory agenda and the user involvement activities of The Urban Mediaspace Aarhus project resonate with participatory design. Although in some contexts it may be valuable to establish clear definitions of what constitutes participatory design, as does Kensing [12], we find that inevitably, such definitions will be challenged or expanded when designers engage in new types of projects, such as The Urban Mediaspace Aarhus case. In order to steer clear of terminological confusion, we have intentionally refrained from labeling The Urban Mediaspace Aarhus project a participatory design project, instead using terms such as "participatory approaches" and "user involvement". We concur with Iversen, Kanstrup, and Petersen [11], who argue that participatory design is more than a set of methods and techniques. They describe it as an approach driven by emancipatory, democratic values, or in other words, the tools and techniques representative of participatory design embody higher layers of concerns and values that can guide, inspire, and focus design. Judging from the findings from The Urban Mediaspace Aarhus project, our position is that both values and methods from participatory design can certainly be employed in large-scale design projects. We therefore see The Urban Mediaspace Aarhus project as a potential source of the inspiration called for by Shapiro [21], who asks the participatory design community to also engage in such projects. Alexander states that "Even in the biggest building, people must be the core" [1], and participatory design can guide the way.

While we have focused on drawing out special characteristics of large-scale projects in the foregoing discussion of key lessons, some of the issues certainly resonate with previous findings in participatory design. This is not surprising, since some of the approaches and methods employed build directly on insights from this field (e.g. cultural probes and collaborative prototyping). However, it is also clear from our studies that it should be carefully considered how importing existing methods can connect to the special challenges of large-scale projects. This indicates general need for revisiting and reconsidering existing methods and techniques, and examining how they may require revision and/or need to be supplemented with new ones, in light of said challenges.

It is worth mentioning that The Urban Mediaspace Aarhus project was initiated before the spread of Web 2.0 and social media. Web 2.0 technologies clearly encompass elements of participation, which extend the reach of the institution. The idea of "Library 2.0" [3] has been proposed as a model for libraries where the community shapes the library content, and stresses the issue of community participation as a cornerstone for re-establishing the role of the libraries. In Library 2.0, this is significantly framed in terms of web-based services, which is the reason we argue that Web 2.0 technology should be considered only a supplement to the existing library services and development methods.

Promoting and Anchoring Participation in the Project

Various sources have influenced the establishment of participation as a central driver of the project. For instance, there has been influence from participatory design research, since researchers have worked with the library for a number of years, and carried out joint projects based on participatory design. Inspiration also stems from the Seattle Public Library, with regard to both the process leading up to the building project, and the development process, in partnership with architects and users. Aarhus's model of public participation has also had an influence, as has the political desire for extensive public involvement. Other important factors that support the participatory agenda include committed leadership, personal conviction/ideals on the part of involved project members, dependence on key people, and a flexible organization (as opposed to an error finding organization). Altogether, many factors have converged to make participation the preferred choice for the process.

During such a long development process, many discussions and battles will occur. From the start, the focus is more on a conceptual level, especially internally, politically, and with partners, but as the process moves into a more concrete phase, there is increased focus on specifics. Using participation as a major driver affects the entire process, so that nobody knows exactly how it will unfold, and what the results will be. A large-scale project like this cannot be led by participatory design alone, as it would probably lose direction and focus quite quickly, but it is clear that it can contribute to and inform the project along the way. In this project, the participatory activities have been vital, and conducted by all involved partners.

The participatory agenda for the project has had a visible impact on many levels, and there is no hesitation in bringing up issues that might cause problems for other partners, as long as there is a consensus that it will make for a better end product. For instance, when the space program had to be tested by the authorities in order to determine that it met the legislation regarding accessibility, the architects were satisfied with an approval, but the library took this process one step further, as their ambitions regarding accessibility for this project are very high. An expert, a handicapped man with extensive experience in accessibility issues, has been invited several times to come up with suggestions for improvements. The outcome of these workshops was passed on to the architects and engineers for further iterations, and some issues were brought into the program.

Design Considerations

If you are a design practitioner about to embark on a large-scale participatory project, the big question is, "what can The Urban Mediaspace Aarhus project teach us?" During our participation in the project, and throughout the analyses presented in this paper, we have formed a series of design considerations. These design considerations incorporate insights from all levels of project partners and stakeholders, and many of them clearly echo the key lessons from the project, as stated by the project manager, principal architect, and library services consultant. As with the discussion of the key lessons above, some of these considerations will resonate with existing findings; this being a case study, our aim has not been to develop entirely novel implications for design, but rather to explore the considerations that spring from this specific case. We have divided the design considerations into four categories: *how and why participatory approaches and values can be incorporated into a large-scale project*, *how participatory activities can be carried out*, *how the knowledge and insights from these activities can inform the project*, and *the outcomes of the participatory approach in practice.*

First, in order to *incorporate participatory approaches and values in a large-scale project*, there should be committed and engaged leadership when it comes to the participatory agenda, also personal conviction among involved project members, and a flexible organization. Establish awareness regarding cooperation, based on different paradigms of inquiry: designer, customer, and user. The dichotomy between user demands and what is technically feasible might lead to conflict. Establish a shared language, in order to achieve a mutual understanding of the agenda and ideals; designers might see the building itself as an experience, while the customers see the services as the experience. A clear focus for the participatory design activities is necessary, since they can both clarify and obscure. Invest time in designing the participatory design process. Reciprocal partnership, good communication, and an understanding of different perspectives between the project partners are essential. For instance, architects should communicate about the architectural process, and the library needs to share its knowledge with architects.

Secondly, there are considerations regarding *how participatory activities may be carried out*: Hold collaborative working workshops with a constructive purpose, and in a language everybody understands. Make use of practical and concrete tools, such as visuals, models, and examples. Participatory events should be orchestrated by different project partners, so that a rich knowledge may be absorbed at all levels of the process. Carefully plan when to involve users and when not; it is difficult to engage people when the goal is too distant. Develop on an appreciative understanding of user insights and input, to create a sense of ownership and responsibility among participants. Reach the mutual understanding that nobody knows exactly how the participatory activity will unfold, or what the result will be. Divide the labor, so that there are clear roles regarding the aim of the participatory activities, for instance between what concerns the building and what concerns the services. Deadlines and deliverables provide direction and purpose, and are crucial to making the participation process concrete.

Thirdly, there are considerations regarding *how the knowledge and insights from these activities may inform the project*: Plan how to capture insights from participatory activities in a structured way, perhaps by best practice examples. Networks and knowledge sharing for inspiration are important. Establish a common plan for the decision-making structure, to establish a connection between data, analysis, and decision. Also establish a plan for how to inform the participatory process, not just the project. Avoid too many compromises, which might indicate a lack of overview.

Fourthly, there are considerations regarding *the outcomes of the participatory approach in practice:* Participatory activities are an ongoing qualification of vision, idea, and product, and gain much in quality and depth, as well as political prestige. Participatory design activities in a large project are expensive, and demand substantial resources, but are worth it. There is a need for a solid program from the start, to prevent the project from slipping when involving user participation. Stay open to changes, even in the space program, as iterations are necessary in participatory projects. Milestones and deadlines in a foreseeable future are important especially in large-scale projects. See milestones as key condensations of insights.

Finally, we do not consider this list of design considerations exhaustive, but rather a series of rough guidelines for venturing into a new area of participation. However, we hope that they may guide and support others who intend to engage in large-scale projects of this character.

CONCLUSIONS

In this paper, we have sought to enrich the discussion of challenges and benefits associated with a participatory approach to large-scale projects through case studies. Our contributions to this discussion are based on eight years of involvement in The Urban Mediaspace Aarhus project, in which our initial focus was on the design of interactive systems, as we came to realize that the participatory agenda of the project makes it a pioneering project of large-scale user involvement. We have discussed the scale and limitations of participatory approaches and user involvement activities, how to anchor participation in the project, and finally, we have formulated a series of design considerations that may guide practitioners in the field. These considerations fall into four categories: how to establish a participatory agenda, how to carry out user involvement activities, how to capture the results of these activities, and finally, what the outcomes of such an approach may be. We hope that this detailed study of The Urban Mediaspace Aarhus project may serve as an exemplar, by providing insights and inspiration for other designers, researchers, and developers when planning, carrying out, and studying user involvement in large-scale development projects.

REFERENCES

1. Alexander, C. The Nature of Order, Book three, A vision of the living world. California, USA. (2005).
2. Buchhave B. Transformationer. Aarhus Kommunes Biblioteker, (2006).
3. Casey, M.E. & Savastinuk, L.C. Service for the next generation library, *Library Journal*, 9(1). (2006).
4. Clemet, A. & van den Besselaar, P. A retrospective look at participatory design projects. *Communications of the ACM*, 36(4), 29-37 (1993).
5. Dalsgaard P. Challenges of participation in large-scale projects. In *Proc. PDC'10*. Sydney, Australia (2010).
6. Eriksson E. U.F.O.scope! - Families Playing Together at the Public Library. *In Proc. DIS'10*, ACM Press (2010).
7. Eriksson E., Lykke-Olesen A. StorySurfer: a playful book browsing installation for children's libraries. *Proc. IDC'07*. ACM Press (2007), 57-64.
8. Eriksson E., Krogh, P., Lykke-Olesen A. Inquiry into Libraries - A Design Approach to Children's Interactive Library. *Proc. NORDES'07*. (2007)
9. Fierro, A. *The Glass State*, MIT Press (2003).
10. Flyvbjerg, B. Five misunderstandings about case-study research. *Qualitative Inquiry*, 12(2), (2006) 219-245.
11. Iversen, O., Kanstrup, A. M. and Petersen, M. G. A visit to the "new Utopia": revitalizing democracy, emancipation and quality in co-operative design. *Proc. NordiCHI 2004*, ACM Press (2004), 171-179.
12. Kensing, F. The Trade Unions Influence on Technological Change, in U. Briefs et al. (Eds.): *Systems Design For, With and By the Users*. (1983).
13. Krogh P.G., Ludvigsen M., Lykke-Olesen A. Help Me Pull That Cursor A Collaborative Interactive Floor Enhancing Community Interaction. In *Australasian J. of Inf. Systems* 11(2), (2004).
14. Kuhn, T.S. *The structure of scientific revolutions*, University of Chicago Press, Chicago. (1962).
15. Lykke-Olesen, A. & Nielsen, J. BibPhone: adding sound to the children's library. *Proc. IDC'07*. ACM Press, (2007).
16. McCrady, E. Bibliothèque Nationale: A Building Hostile to Preservation and Access. In *Abbey Newsletter*, 22(4), Abbey Publications (1998).
17. Oostveen, A. & van den Besselaar, P. From small scale to large scale user participation: a case study of participatory design in e-government systems. *Proc. PDC'04*. ACM Press, 173-182. (2004)
18. Rittel, H.W.J. & Webber, M.M. Dilemmas in a general theory of planning. *Policy Sciences*, 4(2). (1973).
19. Sanders L. Exploring co-creation on a large scale. In *Designing for, with and from User Experience*, StudioLab Press (2010).
20. Simonsen, J. & Hertzum, M. Participative Design and the Challenges of Large-Scale systems: Extending the Iterative PD Approach. *Proc. PDC'08*. ACM Press (2008).
21. Shapiro D. Participatory design: the will to succeed. *Proc. CC '05*, ACM Press (2005), 29-38.
22. The Aarhus public libraries. The library's voice – a guide to user driven innovation, Aarhus (2008).
23. The Aarhus public libraries. Unleash the users – everyone is entitled to a cool library! Aarhus (2009).
24. The Aarhus municipality. Web: http://www.urbanmediaspace.dk/en.
25. The Aarhus public libraries. Transformation Lab – A Report on Forms of Dissemination in the Physical Space. Aarhus, Denmark. (2007).

Probing Bus Stop for Insights on Transit Co-design

Daisy Yoo[1], John Zimmerman[2], Tad Hirsch[3]
1.University of Washington | 2. Carnegie Mellon University
dyoo@uw.edu, johnz@cs.cmu.edu, thirsch@uw.edu

ABSTRACT

Social computing provides a new way for citizens to engage with their public service. Our research investigates how social computing might support citizens co-design their transit service. We conducted a field study with public transit riders, exploring the issues and controversies that reveal conflicting communities. Our analyses revealed three insights. First, encourage citizens to share what they see as the rationale for current service offerings. Second, encourage citizens to share the consequences of current services and of proposed changes and new designs. Third, focus on producing a shared citizen and service provider understanding of what the goals and mission of the public service should be.

Author Keywords

Co-design; service design; transit; public service; social computing; political design; contestational design; eGovernment

ACM Classification Keywords

H.5.m. Information interfaces and presentation (e.g., HCI): Miscellaneous.

INTRODUCTION

Social computing provides a new opportunity for citizens to reach out and change their world. HIC researchers have begun to investigate on how social computing can increase citizen engagement and participation with government. In addition, researchers have recently begun to investigate how social computing can support planning activities around urban infrastructure, giving citizens a greater voice in the planning process that reshapes their world. Even with these research activities, it is an open research question as how to design social systems that really allow citizens to take ownership of and give shape to their world.

Service design is an emerging design practice that has recently embraced by many interaction designers. It is distinctly different from the more product-centric approaches typically followed in user-centered design. Service design takes a systemic view that focuses on the co-production of value between service providers and customers. This approach is a good fit for working on social computing systems, where the goal is often to design *sustainable, social ecologies* rather than a *single computer system* intended to meet a target audience's needs. Service design researchers see public services as a special case. They note that competition often does not drive service innovation because many public services are monopolies. Researchers have speculated that co-design, where customers actively participate in the design of service offerings, could be the best path to public service innovation [3].

Our research attempts to pull these two threads together. We want to apply the power of social computing in order for citizens to engage in the co-design of their public services. We employ a research through design approach [30], designing a *thing* as a method of inquiry. Specifically, we follow a *field* approach to research through design [15]; conducting fieldwork to understand a situation, ideating and then iteratively refining a design intended to improve the state of the world, and them deploying it into the field to understand its effect.

As a first step in a research through design process, we conducted a field study with transit riders in order to gain insights on how they might best engage with their transit service in a dialog to co-design new service offerings. We engaged riders from a single bus stop in interviews about their service experiences, in drawing maps of routes they take and desire to take, and in keeping a journal of their ongoing service experiences. Our analysis revealed three insights for designing social computing systems that support co-design of public services. First, these systems can encourage citizens to share their rationale for current service offerings, revealing what citizens perceive to be the goals and motivators of the service. Second, these systems can encourage citizens to share the consequences of current and proposed service offerings as these help others better empathize with the impact design choices might have. Third, we see that co-design via social computing might best focus on searching for a shared citizen and service provider understanding of the goals and mission for the service as the outcome of this dialog system.

In this paper we provide a brief overview of literature on service design, on citizens' electronic participation, and on advances in HCI related to publics and civic virtues. We then provide an overview of our prior research. Next, we describe our field study with transit riders. This is followed by our findings and a discussion of how these findings might inform the design of a co-design dialog system.

RELATED WORK

Service Design and Co-Design

Service design has recently emerged to address the increasing importance of the service sector [18]. This seems particularly relevant to HCI given the growth of Software as a Service. Service designers have justified the need for a new design discipline by focusing on the differences between products and services [7]. Specifically, they note that products are things that can be stored (warehoused) and that value and ownership is exchanged between the maker and the consumer at the point of purchase. Services on the other hand are processes; they cannot be stored. Instead, value is co-produced between the customer and service provider during a service encounter, and ownership is never transferred.

Service designers work to construct a *service concept*; a description of *what* a service is and *how* it both meets the needs of customers and fulfills a service provider's strategic initiative [10]. One key construct in service design is *customer competence*; how customers can take actions that co-produce value for themselves and for the service provider [20]. This stands in contrast to user-experience design, which focuses almost exclusively on how products and services fulfill a user's needs and desires. Software companies that have select customers beta-test software provide a great example of customer competence and value co-production. Here customers get a preview of new technology and some influence on its design while the company gets free labor to test and improve their software.

Service design researchers view public services as a special case [3]. Public services are often established as monopolies with a mission to increase equity and community perceptions of fairness in contrast to commercial services' focus on profit. In a monopoly there is often no competition to drive service innovation. Service researchers claim co-design, where the customers participate in the design of the service, is the best approach to service innovation for public services [3].

The HCI design community has a long history of co-design that comes from participatory design [1]. However, co-design in service design appears different than co-design in participatory design [11]. Part of this stems from the fact that in service design, a single person often plays both a customer and a service provider role. For example, a discharge nurse at a hospital is a service provider for the patient checking out and also a customer of the medical staff that created the patient's home care plan. Additionally, for many service design practitioners, getting input from customers during a design process often seems to count as co-design, and this seems quite different than participatory design's expectation that users more materially participate in the idea generation and prototyping activities.

Social Computing and Urban Planning

Urban planning has a long history of considering the needs of citizens in the creation of new urban environments [2]. Planners most often use surveys, focus groups, and community meetings to achieve some measure of citizen participation, and they note that these traditional methods can be slow, expensive, and often engage only a tiny fraction of citizens. Recently, they have begun to investigate if social computing can help [2]. The Urban Mediator offers an interesting example [24, 25]. This online tool allows citizens and urban planners to create and share topics. It has been used in Finland as a digital participatory design approach to engage citizens in discussing traffic issues and to share their ideas about design proposals. The work on Urban Mediator is particularly interesting for three reasons. First, it provides a case that shows citizens can and will engage in planning discourse related to their urban services. Second, it frames the citizen participation as co-design from a participatory design perspective. Third, like other ePlanning research, current work has not employed a service design perspective; however, it engages participants in co-design activities more often found in service design (e.g. sharing opinions) than in participatory design (e.g. prototyping new designs).

There have been several new services that, similar to ePlanning, work to engage citizen participation in their urban facilities. For example, FixMyStreet.com [16] is a service that allows people to report problems like potholes to municipal authorities. ParkScan [19] is a service that allows users to report on problems with city parks. ParkScan has a feedback loop that allows users to see how the problems they report have been addressed. In addition, it helps to track the relationship between funding and services. While interesting examples of the potential of social computing to engage citizens in co-design, at this time neither service allows users to make and comment on suggestions posted by other users; to engage in an actual dialog between different citizens and between public service providers and citizens.

A recent paper investigating FixMyStreet [16] offered a 3-stage framework for dialog: Stage 1, electronic communication between citizens and services; Stage 2, analysis of electronic communications to gain insight on services; and Stage 3: citizens share information with other citizens and with the service. The authors claim that FixMyStreet's current design cannot reach Stage 3 because citizens post individually, and cannot unite their voices.

eGovernance

Our research shares a strong connection to work in eGovernance, which aspires to utilize ICTs to transform government towards efficient, effective, and citizen-centric service delivery [22]. A key component of this transformation is "public consultation:" directly engaging citizens in governance by notifying citizens about government decisions, soliciting public opinion, and actively involving the public in planning and policy formation [23]. Public consultation can take a variety of forms, including petitions, voting, and public comment/discussion systems [20]. Regardless of the mechanism, public consultation is generally regarded as a means to broaden public participation in governance, and increase government transparency and efficiency [17].

Prior studies have found that public consultation systems can have a direct impact on top-level decision-making [14]. However, it is also acknowledged that many online deliberation and public consultation efforts have fallen short of expectations (for example, [4]). In particular, there have been challenges in encouraging public trust and confidence in government [28] and in employing transparent decision-making processes that enable citizens to understand the impact of their participation [5]. The failure to deliver has been linked with an overreliance on technical and organizational imperatives, with insufficient involvement of the public in design and implementation [13]. Accordingly, we see a need for public engagement platforms that shift away from only emphasizing information dissemination, and towards enabling co-design.

The politics associated with public transit are often contentious. Conflicts between social groups arise over issues including cost, quality, and perceived inequities of service. These run from large-scale infrastructure decisions to the smallest details of day-to-day operations. As Hirsch observed, "contestational" design activity that explicitly acknowledges and participates in social conflicts is a relatively under-theorized area of design practice [11].

DiSalvo, inpired by Dewey, recently introduced the idea that interaction designers should consider the design of "publics" [6]. This perspective holds that there is no public, but instead many publics that emerge in response to an issue. He suggests that designers might support the formation of publics by getting citizens to "project" future outcomes and to "trace" historical precedent.

Our work attempts to bring these many research threads together. We agree with urban planners, that social computing technology offers an opportunity for a new and more effective practice of co-design. We advance on their work by bringing in a service design approach, an approach optimized for producing a service as a design outcome. In doing so, we investigate what co-design means for large groups of citizens connecting and sharing in an online environment. In addition, our work attempts to operationalize the ideas around contestational design and around publics as a framing for what could make an effective dialog system that allows citizens and service providers to work together in defining the goals of a public service through a design process around service innovation.

OUR PRIOR WORK

The research reported here is part of a larger project focused on co-design of a transit service with the intention that citizens feel ownership for the public services they pay for and use. Previously, we conducted a field study to understand riders' service experiences and to probe on a desire to participate in co-design [30]. Our participants shared that they did not feel a sense of ownership for the transit service and in general they were skeptical of taking on the responsibility that comes with ownership. They did express a strong desire for real-time arrival information, claiming this would significantly improve their service experience. However, the likelihood of this service becoming available seemed small due to its costs in the millions of dollars.

In response, we developed a crowdsourced real-time arrival system. We viewed the location enabled smart phones many riders carry as a type of customer competence, and that they could use this to co-produce a real-time system with the transit service. Our system allows riders to share location traces. Our system takes these traces as input and pushes out real-time arrival estimates. In a field trial of our service, we observed that riders who had rarely if ever reported a problem to the transit service were now much more likely to submit a problem report [31]. Based on this, we view our real-time information service as a platform for a co-design dialog system. We feel that a mobile phone in the hand, that is navigated to a transit information service at the time a person experiences the transit service, significantly reduces the effort required to engage in a dialog. The study reported in this paper is an attempt to gain insights on what a dialog service should be in order to situate it within our current, real-time information service.

BUS STOP STUDY

Our fieldwork study goal was to discover issues that concern riders. In particular, we wanted to understand where they wanted to go but could not get to using the transit service as well as the issues that reveal points of conflict and the groups engaged in this conflict. We wanted to better understand this design space in order to address how information should be structured and displayed within a co-design social computing system. We assumed route planning would be one of the main topics of any co-design system involving transit. Based on this assumption, our fieldwork was framed to elicit issues around the current service offerings and ideas for how routes might be planned differently and preferably in the future.

Research Setting and Data Collection Contexts

We chose to focus on riders at a single bus stop, seeing them as a microcosm of the larger set of riders. This approach made the choice of the bus stop particularly important. We selected a stop that served a number of distinct but overlapping communities. Our study location resides on the edge of a commercial district where it connects with city suburbs. It sits at a busy intersection containing a public library, Christian church, Jewish Community Center, and a drug store. The stop functions as a departure point for people who live in the neighborhood,

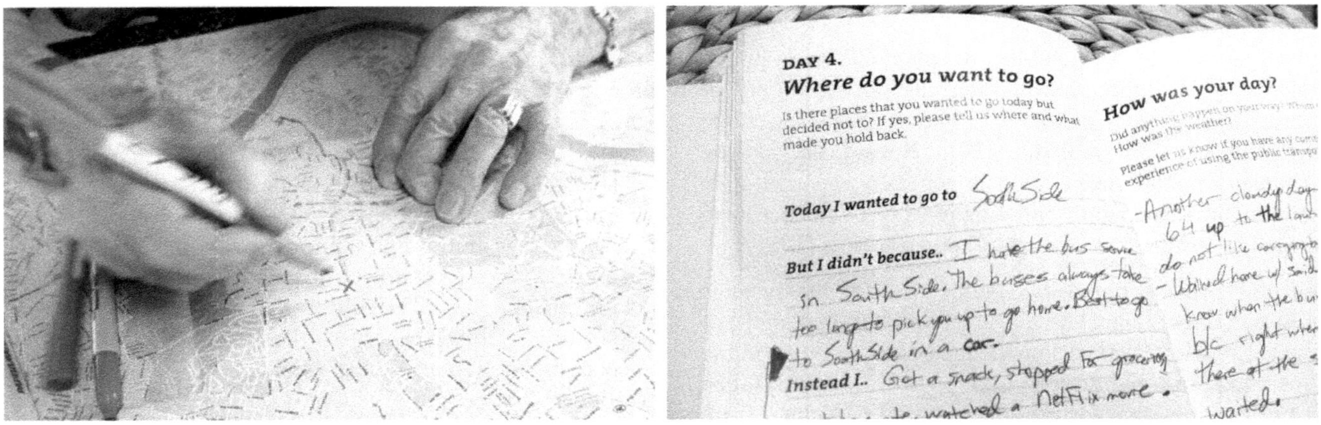

Figure 1. Example Map Study (a) and Journal Study (b).

as a destination for people who work and shop in the commercial district, and as a transfer point for people who live in the suburbs.

To provide context for understanding the data, please note three important aspects of the transit service we studied. First, senior citizens are allowed to use the service free of charge. The state Department of Transportation's Free Transit Program for Senior Citizens, paid for by proceeds from the state Lottery, reimburses the transit authority for all senior rides. All riders age 12 or older pay a full fare unless they qualify for a half fare as a person with a disability. Second, the transit authority carried out a 15 percent reduction in service just prior to our study, which offered a dramatic backdrop to our research. 25 days before our first interview a protest rally was held at our selected stop in the hopes of stopping the service cut before it went into effect. The service cut resulted in elimination of 29 bus routes, reductions in service on 37 routes, and the loss of approximately 270 jobs. Third, this research took place in the US. In the US, the majority of people drive themselves individually to work, and public transit is often viewed as a service intended for the urban poor. In Pittsburgh, where this study takes place, less than 6% of workers commute via transit, which is a fairly typical rate of use in the US [29].

Participants

We carefully selected participants in order to investigate multiple dimensions of potentially contesting communities. One question of interest was whether participants' views differed because of the different payment methods. Therefore, we focused on getting a balance of younger riders (ages 18-30) and senior riders (ages 60+) as well as to highlight potential generational conflict. Within each age group, we included riders who view this stop as a transfer location as well as riders who see it as a home stop. In recruiting we visited the stop during both the morning and evening rush hours and approached people while they waited for their bus to arrive. We recruited six seniors (2 male, 4 female; ages 60-93, M=81.2) who ride for free, eight younger riders (2 male, 6 female; ages 18-27, M=22.4). Additionally, we recruited one wheelchair rider (male, age 58) who qualifies for a reduced fare. Five of the participants (2 young, 3 senior) lived in the suburbs. The rest lived near the stop and considered it their home stop.

Procedures

Participants completed the following tasks: preliminary interview, a weeklong transit usage journal, and an exit interview. During the 60-minute, semi-structured, preliminary interview, we asked participants to describe their routine experiences with the transit service, including experiences that made them happy and experiences they considered service failures. We also asked them to trace the routes they regularly took with public transit, routes they regularly drove or were driven, and routes they regularly walked. This was done on a 24x36 inch paper map using different color highlighters (Figure 1a). Next we asked participants to show us where they wanted do go using public transit that they could not easily get to with current services.

We left participants with a one-week journal to complete (Figure 1b). This journal consisted of open-ended questions inspired by cultural probes [9]. It asked participants to trace where they went and what mode of transportation they took. In addition, it asked them to specify the places they desired to go but did not go. Participants were instructed to write a short narrative based on the following prompts: *Where do you want to go? Are there places that you wanted to go today but decided not to? Today I wanted to go to... But I didn't because... Instead I...* These instructions nudged participants to rationalize their actions, and to link inadvertent consequences that derived from actions.

After completing the journal study, we conducted a 90-minute, semi-structured exit interview. This interview paralleled the preliminary interview. In addition, we shared the traces of where other participants wanted to go and selected personal narratives shared with us by other participants in order to gain insight into what might trigger an effective dialog between transit service users.

To analyze the findings we took the following steps. The recorded interviews were transcribed. We developed coding manuals for both the interview transcripts and journal data, in order to reveal issues and themes across the participants. Themes were developed and refined through an iterative process of evaluation. A single coder manually coded the data. We used open, axial, and selective coding [27] in our analysis. In addition, we laid out the hand-traced maps and made groupings based on where people regularly travel and where they desired to go but could not easily get to using current services.

FINDINGS

Our fieldwork revealed several issues that raised conflicts between different groups. Issues ranged from the daily experience of overcrowded buses to major service reductions to discussions of service goals such as who the service should be serving.

In the following sections, we present selected examples from the field study that illustrate the issues around public transit. We refer to each participant in terms of their group (S for seniors, Y for young, and W for wheelchair) followed by their home location (U for the local urban neighborhood and S for suburbs) followed by the participant number.

Overcrowding as a Daily Service Experience

One common experience all participants reported was overcrowded buses. Participants expressed strong anxiety about not being able to get on the bus because it was full. WU1 (age 58) shared that since the service cuts, buses were always overcrowded; sometimes the bus is so "stuffed to the gills" that it goes right past without stopping. Otherwise, the bus is nearly full, so only a few of the waiting riders can board. The uncertainty created by the crowding provoked substantial tension and revealed contesting groups.

Riders vs. bus drivers

Participants viewed bus drivers as distinctly separate from the transit service. Their narratives showed that they view bus drivers as having agency in making choices to stop or to deviate in their routes. *"Often there would be a nice bus driver that will let* [people] *on when the bus is packed. There are some bus drivers* [that] *are very cruel. And they won't open the door, and many times, early in the morning, they ride right by you"* (SU6, age 88). Participants did not address this as drivers following or deviating from pre-specified procedures, but instead viewed this as a driver's personality trait.

Similarly, WU1, the wheelchair user, viewed drivers as having control over the boarding procedures: *"Imagine that I was waiting at the bus stop and thousands of people are waiting. ...Now the bus driver has a few options – put me on first or last. Okay. Now if there's a ton of people waiting for the bus it makes sense to put me on first because it makes more room for me to maneuver. People who are displaced have options to choose seats. ...Normally, if the space was not* [at a] *premium... drivers prefer to put me on last, and I could care less. But where there's a crowd of people, it matters to me. In the worst-case scenario, what happens is he puts everybody on but me and says it's too full, I can't get you on."*

Wheelchair users vs. non-disabled riders

For WU1, the lack of behavioral conventions surrounding boarding of crowded buses framed non-disabled riders as a contested community. *"There is this quality that we, human beings,* [that] *part of us is cattle. If* [the driver] *opens the door, people... move into their cattle mentality. They just start walking through, tripping over me as if they gotta get on because the door opened, okay? So sometimes no matter what the driver does... the cattle mentality takes over."* Interestingly, this conflict is not discussed as a lack of structure imposed by the transit service on how people should use the service.

Senior citizens vs. young people

The crowded buses also raised a point of conflict flowing from senior riders toward younger riders. Most senior citizens traveled between our selected stop and downtown, passing by three colleges on their way. They identified students as a source of the overcrowding and the backpacks that students carry, which can swing into the space of a seated rider, as a serious safety concern: "*We have college students riding the buses. The buses are jammed now with their backpacks, and a lot of people wouldn't get on because of it. They are very unhappy and they are miserable. They said there's no convenience for older people. ...With their big backpacks they bump people. You can't get through. It was hard for me to get through today to even get off"* (SU2, age 93).

SS3 (age 82) also expressed anxiety with students: *"You can't move on the bus so help me. I'm not lying. When you get the bus downtown and get* [near the colleges], *all these students pile up. They're all over you. They are over your feet. ...I mean it's ridiculous. Really it is."* Unsurprisingly, when asked to project ideal routes, all of the senior participants expressed a desired route that would bypass the universities and take them straight downtown.

Planning, Service Changes and Service Cuts

Participants shared personal narratives that describe what they perceive to be the rationale for the recent service cuts. These narratives reveal their own role in the transit service and they point to many potential points of conflict.

Urban riders vs. suburban riders

Suburban riders felt the service cuts had greater impact on them than on urban riders. Four of our five suburban participants lost their home stops due to the service cuts. In each case participants felt the distance they needed to travel to the nearest stop was impractical. They provided rough estimates for their new home stop being more than a 40-minute walk, at least 20 blocks away, and at least 2 miles away. Moving of the home stop raised issues around safety (e.g. crime, accidents), ease of access (e.g. potholes, hills), and an increased number of transfers or wait times for transfers (e.g., the dread double transfer). While the urban riders complained about inconvenience and lost flexibility due to the reduction in buses that come to the stop, the suburban riders felt a strong sense of loss for the service itself: *"We are being denied. ...Why'd you have all these buses in* [the urban area]*? You have seven buses, which isn't fair"* (SS3). SS1 (age 60) distinguished "feeder routes" that serve the suburbs from the main routes that serve urban areas: *"The point is, they cut the feeder routes. They threw out what they had. They're cutting the feeder routes! There use to be four buses in that area. ...All cut out!"* The conflict appeared to be most directed at the transit service, but some clearly was directed toward the urban riders.

Dangerous neighborhoods. Participants mentioned crime as part of the rationale used for making the service cuts in the suburbs. Several urban participants implicitly or explicitly expressed reluctance to travel through specific suburban neighborhoods. Looking at the city map, they would label certain neighborhoods as very dangerous. SS3 confessed that 20 years ago, living in the city, she had refused to support stops that connected "dangerous" (low-income) suburbs with her home. Now she is living in those suburbs: *"In 1990, I lived there in* [the city] *and* [the transit authority] *wanted to put a stop for people in* [a lower income town] *to get on the bus.* [City residents] *refused. ...They didn't want the people, the crowd, to come in. Those 'characters' come in from* [the lower income town]. *...So this is 1990 and now I'm punished.* [City residents] *would not allow. ...They are denying this old lady."*

YS5 (age 20), who lives in suburbs perceived as dangerous, wanted more stops because it *is* dangerous; she wants to decrease the distance she must walk to get on a bus. She reported that her nearest stop is 2.3 miles away, past a desolate cemetery, a convenient store that functions as a gathering place for "junkies", and past several bars. She wants more bus stops to protect her from exposure to crime. SS3 also asked for more stops and routes in need for protection: *"There are some danger. Very dangerous. ...The characters. ...'Give me some cigarettes, give me some change.' Characters. So you have to be very careful. ...And you can't walk* [to] *your house ten and twelve blocks."* This raises an interesting point of conflict between riders who do not want buses stopping in bad neighborhoods for reasons of safety and riders who want more stops in dangerous neighborhoods to increase safety.

Racial tensions. SS1 speculated that race was another factor in the service cuts. His neighborhood had four routes, which were reduced to one that operates only on weekdays. While the whole neighborhood is perceived as low-income, he viewed the surviving route as covering an African American community: *"They chose ...which is down here* [where the black community is located] *over all the residential areas. Maybe that was a counter.* [If] *they would have cut that one maybe they would have been accused* [of] *racism. ...I don't know why. There's a large black population up here, too. I don't know that, but I'm speculating why they cut the ones they did."*

Senior citizens vs. young people

Reactions to the service cuts raised a point of conflict between senior citizens and youths. Each group characterized the cuts as being driven by the perception that the city has a large senior population. Interestingly, in creating a personal narrative, each group saw themselves as the victim of the large senior population: *"It's a city with a lot of old people in it, you know, a lot of senior citizens. And it tends to be a city that doesn't consider the feelings of young people and young adults as much. And so* [they cut the route] *...because you don't have a lot of senior citizens taking that route. ...That's places where young people went"* (YU8, age 20). As a counter point, SS1 (age 60) shared that the service cuts were intended to keep young people from leaving the city: *"I guess they* [the transit authority] *sort of figured out 'Forget these old people up here.' Seniors, I mean."*

Free transit program for senior citizens. Senior participants speculated that the fact that seniors ride for free influenced the cuts: *"Maybe that's why they were eliminated, because it's a low paying route. The* [other route] *is a paying route. Everybody that takes* [that other route] *are working and buy tickets. This route, a lot of the people probably have the senior citizen passes"* (SS1). SU6 (age 88) was self-conscious about being seen as a free-rider: *"I know. I often heard them say that they should charge the seniors. I feel that I don't want to take a seat from somebody because I'm not paying and they paid ...I'd rather stand because I did not pay than sit down. That's the way I feel about it."*

SS3 also saw the cuts as being driven by money and the fact that seniors ride for free. She argued that this was unfair due to the law requiring lottery proceeds to benefit senior citizens. SS3, a frequent purchaser of lottery tickets: *"It says on these signs that lottery money is allotted to senior citizens. That's my money, pal. And you are not giving me a bus to ride. ...You are getting that money, aren't you? And the signs are posted. The lottery tickets are supposed to be allotted to the senior citizens. Not you young ones. The SENIOR CITIZENS!"* This rationale indicates that participants somewhat viewed the various public services as coordinated; working together.

Contribution to local communities. In reflecting on the rationale for the cuts, senior participants often framed their personal narratives around the service as a right they had earned through many years of contributing to their communities: *"Coming from* [the local university], *I've done these kind of studies in order to help. ...*[I was] *honored by the Order of the May, you know what that is? Those who have contributed at least 25 years or more"* (SS5, age 86); *"I'm 82 and I'm still paying income tax. I'm paying your wages. And I can't get anywhere. ...82 and I worked all my life. I've worked ...and saved lives, took care of the elderly. Did with that never went anywhere. Now I'm free and got a little bit of money, perhaps, and I can't move because of you* [the transit authority]*! Why are you* *punishing me?"* (SS3). In addition to their own time and efforts helping the communities, senior participants often described how much their spouses, parents and children have also contributed through their effort as a police officer, marine, war's battered veteran, government employee, nurse, doctor, educator and so on.

Riders vs. transit authority

Several cases emerged in which the transit authority was viewed as the source of conflict. Some participants viewed the cuts as resulting from poor management. SU6: *"They say they are short of money. They are short of money because they had too many parties and they wasted their money. And the head guy makes $500,000 a year, which we think is ridiculous. Overpaid. And they have parties; they foolishly spend their money. And their wages; it is a difficult job to be a bus driver, but they get like $99 an hour, or a day ...They are VERY, VERY well paid."*

YS5 participated in a rally hoping to save her route and home stop. She felt the protest was dominated by the bus drivers union. *"All they say is 'Jobs, jobs, jobs!' I say 'Home, home, home!'...Nobody listened."* SS1 reported a similar experience: *"They seemed to focus more on the union. And I'm not against the union. I'm good* [that] *bus drivers have the unions. But ...somehow, seemed like we got cut* [out of conversation] *...there is the battle between the union and the* [transit authority]*."* He further elaborates on how riders were neglected in this 'battle': *"And the customers, I don't think it was really a consideration at all! ...That wasn't where the battle was taking place. The battle was taking place in salaries and ...whatever the whole deal. I hate to tell you. I don't think they are worried about trying to serve the most number of people. ...They definitely weren't. Definitely weren't!"* These two groups, the riders and the drivers union, who could have been united in opposition to the cuts never found a way to work together.

Impacts of Service Change

Participants almost never directly addressed the overall purpose for the transit service. However, their personal narratives hinted at this in terms of the consequences they experienced as a result of a transit service action. When we shared the personal narratives of other riders with a participant during the exit interview, the interviewee had the strongest reaction when learning about the consequences others had suffered.

Ripple effect

A story shared by SU2 (age 93) triggered many notes of sympathy. She used to go to the mall with her friends 2-3 times a week. Then her stop was moved from next to the mall to the side of the highway: *"We would have lunch and we would all sit at a table and laugh and talk, and we would talk about good old days.* [Then] *they moved the stop. ...They moved the stop to the bottom of the hill, then you had to walk all the way up through the parking lot and it had large potholes and you had to be careful the cars don't hit you. We no longer hang out."* The consequences of this single change had a huge impact on her and her friends' quality of life. *"Friends don't want to travel to the new place, it's too hard for them. ...The one is using the walker, the other got heavy. ...They said all they do is eat and sleep. My one friend goes to Sears just to get her hair washed and colored at the mall but she don't go either anymore because they moved the bus stops at the bottom; it's too dangerous to walk through a parking lot with large potholes. The cars are backing up and they might not see you. I'm sure there's been some accidents there.* [The transit authority] *should do better. And they haven't"*

We encountered a case in which the suburban citizens were moving to urban areas for access to better education. SS3 reported losing her neighborhood: *"She's gotta move out of town. She's on that bus two or three times a day to pick her son up ...and now she's moving to [an urban neighborhood]. I said, 'You go out there?' and she says, 'Oh! There are all kinds of buses out there!' ...She comes to the library, takes her little boy* [to school] *but now he has to leave the school* [so instead] *she leaves the neighborhood. And it's pitiful."* This story, in particular, raised immediate reactions. All participants, either urban or suburban, agreed on the importance of education for children. YU7 (age 26) immediately connected this story to an article she had read about the service cuts and low-income children being shut out of educational opportunities. She asked if there was anything she could do to save their routes.

Everyday experiences

The journals revealed instances of the transit service influencing moods. Each day, participants were asked to reflect on where they wanted to go but they could not, what actions they took instead, and what the day was like in general. This activity captured some minor but meaningful events in people's lives, which rarely have been perceived as transit service breakdowns. YU1 (age 27) wrote of his desire to visit his mother each day in the journal, but chose to not go. His mother lives in the suburbs, a one and a half hour ride on a crowded bus. Instead he reported that he worked, played Playstation, or slept in. Finally, on the day 5, he went to his mother's. For the first time in the journal, he recorded that his day was good. Accordingly, during the exit interview, he expressed a desire for an express route so he could see his mother more frequently.

SS3 claimed that the service cuts ruined her life: *"I can't get to* [radio] *promotions, can't get to downtown on Saturdays, can't get to the* [local theater]*. ...I can't get to a movie at night. You are denying me all these privileges and I'm bored all the time."* YU8 also could not attend the movies following the cuts. Instead, she reported snacking and watching Netflix movies by herself.

Interestingly, senior participants showed strong customer loyalty to their hair stylists. When asked to indicate important destinations on the map, most seniors marked hair salons. They would stick with the stylist they liked, and would not go anywhere else. For example, SS1 traveled more than 15 miles, approximately 2 hours to get a haircut. SS3's stylist only worked one day a week, on Saturdays. She was devastated that, ever since the service cuts, the bus only runs on weekdays and she would never get her hair done. Not having access to a stylist might lead to rather serious consequences as SU2 reported. Her friend would not come out of her house at all because she lost access to her stylist; she was "disgusted" with her appearance.

Collectively, these cases highlight how the transit service shapes people's everyday practices and feelings, and even their identities and sense of self.

DISCUSSION

Our findings show that there are many different stakeholder groups and there are many issues around which conflicts between these groups may arise. The notion of multiple, conflicting social groups can easily be obscured under the umbrella of "the public". In an ideal world, one might imagine a public service that is "of, by and for the people" united as one. However, the public is neither abstract nor universal [6]. The public actually consists of many "publics" with concrete and individual interests. The complexity hints that a successful co-design social computing system must go well beyond the simplistic handles of "service provider" and "customer" that define the roles used in service design. It forces designers to think of the public in new ways that have been less addressed in the HCI community. A service must support a dynamic set of voices; the ability for new contesting communities to emerge as the issues within the dialog change.

Our findings have several implications for the design of dialog systems for co-designing public services. We analyzed and synthesized the structure of narratives across four themes to understand the functioning of public dialog:

1. observations: what happened
2. emotions: how they felt
3. rationale: what they think motivates the actions of others
4. consequences: how things can be different and what really matters

Riders' narratives generally conveyed observations and emotions while rationales and consequences emerged from responses to probing questions by the interviewer. Although seldom self-externalized, we found that rationales and consequences have crucial roles in advancing the public discourse. Articulating rationales surfaces issues and forms publics by revealing underlying tensions and making dispute visible. Communicating consequences in contrast leads to public consultation of the service goals and mission by co-producing values and calling for a collective action.

In what follows we present a set of design opportunities and challenges for an effective co-design system.

Sharing Rationales

A co-design system can encourage citizens to share their rationales for current service offerings, revealing what citizens perceive to be the goals and motivators driving the public service. It can stimulate dialog by directly asking public service users and stakeholders to share their own rationale for why the service functions the way it functions. The personal narratives we collected showed how different groups could view the same issue and draw wildly different conclusions. For example, both the urban and suburban participants identified certain neighborhoods as dangerous and emphasized safety; yet each group proposed the solutions in very opposite ways. Urban riders suggested eliminating the routes that pass through those neighborhoods while suburban riders suggested locating more stops to increase protection. Both the young and senior participants viewed the city's large community of senior citizens as a driver of the cuts, but each group then viewed the outcome of this in opposite ways. Young riders saw the choices made as benefiting seniors and seniors saw the choices as being made as benefiting the youth. A co-design system that can surface these points of conflict and opposing views of the same reality can be a first step in moving toward consensus. In addition, it can provide the opportunity for the public service to see the complexity with which it is viewed and to see how its actions are both interpreted and misinterpreted.

Sharing Consequences

A co-design system can encourage citizens to share the consequences of current and proposed service offerings as these help others better empathize with the impact design choices might have. Personal narratives shared by participants proved much more effective in their communication when participants detailed the larger consequences and not just the details of the service change. Detailed consequences made it much easier for other participants to take an empathic view of other riders' worlds and to move them toward a collective action. For example, urban and suburban participants came together to save the routes for children in low-income town to have access to better schools in the city. They all valued education. A co-design system could provide a structured interface for capturing people's life stories of how the service influences their everyday. Linking together a chain of consequences from the same issue can be one way to make more effective display of many people's concerns. For example, information on an issue could provide a summary along with a set of consequences, possibly even ranking the consequences based on the number of people that shared them or using social networking tagging conventions using labels such as "like," "agree," or "important."

Taking Actions

We see that co-design via social computing might best focus on searching for a shared citizen and service provider understanding of the goals and mission for the service as the outcome of this dialog system, which can be achieved through structured sharing of rationales and consequences. Furthermore, a successful co-design dialog system should provide feedback on how the participation of citizens and stakeholders in the dialog system influenced the service's actions and offerings. Without any feedback the dialog system could quickly appear as a "black hole" where people seemingly offer complaints and suggestions that are never seen, considered, or acted upon.

We imagine there could be two ways public voices can have impact on service innovation. First, is to participate in the official service development process. This requires active response from the public service providers. Second, is to participate in social action. For example, wheelchair users may share their experiences and concerns about getting on a crowd bus. Shared narratives can raise public awareness to take collective action among riders, in this example, to let wheelchair users get on first. In both cases, the point of the system is not about transparency of decision makers, the service providers. Instead, the point is to let citizens participate in decision-making, particularly when it is about the public's performance of the service.

Identifying Stakeholder Groups

A co-design system needs to support many stakeholder groups and the dynamic formation of groups based on the topic under discussion. Here we note several key design challenges in identifying and engaging multiple groups in dialog. First, for the legibility of narratives and to avoid misuse of a system, it might be required that people share some of their personal information such as their name, age, gender and important affiliations. For example, a system might use a person's name and neighborhood as a signature on a post or response. In addition, the role people associate with a place (e.g., where I live, where I work, where I entertain) may provide a key reference point for interpreting a person's narrative and for organizing and displaying collected narratives. Second, organizations that are not people might also deserve a voice. For example, as illustrated in the SU2's narrative of her stop being moved from next to the mall to the side of the highway, a mall has a stake in how transit vehicles cross its property. Therefore, a system would need to be able to distinguish between an institutional voice and a personal voice. Third, employees of the public service (e.g., the bus drivers) should have a voice, but their participation in the dialog may put their job in jeopardy. It raises a tension around the benefits of anonymity for some participants and the transparent and equal treatment of all participants. Fourth, there is a need to engage indirect stakeholders who do not use the public service but should have a voice in what it does and the services it offers. In the case of the transit service, the challenge is to engage people who regularly drive. These people benefit when others use transit in terms of less traffic, increased parking, and less pollution. In addition, within the US they are much larger group of citizens than transit riders and thus they have a larger political voice.

Visualizing Money Flow

Public services receive money from a variety of sources, often with strict restrictions on how this money can be spent (e.g., The state Department of Transportation's Free Transit Program for Senior Citizens paid for by proceeds from the state Lottery). An effective co-design system could visualize the different sources as well as how the funding is allocated. This could work as a shared frame of reference that citizens, stakeholders, and the service can point to when proposing or critiquing different ideas for service innovation. When funding remains fixed, then each new service offering generally must also result in a service cut. Having a clearer and agreed upon reference for this funding would better support negotiation and investigation by everyone of new design ideas. We observed emergent rationales and behaviors, particularly from the senior participants to understand how their actions and use impacted the financial aspects of the transit service and in rationalizing why they should or should not be provided with the services they desired.

CONCLUSION

Our research probed the opportunity for a social computing system that would allow the public to participate in the co-design of their transit service. We conducted a field study with young and old, and urban and suburban riders soon after a major service cut had taken place. We observed that the personal narratives they shared describing their service experiences could be a rich source of information for a co-design system. These narratives revealed how they perceived the actions of the transit service. In addition, the consequences they shared helped others gain an empathic view of their situation and new insights on what the goals of the transit service should be. Based on findings, we speculate that a co-design social computing system would benefit from a dialog structure that encourages people to share personal narratives, to describe their rationale for transit service actions, and to detail the consequences of service changes. In addition, we recommend that such a system support dynamic user groupings, feedback that indicates how participants' contributions have impacted service's behavior, and visualizations that communicate funding sources and expenditures. We see a real opportunity for social computing technology to support the way people engage with and take ownership of public services, and we encourage other researchers to engage with this emerging topic.

ACKNOWLEDGMENTS

This research was supported by the Rehabilitation Engineering Research Center on Accessible Public Transportation (RERC-APT). The RERC-APT is funded by grant H133E080019 from the US Department of Education through the National Institute on Disability and Rehabilitation Research. Additional support was provided by Traffic21 at Carnegie Mellon University, a program developed with the support of the Hillman Foundation; and a University Transportation Center grant (DTRT12-G-UTC11) from the US Department of Transportation.

REFERENCES

1. Bødker, S., Ehn, P., Sjögren, D. and Sundblad, Y. Co-Operative Design: Perspectives on 20 Years with 'the Scandinavian IT Design Model. In *Proc. of NordiCHI,* (2000) ACM Press, 22-24.
2. Brabham, D. C. Crowdsourcing the Public Participation Process for Planning Projects. *Planning Theory*, *8*, 3 (2009), 242-262
3. Bradwell, P. and Marr, S. *Making the Most of Collaboration an International Survey of Public Service Co-Design.* DEMOS, in association with PriceWaterhouseCoopers Public Sector Research Centre, London, 2008.
4. Chango, M. Challenges to e-government in Africa south of Sahara. In *Proc. of the Conference on Theory and Practice of Electronic Governance,* (2007).
5. Cho, JS., Chun, SA. Towards transparent policy decision making process. In *Proc. of Digital Government Research Conference,* (2011).
6. DiSalvo, C. Design and the Construction of Publics. *Design Issues*, *25*, 1 (2009), 48-63.
7. Edvardsson, B., Gustafsson, A. and Roos, I. Service Portraits in Service Research: A Critical Review. *International Journal of Service Industry Management*, *16*, 1 (2005), 107-121.
8. Evans-Cowley, J. S. Crowdsourcing the Curriculum: Public Participation in Redesigning a Planning Program. Working Paper, (February 12, 2011). Available at SSRN: http://ssrn.com/abstract=1760525
9. Gaver, W.W., Dunne, T., and Pacenti, E. Cultural Probes. *interactions*, *6*,1 (1999) 21-29.
10. Goldstein, S. M., Johnston, R., Duffy, J. A. and Rao, J. The Service Concept: The Missing Link in Service Design Research? *Journal of Operations Management*, *20*, 2 (2002), 121-134.
11. Hirsch, T. Contestational Design: Innovation for political activism. Dissertation. MIT, Dept. of Architecture, Program in Media Arts and Sciences, (2006).
12. Holmlid, S. Participative, Co-Operative, Emancipatory: From Participatory Design to Service Design. In *Proc. of Nordic Conference on Service Design and Service Innovation,* (2009) Oslo School of Architecture and Design.
13. Janowski, T., Ojo, A. and Estevez, E. Rapid Development of Electronic Public Services: A Case Study in Electronic Licensing Service. In *Proc of Conference on Digital Government Research*, (2007) Digital Government Society of North America, 292-293.
14. Kaschesky, M., Riedl, R. Top-level decisions through public deliberation on the internet. In *Proc. Of the Conference on Digital Government Research,* (2009).
15. Koskinen, I., Zimmerman, J., Binder, T., Redstrom, J. and Wensveen, S. *Design Research through Practice: From the Lab, Field, and Showroom.* Morgan Kaufmann, Boston, 2011.
16. King, S. F. and Brown, P. Fix My Street or Else: Using the Internet to Voice Local Public Service Concerns. In *Proc. of Theory and Practice of Electronic Governance*, (2007) ACM Press. 72-80.
17. Matheus, R., Ribeiro, MM. Public online consultation of federal ministries and federal regulatory agencies in Brazil. In *Proc. of the Conference on Theory and Practice of Electronic Governance,* (2009).
18. Ng, I. C. L., Maull, R. S. and Smith, L. Embedding the New Discipline of Service Science. In *The Science of Service Systems*. H. Demirkan, J. H. Spohrer and V. Krishna (eds). Springer, 2009.
19. ParkScan: http://parkscan.org/
20. Petrik, K. Participation and e-democracy how to utilize web 2.0 for policy decision-making. In *Proc. of the Conference on Digital Government Research,* (2009).
21. Prahalad, C. K. and Ramaswamy, V. Co-Opting Customer Competence. *Harvard Business Review, 78*, 1 (2000), 79-90.
22. Qian, H. Global perspectives on e-governance. In *Proc. of the Conference on Theory and Practice of Electronic Governance,* (2010).
23. Rodrigo, D., Amo, PA. (2006): Background Document on Public Consultation. *OECD*, Paris.
24. Saad-Sulonen, J. and Cabrera, A. B. Setting up a Public Participation Project Using the Urban Mediator Tool: A Case of Collaboration between Designers and City Planners. In *Proc. of NordiCHI*, (2008) ACM Press, 539-542.
25. Saad-Sulonen, J., Botero, A. and Kuutti, K. A Long-Term Strategy for Designing (in) the Wild: Lessons from the Urban Mediator and Traffic Planning in Helsinki. In *Proc. of DIS* (2012) ACM Press, 166-175
26. Shostack, G. L. How to Design a Service. In *European Journal of Marketing 16*, 1 (1982), 49-63.
27. Strauss A., Corbin J. *Basics of Qualitative*, 2nd Ed. SAGE Publications, 1998.
28. Tomkins, AJ., PytlikZilllig, LM., Herian, MN., Abdel-Monem, T., Hamm, JA. (2010): Public input for municipal policymaking. In *Proc. of the Digital Government Research Conference on Public Administration Online.*
29. US Census Bureau (2010): http://www.census.gov/prod/2010pubs/acsbr09-5.pdf Accessed: September 1, 2012.Winner, L. “Do Artifacts Have Politics?” in *The Whale and The Reactor: A Search for Limits in an Age of High Technology*, Chicago: University of Chicago Press, 1989.
30. Yoo, D., Zimmerman, J., Steinfeld, A., and Tomasic, A. Understanding the Space for Co-Design in Riders' Interactions with a Transit Service. In *Proc of CHI*, (2010) ACM Press, 1797-1806.
31. Zimmeramn, J., Tomasic, A., Garrod, C., Yoo, D., Hiruncharoenvate, C., Aziz, R., Thiruvengadam, N. R., Huang, Y., and Steinfeld, A. Field Trial of Tiramisu: Crowd-Sourcing Bus Arrival Times to Spur Co-Design. In *Proc of CHI,* (2011) ACM Press, 1677-1686.
32. Zimmerman, J., Forlizzi, J. and Evenson, S. Research through Design as a Method for Interaction Design Research in HCI. In *Proc. of CHI*, (2007) ACM Press, 493-502.

A Value Sensitive Action-Reflection Model: Evolving a Co-Design Space with Stakeholder and Designer Prompts

Daisy Yoo[†], **Alina Huldtgren**[*], **Jill Palzkill Woelfer**[†], **David G. Hendry**[†], **and Batya Friedman**[†]

[†]The Information School
University of Washington
Seattle, WA 98195-2840
{dyoo, woelfj, dhendry, batya}@uw.edu

[*] Interactive Intelligence Group
Delft University of Technology
Delft, The Netherlands
alina@huldtgren.com

ABSTRACT

We introduce a design method for evolving a co-design space to support stakeholders untrained in design. Specifically, the purpose of the method is to expand and shape a co-design space so that stakeholders, acting as designers, focus not only on the form and function of a tool being envisioned but also on the social context of its use and values that lie with individuals, groups, and societies. The method introduces value sensitive stakeholder prompts and designer prompts into a co-design process, creating a particular kind of reflection-on-action cycle. The prompts provide a means for bringing empirical data on values and theoretical perspective into the co-design process. We present the method in terms of a general model, the Value Sensitive Action-Reflection Model; place the model within discourse on co-design spaces; and illustrate the model with a discussion of its application in a lo-fi prototyping activity around safety for homeless young people. We conclude with reflections on the model and method.

Author Keywords

Co-design; creativity; design method; Envisioning Cards; homeless young people; mobile technologies; prototyping; reflection-on-action; safety; security; Value Sensitive Action-Reflection Model; value scenarios; value sensitive design

ACM Classification Keywords

H.5.m. Information interfaces and presentation (e.g., HCI): Miscellaneous.

INTRODUCTION

Tools are not only about acting in the world – they also reflect back the conditions, perceived needs, and values of the people and societies who make, own, and use them. From this perspective, the form and function of tools can tell us a good deal about what is important to the tools' owners and users, including what they care about, what activities they wish to do, what problems they wish to solve, with whom they wish to communicate, with whom they wish to sustain friendship and build community, from whom they wish to remain hidden, and who or what they want to keep safe. As such, the form and function of tools provide a view onto people's values and the intersection of those values with technology.

Analyses grounded in existing tool use provide one such lens, albeit constrained by a range of pragmatic dimensions that include people's resources, infrastructure, and socio-political context. Consider the case of cookies and web browser security and privacy, a complex interaction design problem. A retrospective analysis between the years of 1995-1998 of early web browsers and their cookie settings shows substantial development of technical features to provide users with transparency about and control of cookie settings [15]. Such technical development in response to public outcry about privacy could give the impression that people were interested in managing cookies when they were being set. But such analyses of the deployed technical mechanisms would miss the possibility that what people really cared about was managing cookies at the time of use. That particular technical implementation would have required a major redesign of underlying web protocols.

To understand what is important to people in their lives, it is often helpful to complement analyses of what people do with existing tools with their visions for how tools *could be different*. Therein lies the design turn. By engaging with stakeholders around perceived needs and values in the co-design of yet-to-be-built tools researchers and designers are offered a window into the kind of relationship between technology and values that people and societies might wish to experience. Given this kind of value sensitive envisioning goal for co-design, how might researchers and designers construct a co-design space that would foreground consideration of human values?

In this paper we introduce a Value Sensitive Action-Reflection Model to support such value sensitive envisioning. The model builds from the work of Schön [22,23] and more recent work on co-design spaces [3,5,9,19,20,21], as well as from work in value sensitive design [11,12]. At the outset of this work, the goal was to advance our understanding for how mobile phones might help keep homeless young people safe in their communities. However, in the course of conducting that

CHI 2013, April 27–May 2, 2013, Paris, France.

research, we encountered the need to extend existing co-design methodology. Accordingly, we take this opportunity to report on our methodological innovation. In this paper we strike a balance between introducing the Value Sensitive Action-Reflection Model, our key contribution, and reporting on our co-design study. The reporting of the co-design study helps us examine the model; at the same time, the model helps to provide rationale for the methodological choices made in the study.

BACKGROUND

Spaces for Co-design

Co-design, sometimes called co-creation, emerged in the late 1990s, building on the tradition of participatory design (PD) and user-centered design (UCD). The term co-design, in its broad sense, refers to any act of joint creativity in which designers, end-users untrained in design, and perhaps other stakeholders work together in design processes [21]. Over the past decade co-design has been widely accepted as a valid user study methodology in the fields of product design, service design, interaction design and HCI [16].

More recently, Sanders and colleagues have theorized the concept of *co-design spaces* [19]. In brief, their work foregrounds the importance of scaffolding the co-design space in order to improve the creativity of stakeholders who are less experienced in design. Ideally this scaffolding – that is the materials, structure, and activities of the co-design space – should encourage stakeholders to explore many possible solutions, feel confident to put forward ideas, and eagerly aim for new, creative ideas. Furthermore, Sanders et al. show how common methods – Futures Workshops and design tools for creative exploration – can be understood as co-design spaces [20,21].

We see an important connection between Sanders et al.'s conception of co-design spaces and Schön's foundational analysis of design [22,23]. Here, two points are particularly germane. First, in addition to exploring design as a conversation with materials, as a form of reflection-*in*-action, Schön emphasizes the importance of reflection-*on*-action. He shows how focused comments by teachers can prompt students of architecture to pause and reflect on the current state of a design and then take new action. Accordingly, we ask: how might researchers or designers prompt stakeholders to reflect on action without undermining exploration and creative thinking? Second, Schön also emphasizes that the designer engages in different kinds of "seeing," that is, the designer makes appreciations related to different kinds of object domains (e.g., cost, form, structure, etc.). Accordingly, we ask: how might stakeholders participating in a co-design process be prompted to consider object domains of particular salience to a design project? In the present study the object domain concerns the aspects of society and values along with features of mobile phones; hence, we turn to value sensitive design to address in part both questions.

Value Sensitive Design

In the 1990s value sensitive design emerged with the aim to offer a theoretically grounded approach to the design of technology that accounts for human values in a principled and comprehensive manner throughout the design process [11]. In the design research reported here, we bring two methods developed within value sensitive design into a space of co-design, prompting stakeholders to reflect on the technical and value aspects of their design ideas.

Value Scenarios. Value scenarios, an extension to traditional use and problem scenarios [6], consist of stories that emphasize the social and value considerations of new technologies, especially long-term and potentially negative impacts [17]. In prior work value scenarios have been written by designers for use as an analytic tool to explore values related to good parenting and mobile applications for monitoring teenagers [8]; in other work value scenarios have been written by stakeholders and thereby used as an empirical tool to elicit safety-oriented stories about mobile phone use for homeless young people [24].

Envisioning Cards. The Envisioning Cards [10,12] consist of a deck of 28 themed cards that are intended to raise awareness of long-term and systemic effects of proposed technologies. Each card presents a title and an evocative image related to one of four envisioning criteria – stakeholders, time, values, and pervasiveness [17]. On the flip side, the card offers a theme describing that card's key concept and a focused design activity related to the theme. The cards are intended to be used for various design processes: ideation, co-design, heuristic evaluation, critique, and more. Prior use includes ideation and goal setting with health enterprise systems in Eastern Africa, heuristic value analysis of security in cloud computing, and surfacing value tensions in persuasive profiling [10].

Socio-technical Context: Homelessness, Youth, Safety

As part of a larger movement with the HCI community to engage a more diverse community of users [2], recently studies have examined the use and design of technology by homeless people [14,18], including homeless adults in urban settings who were found to use mobile phones to tap into social networks for basic needs and homeless mothers living in an emergency shelter who were found to benefit from information sharing on public displays.

The socio-technical context for this work entails that of homeless young people, mobile technologies, and safety. In the United States, at any given time during the year it is estimated that 3 million people are both young, up to the age of 30, and homeless [26]. Extensive research reveals that homeless young people are a heterogeneous mix of ages, genders, races and ethnicities [26]. Life can be very difficult when a good deal of time is spent securing basic needs, such as safety, food, and shelter, often while managing physical and mental health problems. At the same time, despite the extraordinary conditions of living on the streets, homeless young people seek ordinary

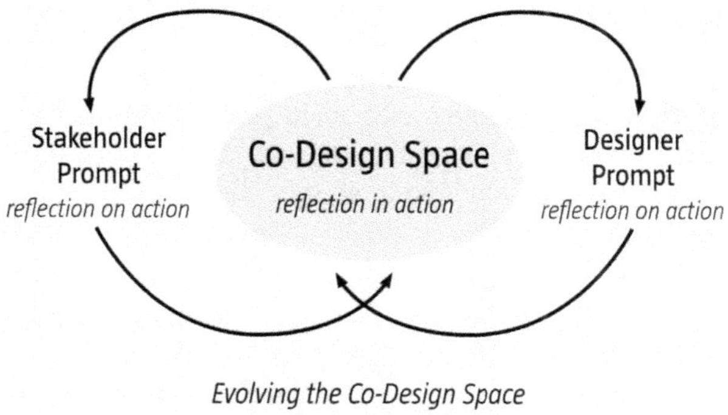

Figure 1. Value Sensitive Action-Reflection Model.

experiences with technology such as music players, social network sites, and mobile phones [25].

SPACES FOR CO-DESIGN: A VALUE SENSITIVE ACTION-REFLECTION MODEL

To bring forward values in what can be an essentially technology-centric co-design process, we developed a Value Sensitive Action-Reflection Model. The model draws in spirit on Schön's attention to reflection-on-action and extends the work of Sanders and colleagues on the construction of co-design spaces.

While co-design can be approached in many ways, co-design spaces at their core typically include creative toolkits (e.g., maketools [20]), designed assignments (e.g., design games [5]), and in-situ ideation and communication among stakeholders to co-create solutions. Traditionally, although co-design has focused on end-user needs and desires, less emphasis has been placed on values and societal concerns.

To the traditional co-design core, the model presented here blends methods from value sensitive design to structure engagement with consideration of values. Specifically as shown in Figure 1, the model begins with the familiar core materials and activities of a co-design space that afford somewhat free-form design in response to an initial design challenge. With initial design ideas in hand, and herein lies the model's innovation, we add two types of structured interventions. One type, known as a *stakeholder prompt*, entails material that by and large originates with the stakeholders and provides a good deal of direct access to stakeholder perspectives. A variety of materials can function as stakeholder prompts such as stakeholder generated value scenarios [17], value sketches [24], or responses to cultural probes [13]. The second type of intervention, known as *a designer prompt*, entails materials that originate largely from a designer or researcher perspective. Similarly, a variety of designer generated materials can function as designer prompts such as Envisioning Cards [12], personas [7] or pastiche scenarios [4]. The model is meant to be fairly general; in its current form, these two types of interventions can be invoked multiple times and used in any order including the use of only stakeholder or only designer prompts. The novelty of our approach is not in the prompts per se but in the constellation of (1) the combination of both stakeholder-led as well as designer-led prompts; and (2) a lens on human values.

METHODS

Researcher Stance

The present research is part of a long-term engagement with a community of homeless young people in Seattle, Washington in which value sensitive design theory and method has been applied in a number of research and design projects. Collectively, the authors have substantial experience working with this community – as volunteer instructors in educational programs, as consultants on IT projects with our principle collaborating organization, and as researchers – and substantial methodological experience with co-design, value scenarios, and the Envisioning Cards.

Participants

Between June-August 2011, sixteen participants worked in pairs, yielding eight co-design groups, six with homeless young people (8 men, 4 women; ages 19-27, M=23), one with police officers (1 man, 1 woman; ages 39, M=39), and one with service providers (2 women; ages 30 and 51, M=41). To create a comfortable co-design environment, separate sessions were held for each of the three population types. All study participants were offered $25.00 gift cards.

Procedures

Participants were oriented to the study and the co-design materials were introduced. These materials included broken-off pieces of cell phones (e.g., screens, keyboards, casings) and craft materials (e.g., cardboard, colored paper, glue, tape, colored modeling clay). Additionally, we included a 11×17 inch spec. sheet that provided a 9×9 inch space for sketching a mobile phone, and prompted participants to name their prototype phone, to list its key functions and features, to specify its look and feel (e.g., color, cost, battery life), and to answer three design questions (e.g., How might the features of the phone help to keep a homeless youth or young adult safe?). Participants were encouraged to be forward looking and assume any idea could be pursued in the co-design process.

Once these materials were introduced, participants were given the following instruction:

> *Homeless youth and young adults may face special challenges in keeping safe from harm. Please make a prototype of a cell phone that might help keep a homeless youth or young adult safe. There are no right answers.*

In the first of three stages, participants were instructed to complete their spec. sheet and develop an initial prototype.

In the second stage, with their initial prototypes in hand and applying the Value Sensitive Action-Reflection Model (see Figure 2), participants were prompted to iterate the design twice, first with a stakeholder prompt and then with a designer prompt. Each of the prompts was intended to promote a cycle of reflection-on-action that expanded the co-design space from the designed artifact to the broader socio-technical context of use.

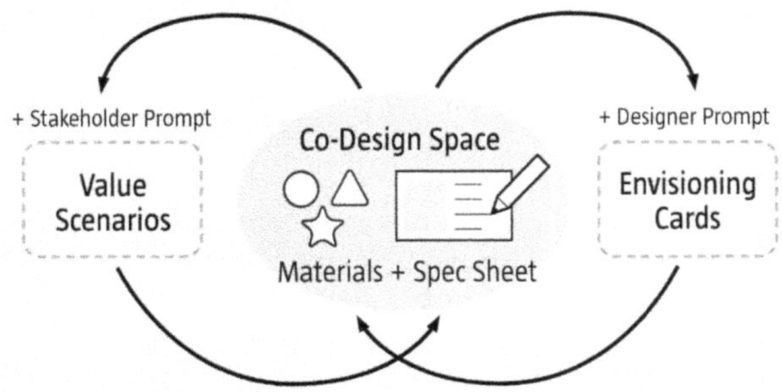

Figure 2. Model applied in the mobile phone study.

Stakeholder Prompt – The Value Scenario

Prior work had elicited 19 value scenarios from homeless young people about how they might use mobile phones to keep safe [24]. A sample of 11 scenarios was selected by the researchers and repurposed on cards as stakeholder prompts. The scenario cards convey situations where safety is at stake, how mobile phones can be used to keep safe, and specific features of mobile phones. For example:

> *Once upon a time a young man went down the alley, he noticed five guys following him, he immediately calls his cousin who lived in a building along the same alley. The upper light turns on and the said cousin appears and calls out, in turn the five guys walk away.*

Participants were instructed to select one value scenario card and to consider their prototypes in light of the situation described in the scenario (see Results for text of participant selected scenarios). Then, they completed a second spec. sheet to record any changes that they would make to their prototypes or to explain why no changes were needed.

Designer Prompt – The Envisioning Card

For the second prompt, participants selected an Envisioning Card from a set of six preselected cards. The six cards were selected by the researchers from the full set of 28 themed cards [12] for their relevance to mobility and sharing. The six cards were: CHANGING HANDS, CONSIDER CHILDREN, CROSSING NATIONAL BOUNDARIES, ONE PERSON MULTIPLE ROLES, SUSTAINED FRIENDSHIPS, and VALUE TENSIONS. As one illustrative example, the CHANGING HANDS card has the following prompt (theme and design activity):

> *A single product can change hands once, twice, or more times during its lifecycle. It may be passed among family members (e.g., coming of age gift) or across town (e.g., consignment). How might use of the system change as the technology changes hands?*
>
> *Design a scenario of your product changing hands. Imagine a specific challenge an individual might face when wanting to shift ownership. What features might make this process smoother?*

Similar to the stakeholder prompt, participants were instructed to complete a third spec. sheet to record any changes or explanations for why changes were not needed.

In the third and final stage, participants gave 3-5 minute demonstrations of their prototypes in use.

The co-design sessions varied in length from 88-168 minutes (M=114 min.). Audio recordings were made of each session and photographs were periodically taken. At the end of each session, the research team collected the physical prototypes and the three spec. sheets.

RESULTS

Participants' co-design ideas were reflected through a diversity of representations including physical prototypes, sketches, textual information written on the spec. sheets, and oral exposition of their designs and design changes that accompanied a demonstration of their devices. Because in this paper we are concerned primarily with the effect of the value sensitive prompts on shaping the co-design space, our reporting and analysis of results will emphasize the changes (if any) that were stimulated by those prompts. That said, participants produced a wide range of rich, creative designs in response to the initial design challenge that, in turn, served as the starting point for the structured design prompts. Thus we first present some results from the overall designs to provide a context for applying the design prompts before turning to examine the specific effects of those prompts. We save a more complete reporting of the co-design outcomes for another paper.

Recall, too, that we did not set out to develop or assess a new model for shaping a co-design space. Rather the model came about as we sought to explore ways to scaffold stakeholders' engagement with safety for homeless young people and other relevant values when envisioning new designs for mobile technology.

Overall Designs

The presentation of our data for the overall designs borrows in concept and form from Agee's and Evans's seminal work *Let Us Now Praise Famous Men* [1]. In reporting their work, Agee and Evans first present an uncaptioned series of striking black and white photographs that record three tenant families in the deep south of the United States during the 1930s and their physical surroundings; followed by words recording, again, people and place, and this time stories of interactions. The prologue of uncaptioned images throws the reader into the visual context of the research with minimal interpretation; the words follow as one way in to understanding those images and their implications.

In a similar vein, to allow the reader to form his or her own impressions of the data, we selected four of the eight designs (three by groups of homeless young people and the fourth by police officers). Photographs of the physical prototypes and sketches of the participants' devices are shown on the next page (Figures 3-6). Building on the gallery of photographs, we next provide holistic written accounts that explain these four devices in terms of what participants chose to recount about them. With this reporting style, we seek to position readers to form their own impressions of the data prior to presenting brief analyses of all eight designs and our interpretation as researchers.

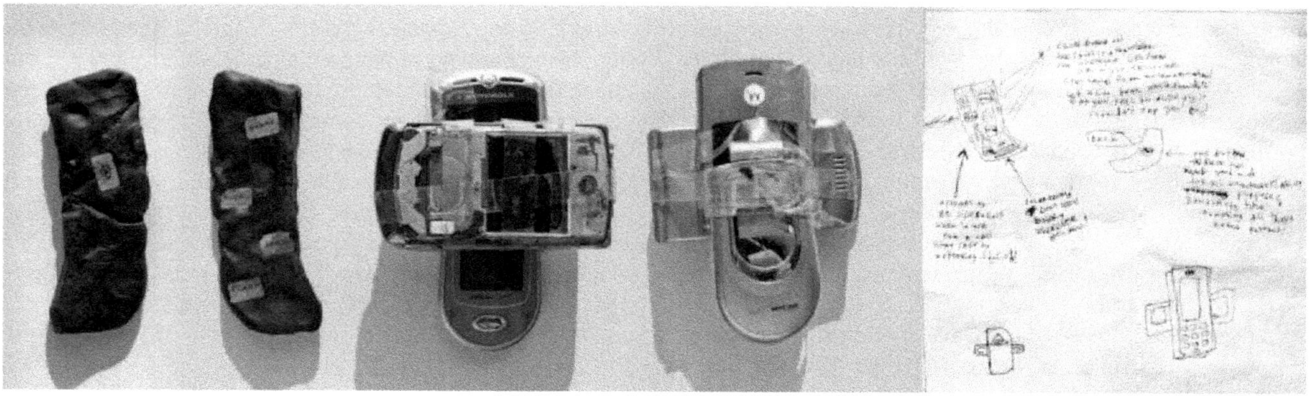

Figure 3. Brittany Futureproof (Homeless Young People).

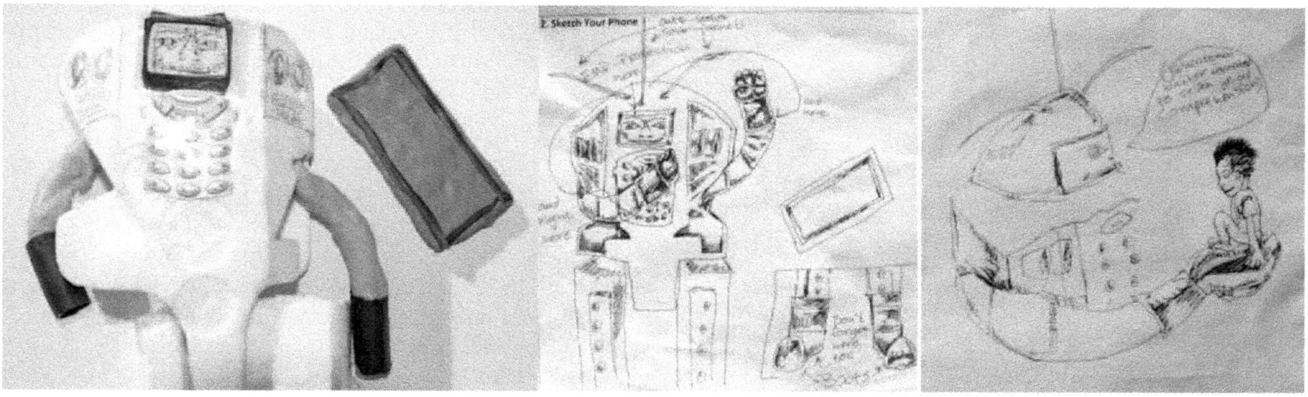

Figure 4. Failed Delusions (Homeless Young People).

Figure 5. Hassle Free (Homeless Young People).

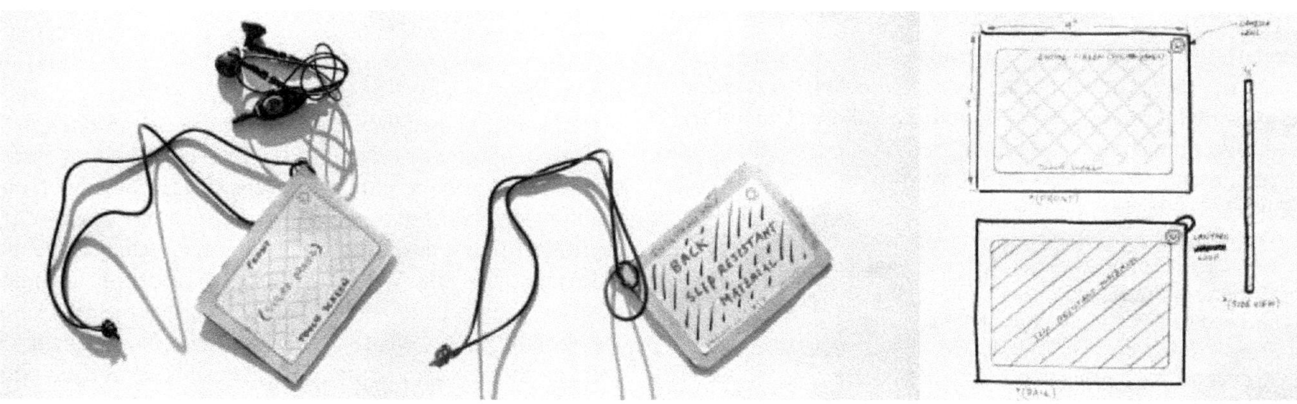

Figure 6. INDESTRUCTABLE (Police Officers).

Holistic Written Accounts of Four Designs

We now present brief holistic written accounts of these four designs, staying close to the language participants used on their spec. sheets and to describe their designs in the audio recordings. These accounts come from an in-depth process of considering each prototype. Specifically, we carefully inspected the spec. sheets, sketches, prototypes and photographs of the prototyping process and listened to the audio recordings of each co-design session. The researchers repeatedly discussed these. Then, iteratively and synthetically, narratives were written, reviewed, and edited for concise reporting. As appropriate, we include fairly lengthy verbatim quotations from the participants.

Brittany Futureproof (Homeless Young People, Figure 3). Brittany Futureproof comes with a swivel screen and a set of advanced technology such as telepathy and alien-plants-animal translation:

> There is actually near infinity number of buttons [on the front] you press the buttons for whatever species of life form you might encounter.... It just translates between you two so that if there's any conflict, you know, say you meet an alien and it's about to zap you and you just press the alien button and then it translates. [It] just mediates.

Beside this important communication feature that helps to mediate social interactions, Brittany Futureproof includes several other safety features. One is a button on the back of the phone that when pressed can read someone's mind in order to give the user an indication of whether she is in danger. This mind-reading function allows for a quick assessment of the situation (no wasting time with translations and pushing several buttons). Another safety feature is making the phone look like "stylish" side-burns:

> It's in the shape of the sideburns. So, if you're using it, it'll blend in.

Failed Delusions (Homeless Young People, Figure 4). This robot can fly to the location of a phone call and has built-in EMP (electro-magnetic pulse) disruption protectors. Among its features:

> It warns of impending law enforcement in the areas and lists the officers' possible offenses. There is also a snitch radar, too, on it. Just in case anybody that works for the police officer, they are immediately, you know their information is immediately broadcasted to everybody in the neighborhood.

Failed Delusions can also "extrapolate" air molecules and reconstruct them into food. It uses solar panels to provide energy and therefore, offers indefinite talk and stand-by times. The phone can easily be shared with other homeless youth, although it is closely tied to its owner:

> It takes a sample of your DNA as well as having a scent detector. So, you can control it pretty much by what you say, because it only has recognition towards you [and] it recognizes other people as being a friend if you consider them to be a friend. It can't get lost, 'cause it's a giant robot. It will find you and fly back to you.... You have like a symbiotic relationship to it to a certain degree.

Hassle Free (Homeless Young People, Figure 5). Hassle Free is a new type of phone that is hands-free and wearable made out of light materials. It is strapped to the user's hand and consists of three components: (1) the basic phone component located between the thumb and index finger including an on/off switch and a microphone; (2) the smaller ear piece attached to the tip of the index finger including a speaker and detachable ear bud; and (3) a fold out screen that can be attached to the outside of the user's hand. Hassle Free will keep its homeless user safe as:

> You don't have to dig into your pocket if you have to dial 911.... Or there might be like a system like if you were to fall it would register that you hit the ground or impacted it or maybe someone pushed you down, you got hit by a car or whatever. As soon as the impact is registered it asks you 'Are you okay?' If you don't respond or if you respond 'No, I'm not ok' some sort of help would be brought your way immediately.

INDESTRUCTABLE (Police Officers, Figure 6). This phone is lightweight, waterproof, and durable, with such safety features as theft prevention, quick access to 911, and built-in camera for making connections with service providers. Input is handled via the touchscreen or voice recognition and it comes with headphones. Worn on the body, the phone is a tool for reaching out to others:

> It's pliable. I can stick it to my shoes, you know, or around your ankle or something on your shoe if I were to go around running. The counselor version 101 is gonna have the camera and, you know, whatever, so next time you come into [a clinic] and you set [the phone] on the charger it's going to automatically update your apps or, give you the new phone numbers to all the shelters or give you the new whatever.

Characterizations of the Eight Mobile Phone Designs

To complement the more impressionistic treatment of the photographs and written accounts above, we next provide some analytic detail on all eight mobile phone designs. We conducted an in-depth examination of the technical features that participants chose to represent in their sketches and prototypes. We also attended to the overall structure of the representation and the form of the mobile phone.

As shown in Table 1, technical features included many familiar ones such as screen type or camera; as well as more unusual ones such as energy sources (e.g., solar and lunar), emergency functions (e.g., rape whistle, taser), and enhanced communication (e.g., real-time translation). In terms of overall representational structure, some participants embedded their technical solutions in a narrative or storyline (e.g., the Failed Delusions group situated their robotic phone in a sense of place and personal relationship with the homeless young person) while others represented their design solutions through technical features only (e.g., the Hassle Free group provided only technical details for their hands-only phone). In terms of the form of the mobile phone, many were used including typical flip and bar phones (e.g., Brittany Futureproof) as well as robots (e.g., Failed Delusions) and wearables (e.g., Hassle Free).

1. Screen Type (e.g., touch, display, foldout)
2. Camera
3. Audio (e.g., ear buds, remote control, mic)
4. Accessory (e.g., bracelet, phone cover)
5. Energy Source (e.g., battery, solar panel, lunar panel, universal charger)
6. LED
7. Can Opener
8. Emergency (e.g., rape whistle, pepper spray)
9. Robot
10. Slip Resistant Pad
11. EMP Protection
12. Product Identifier
13. Buttons
    - 13.1. Lock / Unlock
    - 13.2. On / Off
    - 13.3. Send / End
    - 13.4. Ring of Arrow Keys
    - 13.5. Keypads
    - 13.6. Talk
    - 13.7. Enhanced Communication (e.g., mind-reading, real-time translation)
    - 13.8. Calendar
    - 13.9. Contact List (e.g., key service providers, friends)
    - 13.10. Transportation (e.g., vehicle, map)
    - 13.11. Other services
    - 13.12. Unspecified

Table 1. Coding categories for technical features.

The Effects of the Prompts

We now turn to a methodological view of the data. Recall the model presented in Figure 2 in which reflection-on-action was prompted with stakeholder prompts (i.e., value scenarios) and designer prompts (i.e., Envisioning Cards). These prompts, in short, were intended to trigger the generation of new ideas related to mobile phones and the socio-technical context of safety, youth, and homelessness. To examine the impact of the stakeholder and designer prompts, we analyzed each group's spec. sheets and prototypes before and after each prompt was administered.

As shown in Table 2, the prompts led to the addition of 21 new features in total. Participants chose to represent their changes on the spec. sheets and on the sketches; no changes were made to the physical prototypes. Notably, the majority of new features arose from the design work of the police officers and service providers, and fewer from the design work of the homeless young people (on average 6.5 and 1.3 new features, respectively).

A qualitative analysis of the impact of the prompts shows by and large a coherent relationship between the prompt's content and the proposed change. Moreover, when participants offered no changes in response to the prompts, they typically provided reasonable explanations for why their current designs sufficed. In the material that follows we report in detail on both types of prompts.

Stakeholder Prompt: Value Scenarios

Recall that the value scenarios were generated by other homeless young people in prior research. Across the eight co-design groups, seven unique scenarios were selected, with the service providers choosing two scenarios and one group of homeless young people declining to use a prompt.

The INDESTRUCTABLE (police officer) group selected this scenario:

> *I think it would be useful if you get hurt at night time or need to go to the Hospital and yeah or it could be useful for contacting friends and family. yup!!*

Mobile Phone	Value Scenarios	Envisioning Cards	Total
Hortical	2	1	3
Failed Delusions	1	1	2
Brittany Futureproof	1	1	2
Hassle Free	--	1	1
BOB	0	0	0
The Motorola Stupid Martian	0	0	0
INDESTRUCTABLE (Police Officers)	4	4	8
Squatters Phone (Serv. Providers)	3	2	5
Total	**11**	**10**	**21**

Table 2. Number of new features by prompt.

In response to the scenario, they added several new features: "Touch activated power-up feature;" "Panic button activation;" "Resources icon;" and "Dial-A-Icon (which sets up a speed dial to contact resources for help)."

The Squatters Phone (service provider) group selected two value scenarios:

> *I don't think cell phones keep people safe because if you call the cops for seeing a crime you might get beat up later for snitching.*
>
> *I would use devices in my cell phone to record law enforcement, when they choose to harass me.*

In response to the first value scenario they added: "untraceable way to report crime," and "contacting specific cop who's known to be safe." For the second, they added: "a built-in contact to report complaints/anti-harassment."

Turning to the homeless young people, the Brittany Futureproof (BF) group selected this scenario:

> *I was lost in the mountains, with no means of any gear all I had was my Phone which was used to call for an evacuation.*

In response to the scenario, the group proposed an innovative energy source, lunar panels, in addition to the solar panels in their initial design. Interestingly, the participants did not admit to the change at first; rather, they presented the new feature as if it was part of their initial design. Later they said that the lunar panels were actually a change made in response to the prompt:

> BF: If you're in the mountains, um, there is no outlets to plug your phone to charge it...and our phone has solar panels so uh, it would just, we also have the lunar panels actually. We forgot to tell you. [It] charges off the moonlight, too.
>
> Facilitator: So you, what changes did you decide to make that you wrote on your spec. sheet?
>
> BF: Actually, we uh, we didn't forget to tell you about the lunar panels. That was the change we made.
>
> Facilitator: So you've added...lunar panels to the phone?

The Hortical group selected this scenario:

> *Once upon a time there was three little Pigs, One lived in a house, one lived on the streets, and the last one lived in a squat. One day a big bad wolf was looking for squatter, the big bad wolf was out to get all little pigs. The first little pig called the second pig, and he found the third pig through word of mouth. Thank cell phone.*

In response to the value scenario, the new sketch depicted a wolf and three pigs, the phone's pepper spray was changed to wolf mace, and the beacon "beep" to a "pig squeak."

The Failed Delusions group selected this scenario:

> *I would use devices in my cell phone to record law enforcement, when they choose to harass me.*

Instead of changing the phone functions and features, this group responded with a policy, namely that persons in any form of military or law enforcement role would be prohibited from purchasing their device.

The BOB and the Motorola Stupid Martian groups each selected a value scenario and did not make any changes. Instead of exploring new ideas, both groups used their value scenario as an evaluation tool to highlight key features and functions of their initial designs.

The BOB group selected this scenario:

> *I feel when hitching rides, with a cell phone you can be kept safe. If you're walking down the road with your thumb out and a cell phone to your ear a "weirdo" is less likely to pick you up.*

Not making any changes, the BOB group wrote on their spec. sheet: "Our phone turns into a house-boat-car so hitching is pointless. And we're cool."

The Motorola Stupid Martian group selected this scenario:

> *Keep in touch with friends and family and take pic's for the party when ppl getting mess up.*

On their spec. sheet they wrote: "[Our] phone has two cameras and can download apps without WIFI."

The Hassle Free group declined to select a value scenario, giving the following explanation that surfaces critical aspects of the social conditions for and fundamental concerns of homeless young people:

> Simplicity is the best. It keeps everything cost effective. That way I can actually have this phone, not just be talking about it or hearing about it ... You start adding things to phones it starts to cost you and you start to pay for more services, and you don't have it. If it's still cheap everybody can have one. Everybody can be safe. It's all about price. If you price something too expensive, we can't be safe because we won't have any offers of this.

Designer Prompt: Envisioning Cards

Having completed one iteration in response to a stakeholder prompt, participants were instructed to select an Envisioning Card from a set of six and to iterate again. Across all groups, four cards were chosen. We now briefly summarize responses to the cards.

The Squatters Phone (service provider) group selected the SUSTAINED FRIENDSHIP card. While the theme addresses the issue of a technology effecting people's friendships and family relationships, this group generated new ideas around ways to strengthen relations between homeless young people and the service providers. They added a contacts back-up system "so [that] the service providers can always be contacted." Additionally, they suggested an optional rollover program for the "funders/friends" to help homeless young people by donating extra minutes.

The INDESTRUCTABLE (police officer) group selected the CROSSING NATIONAL BOUNDARIES card. While other groups focused on their card's theme, this group focused on the design activity:

> *Choose three countries across the globe and envision challenges for your system if it was deployed in each of those countries. Label any common concerns across the identified challenges.*

For this design activity, they considered the use of their phone in three countries (India, Finland and Mexico) and added four features reflecting diverse socio-technical aspects including cultural dress code, appropriate size of the phone, charging methods, and software modifications.

Turning again to the homeless young people, the Hortical group selected the CHANGING HANDS card. The theme addresses the issue of a technology changing owners during the device's life cycle. Shifting the intent of the card, this group considered short-term borrowing and added a pin-code to their phone to protect it from unauthorized use.

The Brittany Futureproof group also selected the CHANGING HANDS card. Moreover, they also used this card to consider short-term borrowing, adding a button to deactivate the mind-reading function when sharing.

The Failed Delusions group chose the CONSIDER CHILDREN card. In response to the prompt, they considered how their robot phone would interact with children and decided to add an educational program to their design. In order to illustrate their upgrade they created a new sketch on the spec. sheet, showing a child in the robot's hand, reflecting how the robot would talk to a seven-year old.

The Hassle Free group selected the CROSSING NATIONAL BOUNDARIES card and decided to add linguistic software to their phone to help with translation to other languages. Note that the group had declined to select a Stakeholder prompt.

The same two groups – BOB and The Motorola Stupid Martian – did not make any changes to their designs. As with the Stakeholder prompt, they used the designer prompt as an evaluation tool in order to highlight the phone's existing functionality. The BOB group selected the CHANGING HANDS card and determined no changes were needed. They wrote on the spec. sheet that the phone is DNA sensitive and the phone is free so "get your own one" instead of sharing. The Motorola Stupid Martian group selected the SUSTAINED FRIENDSHIP card and wrote on their spec. sheet: "We have all the equipment to keep in contact with friends and family."

DISCUSSION

Co-design Spaces: Engaged Stakeholders and Meaning

The issue of engagement is important and complex. Of many meaningful forms of assessment, counting the number of new features is one; another is characterizing the complexity and nuance of storytelling related to the artifacts. In terms of the sheer number of new features, Table 2 shows that the police officers and service providers can be seen as more engaged than the young people. At the same time, in terms of complexity and nuance of story, homeless young people can be seen to be quite engaged; for example, assessing arguments for not including new features, expressive depth of the sketches, and so on. Consider the prototypes and accompanying narratives holistically. While sometimes fantastical, they reveal a certain pragmatic intelligence and a good deal of creativity. Furthermore, the co-design activity brought forward vital needs, including, for example, the need to be heard and understood, the need to monitor the environment, the need to dispatch information through social networks, and the need for food, transportation, education, and safety.

We believe, on balance, that the co-design method was engaging because it enabled homeless young people to express intimate concerns about their lives in a relatively playful and comfortable manner. Moreover, speculating, the fantastical aspects of the prototypes may have provided a degree of "distance" between the person and the entrenched issues of homelessness, related to basic needs, human dignity, and social justice. Accordingly, it may be the case that our method – with its creative and reflective aspects – is particularly well suited to surfacing the needs and values of participants in intimate or vulnerable situations.

Reflections on Our Use of the Model

We now consider in greater detail how the stakeholder and designer prompts functioned in the co-design space. One question is: in what ways did the prompts expand the co-design space? First, the model prompted participants to generate new ideas. The use of the prompts not only resulted in an increased number of ideas (see Table 2) but, more importantly, it led to divergent thinking. The prompts drew attention to the particular socio-technical setting of use (i.e., value scenarios) and more generally the social and contextual issues that are easily overlooked (i.e., Envisioning Cards). In addition to generating technical possibilities – form and function – participants explored various problem solving strategies such as service design (e.g., rollover minutes by the Squatters Phone) and policy making (e.g., sales restrictions by the Failed Delusions).

Furthermore, the model expanded the co-design space by prompting participants to evaluate and elaborate their initial ideas. In several cases where no changes were made, the selection and interpretation of the prompt provided a clue for understanding participants' perspectives. Using the prompt, participants constructed rationales for their initial design choices and reaffirmed the most critical values and concerns. Evaluation sometimes led to elaboration of underdeveloped ideas. For example, the BOB group evaluated its DNA sensitive feature in response to the CHANGING HANDS card and elaborated on the obsolescence procedure of a person's biological record: "[when the phone becomes obsolete] it goes back to the factory, melted-down and gets made into a new one."

A second, related question is: how, if at all, did participants appropriate and employ the prompts? Both the value scenarios and envisioning cards proved flexible and suggestive; participants were able to derive meanings from the prompts that were applicable to their participation situations. For example, rather than following what is inscribed, the service providers selected the SUSTAINED FRIENDSHIP card and applied it to the relationship between themselves, homeless young people, and funders. Showing the multiple uses, the Envisioning Cards in particular provoked variety of access. Many participants focused on the theme, while the INDESTRUCTABLE group engaged the design activity, and the Motorola Stupid Martians group focused on the image and the title only: "I totally didn't read the back of that card." In all cases, the prompts allowed interpretive flexibility and multiple uses to evoke relevant concerns from across multiple stakeholders with diverse backgrounds and experiences.

Open Questions

As with the first use of any new method, there are limitations and open questions. Our case is no exception. In particular, the Value Sensitive Action-Reflection Model presented here has only been used once and only with value scenarios and Envisioning Cards for stakeholder and designer prompts respectively.

To begin discussion of the model we raise four open questions and offer some initial responses: (1) *What purposes can the Value Sensitive Action-Reflection Model serve?* Our short answer: many. Depending on the context and co-design goals, the model could be used to stimulate values assessment, envision futures, move toward realizable designs, as well as other aims; (2) *How do you generate effective stakeholder prompts?* Field data collected from stakeholders about their concerns and perspectives can be a rich source for stakeholder prompts. These data can take the form of stakeholder generated scenarios (as in the case reported here), concept maps, anticipated barriers to use from Futures Workshops, metaphors for system design, and so forth; (3) *How do you generate effective designer prompts*? Best practices, design toolkits, and representations from practicing designers and design researchers can provide innovative material for designer prompts. To be effective with individuals untrained in design, the material will likely need to be packaged in a simple format with straightforward directions for use; and (4) *What data should you collect from the co-design activities and for what purposes?* Recall that the stakeholder and designer prompts are structured interventions to elicit perspectives on value and societal concerns. Collecting data to assess change (before and after use) in response to the prompts provides one systematic type of evidence. Of course, there can be a wide variety of data sources including but not limited to drawings, physical prototypes, use cases, stories, and other representations; and how to characterize change across such a wide range of representations can be challenging.

These four questions merely begin the conversation about how to employ, elaborate, and assess meaningful use of the Value Sensitive Action-Reflection Model.

CONCLUSION

In order to position stakeholders to articulate visions of yet-to-be-built tools and to explore how possible tools relate to the values of individuals, groups, and societies we have sought to develop an appropriate method. On reflection, we recognized that the method we developed for one particular study could be generalized and we have sought to do so through the Value Sensitive Action-Reflection Model.

The data and analyses reported in this paper have shown how imagined tools – by their form, function, and narrative – reflect back on the values and needs of their designers; and, how stakeholder and designer prompts can be used to evolve a co-design space. In addition, we have placed our particular method and general model in the ongoing discourse on how designers and researchers might structure and expand spaces for co-design [3,9,16,19]. The model and methodological detail reported in this paper clarify one particular point of view on co-design. We hope that readers will borrow and appropriate and, in turn, report on their methodological innovations.

ACKNOWLEDGMENTS

Special thanks to all participants for their willingness to consider safety and mobile phones. This research was supported in part by NSF Award CNS-0905384.

REFERENCES

1. Agee, J., and Evans, W. *Let Us Now Praise Famous Men*. First Mariner Books, New York, 1939/2001.
2. Bannon, L. Reimagining HCI: Toward a more human-centered perspective. *interactions 18*, 4 (2011), 50-57.
3. Binder, T., De Michelis, G., Ehn, P., Jacucci, G., Per Linde, P., and Wagner, I. *Design Things*, MIT Press, 2011.
4. Blythe, M. A., and Wright, P. C. Pastiche scenarios: Fiction as a resource for user centered design. *Interacting with Computers*, 18, 5 (2006), 1139-1164.
5. Brandt, E. Designing exploratory design games: A framework for participation in participatory design? In *Proc. PDC 2006*, ACM Press (2006), 57–66.
6. Carroll, J. M. Five reasons for scenario-based design. In *Proc. HICSS 1999*, IEEE (1999), 3051-3061.
7. Cooper, A. and Reimann, R.M. *About Face 2.0*. Wiley Publishing, Indianapolis, IN, 2003.
8. Czeskis, A., Dermendjieva, I., Yapit, H., Borning, A., Friedman, B., Gill, B. T., and Kohno, T. Parenting from the pocket: Value tensions and technical directions for secure and private parent-teen mobile safety. In *Proc. SOUPS 2010*, ACM Press (2010).
9. Ehn., P. Design things: Challenges to design thinking in the tradition of participatory design? In *PDC 2008*, ACM Press (2008), 92-101.
10. Friedman, B., and Hendry, D. G. The Envisioning Cards: A toolkit for catalyzing humanistic and technical imaginations. In *Proc. CHI 2012*, ACM Press (2012), 1145-1148.
11. Friedman B., Kahn P. H., Jr., and Borning, A. Value sensitive design and information systems. In *Human-computer Interaction in Management Information Systems: Foundations*, M.E. Sharpe, Armonk, NY, 2006, 348-372.
12. Friedman, B., Nathan, L. P., Kane, S., and Lin, J. *Envisioning Cards*. University of Washington, Seattle, WA, USA, 2011. Available at: envisioningcards.com
13. Gaver, W., Dunne, T., and Pacenti, E. 1999. Cultural Probes. *interactions*, 6(1), 21-29.
14. Le Dantec, C. A., Christensen, J. E., Bailey, M., Farrell, R. G., Ellis, J. B., Danis, C. M., Kellogg, W. A., and Edwards, W. K. A tale of two publics: Democratizing design at the margins. In *Proc. DIS 2010*, ACM Press (2010), 11-20.
15. Millett, L., Friedman, B., and Felten, E. Cookies and Web browser design: Toward realizing informed consent online. In *Proc. CHI 2001*, ACM Press (2001), 46-52.
16. Muller, M. J. Participatory Design: The Third Space in HCI. In Jacko, J.A., and A. Sears (Eds.), Human-Computer Interaction: Development process. Florida, USA: CRC Press (Taylor & Francis), 2009. 161-181.
17. Nathan, L. P., Friedman, B., Klasjna, P. V., Kane, S. K., and Miller, J. K. Envisioning systemic effects on persons and society throughout interactive system design. In *Proc. DIS 2008*, ACM Press (2008), 1-10.
18. Roberson, J., and Nardi, B. Survival needs and social inclusion: Technology use among the homeless. In *Proc. CSCW 2010*, ACM Press (2010), 445-448.
19. Sanders, E. B.-N., and Westerlund, B. Experimenting, exploring and experimenting in and with co-design spaces. In *Nordic Design Research Conference*, Helsinki (2011), 1-5.
20. Sanders, E. B.-N., and William, C. T. Harnessing people's creativity: Ideation and expression through visual communication. In *Focus Groups: Supporting Effective Product Development*. Taylor and Francis, 2001.
21. Sanders, E. B.-N., and Stapper, P. J. Co-creation and the new landscapes of design. *CoDesign*, 4, 1 (2008), 5-18.
22. Schön, D. A. *The Reflective Practitioner: How Professionals Think in Action*. Basic Books, New York, 1983.
23. Schön, D. A. Problems, frames and perspectives on designing. *Design Studies*, 5, 3 (1984), 135-156.
24. Woelfer, J. P., Iverson, A., Hendry, D. G., Friedman, B., and Gill, B. Improving the safety of homeless young people with mobile phones: Values, form and function. In *Proc. CHI 2011*, ACM Press (2011), 1707-1716.
25. Woelfer, J. P., and Hendry, D. G. Homeless young people and technology: Ordinary interactions, extraordinary circumstances. *interactions* 18, 6 (2011), 70-73.
26. Whitbeck, L. B. *Mental Health and Emerging Adulthood among Homeless Young People*. New York: Psychology Press, 2009.

Configuring Participation: On How We Involve People In Design

John Vines[1], Rachel Clarke[1], Peter Wright[1], John McCarthy[2], and Patrick Olivier[1]
Culture Lab,
School of Computing Science,
Newcastle University, UK
{john.vines, r.clarke, p.c.wright,
patrick.olivier}@ncl.ac.uk
School of Applied Psychology,
University College Cork,
Republic of Ireland
john.mccarthy@ucc.ie

ABSTRACT
The term 'participation' is traditionally used in HCI to describe the involvement of users and stakeholders in design processes, with a pretext of distributing control to participants to shape their technological future. In this paper we ask whether these values can hold up in practice, particularly as participation takes on new meanings and incorporates new perspectives. We argue that much HCI research leans towards *configuring participation.* In discussing this claim we explore three questions that we consider important for understanding how HCI configures participation; Who initiates, directs and benefits from user participation in design? In what forms does user participation occur? How is control shared with users in design? In answering these questions we consider the conceptual, ethical and pragmatic problems this raises for current participatory HCI research. Finally, we offer directions for future work explicitly dealing with the configuration of participation.

Author Keywords
Participation; participatory design; performance art; participatory media.

ACM Classification Keywords
H.5.m [Information interfaces and presentation (e.g., HCI)]: Miscellaneous;

INTRODUCTION
Participation is a subject of great interest to the HCI community. A search of the ACM Digital Library for papers using the term "participatory" returns 115 results across CHI 2012's archived and extended abstract papers. Traditionally, the term's use in HCI has been drawn from participatory design, an approach to the design of technology that calls for democratization and end-user involvement in the design process. The use of the term within the HCI research community often refers to this meaning still, describing the involvement of people in a design process [17,21,33,54], or the gathering of insights and requirements to inform future design [24,56]. The underlying claim here is that their participation in design gives users[1] more control in determining the technologies they might eventually use in work or leisure. More recently "participatory" has come to mean considerably more in HCI than its traditional focus on design processes. Participation might also describe ways of distributing the decision making process within organizations or communities [14,15], to refer to audience involvement in the creation of a digital artwork [45,53], to discuss knowledge sharing on social networks [44,51,52] or unwittingly taking part in the collection of data [13,23]. The tenet of giving users more control is often still apparent in these contexts.

At CHI 2012, John Carroll acknowledged the aforementioned diversification of the term and called for some 'policing of participation' by the HCI community [57]. The concern was that within HCI the term 'participation' is becoming meaningless and often poorly articulated and theorized in papers. This paper contributes to this discussion. We argue that the diversification of participatory HCI—to include perspectives from participatory media, social media, crowd-sourcing and the arts—is a benefit to the community. It opens up the space for thinking about participation in design in broader terms than if we were to restrict ourselves to tight definitions or specific traditions. We are equally aware however that the expansion into new contexts can result in loss of the core values that motivated wider user participation in the first instance. In particular, we are concerned that the expansion of participatory HCI can lead to authors not articulating a number of assumptions within research and practice. These include not accounting for the agency of researchers, funders and the locations of engagement as contributing factors to the quality of user participation. This, we contend, can leave to exaggerated claims about the sharing of control with users.

In order to unpack these concerns we structure the paper around the following: First, we ask what has traditionally

[1] We are very aware of the problematic nature of the term 'user', particularly in multi-faceted participatory work. We use it throughout due to its significance within HCI discourse and the equally problematic nature of using encompassing terms such as 'people' and 'participants'.

been the main value of user participation in design processes within HCI? Second, we contextualize *configuring participation* as both a way of problematizing how HCI sometimes frames user participation in design but also as a tool for thinking about the opportunities a broader definition of participation in design might bring. Third, we discuss the three main issues that configuring participation highlights; that participation can occur at multiple forms of engagement; a lack of articulating who initiates, directs and benefits from research where users participate in design; and the danger of ignoring the expertise and agency of researchers who participate in design processes. Finally, we offer summative conceptual, ethical and pragmatic challenges that this raises in relation to the core values of participation in design. This paper is synergetic with a growing body of work within the broader participatory design community that calls for and provides greater critical reflection on how we involve people in design processes [11,31,47]. Here however we focus on and contribute to the growing discourse on user participation in HCI by unpacking some central conceptual problems emerging in the research performed by the community. We highlight the benefits of a more holistic definition of participation, and provide guidance as to how such a holistic stance might be pursued in the future.

GOALS OF PARTICIPATION

First we explore three of the main goals that have motivated user participation in design processes within HCI: sharing control, sharing expertise and inspiring change.

Sharing control with users

Control and agency were explicit motivating factors in the early Scandinavian Co-operative Design movement [15,42]. The introduction of computers into workplaces prompted concern from workers and their unions that they would no longer have control over their roles and duties or that these roles would be deskilled or replaced altogether [28]. As epitomized by Kristen Nygaard's foundational work [42], the focus of early cooperative design actually involved very little design *per se*. Rather it emphasized the importance of providing these workers and union officials the knowledge and skills about the potential of computational systems so that their views would be better articulated when bargaining with management. In this vein, Caroll and Rosson [14] argue that user participation is primarily motivated by the moral proposition 'that the people whose activity and experiences will ultimately be affected most directly by a design outcome ought to have a substantive say in what that outcome is' [14, p.244]. As the participatory design movement gained traction in the United States the notion of sharing control with relevant end users was still of central importance [38]—albeit often motivated by commercial concerns such as developing more appropriate products and interfaces for market (e.g. [20]).

User participation in a design process—be this implied at the boardroom or explicit involvement in design workshops—is heavily oriented towards destabilizing power structures that might enforce ill-considered technologies on groups who are not typically consulted. In HCI direct user participation is often associated with an agenda to empower groups of people whose views, opinions and needs might be the most ignored by mainstream society. Within HCI, many papers describing participatory processes provide examples of working with groups who might normally be excluded [17,29,54,55], people with very specific health and emotional needs [2,33] or in contexts where the introduction of ICT might be in conflict with cultural traditions [58]. Furthermore, as with the wider transition to the third-wave in HCI, participatory processes have moved beyond work-oriented contexts to deal with subjects such as stroke rehabilitation [2], museum exhibitions for children [48] and residential care [7] (among others). Within all of these examples there is an underlying concern that these groups are often disenfranchised by decisions made in the design of most technologies within the associated domains.

Sharing expertise through boundary objects

Leading on from the moral proposition of control, a pragmatic concern for user participation has been establishing ways to elicit knowledge, values and opinions from users in the design process. In this sense users are understood as a source of information and having certain types of expertise that should be intersubjectively shared and exchanged [14]. Therefore, a considerable emphasis has been placed on developing tools and methods for the elicitation of meaningful and useful information.

An omnipresent element of participatory design processes is the 'workshop'. Design workshops are typically gatherings of project teams (researchers, designers, system experts etc.) with users and stakeholders to identify challenges and develop new ideas. Ehn [15,16] refers to how the setting of such workshops is typically situated around the formation of 'boundary objects' [49], which act as shared articulations of knowledge of those participating in the design process. For example, Ehn discusses how participatory design workshops would involve the acting out of scenarios by workers with cardboard boxes that serve as imaginary computers [16]. Over the past two decades a number of workshop techniques have been developed that offer defined structures to the elicitation process. Methods such as future workshops [27], metaphorical design [35], and inspiration cards [20] all offer different approaches to provoke participants to articulate their existing practices and their concerns through such boundary objects.

As HCI has moved beyond workplaces as a focal point of studies researchers have adapted the approaches to eliciting information from users (e.g. [4,6,7,17,56]). Designing with people living with dementia requires a very different approach to designing with factory workers or office staff. As Lindsay et al. [33] discuss at length, the former requires the development of longer-term relationships with participants through regular contact, sessions often need to repeat what was discussed before, and very little 'work' is done at the sessions themselves. Similarly, in residential care homes, participation from residents might be highly passive and researchers must be far more interpretive of and responsive to their needs [7]. In these cases elicitation is still a key quality of user participation but the manner in which it is captured, interpreted and embodied in boundary objects changes radically.

Individual, organizational and technological change

Another set of qualities associated with participation in design is motivating some form of change through the design process. Returning again to the Scandinavian cooperative design work, a key concern was that of reflecting current practices and inspiring subsequent change. Ehn [15] argued that user participation in design is a balance between an articulation of 'tradition' (i.e., what are peoples' current practices, experiences, etc – and how can we make best use of these in design) and 'transcendence' (i.e., how can people imagine possible futures, let go of current 'limiting' practice, or reflect on what they do). Bødker [8] has since argued that her experience as an advocate for participatory design has been to highlight to participants that there are alternatives available to them. This emancipatory view of participation highlights how a central aim was to alert users to their own a voice and enable them to use it.

User participation has been more explicitly design-orientated when introducing new technologies to inspire organizational and community change. Hayes [22] describes participatory approaches as having a lineage in action research, highlighting the significance of organizational and individual change as a key concern of early participatory design research. Here, participation becomes framed as an interventionist practice where new ideas, processes and 'lenses' [8] are introduced to provoke change. As such, approaches such as technology probes [25] and provotypes [37] fit in this space if incorporated into a long-term cyclical approach where the prototype is deployed to provide insight into changing work, home or community practices.

Another motivation behind user participation in design processes is that this will change future technology design to improve peoples' lives [14]. In one sense this implies new designs are improvements over existing technologies as they are more sensitive to the needs and desires of specific user groups. In another sense this also means that these designs, again, act as boundary objects with which to challenge the perceptions of stakeholders or to provoke discussion about key societal issues. Vines et al [55] describe their design work with groups of people aged over 80, with whom they collaboratively designed new payment technologies, which were then used as boundary objects for discussion with the British banking industry. Another example that takes a rather different approach to communicating the outcomes of working with users is Alan F. Newell and colleagues' 'intermediary theater' [40]. Newell et al. work with professional actors to use theatrical performance in order to alter student and professional designers' attitudes towards older people. In these cases the researchers used these intermediaries as tools for communicating the needs of those groups they had been working with to key decision makers and young designers.

Summary: learning and sharing expertise

Central to the above values is that people are resourceful and skillful and researchers should establish ways for this knowledge to be shared, communicated and embodied in technology design. By cooperating and forming boundary objects we provide spaces for knowledge and skills to be shared and inspire preferable future states. We consider these important values for HCI in general—but we also question how these goals have been maintained as the scope for user participation in design has expanded.

CONFIGURING PARTICIPATION

To help us in our exploration of the values of participation in contemporary HCI research, we first make a proposition: rather than engaging in *participatory design* HCI researchers instead engage in acts of *configuring participation*. That is to say that the primary work being undertaken here is the design of the process—i.e. the configuration of the experience of participation itself. Johan Redström's work on 'user design' [43] is a useful starting point for explaining our argument. Redström suggests that although design disciplines (including HCI) have transitioned from considering users as cognitive information processors to generative agents of rich cultural experiences, there is still a predominant interest in 'fitting' people to technologies. While the terminology and models of the world that the discipline uses have diversified, the fundamental drive to ensure technology and people match one-another has not. In particular by focusing on 'users' we do our designing around the notion of 'use' and how we can ensure that people can become 'users' with as much simplicity as possible. He argues:

> '[i]t is user design in the sense that it is design where the processes through which people turn into users are in focus and where the explicit aim is to work with the results of this process, i.e., how use and user should turn out. We, as designers, turn people into users by means of our designs, by presenting a thing to be used. By making the desired interpretation of the objects obvious and impossible to resist, we aim to design not only the object itself but also the perception, and even the experience, of it. Indeed, the terms 'user testing' and 'user evaluations' can be read in two rather different ways.' [43, p.129]

Redström argues against tight couplings between models of users and design outcomes. It echoes long-held arguments that manifest in HCI regarding systems designers who are eager to predict how people will act around their creations and the messiness of the situated actions that occur [50].

Focusing so much on determining who will be the eventual user of a technology leads us to forget that very often much designing occurs during use (as noted by many social historians of technology [41]). However we also believe that this argument provides insight into the problems of participation in design. Redström alerts us to how 'user design' manifests in complex scenarios where multiple disciplinary perspectives and stakeholders come together to determine who it is that is most likely to benefit from technologies in certain domains and contexts. We take Redström's argument further, considering that not only does HCI lean towards 'user design' in respect to the design of new technologies, but 'user design' occurs when we configure the process of participation. That is to say decisions made before and during user participation impact heavily on the quality of their involvement in design. This subsequently raises a number of problems related to the core goals of participation. Specifically, we argue that there are three key issues that need raising:

Forms of participation: It is rarely articulated how user participation in design occurs in different forms of interaction and engagement. This occurs not just when comparing projects but also across the timescale of individual projects and, undeniably, within workshops, meetings and other interactions between participants, researchers, stakeholders and partners.

Initiators and beneficiaries: Very often it is researchers, designers or funders who initiate user involvement, and decisions are made about who should and should not participate in projects. This also raises questions about who it is that benefits from user participation in design.

Sharing control: While a core value of user participation is the sharing of control with users, this can mask the agency, expertise and agendas of the researchers or designers leading or facilitating the participatory process.

These three issues we collectively consider important elements for understanding how HCI engages in configuring participation. In the following sections we go through each of these issues individually. It is our argument that these are issues shared across a number of 'participatory' subjects in HCI. Emerging fields of HCI research such as participatory media, crowd-sourcing and performance art in many ways share the core goals of participation in design: to share control beyond the designer, to elicit and share human expertise and to motivate change. At the same time they provide lenses with which to make these goals somewhat problematic. In discussing these issues we draw upon examples from these fields to illustrate our concerns and to consider future directions for user participation in design.

IN WHAT FORM DOES PARTICIPATION OCCUR?

Our first consideration is that very rarely is it considered that when users do participate in design processes that these can happen at very different degrees of engagement—not just between projects but also often within an individual project over time. In other 'realms' of participation—such as participatory media and the performance arts—there is a critical awareness to the degrees at which people contribute to a particular project. We discuss these in turn below.

Defining participatory media is in itself not a simple task. Most contemporary definitions (e.g. [44]) state that participatory media is 'many-to-many' media where all people connected to a specific network can receive text, images, audio and video (and more) from all others on a network. While there are substantial differences between the notions of participatory media and participatory design, there are also a number of synergies in their underlying principles. For example, much of the rhetoric surrounding participatory media refers to how users are given more of a share in the production of content and become prosumers (producer-consumers) [36]. As such, users of participatory media are both active producers and passive consumers of media. While participatory media can support prosumption, the levels at which users engage with such media can vary dramatically. Bernoff and Li's [5] 'social technographs' framework groups users of participatory media into 6 categories: creators, critics, collectors, joiners, spectators and inactives. Here, users of participatory media range from those who actively upload videos and music or write blogs through to those who just comment on websites and those who just spectate, consuming the media provided by other users. Of course, individuals might blur into multiple categories—but the insight here is that the forms of engagement in participatory media are diverse and continually fluctuate.

This can be illustrated by a common example—YouTube. Although YouTube has over 800 million unique users each month [59] it is estimated that only approximately 20% of these regularly upload content and post comments on the website [5]. The remainder primarily view videos. YouTube's participatory and business model is driven by this spectatorship. Relatively passive interactions such as these add to the view counts of videos, adding to Google's and the video uploader's advertising revenue and, if popular enough, raising it in the 'currently being watched' pages. This, in turn, generates further views. Recommended videos appear to the side, eliciting spectators to continue to watch related videos and, as such, generating further views and revenue. While there is much evidence of user-generated content throughout, the experience of YouTube is very much designed to facilitate the engagement of spectators.

We can also turn to examples from within digital and performance art that explore the different forms of engagement that occurs between performers, spectators and audience members. Benford et al. [3] distinguish the *audience* from *bystanders* in understanding the experiences of spectators of Blast Theory's mixed reality game *Uncle Roy All Around You*. Here, a virtual game is explored and acted out on the streets of a busy city center where players interact with performers acting as characters from the game. Benford et al. describe how the audience are spectators who are 'witting', in the sense that they are aware that the performance is taking place and can attempt to interpret the performers actions. Bystanders are 'unwitting' in that although they are implicated as spectators they are unaware of the performance and therefore unable to interpret actions as that belonging to a performance. This has some resonance with design processes where users unwittingly participate in the development of a new technology. Take, for example, some of the tactics used by Google in their development of their Voice Search [18] functionality on Android's JellyBean operating system. One of the reasons why Google's voice tool is so advanced is that in 2007 they started a freephone business directory service called GOOG-411. The service was popular, possibly due to it being free compared to the relatively expensive services already available in the US and Canada. The primary reason for the services existence, however, was to enable Google to collect a large database of voice and phoneme data to underpin its speech recognition algorithms [39]. Once this was achieved GOOG-411 was closed down. Putting aside Google's ethically suspect data collection methods and the political values associated with this company, there is a sense with this example that users have unwittingly participated in the definition of a new technology.

It occurs to us that these discussions on forms of engagement highlight limitations in the way in which user participation is understood in HCI. First, it alerts us to how user participation in design is much broader in scope than is often maintained. For example, those who happen to be walking to work or doing their shopping become implicated as spectators of performances occurring within the city landscape. The more passive users of YouTube who 'spectate' have a stake in shaping the experience of others who come to use the website. Those who used Google's directory services contribute data that is used to design the architecture for future services. These highlight how users might participate in the design of new systems through unwitting actions. These processes are still participatory in the sense that small contributions hold significant weight on the outcome and experiences of others.

Second, we observe how user participation in design processes is equally as complex in terms of forms of participation as it is in participatory media and performance art. It alerts us to how participation in 'x' process can never be framed as a binary in or out. Users can participate in ways that are witting, unwitting, spectator-like, as a reflexive commentator or as a creator that leads the participation of others. We are not suggesting here that user participation should occur in multiple forms at one time but that it already does so. In design workshops, meetings, interviews and forums individuals engage and contribute in very different ways. Some participants are passive, some vocal. Some engage with the topic at hand, some deviate into unrelated but equally important issues. Perhaps more disconcerting—as with the Google example—participants might contribute to a project under one pretense but their input is extrapolated in new ways. Light [30] alerts us to how in participatory design there is rarely any reflection on the micro-dynamics of interaction between participants and researchers and the impact this has on participatory processes. Articulating these different forms of participation along with the scale of such interactions [30] is a crucial consideration when configuring participation.

WHO INITIATES AND BENEFITS?

Projects of participation require 'actors' to initiate them and to direct them over time. In HCI however it is rarely discussed who initiates participation, who benefits, and how this is directed over time. We might assume that initiation is led by members of the project team performing a study or designing a particular system. It is often these individuals who recruit participants, lead workshops and act as a point of contact for those taking part. If we continue tracing back initiation however, those who write research proposals (such as faculty members) or stakeholders and funding organizations that write the call for proposals and policy documents to which they respond heavily influence this process. Clearly the array of actors implicated in initiating wider user participation in design is complex and diverse. We consider that understanding who it is that initiates and benefits from such action is important as it impacts upon who participates and where it is performed.

First, let us discuss issues to do with who participates. Our contention here is that the settings within which participation is initiated has a significant impact on the quality of participation and also who it is that gets involved. In order to problematize this, we take another example from participatory media. Over the last several years there has been increased interest in 'democratic innovation' sites such as OpenIDEO and Innocentive where members of the public are encouraged to participate in helping to solve societal challenges. Such a challenge might be: 'How might we restore vibrancy in cities and regions facing economic decline?' [34]. Members of the community can then add suggestions in comments, add photos and drawings, comment on ideas and vote ideas up and down until, over time, 'winning' ideas are selected. The point to be made here is that, in reality, such democratic innovation sites tend to draw in those most inclined to participate in design innovations (i.e, designers, creatives, consultants and business people). The language on such sites support this, where 'challenges' go through a temporal sequence of refinement, evaluation, conceptualisation and realisation—the language associated with an expertise in design rather than everyday terminology that is more widely accessible. Therefore, one of the key issues at hand here is that while the provision of new tools imply democratization and giving agency to disenfranchised users, these tools often have a tendency to be most appropriated by those whose voices will likely already be listened to [6].

In contexts where designers, researchers and participants are collocated there are similar issues to be raised about who initiates participation and where. Writing candidly for a moment, the lead author has worked on a project where older participants were invited from an existing advocacy and research panel. These participants—unbeknownst to the researchers at the time—had for over 20 years taken part in studies at a University, which mostly exploring the longitudinal changes on their memory in later life. Although the project in this case was focused on understanding their experiences in a particular domain to inform technology design and policy work, for some time there was some suspicion from participants that researchers were 'testing' them. When given probe-like packs to take home with them they often referred to them as 'homework' and would complete all that was asked. This called into question the knowledge being shared—i.e., how meaningful is probe data if it is considered homework? Furthermore, it heightened attention to the difficulties surrounding the role of participants from advocacy groups and research panels acting on behalf of or as representatives of their peers. These become particularly pertinent issues when claims are made about the inclusion of often excluded members of society—i.e., just how meaningful is this form of participation when the participants have been in and out of Universities for 20 years? This illustrates that very often the manner in which user participation is initiated and the settings it takes place in can heavily shape the design process.

Second, having questioned who it is that initiates user participation in design processes, it is also worthwhile questioning who it is that is benefitting. As we noted at the start of the paper, one key goal of user participation is that it leads to some form of change—to participants, to society, or to organizations. While Ehn [15] aspired for participants to experience transcendence, it is very rare that the benefits for participants are articulated in HCI research. Iversen et al. [26] have called for a return to a focus on the personal gains of participants in participatory design processes. Although there are examples of reflective interviews following up on the experiences of participants (e.g. [10,11,32]) these are rare.

In the aforementioned context of OpenIDEO it is quite transparent as to who gains from user participation. Although the 'contributors' own the ideas proposed in response to challenges, many are sponsored by commercial enterprises (such as Nokia, Barclays Bank) and we might infer that a number of the "better" ideas are placed into practice by these organizations. In the context of academic research it is a little harder to identify the beneficiaries. In the UK context we might ascertain that, again, a number of the beneficiaries are in commercial organizations. In order to be successful in bidding for research grants many projects now have to have industrial partners that are involved in the research throughout. This fits in with a wider agenda within the UK where research councils have to provide evidence to their funders (the Government) as to the wider societal and economic impact the work they pay for has on the nation. In this context understanding whom these beneficiaries are is important as it might identify situations where user participation becomes extrapolated.

Furthermore, it would also be fair to assume that the researchers leading the research gain from user participation. For example, Vines et al. [55,56] briefly refer to how the experience of meeting regularly with eighty year olds to discuss concerns about access to banking made them reflect on their own financial habits. Researchers do nonetheless gain from user participation in many other ways as well. Data from workshops and ethnographies acts as the basis for arguing why certain decisions have been made in the design process ("this feature was incorporated based upon feedback from our co-designers"). Having information from participants—paper prototypes, transcribed data, sketched scenarios—provides not only valuable information for design but for evidencing that these eventual designs represent the views of users. This data is typically included in conference presentations and archived papers, and offers a sense of transparency between the participants and the manner in which this is interpreted and documented by researchers [9]. We do not mean to be overtly critical here—and certainly the authors of this paper have performed this practice in the past and will continue to do so—but it alerts us to how, in Iversen et al's terms, researchers 'gain' from user participation in design.

HOW IS CONTROL SHARED?

Our final issue to consider is the ways in which control is shared with users. Here we do not question whether control *is shared* but to what *degree it is shared* and what role might the researcher play here. The manner in which control is shared can in itself alter significantly depending on the manner in which participation is configured, the methods used and the degree to which the design process is bound. Again, we believe there is insight to be gained here from work just outside the normal HCI literature on participation, in work undertaken in the digital performing arts. We use this to highlight the nuances of sharing control.

One of the primary concerns within the interactive and performance arts is the exploration of the relationships between the triad of the artwork, the artist and those who participate in experiencing the work (the audience, spectator, viewer etc.). Influential semiotics and aesthetic theorists such as Umberto Eco and Ernst Gombrich have long argued that the meaning of works of art—be this literary works, visual art or performance pieces—are shaped by the artist but left incomplete in order for spectators, readers and viewers to complete. These notions have been appropriated *en masse* in the field of digital art, often on the assumption that digital technologies provide a rich ground for exploring more active and interactive spectatorships [19]. These principles have also fed into a number of examples of performance art in HCI (e.g.

[45,53]). One such example is the *humanaquarium*, an interactive installation where two musical performers (a soprano and a synth/mandolin player) sit inside a plain looking box [53]. The acrylic front of the box acts as both a transparent window to the performers and as a touch-enabled surface. On the rear wall behind the performers are projected visualizations that respond to the voice of the soprano. Audience members could interact directly with the touch-sensitive front panel resulting in alterations to the sound outputs and the visualizations on the rear of the box. Furthermore, the *form of engagement* from the audience had a significant affect on the aesthetic quality of the performance. If the audience was less engaged then the enclosed performers would try to entice them in and *initiate* interaction. A third-member would pretend to be an audience member, demonstrating how to interact with the screen. Although the functional qualities of the work changed little over the course of a year, the performers described how they came to understand the piece better over time. They *benefitted* from being sensitized to how their expressivity as performers would often be a hindrance to shyer audience members coming forward to interact directly. They learnt how to adapt their performance to specific contexts and different audiences and start 'designing from within' the box.

As with the goals of user participation, audience involvement in the creation of the *humanaquarium* is crucial. Tensions emerge however regarding how control is distributed to the audience. While it illustrates to us the messy boundary between artist, spectator and artwork whilst the performance is in progress it also emphasizes how the finality of the artwork is in the hands of the artist. Taylor et al. [53, p.1863] explicitly refer to the inherent tensions they faced as artists who desired to 'introduce more complex structures, musical motifs and visual narratives and [... interact ...] with each other musically' and the need to contingently simplify the aesthetic 'product' to facilitate audience interaction. While the artists are reacting to the behaviors of the audience the finality of these interactions—in how they lead to the production of the performance—are interpreted by the practitioner. Similarly, those audience members who reconfigure the visualization and the audio output are operating within a predetermined set of variables that were defined when the system was designed. The performance itself is an *act* of collaboration as those interacting with it are still working within the realms of the artist(s) intent. But at the same time, the piece is not complete without their presence and engagement in the work.

The *humanaquarium* example is useful as it problematizes the relationships between researchers and users in participatory HCI. As alluded to by Brown et al. [12], it is quickly forgotten how researchers themselves have specific sets of expertise, make judgments and have agendas that they bring as co-participants in design. Although researchers act under the pretext of sharing control with users, they still act as interpreters through which activities are organized, discussions facilitated and, typically, sessions are recorded, documented and then archived. While users might be involved in the formation of boundary objects, very often researchers determine the ways in which these are staged. The fact that very often user involvement occurs in 'design sessions' or 'workshops' illustrates some of our issues here—this is the language of the designer and not those of 'users' (and, of course, the same problems can be said of the word 'user'). As such, we might ask here what decisions are being made and by whom—and whether there are ways in which, like the *humanaquarium*, the sharing of questions and decisions might change over time. In long-term participatory work covering months and years such filters might become less evident but undoubtedly still a factor. As such, while control is certainly shared, it must not be forgotten that the researcher is as crucial an agent in the participatory process as any other participant.

PARTICIPATORY CHALLENGES AND FUTURES

Echoing recent calls for greater critique and reflection on how participatory research is performed and communicated [47], we have alerted the HCI community to some problems inherent in research that involves users as participants, partners or collaborators in design. We have suggested that while there is a humanistic and democratic impulse within participatory research, we must be aware of the fundamental agency of the researchers and designers in configuring the process of participation and its outcomes. By alerting the community to issues about control and agency, we by necessity need to ask questions about the motives of involving people in design—particularly who initiates participation, and who benefits from it. Furthermore, we have highlighted the limitations of tight definitions of participation in design as it distracts us from articulating and exploring how participation can occur to varying degrees of engagement and witting-ness. In this concluding section we restate these concerns in the form of conceptual, ethical and pragmatic problems, and suggest some future strategies to navigate through them.

Conceptual challenges: One of the tenets of involving users as partners or collaborators in design processes is that they are given more control in defining their own technological futures. This, we have contended, can fail to acknowledge the still considerable agency of researchers and their responsibilities to funders and other stakeholders. Furthermore, we have highlighted how the changing landscape in HCI through participatory media, performance art and novel data collection techniques necessitates a much broader understanding of what user participation means. Participation can be highly passive and even unwitting but still potentially satisfying for those involved.

Ethical challenges: These are ethical in the sense that when we configure participation we must make explicit the influencing factors that leads to certain individuals participating over others. While strictly determining who can and cannot be involved is often done so to bound the design (and subsequently the use) space, this reduces the potential to incorporate diverse voices in the design process and can lead to the voices that are heard most often being rearticulated. There are also ethical concerns in that it is not always clear to those who participate how their data and 'voices' will be represented and what they will be used for. Furthermore, unwitting participation implies an element of deception or at the very least a lack of full informed consent for those taking part. As such, unwitting forms of participation highlights a lack in existing procedures of ethics committees and review boards in accurately assessing ethical issues in participatory research.

Pragmatic challenges: In not explicitly considering the issues raised in this paper—such as in what form do people engage in design, how is control shared, and who initiates, benefits and leads the research— many research opportunities are lost. By predetermining who participates we immediately limit the potential for our designs. Furthermore, by working with those that best fit our agendas, methods and expertise the research we perform is less challenging, innovative and inclusive.

In response to these challenges we suggest four future strategies.

Transparency in documentation: Configuring participation is often motivated by agendas, either those of researchers, their employers, funders, or project partners and stakeholders. *A priori* agendas can impact upon the outcomes of the project or at the very least how they are documented and archived. This is not to suggest that researchers purposely misrepresent a project or misguide participants—rather we are just aware that it is easy for the agendas and values of researchers to implicitly affect how qualitative work is interpreted. A simple way of maneuvering through these issues is to be more transparent in personal agendas from the start. In view of this we add to the growing call for researchers to make their stance explicitly known from the offset in publications [9] and for greater candor in how processes are documented [1]. Such sincerity however should incorporate multiple perspectives and voices, and not just those of the researchers.

Explore preconceptions: We consider transparency important in the process itself regarding the expertise and preconceptions shared by the researchers and those taking part in the research. The impulse to configure participation leads to a number of assumptions being made about whom should and should not be involved in HCI research. We suggest that this could in itself be looked on positively and integrated into design work. Once we accept that preconceptions exist, then designers and participants can collaborate with one another to identify in what ways these assumptions need to be reconfigured. Here we contend that the participants might need to test their own assumptions as much as the researchers. One example that touches on this is the questionable concept technique, which merges concept designs and prior contextual data (excerpts from interviews) with opportunities for participants to comment on the ideas and, more importantly, the contexts they were inspired from and the values embedded within by the researchers [56].

Configure multiple forms: We have argued that participation in design occurs not just at the state of yes and no, in and out, but across degrees of awareness and engagement within the design process. We have not had the space to fully scope this out, but we consider it important that future work considers configuring participation across all manner of forms. This might include situations where users are involved very passively, to those where activists and advocates direct and shape the agenda, to situations where participants are guided by researchers. Our point here has been that all manner of forms and levels of participation are in play at any moment in time already—it is that these are rarely articulated or made sense of. Furthermore, this reveals opportunities for exploring how participation can be more open and reflexive, to support people to offer as much and as little as they desire but still feel they have contributed. Simon [46] alerts us to how in the context of a museum, visitor participation can occur at a variety of levels—and we contend that having multiple forms in a single project leads to a richer participatory environment. At the same time, this is not to suggest a hierarchy to these forms, and that one form of participation should be given greater credence than others.

Another concern we have raised is that configuring participation might lead to those whose voices are most likely to be heard being listened to again. We consider being flexible in where we set the boundaries for participation important if the voices of those less likely to become involved are to be reached. Those less likely to take part do not always do so because researchers do not identify them—they simply just do not have the motivations and desires to participate. One result of a more lightweight framing of participation might be the opportunity to identify novel and less intrusive ways to bring these views into the design process.

Participants reconfigure the process: Finally, it occurs to us that as well as taking part in the design process, there are opportunities here for users to be given a greater share in *defining* the design process. It is not unusual for researchers to involve users and participants in defining the problem space [6] but it is less often that participants are offered a stake in defining the process and tools that might resolve these problems. We imagine that providing users opportunities to define the methods, tools and techniques used to create boundary objects would be a fruitful area to explore different forms of participation and different degrees of sharing control in the design process. In this sense, while the researcher might come to the users with a configuration in mind, opportunities are provided for it to be reconfigured over time.

CONCLUSION

In this paper our goal has been to bring to attention the plurality of participation in HCI and the problems and possibilities this brings to future research. We have called for a more nuanced understanding about how control is shared between researchers and participants, for the initiators and beneficiaries to be more explicitly revealed and for there to be a broadened and more reflexive understanding regarding the forms which participation can occur in. These issues are currently neglected within HCI literature. Furthermore, neglecting these issues may mean we loose sight of the core goals of user participation in design that the community has articulated for nearly 30 years. Even so, we should also be prepared to allow traditions to develop and change. These are very exciting times indeed, and with new technologies comes new audiences and new perspectives on what design could and should be. These are opportunities not to be missed.

ACKNOWLEDGMENTS

This research was performed as part of 'SALT', funded by the TSB ALIP 3 and 4 programmes (project code 2377-25137). We thank those who through conversation and discussion have inspired this paper, in particular Ann Light, Tuck Leong, Ole Iversen, Jack Carroll, Susanne Bødker and Gary Marsden.

REFERENCES

1. Akama, Y., and Light, A. A candor in reporting: designing dexterously for fire preparedness. In: *Proc. CHI EA '12*, ACM (2012), 281-290.
2. Balaam, M., Egglestone, S., Fitzpatrick, G., Rodden, T., et al. Motivating mobility: designing for lived motivation in stroke rehabilitation. In: *Proc. CHI '11*, ACM, 3073-3082.
3. Benford, S., Crabtree, A., Reeves, S., Sheridan. J., Dix, A., et al. The Frame of the Game: Blurring the Boundary between Fiction and Reality in Mobile Experiences. In: *Proc. CHI '06*, ACM (2006), 427-436.
4. Benton, L., Johnson, H., Ashwin, E., Brosnan, M., Grawemeyer, B. Developing IDEAS: Supporting children with autism within a participatory design team. In: *Proc. CHI '12*, ACM, 2599-2608.
5. Bernoff, G., and Li, C. *Groundswell: Winning in a World Transformed by Social Technologies.* Cambridge, Harvard University Press, 2008.
6. Bjorgvinsson, E., Ehn, P., and Hillgren, P. Agonistic participatory design: Working with marginalized social movements. *CoDesign*, 8 (2-3), 127-144.
7. Blythe, M., Wright, P., Bowers, J., Boucher, A., Jarvis, N., Reynolds., P., Gaver, W. Age and experience: Ludic engagements in a residential care home. In: *Proc. DIS '10*, ACM (2010), 161-170.
8. Bødker, S. A is for alternatives. *Scandinavian Journal of Information Systems*, 15 (1), 1-3.
9. Borning, A., and Muller, M. Next steps for value sensitive design. In: *Proc. CHI '12*, ACM (2012), 1125-1134.
10. Bossen, C., Dindler, C., and Iversen, O. User gains and PD aims: Assessment from a participatory design project. In: *Proc. PDC '10*, ACM (2010), 141-150.
11. Bossen, C., Dindler, C., and Iversen, O. Impediments to user gains: Experiences from a critical participatory design project. In: Proc. PDC '12, ACM, 51-60.
12. Brown, B., Reeves, S., and Sherwood, S. Into the wild: Challenges and opportunities for field trial methods. In: *Proc. CHI '11*, ACM (2011), 1657-1666.
13. Calabrese, F., Di Lorenzo, G., Liu, L., and Ratti, C. Estimating origin-destination flows using mobile phone location data. *Pervasive Computing*, IEEE (2011), 36-44.
14. Caroll, J., and Rosson, M. Participatory design in community informatics. *Design Studies*, 28, 243-261.
15. Ehn, P. *Work-oriented design of computer artifacts.* Arbetslivscentrum, Stockholm, 1989.
16. Ehn, P., and Kyng, M. Cardboard computers: Mocking-it-up and hands-on the future. In: Greenbaum, J and Kyng, M. *Design at work: Cooperative design of computer systems.* Lawrence Erlbaum, Hillsdale, 1991.
17. Frauenberger, C., Good, J., Keay-Bright, W, and Pain, H. Interpreting Input from Children: A Designerly Approach. In: *Proc. CHI '12*, ACM (2012), 2377-2386.
18. *Google Voice Search* http://www.google.co.uk/mobile/voice-search/
19. Graham, B., and Cook, S. *Rethinking curating: Art after new media.* Cambridge, MIT Press, 2010.
20. Gruen, D. *Storyboarding for design: An overview of the process.* Cambridge, Lotus Research, 2000.
21. Halskov, K., and Dalsgard, P. Inspiration card workshops. In. Proc. DIS '06, ACM (2006), 2-11.
22. Hayes, G. The relationship of action research to human-computer interaction. *ToCHI*, 18 (3), 15.
23. Henze, N., Rukzio, E., and Boll, S. Observational and experimental investigation of typing behaviour using virtual keyboards for mobile devices. In: *Proc. CHI '12*, ACM, 2659-2668.
24. Hook, J., Green, D., McCarthy, J., Taylor, S., Wright, P., Olivier, P. A VJ centered exploration of expressive interaction. In: *Proc. CHI '10*, ACM (2010), 1265-1274.
25. Hutchinson, H., Mackay, W., Westerlund, B., et al. Technology probes: Inspiring design for and with families. In: *Proc. CHI '03*, ACM, 17-24.
26. Iversen, O., Halskov, K., and Leong, T. Rekindling Values in participatory design. In: *Proc. PDC '10*, ACM (2010), 91-100.
27. Jungk, R., Mullert, N. *Future workshops: How to create desirable futures.* Institute for Social Inventions, London, 1987.

28. Kensing, F., and Blomberg, J. Participatory design: Issues and Concerns. *Computer Supported Cooperative Work*, 7, 167-185.
29. Le Dantec, C. Participation and publics: Supporting community engagement. In: *Proc. CHI '12*, ACM, 1351-1360.
30. Light, A. The unit of analysis in understanding the politics of participatory practice. In: *Proc. PDC '10*, ACM, 183-186.
31. Light, A., and Akama, Y. The human touch: participatory practice and the role of facilitation in designing with communities. In: *Proc. PDC '12*, ACM Press (2012), 61-70.
32. Light, A., Wakeford, T., Egglestone, P., and Roger, J. research on an equal footing? A UK collaborative inquiry into community and academic knowledge. In: Proc. IKTC '11,
33. Lindsay, S., Brittain, K., Jackson, D., Ladha, C., Ladha, K., and Olivier, P. Empathy, participatory design and people with dementia. In: *Proc. CHI '12*, ACM (2012), 521-530.
34. OpenIDEO. http://www.openideo.com/open/vibrant-cities/brief.html
35. Madsen, K. A guide to metaphorical design. In: *Com. ACM*, 37 (12), 57- 62.
36. Miller, V., *Understanding digital culture*. New York, Sage, 2011.
37. Mogensen, P. Towards a provotyping approach in systems development. *Scandinavian journal of information systems*, 3, 1991, 31-53.
38. Muller, M., and Druin, A. Participatory design: The third space in HCI. In: Sears, A., and Jacko, J (eds.) The Human-Computer Interaction Handbook (3rd Edition). Lawrence Erlbaum, Hillsdale, 2012, 1125-1154.
39. New York Times. *Google's data advantage over Apple's siri*. http://bits.blogs.nytimes.com/2012/07/19/googles-data-advantage-over-apples-siri
40. Newell, A., Morgan, M., Gibson, L., and Forbes, P. Experiences with professional theatre for awareness raising. *Interacting with computers*, 23 (6), 594-603.
41. Nye, D. *Technology matters*. Cambridge, MIT Press, 2006.
42. Nygaard, K. The iron and metal project: Trade union participation. In: Sandberg, A. *Computers Dividing Man and Work – Recent Scandinavian Research on Planning and Computers from a Trade Union Perspective*. Utbildningsproduktion, Malmø, Sweden.
43. Redstrom, J. Towards user design? On the shift from object to user as the subject of design. *Design studies*, 27, 2, 123-139.
44. Rheingold, H. Using participatory media and public voice to encourage civic engagement. In: Bennett, W (ed.). *Civic life online: Learning how digital media can engage youth*. Cambridge, MIT Press, 2008.
45. Sheridan, J., Bryan-Kinns, N., Reeves, S., Marshall, J., and Lane, G. Graffito: Crowd-based performative interaction at festivals. In: *Proc. CHI EA '11*, ACM, 1129-1134.
46. Simon, N. *The participatory museum*. Museum 2.0, Sant Cruz, 2010.
47. Simonsen, J., and Robertson, T. Routledge International Handbook of Participatory Design. Routledge, New York, 2013.
48. Smith, R., and Iversen, O. When the museum goes native. *Interactions*, 18 (5), ACM (2011), 15-19.
49. Star, S., Griesemer, J. Institutional ecology, 'translations', and boundary objects: amateurs and professionals in Berkeley's museum of vertebrate zoology, 1907-39. *Social studies of science*, 19, 3, 387-420.
50. Suchman, L. *Plans and situated actions. The problem of human-machine communication*. Cambridge, Cambridge University Press, 1987.
51. Tausczik, Y., Pennebaker, J. Participation in an online mathematics community: Differentiating motivations to add. In: *Proc. CSCW '12*, ACM, 207-216.
52. Tanenbaum, J., Tanenbaum, K., and Wakkary, R. Steampunk as design fiction. In: Proc. CHI '12, ACM (2012), 1583-1592.
53. Taylor, R., Schofield, G., Shearer, J., Wallace, J., et al.. Designing from within: humanaquarium. In: *Proc. CHI '11*, ACM (2011), 1855-1864.
54. Uzor, S., Baillie, L., and Skelton, D. Senior designers: Empowering seniors to design enjoyable falls rehabilitation tools. In: *Proc. CHI '12*, ACM (2012), 1179-1188.
55. Vines, J., Blythe, M., Dunphy, P., Vlachokyriakos, V., Teece, I., Monk, A., and Olivier, P. Cheque Mates: Participatory design of digital payments with eighty somethings. In: Proc. CHI '12, ACM (2012), 1189-1198.
56. Vines, J., Blythe, M., Lindsay, S., Dunphy, P., Monk, A., Olivier, P. Questionable concepts: critique as a resource for designing with eighty somethings. In: *Proc. CHI '12*, ACM (2012), 1169-1178.
57. Vines, J., et al. *Summary Report on CHI 2012 invited SIG: Participation and HCI: Why Involve People in Design?* http://di.ncl.ac.uk/participation/wp-content/blogs.dir/20/ files/2012/09/CHISIGReportFinal.pdf
58. Winschiers-Theophilus, H., Chivuno-Kuria, S., Kapuire, G., Bidwell, N., and Blake, E. Being participated: A community approach. In: *Proc. PDC '10*, ACM (2010), 1-10.
59. Youtube – frequently asked questions. http://www.youtube.com/t/faq

The Efficacy of Human Post-Editing for Language Translation

Spence Green, Jeffrey Heer, and **Christopher D. Manning**
Computer Science Department, Stanford University
{spenceg,jheer,manning}@stanford.edu

ABSTRACT

Language translation is slow and expensive, so various forms of machine assistance have been devised. Automatic machine translation systems process text quickly and cheaply, but with quality far below that of skilled human translators. To bridge this quality gap, the translation industry has investigated *post-editing*, or the manual correction of machine output. We present the first rigorous, controlled analysis of post-editing and find that post-editing leads to reduced time and, surprisingly, improved quality for three diverse language pairs (English to Arabic, French, and German). Our statistical models and visualizations of experimental data indicate that some simple predictors (like source text part of speech counts) predict translation time, and that post-editing results in very different interaction patterns. From these results we distill implications for the design of new language translation interfaces.

Author Keywords

Language translation, post-editing, experiment, modeling

ACM Classification Keywords

H.5.2 Information Interfaces: User Interfaces; I.2.7 Natural Language Processing: Machine Translation

INTRODUCTION

High quality language translation is expensive. For example, the entire CHI proceedings from 1982 to 2011 contain 2,930 papers. Assuming roughly 5,000 words per paper and $0.15 per word—a representative translation rate for technical documents—the cost to translate the proceedings from English to just one other language is $2.2 million. Imagine: this sum is for one conference in one subfield of one academic discipline. To lower this cost, various forms of machine assistance have been devised: *source* (input) aids like bilingual dictionaries; *target* (output) aids such as spelling and grammar checkers; and *post-editing* (see [2]), the manual correction of fully automatic machine translation (MT) output. Language translation in practice is thus fundamentally an HCI task, with humans and machines working in concert.

CHI 2013, April 27–May 2, 2013, Paris, France.

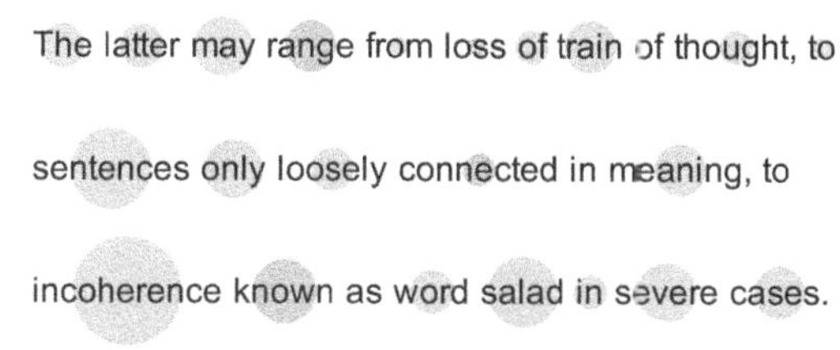

(a) English input sentence with mouse hover visualization

MT:	Celui-ci peut aller de la perte d'un train de la pensée
POST-EDIT:	**Ceux-ci peuvent** aller de la perte **du fil** de la pensée

(b) Post-editing of French MT output

Figure 1: Translation as post-editing. (a) Mouse hover events over the source sentence. The color and area of the circles indicate part of speech and mouse hover frequency, respectively, during translation to French. Nouns (blue) seem to be significant. (b) The user corrects two spans in the MT output to produce a final translation.

Fully automatic MT is almost free, but the output, as represented by state-of-the-art systems such as Google Translate and Bing Translator, is useful for *gisting*—obtaining a rough idea of the translation—but far below the quality of skilled human translators. Nevertheless, the ostensible cost and speed benefits of MT are too appealing to resist, so the translation industry has long incorporated post-editing functionality into translator interfaces. But in terms of translation time and quality—the two variables of primary interest—post-editing has a mixed track record both quantitatively [46, 20] and qualitatively [32, 48]. Some studies have shown decreased translation time but lower quality, and even if speed does increase, translators often express an intense dislike for working with MT output.

This paper presents a controlled experiment comparing post-editing (hereafter "post-edit") to unaided human translation (hereafter "unaided") for three language pairs. We test four hypotheses: (1) post-edit reduces translation time, (2) post-edit increases quality, (3) suggested translations prime the translator, and (4) post-edit results in less drafting (as measured by keyboard activity and pause duration). Our results clarify the value of post-editing: it decreases time and, surprisingly, improves quality for each language pair. It also seems to be a more passive activity, with pauses (as measured by input device activity) accounting for a higher proportion of the total translation time. We find that MT suggestions prime translators but still lead to novel translations, suggesting new possibilities for re-training MT systems with human corrections.

Our analysis suggests new approaches to the design of translation interfaces. "Translation workbenches" like the popular SDL Trados package are implicitly tuned for translation drafting, with auto-complete dialogs that appear while typing. However, when a suggested translation is present, we show that translators draft less. This behavior suggests UI designers should not neglect modes for source comprehension and target revision. Also, our visualizations (e.g., Figure 1) and statistical analysis suggest that assistance should be optimized for certain parts of speech that affect translation time.

We first review prior work on post-editing and machine-assisted translation. Then we describe the translation experiment. Next, we present visual and statistical analyses of the new translation data. Finally, we correlate the visual and statistical results with user feedback, and distill design implications.

RELATED WORK

Translation is a difficult computational task because it is hard to routinize. Consequently, the idea of combining human and machine expertise (see [8, 28]) was one avenue for re-starting machine translation research, which had stalled in the mid-1960s. Industry saw post-editing as one way to aid translators with imperfect contemporary technology, with conferences on the subject convened at least as early as 1981 [33]. Unfortunately, the HCI perspective on MT has been overlooked in natural language processing (NLP), where end-to-end automation of the translation process has been the preeminent goal since the statistical revolution in the early 1990s [35].

This paper unites three threads of prior work: visual analysis of the translation process, bilingual post-editing, and monolingual collaborative translation.[1]

Visual Analysis of the Translation Process

Post-editing involves cognitive balancing of source text comprehension, suggested translation evaluation, and target text generation. When interface elements are associated with these processes, eye trackers can give insight into the translation process. O'Brien [41] used an eye tracker to record pupil dilation for post-editing for four different source text conditions, which corresponded to percentage match with a machine suggestion. She found that pupil dilation, which was assumed to correlate with cognitive load, was highest for the no assistance condition, and lower when any translation suggested was provided.

Carl and Jakobsen [14] and Carl et al. [15] recorded fixations and keystroke/mouse activity. They found the presence of distinct translation phases, which they called *gisting* (the processing of source text and formulation of a translation sketch), *drafting* (entry of the translation), and *revision*, in which the draft is refined. Fixations clustered around source text during gisting, the target text entry box during drafting, and in both areas during revision.

In practice, eye trackers limit the subject sample size due to convenience and cost. We will track mouse cursor movements as a proxy for focus. This data is easy to collect, and correlates with eye tracking for other UIs [16, 26], although we do not explicitly measure that correlation for our task.

[1] See Tatsumi [47] for a broader survey of post-editing.

Bilingual Post-editing

The translation and NLP communities have focused largely on bilingual post-editing, i.e., the users are proficient in both source and target languages. Krings [31] conducted early work[2] on the subject using the Think Aloud Protocol (TAP), in which subjects verbalize their thought processes as they post-edit MT output. He found that the post-edit condition resulted in a 7% decrease in time over the unaided condition on a paper medium, but a 20% increase in time on a computer screen. However, Krings [31] also observed that TAP slowed down subjects by nearly a third.

Later work favored passive logging of translator activity. O'Brien [39] used Translog [27], which logs keyboard and mouse events, to measure the effect of source features on time. Subsequently, O'Brien [42] investigated the hypothesis that longer duration pauses reflect a higher cognitive burden (see [45]) and thus slower translation time. However, both of these experiments focused on the effect of rule-based, language-specific source features (see [7]). For instance, "words that are both adverbs and subordinate conjunctions" (e.g., 'before') were selected. The generality of such rules is unclear.

Guerberof [22] focused instead on comparison of post-edit to unaided. She observed reduced translation time with post-editing—albeit with very high per subject variance—but slightly lower quality according to a manual error taxonomy. However, she used only nine subjects, and did not cross source sentences and conditions, so it was not possible to separate sentence-specific effects.

In contrast, Koehn [29] crossed five blocks of English-French documents with five different translation conditions: unaided, post-edit, and three different modes of interactive assistance. He used 10 student subjects, who could complete the experiment at any pace over a two week period, and could use any type of alternate machine assistance. He found that, on average, all translators produced better and faster translations for the four assisted conditions, but that the interactive modes offered no advantage over post-editing.

Results derived from small data samples and student subjects may not generalize to industrial settings. At Adobe, Flournoy and Duran [19] found that post-editing resulted in a 22-51% decrease in translation time for a small scale task (about 2k source tokens) and 40-45% decrease for a large-scale task (200k source tokens). They also found that MT quality varied significantly across source sentences, with some translations requiring no editing and others requiring full re-translation. Likewise, at Autodesk, Plitt and Masselot [44] found that post-editing resulted in a 74% average reduction in time. Quality was assessed by their corporate translation staff using an unpublished error classification method. The raters found a lower error rate in the post-edit condition.

These large-scale experiments suggested that post-editing reduces time and increases quality. However, at Tilde, Skadiņš et al. [46] also observed reduced translation time for post-edit,

[2] Krings [31] is an English translation of the 1994 thesis, which is based on experiments from 1989-90.

but with a higher error rate for all translators. Like the other industrial studies, they did not report statistical significance.

Garcia [20] was the first to use statistical hypothesis testing to quantify post-editing results. In the larger of his three experiments, he measured time and quality for Chinese-English translation in the unaided vs. post-edit conditions. Statistically significant improvements for both dependent variables were found. Smaller experiments for English-Chinese translation using an identical experimental design did not find significant effects for time or quality. These results motivate consideration of sample sizes and cross-linguistic effects.

Finally, Tatsumi [47] made the only attempt at statistical prediction of time given independent factors like source length. However, she did not compare her regression model to the unaided condition. Moreover, her models included per-subject factors, thus treating subjects as fixed effects. This choice increases the risk of type II errors when generalizing to other human subject samples.

Monolingual Collaborative Translation

In contrast to bilingual post-editing, the HCI community has focused on *collaborative translation*, in which monolingual speakers post-edit human or machine output.[3] Quality has been the focus, in contrast to bilingual post-editing research, which has concentrated on time. Improvements in quality have been shown relative to MT, but not to translations generated or post-edited by bilinguals.

Morita and Ishida [37, 38] proposed a method for partitioning a translation job between source speakers, who focus on adequacy (fidelity to the source), and target speakers, who ensure translation fluency. An evaluation showed that collaborative translation improved over raw MT output and back translation, i.e., editing the input to a round-trip machine translation (source-target-source) until the back translation was accepted by the post-editor. Yamashita et al. [49] also considered back translation as a medium for web-based, cross-cultural chat, but did not provide an evaluation.

Hu et al. [23] evaluated iterative refinement of a seed machine translation by pairs of monolinguals. Collaborative translations were consistently rated higher than the original MT output. Hu et al. [24, 25] gave results for other language pairs, with similar improvements in quality. Informal results for time showed that days were required to post-edit fewer than 100 sentences.

MT seed translations might not exist for low-resource language pairs, so Ambati et al. [3] employed weak bilinguals as a bridge between bilingual word translations and monolingual post-editing. Translators with (self-reported) weak ability in either the source or target language provided partial sentence translations, which were then post-edited by monolingual speakers. This staged technique resulted in higher quality

[3]In NLP, Callison-Burch [9] investigated monolingual post-editing, but his ultimate objective was improving MT. Both Albrecht et al. [1] and Koehn [30] found that monolingual post-editors could improve the quality of MT output, but that they could not match bilingual translators. Moreover, both found that monolingual post-editors were typically slower than bilingual translators.

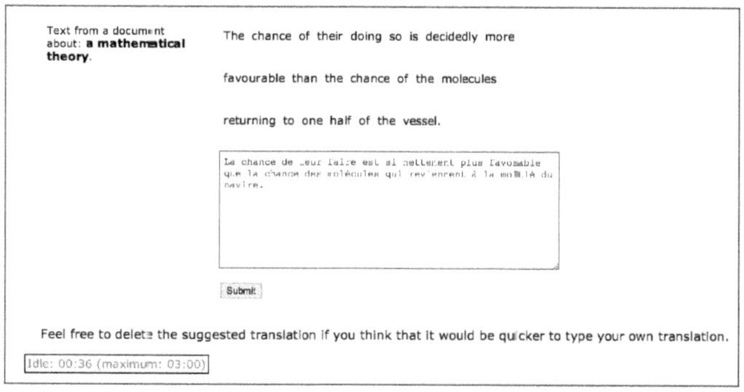

Figure 2: Web interface for the bilingual post-editing experiment (post-edit condition). We placed the suggested translation in the textbox to minimize scrolling. The idle timer appears on the bottom left.

translations (according to BLEU [43], an automatic MT metric) on Amazon Mechanical Turk relative to direct solicitation of full sentence translations.

Experimental Desiderata from Prior Work

Prior published work offers a mixed view[4] on the effectiveness of post-editing due to conflicting experimental designs and objectives. Our experiment clarifies this picture via several design decisions. First, we employ expert bilingual translators, who are faster and more accurate than monolinguals or students. Second, we replicate a standard working environment, avoiding the interference of TAP, eye trackers, and collaborative iterations. Third, we weight time and quality equally, and evaluate quality with a standard ranking technique. Fourth, we assess significance with mixed effects models, which allow us to treat all sampled items (subjects, sentences, and target languages) as random effects. We thus isolate the fixed effect of translation condition, which is the focus of this paper. Finally, we test for other explanatory covariates such as linguistic (e.g., syntactic complexity) and human factors (e.g., source spelling proficiency) features.

EXPERIMENTAL DESIGN

We compared the two translation conditions—unaided and post-edit—with a 2x2 experimental design. Translation conditions, implemented as different user interfaces, and source sentences were the independent variables (factors). Experimental subjects saw all factor levels, but not all combinations, since one exposure to a source sentence would certainly influence another. We used simple web interfaces (Figure 2) designed to prevent scrolling since subjects worked remotely on their own computers. Source sentences were presented in document order, but subjects could not view the full document context. After submission of each translation, no further revision was allowed. In the post-edit condition, subjects were free to submit, manipulate, or even delete the suggested translation from Google Translate (March 2012). We asked the subjects to eschew alternate machine assistance, although we permitted passive aids like bilingual dictionaries.

[4]Recent, unpublished anecdotal evidence and proprietary trials have more consistently shown the effectiveness of post-editing, motivating adoption at some companies (Ray Flournoy, Adobe, *(p.c.)*).

Subjects completed the experiment under time pressure. Time pressure isolates translation performance from reading comprehension [12] while eliciting a physiological reaction that may increase cognitive function [6]. However, a fixed deadline does not account for per-subject and per-sentence variation, and places an artificial upper bound on translation time. To solve these problems, we displayed an idle timer that prohibited pauses longer than three minutes. The idle timer reset upon any keystroke in the target textbox. Upon expiration, it triggered submission of any entered text. The duration was chosen to allow reflection but to ensure completion of the experiment during a single session.

We recorded all keyboard, mouse, and browser events along with timestamps.[5] The source tokens were also placed in separate `<span>` elements so that we could record hover events.

We randomized the assignment of sentences to translation conditions and the order in which the translation conditions appeared to subjects. Subjects completed a block of sentences in one translation condition, took an untimed break, and then completed the remaining sentences in the other translation condition. Finally, we asked users to complete a questionnaire about the experience.

Selection of Linguistic Materials

We chose English as the source language and Arabic, French, and German as the target languages. The target languages were selected based on canonical word order. Arabic is Verb-Subject-Object (VSO), French is SVO, and German is SOV. Verbs are salient linguistic elements that participate in many syntactic relations, so we wanted to control the position of this variable for cross-linguistic modeling.

We selected four paragraphs from four English Wikipedia articles.[6] We deemed two of the paragraphs "easy" in terms of lexical and syntactic features, and the other two "hard." Subjects saw one easy and one hard document in each translation condition. We selected passages from English articles that had well-written corresponding articles in all target languages. Consequently, subjects could presumably generate natural translations irrespective of the target. Conversely, consider a passage about dating trends in America. This may be difficult to translate into Arabic since dating is not customary in the Arab world. For example, the terms "girlfriend" and "boyfriend" do not have direct translations into Arabic.

The four topics we selected were the 1896 Olympics (easy; Example (1a)), the flag of Japan (easy), Schizophrenia (hard), and the infinite monkey theorem (hard; Example (1b)):

(1) a. It was the first international Olympic Games held in the Modern era.

b. Any physical process that is even less likely than such monkeys' success is effectively impossible, and it may safely be said that such a process will never happen.

[5]We did not record cut/copy/paste events [13]. Analysis showed that these events would be useful to track in future experiments.

[6]Gross statistics: 27 sentences, 606 tokens. The maximum sentence length was 43, and the average length was 22.4 tokens.

	Arabic		French		German	
	M	*SD*	*M*	*SD*	*M*	*SD*
Hourly Rate* ($)	10.34	4.88	17.73	4.37	20.20	10.95
Hours per Week*	31.00	26.13	17.19	13.43	18.88	7.72
En level*	4.94	0.25	4.94	0.25	5.00	0.00
En Skills	4.21	0.34	4.28	0.36	4.34	0.34
En Spelling	4.60	0.42	4.79	0.28	4.78	0.21
En Vocabulary	4.41	0.35	4.40	0.34	4.38	0.55
En-Ar Translation	4.93	0.15				
Fr Spelling			4.72	0.15		
Fr Usage			4.49	0.23		
Fr Vocabulary			4.62	0.22		
En-Fr Translation			4.69	0.19		
De Spelling					4.64	0.30
De Vocabulary					4.68	0.22
En-De Translation					4.77	0.16

Table 1: oDesk human subjects data for Arabic (Ar), English (En), French (Fr), and German (De). oDesk does not currently offer a symmetric inventory of language tests. (*self-reported)

Selection of Subjects

For each target language, we hired 16 self-described "professional" translators on oDesk.[7] Most were freelancers with at least a bachelor's degree. Three had Ph.Ds. We advertised the job at a fixed price of $0.085 per source token ($52 in total), a common rate for general text. However, we allowed translators to submit bids so that they felt fairly compensated. We did not negotiate, but the bids centered close to our target price (mean±standard deviation): Arabic, ($M = 50.50, SD = 4.20$); French, ($M = 52.32, SD = 1.89$); German, ($M = 49.93, SD = 12.57$).

oDesk offers free skills tests administered by a third party.[8] Each 40-minute test contains 40 multiple choice questions, with scores reported on a [0,5] real-valued scale. We required subjects to complete all available source and target language proficiency tests, in addition to language-pair-specific translation tests. We also recorded public profile information such as hourly rate, hours worked as a translator, and self-reported English proficiency. Table 1 summarizes the subject data.

Subjects completed a training module that explained the experimental procedure and exposed them to both translation conditions. They could translate example sentences until they were ready to start the experiment.

Translation Quality Assessment

Translation quality assessment is far from a solved problem. Whereas past experiments in the HCI community have used 5-point fluency/adequacy scales, the MT community has lately favored pairwise ranking [11]. Pairwise ranking results in higher inner annotator agreement (IAA) than fluency/adequacy rating [11]. We used software[9] from the annual Workshop on Machine Translation (WMT) evaluations to rank all translations on Amazon Mechanical Turk (Figure 3). Aggregate non-expert judgements can approach expert IAA levels [10].

[7]**http://www.odesk.com**

[8]ExpertRating: **http://www.expertrating.com**

[9]**http://cs.jhu.edu/~ozaidan/maise/**

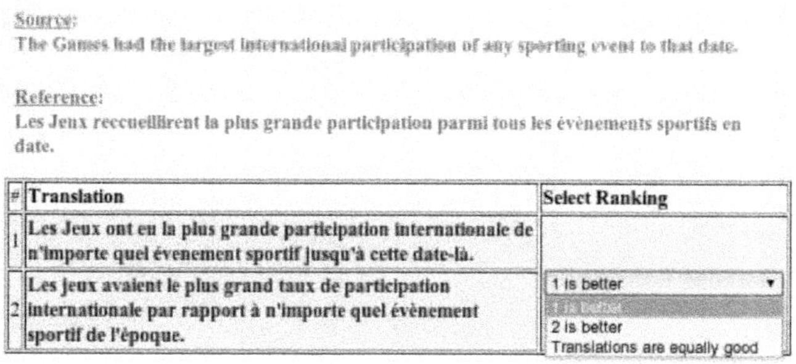

Figure 3: Three-way ranking interface for assessing translation quality using Amazon Mechanical Turk. Raters could see the source sentence, a human-generated reference translation, and the two target sentences. Each HIT contained three ranking tasks.

The combination of pairwise rankings into a total ordering is non-trivial. Currently, WMT casts the problem as finding the minimum feedback arc set in a tournament (a directed graph with $\binom{N}{2}$ vertices, where N is the number of human translators). This is an NP-complete problem, but it can be approximated with the algorithm of Lopez [36].[10]

We performed an exhaustive pairwise evaluation of the translation results for all three languages. For each source sentence, we requested three independent judgements for each of the $\binom{N}{2}$ translation pairs. We paid $0.04 per HIT, and each HIT contained three pairs. Workers needed an 85% approval rating with at least five approved HITs. For quality control, we randomly interspersed non-sensical HITs—the translations did not correspond to the source text—among the real HITs. We blocked workers who incorrectly answered several spam HITs.

Raters were asked to choose the best translation, or to mark the two translations as equal (Figure 3). For each source sentence and each set of N target translations, the procedure resulted in a ranking in the range $[1,N]$, with ties allowed.

VISUALIZING TRANSLATION ACTIVITY

We visualized the user activity data to assess observations from prior work and to inform the statistical models.

Mouse Cursor Movements

Figure 4 shows an example English sentence from the Schizophrenia document with hover counts from all three languages. The areas of the circles are proportional to the square root of the raw counts, while the colors indicate the various parts of speech: noun, verb, adjective, adverb, and "other". The "other" category includes prepositions, particles, conjunctions, and other (mostly closed) word classes.

Nouns stand out as a significant focal point, as do adverbs and, to a lesser degree, verbs. These patterns persist across all three languages, and suggest that source parts of speech might have an effect on time and quality. We assess that hypothesis statistically in the next section.

Huang et al. [26] showed that mouse movements correlated with gaze for search engine UIs. While we did not correlate

[10]`http://github.com/alopez/wmt-ranking`

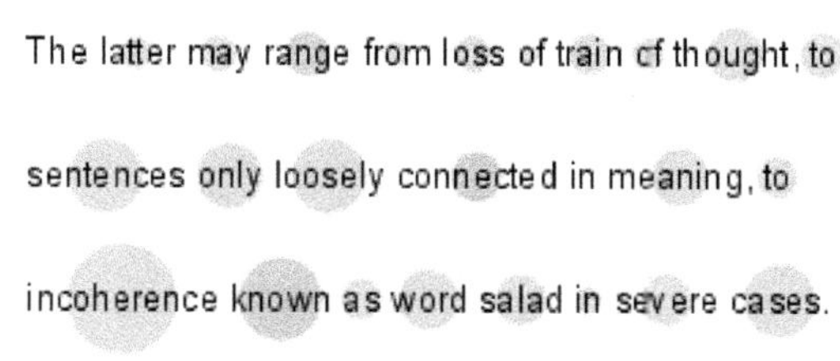

(a) Arabic

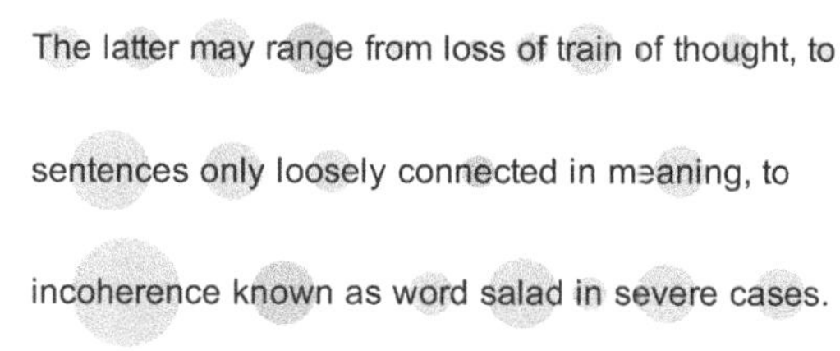

(b) French

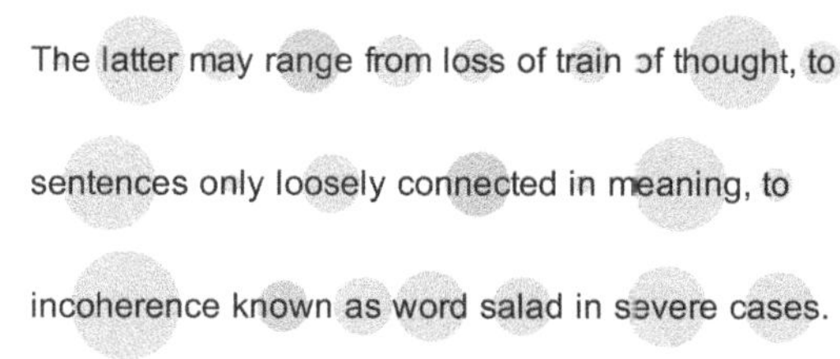

(c) German

Figure 4: Mouse hover frequencies for the three different languages. Frequency is indicated by area, while the colors indicate five word categories: nouns (blue), verbs (red), adjectives (orange), adverbs (green), and "other" (grey). Nouns are clearly focal points.

mouse movements with an eye tracker for our task, the visualization nonetheless shows distinctive patterns that turn out to be significant in our statistical models.

User Event Traces

We also plotted the mouse and keyboard event logs against a normalized time scale for each user and source sentence (Figure 5). Users in the unaided condition demonstrate the gisting/drafting/revising behavior observed in prior work with eye trackers [15]. Initial pauses and mouse activity in the gisting phase give way to concentrated keyboard activity as the user types the translation. Finally, more pauses and mouse activity indicate the revision phase.

The post-edit condition results in drastically different behavior. Phase boundaries are not discernible, and pauses account for a larger proportion of the translation time. Users clearly engaged the suggested translation even though the option to discard it existed. In addition, the post-edit condition resulted in a statistically significant reduction in total event counts: Arabic $t(26) = 16.52, p < 0.001$; French $t(26) = 33.63, p \leq 0.001$; German $t(26) = 37.08, p < 0.001$. At least from the perspective of device input activity, post-editing is a more passive activity than unaided translation.

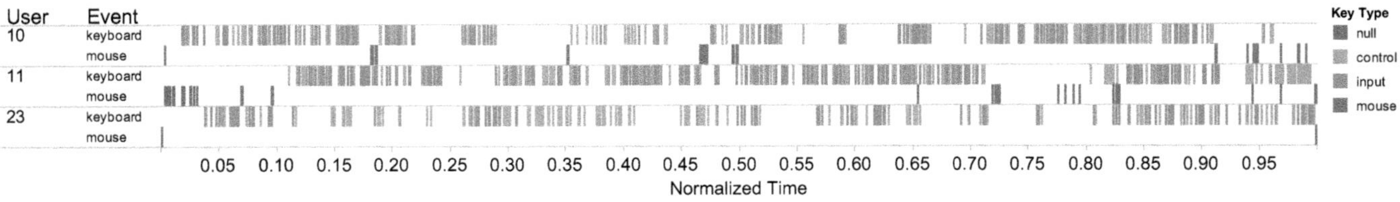

(a) Unaided condition

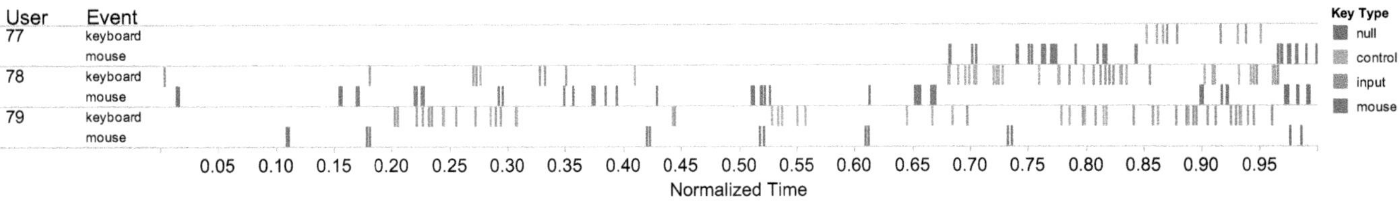

(b) Post-edit condition

Figure 5: Arabic user activity logs for the English input shown in Figure 4. Events are colored according to input type: control keys (e.g., up/down arrows; orange), input keys (green), mouse buttons (red), and "null" (blue), which means that Javascript failed to trap the input character. (a) The unaided condition results in visible gisting, drafting, and revision phases, which are sequential. (b) The post-edit condition does not result in clear phases. Pauses are longer and account for more of the total translation time.

STATISTICAL ANALYSIS

A consistent observation in prior work on MT post-editing has been significant per-subject and per-source-sentence (in terms of the quality of the machine suggestion) variation. Two major statistical mistakes have been made in dealing with this variance. First, Tatsumi [47] used a multiple regression design with predictors for each subject. This is the least effective solution for regression—per-subject regressions or by-item means would be superior [4]—since her model measured significance of each subject relative to the others, but not to the larger human population.

An alternative to multiple regression is analysis of variance (ANOVA), the workhorse of HCI experimental layouts. Per-subject variance could be modeled with a repeated measures design (RM-ANOVA), but our experiment was necessarily a between-subjects design. Nonetheless, we could treat source sentences as a fixed effect and use a two-way, between-subjects ANOVA. However, language is not a fixed effect since we cannot include all possible source sentences in the experiment. The "language-as-fixed-effects fallacy" [18] has been the motivation in psycho-linguistics research for *mixed effects models*, which can incorporate arbitrary fixed effects (e.g., translation conditions) and random effects (e.g., subjects, sentences).[11]

Mixed effects models are not widely used in HCI, but they are preferable to ANOVA whenever experimental factors are sampled from a larger population. In this setting, mixed models reduce the risk of type II errors. Other practical benefits include accommodation of unbalanced designs and longitudinal (dependent) covariates, which can model learning and fatigue. We assess significance with likelihood-ratio (LR) tests.

[11] See Appendix for mathematical details.

Translation Time and Quality

This paper seeks to quantify the effect of post-editing on translation time and quality (Figure 6).[12] Plots showed that time was not normally distributed, so we applied a log transformation and fit linear mixed models.[13] As for quality, our ranking procedure yields discrete ranks, which are obviously not normally distributed. To account for non-normality and to exploit the ordering of the rank response, we built ordinal mixed models.[14]

In addition to the per-subject covariates listed in Table 1, we also included source (English) features. We annotated the source text with Stanford CoreNLP[15] to obtain syntactic complexity [34], number of named entities, and part of speech tag counts. We also included (log transformed) mean lexical frequency[16] and sentence length. We standardized all numeric covariates by subtracting the mean and dividing by one standard deviation [21]. Finally, after fitting models with all of the data, we pruned data points with residuals exceeding 2.5 standard deviations [4] and refit the models.

Monolingual Time and Quality Results

Table 2 shows results for log-transformed time. The standard 2x2 ANOVA model, which treats source sentences as fixed effects, shows a significant main effect for translation condition across all three languages. However, the risk of type II errors is high, since the ANOVA does not account for per-subject or per-sentence variance. The mixed effects model addresses

[12] Intuition suggests that time and quality might be correlated. For each language, we ran Pearson's correlation test for the two response variables: Arabic, $t(430) = 0.739, p < 0.274$; French, $t(430) = 3.71, p < 0.001$; German, $t(430) = 2.49, p < 0.05$. Positive correlations—monotonic increases in time correspond to increases in rank (lower quality)—exist for two languages. Consequently, multivariate models might be a direction for future research.

[13] With the `lme4` R package [5].

[14] With the `ordinal` R package [17].

[15] **http://nlp.stanford.edu/software/corenlp.shtml**

[16] Relative to counts in the English Gigaword corpus (Linguistic Data Consortium catalog number LDC2009T13).

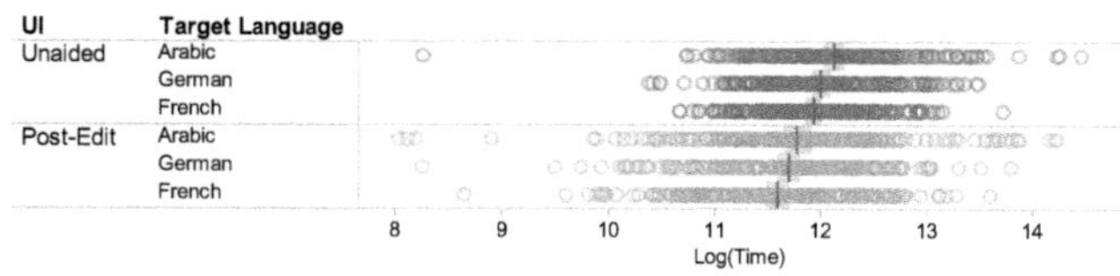

(a) Log-transformed times for each translation. Red bars indicate means for each (UI, language) pair; grey bands show 95% confidence intervals.

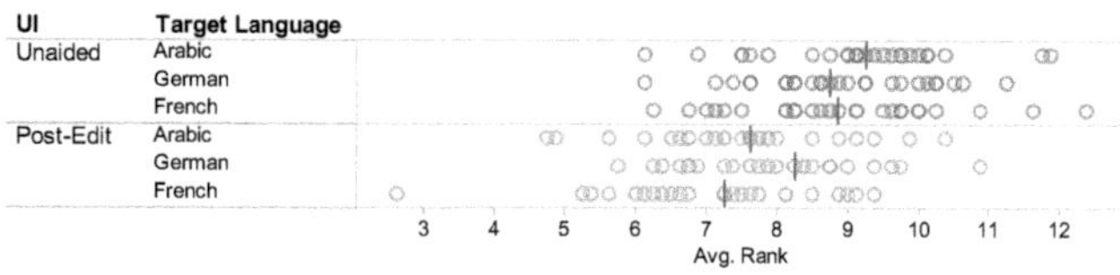

(b) Average rank for each source sentence by language. Red bars indicate the median average rank for each (UI, language) pair.

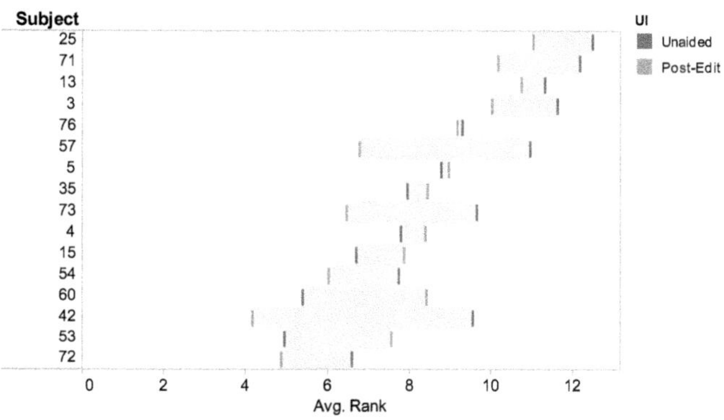

(c) Average rank in each condition by subject (German).

Figure 6: Summarizations of the post-editing experiment data. (a) Mean time is lower for post-edit. (b) Median rank is better for post-edit. (c) Individual responses show high variance. German subjects 4, 5, 15, 35, 53, and 60 are actually faster, on average, in the unaided condition.

these shortcomings with random intercepts for subjects and sentences, and random slopes for translation condition. Informally, the random slopes can be interpreted as follows: translation condition might affect some subjects more than others, and its affect might also depend on the source sentence (Figure 6c). These interpretations account for observations in prior work, namely that MT suggestions help some subjects more than others, and that MT quality varies across source sentences.

The mixed models found significant main effects for translation condition in Arabic $\chi^2(1, N = 432) = 7.54, p < 0.01$, French $\chi^2(1, N = 432) = 10.12, p < 0.01$, and German $\chi^2(1, N = 432) = 19.69, p < 0.001$. [17]

For rank (Table 3), we included random intercepts for subjects and sentences (`ordinal` [17] does not yet support random slopes) in the ordinal models. We found significant main effects for translation condition in Arabic $\chi^2(1, N = 432) = 16.09, p < 0.001$, French $\chi^2(1, N = 432) = 15.24, p < 0.001$, and German $\chi^2(1, N = 432) = 4.03, p < 0.05$.

[17]The data set and scripts to reproduce these experiments (with effect sizes) are available at: **http://www.spencegreen.com/research/**

Model	Factor	Ar	Fr	De	ALL
ANOVA (2x2)	**post-edit**	•••	•••	•••	–
	source sentence	•••	•••	•••	–
Mixed Effects	**post-edit**	••	••	•••	•••
	Hourly Rate* ($)	•			
	En level*		•		
	log source length	•••	•••	•••	•••
	log syntax complexity	•			
	% nouns in source	••	•	•	••
	Translation Test	•			–
	Target Spelling Test			•	–

Table 2: Time results for post-edit and other significant covariates. Insignificant covariates in the full model are not listed. Statistical significance: ••• $p < 0.001$; •• $p < 0.01$; • $p < 0.05$.

Model	Factor	Ar	Fr	De	ALL
Mixed Effects	**post-edit**	•••	•••	•	•••
	Hourly Rate* ($)	•			
	En Skills Test		•		•
	Target Vocab test		•••		–

Table 3: Rank results for post-edit and other significant covariates.

Cross-lingual Time and Quality Results

We also pooled the data for all three languages and built new mixed effects models with target language as an additional random effect. Effects not present in the monolingual models may be detected in the cross-lingual model due to increased statistical power. A 3x3 ANOVA with target language as a fixed effect is possible yet clearly flawed, so we omit it. We also removed the translation and target language test covariates since subjects only took the tests for their target language. For time, we found a significant main effect for translation condition $\chi^2(1, N = 1296) = 11.58, p < 0.001$ ("ALL" in Tables 2 and 3). Source sentence length and the percentage of source noun tokens were significant covariates. For rank, we also found a significant main effect for translation condition $\chi^2(1, N = 1296) = 32.47, p < 0.001$.

Translation Edit Distance

We have shown that translation condition has a significant effect on quality. Does the suggested translation prime the post-editor, thus resulting in a translation that is similar to the suggestion? We computed the Damerau-Levenshtein edit distance[18] between the suggested translation and each target translation, and then averaged the edit distances for each source sentence and translation condition. We then used a paired difference t-test to assess significance. We found statistically significant reductions in edit distance for the post-edit condition: Arabic $t(26) = 68.45, p < 0.001$; French $t(26) = 39.02, p < 0.001$; German $t(26) = 55.65, p < 0.001$.

[18]Extends Levenshtein edit distance with transpositions to account for word order differences.

Response	Likelihood-ratio Test		Sign
Count (300ms)	$\chi^2(1, N = 1296) = 10.22$	$p < 0.01$	−
Count (1000ms)	$\chi^2(1, N = 1296) = 7.12$	$p < 0.01$	−
Mean duration	$\chi^2(1, N = 1296) = 9.37$	$p < 0.01$	+
Ratio (300ms)	$\chi^2(1, N = 1296) = 4.87$	$p < 0.05$	+
Ratio (1000ms)	$\chi^2(1, N = 1296) = 11.06$	$p < 0.001$	+

Table 4: Effect of translation condition on pause count, duration, and ratio (all languages). "Sign" refers to the polarity of the fixed co-efficient for post-edit. The sign indicates that post-editing results in fewer distinct pauses (count), that are longer (mean duration), and account for more of the total translation time (ratio).

Pause Duration and Frequency

In translation process studies, pauses have frequently been used as proxies for cognitive load. Schilperoord [45] used a cutoff of 300ms between input events, while others [29, 42] have used 1000ms. We fit the same mixed effects models used for time to the following response variables: pause count (300ms and 1000ms), mean pause duration (300ms), and pause ratio (300ms and 1000ms). Pause ratio is the total pause time divided by translation time.

We logged all events in the DOM Level 3 specification except: `abort`, `keyup`, `mousemove`, and `wheel`. Pauses are the intervals between these events, a slightly broader definition than past work (see [29, 42]).

Due to space constraints, we only report cross-lingual significance levels for translation condition. Table 4 shows that a significant main effect for the post-edit condition exists for all five response variables. The polarity of the co-efficients indicates that post-edit results in fewer total pauses. These pauses are longer and account for a larger fraction of the total translation time. These results support the differences in user behavior observed in the event visualizations (Figure 5).

DISCUSSION

The triangulation of user activity visualization, statistical modeling, and qualitative user feedback yields new insights into machine-assisted translation.

Translators strongly prefer post-edit

Translators have previously reported a strong dislike of full MT pre-translations [32, 48]. However, our cross-linguistic mixed effects model showed significant main effects for both time and quality. Visualization of the user activity logs showed fewer interactions and longer pauses in the post-edit condition, observations that we verified with mixed effects models (Table 4). Moreover, when asked, "Which interface enabled you to translate the sentences most quickly?", 69% of translators chose post-editing. When asked, "Were the machine translations useful?", 56% responded in the affirmative, 29% were neutral, and only 15% disagreed. One user even responded,

```
Your machine translations are far better than
the ones of Google, Babel and so on.  So they
wered helpfull [sic], but usually when handed
over google-translated material, I find it way
easier end [sic] quicker to do it on my own
from unaided.
```

The subjects did not know that the suggestions came from Google Translate. Users may have dated perceptions of MT quality that do not account for the rapid progress in the field.

Post-edit has measurably different interaction patterns

Post-editing seems like a more passive activity from several angles. We found statistically significant reductions in event counts, visual (Figure 5) and statistical (Table 4) evidence of longer duration pauses, and final translations that were similar to the suggestions. Users did not devote as much time to text generation (Figure 5b). However, we did not find general human factors predictors of translation time or quality. For example, only a few of the oDesk predictors in Table 1 were significant in the monolingual mixed models, and none of them were significant in the cross-lingual models. Of course, we recruited experts, so the scores were near perfect with low variance. Nonetheless, post-edit still had a significant per subject random component, as illustrated by the individual variation in Figure 6c. We used random slopes to account for this variance, but design principles are difficult to infer from random effects. Closer human subjects analysis is needed to isolate fixed predictors of post-edit productivity.

Suggested translations improve final quality

Across languages, we found a very significant main effect ($p < 0.001$) for quality. Machine translation quality has advanced since many earlier post-editing studies were conducted. Nonetheless, even recent research offers a mixed view on the products of post-editing, with [22, 46] reporting lower quality and [20, 44] reporting higher quality. We found very significant effects ($p < 0.001$) for Arabic and French, and a less significant effect ($p < 0.05$) for German. The user survey suggests that the German translators may have been optimizing for time instead of quality. When asked "Which interface enabled you to translate the sentences most quickly?", 75% chose the post-edit condition, the highest proportion among the three language groups. When asked if the suggested translations were "useful," 50% answered in the affirmative, 37% were neutral, and only 12.5% disagreed.

Simple source lexical features predict time

Prior work measured the effect of rule-based, language-specific source-side features [7, 39, 40] that may not generalize across languages and text genres. In contrast, we found that very general linguistic features such as basic part of speech counts and syntactic complexity predict translation time. Across languages, we found a significant main effect for %nouns, the proportion of nominal tokens in the source sentence. One notable omission from this list is %verbs, which we hypothesized would be a salient linguistic feature. The mouse hover patterns showed that users fixated on nouns, and to a lesser degree adjectives. However, the user survey presented a slightly different picture. Across languages, users provided the following ranking of basic parts of speech in order of decreasing translation difficulty: Adverb, Verb, Adjective, Other, Noun.[19] Translators seem aware of the difficulty of adverbs, but apparently underestimate the difficulty of nouns.

[19]The users who ranked "Other" highly were asked to further qualify their response. These responses uniformly demonstrate a basic misunderstanding of the concept of part of speech.

UI DESIGN IMPLICATIONS

Our results and analysis suggest several design principles for new and existing machine-assisted translation systems.

Show Translations for Selected Parts of Speech

Both the activity visualizations and mixed effects models indicate that users struggle with certain parts of speech, such as nouns and adverbs. Verbs, prepositions, and other parts of speech did not affect translation time. While many translation interfaces support dictionary lookup, users may benefit from the automatic display of translations for certain parts of speech.

Avoid Predicting Translation Modes

Conventional wisdom has it that translation consists of gisting, drafting, and revising phases [15]. However, the user activity logs show that these phases are interleaved in the post-edit condition. The system should not be tuned to a specific mode. One option would be to allow the user to toggle specific assistance for each translation phase.

Offer Full Translations as References

We used a simple interface in which the suggested translation appeared in the input textbox. Several translators commented that they pasted the translation elsewhere for reference, using only parts of it in their final submission. The activity visualizations also indicated a significant amount of control key activity in the post-edit condition, meaning that users were navigating with arrow keys through the suggestion. We conclude that the suggested translation should be accessible, but should not impede entry of the final translation.

Use Post-Edit Translations to Improve MT

This paper has concerned itself with assistance to the human translator. However, the edit distance analysis showed that translations produced in the post-edit condition diverged from both the unaided translations and the raw MT output, yet were closer to MT: humans start from MT, then produce a novel output. The words, phrases, and re-orderings applied in that production process could be used as additional training data, thus creating a virtuous cycle in which both humans and machines improve. UI design can play a role in this loop by automating manipulation of the machine assistance, thus encouraging user actions that can be recorded. For example, we have mentioned the utility of the full machine translation as a reference. Instead of allowing uncontrolled copy/paste operations, a UI feature could automate selection of words and phrases. An event trace of these edit operations could be used as features in existing discriminative MT training algorithms. We suggest that UI designers and MT system builders work cooperatively to improve both human and machine translation.

CONCLUSION

Natural language processing systems have entered mainstream use, yet few analyses of human interaction with them exist. Machine translation systems are among the most widely used, and they hold great promise for lowering the high cost of translation. We analyzed MT post-editing, a common feature in commercial translator interfaces. Our results strongly favor the presence of machine suggestions in terms of both translation time and final quality. If translators benefit from a barebones post-editing interface, then we suspect that more interaction between the UI and MT backend could produce additional benefits. While Koehn [29] found that interactive assistance offered no advantage over post-editing, he was less concerned about UI design and human factors. Our results fill that gap, and inform the design of new interactive interfaces, which should be compared to post-editing. Our work also applies directly to existing translator workbenches.

APPENDIX: FROM ANOVA TO MIXED EFFECTS MODELS

Consider a balanced, one-way analysis of variance (ANOVA) model with $i \in \{1, \dots, I\}$ clusters (e.g., translation conditions) and $j \in \{1, \dots, J\}$ observations per cluster:

$$y_{ij} = x_{ij}\beta_i + \epsilon_{ij} \tag{1}$$

where y are normally distributed observations (dependent variables), x are the independent variables (effects), the β_i are the group means for $y_{i\cdot}$, and $\epsilon \sim \mathcal{N}(0, \sigma^2)$ are random per-observation errors (residuals) with common variance. The null hypothesis is that the co-efficients, which are fit with ordinary least squares, are equal for all clusters, i.e. $\beta_1 = \beta_2 = \cdots = \beta_I$. The F-test for this model is a ratio of the between- and within-subjects sum-of-squared (SS) errors, which has the familiar form

$$F = \frac{SS_b(IJ - I)}{SS_w(IJ - 1)} \tag{2}$$

Random differences among clusters are not modeled explicitly, thus increasing the risk of type II errors. One method for separating the per-cluster/subject error is a repeated measures design (RM-ANOVA),[20] which is widely used in HCI. RM-ANOVA differs only in terms of SS_w, which is partitioned into subject-specific error plus some residual error:

$$SS_w = SS_{subjects} + SS_{error} \tag{3}$$

RM-ANOVA effectively adds a per-subject random effect without changing the form of the model in Equation 1. The F-test becomes:

$$F = \frac{SS_b(I-1)(IJ-1)}{SS_{error}(IJ-1)} = \frac{SS_b(I-1)}{SS_{error}} \tag{4}$$

The F-value of Equation 4 will increase if SS_{error} is sufficiently small relative to SS_w (Equation 2) so as to offset the loss in degrees of freedom, thus increasing statistical power.

What if we want to include other random effects like sentences or target languages? *Mixed models* extend the ANOVA model in Equation 1 with an explicit random effects component:

$$y_i = x_i^{\mathsf{T}}\beta + z_i^{\mathsf{T}}b_i + \eta_i \tag{5}$$

where i is now called the *grouping factor*. We now write y_i as a $J \times 1$ vector of responses for the ith cluster/group and x_i as a $J \times p$ vector of covariates with fixed co-efficients $\beta \in \mathbb{R}^{p \times 1}$. Further, $E[y_i] = x_i^{\mathsf{T}}\beta$. The random effects structure is defined by a $J \times q$ vector of covariates z_i with associated random effects $b_i \sim \mathcal{N}(0, \Sigma)$, $\Sigma \in \mathbb{R}^{q \times q}$ and the residuals $\eta_i \sim \mathcal{N}(0, R_t)$, $R_t \in \mathbb{R}^{I \times I}$. The model assumes mutual independence of all random vectors.

The vectors x_i and z_i relate the observations y_i to β and b_i. For significance, F-tests no longer apply, but we can use a likelihood-ratio (LR) test for specific fixed effects. Our analysis used LR testing, so we fit the mixed models by maximizing log-likelihood.

ACKNOWLEDGEMENTS

We thank Ray Flournoy and Roger Levy for helpful discussions. The first author is supported by a National Science Foundation Graduate Research Fellowship.

[20] Also known as a "within-subjects" experimental design.

REFERENCES

1. Albrecht, J. S., Hwa, R., and Marai, G. E. Correcting automatic translations through collaborations between MT and monolingual target-language users. In *EACL* (2009).
2. Allen, J. Post-editing. In *Computers and Translation: A translator's guide*, H. Somers, Ed. John Benjamins, 2003, ch. 16, 297–317.
3. Ambati, V., Vogel, S., and Carbonell, J. Collaborative workflow for crowdsourcing translation. In *CSCW* (2012).
4. Baayen, R., Davidson, D., and Bates, D. Mixed-effects modeling with crossed random effects for subjects and items. *Journal of Memory and Language 59*, 4 (2008), 390–412.
5. Bates, D. M. `lme4`: Linear mixed-effects models using S4 classes. Tech. rep., R package version 0.999999-0, **`http://cran.r-project.org/package=lme4`**, 2007.
6. Bayer-Hohenwarter, G. Methodological reflections on the experimental design of time-pressure studies. *Across Languages and Cultures 10*, 2 (2009), 193–206.
7. Bernth, A., and McCord, M. The effect of source analysis on translation confidence. In *Envisioning Machine Translation in the Information Future*, J. White, Ed., vol. 1934 of *Lecture Notes in Computer Science*. Springer, 2000, 250–259.
8. Bisbey, R., and Kay. The MIND translation system: a study in man-machine collaboration. Tech. Rep. P-4786, Rand Corp., March 1972.
9. Callison-Burch, C. Linear B system description for the 2005 NIST MT evaluation exercise. In *NIST Machine Translation Evaluation Workshop* (2005).
10. Callison-Burch, C. Fast, cheap, and creative: Evaluating translation quality using Amazon's Mechanical Turk. In *EMNLP* (2009).
11. Callison-Burch, C., Koehn, P., Monz, C., Post, M., Soricut, R., and Specia, L. Findings of the 2012 Workshop on Statistical Machine Translation. In *WMT* (2012).
12. Campbell, S. A cognitive approach to source text difficulty in translation. *Target 11*, 1 (1999), 33–63.
13. Carl, M. Translog-II: a program for recording user activity data for empirical reading and writing research. In *LREC* (2012).
14. Carl, M., and Jakobsen, A. Towards statistical modelling of translators' activity data. *International Journal of Speech Technology 12* (2009), 125–138.
15. Carl, M., Kay, M., and Jensen, K. T. H. Long distance revisions in drafting and post-editing. In *CICLing* (2010).
16. Chen, M. C., Anderson, J. R., and Sohn, M. H. What can a mouse cursor tell us more?: correlation of eye/mouse movements on web browsing. In *CHI* (2001).
17. Christensen, R. H. B. `ordinal`: Regression models for ordinal data. Tech. rep., R package version 2012.01-19, **`http://cran.r-project.org/package=ordinal`**, 2011.
18. Clark, H. H. The language-as-fixed-effect fallacy: A critique of language statistics in psychological research. *Journal of Verbal Learning and Verbal Behavior 12*, 4 (August 1973), 335–359.
19. Flournoy, R., and Duran, C. Machine translation and document localization at Adobe: From pilot to production. In *MT Summit XII* (2009).
20. Garcia, I. Translating by post-editing: is it the way forward? *Machine Translation 25* (2011), 217–237.
21. Gelman, A. Scaling regression inputs by dividing by two standard deviations. *Statistics in Medicine 27*, 15 (2008), 2865–2873.
22. Guerberof, A. Productivity and quality in the post-editing of outputs from translation memories and machine translation. *International Journal of Localization 7*, 1 (2009).
23. Hu, C., Bederson, B., and Resnik, P. Translation by iterative collaboration between monolingual users. In *Graphics Interface (GI)* (2010).
24. Hu, C., Bederson, B. B., Resnik, P., and Kronrod, Y. MonoTrans2: a new human computation system to support monolingual translation. In *CHI* (2011).
25. Hu, C., Resnik, P., Kronrod, Y., and Bederson, B. Deploying MonoTrans widgets in the wild. In *CHI* (2012).
26. Huang, J., White, R., and Buscher, G. User see, user point: gaze and cursor alignment in web search. In *CHI* (2012).
27. Jakobsen, A. Logging target text production with Translog. In *Probing the process in translation: methods and results*, G. Hansen, Ed. Copenhagen: Samfundslitteratur, 1999, 9–20.
28. Kay, M. The proper place of men and machines in language translation. Tech. Rep. CSL-80-11, Xerox Palo Alto Research Center (PARC), 1980.
29. Koehn, P. A process study of computer-aided translation. *Machine Translation 23* (2009), 241–263.
30. Koehn, P. Enabling monolingual translators: post-editing vs. options. In *HLT-NAACL* (2010).
31. Krings, H. *Repairing Texts: Empirical Investigations of Machine Translation Post-Editing Processes.* Kent State University Press, 2001.
32. Lagoudaki, E. Translation editing environments. In *MT Summit XII: Workshop on Beyond Translation Memories* (2009).
33. Lawson, V., Ed. *Practical Experience of Machine Translation*, North-Holland (1982).
34. Lin, D. On the structural complexity of natural language sentences. In *COLING* (1996).
35. Lopez, A. Statistical machine translation. *ACM Computing Surveys 40*, 8 (2008), 1–49.
36. Lopez, A. Putting human assessments of machine translation systems in order. In *WMT* (2012).
37. Morita, D., and Ishida, T. Collaborative translation by monolinguals with machine translators. In *IUI* (2009).
38. Morita, D., and Ishida, T. Designing protocols for collaborative translation. In *Principles of Practice in Multi-Agent Systems* (2009).
39. O'Brien, S. Machine translatability and post-editing effort: How do they relate? In *Translating and the Computer* (2004).
40. O'Brien, S. Methodologies for measuring the correlations between post-editing effort and machine translatability. *Machine Translation 19* (2005), 37–58.
41. O'Brien, S. Eye-tracking and translation memory matches. *Perspectives: Studies in translatology 14*, 3 (2006), 185–205.
42. O'Brien, S. Pauses as indicators of cognitive effort in post-editing machine translation output. *Across Languages and Cultures 7*, 1 (2006), 1–21.
43. Papineni, K., Roukos, S., Ward, T., and Zhu, W. BLEU: a method for automatic evaluation of machine translation. In *ACL* (2002).
44. Plitt, M., and Masselot, F. A productivity test of statistical machine translation post-editing in a typical localisation context. *The Prague Bulletin of Mathematical Linguistics 93* (2010), 7–16.
45. Schilperoord, J. *It's About Time: Temporal Aspects of Cognitive Processes in Text Production.* Amsterdam:Rodopi, 1996.
46. Skadiņš, R., Puriņš, M., Skadiņa, I., and Vasiļjevs, A. Evaluation of SMT in localization to under-resourced inflected language. In *EAMT* (2011).
47. Tatsumi, M. *Post-Editing Machine Translated Text in a Commercial Setting: Observation and Statistical Analysis.* PhD thesis, Dublin City University, 2010.
48. Wallis, J. Interactive translation vs pre-translation in the context of translation memory systems: Investigating the effects of translation method on productivity, quality and translator satisfaction. Master's thesis, University of Ottawa, 2006.
49. Yamashita, N., Inaba, R., Kuzuoka, H., and Ishida, T. Difficulties in establishing common ground in multiparty groups using machine translation. In *CHI* (2009).

Same Translation but Different Experience: The Effects of Highlighting on Machine-Translated Conversations

Ge Gao[1], Hao-Chuan Wang[3], Dan Cosley[2], Susan R. Fussell[1,2]

[1]Department of Communication
[2]Department of Information Science
Cornell University
Ithaca NY 14850 USA
[gg365, drc44, sfussell] @cornell.edu

[3]Department of Computer Science &
Institute of Information Systems and Applications
National Tsing Hua University
101, Sec.2, Kuang-Fu Rd. Hsinchu 300, Taiwan
haochuan@cs.nthu.edu.tw

ABSTRACT
Machine translation (MT) has the potential to allow members of multilingual organizations to interact via their own native languages, but issues with the quality of MT output have made it difficult to realize this potential. We hypothesized that highlighting keywords in MT output might make it easier for people to overlook translation errors and focus on what was intended by the message. To test this hypothesis, we conducted a laboratory experiment in which native English speakers interacted with a Mandarin-speaking confederate using machine translation. Participants performed three brainstorming tasks, under each of three conditions: no highlighting, keyword highlighting, and random highlighting. Our results indicated that people consider the identical messages clearer and less distracting when keywords in the message are highlighted. Keyword highlighting also improved subjective impressions of the partner and the quality of the collaboration. These findings inform the design of future tools to support multilingual communication.

Author Keywords
Multilingual communication; brainstorming; machine translation; highlighting

ACM Classification Keywords
H.5.3 [Group and Organization Interface]: Computer-supported cooperative work

General Terms
Experimentation; Human Factors

INTRODUCTION
Globalization, with the increasingly widespread use of the Internet, has created more opportunities for people to interact with others who speak different native languages. Multilingual organizations often choose to use a common language (*lingua franca*), such as English, and provide intensive language training for all employees [9]. Using a common language reduces the need for expensive human or machine translation. However, speaking a common language can have negative consequences for non-native speakers. Non-native speakers may fear speaking up when they have less than perfect fluency in the common language of the organization [10][22]. They may also splinter into subgroups, each speaking a different native language [e.g., 23]. At the same time, native speakers may be hesitant to converse with non-native speakers because of concerns about their addressee's fluency [e.g., 3].

In recent years, machine translation (MT) technology has made it possible, in principle, for members of multilingual organizations to interact via their own native languages [e.g., 15]. MT tools should theoretically be able to eliminate many of the problems created by use of a common language, such as concerns about fluency or subgroup splintering. However, current MT services still sometimes produce erroneous translations (e.g., by translating *computer bug* into the equivalent of *computer insect*), or by forming poor sentence compositions (e.g. by translating the Chinese sentence "*得在北京时间的六点之前把文件发出去*," equivalent to "*Need to send out this document before 6 o'clock Beijing time,*" into the English translation "*Was in Beijing on a six point document send out*").

Problems in translation quality can make it difficult for group members to establish common ground [7], particularly when teams must refer to objects and entities in a workspace. As a result, studies have shown that when communication requires coming to agreement on objects of reference, using MT is less efficient than using a shared second language [28][30].

Although improvements to MT technology will continue to be made, it will likely be a long time until complete and accurate translations can be made between all languages due to the diversity and complexity of human languages. The accuracy of MT can vary with the length of a sentence, the context of use, and the specific language used [2][18].

In this paper, we take an alternative approach: Rather than trying to improve the quality of MT, we consider modifying presentation of translation results to make the output more useful. We look for simple modifications that can detour around the technical limitations of MT, while improving the efficacy of communication at limited cost.

The specific modification we focus on is the addition of keyword highlighting. Such highlighting can be valuable in several ways. It can improve the organization and display of information for people to process [16][25] and support message comprehension [14]. It is possible to highlight keywords in MT-mediated communication through human processing (e.g., manual annotation), by machine processing (e.g., linguistic analysis of semantically centering words [31]), or a combination of the two (e.g., MT-assisted collaboration annotation [4]). By highlighting keywords of translated messages, it may be possible to direct people's attention to words or concepts salient in a sentence and help guide people to correct interpretations, even if the translation is less than perfect. For example, if we highlight the keywords of the translated sentence "*Was in **Beijing** on a **six** point **document send out**,*" its intended meaning might be easier to discern and comprehend.

In the remainder of this paper, we first review literature suggesting that highlighting could increase the value of MT output for real-time communication and outline our hypotheses. We then present a study in which we compare keyword highlighting to two control conditions: no highlighting and random highlighting. Native English speakers performed three collaborative brainstorming tasks, one in each condition, with a Mandarin-speaking confederate. After each task, they rated their understanding of the messages, their impressions of their partner, and the quality of the collaboration. Keyword highlighting led to higher levels of understanding and more positive perceptions of partners and the collaboration versus no highlighting or random highlighting. The results can inspire the future development of MT-based communication tools.

BACKGROUND AND RELATED WORK

Textual Highlighting and Information Processing

Highlighting has been used as a strategy to support people's processing of information. With paper books, researchers noticed that readers preferred to use highlight markers and boxes to organize information on textbooks [e.g., 16]. With the development of digital media, the strategy of using highlighting has been applied to the design of email system interfaces, webpages, search tools, and web-based parallel translation systems (e.g., [1][5][6][24]).

The main function of highlighting is to help redistribute cognitive resources when processing messages. Since meaningful highlighting can improve the way information is organized and displayed, it reduces the cognitive load of information processing [25]. In an information search task, for example, highlighting the target information can improve searching and reading performance. When Web users want to track textual changes on the same web site at different times, highlighting changes can improve users' awareness of the dynamism of the web content [24].

Based on this evidence, we hypothesized that information processing during MT-mediated communication could also be directed by highlighting. The value of the highlighting, however, should differ depending on whether or not the highlighted words are semantically important for understanding the whole message. When key words in a message are highlighted, paying more attention to them should be beneficial to information processing. However, when random words in a message are highlighted, paying attention to them should not be helpful to understanding, and the highlighting can also have negative, distracting effects to information processing.

Textual Highlighting and Understanding

Highlighting may benefit people's understanding of textual material. When reading traditional textual books, doing highlighting (such as underlining) under important words helps improve understanding of the content. But this benefit disappears when unimportant words in the book content are highlighted [e.g., 13]. Kawasaki and colleagues [14] examined the effect of highlighting with computer-based reading tasks, finding that people's understanding of digital articles could be improved when important words, phrases, and sentences in the text were pre-highlighted.

In this study, we were interested in detecting whether highlighting would influence the understanding of messages in MT-mediated multilingual communication. It was worth noting that the semantic understanding under the current scenario would be different from article reading in previous research in several aspects. First, the textual messages would show up within conversation, which makes them more informal and flexible than messages in written articles. Second, the textual messages were generated by machine translation, which means the quality of the language might not be as good as texts written in one's native language. Third, in synchronous conversation, people are expected to understand and respond to others quickly. Overall, the difficulty and cognitive load in processing a machine-translated message during multilingual communication can be much higher than processing messages in an article.

Thus, we argue that the use of highlighting will be especially helpful for MT-mediated multilingual communication. Although imperfect translation between languages can be distracting, highlighting keywords of each

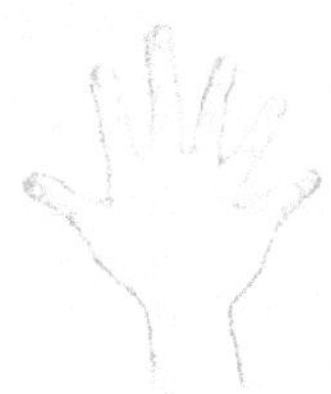

Figure 1. The *extra thumb* task with a brainstorming question of "What are the benefits and difficulties if people had an extra thumb on each hand".

message should help improve the clarity of messages and reduce the distraction of translation errors.

H1: People will find MT-translated messages with keyword highlighting to be more understandable than messages with no highlighting or with random highlighting.

H2: People will find MT-translated messages with keyword highlighting to be less distracting than MT-translated messages with no highlighting or random highlighting.

Random highlighting, on the other hand, could diminish clarity and introduce distractions because it focuses people's attention on possibly irrelevant portions of a message. Alternatively, people might ignore random highlighting altogether after determining it had no value for comprehension. We thus posed the following two research questions:

RQ1: How will random highlighting of a message affect the clarity of a message relative to the same message without any highlighting?

RQ2: How will random highlighting of a message affect ratings of distraction relative to the same message without any highlighting?

Textual Highlighting and Social Experience

In addition to information processing and understanding, we were also interested in examining how different types of highlighting would influence people's social experience during a MT-mediated conversation. Although a small number of recent studies have discussed both shortcomings and benefits of using MT to support social interaction between multilingual dyads, they focused more on analyzing the content rather than improving the presentation of translated messages.

In studies conducted by Yamashita and colleagues [28][30], participants from China, Korea and Japan were asked to collaborate on a tangram task either with a shared second language (English) or with different native languages with MT support. The results indicated that MT hurt the collaboration by making it hard to establish common ground [8]. Other studies, however, suggest that MT can have a positive effect on social experience. In Hautasaari's [11] experiment, for example, participants from Finland and Japan collaborated on a shaping factory game. He found that using MT improved interaction in multilingual dyads by increasing the production of social-emotional messages.

In this study, we go beyond exploring the effect of MT itself by examining how highlighting keywords in a translated message influences social experience during MT-mediated communication. We hypothesized that highlighting keywords in each message would improve social experience during the communication because the highlighting would reduce cognitive load in information processing. Because communication with their partner was smoother and less effortful than with unhighlighted MT output, people would form more positive impressions of their partner and the quality of the collaboration.

H3: People will have more positive impressions of their partners when messages have keyword highlighting rather than no highlighting or random highlighting.

H4: People will have more positive impressions of their collaborations when messages have keyword highlighting rather than no highlighting or random highlighting.

As with comprehension, it is possible that highlighting random words in a message could potentially hurt the establishment of these positive social experiences relative to no highlighting by increasing communication difficulties. It could also have no effect. We thus posed the following two research questions:

RQ3: How will random highlighting affect impressions of a partner in comparison to messages with no highlighting?

RQ4: How will messages with random highlighting affect impressions of the success of the collaboration in comparison to messages with no highlighting?

METHOD

To test our hypotheses and examine our research questions, we conducted a laboratory experiment with a 3-level single factor (non- vs. random- vs. keyword highlighting on the message) within-subject design. Random highlighting was included as a second control condition, to ensure that the effects of keyword highlighting could be attributed to their value in making sense of the messages rather than to their ability to focus peoples' attention on a smaller number of words. All participants were native English speakers from the U.S. who had no knowledge of Mandarin Chinese. Each participant completed three ten-minute brainstorming tasks

Natural English Sentence:
Instead of middle figure pointing, 6th finger at someone might be a new form of insulting.

↓

Manual-translated Chinese Sentence:
第六只手指指人将会取代中指指人成为一种新的侮辱方式。

↓

Machine-translated English Sentence (no highlighting):
Replace with the middle finger to point to others, the sixth finger pointing to the person may be a new kind of insulting way.

↓

Machine-translated English Sentence (keyword highlighting):
Replace with the middle finger to point to others, the sixth finger pointing to the person may be a new kind of insulting way.

Machine-translated English Sentence (random highlighting):
Replace with the middle finger to point to others, the sixth finger pointing to the person may be a new kind of insulting way.

Figure 2. The procedure of generating the machine translated sentences with keywords highlighted (example from the *extra thumb* task).

with his/her Chinese-speaking partner (who was actually a confederate). After each task, the participant was asked about his/her communication experience.

Participants

Thirty-six undergraduate students (20 female) from a U.S. university participated in the study. All had lived in U.S. for more than 10 years and spoke English as their only native language. Their mean age was 20.25 years (SD = 1.66).

Materials

The purpose of this study was to examine how different rules for highlighting text in received messages influenced participants' performance and experience. However, since no current online chat tool or MT module can identify and highlight keywords of a sentence automatically, we developed materials specialized for this study so that the participant could receive instant messages with different types of highlighting during the brainstorming discussion.

Tasks. Three brainstorming tasks asked people to generate ideas about "what are the benefits and difficulties if people had *an extra thumb on each hand / a third eye on the back of head / two wings on the back* in the future" (see Figure 1). These tasks have been used in previous brainstorming studies, and the structure and difficulty of these tasks are considered equivalent [26][27]. During the task, the participant was asked to generate as many different ideas as possible with his/her partner about the given topic. All the brainstorming discussions in this study were text-based. In order to make the best use of time to generate ideas and to rule out alternative explanations for differences such as different amounts of social conversation, participants were asked to follow 2 rules: (1) don't talk about things which are irrelevant to the given topic with the partner (e.g., self-introduction, social chat, etc.), and (2) don't evaluate others' ideas.

Idea pool. An idea pool, from which sentences on the confederate's side were selected, was also developed. Since the participant was told to brainstorm with a Chinese-speaking partner, the messages received by the participant were supposed to be (1) machine-translated English sentences from the partner's Chinese sentences, and (2) with highlighting of particular words in the message depending on the experimental condition.

Thus, we needed to simulate a situation in which the ideas were generated by a Chinese speaker, then passed through machine translation. We started with a pool of ideas collected from a previous brainstorming study [27]. In that original dataset, there were 300 ideas in English, 100 ideas for each brainstorming task. Since our original idea pool was in English, we first asked two native Mandarin Chinese speakers to manually translate all the ideas into Mandarin Chinese. To assess the consistency of translations across translators, we counted the percentage of the sentences receiving the same translation (from English to Chinese) from two native Chinese speakers. During the first round of independent translation, 80% of the messages got the same Chinese translation from both translators. For the remaining 20% of the sentences, the translators discussed the inconsistencies to create a final translation of each message. Next, we used Google Translate to generate English translations of the 300 manually translated Chinese sentences to simulate the quality of translation that people would experience in MT-mediated communication.

Highlighting. Working independently, two native English speakers manually generated the keyword highlighting. Their goal was to identify words that captured the main points of each sentence. Since the Chinese to English machine translated sentences could sometimes be difficult to understand, the two English speakers started from the original English sentences obtained from [27]. They first highlighted the key words in those natural English sentences, then highlighted the counterparts of those keywords in the machine translated English sentences (Figure 2). The consistency between their keywords highlighting on the natural sentences was good (Kappa=0.78). They then discussed their highlighting until they came to agreement.

Random highlighting. The preparation of random highlighting was conducted directly on the machine translated English sentences. To keep the amount of highlighting roughly equivalent, for every idea we randomly selected the same number of words that had been highlighted in the keyword condition. Taking the idea shown in Figure 3, for example, we first counted how many chunks of keywords were highlighted in each idea under the keyword highlighting condition (4 chunks in this example), then randomly highlighted the same number of words in the same idea under the random highlighting condition. We randomized which words to be highlighted in this condition. This randomization was conducted for the purpose of getting a balanced distribution between messages with the entirely nonsensical highlighting and messages with the sporadically sensical highlighting.

Software and Equipment

Chat tool. We developed an online chat tool that could display messages with different types of highlighting (see Figure 3, next page). On the participant's side of the chat interface, the participant could type and receive messages similarly to common IM chat tools such as Gtalk (see the top of Figure 3). After logging in, participants could see if their partner had logged into the same conversation and was available to receive their messages. To input messages, participants typed sentences in the chat box and clicked the enter key.

Confederate interface. Because we wanted the same messages to appear in all conditions, confederates' communication was constrained to the idea pool described earlier. The messages in this pool were already highlighted by color and categorized into no highlighting, random highlighting, and keyword highlighting. The confederate's side of the chat interface allowed him/her to select sentences from the idea pool.

Equipment. Both participants and the confederate were each seated at Dell computers with 25 inch monitors, separated by a divider. They wore headphones during the study so as not to be distracted by outside noise.

Procedure

Participants were brought to the laboratory and instructed about the rules to follow for the brainstorming tasks (no chat on irrelevant topics and no evaluation of one another's ideas). They then worked on three brainstorming tasks, one on each of the three brainstorming topics, and one with each of the three highlighting conditions. The order of tasks and highlighting conditions were counterbalanced across participants using a Latin Square design. Each task took 10 minutes.

Before each task, participants were told that they would have a brainstorming discussion with a partner who spoke Mandarin Chinese as his or her only native language. They were led to believe that they had a different partner for each task, though in reality there was only one partner, the confederate. We did this so that participants would rate their partners and the collaboration independently after each of the three highlighting conditions, rather than being influenced by earlier brainstorming discussions.

Participants typed their own ideas in their native language (that is, English) and received machine translated ideas (also in English but translated from Chinese) from their partners. Participants were made to believe that there was a MT module embedded in the chat tool for translation between English and Chinese.

During the conversation, the confederate selected machine translated English sentences from the pre-existing idea pool and sent these to the participant. The confederate configured the type of highlighting for ideas based on the current experimental condition. The confederate followed the same brainstorming rules as the participants, including no irrelevant chat during the discussion and no evaluation of the other person's ideas.

Measures

Participants answered the same questionnaire after each 10-minute brainstorming discussion. Responses to questions were provided on 7-point scales (1 = strongly disagree; 7= strongly agree). They were led to believe that they had a different Mandarin-speaking partner for each task.

Manipulation checks. Whether participants noticed the highlighted text was assessed by a single 7-point item, "I found some of the words in my partner's sentences were highlighted." Whether they found the highlighting sensible was assessed by a second 7-point item, "I found the highlighted words captured the key meaning of my partner's ideas accurately."

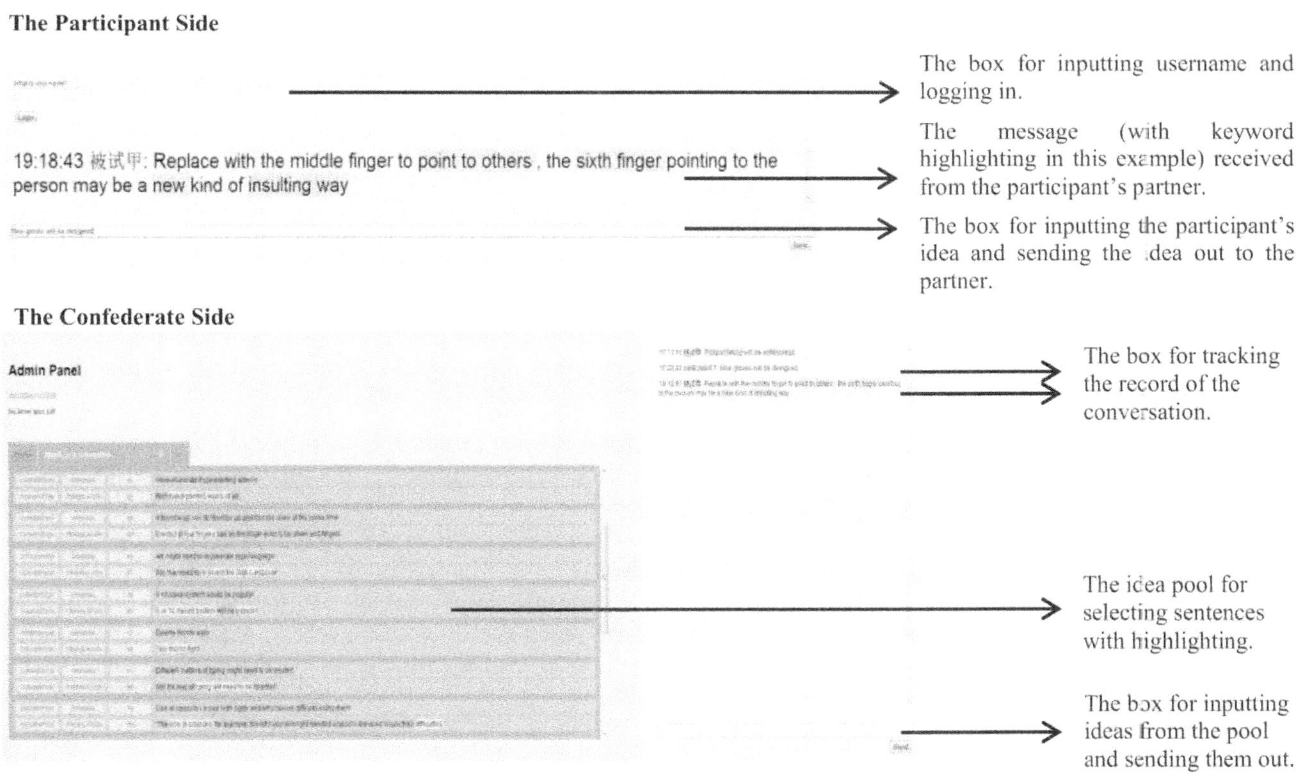

Figure 3. The interface of the chat tool developed in this study (top: participant side; bottom: confederate side).

Clarity of messages. People's understandings of the messages were assessed using a single item, "I felt my partner always expressed his/her idea clearly". Responses were on a scale of 1-7.

Distraction. The extent to which participants found the messages distracting was assessed using two questions ("The unclear information in my partner's ideas was distracting to me," "I had to think harder to understand the ambiguous information in my partner's ideas."). The two questions formed a reliable scale (Cronbach's $\alpha = .79$) and responses were averaged to create a measure of distraction.

Impressions of partner. Participants' impressions of their partners were measured using seven 7-point Likert scales (e.g., "My overall impression of my partner was very positive", "My partner seems friendly"). Factor Analysis with Varimax rotation indicated that these seven questions loaded on a single dimension that accounted for 57% percent of the variance. Scores were averaged to create a measure reflecting the positivity of their impressions of their partner (Cronbach's $\alpha = .88$).

Impressions of collaboration. Participants' impressions of the quality of their collaboration with their partner were measured using four 7-point Likert scales (e.g., "Generally, I'm satisfied with our collaboration on this task"). The questions formed a reliable scale (Cronbach's $\alpha = .73$) and were averaged to create a measure of quality of collaboration.

Cognitive effects of highlighting. The cognitive effects of highlighting were measured using three 7-point Likert scales (e.g., "I paid more attention to the highlighted words rather than other non-highlighted words in the same sentence"). The questions formed a reliable scale (Cronbach's $\alpha = .95$) and were averaged to create a measure of cognitive effects.

RESULTS

To test our hypotheses, we used repeated measures ANOVAs to detect whether participants' responses differed between highlighting conditions (non- vs. random- vs. keyword highlighting). Post-hoc LSD comparisons were used to compare performance between each pair of conditions.

Manipulation Checks

The manipulation checks indicated that participants noticed the highlighting ($F [2, 70] = 562.33$, $p < .0001$). Post-hoc comparisons showed that responses were higher for both keyword highlighting and random highlighting than no highlighting (both $p < .001$). Responses did not differ depending on the type of highlighting ($p = .90$). Participants rated keyword highlighting as significantly better at capturing the meaning of the message than random highlighting ($p < .001$). Therefore both manipulations were successful.

Understanding

H1 and H2 predicted that people's understanding of the messages would vary with different types of highlighting. Among all the three conditions of highlighting, the best understanding would be achieved under the keyword highlighting condition. To test this hypothesis, we examined the main effect of highlighting on ratings of message clarity (H1) and distraction (H2).

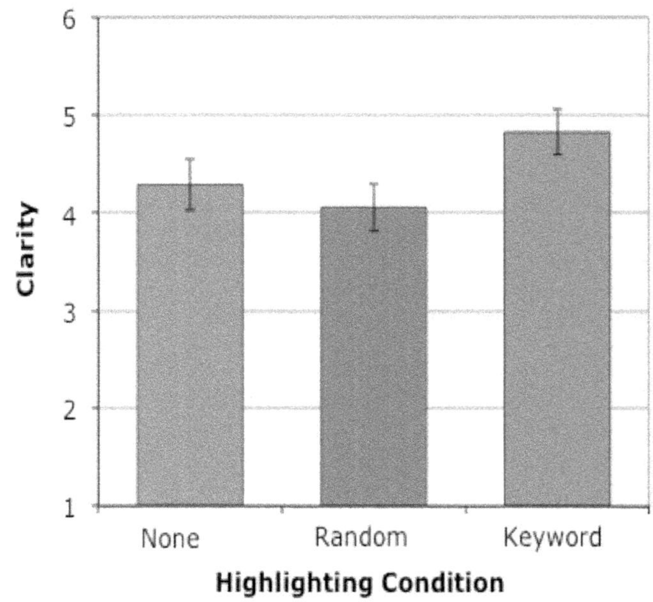

Figure 4. Mean clarity ratings by highlighting condition (error bars represent standard errors of the mean).

As shown in Figure 4, messages with keyword highlighting were better understood than messages with no highlighting or random highlighting ($F [2, 68] = 5.58$, $p = .006$). Post-hoc comparisons showed that clarity was significantly higher in the keywords highlighting ($M = 4.83$, $SD = 1.34$) than in the no highlighting condition ($M = 4.29$, $SD = 1.55$; $F [1, 34] = 5.59$, $p = .02$) or the random highlighting condition ($M = 4.06$, $SD = 1.41$; $p = .004$). These findings provide strong support for H1. RQ1 asked about the effects of random highlighting vs. no highlighting. Our analysis found no significant difference in clarity ratings between the two conditions ($p = .32$).

With respect to distraction, there was a significant main effect of highlighting ($F [2, 70] = 3.82$, $p = .03$) but the pattern of results was only partially consistent with H2 (see Figure 5). Ratings of distraction in the keyword highlighting condition ($M = 3.21$, $SD = 1.28$) were significantly lower than in the random highlighting condition ($M = 3.86$, $SD = 1.45$, $p = .01$) but did not differ significantly from those in the no highlighting condition ($M = 3.49$, $SD = 1.43$, $p = .20$). RQ2 asked about the effects of random vs. no highlighting on distraction ratings. We again found no significant difference in ratings between the two conditions ($p = .16$).

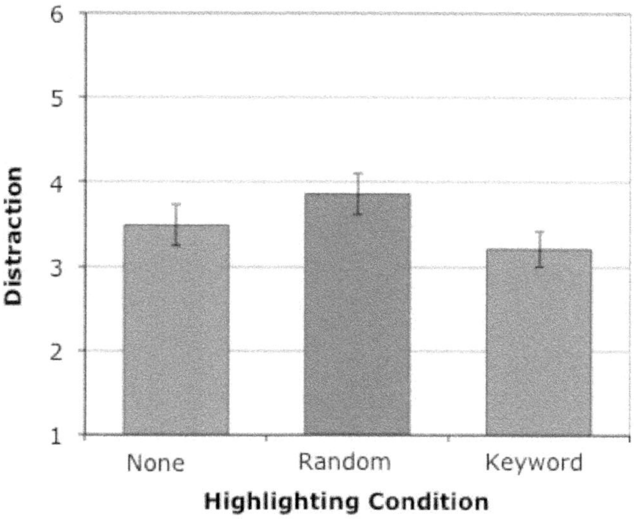

Figure 5. Mean distraction ratings by highlighting condition (error bars represent standard errors of the mean).

Social Experience

H3 and H4 predicted that people would rate their partners and their collaboration more favorably with keyword highlighting than with no highlighting or random highlighting.

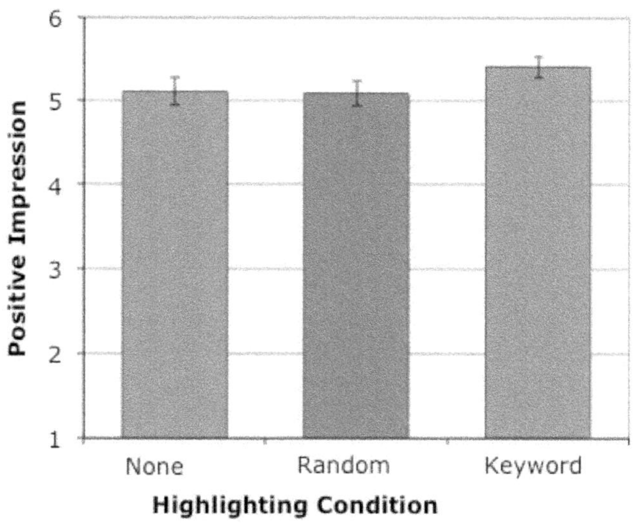

Figure 6. Mean impressions of partner by highlighting condition (error bars represent standard errors of the mean).

Consistent with H3, keyword highlighting led to more positive impressions of one's partner than random or no highlighting ($F [2, 68] = 4.49$, $p = .02$; see Figure 6). Impressions in the keywords-highlighting condition ($M = 5.41$, $SD = 0.77$) were significantly higher than in the no highlighting condition ($M = 5.11$, $SD = 0.94$, $p = .01$) or random highlighting condition ($M = 5.09$, $SD = 0.89$ $p = .02$). RQ3 asked about the effects of random highlighting vs. no highlighting on impressions of the partner. The two conditions did not differ significantly ($p =. 87$).

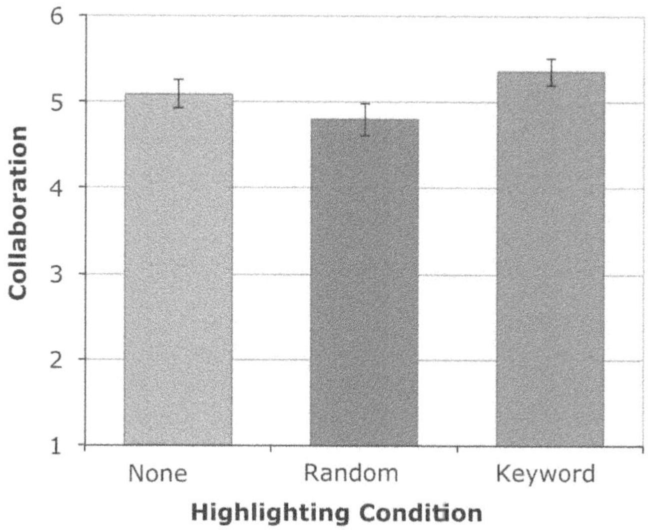

Figure 7. Mean ratings of the quality of the collaboration by highlighting condition (error bars represent standard errors of the mean).

As can be seen in Figure 7, participants' impressions of the success of their collaboration were also influenced by keyword highlighting ($F (2, 68) = 6.13$, $p = .004$), which fully supported H4. Ratings of how well the pair collaborated were significantly higher in the keyword highlighting condition ($M = 5.36$, $SD = 0.92$) than in the no highlighting condition ($M = 5.09$, $SD = 0.90$; $p = .05$) or random highlighting condition ($M = 4.80$, $SD = 1.13$; $p = .003$). RQ4 asked about the effects of random highlighting vs. no highlighting on perceptions of the collaboration. There was a tendency for ratings in the random highlighting condition to be lower than those in the no highlighting condition, but this difference was not significant ($p = .10$).

Effects of highlighting on cognitive processing

To assess whether ease of cognitive processing might explain the benefits of keyword highlighting, we examined people's responses to our measure of cognitive effects (which combined attention, understanding and speed of processing). The result indicated people processed information more effortlessly with keyword highlighting ($M = 4.84$, $SD = 1.49$) rather with random highlighting ($M = 2.72$, $SD = 1.35$; $F [1, 35] = 59.54$, $p < .0001$).

Correlation between understanding and social experience

We further tested the relationship between the understanding measures (clarity and distraction) and the social experience measures (impression of partner and quality of collaboration). As shown in Table 1, there were significant positive correlations between understanding and social experience in this study.

	1	2	3	4
1.Clarity	-			
2.Distraction	-.24*	.79**		
3.Impression	.58**	-.20*	.88**	
4.Collaboration	.64**	-.22*	.65**	.73**

*$p < .05$, **$p<.01$.

Table 1. Correlations between clarity, distraction, impression of the partner and quality of collaboration.

DISCUSSION

Our results suggest that highlighting can be used to facilitate MT-mediated communication. When keyword highlighting was provided, people understood messages better and had a more positive social experience.

The comparison between different types of highlighting with respect to understanding and social experience implied something surprising yet inspirational. As we hypothesized, keyword highlighting led to significant improvement in perceived clarity of messages and social experience. Furthermore, there was a positive relationship between message clarity and impressions of both a partner and the quality of collaboration. The correlation between clarity and quality of collaboration echoes Yamashita and colleagues' studies [28][30] by confirming the fundamental role of message understanding in MT-mediated collaboration. In their studies, the use of MT, as opposed to a shared second language, created confusion about the meaning of referring expressions and hindered group collaboration. Instead of trying to resolve the shortcomings of MT technology, our study focused on exploring an alternative way to support understanding. The results demonstrate the value of using simple designs to support comprehension. When message understanding is improved, we also improve the collaborative and social aspects of communication.

Further, the positive effect of using MT on social aspects of multilingual communication provides complementary knowledge for understanding the relationship between MT mediation and group collaboration. Although some previous studies have shown social benefits of using MT in multilingual communication [e.g., 11], this benefit was attributed to an increased use of social-emotional messages in MT communication. In our study, neither social chat nor idea evaluation was allowed (and we also checked the chat log to make sure participants followed this rule). In this case, the more positive impressions of the partner and of the collaboration can't be attributed to the use of social-emotional messages. Rather, it appears to be due to the ease of understanding a partner's messages. This provides an alternative way to think about how to improve social experience during MT-mediated communication.

Another interesting finding was the similarity of communication experience in the random highlighting and no highlighting conditions. Although random highlighting didn't provide any benefit, it didn't disrupt the communication either. It appears, based on their self-reports about their cognitive processing of the messages, that people didn't pay much attention to the highlighting if it was applied randomly. This suggests that automatic real time keyword highlighting may still be valuable even if the process is less than perfect. People may be able to overlook cases in which words that are not relevant to the meaning of the message are erroneously highlighted.

The mechanisms behind the keyword highlighting effect can also be inferred from people's self-reported cognitive processing in the keyword and random highlighting conditions. Highlighting appears to direct people's attention, but people also evaluate whether the highlighted words are worthy of their attention. The distribution of cognitive sources may be adjusted based on this process. Investigating the learning process in processing highlighted messages can be both of theoretical value to better understand human-information interaction and of practical value to the design of tools to support comprehension.

Design Implications

The findings have several design implications. First, the data indicate that keyword highlighting is an effective way to support MT-based communication at low cost. In the field of natural language processing (NLP), a huge body of work aims to improve algorithms for generating better translation between languages (e.g., [21]). However, the actual experience of using MT to communicate shows that current MT tools still have much space to improve for supporting real time communication.

From the psycholinguistics and communication literature, however, we learn that ambiguous and fragmentary information is a natural part of human language, while processing this imperfect information is part of people's everyday language use [6]. This suggests we could improve MT-mediated communication by not only focusing on the "MT" part, but also the "communication" part, such as developing enriched communication channels to support the processing of imperfect translation. The positive outcomes of simple keyword highlighting support this idea. The value of this communication-oriented approach is multi-faceted, including better understanding and social experience, and it is arguably at lower cost computation- and implementation-wise than traditional NLP work and other research which focuses on translation repair in HCI (e.g., [17][19]).

Further, the similar levels of clarity and experience in the random highlighting and no highlighting conditions suggest that people can tolerate semantically unimportant highlighting. Keyword highlighting may be implemented with simple, cost-effective algorithms, even if these sacrifice some precision in keyword identification. Even if the identification, and thus highlighting, of keywords is imprecise, it doesn't make a message harder to understand than one with no highlighting at all.

Technical Feasibility

The primary goal and contribution of our study was to explore whether working on technical solutions to translation interpretation, such as keyword highlighting, is a worthwhile use of energy by ensuring that highlighting has practical and cognitive value. Thus, we chose manual highlighting as a Wizard of Oz method to ensure high-quality highlighting. We countered this with the random condition to see whether poor-quality highlighting is harmful. Our results show that keyword highlighting is useful and efficient, even when the accuracy of highlighting is compromised. Such evidence makes it more likely that simple techniques can become plausible design solutions.

Our work opens up a design space for exploring technical solutions for tagging keywords in real time. When adding the feature of keyword highlighting to a MT tool, we need to further think about *who* will identify the keywords, *how* the agent performs the processing, and *what* methods can best highlight keywords under the time constraints of real-time communication. For example, it is possible to employ simple heuristics such as treating all verbs and nouns as keywords to obtain initial highlights first, then ask crowdsourcing workers to revise the results by clicking on individual words to add or remove highlights. When multiple workers perform this revision task at the same time, we can count the frequency of highlight-addition and highlight-removal to obtain a majority decision. Because the task that individual workers have to do is greatly simplified, a design of this sort that integrates machine processing and human processing and leverages crowd-based parallelism has the potential to perform quality and efficient highlighting.

Limitations and Future Directions

There were several limitations to our study that leave open important future work. First, the effect of keyword highlighting was gained by a simple form of highlighting, by presenting keywords with a yellow background. Other highlighting methods might weaken or strengthen this effect. In Wu and Yuan's [25] study, they compared the effects of highlighting with different colors on computer-based table content searching. Similar comparisons could be conducted in future studies to get deeper understandings on which visual form(s) of highlighting would be most helpful in supporting MT-mediated multilingual communication. The visualization could be extended to other formats besides color highlighting.

Further, the brainstorming task in our experiment was conducted in English with native English-speaking participants. It is not clear if the effects of keyword highlighting would be different when applied to other populations or to translation between different pairs of languages. People from East Asian cultures tend to distribute their attention to target and background objects more equally during information processing, whereas North Americans pay more attention to the target information rather than the background [20]. Perhaps this difference could weaken the effect of keyword highlighting during the MT-mediated communication among East Asians. Moreover, the culture-based communication style could also impact the understanding of messages in different languages. It will be interesting to see how such factors and the highlighting would interact to influence the quality of multilingual communication.

Further, the brainstorming rules could bring both benefits and limitations to our study. For the purpose of verifying the effects of keyword highlighting through a Wizard of Oz study, such rules were helpful for controlling the pool of sentences that confederates could choose from to present to participants. However, some threats to the generalizability of our findings were also raised from using such rules. As has been pointed out by Clark [7, 8], some conversational moves avoided in our task (e.g., asking questions) could play important roles in the establishment of common ground. To address this point, future studies should go further to examine the effect of keyword highlighting on MT-supported communication in less constrained settings.

CONCLUSION

Our research suggests that keyword highlighting is a useful way to improve the quality of MT-mediated communication. Compared with no highlighting and random highlighting, participants understood messages better and rated their partners and collaboration more highly when keywords in each machine translated message were highlighted. The findings inform the design of new tools to support communication and collaboration across language boundaries.

ACKNOWLEDGMENTS

This research was funded in part by National Science Foundation grant #1025425. The material is also based in part on work supported by the National Science Foundation, while Susan Fussell was working at the Foundation. Any opinion, findings, and conclusions or recommendations expressed in this material are those of the authors and do not necessarily reflect the views of the National Science Foundation. We thank Leslie Setlock, Jean-Carlos Polanco, John Lee and Monica Chen for their assistance and the anonymous reviewers for their valuable comments.

REFERENCES

1. Abu-Hakima, S., McFarland, C., & Meech, J.F. (2001). An agent-based system for email highlighting. In *Proc. AGENTS 2001*, 224–225.
2. Aiken, M., Wang, J., Gu, L., & Paolillo, J. (2011). An exploratory study of how technology supports communication in multilingual groups. *International Journal of e-Collaboration* 7, 1, 17–29.
3. Barner-Rasmussen, W., & Bjorkman, I. (2007). Language fluency, socialization and inter-unit

relationships in Chinese and Finnish subsidiaries. *Management and Organizational Review, 3*, 105–128.

4. Bederson, B.B., Hu, C., & Resnik, P. (2010). Translation by iterative collaboration between monolingual users. In *Proc. Graphics Interface 2010*, 39–46.
5. Chessa, F., & Brelstaff, G. (2011). Going beyond Google Translate? In *Proc. the 9th ACM SIGCHI Italian Chapter International Conference on Computer-Human Interaction 2011*, 108–113.
6. Chi, E.H., Hong, H., L., Heiser, J., Card, S.K., & Gumbrecht, M. (2007). ScentIndex and ScentHighlights: productive reading techniques for conceptually reorganizing subject indexes and highlighting passages. *Information Visualization, 6*, 1, 32–47.
7. Clark, H. H. (1996). *Using Language*. Cambridge Press.
8. Clark, H.H., & Brennan, S.E. (1991). Grounding in Communication. In L.B. Resnick, R.M. Levine & S.D. Teasley (Eds.), *Perspectives on Socially Shared Cognition* (pp. 127–149). Washington, DC: APA.
9. Feely, A.-J., & Harzing, A.W.K. (2003) Language management in multinational companies. *Cross-Cultural Management: An Int'l Journal, 10*, 37–52.
10. Harzing, A-W., & Feely, A.J. (2008). The language barrier and its implications for HQ-subsidiary relationships. *Cross-cultural Management: An International Journal, 15*, 49–61.
11. Hautassari, A. (2010). Machine translation effects on group interaction: an intercultural collaboration experiment. In *Proc. ICIC 2010*, 69–78.
12. Henderson, J.K. (2005). Language diversity in international management teams. *International Studies of Management and Organization, 35*, 66–82.
13. Johnson, D., & Wen, S. (1976). Effects of correct and extraneous markings under time limits on reading comprehension. *Psych. in the Schools, 13*, 454–456.
14. Kawasaki, K., Sasaki, H., & Yamaguchi, H. (2008). Effectiveness of highlighting as a prompt in text reading on a computer monitor. In *Proc. the 8th WSEAS Conference on Multimedia System and Signal Processing 2008*, 311–315.
15. Lim, J., & Yang, Y.P. (2008). Exploring computer-based multilingual negotiation support for English-Chinese dyads: Can we negotiate in our native languages? *Behaviour & Info. Tech., 27*, 139–151.
16. Marshall, C.C. (1997). Annotation: from paper books to digital library. In *Proc. the 2nd ACM international Conference on Digital Libraries 1997*, 131–140.
17. Miyabe, M., & Yoshino, T. (2010). Influence of detecting inaccurate message in real-time remote text-based communication via machine translation. In *Proc. ICIC 2010*, 59–67.
18. Miyabe, M., Yoshino, T., & Shigenobu, T. (2009). Effects of undertaking translation repair using back translation. In *Proc. IWIW 2009*, 33–40.
19. Morita, D., & Ishida, T. (2009). Collaborative translation by monolinguals with machine translators. In *Proc. IUI 2009*, 361–365.
20. Nisbett, R. (2003). *The Geography of Thought: How Asians and Westerners Think Differently and Why*. New York: Free Press.
21. Olive, J., Christianson, C., & McCary, J. (2011). *Handbook of Natural Language Processing and Machine Translation: DARPA Global Autonomous Language Exploitation*. Springer Press.
22. Olson, G.M., & Olson, J.S. (2000). Distance matters. *Human Computer Interaction, 15*, 139–178.
23. Tange, H., & Lauring, J. (2009). Language management and social interaction within the multilingual workplace. *Journal of Communication Management, 13*, 218–232.
24. Teevan, J., Dumais, S.T., & Liebling, D.J. (2010). A longitudinal study of how highlighting web content change affects people's web interaction. In *Proc. CHI 2010*, 1353–1356.
25. Wu, J., & Yuan, Y. (2003). Improving searching and reading performance: the effect of highlighting and text color coding. *Information & Management*, 40, 617–637.
26. Wang, H.C., Cosley, D., & Fussell, S.R. (2010). Idea Expander: supporting group brainstorming with conversationally triggered visual thinking stimuli. In *Proc. CSCW 2010*, 103–106.
27. Wang, H.C., Fussell, S.R., & Cosley, D. (2011). From diversity to creativity: stimulating group brainstorming with cultural differences and conversationally-retrieved picture. In *Proc. CSCW 2011*, 265–274.
28. Yamashita, N., & Ishida, T. (2006). Effects of machine translation on collaborative work. In *Proc. CSCW 2006*, 515–523.
29. Yamashita, N., & Ishida, T. (2006). Automatic prediction of misconceptions in multilingual computer-mediated communication. In *Proc. IUI 2006*, 62–69.
30. Yamashita, N., Inaba, R., Kuzuoka, H., & Ishida, T. (2009). Difficulties in establishing common ground in multiparty groups using machine translation. In *Proc. CHI 2009*, 679–688.
31. Yeh, C-L., & Chen, Y-C. (2004). Topic identification in Chinese based on centering model. *Proc. ACL 2004 Workshop on Reference Resolution and its Applications.*

Improving Teamwork Using Real-Time Language Feedback

Yla R. Tausczik
Human-Computer Interaction Institute
Carnegie Mellon University
ylataus@cs.cmu.edu

James W. Pennebaker
Department of Psychology
The University of Texas at Austin
pennebaker@mail.utexas.edu

ABSTRACT
We develop and evaluate a real-time language feedback system that monitors the communication patterns among students in a discussion group and provides real-time instructions to shape the way the group works together. As an initial step, we determine which group processes are related to better outcomes. We then experimentally test the efficacy of providing real-time instructions which target two of these group processes. The feedback system was successfully able to shape the way groups worked together. However, only appropriate feedback given to groups that were not working well together from the start was able to improve group performance.

Author Keywords
Feedback; linguistic analysis; CSCW; teamwork; CMC.

ACM Classification Keywords
H.5.3 Information Interfaces and Presentation: Group and Organizational Interfaces: CSCW

INTRODUCTION
Using social visualizations to improve group dynamics is a powerful new approach to supporting teamwork. Social visualizations monitor either non-verbal or verbal communication and make subtle aspects of the communication explicit by displaying them in real-time (e.g. [5, 19, 24]). The guiding principle of many of these implementations of social visualizations is that by drawing attention to aspects of the group dynamics, group members will become more aware, and as result will change the way they are communicating in beneficial ways. For example, DiMicco and colleagues [5] designed Second Messenger, a tool that displayed information about the inequalities in participation among group members. In response to their social visualizations, because of greater awareness, over-participators talked less.

Social visualizations provide a good instrument for supporting teamwork in a few ways. By tracking communication patterns, they are able to measure important aspects of group dynamics. Good communication is key to effective teamwork [14]. By providing real-time information on the group dynamics, they provide a mechanism to shape teamwork. Through awareness of the current group dynamics individuals can make continuous adjustments to their behavior in the group.

Leshed and colleagues' GroupMeter, is an especially good example of a social visualization tool [18, 19] . GroupMeter tracks the words people write to each other over chat during the group task. It displays in real-time word use, such as level of agreement, that is relevant to the group's dynamics. Focusing on the words people use to communicate is an especially good source of information on group dynamics. Groups that work well together typically exchange more knowledge and establish good social relationships, which is reflected in the way that they use words [21, 28]. GroupMeter is a special type of social visualization which we will refer to as a **real-time language feedback system**, because it provides group dynamic information based on the words people use during a group interaction.

Despite the tremendous potential of social visualizations to change how groups work together, their advancement has been impeded in a few ways. First, these implementations of social visualizations strive to make members more aware of their group dynamics, yet these systems have focused on very limited dimensions of the group dynamics. Further, the few dimensions that have been displayed, such as balanced participation, are not necessarily the most important group processes. DiMicco and colleagues [5] successfully increased the balance of participation in their groups through social visualizations, however unequal participation may actually be better for producing high quality work [15, 16].

Second, these implementations of social visualizations have relied on individuals to figure out on their own how to change their communication; this is a daunting task. Individuals are already cognitively overloaded during teamwork. Further, individuals may not respond to greater awareness by changing their communication in beneficial ways. For example, Leshed and colleagues [19] found that in response to displaying agreement information group members agreed with each other more. However, more agreement led to lower quality work because group members passively agreed with each other instead of making substantial contributions to the group.

In this paper we tackle these two challenges to advance the design of real-time language feedback systems. Shaping group dynamics relies on understanding the basic question: *Why do some groups of people work well together while others do not?* Despite the substantial amount of research on groups, there is surprising little consistent evidence for which

CHI 2013, April 27–May 2, 2013, Paris, France.

group processes promote good group outcomes [21, 20]. Intelligent Tutoring Systems, which serve a similar purpose for student learning by providing real-time feedback to students to guide their learning, have benefited from sophisticated psychological models of student learning [1, 8]. Without good models of learning they would not have been able to realize substantial gains over traditional classroom teaching. Better models of group dynamics will provide a basis for giving useful real-time group dynamic information. In this paper, we evaluate the importance of four group processes at promoting better group outcomes.

Group interventions have a long history. One technique in experimental psychology has been to use specifically crafted instructions to change group dynamics. For example, Nemeth and colleagues [22] proposed that conflict and dissension in groups was important for promoting group creativity. To test the importance of dissension as a group process they included a direction in the standard instructions for group members to disagree with each other during the group task (i.e. "most studies suggest that you *should* debate and even criticize each other's ideas"). Specific instructions like this one are effective in changing the way that groups work together in a targeted way. In the design of our feedback system, we make use of specific instructions to change group dynamics.

In this paper we describe the development and evaluation of a real-time language feedback system that improves upon Leshed and colleagues' GroupMeter [18, 19]. Like GroupMeter our feedback system monitors the words people write to each other over chat during the group task. However, instead of displaying the group dynamic information visually the feedback system gives instructions that target specifically selected group processes. Our feedback system addresses the problem of monitoring irrelevant group dynamics by targeting two group processes that we show to be related to better group outcomes. It also addresses the problem of relying of individuals to change their communication in beneficial ways by giving groups specific instructions that target these relevant group processes.

"Good" Group Dynamics

The scientific study of groups is messy. There are no standard rules governing the behavior of groups and a web of theories, often with little empirical evidence, have been published that try to explain different aspects of group dynamics [20]. Very broadly, historical small group research has been categorized into three schools of thought [21]. Named after the universities of the main researchers in the 1950s-1980s, each approach adopted a different perspective on the most important aspect of groups to study. This research is informed most strongly by the approaches coming out of two of these schools.

The Harvard school focused on group interactions and processes [2, 3]. Bales and colleagues developed the Interaction Process Analysis to describe the ways in which group members were interacting during group discussions. They used this method to characterize groups along three dimensions: relative dominance, friendliness, and task focus. While these group processes characterize the patterns of interactions in groups well, researchers have been unable to consistently relate these group processes to group outcomes [21]. The Illinois school studied small laboratory groups and focused exclusively on the conditions that increased task performance (e.g. [16]). They found that task performance was dependent on a number of conditions, including group composition, group structure, task type, and communication platform. However, the Illinois school exclusively studied the input conditions (e.g. group composition) under which groups performed well, while ignoring how groups were actually interacting in order to perform well [21]. We combine these two approaches by trying to identify ***group processes***, which we define as patterns of interactions among group members, that produce better group outcomes, such as higher group satisfaction and performance.

The most compelling contemporary theory of group processes focuses on distinguishing between social regulation processes, which describe the social interactions between group members, and information processing processes, which describe how groups gather, organize, and process information as a group [21]. We describe a few of the most commonly discussed group processes as they are relevant to this theory.

Social regulation group processes operate by motivating, regulating, and coordinating groups of individuals through social processes. Groups are hypothesized to perform better, especially in the long run, if they are more cohesive and have deeper social relationships. Creating groups that have stronger social relationships is also an end in itself. Effective teams are ones in which individuals enjoy being a part of the team and want to work together again.

There are a few specific group processes that are relevant to social regulation. *Positivity*, the degree to which group members are encouraging, can enhance interpersonal relationships and motivate individuals to work harder [17]. However, positivity can also detract from task effort when it leads to off-topic conversations. Positivity is reflected in way group members communicate to each other; groups that are positive use more positive emotion words and make more statements agreeing with each other. Empirically when positivity is measured by analyzing communication patterns the outcomes of positivity are mixed. In one study, groups engaged in a flight simulation that used more positive emotion words and agreed with each other more during the simulation performed better at the task [6]. In a different study, successful coalitions of business students agreed with each other more during the negotiation task [12]. However, Leshed and colleagues [18] found that agreement was related to being passive, and led to lower group satisfaction and performance.

Engagement, the degree to which group members are paying attention and connecting with each other, can enhance group cohesion. If individuals are engaged with each other they are more likely to stay motivated and enjoy the task. Engagement is reflected in the degree to which group members tend to converge in the way they talk [13]. In general, groups tend to converge in the way that they talk, this is called Language Style Matching (LSM) [23]. When groups are more engaged their language style converges more [13]. In one study of groups solving puzzles, groups that were more engaged felt greater group cohesion, although they did not perform better on the task [7]. However, in a naturalistic study of real hostage negotiations, higher LSM between hostage takers and police negotiators, which is suggestive of more engagement, was associated with more successful outcomes [29]. Empirical evidence suggests that engagement may be associated with greater group satisfaction and performance, although the results are inconclusive.

One of the most studied aspects of group dynamics, as well as commonly represented in social visualizations, is the balance of participation among group members. *Equal participation*, the degree to which all group members are equally involved, can enable everyone in the group to be active and enjoy the experience [10, 16]. However, equal participation in groups has been associated with both higher and lower quality work [16, 15, 9].

Information processing group processes focus on the cognitive aspects rather than the social aspects of group interactions. Groups can be thought of as information processing systems; through discussion, groups gather, organize, and process information [11, 21]. Limitations and advances in the group processes through which group members share and process information lead to changes in group performance. For example, the degree of *information exchange*, that is the degree to which more information and more relevant information is shared can effect group performance [27]. Despite the fact that all the relevant information to make a decision may be known in a group, group members may not share this information [4]. The degree of information exchange is reflected in group communication in part by the quantity of on task communication. Empirical evidence suggests, information exchange, as measured by quantity of communication and on task communication is related to greater performance. Groups engaged in a flight simulation that communicated more performed better on the task [26]. Groups of students solving problems together that made more task focused statements performed better [14].

We focus on these three social regulation group processes– positivity, engagement, equal participation– and this one information processing group process–information exchange. In theory all four group processes could substantially benefit groups, however there is insufficient empirical evidence examining the impact of these group processes on group outcomes.

THE CURRENT STUDIES

A real-time language feedback system was designed to improve teamwork by targeting specific group processes. This paper had two objectives. The first was to establish which group processes should be targeted. The second was to experimentally evaluate whether our real-time language feedback system could improve teamwork. To address these two goals three studies were conducted: Pilot Study, Study 1, and Study 2. In each study, students took part in small group discussions over instant message to try to better understand a few psychology theories. Students were tested before and after the group discussions to gauge learning. Group work was assessed by using a group discussion task because it is naturalistic, groups are often formed to learn from each other, and it allowed access to a large sample of groups.

Research Objective 1: To identify group processes related to higher quality teamwork

There are many theories about what constitutes good group dynamics. The focus was on four commonly discussed group processes: positivity, engagement, equal participation, and information exchange. These group processes can be measured linguistically and there is some theoretical and empirical evidence to suggest that they encourage better teamwork. However, the relationship between any group processes and effective teamwork is not well established. To address Research Objective 1 we determined which if any of these four group processes, as measured by language use, was correlated with better group satisfaction and performance across the three studies. The Study 1 was specifically designed to test Research Objective 1 (see Table 1), however we analyzed patterns across all three studies to determine the most robust effects.

Research Objective 2: To capitalize on observed differences in group processes to improve teamwork using a real-time language feedback system

By addressing Research Objective 1, it was possible to establish which if any of the four group processes was related to better teamwork. Study 2 was designed to experimentally evaluate whether we could improve teamwork by providing real-time language feedback that targeted these group processes by providing individualized instructions. Two of the group processes, engagement and information exchange, were selected because they were the most strongly related to better teamwork. In Study 2 a controlled experiment with 4 conditions (no feedback, engagement feedback only, information feedback only, both feedback types) was conducted to evaluate the effectiveness of the feedback.

METHOD

A Pilot Study, Study 1, and Study 2 were conducted to develop and evaluate the real-time language feedback system.

Pilot Study

Participants – In the Pilot Study, 494 students from two introductory psychology classes taught in Fall of 2010 participated in the group exercise as part of the class requirements. Of these participants 59 percent were female, they were aged 17 to 34 (M = 19). Participants were randomly assigned to groups of 2-5 students (M = 2.9) based on when they logged in to complete the assignment.

Procedure and Measures – Students logged into an education platform, Texas Online World of Educational Research (TOWER), at specified times to complete the group interaction task [25]. The education platform was an online course center where students took surveys, took quizzes, completed writing assignments, and participated in group chat. Prior to logging into the system students were instructed that in order

	Design	Feedback System	# Participants	# Groups	Satisfaction	Pre-quiz	Post-quiz
Pilot Study	Correlational	Yes	494	173	3.11 (0.98)	76.4% (19.5%)	83.9% (16.9%)
Study 1	Correlational	No	851	183	2.56 (0.80)	35.9% (14.7%)	46.0% (17.5%)
Study 2	Experimental	Yes	816 (621)	210 (160)	3.09 (1.00)	70.2% (16.1%)	72.1% (14.7%)

Table 1. Overview of the three group discussion studies. Means (standard deviations) of group satisfaction as well as performance on quizzes before and after group discussion are given. For Study 2, due to technical errors, only 621 individuals in 160 groups were included in analyses.

to complete the assignment they would need to read supplementary material on a few psychological theories (e.g. 10 pages of the textbook).

Once students logged into the educational platform they were directed to the first quiz. The quiz was 10 multiple-choice questions; it tested students' knowledge of the reading material. After completing the quiz they were randomly matched with other students currently waiting. When there were at least 2 students and no more than 5 students, individuals were directed to an instant messaging platform that was built into the educational platform. The group chat began as soon as someone typed the first message and lasted for 20 minutes.

During the chat groups received feedback messages this will be explained in more detail below. After 20 minutes, the chat window closed automatically. Students took a second 10 multiple-choice question quiz and rated their group members using the Interaction Rating Questionnaire (IRQ) modified to be appropriate for a group [23].

Group Process Variables – Four group processes were predicted to influence group satisfaction and performance based on the previous literature. Language markers were constructed for each of the four variables based on face valid measures and the previous literature. Language was analyzed using Language Inquiry and Word Count (LIWC) at the level of the group and individual as appropriate. Analyses control for group size, which can create statistical artifacts in the language markers.

Positivity Positive emotion words (*nice, good, great*) and assents (*yes, agree*) were converted to z-scores and summed as a measure of positivity [28].

Engagement The degree of language convergence, a proxy of engagement, was measured by calculating Language Style Matching (LSM) among pairs in the group (see [13]) and taking the average among all pairs in the group (see [7]). Pairwise LSM is the average difference of nine function word categories measured by LIWC.

Equal participation The Gini coefficient of individual level word count in the group was taken as a measure of equal participation. It was reverse scored, so that higher numbers show more equal participation.

Information exchange Word count and first-person singular pronouns were converted to z-scores, Word count minus first person singular was taken as a measure of information exchange. Word count is a commonly used crude measure of the total information exchanged (e.g. [26]). First-person singular pronouns suggest self-focus rather than topic focus [28], thus we refined the crude measure by penalized for self-focus rather than topic focus.

Hand coding confirmed that the linguistic markers were adequate proxies for the group processes. Thirty Mechanical Turkers rated a random sample of 30, 5-minute chat samples taken from the middle of the group discussions. Each sample was rated by 5 coders for the group process dimensions. Engagement, equal participant, and information exchange were coded with good inter-rater agreement (ICC = 0.68-0.72) and there was high agreement between the group process variables and their corresponding linguistic markers ($r(28) = 0.49\text{-}0.68, p < 0.01$). Positivity was the most difficult to code; there was only slight agreement between the coders (ICC = 0.49) and rated positivity was not related to the linguistic markers of positivity ($r(28) = 0.06, p = 0.74$). Coders may not have agreed on what being positive meant. The proposed linguistic markers of positivity were used nonetheless as a face valid measure of the number of times that group members agreed with each other and expressed positive emotion.

A Real-time Language Feedback System

A feedback system was designed to shape group dynamics by giving real-time language feedback. Groups were given feedback messages instructing them how to improve their group dynamics. Instructions were created to target a specific group processes. For example, engagement feedback instructed participants to pay more attention to what the other group members were saying (e.g. *"Your group is working OK but could be improved. Be sure and pay attention to what others are saying."*) while information exchange feedback instructed participants to stay on topic and share more material from the readings (e.g. *"You are discussing the relevant material OK, you can improve. Be sure and share information from the readings."*).

Feedback messages provided individualized instructions based on the current group dynamics. Group dynamics were assessed every few minutes; each time the targeted group process (e.g. information exchange) was rated on a 4-point scale from "Poor" to "Good" based on the language markers of that group process. Groups received a different instruction based on their current level of the group process. For example, if a group scored "Poor" on a group process they would be told that they were doing poorly and needed to improve (e.g. *"You are not discussing the relevant material. Focus on the material and share more information from the readings"*). If a group scored "Good" on a group process then they would receive a message telling them they were doing well (e.g. *"You are doing a good job discussing the relevant material. Everyone seems to be paying attention to the topic."*). There were four instructions corresponding to the four ratings for each group process. For the first deployment of the feedback we chose to evaluate a group as a whole, so that group members would have consistent instructions. The instructions were presented to the group using javascript pop-up messages above the chat box and logged for later analysis.

Current group dynamics were assessed by measuring language markers in nearly real time. Group chat messages from the last time interval (e.g. last 2.5 minutes) were collected and processed through LIWC running on the server. A group process for that time interval was rated based benchmarks determined from previous class group discussions. For example, a group was rated as having "Poor" information exchange if their language markers of information exchange ranked in the lower quartile for language markers of information exchange in previous class discussions. This system for rating group processes worked for some group processes and not others, which we will return to later.

In the Pilot Study all groups were given engagement and equal participation feedback.

Group Outcome Variables – Group satisfaction and performance are two outcomes of teamwork, which are only slightly correlated ($r(166) = 0.18$).

Group satisfaction Group satisfaction was operationalized as the average of the group members' rated satisfaction with the group. Each group member rated how well they enjoyed the interaction, how well they 'clicked' with their group, and whether they would work with their group again on 5-point Likert scales [23]. The items were averaged to create an individual level measure of group satisfaction ($\alpha = 0.86$). Individuals rated the group alone, however group members' ratings of the group were related to each other justifying grouping individual level satisfaction scores at the group level ($F(167,312) = 1.43$, $p = 0.02$).

Group performance Group performance was operationalized as the average group members' improvement on the quiz after the group discussion compared to before the discussion. On average students scored better on the quiz after the group discussion than before. Individual level improvement was calculated by taking the individual's score on the post-interaction quiz controlling for the score on the pre-interaction quiz. Individuals took the quizzes alone, however individuals improvement was related to which group they had been apart of justifying grouping individual level improvement scores at the group level ($F(167,312) = 1.84$, $p < 0.001$).

Study 1

Study 1 was conducted to identify which group processes were related to the group outcomes while no group processes were being manipulated. Thus, Study 1 was nearly identical to the Pilot Study, with the exception that there was no real-time language feedback. 851 students from two introductory psychology classes taught in Fall of 2011 participated in the Study 1 as part of the class requirements. Of these participants 62 percent were female, they were aged 17 to 48 ($M = 19$). For Study 1, due to a procedural error group satisfaction was assessed a few days later rather than immediately after the group task.

Study 2

Study 2 was conducted to experimentally evaluate the real-time language feedback system. Thus, Study 2 was also nearly identical to the Pilot Study, except students were randomly assigned to 1 of 4 feedback conditions: no feedback (control), engagement feedback, information exchange feedback, and both feedback types. 816 students from the same classes as Study 1 participated as part of the class requirements. Most of the students were the same in Study 1 and Study 2, however group assignments were different. By Study 2 students had familiarity with group chat, but had no experience with the feedback system.

Due to technical errors with the feedback system in Study 2, some individuals did not receive the appropriate number or type of feedback messages. 13 groups had to be removed because the group received conflicting feedback messages and/or messages at the wrong times. 37 groups were excluded because at least one member of the group received fewer than 50% of the feedback messages they were suppose to have received. This left 621 individuals in 160 groups in Study 2.

IDENTIFICATION OF GROUP PROCESSES RELATED TO HIGHER QUALITY TEAMWORK

All four of the group processes were related to either group satisfaction or performance. There was variability in the relationship between the group processes and better teamwork across the studies, therefore to test for robustness the correlations for all three studies are presented.

Group Satisfaction

All four group processes were significantly correlated with group satisfaction (see Table 2). However, engagement was the most consistent predictor of group satisfaction. There was some variability in which group processes were related to group satisfaction in particular, Study 1 was different from the Pilot Study and Study 2. One explanation is that Study 1 had more difficult quizzes making the task harder than the other two studies.

Group Performance

The relationship between the four group processes and group performance was more complex. Information exchange was the most consistent predictor of group performance (see Table 3). Information exchange was related to better group performance in the Pilot Study and Study 1, however it did not predict group performance in Study 2. The other group processes were occasionally related to group performance. Engagement and equal participation were related to better performance in the Pilot Study and positivity was related to performance in Study 2.

Conclusion

The results show that there are a few identifiable ways in which groups work together that can predict how well the groups are working. In particular, the results suggest that engagement and information exchange are two important group processes that would be good targets of our real-time language feedback system. The results also show that there is

	Pilot Study df=165	Study 1 df=179	Study 2 df=157	Overall df=167
Positivity	0.32***	0.05	0.21**	0.19*
Engagement	0.23**	0.27***	0.25**	0.25**
Equal Participation	0.26***	0.08	0.30***	0.21**
Information Exchange	0.06	0.27***	0.16*	0.16*

Table 2. Linguistic correlates of group satisfaction (* $p < 0.05$, ** $p < 0.01$, *** $p < 0.001$) .

	Pilot Study df=165	Study 1 df=179	Study 2 df=157	Overall df=167
Positivity	0.01	-0.05	0.18*	0.04
Engagement	0.20*	0.12	0.07	0.13†
Equal Participation	0.13†	-0.02	0.13	0.08
Information Exchange	0.14†	0.24***	0.03	0.14†

Table 3. Linguistic correlates of group performance († $p < 0.10$ * $p < 0.05$, ** $p < 0.01$, *** $p < 0.001$) .

variability in whether the group processes affect group outcomes. Variability creates a challenge to a designing a universal system to shape group work. Future work should examine the conditions under which specific group processes are important. Even small differences between the three studies may have influenced which group processes were important. The selected group process variables were better predictors of group satisfaction than group performance. Future work, should focus on other information processing dimensions of group processes rather than social regulation dimensions of group processes in identify stronger predictors of group performance.

CAPITALIZING ON OBSERVED DIFFERENCES IN GROUP PROCESSES TO IMPROVE TEAMWORK

In Study 2 the feedback system was evaluated experimentally. Feedback was expected to change the way groups worked together by changing the group dynamics. It was predicted that engagement feedback would increase engagement and information exchange feedback would increase information exchange.

Feedback was also expected to improve teamwork by creating better group dynamics. Engagement feedback was predicted to increase group satisfaction, because of positive correlations between the two in the Pilot Study and Study 1. While information exchange feedback was predicted to increase group performance, because of positive correlations between the two in the Pilot Study and Study 1. We also speculated that engagement feedback might increase group performance and information exchange feedback might increase group satisfaction because they were sometimes correlated. Finally, we speculated that engagement and information exchange feedback might have synergistic effects by getting students to engage with each other and the material at the same time.

Real-time Language Feedback System

Providing real time language feedback to shape group interactions is a simple concept, yet it requires a large number of technical specifications to work seamlessly. The first full deployment of the feedback system in Study 2 was a good initial trial. Students rated the usefulness of the feedback messages and provided comments on the system. On average they found the feedback to be slightly helpful (M = 3.13, SD = 1.10) along a 5-point scale where 5 corresponded to "very helpful" and 1 corresponded to "it made things worse". There were significant differences based on the feedback type ($F(2, 455) = 10.22$, $p < 0.001$). Those in the information exchange condition found it to be the most helpful (M = 3.37, SE = 0.08); followed by those in the engagement feedback condition (M = 3.16, SE = 0.09); and those in the both feedback types condition found it to be slightly unhelpful (M = 2.80, SE = 0.09).

Those students who liked the feedback made comments about its usefulness such as *"Our group got back on task when the reminder popped up"*. Those that disliked the system provided valid critiques that will need to be addressed in future feedback systems. Many students commented that the messages were distracting: *"I think the feedback that we were getting actually distracted us a little"*. One student objected because they did not believe the feedback they were being given was accurate. He said *"We could have worked better if we actually had more time to finish our last questions and if the pop up window didn't keep claiming we were off subject when our conversation was clearly relevant to the material"*.

There were a few technical issues that reduced the efficacy of the feedback system. The high computational demands of processing language use in real-time and providing feedback for hundreds of groups simultaneously proved to be a challenge and not all feedback messages were given. Missing feedback messages were not associated with feedback condition or feedback level. Also, benchmarks for the feedback messages in Study 2 were established based on the language use in Study 1. These benchmarks worked well for information exchange feedback. However, they did not work well for engagement feedback. Almost all the engagement feedback said the they were doing poorly. This had two consequences. First, groups received very negative messages for engagement feedback; feedback that was basically too harsh. Second, because the benchmarks were too harsh it was difficult to do better over time and receive messages in the "Ok" or "Good" range. This may have been discouraging for groups trying to use the feedback to improve.

Those students that received engagement feedback were more likely to comment about the feedback during the chat. Many of the comments were negative (e.g. *"yo this popup sucks"*, *"death to the green box"*). By calculating the percent of words exclusively making reference to the feedback system (e.g. 'popup') the degree to which groups discussed the feedback can be assessed. Discussion of the feedback system varied by condition ($\chi(2) = 8.86$, $p = 0.01$). 67% of groups that received engagement feedback, alone or with information exchange feedback, commented on the feedback system,

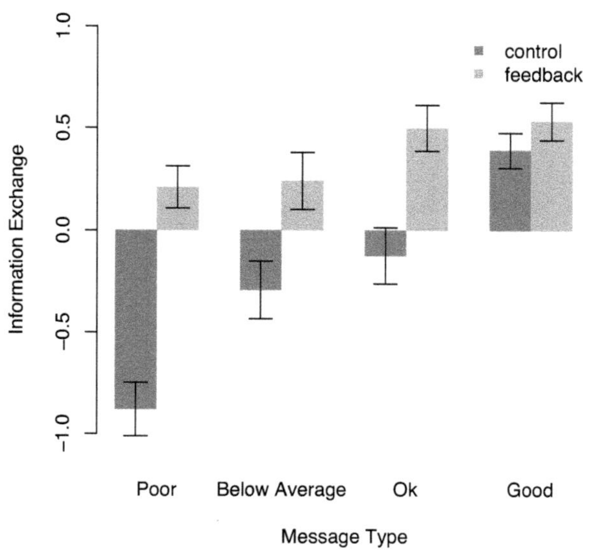

Figure 1. Impact of information exchange feedback messages on information exchange. X-axis displays the level of information exchange in the group in the previous 2.5 minute interval. Y-axis displays the level of information exchange in the group in the current 2.5 minute interval. Those in the feedback group received a message encouraging information exchange while those in the control did not.

whereas only 39% of groups that received information exchange feedback alone commented on the feedback system during the group discussion.

Overall, the Study 2 provided a good initial test of real-time language feedback system as a group intervention. Once some of the technical challenges from Study 2 are addressed, the feedback system is likely to be even more effective.

Impact on Group Dynamics

Both feedback types had a significant impact on language use during the group discussion. Changes in language use suggest that the groups changed the way they were working together in response to the recommendations made by the feedback system. Engagement and information exchange feedback both increased the linguistic marker of engagement, LSM ($F(3, 156) = 3.99$, $p = 0.009$). Groups that received engagement feedback alone ($M = 0.76$, $SE = 0.02$), information exchange feedback alone ($M = 0.78$, $SE = 0.01$), or both feedback types ($M = 0.80$, $SE = 0.01$) all had higher LSM scores compared to groups that received no feedback ($M = 0.72$, $SE = 0.02$). Pairwise t-tests showed that compared to the control, the feedback conditions had at least marginally significantly higher scores ($t_{Eng}(156) = 1.6$, $p = 0.10$; $t_{Inf}(156) = 2.8$, $p = 0.006$; $t_{Bth}(156) = 3.1$, $p = 0.002$).

Information exchange feedback had a significant impact on the linguistic markers of information exchange ($F(3, 156) = 6.14$, $p < 0.001$). Groups that received information exchange feedback alone ($M = 0.46$, $SE = 0.18$) and those groups that received both feedback types ($M = 0.34$, $SE = 0.18$) had higher values for the linguistic measure of information exchange than groups that received no feedback ($M = -0.64$, $SE = 0.23$) or groups that received engagement related feedback alone ($M = -0.22$, $SE = 0.23$). Pairwise t-tests showed that these mean differences between the information exchange feedback conditions and the control were significant ($t_{Inf}(156) = 3.8$, $p = < 0.001$; $t_{Bth}(156) = 3.3$, $p = < 0.001$).

A multi-level model analyzing group dynamics in 2.5 minute time intervals was used to test whether some types of groups benefited from information exchange instructions more. The model tested whether the benefit of receiving feedback depended on the groups' previous information exchange level (e.g. "Poor" vs "Good"). There was a significant interaction between previous information exchange level and whether a group received a feedback message ($t(956) = 2.27$, $p = 0.02$; see Figure 1). Those groups that received feedback messages indicating that their previous level of information exchange was "Poor", "Below average", or "Ok" were able to raise the amount of information exchanged, whereas those not given feedback maintained the same low levels of information exchange. There was not a large impact of giving feedback for those who where categorized as having "Good" levels of information exchange in the previous time interval.

The results show that both feedback types had an impact on the language used. Information exchange and engagement feedback impacted linguistic markers of engagement. Only information exchange feedback impacted linguistic markers of information exchange. Information exchange feedback was most useful for groups with low levels of information exchange.

Impact on Group Satisfaction

Receiving feedback had a significant impact on group satisfaction ($F(3, 156) = 6.24$, $p < 0.001$). Groups that received information exchange feedback alone were marginally more satisfied ($M = 3.34$, $SE = 0.09$) and those that received both feedback types were significantly less satisfied ($M = 2.76$, $SE = 0.08$) compared to those that received no feedback ($M = 3.14$, $SE = 0.10$) or engagement feedback only ($M = 3.10$, $SE = 0.10$; $t_{Eng}(156) = 0.31$, $p = 0.76$; $t_{Inf}(156) = 1.6$, $p = 0.12$; $t_{Bth}(156) = 2.7$, $p = 0.007$). This pattern of effects is consistent with ratings of the feedback systems overall, those in the information exchange condition preferred it to those in the engagement condition, and those that received both feedback types enjoyed the experience the least.

Impact on Group Performance

Receiving feedback had a significant effect on group performance ($F(3, 156) = 1.69$, $p = 0.046$). Those groups that received engagement feedback only performed significantly worse ($M = -0.31$, $SE = 0.14$) than those that received no feedback ($M = 0.05$, $SE = 0.12$), information exchange feedback only ($M = 0.11$, $SE = 0.10$), or both feedback types ($M = 0.13$, $SE = 0.13$). Those that received information exchange feedback, either alone or with engagement feedback, performed slightly better than the control, however the mean differences were not significant ($t_{Eng}(156) = 2.1$, $p = 0.04$; $t_{Inf}(156) = 0.4$, $p = 0.71$; $t_{Bth}(156) = 0.4$, $p = 0.66$).

However, feedback had a different effect depending on groups' initial dynamics. Language analyses showed that feedback messages had a stronger effect on groups that had

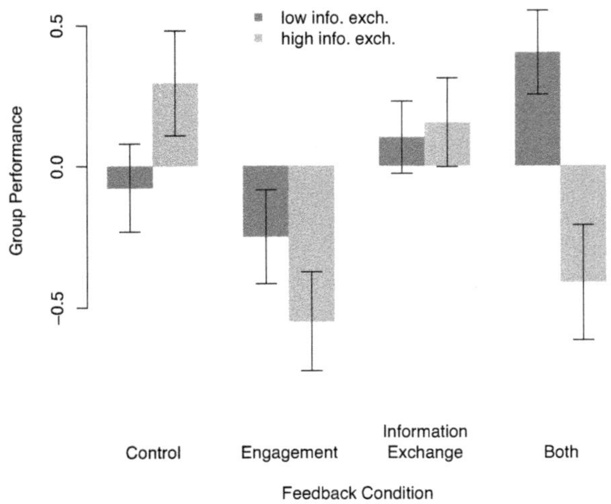

Figure 2. Group performance for groups in different feedback conditions. Groups are divided based on their initial levels of information exchange.

lower levels of information exchange. To better understand how feedback might affect groups with different initial group dynamics, groups were divided based on their level of information exchange in the first 2.5 minutes. Those groups with "Good" levels of information exchange, were considered on task. The groups with "Poor", "Below average", or "Ok" levels were considered to be low in information exchange and to have room for improvement. The feedback condition had a significant effect on group performance depending on whether the groups began the discussion on task or if there was room for improvement. The interaction between feedback condition and levels of information exchange in the first 2.5 minutes was significant ($F(3, 151) = 3.68$, $p = 0.01$; see Figure 2).

Those groups that had high levels of information exchange initially did not benefit from the information exchange feedback and did worse as a result of the engagement feedback. Pairwise t-tests show that the groups with high initial levels of information exchange performed worse when engagement feedback was given alone or with information exchange feedback compared to groups in the control, while those who received information exchange feedback performed the same ($t_{Eng}(40) = 3.1, p = 0.004$; $t_{Inf}(40) = 0.4, p = 0.59$; $t_{Bth}(40) = 2.9$, $p = 0.006$). Getting engagement feedback disrupted groups that were on task and information exchange feedback had no effect.

Those groups that were initially low in sharing information benefited from information exchange and engagement feedback when combined. Pairwise t-tests show that groups given engagement feedback alone or information exchange feedback alone performed no differently than control groups ($t_{Eng}(112) = 0.8$, $p = 0.42$; $t_{Inf}(112) = 0.8$, $p = 0.40$; $t_{Bth}(112) = 2.1$, $p = 0.04$). However, those groups given information exchange feedback and engagement feedback together performed better than control groups.

	Prediction	Result
Engagement Feedback	Increase engagement	Marginal
	Increase group satisfaction	No
	Increase (?) group performance	No
	Prediction	**Result**
Information Exchange Feedback	Increase info. exchange	Yes
	Increase group performance	Some
	increase (?) group satisfaction	Marginal

Table 4. Summary of Study 2 results.

Conclusion
Real-time language feedback shows great potential for shaping group dynamics. Feedback messages targeted at specific group processes were able to change the group dynamics (see Table 4). Engagement feedback led to a marginal increase in engagement. Information exchange feedback led to an increase in information exchange and engagement. Although not all of the changes to the group dynamics were predicted, many of the changes were in the right direction.

Feedback changed the group dynamics, but the changes in group dynamics did not always result in the predicted and desired outcomes. Engagement feedback had no effect of group satisfaction and actually decreased group performance. Engagement feedback failed most likely because it was too harsh. If given correctly engagement feedback might have been able to increase teamwork. However, we did learn a valuable lesson that harsh, negative feedback can be damaging.

Information exchange feedback led to a marginal increase in group satisfaction and had no visible effect on group performance when all groups were examined together. However, when groups were divided based on their initial levels of information exchange, groups that started out with low levels of information exchange benefited from information exchange feedback when combined with engagement feedback, while those with high levels of information exchange did not. This suggests that information exchange feedback may be useful, but only for groups that are not working well together from the start.

We speculated that combining feedback types might have synergistic effects; the results were mixed effects. In general, receiving both feedback types together was likely too cognitively taxing. Students that received both feedback types, liked the feedback the least and and were more dissatisfied with their group experience. However, receiving both feedback types provided the only observable improvement in group performance, most likely because of synergistic effects.

GENERAL DISCUSSION

Toward a Model of Good Group Dynamics
The use of social visualizations to shape teamwork, has been significantly impeded by a poor understanding of the optimal group dynamics. Previous work in psychology, which social visualizations have relied upon, developed complicated theories of important group processes without being able to relate them to important outcomes [2, 21]. We focused on a

contemporary theory of group processes, which distinguishes between social regulation and information processing processes [21]. We found that social regulation processes, including positivity, engagement, and equal participation, were more consistently related to group satisfaction, and only occasionally related to group performance. Whereas, the degree of information exchange, an information processing process, was the group process most consistently related to group performance. However, even information exchange was only weakly related to group performance. A broader exploration of group processes is needed to identify good predictors of group performance.

The results suggest two fruitful paths toward developing a better model of good group dynamics. The selected group processes were more strongly related to group satisfaction than group performance. In part, because the majority of the selected group processes focused on social regulation. Social regulation is important in establishing smooth interactions, but in a short 20 minute group discussion it may not be as important for group performance. Ultimately, group performance is a result of collecting, organizing, and processing information. Thus, the focus should be on group processes involved in information processing. We selected the degree of information exchange as a simple group process involved in information processing. However, staying on task and sharing information was not always enough to promote understanding in the group discussions. It is clear that group processes that produce more complex information processing need to be identified and studied. One group process worth exploring is the development of roles based on expertise. For example, groups which develop roles in which those with less expertise ask questions and those with more expertise answer the questions may process the information that is shared more deeply. Identification of experts within a group was one technique that allowed decision groups to share more information [4].

Social regulation processes may still play an important role when they interact with information processing processes. We found that the feedback system was able to improve group performance for groups that started out exchanging little information when they received feedback that instructed them to stay engaged and exchange more information. In this case, engagement alone may not improve teamwork, however if the group is focused on the task and sharing information engagement may be able to enhance the value of sharing information. Another example of an interaction between social regulation and information processing may be the role of conflict and dissension in a group. Nemeth and colleagues found some evidence that conflict and dissension could improve creativity in a group [22]. Conflict in a group is likely to improve creativity, not because it solidifies relationships or enhances the emotional experience of group members, but because it coordinates individuals, by pitting them against each other, in a way that gets them to think more deeply.

Shaping group dynamics with real-time language feedback, not only has the benefit of improving group dynamics, it provides a strong experimental paradigm for establishing causal relationships between group processes and outcomes. Historically many psychologists have focused on inputs to groups (e.g. group composition) rather than group processes in part because it is difficult to experimentally manipulate group dynamics by changing group processes. This work relied on determining if there was a connection between group processes and outcomes using correlations, which is only a first step. Once the kinks in the feedback system are resolved, it will be possible to systematically test for causal relationships between group processes and outcomes.

Toward the Design of Real-time Language Feedback

Real-time language feedback systems show great potential as group support systems to shape group dynamics. We advanced the design of these feedback systems in two ways. First, we used feedback to target two group processes that we thought could bring about better group satisfaction and performance. Second, our feedback system gave individualized instructions targeting these group processes. Individualized instructions help to explicitly direct groups to change their behavior in beneficial ways. The experimental evaluation of the feedback system provided both promising results as well as many failures.

The results of the evaluation provide strong lessons for the future design of real-time language feedback systems. First, a focus should be on using real-time language feedback to shape group dynamics that are relevant to group performance and not group satisfaction. We found that improving group satisfaction is especially challenging using feedback. Satisfaction or dissatisfaction with the feedback system overshadowed ratings of group satisfaction. Thus, changing group dynamics to improve group performance is a better goal. Many social visualizations have focused on aspects of social regulation, such as the amount agreement and equal participation (e.g. [19, 5]). This is misguided since we found that social regulation processes are more closely related to group satisfaction than group performance. Second, feedback should only be given to groups that are not working well together from the start. Good group dynamics are hard to establish. Feedback has the potential to disrupt groups that are doing well from the start, either because it is distracting or slightly inaccurate. Only those groups that are doing badly from the start may benefit from feedback. Third, providing accurate individualized feedback is important, yet challenging. Engagement feedback because it was too negative may have made groups perform worse. Fourth, providing more than one feedback message at a time may be too cognitively overloading. Once these challenges are overcome the feedback system shows great promise for being able to shape group dynamics and improve teamwork.

ACKNOWLEDGEMENTS

Preparation of this manuscript was aided by funding from the Army Research Institute (W91WAW-07-C-0029) and National Science Foundation (NSCC-0904913).

REFERENCES

1. Anderson, J. R., Corbette, A. T., Koedinger, K. R., and Pelletier, R. Cognitive Tutors: Lessons Learned. *Journal of Learning Sciences 4* (1995), 167–207.

2. Bales, R. F. *Interaction Process Analysis: A method for the study of small groups*. The University of Chicago Press, Chicago, 1950.
3. Bales, R. F., and Strodtbeck, F. L. Phases in group problem-solving. *The Journal of Abnormal and Social Psychology 46* (1951), 485–495.
4. Diehl, M., and Stroebe, W. Productivity loss in brainstorming groups: Toward the solution of a riddle. *Journal of Personality and Social Psychology 53* (1987), 497–509.
5. DiMicco, J. M., Hollenbach, K. J., Pandolfo, A., and Bender, W. The Impact of Increased Awareness While Face-to-Face. *Human-Computer Interaction 22* (2007), 47–96.
6. Fischer, U., McDonnell, L., and Orasanu, J. Linguistic correlates of team performance: Toward a tool for monitoring team functioning during space missions. *Aviation Space and Environmental Medicine 78* (2007), 86–95.
7. Gonzales, A. L., Hancock, J. T., and Pennebaker, J. W. Language style matching as a predictor of social dynamics in small groups. *Communication Research 31* (2010), 3–19.
8. Graesser, A. C., Conley, M. W., and Olney, A. Intelligent tutoring systems. In *APA Handbook of Educational Psychology*, S. Graham and K. Harris, Eds., vol. 2579. American Psychological Association, Washington, DC, 2012, 451–473.
9. Hackman, J. R., and Kaplan, R. E. Interventions into group process: An approach to improving the effectiveness of groups. *Decision Sciences 5* (1974), 459–480.
10. Hare, A. P. *Handbook of Small Group Research*. Free Press, New York, 1962.
11. Hinsz, V. B., Tindale, R. S., and Vollrath, D. A. The emerging conceptualization of groups as information processors. *Psychological Bulletin 121* (1997), 43–64.
12. Huffaker, D., Swaab, R., and Diermeier, D. The language of coalition formation in multiparty online negotiations. In *In Proceedings of the International Communication Association Conference* (Montreal, Canada, 2008), 22–26.
13. Ireland, M. E., and Pennebaker, J. W. Language style matching in writing: Synchrony in essays, correspondence, and poetry. *Journal of Personality and Social Psychology 99* (2010), 549–571.
14. Jonassen, D. H., and Kwon, H. Communication patterns in computer mediated versus face-to-face group problem solving. *Educational Technology Research and Development 49* (2001), 35–51.
15. Kittur, A., and Kraut, R. E. Harnessing the wisdom of crowds in wikipedia: quality through coordination. In *Proc. CSCW 2008*, ACM Press (2008), 37–46.
16. Leavitt, H. J. Some effects of certain communication patterns on group performance. *Journal of Abnormal Psychology 46* (1951), 38–50.
17. Lebie, L., Rhoades, J. A., and McGrath, J. E. Interaction process in computer-mediated and face-to-face groups. *Computer Supported Cooperative Work 4* (1996), 127–152.
18. Leshed, G., Hancock, J. T., Cosley, D., McLeod, P. L., and Gay, G. Feedback for guiding reflection on teamwork practices. In *Proc. GROUP 2007*, ACM Press (2007), 217–220.
19. Leshed, G., Perez, D., Hancock, J. T., Cosley, D., Birnholtz, J., Lee, S., McLeod, P. L., and Gay, G. Visualizing real-time language-based feedback on teamwork behavior in computer-mediated groups. *Proc. CHI 2009* (2009), 537–546.
20. Levine, J. M., and Moreland, R. L. Progress in small group research. *Annual Review of Psychology 41* (1990), 585–634.
21. McGrath, J. E. Small group research, that once and future field: An interpretation of the past with an eye to the future. *Group Dynamics: Theory, Research, and Practice 1* (1997), 7–27.
22. Nemeth, C. J., Personnaz, B., Personnaz, M., and Goncalo, J. a. The liberating role of conflict in group creativity: A study in two countries. *European Journal of Social Psychology 34* (2004), 365–374.
23. Niederhoffer, K. G., and Pennebaker, J. W. Linguistic style matching in social interaction. *Journal of Language and Social Psychology 21* (2002), 337–360.
24. Nowak, M., Kim, J., Kim, N. W., and Nass, C. Social Visualization and Negotiation: Effects of Feedback Configuration and Status. In *Proc. CSCW 2012*, ACM Press (2012), 1081–1090.
25. Pennebaker, J. W., Gosling, S. D., and Ferrell, J. D. Digital in-class teaching using the TOWER system: A pilot project of two 500-student introductory psychology classes. Tech. rep., Technical Report, Department of Psychology, University of Texas at Austin, 2012.
26. Sexton, J. B., and Helmreich, R. L. Analyzing cockpit communications: The links between language, performance, and workload. *Human Performance in Extreme Environments 5* (2000), 63–68.
27. Stasser, G., Taylor, L. A., and Hanna, C. Information sampling in structured and unstructured discussions of three- and six-person groups. *Journal of Personality and Social Psychology 57* (1989), 67–78.
28. Tausczik, Y. R., and Pennebaker, J. W. The psychological meaning of words: LIWC and computerized text analysis methods. *Journal of Language and Social Psychology 29* (2010), 24–54.
29. Taylor, P. J., and Thomas, S. Linguistic style matching and negotiation outcome. *Negotiation and Conflict Management Research 1* (2008), 263–281.

SpatialEase: Learning Language through Body Motion

Darren Edge[1]
[1] Microsoft Research Asia
Beijing, China
darren.edge@microsoft.com

Kai-Yin Cheng[1,2]
[2] National Taiwan University
Taipei, Taiwan
keynes.z@gmail.com

Michael Whitney[1,3]
[3] University of North Carolina Charlotte
Charlotte, NC, USA
mwhitne6@uncc.edu

ABSTRACT
Games that engage both mind and body by targeting users' kinesthetic intelligence have the potential to transform the activity of learning across a wide variety of domains. To investigate this potential in the context of second language learning, we have developed SpatialEase: a Kinect game for the body-based learning of language that is grounded in space and motion. In this game, learners respond to audio commands in the second language by moving their bodies in space, while a game mechanic based on distributed cued-recall supports learning over time. Our comparison of SpatialEase with the popular Rosetta Stone software for learner of Mandarin Chinese showed similar learning gains over a single session and generated several key implications for the future design of mixed-modality learning systems.

Author Keywords
Embodied gaming; Kinesthetic learning; Language learning

ACM Classification Keywords
H5.2 Information interfaces and presentation: User Interfaces

INTRODUCTION & RELATED WORK
Language, thought, and action are inextricably linked. When we learn our first language, we do so by mapping words to abstract concepts that are grounded in our bodily experiences of the world [10]. Total Physical Response (TPR) is an approach to second language learning that aims to replicate such native language development though the co-production of spoken commands and bodily actions [1]. Our aim is to support TPR-style learning in the absence of a human instructor, using embodied interaction [3] to help learners forge associations between new second language expressions and the existing *kinesthetic image schemas* they already use to plan and perform physical actions [10].

To investigate the potential for kinesthetic language learning, we have therefore developed the "SpatialEase" game for Microsoft Kinect (Figure 1). In the game, learners respond to commands spoken by the system (e.g., a translation of "step forward then raise your right hand") with meaningful bodily actions that render learning visible.

Figure 1. SpatialEase Game for Language Learning

Our approach follows that of the Mathematical Imagery Trainer [7] by leveraging kinesthetic learning, but is independently motivated by the observation that gestures and speech express the same or related meanings at the same time [8]. In Second Language Acquisition (SLA) research, Growth Point Theory [12] hypothesizes that speech and gesture interact and influence one another throughout the planning and speaking of utterances, with gestures helping speakers to internalize the abstract via the concrete [6]. The related Information Packaging Hypothesis [9] holds that gestures play a role in conceptualizing information for speaking, and that the more difficult the information is to conceptualize, the more speakers will gesture. Engaging learners' kinesthetic intelligence has also been shown to improve performance for children learning mathematics, adults learning about science and medicine, and for French children learning English vocabulary [6]. In this latter study, findings align with the results from Cognitive Psychology that enacted actions are recalled better than action phrases without enactment [4], and that self-enactment is better than observing enactment by others [5]. By creating a kinesthetic game that leverages these findings, we aim to help learners acquire a second language through constructions grounded in space and motion.

We first outline the design of our SpatialEase game before presenting the results of a study comparing it to the popular Rosetta Stone software, which acted as a benchmark for primarily visual learning. We found the two approaches to be comparable over a single session, with mixed user preferences. From our analysis we contribute three implications for the design of kinesthetic learning games: target relationship recognition over concept recall for engaging game mechanics; adapt game content and complexity based on models of learner memory; and mix kinesthetic learning with visual and auditory modalities to create diverse challenges for all learners.

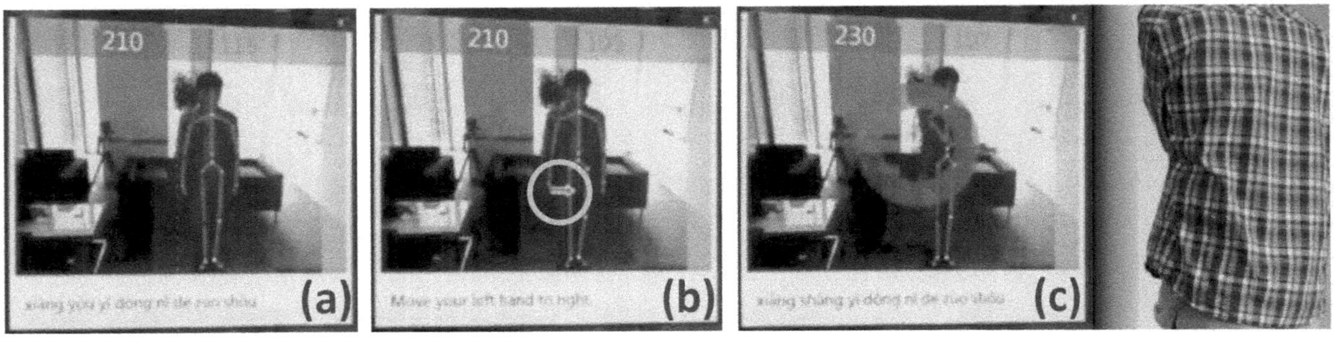

Figure 2. Interactive Flow: (a) SpatialEase issues a command in Chinese; (b) if the user doesn't move or moves incorrectly, arrows are drawn on the video indicating the corresponding action; (c) the user performs the correct action and hear the next command.

DESIGN OF A GAME MECHANIC

The Kinect SDK for Windows[1] has already been used to support learning in physical domains (e.g., sign language[2]). For kinesthetic learning of a second language, we drew inspiration from the Rosetta Stone application[3] in which the learner maps second language sentences to minimally different scenarios, e.g., translations of *"This {boy | girl} is {eating | drinking}"*. As the learner maps the text and sound of these constructions to the corresponding images, they infer the meanings of words and the relationships between them. Our kinesthetic equivalent is to use fast switching of body poses over time, encouraging similar inference across minimally different language constructions.

We were also inspired by the traditional game in which commands should only be followed if accompanied by the prefix "Simon says" (e.g., raise your left hand in response to "Simon says, 'raise your left hand'", but remain still on "Shake your right foot" because "Simon didn't say"). Our adaptation is for learners to only respond to grammatical commands. This focus on sentence form encourages the same beneficial shift from semantic to syntactic processing as when learners progress from listening to speaking.

THE SPATIALEASE KINECT GAME

We developed our SpatialEase game using the Kinect SDK for Windows. The core language of the game is based on phrases used to command bodily movement combined with the language of *kinesthetic image schemas* [10] – recurring patterns of spatial orientation, bodily movement, and object manipulation that give structure and meaning to our experience of reality (e.g., LEFT–RIGHT, UP–DOWN, FORWARDS–BACKWARDS). In our prototype for learners of Mandarin Chinese, successive game levels introduce increasingly complex constructions from core concepts. The first two levels are based on the following patterns:

"Move your {left | right | pair} {hand | foot | head | body}"

"Towards {up | down | left | right | front | back} move your {left | right} {hand | foot | body}"

---

[1] http://www.microsoft.com/en-us/kinectforwindows/

[2] http://cats.gatech.edu/content/copycat-and-kinect/

[3] http://www.rosettastone.com/

The game maintains a queue of language on which to test the learner. This is fed by a set of core concepts (e.g., left hand, right hand) that are so far *untested*. Each level begins with the system randomly selecting one of these and forming a command, such as the translation of "Move your left hand". This command is synthesized as speech and accompanied by a subtitle (Figure 2). If the learner moves their body accordingly, the underlying concept is added to the *correct* set and the next *untested* concept is selected.

If the learner fails to respond, the command is repeated. If they fail to respond a second time, or if their attempt was incorrect, then the concept is added to the *incorrect* set and the system indicates the correct action by drawing arrows on the live video stream of the learner's body (Figure 2b, highlighted). To provide the learner with sufficient practice in support and demonstration of learning, three further tests of that command are then scheduled after one, two, and three intervening tests respectively. These "spacing" tests are based on concepts drawn from the *untested* set if any remain, or else from the *correct* set for extra reinforcement.

Once all concepts are in the *correct* set, the "Simon says" phase begins with three concepts selected for grammar testing. Each concept is presented in either a grammatical construction (with chance 50%), or in one of four ungrammatical constructions. Incorrect responses restart the phase, while three successive correct responses complete it.

At all times, the learner faces time pressure to respond: each command is followed by only a ten second window in which to act, and each level is allocated only three minutes for completion. Completing a level within the time allocation resets the timer to three minutes and advances the learner to the next level. This creates a natural difficulty gradient as well as repetition of key concepts across games – such *distributed cued-recall* is a fundamental learning technique [2]. Learners can also track their performance across games using our simple scoring mechanism, which awards $10 \times N$ points per correct response on Level N.

By integrating learning into the game play mechanics, rather than simply extending them, we follow the "coherent, experimentally verified rule" of successful educational game design as presented by Linehan et al. [11].

USER STUDY

We conducted a user study in which participants used both SpatialEase and Rosetta Stone to learn Mandarin vocabulary and grammar of roughly equivalent complexity[4]. Since both systems employ the pedagogical approach of supporting learning through inference (rather than through direct instruction, e.g., with textbooks), this allowed us to compare the predominantly *visual* Rosetta Stone against the characteristically *kinesthetic* SpatialEase.

Given that there is "virtually no evidence" linking learning style preferences to the effectiveness of learning with different styles (e.g., words versus pictures versus speech) [13], we did not attempt to demonstrate any relationship between preferences expressed prior to system use and final performance. Nor did we attempt to establish the superiority of one modality over another. Rather, our goal was to understand whether the kind of kinesthetic learning embodied in the SpatialEase system has a potential role in future mixed-modality systems for learners of all styles.

Participants & Design

We recruited 8 novice learners of Mandarin Chinese (2 female, mean age 26) from the international staff and visitors to our Chinese lab. Each user study lasted approximately two hours and followed the structure: pre-test, method 1 learning, method 1 post-test, method 2 learning, method 2 post-test, survey. Method order was counterbalanced across participants and learning with each method was limited to 20 minutes.

The test contained four sections covering vocabulary and grammaticality questions for the language taught in both Rosetta Stone and SpatialEase. Both methods introduced 19 Chinese vocabulary items, and in our test participants listened to synthesized speech of each before typing the English translations. For the grammaticality questions, 20 constructions were generated for each method consisting of 10 that were grammatically correct and 10 that were grammatically incorrect. Participants listened to each of these before indicating that they perceived the grammar to be *correct* or *incorrect*, or that they *don't know*.

Results

Learners did not typically know any of the SpatialEase vocabulary before playing the game, but most knew at least one word from Rosetta Stone. Given the varying Chinese language levels of participants, we also observed large differences between individuals. Overall, we found the single-session learning gains from our SpatialEase game to be comparable with those from using Rosetta Stone, with average vocabulary improvements of 6.4 items for SpatialEase and 5.6 for Rosetta Stone, and with grammar improvements of 7.6 and 8.5 respectively (see Table 1).

[4] Rosetta Stone sentences (from level 1, lesson 1) were of the form *{one|this|these} {man|woman|boy|girl} {is|are} {eating|drinking|running|swimming|cooking|reading|writing}*.

User ID	Vocabulary (out of 19)				Grammar (out of 20)			
	Rosetta Stone		SpatialEase		Rosetta Stone		SpatialEase	
	pre-test	post-test	pre-test	post-test	pre-test	post-test	pre-test	post-test
P1	2	12	0	13	7	19	6	16
P2	10	5	0	2	5	11	5	9
P3	2	10	0	3	0	13	0	5
P4	2	2	0	9	10	8	10	8
P5	0	12	0	2	0	11	0	16
P6	11	15	1	16	11	18	10	14
P7	1	10	0	5	0	4	0	14
P8	1	8	0	2	0	17	0	10
mean (*sd*)	3.6 (4.3)	9.3 (4.1)	0.1 (0.4)	6.5 (5.5)	4.1 (4.8)	12.6 (5.2)	3.9 (4.5)	11.5 (4.1)
delta (*sd*)	5.6 (5.7)		6.4 (5.2)		8.5 (6.0)		7.6 (6.0)	

Table 1. Results of study comparing Rosetta Stone (RS) and SpatialEase (SE). Pre/post-tests measure vocabulary and correct grammar recognition after 20 minutes per method.

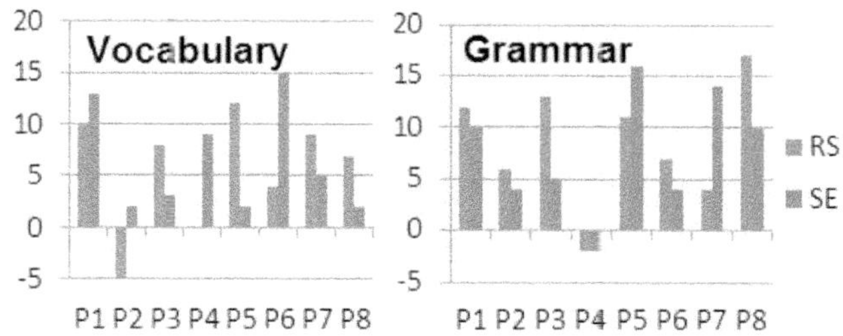

Figure 3. Learner improvements from pre-test to post-test

Figure 3 highlights the large individual differences in learner improvements from pre-test to post-test, for both vocabulary recall and grammar recognition. The same divergence was also seen in subjective preferences – three for SpatialEase, two for Rosetta Stone, and three undecided.

Discussion

While grammar improvements were not affected by method order, for vocabulary the first method resulted in roughly twice the improvement of the second method, for both method orders. This suggests a fatigue effect for vocabulary recall that does not exist for grammar recognition. One interpretation is that since recognition is a sub-process of recall, recognition-based testing is less demanding and thus has a lower threshold for success in the face of fatigue. Another interpretation is that since learners consciously attend to novel vocabulary but unconsciously acquire grammatical relations through induction over experiences, it is this conscious, directed effort that leads to fatigue. In both cases, the implication for the design of educational games is to encourage the fast and accurate recognition of correct relationships between elements. Such game mechanics have applicability beyond the grammatically of syntactic relationships between lexical language items, and could be employed in the learning of relationships in general (e.g., combinations, influences, causes, reactions).

The cases of P2 and P4 are also interesting. After using Rosetta Stone, P2 apparently forgot some vocabulary and

P4 learned no new vocabulary, while P4 became worse at differentiating the grammatical from the ungrammatical after using both methods. These results point to the effects of cognitive overloading and cognitive interference from attempting to pack so much learning into a short time period. Again, individual differences could play a role in determining what constitutes too much attempted learning, but the implication for design is to track performance in real time and stop play when the cost to learning quality outweighs the benefits of practice quantity. Such decisions about what to learn and when to rest should connect game content to learning curricula (e.g., from standard textbooks and personalized flashcards) and be informed by the extensive literature on distributed learning practice [2].

In subjective feedback, one participant highlighted a commonly expressed trade-off: "*The pictures work better in terms of learning as I have a reference to work with and other images to compare. However, the body-based is more engaging as I can visualize myself in the learning and anticipate the results of my actions.*" [P5]. Kinesthetic learning appears to have the advantage in terms of engagement: "*I was getting very tired and bored with Rosetta, but providing engaging experiences seems like the best approach – one where you don't feel so much like you are learning but achieving*" [P6]. Such engagement could also help develop executive motivation for learning in general: "*In SpatialEase, the system could direct me completely in Chinese. This made me already feel more comfortable with the Chinese language and more willing to continue to learn with the Rosetta approach*". Our third implication for design is therefore to share learning material and track learner actions across a range of different systems that combine learning media and modalities in ways appropriate to different goals, devices, and contexts.

Limitations & Future Work

The small sample size and timescale of this initial study prevents us from drawing firm conclusions on learning outcomes, and the large individual differences suggest that a more refined study design is necessary to understand the relative contributions of different modalities to learner engagement in the moment. A larger sample size and longitudinal study design would also be necessary to examine the important question of how kinesthetic learning can transform learner motivation over the long term.

Future design work should explore how the SpatialEase game mechanic can be extended to incorporate more abstract concepts, more complex linguistic structures, and work in concert with other tools like Rosetta Stone. Expanding on the current design, the language of time and sequence could be added to stretch the learner's real-time processing capability (e.g., "Before X, do Y"). The vocabulary could also be extended by virtual objects and actions (e.g., "Put the red ball in the blue bucket") that connect to vocabulary sources like flashcards. Finally, abstract concepts (such as "love") could be incorporated in several forms: on-screen word targets to be selected in the correct order; grammatical constructions to be distinguished from ungrammatical; or the correct visual representation to be selected for a given phrase spoken or shown. This latter mechanic matches that of Rosetta Stone, and demonstrates a possible point of convergence for the two methods.

CONCLUSION

Whereas applications of Kinect technology have helped gamers *learn to move* in activities such as dance and yoga, our SpatialEase game helps people *move to learn* in ways that leverage their kinesthetic intelligence.

Through our user study, we have developed three implications for the design of kinesthetic learning games in general: target relationship recognition over concept recall for engaging game mechanics; adapt game content and complexity based on models of learner memory; and mix kinesthetic learning with visual and auditory modalities to create diverse challenges for all learners.

ACKNOWLEDGEMENTS

We thank the participants in our studies and Enio Ohmaye for the reference to the TPR method of language learning.

REFERENCES

1. Asher, J.J. (1969). The Total Physical Response Approach to Second Language Learning. Modern Language Journal, 53(1)
2. Cepeda, N.J., Pashler, H., Vul, E. & Wixted, J.T. (2006). Distributed Practice in Verbal Recall Tasks: A Review and Quantitative Synthesis. Psychological Bulletin, 132(5)
3. Dourish, P. (2004). Where the Action Is: The Foundations of Embodied Interaction. Cambridge, MA: MIT Press
4. Engelkamp, J. & Cohen, R.L. (1991). Current issues in memory of action events. Psych. Research, 53, 175– 182
5. Frick-Horbury, D. (2002). The use of hand gestures as self-generated cues for recall of verbally associated targets. American Journal of Psychology, 115(1), 1–20
6. Gullberg, M. (2008). Gestures and Second Language Acquisition. In P. Robinson & N.C. Ellis (Eds.) Handbook of Cognitive Linguistics and Second Language Acquisition. New York: Routledge
7. Howison, M., Trninic, D., Reinholz, D. & Abrahamson, D. (2011). The mathematical imagery trainer: from embodied interaction to conceptual learning. CHI 2011, 1989–1998
8. Kendon, A. (1972). Some relationships between body motion and speech. In A.W. Siegman & B. Pope (Eds.), Studies in dyadic communication, 177–210, New York: Permagon
9. Kita, S. (2000). How representational gestures help speaking. In D. McNeill (Ed.), Language and gesture, 162–185, Cambridge, UK: Cambridge University Press
10. Lakoff, G. (1987). Women, Fire, and Dangerous Things: What Categories Reveal about the Mind. Chicago: University of Chicago Press
11. Linehan, C., Kirman, B., Lawson, S. & Chan, G. (2011). Practical, appropriate, empirically-validated guidelines for designing educational games. CHI 2011, 1979–1988
12. McNeill, D. (2005). Gesture and Thought. Chicago: University of Chicago Press
13. Pashler, H., McDaniel, M., Rohrer, D. & Bjork, R. Learning Styles: Concepts and Evidence. Psychological Science in the Public Interest, December 2008, 9(3), 105–119

Using fNIRS Brain Sensing to Evaluate Information Visualization Interfaces

Evan M Peck
Tufts University
evan.peck@tufts.edu

Beste F Yuksel
Tufts University
beste.yuksel@tufts.edu

Alvitta Ottley
Tufts University
alvittao@cs.tufts.edu

Robert J.K. Jacob
Tufts University
jacob@cs.tufts.edu

Remco Chang
Tufts University
remco@cs.tufts.edu

ABSTRACT
We show how brain sensing can lend insight to the evaluation of visual interfaces and establish a role for fNIRS in visualization. Research suggests that the evaluation of visual design benefits by going beyond performance measures or questionnaires to measurements of the user's cognitive state. Unfortunately, objectively and unobtrusively monitoring the brain is difficult. While functional near-infrared spectroscopy (fNIRS) has emerged as a practical brain sensing technology in HCI, visual tasks often rely on the brain's quick, massively parallel visual system, which may be inaccessible to this measurement. It is unknown whether fNIRS can distinguish differences in cognitive state that derive from visual design alone. In this paper, we use the classic comparison of bar graphs and pie charts to test the viability of fNIRS for measuring the impact of a visual design on the brain. Our results demonstrate that we can indeed measure this impact, and furthermore measurements indicate that there are *not* universal differences in bar graphs and pie charts.

Author Keywords
fNIRS; BCI; visualization; brain sensing; evaluation.

ACM Classification Keywords
H.5.2 Information Interfaces and Presentation: User Interfaces

General Terms
Human Factors; Design; Measurement.

INTRODUCTION
The quantitative evaluation of visual interfaces has been a significant goal of both the HCI and visualization community for decades. Numerous quantitative and qualitative approaches have been proposed to peek into the user's cognitive processes during interaction. Nevertheless, there are limitations to evaluating performance in a visual interface without directly monitoring the brain's cognitive processes. Evaluations of basic tasks may not generalize to complex tasks using the same visual forms (i.e. bar graphs and pie charts [6, 28, 32]), and psychology research suggests that evaluating performance without workload may lead to incorrect conclusions about the cognitive efficiency of an interface [3, 17, 23, 40]. Finally, cognitive state can change even as performance remains stable, meaning that performance metrics may not always accurately reflect cognitive processes [7, 37].

As a result, there has been a renewed interest in objective methods to evaluate cognitive processes during interaction with a visual interface [1, 26]. In particular, *functional near-infrared spectroscopy (fNIRS)* (Figure 1) has received increased attention as a lightweight brain sensing technology in HCI because in comparison to other brain sensing methods, it is portable [36], resistant to movement artifacts [19], and observes similar physiological parameters to fMRI [5, 35, 39]. While previous fNIRS experiments in HCI have studied cognitive state at various stages of interaction [2, 12, 15, 16, 29, 31], these experiments largely omit a critical component of interface design: How do different visual designs and interfaces affect the user's ability to perform visual judgment at a cognitive level?

The potential of using fNIRS to inform the design of interactive interfaces for visualization is appealing. If fNIRS can successfully measure the impact of visual design on the user, then it can provide access to physiological parameters that have not previously been analyzed in this context. Furthermore, it can do so in ecologically sound settings that allow users to interact naturally with an interface [30].

However, there are concerns as to whether fNIRS may be capable of monitoring brain activity in these scenarios. The physiological parameters which fNIRS monitors (oxygenated and deoxygenated hemoglobin) typically peak 5-7 seconds after interaction, meaning that the signal is slow-moving in comparison to the massively-paralleled processes employed by the brain's visual system. In addition, tasks that leverage the perceptual system may not induce measurable activity in the prefrontal cortex (PFC), the area of the brain most commonly monitored by fNIRS.

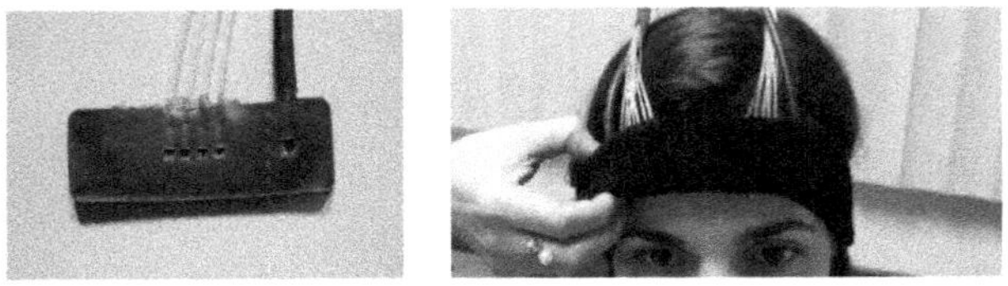

Figure 1. Left: An fNIRS probe with four light source and one light detector. Right: Two fNIRS probes are secured on a participant's forehead using a headband.

In this work, we test the viability of using fNIRS to observe how visual design modifies brain activity in complex tasks. We conducted three experiments to (a) examine how participants process bar graphs and pie charts differently in their brains, (b) determine the efficacy of using fNIRS as a technique for evaluating mental workload in visual tasks, and (c) classify visual tasks that are most suited for using fNIRS in evaluation.

To investigate this, we employ a classical comparison in the field of visualization - bar graphs and pie charts - and ask users to perform a difficult task on the information contained in those graphs. Based on our results, we make three contributions:

- **Our findings suggest that fNIRS can be used to monitor differences in brain activity that derive exclusively from visual design.** We find that levels of deoxygenated hemoglobin in the prefrontal cortex (PFC) differ during interaction with bar graphs and pie charts. However, there are *not* categorical differences between the two graphs. Instead, changes in deoxygenated hemoglobin correlated with the type of display that participants believed was more difficult. In addition, participants reacted differently to pie charts and bar graphs at a cognitive level, but exhibited the same performance characteristics.
- **We propose that the fNIRS signals we observed indicate the amount of cognitive workload induced by interacting with a visual interface.** We conducted an experiment that compares brain activity observed in bar graphs and pie charts with activity from a visuospatial n-back task - a well-characterized task from the psychology literature for modifying load on working memory. Our results are consistent with the existing fMRI literature and agree with participant response data (NASA-TLX), indicating that fNIRS signals correlate with cognitive workload.
- We discuss the benefits of using fNIRS for evaluating visual design and conduct an auxiliary study to identify the limits of using fNIRS in perceptually driven tasks. **We find that fNIRS can provide insight on the impact of visual design during interaction with difficult, analytical tasks, but is less suited for simple, perceptual comparisons.**

BACKGROUND

Brain and Body Sensing in Visualization Evaluation

As Fairclough [10] points out in his seminal review, physiological sensing in HCI has the advantage of having higher temporal fidelity in that it can access data at any time. In contrast, post-hoc questionnaires or recordings of observable behaviors represent discrete and sporadic events that reflect aggregated opinions about a whole experience.

While the field of HCI has seen an increased acceptance of physiological sensing in evaluation, to date, this push has not translated to the evaluation of visual interfaces and visual form. Historically, recording behavioral metrics or administering questionnaires have been used to evaluate visual design. However, Riche [26] notes that the exploratory nature of tasks in infovis systems, coupled with the "the difficulty to decompose [them] into low-level and more easily measured actions" makes analysis problematic. To overcome some of these obstacles, Riche proposes the use of physiological measures to evaluate visual interfaces.

Unfortunately, to our knowledge, there have been only two significant attempts to explore this space. Investigating the impact of visual variables on heart rate, galvanic skin response (GSR), and respiratory rate, Causse and Hurter found that interactions with text v. angle-based visual forms elicited different signals with GSR [4]. Few other significant interactions were observed. Work by Anderson et al. is the most promising example of using physiological signals to evaluate visual interfaces [1]. They used electroecephalography (EEG) to determine that the canonical box plot requires less extraneous load (i.e. the additional load placed on users by the design of a task) than various other box plot designs [1].

However, there are notable caveats to the use of EEG. While EEG has a high temporal resolution, it also has a low spatial resolution, meaning that the origin of recorded electrical activity is difficult to locate. Additionally, EEG has traditionally been considered to be extremely sensitive to movement artifacts, although recent developments have lessened this issue [24].

Brain Sensing with FNIRS

An alternative technology to objectively monitor activity in the brain is *functional near-infrared spectroscopy (fNIRS)*, an optical brain sensing device that has the potential to lend insight to visual interactions [5, 36, 39].

fNIRS uses near-infrared light to measure concentration and oxygenation of the blood in the tissue at depths of 1-3cm [36]. Light is sent into the forehead in the near infrared range (650-900 nm), where it is diffusely reflected by the scalp, skull, and brain cortex. At this wavelength, oxygenated and deoxygenated hemoglobin are the primary absorbers of light. A very small percentage of the light sent into the head returns from the cortex to the detector on the fNIRS probe. By measuring the light returned to the detector, researchers are able to calculate the amount of oxygen in the blood, as well as the amount of blood in the tissue. Since changes in blood flow and oxygenation indicate activation levels in the brain we can use fNIRS to measure activity in localized areas of the brain.

In general, fNIRS is quick to set up and more tolerant of user movement than other brain sensing techniques such as fMRI or EEG - a critical feature for ecologically valid evaluation [30, 35]. Investigating the use of fNIRS in user studies, Solovey et al. [30] found that mouse-clicking, typing, eye

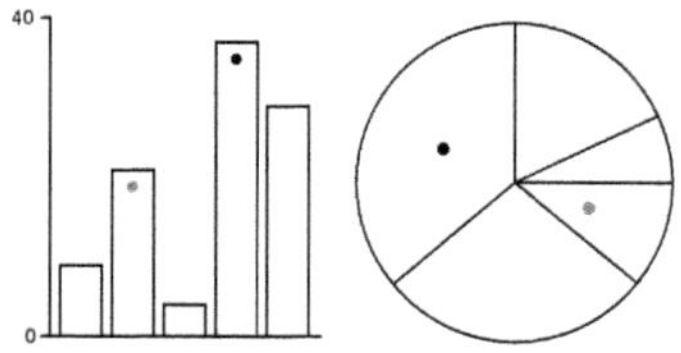

Figure 2. An example bar graph and pie charts from Cleveland and McGill's comparison task. Participants were asked to make a percentage estimation of the smaller section, marked by a red dot, with the larger section, indicated by a black dot.

movement, and blinking do not disrupt the fNIRS signal. Additionally, minor head movement, respiration, and heartbeats are correctable, as they can be filtered out using known signal processing techniques. Only major head and forehead movement (which could be induced by frowning) are disruptive to the signal [30].

FNIRS readings have been validated against fMRI and the device is sensitive to physiological parameters that are not accessible by other brain sensing techniques [35]. Because it measures the relatively slow hemodynamic response of blood to the brain (5-7 seconds), fNIRS has a slow temporal resolution in comparison to EEG, which indirectly measures the electric activity of the brain. However, this light-based sensing technique allows fNIRS to have a spatial resolution of 1-3cm, which is much sharper than EEG (although less precise than fMRI).

As a result, fNIRS has seen increased use for research in HCI as a complementary device to EEG [12]. Hirshfield et al. [16] used fNIRS to create a novel experimental protocol to explore the mental workload of users. They then used that protocol to measure the syntactic workload of users while interacting with two different interfaces. One of the most recent examples is from Solovey et al. [29, 31], who explored the use of fNIRS in designing adaptive interfaces to support multitasking. This led to the system *Brainput* which can identify different brain signals occuring naturally during multitasking and use these to modify the behavior of the interface [29]. FNIRS has also been used to monitor workload changes in air traffic control tasks and piloting a virtual unmanned aerial vehicle (UAV) [2].

These studies have been important in the development of fNIRS within HCI. However, the cognitive effects of different visual displays on the user is a yet unexplored area.

Pie Charts and Bar Graphs

We chose the visualization of bar graphs and pie charts as a suitable testbed for monitoring the user's cognitive processes because it is a familiar, well-studied comparison in the field of information visualization. In this section, we briefly outline the body of research that studies interaction with bar graphs and pie charts.

In Cleveland and McGill's ranking of visual variables, participants were presented with either a bar graph or pie chart (Figure 2) and asked to estimate the proportion percentage of a smaller value in the graph to a larger value [6]. Their results indicated that position judgments (bar graphs) facilitated more accurate visual comparisons than angle judgments (pie charts).

However, Simkin and Hastie found that pie charts and bar graphs performed equally well in part-to-whole comparisons [28]. Spence and Lewandowsky demonstrated that pie charts perform reasonably well in a direct comparison with other basic visual forms [32]. In more complex tasks - when comparisons consist of combined proportions (A+B v. C+D) - pie charts can outperform bar graphs [34]. For a more extensive history of the pie chart, see Spence's article "No Humble Pie: The Origins and Usage of a Statistical Chart" [33].

Recently, there have been a handful of studies that utilize Cleveland and McGill's comparison as a baseline to investigate various dimensions of interaction. Heer et al. replicated Cleveland and McGill's experiment using Mechanical Turk, demonstrating that "crowd sourcing" is a viable mechanism for graphical perception experiments [14]. Using pie charts and bar graphs, Hullman et al. showed that social factors can influence quantitative judgments [18]. For example, showing a user a histogram of previous responses to a visual comparison would dramatically skew the user's own judgment. Finally, Wigdor et al. explored the impact of distortion on angle and position judgments in tabletop displays. They found that varying the orientation of the display surface altered visual comparisons [38].

Despite the sizable body of research that has investigated bar graphs and pie charts, these studies also indicate that as the task or environment change, performance differences between the two forms become less clear. Therefore, we find this familiar comparison to be a sufficient baseline for objectively exploring users' cognitive processes with fNIRS.

RESEARCH GOALS

Our primary goal in this work was to investigate the viability of using fNIRS to evaluate visual design by having participants perform the same complex task on both bar graphs and pie charts. We theorized that in a complex task, bar graphs and pie charts would support the cognitive processes of the user differently. Thus, our principal hypothesis was as follows:

- *Hypothesis:* We will observe different brain signals during interaction with bar graphs and pie charts, indicating that bar graphs are easier to use.

Depending on the outcome of our experiments, our secondary goal was to further specify the use of fNIRS in visualization research. First, we compared fNIRS signals from participants in a well-established psychology task (n-back task) to those observed in bar graphs and pie charts. We combined those observations with previous fMRI literature and participant survey responses to surmise the underlying cognitive processes associated with our fNIRS signal. Additionally, we performed an auxiliary study using simple comparisons on bar graphs and pie charts to identify a lower bound for using fNIRS in visualization research. We present these results below, after the main experiment.

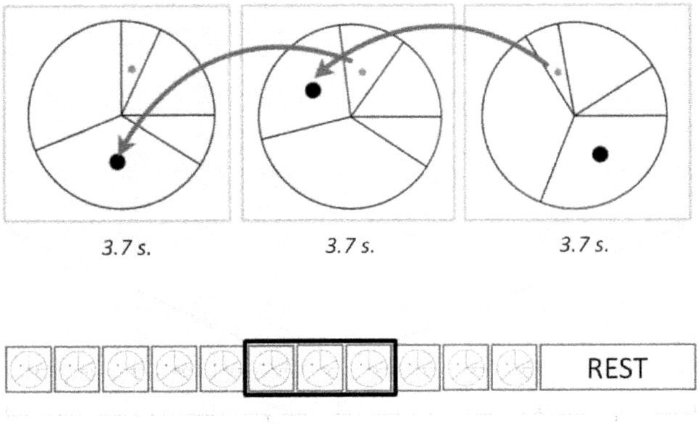

Figure 3. In our modified comparison task, participants compare a slice in the current pie chart to a slice from the previously seen pie chart.

In the following sections, we outline the methodology used for our bar graph v. pie chart experiment, discuss the results of that experiment, and finally, generalize our study to visualization research.

METHODS

Although originally inspired by Cleveland and McGill's classical position v. angle experiment, we modified the complexity of their task in order to reconstruct the memory-intensive, analytical reasoning that is performed on high-performance visual interfaces. For that reason, we modeled our task loosely after the n-back task, a well-characterized psychology task that is meant to increase load on working memory.

In this task, participants were presented a series of slides, each displaying either a bar graph or pie chart, to view sequentially. They were instructed to estimate the size difference to the nearest ten percent of a smaller section of the graph (marked by a red dot) in the current slide to a larger section (marked by a black dot) in the *previous* slide. Estimates were entered using a single keystroke on the keyboard ('1' for 10 percent, '2' for 20 percent, etc). Figure 3 shows an example of three slides using the pie chart condition.

Each trial lasted 40.7 seconds and consisted of 11 slides (or 10 comparisons with the previous slide), with each slide being presented for 3.7 seconds. Participants viewed 8 trials where the task depended on bar graphs and 8 trials where the task depended on pie charts. Trials were shown in random order.

To construct the graphs, 88 datasets (8 trials x 11 slides) were randomly generated at the time of the experiment using the same constraints as those outlined in Cleveland and McGill's classical angle v. position experiment. Accordingly, the same datasets were used for both bar graphs and pie charts. Comparisons were chosen at run-time by randomly selecting one of the largest two graph elements in the current slide and one of the smallest three elements in the next slide. This final constraint was necessary to guarantee that the two marked segments of each graph would not overlap and that percentage estimates would not exceed 100%.

Measures

Questionnaire: NASA TLX

We used an unweighted NASA-TLX questionnaire [20], a subjective rating that has been successfully used to capture workload since the 1980s [13]. The questionnaire collects six components of workload - *mental demand, physical demand, temporal demand, performance, effort,* and *frustration*. In total, we collected two surveys reflecting the two conditions - bar graphs and pie charts. We focus primarily on the questionnaire's mental demand dimension.

Brain Sensing: fNIRS Signal Analysis

We used a multichannel frequency domain OxyplexTS from ISS Inc. (Champaign, IL) for fNIRS data acquisition. Two fNIRS probes were placed on the forehead in order to measure the two hemispheres of the PFC (Figure 1). The source-detector distances were 1.5, 2, 2.5, and 3cm. Each distance measures a difference depth in the cortex. Each source emits two light wavelengths (690 nm and 830 nm) to detect and differentiate between oxygenated and deoxygenated hemoglobin. The sampling rate was 6.25Hz. For each of the two fNIRS probes, we selected the fNIRS measurement channels with source-detector distances of 3cm, as the light from these channels is expected to probe deepest in the brain tissue, while the closer channels are more likely to pick up systemic effects and noise.

To remove motion artifacts and optical changes due to respiration and heart beat we applied a folding average filter using a non-recursive time-domain band pass filter, keeping frequencies between 0.01Hz and 0.5Hz. The filtered raw data was then transformed into oxygenated hemoglobin and deoxygenated hemoglobin concentrations using the modified Beer-Lambert Law [5]:

$$\Delta A = \varepsilon \times \Delta c \times d \times B \quad (1)$$

where ΔA is the change in attenuation of light, ε is the molar absorption coefficient of the absorbing molecules, Δc is the change in the concentration of the absorbing molecules, d is the optical pathlength (i.e., the distance the light travels), and B is the differential pathlength factor. The attenuation of light is measured by how much light is absorbed by oxygenated and deoxygenated hemoglobin (which are the main absorbers of near infra-red light at these wavelengths). As the attenuation of light is related to the levels of hemoglobin, given ΔA, we can derive the changes in the levels of oxygenated and deoxygenated hemoglobin [5]. Finally, to remove noise artifacts, we smoothed the data by fitting it to a polynomial of degree 3 and applied a low-pass elliptical filter [31].

Performance: Speed and Accuracy

We logged all key-strokes and response times. We defined response time as the number of milliseconds from a graph's appearance to the final keystroke (user judgment) before the next graph. For accuracy, we used Cleveland and McGill's log absolute error measures of accuracy [6]:

$$\text{error} = \log_2(|\text{judged percent} - \text{true percent}| + .125) \quad (2)$$

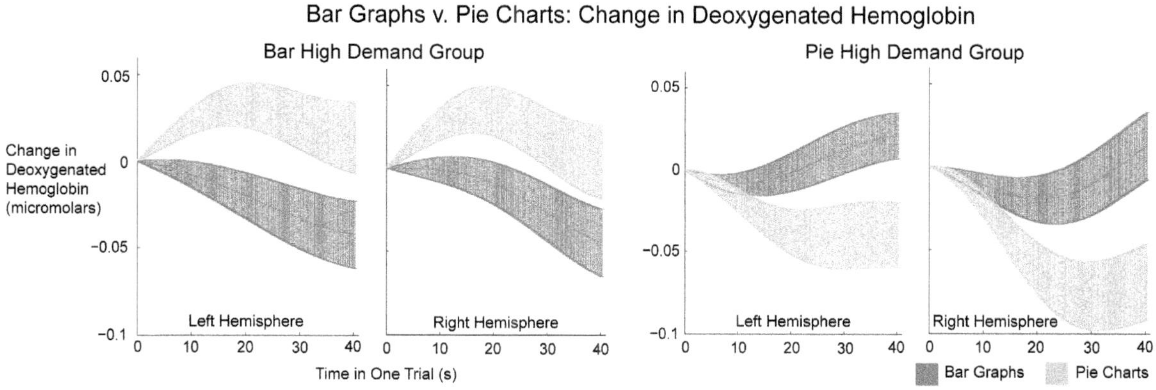

Figure 4. In a user study involving bar graphs (blue) and pie charts (green), we found that a group of participants that subjectively rated bar graphs as more mentally demanding than pie charts (left) exhibited reserved fNIRS signals from those who rated pie charts as more mentally demanding than bar graphs (right). The differences between signals in each graph demonstrate that brain sensing with fNIRS can monitor neural activity derived exclusively from visual. The plots represent the mean change in deoxygenated hemoglobin across all trials of each condition. The width of the line represents the standard error at each time point.

Experimental Design

16 participants took part in the study (7 male, 9 female). Participants had a mean age of 20 years (SD 2.4) and were incentivized $10 for participation. The study used a within-subjects design. All participants completed a fifteen minute bar graph v. pie chart task in which the independent variable was the data visualization technique: *bar graphs*, *pie charts*. Participants also completed a fifteen minute visuospatial n-back task in which the independent variable was the number of slides the participant needed to remember at once: *1-back*, *3-back* (we discuss the results of this experiment in our investigation of fNIRS signals and workload). At the conclusion of each section, participants completed an unweighted NASA-TLX questionnaire for each condition. The order of sessions (n-back, angle vs. position) was counterbalanced and the order of conditions (1-back vs. 3-back, bar graph vs. pie chart) in each session was randomized. The study was conducted in a lab setting, with stimuli presented on a single monitor under controlled lighting conditions.

RESULTS

For the purpose of analyzing the fNIRS signal, we calculated the mean change in deoxygenated hemoglobin ($\overline{\Delta Hb}$) across the duration of each trial (omitting the first 10 seconds[1]) for each participant as shown in equation (3):

$$\overline{\Delta \mathrm{Hb}} = \frac{\sum_{\mathrm{t}=0}^{\mathrm{n}}(\mathrm{Hb_t} - \mathrm{Hb_0})}{\mathrm{n}} \quad (3)$$

where n is the number of time-points, Hb_0 is the level of deoxygenated hemoglobin at the first recorded point (time zero), and Hb_t is the level of deoxygenated hemoglobin at time-point t of a trial. The change in deoxygenated hemoglobin (ΔHb) is calculated by subtracting Hb_0 from the level of deoxygenated hemoglobin at each time-point t. This is one of many techniques that have been used in the fNIRS literature to evaluate changes in oxygenated and deoxygenated hemoglobin [2]. While there may be boundary cases in which this measure is not sensitive to differences between signals, in this case, it captures the clear distinction between conditions.

[1]Omitting the first 10 seconds of the trial is due to the delayed physiological response of sending oxygen to the brain

fNIRS Signal: Bar Graphs v. Pie Charts

Addressing our initial hypothesis, we found no significant differences in deoxygenated hemoglobin between the bar graph ($M = -.0292, SD = .0471$) and pie chart ($M = -.0249, SD = .0679$) conditions ($t(15) = -.280, p = .784$). Contrary to our initial belief, these results indicate that there were no categorical differences in brain activity between the two visual forms. However, during the examination of data from NASA-TLX questionnaires, we encountered an interesting trend. In this section, we discuss and analyze this.

NASA-TLX Results

Isolating the mental demand dimension of the NASA-TLX survey, we found that 7 out of 16 participants believed pie charts to be more mentally demanding than bar graphs while an additional 7 participants expressed that bar graphs were more mentally demanding than pie charts (a remaining 2 participants found the graphs to require equal amounts of mental effort). These responses were largely unexpected, as our hypothesis indicated that we would likely find a categorical difference between bar graphs and pie charts. For the sake of clarity, those who thought pie charts to be more mentally challenging will be referred to as **pie high demand** and those who thought bar graphs to be more mentally demanding will be referred to as **bar high demand**.

fNIRS Signal: Bar High Demand v. Pie High Demand

Investigating the differences in these two groups, we found that the levels of deoxygenated hemoglobin exhibited by participants who found bar graphs more mentally demanding were the *reverse* of those participants who found pie charts more mentally demanding. Figure 4 shows that in the *bar high demand group*, we observed a decrease in deoxygenated hemoglobin in both the left and right hemisphere during tasks completed on bar graphs. In comparison, these same interactions induced a slight increase in deoxygenated hemoglobin in the *pie high demand group*.

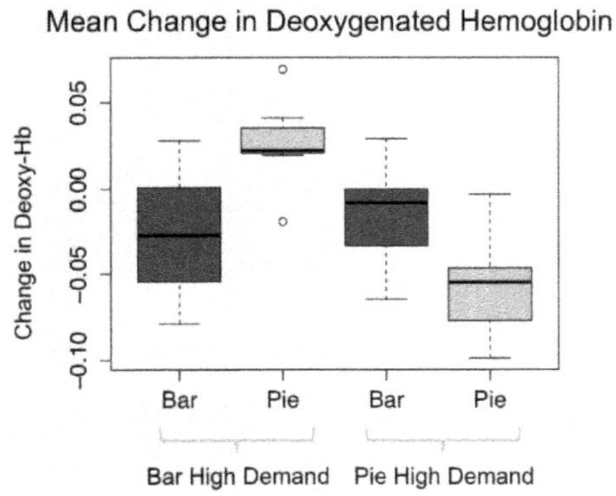

Figure 5. The mean change in deoxygenated hemoglobin for each graph shows that the visual design that partipants found to be more difficult resulted in larger decreases in deoxygened hemoglobin.

Thus, we performed an ANOVA on the mean change in deoxygenated hemoglobin using a 2 (task) x 2 (group) split plot design. The ANOVA revealed a significant difference between groups ($F(1,12) = 9.95, p < .01$), as well as a significant interaction between groups (*pie high demand* and *bar high demand*) and task ($F(1,12) = 16.49, p < .01$). This finding shows that participants in the *pie high demand group* and the *bar high demand group* showed significantly different patterns of deoxygenated hemoglobin while performing the two tasks (Figure 5). Note that while the mean provides a suitable metric for analysis, it can miss some trends in time-series data. Specifically, Figure 5 suggests that both groups recorded similar changes in deoxygenated hemoglobin while interacting with bar graphs. However, Figure 4 shows that the fNIRS signal was trending in opposite directions.

Performance: Bar High Demand v. Pie High Demand

In light of these group differences, we performed another analysis on response times by running a similar ANOVA on mean response time using a 2 (task) x 2 (group) split plot design. After ensuring that the data fit a normal distribution, we found no significant interaction between groups and tasks ($F(1,12) = 2.425, p = .145$). Similarly, an ANOVA on log error as shown in equation (2) found no significant difference in the interaction between group and task ($F(1,12) = .51, p = .4907$). We display a box-plot of log error and response time for each of the two groups in Figure 6.

These results suggest that although there were significant differences in brain activity between bar graphs and pie charts, there was no observable differences in performance, either categorically (bar graphs v. pie charts) or between group (bar high demand v. pie high demand). This is a very different result from those observed by Cleveland and McGill [6], in which position judgments (bar graphs) were found to significantly outperform angle judgments (pie charts). However, given the complex nature of the task, it is not surprising that performance corresponds more closely to findings from Spence and Lewandowsky that pie charts can perform as well, or better than bar graphs in difficult tasks [32, 34].

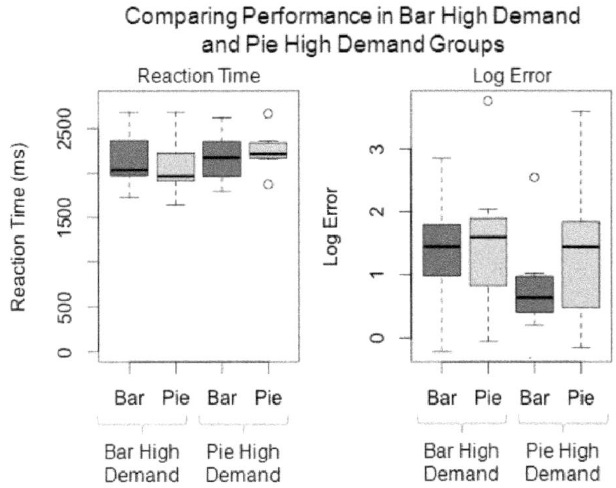

Figure 6. Despite a clear separation in brain activity between the bar high demand group and the pie high demand group, we observe very little difference in response time and error. The whiskers represent the max/min values, excluding outliers. Outliers are assigned by being more/less than 1.5 times the value of the upper/lower quartiles.

DISCUSSION OF BAR GRAPHS AND PIE CHARTS

Our results show that changes in deoxygenated hemoglobin during the use of bar graphs in a complex task are statistically different from those observed during the use of pie charts. However, this distinction was not categorical. Instead, brain activity depended on the individual and correlated with reports of mental demand in a NASA-TLX questionnaire. These differences between participants may call into question the conventional wisdom to *always* use bar graphs instead of pie charts.

Differences in Perceived Mental Demand

In the background, we outlined studies that used performance metrics of speed and accuracy to compare the use of bar graphs and pie charts. We expected that self-reports of mental demand would roughly resemble performance trends, and following previous research, one visual form would be categorically favored over the other. However, we discovered that 14 out of 16 participants found one chart to be more mentally demanding than the other. **Therefore, we reject our initial hypothesis that brain signals would indicate that bar graphs are easier to use for most people**.

Subjectively, there was no indication that either bar graphs or pie charts were superior across all participants on this particular task. 7 participants reported pie charts to be more mentally demanding and 7 participants reported bar graphs to be more mentally demanding (the final 2 reported no noticeable difference). Although we did not investigate the underlying cause of this observation, we suspect that this is due to either differences in cognitive traits (e.g. spatial ability), strategies employed to complete the task, or previous experience with bar graphs and pie charts.

Survey Responses and fNIRS Signals

While surveys can be found to be affected by bias or an inability to accurately externalize cognitive state, we found a surprising correlation between fNIRS readings and mental demand reports on NASA-TLX. **The graph that participants reported to be more mentally demanding recorded decreased levels of deoxygenated hemoglobin, validating the use of fNIRS to procure meaningful information about cognitive state.** Additionally, the results indicate that participants were generally well-tuned to their own cognitive processes and accurately externalized their cognitive load. We discuss the implications of this observation in the following section.

Indistinguishable Performance Between Graphs

A comparison of NASA-TLX responses and speed and accuracy demonstrates a dissociation between performance and cognitive state during the use of bar graphs and pie charts. Performance measures on both graphs were statistically indistinguishable from each other, regardless of whether participants found one graph to be more mentally demanding. However both questionnaire responses and fNIRS readings showed that the two designs influenced brain activity differently.

Given these results, it is possible that participants were exerting different amounts of mental effort on a given graph to achieve the same levels of performance. Furthermore, this observation suggests that evaluating performance metrics without considering cognitive state might have led to different conclusions about the efficacy of bar graphs and pie charts in this experiment. In the next section, we investigate whether the fNIRS signals we observed reflect levels of mental demand.

N-BACK TASK: DETECTING MENTAL WORKLOAD

During the course of this paper, we have been intentionally ambiguous about assigning a specific cognitive state to our fNIRS readings. The brain is extremely complex and it is dangerous to make unsubstantiated claims about functionality. However, for fNIRS to be a useful tool in the evaluation of visual design, there also needs to be an understanding of *what* cognitive processes fNIRS signals may represent. In our experiment, we have reason to believe that the signals we recorded correlate with levels of mental demand. We share three legs of evidence that support this claim:

1. fMRI studies have suggested that decreases in deoxygenated hemoglobin are indicative of increased brain activity [9]. Active regions of the brain require more oxygen to function. Thus, as levels of oxygenated hemoglobin increase to meet these demands, levels of deoxygenated hemoglobin decrease.
2. Self-reports of mental demand from the NASA-TLX results during the bar-graph and pie chart task correlated with levels of deoxygenated hemoglobin. Graphs that were reported to require more mental effort were accompanied by lower levels of deoxygenated hemoglobin.
3. We ran each participant on a well-characterized working memory task from the psychology literature - the visuospatial n-back test - and found that brain activity in the more mentally demanding graph mirrored activity in the more demanding n-back condition. We discuss the details of this experiment in the next section.

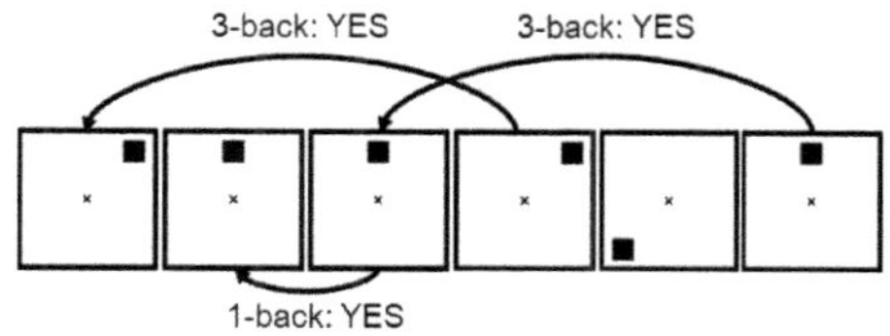

Figure 7. In the visuospatial n-back task, participants view a series of slides and respond whether the current pattern matches the pattern from n slides ago. We show positive answers for both the 1-back and 3-back conditions.

Methods

In the n-back task, participants were shown a series of slides, each with a distinct visual pattern, and asked whether the current slide matched the pattern from either 1 slide previously (1-back) or 3 slides previous to the current slide (3-back). Thus, the 3-back task strains the participant's visuospatial working memory by forcing him or her to constantly remember (and update) 3 images at once. By comparison, the 1-back task is relatively simple, requiring participants to remember only visual pattern from the previous slide.

Figure 7 shows an example of 6 slides from the n-back test. For each slide, the visual pattern remained on the screen for 300ms followed by a blank response screen for 1550ms in which participants answered 'yes' or 'no' using a single keystroke. Participants were given 8 trials of each condition with each trial consisting of 22 slides. Each trial lasted for 40.7 seconds and trials were separated by 12-second rest periods. This experimental timing mirrors the timing in the bar graphs/pie charts task, enabling us to compare equal slices of time for the fNIRS data.

Results

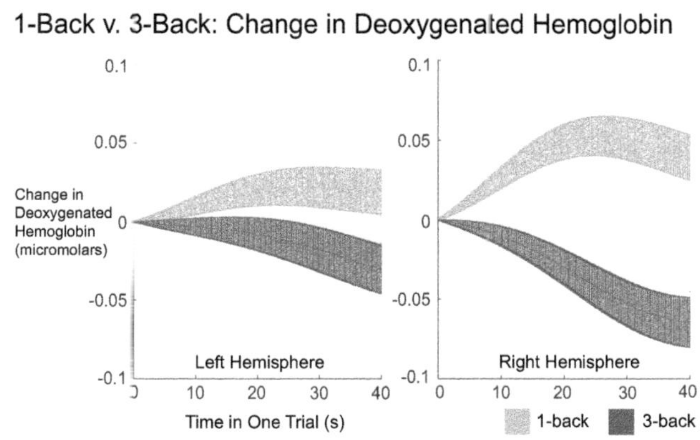

Figure 8. The mean fNIRS signal across all 16 participants in the Baseline Task. We see a clear separation between the 1-back and 3-back conditions participants. The more demanding 3-back condition mirrors signals from the graph design that participants believed was more mentally demanding.

Looking at the results, Figure 8 shows that there is a clear distinction between 1-back (blue) and 3-back (black) trials. These results are expected and resemble previous studies of the n-back task [21]. Additionally, the 3-back task induced lower levels of deoxygenated hemoglobin, agreeing with other observations of deoxygenated hemoglobin from the fMRI literature.

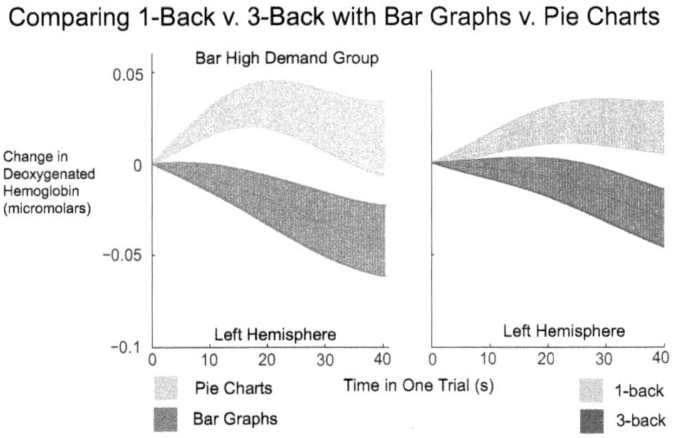

Figure 9. An example of comparing the n-back signal with those recorded in the bar graph v. pie chart experiment. The signal recorded during the more demanding 3-back resembles the signal recorded during bar graphs for the bar high demand group - participants who found bar graphs to be more mentally demanding than pie charts.

When placed side-by-side with the fNIRS readings from out bar graph/pie chart task, we notice that signals from the more mentally demanding 3-back resemble those from the graph that participants identified as requiring more mental effort (Figure 9). Similarly, the signal recorded from the less-demanding 1-back task resembles those observed in the graph that participants identified as requiring less mental effort (Figure 9).

Given these three legs of evidence - previous observations noted in fMRI studies, correlations with survey data, and correlations with signals observed in the n-back task - we feel confident that the fNIRS signals observed during use with bar graphs and pie charts correlate with mental demand in the brain. Furthermore, these results suggest that fNIRS can be used to monitor mental demand in other visual interfaces.

FNIRS: CONSIDERATIONS FOR EVALUATION

We have shown that we can successfully differentiate fNIRS signals during the interaction of bar graphs and pie charts in a complex task and that these signals likely indicate workload in the brain. In this section, we synthesize our results, previous literature, and an auxiliary study to explore *when* fNIRS is an appropriate tool for the evaluation of visual design.

Are Surveys Good Enough?

Cognitive state is often overlooked in evaluation, partially because it is difficult or cumbersome to quantify. We found that a simple survey agreed with fNIRS readings and accurately captured the participant's mental workload. This is good news for simple evaluations of mental demand. Questionnaires do not require an unreasonable time investment, and the strength of our observations were based on a single dimension in the NASA-TLX questionnaire. If more objective measures are not available, questionnaires can provide insight into a user's cognitive state.

Nonetheless, questionnaires can be problematic as they depend on the assumption that people can sense and externalize their subjective feelings without being biased by external influences [8, 22]. In comparison, brain sensing provides an objective snapshot of cognitive state and short-cuts the rating process by directly measuring the brain *during* interaction. As opposed to post-hoc questionnaires, neurophysiological measures require no additional effort or time from the participant. Furthermore, physiological measures can be used in more complex or time-consuming tasks for fine-grained observations of cognitive processes. Instead of a single workload metric for the entirety of a task, physiological measures can provide time-sensitive evaluations, potentially identifying periods of mental demand. We recommend that visualization researchers carefully weigh the nature of their comparison to select an appropriate technique.

Lending Insight to Complex, Analytical Tasks

Given the results of our study, we suggest that fNIRS may be well-suited for the analysis of complex interactions that are common in visual analytic systems. In this section, we highlight three other factors that point to fNIRS being well-suited for analytical tasks:

- The extended timeline of complex tasks mitigates the slow temporal resolution of fNIRS, which occurs because of the delayed (5-7 seconds) physiological response to brain activity.
- The PFC - the region of the brain that fNIRS most easily measures - has been posited to "integrate the outcomes of two or more separate cognitive operations in the pursuit of a higher behavioural goal" [25]. These higher-level cognitive functions typically drive analytical thought and include (but are not limited to) selection, comparison, the organization of material before encoding, task switching, holding spatial information 'online', and introspective evaluation of internal mental states [25, 27].
- The successful examples of applying fNIRS measures to interface evaluation have traditionally leveraged mentally demanding scenarios such as multi-tasking the navigation of multiple robots [29], increasing the difficulty of a video game [11], or reversing the steering mechanism in a driving task [15].

Given these factors, we believe that fNIRS will provide the most insight to visual interfaces that require complex, analytical thought. However, fNIRS is not without its limitations; as we demonstrate in the next section, short, low-level tasks are difficult to detect using fNIRS.

Perceptually-Driven Tasks are Difficult to Monitor

To explore the limits of using fNIRS to evaluate visual interfaces, we constructed an experiment that is closer to Cleveland & McGill's original comparison of position v. angle, which is based on more perceptually-driven interactions. Whereas trials in our previous experiment required participants to make percentage comparisons in graphs across slides, a trial in this modification consisted of 4 percentage comparisons (3.75 seconds per comparison) on the same

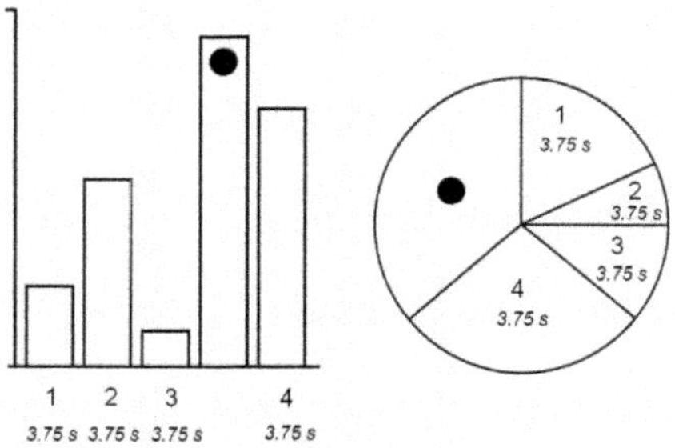

Figure 10. Participants sequentially compared elements of a graph to the largest element of the graph.

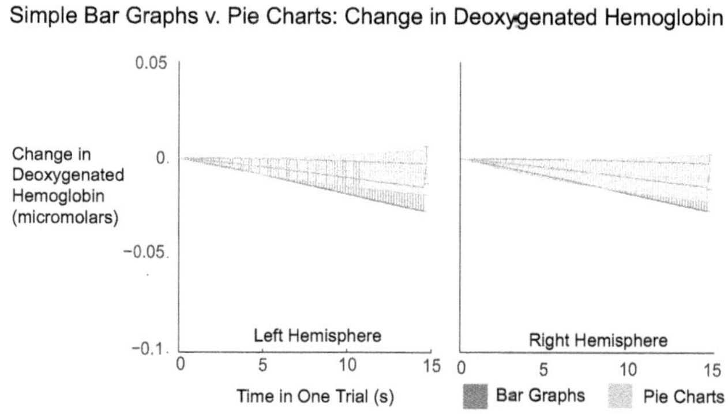

Figure 11. The mean fNIRS signal across all 8 participants in a simple bar graphs and pie charts task. The lack of activation shows that fNIRS may be less suited for simple, perceptual comparisons.

graph and participants interacted with 12 trials of bar graphs and 12 trials of pie charts. Thus, for each trial, four small pieces on a graph were sequentially compared to the largest piece in the graph (Figure 10).

To compare the changes in deoxygenated hemoglobin with our previous study, we ran an additional 8 participants and plotted the fNIRS signal using the axis of the same scale as the complex task. Looking at Figure 11, we can see that both pie charts and bar graphs caused very little activation in the PFC, with little to no differentiation between signals.

These results are not surprising. Quick visual and perceptual tasks are not likely to be observed by fNIRS. Tasks that rely heavily on preattentive processing use very little of the processing power of the PFC. Additionally, it takes a couple of seconds to observe the hemodynamic response resulting from brain activity, and 5-7 seconds in total for the oxygen levels to peak in the brain. This means that we are unlikely to observe quick and subtle interactions with a visualization. We therefore recommend that fNIRS will lend the most insight during more complex analytical interactions.

FINDINGS AND FUTURE WORK

We have demonstrated that fNIRS is a viable technology for investigating the impact of visual design on a person's cognition processes. Using the classical comparison of bar graphs and pie charts, we found that decreasing levels of deoxygenated hemoblogin correlated with the visual form that participants found to be more mentally demanding. We suggest that these changes in deoxygenated hemoglobin, detected in the PFC, indicate the amount of mental effort associated with the visual design. As we demonstrated in our study, these differences in workload are not necessarily reflected in traditional performance metrics.

Exploring the use of fNIRS in visualization research, we suggested that fNIRS is well suited for the evaluation of visual interfaces that support analytical reasoning tasks. This advantage should be particularly appealing for interface designers, as the complexity of visual analytic systems often make it difficult to apply traditional performance metrics. Additionally, the resistance of fNIRS sensors to movement artifacts allows users to interact naturally with an interface, resulting in more ecologically sound evaluations.

Lowering the barrier to monitor cognitive state increases the opportunity to develop adaptive applications that specially calibrate the display of information to the individual. Recently, Solovey et. al [29] used fNIRS to determine *when* the user should be interrupted with new information and built a system that adapted the level of automated assistance in a virtual robot navigation task. While recent work in visualization has begun to pay careful consideration to the impact of a user's personality and cognitive traits, using tools like fNIRS, we hope that visual interfaces can be designed to also be attentive to the user's current cognitive state.

The strengths of fNIRS are appealing, however, there are also limitations. While we identified periods of high or low workload, more specific mappings of fNIRS signals to cognitive states are needed to promote fine-grained evaluations of visual interfaces. Additionally, we found that fNIRS is less suited for quick visual tasks that are driven by the user's perceptual system. Despite these drawbacks, fNIRS provides a suite of benefits that are distinctive and complimentary to those offered by other physiological sensors. With the decreasing cost of brain sensing technology and its increasing use in HCI, we believe that the door has finally opened to directly explore the impact of visual design on cognitive state.

ACKNOWLEDGMENTS

We thank Dan Afergan, Andrew Jenkins, Francine Lalooses, and Garth Griffin who are students in the HCI group at Tufts; Sergio Fantini and Angelo Sassaroli from the Biomedical Engineering Department at Tufts; Jordan Crouser from the VALT group at Tufts; and Erin Solovey from the Humans and Automation Lab at MIT. We thank the National Science Foundation (grant nos. IIS-0713506, IIS-1065154, IIS-1218170) for support of this research.

REFERENCES

1. Anderson, E., Potter, K., Matzen, L., Shepherd, J., Preston, G., and Silva, C. A User Study of Visualization Effectiveness Using EEG and Cognitive Load. In *EuroVis 2011*, vol. 30, Wiley Online Library (2011), 791–800.

2. Ayaz, H., Shewokis, P. a., Bunce, S., Izzetoglu, K., Willems, B., and Onaral, B. Optical brain monitoring for operator training and mental workload assessment. *NeuroImage 59*, 1 (2012), 36–47.

3. Bertini, E., Perer, A., Plaisant, C., and Santucci, G. BEyond time and errors: novel evaLuation methods for Information Visualization. *BELIV* (2010), 4441–4444.
4. Causse, M., and Hurter, C. The physiological users response as a clue to assess visual variables effectiveness. *Human Centered Design* (2009), 167–176.
5. Chance, B., Anday, E., Nioka, S., Zhou, S., Hong, L., Worden, K., Li, C., Murray, T., Ovetsky, Y., Pidikiti, D., and Thomas, R. A novel method for fast imaging of brain function, non-invasively, with light. *Optics express 2*, 10 (1998), 411–23.
6. Cleveland, W. S., and McGill, R. Graphical Perception: Theory, Experimentation, and Application to the Development of Graphical Methods. *Journal of the American Statistical Association 79*, 387 (1984), 531–554.
7. De Waard, D. *The measurement of drivers' mental workload.* PhD thesis, 1996.
8. Dell, N., Vaidyanathan, V., Medhi, I., Cutrell, E., and Thies, W. Yours is Better! Participant Response Bias in HCI. In *ACM CHI 2012* (2012), 1321–1330.
9. D'Esposito, M., Zarahn, E., and Aguirre, G. Event-Related Functional MRI: Implications for Cognitive Psychology. *Psychological bulletin 125*, 1 (1999), 155–164.
10. Fairclough, S. H. Fundamentals of Physiological Computing. *Interacting with Computers 21* (2009), 133–145.
11. Girouard, A., Solovey, E., Hirshfield, L., Chauncey, K., Sassaroli, A., Fantini, S., and Jacob, R. J. Distinguishing difficulty levels with non-invasive brain activity measurements. *Human-Computer Interaction INTERACT 2009* (2009), 440–452.
12. Girouard, A., Solovey, E. T., Hirshfield, L. M., Peck, E. M., Chauncey, K., Sassaroli, A., Fantini, S., and Jacob, R. J. From Brain Signals to Adaptive Interfaces : using fNIRS in HCI. 2010, 221–237.
13. Hart, S. G., and Staveland, L. E. Development of NASA-TLX (Task Load Index): Results of empirical and theoretical research. *Human mental workload* (1988), 139–183.
14. Heer, J., and Bostock, M. Crowdsourcing graphical perception: using mechanical turk to assess visualization design. *ACM CHI 2010* (2010), 203–212.
15. Hirshfield, L. M., Gulotta, R., Hirshfield, S., Hincks, S., Russel, M., Ward, R., Williams, T., and Jacob, R. J. K. This is Your Brain on Interfaces : Enhancing Usability Testing with Functional Near-Infrared Spectroscopy. In *ACM CHI 2011* (2011), 373–382.
16. Hirshfield, L. M., Solovey, E. T., Girouard, A., Kebinger, J., Jacob, R. J. K., Sassaroli, A., and Fantini, S. Brain Measurement for Usability Testing and Adaptive Interfaces: An Example of Uncovering Syntactic Workload with Functional Near Infrared Spectroscopy. In *ACM CHI 2009* (2009), 2185–2194.
17. Huang, W., Eades, P., and Hong, S.-H. Measuring effectiveness of graph visualizations: A cognitive load perspective. *IEEE Transactions on Information Visualization 8*, 3 (2009), 139–152.
18. Hullman, J., Adar, E., and Shah, P. Benefitting InfoVis with visual difficulties. *IEEE Transactions on Visualization and Computer Graphics 17*, 12 (2011), 2213–22.
19. Lloyd-Fox, S., Blasi, A., and Elwell, C. E. Illuminating the developing brain: the past, present and future of functional near infrared spectroscopy. *Neuroscience and biobehavioral reviews 34*, 3 (Mar. 2010), 269–84.
20. Moroney, W. F., Biers, D. W., Eggemeier, F. T., and Mitchell, J. A. A Comparison of Two Scoring Procedures with the NASA Task Load Index in a Simulated Flight Task. *National Aerospace and Electronics* (1992), 734–740.
21. Owen, A. M., McMillan, K. M., Laird, A. R., and Bullmore, E. N-back working memory paradigm: a meta-analysis of normative functional neuroimaging studies. *Human Brain Mapping 25*, 1 (2005), 46–59.
22. Paas, F., Tuovinen, J. E., Tabbers, H., and Van Gerven, P. W. M. Cognitive Load Measurement as a Means to Advance Cognitive Load Theory. *Educational Technology 38*, 1 (2003), 63–71.
23. Paas, F. G., and Van Merriënboer, J. J. The efficiency of instructional conditions: An approach to combine mental effort and performance measures. *Human Factors: The Journal of the Human Factors and Ergonomics Society*, 35 (1993), 737–743.
24. Presacco, A., Goodman, R., Forrester, L., and Contreras-Vidal, J. Neural decoding of treadmill walking from noninvasive electroencephalographic signals. *Journal of Neurophysiology 106*, 4 (2011), 1875–87.
25. Ramnani, N., and Owen, A. M. Anterior Prefrontal Cortex: Insights into Function from Anatomy and Neuroimaging. *Nature reviews: Neuroscience 5*, 3 (2004), 184–94.
26. Riche, N. Beyond system logging: Human logging for evaluating information visualization. In *BELIV* (2010).
27. Rowe, J. B., Toni, I., Josephs, O., Frackowiak, R. S., and Passingham, R. E. The prefrontal cortex: response selection or maintenance within working memory? *Science 288*, 5471 (2000), 1656–60.
28. Simkin, D., and Hastie, R. An Information-Processing Analysis of Graph Perception. *Journal of the American Statistical Association 82*, 398 (1987), 454–465.
29. Solovey, E., Schermerhorn, P., Scheutz, M., Sassaroli, A., Fantini, S., and Jacob, R. Brainput: Enhancing Interactive Systems with Streaming fNIRS Brain Input. In *ACM CHI 2012* (2012), 2193–2202.
30. Solovey, E. T., Girouard, A., Chauncey, K., Hirshfield, L. M., Sassaroli, A., Zheng, F., Fantini, S., and Jacob, R. J. K. Using fNIRS Brain Sensing in Realistic HCI Settings: Experiments and Guidelines. In *ACM UIST 2009* (2009), 157–166.
31. Solovey, E. T., Lalooses, F., Chauncey, K., Weaver, D., Scheutz, M., Sassaroli, A., Fantini, S., Schermerhorn, P., and Jacob, R. J. K. Sensing Cognitive Multitasking for a Brain-Based Adaptive User Interface. In *ACM CHI 2011* (2011), 383–392.
32. Spence, I. Visual psychophysics of simple graphical elements. *Journal of Experimental Psychology: Human Performance and Perception 16* (1990), 683–692.
33. Spence, I. No Humble Pie: The Origins and Usage of a Statistical Chart. *Journal of Educational and Behavioral Statistics 30*, 4 (2005), 353–368.
34. Spence, I., and Lewandowsky, S. Displaying proportions and percentages. *Applied Cognitive Psychology 5* (1991), 71–77.
35. Strangman, G., Culver, J. P., Thompson, J. H., and Boas, D. a. A Quantitative Comparison of Simultaneous BOLD fMRI and NIRS Recordings during Functional Brain Activation. *NeuroImage 17*, 2 (2002), 719–731.
36. Villringer, A., and Chance, B. Non-invasive optical spectroscopy and imaging of human brain function. *Trends in Neurosciences 20*, 10 (1997), 435–42.
37. Wickens, C., and Hollands, J. *Engineering Psychology and Human Performance.* Prentice-Hall, Upper Saddle River, NJ, 1999.
38. Wigdor, D., Shen, C., Forlines, C., and Balakrishnan, R. Perception of elementary graphical elements in tabletop and multi-surface environments. *ACM CHI 2007* (2007), 473–482.
39. Wolf, M., Ferrari, M., and Quaresima, V. Progress of near-infrared spectroscopy and topography for brain and muscle clinical applications. *Journal of Biomedical Optics 12*, 6 (2012), 062104.
40. Yeh, Y., and Wickens, C. D. Dissociation of Performance and Subjective Measures of Workload. *Human Factors: The Journal of the Human Factors and Ergonomics Society 30*, 1 (1988), 111–120.

Weighted Graph Comparison Techniques for Brain Connectivity Analysis

Basak Alper
UCSB
basakalper@gmail.com

Benjamin Bach
INRIA
benjamin.bach@inria.fr

Nathalie Henry Riche
Microsoft Research
nath@microsoft.com

Tobias Isenberg
INRIA
tobias.isenberg@inria.fr

Jean-Daniel Fekete
INRIA
jean-daniel.fekete@inria.fr

ABSTRACT
The analysis of brain connectivity is a vast field in neuroscience with a frequent use of visual representations and an increasing need for visual analysis tools. Based on an in-depth literature review and interviews with neuroscientists, we explore high-level brain connectivity analysis tasks that need to be supported by dedicated visual analysis tools. A significant example of such a task is the comparison of different connectivity data in the form of weighted graphs. Several approaches have been suggested for graph comparison within information visualization, but the comparison of *weighted* graphs has not been addressed. We explored the design space of applicable visual representations and present augmented adjacency matrix and node-link visualizations. To assess which representation best support weighted graph comparison tasks, we performed a controlled experiment. Our findings suggest that matrices support these tasks well, outperforming node-link diagrams. These results have significant implications for the design of brain connectivity analysis tools that require weighted graph comparisons. They can also inform the design of visual analysis tools in other domains, e.g. comparison of weighted social networks or biological pathways.

Author Keywords
Graph comparison; brain connectivity analysis; brain connectivity visualization.

ACM Classification Keywords
H.5.m. Information Interfaces and Presentation (e. g. HCI): Miscellaneous

INTRODUCTION
Understanding brain connectivity can shed light on the brain's cognitive functioning that occurs via the connections and interaction between neurons. The term brain connectivity refers to different aspects of brain organization including *anatomical connectivity* consisting of axonal fibers across cortical regions, and *functional connectivity* defined as the observed statistical correlations between regions of interest (ROIs)—units of neural groupings or anatomically segregated brain regions [26]. Although, the processes for acquiring the two types of connectivity data differ, they can both be expressed as weighted graphs in which nodes represent ROIs and edges can encode the strength of their correlation (*functional*) or the density of fibers connecting them (*anatomical*).

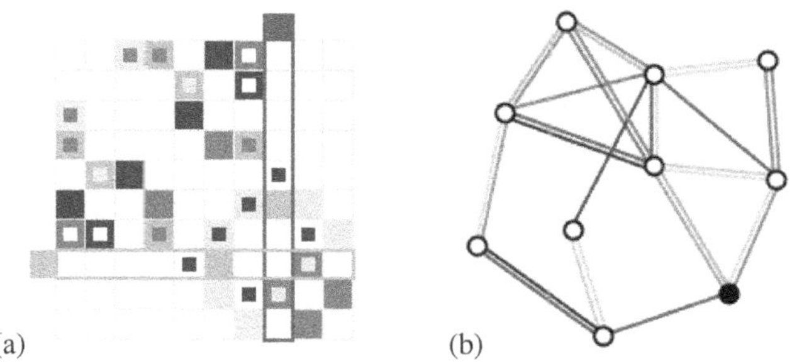

Figure 1. Alternative superimposed (a) matrix and (b) node-link visualizations supporting weighted graph comparisons.

Recent research in neuroscience successfully began to analyze the connectivity data using graph theoretical methods [20] and statistics [43]. However, visualization systems can provide significant insights for the discovery of unforeseen structural correlation patterns, in particular across several datasets. For example, comparing patterns of functional connectivity and anatomical connectivity pre- and post-removal of parts of brain tissue may help neuroscientists to understand how the brain rewires itself to restore its function. Although statistical and graph theoretical methods are available for such analysis, visualization systems featuring connectivity comparison tools can provide significant insights for the discovery of unanticipated correlation patterns. Visual graph comparison, thus, can be an essential tool for comprehensive brain connectivity analysis.

To build effective interfaces for brain connectivity analysis, we identify common visual analysis tasks that neuroscientists carry out in brain connectivity analysis based on interviews with neuroscientists and an in-depth review of the domain literature. By doing so, we provide a link from domain-specific problems in neuroscience to more generic problems in HCI and visualization. Based on this task identification, we also establish that weighted graph comparisons can benefit a group of higher-level tasks in visual brain connectivity analysis. We explored alternative visual encodings that facilitate the comparison of edge weights across two graphs in a superimposed view, both in node-link diagrams and adjacency matrices.

Finally, we report on a controlled experiment comparing two of these representations (Fig. 1) for their ability to encode connection weights of two graphs. Results of the study led us to implications for the design of brain connectivity visualization tools. While weighted graphs are present in a plethora of domains: computer networks, social networks, biological pathways networks, air traffic networks, commercial trade networks; very few tools currently exist to represent and compare them. As we used generic comparison tasks during the study, our results can also inform the design of general weighted graph comparison tools.

HIGH-LEVEL BRAIN CONNECTIVITY ANALYSIS TASKS

Neuroscientists investigate brain connectivity to answer questions such as how brain connectivity changes throughout development, with aging, or with physical injury, what kind of connectivity patterns are required for a particular functionality, and how these connectivity patterns show variances across individuals and across certain anomaly conditions. Some of the subtasks carried out during these explorations can be supported by visualizations. Through a literature survey and a series of one-hour long interviews with seven neuroscientists, we identified a list of major tasks in brain connectivity analysis where visualizations are already in use or can be used to aid and enhance the analysis:

1. *Identify network structures that are responsible for a specific cognitive function:* Neuroscientists examine how our brain carries out specific cognitive functions, identify the regions responsible or involved, and study their interaction with each other while executing these functions [41]. However, significant individual variations exist. These variations require the comparison of connectivity data of large subject groups to be able to identify common network structures.
2. *Identify effects of anatomical structure on functional connectivity:* Understanding the effect of anatomical structure on the formation of functional relations is a key challenge in neuroscience [9, 24, 25]. For this purpose, scientists look for correlated patterns across anatomical and functional connectivity, requiring the simultaneous exploration of the two connectivity data to reveal complex mappings between.
3. *Identify alterations in brain connectivity:* Brain connectivity of an individual changes over time—through development and with aging [14]. Another instance of alteration in brain connectivity is the development of re-routings that restore functionality typically after a local injury [10]. In addition, changes in white matter fiber connectivity following behavioral training of a complex skill have also been reported [35]. In order to understand the temporal evolution of these changes, scientists need to compare connectivity data gathered at different instances in time.
4. *Identify the existence or the loss of patterns in brain connectivity that are associated with anomalous conditions:* Neuroscientists have already shown that certain cognitive anomalies are associated with the loss of specific connectivity patterns [6, 34]. For instance in Alzheimer's disease, it is observed that functional connectivity does not exhibit small-world properties as much as a healthy brain [34]. Identifying such differences in connectivity patterns is essential for the diagnosis and treatment of these anomalies, which can be done by comparing the connectivity of the anomalous brains to healthy ones.
5. *Identify deviation of an individual's connectivity from a population mean:* The aforementioned tasks often utilize an 'average' brain—the term 'average' encompassing connectivities that are common to all individuals. The average brain, in turn, can be used to characterize an individual's brain by studying the deviation of it from the average brain.
6. *Effective brain parcellation and multimodal connectivity analysis:* Identifying brain structures that act as a unit is an important problem. Automatic parcellation algorithms, based on statistical likelihood of synchronized activation, are employed to identify these units. A variety of statistical techniques along with multiple data sources exist each yielding different parcellations. For example, an automatic parcellation based only on functional connectivity data can be refined by taking into account fiber connectivity [29], or anatomy-based parcellation can be validated by functional connectivity relationships between the regions [7]. Thus, different parcellation outcomes are needed to be compared to verify the robustness of a technique [42].
7. *Identify effects of local injury:* In clinical applications it is important to predict the effect of a local injury. A localized damage of anatomical structure can have multiple implications on functional connectivity due to the loss of indirect as well as direct connections. Similarly, in image-guided neurosurgery [4], identifying optimal surgical paths that minimize damage induced by intervention is also important. In order to be able to make these decisions, neurologists look at brain connectivity data in a spatial context and observe which anatomical and functional connections are associated with which specific brain locations.

This summary shows that a large number of neuroscientific problems can be facilitated with weighted graph comparison tools. Apart from the last task, for which connectivity data has to be presented in its spatial context (inside the brain volume), all other tasks can be conducted with non-spatial representations such as 2D node-link diagrams and adjacency matrices. Although it is essential for brain connectivity analysis to communicate spatial context of the data to ease the interpretation, non-spatial representations can prove more effective for communicating changes in complex connectivity data, as they relax a set of strong constraints on the visual representations (such as preserving the exact shape of connections in three dimensions). Hence, tools supporting brain connectivity analysis have to offer multiple visual representations—each of which are optimal for specific set of tasks. In this paper our focus is on connectivity comparison tasks which, at an abstract level, can be expressed as comparison of two weighted graphs.

RELATED WORK

Work relating to our own can be found in three domains: the study of brain connectivity in neuroscience, the use of visualizations within this domain, and research on graph comparison and weighted graph visualizations in information visualization. We review each of these areas below.

Brain Connectivity

Functional connectivity data is derived from functional magnetic resonance imaging (fMRI). Based on the blood oxygen consumption level, fMRI images show active regions of the brain at a given instance. Neuroscientists apply a variety of statistical and computational methods over collections of fMRI images to characterize global structures in the coordinated neural activity [32,37]. Functional connectivity, therefore, can be seen as a relatedness among specific region of interests (ROIs) in the brain which are highly correlated functionally. Thus, functional connectivity among ROIs can be represented as a fully connected, weighted relatedness graph.

White matter fibertracts, the so called *anatomical connectivity* structures, are derived through applying tractography algorithms to diffusion tensor imaging (DTI) data which represents anisotropic diffusion of water through bundles of neural axons. The resulting fibertracts (representing axon bundles) are often clustered based on their trajectory similarities and regions that they connect to [27]. It is possible to define a fiber connectivity measure between all ROI pairs depending on the fibertract density between them [22]. Hence, similar to functional connectivity, anatomical connectivity between regions of the brain can be expressed as a weighted graph.

Use of Visualizations in Brain Connectivity Analysis

Defined as a correlation matrix between specific locations within the brain volume (ROIs), functional connectivity data is often visualized as 3D node-link diagrams: ROIs are shown as nodes and weighted edges denote the pairwise strength of these node relationships (e. g., Fig. 2(a)). Although the edges below a certain strength threshold can be hidden, the resulting images are still cluttered and suffer from the known side effects of 3D rendering such as occlusion [14, 19]. To facilitate comparison, two connectivity datasets can be overlaid within the 3D brain [42], with edge colors denoting correlation and anti-correlation between the end points. However, the clutter and complexity of the visual encoding in these spatial/volumetric representations makes it difficult to perform accurate weighted edge comparison tasks.

An alternative approach is to show the connectivity data as a 2D node-link diagram whose layout is calculated by multidimensional scaling or force-directed algorithms [1] (e. g., Fig. 2(c)). These layouts remedy some of the clutter problems by eliminating overlaps and reducing number of long edges. They are thus adopted especially among those scientists who practice graph-theoretical analysis of brain connectivity. The spatial context of the data, however, is still crucial for an effective interpretation of the data by neuroscientists who are trained to reason with respect to spatial brain regions. Hence, node-link diagrams are often accompanied with a separate spatial rendering of the node positions, with nodes on the two representations being matched by region color and label [31]. To preserve the spatial character of the data to some extent, many 2D connectivity node-link diagrams adopt a biological layout where node positions are projections on 2D planes defined by two of the standard anatomical axes (e. g., ventrodorsal, anteroposterior, left-right; e. g., Fig. 2(b)) [1]. These layouts communicate spatial properties of the data coarsely, helping scientists orient themselves in the graph, while enabling the use of color for encoding other information such as change across two states [6, 33].

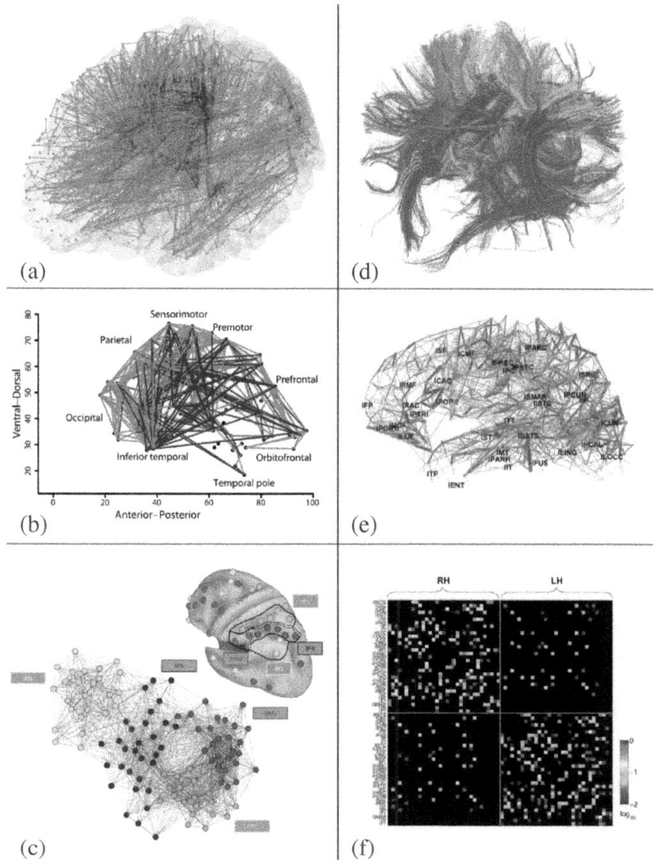

Figure 2. Existing visualization techniques for brain connectivity. Left column, functional connectivity: (a) 3D spatial node-link diagram within the brain volume (courtesy of Erik Ziegler, Cyclotron Research Centre, Univ. of Liège, generated with ConnectomeViewer [19]), (b) 2D node-link diagram with biological layout [1], and (c) force-directed node-link accompanied with a spatial visualization showing actual positions of the nodes [31]. Right column, anatomical connectivity: (d) fibers within the 3D volume of the brain, (e) fiber density ROI graph as a spatial node-link diagram [22], and (f) matrix representation of fiber densities between ROIs [22]. All images reproduced with authors' permissions.

Matrices of functional connectivity as an alternative representation are also popular [1, 19, 34] and are occasionally used in the form of small multiples to illustrate trends across different connectivity datasets [5, 20, 28]. To support direct comparisons, correlation coefficients from multiple scan states can be shown within nested quadrants of a matrix cell [39]. However, this design makes it hard to focus on a single scan state.

Representing physical entities, fibertracts that constitute anatomical connectivity are more frequently visualized within the 3D brain volume [19] (e. g., Fig. 2(d)). Research in fiber connectivity visualization focuses on their similarity clustering, bundling, and selection in 3D space [30, 38] as well as on illustrative depiction [18]. While non-spatial representations for fiber similarity and clustering are also used [27], neuroscientists reported difficulties with interpreting these representations. Related to our work, anatomical connectivity can be reduced to a fiber density graph among ROIs and visualized as a 3D spatial node-link diagram combined with a matrix representation [22] (e. g., Fig. 2(e)–(f)).

So far, the coordinated visualizations of structural and functional connectivity has received little attention, and existing visualizations focus on spatial representations rather than supporting abstract graph comparison tasks. Several tools (e. g., ConnectomeViewer [19, 29]) support visual brain connectivity analysis using spatial 3D node-link and matrix representations for functional connectivity and volumetric fibertract representations for anatomical connectivity. Although it is crucial to communicate the spatial context in brain connectivity analysis for several tasks, 2D non-spatial representations with flexible layouts are more suitable to communicate differences/changes in the connectivity data in an explicit way. To the best of our knowledge, none of the existing brain connectivity tools supports such a visual connectivity comparison.

Weighted Graph Visualization and Comparison

A weighted graph is visualized either as a node-link diagram or an adjacency matrix. In node-link diagrams, weight is either mapped to the length of an edge with inverse proportions [11] or is encoded in the thickness and/or color of an edge [16]. In matrix visualizations, the weight of a connection is mapped either to the color of the corresponding cell or to the size of a glyph inside the cell [40]. Among these representations, people most commonly encode weight as edge thickness in node-link diagrams. However, to the best of our knowledge, there is no study on alternative visual encodings of edge weight for graphs nor their comparison.

Comparison of weighted graphs is an open research question. However, various comparison techniques are proposed for unweighted graphs in a number of domains for problems related to characterization of metabolic pathways [8, 36], business process models [2] and software evolution [11].

We can categorize techniques for comparing unweighted graphs as follows: (i) juxtaposed views where two graphs are presented side-by-side and often complemented with interactive techniques that highlight the matches between the two [2], (ii) superimposed or overlaid views where a single layout is used for both graphs while differing edges and nodes are color coded [2, 17, 23], and (iii) animated views where positions of nodes are interpolated between the two graphs, while added or removed elements are faded in or out respectively [12, 17]. A more detailed categorization of these techniques was presented by Gleicher et al. [21], who also emphasize the continuing necessity of comparison tools in visualization.

Similar techniques exist for depicting dynamic graphs to communicate changes during a graph's evolution. Work in this area focuses on the preservation of a viewer's mental map by restricting layout changes across time steps. This approach facilitates the detection of temporal patterns in both animated and multiple juxtaposed views [3, 13]. Although important, these methods do not easily extend to brain connectivity data where mental map preservation involves spatial aspects of the data, hence requires a deterministic biological layout.

Nevertheless, *weighted* graph comparison—a crucial component in brain connectivity analysis—has yet to be addressed.

VISUALIZATION DESIGN RATIONALE

In the following we discuss our choices for visually coupled presentation of two graphs and visual encodings adopted in node-link and matrix visualizations.

Visually Coupled Graph Representations

Comparing two weighted graphs requires communicating absence or presence of connections, as well as their absolute weights in both graphs. As mentioned above, three alternative representations exist for presenting two graphs: side-by-side (juxtaposed), overlaid (superimposed), and animated views. While smooth animations are effective for observing trends over multiple states, they do not provide information about two graphs in a single image. Additionally, smooth animations may increase the time requirement as the viewer may need to watch the animation repeatedly when multiple elements from both graphs need to be compared. Therefore, we only considered side-by-side and overlaid representations.

From informal feedback on our initial implementations, side-by-side views proved to be much slower and error-prone compared to the overlaid views—likely due to the fact that the distance to be covered even for simple comparison tasks is much higher in the side-by-side view compared to the overlaid views (element lookup). The difference increases tremendously as the graphs get larger. Moreover, side-by-side views necessitate about double the screen space compared to the overlaid or animated views.

The last alternative, overlaid views has the potential drawback of visual clutter due to added visual elements. However, for the data sizes and densities we consider in this work, we found overlaid representations to be better suited for the effective execution of the comparison tasks. We thus decided to base our visualizations on overlaid views.

Edge Weight Visual Encoding in Node-Link Diagrams

The design space for the visualization of weighted graphs is, in fact, limited to the use of color (intensity or hue) or size on edges in node-link diagrams or glyphs inside the cells in matrix visualizations. However, these mappings do not suffice when edge weights from two graphs need to be shown in an overlaid view. Although it is most common to use edge thickness in node-link diagrams for encoding weight, this approach increases the space requirements especially when edges from two graphs need to be shown. Moreover, when node-link diagrams represent dense graphs, it is important to keep edge thickness at a minimum.

We examined two other options for overlaid edge weight encoding. First, we considered two constant width parallel edges with two different color scales—each encoding the edge weight from one graph (Fig. 3(b)). As the alternative, we considered stacking a dashed edge on a normal edge, enabling viewers to see the line underneath the dashed line (Fig. 3(a)). We tried both alternatives with our datasets and found continuous parallel lines to be more legible, especially for dense graphs. Dashed lines caused much change of color through the entire visualization, making the overview seem cluttered and edges of one graph difficult to isolate.

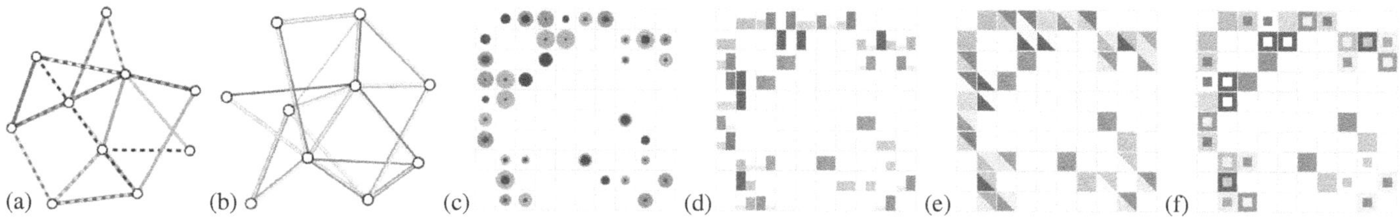

Figure 3. Examples of all visual encodings examined to facilitate the comparison of weighted graphs.

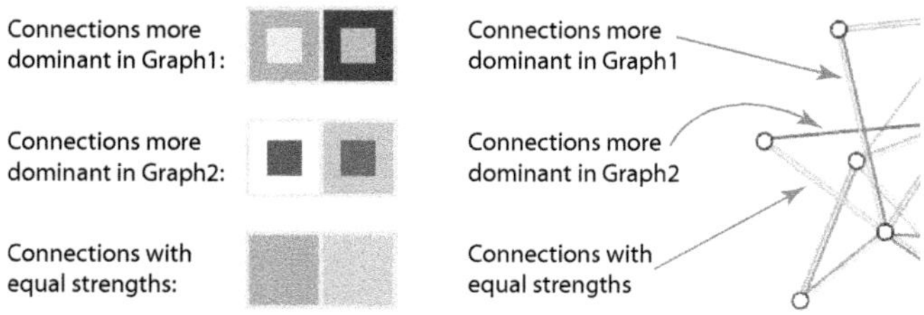

Figure 4. Details of the selected edge weight encoding in matrices (left) and node-link diagrams (right) using superimposition.

Edge Weight Visual Encoding in Matrices

Matrix representations which eliminate occlusion problems that degrade node-link diagrams facilitate the encoding of additional information in cells more effectively [15]. Our initial approach for encoding the weight within a matrix cell was to use scaled glyphs such as concentric circles (Fig. 3(c)). Here the radius of the inner circle is mapped to the union weight and change from one graph to the other is mapped to the outer circle radius, while decrease and increase is differentiated by color. We did not pursue this approach further because of the difficulty of identifying a single connectivity state. Besides, when the difference is minimal, the borders produced between inner and outer circles became illegible within the limited cell space.

Next, we examined color-coded bar charts shown within the cell to show the absolute weight from each graph (Fig. 3(d)). We eliminated this approach due to the horizontal line patterns it produced and also complicated focusing on weights from one graph at a time. We investigated alternative ways of dividing matrix cells into two regions and using a separate color scheme for each region to encode weight from the corresponding graph. We tried vertical, horizontal, and diagonal divisions (Fig. 3(e)) but they all produced patterns interfering with the cell boundaries of the matrix.

Finally, we adopted an inner and outer squares division (Fig. 3(a)) where the edge weight from each graph is mapped to the color density of the corresponding region. We considered this approach useful since it did not obscure the matrix' grid structure. It also allowed us to use brightness alone to encode weight since it was possible to differentiate graphs based on the spatial encoding (inner vs. outer)—freeing up hue to encode other data attributes. As a natural outcome of this encoding, the amount of change is mapped to the contrast between inner and outer regions of a cell, easily enabling viewers to differentiate regions with high and low change.

CONTROLLED STUDY

In this study we investigate the effectiveness (*accuracy*, *task completion time*) of the described node-link diagrams and matrices (Fig. 4) when comparing two graphs (G_1, G_2) with different edge weights. Our goal is to assess how both techniques scale with changing graph sizes and edge densities across different comparison tasks, to inform designs that would utilize both representations. Representative tasks for the study were derived from common tasks in analyzing differences in brain connectivity, as previously described.

Techniques

We used the visual encodings described in the previous section for overlaying two graphs in node-link and matrix visualizations. In all techniques, the entire information is shown in one full-screen window without a need to zoom or pan. This design eliminates any confounds due to navigation issues rather than reading of the visual representation to complete the task.

1. **Matrix—Overlaid** (*M*): A single adjacency matrix representation shows edge weights in both graphs. Each matrix cell (12×12 pixels) contains an inner region encoding the weight of the edge in G_1 and an outer region encoding the weight of the edge in G_2 (Fig. 5(a)). The absolute weight is mapped to the color brightness for which we used a perceptually linear scaling. A cell with a light inner and dark outer regions indicates an edge with a high weight in G_1 and a low weight in G_2. Vice versa, a cell with a dark inner and a light outer region indicates an edge with a high weight in G_2 and a low weight in G_1. Since one of our tasks required identifying a specific region, we reordered rows and columns of the matrix to ensure that nodes were placed in the same regions in both the matrix view and the node-link diagram. To provide users with stable representations across all tasks, we used this ordering for all trials. The tradeoff of this ordering is, however, that it did not ensure a close placement of items that need to be compared during other tasks, as other reordering algorithms could have.

2. **Node-Link Diagram—Overlaid** (*NL*): A single node-link diagram shows edge weights in both graphs using two parallel edges. Connections that are present in G_1 are encoded in green colored edges, while connections that are present in G_2 are encoded with the red colored edges (Fig. 5(b)). Thus, a single green edge represents an edge that was only present in G_1, while a single red edge represents an edge that was only present in G_2. The absolute edge weight is encoded using brightness as in the matrix condition, and we ensured that values for the same edge weight had the same brightness. To ensure the generalizability of our results, we eliminated the fixed biological layout alternative and only used a force-directed layout. We made this choice because fixed layouts produce less optimal arrangements with re-

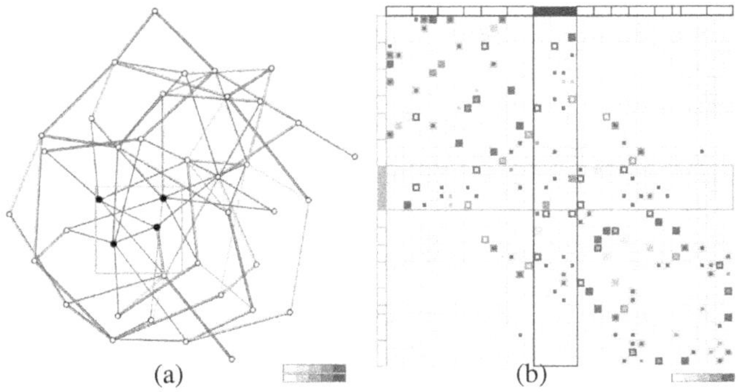

Figure 5. Example from our controlled study: node-link and matrix representation of the same data (small, dense) for the region identification.

spect to edge crossings and visual clutter, thus are likely to decrease the performance of node-link diagrams.

Tasks

Based on our task analysis in this paper's second section, we identified three generic comparison tasks that are required for successfully executing high-level brain connectivity comparisons. These tasks require users to assess changes in edge weights at different level of details: from a single element to the overview of a large portion of the data. Below we describe each task and the optimal strategy for achieving it.

Assess weight change of a node's connections (*Trend*): *Given one highlighted node, does the overall edge weight to all of its neighbors* ***decrease*** *or* ***increase*** *from* G_1 *to* G_2*?* Participants completed this task in three steps: (1) they needed to identify all connections to the highlighted node, (2) they needed to assess the change in weight for each connection, and (3) they needed to estimate the aggregated change for all these connections. To avoid confounds in the study, we made sure all trials exhibited a clear increase or decrease trend. To prevent participants from selecting one option at random, we offered an additional "I don't know" option and instructed them to select it if their confidence was low. We excluded these trials from the analysis.

Assess connectivity of common neighbors (*Connectivity*): *Given two highlighted nodes,* ***how many*** *of their common neighbors in* G_1 *are still common neighbors in* G_2*?* Participants completed this task in two steps: (1) they needed to find common neighbors, meaning the nodes that are connected to both of the highlighted nodes and (2), among them, they needed to count how many are present in both graphs. Participants selected an option from 0 to 6.

Identify the region with most changes (*Region*): *Identify the region showing the* ***most variation*** *between* G_2 *and* G_1*?* For this task we provided users with simple interaction tools to view regions. In the node-link case, we divided the diagram into a 4 × 4 grid and assigned each node to the region it fell into. As participants moved their mouse pointer on the diagram, the corresponding region boundary appeared in light blue and nodes of the region became highlighted (Fig. 5(a)). In the matrix condition, we used the same 16 regions, ordering the nodes linearly according to the regions they belonged to. As participants moved their mouse pointer on the matrix, the region boundaries were highlighted (Fig. 5(b)).

Participants completed this task by browsing each region successively, estimating the region with highest edge weight variation. To avoid confounds in the study, we ensured that all trials presented a region with discernably higher variation than the rest. Participants clicked on a region of their choice.

Data

We used synthetic data in order to ensure generalizability of the results, and to be able to control data size and density. We generated four types of uniform networks with either 40 (*Small*) or 80 (*Large*) number of nodes, and with either 5% (*Sparse*) or 10% (*Dense*) edge density. For each data type, we created four isomorphic networks per trial which were used across all tasks. We created five additional datasets for training with a *Small*, *Sparse* metric. The edge weights were assigned arbitrarily to each of the generated graphs, ranging from 0 to 1 in increments of 0.2. We created comparison graphs by copying the original weighted graphs and then randomly perturbing the edge weights of 70% of the edges in order to ensure edge weights that remain constant across the graphs.

Participants and Setting

11 participants (1 female) participated in the study with a mean age of 30.2 years. All participants had normal or corrected-to-normal vision, without color deficiency. Participants were graduate students or researchers, familiar with graphs. The experiment was conducted in a quiet room during the day. The study computer was a 2.4 GHz Dual-Core HP Z800 workstation equipped with a 30 inch screen with a 2500 × 1600 pixel resolution. The visualization area was restricted to window of 1500 × 1350 pixels. Participants interacted with a mouse and keyboard to complete the tasks.

Experimental Procedure

We used a within-subject, full-factorial design: 2 *Techniques* × 3 *Tasks* × 2 *Sizes* × 2 *Densities*. We repeated each condition four times. We counter-balanced the techniques (*M*, *NL*) using a Latin square. Tasks appeared always in a fixed order of increasing complexity (*Trend*, *Connectivity*, and *Region*). Datasets also appeared in a fixed order from simple (*Small* and *Sparse*) to more complex (*Large* and *Dense*). For each trial, we measured *accuracy* and *task completion time*.

Before the controlled experiment, we instructed participants about the visualizations as well as the weight encoding used in each, making sure none of them had any vision problems. We asked them to complete trials as accurate and as fast as possible. Before each new technique and task, five training trials were provided. Participants completed the first two following the explanations of the instructor. They answered the remaining trials on their own unless they had further questions. Trials were not timed during the training. After training trials, participants completed the 16 timed trials (2 Size × 2 Density × 4 Repeat) required for each condition (technique × task). For all conditions, we collected a total of 96 trials per participant (excluding training).

To keep the experiment within a reasonable time, we limited the time per trial to 30 seconds (measured as a feasible value in a pilot study) and notified participants before the experiment. After 20 seconds, the screen flashed and a time counter appeared below the visualization for the remaining 10 seconds. To provide their answer, participants pressed the space bar to view the dialog box with the answers. After this point, the timer stopped and the visualization disappeared. Participants were instructed to take breaks if needed when no visualization was shown on the display. None of the participants took a noticable break nor reported any fatigue.

Hypotheses

Our hypotheses for the experiment were the following:

- **H1**—For the *Trend* task, we expected Matrix to outperform (*accuracy* and *completion time*) Node-Link for high-density datasets. We expected that occlusion problems in Node-Link would get severe in *Dense* cases, causing more errors. We also believed that the spatial encoding used in Matrix would prove easier to remember than the color encoding used in Node-Link, leading to faster answers.
- **H2**—For the *Connectivity* task, we expected Matrix not to outperform Node-Link because we believed participants might need to compare two distant columns or rows in Matrix, whereas the force-directed layout in Node-Link ensures that connected nodes are in closer proximity.
- **H3**—For the *Region* task, we expected Matrix to outperform Node-Link (*accuracy* and *completion time*). In Matrix, all connections of nodes in one region are contained within the region boundary. However, in Node-Link, participants had to consider links that are drawn across region boundaries, leading to more errors and slower answers.
- **H4**—Overall, we expected Node-Link to decrease in performance (*accuracy* and *completion time*) for *Dense* datasets, as edge density causes many edge crossings, decreasing the legibility of this representation.

Results

We used a repeated-measure analysis of variance (RM-ANOVA) to analyze the collected accuracy and time performance data. We performed the RM-ANOVA on the logarithm of the task times to normalize the skewed distribution, as is standard practice with reaction time data. The analysis of the time performance is reported for correct answers only.

Accuracy. The accuracy results are summarized in Table 1 and Fig. 6(a). We found a significant effect of accuracy for *Technique* ($F_{(1,10)} = 55.32, p < .0001$) with a large effect size ($\eta_p^2 = .85$). Overall, Matrix is about 20% more accurate than Node-Link. The RM-ANOVA also revealed a significant effect of *Task* ($F_{(2,20)} = 28.67, p < .0001$) with large effect size ($\eta_p^2 = .74$), and a significant effect of the interaction *Task*

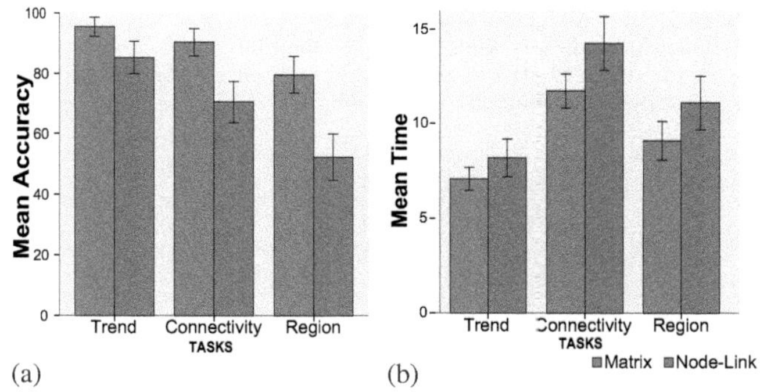

(a) (b)

Figure 6. (a) Mean accuracy in %, (b) and mean completion time in seconds per task for matrix (blue) and node-link (red) techniques. Error bars represent +/– 2 standard errors.

× *Technique* ($F_{(2,20)} = 4.34, p < .05$) with a large effect size ($\eta_p = .30$). Pairwise comparisons revealed that Matrix is more accurate than Node-Link for all three tasks.

We also found a significant effect of *Size* ($F_{(1,10)} = 18.69, p < .01$) with a large effect size ($\eta_p^2 = .65$) and *Density* ($F_{(1,10)} = 61.00, p < .0001$) with a large effect size ($\eta_p^2 = .86$). As expected, accuracy decreases for *Large* or *Dense* networks. The interaction *Technique* × *Size* ($F_{(1,10)} = 6.5, p < .05$) is significant with a large effect size ($\eta_p^2 = .39$). Node-Link is affected by *Size*, losing about 25% accuracy in large datasets compared to small ones. In contrast, Matrix has less than 1% loss in accuracy. Pairwise comparisons indicate that Matrix significantly outperforms Node-Link for large networks across all three tasks. The results indicate that both *Techniques* are affected by *Density*, Matrix losing about 10% accuracy, Node-Link about 20%. Pairwise comparisons indicate that Matrix significantly outperforms Node-Link both for *Sparse* and *Dense* networks across all three tasks.

Completion Time. We analyzed the completion time for correct answers only, using a mixed linear model capable of handling missing data cases. We excluded about 10% incorrect trials for Matrix and 30% for Node-Link (out of 528 total trials per technique).

The completion time results are summarized in Table 2 and Fig. 6(b). We found a significant effect of time for *Technique* ($F_{(1,10)} = 28.40, p < .0001$). Overall, Matrix is 15% faster than Node-Link. We also found a significant effect of *Task* ($F_{(2,20)} = 183.25, p < .0001$) and *Technique* × *Task* ($F_{(2,20)} = 3.82, p < .05$). Pairwise comparisons reveal that Matrix is faster than Node-Link for *Connectivity* and *Region* tasks.

We also found a significant effect of *Size* ($F_{(1,10)} = 139.19, p < .0001$) and *Density* ($F_{(1,10)} = 30.94, p < .0001$). As expected,

Table 1. Means of accuracy in percentages, the standard error is indicated in parentheses. Significant differences in accuracy are indicated by *. More accurate results are highlighted in bold.

	Matrix	Node-Link	p-value
All tasks*	**88.5** (0.9)	69.3 (2.0)	< .001
Trend *	**95.5** (1.2)	85.2 (4.3)	< .05
Connectivity *	**90.3** (1.0)	70.5 (2.5)	< .0001
Region *	**79.6** (2.1)	52.3 (4.5)	< .0001

Table 2. Means of completion times (excluding errors) in seconds, the standard error is indicated in parentheses. Significant differences in completion time are indicated by *. Faster results are highlighted in bold.

	Matrix	Node-Link	p-value
All tasks*	**9.3** (0.3)	11.0 (0.4)	< .001
Trend	7.1 (0.3)	8.2 (0.5)	not significant
Connectivity *	**11.7** (0.5)	14.3 (0.7)	< .0001
Region *	**9.1** (0.5)	11.1 (0.7)	< .01

Table 3. User preference (means of ratings from -2-strongly node-link, -1-somewhat node-link, 0-indifferent, 1-somewhat matrix, 2-strongly matrix), the standard error is indicated in parentheses. Significant differences in user preference are indicated by *.

	Preference	p-value
Overall*	**1.25** (0.26)	< .0001
Trend	0.63 (0.38)	not significant
Connectivity *	**1.31** (0.23)	< .0001
Region *	**1.36** (0.21)	< .0001

completion time increases for *Large* or *Dense* networks. The interaction *Technique* × *Size* ($F_{(1,10)} = 9.84, p < .01$) is significant. Node-Link is particularly affected by *Size*. For *Large* datasets, the completion time increases by about 60% for Node-Link and 40% for Matrix. For *Dense* datasets, the completion time increases by about 25% for both techniques.

User Preference. Users rated their preference on a 5-point scale from -2 (strong preference for Node-Link) to +2 (strong preference for Matrix). We analyzed these ratings using a z-test. Results reported in Table 3 reveals that there is a significant difference in user preference between *Techniques*. Users preferred Matrix overall ($p < .0001$). In fact, 7 out of 11 participants ranked Matrix as the most effective representation (maximum rating of 2). Z-test also showed that the user preference was significantly different for the *Connectivity* ($p < .0001$) and the *Region* tasks ($p < .0001$). For these tasks, Matrix was preferred to Node-Link.

DISCUSSION

The results of our controlled experiment indicate that matrix representations are more effective than node-link diagrams for encoding edge weights and performing comparison tasks. While we expected that it would be the case for the *Trend* (H1) and *Region* (H3) tasks in the *Dense* datasets, we were surprised to find significant differences in accuracy across all tasks for both sparse and dense networks.

We also did not expect a significant performance difference across techniques for *Connectivity* (H2). While we did not find any significant difference in completion time for correct answers, the results indicated that matrix outperformed node-link in accuracy, contradicting (H2).

Although we originally thought that comparison in matrices may be error-prone since the rows or columns to be compared may be far away, we in fact observed that the linear arrangement of the matrix allowed people to inspect each of the candidate neighbors successively. In contrast, despite common neighbors being placed closer together in space in the node-link diagram, performance suffered from the less systematic manner to count them, leading to a decrease in accuracy.

We did not expect the strong performance decrease of node-link diagrams for large networks, in addition to dense ones (H4). We believe that this happened because, although we used a fixed edge density, the total number of edges increases quadratically with a linear increase in number of nodes. The total number of links shown in large sparse datasets, thus, is much higher than small sparse datasets. To offer a similar visual complexity in small and large graphs, we could envision to control the edge density per display area unit.

Implications for design

The findings of the study indicate that, for edge weight comparisons, node-link representations are more error-prone and less readable than matrices. However, node-link diagrams offer a flexible layout that can be adjusted to reflect spatial characteristics of the data much more effectively than the linear matrix orderings allow. Therefore, while scientists should adopt matrix representations to ensure better accuracy when performing comparison tasks, efforts have to be made to augment these visualizations with spatial context or couple them with appropriate spatial representations.

A second point to consider relates to the datasets' density. While we tested graphs with connection densities of 5% and 10%, brain connectivity data is, in fact, a fully connected graph with a wide range of weight values; it becomes spare after *thresholding*: removing edges with weight under a specified threshold. One classical criteria for thresholding is to limit the density of the graph to be readable using a node-link representation. For certain tasks, it may be preferable to analyze the entire connectivity information to spot patterns in weak connections. In such cases, matrix representations are the best choices as they scale better with density. For other cases such as the presentation of key findings, however, node-link diagrams may be a better choice because they are more compact for presenting significant trends and are better at preserving the spatial context.

CONCLUSION AND FUTURE WORK

The comparison of brain connectivity patterns is a general problem in the neurosciences. To address it, we have gathered a list of seven tasks that are very common in this domain, both from interviews with experts and from a literature survey, and shown that most of these tasks can be translated to weighted graph comparisons. To support these tasks, we have explored the design space of applicable visual representations. We chose the two most suitable: one augmenting node-link diagrams and the other augmenting adjacency matrices. We thus designed novel visual representations to depict the edges along with the two weights to be compared between graphs.

Based on this visualization design we performed a controlled study, comparing the two representations using two graph sizes and two graph densities. The results show that matrices outperform node-links for the chosen tasks, especially when the graph becomes dense or large. Our recommendation is thus that matrices should be used unless the graph is small and sparse. To the best of our knowledge, this paper is the first to present visualizations designed for weighted graph comparison tasks as well as a controlled study of their effectiveness.

The tasks that we selected in our study consider the graphs to be non-spatial. Spatial representations, however, are still essential for neuroscientists especially for tasks that rely on spatial locations such as comparing patterns around an injury in the brain. As for future work, we will investigate integration of our proposed non-spatial visualization with spatial visualizations.

Since weighted graphs exist in a wide variety of domains such as social and computer networks, we will also investigate other application areas for our proposed visualization. While some useful tasks for these domains are likely to differ from the ones we considered, we believe our visual representations are still suitable and that our results would still hold, although variations in the visual encodings could certainly improve some particular domain-dependent tasks.

ACKNOWLEDGEMENTS

We would like to thank Thomas Grabowski, Jr., MD, Dr. Tara Madhyashta, Dr. Kayo Inoue from The Integrated Brain Imaging Center (IBIC) at University of Washington, and to Dr. Arjun Bansal from Harvard Medical School for their valuable input that went into this work.

REFERENCES

1. Achard, S., Salvador, R., Whitcher, B., Suckling, J., and Bullmore, E. A Resilient, Low-Frequency, Small-World Human Brain Functional Network with Highly Connected Association Cortical Hubs. *J. Neurosci. 26*, 1 (2006), 63–72. doi> 10.1523/JNEUROSCI.3874-05.2006

2. Andrews, K., Wohlfahrt, M., and Wurzinger, G. Visual Graph Comparison. In *Proc. IV*, IEEE Computer Society (Los Alamitos, 2009), 62–67. doi> 10.1109/IV.2009.108

3. Archambault, D., Purchase, H., and Pinaud, B. Animation, Small Multiples, and the Effect of Mental Map Preservation in Dynamic Graphs. *IEEE TVCG 17*, 4 (2011), 539–552. doi> 10.1109/TVCG.2010.78

4. Archip, N., Clatz, O., Whalen, S., Kacher, D., Fedorov, A., Kot, A., Chrisochoides, N., Jolesz, F., Golby, A., Black, P., et al. Non-Rigid Alignment of Pre-Operative MRI, fMRI, and DT-MRI with Intra-Operative MRI for Enhanced Visualization and Navigation in Image-Guided Neurosurgery. *NeuroImage 35*, 2 (2007), 609–624. doi> 10.1016/j.neuroimage.2006.11.060

5. Bassett, D., Brown, J., Deshpande, V., Carlson, J., and Grafton, S. Conserved and Variable Architecture of Human White Matter Vonnectivity. *NeuroImage 54*, 2 (2011), 1262–1279. doi> 10.1016/j.neuroimage.2010.09.006

6. Bassett, D., Bullmore, E., Verchinski, B., Mattay, V., Weinberger, D., and Meyer-Lindenberg, A. Hierarchical Organization of Human Cortical Networks in Health and Schizophrenia. *J. Neurosci. 28*, 37 (2008), 9239–9248. doi> 10.1523/JNEUROSCI.1929-08.2008

7. Beckmann, M., Johansen-Berg, H., and Rushworth, M. Connectivity-Based Parcellation of Human Cingulate Cortex and Its Relation to Functional Specialization. *J. Neurosci. 29*, 4 (2009), 1175–1190. doi> 10.1523/JNEUROSCI.3328-08.2009

8. Brandes, U., Dwyer, T., and Schreiber, F. Visual Understanding of Metabolic Pathways Across Organisms Using Layout in Two and a Half Dimensions. *Journal of Integrative Bioinformatics 1*, 1 (2004), 2:1–2:16. doi> 10.2390/biecoll-jib-2004-2

9. Bullmore, E., and Sporns, O. Complex Brain Networks: Graph Theoretical Analysis of Structural and Functional Systems. *Nature Reviews Neuroscience 10*, 3 (2009), 186–198. doi> 10.1038/nrn2618

10. Cao, C., and Slobounov, S. Alteration of Cortical Functional Connectivity as a Result of Traumatic Brain Injury Revealed by Graph Theory, ICA, and sLORETA Analyses of EEG Signals. *IEEE Transactions on Neural Systems and Rehabilitation Engineering 18*, 1 (2010), 11–19. doi> 10.1109/TNSRE.2009.2027704

11. Collberg, C., Kobourov, S., Nagra, J., Pitts, J., and Wampler, K. A System for Graph-Based Visualization of the Evolution of Software. In *Proc. SoftVis*, ACM (2003), 77–86. doi> 10.1145/774833.774844

12. Diehl, S., and Görg, C. Graphs, they are Changing: Dynamic Graph Drawing for a Sequence of Graphs. In *Proc. Graph Drawing*, Springer (2002), 23–31. doi> 10.1007/3-540-36151-0_3

13. Diehl, S., Görg, C., and Kerren, A. Preserving the Mental Map using Foresighted Layout. In *Proc. VisSym*, Eurographics Association (2001), 175–184.

14. Dosenbach, N., Nardos, B., Cohen, A., Fair, D., Power, J., Church, J., Nelson, S., Wig, G., Vogel, A., Lessov-Schlaggar, C., et al. Prediction of Individual Brain Maturity Using fMRI. *Science 329*, 5997 (2010), 1358–1361. doi> 10.1126/science.1194144

15. Elmqvist, N., Do, T.-N., Goodell, H., Henry, N., and Fekete, J.-D. ZAME: Interactive Large-Scale Graph Visualization. In *Proc. PacificVIS*, IEEE Computer Society (2008), 215–222. doi> 10.1109/PACIFICVIS.2008.4475479

16. Epskamp, S., Cramer, A., Waldorp, L., Schmittmann, V., and Borsboom, D. qgraph: Network Visualizations of Relationships in Psychometric Data. *Journal of Statistical Software 48*, 4 (2012), 1–18.

17. Erten, C., Harding, P., Kobourov, S., Wampler, K., and Yee, G. GraphAEL: Graph Animations with Evolving Layouts. In *Proc. Graph Drawing*, Springer (2004), 98–110. doi> 10.1007/978-3-540-24595-7_9

18. Everts, M. H., Bekker, H., Roerdink, J. B. T. M., and Isenberg, T. Depth-Dependent Halos: Illustrative Rendering of Dense Line Data. *IEEE TVCG 15*, 6 (2009), 1299–1306. doi> 10.1109/TVCG.2009.138

19. Gerhard, S., Daducci, A., Lemkaddem, A., Meuli, R., Thiran, J., and Hagmann, P. The Connectome Viewer Toolkit: An Open Source Framework to Manage, Analyze, and Visualize Connectomes. *Frontiers in Neuroinformatics 5* (2011), 3:1–3:15. doi> 10.3389/fninf.2011.00003

20. Ginestet, C., and Simmons, A. Statistical Parametric Network Analysis of Functional Connectivity Dynamics during a Working Memory Task. *NeuroImage 55*, 2 (2011), 688–704. doi> 10.1016/j.neuroimage.2010.11.030

21. Gleicher, M., Albers, D., Walker, R., Jusufi, I., Hansen, C., and Roberts, J. Visual Comparison for Information Visualization. *Information Visualization 10*, 4 (2011), 289–309. doi> 10.1177/1473871611416549

22. Hagmann, P., Cammoun, L., Gigandet, X., Meuli, R., Honey, C., Wedeen, V., and Sporns, O. Mapping the Structural Core of Human Cerebral Cortex. *PLoS Biology 6*, 7 (2008), e159. doi> 10.1371/journal.pbio.0060159

23. Hascoët, M., and Dragicevic, P. Interactive Graph Matching and Visual Comparison of Graphs and Clustered Graphs. In *Proc. AVI*, ACM (2012), 522–529. doi> 10.1145/2254556.2254654

24. Honey, C., Kötter, R., Breakspear, M., and Sporns, O. Network Structure of Cerebral Cortex Shapes Functional Connectivity on Multiple Time Scales. *PNAS 104*, 24 (2007), 10240–10245. doi> 10.1073/pnas.0701519104

25. Honey, C., Sporns, O., Cammoun, L., Gigandet, X., Thiran, J., Meuli, R., and Hagmann, P. Predicting Human Resting-State Functional Connectivity from Structural Connectivity. *PNAS 106*, 6 (2009), 2035–2040. doi> 10.1073/pnas.0811168106

26. Horwitz, B. The Elusive Concept of Brain Connectivity. *Neuroimage 19*, 2 (2003), 466–470. doi> 10.1016/S1053-8119(03)00112-5

27. Jianu, R., Demiralp, C., and Laidlaw, D. Exploring 3D DTI Fiber Tracts with Linked 2D Representations. *IEEE TVCG 15*, 6 (2009), 1449–1456. doi> 10.1109/TVCG.2009.141

28. Kramer, M., Eden, U., Lepage, K., Kolaczyk, E., Bianchi, M., and Cash, S. Emergence of Persistent Networks in Long-Term Intracranial EEG Recordings. *J. Neurosci. 31*, 44 (2011), 15757–15767. doi> 10.1523/JNEUROSCI.2287-11.2011

29. Li, K., Guo, L., Faraco, C., Zhu, D., Chen, H., Yuan, Y., Lv, J., Deng, F., Jiang, X., Zhang, T., et al. Visual Analytics of Brain Networks. *NeuroImage 61*, 1 (2012), 82–97. doi> 10.1016/j.neuroimage.2012.02.075

30. Moberts, B., Vilanova, A., and van Wijk, J. Evaluation of Fiber Clustering Methods for Diffusion Tensor Imaging. In *Proc. Visualization*, IEEE Computer Society (2005), 65–72. doi> 10.1109/VISUAL.2005.1532779

31. Nelson, S., Cohen, A., Power, J., Wig, G., Miezin, F., Wheeler, M., Velanova, K., Donaldson, D., Phillips, J., Schlaggar, B., and Petersen, S. A Parcellation Scheme for Human Left Lateral Parietal Cortex. *Neuron 67*, 1 (2010), 156–170. doi> 10.1016/j.neuron.2010.05.025

32. Rajapakse, J., and Zhou, J. Learning Effective Brain Connectivity with Dynamic Bayesian Networks. *NeuroImage 37*, 3 (2007), 749–760. doi> 10.1016/j.neuroimage.2007.06.003

33. Richiardi, J., Eryilmaz, H., Schwartz, S., Vuilleumier, P., and Van De Ville, D. Decoding Brain States from fMRI Connectivity Graphs. *NeuroImage 56*, 2 (2011), 616–626. doi> 10.1016/j.neuroimage.2010.05.081

34. Sanz-Arigita, E., Schoonheim, M., Damoiseaux, J., Rombouts, S., Maris, E., Barkhof, F., Scheltens, P., and Stam, C. Loss of 'Small-World' Networks in Alzheimer's Disease: Graph Analysis of fMRI Resting-State Functional Connectivity. *PloS one 5*, 11 (2010), e13788. doi> 10.1371/journal.pone.001378

35. Scholz, J., Klein, M., Behrens, T., and Johansen-Berg, H. Training Induces Changes in White-Matter Architecture. *Nature Neuroscience 12*, 11 (2009), 1370–1371. doi> 10.1038/nn.2412

36. Schreiber, F. Comparison of Metabolic Pathways using Constraint Graph Drawing. In *Proc. APBC*, Australian Computer Society, Inc., Australian Computer Society, Inc. (2003), 105–110.

37. Seth, A. A MATLAB Toolbox for Granger Causal Connectivity Analysis. *J. Neurosci. Methods 186*, 2 (2010), 262–273. doi> 10.1016/j.jneumeth.2009.11.020

38. Sherbondy, A., Akers, D., Mackenzie, R., Dougherty, R., and Wandell, B. Exploring Connectivity of the Brain's White Matter with Dynamic Queries. *IEEE TVCG 11*, 4 (2005), 419–430. doi> 10.1109/TVCG.2005.59

39. Thomason, M., Dennis, E., Joshi, A., Joshi, S., Dinov, I., Chang, C., Henry, M., Johnson, R., Thompson, P., Toga, A., Glover, G. H., Horn, J. D. V., and Gotlib, I. H. Resting-State fMRI Can Reliably Map Neural Networks in Children. *NeuroImage 55*, 1 (2011), 165–175. doi> 10.1016/j.neuroimage.2010.11.080

40. van Ham, F., Schulz, H., and Dimicco, J. Honeycomb: Visual Analysis of Large Scale Social Networks. In *Proc. INTERACT*, Springer (2009), 429–442. doi> 10.1007/978-3-642-03658-3_47

41. Vidal, J., Freyermuth, S., Jerbi, K., Hamamé, C., Ossandon, T., Bertrand, O., Minotti, L., Kahane, P., Berthoz, A., and Lachaux, J. Long-Distance Amplitude Correlations in the High Gamma Band Reveal Segregation and Integration within the Reading Network. *J. Neurosci. 32*, 19 (2012), 6421–6434. doi> 10.1523/JNEUROSCI.4363-11.2012

42. Worsley, K., Chen, J., Lerch, J., and Evans, A. Comparing Functional Connectivity via Thresholding Correlations and Singular Value Decomposition. *Philos. Trans. R. Soc. Lond. B Biol. Sci. 360*, 1457 (2005), 913–920. doi> 10.1098/rstb.2005.1637

43. Zalesky, A., Fornito, A., and Bullmore, E. Network-Based Statistic: Identifying Differences in Brain Networks. *NeuroImage 53*, 4 (2010), 1197–1207. doi> 10.1016/j.neuroimage.2010.06.041

At the Interface of Biology and Computation

Alex S. Taylor[1], Nir Piterman[2], Samin Ishtiaq[1], Jasmin Fisher[1]
Byron Cook[1], Caitlin Cockerton[1], Sam Bourton[3], David Benque[4]

[1] Microsoft Research
21 Station Road,
Cambridge, CB1 2FB, UK
[ast; sishtiaq; jfisher; bycook,
v-caitc]@microsoft.com

[2] Department of Computer Science
University of Leicester
University Road
Leicester, LE1 7RH, UK
nir.pieterman@le.ac.uk

ABSTRACT
Representing a new class of tool for biological modeling, *Bio Model Analyzer* (BMA) uses sophisticated computational techniques to determine *stabilization* in cellular networks. This paper presents designs aimed at easing the problems that can arise when such techniques—using distinct approaches to conceptualizing networks—are applied in biology. The work also engages with more fundamental issues being discussed in the philosophy of science and science studies. It shows how scientific ways of knowing are constituted in routine interactions with tools like BMA, where the emphasis is on the practical business at hand, even when seemingly deep conceptual problems exist. For design, this perspective refigures the frictions raised when computation is used to model biology. Rather than obstacles, they can be seen as opportunities for opening up different ways of knowing.

Author Keywords
Computational biology, ethnography, philosophy of science, science studies, epistemology, materiality.

ACM Classification Keywords
H.5.m. Information interfaces and presentation (e.g., HCI): Miscellaneous.

General Terms
Design; Human Factors.

INTRODUCTION
Recent advances in computer science (CS) have led to a new class of tool for reasoning about the theoretical behaviors of complex and infinite systems. Unfortunately, these powerful computational tools can require some fundamentally different ways of conceptualizing and approaching established problems. The kind and format of questions that can be asked present several difficulties for end users, as do the results the tools produce. In this paper, we describe an ongoing project in which we are designing the user interface for one such tool and our efforts to tackle some of the attendant difficulties. The tool, called *Bio Model Analyzer* (*BMA*), supports the modeling and analysis of what in biology are called gene regulatory networks.

Surprisingly, the new wave of computational tools being pioneered in CS and operationalized in the sciences has been a neglected topic in HCI. Research has focused on the collaborative aspects of scientific (and in some cases biological) tools, often looking to support the sharing of data, analysis and results (e.g. [4,5]). However, the role computation plays in interaction and design has had little if any immediate attention. This absence is understandable given the depth of technical understanding demanded and, it must be said, the apparent dryness of the subject area. However, as we'll show, the peculiarities of computational techniques do have consequences for interaction, and these seem particularly relevant to design and HCI in light of the claims coming from some quarters—somewhat grandiose, perhaps—of biology presenting the next wave of technology [7].

The design of BMA, a software tool that determines the stability of biological networks, is thus offered as a way into thinking about the emerging role computation is playing in biology and the sciences more broadly, and how HCI might usefully contribute. Our focus details attempts to design a tool that appeals to a range of users, from the computationally savvy to experimental biologists with no background in computer programming. It also, however, raises what we see to be some fundamental issues with wider implications. It animates a deeper discussion around some of the tensions or frictions that can arise when new computational techniques are introduced into established scientific practices, and what these frictions might mean for tool design.

Succinctly, the contributions we wish to draw out of this work can be summarized in three points. The first is narrow addressing, specifically, the design of interactive tools for computational biology. It aims to show there are good reasons for displaying the multiple perspectives that appear intrinsic to the new class of computational tools—tools like BMA—even though they can introduce conceptual tensions. The other two contributions open the work up to the broader relations between HCI and the sciences. With the second, we'll aim to show that HCI has an important con-

CHI 2013, April 27–May 2, 2013, Paris, France.

3 Quantum Black, 4-5 Bonhill, London EC2A 4BX UK
4 Royal College of Art, Kensington Gore, London, SW7 2EU, UK

tribution to make in the uptake of computation in the sciences, and crucially how computation becomes entangled in the ways scientific knowledge is constituted. We'll show that HCI has the potential to intervene at the intersections of computation and science, where new findings are being made, but also where the frictions between users and tools can be at their most acute. Relatedly, the third contribution is to tie HCI's potential interventions into broader questions about how tools prioritize certain ways of knowing. BMA aims to make visible the conceptual frictions that can arise in computational biology by allowing results to be seen from heterogeneous perspectives. Thus it aims for an openness to ways of knowing. For HCI, we hope to invite questions about design's role in achieving such an objective.

To begin, we first outline the empirical materials that have contributed to this paper and also give some background to the theoretical arguments that have informed it. We then discuss computation in biology and describe BMA's computational underpinnings. The body of the paper turns to a problem that has been central to BMA's design, one we've called the *proof-mode problem*. At this stage, suffice to say this is something that has been repeatedly returned to during the tool's development and provoked much discussion amongst the project members. Having discussed this problem from two particular viewpoints, we will then return to the paper's overall contributions in an implications and general conclusions section.

Research Approach and Orientation

The presented work is taken from an extended and on-going project in which a core team of eight members from biology (1), CS (2), social science (2), design (1) and software engineering (2) have collaborated on the implementation and design of BMA. Specifically, we use materials from a design phase spanning eighteen months, in which: group members regularly attended (bi-weekly and sometimes weekly) meetings to discuss the tool's design; preliminary one-on-one interviews were undertaken with six biologists invited to test BMA and give detailed opinions about its design and purpose; and two non-team members trialed the tool, intensively, in their own research. Alongside this, a number of iterations of the tool were internally implemented and trialed, with numerous features added and modified.

For the purposes of this paper, dominant use is made of the in-house, one-on-one interviews with the team's members, the transcripts and field notes taken in team meetings, and interviews and written materials from one of the non-team members who participated in a full trial of BMA. Although the general thrust of the comments from the early, one-on-one interviews with the six biologists is captured, only passing reference is made to the extensive transcripts we compiled. Together, the materials used are assembled to construct what we call two 'viewpoints'. Both of these elaborate on particular aspects of the proof-mode problem, weaving together a story about the issues it raised and a design perspective it precipitated.

As this use of two viewpoints to study tool use might be seen to deviate from the norm in HCI, some explanation is called for. The approach has been broadly motivated by three factors. Most superficially, the first is to do with the limitations of space and thus an effort to choose the most informative way of introducing the tool and the kinds of problems faced. Secondly (and still practically motivated), the materials used have been chosen to string together a coherent narrative from what—even for the team members—has become a convoluted project. The focus on a singular problem will limit, it is hoped, the amount of technical terminology and domain specific knowledge needed to engage with the text. We're acutely aware that the technical details discussed below will be unfamiliar to many and thus our hope is the viewpoints will make the trajectory of our work and problems faced easier to follow. Thirdly and most significantly, the viewpoints and narrative have helped piece together a distinctive position on tool use and design, one we will turn to next. It should be said at this stage, however, that the position emerged from the interplay of empirical work and reading around the relevant topics in biology, the philosophy of science and science studies. The objective with this was not, purely, to prescribe functions and features for BMA, but to enliven a dialogue around the broader role of computational tools and an orientation to their design.

The thrust of the paper's arguments, then, draws on a literature concerned with how scientific knowledge is constituted. Much of this research has its origins in seminal work in science and technology studies such as Bowker and Star's investigations into the social character of scientific categories [6] and Pickering's insights into the complex and intertwined trajectories of knowledge production [24]. More particularly, though, our work has come to be shaped by recent research in feminist technoscience and a turn to a 'new' or socio- materialism [27]. Specific references will be made below, but the gist of this broad movement is that the separations between knowledge, knower and object/matter are part of a long-established but problematic metaphysics of scientific ways of knowing [2,28,31]. Accordingly, to really get to grips with how knowledge is constituted, it is argued one must see these three things as inexorably enmeshed, continually being assembled and forming particular relations. Knowledge is thus seen as a relational achievement, always in a state of becoming, of moving on.

Another strong influence has been from a related literature in science studies and the philosophy of science looking at the relations between practice and theory [15]. Helping to make sense of BMA's use has been a perspective that sees knowledge as part of a practical endeavor, where materially bound, pragmatic activities and decisions—not overarching abstract theories—are determinants of how scientists see, interact with and go on to make sense of their phenomena [15,18,25]. Furthermore, theory is not seen as the ultimate achievement, outside of or superior to science on the ground. The different materials and ideas scientists such as biologists work with are viewed as continuously transforming in practice, being one moment the objects of study and another the tools or theories used to manipulate and understand them [18]. Again, the always-shifting relations are seen to be the source of these unfolding transformations.

Finally, the paper's arguments are set alongside a more general set of theory-oriented perspectives emerging in HCI in which interactive systems and the material interventions enacted by them—in practice—are being recognized as integral to ways of knowing and being [22,26,29,30,32]. Although the work we present is specific to science and biology, we see our arguments to be situated in this broader intellectual dialogue. Tentatively at this stage, they are intended to offer a way of framing interaction that moves the analytical concerns on from prefigured or essentialist notions of users, tools and the stable interfaces between them; a starting point is articulated that opens up how an assemblage of multiple agencies and emergent entanglements can be investigated, (re)configured and (re)designed.

BMA AND COMPUTATIONAL BIOLOGY

These discussions and how they have provided routes into thinking differently about BMA's design will be returned to in a moment. First, let us backtrack a little and provide some context.

Computation is playing an increasingly significant role in modeling and analyzing biological systems. Systems biology, for instance, attracts those from diverse disciplines such as biology, chemistry, physics, mathematics, electrical engineering and computer science, among others. Harnessing computation, it aims to explain how organisms function by modeling and analyzing the behaviors and relationships of genes, proteins and other biological elements [12]. Tools such as *CellDesigner™* [13] and *Virtual Cell* allow cell network processes to be graphically drawn and simulated, placing an emphasis on the modeling of stepwise processes along biological pathways (i.e., the sequence of molecular events that lead to cellular behavior).

The point has been made well elsewhere that such *in silico* techniques offer ways of abstracting the data and making inferences that obviate the need to manually work through every possible case of a problem (and, for that matter, resort to time consuming and costly experimentation in the lab). Predictably, though, as the area has matured and the requirements have become more specific, distinct computational techniques have emerged to tackle narrowly defined problems. For the purposes of this paper, a helpful way to think about the spectrum of computational techniques is to separate them into *bottom-up functional* and *top-down structural* approaches [12,19].

Bottom-up approaches—seen in software like *CellDesigner* and *Virtual Cell*—construct models directly from experimental evidence, building up representations from discrete biological functions (hence bottom-up functional). Ostensibly, the model represents the way a biological organism works or functions—it *simulates* the biology. So model parts may be cells, genes and/or proteins and the model may, for instance, represent the signaling pathways between them. By necessity, there are omissions, simplifications, and abstractions made in the models, but the aim is to instantiate a one-to-one mapping with the elements of a biological network and the relationships between them.

Top-down techniques employ a significantly different meaning of model. Models may or may not have an immediate correspondence to biological processes. A high-level structure is determined by the computational technique applied, in a sense how the code or program is run to produce them. A model may thus execute a proof, where the relations between a biological elements are systematically checked against testable criteria [11]. The structure is thus imposed top-down by the way particular relationships between entities are formalized and evaluated, programmatically. The key point to recognize here is that the model, and in particular its structure, is derived top-down by the execution of the proof. Again, this contrasts with the bottom-up functional approaches that incrementally build up models based on the way the biology functions.

BMA is an example of this latter approach to modeling. The computational underpinnings of the tool runs what is known in CS as a symbolic model-checking algorithm to prove whether the model achieves *stabilization* [8,9]. It checks, in other words, whether the modeled system will, from every possible starting point, always eventually reach a single 'safe' configuration or equilibrium. In biology, such modeling could offer, for example, a means of assessing whether a cellular system develops in a stable way that is robust to perturbations from the outside environment, and experimenting with interventions that might improve such a robustness.

The innovation here is that BMA is able to prove stabilization for highly complex models that may have a huge number of configurations or states. To work around problems of scale, the tool evaluates symbolic sets of this extremely large state space. Furthermore, rather than analyzing the whole network, it answers questions about discrete components such that stabilization is established as a composition of smaller mathematical arguments (i.e., lemmas). In effect, BMA's analysis results in the quick discovery of components that take initial steps towards stabilization and then determines the mechanism by which other components follow that lead.

It is this that defines the tool's approach as top-down. The structural configurations and sequential path through them are determined not by biological functions *per se*, but by the way the underlying algorithm works. As a matter of fact, the algorithm has its origins in techniques used for model-checking computer code and testing whether, given a particular arrangement of properties, a software program "terminates" without errors or 'bugs' [see 10]. Consequently, the algorithm and its incremental progresses through the

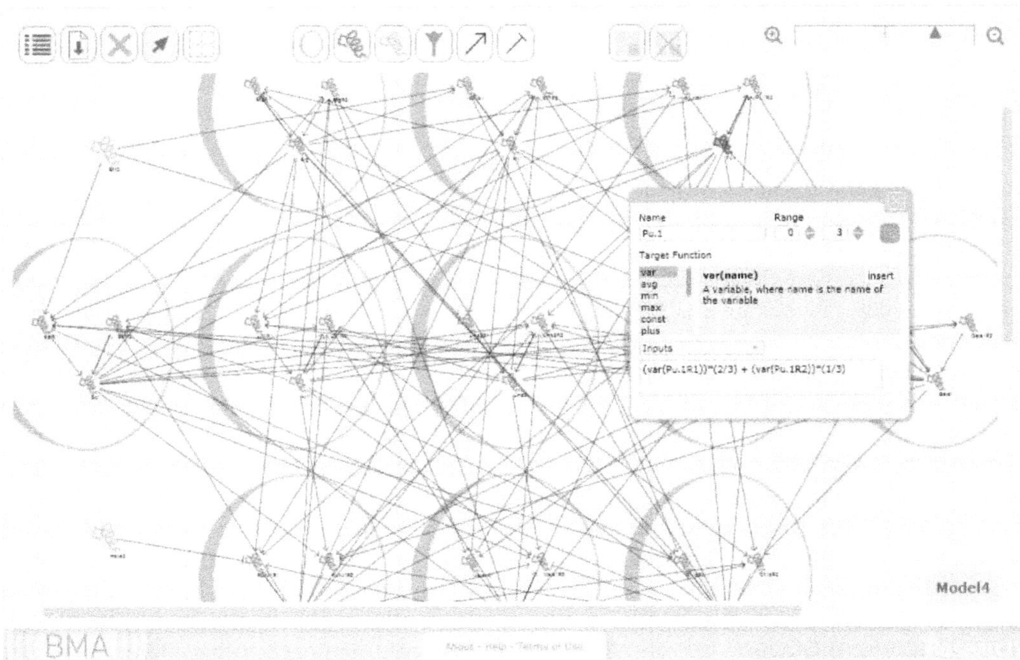

Figure 1. BMA 'mode' for constructing and manipulating regulatory network, with variable panel open for editing parameters.

model has what could be best described as a loose correspondence to the biology and treats it more like a generic network of nodes and connections.

The Proof-mode problem

The computational technique that underpins the BMA tool has been more or less complete since 2011 and shown to successfully replicate the results observed in laboratory experiments with mammalian skin cells and *Caenorhabditis elegans* (*c. elegans*) development [9]. The current emphasis in the project is to develop a graphical user interface so that biologists with little to no programming expertise can use the tool. To this end, a web-based front-end has been designed to support, one, the graphical construction and manipulation of biological networks (Fig. 1) and, two, the execution of the proof and graphical presentation of the results (Fig. 2). (For details of the UI see [3]). Although some sticking points persist, some of which we will come to later, the first of these UI modes has reached a relatively mature stage of implementation. In both our preliminary interviews and trials, respondents found the features for constructing and manipulating the biological networks straightforward to use and compared them, favorably, to familiar graphical layout applications such as Microsoft PowerPoint and Adobe Photoshop.

Less developed is the way the tool displays the results. The most recent complete implementation runs the analysis with the straightforward selection of a 'proof' button in the tool's interface. However, the display of results merely indicates whether the network has stabilized (green highlight) or, if there is instability, which network elements have failed to stabilize (red highlight)(Fig. 2). To add to the paucity of this visual representation, the red highlight may also indicate the analysis having "timed out". This is because the output from the proof originally treated the timing out of the analysis as equivalent to instability. Thus the tool effectively produces a binary output for each element in the model, representing stability or instability. Biologists responding to this part of the tool have been confused by these results and unclear how they might be applied.

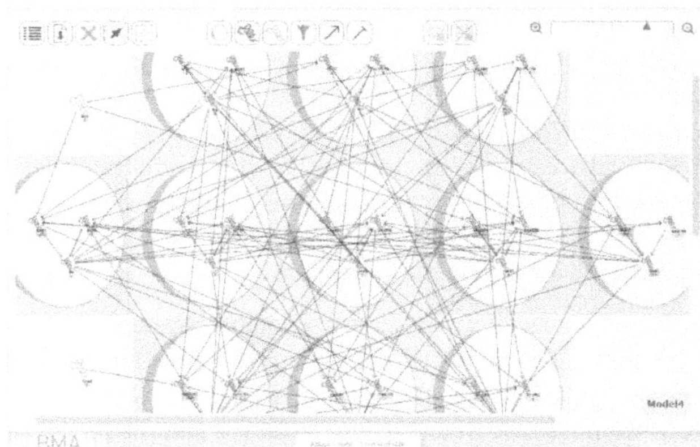

Figure 2. Results of analysis in BMA's 'proof mode' with stability of variables highlighted in green and instability in red.

This evident weakness in the tool, that has come to be known by the project's members as the 'proof-mode problem', has been revisited throughout the work. In project meetings, a host of different designs for representing the proof and its output have been proposed and rejected. On the face of it, the difficulty appears to be the result of the top-down structural approach used in the tool. For the project team, the protracted discussions have, time and again, resorted to, on the one hand, the lead biologist struggling to understand why some aspect of the biological processes can't be represented and, on the other hand, the computer scientists explaining that the computational approach employed doesn't allow for the simulation of biological processes. All too often the outcome of these discussions has been to move on to other less problematic features of the tool's design. It isn't that either side is unaware of the constraints. On the contrary, there is a high degree of understanding of both the biology and computational workings from both sides. At issue appears to be the seemingly intractable problem of visualizing the tool's analysis in a way that usefully represents the biology.

It is worth noting, too, that this tension surfaces with most vigor in the design discussions of the tool's interface. Before the UI design was considered, it seemed the primary achievement was simply to reproduce the results of empirical experimentation. And yet the interface design introduces problems because it situates the tool in use. It demands that beyond demonstrating BMA is capable of replicating the results of experiments, there must be some recognition of the sense-making activities of biologists. Thus the work at and on BMA's interface appears to be about more than designing an easy to use tool. It is through such a concern that we see the multi-disciplined project team coming to terms with what they are developing and how it is of practical use in scientific research. The work at and on the human-machine interface, then, cannot be reduced to, as Suchman richly words it "machinic operations" but on the contrary opens up to inspection "a specifically enacted site of extended, heterogeneously constituted human/nonhuman capacities for thought and action." [27]. Exposed, that is, are the entangled relations between user and tool and these, in turn, invite questions about the doings and knowings enacted through them.

In the following we tease this out a little more, with the aim of illustrating how it is that scientific practices can be further understood and designed for. We recount an issue that revealed itself in our efforts to deal with the computational approach used in BMA and specifically one that arose in tackling the proof-mode problem. Our inclination, early on, was to think of the problem as a weakness in representation: that the tool, because of its top-down approach, misrepresented the biology. We found ourselves adopting what could be fairly described as a realist position, with the implication that there are absolute phenomena to be measured in biology, and, if you will, 'true' ways in which to represent them. This position has been given credence in the philosophy of science with discussions reinforcing the singular 'meaning' of biological phenomena and criticisms of computational techniques for being one-step removed from such 'truths' [14,19].

However, by paying close attention to the tool's use in our early trials, and particularly the efforts to overcome the proof-mode problem, we found the tool being used in practical ways to get on with the business at hand. In other words, the use of the tool and efforts to overcome the proof-mode problem overrode the concerns we had for what was real or true in biology, and shifted the emphasis to the practical business of moving on. The biological models were not enlisted with any strong theoretical motivations or to determine any grand truths in science. Instead, as the historian and philosopher of science Evelyn Fox Keller has observed in remarkably similar work, the modeling seemed pragmatically useful for "designing new kinds of experiments, for posing new kinds of questions, and for guiding new kinds of manipulation of the system itself." [17:S82].

A VIEW OF USE

The first of our viewpoints onto the proof mode problem is centered on the first attempt by a non-member of the BMA team to construct a network and test a model using the tool. So far, two different case studies of this kind have been undertaken. The one considered here, lasting over 3 months and led by a MSc. student Lucy, presents the most discussed by the team and well-documented to date.

Lucy's master's studies are part of a wider program of work at an internationally renowned university's medical research institute. This program applies an "integrated approach" to determining the regulatory networks responsible for blood stem cell development. In biology, blood cell development or *haematopoiesis* constitutes one of the paradigm cases for studying stem cells' peculiar capacity to both self-renew and differentiate into other cell types. A considerable literature therefore exists on the subject and there is plenty of scope for mining extant results and cross-validation. Lucy's use of BMA is thus part of a continued effort to incorporate computational techniques into the institute's integrated approach—alongside other techniques such as *in vitro* experimentation and *high-throughput sequencing*. It also, though, serves as a test case for, (1), confirming BMA's capabilities for modeling known biological phenomena and, (2), determining whether the tool provides the basis for extending know-how in this discrete but important problem area of biology.

With respect to the first of these latter two objectives, Lucy's original aim was to determine whether a regulatory network of what are known as transcription factor proteins and their interconnections, modeled in BMA, exhibited blood cell behaviors observed in the laboratory. Although the number of different proteins involved in blood cell development is known to be in the thousands, a review of the literature had identified thirteen transcription factors as crucial to blood cell differentiation—as their absence precluded normal blood production—and these formed the basis for constructing the network model. Each protein was modeled qualitatively, varying between a small number of levels (e.g. 0-1=low to medium, or 1-2=medium to high). Also incorporated were the complex array of promoting and inhibiting connections. In combination, these interconnections and levels define, if you like, the transcription factors that can communicate with each other and the amount of influence they have over each other. Lucy's use of BMA was to assess whether this network of proteins, connections and value ranges produced a model that was self-contained and did indeed stabilize as expected.

With respect to the second objective, Lucy's hope was that the introduction of perturbations into the BMA model might provide the basis for new hypotheses to be tested in the lab and ultimately new understandings of blood cell development. For instance, Leukemia is known to be associated with particular genes being 'knocked out'. The modeling in BMA was seen as a means of reproducing these knockouts and testing possible counterbalancing interventions, thereby hypothesizing about potential therapies.

Lucy's first problematic encounter with BMA was in configuring the transcription factors and connections in such a way that the proof could be executed. With her initial attempts to compose and test the model, she found that the tool timed out, repeatedly. With help from the team's computer scientists, this was discovered to be because the connections she'd defined between the proteins were too literal and consequently had led to a complexity that was too demanding for the tool. The details behind this are unnecessarily technical for the arguments here, though it is worth noting that to successfully execute the model, Lucy needed to change her approach to modeling by further abstracting the structural configuration to conform to a notion of a model expected by the tool. As Byron, one of the team's computer scientists put it, "she didn't [initially] use it in the spirit it was written" and this necessitated a change in approach with the "right" structure of modeling in mind. The biology, in effect, had to be re-configured, structurally, to be 'readable' in computational terms and this required a change in mindset—or "spirit"—on Lucy's part.

We begin, here, to get a sense of particular frictions that can arise when modeling biology using computational techniques and specifically when a top-down structural as opposed to bottom-up functional approach is applied. Such frictions further manifest themselves in other ostensible limitations to the tool. Although Lucy was eventually able to execute the blood cell network using BMA and prove it stabilized, she found a severe limitation of the tool was the way it accounted for (or to be more precise did not account for) the progression of the biology over time. Quite simply, the tool does not model time. Indeed, it intentionally avoids doing so. To handle highly complex cell systems, and work through an inordinately large number of possible states, BMA, by design, avoids having to simulate cellular development over time. In Byron's words:

> "So we're not running the system; we're more making an argument at a level that is higher than basic time... We just start thinking about how the system is configured and start making logical inferences that are valid about the behavior..."

Here again we are confronted by the peculiarities of the top-down approach applied to model checking in BMA. The "logical inferences" that are made are derived using algorithmic formalisms, not properties purely of the biology and specifically not employing any notion of temporal progression of cellular organisms. In the case of Lucy's blood cell network, the proof did not model the five stages of cell differentiation that have been observed in experiments, nor did it assume any starting points or complete pathways intrinsic to the biology. In simple terms, it took into account the range of variation and tested locally (and algorithmically) defined sets of connections. In the following, Nir, another of the team's computer scientists, patiently explain this:

> "The way I think about [these] models is that they capture all points in time [...] So in these kinds of models there is no element that says, well, I'm allowed to refer to my watch and change my behavior according to time [...] I'm constructing here a static picture of how they change for every possible time and every possible value."

The point to emphasize here is that something ordinarily thought to be intrinsic to biology, time, is not accommodated in the modeling approach used by BMA [18]. The continuous and time-dependent properties of biological organisms (conventionally represented in biology using differential equations [18:250]) are quite simply absent. Conveyed by Nir is that the very power of the tool is achieved because it avoids having to work from any estimated starting points (that could be error-prone) and instead runs through and checks every possible state. So, in BMA, time is abstracted away, eliminated. Indeed, Lucy raises this as a source of confusion in explaining how she imagined using the tool:

> "We weren't really sure what was going to happen initially. We were going to try and get it to go from one start point to the next and then through the stages individually but we couldn't really do that once we'd abstracted everything so then we had to find another way of looking at the different points within it."

She goes onto explain:

> "We ended up using a program based on [the model] in Excel—that Nir created—because a lot of the time it's not actually the endpoint that's most interesting, it's how it got there and the intermediate stages—especially for this project—that we're interested in."

Lucy describes a workaround for the tool's incapacity to simulate the temporal changes within the blood cells. Having proved stability using the tool, she had Nir help put together an Excel table so that she could manually enter and test values in her paired-down model. This enabled her to see, from predefined starting values, how the model progressed. In effect, she required a means of re-introducing and simulating biological time and stepping through the five known stages of blood cell differentiation.

Once again, the use of BMA appears to exemplify the kinds of fundamental breakdowns that can occur between the representational forms considered intrinsic to biology on the one hand, and afforded by computation on the other. Lucy required a solution outside of the tool to re-introduce and observe cell-change over time, even if the temporal delineation was crude.

And yet the actual use of BMA in practice paints a very different picture. Unsurprisingly, perhaps, rather than insurmountable, such frictions on the ground seem to be treated as pragmatic ones (at least in the case of BMA). What appears to have been far more important to the tool's potential users—users such as Lucy as well as others we interviewed—has been its practical value. Lucy's comments on the immediate value of BMA lends some initial support to this:

> "[The tool] confirmed that there weren't any crucial links missing as well and that they weren't the wrong way round cause when we tried switching them it went completely wrong."

So the tool provides a quick if not completely foolproof way of assessing a model's functional connections. Furthermore, as Lucy explains, it sits within a more intertwined set of practices of judgment, understanding and iterative modifications to the model:

> "It is interesting cause you see which ones don't stabilize ... you have to then go back and look at the biology and see if that is interesting [...] [and if] we've missed some connections... Also because we are only using the 13 genes and there are hundreds actually involved in the process like sometimes it would be useful to have other inputs but that's a biological issue so we have to go back and say what is stopping that from stabilizing and it's often because that particular protein is also regulated by something else."

Such pragmatism evidently involves dealing with the limitations of what is known and working with the tools that enable one to "go back" and test out new or alternative possibilities. It seems, modeling tools such as BMA are unremarkably subsumed into an assembled "machinery of seeing" [1] or "reasoning machinery" [25:20], and, in doing so, are less impeded by problems that appear, at first glance, fundamental. As Lucy suggests, her motive is really to be able to revisit the model and/or the biology and test out different ideas to expand what is known. She is relatively unperturbed by, even disinterested in, whether the tools she uses are built on or result in conceptual inconsistencies.

So, from afar, BMA could well be seen as a source of conceptual difficulties (as they were by the team). Moreover, these difficulties or frictions are manifestly born out of the coming together of computation and biology and the representational forms they allow for. Yet, the difficulties, in practice, are centered on getting the results to make sense in practical terms, in short, in using them to determine "what to do", a way to move on. Moving between the various representations of the biology, they provided Lucy with a way to ask more questions about the model represented in BMA and to test-out changes in the blood cell network.

For BMA's design, the issue worth highlighting is how we should understand the output of the analysis. Seen alone as a static image indicating binary outcomes, it appears an object vulnerable to conceptual difficulties. However, situated in use—practical use—we see it, as far as possible, being implicated in and forming a basis for what science studies scholars Amann and Knorr Certina [1] have described as a *sequence of practice*; that is, contributing to "the work of seeing what the data consist of" [1:138] and more particularly for BMA 'what to do with what is seen'. By interleaving the tool's model with a temporal representation in Excel, for instance, the user can see the analysis introducing a way to interrogate and further augment a continually evolving 'picture' of cellular development. The "[i]mage analyzing exchanges are not just "about" an object; they are also "with" an object." [1:140]. The fault lines seem not to hinge on the conceptual consistency of the data and their representations, a strict notion of what is real, or the coherence of the techniques used to produce and represent results. Rather it is whether they enable a trajectory of interpretation and intervention.

A VIEW FROM DESIGN

The second of the two viewpoints we want to consider, that from design, conveys similar points. However, it's also hoped they may introduce an approach for opening up the representations and enabling a heterogeneity of trajectories.

From the outset of the design work (as we've discussed), the apparent incongruity between the computational workings and the biological processes kept the team coming back to questions concerning how the analysis could be revealed to the user and, in particular, how a representation of cell development over time might be incorporated into the 'proof mode'. Much of the motivation for this came from feedback from the initial interviews with BMA users as well as from the two non-team members (including Lucy) who used the tool in anger. Also instrumental, was the team's lead biologist. She, over the course of the project, reiterated the importance of a temporal component in the tool and, if anything, became more vocal about its absence as the project progressed.

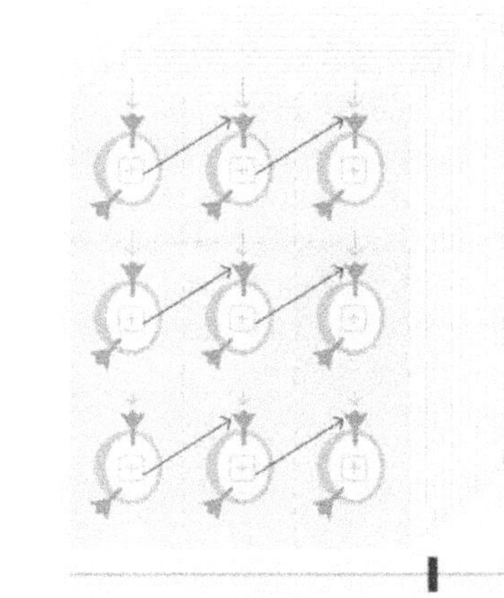

Figure 3. Sketch to visualize proof progression where the user can 'scrub' through pages or steps of the proof.

The proposal repeatedly returned to has been to visualize the temporal progression of the proof—that is, display to the user some representation of execution of the proof over time ('proof time', so to speak, as opposed to 'biological time'). Figure 3 shows a possibility for one such representation that has been envisioned and discussed by the team's members. However, ideas such as these have presented something of a dilemma for the team. The worry has been that proof time might be confused with biological time; all members of the team have been sensitive to the different notions of time at play and weary about introducing any further confusion for users. Figure 3 illustrates how proof time could be a source of confusion; the problem is that the temporal ordering of the steps has no direct mapping to the actual progression of the biology. In strictly realist terms, it misrepresents what is known about the biology and worst still has the potential to lure users into thinking they are seeing something biologically meaningful. Thus, it's evident why representing proof time may have been a concern for the team; there appears an intrinsic conflict or tension.

Yet, the pragmatic perspective we've discussed above has provided a different way of approaching this problem and, as it happens, offered a more constructive starting point for design possibilities. In pragmatic terms, the problem becomes one of whether proof time can be visualized in such a way that allows users to see the analysis as part of a sequence of practice. That is, whether the representation of proof time enables one to take a next step—to move on—in one's trajectory of experimentation and idea generation. This, then, is to see design not as a means to insist on and prioritize a representation that conforms to a singular conception of biology, but, instead, as a means of opening up opportunities for further intervention.

At first glance, such concerns with BMA's interface may themselves seem to be purely pragmatic ones to do with the narrow problems of user interface design. Naturally, there are practical issues concerning visual layout, consistency, intelligibility of the UI, and so on. However, this work of implementing the UI brings us back, again, to questions of knowledge making in science and specifically the interdisciplinary frictions raised in bringing computation and biology together. Relevant to these issues are the ongoing discussions in science studies and the philosophy of science turning on the supposed separation between representation and intervention [15] or, to put it another way, knowing and doing. Such binaries have received considerable attention with scholarly research contesting and refiguring the seemingly incommensurable, such as the divides between subject-object, theory-practice, human-nonhuman, real-unreal, nature-society, etc. [2,15,20,21,28,31]

Although engaged in vastly different realms of scientific life, two relatively recent works provide particularly helpful places to start from here, one the book *Science and an African Logic* [31] by Helen Verran and the other by Karen Barad [2] in her detailed account of the unfolding controversies in quantum physics. Both present an analytic frame in which knower, knowledge and thing (matter) are inseparably entangled and located within ongoing, processual practices. The broad argument made is not whether scientific (or for that matter indigenous) ways of knowing have a special or privileged right to truth claims or reality, but rather how knowing is something enacted through entanglements of people and things in-action.

Verran, for example, weaves her way around and within the muddy separations between relativism and foundationism (the latter being, for our purposes, akin to realism). She disavows both by locating herself "inside" the acts of ordering and knowing. In her studies of Yoruba-speaking children in Southwestern Nigeria, she observes the messiness of experimentation and the energy she invests in putting things in place. This is not to imagine some ideal, cleaner, tidier science and knowledge making, but to understand 'realness as emergent' [31:37], always subject to and entangled in an unfolding assemblage of things being brought into relation to one another. Barad helps make sense of the apparatus *vis-à-vis* this 'relational achievement'. The apparatus, or the tools, are inseparable from the experiment, experimenter and phenomenal world, so that their "intra-action"—as Barad refers to it—are all assembled in what, exactly, the phenomenon is. "Every measurement involves a particular choice of apparatus, providing the conditions necessary to give meaning to a particular set of variables, at the exclusion of other essential variables" [2:115]. The apparatus are thus unavoidably implicated in what is observed (and not observed) and consequently what is known. Crucially, as Barad argues, this is not an anti-realist or relativist position. It is what she calls 'agential realism', a recognition that what is real is actively brought into—or performed in—the world. Through tool use, then, phenomena are understood to be in a continuous state of becoming.

Returning to BMA, these arguments offer an alternative conception of the proof-mode problem. They help to see tools using top-down structural modeling techniques such as BMA as new ways of interacting with and, in a manner of speaking, enacting biology, and thus 'seeing' the phenomena anew. If computational tools are thought not as lenses onto a static phenomenal world—a presupposed ground truth—but instead part of the assemblage of things that constitute the "intra-action" of the experiment, we begin to see how the proof-mode problem is not just an obstacle to be overcome by re-introducing some notion of 'real' or 'natural' processes, e.g., biological time. Rather, the problem becomes one of enabling one particular relational achievement over (or as well as) another. And, critically for design, the challenge becomes how to make such unfolding and emergent relational achievements intelligible so that one is able to 'move on'.

This, then, offers a way of seeing the frictions—apparently rooted in disciplinary and conceptual differences—as opportunities to open up the sequence of practices. Knowing isn't treated as passively waiting to be found in "objects-ready-made", as Verran refers to them [31:152], but contingent and situated in practice. The tool becomes integral to these unfolding enactments, not merely a better or worse lens, but an active agent in constituting what is known. With this, the frictions open up opportunities for representing multiple figurings of phenomena and consequently enabling biology to be enacted in divergent and new ways.

Appropriately, perhaps, the consequence of framing things in these terms on BMA's design is still being worked out by the team. However, as part of the tool's ongoing development, the possibility has led to quite a different approach to designing the output of the analysis. Our efforts have been to test a range of divergent representational forms, some potentially inconsistent. Furthermore, we have experimented with both incorporating a number of these into the tool's proof mode and giving the user a straightforward means of creating mini or sub-experiments. The former has been driven by a goal to offer multiple and in some cases divergent ways of working with and making sense of the model data at the cost of consistency. The latter is intended to encourage a succession of views of the analysis that can be easily compared and contrasted, and that help users piece together a picture of the interventions they've made.

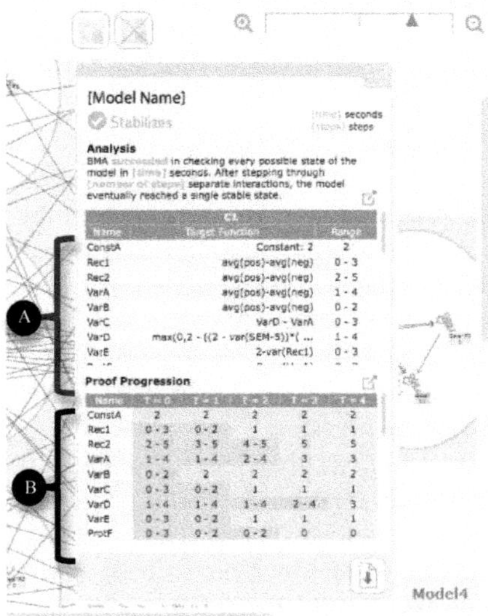

Figure 4. Mock-up of proof mode and output to analysis.

An early mock-up for presenting the results in the UI (Fig. 4) offers an indication of what this might look like. The interface is probably overly formal for one meant to promote open-ended thinking, but the general goal has been to give the user a way of seeing the proof's results differently, allowing them to shift views and easily intervene in the analyses. In the top table (A), the user can edit the network's variables (i.e., functions, ranges, etc.) and the proof is automatically re-executed. As well as the graphical representation of the network being updated, a "Proof Progression" table is displayed (B), representing how the variables' ranges change over a sequence of stages to reach stability. Thus, proof time is visualized in such a way that the graphical/structural and temporal representations are set against each other, encouraging users to try out modifications.

Not shown here are two other additions to the UI that have been conceived of in the same vein. One introduces a means of identifying and graphically representing nodes that are 'key' in the progression of the proof (using *directed acyclic graphs*). These graphs give users an idea of what if any variables are key to the proof's analysis and what modifications may introduce significant changes. A second is a table listing changes made to variables as mini-experiments so that users can quickly switch between different network configurations and make comparisons. Again, the overall intention is to construct a UI for the proof mode that shows different representations of the analysis, but to make this intelligible and as manageable for the user as possible.

IMPLICATIONS AND CONCLUSIONS

On the face of it, this paper has a straightforward message, one showing how a grounded investigation into the practices of computational biology can help with designing constructive tools for biologists. From one viewpoint, we've shown that seeing tools like BMA as part of a set of practices for getting on with scientific work allows apparent problems arising from the use of computational techniques to be constructively refigured. From a second viewpoint, we've shown how UI design might be approached to support this notion of science as a sequence of entangled practices. We've found that opening up the interface to incorporate multiple representational forms resonates with the continuous and unfolding interventions scientists perform in their routine work. In this light, the paper provides an illustrative example of the work at the intersection of computation and biology, the kinds of problems that can be faced, and how in at least one case they might be tackled.

There is, however, a wider message we hope to have conveyed. This is more to do with how HCI approaches building tools in areas where computation is changing the ways scientific questions are being asked and answered. It is worth reiterating, such tools are establishing themselves across the gamut of research from the natural sciences to the social sciences and humanities, as well as into the more familiar domain of social networking/analysis. Seen in terms of pragmatic on the ground work, design in these areas opens up significant opportunities. Room is made for different ways of knowing when it is understood that, to borrow Barad's words, "representations are not (more or less faithful) pictures of what is, but productive evocations, provocations, and generative material articulations or reconfigurations of what is and what is possible" [2:389]. Thus, design has a part to play in showing knowledge to be something underway, and the role tools have in intervening in these processes. BMA hopefully illustrates, for example, how design might be used to resist conformity to a single perspective. This is not just an idea of design that promotes different views onto the same phenomena. It locates design and HCI within an orientation that contests science as a monistic endeavor and supports instead an emergent idea of scientific ways of knowing.

Finally, something that has remained implicit thus far are the motivations behind and implications of an approach that prioritizes an 'entangled co-emergence' of agencies and knowings [2]. By accepting that the phenomenal world out-there is, so to speak, enacted—not merely discovered—we are forced to face the prospect of designing tools that provoke very particular questions and trajectories. As the science and technology studies scholar John Law reasons:

> "[i]f out-therenesses are constructed or enacted rather than sitting out there waiting to be discovered, then it follows that their truth or otherwise is only one of the criteria relevant to their creation... But the moment we acknowledge this we are faced with new questions. What kind of out-therenesses are possible? Which are so embedded that they cannot be undone? Where might we try to undo or redo them? How might we try to nudge research programmes in one direction rather than another?" [21:40]

Thus, in a modest way, what we have presented is motivated by a need to extend the work at the interface beyond the immediate problems of representation. It is driven by a determination to acknowledge and begin taking seriously HCI's role in ways of knowing. With BMA this position has led us, tentatively, to explore ways of revealing the multiple agencies that are assembled to enact biology. The wider programmatic implications for HCI though are to do with the role the field might take in designing tools that offer new ways of both asking and answering questions. Our work hopefully animates a discussion about the knowings we wish to promote in designing these tools, and how we should actively participate in shaping the processes of discovery and invention in science and technology.

ACKNOWLEDGMENTS
We are indebted to all the members of BMA's project team and are grateful to Abigail Sellen and Lucian Leahu for their feedback on early drafts. Special thanks also go to our study's participants for their invaluable time and thoughts.

REFERENCES
1. Amann, K. and Knorr Cetina, K. The fixation of (visual) evidence. *Human Studies 11*, 2 (1988), 133–169.
2. Barad, K.M. *Meeting The Universe Halfway*. Duke Univ. Press, 2007.
3. Benque, D., Bourton, S., Cockerton, C., et al. Bio Model Analyzer: Visual tool for modeling and analysis of biological networks. In *Proc. CAV '12*, Springer-Verlag (2012). 686–692.
4. Bietz, M. J., Ferro, T. and Lee, C. P. Sustaining the development of cyberinfrastructure: an organization adapting to change. *CSCW '12*, ACM Press (2012), 901-910.
5. Bietz, M. J. and Lee, C. P. Collaboration in metagenomics: Sequence databases and the organization of scientific work. *ECSCW '09*, Springer (2009), 243-262.
6. Bowker, G. and Star, S. L. *Sorting Things Out*. MIT Press, Cambridge, 1999.
7. Carlson, R.H. *Biology is Technology*. Harvard Univ. Press, Cambridge MA, 2011.
8. Chabrier, N. and Fages, F. Symbolic model checking of biochemical networks. *CMSB '03*, Springer-Verlag (2003), 149–162.
9. Cook, B., Fisher, J., Krepska, E., and Piterman, N. Proving stabilization of biological systems. *VMCAI '11*, Springer-Verlag (2011), 134–149.
10. Cook, B., Podelski, A., and Rybalchenko, A. Proving program termination. *Comms ACM 54*, 5 (2011), 88-98.
11. Fisher, J. and Henzinger, T.A. Executable Cell Biology. *Nature Biotechnology 25*, 11 (2007), 1239–1249.
12. Fisher, J., Harel, D., and Henzinger, T.A. Biology as reactivity. *Comms ACM 54*, 10 (2011), 72–82.
13. Funahashi, A., Morohashi, M., and Kitano, H. CellDesigner: a process diagram editor for gene-regulatory and biochemical networks. *Biosilico 1*, 5 (2003), 159–162.
14. Giere, R.N. Is computer simulation changing the face of experimentation? *Phil. Studies 143*, 1 (2009), 59–62.
15. Hacking, I. *Representing and Intervening*. Cambridge Univ. Press, Cambridge UK, 1983.
16. Ideker, T., Galitski, T., and Hood, L. A new approach to decoding life: systems biology. *Annu Rev Genomics Hum Genet 2* (2001), 343–372.
17. Keller, E.F. Models of and models for: Theory and practice in contemporary biology. *Philosophy of Science 67*, (2000), S72–S86.
18. Keller, E.F. *Making Sense of Life*. Harvard Univ. Press, London, 2002.
19. Krohs, U. and Callebaut, W. Data without models merging with models without data. In F.C. Boogerd, ed., *Systems biology: Philosophical foundations*. Elsevier, Amsterdam, 2007, 181–283.
20. Latour, B. The whole is always smaller than its parts: A digital test of Gabriel Tarde's monads. *British Journal of Sociology*, (in press).
21. Law, J. *After Method*. Routledge, London, 2004.
22. Leahu, L. Representation without representationalism (Doctoral dissertation). Cornell Univ., Ithaca, NY, 2012.
23. Myers, N. Conjuring Machinic Life. *Spontaneous Generations 2*, 1 (2009), 112–121.
24. Pickering, A. *The Mangle of Practice*. University of Chicago Press, Chicago IL, 1995.
25. Rheinberger, H.J. *Toward a History of Epistemic Things*. Stanford Univ. Press, Stanford, CA, 1997.
26. Rosner, D.K. The material practices of collaboration. *CSCW '12*, ACM Press (2012), 1155–1164.
27. Suchman, L. Agencies in technology design: Feminist reconfigurations. *Workshop on Gendered Innovations in Science and Engineering*, Stanford Univ. (15 April, 2005).
28. Suchman, L. *Human–Machine Reconfigurations: Plans and Situated Actions, 2nd Edition*. Cambridge Univ. Press, Cambridge UK, 2006.
29. Taylor, A.S. Machine intelligence. *CHI '09*, ACM Press (2009), 2109–2118.
30. Taylor, A.S. Out There. *CHI '11*, ACM Press (2011), 685–694.
31. Verran, H. *Science and an African logic*. Univ. of Chicago Press, Chicago IL, 2001.
32. Wiberg, M., Ishii, H., Dourish, P., et al. "Material interactions": from atoms & bits to entangled practices. *EA-CHI '12*, ACM Press (2012), 1147–1150.

Crowdfunding inside the Enterprise: Employee-Initiatives for Innovation and Collaboration

Michael Muller, Werner Geyer, Todd Soule, Steven Daniels, & Li-Te Cheng†
IBM Research, One Rogers Street, Cambridge, MA, USA 02142
{michael_muller, tssoule, danielsa, werner.geyer}@us.ibm.com, lcheng@ieee.org

ABSTRACT
We describe a first experiment in enterprise crowdfunding – i.e., employees allocating money for employee-initiated proposals at an Intranet site, including a trial of this system with 511 employees in IBM Research. Major outcomes include: employee proposals that addressed diverse individual and organizational needs; high participation rates; extensive inter-departmental collaboration, including the discovery of large numbers of previously unknown collaborators; and the development of goals and motivations based on collective concerns at multiple levels of project groups, communities of practice, and the organization as a whole. We recommend further, comparative research into crowdfunding and other forms of employee-initiated innovations.

Author Keywords
Crowdfunding; enterprise; innovation; employee; social

ACM Classification Keywords
H.5.3.Group and organizational interfaces (CSCW).

INTRODUCTION
Crowdfunding – in which consumers directly invest in a proposed undertaking through social media – is a relatively new phenomenon, in which over 80% of crowdfunding sites are less than five years old [4]. And yet, crowdfunding has already become an important resource for initiatives in technology [4], creative arts [1,4,7], journalism [4], and charity [7]. As recently as 2011, Belleflamme et al. described formal research related to crowdfunding as "nascent" [4]. Some of the most integrative and detailed analyses are still in draft or workshop form (e.g., [4,7]). Correspondingly, crowdfunding is a relatively new topic for HCI and CSCW (e.g., [7,17,27]). We believe that this paper is the first investigation of crowdfunding on an organization's Intranet.

In a typical *indirect* crowdfunding paradigm, an online platform serves as a meeting-point for people who *propose* projects and people who *invest* in those projects. Internet sites such as Kickstarter [15] and Indiegogo [13] have been credited with facilitating the funding of large-scale and small-scale proposals. Famous cases include raising over 100 times the needed funding for a charitable purpose [25], over US$10M for a pre-release product [33], and over US$100,000 in a single day for a music project [30].

For HCI and CSCW, the crowdfunding phenomenon suggests new ways to think about innovation [19,37], idea management [2,3,11,21], charitable giving [8,9], and amateur communities [18]. In this paper, we explore the potential of crowdfunding within an organization, highlighting participation rates, inter-departmental collaborations, and the diversity of ideas that were proposed and supported among a community of peers.

BACKGROUND AND RELATED WORK

Crowdfunding Practices and Processes
Crowdfunding sites are organized around shared documents called *proposals*. A proposal is a description of a project to be done, a request for funds for that project, and a claim of the ability of the *proposer* to bring the project to a successful conclusion. If they are interested in the proposal, *investors* make *investments* to it (i.e., contribute funds). People may also *volunteer* to help accomplish the work, or *comment* on the proposal, or *follow* updates, or *view* it.

Often, the proposer specifies *benefits* or *rewards* that will be delivered to people who invest a certain amount. In more financially-oriented sites, what is offered to investors is the possibility of a financial return. In more charity-oriented sites, there is no tangible benefit, but there is the opportunity to contribute to a cause or a social good.

In general, a proposer specifies a *target* amount of funding, and a period of time in which s/he hopes to raise that amount through investments by the crowd. If the specified amount of funds is reached, then the funds are awarded to the proposer, and the benefits (if any) are committed to the investors. If the specified amount of funds is not reached by the deadline, then all the funds are returned to the investors, and all commitments are cancelled.

Varieties of Crowdfunding
Kuo and Gerber reported over 200 crowdfunding sites that are currently or recently active [17]. Ordanini et al.

†Li-Te Cheng is now at Google.

distinguished three major types of crowdfunding sites, each with its own purpose and language ([29]; see also [4,17]):

- **Profit/investment**-focused sites allow people to invest money with a hope of financial return.
- **Creativity**-focused sites ask for contributions toward a cultural, commercial, or civic project. Contributors may receive a reward or benefit, such as a free copy of a CD from a music project.
- **Charity**-focused sites encourage donations toward worthwhile causes.

What we have called *proposing* is sometimes called *creating* or *pitching*. What we have called a *proposal* is sometimes called a *project*, a *pitch*, or a *cause*. What we have called *investing* is sometimes called *backing*.

Crowdfunding as Innovation by the Crowd

Crowdfunding sites allow a kind of collaborative innovation, because proposers can describe new ideas and ask for financial and other kinds of support [17,19]. Peers can invest in the proposal. Each financial support becomes a kind of "vote" in favor of the innovation, in a way that is similar to voting in idea management systems (IMSs) [2,37] and innovation management systems [3,11,21].

However, the IMS literature devotes a great deal of attention to the burdens that IMSs place on facilitators and decision-makers [2,3,11,21]. By contrast, crowdfunding sites generally operate without formal facilitation, and the decision takes place directly as a consequence of the amount of investment.

Motivations for Participating in Crowdfunding

Most production Internet sites do not provide public data about visits or views. There is therefore little information about the *participation rate* in crowdfunding, but there have been several studies of the *motivations* for participating.

In a grounded theory analysis across several crowdfunding Internet sites, Gerber et al. described *proposer* motivations as comprising promotion of their work, raising funds, connecting with investors, and gaining public approval [7]. Along with Harms [10], Gerber et al. also focused on the proposer goal to maintain control of their own project [7]. Belleflamme et al. concur, adding motivations of testing an innovation and gaining customer intelligence [4].

Regarding *investors'* motivations, van Wingerden and Ryan distinguished between intrinsic motivations (control of use of an innovation, improvement of current circumstances, enjoyment, and sense of involvement) vs. extrinsic motivations (financial reward) [35]. Harms adds functional utility (what is the innovation *good* for?), enhancement of self-concept, and self-expressiveness [10]. Ordanini et al. concur about participation in innovation, self-esteem, expressiveness, and add public recognition and patronage [29].

RESEARCH QUESTIONS

Crowdfunding appears to have different dynamics from online discussions [11], idea management [2,37], and other social media [24]. Participation rates in most social software are usually below 20% [24,26]. We ask,

RQ1. How does Intranet crowdfunding participation compare with other social media?

Crowdfunding is a relatively recent phenomenon in social media or "crowdware" [31] on the Internet. Less is known about crowdfunding as a tool within an organization:

RQ2a. What kinds of projects do employees propose when crowdfunding takes place "behind the firewall"?

We wondered whether the goals and motivations found in Internet crowdfunding (summarized above) would apply within an organization:

RQ2b. What are the goals and motivations of employees participating in crowdfunding within their organization?

Crowdfunding has been argued to provide a means for people to work together in the service of a common goal [7,29,35]. Van Wingerden and Ryan claimed that there was a tendency to invest in "regional or local" patterns of crowdfunding [35]. However, Agrawal et al. noted that investors found common cause across obstacles of distance, which they termed "the most striking feature of 'crowdfunding'" [1]. In enterprises, organizational structure can present obstacles to collaboration [11,24]. We ask,

RQ3a. Do people collaborate via crowdfunding *within* departments, or do they collaborate *across* departments?

Crowdfunding has been argued to provide an egalitarian opportunity to invest in projects [3], and a way for "every member of the crowd" to participate [27]. We ask,

RQ3b. Is crowdfunding participation equally distributed across different organizational levels and managerial status?

We suspected that not all proposals would receive their target amount of funds. We therefore wanted to understand

RQ4. What distinguishes successful vs. unsuccessful proposals?

As mentioned above, the IMS literature discusses the difficulties of facilitating idea-generation and idea-selection [2,3,21]. We were interested to know,

RQ5. What are the facilitation needs of enterprise crowdfunding?

1x5, AN INTRANET CROWDFUNDING APPLICATION

We explored these questions by developing "1x5," an experimental web-based application for crowdfunding inside an organization, using the organization's Intranet. The design of the 1x5 Intranet site (Figure 1) was inspired by popular Internet crowdfunding sites. Unlike the Internet sites, access to 1x5 was possible only behind IBM's

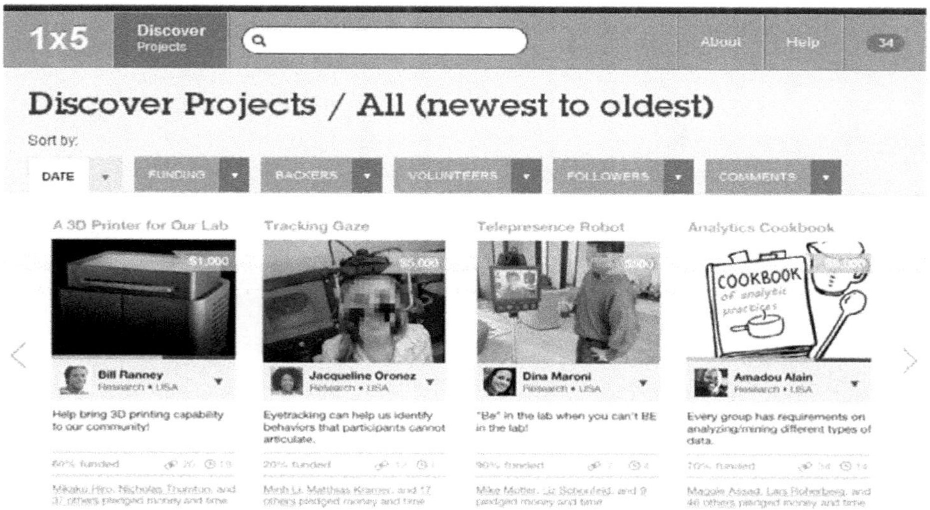

Figure 1. Home page of 1x5.

firewall. Also, each user of 1x5 was authenticated via the organization's online directory, with full non-anonymous information about the employee, including a link to her or his internal social-networking profile page (similar to [3,11,21,24]). 1x5 was built on Node.js and MongoDB with the Express application framework.[2]

We deployed 1x5 for 35 days in IBM. A vice president within the IBM Research organization agreed to provide US$100 per regular full-time employee for the 511 people in his organization. Unlike Internet crowdfunding, our users were entrusted with spending money from a budget instead of using their private funds. This funding was available on a "use it or lose it" basis, only for the duration of the 1x5 trial. Each employee was free to invest any or all of her/his $100 on one or more proposals by other employees (i.e., employees could not invest in their own proposals). Proposers might offer rewards to investors, such as priority usage of a shared resource to be purchased through 1x5 funding.

Because we had only 35 days, we imposed a uniform deadline for full funding on all projects. Also, we did not allow investors to give more than the target amount of funding. By contrast, most Internet crowdfunding sites allow people to invest beyond the funding target of the proposal. However, unlike Internet crowdfunding sites, we knew the exact limit of our funding pool – i.e., $50,000. To give an opportunity to as many proposals as possible, we limited each proposal to receive a maximum of its target amount. Once a proposal was successful, further funding was disabled, although other non-financial actions could continue (e.g., volunteering, commenting, following). We hoped that employees would browse for other projects that they could support.

Access and Permissions

Any employee of IBM could access the 1x5 platform. However, access permissions differed depending on whether s/he was a member of the sponsoring organization. Members of the sponsoring organization had full privileges to write proposals and to invest in other people's proposals in 1x5, as well as to volunteer, comment, follow, and view selected projects and the 1x5 activities of other people. By contrast, non-members were restricted to volunteering, commenting, following, and viewing. In addition, all users could view lists of projects, optionally sorted by funds, number of investors, etc., as shown in Figure 1.

METHOD

We conducted a 35-day trial of 1x5. We imposed the time-limitation following observations of Millen and Fontaine [21] that shorter durations encourage focus and a sense of urgency in large-scale inter-organizational collaborations.

Holtzblatt and Tierney reported on the importance of messaging by senior leadership for social media innovation work [11]. We therefore arranged for the trial to be announced via an email from the sponsoring vice president to the members of his organization. Participation was entirely voluntary. Following advice of Wash and Lampe [36], we also published a one-page newsletter, featuring selected projects and users, on a weekly basis. At the conclusion of the trial, the sponsoring vice president sent a brief thank-you email, encouraging the employees to follow-through with their funded proposals.

Data Collection

We used three types of data for our analysis.

Data Logs. First, we recorded all events within 1x5, including view actions, resulting in a 24,622-event dataset (excluding data related to members of the 1x5 team).

---

[2] http://nodejs.org, http://mongodb.org, http://expressjs.com

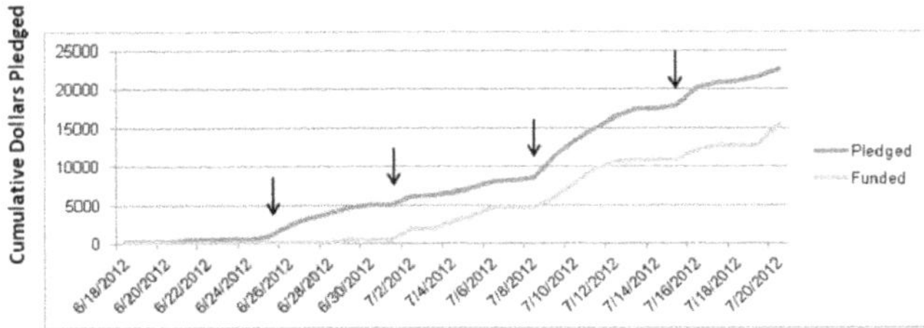

Figure 2. Timecourse of investments. The top line shows the total amount that users pledged. The bottom line shows the total amount that was awarded to projects that met their funding goal.

Interviews. Second, we conducted 24 interviews with a stratified sample of users, including:

- 6 proposers of successful projects (i.e., projects that received the full amount of their requested funds)
- 6 proposers of unsuccessful projects (projects that did not meet their funding goals, and therefore received no funding)
- 6 investors (who did *not* also propose a project)
- 6 viewers (users who viewed, but did not propose, invest, volunteer, or comment)

Most interviews were conducted by telephone (one with a chat channel for disambiguation). Three interviews used email, to accommodate employees' vacation schedules.

Interviews were iteratively coded as our understanding of the 1x5 experience evolved. In the language of grounded theory (e.g., [4]), we moved from open codes to axial codes. However, our analysis was guided by the relatively hypothesis-driven Research Questions described above, so we did not engage in a full grounded theory analysis.

Email Surveys. Third, we conducted several brief email surveys. These included:

- Survey to all project proposers regarding how they had promoted their projects (38% response rate)
- Survey to all project proposers regarding social networking ties to their investors (50% response rate)
- Survey to a random sample of investors about the importance of the projects they had invested in (27% response rate within the sample)

RESULTS

We begin our results with a summary of the trial, followed by answers to the seven Research Questions.

Summary of the Trial

311 employees participated in the 1x5 trial. Collectively, they proposed 34 projects with a total requested funding of US$101,600. Nineteen proposals (56%) were successfully funded (compare to a success rate of 43.89% at Kickstarter [15]). Employees pledged a total of US$22,500 on the 34

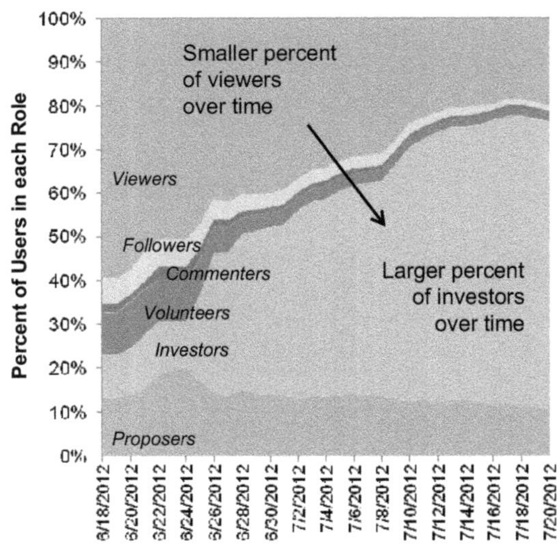

Figure 3. Timecourse of user engagement. Over time, many users "converted" from viewers to investors.

projects (45% of available funds). However, the conventional rules of crowdfunding sites restrict funding to those projects that have *met their funding goals*, and thus only US$15,800 was awarded to the 19 successful projects (32% of available funds). Among the employees who invested, people pledged an average of US$90 (90% of their allowed investments).

Figure 2 presents a timeline of the employees' cumulative investments. Note the periodic increases in investment at roughly weekly intervals. We attribute these increases to the arrival of our email newsletter, which appears to have renewed employee engagement after each distribution.

We coded each participant in terms of the user-selected role that each person achieved. For analytic purposes, we made the roles mutually exclusive – hence, each user was assigned to a single role. Within the value system of our crowd-funding experiment, we considered the role of *proposer* as the "highest" role, because without proposals, there was nothing for other employees to act upon (note that proposers may also have engaged in other types of actions). Also within the value system of the experiment, we considered the role of *investor* to be next highest role, because investing led to the allocation of funds to projects (investors did *not* propose a project, but may have engaged in actions other than proposing or investing). After investors, we coded the roles in descending order of engagement, as *volunteer* (no proposing or investing), *commenter* (no proposing, investing, or volunteering), *follower* (only following or viewing), and finally *viewer* (viewing and no other type of action).[3]

[3] We note that other types of applications may have different implicit or explicit value systems, in which roles such as commenter or viewer/lurker may have higher value (e.g., [28]).

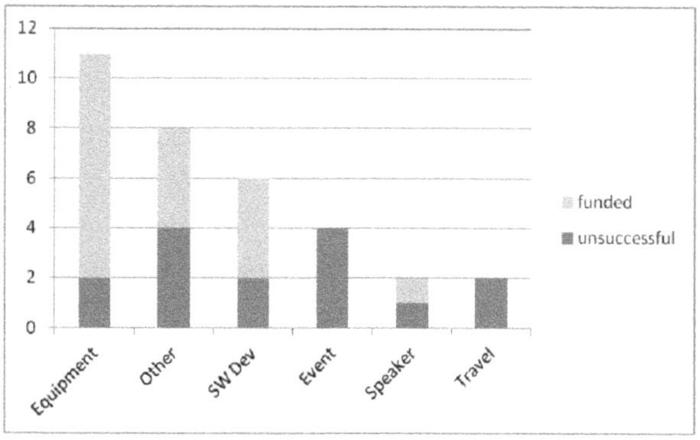

Figure 4. Categories of successful and unsuccessful proposals.

Figure 3 shows a stacked area graph of the daily proportion of users in each participation category over the time course of the 1x5 trial. Note the tendency of viewers to "convert" to investors over time. 70% of the non-converting viewers were external to the organization, and could only view or volunteer. In general, employees appeared to be strongly engaged with the 1x5 project.

Participation – RQ1

Overall, 311 people participated in the 1x5 trial. Among them were 255 members of the sponsoring organization, and 56 employees from outside of the sponsoring organization. For the sponsoring organization, the participation rate was 48%.

To compare these results with other published participation figures, we exclude the action of *viewing*, because most systems and studies do not report viewer or "lurker" data. With this restriction, fully 47.1% of the members of the sponsoring organization participated in 1x5. This participation rate compares favorably with Nielsen's estimates of 10% participation in social Internet applications [26] and our own observation of 13% participation in the 188 most active online communities in IBM's internal communities server [24]. More specific comparison figures may be found in an analysis of participation rates of about 25% in a very large-scale brainstorming activity [21]. Unpublished data from other Intranet applications has showed 5% participation in a structured discussion held during a weekend; 11% participation in a longer-term structured discussion; and 39.7% participation among 26 innovation communities using threaded discussions. The answer to **RQ1** (participation) is that 1x5 garnered more employee participation than any of the previously published reports.

Proposal Contents – RQ2a

We provided six mutually-exclusive categories for proposers to describe their proposals, as shown in Figure 4. Equipment proposals included robotics, a 3D printer, and equipment for morale-boosters (e.g., sports equipment). The "Other" category included Internet accounts for services such as micro tasks and surveys, and miscellaneous morale proposals (e.g., beverages). Software Development was predominantly a matter of sharing information in support of software development. The remaining three categories of "Event", "Speaker", and "Travel" reflect their titles.

The four proposals shown in Figure 1 give an idea of the diversity in employees' ideas. Proposals ranged from tools for work (eye-tracker) to new technology explorations (3D Printer, Telepresence robot) to peer-to-peer support (Analytics cookbook). The answer to **RQ1** (proposals) is that employees proposed diverse concepts with application to work, corporate culture, and morale.

User Goals and Motivations – RQ2b

Why were employees so engaged in 1x5? One component of the motivation appears to have been the experience of using 1x5 itself. Employees described this experience as

> *beautiful wonderful super-easy fantastic*
>
> *a really great project, and I would like to do it again.*

Employee Needs

At a deeper level, 1x5 appears to have answered pent-up employee needs:

> *this would give everyone a chance to enable what they want, for their particular responsibility or the environment in general, that's a good thing*
>
> *people did small projects and they focused on improving the [organizational] environment - I really appreciated it.*

Employees' investment decisions also reflected previously unsatisfied needs:

> *... apps or functions or services that I would be interested in using ...*
>
> *There was an element of "can I take advantage of it"...*
>
> *I used naked self-interest as my [investing] strategy*

Iterative coding led to several axial codes that address the themes of our research questions in greater detail. In their conventional, managed work objectives, employees tended to be assigned specific deliverables for specific clients according to an annual budgeting process. The 1x5 trial appeared to open new opportunities for side-projects or other forms of interest-driven innovation.

Minority Disciplines

One set of comments and projects addressed areas of professionalism that had no funding support. In his concept of the "double-knit organization," McDermott proposed that enterprises would want to support both their conventional "vertical" organizations (e.g., corresponding to business units) and also their diffuse, "horizontal" networks of skilled practitioners [20]. This issue may be particularly important for practitioner communities that are not mainstream to their organizations – the so-called "minority disciplines" ([21]; see [27] for a similar argument applied to crowdsourcing). Members of those communities seemed to use 1x5 to organize community support for resources that served the specific needs of their disciplines.

For example, employees proposed a project to fund survey-based tools on the public Internet, and a project to fund the use of micro-tasking Internet tools – resources that had not been available to them before 1x5. Note the strong motivation based in business needs:

> *HCI researchers in other labs, like [competitors], have easy access to people with whom to test ideas and gather empirical data*
>
> *... a way to treat "the crowd" as if it were another colleague down the hall.*
>
> *we need ... a tight loop of feedback from real people about our products, our potential products and our design ideas... The [micro-task] project is one tool of several required to provide this feedback.*

Technical Interests Beyond Current Assignments.

By contrast, another axial code was the pursuit of technical interests that did not fit within employees' assigned project work. For example, there were two projects in robotics. Neither of these projects, as proposed, addressed novel research concepts. However, each was proposed to be used to achieve primarily *social* goals – one for greater enfranchisement of remote employees, and the other for guiding visitors to employees' specific work locations. One investor in a robotics project said that the project was

> *important for creativity and hacking and thinking beyond boundaries - creative experimentation point of view - hardware would be new for our group – important someday for how we do telepresence in the future*

The theme of creativity was also present in other projects, e.g. the purchase of a 3D printer. Employees commented,

> *hacking, creative spirit...*
>
> *...fun way to learn more about the whole maker culture*
>
> *an important technology to get familiar with ... cutting edge hi-tech. Moreover, they end up producing tangible goods, which is something that many of us at IBM would like to [do]...*

However, the theme of creativity and hacking was strongly related to utility and the development of knowledge that would be valuable for the future:

> *I work in sensors... the problem [is] always to package it in a nice way. I wanted a nice adapter, so I could pack in a sensor and some batteries, like a phone. Having the ability to print out a part...*
>
> *It is usually very difficult to ... create ... the objects of the desired shape. With a 3D printer, this task can be easily done and hence make the research more efficient.*

Some of the research motivations were focused beyond present-day utility and enjoyment, to knowledge that could be important to business opportunities of the future:

> *3D printing is being used to make prosthetics and bone models today. [Someday] We may be able to... print off a new internal organ.*

These two sets of examples are somewhat in contrast – unmet business needs vs. a need for creativity and new learning. What unifies these two sets of examples is that employees felt passionately about areas of professional development that had been unavailable to them. The 1x5 system provided a means to articulate those passions, and to garner support for realizing those passions so as to benefit both employees and their organizations.

Removing Constraints

An over-arching theme for many of the employee decisions – regarding both proposing and investing – was *removing the constraints imposed by corporate processes.* All organizations have work processes and approval chains. In some cases, these requirements can interfere with new initiatives, creative hypotheses, and the aforementioned needs of minority disciplines. 1x5 provided an alternate mechanism for supporting these kinds of needs.

Two other employees said,

> *This is one way to actually get technology here. Actually getting funding from IBM is hard.*

One project proposer (who was also an ardent supporter of related projects) said,

> *[Although] I thought that the most exciting projects were not within the rules... I wanted to make a statement about the things I need that I don't have...*

Both of the projects that she felt so strongly about were funded.

In answer to **RQ2b** (goals and motivations), we believe that 1x5 performed two services simultaneously: Employees were able to articulate diverse unmet needs in new ways, and they were able to satisfy those needs through collaborative action. Of course, not all futuristic concepts lead to valuable outcomes, and we won't know for a while which of these new endeavors (if any) will provide value. The achievement, so far, is that 1x5 could be used to bring people together around their shared needs, and that 1x5 facilitated their taking effective action. Alternative methods such as IMSs or brainstorms usually involve less direct control by employees [2,3,37] and may require staff-weeks to analyze and turn into actionable decisions [11,21].

Inter-Departmental Collaboration – RQ3a

In the preceding section, we concluded that 1x5 brought people together to meet their shared needs. In this section, we formalize that observation quantitatively.

from \ to	DeptA	DeptC	DeptF	DeptG	DeptH	DeptI	DeptJ	DeptP	DeptR	DeptS	DeptW	DeptY	DeptZ
DeptA	12.31%	3.62%	4.10%	1.54%	1.92%	6.67%	2.10%	4.33%	11.97%	23.08%	0.00%	2.21%	0.45%
DeptC	1.81%	2.21%	1.57%	7.06%	3.78%	11.76%	3.21%	5.15%	0.00%	23.53%	0.00%	2.50%	0.69%
DeptF	0.00%	0.00%	0.00%	0.00%	0.00%	0.00%	0.00%	0.00%	0.00%	0.00%	0.00%	0.00%	0.00%
DeptG	8.21%	10.20%	25.78%	79.05%	8.57%	30.22%	9.70%	6.67%	5.93%	0.00%	31.11%	10.91%	6.27%
DeptH	7.14%	17.23%	6.67%	14.76%	31.48%	15.24%	12.99%	10.71%	7.94%	0.00%	2.38%	8.98%	6.72%
DeptI	26.15%	36.86%	16.89%	29.33%	16.67%	125.71%	26.67%	22.50%	10.37%	40.00%	22.22%	15.15%	6.27%
DeptJ	0.00%	0.00%	0.00%	0.00%	0.00%	0.00%	0.00%	0.00%	0.00%	0.00%	0.00%	0.00%	0.00%
DeptP	2.40%	5.15%	0.83%	2.50%	2.23%	11.67%	4.55%	10.83%	0.00%	0.00%	12.50%	4.73%	0.74%
DeptR	0.00%	0.00%	0.00%	0.00%	0.00%	0.00%	0.00%	0.00%	0.00%	0.00%	0.00%	0.00%	0.00%
DeptS	0.00%	0.00%	0.00%	0.00%	0.00%	0.00%	0.00%	0.00%	0.00%	0.00%	0.00%	0.00%	0.00%
DeptW	0.00%	0.00%	0.00%	0.00%	0.00%	0.00%	0.00%	0.00%	0.00%	0.00%	0.00%	0.00%	0.00%
DeptY	6.06%	6.42%	6.06%	6.67%	7.47%	11.11%	7.44%	5.68%	2.69%	9.09%	0.00%	11.47%	2.50%
DeptZ	1.81%	0.00%	0.00%	1.57%	3.36%	3.92%	5.35%	10.29%	0.00%	0.00%	3.92%	2.85%	29.41%

Table 1. Heatmap of inter-departmental collaborations. Rows represent the department in which the proposer was employed. Columns represent the department in which the investor was employed. The color of the cell represents how much greater the cell's value is, in contrast to predicted values based on the number of members of each department.

Table 1 is a "heatmap" that shows inter-departmental collaboration. Each row and each column correspond to a particular department within the sponsoring organization. Each cell represents the strength of collaboration between two departments, expressed as the number of proposer-investor linkages (i.e., User1 from DepartmentA proposes a project, and User2 from DepartmentB invests). Cell totals are normalized by the number of people in each department.

There are several hypotheses to consider. A simple null hypothesis of *parochialism* would state that employees support projects by people in their *own* departments. If that were the case, then the major diagonal of Table 1 would be highly populated, and the remaining cells would be empty. However, Table 1 shows many off-diagonal cells with a great deal of activity, suggesting that people are not behaving in a parochial fashion. We calculated the mean number of departments whose members backed each project, and we conducted a t-test comparing that mean to the value predicted by the extreme parochialism hypothesis, namely that each department's proposal would be supported by exactly *one* department (the same department as the proposer). The mean number of departments that invested

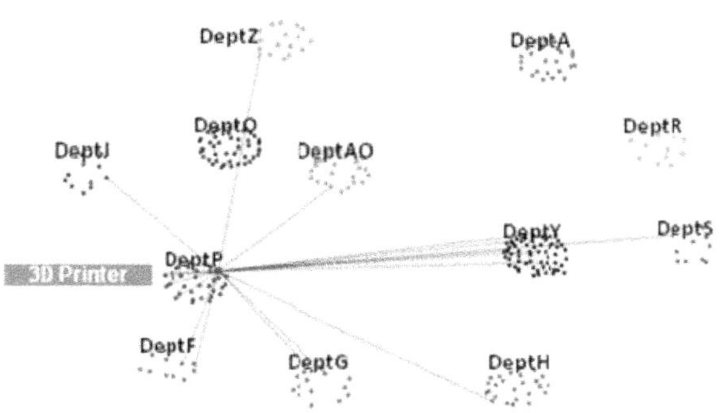

Figure 5. Inter-departmental investing pattern. Each cluster of dots represents the users from a particular department. The blue rectangle indicates the project name, which is listed next to the department of the proposer. For this representative project, investors came from 8 different departments. Table 1 shows a more systematic summary of inter-departmental investment patterns.

in each proposal was 7.71, and the parochialism hypothesis could be rejected with $p<.001$ confidence.

Now that we have established the generality of the inter-departmental collaboration in statistical terms, we briefly examine a representative project graphically. Figure 5 shows the patterns of investments across departments for the 3D Printer proposal. In many cases, a single member of a department made the investment decision, reflecting the diffuse nature of the "horizontal" communities described by McDermott [20]. Proposers reported (via survey) that 42% of their investors were *unknown* to them. The answer to **RQ3a** is that 1x5 appeared to connect people in new ways, focusing on their shared interests and needs.

How well were employees making connections via 1x5? One proposer observed,

> *I felt a certain building of community through the process of participating - there were several things there that could help all of us*

Another proposer noted that 1x5 allowed to

> *facilitate people who are interested in common topics to meet and form research projects*

The proposer of one of the two robotics projects said that

> *there was someone who asked about my proposal and then made a related proposal [both were funded]... There's a budding relationship with this guy.*

Further study will be needed to determine the importance and strength of the ties that may have been developed online [32] among (a) proposers and investors and (b) co-investors in the same project.

Influence of Organizational Level – RQ3b

The preceding section examined the effect of departmental structures. We turn now to the effect of hierarchical levels in the organization.

Bailey and Horvitz proposed a test of the "grassroots" quality of participation in an employee innovation program

[3]. They coded the "depth" of an employee within each organization, measured as the number of steps from the CEO to that employee. We performed a similar analysis of participation rate according to employee "depth." Employees who participated in 1x5 had depths from 4 (department heads) to 7 (individual, non-management contributors). Participation rates per depth varied from 33.3% to 62.2%; chi-square analyses found no significant differences (chi-square(4)=6.053, n.s.). The answer to **RQ3b** (equal participation across organizational hierarchy) is that the high level of participation in 1x5 appears to be generalized through all depths among the employees. Bailey and Horvitz also compared managers and non-managers, as a simpler test of the "grassroots" nature of participation. When we applied the same test, we found no significant participation differences between non-managers and managers (30% and 35% respectively, chi-square(1)=.947, n.s.). Employees appeared to participate at the same rate, regardless of their management status or position in the organizational hierarchy.

Successful vs. Unsuccessful Projects – RQ4

We wanted to understand what factors are associated with the 19 projects that were successful. We compared successful and unsuccessful proposals according to many quantitative attributes (date of proposal, number of investors, number of viewers, etc.), but the only quantitative differentiator was the funding target: successful proposals requested less money than unsuccessful projects (t-test, $p<.01$). One proposer reported that he

> *...set the budget sufficiently low to guarantee success...*

In a recent survey, Kraut and Resnick summarized results showing that higher-status individuals are more influential than lower-status individuals, in online and offline groups [16]. We wondered if proposers who were managers would have greater success than non-managers. The data do not support this hypothesis: even though managers participated at the same rate as non-managers (**RQ3b**), managers' projects were 20% successful, vs. non-managers' projects (50% successful).

We also considered whether the category of the proposal (**RQ2a**) might influence success (Figure 4). The number of proposals is too small for significance testing in the 2x6 design. We note a non-tested tendency toward greater success for proposals related to equipment and software.

Qualitative reports from a survey of proposers gave a different perspective. Proposers told many stories about how they promoted their proposals, ranging from emails and chats with their social networks, to paper advertisements (the proposer of the 3D Printer posted his adverts next to conventional 2D printers), to setting up a table in a high-traffic hallway to discuss the proposal with people. One proposer changed his Intranet microblog status text into a promotional message for his proposal. We did not have a sufficient number of proposals to allow a formal analysis of promotional activities, so we list these strategies as suggestive for future research. The tentative answer to **RQ4** (success factors) is that low target level and promotion activities appear to be important (see also [13]).

Facilitation and Moderation – RQ5

We note informally that many accounts of social media usage, inside and outside of enterprises, focus on needs and strategies for facilitating and moderating the users' activities [2,9,11,11,21,32,35]. By contrast, 1x5 required little manual facilitation. We reviewed each proposal before it was published on the site, but we requested minor changes in only three of the 34 proposals. Content for weekly newsletters could have been automatically populated based on the amount of activity related to proposals and individual users. The informal answer to **RQ5** is that, while proposers may work to promote their projects (**RQ4**) [13], crowdfunding within an enterprise requires little "hands-on" facilitation or moderation by administrators or managers.

DISCUSSION

Our experiences with enterprise crowdfunding were quite promising. Employees successfully proposed diverse projects in areas of equipment, software development tools, and access to resources (**RQ2a**). Proposals spanned multiple employee needs, including new and challenging technologies, resources needed to do work, extensions of cultures of experimentation, and morale boosters (**RQ2b**).

Participation was higher than most forms of social media [21,24,26] (**RQ1**), and was well-distributed across the organizational hierarchy and management structure (**RQ3a, RQ3b**). The high participation appeared to spring from the ability to make real change in employees' work environments, and to satisfy work needs through a channel that was not constrained by corporate expense controls [10] (**RQ2b**). In addition, employees were able to meet the needs of their disciplinary communities [20,21] as well as their larger workplace organization (**RQ2b**).

To accomplish this, employees collaborated across many departmental boundaries, with more than 40% of the funding collaborations occurring among strangers (**RQ3a,RQ3b**). Clever, innovative promotional strategies helped to make proposals successful (**RQ4**). Finally, these results were achieved with far less "overhead" work (facilitation and moderation) than comparable innovation programs [2,3,11,21,37] (**RQ5**).

Some features should be reconsidered. A few employees objected to the timeframe. Also, we noticed that some projects were on track of being funded but given the large amount asked for, never reached their funding goal during the trial period: Perhaps 35 days was too short? Employees also wanted the ability to rescind their investments in proposals that were clearly going to fail, so that they could re-allocate their funds to proposals that had a chance of success. Finally, some employees wished for the Internet model of crowdfunding [13,15], in which it is possible to invest *beyond* a project's funding target. These and other variations may become useful comparisons in future trials.

Limitations and Future Research

These outcomes were achieved in a single research organization. Our experiment involved only one type of crowdfunding (see "Varieties of Crowdfunding," above) [17,29]. More research will be needed to see if this kind of strategy and system will work in other companies, for other types of crowdfunding, and in organizations that provide different support for experimentation and innovation [10].

Also, our trial was conducted at a relatively small scale with a total budget of $50K. With that in mind, our users were well aware that bigger projects were impossible to get funded successfully. Future trials with a larger budget and more participants are planned to see if crowdfunding within the enterprise is viable for larger project proposals, and if this can potentially lead to superior ways of making business investment decisions, leveraging the collective intelligence of an organization's workforce.

Other innovation strategies have been successful in more product- or service- oriented corporate functions in multiple companies. Terveen et al. outlined a research paradigm in which a service of demonstrated value can be systematically modified to test specific hypotheses and theories [34]. We hope to use a variant of this approach to perform direct comparisons of crowdfunding with differently structured IMSs [2,3] and brainstorming solutions [11,21].

Follow-on research will be needed within our own company, to determine how many funded proposals lead to useful outcomes. We are encouraged that most funds have been spent on the proposed resources, and that many proposers are working with their investors and to use the resources in support of research and organizational change.

Implications for Design

Our preliminary results showed that the strategy of crowdfunding can be of value in at least one corporate environment. Reports from employees suggest that overall success was due in part to *concretizing* the innovation process around real money and real change in their workplaces [10,35], as well as the opportunity to join efforts with others (known and unknown) around *employee-initiated* topics of importance (see [7,29]). These conceptual design attributes can be re-used in both (a) extensions of the crowdfunding approach, and (b) other innovation programmes.

We think that our design may have under-emphasized the social context in which people collaborated on their shared interests (e.g., [7,29]). We hope to strengthen linkages to related social resources (e.g., employee profiles) and to spaces for collaboration to support work on the new initiatives. We speculate that a stronger social foundation could enhance both proposal-related work, and other workplace initiatives. Connections formed during these collaboration exercises could become the basis for social recommendations of new collaborations and initiatives.

Implications for Theory

The reported motivations for participating in crowdfunding on the Internet emphasize individualistic gain from financial investments or awards [4,7,10,29,35]. Even the personally-oriented motivations were reported in terms of individual orientations – e.g., *I* can help others or support a cause [7], or *I* can experience a sense of belongingness [29].

Our experiences with 1x5 suggest that, in workplaces, employees may make common cause around a shared purpose that benefits individuals, groups, and their enterprise – moving from "naked self-interest" (**RQ2b**) to "things... that could help all of us" (**RQ3a**). Could this contrast be due to employees spending budgeted money instead of their own funds? It will be interesting to see what new forms of "grassroots" collaborations and employee initiatives occur, in particular at a larger scale compared to our experiment. We will also be interested to explore how these motivations may define new collaborative motivational spaces, first in organizations and later perhaps in among larger-scale Internet communities.

We envision a more daring experiment, such as using a crowdfunding approach to allocate entire budgets of departments or companies. In terms of participatory theory (recently surveyed in [23]), this kind of employee empowerment could provide a new position between conventional executive decisions and workplace democracy concepts such as the Collective Resource approach [6]. More experimentation will be necessary before we take such a step.

CONCLUSION AND CONTRIBUTION

In this paper, we have joined Gerber and colleagues [7,17], and Noble [27], to bring crowdfunding into the CHI domain of study. We presented what we think is the first application for *enterprise crowdfunding*, and we have described a medium-scale trial of this application in an organizational context featuring real funds and real employee concerns. We have shown several strengths of our approach, in terms of ideas proposed, participation, collaboration, and the discovery of new collaboration opportunities.

With due concern for the early state of this research, we have suggested implications for design of other employee-innovation programs, and we have suggested new opportunities for theory development based on employees discovering and jointly satisfying common needs, at multiple organizational levels of groups with shared interests, minority disciplines, and organizations as a whole. Finally, we have outlined a series of additional research questions and opportunities for future work.

ACKNOWLEDGMENTS

We thank Elizabeth Gerber for helpful discussions, and David McQueeney for support.

REFERENCES[4]

1. Agrawal, A., Catalini, C., & Goldfarb, A. (2010). The geography of crowdsourcing. NET Institute Working Paper No. 10-80, 20 October 2010 (revised 9 January 2011). http://papers.ssrn.com/sol3/papers.cfm? abstract_id=1692661
2. Baez, M., & Convertino, G. (2012). Designing a facilitator's cockpit for an idea management system. *CHI 2012 Ext. Abstr.*
3. Bailey, B.P., & Horvitz, E. (2010). What's *your* idea? A case study of a grassroots innovation pipeline within a large software company. *Proc. CHI 2010.*
4. Belleflamme, P., Lambert, T. & Schwienbacher, A. (2011), "Crowdfunding: Tapping the Right Crowd" retrieved from http://www2.dse.unibo.it/dsa/seminari/ 610/Crowdfunding_BLS_13Feb2011.pdf.
5. Charmaz, K. (2006). *Constructing grounded theory: A practical guide through qualitative analysis.* Thousand Oaks, CA, USA: Sage.
6. Ehn, P. & Kyng, M. (1987). The collective resource approach to systems design. In G. Bjerknes, P. Ehn, and M. Kyng (Eds.), *Computers and democracy: A Scandinavian challenge.* Brookfield VT USA: Gower.
7. Gerber, E.M., Hui, J.S., & Kuo, P.-Y. (2012). Crowdfunding: Why people are motivated to participate. Position paper at CSCW 2012 DIST workshop, http://distworkshop.wordpress.com/resources/.
8. Ghosh, A., & Mahdian, M. (2008). Charity auctions on social networks. *Proc. ACM-SODA.*
9. Goecks, J., Voida, A., Voida, S., Mynatt, E.D. (2008). Charitable technologies: Opportunities for collaborative computing in nonprofit fundraising. *Proc. CSCW 2008.*
10. Harms, M. (2007). *What drives motivation to participate financially in a crowdfunding community?* Master's thesis, Vrije Universiteit Amsterdam.
11. Helander, M., Lawrence, R., & Li, Y. (2007). Looking for great ideas: Analyzing the innovation jam, *Proc. KDD 2007.*
12. Holtzblatt, L. & Tierney, M. (2011). Measuring the effectiveness of social media on an innovation process. *Proc. CHI 2011.*
13. Hui, J., Gerber, E., & Greenberg, M. (2012). Easy money? The demands of crowdfunding work. Northwestern University Segal Design Inst. Tech. Rep. 12-04.
14. Indiegogo (n.d.). http://www.indiegogo.com.
15. Kickstarter (n.d.). http://www.kickstarter.com/help/stats
16. Kraut, R., & Resnick, P. (2012). *Building successful online communities: Evidence-based social design.* Cambridge, MA, USA: MIT Press.
17. Kuo, P.-Y., & Gerber, L. (2012). Design principles: Crowdfunding as a creativity support tool. *CHI 2012 Ext. Abstr.*
18. Kuznetsov, S., & Paulos, E. (2010). Rise of the expert amateur: DIY projects, communities, and cultures. *Proc. NordiCHI 2010.*
19. Leigh, K.E., Huber, A.M., & Tremblay, K.R., Jr. (2012). Fostering individual and organizational creativity in design. *Soc. & Info. Tech.* http://www.iiis.org/ CDs2012/CD2012IMC/IREPS_2012/PapersPdf/ IR715DF.pdf
20. McDermott, R. (1999). Learning across teams: How to build communities of practice in team organizations. *Know. Mgmt. J. 8*, 32-36 (May/June).
21. Millen, D.R., & Fontaine, M.A. (2003). Multi-team facilitation of very large-scale distributed meetings. *Proc. ECSCW 2003.*
22. Muller, M., & Carey, K. (2002). Design as a minority discipline in a software company: Toward requirements for a community of practice. *Proc. CHI 2002.*
23. Muller, M.J., & Druin, A. (2012). Participatory design: The third space of HCI. In Jacko, J., *Human Computer Interaction Handbook.* Boca Raton, FL, USA: CRC Press.
24. Muller, M., Ehrlich, K., Matthews, T., Perer, A., Ronen, I., & Guy, I. (2012). Diversity among enterprise communities: Collaborating, teaming, and innovating through social media. *Proc. CHI 2012.*
25. Netburn, D. (2012). Online donations to bullied bus driver top $540,000. *Los Angeles Times,*, 22 June 2012.
26. Nielsen, J., (2006). Participation inequality: Encouraging more users to contribute,' http://www.useit.com/ alertbox/participation_inequality.html.
27. Noble, J. (2012). Minority voices in crowdsourcing: Why we should pay attention to every member of the crowd. *Proc. CSCW 2012.*
28. Nonnecke, B., Andrews, A., & Preece, J., 'Non-public and public online community participation: Needs, attitudes, and behavior. *Elec. Com. Res. 6*(1), 7-20.
29. Ordanini, A., Miceli, L., Pizzetti, M., & Parasuraman, A. (2011). Crowdfunding: Transforming customers into investors through innovative service platforms. *J. Serv. Mgnt. 22*(4), 443-470.
30. Reed, J. (2012). Fans kick in a million to let Palmer make music her way. *Boston Globe* 26 June, 2012.
31. Schneider, D., Mornes, K., Moreira de Souza, J., & Esteves, G.P. (2012). CSCWD: Five characters in search of crowds. *Proc. IEEE CSCWD 2012.* Schuler, D., & Namiaki,
32. Steinfield, C., DiMicco, J.M., Ellison, N.B. & Lampe, C. (2009). Bowling online: Social networking and social capital within the organization. *Proc. C&T 2009.*
33. Tam, F.-W. (2012). Pebble technology becomes Kickstarter's test case. *Wall Street Journal* 2 July 2012.
34. Terveen, L., Riedl, J., Konstan, J., & Lampe, C. (in press). The build to learn genre of social computing research. To appear in Olson, J., & Kellogg, W. (eds.), *Ways of knowing in HCI.*
35. van Wingerden, R., & Ryan, J. (2011). *Fighting for funds: An exploratory study into the field of crowdfunding.* Lund University School of Economics and Management.
36. Wash, R., & Lampe, C. (2012). The power of the ask in social media. *Proc. CSCW 2012.*
37. Westerski, A., Iglesias, C.A., & Nagle, T. (2011). The road from community ideas to organisational innovation: A life cycle survey of idea management systems. *Int. J. Web Based Communities* 7(4), 493-50.

[4] All URLs were checked on 12 September 2012.

Community Insights: Helping Community Leaders Enhance the Value of Enterprise Online Communities

Tara Matthews[1], Steve Whittaker[2], Hernan Badenes[3], Barton A. Smith[1], Michael Muller[4], Kate Ehrlich[4], Michelle X. Zhou[1], Tessa Lau[5]
[1]IBM Research - Almaden, San Jose, CA, USA, {tlmatthe, barton.smith, mzhou}@us.ibm.com
[2]UC Santa Cruz, Santa Cruz, CA, USA, swhittak@ucsc.edu
[3]IBM, Buenos Aires, Argentina, hbadenes@ar.ibm.com
[4]IBM Research - Cambridge, Cambridge, MA, USA, {michael_muller, katee}@us.ibm.com
[5]Willow Garage, Menlo Park, CA, USA, tlau@tlau.org

ABSTRACT
Online communities are increasingly being deployed in enterprises to increase productivity and share expertise. Community leaders are critical for fostering successful communities, but existing technologies rarely support leaders directly, both because of a lack of clear data about leader needs, and because existing tools are *member*- rather than *leader-centric*. We present the evidence-based design and evaluation of a novel tool for community leaders, Community Insights (CI). CI provides *actionable analytics* that help community leaders foster healthy communities, providing value to both members and the organization. We describe empirical and system contributions derived from a long-term deployment of CI to leaders of 470 communities over 10 months. Empirical contributions include new data showing: (a) which metrics are most *useful* for leaders to assess community health, (b) the need for and how to design *actionable* metrics, (c) the need for and how to design *contextualized analytics* to support sensemaking about community data. These findings motivate a novel community system that provides leaders with useful, actionable and contextualized analytics.

Author Keywords
Online communities; community leaders; iterative design; system evaluation; enterprise; workplace.

ACM Classification Keywords
H.5.m. Information interfaces and presentation (e.g., HCI): Miscellaneous.

INTRODUCTION
Online communities are becoming increasingly prevalent in enterprises, with easy-setup social software and increased awareness of benefits to businesses and employees. These benefits include breaking down organizational and distance barriers to knowledge sharing and collaboration [8,35]; improved skills and ability to execute and retain staff [35]; improved sales [3]; improved speed of execution, increased quality, reduced costs [8,39]; and enhanced innovation processes [20]. However, attaining these benefits is no simple matter and an effective community leader is a critical success factor [2,15,35].

Because of their essential role in fostering community success, online community leaders are a growing population in enterprises. Some activities they perform within communities are to encourage contributions and discussion [13,15,27], contribute and read content [5,13], organize and curate content [1,13,27,36], answer questions [13], moderate [1,5,13,15], create a positive environment [1,5,13,15], advertise the community externally [5,15], and maintain infrastructure [1,5,15,27,36]. Prior work documents effective leader strategies for enacting these activities [15,17,19,28,29,35,39].

However, there is a critical gap between these guidelines and the actual practice of facilitating valuable communities. Leaders' unique role involves *assessing* community progress on goals and *intervening* to guide the group towards achieving those goals. Static guidelines cannot help with such assessments; rather dynamic community analysis tools are needed. However, there is virtually no research on tools for community leaders. When community analysis tools have been built and evaluated, they are *member-centric* (focusing on members' not leaders' needs) [4,9,18,24,30] or created for *research* purposes [31,32,34]. Only a few commercial tools explicitly focus on community analysis [21], but they report no motivating research or evaluations. Furthermore, the large online communities literature proposes many possible metrics for assessing community health but we know little about which would be useful to leaders in practice.

Our aim is to develop and evaluate novel tools that facilitate effective leadership in online communities. We present the evidence-based design and evaluation of Community Insights (CI), a new tool to help leaders foster healthy communities that provide value to members and the organization. In contrast to many prior tools, CI was co-developed with leaders using an evidenced-based approach, not intuition about leaders' needs. We deployed CI to leaders of 470 communities over 10 months, gathering detailed feedback. We describe how our final version of CI is a novel system that provides leaders with useful, actionable and contextualized analytics.

RELATED WORK

Understanding Community Leadership to Inform Tools

Much prior research has focused on fostering "successful" online communities, within and outside organizations [15,17,19,28,29,35,39]. It outlines key information for community leaders or best practices that might inform possible tool needs. We summarize key findings from these studies and their implications for designing leader tools. Importantly, prior works don't provide explicit guidelines for designing tools, or predict key system features leaders will actually use and want. Many design implications are derivable from prior work, but it is difficult to know which would *actually* be useful. The present research helps identify which of these prior ideas are useful *in practice*.

Several authors discuss the importance of leaders assessing the health and success of their community [14,15,28,35], both to facilitate improvements and to justify continued funding of the community. But success metrics proposed in prior work are rarely validated. Iriberri and Leroy [14] survey community success factors and metrics. The most common success metrics are: *volume of members' contributions* (e.g. measured as posts per time period) [6,7,14,23,25,27,42], *community size* (i.e. number of members) [14,22,23,25,27,42], and *quality of relationships among members* (e.g. the extent of contact among members or via qualitative feedback) [14,23,27,35,42]. Other common metrics include *number of threads* [7,25,42], *number of replies* [7,25,42], *threads with responses* [7,42], *delay in response time* [7], *reciprocity among members* [27], and *member satisfaction* [27,42].

Other work discusses how leaders can promote successful communities, advocating leader activities including: to encourage contributions and discussion [13,15,17,27], contribute and read content [5,13], organize and curate content [1,13,27,36], deal with disruptive behavior [1,5,13,15,17], create a positive environment [1,5,13,15], foster connections [17,35], manage new members [17], advertise externally [5,15], and maintain infrastructure [1,5,15,27,36]. Again, these works don't directly examine leaders' main challenges, motivate designs for leader tools, or observe how leaders use such tools.

Many authors suggest that identifying social roles helps members know whose posts to read. A role taxonomy for Usenet groups is presented in [11]: Newbie, Celebrity, Elder, Lurker, Flamer, Troll, and Ranter. Social network analysis has identified key roles via "online signatures" [10,31,34]. Other work develops algorithms for identifying experts [10,26,41], who are recognized as important in communities. We test whether and how identifying certain social roles is useful to community leaders.

Tools for Community Maintenance and Analysis

Community analysis tools can be divided into three classes, depending on whom they are designed for: member-centric, researcher-centric, and leader-centric. There are very few leader-centric tools (exceptions include commercial tools like Lithium Customer Intelligence Center [21]) and almost no evaluations of them (an exception being Gurzick et al. [12]). The design and evaluation of CI is our main contribution, addressing the limitations of prior work.

The most common class of community analysis tools is *researcher-centric*. These include interfaces or algorithms to provide researchers with a deeper understanding of community behaviors, but which are not usable by end-users. For example, History Flow visualizes Wikipedia article changes, enabling researchers to study author collaboration [32]. Other researcher tools identify emergent leaders [43] or experts [26], model the evolution of communities [7], and automatically rate contributions [33].

Member-centric tools include UIs for community members as their intended users. For example, Netscan depicts "social accounting metrics" for Usenet to help members "form cooperative relationships by offering a better sense of the other players involved" [4,31]. Brush et al. [4] evaluated the use of social metrics in Netscan in a long-term field study. They found active users were interested in author metrics, whereas light users focused on content metrics. CI includes many similar metrics—top contributors, top posts, statistics about posts and people and detailed descriptive statistics about individuals. However we examine the utility of these metrics for enterprise community leaders.

Other projects aim to increase members' understanding of social dynamics behind Wikipedia articles, to improve member's ability to interpret and trust the information presented [24,30]. Even though community leaders are not the intended users of these systems, they demonstrate the value of social accounting information for end-users. We explore the social accounting information that enterprise community leaders want and their needs surrounding assessments of community health.

Research on *leader-centric* analysis tools is incredibly rare. Gurzick et al. [12] studied moderators using an activity monitoring tool in an online community for teens. The work shows it is important to understand how moderators actually use tools. The monitoring tool affected how moderators operated, allowing them to promote discussion: posting comments about content members were currently viewing. Our work also seeks to explore how tools enhance the activities of enterprise online community leaders.

We are not aware of any leader-centric research systems, but a few commercial tools aim to support leaders. Many commercial tools support web analytics, helping website owners understand visitors' actions on their site, emphasizing metrics like number of visitors, page views, and conversions (when a visit leads to a purchase). Few offer community-specific support and these are marketed to businesses for website monitoring. Closest to our work is Lithium Customer Intelligence Center, which allows leaders to monitor customer communities' health [21]. It includes 6 health metrics—*content value*, *number of members*, *traffic*, *responsiveness*, *interaction*, and *liveliness*—and one combined metric—the *Community Health Index* (CHI). However, the derivations and evaluation of these metrics are not reported. Other commercial analytics tools have the same limitation. We include similar metrics in CI (and others based on our research) but evaluate their usefulness to leaders.

RESEARCH AND ORGANIZATIONAL CONTEXT

This research was conducted in a global enterprise offering technology products and services to businesses. The company widely encouraged employee leadership of, and participation in, internal online communities and made commercial technology, IBM Connections Communities, available to all employees. All communities we studied used this tool, which enabled leaders to easily create a community space with various social tools like forums, blogs, wikis, files, and bookmarks. As a result, there was a proliferation of communities and widespread membership, with 111,557 communities and 487,941 distinct members over four years. Communities ranged in size from a couple to tens of thousands. Many employees were members of multiple communities. Leaders of these internal communities were the subjects of our research.

Communities assigned one of two designated roles to each person in their online space: *owner* or *member*. Members can view and post content, but edit only their own content. Owners have members' rights plus they can edit any content, add/remove members, and configure tools. Formal community leaders, the subject of our research, are always designated as owners, although not all owners are formal leaders. Throughout the rest of the paper, for simplicity we assume that owners are community leaders, using *owner* to refer to a system-designated community leader.

Participants

Our research involved 26 participants: 9 for requirements interviews (conducted before the system was built), 14 for evaluation interviews (conducted after system deployment), and 3 who participated in both. They led communities of different sizes, ages, and types: (CoPs) (12 leaders), teams (4 leaders), or both (10 leaders), as defined in [23]. CoPs tended to have more leaders who posted less often; team communities had fewer leaders who tended to post more and be explicitly assigned to their role [23]. For 13 participants, leadership was a formal job responsibility. Eleven participants chose to enact their job responsibilities by becoming a leader although it was not a formal role (e.g. someone tasked with enabling employees to use a particular methodology, who chose to accomplish this using a community). Three participants assumed their role voluntarily (e.g. they were passionate about a topic and wanted to share their interest). Participants were mainly experienced leaders (20/26), recruited because they had thought deeply about their role. We also recruited a smaller set of inexperienced leaders (6/26), to gain a broader perspective into this growing leader population. Only 4 out of 26 participants were managers.

FORMATIVE RESEARCH TO UNDERSTAND ENTERPRISE ONLINE COMMUNITIES AND LEADERS

To inform CI's design, we conducted initial requirements interviews with 12 leaders. Leaders were recruited in an online forum for people who led online communities of various types. Our goal was to determine how to create leader tools. We asked leaders how they enacted their role, the challenges they faced, and their needs. Interviews were semi-structured, conducted by phone, lasting 60 mins. They were audio recorded and transcribed. Transcriptions were iteratively analyzed by 4 analysts for themes pertaining to our research questions. We summarize key results.

Leader Generated Implications for CI Design

Community leader needs concerned two major questions:
(1) How healthy and successful is my community?
(2) How can I take action to enhance its health and success?

Leaders explained that they currently had very little support for answering these questions, as there were no community analytic tools made available. They had many suggestions about what information would help them. We identified 6 categories of information needs: understanding (1) *people*; (2) *content*; (3) *participation*; (4) *sociability*, how well the community fostered member relationships; (5) *leadership*, the impact of leader's actions; and (6) *comparable communities*, i.e. how the community relates to other communities. The first three categories were discussed as the most critical needs by participants, so we describe these in detail. These needs are consistent with prior literature [6,15,16,17,19].

(1) People: Who are community members and do they form sub-groups? What do members want of the community? Who are the important people, e.g. top contributors, experts, and emerging thought leaders? Leaders believed that answering these questions would help them understand dynamics, distribute information, plan events, and engage with particular people and sub-groups in the community.

(2) Content: What topics are members creating and discussing and which are most valued? What types of value are derived from content? Does content match member needs? Leaders wanted this information to assess the value of content and to provide better content.

(3) Participation: How much are members or sub-groups contributing and reading? What other activities and interactions are taking place? Leaders saw *participation* as a strong indicator of health—and the community's ability to achieve its goals.

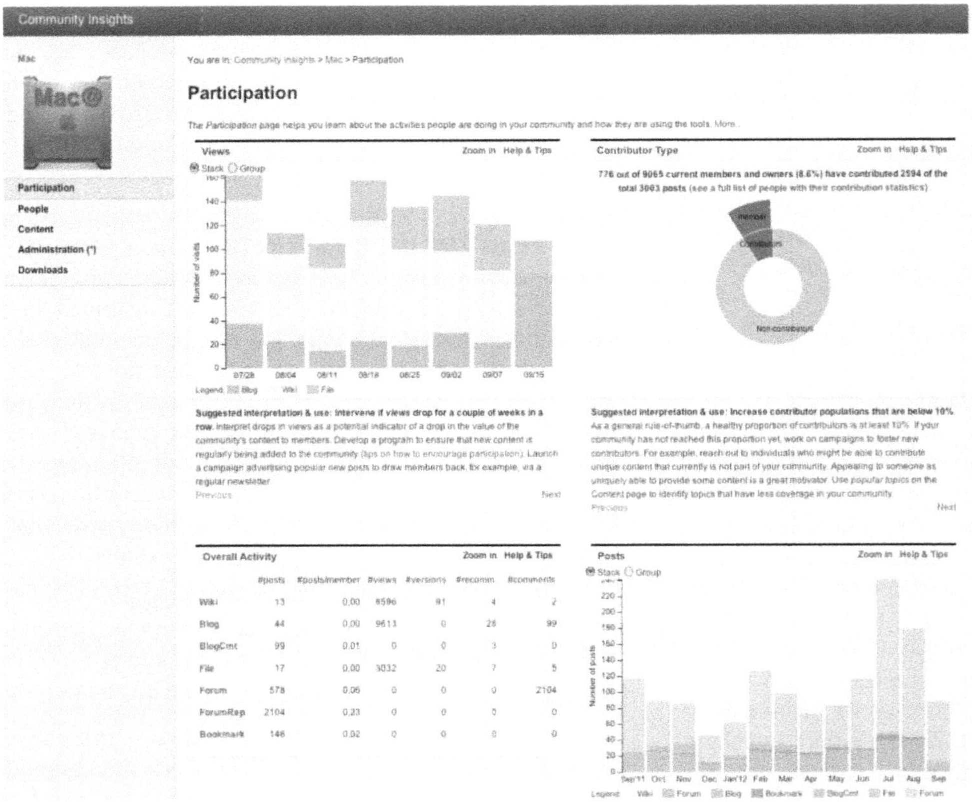

Figure 1. Community Insights screenshot of the *Participation* page for the "Mac" technical support community. Navigation to the *People* and *Content* pages is in the left bar.

Leaders of CoPs and teams had different information needs due to differing goals. CoP leaders were interested in interaction around *end-user generated content*, similar to prior work [6,14,17]. This was a secondary goal for team-based communities, which primarily focused on *publishing* team relevant information. Leaders of both communities types were interested the same information—leading to common needs targeted in our initial version of CI—but team leaders were more interested in consumption activities and CoP leaders in contribution activities.

More critically, unlike prior work, leaders weren't just interested in passive understanding. Instead they wanted information to *inform actions* to improve their community. They wanted to identify potentially transformative information: particular people or sub-groups for proactive engagement; high value content to duplicate; or popular topics to use to organize the site.

Also of interest was information *not* discussed by our leaders but discussed at length in prior work. Dealing with *disruptive* member behavior is a major issue in internet communities [15,17] that enterprise community leaders did not have to confront. Members were all employees, invested in the success of the business, and identified by full names in community spaces, which discouraged disruptive behavior. Finally, although community size has been suggested as a success criterion [14,22,23,25,27,42], many of our leaders were more focused on unusual *changes* in size as a way of identifying possible issues.

THE DESIGN OF CI

The CI design was inspired by these leader interviews. The initial version we evaluate included information about three of the six information categories from the interviews - *participation* (see Fig. 1), *people*, and *content*—since these were the three most desired categories of information from our participants. The final three—*sociability*, *leadership*, and *comparable communities*—were seen as less critical by leaders so were left for future work.

Even within these three categories, prior work has suggested many types of information that might be provided. But which information is actually *useful* and *needed* by leaders to do their jobs effectively? We could not rely on prior work to tell us what information was useful because most tools have not been evaluated with leaders, and because our leaders worked in an enterprise rather than an internet context. For example, if we relied on prior literature, we might have focused on disruptive member behavior [15,17]. However, enterprise community leaders do not have this problem. Also, we may not have realized how critical member demographics were to leaders, since this is not commonly discussed in the literature.

The interviews enabled us to initially prioritize the many metrics suggested in prior literature—we included in CI the highest priority metrics to our leaders. Identifying the most useful subset of metrics in the enterprise represents a contribution of this work.

Participation metrics in CI focus on member contributions as emphasized in prior literature [5,6,7,14,15,17,21,23,25,27,42]: *overall activity* (Fig. 1 bottom-left), *posts* (Fig. 1 bottom-right), *views* (Fig. 1 top-left), and *contributor type* (Fig. 1 top-right).

People metrics in CI include two commonly proposed metrics—*membership change* (Fig. 2) [14,22,23,25,27,42] and *top contributors* (Fig. 3) [4,15,17,26,34,37,38]. Differing demands of enterprise community leaders motivated us to add three *people* metrics not explicitly discussed in prior work: *members' geographic locations* (a map and tiered pie chart showing where members are located in the world), *members' business divisions* (a tiered pie chart showing the part of the organization in which members work), and *manager/non-manager* (a pie chart showing proportions of managers and non-managers).

Content metrics in CI are less commonly discussed in the literature, but of great interest to leaders: *popular topics* (Fig. 4) [4,17,37], value of posts (a stacked bar chart showing how many posts in the past several months were low, medium, and high value—algorithm discussed below) [21,33], and *most valuable posts* (lists showing posts with top value ratings in the last month and of all time) [4,33].

To ensure that CI protected members' privacy and complied with privacy policies enforced by different countries, we consulted with an employee data privacy expert in Europe, where employee privacy laws are the strictest. We modified our interface in the ways this expert suggested to ensure we upheld community members' privacy.

In the following sections, we describe the metrics in more detail to illustrate support for leaders' two major needs: (1) assessing community health and value and (2) determining actions they could take to improve community health.

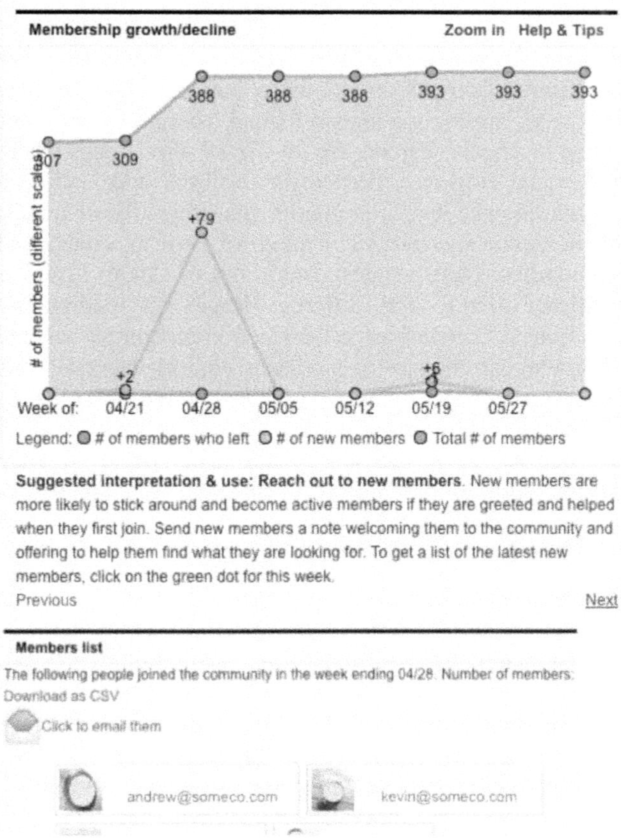

Figure 2. (top) *Membership change* with tips below. (bottom) List of new members appears when leader clicks on the chart's green dot showing that there are 79 new members (shown partially).

Assessing Community Health and Value

Interview participants wanted information to assess community health. CI supported this by including metrics that most leaders emphasized as key health indicators. Some of these overlapped with prior work; one common metric was volume of contributions [6,7,14,23,25,27,42], represented by our *posts* and *overall activity* widgets (bottom two widgets in Fig. 1). Other commonly suggested metrics are community size [14,22,23,25,27,42] (represented over time by our *membership change* widget), proportion of members who contribute [37] (our *contributor type* widget—see upper-right of Fig. 1), and consumption [37,38] (our *views* widget—see upper-left of Fig. 1). These four metrics represent the top requests related to community health from participants.

However, participants wanted to go beyond simple health metrics to assess the value of the community for members' everyday work. We therefore computed metrics for *value of posts* and *most valuable posts*. Value of a post was modeled by a linear regression function combining number of *views*, *comments*, and *recommendations* each post received. Precise weights were determined from community feedback, as members rated in a survey various posts for the value each offered to their job. This is similar to [21,33] except we asked our raters to focus on *extrinsic value of posts in supporting their job*. Posts receiving many views, comments, and/or recommendations were ranked higher than those receiving only a few.

Design for Community Action

Our requirements interviews indicated the importance of providing leaders with *guidance on actions to take* to improve community health and value. However the optimal action might depend on the state of the community. For example, if a community is losing members, leaders want to diagnose why, to reverse the trend. Based on participant feedback, we developed several ways to support remedial action. While other research and commercial systems propose metrics in the *people* and *content* categories [4,10,15,17,21,38], those systems don't explain how this information might be used to *change* community behavior.

(1) Identifying critical contributors and content. Leaders wanted to identify and engage with particular people or

Figure 3. Member profile in *top contributors* list (which lists the top 10 and links to a page listing all contributors). Points leaders to active members who they might engage in volunteer activities.

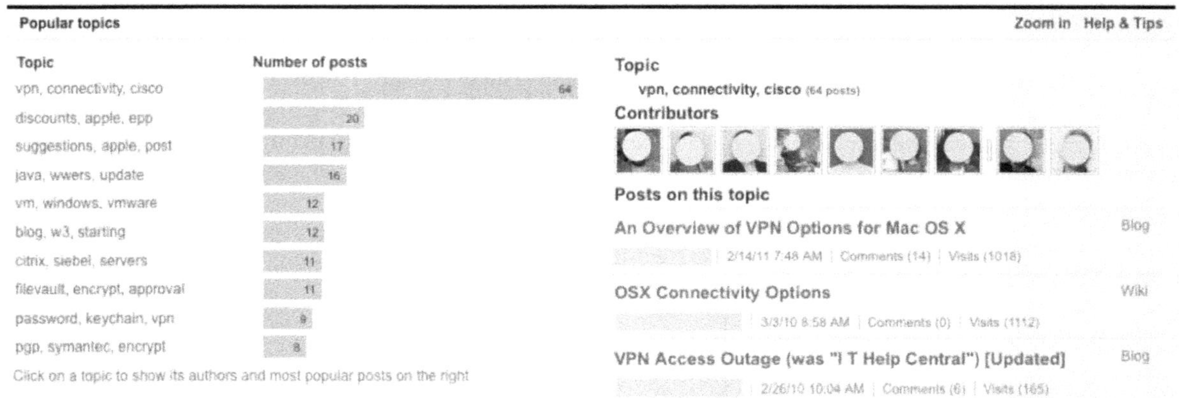

Figure 4. Profiling topics in the *popular topics* widget. (Left) Points leaders to particular topics of interest. (Right) Details the top contributors and the most popular posts (partially shown) for the "vpn, connectivity, cisco" topic.

topics of interest. While prior research argues for the utility of similar information to certify content or expertise [10,11,26,31,41], leaders wanted role information for additional purposes. They wanted to identify and engage with members who might volunteer to generate new content, participate as event presenters, or lead initiatives. They wanted to identify topics or high interest content to promote it in a newsletter or solicit similar content.

Thus, we designed CI to profile particular people, content, and topics of interest, but with the goal of making this information *actionable*. The *top contributors* metric leveraged the *value of posts* metric already described. We analyzed each contributor's posts, ranking their aggregate value using the *value of posts* metric. To provide actionable information, we designed profiles for the top ten contributors, shown in Fig. 3. Profiles help leaders identify core members and potential volunteers, along with tasks the leader might ask the member to do. For example, the profile suggests topics of expertise upon which the person might present. Similarly, CI profiles posts in the *most valuable posts* widget (including name of the post, author name, date posted, number of comments, number of visits, type of post, and a link to the actual post), and particular topics of interest in the *popular topics* widget (see Fig. 4), again offer leaders opportunities to recruit assistance or new content.

(2) Engaging with sub-groups. Leaders wanted to identify and communicate with particular community sub-groups. This included people from a particular geographic region or business unit, those recently joining or leaving the community, and high status people like managers. The *People* page helps leaders identify such sub-groups via the *geographic locations*, *business unit*, *managers/not* and *membership change* widgets. More importantly we facilitate leaders engaging with sub-groups by clicking on elements in these widgets. For example, clicking on a "new members" data-point in the *membership change* chart shows a list of new members for the selected time period (see Fig. 2). The list enables the leader to easily contact the new members, as suggested in prior literature [17].

(3) Tips for using metrics. Leaders requested guidance on actions to help them foster more healthy and valuable communities. CI includes a "help & tips" page for each metric offering concrete suggestions for interpreting and acting upon it. Such action-oriented tips set CI apart from more passive analytic systems, which present data without suggesting how users can act upon it. Tips were seeded by the research team using ideas taken from leader interviews and prior work. Users could also submit their own tips to share with other community leaders and recommend tips (the most recommended tips appeared at the top). An example of a *membership change* tip is shown in Fig. 2.

(4) Visualizing trends. Leaders argued that static data was not as useful as trends, which better indicate when and how to act, e.g., reversing a negative trend, continuing activities leading to a positive trend, etc. In CI, we show trends where appropriate. However, participant feedback and later data analysis showed that community maturity affects trends. For example, *membership change* is tiny in established communities. Thus, we designed a mix of data to illustrate significant trends for different stages of community development. Leaders of established communities wanted to know about changes in members' topical interests; thus we show *most valuable posts* in the *last month,* as well as *of all time*. Similarly, we show *top contributors* not only of *all time*, but also in the *last month* and *last week*, an iterative addition based on user feedback. In both cases, this allows leaders to assess current behavior in the context of the entire history of community interaction.

System Implementation

CI is an interactive web application: its user interface is implemented with the Dojo toolkit (dojotoolkit.org) and d3.js (d3js.org). The backend is a Java application over a relational database (IBM DB2). Data from Communities is only accessed during a batch, import process occurring once a week. The database process models and provides the metrics and analytics needed for the system.

SYSTEM DEPLOYMENT & EVALUATION METHOD

We assessed CI in a 10-month deployment in which we collected log usage data, and iterative evaluation by leaders

Page	Widget	Views, Users	Interpret (help & tips + zoom in)
Participation (default homepage)		5452, 969*	
	Views		304
	Posts		196
	Overall activity		134
	Contributor type		128
People		3665, 484	
	Geo location		297
	Business div		134
	Top contributors		70
	Manager/not		48
	Membership size		39
Content		2383, 405	
	Value of posts		69
	Popular topics		51
	Most valuable posts		42

Table 1. Number of page views and unique users of CI pages, and use of widgets (in 6.5 months of log data). For each widget, *Interpret* is the sum of (1) page views of the widget's *help & tips* page, (2) clicks to toggle tips under the widget (Fig. 3 top), (3) zooming in on the widget (opening a bigger widget view). *Inflated since *Participation* is the default community homepage.

in interviews. In interviews leaders told us which information in CI was most useful. We triangulated interviews with usage data, telling us whether and how leaders were able to interpret and act on CI information.

CI Deployment Process

We deployed CI on our company's intranet in late-October 2011, including data from 45 communities. We advertised the deployment: announcing it on internal social software, notifying community leaders in the company, and demoing it to community leaders. Leaders added their communities to the system throughout the deployment, which is ongoing. In late-August 2012, CI included 470 communities with 2532 unique owners and an average of 9 owners per community. We began logging in February 2012—recording each action (page views, clicks), when the action happened, by what user, and for what community—collecting 6.5 months of CI usage data.

Evaluation Interviews

We conducted 1-hour *evaluation interviews* via phone with 17 active leaders. Participants were chosen to be those who frequently accessed CI (high numbers of page views and days accessed) and represented communities of different sizes, ages, and types. As of the writing of this paper, they had accessed CI pages an average of 176.7 times on 14.8 distinct days for 4.9 distinct communities.

Participants viewed CI while we asked semi-structured questions about health, action, and understanding. *Health*: In what ways did leaders assess community health using CI? Which metrics were most useful? *Action*: In what ways did leaders analyze and act with CI? Which metrics were most useful? *Understanding*: What issues did leaders experience interpreting the community data CI presented, if any? Detailed notes were taken during sessions and analyzed for themes pertaining to these research questions.

RESULTS

Leader response to CI was overwhelmingly positive. Quotes show both that CI was useful, and how it provided value: *"Thank you - we have been looking for something like this, and it will be very useful in monitoring the activity and usefulness of our community (and perhaps help us pinpoint areas that need more work)." E3*

Our interviews showed that leaders were successful in using CI for both major design goals: (1) assessing health and value and (2) determining actions to improve community health. For each, we describe which metrics were most useful. However, we also discovered that understanding community data is incredibly complex, leading to further design iterations. In the rest of this section, we present usage and interview data about whether and how leaders were able to interpret and act on CI information.

Most Useful Metrics for Assessing Community Health

In assessing health, leaders most often discussed *participation* data: views, posts, contributor type, and overall activity. Table 1 (right column) indicates how often users actively examined these. Prior literature emphasizes volume of *posts* and community *size* as key health indicators [4,6,14,15,17,37,38]. Instead our data shows that *member views* was by far the most used health indicator. Leaders wanted consumption data focused on participant *demographics*; i.e. consumption by geographical region, business unit, or other sub-groups over time. *"Very interesting to see the nationality, work functions, etc. of members, and extremely useful to discover what kind of posts they are interested in reading." –E1*

However, leaders aired reservations about simple, one-size-fits-all health metrics, pointing out the need to consider specific community goals when measuring success. Specifically, they questioned "bigger is better" measures advocated by both their management and prior literature [14] *"[My managers] want to know about growth in membership... Just because we're the 64th largest community, does that really mean anything? To the extent... you could tie [stats] to a business goal – if your goal is to get the word out about something, this is the kind of community you should have, and these are the kind of stats you should collect." –P2*

Instead leaders were enthusiastic about *content* data—popular topics, value of posts, and most valuable posts. They asked for more analytics like this: *"Very cool... This helps me understand if the content I'm putting out there (digital reputation, primarily) is providing value to the community – I can see that it is!" –B1*

Beyond Passive Analytics to Supporting Action

Leaders were not just interested in passively understanding raw data. Instead CI successfully helped community leaders determine *remedial actions*. The most commonly discussed actionable information were *people* data (see Table 1 for how often users actively examined these). We now discuss four types of information participants report *led to action*:

(1) Identifying particular sub-groups or members for active engagement. Leaders wanted to intervene most often to *engage* with specific subgroups or members, e.g. asking topic experts to contribute new content, soliciting feedback from people who had left the community, tailoring content to sub-groups. They found this information in the *people* data *"You need to know who the people are visiting your community. I need to do something to get more sales people visiting. I need to send communications to them, specifically." –J1*

Leaders were particularly enthusiastic about the *top contributors* metric, using this list to engage with the most popular contributing members to take on informal leadership roles, elicit their feedback, acknowledge stellar contributions, and evaluate their contributions to a team. *"I've been particularly interested in the 'people' area and 'top contributors.' We're trying to create a council of [volunteers] to make sure content is updated." –M1*

To better support this, leaders asked for new analytics to identify other useful types of people such as "experts," "influencers," top contributors from particular geographies, frequent consumers in particular job roles, and so on.

(2) Identifying community health problems that require facilitation. Leaders actively used CI to *diagnose and address current or potential community health problems*. Leaders wanted long-term trend data (e.g. a decline in activity), but were able to use even static data so long as they had baseline "healthy" thresholds (e.g. 'above 10% contributors is good' [37]). *"I look at the metrics and facilitate discussions with community managers based on the metrics. For example, if there's lots of passive file downloading, I will recommend that they start weekly community discussions to facilitate active participation." –A1*

To better support this, leaders asked for more sophisticated analyses of activity *patterns* to identify potential problems. They wanted guidance on metrics relating to their particular goals, since CI targets communities with a variety of goals.

(3) Identifying successful examples to emulate (e.g., popular posts or topics). Participants were constantly looking for *successful precedents* to *emulate* to improve their own community and leadership skills. *"The 'posts' by application chart... tells me that in certain months, it was a forum reply that really caught on. So then I can go back into my community... and look at it and when I compare it with those forums that I created this month, it reveals whether it was the language of the forum, or if it was the aesthetic beauty of the forum that really made the difference, or was it the positioning of the forum that made the difference. So that comparative study that I could do is really important." –K1*

To better support this, leaders wanted automated ways of identifying "successful" content or actions. They also wanted to look *outside their community*, to identify other communities or community content they might learn from. *"Benchmarking my community against others can help me understand how I am doing... in the area of getting my community members to engage and participate. I might want to contact other community managers who have higher rates of engagement / posting than I do to get some ideas on how to improve participation rates." –W1*

(4) Evaluating effects of particular actions/events in the community to aid future planning. Leaders examined CI to *evaluate the effects of particular actions or events* to *help with future planning.* Most leaders organized regular events involving phone conferences or presentations that members could attend. Leaders logged how many people attended, downloaded event materials, discussed the meeting, and so on. Leaders used this information to select popular topics for future events or modify the format or timing of meetings so more people could attend. *"If we run a call and most of the people who are attending are downloads instead of live attendees, maybe we have a bad meeting time for that particular call." –P2*

Often leaders wanted to evaluate *their own actions*, e.g., sending out a newsletter or creating new content, using uptake data to make improvements. *"We are thinking about writing more blogs. We want to see if writing blogs has an impact in the community. So we want to be able to select a particular day/time when a blog was posted and see what the metrics look like before and after." –M1*

To better understand their impact, leaders wanted to examine data for specific time periods close to an event, to see how their action or event affected long-term trends.

Contextualized Analytics: from Passive Data to Understanding

Interpreting analytics was a major challenge for leaders. We heard many comments like "How does 13% contributors compare with other communities?" and "Now that I know the number of posts, what do I *do* with it?"

We knew from our initial interviews that *interpretation* of analytics was critical, so we designed the "help & tips" to better support interpretation and action. However, help was not enough. Leaders needed *contextualized analytic* support for *sensemaking*, i.e. data presentations that provide context for interpretability. We therefore worked with leaders to identify their main types of sensemaking activities:

(1) *Compare with meaningful general baselines:* compare my community's data with 'good' and 'bad' thresholds derived from norms for the enterprise.

(2) *Compare with related communities:* compare my community's data with other similar communities. *"How healthy is my group compared to the average characteristics of the same category of group (I assume there is some categorization that makes sense)." –D1*

(3) *Relate to critical events:* ability to view data in the context of specific known events (e.g. by looking at the time period during which that event occurred). *"Being able to go in and see changes in activity based on date... That way we could say, 'we tried this on this particular day, and for the next two weeks we saw what were the biggest changes.'" –P2*

(4) *Relate to leader interventions:* ability to view data in the context of one's own activities (which are inherently understandable to people). *"We had no idea what impact if any we were having. Until we came across Community Insights, that let us know that some of the things that we've been trying, and posting, and event managing within the community seem to have some effect." –P1*

(5) *Spot exceptions:* pointing out 'unusual' data (like a spike in readership or a drop in membership). *"If a file suddenly stopped getting downloads or a wiki page suddenly flat lined, maybe we should get rid of the page." –P2*

(6) *Relate to goals:* identifying which metrics answer common leader questions or indicate success on common goals. Participants wanted community data tied to *concrete, positive business outcomes*, like increased sales, productivity, employee skills, relationships, and so on. *"Our*

goals are to drive traffic to build skills, share knowledge, achieve skill enhancement... get the membership to be more social and collaborative... Are there key metrics that help us indicate these goals?" –R1

Interpretation was a challenge for initial interview participants in early email feedback. However as we have already seen, CI did enable leaders to *relate trend data to particular events and interventions*, where leaders explored changes surrounding those events against baseline data. Trend data also enabled leaders to *spot exceptions*, which appeared as spikes and dips in time-based charts, for example, the spike in membership in Fig. 2 (top).

We iteratively updated CI to support some of the other types of sensemaking activities. We added the "suggested interpretation & use" text underneath each widget (Fig. 2, top) as an iterative change, and added tips there that explicitly described *known performance baselines* from prior literature (e.g. the *contributor type* metric has the tip: 'successful communities have about 10% members contributing' [17,37]). We also included *exceptions* that leaders should watch out for (e.g. the *membership change* metric has a tip alerting leaders about drops in membership and to contact members who have left for feedback). (We leave addressing *compare with related communities* and *relate to goals* to future work.) This change met with positive feedback from users: *"One more thing I 'love' on the tool: the interpretation suggestions. One may agree fully or argue... but the thing is that it gives sense and food for thinking about the graphics." –E2*

DISCUSSION AND CONCLUSIONS

Systematically evaluated leader-centric community tool: We have iteratively deployed CI with community leaders from 470 communities over 10 months, gathering detailed feedback. Despite the importance of proactive leader focused efforts [2,15,17,35], as far as we are aware CI is the first leader-centric community tool, and certainly the first one to be actively co-developed integrating leader feedback.

New empirical findings: Our empirical contributions are to (a) *re-evaluate metrics* using leader feedback to determine their utility, (b) show that leaders want actionable data presenting the interventions they want the system to inform, and (c) show that raw data is inadequate to support sensemaking so contextualized analytics are needed. These empirical findings are embodied in our system. Finally our interviews suggested a major difference between enterprise and internet communities as we saw few examples of misbehaviors, e.g. trolling, which are commonly reported in internet communities.

Rethinking metrics – less generic and more actionable: Prior literature emphasizes *growth* in both *volume of posts* and *community size* as key health metrics [4,6,14,37,38]. In contrast our interview and usage data show that leaders were most concerned to see *views* as a health indicator. Overall however, leaders doubted that simple metrics alone were particularly useful, as communities have very different goals overall and are at different phases of their existence [14,37,38]. Instead, leaders found more value in metrics linked to actions that helped them facilitate community goals. While prior work on community building guidelines describes multiple, often conflicting metrics and actions that leaders might take to create "successful" communities, it does not usually evaluate these or link them to system support. Our results suggest the need to develop new metrics focused around achieving specific actions within the community, rather than focusing on overall growth measures. These empirical observations also have direct design implications for tools to help leaders.

New types of action-oriented analyses: We were able to support action-oriented analyses by implementing 'tips' about how leaders could exploit community analytics. In these tips, we guided leaders to the best metrics for identifying: particular members and sub-groups for leaders to engage; problems that require leader remediation; successful examples for leaders to emulate; and ways to evaluate particular events in the community to help future planning. We have also developed algorithms for assessing the value of content and ranking contributors.

Contextualized analytics: Prior work has not provided or evaluated tools for leaders. It therefore neglects to discuss critical challenges in helping leaders *make sense* of community data. Sensemaking is not just about usability (e.g. readable charts), it is about presenting analytics so leaders can understand their application. To address this, we developed *contextualized analytics*, data presentations that provided adequate context to support interpretability, and proposed six instances. Furthermore, we followed this work with the development of new metrics and visualizations to enable leaders to compare their community with others and explore how their actions have impacted member activity. These new features have been evaluated in a separate study [40].

In the future, CI could support further empirical and theoretical work on communities. For example, prior literature has many proposals on tactics to enhance interaction and participation. CI might provide an evaluation environment in which researchers explore the effects of specific interventions on participation. This would help systematize the currently complex and often competing recommendations in the literature around actual data.

CI might also help advance systems work. Currently we have developed our own algorithms for identifying valued content and top contributors. However, other researchers have developed similar algorithms using machine learning methods and evaluated these using corpus based methods. In future work we might explore actual user reactions to competing algorithms in the context of a working tool, CI.

New research is also needed to explore *extrinsic* metrics, e.g. the impact of community interaction on outcomes like worker productivity or networks. While our measures of post values and top contributors indirectly evaluate content and people for their impact on people's work, it is important to develop new metrics to examine a community's effects outside the context of their internal communications.

We developed a novel user tool created via extensive user-led design that enabled leaders to better assess community health. We discovered critical design characteristics for such tools: they need to support action-oriented information and provide contextualized analytics. Further, we advanced theories about community evaluation metrics. In future work we will extend our tool to contribute to theory and practice in this critical area.

REFERENCES

1. Berge, Z.L. Facilitating computer conferencing: Recommendations from the field. *Educ. Tech. 35*, 1 (1995), 22–30.
2. Bourhis, A., Dubé, L., and Jacob, R. The Success of Virtual Communities of Practice: The Leadership Factor. *Electronic J. of Knowl. Mgt. 3*, 1 (2005), 23–34.
3. Brown, S.I., Tilton, A., and Woodside, D.M. The case for online communities. *McKinsey Quarterly 1*, (2002).
4. Brush, A.J.B., Wang, X., Turner, T.C., and Smith, M.A. Assessing differential usage of usenet social accounting meta-data. *Proc. of CHI*, (2005), 889–898.
5. Butler, B., Sproull, L., Kiesler, S., and Kraut, R. Community effort in online groups: Who does the work and why? In *Leadership at a distance*. Erlbaum, 2002.
6. Butler, B.S. Membership size, communication activity, and sustainability: A resource-based model of online social structures. *Info. Sys. Research 12*, 4 (2001), 346–362.
7. Durant, K.T., McCray, A.T., and Safran, C. Modeling the temporal evolution of an online cancer forum. *Proc. of Health Informatics*, ACM (2010), 356–365.
8. Ebrahim, N.A., Ahmed, S., and Taha, Z. Virtual R&D teams in small and medium enterprises: A literature review. *SSRN eLibrary*, (2009).
9. Farzan, R., DiMicco, J.M., and Brownholtz, B. Spreading the honey: A system for maintaining an online community. *Proc. of GROUP*, (2009), 31–40.
10. Fisher, D., Smith, M., Welser, H.T. You are who you talk to: Detecting roles in Usenet newsgroups. *Proc. of HICSS '06*.
11. Golder, S.A. and Donath, J. Social roles in electronic communities. *Proc. of AoIR*, (2004).
12. Gurzick, D. and White, K.F. A view from Mount Olympus: the impact of activity tracking tools on the character and practice of moderation. *Proc. of GROUP*, (2009), 361–370.
13. Holmes, P. and Cox, A.M. 'Every group carries the flavour of the admins': leadership on Flickr. *Intl. J. of Web Based Communities 7*, 3 (2011), 376.
14. Iriberri, A. and Leroy, G. A life-cycle perspective on online community success. *ACM Comput. Surv. 41*, 2 (2009), 1–29.
15. Kim, A.J. *Community building on the web : Secret strategies for successful online communities*. Peachpit Press, 2000.
16. Koh, J., Kim, Y.-G., Butler, B., Bock, G.-W. Encouraging participation in virtual communities. *Com. ACM 50*, 2, 2007.
17. Kraut, R.E. and Resnick, P. *Building successful online communities: Evidence-based social design*. MIT, 2012.
18. Krieger, M., Stark, E.M., and Klemmer, S.R. Coordinating tasks on the commons: Designing for personal goals, expertise and serendipity. *Proc. of CHI*, (2009), 1485–1494.
19. Leimeister, J.M., Sidiras, P., and Krcmar, H. Success factors of virtual communities from the perspective of members and operators: An empirical study. *Proc. of HICSS*, (2004).
20. Li, C. and Bernoff, J. *Groundswell: Winning in a world transformed by social technologies*. Harvard Bus., 2008.
21. Lithium Technologies, Inc. *Community health index for online communities*. 2011.
22. Ludford, P., Cosley, D., Frankowski, D., Terveen, L. Think different: increasing online community participation using uniqueness and group dissimilarity. *Proc. of CHI*, (2004).
23. Muller, M., Ehrlich, K., Matthews, T., Perer, A., Ronen, I., and Guy, I. Diversity among enterprise online communities. *Proc. of CHI*, (2012), 2815–2824.
24. Nunes, S., Ribeiro, C., David, G. WikiChanges: exposing Wikipedia revision activity. *Proc. of WikiSym*, (2008).
25. Van Oostendorp, H. Van Varik, F. Stimulation of activity in online communities. *Proc. of ECCE*, (2011), 163–170.
26. Pal, A., Farzan, R., Konstan, J.A., and Kraut, R.E. Early detection of potential experts in question answering communities. In J.A. Konstan, R. Conejo, J.L. Marzo and N. Oliver, eds., *User Modeling, Adaption and Personalization*. Springer, Berlin, 2011, 231–242.
27. Preece, J. *Online communities: Designing usability and supporting sociability*. Wiley, 2000.
28. Saint-Onge, H. and Wallace, D. *Leveraging communities of practice for strategic advantage*. Butterworth, 2002.
29. Stuckey, B. Making the Most of the Good Advice: Meta-Analysis of Guidelines for Establishing an Internet-Mediated Community of Practice. *Proc. of WBC*.
30. Suh, B., Chi, E.H., Kittur, A., Pendleton, B.A. Lifting the veil: Improving accountability and social transparency in Wikipedia with wikidashboard. *Proc. of CHI* '08, 1037-1040.
31. Turner, T., Smith, M., Fisher, D., and Welser, H. Picturing Usenet: Mapping computer-mediated collective action. *J. of Computer-Mediated Com. 10*, 4 (2005).
32. Viégas, F.B., Wattenberg, M., and Dave, K. Studying cooperation and conflict between authors with *history flow* visualizations. *Proc. of CHI*, (2004), 575–582.
33. Wanas, N., El-Saban, M., Ashour, H., Ammar, W. Automatic scoring of online discussion posts. *Proc. of WICOW*, (2008).
34. Welser, H.T., Gleave, E., Fisher, D., and Smith, M. Visualizing the signatures of social roles in online discussion groups. *J. of Soc. Structure 8*, 2 (2007), 1–32.
35. Wenger, E., McDermott, R.A., and Snyder, W. *Cultivating communities of practice: A guide to managing knowledge*. Harvard Bus., 2002.
36. Wenger, E., Smith, J.D., and White, N. *Digital habitats: Stewarding technology for communities*. CPsquare, 2012.
37. Whittaker, S., Terveen, L., Hill, W., Cherny, L. The dynamics of mass interaction. *Proc. of CSCW* '98, 257–264.
38. Whittaker, S. Talking to strangers: An evaluation of the factors affecting electronic collaboration. *Proc. of CSCW*, (1996), 409–418.
39. Williams, R. and Cothrel, J. Four smart ways to run online communities. *Sloan Mgt. Rev. 41*, 4 (2000), 81–92.
40. Xu, A., Chen, J., Matthews, T., Muller, M., and Badenes, H. CommunityCompare: Visually comparing communities for online community leaders in the enterprise. *Proc. of CHI*, (2013).
41. Zhang, J., Ackerman, M.S., and Adamic, L. Expertise networks in online communities: Structure and algorithms. *Proc. of WWW*, (2007), 221–230.
42. Zhang, W. and Storck, J. Peripheral members in online communities. (2001).
43. Zhu, H., Kraut, R.E., Wang, Y.-C., Kittur, A. Identifying shared leadership in Wikipedia. *Proc of CHI* '11, 3431-3434.

CommunityCompare: Visually Comparing Communities for Online Community Leaders in the Enterprise

Anbang Xu [1], Jilin Chen [2], Tara Matthews [2], Michael Muller [3], Hernan Badenes [4]
[1] Department of Computer Science, University of Illinois, Urbana, IL, USA, xu26@illinois.edu
[2] IBM Research - Almaden, San Jose, CA, USA, {jilinc, tlmatthe}@us.ibm.com
[3] IBM Research - Cambridge, Cambridge, MA, USA, michael_muller@us.ibm.com
[4] IBM, Buenos Aires, Argentina, hbadenes@ar.ibm.com

ABSTRACT
Online communities are important in enterprises, helping workers to build skills and collaborate. Despite their unique and critical role fostering successful communities, community leaders have little direct support in existing technologies. We introduce CommunityCompare, an interactive visual analytic system to enable leaders to make sense of their community's activity with comparisons. Composed of a parallel coordinates plot, various control widgets, and a preview of example posts from communities, the system supports comparisons with hundreds of related communities on multiple metrics and the ability to learn by example. We motivate and inform the system design with formative interviews of community leaders. From additional interviews, a field deployment, and surveys of leaders, we show how the system enabled leaders to assess community performance in the context of other comparable communities, learn about community dynamics through data exploration, and identify examples of top performing communities from which to learn. We conclude by discussing how our system and design lessons generalize.

Author Keywords
Online communities; community leaders; visualization; iterative design; system evaluation; enterprise; workplace.

ACM Classification Keywords
H.5.3 [Information Interface and Presentation]: Group and Organization Interfaces – Collaborative computing.

INTRODUCTION
Online communities have become prevalent in enterprises, with widespread accessibility of social software and increased recognition of their benefits to businesses. These benefits include overcoming geographic and organizational barriers to collaboration and knowledge sharing [10, 34]; enhancing skills and abilities to execute and coordinate tasks [4, 16]; improving quality while reducing cost [10]; promoting internal and external innovation [18]; and so on.

Community leaders are responsible for and critical in enabling such benefits of enterprise communities [3]. Their unique role involves *assessing* community progress on goals and *intervening* in the community to guide the group towards achieving those goals. Such interventions include encouraging contributions and discussion, contributing and reading content, organizing and curating content, answering questions, moderating, creating a positive environment, advertising the community externally, and maintaining infrastructure. While prior work has documented leader strategies for carrying out these interventions that can enhance community operation [14, 16, 17, 26, 34], there is a critical gap between these guidelines and the actual practice of facilitating valuable communities. Static guidelines cannot help; rather dynamic community analysis tools are needed.

In this work, we propose to facilitate community leaders' understanding of communities through a visualization system. Specifically, we present the design and evaluation of CommunityCompare, an interactive visual analytic system aimed to better enable community leaders to make sense of their own community's online activity through comparisons with other communities on multiple metrics. The system was motivated by formative interviews with leaders within our company, which highlighted the need for better tools to understand community metrics in order to inform leadership activities. We chose visualization as our solution as it is known to support digestion of complex multivariate data [15] and rapid learning [28].

There is virtually no research on tools for community leaders [20]. Prior visualization of online communities often focused on uncovering insights for *research* purposes [12, 23, 25, 31], or on supporting *member* needs [4, 29, 30] rather than leader needs. In contrast, CommunityCompare is a tool aimed at *community leaders,* designed to support specific needs and use cases, which were derived from formative interviews. These use cases included (1) contextualizing community performance assessments with comparisons, (2) interpreting community dynamics, and (3) identifying example communities from which to learn.

We evaluated CommunityCompare via interviews with leaders near the end of our design cycle and surveys conducted after a one-month field deployment within our company. This research addresses two questions:

RQ1: *Will a metric-based visual analytic system for comparing communities satisfy community leaders' needs? How will the tool be used?*

RQ2: *How should we design such a system effectively for community leaders? What design lessons can we learn?*

We offer both system and empirical contributions: a novel system that supports critical needs of community leaders, and extensive feedback from community leaders about how they used the system and ways to improve its design.

We begin with a review of prior research. We then present initial interviews that motivated the creation of CommunityCompare, followed by our system design and an example usage scenario. Next, we present the evaluation of CommunityCompare, in the form of additional in-person interviews and post-deployment surveys, including a description of uses and design lessons. We finish with a discussion of how this work can inform future designs.

RELATED WORK

Assessing Community Health and Success

Much research has focused on how to foster healthy and successful online communities, within and outside organizations, e.g. [16, 17, 26, 34]. Active community leaders are responsible for and critical in fostering successful communities [3, 34]. Among the activities successful leaders do, several authors have discussed the importance of assessing community health to motivate improvements [14, 34]. Presenting community leaders with quantitative health or success metrics could help them with this task.

Success metrics have been proposed in prior literature, although they are rarely validated [14, 17]. Some of the more common success metrics include number of members [14, 19, 22, 24, 26], number of contributions [9, 14, 22, 24, 26], number of threads [9, 24], number of replies [9, 24], threads with responses [9], delay in response time to a topic or a reply [9], quality of relationships [14, 22, 26], reciprocity among members [26], and member satisfaction [26]. For comparison purposes, a few researchers propose normalized metrics, such as messages per unit time [26], messages per topic [24] and messages per person [22, 24].

We leverage this work to select metrics for CommunityCompare and go beyond it to validate their usefulness to leaders in community comparisons.

Visualization Systems for Exploring Communities

A variety of systems have been designed to visualize online groups and communities. Whereas most of these systems are aimed at *community members* or *researchers*, our work differs in its focus on *community leaders* as end-users. Leaders' roles and needs are significantly different from members because they are expected to *intervene* in the community to ensure its success. The only other tool we are aware of that was designed to support community leaders is Community Insights [20]. CommunityCompare was added to the Community Insights system and deployed with the same set of users after they described the need to contextualize community metrics through community comparisons, something not supported in the initial Community Insights system [20]. These results, along with our formative interviews presented below, helped motivate this work.

A number of systems have been developed to support the needs of online community *members*. As an early project in this space, Netscan [4, 29] offered visual dashboards for Usenet users to track metrics and contents in newsgroups. Netscan provided a comparison of various Usenet groups so that people could decide which groups they might want to join based on their topic or activeness. More recently, WikiDashboard [30] visualized how other users have edited Wikipedia articles over time, so as to build a user's trust in articles through increased transparency. Many Eyes was proposed as a valuable tool for creating visualizations in a collaborative setting [8].

Researchers have long explored community datasets through visualization. History Flow [31] and WikiChanges [23] visualized a history of content changes in Wikipedia articles to show the evolution of article content over time. Multiple systems, including SocialAction [25] and Vizster [12], visualize the social networks of online groups to uncover the social structure among individuals.

Such visualizations help to enhance our understanding of community dynamics, motivating the present work. The main limitation of these systems is that they were not designed to support the needs of community leaders.

RESEARCH CONTEXT

This research was conducted within a global company offering technology products and services to businesses. The company widely encouraged employee leadership of, and participation in, internal (intranet only) online communities. To support this, the company made available to all employees a software suite that supports the creation of online communities. This software enabled a community leader to configure multiple social and collaboration tools to meet community needs, including: Discussion Forums, Blogs, Wikis, Files (modeled after [27]), Bookmarks (modeled after [21]), Activities [35], Ideation Blogs (posting, commenting on, and voting for "ideas"), Media Gallery (social repository for videos), and Feeds. The major goals of these communities included sharing information, building skills and professional networks, and collaborating on deliverables. Employees participated from diverse organizations, including sales, marketing, consulting, software/hardware development, and customer support. Participation was usually voluntary, although some employees were "strongly encouraged" to participate in specific communities, and some had community leadership in their job responsibilities.

MOTIVATING INTERVIEWS

Our design was motivated by a set of formative interviews with community leaders in our company. We conducted one-hour, semi-structured, phone interviews with 12 community leaders, representing communities of diverse sizes, ages, and types, about their practice and needs. These interviews revealed a broad range of needs and challenges of community leaders. Here, we present a portion of the results focused on community comparisons.

All community leaders we interviewed wanted to compare their community's performance metrics with others for various reasons. Ultimately, the reasons they discussed were all tied to a desire to *take action* to improve their community. The comparative information they desired was intended to help them plan concrete actions in the community, such as improving performance along lagging metrics or reaching out to successful leaders for advice.

One highly discussed reason was assessing community performance in the context of other comparable communities. Leaders discussed how performance metrics, such as percentage of contributors or rate of posting, were difficult to interpret in isolation. In the words of one leader:

> "*As a community manager, I'd like to benchmark my community against other active communities. Where does my community rank? Knowing this information helps me understand how well I am doing to engage my community members...*" [P1]

Several leaders had already adopted a practice of comparing communities, which had helped them better interpret their own community's performance. However, the process was laborious. One leader described her manual comparisons with others and what she learned about participation rates:

> "*There's certain communities I keep an eye on – I poll to see what's trending as far as what seems to be average percentage of members participating. Seems to me based on ones that I look at, 2-3% of your membership participating seems like kind of average right now. Your high performing communities are anywhere from 7-10% other membership participating. And if you have over 10%, chances are you're probably looking at a required space for people being told they have to go and do something.*" [P2]

Meanwhile, leaders also wanted to identify top performing communities through metric comparison, so that they could learn from these communities. According to one leader:

> "*I might want to contact other community managers who have higher rates of engagement / posting than I do to get some ideas on how to improve participation rates.*" [P3]

Many leaders recognized that diversity of communities affected such comparisons. They stressed that comparisons are only meaningful when the communities being compared share key similarities, explicitly discussing their type, size, and maturity level or age as important.

As community leaders currently have no tool to help with these community comparison needs, we set out to address them with CommunityCompare. In particular, we designed for three use cases that community leaders mentioned in interviews:

1) *assess community performance* by comparing a community with other similar communities;

2) *interpret dynamics of communities* so they can plan interventions;

3) *identify top performing example communities* so that they can learn from the leaders of these communities.

SYSTEM DESIGN

We designed CommunityCompare, an intranet application that visualizes a number of communities along multiple metrics, so that a community leader can compare her community with others. Through such comparison we support the three use cases described in the prior section.

We included eight health and success metrics in our system that are commonly proposed in prior literature (Figure 1a). These measure community size [6, 17], community age [14, 34], member activity [6, 9, 14, 22, 26], owner (leader) activity [3], views (the total number of visits) [17], and contributors (the number of members who have contributed at least one piece of content) [1]. Since leaders and members use forums differently from other media such as wikis and blogs [22], we showed activity on forums separately from other media. In our system, *forum activity* is the number of forum posts, while *publication* is the total number of posts on files, blogs, wiki, feeds and bookmarks.

Given the design goals and the selection of metrics, we approached the design of our system by reasoning through four design aspects: (1) *metrics presentation*, i.e. how to present the metrics so as to support assessment and interpretation; (2) *time frame and scales*, i.e. in what time frame and scale metrics are visualized; (3) *selecting communities*, i.e. how leaders select communities to compare in the system; and (4) *identifying examples*, i.e. how leaders can identify top performing example communities from which to learn. Below we describe our design process according to these four aspects.

Metric Presentation

We designed the metrics presentation to support metric-based assessment. We chose an interactive visualization because visualization is known to facilitate digestion of multivariate data [15] and rapid learning [28].

We adopted a parallel coordinates plot (PCP) as the central visualization technique for two reasons: (1) a PCP displays multiple metrics at once allowing efficient assessment [33]; and (2) representing data points as polylines on multiple axes helps leaders reason about the relationship between metrics [13]. Two enhancements were made to PCP [11]: (1) to let leaders easily follow connectivity between axes, we smoothed the poly-line curves in the PCP; (2) to allow easier identification of visual clusters on each axis, we made the curves flat at coordinate intersections.

Throughout the paper, we refer to the PCP as the system's *main chart* (Figure 1a). Leaders can re-arrange the order of the axes through drag-and-drop, so the order of axes for a user may not follow the same order shown in Figure 1a. In the main chart, the community led by the current user of the system is highlighted in orange. The main chart was implemented using the Data-Driven Documents (D3) [2].

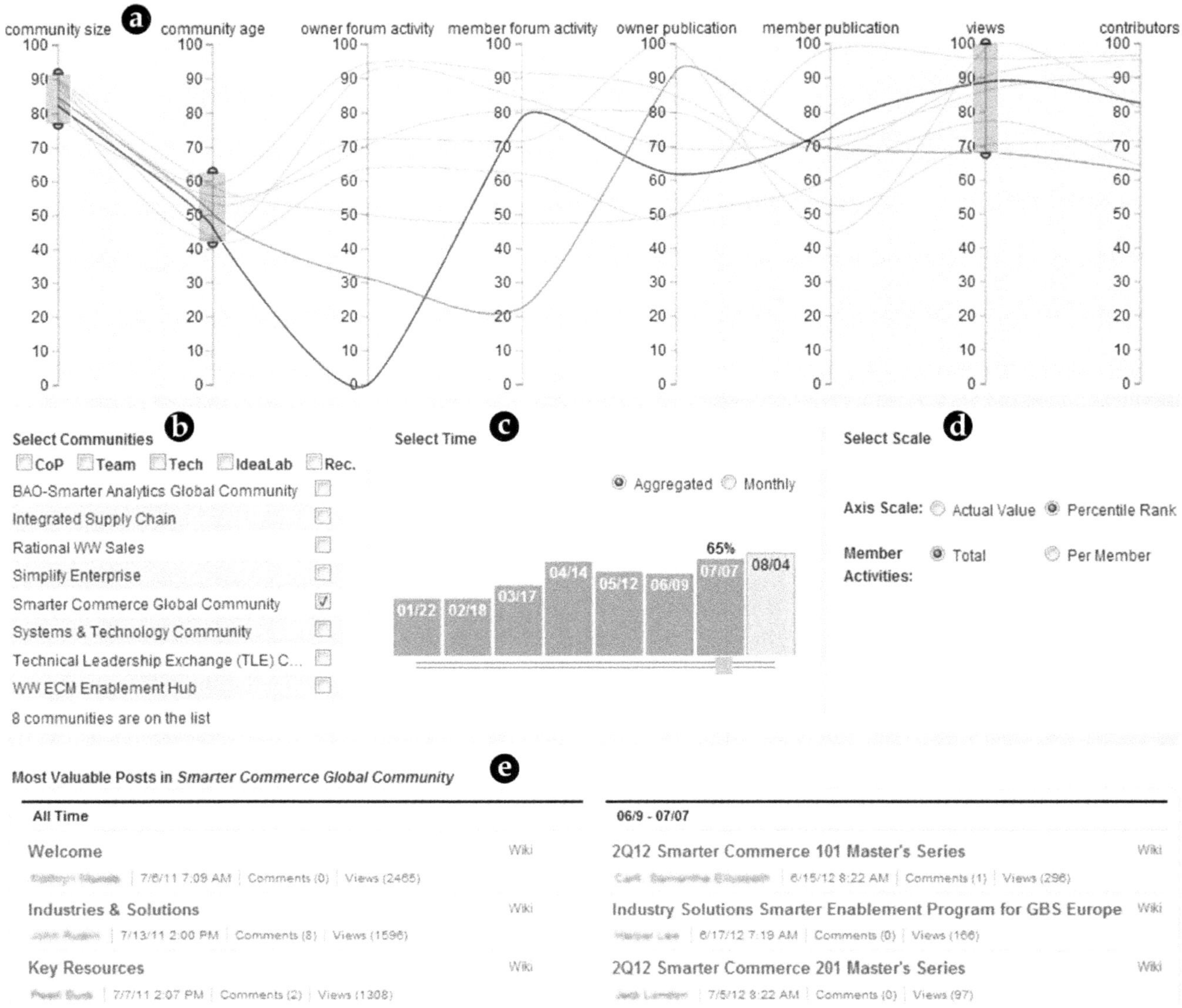

Figure 1. A Screenshot of The CommunityCompare System.

A user tries to find communities of similar *size* and *age* as her community, and with more *views* than hers. Each line in the main chart (a) represents a community; the user's community is highlighted in orange. She creates three visual filters on the main chart (a) to filter communities according to her criteria. The communities shown in (a) are also available as a list (b). Checking a community in the list (b), highlights it in black in the main chart (a). Clicking the name of a community in the list (b) loads its most valuable posts below (e). Two other widgets (c, d) are used to change the time frames and scales in (a). Note that the system will update the axis labels automatically according to the user's "member activities" choice in (d) (e.g. from *views* here to *views per member* in Figure 2).

Time Frame and Scales

The CommunityCompare metrics (see Figure 1a) can be calculated for different time frames and in different scales. For time, each metric can be calculated and viewed in the main chart over the lifetime of a community (*Aggregated*) or on a per month basis (*Monthly*) (Figure 1c). The height of each bar in the timeline in Figure 1c represents the average percentile rank of the metrics of the user's community in the corresponding month.

For scale, prior studies on communities have calculated member activity both in the aggregate and on a per member basis [22], and have made various data transformations [7]. A *Select Scale* widget (Figure 1d) was designed to provide these options for leaders. Users can switch between *Total* and *Per Member*, which makes the main chart display each of the four member metrics (*member forum activity*, *member publication*, *views*, and *contributors*) either as a sum of all members or as a per member average. Leaders can also switch from *Actual Value* to *Percentile Rank*. In the latter option, the main chart displays each metric not in its absolute value, but in its percentile rank against all other communities. This option helps leaders understand the relative position of their community on each metric with respect to all others; and it normalizes the distribution of communities on metrics, thus alleviating visual clutters in the main chart caused by highly skewed distributions (e.g. if many communities had few members they would be clustered at the bottom of the *community size* axis).

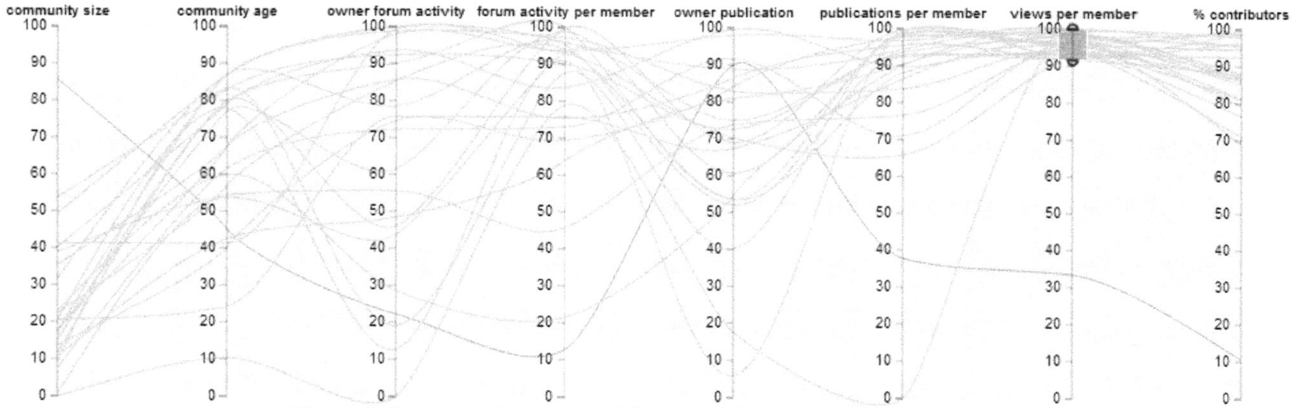

Figure 2. Interpret Dynamics of Communities through Visual Filters.
A user investigates factors related to high member views by creating a visual filter at the top of the *views per member* axis. To explore the relationships among metrics, the user can create one or more visual filters to examine a subset of polylines. She first creates a visual filter on the low end of the *views per member* axis and then drags it from low to high along the axis to see how the distribution changes.

Selecting Communities

CommunityCompare supports *filtering* communities shown in the main chart and list (Figure 1b) and *highlighting* lines in a darker color in the main chart.

Filtering: Our initial motivating interviews suggested that leaders wanted to limit comparisons to other communities similar in size and age to theirs. Thus, we allowed leaders to create visual *filters* on any individual axis in the main chart, by drawing a box around a range on the axis. Communities within the range of the box are highlighted to reflect the selection, while other communities disappear until the box is removed [33]. These filters therefore supported selecting communities not only according to similarity in size and age, but according to arbitrary criteria on any of the eight metrics we provided.

The *Select Communities* list (Figure 1b) names the communities in the main chart. As users create filters to select communities, the set of communities listed changes.

Highlighting: To support comparison with idiosyncratic sets of communities, we enabled users to highlight communities by checking their names in the *Select Communities* list. In initial motivating interviews, leaders also expressed an interest in selecting communities by type. The *Select Communities* list also supports highlighting according to five community types: community of practice (CoP), team, technical support (Tech), IdeaLab and recreation (Rec). Details of these community types can be found in Muller et al. [22].

Identifying Examples

In our initial design we expected leaders to identify top performing example communities from which to learn by creating visual filters on the main chart—leaders can create a filter on the top portion of a metric and the chart and list will show only those communities performing at the top of that metric. However, this solution turned out to be insufficient, because leaders could not fully judge if a community was an appropriate example from metrics alone.

Based on this user feedback, we added the ability to click on a community name in the *Select Communities* list and see that community's most valuable posts in a separate *Valuable Posts* widget (Figure 1e). To support this functionality, we first surveyed community members from a sample subset of communities, asking them to rate a series of community posts on how valuable each was to their work. We then correlated these ratings with objective metrics such as the number of views, recommendations, and replies these posts got, and created a formula to estimate the user-rated value of each post according to the correlation. The system in the end selected the posts to display in the widget according to the formula. Our approach above is comparable to Wanas et al. [32].

USAGE SCENARIO

We demonstrate the use of the CommunityCompare system through a concrete usage scenario of Emma, a hypothetical community leader. Figures 1 and 2 reflect the end-state of this scenario, but many of the earlier steps in the scenario are visible as well.

Assessing Community Performance

Emma knows the total number of posts and views in her community, but is not sure if these reflect a healthy activity level or if she should work harder to facilitate increases. She decides to use CommunityCompare to assess her community by comparing with other communities similar to hers in size and age. She clicks on *Percentile Rank* in the *Select Scale* widget, causing the main chart to show each metric in percentile ranking. She creates a visual filter that covers about 40% on the *community size* axis, with the curve representing her community at the middle of that 40%. She then creates another visual filter on the *community age* axis in a similar fashion. She finds that her community has higher *owner publication* than other communities similar in size, with a percentile rank of 90, i.e. 90% of communities in our system were below hers in *owner publication* (Figure 1a). She is encouraged by the evidence that she is a very active leader compared to leaders in other similar communities.

Emma wonders whether she posts more than her colleague leading the "Smarter Commerce Global Community." She thus chooses this community from the *Select Communities* list (Figure 1b). The main chart then highlights the chosen community in black, and Emma is surprised to find that her colleague does less posting but has higher rates of member activity (see Figure 1a). She makes a mental note to ask her colleague how she accomplished this.

Emma then checks whether members visit her community frequently. She sees that the per member scale is more appropriate here, because this would average out the fact that her community is quite large. So she clicks *Per Member* in the *Select Scale* widget and discovers that the number of *views* of her community is low compared with other communities (see Figure 2).

Interpreting Community Dynamics

Emma is surprised because she had expected her frequent posting to attract member visits. To investigate factors that might increase member visits, she creates a visual filter that covers the top portion of the *views* axis, so as to select all communities with many *views*. As shown in Figure 2, the selected communities spread across the axis on *owner publication*, indicating that communities with high *views* do not necessarily have high *owner publication*. In contrast, the selected communities concentrate at the top of the *% contributors* axis, suggesting that communities with high *views* also tend to have a higher portion of contributing members. Many of these communities also have high *publications per member*. Thus, Emma reasons that perhaps posting more by herself does not attract as many visits as she had thought before; instead it may be more promising to encourage members to share more.

Identifying Top Performing Example Communities

Emma now wants to learn how she might increase member visits by looking at example communities that are doing well on this metric. She wants to find example communities that have similar size and age compared to her community, and at the same time have more views than hers. To achieve this, she creates two visual filters on the *community size* and *community age* axes around her community, and creates another filter on the *views* axis above her community (Figure 1a). Note that since her filter on *community size* has already taken into account the size of her community, the visualization of *views per member* is similar to the visualization of *views* in total. She now sees 8 communities shown in the main chart (Figure 1a) and listed in the *Select Communities* widget (Figure 1b). She wants to know what has been posted in these communities, so she clicks on the name of each community in the list to view their top posts (Figure 1e). She sees several examples of posts that give her new ideas for discussion topics in her community. She then saves the list of communities and decides to contact the leaders to learn more about their activities.

EVALUATION

We evaluated CommunityCompare through both in-person interviews and post-deployment surveys. The in-person interviews helped us obtain detailed qualitative feedback from community leaders and refine our design. The post-deployment surveys helped us obtain feedback from more leaders who had used the system in realistic settings.

a) Learned something new about my community	6.6 (0.6)
Planed actions to improve my community	6.1 (1.2)
Understood communities' performance by comparison	5.8 (1.2)
Explored relationships between metrics I care about	5.4 (1.5)
Identified good examples that I may learn from	5.1 (1.5)
b) CommunityCompare was easy to learn and use	5.5 (1.1)
Easy to find specific other communities to compare	5.2 (1.4)
The system includes metrics that I care about	5.7 (1.1)
Easy to select wanted time spans using *Select Time*	5.0 (1.8)
Understood and used the metric scales in *Select Scales*	5.0 (1.4)

Table 1. Usefulness and Usability of CommunityCompare. Shows the average ratings with standard deviations in brackets from 44 community leaders, where 7 means "strongly agree" with a statement and 1 means "strongly disagree" with it.

In-Person Interviews

We interviewed 15 community leaders near the end of our design cycle. Interviews lasted one hour and were audio recorded and transcribed.

Interviews were split into three parts: a pre-interview (15 minutes), a system walkthrough (30 minutes), and a post interview (15 minutes). In the pre-interview, we asked the participant about their role and community goals. Then we asked the participant to describe the activity levels of their community and how they thought it compared with others. In the system walkthrough, participants were introduced to the system and then explored it openly (i.e., without specific tasks) using a think-aloud protocol. In the post-interview, we repeated the same questions about community activity and how their community compared with others. Then we asked the participants what they did and did not like about the system and how they might use the system in their leadership work.

Post-Deployment Surveys

We deployed the CommunityCompare system within our company on July 16. At the time of this writing the system had been deployed for 10 weeks and served 500 intranet communities.

We conducted a survey one month after the deployment began. We invited 150 community leaders who had used the system at least once (according to log data) to complete the web-based survey and received 44 valid responses (30% participation rate). The survey contained ten seven-point Likert-scale questions about the usefulness and usability of CommunityCompare (see Table 1), and five open-ended questions about how leaders used CommunityCompare and what would make it better.

Participants

Participants for both the interviews and the survey were community leaders within the company studied. Together, these leaders had varied years of experience in community leadership: 28% of participants had been a community leader for more than 2 years, 35% for 1-2 years, and 27% for less than 1 year. Most of participants (86%) stated that community leadership is required or important to their job. A majority of participants (65%) currently led one or two communities.

RESULTS

Overall community leaders responded positively to our system and found it useful for assessing community performance, interpreting community dynamics, and identifying example communities (see survey results in Table 1). Meanwhile, qualitative feedback gathered from the interviews and surveys revealed richer details into the usage of the system. Below we organize these details according to our two design questions: how was the system used and what lessons did we learn for designing a community comparison system for leaders.

Use of the CommunityCompare System

We present qualitative results describing the use of the system around our three use cases: assessing community performance, interpreting community dynamics, and identifying top performing example communities. All the use cases were strongly influenced by leaders' desire to *take action* based on community data. Though CommunityCompare does not support scientifically rigorous interpretations of community data, our participants appreciated that it enabled them to take more informed action than they could without it.

Assessing Community Performance

Participants not only said they found the system highly useful for evaluating their community's performance, they *demonstrated* it with dramatically different descriptions of their community's performance before versus after using CommunityCompare. Before using the system, participants made short and vague evaluations based on impressions from their day-to-day leadership work, e.g., "*If I would guess, I would say it's about average*" [P4]; "*we are pretty active.*" [P5]

In contrast, after using the system, participants were able to concretely discuss a *more thorough and more accurate* understanding of their community's performance.

> "*[Referring to % contributors under the monthly view] we are 90%...We have a high percentage of contributors this month. [Switch to aggregated view] 70% overall.... We have many members that are contributing. That's very positive. My perception was much lower than that. I think I see the same people contributing over and over again in that community. So I would guess that to be much lower.*" [P4]

> "*We are better than I thought. I thought we are insufficient in our usage of forum... Compared to other industry communities, ours is not bad. I think they are struggling on the same stuff we are.*" [P6]

Furthermore, they often described ways they wanted to take action on what they learned in CommunityCompare:

> "*That's interesting to see that our owners are publishing far more than similar size communities and similar age... But we need to think about the forum [Referring to member forum posts]. Ours is zero. I know they [members] are not using it [the forum]... That tells me I still have work to do: getting more people [members] to contribute.*" [P5]

Participants also often referred to numbers in *Percentile Rank* when assessing performance:

> "*Despite my previous opinion on our forum activity that is not very high, it actually is not too bad. I looked at the rank order and aggregated for 63%.*" [P7]

> "*The member publication for that community is close to the 95 percentile... This is not the best community, but overall it gets high marks.*" [P8]

Feedback from the survey echoed the usefulness of the system on assessment and planning action:

> "*I was able to compare metrics across similar communities. It helped me understand areas where I need to focus more going forward.*" [P9]

> "*Able to see trends in key metrics where other related communities are progressing, will help us with planning and strategy to improve participation.*" [P10]

Interpreting Community Dynamics

Community leaders were keen to interpret community dynamics, as this was often necessary to plan their actions. Participants therefore used the visual filters in the system's main chart to create queries on the metrics and to explore the relationships among different metrics of interest. For instance, one participant began the interview with a hypothesis that leaders who post a lot in communities can stimulate member activity. The participant followed our think-aloud protocol when testing this hypothesis in CommunityCompare:

> "*If I draw a little box here to get Top 10 percentile for owner publication, you can see that the member forum activity is all over the place as the member publication activity. So it's not as if I publish more myself, other people will publish too. No, that's not happening. There's no correlated effect there.*"[P11]

The participant then went on to explore other metric relationships that he might use to increase *member forum activity*, by creating another visual filter on that axis and observing common patterns:

> "*So if I want my member forum activity to be in the top 10% percentile... [Draws a box on the top 10th percentile for member forum activity.] What is the common theme here... I can see the size of the community is kinda small. 50 or less [below 50 percentile], right?... % contributors is kinda large. It cannot prove causality here but that's interesting, right?*"[P11]

Explorations like this were not scientifically rigorous, and not all participants were able to learn the system fast enough to explore as such. However, all participants who were able to do so praised the usefulness of the insights they gained, which were previously unavailable to them.

Identifying Top Performing Example Communities

Community leaders were highly interested in finding example communities that they could learn from. A subset of interview participants already had example communities from which they drew lessons, although their assessment of "good" was vague due to lack of quantitative comparison. For instance, one participant told us about a list of successful communities she kept as examples:

> "*I have a deck of examples of good communities. I don't know how I would define 'good.' I think that I define them each differently. They've done example of things that I think are good and I think it could be helpful to their members.*" [P12]

During the interviews, a majority of participants discussed successful example communities they identified using our system. Participants were interested in learning from these example communities, again to inform their own actions.

Importantly, our system allowed participants to identify previously *unknown* example communities in an *easy* and *systematic* fashion—users could simply name a metric to maximize and immediately see the best communities on that metric. If desired, they could make more complex visual filters (like in Figure 1a) so as to find top performing communities satisfying certain constraints:

> "*This is showing me communities that I never would have found on my own. I probably never would come across to actually get some examples like 'Europe Transformation' I would never have found that... It looks like it's a highly successful community and I'd like to learn more about it.*"[P12]

Finding previously unknown, successful communities helped leaders plan how to improve their own communities by example. In the post-deployment survey, several respondents indicated they had learned from example communities, e.g., by identifying "*what kinds of content is being used in high participation communities*"[P22] and "*get[ting a] better sense of how I can add most value content to my own community*" [P23].

Participants also used these example communities to discover new collaboration opportunities. A Marketing community leader described his reflections upon seeing that related Sales communities were performing worse than his:

> "*[Referring to communities just found] As Marketing, one of our objectives is to progress pipeline as related to most Sales and general activities. You know, can I help them [Sales]? Can I contribute to their communities? Or can our community get or use more content [from the Sales communities]?*" [P13]

Design Lessons Learned

The CommunityCompare system was a design exploration—even though we knew about leaders' high-level needs, there were many uncertainties about exactly what comparison capabilities they would want. In this subsection we address our second research question by presenting three main design lessons we learned from users.

Are These Communities Similar? Depends on the Leader

Many leaders in initial motivating interviews mentioned the necessity of comparing with *similar* communities, and used size, age and type as example criteria. These are also common criteria used in the literature to categorize communities [6, 14, 22]. We therefore supported a range of options for selecting communities, including selection by metrics like size and age, by community type, and by choosing individual communities from a list.

Surprisingly, while leaders found these options useful (Table 1b), they were far from satisfied. Leaders often initially selected communities based on metrics like size and age, but they quickly started customizing comparisons by selecting and deselecting communities from the list in the *Select Communities* widget. Leaders explained that selecting by metrics and community types were too coarse grained, and each leader often had a different opinion about exactly what communities were similar or comparable.

We uncovered various notions of similarity that were unknown before designing the system by observing what communities leaders actually selected and asking them to explain. These notions of similarity include shared community goals (e.g. broadcasting information, member discussion), related topical focus (e.g. marketing, sales), and related organizational structures (e.g. within the same business division, managed by a known colleague). However, it was challenging for users to discover other communities with these attributes from the list.

Leaders suggested ways the system could better facilitate comparing with the right set of communities. These included finding communities that shared members with theirs, that shared keywords in titles or tags, or that other leaders had identified. One leader explained the first idea:

> "*Select among my communities and find communities with shared membership using the slide bar range tool to go from 0-100% overlap.*" [P14]

Overall, the notion of "similar communities" contained rich nuances and varied greatly between individual leaders. A dedicated query interface may be needed to fully support all these different notions and ways of selecting communities.

Metrics Are Silver, Content Is Golden

Our initial design of the system focused on exploring metrics through parallel coordinates, and did not contain the *Valuable Posts* widget. Early interview feedback quickly motivated us to add the widget, because *making sense* of metrics without seeing sample content was too challenging. Furthermore, leaders wanted to take the next step beyond assessing their community's relative performance—seeing examples helped them formulate concrete ideas about *how to act* on the comparisons:

> "*You can go and see what maybe a good example is and what best of practices are. That's getting a kind of activity you would hope to mimic. I think that's pretty valuable.*" [P15]

The direct connection between quantitative metrics and actual community content was probably the most effective and well-liked novel feature of CommunityCompare. Leaders were able to filter communities by metrics through the main chart, identifying a subset of high performing communities, and then use the *Valuable Posts* widget to learn why those communities were doing well by examining their most popular content:

> "*What I was most interested in was determining what defined a successful community using the slider bars [visual filters in the main chart]. I'd go over and try to pattern community*

demographics to identify groups like ours, identify high performers in terms of collaboration, and then go and look at observable community characteristics... high-hitting posts in the forum, wiki, etc... and try to observe what made them successful." [P16]

"*One of the features I like is being able to drill down on specific communities. You look at the activities of these communities, you know, like forum activities. Then click on one of these communities and being able to drill down on that. I think that's really impressive.*" [P17]

These observations revealed that we did not fully expect beforehand: quantitative metric exploration combined with qualitative content can be a powerful combo for community leaders to better make sense of data and learn by example.

Too Complex to Use or Too Few Capabilities?

Comparing community data in ways that support a community leader's interpretation of key performance metrics and ability to make action plans is an incredibly complex analytical task. In our design process, we continuously observed a tension between the system imposed learning curve and the richness of its analytic capabilities. Upon first impression, leaders often commented that the system was overly complex:

"*I'm not sure this is the most user-friendly design for presenting information. It may be. But it was initially challenging to read.*" [P18]

"*I had only a quick look at the system but have to confess I didn't really understand how to use it.*" [P19]

Some of the confusion was caused by unfamiliarity with the parallel coordinates visualization—some leaders initially could not read it without explanation. The availability of different time frames and scales also caused problems—in interviews several leaders reached incorrect conclusions, either because they misunderstood the scale or because they forgot they had changed the scale themselves earlier.

However, after becoming familiar with the system, most participants felt comfortable with the visual representation and interaction modality. One leader commented as such on the process: "*My initial thought is that it has all the same data, but I find it is more useful now.*" [P20]

To understand whether users could overcome analytic complexity longitudinally, we asked survey respondents to report on the usefulness of the various analytic options. Overall, 62% of leaders found the *Percentile Rank* option useful vs. 54% for the *Actual Value* option; 66% of leaders found the *Total* option useful vs. 45% for the *Per Member* option. None of these differences were statistically significant, suggesting that the analytic options were similarly useful in longitudinal usage (also see Table 1b).

Many leaders even started requesting additional options after usage, which would make the system more complex. For example, one leader suggested: "*I would like an additional option of being able to more selectively choose granularity of the timescale for metrics and postings being presented.*" [P21]

These results reflect tensions between novice users who thought the system was complex, and experienced users who desired additional analytic capabilities. Designers of complex analytic system could consider designing a range of different interfaces, from a controlled basic version (e.g. a few pre-selected communities on a few metrics) to a more flexible advanced version (e.g. a dedicated query interface for selection and a set of customizable metrics) [5].

DISCUSSION

Our evaluation of CommunityCompare demonstrated the system's power in the hands of practicing community leaders. We believe our system can be immediately useful to community leaders not only in other enterprises, but also outside traditional organizations. We chose commonly used success metrics that have been used to assess internet communities of practice and interest [14] and open collaboration projects, such as Wikipedia and Apache [7]. As a result, our system can likely be used to empower leaders of these groups.

Our usage scenarios revealed interesting details into the needs and practices of community leaders related to *success metrics*. We explored the usefulness of a set of success metrics for communities commonly proposed in prior literature [14]. Our results show that these metrics are more *meaningful* in the context of other comparable communities and when presented with concrete *examples* of content in those communities. Our system also demonstrates community leaders' interest in using metrics to *inform leadership actions* in their community, such as emulating practices exhibited by high performing communities. Metrics used for comparisons might also be expected to generate competition. However, leaders in our study were more likely to want to learn from or collaborate with leaders of more successful communities, possibly due to their shared organizational context.

Our design lessons provide useful knowledge for designers of complex analytic systems aimed at community leaders. Fundamentally, leaders are not necessarily sophisticated data analysts. That they were able to understand a set of fairly complex analytical capabilities and perform sophisticated explorations of metrics is motivating for future community analytic systems. However, it is important to scaffold novice users with simpler interfaces until they become more experienced. To make the metrics more meaningful and actionable, it was effective to pair them with actual content. We also observed that high level categorizations of communities proposed in prior work [14, 22] were not sufficient for the comparisons leaders wanted to do; instead they had idiosyncratic comparison criteria that would require the ability to define custom sets of communities with which to compare.

There are limitations to the work presented here. CommunityCompare only allows leaders to explore communities on multiple *quantitative* metrics. However, qualitative features like the leader's popularity, organizational support, or the community's topic area can also affect community success [17]. To help leaders assess a broader range of success factors, future systems research might explore how to automatically categorize and integrate such qualitative features. Also, on the basis of the preliminary and promising evaluation results, we intend to evaluate CommunityCompare in a multi-year field study to examine whether the system will lead to more successful communities over time and how it helps leaders take specific actions to improve their communities.

CONCLUSION

The primary contributions of this work are twofold: (1) We presented CommunityCompare, a novel system for leaders of enterprise online communities to compare their community against others on multiple metrics. Through interviews and surveys with community leaders, we showed that leaders can gain new insights into their communities in three ways: (a) assessing community performance by comparison; (b) learning about community dynamics through data exploration; and (c) identifying top performing example communities from which to learn. (2) We drew three key lessons for designing analytic tools for community leaders: (a) selecting communities to compare against requires the flexibility to create custom sets; (b) quantitative metric exploration combined with actual content supports leaders' ability to learn by example; and (c) visual analytic systems must strike a difficult balance between novice and experienced users. Future work will enhance the social aspects of the system, connecting related community leaders and better enabling them to share leadership ideas with each other through examples.

REFERENCES

1. Beenen, G., Ling, K., Wang, X., Chang, K., Frankowski, D., Resnick, P., & Kraut, R., Using social psychology to motivate contributions to online communities. In *CSCW*, (2004).
2. Bostock, M., Ogievetsky, V., & Heer., J. D3: Data-Driven Documents. *IEEE TVCG*, *17*, 12, (2011), 2301-2309.
3. Bourhis, A., Dubé, L., & Jacob, R. The Success of Virtual Communities of Practice: The Leadership Factor. *Electronic Journal of Knowledge Management*, *3*, 1, (2005), 23-34.
4. Brush, A.J.B., Wang, X., Turner, T.C., & Smith, M.A., Assessing Differential Usage of Usenet Social Accounting Meta-Data. In *CHI*, (2005).
5. Brusilovsky, P. and Schwarz., E., User as Student: Towards an Adaptive Interface for Advanced Web-Based Applications. In *UM*, (1997).
6. Butler, B.S. Membership Size, Communication Activity, and Sustainability: A Resource-Based Model of Online Social Structures. *Info. Sys. Research*, *12*, 4, (2001), 346–362.
7. Chen, J., Ren, Y., & Riedl, J., The Effects of Diversity on Group Productivity and. Member Withdrawal in Online Volunteer Groups. In *CHI*, (2010).
8. Danis, C.M., Viégas, F.B., Wattenberg, M., & Kriss., J., Your Place or Mine? Visualization as a Community Component. In *CHI*, (2008).
9. Durant, K., McCray, A., & Safran, C., Modeling the Temporal Evolution of an Online Cancer Forum. In *IHI*, (2010).
10. Ebrahim, N.A., Ahmed, S., & Taha, Z. Virtual R&D Teams in Small and Medium Enterprises: A Literature Review. *SSRN eLibrary*, (2009).
11. Graham, M. and Kennedy, J., Using Curves to Enhance Parallel Coordinate Visualisations. In *InfoVis*, (2003).
12. Heer, J. and Boyd, D., Vizster: Visualizing Online Social Networks - In *InfoVis*, (2005).
13. Inselberg, A. and Dimsdale, B., Parallel Coordinates: A Tool for Visualizing Multi-dimensional Geometry. In *Vis*, (1990).
14. Iriberri, A. and Leroy, G. A Life-Cycle Perspective on Online Community Success. *ACM Comput. Surv.*, *41*, 2, (2009), 1-29.
15. Keim, D.A., Mansmann, F., Schneidewind, J., & Ziegler, H., Challenges in Visual Data Analysis. In *InfoVis*, (2006).
16. Kraut, R.E., Resnick, P., et al. *Building Successful Online Communities: Evidence-Based Social Design.* MIT Press, '12.
17. Leimeister, J.M., Sidiras, P., & Krcmar, H., Success Factors of Virtual Communities from the Perspective of Members and Operators: An Empirical Study. In *HICSS*, (2004).
18. Li, C. and Bernoff, J. *Groundswell: Winning in a World Transformed by Social Technologies*. Harvard Bus. Press, '08.
19. Ludford, P., Cosley, D., Frankowski, D., & Terveen, L., Think Different: Increasing Online Community. Participation Using Uniqueness and Group Dissimilarity. In *CHI*, (2004).
20. Matthews, T., Whittaker, S., Badenes, H., Smith, B., Muller, M., E., K., Zhou, M., & Lau, T., Community Insights: Helping Community Leaders Enhance the Value of Enterprise Online Communities. In *CHI*, (2013).
21. Millen, D.R., Feinberg, J., & Kerr, B.D., Social Bookmarking in the Enterprise. In *CHI*, (2006).
22. Muller, M., Ehrlich, K., Matthews, T., Perer, A., Ronen, I., & Guy, I., Diversity among Enterprise Online Communities: Collaborating, Teaming, and Innovating through Social Media. In *CHI*, (2012).
23. Nunes, S., Ribeiro, C., & David, G., WikiChanges: Exposing Wikipedia Revision Activity. In *WikiSyms*, (2008).
24. Oostendorp, H.v. and Varik, F.v., Stimulation of Activity in Online Communities. In *ECCE*, (2011).
25. Perer, A. and Shneiderman, B. Balancing Systematic and Flexible Exploration of Social Networks. *IEEE TVCG*, *12*, 5, (2007), 693-700.
26. Preece, J. *Online Communities: Designing Usability and Supporting Sociability*. John Wiley & Sons, 2000.
27. Shami, N.S., Muller, M., & Millen, D., Browse and Discover: Social File Sharing in the Enterprise. In *CSCW*, (2011).
28. Shneiderman, B. and Maes, P. Direct Manipulation versus Interface Agents *Interactions*, 1997, 42-61.
29. Smith, M. Tools for Navigating Large Social Cyberspaces. *Commun. ACM 45*, 4, (2002), 51-55.
30. Suh, B., Chi, E., Kittur, A., & Pendleton, B., Lifting the Veil: Improving Accountability and Social. Transparency in Wikipedia with WikiDashboard. In *CHI*, (2008).
31. Viégas, F.B., M., W., & Dave, K., Studying Cooperation and Conflict between Authors with history flow Visualizations. In *CHI*, (2004).
32. Wanas, N., El-Saban, M., Ashour, H., & Ammar, W., Automatic Scoring of Online Discussion Posts. *WICOW*, '08.
33. Ward, M.O., XmdvTool: Integrating Multiple Methods for Visualizing. Multivariate Data. In *Vis*, (1994).
34. Wenger, E., McDermott, R.A., & Snyder, W. *Cultivating Communities of Practice: A Guide to Managing Knowledge*. Harvard Business Press, 2002.
35. Yarosh, S., Matthews, T., Moran, T.P., & Smith, B., What Is an Activity? Appropriating an Activity-Centric System. In *INTERACT*, (2009).

Analyzing Crowd Workers in Mobile Pay-for-Answer Q&A

Uichin Lee, Jihyoung Kim[†], Eunhee Yi[‡], Juyup Sung, Mario Gerla[†]
KAIST Knowledge Service Engineering, [†]UCLA Computer Science, [‡]LG UX R&D Lab
{uclee, juyup.sung}@kaist.ac.kr, {jhkim, gerla}@cs.ucla.edu, eunhee2.yi@lge.com

ABSTRACT
Despite the popularity of mobile pay-for-answer Q&A services, little is known about the people who answer questions on these services. In this paper we examine 18.8 million question and answer pairs from Jisiklog, the largest mobile payforanswer Q&A service in Korea, and the results of a complementary survey study of 245 Jisiklog workers. The data are used to investigate key motivators of participation, working strategies of experienced users, and longitudinal interaction dynamics. We find that answerers are rarely motivated by social factors but are motivated by financial incentives and intrinsic motives. Additionally, although answers are provided quickly, an answerer's topic selection tends to be broad, with experienced workers employing unique strategies to answer questions and judge relevance. Finally, analysis of longitudinal working patterns and community dynamics demonstrate the robustness of mobile pay-for-answer Q&A. These findings have significant implications on the design of mobile pay-for-answer Q&A.

Author Keywords
Mobile Pay-for-Answer Q&A; User Behavior

ACM Classification Keywords
H.5.3 Information Interfaces and Presentation (e.g., HCI): Group and Organizational Interfaces

INTRODUCTION
Mobile devices have significantly changed the way we seek information. People can now search large repositories like the web from anywhere. Additionally, mobile Q&A services like Naver Mobile Q&A, ChaCha, and Jisiklog make it possible to quickly and easily find information by asking questions via instant messaging or SMS. This paper focuses on mobile Q&A, which has experienced significant growth in recent years. For instance, as of December 2012, ChaCha answered more than 4.5 billion questions, far surpassing the number of questions answered in Yahoo! Answers. When compared with traditional web-based Q&A, mobile Q&A users tend to ask a broad range of questions attributed to everyday life situations [17]. For example, users might use text messaging to check a bus schedule or asking for quick restaurant suggestions. The key drivers of mobile Q&A usage include accessibility, availability, and promptness [17].

Most popular mobile Q&A sites are based on pay-for-answer services where answerers receive monetary incentives either from the askers (e.g., Jisiklog, AQA, KGB Answers) or their employers (e.g., ChaCha). Unlike web-based pay-for-answer Q&A where askers can offer as much as they like to pay (e.g., Google Answers: $2–$200), in mobile pay-for-answer Q&A, payment is typically a fixed rate per task. For instance, ChaCha workers are paid $0.10–$0.20 for an answer based on answerer level and $0.01 for vetting answers. Jisiklog workers receive 80 KRW (approximately $0.08) for answering and 20 KRW (approximately $0.02) for vetting answers.

Existing mobile pay-for-answer Q&A services are unique in that they provide a structured workflow, breaking question answering into real-time micro-tasks to generate answers, and perform quality control using piece-rate financial incentives. Mobile Q&A services also provide limited opportunity for interaction between answerers and askers, as text input and output is challenging on mobile phones, and messages are often length limited and expensive. Mobile pay-for-answer Q&A services have evolved over many years (with ChaCha and Jisiklog established in 2006) to become real-time knowledge marketplaces for mobile information seekers.

Our goal in this paper is to investigate the behaviors and strategies of crowd workers who answer questions in mobile pay-for-answer Q&A. While this has been investigated extensively in existing web-based Q&A sites, little is known about the mobile pay-for-answer Q&A. We analyze a longitudinal Q&A dataset from Jisiklog spanning over 60 months and the results of a supplementary online survey study of 245 Jisiklog answerers. To the best of our knowledge, this work is the first large scale study on mobile pay-for-answer Q&A.

From the analysis, we find that while previous work on traditional Q&A sites has shown that social factors are important motivators [21, 22, 7], in mobile pay-for-answer Q&A sites answerers are instead mostly motivated by financial and intrinsic factors. Additionally, unlike traditional Q&A sites where users mostly focus on a few topics of interest [19, 3], mobile Q&A answerers tend to respond to a broader range of topics. Response times are fast, with experienced users answering particularly quickly and using unique strategies. Experienced workers also invest a significant amount of time daily, dispersed over multiple work periods. We believe that this understanding of the behavior and strategies of answerers can be used to improve existing mobile Q&A system design, and, more broadly, real-time crowdsourcing systems that leverage the wisdom of crowds.

RELATED WORK

We begin our discussion of mobile pay-for-answers Q&A by giving an overview of existing related research studying user interactions in social Q&A, pay-for answer Q&A, and online labor markets.

User Interactions in Social Q&A

Social Q&A sites like Yahoo! Answers and Naver KiN use the wisdom of crowds to answer questions. Adamic et al. [3] studied the asker-answerer social network on Yahoo! Answers and users' interests across various topic categories. They found that participation is highly skewed, with answerers tending to focus on just a few categories. Nam et al. [19] found a similar trend in Naver KiN; answerers' participation on Naver KiN is intermittent, and their expertise lower than is in often found in specialized online forums [19]. This trend persists in mobile Q&A [17]. The time it takes for questions to be answered on social Q&A sites tends to be fairly long. Hsieh et al. [13] showed that in Microsoft Live Q&A, the average time was almost 3 hours, with 20% of questions never even receiving an answer. The average time in Naver's mobile Q&A was 15.5 minutes, and 34% of the questions were not answered; unlike traditional social Q&A, mobile Q&A users often repeat or refine their information needs over a series of questions as coping strategies [17]. Yang et al. [26] studied two-year-long Q&A datasets from multiple social Q&A sites to understand user lifespan and community stability. The lifespan distribution shows that a large fraction of users leave (30%–70%) after a single post, and only a small fraction of users stay longer than 200 days (3%–10%).

How long people remain active in a social Q&A system varies by their role, with answerers staying longer than askers [26]. People's motivation for answering can be classified into intrinsic and extrinsic factors [20]. Intrinsic motivations include information ownership, perceived benefits (e.g., enjoyment, altruism, learning), and individual attitudes [19, 20, 23]. Extrinsic motivations includes social recognition (e.g., points/levels, leaderboards), social norms (e.g., interest votes), and financial incentives. Like existing research in social Q&A, in this paper we look at the motivations of answerers, the topics of questions that a user chooses to answer, answering delay, answering strategies, and community stability. We do so specifically within a system that provides answers in return for financial compensation.

User Interactions in Pay-for-Answer Q&A

Prior work to understand user interaction on pay-for-answer Q&A sites has focused on web-based pay-for-answer Q&A sites such as Mahalo Answers [14], Uclue, and Google Answers (discontinued in December 2006) [7, 22, 20]. Research from psychology and behavioral economics shows that monetary incentives can crowd-out intrinsic and social motivators [10]. In reality, given that individual motivations are diverse, only a subset of the population may be motivated by financial rewards, and the crowding out effect may not be critical. For instance, Raban et al. [21] analyzed a Google Answers dataset and showed that social features (e.g., social approval and observational cooperation) have a positive impact on the number of answers per user. Even with monetary incentives, researchers found that, similar to free systems, the level of participation in Google Answers followed a power-law, with a small fraction of users answering the majority of questions [21, 7], and most askers posting only a few questions [22]. The median delay for receiving answers on Google Answers was less than three hours which is comparable to online social Q&A; fewer questions were posted during the weekends, and questions posted between 8-10PM received the fastest responses [7]. Since the interaction environments of mobile Q&A are very different from those of existing web-based pay-for-answer Q&A (e.g., real-time, via instant messaging or SMS, piece-rate payment), we are interested in characterizing interaction patterns of answerers and their motivations by studying the Jisiklog dataset and the survey results of Jisiklog workers.

Prior work on the impact of financial incentives on answers has arrived at conflicting conclusions. Harper et al. [9] showed that pay-for-answer sites elicit better answers than free sites (e.g., Google Answers vs. Yahoo! Answers), and that higher quality answers can be acquired by paying more money. In contrast, Chen et al. [6] showed that paying more only elicits longer answers, and not better answers. Hsieh et al. [14] analyzed Mahalo, a pay-for-answer Q&A site, and showed that askers wish to pay when requesting facts and will pay more when asking difficult questions.

User Interactions in Online Labor Marketplaces

Pay-for-answer Q&A can be considered as a special form of online labor marketplaces in which people perform a variety of human intelligence tasks, ranging from simple image labeling and transcription to complex information seeking and graphic design. In recent years, several popular online labor marketplaces such as Amazon Mechanical Turk (M-Turk) and Taskcn have been extensively investigated [15, 25, 24]. In their analysis of M-Turk, Ipeirotis [15] found that the number of posted tasks per requester follows a power-law distribution. More than 90% of tasks paid less than $0.10, and the median delay for task completion was about 16 hours. This level of payment is quite comparable to that in mobile pay-for-answer Q&A services, but, unfortunately, M-Turk does not reveal any information from which we can analyze the longitudinal behavior of workers. Recently, Yang et al. [25, 24] analyzed Taskcn, an online marketplace for specific task categories requiring some level of technical skills (i.e., graphic design, web site design, writing, and programming). Unlike M-Turk, a requester can receive submissions from multiple users and then select the best submission to which the bounty is awarded. In Taskcn, the level of participation is highly skewed such that the majority of users submitted or won a very small number of tasks [25, 24].

In a study of M-Turk, Mason and Watts [18] found that paying more will increase the quantity, but not the quality of work. As the rational choice theory in economics informs, experienced workers in Taskcn often choose to improve their per-

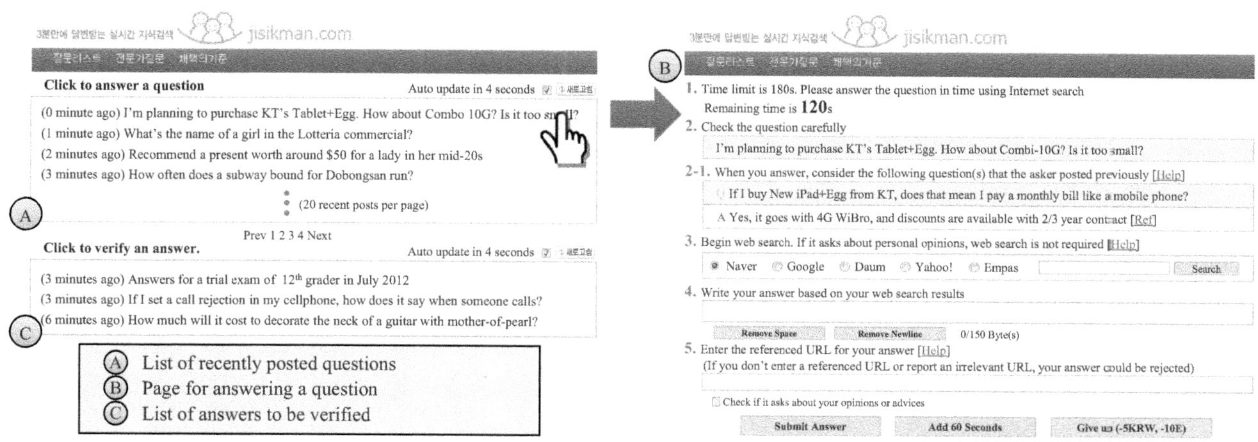

Figure 1. Main page (left) that lists newly posted questions (A) and answers to be verified (C); and an answer page (B) with a five-step guide for answering (URL: `http://answer.jisikman.com`). Here, the text was translated into English for illustration

formance with financial gain (e.g., selecting less competitive tasks) [25]. According to the survey results of M-Turk workers [15], about 40% of US workers expressed that fun and enjoyment is a key motivating factors. It is less clear how the intrinsic and social factors of knowledge sharing (e.g., altruism, learning) co-exist in a knowledge marketplace with piece-rate wage; identifying these factors is one of the primarily goals of this work. Since the amount of work and the level of payment in mobile pay-for-answer Q&A are comparable to those in M-Turk, some of our findings may provide valuable insights into understanding the dynamics in online labor marketplaces.

USER INTERACTIONS IN JISIKLOG

We study the online labor marketplace of mobile pay-for-answer Q&A by looking at the Jisiklog system. Jisiklog was first launched for SKT mobile subscribers in October 2006, and the service was opened to other mobile service providers (e.g., KT, LG) in April 2007 [1]. The Q&A data are publicly available, and major search engines including Google and Naver have been using the dataset for Q&A search.

Askers post questions by sending SMS messages. As shown in Figure 1, an answerer (also called a *jisikman*) can browse a list of recently posted questions (top-left, A) and the answers that need to be verified (bottom-left, B). There are two answerer classes, namely amateur and expert jisikmen. Experts' answers are immediately delivered to askers, while amateurs' answers are first verified by an expert (see a simplified workflow chart in Figure 2). Answers by amateurs are routed to the verification section (located at the left-bottom, C), and experts can either accept or reject these answers after review. An asker pays 200 KRW (approximately $0.20) for an answer; a jisikman receives 80 KRW (approximately $0.08) for answering a question and 20 KRW (approximately $0.02) verifying an answer.

To preserve answer quality (both for amateurs and experts), Jisiklog runs an answer review board. Any members whose level is at least 10 with a weekly acceptance rate of 80% or higher can file an objection to a posted answer. If the objection is sustained (determined by a majority vote by the expert jisikman; 5 KRW per vote), 100 KRW ($0.10) and 200 points

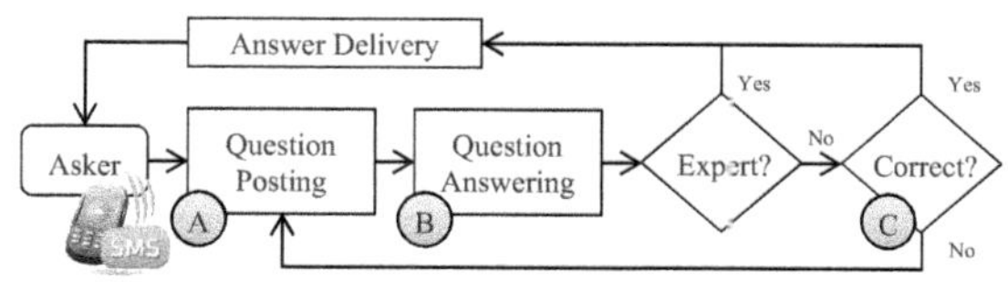

Figure 2. Simplified workflow of Jisiklog (the numbers correspond to the web pages in Figure 1)

deducted from the answerer are awarded to the objector. Conversely, if overruled, 165 KRW ($0.165) and 330 points deducted from the objector are awarded to the answerer. Note that askers can also file an objection for unsatisfactory answers, and they receive a voucher for a free answer if sustained. Workers can transfer the earned money to their bank account, and a unit of transfer is 10,000 KRW (approximately $10.00).

Along with monetary incentives, Jisiklog also has a leveling system based on a jisikman's earned points. Workers earn 100 points for each answer, and there are other activities and events from which they can either earn or lose points [1]. Jisiklog has a conversion table that maps points to a level. The conversion is roughly exponential ($R^2 = 0.997$), with users needing to earn approximately $\exp(5.25+129\ell)$ to increment a level for a given level ℓ. An amateur jisikman whose level is above 20 ($\geq$ 18,685 points) can become an expert jisikman if, in a given week, that jisikman answers at least 10 questions, 90% of their answers are verified, and no objections are received.

The page for creating an answer contains a five-step guide (see Figure 1, B). In Step 1, the answerer is informed that the question needs to be answered in 3 minutes; the remaining time is counted down in the Step 1 slot. Step 2 displays the current question, and the user is asked to consider several recent questions posed by the asker when answering. Step 3 provides a list of popular search engine links, asking an answerer to search the Internet. In Step 4, the answerer fills in an answer (minimum length of 50 bytes, maximum length of 150 bytes), and in Step 5, the answerer enters a referenced URL based on which the answer was made. The worker can skip this step if the asker is seeking an opinion or advice. If

	Fruitful*	\$Major	\$Minor***	KillTime	Help	Fun	Learn	LevelUp	Accept	Expert	Rank	N
Exp.	53.4%	4.2%	77.1%	14.4%	16.9%	26.3%	30.5%	3.4%	3.4%	5.1%	2.5%	118
Novice	40.3%	1.6%	57.3%	16.9%	16.1%	33.9%	21.8%	4.0%	6.5%	3.2%	0.8%	124
Overall	46.7%	2.9%	66.9%	15.7%	16.5%	30.2%	26.0%	3.7%	5.0%	4.1%	1.7%	242

Table 1. Distribution of motivation items, and distribution based on experience level ($^{*}p < 0.05$, $^{**}p < 0.01$, $^{***}p < 0.001$)

more time is needed, an additional minute can be granted by clicking the "Add 60 seconds" button (bottom-right)—a user is given at most 3+1 minutes in total. The answerer can give up by clicking the "give up" button. No penalty is levied for this before 5 seconds, but after 5 KRW and 5 points are deducted, and after 10 seconds, additional 5 points are deducted.

METHODOLOGY

To learn more about how people answer questions on Jisiklog, we downloaded the entire Q&A dataset from the period of May 1, 2007 to April 22, 2012 (about 60 months), for a total of 18,869,566 question-answer pairs. For a given question-answer pair, we also collected associated metadata such as the answerer ID and posting timestamps of questions.

We supplemented the crawled data with an online survey of Jisiklog answerers. We posted a link to the survey to the jisikman community website on May 18, 2012, and left it available for a month. After removing duplicate and erroneous responses, we received a total of 245 responses. The survey was composed of four parts: (1) demographics (e.g., age, gender, job, computer usage, income, user ID), (2) motivating factors (e.g., financial, altruistic), (3) answering strategies (e.g., topic focus, information resource usage, answering knowhow), and (4) feelings around financial incentives and quality (e.g., appropriateness, perceived quality).

A participant's user ID was used to identify the respondent in the crawled dataset, and to classify answerers as experienced and novice based on the number of answered questions. The threshold number was set to 200, corresponding with the number of questions required to be above Level 20, the minimum level to become an expert jisikman (although results are consistent across different thresholds).

Most participants were in their 10s (41.8%), 20s (43.9%), and 30s (11.9%), with only a small number above 40 (2.4%). Participants were mostly single (91.8%), and females were dominant (60.0%). Occupations ranged from junior high school students (10.2%), high school students (29.7%), college students (26.5%), graduate students (2.0%), homemakers (2%), engineering (10.2%), service/finance/education (9.3%), and miscellaneous (5.7%); 3.7% were unemployed. Since a large fraction of participants are students, the distribution of monthly income was highly skewed; < 50K (approximately \$500): 68.2%, 50K–100K (approximately \$500-\$1000): 5.7%, 100K–150K (approximately \$1000–\$1500): 7.8%, 150K-200K (approximately \$1500–\$2000): 6.5%, > 200K (approximately \$2000): 11.8%. The average usage time of computers per day was 4.27 hours (SD: 3.44).

We structured the data analysis along the following aspects of user interaction in mobile pay-for-answer Q&A: (1) key motivators of user participation (including intrinsic and extrinsic factors); (2) working strategies of experienced users (including topic selection, information seeking, and answer assessment); and (3) longitudinal interaction dynamics (including work frequency and duration, contribution, and attrition).

KEY MOTIVATORS

We begin our analysis of the data collected by investigating how the intrinsic and social factors of knowledge sharing (e.g., altruism, learning) co-exist with monetary incentives in Jisiklog. We find that while previous work on traditional Q&A sites has shown that social factors like levels and ranks are important motivators [21, 22, 7], in mobile pay-for-answer Q&A users are rarely motivated by social factors. Instead, they are motivated by intrinsic factors such as altruism, fun, and learning, in addition to the major motive of financial gain.

To explore motivation, we designed the survey questions related to motivation by building on key motivational factors in online labor marketplaces [15] and including additional motivations related to intrinsic and social motivations of social Q&A [19, 21]. The survey contained 11 potential motivation items, and participants were asked to select a set of items that best described their motivations. The following are the motivation items, shown in Table 1: fruitful way of spending free time (Fruitful); for primary income sources (\$Major), for minor income sources or pocket change (\$Minor); to kill time (KillTime); to help other people (Help); I find the tasks to be fun (Fun); to learn things while answering (Learn); to increase the level (LevelUp); to improve acceptance rate (Accept); to become an expert jisikman (Expert); and to be listed on a leaderboard (Rank).

Table 1 shows the distribution of responses. As expected, the strongest motivating factor is monetary incentives (total 69.8%). However, 31.0% of users were not motivated by monetary incentives. Unlike the results of Google Answers by Raban et al. [21], intrinsic motivators were considered more important than social motivators. Intrinsic motivators such as altruism (16.5%), fun (30.2%), and learning (26.0%) were marked by a considerable number of participants. These factors did not show a significant correlation between age groups (teenagers vs. adults). In contrast, social motivators like leveling-up (3.7%), becoming an expert jisikman (4.1%), and making the leaderboard (1.7%) were regarded as less important.

We hypothesize that a combination of several unique characteristics of mobile Q&A such as real-time constraint, workflow design, and piece-rate incentives, influences users to pay more attention to intrinsic factors than social factors. For example, the lack of social motivation may derive from the limited forms of user interactions that are possible within the system (e.g., only one answer, verification by professional jisikmen). Participants expressed a fairly low sense of belonging to the community, asked using a 5-point Likert scale (average 2.08, SD: 0.98).

We further divided participants into experienced and novice answerers. A Chi-square test with Yates' continuity correction revealed that the distribution of motivation is significantly differentiated by experience ($\chi^2 = 238.5$, $p < 0.001$, Cramer's V = 0.67). The difference comes from two sources, namely fruitful use of free time ($p < 0.05$), and income sources or pocket change ($p < 0.001$). It appears that while experienced users were more motivated by monetary incentives (77.1% vs. 66.1%), these monetary incentives did not crowd-out the intrinsic and social motivation of experienced users. Our findings suggest that even with two market norms, intrinsic and social motivators can co-exist with monetary incentives and play an important role in long-term participation. Moreover, the faction of participants who did not select monetary incentives as a motivation factor is not statistically different across different groups (28.8% and 33.06% in experienced and novice groups, respectively).

USER WORKING STRATEGIES

We next look at answerer behavior as it relates to topic selection, answering strategies, and quality assessment. Unlike traditional Q&A sites where users mostly focus on a few topics of interest (e.g., Naver KiN [19], Yahoo! Answers [3]), we see that Jisiklog answerers tended to respond to a much broader range of topics, possibly to increase earnings or learn more. Experienced users tended to answer faster, but there was significant variation in answer speed partly due to diverse skill levels and individual attitudes (e.g., valuing fast responses vs. witty or accurate answers). Overall, the time to response was very fast, which suggests an efficient real-time knowledge marketplace. Experienced answerers were likely to refer to diverse web information sources and to assess answer quality mainly based on accuracy, source quality, and specificity.

Topic Selection

To understand the variation in topic of the questions answerers selected to answer, we asked answerers in the survey whether they tended to focus on specific topics of interest when selecting questions to answer on a 5-point Likert scale (1: never to 5: always). Participants expressed moderate level of focus on topic selection (average: 2.67, SD: 1.06). For example, one person responded, "*I usually select questions that fit into my major.*" There was no significant difference in topic selection between experienced and novice answerers (U = 7360.5, p-value = 0.8043).

Since participants reported a moderate level of topic preference, we decided to quantify the spectrum of their topic preferences in the crawled data. Unlike traditional social Q&A, Jisiklog askers do not specify a topic when they text questions via SMS. To automatically classify topic categories, for a given question we extracted the key words using a Korean parser called KKMA (Kokoma Korean Morpheme Analysis) [2]. We then searched the extracted keywords using Naver KiN, a popular social Q&A service in which askers manually select the relevant topics when posting questions. From the top 10 search results, the most frequent topic category was selected as the topic category for the question; Naver KiN has 13 major topic categories.

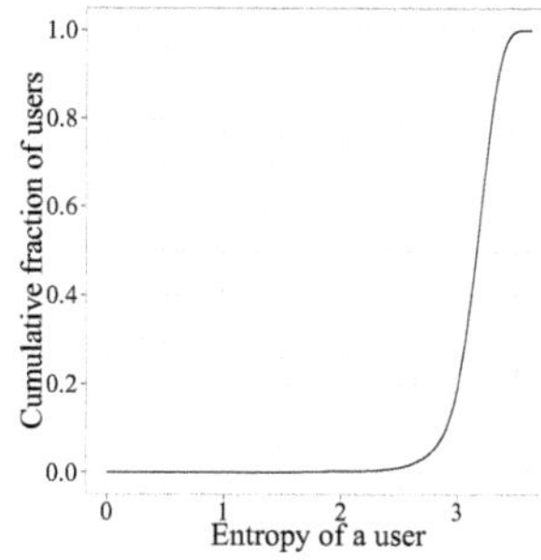

Figure 3. Topic entropy of users

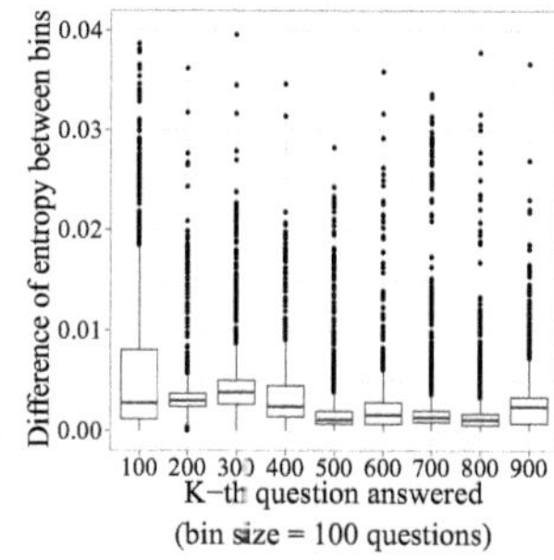

Figure 4. Entropy changes

The classified results are given as follows: computer (2.2%), games (4.6%), entertainment/art (19.3%), economy (3.7%), shopping (5.7%), society/politics (9.2%), health (7%), life (22.7%), travel (2.4%), sports (2.7%), education (10.2%), regional (5.0%), and counseling (6.0%).

To capture the degree of focus on particular topics by an answerer, we use an entropy measure—the lower the entropy, the higher the level of focus on certain topics. Consider an answerer i who made p_k faction of answers on topic k (for all $k = 1, \cdots, 13$). An answerer i's entropy is $-\sum_k p_k \log p_k$. If a user answered only a single category (say topic j, $p_j = 1$ and $p_i = 0$ for all $i = 1, \cdots, j-1, j+1, \cdots, 13$), the entropy is zero. Entropy is maximized when any topic is equally likely to be selected by a user (i.e., a uniform distribution). The cumulative distribution of topical entropy for all answerers who posted more than 100 answers can be seen in Figure 3. The shape of the distribution is very narrow and highly skewed, with average entropy of 3.14. To place this value in context, we calculate the entropy of a hypothetical random answerer who randomly selects questions from the list, and find that it is very close to the observed data (3.32). This result is very different from what has been observed in traditional social Q&A, where answerers tend to focus on several topic categories of interest [3, 19].

We also analyze whether experienced answerers' topic entropy changed over time, and found considerable consistency. For those who answered more than 1000 questions, we calculate the entropy difference between two consecutive bins (e.g., 1–100th questions vs. 101–200th questions) and plot the results in Figure 4. The figure clearly shows that a user's topic entropy rarely changes over time (within 0.04).

Answering Strategies

To better understand how answerers create their responses, we asked participants to report: (1) what effective answering strategies they used (free-text); (2) what kinds of information resources they used when answering (e.g., web search, Jisiklog search, dedicated web sites like maps and weather, personal experience), and how frequently each was used (on a 5-point Likert scale); (3) whether their strategies changed over time (free-text); and (4) whether they found that 3+1 minutes are enough time to answer (on a 5-point Likert scale). Additionally, we analyzed the Q&A dataset to measure the average time it took to answer a question.

To analyze the free-text answering strategies reported by our participants, we performed open coding and identified common themes. The four main strategies that emerged include: (1) choosing the type of question to answer (e.g., based on expertise or difficulty); (2) effectively using various information resources (e.g., web search, Jisiklog, dedicated web services) based on question content; (3) developing thoughtful and sincere answers; and (4) actively maintaining question-answering resources (e.g., bookmarks, summaries of frequently asked questions and frequently used sentences). Our manual classification with two coders shows that the participants' strategies can be reliably classified (Cohen's kappa: 0.8). The four categories have the following distribution: (1) 15.9%, (2) 67.7%, (3) 16.9%, and (4) 10.0%.

Participants reported being selective about the type of questions they chose to answer 15.9% of the time, with one participant saying, "*I wait until there are questions that I would like to answer.*" As discussed in the previous section, participants sometimes looked for topics of interest or topical diversity. For example, one reported, "*Since I'm majoring in chemistry in college, I prefer answering science questions. I usually refer to my textbook and several online forums to answer questions.*" This may be because these questions are easier for the individual to answer, and ease was a common theme (e.g., "*I prefer answering easy questions like TV schedules, restaurant recommendation, SAT answers, etc.*"). One participant reported actively seeking questions that could be addressed via a particular resource ("*I select a topic category that I can answer using Naver web search.*").

Regardless of the question selected, most questions asked on Jikilog require outside resources to answer, and resource selection was the most common aspect of question answering mentioned by participants (arising in 67.7% of responses). For example, one participant said, "*For study and college entrance related questions, I use search results from Naver KiN and add some personal comments. For direction and health questions, I use Naver Map and Encyclopedia. For computer related questions, I use Naver KiN and Jisiklog. I have a list of dedicated web sites for various kinds of questions.*" Another said, "*For questions on last bus schedules or directions, I usually use Naver Map or Naver Public Transit Info.*"

When asked directly about what information resources they used, participants answered that web search was the most frequently used (average 4.54, SD: 0.82) with other resources rating below 3.3 on average (SD < 1.25). To check whether the usage of information resources differed on the basis of experience level (experienced vs. novice), we ran a Mann-Whitney's U test. We found that experts were more likely to search using web search (Exp. 4.66 vs. Novice 4.43; $U = 8538$, p-value < 0.05) and Jisiklog search (Exp. 3.37 vs. Novice 2.74; $U = 9607.5$, p-value < 0.001), and were more likely to use dedicated web sites (Exp. 3.54 vs. Novice 3.07; $U = 9096$, p-value < 0.01).

The third common theme emerged among answering strategies related to developing thoughtful and sincere responses, occurring 16.9% of the time. For example, one participant stated, "*Instead of simply copying and pasting the answers from a web search, I try my best to explain the answer in detail such that if I were the askers, I could also easily understand the answer.*" Another said, "*For sports related questions, I try to provide as much detail as possible; like the bottom of 8th inning, 1 out, bases loaded, the next batter is Daeho Lee. For counseling questions, I try to analyze the asker's characteristics and give personalized answers as much as possible.*"

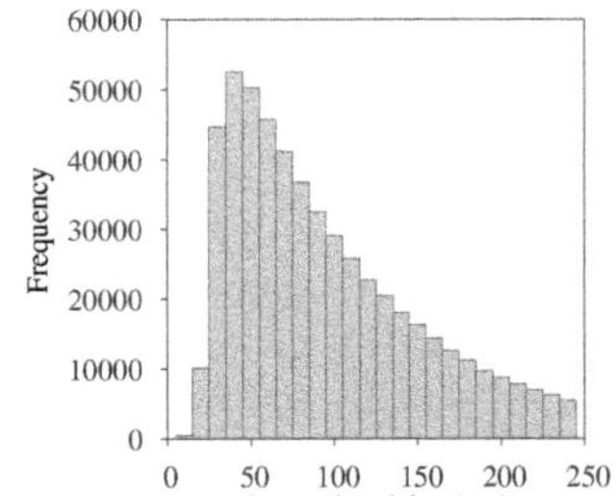

Figure 5. Answer delay dist.

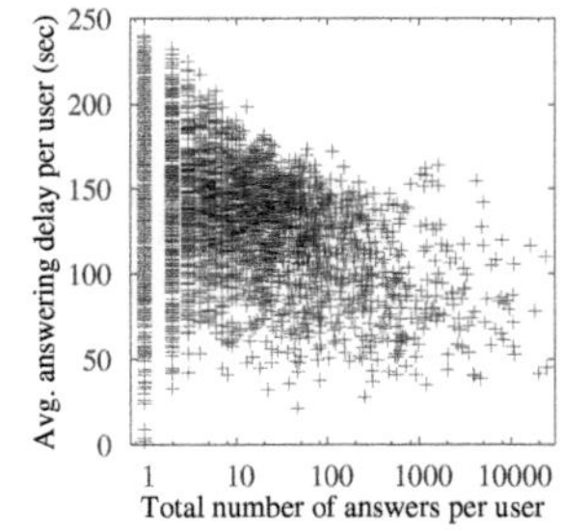

Figure 6. Answer delay per user

To support question answering 10.0% of participants reported active maintenance of question answering resources, ranging from bookmarks ("*I came up with question categories and arranged the bookmarks of frequently visited web sites based on those categories.*") to common questions and answers ("*I maintain frequently asked questions or expected answers in my memo pad.*").

When asked how their answering strategies developed over time, participants gave examples of how they arrived at the above strategies, from question selection ("*In the beginning, I had quite a few cases of having difficulties in finding answers in three minutes. As time passed, I gained a sense of what questions I can answer and learned how to utilize various dedicated web sites.*") to resource selection ("*I used to search mainly web portals, but now I use various web sites simultaneously to answer questions.*") to more answer generation ("*I changed my strategy from simply copying/pasting answers to providing more reliable/accurate answers.*"). We also observed that experienced users were more likely than novice users to maintain their own answer resources, as such require time and experience to construct. Overall, as time passes, it appears that users become more skillful at answering questions from the web.

In general, the labor market literature shows that this kind of on-the-job learning plays a significant role in developing worker skills and facilitating worker productivity [16]. Consistent with this, we found that experienced users in Jisiklog felt less time pressure when compared with novice users. When asked whether the time limit for answering (3+1 minutes) was appropriate, participants generally felt that they need more time (average 2.5, SD: 0.94). However, when experienced and novice users were compared, the novice group (average 2.38, SD: 0.91) reported feeling more time pressure than the experienced group (average 2.65, SD: 0.95), as confirmed by a Mann-Whitney's U test ($U = 9035$, p-value < 0.01).

We also looked at the amount of time that answerers invested in answering questions. The crawled dataset only contains the timestamp of question pickup from the main page in Figure 1 and does not have an actual timestamp of answer submission. However, since newly posted answers are immediately displayed on the peer review board (in which users can file an objection), we can use this information to measure the time it takes to answer a question. To this end, we monitored the board for 7 months, from November 1, 2011 to April 31, 2012. The total number of dowloaded questions was 529,581, and the average answering delay was 88.6 seconds (SD: 54.5). The delay histogram is depicted in Figure 5. The shape of the distribution is quite smooth with a near linear tail (cut-off value of 4 minutes).

We also looked at whether the time it took to generate an answer was dependent on the total number of answers given by a user, and found experienced answerers required less time. Figure 6 shows a scatter plot of all the users. The overall delay dispersion of novice users (less than 200 questions) varies widely, whereas the average delay of experienced users is mostly below 150 seconds. Nonetheless, the average answering delay of experienced individuals still sometimes differed significantly. As shown in the figure, the following are the average delays of top seven users (located at the bottom right): 45.0 (SD: 27.2), 109.9 (SD: 50.4), 41.6 (SD: 30.3), 78.0 (SD: 45.7), 116.6 (SD: 50.3), 52.7 (SD: 33.5), 105.6 (SD: 51.7).

Two of the top seven users participated in the survey, and provided comments about their answering strategies. One reported, "*Speed is the most important thing; first pickup a question and answer as soon as possible.*" The other said, "*For direction questions I usually get directions from maps, but I would prefer giving more detailed answers based on my experience. I'm quite knowledgeable with directions. People frequently ask about song titles, but to improve satisfaction of askers I try to include witty remarks.*" These individuals have different perspectives on giving answers, with one valuing speed, and the other satisfaction. This in turn leads to very different answering delay (41.6 seconds versus 105.6 seconds). These findings are consistent with Wang et al.'s [23] observation that individual attitudes are important factors of information sharing.

Assessing Answer Quality

There are two ways answer quality is assessed on Jisiklog; pending answers are verified by an expert jisikman, and objections can be filed to delivered answers. In the survey, we asked open-ended questions on the criteria participants used to assess answers for these tasks. We used criteria proposed by Barry and Schamber [4], including: (1) depth, scope, and specificity, (2) accuracy and validity, (3) clarity, (4) currency (up-to-date), (5) tangibility (proven with real data or numbers), (6) source quality (reputable, trusted, accurate, expert), (7) accessibility (costs of access), and (8) availability. For verification (total 87) and objection (total 67), two raters classified the responses. The reliability of the ratings in each category was checked with Cohen's kappa; most of our ratings had a kappa value greater than 0.7, meaning substantial agreements. For verification, the primary factors that participants consider important include accuracy and validity (59.8%), source quality (47.1%), and depth, scope, and specificity (36.8%). For example, one participant responded, "*1. Correctly answered, 2. Used correct reference, 3. Correctly understood the user's needs, 4. Sincerely gave answers. Also, check whether the answer is too short or content in the reference page is well reflected.*" Another said, "*I consider trustworthiness (accuracy) of an answer most important. Askers are paying money for answers. If accuracy is low, it is hard to differentiate Jisiklog from other free services on major portals like Naver KiN.*" The same criteria were important when filing an objection.

The remaining criteria for assessment were rarely mentioned, including tangibility (3.4%), clarity (2.3%), currency (2.3%), availability (2.3%), and accessibility (0.0%). While currency is mentioned by few participants, it is closely related to accuracy and validity, and its importance may have discounted. In fact, quite a few questions in Jisiklog are time sensitive, including questions for sports scores, TV schedules, and traffic information. This suggests that currency may in reality be an important factor. One of our participants states the following reason for filing currency-related objections: "*Traffic related information changes quite often and updates may be slow, and I found many cases of wrong answers. I have been mainly filing objections on direction questions. Since I joined this community, I filed more than 6000 cases. I think that this is the largest number of objections in Jisiklog.*"

INTERACTION DYNAMICS

We investigate longitudinal user interactions by corroborating the analysis results of five-year-long Q&A dataset with the survey results. In particular, we study longitudinal working patterns of answerers (i.e., working hours, frequency) and community dynamics (i.e., churning and dropouts). We find that experienced answerers invest a significant amount of time daily (on average 8 hours), and their daily working hours are likely dispersed over multiple work periods. There is a tendency that the longer the daily working hours, the larger is the number of work periods (e.g., heavy users work more hours more frequently). Further, while answerers' monthly churning rate is fairly high, the contribution of top-k% answerers is quite consistent over time, showing the robustness of Jisiklog.

Longitudinal Working Patterns

We begin by looking at peoples working patterns on Jikislog, including the hours spent working and the frequency of work blocks. We tracked the activity of workers who answered more than 100 questions over the entire period. For a given worker, we define a work block as a series of answers where the inter-answer time of any pair of consecutive answers is no greater than 30 minutes. The assumption is that the worker is likely to do other things besides working in Jisiklog if the break time is longer than 30 minutes. To measure how frequently an individual worked for a given day, we use a metric of the number of work blocks per day. The duration of a work block (in hours) is the difference of posting times between the first and last questions in a work block. If a work block contains only one question, we treat it as a singular work block and fix the duration as three minutes.

We present the cumulative distribution of work hours per day in Figure 7. The shape of the distribution is quite narrow and skewed (average: 8.55 hours). We also present the boxplot

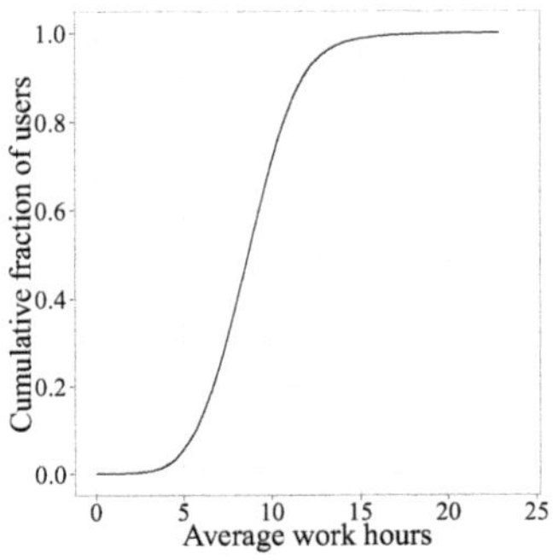

Figure 7. Daily work hours per user

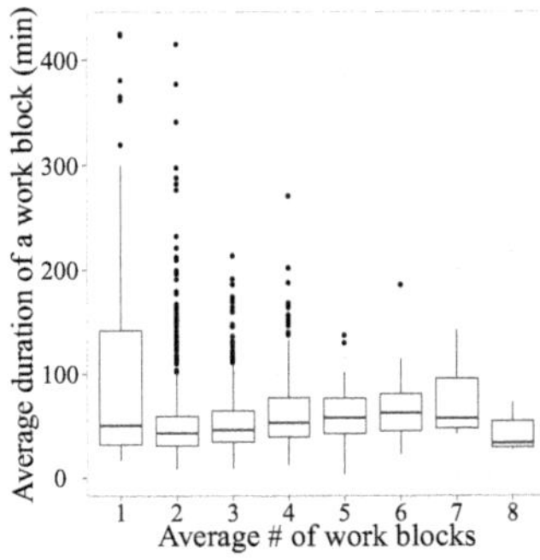

Figure 8. Num. work blocks vs. block duration

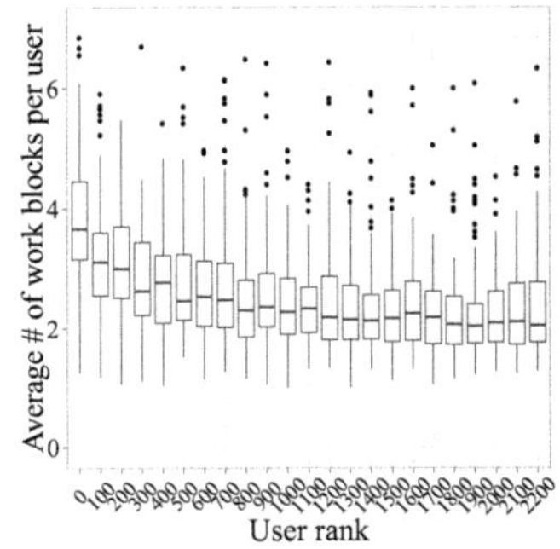

Figure 9. Rank vs. num. work blocks

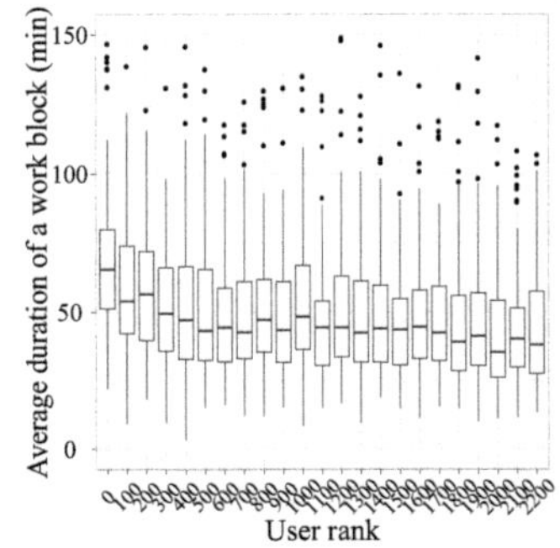

Figure 10. Rank vs. block duration

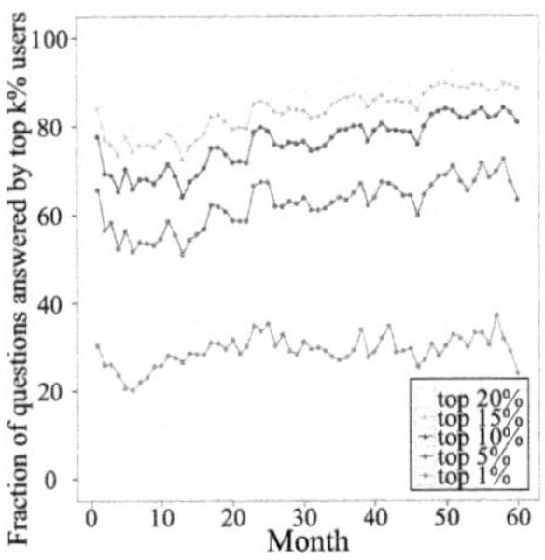

Figure 11. Top-$k\%$ contribution

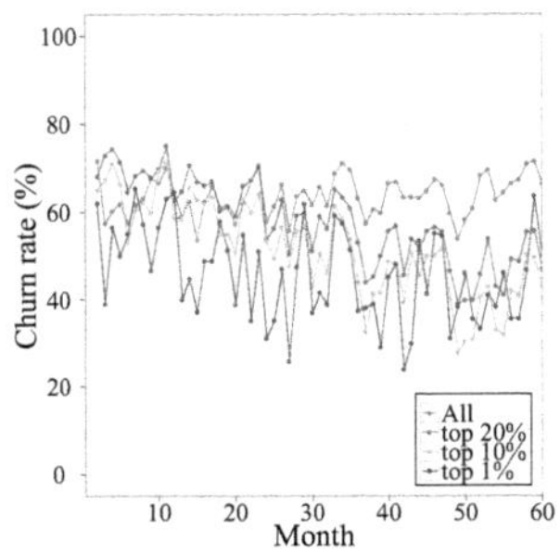

Figure 12. Top-$k\%$ churning

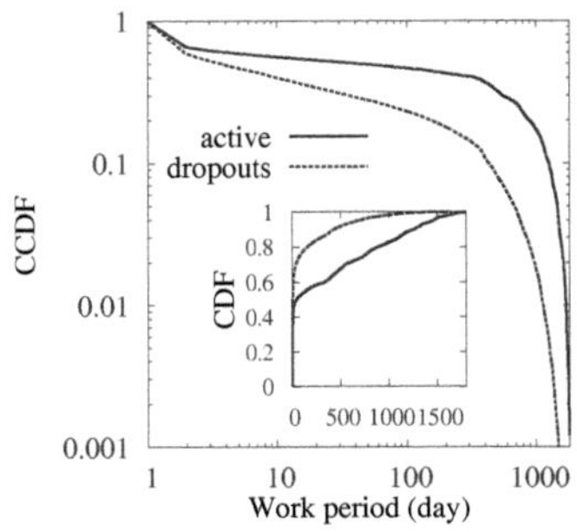

Figure 13. Work periods

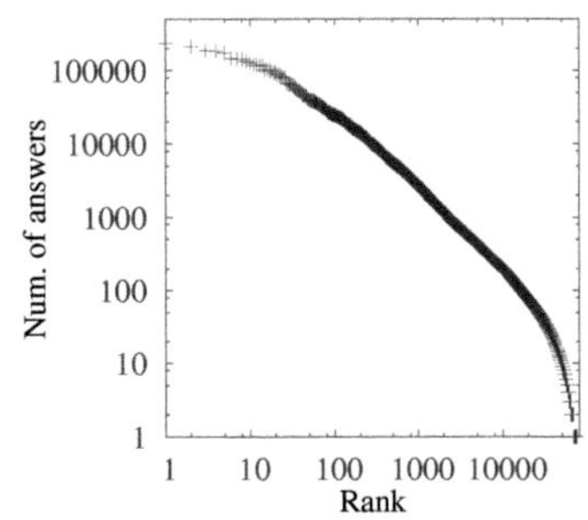

Figure 14. Rank vs. contribution

of the average duration of a work block per user as a function of the average number of work blocks per user in Figure 8. This figure clearly shows that many answerers attempt to work over the course of a day as time permits, consistent with our survey results—one of the leading motivators was to make fruitful use of spare time. For the workers who work only once per day (the number of blocks = 1), the dispersion of work block duration is much wider than that of the other workers. For the other workers who work more than once, there is a tendency of working more hours and more frequently; as the number of work blocks increases, the median work duration also increases. To explore whether this pattern appears in the experienced worker group (top 2000 users), we also plot the number of work blocks (Figure 9), and the average work block duration (Figure 10) as a function of worker rank (with a bin of 100 workers). The graphs clearly show that the higher the rank, the longer the work duration and the larger the number of blocks.

Community Dynamics

We investigated the community dynamics by examining the temporal changes of contribution and churning rates of top-$k\%$ answerers. We also studied the work periods of individual workers (active vs. dropout) and identified the major reasons why some participants temporarily stopped from work.

We first present the contribution of top-$k\%$ answerers over the five-year period (k = 1–20%) in Figure 11. For a given month, we rank all the workers, and the contribution of top-$k\%$ answerers is plotted. The average contributions of top-1%, top-5%, top-10%, top-15%, and top-20% answerers are 29.3%, 62.4%, 76.1%, 83.2%, and 87.6%, respectively. We also analyze the monthly churn rate (or attrition), which measures the fraction of workers who are active in one month becomes inactive in the following month. For example, assume that 4 users (A, B, C, D) are active in the first month, and 4 users (C, D, E, F) are active in the second month. Since two users (A, B) are left, the churn rate of active workers in the first month is 0.5. The churn rates of the top-$k\%$ active answerers in each month (k = 1–20, 100) are plotted in Figure 12. The average churn rate of top 1%, top 10%, top 20%, and 100% is 45.7%, 51.6%, 57.8%, and 63.5%, respectively. Even with high churning in each month, the contribution of top-$k\%$ answerers does not dramatically change over time, which partly demonstrates the strength of power-law networks [8, 20].

Since a large fraction of survey participants are students, we examined whether school schedules such as back-to-school affected the churn rate, but we do not find any significant correlation. Instead, we find that some of the promotion events by Jisiklog have great impact on churning rates. For example, when the piece-rate was increased in the 12th month as seen in Figure 12, the churn rate of top 1% and top 10% decreased from 64.5% and 58.9% to 40% and 58.3% in the following month, respectively. Also, when Jisiklog announced that they would give more experience points, which helped users raise their levels easily in the 14th month, the churn rate of top 1% and top 10% was decreased from 44.7% and 65.4% to 37.1% and 62.8%, respectively.

To understand how long workers stay in the system, we calculate the work period of individual workers. We divided workers into two groups, namely active and dropout. If a worker is not active in the last 6 months, we assume that the worker has dropped out of the system. Note that there are some users who are not active for more than 6 months and become active again, but such cases are quite rare in our dataset. We plot the cumulative distribution of the work periods for both groups in Figure 13. The distribution for dropouts approximately follows a power-law distribution with an exponential cutoff due to the 54 month limit. This means that quite a large fraction of people leave quite early (e.g., about 41% in 1 day, 80% in 154 days, and 90% left in 400 days), whereas once they are committed, they tend to stay longer and consistently contribute as shown in Figure 14. This phenomenon is also observed in traditional social Q&A sites such as Yahoo! Answers and Naver KiN [26]; it appears that monetary incentives do not significantly increase user activity lifespan as opposed to social motivators.

In our survey, we asked the participants whether they had experiences of stopping from work (for example, for a week to a few months) and if so, what the reasons were. 77.1% of the participants said they had such experiences. The following are the major reasons that emerged from the responses: (1) too busy with primary work (46.8%); (2) lack of motivation due to low financial incentives (11.2%); (3) tiresome to answer questions (8.1%); (4) too competitive to pick up questions (7.5%); (4) low acceptance rate and frequent objections (7.0%); and (5) difficult to answer questions or/and to provide good references (4.3%). These reasons partly explain the findings about community dynamics. The entry barrier of novice users is fairly high; a large portion of users tend to drop out of the systems at an early stage since the work environment is quite competitive and demanding and the compensation is low. Once users are committed to working (e.g., successfully surviving the on-the-job training period, and having become an expert jisikman), they tend to stay longer. However, their contributions could be intermittent, as a large portion of users are doing this work during their spare time; Jisiklog nonetheless has enough committed workers who can sustain the overall community.

DISCUSSION

We discuss in this section several design implications on the basis of our findings, namely designing assistive tools for answerers and employing mechanisms for improving intrinsic/extrinsic motivations. We also discuss the limitation of this work and possible directions of future work.

There are several ways of designing effective assistive tools for answerers. First, we found that the answerers in the current system lack a sense of belonging to the community, and thus they are not inclined to share knowledge (e.g., tips, bookmarks) with other answerers. Introducing sharing mechanisms as in social bookmarking (e.g., del.icio.us, Digg) would not only improve the efficiency of workers but also stimulate social interactions, thus enhancing the sense of belonging. In the case of bookmarks, it is possible to use machine learning algorithms for automatic web link recommendation. Second, since a majority of answerers are part-time workers, and their interaction patterns are quite intermittent, another effective assistive tool would be supporting work scheduling functions on the basis of detailed analysis of working patterns; e.g., efficiently reminding users of the importance of their contributions. Finally, helping users to track work related activities would be very useful to improve work efficiency and participation (e.g., validation/objection event tracking, extra audio/visual cues on remaining time).

We showed that both intrinsic motivators (e.g., enjoyment, learning, altruism) and monetary incentives play important roles, but the social motivation is quite weak in Jisiklog. We suggest introducing mechanisms that can improve perceived values of learning and altruism and also facilitate social interactions. One way of increasing a user's perception of learning would be to permit the user to browse a list of answers or visualizing tags/keywords based on interaction history (or topics). We could enhance a user's feeling of altruism by enabling a donation feature; e.g., directly transferring earnings to a charity foundation—in this case, answerers are helping both the askers and other people in need. A community-wide donation campaign would improve the sense of belonging to the community. The current system lacks features that can facilitate social interactions; some well-known features can be integrated (e.g., sharing awareness information of other workers, displaying performance in leaderboards, etc.). With piece-rate wages, goal setting happens quite naturally [12]. We can elicit such behavior by introducing related features, and designing more effective financial incentive mechanisms for mobile pay-for-answer Q&A is part of our future work.

In mobile pay-for-answer Q&A, most activities are time critical (e.g., question pick-up/answering). While this level of interactivity would provide a feeling of engagement, it would be cognitively demanding and could result in reduced long-term participation. Gamifying some of the activities or introducing social awareness (e.g., online chatting) could lower this burden. Our analysis showed that labor supply and demand dynamically change over time in Jisiklog. Further investigation of the dataset is needed to better understand the ecology of an online labor marketplace using economic theories [11]. For instance, labor oversupply creates a competitive work environment (leading to high entry barriers to newcomers and high cognitive loads to workers that are due to the attrition of workers). On the other hand, because of the real-time nature of question asking [17], labor undersupply may lower service quality (e.g., large response delay), thus causing asker attrition.

The main findings on Jisiklog can be used to understand other mobile pay-for-answer Q&A sites that share the same design characteristics. For instance, ChaCha has a very similar workflow/incentive structure as that of Jisiklog. More broadly, mobile pay-for-answer Q&A can be thought of as a real-time knowledge marketplace for mobile information seekers. Our findings will thus provide valuable insights into the design of real-time crowdsourcing systems that exploit the wisdom of crowds such as real-time visual Q&A like VizWiz [5] (e.g., designing a workflow for real-time quality control, assistive tools for creating efficient work environments, and mechanisms of accommodating diverse motives).

However, as with any qualitative or single-site work, the generalizability of this work is limited such that additional research on similar mobile Q&A services is necessary. For this reason, we have performed a preliminary study on the user behavior of ChaCha based on a trace dataset for almost a one year period. Due to limited availability of public information, thus far we have only been able to confirm that user contribution and topic selection patterns are similar to those of Jisiklog. Further investigation is needed to compare the findings with those related to ChaCha and other sites. Another aspect worth exploring is the investigation of the cultural implications on the online labor marketplaces; identifying key differences between different cultures will help in generalizing the results.

CONCLUSION

We studied the behaviors and strategies of crowd workers in mobile pay-for-answer Q&A using the longitudinal Q&A dataset from Jisiklog and the results of a complementary survey study of Jisiklog workers. The following findings were derived from our analysis structured along the key aspects of user interactions, namely major motivators of user participation, working strategies of experienced users, and longitudinal interaction dynamics. First, unlike traditional Q&A sites, we found that users are rarely motivated by social factors, but are more motivated by financial incentives and intrinsic factors (e.g., altruism, fun, and learning). Second, experienced users have fairly unique working strategies on topic selection, answer search, and answer quality assessment. Unlike traditional Q&A sites, an answerer's topic selection tends to be broad, and yet, answers are provided quickly (taking less than 90 seconds on average). Experienced users have several common answering strategies (e.g., referring to diverse web resources), and the primary factors of quality assessments include accuracy/validity, source quality, and specificity. Third, we found that even with high churning in each month, the contribution of top-$k\%$ answerers is quite consistent over time, showing the robustness of mobile pay-for-answer Q&A.

ACKNOWLEDGEMENTS

This work was supported by the National Research Foundation of Korea Grant funded by the Korean Government (MEST) (NRF-2012R1A1A1008858). We would like to thank Jisiklog for providing the dataset, Dr. Jaime Teevan for shepherding the manuscript through the revision process, and the anonymous reviewers for their helpful comments.

REFERENCES

1. Jisiklog Service Guide. `http://cs.jisikman.com/cs/h_info/info.jsp`.
2. Kokoma Korean Morpheme Analysis. `http://kkma.snu.ac.kr/`.
3. Adamic, L. A., Zhang, J., Bakshy, E., and Ackerman, M. S. Knowledge Sharing and Yahoo Answers: Everyone Knows Something. In *WWW* (2008).
4. Barry, C. L., and Schamber, L. Users' Criteria for Relevance Evaluation: A Cross-situational Comparison. *Information Processing & Management* (1998).
5. Bigham, J. P., Jayant, C., Ji, H., Little, G., Miller, A., Miller, R. C., Miller, R., Tatarowicz, A., White, B., White, S., and Yeh, T. VizWiz: Nearly Real-time Answers to Visual Questions. In *UIST* (2010).
6. Chen, Y., Ho, T.-H., and Kim, Y.-M. Knowledge Market Design: A Field Experiment at Google Answers. *Journal of Public Economics Theory* (2010).
7. Edelman, B. Earnings and Ratings at Google Answers. *Economic Inquiry* (2012).
8. Granovetter, M. The Strength of Weak Ties: A Network Theory Revisited. *Sociological Theory* (1983).
9. Harper, F. M., Raban, D., Rafaeli, S., and Konstan, J. A. Predictors of Answer Quality in Online Q&A Sites. In *CHI* (2008).
10. Heyman, J., and Ariely, D. Effort for Payment: A Tale of Two Markets. *Psychological Science* (2004).
11. Horton, J. J. Online Labor Markets. In *WINE* (2010).
12. Horton, J. J., and Chilton, L. B. The Labor Economics of Paid Crowdsourcing. In *EC* (2010).
13. Hsieh, G., and Counts, S. mimir: A Market-Based Real-Time Question and Answer Service. In *CHI* (2009).
14. Hsieh, G., Kraut, R. E., and Hudson, S. E. Why Pay?: Exploring How Financial Incentives are Used for Question & Answer. In *CHI* (2010).
15. Ipeirotis, P. G. Analyzing the Amazon Mechanical Turk Marketplace. *Journal XRDS: Crossroads* (2010).
16. Jovanovic, B., and Nyarko, Y. Learning by Doing and the Choice of Technology. *Econometrica* (1996).
17. Lee, U., Kang, H., Yi, E., Yi, M. Y., and Kantola, J. Understanding Mobile Q&A Usage: An Exploratory Study. In *CHI* (2012).
18. Mason, W., and Watts, D. J. Financial Incentives and the "Performance of Crowds". In *KDD-HCOMP* (2009).
19. Nam, K. K., Ackerman, M. S., and Adamic, L. A. Questions in, Knowledge iN?: A Study of Naver's Question Answering Community. In *CHI* (2009).
20. Raban, D., and Harper, F. M. Motivations for Answering Questions Online. In *New Media and Innovative Technologies* (2008).
21. Raban, D. R. The Incentive Structure in an Online Information Market. *JASIST* (2008).
22. Shah, C., Oh, J. S., and Oh, S. Exploring Characteristics and Effects of User Participation in Online Social Q&A Sites. *First Monday* (2008).
23. Wang, S., and Noe, R. A. Knowledge Sharing: A Review and Directions for Future Research. *Human Resource Management Review* (2010).
24. Yang, J., Adamic, L. A., and Ackerman, M. S. Competing to Share Expertise: the Taskcn Knowledge Sharing Community. In *ICWSM* (2008).
25. Yang, J., Adamic, L. A., and Ackerman, M. S. Crowdsourcing and Knowledge Sharing: Strategic User Behavior on Taskcn. In *EC* (2008).
26. Yang, J., Wei, X., Ackerman, M., and Adamic, L. Activity Lifespan: An Analysis of User Survival Patterns in Online Knowledge Sharing Communities. In *ICWSM* (2010).

Octopus: Evaluating Touchscreen Keyboard Correction and Recognition Algorithms via "Remulation"

Xiaojun Bi[1] Shiri Azenkot[2] Kurt Partridge[1] Shumin Zhai[1]
[1]Google Inc.
Mountain View, CA, USA
{bxj, kep, zhai}@google.com
[2]University of Washington
Seattle, WA, USA
shiri@cs.washington.edu

ABSTRACT
The time and labor demanded by a typical laboratory-based keyboard evaluation are limiting resources for algorithmic adjustment and optimization. We propose *Remulation*, a complementary method for evaluating touchscreen keyboard correction and recognition algorithms. It replicates prior user study data through real-time, on-device simulation. To demonstrate remulation, we have developed Octopus, an evaluation tool that enables keyboard developers to efficiently measure and inspect the impact of algorithmic changes without conducting resource-intensive user studies. It can also be used to evaluate third-party keyboards in a "black box" fashion, without access to their algorithms or source code. Octopus can evaluate both touch keyboards and word-gesture keyboards. Two empirical examples show that Remulation can efficiently and effectively measure many aspects of touch screen keyboards at both macro and micro levels. Additionally, we contribute two new metrics to measure keyboard accuracy at the word level: the *Ratio of Error Reduction (RER)* and the *Word Score*.

Author Keywords
Simulation; Text Entry; Touch Screen Interaction

ACM Classification
H5.2 [Information interfaces and presentation]: User Interfaces. - Graphical user interfaces.

General terms
Design; Human Factors

INTRODUCTION
Today, touchscreen keyboards are used by hundreds of millions of people around the world as their default text entry method. To reduce typing errors, most of these "Smart Touch Keyboards" (STKs) correct errors automatically as users type. However, occasionally the error correction system itself makes a mistake, with undesirable and sometimes humorous consequences [6,20].

An increasingly popular alternative to the STK is the smart gesture keyboard (SGK). An SGK recognizes words based on the user's finger gestures (Figure 1, right). SGK's are also known as Shape Writing keyboards [21, 28], gesture keyboards [5] or word-gesture keyboards [29] in the literature. Different forms of SGKs have been commercially distributed in many products such as ShapeWriter, SlideIT, Swype, Flex T9, TouchPal, and the Android 4.2 stock keyboard (Gesture Typing) [2]. SGKs face the same correction challenges as STKs because they must map ambiguous finger gestures to words.

Figure 1. Illustrations of Smart Touch Keyboard (Left) and Smart Gesture Keyboard (Right)

HCI research has explored various techniques for error prevention, including adapting decoding algorithms to hand posture [4], and personalizing ten-finger typing for large touchscreens [7].

As with other advanced UI technologies such as speech recognition, effective and efficient evaluation is critical to the improvement of smart keyboards. An evaluation generally consists of (1) data collection and (2) data analysis. Our goal is to facilitate both stages of the process. Collecting keyboard output data typically involves a laboratory experiment with a dozen or more participants. The time and labor required by these experiments make frequent evaluation of small algorithmic changes infeasible.

Moreover, current data analysis techniques do not provide important information about keyboard algorithms. For example, they do not explicitly and quantitatively measure an STK's ability to correct user errors, and the typical accuracy metrics (e.g., the MSD error rate [16]) examine output at the character-level, and do not reflect today's keyboards' word-level behaviors.

To expand the repertoire of tools and methods for evaluating STKs and SGKs, we propose *Remulation,* a novel keyboard evaluation approach that measures correction and recognition algorithms of keyboards by *re*playing previously collected user data through real-time on-device si*mulation*. It takes touch screen events recorded

CHI 2013, April 27–May 2, 2013, Paris, France.

during prior user studies as input, and injects them into a live mobile keyboard, at the same rate as they were collected. The original experiment is thereby replicated on a working keyboard. Remulation can efficiently evaluate many (not all) aspects of both STKs and SGKs without conducting laboratory experiments, and can be done repeatedly as if the same group of participants were employed to type the same input tirelessly over and over on different keyboards.

Typical use cases for Remulation include: (1) a developer seeks to evaluate the impact of an algorithmic change to her keyboard, (2) a researcher seeks to evaluate different versions of the same third-party keyboard, and (3) a device manufacturer wants to select a third-party keyboard to embed in its devices without inspecting the keyboards' proprietary source code or algorithms.

To effectively measure the accuracy of a keyboard algorithm, we introduce the metrics of *Word Score*, which reflects the number of correct words out of every 100 input words from a given test dataset, and *Ratio of Error Reduction* (RER), which quantifies an STK's error prevention and correction ability. Both metrics measure keyboard accuracy at the word level.

In the rest of this paper we demonstrate the Remulation approach and its corresponding data analysis methods by designing and implementing Octopus, a Remulation-based keyboard evaluation tool. We put Remulation and Octopus into practice by applying them to two STKs and two SGKs, revealing various insights at both the macro and micro levels.

In summary, this work contributes a novel approach to evaluating touchscreen keyboards, which includes:

- *Remulation*, a new approach for evaluating keyboard correction and recognition algorithms by replicating prior user study data with real-time simulation
- The design and implementation of Octopus, a Remulation-based keyboard evaluation tool and system
- A demonstration of Remulation and Octopus in real use, with evaluations of two STKs and two SGKs
- *RER* and *Word Score*, new metrics for evaluating keyboard accuracy.

RELATED WORK

Collecting natural use data and applying them to train recognition algorithms has been widely adopted as a research methodology in AI (e.g., speech and handwriting recognition). Recently, it has also been employed to design keyboard algorithms. Gunawardana et al. [9] used pre-recorded data on a keyboard to train and evaluate their own error correction algorithm. Remulation uses some of the same techniques for the different problem of comparing two or more third-party keyboards when the source code or algorithm is unavailable. Our work shows that it is possible to send "fake" touch events to today's mainstream devices (Android in particular but other OSs in principle) and evaluate keyboards in a "black box" fashion.

In what follows we discuss relevant prior work on (1) simulating human text entry for evaluating keyboard performance without traditional laboratory studies, and (2) current analysis techniques used for assessing a text entry method's accuracy.

Simulating Text Entry

In 1982, Rumelhart and Norman [23] described a model for simulating skilled typists on physical typewriters, with the goal of understanding human typing behavior. Their model focused on predicting keystroke timing and simulated key transposition and doubling errors. In our work, we rely on direct data replication rather than complex modeling of human performance, and seek to evaluate keyboard algorithms rather than theorize user behavior.

Since the early 1990's, research interest has shifted from studying physical typewriters to soft keyboards. The Fitts-digraph model, first proposed by Lewis [12], was used to estimate average text entry speeds based on movement time between pairs of keys and digraph frequencies. This model has been a popular performance prediction tool for keyboard evaluation with different layouts using a single finger or a stylus [12,13,14,19], and has been used as an objective function for keyboard optimization [26]. A two-thumb physical keyboard predictive model has also been proposed [15]. Unlike these models, which predict an upper bound for average text entry speed assuming a certain error rate implied by Fitts' law (4% per target), our Remulation and analysis method assesses keyboard error rates and accuracies using the same speed that had naturally occurred in the data collection experiment. Also, we focus on evaluating keyboards with similar appearances but different algorithms, instead of different layouts.

Measuring Accuracy in Text Entry

Standard text entry accuracy metrics compare the transcribed and presented strings. The Minimum String Distance (MSD) [16] is often used to measure the "distance" between the two strings, based on the number of character insertions, deletions, and replacements needed to turn one string into another. While this has been effective in measuring traditional physical keyboards that literally output every letter typed, it is insufficient for measuring STKs. STKs embed a dictionary or language model and do not necessarily map touch points to text on an individual letter basis. Similarly, SGKs usually work at the word level: they recognize a continuous finger gesture to output a single word [21, 28, 29]. Since both SGKs and STKs operate at word-level, it is more meaningful to adopt the word-level metrics. Furthermore, although word-level metrics (e.g., WER) are common in other fields such as speech recognition [1], they are rarely used to measure keyboard performance.

Wobbrock and Myers [25] analyzed the character input stream in addition to the presented and transcribed strings. They assume that text flows serially character by character.

This assumption does not hold for STKs, in which whole words may be algorithmically modified after they are entered. The character-level metric also does not suit SGKs well.

Building upon this prior work, we develop new word-level metrics to measure keyboard accuracy.

OCTOPUS: A REMULATION-BASED KEYBOARD EVALUATION SYSTEM

Based on the Remulation concepts described earlier, we designed and implemented Octopus (named after the conference room "Dr. Octopus" where the concept was first discussed). Octopus is a Remulation-based touchscreen keyboard evaluation tool. Figure 2 shows its architecture, which consists of (1) the Simulator, (2) Dataset, and (3) the Keyboard Output Receiver.

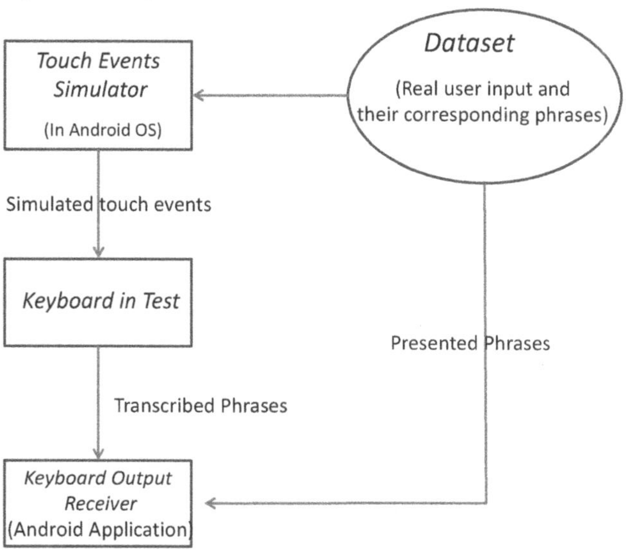

Figure 2. The architecture of the Octopus System.

(1) Touch events simulator. This component simulates touch actions on a mobile device in real time according to the dataset. It can simulate TOUCH_DOWN, TOUCH_MOVE, and TOUCH_UP events, which are the three basic touch operations on a mobile device. Using these events as building blocks, Octopus can simulate all the typical touch interactions. For example, a quick tap usually consists of a TOUCH_DOWN event immediately followed by a TOUCH_UP event, and a gesture usually consists of a TOUCH_DOWN event followed by several TOUCH_MOVE events and a TOUCH_UP event.

The Simulator accurately specifies the interval between every two touch events. The precision of such intervals between two events is less than ±10 ms. It can also simulate multi-finger interaction by specifying the finger ID of a touch event. These features allow Octopus to keep fidelity high in simulation, which is critical for evaluating modern soft keyboards. For example, a keyboard might adjust its algorithm according to the typing speed of a user. Simulating touch actions in real time is critical to measure such algorithms. When a user quickly types with two thumbs, she might land the second thumb before lifting the first one, generating multi-touch events. Octopus enables us to investigate how a keyboard handles these situations.

(2) Dataset. The dataset is fed into Octopus to simulate real users' text entry actions. The datasets consist of touch events and their corresponding phrases in *presented phrases*. Each touch event includes the event type (i.e., TOUCH_DOWN, TOUCH_MOVE, or TOUCH_UP), the (x,y) screen coordinates, the timestamp, and the finger identifier.

The collected data aims to reflect fundamental human performance, independent of particular visual design elements, keyboard features, or algorithms. Also, to challenge keyboards' algorithms and better discriminate different keyboards, the dataset strives to capture users' relaxed, natural and uncorrected typing behaviors.

In the current implementation of Octopus, the dataset is collected through lab studies in which participants type or gesture the presented phrases on a mobile device as naturally and as quickly as possible, using a collector keyboard. The collector keyboard provides users with only asterisks as feedback when they enter text, to prevent them from adjusting their input behaviors to take advantage of certain keyboard algorithms and features (such as deleting a whole word at a time).

Ideally, the layout and dimensions of the collector keyboard are identical to the test keyboard used during Remulaiton. If the test keyboard has slightly different dimensions, touch points can be scaled and translated according to the target keyboard's height, width, and top-left corner location. The validity of such transformations should be further empirically verified in future research, particularly when the transformation is large.

(3) Keyboard Output Receiver. This is an application (Figure 3) that runs on the touch screen device at the same time as the Simulator that generates the touch events.

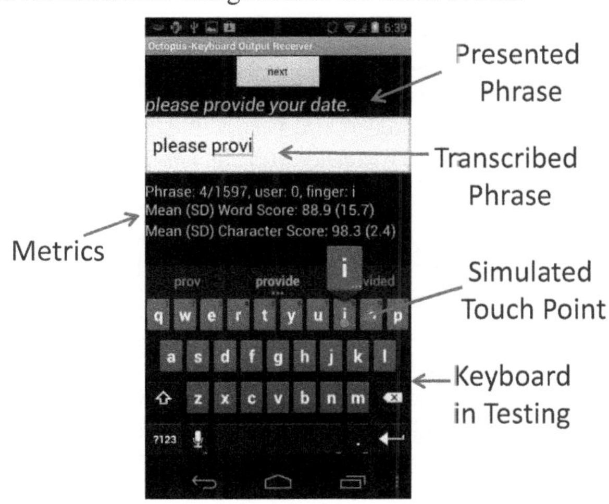

Figure 3. The UI of Keyboard Output Receiver as Octopus *remulates* the phrase "please provide your date." The red dot marks a simulated touch point.

The Keyboard Output Receiver includes a standard text view widget that receives the *transcribed phrases* from the keyboard. The communication between the keyboard and the Keyboard Receiver is through the mobile OS input method framework, so Remulation can be performed on any keyboard that is installed on the device. The Keyboard Output Receiver logs the *transcribed phrases* generated by the keyboard, compares them with the *presented phrases* from original Dataset, and then calculates and displays the quality measures of the keyboard being tested (Figure 3).

STRENGTHS AND LIMITATIONS

The Octopus *remulation* method is but one method of keyboard evaluation. Text entry is a complex process and no single method, such as a laboratory experiment, instrumented field deployment, or modeling and prediction, can provide a complete understanding of a keyboard. In our view, the Remulation-based approach offers another method that has both strengths and limitations.

Strengths. The advantages of this method include:

1. *Efficiency.* Empirical data can be used and reused multiple times to evaluate different keyboards. Efficiency is important for rapid algorithm iteration, since a developer can determine the impact of algorithm changes without new human participants.
2. *Fidelity.* This approach faithfully replicates participants' behavior in real time during the user study. It can precisely specify the time intervals between touch events, and also can support multi-touch input.
3. *Sensitivity.* Running Octopus is like employing the same group of participants typing over and over on multiple keyboards. There are no confounding variables like time of day, fatigue, or learning effects, so the impact of small algorithm tweaks can be measured reliably.
4. *No source code required.* This approach offers a "black box" evaluation: one must only install a keyboard on a mobile device to evaluate it. This enables evaluation of third-party keyboards without accessing their proprietary algorithms or source code.

Limitations. Octopus focuses on correction and recognition algorithms of keyboards. It does not evaluate the entire user experience of a touchscreen keyboard. In particular, it does not evaluate UI-related interaction behaviors, such as selecting the target via the suggestion bar or using the backspace key. Also, it is limited to keyboards with the same layout as the one used in data collection (e.g., Qwerty).

Because the user data is collected a priori and the keyboard for data collection does not provide the user with feedback for correct or erroneous input, Octopus does not account for changes in user behavior in response to keyboard output. Octopus focuses on "open loop" typing aspects in which the user types ahead and trusts the keyboard to correct their imprecise input (be it touch or gesture). This type of data reflects the most basic and natural input behaviors, unencumbered by the UI and algorithms, but does not capture feedback-driven behavior adjustments.

IMPLEMENTATION

We implemented Octopus on the Android operating system. The initial simulator was implemented on a desktop machine. It constructed touch events according to the Android protocol and sent them to the device using Android Debug Bridge (ADB) [3] via a USB cable. The limitations of this approach were 1) it was difficult to accurately control time intervals between simulated events because of the latency variance between the device and the machine; 2) simulated events occasionally went missing due to disruptions in the USB connection; and 3) the protocol for constructing touch events varied across devices, requiring extra engineering per device.

The current Simulator was implemented on top of Android's Monkey event simulation tool. It runs on a device without direct connection to a host computer. Since it simulates touch events at the OS level, it works on any Android device. From the perspective of a keyboard application, events from the simulator are indistinguishable from events that are generated by the device's touch screen.

The Keyboard Output Receiver is a standard android application developed in Java.

METRICS FOR MEASURING KEYBOARD ACCURACY

Octopus is designed to evaluate the effectiveness of keyboard algorithms. This section introduces the measures used: *Character Score*, *Word Score*, and *Ratio of Error Reduction.*

Character Score

Character Score is based on Minimum String Distance, (MSD) [16], which is the smallest number of character insertions, deletions, and replacements needed to transform one string into another:

$$MSD\ error\ rate = \frac{MSD(P,T)}{MAX(|P|,|T|)} \quad (1)$$

where P is the presented phrase and T is the transcribed phrase. To more intuitively and directly reflect accuracy, we convert the error rate to *character score*:

$$Character\ Score = (1 - MSD\ error\ rate) \times 100 \quad (2)$$

The character score is between 0 and 100, and approximately indicates the percentage of correct characters. The higher the score, the more accurate the keyboard. A keyboard with a score of 100 is error-free. However, note that this score depends on the test dataset. A dataset could include fundamental errors (e.g. input based on misread words from *presented text*), so a score of 100 may not be achievable.

Word Score

Word Score is based on Minimum Word Distance (MWD), which is the smallest number of word deletions, insertions, or replacements needed to transform one string into another.

$$MWD\ error\ rate = \frac{MWD(P,T)}{MAX(|P|,|T|)} \quad (3)$$

A word is defined as a string of characters entered between one or more continuous spaces. $|P|$ and $|T|$ are the lengths of the presented and transcribed phrases, measured in number of words.

Similar to Character Score, Word Score is defined as:

$$Word\ Accuracy\ Score = (1 - MWD\ error\ rate) \times 100$$

It approximately represents the percentage of correct words for a given dataset. Like Character Score, it is also dataset-dependent.

Ratio of Error Reduction (RER)

Character and *Word Scores* measure the overall accuracy of a given dataset, but they do not specifically measure a keyboard's correction and recognition capabilities. Comparing transcribed to presented text does not provide information about how many of a user's errors were corrected by the touch keyboard.

Figure 4 shows an example of user touch input on a soft keyboard. The presented text is "home," but the user touches the keys "h", "o", "m", and "w." A naïve keyboard that does not attempt to correct user imprecision may output "homw," but the keyboard in the figure has successfully corrected the user's input and output the text "home." However, if we compare the presented text to the transcribed text, we do not learn about the successful error correction. If the user's input had been precise (hitting the "h," "o," "m," and "e" keys), the naïve keyboard would have produced the same transcribed text. A Word Score comparing presented text with transcribed text will give the same result for the two scenarios.

presented: home

transcribed: home

Figure 4. A user touches the screen when entering the word "home." The touches are labeled in the order entered. The user imprecisely entered the "e," touching above the "w" key instead.

We thus propose to compare the presented and transcribed text to *baseline* text, which reflects a user's uncorrected keyboard output. The baseline text is generated from the closest key labels on the keyboard to the users' actual touch points. This is a naïve key-detection algorithm that offers no error correction, and literally transcribes the user's touch points. Comparing the *baseline* text to the presented text provides information about a *user's* accuracy; comparing the *baseline* text to the transcribed text provides information about the *keyboard's* ability to correct user errors.

To quantify a touch keyboard's ability to correct user error into correct words, we propose another metric, the *Ratio of Error Reduction* (RER). This metric is defined as the proportion of errors in the baseline string that were fixed by the keyboard. The RER is calculated as follows:

$$RER = \frac{E_{baseline} - E_{transcribed}}{E_{baseline}} \times 100\% \quad (4)$$

where $E_{baseline}$ is the error rate of the baseline text and $E_{transcribed}$ is the error rate of the transcribed text. *RER* is applicable only when $E_{baseline} > 0$. We can use either the MSD or the MWD to express the error rates.

EVALUATING STKS

We used Octopus to evaluate two touch keyboards on Android phones. Since the purpose of the current work was to research and demonstrate an evaluation method and a tool, not to report the relative merit and quality of different commercial products, we anonymously refer to the two keyboards as STK-A and STK-B. The dimensions of the two are identical, but the algorithms that determine keyboard output for given touch input are different. Since STK-B was developed a bit later than STK-A, it was expected that it would perform slightly better than STK-A.

Method

Collecting Typing Data

To evaluate the keyboards with Octopus, we collected text input data from users in a laboratory study we called "Salt." The study was similar to the dataset used in Azenkot and Zhai [4], but with different conditions for different hand postures, and different instructions to encourage the users to type more quickly.

A wizard of Oz keyboard was used in the study (Figure 5), which provided users with only asterisks as feedback when they entered text. After a user finished a phrase, she pressed the "next" button to proceed to the next phrase.

We recruited 40 participants. The average age was 32 (the youngest was 18 and the oldest was 59). Five were left-handed. All had experience with text entry on smartphones. The average level of self-rated proficiency with STKs was 5.5 (SD = 1.2) according to a pre-study questionnaire (1 – 7, 1 = no experience, 7 = expert).

Unlike the study in Azenkot and Zhai [4], which specified a hand posture for every participant, this study allowed the participants to text with two thumbs, one finger, or one thumb on the dominant hand according to their preference. A Galaxy Nexus phone was used throughout the study.

Twenty-four users entered text with two thumbs, 4 with one thumb, and 12 with the index finger.

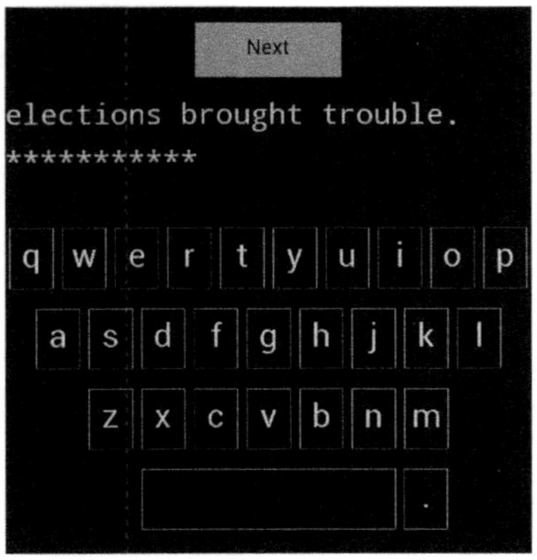

Figure 5. The WOZ keyboard we used to collect data for evaluating STKs. The keyboard design aims to capture fundamental text entry behavior.

Each participant entered the same set of 50 phrases randomly chosen from the MacKenzie and Soukoreff phrase set [17, 25]. All touch events were logged. Participants were asked to enter text "as naturally and as fast as possible." The first 10 phrases for each user were considered a warm-up and excluded in the dataset. Overall, we collected input for 1,597 phrases with 7,106 words.

Running Octopus

We ran Octopus using the Salt dataset on two Galaxy Nexus phones, the same type of phone used to collect the data. A complete run of Octopus with the Salt data took about 212.8 minutes (about 3.5 hours) on each keyboard.

Results and Discussion

Character and Word Scores

The mean *Word Scores* across the 40 participants were 83.7 (SD = 11.0), and 84.7 (SD = 10.2). The *character scores* were 94.6 (SD = 4.4) and 94.5 (SD = 4.6), for STK-A and STK-B, respectively (Figure 6). A paired t-test did not show a significant difference between these two keyboards on either of the two measures, indicating that the overall accuracies of these keyboards were similar.

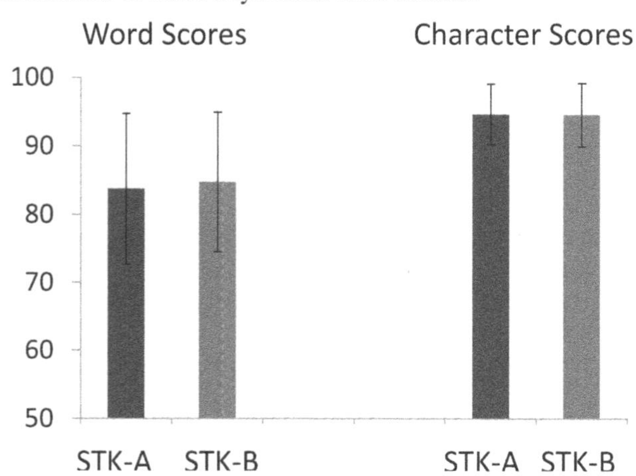

Figure 6. Mean (SD) of Word and Character Scores.

A detailed analysis, however, shows important differences between the two keyboards. The same correct output were generated from the two keyboards on 5,401 (of 7,106) words from the Salt dataset. There were 1,000 cases of touch input in Salt in which both STKs failed to generate correct target words. There were 438 word cases in which STK-B succeeded but STK-A failed. By visually inspecting the output, we discovered that STK-B seemed better at handling missing spaces than STK-A. The top three rows in Table 1 show examples. Conversely, there were 267 cases where STK-B failed but STK-A succeeded, as shown by the bottom three rows of Table 1. STK-B seemed to be more conservative than STK-A in auto-correcting spatial proximity errors.

Output on STK-A	Output on STK-B
pleasevorovife your date	please provide your date
my gagoritevsibjevy	my favorite subject
an offervyoy cannot refus	an offer you cannot refuse
three two one zero	three twp one zero
are you talking to me	are yiy talking to me
hair gel is very greasy	hair gel is very greadu

Table 1. Examples of Salt output from STK-A and STK-B. The phrases on the same row were generated on the same set of touch points.

Here we can see the Octopus *remulation* approach not only generated global metrics, but also afforded inspection of specific error cases. The latter capability enables the kind of micro-level analysis critical for more detailed insights into a keyboard's characteristics.

RER Rates

The word and character scores of baseline text of the Salt dataset were 38.9 (SD = 15.3) and 80.6 (SD = 8.6) respectively, indicating that users' input was very sloppy. More than 60% of words would have been incorrect if the touch input were decoded with a naïve closest-label keyboard algorithm.

Both STK-A and STK-B keyboards markedly reduced the errors due to imprecise input. As shown in Table 2, the *Ratio of Error Reduction* (RER) was 72.6% and 75.1% for MWD, and were 72.2% and 71.6% for MSD, for STK-A and STK-B, respectively. Approximately 7 out of 10 word errors in the Salt dataset were corrected by each keyboard.

	MWD	*MSD*
STK-A	16.3%	5.4%
STK-B	15.2%	5.5%
Baseline	61.1%	19.4%
RER of STK-A	**72.6%**	**72.2%**
RER of STK-B	**75.1%**	**71.6%**

Table 2. Ratio of Error Reduction (RER) for both keyboards, using the MSD and MWD to measure error.

When a keyboard attempts to correct user errors, a word undergoes a transition between two possible states: *correct* (no errors) and *incorrect* (contains some errors). There are four such transitions: *incorrect* to *correct*, *incorrect* to *incorrect*, *correct* to *incorrect*, and *correct* to *correct*. Table 3 shows examples of the transitions for the presented text "home."

Ideally, all transitions are either *correct* to *correct*, where the keyboard algorithms recognize the input is correct and do not modify it, or *incorrect* to *correct*, where the keyboard algorithms identify "sloppy" input and modify it to the target word. *Correct* to *incorrect* transitions are likely to occur when a user enters a string that is OOV (out of vocabulary). Transitions that move from *Correct* to *Incorrect* have been found in prior work to be disruptive and frustrating to users [9].

	Baseline	*Transcribed*
Incorrect → Correct	homw	Home
Incorrect → Incorrect	hone	Gone
Correct → Incorrect	home	homw
Correct → Correct	home	home

Table 3. Examples of transitions from the baseline to the transcribed text for the presented text "home." A "correct" state indicates the transcribed text is the same as the presented text, and an "incorrect" state indicates they are different.

To deeply understand the keyboard's error correction behavior, we investigate the composition of these four types of transitions (Figure 7). 3,297 words (46.4%) on STK-A and 3,425 words (48.2%) on STK-B keyboards underwent an *incorrect* to *correct* transition, demonstrating strong auto-correction performance for both keyboards. STK-A and STK-B falsely changed 1.5% and 0.8% of words from correct to incorrect. Although small in number, in this very critical category of errors, STK-B made only about half the errors that STK-A did. Table 4 shows examples of successful corrections.

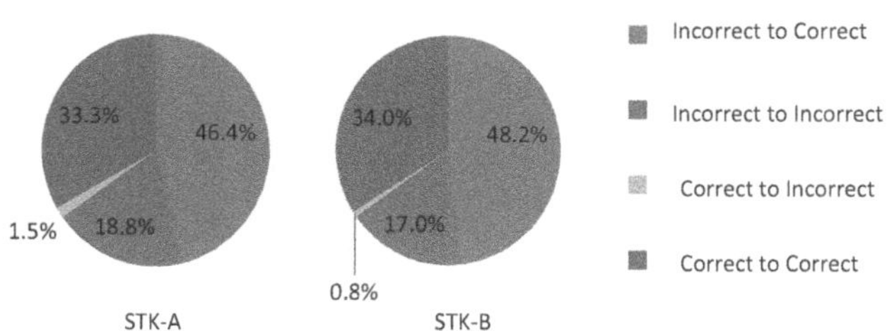

Figure 7. Percentages of Four Types of Transitions on STK-A (left) and STK-B (right) keyboards

Baseline	Corrected output on STK-A and STK-B
he s jst kr everone	he is just like everyone
nofer youcannot refuse	an offer you cannot refuse
pleae orovife our aye	please provide your date

Table 4. Examples of Successful Corrections. Words in red are erroneous words.

EVALUATING WORD-GESTURE KEYBOARDS

In addition to evaluating STKs, we used Octopus to evaluate two SGKs, SGK-A and SGK-B. SGK-B was developed later than SGK-A, so we expected it to perform better.

Method

Collecting Gesture Data

The Salt study described earlier also collected gestures. The experiment balanced the order of gesture and touch data collection. The WOZ keyboard in the study was the same as the one used in touch data collection (720 × 414 pixels). It was identical to SGK-B in dimensions, but slightly different from SGK-A in height (720 × 398 pixels).

The gesture data collected were therefore slightly scaled to match SGK-A when running Octopus.

The same 40 subjects participated in the study. The levels of proficiency of these participants reflected the partial adoption of SGKs: half of the participants were proficient users who used SGKs at least 5 days a week; the other half had never used an SGK.

Unlike STK data collection in which participants freely chose the preferred input finger, hand posture was a two-level, within-subject factor (i.e., thumb or index finger). Each participant gestured a set of 50 phrases by index finger and the same set of phrases by the thumb. The device used in this study was the same as the one used in the typing data collection study. A user's finger gesture trace was shown using a blue stroke, and only minimal output feedback was provided. The current target word was underlined and the previously gestured words were dimmed (Figure 8). Our purpose was again to capture the most natural input behaviors, and to avoid interference from any particular recognition algorithm.

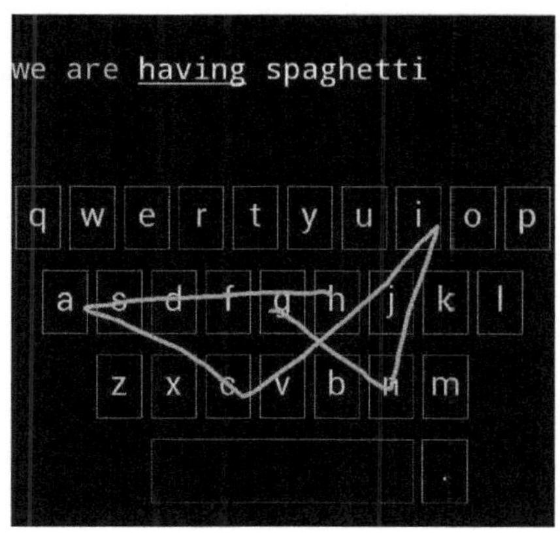

Figure 8. Keyboard Layout for Gesture Data Collection. The participant was gesturing the word *having*.

The first 10 phrases for each posture and each user were treated as a warm-up and excluded from the dataset. In the entire study, we collected data for 40 × 2 (finger postures) × 40 (participants) = 3,200 phrases with 14,235 words.

Running Octopus

We ran Octopus using the Salt gesture data described above on a Galaxy Nexus phone to evaluate SGK-A and SGK-B. The study had two within-subject factors: input finger (thumb and index finger) and keyboard (SGK-A, and SGK-B). A complete run of Octopus took approximately 400 minutes (around 7 hours).

Results and Discussion

Since gesture input does not have *baseline* text, the RER measure is not applicable for evaluating SGKs. We therefore focus on the word and character scores.

An ANOVA showed that both word ($F(1,39) = 155.5$, $p < .001$) and character ($F(1,39) = 134.6$, $p < .001$) scores of SGK-B were significantly higher than those for SGK-A. The mean word scores were 73.0 (SD = 12.2) and 81.9 (SD = 10.0), and the mean character scores were 83.8 (SD = 8.8) and 89.7 (SD = 7.0) for SGK-A and SGK-B respectively (Figure 9). SGK-B generated about 10 more correct words in every 100 gestures than SGK-A.

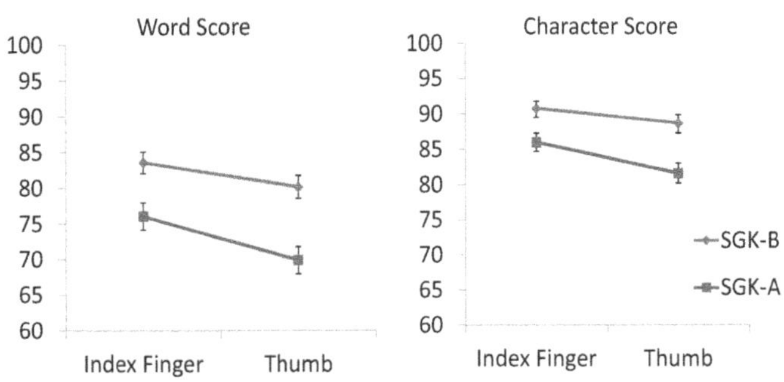

Figure 9. Mean (Std. Error) Word and Character scores by Keyboard and Posture.

The analysis also showed a significant main effect of input finger on word ($F(1, 39) = 14.6$, $p < 0.01$) and character ($F(1, 39) = 11.0$, $p < 0.05$) scores. The participants were more accurate gesturing with the index finger than with the thumb.

ANOVA showed significant interactions for keyboard × input finger on both word ($F(1,39) = 10.0$, $p < .005$), and character scores ($F(1,39) = 12.1$, $p < .005$). As illustrated in Figure 9, SGK-B was especially more accurate than SGK-A in the thumb condition, in which the input was more "sloppy" than in the index-finger condition.

Figure 10 shows the mean word score for each participant. As illustrated, SGK-B is more accurate then SGK-A for 39 out of 40 participants (and the remaining participant had the same score on both). It confirms the finding from the ANOVA analysis: SGK-B is significantly superior to SGK-A.

By comparing the output of both keyboards with presented phrases, we discovered some limitations of each keyboard. These findings could help developers to further improve the algorithms.

One interesting observation of SGK-A's performance was that it tended to mistakenly include unintended letters adjacent to the target letter in the recognition results. As shown in the first three rows of Table 5, SGK-A misrecognized *provide* as *provides, are* as *ate*, and *smart* as *smarty*. Unintended letters *s* (close to *e*), *t* (close to *r*), and *y* (close to *t*) were mistakenly included.

SGK-A Output	SGK-B Output
please provide your date	please provides your date
you are not a jedi yet	you ate not a jedi yet
yes you are very smart	yes you are very smarty
a great dissonance	a great disturbance
you must be hefting old	you must be getting old
a quezon to answer	a question to answer

Table 5. Examples of Output Phrases on SGK-A and SGK-B. Erroneous words are in red.

Unlike SGK-A, one potential problem for SGK-B was its large vocabulary. It contained obscure words that distracted a sloppy gestures from their intended word. For example, it falsely recognized the target words *disturbance* as *dissonance, getting* as *hefting*, and *question* as *quezon* (see the bottom three rows of Table 5).

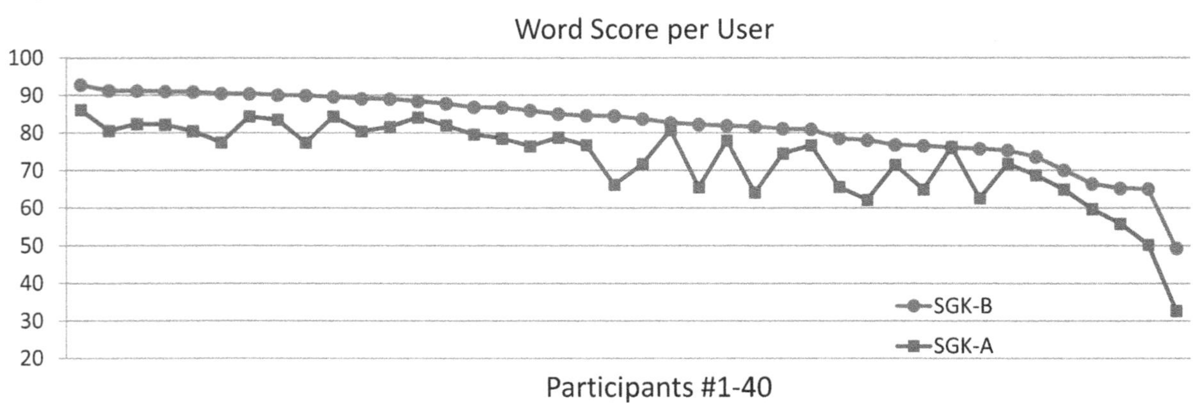

Figure 10. Mean Word Score for Each Participant (Sorted in Descending Order on SGK-B).

LIMITATIONS AND FUTURE WORK

We note again that the performance measures from Octopus Remulation depend on the test dataset. A dataset can be either too easy (nearly perfect input) so all keyboards can give high word scores (a ceiling effect), or too difficult (all input hopelessly sloppy and erroneous) so no keyboard can do well on it (a floor effect). We have collected a dataset, Salt, that is natural and sloppy, so it can discriminate among different keyboards. Indeed our word scores were in 70's and 80's, close neither to the ceiling (100) nor the floor (0). However whether the Salt data closely resembles users' "natural" behavior on real keyboards is debatable. We suspect there may not be a "perfectly natural" behavior when it comes to interacting with real UI technologies. The better the recognition technology gets, the sloppier the user may behave to take advantage of the technology. It will therefore be necessary to collect different datasets that reflect different ranges of user expertise and behavior.

Octopus can be used and enhanced in several ways. We described only two applications of Octopus for evaluating touch and gesture keyboards. With a new set of data, Octopus can be used to evaluate keyboards with different layouts on various devices, including tablets. With appropriate operating system support, the Remulation approach can also be implemented on platforms other than Android, such as Apple's iPhone and Microsoft's Windows Phone, enabling comparison across platforms.

CONCLUSION

We have presented *Remulation*, a novel approach to evaluating keyboard correction and recognition algorithms by replicating prior user study data via real-time simulation. It contributes to the wide spectrum of user interface evaluation methods, ranging from A/B testing in laboratory experiments to model-based prediction. We have also contributed two new metrics, *Word Score* and *Ratio of Error Reduction* (RER), to measure keyboard accuracy at the word level, and to quantify STK error-correction capability.

Based on the *Remulation* approach and new data analysis methods, we have designed and implemented Octopus, a keyboard evaluation tool. Powered by the Salt dataset we collected, we used Octopus to evaluate two smart touch keyboards and two smart gesture keyboards. The results clearly demonstrated the value of the *Remulation* approach, the Octopus tool, and the metrics of *Word Score* and *RER*. For example, Octopus showed that today's STKs can correct over 70% of the word errors that a naïve touchscreen keyboard would produce on the Salt dataset. Octopus also exposed different types of errors made by the tested STKs, even though standard metrics showed that the keyboards performed identically. We have shown that Octopus remulation can also be applied to continuous word gesture-based keyboards, and found that one SGK is much stronger than another, which in turn suggests that this novel input paradigm [29] may progress even further with future research.

ACKNOWLEDGEMENTS

We thank participants in our studies, and the CHI paper reviewers for the insightful comments.

REFERENCES

1. Andrew, C. W., Maier, V., Green, P. (2004). From WER and RIL to MER and WIL: improved evaluation measures for connected speech recognition. *Proc. of INTERSPEECH.* 4 pages.
2. Android 4.2 http://www.android. com/whatsnew/
3. Android Developers. Tools: Andorid Debug Bridge. Accessed April 13, 2012. http://developer.android.com/guide/developing/tools/adb.html.
4. Azenkot, S. and Zhai, S. (2012). Touch Behavior with Different Postures on Soft Smart Phone Keyboards. *Proc. of MobileHCI'12.* 251-260.
5. Bi, X., Chelba, C., Ouyang, T., Partridge, K., and Zhai, S. (2012). Bimanual gesture keyboard. *Proc. of UIST'12.* 137-146.
6. Damn You, Auto-Correct! http://www.damnyouautocorrect.com/. Accessed April 13, 2012.
7. Findlater, L., and Wobbrock, J.O. (2012). Personalized input: improving ten-finger touchscreen typing through automatic adaptation. *Proc. of CHI '12.* 815-824.
8. Goodman, J., Venolia, G., Steury, K., and Parker, C. (2002). Language modeling for soft keyboards. *Proc. AAAI '02*, Menlo Park, CA, USA, 419-424.
9. Gunawardana, A., Paek, T., and Meek, C. (2010). Usability guided key-target resizing for soft keyboards. *Proc. IUI '10.* ACM, New York, NY, USA, 111-118.
10. Kristensson, P.O. and Zhai, S. 2004. SHARK: a large vocabulary shorthand writing system for pen-based computers. *Proc. of UIST '04.* ACM Press: 43-52.
11. Lewis, J. R. (1992). *Typing-key layouts for single-finger or stylus input: initial user preference and performance* (Technical Report No. 54729). Boca Raton, FL: International Business Machines Corporation.
12. Lewis, J. R., Kennedy, P. J., & LaLomia, M. J. (1999). *Development of a Digram-Based Typing Key Layout for Single-Finger/Stylus Input.* Proceedings of The Human Factors and Ergonomics Society 43rd Annual Meeting.
13. Lewis, J. R., LaLomia, M. J., & Kennedy, P. J. (1999). *Evaluation of Typing Key Layouts for Stylus Input.* Proceedings of The Human Factors and Ergonomics Society 43rd Annual Meeting.

14. Lewis, J. R., Potosnak, K. M., & Magyar, R. L. (1997). Keys and Keyboards. In M. G. Helander, T. K. Landauer & P. V. Prabhu (Eds.), *Handbook of human-computer interaction* (2nd ed., pp. 1285-1315). Amsterdam: Elsevier Science.
15. MacKenzie, I. S. and Soukoreff, R. W. (2002). A Model of Two–Thumb Text Entry. In Proceedings of Graphics Interface '02, pp. 117–124.
16. MacKenzie, I. S. and Soukoreff, R. W. (2002). A chracter-level error analysis technique for evaluating text entry methods. In Proceedings of the 2nd Nordic Conference on Human-Computer Interaction (NordiCHI). Arhus, Denmark (Oct. 19–23). 243–24.
17. MacKenzie, I. S., and Soukoreff, R. W. (2003). Phrase sets for evaluating text entry techniques. *Proc. of CHI EA '03*, pp. 754-755. New York: ACM.
18. MacKenzie, I. S., and Tanaka-Ishii, K. (Eds.). (2007). *Text Entry Systems: Mobility, Accessibility, Universality*: Morgan Kaufmann Publishers.
19. MacKenzie, I. S., and Zhang, S. X. (1999) The design and evaluation of a high-performance soft key-board. Proceedings of the ACM Conference on Human Factors in Computing Systems CHI '99, pp. 25-31. New York: ACM.
20. The New York Times, iPhone Keyboard Secrets. http://pogue.blogs.nytimes.com/2007/06/27/iphone-keyboard-secrets/
21. Rick, J. (2010). Performance optimizations of virtual keyboards for stroke-based text entry on a touch-based tabletop. *ACM UIST*, 77-86.
22. Rudchenko, D., Paek, T., and Badger, E. (2011). Text Text Revolution: A game that improves text entry on mobile touchscreen keyboards. *Proc. Pervasive '2011.*
23. Rumelhart, D. E. and Norman, D. A. (1982), Simulating a Skilled Typist: A Study of Skilled Cognitive-Motor Performance. Cognitive Science, 6: 1–36.
24. Wobbrock, J.O. (2007). Measures of text entry performance. Chapter 3 in I.S. MacKenzie and K. Tanaka-Ishii (eds.), Text Entry Systems: Mobility, Accessibility, Universality. San Francisco: Morgan Kaufmann, pp. 47-74.
25. Wobbrock, J.O. and Myers, B.A. (2006). Analyzing the input stream for character-level errors in unconstrained text entry evaluations. ACM Transactions on Computer-Human Interaction 13 (4), pp. 458-489.
26. Zhai, S., Hunter, M., & Smith, B. A. (2002). Performance optimization of virtual keyboards. *Human-Computer Interaction, 17*(2,3), 89-129.
27. Zhai, S. and Kristensson, P.O. 2003. Shorthand writing on stylus keyboard. *Proc. of CHI '03*. ACM Press: 97-104.
28. Zhai, S. and Kristensson, P.O. Introduction to Shape Writing (2006) *IBM Research Report* RJ10393 (A0611-006), November.
29. Zhai, S. and Kristensson, P.O. (2012). The word-gesture keyboard: reimagining keyboard interaction. *Commun. ACM* 55, 9 (September 2012), 91-101.

TapBoard: Making a Touch Screen Keyboard More Touchable

Sunjun Kim, Jeongmin Son, and Geehyuk Lee
Human-Computer Interaction Lab, KAIST
291 Daehak-ro, Yuseong-gu, Daejeon, South Korea
{kuaa.net, jmin.sohn, geehyuk}@gmail.com

Hwan Kim, and Woohun Lee
Department of Industrial Design, KAIST
291 Daehak-ro, Yuseong-gu, Daejeon, South Korea
{hwan.kim, woohun.lee}@kaist.ac.kr

ABSTRACT
A physical keyboard key has three states, whereas a touch screen usually has only two. Due to this difference, the state corresponding to the touched state of a physical key is missing in a touch screen keyboard. This touched state is an important factor in the usability of a keyboard. In order to recover the role of a touched state in a touch screen, we propose the TapBoard, a touch screen software keyboard that regards tapping actions as keystrokes and other touches as the touched state. In a series of user studies, we validate the effectiveness of the TapBoard concept. First, we show that tapping to type is in fact compatible with the existing typing skill of most touch screen keyboard users. Second, users quickly adapt to the TapBoard and learn to rest their fingers in the touched state. Finally, we confirm by a controlled experiment that there is no difference in text-entry performance between the TapBoard and a traditional touch screen software keyboard. In addition to these experimental results, we demonstrate a few new interaction techniques that will be made possible by the TapBoard.

Author Keywords
TapBoard; text-entry method; touch screen keyboard.

ACM Classification Keywords
H.5.2. Information Interfaces and Presentation: User Interfaces - Input devices and strategies.

General Terms
Design; Human Factors.

INTRODUCTION
Tablet computers with multi-touch screens are increasingly popular. As more applications are being designed for tablets, the role of the touch screen software keyboard is becoming more important. Tablet computers with large touch screens, such as the Apple iPad and the Samsung Galaxy Tab, have software keyboards with a full-size, complete QWERTY layout, similar to that of a laptop. Because of the similarity between the software keyboard and the laptop keyboard in terms of both form and size, users tend to type on the touch screen software keyboard with all ten fingers and attempt to touch-type, as they do on a physical keyboard [2].

An intrinsic problem in the design of touch screen software keyboards is that touch screens usually have only two states (released and touched), whereas real physical keys have three states (released, touched, and pressed). Due to this mismatch in the number of states, touch screen keyboard designs have had to disregard the touched state of physical keys, simulating only the released and pressed states, as illustrated in Figure 1. As the result, touch screen software keyboards do not currently have a state that corresponds to the touched state of physical keys.

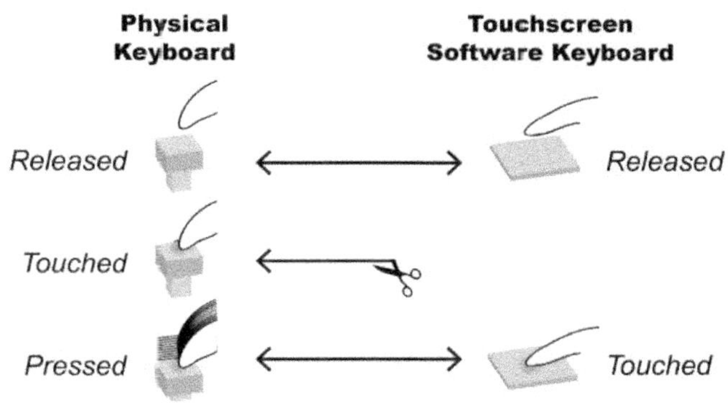

Figure 1. Mapping between the states of physical keys and the states of touch screens. Due to the mismatch in the number of states, the touched state of physical keys is not mapped to any state in touch screens.

The touched state actually plays an important role in the usability of physical keyboards [6, 10, 18, 23]. For instance, a keyboard user can rest their fingers in the touched state during typing. Users can also feel the texture of the keys, allowing the chance to align their fingers. An ultimate solution to restore the role of the touched state in a touch screen keyboard seemed to be the use of a three-state touch screen [4, 11], but the relevant technology is not yet ready for the market. As a currently feasible solution, we consider the alternative mapping illustrated in Figure 2, where the released and touched states of physical keys are mapped to the released and touched states of touch screens, respectively. In contrast to the case in Figure 1, the pressed state of physical keys is disregarded instead of the touched state. In fact, the role of the pressed state of physical keys is not as important as that of the touched state. The pressed state is usually a transient state that is visited only briefly during a keystroke event. A keystroke event, which is not a state, is more important than the pressed state. Therefore, we decided to disregard the pressed state, and simulate a keystroke event with a tapping event. A consequence of this mapping is that there will be some restriction in utilizing the touched state, as a brief touch will be interpreted as a tapping action. If one wishes to rest their fingers on the touch screen keyboard, the duration should be longer than a certain threshold. Despite this small limitation, the touched state of a touch screen has now become available for other purposes. The result is the TapBoard, a touch screen software keyboard that can be operated by a tapping action. A tapping event, as will be defined precisely later, is defined not only by its short duration, but also by a small movement on the screen.

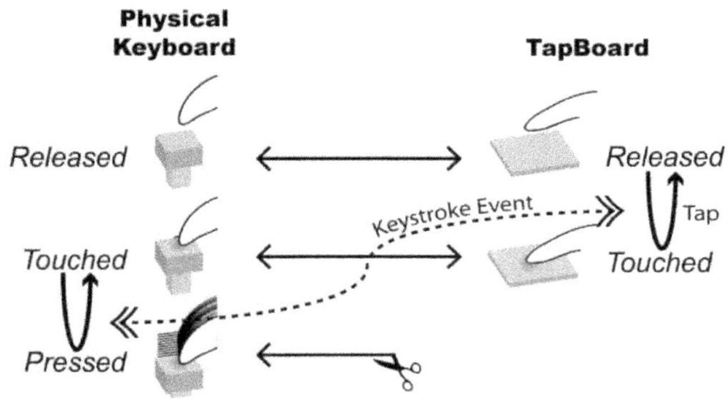

Figure 2. Mapping between the states of a physical key and the states of a touch screen in TapBoard. The pressed state of a physical key is disregarded, and the keystroke event of a physical key is now mapped to the tapping event of a touch screen.

We made a few assumptions when we first conceived the TapBoard. First, we could observe that people do use tapping when they type on a touch screen keyboard, and therefore we expected that TapBoard would be compatible with users' existing typing skills. Second, we expected that users will quickly be able to adapt to TapBoard and utilize the touched state, e.g., for resting their fingers on the screen. Third, we expected that TapBoard will be as efficient as an ordinary touch screen keyboard, because it is compatible with the existing typing skill of most users. All these assumptions require experimental support; hence, we conducted three user studies to collect experimental data. In the first, we verify the first assumption that underlies the TapBoard design, and observe user behavior on both physical and touch screen software keyboards. In the second study, we elicit several behavioral observations to support the second assumption and fine-tune the parameters of TapBoard. In the third study, we compare the text entry performance of a traditional touch screen software keyboard and TapBoard, and obtain experimental support for the third assumption.

In the following, we first summarize related works on touch screen text-entry methods and user typing behavior. We then present the detailed design of TapBoard, and describe three empirical studies. After the experimental results, we introduce some new possibilities enabled by the recovered touched state of TapBoard. Finally, we conclude the paper by summarizing the contributions of the current research.

RELATED WORK

Because typing skills transfer from the physical to software keyboards [20], we introduce a number of relevant studies on the characteristics of text entry on a physical keyboard and a touch screen software keyboard. In the following subsections, we discuss the importance of the touched state in physical keyboards and why it should be offered in large-size touch screen devices.

Text Entry Using Physical Keyboards

Expert touch-typists can type very quickly on physical keyboards without any visual attention. Several studies targeting such typists have pointed out that the removal of kinesthetic and tactile feedback significantly reduced the typing performance [2, 6]. In particular, Crump and Logan claimed that simply removing the keycaps, which takes away only tactual information and not kinesthetic movement, also had a negative influence on performance [6]. Other studies confirm that tactile information from the keys is the main factor in finger motion planning [6, 10, 18]. It seems clear that touch-typing and fast typing exploit the tactile cues provided by the touched state of physical keyboards.

Text Entry using Touch Screen Software Keyboards

As physical keyboards come in different sizes, touch screen software keyboards are implemented in various forms, from 3-inch devices to full-sized tabletops. Compared to physical keyboards, touch screen software keyboards are known to suffer from poor performance [2, 5, 9, 26, 32]. Interestingly, however, well-designed touch screen software keyboards offer comparable performance to that of physical keypads in small-size devices such as smartphones [13, 15]. Because both keyboards rely heavily on the user's intensive visual attention, the typing skill required for them is similar. In this case, the experience of physical keyboards can be easily transferred to software keyboards.

In contrast, typing performance on touch screen devices larger than a tablet is considerably worse than that on physical keyboards [5, 9, 24]. A number of studies have attempted to overcome the performance limitation using layout adaptation [8, 25], different layouts and sizes [17, 19, 26], and tactile feedback [22]. However, even in the best possible condition, where participants could ignore typing errors, results with touch screen keyboards were still 31% slower than with physical keyboards [9].

Possible Feedbacks for Touch Screen

As discussed in the previous subsection, the touched state plays a critical role in the use of physical keyboards. Therefore, we expect solutions providing the touched state in software keyboards [29, 30, 31] to be a strong candidate for improving their performance. TouchFire [30] and SLAP Widget [31] offer a tangible keyboard object on the touch screen. Only keystrokes are transferred to the touch screen by a mechanical structure, and other touches are blocked. Tactus technology [29] developed a deformable touch screen surface, which generates physical bumps dynamically. TeslaTouch [3] LATPaD [16], and STIMTAC [1] exhibit a dynamically changeable surface texture. The above techniques enable users to get information from the surface of the screen while sweeping their fingers across it.

TAPBOARD

TapBoard should accept only brief touches within the size of a key as valid keystrokes and ignore other touches. In order to do so, TapBoard runs a state machine, as shown in Figure 3, for each touch point. The state machine, which is initially in the [Idle] state, makes a transition to the [Touched] state on a [Touch(i)] event, where i is the index of the current touch point. On this transition, it resets a timer t and displacement d, creates a key-input object k, and outputs a [Preview(k)] event. The state machine returns to the [Idle] state when one of the following three events occur. (1) The timer t exceeds a timeout threshold τ. (2) The displacement d exceeds a displacement threshold δ. (3) A [Release(i)] event occurs. In the first two cases, a [Cancel(k)] event is output for the key-input object k. In the third case, a [Complete(k)] event is output for the key-input object k. Only a [Complete(k)] event is considered as a keystroke.

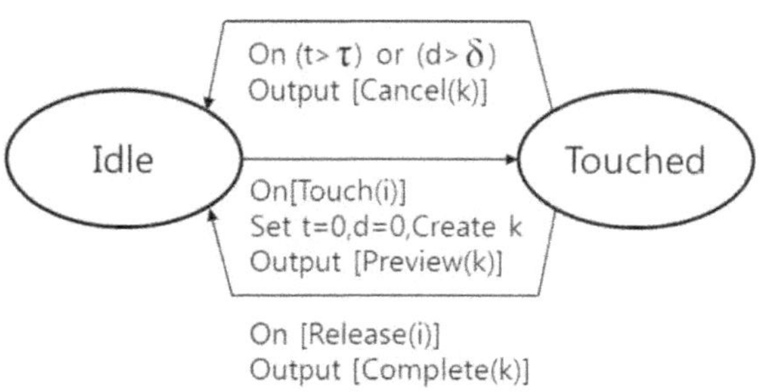

Figure 3. State machine of each touch point in TapBoard.

A TapBoard prototype was implemented in C# so that it can run on both the Samsung Slate 7 and Samsung SUR40. The prototype does not support all the keys of a standard full keyboard, offering only the alphabet keys, shift keys, a space bar, enter key, and backspace key, as shown in Figure 4. The TapBoard algorithm applies to all keys except the backspace and shift keys. These are excluded based on the results of experiment 1, which is described later.

As shown in Figure 4, the TapBoard layout replicates the dimensions of a physical keyboard. The timeout parameter τ was initially set to 300 ms, but was changed to 450 ms based on the result of experiment 2, which is described later. The distance threshold parameter δ was initially set to the width of an alphabet key, which is 80 pixels (about 15 mm). In addition to implementing the basic logic shown in Figure 3, we had to find some workarounds to handle the non-ideal behavior of the touch screen device, e.g., occasional spurious touch-and-release events, when five or more fingers are touching the screen. We handled at most five touch events simultaneously to prevent such erroneous behavior.

Figure 4. Screen snapshot showing the design of the prototype touch screen keyboard.

EXPERIMENTS

In a series of experiments, we validated the effectiveness of the TapBoard concept. First, we collected typing logs from physical keyboards and touch screen software keyboards to set the initial parameters for TapBoard. Second, we investigated whether users can adapt to the TapBoard concept. Finally, we studied whether there is a performance difference between using TapBoard and a conventional touch screen keyboard.

Experiment 1: Inspecting Typing Behavior

We conducted a within-subjects experiment with three different keyboard conditions: an instrumented physical keyboard with touch sensors (*physical*), a software keyboard typical of tablet PCs (*tablet*), and a software keyboard typical of tabletop PCs (*tabletop*). The experiment was carried out to measure the keystroke durations, i.e., key press durations on *physical* and touch durations on *tablet* and *tabletop*. We also observed the variation in typing behavior with conditions. For this experiment, 12 university students (six males and six females, mean age 22.7 years) were recruited. All of them were touch typists with traditional physical keyboards, but did not have much typing experience with software keyboards on tablet or tabletop computers.

Apparatus

We used a Samsung Slate 7 as the *tablet* and a Samsung SUR40 as the *tabletop*. The Samsung SUR40 uses an optical touch screen that is sensitive to hovering objects, and therefore, in the case of the Samsung SUR40, participants had to wear black-painted cotton gloves that left only their fingers uncovered. These gloves prevented erroneous touch inputs from the palm of the hand.

In the *physical* keyboard, we implemented a conductive touch sensor using similar techniques to [12]. Participants wore a conductive pad connected to a function generator producing a 1 MHz sine wave. The touch sensor scanned the transferred signal through the human body. We multiplexed the touch sensor input with six 74HC4051 8-channel analog multiplexers, so the sensor unit was capable of sensing 48 touches individually. We attached copper tapes to the alphabet keys, shift keys, backspace key, space bar, and enter key, and wired them to the touch sensor unit to capture touch events (Figure 5).

Figure 5. Implementation of the *physical* condition, which is an instrumented physical keyboard with touch sensors.

In all conditions, we developed a transcription test program (Figure 4) in which participants must transcribe test phrases shown at the top of the screen. For the *tablet* and *tabletop* conditions, the software keyboard was shown below the textbox. Each key on the software keyboard changes color when touched. Software keyboards are programmed to record touch and release events with timestamps and corresponding characters. For the *physical* condition, only the given text and a transcription textbox were shown on the screen, and participants were asked to transcribe the words using the instrumented keyboard. Touch and release events from the touch sensor, as well as key press and release events from the keyboard itself, were recorded with timestamps and corresponding characters. The keyboard dimensions, such as key size and distance between keys, were controlled to be identical in all three conditions.

Procedure

Each participant was asked to transcribe 50 sentences that were selected randomly from the MacKenzie and Soukoreff phrase sets [21] for each condition. They were required to type as fast and as accurately as possible. Participants typed 10 sentences in a training session, and 50 sentences in a test session. The order of devices was fully counterbalanced across participants to avoid carryover effects. Each participant took 40 min to finish the entire typing session.

Result

We recorded all touches from *tablet* and *tabletop*, and all touches (*touch*) and key presses (*press*) from *physical*. For touch data in the *physical* condition, we excluded touch durations of less than 10 ms, which were considered to be due to device noise. A total of 24058 touches on *tablet*, 24262 touches on *tabletop*, and 21796 key presses and 39366 touches on *physical* were collected.

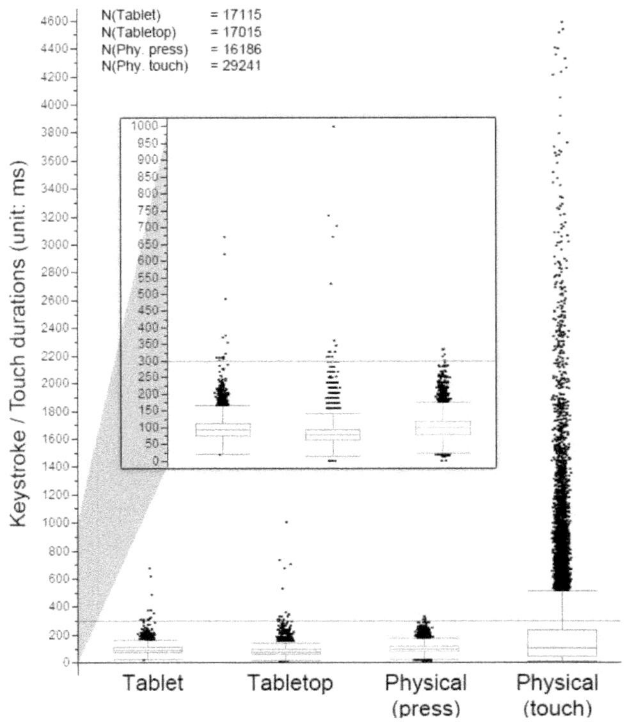

Figure 6. Box plots of touch duration and keystroke duration for alphabet keys. Touch durations of the touch screen devices and keystroke durations of the physical keyboard have similar distributions under 300 ms, while touch durations of the physical keyboard exhibit a significant tail over 300 ms.

We first analyze alphabet keystrokes. In total, 17162 touches on *tablet*, 17015 touches on *tabletop*, and 16186 key presses and 29241 touches on *physical* are analyzed. Figure 6 illustrates the distribution of keystrokes from each device. The 99.9 percentile values for *tablet*, *tabletop*, and *physical press* were 296 ms, 267 ms, and 285 ms, respectively. Most keystrokes took less than 300 ms. However, *physical touch* exhibits a significantly different distribution. More touches were counted than *physical presses* because fingers tend to touch surrounding keys during typing. Only 81% (23675 touches) of them fall within 300 ms. Short touches (<300 ms) are mainly induced by keystrokes. Long touches (>300 ms), which are of most interest, are mainly induced by resting or home-row searching.

Next, we analyze the other keys. The enter, space, and backspace keys exhibit similar distributions to the alphabet keys. For the shift keys, we observed a significant increase in touch duration and keystroke duration (Figure 7) compare to those for the alphabet keys. Additionally, users activated the shift key longer on *tablet* and *tabletop* than on *physical*. Therefore, we cannot apply the TapBoard concept to the shift key. In addition, although it is not observed in this experiment, the backspace key often requires auto-repeat functionality. Thus, TapBoard is not suitable for the backspace and shift keys.

Finally, we inspected logs from the touch sensor and found some interesting patterns. (1) The number of simultaneously touched keys varied by participant. Figure 8 plots two extreme participants. P1 tends to touch and press exactly one intended key. In contrast, P12 often rested all fingers (nine touch counts). (2) Participants often realigned their fingers. Figure 9 shows a representative aligning pattern. (3) Resting touches were concentrated on home-row keys (ASDFGHJKL) and the space bar (70.8%), followed by upper-row keys (QWERTYUIOP, 21.8%). Fingers rarely rested on lower-row keys (ZXCVBNM, 1.4%). Figure 10 plots the distribution of resting touches.

In summary, most of the keystrokes are short (<300 ms), which supports our assumption. We also found that the touched state of physical keyboards exhibits totally different characteristics. Participants mainly utilize the touched state for aligning their fingers on the home row.

Experiment 2: Typing behavior with TapBoard

We conducted an observational study with two different touch screen devices: a tablet PC (*tablet*) and a tabletop PC (*tabletop*). We designed an experiment in which participants typed and waited during conversations. We expected TapBoard to lead users to rest their fingers on the touch screen keyboards and find the home row while waiting. For this experiment, five participants were recruited. All of them were university students (two males and three females, mean age 23.0 years). All of them were touch typists with traditional physical keyboards

Apparatus

This experiment again used the Samsung Slate 7 and Samsung SUR40. Subjects were provided with a simple chat program in both conditions. The program layout was identical to the transcription program of experiment 1, except that the software keyboard adopted the TapBoard algorithm with timeout threshold τ = 300 ms and distance threshold δ = 80 px. For a more natural typing experience, we allowed the participants to type in their mother tongue (Korean). The program recorded touch and release events with timestamps and corresponding characters. In addition, the software keyboard gave additional visual feedback when subjects put at least four fingers on the home-row.

Procedure

The participants were asked to chat with a moderator. The moderator and each participant talked about their daily life and interests. e.g., "what is your hobby?" or "please describe Mr./Miss Right." In addition, we gave the following instruction.

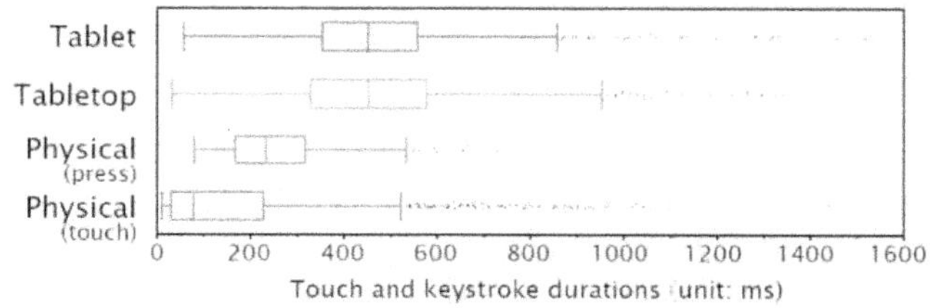

Figure 7. Box plots of touch durations and keystroke durations for the shift key.

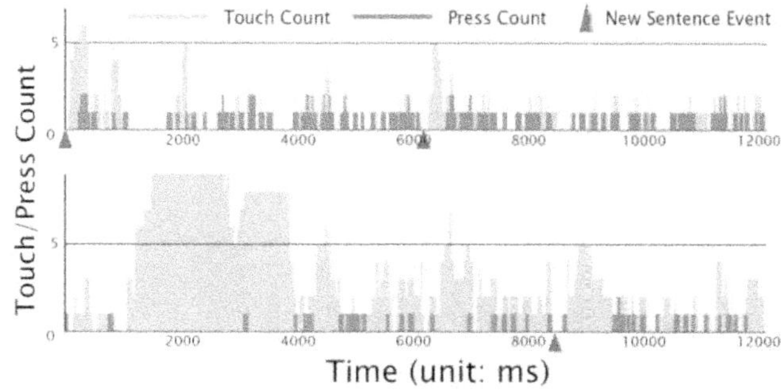

Figure 8. Typing behavior plot. Touch count represents number of touched keys, and press count represents number of pressed keys at a certain time. New sentence events take place when participants are given a new sentence to be transcribed.

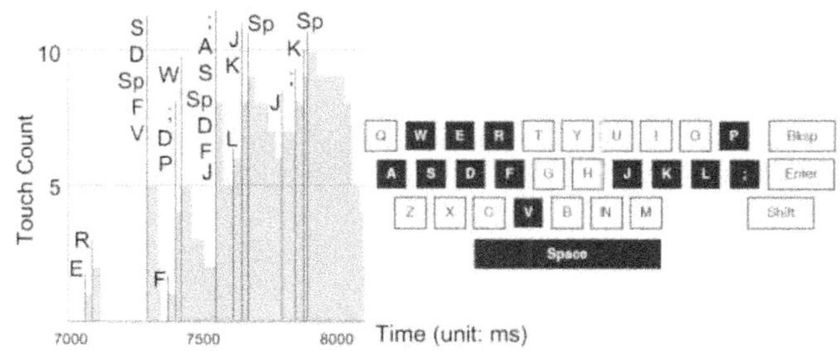

Figure 9. An aligning behavior pattern (P4).

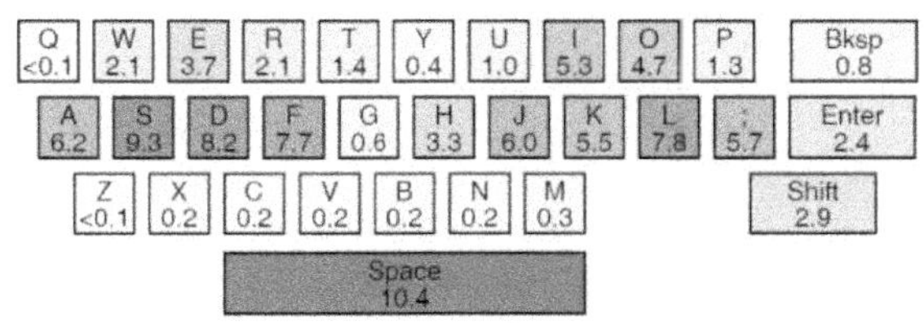

Figure 10. Distribution of resting touches. (unit: %)

> *"This chat session will be conducted through a special keyboard called TapBoard. Its appearance is not very different from that of a general keyboard, but it will cancel your input if you touch the surface for longer than 300 ms."*

We conveyed this instruction just once before the start of each session in order that the participants understood the key feature of TapBoard naturally without any enforcement. After receiving this instruction, they tried cancelling their touches with one finger, two fingers, five fingers, and then eight fingers. Then, they conducted a 10 min chat session. Each participant had a session with both the *tablet* and *tabletop* conditions. Three participants started with *tablet*, and the other two started with *tabletop* in their first session.

Result

We observed resting behavior from four out of five participants. Figure 11 illustrates the representative resting behavior from one participant. Participants tended to rest their fingers (represented by *Canceled touch count*) while the moderator was typing questions (represented by *Moderator*). Similar behavior was observed for four participants across both devices. The exception was P2, who did not rest his fingers at all. P2 leant against the chair backrest during the whole of the chat sessions, and crossed his arms after he finished his replies. The debriefing with P2 revealed that he did not realize that TapBoard allowed him to rest his hands on the device.

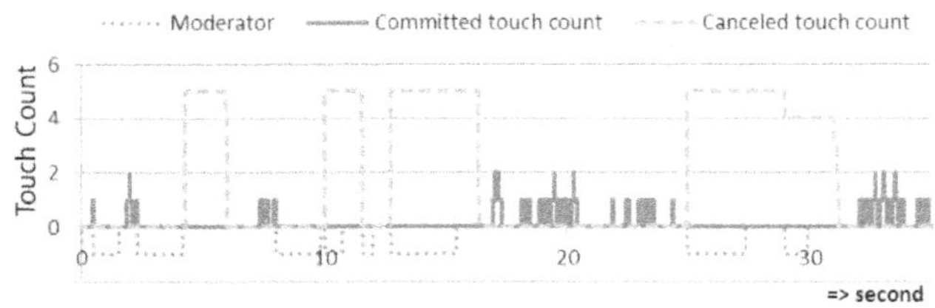

Figure 11. Resting behavior observed in participant P1.

Accumulated resting time percentages (canceled touches) are shown in Figure 12. With the exception of P2, participants actively rested for up to 29% of the total experiment time. We observed an interesting result related to the order of the conditions. P1 and P3 show a lower resting rate with the *tablet*, which was their starting condition. However, P4 and P5 show a higher resting rate with *tabletop*, which was their starting condition. We cautiously claim that *tabletop* induces more resting behavior due to its affordance.

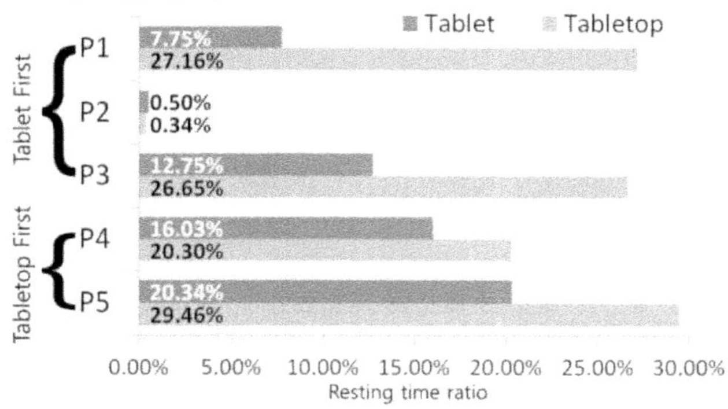

Figure 12. Resting time ratio within total experiment time for each participant and condition.

The timeout threshold τ is the dividing line between typing and resting, and there is a tradeoff. As we increase the threshold value, typing becomes easier, and as we decrease it, resting becomes easier. We collected canceled touches during typing and resting, and calculated the expected error rates along with different timeout thresholds from 300 ms to 1000 ms. We added two error rates and found the minimum point: 470 ms for *tablet* and 440 ms for *tabletop* (Figure 13). As a result, we conclude that 450 ms would be the balanced timeout threshold value, i.e., the tradeoff between typing and resting.

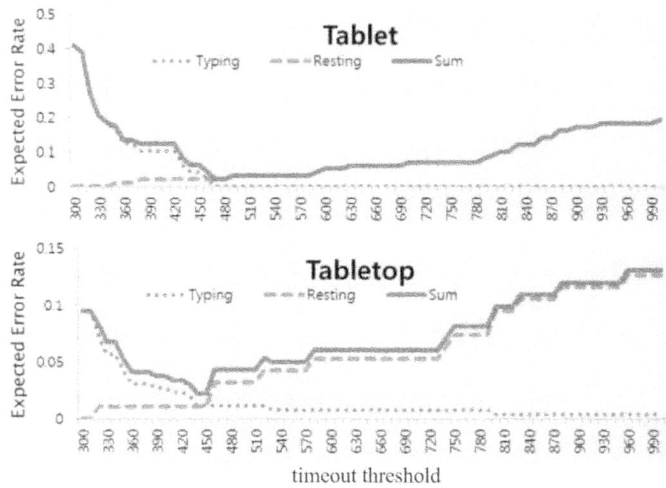

Figure 13. Expected error rates for different values of the timeout threshold parameter.

Experiment 3: Text Entry Performance

We conducted a comparative study with TapBoard keyboards (*TapBoard*) and traditional touch screen software keyboards (*Normal*) to measure text entry performance. The goal of this experiment was to show that TapBoard does not have an adverse effect on text entry performance. We expected participants to find the two conditions indistinguishable during the consecutive typing sessions. For this experiment, 10 university students were recruited (four males and six females, mean age 22.4 years). All of them were touch typists with traditional physical keyboards, but did not have a lot of experience with software keyboards on tablet computers.

Apparatus

In this experiment, transcription programs on the Samsung Slate 7 were given to subjects for both conditions. For the *TapBoard* condition, the timeout threshold τ was set to 450 ms based on the results of experiment 2.

Procedure

The participants were asked to perform transcription tasks with both *TapBoard* and *Normal*. They transcribed sentences randomly picked from the MacKenzie and Soukoreff phrase sets [21]. Each session consisted of continuous transcription for 20 min. Typing sessions alternated between *TapBoard* and *Normal*. Participants performed five sessions for each condition, thus giving a total of ten sessions per participant. The order in which the devices were used was counterbalanced. The ten sessions were spread over three consecutive days to prevent fatigue.

Result

We measured the typing speed and error rates according to metrics proposed by Soukoreff and MacKenzie [27]. Figure 14 shows the results for each condition. We then analyzed the results using two-way repeated measure ANOVA. *Session* and *Condition* are within-subject factors.

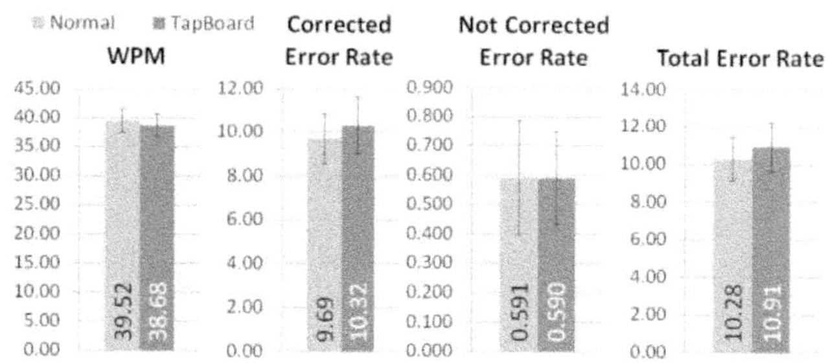

Figure 14. Performance measurements for *Normal* and *TapBoard* keyboards. Error bars represent the 95% confidence interval.

Typing Speed is measured in Words Per Minute (WPM), which is defined by Characters Per Second (CPS) * 60 / 5. The *Corrected Error Rate* (CER) is the frequency of errors committed but corrected during typing. *Not Corrected Error Rate* (NCER) is the frequency of errors left in the transcribed text. Finally, *Total Error Rate* (TER) is the unified error metric that combines these two error rates. Table 1 presents statistical test results for each performance metric.

	Condition ($F_{1,9}$ / p-value)	*Session* ($F_{4,36}$ / p-value)	Interaction ($F_{4,36}$ / p-value)
WPM	2.76 / .13	**10.50 / <.0001**	1.30 / .29
CER	1.52 / .25	**3.52 / <.05**	1.61 / .19
NCER	0.0003 / .998	**2.84 / <.05**	1.74 / .16
TER	1.36 / .27	**3.08 / <.05**	2.04 / .11

Table 1. Two-way repeated measure ANOVA results. *Condition* has two levels (*TapBoard* and *Normal*), and *Sesssion* has five levels (five sessions for each condition). Bold text represents significant main effect.

In summary, *Session* has a significant main effect, and *Condition* and *Condition*Session* interactions do not exhibit significant effects for all performance metrics. We conclude that *TapBoard* and *Normal* are not statistically different in their performance. To examine the equivalence of the performance of the two methods more rigorously, we picked two consecutive sessions and examined their equivalence using Two One-Sided t-Tests (TOST). For example, we compared session one and session two, session three and session four, and so on. Because we alternated the conditions, any two consecutive sessions consist of one *TapBoard* session and one *Normal* session. At the 95% confidence level, the test result indeed exhibited statistical equivalence for all session pairs.

Additional session

In the experiments thus far, the distance threshold δ was 80 px. A smaller δ value will enable better utilization of the touched state, but may increase the chance of canceling a legitimate keystroke. The value of 80 px worked well, but we hope to minimize δ for better utilization of the touched state, e.g., for better gesture operation. This, however, should be possible without degrading typing performance.

In order to estimate the touch displacement while typing on a touch screen, we conducted a pilot study with four graduate students (all male, ages from 23 to 28 years). They typed for 5 min in the *Normal* condition and we collected 5297 touch data. A maximum 50 px displacement between a touch and a release was observed (Max = 49.04 px, Mean = 7.94 px, SD = 6.07). Based on this result, we set δ = 50 px and conducted an experiment to see whether this reduction affected the typing performance. The experiment was a continuation of experiment 3. We conducted one additional session with *TapBoard* and *Normal* with the same participants (except P8, whom we could not contact). Then, we compared the new results with those of the last sessions of experiment 3. We analyzed the results with two-way repeated measure ANOVA. Within-subject factors are the two-level *Threshold* (δ = 80 px and δ = 50 px) and two-level *Condition* (*TapBoard* and *Normal*). Table 2 presents the results.

	Condition ($F_{1,8}$ / p-value)	*Threshold* ($F_{1,8}$ / p-value)	Interaction ($F_{1,8}$ / p-value)
WPM	.59 / .49	.21, .66	.52 / .49
CER	.33, .58	.12 / .73	.58 / .47
NCER	.04 / .85	1.89 / .21	2.21 / .18
TER	.32 / .59	.21 / .66	1.09 / .33

Table 2. Two-way repeated measure ANOVA results for the additional session.

None of the factors exhibit significant effects for any performance metric. Thus, we conclude that TapBoard with δ = 50 px would be as effective as with δ = 80 px.

UTILIZATION OF TAPBOARD TOUCH STATE

As we have shown that TapBoard does not adversely affect typing performance on a touch screen, the next step is to show how the touched state of TapBoard may be utilized to enhance the touch screen keyboard experience.

Resting While Typing

As in the case of a physical keyboard, TapBoard users will be able to rest their fingers between typing operations. This possibility was in fact verified in the second experiment. Most of the participants in the experiment would rest their fingers on the touch screen while they waited for their turn to type in a conversation session. We expect that this feature of the TapBoard will be better appreciated when people are involved in a careful writing task, as they have to pause frequently between typing operations in order to find the best words or expressions for their work. We also expect that this feature will be more useful for a tabletop computer with a large touch surface, because a large and stable surface has the affordance to invite resting behavior [9]. This was the reason why we chose a tabletop computer as well as a tablet computer in experiments 1 and 2. The results of experiment 2 actually support this expectation, i.e., participants showed a stronger tendency to rest on the keyboard in the case of a tabletop computer.

A closely related possibility is "anchored typing." By anchored typing, we mean a typing operation with one finger while the other fingers rest on the touch screen, as shown in Figure 15. This behavior is commonly observed when a user is repeatedly using special keys, such as a shortcut key or an arrow key. For instance, in order to read a long web page, one would use a page-down key repeatedly. Anchored typing is often a comfortable and stable typing technique for this kind of task. This scenario may sound somewhat outdated, as page turning is now usually done with a finger gesture on a touch screen. However, applications for which text-entry is a primary operation will need a software keyboard as a major input tool, and then the use of special keys will continue to be a viable interactive option.

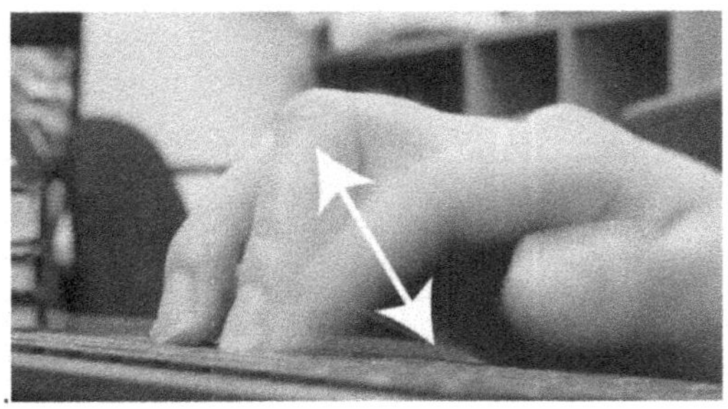

Figure 15. Anchored typing. One finger is repeating keystrokes while the other fingers are resting on the keyboard.

Tactile Feedback

The importance of tactile feedback in the use of a physical keyboard cannot be overemphasized. Users can feel the texture of the keys, and have a chance to align their fingers before starting to type. The touched state of TapBoard will enable users to feel the texture of the keyboard on a touch screen. This may sound meaningless, as there is no texture on a touch screen. This is true at present, but we anticipate that touch screens will have texture in the near future. There are already some early studies toward this goal, such as TeslaTouch [3], LATPaD [16] and STIMTAC [1]. One company is also presenting an early prototype of a programmatically deformable touch screen [29]. All of these tactile feedback technologies may only be meaningful when a user can touch and feel the surface.

Even before such an advanced tactile feedback technology becomes available, some researchers have begun studying the benefit of fine textures on a touch screen for typing performance. Kim and Lee [14] studied the effect of a thin, tactile overlay on a screen keyboard on typing performance. With a combination of a tactile overlay and clicking sound feedback, text entry performance and user preference were significantly improved. There is also a commercial product with a similar goal, known as TABLSKIN [28]. In order to study the benefit of being able to feel a touch screen keyboard, we constructed a tactile overlay using urethane film stickers (0.2 mm thick) on an ordinary OHP film, as shown in Figure 16a. In a pilot study, we could observe that participants were able to "blind-type" on the touch screen after approximately 10 min training. Another interesting possibility is typing with only a transparent template, i.e., without a graphical representation of a keyboard on the screen, as shown in Figure 16a. A clear advantage of this "texture-only" typing is that a software keyboard is not occluding an application window. In Figure 16b, for example, a user is typing on a web page using only the tactile overlay while reading the web page using the whole screen area.

Figure 16. (a) Transparent template, (b) template on contents.

Adaptive Keyboard

As TapBoard allows users to feel a touch screen more, it will also allow a touch screen to feel the users' touch more. A screen keyboard will be able to track the positions of hands and fingers when users rest their hands on the screen keyboard. A software keyboard may be instantiated under the hands when users rest their hands on a touch surface such as on a tabletop computer. The keys of a screen keyboard may adjust their positions to conform to the finger positions of individual users better. This concept, an adaptive screen keyboard, was in fact shown in [25]. In their design, the touch screen instantiates a left or right half of the keyboard when it detects four touch points of a hand. However, they confess to a usability problem due to the difficulty of distinguishing an intentional typing touch and an unintentional touch on the home row by a returning finger. This problem does not exist in the case of TapBoard, because only tapping is regarded as an intentional typing touch. The TapBoard will be a more effective basis for a robust realization of an adaptive screen keyboard. A basic implementation of an adaptive touch screen keyboard based on the TapBoard is shown in Figure 17. In the figure, a software keyboard is following the hands as a user aligns their fingers on the touch screen.

Figure 17. Adaptive touch screen keyboard implementation.

TapBoard Gestures

The most useful possibility enabled by TapBoard is that of using typing operations and gesture operations seamlessly. This is possible because only tapping is regarded as a typing operation, and all other movements on the screen can be utilized as gestures. For example, it will be possible to move the text cursor by a dragging action between typing operations without leaving the keyboard. In the following, we summarize some representative examples.

Text cursor control: It is often necessary to move a text cursor while typing in order to insert or delete a word. Instead of reaching for arrow keys or pointing with a thick finger in a textbox, a dragging gesture on the TapBoard may be used to move the text cursor (Figure 18a). As one drags further, the cursor will move further. Similarly, a dragging gesture with two fingers may be used for backspace operations (Figure 18b).

Text selection and formatting: Text selection may be done by combining the same cursor control gestures and a modifier gesture by the non-dominant hand. For instance, one may be able to select a portion of text by moving the text cursor with one of the fingers of the non-dominant hand anywhere on the keyboard (Figure 18c). This may sound like selecting words using arrow keys with a shift-key down, which is true, but the static gestures of the non-dominant hand can be more diverse. For instance, with two fingers, it may be possible to emphasize formatting (changing the font to italic or bold style) instead of text selection when the text cursor moves (Figure 18d).

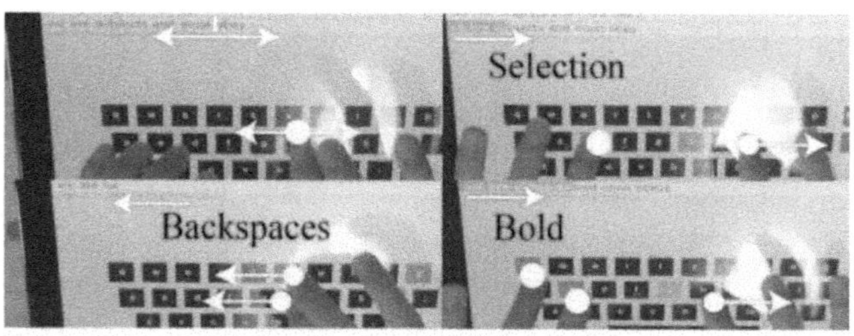

(a) Cursor movement gesture (c) Selection gesture
(b) Backspace gesture (d) Emphasizing gesture

Figure 18. Text cursor control, selection, and formatting implementation.

GUI widget control: It is often necessary to mix typing and GUI widget control. In a form-filling task, e.g., on a web page, it is necessary to jump between different text fields. The gesture for text cursor control may be extended to deal with this problem. In fact, the design of TapBoard gestures to cover all of the primary operations will be a non-trivial design problem, and is not pursued in this paper. Instead, we implemented an example where one can mix typing operations and simple gestures to selectively accept the suggestion of a text box, such as that of Windows Explorer. A screen shot of an example implementation is shown in Figure 19. As users type an initial keyword, the text box shows a list of suggestions. They may select one of them using a vertical gesture and change the last word in the suggestion using a backspace gesture and typing. At this point, the text box will show an updated suggestion list. This cycle of interaction between users and the search box continues until they are satisfied with the current input. This is just an example of a new interaction style that may become possible when it is possible to conveniently switch between typing and GUI control.

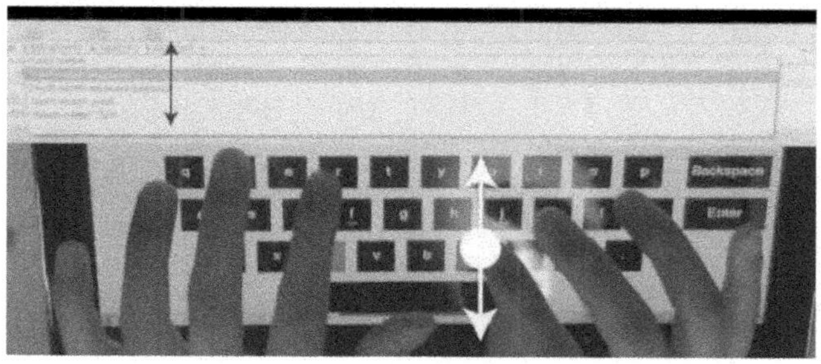

Figure 19. GUI widget control implementation.

Writing while typing: A keyboard may not provide all of the symbols that a user wants to input. In this case, writing (drawing) a symbol may be a more effective alternative. A writing operation may be performed with the dominant hand while all of the non-dominant hand fingers are down (a modifier gesture). Writing input may be translated into a symbol by a gesture recognizer, as in [7], or may be used as it is, i.e., as a handwritten symbol. We did not implement an example for this scenario, as a similar scenario has already been extensively discussed by Findlater et al. [7].

CONCLUSION

We proposed the concept of TapBoard, and verified its feasibility in a series of experiments. First, we showed that TapBoard is compatible with the existing typing skill of users. Second, we showed that users can adapt to TapBoard easily and utilize the touched state, e.g., for resting their fingers. Third, we showed that TapBoard is as efficient as an ordinary touch screen keyboard. After these experimental verifications, we demonstrated new interaction techniques that will be made possible by TapBoard. We expect TapBoard to enhance the touch screen interaction experience significantly, especially by enabling seamless integration of typing operations and GUI operations. An immediate next step is to extend the concept of TapBoard beyond a keyboard and make the whole touch screen more "touchable."

ACKNOWLEDGEMENT

This work was supported by the IT R&D program of MKE/KEIT. [KI10041244, SmartTV 2.0 Software Platform]

REFERENCES

1. Amberg, M., Giraud, F., Semail, B., Olivo, P., Casiez, G., and Roussel, N. Stimtac: a tactile input device with programmable friction. In *Proc. UIST '11 Adjunct*, ACM (2011), 7–8.
2. Barrett, J., and Krueger, H. Performance effects of reduced proprioceptive feedback on touch typists and casual users in a typing task. *Behaviour & Information Technology 13*, 6 (1994), 373–381.
3. Bau, O., Poupyrev, I., Israr, A., and Harrison, C. Teslatouch: electrovibration for touch surfaces. In *Proc. UIST '10*, ACM (2010), 283–292.
4. Buxton, W. A three-state model of graphical input. In *INTERACT*, vol. 90, Citeseer (1990), 449–456.
5. Chaparro, B., Nguyen, B., Phan, M., Smith, A., and Teves, J. Keyboard performance: ipad versus netbook. *Usability News 12*, 2 (2010).
6. Crump, M., and Logan, G. Warning: This keyboard will deconstruct - the role of the keyboard in skilled typewriting. *Psychonomic Bulletin & Review 17* (2010), 394–399.
7. Findlater, L., Lee, B., and Wobbrock, J. Beyond qwerty: augmenting touch screen keyboards with multi-touch gestures for non-alphanumeric input. In *Proc. CHI '12*, ACM (2012), 2679–2682.
8. Findlater, L., and Wobbrock, J. Personalized input: Improving ten-finger touchscreen typing through automatic adaptation. In *Proc. CHI '12*, ACM (2012), 2453–2462.
9. Findlater, L., Wobbrock, J. O., and Wigdor, D. Typing on flat glass: examining ten-finger expert typing patterns on touch surfaces. In *Proc. CHI '11*, ACM (2011), 2453–2462.
10. Gordon, A., and Soechting, J. Use of tactile afferent information in sequential finger movements. *Experimental brain research 107*, 2 (1995), 281–292.
11. Heo, S., and Lee, G. Forcetap: extending the input vocabulary of mobile touch screens by adding tap gestures. In *Proc. MobileHCI '11*, ACM (2011), 113–122.
12. Hinckley, K., and Sinclair, M. Touch-sensing input devices. In *Proc. CHI '99*, ACM (1999), 223–230.
13. Hoggan, E., Brewster, S., and Johnston, J. Investigating the effectiveness of tactile feedback for mobile touchscreens. In *Proc. CHI '08*, ACM (2008), 1573–1582.
14. Kim, S., and Lee, G. Typing on a touch surface: Effect of feedback with horizontal touch keyboard and vertical display setup. In *Proc. APCHI '12*, ACM (2012), 525–530.
15. Lee, S., and Zhai, S. The performance of touch screen soft buttons. In *Proc. CHI '09*, ACM (2009), 309–318.
16. Levesque, V., Oram, L., MacLean, K., Cockburn, A., Marchuk, N. D., Johnson, D., Colgate, J. E., and Peshkin, M. A. Enhancing physicality in touch interaction with programmable friction. In *Proc. CHI '11*, ACM (2011), 2481–2490.
17. Li, F., Guy, R., Yatani, K., and Truong, K. The 1line keyboard: a qwerty layout in a single line. In *Proc. UIST '11*, ACM (2011), 461–470.
18. Logan, G., and Crump, M. Hierarchical control of cognitive processes: The case for skilled typewriting. *Psychology of Learning and Motivation-Advances in Research and Theory 54* (2011).
19. MacKenzie, I., and Zhang, S. The design and evaluation of a high-performance soft keyboard. In *Proc. CHI '99*, ACM (1999), 25–31.
20. MacKenzie, I., Zhang, S., and Soukoreff, R. Text entry using soft keyboards. *Behaviour & information technology 18*, 4 (1999), 235–244.
21. MacKenzie, I. S., and Soukoreff, R. W. Phrase sets for evaluating text entry techniques. In *Ext. Abstracts CHI '03*, ACM (2003), 754–755.
22. McAdam, C., and Brewster, S. Distal tactile feedback for text entry on tabletop computers. In *Proc. BCS HCI '09*, British Computer Society (2009), 504–511.
23. Rekimoto, J., Ishizawa, T., Schwesig, C., and Oba, H. Presense: interaction techniques for finger sensing input devices. In *Proc. UIST '03*, ACM (2003), 203–212.
24. Ryall, K., Morris, M., Everitt, K., Forlines, C., and Shen, C. Experiences with and observations of direct-touch tabletops. In *Proc. Tabletop '06*, IEEE (2006).
25. Sax, C., Lau, H., and Lawrence, E. Liquidkeyboard: An ergonomic, adaptive qwerty keyboard for touchscreens and surfaces. In *Proc. ICDS '11* (2011), 117–122.
26. Sears, A. Improving touchscreen keyboards: design issues and a comparison with other devices. *Interacting with Computers 3*, 3 (1991), 253 – 269.
27. Soukoreff, R. W., and MacKenzie, I. S. Metrics for text entry research: an evaluation of msd and kspc, and a new unified error metric. In *Proc. CHI '03*, ACM (2003), 113–120.
28. TABLSKIN. http://tablskin.com/.
29. Technology, T. http://www.tactustechnology.com/.
30. TouchFire. The screen-top keyboard for ipad. http://www.kickstarter.com/projects/740785012/touchfire-the-screen-top-keyboard-for-ipad.
31. Weiss, M., Jennings, R., Wagner, J., Khoshabeh, R., Hollan, J., and Borchers, J. Slap: Silicone illuminated active peripherals. *Ext. Abstracts of Tabletop 8* (2008).
32. Wigdor, D., Perm, G., Ryall, K., Esenther, A., and Shen, C. Living with a tabletop: Analysis and observations of long term office use of a multi-touch table. In *Proc. Tabletop '07*, IEEE (2007), 60–67.

Métamorphe: Augmenting Hotkey Usage with Actuated Keys

Gilles Bailly[1] Thomas Pietrzak[2] Jonathan Deber[3] Daniel Wigdor[3]

[1] Quality and Usability Lab, Telekom Innovation Laboratories, TU Berlin, Berlin, Germany
[2] Université Lille 1, Lille, France
[3] Department of Computer Science, University of Toronto, Toronto, Canada
gbailly@mpi-inf.mpg.de pietrzak@lifl.fr {jdeber, dwigdor}@dgp.toronto.edu

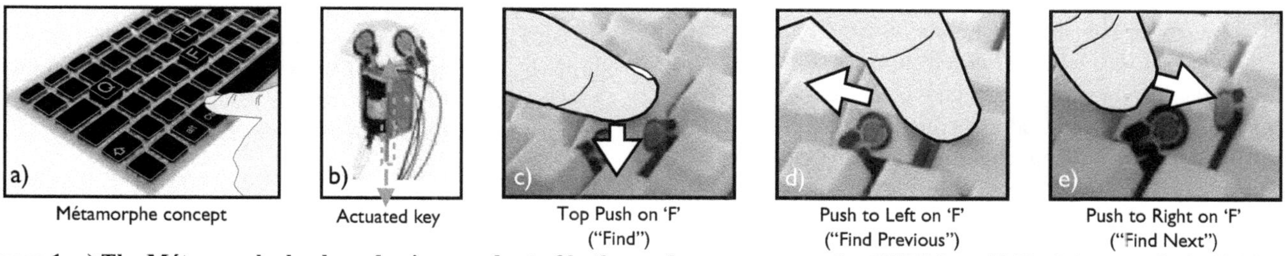

Figure 1. a) The Métamorphe keyboard raises a subset of hotkeys when users press the CTRL key. b) Each key can be individually raised with an embedded solenoid, and contains force sensors that allow a variety of novel gestures to be performed on the key. c-d-e) For example, the 'F' key can be pushed down to select "Find", or pushed left or right to select variations of that command.

ABSTRACT

Hotkeys are an efficient method of selecting commands on a keyboard. However, these shortcuts are often underused by users. We present Métamorphe, a novel keyboard with keys that can be individually raised and lowered to promote hotkeys usage. Métamorphe augments the output of traditional keyboards with haptic and visual feedback, and offers a novel design space for user input on raised keys (e.g., gestures such as squeezing or pushing the sides of a key). We detail the implementation of Métamorphe and discuss design factors. We also report two user studies. The first is a user-defined interface study that shows that the new input vocabulary is usable and useful, and provides insights into the mental models that users associate with raised keys. The second user study shows improved eyes-free selection performance for raised keys as well as the surrounding unraised keys.

Author Keywords

Augmented keyboard; height-changing keys; hotkeys; shape-changing interfaces; user-defined gestures.

ACM Classification Keywords

H.5.2. Information interfaces and presentation (e.g., HCI): User Interfaces – Interaction Styles.

INTRODUCTION

Hotkeys are an efficient way to select commands with a keyboard. In comparison to mouse-based techniques such as pull-down menus or toolbars, hotkeys offer several advantages: they are fast, particularly for repetitive actions (e.g., multiple "Copy"/"Paste" operations [18,19,26]); they let users interact "in place", minimizing mouse movements between graphical widgets [8]; and they do not consume valuable screen real estate [18]. Additionally, hotkeys can reduce hand movements between the keyboard and the mouse [26], increasing the speed of text entry and reducing the risk of musculoskeletal inflammation of the hand [14].

Despite these advantages, many users – even experienced ones – do not transition from the use of a GUI to the use of hotkeys [19]. This failure to transition has been attributed to an anticipated temporary "performance dip" (also known as the "gulf of incompetence") that users may not wish to attempt to bridge [37,41]. In addition, some users are not aware of hotkeys, while others find them a challenge to learn due to non-intuitive mappings [9,19]. Mapping issues may be due, in part, to the fact that any given key could be considered suitable for more than one command, forcing some commands to move to less intuitive keys [41]. Such challenges mean that many users choose traditional menus over hotkeys, ultimately preferring to maintain short-term productivity over long-term efficiency [6].

To overcome some of these challenges, we designed and built Métamorphe (see Figure 1), a novel shape-changing keyboard. While Métamorphe retains the form factor, layout, and tactile qualities of a traditional keyboard, it embeds solenoids that can raise individual keys, and adds force sensors to the sides of the keys, allowing a variety of novel gestures to be performed, increasing expressiveness.

These novel capabilities also provide new input and output channels that favor the guessability, learnability, and eyes-free selection of hotkeys.

The novel input and output capabilities raise interesting research questions: Is the increased interaction vocabulary useful and usable? How should designers assign commands to the new input primitives? Do raised keys improve performance for eyes-free key selection? To answer these questions we conducted two user studies. The first was a user-defined interface study that 1) demonstrated that users readily incorporate the novel input capabilities of raised keys, 2) provided insight into the mental models associated with their use, and 3) provided a set of user-defined hotkeys for Métamorphe. The second study evaluated the impact of raised keys on the eyes-free selection of hotkeys, and showed that 1) raised keys themselves are easier to locate on a keyboard than unraised keys, and 2) raised keys act as haptic landmarks, making it easier to locate neighboring, unraised keys. Finally, we present future directions for Métamorphe with potential scenarios.

RELATED WORK

In creating Métamorphe, we sought to build on related work in the areas of hotkey learning, enhanced keyboards, and shape-changing interfaces.

Hotkey Learning

While numerous studies suggest the importance of hotkeys as a keyboard tool [18,26], only a few solutions have focused on supporting hotkey learning [9,17,28]. Grossman *et al.* introduced audio feedback after the selection of a menu item to expose users to hotkeys [9]. They also proposed cost-based approaches, which disable the menu in order to force users to use hotkeys. While efficient [37], this strategy can frustrate users. HotkeyCoach combined feedback with a cost-based approach [17]: after every mouse-activated command, a pop-up window appeared illustrating the corresponding hotkey. Users could not continue until they used the hotkey or closed the pop-up.

Métamorphe aims to encourage hotkey usage by expanding the space of possible mappings between key and function, thus providing a richer input vocabulary to promote both the guessability and selection of hotkeys.

Enhanced Keyboards

Over the past 30 years, keyboards have remained essentially the same, despite increases in the variety and complexity of software [2,24]. Research on keyboards has investigated ergonomic designs, enhanced layouts, and new capabilities [21,24]. In this section, we review two areas of keyboard work: keyboards with novel input capabilities, and those with novel output capabilities.

Keyboard Input Capabilities

Dedicated function keys. The Xerox Star keyboard [3] and Microsoft's Office Keyboard [24] improve hotkey selection by providing keys dedicated to particular functions. Through haptic feedback, users are able to locate and select these keys eyes-free. While useful, maintaining a 1:1 mapping between functions and dedicated keys is realistic only for a small number of functions. In contrast, Métamorphe uses existing keys, supports both system-wide and application-specific hotkeys, and provides additional expressiveness by enabling different gestures on keys.

Finger-sensing and pressure input. Finger-sensing capabilities allow keys to not only be *pushed* and *released*, but also *touched*. This additional input state can be used to preview information, manipulate virtual objects, or perform gestures [4,15,33,40,42]. Force sensors further extend finger-sensing capabilities by offering a continuum of states between *touched* and *pushed*. Keyboards with force sensors have been used in various contexts such as gaming [7], user authentication [22], and emotional instant messaging [7]. Similarly, Métamorphe augments existing keys with force sensors, but places them on the sides of the keys to allow new gesture capabilities and new interactions.

Other additions to the keyboard have generally served specialized roles. The IBM TrackPoint [35] added a small rubber nub to the center of the keyboard, which is used as an isometric joystick to control the cursor in the absence of the mouse. Some proposed variations used a key instead of the nub [35], or provided vibratory haptic feedback [5].

Keyboard Output Capabilities

Visual Keyboards. The Optimus [27], Microsoft Adaptive Keyboard [25], and TDK [4] keyboards contain small screens on each key that can display application-specific icons or information. While these visual enhancements encourage the recognition of hotkeys, they also force users to divide their attention between the screen and the keyboard, which can be tiring and time-consuming [24].

Haptic feedback. Active haptic feedback is often used to increase the accuracy of virtual keyboards [12] or non-physical buttons [23] on touch surfaces. In the context of physical keyboards, force feedback has been proposed as a means to improve a user's comfort [36] and to prevent errors during text entry [11]. Métamorphe builds on this work by dynamically changing the height of raised keys.

Shape Changing

"A shape-changing interface uses physical change of shape as input or output" [31]. Shape-changing versions of mice [16], displays [1,29,34], keyboards [32], and interactive surfaces [10,38,39] have been proposed. Lumen [29] is a low-resolution interactive display where each pixel can move up and down. The Reflex Keyboard [32] changes shape, but does so by altering the relative positions of the two halves of the keyboard, with the goal of diminishing wrist pain. The Métamorphe's shape-changing keyboard differs from these earlier offerings, as its rising keys and force sensors provide a unique modality of shape changes.

In summary, Métamorphe offers an enhanced keyboard to promote hotkey usage. It differs from existing keyboards by providing a novel, height-changing mechanism that provides haptic feedback and enables new key gestures.

THE MÉTAMORPHE PROTOTYPE

The Métamorphe prototype is shown in Figure 2-bottom. It can individually raise any subset of keys (e.g., common hotkeys when a user presses the Control key). In this section we describe this height-changing mechanism, its integration into a traditional keyboard, and the various human factors that informed its design.

Métamorphe keys are raised and lowered using BLP Series 134 6V (30Ω) push-type solenoids mounted under each key (Figure 1-b). While other technologies, such as linear motors, shape memory alloys, or piezo ceramics can also provide linear motion, solenoids were selected because they are inexpensive, fast, stiff, small enough to fit under each key, and provide sufficient motion. However, solenoids have two limitations: they make a noise when actuated (roughly the same volume as a keystroke), and require continuous power to maintain a key in the raised position, necessitating heat dissipation. Despite these limitations, solenoids were ideal for the creation of our prototype, but further research and development would be required for a shelf-ready commercial implementation.

Each Métamorphe key has four functional positions. One dimension is set by the computer: *raised* (the key is higher than the rest of the keys) or *unraised* (the key is in its regular position). The other dimension (*pushed* or *not pushed*) is controlled by the user's input. We equipped our prototype with eight functioning dynamic keys, which is sufficient to allow a thorough exploration of the Métamorphe design space, and to conduct user studies.

In addition to *pushing*, dynamic Métamorphe keys allow users to perform a large inventory of key gestures, as shown in Figure 2-top. Gestures are detected by force sensors attached to the four side faces of the keys (see Figure 2).

Keyboard Integration

The Métamorphe prototype is built atop a regular HP KU-0316 USB keyboard. It reuses both the mechanical (i.e., the collection of switches) and the electronic (i.e., the circuitry that converts the output of those switches to the appropriate USB signals) components of the original keyboard.

Switches. The existing keyboard uses a dome switch to detect the *pressing* of each key. A dome switch contains a 4 mm dome that acts as a spring to push the key back to the default position when a user removes their finger. Our solenoids are positioned on top of these springs, allowing the keyboard's existing components to detect key presses in both the raised and unraised states.

Keyboard frame. We designed and 3D-printed a custom keyboard frame to vertically guide the solenoids. The actuated keys can be placed in any position on the keyboard. We also 3D-printed non-dynamic keys that fit into the frame to fill in the remaining spaces.

Electronics. Because Métamorphe reuses the existing keyboard's circuitry, it appears to its host computer as a regular USB keyboard and is compatible with all applications. An Arduino Nano, connected via a second USB cable, controls the solenoids and relays force sensor data.

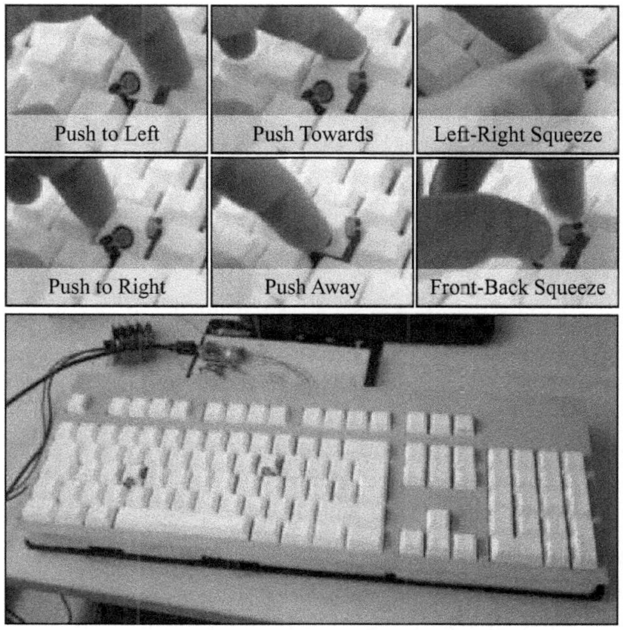

Figure 2. Top: the physical manipulations that can be detected on each key. Bottom: our Métamorphe prototype.

Firmware and API. We developed a communication protocol between the keyboard and the computer, and wrote a C++ library for Linux, OS X, and Windows that encapsulates the communication and handles the mapping between the key IDs and the solenoids.

Human Factors

Actuation force. We conducted a series of tests to determine the ideal voltage to power the solenoids. They require sufficient mechanical power to lift the key cap, their own weight, and the sensors. 6V (suggested by the solenoid's specifications) is sufficient to hold the key in the raised position, but it is not sufficient to lift it. Thus, we briefly power the solenoids with a higher voltage (19V for 50ms) to raise the key, and then switch to 5V to maintain its position. We found that this provided sufficient force to raise the key, without fear of damaging the solenoids.

Which keys. Availability of parts limited the number of actuated keys in the prototype. This led us to consider what might otherwise have escaped notice: it may make sense to restrict the number of raised keys. Certainly, if all keys rise simultaneously, the value of the actuation is nil. Our two studies provide guidance in selecting keys for actuation.

How far to rise. The magnitude of the height change for actuated keys posed a critical design factor for Métamorphe. A key that is not raised enough may be overlooked, while a key that rises too much may impede ease of use, or interfere with unraised keys on the keyboard. We conducted a pilot study with 12 participants to evaluate key heights. We found that 1) at a height of less than 3 mm, the difference in height becomes difficult to perceive haptically, and that the comfort of the side push gestures decreases, and 2) the comfort of a *Top Push* decreases as the height increases to more than 4 or 5 mm. Based on these findings, we concluded that an optimal compromise would be a key height of 4 mm.

Retaining the properties of a keyboard. Métamorphe retains a similar form factor, layout, and tactile quality to a traditional keyboard. It functions normally as a text-entry device, and its spring threshold allows users to rest their fingers on the keys without triggering input [21,44]. When all the keys are in the lowered state, Métamorphe is virtually indistinguishable from a regular keyboard.

Passive-haptic feedback. Keyboards inherently provide some haptic feedback because of their physical keys. Métamorphe expands the range of possible haptic feedback. While it would be possible to use the raising of a key as a source of active haptic feedback (e.g., moving a key under the user's finger to attract their attention), we instead focus on using the raised/unraised state as a source of passive haptic feedback for haptic exploration (e.g., allowing a user to feel which keys are available as hotkeys by their state).

MÉTAMORPHE AND HOTKEYS

Métamorphe promotes hotkey selection in two fundamental ways. First, it applies lessons from prior work to make hotkeys easier to learn. Second, it increases expressiveness by adding raised keys, enabling new gestures that allow more hotkey actions to be defined.

Hotkey Finding

Métamorphe assists novices in identifying favorite or frequent hotkeys through both haptic and visual feedback.

Haptic Feedback

Haptic feedback has been shown to be remarkably fast and accurate as a tool to locate and recognize objects by touch alone [20]. On all keyboards, users can use their spatial memory and proprioception to develop a rough idea of the physical location of keys. However, Métamorphe's haptic feedback is able to provide additional assistance to accurately relocalize hotkeys.

Huynh *et al.* identify three haptic search methods: *scan*, *direct*, and *landmark* [13]. The *direct* and *landmark* search strategies are relevant for the relocalization of hotkeys.

The *direct* strategy uses a tactile or kinesthetic cue for error correction and confirmation of the target location [13]. When a key is raised, the height difference compared to other keys provides haptic feedback and confirms to users that the correct key has been reached.

The *landmark* strategy uses a raised key as an eyes-free landmark to help locate a nearby unraised target key. Users reach the raised haptic landmark, and then perform a quick ballistic movement towards the target location [13].

Visual feedback

In addition to its haptic feedback, a raised key also provides visual feedback, since it looks distinct from the surrounding keys. Although expert users generally prefer to focus on the screen and select hotkeys eyes-free, visual cues can be useful, particularly for novice users [4,27].

Expanded Hotkey Vocabulary

In addition to haptic and visual feedback, raised keys also introduce a novel design space for hotkey input.

Pressing and Squeezing of Raised Keys

On a standard keyboard, a key can be *pushed*, *held*, and *released*. However, Métamorphe's raised keys allow users to interact with several faces of the raised keys, enabling the 9 new gestures shown in Figure 3. Six of these new gestures have been implemented in our current prototype (Figure 2).

Users can *directionally push* (or *side push*) any of the four sides of a key, as illustrated in Figure 3-c-f. Directional pushes require only one finger, and allow for varying placement of the finger on the side of the raised key. Users can also *squeeze* a key with two fingers along the X-axis (a *Left-Right Squeeze* (*LR*), Figure 3-g) or the Y-axis (a *Front-Back Squeeze* (*FB*), Figure 3-h). Raised keys can also be rotated *Clockwise* (*CW*) and *Counterclockwise* (*CCW*) (Figure 3-i-j). Finally, users can *Pull* a raised key a small distance upwards (Figure 3-b). This novel vocabulary of gestures dramatically increases the expressiveness of the keyboard's input.

Number of Hotkeys

The number of single-key hotkeys is constrained by the number of keys available on a keyboard. This pool can be increased with multi-key hotkeys (e.g., using not only Control and another key, but also Control-shift and another key). However, multi-key hotkeys require additional finger coordination [24]. By allowing four new single-finger side push gestures per key, Métamorphe increases the number of available single-finger hotkeys. Two finger gestures (e.g., the squeezes) further expand the number of available hotkeys without requiring additional modifier keys.

Discrete & Continuous Control

Each gesture on our raised keys can be performed with different levels of force, offering two potential advantages. First, setting a force threshold allows the system to ignore false-positive activations when the user touches a key but does not mean to select it. Second, force sensors allow a user to select a command and *continuously control* a parameter in the same gesture. For instance, a *FB squeeze* of the 'Z' key could select a zoom command, while the level of force applied could control the rate of zooming. Other parameters (e.g., velocity or duration) could also provide additional customization of the command.

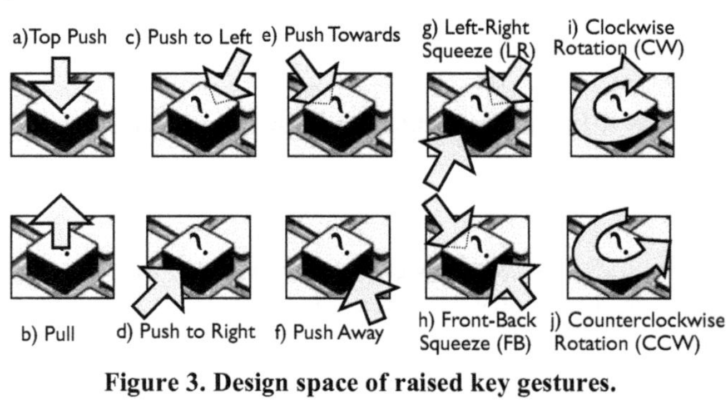

Figure 3. Design space of raised key gestures.

USER STUDY 1: USER-DEFINED HOTKEYS

Increasing the input vocabulary offers increased flexibility to map commands to hotkeys. For example, semantically-related commands could be assigned to a single raised key (e.g., "Save" and "Save As" could be assigned to different gestures on the same key 'S'). Symmetric gestures (e.g., opposing pushes on the same key) could also be assigned to dichotomous commands (e.g., "Previous" and "Next") [43].

We conducted a study to 1) determine how users would make use of the increased vocabulary afforded by the raised keys, 2) investigate the mental models associated with them, and 3) provide guidance to designers about how commands could be assigned to them. We adopted a user-defined interface approach, which involves presenting "the *effects* of actions to participants and elicits the *causes* meant to invoke them" [43]. Simply put, users are shown a video of the results of a command, and are then asked to indicate the input (i.e., the key and gesture) that they thought should elicit that result. This approach can be helpful in identifying users' underlying mental models since participants suggest their own commands, metaphors, and logical groupings.

We followed a similar methodology to Wobbrock *et al.* [43], but made one important modification. The existing methodology did not inform participants of the entire set of commands at the start of the study, causing participants to attempt to locally optimize individual mappings without considering the other commands they had yet to encounter. However, we believed that participants would likely choose to group semantically similar commands to the same gesture or key if they were aware of all of the commands. Thus, we modified the procedure from the previous work such that: 1) participants were shown every command *before* they began defining their hotkeys; and 2) participants were given a worksheet where they recorded their desired keys and gestures, and could modify their choices as new information became available. This may come at the cost of reducing one form of "guessability" of our user-defined hotkey set, since we no longer report users' first, independent guesses. However, we believe that this will trade-off with an accelerated learning of subsequent commands (e.g., if the hotkey to "Align Left" is a *Push to Left* on the 'A' key, users will likely propose that "Align Right" is a *Push to Right* on the same key).

Participants and Apparatus

Twenty participants (11 females), ages 19 to 70 (mean=29, sd=12), were recruited via posters and word-of-mouth, and paid $20 for participation. All were infrequent hotkey users, self-reporting the use of an average of 4.8 (sd=2) hotkeys.

Stimulus videos were presented using a 20″ monitor and standalone speakers. Following the protocol of Wobbrock *et al.* [43], we used a mockup, rather than the actual prototype, to avoid creating participant bias due to any particular design elements of the Métamorphe prototype. The mockup consisted of a sheet of paper printed with an American laptop-style keyboard layout and a transparent 16x16x4 mm plastic square that could be placed anywhere on the keyboard to simulate a raised key.

Procedure

An experimenter briefed each participant, and demonstrated a set of 10 gestures that can be performed on raised keys (shown in Figure 3). The experimenter explained the concept of *thinking-aloud*, and asked the participant to do so during the experiment. He then presented the participant with the 42 stimulus videos to familiarize the participant with the complete set of commands.

Our set of 42 commands (shown in Table 2) consisted of 25 commands used by Wobbrock *et al.* [43] (two commands specific to direct-manipulation were removed) and 17 new commands, organized in five semantic groups: *alignment* ("Align Top", "Align Bottom", "Align Left", "Align Middle", "Align Right", and "Align Justify"), *finding* ("Find", "Find Previous", and "Find Next"), *saving* ("Save", "Save All", and "Save As"), *audio* ("Increase Volume", "Decrease Volume", "Play", and "Pause"), and *clipboard* ("Copy", in addition to Wobbrock *et al.*'s existing "Cut" and "Paste"). The new commands were chosen to reflect traditional menu-based commands with semantically related groups and collisions (i.e., multiple commands beginning with the same letter).

Commands were then presented again, one-at-a-time. For each command, participants were asked to choose a key and a gesture they felt best *fit* with that command. They would then 1) demonstrate the gesture (placing the plastic square on the keyboard layout and performing the gesture); 2) fill in the worksheet with their chosen key and gesture; and 3) think-aloud their reasoning in order to provide the experimenter with an understanding of their mental model and selection strategies. If participants failed to think-aloud, they were prompted to do so by the experimenter. At any time, they were permitted to return to a previous command and modify their choice of key or gesture.

Design

Commands were presented to each participant in a randomized order (without replacement). The overall design of the experiment was: 20 participants x 42 commands = 840 hotkey selections.

Results

We first report quantitative findings from the study, followed by a qualitative discussion of the participants' mental models and selection strategies. Finally, we report a set of user-defined hotkeys.

Quantitative Results

Agreement. Wobbrock *et al.* define agreement as a score between 0 and 1 "that reflects, in a single number, the degree of consensus among participants" [43]. In our work, we distinguish three types of agreement for each command: 1) *key agreement* (participants selected the same key), 2) *gesture agreement* (selection of the same gesture), and 3) *combined agreement* (selection of the same key and gesture). Using Wobbrock *et al.*'s method, we calculated the three agreement scores for each command, which are summarized in Figure 4. We noted that highly directional commands (e.g., "Align Left") tended to have a high gesture agreement, while strongly mnemonic commands (e.g., "Copy") tended to have a high key agreement.

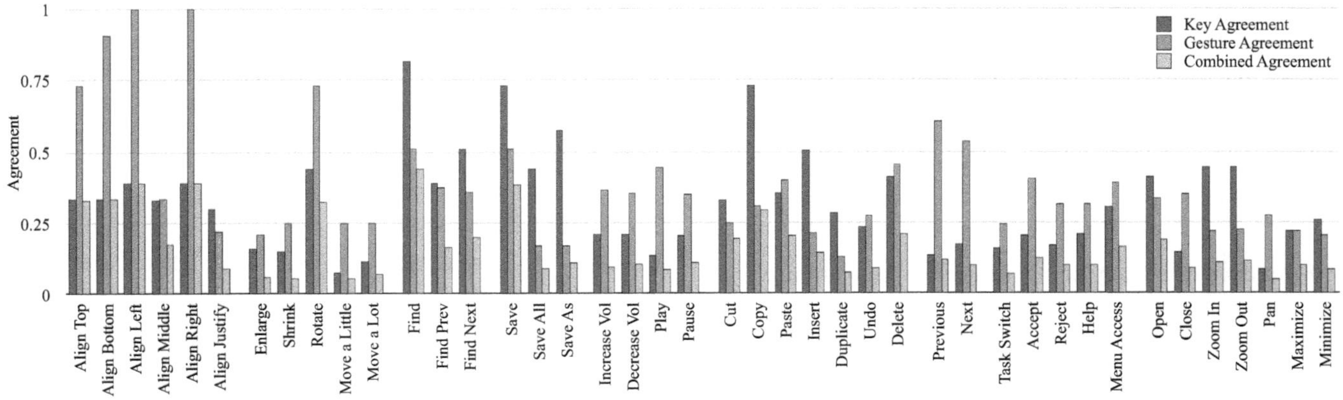

Figure 4. Key, gesture, and combined agreement scores for each command, sorted by semantic group.

Distribution of Keys and Gestures. Excluding two participants that explicitly tried to minimize the number of keys used (using 4 and 7 keys for the entire set of commands), the average number of keys used was 21.6 keys (sd=2.9), a mean of 1.94 commands per key. The average number of different gestures used was 9.3 (sd=1.2); 11 of 20 participants used all 10 gestures. However, some gestures were clearly preferred, as shown in Figure 5.

Grouped Commands. Our command set included two groups containing a primary command and two variants: the *finding* group ("Find", "Find Next", and "Find Previous"), and the *saving* group ("Save", "Save As", and "Save All"). In both cases, participants tended to assign the primary command (e.g., "Save") to *Top Push*, and the variants to different gestures on the same key. For example, 18 participants assigned at least two of the saving commands to the same key, with 14 of them assigning all three commands to the same key. 13 of the 18 that assigned multiple commands to one key picked *Top Push* for the primary command.

Directional Commands. For highly directional commands (e.g., "Pan" or "Move a Lot"/"Move a Little"), participants tended to interact with a raised key as a rate-controlled pointing device (several participants explicitly termed it a "joystick"), and mentioned that they would like to use it to move the view or object. For instance, 15 participants used a key as a joystick when panning. Similarly, 15 participants assigned multiple "Align" commands to a single key, pushing the key in the direction of the desired alignment. These results are consistent with previous findings that participants in user-defined gesture studies tend to gravitate towards physical manipulation metaphors [43].

Dichotomous Commands. Some commands can be classified as dichotomous pairs (e.g., "Shrink"/"Enlarge", "Previous"/"Next", *etc.*). Each pair of keys and pair of gestures associated with dichotomous commands can be divided into three categories: 1) *identical* (i.e., they use the same key or the same gesture), 2) *opposite* (e.g., '<' and '>', or *Push to Left/Right*), or 3) *different*. An ANOVA reveals a significant effect for the gesture*key interaction on the percentage of hotkeys used for dichotomous commands ($F_{4,76}$=52.6, $p<0.0001$). Pair-wise comparisons indicate that participants use opposite gestures on the same keys significantly more often than all other strategies to map dichotomous commands (Table 1). For such commands, participants preferred directional pushes (36 occurrences of *Push to Left/Right* and *Push Away/Towards*), although *CW/CCW* (24 occurrences) and *Top Push/Pull* (16 occurrences) were also used.

		Gesture		
		Identical	**Opposite**	**Different**
Key	**Identical**	4.0%	56.0%	6.0%
	Opposite	7.0%	8.0%	1.5%
	Different	3.0%	9.0%	5.5%

Table 1. Breakdown of key and gesture assignments for dichotomous commands.

Mental Models and Selection Strategies

Having reviewed quantitative results, we now examine strategies employed by participants in making their selections of keys and gestures, in order to gain insight into the mental models associated with the mappings.

For the majority of the 42 commands, most participants decided on an appropriate key first, and then chose an appropriate gesture, although some commands (e.g., "Rotate"), tended to elicit a gesture choice first.

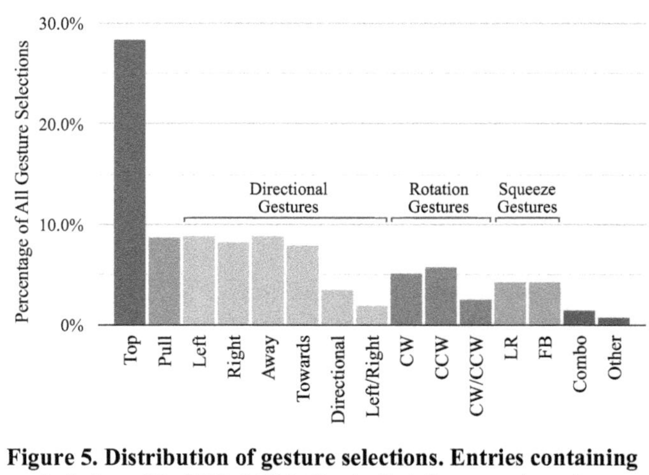

Figure 5. Distribution of gesture selections. Entries containing a slash (e.g., "Left/Right") indicate that the user chose to use either of the listed gestures for a command.

Strategies for Key Selection

An analysis of the think-aloud data revealed six primary strategies for key selection.

Mnemonics. This was the most common basis for choosing a key. Participants selected keys based on the command's first letter (e.g., 'S' for "Save"), significant letter (e.g., 'L' for "Align Left", or 'W' for "Task Switch"), or synonym (e.g., 'D' for "Shrink" and "Enlarge" because both are forms of "dilation").

Prior Experience. Many selections were based on previous experience (e.g., 'V' for "Paste"), although a few participants used the opportunity to "correct mistakes" in existing hotkey assignments, or take better advantage of the raised keys (e.g., moving "Paste" to an opposing gesture on 'C').

Physical Location. Participants used the physical location of a key on the keyboard (e.g., F5 for "Menu Access" because the key is located at the top of the keyboard, mirroring the location of the menu bar).

Glyph Affordances. Participants considered the glyphs printed on a key (e.g., '%' for "Align Middle" because "it's like two circles with a line in the middle"). Participants often selected keys based on their secondary symbols, despite the fact that they did not use the shift key as part of their hotkey. However, some participants used gestures to disambiguate symbols on keys (e.g., P6 picked *Push Away* on '6' because he wanted to use the '^' symbol).

Physical Constraints. Some participants considered a key's physical constraints (e.g., the difficulty of rotating the spacebar) and some used placement strategies designed to reduce the risk of accidently hitting a "dangerous" key.

Semantic Grouping. Finally, semantic groupings were also common. Participants would make one key assignment based upon one of the above strategies, and then assign semantically related commands to the same key (e.g., the aforementioned assignment of "Paste" to 'C', or picking 'V' for "Increase Volume", followed by the subsequent assignment of "Play" to the same "music functions" key).

Strategies for Gesture Selection

Participants typically used *Top Push* as their default gesture, and opposing gestures for dichotomous commands (see Figure 4 and Table 1). We also identified three other gesture selection strategies.

Avoiding Errors. Some participants intentionally chose gestures they saw as difficult or ergonomically challenging (e.g., *Pull* or *LR*) to invoke commands deemed to have significant or irreversible actions (e.g., "Delete").

Directional Gestures. Participants used directional gestures for a variety of actions, but some expressed a reluctance to use directional gestures for non-directional actions (e.g., assigning "Copy" to a *Push to Left*).

Metaphors. Participants frequently used analogies and metaphors for selecting gestures, including physical gestures (e.g., *CW/CCW* for "Rotate") and metaphorical gestures (e.g., *Pull* to summon a help system based on the concept of pulling an emergency assist cord in a hospital, or *FB* to "squish" text). Some also chose gestures based on similarities to multitouch gestures they already knew (e.g., *LR* uses a finger motion that is similar to pinch-to-zoom).

Finally, some participants proposed novel combinations of gestures, extending the expressiveness of the initial gesture set. These included wiggling keys (i.e., rapidly moving the key left and right), combining a squeeze with a rotation to make the rotation "more powerful", and combining a *Top Push* with a directional movement to provide additional context for the operation (e.g., using a directional push to align a single object, but a *Top Push* combined with a directional push to "select all" and align every object at once). Other participants introduced concepts such as pressure (pushing harder implied a greater magnitude for an operation), duration (long pushes vs. short pulses), and repeated gestures (e.g., a pair of *Top Pushes* for "Duplicate"). We found that the open-ended nature of the user-defined gesture methodology with a paper prototype was an extremely productive tool to elicit these extensions.

Due to the finite size of our command set, we of course could not encompass all of the activities that users perform on a computer. Although we attempted to create a representative set of commands, there were some commands that many or most participants indicated that they would not normally use (e.g., "Save All"), and some commands that some felt were missing (e.g., "Print"). It is possible that the presence or absence of additional commands could impact the set of key assignments (e.g., the presence of "Print" might have impacted the use of 'P'). We leave this question to be answered in future work.

A Set of User-Defined Métamorphe Hotkeys

To determine the most common key and gesture selections for each command, we analyzed the data in two ways. First, we evaluated the key and gesture independently (i.e., for each command, pick the most common key, and then pick the most common gesture). In cases where multiple keys or gestures were selected the same number of times, we considered all possible permutations (e.g., for "Align Middle", both *FB* and *Top Push* were each selected 8 times; since 'A' was the most frequent key, we consider both A-*FB* and A-*Top*). The second analysis considered the key and gesture as a pair (i.e., for each command, select the most common tuple of key and gesture). The former approach more accurately captures the individual keys and gestures, but could result in hotkey assignments that were not actually chosen by any users, while the latter could result in a simple plurality of a small number of users overriding the general trends of the remaining pool.

We compared the resulting sets and developed the user-defined hotkey set shown in bold in Table 2. For 30 of 42 commands, both methods yielded a single identical hotkey. For eight commands, although one or both methods yielded multiple hotkeys with the same number of occurrences, there was only a single hotkey that was obtained by both methods, which was selected for our set.

For the remaining four commands, there was no clear agreement between the two methods. As such, while an HCI practitioner could certainly select an appropriate compromise as a hotkey, based on our dataset there does not appear to be a purely user-defined alternative that is dominant. In addition, it is interesting to note that there are some choices that appear actively suboptimal. For example, "Previous" and "Next" have opposite gestures, but are placed on different keys. More significantly, "Accept" and "Reject" have mixed mental models; "Accept" has been assigned to 'Y' (based on a yes/no mental model), while "Reject" has been assigned to 'R' (based on an accept/reject mental model); this hybrid mental model would never be chosen intentionally. Although these inconsistencies demonstrate some of the limitations of a strictly user-defined interface, the approach still provides invaluable insight into users' mental models.

In conclusion, this user study shows: 1) participants readily assign multiple commands to the same key, and 2) participants exploit the range of novel gestures introduced by a raised key, particularly to highlight semantic relationships (e.g., dichotomous commands). Additionally, it provides an example of a set of user-defined hotkeys for Métamorphe.

USER STUDY 2: EYES-FREE SELECTION

We also conducted a user study to compare the speed and accuracy of eyes-free hotkey selection on Métamorphe and a traditional keyboard. Specifically, our research questions were: 1) Do raised keys improve performance for eyes-free selection? 2) Do raised keys impact the performance of selecting surrounding unraised keys? 3) How easy is it to push the side of a raised key?

Procedure

On Métamorphe, users were asked to perform the following actions: *Top Push* on both a raised and unraised key, and the four side pushes on a raised key. On the regular keyboard without raised keys, we replaced the side pushes with additional *Top Pushes*. The stimulus for each trial was a visual depiction of a keyboard that highlighted the target key, as well as the locations of all raised keys. We used this visual depiction to simulate the case where a user is already familiar with the command-to-hotkey mapping, and has a rough idea of the location of the target on the keyboard. The 20 different target hotkeys used in the experiment are shown in Figure 6. There were two raised keys ('D' and 'O', yielding 4 x 2 = 8 possible side pushes) and 18 lowered keys distributed near the raised keys.

Participants received a 5 min. training phase, which allowed them to select each target once. They began each trial by pressing the spacebar with both hands. A stimulus appeared on-screen, and participants selected the indicated hotkey by pressing Control and the specified key. Participants were asked to select hotkeys eyes-free as quickly and accurately as possible. As soon as the top or side of a key was pressed, the trial was completed. They then moved their hands back to the spacebar, and began the next trial.

Participants & Apparatus

Twelve right-handed volunteers from our institution, ages 23 to 39 (mean=28.3, sd=5.2) participated in the experiment. We used a black box to mask Métamorphe from the participants to ensure eyes-free selection of keys.

Design

We used a within-subject design. Participants performed 4 blocks of 28 key selections for each keyboard. The order of keys within each block was randomized. The order of presentation of keyboards was counter-balanced between participants. The overall design was: 12 users x 2 keyboards x 28 targets x 4 blocks = 1344 selections.

Results

Keyboard. An ANOVA reveals a significant effect for *keyboard* on accuracy ($F_{1,11}$=19.01, p<0.001) A *post hoc* Tukey test shows that Métamorphe is significantly more accurate than the traditional keyboard (95% vs. 80%). An ANOVA also reveals a significant effect for *keyboard* on speed ($F_{1,11}$=54.14, p<0.0001). A *post hoc* Tukey test shows that Métamorphe is also significantly faster (2.6 s vs. 3.9 s).

Command	Top Key(s) + Top Gesture(s)	Top Tuple(s) (if different)	Command	Top Key(s) + Top Gesture(s)	Top Tuple(s) (if different)	Command	Top Key(s) + Top Gesture(s)	Top Tuple(s) (if different)
Align Top	**A-*Away***		Save	**S-*Top***		Previous	**P-*Left***	
Align Bottom	**A-*Towards***		Save All	**S-*Pull***	**S-*Pull***, S-*LR*	Next	**N-*Right***	
Align Left	**A-*Left***		Save As	**S-*Right***		Task Switch	tab-*Left/Right*	[4 tuples tied]
Align Middle	**A-*FB***, A-*Top*	**A-*FB***	Increase Vol	**V-*CW***		Accept	**Y-*Top***	
Align Right	**A-*Right***		Decrease Vol	**V-*CCW***		Reject	**R-*Top***	
Align Justify	J-*Pull*	J-*Top*, A-*Pull*	Play	**P-*Left***		Help	**H-*Top***	
Enlarge	**+-*Pull***, +-*CW*	**+-*Pull***, S-*CW*	Pause	**N-*Right***		Menu Access	**menu-*Top***	
Shrink	**S-*CCW***, --*CCW*	**S-*CCW***	Cut	**X-*Top***, C-*Top*	**X-*Top***	Open	**O-*Top***	
Rotate	**R-*CW/CCW***		Copy	**C-*Top***		Close	**C-*Top***	
Move a Little	M-directional	N-directional	Paste	**V-*Top***		Zoom In	**Z-*CW***	
Move a Lot	**M-directional**		Insert	**I-*Top***		Zoom Out	**Z-*CCW***	
Find	**F-*Top***		Duplicate	**D-*Top***		Pan	P-directional	[20 tuples tied]
Find Prev	**F-*Left***		Undo	**U-*Top***	**U-*Top***, Z-*Top*	Maximize	**M-*Pull***	
Find Next	**F-*Right***		Delete	**backspace-*Top***, D-*Top*	**backspace-*Top***	Minimize	**M-*Towards***, M-*CCW*, M-*Top*	**M-*Towards***, --*CCW*

Table 2. The most common hotkeys (using the *key + gesture* and *tuple* methods) for all 42 commands. Hotkeys in bold are our user-defined set. A blank entry in the *tuple* column indicates that this hotkey was the same as the *key + gesture* hotkey.

Distance from raised keys on Métamorphe. An ANOVA reveals a significant effect for *distance* (from the target to a raised key) on accuracy ($F_{2,33}$=7.78 p<0.001). A *post hoc* Tukey test shows that the accuracy at a distance of 0 keys (i.e., selecting a raised key) (98%), 1 key (95%), and 2 keys (97%) is significantly greater than 3 keys (82%). There is a significant effect for *distance* on time ($F_{3,33}$=58.56 p<0.0001). A *post hoc* Tukey test shows that time increases with the distance (d) from the raised key (d = 0: 1.7 s; d = 1: 2.4 s; d = 2: 2.8 s; d = 3: 3.6 s), indicating that users are indeed using the raised key as a landmark.

Side Pushes. An ANOVA reveals a significant effect for *gesture* on accuracy ($F_{4,44}$=7.19, p<0.0001). A *post hoc* Tukey test shows that *Top Push* is significantly more accurate (98%) than the other gestures (*Push to Right*: 88%; *Push to Left*: 74%; *Push Away*: 78%; *Push Towards*: 79%). An ANOVA also reveals a significant effect for *gesture* on time ($F_{4,44}$=10.03, p<0.0001), with a *post hoc* Tukey test showing that *Top Push* is significantly faster (1.8 s) than the other gestures (*Push to Right*: 2.4 s; *Push to Left*: 3.0 s; *Push Away*: 2.5 s; *Push Towards*: 2.1 s).

Observations.

Raised keys. While the quantitative results did not show differences between the different side pushes, participants reported that some gestures were more challenging to perform. 7 participants mentioned that *Push to Right* with the right hand or *Push to Left* with the left hand was slightly more difficult to perform because it requires an unnatural posture. However, one user also mentioned "it was easier to select a hotkey on the side of a [raised] key than a lowered key far from a raised key".

Unraised keys. All users first reached for the closest raised key before moving to the target unraised key, even if the use of this landmark required them to initially overshoot the target key. However, they adopted two different strategies of haptic exploration to perform the final movement from the raised key to the unraised key. The first strategy used a single finger, which was simply moved from one key to the other. The second strategy used two fingers. One finger (e.g., the ring finger) is used as a pivot on the raised key, while a second finger (e.g., the index finger) directly reaches for the unraised key. The distance between fingers is used as an indicator to approximate the distance between the raised key and the unraised key.

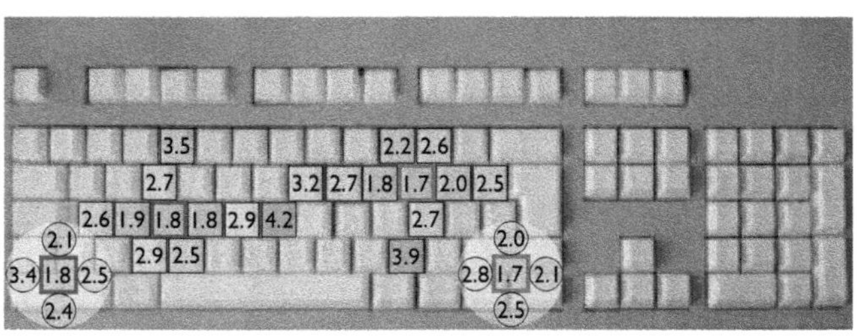

Figure 6. Heat map of selection speed (in s) for each target keys. The two raised keys are outlined. Insets show speeds for *Top Push* and the directional pushes on the raised keys.

Discussion

Performance. Our results show that Métamorphe improves eyes-free selection in both time (improvement of 33%) and accuracy (improvement of 18%) over a traditional keyboard. These results confirm that the additional passive haptic feedback provided by Métamorphe can help users to select hotkeys eyes-free.

Haptic exploration. Our observations confirm that users use the raised keys as haptic landmarks [13] to select unraised keys in proximity to a raised key. We also observed that users combine haptic exploration and proprioception to select hotkeys.

Neighborhood. The accuracy decreases significantly when the distance from the raised key is more than two keys; we therefore recommend placing raised key landmarks within that distance of any desired unraised key targets.

Sides of Keys. Finally, our results confirm that *Top Push* is faster and more accurate than the side pushes. Additionally, they do not reveal any performance differences among the side pushes. However, *Push to Right* with the right hand or *Push to Left* with the left hand were perceived as slightly more difficult.

FUTURE WORK

We envision several future applications for Métamorphe.

Discoverability of hotkeys. Métamorphe could enhance hotkey learning by raising applicable hotkeys (e.g., when the cursor hovers over an object). This could also help visually impaired users to explore available hotkeys.

Text input. Métamorphe could be adapted to predict the next character in a string of text and automatically raise that key to (subtly) prompt the user and avoid spelling errors. This capability would be most appropriate with short and constrained text entry (e.g., city names). In addition, rising keys could provide tactile hints when learning typing skills.

Security. Métamorphe could provide additional security features for password entry, since passwords could consist of both characters and gestures. This would increase the keyspace of inputs to the system, increase the difficulty of shoulder surfing, and could make passwords easier to remember because users could incorporate spatial memory.

Gaming. Raised keys could indicate a ready to use action (e.g., a spell), and the increased vocabulary could provide additional game controls.

Tangible Interfaces. Physical controls could be provided on-demand for a wide variety of tasks. For instance, an on-screen dialog with three slider widgets could raise three keys to provide tangible controls for each widget.

CONCLUSION

We have presented Métamorphe, a novel keyboard with height-changing keys that provides haptic and visual feedback. As an input device, Métamorphe also offers a novel vocabulary of gestures, which increases the number of available hotkeys and their expressiveness. To validate

Métamorphe, we conducted two user studies. The first study 1) showed that users chose to exploit the novel capabilities of the keyboard when assigning hotkeys, 2) provided us with insight into users' mental models, and 3) produced a set of user-defined hotkeys. A second user study 4) found that Métamorphe's raised keys are easier to select eyes-free than unraised keys, and 5) raised keys positively impact the ease of selection of nearby unraised keys. Finally, we defined promising areas for development for shape-changing keyboards.

ACKNOWLEDGEMENTS

This work was funded in part by the Alexander von Humboldt Foundation. We thank Michel Amberg, Jörg Müller, Matthieu Lorenzo, Vincent Meunier, Benoit Legouis, John Hancock, Kim Wright, and Ines Ben Said.

REFERENCES

1. Bau, O., Petrevski, U., and Mackay, W. (2009) BubbleWrap: A Textile-Based Electromagnetic Haptic Display. *CHI EA '09*, 3607–3612.
2. Beaudouin-Lafon, M. (2004) Designing Interaction, not Interfaces. *AVI '04*, 15–22.
3. Bewley, W. L., Roberts, T. L., Sehroit, D., and Verplank, W. L. (1983) Human Factors Testing in the Design of Xerox's 8010 "Star" Office Workstation. *CHI '83*, 72–77.
4. Block, F., Gellersen, G., and Villar, N. (2010) Touch-Display Keyboards: Transforming Keyboards into Interactive Surfaces. *CHI '10*, 1145–1154.
5. Campbell, C. S., Zhai, S., May, K. W., and Maglio, P. P. (1999) What You Feel Must Be What You See: Adding Tactile Feedback to the Trackpoint. *INTERACT '99*, 383–390.
6. Carroll, J. M., and Rosson, M. B. *Paradox of the Active User*. MIT Press, Cambridge, MA, USA, 1987, pp 80–111.
7. Dietz, P. H., Eidelson, B., Westhues, J., and Bathiche, S. (2009) A Practical Pressure Sensitive Computer Keyboard. *UIST '09*, 55–58.
8. Fitzmaurice, G., Matejka, J., Khan A., Glueck M., and Kurtenbach, G. (2008) PieCursor: Merging Pointing and Command Selection for Rapid In-place Tool Switching. *CHI '08*, 1361–1370.
9. Grossman, T., Dragicevic, P., and Balakrishnan, R. (2007) Strategies for Accelerating On-line Learning of Hotkeys. *CHI '07*, 1591–1600.
10. Harrison, C., and Hudson, S. E. (2009) Providing Dynamically Changeable Physical Buttons on a Visual Display. *CHI '09*, 299–308.
11. Hoffmann, D., Spelmezan, D., and Borchers, J. (2009) TypeRight: A Keyboard with Tactile Error Prevention. *CHI '09*, 2265–2268.
12. Hoggan, E., Brewster, S. A., and Johnston, J. (2008) Investigating the Effectiveness of Tactile Feedback for Mobile Touchscreens. *CHI '08*, 1573–1582.
13. Huynh, K., Stepp, C.E., White, L.W., Colgate, J.E., and Matsuoka, Y. (2010) Finding a feature on a 3D object through single-digit haptic exploration. *IEEE Haptics Symposium '10*, 83–89.
14. Jorgensen, A., Garde, A., Laursen, B., and Jensen, B. Using Mouse and Keyboard Under Time Pressure: Preference, Strategies and Learning. *Behavior and Information Tech. 21*, 5 (2002), 317–319.
15. Kato, J., Sakamoto, D., and Igarashi, T. (2010) Surfboard: Keyboard with Microphone as a Low-cost Interactive Surface. *UIST '10*, 387–388.
16. Kim, S., Kim, H., Lee, B., Nam, T.-J., and Lee, W. (2008) Inflatable Mouse: Volume-adjustable Mouse with Air- pressure-sensitive Input and Haptic Feedback. *CHI '08*, 211–214.
17. Krisler, B., and Alterman, R. (2008) Training Towards Mastery: Overcoming the Active User Paradox. *NordiCHI '08*, 239–248.
18. Kurtenbach, G. *The Design and Evaluation of Marking Menus*. Ph.D. Thesis, Dept. of Computer Science, University of Toronto, 1993.
19. Lane, D. M., Napier, A. H., Peres, C. S., and Sándor, A. The Hidden Costs of Graphical User Interfaces: The Failure to Make the Transition from Menus and Icon Tool Bars to Keyboard Shortcuts. *International Journal of Human-Computer Interaction 18*, 2 (2005), 133–144.
20. Lederman, S. J., and Klatzky, R. L. Hand Movements: A Window Into Haptic Object Recognition. *Cog. Psych. 19*, 3 (1987), 342–368.
21. Lewis, J. R., Potosnak, K. M., and Magyar, R. L. Keys and Keyboards. In M. Helander, T. K. Landauer, P. V. Prabhu. *Handbook of Human-Computer Interaction*. Elsevier, 1997, 1285–1311.
22. Loy, C., Lai, W., and Lim, C. Development of a Pressure-based Typing Biometrics User Authentication System. Tech. rep., University of Science Malaysia & MIMOS Berhad, 2005.
23. Lylykangas, J., Surakka, V., Salminen, K., Raisamo, J., Laitinen, P., Rönning, K., and Raisamo, R. (2011) Designing Tactile Feedback for Piezo Buttons. *CHI '11*, 3281–3284.
24. McLoone, H., Hinckley, K., and Cutrell, E. (2003) Bimanual Interaction on the Microsoft Office Keyboard. *INTERACT '03*, 49–56.
25. Microsoft Adaptive Keyboard. http://www.microsoft.com/appliedsciences/content/projects/uist.aspx
26. Nielsen, J. *Usability Engineering*. Morgan Kaufman, 1993.
27. Optimus Maximus Keyboard, ArtLebedev Studios. http://www.artlebedev.com/everything/optimus/
28. Peres, S.C., Ii, F.P.T., Fleetwood, M.D., Chung, P., & Paige-Smith, D.L. Keyboard Shortcut Usage: The Roles of Social Factors and Computer Experience. In *Proc. of Human Factors and Ergonomics Society 48th Annual Meeting 2004*, 803–807.
29. Poupyrev, I., Nashida, T., Maruyama, S., Rekimoto, J., and Yamaji, Y. (2004) Lumen: Interactive Visual and Shape Display for Calm Computing. *SIGGRAPH '04*, 17.
30. Poupyrev, I., Nashida, T., and Okabe, M. (2007) Actuation and Tangible User Interfaces: The Vaucanson Duck, Robots, and Shape Displays. *TEI '07*, 206–212.
31. Rasmussen, M. K., Pedersen, E. W., Petersen, M. G., and Hornbæk, K. (2012) Shape-Changing Interfaces: A Review of the Design Space and Open Research Questions. *CHI '12*, 735–744.
32. Reflex Keyboard, Smartfish Technologies.
33. Rekimoto, J., Ishizawa, T., Schwesig, C., and Oba, H. (2003) PreSense: Interaction Techniques for Finger Sensing Input Devices. *UIST '03*, 203–212.
34. Richter H., and Wiethoff, A. (2011) EdgeMatrix: Remote Tactile Feedback on Interactive Surfaces Using a Shape Display. *TEI '11*.
35. Rutledge, J. D., and Selker, T. (1990) Force-to-Motion Functions for Pointing. *INTERACT '90*, 701–706.
36. Savioz, G., Markovic, M., and Pierrard, Y. (2011) Towards multi-finger haptic devices: A computer keyboard with adjustable force feedback. *ICEMS '11*, 1–6.
37. Scarr, J., Cockburn, A., Gutwin, C., and Quinn, P. (2011) Dips and Ceilings: Understanding and Supporting Transitions to Expertise in User Interfaces. *CHI '11*, 2741–2750.
38. Weiss, M., Schwarz, F., Jakubowski, S., & Borchers, J. (2010) Madgets: Actuating Widgets on Interactive Tabletops. *UIST '10*, 293–302.
39. Weiss, M., Remy, C., and Borchers, J. (2011) Rendering Physical Effects in Tabletop Controls. *CHI '11*, 3009–3012.
40. Westerman, W. *Hand Tracking, Finger Identification, And Chordic Manipulation On A Multi-Touch Surface*. Ph.D Thesis, Dept. of Electrical Engineering, University of Delaware, 1999.
41. Wigdor, D., and Wixon, D. *Brave NUI World: Designing Natural User Interfaces for Touch and Gesture*. Morgan Kaufman, 2011.
42. Wilson, A. D. (2006) Robust Computer Vision-Based Detection of Pinching for One and Two-Handed Gesture Input. *UIST '06*, 255–258.
43. Wobbrock, J. O., Morris, M. R., and Wilson, A. D. (2009) User-Defined Gestures for Surface Computing. *CHI '09*, 1083–1092.

Promoting Hotkey Use through Rehearsal with ExposeHK

Sylvain Malacria[1] **Gilles Bailly**[2] **Joel Harrison**[1] **Andy Cockburn**[1] **Carl Gutwin**[3]
[1]University of Canterbury, Christchurch, New-Zealand
[2]Quality and Usability Lab, Telekom Innovation Laboratories, TU Berlin, Berlin, Germany
[3]Department of Computer Science, University of Saskatchewan, Saskatoon, Saskatchewan, Canada
sylvain@malacria.fr, andy@cosc.canterbury.ac.nz, gillesbailly1@gmail.com, gutwin@cs.usask.ca

Figure 1. The user wants to open a new tab but is not sure of the hotkey. He visually locates the button in the toolbar (boxed on left), then presses the Command key (⌘) to activate ExposeHK, which overlays toolbar items with available hotkeys (right). He completes the command by pressing ⌘ T.

ABSTRACT

Keyboard shortcuts allow fast interaction, but they are known to be infrequently used, with most users relying heavily on traditional pointer-based selection for most commands. We describe the goals, design, and evaluation of ExposeHK, a new interface mechanism that aims to increase hotkey use. ExposeHK's four key design goals are: 1) enable users to browse hotkeys; 2) allow non-expert users to issue hotkey commands as a physical rehearsal of expert performance; 3) exploit spatial memory to assist non-expert users in identifying hotkeys; and 4) maximise expert performance by using consistent shortcuts in a flat command hierarchy. ExposeHK supports these objectives by displaying hotkeys overlaid on their associated commands when a modifier key is pressed. We evaluated ExposeHK in three empirical studies using toolbars, menus, and a tabbed 'ribbon' toolbar. Results show that participants used more hotkeys, and used them more often, with ExposeHK than with other techniques; they were faster with ExposeHK than with either pointing or other hotkey methods; and they strongly preferred ExposeHK. Our research shows that ExposeHK can substantially improve the user's transition from a 'beginner mode' of interaction to a higher level of expertise.

Author Keywords

Hotkeys; Keyboard Shortcuts; Rehearsal; Menus; Command Selection; Novice Mode; Expert Mode.

ACM Classification Keywords

H.5.2. Information Interfaces and Presentation: User Interfaces. – Graphical user interfaces (GUI).

INTRODUCTION

Hotkeys, also called keyboard shortcuts or accelerators, offer a shortcut alternative to pointer-based selection of commands from toolbars and menus. Their efficiency stems from three mechanical advantages over pointing: first, in many tasks such as word-processing, the hands rest on the keyboard, so hotkeys eliminate the need to move the hand to a pointing device and back; second, they eliminate the need for a pointing round-trip from the workspace to the control widgets and back; and third, they allow a wide range of commands to be selected with a single key combination, thus removing the need to traverse a menu or tab hierarchy. A variety of theoretical models (e.g., KLM [7]) and empirical studies (e.g, Odell et al. [24]) demonstrate that hotkeys improve user performance.

Despite this potential, hotkeys are under-used: several studies have demonstrated that few users employ any form of shortcut interface [1, 5, 9, 19, 20]. Carroll's 'paradox of the active user' [9] suggests that users are simply too engaged in their tasks to consider learning alternative strategies or methods, even if these methods may eventually improve performance. In addition, keyboard shortcuts require that users learn hotkeys beforehand, potentially resulting in errors due to incorrect hotkey/command memory associations.

The poor adoption of hotkeys and other high-performance interface techniques creates a substantial usability problem. While the performance difference between hotkeys and pointer-based commands may be small for some actions, it can be large when command activation involves hierarchical navigation (such as a menu-cascade) or when selecting widgets located far from the workspace. These small performance differences can compound into substantial effects when multiplied across thousands of daily repetitions. It is therefore important to find ways of helping users transition from the pointer to hotkeys.

Two recent studies show the state of the art in encouraging hotkey use. Grossman et al. [12] and Krisler and Alterman [17] investigated the use of feedback (emphasising the hotkey after pointer selection) and cost (imposing additional steps to complete pointer selections) as mechanisms for encouraging adoption and use of hotkeys, with positive results.

However, these approaches have three substantial limitations. First, they use pointer-based selection as the starting point for hotkey presentation (i.e., the hotkey is only shown after mouse-based selection). Consequently, users reinforce pointing even while trying to learn a faster non-pointer method. Second, cost-based techniques work by penalising pointer selections, rather than by making hotkeys more attractive. For example, one of Grossman's successful techniques imposed a delay after pointer-based selection: the hotkey 'incentive' was turning users away from the old technique, rather than actually improving performance. Third, users are unable to exploit the spatial-location knowledge developed through prior pointer-based selection. Users must switch entirely to the new approach, which usually implies a temporary but substantial reduction in performance (a 'performance dip' [31]) that is likely to deter hotkey use.

We have developed and evaluated a new method for encouraging and improving hotkey use – called ExposeHK (EHK) – that addresses these issues. When activated with a modifier key (e.g., the Control key), EHK displays the hotkeys in the application's toolbar (see Fig.1), menu, or ribbon. Importantly, EHK is compatible with existing toolbar and ribbon designs, and it can be readily adapted to menus.

This work makes three main contributions. First, it describes design principles for promoting hotkey use. Second, it presents ExposeHK (EHK) – a system instantiating the principles with toolbar, menu and ribbon designs. Third, it presents empirical results showing that EHK promotes earlier and higher levels of hotkey use, that participants are faster with it, and that they strongly prefer EHK.

EXPOSEHK: DESIGN GOALS AND RELATED WORK

EHK uses a simple interaction mechanism to promote hotkey use. While a modifier key is held down, all hotkeys are concurrently displayed on top of their graphical controls. Selections are completed using the hotkey or by pointing.

We implemented and evaluated three forms of the technique for toolbars (ExposeHK$_T$, see Fig.1), menus (ExposeHK$_M$, see Fig.6), and ribbons (ExposeHK$_R$, see Fig.9), with details presented later. This section describes the design goals for EHK, as well as key associated prior work.

Design Goals

The ultimate objective of EHK is to improve the rate at which users attain expertise with interfaces, by promoting hotkey use. Figure 2, adapted from [31], illustrates this idealised objective. It shows that switching to traditional shortcuts involves a temporary 'performance dip' that discourages their use. The dip occurs because users who are competent with pointer-based

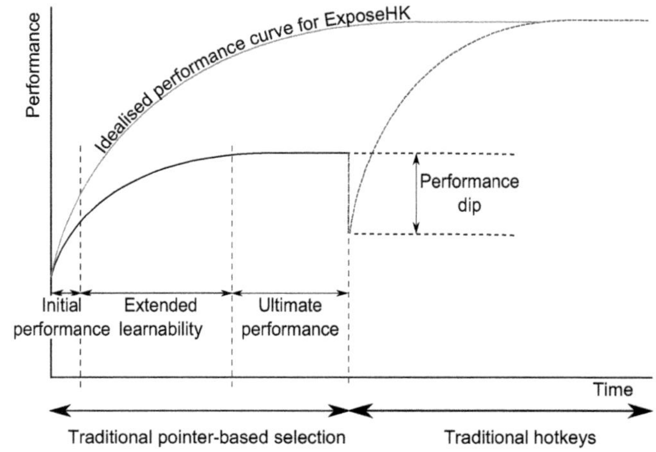

Figure 2. Intended learning curve for ExposeHK, compared with modality switching (adapted from [31]).

selection must pause, display the hotkey, learn it, and rehearse the key sequence. With EHK we aim instead to support a smooth and continual transition to expert performance. We have four goals to help EHK achieve this objective, as follows.

Goal 1: Enable hotkey browsing

In most contemporary interfaces hotkeys are not displayed until the user posts a menu item or dwells on a toolbar item (exceptions, such as Alt keys, are discussed with goal 4 below). Consequently, learning hotkeys involves moving the cursor to the point where a simple click would complete the selection – but then pausing, awaiting the shortcut feedback, and committing it to memory before proceeding (possibly by clicking rather than by using the shortcut). These actions can induce a performance dip (Fig. 2) that discourages hotkey use and traps the user in pointer-based 'beginner mode' [31]. Any memory errors while learning hotkeys will further inhibit performance.

To avoid this trap, systems should allow users to browse hotkeys *without requiring* a pointing action. ExposeHK meets this goal by showing the hotkeys when a modifier key is pressed, as shown in Figures 1 and 6. Users can therefore initiate their command actions using the *same modality* that they will ultimately use as experts. Novice users will still need to visually search for the target interface control, but once identified, they can press the EHK modifier key to display the hotkeys underlying the control, avoiding the need to move the hand to the mouse and point to the target. Furthermore, EHK does not require that users learn hotkeys beforehand, avoiding errors due to incorrect hotkey/command memory associations. By providing a single modality that removes the need to pre-learn the hotkeys we aim to minimise the magnitude and deterrent effect of the performance dip (Fig. 2).

Goal 2: Support physical rehearsal

In analysing factors influencing the development of expertise, Kurtenbach [19] proposed the principle of *rehearsal*: *'guidance should be a physical rehearsal of the way an expert would issue a command'*. He deployed this principle in marking menus, which allow novices to select items by moving the cursor into one segment of a visually displayed 'pie menu' [6] (a cursor-centred circular arrangement of menu items). Experts select items using exactly the same physical action (a directional gesture), but without waiting for feedback.

The potential value of using the same physical action for novice and expert selections is supported by psychology literature on automaticity and the power law of practice (see [32] for a comprehensive review of motor control and learning). *Automaticity* [33] represents a high level of attainment in motor learning, allowing controls to be manipulated without substantial conscious deliberation. It is characterised by fast and parallel processing. The key determinant in the development of automatic performance is extreme repetition, although repetition alone is not sufficient for some tasks (e.g., Card et al. [8] studied one user repeating a text editing task 1100 times, without observing automaticity). These effects support Kurtenbach's principle of rehearsal, yet few shortcut interfaces (other than marking menus and their variants) exploit the principle. Traditional hotkey methods require users to discover hotkeys using a non-hotkey modality (pointing), and consequently users rehearse pointing, not hotkey use. EHK, in contrast, allows users to discover and rehearse hotkeys using only the hotkey modality. Furthermore, EHK is compatible with traditional interfaces, whereas systems like marking menus require interface changes (i.e., non-traditional circular menu layouts).

Goal 3: Rapid hotkey identification for intermediate users

When users have an intermediate level of skill, they are likely to have partial knowledge of their interaction environment. For example, users may know the spatial vicinity of controls, even if not their exact location; or they may suspect that a particular hotkey sequence triggers a needed command, but be unwilling to execute it without confirmation. EHK leverages human spatial memory by ensuring that hotkeys are displayed at the spatial location of the underlying visual control, which reduces visual search time and allows rapid confirmation of hotkey bindings.

Goal 4: Stable commands in a flat hierarchy

A key reason for hotkeys' efficiency is that most hotkey interfaces use a single key combination to select a command, instead of a series of several point-and-click activities to traverse the command hierarchy. For example, the hotkey CTRL-B may replace two pointing actions for the 'Font' menu and 'Bold' item. Importantly, not all hotkey methods support hierarchy flattening. For example, Alt-Key navigation (part of the accessibility interface in Microsoft Office) displays hotkeys associated with successive levels of the interface hierarchy when the 'Alt' key is pressed, allowing users to traverse the interface. Theoretical and empirical results tend to show that selection time increases with the number of menu levels for experts [10, 31]. In addition, it has been shown that it is difficult to chunk a multiple-keys sequence into one single cognitive unit when using Alt-Key navigation [23].

ExposeHK's hotkey bindings are also stable across invocations (within an application), which allow users to learn and rapidly reproduce key sequences. While this may seem an obvious feature of hotkey interfaces, there are interesting accessibility interfaces that support some of EHK's characteristics, but violate this goal. In particular, the 'show numbers' [11] interface in Windows 7 visually overlays each widget with a number that fades in and out (similar to EHK). Speech input then allows any widget to be selected by reading the number. While this is a powerful accessibility tool, it violates goal 4 because the activation numbers change across invocations.

Other related work

There is extensive literature on understanding and supporting expert performance with user interfaces. This includes work on user strategies (e.g., [5]), interface techniques that optimise expert performance (e.g., Flower Menus [3]), techniques supporting transitions from novice to expert performance (e.g., Blur [31], Marking Menus [18, 19], and Octopocus [4]), understanding collaborative skill sharing [25], and supporting community expertise [22].

Key prior work specifically on hotkeys includes empirical performance comparisons between shortcut techniques including hotkeys (e.g., [16, 20, 24, 15, 2]) and specialised hardware promoting hotkey use (e.g., a touch-sensitive keyboard that highlights on-screen widgets before a key is pressed [28]). Finally, the two studies most closely related to our objectives concern the use of interaction cost as a disincentive for pointer-based selection [12] and the use of feedback to help users learn hotkey bindings [12, 17]. As summarised in the introduction, we want to promote hotkeys without requiring pre-learning, without imposing an explicit cost on pointer-based techniques, and without the potential distraction of post-action feedback.

USER STUDIES RATIONALE

We conducted three studies to deploy and evaluate ExposeHK with traditional organizations of commands in graphical user interfaces: toolbars, menus, and ribbons. Studies 1 and 2, which respectively used toolbar and menu adaptations of ExposeHK, focus on goals 1 to 3, which concern promoting transitions to hotkey use. The primary measure of studies 1 and 2, therefore, is the proportion of commands completed using hotkeys – these studies answer the question, 'does ExposeHK promote earlier and increased hotkey use compare to other methods?' Study 3 then focuses on goal 4, examining the performance improvements that ExposeHK can provide when applied to the Microsoft Ribbon user interface, in comparison to existing methods.

STUDY 1: TOOLBARS (EXPOSEHK$_T$)

The toolbar version of ExposeHK (ExposeHK$_T$), shown in Figure 1, overlays the hotkey associated with each toolbar item when a modifier key is pressed. Study 1 focuses on hotkey adoption with ExposeHK$_T$ compared with traditional tooltips and audio feedback. Traditional tooltips provide baseline comparison with a commercial standard, and audio feedback was used because Grossman et al. [12] showed it to be an effective method for promoting hotkey use. The audio feedback condition used voice synthesis to read the hotkey binding when the pointer clicked the item. Participants in the study were free to complete selections by pointing to toolbar items or by invoking hotkeys.

The study was designed to answer several questions about ExposeHK$_T$ in comparison to traditional tooltips and audio-supplemented hotkey feedback:

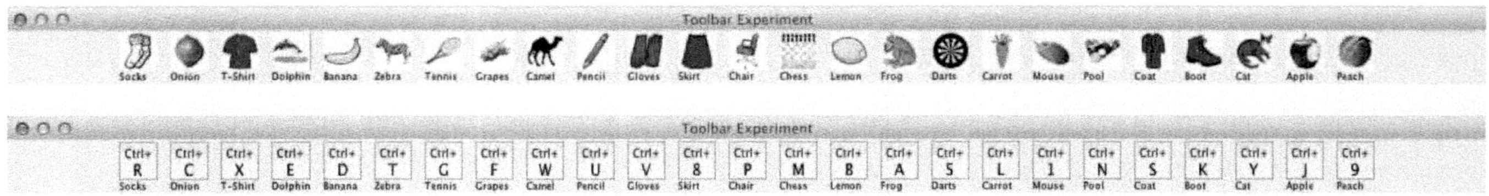

Figure 3. Example of a toolbar used in the study (top), and with the ExposeHK$_T$ mode on (bottom)

- does ExposeHK$_T$ result in earlier and higher levels of hotkey use?
- how does hotkey use with the three interfaces (ExposeHK$_T$, audio, tooltips) change with experience and frequency of item selection?
- does ExposeHK$_T$ support faster command selection?
- are errors affected by interface or selection mechanism?
- how are the systems subjectively perceived?

Experimental method

The method was based on Grossman et al.'s [12] hotkey study with some modifications, as described below.

Task and stimulus. Each task involved selecting a toolbar item in response to a voice-synthesised audible stimulus that read the name of one of the targets – Figure 3 shows a toolbar used in the study. Voice-synthesis was used to ease risks of confounds stemming from factors such as visual pop-out effects due to exact matches between the stimulus (e.g., a cat icon) and its representation in the interface.

The audio stimulus was produced, and task timing began, when the cursor was inside a 70×70 pixel box in the center of the screen and the space bar was pressed. The participant then selected the corresponding item, either by clicking on the target or by selecting the correct hotkey. As in Grossman et al.'s study, timing stopped when the user moved the cursor back to the box and pressed the spacebar, which simulates a pointing round-trip from the workspace to a control and back to the workspace. Completing one trial immediately initiated the next. All user events were logged, including mouse movement and incorrect selections.

Procedure. Participants completed tasks with all three interfaces: *ExposeHK$_T$*, *audio feedback*, and *tooltips*. In the *ExposeHK$_T$* condition, the hotkey binding replaced the corresponding toolbar icon when the control key was pressed. In the *audio feedback* condition, voice-synthesis read the hotkey binding when the user clicked on the item (i.e, after selection). In the *tooltip* condition, a tooltip showed the hotkey immediately when the cursor entered a toolbar item. Immediate display was used (rather than the traditional method of awaiting a dwell timeout) to maximise hotkey exposure and minimise the performance penalty for awaiting the tooltip.

Before using each interface participants received brief training (approximately 30 seconds; data discarded) in which they were prompted to select one item from a toolbar containing four items, first using the pointer, and then selecting the same item using a hotkey. During training, a single sentence was shown describing how to use the hotkeys: either 'Hover over the toolbar item to display the hotkey', 'Voice synthesis will read the name of the hotkey when you select the item', or 'Press the Control key to show the hotkeys'. The potential benefits of using hotkeys were not mentioned to the participants.

The toolbar used in the study consisted of 25 buttons, with a different set of buttons for each interface (e.g., Figure 3). Participants completed six blocks of trials with each interface. Each block consisted of 24 selections, comprising 12 different targets that were selected 8, 4, 2, 2, 1, 1, 1, 1, 1, 1, 1, 1 times each, giving a near-Zipfian distribution (commonly exhibited with command selections, and also used by Grossman et al. [12]). The same 12 targets with the same frequencies were repeated in each block. Targets within this distribution were controlled so that the target appearing 8 times was activated by holding the control key and pressing a hotkey in the left-hand side of the keyboard (Control plus one character among q,w,e,a,s,d,z,x,c), the target appearing 4 times was selected by a key in the right set (u,i,o,p,j,k,l,m), and a target selected twice was in the middle-keyboard (r,t,y,f,g,h,v,b,n). The remaining targets were evenly distributed across the left, middle, and right keyboard sides. Finally, the physical location of targets in the toolbar was controlled to balance the pointing distance for each target of a particular frequency across interface conditions.

Participants were instructed to complete selections as quickly and accurately as possible. To discourage 'racing through' the study irrespective of errors, each erroneous selection incurred a 3 second delay prior to initiating the next task. Once all blocks with an interface were complete, participants completed NASA-TLX worksheets [13] for the technique and gave comments. At the end of the experiment, which lasted approximately 30 minutes, participants ranked their preference for the interfaces and gave final comments.

Design. The experiment used a 3×6×4 analysis of variance for within-subjects factors *technique* (*ExposeHK$_T$*, *audio*, and *tooltips*), *block* (levels 1-6), and *frequency* (whether the item was selected 1, 2, 4, or 8 times in the block). Order of *technique* and the dataset used with the toolbar were counterbalanced across the participants using a Latin Square. The primary dependent measure was the proportion of trials completed using hotkeys. Additional dependent measures included selection time (with error trials removed) and error rate.

Although the within-subjects factor *technique* was counterbalanced, we anticipated the possibility of asymmetric skill transfer, with particular technique orders differently influencing performance in subsequent conditions (see [26]). We therefore analysed factors *order* and *technique*, and found a significant interaction. The results analysis therefore reports

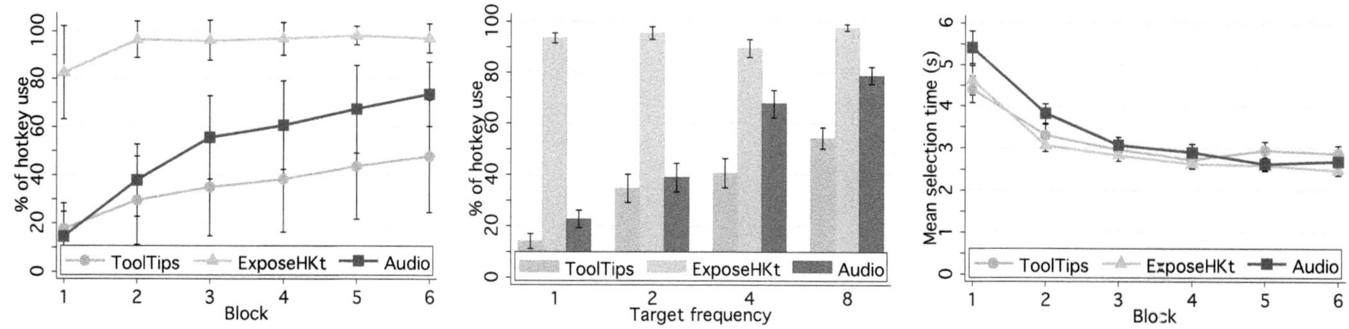

Figure 4. Results of Study 1. Left: % hotkey use by block; Center: % hotkey use by frequency; Right: mean time by block. Error bars $\pm 1 s.e.$

between-subjects treatment of *technique*, discarding data from all but the first technique for each participant. For significant ANOVA effects, we include partial eta-squared (η^2) as a measure of effect size [29].

Participants and Apparatus. 36 university staff and students participated, aged 20-45, 6 female. Experimental software, implemented in Java Swing, ran on Windows XP, using a 1680×1050 22" display, optical mouse, standard QWERTY keyboard, and earphones.

Results

The overall mean time for a correct item selection was 3.37s (σ 1.5), with a low overall error rate of 2.8%. Across all conditions, the mean time to select an item using a hotkey was 2.74s (σ 0.19), which was 35% faster than pointer-based selections (4.16s, σ 0.27). The following paragraphs describe analysis of the dependent measures. Subjective responses for all studies are reported after Study 3.

Proportion of hotkey use. Figure 4 (left) shows the proportion of command selections completed using hotkeys with the three *techniques* across blocks. With ExposeHK$_T$, 94% of correct selections were completed using hotkeys, compared with 50% with *audio* and only *35%* with *tooltips* ($F_{2,33} = 21.7, p < .001, \eta^2 = .57$). As expected, hotkey use progressively increased across *blocks* ($F_{5,165} = 39.6, p < .001, \eta^2 = .54$) and across all *item frequencies* ($F_{3,99} = 31.7, p < .001, \eta^2 = .49$), with infrequent items having lower hotkey selection rates.

Importantly, there was a significant *technique*×*block* interaction ($F_{10,165} = 6.3, p < .001, \eta^2 = .27$). Figure 4 (left) shows that ExposeHK$_T$ users made an early and sustained switch to hotkeys, contrasting with other techniques' gradual increase. This suggests that ExposeHK$_T$ fulfills goal 1 (supporting hotkey browsing by novices), as over 81% of first block selections were completed using hotkeys.

Figure 4 (center) shows a significant *technique*×*frequency* interaction ($F_{6,99} = 9.2, p < .001, \eta^2 = .36$). While hotkeys were consistently employed regardless of item frequency with ExposeHK$_T$, low-frequency items were seldom selected using hotkeys with *tooltip* and *audio* conditions.

Finally, our study replicates Grossman's finding [12] that *audio* feedback outperforms standard tooltips.

Item selection time. Figure 4 (right) shows mean selection times with the different *techniques* across *block*. While there was no significant main effect of *technique* ($F_{2,33} = 1.09, p = .34$), there was a significant *technique*×*block* interaction ($F_{10,165} = 1.99, p < .05, \eta^2 = .10$), stemming from *audio*'s slower selection times initial blocks. As expected, *block* ($F_{5,165} = 82.8, p < .001, \eta^2 = .71$) and *frequency* ($F_{3,99} = 89.7, p < .001, \eta^2 = .73$) showed significant effects. Finally, the mean time for pointer-based selections in the final block (for those who continued to use the mouse with any technique) was 3.53s, compared to 2.38s with hotkeys.

Error rate. Tooltips, audio, and *ExposeHK$_T$* had similar error rates (for both mouse and hotkey selection) of 2.6%, 3.3% and 2.7% respectively, showing no significant main effect ($F_{2,70} = 1.3, p = .28$). There was no effect of *block* ($p = 0.24$) .

STUDY 2: MENUS (EXPOSEHK$_M$)

Deploying ExposeHK with toolbars is simple because each icon has a unique spatial location, giving an unambiguous position for each hotkey when ExposeHK is activated. However, extending ExposeHK to the large command sets offered by menus raises design challenges because items can share the same display location. For example, Figure 5 (left) shows that the 'Safari' menu extends horizontally across 'File', 'Edit', 'View' and 'History' menus.

Characterising menu hotkeys

To understand how hotkeys are used in existing menus, and the degree of overlapping, we wrote a program using the Mac OS accessibility API to inspect the structure and location of menus in 30 mainstream Mac applications such as Microsoft Word and Adobe Photoshop.

The mean number of top-level menus (excluding the global Apple menu) was 8.97 (σ 1.77), and the mean number of items in one top-level menus was 10.48 (σ 5.9). The total number of hotkeys offered by applications ranged from 15 to 112 (mean 55.31, σ 20.53). Across applications, a mean of 77.8% of hotkeys were located in top-level menus, and 22.1% in second-level menus. The proportion of menu items with associated hotkeys is 47.6% in top-level menus and 15.4% in second-level menus.

We calculated the degree of spatial overlapping between items with hotkeys using heatmap-style data similar to that shown in Figure 5 (right) for each application. The mean number of spatial collisions (two overlapping items) between hotkey items per application was substantial at 23.93 (σ 10.35), and 44.9 (σ 18.78) between a hotkey item and a normal item.

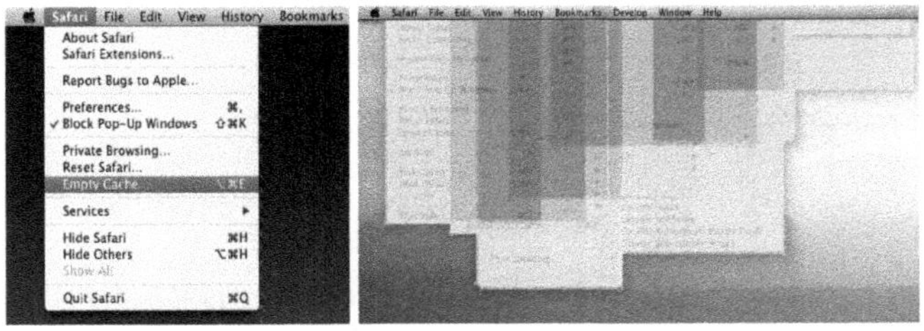

Figure 5. Left: The Safari menu would overlap with File, Edit, View and History menus. Right: heat map of Safari menus overlapping (red/dark means more overlap).

Adapting ExposeHK to menus

The primary design concept of ExposeHK$_M$ is similar to ExposeHK$_T$ – pressing a modifier key exposes all of the menu items with associated hotkeys overlaying items, as shown in Figure 6. Command selections can be completed by pressing the hotkey or by using the pointer. Second-level menu cascades are not displayed, so some degree of pointer-based selection is still necessary.

ExposeHK$_M$ modifies the visual layout of menus to remove spatial overloading. This is necessary to support hotkey browsing (goal 1) and to help intermediate users exploit their spatial memory (goal 3). With ExposeHK$_M$, the width of the gap between top-level menu items is determined by the width of the longest item with a hotkey in each menu. If a longer item without a hotkey exists within the menu, the name is truncated until the cursor hovers over it.

An obvious consequence of this design is that the menubar width increases. Using data from our menu structure analysis, we calculated a mean menubar width of 1204 px for the 30 applications (using the default system font), ranging from 722 px to 1736 px. This raises interesting issues for deployment – ExposeHK$_M$ can be readily adapted to Mac OS X menus because they extend across the width of the primary screen; however, it would be more difficult to deploy in small windows where the menubar resides within the window. We return to issues of deployment in the discussion.

Although ExposeHK$_M$ is intended to promote hotkey use, it is compatible with pointer-based interaction and users can select items using the pointer if preferred. Doing so should be more efficient than traditional menus because it removes the requirement to first point to a menu to post it (pressing the modifier key posts all menus at once), thus replacing two pointing actions with a single one. Although this design risks giving an initial impression of visual clutter, studies suggest that similar methods of parallel presentation can improve pointer-based selection performance [30] and reduce visual search times because rapid eye saccades can replace comparatively slow pointer-based manipulation [14, 27]. Finally, users can still browse the menus and select the items using the pointer only as with a regular menubar if preferred.

Experimental method

Study 2 examined hotkey use with ExposeHK$_M$ in comparison to traditional menus supplemented with audio feedback (preference results are deferred until after Study 3). Audio feedback was used because it succeeded in promoting hotkey use in [12] and in Study 1. The method was based on Study 1 (in turn based on [12]), with modifications described below.

Task and stimulus. Tasks involved selecting a menu item in response to an iconic target stimulus (e.g., a hat icon for the target 'Hat'). Iconic stimuli were used instead of text because pilot studies suggested that long and short word stimuli were easier to visually identify in the menu; iconic stimuli removed this confound: Figure 6 shows a menu and stimulus used in the study. The mechanism for presenting stimuli and completing selections was otherwise identical to Study 1.

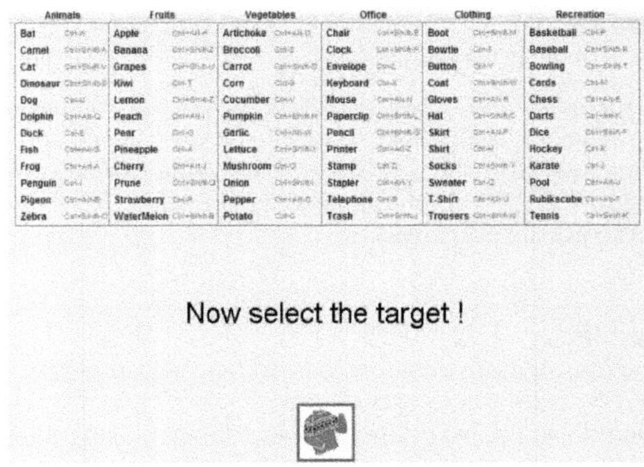

Figure 6. Example menu and stimulus used in Study 2.

Procedure. All participants completed the tasks using *ExposeHK$_M$* and *audio feedback.* When using *ExposeHK$_M$*, all the menus concurrently appeared when the Control key was pressed (Fig. 6). With both interfaces selections could be completed by pointing or by using a hotkey. In the *audio feedback* condition voice-synthesis read the hotkey binding (e.g., 'Control-D') whenever a selection was made using the pointer. The hotkeys associated with target items all consisted of a single letter plus the Control key. The menus were populated using Grossman et al.'s dataset, consisting of 6 menu categories, each containing 12 items (Fig. 6).

Participants received brief training prior to using each interface, which involved selecting an item 4 or more times using the pointer and hotkey (data discarded). They then completed six blocks of trials, with each block consisting of 24 selections, using the same distribution as Study 1.

Design, Participants and Apparatus. The experiment was designed as a 2×6×4 repeated-measures design for within-subjects factors *technique* (levels *ExposeHK$_M$* and *audio*), *block* and *frequency* (as for Study 1). Order of *Technique* was counterbalanced. The target sets used in the menus were also counterbalanced. All participants from Study 1 proceeded immediately to Study 2 using the same apparatus.

We inspected the data for evidence of asymmetric skill transfer, and proceeded with within-subjects ANOVA having found

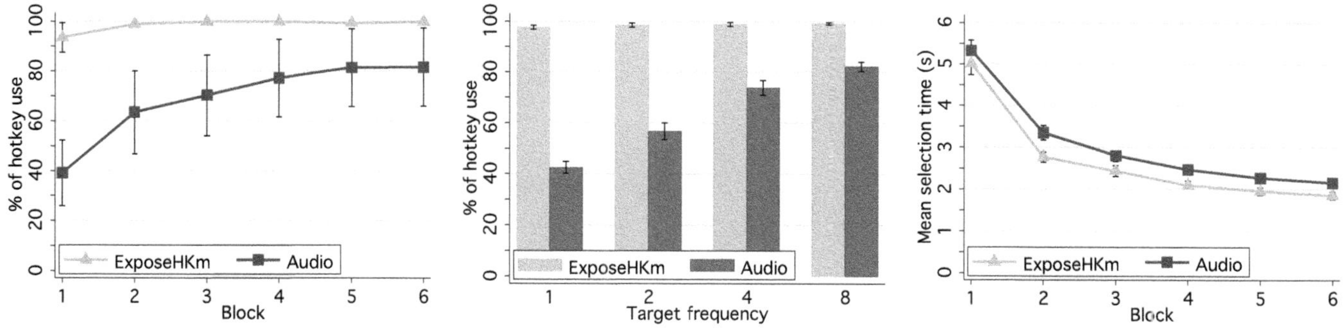

Figure 7. Results of Study 2. Left: % hotkey use by block; Center: % hotkey use by frequency; Right: mean time by block.

none (between-subjects analysis does not substantively change the results of significance tests).

Results

Proportion of hotkey use. There were strong main effects for *technique* ($F_{1,35} = 45.2, p < .001, \eta^2 = .56$), *frequency* ($p < .001, \eta^2 = .51$), and *block* ($p < .001, \eta^2 = .64$), as shown in Figure 7 (left and center). With ExposeHK$_M$, 99% of selections were completed using hotkeys, ranging from 93% in block 1 to 100% in block 6, compared with 64% with *audio*, ranging from 37% in block 1 to 77% in block 6. The continuous high hotkey use with ExposeHK$_M$, compared to the gradual increase with *audio* caused a significant *technique×block* interaction ($F_{5,95} = 20.3, p < .001, \eta^2 = .46$). There was also a significant *technique×frequency* interaction ($F_{3,105} = 32.6, p < .001, \eta^2 = .48$) caused by ExposeHK$_M$'s consistently high hotkey use across frequencies, but only 42% hotkey use for infrequent targets with *audio*.

Item selection time and errors. Figure 7 (right) shows the mean selection time (errors removed) with the different *techniques* across *block* (including both pointer-based and hotkey-based selections). Mean selection times with ExposeHK$_M$ (2.78s σ 1.8) were faster than *audio* (3.16s σ 2.02): $F_{1,35} = 15.06, p < .001, \eta^2 = .30$. As anticipated there were significant main effects of *block*, and *frequency* ($p < .001$), but *technique* did not interact with either.

Error rates were marginally lower with ExposeHK$_M$ (2.4%) than *audio* (3.0%): $F_{1,35} = 3.32, p = .08$.

Regardless of *technique*, the mean hotkey selection time was 2.53s, which was less than half that of pointer selections (5.9s). Hotkey error rates (2.4%) were also lower than pointer selections (5.9%), which we attribute to the narrow height of menu items causing relatively frequent 'off by one' errors.

In summary, the results provide similar validation to that of Study 1. With ExposeHK$_M$, participants chose to use hotkeys for nearly all commands almost immediately. In contrast, with audio feedback the transition to hotkeys was more gradual: hotkey use reached a lower maximum level, and hotkeys were comparatively rarely used with infrequent items.

STUDY 3: RIBBONS (EXPOSEHK$_R$)

Microsoft's Office 2007 'fluent' user interface merges toolbar and menu designs, using a tabbed 'ribbon' to separate multiple toolbars. Adapting EHK to the ribbon is challenging because each of several tabs places different items in the same spatial location. Also, the ribbon supports an Alt-key method for navigating its ribbon that is superficially similar to EHK. This raises two questions: can EHK be adapted to the ribbon, and does it improve performance over the Alt-key technique?

The ribbon adaptation, called ExposeHK$_R$, is visually similar to ExposeHK$_T$, but it additionally allows users to move between tabbed toolbars using the scrollwheel (as does the current Microsoft Ribbon interface) or arrowkeys. To remain consistent with the Ribbon's tabbed subsets, ExposeHK$_R$ relaxes goal 1, which motivated the concurrent presentation of all items with toolbars and menus.

There are two key differences between Microsoft's Alt-key interface and ExposeHK$_R$, both arising with respect to goal 4 (stable commands in a flat hierarchy). First, every selection with Alt-keys is necessarily hierarchical, involving a hotkey specification of the target tab and then the target item within the tab. Multi-level selections are necessary even when the correct target tab is pre-selected. With ExposeHK$_R$, in contrast, hotkeys are globally available in a flat hierarchy. Furthermore, selecting a hotkey with ExposeHK$_R$ has the side effect of switching to the tab that contains the target item, which is intended to assist with browsing hotkeys when users make a series of selections within the same tab. Second, Alt-keys are unstable, with the same letter representing different meanings in different modes (e.g., in Microsoft Word 'H' is used for Home, Shading, Header, and more), whereas ExposeHK$_R$'s commands are stable and mode-insensitive. These design differences have implications for the designer's choice of hotkey bindings, as discussed later.

Experimental method

Studies 1 and 2 focused on the proportion of hotkey use resulting from techniques that aim to promote them. In Study 3, the primary concern is the ultimate objective of hotkey interaction – improved performance – compared across three ribbon methods: ExposeHK$_R$, mouse selection, and Alt-keys.

Task and stimulus. Each task involved selecting an item within a ribbon-like interface (Figure 8) in response to a text stimulus representing the target. The mechanism for presenting stimuli and handling errors was otherwise identical to Study 2. The key-bindings used with Alt-keys all used Alt, then a

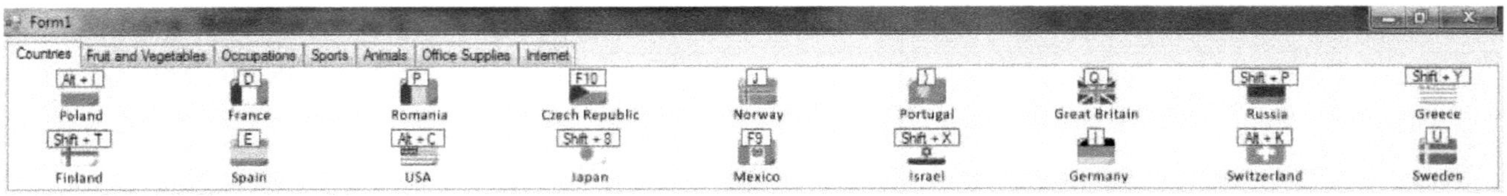

Figure 8. Example of a ribbon used in our experiment, with the ExposeHK$_R$ mode on.

single keypress for each of two levels (tab, then item). The key-bindings for ExposeHK$_R$ all used Control then a single keypress.

Procedure. All participants completed the tasks using *ExposeHK$_R$*, *Alt Keys* and *pointer* (mouse selection). With each condition they were required to complete selections using the primary interaction modality in order to get them to a performance maximum with that modality. Therefore, with ExposeHK$_R$ and *Alt Keys* they were required to use hotkeys and with *pointer* hotkeys were disabled. Before using each technique, participants received brief instruction and then completed eight random selections from a ribbon populated with a training set of items (data discarded). They were instructed to select targets as quickly and accurately as possible.

The ribbon used in the experiment consisted of 7 tabs with 18 items each. Participants completed 8 blocks of 12 selections with each interface. Each block comprised 2 selections of the same 6 targets, allowing participants to gain expertise across blocks. Half of the selections in each block involved switching to a different tab, allowing us to inspect the impact on performance of tab-switching with the different interfaces.

Design, Participants and Apparatus. Selection time data was analysed using a 3×8×2 analysis of variance for within-subject factors *technique* (*ExposeHK$_R$*, *Alt Keys* and *pointer*), *block* (levels 1-8), and *tab switch* (yes or no). Order of *technique* and the dataset used with each technique were counterbalanced across participants. 18 volunteers (aged 21-45, 1 female) participated. Experimental software, written in C#, ran on Windows 7 with a 1280×1024 22" display, optical mouse, and QWERTY keyboard.

Results

Figure 9 summarises the selection time results for the three *techniques* across *block* (left) and *tab switch* (right). Analysis of variance showed significant main effects for all factors: *technique* ($F_{2,34} = 34.5, p < .001, \eta^2 = .67$), *block* ($F_{7,119} = 111.2, p < .001, \eta^2 = .87$), and *tab switch* ($F_{1,17} = 282.5, p < .001, \eta^2 = .94$).

The overall mean selection time with ExposeHK$_R$ (2.86 s, σ 1.6) was 8.6% faster than pointer selections (3.13 s, σ 0.97), and 36% faster than Alt Keys. However, Figure 9 (left) shows a significant *technique*×*block* interaction, with ExposeHK$_R$ slightly slower than pointer in the first two blocks, but substantially faster (30%) than pointer by the final block (posthoc Bonferroni, $p < .05$). Pairwise comparison of performance in the final block shows significant differences between all three interfaces. The early asymptote of the pointer performance curve suggests that pointer selection rapidly reaches a relatively low performance ceiling.

Figure 9 (right) shows the significant *technique*×*tab switch* interaction ($F_{2,34} = 10.6, p < .001, \eta^2 = .67$), which is best attributed to the contrast between the pointer and ExposeHK$_R$ being similarly affected by the need to switch tabs, while performance with Alt Keys was more consistent across the tab switch levels. This is explained by the Alt Key mechanism requiring users to carry out identical hierarchical actions regardless tab switch state, whereas pointer and ExposeHK$_R$ actions are different depending on the need to switch tabs (they need to carry out additional actions to click on the item or to view the hotkey). With experience, however, once hotkeys are well learned, ExposeHK$_R$ users do not need to switch tabs, which best explains the three-way significant *technique*×*block*×*tab switch* interaction ($F_{14,238} = 2.81, p < .001, \eta^2 = .14$).

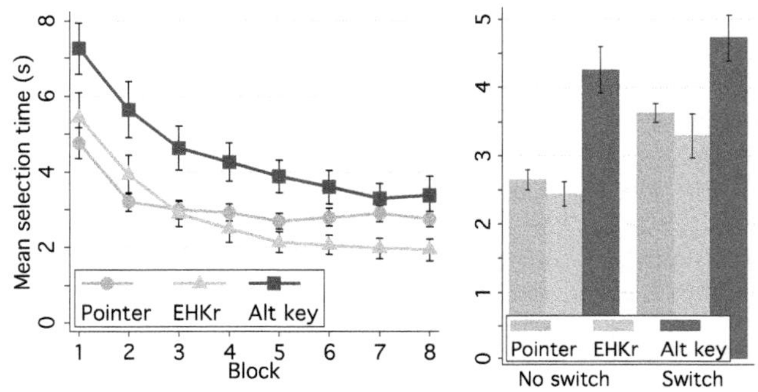

Figure 9. Mean selection time (s) per block (left) and condition (right)

SUBJECTIVE RESULTS (ALL STUDIES)

After each study participants completed NASA-TLX worksheets to assess subjective workload with each interface, they ranked the interfaces for overall preference, and they provided comments. In all cases, the participants' subjective responses strongly favoured EHK – 66.7% ranked it first for overall preference in Study 1, 77.8% preferred it over *audio* in Study 2, and 88.9% ranked it first in Study 3. Mean responses are shown in Table 1, with significant differences shown in bold (Friedman and Wilcoxon tests).

In studies 1 and 2, NASA-TLX measures showed that EHK had the lowest or equal-to-lowest workload measure in all categories. Several participants also commented that the audio feedback method was "annoying", and that they intentionally decided ignore its feedback. In study 3, EHK was assessed as resulting in lower physical demand, less frustration, and higher perceived success than pointing, but it had higher mental demand. We suspect that the low mental demand of pointing is a key factor in users failing to migrate to hotkeys, but we also suspect that once practiced, hotkeys require similar mental demand to pointing (e.g., using Control-C for copy no longer requires much thought for most users). We return to this issue in the discussion.

	Study 1			Study 2		Study 3		
	eHK	T	A	eHK	A	eHK	Alt	P
Mental demand	**2.7**	**3.2**	**3.4**	2.6	2.9	**2.9**	**4.0**	**1.9**
Physical demand	**2.4**	**3.0**	**2.7**	**2.1**	**2.7**	**1.8**	**2.5**	**3.1**
Temporal demand	2.6	2.7	2.6	2.5	2.7	2.3	3.0	2.1
Hard work	**2.6**	**3.2**	**3.1**	**2.4**	**3.0**	**2.9**	**3.8**	**2.9**
Frustration	**2.1**	**2.6**	**3.0**	**2.0**	**2.7**	**1.9**	**3.2**	**2.7**
Successful	3.8	3.4	3.5	**4.0**	**3.7**	**4.2**	**3.0**	**3.2**

Table 1. Mean NASA-TLX and other values (1=low, 5=high) per experiment (Toolbars, Menus or Ribbon) and techniques (eHK: ExposeHK; T: Tooltips; A: Audio; Alt: Alt keys; P: Pointer). Significant effects for ExposeHK in bold.

DISCUSSION

Design goals 1-3 address issues in promoting users' transition to using hotkeys: helping novices browse hotkeys (goal 1), using physical rehearsal (goal 2), and drawing on spatial memory to assist hotkey identification and confirmation for intermediate users (goal 3).

Studies 1 and 2 showed that toolbar and menu adaptations of EHK improved on the state-of-the-art systems for promoting hotkey use. Participants made an early, comprehensive, and sustained switch to hotkeys when using EHK, whereas standard tooltips and post-selection audio feedback resulted in slower hotkey adoption and lower levels of use. Participants, mostly university staff and students, were almost certainly aware of keyboard shortcuts as an interface mechanism, possibly increasing hotkey use for all conditions. Finally, participants also strongly preferred EHK to the other conditions tested (audio feedback and contemporary designs).

Design goal 4 addresses ultimate performance with hotkeys by advocating stable bindings that are globally applicable in a flat interface hierarchy. Study 3 therefore examined user performance with EHK when adapted to a contemporary 'ribbon' design of tabbed toolbars, comparing performance with standard pointer-based selection and with a commercial hierarchical 'Alt' Keys interface. Results showed that EHK quickly outperformed the pointer by up to 30% on selection time. EHK substantially outperformed the Alt keys interface throughout.

Together the studies suggest that user performance in command selection can be improved by incorporating EHK in standard toolbar, menu, and ribbon interfaces. With EHK novice users have a mechanism to browse hotkeys without using the pointer, and they can issue hotkey commands as a rehearsal of the expert mechanism. Intermediate users can draw on their spatial knowledge of commands to rapidly find hotkey bindings. Finally, the ultimate performance of experts is improved through stable bindings and flat hierarchies.

The following subsections discuss issues of deployment and identify promising areas for further work.

Discoverability and pointer compulsion

The studies show that when participants are aware of EHK they use it to their advantage and are enthusiastic about it. However, all three studies included explicit instruction and practice with EHK prior to experimental tasks, which raises questions of how it will be discovered and used in practice. We see two challenges for practical deployments, related to its *discoverability* and to the need to break users' inertia in continuing with pointer-based selections (or *pointer compulsion*).

Discoverability. Interactions such as EHK have no visual representation to aid their discovery until the user accidentally or deliberately presses its modifier-key trigger. Similar problems of weak affordances are present in many forms of interaction, such as touchscreens, where the number of taps, the number of fingers, the tap location, or press duration can be used to control different interactive effects, without any visual representation. In such cases designers often use techniques such as on- and off-line tutorials, 'tip of the day' utilities, and general marketing to promote discovery and awareness.

Social interactions around computing (e.g., over-the-shoulder observation) also play a major role is disseminating useful system capabilities [25]. Consequently, useful facilities can become widely known even when their presentation is subtle or relatively cryptic.

Pointer compulsion. Studies 1 and 2 explicitly instructed users to make a series of pointer-based and hotkey-based selections with each interface prior to beginning experimental tasks. However, in pilot studies, some participants completed selections using the pointer despite clearly displayed instructions to use hotkeys, and they continued to do so until verbally instructed to use the hotkeys. Breaking this inertia of pointer-based interaction is challenging, but doing so is a primary objective of goals 1-3.

Regardless of these challenges to adoption, it is important to note that EHK is largely compatible with existing designs – it supplements their functionality without changing their basic behavior, allowing users to maintain existing interaction strategies without performance detriment, but also offering a higher performance ceiling if used.

In on-going work we are developing an application that will incorporate ExposeHK$_M$ into Mac OS X menus. This will allow us to gain insights into longitudinal use of EHK in real-world deployments.

Modifier keys and vocabulary

The hotkeys in our experiments used only the Control key as a modifier. However, some applications use multiple modifiers and modifier combinations to increase hotkey vocabulary (e.g. Control, Alt, and Control+Alt). Although we have not yet evaluated multiple modifiers, we suspect that the results will generalise to modifier key combinations. Importantly, design guidelines advocate using single modifier keys (like those evaluated) for important commands: for example, Apple recommends that developers "use the Command key as the main modifier key in a keyboard shortcut" [21]. Furthermore, our analysis of how hotkeys are used in 30 mainstream applications showed that 93.4% (sd 12.7%) of commands use the Command key, suggesting that our method is representative of contemporary hotkey deployments.

When multiple modifiers are required, EHK could be further adapted to help users learn the modifier key bindings. For example, the display mechanism for exposing hotkeys could highlight the items accessed with the currently depressed modifier key (e.g., using a different color or opacity), while also showing all other hotkey bindings to assist users who are unsure of the required modifier for their target.

By advocating for stable hotkey bindings in a globally accessible flat hierarchy, goal 4 limits the number of commands accessible through a single hotkey character with each single modifier key to ≈ 45 (alphanumerical plus special characters). In contrast, a two-level Alt hierarchy that uses a single character at each level gives access to up to $t \times 45$ (plus numbers and special characters) commands (where t is the number of top-level tabs). Pragmatically, though, we suspect that very few users know as many as 45 hotkeys in any existing system.

Adaptation to other interfaces

Several design solutions could be used to adapt EHK to menu and toolbar combinations. Most toolbar items are replicated in menus, so the simplest solution would be to allow the menus to occlude the toolbar. However, this would impair intermediate users' ability to use their spatial memory of items in the toolbar (opposing goal 3). Alternatively, different modifier keys, or different actions on the same modifier key, could be used to trigger toolbar and menu hotkey exposure: for example, a single Control key press might show ExposeHK_T, and a second one ExposeHK_M.

By displaying all of the available menu commands at once, ExposeHK_M effectively turns the command-access interface into a CommandMap [30]. Scarr et al. demonstrated that pointer-based interaction with CommandMaps substantially outperforms ribbon and menu designs because it replaces two actions (each involving search, decision, and pointing) with a single one. Consequently, even when items within ExposeHK_M have no associated hotkey, ExposeHK_M should improve performance over traditional schemes.

CONCLUSION

Keyboard shortcuts such as hotkeys are widely deployed in current applications but they are known to be underused. We presented ExposeHK, a simple interactive technique that overlays hotkeys onto existing widgets when a modifier key is pressed. Its design promotes hotkey use and enhances efficiency through four goals: enable hotkey browsing; support physical rehearsal; support rapid hotkey identification; and support stable commands in a flat hierarchy. We presented three ExposeHK exemplars that work with the main methods for organising commands in graphical user interfaces: toolbars, menus, and tabbed 'ribbon' toolbars. Three studies, one with each of the designs, demonstrated that the adaptations succeed in promoting earlier and higher levels of hotkey use than other methods, that they improve user performance, and that they are subjectively preferred to alternatives.

REFERENCES

1. Alexander, J. *Understanding and Improving Navigation Within Electronic Documents*. PhD thesis, University of Canterbury, Christchurch, New-Zealand, 2009.
2. Appert, C., and Zhai, S. Using strokes as command shortcuts: cognitive benefits and toolkit support. *CHI '09*, ACM, 2289–2298.
3. Bailly, G., Lecolinet, E., and Nigay, L. Flower menus: a new type of marking menu with large menu breadth, within groups and efficient expert mode memorization. *AVI '08*, ACM, 15–22.
4. Bau, O., and Mackay, W. Octopocus: a dynamic guide for learning gesture-based command sets. *UIST '08*, ACM, 37–46.
5. Bhavnani, S. K., and John, B. E. The strategic use of complex computer systems. *Hum.-Comput. Interact. 15*, 2 (Sept. 2000), 107–137.
6. Callahan, J., Hopkins, D., Weiser, M., and Shneiderman, B. An empirical comparison of pie vs. linear menus. *CHI '88*, ACM, 95–100.
7. Card, S., Moran, T., and Newell, A. The keystroke-level model for user performance time with interactive systems. *Commun. ACM 23* (July 1980), 396–410.
8. Card, S., Newell, A., and Moran, T. *The Psychology of Human-Computer Interaction*. L. Erlbaum Associates Inc., 1983.
9. Carroll, J. M., and Rosson, M. B. *Paradox of the active user*. MIT Press, Cambridge, MA, USA, 1987, 80–111.
10. Cockburn, A., and Gutwin, C. A predictive model of human performance with scrolling and hierarchical lists. *HumanComputer Interaction 24*, 3 (2009), 273–314.
11. Common commands in speech recognition. http://windows.microsoft.com/en-NZ/windows-vista/ Common-commands-in-Speech-Recognition.
12. Grossman, T., Dragicevic, P., and Balakrishnan, R. Strategies for accelerating on-line learning of hotkeys. *CHI '07*, ACM, 1591–1600.
13. Hart, S., and Staveland, L. Development of nasa-tlx (task load index): Results of empirical and theoretical research. *Human mental workload*, Elsevier, 139–183.
14. Hornof, A. Visual search and mouse-pointing in labeled versus unlabeled two-dimensional visual hierarchies. *ACM Trans. Comput.-Hum. Interact. 8*, 3 (Sept. 2001), 171–197.
15. Howes, A., Payne, S. J., and Woodward, A. The trouble with shortcuts. *CHI '00 Extended Abstracts*, CHI EA '00, ACM, 267–268.
16. Jorgensen, A., Garde, A., Laursen, B., and Jensen, B. Using mouse and keyboard under time pressure: Preference, strategies and learning. *Behaviour & Information Technology 21*, 5 (2002), 317–319.
17. Krisler, B., and Alterman, R. Training towards mastery: overcoming the active user paradox. *NordiCHI '08*, ACM, 239–248.
18. Kurtenbach, G., and Buxton, W. Issues in combining marking and direct manipulation techniques. *UIST '91*, ACM, 137–144.
19. Kurtenbach, G. P. *The design and evaluation of marking menus*. PhD thesis, University of Toronto, Ontario, Canada, 1993.
20. Lane, D., Napier, A., Peres, C., and Sandor, A. The Hidden Costs of Graphical User Interfaces: The Failure to Make the Transition from Menus and Icon Tool Bars to Keyboard Shortcuts. *International Journal of Human-Computer Interaction 18* (2005), 133–144.
21. Mac os x human interfaces guidelines. https://developer.apple.com/library/mac/#documentation/ UserExperience/Conceptual/AppleHIGuidelines/Intro/Intro.html.
22. Matejka, J., Li, W., Grossman, T., and Fitzmaurice, G. Communitycommands: command recommendations for software applications. *UIST '09*, ACM, 193–202.
23. Miller, C. S., Denkov, S., and Omanson, R. C. Categorization costs for hierarchical keyboard commands. *CHI '11*, ACM, 2765–2768.
24. Odell, D., Davis, R., Smith, A., and Wright, P. Toolglasses, marking menus, and hotkeys: a comparison of one and two-handed command selection techniques. *GI '04*, 17–24.
25. Peres, C., Tamborello, F., Fleetwood, M., Chung, P., and Paige-smith, D. Keyboard shortcut usage: The roles of social factors and computer experience. *HFES '04*, 803–807.
26. Poulton, E., and Freeman, P. Unwanted asymmetrical transfer effects with balanced experimental designs. *Psychological Bulletin 66*, 1 (1966).
27. Quinn, P., and Cockburn, A. The effects of menu parallelism on visual search and selection. *AUIC '08*, Australian Computer Society, 79–84.
28. Rekimoto, J., Ishizawa, T., Schwesig, C., and Oba, H. Presense: interaction techniques for finger sensing input devices. *UIST '03*, ACM, 203–212.
29. Richardson, J. T. Eta squared and partial eta squared as measures of effect size in educational research. *Educational Research Review 6*, 2 (2011), 135–147.
30. Scarr, J., Cockburn, A., Gutwin, C., and Bunt, A. Improving command selection with commandmaps. *CHI '12*, ACM, 257–266.
31. Scarr, J., Cockburn, A., Gutwin, C., and Quinn, P. Dips and ceilings: understanding and supporting transitions to expertise in user interfaces. *CHI' 11*, ACM, 2741–2750.
32. Schmidt, R. A., and Lee, T. D. *Motor control and learning: A behavioral emphasis*, vol. 3. Human Kinetics, 2005.
33. Schneider, W., and Chein, J. Controlled & automatic processing: behavior, theory, and biological mechanisms. *Cognitive Science 27*, 3 (2003), 525–559.

MorePhone: A Study of Actuated Shape Deformations for Flexible Thin-Film Smartphone Notifications

Antonio Gomes
Human Media Lab
Queen's University
Kingston, ON, Canada, K7L3N6
gomes@cs.queensu.ca

Andrea Nesbitt
Human Media Lab
Queen's University
Kingston, ON, Canada, K7L3N6
nesbitt@queensu.ca

Roel Vertegaal
Human Media Lab
Queen's University
Kingston, ON, Canada, K7L3N6
roel@cs.queensu.ca

ABSTRACT
We present MorePhone, an actuated flexible smartphone with a thin-film E Ink display. MorePhone uses shape memory alloys to actuate the entire surface of the display as well as individual corners. We conducted a participatory study to determine how users associate urgency and notification type with full screen, 1 corner, 2 corner and 3 corner actuations of the smartphone. Results suggest that with the current prototype, actuated shape notifications are useful for visual feedback. Urgent notifications such as alarms and voice calls were best matched with actuation of the entire display surface, while less urgent notifications, such as software notifications were best matched to individual corner bends. While different corner actuations resulted in significantly different matches between notification types, medium urgency notification types were treated as similar, and best matched to a single corner bend. A follow-up study suggested that users prefer to dedicate each corner to a specific type of notification. Users would like to personalize the assignment of corners to notification type. Animation of shape actuation significantly increased the perceived urgency of any of the presented shapes.

Author Keywords
Flexible Displays; Shape Changing Interfaces; Actuation; Notification; Organic User Interfaces.

ACM Classification Keywords
H.5.m. [Information interfaces and presentation (e.g., HCI)]: Miscellaneous.

General Terms
Human Factors; Experimentation.

INTRODUCTION
In the future, the physical form of computing devices might become as mutable as that of software data in terms of shape, behavior and movement, allowing devices to form a more dynamic relationship with the user's environment [15]. The reason for this is the emergence of new advanced technologies and materials for computer input and display that can be used for designing flexible computers. Thin-film electrophoretic displays (Flexible E Ink) [18], flexible organic light emitting diodes (FOLEDs) [16], and surface mountable thin film bend, pressure and touch sensors have resulted in a surging interest in exploring the possibilities of flexible, more organic [32] computer interfaces, such as Gummi [28], PaperWindows [13], PaperPhone [18] and Nokia's Kinetic [16]. A number of benefits have been attributed to flexible interfaces in literature, including: increased mobility, flexible screen real estate, better ergonomic fit to the body, increased robustness, light-weight multi-display operation for multitasking, and natural support for haptics. While one might debate the benefits provided by thin-film flexible computer prototypes over rigid form factors, the usability of flexible computer interfaces has become an active topic of research in HCI over the past few years [13,18,19,28].

CHI 2013, April 27–May 2, 2013, Paris, France.

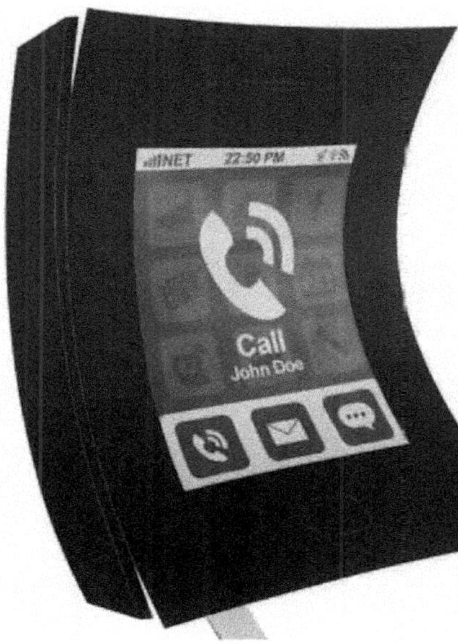

Figure 1. MorePhone actuated shape changing phone.

Actuated Flexible Display Interfaces
While studies have been conducted on the use of actuation in rigid mobile bodies [11], input devices [30], pixelated actuated displays [20,24], actuated paper [25] and shape changing interfaces [5], one area that has received little attention to date is the actuation of flexible display surfaces.

Flexible displays provide a natural platform for actuation compared to rigid displays as they can be deformed with ease. The purpose of such actuated physical deformations is to communicate the state of the computer system through a change in the *visual* or *haptic* appearance of the device's shape.

Using Shape Change for Ambient Notifications

A common problem with auditory notifications is their general disruptiveness, both in terms of single user attention and in terms of interference with social interactions [29]. Visual notifications can be distracting [22] and easily missed when the user is not actively attending to the display. For this reason, vibro-tactile feedback has become a popular way of notifying users [4]. However, like visual notifications, vibro-tactile notifications are easily missed when the user is not in direct contact with the device. By contrast, actuated shape notifications provide a means for tactile notification that does have a distinct visual correlate [1]. Actuated shape notifications also provide a design space in between *visual* and *tactile* methods of feedback that is potentially rich in terms of communicating various states of the system.

Contributions

In this paper we present MorePhone, a prototype smartphone that uses shape deformations as its primary means of both *haptic* and *visual* notifications (Figure 1). We present a study of the semantics of a shape notification design language through a participatory study, matching urgency and notification types to full screen, 1 corner, 2 corner and 3 corner bends. An informal follow up study ascertains if shape actuation requires pairing with visual cues to convey information. We conclude with design recommendations for the presentation of actuated shape notifications on smartphones.

RELATED WORK

We will first discuss work related to *auditory*, *visual* and *tactile* notification cues. We will then discuss studies of actuated, shape-changing devices.

Auditory Notification Cues

Auditory notification cues can be attention demanding, intrusive, and often perceived as inappropriate. "Beeping and ringing is by nature an intrusive sound not unlike the sound of an alarm clock" [21]. According to Shell et al. [29], when many ubiquitous devices simultaneously demand full attention from the user, this may lead to attention overload. Hansson [10] describes attention overload as being obtrusive not only to the owner of the device, but also those in her vicinity.

Visual Notification Cues

Visual cues are useful in contexts that demand no disruption. However, they can be easily missed, as their effectiveness relies on users active engagement with the display device [10]. According to McCrickard [22], visual cues demand a high cognitive load and critical notifications may be lost over the users current activity.

Vibro-tactile Notification Cues

Vibro-tactile notifications effectively limit notification to one's own personal space. Brown and Brewster [4] evaluated vibro-tactile notification cues and their appropriateness to convey information when visual displays are not available. However, it is not always easy to distinguish between various vibro-tactile alerts, as they are invisible, thus hard to interpret, and their design space has been mostly limited to time-based vibration patterns [10,27]. Vibro-tactile notifications are also invisible to social contexts, increasing the risk for misinterpretations of a user's actions. Actuated shape notifications provide silent yet public notification cues that are visible to others. Because they offer a richer repertoire of visible shapes, they may also provide a larger semantic space for interpreting the type of notification.

Actuated Mobile Shape-Changing Interfaces

While research in the domain of ambient user notifications has been extensive, we find few projects where actuated notifications where seamlessly integrated in a shape changing mobile device. Dynamic Knobs [12] evaluated the concept of a rigid mockup phone capable of changing shape in a small extension on one of its sides. Hemmert et al. [11] also explored the concept of a shape-changing device that uses two-dimensional tapering to display the directionality of off-screen contents. We believe actuated notifications in flexible mobile devices might also be useful for displaying this type of notification. Horev [14] investigated the use of actuated pixel matrices in mobile phones. Although these can provide the user with simultaneous tactile matrices, the interpretation requires high tactile attention, drawing on abstract languages that users need to learn how to decode. Coelho and Maes [6] presented Surflex, a programmable surface for the design and visualization of physical forms. Surflex provides a notification platform that inspired our design. Note that none of the above projects included a high resolution display in the actuation surface.

Actuated 3D Displays

Actuated 3D displays serve to provide 3D graphics by dimensioning the actual display through actuation. Poupyrev et al.'s [24] Lumen explored the design of an actuated pixelated information display. Lumen used light and shape memory alloys to lift pixels in the z dimension of the screen to display 3D movement and simple 3D shapes. Similarly, ShadePixel [17] demonstrated a foam skin actuated by solenoids to produce shadow effects that visualize pixels using ambient light. By contrast, Leithinger and Ishii [20]'s Relief's main purpose was to allow high resolution images to be visualized in 3D. Their system uses a series of rods that actuate a fabric display that is top projected with 2D images.

Studies of Actuated Shape Interfaces

To our knowledge, there are few empirical studies that explored effects of shape-changing in a flexible mobile device context. However, studies have been conducted on designing gestures for such devices and we borrow from their methodology. Lahey et al. [18] evaluated the effectiveness of bend gestures to execute tasks in a flexible mobile device. In this study, users designed bend gestures for common computing actions deployed on a flexible E Ink smartphone. They identified the most frequently used bend gesture pairs and observed that bend gestures that take directional cues into account are more natural to users. Lee et al. [19] conducted a study to generate a set of interaction gestures for mockup deformable displays as input devices. In this study, participants were given 11 specific interaction tasks, such as zooming or navigating, and were instructed to deform the displays in ways that would execute these tasks. They found that users preferred pairings of closely related but opposite actions and gestures. Rasmussen et al. [26] conducted a review of the design space of shape-changing materials and proposed guidelines for designing mutable interfaces.

DESIGN SPACE OF SHAPE CHANGING NOTIFICATIONS

To inform the design of a flexible mobile device that uses shape changes for the purpose of notifications, we used the following design criteria:

Lessen Reliance on Screen Real Estate for Notification

Visual notifications use valuable real estate on the display. While they provide easy access to contextual semantics of a notification, they are easily missed when eyes are off the display. When minimal pixels are used to provide notifications much of the semantics of notification is lost.

Lessen Reliance on Auditory Notifications

Auditory notifications demand immediate attention and are disruptive to others. Using alternate channels of notification provides means for designing notifications that are less disruptive.

Introduce Actuated Shape Changes for Notification

Vibro-tactile cues are easily missed when the user is not in contact with the device. Use of actuated shape notifications potentially allows for a notification platform that is simultaneously *tactile and visual.*

Design for Ambient-Foreground Transitions

The use of actuated shape notifications allows a device to communicate state from a distance or the periphery of interaction, and provide a smooth trajectory towards focused interactions with the notification source.

Richer Forms of Tactile-Visual Feedback

Vibro-tactile notifications provide minimal means of distinguishing between different notifications. As such, they often require visual notification to contextualize the semantics of the notification. Actuated shape notifications may offer a potential for exploring the sweet spot between visual and tactile notification design.

Kinetic Properties

Changes in the speed and intensity of an object's movement can be explored to express emotional connotations [26]. Surflex [6] used changes in tempo and intensity of its actuation to express dynamic emotional contexts. Thrifty Faucet [31] used random movements to express personality traits.

Expressive Properties

Repeated animation of any particular shape may increase its perceived urgency (i.e. a fast, pumping motion might be perceived as something that requires immediate attention). Changes in shape attract more attention in peripheral vision than do static notifications.

Mapping Shape Changes to Notifications

To inform our design of the semantic mapping between actuated shape changes and specific notifications, we designed a participatory study that allowed users to indicate the perceived urgency of various changes in shape, and associate them with common smartphone notifications to find patterns of semantic relationships. In general, we hypothesized that gross shape changes would be perceived as pertaining to more urgent notifications, such as phone calls. We also hypothesized that different shapes might convey different meanings to users in terms of their appropriateness for a particular notification. We were interested in understanding if the curling of more than one corners of the display would be perceived as indicating multiple, less urgent, simultaneous notifications.

Visual vs. Shape-only Notifications

We were also interested in understanding whether users would prefer to dedicate a particular corner of the display to a particular notification, or whether they would prefer to use a single corner for notifications in conjunction with visual notifications. This question is particularly relevant in the case of multiple simultaneous notifications. We designed a second, more informal, study with a fully functional prototype to determine appropriate design recommendations in this regard.

MOREPHONE IMPLEMENTATION

Before we discuss our first study, we will discuss the implementation details of our shape changing smartphone prototype. MorePhone (Figure 1) is a 14.4 x 9 *cm* flexible smartphone prototype that actuates its display as a means of providing user notifications. Our prototype consists of 3 layers: a flexible E Ink display augmented with a layer of bi-directional bend sensors and an actuation layer with Flexinol shape-memory alloys (Figure 2**Error! Reference source not found.**) [25]. MorePhone bend and actuation layers are tethered to an Arduino board [2] that is connected to a MacBook Air laptop running a simple Processing application allowing the laptop to send actuations to the prototype, and respond to user bend inputs.

Flexible Display

The first layer of our prototype consists of an Arizona State University 3.7" Bloodhound flexible electrophoretic display (Figure 2a) [3]. This display is driven by an E Ink Broadsheet AM 350 Kit [8] connected to a MacBook Air laptop running a Processing application that provides full screen gray scale images to the AM 350. The flexible

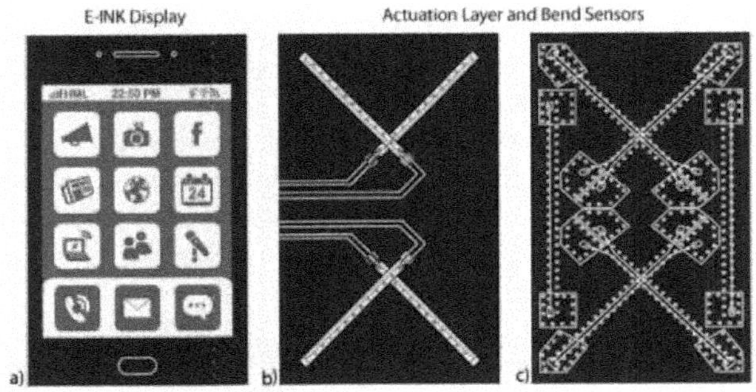

Figure 2. MorePhone layers of flexible cardboard circuitry.

display is glued to cardboard substrates containing the bend sensing and actuation layers (Figures 2b and c).

Bend Sensor Layer

Figure 2b shows the second layer, containing 4 Flexpoint 2" bidirectional bend sensors [9] that are used to gauge user responses to shape actuation notifications. These bend sensors are glued to a 14.4 x 9 *cm* 110 *lbs* cardboard substrate and soldered to a printed circuit. Bend data is processed by an Arduino, and interpreted by a Processing application on the laptop to control actuation.

Shape Actuation Layer

Figure 2c shows the third layer, which contains an actuation circuitry made of Flexinol [7] shape-memory wire. Flexinol wire contracts upon heating, which is achieved by putting a current on the wire. The wire was sewed with Kevlar threading to a second layer of cardboard substrate via small lasercut holes, allowing for its expansion and contraction (Figure 3) [25]. We used 0.006' low-temperature Flexinol wire using a current of 410 *mA* to produce a full contraction in 1 *s*. We controlled the degree of actuation as well as the velocity of actuation by altering the voltage via the Arduino board. Use of a single 0.006' wire provides a maximum pulling force of 321 g, which is not enough to provide a noticeable change of shape in our flexible phone prototype. We therefore used 2 parallel wires for each actuated section, allowing it to produce distinct and reliable curls of up to 1.5 cm at each of the four corners, as well as the entire display.

Shape Notification and Visualization

Figure 1 shows MorePhone actuating the entire screen up to 1.5 *cm* on each side. MorePhone also can actuate each of the 4 corners of the display independently from one another, providing a total of 17 possible shape combinations (including flat). Figure 4 shows MorePhone actuating the top right corner of the display. To provide additional feedback on the type of notification, MorePhone can pop up a visual notification balloon in the actuated corner. In the example shown in Figure 4, actuation of the top-right corner also pops up a notification balloon that contextualizes the notification as a text message. Users can open the text message and cancel the notification by pressing the actuated corner. The current prototype allows

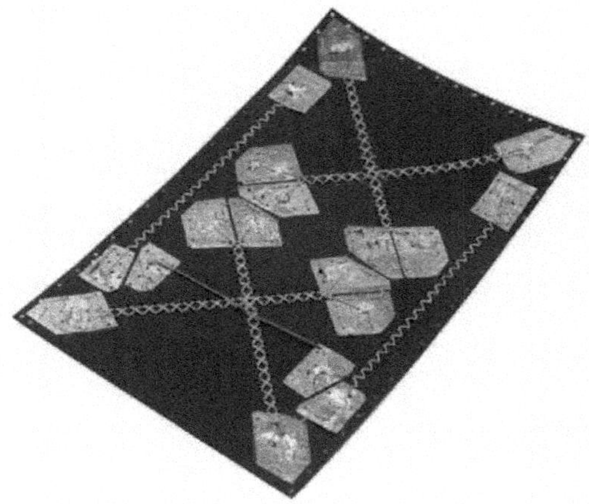

Figure 3. Cardboard actuation layer with Flexinol wires affixed to a copper substrate.

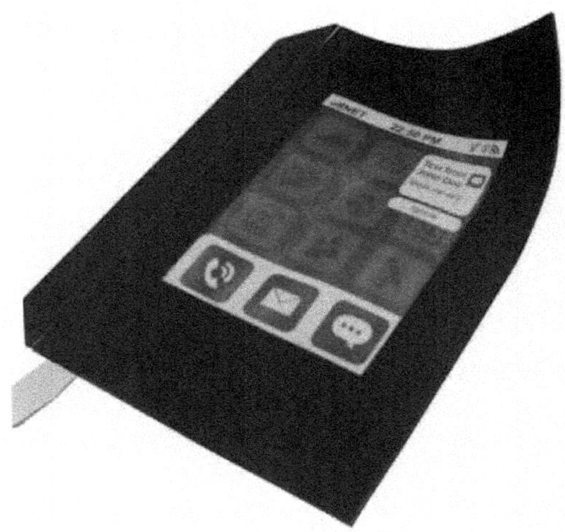

Figure 4. MorePhone displaying shape actuation in the top right corner, with on-screen notification popup.

any shape actuation to be animated with .5 *s* pulses, e.g., to convey urgency.

USER STUDY 1: SHAPES AND NOTIFICATION TYPES

Our first user study had a two-fold objective: First, we wanted to determine how users perceive the urgency of shape configurations provided by MorePhone. Second, we were interested in determining whether and how users would relate particular shape configurations to specific types of notifications. Our design was based on studies by Lee et al. [19], who studied the participatory design of bend interactions with mockup displays, Morris et. al. [23], who designed multitouch gestures to perform operations in a Microsoft Surface table based on user agreement, and Lahey et al. [18], who studied participatory design of bend interactions with flexible smartphones.

Overview

We showed participants the subset of MorePhone shapes illustrated in Figure 5 for two cases: where MorePhone was held in the hand, and where it was placed on the table. We

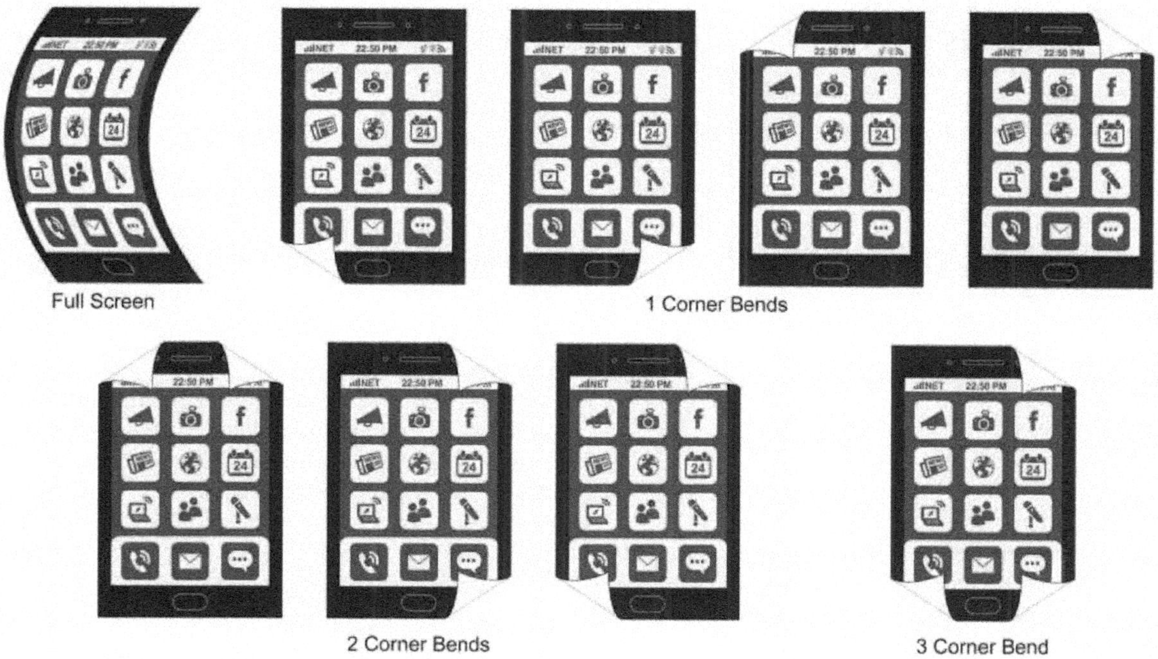

Figure 5: Subset of MorePhone shape actuations as experienced by participants of our experiment.

subsequently asked them to rate the perceived urgency of each shape, after which we asked to rate the correspondence of each shape to a set of notification types.

Participants

14 participants volunteered for this study (5 females, 9 males). The participants were between the ages of 19 and 37 (mean 26 years). All participants were students, and received $10 for 1 hour of participation.

Experimental Design

We used a within-subjects design for our study, in which each participant was asked to evaluate each shape in both conditions: where the device was handheld (VT: visuo-tactile) and where it was on a table (VO: visual-only). Shapes were presented in random order. Condition order was counterbalanced between subjects.

Shape Condition

The 9 shapes presented during the study, in addition to flat, are shown in Figure 5. To limit the amount of time required per trial, we removed the 4-corner bend, and only showed one 3-corner bend and half of all possible 2-corner combinations. The first shape was the baseline of a flat display with no actuation (not shown). The second shape, Full Screen, was a bending of the entire display along its horizontal axis. The next set of four shapes, 1 Corner Bends, curled each of the four corners of the device. The next set of three shapes, 2 Corner Bends, simultaneously curled two opposing corners of the device. In the final shape, 3 Corner Bend, three corners of the device were curled. In all shape conditions, the display was bent into a concave shape with the tip of the display curling 1.5 *cm* upwards, as measured vertically from the flat shape. The shape was actuated from flat to shape in 1 *s*.

Shape Animation

We animated each shape group to evaluate whether this would increase the perceived urgency of the shape. Each animation consisted of 5 pulses from flat to shape, each of 0.5 *s* duration. We then asked subjects how appropriate animation was for each notification type, using a 5 point Likert scale.

Visuo-tactile vs. Visual-only Condition

To ascertain the effect of visual-only versus visual-tactile feedback of MorePhone, shapes were presented in two different conditions, one where the prototype was held in the non-dominant hand, and one where it was placed on the table. In the visuo-tactile condition, users were asked whether they could see and feel the shape after actuation. The users held the prototype such that all shapes were able to touch the skin. In the visual only condition, they were only asked if they could see the shape after actuation.

Notification Types

We selected notification types commonly present in standard smartphone devices: *voice call, text message, email, voicemail, alarm/reminder, social notification* and *software update*. Prior to the session, users were asked to rate each notification type on urgency using a 5-point Likert scale (strongly agree-strongly disagree), evaluating the statement *"A [notification type] is urgent and requires my immediate attention"*. They also ranked the urgency of calls, text messages and emails by specific people.

No Visual or Auditory Notifications
The goal of our experiment was to discover possible mappings between various shapes and various notification types, rather than comparing the efficacy of shape notifications versus *visual*, *auditory* or *tactile* notifications. To avoid confounding effects of display design on the outcome of this experiment, the flexible display showed a neutral and static home screen in all conditions.

Task and Questionnaire
During the session, subjects were presented with a random shape for 2 *s*, after which they were asked to rank this shape for agreement with statements using a 5-point Likert scale (strongly disagree–strongly agree), pertaining to a) the perceived *urgency* of the notification, and b) the *appropriateness* of the shape for a particular notification type.

Ranking Urgency of the Shape
The first question evaluated the perceived urgency of the shape, measuring agreement with statement *"This shape indicates something urgent has happened that requires my immediate attention"*.

Mapping Shape to Notification Type
The remaining 7 questions evaluated the perceived appropriateness of the shape for each of the notification types. We measured agreement with the statement *"This shape indicates [notification type]."*

Personalization
To examine whether shape actuations might provide participants with associations of individual persons, participants were asked to evaluate the statement *"I think this shape signifies an incoming email from someone specific"* using the same Likert scale format, and were then asked to specify whom they were referring to.

Responding to Notifications
For each shape, users were asked how they would respond to the notification.

Usefulness
At the end of the session participants were asked: (1) *"In what ways do you think actuated notifications are useful?"* (2) *"In what ways do you think actuated notifications are not useful?"* and (3) *"Would you use an actuated mobile device if it was widely available?*

Training and Procedure
After completing the information and consent forms, participants were shown a subset of random shapes to allow them to become familiar with the MorePhone prototype. We demonstrated these actuations asking participants to *"Imagine this is your future phone: it does not just notify you by ringing and vibrating – but by changing shape."* We instructed users to avoid folding or twisting the device, due to the fragile nature of the prototype. We guided the participants to hold the display as if it was wireless, and to ignore the single connector cable. Aside from this, we did not instruct participants on shape changing notifications. Throughout the experiment, participants were encouraged to think aloud, so as to verbalize their thought processes, which were noted by the experimenters.

RESULTS
All subjects taking part in our study stated they were able to distinguish all 10 variations in shape that they were presented with, both with the device resting on a table (visual-only) or handheld (visuo-tactile). In the visuo-tactile condition, all participants indicated they were able to feel and see the shapes. In the visual-only condition, all participants indicated they were able to see the shapes.

Statistical Analysis
We analyzed results from our questionnaire data using a one-way Friedman's non-parametric analysis of variance based on ranked order of the questionnaire items, and with Bonferroni corrected one-tailed Wilcoxon Signed Rank post-hoc tests. Bonferroni correction was applied by evaluating the standard alpha level of .05 divided by the number of comparisons.

Grouping of Shapes
In both visuo-tactile (VT) and visual-only (VO) conditions, there were no significant differences between shapes with a single corner (VT: Friedman's χ^2 (3)=1.679, p=.642; VO: Friedman's χ^2 (3)=2.305, p=.512). There were no significant differences between shapes with two corner bends in the visual-only condition (Friedman's χ^2 (2)=.867, p=.648). There was a small but significant difference between shapes with two corner bends in the visuo-tactile condition (Friedman's χ^2 (2)=9.091, p=.011). To simplify analysis and reduce the chance of Type II errors upon posthoc analysis, we subsequently grouped shapes into five groups: Flat, Full Screen, 1 Corner Bend, 2 Corner Bend, and 3 Corner Bend. Because we focused on the visual-only condition for further analysis, the significant difference between 2 Corner Bends in the visuo-tactile condition did not affect further results.

Visuo-tactile vs. Visual-only
In the present scenario, differences between visuo-tactile and visual-only conditions were very small, and not significant for any shape group (2-tailed Wilcoxon Signed Rank at alpha of 0.05): Flat: Z=-1.732, p=.083; Full Screen: Z=-.289, p=.773; 1 Corner: Z=-1.655, p=.098; 2 Corner: Z=-1.706, p=.088; 3 Corner: Z=-.730, p=.465. Since results were very similar between VT and VO on all measures, we chose to present further statistical analyses for the visual-only condition only. There appeared to be little effect of tactile feedback on the choice of notification style. This limitation might be caused by the usage of an actual display. Alternative methodologies and materials could lead to different results.

Flat vs. Shape Notifications
A planned comparison showed a large and significant difference in ratings on all questionnaire items between the mean baseline flat condition and the average score over all

Shape	1 Corner	2 Corner	3 Corner	Full Screen
Urgency	3.07 *(0.15)*	3.40 *(0.17)*	3.71 *(0.29)*	4.43 *(0.17)*

Table 1. Mean *(s.e.)* urgency score for each shape group .

shape groups (Z=-3.298, p<.001). The flat condition was rated the lowest on all items, with a mean score of 1.3 across items. We subsequently discarded this flat baseline condition from further analysis, so as to avoid biasing results between shape groups. This means all subsequent comparisons were between shapes other than flat.

Shape and Urgency

Table shows the means and std. errors for each questionnaire item, per shape group, for the visual-only condition. Differences in urgency ratings were highly significant between shape groups (Friedman's χ^2 (3)=25.272, p<0.001). Bonferroni corrected post-hoc comparisons (evaluated at an alpha level of 0.0083), show Full Screen Bends were rated significantly more urgent than 2 Corner Bends (Z=-3.204, p<0.0002) and 1 Corner Bends (Z= -3.308, p<0.002), but not 3 Corner Bends (Z= -1.263, p=0.02). When Bonferroni corrected, there were no significant differences in urgency ratings between any other shape groups.

Shape and Notification Type

Table shows the means and std. errors for each notification type, per shape group, for the visual-only condition. Differences between shape groups in matching scores for text (Friedman's χ^2 (3)=7.639, p=.054), email (Friedman's χ^2 (3)=1.439, p=.696), voicemail (Friedman's χ^2 (3)=1.950, p=.583) and social network notifications (Friedman's χ^2 (3)=7.421, p=.060) were not significant.

Call Notifications and Shape Group

Differences between shape groups in matching scores for voice call notifications were highly significant (Friedman's χ^2 (3) =22.451, p<.001). Bonferroni corrected post-hoc comparisons (evaluated at an alpha level of 0.0083) show Full Screen Bends were rated significantly higher in terms of matching Voice Call notifications than 1 Corner Bends (Z=-3.329, p<.0002), 2 Corner Bends (Z=-3.084, p=.0002) or 3 Corner Bends (Z=-2.041, p=.0035). 1 Corner Bends were rated significantly higher than both 2 Corner Bends (Z=-2.374,p=.0015) and 3 Corner Bends (Z=-2.249, p=.002). There were no significant differences between 2 Corner Bends and 3 Corner Bends (Z=-1.069, p=.024).

Alarm/Reminder Notifications and Shape Group

Differences between shape groups in appropriateness ratings for Alarm/Reminder notifications were highly significant (Friedman's χ^2 (3) =18.139, p<.001). Bonferroni corrected post-hoc comparisons (evaluated at an alpha level of 0.0083) show Full Screen Bends were rated significantly higher in terms of matching Alarm/Reminder notifications than 1 Corner Bends (Z=-2.938, p=.0003), 2 Corner Bends (Z=-2.812, p=.0003) and 3 Corner Bends (Z=-2.588,

Notification Type	Shape			
	1 Corner	2 Corner	3 Corner	Full Screen
Alarm	2.05 *(0.28)*	2.38 *(0.25)*	2.71 *(0.41)*	3.57 *(0.33)*
Call	2.89 *(0.20)*	3.33 *(0.23)*	3.71 *(0.29)*	4.43 *(0.14)*
Voicemail	3.32 *(0.23)*	3.40 *(0.22)*	3.50 *(0.25)*	3.14 *(0.27)*
Text	3.66 *(0.15)*	3.48 *(0.16)*	3.50 *(0.27)*	3.86 *(0.25)*
Email	3.52 *(0.17)*	3.33 *(0.19)*	3.21 *(0.26)*	3.14 *(0.29)*
Social	3.41 *(0.21)*	2.90 *(0.22)*	3.00 *(0.31)*	2.71 *(0.24)*
Software	2.88 *(0.23)*	2.50 *(0.23)*	2.29 *(0.22)*	1.79 *(0.19)*

Table 2. Mean *(s.e.)* score for matching each shape group to each notification type .

p=.00083). There were no significant differences between 1 Corner Bends and 2 Corner Bends, (Z=-1.483, p=.0115), 1 Corner Bends and 3 Corner Bends (Z=-1.610, p=.009), and 2 Corner Bends and 3 Corner Bends (Z=-.827, p=.034).

Software Update Notifications and Shape Group

Differences between shape groups in matching scores for software update notifications were highly significant (Friedman's χ^2 (3) =21.690, p<.001). Bonferroni corrected post-hoc comparisons (evaluated at an alpha level of 0.0083) show 1 Corner Bends were rated significantly higher in terms of matching software notifications than 2 Corner Bends (Z=-2.533, p=.001), 3 Corner Bends (Z=-1.933, p=.0045) and Full Screen Bends (Z=-3.187, p=.0002). 2 Corner Bends were rated significantly higher than 3 Corner Bends (Z=-.680, p=.0041) and Full Screen Bends (Z=-2.542, p=.0018). 3 Corner Bends were rated significantly higher than Full Screen Bends (Z=-2.942, p=.00034).

Animation and Urgency of Notification Types

Figure 6 shows the results for matching animated shapes with notification types. Results show a significant and strong correlation (r^2=0.85, p<0.001) between the notification type matching scores for animated shapes, and the pre-session notification type urgency scores. By contrast, correlations between non-animated shape group matching scores and pre-session notification type urgency scores were not significant for any of the shape groups.

Personalization of Shape

There were no clear results with regards to personalization of shapes or shape groups to persons. 70% of participants had no preference for a person they would associate with 1 Corner Bends, 79% of the responses indicated no

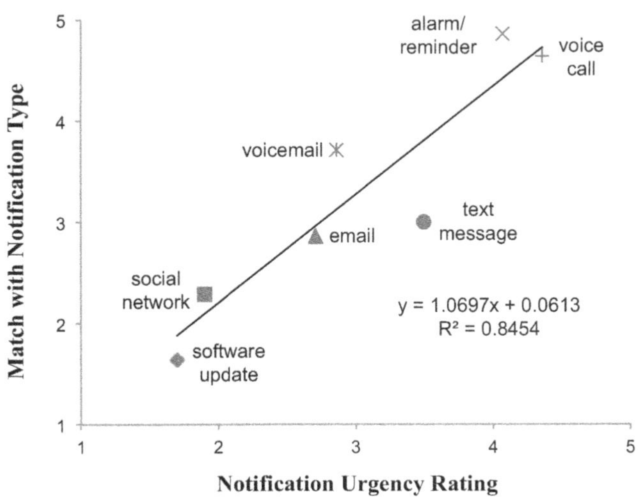

Figure 6. Match scores against pre-study ratings of notification types for animated shape notifications.

preference for 2 Corner Bends, 64% for 3 Corner Bends, and 54% for Full Screen Bend.

Responding to Notifications
Most participants, when asked how they would respond to a shape notification, answered that they would simply touch the screen of the device. One participant remarked they would touch the shape changing corner(s) of the device.

Usefulness and Participant Comments
13 of 14 participants said they would use this technology if it was widely available, and seek it out. 1 participant indicated no preference. Some concerns were voiced about the durability of the current prototype.

Silent and Noisy Usage Scenarios
Participants said the actuated shape notifications would be useful in situations where silence is necessary. Scenarios mentioned included: meetings, movies, or when concentrating. Another benefit identified is the ability to receive notifications in noisy environments. *"I listen to music all the time, and I usually miss notifications even if my phone is on high volume. If this was beside me while I worked I would notice my phone moving, and probably respond to people a lot more frequently."*[P13].

Visual Communication at a Distance
A common useful feature participants noted was the ability to receive notifications from a distance. Due to the device's capacity to hold shape, participants noted they could identify the notification and decide whether to attend to this notification or ignore it, without ever going to the phone. Participants commented that shape notifications would not be useful if the phone was in another room: *"I would want to pair the movement with the sounds phones have now."* [P3]. The addition of sound was a popular comment among participants, as: *"For really demanding notifications, I do not think movement would be enough."* [P2,P7,P11].

Shape Animation
All participants were enthusiastic about animating the phone, but the majority mentioned the desire to personalize these animations: *"Pulsing very gently would be more suitable for secondary notifications."*[P6]; *"I'd like to specify contacts and associate pulsing with a very close friend or a very urgent notification."*[P8]; *"Different pulsing patterns could provide information in a similar sort of way that the shapes provide information."*[P12].

Corners and Notifications
Participants commented on the shapes presented, mentioning an affinity for the shapes that moved one corner, and the shape that actuated the full-body of the device: *"The single corners are very clear, they're simple; I would want to assign a notification to each one. Simultaneous corners are a bit confusing: it's more like it's saying I've received two or three notifications. But it did get my attention."*[P4]

DISCUSSION
Results suggest that generally speaking, tactile feedback appears to have little effect on the appreciation of particular shapes for various types of notifications. We believe there are a number of explanations for this. Firstly, all deformations of the device were away from the hand (the corners pointed upwards). While users reported to be able to feel these deformations, this meant there was no positive pressure exerted on the hand during the presentation of any of the shape notifications. Secondly, the forces exerted by this MorePhone prototype are insufficient to provide significant kinesthetic cues. Thirdly, comments indicated that participants considered shape deformation as a means of visually drawing their attention (as opposed to tactilely). The latter can be explained by the fact that movement in the user's peripheral vision upon shape actuation provides a powerful yet subtle and ambient means to signify a status change in the phone's notification state. Although there was a significant difference between notification type matching scores for various 2 Corner Bends in the visual-tactile condition, this was not significant in the visual-only condition, and this was not significant in either condition for 1 Corner Bends. We believe that, while subtle, this effect was due to participants perhaps experiencing more of the shape change through tactile sensations in 2 Corner conditions.

Shape and Urgency
Our hypothesis that different shapes would be rated with different urgency was partially confirmed. While there were significant differences in urgency ratings between Full Screen, 2 and 1 Corner bends, there was no significant correlation between pre-study urgency and notification type match for shape groups. While Table suggests a small but insignificant trend between urgency rankings and surface area of shape groups, this is not substantiated by a clear association between pre-study urgency scores and notification type matches for shape groups. Any connection between urgency and area in shape groups appears largely

associated with full screen actuation as opposed to other, smaller, surface area actuations.

Shape and Notification Type

Our hypothesis that different shapes convey different meanings to users in terms of their appropriateness for a particular notification was confirmed. Participants, however, indicated no particular preference of any one shape group for text, voicemail, social or email notifications. Comments by participants suggested that all message notifications were best matched with a single corner bend, using multiple corners for multiple simultaneous notifications. As such, for these categories, we believe they interpreted the shapes differently, and rather than using shape to identify what message type they would receive, they were more interested in determining how many simultaneous notifications there would be.

Animation of Shapes

Results for animation of actuated shape notifications strongly suggest that animation is aligned with urgency. Approximately *85%* of the variance in matching of notification types with animation was explained by pre-study urgency rankings alone.

USER STUDY 2: DISPLAY VERSUS SHAPE

In our second, more informal study, we used MorePhone with an active display providing visual popup notifications in two corners of the flexible display: top right and bottom right. 6 participants volunteered for this study (3 females, 3 males, mean 27.5 years). The purpose of this follow-up study was to ascertain if users would require visual notifications to ascertain notification type, and whether they would touch the actuated corner to attend to the notification. We were also interested to know whether they wanted to dedicate particular corners of the display to particular notifications, as suggested by their comments in the first study, or whether they would prefer to have the entire display signify the notification type. We used the same apparatus as in the first study, but with active graphical notifications.

Task

We first showed a shape actuation in the top right corner, with a visual notification popup of a text message, and asked participants where they would touch the display upon a shape notification. We subsequently also actuated the bottom-right corner with a visual notification popup of a Facebook update. After this, we showed them the same sequence, without visual notification, and asked participants what they thought these notifications meant, and whether they thought the visual popup was helpful. We again repeated the sequence with visual notification, this time reversing the corners for each visual notification type. We subsequently asked them if they preferred dedicating corners to a notification type, and if so, whether they wanted to personalize which corner. Finally, we repeated the same sequence without visual notification, telling participants that a one-corner bend indicated a text message, and a two corner bend a Facebook message. We asked them if they preferred to be able to tell from a distance by the number of actuated corner what kind of notification they received.

Results and Discussion

Results from the follow-up study showed 4/6 participants touching the display on the curled tip to address the notification. The remaining participants simply touched the display. After having been shown which corner pertained to which notification, all participants were able to determine the notification type based on shape-only notifications. 5/6 participants preferred notifications in a dedicated corner as they found arbitrary corners confusing. *"There should be an option allowing user to set for each corner which alerts should be displayed."* [P2]. 4/6 Participants indicated they saw little to no value in determining the type of notification by the shape of the screen. Results clearly point in the direction of the use of customizable dedicated corners with visual notifications for actuated shape notifications. All participants wanted to be able to personalize in which corner each notification type would appear. There were also benefits identified for using shape notifications without visual cues. *"I see this being useful in social contexts, because it is less disruptive and favors privacy. I don't like keeping my phone face up in public as I don't want people to be able to read every text I receive."* [P1].

DESIGN RECOMMENDATIONS

From the above discussion, we derived a number of design recommendations for actuated smartphone notifications:

1. Use Animation to Increase Urgency of Notifications

We recommend that animation of actuated shape notifications is used to increase the urgency of any type of notification. This may be particularly appropriate for alarms and urgent voice calls.

2. Full Screen for the Most Urgent Notifications

We recommend that in static cases, actuation of the full surface of the display is best used for the most urgent category of notifications. This includes alarms and reminders, as well as voice calls.

3. Multiple Corners for Simultaneous Notifications

Notifications other than alarms and voice calls best rely on 1 Corner bends. Multiple corners are best used to indicate multiple parallel notifications, by type.

4. Dedicate Corners to Notification Type

Corners are best dedicated as pertaining to a particular notification type, and should be personalizable by users.

5. Provide Visual Notification Popups

Actuated shape notifications are best augmented with co-situated visual notifications. This supports learning which notification pertains to which corner, and allows for cases in which there are more alerts than corners available.

6. Filling the Gap between Visual & Tactile Notifications
Flexible smartphones support new notification paradigms that can use deformation to convey information. While more research is needed to ascertain the efficacy of shape actuation for tactile feedback, the capacity to actively change shape provides an extra design vocabulary that fits between current visual and vibratory notification methods.

LIMITATIONS AND FUTURE DIRECTIONS

While we expect future MorePhone prototypes to be highly customizable, allowing users to design their own actuated shape vocabulary, current hardware limitations prevented such customization. The current prototype is limited in terms of the amount of force it can exert on the body which constrained the expression of shape actuation for kinesthetic feedback. These limitations may be due to present display technology and results may vary with different actuation or display methods and materials. There appears to be a tradeoff between visual and tactile actuated shape notification design: in order for shapes to be clearly visible, they are best actuated outwards. Haptic perception is, however, best served through inward actuation. Our results may, as such, be limited by the choice for our prototype to actuate outwards. We aim to reduce the need for power cables in future designs.

CONCLUSION

In this paper, we presented MorePhone, a prototype flexible smartphone that changes shape to provide notifications. We studied how users perceive the urgency of full screen, single corner and multiple corner shape notifications. Results suggest full screen notifications are best used for the most urgent notifications, such as phone calls and alarms. Single corner notifications were best matched to notifications that were ranked as less urgent, such as emails and messages. Users preferred using multiple corner actuations to service multiple notifications, dedicating each corner to a particular notification type.

REFERENCES

1. Alexander, J., Lucero, A. and Subramanian, S. Tilt Displays: Designing Display Surfaces with Multi-axis Tilting and Actuation. In Proc. MobileHCI'12, ACM.
2. Arduino. http://www.arduino.cc (2012).
3. Arizona State University, Flexible Display Center. http://*flexdisplay.asu.edu* (2012).
4. Brown, L. M., Brewster, S. a., & Purchase, H. C. (2006). Multidimensional tactons for non-visual information presentation in mobile devices. *MobileHCI '06*, 231.
5. Coelho, M. and J. Zigelbaum. Shape-changing interfaces. *Personal Ubiquitous Computing* 15, 2 (2011), 161-173.
6. Coelho, M., Ishii, H., and P. Maes. Surflex: a programmable surface for the design of tangible interfaces. In *Ext Abstracts CHI'08*. ACM Press (2008), 3429-3434.
7. DynAlloy Inc. Technical characteristics of Flexinol actuator wire. *http://www.dynalloy.com* (2011).
8. E Ink Inc. *http://www.eink.com* (2010).
9. Flexpoint Inc. *http://www.flexpoint.com* (2012).
10. Hansson, R., Ljungstrand, P. and J. Redström. Subtle and public notification cues for mobile devices. In *Proc UbiComp'01*. Springer-Verlag (2001), 240-246.
11. Hemmert, F., Hamann, S., Löwe, M., Wohlauf, A., and Joost, G. Shape-changing mobiles: tapering in one-dimensional deformational displays in mobile phones. In *Proc TEI'10*, ACM Press (2010), 249-252.
12. Hemmert, F., Joost, G., Knörig, A. and Wettach, R., Dynamic knobs: shape change as a means of interaction on a mobile phone. In *Ext. Abstracts CHI'18*, ACM, 2309-2314.
13. Holman, D., Vertegaal, R., Altosaar, M., Troje, N. and D. Johns. PaperWindows: Interaction techniques for digital paper. In *Proc CHI'05*, ACM Press (2005), 591-599.
14. Horev, O. Talking to the hand – the interactive potential of shape-change behavior in objects and tangible interfaces. In *Proc DESFORM'06*, (2006).
15. Ishii, H., Lakatos, D., Bonanni, L., and J-P. Labrune. Radical atoms: Beyond tangible bits, toward transformable materials. *interactions* 19, 1 (2012), 38-51.
16. Kildal, J., Paasovaara, S., and V. Aaltonen. Kinetic device: designing interactions with a deformable mobile interface. In *Ext Abstracts CHI'12*. ACM Press (2012), 1871-1876.
17. Kim, H. and W. Lee. Shade Pixel. In *ACM SIGGRAPH'08 Posters*. ACM Press (2008), 34.
18. Lahey, B., Girouard, A., Burleson, W., and R. Vertegaal. PaperPhone: Understanding the use of bend gestures in mobile devices with flexible electronic paper displays. In *Proc CHI'11*. ACM Press (2011), 1303-1312.
19. Lee, S. et al. How users manipulate deformable displays as input devices. In *Proc. CHI'10*, ACM Press (2010), 1647-1656.
20. Leithinger, D. and H. Ishii. Relief: A scalable actuated shape display. In *Proc TEI'10*. ACM Press (2010), 221-222.
21. Ling, R. "One can talk about common manners!": The use of mobile telephones in inappropriate situations. In: *Telektronikk (Telenor R&D Journal) 2*, (1998), 65-76.
22. McCrickard, D.S. and C. M. Chewar. Attuning notification design to user goals and attention costs. *Comm. ACM* 46, 3 (2003), 67-72.
23. Morris, M.R., Wobbrock, J.O., Wilson, A.D. Understanding users' preferences for surface gestures. In *Proc. Graphics Interface GI'10*, (2010), 261-268.
24. Poupyrev, I., Nashida, T., Maruyama, S., Rekimoto, J. and Y. Yamaji. Lumen: Interactive visual and shape display for calm computing. In *Proc SIGGRAPH'04*, ACM Press (2004), 17.
25. Qi, J. and Buechley, L. Animating paper using shape memory alloys. In *Proc CHI'12*. ACM Press (2012), 749-752.
26. Rasmussen, M. K., Pedersen, E. W., Petersen, M. G., & Hornbæk, K. (2012). Shape-Changing Interfaces : A Review of the Design Space and Open Research Questions, 735–744.
27. Sahami, A., Holleis, P., Schmidt, A., and J. Häkkilä. Rich tactile output on mobile devices. In *Proc European Conference on Ambient Intelligence*. (2008), 210-221.
28. Schwesig, C., Poupyrev, I., and E. Mori. Gummi: A bendable computer. In *Proc CHI'04*. ACM Press (2004), 263-270.
29. Shell, J.S., Selker, T. and R. Vertegaal. Interacting with groups of computers. *Comm. ACM* 46, 3 (2003), 40-46.
30. Tang, S.K. and W.Y. Tang. Adaptive mouse: a deformable computer mouse achieving form-function synchronization. In *Ext. Abstracts CHI'10*. ACM Press (2010), 2785-2792.
31. Togler, J., Hemmert, F., and Wettach, R. Living Interfaces: The Thrifty Faucet. TEI'09, (2009), 43-44.
32. Vertegaal, R. and I. Poupyrev. Organic User Interfaces: Introduction to special issue. *Comm ACM* 51, 6 (2008), 26-30.

Morphees: Toward High "Shape Resolution" in Self-Actuated Flexible Mobile Devices

Anne Roudaut[1], Abhijit Karnik[1], Markus Löchtefeld[2], Sriram Subramanian[1]

[1]Department of Computer Science,
University of Bristol, UK
{anne.roudaut, karnik, sriram}@cs.bris.ac.uk

[2]German Research Institute for Artificial Intelligence (DFKI), Saarbrücken, Germany
markus.loechtefeld@dfki.de

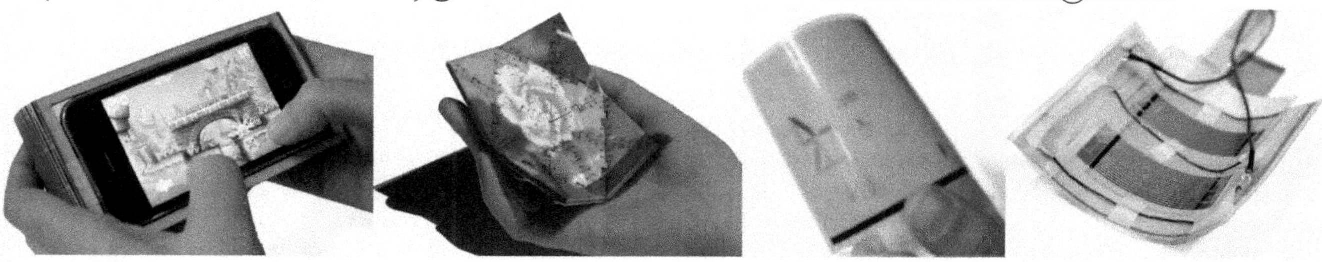

Figure 1. Morphees are self-actuated flexible mobile devices that adapt their shapes to offer better affordances. (a) E.g a mobile device can shift into a console-like shape by curling two opposite edges and be easily grasped with two hands. Among the six strategies we built to actuate Morphees, here are two high-fidelity prototypes using Shape Memory Alloys (SMA): (b) one using projection and tracking on wood tiles that are actuated with thin SMA wires; and (c) one directly bending a flexible touchscreen (E-Ink and Unmousepad) by using (d) SMA wires that we educated (forged) to remember the shape we needed.

ABSTRACT

We introduce the term *shape resolution*, which adds to the existing definitions of screen and touch resolution. We propose a framework, based on a geometric model (Non-Uniform Rational B-splines), which defines a metric for *shape resolution* in ten features. We illustrate it by comparing the current related work of shape changing devices. We then propose the concept of *Morphees* that are self-actuated flexible mobile devices adapting their shapes on their own to the context of use in order to offer better affordances. For instance, when a game is launched, the mobile device morphs into a console-like shape by curling two opposite edges to be better grasped with two hands. We then create preliminary prototypes of *Morphees* in order to explore six different building strategies using advanced shape changing materials (dielectric electro active polymers and shape memory alloys). By comparing the shape resolution of our prototypes, we generate insights to help designers toward creating *high shape resolution Morphees*.

Author Keywords

Shape resolution, organic user interface, shape changing, flexible touchscreen, haptic feedback.

ACM Classification Keywords

H5.2 [Information interfaces and presentation]: User Interfaces - Graphical user interfaces, Input devices and strategies, Haptic I/O.

INTRODUCTION

There are a growing number of shape-changing devices [20, 39, 42, 51]. However, most research has focused on demonstrating point-designs, i.e. illuminating a spot, in the space of possible shape-changing devices. We have reached a point in the evolution of these devices where it is necessary to be able to articulate how the devices compare and contrast with each other. If we take the analogy of a display device, we can express (and thereby compare and contrast) new display devices in terms of the number of pixels available, the pixel density, the screen size, screen refresh rate and number of bits per pixel. This tuple provides a rich space within which we can situate the different display devices built and identify gaps in the innovation cycle.

In contrast, we have no equivalent metric to describe shape-changing devices. Hence it is not clear how one prototype differs from another or what opportunities exist for new devices in this landscape. To address this gap, we introduce *shape resolution,* a tuple with ten features that we derive from Non-Uniform Rational B-splines (NURBS), a geometrical model able to describe most shapes. These features such as *Area, Closure and Zero-crossing* describe the features of a shape and also explain why they are desirable in a shape-changing device.

To explore a portion of the large design space that our framework offers, we propose and study the concept of *Morphees*, the next generation of flexible mobile devices that adapt their shapes on-demand to better fit the myriad of services they are likely to support. *Morphees* allows users to download applications that embed a dedicated form factor, for instance the "stress ball app" collapses the device on itself, or the "game app" makes it to adopt a console-like shape (Figure 1a).

We concretize our concept of *Morphees* by implementing preliminary prototypes that help us to explore six building strategies using different shape changing materials. For instance one uses tiles of wood that are actuated with thin Shape Memory Alloys (SMA) wires (Figure 1b) and the other bends a flexible touchscreen (E-Ink and Unmousepad [43]) using SMA wires that we forged to return to the shape we needed (Figure 1c). We compare the *shape resolution* of each design strategies and generate insights into creating *high shape resolution* self-actuated flexible devices.

Our main contribution is to offer the first metric for comparing shape-changing devices in term of shape by introducing the term *shape resolution* and its definition in ten features. We also contribute the concept of *Morphees*, the next generation of self-actuated flexible mobile devices, and show six technological approaches for building them. By evaluating the *shape resolution* of these strategies, we present informative insights for builders toward creating *high shape resolution* shape-changing devices.

THE FRAMEWORK OF SHAPE RESOLUTION

Our definition of *shape resolution* is based on the model of Non-Uniform Rational B-splines (NURBS) and has ten features (Figure 2) that are analogous to the ones used for display resolution such as number of pixel, size of pixel, bit per pixel etc. However, *a high resolution* feature is not about maximizing its value but **maximizing the range of its possible values**. For instance, a shape has a *high-curvature resolution* if its surface has range of curvatures comprised between $-\pi$ and π (concave to convex spike).

Our features complement Coelho's properties [7] that describe the technological properties of shape-changing devices. Examples include power requirement, ability to memorize new shapes, input stimulus such as voltage potential or ability to sense deformations. This approach differs from ours in that these properties describe the object material and not the possible shapes it can adopt. To give a simple analogy, a display resolution is given by features such as pixel count, screen size or bits per pixel but not features such as power consumption or display technology (e.g. LCD), that, even if useful, relate to the underlying technology. Our approach follows the same line than the display resolution definition while Coelho's approach informs the technological description of the device.

NURBS principle

Invented in the 70s, NURBS is the geometrical model used to represent shapes from straight lines, to conic sections to free-form curves. A way to understand it is to see the shape as a grid of **control points** (a mesh), with particles traveling across it to trace the surface of the shape. At any time t, the particles' positions are an average of all the control points that attract them. The attraction depends on other attributes: the **weights** that can be seen as the amounts of attraction each control point has; the **degree** of freedom that can be seen as the size of the attraction effect: the more degrees, the more control points affect the particles, thus flattening the overall surface (e.g. a NURBS surface of degree 1 is a combination of lines). The **knot vector** allows some control points to affect the surface more strongly than others by partitioning the time into intervals. By varying the relative lengths of the intervals, it varies the amount of time each control point affects the particles, thus creating a surface less smooth. When the knot vector contains several consecutive knots of the same value (knot-multiplicity), it forces the curve to go through the associated control point, and create a kink in the surface [21].

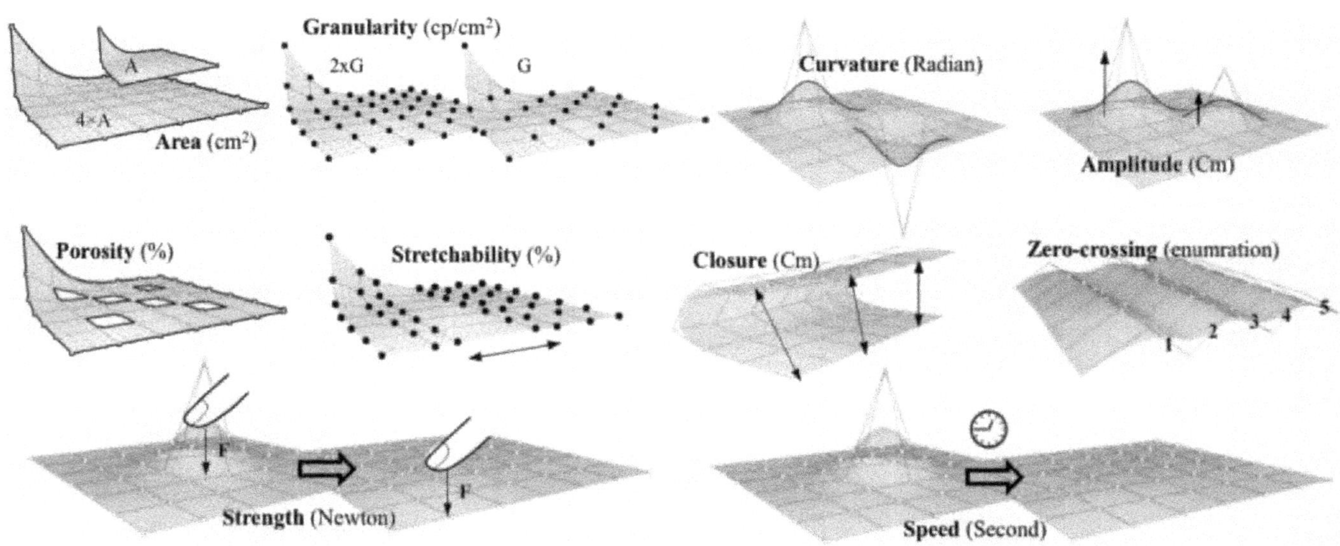

Figure 2. Summary of the 10 features of *shape resolution*. Contrary to the display or touch resolution, high resolution is not about maximizing each features, but rather maximizing the possible range of values.

NURBS can describe shapes but do not take into account physical constraints such as time, mass distributions, and internal deformation energies. Dynamic-NURBS [49] incorporates these and other physical quantities into the NURBS geometric equations. A detailed description of NURBS and Dynamic-NURBS can be found in [21, 49].

Simplified version of NURBS

The features of NURBS (control points, weight, degree, knot vector) are at a level of abstraction that does not help comparing shape-changing devices from a design perspective. At the same time, these models are powerful tools that can describe any shape. Given these arguments, our approach is to use a simplified version of NURBS and to extract features at a level of abstraction that is intuitive and descriptive to designers and practitioners. We choose to use a uniform weight across control points, with a fixed degree of freedom of two, allowing the creation of almost all possible shapes. By using a simplified version of NURBS, we lay down the foundation to extend our feature set in the future by using the complete NURBS model.

Advantages of using NURBS

There are other geometrical model for representing shapes (e.g. using volumetric representation) but we believe that NURBs model represents a good approach to describe topographies of deformable devices for the following reasons: (1) It gives a precise and uniform metric for computing the value of the features. For instance, a designer can easily compute them in a CAD tool (e.g. Maya deals with NURBs and a script can easily compute values for these features); (2) Its foundations are deeply rooted in the physical word: In the bygone days before computers, draftsmen (for shipbuilding) were drawing smooth curves using a splines, thin rods of flexible material held in place with lead weights called ducks (the equivalent of control points in NURBs); (3) It can accurately describe any shapes and thus allows us to explore a conceptual space, which not only copes with existing technologies but that also encompasses enhancements in material development.

THE TEN FEATURES OF SHAPE RESOLUTION

A way to understand the generation of our ten features is to see the shape as a mesh: a shape is made of (a grid of) control points as a display is made of pixels. Finding features is then describing the possible ways this mesh can deform. Our approach was first to list usual mathematical operations we can perform on a grid of points (e.g. area, angles, sum of angles, altitudes, distances etc.); secondly we generated the shapes created by varying these measures; finally we grouped shapes by similar characteristics that lead to our features that are illustrated in Figure 2 and for which we give the computation metrics in Table 1. In this section we define and illustrate them using the related work.

Our features work with both uniform and non-uniform shapes. With a uniform shape, the same values apply for each feature all over the surface, whereas with a non-uniform shape, the values of each feature are defined per part.

Area

The *Area* of the shape is its surface area. A way to approximate it is to compute the surface area of the mesh convex hull. With NURBS, it is equivalent to computing the surface area of the controls points since a NURBS surface is contained in the convex hull of these points.

There are several manually changeable *Area* devices. For instance Xpaaand [24] is a display that can roll on itself and that the user extends by pulling its edges ([90C m^2;720 Cm^2]). Actuated 3D construction kits such as Bosu [37], Topobo [41] or Kinematics [35] have a potentially infinite, extendable *Area* since users can always manually attach a new block to the entire assembly.

Automated changeable *Area* devices include large architectural structures [34, 1] and small systems such as the Inflatable Mouse [26]. The BMW kinetic sculpture [1] consists of balls hanging from a ceiling and moving vertically to create a shape. As the shape fits in a room, the *Area* varies from the surface of the floor to the surface area of the room itself. The Inflatable Mouse [26] is a relatively small device that inflates and deflates for ergonomic purposes. Its *Area* changes as a function of the pressure in a balloon placed inside. The maximum *Area* is nearly five times the minimum. A similar deformation is used in Ambient Life [15], where a mobile device has a soft casing that inflates to mimic breathing when air flows back and forth in it. Among his other works on shape changing devices, Hemmert also propose a device whose casing tapers downwards when held in hand, thus increasing its *Area* by a factor of ~3 (the back plate tilts by 10° into each direction, extending by up to 15mm in depth) [16].

Name	Type, unit	Computation
Area	$[\mathbb{R}^+]$ (cm^2)	surface area of the total convex hull
Granularity	$[\mathbb{R}^+]$ (cp/cm^2)	number of control points / *Area*
Porosity	$[0;\mathbb{R};100]$ (%)	100×(Σ holes *Area* / *Area*)
Curvature	$[-\pi;\mathbb{R};\pi]$(rad)	angle between 3 consecutive control points - π
Amplitude	$[\mathbb{R}^+]$ (cm)	distance between rest and actuated position of a point on the surface
Zero-crossing	$[\mathbb{N}^+]$ (Enum)	Σ sign changes between each consecutive angles
Closure	$[0;\mathbb{R}^+;100]$ (%)	100×(*Area*-boundaries *Area*) / *Area*
Stretchability	$[-100;\mathbb{R};\infty]$ (%)	100×(final-initial) / initial distance between 2 control points
Strength	$[\mathbb{R}^+]$ (Newton)	force to move a control point from 0 to max *Amplitude*
Speed	$[\mathbb{R}^+]$ (Second)	time to automatically move a control point from 0 to max

Table 1. Metrics of the ten features of *shape resolution.*

Granularity

Granularity measures the density of physical actuation points. We assume that these physical actuation points have a 1:1 relation to NURBS control points and hence granularity is computed by dividing the number of control points (cp) by the *Area* of the shape in rest state.

Granularity is generally fixed. E.g. Surflex [6] (Figure 3a) or programmable blobs [53] are actuated materials with four control points. BMW kinetic sculpture [1] (714 metal balls, *Area* not given) has higher *Granularity* followed by actuated-pin displays. Such devices are made of an array of linear actuators that move up and down to create a shape above a plane. Examples include Popup [32] with a *Granularity* of 0.4 cp/cm^2 (4x4 pins on 64x64mm), FEELEX [22] with a *Granularity* of 0.063 cp/cm^2 (6x6 pins on a 24x24cm), Lumen [38] with a *Granularity* of 2.4 cp/cm^2 (13x13 pins on 84x84mm), Relief [28] with a *Granularity* of 0.07 cp/cm^2 (12x12 pins on 45x45cm).

To our knowledge there are no objects that change granularity on-demand, except actuated-pin displays that can simulate this by actuating groups of pins as one.

Porosity
The surface of a shape can be discontinuous or perforated. The related feature is *Porosity* and is the ratio of the *Area* of perforated parts to the total *Area* of the shape. Computing the surface areas in done by using the convex hull made by the control points of the perforated and non-perforated parts of the surface. Thus the porosity can be computed by the following formula: 100×(Σ holes *Area* / *Area*).

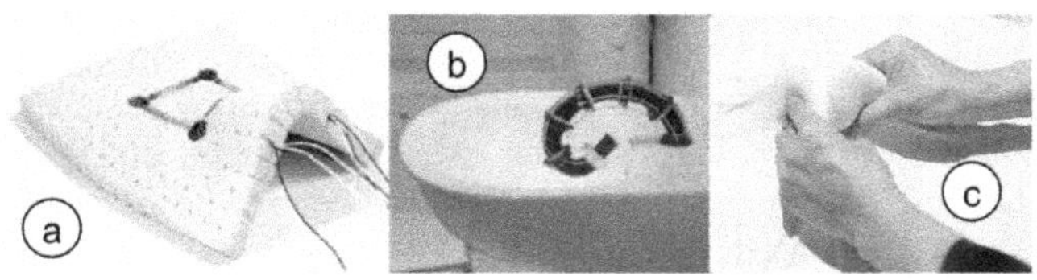

Figure 3. (a) Surflex is an actuated material whose mesh is base on four control points; (b) The trinity Faucet has a null *Zero-crossing*, it can curl on itself; (c) ClaytricSurface is a surface, filled wit Polysterene balls, that can increases its *Strength* by sucking air out of the material.

Changing the *Porosity* of a material is difficult since this deformation is not homeomorphic, i.e. not a result of a continuous stretching or bending of the original shape. Thus it is necessary to pre-perforate the material and close the hole when needed. This mechanism has for instance been used to create automated blinds to regulate the flow of air and light. Examples include Homeostatic facade [57] which *Porosity* goes from 0% to theoretically ~90% or Shutters [5] which *Porosity* goes from 0% to ~50%.

Curvature
The *Curvature* intuitively describes the curviness of the surface. It is computed by removing π from the angle between 3 consecutive control points. Thus, the *Curvature* is positive for convex shapes, negative for concave shapes and zero for planes. For instance, a unit sphere has π/2 *Curvature* since the control points of a sphere form a cube.

Examples of fixed *Curvature* devices include spherical devices (*Curvature* π/2) such a Sphere [3] and FlyEye [55], or arc shapes (Curvature also ~π/2) such as pointing devices proposed in Mouse 2.0 [52].

There are manually changeable *Curvature* devices such as Speakup [58] that changes its shape from convex to concave. Note, however, that curve deformations are not trivial due to the intrinsic properties of material: a non-stretchable plane cannot be deformed into a sphere. Such planes may be deformed into cylinders. This is seen in Gummi [45], a thin touchscreen device that users can manually and continuously bend in one dimension. Other devices using E-ink flexible touchscreen allowing similar deformations include the PaperPhone [27], DisplayStacks [11] or FlexCam [8]. Bookisheet [54] reports a maximum bending of ± π/2 that corroborates our own measures using an 8x10cm E-ink display. Curving more than the material limits causes damage. In order to increase the maximum *Curvature*, alternative materials have to be considered, for instance paper as in Paper Window [18].

Finally, few works have investigated automated changeable *Curvature*. Haptic Chameleon [30] is a widget for navigating video that changes shape depending on its functionality. For instance, when circular (*Curvature* π/2) it plays the video frame by frame, and when rectangular (*Curvature* 0 on each edges) it plays the video scene by scene. Harrison [13] demonstrates a touchscreen that creates bumps and valleys on a seamless surface. They created air chambers by layering several specially cut pieces of clear acrylic. A thin sheet of latex is draped on top. Inflating or deflating the cavities allows a *Curvature* range from -π/2 to π/2 for each cavity. A similar mechanism is presented in [46]. Reverse *Curvatures* (concave and convex) are also possible with Surflex [6] since it has actuators on both sides of a material (Figure 3a).

Amplitude
The *Amplitude* intuitively describes the range of displacement of control points. It is computed as the distance between the rest position and the actuated position of a point on the surface. For instance, a rigid plane has zero *Amplitude* and a unit sphere has an *Amplitude* of 1.

Examples of automated changeable amplitude include actuated-pin displays already presented earlier. For instance Popup [32] has a maximum *Amplitude* of 12cm, FEELEX [22] 8cm, Lumen [38] 6cm and Relief [28] 13cm. In comparison, BubbleWrap [3] or ShadePixel [25], that are also actuated-pin displays, operate at a smaller *Amplitude* (<1cm) and are rather used to simulate texture on a surface.

Note that actuated-pin display are 2.5D, meaning that they have a planar base. But the computation of the *Amplitude* also applies for any 3D shapes. The shape on Figure 3b can be used to illustrate how to proceed: each visible joint being assimilated as a control point, the *Amplitude* is thus given by the altitude between each triplet of consecutive joints.

Zero-crossing
Zero-crossing describes the capability of a shape to have wave-like forms. It is the number of sign-changes between each pair of consecutive angles across the surface. A shape with a large *Zero-crossing* can have a wave pattern. A

sphere has zero Zero-crossing. Note that there is a relation between *Granularity* and *Zero-crossing*; a high *Granularity* implies a possible high value for *Zero-crossing*.

There are few works investigating changeable Zero-Crossing devices. Harrison [13] demonstrates one of them with a touchscreen that creates bumps and valleys. When the touchscreen is flat the Zero-Crossing value is *null* but when air is pumped into the preformed cavities, the Zero-crossing reached a value that depends on the number of cavities; two in their example. With Pinoky [47] it is possible to increase this number. Pinoky is a ring-like device that can be attached to a plush toy for instance. By attaching the devices in several points of the plush and by alternating the direction of the actuation, it is thus possible to achieve variable *Zero-crossing*. However Pinoky has a low *Granularity* as the actuator are substantially large. Paik et al. demonstrate how to fold a surface into a set of shapes such as a boat or an airplane using the art of Origami [36]. Finally, the Thrifty Faucet [50] (Figure 3b) shows water consumption and hygiene to the user through deforming its shape into various postures. The Faucet can curl on itself or form a wave pattern (from zero to three Zero-crossing).

Closure

Closure intuitively describes how "closed" a shape is. It is computed as 100×(Area- boundaries Area) where boundaries *Area* is the surface area of the shape created by using the control points situated on the edges. A Plane has 0% Closure while a Sphere has 100% closure.

Thrifty Faucet [50] (Figure 3b) illustrates changeable *Closure*. The Faucet is flat at rest and can form a spiral when actuated. Topobo [41] also achieves this circular deformation. Tilt display [1] illustrates an actuated-pin display with higher *Closure* than other pin-displays: the screen placed on each pin can tilt, thus offering control over the *Closure* of the shape. Finally, Qi [40] demonstrates how to curl and flip pieces of paper on themselves by sewing Shape Memory Alloy directly on them.

Stretchability

Stretchability describes how much the surface distorts between two control points. It tells how far apart (stretching) or close (compressing) two control points can move. It is computed as $100\times(d_{final}-d_{initial})/d_{initial}$ where d_{final} is the final distance and $d_{initial}$ the initial distance between two control points. 0% means that a shape is not stretchable. A purely compressible shape has a negative *Stretchability* value up to -100% and a purely stretchable shape has a positive value limited by the physical characteristics of the material.

Shape changing objects relying on solid materials have a fixed *Stretchability* of 0%. Inflatable devices have a fixed positive *Stretchability*. For instance the Inflatable Mouse [26] (~500%), Ambient Life [15] or inflatable buttons [13].

An example of a device with changeable *Stretchability* is Mudpad [23]. It is a surface that can change viscosity under the effect of an electromagnetic field in order to provide haptic feedback. The viscosity levels range from low viscocity fluids like water to highly viscous peanut butter. The liquid is embedded in a latex casing that can be deformed when users are pressing the surface.

Strength

The *Strength* is the force needed to move a control point from the minimum *Amplitude* position to the maximum *Amplitude* position of the shape. Note that we define a difference in *Amplitude* as the reference point to compare *Strength* of devices. For instance a shape with a fixed high *Strength* is a rigid shape, i.e. it requires a large amount of force to deform (or break).

For decades, haptic feedback researchers have been investigating automated changeable *Strength* using device such as articulated arm. One example of manipulating physical shape with an articulated arm is the Haptic Chameleon presented earlier [30]. The changes in shape that the controller undergoes (circle to rectangle) create a force feedback (*Strength* is not specified).

Examples of haptic feedback devices are ClaytricSurface [29] (Figure 3c) or Jamming UI [10] that are surfaces filled with Polysterene balls. By changing the air pressure inside the box, the particles compress, thus changing the softness of the overall material. This mechanism, called jamming, provides high *Strength* and is used to allow robots to grab heavy objects. MimicTile [31] is a flexible actuator placed on the side of a device that can dynamically change it stiffness by using an assembly of Shape Memory Alloy (the nominal practical force produced is 150 gf). SqueezeBlock [12] enables eye-free interaction with a mobile device by altering the stiffness and size of the virtual spring. Dynamic Knobs [17] is a knob, placed on the side of a mobile phone, which alters it shapes so that the user can explore the phone status by touching it (no *Strength* values given).

Speed

The *Speed* is the time needed to move a control point from the rest position to the maximum *Amplitude* position of the shape under self-actuation. As with *Strength* the difference in *Amplitude* serves as the reference point to compare *Speed* of devices. To draw an analogy with displays, *Speed* can be seen as the refresh rate of a shape. Note that deformable-only devices such as bendable touchscreens (Gummi [45], PaperPhone [27], DisplayStacks [11] FlexCam [8] or Bookisheet [54]) are characterized by 0 *Speed*. In other words they are not self-actuated.

The range of *Speed* covered by shape changing devices depends on the actuator technology. For instance devices using thin SMA wires, such in Animating Paper [40] or Shutters [5], can change shape very quickly even so they do not investigate variable *Speed*. Actuated-pin displays based on motors allow for more control over the Speed. For instance the triggering speed of FEELEX [22] pins is 100ms. We did not find any values of variable *Speed* in the literature of shape changing objects we reviewed.

Summary of current related work shape resolution

We explained the ten features that describe the resolution of a shape and illustrated these features with existing related work. Based on this we observe that:

- Changeable *Area* devices are either very large and allow a large range of values, or small but only allow a small variation of *Area* (5 times for the highest resolution one).
- *Granularity* is still low for most hand sized devices, and there are no devices with changeable *Granularity*.
- Change in *Porosity* has not been widely studied. Existing works only include large *Area* devices (window blinds).
- There are devices with fixed or manually changeable *Curvature* but few have changeable *Curvature*.
- Few systems have investigated changeable *Amplitude*.
- Changeable *Zero-crossing* has not been investigated fully. To our knowledge there are no shape changing devices that allow a wide range of *Zero-crossing* combined with high *Granularity*.
- Changeable *Closure* has not been intensively investigated either, especially combined with high *Granularity*.
- *Stretchability* devices are not mainstream. In particular we found only one example of a device with automated changeable *Stretchability*.
- Haptic feedback research has investigated high *Strength* resolution. There are however a few small *Area* devices (mobile) providing high *Strength*.
- *Speed* has currently been investigated as a value to maximize but we did not find shape changing with variable deformation *Speed*.

In summary, we observe that work on shape changing devices have concentrated on increasing the shape resolution for specific features, but few combine multiple high resolution features. In particular we see several gaps: (1) there are no small *Area* and high *Granularity* devices with changeable *Zero-crossing* and *Closure*; (2) there are few devices that change their *Porosity* or *Stretchability*. This is probably due to the intrinsic limitations of materials that are hard to deform; (3) there are few small Area devices with high resolution *Strength*. The main issue is that force-feedback actuation is difficult to miniaturize, as it requires physical motors; (4) there are no devices with changeable *Speed*, i.e. that investigate the animation of the deformation (this corroborates with Rasmussen [42]).

MORPHEES: CONCEPT AND PROPERTIES

A *Morphee* is a self-actuated flexible mobile device that address the multiple affordance desired by any applications and transform itself into desired shapes. We envision that app stores can potentially evolve to give opportunities to developers to create practical applications with their specific form factors. Using the Norman's definition of affordance [33], we present two main properties that such devices offer.

Perceived affordance on-demand

A *Morphee* changes shape to suggest the way it should be operated. For instance, the two sides of a *Morphee* can curl outward to mimic a console, thus suggesting users to grab the device with two hands. In Figure 4b, the top edges of a *Morphee* curls inward when the user is typing a password, thus suggesting a private operation to others in the vicinity (e.g. when typing a password).

Actual affordance on-demand (tactile & force feedbacks)

A *Morphee's* physical properties change during the interaction to help users perform actions. In other words, it offers *tactile and force feedback*. For instance, in Figure 4b, the curled edge of a *Morphee* becomes a gun trigger in a shooting game, i.e. it offers resistance and a detent sensation when pushed by users. Figure 4c instantiates the inflatable buttons by Harrison [13]: the surface creates bumps and valleys to mimic a physical keyboard, thus helping the user to enter text.

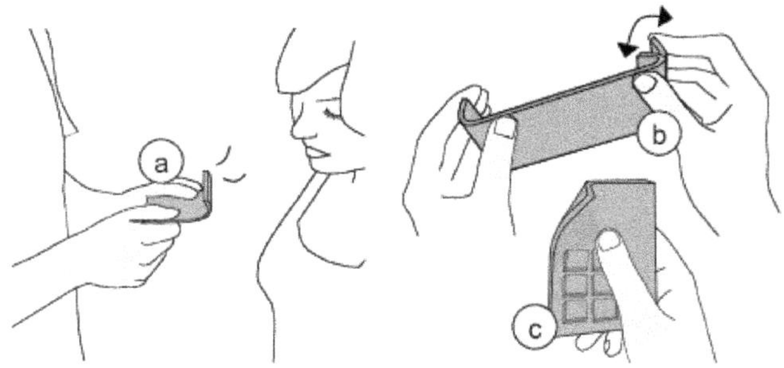

Figure 4. (a) The *Morphee* top edge bends inward to hide screen content to other users when typing a password. (b) a curled edge of the *Morphee* can be pushed to serve as trigger in a shooting game; (c) Bumps appear on the surface of the *Morphee* to mimic a physical keyboard to help the user typing.

Implementing Morphees

A Morphee has to be as thin and flexible as possible, with no physical switches or dials that could prevent shape deformations. It has several layers of flexible components: the computation circuits, the display and a 2D touch sensor and a shape-shifting layer. The shape-shifting layer morphs (and also senses its deformation), thus affecting the entire assembly. The key point is that the shape-shifting layer is a grid of physical control points, which can be actuated to form the desired shape. It implies that Morphees **physically instantiate our framework**. Actuating control points in the middle of the layer creates bumps and valleys while actuating control points in the periphery curl the layer. To realize these actuations there are various strategies possible, which we now investigate.

MORPHEES: SIX ACTUATION STRATEGIES

We compare six actuation strategies, five using advanced technologies in morphing materials: Dielectric Electro Active Polymers (DEAP) and Shape Memory Alloys (SMA). We start with the simple strategies and then progress to more complex and higher shape resolution strategies. For each strategy we present their principle of actuation and the prototypes we built. We then evaluate the strategy with the ten features we proposed to define the *shape resolution* (see summary in Table 2).

Morphee-motor: Linear actuation using motors

Principle: Morphee-motor is inspired by the SPIDAR system [44]: it uses motors and guitar strings to actuate control points. Actuating one motor decreases or increases the length between two corresponding nodes, thus bending the underlying part of the screen. The motor-strings couple is only placed on one side of the device so that strings do not prevent touch interaction when extended.

Low-fidelity prototype: The prototype shown in Figure 5a consists of two servo motors, two guitar strings and four control points on a 8x10cm sheet of plastic that has the same thickness than a flexible touchscreen (An E-ink flexible display being ~2mm thick and a flexible touch sensor ~1mm) and approximately the same flexibility. The strings are attached on diagonally opposite corners of the device. A set of 6 rings serves as guides for the strings along each diagonal (see a). When a motor turns in one direction it bends the screen inward, otherwise the screen goes back to its initial flat shape.

Shape resolution: The main advantage of Morphee-motor is the *Strength* it provides due to the motors. It also allows for high *Amplitude* and *Curvature*. One drawback of this approach is that increasing the *Granularity* of it would increase the number of motors needed and thus decrease the overall flexibility of the device. Also *Curvature* depends on the underlying material, a common issue we found recurrent with other strategies. A workaround is described in the section "Toward high resolution Morphees".

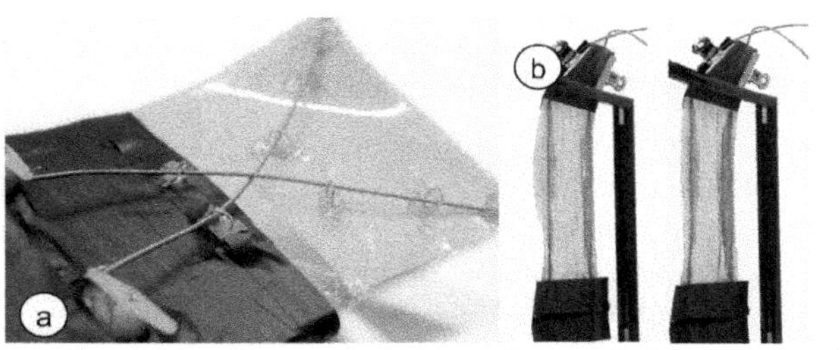

Figure 5. (a) Morphee-motor uses motors and strings to bend a piece of plastic that mimics the property of a flexible touchscreen. (b) Morphee-polymer uses Dielectric Electro Active Polymer to bend a sheet of paper.

Morphee-polymer: Linear actuation using DEAP

Principle: Morphee-polymer uses Dielectric Electro Active Polymers (DEAP). It consists of an elastomer sheet sandwiched between two electrode layers. When voltage is applied to the electrodes, electrostatic forces squeeze the sheet causing expansion in the perpendicular direction. Actuating the material decreases or increases the length between two corresponding nodes, thus bending the underlying part of the screen. The actuators are only placed on one side of the device so that the actuators do not prevent touch interaction when in their extended form.

Low-fidelity prototype: The prototype shown in Figure 5b consists of a sheet of polypower DEAP material (www.polypower.com) attached to a piece of classic paper (7×12cm). The actuation is done by using a switched-mode power supply that delivers voltages between 1000-2500V.

Shape resolution: The main advantage of Morphee-polymer is that *Granularity* can be increased without loss of flexibility. However it has less Strength, *Curvature* and *Amplitude* range, and it also has a fixed *Speed.* Lastly the power supply (~2500V) poses a challenge for miniaturization and safety.

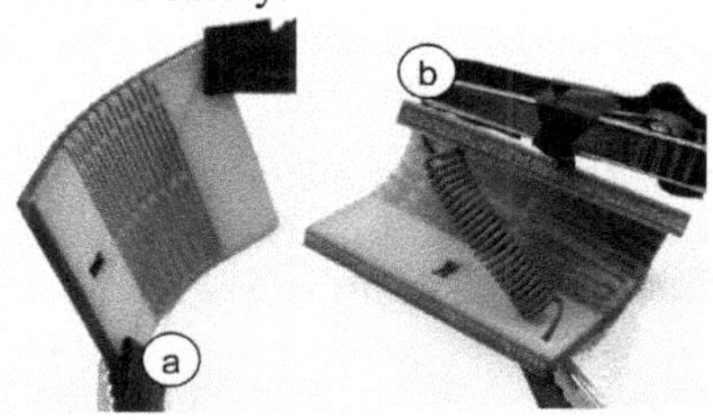

Figure 6. (a) Morphee-wire: It uses SMA in the form of wires. Here our prototype consisting of a flexible piece of wood. (b) Morphee-spring: It uses SMA in the form of springs.

Morphee-wire: Linear actuation using SMA wires

Principle: Morphee-wire uses Shape Memory Alloys (SMA) in the form of wires. SMA is a special metal alloy that "remembers" its original *educated* shape when deformed within limits, and returns to this *educated* shape when heated (70° to 90° C). SMA wires are special cases of SMA. They are educated to return to a smaller length than their original one (5% less length). A common way to actuate SMA is by passing current through them, which causes them to heat up. The actuators are only placed on one side of the device so that they do not prevent touch interaction when in their extended form.

Low-fidelity prototype: The prototype shown in Figure 6a consists of a piece of wood with a laser cut pattern allowing it to bend. Each edge of the wood is linked to a 0.06mm diameter 7cm SMA wire.

Shape resolution: Morphee-wire offers a reliable way to create a high *Granularity* shape. However, it does not provide enough *Strength* (more than Morphee-polymer), *Amplitude* or *Closure* as the wire can only shrink 5%. An alternative way is to use SMA springs (see Morphee-spring) or by combining it with a pulley system (see Morphee-sewn-wire). One advantage of using thin SMA wires is the *Speed* of the deformation (<1 second).

Morphee-spring: Linear actuation using SMA springs

Principle: Morphee-spring uses SMA springs which are educated to return to a compact spring when heated. As with SMA wires, a way to actuate them is to apply a voltage to heat them up. Because of their specific educated shape, SMA springs shrink more than wires. The actuators are only placed on one side of the device so that they do not prevent touch interaction when in their extended form.

Shape resolution: Morphee-spring provides more *Strength*, *Amplitude* and *Curvature* than Morphee-wire and Morphee-polymer. One drawback is the *Speed* that is quite slow (>1s second). In addition the springs are much thicker than actuators used in other strategies, this can prevent the creation of a thin flexible device. With our high-fidelity prototype, *Curvature* is affected in a similar way as in Morphee-motor.

Low and high fidelity prototypes: The first prototype (Figure 6b) consists of a bendable piece of wood (3mm). Each edge is linked to a SMA spring (1mm diameter wire and 5mm diameter for the spring). As springs shrink more than wires, we built another prototype with higher *Granularity* using a grid of 9 springs. We coupled springs with a Darlington pair transistor, which acts as a current driver and was controlled through an Arduino board.

Morphee-forged: "Home-educated" SMAs

Principle: Morphee-forged uses SMA wires that bend to a certain angle. This mechanism is possible by educating the SMA wires as bent shapes and to attach them to the device. When cold the wires are straight but when heated they bend. The set up is **reversible**: it is possible to place educated SMA on both sides of the device, as their deformation will follow the deformation of the screen.

Low and high fidelity prototypes: The low-fidelity prototype (Figure 1a) consists of a piece of wood with flexible edges. We attached two educated SMA to each edge to allow them to curl. The high-fidelity prototype (Figure 1c) combines an E-ink display (2mm thick) with an unmousepad touchsensor [43] (1mm thick). We attached our educated SMA to the devices using heat-insulated tape. The device can thus be in two shapes: flat or cylinder. Off-the-shelf SMA are educated to a certain shape (shrinking in size, springs, or straight shapes) but it is possible to educate them by heating (>500° C). We thus used SMA wires (1mm thick) that we maintained in the appropriated shape we needed while heating them up using a propane gas stove.

Shape resolution: Morphee-forged has advantages over other strategies. It allows concave and convex *Curvatures*, multiple Zero-Crossing and strong *Strength* and *Amplitude*. One drawback is the *Speed*: as it uses relatively thick SMA, the heating time is longer (the resistance of the wire is larger), thus increasing the actuation time.

Morphee-couture: Wood structure sewn with SMA

Principle: Morphee-couture uses the same SMA wires than Morphee-wire. The difference is that the wires are sewn into a tiled structure with inter-locking edges. The special pattern shown in Figure 7 acts as a lever that multiplies the shrinkage to give large actuation (5% shrinkage gives 90° bend). Note that the tiled structure is made of heat resistant material and that we added metal crimps in each hole to avoid the SMA burning the wood. The set up is **reversible**: inverting the pattern allows bends in the opposite direction.

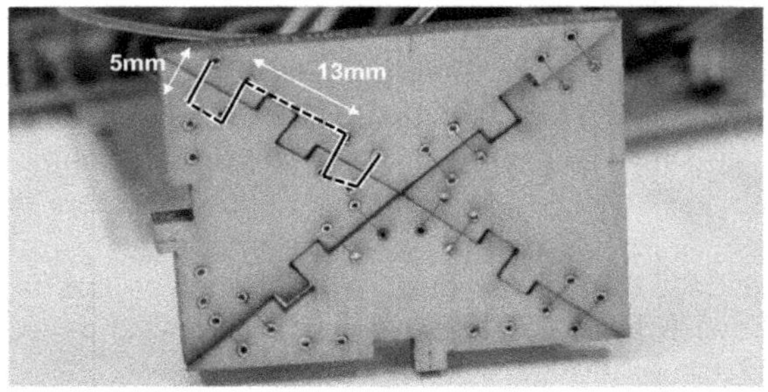

Figure 7. With the Morphee-couture, the sewing pattern allows to gain more from the SMA wires, i.e. that it allows each pieces of wood (3mm thick) to bend at 80°.

High-fidelity prototypes: Our prototype (Figure 1b) is based on a structure of 8 wood tiles. We coupled each wire with a Darlington pair transistor, which acts as a current driver and was controlled through an Arduino board. Using a projector we implemented three applications to illustrate *Morphees*: (1) one that bends the top of the device toward the user to hide the screen content; (2) one that bends the four corners in the same fashion that a flower blooming or closing; (3) one that actuates any hinges that users choose.

Shape resolution: Morphee-couture has numerous advantages over the previous strategies. It allows for concave and convex *Curvature* as well large *Amplitude*. It has a faster *Speed*, but less *Strength* than Morphee-forged.

Feature	Morphee-motor	Morphee-polymer	Morphee-wire	Morphee-spring	Morphee-forged	Morphee-couture
Area	54cm² (9×6cm)	84cm² (7×12cm)	20cm² (5×4cm)	p1: 20cm²(5×4cm) p2: 80cm²(10×8cm)	p1: 42cm² (6×7cm) p2: 70cm² (10×7cm)	80cm² (10×8cm)
Granularity	0.15 cp/cm² (8cp)	0.04 cp/cm² (3cp)	0.15 cp/cm² (3cp)	p1: 0.15 cp/cm² (3cp) p2: .23 cp/cm² (18cp)	p1: .14 cp/cm² (6cp) p2: .04 cp/cm² (3cp)	0. 45 cp/cm²(36cp)
Porosity	0%	0%	0%	0%	0%	0%
Curvature	[0;π/8] can be increased with DC motors	[0; π/12], limited by maximum voltage for DEAP material	[0; π/12] limited by SMA	p1: [0; π/2] p2: [0; π/12] limited by SMA	p1: [-2π/3; 2π/3] p2: [-π/2; π/2] limited by SMA	[-2π/3; 2π/3] limited by SMA
Amplitude[1]	[0;6cm]	[0;1cm]	[0;0.5cm]	p1: [0;2cm] p2: [0;2cm]	p1: [0;1.5cm] p2: [0;3.5cm]	[0;4cm]
Zero-crossing	0. Actuators only on one side	0. Actuators only on one side	0. Actuators only on one side	0. Actuators only on one side	0	[0;3]
Closure	[0;6.2%]	[0;4.2%]	[0;10%]	P1: [0;50%] p2: [0;15%]	P1: [0;56%] p2: [0;55%]	[0;25%]
Stretchability	0%	0%	0%	0%	0%	0%
Strength[1]	170gf	50gf	150gf	500gf	500gf	150gf
Speed	0.5s, variable Speed depending on motors	0.04s depends on charge time	[1s;3s] depends on SMA heat-up and cool-down times	[1s;5s] depends on SMA heat-up and cool-down times	[1s;3s] depends on SMA heat-up and cool-down times	[1s;3s] depends on SMA heat-up and cool-down times

[1] Limits on values are similar to ones described for Curvature

Table 2. Evaluation of the 10 features for the prototypes we built using the six-actuation strategies we explored.

TOWARD HIGH SHAPE RESOLUTION MORPHEES

By evaluating our prototypes we gathered insights to help future builders. There are three main challenges to consider. First at the shape level, it is hard to have all features with high resolution. Secondly we discuss device's life cycles and the possibility of creating bistable devices. Finally, we argue that it is difficult to combine high shape resolution with high display and touch resolution.

High shape resolution

As demonstrated with our prototype and the examples from the related work, it is difficult to create devices with high resolution for all features. E.g. we need to optimise the compromise between *Curvature*, *Strength* and *Speed*: SMA wires are fast to actuate but have less *Strength* and *Curvature*. Morphee-couture offers a way to overcome this issue using a pulley system. It however does not increase the *Strength*. In comparison, Morphee-forged offers large *Curvature* and *Strength* but is much slower.

The tradeoffs between features are not specific to shape resolution, but also apply to display resolution. E.g. It is hard to create displays with a high refresh rate, high pixel density, high bits per pixel etc. For shapes, each feature is likely to be more important than others in various context. For instance a device with high *Strength* can be adapted for force feedback applications, while a device with high *Speed* can be used to create animated shape notifications to users. The choice of the device shape changes has thus to be dictated by the range of applications it can support, therefore maximizing the resolution of specific features.

Figure 8. Bistable shape can be achieved using heat deformable plastic.

Device life cycle and bistability

Another challenge is the life cycle. Maintaining a device in a shape requires the material to be constantly on, drawing significant power. In addition, shape-changing materials have a life cycle as well. They can potentially be triggered hundreds of thousands of times. But if the strain overcomes a certain ratio (depending on the material), it reduces their life cycle. For example we experienced this phenomenon with home-educated SMA: we educated some SMAs in a 90° bending shape and actuated them several times to test it. During the process we manually unbend the wire several time to force it to form a line. This caused a lot of stress in the material, thus reducing its life cycle. After several actuations, the SMA was only able to bend at 45°.

One solution is to use bistable materials. Similar to a bistable screen that can stay in one state when no power is provided (E-Ink), a bistable device can stay in one shape when no power is provided. A way to achieve this is to use heat deformable plastic (Figure 8) that becomes malleable when heated, and retains their shape when cooling down. Another example of bistable structure has also been proposed in the shape memory polymer chair [9].

High shape-display-touch resolution

Another big challenge is to combine high resolution for the shape layer but also for the display and touch ones. However, this is difficult given that the flexibility of the display and touch sensor will impact the way the shape layer can deform. As we experienced, the E-ink flexible display is quite stiff and reduces the possible Curvature that the device can have. A way to alleviate these issues is to use projection and tracking as in our Morphee-couture and as suggested in a recent vision of mobile computing [14]. In this case the display and touch layer does not add any constraint on the shape-changing layer. Another way to overcome this issue is to consider tiling the touch sensor and display as in the tiles of Morphee-couture.

Another issue is that the deformation can impact the data retrieved by the touch sensor. For instance, bending a resistive touch sensor is likely to trigger touch events while no fingers are in contact as it relies on pressure. The same problem would happen with optical sensing or TDR [56]. Thus the touch sensor technology has to be appropriately chosen to avoid this phenomenon. For example this is possible with capacitive touch sensing as used in Mouse 2.0 [52]. Some resistive technologies are also promising, such as TactileTape [19] that supports bends up to 85° .

CONCLUSION

In this paper we contributed a new metric to define the resolution of an interactive device: in addition to display and touch resolution, we proposed "shape resolution". We believe our work lay down the foundation for creating future high shape resolution devices. One example of such devices is our concept of *Morphees*, self-actuated flexible mobile devices that can change shapes on their own to offer better affordances. We envisage *Morphees* to be the next generation of mobile devices, with which users can download applications with their own form factor. In future work we are thus interested in building higher shape resolution *Morphees* by investigating further the flexibility of materials. We are also interested in exploring other kind of deformations that our prototypes did not yet explore, such as *Porosity* and *Stretchability*.

ACKNOWLEDGEMENTS

This work has been supported by the EC within the 7th framework programme through the FET Open scheme under grant agreement no. 309191.

REFERENCES

1. Alexander, J., Lucero, A., Subramanian, S. Tilt Displays: Designing Display Surfaces with Multi-axis Tilting and Actuation, MobileHCI12.
2. Artcon: www.artcom.de
3. Bau, O., Petrevski, U., Mackay, W. BubbleWrap: a textile-based electromagnetic haptic display. CHI EA '09, 3607-3612.
4. Benko, H., Wilson, A.D., Balakrishnan, R. Sphere: multi-touch interactions on a spherical display. UIST'08. 77–86.

5. Coelho, M. and Maes, P. Shutters: A Permeable Surface for Environmental Control and Communication. TEI'09, 13
6. Coelho, M., Ishii, H., Maes, P. Surflex: a programmable surface for the design of tangible interfaces. CHI'08, 3429.
7. Coelho M., Zigelbaum, J. 2011. Shape-changing interfaces. Personal Ubiquitous Comput. 15, 2, 161-173.
8. Dickie, C., Fellion, N., Vertegaal, R. FlexCam: using thin-film flexible OLED color prints as a camera array. CHIEA'12
9. Fan J-N, Schodek D. Personalized furniture within the condition of mass production. Ubicomp'07.
10. Follmer S., Leithinger, D., Olwal, A., Cheng, N., Ishii, H. Jamming user interfaces: programmable particle stiffness and sensing for malleable and shape-changing devices. UIST'12.
11. Girouard, A., Tarun, A., Vertegaal, R. DisplayStacks: interaction techniques for stacks of flexible thin-film displays. CHI '12, 2431-2440.
12. Gupta, S., Campbell, T., Hightower, J.R., Patel. S.N. SqueezeBlock: using virtual springs in mobile devices for eyeMorphee-free interaction. UIST '10.101-104.
13. Harrison, C. Hudson, S. E. Providing Dynamically Changeable Physical Buttons on a Visual Display. CHI '09, 299-308.
14. Harrison, C., Benko, H., Wilson, A.D. OmniTouch: wearable multitouch interaction everywhere. UIST '11, 441-450.
15. Hemmert, F. Ambient Life: Permanent Tactile Life-like Actuation as a Status Display in Mobile Phones. UIST EA'08.
16. Hemmert, F., Hamann, S., Löwe, M., Wohlauf, A., and Joost, G. Shape-changing mobiles: tapering in one-dimensional deformational displays in mobile phones. TEI'10, 249-252.
17. Hemmert, F, Gesche, J., André, K., Reto, W. Dynamic Knobs: Shape Change as a Means of Interaction on a Mobile Phone. CHIEA'08, 2309-2314
18. Holman, D., Vertegaal, R., Altosaar, M., Troje, N., Johns, D. Paper windows: interaction techniques for digital paper. CHI '05, 591-599.
19. Holman D., Vertegaal, R.. TactileTape: low-cost touch sensing on curved surfaces. UIST '11 Adjunct, 17-18.
20. Ishii H., Lakatos, D., Bonanni, L. Labrune, J.B. Radical atoms: beyond tangible bits, toward transformable materials. interactions 19, 1 (January 2012), 38-51.
21. Issa, R., Essential Mathematics for Computational Design, Robert McNeel & Associates
22. Iwata,H.,Yano,H.,Nakaizumi,F., Kawamura,R.Project Feelex: adding haptic surface to graphics. SIGGRAPH'01, 469-476.
23. Jansen, Y. Mudpad: Fluid Haptics for Multitouch Surfaces. CHI EA'10, 4351-4356.
24. Khalilbeigi, M. Lissermann, R., Mühlhäuser, M., Steimle, J. Xpaaand: interaction techniques for rollable displays. CHI '11.
25. Kim, H., Lee, W. Shade Pixel. SIGGRAPH '08, 34.
26. Kim, S., Kim, H., Lee, B., Nam, T.J., Lee, W. Inflatable mouse: Volume-adjustable Mouse with Air-pressure-sensitive Input and Haptic Feedback. CHI'08, 211-214.
27. Lahey, B., Girouard, A., Burleson, W., Vertegaal, R. Paper-Phone: understanding the use of bend gestures in mobile devices with flexible electronic paper displays. CHI '11. 1303-1312.
28. Leithinger, D., Lakatos, D., DeVincenzi, A., Blackshaw, M., Ishii, H. Direct and gestural interaction with relief: a 2.5D shape display. UIST '11, 541-548.
29. Matoba, Y. Sato, T., Takahashi, N., Koike, H. ClaytricSurface: An Interactive Surface With Dynamic Softness Control Capability, SIGGRAPH'02 Emerging Technologies.
30. Michelitsch G, Williams J, Osen M, Jimenez B, Rapp S. Haptic chameleon: a new concept of shape-changing user interface controls with force feedback. CHIEA'04, 1305-1308.
31. Nakagawa, Y., Kamimura, A., Kawaguchi, Y. MimicTile: a variable stiffness deformable user interface for mobile devices. CHI '12, 745-748.
32. Nakatani, M., Kajimoto, H., Sekiguchi, D., Kawakami, N., Tachi, S. 3D Form display with shape memory alloy, ICAT'03.
33. Norman, D. A. The Design of Everyday Things. New York, Doubleday.
34. Oosterhuis, K., Biloria, N. Interactions with proactive architectural spaces: the muscle projects. Com. ACM 2008, 70.
35. Oschuetz, L., Wessolek, D., and Sattler, W. 2010. Constructing with movement: Kinematics. TEI'10, 257-260.
36. Paik, J., An, B., Rus D., Wood, R. Robotic origamis: self-morphing modular robots Actuated origami. Proc. Int. Conf. on Morphological Computation, Venice, Italy, Sept., 2011.
37. Parkes, A., Ishii, H. Bosu: a physical programmable design tool for transformability with soft mechanics. DIS'10, 189-198.
38. Poupyrev, I.,Nashida,T.,Maruyama,S.,Rekimoto,J., Yamaji, Y. Lumen: interactive visual and shape display for calm computing. SIGGRAPH '04, 17.
39. Poupyrev, I., Nashida, T., Okabe, M. Actuation and tangible user interfaces: the Vaucanson duck, robots, and shape displays. TEI'07, 206-212.
40. Qi, J., Buechley, L. Animating paper using shape memory alloys. CHI '12, 749-752.
41. Raffle, H.S, Parkes, A.J., and Ishii, H. Topobo: A Constructive Assembly System with Kinetic Memory. CHI'04, 647-654.
42. Rasmussen, M.K, Pedersen, E.W., Petersen, M.G., Hornbæk. K. Shape-changing interfaces: a review of the design space and open research questions. CHI'12, 735-744
43. Rosenberg, I., Perlin, K. The UnMousePad: an interpolating multi-touch force-sensing input pad. SIGGRAPH'09, 65.
44. Sato M., Development of String-based Force Display: SPIDAR. VSMM'02. 1034-1039.
45. Schwesig, C., Poupyrev, I., and Mori, E. 2004. Gummi: a bendable computer. CHI '04, 263-270.
46. Stevenson, A., Perez, C., Vertegaal, R. 2010. An inflatable hemispherical multi-touch display. TEI '11.289-292.
47. Sugiura, Y. Lee, C., Ogata, M., Withana, A., Makino, Y., Sakamoto, D., Inami, M. Igarashi, T. PINOKY: a ring that animates your plush toys. CHI'12, 725-734.
48. Sutherland, I. E. 1965, The Ultimate Display, in IFIP Congress, 506-508.
49. Terzopoulos, D., Qin, H. Dynamic NURBSS with geometric constraints for interactive sculpting. ACM ToG'94.
50. Togler, J., Hemmert, F., and Wettach, R. 2009. Living interfaces: The Thrifty Faucet. TEI'09, 43-44.
51. Vertegaal, R., Poupyrev, I. Organic User Interfaces: Introduction to Special Issue. ACM 51(6). 2008: pp. 26-30..
52. Villar, N., Izadi, S., Rosenfeld, D., Benko, H., Helmes, J., Westhues, J., Hodges, S., Ofek, E., Butler, A., Cao, X. Chen, B. Mouse 2.0: multi-touch meets the mouse. UIST '09, 33–42.
53. Wakita, A., Nakano, A., Kobayashi, N. Programmable blobs: a rheologic interface for organic shape design. TEI'11, 273-276.
54. Watanabe, J., Mochizuki, A., and Horry, Y. Bookisheet: bendable device for browsing content using the metaphor of leafing through the pages. UbiComp'08, 360-369.
55. Wimmer, R. FlyEye: grasp-sensitive surfaces using optical fiber. In Proc. TEI '10, 245–248.
56. Wimmer, R., Baudisch, P. Modular and deformable touch-sensitive surfaces based on time domain reflectometry. UIST'11.
57. www.deckeryeadon.com
58. Zigelbaum, J., Chang, A., Gouldstone, J., Monzen, J., Ishii, H. SpeakCup: Simplicity, BABL, and Shape Change. TEI'08.

LightCloth: Sensible Illuminating Optical Fiber Cloth for Creating Interactive Surfaces

Sunao Hashimoto[1] Ryohei Suzuki[1&2] Youichi Kamiyama[1]
Masahiko Inami[1&3] Takeo Igarashi[1&2]

[1]JST ERATO IGARASHI Design Interface Project, 7-3-1 Hongo, Bunkyo-ku, Tokyo, 113-0033, Japan

[2]The University of Tokyo, 7-3-1 Hongo, Bunkyo-ku, Tokyo, 113-0033, Japan

[3]Graduate School of Media Design, Keio University (KMD) 4-1-1 Hiyoshi, Kohoku-ku, Yokohama, 223-8526, Japan

hashimoto@kougaku-navi.net, {suzuki | kamiyama | inami}@designinterface.jp, takeo@acm.org

ABSTRACT
This paper introduces an input and output device that enables illumination, bi-directional data communication, and position sensing on a soft cloth. This "LightCloth" is woven from diffusive optical fibers. Since the fibers are arranged in parallel, the cloth has one-dimensional position information. Sensor-emitter pairs attached to bundles of contiguous fibers enable bundle-specific light input and output. We developed a prototype system that allows full-color illumination and 8-bit data input by infrared signals. We present as an application a chair with a LightCloth cover whose illumination pattern is specified using an infrared light pen. Here we describe the implementation details of the device and discuss possible interactions using the device.

Author Keywords
Soft deformable user interface; diffusive optical fiber; illumination; light communication; position sensing.

ACM Classification Keywords
H.5.2. Information interfaces and presentation (e.g., HCI): User Interfaces.

General Terms
Design; Measurement.

INTRODUCTION
An optical fiber is a flexible transparent fiber made of glass or plastic. It typically has a transparent core surrounded by a transparent cladding material with a lower refractive index. Light entering one end is kept in the core by total internal reflection, and the fiber acts as a waveguide from one end to the other. This physical property is widely used in various applications such as data communication, sensing devices, and illuminating toys. Another type of the fiber is "diffusive" optical fiber which leaks some light through micro-scratches on its surface. A cloth woven from such

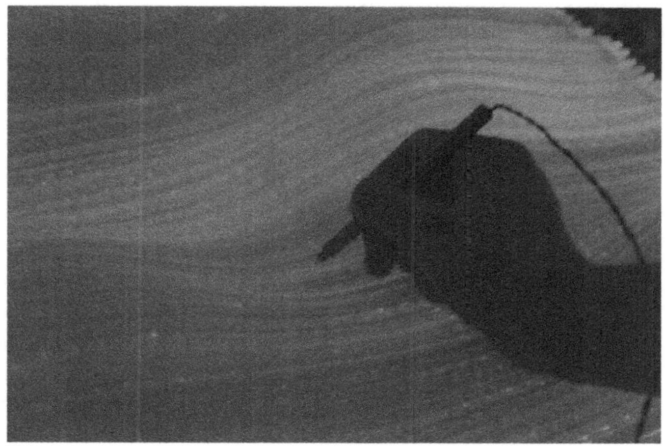

Figure 1. LightCloth enables full-color illumination, bi-directional data communication and position sensing on soft surfaces.

diffusive optical fibers has been used in fashion and spatial design fields for making light-emitting fabric products, e.g. dresses, ties, bags, curtains, and cushions [6, 7]. A diffusive optical fiber not only leaks light but also receives light incident on its surface. The light entering from the scratches on the surface goes through the core and leaks out from the ends. Focusing on this property, we developed a new fabric I/O (input and output) device, called "LightCloth," that enables illumination, bi-directional data communication, and position sensing.

LightCloth is a fabric made of parallel diffusive optical fibers tied together with threads, and each fiber can emit and receive light signals from its surface (Figure 1). This property enables new kinds of interaction via the fabric (e.g., painting the illumination pattern with a light pen). LightCloth is flexible and can be put on nonplanar surfaces and flexible objects. This differentiates our device from other interactive surfaces.

The system consists of a cloth woven from diffusive optical fibers, a light-emitter array, and a light-sensor array. Both visible and invisible rays can be used for input and output. The separation of the interactive surface from the control circuit makes LightCloth resilient to physical impact and water drops. Another advantage is that the surface is unaffected by metal, magnetism, and electric wave because it uses an optical method.

We developed a prototype system that allows full-color illumination and 8-bit data input by infrared signals. As an application, we made an illuminated chair whose illumination pattern can be designed by its user and specified by using an infrared light pen. In this paper, we describe the overview of the proposed system and discuss the interactions possible when using the system.

RELATED WORK

The waveguide property of optical fibers has been used for sensing devices and display devices in the field of human interface technology. In the Data Glove [3], a well known hand gesture input device for virtual reality, an optical flex sensor is mounted in a glove. It measures finger bending by using the property that light leaks out of a scratched optical fiber when the fiber is curved by finger bending. Baudisch et al. proposed a tangible building block, called Lumino [2], containing a glass fiber bundle. The block works as a TV rock, displays the underlying image on the top and transmits visual markers placed on the top to the under surface. Lumino blocks have display and marker-detection functions and can be piled. Nakajima et al. developed a fibratus multi-touch display device, called the Fusa^2 touch display, that uses optical fiber bundles to display an image and recognize touch input [8]. In this system, a projector and an infrared camera are placed behind the fiber bundles. Jackson et al. developed infrared-sensing multi-touch display, called FiberBoard [4]. In this display, a light reflected by finger is transported to a camera through an array of optical fibers. As the fibers are flexible the camera is free to be positioned so as to minimize the depth of the device. This technique is also used in Mudpad [5]. These projects use the ends of fibers as a display and a sensor. LightCloth, in contrast, uses the entire length of the fibers, so it is thin and flexible.

There are various methods for providing an input-output function to fabric materials in the field of e-textiles. Wakita et al. proposed a kinetic textile having input and output functions [13]. In their system, shape memory alloys and electrical flex sensors are attached to soft cloth, so it changes shape like a free-form surface and allows the user to input a form by simply manipulating the textile. Nakatsuma and Shinoda proposed a two-dimensional communication technology for surface networking [9]. They designed a special sheet across which electromagnetic waves can propagate two dimensionally. It enables data and power transmission and position sensing through a thin sheet. Ueoka et al. developed an RFID woven textile and a customized textile inspection machine with an automatic map-making function [12]. They were able to track people's positions on a large carpet with massively distributed tags. Our system is different from these existing systems in that we realize illumination, data communication, and position sensing on flexible surfaces.

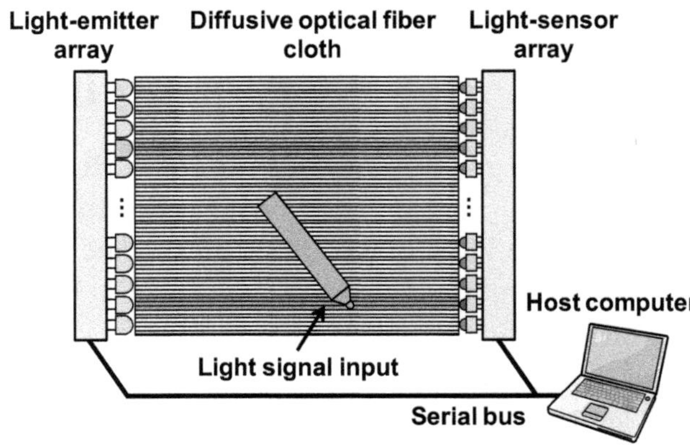

Figure 2. Overview of the system.

LIGHTCLOTH ARCHITECTURE

The overview of the proposed system is shown in Figure 2. LightCloth consists of a diffusive optical fiber cloth, a light-emitter array, a light-sensor array, a light-signal input, and a host computer.

All the diffusive optical fibers in the cloth are arranged in one direction, and this means the cloth becomes a one-dimensional positional I/O. The fibers are bundled into clusters several millimeters wide, and a sensor-emitter pair consisting of a light sensor and a light emitter is attached to each bundle. The width of a bundle limits the resolution of positional information, and the resolution is highest when a sensor and emitter are attached to every fiber.

The light emitter is a source of colors and coded signals. Basically, a light-emitting diode (LED) is used for the light emitter. The light sensor receives the user's input signal and can be either phototransistor, photodiode, or infrared receiver module. A camera and a projector can be used as the sensor-emitter pair, but that requires fiber bundles to be gathered in one place and optics for focusing there to be designed. The coded input light signals can be delivered by a light pen or laser pointer. The light-emitter array and light-sensor array are connected to a computer via a serial bus. The computer controls the illumination pattern based on the received data and the positional information.

The system can use both visible rays and invisible rays for the input/output lights, depending on the purpose. For example, it is possible to use a normal visible light for the output so people can see it, and use infrared light for invisible input. The light from emitters reaches the sensors, so to crosstalk should be prevented by using different wavelengths for the input and output. The sensor is affected by environmental light, especially light of the sun and fluorescent lamps. To avoid such interference, the system needs to use modulated light signals.

PROTOTYPE SYSTEM

We made a prototype system (Figure 3) using a 600 mm × 600 mm diffusive optical fiber cloth. The fibers coming out

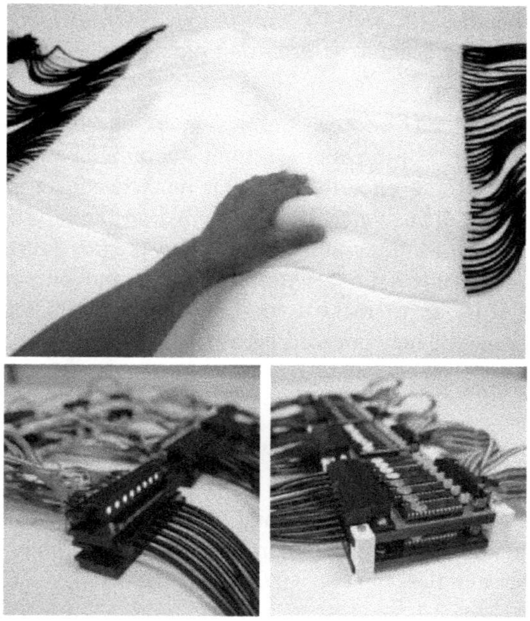

Figure 3. Prototype system. Diffusive optical fiber cloth (top), light emitter array (bottom-left) and light-sensor array (bottom-right).

of both ends of the cloth are bundled unto units 10 mm wide (25–30 fibers), so there are 60 I/O segments (lines). Each bundle is in a protective vinyl tube and is connected to the light-emitter array and the light-sensor array.

The light-emitter array has three LEDs (red, green, blue) for each line, so $3 \times 60 = 180$ LEDs are used. LEDs are driven by microcontrollers (PICs). Each line provides computer-controlled full-color illumination. The light-sensor array has an infrared receiver module for each line, so 60 modules are used. The infrared receiver module we used is the kind generally used for remote-controlling home appliances such as TVs and air-conditioners, and it receives infrared signals modulated at 38 kHz. For the infrared communication, we used general 8-bit serial communication at 2400 bps. In the current implementation, one microcontroller is given to each receiver module to achieve parallel processing. The light signal input is given by the pen-type device shown in Figure 4. It consists of an infrared LED, a microcontroller (Arduino), and a battery. The infrared LED used as the nib outputs infrared signals modulated at 38 kHz. In the current implementation, the data given by the pen-type device designates a color. The light-emitter array and the light-sensor array are connected to the host computer by an 115,200-baud serial link. The host computer controls the LED color corresponding to the input signals, line by line. The result using the first prototype is shown in Figure 5. We used two pens that emit fixed color codes. One of them outputs "green" and the other outputs "red".

Our target application is furniture design, therefore we developed an interactive illumination chair (Figure 6). The

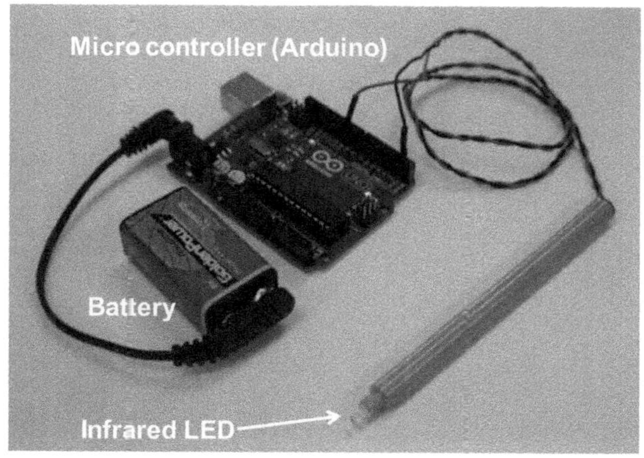

Figure 4. Infrared signal input device.

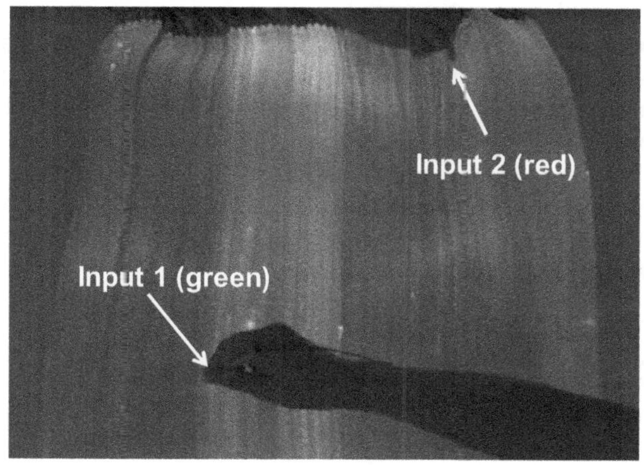

Figure 5. Painting the illumination with two pens.

LightCloth is used as part of the seat that can deform softly, so the user can sit. For this application, we made a special pen having four buttons (red, green, blue and erase). On this pen, color is selectable. The combination of pushing three color buttons makes eight color signals. The user can design the illumination of the chair while sitting on it.

DESIGN ISSUES

In the current design, the emitting and sensing modules are attached to the opposite sides of the fiber cloth, and when constructing the system we need to find both ends of each bundle. This is very tedious work. We expect that the emitter module and sensor module can be unified by putting an emitter and a sensor in the same side. Furthermore, an LED can also be used as a photodiode light detection [1], and we think doing so will make it easier to unify the two modules. If the system can be constructed by just attaching one module to the fiber cloth, finding correspondence between ends will be unnecessary and the design flexibility will be greater. One could then use LightCloth in something that flutters, like a curtain or scarf. In the current implementation, one cloth has one-dimensional information because the fibers are arranged in parallel.

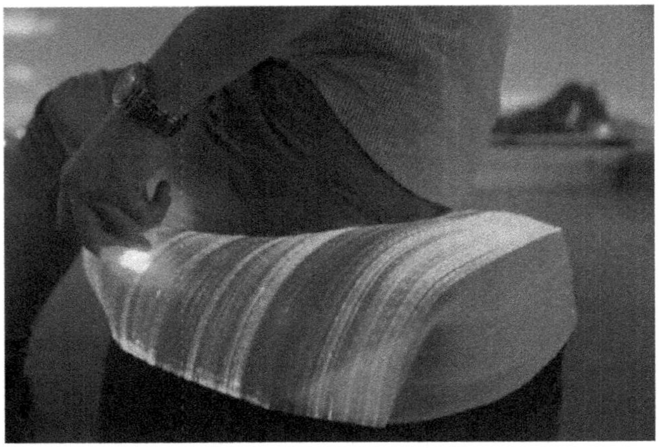

Figure 6. Interactive illumination chair.

To enable two-dimensional information, two cloths would need to be layered orthogonally. Then, though, the illumination pattern would be crossed lines, not an arrangement of pixels. Another possible way is to use photodetecting fibers [10]. This fiber is constructed from glass, metal and semiconductor, and can detect one-dimensional position along single optical fiber. We expect that a cloth woven from this fiber would enable detecting two-dimensional information.

POSSIBLE INTERACTIONS AND POTENTIAL APPLICATIONS

Various forms of input are conceivable other than that from the infrared light-pen we used in the prototype form. We have already started using laser pointers as LightCloth input. We expect that a combination of laser pointers and clothing using LightCloth could enable interesting novel interactions. For example, in a fashion show, when a model wearing a dress using LightCloth passes an invisible laser beam arranged in the runway, the illumination pattern could be changed automatically. This means that designs could be embedded in space. This strategy would also be applicable in various kinds of stage performances, such as dance and drama. A laser gun shooter game is also a possible application. If a line laser were used, the distance between the cloth and the source of the laser light could be estimated. In addition, we could create musical instruments such as a fabric illuminated xylophone with a drumstick giving light signals. We could also create a gaming interface throwing a ball giving light signals at a soft object using LightCloth. As other interesting input form, we are considering using an illuminated water jet provided by a laminar fountain involving a light source.

The LightCloth surface can output multiple light signals, so existing visible/invisible light communication methods using displays and projectors will be applicable on our platform. We are considering applying a display-based computing technique [11] in two-dimensional version in which two cloths are layered orthogonally. Instead of fiducial marker, we will output coded light signals from two fiber bundles (X and Y), and output different signal for each crossing point to control multiple robots.

CONCLUSION

We developed a new fabric interface that enables illumination, bi-directional light communication, and position sensing on soft cloth. Our method adds a sensory function to diffusive optical fibers that are mainly used as materials for illumination, and it widens the possibilities for new fabric interactions with both input and output. Our future work is to make two-dimensional LightCloth and investigate the new interactions available on it.

REFERENCES

1. Akita, J. Interactive Block Device System with Pattern Drawing Capability on Matrix LEDs, In *Proc. CHI EA2012*, 1059-1062.
2. Baudisch, P., Becker, T., and Rudeck, F. Lumino: tangible blocks for tabletop computers based on glass fiber bundles. In *Proc. CHI2010*, 1165-1174.
3. Harvill, Y.L., Zimmerman, T. G., and Grimaud, J.G. Motion sensor which produces an asymmetrical signal in response to symmetrical movement. U.S. Patent 5097252, (1989).
4. Jackson, D., Bartindale, T., and Olivier, P. FiberBoard: compact multi-touch display using channeled light. In *Proc. ITS2009*, 25-28.
5. Jansen, Y. Mudpad: fluid haptics for multitouch surfaces. In *Proc. CHI EA 2010*, 4351-4356.
6. Lumen. http://www.lumen.jp/
7. LumiGram. http://www.lumigram.com/
8. Nakajima, K., Itoh, Y., Tsukitani, T., Fujita, K., Kitamura, Y., and Kishino, F. FuSA^2 Touch Display: Furry and Scalable Multi-touchable display. In *Proc. ITS2011*, 35-44.
9. Nakatsuma, K. and Shinoda, H. High accuracy position and orientation detection in two-dimensional communication network. In *Proc. CHI2010*, 2297-2306.
10. Sorin, F., Lestoquoy, G., Danto, S., Joannopoulos, J.D., and Fink, Y. Resolving optical illumination distributions along an axially symmetric photodetecting fiber, *Optics Express*, 18 (23), (2010), 24264-24275.
11. Sugimoto, M., Kodama, K., Nakamura, A., Kojima, M., and Inami, M. A Display-Based Tracking System: Display-Based Computing for Measurement Systems, In *Proc. ICAT2007*, 31-38.
12. Ueoka, R., Masuda, A., Murakami, T., and Hirose, M. RFID Textile and Map Making System for Large Area Positioning. In *Proc. ISWC2009*, 41-44.
13. Wakita, A., Ueno, M., and Nakano, A. pSurface: Fabric I/O Device for Architectural Algorithmic Design. In *Proc. ALGODE TOKYO2011*.

Bending the Rules: Bend Gesture Classification for Flexible Displays

Kristen Warren, Jessica Lo, Vaibhav Vadgama and Audrey Girouard
Carleton University
Ottawa, Ontario, K1S 5B6, Canada
{kristen_mitchell, jessica_lo, vaibhav_vadgama, audrey_girouard}@carleton.ca

ABSTRACT
Bend gestures have a large number of degrees of freedom and therefore offer a rich interaction language. We propose a classification scheme for bend gestures, and explore how users perform these bend gestures along four classification criterion: location, direction, size, and angle. We collected 36 unique bend gestures performed three times by each participant. The results suggest a strong agreement among participants for preferences of location and direction. Size and angle were difficult for users to differentiate. Finally, users performed and perceived two distinct levels of magnitude. We propose recommendations for designing bend gestures with flexible displays.

Author Keywords
Deformable User Interface; Flexible Display; Affordance; Bend Gesture; Organic User Interface

Classification Keywords
H.5.2 User Interfaces - Evaluation/Methodology, Haptic I/O, Interaction Styles, Prototyping

INTRODUCTION
With the emergence of flexible displays, researchers are increasingly exploring the use of bend gestures as an input technique [2,4,5,6,8]. Bend gestures have their roots in paper documents, where one may flip the corner of a page to turn it [7], and their success is largely due to the inherent tactile feedback. Bend gestures are most successful in the context of e-book readers or maps [4,6,8].

One of the main features of bend gestures is their large number of degrees of freedom: location, direction, size, angle, and speed, to name a few. Such variety offers a rich interaction language, yet can be overwhelming to users. When using PaperPhone, a flexible smartphone prototype, some users had trouble precisely repeating the same gesture, even given the use of limited bend classifications [4]. Bend gestures can be difficult to execute precisely, especially if users are required to distinguish between collocated gestures (Figure 1). Therefore, it is paramount to determine how users perform bends to create and implement appropriate bend gestures.

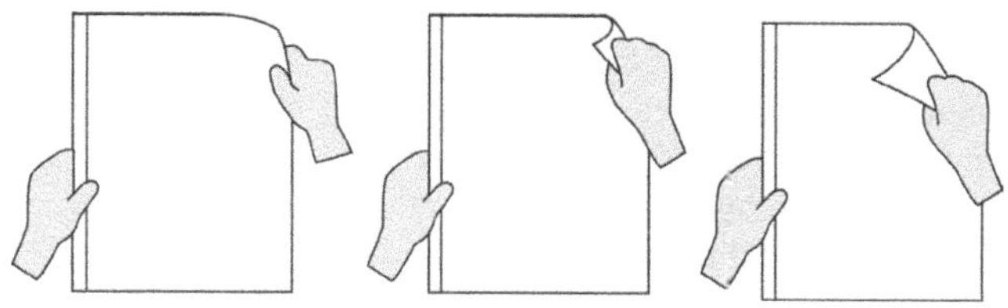

Figure 1. Collocated gestures, e.g. a small, medium and large angle bend, may be difficult to distinguish in practice.

In this paper, we propose an extended bend gesture classification scheme and we evaluate how users naturally perform bend gestures with minimal instruction. By observing gestures classified using location, direction, size and angle, we determine which degrees of freedom can be differentiated by users. We identify strong user preferences for bend gestures and offer design recommendations for future flexible displays.

RELATED WORK
This prior work section is focused on prototypes that introduced different categories of bends. Some of these prototypes are input devices separate from the display [1,2], others bend an extended display bezel [6] while the rest bend a flexible display, either functional [3,4] or projected [8]. Their findings are leveraged in our classification scheme and in this current study, informing which classifications of bend gestures should be examined.

Pioneering the flexible display research field, Schwesig et al. [6] created Gummi, a compact, flexible mobile computing system using bend gestures as input. As they used a rigid display, users navigated the content by bending both sides of the device, made to be an extended bezel. Gummi integrated single and double bends, and used the flat state to distinguish between actions.

Twend investigated the use of deformation as input, and presented a prototype which allowed for the measurement of at least eighteen unique bends, mostly located along the sides and the middle axis of the rectangular prototype [2]. Similar to Gummi, the authors used both analogue and discrete bends. They found bends to be preferred over familiar input methods in certain contexts such as zooming. While the Twend prototype was thick and sponge-like, Watanabe

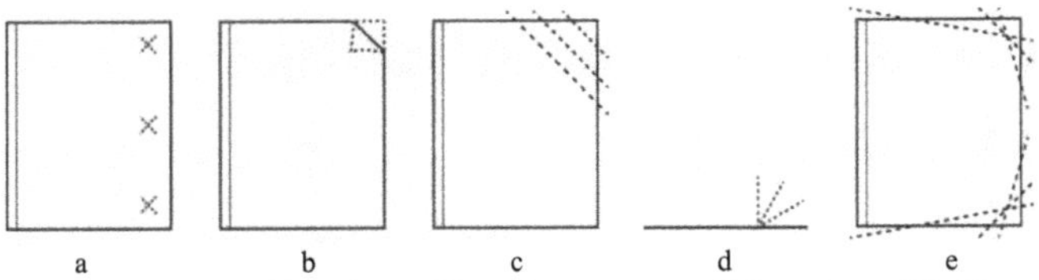

Figure 2. Classification of bend gestures: (a) location, (b) direction, (c) size, (d) angle, (e) edge. Size and Angle illustrate 3 magnitude levels.

et al. [8] created Bookisheet, a thin bendable input device using acrylic sheets, which leverages the metaphor of turning book pages. In Bookisheet, users leafed through a book by bending the side of the device. With its Foldable Input Device [1], Gallant et al. introduced the metaphor of flipping a page by bending the top corner of a page. Their interaction techniques were based on the qualities of paper, as studied by Sellen and Harper [7].

Lee et al. [5] generated a set of interaction gestures for deformable displays. In this study, participants were given paper, plastic and elastic cloth as imaginary displays. The participants were instructed to deform the displays to execute specific tasks, e.g. zooming or navigating to the next page. Their results included a number of bend gestures, such as bending upwards, downwards; bending the middle, the side or the upper corner of the artificial display.

PaperPhone was the first prototype to use a fully functional flexible display [4]. With this smartphone prototype, Lahey et al. asked participants to define bend gestures, and associate those gestures with functionalities. They proposed a classification scheme that categorized bend gestures by location (top corner, side, or bottom corner) and their polarity (up or down). More recently, Nokia presented the Kinetic device [9], a deformable mobile phone which has rubber-like properties. Using this device, Kildal et al. [3] explored bending and twisting, and proposed a set of design guidelines with deformable devices, such as the appropriateness of discrete bend gestures to trigger discrete functionality.

BEND GESTURE CLASSIFICATION SCHEME

Bend gestures can have a variety of complexities: they can be defined according to a simple classification scheme composed of *location* and *polarity* of the force, such as in PaperPhone [4], but their large number of degrees of freedom suggests more complex gestures can be implemented. We build on PaperPhone's initial bend gesture definition to create a classification of bend gestures. Figure 2 illustrates five characteristics. We work with design constraints of current flexible displays, which contain a rigid bezel, but we believe our classifications can be extended to devices without rigid elements.

- **Location**: Where the bend takes place on the device: e.g. top corner, side, bottom corner (Figure 2a).
- **Direction**: The direction of the bend: upwards (toward the user), or downwards (away from the user) (Figure 2b). This was referred to as polarity in PaperPhone.
- **Size of the Bent Area**: The bent surface area of the device, e.g. 1/5th of the device bends (Figure 2c).
- **Angle**: The degree of perpendicularity of the bend in relation to the device plane. These bends can be spoken of in terms of angle in relation to the plane (Figure 2d).
- **Edge**: A bend performed by holding an edge of the device (Figure 2e).
- **Speed of Bend**: The time taken to move the device from the neutral position to the bend position.
- **Duration of Bend**: The length of time the bend is held in place before returning to neutral position.

To determine the subset of classifications to use in the current study, we first performed a pilot study where we observed users bend pieces of paper. We saw users naturally performing gestures based on location and direction (also found by Lee [5] and Lahey [4]). The next most common variables were size and angle. We find that our classification yields a hierarchy of importance: one must first classify a bend by location and direction, then by size and/or angle, before discussing speed and duration of bend. To create a succinct study, we concentrated on the higher level descriptors of natural bend gestures: location, direction, size and angle.

EXPLORING BEND GESTURES STUDY

While computers may be able to recognize even the smallest movement in a bend sensor, human abilities are not as precise. The goal of this study is to determine how many degrees of freedom individuals can consistently differentiate within the four classifications chosen.

Prototype

We created a prototype to detect the location, direction, size, and angle of bends (Figure 3). We used six 3" Flexpoint bidirectional bend sensors. Sets of sensors were placed in three *locations* (top right corner, right side, and bottom right corner). By design, the sensors provide us with the *directionality* of the bend (up or down). However, the value obtained from the sensor is a combination of size and angle. To distinguish between size and angle, we used pairs of sensors in each location. We partially overlapped them to create three zones per pair. We determined the *size* of the bend by observing which bend sensors are activated (the inner sensor, both sensors, or the outer sensor). We correlate the sensor values to obtain *angle*.

We designed the letter sized prototype to be thin and flexible to minimize the physical constraints of performing bend gestures. In this sense, our prototype was closer to that used in the participatory session of Lee et al. [5] than the more rigid PaperPhone [4]. A bezel was affixed to the left side of the device, similar to current deformable display prototypes such as PaperPhone [4]. We fabricated a flexible printed circuit (FPC) to minimize the device's thickness. The bend sensors are connected to an Arduino Uno microcontroller through the FPC.

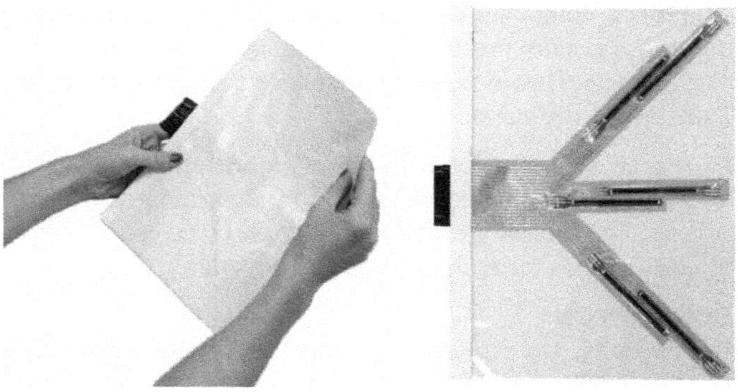

Figure 3. Left: the prototype used in the study. Right: the bend sensors layout at the back of the prototype.

Study Design

Participants were 13 university students and employees (9 males, overall mean age of 25). All but one were right handed. None had prior experience with flexible devices.

Participants were asked to perform a series of bend gestures with minimal instruction. They were given a magnitude (small, medium or large), a characteristic (angle or size), a direction (up or down), and a location (top corner, side, bottom corner), for instance, "large size, bend down, bottom corner". Participants were directed to perform the bend gestures naturally. They performed 36 unique bends during each of three trials for a total of 108 bends per participant. In the first trial, participants performed the bend gestures grouped by direction, then size or angle, then location, and finally magnitude (e.g. small size bend up with the top corner, medium size bend up with the top corner, large size bend up with the top corner, etc.). The remaining sets of trials were presented in a random order. At the end of the study, a semi-structured interview was conducted to measure user preferences. Participants were asked questions regarding their experience relating to preferred location, direction, size, angle, and overall bend.

Hypotheses

We hypothesized that bending down would result in smaller bends than bending up (H1) since bending down presents a larger ergonomic challenge. We expected small and large size bends to be easy to complete and interpret, but medium size bends to often be mislabeled, as their sensor values would overlap with large bend values (H2). We predicted that bending the top corner up would be the preferred bend for users (H3), and similarly, that the bottom corner down would be the most difficult or least preferred (H4). Finally, we hypothesized that small size and angle bends would be preferred over medium or large (H5), as they require the least amount of wrist movement and visual occlusion of the screen is minimal.

RESULTS

Quantitative

We analyzed the bend sensor values by performing a repeated measures factorial analysis of variance using bend location (3) * bend direction (2) * bend magnitude (3) for angle and size. We transformed the data so a value of zero represents flat. A higher value meant a larger activation, independent of the direction of the data. We examined only the two sensors corresponding to the location of the bend.

Results showed that users performed larger bends in the top location, followed by the side and the bottom location, for size ($F(2, 22)=4.645$, $p=0.031$) and angle ($F(2, 18)=4.648$, $p=0.024$). Users performed smaller downward bends than upward for size ($F(2, 18) = 4.648$, $p=0.024$) as well as angle ($F(2, 22)= 4.645$, $p=0.031$). We found a significant effect for angle magnitude ($F(2, 22)=14.403$, $p=0.001$), indicating that users can differentiate between three angle magnitudes. This holds true for each location ($F(4, 44)=3.064$, $p=0.041$).

We used the Friedman test to evaluate the size magnitudes using zone values. The difference between zones was significant for each location (top corner: $X^2=12.056$, $p=.002$; side: $X^2=26.694$, $p=.000$; bottom: $X^2=32.263$, $p=.000$).

Qualitative

The majority of participants indicated the top corner was their preferred *location* for bends (69%), followed by the side location (31%). The majority of users preferred the small *size* of bend (54%), versus 15% preferring the medium size and 15% preferring the large size (15% of participants indicated no preference). The majority of users preferred also a small *angle* bend (62%), versus 15% preferring a large angle. Finally, 31% participant had no preference about angle. When asked about their *overall bend* preference, the majority of participants indicated a combination of top corner location and up direction (77%), with significant variability in size and angle preferences. 40% of participants indicated difficulty differentiating between three magnitudes and would prefer two.

DISCUSSION

The results showed support for most of our hypotheses, with strong agreement on bend gesture preferences. Our quantitative results supported our first hypothesis, participants did perform smaller bends downward than upward. We also found that many users indicated bending downward to be more awkward than upwards. Participants performed the largest bends in the top corner location, followed by side. This may be due to the ease of bending in the top corner and side locations reported by participants.

Users showed a preference for the top location, followed closely by the side location. This preferred location corresponds to that of previous work [4,5]. The overall preferred gesture, the top corner upwards, supports H3, but differs from that noted in PaperPhone, i.e. the side location [4]. We also confirm H4, users found the bottom corner bends most difficult to perform. Participant observations revealed an ergonomic explanation for this trend, as most participants attempted several hand positions in the bottom corner location before settling on the most comfortable to perform the bend. This suggests the bottom corner to be the least ergonomic. Finally, we confirm that small angle and size bends are preferred over medium or large (H5), being more ergonomic and providing the least amount of screen occlusion.

In general, we observed a disconnect between the user perception of accurate bends performed and their actual performance. For instance, our results both support and counter H2, where we hypothesized that users would have difficulty differentiating between three levels of magnitude. While the statistical analysis supported the use of three levels of magnitude, this result is not meaningful once we observe the zones activated, and how users performed bends. Our participants typically performed small and medium size bends at a sharp angle, activating the outer zone for small size bends (48%) and the outer and middle zones for medium size bends (28% and 65% respectively). However, their large size bends were quite curved (instead of sharp), often activating both sensors, which activates the middle zone (68%), instead of the inner zone (17%). Hence our current prototype cannot reliably detect large bends (inner zone only). In addition, many users indicated a preference for two magnitudes rather than three for both size and angle. Therefore, we recommend only two magnitudes, to improve accuracy and user experience.

Limitations

It is important to note the impact of physical constraints of the prototype. The bezel led the user to only manipulate the device with their right hand, which is not ideal for all users. The prototype's size and rigidity had a large impact on the gestures produced. However, we believe our results generalize to other sizes. In addition, we acknowledge that visual feedback is important to bend-gesture research and that it was omitted here: we chose to focus our study on the attributes of physical deformations without the potential bias of visual feedback (similar to Lee et al. [5]).

DESIGN RECOMMENDATIONS

When designing bend gestures the function and complexity of the application should be taken into careful consideration. The following are general design recommendations:

Map frequently used functions to the top corner

The top corner was the most preferred location followed by side and then bottom corner. We recommend mapping frequently used functions the top corner to optimize usability.

Use two levels of magnitude

We recommend two levels of magnitude to increase the distinction between bend gestures for deformable devices with similar physical attributes to our prototype. While users of a different prototype design may be able to detect three levels reliably, we base this guideline on our results, which include users reporting confusion relating to three levels of magnitude, and a strong preference for two.

Select either size or angle, unless using expert users

The distinction between concepts of size and angle was often unclear to users, based on how users performed bend gestures, as well as their interview comments. For instance, several users described bends using the term "curvature", which is a combination of size and angle. If one needs to describe a gesture precisely, we recommend selecting either size or angle. However, we predict expert users will be able to make this distinction.

Create an adaptable classification algorithm

We suggest developing classification algorithms that take into account the significant variability observed in the magnitude of bends for each location and direction.

CONCLUSION

In this study, we explored how users performed bend gestures using four criteria: location, direction, size and angle. Our study identified that the top corner was preferred of the three locations. We observed that upward bends were larger than downward bends. Two levels of magnitude showed optimal distinction with our prototype. Lastly, we recommend the use of size or angle for clarity with novice users. The granularity achieved by our study further extends past research done on bend gestures.

Given that most users are unfamiliar with bending as an input method, it is worthwhile to investigate user's bend gesture performance and preference with a longitudinal study. It would also be valuable to determine how to effectively guide users when performing bend gestures as well as how to indicate when a bend is available. A study of the use of visualizations to inform and guide users to perform correct bends in cases of collocated gestures is warranted.

ACKNOWLEDGEMENTS

This work was supported is funded by the National Sciences and Engineering Research Council of Canada (NSERC).

REFERENCES

1. Gallant, D., Seniuk, A., and Vertegaal, R. Towards more paper-like input: flexible input devices for foldable interaction styles. *Proc. UIST*, (2008), 283–286.
2. Herkenrath, G., Karrer, T., and Borchers, J. Twend: Twisting and Bending as new Interaction Gesture in Mobile Devices. *Proc. CHI*, (2008), 3819–3824.
3. Kildal, J., Paasovaara, S., and Aaltonen, V. Kinetic Device : Designing Interactions with a Deformable Mobile Interface. *Proc. CHI EA*, (2012), 1871–1876.
4. Lahey, B., Girouard, A., Burleson, W., and Vertegaal, R. PaperPhone: Understanding the Use of Bend Gestures in Mobile Devices with Flexible Electronic Paper Displays. *Proc. CHI*, (2011).
5. Lee, S.-S., Kim, S., Jin, B., et al. How users manipulate deformable displays as input devices. *Proc. CHI*, (2010), 1647.
6. Schwesig, C., Poupyrev, I., and Mori, E. Gummi: a bendable computer. *Proc. CHI*, (2004), 263 – 270.
7. Sellen, A.J. and Harper, R.H.R. *The Myth of the Paperless Office*. MIT Press, 2003.
8. Watanabe, J., Mochizuki, A., and Horry, Y. Bookisheet: bendable device for browsing content using the metaphor of leafing through the pages. *Proc. UbiComp*, (2008), 360–369.
9. NRC developed Nokia Kinetic prototype demoed at Nokia World 2011. http://research.nokia.com/news/12110.

Turkopticon: Interrupting Worker Invisibility in Amazon Mechanical Turk

Lilly C Irani
UC Irvine, Department of Informatics
Irvine, CA 92697
lirani@ics.uci.edu

M. Six Silberman
Bureau of Economic Interpretation
six@economicinterpretation.org

ABSTRACT
As HCI researchers have explored the possibilities of human computation, they have paid less attention to ethics and values of crowdwork. This paper offers an analysis of Amazon Mechanical Turk, a popular human computation system, as a site of technically mediated worker-employer relations. We argue that human computation currently relies on worker invisibility. We then present Turkopticon, an activist system that allows workers to publicize and evaluate their relationships with employers. As a common infrastructure, Turkopticon also enables workers to engage one another in mutual aid. We conclude by discussing the potentials and challenges of sustaining activist technologies that intervene in large, existing socio-technical systems.

Author Keywords
Activism; infrastructure; human computation; Amazon Mechanical Turk; design; ethics

ACM Classification Keywords
H.5.m. Information interfaces and presentation (e.g., HCI): Miscellaneous.

INTRODUCTION
Crowdsourcing and human computation are often described as a new frontier for HCI research and creativity, and for technological progress more broadly. CHI researchers have built word processors powered by crowds. Others have shown how usability and visualization evaluations can be taken out of the lab and into the natural environments of crowdworkers.

These frontiers, however, are enabled by the novel organization of digital workers, distributed across the world and organized through task markets, APIs, and network connections. This paper looks behind the walls of abstraction that enable human computation in one specific system, Amazon Mechanical Turk (AMT). We present workers' occupational hazards as human computers, and explain the activist project we developed in response. Turkopticon, the project we present, is a tool in its fourth year of deployment. The system receives 100,000 page views a month and has become a staple tool for many AMT workers, installed over 7,000 times at time of writing.

CHI 2013, April 27–May 2, 2013, Paris, France.

Turkopticon allows workers to create and use reviews of employers when choosing employers on AMT. Building and maintaining the system, as well as communicating about the system with workers, has offered us a distinct vantage point into the social processes of designing interventions into large-scale, real world systems. Turkopticon supports a thriving collective of workers engaged in mutual aid, brought together by our simple browser extension and web-based technology.

This paper makes several contributions. First, it offers a case study designing an intervention into a highly distributed microlabor system. Second, it shows an example of systems design incorporating tools feminist analysis and reflexivity. Rather than conducting HCI research to reveal and represent values and positions, and then building systems to resolve those political differences, we built a system to make worker-employer relations visible and to provoke ethical and political debate. Third, this paper contributes lessons learned from intervening in existing, large-scale socio-technical systems (here, AMT) from its margins.

METHOD AND OUR STANCE
This paper draws on four years of participant-observation as design activists within AMT worker and technologist communities. Turkopticon grew out of a tactical media art project intended to raise questions about the ethics of human computation. Tactical media, one tradition within activist art, emphasizes developing urgent, culturally provocative interruptions and resistance through the design of media [13, 19, 21]. In addition to the interviews, observation, and casual conversation that feature in many HCI ethnographies, our encounters with Turk workers began through highly mediated "Human Intelligence Tasks" and feedback around Turkopticon. (We began this research in 2008, prior to the growth of popular online worker forums turkernation.com and mturkforum.com.)

We conducted several informal surveys through Mechanical Turk. 67 respondents answered our open-ended question survey about what they would desire as a "Workers' Bill of Rights." Points of agreement among worker respondents on this survey became the basis for the design of Turkopticon.

The first author complements participant-observation, as a system builder of Turker tools, with observation and open-ended interviews with AMT employers. She attended a major crowdsourcing conference as well two smaller crowdsourcing meetups. She also conducted open-ended interviews with four employers on AMT and numerous conversations with other employers. These ethnographic data contextualize the data we generate as we design and maintain Turkopticon.

Over the course of this research, each of our stances developed as a result of our own involvement with the workers through the project, and through our evolving understandings of the broader crowdsourcing community. We began highly critical of the fragmentation of labor into hyper-temporary jobs, seeing them as an intensification of decades-old US trends toward part-time, contingent work for employer flexibility and cost-cutting [3, 35]. AMT, it seemed to us produced temporary employees at "the speed of thought," to borrow Bill Gates' promissory turn of phrase, precisely by forgetting about ergonomics, repetitive stress injuries, and minimum wage laws. We were biased – decidedly so.

Our biases were validated by some workers and challenged by others. For each one who reported needing the money to pay for rent or groceries, there was another who did it for fun or to "kill time."

We highlight our own stances under advisement of Borning and Muller who, with many feminist scholars, call for researchers to shed trappings of objective authority and account for how our own contexts and assumptions shape our research practices [7]. However, it is not only that our biases distort our perception of reality that is out there in the world of AMT work. Certainly, we have much to learn about how workers feel about their work and the problems they encounter, as we have published. But we also intervene in AMT by building a technology used by its workers. By intervening in the system as designers and as observers, we change the reality of the system itself [4, 29, 41]. The ethical challenges and issues faced by workers, and the ethical issues we face as researchers, are produced in the encounters between us, the workers, and Turkopticon. This paper offers a snapshot of the lessons we have learned and their implications for design practice at this point in the evolving socio-technical system.

First, we explain AMT, focusing on the kinds of worker-employer relationships enabled by the system. We then describe our motivations for building Turkopticon, the design of the system, and learnings relevant to the design of political and activist technologies.

BACKGROUND: AMAZON MECHANICAL TURK (AMT)

Amazon Mechanical Turk is a website and service operated by Amazon as a meeting place for requesters with large volumes of microtasks and workers who want to do those tasks, usually for money [24]. These tasks often add up to a few dollars an hour for those experienced with the platform. Amazon legally defines the workers as contractors subject to laws designed for freelancers and consultants; this framing attempts to strip workers of minimum wage requirements in their countries. United States workers are a significant minority, numbering at 46.8% in recent surveys [24]. This framing, however, has not been tested in courts, and courts have deemed similar framings of distributed, non-computer data work illegal [18].

AMT can be described many ways. Explaining it as a microlabor marketplace draws attention to pricing mechanisms, how workers choose tasks, and how transactions are managed. Explaining it as a crowdsourcing platform draws attention to the dynamics of mass collaboration among workers, the aggregation of inputs, and the evaluation of the crowdsourced outputs. Explaining AMT as a source of human computation resources, however, is consistent with how both the computing research community and Amazon's own marketing frames the system [e.g. 28].

Dividing data work into small components is not itself new. A 1985 case, *Donovan vs DialAmerica*, tells of an earlier version of AMT-style labor. An employer sent cards with names to home workers hired as independent contractors. These contractors had to ascertain the correct phone number for each name; they were paid per task. Courts decided that these workers were in fact employees entitled to minimum wage under the Fair Labor Standards Act (FLSA) [18, p.136]. Since the late 1990s, American companies have hired Business Process Outsourcing firms in English-speaking countries with lower costs of living to perform large volumes of data processing tasks that cannot be fully automated.[1]

Humans-as-a-service

AMT jumps beyond these older forms of information work by setting workers up as resources that can be directly integrated into existing computer systems as "human computation." When Jeff Bezos launched AMT to an MIT audience in 2006, he announced: "You've heard of software-as-a-service. Now this is human-as-a-service" [5]. Since launch, AMT has been marketed as one of Amazon's Web Services, alongside silicon computational cycles and data storage in the cloud. Bloggers and technologists have followed suit, both in published sources and conferences and meetups we attended, calling AMT a "Remote Person Call" (playing off of "Remote Procedure Call") and "the Human API." Crowdsourcing company CrowdFlower even coined the neologism "Labor-as-a-service (LaaS)" to market the value of crowdsourced workforces to companies.

This combination of abstraction and service orientation in both the metaphors and infrastructural forms suggest a particular kind of social relationship. "As-a-service" draws

[1] In 2012, a US Mechanical Turk worker filed a class action suit against Crowdflower for violations of FLSA. The outcome of the suit was unknown at time of press.

meaning from commonplace resonances of service. To serve is to make labor and attention available for those served; to promise service is to be bound, by duty or by wage, to the will of the served. Among computer scientists, "as-a-service" builds off of this common sense meaning and more specifically suggests a division of technical labor by which programmers can access computational processing functions housed and maintained on the Internet and by someone else. As long as the service keeps running, programmers need not concern themselves with where the code is running, what kind of machine it runs on, or who keeps the code running, but only the proper protocol for issuing the call through a computer and receiving the response. As-a-service suggests an arrangement of computers, networks, system administrators, and real estate that allows programmers to access a range of computer services remotely and instantly.

Framing workers on AMT as computational services is more than just rhetorical flourish. Through AMT, employers can literally access workers through APIs. Though a web form-based interface is available, the API allows AMT employers can put tasks into the workforce and integrate worker output directly into their algorithms. Techniques for integrating workers into computational technologies in this way have been pioneered in HCI, in databases research, and in industry (see [42] for a summary). Twitter, for example, has recently open sourced a visual toolkit for running human judgment experiments on AMT [12]. These experiments are a key component of developing, evaluating, and training search and ranking algorithms. Twitter's toolkit offers an interface for building these experiments, providing monitoring tools and visualizations interfacing with AMT's 24/7, massively distributed workforce through APIs. CrowdFlower also builds atop AMT's APIs, offering crowdsourced data processing tools tailored to needs common to different industries.

We see here, then, that AMT brings together crowds of workers as a form of infrastructure, rendering employees into reliable sources of computation. As established organizations develop and publicly release tools for the system, they embed computational microwork firmly in existing technological practices and systems. AMT is becoming infrastructure in the sense that Star & Ruhleder have analyzed it: AMT is shared, AMT is incorporated into existing shared practices, and ideally, AMT is ready-to-hand and worked *through* not *on*. Working technological infrastructures, in Star & Ruhleder's analyses, are used with such fluency that they become taken-for-granted, humming quietly and usefully in the background. The infrastructures kept humming dutifully in the background in AMT are the socio-technical system of workers interacting with employers through APIs, spreadsheets, and minimal web-based task forms.

Ruhleder and Star famously called for going beyond a consideration of *what* is infrastructure to a consideration of *when* is infrastructure [34]. Asking *when* is infrastructure recognizes that systems that might hum along beyond notice in one moment might break down and require maintenance and repair in another. And a system that might hum along beyond notice for an end-user might be very much the focus of attention for those in charge of maintaining it. The question "when is infrastructure?" then, suggests also asking, "for whom is infrastructure?" When it is working as infrastructure, AMT platform clearly hums along supporting the work of employers — the programmers, managers, and start up hackers who integrate human computation into their technologies. In this light, that the design features and development of AMT has prioritized the needs of employers over workers is not surprising.

Further, by hiding workers behind web forms and APIs, AMT helps employers see themselves as builders of innovative technologies, rather than employers unconcerned with working conditions. Suchman argues that there are "agencies at the interface" that reconfigure the relations among humans and machines, making both what they are [40]. AMT's power lies in part in how it reconfigures social relations, rendering Turk workers invisible [37], redirecting focus to the innovation of human computation as a field of technological achievement.

Employing Humans-as-a-Service

In this section, we explain basic features of AMT and show how the design prioritizes the needs of employers.

AMT employers define HITs on AMT by creating web-based forms that specify an information task and allow workers to input a response. Tasks include structuring unstructured data (e.g. entering a given webpage into an employer's structured form fields), transcribing snippets of audio, and labeling an image (e.g. as pornography or violating given Terms of Service). Employers define the structure of the data workers must input, create instructions, specify the pool of information that must be processed, and set a price. (Ipeirotis [22] offers an excellent background.)

The employer then defines criteria that candidate workers must meet to work on the task. These criteria include the worker's "approval rating" (the percentage of tasks the worker has performed that employers have approved and, by consequence, paid for), the worker's self-reported country, and whether the worker has completed certain skill-specific qualification exams offered on the platform. This filter approach to choosing workers, as compared to more individualized evaluation and selection, allows employers to request work from thousands of temporary workers in a matter of hours.

Once a worker submits work, the employer can choose whether to pay for it. This discretion allows employers to reject work that does not meet their needs, but also enables wage theft. Because AMT's participation agreement grants employers full intellectual property rights over submissions regardless of rejection, workers have no legal recourse against employers who reject work and then go on to use it.

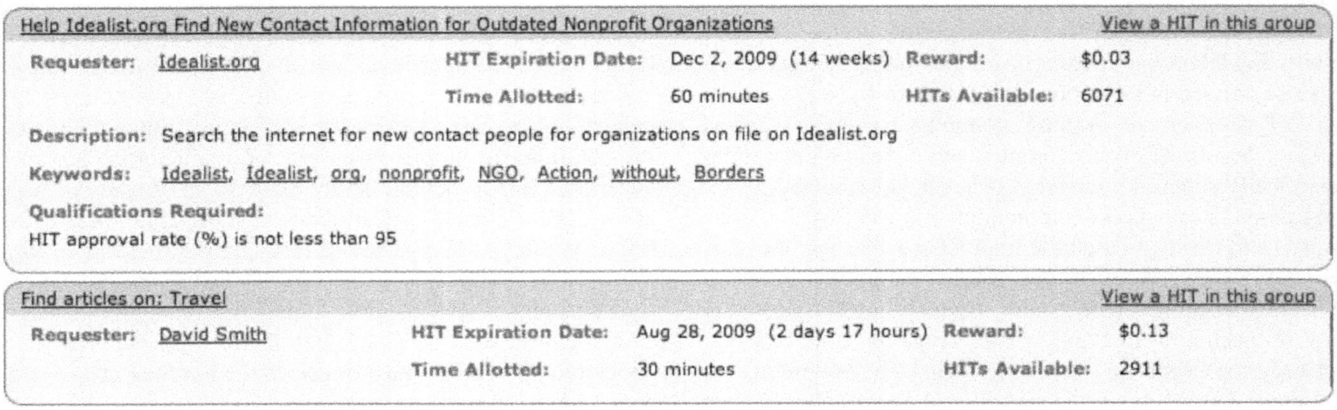

Fig. 1: What a worker sees: the Human intelligence Tasks (HITs) list on AMT.

Employers vet worker outputs through automated approaches such as qualifying workers through test tasks to which the correct answer is known or requesting responses to a single input from several workers and algorithmically eliminating any answers that do not agree with the majority.

Within this large scale, fast moving, and highly mediated workforce, dispute resolution between workers and employers becomes intractable. Workers dissatisfied with a requester's work rejection can contact the requester through AMT's web interface. Amazon does not require requesters to respond and many do not; several requesters have noted that a thousand to one worker-to-requester ratio makes responding cost prohibitive. In the logic of massive crowd collaborations, dispute resolution does not scale. Dahn Tamir, a large-scale requester, explained a logic the first author heard from several Turk employers:

"You cannot spend time exchanging email. The time you spent looking at the email costs more than what you paid them. This has to function on autopilot as an algorithmic system…and integrated with your business processes."

Instead of eliciting a response, workers' dispute messages become signals to the employer. Rick, a CEO of a crowdsourcing startup, explained to me that messages from workers signal the algorithm's performance in managing workers and tasks. If a particular way of determining "correctness" for a task results in a large number of disputing messages, Rick's team will look into revising the algorithm but rarely will retroactively revise decisions. Algorithmic management, here, precludes individually accountable relations.

Workers have limited options for dissent within AMT itself. Resistance through incorrect answers can simply be filtered out through employer's algorithmic tests of correctness. Dissatisfied workers' within AMT had little option other than to leave the system altogether. Because AMT treats workers interchangeably and because workers are so numerous (tens of thousands by the most conservative estimates), AMT can sustain the loss of workers who do not accept the system's terms.

Turkopticon has been designed to offer workers a way to dissent, holding requesters accountable and offering one another mutual aid.

MOTIVATING TURKOPTICON

Turkopticon developed as an ethically-motivated response to workers' invisibility in the design of AMT. We were troubled by a number of issues in our first encounters with AMT, not only worker invisibility. Workers, even in the US, are paid below minimum wage in many cases. Technologist and research discourse seemed unconcerned with the human costs of human computation. Individuated workers had little opportunity to build solidarity, offering them little chance of creating sufficiently coordinated actions to exert pressure on employers and Amazon.

Rather than working from our own intuitions, however, we took seriously the possibility that this new form of work also might offer workers benefits and pleasures that we did not understand, or cause troubles we could not anticipate. Survey research on Turk worker motivations, for example, reports that though a significant minority of workers rely on their income from the platform to pay for household expenses. At the same time, other workers report working for fun or to pass the time while bored (sometimes even at another job) [23, 22, 33].

Workers' "Bill of Rights"

To provoke workers' imaginations about the infrastructural possibilities, we placed a task onto AMT asking workers to articulate a "Worker's Bill of Rights" from their perspective. We chose this approach over a more neutral battery of questions because of the highly mediated nature of our interactions with workers through the medium of the HIT. Workers paid per task — of which our question was one — provided short answers to open-ended questions based on our past experiences questioning workers in the platform. Asking a provocative question drew stronger, more detailed responses oriented towards concerns of crowdsourcing ethics. We also sought permission from workers to publish their responses on the web in hopes of generating interaction between workers and broader publics concerned with crowdsourcing.

Our work treated crowdsourcing ethics as an open question about a new technology, still under negotiation. In structurationist terms, practices and meanings of the technology had not yet stabilized [32]. Our ethical questions, then, were not trying to get at some underlying, stable truth, but rather at ongoing ethical and political negotiations among participants in crowdsourcing systems. Like Bruckman and Hudson, we gathered empirical data on workers' ethics — here framed as rights — to explore the ethical dimensions of crowdsourcing [9]. Rather than draw firm conclusions here, however, we continue to keep the debate open. We grapple with the problem of advocacy as explained by Bardzell [2], in which Feminist HCI practitioners both seek to bring about social progress, but also question their own images of what such social progress looks like. By publishing responses to our questions and building Turkopticon, as we will discuss, we sought to provoke debate about progress in crowdsourcing and make questions of work conditions visible among technologists, policy makers, and the media.

Workers' responses to the question of a "Bill of Rights" revealed a range of concerns, some broadly expressed among workers and others that polarized.

Of our 67 responses [42], workers recurringly raised a number of issues:

- 35 workers felt that their work was regularly rejected unfairly or arbitrarily
- 26 workers demanded faster payment (Amazon allows employers 30-days to evaluate and pay for work)
- 7 explicitly mentioned a "minimum wage" or "minimum payment" per HIT
- 14 mentioned "fair" compensation generally
- 8 expressed dissatisfaction with employers' and Amazon's lack of response to their concerns

The consequences of these occupational hazards for workers included lost or delayed income, accidental download of malware that damaged their computers, and reduced worker "approval ratings." Approval ratings are one of the few ways employers can filter workers. When an employer rejects an employer's work, whether because it did not meet their needs or simply so they employer did not have to pay, the worker's approval rating goes down. If the rating goes too far down, AMT will hide tasks requiring high ratings from the worker. Lost approval ratings, then, are lost opportunities for work which make it even more difficult to accumulate experiences to raise the rating again.

A Sense of Fairness

Beyond the inconveniences and dangers of doing Turk work, several workers articulated a more general frustration we characterize as a sense of fairness. This sense came through in numerous responses that requesters ought to respond to questions from workers, that requesters ought to justify their rejections, and that workers have the right to confront employers about those rejections.

A number of workers directed their frustrations towards Amazon itself. One worker was so frustrated that he or she thanked the first author by name for posting the HIT and offering an opportunity to express his anger: "I don't care about the penny I didn't earn for knowing the difference between an apple and a giraffe, but I'm angry that MT will take requester's money but not manage, oversee, or mediate the problems and injustices on their site."

Another worker noted the imbalance in Amazon's priorities as they developed the AMT platform:

"I would also like workers to have more of a say around here, so that they can not easily be taken advantage of, and are treated fairly, as they should be. Amazon seems to pay more credence to the requesters, simply ignoring the fact that without workers, nothing would be done!"

We confirmed this priority with prominent requesters as well as a source close to Amazon who wished to remain anonymous. Because Amazon collects money for task volume, Amazon has little reason to prioritize worker needs in a market with a labor surplus.

Mutual Aid for Accountability

Our exploratory interactions with workers left us with no unified image of what workers are like and what intervention might be "appropriate." Those workers who suggested action offered diverse ways forward. Some were interested in a forum in which Turkers could air concerns publicly without censorship or condescension, and worker visibility and dignity more generally. Others were interested in a way to build long-term work relationships with prolific requesters, and worker-requester relations generally. Several respondents asked for unionization, while several others volunteered their aversion to unions.

There were few shared values and priorities that could guide the development of an infrastructure of mutual aid. There were, however, possibilities for creating partial alliances — points of common cause across diverse workers. Donna Haraway, a feminist STS scholar, argues for partial connections — alliances built on common cause rather than common experience or identity — as a way to sustain political and ethical action across people with irreducible differences [20].[2] We took inspiration from this approach.

---

[2] Haraway's argument responded to criticisms that socialist feminism, a Marxist analysis of gender, claimed white women's experiences of gender marginalization as common cause for *all* women. Crenshaw, for example, countered that women exist at the intersection of race, class, and gender categories; each intersection created specific kinds of vulnerabilities. What Haraway proposed was a way to make progressive interventions without making universalizing claims about the issues of all women. She did this by proposing that women, as irreducibly different "cyborgs," build alliances based on common cause and partial connections [20].

Motivated by responses to the "Bill of Rights," we designed and built Turkopticon. Turkopticon responded in part to the occupational hazards of Turking listed above. We also built Turkopticon to offer workers ways of supporting one another in context of their existing practices. The system allows workers to make their relationships with employers visible and call those employers to account. As workers build up the record of relationships with employers, they also build up a commons together with other contributors. By explicitly designing for scales beyond the individual or the dyadic relationship, we sought to build up a group of people who see their interests as aligned with others [16, 31]. Dourish called this the design of politics; he calls for moving beyond the user-technology dyad that often defines design interventions to the creation of larger scale collectives and movements building on social software.

The crowd we wanted to mobilize into a collective, however, was constituted by an infrastructure we had no control over – the AMT platform itself. In contrast to the collectives Dourish seeks to mobilize through Facebook, or the Internet hackers Chris Kelty describes as building the infrastructure that make their association possible [26, p.3], our task was to create a means of association people whose common cause was their work on AMT but who lack the technical skills to build infrastructures of assembly. Rather than design a system anew, our work was to graft a new infrastructure onto an existing one.

TURKOPTICON: THE SYSTEM

Turkopticon is a browser extension for Firefox and Chrome that augments workers' view of their AMT HIT lists with information other workers have provided about employers ("Requesters" in AMT parlance). Workers enter reviews of employers that they have worked with, entering ratings of four qualities of employers as well as an open-ended comment explaining their rating. These reviews are available on the Turkopticon website; workers can view both recent reviews, as well as all reviews for a particular requester, identified by a unique Amazon requester ID.

Turkopticon is named for panopticon, a prison surveillance design most famously analyzed by Foucault. The prison is round with a guard tower in the center. The tower does not reveal whether the guard is present, so prisoners must assume they could be monitored at any moment. The *possibility* of surveillance, the theory goes, induces prisoners to discipline themselves. Turkopticon's name cheekily references the panopticon, pointing to our hope that the site could not only hold employers accountable, bu induce better behavior.

Going beyond simply a review site, we designed Turkopticon to fit into workers existing Turking workflow. The browser extension – a Javascript userscript packaged for both Firefox and Chrome – works by searching the document object model (DOM) of AMT pages as the worker browses. We locate links that contain requester IDs in their target URLs, choose the link that is a requester name, and insert a small CSS button next to the name that, on mouse-over, launches more details on that requester. The extension issues an XMLHTTP request for details we have on the requester that then load in the background as the rest of the "Available HIT" page renders.

The embedded review overlay contains both averaged ratings of the requester, and a link to view all reviews and open-ended comments on the requester on our website. (See figure 2.) From this overlay, workers can also review requesters. When the worker clicks the requester review link, we take them to Turkopticon's requester review form with the requester ID we strip from page's underlying HTML pre-populating the review's form field. The embedded overlay is available anywhere in the AMT interface where a worker might see a requester: both at points where they are selecting HITs and where they are checking approval and payment status for submitted HITs.

Standardizing Requester Reputations

We now turn to how the kind of data we decided to collect on requesters. Because the AMT model often has workers doing HITs from a large number of employers in a session, we needed to offer workers a quick way to assess employers. We also saw in the Bill of Rights that workers were not unified in what they valued in an employer. Some wanted a short response time while others did not care, for example. By taking ratings on various qualities rather than taking an aggregating rating in the style of product review sites, we offered workers discretion in evaluating the ratings.

Turkopticon collects quantitative ratings from reviewers on four qualities that we hypothesized would be relevant based on the Workers' Bill of Rights survey.

- Communicativity: How responsive has this requester been to communications or concerns you have raised?
- Generosity: How well has this requester paid for the amount of time their HITs take?
- Fairness: How fair has this requester been in approving or rejecting your work?
- Promptness: How promptly has this requester approved your work and paid?

A score of "0" means we have no data for that attribute

We also require workers to enter a free-form text comment to contextualize their scores. We provide the free-form box so that workers can share more nuanced, fine-grained stories of their experiences. We require workers to fill it, however, because the substance of testimonials is one of the ways other workers can evaluate other workers credibility.

Bootstrapping a Collective System

Turkopticon is nothing without users and their reviews; like many CSCW systems, it requires a "critical mass" to serve users at all [1]. How to launch a brand new system when the system has no content? Generating community around the project was difficult because workers were so invisible,

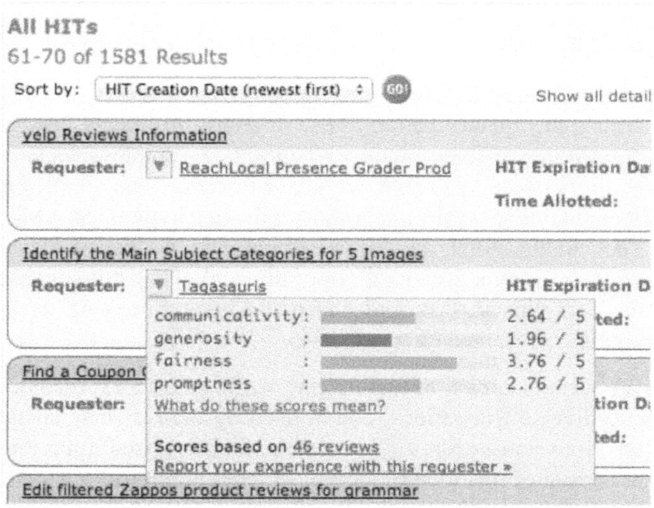

Fig. 2: The Turkopticon browser add-on adds information about requesters provided by other workers.

largely separated from one another, and today's prominent worker forums (e.g. TurkerNation or mturkforum) were much smaller.

We overcame this problem by enlisting the support of DoloresLabs, a crowdsourcing company that builds custom toolkits for employers wishing to employ Mechanical Turk labor. DoloresLabs created a task for our team with a list of prominent requesters and solicited 300 initial reviews for which it compensated workers. The initial reviews seeded our database so new users installing Turkopticon could immediately integrate the tool into their workflow. Rather than requiring initial users to produce reviews, our bootstrapping allowed for users to consume the reviews we hoped they would eventually produce and improve upon.

Making alliance with a prominent employer in the Mechanical Turk system was a double-edged sword. DoloresLabs supported us because they believed that crowdlabor industries would benefit from a fairer labor market; Turkopticon promised to remedy the information asymmetry between workers and employers, repairing Mechanical Turk into a more "transparent" marketplace [6]. Our team, by contrast, built Turkopticon in part to draw attention to commodification and exploitation in large-scale crowdsourcing markets. Just as the Turkopticon tool was a way of building partial connections across workers, the Turkopticon design process made partial connections despite different visions for the future of crowdsourcing.

Reputation without Retribution

Turkopticon attempts to prevent employers from retaliating against workers writing reviews by obfuscating workers' email addresses. As we designed Turkopticon, we anticipated that workers would fear retribution for writing critical reviews. Our discussions with workers on forums have confirmed this at least for some workers. At tension with the need for anonymity, however, is the need for reputation among users of the system. There are high

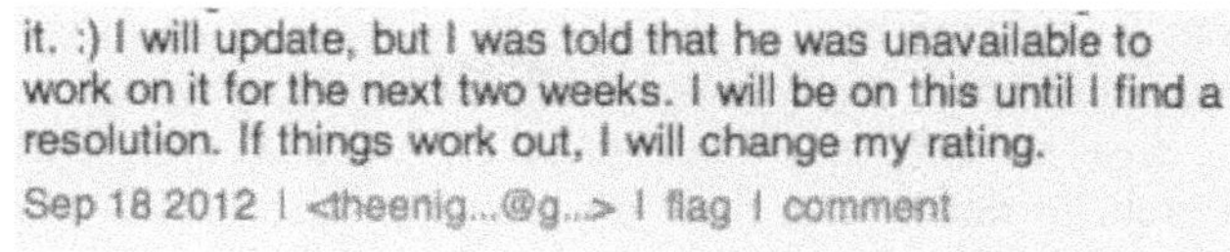

Fig. 3: Workers are protected from retribution by the obfuscation of their email addresses.

incentives for requesters to write positive reviews for themselves and, in practice, requesters attempt to do this.

We balanced the need for anonymity with reputation by displaying users' reviews signed with a partially obfuscated email address. This email address is then linked to a page that shows all reviews written by that user. Readers of reviews can make judgments about the credibility of workers by evaluating other contributions by the user and making their own decision about whether to engage the employer.

Comment Moderation

After two years of running the tool unmoderated, we developed a set of user interface designs to allow selected users to moderate comments on the site. The mechanism is technically simple, leaning on existing social practices and community reputation. Any Turkopticon user can flag a review. A moderator has to add a second flag to hide the review from the site.

We selected our first cohort of moderators by calculating the most prolific reviewers on the site, emailing them invitations to moderate Turkopticon, and posting the list of those who accepted invitations to a widely read worker forum. We left nominations up for a week and received no objections, so we proceeded.

In selecting moderators, we also attempted to align Turkopticon with other worker forums in two ways. First, we selected moderators from the worker community who were engaged in debates and movements in worker forums that we, as non-workers, had little visibility into. By letting moderators in, we also gave them visibility and input into our design processes; based on this inside view, these moderators have been able to vouch for us during critical junctures where a bug or misunderstood feature triggers suspicions among users.

Along with moderation, we also introduced an option for workers to take on screen names – self-chosen identifiers – in place of their obfuscated email addresses. This simple measure has made it possible for reviewers to choose to harmonize their Turkopticon identity with their identity in other forums. We do not, however, force any harmonization.

We rely on primarily social moderation, by a small number of moderators, for several reasons. First, automated approaches are difficult to implement in practice because they cannot account for community-specific and emergent norms [38]. Within the space of social moderation, broad-based community moderation (e.g. Slashdot [27]) is susceptible to vandalism because our users are potentially from two competing classes with opposed incentives. Requesters could easily make an account and begin flagging negative reviews they have received, or even pay Turk workers to down vote their reviews. Moderators draw on knowledge from their involvement in other worker forums to judge the credibility of reviews in question.

DISCUSSION

Strengthening Ties Through Maintenance and Repair

Though HCI has conventionally been concerned with the design, deployment, and evaluation of technological artifacts, the social and technical life of Turkopticon, like any technology, depends on ongoing maintenance and repair [25]. Certainly, we do ongoing technical maintenance. For example, we have to rebuild the extension when Firefox and Chrome release versions with new requirements of add-ons; server load that grew with use demanded that we rewrite code to make more efficient use of our servers resources.

Less remarked on, however, is the work of keeping up with changing design requirements as worker and requester practices change. Comment moderation to cull increasing requester reviews and profanity was one such change, already discussed. We also recently augmented the requester review form with a toggle indicating whether a requester violates Amazon's Terms and Conditions. These design changes reflect changing norms as the kinds of tasks and practices on AMT shift.

As important as the specific design features that we add and upkeep are the community relationships we build and strengthen through this ongoing maintenance of Turkopticon. We learn of concerns and confusions through our user support forum, through our email, and through our moderators who face emerging review practices on the frontline of the Turkopticon reviews page. We, as systems designers and maintainers, gain from highly engaged workers who help us understand what it means to see like a Turk worker and keep up with changes to their evolving practices. We enlist moderators in discussions of web site policy and interaction design, and alter and repair the technology in response to their requests and observations. Moderators here are not objects to be observed by us, but experts in their own right who participate in the collective activism of keeping Turkopticon thriving. (Bardzell and Bardzell have also argued for the incorporation of experts into activist design.)

This work of maintenance and upgrading, undertaken with the participation of workers, does more than offer insight into needs and requirements. This work strengthens ties and builds solidarity among workers collaborating on the practical, shared, and political circumstances they face as crowdworkers. Dourish has argued that HCI research often takes market framings for granted, individuating users as decision-makers to be persuaded or empowered [16]. Framings of social computing that emphasize networks and interaction can similarly frame collectivity as an aggregation of individuals. We call on HCI researchers to instead see technology design's potential for sustaining new polities that can become powerful foundations for social change.

Tactical Quantification

Although quantification has myriad problems as a description of lived practice, Turkopticon employs *tactical quantification* to enable worker interaction and employer accountability while integrating into the rhythms of AMT. Tactical quantification is a use of numbers not because they are more accurate, rational, or optimizable [10], but because they are partial, fast, and cheap – a way of making do in highly constrained circumstances.

We were skeptical of quantifying workers' rich experiences and diverse frustrations, conditioned by their diverse social positions and needs. HCI researchers have raised a number of critiques of quantification in computational systems. Quantification has been associated with failed, injurous modernist attempts to model, rationalize, and optimize messy real world systems. These models necessarily universalize and simplify [10]. In the hands of powerful actors, quantifying, approximate models can drive policies that attempt to form the world in models' images [17].

The use of Turkopticon in the wild has, unsurprisingly, borne out some of these concerns. The "generosity" category, for example, has strained under the weight of representing such a subjective assessment. Workers in India accustomed to much lower salaries and cost of living than Americans may feel that a job averaging $2 an hour is generous, while an American might balk at such a rate.

Standardizing ratings into quantified buckets was instead a compromise we made to our own values as designers in negotiating the power relations of the AMT ecosystem. AMT emphasizes speed and scale [11, 36]. To attract and retain users, we had to begin with the norms of the infrastructure in which we intervened, lest we push too far and become incompatible.

In this sense, Turkopticon is not an expression of our own values, or even the values of the users we interviewed, but a compromise between those values and the weight of the existing infrastructural norms that torqued our design decisions as we intervened in this powerful, working real world system. In their analyses of the consequences of infrastructural classifications, Bowker and Star use the concept of torque to describe the way people's lives can be twisted and shaped as they are forced to fit classification systems and infrastructures, such as racial classifications on government documents or disease categorizations. People live messy, fluid lives that can fall out of sync with the rhythms, categories, and temporality of the infrastructure [8,p.190]. Bowker and Star note that more powerful actors do not experience torque as they determine the categories of the infrastructure and often experience those categories as natural. We were situated at the margins of a large, working sociotechnical system, trying to insert ourselves in. The design of Turkopticon, then, had to be as much an expression of the standards and rhythms set by a large, corporate infrastructure as it was of designer and user values, desires, and politics. By intervening in a working, real world collaborative technological system, we did not enjoy the luxuries of ethics- and values-oriented design projects that design technologies anew.

Publics and their Means of Assembly

A number of researchers have argued that design activities can generate publics – groups that coalesce around identification with a common problem and a shared effort to resolve the problem [14, 30]. Activities such as exploratory prototyping or future-envisioning engage diverse stakeholders in identifying causes of common concern. Design engagement offers one way of collectively inquiring into assumptions, dependencies, and paths forward.

Our early work on Turkopticon – especially the Workers' Bill of Rights – shared this spirit of engaging workers in imagining alternative ways of doing microlabor. Workers' responses revealed vastly disparate visions and self-understandings when it came to issues of minimum wage, relations with requesters, and desire for additional forms of support. Moreover, workers distributed across the world faced vastly different circumstances. Indian Turkers, for example, tend to be highly educated and face lower costs of living than Americans. Bringing these workers together as a public to engage in shared inquiry and democratic interchange would require speaking across cultures, ideologies, and vastly different life circumstances. Turkopticon performs an intermediate step in the formation of publics by bringing people together around practical, broadly shared concerns. By creating infrastructures for mutual aid, we bolster the social interchange and interdependency that can become a foundation for a more issue-oriented public. There have been calls in HCI for *representing* interdependence as a way of working towards more ethical and sustainable practices [31]. AMT's labor market, however, individuates by design; workers are independent by default. Turkopticon provides an infrastructure through which workers can engage in *practices of interdependence*, here as mutual aid.

THE AMBIVALENCE OF SUCCESS IN ACTIVIST TECHNOLOGIES

Turkopticon has succeeded in attracting a growing base of users that sustain it as a platform for an information-sharing community. In part because of its practical embeddedness, it has drawn sustained attention to ethical questions in crowdsourcing over the course of its operation. This attention comes not only in the crowdsourcing community, but also in broader public fora. We have been invited to speak at industry meetups and on Commonwealth Club panels on crowdsourcing. We have also attracted attention from journalists writing pieces on crowdsourcing in venues such as *O'Reilly Radar*, *The Sacramento Bee*, *AlterNet,* and *The San Jose Mercury News*. As a media piece, Turkopticon's sustained dissent over the last four years has qualities of adversarial design [15]; the system stands as a visible reminder of the microlabors that sustain crowd platforms. This agonistic reminder disrupts the optimism that surrounds crowdpowered systems.

However, Turkopticon's existence sustains and legitimizes AMT by helping safeguard its workers. AMT relies on an ecosystem of third party developers to provide functional enhancements to AMT (e.g. CrowdFlower, SamaSource, Twitter). Turkopticon is a squeaky but reliable part of this ecosystem. Ideally, however, we hoped that Amazon would change its systems design to include worker safeguards. This has not happened. Instead, Turkopticon has become a piece of software that workers rely on funded through subsidies from academic research – an unsustainable foundation for such a critical tool.

To stay vital, our team plans on developing new media interventions to give the Turkopticon community greater visibility to the press, to policy makers, and to organizers. Through the design of layered infrastructures, we can support complex and overlapping publics that open up questions about possible futures once again.

This paper has offered an account of an activist systems development intervention into the crowdsourcing system AMT. We argued that AMT is predicated on infrastructuring and hiding human labor, rendering it a reliable computational resource for technologists. Based on a "Workers' Bill of Rights" meant to evoke workers' imaginations, we identify hazards of crowdwork and our response as designers to those hazards – Turkopticon. The challenges of developing Turkopticon shows the challenges of developing real-world technologies that intervene in existing, large-scale sociotechnical systems. Such activism takes design out of the studio and into the wild, not only testing the seeds of possible technological futures, but attempting to steer and shift the existing practices and infrastructures of our technological present.

ACKNOWLEDGEMENTS

We dedicate this paper to the memory of Beatriz da Costa, the tactical media artist and professor who pushed us to take the plunge from imagining to building and maintaining. We thank Chris Countryman, Paul Dourish, Gillian Hayes, Lynn Dombrowski, Karen Cheng, Khai Truong, and anonymous reviewers for feedback. This work was supported by NSF Graduate Research Fellowship and NSF award 1025761.

REFERENCES

1. Ackerman, M. 2000. The intellectual challenge of CSCW: The gap between social requirements and technical feasibility. *Human-computer interaction*, 15(2), 179–203.
2. Bardzell, S. 2010. Feminist HCI : Taking Stock and Outlining an Agenda for Design, *Proc. CHI*, 1301–1310.
3. Barley, S.R. and Kunda, G. 2004. *Gurus, hired guns, and warm bodies: itinerant experts in a knowledge economy*. Princeton University Press.

4. Berg, M. 1998. The politics of technology: On bringing social theory into technological design. *ST&HV*, 23(4), 456–490.
5. Bezos, J. 2006. Opening Keynote. *MIT Emerging Technologies Conference*. Accessed: http://video.mit.edu/watch/opening-keynote-and-keynote-interview-with-jeff-bezos-9197/
6. Biewald, L. 2009. "Turkopticon." *Crowdflower Blog*. Accessed: http://blog.crowdflower.com/2009/02/turkopticon/
7. Borning, A. and Muller, M. 2012. Next steps for value sensitive design. *Proc. CHI*, 1125-1134.
8. Bowker, G. & Star, S.L. 2000. *Sorting Things Out: Classification and Its Consequences*. MIT Press.
9. Bruckman, A. and Hudson, J.M. 2005. Using Empirical Data to Reason about Internet Research Ethics. *Proc. ECSCW*, 287-306.
10. Brynjarsdottir, H., Håkansson, M., Pierce, J., Baumer, E., DiSalvo, C., and Sengers, P. 2012. Sustainably unpersuaded. *Proc. CHI*, 947–956.
11. Crenshaw, K. 1991. Mapping the Margins: Intersectionality, Identity Politics, and Violence Against Women of Color. *Stanford Law Review*, 43(6), 1241-1299.
12. Crowdsourced data analysis with Clockwork Raven. Accessed at http://engineering.twitter.com/2012/08/crowdsourced-data-analysis-with.html
13. da Costa, B. and Philip, K., eds. 2008. *Tactical Biopolitics: Art, Activism, Technoscience*. MIT Press.
14. DiSalvo, C. 2009. Design and the Construction of Publics. *Design Issues*, 25(1), 48–63.
15. DiSalvo, C. 2012. *Adversarial Design*. MIT Press.
16. Dourish, P. 2010. HCI and environmental sustainability: the Design of Politics and Politics of Design. *Proc. DIS 2010*, 1–10.
17. Dourish, P. and Mainwaring, S. 2012. Ubicomp's Colonial Impulse. *Proc. Ubicomp*.
18. Felstiner, A. 2010. Working the Crowd : Employment and Labor Law in the Crowdsourcing Industry. *Berkeley Journal of Employment & Labor Law*, 32 (1), 143–204.
19. Garcia, D. and Lovink, G. 1997. The ABC of tactical media. nettime listserv. Accessed: http://www.nettime.org/Lists-Archives/nettime-l-9705/msg00096.html
20. Haraway, D.J. 1990. *Simians, Cyborgs, and Women: The Reinvention of Nature*. Routledge.
21. Hirsch, T. 2009. Learning from activists. *Interactions*, 16(3), 31–33.
22. Ipeirotis, P. 2010. Demographics of Mechanical Turk.. NYU Working Paper No. CEDER-10-01
23. Ipeirotis, P. 2010. Analyzing the Mechanical Turk Marketplace. *XRDS*, 17(2), 16-21.
24. Ipeirotis, P. 2008. Why People Participate in Mechanical Turk? Accessed: http://www.behind-the-enemy-lines.com/2008/03/why-people-participate-on-mechanical.html
25. Jackson, S., Pompe, A., and Krieshok, G. 2011. Things fall apart: maintenance, repair, and technology for education initiatives in rural Namibia. *Proc iConference*, 83–90.
26. Kelty, C. 2012. *Two Bits: The Cultural Significance of Free Software*. Duke University Press.
27. Lampe, C. and Resnick, P. 2004. Slash(dot) and burn. *Proc SIGCHI 2004*, 543–550.
28. Law, E. and Von Ahn, L. 2011. *Human Computation*. Morgan Claypool Publishers.
29. Law, J. 2004. *After method: mess in social science research*. Routledge.
30. LeDantec, C. 2012. Participation and Publics: Supporting Community Engagement, *Proc. CHI 2012*, 1351-1360.
31. Light, A. 2011. Digital interdependence and how to design for it. *Interactions*, 18 (2), 34.
32. Orlikowski, W.J. 1992. The Duality of Technology: Rethinking the Concept of Technology in Organizations. *Organization Science*, 3(3), 398–427.
33. Ross, J., Irani, L., Silberman, M.S., et al. 2010. Who are the crowdworkers?, *EA CHI 2010 (alt.chi)*, 2863-2872.
34. Ruhleder, K. and Star, S.L. 2001. Steps Toward an Ecology of Infrastructure: Design and Access for Large Information Spaces. In J. Yates and J. Van Maanen, eds., *Information Technology and Organizational Transformation: History, Rhetoric, and Practice*. Sage, 305–343.
35. Smith, V. 1997. New Forms of Work Organization. *Annual Review of Sociology*, 23, 315–339.
36. Snow, R., O'Connor, B., Jurafsky, D., & Ng, A.Y. 2008. Cheap and fast---but is it good?: Evaluating non-expert annotations for natural language tasks. *Proc. EMNLP*, 254–263.
37. Star, S.L. and Strauss, A. 1999. Layers of Silence, Arenas of Voice: The Ecology of Visible and Invisible Work. *Proc. CSCW*, 8, 9–30.
38. Sood, S., Antin, J., and Churchill, E. 2012. Profanity use in online communities. *Proc. CHI 2012*, 1481–1490.
39. Suchman, L. 1995. Making Work Visible. *CACM*, 38(9).
40. Suchman, L. 2006. *Human Machine Reconfigurations*, Cambridge Univ. Press.
41. Taylor, A. 2011. Out There. *Proc CHI*, 685–694.
42. TurkWork. http://turkwork.differenceengines.com

Don't Hide in the Crowd! Increasing Social Transparency Between Peer Workers Improves Crowdsourcing Outcomes

Shih-Wen Huang and Wai-Tat Fu
University of Illinois at Urbana-Champaign
Department of Computer Science
Urbana, IL 61801
{shuang51,wfu}@illinois.edu

ABSTRACT
This paper studied how social transparency and different peer-dependent reward schemes (i.e., individual, teamwork, and competition) affect the outcomes of crowdsourcing. The results showed that when social transparency was increased by asking otherwise anonymous workers to share their demographic information (e.g., name, nationality) to the paired worker, they performed significantly better. A more detailed analysis showed that in a teamwork reward scheme, in which the reward of the paired workers depended only on the collective outcomes, increasing social transparency could offset effects of social loafing by making them more accountable to their teammates. In a competition reward scheme, in which workers competed against each other and the reward depended on how much they outperformed their opponent, increasing social transparency could augment effects of social facilitation by providing more incentives for them to outperform their opponent. The results suggested that a careful combination of methods that increase social transparency and different reward schemes can significantly improve crowdsourcing outcomes.

Author Keywords
Crowdsourcing; human computation; social transparency; social facilitation; social loafing

ACM Classification Keywords
H.5.m. Information Interfaces and Presentation (e.g. HCI): Miscellaneous

INTRODUCTION
Crowdsourcing has been proven as an effective way to solve various kinds of problems [8]. One of the most notable examples is the ESP game [26], which recruits people to generate image labels while playing an online game. By 2008, this game had recruited 200,000 players and collected more than 50 million labels [27]. In addition, individuals can also easily recruit online workers from Amazon Mechanical Turk (AMT)[1] to solve problems that are difficult for digital computers (e.g., collecting labeled data for natural language processing [23] and relevance evaluation [1]) at a very low cost. These examples have merely begun to demonstrate the potential of crowdsourcing as a social computing technique that can be applied in a wide range of situations.

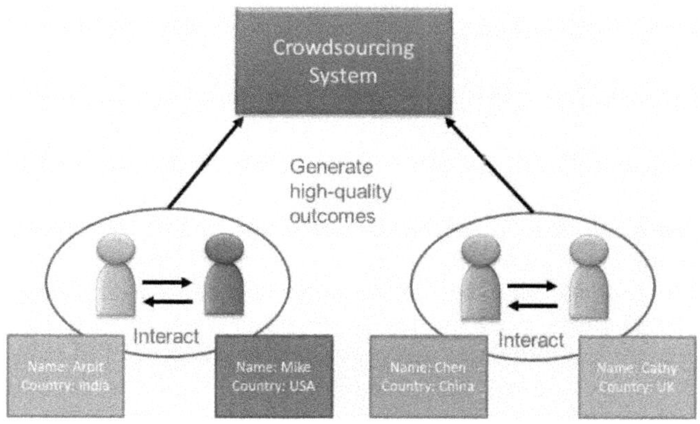

Figure 1. Sharing demographic information between paired workers allows the crowdsourcing system to collect outcomes with higher quality.

However, quality control is still one of the biggest issues for crowdsourcing[2] [11]. For example, although the ESP game can successfully recruit players to create a large amount of image labels, a study [22] showed that many of these are low-quality labels that can be generated by robots with little real world knowledge. Moreover, the reliability of workers recruited from AMT is also questionable. People have found that there are many spammers or even robots in AMT, which greatly reduce the quality of the outputs collected from this platform [8]. As a result, designing mechanisms that can ensure the quality of crowdsourcing outcomes is crucial to its success.

[1] https://www.mturk.com/mturk/welcome

[2] Crowdsourcing and human computation are two highly overlapped fields. Though the foci of these two fields are slightly different, researchers sometimes use these two terms interchangeably. We use the term crowdsourcing throughout because the findings of our study can be applied to diverse applications; however, research in human computation is also highly related to this study. For more discussion about the similarities and differences between crowdsourcing and human computation, please see Quinn *et al.* [21].

Increasing social transparency as a possible way to enhance quality of collaborative work

The term social transparency has been well studied. For example, the survey in Stuart *et al.* [24] provided a framework that defines various kinds of social transparency (i.e., identity transparency, content transparency, and action transparency) in networked information exchange. The kind of social transparency discussed in this paper is similar to the identity transparency according to their definition. Specifically, Stuart *et al.* [24] suggested that identity transparency (e.g., real name, persistent identity in applications) can make online information more useful and better evaluated. For instance, a study [19] on an online suburban community network showed that using real name not only created accountable online information exchange but also helped promote local commerce in the community.

The idea of increasing social transparency to enhance accountability in collaborations was first introduced by Erickson and Kellog [5]. They argued that in the physical world, people make everyday decisions based on various "social cues." Some of these social cues allow people to perceive the extent to which their behavior is acceptable for others (e.g., smiles, frowning, etc), and people often learn to adjust their behavior based on the perception of these social cues. In addition, the more that two persons know each other, the more likely people will be influenced by the social cues. In other words, the availability of social cues often increases the perception that a person is accountable for his or her actions. However, these social cues are often missing when people collaborate with each other remotely through a digital system. To address this problem, they implemented a social translucent system that made social cues salient to the collaborators using the system. They showed that a social translucent system can make the users more aware of the presence of others, and as a result, the users can know that they are accountable for their actions.

Kittur *et al.* [15] studied how social transparency help Wikipedia readers adjust their trust toward the information. They designed WikiDashboard [25], a visualization tool that helps users identify the page that was edited by which editors and when the edits were made. Their study [15] showed that manipulating the editor-accountable visualization significantly affected the trust of the readers. Therefore, they argued that their visualization can improve the trustworthiness of Wikipedia articles. They also mentioned it is possible that this social transparency created by their visualization tool can encourage writers to be more responsible [25]. As a result, the quality of the articles also improves.

In addition, research in social identity theory [20] suggests that identity formation process (e.g., information sharing) makes group members more commit to their group.

These studies have demonstrated that social transparency can effectively improve online collaborative work. Because crowdsourcing also utilizes the power of multiple workers to complete a collective task, it is reasonable for us to hypothesize that increasing social transparency (either between colleagues or between requesters and workers) in crowdsourcing can also enhance outcome quality. To test this hypothesis , we designed a study to test how increasing social transparency would affect the quality of outcomes generated by crowd workers. We are also interested in how social transparency may interact with different reward schemes to influence outcomes. Before we discuss the details of the study, we will first review how different reward schemes can affect the performance of crowd workers below.

Three possible effects of peer-dependent reward schemes on motivating crowd workers

Micro-tasks in crowdsourcing typically are trivial and tedious to workers. Therefore, one notable reason that crowd workers fail to generate high-quality work is the lack of motivation [21]. Therefore, it is important for requesters to design a crowdsourcing system that can offer enough incentives to workers [16]. The most common incentive used to recruit workers in crowdsourcing is monetary reward. Nevertheless, previous research on financial incentives [18] in crowdsourcing suggested that increasing monetary reward seemed to augment the amount of work produced but not the quality. This finding implies that monetary reward alone might not be enough to motivate workers to generate high-quality work. Interestingly, [10] found that making the reward of the workers codependent on each other can significantly increase the quality of their work. Specifically, the crowdsourcing system created by them used the answers of its workers to evaluate future workers of the system. Every worker in the system knew that his/her answer would be used to evaluate the answer of future workers. Therefore, since the chance that two workers generated the same wrong answer was small, if a worker produced a wrong answer, the workers that were evaluated by this erroneous answer could not earn rewards regardless of whether or not they generated the correct answer. Their study showed that workers put more effort in solving the task to prevent other workers from being penalized unjustly. This study suggests that it is possible to design other peer-dependent reward schemes to enhance the performance of crowd workers.

However, not all peer-dependent reward schemes can motivate workers to perform better. Previous research has shown that poor designs of peer-dependent reward schemes in a collaborative work environment could even lead to worse outcomes [12]. We summarized three possible effects of peer-dependent reward schemes between crowd workers on their motivations below:

- **Social loafing:** Previous studies have shown that when individuals work in a group and only the outcome of the group is evaluated, individual performance becomes significantly worse than when they work alone [12]. For example, an experiment showed that when subjects conducted a rope pulling task, individual effort decreased as the group size increased. Harkins [7] argued that because it is difficult to evaluate each individual in the group when working on a collective task, people feel that they can *hide in the crowd* such that there is a diffusion of responsibility from the individuals to the group. As a result, their effort levels tend to drop. Kerr *et al.* [13] argued that people exert less effort when working in groups because they may feel that their inputs are not essential to the collective outputs of the group.

Since crowdsourcing is essentially a large collective task, this phenomenon of *social loafing* can decrease the motivation of workers to do well. Therefore, it is important for researchers to study how social loafing can impact the performance of crowd workers and design mechanisms to mitigate its potential negative effects.

- **Altruistic motives:** In contrast to social loafing, the existence of *altruistic motives* is believed to lead to better performance when workers are encouraged to work collaboratively [10]. Altruistic motives refers to the ideas that workers have the tendency to behave so as to benefit their colleagues, even if the behavior entails a negative utility for themselves. Studies [2, 17] have shown that workers will adjust their effort level when the rewards of other workers depend on them. Previous research [10] also showed that when workers in a crowdsourcing system know that their answers will be used as evaluation standards by the system, they work harder to prevent other crowd workers from being unjustly penalized due to their errors.

- **Social facilitation:** The other possible social effect that encourages workers to generate better crowdsourcing outcomes is *social facilitation*. Social facilitation is an effect occurs when that individuals are motivated to perform better when they know they can be compared to others[3]. A study [7] showed that when conducting a brainstorming task, subjects who were paired with another subject and knew their individual work would be evaluated generated significantly more ideas than subjects who worked alone. Harkins [7] suggested that social facilitation can be conceived as the complement of social loafing. That is, when the outcomes of each individual in the group are evaluable, the workers are motivated to outperform other members in the group. As a result, the collective outputs of the entire group are also better. Study [17] also highlighted that worker effort is positively related to the performance of workers who see the work being executed. Similarly, social comparison theory [6] suggests that people have the tendency to compare their own work to others. These results suggest that social facilitation can effectively enhance individual performance in collaborative work.

To summarize, previous research has shown that a set of complex social effects may interact to influence the motivation of the workers. It is not clear, however, how directly manipulating social transparency and reward schemes may make each of these social effects more or less salient, such that a designer of a crowdsoucing system can more reliably predict how these effects can be utilized to improve outcomes. To this end, we design our experiments by focusing on two common reward schemes: a teamwork scheme and a competition scheme. In a teamwork scheme, in which workers in a group are rewarded based on the collective outcomes of the group, there are two possible effects that may influence the motivation of the workers. First, social loafing can negatively impact the performance of workers because they feel that they can hide in the crowd and rely on their partner's effort. If this is the case, we should find that social loafing is more salient when a worker perceives that their partner is already at a high level of performance. In such situation, the worker may not be motivated to put extra effort in the task as the collective outcome is likely to be good. In contrast, a second factor, altruistic motives, can positively impact the performance of workers in the same reward scheme because a worker may not want their partner to feel that his or her poor performance may impact their collective reward. If this is the case, we should find that altruistic motives may be more salient when social transparency is high, as the perception of the presence of their partner may enhance the effect of altruistic motives. In a competition scheme, in which rewards of workers depend on the differences between the outcomes of the workers and their colleagues, it is possible that social facilitation can improve their performance because they are motivated to outperform each other. If this is the case, we should find that pairing with a worker with a high level of performance should motivate a worker to work even harder.

To investigate how different peer-dependent reward schemes improve of degrade the performance or crowd workers, we created three conditions that differ in the reward schemes. Specifically, the way the reward of the workers in our experiment depend on 1) *only the worker's performance*, 2) *the collective outcomes of paired workers*, or 3) *the difference between the performance of paired workers*.

EXPERIMENTAL DESIGN

We used a 3x2 design to see how different peer-dependent reward schemes and social transparency levels affect the performance of crowd workers. 300 subjects were recruited from AMT. We asked the workers to perform tasks individually (**I**), paired with another worker as a team (**T**), and competitively against another paired worker (**C**). Half of the workers worked anonymously (**A**), and the other half of them were asked to report their demographic information (i.e., name, gender, age, and nationality) (**D**). When the workers who revealed their demographic information were paired with another worker, their demographic information was shared with their paired workers. We also examined if there was any interaction effect between social transparency levels and reward schemes.

Noun counting task

The workers in our experiment were asked to count the words with a particular part-of-speech (noun) in a list of 30 words. Each word in the word list had equal probabilities to be a noun or not a noun. There were two advantages of this task that made it a very good test-bed for us to examine how the factors affected the quality of the outcomes. First, it had a ground truth (objectively correct answer) to serve as the gold standard, making it feasible to measure the quality of an answer by observing the difference between the answer and the

[3]There was a controversy in the literature whether social facilitation includes solely the mere presence of others [28] or should also include comparisons between peers [7]. In this paper, we adopted Harkins' [7] definition of social facilitation, which includes the effect of peer comparison.

gold standard. Moreover, the workers needed to put in a certain level of effort to solve the task, and to a large extent, outcome quality increases with the level of effort. This task is also representative of the tasks used in previous crowdsourcing systems (e.g., [14, 23]).

To evaluate the performance of the workers, we first computed the label accuracy of each collected label. The label accuracy shows how close the label is to the gold standard answer. Therefore, the formula for label accuracy is:

$$Label\ Accuracy = 1 - \frac{|N_{GS} - N_{worker}|}{Max(30 - N_{GS}, N_{GS})}$$

where N_{GS} is the correct number of nouns in the list and N_{worker} is the number of nouns in the list reported by the worker. Therefore, the numerator of the second term in the formula is the distance between the label generated by the worker and the gold standard answer, and the denominator is the distance between the worst possible answer and the gold standard answer. (If $N_{GS} > 15$, the worst possible answer is 0; otherwise, it is 30.) Therefore, the label accuracy is a number between 1 and 0, where 1 represents that the label is exactly the same as the gold standard, and 0 means that the answer is the worst possible answer. Then, the average label accuracy of each worker was computed by averaging the label accuracy of the ten labels generated by the worker. We used the average label accuracy of the workers to measure their work quality.

Variable 1: Peer-dependent reward schemes

In our experiment, we compared the performance of workers under three different peer-dependent reward schemes:

- **Individual (I):** This system was used to imitate traditional crowdsourcing systems, where the bonus of workers only depends on their own performance. Therefore, in this system, worker performed the task individually, and their bonus did not depend on other peer workers.
- **Teamwork (T):** The workers within this reward scheme were paired with another worker as a team. Their bonus was decided by the average of the performance of both workers. In other words, the workers on a team were codependent on each other because only the collective outcomes were evaluated. This allowed us to examine whether social loafing (negative) or altruistic motives (positive) really created an effect on worker performance in a team environment.
- **Competition (C):** This reward scheme aims to test the effect of social facilitation. The workers under competition reward scheme were also paired with another worker. However, unlike the previous condition, the paired workers were opponents. The bonus of a worker was decided by the positive difference between the worker and his/her opponent.[4] Therefore, the workers would have the incentives to outperform their opponents in order to earn more monetary reward.

[4]The worker could not earn bonus if his/her performance was worse than the opponent.

Variable 2: Social transparency levels

In our experiment, we also controlled the levels of social transparency of the workers. The two levels of social transparency used in our experiment were the following:

- **Anonymous (A):** This was the lowest level of social transparency; the only information shared by workers and the system was the worker ID in AMT. If the system paired the workers, the paired workers cannot get any information from each other.
- **Demographic information revealed (D):** Under this level of social transparency, the workers were asked to reveal their demographic information, which included their name, gender, age, and nationality. When the workers worked with another worker, this information was also shared with their teammate or opponent.

Subject recruitment on Amazon Mechanical Turk

We published our HITs on AMT from 8/25/2012 to 9/4/2012. The title and the description of these HITs were both "Count the nouns in a word list". We did not require our workers to pass any qualification tests. The price tags for the HITs were $0.05, which were the rewards the workers could earn regardless of their performance. On the HIT page, we provided a link to route the workers to our experiment website and a text area for the workers to enter an eight-digit completion code. When the workers completed their jobs, our website showed them the total bonus they could earn for their performance and the unique completion code that they would have to enter on the original HIT page on AMT. We then paid the workers both of their rewards (performance independent) and bonuses (performance codependent) based on the completion codes they entered. The system also automatically rejected repeated workers by checking if their AMT worker ID already existed in the database.

Experimental interface

When the workers visited the experiment website, they were randomly assigned to one of the 6 conditions (**IA, TA, CA, ID, TD,** or **CD**). On the introduction page (Figure 2.a), the system told the workers that they had to answer 10 questions about counting the nouns in a word list[5]. It also showed how the bonuses for the workers were decided; the exact words we used for each condition in the introduction were as follows:

- **IA, ID:** When you finish the task, you can earn a bonus which is your accuracy times 0.1. EX: If your accuracy is 0.73, you can earn $0.07 bonus (rounded to the closest 0.01 level)
- **TA, TD:** You will be paired with another worker in the system as a team. Your bonus will be decided by the average of your accuracy times 0.1. EX: If your teammate's accuracy is 0.93 and your accuracy is 0.53. The average

[5]We used the same 10 word lists for all workers. One possible concern is that some of the workers released the information to others. However, we found that the correlation between the performance and the arrival time of the worker was very low ($r = 0.04$), which shows that the workers should not get extra information because the average accuracy didn't go up.

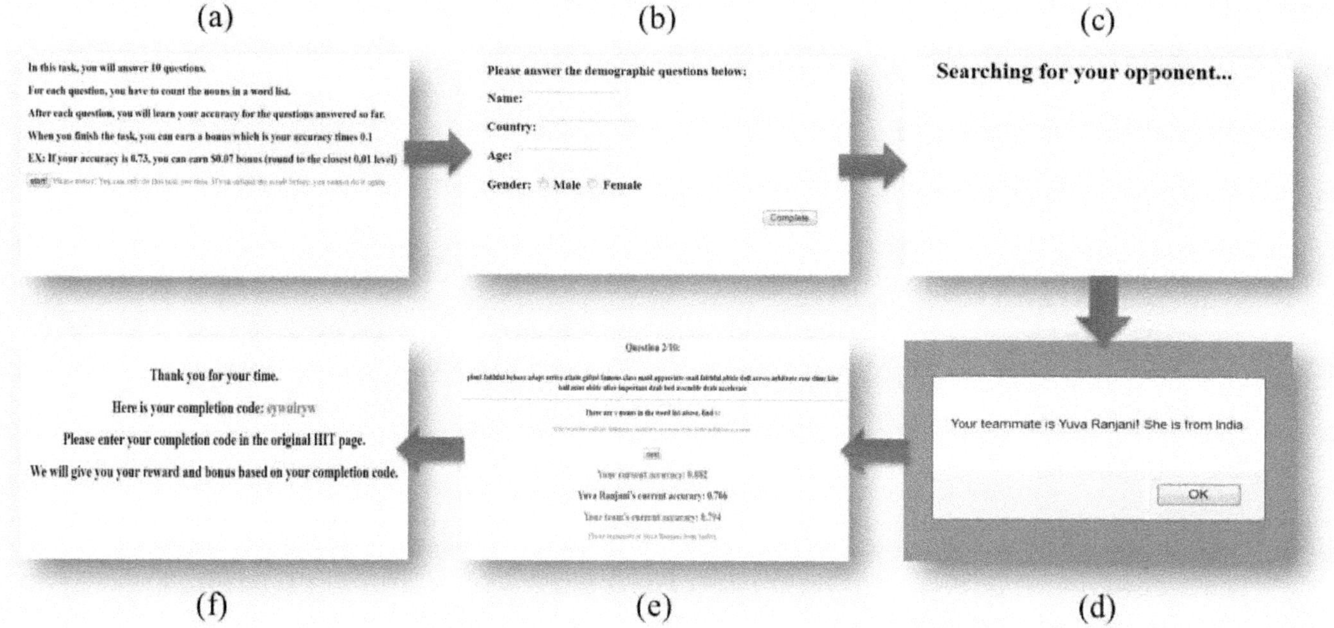

Figure 2. Experimental interfaces used in our experiment: (a) Introduction page (b) Demographic information collection (c) Asynchronous interaction design (d) Information sharing between workers (e) Noun counting page (f) Completion page

accuracy of your team is 0.73. Therefore, you and your teammate can get $0.07 bonus each (rounded to the closest 0.01 level)

- **CA, CD:** Another worker will be chosen to be your opponent. Your bonus will be the positive difference between your accuracy and your opponent's times 0.5. EX: If your opponent's accuracy is 0.79 and yours is 0.93, your bonus will be 0.14*0.5=0.07 (rounded to the closest 0.01 level) However, if your performance is worse than your opponent, you won't earn the bonus.[6]

After workers read the introduction, those that needed to reveal their demographic information (**ID, TD,** and **CD**) were asked to enter their information (Figure 2.b). The anonymous workers (**IA, TA,** and **CA**) skipped this step and went to the next step directly.

	IA	ID	TA	TD	CA	CD
Introduction Page	✓	✓	✓	✓	✓	✓
Demographic Info Collection	✗	✓	✗	✓	✗	✓
Asynchronous Interaction Design	✗	✗	✓	✓	✓	✓
Info Sharing between workers	✗	✗	✗	✓	✗	✓
Noun Counting Page	✓	✓	✓	✓	✓	✓
Completion Page	✓	✓	✓	✓	✓	✓

Figure 3. Summary of experimental interfaces used in the six conditions.

Then, we used an asynchronous interaction design [9] to make workers in conditions **TA, CA, TD,** and **CD** feel that they were matched with another worker. Instead of really matching the workers, we provided recorded data from a randomly selected previous worker in the same condition[7]. We adopted this asynchronous interaction design to prevent the workers from gaming the system by starting multiple tasks concurrently in the experiment website, which allowed them to be paired with themselves. This design has been adopted by many GWAPs (e.g., ESP game), and previous research [9] has shown that this asynchronous interaction design can effectively create the perception that workers are actually working with another worker concurrently. In this design, the workers were redirected to a worker matching page (Figure 2.c). This page paused for a few seconds and indicated that the system was trying to match the worker with another worker (either teammate or opponent). These workers also were redirected to a waiting page after each question to wait for the paired worker to respond. The workers who revealed their demographic information and were paired with another worker (**TD** and **CD**) also received a message that showed the demographic information of their paired worker before the task began (Figure 2.d).

After that, the workers in all conditions would see the interface for performing the noun counting task (Figure 2.e). In

[6]This design was based on a pilot study that an average worker's accuracy is around 0.8; therefore, it adjusted the amount of bonus to be similar to other conditions.

[7]The first worker in the paired conditions received data from randomly selected individual worker

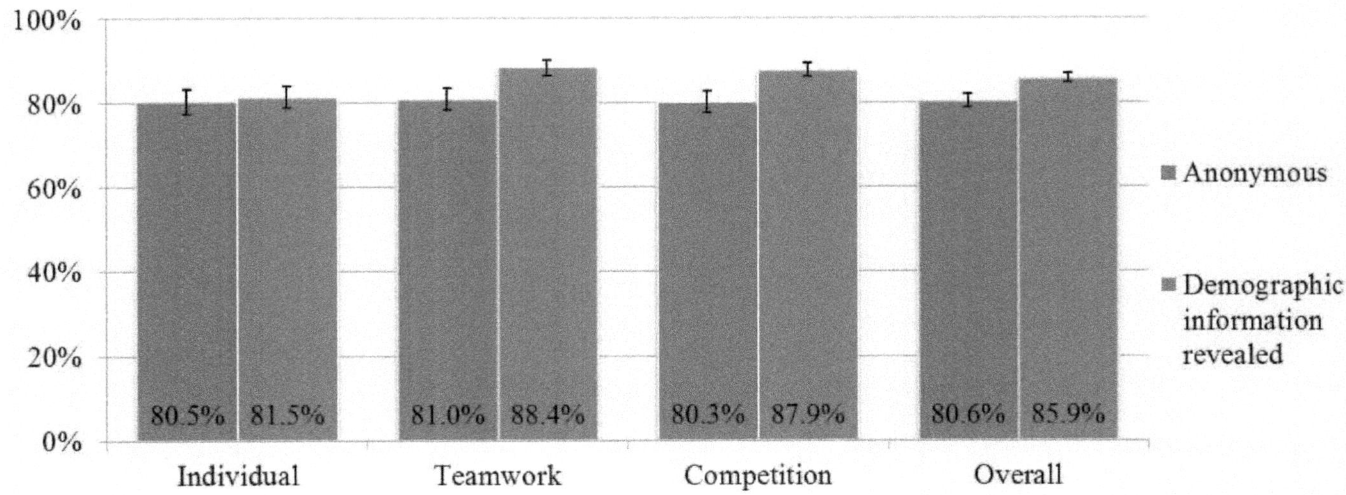

Figure 4. The mean of the average label accuracies of the workers under different peer-dependent reward schemes and social transparency levels (with standard error). In general, the workers who revealed their demographic information outperformed the ones who worked anonymously.

	Individual vs. Teamwork	Individual vs. Competition	Teamwork vs. Competition
Anonymous	80.5%(20.6%) vs. 81.0%(17.6%) (t(96) = 0.13, p = 0.45)	80.5%(20.6%) vs. 80.3%(18.6%) (t(97) = 0.06, p = 0.48)	81.0%(17.6%) vs. 80.3%(18.6%) (t(98) = 0.20, p = 0.42)
Demographic info. revealed	81.5%(17.6%) vs. 88.4%(13.0%)* (t(90) = 2.25, p < 0.02)	81.5%(17.6%) vs. 87.9%(11.7%)* (t(86) = 2.15, p < 0.02)	88.4%(13.0%) vs. 87.9%(11.7%) (t(97) = 0.22, p = 0.41)

Table 1. The comparison between the mean (standard deviation) of the average label accuracy of workers with different peer-dependent reward schemes with social transparency level fixed and their t-test statistics. The significant results (p-value < 0.05) are marked with *.

the upper part of the interface, the system showed a word list and an input box for them to provide their answers. The system specifically told the workers to count a word as a noun if one of its definitions is a noun because it is possible for a word to have multiple definitions and only some of them are nouns. This made the gold standard answer of the question clearer to the workers. At the bottom part of the interface, it showed the workers their current label accuracy for the questions they had answered. The workers within the teamwork reward scheme could see their teammate's current label accuracy and the current average label accuracy for their team (**TA** and **TD**). The workers under the competition reward scheme could see their opponent's current label accuracy and the current difference between them (**CA** and **CD**). The workers that were paired with another worker and shared demographic information could also see their colleague's information at the bottom of the interface (**TD** and **CD**).

Finally, after the workers completed 10 questions, they would be redirected to the completion page that showed the completion code (Figure 2.f). The design of the experimental interface of the six conditions is summarized in Figure 3.

RESULTS

300 subjects (50 subjects per treatment) were recruited from AMT; each of them completed 10 noun counting tasks and generated 10 labels; therefore, 3,000 labels (500 labels per treatment) were collected for our results analysis.

We conducted a 3X2 Two-Way ANOVA to see if there were significant effects from the peer-dependent reward schemes, social transparency levels, and their interaction. The results showed that social transparency level did significantly affect the performance of workers ($F(1, 294) = 7.58, p < 0.01$). However, the effect of peer-dependent reward schemes was not significant ($F(2, 294) = 1.41, p = 0.24$). Moreover, the effect of the interactions between the two factors was also insignificant ($F(2, 294) = 1.26, p = 0.28$).

Social transparency effectively improved outcome quality of crowdsourcing

The mean of the average label accuracies for the workers with different social transparency levels and peer-dependent reward schemes are summarized in Figure 4. The results show that the average label accuracy of the workers who revealed their demographic information ($\mu = 85.9\%$, $SD = 14.5\%$) was significantly higher than those who did not ($\mu = 80.6\%$, $SD = 18.9\%$) ($t(280) = 2.75$, $p < 0.01$). This result supports our hypothesis that increasing the social transparency of workers makes them more accountable. Therefore, the quality of outcomes of crowdsourcing system also became better.

Moreover, although the ANOVA shows that the interaction effect between social transparency levels and peer-dependent reward schemes was not significant, we did find some interesting patterns in the result. Specifically, when the workers did not reveal their demographic information, there were no significant differences between the workers under the three reward schemes, which means that neither teamwork nor competition motivated the workers to perform better when the workers knew that they were working anonymously.

On the other hand, when the workers revealed their demographic information, the differences between the workers whose rewards were codependent on their peers and those who worked individually became significant (i.e., between **TA** and **TD** and between **CA** and **CD**). The average label accuracies of the workers who worked as a team and competed against each other were both significantly higher than individual workers. (The comparisons and their t-test statistics are summarized in Table 1)

These differences, of course, need to be interpreted cautiously, as the overall interaction effect between social transparency levels and peer-dependent reward schemes was not significant. Nevertheless, we can see that social transparency had a better ability to enhance outcome quality when the workers felt that their information was shared with their colleagues. In contrast, if they felt that their information was only shared with the system (requester), social transparency did not have a significant effect on enhancing the performance of crowd workers.

Effects of different peer-dependent reward schemes

The overall performance of the workers suggests that the two different peer-dependent reward schemes (i.e., teamwork and competition) used in our experiment had no significant difference on enhancing worker performance. They both worked well when the workers revealed their demographic information and did not have significant effects when workers worked anonymously.

To gain more insight about how these two reward schemes differed, we measured how workers reacted to feedback with different accuracy levels. If social loafing created a negative effect on workers in teamwork conditions, then one would expect that when workers received high-accuracy feedback from their teammates, their effort levels should decrease because they already could earn a high bonus by relying on the performance of their teammates. In contrast, workers who received high-accuracy feedback from their opponents in the competition conditions should perform better because social facilitation suggests that workers were motivated to outperform their colleagues.

To test if these hypotheses are true, we divided the feedback into two levels (high, low) using the median label accuracy of all feedback.[8] We then calculated the average label accuracy of the next question based on the feedback accuracy level of the previous question. We then performed a three-way ANOVA on accuracies with label accuracy level (low vs high), reward schemes (teamwork vs competition), and social transparency (anonymous vs sharing demographic information) as independent variables. Results showed that the three-way interaction was significant ($F(1, 1782) = 6.831, p < 0.01$). As shown in Figure 5 & 6, the three-way interaction was caused by the differential effects of social transparency on how workers performed in each reward scheme when received with a low or high accuracy feedback. We will performed separate two-way ANOVAs on these to understand this three-way interaction below.

[8]Across all conditions, 88.5%.

Social loafing made workers who received high-accuracy feedback from teammate perform worse

A 2X2 two-Way ANOVA (social transparency level and feedback accuracy level) for the workers who cooperated with the paired worker (teamwork) showed that social transparency significantly affected the performance of the workers ($F(1, 896) = 34.23, p < 0.01$). Moreover, the effect of the accuracy level of feedback from teammates was also significant ($F(1, 896) = 6.43, p < 0.02$). However, the effect of the interaction of these two factors was not significant ($F(1, 896) = 0.15, p = 0.70$).

This result has two important implications. First, it indicates that social loafing negatively affected worker performance in teamwork conditions. That is, team members were less diligent when they found that they could earn a higher bonus because their teammates already performed very well. Second, social transparency between team members can enhance the performance of the workers regardless of their teammates' performance. This shows that sharing demographic information between team members increased social transparency, which possibly increased the motivation of the workers through altruistic motives to put more effort into the task. As a result, simply asking workers to share demographic information before the tasks was enough to motivate workers in teamwork conditions to perform better than workers in individual conditions.

Social transparency enhanced social facilitation in competition conditions

A 2X2 Two-Way ANOVA (social transparency level and feedback accuracy level) for the workers who competed against their paired worker (competition) showed that the effect of social transparency was significant ($F(1, 896) = 20.92, p < 0.01$). However, the accuracy level of the feedback from opponents did not significantly affect the average label accuracy of workers ($F(1, 896) = 0.12, p = 0.91$). Finally, the effect of the interaction between these two factors was significant ($F(1, 896) = 17.19, p < 0.01$). Simple effects analysis showed that the difference between low and high accuracy of feedback was significant in both the anonymous condition ($t(444) = 3.04, p < 0.001$) and in the high social transparency condition ($t(425) = 2.09, p < 0.05$)).

This interesting result shows that when workers competed against each other anonymously, performance was better when they received a low accuracy feedback. However, when the social transparency was high, their performance was significantly higher when they received a high accuracy feedback. This suggested that social transparency had a significant interaction with the level of accuracy of the feedback provided by their opponents in the competition reward scheme. It appears that social transparency was key to the social facilitation in the competition conditions. It is possible that when the workers did not share their information with

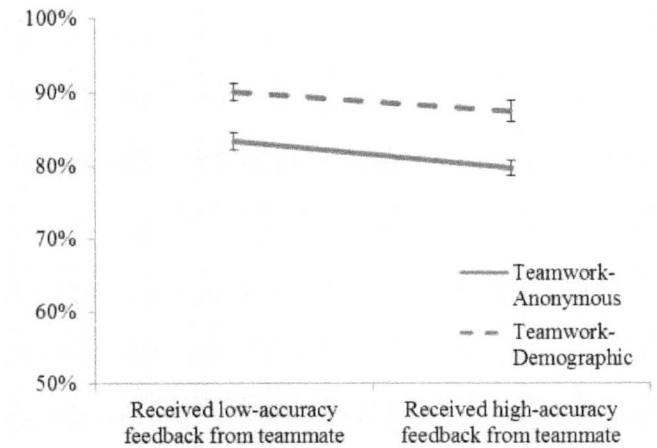

Figure 5. When workers who worked in the teamwork condition received high-accuracy feedback from teammates, they performed significantly worse, which validates the negative effect of social loafing on crowd workers.

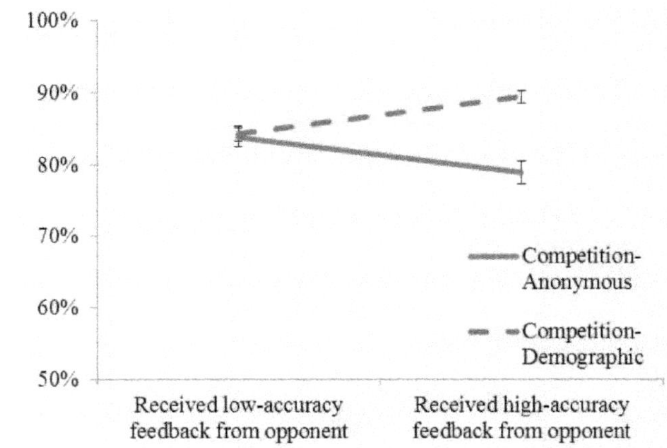

Figure 6. Workers who shared their demographic information performed significantly better when they received high-accuracy feedback from opponents. This shows that social transparency helped enhance the effect of social facilitation.

each other, they in general were less motivated than when social transparency was high. As a result, they were more likely to work harder when they received a low accuracy feedback than when they received a high accuracy feedback. On the other hand, our analysis showed that when the workers received high-accuracy feedback from their opponent, they were motivated to perform even better than their opponents. This led to better overall performance for workers in the high social transparency competition conditions.

DISCUSSION

Social transparency makes social interactions between crowd workers more realistic

Our analysis shows that revealing demographic information can increase social transparency, thereby motivating workers to put more effort into the task when interacting with their teammates. Moreover, in a competition reward scheme, workers who share their information also have more incentives to outperform each other. This suggests that social transparency can make social interactions between crowd workers more engaging. Therefore, it is possible that the strategy of increasing social transparency can be applied to other reward schemes that hinge on social interactions between crowd workers. For example, this strategy can be applied to the external assessment scheme proposed by Dow *et al.* [3]. Asking crowd workers who served as assessors to provide their own personal information is possible to make them provide more responsible feedback and assessment and therefore became better shepherds for other workers. Furthermore, workers in peer consistency evaluation [?] can also work harder if they know that their work will be used as evaluation standards with their personal information attached. We believe that the findings of our experiment could be applied to various mechanism designs that involve social interaction between workers.

Better utilizing the power of altruistic motives

When workers collaborated with a teammate, the workers with a high-accuracy teammate performed worse than those with a low-accuracy partner regardless of whether they revealed their demographic information or not. This shows that the effect of social loafing was stronger than the effect of altruistic motives when the bonuses depend on the collective outcomes. However, this does not mean that altruistic motives cannot improve worker performance. In future, mechanisms that better utilize altruistic motives and prevent the system from suffering social loafing could be designed. For instance, the system could make workers feel that their performance can affect the bonus of other workers but does not let them benefit from the good performance of others (e.g., the altruistic motives condition used in [10]). This would allow us to separate the effects of social loafing and altruistic motives so that the system could better utilize the power of altruistic motives.

How does the original motivation influence the effect of social transparency?

The results of our experiments show that social transparency between paired workers made them perform significantly better. However, a limitation to our study is that we didn't vary the level of financial incentive or the task design. Therefore, it is not clear if the result of our experiment can be applied to diverse settings. Especially, the task used in our experiment offered only a small amount of payment and allowed workers to guess the answer without putting much effort. This could make our experiment attract some spammers which skewed the results. As a result, it is possible that the mechanism of reducing anonymity used in our experiment only works for workers with low motivation.

Though this is an important limitation to our study, given the random assignment, if there really was such effect, it should had influence all the conditions[9]. Since we have found some

[9] We tested if there was a selection effect by calculating the drop-out rates (the percentages of participants dropped after they saw the instruction). It shows that there was no significant difference between conditions.

significant differences between conditions, the effects should not affect the comparisons presented in this paper.

In the future, it is valuable to vary the settings of our experiment to see if workers with different original motivation react to the mechanism of reducing anonymity.

Privacy issues and utilizing social translucence

The results of our experiment showed that social transparency between paired workers (i.e., sharing workers demographic information) significantly improved outcome quality. However, increasing social transparency between crowd workers also raised the concern for privacy issues [4]. Some online labor markets do not allow requesters to gather personal information from workers in order to protect the workers. For example, AMT prohibits requesters to collect personal identifiable information[10] (e.g., email) from workers. Reducing the anonymity of crowd workers might even make some of them unwilling to work on HITs. This could decrease the efficiency, which is one of the biggest advantages of crowdsourcing.

One possible way to address this issue is to utilize the idea of social translucence as mentioned in Erickson *et al.* [4], in which they designed graphical interfaces that presented only the social cues of the colleagues without sharing their identifiable information. This could help requesters ensure outcome quality by strengthening the social connections between workers and preventing the workers from feeling that their privacy was invaded. We believe this "virtual workspace" idea can be useful to crowdsourcing researchers and practitioners and is worth further investigation in the future.

CONCLUSIONS AND FUTURE WORK

This paper found that increasing social transparency between workers effectively enhanced the quality of crowdsourcing outcomes. That is, when workers were asked to provide their demographic information (i.e., name, nationality, gender, and age) to their teammates or opponents, they performed significantly better than those who worked anonymously. Since there are many possible social interactions between the workers in a crowdsourcing system, we believe our findings present a novel way to enhance outcome quality of crowdsourcing systems.

Moreover, we found that social loafing created a negative effect on the performance of team members. When the workers received high-accuracy feedback from their teammates, they put less effort in their work because they realized that they could already reap a bonus based on the performance of their teammate. However, social transparency was able to make the workers more accountable to their teammates, so the workers performed significantly better when they revealed demographic information to their teammates.

In addition, our results suggest that social transparency also made the effect of social facilitation significant. When two anonymous workers competed against each other, the workers were not motivated to perform better. In contrast, when the paired workers shared their information, the workers had more incentive to outperform their opponents. As a result, when they received high-accuracy feedback from their opponent, the worker put more effort in performing better. This made the workers within the competition reward scheme perform significantly better than those who work individually.

[10]https://requester.mturk.com/help/faq

These results suggest that designing various peer-dependent reward schemes can successfully motivate workers to generate outcomes of higher quality. Since previous research [18] has proven that increasing financial incentive does not always motivate workers to perform better, the reward schemes that utilize the existence of peer workers can be both more useful and more cost-effective.

In future studies, we would like to tease out the effects of self-identifiability and peer-identifiability. The information sharing conditions share both the information of the worker and his/her peer. This makes it difficult to know if the better performance is because of the worker shared the information or learned the information from the peer. Therefore, separating the effects will help us gain more insight on how social transparency affect the motivation of crowds. In addition, we would like to examine whether strategically selecting the paired workers can further enhance the performance of crowd workers. Previous research [26] has shown that it is not necessary to really pair two online workers to create social interaction. Using interface design (i.e., worker searching page and worker waiting page) alone can make workers feel that other workers are working with them concurrently. This design allows the system to actively select the opponents or teammates for the workers. For example, since our results have shown that high-accuracy feedback from opponents can motivate the workers in competition conditions perform better, we can strategically select one of the high-accuracy workers as an opponent to the new worker. In addition, we can also deliberately select one of the workers with low-accuracy to be the teammate of the new worker in teamwork mode to reduce the effect of social loafing. Moreover, it is also possible to vary the level of financial incentive to see how it affects the performance of workers with different social transparency levels. The higher financial incentive can make the workers more accountable for their actions, but it also can reduce the intrinsic value of the workers and makes the effect of social loafing even stronger. To understand the effect, a systematic study that involves different levels of financial incentive can be conducted to tease apart the complex interactions of these effects.

ACKNOWLEDGEMENTS

Many thanks to the anonymous reviewers for their valuable comments for us to improve the earlier draft of this work. This paper is also benefited from the discussion with Pei-Fen Tu, Jessie Chin, and Vera Liao.

REFERENCES

1. Alonso, O., Rose, D. E., and Stewart, B. Crowdsourcing for relevance evaluation. *SIGIR Forum 42*, 2 (Nov. 2008), 9–15.

2. Bandiera, O., Barankay, I., and Rasul, I. Social preferences and the response to incentives: Evidence

from personnel data. *The Quarterly Journal of Economics 120*, 3 (2005), 917–962.

3. Dow, S., Kulkarni, A., Klemmer, S., and Hartmann, B. Shepherding the crowd yields better work. In *Proceedings of the ACM 2012 conference on Computer Supported Cooperative Work*, CSCW '12, ACM (2012), 1013–1022.
4. Erickson, T., Halverson, C., Kellogg, W. A., Laff, M., and Wolf, T. Social translucence: designing social infrastructures that make collective activity visible. *Commun. ACM 45*, 4 (Apr. 2002), 40–44.
5. Erickson, T., and Kellogg, W. A. Social translucence: an approach to designing systems that support social processes. *ACM Trans. Comput.-Hum. Interact. 7*, 1 (Mar. 2000), 59–83.
6. Festinger, L. A theory of social comparison processes. *Human relations 7*, 2 (1954), 117–140.
7. Harkins, S. G. Social loafing and social facilitation. *Journal of Experimental Social Psychology 23*, 1 (1987), 1 – 18.
8. Howe, J. The rise of crowdsourcing. *Wired Magazine* (06 2006).
9. Huang, S.-W., and Fu, W.-T. Systematic analysis of output agreement games: Effects of gaming environment, social interaction, and feedback. In *Proceedings of HCOMP12: The 4th Workshop on Human Computation* (2012).
10. Huang, S.-W., and Fu, W.-T. Enhancing reliability using peer consistency evaluation in human computation. In *Proceedings of the ACM 2013 conference on Computer Supported Cooperative Work*, CSCW '13, ACM (2013).
11. Ipeirotis, P. G., Provost, F., and Wang, J. Quality management on amazon mechanical turk. In *Proceedings of the ACM SIGKDD Workshop on Human Computation*, HCOMP '10, ACM (2010), 64–67.
12. Karau, S., and Williams, K. Social loafing: A meta-analytic review and theoretical integration. *Journal of Personality and Social Psychology 65*, 4 (1993), 681–706.
13. Kerr, N. L. Motivation losses in small groups: A social dilemma analysis. *Journal of Personality and Social Psychology 45* (1983), 819–828.
14. Kittur, A., Smus, B., Khamkar, S., and Kraut, R. E. Crowdforge: crowdsourcing complex work. In *Proceedings of the 24th annual ACM symposium on User interface software and technology*, UIST '11, ACM (2011), 43–52.
15. Kittur, A., Suh, B., and Chi, E. H. Can you ever trust a wiki?: impacting perceived trustworthiness in wikipedia. In *Proceedings of the 2008 ACM conference on Computer supported cooperative work*, CSCW '08, ACM (2008), 477–480.
16. Law, E., and Von Ahn, L. *Human Computation.* Synthesis Lectures on Artificial Intelligence and Machine Learning. Morgan & Claypool Publishers, 2011.
17. Mas, A., and Moretti, E. Peers at work. Working Paper 12508, National Bureau of Economic Research, September 2006.
18. Mason, W., and Watts, D. J. Financial incentives and the "performance of crowds". *SIGKDD Explor. Newsl. 11*, 2 (May 2010), 100–108.
19. Millen, D. R., and Patterson, J. F. Identity disclosure and the creation of social capital. In *CHI '03 extended abstracts on Human factors in computing systems*, CHI EA '03, ACM (2003), 720–721.
20. Postmes, T., Spears, R., Lee, A., and Novak, R. Individuality and social influence in groups: inductive and deductive routes to group identity. *Journal of personality and social psychology 89*, 5 (2005), 747.
21. Quinn, A. J., and Bederson, B. B. Human computation: a survey and taxonomy of a growing field. In *Proceedings of the 2011 annual conference on Human factors in computing systems*, CHI '11, ACM (2011), 1403–1412.
22. Robertson, S., Vojnovic, M., and Weber, I. Rethinking the esp game. In *Proceedings of the 27th international conference extended abstracts on Human factors in computing systems*, CHI EA '09, ACM (2009), 3937–3942.
23. Snow, R., O'Connor, B., Jurafsky, D., and Ng, A. Y. Cheap and fast—but is it good?: evaluating non-expert annotations for natural language tasks. In *Proceedings of the Conference on Empirical Methods in Natural Language Processing*, EMNLP '08, Association for Computational Linguistics (Stroudsburg, PA, USA, 2008), 254–263.
24. Stuart, H. C., Dabbish, L., Kiesler, S., Kinnaird, P., and Kang, R. Social transparency in networked information exchange: a theoretical framework. In *Proceedings of the ACM 2012 conference on Computer Supported Cooperative Work*, CSCW '12, ACM (2012), 451–460.
25. Suh, B., Chi, E. H., Kittur, A., and Pendleton, B. A. Lifting the veil: improving accountability and social transparency in wikipedia with wikidashboard. In *Proceedings of the twenty-sixth annual SIGCHI conference on Human factors in computing systems*, CHI '08 (2008).
26. von Ahn, L., and Dabbish, L. Labeling images with a computer game. In *Proceedings of the SIGCHI conference on Human factors in computing systems*, CHI '04, ACM (2004), 319–326.
27. von Ahn, L., and Dabbish, L. Designing games with a purpose. *Commun. ACM 51* (Aug. 2008), 58–67.
28. Zajonc, R. Social facilitation. *Science 17* (1965), 65.

Combining Crowdsourcing and Google Street View to Identify Street-level Accessibility Problems

Kotaro Hara, Victoria Le, Jon E. Froehlich
Human-Computer Interaction Lab (HCIL)
Computer Science Department, University of Maryland, College Park
{kotaro, jonf}@cs.umd.edu; vnle@umd.edu

(a) *Object in Path* (b) *No Curb Ramp* (c) *Surface Problem* (d) *Prematurely Ending Sidewalk*

Figure 1: In this paper, we propose and investigate the use of crowdsourcing to find, label, and assess sidewalk accessibility problems in Google Streetview (GSV) imagery. The GSV images and annotations above are from our experiments with Mechanical Turk crowd workers.

ABSTRACT
Poorly maintained sidewalks, missing curb ramps, and other obstacles pose considerable accessibility challenges; however, there are currently few, if any, mechanisms to determine accessible areas of a city *a priori*. In this paper, we investigate the feasibility of using untrained crowd workers from Amazon Mechanical Turk (turkers) to find, label, and assess sidewalk accessibility problems in Google Street View imagery. We report on two studies: Study 1 examines the feasibility of this labeling task with six dedicated labelers including three wheelchair users; Study 2 investigates the comparative performance of turkers. In all, we collected 13,379 labels and 19,189 verification labels from a total of 402 turkers. We show that turkers are capable of determining the presence of an accessibility problem with 81% accuracy. With simple quality control methods, this number increases to 93%. Our work demonstrates a promising new, highly scalable method for acquiring knowledge about sidewalk accessibility.

Author Keywords
Crowdsourcing accessibility; accessible urban navigation; Google Street View; Mechanical Turk; image labeling

ACM Classification Keywords
H.5.m. Information interfaces and presentation (e.g., HCI)

INTRODUCTION
According to the most recent US Census (2010), roughly 30.6 million individuals have physical disabilities that affect their ambulatory activities [32]. Of these, nearly half report using an assistive aid such as a wheelchair (3.6 million) or a cane, crutches, or walker (11.6 million) [32]. Despite aggressive civil rights legislation for Americans with disabilities (*e.g.*, [3, 21]), many city streets, sidewalks, and businesses in the US remain inaccessible [24].

The problem is not just that sidewalk accessibility fundamentally affects *where* and *how* people travel in cities but also that there are few, if any, mechanisms to determine accessible areas of a city *a priori*. Indeed, in a recent report, the National Council on Disability noted that they could not find comprehensive information on the "degree to which sidewalks are accessible" across the US [24]. Traditionally, sidewalk assessment has been conducted via in-person street audits [17,29], which are labor intensive and costly [25], or via citizen call-in reports, which are done on a reactive basis. As an alternative, we propose the use of crowdsourcing to locate and assess sidewalk accessibility problems *proactively* by labeling Google Street View (GSV) imagery (Figure 1).

We report on two studies in particular: a feasibility study (Study 1) and an online crowdsourcing study using Amazon Mechanical Turk (Study 2). Because labeling sidewalk accessibility problems is a subjective and potentially ambiguous task, Study 1 investigates the viability of the labeling sidewalk problems amongst two groups of diligent and motivated labelers: three members of our research team and three "sidewalk accessibility experts"—in this case, wheelchair users. We use the results of this study to: (i) show that the labeling approach is reliable, with high intra- and inter-labeler agreement within and across the two groups; (ii) acquire an understanding of baseline performance—that is, what does good labeling performance look like? (iii) provide validated ground truth labels that can be used to evaluate crowd worker performance.

For Study 2, we investigate the potential of using crowd workers on Mechanical Turk (turkers) to perform this labeling task. We evaluate performance at two levels of labeling accuracy: *image level*, which tests for the presence or absence of the correct label in an image, and *pixel level*, which examines the pixel-level accuracies of the labels provided (as in Figure 1). We show that, when compared to ground truth, turkers are capable of determining that an accessibility problem *exists* in an image with 80.6% accuracy (binary classification) and determining the correct *problem type* with 78.3% accuracy (multiclass classification). Using a simple majority voting scheme with three turkers, this accuracy jumps to 86.9% and 83.8% respectively. We also examine the effect of two quality control mechanisms on performance: statistical filtering and multilevel review (see [22]). Our findings suggest that crowdsourcing both the labeling task and the verification task leads to a better quality result. We also demonstrate the performance/cost tradeoffs therein.

The primary contributions of this paper are threefold: (i) the first step toward a scalable approach for combining crowdsourcing and existing online map imagery to identify perceived accessibility issues, (ii) measures for assessing turker performance in applying accessibility labels, and (iii) strategies for improving overall data quality. Our approach could be used as a lightweight method to bootstrap accessibility-aware urban navigation routing algorithms, to gather training labels for computer vision-based sidewalk assessment, and as a mechanism for city governments and citizens to report on and learn about the health of their community's sidewalks (*e.g.*, through accessibility scores similar to *walkscore.com*).

BACKGROUND AND RELATED WORK

We provide background on sidewalk accessibility and sidewalk audit methods, in addition to related work on crowdsourcing and image labeling.

Factors Affecting Street-Level Accessibility

The US Department of Transportation [33] and the US Access Board [20] describe common problems that inhibit pedestrian access, including: (i) no place to walk—paths are either non-existent or not well-connected to destinations such as schools and transit; (ii) poor walking surfaces; (iii) blocked pathways, either temporarily (*e.g.*, by a vehicle) or permanently (*e.g.*, by a utility pole); (iv) difficult street crossings (*e.g.*, long walkway with no median, no curb ramps); (v) narrow sidewalks: wheelchair and scooter users require a wider path than ambulatory pedestrians, with most guidelines suggesting at least 60 inches.

Existing Sidewalk Audit Methods

In the US, state and federal departments conduct and encourage road safety audits that can also include walkability and pedestrian access (*e.g.*, [17,34]). Less formally, community organizations organize "Walk Audits" to find and assess deficiencies such as missing sidewalks, curb ramps, and/or dangerous street crossings (*e.g.*, [29]). Participatory reporting of accessibility problems has also been accomplished through applications that allow citizens to report non-emergency neighborhood issues to local government agencies (*SeeClickFix.com*) or to share information on wheelchair accessibility of businesses (*Wheelmap.org*); however, these applications do not support remote, virtual inquiry and have not been shown to scalably collect data on accessible public rights-of-way.

Street and neighborhood audits are also conducted by researchers in public health, sociology, and urban planning with the goal of studying the built environment and its impact on human behavior (*e.g.*, [12,17,27,30]). Since physical audits are often time-consuming and expensive [25], some studies have explored more efficient methods including recording video while driving for later review [27], or using satellite imagery and other map tools (*e.g.*, [19,30]). Omnidirectional streetscape imagery such as that in GSV has recently been used to perform *virtual* audits [5,11,25]. Reported benefits include time-savings and the ability to monitor and analyze multiple cities from a central location [5,25]. As an emerging area of research, work thus far has focused on the robustness and reliability of such approaches. Most importantly for our work, high levels of concordance have been reported between GSV *vs.* physical audit data for measures including pedestrian safety, traffic and parking, and pedestrian infrastructure [5,11,25].

Finally, most relevant to our work is the recent *CrossingGuard* paper by Guy and Truong [14], which focuses on navigation aids for visually impaired pedestrians and includes a small-scale study of GSV with three turkers. While similar in spirit, Guy and Truong focus exclusively on intersections for the visually impaired while we examine sidewalks for people with mobility impairments. More importantly, we ask turkers to mark *perceived* accessibility problems (*i.e,* perform judgments of accessibility) while [14] asks turkers to "check-off" the existence of traffic objects (*e.g.*, left turn signal, stop sign). Lastly, we ask turkers to directly label pixels, which helps establish an important initial baseline for collecting streetview accessibility training examples for computer vision.

Crowdsourcing and Image Labeling

Our image labeling task is analogous to that commonly performed in computer vision research for image segmentation, and object detection and recognition [6,26, 28,35,1]. Since manually building a large dataset of annotated images for training computer vision algorithms is expensive and time consuming [26], a number of web-based image labeling tools have been developed to capitalize on the large user population accessible over the

Figure 2: Labeling GSV images is a three step process consisting of *marking* the location of the sidewalk problem in the image, *categorizing* the problem into one of five types, and *assessing* the problem's severity. Here, the utility pole is labeled *Object in Path* and rated 5 (*Not Passable*).

Internet (e.g., [1,2,26,28]). These tools differ in the level of information acquired about each image and their userbase.

For example, in von Ahn *et al.*'s work, textual labels are provided for images through a clever collaborative game-with-a-purpose, where users provide captions to describe objects in an image [1] or draw bounding boxes around specific items [2]. *LabelMe* [26] provides even more granular segmentation by allowing users to draw polygonal-outlines around objects, which are publically viewable and editable. Finally, to our knowledge, Sorokin and Forsyth [28] were the first to experiment with "outsourcing" image labeling to Mechanical Turk. In a series of experiments, they showed that a large number of high quality image annotations could be acquired relatively cheaply and quickly. Others have successfully used Mechanical Turk for a variety of purposes including document editing [7], graphical perception experiments [16], and near real-time assistance with visual problems for blind people [8].

ANNOTATION INTERFACE AND DATASET

To collect geo-labeled data on sidewalk accessibility problems in GSV images, we created an interactive online labeling tool in JavaScript, PHP and MySQL (Figure 2). We also created a verification interface (Figure 3) where users could accept or reject previously collected labels. Below, we describe the annotation interface and the primary dataset used in our studies. We return to the verification interface in the Study 2 section.

For the annotation interface, labeling is a three-step process consisting of *marking* the location of the problem (if one exists), *categorizing* it into one of five types, and *assessing* its severity. For the first step, the user draws an outline around the perceived accessibility problem in the image (similar to LabelMe [26]). A pop-up menu then appears with five problem categories: *Curb Ramp Missing, Object in Path, Surface Problem, Prematurely Ending Sidewalk,* and *Other*. After a problem category has been selected, a five-point Likert scale appears, asking the user to rate the severity of the problem where 5 is most severe ("not passable") and 1 is least severe ("passable"). The label is then complete. After all identified sidewalk problems have been labeled in a given image, the user can select "submit labels" and another image is loaded. Images with no apparent sidewalk problems can be marked as such with a button labeled "There are no accessibility problems in this image." Users can also skip images and record their reason (*e.g.*, "image too blurry", "sidewalk not visible"). Other labeling techniques were explored in early prototypes [15].

The test dataset used in the labeling interface consists of 229 images manually scraped by the research team using GSV of urban neighborhoods in Los Angeles, Baltimore, Washington DC, and New York City. We attempted to collect a balanced dataset. Of the 229 images, 179 contained one or more of the aforementioned problem categories; 50 had no visible sidewalk accessibility issues and were used, in part, to evaluate *false positive* labeling activity. Based on our majority-vote ground truth data (described later), we determined the following composition: 67 images with *Surface Problems*, 66 images with *Object in Path*, 50 with *Prematurely Ending Sidewalk*, and 47 with *Curb Ramp Missing*. This count is not mutually exclusive—48 images in total included more than one problem type. The label *Other* was used 0.5% of the time in Study 1 and 0.6% in Study 2 and is thus ignored in our analyses. As of September 2012, the average age of the images is 3.1 years old (*SD*=0.8 years). We return to the potential issue of image age in the discussion.

EVALUATING ANNOTATION CORRECTNESS

In this section, we provide an overview of the correctness measures used in our two studies. Because this is a new area of research, we introduce and explore a range of metrics—many of which have different levels of relevancy across application contexts (*e.g.*, calculating the accessibility score of a neighborhood *vs.* collecting training data for a computer vision algorithm).

Defining Levels of Annotation Correctness

Assessing annotation correctness in images is complex. To guide our analysis, we derived two spectra that vary according to the type and granularity of data extracted from each label: the localization spectrum and the specificity spectrum. The *localization* spectrum describes the positioning of the label in the image, which includes two discrete levels of granularity: *image level* and *pixel level*. For image level, we simply check for the absence or presence of a label anywhere within the image. Pixel level is more precise, examining individual pixels highlighted by the label outline. Our pixel-level analysis is analogous to image segmentation in computer vision and, indeed, our evaluation methods are informed from work in this space.

The *specificity* spectrum, in contrast, varies based on the amount of descriptive information evaluated for each label.

Figure 3: The verification interface used to experiment with crowdsourcing validation of turker labels—only one label is validated at a time in batches of 20. (a) A correctly labeled *No Curb Ramp* problem; (b) A false positive *Object in Path* label (the utility pole is located in the grass and not in the sidewalk); (c) A false negative example: The cars should have been marked as *Object in Path*.

At the finest level of granularity, we check for matches based on the five label categories as well as corresponding severity ratings: *Object in Path*, *Prematurely Ending Sidewalk*, *Surface Problem*, *Curb Ramp Missing*, and *No Problem* (indicating the user had clicked "no accessibility problems found"). Note that *Curb Ramp Missing* and *No Problem* were exempt from severity ratings. At the next level of granularity, we only examine problem types, ignoring severity ratings; we refer to this level as *multiclass*. Finally, at the coarsest level of granularity we group all problem categories into a *binary* classification of problem vs. no problem.

As the first work in the area, these dimensions of analysis are important for understanding crowd worker performance across various measures of correctness. Identifying an appropriate level of correctness may depend on the specific application context. For example, because of the focal length and camera angles used in GSV imagery, simply identifying that an accessibility problem exists in an image (*i.e.*, image-level, binary classification) localizes that problem to a fairly small geographic area: a specific street side and sidewalk within a city block. This level of geographic precision may be sufficient for calculating accessibility scores or even informing accessibility-aware routing algorithms. Binary classification—whether at the image level or the pixel level—also helps mitigate the subjectivity involved in selecting a label type for a problem (*e.g.*, some persons may perceive a problem as *Object in Path* while others may see it as a *Surface Problem*). In other cases, however, more specific correctness measures may be needed. Training computer vision algorithms to segment and, perhaps, automatically identify and recognize obstacles, would require pixel-level, multiclass granularity.

Image-Level Correctness Measures

For image-level analysis, we computed two different correctness measures: a straightforward accuracy measure and a more sophisticated measure involving precision and recall. For *accuracy*, we compare ground truth labels with turker labels for a given image and calculate the percentage correct. For example, if ground truth labels indicate that three problem types exist in an image: *No Curb Ramp*, *Object in Path*, and a *Surface Problem*, but a turker only labels *No Curb Ramp*, then the resulting accuracy score would be 50% (1 out of 3 problems identified correctly and 1 correct for *not* providing *Sidewalk Ending*). Though easy to understand, this accuracy measure does not uncover more nuanced information about *why* an accuracy score is obtained (*e.g.*, because of false positives or false negatives).

As a result, we incorporated a second set of correctness measures, which extend from work in information retrieval: *precision*, *recall*, and an amalgamation of the two, *f-measure*. All three measures return a value between 0 and 1, where 1 is better:

$$Precision = \frac{\#\ of\ True\ Pos\ Labels}{\#\ of\ True\ Pos\ Labels + \#\ of\ False\ Pos\ Labels} \qquad \text{(Eq. 1)}$$

$$Recall = \frac{\#\ of\ True\ Pos\ Labels}{\#\ of\ True\ Pos\ Labels + \#\ of\ False\ Neg\ Labels} \qquad \text{(Eq. 2)}$$

$$F\text{-}measure = 2 * \frac{Precision * Recall}{Precision + Recall} \qquad \text{(Eq. 3)}$$

True positive here is defined as providing the correct label on an image, *false positive* is providing a label for a problem that does not actually exist in the image, and *false negative* is *not* providing a label for a problem that *does exist* in the image. In this way, precision measures the accuracy of the labels actually provided (*i.e.*, a fraction expressing the ratio of correct labels over *all labels provided*) while recall measures the comprehensiveness of the correct labels provided (*i.e.*, a fraction expressing the ratio of correct labels over all *possible correct labels*). For example, a precision score of 1.0 means that every label the turker added was correct but they could have missed labels. A recall score of 1.0 means that the turker's labels include all of the actual problems in the image but could also include non-problems. Given that algorithms can be tuned to maximize precision while sacrificing recall and vice versa, the f-measure provides a single joint metric that encapsulates both. We use accuracy, precision, recall, and f-measure to describe our image level results.

Pixel-Level Correctness Measures

Pixel-level correctness relates to image segmentation work in computer vision. Zhang [1] provides a review of methods for evaluating image segmentation quality, two of which are relevant here: the *goodness method*, which examines segmentation based on human judgment and the *empirical discrepancy method*, which programmatically calculates the difference between test segmentations and "ground truth" segmentations for a given image. The goodness method can be advantageous in that it does not require ground truth; however, it is labor intensive because it relies on human judgment to perceive quality. Though judging the quality of segmentations can also be crowdsourced, partly mitigating the labor concern (*e.g.*, [7]), the quality of the judgment itself remains an issue.

Thus, we also explored two empirical discrepancy methods: *overlap* (or area of intersection) [2,31] and, again, precision/recall combined with f-measure [9,10], which is similar to that explained above though applied at the pixel level rather than the image level. For our first discrepancy method, overlap is defined as:

$$Overlap(A,B) = \frac{Area(A \cap B)}{Area(A \cup B)} \quad \text{(Eq. 4)}$$

where A and B are the pixel outlines. Note that if the outline A is perfectly equal to the outline B, then $Overlap(A,B)=1$. If A and B are disjoint, then $Overlap(A,B)=0$. Although this metric is easy to understand, similar to the straightforward accuracy measure for image-level analysis, it fails to capture nuances in correctness. Thus, for our second discrepancy metric we define precision, recall, and f-measure at the pixel level. From the image segmentation literature [6], *precision* is defined as the probability that a generated outline-fill pixel area correctly highlights the target object and *recall* is the probability that a true outline-fill pixel is detected. Thus, in order to calculate precision and recall at the pixel level, we need to compute three different pixel counts for each image:

1. **True positive pixels:** number of overlapping pixels between the ground truth segmentation and the test segmentation;
2. **False positive pixels**: number of pixels in the test segmentation *not* in the ground truth segmentation;
3. **False negative pixels:** number of pixels in the ground truth segmentation *not* in the test segmentation.

Precision and recall can then be computed by the following formulae (f-measure is the same as *Eq. 3* above):

$$Precision = \frac{\#\,of\ True\ Pos\ Pixels}{\#\,of\ True\ Pos\ Pixels + \#\,of\ False\ Pos\ Pixels} \quad \text{(Eq. 5)}$$

$$Recall = \frac{\#\,of\ True\ Pos\ Pixels}{\#\,of\ True\ Pos\ Pixels + \#\,of\ False\ Neg\ Pixels} \quad \text{(Eq. 6)}$$

Before calculating pixel-level correctness for any of the measures, we flatten all labels with equivalent type into the same layer and treat them as a single set of pixels. This allows us to more easily perform pixel-by-pixel comparison between ground truth labels and test labels marked with the same problem type.

STUDY 1: ASSESSING FEASIBILITY

Labeling accessibility problems perceived in streetscape images is a subjective process. As such, our first study focused on demonstrating that informed and well-motivated labelers could complete the labeling task and produce consistent results. We had two additional goals: (i) to produce a vetted ground truth dataset that could be used to calculate turker performance in Study 2, and (ii) to help contextualize Study 2 results (*i.e.*, what does "good" performance look like?).

We collected independently-labeled data from two groups: three members of our research team and three wheelchair users (who served as "sidewalk accessibility experts"). We then computed intra- and inter-annotator agreement scores for within and between each group respectively. We explore agreement at both the image level and the pixel level across binary and multiclass classification.

Collecting Wheelchair User Ground Truth Data

Three wheelchair users were recruited via listservs and word-of-mouth: two males with spinal cord injury (tetraplegia) and one male with cerebral palsy. All three used motorized wheelchairs; one also used a manual wheelchair but rarely. Each wheelchair user took part in a single labeling session at our research lab. Participants were asked to label the images based on their own experiences and were instructed that not all images contained accessibility problems. They were also asked to "think-aloud" during labeling so that we could better understand the rationale behind their labeling decisions.

The sessions lasted for 2-3 hours and included a short, post-labeling interview where we asked about the participant's personal experiences with sidewalk/street accessibility and about potential improvements to our labeling tool. In consideration of participant time and potential fatigue, only a subset of the total 229 image dataset was labeled: 75 in total. These images were selected randomly from each of the four problem categories (*4 categories x 15 images = 60*) plus an additional 15 randomly selected "no problem" images. Participants were compensated $25-35 depending on session length. Below, we report on evaluating agreement between the researchers, the wheelchair users, and the researchers *compared* to the wheelchair users. For the latter calculation, we compare *majority vote* data from each group so N=2 rather than N=6. We describe both image-level and pixel-level performance.

Evaluating Image-Level Agreement and Performance

We computed inter-rater agreement on labels at the image level using Fleiss' kappa [18], which attempts to account for agreement expected by chance. As this was an image-level analysis, we tested for agreement based on the absence or presence of a label in an image and not on the label's particular pixel location or severity rating. Multiple labels of the *same type* were compressed into a single "binary presence" indicator for that label. For example, if three individual *Surface Problems* were labeled in an image, for our analysis, we only considered the fact that a *Surface Problem* was detected and not how many occurrences there were exactly. This helped control for different annotator tendencies—some who would provide one large label to cover contiguous problem areas and others who would provide separate labels. Results are shown in Table 1 for both binary and multiclass classification (N represents the number of annotators and I the number of images, Table 2 uses the same notation).

Three key results emerge: first, both the researchers and the wheelchair users had moderate to substantial levels of agreement [18], which indicates that the labeling task, at least at the image-level, is feasible and that the labels are

Image-Level Label Specificity	Label	Researchers (*N*=3, *I*=229)	Wheelchair Users (*N*=3, *I*=75)	Researchers vs. Wheelchair Users (*N*=2 groups, *I*=75)
Binary Classification	No Problem vs. Problem	0.81	0.68	0.79
Multiclass Classification	No Curb Ramp	0.81	0.82	0.83
	Object in Path	0.56	0.55	0.62
	Sidewalk Ending	0.86	0.71	0.78
	Surface Problem	0.62	0.40	0.74
	Overall	0.69	0.62	0.74

Table 1: Fleiss' kappa annotator agreement scores for image-level analysis between the researchers, the wheelchair users, and the researchers compared to the wheelchair users (this lattermost comparison is based on majority vote data within each group).

fairly consistent across labelers; second, and just as importantly, the third column in Table 1 shows high agreement *between* the majority vote data of the research team and the wheelchair users, which indicates that the accessibility problems identified by the research team are consistent with "experts"; and, finally, the multiclass agreement results show that *Object in Path* and *Surface Problem* have more disagreement than *No Curb Ramp* and *Sidewalk Ending*. This is likely because *Object in Path* and *Surface Problems* are often less salient in images and because they are occasionally substituted for one another (*e.g.*, some labelers perceive a problem as *Object in Path* while others as a *Surface Problem*).

Evaluating Pixel-Level Agreement and Performance

Calculating pixel-level agreement is more challenging. Because no widespread standards exist for evaluating pixel-level agreement for human labelers, we followed the process prescribed by Martin *et al.* [23]. We verify the labeling process by showing that pixel-level label overlap and f-measure scores are higher between labelers on the *same* image than across *different* images. These scores will later act as a baseline for defining good pixel-level performance when evaluating turker labels. To compare between the *same* images, 678 comparisons are required (3 annotators x 229 images). For *different* images, 156,636 comparisons are required (3 annotators x (229 x 229 – 229)). Because the wheelchair users only labeled 75 of the 229 images, their comparison count is correspondingly lower (225 for same, 16,650 for different). We ignore images for which all annotators labeled *No Problems Found* (as no pixel labels exist in these images). Our results are shown in Table 2.

From these results, we conclude that our pixel level annotations across labelers are reasonably consistent, although less so than for image level. Unsurprisingly, agreement is higher for binary classification than for multiclass, though not substantially. This indicates that a major source of disagreement is not the label type (*e.g.*, *Object in Path* vs. *Surface Problem*) but rather the pixels highlighted by the outline shape. We emphasize, however, that pixel outlines for even the same object across labelers will rarely agree perfectly; the key then, is to determine what level of overlap and f-measure scores are acceptable and good. Our results suggest that overlap scores of 0.31

Pixel-Level Label Specificity	Correctness Measure	Image Comparisons	Researchers (*N*=3, *I*=229)	Wheelchair Users (*N*=3, *I*=75)	Researchers vs. Wheelchair Users (*N*=2 groups, *I*=75)
Binary Classification	Area Overlap	Same	0.31 (0.21)	0.26 (0.22)	0.27 (0.21)
		Different	0.02 (0.05)	0.01 (0.04)	0.01 (0.04)
	F-Measure	Same	0.43 (0.25)	0.37 (0.26)	0.38 (0.26)
		Different	0.03 (0.08)	0.02 (0.06)	0.03 (0.07)
Multiclass Classification	Area Overlap	Same	0.27 (0.21)	0.22 (0.22)	0.23 (0.21)
		Different	0.01 (0.03)	0.00 (0.02)	0.00 (0.02)
	F-Measure	Same	0.38 (0.26)	0.32 (0.27)	0.33 (0.27)
		Different	0.01 (0.05)	0.01 (0.04)	0.01 (0.04)

Table 2: The results of our pixel level agreement analysis (based on [23]) between the researchers, wheelchair users, and researchers compared to wheelchair users. Similar to Table 1, the rightmost column is majority vote data. Cell format: average (stdev).

and 0.27 and f-measure scores of 0.43 and 0.38 for binary and multiclass classification respectively are indicative of what a motivated and diligent annotator can achieve. We emphasize that even 10-15% overlap agreement at the pixel level would be sufficient to confidently localize problems in images and highlight these areas in accessible map routing interfaces. This level of consistency, however, may not be sufficient for training computer vision. We return to this point in the discussion.

PRODUCING GROUND TRUTH DATASETS

Finally, now that we have shown the feasibility of the labeling task and found reasonably high consistency amongst labelers, we can use these Study 1 labels to produce a ground truth dataset for evaluating turker performance. We consolidate the labeling data from the three researchers into four unified ground truth datasets: binary and multiclass at both the image and the pixel level

Consolidating Image-Level Labels: To combine image-level labels across the three labelers, we simply create a majority-vote "ground truth" dataset. Any *image* that received a label from at least two of the three researchers was assigned that label as "ground truth."

Consolidating Pixel-Level Labels: Combining labels from the three researchers at the pixel level is less straightforward. The consolidation algorithm will directly impact the results obtained from our correctness measures. For example, if we combine highlighted pixel areas across all three researchers (union), then turker precision is likely to go up but recall is likely to go down. If, instead, we take the intersection across all three labelers, the ground truth pixel area will shrink substantially, which will likely increase turker recall but reduce precision. Consequently, we decided to, again, adopt a majority vote approach. To produce the majority vote pixel-level dataset, we look for labels from at least two of the three researchers that overlap by 15% of their unioned area. The value of 15% was chosen because it is the lower-quartile cutoff using researcher overlap data. For binary classification, the label type was ignored—thus, any labels that overlapped by 15% or more were combined. For multiclass, the labels had to be of the same type.

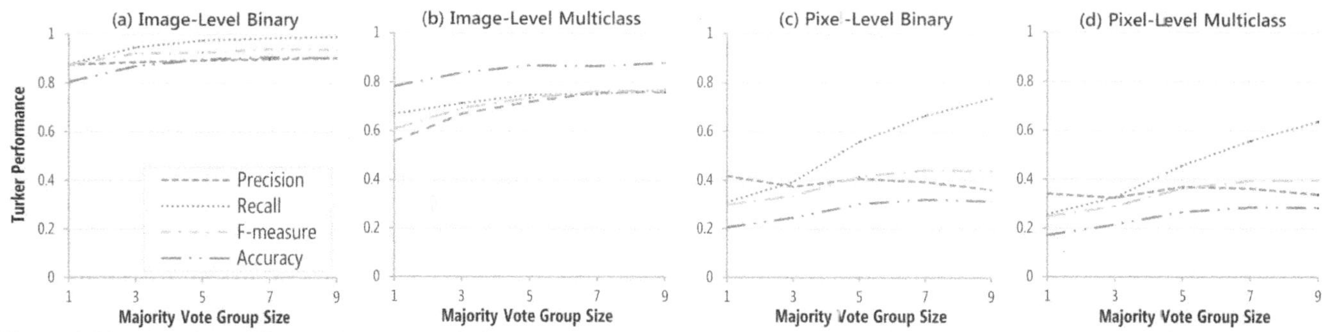

Figure 4: Binary and multiclass performance at the image- and pixel-levels with varying majority vote group sizes. Each graph point is based on multiple permutations of the majority vote group size across all 229 images. Standard error bars are in black (barely visible due to low variance).

STUDY 2: CROWD WORKER PERFORMANCE

To investigate the potential of using untrained crowd workers to label accessibility problems, we posted our task to Mechanical Turk during the summer of 2012. Each "hit" required labeling 1-10 images for 1-5 cents (0.5 to 5 cents per image). Each turker new to the task was required to watch at least half of a 3-minute instructional video, after which the labeling interface automatically appeared. Note: one task encompasses labeling one image.

We first describe high-level results before performing a more detailed analysis covering labeler count *vs.* accuracy, two quality control evaluations, and the best and worst performing images. For the analysis below, we do not consider severity ratings. Instead, we leave this for future work. However, given that we found a high rate of false positives amongst the turker data, we did examine the effect of removing labels that received a severity rating of a 1 (*Passable*) or a 2 (*Fairly Passable*). Our findings did not change significantly as a result.

High-Level Results

In all, we hired 185 distinct turkers who completed 7,517 image labeling tasks and provided a total of 13,379 labels. Turkers completed an average of 40.6 tasks (*SD*=61.2); 20 turkers labeled only 1 image and 10 turkers labeled all 229. The median image labeling time was 33.3s (*SD*=89.0s) and the average number of labels per image was 1.79 (*SD*=1.27). When compared with our ground truth dataset, overall turker accuracy at the *image* level was 80.6% for binary classification and 78.3% for multiclass classification. At the pixel level, average area overlap was 20.6% and 17.0% for binary and multiclass, respectively. These numbers are reasonably close to the values of 27% and 23% that we saw for wheelchair users *vs.* researchers.

Accuracy as a Function of Turkers per Image

Collecting multiple annotations per image helps account for the natural variability of human performance and reduces the influence of occasional errors; however, it also requires more workers [28]. Here, we explore accuracy as a function of turkers per image. We expect that accuracy should improve as the number of turkers increases, but the question then, is by how much? To evaluate the impact of the number of turkers on accuracy, we collected labels from 28 or more turkers for *each* of our 229 images. We compare our majority vote ground truth data with majority vote data

Image-Level Label Specificity	Label	Maj Vote Size: 1	Maj Vote Size: 3	Maj Vote Size: 5	Maj Vote Size: 7	Maj Vote Size: 9
Binary	No Prob vs. Prob	80.6 (0.1)	86.9 (0.3)	89.7 (0.2)	90.6 (0.2)	90.2 (0.2)
Multiclass	No Curb Ramp	78.6 (0.1)	86.0 (0.1)	90.2 (0.3)	91.6 (0.2)	93.7 (0.3)
	Object in Path	73.0 (0.1)	78.1 (0.2)	81.3 (0.3)	82.2 (0.1)	83.4 (0.2)
	Sidewalk Ending	84.7 (0.1)	88.3 (0.1)	88.5 (0.4)	89.5 (0.4)	89.8 (0.3)
	Surface Problem	77.0 (0.1)	82.1 (0.2)	84.9 (0.3)	85.9 (0.4)	88.4 (0.3)
	Overall	78.3 (0.0)	83.8 (0.1)	86.8 (0.2)	86.6 (0.2)	87.9 (0.1)

Table 3: Binary and multiclass label type accuracy at the image level across five majority vote group sizes. Cell format: avg% (stderr %).

across five turker group sizes: 1, 3, 5, 7, and 9. Because we have 28 turkers per image, we can run the analysis multiple times for each group size, average the results, and calculate error margins (which produces a more accurate portral of expected future performance for each group size). For example, when we set the majority vote group size to three, we randomly permute nine groups of three turkers. In each group, we calculate the majority vote answer for a given image in the dataset and compare it with ground truth. This process is repeated across all images and the five group sizes, where (*X=majority vote group size, Y=number of groups*): (1,28), (3, 9), (5,5), (7, 4), (9, 3). To compute the majority vote *answer* for each group size, we use the same label consolidation process as that used for the researcher majority vote labels.

We conducted this analysis at the image and pixel levels for binary and multiclass classification across our multiple correctness measures. Results are shown in Figure 4 (image and pixel level) and Table 3 (image level only). As expected, performance improves with turker count but these gains diminish in magnitude as group size grows. For example, at the image level, binary accuracy improves from 80.6% to 86.9% with 3 turkers and to 89.7% with 5 turkers but only to 90.2% with 9 turkers. For image-level multiclass, we see a similar trend. At the pixel level, the binary area overlap measure improves from 20.6% to 30.3% with 5 turkers but only to 31.4% with 9 turkers. Again, multiclass performance is similar (see Figure 4d). Even though group sizes beyond 5 continue to improve results at both the image and pixel level, this benefit may not be worth the additional cost.

Note that for the pixel level, the recall score rises dramatically in comparison to other metrics. This is because the consolidated majority vote pixel area tends to grow with turker count (with more pixels labeled, recall will go up).

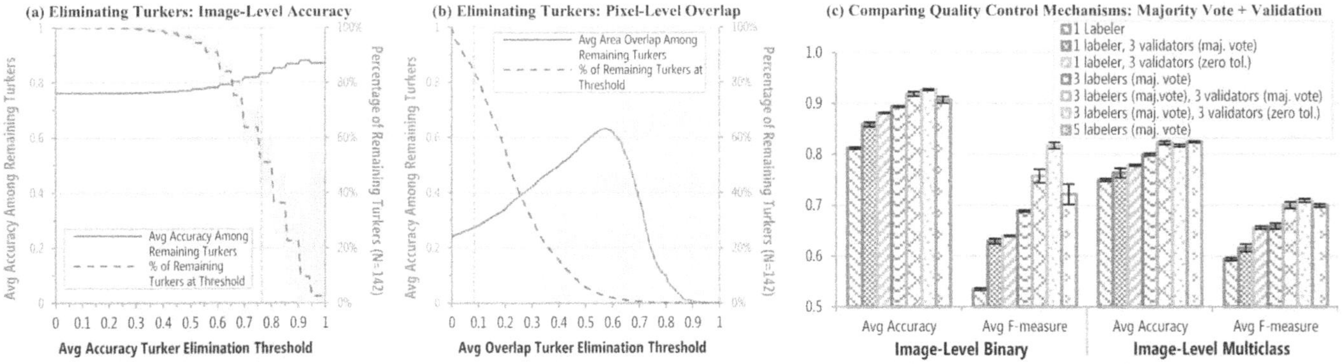

Figure 5: (a and b) Show the effect of increasingly aggressive turker elimination thresholds at the image- and pixel-levels based on average multiclass performance of 5 images. Error bars are standard deviation (for blue) and standard error (for red). As the threshold increases, fewer turkers remain and uncertainty increases. (c) Compares the effectiveness of various quality control mechanisms on performance at the image level.

Different consolidation processes will produce different results. Finally, similar to Study 1, *Sidewalk Ending* and *No Curb Ramp* labels performed better than *Object in Path* and *Surface Problem* (Table 3).

Quality Control Mechanisms

We explore two quality control approaches: filtering *turkers* based on a fixed threshold of acceptable performance and filtering *labels* based on crowdsourced validations collected through our verification interface. In both cases, we perform our analyses offline, which allows us to simulate performance with a range of quality control mechanisms.

Statistical Filtering: For the first approach, we explored the effect of eliminating turkers based on their average multiclass performance at both the image and pixel level. The goal was to uncover effective performance thresholds for eliminating poor quality turkers. We assign measure of errors to image-level and pixel-level correctness by using a Monte Carlo-based resampling approach called Bootstrap [13]. We first eliminate all turkers from our dataset who had completed fewer than five tasks. We then take samples of the remaining 142 turkers with replacement. For each sampled turker we randomly select five tasks that s/he completed to measure their average multiclass accuracy (for image level) or multiclass overlap (for pixel level). We shift our elimination threshold by increments of 0.01 and reject turkers if their average performance is lower than this threshold. At each increment, we also calculate overall performance across *all tasks* among the remaining turkers. We repeat this process independently at the image and pixel levels N=1000 times to calculate error bars.

Results are shown in Figure 5 (a and b). In both figures, we see overall performance steadily increase as poor performing turkers get eliminated. However, the threshold where elimination takes effect differs between the two mechanisms due to differences in difficulty. For example, to achieve the same accuracy level as we would expect from majority vote with 3 turkers (0.84), the average performance elimination threshold needs to be 0.76 (marked in orange in the graph). At that threshold, image-level multiclass accuracy amongst the remaining turkers goes up to 0.84, but at a cost of eliminating 51.2% of our workforce. For pixel-level data, to achieve a score similar to the average area overlap between researcher labels (0.27), the elimination threshold needs to be set to 0.08, which increases the overlap score from 0.24 to 0.27 but reduces our workforce by 15% (again, orange line in graph). Thus, as expected, our results show accuracy gains with increasingly aggressive elimination thresholds; however, these accuracy gains come at a cost of reducing the effective worker pool. We expect that future systems can use these results to identify poor performing turkers *proactively* during data collection via ground truth seed images (*e.g.*, see [22]), and either offer additional training, or, in the extreme case, rejecting the work outright and blacklisting the turker. The threshold used depends on the accuracy needs of the application.

The Verification Interface: For the second quality control approach, we use our verification interface (Figure 3) to subjectively validate labels via crowdsourcing. Here, turkers validate existing labels rather than provide new ones. We ensured that the same turker did not label and validate the same image. As the validation task is simpler than the labeling task, we batched 20 validations into a single hit at a cost of 5 cents. We collected three or more validations per label across 75 images (the same subset used by the wheelchair users in Study 1). In all, we collected 19,189 validations from 273 turkers. Whereas the median time to label an image was 35.2s, the median time to validate a label was 10.5s. Thus, collecting validations is quicker and cheaper than collecting new labels.

We performed a series of analyses with the validation data, using both majority vote validation and zero tolerance validation. For the latter, if any validator down-votes a label, that label is eliminated. We compare these results to no quality control (baseline), the use of majority vote labels, and a combination of majority vote labels plus subjective validation. Results are in Figure 5. As before, performance improves with additional turkers—either as labelers *or* as validators. The best performing quality control mechanism was 3 labelers (majority vote) plus 3 validators (zero tolerance) beating out 5 labelers (majority vote). This suggests that it is more cost effective to collect 3 labels *with* validation than 5 labels total per image, particularly given that validation requires less effort.

(a) 0.80, 0.59; 0.20, 0.0 (b) 0.81, 0.70; 0.0 , 0.0 (c) 0.86, 0.59; 0.15, 0.0 (d) 0.74, 0.89; 0.52, 0.52 (e) 0.97, 0.79; 0.58, 0.55 (f) 0.94, 0.96; 0.63, 0.61

Figure 6: A selection of the bottom and top three performing images in our dataset based on *multiclass* pixel-level area overlap. Top row: original GSV image; middle row: majority vote ground truth from researchers using 15% overlap; bottom row: turker labels. Numbers show turker performance results for that image, from left to right: image-level binary, image-level multiclass; pixel-level binary, pixel-level multiclass.

Best and Worst Performing Images

Finally, to uncover what aspects of an image make it particularly easy or difficult to label, we sorted and visually inspected images in our dataset by multiclass pixel-level area overlap performance. Figure 6 shows a selection of the bottom and top performing images (left 3, right 3). For the worst performing images, there are many false positives: for example, utility poles and stop signs labeled as obstacles even though they are not in the sidewalk path. Figure 6c highlights two additional common problems: first, problem types can have ambiguous categories—in this case, the ground truth label indicates *Sidewalk Ending* while many turker labels selected *Surface Problem*; second, it is unclear *how much* of the problem area should be highlighted. For *Sidewalk Ending*, the ground truth labels highlight only the sidewalk termination point—some turkers, however, would label this section *and* any beyond it with no sidewalk (thereby greatly reducing their pixel-level scores). Future interfaces could detect these mistakes and provide active feedback to the turker on how to improve their labeling. In contrast, for the best performing images, the accessibility problems are, unsurprisingly, more salient and the camera angle provides a relatively close-angle shot.

DISCUSSION AND CONCLUSION

We have shown that untrained crowdworkers could find and label accessibility problems in GSV imagery. We also highlighted the effect of common quality-control techniques on performance accuracy. Here, we discuss limitations of our study and opportunities for future work.

Our prototype labeling system relied on a manually curated database of images selected by the research team. This approach was sufficient to demonstrate the feasibility of our idea but ignored important practical aspects such as locating the GSV camera in geographic space and selecting an optimal viewpoint. These challenges clearly need to be solved to produce a scalable approach. We are currently working on multiple solutions including: (i) a software agent that virtually "drives" through city streets in GSV and attempts to snapshot optimal angles of sidewalks and street intersections and (ii) deferring this complexity to the crowd worker by allowing them to control camera angle and zoom level in an updated labeling interface.

An additional limitation relates to the GSV images themselves. Image quality can sometimes be poor due to lighting conditions, which can often be auto-corrected, or blurriness. More work is also needed to assess the degree to which sidewalk occlusion (*e.g.*, parked cars) is an issue in GSV images across different regions. Finally, GSV image age is also a potential problem (recall that images were 3.1 years old on average in our dataset). The following factors should mitigate this lattermost issue: (i) as noted earlier, virtual GSV neighborhood audits and physical audits have resulted in high concordance for pedestrian infrastructure data [5,11,25]; (ii) GSV is already being treated as a valuable resource by the accessibility community—*e.g.*, one of our mobility-impaired participants mentioned that he uses GSV to examine an area for traversability before leaving his house; (iii) GSV imagery is often updated as the GSV technology improves or simply to ensure accuracy *e.g.*, Google updated 250,000 miles of roads in early Oct 2012 (http://goo.gl/hMnM1). Moreover, all of the above GSV limitations may be potentially resolved through other data sources such as high-resolution top-down satellite or fly-over imagery [30], volunteer-contributed geo-located pictures (*e.g.*, *SeeClickFix*), or government 311 databases.

While we captured important accessibility characteristics of sidewalks, other problems may exist. For example, the wheelchair users in Study 1 indicated that sidewalk narrowness can also reduce accessibility. We did not have a means of measuring sidewalk width or assess narrowness. Future work should look at the ability to calculate widths (*e.g.*, via computer vision-based mensuration), which could, perhaps, be reconstructed via the multiple camera angles offered by GSV or derived from the 3D-point cloud data that modern GSV cars collect (see [4]). While this 3D data is not yet publicly available, it could also be useful in object detection for automatically identifying problems.

We intend to integrate computer vision (CV) into our approach primarily for image triage, view selection, mensuration, and semi-automatic object detection. Doing so will allow for further scalability, for example, where turkers verify automatically generated labels. However, while our current pixel-level results should be useful for *localizing* where problems exist in images, they may not be sufficient for training CV algorithms. To capture higher quality training data for CV, a future labeling tool should provide finer granularity outlines, feedback to turkers about their performance, proactive quality control, and better training.

For quality control, future applications will be using images where ground truth is *unknown*. Instead, "ground truth" seed images will need to be injected into the labeling dataset to actively measure turker performance (see [22]). Active monitoring will allow turkers to receive performance feedback, help assist them when they make common mistakes, and warn and, eventually, eliminate poor quality workers if they do not improve. Beyond turkers, we also plan to build a volunteer-based participatory website to both visualize our results and highlight areas that need data collection. In contrast to our current interface, we could allow for collaborative editing (*e.g.*, [26]) and experiment with incentivizing volunteers (*e.g.*, through gamification).

Our general approach of collecting useful, street-level information in a scalable manner from GSV images has application beyond sidewalks. We would like to expand our approach to assess the accessibility of building fronts, friction strips and stop lights at intersections (similar to [14] but with pixel-based labeling), and non-accessibility related topics such as tracking and labeling bike lanes in roadways.

REFERENCES

1. von Ahn, A. & Dabbish, L. (2004). Labeling images with a computer game. *CHI '04*, 319-326.
2. von Ahn, L., Liu, R., & Blum, M. (2006). Peekaboom: a game for locating objects in images. *CHI'06*, 55-64.
3. Americans with Disabilities Act of 1990, Pub. L. No. 101-336, 104 Stat. 328.
4. Anguelov, D., Dulong, C., *et al.* (2010). Google Street View: Capturing the World at Street Level. *IEEE Computer*, V.43, 32-38
5. Badland, H., Oplt, S., Witten, K., Kearns, R., & Mavoa, S. (2010). Can virtual streetscape audits reliably replace physical streetscape audits? *Journal of Urban Health*, 1007-1016.
6. Berkeley Segmentation Dataset and Benchmark (2007), http://www.eecs.berkeley.edu/Research/Projects/CS/vision/bsds/
7. Bernstein, M., Little, G., *et al.* (2010). Soylent: a word processor with a crowd inside. *UIST'10*, 313-322.
8. Bigham, J., Jayant, C., *et al.*, 2010. VizWiz: nearly real-time answers to visual questions. *UIST'10*, 333-342.
9. Chen, D., Bilgic, M., Getoor, L., and Jacobs, D. (2011). Dynamic Processing Allocation in Video. *IEEE Trans. Pattern Anal. Mach. Intell.* 33, 11, 2174-2187.
10. Cheng, C., Koschan, A., *et al.*(2012) Outdoor scene image segmentation based on background recognition and perceptual organization. *IEEE Trans Image Process*. 21(3):1007-19
11. Clarke, P., Ailshire, J., *et al.* (2010). Using Google Earth to conduct a neighborhood audit: Reliability of a virtual audit instrument. *Health & Place*, *16*(6), 1224-1229.
12. Clifton, K., Smith, A., & Rodriguez, D. (2007) The development and testing of an audit for the pedestrian environment. *Landscape and Urban Planning*; 80(1–2):95-110
13. Efron, B. & Tibshirani, R. (1994) An introduction to the Bootstrap. New York: Chapman & Hall.
14. Guy, R. & Truong, K. (2012). CrossingGuard: exploring information content in navigation aids for visually impaired pedestrians. *CHI'12*, 405-414.
15. Hara, K., Le, V., & Froehlich, J. (2012). A feasibility study of crowdsourcing and google street view to determine sidewalk accessibility. *ASSETS '12 Poster*. 273-274.
16. Heer, J. & Bostock, M. (2010). Crowdsourcing graphical perception: using mechanical turk to assess visualization design. *CHI'10*, 203-212.
17. Institute of Transportation Engineers, Pedestrian mobility and safety audit guide, http://www.ite.org/PedAudits/AuditGuide.pdf
18. Landis, R. & Koch, G. (1977). The measurement of observer agreement for categorical data. *Biometrics*; 33:159 –74.
19. Leslie, E., Coffee, N., Frank, L., Owen, N., Bauman, A., Hugo, G. (2007) Walkability of local communities: Using geographic information systems to objectively assess relevant environmental attributes. *Health Place*. 3(1):111–22.
20. Public Rights-Of-Way Access Advisory Committee (PROWACC). (2007). Special Report: Accessible Public Rights-of-Way Planning and Design for Alterations, http://www.access-board.gov/prowac/alterations/guide.htm
21. Kinney *et al.* *vs.* Yerusalim & Hoskins. 93-1168 U.S. (1993). http://www.access-board.gov/PROWAC/yerusalim.htm
22. Quinn, A. & Bederson, B. 2011. Human computation: a survey and taxonomy of a growing field. *CHI'11*, 1403-1412.
23. Martin, D., Fowlkes, C., Tal, D., Malik, J. (2001) A database of human segmented natural images and its application to evaluating segmentation algorithms and measuring ecological statistics. *ICCV'01*. 2: 416-23
24. National Council on Disability. (2007) The impact of the Americans with Disabilities Act: Assessing the progress toward achieving the goals of the ADA.
25. Rundle, A., Bader, M., Richards, A., Neckerman, K., & Teitler, J. (2011) Using Google Street View to audit neighborhood environments. *Am J Prev Med*; 40(1):94-100
26. Russell, B., Torralba, A., Murphy, K., & Freeman, W. (2008). LabelMe: A Database and Web-Based Tool for Image Annotation. *Int. J. Comput. Vision* 77, 1-3, 157-173.
27. Sampson, R. & Raudenbush, S. (1999) Systematic social observation of public spaces: a new look at disorder in urban neighborhoods. *Am J Social*; 105(3):603–51
28. Sorokin, A., Forsyth, D. (2008) Utility data annotation with Amazon Mechanical Turk. *CVPR'08*. 1-8.
29. StreetsWiki, Walk Audit, http://streetswiki.wikispaces.com/Walk+Audit
30. Taylor, B., Fernando, P., Bauman, A., Williamson, A., Craig, J., Redman, S. Measuring the quality of public open space using google earth. American Journal of Preventive Medicine 2011; 40(2):105-12
31. Timp, S. & Karssemeijer, N. (2004) A new 2D segmentation method based on dynamic programming applied to computer aided detection in mammography. *Medical Physics*. 31(5):958-72
32. U.S. Census Bureau (2010), Americans with Disabilities: 2010 Household Economic Studies, http://www.census.gov/prod/2012pubs/p70-131.pdf
33. U.S. Department of Transportation, Designing Sidewalks and Trails for Access, http://www.fhwa.dot.gov/environment/bicycle_pedestrian /publications/sidewalks/index.cfm
34. U.S. Department of Transportation, Road Safety Audits (RSA), http://safety.fhwa.dot.gov/rsa/
35. Yao, B., Yang, X., & Zhu, S. (2007). Introduction to a large-scale general purpose ground truth database: methodology, annotation tool and benchmarks. *EMMCVPR'07*, 169-183.
36. Zhang, Y. (2001) A review of recent evaluation methods for image segmentation. *ISSPA'01*. 1:148-51.

Labor Dynamics in a Mobile Micro-Task Market

Mohamed Musthag, Deepak Ganesan
Department of Computer Science
University of Massachusetts, Amherst, MA 01003
{musthag, dganesan}@cs.umass.edu

ABSTRACT

The ubiquity of smartphones has led to the emergence of mobile crowdsourcing markets, where smartphone users participate to perform tasks in the physical world. Mobile crowdsourcing markets are uniquely different from their online counterparts in that they require spatial mobility, and are therefore impacted by geographic factors and constraints that are not present in the online case. Despite the emergence and importance of such mobile marketplaces, little to none is known about the labor dynamics and mobility patterns of agents.

This paper provides an in-depth exploration of labor dynamics in mobile task markets based on a year-long dataset from a leading mobile crowdsourcing platform. We find that a small core group of workers ($< 10\%$) account for a disproportionately large proportion of activity ($> 80\%$) generated in the market. We find that these *super agents* are more efficient than other agents across several dimensions: a) they are willing to move longer distances to perform tasks, yet they amortize travel across more tasks, b) they work and search for tasks more efficiently, c) they have higher data quality in terms of accepted submissions, and d) they improve in almost all of these efficiency measures over time. We find that super agent efficiency stems from two simple optimizations — they are $3\times$ more likely than other agents to chain tasks and they pick fewer lower priced tasks than other agents. We compare mobile and online micro-task markets, and discuss differences in demographics, data quality, and time of use, as well as similarities in super agent behavior. We conclude with a discussion of how a mobile micro-task market might leverage some of our results to improve performance.

Author Keywords

crowdsourcing; mobile crowdsourcing; micro task markets; labor mobility

ACM Classification Keywords

H.5.m. Information Interfaces and Presentation (e.g. HCI): Miscellaneous

Platform	Tasks
Field Agent [2]	Price checks, Service Assessment, Photography, Verification, Property Evaluation
Gigwalk [3]	Data collection, Photography, Focus Groups, Store Audits, IT, Financial Services
NeighborFavor [4]	Deliveries, Rides, Groceries
TaskRabbit [5]	Odd Errands, Groceries, Moving, Deliveries, Cleaning
WeGoLook [6]	Verify Properties, Automobiles, Dates, Boats, Heavy Equipment before purchase

Table 1. Some Active Mobile Crowdsourcing Platforms

General Terms

Human Factors; Measurement.

INTRODUCTION

The past decade has seen unprecedented growth in smartphones, with millions of these devices becoming first-class citizens of the Internet. The growing smartphone user base has enabled new paid mobile crowdsourcing marketplaces, where individuals are paid to perform tasks using their mobile phones as they move around in their day-to-day lives. Such task markets represent the mobile equivalent of online task markets such as the Amazon Mechanical Turk [1], and provide an exchange for short and generic micro-tasks that can be performed by any individual with a smartphone. Several instances of such mobile crowdsourcing markets have emerged commercially including Gigwalk [3], FieldAgent [2], and TaskRabbit [5] (see Table 1)— typical tasks pay users a few dollars for capturing photos of buildings or sites, price checks, product placement checks in stores, traffic checks, location-aware surveys, and so on.

While there has been significant prior work on online microtask markets such as the Amazon Mechanical Turk, they do not capture several unique characteristics of mobile crowdsourcing markets. These markets are different from their online counterparts in that they involve *mobility* in the physical world. As a consequence, they are influenced by a host of location-dependent factors such as population density, transportation modes, commute costs, and geographically scoped supply and demand, none of which play a role in online task markets. Such mobile task markets provide valuable and unique insights into the labor dynamics for micro-tasks in the physical world, and our understanding of how location-dependent factors influence individual agent behavior as well as overall system dynamics.

In this paper, we leverage a large dataset of several hundreds of thousands of mobile micro-tasks and tens of thousands of agents from a popular mobile crowdsourcing platform. Our contributions are three-fold. First, we mine the dataset to answer several questions about spatio-temporal labor dynamics of agents in a mobile task market. We look at how far agents are willing to move to perform tasks, how they amortize the costs associated with travel across tasks that they perform, how efficient they are in locating tasks that they wish to perform and in actually executing the tasks, and the quality of data that they provide. We look at temporal trends across all of these metrics to understand whether their efficiency tends to improve or reduce over time. Our analysis reveals that a small fraction of agents ($< 10\%$ of all agents), whom we refer to as *super-agents*, perform more than 80% of the tasks and earn more than 80% of the total earnings. We track these super agents to understand what makes them so good at leveraging a mobile crowdsourcing system. We find that super agents are willing to travel longer distances to reach jobs and thereby incur larger fixed travel costs, yet they are more efficient and amortize the fixed costs by performing several back-to-back jobs at locations that they travel to as well as by optimizing the time spent in searching and completing jobs. We also find that super agents are constantly improving in their efficiency across spatial and temporal dimensions, as well as improving the quality of data they provide.

Second, we contrast mobile crowdsourcing and online crowdsourcing markets in terms of demographics, super agent behavior, data quality and other metrics. We find that mobile markets have more male, educated, and younger agents in comparison with online task markets. We also see fewer data quality issues in mobile crowdsourcing markets compared to the online case, perhaps because of location-based validation and the high commute costs. We find similarities in super agent behavior across these task markets but differences in usage behavior.

Third, we discuss implications of our analysis for the design of mobile task markets, how to design these markets to make them more effective, and how to use our findings about super agent behavior to enable other agents to be more efficient and productive. Our analysis provides a valuable first look at labor dynamics in a large-scale mobile crowdsourcing system.

MOBILECROWD PLATFORM & DATASET

MobileCrowd (real name hidden for anonymity) is a smartphone-based crowdsourcing platform. It allows individuals with smartphones easy access to flexible work, while allowing businesses to tap into a mobile workforce. MobileCrowd is active in several major metros in the US including Los Angeles, New York City, San Francisco Bay Area, Seattle, among others. MobileCrowd customers post tasks, which usually have more than one instantiation and may be assigned in various locations. For example, a task could be to try a product and report on the customer experience and this task may be assigned for multiple stores in different locations. Cafe and restaurant tasks have agents visit cafes or restaurants, take pictures of their menus, and may involve reviewing the quality of service, food, and atmosphere. One of the biggest categories of tasks in the dataset is the Photosynth category. It requires agents to capture high quality panoramic images using the Microsoft Photosynth[1] app. Traffic tasks may have agents investigate the existence of a roadblock at a particular location.

Workers can search for tasks easily on a map, clicking through to view details of the task. Almost all tasks ($>99.8\%$) required agents to be present at the location of the task before they can accept one. Upon downloading the app, agents report their gender, age, highest level of education, and current profession, providing valuable information about the demographics of the agents on MobileCrowd. All activity generated by the agent on the app is logged with a timestamp and location. This includes agent authentication events, profile update events, task downloads and views, starting and completion of tasks, acceptance and rejection of tasks by task posters, etc. Overall, the dataset contained over 28 million log entries, providing a wealth of data about agent behavior that forms the basis of our analysis.

MobileCrowd was initially released on the Apple iPhone, and has subsequently been released for the Android OS. We have data for over 400 days of MobileCrowd agent activity ending in September 2011. Our trace ended before the Android app was released so the dataset contains only iPhone users. Hundreds of thousands of different assignments were posted over this period, out of which tens of thousands had been completed by the end of our trace[2]. Out of the tens of thousands of unique agents who were registered to use the service, several thousand agents successfully completed at least one assignment, whom we call *active* agents. All analyses presented in the paper are over these active agents, and a subset of these active agents whom we refer to as super-agents, unless mentioned otherwise.

SUPER AGENTS AND THEIR BEHAVIOR

While examining MobileCrowd user behavior, we observe an interesting trend — a relatively small core-group of users generate a disproportionately large fraction of the activity. Figure 1 shows that 10% of active agents are responsible for a remarkable 84% of total earnings, and for 80% of the total tasks done on MobileCrowd. The existence of such heavily skewed behavior on MobileCrowd makes it important to focus on this critical group of users since they play a dominant role in the overall dynamics of the system and contribute the most value to task posters in such a marketplace. We refer to this top 10% of active agents as *super-agents*, a term that we will use throughout this paper to refer to this group.

Our analyses in the rest of this section examines several questions pertinent to user behavior through a super agent lens. Why are super agents significantly more effective at performing tasks and earning money through mobile crowdsourcing?

[1] http://itunes.apple.com/us/app/photosynth/id430065256?mt=8

[2] At the request of MobileCrowd, we do not provide precise numbers of the size of the task market in terms of the agents, tasks, and revenue. Rather, we focus on understanding performance of agents, and comparing different groups in terms of their efficiency.

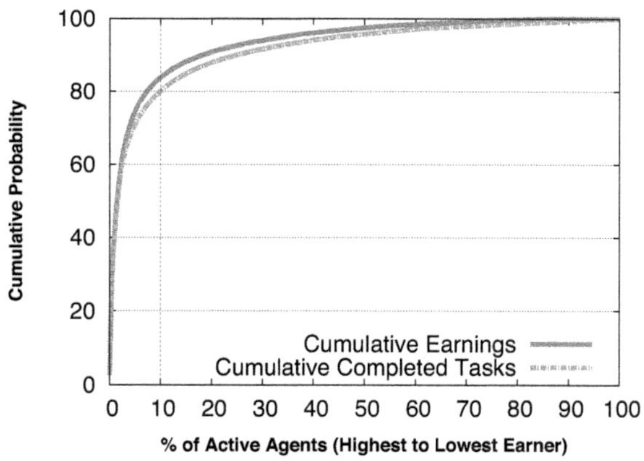

Figure 1. Top 10% of active agents responsible for 84% of total earnings and 80% of all completed tasks on MobileCrowd

Do super agents earn more simply because they perform more tasks or do they have any tricks that make them more efficient in performing these tasks? How far are agents willing to travel to perform tasks? Are the amounts earned on tasks sufficient to amortize commute costs? Are there any demographic differences between super agents and other agents? Through the process of answering these questions, we hope to identify characteristics that distinguish this group, and that could provide useful insights for task posters and agents.

We use mixed-effects regressions analyses, which account for correlation of observations within individuals, to test for significant differences. Where useful, p-values are reported with the means and confidence bounds of the corresponding distributions.

How efficient are super agents?

In this section, we look at the efficiency of agents on the MobileCrowd platform. Since mobile tasks involve both physical mobility as well as time spent on the app to perform the task, we need to consider both the spatial and temporal efficiency of an agent. From a spatial perspective, Labor Economists have argued that higher labor mobility, either in the form of occupational mobility (changing jobs) or geographic mobility (changing work location), contributes to economic growth by eliminating inefficiencies in the economy [8]. In the context of mobile crowdsourcing, we see a lot of geographical labor mobility. While this does not manifest in the sense of uprooting livelihoods and relocating as commonly understood by Economists, willingness to move longer distances generally makes more tasks accessible to workers provided that there are tasks available further away. From a temporal perspective, a pertinent question is how efficiently agents perform work in a mobile task market. Just as labor mobility incurs the overhead of moving to the task location, there is also temporal overhead incurred in searching across the list of available tasks in an area, and deciding which tasks to perform. In the rest of this section, we look at these two aspects of efficiency of mobile agents.

Distance Efficiency

Given evidence of the benefits of labor mobility in the Economics literature, we would like to capture how these benefits manifest themselves, and to what degree they extend to the present context of mobile crowdsourcing. Is traveling longer distances correlated with higher activity on MobileCrowd? Do agents who have larger geographically "active" regions perform better? Can the success of super agents be explained by their willingness to travel larger distances? Are agents able to recoup the additional travel time and monetary cost associated with geographical mobility to tasks (e.g. fuel cost, bus/subway tickets, parking fees, etc)?

The metric that we use for capturing these tradeoffs is *distance efficiency*, which we define as the number of dollars earned per mile traveled in a day. A higher distance efficiency means that an agent earned more dollars per mile, which is preferred irrespective of the transportation mode that the agent used.

Estimating distance traveled: To compute distance efficiency, we must first estimate the distance traveled in a day to perform the tasks. However, measuring the total distance traveled by a super-agent is not straightforward since we first need to identify the "home" location for each agent, and then calculate the round-trip distance between home and the tasks that were performed in the day. In addition, it is possible that agents further amortize travel costs by performing tasks that are closer to their "work" location or other meaningful locations where they may be visiting.

We approximate the total distance traveled by an agent as follows. We look at all the locations at which the app was used but where a task was not actually completed — this includes browsing for tasks, updating profile, or viewing earnings, but does not include working on and submitting tasks. We assume that most of these points are likely to emerge from the "planning" location i.e. the location from where a user plans the travel circuit for the day. We identify this planning location for each active agent as the largest cluster among the non-worked location samples, generated by running an hierarchical clustering algorithm on the dataset, where clusters are not allowed to span more than a mile in radius.

Once the *planning* location is identified, our estimate for the daily distance travelled is the length of the simple cycle starting from the planning location, and visiting all completed assignments in a day. For example, if an agent does most of his planning in location A and in one day completed a task in location B and another in location C, the daily distance traveled would be the sum of the distance between A and B, B and C, and C and A, where each distance is the great circle distance between the two points. We filtered out cases where agents traveled more than 100 miles since agents sometimes performed work in other cities while traveling.

Figure 2 shows the CDF of the daily distances travelled on days where at least one task was completed. We find that super-agents travel on average 14.07 miles each day in-order to complete tasks, which is 2.91 miles longer in a day than other agents ($p < 0.000$).

Distance efficiency: We have seen that super agents are willing to travel longer distances, but does the extended travel

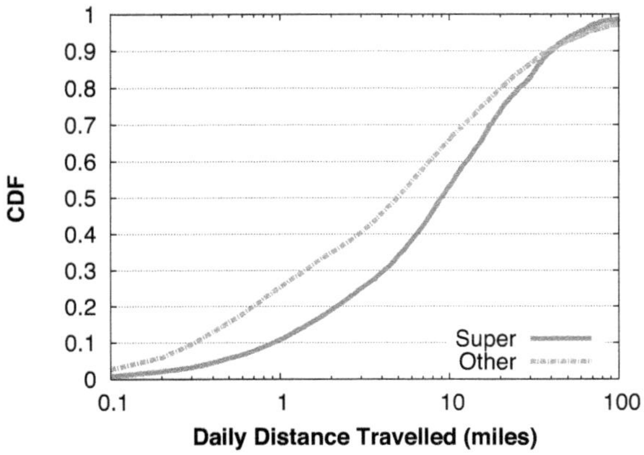

Figure 2. Distance travelled (log scale) in a day CDF. Super agents travel larger distances daily

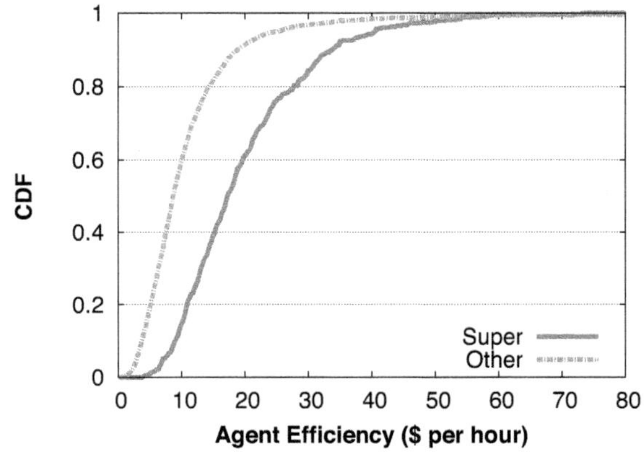

Figure 4. Working Efficiency CDF. Super agents are more efficient working on tasks

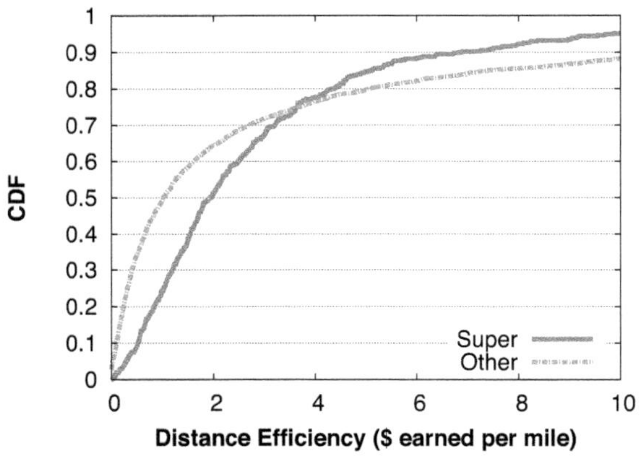

Figure 3. Distance Efficiency CDF. Super agents earn more per mile than a majority of other agents.

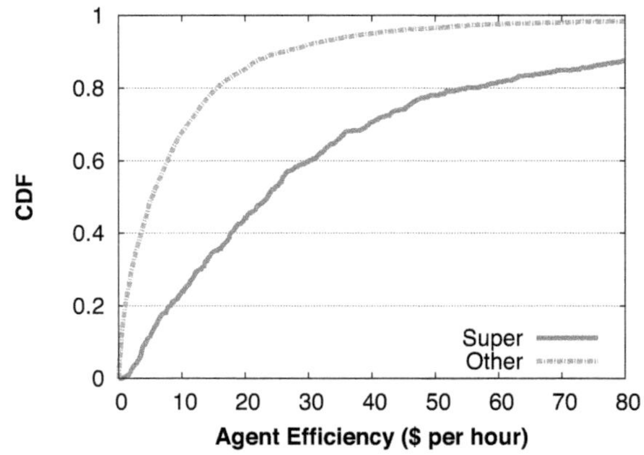

Figure 5. Searching Efficiency CDF. Super agents are more efficient searching and planning

lead to more earning opportunities? Figure 3 shows the CDF of distance efficiency for all active agents. The graph shows that super agents have higher distance efficiency in all except the last quartile of agents, where the trend flips. This demonstrates that longer distances that super agents are willing to travel occasionally hurts their distance efficiency. The higher distance efficiency for some of the other agents also arises from the fact that they perform only a few tasks that are very proximate to their residences, leading to high efficiency. In terms of average earnings, super agents and other agents are similar earning on average 6.51 and 6.57 dollars per mile respectively.

In summary, we see that even though super agents travel longer distances, they earn more in their travels, thereby making their distance efficiency higher than a majority of other agents.

Temporal Efficiency
Having looked at the mobility patterns of agents in MobileCrowd, we turn to the temporal aspects of their behavior. Specifically, we look at how efficiently they use their *time* on MobileCrowd. The time that a user spends on the MobileCrowd app can be split into two parts: a) the time that a user spends doing a task, whether it involves capturing pictures or answering questions, and b) the time that a user spends perusing through available jobs to search for an appropriate one. Since our dataset includes details on exactly what action was performed on the app each time it was used, it allows us to precisely separate the two metrics. Together, these metrics capture the temporal efficiency of a user.

Working efficiency: In order to measure how well an agent uses her time while working, we define *working efficiency* as the number of dollars earned per hour spent working on assignments. Figure 4 shows the CDF of working efficiency for all active agents. Super agents earn on average 19.84 dollars per hour, while other agents earn 10.82 dollars per hour ($p < 0.000$)

Searching efficiency: The temporal efficiency of a mobile agent depends not only on the time spent working on assignments, but also the time agents spend planning and looking for tasks to perform. In this section we look at these sessions in which agents do no work, but spend searching and planning. Similar to *working efficiency*, we define *searching efficiency* as the dollars earned per hour that an agent spends planning and searching for tasks. Figure 5 shows the CDF of *searching efficiency* of agents. We find that super agents earn on average 40.19 dollars per minute spent plan-

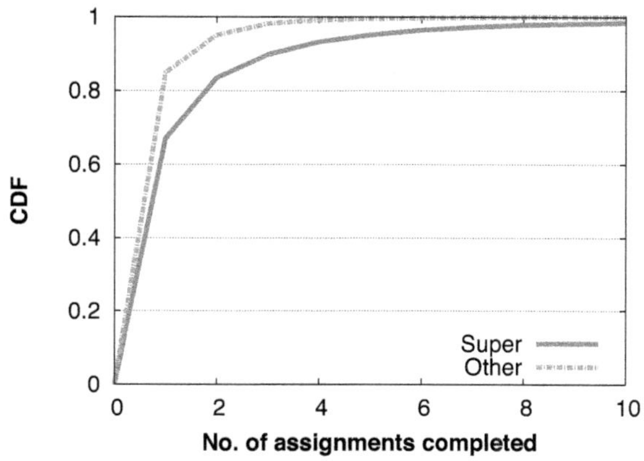

Figure 6. Session Worked Count CDF. Super agents chain more than one assignment in almost 20% of sessions

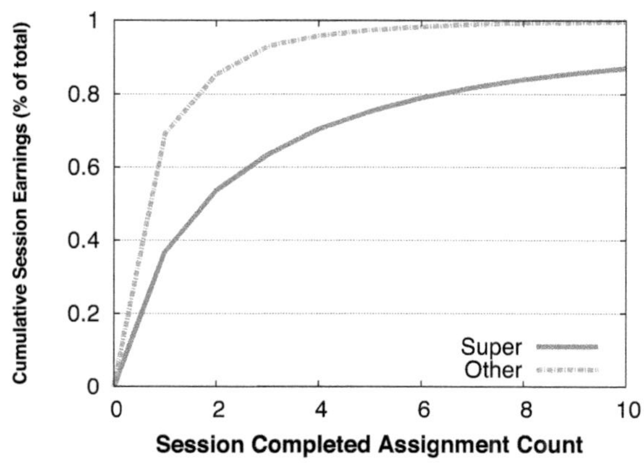

Figure 7. Cumulative Session Earnings. Nearly 50% of total super agent earnings is generated by sessions in which agents chained at least 2 tasks

ning and searching, whereas other agents earn 16.46 dollars per minute. ($p < 0.052$)

Thus, not only are super agents traveling more distances to improve distance efficiency, they are also planning and searching for tasks more efficiently to improve temporal efficiency.

Why are super agents more efficient?

Our results so far have demonstrated that super agents are more efficient along the spatial and temporal dimensions. We now ask "how" they achieve higher efficiencies. Are there any specific techniques that super agents utilize to improve their efficiencies?

Chaining Tasks: One intuitive method by which super agents may be improving efficiency is by working on several spatially proximate tasks each time they travel to a location. Since many tasks involve photos and information about businesses, they tend to be clustered in downtown areas and malls where several businesses are present. This provides an opportunity to "chain" several tasks and perform them in a single batch.

To understand if this behavior is present, we divide the agent activity logs into segments of activity, which we refer to as sessions. A session is defined as a series of agent activity events whose inter-event gap is not longer than ten minutes and the inter-event distance is not more than half a mile. A worked session is a session during which at least one task was attempted.

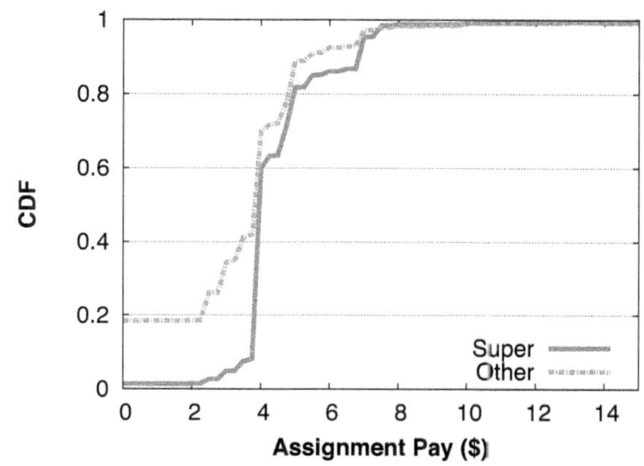

Figure 8. Completed Assignment Pay CDF. Super agents complete fewer lowly paid tasks

Figure 6 shows that while non-super agents chained more than one assignment in only 5% of worked sessions, super agents chained more than one assignment in almost 20% of worked sessions - a four-fold difference. Indeed, we find super agents are $3\times$ more likely to chain multiple assignments into one ($p < 0.000$).

This difference is even more significant if we look at the proportion of total earnings generated by sessions where chaining occurred. Figure 7 shows the cumulative fraction of the agents' earnings produced by sessions where they completed one assignment, two assignments, and so on. For super agents, this plot shows that this 20% of worked sessions, where more than one assignment was completed, is responsible for nearly 50% of total super-agent earnings. For the rest of the agents, this plot shows that the corresponding 5% of sessions generated only about 15% of non-super-agent earnings.

This explains why, in a majority of cases, super agents have higher distance efficiency even though they travel longer distances — they amortize the travel costs better by chaining multiple tasks into one worked sessions. These results are in line with labor economic theories about the impact of mobility on overall economic activity — more willingness to move can provide larger rewards in terms of earnings.

Higher paid tasks: The above result explains how super agents are more efficient along the spatial dimension but how do they improve temporal efficiency?

First, we look at the rewards for tasks that agents perform, and see if there is a difference in rewards for tasks that are selected by super agents v.s. other agents. Figure 8 shows the CDF of offered rewards on completed assignments. We see that the super agent distribution is to the right of that for the other agent, implying that super agents do in fact work on higher priced tasks in comparison with other agents ($p < 0.000$).

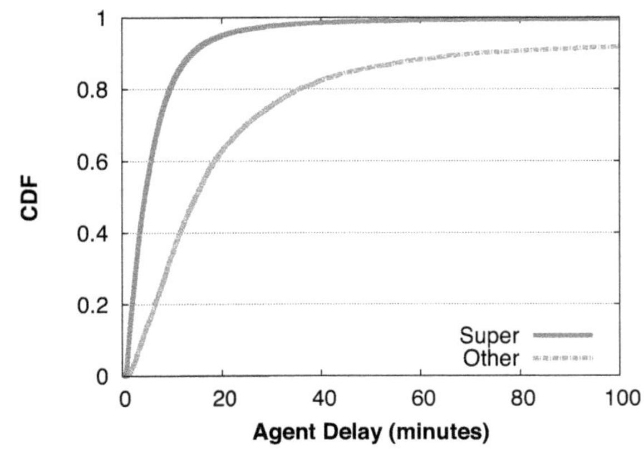

Figure 9. Completion Delay CDF - Photosynth tasks. Super agents are $3\times$ faster at completing Photosynth tasks

Second, we look at the rate at which super agents perform tasks and see if there are intrinsic differences in the rate at which work is done by different agent groups. In order to understand this behavior, we look at the largest category of tasks in MobileCrowd, which are the Photosynth tasks and check if super agents are quicker to complete these tasks. We fix the category of tasks to control for any differences between tasks in terms of the amount of work involved. Figure 9 shows the CDF of time taken by agents to complete these Photosynth assignments. While the rest of the crowd takes 14.75 minutes on average to complete these Photosynth tasks, super agents take merely 4.58 minutes on average to complete these tasks ($p < 0.001$). Super agents are more than 3 times more efficient at doing Photosynth tasks than the rest of the agents!

Thus, the high temporal efficiency of super agents is a combination of selection of higher paid tasks as well as being faster in completing these tasks.

How does efficiency change over time?

An important question in a crowdsourcing task market is how agents change their behavior over time. We discussed several measures of agent efficiency, but do these efficiency measures improve over time or do they wane? In addition to providing insights into how agents learn methods to utilize the system more effectively, perhaps a bigger reason to analyze trends is to understand if the market place remains attractive for agents over a long term. Retention of important personnel is critical to any organization, and particularly to a task market where an agent can leave at any time. If the efficiency numbers remain steady or rise over time, that suggests a vibrant marketplace, and if the efficiency numbers dip, it suggests a marketplace in decline. To understand such "retention" aspects of MobileCrowd, we look at trends in efficiency i.e. how do the spatial and temporal efficiency metrics change over time for super agents.

Spatial efficiency trends: First, we look at the distance agents travel to do tasks and its variation over time. To do this analysis, we take the time every assignment was completed and normalize by the day they joined MobileCrowd. So, if two agents A and B completed two assignments on the same day, and A had joined MobileCrowd 5 days ago and B, 25 days ago, then these assignments would be marked as been completed on day 5 for agent A and day 25 for agent B. We find that super agents travel larger distances to complete tasks over time ($p < 0.000$). This indicates increasing involvement in MobileCrowd as super agents continue to use the system.

Second, we look at whether agents learn to improve their distance efficiency score over time. For both super agents ($p < 0.000$) and other agents ($p < 0.021$) we find a positive effect of time on distance efficiency. This implies that all agents on average improve their distance efficiency score as they continue to participate in MobileCrowd.

Temporal efficiency trends: We now turn to trends in temporal efficiency. We look at whether agents are able to improve their working and searching efficiency over time. We find that all agents, not just super agents, improve their working efficiency over time ($p < 0.000$). This indicates that agents are either chaining more tasks over time, shifting to higher paid tasks, getting faster in completing tasks, or any combination thereof. In terms of searching efficiency, we find no statistical evidence to suggest that super agents improve on this dimension, whereas other agents improve searching efficiency over time ($p < 0.005$).

Thus, we see that super agents, and other agents as well, generally improve in their efficiency as they continue to use the mobile task market. This improvement in efficiency is both a sign of increasing engagement in the system, and a sign that they are learning ways to reduce the overhead of using such a platform. In particular, the fact that super agent participation increases over time suggests that the demand side of such a market place is steady — once agents become active participants in such a system, they remain active.

How does efficiency depend on location?

Our analysis of spatial efficiencies assumed that agents across the country were homogeneous in their travel patterns, and efficiencies. We now separate agent behavior across different geographies to understand whether there are differences across different metros and/or states, and how we might understand agent behavior in different geographies.

First, we look at how travel distances and distance efficiencies vary across metros in the U.S. We pick five metros where a significant fraction of tasks were located, and compare them across the two metrics. Major metros in the U.S. differ widely in their geographic spread and urban sprawl, typical commute patterns and transportation modes, availability and popularity of public transportation, proximity between downtowns (where tasks are located) and residential areas (where agents live), and so on.

Figure 10 shows a box plot of distances traveled by agents on days where at least one task was completed broken down by five major metros in the U.S. We observe some interesting trends — commute in LA is double that of NYC, and easily the largest across all metros. Miami is the second highest in terms of commute, followed by SF, Chicago, and the lowest being NYC. The trend generally reflects the urban sprawl of

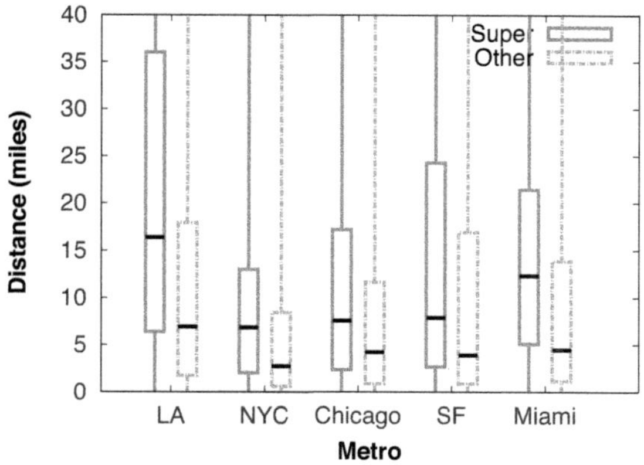

Figure 10. Daily distance traveled by 5 of the most active metros. Super agents in LA travel on average 27 miles daily, whereas agents in NYC travel only 10 miles daily

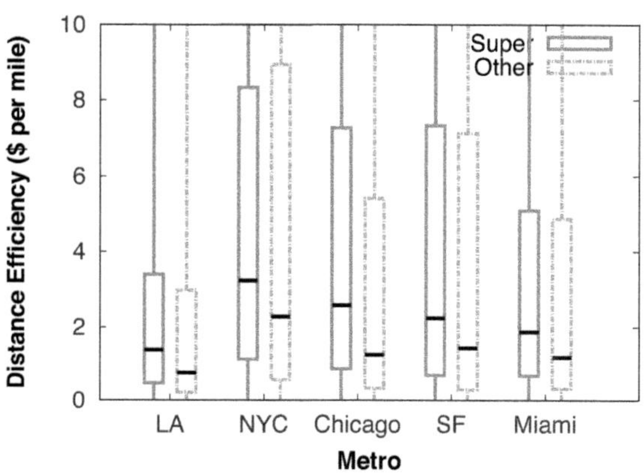

Figure 11. Distance efficiency by 5 of the most active metros. Super agents in NYC make almost double per mile traveled compared to super agents in LA

these metros — LA and Miami are sprawling cities spread over large regions with people largely living in the suburbs, whereas NYC is less sprawling, more dense with many residents in high-rises proximate to the downtowns. Other cities fall in between these extremes. Regardless of the metro, however, we find that super agents are willing to move more, meaning that they are willing to incur more travel costs (and associated time) for performing tasks each day.

The differences in distance traveled is reflected in the distance efficiencies of agents in the different metros. Figure 11 show that agents in NYC have the highest efficiency, followed by Chicago, SF, Miami and the lowest being LA. This reflects the fact that the super agents in LA or Miami are not able to amortize their travels over more tasks than their counterparts in NYC or Chicago. Thus, the overall earnings per trip remains roughly the same across the metros, leading to lower distance efficiency for some of the cities. As with distance traveled, we find that super agents have higher distance efficiency than other agents in all except the third quartile for NYC.

Second, we look at travel distances and distance efficiencies across states in the U.S. We summarize the results but do

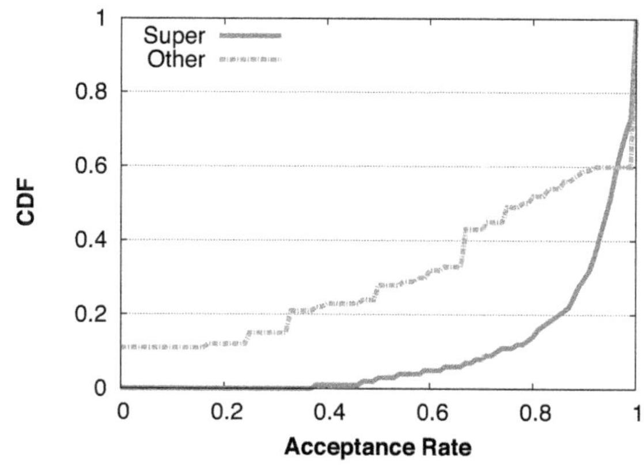

Figure 12. Acceptance Rate CDF. Super agents' submissions have a higher accpetance rate

not show graphs in the interest of space. We find trends that are similar to those observed for the key metros. In general, agents in FL and CA earn less per mile traveled compared to agents in the other states, and agents in NY and MA earn the most per mile traveled, reflecting the sprawl of cities in the corresponding states. However, regardless of the state, super agents have better distance efficiency numbers compared to the rest of the agents as they are able to amortize travel costs over their comparatively larger daily earnings.

The results show that while there are differences across metros/states as might be expected based on the differences in population spread and urban sprawl, the overall conclusion remains remarkably consistent — super agents travel more than other agents but they have higher distance efficiency.

Does efficiency impact quality?

Our results thus far have shown that super agents are more efficient in spatial and temporal dimensions, but is the data quality good or do they submit low quality responses in their effort to make more money? To understand the difference in data quality between super agents and the rest, we look at whether the domain expert who requested the job accepted or rejected the submission. If accepted, the agent who completed the task is paid. Otherwise, it is automatically reposted allowing agents to reattempt the task. The acceptance rate for an agent is defined as the fraction of the tasks completed by the agent that has been accepted by the requester.

Figure 12 shows the CDF of acceptance rates broken down by agent class. We find that super agents on average have an acceptance rate of 90.73% while other agents have an acceptance rate of 69.58%. Furthermore, we find that super agents tend to improve their acceptance rate over time ($p < 0.000$). These result shows that super agents are not only more efficient, but also provide higher quality responses than the rest of the agents. Perhaps this is unsurprising, since rejected responses would reduce the overall efficiency of super agents since the time/cost of searching, working, and traveling would have been wasted. In their effort to maximize overall efficiency, they provide good data to ensure that their responses are not rejected.

Education	Super	Other	Total
Some High School	0.93%	1.02%	1.02%
High School	3.70%	5.79%	5.58%
Some College	14.81%	17.52%	17.25%
College	55.79%	54.36%	54.5%
Some Graduate School	4.86%	4.99%	4.98%
Graduate School	19.91%	16.31%	16.67%

Table 2. Proportion of active agents by highest education level

Age	Super	Other	Total
Under 18	1.16%	1.21%	1.20%
18-35	57.64%	68.66%	67.56%
35-50	34.26%	24.98%	25.91%
50-65	6.48%	4.84%	5%
Over 65	0.46%	0.26%	0.28%

Table 3. Proportion of active agents by age-group

Who are the super agents?

The super agents are clearly more efficient in every dimension — spatial, temporal and quality. So, who are these people? How do they differ from the other agents?

Table 2 shows that agents on MobileCrowd are highly educated. Over 75% of agents hold a college degree, and over 20% hold an advanced degree. We find that more educated agents are significantly more likely to become super agents ($p < 0.010$).

Table 3 shows that most agents are young. Almost 70% of active agents are under 35 years of age. However, we find that older agents are more likely to become super agents ($p < 0.000$).

Table 4 shows two groups of agents: students (16.32% of active agents), who made up the largest profession on MobileCrowd, and photographers (3.75% of active agents), who had the highest completed assignment yield, i.e. average number of assignments completed per agent. Despite being the largest profession on MobileCrowd, students are less likely to become super agents ($p < 0.009$). In contrast, we find photographers to be more likely to become super agent ($p < 0.036$). Photographers had a completed assignment yield of 23.57 assignments/agent, while the overall active agent population had a yield of 6.93 assignments/agent.

The fact that photographers are more likely to become super agents may be attributed to the fact that a large fraction of mobile crowdsourcing jobs involved capturing images of a physical location or building (83% of all tasks). Photographers have a natural inclination for such jobs, and seemed to be better suited for them. Thus, even though mobile crowdsourcing jobs are simple enough to be performed by any user with a smartphone, the nature of the job tends to attract users with certain types of interests and skillset more than others.

ONLINE VS. MOBILE CROWDSOURING MARKETS

While our work represents perhaps the first view into user behavior in mobile crowdsourcing systems, there is extensive literature on worker behavior in online crowdsourcing systems such as the Amazon Mechanical Turk, TopCoder, Witkey, etc [7, 9, 10, 12, 13, 17, 18, 19]. In this section, we contrast some of the results that we have observed with observations made in online crowdsourcing counterparts. While location-related aspects are unique to mobile crowdsourcing, we find commonalities in super agent behavior and differences in the demographics of users who participate in mobile v.s. online task markets.

Occupation	Super	Other	Total
Student	11.81%	16.83%	16.32%
Photographer	5.79%	3.52%	3.75%

Table 4. Proportion of active agents who are students and photographers

Comparing Demographics

While a few of the demographic make up and behavioral patterns we observe on MobileCrowd are consistent with their online counterparts, many are different. Whereas women (65%) outnumbered men (35%) amongst *MTurkers* in the U.S. [13], we find the opposite on MobileCrowd, there are signficantly more male (71%) agents than female (29%) agents. Perhaps this difference is due to the high mobility requirement in mobile crowdsourcing markets. Yet, we did not find evidence that suggested that active male agents had any higher probability of success on MobileCrowd.

[13] found that 54% of MTurkers in the U.S. to be between 21-35 years old. In MobileCrowd, the corresponding figure is over 62%, suggesting that whilst crowdsourcing in general is most popular amongst the young, *mobile* crowdsourcing is slightly more so. Despite this skew, and somewhat surprisingly, we find that the older agents have a higher probability of success on MobileCrowd.

Whereas [13] found 55% of MTurkers in the U.S. reported they hold at least a college degree, in MobileCrowd, over 75% reported holding at least a college degree, indicating a significantly more educated labor market in the mobile crowdsourcing sphere. These last two findings may be the result of the higher barrier to entry into the mobile crowdsourcing market. Many have access to the web, but not as many have access to smartphones.

Comparing Super Agent Behavior

A heavy tail of participants who have a significantly lower level of activity compared to the top contributors is not uncommon for any online community [12]. In *online* crowdsourcing, MTurk, one of the most well-studied platforms, was found to exhibit this heavy-tail characteristic [12]. In one longitudinal study [13], 10% of the most active MTurkers were found to complete 75% of the HITS. (In MobileCrowd, 10% of the most active agents completed 80% of all completed tasks.) The same study reported that 16% of the most active MTurkers earned 70% of total income. (In MobileCrowd, 16% of the most active agents accounted for 89% of total earnings.) This characteristic has been independently verified in [10], which found that the top 22% of MTurkers on AMT completed 80% of the HITs. Such a long-tail phenomenon is not only exhibited by the MTurkers [13, 19], but also seen on the part of *requesters* [12]. Indeed, it was observed by [12] that 0.1% of total requesters on AMT accounted for more than 30% of the overall tasks posted on the market.

Yang et. al found a similar effect on a popular WitKey website – Task.cn. A WitKey website is an online knowledge market where users post questions or problems and other users provide solutions competing for a monetary award. Task.cn is one of the biggest WitKey websites in China with millions of registered users. They found that 0.1% of active users were responsible for proposing 20% of the winning solutions[19] (by comparison, 0.1% of workers were responsible for 10.78% of earnings, and 11.12% of completed tasks in MobileCrowd) This 0.1% of users were additionally found to increase their win to submission ratio over time, similar to efficiency trends that we observed about super agents.

Comparing Data Quality

One of the challenges in online crowdsourcing is obtaining high quality data from agents. This is the result of the difficulty involved in manually verifying the quality of submitted responses, which can be time-consuming and can negate the benefits of crowdsourcing. As a consequence, many requesters only sample some of the results, and are more likely to automatically pay workers since the price is low. Malicious workers (or bots pretending to be workers) can take advantage of the verification difficulty, and submit low-quality responses in the hope that they will not be checked [15]. For example, [15] cites an example where users are required to classify a website into G/PG/R or X categories, but it is difficult to verify if the worker actually visited the site.

We find that the difficulty with verifying data quality is less prevalent in mobile crowdsourcing systems. Most submissions are of high quality, and the rejected submissions are often because users did not provide high-quality photos or fill out all fields rather than malicious intent. Our hypothesis is that this is because of two reasons. First, since the mobile application records location and time data from users' smartphones, verification of the fact that agents visited the location where they were supposed to perform tasks is trivial. Second, the cost of doing a task is significantly higher compared to online tasks because of additional travel and commute costs associated with moving to task locations. The effect of this overhead can be be better understood using a game theoretic model of crowdsourcing systems (Ho et. al [11]). Intuitively, by expending low effort, agents incur a higher risk of not getting paid, and given the higher cost of doing tasks on mobile task markets, the expected payoff is significantly less. Thus, agents have limited incentive to submit low-quality results, leading to higher quality of work in a mobile task market.

Comparing Time of Use

Another difference that we find between the two task markets is when workers/agents are likely to use the market. Studies of online labor markets have found that the workforce peaks in early afternoon times [14]. The reasons for this behavior vary, but often is due to the availability of high-speed internet access from workplace rather than home. The corresponding time-of-day usage pattern for MobileCrowd is shown in Figure 13. We see that the peak is shifted towards later in the evenings, typically between 4–7pm, which corresponds to the likely time when agents leave their day job and are able to travel to the location where they perform the tasks.

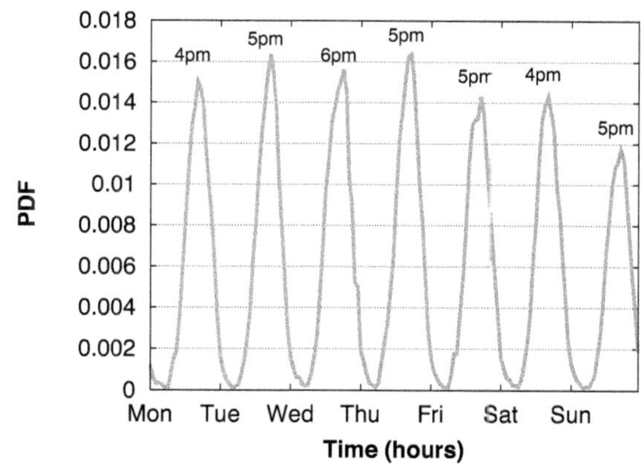

Figure 13. Time of work in MobileCrowd. Activity peaks daily between 4-7pm

DISCUSSION

Our analysis of labor dynamics in mobile crowdsourcing markets reveals several opportunities for improving the design of such systems. We outline some techniques that can be used to improve agent performance.

Providing Routes: We found that super agents optimize their efficiency by planning their routes efficiently, and chaining tasks to perform a sequence of tasks. In contrast, other agents are less likely to strategize as carefully and therefore have lower efficiency across the board.

These observations suggest an opportunity for a mobile crowdsourcing platform to improve how it presents tasks to users. Rather than just listing each task separately, a mobile task market can automatically identify routes that involve chaining of tasks, and provide recommendations to agents about these routes. Such recommendations may be particularly useful to agents who are less likely to identify such opportunities by themselves, and would serve two purposes: a) it can improve the efficiency of a non super agent, and b) the aggregate revenue over a route is likely to be more attractive than the incentive for a single task. Providing such "action plans" has been shown to be useful to workers in online crowdsourcing systems [16], and can be utilized to improve agent performance in mobile task markets as well.

Travel surcharges: One of the questions that a mobile agent faces is whether earnings from performing a task covers the aggregate travel costs of commuting to the task location. The analysis in this paper provides insights into how a mobile crowdsourcing system may be able to simplify this decision for an agent.

The first option is to provide agents with a rough estimate of travel costs by leveraging online "travel cost calculators" that use information about gas prices, traffic, and local public transportation costs[3]. Together with travel costs, the agent

[3]http://fuelcostcalculator.aaa.com/

can be provided an estimate of the true profit that they stand to make if they perform a task (or a chain of tasks). Our intuition is that presenting such options with greater transparency can perhaps influence agents to increase the range that they cover. For example, they may travel more if they see that traveling an additional 10 miles beyond their normal commute can be amortized over a larger incentive across a chain of tasks.

The second option is for the system to encourage requesters to explicitly incorporate such travel costs in pricing tasks. A rough estimate of travel costs may be obtained by identifying typical travel distances for super agents in the geographic region where task is to be posted (similar to our breakdown by metro/state), and estimate typical agent travel costs. This can be provided to requesters as a hint to decide how to price their tasks to attract maximum interest from nearby super agents.

Hints for task poster: In this work, we have shown that super agents play a dominant role in the operation of the system, and perhaps provide the best indicator of the steady state demand for tasks in a mobile crowdsourcing system. Thus, by tracking the number of super agents and their frequency of work, we can obtain a robust estimate of the demand for tasks in a geographic area.

This information can be valuable to a task poster. If a new task is being posted at a location, a task poster could be presented with information about the number of super-agents who are "in range" of the task location as well as other tasks in the vicinity of the same super agents. Such geo-scoped supply-demand information can be useful for task posters to estimate how long a task may take to complete as well as to provide an idea of how to price a task competitively to attract sufficient interest from the super agents.

CONCLUSIONS

"Mobile crowdsourcing" using smartphones is becoming an increasingly important tool for a variety of application domains where small jobs need to be done in the physical world. However, little is known about labor dynamics in micro-task markets that require physical mobility of agents. In this paper, we analyze user behavior on one of the largest and most popular mobile task markets. We analyzed efficiency of mobile agents in terms of how much distance they travel and time they spend for each dollar earned, and understand how a few agents (super agents) manage to perform much more efficiently than others. We looked at the behavior of these agents across metros/states with vastly different population spread and transportation modes, and across time to understand trends. In addition to analyzing agent behavior in a mobile task market, we also looked at how such markets differ from online crowdsourcing markets such as the Mechanical Turk that have been extensively analyzed over the last several years. We find significant differences in demographics, data quality, and other factors, reflecting the differences in the costs involved, and smartphone-using agent population. Finally, we draw lessons to improve the design of mobile task markets and improve efficiency of new agents. Our findings provide a valuable first look at spatio-temporal labor dynamics in mobile task markets.

While our analysis provides extensive insights into mobile task markets, it also opens up several interesting directions. One direction is modeling completion delay for tasks, based on super-agent and task availability in the geographic vicinity. Another direction is exploring the dynamics on the demand side of the market. What is the arrival rate of new tasks? Is there a stable flow? While some of these questions have been explored in the context of online markets, location provides a new dimension to explore behavior in mobile task markets.

ACKNOWLEDGEMENTS

This work was funded by NSF grants CNS-0910900, CNS-0855128, and a Google grant. We thank the anonymous reviewers for their insightful comments.

REFERENCES

1. Amazon Mechanical Turk. **https://www.mturk.com/**.
2. Field Agent. **http://www.fieldagent.net/**.
3. Gigwalk. **http://www.gigwalk.com/**.
4. NeighborFav. **http://www.neighbfav.com/**.
5. TaskRabbit. **http://www.taskrabbit.com/**.
6. WeGoLook. **http://www.wegolook.com/**.
7. Adda, G., and Mariani, J. Language resources and amazon mechanical turk: Legal, ethical and other issues. In *Legal Issues for Sharing Language Resources workshop*, LREC 2010 (Malta, 2010).
8. Borjas, G. J. The economic benefits from immigration. In *Journal of Economic Perspectives 9 (2)*, vol. 9 (1999), 3–22.
9. Brabham, D. Moving the crowd at istockphoto: The composition of the crowd and motivations for participation in a crowdsourcing application. In *First Monday 13, 6* (2008).
10. Deneme. How many turkers are there? In *Deneme Blog*, http://groups.csail.mit.edu/uid/deneme/?p=502 (Dec. 2009).
11. Ho, C.-J., Zhang, Y., Vaughan, J., and van der Schaar, M. Towards social norm design for crowdsourcing markets. In *AAAI Workshops* (2012).
12. Ipeirotis, P. G. Analyzing the amazon mechanical turk marketplace. In *XRDS*, vol. 17, ACM (New York, NY, USA, Dec. 2010), 16–21.
13. Ipeirotis, P. G. Demographics of mechanical turk. New York University, Stern School of Business (New York, NY, USA, 2010).
14. Ipeirotis, P. G., and J., H. Visualizations of the odesk "oconomy": Exploring our world of work. In *oDesk Blog*, https://www.odesk.com/blog/2012/07/visualizations-of-odesk-oconomy (2012).
15. Ipeirotis, P. G., Provost, F., and Wang, J. Quality management on amazon mechanical turk. In *Proceedings of the ACM SIGKDD Workshop on Human Computation*, HCOMP '10, ACM (New York, NY, USA, 2010), 64–67.
16. Kokkalis, N., Huebner, J., Diamond, S., Becker, D., Chang, M., Lee, M., Schulze, F., Koehn, T., and Klemmer, S. Automatically providing action plans helps people complete tasks. In *AAAI Workshops* (2012).
17. Mason, W., and Watts, D. J. Financial incentives and the "performance of crowds". In *SIGKDD Explor. Newsl.*, vol. 11, ACM (New York, NY, USA, May 2010), 100–108.
18. Ross, J., Irani, L., Silberman, M. S., Zaldivar, A., and Tomlinson, B. Who are the crowdworkers?: shifting demographics in mechanical turk. In *Proceedings of the 28th of the international conference extended abstracts on Human factors in computing systems*, CHI EA '10, ACM (New York, NY, USA, 2010), 2863–2872.
19. Yang, J., Adamic, L. A., and Ackerman, M. S. Crowdsourcing and knowledge sharing: strategic user behavior on taskcn. In *Proceedings of the 9th ACM conference on Electronic commerce*, EC '08, ACM (New York, NY, USA, 2008), 246–255.

Creativity Support for Novice Digital Filmmaking

Nicholas Davis, Alexander Zook, Brian O'Neill, Brandon Headrick, Mark Riedl
School of Interactive Computing
Georgia Institute of Technology
{ndavis35; a.zook; boneill; brandonheadrick; riedl}@gatech.edu

Ashton Grosz, Michael Nitsche
School of Literature, Media, and Communication
Georgia Institute of Technology
{grosz; michael.nitsche}@gatech.edu

ABSTRACT
Machinima is a new form of creative digital filmmaking that leverages the real time graphics rendering of computer game engines. Because of the low barrier to entry, machinima has become a popular creative medium for hobbyists and novices while still retaining borrowed conventions from professional filmmaking. Can novice machinima creators benefit from creativity support tools? A preliminary study shows novices generally have difficulty adhering to cinematographic conventions. We identify and document four cinematic conventions novices typically violate. We report on a Wizard-of-Oz study showing a rule-based intelligent system that can reduce the frequency of errors that novices make by providing information about rule violations without prescribing solutions. We discuss the role of error reduction in creativity support tools.

Author Keywords
Creativity Support Tools; Digital Filmmaking.

ACM Classification Keywords
H.5.m. Information interfaces and presentation (e.g., HCI): Miscellaneous.

General Terms
Human Factors; Experimentation.

INTRODUCTION
Machinima is a new form of creative digital filmmaking that leverages the real time graphic rendering capabilities of video game engines to create high fidelity animations. In its most rudimentary form, a machinima film is a recording of scripted video game characters with audio overlay. However, the tools of the trade have expanded beyond the initial confines of early video game engines to introduce much more complexity and nuance and include control of lighting, set and character design, and cinematography. This creative reuse of technology has opened a door to individuals with no experience in animation or filmmaking to create professional looking animated films.

The proliferation and open nature of machinima tools have introduced many new avenues for creative expression and significantly lowered the barrier to entry for digital filmmaking. These tools have empowered individuals to creatively express themselves in ways that were prohibitively expensive a decade ago. Machinima has been hailed as filmmaking for the masses [11]. However, no matter how powerful the tools have become, there are still elements of the filmmaking craft that remain unknown to novices. For this reason, their productions often suffer and fail to make creative contributions to the film domain.

In his systems model of creativity, Csíkszentmihályi [6] explains that the individual, field, and domain all play a role in evaluating creative contributions through social consensus. Individuals provide novel products, the field consists of respected leaders in a domain, and the domain is the accepted knowledge, rules, and procedures used by the community. Domain experts act as gatekeepers to filter contributions from individuals according to accepted conventions. In film, established cinematographic norms help audiences experience the illusion that they are watching a continuous narrative rather than a sequence of strung together camera shots. To achieve this, expert machinima makers ("machinimators") leverage (a) domain knowledge of conventional cinematography techniques and (b) skills in digitally manipulating and arranging cameras in machinima tools. They develop these skills through extensive practice and familiarization with the tools of the domain. We aim to support novices by providing systems that support this domain knowledge required for acceptance by gatekeepers and providing it as guidance on demand.

Our long-term goal is to address the question of whether creativity support tools (CSTs) decrease the divide between expert machinimators and novices. Creativity support tools can enhance peoples' creative abilities in a number of ways: they can scaffold standard procedures, facilitate peer collaboration, teach creativity techniques, or directly assist with the creation of artifacts through mixed-initiative artificial intelligence [17]. In this paper we concern ourselves with the divide between experts and novices with regard to domain knowledge of conventional cinematography. Machinima adopts a set of "filmic language" conventions from Hollywood-style filmmaking. We hypothesize that an intelligent creativity support tool can interact with novices to improve the quality of machinima artifacts by offloading the need to possess conventional filmmaking knowledge. To scope the problem, we specifically focus on the cinematographic knowledge of camera placement and cut timing that are both central aspects of filmic language.

We report on a pair of studies leading to the development of a creativity support tool for novice machinimators. Our first exploratory study examines what filmmaking skills novices do and do not possess. This study shows novices are unable to consistently follow key rules of a conventional filmic language. This in turn results in films expert machinimators deem unacceptable. To our knowledge, this is the first empirical study of novice machinimation abilities and the cinematic conventions they most often violate. From these results we hypothesize that a rule-based feedback system can support novices by alerting them to violations of these cinematic conventions and explaining their purposes.

Our second, evaluative study confirms this hypothesis, showing that novices with rule-based support are able to eliminate nearly all violations of cinematic conventions. Novices are able to improve their cinematography when informed only of errors and their definitions, without direction as to how to make corrections. Thus, a rule-based system can support novices by offloading the need to initially know film conventions without constraining novices' creativity by enforcing particular ways of realizing those conventions. This paper concludes with a discussion of our system in relation to the domain of creativity support tools, suggesting directions for further development of this work to better support novice filmmakers.

BACKGROUND

Machinima as Digital Filmmaking

Like other digital art forms, such as net art or collaborative online authoring, machinima evolved largely bottom-up, driven by users who wanted to use the new venues to express themselves in novel ways. In the case of machinima, defined as "animated filmmaking within a real-time virtual 3D environment" [18], the new artistic expressions are an expansion of the moving image through emergent creative practices. Machinima references existing forms of visual storytelling in cinema and expands them through the affordances of the evolving digital media.

Video games have been the most important digital media form for the evolution of machinima, which takes advantage of the technical features present in games, such as real-time rendering and easy control of animation and camera. Because machinima builds on existing game engines it is less code-based and more focused on using virtual game worlds as accessible production stages for filmmaking [16]. This game-based approach to machinima requires fewer programming skills because the underlying game already provides supporting technology, such as real-time rendering, sound management and lighting. It also includes a range of content in the form of 3D levels and animated character models. Players use these elements to become creative producers of novel digital art pieces using video games as expressive tools. As a result, machinima has enabled techniques for virtual performances [5], fan-media distribution [12], and has evolved into an emerging format for media production across narrative genres [16].

Because games are easily accessible and widely available, machinima creation rapidly grew in the gaming community into a vibrant form for visual exchanges of gameplay and game-based storytelling. Machinima.com's YouTube channel alone claims 9 billion views in 2011-2012. The creative value of machinima has been noticed—and to some extent supported—by game companies that have started to include machinima production tools in their game releases, such as Valve's Filmmaker or Epic's Unreal Development Kit. Newer machinima tools such as *Moviestorm*, *iClone*, and *Xtranormal* have expanded beyond game engines to become freestanding software interfaces that leverage real-time rendering of 3D virtual worlds as dynamic stages. These tools further remove the machinimator from programming, scripting, and needing to understand the internals of the underlying game engine technology. Machinima, thus, bridges the "digital divide" through easy access, supporting new media literacy and providing what Payne [21] identifies as a new media production practice that "allows students to find their own artistic voices while becoming increasingly well versed in the representational strategies, storytelling techniques, and formal aesthetic devices of narrative film and television."

One of the most striking differences between machinima filmmaking and more traditional animation techniques is the real-time nature of machinima tools. Davis et al. [7] found that the creative practices of expert machinimators are structured around this feedback mechanism in such a way that the creative process is more heavily based on exploration and evaluation than careful pre-planning, which is accomplished through storyboards (a visual sketch of each camera shot) in traditional animation. In contrast, expert machinimators use their tools to playfully explore different ideas and evaluate them on the fly. In many instances critical creative discoveries only occur as a result of the playful and creative exploration of the scene using a kind of "walkthrough evaluation" method. Video games allow the machinimator to explore a scene and look around. This immersion enables filmmakers to situate themselves within the scene to evaluate different camera angles, mise-en-scene, and staging considerations, which can lead to impromptu discoveries and situated creativity [7].

The particular creative potential of machinima is widely acknowledged [21]; however, the format is often perceived as stuck in a form of "arrested development" where "machinima seems to live in a state of suspended animation, growing in size but not in maturity" [23]. Its open access and easy distribution method allow anyone to produce machinima pieces, but ease of use does not mean that the results are always notable for their artistic value.

Typical machinimators lack formal training in the art form of traditional cinema. Thus, we seek to support these novice machinimators, focusing on cinematic camera work.

Cinematic Rules: A Film Language

Machinima borrows its conventions from cinema. Over time and through practice, film has evolved from its crude roots as a visual medium that titillated nineteenth century audiences by capturing in one continuous shot the train arriving at the station of La Ciotat [15]. Film today is a mature narrative format with a language of conventional cinematography to describe the placement and pacing of shots. Although experienced filmmakers violate these rules for stylistic purposes, the rules comprise guidelines for novices to construct a cinematic reality in line with viewers' expectations. By following these rules, spatial orientation, visual continuity and temporal rhythm can be achieved without drawing attention to the seams between shots in a scene. There are many rules in the modern filmic language with some emphasized more than others by different filmmakers.

There are too many rules and conventions to enumerate here. We focus on four rules that are commonly acknowledged as important by filmmakers. These rules were identified in the results of our first study to be those most egregiously violated by novice machinimators and are overviewed here to give a sense of the filmic language.

- *The 180-Degree Rule.* This rule establishes a conceptual line between two characters' line of sight that the camera should not cross. Violation of this rule can result in disorientation due to a reversal of space that changes the left-right relationship [13].
- *The 30-Degree Rule.* With a continuous object in focus, sequential cameras should be placed more than 30 degrees apart. Violating this rule results in a noticeable jump in the action, called a "jump cut" that interrupts the illusion of continuity and draws attention to the camera work itself [10].
- *Cutting on Action.* Viewers are least likely to notice cuts between camera angles if the action initiated in the first shot is carried over into the next. Not cutting on the initiation of an action creates the impression that one action (e.g., a man getting up from an armchair) shot from two different perspectives (front and behind) appears to be one fluid movement [3].
- *Pacing.* Shots should change at a regular pace, and abrupt changes should only occur at moments of high emotion or drama. While not strictly a rule, most filmmakers try to preserve a particular cinematic rhythm that can often reflect the emotional and dramatic state of the characters [14].

These conventions focus on the most basic forms of continuity. Other rules tie the cinematography to the story content. For example, a common pattern of camera cuts for filming a dialogue between two actors is the "shot reverse shot" in which a sequence of shots alternates between characters (typically shot from over the characters' shoulders) to convey direct conversation. Arijon [1] attempts to enumerate many of these conventional patterns and establish a grammar of filmmaking.

Creativity Support Tools

Our work focuses on developing creativity support tools aimed specifically at novices within the machinima domain. Shneiderman [24] distinguishes creativity support tools (CSTs) from productivity support tools through three criteria: clarity of task domain and requirements, clarity of success measures, and nature of the user base. Productivity support tools are designed around a clear task with known requirements, have well-defined success metrics, and are characterized by a known and relatively well-understood set of users. In contrast, CSTs often work in ill-defined domains with yet-unknown or unknowable requirements, have vague success measures, and have an unknown user base or one that behaves in unorthodox manners. For example, consider support tools for the well-defined goals of product supply scheduling, which include many clearly defined variables like cost metrics for shipping efficiency. Contrast this with a machinima creation support tool. Here, task requirements consist of a plethora of elements that define a "good" machinima film, success is measured by user acceptance of their final product, and users potentially range from professional filmmakers to high-school game players, all of whom may use the tool in unexpected ways.

Creativity support tools can take many forms. Nakakoji [19] organizes the range of creativity support tools with three metaphors: *running shoes*, *dumbbells*, and *skis*. Running shoes improve the abilities of users to execute a creative task they are already capable of—they improve the results users get from a given set of abilities. Dumbbells support users learning about a domain to become capable without the tool itself—they build users' knowledge and abilities. Skis provide users with new experiences of creative tasks that were previously impossible—they enable new forms of execution. A contemporary text editor that highlights grammar mistakes is a running shoe; explaining why those wordings are ungrammatical makes the tool a dumbbell. Machinima creation tools were once skis—enabling a new class of digital animation. Now, with commercial support tools, machinima has shifted to the role of running shoes for experts by easing editing compared to the initial game engine modifications. Yet novices struggle to employ these tools as dumbbells and few existing tools enhance the creative products of novices like running shoes.

Bardzell has shown that fostering creativity in amateur machinima creation tools often goes hand in hand with limiting their functionality to fit the expertise of users and conditions of distribution. The "authoring tools themselves are built on a shared, implicit language of creativity" [2]. Respecting the potential challenges of increasingly complex tool features, we aim to provide dumbbells and running shoes to novice machinimators by adding advisory capabilities to machinima creation tools. Rather than extend the functionality of machinima creation tools through more advanced controls, we provide on-demand feedback to users that notifies them of cinematic mistakes (running shoes) and explains the nature of these errors (dumbbell).

Lubart [17] enumerates four ways a computer interface may support creativity. A computer *nanny* provides tools to organize machinima content to use, but does not help novices select and use the appropriate content. We do not aim to enforce a particular workflow in creative practice, but to reduce the knowledge barrier to entry. A computer *pen-pal* supports collaboration within teams, but is less important to an independent individual or novices lacking the ability to implement their own or teammates' ideas. Computer *coaches* emphasize teaching a domain and supporting novice users in meeting the demands of a field they are unfamiliar with. Computer *colleagues* may meaningfully contribute to tasks so a human-computer team becomes a contributor to a domain. Both computer coaches and colleagues have the potential to support users in overcoming domain gatekeepers. Riedl and O'Neill [22] have proposed a fifth role of computer as *audience*, where the computer simulates the cognitive and affective responses of the recipient of a creative artifact, which can in turn provide valuable insight to creators.

Computer-Aided Critiquing Systems

Computer-aided critiquing systems—also known as *critics*—are a type of computer colleague that employ rule-based feedback to users about violations of domain rules in their design [9, 20]. A critic continuously compares the current state of a design against a set of rules encoding expert knowledge. Rules for design domains specify a set of preconditions indicating when a convention is violated and include information explaining the violation and potentially offering suggestions to fix it. Critics help users avoid mistakes, enabling them to reach a baseline product quality that makes creative results possible. Fischer et al. [9] note computer critics can enhance both user performance and user learning, aligning with Nakakoji's discussion of CSTs as running shoes that enhance performance and dumbbells that instruct the user. As distillations of encoded domain expertise, critics represent Lubart's coaches by alerting users to errors and explaining the nature of the problem. The critic we present in this paper provides on-demand expert feedback on cinematic rule adherence.

We hypothesize that in the domain of machinima film production a critic may be able to aid novices by offloading domain knowledge about cinematic conventions and therefore help them meet baseline artifact quality. In the next section we report on a study that finds that novices can make machinima films but frequently violate cinematic conventions and a study that demonstrates the feasibility of using a rule-based critic to reduce errors in novice machinima films. We discuss the implications of our studies for CSTs and novice machinima creation support.

MACHINIMATOR STUDIES

In the course of our research on novice creation of machinima, we conducted two studies. The first study—an exploratory investigation of novice machinima creation—sought to identify the aspects of the cinematic process that would benefit most from computational support. Qualitative expert analysis of machinima scenes created by novices uncovered a set of cinematic conventions novices frequently violated. A second study was designed to test the hypothesis that a critic could reduce the rate at which novice machinima creators violate these basic cinematographic rules. In a Wizard-of-Oz study of such a critic, we found novices violated significantly fewer cinematographic rules when allowed to ask what shots violated such rules.

Study 1: Exploratory Study of Novice Machinima Creation

In this exploratory study, we investigated the abilities of novice machinimators. Since we are developing tools to support creative digital filmmaking, we wanted to investigate how well novices could make films given the proper tools, and where the novices needed improvement. To understand the creative practices of novice machinimators, we invited seven individuals with no experience in filmmaking to edit the cinematography of two pre-scripted narrative scenes. We used an easy to use and freely available software platform called *Xtranormal* (http://www.xtranormal.com) for the study.

Xtranormal is a commercially available machinima creation tool. It is based on a freemium business model by which users make movies with free assets but are charged to publish them. Individuals choose which assets they would like to use, such as characters and settings. Users can position characters and script them to perform actions within the scene, such as walking, jumping, and waving. To make each character speak, a line of dialog can be created for that particular character. The entire dialogue is displayed as a script on the bottom half of the interface. To create an action or facial expression, the user finds that action in the menu and inserts it at the proper point in the script. Similarly, users can create and insert cameras into the dialogue to make the cinematography for a scene. When the play button is pressed, the scene begins playback from the beginning of the script and proceeds until paused or until the end of the movie. When the system reaches an action or a change in camera angle during playback, *Xtranormal* shows the corresponding animation or changes the view to the designated camera.

We selected *Xtranormal* as the machinima tool for our study because it was designed for inexperienced creators. Unlike game engines, *Xtranormal* does not require knowledge of scripting or programming game engines. The tool has successfully been marketed to novice machinima creators, in part due to its ease of use when compared to game engines. Although the software is not difficult to learn, there is a considerable learning curve associated with creating one's first movie. For example, understanding how to properly move the cameras around the scene to create the desired angle requires some familiarity with the camera controls. Furthermore, searching through all the available actions and testing them out takes time. For the purposes of our research, we were only interested in the ability of novice filmmakers to assemble the cinematography for a scene. The overall usability of *Xtranormal* as a filmmaking tool was not our primary concern. In order to isolate and study cinematography, we created two stock scenes (stories) with 23 pre-selected camera angles that participants were required to choose from.

Method

We recruited seven participants with no professional experience or formal training in filmmaking to edit the scenes by choosing camera angles from the 23 angles available, thus deciding when to cut between those cameras. Participants underwent an orientation to familiarize them with the functionality of the *Xtranormal* interface. Orientation included tasks such as placing cameras, deleting cameras, playing a scripted scene from the start, and playing specific portions of the scene.

Experimenters provided two isomorphic scenes in *Xtranormal* (each approximately one minute long), complete with dialogue, actions, scripted characters, and 23 pre-selected static cameras. We instructed participants to select the camera angles for the scene and to specify where the camera angles should change in order to create the best possible scene. Participants were given up to 20 minutes to complete this task for each scene. All participants received a $10 gift card as compensation. As an incentive, experimenters offered $15 of additional compensation for the top 25% of films judged externally by a panel of experts.

Results

To evaluate the movies, we invited three film experts to watch the seven pairs of movies and evaluate the cinematography. Experts watched each pair of scenes created by an individual participant, selected the scene they thought was better and verbally explained why. In order to control for differences in baseline skills among participants, we used pairs of scenes from the same participant. The comparison task was meant to force the experts to consciously think about and explain what factors they think make the cinematography good or bad. The results from this evaluation were coded and analyzed using thematic analysis. Thematic analysis [4] is a qualitative data analysis method where the researcher codes data based on themes identified in research questions. Coded data is then analyzed to find patterns and describe relationships.

The analysis revealed that expert evaluations aggregated around three categories of content: (1) adhering to conventional shot framing, (2) maintain spatial continuity, and (3) aligning cinematography with semantic scene information. Conventional shot framing consists of avoiding occlusion of characters and placing cameras an appropriate distance from characters. Spatial continuity between shots is laid out in conventions related to ways of organizing a series of shots such as the 180 Degree Rule (described in the cinematic rules background section) or using a sequence of shots that alternates between characters to convey direct conversation, known as "shot reverse shot." Aligning cinematography and scene semantics entails introducing and shifting screen time among characters and objects as relevant to the story, employing camera angles relevant to story structure, and timing cuts to align with story content. Experts commonly mentioned the need to show characters when they are introduced to the scene, use camera angles to align with character status and dialogue tone, or adjust camera angles to convey a coherent point of view of a single character. Timing camera cuts on relevant actions, dialogue points, or shifts in characters' knowledge pertinent to the story were also important.

Thematic analysis further revealed that experts differed in which aspects of films they praised. Opinion on what made a film "good" differed, but there was clear consensus on mistakes, particularly relating to shot structure (categories 1 and 2). Experts diverged more widely on mistakes when connecting cinematography and story, often noting these were choices of personal style. Errors of cinematographic rules were frequent and substantial enough to distract from the film content and result in highly negative film evaluations. This pattern aligns with Shneiderman's description of ill-defined success evaluation criteria for a domain [24]. We infer that machinima success is complex and depends on author style and intent, but violations of baseline norms are striking.

The errors the judges found most distracting involved (a) breaking the 180-Degree Rule and (b) "jumpy" or "jittery" camerawork, which we interpreted to refer to 30-Degree Rule violations. Breaking the 180-Degree Rule is confusing because characters switch places on the screen without any explanation. Expert 1 describes this phenomenon:

> *There was one shot where you are looking at the mother and it flips to another shot, which is completely flipped her direction on screen, and your focus is on the same exact spot when that happens, it is breaking all kinds of rules, and you would never want to do that.*

It is true that these rules are not steadfast; filmmakers routinely break the rules, but they do so deliberately with a particular effect in mind. In some cases, the novices would break a rule, and the experts would forgive the error if it was justified in context. With respect to one participant's scenes, Expert 1 notes "The line of action stuff that happened in both clips seems to be more justified in [clip] B because it introduced [one of the other characters]."

This quote illustrates that the 180-Degree Rule is an important factor in evaluating a film, and it also demonstrates that there is not a uniformly correct way to film a scene. Although this instance shows an example where the participant happened to get lucky and justifiably break a rule, it does not change the fact that rule violations tend to distract the experts and cause them to view the clip negatively.

Experts noted issues with cut timing related to dialogue and actions often disrupted the flow of the scene. Expert 1 explained:

> *[T]here's some weird timing in the dialog. Usually when you do dialog, you have the first syllable still in the same cam[era] position in the old one and then cut, everything gets a lot more fluid, but that was still fine.*

Cutting at odd points in events confuses viewers by making it hard to follow which actions are occurring and which are the most relevant to the scene.

Pacing and timing issues were another source of distraction for the experts. Pacing errors can occur when the camera changes too abruptly or one shot lasts too long. Expert 2 explains how pacing factored into his/her decisions:

> *There were a couple of times where some of the shots were in there for a second or two, and it was more awkward than adding anything to the scene. Clip A did that too, although it wasn't quite as distracting.*

Here, clips A and B both made similar pacing errors that distracted the expert, and the degree of distraction directly influenced the evaluation of these clips. Expert 3 also notes how pacing can be a distraction: "the cut to the third party robot was half a second, it was very abrupt and weird." Jumpy or jittery shots were not the only pacing problems; Expert 3 also disliked that there were "some long shots that went on quite long."

In Study 1, the experts were not probed to scrutinize the films based on the rules and conventions we highlighted in the background section of this paper. However, their comments converged on these rules as being critical weaknesses for novices applying a visual film language. The main sources of problems were camera choices that distracted experts from the story itself. While there is no "right" way to place cameras, there are certainly errors that prevented experts from being completely immersed in the story, typically due to violations of cinematographic norms. To our knowledge we are the first to empirically document key novice machinima creation abilities. These results highlight expert emphasis on avoiding errors as opposed to any specific guidelines for success and led us to conclude that a machinima creation CST could assist and not simply prescribe solutions to novice machinimators. In the subsequent study we considered a rule-based CST tool based around four cinematic rules: the 180-Degree Rule, the 30-Degree Rule, pacing, and cutting on action.

Study 2: Wizard-of-Oz

Based on the findings from Study 1, we explored ways to help individuals avoid violations of the basic rules of filmmaking that experts perceived as a baseline for visual storytelling. To explore a rule-based critic approach before developing a complex system we performed a Wizard of Oz (WOZ) study focused on four rules: the 180-Degree Rule, the 30-Degree Rule, pacing, and cutting on action. We hypothesized that a rule-based critic would be able to detect and reduce the number of errors that users make in the filmmaking process by informing users when they are making an error of a specific type. Our WOZ study aimed to help the user avoid basic cinematographic mistakes through providing information on rule violations without directing users to any particular way of addressing those violations.

Method

In this study, 20 participants with no professional experience or formal training in filmmaking performed a cinematography task similar to the *Xtranormal* scene construction exercise described in the first study. As before, a scene was pre-scripted with dialogue, characters, and a selection of pre-existing cameras to choose from. The participant was first familiarized with the software and shown the entire pre-staged scene from a fixed single-camera perspective. They were then instructed to create the best scene by selecting from 23 pre-existing camera angles and temporally and spatially placing them using *Xtranormal*'s script editing interface. Participants were given 40 minutes to complete this task. We pre-selected the set of camera angles to provide novices with some structure for this complex and time-constrained task without unduly limiting their possible actions. All participants received a \$10 gift card for their time. As an additional incentive, we offered an extra \$15 compensation for participants whose movies were evaluated as being in the top 25%.

In the control condition, participants (n = 10) were timed and given up to 40 minutes to complete the film-editing task without any additional intervention. In the experimental condition (n = 10), participants were given access to an additional resource that they could use to analyze their movie and determine errors. After the first 20 minutes of editing and camera adjusting, the participant was informed that they had access to an automated system to analyze their movie for errors over the remaining period of up to 20 additional minutes. Participants in this condition were required to press an "analyze" button at least once during their creative process and were allowed to press the button as many times as they wanted from that point forward. The analyze feature was turned off for the first 20 minutes in order to provide a baseline performance with which to compare the performance after the intervention.

We used a Wizard-of-Oz (WOZ) study design wherein a film expert and an assistant imitated the functionality of a hypothetical intelligent rule-based critic whenever the

Figure 1: Interface used by Study 2 participants

"analyze" was pressed. Our film expert has a degree in film, extensive experience in filmmaking, and is prominent within the machinima community. While the expert identified rule violations, an assistant prepared the notifications that would be sent to users. During the study, participants were unaware that the critic was not automated. As far as the user was concerned, an actual rule-based critic provided feedback about their film.

Figure 1 shows the interface used by participants in Study 2. The *Xtranormal* interface is on the left and an IRC client on the right. The expert and assistant watched a live video feed of the participant's screen and graded each shot as it was created in the film, looking only for violations of the four rules. The expert prepared a list of errors from a pre-compiled list. The assistant entered this error list into the WOZ interface and waited for the user to press "analyze." When that occurred, the assistant sent a message containing all of the errors and stock notification messages describing those errors. The message was sent from the WOZ interface to the user's computer using a custom IRC chat client that the participant was told was part of the critic.

At the end of the list of violations, an explanation was provided for each rule that was violated. An example of a violation notification is: "The first shot in dialog line 2 breaks the 180-Degree Rule." An example of an explanation is:

The 180 degree rule: The imaginary line between two characters is called the line of action. Once a camera is placed on one side of the line of action it cannot cross this line.

The WOZ informed the participants of rule violations and provided generic explanations of the rule definitions, but did not otherwise provide any information on how to correct the violations. Thus, all manipulations of the cameras were explicit creative choices of the participants.

Results

Three analysts who were involved in the experimental design conducted the evaluation. All three evaluators were members of the research team and trained to recognize violations of the four key rules and the conditions under which violating those rules is acceptable. To prevent bias during the evaluation, the order of the films was randomized. The only differences between films were the specifically selected shots and each cut; story and dialogue were held constant.

Each shot was evaluated against the one that came before it. For example, only the second cut could break the 180-Degree Rule because it is related to the previous shot. However, once the line is broken, all subsequent shots on that side of the line are not marked as errors. Once the user inserts a camera that jumps back over the line, this jump will only count as one error. Pacing issues were judged

Table 1: Number of rule violations in each condition in Study 2

Rule	Control Mean (SD)	Pre-Intervention Mean (SD)	Post-Intervention Mean (SD)	Control vs. Post	Pre vs. Post
180-Degree Rule	4.8 (1.75)	4.0 (3.05)	2.1 (2.99)	$p < .05$	$p < .01$
30-Degree Rule	1.3 (1.25)	1.2 (2.15)	1.3 (2.79)	n.s.	n.s.
Cutting on Action	3.9 (1.29)	4.1 (1.52)	1.4 (1.58)	$p < .001$	$p < .01$
Pacing	0.6 (1.58)	1.3 (2.06)	1.8 (2.57)	n.s.	n.s.
Number of cuts	13.9 (4.09)	11.9 (4.56)	9.7 (5.62)	$p < .05$	$p < .05$

more leniently and were generally coded for clusters of shots that were less than 1 second long. If three shots in a row were less than one second long, only one pacing error was generated.

Each of the three evaluators independently checked each cut in each of the 30 films (10 control, 10 in the experimental condition before WOZ intervention, and 10 after the experimental intervention) for violations of the rules. Afterward, the raters met and came to consensus on each individual cut; detecting, counting, and judging each individual cut is a difficult and nuanced process that can be easily overlooked on an individual basis. During the consensus process, each scene was watched in its entirety and then re-evaluated. Those evaluations were compared to the individual evaluations and any discrepancies were analyzed and discussed among the group. Disagreements were settled through a majority rules system.

Table 1 shows the results of Study 2. We conducted a between-subjects comparison between the control group and the final scenes produced by the experimental group using a one-tailed independent-samples t-test. We also conducted a within-subjects comparison between the scenes created in the experimental condition prior to and after enabling the "analyze" function and critic intervention using a one-tailed paired-samples t-test.

After the WOZ intervention, participants in the experimental condition produced films with fewer violations of the 180-Degree Rule than those in the control condition ($p < .05$), as well as fewer violations of the Cutting on Action Rule ($p < .001$). No significant differences were found in the number of violations of the 30-Degree Rule or Pacing. However, we did find that films produced in the WOZ condition had fewer cuts than those in the control condition ($p < .05$).

Within the WOZ condition, participants showed improvement from their pre-intervention films to their final products. Overall, films had fewer violations of the 180-Degree Rule ($p < .01$) and the Cutting on Action Rule ($p < .01$). While there was no significant difference in the number of violations of the 30-Degree Rule or Pacing, the final films did have significantly fewer cuts than the same films before the WOZ intervention ($p < .05$).

Analysis

Rule-based feedback virtually eliminated novice mistakes of all forms in both the between-subjects and within-subjects comparisons. For the 180-Degree Rule and the Cutting on Action Rule novices moved from initially high rule-violation rates (4.8 and 3.9 mean violations in the control condition, respectively) to lower rates (2.1 and 1.4 mean violations in the post-intervention condition, respectively). Both the 30-Degree Rule and Pacing Rule had few violations initially (1.3 and 0.6 mean violations in the control condition, respectively) and thus were unlikely to show significant improvements with further feedback (1.3 and 1.8 mean violations after intervention, respectively). The reduced number of overall cuts made when comparing the pre- and post-intervention conditions is likely due to novices removing extraneous cuts that introduce errors. Overall our results show the rule-based feedback enables novices to detect and correct violations of basic cinematographic conventions. These results are particularly encouraging given the tight time constraints and relative complexity of the task.

We conclude that a rule-based critic is well suited to handle the task of providing feedback to novice machinima creators. Filmmaking has been described as a constraint satisfaction process involving hard and soft constraints derived from a variety of sources including the story, the filming environment, and cinematographic conventions and rules [8]. As a constraint satisfaction task, novices must produce a film that does not violate any of the film rules, unless justified by circumstances. These tasks are not easy for novices because they may not be used to these types of decisions and may not be aware of all the rules involved. The critic is well suited for an individual novice user who wants to create a film clip that has a minimal amount of errors without studying all the rules of film. Importantly, Study 2 demonstrates that providing novices on-demand feedback for what violations have occurred—without information on *how* to correct those violations—is sufficient for novices to significantly improve their films. A rule-based critic can thus support novices' skills without constraining their creative freedom.

DISCUSSION

We have framed supporting creative filmmaking in terms of film conventions realized as a system of rules. There is often a fine line between productivity support and creativity support defined by: (a) how ill-defined the task is, (b) the ambiguity of success, and (c) the diversity of potential users and their behaviors [24]. Unlike a spell-checker, a machinima CST has to deal with an ill-defined goal in the sense that an animation can routinely violate the rules and conventions of cinematography and still be accepted. Study 1 highlights the ill-defined nature of the machinima creation task by showing how experts in the domain diverge on success criteria but achieve consensus on rule violations. For a diverse population of potential users such as the community of machinimators, the rules have to be known in order to be broken for cinematic effect. For novices, these rules are not intuitively known – they cannot explore a creative domain as they are unaware of the nature of that domain.

Given the ill-defined nature of machinima production, we cast the machinima cinematography task as achieving a sense of "syntactic" correctness, providing a minimal definition of success amenable to computational support. Experts speak of success in terms of conventional rules, and we consequently designed our creativity-support system, evaluated in Study 2, as a rule-based system. Focusing on conventional rule adherence allows our tool to address the ambiguous nature of success for machinima creation without subscribing to any single creative goal for machinima creation. An inherent weakness of a rule-based system is its inflexibility. However, in creativity support, an intelligent system is not designed to automate the filmmaking process, but instead to support human decision-making. Machinimators value their ability to make their own creative choices when making films. Our approach enables individuals to retain their creative freedom while making informed decisions. This perspective implies supporting novice creativity in filmmaking requires novices to first become aware of these rules and then ultimately reflect on and selectively ignore or modify these rules.

Our critic helps novices create syntactically correct scenes to fit into an existing cinematic tradition. Following Nakakoji [19], our critic aims to be both running shoes that enhance novice's abilities to produce machinima and a dumbbell to convey important cinematographic knowledge. Drawing from Lubart, our critic can support understanding rules through coaching users on cinematography. At this time we have focused specifically on informational feedback, leaving the question of its educational efficacy for future work. An important feature of our approach is that we do not attempt to replace the human creator.

Csíkszentmihályi's systems theory of creativity [6] justifies the need for domain knowledge to make creative contributions to the film domain. Minimizing substantial errors can enhance social acceptance and success of novices' creations within the machinima field, without limiting user abilities to explore alternatives. By providing feedback on when a camera placement violates various cinematic rules, the critic enables a user to compare the trade-offs between achieving certain visual effects and adherence to film conventions. The system becomes a tool for informed creative experimentation. It does not replace human creativity. Study 2 found this coaching to reduce errors. Future work remains to investigate whether this technique leads to creative rule breaking or merely constrains users to obey the rules handed down to them.

Targeting novice machinima creation guided us to limit the complexity of our critic tool to simple on-demand requests with error highlighting and explanations. These steps ensure that our tool supports creativity, even across a diverse user base, rather than enforcing a particular machinima productivity pipeline. Taking these measures allows us to sidestep frequent tool turnover in the still-evolving machinima domain by targeting the underlying domain conventions and creativity support techniques at stake. We see great potential for future computer colleagues to collaborate with users in genuinely novel machinima creation tools [17]. Such tools could leverage the complementary strengths of humans in making holistic judgments and computers in performing brute-force optimization or constraint satisfaction to create new machinima creation skis.

CONCLUSIONS

Machinima offers exciting new possibilities for creative expression. By significantly lowering the entry barrier for digital filmmaking, machinima can provide a cinematic voice to the masses. However, powerful tools alone do not ensure that novices can effectively tell their story through the medium of film. There are nuances of the craft that expert filmmakers have learned through schooling and experience. In this paper, we explored how a rule-based critic can help novices meet the basics of cinematographic convention while producing machinima.

Our first exploratory study sought to understand what kinds of challenges novices face when creating the cinematography for a short film scene. We found that novices routinely make errors that violate established filmic convention. Experts who evaluated these film clips stated that the basic rules of what is referred to as a "film language" had been violated. We documented a set of several of the most important of these rules. Based on these findings, we designed a rule-based critic that analyzed users' cinematography decisions and provided feedback when individuals violated basic cinematography rules. The second study showed that this rule-based critic significantly reduced the errors that novices made without forcing particular corrections to those errors.

The on-demand and immediate nature of our critic complements the real time rendering capabilities of machinima. This type of intelligent creativity support tool may support learning by encouraging users to creatively explore and evaluate different cinematography configurations while minimizing distracting errors.

ACKNOWLEDGEMENTS

This material is based upon work supported by the National Science Foundation under Grant No. IIS-1002768. Any opinions, findings, and conclusions or recommendations expressed in this material are those of the author(s) and do not necessarily reflect the views of the National Science Foundation.

REFERENCES

1. Arijon, D. Grammar of the film language. Focal Press, Boston, 1976.
2. Bardzell, J. Creativity in Amateur Multimedia: Popular Culture, Critical Theory, and HCI. *Human Technology*, 3, 1 (2007), 12-33.
3. Beller, H. *Handbuch der Filmmontage. Praxis und Prinzipien des Filmschnitts.* Tr Verlagsunion , München, 1999.
4. Braun, V. and Clarke, V. Using thematic analysis in psychology. *Qualitative Research in Psychology 3*, 2 (2006), 77–101.
5. Carroll, J. and Cameron, D. Machinima: Digital Performance and Emergent Authorship. In *Proc. DiGRA 2005,* (2005), 1-9.
6. Csikszentmihalyi, M. (1999). Implications of a Systems Perspective for the Study of Creativity. In R. J. Sternberg (Ed.), *Handbook of creativity* (p. 313). Cambridge Univ Pr.
7. Davis, N., Li, B., O'Neill, B.., Nitsche, M., and Riedl, M. Distributed Creative Cognition In Digital Filmmaking. In *Proc. Creativity & Cognition 2011*, ACM Press (2011), 207–216.
8. Elson, D.K. and Riedl, M.O. A Lightweight Intelligent Virtual Cinematography System for Machinima Production. *Proceedings of the 3rd Conference on Artificial Intelligence and Interactive Digital Entertainment.*
9. Fischer, G., Nakakoji, K., Ostwald, J., Stahl, G., and Sumner, T. Embedding critics in design environments. *The Knowledge Engineering Review* 8, 4 (2009), 285.
10. Hayward, S. *Cinema Studies: The Key Concepts*. Routledge, London, 2000
11. Hancock, H. and Ingram, J. Machinima for Dummies. Wiley Publishing Inc., Hoboken, 2007.
12. Ito, M. Machinima in a Fanvid Ecology. *Journal of Visual Culture* 10, 1 (2011), 51-54.
13. Katz, S. D. *Film Directing Cinematic Motion: A Workshop for Staging Scenes*. Michael Wiese Productions, Studio City, 2004.
14. Kindem, K. and Musburger, R. *Introduction to Media Production: The Path to Digital Media Production.* Focal Press, Burlington, 2009.
15. Loiperdinger, M. Lumière's Arrival of the Train: Cinema's Founding Myth. *The Moving Image*, 4(1), 89–118
16. Lowood, H. and Nitsche, M. The Machinima Reader. The MIT Press, Cambridge, 2011.
17. Lubart, T. How can computers be partners in the creative process: Classification and commentary on the Special Issue. *International Journal of Human-Computer Studies 63*, 4-5 (2005), 365–369.
18. Marino, Paul. *3D Game-Based Filmmaking: The Art of Machinima*. Scottsdale: ParaglyphAnderson, 2004.
19. Nakakoji, K. Meanings of tools, support, and uses for creative design processes. In *Proc. International Design Research Symposium* (2006), 156-165.
20. Oh, Y., Gross, M., and Do, E.Y.-L. Computer-Aided Critiquing Systems. In *Proc. CAADRIA (Computer Aided Architectural Design Research in Asia)*, (2008), 161–167.
21. Payne, M. T. *Everything I Need to Know about Filmmaking I Learned from Playing Video Games: The Educational Promise of Machinima*. In H. Lowood, M. Nitsche (Eds.) *The Machinima Reader*. The MIT Press, Cambridge, 2011, 241-256.
22. Riedl, M. O. and O'Neill, B. Computer as audience: A strategy for artificial intelligence support of human creativity. In *Proc. CHI Workshop of Computational Creativity Support*, (2009).
23. Salen, K. *Arrested Development: Why Machinima Can't (or Shouldn't) Grow Up.* The MIT Press, Cambridge, 2011.
24. Shneiderman, B. (2007). Creativity support tools: accelerating discovery and innovation. *Communications of the ACM*, 50(12), 20-32.

AutoGami: A Low-cost Rapid Prototyping Toolkit for Automated Movable Paper Craft

Kening Zhu[1,2,3], Shengdong Zhao[1,2]
[1]NUS-HCI Lab, [2]NGS, [3]Keio-NUS CUTE Center
National University of Singapore, Singapore
zhukening@nus.edu.sg, zhaosd@comp.nus.edu.sg

ABSTRACT
AutoGami is a toolkit for designing automated movable paper craft using the technology of selective inductive power transmission. AutoGami has hardware and software components that allow users to design and implement automated movable paper craft without any prerequisite knowledge of electronics; it also supports rapid prototyping. Apart from developing the toolkit, we have analyzed the design space of movable paper craft and developed a taxonomy to facilitate the design of automated paper craft. AutoGami made consistently strong showings in design workshops, confirming its viability in supporting engagement and creativity as well as its usability in storytelling through paper craft. Additional highlights include rapid prototyping of product design as well as interaction design such as human-robot interactions.

Author Keywords
Automated paper craft, paper computing, toolkit, selective inductive power transmission.

ACM Classification Keywords
H.5.2. User Interfaces: Interaction styles, Prototyping

INTRODUCTION
In 1998, Wrensch and Eisenberg embedded computation in arrays of low-cost material substrates available to crafters to enable enhancement of our daily lives through the easy and economic design of intelligent everyday objects [28]. Among low-cost materials, paper stands out because of its unique advantages: it is easy to use, flexible, lightweight, and readily available. As a traditional medium for art and communication, it has long been popular for creating 2D and 3D models as well as paper craft.

To embed computation and interactivity in paper crafts, researchers have explored the use of shape-memory alloy (SMA) [8] in triggering the movements of paper electrically. This lightweight, flexible metal alloy can be directly integrated with paper, which makes it a preferred material in movable paper craft [16]. Using SMA, it is possible to incorporate mechanisms such as flaps, pull tabs, and volvelles (rotary wheels) that cause movement on the 2D paper surface or above the surface in 3D space [25].

In the past few years, a number of studies have focused on generating and enhancing paper movements using digital technology [6, 9, 10, 13, 14, 17, 20]. This body of research ranges from simple movement to relatively complex shape-changing using microelectromechanical systems (MEMS), which significantly advanced the technology for movable paper craft. Current research development for movable paper craft can benefit from the systematization of existing research results and the creation of a unified body of engineering and design knowledge.

We analyzed the design of movable paper craft and developed a taxonomy that focuses on the movements of single and multiple pieces of paper; subsequently, we generated a pattern language for automated movable paper craft.

More importantly, we developed AutoGami, a toolkit that allows users with no prior knowledge of electronics to design automated paper craft by using the taxonomy as a guide. AutoGami's software interface allows users to plan a variety of paper craft movements: its use of selective inductive power transmission [29] allows users to control aspects of movement such as duration, amplitude, and sequence without concerning themselves with technical implementation. Compared with previous work on automated paper craft (Table 1 and Table 2), AutoGami provides additional controllability and customizability.

This paper provides the following contributions.

- A systematic analysis of the design space for automated movable paper craft.
- A low-cost rapid prototyping toolkit for automated movable paper craft using the technology of selective inductive power transmission.

Usage Scenario
To highlight the main features of AutoGami and to demonstrate how the toolkit can help enrich people's daily lives and improve their efficiency at work, we first describe three usage scenarios. These scenarios are carefully selected based on the feedback and observation of over 400 people from demonstrating AutoGami on many occasions,

including five workshops (described in more details in the evaluation section), a two-day local Maker Faire, a three-day interior design exhibition, a one-day open house exhibition, and two peer laboratory visits.

Storytelling Using Automated Paper Craft

Jean is a housewife and mother of a five-year-old boy, Tom, and a three-year-old girl, Kate. Just like most kids, both Tom and Kate love to hear stories from their mother. But because they are very young, some of the concepts in the story are difficult for them to grasp. Jean wants to enrich the stories with visual animation. Inspired by the traditional Chinese shadow puppet, she decides to create an animated paper puppet theater and invests in the AutoGami toolkit. She animates the story of The Hare and The Tortoise by first making the characters on paper (Figure 1) then using AutoGami's software and hardware to design simple movements.

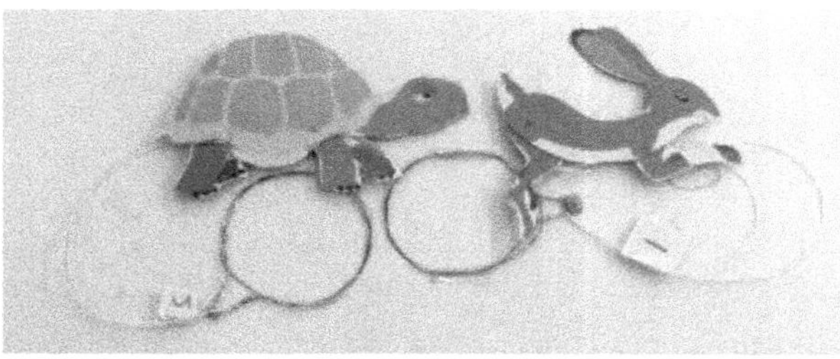

Figure 1: Movable paper characters for telling the story, The Hare and The Tortoise using AutoGami

While she tells the story, she makes the paper characters move accordingly: Hare moves fast in the beginning but slows down after a while. Tortoise, on the other hand, moves slowly but consistently. As time passes, Tortoise surpasses Hare and wins the race. Both Tom and Kate are engaged in the story, cheering for the Tortoise as it moves, and clapped when it wins. Because of AutoGami, Jean can tell stories in a much more vivid way. And since it is simple and easy to use, telling animated stories can be a daily activity that is enjoyed by all members of the family.

Rapid Prototyping in Intelligent Devices

John is a researcher specializing in social robotics and intelligent environments. In his next project, he will be creating social robots that have different personalities and look and feel. The movements he needs to design range from saying greetings, nodding and shaking the heads, and facial expressions.

John needs to test different types of movement so that he can assign the appropriate one for each robot. After making the paper models for each robot, as shown in Figure 2(a), he uses AutoGami to design movements, test their various types, and study each one's different patterns by adjusting parameters such as the duration and the range of movement. AutoGami's rapid prototyping system made it possible for John to identify specific types of movement appropriate for each robot, which in turn allowed him to determine the most suitable hardware to support each type of movement. He was able to save both time and money because the toolkit was easy to use, he was able to create prototypes using accessible material, and he was able to conduct tests before purchasing the necessary hardware.

John also uses AutoGami to simulate smart home behaviors. He builds a 3D paper model of a house (Figure 2(b)). Using AutoGami software, he designs the movement of the door and the window. John found the automated paper craft prototypes a very useful and effective means for both previewing the intelligent behavior and to communicating the idea with his colleagues.

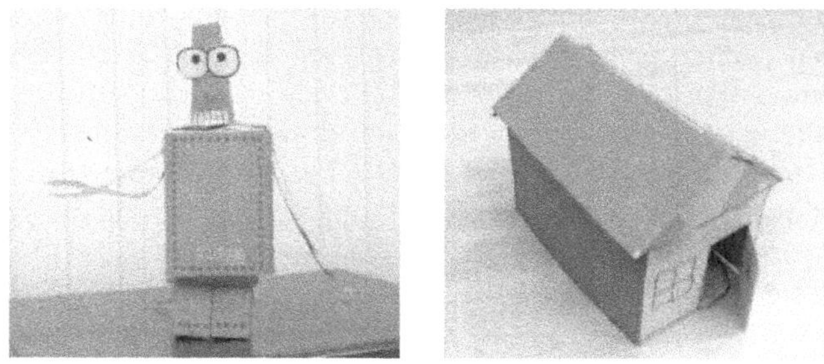

(a) (b)

Figure 2: (a) Robot prototyping using AutoGami; (b) Smart home prototyping using AutoGami

Interactive Art Design

Mary, a paper craft artist, was invited to exhibit her work in the city museum. To make her artwork more engaging, the museum suggested using digital technology. Mary, who has limited knowledge in technology, uses AutoGami to automate her paper craft. After trying out the toolkit for the first time, she finds that it can trigger movements in different origami without the need to connect them to complex circuits. She creates different origami, such as a crane with flapping wings and a dog with a moving mouth. She also creates an array of origami flowers that she will arrange to depict pixels in a matrix display. She designs movements so that groups of flowers bloom at different intervals, creating different patterns that display in a sequence.

AutoGami made the design process efficient because Mary could arrange and rearrange the position of the flowers and test the different parameters for blooming. Automating paper craft was easy and fast because Mary only needed to attach actuators to the origami and plan the sequence of blooming in the GUI. At the exhibition, the automated artwork was well-received by the audience, who were amazed by how the paper craft was animated without the use of electronic wires.

The above scenarios illustrate the capabilities and potential of our toolkit. We now discuss the background and related work that motivate us to create AutoGami.

BACKGROUND AND RELATED WORK

Throughout the evolution of paper, artists and designers have created various art forms through techniques such as folding, bending, and pop-up [22]. Today, paper craft is used in many other areas, such as storytelling, education, and medical treatment. Making paper craft has shown to improve children's creativity, spatial reasoning skills, and performing ability [21]. Paper craft can also be used to enhance in-class communication among teachers and children, and to help develop cognitive and language abilities necessary for reading and writing [7, 15]. However, while traditional paper craft have played an essential role in enriching art and culture, they are generally static; at most, they allow only manual or mechanical interaction, limiting their potential in the digital age.

Our work was inspired by various efforts toward the integration of the physical and virtual worlds, including tangible and physical computing [11], augmented reality environments [27], ubiquitous computing [26], and the emerging digital art-related research in the CHI community (i.e., [18, 19]). It is a contribution to the research on automated movable paper craft using SMA and to toolkits for creating movable craft.

Automated paper craft using SMA has drawn interest from researchers since the late 1990s and early 2000s. The first project that used SMA in paper craft we aware of was the Programmable Hinge [28], wherein SMA was attached to a paper-made hinge structure and controlled by an external microcontroller. The Programmable Hinge set an early example of implementing automated movable paper craft for the following projects. In the Interactive Paper Devices project [20], Greg Saul et al. introduced a method of embedding electrical circuits with sensors and actuators using conductive gold leaf gilding. They also presented paper prototypes of a robot, speakers, and LED lamps.

Coelho et al. [6] improved on the method of embedding electrical circuits by developing pulp-based computing, a set of techniques for building sensors, actuators, and circuit boards that behave, look, and feel like paper. Jie Qi et al. [17] created Electronic Popables, an interactive pop-up book that integrates electronics and pop-up mechanisms as a unified story book. Animated Paper [14] is a hardware platform created from paper and shape memory alloy (SMA), which is easy to control using different energy sources ranging from sunlight to lasers. Paper craft is actuated by SMA and its movements controlled with a high-power laser pointer.

In 2012, Jie Qi et al. [16] presented a set of mechanisms for actuating paper with SMAs that produced, among other things, the folding flap, parallelogram, curling flap, and clam shell, and tested one of these mechanisms in workshops. A few projects on automated paper craft used motors (Oribotics [9], Adaptive Blooming [13]) and MEMS (Programmable Matter [10]) instead of SMAs. However, SMA has the advantage of being low-cost, lightweight, and easily integrated with paper.

Leah Buechley et al. [3] used the extended LilyPad Arduino to introduce one of the first paper computing kits, which could be attached to the book page by magnetic snaps. It needs circuit planning for creating paper books that produce light and sound. Designing the output circuit also requires users to have prerequisite knowledge and experience in electronics. In addition, the complex circuitry and massive wiring increases the bulkiness of paper.

We developed our toolkit based on the technology of selective inductive power transmission [29]. Compared with the movable craft toolkits we described previously, ours doesn't require users to consider the design of the circuit and wire connection. They only need to attach the power receiver with actuator to the paper to implement their design. In addition, AutoGami has a software interface that allows users to plan and preview the movements before implementing them on paper.

ANALYSIS OF MOVABLE PAPER CRAFT

To understand the capability and limitation of prior work in movable paper craft, we conducted a detailed analysis, including the literature on traditional movable paper craft [12, 23, 24] and nine papers on automated movable paper craft that have been published in the past ten years [6, 9, 10, 13, 14, 16, 17, 20, 28]. Based on the analysis, we developed a simple taxonomy to classify the types of movement supported by existing movable paper crafts (Figure 3) and a pattern language to formally analyze and compare the existing systems.

Taxonomy of Paper Movement

Taking our cue from the motion-centric taxonomy for classifying human manipulation behavior created by Bullock et al. [4], which divides hand motion into *Within Hand* and *Not Within Hand*, we classified the movements of paper craft in two main categories: *Single Paper*, which consists of movements created by one piece of paper, and *Multiple Paper*, which consists of movements created by multiple pieces of paper (Figure 3).

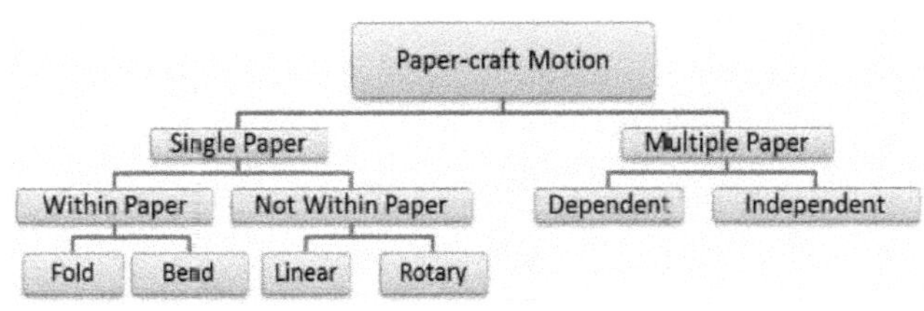

Figure 3: Classification of paper movement

Single Paper has two subcategories, which are defined by where the movement occurs:

Within Paper - Movement that occurs in parts of the paper, such as folding or bending paper (Figure 4) to further classify the more complicated movements of paper craft under subcategories of *Within Paper* and *Not Within Paper*.

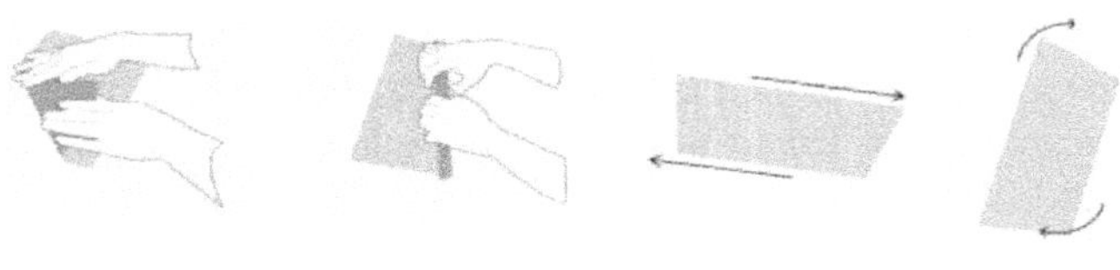

(a) (b) (c) (d)

Figure 4: Movement primitives of single piece of paper: (a) fold, (b) bend, (c) linear translation, (d) rotation

Fold - creates a crease; a combination of creases creates origami. Fold refers to folding in one direction and multiple directions (Figure 4(a)).

Bend - changes the paper's shape without creating creases; because of its texture, the paper usually reverts to its original shape after the bend is released. Bend includes bending forward and backward (Figure 4(b)).

Linear - movement in 1D, 2D, and 3D space (Figure 4(c)).

Rotation refers to the orientation of the paper craft. Movement along the axis can occur in 2D and 3D space (Figure 4d).

Multiple Papers also has two subcategories:

Dependent - The movement of one paper could trigger the movement of another paper. This type of movement is common in movable paper craft [12], which uses traditional mechanical structures such as gears and pulling bars. In movable paper craft, we can equate dependent movement in terms of input-output relationship.

Independent - The movements of multiple papers have no cause and effect relationship. Each paper's movement is triggered by different sources.

Pattern Language for Automated Paper Craft

The taxonomy of paper movement describes one important dimension a movable paper craft system can support. To comprehensively classify a system, a more systematic description is needed. Thus, we designed a pattern language as inspired by Card et al. [5].

In our pattern language, an automated movable paper craft can be abstracted into a four-dimension vector:

$$(\textit{Movement, MovementStyle, R, W})$$

Where: *Movement* is the possible movements generated in the paper craft. It includes all the movement primitives mentioned above in the subcategories of *Within Paper* and *Not Within Paper*.

MovementStyle is either *continuous* (perpetually moving) or *binary* (moving or not moving).

R is the dependency between different movements.

W is a set of general rules that describes the properties of the paper craft, how the system works, and its constraints.

Our pattern language uses the following set of operators:

$$< \&, |, \rightarrow, \neg >$$

Where: & (*and*) means the output movements can be performed at the same time. For instance, a paper craft can be folded and perform linear movement on a surface at the same time with any system-mode changing, such as button pressing.

| (*or*) means the system can only process a single output at a time, which would lead the mode-changing of the system.

→ (*dependent*) shows the connection between input and output, where the starting point is the input method, and the end point is the output result.

¬ (*binary*) means the movement is performed in continuous or binary style.

We then used this pattern language to analyze four existing automated paper crafts as examples.

The *Programmable Hinge* [28] can control the rotation angle of the hinge through a microcontroller. Using the pattern language, we can describe it as:

$$\textit{ProgrammableHinge} = (\textit{Movement: 2DRotary, MovementStyle: Continuous, R: \{\}, W: \{\}})$$

In *Animated Paper* [14], SMA animates paper craft by bending, which causes it to move on a flat surface:

$$\textit{AnimatedPaper} = (\textit{Movement: Bend, Linear, MovementStyle: Binary, R}: \neg \textit{Bend} \rightarrow \neg \textit{1DLinear} | \neg \textit{2DLinear, W: \{\}})$$

In *Animating Paper with SMA* [16], there is multiple bending and folding. Since they cannot be performed at the same time, the movements have an | (or) relationship:

$$\textit{AnimatingPaperWithSMA} = (\textit{Movement: Fold, Bend, MovementStyle: Binary, R}: \neg \textit{Fold} | \neg \textit{Bend, W: \{\}})$$

In *Interactive Paper Devices* [20], the movement of the paper robot was triggered by bending the SMA.

$$\textit{InteractivePaperDevices} = (\textit{Movement: Bend, MovementStyle: Binary, R}: \neg \textit{Bend, W}: \{\})$$

Table 1 shows the analysis of these examples and other related work in automated movable paper craft, including the use of SMAs, motors, and MEMS as movement actuators. The dashed line indicates the | (*or*) relationship between two movements.

The taxonomy and pattern language helped us understand the capabilities of the prior work and allowed us to identify a number of areas for improvement. First, we find the number of movement types supported by previous systems cover different and often limited number of cells in Table 1. Most of them only support binary movement (i.e., [6, 14, 16, 17, 20]). In Animating Paper with SMA, for instance, movement is still relatively unsophisticated: it is controlled by switching the power supply on and off. A power on/off

①: Programmable Hinge [28]
②: Interactive Paper Devices [20]
③: Animated Paper [14]
④: Electronic Popables [17]
⑤: Animating Paper with SMA [16]
⑥: Pulp-based Computing [6]
⑦: Oribotics [9]
⑧: Adaptive Bloom [13]
⑨: Programmable matter by folding [10]
⑩: AutoGami

Not Within Paper					Within Paper				
Rotary Motion		Linear Motion			Bend		Fold		
2D	3D	1D	2D	3D	Single Direction	Multiple Directions	Single Direction	Multiple Directions	Style
		③	③		③ ⑤ ④		⑥ ⑤② ④		Binary
⑩			⑩		⑩	⑩	① ⑨ ⑩	⑦⑧ ⑨ ⑩	Continuous

Table 1: Comparison of related works using the taxonomy of paper movement. This table shows that AutoGami supports a large range of movements as compared with other alternative systems.

pattern is used, for example, to flap the wings of a paper crane.

Second, the support for designing movement is limited. Except for Interactive Paper Devices [20], others do not have a graphical user interface for designing movement.

Third, existing toolkits either support rapid prototyping without sufficient controllability and customizability (Programmable Hinge [28] and Animating Paper with SMA [16]) or require electronic knowledge on the part of users in order to create circuits for programming and controlling the movement of paper craft (Interactive Paper Devices [20]).

Fourth, some use expensive and proprietary technologies (i.e., Animated Paper uses a high-power laser for heating up the SMA), making them less accessible.

To overcome some of the above limitations and to make automated movable paper craft accessible to more users, we developed AutoGami.

AUTOGAMI: A TOOLKIT FOR CONSTRUCTING AUTOMATED MOVABLE PAPER CRAFT

AutoGami is a low-cost and easy to use toolkit that runs on selective inductive power transmission [29], which allows paper craft to make more types of movements, and fully explores the taxonomy of automated paper craft. Its graphical interface makes designing and programming easier as it requires little or no engineering knowledge, supports rapid trial-and-error testing via simulation. Compared with existing systems and toolkits, AutoGami can support more movement types, as specified using the pattern language below.

AutoGami = (Movement: Rotary, Linear, Fold, Bend,

MovementStyle: Continuous, R: Rotary|Linear|Fold|Bend, W: {})

Implementation

Figure 5 shows an overview of AutoGami toolkit. The AutoGami hardware is developed based on the technology of selective inductive power transmission, which consists of controllable power transmitter and power receivers. In addition, the hardware part is connected to the controlling software through Arduino interface.

Hardware

The transmitter has a push/pull MOSFET oscillator with high output power. The LC tank in the system generates the oscillation, and two power MOSFETs amplify it to enable the system to transfer more energy wirelessly. As shown in Figure 6, a one-turn antenna with a diameter of 100 mm is made of a 6-mm diameter copper loop. The power transmitter in AutoGami contains customizable slots that enable users to design their own wireless power transmitter by connecting different capacitors. In terms of controllability, the transmitter circuit could be connected to Arduino output through connection slots, or directly through the on-board switches, to turn the relays on or off and generate different output frequencies.

For the structure of the power receiver and movement actuator, we used LC tank to harvest energy at its resonance frequency. The inductor L in the system refers to coil made of 0.5mm enameled copper wire; it is circular with diameter of 5cm and has only 2 turns to match the small resistance of the SMA wire. The capacitor and the SMA are attached to 2 nodes of the copper coil. Each coil will have a different value capacitor attached, thus each will have different resonance frequency. For the movement actuator, we used spring-shaped SMA with the model of BMX100500 from TOKI Cooperation [1].

Software

AutoGami comes with software (Fig. 6) that facilitates the design of paper craft movements. Its GUI enables users without programming experience to draw the shape, and design the movements of the paper craft, assign actuators to the different movements, and set the sequence of those movements. The software allows the user to simulate movement using SMA before the automated paper craft is implemented in paper and SMA.

To automate paper craft with AutoGami, the user first creates the physical prototype of the movable paper craft, and then draws a model of it using the software, and designs movements by setting the amplitude and duration of different motions in the GUI. According to the IDs of the receivers, the user then attaches SMAs to different parts of

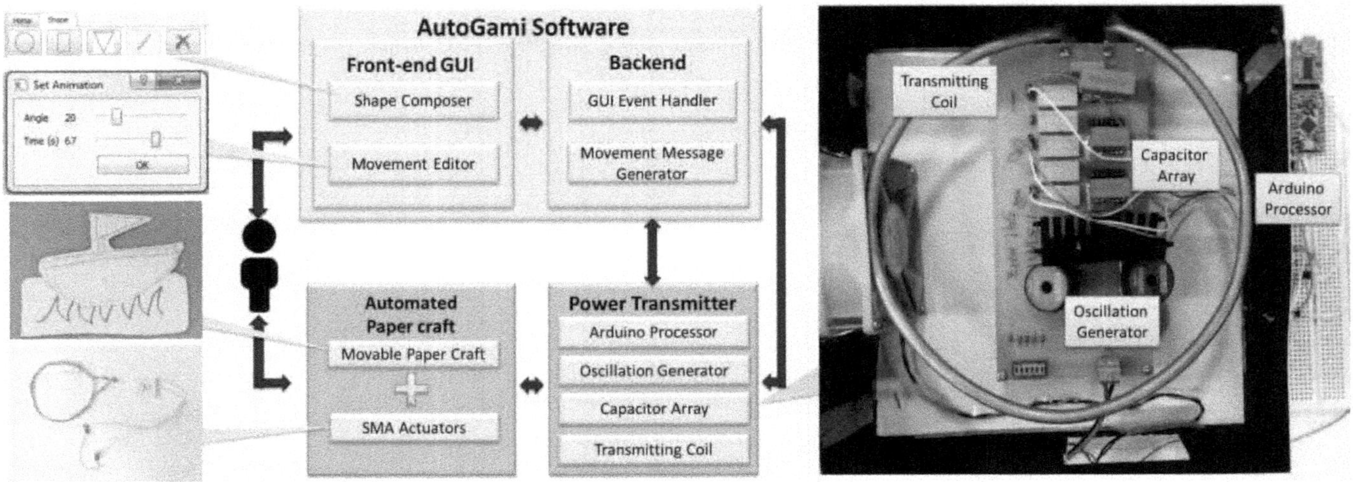

Figure 5: Overview of AutoGami's hardware and software

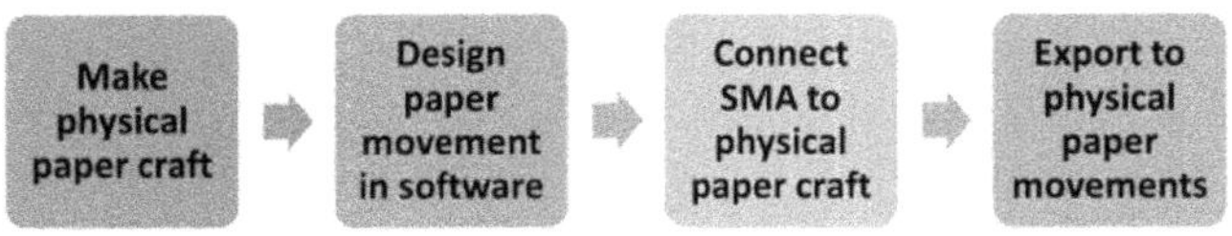

Figure 6: Steps of using AutoGami to create automated paper craft.

the paper craft, where movement will be triggered. When the power transmitter is on, the Arduino processor analyzes the information sent by the software and triggers a specific movement in the appropriate output frequency. Figure 6 is a step-by-step illustration of this process.

Features of AutoGami

AutoGami's software and hardware support features ranging from movement of different parts of a paper craft to creating a new type of movement using multiple actuators. We use a paper puppet of a bear (Figure 7(a)) to illustrate the toolkit's main features.

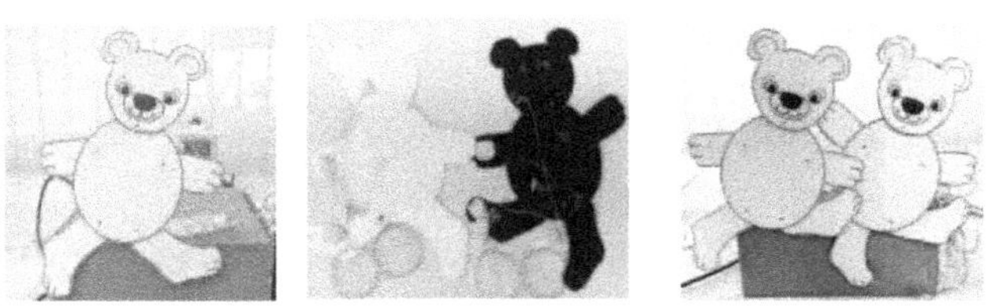

(a) (b) (c)

Figure 7: (a) A paper puppet made in AutoGami; (b) Replicating movements to another paper craft using the copy and paste method; (c) Final product of copy and paste

Moving different parts of the paper-craft separately

Selective inductive power transmission can activate different power receiving coils in different output frequencies. This allows users to assign a frequency to a movement that will be implemented in a particular part of the paper craft. The IDs of the joints in the drawing are mapped to power receivers with different resonant frequencies so that the user could identify the joint in the paper craft where he wants to trigger movement. In the case of the paper bear, the arm can be moved while the leg is static, and vice versa.

Adjusting the amplitude and the duration of different movements

AutoGami allows the user to set the amplitude, or range, of the movement, as well as how long the movement is performed. For example, the angle of a waving arm can be set to a certain degree, or a car can be set to move a certain distance. In Figure 5, slide bars are adjusted to set the amplitude and duration of a movement so that the paper bear waves hello by moving the arm at a small angle (20 degrees) for about 60 seconds, or waves goodbye by moving the arm at a wider angle.

Defining a sequence of movements

Users can define which movement is played before or after another movement. The sequence of movements can be arranged by setting the parameters of each movement (amplitude and duration) in a particular order. In the example of the paper bear, the user can set a sequence of movements so that the arm first waves goodbye then the legs move so that the bear walks away.

Replicating movement in another paper craft

Movements of one paper craft can be implemented in another through a physical copy-and-paste method. When two paper crafts have the same structure and are supposed to execute the same movements, the SMAs are simply attached to the same joints in the new paper craft. The sequence of movements that was created in the software

		AutoGami	Interactive Paper Devices [20]	Animated Paper [14]	Animating Paper with SMA [16]
Cost		~$100	~$200	>$1000	~$20
Knowledge Required		Paper craft making	Advanced electronics	Paper craft making	Soldering
Hardware Technology	Power Source	Inductive Power	Wire connection	Laser	Wire connection
	Hardware complexity	Low	High	Low	Medium
Controllability		Adjust the parameters of different motions	No	Binary on and off	No
Programmable		Yes	No	No	No
User interface	Paper craft Design	GUI	GUI	No	No
	Motion Design and Control	GUI	No	GUI	No

Table 2: Comparison of AutoGami and existing method for automating paper craft using SMA

interface is played to generate the same movements of the original paper craft. Figure 7(b) and Figure 7(c) show that the user only needs to set up the software once to make two or more paper bears execute the same movements.

Combining multiple actuators in one movement
The ability to selectively activate different SMAs allows the user to attach multiple SMAs to one movable part in the paper craft and set them up to move in different directions at the same time. This results in a new pattern of movement.

Comparison with Existing Toolkits on Paper Movement
We compared AutoGami with other toolkits in terms of expressiveness (customizability), cost, hardware interface, software interface, and prerequisite knowledge from users (see Table 2). With AutoGami, designing paper craft can be done at a lower cost, and knowledge in electronics is not required. There is higher controllability in designing movements, and the complexity of the hardware embedded in the paper craft is lesser.

Cost
AutoGami reduces the cost of hardware implementation by eliminating expensive processes and equipment such as gold leaf gilding and laser generators.

Prerequisite Knowledge from Users
AutoGami's design interface and attach-and-play method of implementation do not require advanced knowledge in electronics unlike Interactive Paper Devices, which require expert knowledge in circuit design and programming, and Animating Paper with SMA, which requires soldiering skills.

Hardware Technology
Interactive Paper Devices integrates an electronic circuit with a PIC controller into the paper material, which increases the complexity of the paper craft. Animating Paper with SMA also requires a copper-tape-based circuit to be embedded in the paper. On the other hand, AutoGami—like Animated Paper—uses attach-and-play, which merely requires the SMA to be attached to the paper to generate the movement.

AutoGami's use of inductive power has the advantage of eliminating massive wire connections to the external power source. Although Animated Paper also uses SMAs, it heats and powers up the SMA actuator with a high-power laser, an item that is not as readily procured and thus reduces the toolkit's accessibility.

Controllability and Programmability
The expressiveness of a toolkit refers to the extent it allows users to customize different movements, i.e., speed, time, sequence, and direction. Our experiment-based data shows that the speed of SMA contracting increases linearly with the current (in *Ampere* or *A*), as illustrated by the following mathematical equation:

$$Speed\ (cm/s) = 0.3218 * Current\ (A) + 0.0725$$

Animated Paper only allows binary control of the movement, which is triggered by switching the power on or off. Interactive Paper Devices and Animating Paper with SMA are more expressive than this, but AutoGami has higher controllability and programmability than these three toolkits because it can activate different actuators at different times.

Software and User Interface
Unlike other toolkits, AutoGami uses both GUI and physical interface in designing and controlling movements. This feature allows users to simulate the movements before implementing them to the paper craft.

WORKSHOP STUDIES
To evaluate the usefulness and usability of AutoGami, we conducted five workshops with an emphasis on the following questions:

How do users evaluate the intuitiveness and learnability of AutoGami?

Do users find the toolkit useful and engaging?

Is there evidence that the toolkit facilitates creativity?

We initially hoped to perform a comparison study with one of the three existing toolkits [14, 16, 20] listed in Table 1. However, Animated Paper [14] is a more costly, higher-end toolkit while Animating Paper with SMA [16] is simpler and less expressive than AutoGami. Thus, both are less than ideal for the purposes of comparison. Interactive Paper Device [20] is comparable to AutoGami in terms of cost and supported functionalities, but its software is not available for download and we don't have enough details to replicate the system.

Therefore, we have adopted the evaluation strategy followed by other creative systems, such as SandCanvas [18], and procedures used by Buechley et al. [2] for our evaluation.

Participants

Our workshops had a total 10 participants (2 people per workshop) consisting of five males and five females with ages ranging from 23 to 39 years (M=27.5, SD=4.81). The workshops were held in a meeting room with a dimension of 10 m x 7 m. Prior to conducting the workshops, we recorded the information on each participant's background skills in electronics and paper craft. Eighty percent of the participants considered their experience of electronics to be of intermediate level or lower, while 20% of them considered their background of paper craft to be of expert level but their experience in it to be at a lower level.

Apparatus

As shown in Figure 8, each participant worked with an AutoGami toolkit, which consisted of hardware (a transmitter connected to a power supply and two power receivers with SMAs in different resonant frequencies) and a software interface installed in a Lenovo ThinkPad X220. They were supplied with tools for making paper craft, such as paper, colored pens, scissors, needle, and wire. They were also provided with some premade paper crafts that they could examine and get inspiration from.

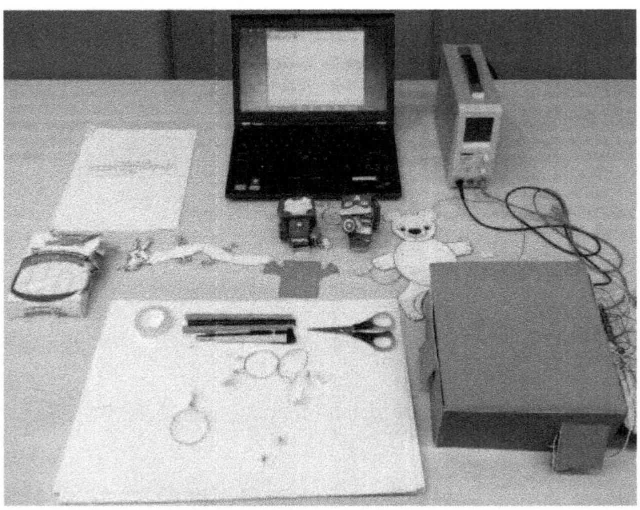

Figure 8: Setup of the workshop environment

Method

The workshop was conducted in four sessions:

1. Introduction. (*10 minutes*) The workshop facilitator gave a brief introduction of AutoGami and the technology of selective inductive power transmission, and showed a few examples of automated movable paper craft that can be made using AutoGami. The objective was to give the participants a brief understanding of the toolkit and the technology.

2. Guided Task. (*15–20 minutes*) After being introduced to AutoGami, the participants were given a printed tutorial on how to make an automated movable paper craft. The participants were asked to recreate this example to familiarize themselves with the AutoGami toolkit. The activity involved creating paper craft from scratch and planning the movements of two independent parts using the software interface.

3. Free Task. (*30–40 minutes*) Participants were grouped in pairs and were asked to explore their creativity and imagination by creating a new automated movable paper craft. This session aimed to provide us insights on how AutoGami allows users to explore their creativity.

4. Demo. (*10 minutes*) After making their own paper craft, each pair was asked to show a demo of the automated paper craft and explain the design rationale.

The workshop process was video recorded with the participants' consent. After the workshop, the participants answered a questionnaire on their impressions of the toolkit.

Results

User Evaluation of AutoGami's Intuitiveness and Learnability

Participants found AutoGami's hardware and software interfaces intuitive and easy to learn. One participant reported that it was *"easy to get used to the system"* and to working with the toolkit. Other participants commented: *"It is amazing to [familiarize myself] with a new technology and create an automated movable paper craft in less than one hour,"* that AutoGami can be easily and quickly understood, and that *"it is like the LEGO [of paper craft]."* The results of the questionnaire showed that intuitiveness earned a score of 4.5/5 while learnability scored 4.7/5.

All the participants were able to finish the guided task within the allotted time of 20 minutes. In the 40-minute free task, the participants were able to come up with different ideas for automated paper craft and implement them using AutoGami. They were allowed to ask questions when they faced difficulties, but very few did. There were, at most, two questions asked during each of the five workshops, which suggested that the toolkit was self-explanatory.

Nonetheless, the questions posed did help us to identify minor usability problems of the interface. Examples were *"Do I need to draw the exact shape of my paper craft? It seems I can only draw some simple shapes here,"* and *"What are the exact positions to attach the two ends of SMA?"* which indicate that the free-drawing function and the instructions on how to attach SMAs can be improved.

Figure 9: Automated paper craft created in AutoGami workshops

User Opinions on the Toolkit's Usefulness and Capacity to be Engaging

Workshop participants unanimously agreed that the toolkit is useful and that it can be employed in the following: teaching electronics, software, and interaction design to children; interactive storytelling; rapid prototyping for robot movements; designing smart furniture; and pure entertainment.

Overall enjoyment scored 4.5/5. It was observed that enjoyment increased when the participants were allowed to be creative. They were excited by the opportunity to create movable paper craft. This is reflected in the higher rating of enjoyment for the free task (4.7/5) as compared to the guided task (4.2/5).

Participants liked the toolkit, and most of them strongly agreed (4.4/5) that they wanted to recommend it to their friends. According to feedback, the toolkit is fun for introducing children to electronics, software, and movable paper craft; as one participant said, *"I had a great time playing with movable paper craft."*

Evidence of the Toolkit's Ability to Facilitate Creativity

Six pieces of automated paper craft were created during the five workshops, ranging from a natural scene to animals and from cartoon characters to architecture (Figure 9). A pair of girls used the copy-and-paste method to apply the same movements to a different paper craft. They used the same pulling movement on their cat's mouth and their elephant's nose. Another pair—an animation designer and an electronic engineer—adjusted the amplitude and duration of a movement to create a boat that moved in the waves. The boat's big movement depicted a bigger wave while a small movement depicted a smaller wave.

The post-workshop questionnaire also showed positive results in the area of facilitating creativity. The participants said that the toolkit allowed them to easily explore different possibilities of automatic movable paper craft, as evidenced by the score of 4/5 for this statement. Similarly, the statement "I became creative in automated movable paper craft using this toolkit" earned a score of 4.4/5.

In summary, the distributions of the scores for selected key questions are illustrated in Figure 10.

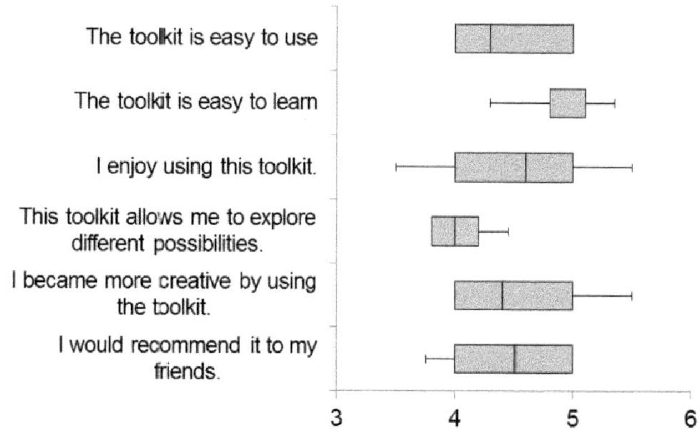

Figure 10: Score distribution for selected questions in the post-workshop questionnaire

Other Insights

Every group in the workshop used a similar process for designing automated paper craft. During the free task, most groups first decided on what real-world example to use for the automated paper craft. They then decided on the color of each part of the paper craft, as they identified color as an important characteristic. Finally, they decided on the movement the paper craft should make. This process motivated us to look at the properties of traditional paper craft—such as real-world examples, color, texture, and shape—in more detail as we improve the analysis of the design space on automated paper craft and further develop our toolkit.

LIMITATIONS

The current AutoGami hardware has limitations that prevent it from performing very complex, fast, and precise movements. AutoGami's software interface only supports drawing with simple shapes (e.g., circle, rectangle, and triangle). Thus, when using the GUI to draw a paper craft, the user can only draw its general shape. In addition, the size of the power-receiving coil needs to be optimized. It is relatively big compared to the size of the transmitter; as a result, it limits the number of receivers that can be placed on the inductive surface.

CONCLUSION AND FUTURE DIRECTIONS

In this paper, we have analyzed the research on movable paper craft by presenting a taxonomy and pattern language for this field. Our taxonomy can help researchers and designers to better understand previous work and to identify promising opportunities for new design. Motivated by our analysis, we developed AutoGami, a low-cost rapid prototyping toolkit for automated paper craft. Its software and hardware interfaces support the design of different patterns of automated movements in paper craft. The results of workshops have proven the usefulness of AutoGami, as users can create diverse, meaningful automated paper craft using the toolkit. Additionally, participants felt highly engaged in using AutoGami to create automated paper craft.

AutoGami provides a unique platform with rich capabilities, controllability, and expressiveness; it can also support various applications of automated paper craft such as storytelling, artwork design, and product prototyping. With further development of the toolkit, we aim to bring the joy of exploring and using automated paper craft to more users.

ACKNOWLEDGMENTS

We would like to thank Hideaki Nii for his guidance in designing and building the hardware prototype. We also thank members of the CUTE center and NUS-HCI lab for their generous help and support. This research is supported by the Singapore National Research Foundation under its International Research Centre @ Singapore Funding Initiative and administered by the IDM Programme Office.

REFERENCES

1. BioMetal, Toki cooperation. http://www.toki.co.jp/biometal/index.php.
2. Buechley, L., Eisenberg, M., Catchen, J., and Crockett, A. The lilypad arduino: using computational textiles to investigate engagement, aesthetics, and diversity in computer science education. In *Proc. of CHI 2008*, ACM Press (2008), 423–432.
3. Buechley, L., Hendrix, S., and Eisenberg, M. Paints, paper, and programs: first steps toward the computational sketchbook. In *Proc. of TEI 2009*, ACM Press (2009), 9–12.
4. Bullock, I., and Dollar, A. Classifying human manipulation behavior. In *Proc. of ICORR 2011*. 1- 6.
5. Card, S. K., Mackinlay, J. D., and Robertson, G. G. The design space of input devices. In *Proc. of CHI 1990*, ACM Press (1990), 117–124.
6. Coelho, M., Hall, L., Berzowska, J., and Maes, P. Pulp-based computing: a framework for building computers out of paper. In *Proc. of CHI 2009*, ACM Press (2009), 3527–3528.
7. Deborah, F, Origami and Communication Strategies. *Doshisha Studies in Language and Culture* 1-2, 315 – 334. 1998.
8. Falcioni, J. G. Shape Memory Alloys. *Mechanical Engineering*. April 1992, 114.
9. Gardiner, M., and Gardiner, R. The functional aesthetic of folding, self-similar interactions. In *Proc. of TEI 2012*, ACM Press (2012), 19-22.
10. Hawkes, E., An, B., Benbernou, N. M., Tanaka, H., Kim, S., Demaine, E. D., Rus, D., and Wood, R. J.., Programmable matter by folding, *In Proc. of NAS*, vol. 107, no. 28, 2010.
11. Ishii, H., and Ullmer, B. Tangible bits: towards seamless interfaces between people, bits and atoms. In *Proc. of CHI 1997*. ACM Press (1997), 234-241.
12. Ives, R., Ed. *Paper Engineering and Pop-ups FOR DUMMIES*. Wiley Publishing, 2009.
13. Justin Goodyre -- Constructing Realities | ARUP Phase 2 Gallery | London 2010. http://www.constructingrealities.com/?p=5.
14. Koizumi, N., Yasu, K., Liu, A., Sugimoto, M., and Inami, M. Animated paper: a moving prototyping platform. In *Adjunct Proc. of UIST 2010*, ACM Press (2012), 389–390.
15. McGee, L. M., Charlesworth, R., Books with movables: More than just novelties, *The Reading Teacher* 37 (9) 853-859.
16. Qi, J., and Buechley, L. Animating paper using shape memory alloys. In *Proc. of CHI 2012*, ACM Press (2012), 749–752.
17. Qi, J., and Buechley, L. Electronic popables: exploring paper-based computing through an interactive pop-up book. In *Proc. Of TEI 2010*, ACM Press (2010), 121–128.
18. Rubaiat, H. K, Chua, K. C., Zhao, S., Davis, R., Low, K.. SandCanvas: a multi-touch art medium inspired by sand animation. In *Proc. of CHI 2011*, ACM Press (2011), 1283-1292
19. Rubaiat, H. K, Igarashi, T., Zhao, S., Davis, R. Vignette: interactive texture design and manipulation with freeform gestures for pen-and-ink illustration. In *Proc. of CHI 2012*, ACM Press (2012), 1727-1736
20. Saul, G., Xu, C., and Gross, M. D. Interactive paper devices: end-user design and fabrication. In *Proc. of TEI 2010*, ACM Press (2010), 205–212.
21. Shumakov, K. and Shumakov, Y., Functional interhemispheric asymmetry of the brain in dynamics of bimanual activity in children 7-11 year old during origami training. PhD dissertation, Rostov State University, 2000.
22. Sloman, P., Ed. *Paper: Tear, Fold, Rip, Crease, Cut*. Black Dog Publishing, 2009.
23. Snyder, C., Ed. *Paper Prototyping: The Fast and Easy Way to Design and Refine User Interfaces*. Morgan Kaufmann, 2003.
24. Thelma R. Newman, Jay Hartley Newman, L. S. N., Ed. *Paper as Art and Craft: The complete book of the history and processes of the paper arts*. Crown Publishers, 1973.
25. Van S. D., Broman, E., E. G. K. R. A. M., Ed. *Paper Engineering: Fold, Pull, Pop and Turn*. Smithsonian Institution Libraries, 2010.
26. Weiser, M. The computer for the 21st century. *SIGMOBILE Mob. Comput. Commun.* Rev. 3, 3 (July 1999), 3-11.
27. Wellner, P. Interacting with Paper on the Digital Desk. In *Commun. ACM* 36(7): 86-96 (1993)
28. Wrensch, T. and Eisenberg, M. 1998. The programmable hinge: toward computationally enhanced crafts. In *Proc. of UIST* 1998. ACM Press (1998), 89-96.
29. Zhu, K., Nii, H., Fernando, O. N. N., and Cheok, A. D. Selective inductive powering system for paper computing. In *Proc. of ACE 2011*, ACM Press (2011), 59:1–59:7.

HyperSlides: Dynamic Presentation Prototyping

Darren Edge[1] **Joan M. Savage**[1,2] **Koji Yatani**[1]
[1] Microsoft Research Asia, Beijing, China
[2] Indiana University-Purdue University, Indianapolis, IN, USA
darren.edge@microsoft.com, joanmariesavage@gmail.com, koji@microsoft.com

ABSTRACT
Presentations are a crucial form of modern communication, yet there is a dissonance between everyday practices with presentation tools and best practices from the presentation literature. We conducted a grounded theory study to gain a better understanding of the activity of presenting, discovering the potential for a more dynamic, automated, and story-centered approach to prototyping slide presentations that are themselves dynamic in their ability to help presenters rehearse and deliver their story. Our prototype tool for dynamic presentation prototyping, which we call HyperSlides, uses a simple markup language for the creation of hierarchically structured scenes, which are algorithmically transformed into hyperlinked slides of a consistent and minimalist style. Our evaluation suggests that HyperSlides helps idea organization, saves authoring time, creates aesthetic layouts, and supports more flexible rehearsal and delivery than linear slides, at the expense of reduced layout control and increased navigation demands.

Author Keywords
Presentations; Slideware; PowerPoint; Grounded Theory

ACM Classification Keywords
H5.2 Information interfaces and presentation: User Interfaces

INTRODUCTION
The activity of preparing and delivering presentations, whether to teach, inform, or persuade, is of critical importance across education, academia, and business. Current presentation software is dominated by Microsoft PowerPoint [29], but this application has given rise to a whole family of slideware including Apple Keynote [1]. The success of slideware can be measured by the 60 million monthly visitors to the SlideShare platform for web-based presentation sharing [43] and the 12 million English PowerPoint files indexed by Google as of January 2013.

Nevertheless, while slideware can lift the floor of public speaking, it can also lower the ceiling [37] by creating a dependency on slides that in many cases resemble text documents ("slideuments") [10]. Far from Dale Carnegie's 1930s ideal that visual materials will promote clarity [6], this has led to the problematic practice of peripheral computing by audience members [19] who can simply read along rather than listen. In a critique of "The Cognitive Style of PowerPoint" [48], Edward Tufte further attacks the foreshortening of evidence and thought, low spatial resolution, single-path hierarchy, fragmented narratives, rapid temporal sequencing, chartjunk, formatting, and commercialism of PowerPoint. Don Norman makes the counterargument "In Defense of PowerPoint" [33], however, that "most people give poor talks" and the problem lies with the talk, not with the tool. Empirical studies also suggest that slides have a positive effect on learning outcomes when they are shared or printed for offline reading and review [22].

Even so, a wide range of technologies have been created to augment or replace slide presentations. Following Zoomable User Interface (ZUI) research [5] applied to presentations [15], the commercial Prezi application [40], the Fly research application [25], and the pptPlex add-in for PowerPoint [39] present alternatives to the 35mm slide metaphor in the form of zoomable canvases. As yet though, experimental comparisons of slide versus canvas presentations have not yielded significant differences in the recall of facts or structure [23], while decorative use of rotation has been shown to negatively impact spatial understanding [24].

Various projects have explored other aspects of presenting, including authoring with scanned paper [36]; interaction with paper representations of slides [31, 42]; gestural interaction [13]; non-linear navigation [30, 45]; multi-screen content [21]; mobile "crowd" feedback during delivery [47]; and automatic feedback on speech during rehearsal [20]. However, very few works have attempted to address all five canons of rhetoric formulated by Cicero [9], from the *invention* and *arrangement* of arguments through their elaboration in *style* and *memory* before final *delivery*. Similarly, presentation tools are "simply containers for ideas and assets" [10] and offer no guidance about how to communicate using such devices as the ethical, emotional, and logical means of persuasion defined by Aristotle [3].

Our goal was therefore to uncover the gap between actual presentation practices and the "best practices" advocated in the presentation literature, before designing tools that help presenters to bridge that gap. We began by conducting a grounded theory study [8], interviewing 20 people for whom presenting was a core competency. In this study, we identified the need for a more dynamic approach towards the rapid and iterative prototyping of slide presentations that themselves offer greater dynamism and flexibility in their support for planning, rehearsing, and delivering a story.

From the results of our grounded theory study we derived four implications for the design of dynamic presentation prototyping systems. We use these to motivate the design of our HyperSlides system, which leverages the PowerPoint application and document format for dynamic prototyping, while transforming the conventional slide metaphor to support more dynamic forms of rehearsal and delivery:

1. *Planning with points.* In HyperSlides, points to be communicated are hierarchically organized into scenes of a storyline using a lightweight text markup language.
2. *Styling as a service.* In HyperSlides, slides are generated from scenes, styled based on general design principles, and automatically hyperlinked to one another.
3. *Linking between scenes.* In HyperSlides, scenes connect to one another via verbal linkages and to a visual overview of the storyline for non-linear navigation.
4. *Expanding on demand.* In HyperSlides, scenes expand into points and points into supporting details that can be shown dynamically without breaking presentation flow.

To understand the experiences of approaching presentations in such a dynamic manner, we observed the use of HyperSlides in a 5-hour workshop with 12 students. We found that HyperSlides encourages many of the best practices for presentations identified through our grounded theory study and literature review, helping presenters to organize their thoughts, saving them authoring time, creating aesthetic layouts automatically, and supporting more flexible rehearsal and delivery than linear slides. These benefits come at the expense of reduced layout control during presentation authoring and increased navigation demands during delivery.

The contributions of this work are therefore: 1) the development of categories and implications from our grounded theory study, culminating in the notion of dynamic presentation prototyping; 2) the design of the HyperSlides system; and 3) the validation of HyperSlides in a user study that demonstrated dynamic practices in the authoring, rehearsal, and delivery of presentations under time pressure.

UNDERSTANDING THE ACTIVITY OF PRESENTING

To enrich our understanding of presentions, we conducted qualitative research with people for whom presenting was a practised (even if underdeveloped) competency. We adopted the constructivist approach to grounded theory [8], acknowledging that both researchers and participants construct theories through the analytic lens of their past interactions with people, perspectives, and practices. As such, we offer an interpretive and provisional account that helps us to understand the fundamental concerns and processes that constitute the activity of presenting.

Procedure

We began with eight interviews structured around open-ended questions eliciting reflections on participants' presentation experiences. These were recorded and transcribed for analysis. Line-by-line coding of theses transcripts resulted in 162 short, active phrases that distilled and defined processes in action and patterns between them.

Following initial interviews, we used affinity diagramming to cluster initial codes into related groups. We then created synthesized category labels as focused codes to be used in subsequent analysis. Reexamination of existing data confirmed our categorization had high levels of fit, relevance, and coverage. We then continued with 12 further interviews until we had saturated each of these categories.

Participants

We recruited 20 participants (5 female), of ages 25–55 (mean 35), from 10 nationalities. They comprised 6 industrial researchers working in design, development, and management, 6 student research interns with backgrounds in engineering and computer and social sciences, and 8 people working as teachers, pastors, and sales and business professionals. Our initial and subsequent theoretical sampling prioritized diversity of profession but unity of professional need to prepare and deliver presentations.

Categories

Through our grounded theory analysis, we developed eight categories that characterized the activity of presenting as experienced by our participants. All were used to inspire the design of the HyperSlides system, but here we present only the five categories that most directly illustrate the need for a more dynamic approach to presenting. Direct quotes are attributed to participants using the notation [PX] to refer to participant X, but all analysis closely follows participant quotes grounded in presentation experiences.

1. Setting goals given constraints

Presentations result from goal-directed activity constrained by parameters of the content, the audience, the schedule, the event, and the contexts of preparation and delivery. Mismatched goals and constraints cause problems, e.g.:

"I don't want to spend more time on my slides than the actual intellectual work I've put into it – it's like you see those presentations where people look like they obviously spent more time on their slides than the actual work." [P7]

Presentation goals can be explicitly constrained by event rules, either in time or slides (or both, as in the Pecha Kucha style of 20 slides for 20 seconds each [38]). They can also be influenced by the relative performance of peers and the intrinsic desire of the person to present.

For a presentation, "the message depends on the audience" [P4]. Presenters should therefore reflect on the relationship between different kinds of audience members and the content to be presented, anticipating and formulating responses to questions that could arise as a result.

However, sometimes "the audience is not big enough or the issue not large enough to use a lot of time on it" [P6]. Preparation time can be affected by anticipated differences in audience expertise, culture, language, and learning-style. The effort required depends on the readiness of content – "sometimes you are just scrambling to put something together" [P9] – as well as presenter – "if I'm forced to do something on short notice I feel very uncomfortable" [P4].

2. Telling stories with slides

Information and examples can be wrapped in a narrative and delivered through the interplay of visuals and speech. Successful communication has multiple points and layers that are connected by a sense of coherence and flow:

"I prefer to do very focused slides – images, words that are very brief and to the point so it avoids people spending all their time looking at the PowerPoint while you're talking and trying to communicate. Ideally it needs to be seamless in a transition, where if you are moving from three different points... your first point should logically lead into the second point... all three of them really work together to drive at the final conclusion or the original question. So really it should work together as a unit – three pieces of the same idea, just broken down." [P13]

Story development should begin before slide building. Starting with the goal in mind can help guide all subsequent activity, including crafting implicit messages, explicit takeaways, or rhetorical questions. Mapping points to slide titles also gives a provisional structure for elaboration.

Images and graphics can replace text in ways that "hit the right tones – inspiring, motivational" [P11]. The addition of a few words can aid communication clarity as well as helping people come up with questions. Effectiveness rises when such slides are concluded with "a powerful point or a summation that is left to sink in before moving on" [P5].

Presenters can "spend a lot of time on how to connect slides" [P8]. Leading with a question, hint, or concern prior to changing slides shows that the presenter is in control and avoids breaking the flow. Planning transition words helps both the presenter to consider why they are moving to the next topic and the audience to follow the progression.

Seeing and rearranging content in overview helps create a sense of flow, whether looking for stories in images or connecting descriptions of slide contents. Finally, the technique of "tying back to a general story or idea helps keep people in the outline of what's going on" [P6].

3. Preparing for structured spontaneity

Cycles of rehearsal and refinement can help consolidate the presentation structure in the mind of the presenter, encouraging a natural delivery free of reading and recital:

"I can sort of read stuff and without thinking about how to connect them – thinking I've connected them once, therefore they should make sense. But it's a lot less effective to the audience – I think it's a lot better if I'm delivering, making sense and connecting each point at a time. Then I think the audience has an easier time. It's a degree of familiarity but it's also the ability to talk about something and thinking ahead." [P9]

High-level rehearsal involves going back and forth at the macro level to internalize the presentation outline, and doing this many times "until you know in your head how you will transition from this idea to that idea" [P3]. This helps presenters to not think about the words but the flow, because "If you don't depend on the words then you don't have to worry about memorizing anything" [P15]. Memorization is sometimes employed just for the wordings of strong slide conclusions that set up the following slide.

Lower-level rehearsal uses slide visuals as cues for the recall of points to make verbally, treating the presentation as a "cheat sheet of minimum clues" [P14]. Strategies for learning these associations include the use of presenter notes, physical flashcards to drill points into short-term memory, and making redundant changes across notes and slideware. While more practice makes the delivery more intuitive, "the best thing is a well-spaced work flow that isn't consolidated into a single session of cramming" [P5]. While rehearsing, practicing speaking slides out loud highlights differences between written and spoken language, which supports rephrasing of notes to be spoken. A clear mental structure also supports performance-oriented rehearsals such as practice walking around, in front of a mirror, gesturing, or visualizing the delivery in their mind.

Reading from presenter notes typically results in "not a really good experience – it really stops the flow of things, the human-to-human interaction" [P17]. Instead, many presenters printed back-up information that could be re-read to remind the presenter just before the presentation, then left "lying on the podium just to be safe" [P14].

4. Orchestrating focus and flow

During delivery, the presenter must orchestrate the audience's attention using the combination of visuals, gestures, and speech, directing focus at key points and communicating a clear, purposeful flow from start to finish. Since breaking the flow is highly detrimental, presenters have devised coping strategies, e.g., preparing hyperlinks:

"I use a lot of references as well this one feature in PowerPoint that's very useful – I'm talking about a certain point and I need to develop it further so I just click at that point with the mouse and it jumps all the way to back-up pages with detailed information. I click another button and it goes back to the original page so it doesn't interrupt the whole sequence of the presentation." [P16]

Many presenters prepare such extra slides like an appendix at the end of their presentation. Such slides can be useful "in case people ask you for more data, more proof – you should always be able to support what you say" [P3]. Sometimes it is also desirable to show slides out of linear order as a way of making points spontaneously or in response to audience questions. It is possible to memorize slide numbers for direct keyboard navigation rather than skipping through slides in sequence, but this is onerous and can still result in "hopping around" when slide numbers are misremembered. Exiting a presentation to access additional files can result in "losing the whole audience while showing everyone how you organize your files" [P2]. Impromptu whiteboard sketches were often used as a fallback [P10].

One tactic to prevent the audience reading ahead is to show a headline as a reminder that prompts the presenter to speak freely about a topic, only showing bullet points afterwards as a recap. However, anxious presenters often forget what to say and prefer glancing back at detailed slides. Sometimes presenters also need to see the next slide before they know what to talk about, which can cause even larger problems if the presenter is surprised by what appears.

5. Influencing audience with timing

Communication takes place over time, and the presenter's timed rehearsals, attention to timekeeping, and rhythm of spoken delivery all affect audience perceptions. Even with good timekeeping, problems like slide skipping still occur:

"I don't often go over. I pay attention to presenter mode in PowerPoint – I do know how much time I have left. Very often they'll have questions – they'll just jump right into questions and so I'll just cut – I'll dynamically cut out material or I'll just be like, okay we don't have time for this stuff. And I'll just skip, skip, skip. Then I'll just get over to the important points." [P17]

The converse problem is also possible – stressed presenters can speak too fast, exhausting their slides and having to fill the remaining time unaided. Automatically advancing slides can help in some ways but become problematic as soon as there is deviation from the original plan.

During delivery, presenters can aim to hit particular topics by particular times. To end a talk gracefully, some presenters use handheld "clickers" that vibrate at fixed intervals (e.g., 5 or 2 minutes) before the end of the allotted time, letting you "feel when you are getting there" [P2]. Finishing on time can be seen as a measure of success for any presentation, but for some talks, this is even more critical when the alternative is being told to stop speaking.

Rapid transitions between slides can also be used to visually reinforce the logic of spoken arguments. For persuasive presentations in general, the main challenge is often not about content, but "building the right tones and crescendos" [P11] by varying the rhythm over time.

The density of slides or script text can also be used to make projections of the final speaking time, while iterative timed rehearsals reduce the uncertainty of how long each slide will take. Presenters who do not rehearse can overestimate the points they can cover and "end up skipping most of the bullet points on the slides" [P12].

The need for dynamic presentation prototyping

The categories presented in the previous section describe fundamental processes in the activity of presenting, many of which were described in terms of actions with slides in conventional slideware applications such as PowerPoint. The fundamental concern arising from this analysis can be expressed in terms of how interaction affordances and constraints shape the nature of presentation authoring, rehearsal, and delivery. In particular, the authoring environment of conventional slideware offers many affordances for graphical manipulation, while the slideshow mode is highly constrained by the linear way in which presentation slides are built and navigated, as well as the literal way in which all slide content must be presented (even during rehearsal when testing might be more valuable [7]).

Our notion of a dynamic approach to presentation prototyping reverses this balance by promoting tight constraints on authoring possibilities while opening up rich and differentiated interaction affordances for presentation rehearsal and delivery. Our argument is that given a fixed amount of time to prepare a presentation, the time saved by not directly manipulating text, images, and other slide "shapes" can be reallocated to two of the sub-activities shown by the grounded theory study to be of critical importance: *telling stories with slides* by thinking about the sequence, structure, and purpose of points to make; and *preparing for structured spontaneity* by mentally and verbally rehearsing how to add value to the points shown on the slides. Time spent on these sub-activities should result in better mastery of better material, creating freedom to be more dynamic, responsive, and improvisational during delivery: *orchestrating focus and flow*. All of these categories suggest some kind of prepared connection between points that can be dynamically revealed on demand either to test the presenter (during rehearsal) or share with the audience. This is further supported by the ability to show content in time with speech or pass over it due to time constraints: *influencing audience with timing*. When *setting goals given constraints* while planning and rehearsing the presentation, dynamic presentation prototyping should support the same kind of early, iterative, and responsive prototype delivery that characterizes agile software development practices [2].

Implications for design & Supporting literature

In the following sections, we map the concept of dynamic presentation prototyping onto four implications for the design of future tools. We motivate each with ideas from the popular and scientific literature we reviewed subsequently.

A. Planning with points

Presentation tools should help people to organize the points they wish to communicate, and "every once in a while being able to spit out a presentation" [P9]. Through lightweight authoring and the automatic generation of presentation documents that are sensitive to variations in audience and timing, planning and authoring should be possible even when distributed across devices and contexts.

Planning with points before committing them to slides avoids the problem of never seeing the whole story at once [49]. It also avoids slide procrastination – "fidgeting with and worrying about bullets and images on slides [...] instead of how we craft the story that is most effective, memorable, and appropriate for our audience" [41]. Crafting messages should precede visual design [10], and each message should propel the audience closer to the destination of their "journey" [11].

Doing the "data dump" outside slideware supports the distillation and organization of ideas and helps the presenter to check whether their sequence of slides titles creates a meaningful "flow" [49]. The lightweight nature of such planning is well supported by the analog tools of "paper, a whiteboard, post-it notes, or a stick in the sand" [41]. Presentation applications are "simply containers for ideas and assets" generated through these creative processes [10].

An early focus on communicative substance without the distractions of visual style also allows greater attention to the language used, for example the crafting of "twitter-like headlines" that are concise, specific, and memorable [14].

B. Styling as a service
Presentation tools should be able to take a collection of points sourced from multiple people and documents and generate a presentation of those points with consistent styling. This styling should be quickly and easily customizable while conforming to best practices in the visual design of presentations.

Several existing presentation tools offer different environments for authoring and presentation. Beamer [4] and Slidy [44] use LaTeX and HTML markup respectively to specify the logical structure of a presentation before combining with a visual theme and "compiling" into slides. In code-based approaches, Impress.js [18] uses JavaScript to specify zoomable canvas presentations, and Slithy [52] uses Python to generate rich parameterized animations. Such textual specifications support a smooth transition from point outlines created in collaborative text editors such as Google Docs [16] to the markup of those points with styles.

Styling as a service should encourage the use of images as a way to have the audience "not only understand your point better but also have a more visceral and emotional connection to your idea" [41]. This view is supported by the Picture Superiority Effect: concepts presented as images are remembered for longer than concepts presented as words [32]. The Dual Coding theory of memory [35] – that information has both visual and verbal components that form separate representations in the mind, each of which can act as a cue for retrieval – adds that words and images used together will amplify their joint message. This Multimedia Effect has been demonstrated experimentally [26] and encoded in two principles of multimedia learning [28]: the Multiple Representation Principle (use both pictures and words) and the Continuity Principle (use them together). The remaining principles are the Split-Attention Principle (when using visual explanations, augment with speech rather than text), the Individual Differences Principle (these effects apply more for low-knowledge and high-spatial learners), and the Coherence Principle (use fewer rather than more words and pictures). These are based on theories of Cognitive Load [46] and ways of reducing it [27]. In other words, "only put elements on your slides that help the audience recall your message" [11].

In general, styling as a service should automatically exploit all of the "big four" principles of visual design: contrast, repetition, alignment, and proximity [41]. For example, when displaying text bullets, it should also use proportional spacing to "avoid anticipation of bullets to come" and avoid line-wrapping to "minimize eye sweeps" [49].

C. Linking between scenes
Presentation tools should help presenters to craft and connect the central "scenes" of a high-level narrative, encouraging planning of verbal linkages between scenes and striking the right balance between "storytelling and analysis" [P7]. Organization of points into scenes should also guide presenter choices about how deeply to explore each scene while completing their narrative on time.

The notion of a scene is borrowed from the dramatic arts as a coherent set of points that advance the higher-level story. Scenes are the foundations of the 16 "flow structures" presented in [49], examples of which include chronological, problem/solution, and opportunity/leverage. Appropriate scenes for a presentation can be discovered by clustering related points into 3-5 "Roman columns" of the presentation, providing a mental focus for both presenter (when learning the presentation) and audience (when following it) [49]. A hierarchical organization of both scenes and the points within them ensures that "all the supporting information hangs off one big idea" [11]. One pattern to organize groups of slides into higher-level scenes is bumper slides that give visual closure between sections [41, 49].

Various ways of verbally linking scenes, or using "internal linkages", include using an opening gambit (such as a question, factoid, or anecdote), making repeated references to the flow structure, making logical transitions between outbound and inbound topics, and closing with your call to action [49]. Presenting a visual road map or outline near the start and end of the presentation can help the audience create and retain a mental model of the presentation [49].

Linking between scenes both visually and verbally creates dynamic tension through contrast, especially when scenes alternate between "what is" and "what could be" [11]. Based on insights from mythological, literary, and cinematic structures, this "presentation form" uses these contrasts to create a clear beginning, middle, and end, via turning points that help to inject energy and emotion [11].

D. Expanding on demand
Presentation tools should support the dynamic expansion of points into sub-points, notes, media, files, or web pages that support the point being presented. As a presenter, the expansions of points and connections between scenes during rehearsal should help "get the structure in your head" [P3]. During delivery it can support dynamic content control in response to forgetting or audience reactions.

The flashcard-like method of testing recall of some target information given an initial cue is called cued-recall learning, and has been studied extensively [7]. The most family of virtual flashcard applications are based on the SuperMemo algorithm [51], and recent HCI work has explored the use of contextual flashcards to prepare to speak in a second language [12]. However, current presentation software does not support cued-recall learning.

Rehearsal practice is recommended to follow the "3 Rs of letting go" [10]: Reducing slide or script text after each rehearsal; Recording the verbalization of each rehearsal (speaking words aloud to slides [49]); and Repeating rehearsals over time. Expanding on demand would bring cued-recall testing of points and linkages to presentation rehearsal, supporting finer-grained testing than is possible with slide notes. Such planned practice is the only way to achieve effective spontaneity [10], while letting the presenter "add value beyond each bullet by discussing, interpreting, and providing supporting evidence" from memory [49].

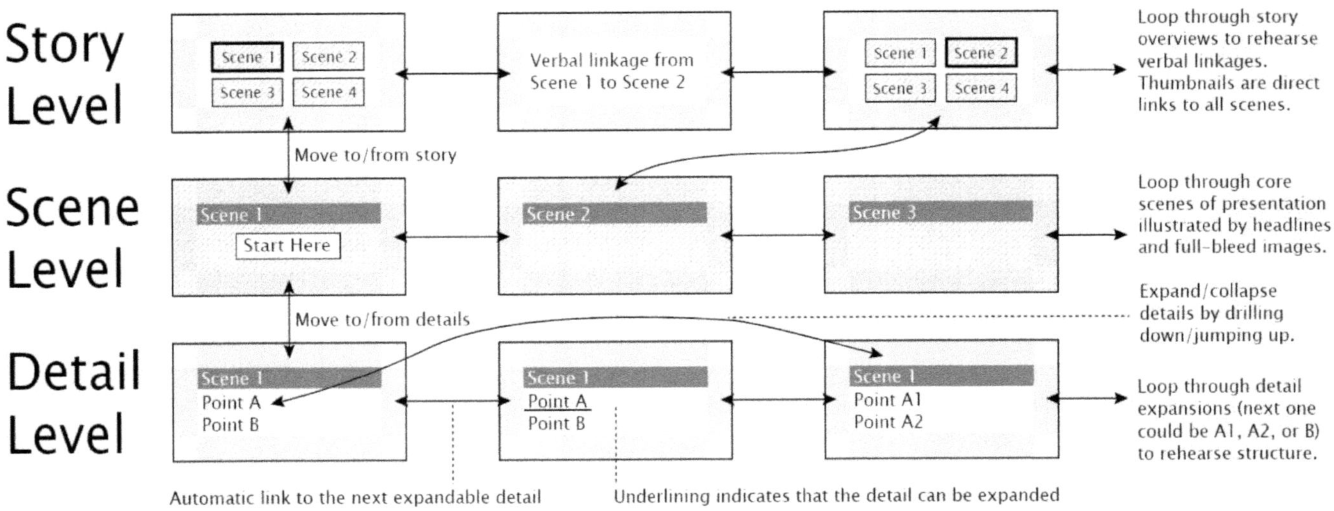

Figure 1. Topology of a HyperSlides presentation. Slide borders act as hyperlinks that support presentation traversal at three levels: core illustrated scenes, the high-level storyline, and low-level details expandable on demand

During delivery, the ability to expand points on demand gives the presenter freedom and flexibility to read the audience and present the right points to the right depth. This can occur following advice to "always speak 1:1" with audience members, "phrasing and pausing" to check understanding through eye contact and head nods [50].

DESIGN OF HYPERSLIDES

We designed our prototype HyperSlides system around the implications for design presented in the previous section. This system uses the Microsoft PowerPoint application and slide document format as a platform for prototyping presentations that are algorithmically transformed into slides but neither conceived nor navigated in the manner of conventional linear slides presentations. In the following sections, we describe the features of HyperSlides that support the dynamic prototyping of dynamic presentations.

A. Planning with points in HyperSlides

The title and bullet-like points of a HyperSlides presentation are created in a text file using a simple markup language (see Table 2). This supports the development of high-level scenes illustrated with full-bleed images, the expansion of scenes into points, the expansion of points into sub-points and supporting files, media, and web pages, and the preparation of verbal linkages between scenes. Such a text format supports highly lightweight authoring, but in the future could be performed through more visual means in a GUI or IDE.

B. Styling as a service in HyperSlides

The specification of a variety of style options is possible, including the font types and colors of title and body text, the size and color of the title background to create contrast when overlaid on a background image (as in Haiku deck [17]), and the slide aspect ratio and background color. Slide titles are automatically scaled to fill the space available. It is also possible to adjust the width of a special "hyperframe" – a set of transparent boxes added to the four edges of each slide, each of which can hyperlink to other slides in a richly interconnected slide network (see scene level of Figure 1).

Action	Syntax	Explanation
Create scenes	[Scene 1 < image1.jpg] [Scene 2 < image2.jpg]	Create scene slides with titles "Scene X" that have the background imageX.jpg.
Add details	[Scene 1 < image1.jpg] [> Point A] [>> Point A1] [>> Point A2] [> Point B]	Add Point A and Point B as details of Scene 1, with Point A1 and Point A2 sub-details of Point A. A third level of detail is possible using [>>>...], and so on.
Add hyperlinks	[> Point A >> http://url.tld] [> Point B >> anyfile.ext]	Link from Point A to a URL. Link from Point B to a file.
Embed media	[> Point C > media.ext]	Embed image or video into a slide linked from Point C.
Add verbal linkages	[Scene 1] {Linkage from Scene 1 to 2} [Scene 2]	Add verbal linkage from Scene 1 to Scene 2 (see Figure 1 for details).
Adjust styles	*styleParameter styleValue	Adjust visual properties (fonts, colors, spacing, etc.)
Add notes	This is a note.	Anything outside [...] or {...} is ignored.

Table 2. HyperSlides markup language.

These hyperlinks provide the mechanism for more dynamic navigation between slides. They are generated according to a HyperSlides specification using the Open XML SDK 2.0 for Microsoft Office [34], which supports strongly-typed generation of the XML elements underlying the .pptx file format of PowerPoint 2007 onwards. In slideshow mode, these hyperlinks can be navigated using the mouse or touch.

C. Linking between scenes in HyperSlides

The scene level of Figure 1 shows how the core, illustrated scenes of the presentation connect to one another horizontally. Clicking the top border of a scene slide jumps to a hyperlinked "storyline" slide with the outbound scene highlighted. Clicking on any scene thumbnail jumps directly to that scene, while horizontal navigation reveals the verbal linkages planned for transitions between scenes. We call this the "story rehearsal path", intended for use during preparation but not delivery. From an illustrated scene, clicking the bottom border drops down to reveal the top level of points for that scene. If the presenter reveals these points (rather than speaking to just the illustrated scenes), they must navigate back up to the scene level before advancing. This gives closure to each scene and prompts the speaker to say their prepared verbal linkage without slide text competing for the audience's attention.

D. Expanding on demand in HyperSlides

Any point can act as a hyperlink to an external file or web page. The detail level of Figure 1 shows how points can also act as internal hyperlinks to supporting points, descriptions, or media (images or videos). Once points have been expanded, clicking on the top border of the each slide will navigate back up the hierarchy. Navigating horizontally at the detail level follows the "detail rehearsal path", performing a depth-first traversal of all expandable points in the presentation, with "cue" slides using text underlines to indicate which point expansion the presenter should attempt to recall. The presenter should keep traversing this path until they can comfortably recall the structure and content of the points to be communicated. Slide notes are also generated automatically to show the inbound and outbound scene linkages and previews of point expansions.

HyperSlides Illustration

To generate a HyperSlides presentation, the HyperSlides executable file, the input text file named input.txt, and any hyperlinked files or media to embed in the presentation must be placed in the same folder. Double clicking on the executable regenerates the output.pptx file, which is then automatically opened in the installed version of PowerPoint (PowerPoint 2007 onwards). The annotated markup to the right could be used in as input.txt file that the HyperSlides executable would transform into the presentation in Figure 2.

Example input.txt file for a presentation about HyperSlides

{A new way to think about presentations}
⤷ *opening verbal introduction*
[Presenting with HyperSlides < Presenting.jpg]
⤷ *title and image of scene 1*
[> Dynamic Presentation Prototyping]
[>> Dynamic Prototyping of Presentations]
[>> Prototyping of Dynamic Presentations]
[> Practical Guidance > PresentationZen.jpg]
[> Empirical Grounding >> GroundedTheoryStudy.docx]
⤷ *hyperlinked bullets, slides, and files of scene 1*
{Presentation slides are prototyped dynamically}
⤷ *verbal transition to scene 2*
[Authoring < Prototyping.jpg]
[> Setting Goals given Constraints]
[> Telling Stories with Slides]
[> Planning with Points]
[> Styling as a Service]
[> Linking between Scenes]
{Presentation links are rehearsed dynamically}
[Rehearsal < Rehearsing.jpg]
[> Preparing for Structured Spontaneity]
[> Linking between Scenes]
[> Expanding on Demand (to learn the story)]
{Presentation itself is delivered dynamically}
[Delivery < Delivering.jpg]
[> Orchestrating Focus and Flow]
[> Influencing Audience with Timing]
[> Expanding on Demand (to tell the story)]
{Rapid iterative prototyping of flexible presentations}
⤷ *closing verbal takeaway message*

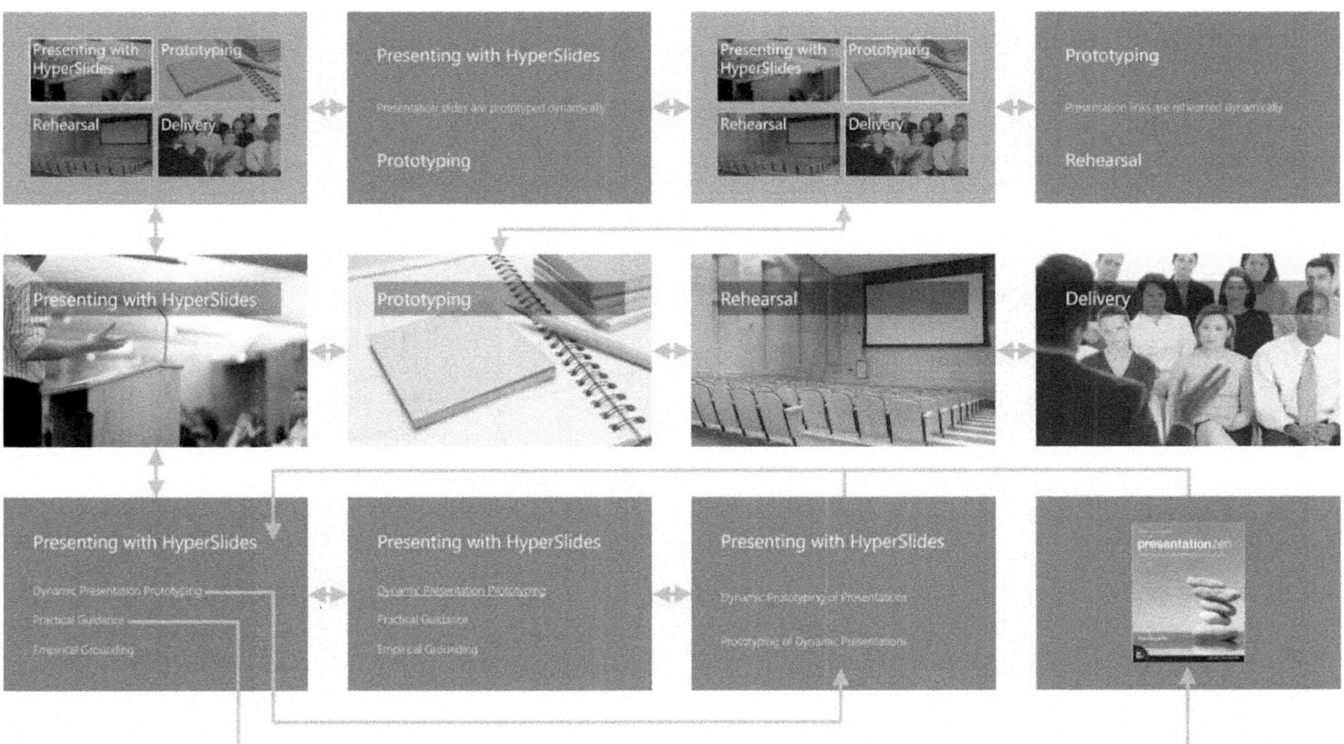

Figure 2. Example slides and navigation paths of a HyperSlides presentation in the default visual style

EVALUATION OF HYPERSLIDES

We were interested in understanding how dynamically prototyping, rehearsing, and delivering presentations could be beneficial to presenters and the extent to which HyperSlides supports such dynamism in practice.

Procedure

We ran a 5-hour workshop in which 12 participants:

1. Learned the technical use of HyperSlides through a series of per-feature mini-lessons (30 minutes);
2. Authored and rehearsed an 8-10 minute HyperSlide presentation on a topic of their choice (2 hours);
3. Took turns delivering their HyperSlide presentation to the remaining workshop participants (2 hours);
4. Provided feedback through two 6-participant focus group discussions held in parallel (30 minutes).

Participants also voted for the top three presentations, with the three presentations receiving the most votes winning prizes equivalent to 150, 50, and 30 USD respectively. All participants received a free lunch and a 15 USD gift card.

Participants

We recruited 12 participants (5 female) of ages 22–26 (mean 23) who did not participate in our grounded theory study. All were students working in our lab from a variety of research, engineering, and design backgrounds. These students – speakers of English as a second language at the beginning of their careers – represent ideal candidates for evaluating tools that aim to support the development of better presentation communication skills. All were proficient in the technical use of PowerPoint or Keynote or both, but wanted to develop their presentation skills further.

Findings

Our high-level finding is that HyperSlides encourages many of the best practices for presentations identified through our grounded theory study and literature review, and that injecting dynamism into the processes of presentation authoring, rehearsal, and delivery resonates with presenter needs. We now discuss participant feedback in terms of our four motivating implications for design.

Planning with points

Participants reported that "writing the script is very simple and easy to learn" and it "definitely saves time compared to building your presentation with normal PowerPoint" – "if you want to make a quick presentation it's the easiest way". This might be due to lower start-up costs and greater fluidity – "it is very easy to get started from scratch. I just define the titles and it is very easy to change their order". Another positive aspect is that "you just think the structure and words you are going to say", not about the final styling.

The hierarchical structuring in particular was well received. One participant described how "the structure is very helpful in helping me organize my thoughts", while another said it makes them "think in a tree way, an organized way". Another described how it helps them to "see the tree and the flow of the presentation more easily than in normal PowerPoint" where "the content easily gets messed up". In contrast, HyperSlides "naturally makes a well-organized presentation. It's just like a mind map – it makes me think".

One suggested improvement to planning with points was to incorporate syntax highlighting into the text editor to support visual parsing of otherwise similar-looking text elements, or to develop a custom graphical editor that supported the mapping out of points and their relationships in space.

Styling as a service

Participants appreciated the style of the automatically generated PowerPoint files. In such HyperSlides presentations, "the title and images and items are very clear", "the layout is beautiful", and "you get all that from a list of points". In other words, "you can just type a few words and have a great PPT".

However, more work is needed to meet the expectations of experienced PowerPoint users. One noted that HyperSlides "has some restrictions on design", such as not being able to add background images to all slides. This design decision was deliberately taken to create contrast between illustrated scenes and subordinate slides of text points and embedded media. The addition of a template using a not-quite-full-bleed background image for text was the most highly requested additional feature, which was promising since participants rarely created such slides in their prior practice.

On the theme of "the templates were really great but maybe you could do more", participants suggested that it would be good to choose from designer-crafted visual styles, to help the user choose complementary style options, and to automatically match pictures to words.

Our participants also commented "perhaps HyperSlides makes things too simple" and that "(HyperSlides is) good to generate a PPT quickly then edit with PowerPoint". This is currently necessary to use advanced features like animation, smart art, and equations. As an alternative to opening the full PowerPoint application, users could "just use a GUI for just the little things, like arranging words with images".

These constraints of the current HyperSlides prototype mean that "the best case for this is a presentation we make in 30 minutes or so – not the super important one". Another participant said that "for a conference talk, I would use this to make prototypes until I had fixed the flow of the presentation, then copy and paste into a regular PPT to make it fancy". Even then, the fact that participants would consider real use of the current, early prototype in their everyday presentation practices is highly encouraging.

Linking between scenes

For one participant, "the most useful feature is the overview to learn and navigate through the structure" of the HyperSlides presentation. Another described how "the biggest difference is how we use the tree structure to navigate between slides", which "provides a great way to explore multimedia" organized into scenes. The verbal linkages between scenes were also found to be useful: "we can see the script of what we should talk about between slides. This can be not only for you, but also for other people who want to understand your thoughts more".

During the presentations, we observed presenters frequently navigating between scenes not horizontally, but vertically via the storyline overview. This was seen as helpful to the audience because "the tree structure is the real structure of slides", but ordinarily it is only the "linear structure" of slide sequences that is ever communicated to the audience. This structure was also seen to be of value to the presenter, who could use the combination of the presentation timer and the "current location" to "work out where to go next".

Expanding on demand

The ability to expand scenes and points on demand was found to be "more flexible than regular slides because it can go from this slide to A, or B, or C. That's really helpful". This technique is "better than the usual approach of hiding slides", and when used for rehearsal, it is "better than the normal way" of adding notes to the slides because this "cannot possibly just remind you about what you are going to say. Making the slide and the notes into two separate slides is much better". Another participant described how they "love" the simple rehearsal traversal just by "clicking right". An advantage for presentation delivery is that expansion can be used "whenever we forget what we want to say next".

However, while many participants "like the idea of combining your notes with your formal slides", some also accidentally navigated into the rehearsal path (revealing underlined points) during their presentations. Although this problem may disappear with additional practice, multiple participants suggested that we "separate the rehearsal mode and the delivery mode" because "during the presentation, if you make a mistake, it's not that easy to undo". One cause of navigation errors could be that "with a mouse, it's not always easy to get into a hot region", a problem that "would be better with a touch device" or using arrow keys to navigate. On any platform, the tree structure always carries the risk that "it's possible to get lost", so "maybe two levels of details are enough". A "breadcrumb trail you can hide" might also support location awareness – addressed by one participant by explicitly enumerating his points hierarchically. Tooltip navigation hints would also avoid exploratory clicks down the tree and back up again, although extra rehearsal could well ameliorate this problem.

Discussion

Our study confirmed the strength of a dynamic approach to presentations. Participants were able to naturally exercise some best presentation practices using HyperSlides, which was described as "like a textbook telling people how to give a presentation". The approach was found to be "suitable for more informal and flexible talks" compared with conventional linear presentations. Participants also found the resulting talks to be clear in both structure and style.

The main improvement suggested by study participants was the ability to generate different presentations for rehearsing, delivering, and sharing, to avoid the problems of accidentally navigating to slides intended only to support presentation rehearsal, or sharing media unnecessary for the core communication. A potential compromise is to mark up "next points" in a way that combines the simplicity of linear slides with the power of tree structures that expand on demand.

Another option, which we have implemented in a simplification of HyperSlides, is to omit dedicated rehearsal paths in ways that reduce the chances of novice users making navigation errors. This has several additional advantages:

1. At the detail level, the left hyperframe edge can be used to navigate up the hierarchy. This was suggested in the study as feeling more natural than using the top edge.
2. This frees the top hyperframe edge to link directly to the overview, no matter what the current detail level.
3. At the top-level of details directly beneath the scene slide, the right hyperframe edge is free to link to the next scene. This was suggested as an alternative to navigating up through the current scene when undesirable to do so.
4. The bottom edge of the top-level detail slide can link to the top edge of verbal linkage slide, whose bottom edge can then link to the next scene slide. This scene-detail-linkage-scene "downwards" rehearsal loop tests presenters in a way that complements bullet expansions.

CONCLUSIONS AND FUTURE DIRECTIONS

Following our grounded theory study and literature review, we propose a *dynamic approach* to presentation prototyping, rehearsal, and delivery that touches upon each of Cicero's five canons of rhetoric: invention and arrangement (*planning with points*), style (visual *styling as a service* and verbal *linking between scenes*), and memory and delivery (*expanding on demand*). In HyperSlides, the explicit encouragement of supporting links, illustrated scenes, and verbal linkages also promotes Aristotle's *ethos*, *pathos*, and *logos* to a greater extent than bullets and slide templates.

As we move forwards, we will continue to build tools that embody the ancient art of persuasion while advancing the state of the art in presentation technology. However, more work is required to address the limitations of the current system. For users with more demanding requirements on graphic design, animation, and layout, a more visual authoring environment might help. In the spirit of dynamic prototyping, algorithmic generation of "small multiples" – alternative design candidates shown side-by-side for comparison – could support the transformation of logically-structured points into expressive slides. Moving beyond slides, similar specifications could also be transformed into other multimedia representations (e.g., canvas-based). For all such approaches, more interactive guidance about how to construct the story behind the visuals could also be incorporated into the authoring process. In addition, more progressive guidance about how to move from a finished document to a prepared presentation should be investigated as a way to encourage greater investment in presentation rehearsal, with greater returns gained more efficiently. As with the HyperSlides system, our study also needs to be extended to fully examine the consequences of HyperSlides use in practice and to understand how and when it should be used in preference to more conventional slide authoring, as well as to suggest further implications for design. For now, the HyperSlides prototype represents a promising first step towards more dynamic prototyping of presentations that themselves offer greater dynamism and flexibility in their support for planning, rehearsing, and delivering a story.

ACKNOWLEDGMENTS

We would like to thank the participants in our studies.

REFERENCES

1. Apple Keynote. http://www.apple.com/iwork/keynote/
2. Agile Manifesto. http://agilemanifesto.org/principles.html
3. Aristotle (1954). Rhetoric. W. Rhys Roberts translation. http://rhetoric.eserver.org/aristotle/
4. Beamer. http://en.wikibooks.org/wiki/LaTeX/Presentations
5. Bederson, B.B., Stead, L. & Hollan, J.D. (1994). Pad++: Advances in Multiscale Interfaces. CHI'94, 315-316.
6. Carnegie, D. (1962). The Quick and Easy Way to Effective Speaking: Modern Techniques for Dynamic Communication. Pocket Books.
7. Carpenter, S.K., Pashler, H. & Vul, E. (2006). What types of learning are enhanced by a cued recall test? Psychonomic Bulletin & Review, 13(5), 826-830.
8. Charmaz, K. (2006). Constructing Grounded Theory: A Practical Guide through Qualitative Analysis. Sage.
9. Cicero (1888). De Inventione. C.D. Yonge translation. http://www.classicpersuasion.org/pw/cicero/dnvindex.htm
10. Duarte, N. (2008). Slide:ology: The Art and Science of Creating Great Presentations. O'Reilly Media.
11. Duarte, N. (2010). Resonate: Present Visual Stories that Transform Audiences. Wiley.
12. Edge, D., Searle, E., Chiu, K., Zhao, J. & Landay, J. (2011). MicroMandarin: Mobile Language Learning in Context. CHI 2011, 3169-3178.
13. Fourney, A., Terry, M. & Mann, R. (2010). Gesturing in the wild: understanding the effects and implications of gesture-based interaction for dynamic presentations. BCS'10, 230-240.
14. Gallo, C. (2010). The Presentation Secrets of Steve Jobs: How to be Insanely Great in Front of Any Audience. McGraw Hill.
15. Good, L. & Bederson, B.B. (2002). Zoomable user interfaces as a medium for slide show presentations. Information Visualization 1, 1 (March 2002), 35-49.
16. Google Docs Presentations. http://www.google.com/google-d-s/presentations
17. Haiku deck. http://www.haikudeck.com/
18. Impress.js. http://bartaz.github.com/impress.js/
19. Iqbal, S.T., Grudin, J. & Horvitz, E. (2011). Peripheral computing during presentations: perspectives on costs and preferences. CHI'11, 891-894.
20. Kurihara, K., Goto, M., Ogata, J., Matsusaka, Y. & Igarashi, T. (2007). Presentation sensei: a presentation training system using speech and image processing. ICMI'07, 358-365.
21. Lanir, J., Booth, K.S. & Findlater, L. (2008). Observing presenters' use of visual aids to inform the design of classroom presentation software. CHI'08, 695-704.
22. Levasseur, D.G. & Sawyer, J.K. (2006). Pedagogy Meets PowerPoint: A Research Review of the Effects of Computer-Generated Slides in the Classroom. The Review of Communication, vol. 6(1), 101-123.
23. Lichtschlag, L., Hess, T., Karrer, T. & Borchers, J. (2012). Fly: studying recall, macrostructure understanding, and user experience of canvas presentations. CHI'12, 1307-1310.
24. Lichtschlag, L., Hess, T., Karrer, T. & Borchers, J. (2012). Canvas Presentations in the Wild. CHI'12 EA, 537-540.
25. Lichtschlag, L., Karrer, T. & Borchers, J. (2009). Fly: a Tool to Author Planar Presentations. CHI'09, 547-556.
26. Mayer, R.E. (1997). Multimedia Learning: Are we asking the right questions? Educational Psychologist, 32(1), 1-19.
27. Mayer, R.E. & Moreno, R. (2003). Nine Ways to Reduce Cognitive Load in Multimedia Learning. Educational Psychologist, 38(1), 43-52.
28. Mayer, R.E. (2001). Multimedia learning. New York: Cambridge University Press.
29. Microsoft PowerPoint. http://office.microsoft.com/en-us/powerpoint
30. Moscovich, T., Scholz, K., Hughes, J.F. & Salesin, D.H. (2003). Customizable Presentations. ICMI'03.
31. Nelson, L., Ichimura, S., Pedersen, E.R. & Adams, L. (1999). Palette: a paper interface for giving presentations. CHI'99, 354-361.
32. Nelson, D.L., Reed, U.S., & Walling, J.R. (1976). Pictorial superiority effect. Journal of Experimental Psychology: Human Learning & Memory, 2, 523-528.
33. Norman D. In defense of PowerPoint. (2004). http://www.jnd.org/dn.mss/in_defense_of_p.html
34. Open XML SDK 2.0 for Microsoft Office. http://msdn.microsoft.com/en-us/library/office/bb448854.aspx
35. Paivio, A. (1990). Mental Representations: A Dual Coding Approach. Oxford University Press.
36. Panjawi, S., Samdaria, N., Gupta, A., Cutrell, E. & Toyama, K. (2010). Collage: A Presentation Tool for School Teachers. ICTD'10.
37. Parker, I. (2001). Absolute PowerPoint: Can a software package edit our thoughts? The New Yorker.
38. Pecha Kucha 20 × 20 = 6:40. http://pecha-kucha.org/
39. pptPlex PowerPoint add-in. http://www.microsoft.com/en-us/download/details.aspx?id=28558
40. Prezi. http://prezi.com/
41. Reynolds, G. (2012). Presentation Zen: Simple Ideas on Presentation Design and Delivery. New Riders.
42. Signer, B. & Norrie, M.C. (2007). PaperPoint: a paper-based presentation and interactive paper prototyping tool. TEI'07, 57-64.
43. SlideShare. http://www.slideshare.net
44. Slidy. http://www.w3.org/Talks/Tools/Slidy2/
45. Spicer, R., Lin, Y-R, Kelliher, A. & Sundaram, H. (2012). NextSlidePlease: Authoring and delivering agile multimedia presentations. TOMCCAP, 8(4)
46. Sweller, J. (1988). Cognitive load during problem solving: Effects on learning. Cognitive Science, 12(2), 257–285.
47. Teevan, J., Liebling, D.J., Paradiso, A., Suarez, C.G.J., von Veh, C. & Gehring, D. (2012). Displaying Mobile Feedback during a Presentation. MobileHCI'12.
48. Tufte, E.R. (2003). The Cognitive Style of PowerPoint: Pitching Out Corrupts Within. Graphics Press.
49. Weissman, J. (2009). Presenting to Win: The Art of Telling Your Story. FT Press.
50. Weissman, J. (2009). The Power Presenter: Technique, Style, and Strategy from America's Top Speaking Coach. Wiley.
51. Wozniak, P.A. & Gorzelanczyk, E.J. (1994). Optimization of repetition spacing in the practice of learning. Acta Neurobiologiae Experimentalis, 54.
52. Zongker, D. (2003). Creating Animation for Presentations. PhD thesis, University of Washington. http://grail.cs.washington.edu/theses/ZongkerPhd.pdf

SidePoint: A Peripheral Knowledge Panel for Presentation Slide Authoring

Yefeng Liu[1,2], Darren Edge[1], Koji Yatani[1]

[1]Microsoft Research Asia
Beijing, China
{darren.edge, koji}@microsoft.com

[2]Waseda University
Tokyo, Japan
yefeng@dcl.info.waseda.ac.jp

ABSTRACT

Presentation authoring is an important activity, but often requires the secondary task of collecting the information and media necessary for both slides and speech. Integration of implicit search and peripheral displays into presentation authoring tools may reduce the effort to satisfy not just active needs the author is aware of, but also latent needs that she is not aware of until she encounters content of perceived value. We develop SidePoint, a peripheral panel that supports presentation authoring by showing concise knowledge items relevant to the slide content. We study SidePoint as a technology probe to examine the benefits and issues associated with peripheral knowledge panels for presentation authoring. Our results show that peripheral knowledge panels have the potential to satisfy both types of needs in ways that transform presentation authoring for the better.

Author Keywords

Presentation authoring; peripheral displays; natural language processing

ACM Classification Keywords

H5.2 Information interfaces and presentation: User Interfaces.

INTRODUCTION & BACKGROUND WORK

Preparing for presentations is of critical importance for many people, but often complicated by the need to collect necessary information during the authoring of slides. To understand how this affects user behavior, we conducted an exploratory study with 8 students, each spending an hour to prepare for a 5-minute presentation of their research. We observed participants spending a substantial amount of time using the Web to find both informational and inspirational content, with constant switching between the Web browser and the presentation environment. Presentation authors thus have both *active needs* (typical of what they would attempt to satisfy through proactive Web search), and *latent needs* (previously unanticipated by the author and often identified and satisfied simultaneously when browsing).

Our exploratory study also showed that the unstructured nature of Web search results and the density of Webpages often made it hard to isolate relevant and usable information. As a result, participants often had to spend more time in the Web browser than in PowerPoint. We can interpret this through the lens of Information Foraging Theory [13], which suggests people naturally adapt their environments to maximize the gain of valuable information per unit cost of time and attention. We therefore identified a design opportunity to embed implicit search into the presentation authoring environment, reducing the cost of information finding and supporting both kinds of information needs.

Figure 1 shows our SidePoint add-in for PowerPoint – a peripheral panel that shows concise knowledge items relevant to the content of the current slide as it is being created. We source these knowledge items from NeedleSeek [15, 16, 17] – which offers semantically relevant facts and descriptive sentences – before processing and displaying them in a concise, browsable format. These items can provide value in two ways. The first is directly by left-clicking an item to copy to the notes section of the slide. The second is indirectly through item information-scent [13]: right-clicking on an item loads a Web browser showing literal search results for that item to explore details of the information. Future improvements in knowledge base technologies can directly transfer to interfaces like SidePoint.

Using SidePoint as a technology probe [8], we examine the potential benefits and issues associated with peripheral knowledge panels for presentation slide authoring. This work contributes to the understanding of the needs of presentation authors, demonstrates the feasibility of peripheral knowledge panels, and offers future design directions for such systems.

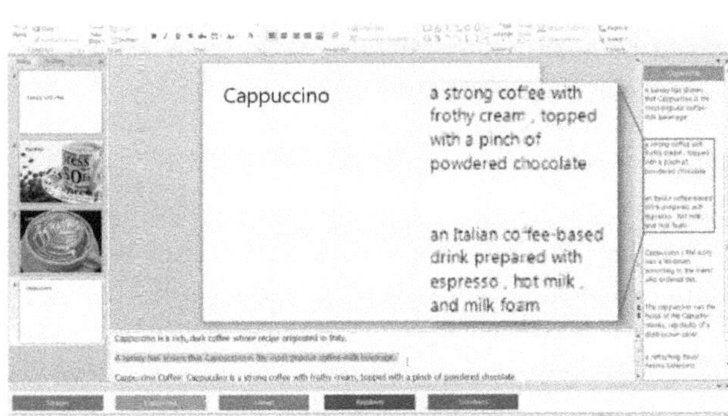

Figure 1. SidePoint interface showing concise knowledge items relevant to the slide content ("Cappuccino"). We use SidePoint as a technology probe to examine how peripheral knowledge panels can support presentation authoring.

RELATED WORK

Implicit search has been investigated as a way to improve Web search experience [9] and advertisement accuracy [2], as well as interactive systems more generally. Information retrieved by implicit search is often presented in ambient and peripheral displays [12]. Such displays offer non-critical or secondary information [3] without significantly distracting the user's focus from the main task. Thus, peripheral displays are used as an appropriate design for implicit search results.

The Remembrance Agent [14] is an implicit search engine for Emacs showing documents related to the current one the user is reading or writing. Dumais et al. extended this idea to the context of email authoring [5]. Their system offers information relevant to the current email retrieved from other emails, the calendar, Webpages, files, and instant messaging history. Similarly, implicit search has been applied to support information management and retrieval tasks with Webpages [4], answer discovery for questions posted in online social network status updates [7], software development [1], and the user's learning of complex software [11].

Implicit search can include user context beyond interaction within one application. Henzinger et al. [6] built a system offering Webpages that the user might want to read based on TV programs she is watching. With sensors in the environment, the system built by Maekawa et al. [10] shows tips relevant to the user's current activity in the real world. Our work contributes to further understanding of benefits and design challenges of implicit search and peripheral displays focusing on presentation authoring.

SIDEPOINT IMPLEMENTATION

SidePoint is a peripheral interactive panel that displays knowledge relevant to current slide content. Our design allows SidePoint to be integrated into existing tools (e.g., PowerPoint) without interfering with the main workspace.

Text Parsing

SidePoint infers what topic the user is considering for her presentation based on her text input. When the user finishes entering words or sentences in a textbox, SidePoint analyzes them with the Splat parser [18]. This parser returns a dependency tree (a tree representing a grammatical structure), and the system extracts nouns and noun phrases (e.g., adjective + noun, or noun + preposition + noun) as a keyword set. SidePoint then retrieves knowledge about each keyword set through NeedleSeek [17] (technical details of NeedleSeek are available in [15, 16]).

When the keyword is too specific or too long, NeedleSeek may not offer any result; in this case, SidePoint uses Web search results. Although these results are not necessarily optimal, our pilot studies indicated that people would still want to see some information about such keywords.

Knowledge Panel

After SidePoint collects knowledge from NeedleSeek, it shows the results in a knowledge panel on the right side of the PowerPoint window. These are derived from key sentences

Figure 2. Concept Panel for the term "espresso". The user can simply click an image to import to the slide.

describing the keywords. These sentences in general have a structure of *[keywords]-[Be verb]-[description]*. SidePoint parses the sentences with Splat to extract the subject complement of the keywords as a concise description. It then orders all descriptions by increasing length. In this manner, SidePoint prioritizes descriptions that are quick to browse. Some NeedleSeek results are short facts related to the keyword (e.g., demographic information of a city), which we list first.

Left-clicking on an item in the panel imports that fact or description into the note section of the current slide. Items can thus be stored for reference or copied onto the slide itself. Right-clicking on an item navigates the user to the Web browser and automatically shows literal Web search results for that item, revealing its source. In this way, the system offers a smooth transition from glanceable facts and descriptions to deeper exploration on the Web. When NeedleSeek returns no results, SidePoint simply lists Web search result summaries in the knowledge panel. They link to search results in the browser in the same way.

Concept Panel

In addition to the knowledge panel on the right side of the interface, SidePoint also incorporates a concept panel that runs along the bottom of the interface and shows alternative concepts that can populate the knowledge panel if selected. This panel displays three different kinds of concept. The first is images: clicking on the image concept appropriates the space of the knowledge panel to display categories of image search results (photos, monotones, graphics, and people). Clicking on any of these shows results of that type; clicking on a desired image automatically adds it to the current slide. Semantically related concepts retrieved from NeedleSeek and alternative nouns and noun phrases from Splat make up the final two concept types. Clicking on any of these updates the knowledge panel results accordingly.

USER STUDY

We examined the benefits and problems of SidePoint in the context of presentation authoring – in particular, how they could satisfy active and latent needs. Our integration of NeedleSeek knowledge allowed us to investigate the satisfaction of both need types and observe how it would support slide authoring. We recruited 12 participants (8 male, 4 female, P1-P12) of age 21-44 (mean 24), with 5+ years

PowerPoint experience and backgrounds in engineering, design, and finance, from our laboratory. None of them knew the SidePoint system before the experiment.

Procedure

The main task in our experiment was to build a 5-minute presentation about their life (e.g., places lived, schools or universities attended, and countries visited). The experimenter first guided the participant through an example presentation showing SidePoint functionality, before participants progressed through three stages:

1. **Plan**. Plan key points to present by typing them in the notes of empty slides; e.g., in a slide on Paris, these might be food, culture, landmarks, or examples thereof.
2. **Build**. Use SidePoint while authoring slides. As our focus was to observe the user experience of SidePoint, we did not allow Web search or free browsing.
3. **Discuss**. Describe how SidePoint supported both planned and unplanned key points, and discuss how SidePoint affected the overall authoring experience.

Findings

On average, participants planned 9 key points per 5-minute talk, found supporting information from SidePoint for 5 of them, and incorporated 2 additional items. However, there were large individual differences, shown in Figure 3.

P1, P3, P5, and P12 had detailed preliminary ideas about what key points to discuss (e.g., weather, culture), finding supporting information for about half of those points. On the other hand, P7 and P9 decided immediately what to say and wrote detailed scripts up front, and did not use SidePoint often. Uniquely, P8 found greater inspiration from suggested items than in her initial planning. We now explain these behaviors by grouping into four themes.

Saving author's time vs. using authoring space

Participants positively mentioned the time-saving nature of peripheral knowledge panels. For example, P11 commented *"if you want to add information or add images, it really saves time"*, referring to how she was pleased to find and use directly an image of her favorite building. This process was *"really convenient, much better than searching on the Internet, saving to my local desktop, and dragging onto slides"*. Along with other participants, she also described the images and text as inspirational: *"this kind of text* (description points) *is helpful for my presentation. It helps me to explore the topic. I got inspiration from this"*.

SidePoint was also described as a beneficial use of the authoring space. For P5, *"this design is not distracting, the image search is convenient, and automatically adding a reference into notes is good too"*. For P8, *"the ambient display design is good, it only takes up a very small space. I don't feel it is distracting"*. These descriptions suggest that relatively small embedded knowledge panels can save time and support fluid authoring when they reduce application switching costs and automate otherwise manual actions.

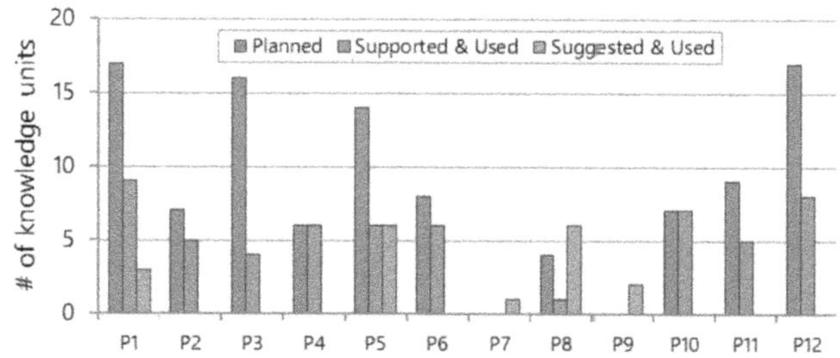

Figure 3. Numbers of planned key points and used knowledge items during the user study.

Triggering implicit vs. explicit search

Several participants remarked that SidePoint felt like search without searching. For P11, *"when I want to get some information, I don't need to go to the Web browser and search, I can just input something here... I don't even need to input really"*. She continued that *"If I just describe places I have been, I don't want to go and search them on the Internet. It's too boring. So if you show them on this place* (the panel)*, it gives me inspiration, I can see more about it"*. In particular, she was inspired by the description of her hometown as *"a beautiful and romantic city with countless stories and fascinating scenery"* and used it on her slide. In another example, P2 noted *"I don't have particular goals or expected topics in mind. I just want to input the words and see what information returns, then choose the ones I feel are good for this slide, and then think about what else I may need"*. This approach created opportunities to satisfy latent needs, e.g., for P3, *"the 'surprising result' moment happened several times, which is really good for me"*. This demonstrates the potential value of implicit search to support thought processes without losing attention to slides.

Although participants agreed that implicit search helped their presentation slide authoring, some requested greater control over what would be searched for and when, e.g., for P3, *"I want to have a button or something to trigger search when I need it, and to stop or refresh the search as I want"*. Satisfying both active and latent needs is difficult, but one behavior in particular linked the two and demonstrated our intended crafting of information scent: *"I didn't find what I wanted from the results, but I did find them by right-clicking and jumping to web sites... hmm... just by right click I could arrive at the content, in that sense it is quite useful"*. For example, the description *"Tianjin dining culture is renowned throughout China, and not only the traditional Tianjin snacks, but the cuisines from other regions of China can also be found"* linked to a website listing all of the different kinds of such regional snacks.

Finding the right facts vs. descriptions

Some participants appreciated knowledge presented as facts; e.g., for P5, *"the fact data is good... it basically provides most of the information I want to introduce my city"*. For others like P6, however, *"the facts are not interesting. I don't think people will be interested in the population or GDP of my hometown"*. This highlights how the value of such facts can be subjective and relative to the specific purpose of the talk, whether to inform or entertain.

Many participants found more value in the description points. For P8, *"the descriptions aren't bad and did suggest some useful aspects I didn't think of"*. During the study, he read through the text points while repeatedly commenting that *"this is good"*, *"this is right"*, and *"this is very true"*. He particularly liked the precise and succinct descriptions of his research area, e.g., *"the study of how knowledge about the world can be represented and what kinds of reasoning can be done with that knowledge"*.

Exploring related concepts vs. attributes

Some participants appreciated the display of related concepts in the concept panel, e.g., for P1, *"the related concepts are useful. I want to show places to travel when I introduce my city, and it suggested nearby cities"*. P9 remarked how the system was "*smart*", offering Graphic Design after she had entered Industrial Design on her slide.

However, participants also found that the related concepts offered by NeedleSeek were often too tangential to be relevant in a talk about a particular topic. A suggested alternative to related concepts is to reveal more of the attributes of the current concept. For P11, *"it's better if they have any kind of filter, like if I input a place, I can chose people or scenery"*.

Design Considerations

Based on our results, we propose four design considerations for peripheral knowledge panels that support slide authoring:

1. Trade interface space for time saving until the complexity of the transformed task requires tool switching, providing information-scent-rich entry points for tool switching.
2. Show implicit knowledge results for visual and verbal inspiration, but appropriate the display space for search results when information needs are expressed explicitly.
3. Show a variety of knowledge types at the beginning of the task (e.g., facts, descriptions), but improve relevance over time by adapting to author behavior and content.
4. Support attribute-driven idea refinement through both structured exploration of known attributes and dynamic combination of cues to test for possible attribute relationships (e.g., by searching "{bullet} of {title}").

Together, these directions characterize the ways in which peripheral knowledge panels can become pivotal in their support of presentation authoring – helping authors to pivot between different applications, search modes, result types, and knowledge levels in the increasingly semantic Web.

CONCLUSION AND FUTURE WORK

The core design problem of the information age is to increase the relevant information encountered by a user as a function of the amount of time they invest in interaction [13]. Our SidePoint prototype aims to maximize such exposure to relevant content during time already committed to the primary task of authoring presentation slides. Through our study of SidePoint as a technology probe, we have shown that peripheral knowledge panels have the potential to satisfy both active and latent information needs in ways that transform presentation authoring for the better.

Future work should investigate peripheral knowledge panels in broader contexts and over longer timescales. Comparative studies with other intelligent search tools would also help identify the characteristic benefits and issues of peripheral knowledge panels. In addition, the present study only examines the effect of peripheral knowledge panels on specific presentation topics. Our criterion for the topics was something the user was familiar with but does not necessarily remember all details about. This type of topic frequently generated both active and latent information needs as seen in our experiment. Future studies should examine how frequently other kinds of topic raise active and latent needs and how this affects the use and value of peripheral knowledge panels in general.

REFERENCES

1. Brandt, J., Dontcheva, M., Weskamp, M. & Klemmer, S.R. (2010). Example-centric programming: integrating web search into the development environment. CHI'10, 513-522.
2. Broder, A., Fontoura, M., Josifovski, V. & Riedl, L. (2007). A semantic approach to contextual advertising. SIGIR'07, 559-566.
3. Cadiz, J.J., Venolia, G. D., Jancke, G. & Gupta, A. (2002). Designing and deploying an information awareness interface. CSCW'02, 314-323.
4. Czerwinski, M., Dumais, S., Robertson, G., Dziadosz, S., Tieman, S.L. & van Dantzich, M. (1999). Visualizing implicit queries for information management and retrieval. CHI'99, 560-567.
5. Dumais, S., Cutrell, E., Sarin, R. & Horvitz., E. (2004). Implicit queries (IQ) for contextualized search. SIGIR'04, 594.
6. Henzinger, M., Chang, B., Milch, B. & Brin, S. (2005). Query-Free News Search. WWW'05, 1-10.
7. Hecht, B., Teevan, J., Morris, M.R. & Liebling, D. (2012). SearchBuddies: bringing search engines into the conversation. ICWSM'12, 138-145.
8. Hutchinson, H., Mackay, W., Westerlund, B., Bederson, B.B., Druin, A., Plaisant, C., Beaudouin-Lafon, M., Conversy, S., Evans, H., Hansen, H., Roussel, N. & Eiderbäck, B. (2003). Technology probes: inspiring design for and with families. CHI'03, 17-24.
9. Kraft, R., Mahoul, F., and Chang, C.C. (2005). Y!Q: contextual search at the point of inspiration. CIKM'05, 816-823.
10. Maekawa, T., Yanagisawa, Y., Sakurai, Y., Kishino, Y., Kamei, K. & Okadome, T. (2009). Web searching for daily living. SIGIR'09, 27-34.
11. Matejka, J., Grossman, T. & Fitzmaurice, G.W. (2011). Ambient help. CHI'11, 2751-2760.
12. Matthews, T., Rattenbury, T. & Carter, S. (2007). Defining, designing, and evaluating peripheral displays: an analysis using activity theory. Human-Computer Interaction, 22 (1).
13. Pirolli, P. (2003). Exploring and Finding Information. In HCI Models, Theories, and Frameworks, M. Kaufmann, 157-191.
14. Rhodes, B. & Maes, P. (2000). Just-in-time information retrieval agents. IBM Systems Journal, 39(3-4), 685-704.
15. Shi, S., Zhang, H., Yuan, X. & Wen, J-R. (2010). Corpus-based semantic class mining: distributional vs. pattern-based approaches. COLING'10, 993-1001.
16. Zhang, F., Shi, S., Liu, J., Sun, S. & Lin, C-Y. (2011). Nonlinear evidence fusion and propagation for hyponymy relation mining. ACL'11, 1159-1168.
17. NeedleSeek http://needleseek.msra.cn/
18. Splat. http://msrsplatdemo.cloudapp.net/

Control Your Game-Self: Effects of Controller Type on Enjoyment, Motivation, and Personality in Game

Max Birk and Regan L. Mandryk
Department of Computer Science
University of Saskatchewan
110 Science Place, Saskatoon, SK, S7N 5C9
max.birk@usask.ca, regan.mandryk@usask.ca

ABSTRACT
Whether they are made to entertain you, or to educate you, good video games engage you. Significant research has tried to understand engagement in games by measuring player experience (PX). Traditionally, PX evaluation has focused on the enjoyment of game, or the motivation of players; these factors no doubt contribute to engagement, but do decisions regarding play environment (e.g., the choice of game controller) affect the player more deeply than that? We apply self-determination theory (specifically satisfaction of needs and self-discrepancy represented using the five factors model of personality) to explain PX in an experiment with controller type as the manipulation. Our study shows that there are a number of effects of controller on PX and in-game player personality. These findings provide both a lens with which to view controller effects in games and a guide for controller choice in the design of new games. Our research demonstrates that including self-characteristics assessment in the PX evaluation toolbox is valuable and useful for understanding player experience.

Author Keywords
Personality: motivation; self-discrepancy theory; self-determination theory; games; controller

ACM Classification Keywords
H.5.m. Information interfaces and presentation (e.g., HCI): Miscellaneous.

General Terms
Human Factors; Design; Measurement.

INTRODUCTION
Whether they are made to entertain you, or to educate you, good video games engage you. Good games draw the player in and keep them engaged during play, and an engaged player will give the game a better chance of success at its intended purpose, irrespective of whether that be to divulge or divert. Because it is so important for games to be engaging, there has been significant effort from researchers and practitioners in identifying and distilling the essential ingredients for successful and engaging game design. These efforts have taken both a prescriptive approach (i.e., attempting to formulate rules for game design), and an analytic perspective (i.e., measuring play experience).

The analytic approach to understanding player experience (PX) has taken many forms. Significant research has been conducted on operationalizing concepts important to PX (e.g., engagement, flow) [4], and measuring these concepts by instrumenting [16], observing [13], and surveying [11] the player. Although prior research on measuring PX applies various methodological approaches, what previous work has in common is that it all attempts to quantify or qualify the player's experience. However we suggest that to fully understand PX, we must understand both how a player feels about a game and how they feel about themselves during gameplay. For example, consider a role-playing game that rewards players who steal items from their teammates. A player might be engaged and get satisfaction from exercising their stealth inside the boundaries of the game, but quit playing, because succeeding makes them feel sleazy. In this case, the important information is not *how the player feels about the game*, but about *how the game makes them feel about themselves.*

Previous work has introduced the idea of considering a user's experience of themselves during play by investigating a user's in-game trait personality; however, this application of in-game personality has been only in the context of sociological exploration of virtual worlds [39], association with in-game avatars [2] or preference of game genre [23], and not for the purpose of PX evaluation. To investigate the relationship between player experience of a game and a player's in-game personality (how they felt about themselves), we chose to compare the effects of different game controllers. Studying game controllers is a natural choice for this research as the controller acts as the interface between the player and the game – it is the device through which players engage with the game. Previous work comparing input devices in gameplay has focused on measuring performance differences in terms of targeting [20] or steering [1], or player experience differences in terms of spatial presence [34, 36] or immersion [25]. These studies show that controller does affect PX, making controller a good experimental manipulation – we assume that different controllers will elicit different play experiences; however, in this research we ask the question: *could the choice of game controller have an impact on the player's perception of themselves during play?*

We explore how the type of controller used during game play affects the player's game experience in terms of their enjoyment and their motivation. More importantly, we show how controller choice affects a player's perception of themselves and how their perceived personality (using the five factor model [10]) within the game (*game-self*) compares to their idealized version of themselves (*ideal-self*) and their reality (*actual-self*) [8]. To experimentally determine the role of controller on PX, we designed and implemented a custom game that allowed us to compare three controller types (Microsoft Kinect, PlayStation Move, and Xbox GamePad).

Our results show that the choice of controller affects our enjoyment and motivation to play. Further, we show how playing with different types of controllers changes how we satisfy our needs within game play and how we perceive ourselves in a game. Specifically, the choice of controller affects our perceived Agreeableness and Neuroticism. In addition, we show that change in game-self is the biggest predictor of both enjoyment and motivation to play. These findings provide both a lens with which to view controller effects in games and a guide for controller choice in the design of new games. Our research demonstrates that including personality assessment in the PX evaluation toolbox is valuable for understanding player experience.

RELATED WORK

In this section we provide an overview of existing approaches to evaluating PX, the application of cognitive evaluation theory and personality theory to understanding PX, and previous work on how controller affects PX.

Evaluating Player Experience

Early attempts at game experience evaluation appropriated methods from classic usability evaluation, but researchers quickly discovered that games have different goals (e.g., to challenge the user) and constraints (e.g., interrupting players would break the experience) than productivity software [9]. To combat these differences, researchers proposed revising methods of traditional user experience evaluation for use in games, including revised heuristics for playability evaluation [26] and revised questionnaires appropriate for the gaming context [27]. In addition, new methods were created, including new survey instruments (e.g., [11]), psychophysiological methods of evaluation [16], and event log analysis [12] (what has now become known as telemetry, game metrics, or game analytics [33]).

An increasingly active field of research, the goal of game experience evaluation is to understand how the game affects the emotional and cognitive experience of the player to produce the desired outcome of 'fun' [5]. Although a few evaluation approaches have been based on theory [37], the grounding of PX evaluation in established theories of human behaviour is lacking. Furthermore, a majority of studies that measure game experience do not leverage the research in validated evaluation approaches and instead apply ad-hoc surveys to gather participant responses.

Self Determination Theory for PX Evaluation

The first psychological theory with validated scales that we explore for understanding PX is Self Determination Theory (SDT) [31]. We first describe the general theory and then provide examples of its use in understanding PX.

Overview of SDT

SDT is comprised of several mini-theories and focuses on factors that influence motivation. One mini theory, Cognitive Evaluation Theory (CET) [31], describes intrinsic motivation in terms of competence and autonomy. To assess the factors that support intrinsic motivation in games, the concept (and evaluation instrument) of Player Experience of Needs Satisfaction (PENS) [32] was developed. We next describe the concepts within PENS.

Intrinsic Motivation. In terms of SDT, intrinsic motivation (IM) is defined by a locus of control inherent in the person, and an outcome attributed to volition and achievement. IM is distinct from external motivation, which is defined by an external locus of control, e.g., deadlines. CET proposes that IM is a function of autonomy, and competence.

Competence. CET proposes that the experience of competence derives from challenge, and the personal effort of mastering challenges. For example, the laddering used in many games provides a structure for players to exert effort to master successively harder challenges.

Autonomy. CET proposes that the experience of autonomy derives from volition and willingness to perform a task. For example, multiple in-game options give players cause to experience autonomy through willing decision-making.

Relatedness. Within SDT, relatedness is defined as the feeling of belonging to a group, and is an important factor for psychological well-being. Social games like FarmVille and massively multiplayer online role-playing games (MMORPGs) make extensive use of this concept.

Presence. PENS defines presence as "the sense that one is within the world". Presence is fostered by competence and autonomy, and related to the flow concept [4] as the highest state of presence.

Intuitive Controls. PENS defines controls as intuitive, when they do not interfere with one's sense of presence, are easily mastered, and make sense in context of the game.

Use of SDT in PX Evaluation

SDT has been applied in many psychological studies of motivation (see [31]), but has recently been extended to virtual environments and games. SDT was applied (using PENS) to identify how different game genres satisfy needs differently (e.g., experienced autonomy is highest in roleplaying and strategy games) [11]. In the context of game-based learning, [32] shows that experienced competence, autonomy, and relatedness increase motivation, positive mood, and the recommendation of a game. Finally, in [24], the authors validate the application of SDT (using PENS) to the domain of exergames, showing that SDT-guided game feature choices result in improved game enjoyment, game recommendation and game rating. Specific to the evaluation of input, [17] applied PENS to show that realistic and tangible controller mappings led to higher experienced autonomy and presence.

Self-Discrepancy Theory for Understanding Gameplay

The second psychological theory that we explore for understanding PX is Self-Discrepancy Theory [8]. Although it has not been applied directly to PX evaluation, it has been used to understand play. We first explain the general theory and then give examples of its use in games.

Overview of Self-Discrepancy Theory

Self-discrepancy theory is based on the assumption that people compare themselves to so called *self-guides*, or internalized standards [8], and has been applied in fields such as mental health and work-life balance (see [31]). Self-guides represent three domains of the self, namely the *actual-self* (i.e., the attributes we actually possess), the *ideal-self*, (i.e., the attributes or characteristics we ideally want to possess), and the *ought-self* (i.e., the attributes we – or another person – believe we should have).

A common way to assess self-guides is to use the five factor model of personality, commonly referenced as the Big Five [10]. Usually used to assess personality traits, the instructions are rephrased to use the following five factors to assess different states of self-characterization.

Extraversion (*E*) is a tendency to be energetic, outgoing, and assertive. People who score high on *E* tend to be involved in social activities, rather than spend time alone.
Agreeableness (*A*) is a tendency to be friendly, caring, and conflict avoiding. People who score high on *A* prefer co-operation to competition and are not likely to be aggressive.
Conscientiousness (*C*) is a tendency to show self-discipline, act dutifully, and aim for achievement. People who score high on *C* plan activities rather than engaging in spontaneity, and tend to be organized and dependable.
Neuroticism (*N*) is a tendency to be nervous, sensitive, and emotionally unstable. People who score high on N respond poorly to environmental stress, and are likely to experience stress and frustration in minor situations.
Openness to Experience (*O*) is a tendency to be intellectually curious, think abstractly, and to explore. People who score high on *O* are likely to try something new, rather than sticking to old beliefs and tradition.

Use of Personality Theory in Game Research

The use of personality theory in general – and the five factors in particular – have been useful for understanding play in several contexts. For example, the five factors of personality have been shown to correspond with a player's preferred genre [23] and motivation to play [21]. In the area of player taxonomies, research has shown that player type can be predicted from the personality traits of the player [19], and that considering personality traits in combination with player taxonomies and game design elements can inform the understanding of enjoyment in game play [29]. Additionally, research has shown that personality traits carry into general behavior in virtual worlds [7].

Use of Self-Discrepancy Theory in Game Research

In contrast to the direct application of personality traits (e.g., Big Five factors), self-discrepancy theory considers the difference between self-guides (e.g., the discrepancy between actual-self and ideal-self), and has been applied successfully to understand games. For example, research on character choice in World of Warcraft has shown that players create characters closer to their ideal-selves than to their actual-selves [2], and that this trend was stronger for those with higher depression scores. Additionally, research has shown that the discrepancy between actual-self and ideal-self is related to game enjoyment, especially when convergence between *game-self* (self rated in the context of game play) and ideal-self is high [28]. Finally, self-discrepancy has been used to explain game addiction [14].

Effects of Controller Choice on PX

Previous work comparing input devices in gameplay has focused on measuring performance in terms of targeting [20] or steering [1]. At the level of PX, research has shown that movement-based input enhances engagement and social interaction [15] in collaborative games. Others have shown that controllers differ in terms of spatial presence [36] and immersion [25] within games. It is important to understand the spatial presence of controllers, because research has shown that presence can predict enjoyment in game play [34]. Finally, as noted in the section on the use of SDT in PX evaluation, a realistic mapping between controller and task leads to a higher experience of autonomy and presence, but not competence [17].

EXPERIMENT DESCRIPTION

The goal of our study was to understand how playing a game with different controllers alters our game experience and our view on game-self characteristics. We compared three controller types in a targeting game.

Game, System, and Apparatus

We designed a simple 3D game where the premise was that the user was flying inside of a tornado in a ship and the goal was to collect spinning items (Figure 1). Collection was accomplished using a 'tractor beam' by hovering over the item for 0.8 seconds. The beam changed colour to provide feedback on successful hovering, and feedback on the number of collected items were displayed in a gauge on the ship's console. Items appeared in waves of related items (e.g., vegetables, construction items), and the player was instructed to collect 10 items from each wave of 30 items. Collecting 10 items allowed the player to speed in the ship to the next wave. The number of waves in each game depended on the success of the player and each game ended after five minutes. Our design goal was to create a game that was playable with a variety of controller types, while keeping difficulty constant to allow inexperienced gamers – or gamers inexperienced with a particular controller – the opportunity to succeed in the task. Although complete in terms of the formal elements of game design, our game was specifically designed to be stripped of dramatic elements – such as characters, story, and dramatic arc – to study how controller choice affects self-perception and PX without interference from dramatic effects, (such as an unfolding narrative), or confounding effects, (such as how much the player identifies with their in-game avatar) [2].

Figure 1. Screenshot of TornadoTwister.

The game was built using C# and XNA 4.0. We used the Sony Move CL Eye Platform Driver and the Microsoft Kinect SDK 1.5. The system ran on a Windows 7 PC with a 22" monitor with a resolution of 1680 by 1050. Players stood 1.5 meters from the display in all conditions.

Controller Conditions

Our game required only that the player target objects by manipulating the x- and y-position of the tractor beam; there was no binary input necessary. We compared three popular controller types (traditional, positional, and gestural) represented by the Microsoft XBox GamePad, the Sony PlayStation Move, and the Microsoft Kinect.

GamePad (GP): We used an Xbox360 standard controller. For our study we used the A-Button to start the game and the right analog stick to position the tractor beam.

Move (MO): The PlayStation Move is a position-based controller, using a wand with a coloured light orb on top, which is tracked by the PlayStation "Eye" Camera. The PlayStation Eye was set to capture the scene at 60 Hz with a resolution of 640 x 480, and a 76° field of view. The location of the orb can be determined with an accuracy of 1mm and a latency of 22 ms. For our study, we used the PlayStation Move button to start the game and the x- and y-position of the controller to position the tractor beam.

Kinect: The Microsoft Kinect is a gesture-based controller developed for Xbox360. The device uses one camera that detects x- and y-position and another infrared receiver camera that detects depth through the dispersion of dots displayed via an infrared transmitter – for a detailed specification see [34]. In our study the experimenter started the game; the x-position of the tractor beam was controlled by the relative position of the left and right shoulder to the Kinect; the y-position was controlled by the relative position of hip and shoulder to the Kinect.

Training

Players completed a training condition consisting of aiming at 8 targets positioned around the display using the same selection mechanic as in the game (0.8-second dwell) prior to each controller condition.

Participants and Procedure

The experiment was conducted with 78 students from the University of Saskatchewan (38 female, mean age=25.8, SD=6.6). Students were recruited via mailing lists and notices on bulletin boards, and represented a variety of disciplines of study. Most participants played games (94%): 73% played on computers, 44% on consoles, and 45% on mobile devices. In terms of controller expertise, 51% were experienced with the GamePad, 53% with the PlayStation Move or Nintendo Wii, and 9% with Kinect[1].

Participants began by completing an informed consent and a questionnaire about their actual-self, ideal-self, and their current affective state. They then played one game (exactly 5 minutes) with each of the three different controller types. After each controller condition the players completed questionnaires assessing their experience of the game and of themselves within the game (game-self). At the end of the experiment, players completed demographic questions.

The experiment was a within-subject design, with all participants using each of the three controllers. Order of presentation of controller was fully counterbalanced.

Measures

We collected all dependent measures using validated scales. Cronbach's-α is reported for PANAS, IMI, and PENS in Table 1. For BFI, $\alpha_{actual\text{-}self}$=.641, and $\alpha_{ideal\text{-}self}$=.669; $\alpha_{game\text{-}self}$ is not reported because of the use of randomized subscales; imputation would overestimate $\alpha_{game\text{-}self}$.

[1] Note that the novelty of the Kinect among our sample is a potential confound. As such, we replicated our analyses for a subgroup where players were unfamiliar with all devices (N=31; 19 female). Our main results are all confirmed in this subgroup, with two exceptions (flagged in the results), where the trends of the results remain, but $p_{MainEffect}$>.05.

Game Enjoyment

Enjoyment of game was measured using two scales.

PANAS: Positive Affect and Negative Affect were assessed using the Positive Affect Negative Affect Schedule-Expanded (PANAS-X) [38]. In the PANAS-X, participants are asked to agree with 20 emotion adjectives on a Likert-scale ranging from 1 (very slightly or not at all) to 5 (extremely). Half of the adjectives are positive (e.g., 'active') and half are negative (e.g., 'guilty'). Ratings are merged to create a composite score for negative affect and one for positive affect. The PANAS-X has been used to evaluate the enjoyment of video games (e.g., [28]).

IMI: Intrinsic Motivation was assessed using the 18-item Intrinsic Motivation Inventory [30], which has been used to evaluate experience with video games (e.g., [32]). A series of items are rated on 5-point Likert-scale, ranging from 1 (not at all) to 5 (quite a bit). Example items are "I enjoyed this game very much" and "I think I am pretty good at this game". Data is merged to create four scores for each of interest-enjoyment, competence, effort-importance, and tension, and also an overall score of intrinsic motivation.

Need Satisfaction

The Player Experience of Need Satisfaction Scale (PENS) [32], was designed to understand game experience from the perspective of SDT [31], and has been used to evaluate games (e.g., [32]). We used PENS after each condition to assess if the game satisfied the players' needs for Competence, Autonomy, Relatedness, Immersion and Intuitive Controls. A series of statements was agreed with using a 5-point Likert-scale from 1 (not at all) to 5 (quite a bit). Example items include "I feel competent at the game" or "Learning the game controls was easy". Data are merged to create a score for each of the five underlying constructs. Although some have argued for leaving out the subscales on Relatedness if the game is for a single player [11], it is possible that different controller types could differentially satisfy the need for relatedness, so we included it.

Personality

The player's trait personality was assessed using the Big Five Inventory (BFI) [10]. The BFI is a standard instrument to assess personality dimensions and has been used in the context of games [6]. Data are merged to create a score for each of the underlying dimensions and for an overall score. Self-Discrepancy Theory assumes that the distance between self-concepts is predictive for psychological well-being. There are many ways to measure differences between self-concepts, including personality questionnaires, which easily assess personality constructs and get a measure for Self-Discrepancy at the same time. We use the overall score from the BFI to give a simple estimate for Self-Discrepancy by calculating divergence (see [28] for further explanation).

Participants completed the BFI five times. At the beginning of the experiment, participants were asked to reflect on their actual-self and rated their agreement with 44 statements of the form, "The type of person you are...", with answers such as "is talkative" or "likes to cooperate with others". Ratings used a 5-point Likert scale from 1 (strongly disagree) to 5 (strongly agree). Participants also reflected on their ideal-self, by completing items of the form "The type of person you wish, desire, or hope to be...", with the same items as used for assessing actual-self. After each game condition, participants were asked to assess their game-self using a short form (15 questions). Participants were asked to answer the questionnaire by completing the sentence "Reflect on the characteristics you see yourself having during the game – the type of person you were playing the game". Items in the short version covered all 5 aspects of personality, the number of items representing the scales E, A, O, N, C per questionnaire were stable, and we fully counterbalanced the presentation. Drawing items from a longer questionnaire is an established approach [39].

Data Analyses

All analyses were conducted using RM-ANOVA in SPSS 20. All parametric tests were performed after validating the data for assumptions of ANOVA use. Degrees of freedom were corrected using the Huynh-Feldt method, if the condition of sphericity was not satisfied. Pairwise comparisons used the Bonferonni method of adjusting the degrees of freedom for multiple comparisons, with the exception of the self-discrepancy measures, which used Tukey's LSD to avoid potential Type II errors resulting from small effect sizes. Significance was set at α=.05.

RESULTS

We first present the results of PX as traditionally measured by positive affect and intrinsic motivation. We extend this traditional analysis of PX by presenting the results of need satisfaction. We then explore how the controller conditions changed how players feel about themselves within the context of the game through presentation of the personality results. Finally, we investigate how the use of personality as a measure of *player experience* compares with the use of measures of *play experience* through a regression analysis.

Affect and Intrinsic Motivation

When evaluating PX, the first question of interest is usually whether or not the experience was fun, often measured as the degree of positive affect (e.g., [28]), mediated by the degree of Intrinsic Motivation (e.g., [32]) – especially the motivational component of interest/enjoyment.

Our results show a significant main effect of controller on positive affect ($F_{2,154}$=29.1, $p\approx$.000, η^2=.27). Pairwise comparisons show that the Kinect produced the highest Positive Affect, then the Move then GamePad (see Figure 2). All differences were significant at p<.006. There was no controller effect on Negative Affect ($F_{1.9,145.5}$=2.4, p=.101).

When considered as a whole, there was no effect of controller on overall Intrinsic Motivation ($F_{2,154}$=1.1,

p=.352); however, controller did affect the Interest-Enjoyment subscale ($F_{2,154}$=9.4, p=.001, η^2=0.10) and the Competence subscale ($F_{1.9,144.2}$=8.9, $p\approx$.000, η^2=0.10). Pairwise comparisons show that the GamePad was less enjoyable than the Move (p=.031) or Kinect (p=.001), which were not different from each other (p=.148). For competence, the Move produced greater confidence than the Kinect ($p\approx$.000) or the GamePad (p=.002), which were not different from each other (p=1.0). See Figure 3. There were no main effects of controller on the Effort ($F_{2,154}$=1.7, p=.183) or Tension ($F_{2,154}$=1.9, p=.147) subscales.

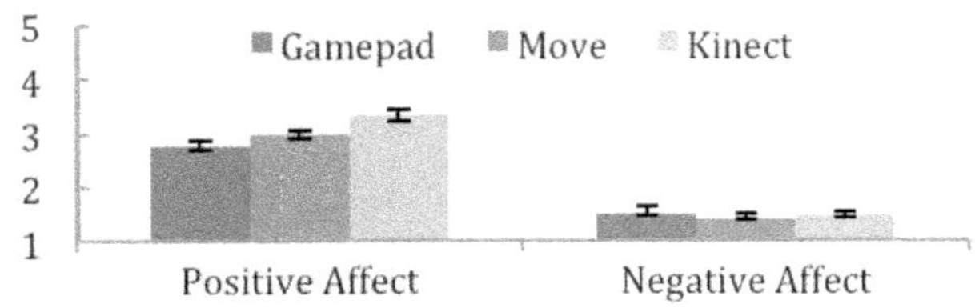

Figure 2. Means (±SE) for positive affect and negative affect on a scale of 1 (low) to 5 (high).

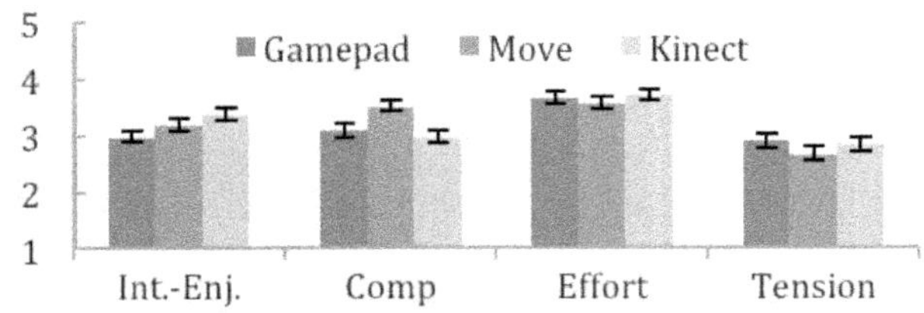

Figure 3. Means (±SE) for subscales of intrinsic motivation on a scale of 1 (low) to 5 (high).

Player Experience of Need Satisfaction

Although the analysis of affect and motivation provide insight into the game experience provided by different controllers, we used PENS, as it has been shown to provide a deeper understanding of game experience [32]. See Table 1 for descriptive statistics, and Figure 4.

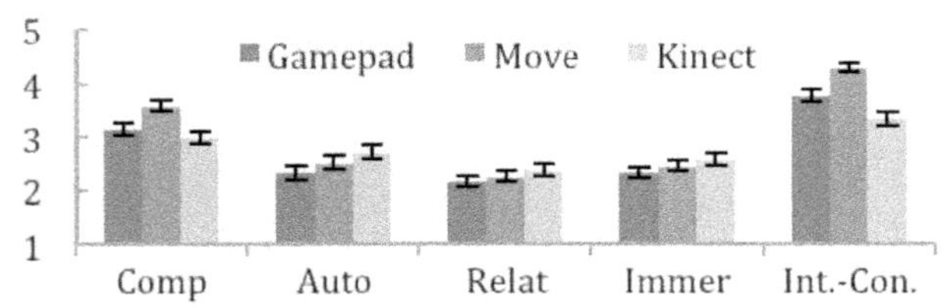

Figure 4. Means (±SE) for subscales of PENS on a scale of 1 (low) to 5 (high).

There was a main effect of controller on Competence ($F_{1.9,145.2}$=11.4, $p\approx$.000, η^2=0.13). Pairwise comparisons revealed that the Move provided higher Competence than the GamePad (p=.001) or Kinect ($p\approx$.000), which were not different from each other (p=.702).

There was a main effect of controller on Autonomy ($F_{2,154}$=9.3, $p\approx$.000, η^2=0.11). The Kinect provided higher Autonomy than the Move (p=.044) and GamePad (p=.001), which were not different from each other (p=.119).

There was a main effect of controller on Relatedness[1] ($F_{2,154}$=4.3, p=.016, η^2=0.05). The Kinect provided higher Relatedness than GamePad (p=.014); the other differences were not significant (MO-KI: p=.281; MO-GP: p=.732).

There was a main effect of controller on Immersion ($F_{2,154}$=5.9, p=.003, η^2=0.07). The Kinect provided higher Immersion than GamePad (p=.004); the other differences were not significant (MO-KI: p=.240; MO-GP: p=.272).

There was a main effect of controller on Intuitive Controls ($F_{1.8,137.0}$=25.2, $p\approx$.000, η^2=0.25). The Move was most Intuitive, followed by the GamePad, then Kinect. All differences were significant (MO-GP: $p\approx$.000; MO-KI: $p\approx$.000; GP-KI: p=.025).

	GamePad		Move		Kinect		
	M	*SD*	*M*	*SD*	*M*	*SD*	*α*
IMI							
Combined	3.15	0.52	3.23	0.60	3.22	0.60	
Interest-Enj.	2.96	0.86	3.19	0.93	3.37	1.06	0.82
Competence	3.08	1.05	3.51	0.92	2.97	1.04	0.90
Effort-Imp.	3.66	0.91	3.55	1.00	3.71	0.86	0.83
Tension	2.90	1.12	2.66	1.04	2.83	1.09	0.86
Affect							
Positive	2.76	0.89	2.98	0.93	3.33	0.91	0.90
Negative	1.52	0.67	1.41	0.51	1.46	0.55	0.86
PENS							
Competence	3.15	1.02	3.56	0.91	2.97	1.06	0.83
Autonomy	2.31	1.14	2.49	1.13	2.70	1.22	0.85
Relatedness	2.15	0.93	2.24	0.92	2.36	1.06	0.67
Immersion	2.32	0.91	2.44	0.97	2.56	1.08	0.89
Intuitive Cont.	3.75	1.06	4.29	0.69	3.32	1.11	0.72

Table 1. Means and SD for intrinsic motivation, affect and PENS on a scale from 1 (low) to 5 high. Cronbach's-α shows the consistency of the scale items for each construct.

Perceived in-game Personality

The results for self-characteristics are presented overall and for the five subscales (see Table 2 for descriptive statistics).

	Actual-self		Ideal-self		GamePad		Move		Kinect	
	M	*SD*	*M*	*SD*	*M*	*SD*	*M*	*SD*	*M*	*SD*
CS	3.41	0.26	3.80	0.19	3.16	0.37	3.26	0.39	3.14	0.43
E	3.27	0.72	4.16	0.46	2.94	0.82	3.15	0.87	2.97	0.84
A	3.78	0.54	4.45	0.46	3.49	0.67	3.77	0.72	3.50	0.72
C	3.53	0.64	4.66	0.29	3.49	0.69	3.55	0.71	3.50	0.81
N	2.78	0.71	1.39	0.34	2.68	1.02	2.37	0.83	2.42	0.84
O	3.70	0.53	4.34	0.40	3.20	0.70	3.44	0.68	3.30	0.76

Table 2. Means and SD for personality by context (CS: composite score, E: Extraversion, A: Agreeableness, C: Conscientiousness, N: Neuroticism, O: Openness).

There was a main effect of controller on overall in-game personality ($F_{2,78}$=3.06, p=.050, η^2 =0.04). The Kinect was higher than the GamePad (p=.050) or the Move (p=.021), which were not different from each other (p=.708). Subscale analysis revealed a main effect of controller on Agreeableness ($F_{1.9,145.3}$=6.05, p=.004, η^2=0.07) and Neuroticism[1] ($F_{2,154}$=3.4, p=.038, η^2=0.04), but not on Extroversion ($F_{2,154}$=2.4, p=.100), Conscientiousness

($F_{2,154}$=0.2, p=.795), or Openness ($F_{2,154}$=2.7, p=.071). Pairwise comparisons show that the Kinect yielded more Agreeableness than both the Move (p=.004) and GamePad (p=.001), which were not different from each other (p=.915). Experienced Neuroticism was higher for the GamePad than the Move (p=.047) or Kinect (p=.031), which were not different from each other (p=.687).

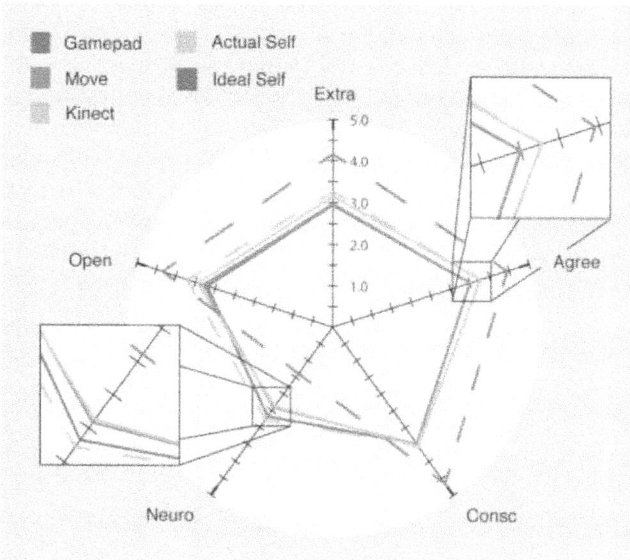

Figure 5. Personality dimension means for: actual-self, ideal-self, and the game-selves (GP, MO, KI) of 1 (low) to 5 (high).

Figure 5 shows the differences in perceived personality in game for the different controllers in the context of perceived actual-self and ideal-self. Interestingly, the in-game personalities are contained within the boundaries of actual-self. Contrary to expectations of game play, the game did not produce more idealized versions of players, but moved their perceived personality further from their ideal than their actual-self (with the exception of neuroticism). This ideal-self-game-self discrepancy is significantly larger for all controller types than for ideal-self-actual-self (all p<.001). We revisit this interesting result in the discussion.

Personality and Need Satisfaction

Figure 5 shows how in-game personality characteristics change with controller type, but also shows how game-self is fairly similar to actual-self. To determine whether the differences in game-self are meaningful for game evaluation, we conducted two-tailed Pearson correlations for game-self and the PENS dimensions separately for each controller. We also calculated the correlations for actual-self and the PENS dimensions across the three controllers. Correlations are displayed in Table 3.

The results show that there are no significant correlations between actual-self and any of the PENS dimensions; however, there are correlations between the PENS dimensions and game-self. For the GamePad condition, the correlation is significant with Autonomy, Relatedness, and Immersion. For the Move condition, the correlation is significant with Competence and Relatedness, and for the Kinect condition, the correlation is significant with Competence, Autonomy, and Relatedness. These results reveal that PX is not related to players' overall personality traits, but is related to their experienced personality within the context of game play, demonstrating that the use of game-self-characteristics for PX is meaningful.

	Actual-self		*GS: GamePad*		*GS: Move*		*GS: Kinect*	
	r	*p*	*r*	*p*	*r*	*p*	*r*	*p*
Com.	.047	.479	.170	.070	.294	.005	.295	.004
Aut.	-.054	.415	.271	.008	.130	.121	.276	.007
Rel.	-.014	.837	.314	.003	.272	.008	.340	.001
Imm.	-.069	.296	.233	.020	.140	.106	.191	.047
Int.	-.031	.635	.150	.097	.050	.319	.150	.088

Table 3. r and p values for correlations between PENS dimensions and personality characteristics.

Added Value of Personality Analysis

The results of the personality analysis show that a choice as simple as which controller is used can affect our in-game personality, and that in-game personality correlates with need satisfaction, whereas actual-self does not; however to understand the role that in-game personality plays in game experience evaluation, we must know the relative contribution of the need satisfaction variables and the personality variables to the overall outcome of increased positive affect or motivation to play. We conducted an analysis of regression with game-self, Competence, Autonomy, Relatedness, Immersion, and Intuitive Control on Positive Affect and overall Intrinsic Motivation (see Table 4 for standardized β-coefficients and p-values). Personality was included as a single factor, indicating overall game-self, whereas the individual contributions from PENS were included individually because they measure distinct dimensions; there is no meaning of an overall PENS score.

	Positive Affect		Intrinsic Motivation	
	β	*p*	*β*	*p*
Game-self	**0.31**	**.000**	**0.18**	**.000**
Competence	**0.23**	**.001**	0.11	.100
Autonomy	**0.28**	**.000**	0.11	.128
Relatedness	0.05	.538	-0.01	.918
Immersion	0.09	.296	**0.46**	**.000**
Intuitive Control	-0.06	.396	0.12	.057

Table 4. Standardized beta coefficients and p values for regression of game-self and PENS dimensions on positive

Our results show that game-self, Competence, and Autonomy predict Positive Affect, with changes in game-self yielding the biggest contribution. In addition, game-self and Immersion predict Intrinsic Motivation, with Immersion providing the larger contribution. These results show that changes to game-self as a result of controller predicts positive affect and intrinsic motivation during game play, and confirm that analysis of in-game personality is a valuable tool to understand PX.

DISCUSSION

Our study shows that there are a number of effects of controller on PX and in-game personality. We describe the significance of the findings, discuss the implications for game design, and finally present the limitations of our study and the future opportunities that our findings provide.

Significance of the Findings

Other researchers have previously applied theories of needs satisfaction to understand and explain player motivation and user experience within a game (e.g., [11, 17, 32]). We do the same in our work but add to the literature with our findings on how controller choice differentially affects our satisfaction of needs. In addition, we demonstrate that the application of self-discrepancy theory to game evaluation adds value to our understanding of PX. Game-self changed significantly with use of a different controller, and the change in game-self as a result of controller choice is a bigger predictor of positive affect than the components of need satisfaction theory. These findings confirm that including trait personality assessment in the PX evaluation toolbox is valuable for understanding player experience.

Our findings also have practical importance. For instance, we use games to escape reality, whether through a fantasy-based role-playing experience (e.g., World of Warcraft) or not (e.g., Bejeweled). We show that controller choice affects game-self, thus it is important for game designers to consider controller choice, to ensure that the escapism provided by games is not unintentionally damaged.

Implications for Game Design

Although the primary purpose of computer and video games has been to entertain, games have also been used to persuade a player to change their attitudes or opinions (e.g., The Cat and the Coup, A Closed World), to inspire behaviour change (e.g., Evoke, Fatworld), and to teach concepts, skills and tools (e.g., Math Blaster, Typing of the Dead, RibbonHero) [18, 3]. Regardless of whether a game is intended to entertain or educate, players will enjoy the experience of play if they are motivated to make progress [32]. Good games draw the player in and keep them engaged during play, and an engaged player will give the game a better chance of success at its intended purpose, irrespective of whether that be to divulge or divert.

Our results demonstrate how the choice of controller in a game mediates the experience, not only for the satisfaction of needs, but also for perceived personality. These findings related to game-self and controllers are useful both as a *lens with which to understand* controller effects in games and as a *guide for choices* on controller in new games.

Findings as a Lens to View Existing Games

Our findings on controller and game-self could be used to understand player experience in a variety of games and situations. For example, consider games where the player must help the character overcome obstacles and prevail (e.g., Deus Ex series, Mass Effect series). In these games, the character begins with vulnerabilities (e.g., low skills) that are resolved through interacting with environmental threats. The designer's intention is that players experience the fragility of the hero and surmount the odds; the goal is to become strong and overcome the feelings of being weak. Players accomplish this through leveling up (which happens to also satisfy our need for Competence). Many of these types of games use traditional controllers (e.g., GamePad), which is shown in our study to increase Neuroticism. By using the GamePad for these types of interactions, the experience of anxiety and instability might be heightened; users may be more likely to experience stress from minor events. It could be that in playing these games with a GamePad, the designer's intention of having players experience the character's fragility is effectively translated.

In another example, consider games designed as social icebreakers or to promote social connectedness (e.g., party games such as Wario's Smooth Moves). Games that target a friendly play environment benefit when players' game-selves are Agreeable. Our results suggest that the Kinect is preferred for enhancing Agreeableness, matching what is working in the games industry; the success of the Kinect has largely been for these types of social games.

Findings as a Guide to Inform New Game Design

Our findings related to in-game personality as a result of controller choice could also be applied to guide controller choice in the design of new games.

For example, consider a game designed to help players learn empathy. Our findings show that using the GamePad heightens the experience of Neuroticism, reinforcing feelings of being uncomfortable with strangers and difficult social situations, and causing players' game selves to be more likely to lose their temper and be prone to annoyance. Our results suggest that using the GamePad would decrease the game-self's natural inclination towards empathy, thus increasing the challenge of experiencing empathy; therefore, it could be a good choice for this application.

In another example, consider a game that encourages deception and betraying others for personal gain (e.g., DayZ). Although the Kinect is a general choice for collaborative or social games, our results show that the Kinect enhances players' Agreeableness within the context of play, reducing willingness to take advantage of others, insult others, and invite conflict. Thus, our findings suggest that the Kinect may not be a good controller choice when designing a game where the mechanics incite low Agreeableness (e.g., by focusing on personal advantage and conflict). The mismatch between the personality affordances of the controller and the intended in-game personality of the player may result in poor PX.

On the other hand, as previously noted, our findings suggest that games designed as social icebreakers or to promote social connectedness would benefit from the Kinect.

Opportunities for Future Work

Our study provides interesting findings for PX research; however, there are some limitations that raise questions for future work. First, our game was intentionally designed to be void of dramatic elements related to story arc or character progression. How our results extend to games where the player relates to their character is unknown. Our results that show how game-self is subsumed by actual-self likely do not extend to situations in which a player interacts via a character with personality traits closer to the player's ideal-self [2]. Second, although our game was engaging, it was not designed to draw a player in like an off-the-shelf game. Our results may differ when applied to games engineered to produce engagement and flow. On the other hand, the underlying mechanism of pursuit tracking used in our game is a common mechanic in a variety of game genres (e.g., first-person shooter), and thus our results related to controller choice have general application. Third, we tested three controllers; extending our results to other game input (e.g., mice, joysticks, touch) is needed. Also, we created a specific control mechanism for Kinect interaction (using torso movement); a different control mechanism (e.g., hand position) may produce different effects on game-self. Finally, our analysis considers all participants as a group. Examining results by demographic factor, such as age, sex, personality traits, or game expertise could produce interesting interactions.

Our findings produce many future opportunities for research, of which we present a few examples. First, we investigated a single-player game; applying our approach to collaborative or competitive play could inform the choice of controller for this popular genre. Second, we look specifically at controller choice in digital games; our analysis could be extended to artifact use in board game play. Finally, our findings can be used as a lens to view existing game success. Relating the predictions of positive affect based on changing game-self to market success of games would provide commerce-based validation of our research.

CONCLUSIONS

Traditional game evaluation focuses on the enjoyment provided by a game (i.e., positive affect). We apply satisfaction of needs theory (using PENS) to explain the underlying components of game enjoyment in an experiment with controller type as the manipulation. In addition, we explore the use of game-self as an additional level of PX evaluation to investigate the difference between how a play experience makes a player feel about the game and how the experience makes them feel about themselves. Our study shows that there are a number of effects of controller on PX and player personality within a game. These findings provide both a lens with which to view controller effects in games and a guide for controller choice in the design of new games. Finally, our research demonstrates that including self-characteristics assessment in the PX evaluation toolbox is valuable and useful for understanding player experience.

ACKNOWLEDGEMENTS

Thanks to reviewers for their feedback, the GRAND NCE for funding, and Kristen Dergousoff, Roxanne Dowd, Jared Cechanowicz, and the rest of the Interaction Lab at the UofS for support.

REFERENCES

1. Bateman, S., Doucette, A., Xiao, R.B., Gutwin, C., Mandryk. R.L., & Cockburn, A. Effects of View, Input Device, and Track Width on Video Game Driving. In *Proc. GI*, 2011, 207-214.
2. Bessiere, K., Seay, & F. Kiesler, S., The Ideal Elf: Identity Exploration in World of Warcraft. *CyberPsychology & Behavior*, 2007, 10(4), 530-535.
3. Bogost, I., *How To Do Things With Videogames*, 2011.
4. Csíkszentmihályi, M., *Beyond Boredom and Anxiety*, 1975.
5. Fernandez, A., Fun Experience with Digital Games: A Model Proposition. In *Extending Experiences: Structure, Analysis and Design of Computer Game Player Experience*, 2008, 181-190.
6. Gilbert, R. L., Foss J.A., & Murphy, N.A., Multi Personality Order: Physical and Personality Characteristics of the Self, Primary Avatar and Alt. In *Reinventing Ourselves: Contemporary Concepts of Identity in Virtual Worlds*, 2011, 213-234.
7. Hefner, D., Klimmt, C. and Vorderer, P., Identification with the player character as determinant of video game enjoyment. In *Proc. of ICEC*, 2007, 39-48.
8. Higgins, E.T., Self-Discrepancy: A theory relating self and affect. *Psychological Review*, 1987, 94(3), 319-340.
9. Isbister, K., & Schaffer, N., *Game Usability: Advice from the Experts for Advancing the Player Experience*, 2008.
10. John, O. P., Naumann, L. P., & Soto, C. J., Paradigm Shift to the Integrative Big-Five Trait Taxonomy: History, Measurement, and Conceptual Issues. In *Handbook of personality: Theory and research*, 2008, 114-158.
11. Johnson, D., & Gardner, J., Personality, Motivation and Video Games (2010). In *Proc. OZCHI*, 2010, 276-279.
12. Kim, J., Gunn, D., Schuh, E., Phillips, B., Pagulayan, R., & Wixon, D. Tracking Real-Time User Experience (TRUE): A comprehensive instrumentation solution for complex systems. In *Proc. SIGCHI*, 2008, 443-452.
13. Lazzaro, N., Why we play games: 4 keys to more emotion. In *Proc. GDC*, 2004.

14. Li D., Liau A., & Khoo A., Examining the Influence of Actual-Ideal-Self-Discrepancies, Depression, and Escapism, on Pathological Gaming Among Massively Multiplayer Online Adolescent Gamers *Cyberpsychology, Behavior, and Social Networking*, 2011, 14(9), 535-539.

15. Lindley S. E., Le Couteur J., & Berthouze N. L, Stirring up experience through movement in game play: effects on engagement and social behaviour. In *Proc. CHI*, 2008, 511-514.

16. Mandryk, R.L., Atkins, M., & Inkpen, K., A Continuous and Objective Evaluation of Emotional Experience with Interactive Play Environments. In *Proc. CHI*, 2006, 1027-1036.

17. McEwan, M., Johnson, D., Wyeth, P. & Blacker, A. Videogame Control Device Impact on the Play Experience. In *Proc. IE*, 2012, 1-3.

18. McGonigal, J., *Reality Is Broken: Why Games Make Us Better and How They Can Change the World,* 2010.

19. McMahon, N., Wyeth, P. & Johnson, D., Personality and Player Types in Fallout New Vegas. In *Proc. FNG*, 2012, 113-116.

20. Napatov, D.,Castellucci, S.J., & MacKenzie, I.S., ISO 9241-9 evaluation of video game controllers. In *Proc. GI, 2009,* 223-230.

21. Park J., Song Y., & Teng C., Exploring the Links Between Personality Traits and Motivations to Play Online Games. *Cyberpsychology, Behavior, and Social Networking*, 2011, 14(12) 747-751.

22. Partala, T., Psychological needs and virtual worlds: Case Second Life, *IJHCS*, 2011, 69(12), 787-800.

23. Peever, N., Johnson, D., & Gardner, J., Personality and Video Game Genre Preferences. In *Proc. IE*, 2012

24. Peng, W., Lin, J., Pfeiffer. P., & Winn, B., Need Satisfaction Supportive Game Features as Motivational Determinants: An Experimental Study of a Self-Determination Theory Guided Exergame, *Media Psychology*, 2012, 15(2), 175-196.

25. Pietschmann D., Valtin, G., & Ohler O., The effect of Authentic Input Devices on Computer Game Immersion. In *Computer Games and New Media Cultures: A Handbook of Digital Games Studies*, 2012.

26. Pinelle, D., Wong, N., Stach, T., & Gutwin, C., Usability Heuristics for Networked Multiplayer Games, In *Proc. GROUP*, 2009, 169-178.

27. Procci, K., Singer, A. R., Levy, K. R., & Bowers, C., Measuring the flow experience of gamers: An evaluation of the DFS-2. *Computers in Human Behavior*, 2012, 28(6), 2306-2312.

28. Przybylski, A.K., Weinstein, N., Murayama, K., Lynch, M.F., & Ryan, R.M., The ideal-self at play: The appeal of video games that let you be all you can be. *Psychological Science*, 2011, 23 (1), 69-76.

29. Quick, J. M., Atkinson, R. K., & Lin, L., Empirical Taxonomies of Gameplay Enjoyment: Personality and Video Game Preference. *International Journal of Game-Based Learning*, 2012, 2(3), 11-31.

30. Ryan, R. M., Control and information in the intrapersonal sphere: An extension of cognitive evaluation theory. *Journal of Personality and Social Psychology*, 1982, 43, 450-461.

31. Ryan, R. M., & Deci, E. L., Self-determination theory and the facilitation of intrinsic motivation, social development, and well-being. *American Psychologist*, 2000b, 55, 68-78.

32. Ryan, R. M., Rigby, C. S., & Przybylski, A. K., Motivational pull of video games: A self-determination theory approach. Motivation and Emotion, 2006, 30, 347-365.

33. Seif El-Nasr, M., Drachen A., Canossa A., Game Analytics: Maximizing the Value of Player Data. Springer, (to appear).

34. Shafer, D.M., Carbonara, C.P., & Popova, L., Spatial Presence and Perceived Reality as Predictors of Motion-Based Video Game Enjoyment, *Presence*, 2011, 20(6), 591-619.

35. Sheldon, K. M., & Filak, V., Manipulating autonomy, competence and relatedness support in a game-learning context: New evidence that all three needs matter. *British Journal of Social Psych.*, 2008, 47, 267-283.

36. Skalski, P., Tamborini, R., Shelton, A., Buncher, M. & Lindmark, P., Mapping the road to fun: natural video game controllers, presence, and game enjoyment. *New Media & Society*, 2010, 224-242.

37. Sweetser, P. & Wyeth, P., GameFlow: a model for evaluating player enjoyment in games. *Computer Entertainment,* 2005, 3-3.

38. Watson, D., & Clark, L. A. *The PANAS-X: Manual for the positive and negative affect schedule-Expanded Form*, 1994.

39. Yee. N., Ducheneaut, N., Nelson, L., & Likarish, P. Introverted Elves & Conscientious Gnomes: The Expression of Personality in World of Warcraft. In *Proc. CHI*, 2011, 753-762.

Mastering the Art of War: How Patterns of Gameplay Influence Skill in Halo

Jeff Huang
Information School
University of Washington
chi2013@jeffhuang.com

Thomas Zimmermann
Nachiappan Nagappan
Microsoft Research

Charles Harrison
Bruce Phillips
Microsoft Games Studios

{tzimmer,nachin,charlesh,bphil}@microsoft.com

ABSTRACT
How do video game skills develop, and what sets the top players apart? We study this question of skill through a rating generated from repeated multiplayer matches called TrueSkill. Using these ratings from 7 months of games from over 3 million players, we look at how play intensity, breaks in play, skill change over time, and other games affect skill. These analyzed factors are then combined to model future skill and games played; the results show that skill change in early matches is a useful metric for modeling future skill, while play intensity explains eventual games played. The best players in the 7-month period, who we call "Master Blasters", have varied skill patterns that often run counter to the trends we see for typical players. The data analysis is supplemented with a 70 person survey to explore how players' self-perceptions compare to the gameplay data; most survey responses align well with the data and provide insight into player beliefs and motivation. Finally, we wrap up with a discussion about hiding skill information from players, and implications for game designers.

Author Keywords
video games; learning; gaming skill; online multiplayer.

ACM Classification Keywords
K.8.0 Personal Computing: General—*Games*

INTRODUCTION
Competitive games are a thriving industry, played by millions, and watched by millions. Tournaments and televised game matches are popular among those skilled enough, and spectators enjoy watching the best players compete in high-stakes tournaments [3]. But the skilled were once unskilled; the best players get there with dedicated practice and determination. So we ask, how do skills in a game develop, and what differentiates the top players? This leads to interesting questions about patterns of play and its relationship with skill. To explore these questions, we use a well established metric of skill from a current popular video game, Halo Reach.

Millions of people play Halo Reach, a first-person shooter on the Xbox game console. From records of their online matches, we study their TrueSkill rating [8], a Bayesian scoring system similar to the Elo rating in chess. This rating provides us with a proven metric for representing skill in scenarios where people are actively trying to improve and outmatch their opponents. Players play online matches over and over, providing a controlled set of repeated trials that can give us insight into playing as a form of practice. Aggregated, this amounts to a large set of objective skill measurements over a 7 month period.

Using this data, we look at what factors affect players' skills and their learning ability, a topic studied across many domains. Having a large dataset of complete game histories from over 3 million players allows us to measure and analyze skill from many dimensions and compare skill gain in Halo with experiments from sports training and learning sciences. For example, people who lift weights at the gym are keenly aware that inactivity (i.e., detraining) reverses muscle gains, but restarting a training regime after inactivity replenishes strength quicker than previously untrained people [16]. We see similar effects of playing breaks occurring in Halo Reach.

To study these factors from multiple perspectives, we take a mixed methods approach, like Halo researchers before us [14, 19]. A quantitative data analysis finds robust trends in a large-scale 3 million player dataset, and allows us to also examine the best players in the cohort we study; surveys explain the observed behavior we see in the quantitative analysis as well as provide insight into players' self-perceptions in learning. Put together, we go beyond identifying *how* and *what* players are doing in the game, to understand *why* players act in a particular way.

We contribute an exploration of skill progression and factors affecting skill. The factors we study are diverse, including: play patterns, demographics, skill change in early matches, and other game titles played. Our secondary contribution is providing implications for the game designers and game system on dealing with these factors' effect on skill, and a discussion of whether players should be provided with skill information.

RELATED WORK

Data Analysis in Games
Our study uses a similar methodology as two other studies of multiplayer Halo, both of which use gameplay records and either player surveys or interviews. Mason

and Clauset [14] use the same data source as us—the Halo Reach multiplayer records, and supplement them with a survey. They find that players with more friends on their team perform better individually, while also performing better as a team. Xu et al. [19] take a different approach on studying social motivations, where they aim to understand the social relationships between Halo 3 players through the gameplay records and interviews. They found that players were well aware of who they played with, and rather than only playing to win, also sought to enjoy the social experience of the game. While we employ similar methods and data as these two studies, our focus is on player skill and the change in expertise rather than social relationships.

Game data can also be used for visualizations, such as Wallner and Kriglstein's implementation that overlays gameplay data from replay files over the in-game map [17]. These visualizations allow players to view a previous match at a glance, but there are also applications that benefit the game designers. By constructing player transition models, Harrison and Roberts could predict a players' next action before it happened. Their model of World of Warcraft players' achievement data used a correlation network to predict which achievement they are most likely to earn next [7].

Prior work on characterizing Project Gotham Racing 4 [10] explained the diverse and extensive amount of data that is collected due to the constantly connected nature of the game consoles. The results of this analysis helped provide a better understanding of the differences between long-term and short-term players, the choices they make, their retention and the extent to which various options in the game are utilized (in this case for example, the type of track, vehicle class, or weather conditions). This led to recommendations for ways to reduce development costs by eliminating unused or unpopular options and to help keep new players engaged.

Users' Learning and Skill from Repetition

People acquire skill from frequent use outside of games. An early and well-known study is that of American telegraphers by Bryan and Harter [1]. The sending and receiving rates, measured in characters per minute, are plotted over time to produce figures showing different rates of acquiring expertise among the two tasks, and particularly a plateau in the middle of the receiving plot. This plateau has incited discussion in follow-up work, where the original authors believed that multiple practice curves existed [2], characterized by the two separate skills of mapping Morse code into letters and predicting the word from the initial letters. However, Keller counters in a later study that there is no plateau effect [11], citing unpublished studies by Tulloss, where "there is no sign of a plateau in any of the Tulloss curves".

Other studies in software have looked at motivators for skill acquisition and differences between experts and non-experts in searching the Web. In a study of non-programmers playing a game that teaches programming, Lee and Ko found that participants completed more levels of the game, and thus acquired additional skill in programming, if the goal was framed in terms of helping a personable robot rather than an inanimate terminal [12]. In another study, White et al. examined experts and non-experts behavior over a 3 month period of search logs. They found that expert searchers differed in terms of query vocabulary, sites they visited, and patterns of search behavior [18]. The authors were also able to predict the expertise of a user with modest success; computer science experts were found to be easier to predict than medicine, finance, or legal experts. In our work, we focus less on predicting skill, and more on explaining factors that affect skill.

Case Studies of Video Game Expertise

Case studies situate the researcher inside the gaming experience, either as observers or as players themselves. Reeves et al. take an ethnomethodological approach to analyzing expertise in the first-person shooter, Counter-Strike, by watching an expert *in situ* [15]. They find that expert play constitutes an understanding of the terrain and a sense of where other players are in the environment. Reeves et al. also suggest regarding gameplay holistically, as it does not make sense when taken in pieces. Another researcher, Hock-Koon, becomes an expert himself in the game Alien vs. Predator [9]. He rigorously kept a journal of his training and lessons learned, and developed a theory of elliptical learning. Hock-Koon argues that learning encompasses multiple levels of understanding for a single mechanism in the game. In contast to these case studies that put the researcher into the game, we step back and look at aggregate data from millions of players to seek generalizable patterns.

TEAM SLAYER IN HALO REACH

Halo Reach is the latest version of the popular Halo franchise on the Xbox console, with over 9 million copies sold[1]. It is a first-person shooter, where players battle with rifles, grenades, plasma weapons, and swords. The games start with the player spawning with initial weapons somewhere on a map; additional weapons, health, and other power-ups are available elsewhere. There are both single-player and multi-player components, where the multi-player games are played on Xbox Live, on a local network, or single Xbox with split-screen.

In Team Slayer, by far the most popular multiplayer playlist (a set of game types with similar rules), teams gain a point whenever a member of their team kills an enemy. When a player dies, they respawn at a random spawn location on the map. The team with the most points at 15 minutes or the first team to reach 50 kills wins the match. Thus, each match typically takes 12–15 minutes, with about 5 minutes following the match to view post-game statistics, to assign the next teams and map, and load the next game. In this paper, we focus on studying skill in Team Slayer because of the simplicity

[1] `http://www.vgchartz.com/game/35024/halo-reach/`

of the game, its popularity, and its consistency of play from match to match. While half the players only play 40 or fewer matches of Team Slayer, the vast majority of the matches are from the minority of players who play hundreds of matches (Figure 1).

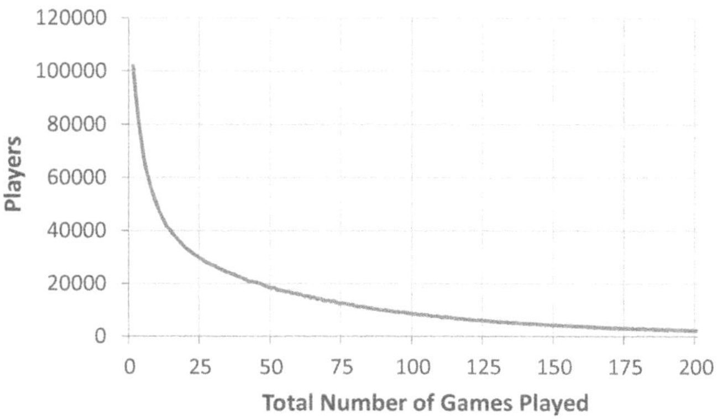

Figure 1. In Team Slayer, half the players played at least 40 matches, and a quarter played 95 matches or more. The chart extends beyond 200 matches as some people played over 1,000 matches during the 7 month period.

TrueSkill

Halo Reach uses a skill rating system called TrueSkill [8], a generalization of the Elo chess rating [6]. TrueSkill is currently used for matchmaking across numerous Xbox titles. The matchmaking system attempts to maximize the probability a match will end in a draw, which generally makes for an exciting match; of course, this is subject to practical constraints such as which players are currently looking for new matches. Halo Reach does not show players their current TrueSkill rating—a design decision we discuss later—so there is little incentive for players to manipulate this rating.

TrueSkill represents a player's skill as a Gaussian distribution, parameterized with a mean μ and standard deviation σ; μ represents the best guess of that player's skill, and σ represents the variation in that guess. The σ generally decreases over time as the player plays more matches since there is more information about their skill. μ starts with an initial value (a prior of 3), that adjusts to a player's "true" value for each multiplayer playlist. The matchmaking system attempts to pair up teams with equal skill (using a conservative estimate of skill computed by $\mu - C\sigma$), striving for balanced matches.

Player performance has been studied retroactively using TrueSkill for games of chess, showing that it can accurately predict the outcome of matches better than other rating systems [4], and in StarCraft, where it agrees with public opinion about the top players in history [5].

METHOD

Data Analysis

We use the TrueSkill "best guess" rating μ as the estimate of a user's skill. The ratings were retrieved from the official Halo servers that compute them for matchmaking. Our dataset consists of the complete first 7 months of games from the 3.2 million Halo Reach players on Xbox Live in its first week of release (September 13–20, 2012). We selected this cohort of players to control for the time when a person starts playing Halo Reach, and the remainder of this paper uses this cohort's historical game records for the 7 month period. Note that we are not sampling—this is the *complete population of players in this cohort*, and our dataset comprises every match played by that population. However, from this data we still know little about the mechanisms through which players improve their skills, which may require alternate methodological approaches (e.g., [15, 9]).

Our analysis can be reproduced by other researchers who download game histories from the Halo Reach API such as Mason and Clauset [14], and the TrueSkill ratings can be recomputed using the published equations [8]. When plotting the players' skill in the charts, the median skill at every point along the x-axis was taken for each group. The median reduces the bias that occurs when plotting μ, a skewed variable that makes taking the mean exaggerate the effect of each factor.

Survey

We supplement the large-scale data analysis results with a survey of a random sample of Halo Reach players who opted-in to be asked about their player experience on the Xbox. These participants were from the United States and were rewarded with a chance to win Microsoft software. We asked a dozen open-ended and multiple-choice questions to 300 players and received 70 responses relating to players' perceptions of skill. The multiple choice questions were often followed up with an open-ended question to allow the participant to elaborate on their response, particularly why they chose an answer.

From this survey, we sought to discover how participants' self-perceptions matched the data analysis results. We wanted to know which behaviors they reported confirmed what we found in the gameplay data, and which ones disagreed with the analysis. We believe that such a mixed-method approach could compensate for some of the weaknesses inherent in both methods. For example, the survey responses could shed light on why players behaved a certain way while the gameplay data could not, but the gameplay data could show patterns for different segments of people that would be difficult to identify in a small-scale survey. However, we did not cross-reference the players in the survey with their data for their privacy.

PATTERNS OF PLAY AND LEARNING

An overarching research question we explored is how players' patterns of play affected their skill. Improving one's skill is tantamount to learning, and we wanted to look at specifically how *play intensity*, *breaks between games*, *playing other games*, and *initial skill change* related to a player's skill in Halo Reach Team Slayer. These factors were chosen during discussion among the authors as common beliefs among gamers as chief determinants of skill.

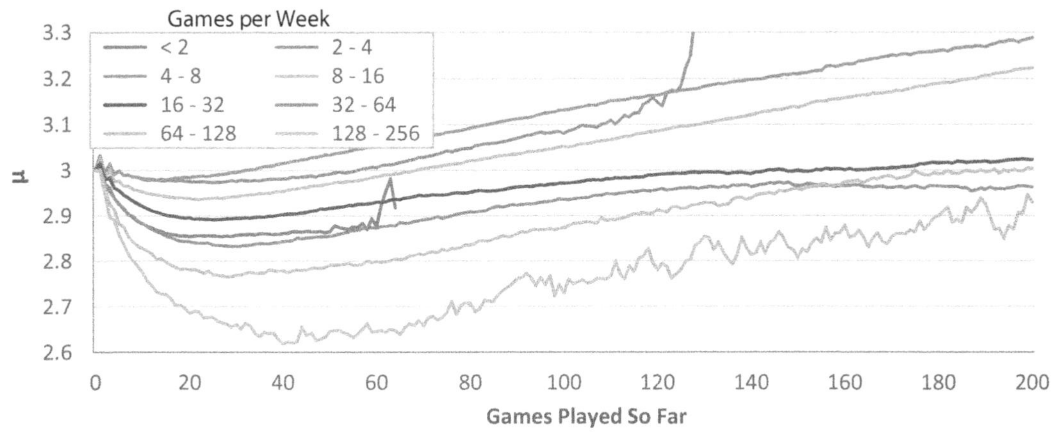

Figure 2. Players who play different numbers of matches per week gain expertise at different rates, generally trending towards higher skill for each match played.

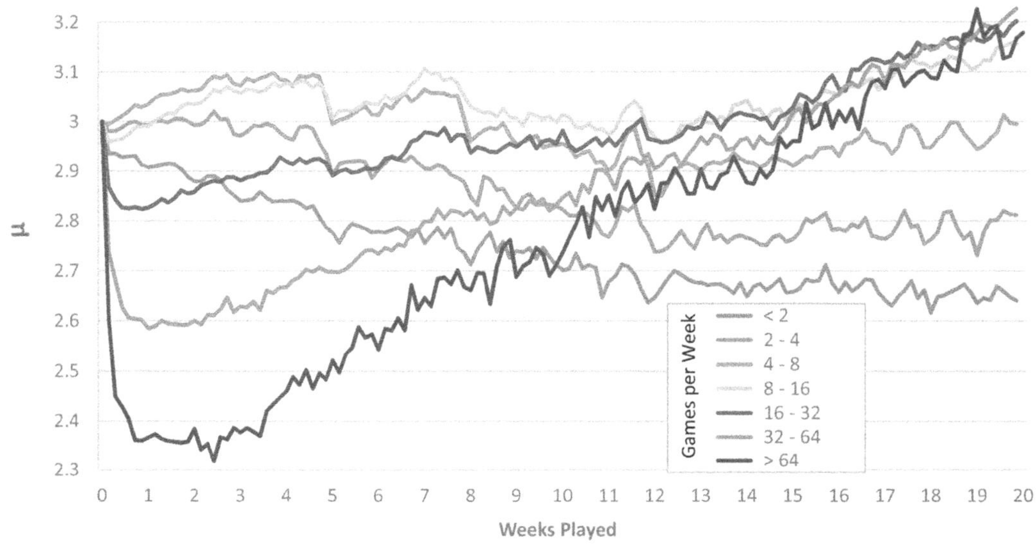

Figure 3. When looking at the skill over the number of weeks played, the more frequent players gain skill faster, even though it takes more matches to reach that level.

Play Intensity

We first investigated how skill is affected by a player's play intensity. Do players improve more if they play the same number of games spread out over more weeks or played more compactly in fewer weeks? Do those who play more games per week improve faster than those who play fewer, and is there a plateau of improvement? To explore these questions, we plot TrueSkill for different players, grouped according to their play intensity measured by games per week.

From looking at the players as a whole, two perspectives are needed. One perspective is at what rate of play intensity do players improve the quickest *per game*. Figure 2 presents in this information by plotting skill over games for players grouped according to games per week. The figure shows that those who play 4–8 games per week seem to do best compared to other groups. However, from a different perspective of which players improve quickest *over time*, Figure 3 reveals that players who play more than 8 games per week can surpass the less frequent players. Despite learning at a lower rate per game, the additional games they played more than compensated for their slower skill gains. Interestingly, those who play more frequently per week tend to start as less skilled players, but improve more rapidly, as shown by the 32–64 and >64 games per week groups (i.e., players who logged over 8 hours a week of multiplayer Team Slayer).

Breaks in Play

Another aspect to the play patterns of players is breaks. Players commonly took breaks of days, weeks, or months due to vacation, to play other games, real life distractions, or just temporary boredom with one game. Here we look at skill change preceding the break to understand why a player took a break, and skill changes in games when the player returns to understand how much skill is lost during a break and how long it takes to recover.

Skill Change Preceding Breaks

We hypothesized from some preliminary discussion with players that they are more likely to continue playing if they are winning, and stop playing after bad losses.

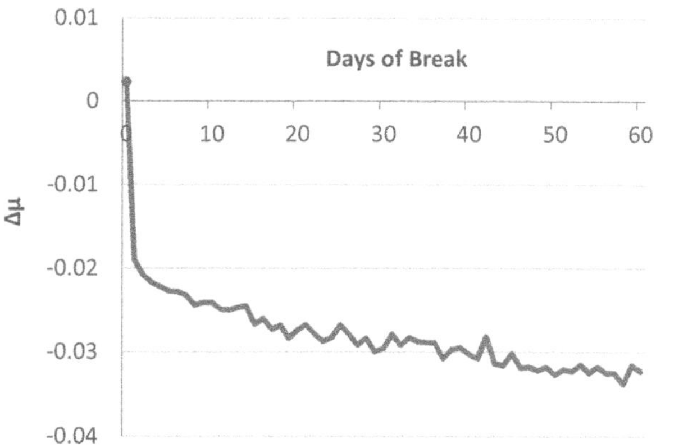

Figure 4. Skill change in the game preceding a break. When there is no break, skill change is barely positive, while breaks are correlated with a drop in skill (caused by a loss in the prior game).

Figure 4 shows evidence of a few behaviors that agree with our hypothesis. Skill gains correlate with no breaks (i.e., 0 day breaks), but only slightly; breaks of a day or more correlate with a decline in skill in the past game, which are caused by losses and longer breaks correlate more with larger skill drops in the past game (possibly losses against weaker opponents). This means players take breaks more often when they lose, which may be instances of frustration.

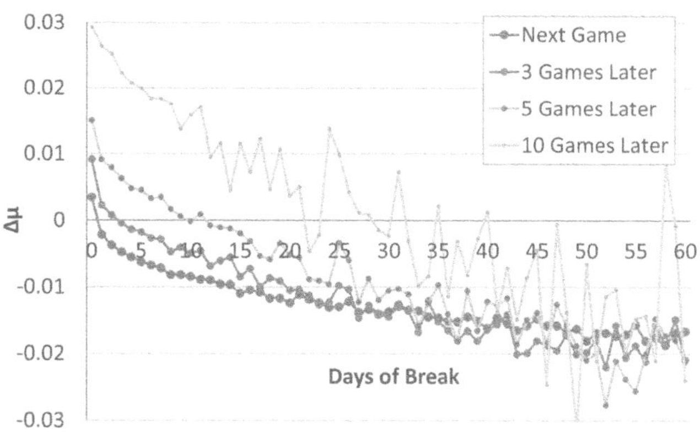

Figure 5. Skill change after different lengths of breaks for the next match, 3 matches after, 5 matches after, and 10 matches after. Larger drops in skill typically follow longer breaks, but players can catch back up quickly.

Skill Change Following Breaks

Figure 5 shows a few behaviors that players exhibit after breaks. The change in skill from before the break to after the break is illustrated by the 4 lines representing the next 1, 3, 5, and 10 matches after the break. When players are not taking breaks (breaks of 0 days), skill generally increases, evidenced by the climbing intercepts on the y-axis. Breaks of 1–2 days correlate with a small drop in skill in the next match played after the break, but has little long-term effect. Longer breaks correlate with larger skill decreases, but the relationship is not linear (60 day breaks do not seem to reduce skill twice as much as a 30 day break). More concretely, a 30 day break correlates with a skill drop of 10 matches of play (10 matches later, the skill returns to the value before the break ($\Delta\mu = 0$)); this is shown by the intersection of the 10 game later line with the x-axis. Thus, the amount of time required to regain skill following a 30 day break is only about 3 hours of gameplay.

Compared to retraining in sports, this catch-up time is short; this may be because there is little physical catch-up required. The player only has to refamiliarize themselves with the controls, and regain the mindset of their previous play.

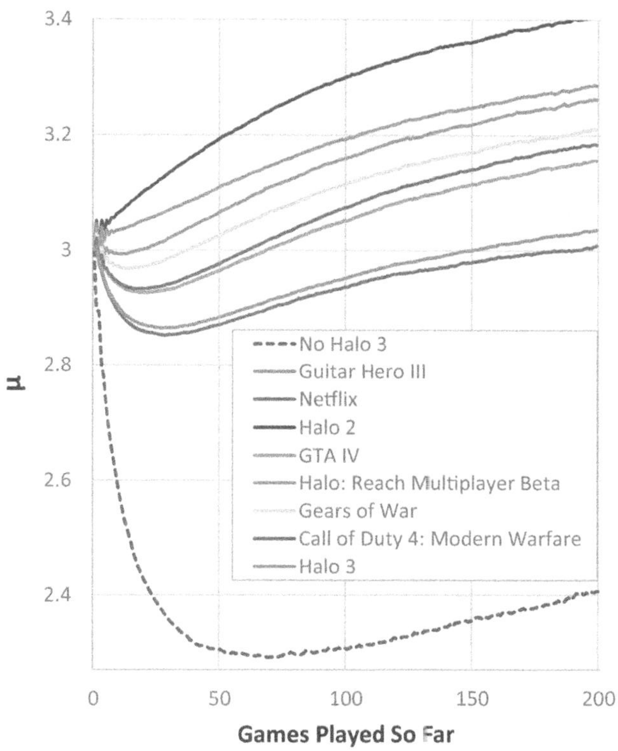

Figure 6. The performance of players who played other games *before* playing Halo Reach; these groups are not mutually exclusive so GTA IV players could also have played Halo 3.

Other Games Played Before Halo Reach

Figure 6 depicts the skill trajectories of players who played game titles before Halo Reach. The figure shows games that were popular among Halo Reach players on Xbox Live[2]. Players who did not play Halo 3 previously are less skilled but gain skill at about the same rate as everyone else. The title that correlates highest with skill is Halo 2 (even more so than Halo 3), but perhaps this is because those players have been engaged with the Halo

[2]The games did not include the original Halo (Halo 1) which was played on an older generation of Xbox Live servers.

franchise longer. Players who participated in the multi-player beta of Halo Reach also performed well. Surprisingly, other first-person shooters and even Guitar Hero III correlated with higher skill, and Netflix and Halo 3 had similar effects on skill. This seems to be due to a large proportion of players in our study cohort (the players who started playing in the first week of Halo Reach) being Halo 3 players. These observations suggest that the number of game titles played before has an effect on skill development as well and that effect may even be stronger than the skill transfer from individual titles.

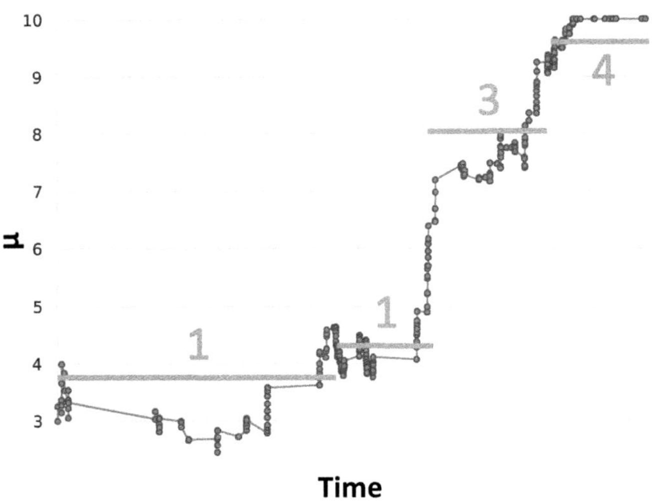

Figure 7. The skill plotted over time for an example individual player. The SAX representation is overlaid, creating the sequence "1134" indicating the player improved drastically in the second half of their matches, eventually becoming one of the best players.

Skill Change

While the median player's skill increases over time, this is not true for every player. We can classify different players' skill change over time and look into each group more closely. We converted the skill time-series into a symbolic representation of 4 levels and 4 time segments (4×4) using SAX (Symbolic Aggregate approXimation) [13]. SAX is a popular algorithm for discretizing time-series data. A player's skill over time is normalized, and divided into equal segments; each segment is then converted into a symbol depending on how much it deviates from the expected mean (Figure 7 shows an example). The segments used in our study were the four periods between the first game and the 100th game (to control for the same number of games per player). Applying SAX to the skill over gameplay data allowed us to aggregate the different patterns of skill change from multiple players.

Table 1 shows that the most common pattern in skill change was a slow steady increase in skill. The second most common pattern showed the opposite trend—a slow decline in skill in the first 100 games. Additionally, numerous other patterns were common, including sharp rises and drops in skills, and improvement followed by decline and vice versa. The most surprising finding is

Pattern	# Players	Total Games
	61791	217
	45814	252
	36320	257
	27290	219
	22759	216
	22452	253
	20659	260
	20633	222
	19858	247
	19292	216
	17573	219
	17454	245
	17389	260
	15670	215
	13692	236
	12516	239

Table 1. Skill change patterns (top 15 most common patterns) for players that played at least 100 games. The total games is the mean number of games played in the entire 7 month period that we have data.

that players who improved in the first 100 games actually ended up playing fewer total games in the entire 7 month period than players with declining skill. We believe two factors play a role in this effect: 1) players that improve are more aggressive and hardcore gamers, who switch to other games earlier; 2) a skill improvement is not obvious to the player, but they do notice themselves performing worse against (unknown to them) stronger opponents, and the additional challenge may cause additional stress and frustration, provoking them to quit.

MODELING SKILL AND TOTAL GAMES

The previous analyses provided descriptive insight into how particular factors in patterns of play affected skill. We wanted to consider the factors holistically, and together, see how well they could predict their 1) *final skill rating* μ and 2) *number of games played* at the end up the 7-month period. This would provide information about how strong each factor comparatively correlates with skill, and may tell us what players are likely to play more games later. This investigation is relevant to game developers who have business needs such as determining the longevity of a game title, what load a server should expect, or whether particular patterns of play give certain players advantages in learning the game. For example, a player who is likely to play fewer games in total and end up with a low TrueSkill rating may have become frustrated with the game at a particular point because they were not improving.

Model Factors and Evaluation

To build the model comprising multiple factors, we looked at the players' game histories. We used the explanatory power of different types of factors to identify which factors best explain the skill and total games of a player. A multiple linear regression computes an R^2 value measuring how much of the variance was explained by a particular combination of factors. An adjusted R^2 is reported in Table 2, which compensates for the number of terms in the model; the adjusted R^2 is a modified R^2 in which the value represents only the factors' improvement over the model that are better than chance.

We looked at four types of features: play intensity in the first 100 games, player demographics, skill change in the first 100 games, and other games played. For *player demographics*, there were four variables: country, age on the Halo Reach release date, how long they had been on Xbox Live, and the number of friends they had on Xbox Live. For *play intensity*, we looked at the number of days it took to reach 100 games, the standard deviation of the timestamps of the games played, and the number of games played per week. For *skill change*, we the player's first 100 matches, and extracted its 4×4 SAX representation as well as a 3×3 SAX representation of its last 30 matches. Finally, for *other games* played, we looked at whether they had played a prior version of Halo before, and whether they had played other first-person shooter titles before; however, most players did indeed have experience with both Halo and other first-person shooters which may have rendered this factor less effective.

Results

We noticed that the *final skill* for players was relatively predictable given knowledge of a player's discretized skill changes in their first 100 games. This leads us to believe that the most common patterns of steady improvement or decline in skill continue in a player's future games. However, demographics had little correlation with skill—it is difficult to predict how well a player performs from their age, country, number of friends, and join date on Xbox Live. These demographics did slightly improve the prediction over using just the SAX skill change factor, when combined with the skill change feature.

For explaining the *total number of games played*, the most important factor was the number of games played per week during the first 100 games. This seems obvious in retrospect since a player playing at a particular rate during the first 100 games is likely to continue at that rate and so it is possible to extrapolate how many games they will eventually play. Other factors of play intensity did little to improve the model once the games per week factor was incorporated, and other types of factors also had little effect. However, there was still a slight improvement to the model when all factors were combined, suggesting that the types of factors are relatively independent from one another.

MASTER BLASTERS

While we identified factors that correlated with performance, it is still unknown what leads to becoming highly skilled. A secondary objective we had is focusing on the subgroup of players who ended the 7-month period with

	Adjusted R^2	
	Final Skill	Total Matches
Demographics	0.050	0.008
Skill Change	0.470	0.005
Other Games	0.010	0.006
Play Intensity	0.009	0.453
Combined Model	0.490	0.471

Table 2. Explanatory power of skill for different groups of factors from our analysis. The Adjusted R^2 value measures the variability in the data that can be accounted for by the model.

the highest TrueSkill μ ratings. From the over 3 million players who began playing Halo Reach in its first week of release (a cohort which is a fairly large portion of overall players), we selected the top 100 players for individual analysis. We call these players "Master Blasters" for their mastery of the game.

Master Blasters possessed some unique characteristics:

- 85 Master Blasters used the DMR weapon to make the most kills. In fact, 40 of the 100 masters used the DMR, sniper rifle, and melee as the top 3 weapons.
- Many Master Blasters had kill/death ratios[3] of 1.6, representing 5 kills for every 3 deaths on average, and nearly all Master Blasters played other multiplayer game types.
- The acquisition of skill for each Master Blaster varied substantially. Several improved drastically after short breaks (Figure 7), unlike the typical player, and others immediately jumped to a high skill rating within a few weeks of play.

However, looking at the individual player records did not show direct evidence of why they became the best. They certainly played more games than average, performed better in the games, and used particular weapons, but this could be said for a hundred thousand other players. They did not differ from the general population in demographics either (in terms of country and friends), although Master Blasters were more likely to be 18–25 years old. The answer to what makes the best players in Halo Reach seems to be absent from the factors we studied; this question continues to elude us, and further investigation is needed.

SURVEY RESULTS

We wanted to present a comparative view to complement our data analysis with opinions from actual Halo Reach players. Thus, we contacted 300 participants who had opted-in to be contacted about their player experience by Microsoft via a survey. The participants had played at least one match of Team Slayer in Halo Reach. Having quantitative data and qualitative opinions via the survey cross-validates the perceptions of the actual players with the in-game data that is collected, providing valuable

[3]Kill/death ratios are a common way to compare players because the TrueSkill rating is hidden. A player must die for every kill, the average kill/death ratio is 1.

empirical strength of our data analysis results. Of the 300 people contacted, 70 people responded to the survey and answered at least one question; 65 people answered questions through to the end.

More than half the participants played the majority of their multiplayer games on the Team Slayer playlist (the game type used in this study). Nearly all participants also played other types of multiplayer game types. Half the participants reported playing fewer than 12 matches each week, while the other half played between 13 and 100 per week. 71% of the participants reported noticing a change in their skill during the period they played Halo Reach. Only 13% did not think their skill changed, while the rest were unsure.

Do you improve by playing with better players?

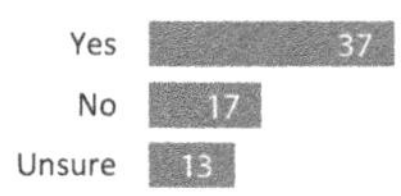

Do you improve by playing against better players?

Participants had diverse opinions about what contributed to improving their skill in Halo. 71% of participants believed they would improve faster by playing more games each week. They noted that familiarity with maps and weapons contributed substantially to their improvement. Additionally, many players noted that slowing down their game in terms of pacing their shots and thinking more during the match was an intentional act they did to improve their skill. Almost all participants thought they improved when playing with better players than themselves, and most (but fewer) thought they improved when playing against better players than themselves.

Emotional effects of playing Halo were frequently mentioned in the responses. Many participants reported feeling frustrated when they knew they could do better, particularly when their perceived skill declined from before. One participant remarked, "when I know I was supposed to be able to make that kill, or use that vehicle effectively, that generates a lot of disappointment."

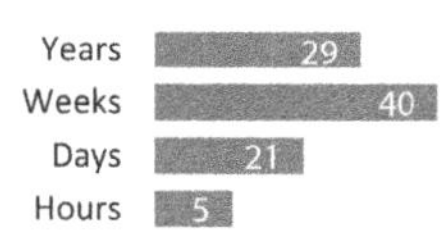

How long of a break will impact your skill?

Participants felt taking breaks hurt their skill once they returned to the game. One participant attributing this phenomenon to reaction time and loss of familiarity with the controls, "When I return after a prolonged absence my aim is less sharp and I play rubbish for a while which is obviously less fun. I sometimes get the added bonus of my creaky brain forgetting the buttons which is never fun either!" The most common response to how long of a break would be needed to impact their skill was several weeks of break. This matches our results from the data analysis where a several week break produced a noticeable decline in skill when the participants returned, although in the analyses we noticed a decline of skill in even a single day of absence. In terms of causes of breaks, one participant described a "string of bad games" would cause them to take breaks, agreeing with our analysis of the pre-break match.

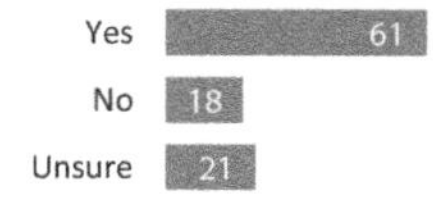

Would you consider buying other games that may improve your skill?

Participant opinion was split on whether they thought other games influenced their skill in Halo. Some participants thought they became worse in Halo by playing other first-person shooters because those other first-person shooters required different techniques, but an almost equal number thought other FPSes helped them improve hand-eye coordination (and other "FPS skills"). However, most participants reported that they would consider buying other game titles if they thought playing those games would improve their skill in Halo.

The most common reasons participants stopped playing was due to boredom and other life issues (family, etc.). Rarely did it have to do with skill; in fact, most participants said they would not stop playing even if they were not improving, which agreed with our data (declining skill did not negatively influence the total number of games the players played).

Overall, the survey responses agreed with the in-game data analysis. Participants felt they were keenly aware of their skill, and it was an important determinant of how much they played, their enjoyment, and their in-game behavior.

DISCUSSION

Learning and Expertise

After analyses of the different factors and looking individually at the Master Blasters, what have we learned about skill? Certainly, the concept of skill varies for every task, as telegraphy or sports training is a very different activity than blasting enemies on a screen. Some factors we examined span multiple activities: frequency of performing the activity correlate with higher performance up to a point and a catch-up period follows long breaks. But among the top 100 players, skill is acquired differently: some are long-time players of the Halo franchise while others started with Halo Reach; some players gain skill rapidly the moment they start playing, and others reach a plateau and only become the best after a break. Our model shows that skill can be measured and quantified, but even when putting together numerous factors, our explanations (represented by adjusted R^2) can only go half-way.

Handling the Effect of Time on Skill

What might game designers do to deal with the effects of play patterns on skill? One direct approach is to incorporate patterns of play directly into the TrueSkill rating system. For example, some rating systems reduce a player's skill rating during periods of inactivity, which also eliminates players who "camp" high ratings they may be undeserved. One participant acknowledged the decline in skill following a break, and the frustration of being expected to perform at their pre-break level, "Because the matchmaking system still thinks I am at level xx, so I should be matched against level xx players - even though I am rusty and need a few games to get back into the groove. This results in team mates just being overall d-bags and talking crap because you have a bad game since you havent played in a while." By changing a player's TrueSkill depending on when their most recent activity took place, the rating system can bias TrueSkill towards players who have played recently. Prior game data can be used to deduce the amount of reduction in TrueSkill that would accurately reflect their probability of winning after breaks.

The game can also take a proactive approach to informing the player. During periods of inactivity, a game system can remind the player that their skill may be declining and by returning to the game sooner rather than later, the player will stem the loss of skill. Another proactive task the system can perform is looking at players' skill change over time, represented by the SAX patterns previously. For players who are not predicted to improve on their own, the system may gently provide tips; most participants (78%) responded positively to receiving practical tips to improve their play.

Hidden Truths about Skill

One design consideration in multiplayer games is whether to show the user their skill rating. The designers of Halo switched between showing the TrueSkill in Halo 3, to replacing it with an experience score that only goes up in Halo Reach. Many survey responses noted the displeasure in losing skill, and the frustration caused by seeing a lowered rating may be a bad experience for competitive players. However, players remarked enjoying seeing their skill increase, which gave them a feeling of satisfaction. The lack of a public skill rating prevents the game from providing positive feedback to the player, who may then become frustrated when they feel like they're not improving when in fact they are simply being matched against stronger opponents.

In cases where the game designers decide not to reveal a player rating, perhaps there may be some benefit to unevenly balanced matches. When a player has improved their skill, rather than pitting them against tougher opponents who may make them feel more frustrated, the players could be matched against the same caliber of opponents before their increase in skill, i.e., slightly weaker opponents. This allows the improving player to enjoy the spoils of expertise for a bit. Another manipulation is when the game notices players declining in skill, the game may want to stop them before they reach a "pain point", where they may become so frustrated with the game they may give it up permanently. This is more useful when the skill ratings are public, as the large drop in skill may leave the player feeling helpless and unable to recover. The hiding of information from the players for their own benefit relates to Cheung and Huang's suggestion that the decision about what information to reveal to stakeholders in a game can have substantial implications for how much the stakeholders enjoy the game (in their case, revealing game information and events to spectators of the game StarCraft) [3]. These questions of hiding and showing skill information and their affect on player emotions are promising areas of further investigation.

Limitations

One common limitation of post-hoc data analysis is the inability to claim causation effects since the game variables unavailable for manipulation to create a controlled experiment. When two variables such as gameplay intensity and skill are correlated, it cannot be determined whether increased gameplay intensity caused an increase in skill or whether some external factor caused both factors to increase; for example, this external factor may be that those players who play more frequently are naturally capable of gaining expertise quicker. The third possibility, that an increase in skill causes more gameplay intensity is also possible, but is unlikely in our study since the player's TrueSkill is not shown to the player. Regardless, we caution claiming that particular factors will cause an increase in skill, but rather our findings describe the nature of players who have higher skill.

TrueSkill starts with an initial prior, and it also takes some time to adjust to a new skill rating. The lag may result in an inaccurate rating in the beginning (due to the prior) or if a player's skill changes substantially. We observed the median TrueSkill decreases from the starting value $\mu = 3$ initially probably because a player's actually skill is lower than that, and it's not until about 30–35 games later that the TrueSkill μ rises again.

User-reported data from 300 players when they signed up for the opt-in player experience panel showed that 18 of them (6%) reported sharing their Xbox live account with other people. When those sharing an account play the same game, and particularly the same playlist in Halo Reach, their different skills will confuse the TrueSkill rating system. The better player may raise the skill rating when they are playing, while the worse player will tend to lower the skill rating, causing it to be highly variable. Thus, during matchmaking, the TrueSkill μ may not accurately reflect the skill of the current player. Additionally, Xbox Live accounts can be handed off to another person, resulting in a similar inaccurate reflection of skill in the TrueSkill rating; it would take a number of games for the rating to readjust to the new player's skill.

Our study did not incorporate the TrueSkill rating from playlists other than Team Slayer. While Team Slayer is the most popular multiplayer variant, players may be learning relevant skills for Team Slayer from similar variants or playlists (for example, by gaining familiarity with maps or weapons in both playlists). Because the TrueSkill ratings are independent from playlist to playlist, TrueSkill does not capture this learning effect either. Players who are playing a variety of multiplayer game types to be technically improving their skill faster than what the TrueSkill system knows from their matches on Team Slayer.

Players may drop out of games due to connection issues, to avoid losing, or because they have to do something else. Halo penalizes those players by marking a drop-out as a loss, even when the team the player was on wins the game. Additionally, players who drop out frequently may be matched up with others who do the same, and eventually the players will be banned from playing online if they drop out too frequently. These drop-outs may affect the assigned TrueSkill ratings for a player, whether deservedly or not.

CONCLUSION

Our study reported numerous findings relating gamers' patterns of play with their skill as computed by the TrueSkill rating system. Through the large data available, we were able to conduct detailed controlled analyses of how particular factors correlated with skill in Halo Reach's Team Slayer playlist. Our primary findings show that play intensity, breaks, and skill changes in early matches may affect the skill level of the player. The factors put together have a moderate ability to explain the variation in skill between players. We supplemented the data analysis with a survey that included open-ended questions; this provided insight into what players themselves felt were determinants of skill.

Overall, we believe our contribution informs the exploration of skill and expertise in a novel domain—video games. Large scale studies where people are highly motivated and meticulously measured are difficult to conduct in real world settings. Our findings participate in the conversation of expertise and learning behavior common in domains such as sports training and education. Additionally, leveraging in-game data can help game designers create better experiences for players, increasing their enjoyment and eliminating frustrating scenarios.

ACKNOWLEDGMENTS

The authors thank Thore Graepel and Tim Menzies for advice during early stages of the work, Coco Inoue for assistance in providing data and continual feedback, and Tom Ball, Venkatesh-Prasad Ranganath, Ramarathnam Venkatesan, and Ben Zorn for feedback during the study. We also thank the Halo Reach players who participated in our survey. Jeff Huang performed this work during a summer internship at Microsoft Research.

REFERENCES

1. Bryan, W. L., and Harter, N. Studies in the physiology and psychology of the telegraphic language. *Psychological Review 4*, 1 (1897), 27–53.
2. Bryan, W. L., and Harter, N. Studies on the telegraphic language: The acquisition of a hierarchy of habits. *Psychological Review 6*, 4 (1899), 345–375.
3. Cheung, G., and Huang, J. Starcraft from the stands: understanding the game spectator. In *Proc. of CHI* (2011), 763–772.
4. Dangauthier, P., Herbrich, R., Minka, T., and Graepel, T. Trueskill through time: Revisiting the history of chess. In *Proc. of NIPS* (2007), 337–344.
5. d_ijk_stra. Statistical bonjwa theory: the history of bw. Retrieved August 1, 2012 from `http://www.teamliquid.net/forum/viewmessage.php?topic_id=357124` .
6. Elo, A. E. *The rating of chessplayers, past and present.* Batsford, 1978.
7. Harrison, B., and Roberts, D. L. Using sequential observations to model and predict player behavior. In *Proc. of FDG* (2011), 91–98.
8. Herbrich, R., Minka, T., and Graepel, T. Trueskill™: A bayesian skill rating system. In *Proc. of NIPS* (2006), 569–576.
9. Hock-koon, S. Affordances of elliptical learning in arcade video games. In *Proc. of DiGRA Nordic* (2012).
10. Hullett, K., Nagappan, N., Schuh, E., and Hopson, J. Empirical analysis of user data in game software development. In *Proc. of ESEM* (2012), 89–98.
11. Keller, F. The phantom plateau. *Journal of the Experimental Analysis of Behavior 1*, 1 (1958), 1–13.
12. Lee, M. J., and Ko, A. J. Personifying programming tool feedback improves novice programmers' learning. In *Proc. of ICER* (2011), 109–116.
13. Lin, J., Keogh, E., Lonardi, S., and Chiu, B. A symbolic representation of time series, with implications for streaming algorithms. In *Proc. of SIGMOD Workshop on Research issues in data mining and knowledge* (2003), 2–11.
14. Mason, W., and Clauset, A. Friends ftw! friendship and competition in halo: Reach. In *Proc. of CSCW* (2013).
15. Reeves, S., Brown, B., and Laurier, E. Experts at play understanding skilled expertise. *Games and Culture 4*, 3 (2009), 205–227.
16. Staron, R. S., Leonardi, M. J., Karapondo, D. L., Malicky, E. S., Falkel, J. E., Hagerman, F. C., and Hikida, R. S. Strength and skeletal muscle adaptations in heavy-resistance-trained women after detraining and retraining. *Journal of Applied Physiology 70*, 2 (1991), 631–640.
17. Wallner, G., and Kriglstein, S. A spatiotemporal visualization approach for the analysis of gameplay data. In *Proc. of CHI* (2012), 1115–1124.
18. White, R. W., Dumais, S. T., and Teevan, J. Characterizing the influence of domain expertise on web search behavior. In *Proc. of WSDM* (2009), 132–141.
19. Xu, Y., Cao, X., Sellen, A., Herbrich, R., and Graepel, T. Sociable killers: understanding social relationships in an online first-person shooter game. In *Proc. of CSCW* (2011), 197–206.

Villains, Architects and Micro-Managers: What Tabula Rasa Teaches Us About Game Orchestration

T.C. Nicholas Graham[1], Irina Schumann[1,2], Mrunal Patel[1], Quentin Bellay[1], Raimund Dachselt[3]
[1]School of Computing, Queen's University, Kingston, ON, Canada
[2]Faculty of Computer Science, University of Magdeburg, Magdeburg, Germany
[3]Interactive Media Lab, Technische Universität Dresden, 01062 Dresden, Germany
{graham, mrunal}@cs.queensu.ca, schumannirina@aol.com, dachselt@acm.org

ABSTRACT
Players of digital games are limited by the constraints of the game's implementation. Players cannot fly a kite, plant a tree or make friends with a dragon if these activities were not coded within the game. Game orchestration relaxes these restrictions by allowing players to create game narratives and settings as the game is being played. This enables players to express their creativity beyond the strictures of the game's implementation. We present Tabula Rasa, a novel game orchestration tool based on an efficient tabletop interface. Based on a study of 20 game orchestration sessions using Tabula Rasa, we identify five behavioural patterns adopted by orchestrators, and four styles of collaborative interaction between orchestrators and players. Finally, we present recommendations for designers of game orchestration systems.

Author Keywords
Game orchestration, game design, tabletop gaming.

ACM Classification Keywords
H.5.3. Collaborative computing.

INTRODUCTION
In many traditional forms of gameplay, design is intermingled with play. Children create games on the fly, establishing the rules as they play [3]. Groups adapt games via house rules and handicaps [14]. In roleplaying games such as Dungeons and Dragons, a game master creates the game narrative for players through an interactive process of describing what the players see and responding to the players' actions [18]. In short, players feel free to invent and modify games as they play them.

In contrast, most digital games separate design and play. Developers ship games as static products. The creativity and flexibility of traditional games, where players fluidly switch between design and play, is simply not supported.

In this paper, we explore *game orchestration,* where a special class of player, the game orchestrator, is given the power to create and modify a digital game world at the same time as others are playing. We show how game orchestration enables creativity in gameplay, by supporting a real-time dialogue between designer and player.

Figure 1: Tabula Rasa: a player (right) engages in a game created in real-time by an orchestrator (left)

To illustrate these concepts, we present Tabula Rasa, a tool for game orchestration (shown in Figure 1). Orchestrators use a digital tabletop to manipulate the game world in real time, using finger painting-like interactions. Orchestrators can change the game to adjust difficulty in response to players' frustration or boredom, and can create new parts of the world for players to explore. In sum, Tabula Rasa brings design-like activities to the runtime of digital games.

We have used Tabula Rasa to study how people use the ability to manipulate players' experiences at runtime. We were interested in questions such as: do orchestrators work quietly in the background, silently manipulating experiences, or do they verbally interact with players? Do orchestrators directly help players, or do they create situations and leave the players to succeed or fail on their own? Do orchestrators view themselves as collaborators, or as antagonists? In fact, we saw all of these behaviours and more, including the "helicopter parent" who rescues the player at the first hint of challenge, the "villain", who enjoys tormenting the player, and the "architect", who creates interesting locales for the player to discover.

The paper makes the following contributions: We show how game orchestration represents a new form of collaborative gameplay. We provide a comprehensive study of how people orchestrate games, in which we identify five behavioural patterns that orchestrators adopt, and four interaction styles within groups of orchestrators and players. Finally, we provide advice to designers of game orchestration systems.

BACKGROUND

"Orchestration" is the act of arranging or directing, often surreptitiously, to produce a desired effect [9]. The term *game orchestration* is therefore used to describe the creation and guiding of experiences for players as a game is being played [2, 7]. The notion of orchestrating games has existed in various forms over many years. Mulcaster described in 1581 the role of a referee in the game of "footeball" as a person who enforces rules and standards of play [6]. Since the mid 1970s, "game masters" or "dungeon masters" have been a critical component of pen-and-paper role-playing games such as Dungeons and Dragons [18]. A game master engages in a conversation with players, describing what the players see, playing the role of people that players encounter, and adjudicating combat. Thychsen et al. describe the role of the game master as maintaining the narrative flow of the game, enforcing rules, engaging the players, and managing the fictional environment [18].

More recently, game orchestration has been used in digital settings. Salovaara et al. provide a series of case studies of orchestration in digital games, identifying a range of roles including moderators, game masters, and people enabling infrastructure behind the scenes [15]. Crabtree et al. introduce the term "game orchestration" to describe the activities of operators of a mobile game based on SMS communication [2]. These operators interpret players' messages, tailor interaction with the player, pace the narrative flow, and guide players to effectively collaborate. Thus orchestrators work "behind the scenes", guiding players' experience. Neustaedter et al. use the term orchestration to describe the ongoing process of managing geocaching games [7]. Orchestrators engage in monitoring caches, players and non-players to ensure the game's smooth operation. As we see from these examples, game orchestration involves runtime manipulation of the game to guide the players' experience. We term the person carrying out these orchestration activities a "game orchestrator". (Note that this usage is unrelated to the body of literature on web service orchestration [11].) More concretely, we identify four ways in which games may be orchestrated:

Orchestrator as game master: This approach attempts to bring the experience of pen-and-paper roleplaying games (such as Dungeons and Dragons) to the digital world. Players gather around a digital table, which portrays maps and tokens for players in the game. A game master guides the story. The intimate feel of traditional roleplaying is preserved by the colocation of players around a table. Examples include TViews [5] and Wizard's Apprentice [9]. Game masters can be seen as a special kind of player, directing the game for their own enjoyment as well as that of the players. In Wizard's Apprentice, players can dynamically shift between orchestrator ("wizard") and player ("apprentice") roles.

Orchestrator as stage manager: Here, the orchestrator acts behind the scenes, manipulating the players' experience without their knowledge. Examples include the performers in the Desert Rain mixed reality performance [4] and Crabtree's "Day of the Figurines" described earlier [2]. Unlike the "orchestrator as game manager" approach described above, stage managers are hidden from the players, and roles are fixed – participants do not migrate between the player and stage manager roles.

Orchestrator as game designer: Orchestration can help in the game design process by allowing rapid sketching of game ideas before they are implemented in code [1]. An orchestrator uses a special interface to manipulate terrain and non-player characters, allowing design concepts to be quickly tested without the cost of implementing them. In the Raptor system, orchestrators use a digital tabletop surface to rapidly manipulate game content for players seated at a traditional PC and game controller [16].

Purposeful orchestration: Here, the orchestrator's goal is to create an experience that is helpful to its players. For example, in SIDES, an orchestrator guides the gameplay to provide therapeutic benefit to children with Asperger's syndrome [12]. In simulation-based training for military officers, orchestrators guide a training exercise behind the scenes, using a digital simulation environment to enact the role of personnel in the field [13].

A number of commercial digital games use orchestration techniques. Bioware's Neverwinter Nights provides a Dungeon Master interface, implementing a simple version of Dungeons and Dragons over the internet. Super Mario Brothers U for Nintendo's Wii U console features a limited version of orchestration, where one player using a touch tablet interface can help another player by modifying the world that she is traversing.

We distinguish game orchestration from the limited ability some games provide to players to modify the game world while playing. For example, in EA's Ultima Online, players can construct houses that others can visit, and in CCP's Eve Online, players can create missions for other players to carry out. In general, game mechanisms allowing players to direct the experience of other players differ over three axes:

Goal: In true orchestration, the goal is to create interesting experiences for the player. In contrast, for example, in Unknown Worlds' Natural Selection game, a "Commander" uses a special interface to provide move and attack orders to other players. For the Commander, the goal is to collaboratively win the game, and the players' enjoyment is incidental.

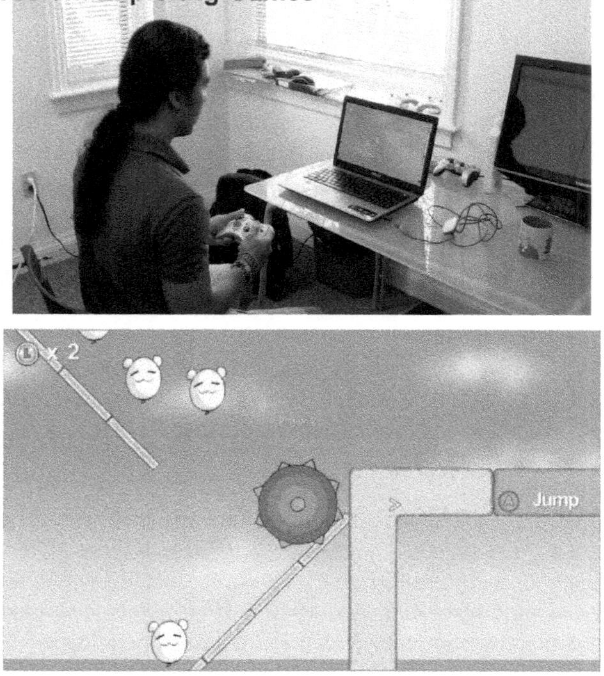

Figure 2: Player's view of Tabula Rasa. The player traverses a maze of platforms and ramps and collects balloons.

Interface: Orchestration systems typically provide a custom interface for orchestrators, as opposed to, for example, Ultima Online, where all players use the same interface.

Time: Although preparation may be performed in advance, orchestration is ultimately a play-time activity, as opposed to, for example, creating a modification ("mod") for the Half-Life 2 game for players to enjoy at a later time.

Despite that fact that game orchestration has been found useful and exciting in a number of contexts, there has been little study of how players use such a facility if available. This paper helps toward answering these questions.

TABULA RASA

To illustrate the concept of game orchestration, we created the Tabula Rasa game orchestration tool. The name comes from the Latin for "clean slate", indicating that the game can be arbitrarily created, modified and guided at runtime. Tabula Rasa takes place in a simple two-dimensional world where players use a standard Xbox 360 game controller to run, jump, pick up and use items (Figure 2). Tabula Rasa best supports action-based platform and puzzle games. Orchestration uses natural interaction, with a finger-painting style of interface for manipulating the game world. Tabula Rasa was implemented in C# using the Meerkat and XNA game development frameworks.

Game orchestrators guide the player's experience by creating and modifying the virtual world, adding or removing platforms and placing treasure in the world. An orchestrator uses a digital tabletop to rapidly create and modify terrain (Figure 1). Game players themselves do not use a tabletop, but play on a normal PC.

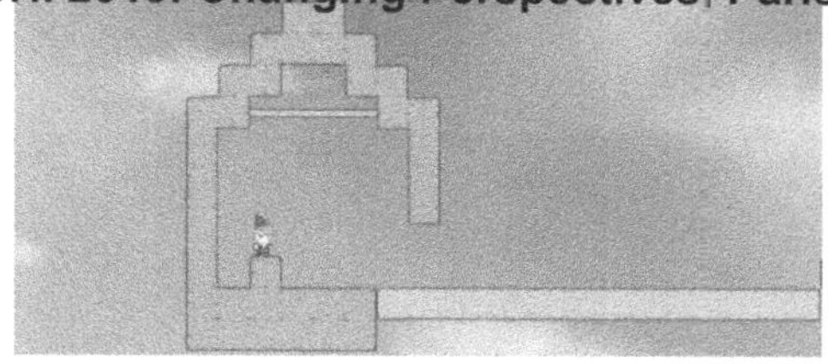

Figure 3: An orchestrator has created a simple house for a "wise old man"

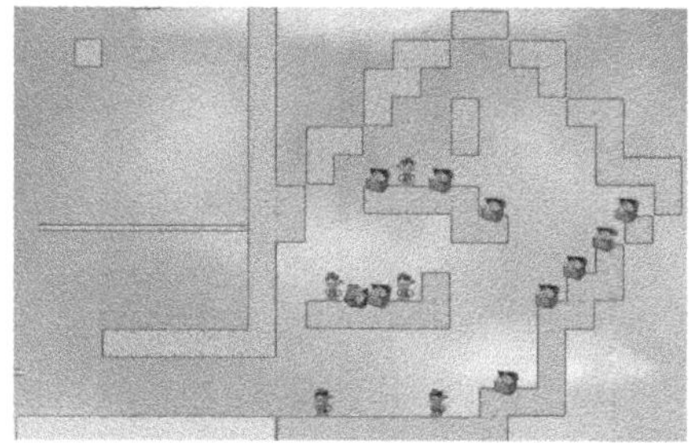

Figure 4: A treasure cave is heavily guarded by bandits

Player's Perspective

Figure 2 shows Tabula Rasa from a player's perspective. The player controls a spiky ball. A joystick on an Xbox 360 controller is used to move left and right. Pressing and holding the controller's "A" button causes the ball to jump. The player traverses a maze of ramps, platforms and jumping pads. Along the way, s/he can collect balloons for points. The challenge for the player is to find a way of traversing the complete level while collecting all balloons.

Orchestrator's Perspective

The orchestrator has a separate user interface dedicated to manipulating the game world itself. The orchestrator does not play the game, but modifies the game at runtime to enhance the player's experience. Specifically, the orchestrator can add and remove ramps, terrain blocks, balloons and non-player characters. If the modifications are in the player's field of view, the player sees them in real-time. The orchestrator may choose to make modifications off-screen to preserve the player's sense of immersion. By modifying the game world, the orchestrator can help the player past obstacles that are proving too difficult and can add completely new parts to the maze.

Figures 3 and 4 show examples of what an orchestrator can create using Tabula Rasa. Terrain blocks have been placed to create interesting structures. In Figure 3, a "wise old man" is located in a crudely drawn house. Figure 4 shows a cave containing bandits and treasure chests.

Orchestration Interface

The key to successful game orchestration is the provision of an interface allowing rapid creation and modification of the game world. If the player suffers lengthy waits while the orchestrator catches up, the illusion of the game can be broken. To support rapid orchestration, Tabula Rasa keeps the game world simple, so that it is easier to modify. As

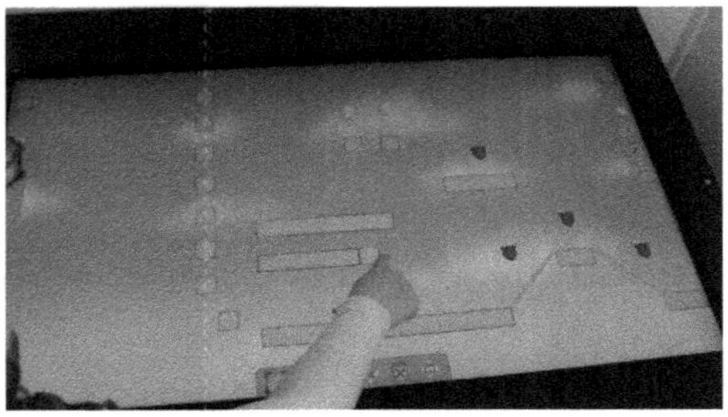

Figure 5: Finger-painting terrain

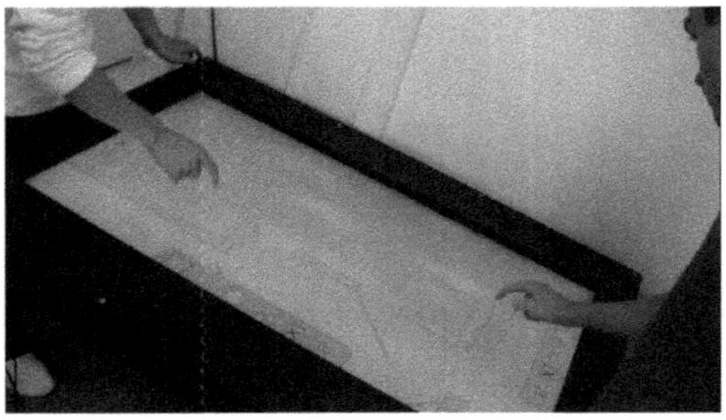

Figure 6: Two orchestrators working at the same time

shown in the earlier examples, the world is two-dimensional, based on a set of simple, pre-defined blocks. The orchestration tool is based on a finger-painting metaphor using a multi-touch digital tabletop. The orchestrator selects a drawing tool from a palette and drags her finger over the tabletop to create new terrain (Figure 5). The palette uses a set of drop-down menus to allow rapid selection of tools. Three palettes are arranged around the table, allowing groups of orchestrators to work together (Figure 6).

In addition to terrain, orchestrators can add objects to the world (e.g., a chest of gold), and non-player characters (NPCs). The world obeys standard physics, meaning that an object will fall to the floor when placed. This reduces the need for precise placement. NPCs can be moved by dragging out a path that the NPC will follow, allowing the orchestrator to quickly add life to a scene.

The use of a digital tabletop surface affords natural manipulation of the game scene. Orchestrators reported this interface to be enjoyable and intuitive, and to afford rapid manipulation of the game world.

This interface supports the forms of orchestration identified earlier. Orchestrators can act as "game masters", communicating with players while modifying the world, and dynamically changing between player and orchestrator roles by changing who is using the table. Or orchestrators can act as "stage managers", restricting players from seeing the table or actions they carry out. An orchestrator can restrict her actions to parts of the world that the player cannot see in order to reduce the players' awareness that the game is orchestrated. Orchestration can be collaboratively used by "game designers", where orchestrators and players sketch interesting play experiences that can later be coded into a standalone game. Because of this flexibility, Tabula Rasa makes an interesting platform for exploring how people use an orchestration system.

STUDY: GAME ORCHESTRATION WITH TABULA RASA

We used Tabula Rasa to explore how people play a game where orchestration is possible. We conducted an observational study to answer the following questions: How do players and orchestrators behave? What kinds of gameplay emerge? Can game orchestration be a fun experience for both orchestrator and player?

Equipment

The orchestrator used a 46" multi-touch display based on a PQ Labs G4 sensor. The display was mounted in a 30" high table, allowing comfortable use while seated or standing. The display resolution was 1920 x 1080 pixels. The player used a laptop computer with a 17" display operating at 1920 x 1080 pixels, and an Xbox 360 wireless game controller to control the game avatar.

The game world was partially populated with platforms, ramps and bouncing blocks. Large sections of the world were left empty. To give the game a goal, balloons were provided that, when popped, increased the player's score.

The player and orchestrator were in the same room. They were physically close enough to converse comfortably, but could not see the other's display. Two video cameras were used, recording the player and the orchestrator.

Recruiting

We recruited ten pairs of participants from the university community. Participants ranged from 18 to 40 years old, with a mean age of 25. Seven participants were female and 13 male. All 20 participants reported that they use a computer for at least two hours per day. All participants reported having played games on a multi-touch device.

Method

At the beginning of the session, the participants were read a letter of information describing the study, signed a consent form, and completed a demographic questionnaire. The concept of game orchestration was explained, and participants were introduced to the digital tabletop. The orchestration interface was demonstrated, and players were permitted to experiment with it until they were comfortable with its functionality.

One participant was randomly chosen to take on the orchestrator role, and the other acted as player. The participants were instructed to play for ten minutes. The only direction provided was that the orchestrator should create a fun experience for the player. Once the ten minutes had elapsed, participants completed a custom questionnaire reporting their experience. The participants then changed roles, and repeated the play session.

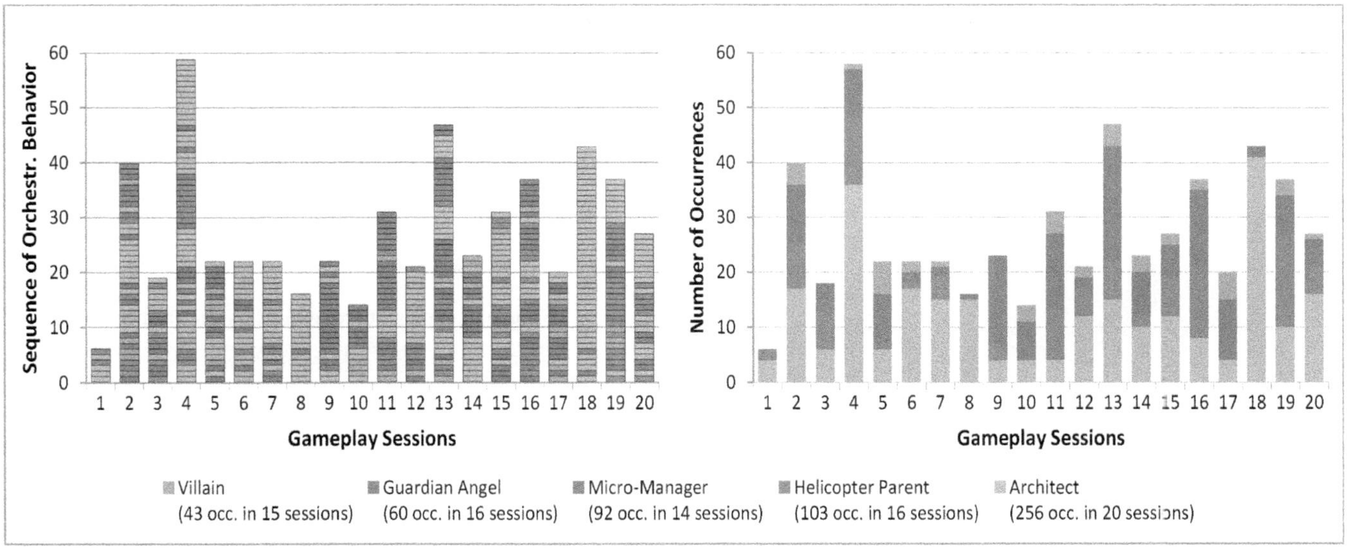

Figure 7: Types and distributions of orchestrator behaviours over all 20 sessions

Finally, a semi-structured interview was conducted to address interesting situations observed during the game.

Analysis

We used an open coding process [17] to identify behaviours and events of interest during the orchestration sessions. The videos for all 10 sessions were analyzed by two coders. Because participants acted as both player and orchestrator for 10 minutes each, there were 20 videos, for a total of 200 minutes. The player and orchestrator videos were viewed side by side to make it easy to see the interplay between the two participants, e.g., to see how a player reacted to an orchestrator's actions. Two meetings were held to review and adjust the list of codes and to resolve disagreements between the two coders. The codes were grouped into three categories: communication, orchestrator actions and player actions. For example, codes were identified which captured when an orchestrator built an area of the world that the player currently could not see, when an orchestrator modified the terrain to directly help a player, and when the orchestrator and player talked with each other. 25 codes were identified, and a total of 1,282 codes were assigned over the 200 minutes of video analyzed.

Groups of codes were identified as markers for interesting orchestrator behaviours and interesting styles of interaction between orchestrators and players. Each occurrence of an interesting behaviour or style was hand-verified by re-examining the videos.

RESULTS

The interviews and questionnaires showed that most orchestrators and players enjoyed their experience. From analysis of the videos, we identified five behavioural patterns that orchestrators adopt, and four styles of interaction between orchestrators and players.

Participant Experience

During the interview, orchestrators were asked whether they succeeded in creating a fun experience for the player. All 20 answered in the affirmative, indicating that orchestrators believed that Tabula Rasa allowed them to achieve the core goal of game orchestration. Participants' comments were highly positive, saying for example "I really enjoyed it" and "I love it". All 20 participants agreed that "It was easy to use the orchestration tool."

Impressions about the player role were positive, but not unanimously so. 18/20 participants agreed with the statement "I enjoyed playing the game while it was orchestrated" (responding 5 or higher on a 7-point Likert scale), and 10/20 strongly agreed with this statement (score of 7 on the 7-point scale). 19/20 agreed that "I would like to play games again that are manipulated by an orchestrator". This implies that most players found this an enjoyable experience, but that a minority did not. One of the two players reporting a negative experience complained that there were no concrete goals, and that the orchestrator's intervention removed any sense of challenge: "You have an infinite amount of coins. You have no goals. Talking with the orchestrator you can get anything you want, design everything that you want. There are no goals or anything to attain."

Orchestrators did not attempt to disguise their actions; all 20 participants agreed with the statement "The changes to the game by the orchestrator were very noticeable." Players largely appreciated the orchestrator's interventions, with 19 of 20 agreeing that "I liked that the orchestrator was there to help with difficult situations." However, a small minority (2/20) agreed that "I was annoyed because of the changes that were made by the orchestrator."

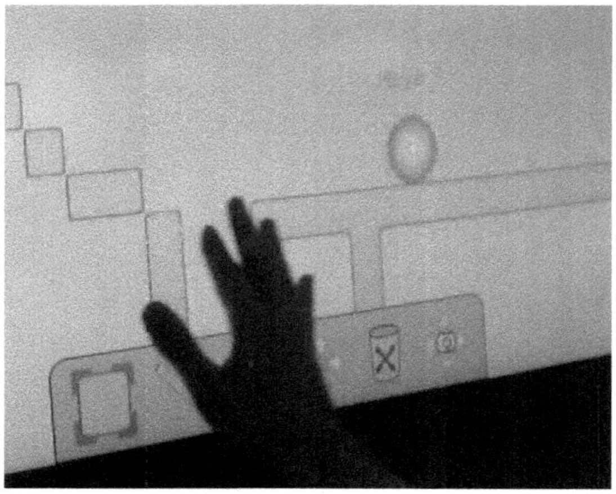

Figure 8: Helicopter Parenting: the orchestrator is closing off a pit before the player falls into it

Orchestrator Behavioural Patterns

During a session, orchestrators moved between a set of five behavioural patterns. These included the "helicopter parent", buzzing around the player to ensure he could make no errors, the "guardian angel" who kept the player out of trouble, the "architect", who worked independently of the player to create new and interesting terrains, the "micro-manager", who enforced his will at ever step, and the "villain", who aimed to spoil the player's fun. Each pattern was used by at least six orchestrators and was seen dozens of times over all sessions. Figure 7 summarizes the patterns that were seen in each of the 20 sessions. The left part of the figure shows the progression from one behaviour to the next, showing how frequently orchestrators changed their behaviour. The right part summarizes the number of occurrences of each behaviour.

Helicopter parent: This pattern involved "hovering" around players like a helicopter, ensuring that the player was never challenged by difficulties. If the player encountered a jump that required careful timing, the helicopter parent would quickly insert a ramp. If the player became stuck on complex terrain, the helicopter parent would immediately smooth the terrain to allow easy passage. We defined a helicopter parent as an orchestrator who would not permit players to ever fail, or even to experience the frustration of a challenge that needed to be resolved. An example of helicopter parenting is shown in Figure 8.

Helicopter parenting was observed frequently, with 16 of 20 orchestrators exhibiting this behaviour at some point in their session. For three of 20 orchestrators, this style dominated play, with more than ten instances observed throughout the ten-minute session.

Players' comments were mixed regarding helicopter parenting. Players described positively that this style of orchestration "makes it easier" and is "helpful" and that the orchestrator's intervention meant they "get to collect more points". Another complained that orchestration made the game "too easy".

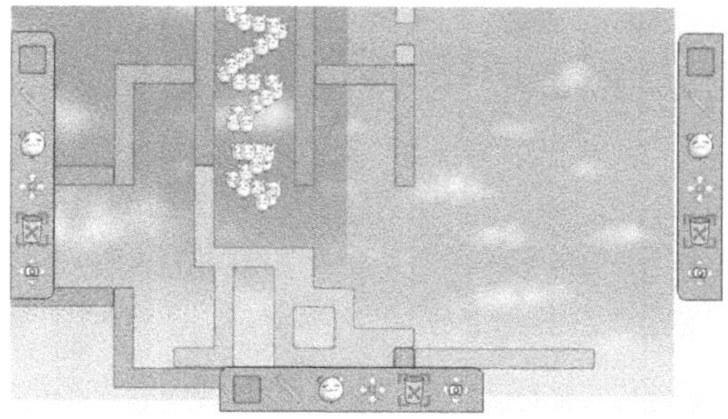

Figure 9: Pipe structure built by an architect

Figure 10: Arch-like structure built by an architect

Guardian angel: This type of orchestrator helped players when they encountered difficulty, but unlike the helicopter parent, permitted the player to struggle before intervening. In some cases, the guardian angel waited until the player clearly could not proceed; in others, the angel acted following a verbal request for help from the player.

In one example, a player fell into an impossibly deep pit. The guardian angel permitted the player to try several times to exit the pit, and only when it became clear that it was not possible to jump out did the orchestrator provide a ramp.

Guardian angel behaviour was frequently observed, with 16 of 20 orchestrators taking on this role at some point during their session.

Players' comments on the role of the guardian angel were positive, including that "it is nice to get help to reach places" and "it's nice to get help when you are stuck". One player commented that orchestration is "different from a computer manipulating the game; a person is more kind."

Architect: The architect operates in a part of the world that the player cannot see, creating interesting structures for the player to find and explore. Examples created by architects include a vertical pipe with bouncy walls filled with balloons (Figure 9) and a balloon arch (Figure 10). The architect pattern was seen in all 20 sessions. It was the most frequently adopted pattern, seen 256 times in total.

Architects operate surreptitiously, out of the player's view. This helps to provide the illusion that the world is static, not being modified under the player's feet.

Architects may suffer time pressure, as they need to complete their creations before the player arrives and starts interacting with them. Architects largely did not experience

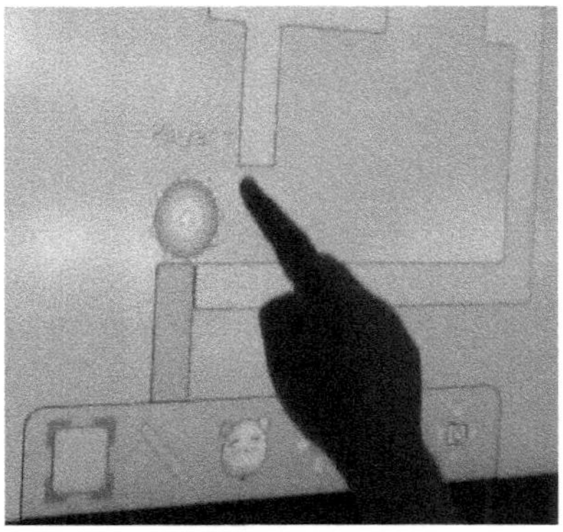

Figure 11: Micro-managing orchestrator draws a wall blocking the player's path, forcing her to go in the other direction

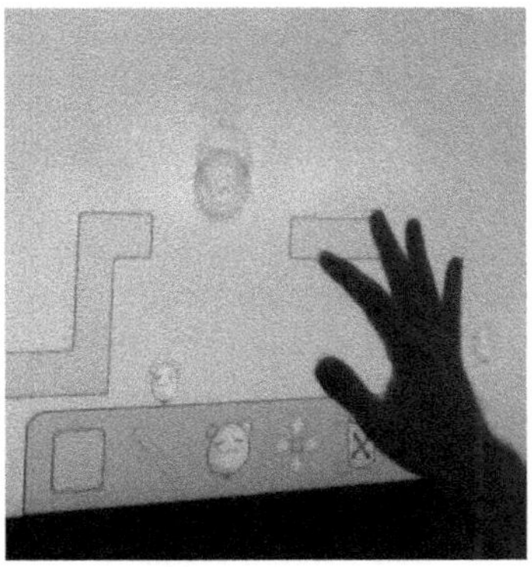

Figure 12: Villainous orchestrator removes the terrain underneath the player, causing him to fall

a sense of haste, however, with 18/20 agreeing that "I had enough time to do the changes I wanted to do."

Players responded positively to the actions of architects, specifying that it makes the world "more dynamic", and that the player "never knows what to expect". A minority found that architectural changes could be too far-reaching, for example saying that "changes were too quick; you need to go back and look", and "if there are too many changes, there is too much to adapt to".

Micro-manager: The micro-manager attempts to directly control the player's experience. For example, a micro-manager might wish a player to travel towards a new area that he has just created. The micro-manager may verbally instruct the player which way to go, or may even modify the terrain of the game world so that the player has no choice but to go in this direction.

In one session, the orchestrator found a tower of balloons on the left-hand side of the player. The orchestrator verbally instructed the player to keep jumping. While the player was jumping, the orchestrator inserted blocks underneath the player, and then directed her to free-fall right on the tower of balloons. Figure 11 shows the orchestrator drawing a wall in front of the player, giving her no choice but to move toward the tower of balloons.

Micro-management was seen in the majority of play sessions (14 of 20). Players' reactions were mixed. For example, one reported that "the orchestrator has too much power", and another "didn't know if the orchestrator helps or not". Micro-management was seen particularly frequently in two of 20 sessions, with more than ten occurrences in each. Surprisingly, in both cases, the players strongly agreed that it was enjoyable to play when the game was orchestrated, and strongly disagreed that orchestration was annoying. This implies that micro-management need not negatively affect the players' experience.

Villain: A villain attempts to spoil the player's fun. Examples of villainous behaviour include completely blocking the player with terrain so he cannot move, or removing the floor below a player just as he is about to complete a jump (Figure 12).

Villainous behaviour was common, seen in 15 of 20 sessions, but only two orchestrators repeatedly acted as a villain (6 times in one session and 5 in another). Following one such session, the player commented that orchestration is "bad if you are stuck with a mean orchestrator." Normally, however, orchestrators appear to have taken on the villainous role without malicious intent, as a prank or joke. Such jokes grow stale with repetition, explaining why the behaviour was rarely repeated.

Interaction Styles

Additionally, our observations revealed four distinct ways in which the player and the orchestrator interacted. These provide insights into the interpersonal dynamics involved in orchestrated gameplay. The interaction styles ranged from subtle manipulation behind the scenes, where the orchestrator attempted to keep her actions secret from the player, to full-on collaboration where the orchestrator and player worked together to achieve a goal in the game.

Orchestrator-dominant: By far the most frequent form of collaboration was "orchestrator dominant", where the orchestrator directs the progression of gameplay. The orchestrator may enforce this dominance either verbally or via the orchestration tools. This form of orchestration was seen in 19 of 20 sessions.

Orchestrators adopted both controlling and helpful forms of dominance. The micro-management of Figure 11 shows the controlling form. In a different session, the orchestrator helped a player who was unfamiliar with the use of a game controller, verbally directing him, and manipulating the terrain to ensure that he could progress.

Orchestrators commented that "it's fun that you can do whatever you want", and "[you're] playing god". One player characterized orchestrator dominance as an antagonistic relationship, where it is "the orchestrator versus the player". Another described the orchestrator as "helpful".

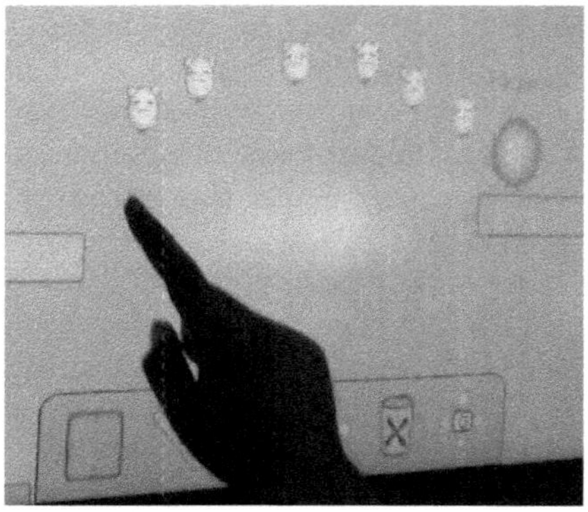

Figure 13: Orchestrator guiding the player with a trail of balloons

Guided: A second form of collaboration in which the orchestrator remains in control is "guided" interaction. Here, the orchestrator subtly directs the player where to go, in contrast to the heavy-handed approach of orchestrator dominance. In one example, the orchestrator wished to guide the player to a newly created part of the level. She did this using in-game cues, providing a trail of balloons leading in the correct direction (Figure 13). This gave the player a hint that there might be something interesting to find if the balloons were followed. Guides may spend significant time working "off screen", creating and modifying parts of the level that the player cannot see.

Guiding differs from orchestrator dominance in that the orchestrator does not directly insert herself into the game, but uses the game itself to guide the player's actions.

Guided orchestration was seen in 17/20 sessions, with a mean of 5 times per session.

Team: Here, the orchestrator and player establish a goal together, and verbally communicate to achieve this goal. Some examples of teamwork that were seen were:

- Climbing as high as possible (seen in two sessions), requiring the orchestrator to build platforms and ramps allowing the player to climb.
- Collaborating to get balloons that are out of the player's reach (seen three times). For example, an orchestrator and player collaboratively developed a plan to get the player over a high wall to retrieve a balloon on the other side.
- Collecting balloons in an acrobatic style (seen twice). The orchestrator and player collaborated on how to use bouncing blocks to allow a player to drop from a height and ricochet over an obstacle to collect a balloon.

Teamwork was the least frequently observed style, seen in 6/20 sessions. This was a particularly social activity, leading one participant to comment that orchestration is "fun depending on the kinds of friends you have".

Player-driven: Here, players dominate the collaboration, instructing the orchestrator what to do. This is distinguished from teamwork in that the player alone determines the goals, and that communication is limited to instructions from player to orchestrator.

Player-driven orchestration was seen in 10/20 sessions, and was used a mean of 4 times in sessions where it occurred. Typically, this form of orchestration arose when the player had a particular goal she wished to achieve, and enlisted the orchestrator's help. For example, one player wished to understand exactly how the game's physics worked. This player instructed the orchestrator where to build terrain in order to allow him to experiment with these mechanics.

Summary

We have described five orchestration behavioural patterns and four styles of interaction between orchestrator and player. All were derived from observation during our study.

It is important to note that orchestrators are not rigidly defined by a single pattern. On average, orchestrators changed type 27 times over their ten-minute session. Furthermore, on average, orchestrators took on four of the five types at some point during the session.

All 20 orchestrators acted as architects for a significant part of their session, implying that it was natural for them to create parts of the level off-screen so that players could encounter a completed design. Equally, most orchestrators also spent significant time closely helping or directing the player; 16/20 acted as helicopter parents, 16/20 acted as guardian angels, and 14/20 as micro-managers. Of these, the guardian angel was the least frequent (60 occurrences), while helicopter parent (103 occurrences) and micro-manager (92 occurrences) were more frequent. This implies that when directly observing players, orchestrators were inclined to significantly intervene in play, either by making sure they made no mistakes, or by forcing the player to play in the way the orchestrator has envisioned. It is interesting that relatively fewer orchestrators were content to let the player play uninterrupted.

Similarly, groups frequently changed their interaction style. On average, each session used 2.6 interaction styles, and groups changed style on average 20 times over the ten-minute session. Unsurprisingly, the dominant interaction styles were those where the orchestrator led. The orchestrator-dominant style was seen 276 times over 19/20 sessions. The guided style was seen 72 times over 17 sessions. The player-driven style was seen in half of the sessions, but with a much lower 29 occurrences. The team style was seen in six sessions, with a total of 24 occurrences. From this we conclude that orchestrators tend to control the session most of the time, but that many groups discovered other means of collaborating for a minority of the time.

This analysis helps in understanding why, as discussed earlier, one participant strongly agreed that "I was annoyed because of the changes that were made by the orchestrator."

The orchestrator in question exhibited six cases of micro-management, four instances of villainous behaviour, and 25 instances of orchestrator dominance, all within a ten-minute session – annoying behaviour indeed!

In sum, the study revealed a rich set of ways in which orchestrators create experiences for players, and varied ways in which the orchestrator and player interact.

ANALYSIS AND DISCUSSION

The study shows that orchestrators exhibit numerous behaviours, and frequently change between them. As was seen in Figure 7, some orchestrators tend to work quietly in the background (e.g., as architect), while others frequently intervene (as guardian angel or helicopter parent), often in a dominant or even villainous way. But in most cases, orchestrators follow all of these behavioural patterns over the course of a single session.

In our questionnaires and interviews, players did not complain about the intervention of orchestrators. We conclude that participants viewed orchestration as another form of playing the game, rather than as selflessly creating experiences for the player. During the frequent occurrences of orchestrator-dominant play and the occasions of villainous play, orchestrators appear to be valuing their own entertainment at least as highly as that of the players. Players also clearly did not expect the orchestrator to quietly remain in the background, as evidenced by the widespread occurrences of team and player-dominant interaction styles. The player viewed the orchestrator as a playmate to be engaged in a fun, collaborative activity. This differs considerably from the "stage manager" style of orchestration seen in, for example, Day of the Figurines [2], where orchestration is considered to be a strictly behind-the-scenes activity, and is closer to the game-master form of orchestration of pen-and-paper role-playing games.

We found that a digital tabletop surface has significant promise for game orchestration. The finger-painting approach allows smooth and fluid creation and deletion of terrain, and allows multiple orchestrators to modify the terrain at once. One major limitation that we have not explored is that the current system can provide only a few dozen tools before the palette becomes clumsy. We believe that this limitation is not critical, however, as interesting terrains and stories can be created even with only a small palette. Additionally, predefined palettes could easily be selected based on the kind of gameplay that is anticipated (e.g., an exterior fantasy setting or a modern building interior), or even switched at runtime. While large tabletop displays are not yet common, many forms of touch-sensitive surfaces have become available at consumer prices, including tablet computers with up to 27" surfaces.

Another limitation of our approach is the restriction of games to two dimensions. The earlier Raptor system [16] has shown that it is possible to sketch 3D games using a 2D top-down view, making it possible to orchestrate, for example, a 3D racing game. This top-down approach is also used in some commercial tools, notably the Neverwinter Nights Aurora Engine. A more general approach would be to use a 3D editor such as in commercial tools like Autodesk Maya and 3DS Max. These full-featured tools, designed for professional artists, do not support the speed of editing required for orchestration. Simplified 3D editing tools can reduce expressiveness in favour of simplicity and fast editing [7]. There is room for study of the tradeoffs involved in these different approaches for presenting the game world to the orchestrator.

Our study picked one of many possible group structures, with only one orchestrator and one player, co-located in the same room. Anecdotally, we have discovered that the positioning of the participants can have a significant effect on the interaction style.

LESSONS FOR GAME DESIGNERS

Our study has shown that game orchestration is a novel and interesting way of bringing design-like activities to runtime. The existence of commercial games like Neverwinter Nights and Super Mario Brothers U implies that game orchestration is an exciting way to provide novel and creative gameplay. Drawing from our study, we therefore propose specific lessons for designers of games incorporating orchestration features:

- *Don't design for a single behavioural pattern.* As we have seen, orchestrators change behaviour frequently and fluidly over the course of the orchestration session. Game orchestration systems should permit easy adoption of the full range of patterns.
- *Support flexible asymmetry.* In a minority of our sessions, villainous or micro-managing orchestrators created a negative experience for players. It should be easy for participants to change who is player or orchestrator, so that no player is held hostage by a malevolent orchestrator. In Tabula Rasa, this is as easy as changing who is sitting at the table and who is holding the game controller.
- *Support speed over expressiveness.* It is critical to be able to create new terrain and structures quickly, so that the player is not forced to wait. In Tabula Rasa, the use of a limited palette of blocky graphics and the use of a finger-painting style of interface allowed rapid manipulation of the world. No participants commented negatively about this limited palette, indicating that players did not view these crude graphics as overly limiting.
- *Consider orchestrators as players.* We saw strong evidence that orchestrators viewed themselves as a special kind of player. Rather than viewing their own entertainment as subsidiary to that of the player, they expected to be entertained in their own right. Game designers could consider ways of providing structured

goals in the game that will engage both orchestrator and player. For example, a game might include prizes for completing a level in a particular way – e.g., completing it quickly or using the fewest blocks.

CONCLUSION

In this paper, we have presented a study of game orchestration based on our Tabula Rasa tool. We have shown that when given game orchestration facilities, people take on a surprising range of behaviours. We identified five different behavioural patterns and observed that people frequently change between these behaviours over an orchestration session. We identified a range of collaboration styles between orchestrators and players, and found that these also change frequently during play sessions. Both orchestrators and players enjoyed this style of play. This study represents a first step in understanding the ways in which creative gameplay can be enabled by bringing design-like activities to a game's runtime. Our orchestrator patterns and interaction styles can now be used to creatively design novel games which take them into explicit consideration.

ACKNOWLEDGEMENTS

We would like to acknowledge the technical help provided by Ameer Hamza, Zi Ye and Christophe Bortolaso. This work was funded by the NSERC SurfNet Strategic Network and the LEIF Transatlantic Student Exchange Program. The paper benefited greatly from the reading of the reviewers.

REFERENCES

1. Agustin, M., Chuang, G., Delgado A., Ortega, A., Seaver, J. and Buchanan, J.W., Game sketching. In *Proc. Digital Interactive Media in Entertainment and Arts,* ACM Press (2007), 36-43.

2. Crabtree, A., Benford, S., Rodden, T., Capra, M., Flintham, M., Drozd, A., Tandavanitj, N., Adams, M. and Row Farr, J., The Cooperative Work of Gaming: Orchestrating a Mobile SMS Game. *Computer-Supported Cooperative Work* 16 (2007), 167-198.

3. Evaldsson, A.-C. and Corsaro, W.A., Play and Games in the Peer Cultures of Preschool and Preadolescent Children: An Interpretive Approach. *Childhood* 4:377 (2008), 377-402.

4. Koleva, B., Taylor, I., Benford, S., Fraser, M., Greenhalgh, C., Schnaedelbach, H., vom Lehn, D., Heath, C., Row-Farr, J. and Adams, M. Orchestrating a Mixed Reality Performance. In *Proc. Human Factors in Computing Systems,* ACM Press (2001), 38-45.

5. Mazalek, A., Mironer, B., O'Rear, E. and Van Devender, D. The TViews Table Role-Playing Game, *Journal of Virtual Reality and Broadcasting,* 5(2008):8, (2008).

6. Mulcaster, R., *Positions Wherein Those Primitive Circumstances Be Examined, Which Are Necessarie for the Training up of Children,* originally published 1581, available in reprinted form by Thoemmes Press (1995).

7. Neustaedter, C., Tang, A. and Judge, T.K., Creating scalable location-based games: lessons from Geocaching. Personal and Ubiquitous Computing (2011), 1-15.

8. Oh, J.-Y., Stuerzlinger, W. and Danahy, J., SESAME: Towards Better 3D Conceptual Design Systems, In *Proc. Designing Interactive Systems,* ACM Press (2006), 80-89.

9. *Oxford English Dictionary,* Third Edition, Sept. 2004.

10. Peitz, J., Björk, S. and Jäppinen, A. Wizard's Apprentice - Gameplay-Oriented Design of a Computer- Augmented Board Game. In *Proc. Advances in Computer Entertainment Technology,* ACM Press (2006), article 18.

11. Peltz, C., Web Services Orchestration and Choreography, *Computer* 36:10 (2003), 46-52.

12. Piper, A.M., O'Brien, E., Ringel Morris, M. and Winograd, T., SIDES: A Cooperative Tabletop Computer Game for Social Skills Development, In *Proc. Computer Supported Cooperative Work,* ACM Press (2006), 1–10.

13. Roman, P.A. and Brown, D., Games – Just How Serious Are They? In *Proc. Interservice/Industry Training, Simulation & Education Conference,* MetaPress (2008), article 8013.

14. Salen, K. and Zimmerman, E., Rules of Play: *Game Design Fundamentals.* MIT Press (2003).

15. Salovaara, A., Johnson, M., Toiskallio, K., Tiitta, S. and Turpeinen, M., Playmakers in Multiplayer Game Communities: their Importance and Motivations for Participation. In *Proc. Advances in Computer Entertainment Technology* (2005), 334-337.

16. Smith, J.D. and Graham, T.C.N. Raptor: Sketching Games with a Tabletop Computer. In *Proc. Futureplay,* ACM Press (2010), 191-198.

17. Strauss A.L. and Corbin J. *Basics of Qualitative Research: Techniques and Procedures, 2nd ed.* Sage (1998).

18. Tychsen, A., Hitchens, M., Brolund, T. and Kavakli, M., The Game Master. In *Proc. Australasian Conf. on Interactive Entertainment* (2005), 215-222.

19. Wong, N. and Gutwin, C., Controlling an Avatar's Pointing Gestures in Desktop Collaborative Virtual Environments. In *Proc. Group,* ACM Press (2012).

Playing with Leadership and Expertise: Military Tropes and Teamwork in an ARG

Tamara Peyton
Penn State University
University Park, PA 16802
tpeyton@psu.edu

Alyson L. Young
UMBC
Baltimore, MD 21250
alyson1@umbc.edu

Wayne Lutters
UMBC
Baltimore, MD 21250
lutters@umbc.edu

ABSTRACT
Ad-hoc virtual teams often lack tools to formalize leadership and structure collaboration, yet they are often successful. How does this happen? We argue that the emergence of leadership and the development of expertise occurs in the process of taking action and in direct response to a lack of structure. Using a twinned set of eight modality sliders, we examine the interactions of fourteen players in an alternate reality game. We find that players adopted military language and culture to structure and arrange their play. We determine that it is critical to account for the context of play across these modalities in order to design appropriately for effective in-game virtual organizing.

Author Keywords
Alternate reality games, computer-supported cooperative work, expertise, leadership, team work, qualitative research

ACM Classification Keywords
H.5.3.m. Group and Organizational Interfaces: Miscellaneous

INTRODUCTION
The player looks around cautiously, noting the positions of guards at the door, non-players massing near the slot machines, a waitress circulating with drink orders. Spotting the bank of payphones across the room, she checks her watch. 17:35. She is late and she knows it, but the wrong information provided to her by a teammate was out of her control. Despite the setback, can she get this axon today and help her team advance? She darts across the room, and places her hand on the phone just as it rings. She jumps, nerves jangled, then takes a deep breath and picks up the receiver... "Hello?..."

This could be a cut scene from any number of video games. In fact, it is from the physical world – one player's interaction in an alternate reality game (ARG). ARGs operate at the liminal juncture of the global online world of the Web and the local offline worlds of cafes, casinos, zoos, museums and homes. Set in a fictional world overlaid onto the actual one, ARG gameplay is the result of ongoing co-construction between players and designers. All ARGs are characterized by collective storytelling and group sensemaking activities. ARGs require players to work collectively to solve tasks in order to advance the game's storyline [17,18].

ARGs are play systems that form a part of the ludological culture of today. "Ludology" is the study of the logic and practices of play; a contested term that is synthesized from the work of three prominent play theorists [4,14,22]. Drawing from the Latin term *ludus* meant as games, fun or play, the intent of understanding the logic of ludus is to reveal the purposeful, instrumental and/or externally directed play of (primarily) adults. Therefore, "ludological culture" is a term invoked in [10] to describe the penetration of a playful mindset into everyday life, increasingly as a result of the popularity of videogames on consoles, computers and smartphones. Ludological elements are now appearing as part of advertising, public politicking and public relations. As such, designing for ludological systems requires a specific attention to the interactive, contextual, and fluid nature of play in practice.

One of the most successful ARGs is I Love Bees (ILB). Developed by 42 Entertainment to promote Microsoft's first-person shooter game, Halo 2, ILB required the collective intelligence of its players to solve intricate puzzles that extended across the physical and online world. Given that there was no game-provided place to converge or tools for collaboration, players had to self-organize into teams to develop creative solutions and assemble their own infrastructure. How did they do this? What team dynamics emerged? What were the markers of leadership and expertise? We address these questions in this study, focusing in particular on the latter.

APPROACH & METHODS
This paper is an analytical report on project work from a larger study examining the practice of collective problem-solving. Using the ARG ILB as an exemplar, the larger project is concerned with how voluntary virtual organizations (VVOs) collaborate in order to collectively solve complex problems. VVOs depend on far-flung volunteers, negotiation of group dynamics, on-going problem definition and problem resolution. We see ARGs as a form of VVO, and we take them to be a prime site for examining collective complex problem solving.

ILB was one of the earlier ARGs and it was influential at setting the paradigm for future ARG design. Mystery and intrigue are central to ILB play, and both the draw and the frustration of the game was its lack of designed tools for coordination, collaboration and teaming. Teams were formed ad-hoc, often around geographical regions, in order to maximize a key game challenge: axon hunting. This involved an ongoing series of challenge/response questions posed to players at a set of coded GPS coordinates. Early in the game, players correctly determined that these represented the latitude and longitude of payphones. These were referred to in game mythology as "axons". At a predefined time, the payphones would ring. If players answered the proper phone at the right time they would receive a question. If answered correctly, an axon would be activated, unlocking clues in the form of short sound clips – puzzle pieces that, when correctly assembled, revealed the next chapter in the unfolding story of the game.

In the absence of an official site to coordinate this teamed axon hunting, players used the ARG fansite, Unfiction.com. It hosted the Haunted Apiary message board, which served as the primary communication hub for ILB. This hub grew to contain more than 54,000 posts by more than 2,700 players. Over the four months of ILB gameplay, players dedicated one of the Haunted Apiary forums to the task of coordinating the ILB axon hunt. This forum conversation was often threaded by geographic region, as specific as a city (e.g., Portland) or as general as a state (e.g., Washington).

Using a grounded theory approach, we investigated axon hunt coordination forum threads in order to gain insight into aspects of virtual teaming and coordination. In our inductive coding process, we saw the emergence of leadership and expertise, as players went about coordinating their efforts around a similar task. Delving into this phenomenon deeper, and following the assertion of [23] that the most active forum posters are those who display leadership and expertise indicators, we selected a subset of fourteen players from the axon coordination threads who had contributed the largest number of postings (N=4705) in their geographic region. They were responsible for more than twenty percent of the forum post activity around axon hunting, and they also accounted for just over nine percent of the overall forum posting activity on the Haunted Apiary generally.

During a second coding pass by two researchers, we realized that the forum posts of our fourteen player subset constructed a set of stories of players' approaches, processes, difficulties and successes when read in their full discursive theme. These stories aligned nicely with the notion of "war stories" – a qualitative data collection and analytical technique that provide "handles" into the data that bring to life specific struggles and accomplishments of a study's participants [15]. In research accounts, war stories are told in such a way that informants are placed in central positions as protagonists. The storytelling inherent in the war story reporting method affords the researcher access to both participants' internal states, as well as any external environmental influences on participants. We noted that axon hunting forum post threads often held markers of war stories, given the way players shared personal hopes, frustrations and desires in forum posts around what transpired during their axon hunting activity.

With the war stories approach in mind, we coded forum posts across player and team narratives. Following case study methodology of [27] and adapted by [31], we assembled fourteen illustrative and exemplary case studies that tell the story of the three prevalent themes of interest: militarization, leadership and expertise. Through our cases, we are able to identify and present rich descriptive accounts of player actions, perceptions and struggles around information seeking, information management and ad-hoc teamwork within the ILB ARG. This approach is consistent with qualitative analytical approaches on unstructured datasets as described by [11], and as exemplified in [19].

From this inductive approach to analysis, we created our research questions for this paper:

1. Can discursive streams from ILB forums provide sufficient detail to be read as "war stories" that illustrate the action of the game?
2. What do these war stories tell us about ad-hoc teamwork, community leadership and group expertise?
3. What design recommendations can be derived from the loosely knit ludological culture of ILB?

BACKGROUND

We consider how people work together within and across geographies to solve complex problems, as part of an ARG team. Consequently, we draw on literature from the fields of qualitative research methods, game studies, and CSCW. With our research goals in mind, we examined the virtual coordination and ad-hoc teaming characteristics identified in the CSCW literature on editing in Wikipedia [32], open-source software development [9], community crisis response [20] and software maintenance [15]. The latter researchers identified leaders, gatekeepers and followers as three types of participants in collaborative information management, and these types were influential in our inductive coding to help identify markers of participation.

An ARG is a ludic digital environment in which people learn things that are generalizable to everyday living [12,17]. To address the question of what sort of collaborative play happens in ARGs, we consulted work that articulates the nature of play and playfulness generally [4,14], as well as within digital games [5,6,29], digital worlds [8] and gamified spaces [3,10].

Leadership and expertise indicators in our data set were important for this paper. We drew from research work that looked at these generally [2,33] and specifically, both within digital games [5,6,13,16,17,24,25,28], and in online forums [23,33].

DISCOVERIES & ANALYSIS

Overview of Key Discoveries

There were four categories of discoveries in our project:

1. the self-organization of players into teams within geographical regions, and their management of the axon hunting tasks within those teams
2. the militarization of play, based on players' use of military tropes, language and organizational ideas
3. the demonstration of expertise and leadership modalities, drawn from communicative distinctions between players as they evolved from privates into lieutenants and generals
4. the design implications of providing an open unstructured environment for task management and teamwork across geographies

Self-Organization, Teaming & Tasking

Players volunteered for tasks. In the early stages of the game, volunteering was often influenced by location and time of task, rather than strategic thinking, with players selecting axons that were close to home, work or school. In many cases, players volunteered for the same axon hunting task each week, claiming responsibility for a specific axon location.

Through our case studies, we note that as the game progressed, players started to identify patterns and to suggest strategies that would maximize their efforts:

> *"I'm thinking I should still concentrate on Union Station, only because there are so many axons in one place at one time (and optical.wav will depend on it). But my priorities will change if getting the low hanging fruit means activating a sound file" (C12)*

Due to the voluntary nature of participation in the game, conditional volunteering behaviour was frequently observed:

> *"If I can take an early dinner on Tues, I'll go on down to help you cover the phones." (C8).*

In the event players were unable to attend to their weekly tasks, they often posted their conflict on the discussion forum to make other players aware and to assist with coordination efforts:

> *"I wish I could go to that one, just because I have the most time invested in it... and because Po Folks has great friend green tomatos![sic] But I'm working" (C8).*

Once tasks were claimed, the act of performing a task, particularly in the initial stages of the game, was an iterative process in which players scoped out a location, narrowed down perspective payphones, tested the payphones to ensure they were functional, and then waited for the expected call. Following completion of a task, players would post their experiences in situation reports on the discussion threads, providing documentation for future task coordination:

> *"Well, it wasn't the three phones on the southwestern end of the first floor of the Glendale Galleria, between JC Penney and Zales. At least, I sure hope it wasn't. The one on the left did not ring, and the one in the middle -- which accepts incoming calls but doesn't ring audibly -- still had a dial tone at 19:13:30. The one on the right -- which accepted incoming calls on Tuesday even though it didn't ring audibly -- was busted. It would not connect to incoming calls today, and didn't even have a dial tone" (C13).*

The iterative, trial-and-error nature of the game meant that players often failed tasks on their first few attempts. In areas with vast numbers of geographically dispersed payphones, this failure was often the result of inadequate coverage, making it difficult to eliminate incorrect payphones:

> *"No dice at Caesar's (really hard to canvas an entire casino the size of Caesar's by yourself... Anybody else have any luck?) [...] ah well... the quest continues" (C9).*

Players also faced issues when phones were in use. An occupied phone meant that players were unable to test the phone during a scouting expedition or to confirm if it would ring during the scheduled time:

> *"I tried the Media City Center axon (i_hate_you) three times last week. I can verify that the group of three pay phones on the third floor at the far back end of the mall -- that is, not directly adjacent to the Magnolia entrance -- are not the ones we want. Other than that, I kept running into people who wouldn't get off the phones, so I have no idea whether we want the ones on the first floor or the ones on the third floor" (C13).*

Traffic also posed a problem for players. C14 reported such issues impacting her ability to reach a location in time:

> *"I also discovered it's impossible to make it from the Gallery of Art to the National Building Museum on foot in 8 minutes (traffic sucks, even for pedestrians). I missed the 10:23 call there by about a minute and a half" (C12).*

Unless players chose to abandon an axon, the process of trial-and-error usually lead to eventual success, especially in instances where situation reports were provided. Keeping the lines of communication open between players via the discussion forum appears to have contributed to greater instances of success. Once an axon task was successfully completed, players would post a description of the task location in order to assist other players in locating the axon in the future. In some cases, players also posted a tally of all successfully completed tasks either for the day or for the week, effectively creating a documentation trail of all tasks completed for a specific time period.

Given that ILB did not provide players with guidance or infrastructure for completing game tasks, players assembled their own strategies and tool sets [32]. These tools were used to document locations, report incomplete tasks, and to provide players with general information on how to perform a task. C12 created a status website to document both location information and completed axon status for his Washington, DC team. Supplementing this site, C14 managed a spreadsheet, which outlined weekly status information on the completed and outstanding axons.

Militarization of Play

Both our master data set and our case study data subset bears out the 'militarization of society' thesis, which argues that military culture has inflected everyday North American life in the post-9/11 Homeland Security era. In particular, evidence exists that suggests the use of military language has intensified post-9/11, and is visible in many of the entertainment artifacts of the early 21st century, from movies to television to video games [7].

Many of the ILB players tended to adopt military language, cultural tropes and organizational concepts to understand and to describe their ILB play. This is perhaps due to the fact that Halo is a militaristic science fiction first person shooter game, and as such military culture is part of the game mythology. Players spoke of organizing their groups into 'armies", "platoons' and "companies. They advocated the appointment or promotion of certain teammates to the 'rank' of 'general' or 'colonel'. Their speech was peppered with terms like "nav com" and "stat". C5 exclaimed that it would be "totally cool" if they could name their main group a "company" with subgroups called "squads" or "armies". C2 spoke of naming their group the army of their city, and she enthusiastically discussed a possible game task in which each team was supposed to take a picture of key team members saluting in front of an axon. C3 congratulated a teammate on their promotion to Lieutenant and also advocated naming their team a "company". C4 spent time educating his team on the proper use of military jargon, going so far as to link to an About.com glossary page on American military language.

Given players' preferences towards military tropes, we have chosen to adopt the same US military ranking system identified by C4 to tag the leaders, gatekeepers and followers in our case studies. It is true that the militarized language and rank assignations players used to structure their play, and which we have extended to structure our discussion, is not fully synchronous with that of actual militaries. However, we see the practice of voluntary militarization of play to be a finding of note. We suggest that the ludological structuring of teamwork and tasking around military tropes in gamified worlds warrants future research.

Leadership & Expertise Frameworks

In relation to leadership, we distinguish between the leaders of a group and the markers of leadership possibly present in individuals. We also distinguish between traditional organization ideas of leadership typically studied and discussed in organization literature, and the under-defined and emergent style of leadership found in online spaces such as ARGs. There are aspects of leadership visible in the ludic digital environments of ARGs that are not well-addressed in existing work around leadership in online spaces. The first is the lack of any requirement to formally identify, designate and formalize a leadership structure within ad-hoc teams. Outside of commercial massively multiplayer gameworlds (MMOGs) such as World of Warcraft with its guild system, leadership in ARGs is an informal, unacknowledged yet crucial part of play. Leaders self-designate themselves through their play style, but rarely do they call out "hey! I'm the leader and y'all follow me!" They wear no "I'm the leader" badge and can only be identified as such through the traces left by their actions.

Leading is accomplished through the execution of tasks, the strategic directing of other players and use of a skilled tactical communication style. Thus, it is an emergent property of play, rather than a role formalized by game designers. While other players seem to acknowledge the leadership of certain players, it is rare that they openly designate someone as *the* leader of their group or team. Our case studies also show us that the self-proclaimed leaders, the ones who do openly ask to be seen as leaders, often are marginalized by other players and can end up feeling unsatisfied with the looser tacit team structures.

Our fourteen case studies also show us that popular ideations of leadership as being aspects of high performing players [5,6] or of only certain kinds of players (such as lieutenants, but not privates) was not applicable in ILB. Based on our cases, even privates demonstrate aspects of leadership modalities and mindsets. This suggests to us that leadership in ludic environments needs to be better understood and studied as a contingent assemblage of possibility. Leadership can be actualized, neutralized or negated by a variety of other modes, contexts, and design decisions. These diversities include: geographic location; other players' modalities; game goals; gaming expertise; social norms and social sanctions; and technological prowess. Designing systems and interfaces for these ludic environments requires sensitivity to this multi-modal nuance. We call this assemblage a ludic ecology and identify this as another opportunity for future work.

Modalities, not Typologies

Following from [2] and [28], we identified two sets of modalities within ILB game practice, which are grouped within practices that we find demonstrate leadership and expertise. However, unlike some game studies work, we highlight the fact that modalities are quantifiably and qualitatively different than a typology of either players [1] or organizational practice [2]. A typology is a fixed and bounded category. Types are inherently reductionist and their use artificially reifies the contingent, messy and personal nature of play. Instead, we adopt the idea of modalities of play. Noting that the term modality has various inflections in HCI work, we use the term in the same sense as it was employed by [28] and [16] to describe patterns of behaviour within sets of practices. We derive it from the term mode, understood as being a factor or an influence in the actions used in a practice. An important caveat noted by [28] is the sense of the multiple and overlapping character of a modality, so that a modality is never a fixed, perfect or exclusive pattern of action. Most modalities are part of a continuum of behaviour, and as such, identifying specific play modalities is done using a set of "sliders". A modality is intended to be part of an inflected and highly individual action pattern within specific sets of play.

Leadership Modalities

Aspects of leadership in digital teams have been described by [2]. Drawing from a cross section of management literature, they identified five facets of leadership in digital teams: team process management; team motivation and new member assimilation; team monitoring and individual accomplishment recognition; appropriate intervention to overcome challenges; and the maintenance of a strategic sense of a team's needs relating to their overarching goals.

Behaviours	Leadership Type & Message
Positive Feedback	**Transactional Leadership:** Energize people through acknowledging work and provides reward **Example:** *This was a great day in DC, congratulations all! (C12)*
Negative Feedback	**Adverse Leadership**: Regulate people through reprimands **Example:** *I hope somebody recorded the unavailable .wavs, because I would be really pissed off if we missed some of the story due to people being too lazy (C1)*
Directing	**Directive Leadership:** Direct people through issuing instructions, commands, assigning tasks, setting goals **Example:** *We know exactly where these phones are. Do not reinvent the wheel. (C14)*
Social Exchange	**Transformational Leadership:** Promote emotional engagement through for example nice talking, starting off-topic conversation,etc. **Example:** *I was thinking about having some dinner up there. If enough people PM me that they are interested I'll get a big table and tell the host/ess to seen anybody looking for Beekeepers my way. (C8)*

Table 1: Leadership modalities [33] with case examples

Our analysis looked for markers of these leadership indicators to select out our specific cases and match them to their leadership style. We also looked for markers devised by [33], focusing specifically on the distinctions between tactical, strategic and person-focused aspects of leadership. We align to their argument that leadership in online communities is based on a shared process of contextual contribution over time, individual positioning relative to group tasks and goals, and attention to team and individual position, strategies and accomplishments.

While the work of [33] is intended for quantitative studies, we found their theorization and exposition to be fruitful for our qualitative approach. Synthesizing their framework with the four facets of digital leadership we adopted from [2], along with ideas on the roles of providers-of-and-pointers-to-information and of gatekeepers in [15], we created a set of four sliders for leadership, called Positive Feedback, Negative Feedback, Directing and Social Exchange (see table 1). These evaluated the appearance of the modality in terms of high, medium, or low behaviour. We employed these to identify the leadership modalities in our case study dataset, expressed as features and degrees of play.

Expertise Modalities

We adopt the idea of gaming expertise as a situated multimodal expression from [16] and [28]. Both papers argue that expertise in gaming practice is not fully visible through simplistic binary constructs analyzed through single modes of play. Contrary to other notions of gaming expertise as encapsulated solely in elapsed time [17], achievement [26], or optimal efficiency [13], it has been argued that an experienced player demonstrates their ludic expertise through four modalities of play: investment, skill, discourse, and game knowledge [28]. All four modalities must be considered when examining individual player's skill levels, and each modality must be taken into account when constructing an analytical framework to understand in-game practice.

Using the four modalities (see figure 1), we analysed the ILB play data from our 14 case studies, coded it for the modalities, and then used a slider system to rank each case's modality expression in terms of high, medium and low appearance. Similar to [16], this modality slider approach gave us a situated analysis of each player's primary and secondary expertise modality.

Merging these modes with the four modes of leadership, we have an integrated framework for analyzing leadership and expertise capabilities within and across our 14 cases.

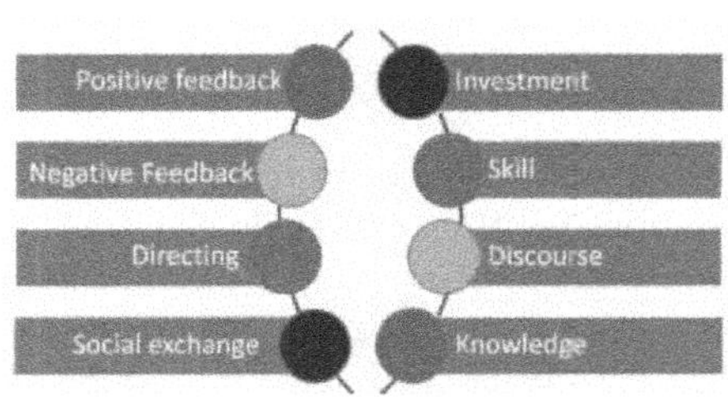

Figure 1. Leadership & Expertise Framework

Modalities & Ranks

After creating a leadership and expertise profile for each player in our fourteen cases, we followed the military structure adopted by ILB players themselves, and assigned each case a rank. These definitional rank categories were based on our interpretation of players' worldview. This resulted in: 1 general, 5 lieutenants, 7 privates, and one "transitional" player, who started as a private and rose to the rank of a lieutenant during the game's lifecycle.

- Generals: C14
- Lieutenants: C2, C4, C5, C6, C11
- Privates: C1, C3, C7, C8, C9, C10, C13
- Transitional: C12

The transitional player is an interesting exceptional case. He personifies the ways in which leadership and expertise modalities are not solely individual player characteristics. His play style and communicative approaches demonstrate that ARG play must be understood contextually.

While we do not separate out the exception represented by C12 from the other privates in the following discussion of each rank's actions and stories, we assert that our understanding of C12's emergent leadership style shows to us that system designers must understand leadership and expertise as modalities, not typologies.

Generals

A general is an individual who possesses the characteristics of a leader most often identified in research literature [2,15]. She demonstrates high-level, strategic thinking and exhibits extensive use of directive language, using both game jargon and politically neutral phrasing. Even on occasions where the situation is tense between her and her squad, she keeps a calm countenance and polite but strong demeanor. A general is an expert at providing positive feedback, acknowledging players' work and providing rewards. She also promotes emotional engagement via social exchange. In traditional MMOG systems, this individual would most closely align with a guild master.

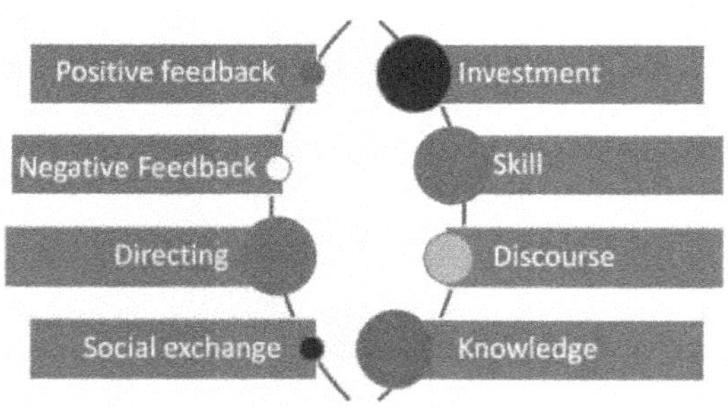

Figure 2. C14 General L&E Profile

In our cases, we have a single example of a general (C14), a coincidental finding that aligns with the relative rarity of generals in actual world militaries (e.g.: In the US Army, there is one general for every 2444 active duty soldiers [21]). Figure 4 shows our general's leadership and expertise (L&E) profile. This player displays extensive use of directive language, for example exhorting players to post information on what phones they covered, to focus on the most obvious axons, and to reuse prior information.

> *"We know exactly where these phones are. Do not reinvent the wheel. Look up this thread for links to C12's page - it has the exact locations and consolidated map info and a description of exactly which phone it is (there's multiple phones some places). He may not have updated the times and axon order to the new list but the location info is ALL YOU NEED" (original emphasis)*

This player employs strategic thinking, particularly with regards to knowledge of the game, axon hunting and coverage strategies, and player coordination:

> *"If you meet someone there that can commit to cover another one, get their nickname and a way to reach them so we can add them to the team and save someone else the trouble of getting to an axon that is covered".*

> *"If you can, let people know here which ones you are definitely going to try so, if schedules are tight, others with a little time can focus on ones you aren't planning to get to."*

C14 demonstrates a high level of skill, using both her geographic and civic knowledge of the area to point out potential challenges (i.e., traffic and road closures) as well as to suggest potential tactics to overcome these challenges (i.e., leaving more time to reach a location):

> *"The Marine Corps Marathon and a couple disease marches take place Sunday so traffic, esp. around the Mall, will be disastrous. Whatever you plan to do, LEAVE EARLY, because if traffic is screwed up by the marathon it will all default to other access points to DC and THOSE will be very busy too."*

In addition, she uses team-created tools to apply previous knowledge obtained in the game to current situations (i.e., information on how to do a task), and she speculates on the difficulty level of a task based on challenges faced at previous, similar location:

> *"At a guess - since it looks like an apartment building - this may be hard to find. The coordinate is probably for the address generally and not for the phone specifically, although it never hurts to scope out the exact spot just in case. But assuming it's the coordinate for the entire property -- you're looking for a payphone. Presumably in a public area. Check the payphone directories to see if one is listed for that address - that is a good (not perfect) indicator that it MAY be the phone [a PM] will call. Otherwise, follow your nose. Can you get into the building lobby to check (maybe not, security in many such buildings would not let you that close)? If not, you may be SOL. Is there a payphone by the tennis courts and/or pool you see on*

the acme map off to the side? Assuming they are still open?"

She goes beyond situation reports to provide theories and strategies based on previous attempts. She also recruits players to take on tasks, as well as suggests who should do which tasks based on the previous week's activities:

"We had an axon in Virginia that was never gotten - we THINK it was in the pool area of an apartment complex, but the pool shut for the season before it could be tested. Get there early - scout all possibilities. If you find a phone, call it from your cell to make sure it takes incoming calls. If there's no number on it, use it to call your cellphone to get the number, then call it back. If it does not take incoming (don't believe what the phone signs may say - test it yourself), move on to the next phone. If you strike out on the first phone (that's 10:57 AM tomorrow our time), [the game designer] apparently will keep calling it all week, even if the axon is reported as ""cancelled"" when the sound clip is released. So you'll have a second chance if there are other possible phones.

C14 manages a resource list of axons that she expected her team to reference and use:

"If you are submitting a new axon, find one that is convenient for you, near home or work so you can get it any time of day. No need to focus on whether you are also replacing a nonfunctional axon; just supply pictorial proof of another payphone that works. Also, my axon list (previous page of thread) is fixed for now (thx C20), also removed distracting but fun references to international axons."

Lieutenants

Based on the L&E modalities framework, a lieutenant is an individual who is leadership-oriented but who tends to escalate issues to a higher rank rather than take charge of issues. While he displays some strategic thinking, he predominantly focuses on tactics to solve more immediate, short-term problems, rather than employing strategies for long-term objectives. While there are some differences, the closest approximation we can make between the lieutenants in our cases and the existing literature would be the roles of gatekeeper and provider-of and pointer-to information, found in [15]. We found that lieutenants use directive language similar to that of a general, but that they are more prone to performing tactical team management, especially as it relates to the provision of feedback with lower level players. This individual is also less likely than the general to promote emotional engagement via social exchange. In a traditional MMOG play, this individual would most closely align with a guild officer.

In our cases, we have five examples of lieutenants. However, when a temporal aspect to each L&E modality is closely examined, we found that only two of the five cases of lieutenants showed stability in their L&E modalities (C2, C11). Three cases (C4, C5, and C6) all displayed emerging properties of generals. In C4's case, it is our contention that he would have become a general if the game had lasted longer than four months. C5 wanted to be a general and was frustrated with his team role as a lieutenant. This led him to abandon the game early. C6 showed many possible L&E markers of a general, similar to C4. However, because C6 was in the same geographic location as C14, the only full general in our dataset, this player did not progress to general.

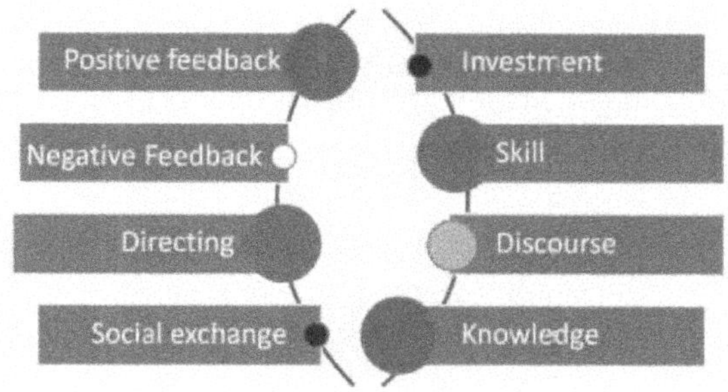

Figure 3. C4 Lieutenant L&E Profile

In line with our L&E framework, these players focused predominantly on the use of tactics to address immediate problems, thus demonstrating a high level of skill. For example, C6 provides detailed information from scouting activities as a means to narrow down the location of a task:

"I estimate that covering the back wall would take at least two, probably three people for a single axon, or one person over two or three different tries. The last group on street level is inside the triangle formed by Gate G, the rental car counters, and McDonald's. There are about twelve phones there as well. The final set of three phones is on the lower level just at the entrance to the Metro.

C6 also exhibits transactional leadership, suggesting players meet for lunch while on axon monitoring duties:

"If anyone else wants to join me we should cover the largest banks first since the odds seems best there. C20 and I are planning some lunches there next week to keep coverage up. PM or AIM me if you'd like to come along; we can exchange cell phone numbers."

C6 further demonstrates their skill by providing tactical information on how to best complete a task, informing players to use maps and satellite images of the location:

"Go ahead of time armed with your maps and satellite photos. It shouldn't be too difficult to scout out; the all the axons on that campus seem to fairly well represented by their coordinates. Have someone reachable by cell phone who can access the IRC Channel and online maps and charts if need be."

C2 also exhibits a number of examples of tactical thinking. She identified game mechanic patterns of axon releases and time periods, enabling her to suggest plans of action for axon hunting. She coordinated group coverage of axons in a way designed to maximize group benefit while minimizing group effort. She was an advocate of team task tracking, using a group list maintained in the team forum as way of knowing who was doing what and when. She also directed others in her team to document their activities by providing frequent situation reports:

"Do you mean you'll be backing up C3, downtown? I'll add you to the list. Thanks! Edit: Err, what I meant to ask was, once you've gotten the 4th and Stark phone (thank you thank you) are you going to take the rest of the downtown phones along with C3, or are you going up to 23rd to take those phones with C1? Either way, it's great, I just want to know so I can update the list accordingly"

Players who exhibited traits of a lieutenant also frequently made tactical suggestions for successful axon hunting. For example, C12 suggests that if players are alone to listen to the beginning of the recording and then drop the receiver in order to answer the next call:

"If it's just one person, don't bother listening to the recording, the calls come every minute. Once a call is hot, drop the receiver and move on. If the earlier patterns hold, the first one or two calls will go to the au bon pain phones; skip them if you're alone."

Moreover, C11 suggests telling non-player civilians who want to use the payphone that it is out of order to keep them off the phone during the designated time, indicating that it had worked when he had tried it previously:

"I'm telling you, what worked for me is this: Someone approaches the phone, and just tell them, very authoritatively, 'These phones don't work'. Amazingly, the person will invariably take what you say as gospel. I mean, why would a stranger lie about something like that?"

In keeping with their 'middle management' style, lieutenants were the individuals most likely to create and maintain team task lists. These lists were managed in a variety of ways through a variety of technologies, including excel lists, web pages, and internal forum lists, and were used to kept track of not only the task to be accomplished, but also to who had signed on for each task within each week. C12, for example, created a Washington, D.C only status website to document both location information and completed axon status. In the following quote, C12 explains the multiple roles of the website, but does not explain the potential use of the site, nor its advantage to the group (which would be a general's strategic task):

"Each location has a graphic created from street maps and satellite imagery; both the mapquest star and acme crosshair locations are present. If a phone was positively identified, I've marked that with a white phone icon. Notes from previous forum posts are included, please let (sic) any updates from previous or new visits and I'll incorporate the information. If someone has said they'll be visiting a particular axon, I'll add that information (in red text).

Overall, the lieutenant's role seemed to fit a middle manager straddling the fine line between "doer" and "thinker".

Private

We view a private as an individual who displays minimal strategic or tactical thinking. She takes orders and provides situation reports on tasks accomplished, but does not offer a lot of insight on how to approach a task or solve a problem. This individual is also more likely to receive than to give both positive and negative feedback. In a traditional MMOG, this individual would be characterized as a guild member. Figure 6 provides the leadership and expertise profile for C13. This private's L&E profile was reasonably consistent with the other privates in our cases,.

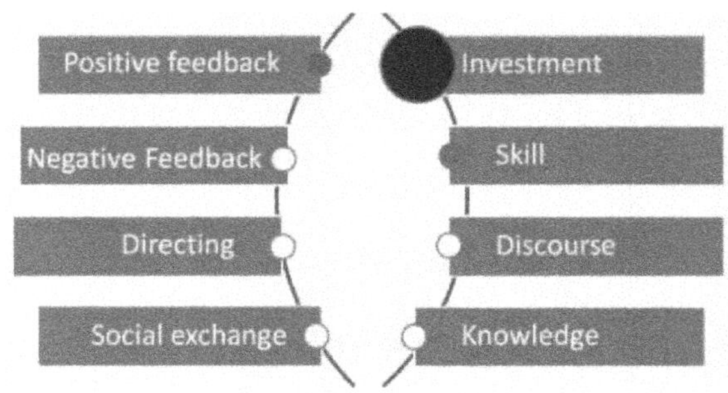

Figure 4. C13 Private L&E Profile

In our cases, we have five examples of privates. In line with the L&E framework, these individuals exhibited very little strategic or tactical thinking. Indeed, their primary function in the game was to take orders or to volunteer for tasks, complete tasks and report back via situation reports.

C13 showed a high investment in the game, but his investment came mainly in the form of providing reports on his axon hunting activities, and also providing recognition for the efforts of fellow teammates. While he uses the common game term of axons occasionally, he tended to use the 'real world' term payphone more often:

C22 and I hit the 17:59 ""creepy"" axon. It's the third pay phone from the left in the Convention Center, which is just east of the Burbank Airport Hilton. Full credit to C22 for actually making the connection; I was watching the bank of phones in the hotel itself./me objects to paying for parking just to hit an axon."

C1 provides information on the location of a task, pointing out that a particular axon (or rather phone) does not exist:

"Just wanted to give a heads up for the SW 107th & Allen axon... it doesn't exist. At least, there's no phone out in the open that I can spot. On the one side of allen there's a hotel called the Greenwood Inn (or something

to that effect), and on the other side is some trucking company, neither of which I could see a phone, especially near the road."

In addition, players who exhibited the traits of a private also provided information to help players successfully locate and activate axons. C8, for example, offers details on particular challenges with parking. She also provides players with an annotated map of the area and a link to a PDF version of the map, which provides detailed information on the campus and the surrounding area:

"Here's a map of campus that I've marked up with important locations. Here's a link to the actual pdf of the map where you can actually read things. [...] This page is very useful in finding UCI [...] Do NOT park at the University Center strip mall and walk over the bridge... This is Irvine, they ARE watching you and the WILL tow your car. Parking lot 16 is $1 for an hour, $2 for 2 hours, and $5 all day [...] I've taken to parking at SPSS 58/79 (Across the street from University Center.) It's more expensive but much more convenient to the axons.

Similarly, C10 informs fellow players that the location of a task will be closed during the time the payphone is scheduled to ring, and to therefore bring snacks along and use the restroom before heading to the location:

"Make sure you don't need restrooms or snacks before going up there, since the place closes at 5:15PM (grounds are still open until sunset, however)."

In a few instances, players who exhibited the traits of a private asked other players to document any information that could assist future axon hunting. C13 for example, asks C21 if he was able to make it to a particular location, suggesting that the information would help ensure that efforts were not duplicated:

"C21, were you able to make it over there? If so, which phones did you rule out, so we don't duplicate efforts?"

IMPLICATION OF FINDINGS

In our data, players enjoyed being able to self-organize into teams, and to group, rank and manage each other based on their expressed teamwork tendencies and styles. Players also criticized the game designers for ILB's lack of tools to facilitate teamwork, reporting, and communication, and they decried the lack of workflow and web publishing capabilities built into the ad-hoc tools they did employ, such as spreadsheet applications.

We therefore find that tool choice and use within ludological teams is based on leadership modalities. The choice of tool is based on the different types of task that are taken on by the different leadership rank tendencies. In ILB, privates tended to concern themselves with task completion, whereas lieutenants addressed tactical task management, and the general determined strategic task direction, managed group identity and oversaw strategic communication. Teamwork, communication and collaborative tools in a game system must therefore be flexible, and enable their contextual deployment. Providing tools based on players' demonstrated needs, and their demonstrated leadership modalities would inform sensitive contextual design around tool design.

We suggest that future ARG designers, or designers of systems that contain ludic elements, take this infrastructure tension under advisement. We further suggest that interface designers can use the leadership and expertise modalities detailed here as a way of understanding the contextual requirements for interaction, communication or progression within the systems they design. We believe that the L&E modalities can be used to craft system elements that can foster and support specific ludological leadership and expertise modalities.

CONCLUSIONS

Our research was driven by three research questions around themes of military tropes, leadership and expertise. Through our construction of fourteen illustrative case studies, which presented the *in situ* stories of fourteen players across more than 4,700 posts, we confirmed that we can read these discursive streams as war stories. Synthesizing a leadership and expertise modalities framework out of existing work, we used the L&E modalities as analytical tools to understand our case studies, and we found clear indicators of contextual leadership and expertise behaviour. The strongest leader was the general, who used a strategic management style and directive language to organize and control her team's play. Our lieutenants straddled the strategic and tactical behaviours, showing high indications of social management communication styles, and tactical skill. The privates exhibited primarily operational behaviour, providing 'sit rep' task reports of accomplishments and challenges, and demonstrating levels of investment through finishing axon hunting tasks. The accomplishment of game successes despite a lack of formal team and task management tools suggests to us that strongly formalized game systems are not always necessary for computer-supported cooperative play. We advise designers of ludic systems to take into account the context of play, and to design for the emergent properties of leadership and expertise modalities

ACKNOWLEDGMENTS

This research is supported by the National Science Foundation (OCI# 0943184). Any opinions, findings, or recommendations expressed here are those of the authors, and do not necessarily reflect the views of the NSF.

REFERENCES

1. Bartle, R. Hearts, clubs, diamonds, spades: Players who suit MUDs. *Journal of MUD Research*, (1996).
2. Bell, B.S. and Kozlowski, S.W.J. A typology of virtual teams: Implications for effective leadership. *Group and Organization Management 27*, 1 (2002), 14-49

3. Bogost, I. *How to do things with videogames.* University of Minnesota Press, MN, 2011.
4. Callois, R. *Man, play and games.* Thames and Hudson, London, 1962.
5. Chen, M. *Leet noobs.* Peter Lang Publishing, New York, 2011.
6. Chen, M. Communication, coordination and camaraderie in World of Warcraft. *Games & Culture 4,* 1 (2009), 47-73.
7. Chilton, P. Metaphor euphemism and the militarization of language. *Current Research on Peace and Violence 10,* 1 (1987), 7-19.
8. Consalvo, M. There is no magic circle. *Games and Culture 4,* 4 (2009), 408-417.
9. Crowston, K., Li, Q., Wei, K., Eseryel, Y., and Howison, J. Self-organization of teams in free/libre open source software development. *Information and software technology journal 49,* 6 (2007), 564-575.
10. Deterding, S., Dixon, D., Khaled, R. and Nacke, L. From game design elements to gamefulness: Defining "gamification." In *Proc. MindTrek '11,* ACM (2011), 9-15.
11. Eisenhardt, K.M. Building theories from case study research. *The Academy of Management Review 14,* 4 (1989), 532-550.
12. Gee, J.P. *What video games have to teach us about learning and literacy (2nd Ed).* Palgrave Macmillan, New York, 2007.
13. Huffaker, D., Want, J., Treem, J., Ahmad, M., Fullerton, L., Williams, D., Poole, M., and Contractor, N. The social behaviours of experts in massive multiplayer online role-playing games. In *Proc. CSE'09,* IEEE (2009).
14. Huizinga, J. *Homo Ludens: A Study of the Play-Element in Culture.* Beacon Press, 1971.
15. Lutters, W. and Seaman, C. Revealing actual documentation usage in software maintenance through war stories. *Information and Software Technology 49,* 6 (June 2007), 576-587.
16. McArthur, V., Peyton, T., Jenson, J., Taylor, T., & de Castell, S. Knowing, not doing: Modalities of gameplay expertise in World of Warcraft addons. *Ext. Abstracts CHI 2011,* ACM Press (2011), 100-110.
17. McGonigal, J. *Gaming can make a better world.* Long Beach, CA, 2010.
18. O'Hara, K., Grian, H., and Williams, J. Participation, collaboration and spectatorship in an alternate reality game. In *Proc. OZCHI'08,* ACM Press (2008), 130-138.
19. Orr, J.E. Narratives at work: story telling as cooperative diagnostic activity. *Proceedings of the 1986 ACM conference on Computer-supported cooperative work,* ACM (1986), 62–72.
20. Palen, L., and Vieweg, S. The emergence of online widescale interaction in unexpected events: Assistance, alliance and retreat. In *Proc. CSCW'08,* ACM Press (2008), 117-126.
21. *Population representation in the military services: Executive Summary.* Office of the Undersecretary of Defense, Personnel and Readiness, 2010.
22. Piaget, J. *Play, dreams and imitation in childhood.* Taylor & Francis, 1999.
23. Preece, J. and Shneiderman, B. The reader-to-leader framework: Motivating technology-mediated social participation. *AIS Transactions on Human-Computer Interaction 1,* 1 (2009), 13-32.
24. Reeves, S., Brown, B., and Laurier, E. Experts at play: Understanding skilled expertise. *Games and Culture 4,* 3 (2009), 205-227.
25. Sherlock, L. Genre, activity and collaborative work and play in World of Warcraft: Places and problems of open systems in online systems in online gaming. *Journal of Business and Technical Communication 23,* 3 (July 2009), 263-293
26. Shim, K.J., Ahmad, M.A., Pathak, N., and Srivastava, J. Inferring player ratings from performance data in massively multiplayer online role-playing games (MMORPGs). In *Proc CSE'09,* IEEE (2009), 119-1204.
27. Stake, R.E. Case studies. in Denzin, N.K & Lincoln, Y.S. eds *Handbook of qualitative research,* Sage, NY, 1994, 236-247.
28. Taylor, N., de Castell, S., Jenson, J., and Humphrey, M. Modeling play: Re-casting expertise in MMOGs. in *Proc. SIGGRAPH 2011,* ACM Press (2011), 49-53.
29. Taylor, T. L. The Assemblage of Play. *Games and Culture 4,* 4 (2009), 331–339.
30. Viegas, F.B., Wattenberg, M., Kriss, J., and Van Ham, F. Talk before you type.: Coordination in Wikipedia. In *Proc. HICSS 2007,* IEEE (2007), 78-87.
31. Yin, R.K. The case study crisis: Some answers. *Administrative Science Quarterly 26,* 1 (1981), 58–65.
32. Young, A.L., Gurzick, D., Lutters, W., Dombrowski, C., and Kim, J. Exploring infrastructure assemblage in virtual volunteer organizations. *Ext. Abstracts CHI 2011,* ACM Press (2011), 2649-2654.
33. Zhu, H., Kraut, R.E., Kittur, A., and Wang, Y-C. Identifying shared leadership in Wikipedia. In *Proc. CHI'11,* ACM Press (2011), 3431-3434.

GravitySpace: Tracking Users and Their Poses in a Smart Room Using a Pressure-Sensing Floor

Alan Bränzel, Christian Holz, Daniel Hoffmann, Dominik Schmidt, Marius Knaust, Patrick Lühne, René Meusel, Stephan Richter, Patrick Baudisch
Hasso Plattner Institute, Potsdam, Germany
{firstname.lastname}@student.hpi.uni-potsdam.de
{christian.holz, dominik.schmidt, patrick.baudisch}@hpi.uni-potsdam.de

ABSTRACT

We explore how to track people and furniture based on a high-resolution pressure-sensitive floor. Gravity pushes people and objects against the floor, causing them to leave imprints of pressure distributions across the surface. While the sensor is limited to sensing direct contact with the surface, we can sometimes *conclude* what takes place *above* the surface, such as users' poses or collisions with virtual objects. We demonstrate how to extend the range of this approach by sensing through passive furniture that propagates pressure to the floor. To explore our approach, we have created an 8 m^2 back-projected floor prototype, termed *GravitySpace*, a set of passive touch-sensitive furniture, as well as algorithms for identifying users, furniture, and poses. Pressure-based sensing on the floor offers four potential benefits over camera-based solutions: (1) it provides consistent coverage of rooms wall-to-wall, (2) is less susceptible to occlusion between users, (3) allows for the use of simpler recognition algorithms, and (4) intrudes less on users' privacy.

Author Keywords

Interactive floor; smart rooms; ubicomp; multitoe; multi-touch; FTIR; tabletop; vision.

ACM Classification Keywords

H.5.2. [Information Interfaces and Presentation]: User Interfaces–Input devices and strategies, interaction styles.

General Terms

Design; Human Factors.

INTRODUCTION

Brummit et al. define self-aware spaces as "… [a space that] knows its own geometry, the people within it, their actions & preferences, and the resources available to satisfy their requests" [5]. Such smart rooms support users by offering not only a series of convenient functions, like home automation, but also by acting pro-actively on the user's behalf. Similar systems have been proposed to monitor the wellbeing of (elderly) inhabitants [15].

In order to provide this support, smart rooms track users and try to automatically recognize their activities. In systems like EasyLiving, this was done by pointing tracking equipment, such as cameras, at the interior of the room [5]. The direct observation of scenes using computer vision is of limited reliability, because of illumination and perspective effects, as well as occlusion between people. The latter also affects more recent approaches based on depth cameras (e.g., *LightSpace* [43]).

We propose an alternative approach to tracking people and objects in smart rooms. Building on recent work on touch-sensitive floors (e.g., *Multitoe* [1]) and pose reconstruction, such as [44], we explore how much a room can infer about its inhabitants solely based on the pressure imprints people and objects leave on the floor.

Figure 1: GravitySpace recognizes people and objects. We use a mirror-metaphor to show how GravitySpace identifies users and tracks their location and poses, solely based on the pressure imprints they leave on the floor.

GRAVITYSPACE

Figure 1 shows our floor installation *GravitySpace* with three users and three pieces of furniture. To illustrate what the system senses and reconstructs about the physical world, the prototype displays its understanding of the physical world using a mirror-metaphor, so that every object stands on its own virtual reflection. Based on this mirror world, we see that GravitySpace recognizes the position and orientation of multiple users, the identity of users as demonstrated by showing their personalized avatars, selected poses, such as standing and sitting on the floor and on furniture, and tracking of leg movements to interact with virtual objects, here a soccer ball. GravitySpace updates in real-time and runs a physics engine to model the room above the surface. To convey the 3D nature of the sensing, this photo was shot with a tracked camera—this camera tracking is *not* part of GravitySpace.

GravitySpace consists of a single sensor, namely the floor itself which is pressure-sensitive, while the seating furniture passively propagates pressure to the floor. All the tracking and identification shown in Figure 1 is solely based on pressure imprints objects leave on this floor as shown in Figure 3.

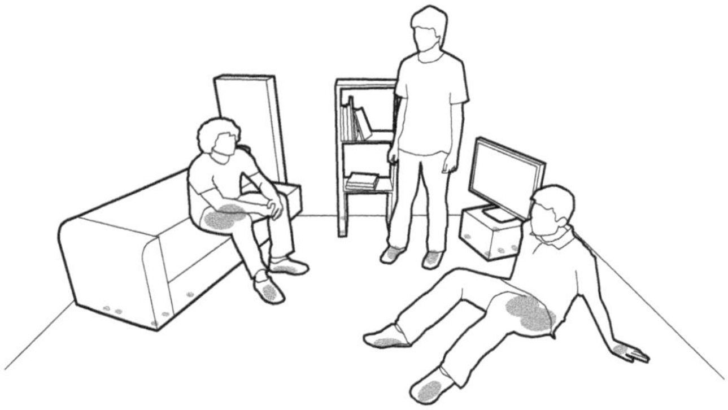

Figure 2: Gravity pushes people and objects against the ground, where they leave *imprints* that GravitySpace can sense.

Our approach is based on the general principle of gravity, which pushes people and objects against the floor, causing the floor to sense pressure imprints as illustrated in Figure 3. While the pressure sensor is limited to sensing *contact* with the ground, GravitySpace not only tracks what happens in the floor plane (such as shoeprints), but is able to draw a certain amount of *conclusions* about what happens in the space *above* the floor, such as a user's pose, or the collision between a user and a virtual ball. In addition, GravitySpace senses what takes place on top of special furniture that propagates pressure to the floor.

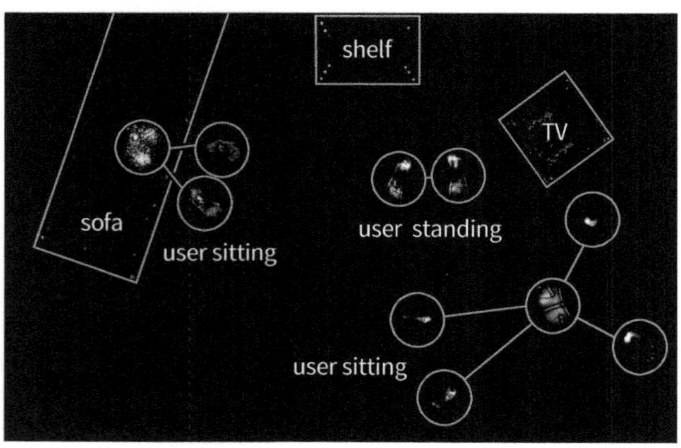

Figure 3: GravitySpace sees the scene from Figure 1 as a set of imprints (circles, lines, and text added for clarity).

Figure 3 shows the scene from Figure 1 as perceived by GravitySpace. This is the information GravitySpace uses to reconstruct the scene above the ground. We see four concepts here, which are detailed in Section *Algorithms*: (1) recognition of poses (86.12% accuracy) based on classifying contact types, such as hands or buttocks, and their spatial arrangement, (2) prediction of leg movements by analyzing pressure distributions, and (3) pressure-based markers that allow GravitySpace to detect objects, such as furniture. In addition, GravitySpace recognizes users based on their shoeprints, similar to *Multitoe* [1], but optimized for the 20 times larger floor size and a larger number of simultaneous users (99.82% accuracy with 120 users in real time).

Prototype Hardware

Figure 4 shows our current GravitySpace prototype hardware. It senses pressure based on FTIR [13], using a camera located below the floor. It provides an 8 m^2 interaction surface in a single seamless piece and delivers 12 megapixels overall pressure sensing resolution at a pixel size of 1×1 mm. Our prototype also offers 12 megapixel back projection. While not necessary for tracking, it allows us to visualize the workings of the system, as we did in Figure 1.

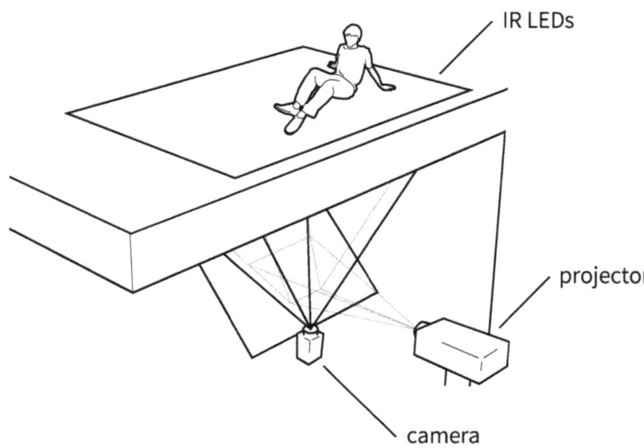

Figure 4: The GravitySpace prototype senses 25 dpi pressure and projects across an active area of 8 m^2 in a single seamless piece.

We expect sensing hardware of comparable size and resolution to soon be inexpensive and mass available, for example in the form of a large, thin, high-resolution pressure sensing foil (e.g., *UnMousePad* [34]). We envision this material to be integrated into carpet and as such installed in new homes wall-to-wall. Since the technology is not quite ready to deliver the tens of megapixel resolution we require for an entire room, our FTIR-based prototype allows us to explore our vision of tracking based on pressure imprints *today*.

CONTRIBUTION

The main contribution of this paper is a new approach to tracking people and objects in a smart room, namely based on a high-resolution pressure-sensitive floor. While the sensor is limited to sensing *contact* with the surface, we demonstrate how to conclude a range of objects and events that take place *above* the surface, such as a user's pose and collisions with virtual objects. We demonstrate how to extend the range of this approach by sensing *through* passive furniture that propagates pressure to the floor.

To explore this approach, we have designed and implemented a fully-functional room-size prototype, which we use to demonstrate our vision true to scale. We have also implemented algorithms for tracking and identifying users, furniture, and poses.

Our main goal with this paper is to demonstrate the technology. We validate it using a technical evaluation of user identification and pose recognition accuracy. The philosophy behind smart rooms, their applications and usability, however, are outside the scope of this paper.

Benefits and Limitations

Compared to traditional camera-based solutions, the proposed approach offers four benefits:

(1) It provides consistent coverage of rooms, wall-to-wall. Camera-based systems have a pyramid-shaped viewing space. Motion capture installations resolve this by leaving space along the edges, but that is impractical in regular rooms, leading to uneven or spotty coverage. Floor-based tracking in contrast, can be flat, integrated into the room itself, and provides consistent coverage across the room.

(2) It is less susceptible to occlusion between users. The perspective from below is particularly hard to block—simply because people tend to stand next to each other, resulting in discernible areas of contact. From a more general perspective, the benefit of pressure sensing is that mass is hard to "hide". Mass has to manifest itself somewhere, either through direct contact or indirectly through another object it is resting on. Camera-based systems, in contrast, may suffer from users occluding each other if the cameras mounted in one spot (e.g., [43]). Systems distributing multiple cameras around a room (e.g., [21]) still suffer from dead spots (e.g., in the midst of groups of users).

(3) *It allows for the use of simpler, more reliable recognition algorithms.* Our approach reduces the recognition problem from comparing 3D objects to comparing flat objects, because all objects are flat when pressed against a rigid surface. This limits objects to three degrees of freedom (translation and rotation in the plane) and allows us to match objects using simple, robust, and well-understood algorithms from digital image processing [8, 11].

(4) *Pressure-based tracking is less privacy-critical.* While floor-based sensing captures a lot of information relevant to assisted living applications (e.g., [15]), it never captures photos or video of its inhabitants, mitigating privacy concerns (e.g., while getting dressed or using the bathroom).

On the other hand, our floor-based approach is obviously limited in that it can recognize objects only when they are in direct contact with the floor. While we reduce the impact of these limitations using 3D models based on inverse kinematics, events taking place in mid-air can obviously not be sensed, such as the angle of an arm being raised or a user's gaze direction. The approach is also inherently subject to lag in that the floor learns about certain events only with a delay. We cannot know the exact position of a user sitting down until the user makes contact with the seat. As we place the avatar in between, it is subject to inaccuracy.

RELATED WORK

The work presented in this paper builds on smart rooms, interactive floors, and user identification in ubiquitous computing.

Multi Display Environments and Smart Rooms

The concept of integrating computing into the environment goes back as far as Weiser (*Ubiquitous computing* [42]). The concept has been researched in the form of smart components in a room, e.g., in multi-display environments such as the Stanford *iRoom* [4] or roomware (*iLand* [37]). Alternatively, researchers have instrumented the room itself, e.g., using cameras and microphones (e.g., *EasyLiving* [5]), making user tracking a key component of the system. The *Georgia Tech Aware Home* [15] tracks users based on multi-user head tracking and combined audio and video sensing. Most recently, Wilson and Benko demonstrated how to instrument rooms using multiple depth cameras (*Lightspace* [43]).

Pressure-Sensing Floors

A series of floor prototypes have used a range of pressure sensing technologies offering a variety of resolutions. The projection-less *magic carpet* senses pressure using piezoelectric wires and a pair of Doppler radars [27] *Z-tiles* improved on this by introducing a modular system of interlocking tiles [32]. Pressure sensing has been implemented using force-sensing resistors [41]. FootSee [44] matches foot data from a 1.6 m^2 pressure pad to pre-recorded pose animations of a single user with in a fixed orientation.

In the desktop world, the *UnMousePad* improves on resistive pressure sensing by reducing the number of required wire connections [34]. Based on this, Srinivasan et al. built larger-scale installations, combined with marker-based motion systems, as well as audio and video tracking [36].

Since none of the existing technologies scale to the megapixel range of resolution, GravitySpace is built on an extension of the *Multitoe* floor. *Multitoe* uses high-resolution FTIR sensing and allows users to interact using direct manipulation [1]. Other instrumented floors are tracked using ceiling-mounted cameras (e.g., *iFloor* [16]) or *front diffuse illumination* (*IGameFloor* [12]). Purposes of interactive floors include immersion (also as part of *CAVEs* [6, 17]), gaming [12], and multi-user collaborative applications [16].

Furniture that Senses Pressure

A series of research and products use pressure-sensitive devices and furniture to monitor health, for instance, to prevent Decubiti (e.g., [39]), orthopedic use inside of shoes (e.g., [10]), and to sense pose while sitting (e.g., [23, 24]).

Sensing through Objects

The pressure-transmitting furniture presented in this paper builds on the concept of sensing *through* an object. The concept has been explored in the context of tangible objects. Mechanisms include the propagation of light through holes (*stackable markers* [3]) and optical fiber (*Lumino* [2]) and the propagation of magnetic forces, sensed using pressure sensors (*Geckos* [18]).

Matching Objects in 2D

The presented work essentially reduces a 3D problem to a 2D problem, allowing us to apply well-explored traditional algorithms from *digital image processing* [8, 11].

Identifying Users

The majority of large-scale touch technologies, such as *diffused illumination* (*DI* [20]), *front-DI* [12], and *FTIR* [13] are ignorant of who touches. *DiamondTouch* improved on this by mapping users to seat positions [9]. Bootstrapper identifies tabletop users by observing the top of their shoes [33]. Recognizing fingerprints has been envisioned to identify users of touch systems [38]; Holz and Baudisch implemented this by turning a fingerprint scanner into a touch device [14]. Schmidt et al. identify tabletop users by the size and shape of their hands [35].

User identification has been used for a variety of applications including the management of access privileges [22] and to help children with Asperger syndrome learn social protocol [30]. Olwal and Wilson used RFID tags to identify objects on the table [25]. The screen-less *Smart Floor* identifies users by observing the forces and timing of the individual phases of walking [26]. While floors so far did not have enough resolution to distinguish soles, footprints have been analyzed as evidence in crime scene investigation [28]. Sole imprints and sole wear has been used to match people either by hand and using semi-automatic techniques based on local feature extractors, such as *MSER* [28, 29]. *Multitoe* distinguishes users based on their shoeprints using template-matching [1].

WALKTHROUGH

In the following walkthrough, we revisit the elements from Figure 1 including user identification and tracking, pose detection, and pressure-transmitting furniture. Given that this paper is about a new approach to tracking, this walkthrough is intended to illustrate GravitySpace's tracking capabilities; it is not trying to suggest a specific real-world application scenario. As before, we render GravitySpace's understanding of users and furniture as a virtual 3D world under the floor. A detailed description of the shown concepts and their implementation can be found in Section *Algorithms*.

Figure 5: GravitySpace detects Daniel sitting on the sofa, and identifies and tracks René walking across the floor.

Figure 5 shows Daniel on the left as he is relaxing on the sofa and GravitySpace's interpretation of the scene in the mirror world. The same scene is shown from a pressure-sensing perspective in Figure 6. GravitySpace parses this pressure image to identify the sofa based on embedded pressure markers and to locate *someone* sitting on top of the sofa based on the pressure imprint of Daniel's buttocks. The sofa is filled with elements that transmit pressure to the floor. GravitySpace combines buttocks and the two feet next to the sofa into a pose. It also identifies Daniel based on his shoeprints. Using this information, Daniel's avatar is selected from a user library and positioned onto the imprints of feet and buttocks.

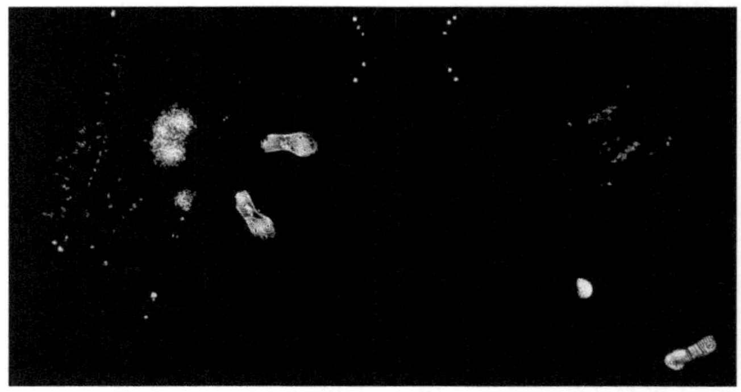

Figure 6: The scene from Figure 5 as seen by the system.

When Daniel's friend, René, comes in he is likewise identified. GravitySpace positions his personalized avatar by fitting a skeleton to René's pressure imprints using inverse kinematics, based on three control points: the two imprints of René's feet in their respective orientation, as well as René's center of gravity. The latter it placed above the center of pressure between René's shoes.

As René walks across the room, GravitySpace continuously tracks his position. By observing the pressure distribution of the foot on the ground, GravitySpace predicts where the foot currently located in midair is expected to come down. This allows it to animate the avatar without having to wait for the foot to touch down.

Figure 7: Daniel and René are controlling a video game by simply leaning over, tracked by observing varying centers of pressure. GravitySpace also detects that Andreas sits down, based on the body parts in contact with the floor.

René and Daniel decide to play a video game. As shown in Figure 7, they interact with the game without a dedicated controller by simply shifting their weight to control virtual racecars. René and Daniel accelerate and brake by leaning forward or backward; they steer by leaning left and right. GravitySpace observes this through the sofa and the cube seat. Also shown in Figure 7, Andreas, a common friend has sat down on the floor to watch the other two playing. GravitySpace determines his pose based on the texture and spatial arrangement of contact points on the floor.

Figure 8: GravitySpace allows for interaction with virtual objects as leg movement is tracked above the floor by analyzing the center of pressure of the other foot.

The three friends then decide to play a round of virtual soccer (Figure 8). The game requires them to kick a virtual ball. GravitySpace cannot directly observe what happens *above* the surface. Instead it observes weight shifts within the *other* foot, and *concludes* where the kicking foot must be located. Using inverse kinematics, it places the avatars and GravitySpace's physics engine computes how the avatar kicks the ball.

PRESSURE-TRANSMITTING FURNITURE

While it is quite possible to create furniture with active pressure sensing (e.g., [24]), we have created *passive* furniture that transmits high-resolution pressure, rather than sensing it. This offloads sensing to a single centralized active sensing component, in our case the floor. Passive furniture also reduces complexity and cost, while the absence of batteries and wires makes them easy to maintain [2].

Everyday furniture already transmits pressure. Furniture imprints, however, are limited to representing overall weight and balance. While locating the center of gravity has been demonstrated by many earlier systems (e.g., VoodooIO [40] or commercial systems, such as the Wii Balance board), this limits our ability to detect activities taking place on top of the furniture (e.g., sitting on a sofa).

In order to recognize identity and poses of the object on top in more detail, we have created the furniture pieces featured in Figure 1 and the walkthrough. They transmit pressure in comparably high resolution. We accomplish this by using an array of "transmitters". Transmitters have to offer sufficient stiffness to transmit pressure (and also to support the weight of the person or object on top). Figure 9 shows how we constructed a cube seat. We use regular drinking straws as transmitters, making the furniture light and sturdy. 1,200 straws (8 mm in diameter) fill each cube seat; 10,000 fill the sofa, which is based on the same principle. Straws are inexpensive (e.g., 80 EUR for filling the sofa). The backrest and armrest of the sofa are pressure-sensitive as well—they are filled with longer "sangria" drinking straws. We obtain the desired curved shape by cutting the straws to length a layer at a time using a laser cutter.

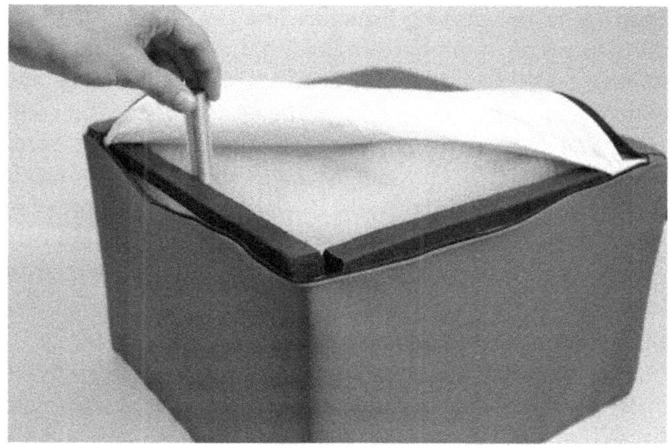

Figure 9: Each cube seat is filled with 1,200 drinking straws. Here one of the steel rods that form the markers is inserted.

Straws are held together by a frame made from 15 mm fiberboard. We stabilize the straws in the box using a grid made from plywood connected to the frame, which essentially subdivides the box into 3×3 independent cells. The grid minimizes skewing, thus prevents the box from tipping over. We cover the bottom of the box with Tyvek, a material that crinkles but does not stretch, which prevents the bottom from sagging, yet transmits pressure. In addition to the leather we added a thin layer of foam as cushioning to the top of the cube seats for added comfort.

Weight shifts on top of the box can cause the box to "ride up" on the straws, which can cause an edge of the box to lose traction with the ground. To assure reliable detection, we create markers from weight rods that slide freely in plastic tubes and held in by the Tyvek. We use an asymmetric arrangement of rods to give a unique ID to each piece.

ALGORITHMS

Figure 10 summarizes the pipeline we implemented to process touches that occur on our floor, including recognizing, classifying and tracking events, users and objects based on the pressure patterns they leave. We optimized our pipeline to process the entire 12 megapixel image in real-time (25 fps).

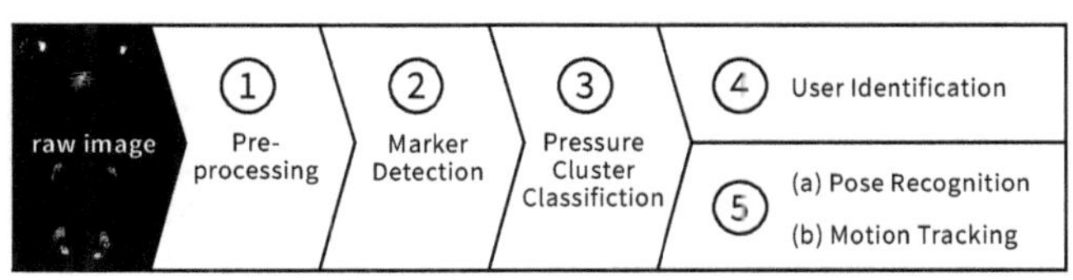

Figure 10: GravitySpace processes all input using this pipeline to recognize and track users and objects.

GravitySpace recognizes objects with texture (e.g., body parts or shoeprints) by extracting the imprint features they leave in the raw image. For objects with little discernible texture or changing texture (e.g., due to users sitting on furniture), we add features using pressure-based markers.

Our GravitySpace implementation supports three key elements: (1) Pose reconstruction using pressure cluster classification, (2) joint estimation based on pressure distributions and inverse kinematic, and (3) user identification based on shoeprints.

Step 1: Pre-Processing Pressure Images

All processing starts by thresholding the pressure image to remove noise. Our algorithm then segments this image and extracts continuous areas of pressure using a connected component analysis. In the next step, GravitySpace merges areas within close range, prioritizing areas that expand towards each other. We call the result *pressure clusters*. A pressure cluster may be for example a shoeprint or the buttocks of a sitting user. GravitySpace then tracks these clusters over time.

Step 2: Identifying Furniture Based on Markers

Pressure imprints of larger objects, such as furniture, provide little distinguishable texture on their own. In addition, the overall texture of seating furniture changes substantially when users sit down. GravitySpace therefore uses dot-based pressure-markers to locate and identify furniture. Figure 11 shows the imprint of a cube that we equipped with a marker. This particular marker consists of five points. Marker points are arranged in a unique spatial pattern that is rotation-invariant. We designed and implemented marker patterns for a sofa, several sitting cubes, and shelves.

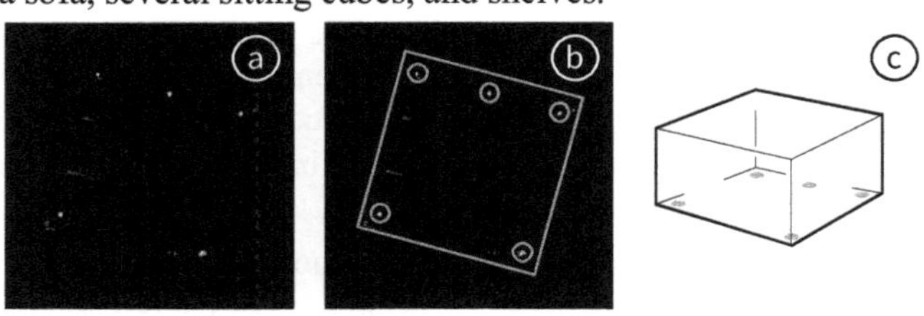

Figure 11: (a) Pressure imprint and (b) detected marker points (c) of marker-equipped cube.

To recognize markers, GravitySpace implements brute-force matching on the locations that have been classified as marker points, trying to fit each registered piece of furniture into the observed point set and minimizing the error distance. To increase the stability of recognition, our implementation keeps objects whose marker patterns have been detected in a history list and increases the confidence level of recently recognized objects. We also use hysteresis to decide when marker detection is stable based on the completeness of markers and their history confidence.

Step 3: Classifying Pressure Clusters Based on Image Analysis

For each pressure cluster in the camera image, GravitySpace analyzes the probability of being one of the contact types shown in Figure 12. GravitySpace distinguishes hands, knees, buttocks, and shoes, thereby further distinguishing between heel, tip, and edge of a shoe. These probability distributions are an essential part of the subsequent pose recognition. Areas covered by furniture pieces are ignored for this classification in order to minimize noise.

In order to classify each pressure cluster, GravitySpace extracts 16 fast-to-compute image features from the respective area in the image, including image moments, structure descriptors using differences of Gaussians, as well as the extents, area, and aspect ratio of the bounding box around the cluster. We trained a feedforward neural network, which assigns probabilities for each type of contact to each cluster.

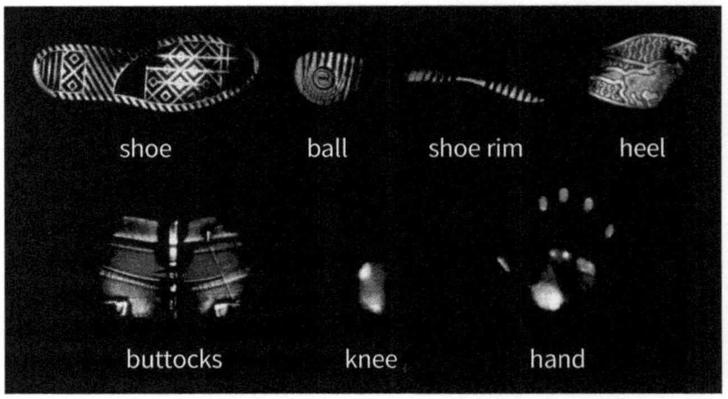

Figure 12: GravitySpace assigns each pressure cluster the probability of being one of the contact types shown above.

Step 4: Identifying Users Based on Shoeprints

Whenever the users' feet are in contact with the ground—for example when standing or sitting, but not when lying—GravitySpace will recognize users by matching their shoeprints against a database of shoes associated with user identities. As users register with both of their shoes, our approach also distinguishes left and right feet.

Due to the large floor area, previous approaches to user identification on multi-touch floors are not sufficient on GravitySpace, such as template matching in *Multitoe* [1], which observed an area of only a 20th of the size.

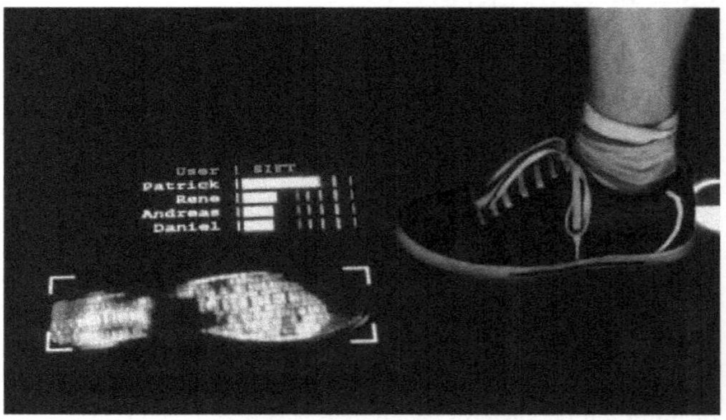

Figure 13: GravitySpace uses SIFT to match detected shoeprints against a database of registered users.

To match shoeprints with the same resolution as previous systems (1 mm per pixel), GravitySpace uses an implementation of SIFT [19] that runs on the GPU. Using SIFT as the feature detector and descriptor algorithm allows us to match shoes with rotation invariance. To identify a user by the shoe, GravitySpace counts the number of features that match in each of the shoe images in the database and the observed shoeprint as shown in Figure 13. A feature thereby matches if the angular distance between the two descriptor vectors is within close range. As the number of detected features varies substantially between different sole patterns, we normalize the distance (i.e., we divide by the maximum number of features in either observed or database image).

Stitching a Shoe Imprint from a Sequence of Frames

When a user walks on the floor, only a small part of their shoe appears in the image at first and then becomes larger as their shoe sole rolls over the floor from heel to toe. Since the camera consecutively captures images of each such partial shoe imprint, GravitySpace merges all partial observations in successive frames into an aggregated imprint, which allows us to capture an almost complete shoe sole. This concept is also commonly used to obtain a more encompassing fingerprint by rolling a finger sideways while taking fingerprints.

Recovering Shoe Orientation Based on Phase Correlation

To predict the location of users' next steps when walking, GravitySpace leverages the orientation of the shoes on the floor. GravitySpace determines shoe orientations directly after matching shoeprints by registering front and back of each database shoeprint with the observed shoe on the floor. Our system transforms both shoeprints into spectrum images and applies log polar transforms to then compute the translation vector and rotation angle between the two shoeprints using phase correlation. All shoes in the database thereby have annotated locations of heel and toes, which happens automatically upon registration by analyzing the direction of walking.

Step 5a: Pose Recognition Based on Spatial Configurations of Pressure Clusters

To classify body poses from the observed pressure imprints, GravitySpace performs pose matching based on the location and classified type of observed pressure clusters. For example, GravitySpace observes the spatial configuration of pressure clusters shown in Figure 14, i.e., the imprints of buttocks, two feet, and two hands as a user is sitting on the floor.

To match a pose, GravitySpace uses a set of *detectors*, one for each pose that is registered with the system. Each detector is a set of rules based on contact types and their spatial arrangement. GravitySpace currently distinguishes five poses: standing, kneeling, sitting on the floor, sitting on cube seat or sofa, and lying on a sofa.

GravitySpace feeds all pressure clusters to all detectors. Each detector creates a set of hypotheses. Each hypothesis, in turn, contains a set of imprints that match the pose described by the detector. For example, hypotheses returned by the sitting detector contain buttocks and two feet. Optionally, there may also be two hands if users support themselves while leaning backwards as shown in Figure 14. Each detector returns all possible combinations (or hypotheses) of imprints that match the pose implemented by this detector. Each hypothesis thus explains a subset of all imprints. We compute the probability of a hypothesis by multiplying the classification probabilities of all contained imprints with a pose-specific prior.

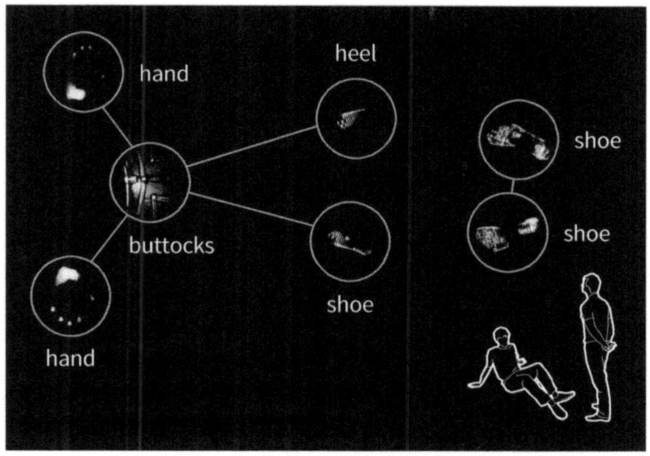

Figure 14: Based on pressure clusters types and their spatial arrangement, GravitySpace recognizes a sitting and a standing user.

From these *individual* hypotheses (explaining a single pose), we compute a set of *complete* hypotheses; each complete hypothesis explains all detected imprints by combining individual hypotheses. We calculate the probability of a complete hypothesis as joint probability of individual hypotheses, assuming that individual poses are independent from each other. We track complete hypotheses over multiple frames using a Hidden Markov Model with complete hypotheses as values of the latent state variable.

Step 5b: Tracking Based on Pressure Distributions

GravitySpace also tracks body parts that are *not* in contact with the floor, such as the locations of feet above the ground while walking or kicking. Our system also tracks general body tilt, for example when a user leans left or right while sitting. This allows for predicting steps before making contact with the floor to reduce tracking latency or to interact with virtual objects on the floor. Obviously, our approach cannot sense events taking place in mid-air, such as raising an arm or changing the gaze direction.

We estimate the location of in-air joints by analyzing the changing centers of gravity within each pressure cluster. We then try to best fit a skeleton to the computed locations of all joints using a CCD implementation of inverse kinematics. GravitySpace finally visualizes the reconstructed body poses with 3D avatars.

Deriving the Location of Feet above the Ground

GravitySpace enables users to interact with virtual objects, such as by kicking a virtual ball as shown in Figure 8. To simulate the physical behavior of virtual objects, GravitySpace first computes the position of feet above the ground. Since a foot is not in contact with the ground when kicking, GravitySpace reconstructs its location by analyzing the changing pressure distribution of the *other* foot, which is on the ground as shown in Figure 15. Our algorithm first calculates the vector from the center of pressure of the cluster aggregated over time to the center of pressure of the current cluster. This vector corresponds to the direction that a person is leaning towards, and is used to directly set the position of the foot in mid-air. We again derive a skeleton using inverse kinematics, which enables animating the remaining joints of the avatar for output.

Tracking body tilt

To track a user's body tilt, for example when leaning left or right when playing the video game described in the walkthrough, GravitySpace observes multiple pressure clusters as shown in Figure 16. The system first computes the joint center of pressure over all pressure clusters of a user by summing up zero and first order moments of the individual pressure images. We then exploit that the center of pressure directly corresponds to a body's center of gravity projected on the floor. Once the center of gravity is determined, GravitySpace sets the corresponding endpoints of the skeleton's kinematic chains; all other joints then follow automatically based on the inverse kinematic.

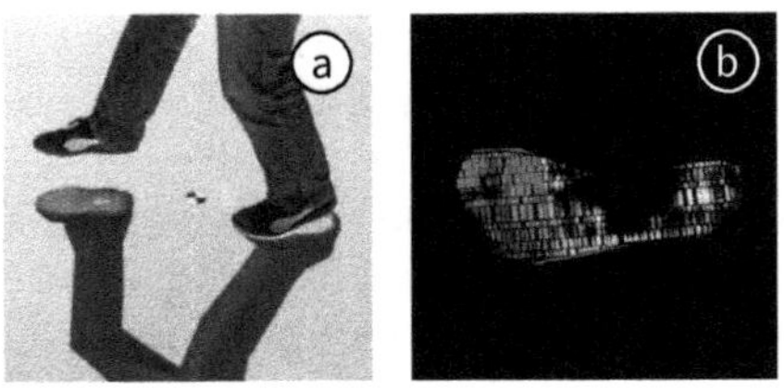

Figure 15: GravitySpace (a) derives the foot location above the floor based on (b) pressure distributions of the other foot.

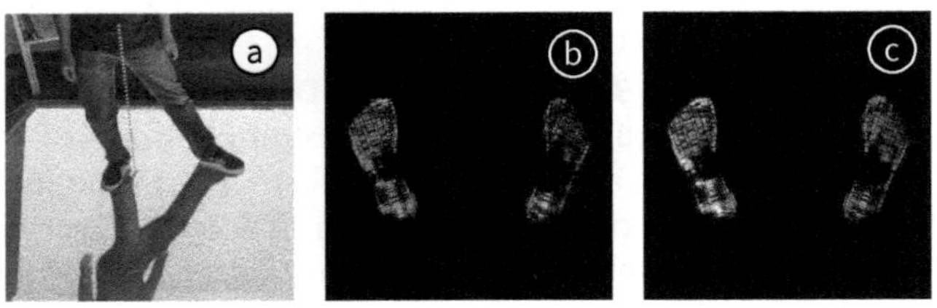

Figure 16: (a) Tracking a user's center of gravity based on (b) and (c) the joint center of pressure of both feet.

EVALUATION

We conducted a technical evaluation of three system components, namely pressure cluster classification, user identification, and pose recognition. In summary, the algorithms of our prototype system allow for (1) distinguishing different body parts on the floor with an accuracy of 92.62% based on image analysis of pressure clusters, (2) recognizing four body poses with an accuracy of 86.12% based on type and spatial relationships between pressure clusters, and (3) identifying 20 users against a 120-user database with an accuracy of 99.82% based on shoeprint matching.

Pressure Cluster Classification

To evaluate pressure cluster classification, we trained a feedforward neural network with data from 12 participants, and tested its classification performance with data from another four participants.

Training Data: We asked 12 participants to walk, stand, kneel, and sit on the floor, in order to collect data of the seven different contact types required for pose recognition, namely hand, shoe (we distinguish between the entire shoe, ball, rim, and heel), knee, and buttocks. In total, we collected 18,600 training samples.

	shoe	ball	shoe rim	heel	buttocks	knee	hand
shoe	1088	1	2	0	0	0	1
ball	17	200	2	18	1	0	12
shoe rim	14	1	297	5	0	0	1
heel	2	83	35	101	0	0	0
buttocks	23	3	0	1	254	3	6
knee	0	17	3	3	0	366	2
hand	7	0	31	21	41	58	459

Figure 17: Confusion matrix for pressure cluster classification.

Test Data: Following the same procedure, we collected data from another four participants, for testing. This resulted in 3,127 samples.

Evaluation Procedure: We manually annotated all training samples to provide ground truth. We then fed the test data into the trained neural network, taking the contact type with the highest probability as outcome. Note that our algorithm does not discard the probability distributions provided by the neural network, but feeds them into the following pose recognition as additional input.

Results: Our approach achieved a classification accuracy of 86.94% for the seven contact types shown in the confusion matrix of Figure 17. If the entire shoe, ball, rim, and heel are grouped and treated as a single contact of type "shoe", as done by the pose recognition, classification accuracy reaches 92.62%.

Pose Recognition

We evaluated our pose recognition implementation with five participants. As pose recognition is based on descriptors of spatial contact layouts, no training data is required for this evaluation.

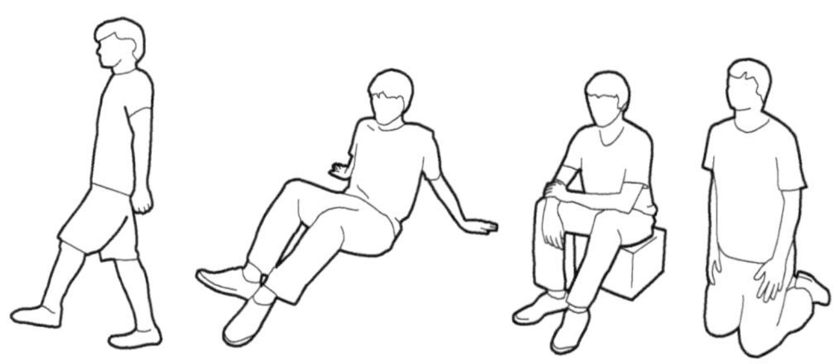

Figure 18: We tested identification of four poses: standing/walking, sitting, sitting on furniture, and kneeling.

Test Data: We collected data from five participants, who each performed the four poses shown in Figure 18, namely standing/walking, sitting on the floor, sitting on furniture, and kneeling. For each participant and pose, we recorded a separate pressure video sequence.

Evaluation Procedure: To provide ground truth, we manually annotated all frames with the currently shown pose. We then ran our algorithm on all frames of the recorded videos, and compared the detected poses to ground truth annotations.

Results: 86.12% (SD=13.5) of poses were correctly identified within a time window of 1.5 s as tolerance. In comparison, FootSee achieves recognition rates of 80% (tested with a single subject) for five standing only activities [44].

User Identification

We determined the user identification accuracy of our implementation with 20 users.

Registration: To populate the user database, each participant walked in circles for about 35 steps on the floor. GravitySpace now selected one left and one right shoeprint for each participant, choosing the shoeprint with the minimum distance in the feature space compared to all other shoeprints of the same participant and foot.

Test Data: After a short break, participants walked a test sequence of about 60 steps. Shoeprints were in contact with the floor for an average of 0.92 s (SD=0.13). Participants then did another round. This time, however, they were instructed to walk as fast as possible, resulting in a sequence of about 70 steps with a lower average duration of 0.38 s (SD=0.11).

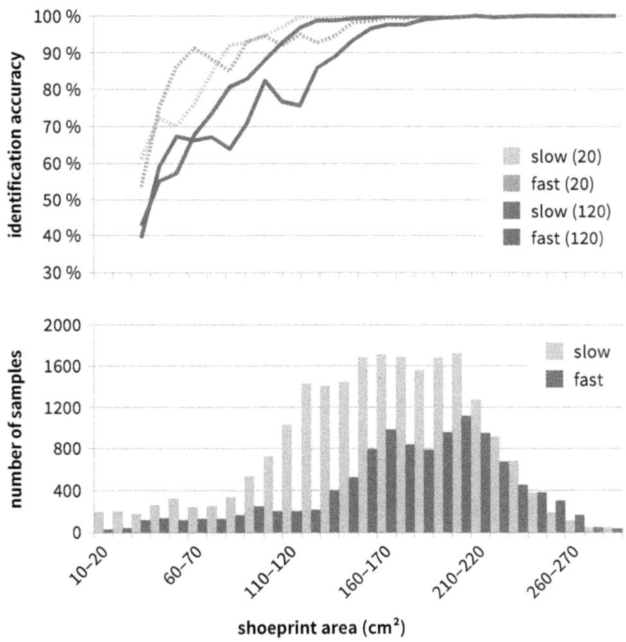

Figure 19: Identification accuracy for walking slow and fast, using databases of 20 and 120 users. Aggregating multiple frames leads to more complete shoeprints and better identification accuracies.

Evaluation Procedure: We evaluated the identification performance by running our algorithms on the recorded test data. Obviously, the slower participants walked, the longer their feet were in contact with the floor, and the more frames were available. The foot part in contact with the floor varied while walking, rolling from heel to toe. As described above, our algorithm reconstructed shoeprints by merging successive pressure imprints. We ran our identification algorithms on all aggregated imprints with an area greater than 30 cm^2, which is the minimum area for discernible shoe contacts as determined during the previous pressure cluster evaluation.

Results: We evaluated the test set against two databases, one containing 20 study participants, and one enlarged with data from 100 additional people (i.e., lab members and visitors). Figure 19 shows the identification accuracy using these two databases for both walking slow and fast. As expected, larger shoeprints aggregated from more frames resulted in better recognition. For the 20-user database, the classification accuracy reached 99.94% for shoeprints with an area between 180 and 190 cm^2 (the average area of shoeprints). When walking fast, recognition rates slightly dropped to a maximum classification accuracy of 99.19%. This is expected as shoeprints were more blurry.

We then reran the classification against the 120-user database. Our approach correctly identified 99.82% shoeprints when walking slowly, and 97.56% when walking fast. In comparison, Orr et al.'s Smart Floor identifies users based on their footstep force profiles and achieves recognition rates of 93% for 15 users [26]. Qian et al. correctly recognize 94% of 10 users based on gait analysis [31].

Speed: Feature extraction took 47.7 ms (SD = 11.4) per shoeprint, which is independent of the number of registered users. Identification took 251.4 ms (SD = 81.2) using a database of 120 users. Each additionally registered user increases the runtime by 2 ms.

To maintain a frame rate of 25 fps, GravitySpace runs user identification asynchronously. Before identification is completed, users are tracked based on heuristics (e.g., distance and orientation of shoeprints). Once identified, user tracking relies on this information. To reduce delays due to identification, GravitySpace caches recently seen users: new contacts are first compared to this short list of before falling back to the entire participant database.

CONCLUSIONS AND FUTURE WORK

We have demonstrated how to track people and furniture based on a high-resolution 8 m^2 pressure-sensitive floor. While our sensor is limited to sensing *contact* with the surface, we have demonstrated how to conclude a range of objects and events that take place *above* the surface, such as user pose and collisions with virtual objects. We demonstrated how to extend the range of this approach by sensing *through* passive furniture that propagates pressure to the floor. As future work, we plan to combine GravitySpace with other touch-sensitive surfaces into an all touch-sensitive room, and explore the space of explicit interaction across large floors.

ACKNOWLEDGMENTS

We thank Martin Fritzsche, Markus Hinsche, Ludwig Kraatz, Jonas Gebhardt, Paul Meinhardt, Jossekin Beilharz, Nicholas Wittstruck, Marcel Kinzel, Franziska Boob, and Jan Burhenne for their help and Microsoft Research Cambridge for their support.

REFERENCES

1. Augsten, T., Kaefer K., Meusel R., Fetzer C., Kanitz D., Stoff T., Becker T., Holz C., and Baudisch P. Multitoe: High-precision interaction with back-projected floors based on high-resolution multi-touch input. In *Proc. UIST'10,* 209–218.
2. Baudisch, P., Becker, T., and Rudeck, F. Lumino: Tangible blocks for tabletop computers based on glass fiber bundles. In *Proc. CHI'10,* 1165-1174.
3. Bartindale, T. and Harrison, C. Stacks on the surface: Resolving physical order with masked fiducial markers. In *Proc. ITS'09*, 57–60.
4. Borchers, J., Ringel, M., Tyler, J., and Fox, A. Stanford Interactive Workspaces: A framework for physical and graphical user interface prototyping. *IEEE Wireless Communications, Vol. 9,* No. 6, IEEE Press, December 2002, 64–69.
5. Brumitt, B., Meyers, B., Krumm, J., Kern, A., and Shafer, S. A. EasyLiving: Technologies for intelligent environments. In *Proc. Ubicomp'00*, 12–29.
6. Cruz-Neira, C., Sandin, D.J., and DeFanti, T.A. Surround-screen projection-based virtual reality: The design and implementation of the CAVE. In *Proc. SIGGRAPH'93*, 135–142.
7. Davidson, P., Han, J. Extending 2D object arrangement with pressure-sensitive layering cues. In *Proc. UIST'08*, 87–90.
8. Davies, E. Roy (2005). *Machine Vision: Theory, Algorithms, Practicalities (3rd ed.).* Amsterdam, Boston: Elsevier. ISBN 9780122060939.
9. Dietz, P. and Leigh, D. DiamondTouch: A multi-user touch technology. In *Proc. UIST'01*, 219–226.
10. F-Scan® System in-shoe plantar pressure analysis http://www.tekscan.com
11. González, R., and Woods, R. *Digital image processing.* Addison-Wesley Longman Publishing Co., Inc. Boston, MA, USA ©1992 ISBN:0201508036.
12. Grønbæk, K., Iversen, O. S., Kortbek, K. J., Nielsen, K. R., and Aagaard, L. IGameFloor: A platform for co-located collaborative games. In *Proc. ACE'07*, 64–71.
13. Han, J. Y. Low-cost multi-touch sensing through frustrated total internal reflection. In *Proc. UIST'05*, 115–118.
14. Holz, C. and Baudisch, P. The generalized perceived input point model and how to double touch accuracy by extracting fingerprints. In *Proc. CHI'10,* 581–590.
15. Kientz, J. A., Patel, S. N., Jones, B., Price, E., Mynatt, E. D., and Abowd, G. D. The Georgia Tech aware home. In *CHI'08 EA,* 3675–3680.
16. Krogh, P. G., Ludvigsen, M., Lykke-Olesen, A. Help me pull that cursor. A Collaborative Interactive Floor Enhancing Community Interaction. In *Proc. OZCH'04*, 22–24.
17. LaViola, J. J., Feliz, D. A., Keefe, D. F., and Zeleznik, R. C. Hands-free multi-scale navigation in virtual environments. In *Proc. I3D'01*, 9–15.
18. Leitner, J. and Haller, M. Geckos: Geckos: Combining magnets and pressure images to enable new tangible-object design and interaction. In *Proc. CHI'11*, pp 2985–2994.
19. Lowe, D. Object recognition from local scale-invariant features. *IEEE Comp. Vision 2.* (1999), 1150–1157.
20. Matsushita, N., and Rekimoto, J. *HoloWall*: Designing a finger, hand, body, and object sensitive wall. In *Proc. UIST'97*, 209–210.
21. Molyneaux, D., Izadi, S., Kim, D., Hilliges, O., Hodges, S., Cao, X., Butler, A., and Gellersen, H. Interactive environment-aware handheld projectors for pervasive computing spaces. In *Proc. Pervasive'12*, 197–215.
22. Morris, M.R. Designing tabletop groupware. In *UIST'05 Doctoral Symposium.*
23. Mota, S. and Picard, R.W. Automated posture analysis for detecting learner's interest level. In *Proc. CVPRW'03*, 49–56.
24. Mutlu, B. and Krause, A. and Forlizzi, J. and Guestrin, C. and Hodgins, J. Robust, low-cost, non-intrusive sensing and recognition of seated postures. In *Proc. UIST'07*,–158.
25. Olwal, A. and Wilson, A.D. SurfaceFusion: Unobtrusive tracking of everyday objects in tangible user interfaces. In *Proc. GI'08*, 235–242.
26. Orr, R. J. and Abowd, G. D. The Smart Floor: a mechanism for natural user identification and tracking. In *CHI'00 EA*, 275–276.
27. Paradiso, J., Abler, C., Hsiao, K., Reynolds, M. The Magic Carpet: Physical sensing for immersive environments. In *Proc. CHI'97,* 277–278.
28. Pavlou, M. and Allinson, N.M. Automatic extraction and classification of footwear patterns. In *Proc. IDEAL'06*, 721–728.
29. Pavlou, M. and Allinson, N.M. Footwear Recognition. In *Proc. Encyclopedia of Biometrics'09*, 557-562.
30. Piper, A., O'Brien, Ringel Morris, M., and Winograd, T. SIDES: A cooperative tabletop computer game for social skills development. In *Proc. CSCW'06,* 1–10.
31. Qian, G., Zhang, J., Kidane, A. People identification using gait via floor pressure sensing and analysis. In *Proc. SCC'08*, 83–98.
32. Richardson, B., Leydon, K., Fernstrom, M., and Paradiso, J. A. Z-Tiles: Building blocks for modular, pressure-sensing floorspaces. In *CHI'04 EA*, 1529–1532.
33. Richter, S., Holz, C., and Baudisch, P. Bootstrapper: Recognizing tabletop users by their shoes. In *CHI'12*, 1249–1252.
34. Rosenberg, I. and Perlin, K. The UnMousePad: An interpolating multi-touch force-sensing input pad. In *Proc. SIGGRAPH'09/ACM Trans. Graph.* (Vol. 28, No. 3, Article 65), 1–9.
35. Schmidt, D., Chong, M., and Gellersen, H. HandsDown: Hand-contour-based user identification for interactive surfaces. In *Proc. NordiCHI'10*, 432–441.
36. Srinivasan, P., Birchfield, D., Qian, G. and Kidan, A. A pressure sensing floor for interactive media applications. In *Proc. ACE'05*, 278–281.
37. Streitz, N., Geißler, J., Holmer, T., Konomi, S., Müller-Tomfelde, C., Reischl, W., Rexroth, P., Seitz, P., and Steinmetz, R. i-LAND: An interactive landscape for creativity and innovation. In *Proc. CHI'99*, 120–127.
38. Sugiura, A. and Koseki, Y. A user interface using fingerprint recognition: holding commands and data objects on fingers. In *Proc. UIST'98*, 71–79.
39. Verbunt M, Bartneck C. Sensing senses: Tactile feedback for the prevention of decubitus ulcers. In *Appl Psychophysiol Biofeedback.* 2010 Sep, 35(3):243–50.
40. Villar, N., Gilleade, K., Ramduny-Ellis, D., and Gellerson, H. The VoodooIO gaming kit: A real-time adaptable gaming controller. In *Proc. ACE'06*.
41. Visell, Y., Law, A., and Cooperstock, J. R. Touch is everywhere: Floor surfaces as ambient haptic interfaces. *EEE Trans. Haptics 2, 3 (Jul. 2009)*, 148–159.
42. Weiser, M. The computer for the 21st century. *Scientific American,* Sep. 1991, 66–75.
43. Wilson, A. and Benko, H. Combining multiple depth cameras and projectors for interactions on, above and between surfaces. In *Proc. UIST'10,* 273–282.
44. Yin, K. and Pai, D. FootSee: An interactive animation system. In *Proc. SCA'03*, 329–338

Improving Digital Object Handoff Using the Space Above the Table

Steven W.T. Sutcliffe, Zenja Ivkovic, David R. Flatla, Andriy Pavlovych, Ian Stavness, and Carl Gutwin
Department of Computer Science, University of Saskatchewan
110 Science Place, Saskatoon, SK, Canada, S7N 5C9
{steve.sutcliffe, zenja.ivkovic, david.flatla, andriy.pavlovych, ian.stavness, carl.gutwin}@usask.ca

ABSTRACT
Object handoff – that is, passing an object or tool to another person – is an extremely common activity in collaborative tabletop work. On digital tables, object handoff is typically accomplished by sliding them on the table surface – but surface-only interactions can be slow and error-prone, particularly when there are multiple people carrying out multiple handoffs. An alternative approach is to use the space *above* the table for object handoff; this provides more room to move, but requires above-surface tracking. We have developed two above-the-surface handoff techniques that use simple and inexpensive tracking: a force-field technique that uses a depth camera to determine hand proximity, and an electromagnetic-field technique called ElectroTouch that provides positive indication when people touch hands over the table. We compared the new techniques to three kinds of surface-only handoff (sliding, flicking, and surface-only Force-Fields). The study showed that the above-surface techniques significantly improved both speed and accuracy, and that ElectroTouch was the best technique overall. This work provides designers with practical new techniques for substantially increasing performance and interaction richness on digital tables.

Author Keywords
Digital tables, coordination, digital object handoff

ACM Classification Keywords
H.5.2. Information interfaces (e.g., HCI): User Interfaces

INTRODUCTION
When people interact around a table they often pass objects to others – this object transfer is called 'handoff', and occurs in many situations, such as when a desired object is out of reach but close to someone else, and when an object is within someone else's personal territory [19]. Handoff can be initiated by the giver ("I think you need this") or the receiver ("May I have that?"), and can be performed with little to no verbal coordination (e.g., exchanging cards during a card game, or passing tools during a work session).

Handoff is also common in digital tabletops, but has traditionally been limited to surface-based interactions where users transfer objects by sliding them across the table surface. However, surface-based handoff can be slow and difficult in some cases. First, handoff speed can be reduced because of *friction*, since users' fingers must be in contact with the surface throughout the action [3]. Second, when there are several people working in the space, handoff can be impaired by *interference* – either occlusion of objects or collision with others' hands and arms. Both of these factors lead to longer completion times, coordination difficulties, and increased errors, and since handoff is a common task in tabletop collaborative work, even small reductions in performance can have a substantial effect on the overall usability of the groupware system.

Researchers have proposed new on-the-surface techniques such as object flicking (e.g., [18]) or force-field transfer [14] that could improve on these problems, but there is very little evaluation of these techniques for object handoff. In addition, new types of table workspaces that are based on physical simulation (e.g., BumpTop [1]) make surface-based transfer techniques even more difficult.

An alternate approach for digital handoff is to use the space above the table rather than just the surface. This has the potential to solve both the friction and interference problems. At real world tables, people naturally and easily overcome many of the limitations of surface-based handoff by simply raising the location of the handoff. This approach can also work at digital tables, but it does present an additional challenge – the handoff action must now be tracked above the table. 3D tracking technologies have existed for some time, but are traditionally both expensive and immobile, limiting their use for practical deployment.

We have developed two new above-the-surface handoff techniques, both of which address the problems of friction and interference, and require only simple and inexpensive above-table tracking. Our first technique extends Force-Field transfer [14] to three-dimensional use, by using a Kinect depth camera to track hand location and proximity. Second, we developed ElectroTouch, which senses physical touches through changes to electromagnetic fields – allowing users to perform handoffs by touching hands over the table. ElectroTouch uses similar technology to the identity-touch sensors of the DiamondTouch table [4], but uses the sensory capability in a novel way – to determine person-to-person touches rather than touches on a table.

We tested the effectiveness of our new techniques by conducting a study that compared them to three existing surface-only handoff methods: traditional sliding, object flicking, and surface-based force-fields [14]. Thirty-two participants carried out repeated handoffs to a partner by themselves or with multiple people working at the same time. Our study provides five main results:

- the above-the-surface techniques resulted in the fastest completion times and the lowest error rates;
- ElectroTouch was significantly faster and significantly more accurate than any other technique;
- depth-based sensing is prone to error when there are four people at the table, but ElectroTouch is robust to increased group size;
- object flicking was the best of the surface techniques;
- participants rated both ElectroTouch and object flicking best for effort and preference.

This work makes four main contributions. First, we introduce two new techniques for object handoff at digital tables, and provide empirical evidence about the performance characteristics of those techniques as well as three traditional transfer techniques. Second, we demonstrate a new tracking technology – ElectroTouch – that can provide physical contact sensing easily and inexpensively. Third, we indicate some of the limitations of depth-camera-based sensing, and show that a low-bandwidth but high-confidence sensor can be better for tasks like object handoff that require conclusive feedback. Fourth, we show the value of object flicking for surface-only handoff when several people are working at the table. Overall, our work provides several new insights and new practical techniques that designers can use to improve collaborative work at tabletop groupware systems.

RELATED WORK

Digital Tabletops

A number of recent studies have explored ways in which digital tabletops can support co-located collaboration [2; 5; 17]. When people work together around a digital tabletop, their awareness of each other's actions is improved by the physicality of pointing, reaching, and using direct touch input [7]. Previous work has also shown that participants were more effective at a collaborative memory game using Stylus input rather than mouse input [13]. While direct touch input enhances certain aspects of co-located collaboration, it may lead to interference between multiple users' actions when many users are working at the same digital table.

Interference

Horneker et al. [11] define interference as, "unintended negative influence on each others' action." In a two-person puzzle task Müller-Tomfelde and Schremmer [16] observed interference (physical collisions) when both people used direct touch, but not when one or both people used mouse input. In a three-person collaborative task to design a floorplan, Horneker et al. [11] found that direct touch input had a positive influence on interaction, including un-requested assistance and non-verbal handoffs, but caused increased rates of interference and user effort. For example, re-negotiation was required between users when conflicts occurred during handoffs. They also note that forced turn taking, or pre-defined personal territories [22], "might interfere with fluent and dense interaction."

Handoff

The transfer of artifacts between people is basic mechanism of collaboration. Such a transfer can be performed synchronously or asynchronously, and Pinelle et al. [17] defined these two interactions as *handoff* and *deposit.* While asynchronous depositing of artifacts is less prone to physical interference during collaborative work, previous work has suggested that synchronous handoff is important for digital tabletops both because it is faster, and because users are reluctant to deposit or retrieve artifacts in other's private areas on the tabletop [19].

In real world handoff, people can exchange objects with little negotiation, planning, or attentive effort. Huber et al. [12] used motion analysis of person-to-person handoffs to show that the basic mechanism of transferring an object exhibits a high degree of temporal and spatial coordination and is organized into three principal phases: reaction, manipulation, and finally post-handover recovery. Also, using motion analysis, Basili et al. [2] found that person-to-person handoff of a physical object is not well modeled by Fitts' law due to prehension, precision grip, and complexity of the motor task. They suggest that digital handoff techniques involving tangible objects may be slower than those based on pointing or aiming interaction. In a pointing-based handoff interaction, Sallnäs and Zhai [20] found that haptic feedback reduced handoff errors.

For collaborative work with many people, synchronous handoff of digital objects can be disrupted due to interference; therefore, interaction techniques are needed to support digital handoff while minimizing interference.

On-The-Tabletop Interaction Techniques

A number of techniques are commonly used for interacting with digital artifacts on a digital tabletop. Surface-only sliding is common on handheld tablets, but sliding objects on a large digital tabletop can be slow due to the friction of fingertips on glass surfaces [3]. Also, when working with multiple people, the active sliding artifacts can interfere with each other, due to occlusion and collisions from simultaneous reaches.

Flicking is another interaction that is widely used on tablets, typically to scroll through documents. It is more effective than sliding input for long distances because of the lack of friction. Reetz et al. [18] evaluated flicking for depositing objects at long distances on tabletops. However, flicking has not been evaluated as a handoff mechanism.

Jun et al. [14] invented a novel handoff technique called surface-only Force-Field (SurfaceFF) in which objects are attracted to the reaching hand of the receiver. Their evaluation of a two-person task showed that SurfaceFF was faster than sliding-based handoff. In situations with more than two people, SurfaceFF may be more prone to negative interference, since there may be more than one reaching hand to which an object is attracted. Another potential drawback of the technique is that it requires sensing hardware to detect the receiver's hand above the surface in addition to the surface touch point. As a result, there is recent interest in using the space above digital tabletops for interaction in addition to touch on the surface.

Above-The-Tabletop Interaction Techniques

A number of recent studies have proposed new interaction techniques based on tracking gestures and motions above a digital tabletop, in addition to touch-based interaction on the surface. Genest and Gutwin [6] and Marquart et al. [15] have explored conceptual gestures for interaction above digital tabletops. High-bandwidth sensors such as the Kinect enable rich single-user interactions, by projecting shadows onto the surface [23], and by tracking hands above the surface [10]. Less work has been reported for above the table gestures for interactions with multiple users.

Robustness is a critical factor for multi-person interactions such as handoff. Interactions that fail to register, or that register inadvertently, can be highly disruptive to fluid person-to-person interactions. Direct-touch sensing between users shows promise as a low-bandwidth but highly robust solution for sensing interactions between users.

Direct-Touch Interaction Techniques

Direct touch sensing was first demonstrated in the DiamondTouch table [4]. It used capacitance-based touch sensing to identify the touch input of specific users in a multi-user digital tabletop. Touché [21] extended capacitance-based touch sensing for use with everyday objects of any variety. Skinput [8] is a direct-touch system that uses acoustic transmission to identify the location of taps on one's own body. While direct touch sensing has been used to interact with tabletops, real-world objects, and one's own body, it has not been adopted for sensing touch between people. As described below, we extend previous work in the development of a new direct-touch system – ElectroTouch.

FORMATIVE STUDY OF HANDOFF ABOVE THE TABLE

To better understand how people exchange objects in the real and digital worlds, we carried out three small observational studies. In the first study, we created a game that required the exchange of different types of real-world objects. From this, we made two observations. First, people are able to give and receive a wide variety of objects that require different hand positions without expending much mental effort. Second, people use a wide array of hand gestures to give and receive even the same object. These observations revealed that a digital object handoff system must be very flexible (able to handle a variety of gestures), and natural, so as to not create an unacceptable increase in effort or mental demand.

In the second study, we examined how people would transfer digital objects if they were not confined to the surface of the table. We created a system that had a variety of digital objects and asked people to exchange those objects in the space above the table in any manner that felt natural to them. In this Wizard-of-Oz system, we had the experimenter manually trigger events to give the illusion of a fully working system. We observed people using a variety of hand positions when exchanging objects as they maintained mental models of the digital objects once they were removed from the surface. We additionally observed that individuals would often make physical contact when exchanging the intangible objects, and that the actions for picking up and putting down digital objects frequently involved touching the surface of the table (i.e., tap-to-pick-up and tap-to-put-down). From these observations, we concluded that physical contact between people may be useful when exchanging digital objects in the space above the table, and that touching the surface of the table would be an appropriate indicator for picking up and putting down the digital object.

In a final study, we examined how people exchanged digital objects if they were required to do so quickly and repeatedly without any visual representation. We again observed that physical contact was very frequently used as a transfer mechanism: for example, people bumped fists or slapped hands in the space over the table. We also noted that the slapping-hand technique was extremely fast, that people did not seem to mind touching in order to complete the handoff, and that a visible representation of the object being transferred was not needed when physical touch was used. From this exploratory experiment, we concluded that physical contact could be a useful mechanism for carrying out above-the-table handoff.

ABOVE-THE-SURFACE HANDOFF TECHNIQUES

We developed two new techniques to enable handoff above the table surface: a force-field technique, and ElectroTouch. Both use the tap-to-pick-up and tap-to-put-down mechanisms determined by the formative study (see above), but differ in the way that the transfer action is achieved.

Above-the-surface Force-Field (AboveFF)

This technique, first introduced (without implementation details or evaluation) by Jun et al. [14], extends the surface-based Force-Field such that both the giver and the receiver use the space above the table for the handoff. Jun et al. implemented a version of AboveFF using pen input, requiring users to press a button to exchange objects. Our AboveFF technique uses a Microsoft Kinect to sense hand locations and proximity by performing depth-image edge detection (ignoring the table surface) to capture only the participants' arms. This makes our implementation more practical (via inexpensive sensing equipment) and more natural (i.e., no trigger is required). The detected arms are assigned to participants using anchor points set in Kinect (3D) space. The furthest point from the user's body (i.e., the point furthest from the anchor point) is classified as the 3D hand location. A handoff occurs if the distance between two hands is 20 cm or less in 3D space (approximately 1.5 times the diameter of the digital object). Note that the use of 3D distance allows one person to cross above or below another's arm without unintentionally triggering a handoff. Additionally, hysteresis is applied so that additional transfers do not occur until the hands are more than 13 cm apart for at least one frame.

The Kinect depth camera is a high-bandwidth sensor that provides a large amount of information about the scene; however, this information can complicate the process of determining handoff. For example, vision algorithms are needed to filter out objects that intrude into the space of interest (e.g., people's heads), to determine the likely body location of each participant, and to determine arm identities. In addition, arms can block the depth camera's view, preventing good sensing of a proximity event (e.g., if the event happens below another person's arm).

ElectroTouch

ElectroTouch provides an interaction technique and an accompanying hardware sensor for sensing handoffs that use physical touch above the table. The sensing system is much lower bandwidth than the Kinect sensor, but provides a much more robust indication of person-to-person touches.

ElectroTouch detects small electrical signals flowing through users' bodies when they make physical contact. Users stand on wire 'antenna pads' to create a capacitive connection; these pads are about 0.5 × 0.5 m, and have two sets of conductors arranged on a dielectric base: one set for transmitting and one for receiving. The wires from the pads are connected to line inputs and outputs of a common computer sound card using a shielded electrical cable. The computer continuously sends a different frequency sinusoidal signal, in the range of 16–19 kHz, to each pad

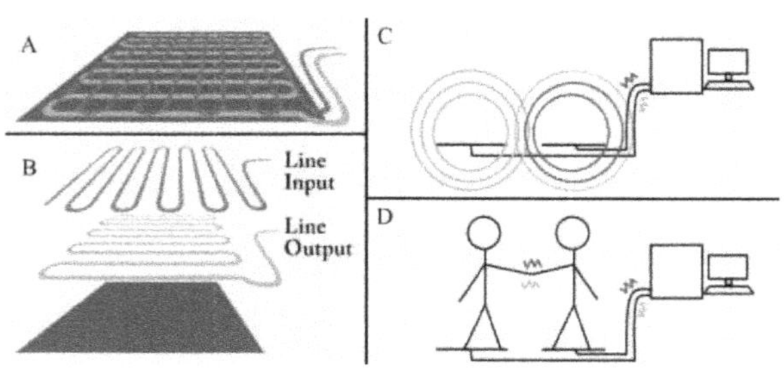

Figure 1: The ElectroTouch system built using cost-effective pads (A) connect to the line input/output (B) of a soundcard transmit EM waves (C) which are transmitted through a person's body and can be detected when two people touch (D).

and senses the signal coming back. Normally, the pads will send back the same signal that they receive. However, when two users make a physical contact, they will also establish a weak electrical circuit connecting the corresponding pads. In this case the sound card receives more than one signal from the pad. The system uses a Fast Fourier Transform to determine if the signal for a touch is above a threshold; these events are interpreted as touches between the users standing on the corresponding pairs of pads.

The system uses only the voltage produced by a standard sound card, and the electromagnetic exposure is comparable to that experienced when wearing wired headphones (and is far below that of a mobile phone). The underlying technology in ElectroTouch was seen in the DiamondTouch table [4], where it was used as an identity-based touch mechanism on a tabletop display. ElectroTouch differs from this work in that it is used for person-to-person touch sensing, and in our use of simple and inexpensive components (the system can be made for a few dollars with wire, cardboard, and a standard multi-port sound card).

With this touch-sensing technology in place, the ElectroTouch handoff technique is simple. Users pick up an object by tapping it on the table, touch hands above the table, and put the object back down by tapping again.

EVALUATION OF ABOVE-THE-SURFACE TECHNIQUES

We conducted a user study to compare the performance of surface-only handoff techniques (Slide, surface-only Force-Field, Flick) to above-the-surface Force-Field and ElectroTouch. We were interested in both time and accuracy: the time needed to carry out handoff actions, and the number of times a handoff went to the wrong person.

Apparatus and Setup

The study was carried out on a custom-built table that uses a 60″ 1920x1028 LCD TV as its surface. A G3 PQLabs overlay frame provides multi-touch sensing, which caused a latency of 85ms between touch and display update. For tracking of arm locations for the Force-Field techniques, a Microsoft Kinect sensor was placed 120 cm above the table,

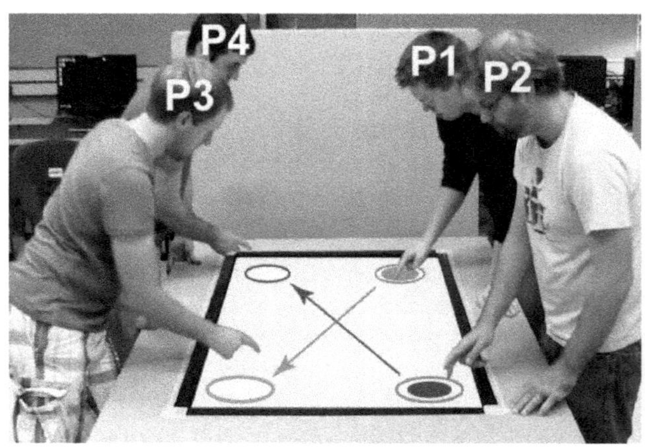

Figure 2: Participant locations and study interface. Handoffs always occurred diagonally across the table.

pointing down at the table surface. Four ElectroTouch pads, one for each participant, were situated around the table (see Figure 1 A). The study used custom software built in C++, and ran on a Core i5 Windows PC. Participants were located as shown in Figure 2 and saw a simple interface with coloured transfer objects and circular drop zones (Figure 2, without the arrows).

Handoff Techniques

We implemented five techniques for the study: three surface-only techniques, and two above-surface techniques.

Slide. The Slide technique is performed as typically seen in many touch-based systems. Object exchange can be performed in two ways. The receiver can touch and drag the object to take possession while it is still being dragged by the original holder. Alternately, the giver can release the object and thereafter have the receiver take it.

Figure 3: Slide technique

Flick. Flicking is similar to sliding except that objects can continue moving after being released. Velocity and direction are calculated using the three previous positions for the object before release. Friction is applied to the object such that it loses 20 pixels per second of velocity. If an object collides with a table edge, it bounces off and loses 20% of its velocity in the bounce direction. The values for friction were chosen through extensive informal testing to ensure this technique performed as well as possible. Exchange occurs when the receiver touches and drags the object at any point during its travel.

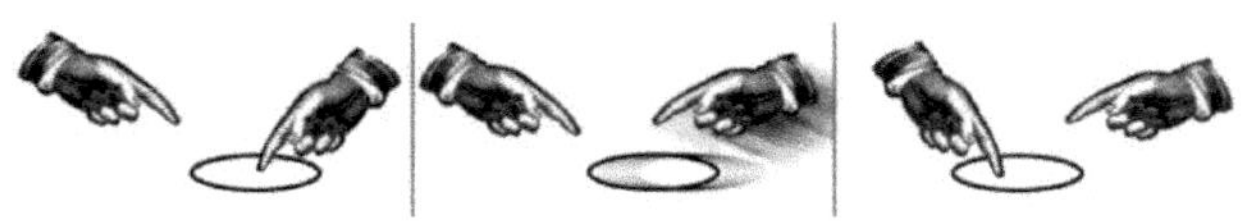

Figure 4: Flick technique

Surface-only Force-Field (SurfaceFF). This technique is similar to sliding, but contains a force-field effect in which the object drifts towards any other hand that is within a 13 cm proximity (based on Jun et al. [14] and refined through pilot studies). The implementation of the Force-Field is similar to that described above for AboveFF, using the Kinect to track receivers' hands and calculate a proximity matrix. The force-field effect is similarly applied to all hands in the space that are within the 13 cm threshold.

Figure 5: Surface-only Force-Field technique

Above-the-surface Force-Field (AboveFF). This technique was implemented as described in the design section above; in addition, the system provided coloured indicators to show who was 'holding' the object that had been picked up.

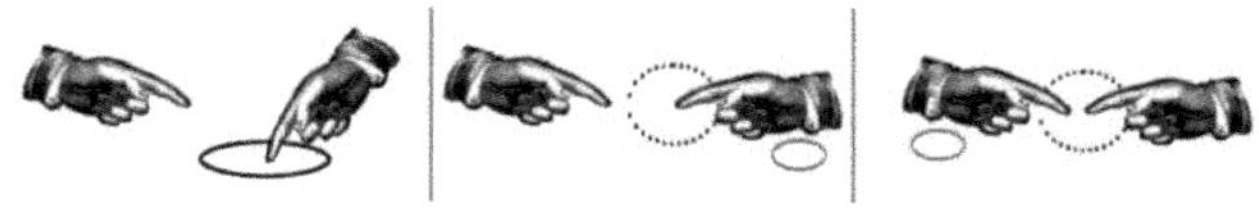

Figure 6: Above-the-surface Force-Field

ElectroTouch. ElectroTouch was implemented as described above (participants removed their shoes while standing on the antenna pads to ensure a good capacitive connection, but this is not a requirement for the technique). The 'picked-up' indicators were also used as with AboveFF. For both above-the-surface techniques, the 85ms latency of the display was an insignificant factor since visual feedback was not a requirement for a transfer to take place.

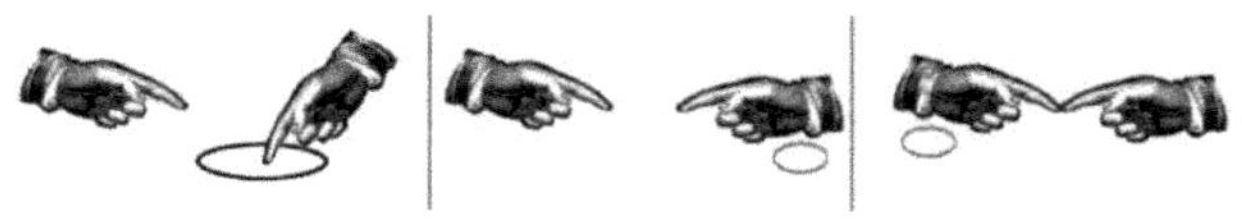

Figure 7: ElectroTouch technique

Participants

We recruited eight groups of four participants (mean age 25.9, 15 male, 29 right-handed) from the local community. 23 of the participants had never used a digital tabletop, while 20 reported frequent use of other touch devices. Each group of four participants was randomly divided into pairs.

Both members in a pair acted as sender and receiver an equal number of times during the study and performed both tasks from the left and right side of the table. Participants were located at the corners of the table during the study and were required to use only their right hand for all tasks.

Task

We chose a task that was representative of the basic interaction underlying natural handoffs. People commonly execute handoffs without switching attention. This is particularly true for the person who does not initiate the handoff. We define the basic mechanism of handoff as a largely autonomous interaction involving four atomic actions: pick-up, give-to, take-from, place-down. This basic handoff mechanism underlies a wide range of possible handoff situations. Any disruption to the basic handoff mechanism in a digital context is likely to have a substantial impact on handoff performance and acceptance of the technology enabling handoff. Disruptions to the basic handoff mechanism are also likely to complicate other situation-specific handoff tasks, such as determining which object to pick up, deciding who to give the object to, and other decision-making processes.

In the study, pairs carried out repeated handoff actions as shown in Figure 2. In each task, one person picked up or selected the 13 cm-diameter coloured object on the table, and transferred it to their partner located diagonally across the table; the partner would then put the object into a circular drop zone 14 cm in diameter (sizes based on Jun et al.'s work [14] and refined through pilot studies). Tasks were successful if the receiver released his or her finger anywhere inside the target zone while dragging or putting down the object. If an object was left untouched on the table (other than in the start state) for more than one second, the trial was reset.

Procedure

Participants carried out trials with all handoff techniques, in both one- and two-pair conditions. Each session was split into two one-pair blocks and one two-pair block. A one-pair block consisted of two participants performing a series of object transfers for each of the five techniques, whereas the two-pair block involved four participants completing object transfers simultaneously. To encourage participants to perform quickly and accurately, a small element of competition was added: the system displayed the scores of the participants at the end of each series. Participants were given the impression that it was a timed event even though the session ended when the players (the losing team in the two-pair case) reached the minimum number of object transfers (ensuring we had enough trials for each pair). The object transfers always occurred from corner to corner (e.g., from P1 to P3 or P2 to P4 in Figure 2). For each technique, a series of at least 10 training trials were performed in both directions (e.g. participant A as giver, then participant A as receiver) for a total of a minimum of 20 training trials. This was followed by a minimum of 12 actual trials in each direction (participant A as giver, then participant A as receiver) from both ends of the table (left position and right position) for a total of 48 actual trials. After each technique, each participant completed a NASA Task Load Index (TLX) survey [9]. When a pair finished the one-pair block (all five techniques), and again after finishing the two-pair block, they individually filled out a subjective-response questionnaire, ranking the five techniques on scales of naturalness, preference, and learnability. Once all trials were complete, participants stated overall preferences for the techniques in the one- and two-pair scenarios.

Each participant performed a minimum of 680 trials (20 training + 48 transfers) × 5 techniques × 2 blocks/participant. Order of technique was counterbalanced using a Latin square design.

Study Design

We used a repeated-measures factorial design with two within-participants factors: *Handoff technique* (Slide, Surface-Force-Field, Flick, Above-Force-Field, and ElectroTouch) and *Number of pairs* (one or two pairs).

Two dependent variables were recorded by the system: *mean object transfer time* (for all conditions) and *accidental handoff rate* (for two-pair conditions).

- Mean object transfer time was calculated by dividing the total elapsed time between each consecutive pair of successful deposits by the total number of successful deposits. Measuring elapsed time between deposits is crucial in the two-pair conditions, since the sender commonly waited to pick up the object in order to avoid a collision with the other pair. These pre-pickup delays are indicative of increased coordination effort (turn-taking), reduced fluidity of handoff, and reduced handoff throughput. As this measure utilizes successful deposits, it incorporates time added due to errors.
- Accidental handoff rate is used only for the two-pair conditions, and is defined as the total number of times the object was transferred to the wrong person, divided by the total number of successful deposits.

We used RM-ANOVA to test for the effects of handoff technique and number of pairs on time per handoff and accidental handoff rate, and to look for interactions. We used planned Bonferonni-corrected post-hoc t-tests to analyze interactions between the surface-based techniques, between the above-the-surface techniques, and between the best surface-only and the best above-the-surface techniques.

Subjective analysis used NASA TLX ratings from each participant for each technique (in the one-pair and two-pair conditions), as well as participant rankings of subjective preference, naturalness, and learnability for each technique in the one and two-pair conditions. We report summary statistics of these findings below.

Results

Handoff time

Mean object transfer times with outliers removed (outside 3 standard deviations, 156 of 8040 samples removed) for each technique and group size are shown in Figure 8. RM-ANOVA found main effects of *Handoff technique* ($F_{4,28} = 261.96, p < .001$) and *Number of pairs* ($F_{1,7} = 18.62, p < .001$), as well as an interaction ($F_{4,70} = 86.11, p < .001$).

Planned post-hoc *t*-tests (Bonferroni-corrected, $\alpha = 0.003$) indicated that Slide and Flick were not significantly different in either group size (one-pair $p = 0.16$, two-pair $p = .06$), but that Flick was faster than SurfaceFF in both group sizes ($p < .001$) and Slide was faster than SurfaceFF for two-pairs ($p < .001$).

For above-the-surface techniques, ElectroTouch was faster than AboveFF (both $p < .001$), and ElectroTouch was also faster than the fastest surface-based technique (i.e., Flick) for both one and two-pairs (both $p < .001$).

Comparing the techniques within the group sizes, there were no significant differences for Slide ($p < .05$) or SurfaceFF ($p > .05$). Flick ($p < .001$) and ElectroTouch ($p < .001$) were faster in the two-pair condition, and AboveFF was slower ($p < .001$).

In summary, we found that ElectroTouch was the fastest technique for both one and two-pair conditions. AboveFF was the second-fastest technique for one pair, but the slowest technique for two pairs. All of the surface-only techniques showed similar mean transfer times, with Slide and Flick being slightly faster than SurfaceFF.

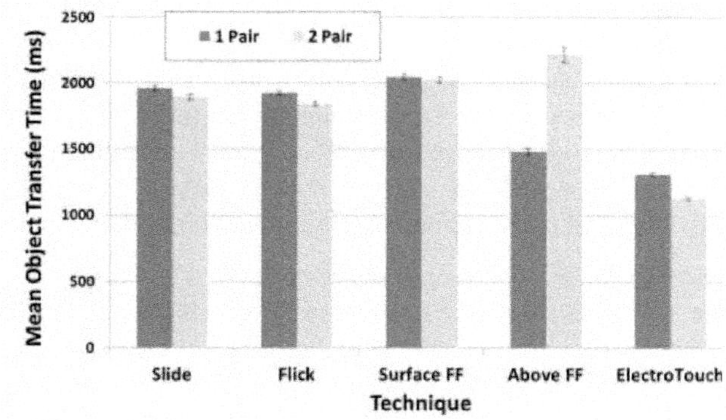

Figure 8. Mean object transfer time (ms) ±s.e. for each technique for one and two pairs.

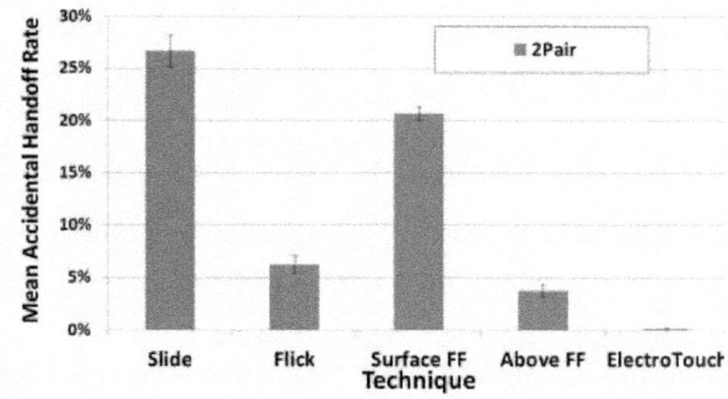

Figure 9. Mean accidental handoff rate (%) ±s.e. for each technique (two-pair condition).

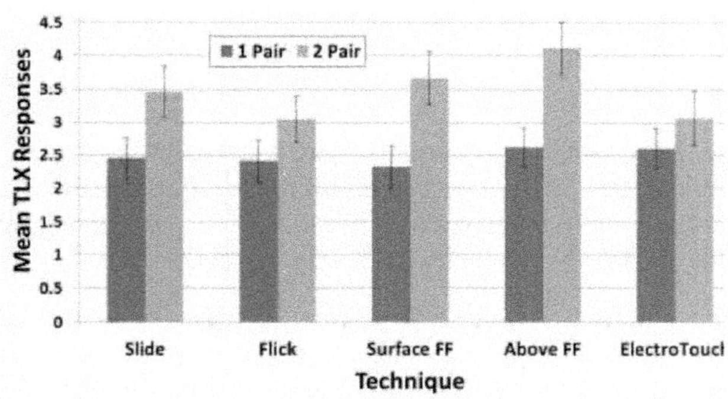

Figure 10. Mean TLX responses (±s.e.) for all TLX columns and participants per technique for one and two pairs.

Accidental handoff rate

Mean accidental handoff rates for each technique are shown in Figure 9. Using RM-ANOVA, we found a main effect of *Handoff technique* ($F_{4,28} = 199.33$, $p < .001$). Planned post-hoc t-tests (Bonferroni-corrected $\alpha = 0.002$), showed significant differences between all techniques except Flick and AboveFF ($p = .03$). These results show that ElectroTouch has the lowest accidental handoff rate.

TLX responses

Each participant completed a NASA TLX task load self-report when they finished each technique in the one and two-pair conditions. We averaged all TLX responses for each technique for all participants and present these results in Figure 10. RM-ANOVA found a significant effect for number of pairs ($F_{1,7} = 19.95$, $p < .001$), and a post-hoc Tukey HSD test showed that above-the-surface Force-Field was rated as having a higher average load than Slide, Flick, and surface-only Force-Field (all $p < .05$). Visually inspecting Figure 10, it is evident that participants rated the two-pair condition as higher demand for each technique.

Subjective responses

We also had participants rank each technique in terms of learnability, naturalness and preference. These results are presented in Figure 11 and show that people generally favoured Flick and ElectroTouch in both group sizes. Participants' overall subjective rankings of which techniques worked best are shown in Figure 12.

DISCUSSION

Summary of Results

Our study showed five main findings:

1. Above-the-surface handoff techniques are faster than surface-only techniques;
2. ElectroTouch was better than any other technique both for speed and accuracy;
3. Flick was the best of the surface-only techniques;
4. There was no substantial work load increase in using above-the-surface techniques based on TLX surveys;
5. There was no substantial difference in the preference, learnability, and naturalness of the various techniques.

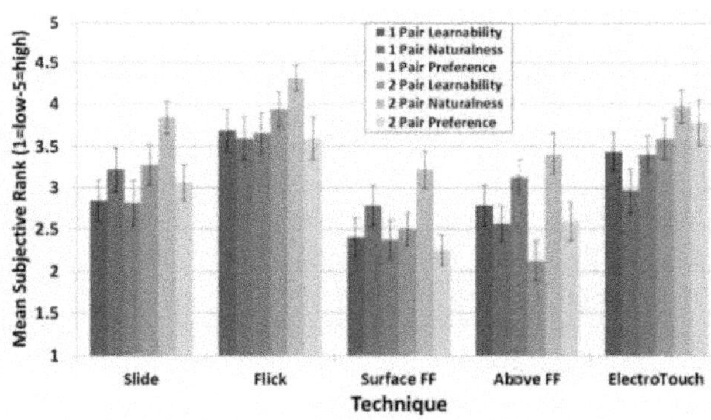

Figure 11. Mean subjective rankings (±s.e.) for each technique for one and two pairs (1=low, 5=high).

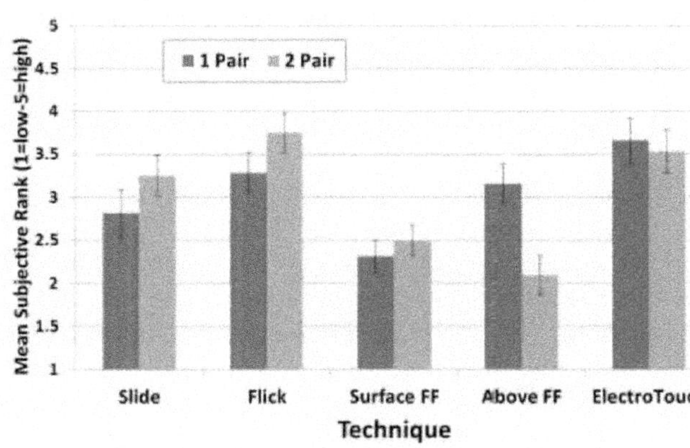

Figure 12. Mean subjective rankings (=s.e.) for each technique of how well each technique worked for one and two pairs.

In the following sections, we interpret and explain these results, discuss how they can be generalized to other contexts, and indicate future possibilities for above-the-surface interaction techniques.

Explanation of Results

Why were above-the-surface techniques better?

Our above-the-surface handoff techniques had shorter completion times and reduced errors compared to surface-only techniques. We believe the performance gains for the above-the-surface technique are due to these techniques' success in solving the two main problems of surface-based handoff – friction and interference. Friction was a noticeable problem in the study, and a main cause of poor performance. This is a significant concern, because object transfer often happens in an outward direction; this requires that people carry out a 'pushing' action with their finger, which incurs much higher friction than a 'dragging' action [3]. Similarly, interference was clearly a common problem for the surface techniques in the two-pair condition: there were many situations where all four hands were in close proximity to one another, forcing people to wait and causing accidental handoffs. In contrast, the above-the surface techniques allowed participants to move quickly to their chosen handoff location in 3D space, and to choose that location so that there was no interference from the other pair.

Why was ElectroTouch best overall?

ElectroTouch performed well for several reasons. First, accidental handoffs rarely occurred – the positive tactile feedback that participants received when transferring an object (via touching their partner's hand) made it much easier for them to carry out the handoff, and much easier to determine that a handoff had happened correctly. Also, the touch sensor was sufficiently robust that people were confident that their touches would be registered. Second, tactile feedback also allowed participants to speed up their transfers: it allowed people to focus on the task of pick-up or put-down rather than on the exchange itself – touch notified the participant that the exchange had taken place and that they could proceed with the next stage of the transfer. Third, ElectroTouch allowed for a wide variety of hand postures and methods for touching, such as the fist bump or the hand slap. This provided users with considerable flexibility when exchanging digital objects.

Why was Flicking the best surface-only technique?

Flick was the best-performing and most-preferred of all the surface-only techniques. It was not remarkably faster than the other surface-only techniques, but it had substantially fewer errors. The reason for the low accidental-transfer rate arises from the technique's design – people were able to stay out of each others' way by flicking the object from their own side of the table. We did notice other types of errors, however – in particular, when users missed 'catching' the flicked object (suggesting that although the handoff speed of Flick could be increased with higher-velocity motion, this could cause other difficulties for the technique). Participants also enjoyed the Flick technique: we received several positive comments from participants, such as "Flick is the most fun and natural", and "Flick works very well because the [objects] don't get in the way". We also observed that people tended to play with Flick much more than the other surface-based techniques.

Which technique requires the most effort?

The NASA-TLX surveys revealed no substantial difference in the workload for all of the techniques with the exception of temporal demand. The TLX results in the one-pair condition showed an increase in temporal demand for the above-the-surface techniques. Participants were required to complete the same number of trials with each technique. We expect that the high TLX score for temporal demand with above-the-surface techniques may be related to the high transfer rate achieved with those techniques, i.e. participants completed the task faster and therefore they may have perceived that the task was more temporally demanding. Apart from this anomaly, there are few differences between the techniques, suggesting that the fastest and least error-prone technique should be used.

Main types of errors for each technique

Although the most important kind of error for a transfer technique is whether the object is given to the correct person, there are other error types that we noted that differed between the techniques.

Slide suffered from accidental contact with the surface with other fingers or wrists, causing the object to stop part way through the transfer. Additionally, taking the object from the giver would occasionally fail if the participant placed their finger at the same approximate location as their partners, or if other parts of the hand touched the surface first outside the boundary of the digital object.

Flick performed well, except when the sender 'threw' the object too fast, which caused the receiver to miss the 'catch'. In addition, the algorithm used to calculate exit velocity uses the previous three locations, so flicking is not as responsive to quick motions as it is in the real world.

Surface-only Force-Field performed reasonably well in the one-pair scenario. However, in the two-pair trials, this technique suffered from interference where objects drifted toward the wrong participant as everyone reached in towards the center of the table. The Force-Field interference resulted in participants ignoring the force fields almost entirely and treating the technique similar to Slide.

Above-the-surface Force-Field encountered errors due to the occlusion of participants hands (i.e., higher-up arms blocking the Kinect camera), which sometimes led to handoffs to the wrong participant. This type of error was avoidable with correct coordination between participants, but required more practice and understanding.

ElectroTouch encountered the least errors of any technique. Accidental handoffs did occur, but were rare. People are quite good at avoiding accidental touches and our results show that this type of error did not occur frequently. We did observe participants attempting to pick up the object too early in the process, and placing the object down in the incorrect location. We attribute these errors to the high transfer rate achieved by participants using ElectroTouch.

Generalizability

Both ElectroTouch and above-the-surface Force-Field are easy and cheap to implement both in terms of software and hardware. Therefore, adding these capabilities to any touch table or other large display device is relatively straightforward. The ElectroTouch pads are flexible and could be placed on any surface where a person may be sitting or standing. The Kinect is a relatively cheap device that can be mounted above or in front of the interaction surface, providing depth information in order to determine the proximity of the hands. While both techniques are practical, our study demonstrates that the direct touch feedback provided by ElectroTouch is an effective cue for handoff without tangible objects.

Our findings for the AboveFF technique (both the speed and the high error rate) will likely generalize to other implementations and sensors as well. The Kinect is a low-resolution device compared to other sensors (such as a Vicon tracker), but the Kinect was sufficient in our implementation of AboveFF to provide reliable arm tracking and an effective force-field mechanism. The main problem with the AboveFF technique was occlusion, and this issue will arise even with much more expensive sensors which also rely on line-of-sight cameras (multiple cameras will reduce but not remove occlusion).

In terms of the generalizability of the techniques to other tasks and table scenarios, one obvious issue is the effective range of the techniques. ElectroTouch, sliding, and the Force-Field techniques all rely on people being able to bring their hands into touch or close proximity; this means that on large tables, it will be difficult or impossible to transfer objects with these methods. The Flick technique, however, is not overly affected by distance (depending on the amount of virtual friction), and could easily be used to transfer objects over larger distances.

It is also clear that the handoff techniques used here are not mutually exclusive, and that the best way to improve handoff performance in real-world situations is likely to implement multiple techniques that can be used in different work contexts. For example, Slide and Flick can easily be merged into one technique, and ElectroTouch can work well with surface based techniques – sliding actions can be easily differentiated from pickup actions, and so the system would be able to support both kinds of interaction.

Limitations

Our system provided a visual representation of who was 'holding' an object that had been picked up from the table surface (a small, semi-transparent version of the object near the person who possessed the object). This visual representation is an important consideration for the practical application of above-the-surface handoff. This visualization occasionally led to confusion, and will need to be carefully designed in future applications. In general, any system that uses virtual pick-up from the table surface needs to provide feedback about the state of that activity; there are several possibilities that would work well for different applications (e.g., a marker object as used here, or a dynamic arm 'shadow' cast on the table and holding a semi-transparent version of the object).

The Kinect subsystem presented a number of technical limitations, as discussed above, including resolution, frame rate and occlusion. These drawbacks reduced the robustness of the system and caused both unintended handoffs and intended-handoff failures. A number of these issues are not easily resolved, even with other types of sensors, such as infrared trackers, due to the occlusion that occurs with multiple people in a small workspace, such as around a tabletop. In our assessment, if systems to support collaborative interactions are to remain trackerless and not rely on touch, then a novel sensing technology is required. These problems with the depth-based sensor argue for systems like ElectroTouch that provide robust sensing of a very particular event, rather than a general-purpose sensor like the Kinect that provides a great deal of information that must be processed in order to be useful. In the case of object transfer, our low-bandwidth but robust sensor proved to be the better approach.

ElectroTouch is limited by the requirement that people stand on the antenna pads, reducing their ability to walk around the table. However, the technology underlying ElectroTouch is not tied to these fixed pads, and could be made mobile to allow user movement. For example, a set of smaller pads could be joined together to cover a much larger area, allowing user movement anywhere around the table. Also, a mobile version of the device could be produced using a smartphone and a smaller antenna, where the smartphone processes the electromagnetic signals and sends touch events to the table computer.

Finally, the type of errors varied across technique, which made identifying and comparing errors difficult in practice. Future studies would benefit from having these error types categorized and quantitatively assessed.

CONCLUSION AND FUTURE WORK

Current handoff techniques over digital tabletops are restricted to surface-only gestures. When multiple people need to exchange digital objects, friction and interference can cause slow performance and frustration. To address the problems of surface-based handoff, we developed two new above-the-table handoff techniques. We evaluated these techniques and found them to be significantly faster and less error-prone. One technique in particular that senses actual person-to-person touch in order to carry out the handoff – ElectroTouch – was the best of all techniques, with fast performance and very few accidental transfers.

In the future, we plan to extend our results in several ways. First, we are building extended versions of the ElectroTouch technology as described above. Second, we will refine AboveFF to utilize an adaptive force-field that shrinks as the number of arms in the above-table space grows, to reduce the frequency of handoff errors. Third, we will develop combinations of the techniques and test them in a variety of large and small tabletop environments.

ACKNOWLEDGMENTS

This research is supported by NSERC, the SurfNet research network, and the GRAND NCE.

REFERENCES

1. Agarawala, A. and Balakrishnan, R. Keepin' it real: pushing the desktop metaphor with physics, piles and the pen. *Proc. ACM CHI 2006*, 1283-1292.
2. Basili, P., Huber, M., Brandt, T., Hirche, S. and Glasauer, S. Investigating human-human approach and hand-over. *Hum. Cent. Robot Sys.*, 6, 2009, 151-160.
3. Cockburn, A., Ahlström, D., and Gutwin, C., Understanding performance in touch selections: Tap, drag and radial pointing drag with finger, stylus and mouse. *IJHCS*, 70, 3, 2012, 218-233.
4. Dietz, P. and Leigh, D. Diamondtouch: a multi-user touch technology. *Proc. UIST 2001*, 219–226.
5. Fleck, R., Rogers, Y., Yuill, N., et al. Actions speak loudly with words: unpacking collaboration around the table. *Proc. ACM ITS 2009*, 189–196.
6. Genest, A. and Gutwin, C. Characterizing Deixis over Surfaces to Improve Remote Embodiments. *Proc. ECSCW 2011*, 253-272.
7. Gutwin, C. and Greenberg, S. A descriptive framework of workspace awareness for real-time groupware. *JCSCW*, 11(3), 2002, 411-446.
8. Harrison, C., Tan, D., and Morris, D. Skinput: appropriating the body as an input surface. *Proc. CHI 2010*, 453-462.
9. Hart, S., and Staveland, L. Development of NASA-TLX (Task Load Index): Results of empirical and theoretical research. In P. Hancock and N. Meshkati (Eds.) Human Mental Workload. Amsterdam: North Holland, 1988.
10. Hilliges, O., Kim, D., Izadi, S., Weiss, M. and Wilson, A. HoloDesk: direct 3d interactions with a situated see-through display. *Proc. CHI 2012*, 2421-2430.
11. Hornecker, E., Marshall, P., Dalton, N., and Rogers, Y. Collaboration and interference: Awareness with mice or touch input. *Proc. CSCW 2008*, 167-176.
12. Huber, M., Rickert, M., Knoll, A., Brandt, T. and Glasauer, S. Human-robot interaction in handing-over tasks. *Proc. IEEE Robot and Human Interactive Communication 2008*, 107-112.
13. Inkpen, K., Hancock, M., Mandryk, R., and Scott, S. *Collaboration around a Tabletop Display: Supporting Interpersonal Interactions*, SFU Tech Report, 2002.
14. Jun, L., Pinelle, D., Gutwin, C., and Subramanian, S. Improving digital handoff in shared tabletop workspaces. *Proc. Tabletop 2008*, 9-16.
15. Marquardt, N., Jota, R., Greenberg, S. and Jorge, J. The continuous interaction space: interaction techniques unifying touch and gesture on and above a digital surface. *Proc. INTERACT 2011*, 461-476.
16. Müller-Tomfelde, C. and Schremmer, C. Touchers and mousers: commonalities and differences in co-located collaboration with multiple input devices. *Proc. CHI 2008*, 1149-1152.
17. Pinelle, D., Gutwin, C., and Greenberg, S., Task Analysis for Groupware Usability Evaluation: Modeling Shared-Workspace Tasks with the Mechanics of Collaboration, *ToCHI*, 2003, 281-311.
18. Reetz, A., Gutwin, C., Stach, T., Nacenta, M., and Subramanian, S. Superflick: a natural and efficient technique for long-distance object placement on digital tables. *Proc. Graphics Interface 2006*, 163-170.
19. Ryall, K., Forlines, C., Shen, C., and Morris, M. Exploring the effects of group size and table size on interactions with tabletop shared-display groupware. *Proc. CSCW 2004*, 284-293.
20. Sallnäs, E. and Zhai, S. Collaboration meets Fitts's law: Passing Virtual Objects with and without Haptic Force Feedback, *Proc. INTERACT 2003*, 97-104.
21. Sato, M., Poupyrev, I., and Harrison, C. Touché: enhancing touch interaction on humans, screens, liquids, and everyday objects. *Proc. CHI 2012*, pages 483-492.
22. Tse, E., Histon, J., Scott, S., and Greenberg, S. Avoiding interference: how people use spatial separation and partitioning in SDG workspaces. *Proc. CSCW 2004*, 252-261.
23. Wilson, A. and Benko, H. Combining multiple depth cameras and projectors for interactions on, above and between surfaces. *Proc. UIST 2010*, 273-282.

An Evaluation of State Switching Methods for Indirect Touch Systems

Simon Voelker, Chat Wacharamanotham, Jan Borchers
RWTH Aachen University
52056 Aachen, Germany
{voelker, chat, borchers}@cs.rwth-aachen.de

ABSTRACT
Indirect touch systems combine a horizontal touch input surface with a vertical display for output. While this division is ergonomically superior to simple direct-touch displays for many tasks, users are no longer looking at their hands when touching. This requires the system to support an intermediate Tracking state that lets users aim at objects without triggering a selection, similar to the hover state in mouse-based UIs. We present an empirical analysis of several interaction techniques for indirect touch systems to switch to this intermediate state, and derive design recommendations for incorporating it into such systems.

Author Keywords
indirect touch; three-state model

ACM Classification Keywords
H.5.2 Information Interfaces and Presentation: User Interfaces - Ergonomics, Theory and methods

General Terms
Human Factors, Design, Measurements

INTRODUCTION
Mouse-based UIs distinguish three different input states that the system can react to: Out-of-Range (user's hand not on the device), Tracking (user moving the mouse), and Engaged or Dragging (mouse button is pressed, manipulating the object below the cursor) [3].

Some direct touch systems such as multi-touch screens support richer interactions than the mouse by using multiple fingers and hands, but they mostly lack a Tracking state. Users move from Out Of Range (a finger not touching the surface) directly to Engaged (a finger touching the surface and thus manipulating the objects beneath it). For direct touch systems, this loss is sometimes problematic since it hampers UI techniques such as tooltips, but it is not necessary since users can visually align their finger to the target before touching and thus engaging — the biggest advantage of the Tracking state.

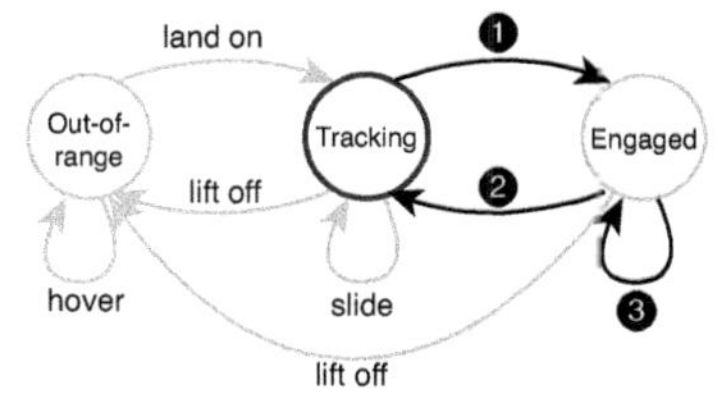

Method	❶	❷	❸
Tapping	one tap	one tap	slide
Hold	hold	–	slide
PS	pressure down-up	pressure down-up	slide
PQ	pressure down	pressure up	slide + pressure

Figure 1. (Top) State transition model for three-state interaction on the indirect touch system [3]. (Bottom) Four methods of state switching.

For indirect touch systems, losing the Tracking state is crucial, since users are usually required to look at the vertical output display and not at their hands on the horizontal input surface while interacting. However, indirect touch systems have many, mostly ergonomic, advantages over horizontal direct touch systems: The users can see the vertical output form a comfortable sitting position without having to lean over a horizontal display [19], which reduces neck muscle strain and neck pain [8, 25]. Furthermore, operating with the hands on a horizontal surface is much less exhausting and faster than on a vertical touchscreen [2, 17]. Traditional desktop computers use the same device arrangement.

The aim of this paper, is to empirically evaluate four different interaction techniques that allow users to enter and leave an intermediate Tracking state on indirect touch systems. After identifying four representative techniques from a review of existing literature, we report results from testing these four techniques in three experiments covering single-touch, multiple-touch, and bi-manual interactions. We conclude with design recommendations for interaction techniques that support a Tracking state in indirect touch systems.

RELATED WORK

Indirect touch
For standard pointing tasks with a stylus, indirect input performed very similar to direct input, in terms of target acquisition and error rates. However, indirect input benefits from

CHI 2013, April 27–May 2, 2013, Paris, France.

less occlusion for difficult targets [7]. While direct touch was faster, indirect touch had a lower error rate and was more precise for 2D/3D rotation, scale, and translation [13].

In a mixed direct and indirect touch environment, indirect input can be used as a high-precision mode because it reduces content occlusion and allows the user to interact with faraway objects in the space near the body [14, 1, 20].

Schmidt et al. [25] showed that the mapping between horizontal and vertical screen for indirect multi-touch input can be easily understood by the users. However, in their study, direct multi-touch input outperformed the indirect multi-touch input for simple aiming and dragging task in terms of task completion times. They also explained that a possible reason for this result could be that the users had to physically hover with their hand above the surface for the Tracking state, which was reported as uncomfortable by the users. This suggests introducing a switching method that allows users to rest their hands while being in the Tracking state and easily change to the Engaged state. The studies in this paper compare four different candidates for such a switching method.

Three-state input in multi-touch systems

While the Tracking state is necessary for indirect touch input, other projects introduced the Tacking state to direct touch input because of benefits of preventing errors or increasing the richness of the input [3]. Therefore, the state switching methods from direct touch systems could inform the design of those in indirect touch systems.

Pressure-based methods

In Pressure-based methods, every lightweight touch is recognized as an input in the Tracking state; the system switches to the Engaged state only when the pressure is increased [4]. Due to friction between the finger and the surface, retaining the pressure while moving the touch on the surface could be uncomfortable. Forlines et al. [8] used the light touches to preview a sequence of actions, and pressured touch to confirm the action.

Gestures

Surface gesturing, e.g., lifting the finger while it is positioned over the target (take-off) [23] or rubbing the target [21] are alternatives. In comparative studies, pressure technique and rubbing outperforms take-off. Multiple finger gestures [18] or a bimanual gesture [21] could also be used for state switching.

While the above-mentioned methods allow single-touch direct-input state switching, there is no comparison of the methods for multi-touch systems. We will now identify design criteria for state switching methods for multi-touch indirect-input systems. These criteria lead to a selection of four representative methods which were tested empirically.

DESIGN CONSIDERATIONS

In our opinion, good state switching methods should meet these properties:

Applicable to individual fingers: Methods that meet this property (1) retain the expressiveness of multi-touch input because all fingers can be used independently, (2) are widely applicable without the need to identify different digits of the hand, and (3) are extendable for multiple-user setups.

Hard to unintentionally switch states: Methods should minimize *slip-ins*, where the user unintentionally switches into the Engaged state from the Tracking state, and *slip-outs*, where the user unintentionally switches out of the Engaged state either into the Tracking or into the Out-of-Range state.

Ergonomic: Methods should allow the user to switch to or to maintain a state for an extended period of time with minimal discomfort.

In the next section, we describe four switching methods that satisfy these design considerations.

STATE SWITCHING METHODS FOR TOUCH INPUT

According to Wang and Ren [26], the fingers have four types of input properties: position, motion, physical, and event properties . On interactive surfaces, position and motion are already occupied for spatial input; therefore, only physical and event properties are left for state switching.

In this paper, we chose *pressure quasimode*, *pressure switch*, *lift-and-tap*, and *hold* as representative methods for state switching. Pressure quasimode spans the dimension of Wang's physical properties because the size, shape, and pressure of the contact area are tightly coupled. Orientation of the finger is not practical for multiple-finger usage because users have to rotate their whole hand to change the orientation. Among event properties, lift-and-tap was chosen over flicking because lift-and-tap provides a stable contact point with the surface after switching into the Engaged state. Pressure switch and hold exploit the time dimension of the physical and event properties, respectively.

An overview of these state switching methods is shown in Figure 1. Only the transitions into and out of the Engaged state differ between the switching methods.

None of these switching methods are new. Pressure quasimode and lift-and-tap have been investigated in [4]. Pressure switch is a minor adaptation of pressure quasimode to overcome the friction problem. Hold is prevalent among commercially available touch systems. However, we looked at these methods in terms of their use with multi-touch input involving multiple fingers and/or hands.

In the remainder of this section, we describe the interaction design, potentials, and limitations of each method. To determine appropriate system specific thresholds for each method, we conducted a preliminary study with five participants for each method.

Common concerns for pressure methods

Pressure Proxy

For both pressure methods, we use the length of the semimajor axis of the touch ellipse as a proxy representing contact pressure. This is supported by the direct relationship between pressure and contact radius of the human finger to a flat surface [22]. The SimPress system used contact area to represent pressure [1]. Since the contact region is always near-elliptical

[5], it is plausible to use an ellipse around the finger tip to represent the pressure. We apply a low-pass filter to the length of the major axis to eliminate jitter.

One-bit Pressure

Although previous work shows that humans can discriminate up to seven levels of pressure with visual feedback [6, 24], a realistic multi-finger switching method would have to be practical with up to 10 fingers. Therefore, for state switching, we chose a one-bit discrete pressure level instead of three bits (seven states) to reduce the mental load and physical effort in maintaining states of all fingers.

Pressure Thresholding by Rate of Change

We used rates of pressure change in thresholding to accomodate the difference among users in their ability to exert pressure. This difference is due to finger size and ability to exert force through hand and finger joints.

Pressure quasimode (PQ)

Interaction design

State switching with pressure quasimode is shown in Figure 2a. To switch into the Engaged state, the user (1) increases pressure faster than a threshold defined by the rate of pressure change $\frac{dP}{dT} > \delta_{engage}$, (2) the centroid of the contact area must still be within a radius r_{max}, and (3) the time of pressure change must not exceed a threshold t_{max}. To switch out of the Engaged state, the user can either release the pressure faster than $\delta_{disengage}$, or reduce it to less than a minimum pressure threshold, P_{min}. The rate thresholds, δ_{engage} and $\delta_{disengage}$ were used to prevent false positive recognition, e.g., the reduction of the pressure while the finger is sliding in the Engaged state. When the users increase the pressure of a finger, the centroid of the contact area drifts towards the palm of the user, the maximum drifting radius r_{max} and the time threshold t_{max} were used to distinguish pressure application from just sliding the finger in the Tracking state. In the implementation, t_{max} was also used as the time to cache touch events for processing. This time frame enables a responsive output of the state switching recognizer.

We found suitable thresholds by letting participants imagine sliding an object on the surface between two designated points on the screen. We processed the data for inflection points (as the first ascent and the last descent) and the peak of pressure.

Potentials and limitations

The benefit of pressure quasimode is that the user is continuously aware of the state of the finger is in because of haptic feedback and proprioception of the fingertip. However, holding pressure with one's finger can become tiring. Since the finger muscles cannot generate enough force, the finger has to receive extra force coming from the forearm muscles. When used repetitively, friction among tendons could cause injuries with this method [17].

Pressure switch (PS)

Interaction design

The pressure switch method is a combination of pressure quasimode and lift-and-tap to overcome the friction problem. The user *toggles* between the Tracking state and the Engaged state by applying a short period of pressure on the screen as shown in Figure 2b. The δ_{engage} of pressure switch were the same as for pressure quasimode.

Potentials and limitations

While the friction problem is alleviated in pressure switch, the feeling of continued pressing during the Engaged state was also taken out. If the user rests the finger on the surface after engaging using momentary pressure, she may not remember that the finger is already in that state.

Lift-and-tap (Tap)

Interaction design

Lift-and-tap [16] involves a sequence of temporary lifting off from the screen and landing back on the screen, as seen in Figure 2c. A user taps once to switch into the Engaged state. The system should use the centroid of the last point before the finger lift-off to determine which control to activate, because a drifting may have occurred at the landing. Once in the Engaged state, the finger remains Engaged until the user lifts the finger out of range. Recognizing lift-and-tap in multi-touch environments must take the drifting of the centroid of the contact point and the time between lifting and landing into consideration. The threshold for the maximum distance of the drifting centroid (r_{max}) and the threshold for maximum time

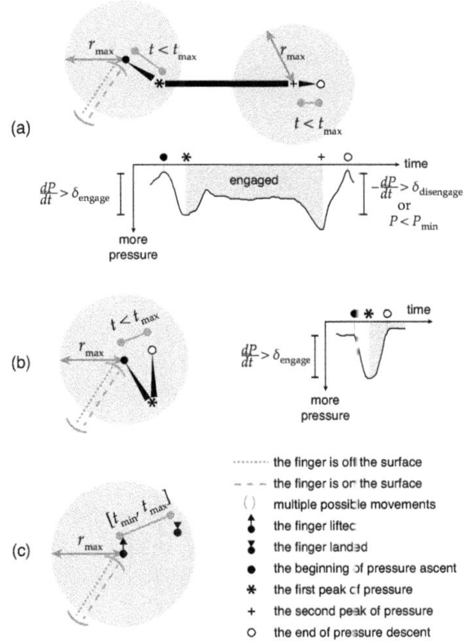

(d)

Threshold	Tap	Hold	PQ & PS
t_{min} (s)	0.09		
t_{max} (s)	1.18	0.50	0.70
r_{max} (mm)	4.14	1.94	7.07
δ_{engage} (mm)			1.30
$\delta_{disengage}$ (mm)			1.14
P_{min} (mm)			0.55

Figure 2. State switching interactions details for (a) pressure quasimode, (b) pressure switch, and (c) lift-and-tap. (d) Threshold values

(t_{max}) allow discriminating tapping from repositioning the finger without any intention to switch into the Engaged state. We determined these thresholds by recording participants tapping on 12 targets spaced evenly across the screen.

Potentials and limitations
Lift-and-tap has the benefit of familiarity since it is widely used in commercially available trackpads. Nevertheless, tapping might not be usable with multiple fingers simultaneously because of the dependencies among fingers in flexion-extension movements [11]. In particular, the middle and the ring finger can move less freely of other fingers, and can stay less still while another finger moves [11].

Hold

Interaction design
Switching into the Engaged state with the hold technique is done by resting the finger on the surface such that the centroid is static within a maximum allowed radius for a certain duration. After the duration, the cursor stays in the Engaged state until the finger is lifted off the surface. There is no direct transition back to the Tracking state. The hold duration (t_{max}) in commercially available touch systems is between 0.5–1 second[1]. We asked participants to hold the finger on the target on the touchscreen and recorded the position of the centroid for 0.5 seconds to determine the maximum distance (r_{max}) that the touch centroid may drift.

Potentials and limitations
Notable limitation of hold is that switching errors may occur easily. While the user is trying to engage one finger, she might engage other fingers resting on the surface as well. To prevent this accidental activation, the user has to either lift or move other fingers; this makes the ergonomical benefit of hold questionable (see: Experiment 2). With this limitation in mind, the hold method may still be suitable for several quasi-mode widgets that require the user to remain Engaged to operate (see: Experiment 3).

EVALUATION OF STATE SWITCHING METHODS

We evaluated the switching errors of the state switching methods in three use cases: single finger, multiple fingers, and bi-manual interaction. For our experiments we adapted the Drag and Drop tasks from [9] because they encompassed Tracking, Engaging, dragging, and disengaging. For the third experiment, we used a task that represents an asymmetric bi-manual interaction.

Our three research questions were:

- Do switching methods differ in switching errors made, subjective perception, and user preference?
- Are these differences consistent over the three use cases?
- Ultimately, which switching method should be recommended for indirect touch systems?

[1]iOS 5.1: 0.5 s. Android 4.1: 0.5–1 s.

Apparatus

Participants sat at a desk with two displays as shown in Figure 3. As a the horizontal touch surface we used a capacitive touch-sensing 27″ Perceptive Pixel display is embedded in a custom-made desk surface. The horizontal display was blank.

The vertical display was used for visual output. The bottom-most pixel of this display was 13 cm above the desk surface. The surface of the display was 47 cm from the topmost touch sensing area used in the horizontal touchscreen. Both displays had the same display area and resolution: 597 $\times$ 336 mm, 2560 $\times$ 1440 pixels. This gave us a 1:1 input:output space size ratio. Both displays were connected to a Mac Pro running the software for the experiments. The effective touch frame rate of our setup was 205 Hz.

For each contact point, a circle cursor with constant diameter of 7 mm (30 px) was visualized with an absolute mapping of the centroid of the contact area to the center of the cursor in 1:1 ratio without any pointer acceleration. The cursors were outlined in the Tracking state and were filled in the Engaged state. We used a 1:1 ratio to avoid precision problems, which occur when the input surface is smaller than the output surface. Furthermore, we used an absolute mapping to prevent confusion when multiple cursors are present on the screen. Especially in multi-touch and bi-manual multi-touch input, cognitive load from mapping multiple touches and multiple cursors would be overwhelming.

Figure 3. The experiment setup. Participants indirectly controlled cursors on the vertical screen by touching the horizontal screen.

Data Analysis

We used Generalized Estimating Equations (GEE)[2] for main analysis of error counts and Wilcoxon signed rank tests with Bonferroni correction for post-hoc (pairwise) comparisons. For the trial time (Experiment 1), a repeated-measure ANOVA and paired t-tests were used.[3]

Note that the error rates reported in the following experiments were calculated as per trial averages. Although the differences may seem small (e.g., 0.1 errors), when projected to the real use—over a longer period and more frequent switching—these small differences are practically significant.

EXPERIMENT 1: SINGLE FINGER

[2]GEE details: Poisson distribution, log link function, and an independent covariance structure.
[3]Statistically significant for all main analyses at $\alpha = .05$ and for all post-hoc tests at $\alpha = .0083$ $(= .05/6)$

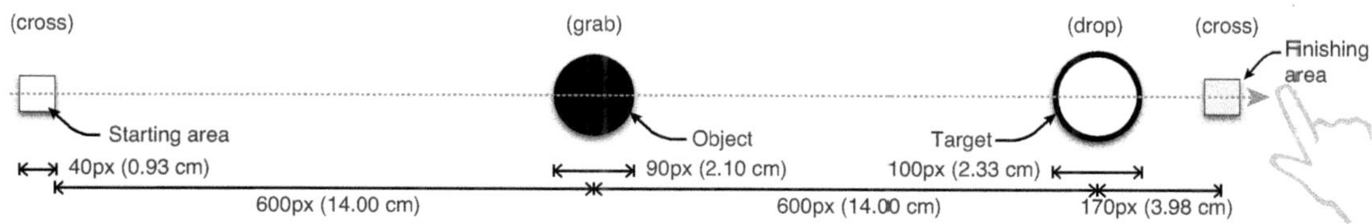

Figure 4. A configuration of the single-finger task. The participant tracks the cursor across the entry, grabs the object, drops the object at the target, and crosses the exit.

In this experiment, we investigated the effect of different switching methods using a single finger, which is the simplest way to interact with a multi-touch screen.

Although a previous investigation of indirect touch object manipulation [20] used only the thumb, the index, and the middle finger, we decided to include all ten fingers in this experiment for three reasons. (1) The ring and the little finger are used to switch states in other input devices, e.g., using the little finger to hold down shift while typing. (2) We did not find any proof in the literature that warrants exclusion of any fingers in the interaction with interactive surfaces.

We counterbalanced the order of fingers and pilot tested the procedure to prevent fatigue effect.

Task

The screen, shown in Figure 4, contained a starting area (left blank square), the object (filled circle), the target (blank circle), and a finishing area (right filled square).

For each of the four techniques, the participants had to execute the following sequence of actions: The participant was first told by the experimenter which finger to use. To start the trial, she had to track the cursor crossing the starting area, and then onto the object, which turned yellow when the cursor was in grabbing range. Here, she had to invoke the switching technique to switch into the Engaged state to grab the object. The participant had to drag the object to the target; the cursor had to remain in the Engaged state until it reached the target. If the object was dropped, she had to re-grab it and resume the task. When the object was in range of the target, the target turned yellow. There, the participant had to switch the state of the cursor to drop the object onto the target. If she accidentally re-grabbed the object after dropping it onto the target, she had to drop it onto the target again. The trial ended after the participant tracked the cursor into the finishing area.

To minimize the time the user took to aim at the targets, which might have confounded the state switching behavior, we used the following specifications: (1) The object and the target were large: 2.1 cm (90 px) and 2.33 cm (100 px) diameter respectively and as such were easy to aim at with a cursor of 7 mm (30 px) diameter. (2) The color of the object and the target changed when the cursor was within range for grabbing or placing the object. (3) The drop was successful when the object was released close to the target within a distance < 1 cm.

Measurements

The recorded raw touch data included timestamps, coordinates, the length of the major and minor axes of the touch ellipse, and its rotation angle. We recorded the cursor position, the object state, and its position at the same frame rate. We distinguished three types of *Switching errors*:

- *Tracking slip-ins (TSI)*: Errors triggered by slipping into Engaged state between starting point and the object.
- *Dragging slip-outs (DSO)*: Errors triggered by slipping out of the Engaged state while dragging the object towards the target. This caused the finger to lose the focus of the object; the participant had to re-grab the object
- *Placement slip-ins (PSI)*: Errors triggered by slipping into the Engaged state after the object was dropped onto the target. This caused the object to be re-grabbed, and the participant needed to drop the object onto the target again.

Experimental Design and Procedure

We conducted the experiment with 8 Computer Science students aged 24–34. They were volunteers from our campus; no monetary compensation was provided. All were right-handed males. Each participant had to conduct four trials with different movement directions (up, down, left, right) for all 10 fingers for each switching technique. This resulted in a total 1280 trials over all users.

The order of switching methods was counterbalanced using a Latin square. The directions and order of the fingers were randomized for each user. After two methods, participants took a five minute break. On average, the experiment took 30 minutes per participant.

During the task, we asked the participants to place all fingers on the screen; this reflected the ergonomical use of an indirect touch setup as we envisioned it. Therefore, multiple cursors were shown. Participants were instructed to avoid using cursors other than the one associated with the finger in use to interact with the object. Each cursor was tracked individually. Only data from the cursor that grabbed the object was used in the analysis. The influence of multiple fingers was investigated in Experiment 2.

At the end of each switching method, we asked the participants to comment on their perception of speed and accuracy of the method and any fatigue of their hand and arm. We asked then to choose the most favorable method.

Result

GEE showed a statistically significant effect of techniques on TSI Wald $\chi^2_{3,N=320} = 32.92$, $p < .001$, on DSO Wald $\chi^2_{3,N=320} = 14.96$, $p < .001$, and on PSI Wald $\chi^2_{3,N=320} = 41.033$, $p < .001$. The detailed result and the post-hoc analysis are shown in Figures 5 and 6. A repeated measures ANOVA shows significant effect of method, $F(3,957) = 3.69, p = .0117$. The details are shown in Figure 7.

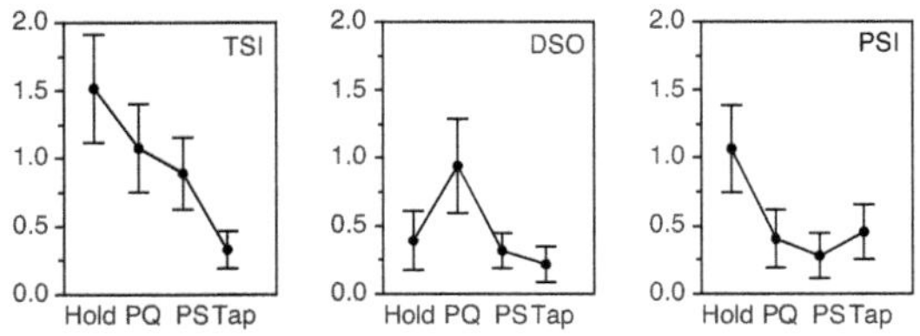

	TSI	DSO	PSI
Hold	1.51 [1.12, 1.91]	0.39 [0.17, 0.60]	1.06 [0.74, 1.38]
PQ	1.08 [0.75, 1.40]	0.94 [0.59, 1.29]	0.40 [0.19, 0.61]
PS	0.89 [0.62, 1.15]	0.31 [0.18, 0.44]	0.28 [0.11, 0.44]
Tap	0.33 [0.19, 0.46]	0.21 [0.08, 0.34]	0.45 [0.25, 0.65]

Figure 5. Error count per trial from Experiment 1 (Mean & 95% CI)

	TSI					
– Hold	−194	.0920	−245.5	<.001	−330	<.001
PS – Hold	−316.5	.0057	−14	.820	−313.5	<.001
PS – PQ	−129.5	.2060	−274	<.001	−19.5	.571
Tap – Hold	−474.5	<.001	−60.5	.107	−335.5	<.001
Tap – PQ	−340	<.001	−281.5	<.001	18.00	.626
Tap – PS	−201	<.001	−58.5	.200	63.50	.181

Figure 6. W statistics and p values of the post-hoc analysis of error counts in Experiment 1. Statistically significant differences are highlighted.

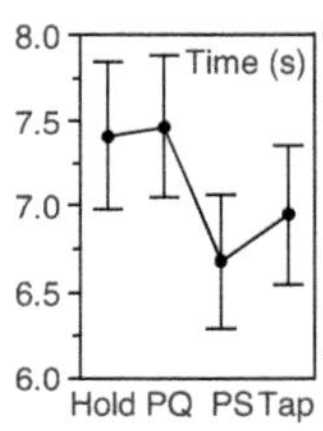

	Trial time (s)
Hold	7.40 [6.97, 7.84]
PQ	7.46 [7.04, 7.87]
PS	6.67 [6.29, 7.06]
Tap	6.94 [6.54, 7.35]

	t_{319}	p
PQ – Hold	0.18	.8542
PS – Hold	−2.64	.0087
PS – PQ	−2.83	.0050
Tap – Hold	−1.67	.0968
Tap – PQ	−1.98	.0487
Tap – PS	0.97	.3311

Figure 7. Experiment 1 trial time (Mean & 95% CI) and post-hoc result.

Participants described that lift-and-tap was natural and intuitive: *"I would use this if there were no instructions"* and *"It's the closest to the mouse."*. In contrast, participants felt that the hold method was unfamiliar, mostly because of slip-ins: *"Hold is the most irritating. You get stuck somewhere all the time."* and *"False activations are annoying, it's prevented me [from moving] faster."*. Participants mentioned tiredness while using the pressure quasimode method: *"This cramps my hands up more than the others."* and *"For long distances the friction could be a problem."*. Four participants chose lift-and-tap as the most favored method, followed by hold (3), and pressure quasimode (1).

Discussion

While Hold yielded a high error rate (TSI & PSI), it was favored by 40% of the participants. We speculate two reasons for this contradiction: (1) During dragging (DSO), hold performed no worse than other methods. With dragging as the main goal, the user may have perceived this technique as better than it was. (2) Inadvertent engaging (TSI) caused no problems here because the screen only contained the target object. In reality, with many onscreen objects, TSI errors would potentially engage unwanted objects.

Although pressure switch, pressure quasimode, and lift-and-tap require users to explicitly switch to the Engaged state, lift-and-tap had lower TSI than the others. While this may have been the result from the lack of familiarity with pressure-based methods, further studies with more repetitions are needed to be conclusive.

The result from pressure quasimode confirms that it is difficult to maintain pressure while dragging across the screen—three times more DSO errors occurred than with lift-and-tap. The participants' comments also supported this.

As expected, the methods with more errors yielded longer trial times. The long time of hold correlates with a high rate of TSI and PSI errors, while the that of pressure quasimode correlates with high TSI and DSO. Although the lower times for lift-and-tap were not statistically significant, we surmise that this effect would be more apparent in real use, in which more errors would require more corrections.

In summary, we recommend the lift-and-tap method for single finger due to its low error rate across the board and the favorable qualitative feedback.

EXPERIMENT 2: MULTIPLE FINGERS

When multiple fingers are used, the fingers may interfere with each other. In the second experiment, we investigated how the performance of switching methods differed when using multiple fingers of one hand.

Task

The task, shown in Figure 8, extends the task from experiment 1 to multiple objects and targets. The participants were instructed to track two cursors crossing both starting areas (shown in the figure as the blank square on the left). Then, the participants had to drag the fingers towards the first object, grab it, drag the cursors towards the second object, and grab it. The participants had to keep both objects Engaged until they were located over their respective targets. Then, they had to move to the finishing areas behind the targets. The distance between both objects and both targets was large enough (10.2 cm; 440 px) to insure that both objects could not be grabbed or released at the same time. The distance between the center of each object to the center of the respective target was constant at 18.6 cm (800px).

To limit the number of trials to be feasible in one experiment session, only the thumb, the index finger, and the middle finger of the dominant hand were tested. The object closest to the user had to be grabbed using the thumb or the index finger with depending the condition. This is the movement that allows the hand to naturally stay in line with the arm.

Measurements

The errors in this experiment may occur in three phases: during object acquisition, during dragging with both fingers,

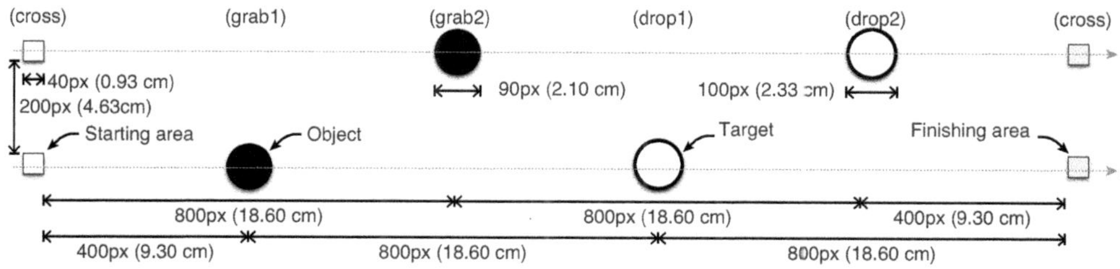

Figure 8. A configuration of multiple-finger task. The participant acquired two objects in order before dropping each of them in their respective targets.

and during object placement onto the targets. In these three phases, errors may occur with the first or the second finger. Therefore, besides *overall errors*, we classified errors into six classes:

- *Acquisition slip-ins (ASI):* The number of errors occured in the second finger while the first finger is acquiring the first object.
- *Acquisition slip-outs (ASO):* The number of errors occured in the first finger while the second finger is trying to acquire the second object.
- *Placement slip-ins (PSI):* The number of errors occured in the second finger while the first finger is trying to place the first object in the target.
- *Placement slip-outs (PSO):* The number of errors occured in the first finger while the second finger is trying to place the second object in the target.
- *Dragging slip-outs in the first finger (DSO1):* The number of errors occured in the first finger during dragging. The participants had to retain all objects for at least 9.3cm (400px).
- *Dragging slip-outs in the second finger (DSO2):* The number of errors occured in the second finger during dragging.

The classification of these errors allows us to pinpoint where the errors occur and to investigate the potential of using different methods for the first and the second finger. Since an error requires the participant to re-grab the object which may cause subsequent errors, only the first error was counted.

Experimental Design

We conducted the experiment with 8 computer science students (age 24–28; one female; all of them right-handed). Each of the participants had to perform two trials in different directions (from left to right, from right to left) for six combinations of fingers (576 trials in total).

The order of switching methods were counterbalanced among participants, while the order of the finger combinations and the direction was randomized. The experiment took 35 minutes on average. We asked for qualitative feedback in the same manner as in Experiment 1.

Result

GEE shows a statistically significant effect of methods on overall errors Wald $\chi^2_{3,N=384} = 58.05$, $p < .001$. The interaction effect of finger order on overall errors was not significant Wald $\chi^2_{5,N=384} = 5.16$, $p = .397$. In break down errors, a significant effect of methods was found only on ASI, Wald $\chi^2_{3,N=384} = 93.24$, $p < .001$, and on PSO, Wald $\chi^2_{3,N=384} = 26.05$, $p < .001$. ASO, DSO1, DSO2, and PSI occured in very small numbers and their effects were not statistically significant. The detailed results and post-hoc analyse are shown in Figure 9 and 10.

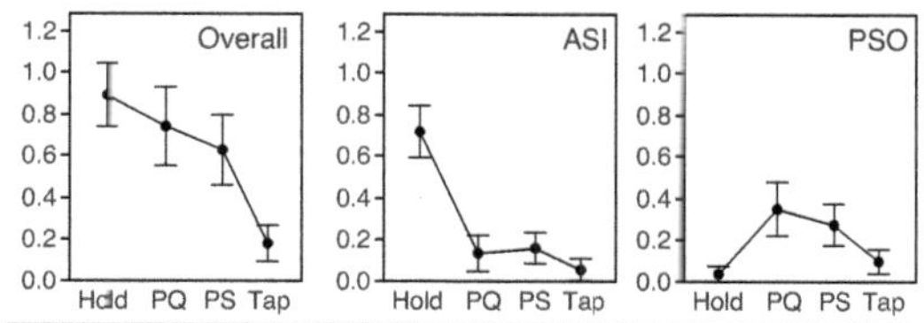

	Overall	ASI	PSO
Hold	0.89 [0.74, 1.04]	0.71 [0.59, 0.84]	0.03 [0.00, 0.07]
PQ	0.74 [0.55, 0.93]	0.13 [0.04, 0.22]	0.35 [0.22, 0.47]
PS	0.63 [0.46, 0.79]	0.16 [0.08, 0.23]	0.27 [0.17, 0.37]
Tap	0.18 [0.09, 0.27]	0.05 [0.00, 0.11]	0.09 [0.03, 0.15]

Figure 9. Error count per trial from Experiment 2 (Mean & 95% CI)

	Overall					
– Hold	−132.00	.2929	−692.50	<.001	192.50	<.001
PS – Hold	−298.00	.0071	−645.00	<.001	116.00	<.001
PS – PQ	−186.50	1.811	19.00	.5262	−77.00	.2143
Tap – Hold	−816.00	<.001	−831.00	<.001	13.00	.3877
Tap – PQ	−604.50	<.001	−14.00	.2676	−206.50	<.001
Tap – PS	−335.50	<.001	−42.50	.0405	−136.00	.0025

Figure 10. W statistics and p value of post-hoc analysis of error counts in Experiment 2. Statistically significant differences are highlighted.

Comments from the participants also indicate a problem with Hold, especially related to slip-ins, *"[Hold] is hard, [I] cannot stop one finger from activating."* and *"You are always pressing something that you don't want."*. Drawbacks of pressure quasimode were also noted by participants: *"[pressure quasimode is] hard to control just one finger"* and *"It's hard to press just the one you want"*. Lift-and-tap was favored by seven participants, follwed by pressure switch (3), and hold (2). None of the participants preferred pressure quasimode. The reason were that lift-and-tap was *"faster"*, *"easier"*, and *"predictable"*.

Discussion

Again, lift-and-tap significantly outperformed the other methods in terms of overall errors. Pressure switch had fewer errors than hold. As seen from the ASI, a lot of slip-in error of the second finger occurred while the participants tried to acquire the first object, which contributes to the high error in hold comparing with other methods. The slip-ins of the first finger when dropping the objects (PSO) occurred more frequently in pressure switch and pressure quasimode than in the other conditions.

Since lift-and-tap had a relatively lower error rate and was more preferred than the other three methods, we recommend tapping as the first choice for multiple-finger uni-manual interaction, especially if the interaction involves frequent state switches.

EXPERIMENT 3: BI-MANUAL

In the last experiment the participants had to to do a asymmetric bi-manual tasks. An example of such a task in conventional desktop computer interfaces is when one hand is using the mouse to manipulate an object on the screen while the other hand presses the keyboard to issue commands. Asymmetric bi-manual tasks are precivied as more complex than uni-manual or symmetric bi-manual tasks [10, 15]. We hypothesize that (1) state switching in one hand influences the state switching in the other hand, and that (2) different state switching methods influence switching errors and switching time differently.

Task

This task was designed to represent translation, scaling, and rotation manipulations on a touch systems. With the dominant hand, the participants had to drag two objects with the thumb and the index finger through a maze. The two objects were two circles with a width of 1.8 cm (80px). The walls of the maze were displayed as 1 cm thick white lines. To move the objects through the maze, the participants had to drag through 8 pairs of gates, which where placed at specific points on the walls. The width of each gate was 2.4 cm (100px), and the distance between the two gates varied between 0 cm and 3.98 cm (170px) to force the participant to pinch the fingers to drag the objects through the gates. The gates were displayed as either blue, red, or yellow areas on the walls, as shown in Figure 11. Each gate differed in gap size, requiring the user to translate each circle individually.

If a dragged object was blocked by a wall the finger could slide off the object. In this case, the object had to be reacquired.

The gates could be opened by holding a correspondingly colored button located at the lower edge of the table on the non-dominant side. Thus, the participants needed to chord single or multiple keys with the non-dominant hand while using the dominant hand to move the objects through the opened gates. To indicate which object should be dragged through which gate, the gates were drawn in the corresponding color of the object.

After the participants had moved both objects through a pair of gates the colored buttons were disabled to enforce an engaging of the hand to open the next pair of gates. A trial was complete when both objects passed the last pair of gates.

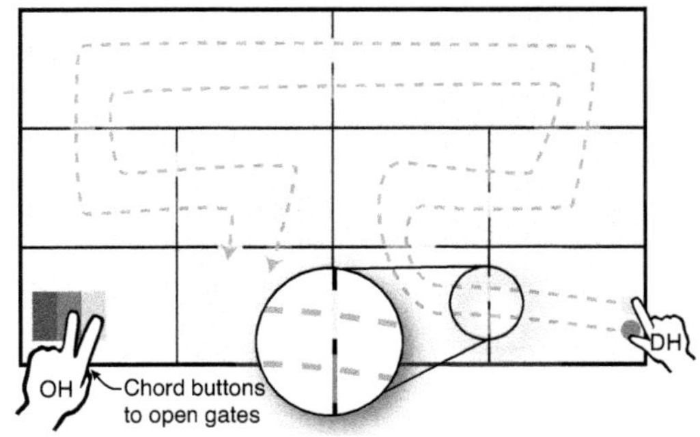

Figure 11. Bi-manual interaction task. The dominant hand (DH) moves a pair of circles through the colored gates while the opposite hand (OH) chords the buttons to open gates of the corresponding colors.

Measurements

In this task, we focus on situations where the user interacts with both hands, specifically, when the objects are within a distance of 1.6 cm (80px) of a gate opening. During this period, the user must move both objects using the fingers of the dominant hand while simultaneously keeping the buttons pressed with the fingers of the non-dominant hand. We measured three types of error:

- *Dominant hand slip-outs (SO_{DH}):* The number of times the dominant hand slips out during bi-manual interaction.
- *Opposite hand slip-outs (SO_{OH}):* The number of times the non-dominant hand slips out during bi-manual interaction.
- *Overall errors:* Sum of both slip-outs.

Methods with low overall errors are preferred. Methods with low SO_{DH} cause fewer error in the main task (object movement) and should be recommended for dominant hand input. Methods with low SO_{OH} cause fewer error in the secondary task (buttons holding) and should be recommended for non-dominant hand input.

Experimental design

We conducted the experiment with 8 computer science students (age 24 to 30; 2 female; all of them right-handed). Each participant conducted two trials in different directions for each switching method, resulting in a total of 64 trials. The order of switching methods and blocks was counterbalanced across participants, while the order of direction was randomized for each user. The experiment took 15 minutes on average. We collected qualitative feedback in the same manner as in Experiment 1.

Result

GEE shows a statitistically significant main effect of switching methods on overall errors, Wald $\chi^2_{3,N=64} = 126.17$, $p < .001$, on non-dominant hand slip-out (SO_{OH}), Wald $\chi^2_{3,N=64} = 25.16$, $p < .001$, and on dominant hand slip-out (SO_{DH}), Wald $\chi^2_{3,N=64} = 23.07$, $p < .001$. The detailed results and post-hoc analysis are shown in Figures 12 and 13.

Participants favored lift-and-tap because it was easy and did not require the user to maintain force: *"You don't waste time and it's easier to apply"*, *"Sometimes I didn't even have to*

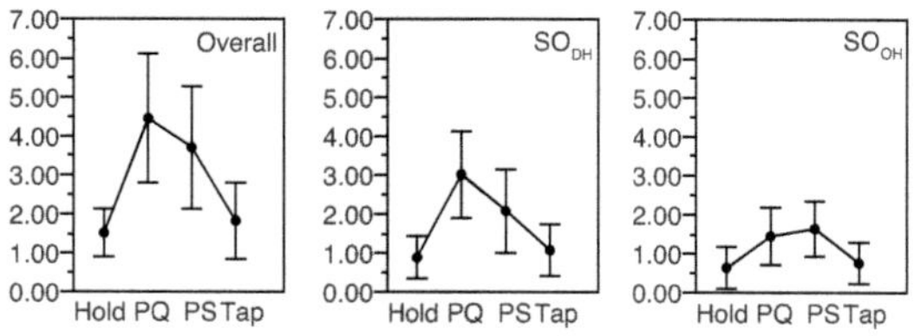

	Overall	SO_{DH}	SO_{OH}
Hold	1.50 [0.88, 2.12]	0.88 [0.33, 1.42]	0.63 [0.08, 1.17]
PQ	4.44 [2.79, 6.09]	3.00 [1.88, 4.12]	1.44 [0.71, 2.16]
PS	3.69 [2.11, 5.26]	2.06 [0.99, 3.14]	1.63 [0.93, 2.32]
Tap	1.81 [0.84, 2.79]	1.06 [0.40, 1.72]	0.75 [0.22, 1.28]

Figure 12. Error count per trial from Experiment 3 (Mean & 95% CI)

	Overall		SO_{DH}		SO_{OH}	
PQ – Hold	49.50	.0032	50.00	0.0070	21.50	.0713
PS – Hold	38.50	.0121	28.00	.0225	28.50	.0488
PS – PQ	−17.50	.3346	−22.50	.2074	3.50	.6250
Tap – Hold	6.00	.6240	4.50	.6719	4.50	.6133
Tap – PQ	−46.00	.0020	−42.50	.0056	−13.00	.0781
Tap – PS	−34.00	.0059	−18.50	.0625	−24.50	.0117

Figure 13. ***W*** **statistics and** ***p*** **value of post-hoc analysis of error counts in Experiment 3. Statistically significant differences are highlighted.**

look [at the non-dominant hand] to select the colors", and *"I'm not forced to press all the time"*. Participants also commented on the potential of hold for long-distance dragging and for the non-dominant hand: *"It's good that you don't have to move your left hand"* and *"You're not losing the targets on accident. You don't have to do anything with the right hand and tap the [buttons] with your left"*. For the ranking, five participants chose lift-and-tap, and three participants chose hold as their most favored method. None of the participants chose pressure switch or pressure quasimode.

Discussion

Less overall errors in lift-and-tap and hold indicate that these methods are suitable for bi-manual interaction. The lower error rate of hold was to be expected because of two reasons: First, in the dominant hand, the user can remain in the Engaged state for the whole task. As seen from the second experiment, only few errors occured while dragging with multiple fingers. Second, the user only has to maintain the finger contacts of the dominant hand with the surface while switching the state using the non-dominant hand. In contrast, it is easier to make mistakes in pressure quasimode and pressure switch because the participants had to maintain the finger pressure.

In summary, the state switching in one hand causes more errors in the opposite hand, especially in pressure quasimode and pressure switch. As switching methods influence switching errors differently, we recommend lift-and-tap and hold to be used in asymmetric bi-manual tasks.

DISCUSSION & CONCLUSION

In this paper, we identified four different switching methods that introduce a third interaction state for indirect touch systems. We conducted three experiments to compare these methods in three interaction scenarios: single finger, multiple fingers, and bi-manual interaction.

Use lift-and-tap as a default state-switching method

Across all three experiments, lift-and-tap outperforms other switching methods in terms of error rate and user preference. We believe the main reason for that is the explicit finger-up movement. It is less likely to be triggered by accident than, e.g., changing pressure or pausing a finger temporarily. This assumption is also supported by qualitative feedback. Therefore, we propose to use lift-and-tap as the switching method for indirect touch systems.

Consider the influence of task & context

While we recommend lift-and-tap as a default method, designers should also consider the influence of the form factor, the UI widgets, and the task. For example, since lift-and-tap loses the touch temporarily, two nearby touches may trade their places, especially in a small device.

The nature of the UI widget and the task should also be considered when choosing a method. For example, hold and pressure quasimode may be more suitable than lift-and-tap for an on screen quasimode modifier key. Interaction designers may allow an alternative switching method on these UI widgets in addition to lift-and-tap.

In some scenarios, a combination of lift-and-tap and hold can be beneficial in bi-manual interaction. As the third experiment showed, hold yielded almost no errors—comparable to lift-and-tap—for targets of which position is fixed, e.g., a button.

For example, in a 3D scene construction application [12], the user could use the non-dominant hand to select a virtual object while placing it on the scene with the dominant hand.

LIMITATIONS

The small number of participants, together with the conservative statistical analysis criteria, may have resulted in a lack of statistical power—some effects of the methods may not have been detected. Despite the clear superiority of lift-and-tap in our experiment, we believe that other methods, especially pressure switch and hold might be useful for some tasks or context-specific applications. Since our participants were from computer science who had experience with touchscreens, the results may not be generalizable for first-time users.

While we determined the thresholds from users' behavior, the thresholds presented were specific to our hardware. Interaction designers can use these thresholds as a starting point for their systems and adjust them according to the temporal and spatial sampling resolution of the sensor.

Of the four methods, participants might not be familiar with pressure switch and pressure quasimode. Although we let the participants familiarize them selfs with each technique, it is hard to beat their experience in lift-and-tap and hold which are ubiquitous on touch screens and track pads. We described the used thresholds and presented all results with CIs to inform future replications, meta-analyses, and design.

FUTURE WORK

In this paper, we only analyzed the methods in terms of the state switching errors. As the next step, we will also address the open question about how precise the users can select objects with each of the methods using a single finger and multiple fingers at the same time. Additional aural and visual feedback in pressure quasimode may allow users to better control the switch. An informal observation among authors indicates a strong learning curve of the switching methods. A further investigation of the performance of trained users could lead to different results. Finally, in this paper, we only used a 1:1 mapping between the input and the output area. In future studies, we also want to investigate how much this ratio can be changed in the way that the output area will be larger than the input area while maintaining nearly the same precision.

ACKNOWLEDGMENTS

This work was funded in part by the German B-IT Foundation.

REFERENCES

1. Benko, H., Wilson, A. D., and Baudisch, P. Precise selection techniques for multi-touch screens. In *Proc. CHI '06*, ACM (2006), 1263–1272.
2. Bi, X., Grossman, T., Matejka, J., and Fitzmaurice, G. Magic desk: bringing multi-touch surfaces into desktop work. In *Proc. CHI '11*, ACM (2012), 2511–2520.
3. Buxton, W. A three-state model of graphical input. In *Proc. INTERACT '90*, North-Holland Publishing Co. (1990), 449–456.
4. Buxton, W., Hill, R., and Rowley, P. Issues and techniques in touch-sensitive tablet input. *SIGGRAPH Comput. Graph. 19*, 3 (1985), 215–224.
5. Cappelli, R., Maio, D., and Maltoni, D. Modelling plastic distortion in fingerprint images. *Advances in Pattern Recognition ICAPR 2001* (2013), 371–378.
6. Davidson, P., and Han, J. Extending 2D object arrangement with pressure-sensitive layering cues. In *Proc. UIST '08*, ACM (2008), 87–90.
7. Forlines, C., and Balakrishnan, R. Evaluating tactile feedback and direct vs. indirect stylus input in pointing and crossing selection tasks. In *Proc. CHI '08*, ACM (2008), 1563–1572.
8. Forlines, C., Shen, C., and Buxton, B. Glimpse: a novel input model for multi-level devices. In *Proc. CHI '05*, ACM (2005), 1375–1378.
9. Forlines, C., Vogel, D., and Balakrishnan, R. HybridPointing: fluid switching between absolute and relative pointing with a direct input device. In *Proc. UIST '06*, ACM (2006), 211–220.
10. Guiard, Y. Asymmetric division of labor in human skilled bimanual action: The kinematic chain as a model. *Journal of Motor Behavior 19*, 19 (1987), 486–517.
11. Hger-Ross, C., and Schieber, M. H. Quantifying the independence of human finger movements: Comparisons of digits, hands, and movement frequencies. *The Journal of Neuroscience 20*, 22 (Nov. 2000), 8542–8550.
12. Kin, K., Miller, T., Bollensdorff, B., DeRose, T., Hartmann, B., and Agrawala, M. Eden: a professional multitouch tool for constructing virtual organic environments. In *Proc. CHI '11*, ACM (2011), 1343–1352.
13. Knoedel, S., and Hachet, M. Multi-touch RST in 2D and 3D spaces: Studying the impact of directness on user performance. IEEE (2011), 75–78.
14. Kosara, R. Indirect multi-touch interaction for brushing in parallel coordinates. In *Proc. VDA '11* (2011), 786–809.
15. Latulipe, C., Kaplan, C. S., and Clarke, C. L. A. Bimanual and unimanual image alignment: an evaluation of mouse-based techniques. In *Proc. UIST '05*, ACM (2005), 123–131.
16. MacKenzie, I. S., and Oniszczak, A. A comparison of three selection techniques for touchpads. In *Proc. CHI '98*, ACM (1998), 336–343.
17. Marras, W. S. Basic biomechanics and workstation design. In *Handbook of Human Factors and Ergonomics*, 3 ed. John Wiley & Sons, Inc., 2006, 340–370.
18. Matejka, J., Grossman, T., Lo, J., and Fitzmaurice, G. The design and evaluation of multi-finger mouse emulation techniques. In *Proc. CHI '09*, ACM (2009), 1073–1082.
19. Morris, M., Brush, A., and Meyers, B. A field study of knowledge workers use of interactive horizontal displays. In *Proc. Tabletop '08*, IEEE (2008), 105–112.
20. Moscovich, T., and Hughes, J. F. Indirect mappings of multi-touch input using one and two hands. In *Proc. CHI '08*, ACM (2008), 1275–1284.
21. Olwal, A., Feiner, S., and Heyman, S. Rubbing and tapping for precise and rapid selection on touch-screen displays. In *Proc. CHI '08*, ACM (2008), 295–304.
22. Pawluk, D. T., and Howe, R. D. Dynamic contact of the human fingerpad against a flat surface. *Journal of biomechanical engineering 121*, 6 (Dec. 1999), 605–611.
23. Potter, R. L., Weldon, L. J., and Shneiderman, B. Improving the accuracy of touch screens: an experimental evaluation of three strategies. In *Proc. CHI '88*, ACM (1988), 27–32.
24. Ramos, G., Boulos, M., and Balakrishnan, R. Pressure widgets. In *Proc. CHI '04*, ACM (2004), 487–494.
25. Schmidt, D., Block, F., and Gellersen, H. A comparison of direct and indirect multi-touch input for large surfaces. In *Proc.INTERACT '09*, Springer (2009), 582–594.
26. Wang, F., and Ren, X. Empirical evaluation for finger input properties in Multi-Touch interaction. In *Proc. CHI '09*, ACM (2009), 1063–1072.

Improving Touch Accuracy on Large Tabletops Using Predecessor and Successor

Max Möllers, Norbert Dumont, Stefan Ladwig, Jan Borchers
RWTH Aachen University, Germany
{moellers, borchers}@cs.rwth-aachen.de, stefan.ladwig@psych.rwth-aachen.de,
norbert.dumont@rwth-aachen.de

ABSTRACT
Touch interfaces provide great flexibility in designing an UI. However, the actual experience is often frustrating due to bad touch recognition. On small systems, we can analyze yaw, roll, and pitch of the finger to increase touch accuracy for a single touch. On larger systems, we need to take additional factors into account as users have more flexibility for their limb posture and need to aim over larger distances. Thus, we investigated how people perform touch sequences on those large touch surfaces. We show that the relative location of the *predecessor* of a touch has a significant impact on the orientation and position of the touch ellipsis.

We exploited this effect on an off-the-shelf touch display and showed that with only minimal preparation the touch accuracy of standard hardware can be improved by at least 7%, allowing better recognition rates or more UI components on the same screen.

Author Keywords
touch; tabletops; offset; accuracy; sequence

ACM Classification Keywords
H.5.2 Information Interfaces and Presentation: Miscellaneous

INTRODUCTION
Touch interfaces are currently the dominant design in mobile computing, and touch-enabled tabletops might become a major computing platform for knowledge workers in the future. However, bad touch recognition often leaves users with frustration regardless of the surface size as not only small targets but also long distances make touching hard [3]. One can increase the target size to compensate for this effect. Another option that even preserves the precious real estate is to correct the user's input for errors. Existing research already tells us how we can do this for single touches on small surfaces [5], yet the correction of touch (sequences) on large-scale surfaces has not been investigated.

CHI 2013, April 27–May 2, 2013, Paris, France.

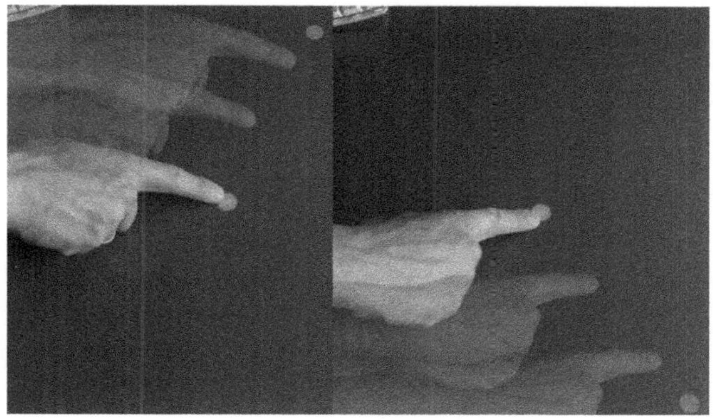

Figure 1. A person hitting the same (green) button, coming from different directions. Although the same target, the person hits it differently.

Also, on larger interaction areas, people have more freedom for touching the surface—different body, arm, finger orientations are possible. However, as people plan actions to be as comfortable as possible [7], we expect a predictable behavior, e.g., changing finger orientation in a sequence of touches depending on the previous or following touch (Fig. 1).

This paper contributes the following: 1) a study on how predecessor and successor location affect touch location and orientation and 2) an application of the predecessor effect to an off-the-shelf touch display showing a significant improvement of accuracy.

RELATED WORK
Several solutions were proposed to solve the problem of inaccurate input as well as occlusion from the finger itself. Some use indirect manipulation by having an input area act as a proxy for the area which is manipulated. This proxy can be located close to the actual input area (*cross-lever*, *precision handle* [1], and *shift* [8]) or farther away, e.g., *back-of-device interactions* [2].

Other methods record more than just the touch point to increase accuracy. Wang and Ren [9] also employed the contact ellipsis. TapSense [4] used the sound of the impact of an object to identify the touch. TouchID Toolkit [6] used gloves with fiducial markers on the finger tips, knuckles, etc. to thoroughly identify fingers and their posture. The *Ridge Pad* is able to track yaw, roll, and pitch from the fingerprint [5].

None of these systems take touch sequences into account. This makes sense for small touch surfaces as only minimal movement inertia is to be expected and limb postures are very similar. However, on larger surfaces limb postures can vary a lot and movement inertia comes into play. In action sequences, Rosenbaum et al. [7] analyzed target acquisitions and showed that subjects seem to plan their actions beyond the first grip, anticipating future states.

TOUCH SEQUENCES ON TABLETOPS

People who work frequently with the same application know which input is required for achieving a goal. They turn this into a sequence of actions, which on a touch device usually consist of a sequence of touches. We assume that individuals plan these sequences of touches by predicting comfortable final limb postures [7].

Thus, given a touch sequence $[\ldots, t_{i-1}, t, t_{i+1}, \ldots]$ our hypotheses are:

H1 Coming from different touch points t_{i-1} changes the angle and offset of the touch at t_i. Predecessor Effect (PE).

H2 Going to different touch points t_{i+1} changes the angle and offset of the touch at t_i. Successor Effect (SE).

We also consider angle (yaw) of the touch ellipsis (Fig. 2, right) as previous work showed a significant effect of this angle on the touch offset.

To evaluate our hypotheses, we let people perform touch sequences on a tabletop in a controlled setting and analyzed our data regarding the PE and the SE.

Setup

We used a 6-ring plus middle button layout for the touch targets (Fig. 2, left). The northernmost button was reachable with no arm stretching or leaning forward. We used round buttons (15 mm diameter) and the ring had a diameter of 40 cm. Dependent on the study condition participants performed up to three touches in a sequence. Only buttons used in the sequence were displayed. These buttons were labeled with "1" to "3" (Fig. 2, right), colored gray, and lit up in green color when they needed to be touched. Users were asked to move their finger to a pre-defined position after performing one touch sequence: a 10 cm by 5 cm wide box on the left half of the table, easily reachable with the right hand.

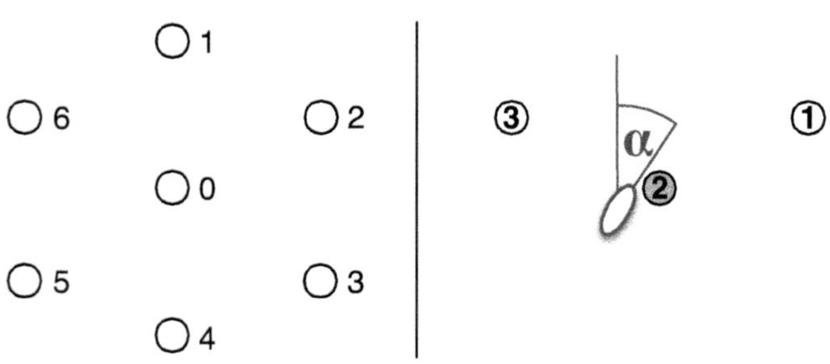

Figure 2. Left) Layout of the buttons in our study. Most touch sequences started on the ring, went to its center and back to the ring. We only look at touches aimed at the center. Right) A participant needs to touch the buttons labeled with "1" to "3": After touching the outer button, he aims at the center button, but overshoots (red ellipsis). We record the location and orientation α w.r.t. the y-axis.

Our experiment used four conditions (cf. video figure):

A first, middle, and last button are displayed simultaneously, i.e., PE and SE should occur.

B first and second are displayed directly at the beginning, then third after the second has been touched, i.e., PE should occur, but SE not as the participant does not know the successor when touching.

C first is not displayed at all, middle and last are displayed directly at the beginning, i.e., PE does not occur as there are no different predecessors (the resting spot is always the same), but SE should happen.

D first is not displayed at all, middle is displayed directly at the beginning, the last after the middle has been touched, i.e., PE and SE should not happen.

Conditions A and B presented sequences of three touches each. Conditions C and D presented sequences of two touches each. Users started with doing one condition, performed latin square balanced order of all touch sequences in this condition, repeated 5 times, and then went to the next condition. This order of the conditions was also latin square balanced among the users.

Task

First, the experimenter gave instructions on how to perform the task and participants were told that their speed and accuracy was a non-important factor. All users were sat at the same predefined position in front of the table and were instructed to use their index finger for touching.

We started the test with a whack-a-mole game for about five minutes in advance of each experiment. This way, participants were able to familiarize themselves with the setting. Then the first touch sequence was presented and participants were asked to press the lit buttons according to their occurrence. Participants took 30 minutes including preparation.

Apparatus & Analysis

We use a multi-touch table with a 3240 × 1920 px display over 140x80 cm. For accurate touch tracking, we use a single camera beneath the table that can be rotated along its axes to be pointed at a specific spot on the screen. This gives us an input resolution of 140 dpi, i.e., sub-pixel accurate tracking for our 59 dpi output resolution.

We collected demographic data before the test using a questionnaire: gender, age, height, and prior experience with touch devices (5-point Likert scale). Our system returned the touch as a contact ellipsis. We record the angle of its main axis and the center of the ellipsis.

We had concerns how the participants height would impact the body posture which might lead to different touch angles. However, arm length scales with height and seemed to counterbalance this effect: we could not see any effect of height.

Participants

14 right-handed people (2 females) took part in the study, aged 20–31, height 163–193 ($M = 181, SD = 7.6$). The questionnaire revealed that participants had experience using

small touch devices such as smartphones ($M = 3.8, SD = 1.2$) but only few had experience with larger touch displays like tables ($M = 1.9, SD = 1.4$) .

Results

To analyze for the PE, we ran a repeated measures one-way ANOVA using data from condition B (where only PE should happen) (Fig. 3, 4, 5). We could see a significant main effect of predecessor on angle ($F_{5,60} = 22.367, p < 0.001$), x-offset ($F_{5,60} = 12.082, p < 0.001$), and y-offset ($F_{5,60} = 6.830, p < 0.001$). Similar results could be seen in condition A (where predecessor and successor should happen): a significant main effect of predecessor on angle ($F_{5,60} = 26.680, p < 0.001$), x-offset ($F_{5,60} = 13.793, p < 0.001$), and y-offset ($F_{5,60} = 7.372, p < 0.001$).

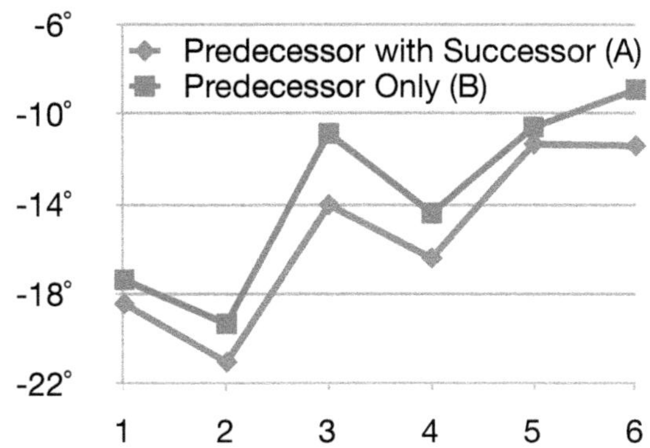

Figure 3. Finger orientation (yaw) depending on the predecessor. It variates similarly in both conditions.

To analyze for the SE, we ran a repeated measures one-way ANOVA using data from condition C (where only SE should happen). It showed no significant main effect of the successor on angle ($F_{5,60} = 1.567, p = 0.183$), x-offset ($F_{5,60} = 1.150, p = 0.344$), or y-offset ($F_{5,60} = 0.932, p = 0.467$). Similar results were seen in the mixed condition A, i.e., no significant main effects.

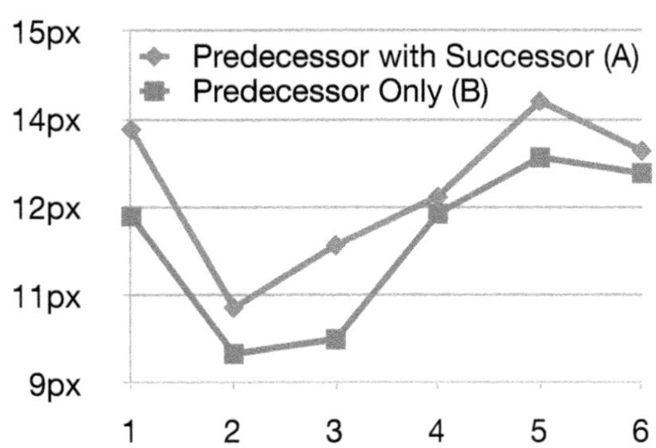

Figure 4. X offset depending on the predecessor. It variates similarly in both conditions.

As expected in the control condition D, neither predecessor nor successor showed any significant main effect.

Discussion

Based on the results, we see that there exists a predecessor effect, i.e., the location of a previous touch in a sequence has an impact on future touches. But we didn't see an effect of succeeding touches. This might be due to the fact that this effect is very small or does not exist. In both cases, we actually welcome this result: We do not need to predict user behavior to get very accurate touches.

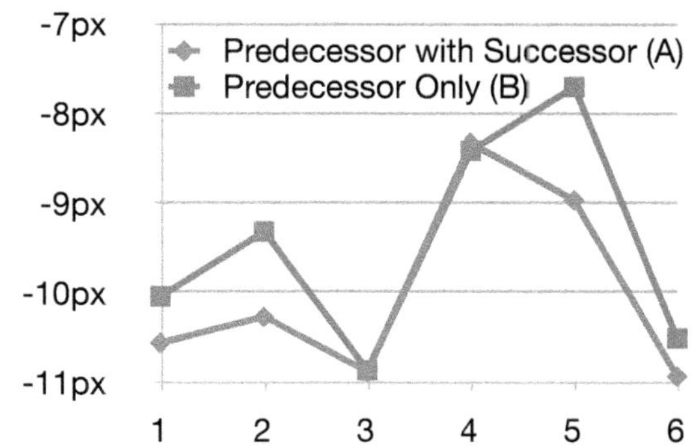

Figure 5. Y offset depending on the predecessor. It variates similarly in both conditions.

Compared to Holz's work, we saw a very low correlation between angle and touch offset ($|r| < 0.1$, cf. Fig. 3 to 4, 5). Thus, we cannot use the yaw angle of the finger to correct offset, but instead need to use the predecessor in this setting.

APPLICATION OF THE PREDECESSOR EFFECT

We showed that the predecessor effect exists. We now apply it to improve the touch accuracy on an off-the-shelf touch display using a simple machine learning approach.

Study Setup

We used a 27" Perceptive Pixel horizontal display with sub pixel accurate tracking on a 110dpi screen. As warm-up, we sat the participants in a fixed spot in front of the display, displayed a round button, and asked them to touch the button 30 times with fixed pitch ("close to horizontal") and roll ("straight on the surface"). Between each touch, they should move their finger to a resting position above the table.

Again, we used a 6-ring plus middle button layout for our application. Users touched a button on the ring first and then touched the middle button. After this, they needed to move their hand to a resting position in front of them in the air. The order of the six buttons was counterbalanced and the full set was repeated 15 times. We measured touch location $\vec{t}$ and angle α, also per participant.

Similar to other machine learning approaches, the data was split randomly and used in two ways: Two thirds were used to generate a model, the other third was used for evaluation.

Offset Model

We correct touches according to which direction they come from as we know that the predecessor has an effect on the touch offset: We take all the touches $\vec{t}$ and put them into 6 buckets according to their predecessor j (cf. Algorithm 1).

For each bucket $BUCK_j$, we then take the median x and median y value of the offsets of the touches, resulting in touch correction vectors $\vec{t}_{BUCK_j}$. They indicate how people typically over- or under-shoot. We chose to use median instead of the average as the former is more outlier-resistant.

Algorithm 1 Correcting for the current predecessor

for all predecessor locations j **do** ▷ *Training*
  $\vec{t}_{BUCK_j} \leftarrow median(\vec{t_i}), \forall \vec{t_i} \in BUCK_j$
end for
for new touch $\vec{t}$ coming from pred j **do** ▷ *Application*
  $\vec{t'} = \vec{t} - \vec{t}_{BUCK_j}$
end for

To evaluate, we subtract the correction term according to the model and get $\vec{t'}$. The correction term can also be based only on per participant data to account for individual behavior. This results in two simple look-up tables.

Participants & Analysis

We recruited 10 right-handed participants (1 female), aged 24-32 ($M = 27.1, SD = 2.9$). The questionnaire revealed that participants had experience using small touch devices such as smartphones ($M = 4.5, SD = 0.7$) and little experience using table-sized touch systems ($M = 2.8, SD = 1.4$). Each participant performed the study in less than 10 minutes.

We create two datasets based on the touch data: corrected for the predecessor as well as the corrected for predecessor and user. For comparison, we calculate the size of a minimal rectangular button that covers at least 95% of the touches, i.e., its width and height is equal to about 1.96 standard deviations of the mean of the x and y data.

Results

Only using the predecessor has no effect, neither good nor bad, on the button size (Fig. 6). Our explanation is that individual differences in touch behavior overshadow the predecessor effect. However, taking individual behavior into account, we can shrink the button by 7%— and we only needed to capture five minutes of user interaction.

FUTURE WORK

We would like to vary more of our parameters: button sizes and shapes, relative user location, targeting speed, etc. We also want to investigate which time is the right threshold to decide whether a touch can affect the next one. Also, more predecessors could explain the sine shape of Fig. 4 and 5.

In a real application, we would extend our 6-ring to a model that stores offset per relative direction (in degrees) and relative distance to every predecessor. This model could even be stored per each pixel to account for potential differences due to the relative location to the user. As this would be a rather big model and thus hard to calibrate beforehand, we want to explore ways to learn this model during the systems usage, similar to what current smartphones do to correct for touch errors and personal touch behavior.

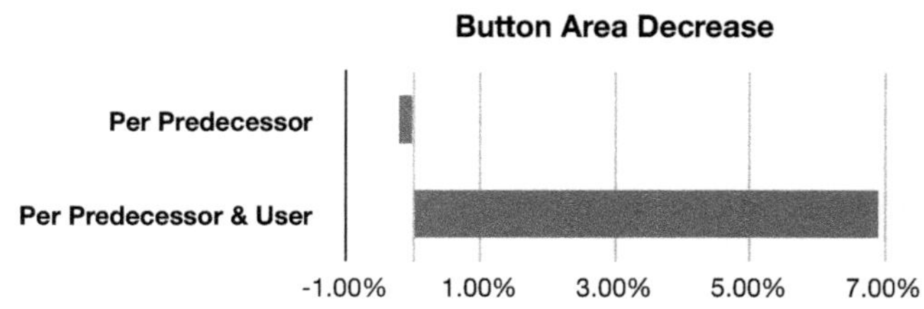

Figure 6. Decrease of minimum button size to allow for 95% touch accuracy. The baseline was the size of a button using raw touch data.

CONCLUSION

We evaluated how touch sequences have an effect on the accuracy of their single touches. We saw that the location of the previous touch affects the location and orientation of the following touch. We applied this knowledge to an off-the-shelf touch table and were able to improve its accuracy with less than 5 minutes of per participant setup. It is quite likely that even this short learning phase can be performed during systems usage, making no setup necessary while improving touch accuracy for any large touch surface.

ACKNOWLEDGMENTS

This work was funded in part by the German B-IT Foundation.

REFERENCES

1. P. Albinsson and S. Zhai. High precision touch screen interaction. *Proc. CHI '03*, 105–112.
2. P. Baudisch. Back-of-device interaction allows creating very small touch devices. *Proc. CHI '09*, 1923–1932.
3. P. M. Fitts. The information capacity of the human motor system in controlling the amplitude of movement. *Journal of Experimental Psychology*, 47(6):381–391, 1954.
4. C. Harrison, J. Schwarz, and S. E. Hudson. TapSense: enhancing finger interaction on touch surfaces. *Proc. UIST '11*, 627–634, October.
5. C. Holz and P. Baudisch. The generalized perceived input point model and how to double touch accuracy by extracting fingerprints. *Proc. CHI '10*, 581–590.
6. N. Marquardt, J. Kiemer, D. Ledo, S. Boring, and S. Greenberg. Designing user-, hand-, and handpart-aware tabletop interactions with the TouchID toolkit. *Proc. ITS '11*, 21–30, November.
7. D. A. Rosenbaum, F. Marchak, H. J. Barnes, J. Vaughan, J. D. Slotta, and M. J. Jorgensen. *Constraints for action selection: Overhand versus underhand grips.* Lawrence Erlbaum Associates, Inc, Mahwah, New Jersey, 1990.
8. D. Vogel and P. Baudisch. Shift: a technique for operating pen-based interfaces using touch. *Proc. CHI '07*, 657–666, April.
9. F. Wang and X. Ren. Empirical Evaluation for Finger Input Properties In Multi-touch Interaction. *Proc. CHI '09*, 1063–1072.

Touchbugs: Actuated Tangibles on Multi-Touch Tables

Diana Nowacka[1], Karim Ladha[1], Nils Y. Hammerla[1], Daniel Jackson[1], Cassim Ladha[1], Enrico Rukzio[2], Patrick Olivier[1]

[1] Culture Lab, School of Computing Science, Newcastle University, Newcastle Upon Tyne, UK
d.nowacka@ncl.ac.uk

[2] Ulm University, Ulm, Germany
enrico.rukzio@uni-ulm.de

ABSTRACT

We present a novel approach to graspable interfaces using Touchbugs, actuated physical objects for interacting with interactive surface computing applications. Touchbugs are active tangibles that are able to move across surfaces by employing vibrating motors and can communicate with camera-based multi-touch surfaces using infrared LEDs. Touchbug's embedded inertial sensors and computational capabilities open a new interaction space by providing autonomous capabilities for tangibles that allow goal directed behavior.

Author Keywords

User interface device; actuated tangibles; interactive tabletops.

ACM Classification Keywords

H.5.2 [Information Interfaces and presentation]: User Interfaces - Haptic I/O.

INTRODUCTION

Tangible user interfaces (TUI) combine the dynamic qualities typical of digital information representations with physical affordances, i.e. "properties of an object that determine how it can be used" [5]. TUIs, in combination with multi-touch tables, provide passive haptic feedback for hand gestures and are augmented by a physical model for visual feedback. This allows people to interact with the input devices in the same way they interact with everyday objects, applying real world skills without the need for training or instructions. The benefits of these user interfaces include the simultaneous reduction of cognitive load placed on users (while they interact with an application) and simplification of the interaction itself. In contexts that are likely to include cognitive overload, time pressure, or stress, this may improve performance and even encourage improvisation and exploration [1].

Actuated TUIs allow data to be connected to, and represented by, physical objects (e.g. dynamic data can be linked to dynamics of the objects). They also facilitate more engaging, playful interaction and afford the use of movement as an expressive output modality. To date, approaches to connect actuated tangible user interfaces with interactive surfaces either require complex modification to, or augmentation of, the interactive surface hardware [4, 6, 8] or use constrained and relatively cumbersome tangible artefacts [2, 7, 10]. For example, Madgets are tangibles containing small magnets that are actuated using an array of electromagnets [8] (yielding a rather discontinuous movement). Marshall et al. [4] facilitate smoother and more accurate motion in their Ultra-Tangibles by applying ultrasound-based air pressure waves to actuate small lightweight objects on an interactive surface. In the few existing actuated tangible systems the possibilities for interaction are limited as the systems are essentially comprised of lightweight passive objects that are manipulated by an external applied force (i.e. electromagnetic or air pressure). Other designs have sought to enhance tangibles with wheels [2, 7, 10]; although wheeled objects are not entirely appropriate for direct interaction on interactive surfaces (i.e. they are not very robust and expose moving parts).

Figure 1. Touchbugs on a multi-touch table.

In this paper we present Touchbugs, an open source hardware and software framework for a novel actuated tangible technology [11]. Touchbugs are small tangibles that use directed bristles and vibration motors for actuation (giving them the ability to move independently). Their infrared LEDs allow multiple Touchbugs to both be spatially tracked (position and orientation) on optical multi-touch tables and to communicate information about their internal state to the table. Embedded inertial sensors, which capture displacement and orientation, provide rich opportunities for interaction design including direct physical manipulation, and symbolic and metaphorical gestures. This novel combination of sensing and actuation capabilities goes beyond simple changes of (virtual) states (e.g. by the use of buttons) offering significantly more potential of expressive interaction [1]. We present the design of Touchbugs and investigate the accuracy of the actuation in a number of experiments. Furthermore, we show how the embedded sensors can be used to stabilize the tangibles movement in an autonomous feedback loop.

MOTIVATION

Our aim was to develop a framework of autonomous, self-contained and controllable actuated tangibles. Our requirements for Touchbugs were: (i) that they are capable of smooth, continuous and controllable movement (both translational and rotational); (ii) that Touchbugs can sense their own movement and maintain internal state information independent of any external system; (iii) that the electronics are robust and compact and can be readily enclosed by cases of different shapes and sizes; and (iv) that the integration of Touchbugs with optical multi-touch tables does not require hardware modifications or augmentations to the table.

TOUCHBUGS

A Touchbug consists of a 40×40mm printed-circuit-board (PCB), as shown in Figure 2, comprising a microcontroller, two vibrating motors, LEDs and several sensors. The PCB is located on two rows of bristles mounted at an angle of approximately 5° to the vertical (see Figure 1). A motor is mounted above each set of bristles, and the vibration generated by these motors causes a high frequency oscillating flexion of the bristles that results in a forward motion (or circular if just one motor is activated). LEDs on the underside of the Touchbug both allow optical multi-touch surfaces (i.e. FTIR or DI) to detect its position, and allow the Touchbug to transmit information to the table (see subsection *Detection on the table*). The embedded sensors (accelerometer and gyroscope) are used to stabilize the movement of the tangible and to sense physical interactions and manipulations (e.g. gestural manipulation). Custom bodies can be readily fabricated to enclose the PCB and the small and compact form factor of the PCB allows a wide variety of appearances and sizes. The Touchbugs shown in Figure 1 are 60×50×20mm; weigh 24g; and have a maximum (straight-line) velocity of 250mm/s.

Figure 2. The Touchbugs PCB (upper and lower surface): (1) micro-controller; (2) left vibration motor; (3) rear LED; (4) right phototransistor; (5) button; (6) accelerometer; (7) gyroscope; (8) battery and (9) right colored LED.

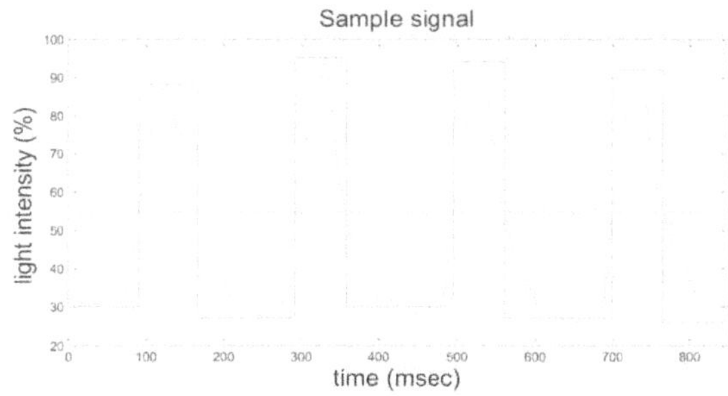

Figure 3. An illustration of the light signal which is sent by the tangibles LEDs.

Detection on the table

An optical multi-touch surface can detect and process the signal from a Touchbug's infrared emitters and thus receive information from them. As illustrated in Figure 3 both amplitude modulation and frequency modulation are employed to communicate information. The amplitude corresponds to the intensity of the infrared diode, and the frequency is the reciprocal of the amount of time between the signal peaks. Additional data (e.g. a button click) can be transmitted by actively modulating the pulse duration (pulse-width). Each LED transmits a distinct signal, which is detected by the camera of the interactive surface as a touch event. The fixed distance between these pseudo-touch events (generated by the LEDs), combined with unique signal frequencies for each LED, allows the detection and identification of multiple Touchbugs (up to half the number of touch events that the interactive surface API supports). Furthermore, by following conventions for setting the two frequencies (i.e. *left* < *right*), the orientation of the tangible can be sensed by the table (to a precision of less than 5°). Parts of the implementation rely on Touchbridge [3].

Actuating the tangibles

We experimented with various different kinds of materials, but discovered that fine and soft bristles worked best. Our final design utilized bristles from consumer off-the-shelf draught excluders that were trimmed to lengths from 7-17mm and attached to the underside of the PCB. Touchbugs can be steered using differential control of the two motors mounted on the top-side of the PCB above the bristles.

Due to factors such as irregular surfaces and slight differences in the lengths of bristles, the Touchbug is unlikely to move by default in a straight line, consequently a feedback control loop is required to stabilize the motion. While the process of control could be managed by the tabletop (indeed, it already measures a Touchbug's orientation), experiments showed that due to latency in the communication between a Touchbug and the table the required control loop could not be maintained. Instead we manage the control of a Touchbug on the tangible itself. A Touchbug senses its deviation from its initial orientation using the gyroscope. The gyroscope measures the angular velocity of the device around three perpendicular axes. However, the measured angular velocity is subject to noise resulting from the vibration of the motors. As illustrated in

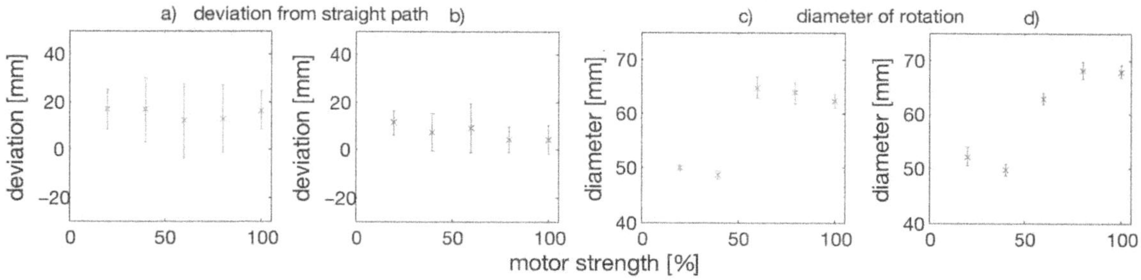

Figure 4. Results from two different experiments. The two leftmost graphs show the absolute deviation from a straight path for 5 different motor settings and 2 different lengths of bristles (red short, blue long). The two rightmost graphs show the diameter for circular motion (just one motor active).

Figure 5, this noise is normally distributed between ± 50°/s. As can been seen in Figure 5, when the tangible is rotating, the measurements significantly exceed this noise-level, although this can be a problem for extremely slow turn rates. We implemented a basic approach to direction control, in which a counter steering motion is induced if the angular velocity exceeds a certain threshold. This counter steering consists of increasing the strength (i.e. speed) of the inside motor (relative to the turn deviation), linearly to the absolute deviation from the initial orientation. This deviation is easily estimated by integrating the rotation measurements over time. Both the threshold from which to start compensating for drift as well as the coefficient that controls the strength of the counter steer, were estimated empirically to work best with medium speed motion.

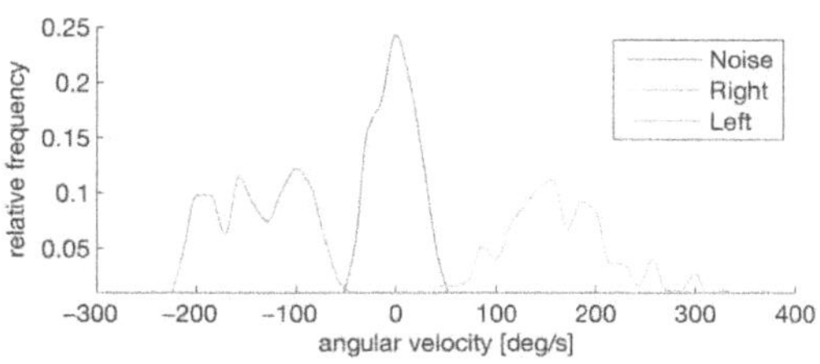

Figure 5. The distribution of angular velocity.

Steering the tangibles

A Touchbug has two phototransistors, one next to each set of bristles on the underside of the PCB (see component 4 in Figure 2). These point towards the interactive surface of the table and are sensitive to both visible and near infrared light. As the phototransistors are affected by ambient and infrared light – and due to the variability in ambient light levels – we restricted ourselves to displaying three light intensities on the surface which the Touchbugs can reliably detect and distinguish: black, grey and white. Displaying these colors is the mechanism by which the table can control the Touchbug. When a light level is detected, the Touchbug sets the strength (speed) of its corresponding motor accordingly. Using white, black and grey semi-circular patterns displayed directly under the Touchbugs, the table is able to start, stop and steer multiple tangibles at the same time. Different configurations of pattern result in different motions as illustrated in Figure 6. In retrospect, to improve the communication channel between the table and the Touchbugs, the phototransistors could have been replaced by ambient light sensors, which are only sensitive to visible light. This would increase the range of detectable intensity levels and therefore afford higher bandwidth and more reliable communication.

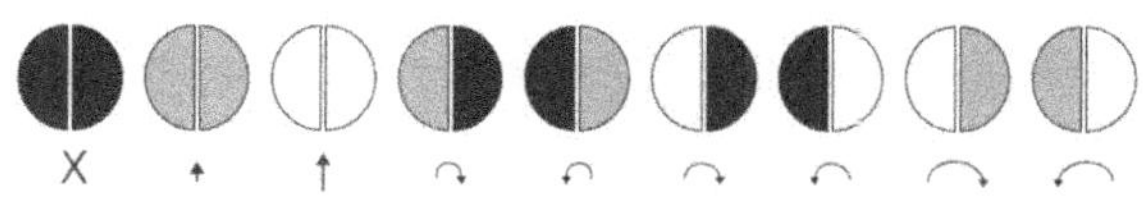

Figure 6. Semi-circles projected below the tangible that can be used for steering. Three colors result in 9 possible motions.

To steer the Touchbug to a specific target, first the angle between the direction of the Touchbug and the direction to the target is calculated using simple trigonometry. However, calculating this angle, rotating the Touchbug accordingly and starting a forward motion is bound to fail, as any rotating motion will also displace the device. Therefore a more sophisticated control mechanism is required. Given the estimated angle it is straight-forward to derive whether the device has to turn left or right to face the target. After initializing the turning motion, the angle between the current direction and the direction to the target is continuously estimated. Once this angle is below a certain threshold the forward motion is initiated. This procedure results in a smooth and natural, slightly curving path from the source position to the target.

EVALUATION OF THE ACTUATION

To assess Touchbug's movement abilities, we conducted two experiments. The first explored the accuracy of the automatic path correction based on the gyroscope measurements for different motor strength settings and bristle lengths. The tangibles were placed on a multi-touch table (SMART™ table) and instructed to cross the available surface by following a straight-line path (10 runs for each motor setting and bristle length, 7mm and 17mm). The results are shown in Figure 4. Graphs (a) and (b) show the absolute deviation from the straight-line path measured after the device travelled for 500mm across the table. Long bristles (b) show less deviation from the path and also a smaller standard deviation compared to short bristles (a). Overall we have not found significant differences in the precision of the automatic path correction for different motor settings. Furthermore, the mean absolute deviation remained below 20mm for all bristle lengths and strength settings tested, less than the size of the actual PCB of the Touchbug.

The second experiment investigated how the motor strength influences the turn-rate of the device. The Touchbug was placed on the multi-touch table and instructed to turn in a circle (just one motor active, 10 runs per motor strength setting and bristle length). The diameter of the resulting circle was measured and the results are reported in Figure 4. Both the short bristles (c) and the long bristles (d) show a very similar relationship between diameter and motor strength setting. When increasing motor strength the diameter initially decreases, after which a sharp jump in circle diameter was observed. We believe this is due to the friction of the bristles on the surface. Up until a medium motor strength setting the friction of the inner, non-vibrating bristle exceeds the drag produced by the forward motion by the vibrating bristle, resulting in a sharp rotation. On higher motor settings the inner bristle begins to slide across the table resulting in a sharp increase in turn diameter.

Limitations of the system

Touchbugs have a number of clear limitations. The tangibles cannot rotate around their center, or move backwards and therefore can get stuck in the corners of a table. Another drawback is the optical tracking of the devices. The infrared diodes have a high intensity; nevertheless the tracking accuracy suffers when the lighting conditions change significantly. The number of Touchbugs that can be used simultaneously is constrained by the number of touch points that the multi-touch surface API can support. Although in theory there are no technical limitations on how many tangibles can be used, to date we have only used five simultaneously. Improvements in table hardware such as increasing the frame rate of the camera, along with more efficient algorithms would reduce latency and increase the bandwidth of the Touchbug-to-table optical communication.

INTERACTION CAPABILITIES

Due to the data set which is transmitted through the accelerometer and the gyroscope a wide range of additional features is in fact available. These sensors allow the recognition of simple motions (like tapping on the device) or gestures such as shaking, which could be used as a direct input or captured for later analysis [9]. Furthermore, we implemented the possibility to couple digital content to the Touchbug – such as 3D objects displayed on the table. When the user rotates the device in his hand, the digital object rotates according to the tangible. The device can also detect if it is laid on its back or if a user is holding it (using simple motion classification). In this case, the vibrating motors can be used as an output to provide variable haptic feedback or to attract the attention of the user. Furthermore, actuated tangibles also have the potential to support collaborative use across more than one remote table (or independent Touchbugs), for example, when a remote user working with the same system moves a tangible, changes can be reflected on a connected table (or Touchbug).

CONCLUSION

In this note we presented Touchbugs, a novel actuated tangible user interfaces framework which can communicate with interactive surfaces. We have characterized Touchbug's actuation and demonstrated its potential as an affordable yet uniquely expressive interaction device for optical multi-touch tables.

ACKNOWLEDGMENTS

This work was part-funded by the RCUK Digital Economy Research Hub on Social Inclusion through the Digital Economy (SiDE) and the Emmy Noether research group Mobile Interaction with Pervasive User Interfaces funded by the German Research Foundation (DFG).

REFERENCES

1. Jacob, R., Girouard, A., Hirshfield, L.M., Horn, M.S., Shaer, O., Solovey, E.T., and Zigelbaum, J. Reality-based interaction: a framework for post-WIMP interfaces. In *Proc. CHI 2008*, 201-210.
2. Krzywinski, A., Mi, H., Chen, W., and Sugimoto, M., RoboTable: a tabletop framework for tangible interaction with robots in a mixed reality. In *Proc. ACE 2009*, 107-114.
3. Ladha, C., Ladha, K., Hook, J., Jackson, D., and Olivier, P. TouchBridge: augmenting active tangibles for camera-based multi-touch surfaces. In *Proc. ITS 2010*, 309-309.
4. Marshall, M., Carter, T., Alexander, J., and Subramanian, S. Ultra-tangibles: creating movable tangible objects on interactive tables. In *Proc. CHI 2012*, 2185-2188.
5. Norman, D.A. The Psychology of Everyday Things. New York, BasicBooks, 1988.
6. Pangaro, G., Maynes-Aminzade, D., and Ishii, H. The actuated workbench: computer-controlled actuation in tabletop tangible interfaces. In *Proc. UIST 2002*, 181-190.
7. Pedersen, E. W., and Hornbæk, K. Tangible bots: interaction with active tangibles in tabletop interfaces. In *Proc. CHI 2011*, 2975-2984.
8. Weiss, M., Schwarz, F., Jakubowski, S., and Borchers, J. Madgets: actuating widgets on interactive tabletops. In *Proc. UIST 2010*, 293-302.
9. Westeyn, T., Kientz, J., Starner, T., and Abowd, G. Designing toys with automatic play characterization for supporting the assessment of a child's development. In *Proc. IDC 2008*, 89-92.
10. D'Ademo, N., Lui, W., et. al. eBug - An Open Robotics Platform for Teaching and Research. In *Proc. ACRA 2011*.
11. http://www.openmovement.co.uk

The Effect of Virtual Achievements on Student Engagement

Paul Denny
Department of Computer Science
The University of Auckland
Auckland, New Zealand
paul@cs.auckland.ac.nz

ABSTRACT
Badge-based achievement systems are being used increasingly to drive user participation and engagement across a variety of platforms and contexts. Despite positive anecdotal reports, there is currently little empirical evidence to support their efficacy in particular domains. With the recent rapid growth of tools for online learning, an interesting open question for educators is the extent to which badges can positively impact student participation.

In this paper, we report on a large-scale ($n > 1000$) randomized, controlled experiment measuring the impact of incorporating a badge-based achievement system within an online learning tool. We discover a highly significant positive effect on the quantity of students' contributions, without a corresponding reduction in their quality, as well as on the period of time over which students engaged with the tool. Students enjoyed being able to earn badges, and indicated a strong preference for having them available in the user interface.

Author Keywords
Badges; achievements; gamification; PeerWise; education; online learning

ACM Classification Keywords
H.5.2 [Information Interfaces and Presentation]: User Interfaces

General Terms
Human Factors; Design

INTRODUCTION
The initial emergence of virtual achievements, sometimes referred to as badges or trophies, awarded to users for completing certain tasks was primarily focused around games. The first large-scale successful implementation of badges to online games was in 2005, when "achievements" were added to the then 3 year old Xbox Live platform [19]. Badges have since been widely implemented on other gaming platforms and have proven extremely successful, leading to increased sales revenues and higher review scores [13]. The potential for this success to transfer to other domains has resulted in a proliferation of the use of badges across a variety of online systems, including question and answer forums (e.g. StackOverflow), social news sites (e.g. Huffington Post), location-based social networking tools (e.g. foursquare) and numerous others. The term "gamification" was coined [12] to describe the general approach of using elements typically seen in games, such as badges, in non-game applications.

Despite the growing utilization of badges, there is little empirical evidence to support their effectiveness at motivating and engaging users. Intuitively, the functionality and user-base of an application are important factors in determining appropriate and effective badges, therefore systematic research is needed to explore their effects across a range of domains. Researchers continue to highlight the importance of ongoing work in this area, and explicitly call for further investigation [15, 3]. We answer this call by conducting a large-scale study that provides empirical evidence of the positive effect that badge-based achievements have on user participation. Given the rapid growth in the use of educational technologies, we focus specifically on examining student interactions with an online learning tool and we discuss the implications of our work for designers of similar systems.

We begin by presenting the tool used in our experiment and then describing the implementation of its badge system. The PeerWise tool is a freely-available, award-winning [1] platform used by more than 300 institutions around the world [25]. Students using PeerWise create their own exam-style questions relevant to the course they are studying and share these via a central repository with other members of the class. This repository then becomes a practice resource with which students can answer and critique their peers' questions. This activity aligns with a "contributing student pedagogy" [18, 21], a recent pedagogical approach in which students take responsibility for creating and moderating learning resources and producing peer feedback. Such approaches are attractive to educators as students become actively involved in the learning process. However, motivating students is a key challenge facing instructors [20], and is of great importance for activities such as this where learning resources are student-generated.

We conducted an experiment over a period of four weeks involving a large class of more than 1000 students using PeerWise as they would in a typical semester. Half of the students, selected at random, had access to the badge system and were able to earn up to 22 distinct badges for their contributions and activity. The other half of the class did not have access to the badges in the user interface, but in all other respects were treated identically. We found the presence of the badges had a clear positive effect on both the number of questions answered and the number of distinct days that students engaged with the tool, yet had no effect on the number of questions authored by students. Students reported enjoying being able to earn badges, and indicated a strong preference for having them available in the interface.

RELATED WORK

Current research into the impact of badges in non-game applications has focused on investigating user perceptions rather than measuring the effect on participation. An early example of this work was conducted by Montola et al. [22] in which an achievement system was added to a location based photo sharing service. The 8 week field trial involved 20 participants using mobile phones to take pictures and record audio clips that were automatically uploaded by an application on the phone to the *Nokia Image Space* service [24]. Individual achievements were awarded for uploading various numbers of photos, sound clips and *scenes* (groups of images), as well as the first upload of each type of content.

Participant interviews indicated that the achievements triggered some friendly competition, however a drawback of the application was that achievements were not visible within the mobile client. Participants did not receive explicit feedback or notification of earned achievements on the device, and were restricted to viewing this information on the web at a later time. The authors conclude that such immediate feedback is a necessity for an effective achievement system.

The authors also noted that achievements in their system appeared to have particular value in assisting users to learn about the features of the application. This is an example of the "instruction" role that badges play in many social systems, as identified by Antin and Churchill [3] in their review of the social psychological functions of badges in social media contexts. Badges serving this "instruction" function help new users learn about the types of activities that are possible in a system as well as those that are highly valued and embody the system's social norms.

A more recent study by Fitz-Walter et al. [15] investigated achievements within a mobile application designed to help University students learn about their campus during the orientation phase of the semester. The application leveraged the GPS and QR-code scanning functionality of smartphones, and achievements were awarded when students physically visited certain parts of their campus and answered questions relating to University services. Several of the achievements, such as those for attending a certain number of events on campus, served the "goal setting" role as described by Antin and Churchill [3]. Goal setting is known to be an effective motivator, and achievements of this type set a target for users that they are challenged to meet.

Almost all students reported that the achievements helped motivate them to explore their campus. The authors identified one flaw in their system, that certain achievements could be easily earned by random guessing (such as requiring a particular floor number in a building to be entered correctly). The authors note that as non-game applications begin to make greater use of achievement systems, there is a need for further research into their design, use and effects.

ENVIRONMENT

We begin by describing the PeerWise environment and giving an overview of the badge system being investigated in our study. PeerWise is an online repository of student-generated multiple-choice questions (MCQs). MCQs consist of a question stem (the introductory text that presents the question) along with a set of (commonly up to 5) alternative answers, only one of which is correct. Creating effective MCQs, particularly designing plausible alternatives, is time-consuming and challenging and requires very good content knowledge [29, 17]. Despite this, MCQs are an attractive option for summative assessment in large classes due to the fact that student responses can be automatically graded.

The challenge of constructing good MCQs can be an advantage if students take the role of question authors. Nicol argues that by being involved in the process of constructing their own questions, rather than simply answering instructor generated questions, students can develop self-regulating skills which are crucial for life-long learning [23]. In addition, research in some disciplines has shown that authoring questions is an effective learning technique. Foos [16] investigated the effect of student-written questions on exam performance, and randomly selected students who created questions as a study technique prior to an exam performed significantly better than those who did not.

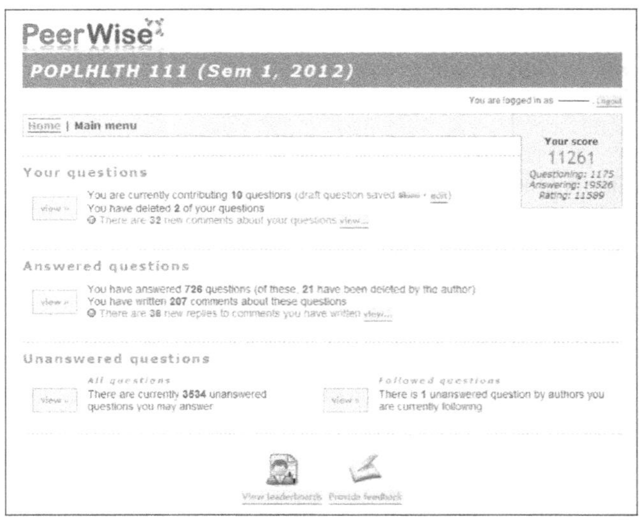

Figure 1. The main menu of the PeerWise tool, prior to the introduction of the badge system

PeerWise

The PeerWise tool supports students in the question authoring process, and enables an entire student cohort to create, share and moderate a repository of their own MCQs [9]. When creating a question, a student must identify a topic or concept to be assessed and consider possible misconceptions when designing the set of alternative answers. In addition, they need to provide an explanation for the correct answer to their question in their own words. This self-explanation step is a key part of the authoring process, and is supported by research demonstrating the benefits of student self-explanation [7, 8, 2] and producing explanations for others [30].

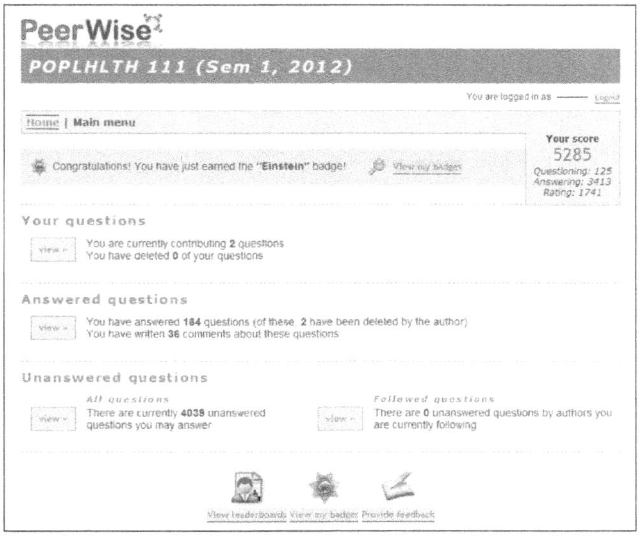

Figure 2. A notification is shown on the main menu when a student earns a new badge

The repository of MCQs developed by a class then becomes a practice resource. Students can answer as many questions as are available and can provide feedback to one another in the form of comments. Students are able to moderate the resource by assigning ratings to individual questions and voting on the most helpful comments. The higher quality questions and comments then become more visible to other students in the class.

Figure 1 shows the main menu of the PeerWise interface from a student's perspective. This menu organizes all of the questions in the repository into three categories: those that have been authored by the student, those that the student has previously answered and all the remaining questions which have not yet been answered.

Prior to the introduction of the badge system, PeerWise already included some game-like elements. For example, each student is shown their PeerWise "score" (visible at the top right of Figure 1), which is calculated by an algorithm that rewards students for authoring, answering and evaluating questions. Rewarding students with points for their actions may help to foster friendly competition which can be a strong motivator [6]. However, one criticism of scoring systems in non-game applications is that certain users may attempt "gaming" of their score by focusing on repetition of non-useful actions which yield points [14]. In the context of educational environments, "gaming" behavior can detract from the learning task and is associated with poor learning outcomes, yet is frequently observed [4]. The PeerWise scoring algorithm attempts to discourage gaming behavior by rewarding students only when *other* students endorse their contributions. An individual student's score does not increase based solely on their own actions, but only when other students indicate their contributions have been of value in some way. The scoring system has been present in the interface for several years.

Figure 3. Clicking the "View my badges" link shows all of the badges the student has been awarded. In this example, the "Author-reply" badge has not yet been earned and so the corresponding icon is not visible

Badges in PeerWise

Implementation of the badge system in PeerWise took place independently of this study. The process began by identifying the core activities that students engage with, and then defining badges for those that instructors wished to encourage. The two key activities are authoring questions and answering questions, and more than half of the badges defined targeted these two activities. In addition to the number of questions answered, students should be encouraged to test their knowledge *frequently* as the benefits, particularly with respect to long-term retention, are well known [27]. Several badges were therefore defined to reward students for returning at regular intervals to practice answering questions and to review and reinforce what they have learned.

Table 1 gives a complete list of the 22 badges made available in PeerWise along with a description of the requirements for earning each. The badges are organized into three categories: "basic", "standard" and "elite", roughly corresponding to the difficulty required to earn them. For example, "basic" badges are primarily designed to highlight the core functionality of the PeerWise tool and can be earned simply for discovering and using different features such as replying to a comment or submitting a rating. In this sense, they satisfy the "instruction" role as defined by Antin and Churchill [3].

Previous research highlighted the necessity of notifying users when new achievements are reached [22]. When a student earns a badge in PeerWise for the first time, a notification message appears on the main menu as illustrated in Figure 2. The notification message includes a link to the "Badges" page which lists all of the available badges highlighting those that the student has currently earned. In this sense, the "Badges" page satisfies certain aspects of the "status/affirmation" role

Table 1. The 22 badges available in PeerWise. The rightmost column highlights those that specifically encourage student activity that is being examined by this research (*=question authoring, **=question answering, *=answering questions on distinct days)**

Category	Badge name	Description	Activity encouraged
Basic	"Question author"	For contributing your first question to PeerWise	*
	"Question answerer"	For answering your first question on PeerWise	**
	"Star-crossed"	For the first time you either "agree" or "disagree" with a comment	
	"Comment"	For the first time you write a comment about a question	
	"Author-reply"	For the first time you write a reply to a comment written about your question	
	"Follower"	For the first time you "follow" a question author	
	"I'll be back"	For correctly answering at least 10 questions, on each of 3 different days	***
Standard	"Helper"	For improving the explanation of an existing question	
	"Popular question author"	For each question you contribute that is answered at least 10 times	*
	"Discussed question author"	For each question you contribute that receives at least 2 comments	*
	"Commentator"	For writing at least 5 comments regarding questions you answer	
	"Critique"	For either agreeing or disagreeing with at least 10 comments	
	"Rater"	For submitting ratings for at least 10 questions	
	"Scholar"	For answering at least 10 questions "correctly" (i.e. receiving a "green" tick)	**
	"Commitment"	For correctly answering at least 10 questions, on each of 5 consecutive days	***
Elite	"Good question author"	For each question you contribute that receives at least 5 "excellent" ratings	*
	"Insight"	For writing at least 2 comments that receive an "agreement"	
	"Conversation"	For replying to at least 5 comments written about your questions	
	"Genius"	For answering at least 10 questions "correctly" in a row	**
	"Leader"	For the first time someone "follows" you as a question author	*
	"Einstein"	For answering at least 20 questions "correctly" in a row	**
	"Obsessed"	For correctly answering at least 10 questions, on each of 10 consecutive days	***

as defined by Antin and Churchill [3], as it highlights a student's personal achievements. This page also displays how many students have earned each of the badges, and the rank in class of the current student's total badge tally, providing them an indication of their relative accomplishments. An example of the "Badges" page is shown in Figure 3. Once the student has viewed this page, the notification message disappears until any subsequent badges are earned. The "Badges" page can be viewed at any time by the student, even in the absence of a notification message, by following the link labeled "View my badges" at the bottom of the main menu. This link is visible at the bottom of Figure 2, where it appears in the middle of the row of three icons.

METHODOLOGY

In this study, we collected data from authentic student use of the PeerWise tool in a large undergraduate course, POPLHLTH111, taught at The University of Auckland in 2012. This course introduces students to frameworks and tools for understanding and controlling the impact of disease in populations. We have two primary reasons for selecting the POPLHLTH111 course for this research. Firstly, it is a particularly large course with more than 1000 students, giving our analyses good statistical power. Secondly, PeerWise has been used in POPLHLTH111 since 2008, prior to the introduction of the badge system, and thus is a regular and expected part of the course for all students. We begin this section with a description of the requirements for students to participate with PeerWise, as determined by the course instructor. We then present our study design and research question, and describe a survey conducted towards the end of the study to investigate student perceptions of the badges and the tool.

Course requirements

The data collected for this study spans the 26-day period from 5th March to 30th March inclusive, corresponding to weeks 2–5 of the 12 week semester. PeerWise was first introduced to students in POPLHLTH111 on Monday 5th March, and they were each asked to author at least 1 question and to answer at least 20 questions before the end of the day on Friday 30th March. Students satisfying these requirements were awarded 1.5% credit towards their final grade in the course. This credit was determined by the course instructor and was consistent with how PeerWise had been used in previous offerings of the POPLHLTH111 course. A mid-term test, contributing 15% to the final grade, was held towards the end of this period on Wednesday 28th March. Earning course credit is a very strong motivator for almost all students and accounts for much of the activity within the system. In this study, we are looking specifically for effects that can be attributed to the presence of the PeerWise badges.

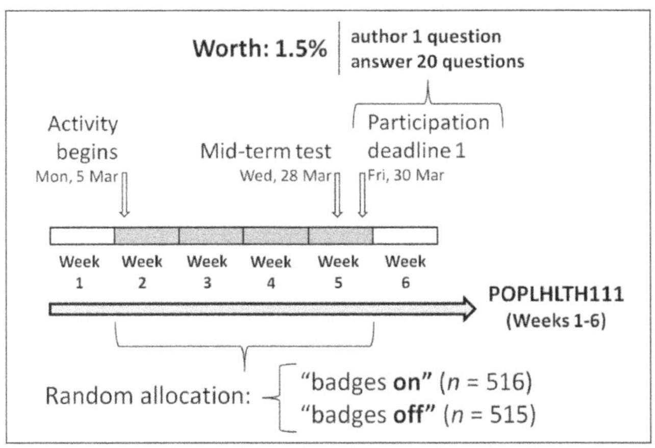

Figure 4. Schematic timeline of course activities (5th – 30th March)

Study design

A total of 1031 students enrolled in the POPLHLTH111 course in 2012. For the purposes of our study, each student was allocated at random to one of two groups. To ensure balanced group sizes, the allocation was performed by generating a random sequence of the integers between 1 and 1031 inclusive [26], and using this sequence to partition the class list into two near-equal sized groups. The first group, labeled "badges on" contained 516 students and the second group, labeled "badges off" contained 515 students.

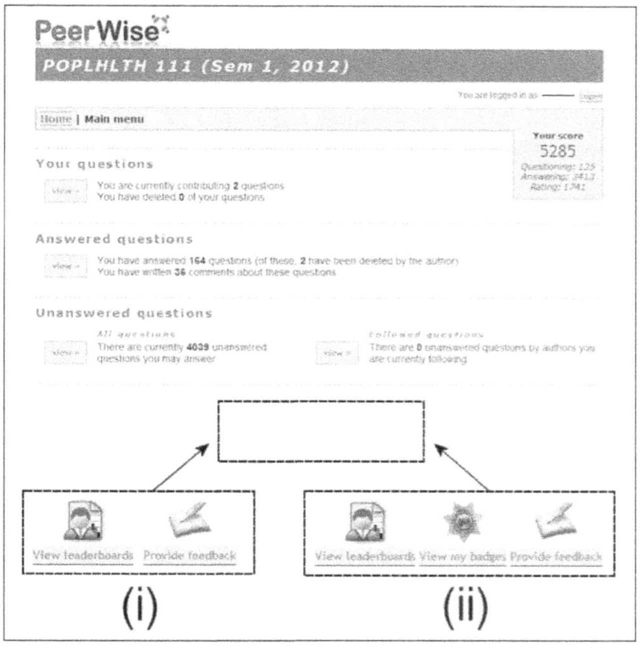

Figure 5. The "View my badges" link is either hidden (i) or visible (ii) at the bottom of the main menu depending on whether badges are enabled or disabled for a given student

On the 5th March, when all students began using PeerWise for the first time, badges were enabled in the user interface only for students in the "badges on" group. Students in this group were able to earn badges, receive notifications for every new badge earned, and see the "View my badges" link at the bottom of the main menu (Figure 5 (ii)) which linked to the "Badges" page. Students in the "badges off" group were not able to earn badges — they did not see the "View my badges" link on the main menu (Figure 5 (i)), did not receive notifications, and were not able to view the "Badges" page. All other features of the tool and requirements for using PeerWise were identical for all students. Figure 4 shows a schematic of the first 6 weeks of the POPLHLTH111 course during which this study was conducted.

Research question

In this study, we set out to investigate whether incorporating a badge system into PeerWise would result in a higher level of participation from students. We defined three measures of participation, the first two of which, the number of questions authored per student and the number of answers submitted per student, reflect the core functionality of the tool. The third measure was the number of distinct days that a student uses the tool. To encourage regular practice, as opposed to completing all required contributions in one sitting, several badges are awarded only when a student interacts with the tool on a number of different days, as well as on a number of consecutive days. The rightmost column of Table 1 highlights the badges that are most closely related to our measures of interest. In particular, there are 5 badges awarded for question authoring and 7 awarded for answering questions. Of these 7 badges, 3 are awarded for answering questions on distinct days. Our specific research question is as follows:

> **Research question**: To what extent does the inclusion of badges (virtual achievements) within PeerWise have an impact on the number of questions a student authors, the number of questions a student answers, and the number of distinct days that a student engages with the tool?

Student perceptions

A survey was conducted online to investigate the perceptions students had regarding the learning value of the PeerWise activity and, for students in the "badges on" group, the motivational effect of the badges. The survey was available from the 26th March, two days before the mid-term test, to the 1st April, immediately following the conclusion of the data collection. Students in both groups were asked to rate the learning value of both authoring and answering questions on PeerWise, as well as provide gender information. In addition, students in the "badges on" group were asked to provide feedback on the extent to which the badges motivated them and indicate their prior experience with badges in the context of online games. Table 2 lists the 7 survey questions shown to students in the "badges on" group, only the first two of which were shown to students in the "badges off" group. Responses to each question were collected on a standard 5-point Likert scale ("Strongly disagree" – "Strongly agree").

Table 2. Survey questions for "badges on" students ("badges off" students were only asked Q1 and Q2)

Q1 (on/off)	Answering questions that were created **by my class mates** was an effective way of learning in this class (POPLHLTH111)
Q2 (on/off)	Creating **my own** questions was an effective way of learning in this class (POPLHLTH111)
Q3 (on)	I found being able to earn "badges" increased my **enjoyment** of using PeerWise
Q4 (on)	The "badges" motivated me to participate **more** than I would have otherwise
Q5 (on)	I regularly play online games where "badges" (or "achievements") are used
Q6 (on)	I would prefer **not** to see "badges" in PeerWise
Q7 (on)	The "badges" awarded for *answering questions* motivated me to answer more questions than I would have otherwise

RESULTS

We observed an excellent rate of participation amongst students, most likely attributed to the course credit associated with the activity. Of the 516 "badges on" students and the 515 "badges off" students, only 12 and 15 respectively did not participate with PeerWise. Therefore, 504 "badges on" and 500 "badges off" students either authored or answered at least one question on PeerWise, leading to a 97% participation rate.

Over the four weeks, a total of 2620 questions were authored and 95685 answers were submitted by all students. The histogram in Figure 6 shows the frequency with which students in the "badges on" group earned various numbers of badges. 80% of students earned more than half of the 22 badges that were available, with only 1 student earning all of the badges. Considering only students who were active, only 3 earned fewer than 7 of the 22 badges.

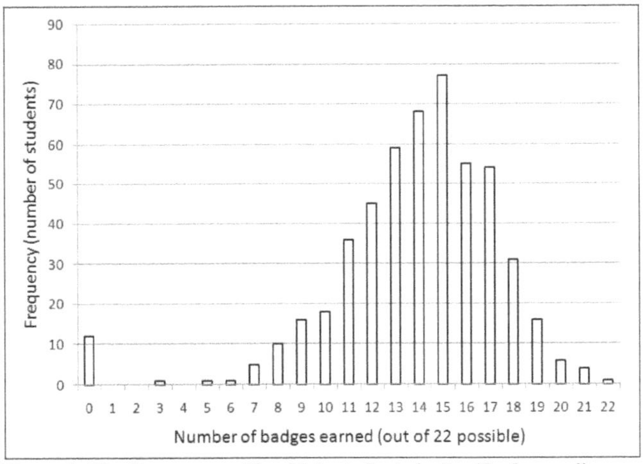

Figure 6. The frequency with which students in the "badges on" group earned various numbers of badges

The effect of the badges

Table 3 gives a summary of the number of questions and answers submitted, as well as the number of distinct days of activity, for students in each group. A student is considered to be active on a given day if they either author or answer at least one question. Totals, averages, medians and standard deviations are given, as is the percentage of all answers submitted by students in each group that were "correct". An answer is deemed to be correct if it matches the answer that the author of the question suggested was correct. This is very often, but not always, the case [5].

Table 3. Comparison of "badges on" and "badges off" activity

		"badges on" (n=516)	"badges off" (n=515)
Totals	Questions	1311	1309
	Answers	52599	43086
	Days active	3617	3199
Averages	Questions	2.54	2.54
	Answers	101.9	83.6
	Days active	7.01	6.21
Medians	Questions	2	2
	Answers	68	60
	Days active	6	6
Std. devs	Questions	2.4	2.2
	Answers	144.0	134.8
	Days active	3.9	3.6
Answers correct (%)		69.29%	69.26%

Several things are apparent in this data. Firstly, despite 5 badges being associated with question authoring, there appears to be no difference between the number of questions authored by students in the "badges on" and "badges off" groups. To the level of significance shown in the table, both the average and median number of questions authored by students in each group is identical. Secondly, there appears to be a large difference between the number of questions answered by students in each group. The total number of questions answered by the "badges on" group over this period represents a 22% increase over the number of questions answered by the "badges off" group. This increase is also reflected in the average (+22%) and median (+13%) number of questions answered.

To visualize *when* these differences occur over the period, Figure 7 plots the total number of answers submitted per day by students in each group. There appear to be two "peaks" in the chart, the most prominent of which (on 28th March) corresponds to the day of the mid-term test. The sharp increase in activity immediately prior to the mid-term test is due to students voluntarily using the tool to practice, which is a pattern consistent with reports of the use of PeerWise in other disciplines [10, 28]. On 25 of the 26 days in this study, students in the "badges on" group submitted more answers than students in the "badges off" group.

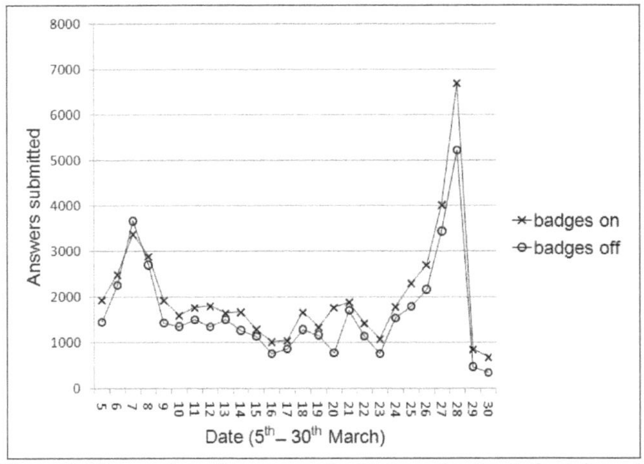

Figure 7. The number of answers submitted per day by students in each group. On all but one day, "badges on" students submitted more answers than "badges off" students

Finally, there appears to be a difference in the number of distinct days that students in each group were active. The average number of distinct days of activity is 13% higher for the "badges on" group, however this does not translate to a difference in the median values.

The data, particularly the number of answers submitted, are heavily skewed as in both groups the most active 10% of students submit approximately one third of all of the answers. For example, the 50 most active students in the "badges on" group submitted 18763 answers (35.7% of all "badges on" answers) compared to 14881 answers (34.5% of all "badges off" answers) submitted by the 50 most active students in the "badges off" group.

To determine the significance of the differences between the groups, we performed a series of Mann-Whitney tests (these are non-parametric and thus robust against skewed data). As indicated by the almost identical totals, the distribution of the number of questions authored did not differ significantly between the two groups (Mann-Whitney U = 131374.5, Z = 0.31, n_{on} = 516, n_{off} = 515, p = 0.7566). The distribution of the number of answers submitted per student did differ significantly between the two groups (Mann-Whitney U = 116386.5, Z = 3.45, n_{on} = 516, n_{off} = 515, $p < 0.001$), with the median number of answers submitted by the "badges on" group being 68 compared with 60 by the "badges off" group.

Finally, the distribution of the number of distinct days of activity differed significantly between the two groups (Mann-Whitney $U = 116584.5$, $Z = 3.41$, $n_{\text{on}} = 516$, $n_{\text{off}} = 515$, $p < 0.001$), with the average number of active days for the "badges on" group being 7.01 compared with 6.21 for the "badges off" group.

One potential concern for the course instructors is that the increase in the number of answers submitted by students in the "badges on" group may have been offset by a corresponding reduction in their quality. For example, perhaps these students were more likely to randomly make selections when answering questions. It appears that this was not the case, as there is no significant difference between the two groups in terms of the correctness of the answers they submitted (just over 69% of all answers submitted by students in either group were correct).

This data provides evidence that the presence of the badges within the PeerWise interface caused an increase in the number of answers submitted by students without a corresponding change in the proportion that were correct. The badges also caused an increase in the number of days for which students were active, however the effect size is quite small and equates to an average of less than one day. The badges did not have any impact on the number of questions authored by students.

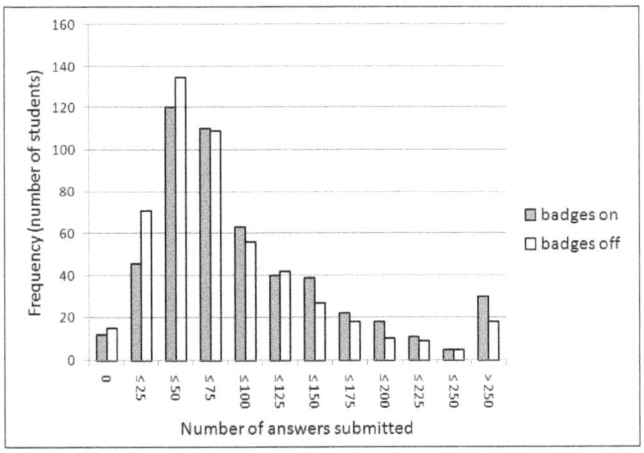

Figure 8. A histogram of the number of answers submitted by students in each group. The "badges on" group is represented by the shaded bars.

Figures 8 and 9 offer alternative ways of visualizing the differences between the groups. In each case, the shaded bars represent the "badges on" group. Students in the "badges off" group outnumber students in the "badges on" group when answering no more than 50 questions or being active on no more than 6 distinct days (corresponding to the first few bars in each Figure). However, when looking at students who answered more than 50 questions or who were active on more than 6 distinct days (the bars towards the right of each Figure), "badges on" students tend to outnumber "badges off" students.

Student perceptions

The online survey, conducted at the end of the four-week period, was voluntary for students to complete. A total of 519 students responded, representing just over 50% of all enrolled students, of which 256 were from the "badges on" group.

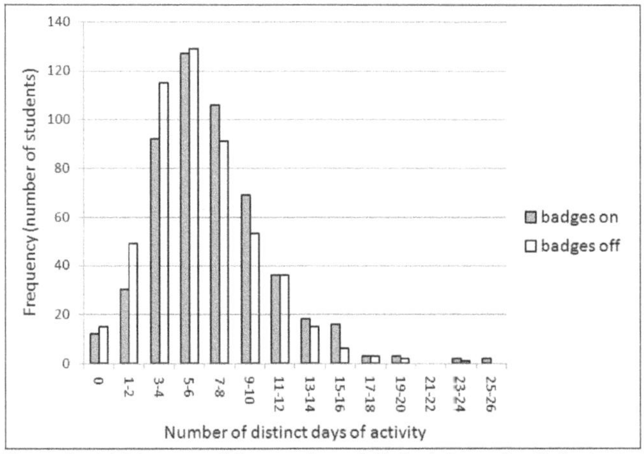

Figure 9. A histogram of the number of distinct days of activity (out of a possible total of 26) by students in each group. The "badges on" group is represented by the shaded bars.

Figure 10 summarizes all student responses to the survey. Each survey question is represented by a horizontal bar, centered at "neutral", with segments proportionate in width to the number of responses of the corresponding type. A bar that is generally positioned further to the right indicates a more positive response to the corresponding question. Note that in the Figure, the survey questions have been edited for length – the full questions can be seen in Table 2.

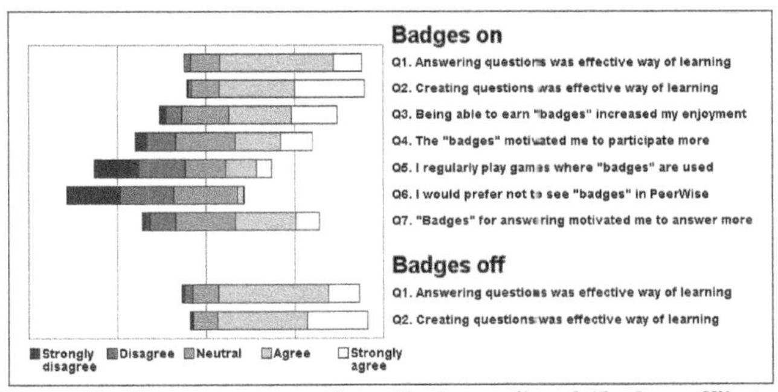

Figure 10. Survey responses from "badges on" and "badges off" students

Students in both groups were positive regarding the learning value of the exercise, however there is no statistical difference between the group responses to Q1 or Q2. Students indicated that authoring their own questions was most beneficial to their learning with 83% of all students in agreement and only 2.5% in disagreement with statement Q2. However, answering questions created by their classmates was also rated as valuable, with 80% in agreement and fewer than 5% in disagreement with statement Q1.

Students in the "badges on" group, who responded to the survey questions regarding the badges, indicated that being able to earn them was enjoyable with more than 60% of responses in agreement and just 12.5% in disagreement with statement Q3. The vast majority of students in this group also indicated that they preferred having badges in the interface, with

60% disagreement and only 4% agreement to the negatively worded statement Q6.

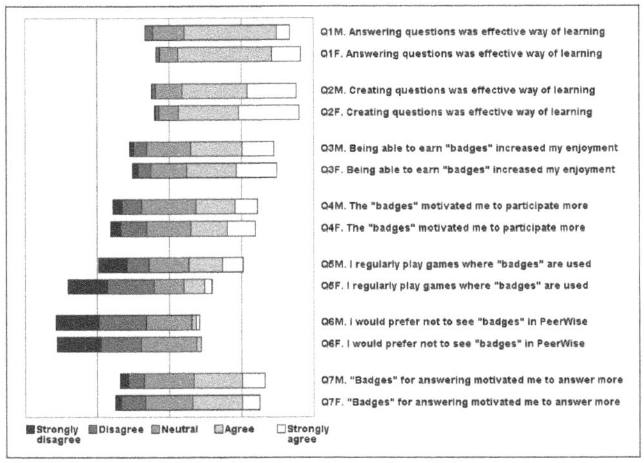

Figure 11. A comparison of male (M) and female (F) responses to the survey, for all "badges on" students

Of all enrolled students, 65.7% were female. The percentage of female survey respondents was 64.9% which is representative of the class as a whole (only 3 respondents did not include gender information). Responses by male students to most questions (except for Q1 and Q5) did not differ from those of female students. Figure 11 compares the responses of all "badges on" students by gender. Identical questions are paired and the question number is suffixed with (M) for male responses and (F) for female responses. With regard to the learning value of authoring questions, female students were more positive than male students when responding to Q1 (Mann-Whitney $U = 6000$, Z = 2.52, $n_F = 163$, $n_M = 91$, $p = 0.012$). Male students had significantly more experience playing online games (that include badge-based achievements) than females (Mann-Whitney $U = 9338.5$, Z = -3.42, $n_F = 163$, $n_M = 91$, $p = 0.001$), with 14% of male students "Strongly-agreeing" with statement Q5 compared to just 5% of female students. However, this had no impact on the reported "enjoyment" of the badges in PeerWise, as the distribution of male and female responses to Q3 did not differ significantly.

DISCUSSION

Our data suggests that the badges had a positive motivational effect, leading to an increase in both the number of answers submitted and the number of distinct days for which students were active. However, the badges did not have an impact on the number of questions that were authored. One explanation for this is that the authoring requirements in this course were low (a single question was required per student) and most students do not typically author more questions than they are required. As a result, there is very little variability in the number of questions authored across all students in the class.

This phenomenon, of students preferring to answer rather than author questions voluntarily, has been previously reported [10] and is likely due to the greater effort and time required to author questions. Answering questions is also a more authentic practice technique for students, which explains the large spikes in voluntary use leading up to formal examinations such as the POPLHLTH111 mid-term test. These voluntary contributions suggest that students already find some intrinsic value in answering questions, as even in the "badges off" group more than four times the required number of answers were submitted. That the badges appear to have an impact on this activity is consistent with Rajat Paharia's observation that the "entity being gamified needs to have some intrinsic value already" [11].

Not all students are motivated by badges to the same extent. One way to gauge a student's interest in the badges is to examine the number of times they view the "Badges" page shown in the screenshot of Figure 3. When a student earns a new badge, they are notified of this by a message that appears on the main menu. This notification message prompts the student to view the "Badges" page, and the message disappears once the "Badges" page is viewed. If the student earns additional badges before visiting the "Badges" page, the notification message simply changes to state how many new badges have been earned. Figure 12 plots, for every student in the "badges on" group, the number of badges they earned against the number of times they viewed the "Badges" page. While most students did not view the Badges page many times, a small number of students were clearly drawn to it, with 10 students viewing the page more than 40 times.

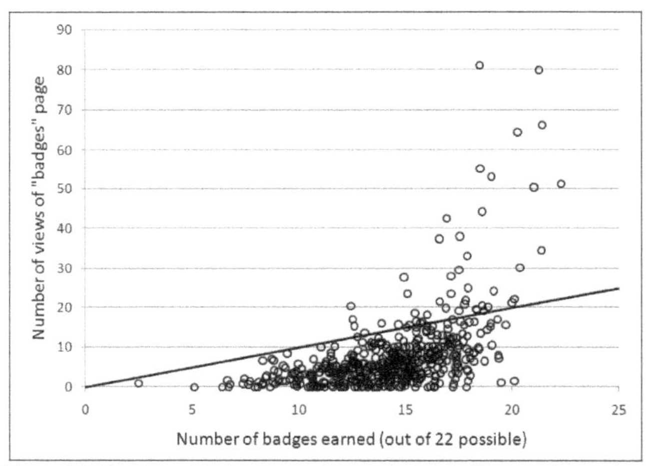

Figure 12. Number of badges earned (out of a total of 22) plotted against the number of times the badge page was viewed for each "badges on" student (a small random jitter has been used to separate data points)

Also evident in Figure 12 is the fact that many students viewed the "Badges" page without being notified of having earned a badge. This may indicate an interest in learning which badges are available and within reach, or simply reflect curiosity regarding how many other students have earned badges. The maximum number of distinct notification messages any student can receive is equal to the number of badges they earn. In practice, a student is likely to receive fewer notification messages than the number of badges they earn, as would be the case if they earn more than one badge prior to visiting the "Badges" page. A common example of this is when a student answers a question for the first time and also rates the question, for which two separate badges are awarded. However, even using the number of badges earned as a conservative upper bound on the number of notifications received, 43 students viewed the "Badges" page at least once without being prompted and are represented by the data points lying above the straight line. Only 49 students never visited the "Badges" page. As we know all 504 students in the "badges on" group who were active earned at least one badge, this indicates that approximately 1 in 10 students simply ignored the badges altogether.

Finally, although the badges did have an effect on participation, they did not impact student perceptions of the learning value of the exercise. The two groups were equally positive on the benefits of both authoring and answering questions.

Threats to validity

In this section, we consider possible threats to the validity of our results. Students in the "badges on" group were selected at random from more than 1000 students. There were no other differences between the treatment of students in each group, and so in this course the presence of the badges appears to have caused the observed increase in student participation.

However, we need to be careful not to overgeneralize this result. Firstly, POPLHLTH111 is a competitive course and students are typically very focused on achieving good grades and therefore tend to participate well with class activities. The students in this experiment may not be representative of another cohort for a different class. Also, the specific badges available in PeerWise were defined prior to our study and it is possible that a different set of badges may be more or less effective than the current set. The requirements that an instructor places on students may also have an impact. For example, students in POPLHLTH111 were required to author 1 and answer 20 questions for 1.5% course credit. Simply meeting these minimum requirements would have at least earned students the first two "Basic" badges, and potentially an additional 3 badges if all questions were answered correctly.

Most students enrolled in POPLHLTH111 study a common set of subjects. In the semester that this study took place, the vast majority of POPLHLTH111 students were concurrently enrolled in a first-year Biology course for which PeerWise was also being used. At the request of the Biology instructor, the badges were enabled for all students for the duration of the course. While it was not compulsory for students to engage with PeerWise in the Biology course, around three-quarters of all students did participate voluntarily. It therefore must be noted that many students in the "badges off" group in our study would have experienced the PeerWise badges for this other course. However, we do not believe that having access to the badges for the Biology course would have greatly influenced student engagement with the POPLHLTH111 repository. Badges are awarded based on participation with a specific course and it is very clear within the interface which course is being interacted with at any one time.

Lessons learned

Although we have shown that a badge-based achievement system can have a measurable effect on student participation, our data also highlights that certain actions (such as students answering questions) are impacted significantly, while others (such as authoring questions) are not, despite both having associated badges. As discussed, a possible explanation is that answering questions is a more familiar activity for students and one in which they immediately see value. The implication for designers of similar systems is that defining badges that reward students for actions in which they already see value may have the greatest impact.

Our data also shows that across each measurable action, student activity either increased or was unchanged by the presence of the badges. For example, both the number of questions authored, and the proportion of answers submitted that were correct were identical for students in both groups. Reinforced by the very positive attitudes our survey revealed, the implication is that utilizing badges in similar contexts is a low-risk proposition for educators as they do not appear to negatively affect student participation.

CONCLUSIONS AND FUTURE WORK

This paper presents the first large-scale study providing empirical evidence of the impact of a badge-based achievement system within an online learning tool. The badges had a significant positive effect on the number of questions answered and the number of distinct days that students were active with the tool, and did not lead to a reduction in the accuracy of student answers. In addition, students enjoyed being rewarded with badges for their contributions and indicated a strong preference for having them in the interface. Although increases did not exist across all measures of activity, such as the number of questions authored by students, no negative effects were observed. Badges therefore can act as powerful motivators in educational contexts of this kind and may be integrated with little risk into similar environments.

Activity in PeerWise is currently anonymous, and so students who have earned the greatest number of badges cannot be identified by their peers. As a result, the badges currently provide personal affirmation rather than status amongst peers. An interesting area for future work will be exploring what it means to publicize these achievements more openly. Allowing a student to display their badges to the rest of the class, or perhaps to a subset of friends who approve, may introduce a competitive element that further impacts engagement. Future work will also explore why earning badges encouraged students to participate in certain ways, but not in others.

In general, the efficacy of a badge-based achievement system depends on many factors. These include user demographics, the purpose of the tool, and the relevance of the badges for encouraging appropriate user behavior. While this work has examined the implementation of one badge system and one particular set of badges in a specific domain, more work is needed to assess the impact of badges and achievements within a range of contexts.

REFERENCES

1. Australasian Association for Engineering Education, Award for innovation in curricula, learning and teaching, "PeerWise", 2009.

2. Aleven, V., and Koedinger, K. An effective metacognitive strategy — learning by doing and explaining with a computer-based cognitive tutor. *Cognitive Science 26*, 2 (2002), 147–179.

3. Antin, J., and Churchill, E. Badges in social media : A social psychological perspective. In *CHI 2011 Gamification Workshop Proceedings* (Vancouver, BC, Canada, 2011).

4. Baker, R., Walonoski, J., Heffernan, N., Roll, I., Corbett, A., and Koedinger, K. Why students engage in "gaming the system" behavior in interactive learning environments. *Journal of Interactive Learning Research 19*, 2 (April 2008), 185–224.

5. Bottomley, S., and Denny, P. A participatory learning approach to biochemistry using student authored and evaluated multiple-choice questions. *Biochemistry and Molecular Biology Education 39*, 5 (2011), 352–361.

6. Burguillo, J. C. Using game theory and competition-based learning to stimulate student motivation and performance. *Comput. Educ. 55*, 2 (Sept. 2010), 566–575.

7. Chi, M., Bassok, M., Lewis, M., Reimann, P., and Glaser, R. Self-explanations: How students study and use examples in learning to solve problems. *Cognitive Science 13* (1989), 145–182.

8. Chi, M., Leeuw, N., Chiu, M.-H., and LaVancher, C. Eliciting self-explanations improves understanding. *Cognitive Science 18* (1994), 439–477.

9. Denny, P., Luxton-Reilly, A., and Hamer, J. The PeerWise system of student contributed assessment questions. In *Proceedings of the tenth conference on Australasian computing education - Volume 78*, ACE '08, Australian Computer Society, Inc. (Darlinghurst, Australia, Australia, 2008), 69–74.

10. Denny, P., Luxton-Reilly, A., and Hamer, J. Student use of the PeerWise system. *SIGCSE Bull. 40*, 3 (June 2008), 73–77.

11. Deterding, S. Gamification: designing for motivation. *interactions 19*, 4 (July 2012), 14–17.

12. Deterding, S., Khaled, R., Nacke, L., and Dixon, D. Gamification: Toward a definition. In *CHI 2011 Gamification Workshop Proceedings* (Vancouver, BC, Canada, 2011).

13. Electronic Entertainment Design and Research. EEDAR study shows more achievements in games leads to higher review scores, increased sales. Press release, Oct. 2007.

14. Farzan, R., DiMicco, J. M., Millen, D. R., Brownholtz, B., Geyer, W., and Dugan, C. When the experiment is over: Deploying an incentive system to all the users. In *Proceedings of the Symposium on Persuasive Technology, In conjunction with the AISB 2008 Convention* (2008).

15. Fitz-Walter, Z., Tjondronegoro, D., and Wyeth, P. Orientation passport: using gamification to engage university students. In *Proceedings of the 23rd Australian Computer-Human Interaction Conference*, OzCHI '11, ACM (Canberra, Australia, 2011), 122–125.

16. Foos, P. W. Effects of student-written questions on student test performance. *Teaching of Psychology 16*, 2 (1989), 77–78.

17. Haladyna, T., and Downing, S. How many options is enough for a multiple-choice test item? *Educational and Psychological Measurement 53*, 4 (1993), 999–1010.

18. Hamer, J., Cutts, Q., Jackova, J., Luxton-Reilly, A., McCartney, R., Purchase, H., Riedesel, C., Saeli, M., Sanders, K., and Sheard, J. Contributing student pedagogy. *SIGCSE Bull. 40*, 4 (Nov. 2008), 194–212.

19. Jakobsson, M. The achievement machine: Understanding Xbox 360 achievements in gaming practices. *The International Journal of Computer Game Research 11*, 1 (2011).

20. Lee, J. J., and Hammer, J. Gamification in education: What, how, why bother? *Academic Exchange Quarterly 15*, 2 (2011).

21. Luxton-Reilly, A., and Denny, P. Constructive evaluation: a pedagogy of student-contributed assessment. *Computer Science Education 20*, 2 (2010), 145–167.

22. Montola, M., Nummenmaa, T., Lucero, A., Boberg, M., and Korhonen, H. Applying game achievement systems to enhance user experience in a photo sharing service. In *Academic MindTrek 2009 Conference*, ACM Press (Tampere, Finland, 2009), 94–97.

23. Nicol, D. E-assessment by design: using multiple-choice tests to good effect. *Journal of Further and Higher Education 31*, 1 (Feb. 2007), 53–64.

24. Nokia. Nokia Image Space. `http://research.nokia.com/page/4987`, 2009. [Online; accessed 20-March-2012].

25. PeerWise. Online learning tool (http://peerwise.cs.auckland.ac.nz/).

26. Random.org. True random number service (http://www.random.org/).

27. Roediger, H. L., and Karpicke, J. D. Test-enhanced learning: Taking memory tests improves long-term retention. *Psychological Science 17* (2006), 249–255.

28. Sykes, A., Denny, P., and Nicolson, L. PeerWise — the marmite of veterinary student learning (Brighton Business School, University of Brighton, Brighton, UK, Nov. 2011). 820–830.

29. Vyas, R., and Supe, A. Multiple choice questions: a literature review on the optimal number of options. *The National Medical Journal of India 21*, 3 (June 2008), 130–133.

30. Webb, N. Peer interaction and learning in small groups. *International Journal of Education Research 13* (1989), 21–39.

A Trace-based Framework for Analyzing and Synthesizing Educational Progressions

Erik Andersen[1], **Sumit Gulwani**[2], **and Zoran Popović**[1]

[1]Center for Game Science
Computer Science & Engineering
University of Washington
{eland,zoran}@cs.washington.edu

[2]Microsoft Research
Redmond, WA
sumitg@microsoft.com

A key challenge in teaching a procedural skill is finding an effective progression of example problems that the learner can solve in order to internalize the procedure. In many learning domains, generation of such problems is typically done by hand and there are few tools to help automate this process. We reduce this effort by borrowing ideas from test input generation in software engineering. We show how we can use execution traces as a framework for abstracting the characteristics of a given procedure and defining a partial ordering that reflects the relative difficulty of two traces. We also show how we can use this framework to analyze the completeness of expert-designed progressions and fill in holes. Furthermore, we demonstrate how our framework can automatically synthesize new problems by generating large sets of problems for elementary and middle school mathematics and synthesizing hundreds of levels for a popular algebra-learning game. We present the results of a user study with this game confirming that our partial ordering can predict user evaluation of procedural difficulty better than baseline methods.

Author Keywords
education; problem generation; execution traces; games

ACM Classification Keywords
H.5.0 Information interfaces and presentation: General

INTRODUCTION

One of the most important domains of human learning is procedural task learning, which spans a wide range of human activities. Humans learn to execute procedures that range from a simple list of actions, such as a cooking recipe, to more complex procedures involving loops and conditionals, such as prime factorization, long division, and solving systems of equations. The standard human practice of learning such procedures is by solving a sequence of training problems. This sequence of problems allows a learner to develop an internal model of the procedural algorithm over time, so that ultimately it can be applied correctly to all possible inputs for that procedure.

CHI 2013, April 27–May 2, 2013, Paris, France.

Procedural learning has been studied in HCI as part of software learnability [13, 23, 26]. Many study designs evaluate application usability by measuring whether a user can successfully execute a target procedure in that application. HCI researchers frequently wish to evaluate the degree to which a user interface design facilitates the learning of such procedures.

A fundamental problem of teaching procedural tasks in both HCI and education is determining the optimal sequence of training problems. Textbooks for elementary and middle school mathematics typically start with problems that only require a few steps to solve and grow to more complex multistep problems that vary based on the input. These progressions often vary widely and many of them are likely suboptimal. The quality of a training sequence depends on many factors, such as the structure of the target procedure, cognitive processes that lead to the creation of procedural models in the mind, level of engagement towards the task, learner background, and learning preferences.

There are a number of guiding principles for learning progressions. Reigeluth and Stein's Elaboration Theory [24] argues that the simplest version of a task should be taught first, followed by progressively more complex tasks that elaborate on the original task. Csikszentmihalyi's theory of flow [7] suggests that we can keep the learner in a state of maximal engagement by continually increasing difficulty to match the learner's increasing skill. By considering Vygotsky's zone of proximal development [33], we can avoid overloading the learner by introducing so many concepts at the same time that the learner cannot create a consistent internal representation. Nevertheless, many important details of optimal progression design are not covered by general principles. It has been estimated that 200-300 hours of expert development are necessary to produce one hour of content for intelligent tutors [2], of which problem ordering is a key part.

In this paper, we create a framework for reasoning about the space of possible progressions as defined by the procedural task itself. Our goal is to create a representation of the space of progressions using only a specification of the algorithmic procedure, defined directly as a computer program. We propose categorizing a procedural task based on features of the program trace obtained by executing the procedure on that task. We show how this trace-based measure can be used to measure the quality of a progression and compare the relative difficulty of two problems.

The use of a trace-based framework for characterizing procedural tasks allows us to borrow well-established techniques from the software engineering community related to software testing. In particular, it allows us to use test input generation tools [31] for generating problems that have certain trace features. It also allows us to use notions of procedure coverage [34] to evaluate the comprehensiveness of a certain progression. Furthermore, we are able to borrow techniques from the sequence comparison literature to compare two different problems, in particular n-gram models [35].

We demonstrate our method by analyzing the space of progressions for two different domains. One domain is early math procedures, such as addition, adding fractions, and comparing integers. The other domain is a well-known interactive math puzzle game. We show how we can generate large sets of practice problems for these procedures. We also show how our framework can be used to analyze and compare expert-designed progressions in terms of thoroughness and aggressiveness. Determining which kinds of progressions are more effective is beyond the scope of this paper. Our goal is to automatically discover the coverage achieved by a progression, and generate additional problems to supplement the areas that it covers sparsely.

To assess our partial ordering measures of problem difficulty, we conducted a pilot user study in which we generated several levels for an algebra-learning game and asked participants to compare these levels to those in the expert-designed progression. We found that our model was better able to predict participant responses than other baseline metrics.

We believe that our framework contributes to HCI by using procedure analysis to reason about the space of possible problems and how they relate to learning. We believe that this will reduce the effort required to create such problem sets. We intend to comprehensively study variations in progressions using our framework, and we hope that other researchers can use the same formalism to discover general principles of problem progressions for procedural tasks.

RELATED WORK

Usability and Learnability in HCI

Effective learning progressions are important not just for school-based learning; they are a key cornerstone of usability and learnability within user applications. Many modern user applications have advanced features, and learning these procedures constitutes a major effort on the part of the user. Therefore designers have focused their energy on trying to reduce this effort. For example, Dong et al. created a series of minigames to teach users advanced image manipulation tasks in Adobe Photoshop [9]. Grabler et al. created a system that allows a user to program a tutorial for image-manipulation tasks through demonstration in GIMP and Adobe Photoshop [12]. We extend these efforts by proposing a basic theory of increasing procedural complexity that may someday reduce the effort of creating such tutorials and games. We envision a methodology in which designers specify a procedure and receive an automatically generated set of tasks that are organized into a progression.

There has also been work in HCI on sociocultural bases for learning. For example, Rieman [25] examined how humans learn to perform procedural tasks through exploratory learning. Linehan et al. [19] provide a series of guidelines for designing effective educational games. Andersen et al. showed that video game tutorials are only effective when the game is too complex for players to learn through experimentation [5] and that changing a progression by introducing secondary game objectives can negatively impact engagement and retention [3, 4]. We attempt to supplement such perspectives with pragmatic approaches to designing learning systems.

Education and Intelligent Tutors

McArthur et al. [21] automatically generate algebra problems as part of an intelligent tutor for algebra. They first collect and annotate problems by what skills they use, such as isolating positive terms, and multiplying both sides of an equation by -1. They then indicate relationships between these skills, such as that one is a prerequisite for another, or that one is a generalization of another. Since each of these skills is essentially a production rule, they specify a grammar for how these rules can transform a problem state into another problem state, and use random values to generate problems. Sleeman [28] used a similar approach of specifying a grammar for algebra problems and used this to generate new problems. We expand on this work by using the idea of procedure traces to automate the identification of relationships between problems and generalize it to a larger class of problem domains. We also show how these ideas allow us not only to generate problems and progressions but also to evaluate existing progressions.

Li et al. studied problem orderings by examining them with a machine learning agent called SimStudent. They found that interleaved problem orderings led to faster learning than blocked orderings [18]. We extend this work by creating a framework in which interleaved or blocked problem progressions can be created for any procedural task. VanLehn [32] has extensively studied student acquisition of the subtraction procedure and analyzed the bugs that children display while learning this procedure. We focus on a larger domain of procedural tasks and show how these procedures can be used to generate practice problems.

Gulwani [14, 15] has applied techniques from formal methods, and in particular program synthesis, to various aspects of intelligent tutoring systems including solution generation [16], problem generation [27], automated grading, and content entry. In this work, we use test input generation techniques from formal methods for problem generation.

Problem Generation

There have been two approaches to generating problems for procedural mathematical content. In one approach, flexibility is provided for instantiating parameters of a problem with random constants [17]. In contrast, for our domain of middle school procedural problems, the choice of the constants makes all the difference in the difficulty level of a problem.

In another approach, certain features of the problem domain are provided as hard-coded options and users are able to choose among these options and generate problems. For instance, in the domain of quadratic equations, some interesting features could be whether the equation is "simple factorable", "difficult factorable, where the leading coefficient is not 1", or "requires use of general quadratic formula". Another interesting feature can be whether or not it has imaginary solutions. Several math worksheet generator websites are based on this approach. The Microsoft Math-Worksheet Generator goes a step ahead and automatically infers such features from a problem instance [22]. Each domain has its own set of features that needs to be defined separately. Our system can infer such features from a problem instance to generate similar problems. However, more significantly, a procedural description of the problem domain leads to automatic definition of such features. Furthermore, our system considers more complicated features, such as n-grams, that relate to a sequence of decisions required to solve a problem as opposed to a single decision.

Recently, there has been some progress in generating problems in non-procedural mathematical domains. Singh et al. [27] proposed a semi-automatic template-based approach to problem generation for the domain of high-school algebra proof problems. The teacher semi-automatically generalizes a given seed problem into an abstract template. However, not all instantiations of those templates are valid proof problems. The underlying system performs a brute-force enumeration over all possible instantiations and uses novel results from randomized algebraic identity testing [16] to filter those instantiations that yield valid problems. They can generate impressive and non-trivial problems; however, there is no guarantee of the difficulty level associated with each problem.

Cerny et. al. [6] also proposed a template-based approach to problem generation for the domain of automata theory problems. A given seed problem is abstracted into a template, and most instantiations, if not all, are actually correct problems. The system then uses a sophisticated solution generation technology based on novel results in automata theory to compute the solutions for various instantiations and then partitions the problems into different equivalence classes based on some user-defined similarity metric. However, no attempt is made to compare the problems across different equivalence classes or different seed problems.

Procedural Content Generation in Games

Smith et al. used answer-set programming to generate levels for the educational puzzle game Refraction (Center for Game Science 2010) that adhered to prespecified constraints written in first-order logic [29]. Similar approaches have also been used to generate levels for platform games [30]. In the majority of existing approaches, designers must explicitly specify constraints that the generated content must reflect, for example, "the tree needs to be near the rock and the river needs to be near the tree". There has been much less work in guiding the generation based on a description of what the player needs to do. Dormans generated levels for puzzle-platform games [10] through grammars that could build a "mission" for the desired tasks the player needed to perform. We expand on these methodologies by generating not only levels but also level progressions directly from a procedure that solves those levels. Although previous work has typically considered level solvers and level generators to be separate entities, our framework unifies them.

A TRACE-BASED FRAMEWORK

We present a trace-based framework for characterizing practice problems and estimating their relative difficulty level. For example, consider the standard addition algorithm for adding any number of positive integers:

Algorithm 1 Addition: Given as input a sequence of sequences of digits $n_i = [n_{i_q}, ..., n_{i_0}]$, add them:

```
procedure ADD(n_1, ..., n_m)
    a ← 0
    maxLen ← max(len(n_1), ..., len(n_m))
    for i ← 0, maxLen − 1 do                ▷ Loop over digits (D)
        k ← 0
        for all n_j do                       ▷ Loop over inputs (N)
            if len(n_j) > i then
                k ← k + n_j[i]               ▷ If digit exists (A)
            end if
        end for
        if c[i] ≠ null then
            k ← k + c[i]                     ▷ If carry exists (C)
        end if
        if len(k) = 2 then
            c[i + 1] ← k[1]                  ▷ If we need to carry (O)
        end if
        a[i] ← k[0]
    end for
    if c[maxLen] = 1 then
        a[maxLen] ← c[maxLen]                ▷ If final carry (F)
    end if
    return a
end procedure
```

We believe that one of the best categorizations of the difficulty of a particular addition problem is the pathway or the trace that the procedure takes while solving that problem. A quick analysis of addition problems in any textbook will likely show many such traces. We use sequences of letters to indicate traces; these letters are output when the program executes commented lines in the above procedure.

Valid inputs to this problem have two or more input numbers and these numbers can have any number of digits. The simplest possible trace under these constraints is the trace corresponding to one-digit number plus a one-digit number where the sum is less than 10: "DNANA". In this trace, the carry branch "C" does not execute because there is no existing carry, the "O" overflow branch does not execute because there is no overflow, and there is no final carry so the final carry branch "F" also does not execute. The digit existence branch must execute because otherwise the addend would be invalid.

The following table shows several problems and their traces:

Problem	Trace
$1+1$	DNANA
$11+1$	DNANADNAN
$1+11$	DNANADNNA
$11+11$	DNANADNANA
$9+1$	DNANAOF
$19+1$	DNANAODNANC
$1+2+3$	DNANANA
$1+2+3+7$	DNANANANAOF
$333+444$	DNANADNANADNANA

Characterizing problems by their execution traces has several implications. It allows us to measure the program coverage of a problem, which can be used to evaluate the comprehensiveness of a progression. It allows us to compare problems, a notion more formally captured in the next section, based on how the procedure executes. It does *not* take into account differences in perceived difficulty that may arise from differences in the input values. For example, students may be much more comfortable with adding $1+1$ than $5+4$, and our model will not take this into account. However, such differences are generally domain-specific and cannot be identified without gathering data. Our model can easily grow to accommodate such distinctions. If a teacher or designer wants to distinguish two classes of inputs, he or she can add a conditional branch to the program that will separate these two classes.

PARTIAL ORDERINGS OVER TRACES

In order to assemble practice problems into progressions that begin simply and grow more difficult, we define a methodology for comparing two different problems. To do this, we define partial orderings over problems based on features of their corresponding traces. We can use this partial order relationship to compare two problems and determine if they are similar in difficulty, if one problem is more difficult than the other, or if no determination can be made using our model. Once we have such a partial ordering, we can identify simpler or more complex variations of a particular problem, and we can use it to sequence multiple problems together into a progression.

There are many possible ways to define a partial ordering over execution traces. Here, we define two partial orderings that we have found useful in analyzing and synthesizing progressions.

Path-based Partial Ordering

We use the following trace features to define our first partial order over traces:

- the number of times a certain loop in the procedure was executed
- whether or not the non-skip branch of a certain exceptional conditional was executed; we define a conditional to be *exceptional* if one of its branches contains no instructions and is equivalent to "skip".

We now use the following recursive definition to define a partial ordering:

Definition 1a: *A trace T_1 that contains loops is as least as complex as trace T_2 if for every loop L in the procedure, the trace T_1 has at least as many iterations of loop L as in trace T_2, and for each subtrace T_2' in T_2 that corresponds to an iteration of loop L, there exists a subtrace T_1' in T_1 that is at least as complex as T_2'.*

We also define the following base case:

Definition 1b: *A non-loopy trace T_1 is at least as complex as trace T_2 if for every exceptional condition in the procedure, if the non-skip branch of the exceptional condition was executed in T_2, then it was also executed in T_1.*

We now give some examples of trace comparisons based on the above-defined partial order.

Example 1: *Loops that execute longer are more complex.* If we compare the traces "DNANA" and "DNANANA", corresponding to the problems $1+2$ and $1+2+3$, respectively, the only difference is that the inner "N" loop executed one more time. Therefore, "DNANANA" subsumes "DNANA".

Example 2: *A conditional branch that executes some statements is more complex than a conditional branch that executes no statements.* If we compare "DNANA" and "DNANAOF", corresponding to the problems $1+2$ and $9+1$, respectively, "DNANAOF" contains all of the "work" of "DNANA", plus the additional step that there is an overflow and the 1 must be carried over to the next digit. Therefore, "DNANAOF" also subsumes "DNANA".

Example 3: Since loops can contain conditionals and other loops, each iteration of a loop that execute multiple times may vary in complexity. Our partial order also allows us to compare such traces. For example, consider the two traces "DNANADNANA" and "DNANADNAN", corresponding to the problems $11+11$ and $11+1$, respectively. In both cases, the outer "D" loop executes twice. The first iteration of this loop is the same but the second iteration is different. The second iteration for "DNANADNANA" executes a final "A" statement in an exceptional condition that "DNANADNAN" skips. Therefore "DNANADNANA" subsumes "DNANADNAN".

The notion of partial order also allows us to take a given trace and build more complex variants. For example, consider again the trace "DNANA" from the above addition example. There are three obvious ways in which this trace can expand. The first is by flipping conditional branches that executed no statements so that they do execute statements. One such trace is "DNANAOF", corresponding to problems in which there is a carry such as $1+9$. Another possible expansion is to increase the number of iterations of the "N" loop by 1, yielding the trace "DNANANA" that corresponds to problems with three one-digit numbers and no carries like $1+2+3$. Another way to expand the problem is to increase the "D" loop by one iteration, perhaps yielding the trace "DNANADNANA" corresponding to two-digit addition problems with no carries like $12+34$.

Figure 1. We can use our trace-based framework to compare progressions. The Singapore Math Sprints books organize worksheets into pairs of "A" worksheets and "B" worksheets, stating that the B side is "intended for more advanced students". The above figures compare the "A" and "B" progressions for two different problem domains. In both figures, the green solid arrows correspond to the "A" progression, and the blue dashed arrows correspond to the "B" progression. Self-edges are removed for clarity. The left side shows a worksheet pair for addition, corresponding to Algorithm 1. The right figure shows a different worksheet pair for fraction computation, corresponding to Algorithm 2. In both cases, we see that the "advanced" progression spends less time in the easier regions and quickly moves into longer pathways that require additional steps. In the case of addition, the "B" problems have more addends, and in the case of fraction computation, the "B" problems have more input fractions.

N-gram-based Partial Ordering

We now define a second partial ordering by utilizing n-grams [35]. This method defines a family of partial orderings depending on the value of positive integer n. n-gram models have been used extensively in natural language processing and search engines, where the meaning of a word can be uniquely defined by just looking at a small context around it in the parent sentence. In the case of procedural execution traces, the intuition is that students can only remember a certain amount of context, and it is most useful to test students on their ability to execute small sequences of algorithmic decisions within a larger execution trace.

The n-gram abstraction of a trace also provides a nice continuum between the standard notions of *statement coverage*, which corresponds to a uni-gram model, and *path coverage*, which corresponds to ∞-gram model in the software engineering literature [34].

Definition 2: *Let n be any positive integer. We say that a trace T_1 is at least as complex as trace T_2 if every n-gram of trace T_2 is also present in trace T_1.*

ANALYSIS OF PROGRESSIONS

In order to test the ability of our framework to analyze progressions, we gathered problems from three different workbooks for elementary and middle school mathematics:

- Math Sprints series from Singapore Math Inc.[1]. These books include many worksheets that are intended to be completed in rapid one-minute sessions. They tend to involve lots of repetition and not too much difficulty.
- JUMP Math curriculum[2]. This Canadian curriculum was able to raise at-grade-level performance from 12% to 60% in a study in Lambeth, England [1].
- Skill Sharpeners: Math[3] by Evan-Moor Educational Publishers.

Evaluating Progressions

We can use our framework to explore interesting patterns in a progression. We first define an algorithm for performing multiple addition and subtraction operations on fractions:

Algorithm 2 Fraction Computation: Given as input a set of fractions $f_1, ..., f_n$ and a set of $+$ and $-$ operations $o_1, ..., o_{n-1}$, execute these operations:

procedure FCOMPUTE($f_1, ..., f_n, o_1, ..., o_{n-1}$)
  if $\exists f_i, f_j : f_i.d \neq f_j.d$ **then**
    $lcm \leftarrow max(d \in f_i.d)$ ▷ Denom. diff. (D)
    while $\exists f_i : lcm \bmod f_i.d \neq 0$ **do**
      $lcm \leftarrow lcm + max(d \in f_i.d)$ ▷ (M)
    end while
    for all f_i **do**
      $s \leftarrow lcm \div f_i.d$
      $f_i.n \leftarrow f_i.n * s$
      $f_i.d \leftarrow f_i.d * s$
    end for
  end if
  $n \leftarrow 0$
  for all o_i **do** ▷ For each operation (O)
    if $o_i = +$ **then**
      $n \leftarrow n + f_{i+1}.n$ ▷ Add (A)
    else if $o_i = -$ **then**
      $n \leftarrow n - f_{i+1}.n$ ▷ Subtract (S)
    end if
  end for
end procedure

Figure 1 shows progressions from the Singapore Math Sprints workbooks for Algorithms 1 and 2. These worksheets are organized into pairs of "A" and "B" worksheets. The instructions state that the "A" progression is intended for weaker students and the "B" progression is intended for stronger students. For most of these pairs, the two worksheets cover the same set of concepts. However, we can see that the "A" progressions spend more time moving back and forth between simple traces and the "B" progressions move into more complicated traces that subsume the early traces.

[1] http://www.singaporemath.com/Math_Sprints_s/184.htm
[2] http://jumpmath1.org/
[3] http://www.evan-moor.com/Product.aspx?SeriesID=122

Figure 2 shows a larger-scale analysis of progressions from all of these books. For each progression that we chose to analyze in each book, we first categorized all of the problems by trace. We can see that for most of these problem types, the number of traces is much less than the number of problems. However, there are differences between progressions; for example, the Singapore Sprints progression for addition has many more unique traces than the Skill Sharpeners progression.

Making progressions more systematic

We can use our framework to identify pathways a progression does not cover and suggest problems to fill that gap, if desired. We first define an algorithm for comparing two integers:

Algorithm 3 Integer Comparison: Given as input two sequences of digits $a = [a_0, ..., a_m]$ and $b = [b_0, ..., b_n]$, determine if $a > b$, $a < b$, or $a = b$:

```
procedure COMPARE(a, b)
    if len(a) > len(b) then
        return more                          ▷ More digits (H)
    else if len(a) < len(b) then
        return less                          ▷ Fewer digits (L)
    end if
    for i ← 0, len(a) − 1 do                 ▷ For each digit (D)
        if a_i > b_i then
            return more                      ▷ Digit is larger (G)
        else if a_i < b_i then
            return less                      ▷ Digit is smaller (S)
        end if
    end for
    return equal                             ▷ Equal (E)
end procedure
```

Figure 3 compares the Skill Sharpeners and JUMP Math progressions for Algorithm 3. Since there are too many nodes in the JUMP Math progression to visualize here, only the first third of the progression is shown. We can see that there is a considerable difference in how these progressions proceed. The JUMP Math progression, indicated in green, goes more quickly into more complex traces. The Skill Sharpeners progression spends more time going back and forth between simple problems, and never reaches some of the longer traces. We can also see that the first third of the JUMP Math progression omits a class of problems indicated by the traces "H" and "L". The JUMP progression eventually includes a problem in the "L" class but not until late in the progression. These traces correspond to problems in which a number is greater than another number because the number of digits is larger. Whether or not this omission is desirable is up to the educator; however, this example shows how a procedural analysis can find holes in progressions.

We can use the n-gram model presented in the partial ordering section to look for missing traces even more deeply. Figure 4 shows an analysis of the n-grams for four progressions for different problems. We compute all of the trace n-grams for each level for each progression, and identify missing n-grams by comparing them to a complete progression. Note

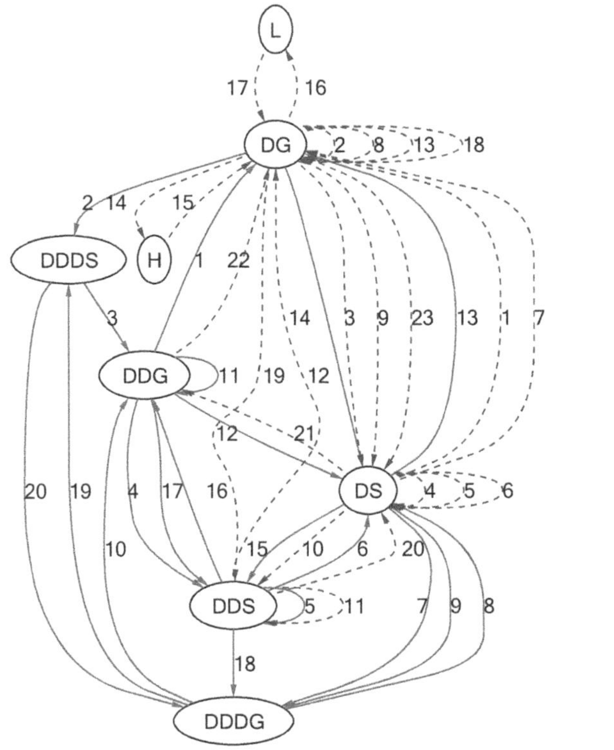

Figure 3. Filling in holes in progressions. This figure compares two progressions for integer comparison (Algorithm 3). "H" corresponds to the trace that gets executed when the first number has more digits than the other and is therefore greater. "L" corresponds to the trace that gets executed when the first number has fewer digits. "D" signifies that the number of digits is the same and that the execution path moves down the digits from left to right. "G" signifies that the digit under examination was smaller and "S" means that the digit under examination was bigger. Therefore, "DG" means that the first number is greater than the second because the first digit was greater. The blue dashed arrows indicate the Skill Sharpeners: Math progression and the green solid arrows indicate the JUMP Math progression. The JUMP Math progression quickly reaches more difficult problems than the Skill Sharpeners progression. The Skill Sharpeners progression never reaches traces longer than "DDG" and "DDS". It also omits problems in which the first number is greater or less than the second number because the number of digits is different. We can "repair" such holes by borrowing problems from other progressions or generating them automatically.

that not all combinations of all letters are possible. For example, the integer comparison trace "H" cannot combine with any other letters because the program returns immediately after that statement.

SYNTHESIS OF PROGRESSIONS

We employ four different strategies for generating and gathering problems: (i) conducting brute force enumeration over inputs, (ii) using test input generation tools to explore the space of execution paths, (iii) using test input generation tools to generate problems that lead to the execution of a desired path by writing a straight-line program with assertions corresponding to that path, and (iv) collecting problems from textbooks.

Large-scale exploration of execution paths

Manual software testing, in general, and test input generation, in particular, are labor-intensive processes. The need

Problem	Book	# problems	# unique traces	% generated
Addition	Skill Sharpeners: Math	584	17	88%
	Singapore Math Sprints	576	48	64%
Fraction Computation	Skill Sharpeners: Math	66	13	100%
	Singapore Math Sprints	248	15	100%
	JUMP Math	131	11	95%
Fraction Reduction	Skill Sharpeners: Math	66	13	100%
	JUMP Math	56	11	100%
Integer Comparison	Skill Sharpeners: Math	24	6	100%
	JUMP Math	88	12	100%

Figure 2. Summary of textbook progression analysis. We analyzed progressions from three textbooks for four different problem domains. We partitioned problems into groups based on their execution trace. The final column shows how many of these traces we were able to generate using Pex, a test input generation tool.

Problem	Book	n-gm.	% Cov.	Missing Traces
Frac. Comp.	JUMP	1	100%	
		2	100%	
		3	93%	SOA
		4	65%	MOAO, OSOA, MOSO, DOSO, SOSO, AOSO, SOAO
	S.S.	1	100%	
		2	75%	OA, OS
		3	50%	DMO, OAO, AOA, OSO, SOA, AOS, SOS
		4	30%	DMOS, DMOA, MOAO, OAOA, OSOA, MOSO, DOAO, AOAO, OSOS, DOSO, SOSO, AOSO SOAO
Int. Comp.	JUMP	1	80%	H
		2	100%	
		3	100%	
		4	100%	
		5	100%	
		6	100%	
	S.S.	1	100%	
		2	100%	
		3	67%	DDD
		4	0%	DDDG, DDDS, DDDD
		5	0%	DDDDG, DDDDS, DDDDD
		6	0%	DDDDDG, DDDDDS, DDDDDD

Figure 4. We can use the n-gram model to evaluate progressions. This table shows an analysis of progressions from JUMP Math and Skill Sharpeners (abbreviated as S.S.) for both fraction computation (Algorithm 2) and integer comparison (Algorithm 3). The table lists what percentage of the feasible n-grams, for various values of n, were covered by all problems together in the progression. The table also lists the missing n-grams. Integer comparison traces involving "E" are omitted because the goal of the exercise was to determine which number is larger.

to reduce the cost of software testing and maintenance has led to development of automated tools for generating test inputs that achieve a high level of coverage. Pex [31] is one such tool that automatically produces a small test suite with high code coverage for a .NET program. It performs path-bounded model-checking by repeatedly executing the program and solving constraint systems to obtain inputs that will steer the program along different execution paths, following the idea of dynamic symbolic execution [11]. Pex uses the theorem prover and constraint solver Z3 [8] to reason about the feasibility of execution paths, and to obtain ground models for constraint systems.

We applied Pex to generate problems for several elementary school mathematics procedures, shown in Figure 5. For each of these problems, we let Pex run for a certain length of time that we varied depending on how many paths we wanted to generate for a particular problem. We then analyzed the execution pathways of each of the problems that Pex generated and partitioned them by trace.

Generating problems to exercise a specific pathway

Pex's goal is to achieve high code coverage. While this allows Pex to generate a large variety of pathways quickly and efficiently, it also creates the possibility that it may not find certain pathways because its goal is statement coverage, not path coverage. However, we can still use Pex to generate problems for a specific trace by converting the procedure to a straight-line procedure. Essentially, we take the desired path and instrument the procedure with assertions that will constrain the execution of the procedure along that particular path.

Using this method on Algorithm 2, we were able to generate an input problem that creates the trace "DAAA" in 40 seconds and "DMMMMMMS" in 35 seconds.

EVALUATION OF OUR SYNTHESIS TECHNIQUES

Textbook problems

Figure 5 shows how we were able to generate large numbers of unique traces with Pex for several math topics. This table indicates how long we let Pex run and how many unique traces it produced. Figure 2 shows what percentage of the set of traces found in the textbooks we were able to generate. It is not 100% for all problems, but we can use the straight-line program method to generate the missing buckets. These results show that using test input generation tools is sufficient for generating problems in this domain.

An Algebra-based Learning Game

In order to validate our framework on a different procedural task domain, we conducted a user study by using Pex to generate several levels for a video game.

DragonBox (WeWantToKnow 2012), shown in Figure 6, is a video game that became the most purchased game in Norway on the Apple App Store [20]. It features game mechanics that involve solving algebra equations. The game does not appear to be an algebra lesson, but the player cannot succeed without learning algebraic simplification and variable isolation. These topics are learned through the level progression. DragonBox represents algebraic expression trees visually as a set

Problem	Time	# unique traces	Constraints
Addition	64 min	1433	# digits ≤ 4, # addends ≤ 6
Fraction Computation	16 min	72	# fractions ≤ 4, numerator ≤ 20, denominator ≤ 20, operations $\in$ addition, subtraction
Fraction Reduction	2 min	29	numerator ≤ 50, denominator ≤ 50, numerator $\leq$ denominator
Integer Comparison	2 min	26	# digits ≤ 8
Subtraction	2 min	157	# digits ≤ 6, difference ≥ 0
Prime Factorization	2 min	70	number ≤ 100000

Figure 5. We used Pex to generate many practice problems for these mathematical procedures. In each exploration, we let Pex run for the indicated length of time and it produced the indicated number of unique traces for that problem. Pex can clearly generate many interesting inputs by directly exploring traces through the procedure. Figure 2 shows the percentage of each textbook progression that this exploration was able to cover.

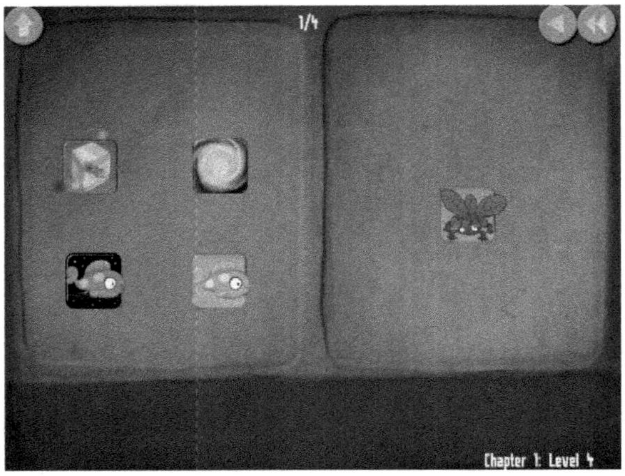

Figure 6. A level of DragonBox. The goal is to simplify an algebraic equation by isolating the variable, indicated by a box. Each half of the screen represents a side of the equation. The green spiral represents a zero and the two fish cards represent 5 and -5. The bug card represents 10. The player can solve this level by executing the following three rules: $+0 \rightarrow \emptyset$, $a + (-a) \rightarrow 0$, and $+0 \rightarrow \emptyset$. ©WeWantToKnow

of cards that represent numbers and variables. On each level, the screen is divided into two halves that represent the two sides of an equation. By dragging cards around, the player can add, multiply, or divide both sides of the equation by a number or a variable, and perform algebraic simplifications. The goal for each level is to isolate the DragonBox card, which represents an unknown variable.

Level Synthesis

DragonBox levels are essentially expression trees that represent algebraic equations. Leaf nodes can be a variable "x" or an integer. Integers can have multiple forms. They can either be an animal card with a unique picture, a number, or a constant like "a" or "c". Since these forms are essentially equivalent, we only focused on generating integer values and rendered all of these values with an animal card. Internal nodes can be either addition, multiplication, or division. The DragonBox interface imposes an ordering on these operations: addition cannot appear below multiplication or division, and division cannot appear below multiplication.

The procedure we wrote to solve DragonBox levels is described in Algorithm 4 in the Appendix. This algorithm is sufficient to solve all of the levels of the expert progression except for three at the end, which require a more complex algorithm that we leave for future work.

Because there are a huge number of possible expression trees for both the left and right-hand sides of the equation, we used Pex to rapidly explore pathways and generate a good coverage of test levels. Pex ran for two hours and generated 781 unique levels. These levels corresponded to 152 unique traces. These traces covered roughly 45% of the original progression traces, but represented a large number of unique and interesting levels.

Synthesis User Study

In order to evaluate the synthesized levels and determine whether or not they were equivalent to the expert-designed levels, we conducted a user study. Twenty participants were recruited through an internal email list at the University of Washington that is read by faculty, staff, and students.

Each participant played 30 levels of DragonBox. These levels were organized into fifteen pairs, each consisting of one automatically generated level and one expert-designed level from the original progression. After playing the two levels in the pair, each participant was asked to judge the difficulty of the first level compared to the second level. Five options were given: "much easier", "slightly easier", "about the same", "slightly harder", and "much harder". Participants played the pairs in a random order and the order of levels within each pair was also randomized.

We organized the levels such that five of the pairs contained levels that our model considered to be equivalent. For these pairs, the traces were exactly the same. In four of the level pairs, the trace of the original level subsumed the trace of the generated level according to our path-based partial ordering, and therefore our model considered the original level to be more difficult. In another three level pairs, the trace of the generated level subsumed the trace of the original level, and the original level was considered to be easier. For the final three pairs, we picked a generated level and an original level with the same trace length but different actions, indicating different conditional branching in the trace. As a result, our model specified no partial ordering for these pairs. Within each category, we tried to pick pairs so that the set would have a range of trace lengths and actions (like "add a to both sides"). For the "easier" and "harder" categories, the more difficult trace included one to three more actions than the easier trace.

Partial ordering was better than random by factor of 3

We first tried to determine whether our partial ordering could predict whether the level pairs were equal in difficulty or not. We found that the percentage of participants who considered a level pair to be equal increased from 25% when our model predicted that the pair was unequal to 62% when our model predicted that the pair was equal. This was statistically significant, $\chi^2(1, 241) = 33.97$, $p < 0.0001$. This indicates that our model reflects some human intution about level equality.

We then compared the root-mean-square error of our model's predictions with that of other baselines. We first grouped the "slightly harder" and "much harder" responses together, giving them a value of 1, and we did the same for "slightly easier" and "much easier" giving those responses a value of -1. We assigned a value of 0 to an equal response. We then measured the average response for each level, and computed the root-mean-square error of our model's predictions for each level. The root-mean-square error of our model overall was 0.35, whereas the error for making random predictions each time was 1.00, roughly three times as much.

Just using the trace length is insufficient

We observed that a simpler metric, the trace length, makes many of the same predictions as our path-based partial ordering. Therefore, to motivate the need for our more complex partial ordering, we compared it with this simpler model. In Algorithm 4, whenever our model predicts that level L_1 is harder than level L_2, it is always the case that the trace of L_1 has more statements than the trace of L_2. Therefore, for this particular procedure, a simpler model that just compares the length of these traces makes similar predictions, and actually makes the same predictions as our path-based partial ordering in cases where one trace subsumes another.

However, our partial ordering does not make a prediction when one trace does not clearly subsume the other, indicating where more data is needed. One such case is when two traces have the same number of actions but the actions themselves are different. In this event, a trace-length metric would predict that these levels are equal, although this is likely naïve because the actions themselves are different and those differences would likely cause a human to feel that the levels are different.

To examine this, we calculated the error for the trace-length metric on the three level pairs with the same trace length but different actions. This error was 0.51, which is higher than the 0.35 error that the path-based partial ordering achieved on the rest of the problems. This suggests that looking at trace length alone is not sufficient, and we need a model that carefully examines the sequence of statements within a trace.

CONCLUSION

We have defined a trace-based framework for using execution traces to explore the space of problem progressions for any procedural task that can be specified as a computer program. We have shown how this trace-based framework can categorize problems according to their traces, define partial orderings that can compare two problems and assemble a set of problems into a progression, and analyze the thoroughness and depth of existing progressions.

Our framework has allowed us to borrow ideas from test input generation in software engineering and apply them to problem generation. Test input generation tools can automatically explore pathways through a procedure, systematically generate large sets of problems that correspond to various unique pathways through this procedure, and generate problems that follow a particular desired path. We applied the framework to two domains: early mathematics education, and level generation for a interactive puzzle game. Our framework synthesized hundreds of unique levels for a popular algebra puzzle game and we conducted a user study to confirm that these levels are similar to the expert-designed progression.

Although most of grade-school mathematics education is procedural in nature, some of it also involves conceptual elements that our framework does not fully address. Future work will allow us to include some of these conceptual elements.

In the future, we plan to address student misconceptions and errors. We believe that our framework can be extended to automatically identify likely errors, generate problems that can isolate such errors, and possibly even preempt them by synthesizing interventions in the form of animations or additional problems. We also intend to collect learning data from multiple problem progressions and use machine learning to learn features of these progressions that are predictive of success.

ACKNOWLEDGMENTS

The authors would like to thank the creators of DragonBox, David Yamanoha for his help in implementing the DragonBox user study, and Ryoko Nozawa for digitizing many problems from the textbooks. This work was supported by Bill and Melinda Gates Foundation grant OPP1031488, Office of Naval Research grant N00014-12-C-0158, Hewlett Foundation grant 2012-8161, Adobe, and Intel.

REFERENCES

1. N. Aduba. JUMP Mathematics in Lambeth: Impact on KS2 National Tests 2009. `http://jumpmath1.org/research_reports`, Nov. 2009.
2. V. Aleven, B. M. McLaren, J. Sewall, and K. R. Koedinger. The cognitive tutor authoring tools (CTAT): preliminary evaluation of efficiency gains. In *Proceedings of the 8th international conference on Intelligent Tutoring Systems*, ITS'06, pages 61–70, Berlin, Heidelberg, 2006. Springer-Verlag.
3. E. Andersen, Y.-E. Liu, R. Snider, R. Szeto, S. Cooper, and Z. Popović. On the harmfulness of secondary game objectives. In *FDG '11: Proceedings of the Sixth International Conference on the Foundations of Digital Games*, New York, NY, USA, 2011. ACM.
4. E. Andersen, Y.-E. Liu, R. Snider, R. Szeto, and Z. Popović. Placing a value on aesthetics in online casual games. In *CHI '11: Proceedings of the SIGCHI conference on Human factors in computing systems*, New York, NY, USA, 2011. ACM.
5. E. Andersen, E. O'Rourke, Y.-E. Liu, R. Snider, J. Lowdermilk, D. Truong, S. Cooper, and Z. Popović. The impact of tutorials on games of varying complexity. In *CHI '12: Proceedings of the SIGCHI conference on Human factors in computing systems*, New York, NY, USA, 2012. ACM.
6. P. Cerny, S. Gulwani, T. Henzinger, A. Radhakrishna, and D. Zufferey. Specification, verification and synthesis for automata problems. Technical report, 2012.
7. M. Csikszentmihalyi. *Flow: The Psychology of Optimal Experience*. Harper & Row Publishers, Inc., New York, NY, USA, 1990.
8. L. M. de Moura and N. Bjørner. Z3: An Efficient SMT Solver. In *TACAS*, pages 337–340, 2008.
9. T. Dong, M. Dontcheva, D. Joseph, K. Karahalios, M. Newman, and M. Ackerman. Discovery-based games for learning software. In *Proceedings of the 2012 ACM annual conference on Human Factors in Computing Systems*, CHI '12, pages 2083–2086, New York, NY, USA, 2012. ACM.

10. J. Dormans. Adventures in level design: generating missions and spaces for action adventure games. In *PCGames '10: Proceedings of the 2010 Workshop on Procedural Content Generation in Games*, pages 1–8, New York, NY, USA, 2010. ACM.
11. P. Godefroid, N. Klarlund, and K. Sen. DART: directed automated random testing. In *PLDI*, pages 213–223, 2005.
12. F. Grabler, M. Agrawala, W. Li, M. Dontcheva, and T. Igarashi. Generating photo manipulation tutorials by demonstration. In *ACM SIGGRAPH 2009*, New York, NY, USA, 2009. ACM.
13. T. Grossman, G. Fitzmaurice, and R. Attar. A survey of software learnability: Metrics, methodologies and guidelines. In *CHI '09: Proceedings of the 27th international conference on Human factors in computing systems*, New York, NY, USA, 2009. ACM.
14. S. Gulwani. Synthesis from examples. *WAMBSE (Workshop on Advances in Model-Based Software Engineering) Special Issue, Infosys Labs Briefings*, 10(2), 2012. Invited talk paper.
15. S. Gulwani. Synthesis from examples: Interaction models and algorithms. *14th International Symposium on Symbolic and Numeric Algorithms for Scientific Computing*, 2012. Invited talk paper.
16. S. Gulwani, V. A. Korthikanti, and A. Tiwari. Synthesizing geometry constructions. In *PLDI*, pages 50–61, 2011.
17. N. Jurkovic. Diagnosing and correcting student's misconceptions in an educational computer algebra system. In *ISSAC*, pages 195–200, 2001.
18. N. Li, W. W. Cohen, and K. R. Koedinger. Problem order implications for learning transfer. In *ITS*, pages 185–194, 2012.
19. C. Linehan, B. Kirman, S. Lawson, and G. Chan. Practical, appropriate, empirically-validated guidelines for designing educational games. In *Proceedings of the SIGCHI Conference on Human Factors in Computing Systems*, CHI '11, pages 1979–1988, New York, NY, USA, 2011. ACM.
20. J. Liu. Dragonbox: Algebra beats angry birds. *Wired*, June 2012.
21. D. McArthur, C. Stasz, J. Hotta, O. Peter, and C. Burdorf. Skill-oriented task sequencing in an intelligent tutor for basic algebra. *Instructional Science*, 7(4):281–307, 1988.
22. Microsoft. Math Worksheet Generator. `http://www.educationlabs.com/projects/MathWorksheetGenerator/Pages/default.aspx`.
23. J. Nielsen. *Usability Engineering*. Morgan Kaufmann, San Francisco, CA, USA, 1993.
24. C. M. Reigeluth and F. S. Stein. The elaboration theory of instruction. In *Instructional Design Theories and Models: An Overview of their Current States*, Hillsdale, NJ, 1983. Lawrence Erlbaum.
25. J. Rieman. A field study of exploratory learning strategies. *ACM Trans. Comput.-Hum. Interact.*, 3(3):189–218, Sept. 1996.
26. B. Shneiderman. *Designing the User Interface: Strategies for Effective Human-Computer Interaction*. Addison-Wesley Longman Publishing Co., Inc., Boston, MA, USA, 1986.
27. R. Singh, S. Gulwani, and S. Rajamani. Automatically generating algebra problems. In *AAAI*, 2012.
28. D. H. Sleeman. A rule-based task generation system. In *Proceedings of the 7th international joint conference on Artificial intelligence - Volume 2*, IJCAI'81, pages 882–887, San Francisco, CA, USA, 1981. Morgan Kaufmann Publishers Inc.
29. A. M. Smith, E. Andersen, M. Mateas, and Z. Popović. A case study of expressively constrainable level design automation tools for a puzzle game. In *FDG '12: Proceedings of the Seventh International Conference on the Foundations of Digital Games*, New York, NY, USA, 2012. ACM.
30. G. Smith, M. Treanor, J. Whitehead, and M. Mateas. Rhythm-based level generation for 2D platformers. In *Proceedings of the 4th International Conference on Foundations of Digital Games*, FDG '09, pages 175–182, New York, NY, USA, 2009. ACM.
31. N. Tillmann and J. de Halleux. Pex-white box test generation for .NET. In *TAP*, pages 134–153, 2008.
32. K. VanLehn. *Mind Bugs: The Origins of Procedural Misconceptions*. MIT Press, Cambridge, MA, USA, 1991.
33. L. S. Vygotsky. *Mind in Society: The Development of Higher Psychological Processes*. Harvard University Press, November 1980 / 1930.
34. Wikipedia. Code coverage. `http://en.wikipedia.org/wiki/Code_coverage`.
35. Wikipedia. N-gram models. `http://en.wikipedia.org/wiki/N-gram`.

APPENDIX

Algorithm 4 Dragon Box

```
procedure DRAGONBOX(left, right)
    simplify(left, right)
    if x ∈ denom(left) ∨ x ∈ denom(right) then
        multiply(left, right, x)
        simplify(left, right)
    end if
    if x ∈ num(left) then
        variableSide ← left
        otherSide ← right
    else
        variableSide ← right
        otherSide ← left
    end if
    while variableSide ≠ x do
        isolate(variableSide, otherSide)
        simplify(otherSide, variableSide)
    end while
end procedure
procedure SIMPLIFY(node)
    if node = + ∧ child = 0 then
        child ← null                                  ▷ Remove +0
    else if node = + ∧ a ∈ child_1 ∧ −a ∈ child_2 then
        child_1 ← 0                                   ▷ Remove a + (−a)
        child_2 ← null
    else if node = × ∧ child = 1 then
        child ← null                                  ▷ Remove ×1
    else if node = ÷ ∧ a ∈ child_1 ∧ a ∈ child_2 then
        child_1 ← 1                                   ▷ Remove a ÷ a
        child_2 ← null
    end if
end procedure
procedure ISOLATE(varSide, otherSide)
    varChild ← varSide.child with variable
    nonVarChild ← other child
    if varSide = + then
        subtract(varSide, otherSide, nonVarChild)
    else if varSide = × then
        divide(varSide, otherSide, nonVarChild)
    else if varSide = ÷ then
        multiply(varSide, otherSide, nonVarChild)
    end if
end procedure
```

Wikipedia Classroom Experiment: Bidirectional Benefits of Students' Engagement in Online Production Communities

Rosta Farzan
University of Pittsburgh
rfarzan@pitt.edu

Robert E. Kraut
Carnegie Mellon University
robert.kraut@cmu.edu

ABSTRACT
Over the last decade, a citizen science movement has tried to engage students, laymen and other non-scientists in the production of science. However, there has been less attention in citizen science projects to use the public to disseminate scientific knowledge. Wikipedia provides a platform to study engagement of citizen scientists in knowledge dissemination. College and university students are especially appropriate members of the public to write science articles, because of the course-work and mentorship they receive from faculty. This paper describes a project to support students' writing of scientific articles in Wikipedia. In collaboration with a scientific association, we involved 640 students from 36 courses in editing scientific articles on Wikipedia. This paper provides details in the design of the program and our quantitative and qualitative approaches to evaluating it. Our results show that the Wikipedia classroom experiment benefits both the Wikipedia community and students. Undergraduate and graduate students substantially improved the scientific content of over 800 articles, at a level of quality indistinguishable from content written by PhD experts. Both students and faculty endorsed the motivational benefits of an authentic writing experience that would be read by thousands of people.

Author Keywords
online volunteer community; socialization; experiment

ACM Classification Keywords
H.5.3 Information interfaces and presentation: Group and Organization Interfaces: Computer-supported cooperative work

INTRODUCTION
Over the last decade, a citizen science movement has tried to engage students, laymen and other non-scientists in the production of science. Citizen science aims to enable volunteers to contribute to real-world research problems, as well as to promote public understanding of science [14]. For example, the Great Sunflower project [1] has recruited gardeners to study the distribution of bees and other pollinators; the Galaxy Zoo project [2] recruits amateur astronomers to help identify galaxies in satellite images; and the E-birds project [3] uses bird watchers to plot distribution and migration. An important goal of many citizen science projects is to educate the public in the process of collecting scientific observations. For example, the Galaxy Zoo project provided tutorials and instructions to the public to increase their knowledge about different kinds of galaxies.

Perhaps because citizen science projects have mainly been initiated by professional scientists seeking data, they have rarely engaged the public in another phase of the scientific process - the dissemination of scientific knowledge. However, doing so would serve an important public good. Writing about science would probably educate those citizen scientists involved far better than would limited data collection. In addition, the product of their work, scientific articles written for the general public, would serve the goal of promoting public understanding of science far beyond the small group of citizen scientists involved in the writing.

Wikipedia, the highly-popular online encyclopedia anyone can edit, provides a platform to study how to engage citizen scientists in knowledge dissemination. With over four million content pages in the English version, Wikipedia is a very important source of information about science for the general public. It is among the five most popular websites on the Internet and is a major resource for the general public trying to learn about science. An early evaluation in the domain of biology showed that the articles in Wikipedia were almost as good as the Encyclopedia Britannica's [6]. Moreover, Wikipedia is far more popular than perhaps more vetted sources of scientific knowledge for the general public, such as the Encyclopedia of Life[4].

Despite these qualities, Wikipedia has major limitations as a source of trusted scientific information. As the Wikimedia Foundation's strategic plan notes, "Wikipedia's coverage is skewed toward the interests, expertise, and language skills of the people who created it. For example, our coverage of biographical and pop culture topics is very strong." Although Wikipedia has many good articles on technology, engineering and the hard sciences, its coverage and quality of articles in the social sciences are substantially weaker. For many topics, the coverage is so poor that even very important articles visited by thousands of people do not have enough content to be useful. For example, Wikipedians themselves have assessed over 65% of psychology-related articles in the

[1]The Backyard Bee Count: The Great Sunflower Project (http://www.greatsunflower.org/)

[2]Galaxy Zoo (http://www.galaxyzoo.org/)

[3]http://ebird.org/content/ebird/

[4]http://eol.org/

English-language Wikipedia as "Start" or "Stub" quality. According to Wikipedia's assessment rubric, "Start" quality articles "provide some meaningful content" but are "quite incomplete" and "the majority of readers will need more," while "Stub" quality articles "provide very little meaningful content." Moreover, most articles in scientific disciplines such as psychology have not generally been reviewed by subject matter experts. This problem stems from a lack of contributions by the most qualified users–domain scientists.

Wikipedia can serve as an appropriate research platform to study how to engage university students to contribute to an online production community while at the same time providing useful educational experiences to the students involved. Although they are not themselves domain experts in a scientific discipline, their course work provides them with relevant subject knowledge in a domain, their access to academic libraries and their library skills potentially makes more up-to-date scientific knowledge more accessible to them compared to less well-connected members of the general public. Moreover, if Wikipedia writing assignments are integrated into a course curriculum, mentorship by expert faculty members can provide quality control, enhance students' education and efficiently leverage the time experts might commit to educating the general public about science.

This paper describes a project to encourage students to participate in writing scientific articles in Wikipedia in ways that benefit the students, the Wikipedia community and the general public. Our goal closely resonates with the outreach missions of many scientific societies to portray a complete and accurate image of their science to the public. Several scientific associations have been trying to encourage their members to contribute to Wikipedia to improve the way it represents scientific knowledge to the general public. In collaboration with the Association for Psychological Science (APS), we designed an initiative to invite the members of APS to harness the power of Wikipedia as a vehicle for disseminating scientific knowledge about psychology in part by using Wikipedia writing assignments in their classes. With this pilot, we were interested in developing a scalable model through which scientific societies could partner with Wikipedia or similar efforts, such as the Encyclopedia of Life, to write, assess and improve publicly-available scientific information. Particularly, we aim at addressing the following research questions:

RQ1: What are the benefits to an online production community of recruiting students from educational programs to contribute to an online production community for a limited term? How does their contribution influence the community and how is the quality and quantity of what they produce?

An influx of outsiders could benefit or harm the community. Although students mentored by faculty could potentially contribute valuable domain knowledge to Wikipedia, they are unfamiliar with the Wikipedia culture and have personal goals that may not overlap with community goals. Our research aims to assess the value of their contribution for the community.

RQ2: How do the classroom and community environments in which students participate influence quality and quantity of their contribution to Wikipedia? Particularly, what is the value of presence of a cohort and peer feedback specific to these classroom experiments on students participation in Wikipedia.

The impact of student involvement on both the community and their own education is likely to depend upon the support they receive in their classrooms and by the larger Wikipedia community. The second goal of our research is to examine how cohort and community support influence students contribution, knowledge and motivation.

RQ3: What value do students receive from contributing to an online production community for a limited time period?

With any educational experiment, it is important to ensure the learning value for the students. Our third research goal is to assess how contribution to an open production community such as Wikipedia contributes to students learning experience. In contributing to Wikipedia, students have to learn about how Wikipedia works, which takes time away from their educational goals.

APS/WIKIPEDIA INITIATIVE

The Association for Psychological Science started a Wikipedia initiative to call on its members to deploy the power of Wikipedia to represent scientific psychology as fully and as accurately as possible, in service of its mission to promote the free teaching of psychology worldwide [1]. APS's invitation included a pair of columns by the APS president that stressed how the initiative fit with both APS's outreach mission and members' sense of identity. The initiative invited psychologists to make three types of contributions: editing Wikipedia articles in their area of expertise, providing feedback on the quality of existing Wikipedia articles, and leveraging their positions as instructors by assigning Wikipedia writing assignments in their classes. Because psychologists could expand their impact by encouraging their students to edit Wikipedia articles, we focused our effort on engaging psychologists in Wikipedia through their classes of undergraduate and graduate students.

To support the initiative, we implemented a portal designed to improve the experience of psychologists and their students as newcomers to Wikipedia. The portal followed the design theme of the APS website and on its homepage, we highlighted the association's call for action. The portal was designed to assist psychologists in finding Wikipedia articles in their areas of expertise that needed improvement, tutorials and other help pages, and information about activities of other members. The portal provided support for students to learn the Wikipedia culture and for faculty to integrate Wikipedia writing assignment in their classes.

Through the APS/Wikipedia Initiative, we encouraged faculty to assign Wikipedia writing assignments in their classes. In a preliminary phase, we organized several information sessions during the annual APS convention that many psychologists attend. Additionally, APS publicized Wikipedia in classroom programs by sending emails to its members, posting advertisements about the initiative in flagship journals and publishing on the APS website testimonials written by faculty who had already introduced Wikipedia assignments in their classes. We also highlighted the benefits of Wikipedia assignments and provided support through the portal we developed.

CLASSROOM ENGAGEMENT

The Wikimedia Foundation started an education program in 2010 which, in its first year, encouraged students from 33 classes at 22 U.S. universities in government, law and public policy programs to write for Wikipedia [5]. Students in this program were highly motivated to write Wikipedia articles because their work could reach a much wider audience and could be more influential than a traditional term paper [12]. Lampe et al. conducted a survey among 463 students who participated in the public policy program to examine factors influencing their intention to contribute to Wikipedia beyond the classroom [11]. Classroom characteristics, and especially the level of class engagement, strongly influenced students' intention to contribute in the future. Although their results highlighted the importance of identifying effective classroom strategies to make students more interested in the assignment, evaluations of the Wikimedia education program did not collect data on the design of the assignment and did not examine the classroom-level factors contributing to success in a class.

An important goal of our project was to investigate how variations in the program implementation across classrooms would influence students' satisfaction with the assignment, the quality of students' work in the assignment, and their future commitment to contributing to Wikipedia. We based our design of the APS/Wikipedia classroom program on prior research in organizational socialization that suggests best practices for bringing newcomers into an existing organization and improving their competence and commitment [13], [2]. We also incorporated training materials from the Wikimedia Foundation's public policy program. We discuss the design rationale for the APS/Wikipedia classroom program in more detail in the sections below.

Providing feedback

Research on organizational socialization shows that mentorship and receiving feedback from experienced role models are associated with positive socialization outcomes [2],[13]. An important advantage of Wikipedia classroom assignments is that students receive feedback on their work from the professor, who is an expert in the field. To support faculty providing feedback to students, the portal presented information about students' activity. Faculty were able to register their courses with the portal and have their students sign up for the courses through the portal. Once these processes were complete, the portal automatically kept track of all students' activity on the portal and on Wikipedia, as shown in Figure 1.

Faculty could view the list of students in the class and a quantitative summary about their activities, including the number of times they edited any Wikipedia page, time they spent editing, and the number of words they added or deleted. The portal also provided a list of pages each student edited, number of edits for each page, and number of words added and deleted. Once students chose specific article pages to improve, the faculty could view a list of all the students who worked on that article and view the additions and deletions that each individual student or the whole group made to the article, as shown in Figure 2. This tool for viewing the details of students' contributions is especially important in the context of Wikipedia, where articles are collaboratively written. Although some students wrote articles from scratch, more typically they started with existing material. As they wrote, other community members could simultaneously edit the article, including enhancing or removing the students' work.

Newcomers who receive feedback from the existing members of a community, both in the form of positive feedback or constructive criticism, are more likely to contribute and feel more committed to the community [5]. To receive feedback from the community, we encouraged the faculty to ask students to post on article talkpages [6] before editing the article and to ask for feedback from editors who already edited the page. As we discuss in more detail in the section on"Community acceptance," some members of the Wikipedia community are hostile to newcomers, and their feedback had negative consequences for student motivation and commitment.

Peer review

Research in peer-evaluation has shown that students learn from providing feedback to their peers and benefit from receiving feedback from others with similar experiences, especially when the review process is structured, anonymous, and reciprocal [4]. Additionally, peer reviewing can increase interaction among the newcomers and therefore improve their sense of community. We encouraged the faculty to ask students to review works of other students as part of the assignment. We provided support in the portal for faculty to assign peer reviews. Faculty can specify the number of reviews per student and decide to assign specific reviews to students or allow the students to sign up for reviews. Once the assignment is done, the system informs the students of their review assignments. Students can view articles edited by their peers including particular edits done by the student. The review form asks students for an overall score as well as free-format comments regarding strengths of their peers' edits and comments suggesting ways their peers can improve their articles.

Cohort support and group work

According to previous research on organizational socialization, newcomers to organizations are more likely to know what they should do, become more productive, be more satisfied and stay longer if they join in a group with other newcomers and go through early socialization experiences with others in their cohort [2] [13]. Being part of a cohort helps newcomers share their experiences, collectively discover the organization's values and work procedures, receive social support

[5] http://outreach.wikimedia.org/wiki/Public_Policy_Initiative

[6] Wikipedia pages dedicated to discussions around the topic of the article page

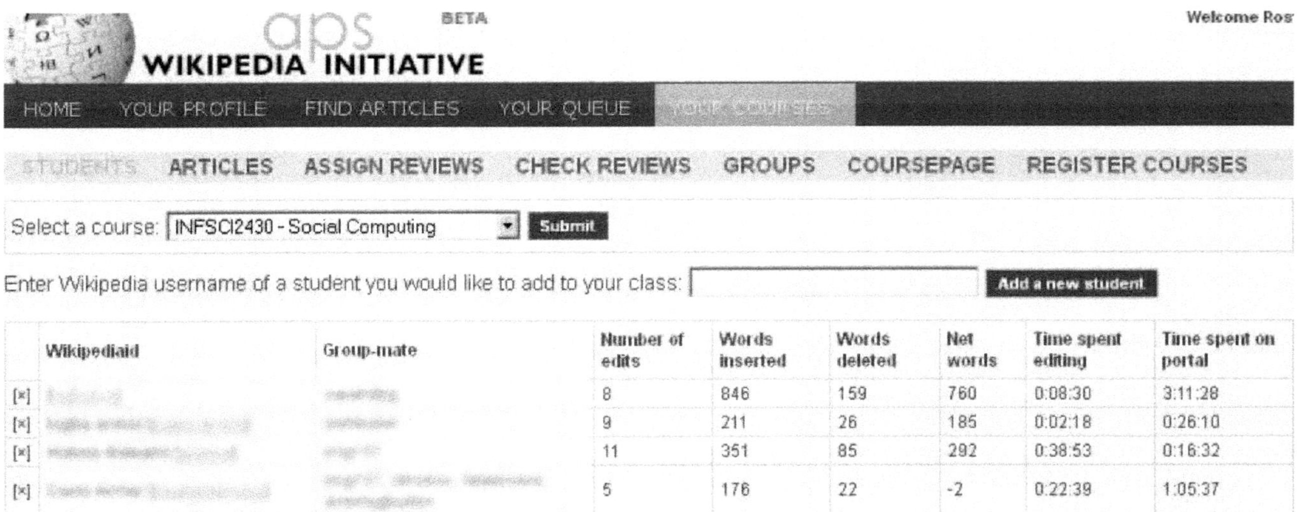

Figure 1. List of students in a class with quantitative information about number of edits, words added and deleted, and time spent editing and on the portal

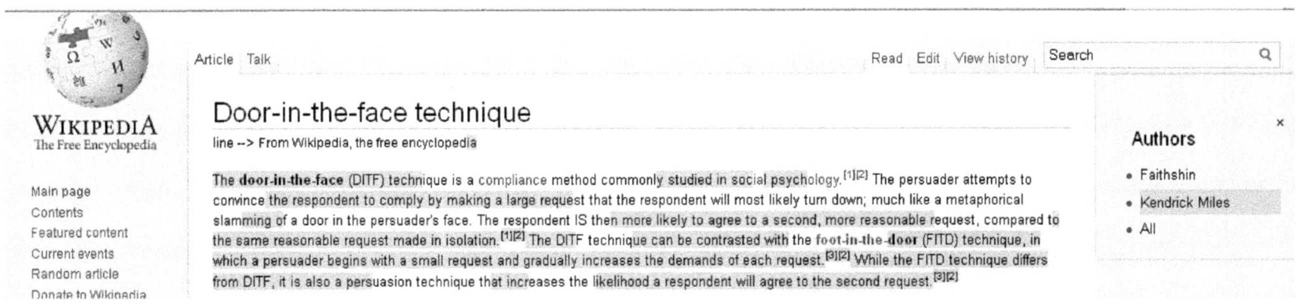

Figure 2. Changes made to the article by students in the class

from their peers and build a long term social support network. In contrast to individual APS PhD psychologists who might identify articles and edit them individually, a classroom assignment naturally provides students a cohort who go through their first experiences of editing Wikipedia together. Each can receive support from other students who experience the same challenges. To enhance the effect of cohort-based socialization, we recommended that faculty assign a small group of students to work together on the same article. Group work can help students to make sense of the new environment together, which can increase their role clarity and self-efficacy. The portal allowed students to select a collaborator from the list of students in their class. Faculty were able to see the group assignments in the portal as well as the activity of both the group and individual members on each article they had edited.

EVALUATION

To address our research questions, we used qualitative and quantitative research methods to understand how a program designed to engage students in Wikipedia authoring influenced Wikipedia and their own education.

Quantitative methods

To answer our first research question about the benefits of students' contributions to Wikipedia, we measured quantity and quality of students' contribution in Wikipedia. As simple measures of quantity, we examined the number of words they contributed. These measures correlate highly with more differentiated measures, including the number of references, inline citations, sections, links and pictures editors added.

Measuring the quality of contributions is more difficult. Ideally, one would like human judgments of the quality of articles before and after contributions have been made to it. Wikipedia's 1.0 Assessment [8] ratings would be appropriate, but only 52% of psychology articles have been assessed as of June, 2012, and these assessments are infrequently updated. Therefore, we use as an index of quality the proportion of words that were added by initiative members and were not deleted by another Wikipedian. Each change made by one Wikipedian to another's work is behavioral evidence that the changer was not satisfied with the original work. Editors frequently change others' work to improve it, because it failed to include proper citations, used copyrighted materials, was poorly written or due to other infractions. However, this measure is by no means perfect. The quality of judgments depends on both the motivation and expertise of the editor making changes, and editors may change another's work because they have ideological disagreements with the

[8] http://en.wikipedia.org/w/index.php?title=Wikipedia:WikiProject_Psychology/Assessment_summary

other editor [10], because it impinges on what they consider their territory [7] or because they are not familiar with content or norms of the scientific disciplines from which the new material came, among other reasons. While this is an imperfect measure of quality, it provides a practical basis for judging the quality of edits done by the students. Especially when interpreted as a contrast measure, comparing students to experts and newcomers in comparable fields. To assess the quality of contribution, for each article, we calculated the percentage of the words they added that remained in the article until our data collection date in June 2012.

Qualitative methods

To answer our second and third research questions, we employed qualitative methods to collect data about the educational value of Wikipedia and different characteristics of classrooms through surveys and interviews with students and faculty.

Even though we provided a common timeline and guidelines to faculty, they varied widely in how they taught their courses, how central the Wikipedia assignment was to them, and which elements of the timeline and guidelines they adopted. At the end of each semester we surveyed students to collect information about different classroom characteristics that prior research suggested would improve the quantity and quality of students' contributions and their future commitment to contributing to Wikipedia. We sent a questionnaire by email to the students at the end of the semester, with two reminders. One hundred and twenty-seven students responded to the questionnaire for a response rate of 18%. We collected information on the following:

- **Peer review**: Whether students were required to review works of their classmates or not. Among 127 students who responded to the survey, 73 reported reviewing other students' work.
- **Group work**: Whether students worked individually or in groups and when working in groups, what was the level of collaboration with their teammates. Sixty-four of the 127 students reported working in groups with other students on the same article.
- **Instruction**: whether students received particular instruction in class regarding their Wikipedia assignment, e.g. in class-editing sessions. Eighty-six of the 127 students reported having in class instruction or editing sessions.
- **Expert Feedback**: Amount and quality of feedback students received from their professor as an expert in the field.
- **Community Feedback**: Amount and quality of feedback students received from the Wikipedia community. We also asked students whether they posted on article talk pages to elicit feedback from Wikipedia editors and whether they received any feedback in response to their posts.
- **Students' communication**: Amount and quality of communication from classmates through different media, including face-to-face meetings, computer-mediated communication (e.g. emails and IMs), social media websites (e.g. Facebook groups), and interaction during the class.

Students reported receiving feedback from their professor several times during the semester and reported significantly less feedback from other students or from the Wikipedia community (on average about once during the semester). Moreover, they valued feedback from their professor more than feedback from these other sources (Wilcoxon signed rank test, Z=4.115, Sig. < .0001). They valued feedback from students significantly more than feedback from the Wikipedia community (Wilcoxon signed rank test, Z=-1.912, Sig. = .056). Table 1 shows the students' average rating of the value of the feedback they received from different sources.

Table 1. Average students' rating of value of feedback from different sources

	Professor	Students	Wikipedia
Mean (Std. Deviation)	3.65 (2.11)	2.78 (2.14)	2.33(2.19)

† Feedback was rated on 5-point Likert scales, with 1 being the lowest and 5 being the highest rating.

Students reported minimal communication with other students. The questionnaire asked them to estimate the frequency of communication from never to very frequently. Communication with other students was generally infrequent. When students communicated with other students about the assignment. it tended to be face-to-face, during and surrounding class sessions. They rarely used Wikipedia talkpages or social media, such as Facebook.

General Statistics

A total of 36 classes with 640 students participated in the APS Wikipedia Initiative in the Fall 2011 and Spring 2012 semesters. Together, they edited a total of 840 articles, adding 442,218 words. In terms of the quantity of work, this is the rough equivalent of writing a 1,200 page textbook in psychology. At the time that the APS/Wikipedia initiative was started, members of WikiProject Psychology had tagged 5,411 articles as associated with psychology. Student members of the APSWI edited 840 articles, about 13% of all articles associated with psychology prior to the initiative. In Wikipedia, WikiProjects are collections of editors interested in specific topics such as psychology, biology, military history, or various music genres. WikiProject Psychology [7] is a subgroup of Wikipedians organized around curating articles in the domain of psychology. WikiProject members place a psychology tag on articles within the scope of psychology.

Classroom characteristics

To evaluate the effect of classroom characteristics on students' performance and satisfaction, we first grouped co-occurring classroom characteristics together using principal component analysis with Varimax rotation. As shown in Table 2, 12 classroom characteristics load on three components.

Peer review, feedback from fellow students, feedback from professor, and in-class instruction and editing are grouped

[7] http://en.wikipedia.org/wiki/Wikipedia:WikiProject_Psychology

into one factor which represents all forms of classroom feedback and instruction that students received to improve their work. We denote this factor as **"Classroom feedback"**. Working in groups and the communication variables are loaded into the second factor. Conceptually, they represent the cohort support that students received from collaboration and communication with others. We denote this factor as **"Cohort"**. Feedback from Wikipedians, and posting on talk-pages are grouped together. Conceptually, these variables represent the external feedback that students received as well as social acceptance and approval of their work. We denote this factor as **"Social acceptance"**. To aggregate classroom characteristics into components, we standardized all the variables and summed variables in each group; we dichotomized each factor based on median split.

Table 2. Principal component analysis - Rotated component matrix

	Component		
	Classroom feedback	Cohort	Community acceptance
In-class instruction	.77	-.13	-.10
In-class editing	.76	-.05	.12
Feedback from students	.68	.19	.35
Feedback from prof	.65	-.00	.58
Peer review	.52	.43	-.21
Face-to-face communication	-.01	.84	.00
Before & after class communication	-.01	.73	.15
Computer-mediated Communication	-.06	.69	.13
Working in groups	.09	.67	.01
Feedback from Wikipedia	.22	.20	.78
Posting on article talkpage	-.02	.07	-.74

† Rotation converged in 5 iterations.

RESULTS

We report the result of our analysis in response to our three research questions in the following sections:

RQ1: Value of students' contribution for Wikipedia Community

One of the challenges of conducting interventions in an ongoing online production environment is evaluating the effects of the intervention. The current research is not a true experiment, in which articles were either randomly assigned to be edited by APSWI students or not. As a result, we relied on a far weaker research design, a matched control design, to understand the effects of this intervention [3]. We contrasted work done by students to work done by relevant comparison samples, including PhD psychologists, other Wikipedians editing psychology articles, and members of WikiProject Sociology and WikiProject Neuroscience. We focused the analysis on the quantity and quality of these editors' contribution.

Comparison with experts

We expected that students' contributions would be as good as those made by expert psychologists since they receive direct feedback from their faculty who are experts in the field. However, a priori, it was not clear whether the quality of their work would match that produced by expert PhDs. We therefore compared the contributions of students writing as part of classroom assignments with the contributions of PhD psychologists who are writing by themselves. Because students had well-defined goals (e.g., to improve an article to "Good Article" status) and because they were working for an external incentive, their classroom grade, we also expected them to have contributed more to the articles than the PhDs, who had no externally imposed goals or incentives. As shown in Table 3, students added 3.4 times more words to the articles than the PhDs, and their contribution had the same survival rate as those made by PhDs. These results support our expectation that classroom training and socialization can help relatively naive students to contribute high-quality content to Wikipedia.

Table 3. Comparison of classroom contribution versus expert contribution

	Classroom students	PhDs	Sig.
Mean # of words added (STD)	598.66 (25.64)	177.09 (12.20)	<.001
Mean % of words surviving (STD)	66.99% (.03)	66.38% (.05)	

Comparison with non-initiative members of WikiProjects

We compared quality and quantity of contributions made by students to contributions made by editors who joined Wikipedia at the same time as students but were not part of the initiative and who edited articles associated with WikiProject Psychology, Sociology, and Neuroscience on Wikipedia. We selected these disciplines because they are likely to have content that is similar to that edited by the students in the initiative. Editors can explicitly join WikiProjects, but only a subset of those who edit relevant articles actually do so. To include a more complete list of editors, we defined an editor as associated with a WikiProject as long as they edited at least one article tagged with that WikiProject label. By this definition, 2,066 new editors were associated with WikiProject Psychology, 2,148 new editors were associated with WikiProject Sociology, and 276 were associated with Neuroscience. To compare the quantity of contributions of students versus non-initiative members associated with these WikiProjects, we conducted a regression analysis with group membership as an independent variable and number of words added as the dependent variable. We used a negative binomial model to account for skewness of the data. Compared with members of these WikiProjects, students added significantly more words to the articles they edited. The mean of number of words added by each group is presented in Table 4.

As described earlier, we measured the quality of contribution as the percentage of words surviving revisions. We conducted a regression analysis with group membership as the

Table 4. Comparison of contribution of students versus non-Initiative members of WikiProjects

	New editors since Sep 2011	Mean words added	Mean % of words surviving
Students	707	484.28	66.62%
Psychology	2,066	133.38	55.17%
Sociology	2,148	112.32	54.49%
Neuroscience	276	138.32	54.98%

independent variable and percentage of words remaining as the dependent variable. More of the words added by students remained than words added by new editors associated with the WikiProjects. The mean percentage of words remaining for each group is presented in Table 4.

RQ2: Effect of classroom factors on students' contribution

We were interested in assessing the effect of classroom characteristics on the quantity and the quality of students' contributions. The 127 students who responded to our survey edited 327 articles. We conducted a regression analysis with the dichotomized classroom characteristics as the independent variables and the number of words added and the percentage of words remaining as the dependent variables.

The results show that students who had more cohort support added 1.6 times more words than those with less support (IRR=1.66, SE=.15, Sig.<.001). On the other hand, students who received more feedback from instructors and peers added fewer words (IRR=.71, SE=.14, Sig.=0.02). This reduction in editing quantity could arise because feedback causes students to revise and delete some of their own work. Alternatively, the requirement in these classes for students to review each others' work may have left them with less time for writing. As shown in Figure 3, however, getting more cohort support in writing mitigated this effect. The effect of cohort support also mitigated the effect of feedback from the Wikipedia community. Students who received more feedback from the Wikipedia community, but did not have cohort support, contributed significantly fewer words, but not when they received cohort support.

Previous research has shown that when new Wikipedia editors receive negative feedback from the community, they reduce the amount of work they do or stop participating [8], [15]. The results of the current research suggest that cohort support may help students to make sense of the feedback they receive from domain experts and the Wikipedia community or to withstand the feelings of rejection or decrease in their self-esteem resulting from negative feedback.

In terms of quality of students' contribution, while there is a trend towards a positive effect of feedback (Means: more feedback=71.2%, less feedback=63.3%, p=0.24) and social acceptance (Means: more Wikipedia feedback=70.5%, less Wikipedia feedback=64.2%, p=0.37) on the quality of students' work, none of the effects is statistically reliable.

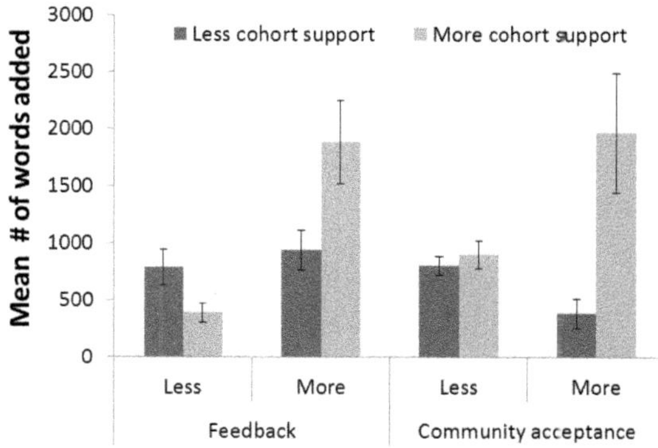

Figure 3. Effect of feedback and cohort support on students' quantity of contribution

RQ3: Educational value of Wikipedia assignment for students

To understand the value of the Wikipedia assignment for students, we conducted surveys and interviews among students and faculty. The questionnaire included several questions about students' educational experience as a result of Wikipedia assignment. Moreover, we conducted interviews with ten faculty to understand the educational value of Wikipedia assignment for students from their perspective. These faculty taught classes ranging from four to 150 students from lower division, senior undergraduate, and graduate classes in different areas such as "History and Psychology", "Psychology of Language", and "Psychology and Neuroscience". The assignment varied in terms of scope and ranged from writing a new article, or making substantial changes to an existing article, to adding only one paragraph.

Faculty perspective

The faculty without exception reported that the assignment was very motivating for students. They reported that students exerted more effort in the Wikipedia assignment than other assignments in the class. For example, according to one interviewee the assignment encouraged students to "work hard and their level of engagement was higher". Students were particularly motivated because they knew many would read their work rather than it only being read by their instructor at the end of the term. According to one of the interviewees, students were motivated "to tackle new challenges because the assignment was meaningful for them" and they were proud of sharing what they learned with others.

Faculty repeatedly reported that students (1) learned "new styles of writing" which focused on explaining scientific topic with a language targeted at the general public as audience; (2) achieved what faculty described as "deeper understanding" of their topic because they had to dig deeper into the topic to provide comprehensive coverage of the topic for the general public; (3) achieved a new "perspective on psychological theory"; (4) improved their abilities of "critical thinking" as they were often criticized by Wikipedia community and they learned to provide evidence from valid sources for every claim they made to support them; (5) improved their"digital literacy" and increased their awareness of Wikipedia and digital sources. They learned about the culture of Wikipedia, what happens behind the scenes in Wikipedia and how much to trust it as a reader.

Students perspective

The questionnaire included several questions designed to measure students' knowledge of editing Wikipedia content and Wikipedia's rules and norms, their intention to continue to edit Wikipedia articles in future, and how the Wikipedia assignment contributed to their learning about the topic of the articles they edited, and the technical aspects of editing Wikipedia articles, and norms and rules of Wikipedia community. Because students within a class were not independent of each other, to assess the effect of classroom characteristics on these attitudinal outcome measures, we conducted a regression analysis with a hierarchical linear model. The model included students nested within courses, which was treated as a random effect. We also controlled for the size of the class by including the number of students of each class in the model.

Wikipedia knowledge: The questionnaire included six factual questions about Wikipedia rules and the syntax of the Wiki markup language (e.g. "What are the "Wikipedia:Did You Know" rules? " or "What does ~~~~ mean in wiki markup language and when do you use it?"). On average, students scored 42.4% (STD=22.31) with a median of 37.5%. The results of a regression analysis show no effect of classroom characteristics on the accuracy of students' responses. Students in smaller size classes performed better on the test, i.e. every additional student in the class decreased the students' performance by 1% (B=1.01, SE=0.004,Sig.=0.005).

Future commitment: We asked students whether they would be interested in editing Wikipedia articles in the future. Sixty-five percent of students expressed some level of interest in contributing to Wikipedia after their class assignment was over. Analysis of the effects of classroom characteristics on students' future commitment shows that students who had stronger cohort support were twice as likely to express interest in future contribution (B=1.99, SE=.39, Sig.=.077). When we examined their actual behavior, students continued to work on Wikipedia less than they predicted they would. After the last day of their class, 13.6% edited at least one Wikipedia page. While a modest number, it is three times larger than the 4.1% of student editors who Lampe et al. reported remained active after the end of classes associated with the Wikimedia Foundation's Public Policy Initiative [11].

Learning: On three Likert questions probing the areas students learned most from the initative, they reported that the Wikipedia assignment helped them to learn about the topic of the article they edited, the norms and culture of Wikipedia community, and the technical aspects of Wikipedia. They believed that the assignment was more effective in helping them learn about the topic of the article and the technical aspects of Wikipedia than about the norms and culture of Wikipedia (Wilcoxon signed rank test: Norms vs Topic: Z=-2.109, Sig=.035, Norms vs Tech: Z=-1.973, Sig=.049). Cohort support and classroom feedback improved students' perception of learning about Wikipedia norms and rules as shown in Figure 4 (Cohort: B=.124, SE=.06, Sig.=.024, Classroom feedback: B=.107, SE=.06, Sig.=.061). There was no significant effect of classroom characteristics on students' perception of learning about the topic of the article, but larger class size had a negative effect. Students in smaller classes reported learning more about their psychology topic (Size: B=1.04, SE=.014, Sig.=.006). Consistent with the results from the Wikipedia knowledge test, there was no effect of classroom characteristics on students' perception of learning about the technical aspects of Wikipedia.

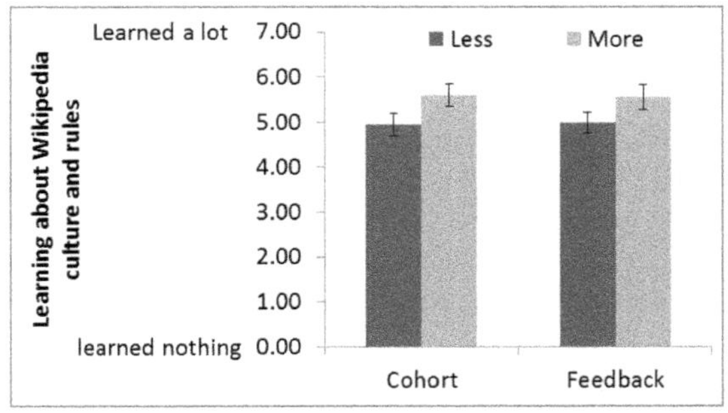

Figure 4. Students' perception of learning about Wikipedia culture and norms.

Other anecdotal evidence from some of these classrooms is consistent with these findings. Students in a small psychology class on Language Acquisition[9] worked in two groups focusing on improving articles on "Vocabulary development" and "Joint attention". By the end of the semester, students were successful in improving both articles to "Good Article" status. Achieving this status is very challenging. At the time the ASPWI started, there were only 19 psychology articles with "Good Article" status; the seven students from this class were able to add two to that list. A faculty member from Davidson College engaged 41 students from two undergraduate classes in Wikipedia assignments [10]. Her students substantially improved the quality of 26 articles, increasing the length of the articles from one paragraph with a few references to a full multi-page article with dozens of references. All in all they added more than 400 peer-reviewed sources to psychology articles on Wikipedia.

COMMUNITY ACCEPTANCE

Although students found feedback from their professors and classmates more valuable than feedback from members of the Wikipedia community, some students did receive useful feedback from existing members of the community. One of the guiding principles of Wikipedia is that all material must be verifiable and attributable to a reliable source. Experienced Wikipedians gave guidance to students to make sure that all the materials that they added were cited properly. Figure 5 shows an example of an encouraging message from one of the Wikipedians to a student. The message provides clear directions for adding citations while giving reassuring feedback to the student about the content they added.

However, not all the feedback from existing members was as constructive, and some established Wikipedia editors were

[9] `Wikipedia:Canada_Education_Program/Courses/Language_Acquisition_(Paula_Marentette)`

[10] `Wikipedia:Ambassadors/Courses/Cognitive_Psychology_(Greta_Munger)`

New material - origin? [edit]

The stuff added in recent days is great (if it's correct). But there's no indication of where it came from. Is this sourced/sourceable or unreferenced (original research) material? If the former, please get the refs in here. thx $\Psi\nu^{Psi}{}_{nu}$ 06:57, 11 April 2011 (UTC)

Hi, I've been updating this page as part of a class project. I will have the refs up in the next couple of weeks. Thanks! —Preceding unsigned comment added by 128.2.247.150 (talk) 17:34, 21 April 2011 (UTC)

Figure 5. Feedback from Wikipedia editors to students

hostile about newcomers playing in their turf. In an essay describing his Wikipedia editing experience, one PhD student complained about an experienced editor who deleted a large proportion of his team's editing with the comments, "Please fully source the article at the VERY least," even though the team had added 20 citations to an existing article, and "Blech. This really needs [[WP:TNT]]," which is Wikipedia's jargon for "Blow it up and start over." An article on "Dimensional models of personality disorders," which a PhD student in another class had substantially improved, was proposed for deletion by an experienced Wikipedia editor. Her rationale was that the article did not meet Wikipedia's standards for general notability, even though, according to the course instructor, "dimensional models of disorders may be the hottest topic in abnormal psychology for the past ten years." The nomination for deletion led to a vigorous debate, consisting of rational argument, references to policy, presentation of evidence as well as vicious name-calling. In both of these cases, students who were the targets of these attacks were understandably upset. As one student remarked, "To have as much work as we did deleted, and then to hear the suggestion that the rest of it be removed as well, from someone who does not appear to be an expert in the field, is disheartening, aggravating, de-motivating and representative of all of these things as we have discussed them [in class] as being detrimental to newcomers on a site over the course of the class."

Some of these conflicts between experienced editors and the students represent fundamental culture clashes on the credibility of different sources. Students and faculty in several of the psychology classes had problems with justifying their use of research literature in the Wikipedia articles. The Wikipedia community requires articles to be based mainly on reliable secondary sources and to avoid original research. However, in many scientific fields, using primary sources such as peer-reviewed journal articles is unavoidable. These primary sources are considered by experts in the field to be the most reliable sources of up-to-date information before it has been synthesized in review articles or textbooks. As a result, in some cases students in the initiative received strongly negative feedback from the Wikipedia community, including deletion of most of their work. Very often the feedback was from Wikipedia editors who were familiar with the rules of Wikipedia but not an expert in the domain of psychology. The feedback these experienced Wikipedians provided tended to be based on superficial aspects of the article and were not very constructive. For example, one editor critiqued students who documented an idea in an article with several citations. This editor complained that the students were synthesizing evidence from the original source, when in fact the students were intending to document that several empirical studies had found support for the idea. This editor was satisfied when the students removed some of the supporting evidence and included only a single citation.

It is important for the health of the Wikipedia community to show acceptance towards newcomers and to strive to incorporate them into the community. Newcomers are sources of new content and new ideas, and their contributions can enrich the existing content in new ways. The Wikipedia community is aware of this problem, and one element in its strategic plan[11] through 2015 is to "[s]upport the recruitment and acculturation of newer contributors by encouraging a welcoming environment on the Wikimedia projects, as well as supporting community leaders who are eager to serve as recruiters, guides and mentors for newer volunteers." (p. 9)

Our current work suggests that stronger cohort support can assist in dealing with some of these challenges. We are interested in capitalizing on the effectiveness of cohort support and creating a self-sustained community of newcomers in which the senior members support future members. In a preliminary intervention, we invited a small group of students who exhibited high-quality performance in their Wikipedia assignment in the Fall 2011 semester to support students in the Spring 2012 semester. Students responded to our invitation enthusiastically: 6 out of 14 agreed to participate, and they participated actively. They reviewed the work of the new students and provided valuable feedback to them. This was a small trial towards the end of the semester; students receiving mentorship were not able to take full advantage of the help since most of them were too far along in their assignment. However, the results are promising, and we will try to extend this trial in future work to design an effective system of peer-mentoring among newcomers, and carefully assessing its value.

CONCLUSION

The APS Wikipedia Initiative has been successful in recruiting psychologists and their students to Wikipedia. In the eight months the initiative has been active, at least 36 classrooms involving 640 students have used article-writing assignments. In addition, other classes used article-writing assignments because of the APSWI, but did not use the tools we provided; therefore, the behavior of the students in their classes was not recorded in our data. For example, we know of the instructor

[11] http://upload.wikimedia.org/wikipedia/commons/c/c0/WMF_StrategicPlan2011_spreads.pdf

of an introductory psychology class of 1,700 who had students read some primary research related to a Wikipedia article and add a citation to the article [9]. Overall, the students whose behavior we captured have improved over 840 Wikipedia articles and have written over 1,200 pages of text, more than the content of a psychology textbooks. Classroom experiments have been successful in encouraging undergraduate and graduate students to substantially improve the quality of psychology articles. Our results suggests that an online production community such as Wikipedia can greatly benefit from incorporating well-structured and guided group of newcomers. On the other hand, contribution to a broader context and sharing knowledge with the general public strongly motivates students. As suggested by prior work in offline organizations, cohort support can further improve students' experience and their commitment and contribution to Wikipeida. Stronger cohort support in classrooms improved students' learning about Wikipedia norms and culture and it increased students' contributions and future commitment to Wikipedia.

The APS Wikipedia Initiative has also started to form a model for how other scientific societies can involve their members in disseminating their science to the general public by getting their members to contribute to Wikipedia and similar encyclopedias. As a result of this initiative, the American Sociological Association, the National Communication Association and five other associations are starting similar initiatives.

Despite this success, there is much to be done to extract lessons from this initiative, to better understand what worked and what needs improvement, and to smoothly roll out similar initiatives for other constituencies on Wikipedia and to generalize them to other online production environments. The case study we provided in this paper is a formative evaluation, designed to give us feedback about how to improve the initiative. It was not intended as a summative evaluation to demonstrate the value of the initiative compared to other ways of engaging citizen scientists or the value of Wikipedia writing for student learning. At a minimum, this research has shown that it is possible to recruit and socialize at least one type of citizen scientists, students, into an existing online production community to the extent that they can operate productively in it. We still need better tools and processes to help the newcomers get up to speed more quickly. But we also need a better understanding of the reaction that an existing community may have towards newcomers and ways to temper that reaction when it is hostile.

ACKNOWLEDGMENT

This work was funded by NSF grant #: IIS-1111166 and a gift from Google. We thank the Association for Psychological Science for their support in running the APS-Wikipedia initiative and especially Brian Weaver for his continuous assistance throughout this research. We also thank Yla Tausczik, Greta Munger, and Paula Marentette for their feedback.

REFERENCES

1. BANAJI, M. Harnessing the power of wikipedia for scientific psychology: A call to action. *APS Observer* (2011).
2. BAUER, T. N., BODNER, T., ERDOGAN, B., TRUXILLO, D. M., AND TUCKER, J. S. Newcomer adjustment during organizational socialization: A meta-analytic review of antecedents, outcomes, and methods. *Journal of Applied Psychology 92*, 3 (2007), 2707–2721.
3. CAMPBELL, D. T., STANLEY, J. C., AND GAGE, N. L. *Experimental and quasi-experimental designs for research*. Houghton Mifflin Boston, 1963.
4. CHO, K., AND SCHUNN, C. D. Scaffolded writing and rewriting in the disipline: A web-based reciprocal peer review system. *Computers and Education 48*, 3 (2007), 409–426.
5. CHOI, B., ALEXANDER, K., KRAUT, R. E., AND LEVINE, J. M. Socialization tactics in wikipedia and their effects. In *Computer Supported Collaborative Work* (2010).
6. GILES, J. Internet encyclopaedias go head to head. *Nature* (2005).
7. HALFAKER, A., KITTUR, A., KRAUT, R. E., AND RIEDL, J. A jury of your peers: Quality, experience and ownership in wikipedia. In *WikiSym09* (2009).
8. HALFAKER, A., KITTUR, A., AND RIEDL, J. Don't bite the newbies: how reverts affect the quantity and quality of wikipedia work. In *Proceedings of the 7th International Symposium on Wikis and Open Collaboration* (2011), ACM, pp. 163–172.
9. JOORDENS, S. Using wikipedia in a mega classroom: A 1,700 student case study. Wikipedia Symposium, 2012.
10. KITTUR, A., SUH, B., PENDELTON, B. A., AND CHI, E. H. He says, she says: Conflict and coordination in wikipedia. In *CM Conference on Human Factors in Computing Systems* (2007), ACM Press, pp. 453–462.
11. LAMPE, C., OBAR, J., OZKAYA, E., ZUBE, P., AND VELASQUEZ, A. Classroom wikipedia participation effects on future intentions to contribute. In *Proceedings of International Conference on Computer Supported Collaborative Work* (2012), pp. 403–406.
12. ROTH, A. Student contributions to wikipedia. Tech. rep., Wikimedia Foundation, 2011.
13. SAKS, A. M., UGGERSLEV, K. L., AND FASSINA, N. E. Socialization tactics and newcomer adjustment: A meta-analytic review and test of a model. *Journal of Vocational Behavior 70* (2007), 413–446.
14. WIGGINS, A., AND CROWSTON, K. From conversation to crowsourcing: A typology of citizen science. In *Proceedings of the 44th Hawaii International Conference on System Sciences* (2011).
15. ZHU, H., KRAUT, R., AND KITTU, A. Effectiveness of shared leadership in online communities. In *Proceedings of the ACM 2012 conference on Computer Supported Cooperative Work* (2012), ACM, pp. 407–416.

TypeRighting: Combining the Benefits of Handwriting and Typeface in Online Educational Videos

Andrew Cross[1*], Mydhili Bayyapunedi[1], Edward Cutrell[1], Anant Agarwal[2], and William Thies[1]

[1] Microsoft Research India [2] edX *Corresponding author: t-across@microsoft.com

ABSTRACT

Recent years have seen enormous growth of online educational videos, spanning K-12 tutorials to university lectures. As this content has grown, so too has grown the number of presentation styles. Some educators have strong allegiance to handwritten recordings (using pen and tablet), while others use only typed (PowerPoint) presentations. In this paper, we present the first systematic comparison of these two presentation styles and how they are perceived by viewers. Surveys on edX and Mechanical Turk suggest that users enjoy handwriting because it is personal and engaging, yet they also enjoy typeface because it is clear and legible. Based on these observations, we propose a new presentation style, TypeRighting, that combines the benefits of handwriting and typeface. Each phrase is written by hand, but fades into typeface soon after it appears. Our surveys suggest that about 80% of respondents prefer TypeRighting over handwriting. The same fraction of respondents prefer TypeRighting over typeface, for videos in which the handwriting is sufficiently legible.

Author Keywords

Online education; massive open online course; handwriting

ACM Classification Keywords

K.3. Computers and Education

INTRODUCTION

While educational technology has been an active area of research for decades, currently we are witnessing an unprecedented surge in the amount of course content that is available online. Initiatives such as Coursera, Udacity, and edX are collectively offering over 250 "massive open online courses", enabling online audiences to learn from top university professors for free. Meanwhile, the Khan Academy has logged over 225 million views of free video lessons, mostly targeted at K-12 learners.

Despite the momentum surrounding online education, to date there has not been consensus on one of the most basic questions: what is the best format for a video lecture? Sites such as the Khan Academy and edX rely mainly on handwritten tutorials, produced using a digital pen and tablet, with an audio voice-over from the lecturer. In contrast, Coursera content is typically structured around typed (PowerPoint) presentations, sometimes with pen annotations, and often with a visual view of the lecturer. Udacity content is mostly handwritten, and includes a semi-transparent view of the lecturer's hands. Content from NPTEL, a collection of 136 video courses from top universities in India, includes a mix of handwritten and typed content.

Figure 1: TypeRighting example. Typeface fades in to replace each handwritten phrase soon after it is drawn[1].

The first goal of this paper is to understand the benefits and drawbacks of handwritten tutorials versus typed presentations for online educational videos. We conduct such a comparison using three videos drawn from edX and the Khan Academy, and opinions gathered from almost 150 survey respondents on edX and Mechanical Turk. Our results are mixed: sometimes handwriting is preferred for its personal and engaging style, but sometimes typeface is preferred for its clarity and legibility. Our first contribution is demonstrating this variation of opinion – both across respondents and across videos – suggesting that neither handwriting nor typeface is the best solution for all cases.

Building on these observations, our second contribution is to define and evaluate a new style of presentation, TypeRighting, that combines the benefits of handwriting and typeface. The idea behind TypeRighting is simple: words are handwritten by the lecturer, but soon after they appear, they morph into typeface (see Figure 1). This video style preserves the personality and engagement of handwriting, while also enabling a legible display as soon as each handwritten phrase is fully drawn. We evaluate TypeRighting via surveys on edX and Mechanical Turk. Results show that about 80% of respondents prefer TypeRighting to the handwritten videos, and the same fraction prefers TypeRighting to typeface when the handwriting is of sufficient quality. While this study is exploratory in nature, we conclude that TypeRighting is a promising video style for online educational content.

CHI 2013, April 27 – May 2, 2013, Paris, France.

[1] Please see http://www.youtube.com/watch?v=RCihSaGX0WE for a video example of TypeRighting.

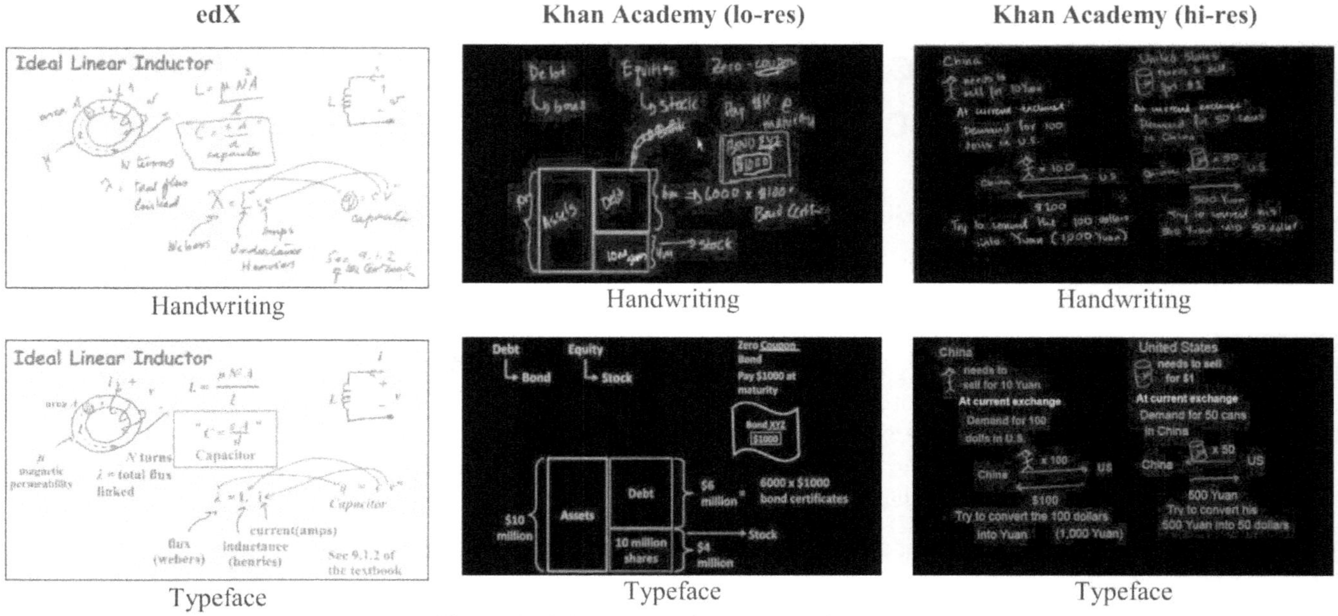

Figure 2: Videos used in the experiments.

RELATED WORK

Prior work has considered student preferences in classroom lectures, comparing PowerPoint slides with writing on a chalkboard, whiteboard, or overhead projector. Studies consistently show students' overall preference for PowerPoint slides, when used appropriately, citing benefits such as improved organization of the lecture, improved legibility compared to handwritten notes, and availability of slides before and after class [3,5,8]. These results may or may not extend to the online scenario, as classroom lectures retain personal interactions between lecturers and students; in the online context, handwriting may help to preserve this personal connection more than PowerPoint slides.

Other studies on multimedia use in learning have shown that blending PowerPoint slides with ad-hoc handwritten notes offers similar benefits [1,7]. Extensive research has been done on best practices for multimedia e-learning, adding the caveat that lecturers must be aware of the cognitive load put on viewers by multimedia presentations [6]. These works emphasize using multimedia in a way that is clear, emphasizes key points, and avoids excessive or distracting content or animations.

HANDWRITING VS. TYPEFACE

The goal of our first experiment is to assess preferences for handwriting versus typeface in online educational videos. The "handwritten" condition corresponds to videos recorded using a digital pen and tablet, as is customary on popular sites such as the Khan Academy. The "typeface" condition represents animated text and graphics, as is often produced using PowerPoint. Our goal is to assess only the viewer's preference for each of these alternatives. While the ultimate aim is to improve learning outcomes, an important prerequisite to learning is retaining the viewers' attention and interest in the video – something that vitally depends on understanding and satisfying their viewing preferences.

Videos

We selected three videos for the study (see Figure 2). The first video is drawn from edX, and explains the concept of an inductor. The second and third videos are drawn from the Khan Academy; one explains the difference between stocks and bonds, while the other explains the effect of trade imbalances on exchange rates. After shortening one of the videos slightly, all are between 7 and 10 minutes long.

The handwritten videos have varying visual quality, reflecting differences in handwriting, resolution, and overall style. In particular, we deliberately selected Khan Academy videos with different resolutions: one is 240p (an older video) and one is 360p (a recent video). To quantify the differences in visual quality, we ran an experiment on Turk (a methodology that has been validated on similar tasks [4]). We asked 50 workers to rate the "quality and clarity" of a still frame from each video on a scale from 1 to 10. The results confirm that the high-resolution Khan Academy video is perceived as having higher visual quality (6.9/10) than the low-resolution Khan Academy video (5.0/10) or the edX video (5.2/10). The difference is significant between the high-resolution Khan Academy video and each of the others (vs. low-res Khan Academy, $t(49)=-5.65$, $p<0.001$; vs. edX, $t(49)=-6.39$, $p<0.001$). The difference observed between the low-resolution Khan Academy video and the edX video is not significant ($t(49)=0.80$, $p=0.43$).

Using the handwritten videos as templates, we used PowerPoint to manually construct videos utilizing typeface in place of handwriting. Each typed phrase appeared independently, in sync with the audio track from the original video. While the typeface videos preserve the overall visual style and color scheme of the handwritten videos, we made minor adjustments to the arrangement of text and drawings. Adjusting the layout is a natural affordance and benefit of using typed slides.

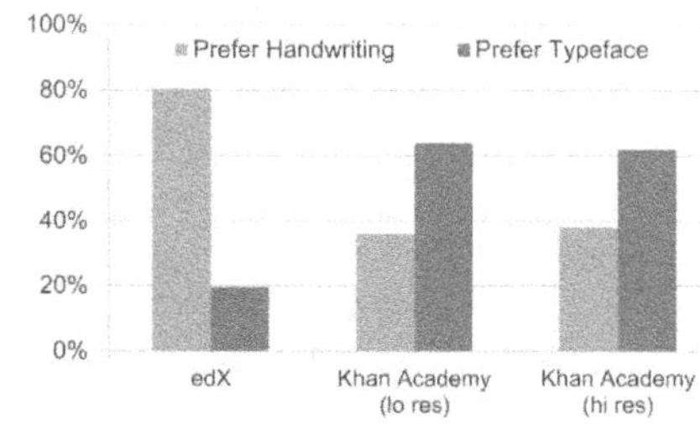

Figure 3: Preferences for Handwriting vs. Typeface

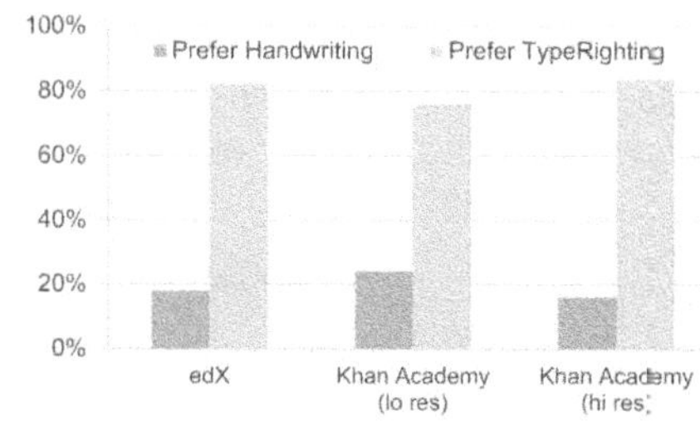

Figure 4: Preferences for Handwriting vs. TypeRighting

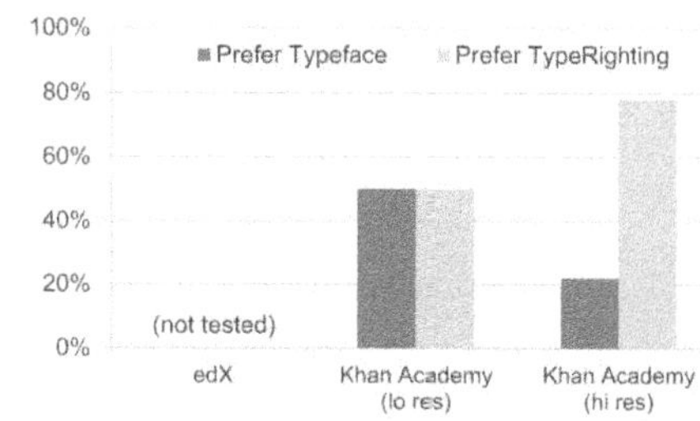

Figure 5: Preferences for Typeface vs. TypeRighting

Participants

We drew participants from different sources, depending on the source of the video. For the edX video, we posted a survey (with permission) in the edX discussion forum. The survey linked to both videos and asked respondents to indicate which video they preferred, and why. We received 46 responses, and 4,000 words of comments in the forum.

To evaluate the Khan Academy videos, we utilized MTurk to recruit participants. Turkers may have some similarity to viewers of online educational videos: they are young, have access to computers, have some free time, and are arguably aspiring to 'better themselves' via education or income generation. We ensured that Turkers were attentive to the video (something that was not ensured for edX participants) by promising a monetary bonus ($0.10 on top of the $0.25 payment for the task) if they passed a short quiz, to appear following the video. Also, to make it easy for participants to evaluate both designs, we provided a "toggle" button that switched between handwriting and typeface in real-time, as the video played. Participants could toggle between the video styles at any time, as often as they wanted.

We included Turk participants in our analysis if they watched at least 30 seconds of each video. We ran the experiment until we collected 50 such responses. Because Turkers from the United States and India can display systematic differences in their responses [1], we ensured that the proportion from each country stayed constant across trials. The proportion enforced came from the results of our first trial: 15 from the U.S. and 35 from India. Final respondents had an average age of 29, and 57% were male.

Results

Results of the experiment appear in Figure 3. For the edX video, 80% of respondents preferred handwriting. However, for the Khan Academy videos, the majority (about 63%) preferred typeface, and this preference was almost identical across the two videos. The preferences are significantly different from even proportions: for edX (binomial test, $p<0.001$) and for the Khan Academy videos, combined (binomial test, $p<0.01$). Preferences did not have significant correlation with gender, age, or country of residence.

Those who preferred handwriting described it as "more personal", "more natural", and "more engaging". They also noted that the cursor (not visible in the typeface version) helped them to follow the current point of interest on the slide. The most up-voted comment on the edX forum wrote, "It reminds me of blackboards... written materials have more personality." A Turker also commented, "The handwriting kept my attention. It felt more authentic. I felt as if I was in a class and it made it more 'fun'".

Those who preferred typeface commented that it was clearer, neater, and easier to read. Some wrote that typeface can be especially helpful for symbols, such as *u* vs *v*, *O(n)* vs *o(n)*, and subscripts / superscripts. The most up-voted edX comment in favor of typeface was, "I much prefer the cleaner PowerPoint text as one of my complaints has been the messy scriblings in the videos." A Turker wrote, "I am a longtime follower of Khan Academy videos and have always been bothered by the handwriting aspect. The typeface version looks much neater and more professional."

Discussion

Our conclusion from this experiment is that there is varying preference for handwriting and typeface in online educational videos. While this might seem like an inconclusive result, it provides important context for our primary contribution, which comes in the next section.

Why did the edX experiment show a preference for handwriting, while the Khan Academy experiment showed a preference for typeface? We can only speculate. It seems that handwriting and/or resolution are not responsible for this difference, as our study of visual quality shows that the handwritten edX video is amongst the pair of lower-quality videos. Moreover, despite significant differences in visual quality, the two Khan Academy videos led to a similar preference for typeface over handwriting. There are several differences between the edX experiment and the Khan experiment that could explain the results, including the lecturer. One edX respondent favored handwriting because they "would not wish to diminish the experience of receiving personal tutorial with Prof. Agrawal".

In addition, an important observation grew out of the edX survey: participants do prefer typeface to handwriting for review of lecture materials. In the words of one respondent, "I like the handwriting when watching the lecture videos. But when I go back to review the lectures I have trouble reading the notes again because there is scribble everywhere." To quantify this sentiment, we augmented our survey with a second question, asking whether handwriting or typeface is preferred for reference notes. Out of 44 responses, 64% indicated a preference for typeface, while 27% preferred handwriting, and 9% were indifferent.

This result led us to the question: is it possible to combine the benefits of handwriting (during the presentation) with the benefits of typeface (for the sake of review)? To use the words of an edX respondent, "It would be nice if the handwritten presentation of the lectures could be somehow combined with the clearer lecture notes for reviewing."

COMBINING HANDWRITING AND TYPEFACE

To combine the benefits of handwriting and typeface, we propose TypeRighting: a style of visual presentation in which each handwritten phrase is replaced by typeface soon after it appears. This simple concept is illustrated in Figure 1. TypeRighting preserves the engaging and personal style of handwriting, as the animation of pen strokes remains the same. However, when a handwritten phrase is fully written, its static image is replaced by typeface, thereby enhancing legibility for the remainder of the video.

To evaluate TypeRighting, we followed the same methodologies described previously. We manually constructed videos in the TypeRighting style by embedding the handwritten videos in PowerPoint and drawing typeface animations as overlays. We posted surveys on edX and MTurk, asking participants to compare either: (i) the TypeRighting video to the handwritten video, or (ii) the TypeRighting video to the typeface video. The second test was done on MTurk only, due to time constraints. The edX survey drew 28 responses (and 2,000 words of comments), and each task on Turk was completed by 50 workers. The parameters of the tasks, including the balance between India and the U.S., were the same as before.

As shown in Figure 4, TypeRighting is consistently preferred to handwriting by a wide margin, even in the case (edX) where typeface is not preferred. Overall, 80% of participants prefer TypeRighting to the handwritten version.

Comments received in support of TypeRighting mirrored our expectations of combining the benefits of handwriting and typeface. One participant wrote, "It had a personal touch, but still was easy to read and comprehend." Another commented, "Things that were not clear became clear in this mode. There I had to strain my eyes to understand but the moment it became bold, it was so clear." Overall, TypeRighting was said to preserve the most beneficial aspects of handwriting, notably the authentic feeling of a classroom lecture, the engaging aspect of visuals changing with the narration, and the helpful visualization of the lecturer's cursor to focus attention.

The small minority of respondents who favored handwriting over TypeRighting sometimes found the transition to typeface to be distracting. A respondent on edX wrote, "I found myself slightly distracted waiting for the transition." However, this respondent and others noted that TypeRighting might feel more natural over time: "I think that issue would resolve after the novelty wears off."

With respect to TypeRighting versus typeface, the results (Figure 5) depend on the video. For the high-resolution video, 78% of respondents prefer TypeRighting. However, for the low-resolution video, only 50% of participants preferred TypeRighting. We believe this difference is due to the low quality of handwriting in the low-resolution video. Several participants wrote that the handwriting did more harm than good in the low-resolution case, e.g., "The handwriting was too messy and unreadable, so it might as well just be skipped." Our conclusion is that TypeRighting offers benefits over both handwriting and typeface, so long as the handwriting is of sufficient visual quality.

CONCLUSIONS

Despite the burgeoning usage of online educational videos, there has been little study of how best to present lessons in video format. This paper helps to fill this gap by conducting a methodical comparison of handwriting versus typeface in educational videos. Our first contribution is to demonstrate that these formats are preferred at different times, and for different reasons: handwriting is personal and engaging, of particular value during the lecture, while typeface is clear and legible, of particular value during review.

Our second contribution is a novel presentation style, TypeRighting, that combines handwriting and typeface while preserving the benefits of each. Our experiments show that TypeRighting is highly preferred over handwriting, even in cases where typeface alone is not preferred. Our results on Khan Academy videos suggest that 80% of lessons delivered – a sum of 180 million to date – would have been improved via adoption of TypeRighting.

This exploratory paper has some limitations that will be important to address in future work. We evaluated only a small number of videos (and limited subject matter) and used audio tracks from handwritten videos, which likely have different pauses in speech, etc., than audio from a slide-based lecture. Also, all videos in TypeRighting format were constructed manually by the authors. In ongoing research, we are developing new ways to simplify construction of videos in this format. Just as video subtitles are often provided by volunteers, we believe that typeface annotations can be quickly generated by the crowd.

REFERENCES

1. Andreson, R. et al. A Study of Digital Ink in Lecture Presentation. *CHI*, (2004).
2. Antin, J. and Shaw, A. Social desirability bias and self-reports of motivation: a study of Amazon Mechanical Turk in the US and India. *CHI*, (2012).
3. Apperson. The Impact of Presentation Graphics on Students' Experience in the Classroom. *Computers and Education 47*, 1 (2006).
4. Heer, J. and Bostick, M. Crowdsourcing Graphical Perception: Using Mechanical Turk to Assess Visualization Design. *CHI*, (2010).
5. Levasseur, D.G. and Kanan Sawyer, J. Pedagogy Meets PowerPoint: A Research Review of the Effects of Computer-Generated Slides in the Classroom. *Review of Comm. 6*, (2006).
6. Mayer, R. and Moreno, R. Nine Ways to Reduce Cognitive Load in Multimedia Learning. *Educational Psychologist, 38(1)*, (2003), 43-52.
7. Mock, K. Teaching with Tablet PC's. *J. Com. Sci. in Colleges*, (2004).
8. Seth, V. PowerPoint or chalk and talk: Perceptions of medical students versus dental students in a medical college in India. *Advances in Medical Education and Practice*, (2010), 11.

Tweeting for Class: Co-Construction as a Means for Engaging Students in Lectures

Jeremy Birnholtz
Communication Studies Dept.
Northwestern University
Evanston IL 60208
jeremyb@northwestern.edu

Jeff Hancock
Depts. of Communication and Information Science
Cornell University
Ithaca, NY 14853
jeff.hancock@cornell.edu

Daniela Retelny
Dept. of Management Science & Engineering
Stanford University
Palo Alto, CA 94305-4121
dretelny@stanford.edu

ABSTRACT
Motivating students to be active learners is a perennial problem in education, and is particularly challenging in lectures where instructors typically prepare content in advance with little direct student participation. We describe our experience using Twitter as a tool for student "co-construction" of lecture materials. Students were required to post a tweet prior to each lecture related to that day's topic, and these tweets – consisting of questions, examples and reflections – were incorporated into the lecture slides and notes. Students reported that they found lectures including their tweets in the class slides to be engaging, interactive and relevant, and nearly 90% of them recommended we use our co-construction approach again.

Author Keywords
Education; Twitter; Engagement; Lecture; Co-construction.

ACM Classification Keywords
H.5.3 Group and Organization Interfaces

INTRODUCTION & BACKGROUND
Today's undergraduates – members of the "millennial generation" – are particularly motivated by opportunities to customize their experiences with media, consumer products, and learning [10]. As such, engaging and motivating undergraduates can be difficult in traditional lecture formats [1], where there may be few opportunities for direct customization, especially when slides and materials are reused from year to year. This becomes even more challenging as novel courses, such as the recent boom in Massively Open Online Courses (MOOC) (e.g., [5]), expand the traditional classroom to include audiences of thousands.

Student engagement is defined as the level of energy students devote to in-class and out-of-class activities linked to desired outcomes, and has been shown to be a key factor in learning [6]. According to connectivist theories of learning (e.g., [9]) that underlie many online courses such as MOOCs, learning is best enabled by allowing students to pose questions, share ideas and discover connections between concepts.

CHI 2013, April 27 – May 2, 2013, Paris, France.

In addition to MOOCs that are exclusively or primarily online, there has been substantial research on using social media tools (e.g., clickers, online discussion forums, blogs, Facebook groups and chat rooms) to increase opportunities for student engagement in traditional classes [2, 3, 8].

Clickers, for example, allow students to respond to instructor-posed questions during class. These give the instructor substantial control, but only permit sharing aggregated student responses with the entire class. A wiki-like approach to course construction, on the other hand, motivates students outside of class and allows them to contribute, but may be less appropriate for classes where certain content or ideas must be covered as a foundation for later coursework.

Blogs or other long-format online forums are a common hybrid and allow students to present their own ideas and content. However, integrating these into classroom discussion can be difficult for instructors due to constraints on time and space in formal lectures and presentations.

Microblogging sites (e.g., Twitter), facilitate a unique hybrid, which we conceptualize as *"co-construction."* The goal in co-construction is to facilitate direct student engagement with each other and the content [9], but also allow for editorial control by the instructor and incorporation of students' contributions in a traditional lecture.

Twitter works well for this because it constrains messages to 140 characters and compiles them into one feed, which allows for public, continuous and real-time conversation [4]. Short student contributions can be quickly read by instructors and easily incorporated into lecture materials such as slides. Twitter is also easily accessible and widely used, so experience with it is a practical skill. Previously, Twitter has been used in teaching contexts to enable backchannel discussions during class, deliver reminders and announcements, stimulate discussions, and increase interaction opportunities [3, 4].

For our course, a 150-student undergraduate lecture that two of us teach (in alternating years), we used Twitter for what [7] refers to as meta-cognitive and reflective activities, such as articulating difficulties or applying key concepts. We developed a teaching model that integrated Twitter in a particular type of "co-construction" of lectures. We had three goals, related to student engagement: 1) make lectures more relevant to students by incorporating questions and examples, 2) improve student preparation for class by motivating reading and thinking outside the classroom, and 3) provide new ways to participate via customizing slides.

To accomplish these goals, we had students post tweets prior to each class that were related to that day's topic. We then integrated these directly into the lecture slides and materials. Importantly, we used Twitter alongside assessment tools such as exams and homework essays. We report here on Twitter, but note that it was not the only way students interacted with the material and each other.

METHOD

Research Context: How We Used Twitter

Our course is a 150-student lecture on communication technology at a large university in the northeast United States. The course primarily draws students majoring in Communication and Information Science, plus a range of students from other majors. Students typically are assigned to read one book chapter or empirical study prior to each lecture, and this reading is the focus of lecture.

By midnight on the night before each lecture (i.e., twice weekly), students had to submit one tweet related to the day's assigned reading. It could be an observation, reflection, question, or anything they deemed on-topic.

Tweets were submitted from course-specific Twitter accounts set up by each student. This simplified access to tweets for us and preserved student privacy. To collect student tweets, we set up a separate Twitter account that compiled the tweets in one public feed using GroupTweet, an application which retweets all tweets sent to the class account and made them visible to all students in the class.

After the deadline, one teaching assistant created a "Tweet Report," which was sent to the instructors. This contained all of that day's tweets, a Wordle visualization of all words used in the tweets (sized according to use frequency, see Figure 2), and a curated set of tweets illustrating common themes, key concepts, and questions or points of confusion.

Before class, the professor used the Tweet Report in assembling the day's lecture slides, including content directly from the tweets. The tweets helped us in three key ways: 1) "troubleshooting" student understanding, 2) illustrating key concepts, and 3) including student questions. Tweets appeared in a colored rectangle (Figure 1) to distinguish them from instructor-generated content.

Identifying information has been removed from tweets in this paper, but those used in class usually had students' usernames attached to them unless it could embarrass the student publicly (i.e., if it revealed a misunderstanding).

Research Methods

We base this paper on our experience in teaching this course three times, responses to a questionnaire at the end of 2009 and 2010, and content coding of tweets from all three years. The questionnaire had 42 items about student experiences with Twitter, using it for class, and perceptions of its effects. Items most relevant to our research goals here are shown in Table 1, with other items measuring factors not discussed here directly. Scales had not been formally validated, but accurately reflected informal feedback we received from students and was consistent from year to year. Most items used 5-point Likert scales anchored by "strongly agree" (5) and "strongly disagree" (1). There were also free-response items inviting general comments. Students received 1 extra credit point for completing the questionnaire. To avoid possible positive response bias, they were told (truthfully) that data would not be analyzed until grades were submitted. 173 students (of 180 enrolled, 86 Female) completed the 2009 questionnaire, and 111 (of 137 enrolled, 61 female) in 2010.

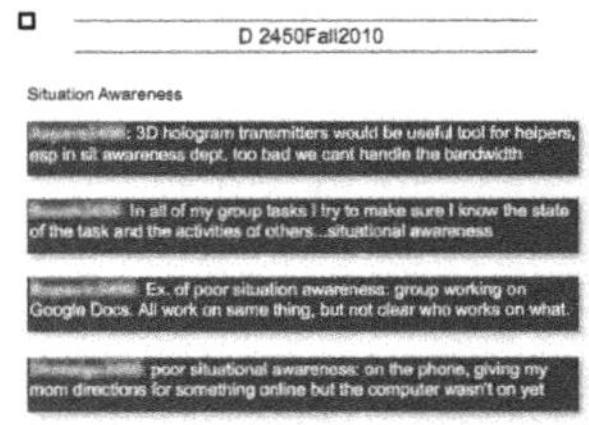

Figure 1. Slide with Tweets

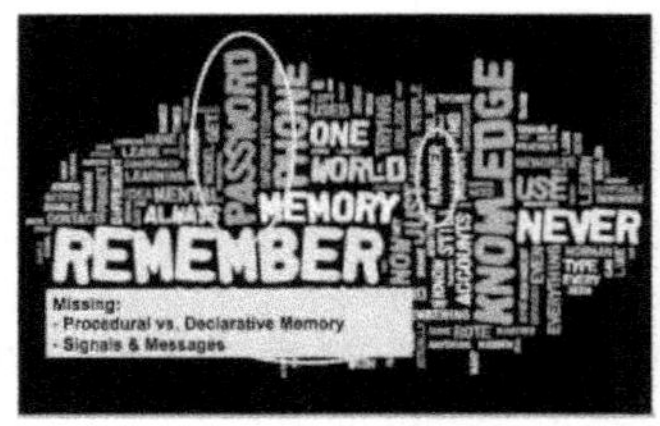

Figure 2. Wordle visualization

Content coding of tweets from all years was done in summer 2012. The data set included 9180 tweets (3657 from 2009, 2456 from 2010 and 3067 from 2011, with enrollment accounting for variance). Three coders coded the tweets, with each tweet coded by two of the coders. Coders iterated on subsets of tweets until agreement was better than 80%. Coding categories included: examples/applications of concepts, questions, comments on the reading content (without application or questions), comments on the course structure/logistics, comments directed at other students (i.e., '@ replies'), jocular comments intended purely for humor, and those that did not fall into one of these categories.

RESULTS

On the whole, students were enthusiastic about co-construction via Twitter. When asked if they recommended future Twitter use , 93% (2009) and 86% (2010) approved.

Making Lecture More Relevant and Interesting

Our first goal was to make lectures more interesting and relevant, ideally also helping students understand course concepts. We measured this in several ways.

	2009 (N=175)			2010 (N=111)		
	Disagree	**Neutral**	**Agree**	**Disagree**	**Neutral**	**Agree**
I enjoyed seeing my own and classmates tweets	5%	6%	89%	5%	4%	91%
Tweets made class more interactive	6%	9%	85%	6%	9%	85%
Answering tweeted questions was helpful	4%	7%	89%	5%	8%	86%
Examples in tweets helped me grasp concepts	3%	15%	81%	9%	12%	79%
Overall I enjoyed discussion of tweets	5%	10%	85%	9%	9%	82%

Table 1. Questionnaire results (full scales compressed to 3 categories)

First, 81% of students in 2009 and 79% in 2010 felt that our incorporation of examples and explanation from the tweets helped them grasp course concepts (see Table 1). We also examined their free-response comments. Many appreciated the perspectives of their fellow students, feeling their peers offered insights on understanding a difficult theory:

> Really was a tool to explain what the readings were saying. The class tweets that were put up helped make a complicated theory more clear and to the point.

This student said tweets raised issues she hadn't considered:

> Other people would bring up problems or examples that I hadn't recognized, which would help me get a better grasp of the material.

Second, this comment reflects that in most tweets (2009: 57%; 2010: 68.6%; 2011: 62.6%), students applied course concepts to examples from their lives. This got them thinking about how to apply concepts, and enabled us to use examples that were likely to be relevant to students.

Twitter also commanded student attention during lecture, particularly as they watched for the appearance of their own and others' tweets: 92% of 2010 and 89% of 2009 students reported that they enjoyed seeing their own contribution to lecture materials. We also observed students quietly cheering or taking photos of their tweets when they appeared on the slides. As one student noted:

> The best thing about tweeting was seeing your own tweets in class. It made you feel famous.

Students also reported that tweets helped make the lecture slides more understandable as they studied for exams.

Improving Preparation and Non-Classroom Time

Our next goal was to improve use of non-classroom time. To understand how our co-construction technique affected this goal, we examined student comments about their tweeting behavior. In terms of improving preparation for lecture, many students reported that one of the strengths of Twitter was that it encouraged them to keep up with readings and engage with the material actively. As this student notes:

> Tweeting really made me keep up with the reading. Made me not just read passively, but actively think about it enough to be able to tweet.

Many others appreciated that it was a low-effort assignment that motivated them to understand some of the material:

> Quick assignment that is not difficult and motivates me to understand at least one of the concepts before each lecture so that I can tweet about it.

This was reflected in the tweets themselves, as the majority were examples of class concepts. An additional fraction (2009: 27.1%; 2010: 20.4%; 2011: 21.3%) were related to readings, but did not include examples. Some students said, however, that reading with an eye toward tweeting sometimes meant not focusing on the entire article:

> Sometimes I would focus on what I would tweet about more than the reading. Once I found an interesting topic to tweet it was hard to stay focused and finish reading the whole article.

In terms of getting students to think about the material, their tweets clearly indicate that they were applying course concepts to their experiences. Here, a student discusses her Facebook ("fb") behavior in terms of the impression formation research covered that week in class:

> *i hate to admit that I "fb stalk" but now everyone makes judgments off of fb profiles (doesn't matter if I've met you yet).*

Another talks about the downfalls of communicating with reduced contextual cues, an important concept covered in the class:

> *I have gotten into unnecessary little fights with friends over taking something that was texted the wrong way.*

Other examples were extremely concise, but indicated clearly that students understood and had thought about a concept, as in this student's brief tweet on "critical mass:"

> *RIP GOOGLE WAVE #criticalmassproblem*

Providing New Ways for Students to Participate

Our third goal in experimenting with Twitter was to enable new ways for students and faculty to interact. On the whole, students took advantage of and appreciated this opportunity, as the vast majority of tweets were deemed relevant to the course (2009: 98.5%; 2010: 98.3%; 2011: 97.7%).

Participation occurred in three ways: direct questions for the instructor, instructor reading of student tweets, and student suggestions about the course.

As Table 1 shows, 85% (both years) of students felt incorporating tweets made class more interactive; and 86% (2010) and 89% (2009) of students felt featuring and answering Twitter questions in class was helpful. Student comments also reflect this, as indicated by this student:

> The best thing about tweeting was being able to ask questions in a huge class. In most lectures that are as large as <course>, individual concerns/opinions are not heard, and tweets really enabled us to interact with one another and <instructor> in a more intimate way than one would expect for such a large lecture.

Despite these positive perceptions, however, a relatively small fraction of tweets were questions (2009: 12.8%; 2010: 7.4%; 2011: 10.6%). Still, even with the 140-character limit, students were able to ask substantive questions, as in this case about deindividuation effects:

> *Are the depersonalization and deindividuation effects measured by degree? It seems like it would depend on the CMC medium.*

There was also some limited evidence of students interacting with each other. Interestingly, this increased substantially over time. In 2009 and 2010, student-directed tweets consisted of 0.4 and 0.5% of tweets, respectively. In 2011, this increased to 2.1%. While still a small fraction, this is a substantial increase; possibly due to increased student familiarity with Twitter conventions.

This was also reflected in student feedback. One student appreciated the ability to interact simultaneously with peers and the instructor:

> Tweeting allowed us to talk about our questions with the material, while notifying the professor at the same time. It allowed us to really get into it.

The key point here is that students used Twitter as a way to interact with each other as well as instructors.

The second way that Twitter enabled novel student-instructor interactions was that instructors could use the content of tweets to assess student (mis)understanding. Some tweets in the example/application category allowed us to see cases where students believed they understood the material, but were actually misinterpreting it. These misunderstandings traditionally wouldn't surface until after homework or exams are graded. In these cases we could display the tweet anonymously and clarify the concept.

A third mode of participation involved students providing feedback about course details on a much more regular basis than is enabled by typical end-of-term feedback. This was a very small number of tweets proportionally (2009: 1.1%; 2010: 1.5%; 2011: 1.2%), but the suggestions were helpful. Some students, for example, thought the text was outdated:

> *another example of how dated the book is-"there won't be any film, just videotape"...or now DVDs and blu ray?*

Finally, the Wordle provided a way for the class to interact in the aggregate with the instructors. It provided a concise visual snapshot of what students were thinking as they tweeted, and importantly, what they were avoiding (see Figure 2). In these cases, we could open the lecture by asking "Does anybody notice anything missing from today's Wordle?" and then discuss why a concept or topic was absent, often because it was poorly explained in the readings. In some ways, this is similar to using clickers, but the Wordle provided a more diverse range of responses.

DISCUSSION

First, we note that students were enthusiastic about using Twitter and having a role in co-constructing the lecture. In their own words, this motivated them in preparing for and during class, and also led to perceptions of better understanding and inclusion of more relevant material. Thus, our goal of improving engagement was realized.

Twitter provided an infrastructure for sending, receiving and aggregating short messages that were easy for the instructors and TAs to read quickly and incorporate into lecture. In this way, the 140-character limit was critical. While students were sometimes frustrated by this limit, we feel that the large number of effective tweets is testament that this was not a debilitating constraint. At the same time, one would need other ways to engage students for more difficult questions or exploration of concepts.

In addition to allowing for more direct involvement, tweets also provided us with another avenue for assessing student understanding of the content. We found this to be helpful in tailoring content to the students' specific needs, and in being able to do so prior to the start of a class period.

We also found that Twitter was not very effective at getting students to interact with each other. This is likely the partial result of an incentive scheme requiring only one tweet per lecture and the clear desirability of having one's tweet selected by the instructor for the day's slides. These parameters could be experimented with to encourage more interaction among students in future work.

Another limitation to this work is that co-construction as presented here was effortful, as tweets had to be manually parsed. This clearly would not scale directly to a MOOC scenario. We believe, however, that a combination of automated text analysis and letting students read and rate others' tweets would allow scaling and provide a useful way to engage a large population of lecture participants.

In interpreting our results, it is also important to consider that our design relies on self-reported data and had no control case for experimentally assessing impact on student performance. This would be useful in future work.

ACKNOWLEDGMENTS

We thank Catherine Ho, Amanda Klopp, and Patrice Lawless for their analysis assistance, and the undergraduate and graduate teaching assistants for our course.

REFERENCES

1. Astin, A. Student involvement: a developmental theory for higher education. *Journal of College Student Personnel*, 25(1984), 297-308.
2. Chen, P. S. D., Lambert, A. D. and Guidry, K. R. Engaging online learners: the impact of web-based learning technology on college student engagement. *Computers & Education*, 55(2010), 92-100.
3. Ebner, M., Lienhardt, C., Rohs, M. and Meyer, I. Microblogs in higher education – a chance to facilitate informal and process-oriented learning. *Computers & Education*, 55(2010), 92-100.
4. Junco, R., Heiberger, G. and Loken, E. The effect of Twitter on college student engagement and grades. *J. of Computer Assisted Learning*, 27(2011), 119-132.
5. Lewin, T. *Instruction for masses knocks down campus walls. New York Times*, March 5, 2012, p. A11.
6. Pascarella, E. T. and Terenzini, P. T. *How College Affects Students: A Third Decade of Research*. Josey-Bass, San Francisco, CA, 2005.
7. Sample, M. A Framework for Teaching with Twitter. *Chronicle of Higher Education*, 2010.
8. Schroeder, A., Minocha, S. and Schneider, C. The strengths, weaknesses, opportunities, and threats of using social software in higher and further education teaching and learning. *Journal of Computer Assisted Learning*, 26(2010), 159-174.
9. Siemens, G. Connectivism: A learning theory for the digital age. *International Journal of Instructional Technology and Distance Learning*, 2, 1 (2005).
10. Tapscott, D. *Grown up digital: How the net generation is changing your world.* McGraw-Hill, 2009.

Delivering Patients to Sacré Coeur: Collective Intelligence in Digital Volunteer Communities

Kate Starbird
Department of Human Centered Design & Engineering
University of Washington
kstarbi@uw.edu

ABSTRACT
This study examines the information-processing activities of digital volunteers and other connected ICT users in the wake of crisis events. Synthesizing findings from several previous research studies of digital volunteerism, this paper offers a new approach for conceptualizing the activities of digital volunteers, shifting from a focus on organizing to a focus on information movement. Using the lens of distributed cognition, this research describes collective intelligence as transformations of information within a system where cognition is distributed socially across individuals as well as through their tools and resources. This paper demonstrates how digital volunteers, through activities such as relaying, amplifying, verifying, and structuring information, function as a collectively intelligent cognitive system in the wake of disaster events.

Author Keywords
Crisis informatics; collective intelligence; distributed cognition; crowdsourcing

ACM Classification Keywords
H.5.3 [Groups & Organization Interfaces]: Collaborative Computing, Computer-Supported Cooperative Work; K.4.2 [Social Issues].

INTRODUCTION

Bringing Patients to Hôpital Sacré Coeur
On January 12, 2010, a 7.0 earthquake struck Haiti, causing catastrophic damage and leaving in its wake great humanitarian need. In the days after the earthquake, over 300,000 injured people required medical care, a concern made logistically complex by widespread destruction to the country's infrastructure [19,23]. The epicenter of the earthquake was in southern Haiti, near the town Léogâne, and consequently the greatest need resided in the southern regions of the country where many hospitals were either destroyed or seriously damaged [19]. Mobile clinics and field hospitals were quickly established near the most affected areas [19,23], but medical teams there struggled to keep up with the volume of injured patients [24].

CHI 2013, April 27–May 2, 2013, Paris, France.

Meanwhile, in the far north of the country in Milot, about 120km from Port-Au-Prince, the Hôpital Sacré Coeur suffered mild damage, but remained fully functional. In the first few days after the quake, while injured people awaited care in other parts of the country, Sacré Coeur had capacity—74 empty beds, a medical staff on hand with more on the way, and two helipads for receiving patients by air—but no patients (personal communication, Tim Traynor). Traynor, Onsite Coordinator at the Center for the Rural Development of Milot (CRUDEM), the organization that runs Sacré Coeur, reports that the hospital tried to communicate with response agencies that it could accept and treat patients, but representatives of the large NGOs who did assess their facility determined that it was too small and too far away to meet their needs.

Believing that their hospital could help people awaiting treatment for in some cases life-threatening injuries, Sacré Coeur staff and volunteers turned to the Internet to get the word out about their facility. On January 13, they posted to their website that the hospital was open, functional, staffed, and ready for patients. Hospital representatives also turned to email, social media, and mainstream media to spread their message. Soon, other social media users, some of them *digital volunteers,* began to help promote their cause. A CRUDEM Facebook post explains what happened next:

> *Then, through a chain of social networking correspondences, board member Sarah Kane made an online introduction to a Coast Guard commander stationed off Haiti. [They] answered the call for assistance and began the transport of patients from Port au Prince to Milot.*

Soon, patients began to stream in, including many airlifted by the US Coast Guard (USCG). On January 16, they received four patients. By the afternoon of January 18, occupancy had increased to nearly 30, and the next day 44 patients were airlifted to their hospital. They were quickly compelled to expand their capacity to accommodate increasing numbers of patients. Eventually, Sacré Coeur performed over 200 amputations for injuries suffered during the quake and treated more than 800 patients (personal communication, Traynor). Traynor claims that this would not have been possible—that his hospital would not have been able to connect with all of these patients—without social media. But what role did social media and social media users play in this incident? This paper addresses this question, exploring the use of social media, especially the role of digital volunteers using these tools, during this and other crisis events.

Social Media Use during Crisis Events

This research contributes to the expanding literature on the use of social media during crises [e.g. 9,11,20,23,25, 26,31]. Among other uses, social media have begun to play host to *digital convergence* behavior; just as people have been known to converge physically onto the scenes of disaster events [5,15], people are now using social media and other information and communications technology (ICT) to converge "digitally" in the aftermath of disasters [11,20,26], and, like many convergers in the offline context who begin to act as volunteers [5,15], some digital convergers are taking on roles as digital volunteers [26].

The 2010 Haiti earthquake marked a turn for humanitarian responders in recognizing an emerging role for social media and its users in disaster response efforts. The Disaster Relief 2.0 Report explained, "...access to mobile and online communication enabled a kind of *collective intelligence* to emerge—when thousands of citizens around the world collaborated ... to help make sense of a large-scale calamity and give voice to an affected population" [7, p. 11].

Previous work on social media use during the aftermath of the Haiti earthquake has examined the self-organizing of digital volunteers, describing how a group of volunteer Twitterers came together to function as an emergent response organization [26]; and analyzed digital traces left by Twitter users who authored medical-themed tweets, finding the Twitter platform to have been used by smaller organizations for "beaconing" behavior—reaching out to connect to others who could help them do their work [23]. Both of these studies [23,26] focused on how Twitter was used to coordinate and organize. This research takes a slightly different perspective, shifting from a focus on organizing to a focus on information. By looking at the movement and manipulation of information shared in social media spaces after disaster events, this paper describes how "collective intelligence" emerges and offers a conceptual framework for understanding what it is and how it works.

Collective Intelligence

Lévy defines collective intelligence as "a universally distributed intelligence, constantly enhanced, coordinated in real time, and resulting in the effective mobilization of skills [distributed across individuals]" [16, p. 13]. The term has been offered as an explanation for seemingly intelligent behavior in large-scale interaction for both humans [16,17] and non-humans [e.g. 4]. Citing phenomena that occur in army ant colonies, Franks described collective intelligence as problem-solving ability within the group that exceeds the capacity of an individual, noting that, "through communication and mass action, army ants find flexible solutions to complex problems" [4, p. 139]. Though Lévy contests the attribution of collective intelligence to non-humans, suggesting a distinction between instinctive crowd behavior and the conscious and constructive participation he claims collective intelligence requires [16], this paper resists the intentionality embedded in that claim. Though crowd work in this context is almost always intentional, individual actions often have broader effects than those intended. Here, collective intelligence is defined as a shared intelligence that is distributed across groups of individuals [16], where the problem-solving capacity of the group is greater than the capacity of a single individual [4].

Though collectively intelligent behavior in humans can be observed offline, the connected interaction enabled by ICT has opened up new ways for the phenomenon to both occur and to be observed [e.g. 16,28]. Early hints of machine-connected, collective intelligence appear in Engelbart's ideas for augmenting the human intellect using machines; e.g. through collaborative online workspaces and hyper-linked documents [2]. Engelbart was influenced by Bush's proposed Memex machine, which described a knowledge system based on the associative nature of human cognition [1]. Using the "trails" of hypertext, people could tap into existing knowledge in a manner more closely related to their own ways of thinking [1,2]. In recent work, Engelbart extends these views into a vision of "collective IQ," that increases humanity's ability to solve complex problems [3].

Real-time coordination of humanitarian response in the wake of crisis events is one of these complex problems to which the collective intelligence of the crowd can be, and is indeed already being, productively applied. This paper aims to extend our understanding of how collective intelligence manifests during crises by analyzing information trails left behind in our hyperlinked information-interaction space.

DATA AND METHODOLOGICAL FRAMEWORK

This research draws from data collected during several studies of remote crowd work during disaster events. These include an extended investigation of the "Tweak the Tweet" project [29], a study of digital volunteers during the aftermath of the Haiti earthquake [26], and long-term participant-observation of Humanity Road, a virtual volunteer organization that responds to disasters [28].

Twitter as a Tool for Digital Volunteers

Twitter has become a popular platform among digital volunteers, for whom it acts as a source of information—including information coming from the ground, a site for working on that information, and a platform for communicating with and connecting to other volunteers, affected people and response agencies [26,28]. Several affordances of Twitter contribute to its utility as a real-time, information-sharing platform during crisis events, including the fact that the vast majority of tweets are public and searchable and that social networking features of the platform allow users to follow anyone they like and permit non-reciprocal ties. Additionally, user-driven linguistic conventions—e.g. mentions, retweets, and hashtags—have served to expand Twitter's usability and functionality.

Tweak the Tweet

The Tweak the Tweet (TtT) project proposed an extension to the functionality of the hashtag, incorporating it into a crisis-reporting microsytnax [28]. TtT asks users to place certain hashtags in front of specific pieces of information, rendering tweets not just searchable, but machine-readable. From its first deployment, TtT has been adopted by remote Twitterers who work to "translate" information they find elsewhere on Twitter or the web into TtT syntax [26].

Data

This research draws from four distinct datasets.

Dataset	Data Description
Contextual Streams of Haiti Voluntweeters	Twitter data. Every tweet sent by 339 Haiti voluntweeters from Jan 10-Feb 1, 2010. 292,928 tweets.
Interviews w/ Voluntweeters	Interviews with 19 Haiti voluntweeters. Completed in July and Aug 2010.
Participant Observation in Virtual Volunteer Org	Varied digital traces. Collected on Skype, Twitter & Google Docs. Jan 2011-Jul 2012.
Keyword Tweets from TtT Deployments	Twitter data. Collected during TtT deployments for 2011 tornados in Alabama (Apr 28-May 12, 102,395 tweets) and Joplin, MO (May 23-Jun 13, 904,710 tweets)

Contextual Streams of Haiti Voluntweeteers

During the TtT deployment for the Haiti earthquake (January 14-24) [26], we used the Twitter Search API to collect tweets that contained hashtags related to Tweak the Tweet, and from that set identified every Twitterer who sent a tweet or retweet in TtT syntax (339 accounts). Previous research indicates that this dataset includes a subset of an emergent digital volunteer network, many of whom identified as "voluntweeters" [26]. Using the Twitter REST API, we collected the full *contextual* stream—every tweet sent between January 10 and February 1—for each of these TtT Twitterers (292,928 total tweets).

Interviews with Haiti Voluntweeters

From the *Contextual Streams of Haiti Voluntweeters*, researchers identified 74 TtT translators [26]. 19 of these Twitter users were interviewed about their TtT use as well as their broader digital volunteer behavior.

Participant Observation in a Virtual Volunteer Organization

The author of this paper has been a participant-observer within a virtual volunteer organization, Humanity Road (HR), for 19 months (January 2011 to July 2012). The organization is a first-of-its-kind formal non-profit in the domain of digital disaster response [28]. This research relies primarily on the digital traces of HR's activity, almost all of which is mediated by ICT.

Keyword Tweets from TtT Deployments

During each TtT deployment, as part of the infrastructure for running the project, tweets were collected using the Twitter Streaming API to "track" keywords identified by researchers to be related to the event. This research includes tweet data collected during TtT deployments for two tornado events in the U.S. in 2011.

Using Tweets to Navigate the Larger Information Space

The majority of information on Twitter can be considered "derivative"—retweeted or otherwise repeated information that can be found elsewhere on the web [25]. Much of this derivative information points to a previous source through original author attribution or URL links. Following the methodological strategy employed by Sarcevic et al. [23], this research follows links, retweet attributions and conversations within tweet text to investigate upstream sources. This paper therefore uses tweet data to navigate the larger information space, a strategy that complements an analytical focus on information trajectories.

Note on Tweet Excerpts

Twitter accounts names are anonymized here, except where owners gave permission for direct attribution. Tweet times are in the local time of the event. Approximate times are for tweets where our data collection did not capture the original tweet, but found it through its traces, i.e. retweets.

Distributed Cognition as a Methodological Framework for Analyzing Collective Intelligence in Action

The theory of distributed cognition [10,12,22] provides a methodological framework for examining connected crowd work from an information-centered perspective. Distributed cognition (dCog) is a theory that claims cognition does not exist solely within individual minds, but is instead distributed socially, across groups of people, as well as physically (and digitally) across tools and artifacts.

A previous study examining "collective intelligence" in the crisis space noted approaching analysis from a dCog view [31], but did not elucidate how this perspective contributed to the understanding of this phenomenon. This paper aims to address that explicitly—to illustrate how dCog can help us understand and describe collective intelligence.

Though presented as a theory of cognition, research studies [e.g. 14,22] have employed distributed cognition as a methodological framework, within which "the unit of analysis is a culturally constituted functional group rather than an individual mind... (permitting researchers) to describe cognitive processes by tracing the movement of information through a system and characterize the mechanisms of the system which carry out the performance, both on the individual and the group level" [14, p. 15]. Cognition, in the dCog view, occurs as transformations of representations, and this model provides an approach for analysis at the level of these transformations. Hutchins has outlined a simple strategy for this, asking, "What information goes where, when and in what form?" [13].

FINDINGS

This paper expands on previous studies, drawing out new findings from existing data sets, and incorporating new data sets for analysis. Importantly, it offers a alternative approach for conceptualizing the activities of digital volunteers, shifting from a focus on organizing to a focus on information movement, and using the lens of distributed cognition to describe collective intelligence in action.

The Information-Processing Work of Digital Volunteers

Earlier work examined the self-organizing of digital volunteers in the wake of the Haiti earthquake, explaining how a group of previously unconnected remote volunteers came together as an emergent organization to help affected people [26]. While that original study described a range of volunteer activities—from performing as "remote operators" to organizing a campaign to fill the cell phones of affected people—this work concentrates primarily on the information-processing work of digital volunteers, activities that we see across individuals and events that have become foundational activities of an emerging practice of "crisis tweeting" and the larger sphere of digital volunteerism [28].

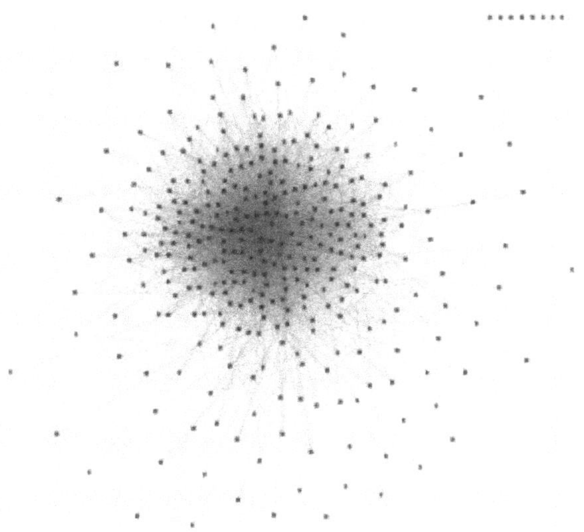

Figure 1. Network of Haiti Voluntweeters

Digital Volunteerism within an Emergent Network

The emergent organization of digital volunteers can be visualized as a network, with volunteers as nodes in that network performing information-processing tasks. Figure 1, a diagram showing connections between Haiti voluntweeters determined through analysis of their *Contextual Streams,* provides an initial abstraction for examining digital volunteer work in this way.

In this image, dark nodes represent the 339 voluntweeters identified during the TtT collection. Grey edges connect Twitterers who retweeted or otherwise mentioned another voluntweeter's account during the Haiti response; this diagram shows a dense network, with all but eight voluntweeters connected to others in the dataset through their tweets. The network can be imagined as one subsection in a much larger information space that contains other individuals, platforms, tools and resources.

Identifying and Amplifying Actionable Information

The most simple and most common form of crowd work during disaster events is amplification. For many Twitter users who later become digital volunteers, amplification acts as an entry-point to volunteerism. Evidence within the *Contextual Steams* and *Interviews with Haiti Voluntweeters* suggests that many began to attempt to help by retweeting information they thought was important. Others learned the behavior by seeing other Twitterers retweeting actionable information, and then adopted that strategy themselves.

Amplifying occurs as the combination of two separate actions: first, identifying actionable information or information deemed relevant to affected people or responders; and second, rebroadcasting that information to increase its range of exposure. The example below demonstrates how the crowd does this:

```
@sergegilles (Jan 26, 3:03pm): I Heard that
there is a Human Traffic of children in Hopital
Espoir, Delmas 75. Can @UNICEF Check this out?
```

This tweet, a report of human trafficking, was sent by a Haitian Twitterer who was in the country during the response period. The Twitter crowd quickly amplified this tweet, retweeting it in a variety of forms. Within the *Contextual Steams of Haiti Voluntweeters*, this tweet was retweeted 16 times—most in the first hour after the original. 118 other tweets were sent referencing the same report, but with slightly different content from the original. 42 of 339 Twitterers in the set of voluntweeters we identified—or 12% of the network—sent at least one tweet about this report of child trafficking. This collective activity by separate nodes within a network of digital volunteers functioned to amplify relevant, actionable information, in this case information from a trusted source who was on the ground at the time. This example is one among hundreds of mass amplification efforts—for other reports—in the *Contextual Steams of Haiti Voluntweeters*.

In addition to functioning to identify good information, i.e. first-hand information that is actionable or helps to improve situational awareness, amplifying also works by identifying good information sources, i.e. people who are on the ground, have special insight on conditions in the affected area, or represent an official voice.

> *"I quickly identified the sources of good information ... the people who meant well but got tricked by hoaxers and tricksters ... and the people actually IN Haiti, both locals, journos and aid workers."*

This interview response reveals how some voluntweeters approached this aspect of their work intentionally, but other research suggests Twitterers can also perform this identification function less purposefully [27]. That study shows how seemingly uncoordinated activity of amplification across a large crowd can have an aggregate effect of adding organization to the information space, performing as a sensor network for relevant, actionable information during mass disruption events.

Identification and amplification fits within the first part of Hutchins' leading question for analyzing dCog, "What information?" These information-processing actions also function to feed other parts of the cognitive system, for instance by providing source material for routing, verifying, and structuring activities described next.

Routing Information

Evidence within the *Contextual Streams* and *Interviews with Haiti Voluntweeters* suggests that many saw routing information as an important task within their digital volunteer work. Routing addresses the next part of Hutchins' question: "What information goes where?" Voluntweeters worked to connect certain information with people who needed or could use it. Though other channels including emails and phone calls were used as well, on the Twitter platform routing was often done using @mentions, public tweets addressed to specific accounts. The following example highlights routing behavior that occurred in the response to the report of human trafficking:

> **@MarkJones** (Jan 26, 3:28pm): @navynews My friend @Sergegilles is getting reports of kids being trafficked @ Hopital Espoir, Delmas 75. Please contact authorities NOW!

> **@skinterfy** (Jan 26, 4:51pm): @redcross RT @MarkJones 100% sure of source. It may be too late by the time we get there. Kids being sold @Hopital Espoir, Delmas 75

These tweets are selections from 64 different tweets sent in the wake of the trafficking report and during the resulting amplification efforts, directing that information to specific accounts. The recipient accounts were typically ones that voluntweeters thought could act on the information. In the cases of @navynews and @redcross, those accounts belonged to organizations with people in Haiti, and voluntweeters might have believed account monitors could pass the information to operatives on the ground. Below, a high-volume and highly-connected voluntweeter describes how she attempted to send actionable information to people on the ground by combining strategies for finding on-the-ground Twitterers with directing behavior:

> *"By searching Twitter and finding these ppl, we could send them details on where to go and who needed what... If we saw that they were headed to a particular area..."*

Directed-to accounts also included media and celebrities who voluntweeters felt could further amplify the report—e.g. several directed tweets went out to @andersoncooper, a CNN reporter who covered the Haiti response. Twitterers also passed tweets on to accounts of other voluntweeters, hoping to continue to move the information if not directly to, then at least closer to someone who could use it.

Voluntweeters intentionally moved information across nodes in the network, attempting to push it directly to nodes that could use it, or move it closer to such nodes. While amplification activity is a mass broadcast out to every node in the network that an account can reach, routing includes identifying *what information* as well as *where* to send it. Routed tweets may carry a stronger, more focused signal than mass broadcasts, with recipients being more likely to tune in—while a typical Twitterer may see thousands of tweets a day while monitoring a popular hashtag stream, they will receive a much smaller number directed to them.

Verifying Information

Another way voluntweeters help shape the information flowing through Twitter and other channels is through verifying information [26]. Many of the interviewed voluntweeters reported that verifying information became an important aspect of their work. Like many other incidents, the report of child trafficking eventually became a focus of this work. Several hours after the initial tweet and after most of the amplification efforts faded, a few voluntweeters began to question the validity of the report and attempted to have someone confirm it.

> **@JaneSM** (Jan 26, 8:31pm): @sergegilles my friend can you please elaborate on the source that came to you with the trafficking report. We thank you

> **@radioto** (Jan 27 12:15am): Is this story is true or not ? "...Heard that there is a Human Traffic of childen in Hopital Espoir, Delmas 75..." PLEASE OFFICIAL SOURCE

In this case, verification work took place across a section of the digital volunteer network, with multiple volunteers joining in on a collaborative effort. At times, interactions like these could be contentious, because reputations were on the line. Digital volunteers may lose the trust of others if they are thought to be passing along bad information. When one openly questions information, others sometimes step in publicly to support the questioner, as did the two in this example. This verifying work had direct impact on the spread of this report. Some time later, after attempting to confirm the information by contacting his source, @sergegilles determined it to be a rumor and shared that with the network, which then worked to spread the retraction—though significantly less broadly than the original report.

Within a dCog perspective, the work of verifying speaks to the issue of "what information?" Through their public, collective work to confirm information, the crowd works as a collaborative sensor network for good and bad information as well as relevant and actionable information. The descriptive account corroborates previous quantitative research suggesting that large-scale patterns of activity can be used to identify rumors on Twitter after a disaster [18].

Though the examples presented here all revolve around the Twitter platform, verifying work moves to (and originates in) other parts of the information system as well, as volunteers look to triangulate reports and find outside sources to confirm. In interviews, some voluntweeters reported calling numbers listed as contact information in tweets to verify that information was true and still valid.

Structuring Information

Structuring, or adding structure to information, is another component of crowd work, one that addresses both "What information?" and the last component of Hutchins' question, "In what form?" Adding metadata to information and entering it into a form or a spreadsheet are types of structuring, as is TtT translation.

Focusing on individual transformations, each act of translation into TtT syntax takes place as a combination of first, the identification of actionable or otherwise relevant information; and second, the performance of one or more transformations that reconfigure the information into a state of increased structure. The following example from the *Joplin TtT Collection* demonstrates:

@TVJoe (May 23, 2011 ~12:20am): Animal shelter established in #Joplin, Missouri. Call (620) 674-3634 if you need animal shelter services.

@TheFireTracker2 (May 23, 2011 12:21:54am): MT @TVJoe: #Offer Animal shelter #Loc Joplin, Missouri. #contact Call (620) 674-3634 if you need animal shelter services. #Joplin

Shortly after the Joplin tornado in May 2011, a handful of TtT translators, many with previous experience using the syntax, worked to identify tweets with actionable information and translate them into TtT syntax. In the above example, a veteran digital volunteer, identifies information that might be useful to affected people and creates a TtT tweet by adding three TtT tags (`#offer`, `#loc`, and `#contact`) and reorganizing the tweet text to match the prescribed format. The consistent word order between the original and the translation suggests a copy and paste technique. @TheFireTracker2 uses "MT" to indicate a "modified tweet," a strategy adopted by TtT translators to give attribution and note that text has been changed. For practiced TtT translators, using a series of micro-structuring actions like adding a few tags and copying-pasting pieces of text, it can take several seconds to a few minutes to generate a tweet like this. These transformations create new representations that are later circulated through the system. During TtT deployments, software processes TtT-formatted tweets into public spreadsheets and Google Maps.

Few cases of TtT translation are as simple as the base translation case: TtT translators recognizing information entering the system for the first time and rapidly translating it into the format. Information often takes a less direct route from original source to structured state. The following example demonstrates this effect, revealing an important role that the larger network plays in relaying the signal through the information space until it reaches a node with the potential to process it.

@medmrsmith (May 23 01:22): #joplin Emergency Animal Hosp on 7th and Illinois behind Sonic is OPEN and taking found animals

@klboard (May 23 01:25): RT @medmrsmith: #joplin Emergency Animal Hosp on 7th and Illinois behind Sonic is OPEN and taking found animals

@Jeannie_Hartley (May 23 01:37): RT @klboard: #joplin Emergency Animal Hosp on 7th and Illinois behind Sonic is OPEN and taking found animals @franyafranya

@maryslate (May 23 01:42): RT @Jeannie_Hartley: RT @klboard: #joplin Emergency Animal Hosp on 7th and Illinois behind Sonic is OPEN and taking found animals ...

@SoutholdSMEM (May 23 01:47): RT @maryslate: RT @klboard: #joplin Emergency Animal Hosp on 7th and Illinois behind Sonic is OPEN and taking found animals

@CrisisMappers (May 23 02:57): #tornado #offer Emergency Animal Hosp behind Sonic is OPEN & taking found animals #loc 7th & Illinois #Joplin #src @medmrsmith @SoutholdSMEM+

In this example, @medmrsmith initially tweets this report of an emergency animal hospital announcing that it will accept animals. Within minutes, the information bounces off three other Twitterers who retweet the text and give attribution to an upstream author, though the original author is soon excluded. Eventually the tweet is translated into TtT syntax by @CrisisMappers, who tracks down the original author and also cites the author immediately upstream.

Here the cognition is two-fold, measurable in both the form of the information and the movement of information across different nodes in the network. @CrisisMappers' TtT translation at the end of this excerpt demonstrates dCog as transformation of representation. Cognition also occurrs through the actions above—the many retweets whereby nodes in the network acted to pass on the information. This relaying activity, a product of amplification, is a feature of a collaborative information-processing system where different nodes have different information-processing capabilities. Tweets are essentially ephemeral, but retweets serve to keep information alive by repeatedly posting it to the public stream [25]. Though the intermediary accounts might not have used the information themselves, their work to rebroadcast information can be seen to increase the odds that it will reach the account of someone who can use it.

Though TtT is one (relatively complex) way of structuring tweets, it is not the only way. The most common form of structuring on Twitter is simply adding hashtags. Often, volunteers comb the Twitter stream and add event hashtags to relevant information before retweeting. *Tag-added RTs* allow the original content to show up in hashtag searches. Digital volunteers can also be seen, across events, developing their own, more complex hashtagging systems. An interview with one voluntweeter revealed a subgroup of those volunteers to have created a system where they would tag tweets with `#rescuemehaiti` to call them to the attention of response agencies and other digital volunteers. Members of that sub-community tuned into this stream of `#rescuemehaiti` for source information for their other coordination activities. This example of user-driven structuring shows activity similar to TtT translation work occurring "naturally" within digital volunteer communities.

During response efforts after the Alabama tornados in the Spring of 2011, Twitterers introduced special hashtags for categorizing certain types of response-related information.

@jsandford (May 3 7:27pm): Please use #ALHaves or #ALNeeds if you have or need supplies in Alabama storm recovery to help better org tweets. #WeAreAlabama @spann

@two_slice (May 6 8:55pm): Theres a need for doctors to help National Guard soldiers w/ meds and such, in Greensboro. #WeAreAlabama #ALneeds

More than 1000 tweets were sent containing one of the two suggested terms (#ALHaves or #ALNeeds). Weeks later, when Joplin, MO was struck by a devastating tornado, digital volunteers from Alabama encouraged those responding to the Joplin event to use variations of those earlier tags (`#MOneeds` and `#MOhaves`), which many new volunteers did.

User-driven tweet structuring can be seen as a self-organizing human computation system providing real-time information processing. Structuring also taps into previous work, like amplification and verification, of other volunteers in the network:

> *There were some ppl that were REALLY good at [TtT translation] and they would catch many of our forgotten tweets and redo them. Sometimes we were going so fast that it was hard to remember to use it.*

This suggests the emergence of a multi-tiered system where some volunteers monitor incoming streams to identify and amplify actionable information and other volunteers tune in to those amplification efforts and then add structure to the information, sometimes through multiple transformations. The cognitive system works to process information in real-time during crisis events through the collective action of individual nodes that transform information by moving it from one place to another, rebroadcasting it to keep it alive in a temporal context, or altering its form by adding micro-structure to its textual content.

Synthesizing Information into Resources

Synthesizing information is a primary activity of the Humanity Road organization. HR devotes considerable effort to creating "situation reports" during active disaster events, where they bring together multiple types of information, including damage reports, nearest airports, location and capacity information for hospitals and shelters, lists of local government and response media accounts, etc.

Synthesizing is the work of pulling information together from disparate sources to create more complete representations of an unfolding event. At the micro level, synthesis work is again enacted as transformations of representations, and like many of the activities described above—e.g. amplifying, verifying, and routing—it relies first on the work of identifying actionable or otherwise useful information during an event. The HR team works together to filter information, identify important pieces, synthesize them into a single resource, and publicize that product of their work to affected people, responders, and other digital volunteers. They complete this work together within conversations in Skype windows as well as through tweets, emails, and other channels.

Significantly, the synthesizing work of Humanity Road volunteers is also embedded within and connected to other digital volunteer communities and the massive connected crowd surrounding them. Volunteers pull information from other Twitter accounts, media reports, official websites, and blogs. Many are connected through Twitter to other digital volunteers and in many cases, to other communities to which those volunteers belong—e.g. CrisisMappers, who work by structuring and synthesizing information into maps [7]. Information filtered by one network or community becomes input for another. HR volunteers often notice new events by seeing tweets from others in their personal networks. They also incorporate information gleaned from these connections into their resources. And other groups may get information for their resources from HR. The cognitive system of HR is plugged into a much larger system that works to process information during crises.

Emergent Organization as Cognitive Architecture

Figure 1 shows the network of connections between the 339 Haiti voluntweeters. Previous research suggests this network was as an emergent one—only a small portion of links between voluntweeters for Haiti had been established before that event [26]. Within the dCog view, these connections and this emergent organization can be seen as (part of) a "cognitive architecture" [10,12], a collection of features of the physical-social-digital environment that shapes the cognitive processes of the group. The emergence of this organization shows this architecture to also be *shaped by* the activities of the group.

Due to the public nature of tweets, the affordance of non-reciprocal ties, and the ability to send public tweets to the attention of any account, connections can and do develop between people who were previously strangers. Across the entire network, many nodes are already connected, but there remain an immense number of potential connections. For voluntweeters, their digital volunteer work—i.e. amplifying information through retweeting, directing information through mentions, marking up tweets with the "correct" hashtags—are all catalysts for creating new connections between nodes. In another view, these activities *are* these connections. And once connections are established between nodes, information may move more freely between them. Thus, the practice of crisis tweeting determined how this structure (see Figure 1) emerged *and what it looked like.* The structure, in turn, shaped how information moved during the event, demonstrating a reciprocal relationship between action and structure, one described by Giddens [6].

The Case of Hôpital Sacré Coeur in Milot, Haiti

The cognitive architecture of digital disaster response extends across networks and platforms. Returning to the example in the Introduction, the account of how Hopital Sacré Coeur used social media to connect with patients, demonstrates this.

Beaconing: Broadcasting an Urgent Message

Sarcevic et al. [23] describe how medical organizations used Twitter for *beaconing* behavior, to broadcast their message as widely as possible. Though CRUDEM did not use Twitter directly, one volunteer there, Sarah Kane, turned to ICT to beacon, sending mass email messages and posting to forums in an attempt to bring patients to the hospital. Kane was "responding" virtually, from outside

Haiti, in the days after the earthquake. This text excerpted from one of her email messages was posted January 15 to a website set up to assist in the response (www.rockmasters.com/haiti-earthquake/communications.htm):

> ***URGENT***: *We have a full-service hospital in Milot, Haiti that is *not* being utilized!! Hopital Sacre Coeur... We can take up to *200 injured patients* immediately! We have operating rooms and beds. ... We have cleared a soccer field for helicopter landing. ... We cannot understand why our facility is not being utilized! As of yesterday, we have received only two patients that came by car. ... Please get the word out to news organizations to get rescue teams... It makes no sense to be 25 minutes away by chopper with beds and doctors waiting to help! ...*
>
> *Sarah Kane - Crudem Support*
> *Hopital Sacre Coeur in Milot, Haiti, 555 555-5555*

CRUDEM, perhaps through Kane, also posted information to their website and made periodic updates to their Facebook page, including this one on January 17:

> *People are dying in the streets AND in the hospitals in Port au Prince. We have a full-service hospital with two ORs, trauma team and ortho team waiting for patients!*

Kane continued to send email messages, until at least January 18, pleading for organizations to bring patients to Sacré Coeur. Many of these were directed to media outlets, urging them to "please broadcast this anywhere you can in media & send to everyone you can" (www.thetakeaway.org/blogs/takeaway/2010/jan/17/aid-agencies-struggle-bring-help) and suggesting that she needed help getting her message to the "highest levels of U.S. government" (Caribbean Free Radio website).

Relaying, Amplifying and Structuring across Platforms

Echoes of these posts show up in several different interactive spaces on the web. As with the excerpts above, several of Kane's email messages were posted within the content of blogs and websites of other small organizations and media outlets. In at least three instances, individuals who were not connected to the organization posted information about Sacré Coeur as comments to other blogs and articles in mainstream media. For example, the following was added as a comment to a New York Times blog on January 15 (cityroom.blogs.nytimes.com/2010/01/15/the-spirit-of-port-au-prinmce-now-broken/):

> *A University of Iowa physician in Haiti now has found a 200-bed hospital, fully equipped, in Milot with no patients in it. He's asking us to try to get the word to people in Haiti. Contact there is Sarah Kane, Crudem Support, Hopital Sacre-Coeur in Milot. 555-555-5555, Sarah@email.net.*

This activity shows digital volunteerism in the form of relaying and amplifying, similar to what this paper has demonstrated on Twitter, occurring elsewhere online.

Not surprisingly, traces of CRUDEM's beaconing behavior also show up on Twitter. The first tweets with links pointing to the CRUDEM website appear on January 13, and more than 600 tweets were sent about the hospital between that day and February 1. Most involved trying to get patients to the facility, though some tweets in the latter part of the collection window dealt with a new issue of obtaining resources (food, cots, etc.) for the hospital. Volunteers worked to move information from other sites onto Twitter and also to amplify messages posted there. Over time, they added more information to the tweets, e.g. listing the contact info for Kane, noting the availability of a landing pad, and including GPS coordinates:

> **@rqskye** (Jan 15): @carelpedre-SacredHeart Hosp, Milot, also has landing pad cleared to accept 200 patients NOW. Call Sarah Kane Crudem 555-555-5555
>
> **@redcrossmom** (Jan 18): @firesideint Milot (19° 37' 0" N, 72° 13' 0" W) Sacre Coeur is open #Haiti Milot,555-555-5555:FullStaff, 2ORs,TeamsWAITING.

As these tweets show, volunteers often directed information about Sacré Coeur to those they thought could help. They also used TtT syntax to structure tweets, sending 66 TtT tweets and retweets about the hospital.

Other structuring activity moved to Ushahidi, a "crisis mapping" platform that was accepting reports about Haiti via SMS and a web portal [7]. Someone, perhaps a digital volunteer, added information about Sacré Coeur to the map on January 16. Later tweets linked to this Ushahidi report.

In addition, two CNN iReports were created about Sacré Coeur, both by individuals unaffiliated with CRUDEM. The first was posted by a woman in Haiti on the morning of January 15. Later that morning, information in that post began to spread through the tweet streams of digital volunteers. CNN picked up the story of Sacré Coeur for the first time that evening, mentioning the hospital on air during the AC360 program. From their transcript:

> *There's apparently a hospital north of here that actually has room for patients. It's a hospital called Sacre-Coeur, it's located in Milot...80 miles north of Port-au-Prince...We are told, I've not seen this with my own eyes but we're told that it's fully operational ...but again, it's far away. A lot of people can't get there.*

It is not clear how CNN reporters first heard about Sacré Coeur, but they and other mainstream media were often the focus of CRUDEM's beaconing as well as digital volunteers' directing activities. Both groups appear to have perceived those channels as having the ability to further amplify their messages.

Delivering Patients to Milot

Eventually, patients began to arrive in Milot. On January 16, the day after the CNN report, the U.S. Navy delivered one group of injured people to Sacré Coeur, an event remarked upon in a Facebook post by CRUDEM that also included another plea for more patients—suggesting that the coordination problem had not yet been fully resolved.

The USCG airlifted two groups of patients, nine total, to Sacré Coeur on the 17th, a day that witnessed the most Twitter activity about the hospital (155 tweets). Though there is no evidence of a direct or causal relationship in the tweet streams, it is possible that Twitter activity and the delivery of patients are themselves related to a common factor: the information, moving in and across networks of social media users and digital volunteers, was beginning to reach nodes that could use it in forms that were usable.

On January 18, while Kane's pleas for patients continued to spread throughout the web, the USCG began to deliver a steady stream of patients. Others arrived via automobile. On the 23rd, tweets began to contain requests for supplies for the facility, which had by then begun to exceed capacity.

Previous studies were careful to avoid claims of impact by digital volunteers during Haiti [23,26], as it is difficult to connect social media activity to actions on the ground. However, evidence in the digital traces analyzed here suggests a role for social media and digital volunteers in delivering patients to Sacré Coeur. According to CRUDEM's Facebook page, Kane eventually made contact with a USCG Commander, and after that the USCG began to coordinate a steady flow of patients to the facility. It is unclear in the digital traces exactly when or how the connection was made, but CRUDEM credits social media. That the USCG first contacted CRUDEM through Kane, a volunteer who was neither located in Haiti nor acting as an official leader of the organization, suggests that Kane's social media posts—and the efforts by others to help distribute the information in those posts—played a role.

It is likely that CRUDEM's message reached people who could act on it through multiple paths. With repeated movement across platforms and media, there was considerable redundancy in the network. It may be hard to assign credit for generating this connection to a single node of the digital volunteer network or to a single post or digital artifact. However, if digital volunteers had not been acting on this information, the connection may not have happened, or it may not have happened as quickly—a critical concern. Traynor recalls that a member of one USCG helicopter team, during one of their first patient deliveries, remarked, "God, had we only known you were here earlier!"

To answer the question posed earlier, social media did not deliver patients to Sacré Coeur, but volunteers did use these tools to coordinate action that saved lives. The perspective advocated here views this not as any individual act by any one person, but collective action by—and collective intelligence within—a network of people, connected through ICT, who helped organize the information space through many small acts of transformation.

CONCLUSION

Collective intelligence, along with the related concept of "crowdsourcing," has become a popular term for characterizing crowd activity online. But what is collective intelligence and how does it work?

Describing his view, Franks wrote, "all intelligence involves rational manipulation of symbolic information" [4, p. 139, citing 8]. Aligned with this view, this empirical analysis of digital traces within the domain of digital disaster response demonstrates how collective intelligence manifests as transformations of information across an ICT-connected crowd. Using the theory of distributed cognition as a methodological framework, this paper shows how seemingly simple actions from individuals collectively organize the information space.

Though the theory of distributed cognition is intended to apply to all systems, the methodological framework has most often been employed to examine interactions between groups of individuals—and their tools—collocated in physical space [e.g. 10,12,14,22]. This research extends the dCog perspective to examine collective action within the massively connected information space of social media and the surrounding Internet. Though a previous study on collective intelligence in social media spaces used this theory as part of a broader analytical frame [31], this paper explicitly employs dCog as a methodological framework for examining the work of digital volunteers.

The dCog framework offers an effective tool for thinking about how this work is coordinated and organized—how these individuals are able to come together as remote response organizations in some instances and massive sensor networks in others. It allows us to conceptualize how this organization emerges without preplanning and without any single individual or node having a complete grasp of the entire system. Heverin and Zach describe how, in the wake of violent crises, individuals come together on social media sites to make sense of the event, a collective sense that can only develop in interaction with others [9]. Digital volunteers go beyond collective sensemaking to collective action, so their goals may be different, but the processes whereby they achieve those goals are similar. Using the dCog methodological framework, we see how local actions create global effects, and how the cognition of the system extends far beyond the cognition of any individual.

DCog also gives us a lens through which to view this emergent activity, by focusing on transformations of information. This approach fits well with the affordances of social media platforms that leave the digital traces of many of these transformations in public view and allow us to easily "step inside the cognitive system" [12].

Collective intelligence can be seen to emerge from the individual actions of digital volunteers to relay, amplify, verify, structure and synthesize information. These actions also form a cognitive architecture [12] for the volunteer network, one that is itself plugged into the cognitive architecture of the larger information space, and one that structures future actions, e.g. by establishing information pathways between trusted volunteers.

Digital volunteerism is becoming an established feature of the online ecosystem after disaster events. It has begun to stabilize, somewhat, as volunteers establish commonly understood ways of doing things and organize into formal virtual volunteer organizations. But it also continues, in event after event, to take on new forms and emerge within new networks of individuals. This research offers a detailed description of the core activities of digital volunteerism and explores the utility of using dCog to both analyze and conceptualze this collective activity online.

ACKNOWLEDGMENTS

This work would not have been possible without the support of Project EPIC at the University of Colorado. I thank Leysia Palen for her guidance throughout this multi-year research effort, and Ken Anderson and Aaron Schram for helping collect the Twitter data used in this analysis. I also thank Ed Hutchins for his early guidance, the reviewers of this paper for their thoughtful feedback, and Taylor Scott for his feedback on a late draft. Early research for this paper was supported by an NSF Graduate Research Fellowship and NSF grants IIS-0546315 and IIS-0910586.

REFERENCES

1. Bush, V. As We May Think, *Atlantic Monthly*, (July 1945), 101-108.
2. Engelbart, D. *Augmenting Human Intellect: A Conceptual Framework*. AFOSR-3233, Summary Report. Stanford Research Institute, 1962.
3. Engelbart, D. Augmenting society's collective IQs. *Proc. of Hypertext and Hypermedia* (2004). New York: ACM, 1-1.
4. Franks, N. Army Ants: A Collective Intelligence: A neural network seems an apt analogy as a colony of army ants navigates the tropical rain forest. *American Scientist*, *77*, 2 (March-April 1989), pp. 138-145.
5. Fritz, C. E. & Mathewson, J. H. *Convergence Behavior in Disasters: A Problem in Social Control, Committee on Disaster Studies*, National Academy of Sciences, National Research Council, Washington DC, 1957.
6. Giddens, A. *Central problems in social theory: action, structure and contradiction in social analysis*, University of California Press, Berkeley, 1979.
7. Harvard Humanitarian Initiative. Disaster Relief 2.0: The Future of Information Sharing in Humanitarian Emergencies. Washington, D.C. & Berkshire, UK: UN Foundation & Vodafone Foundation Technology Partnership, 2011.
8. Haugeland, J. *Artificial Intelligence: The Very Idea*, MIT Press, 1986.
9. Heverin, T. & Zack, L. Use of Microblogging for Collective Sense-making during Violent Crises: A Study of Three Campus Shootings. *J. Am. Soc. Inf. Sci. Technol.* 63, 1 (January 2012), 34-47.
10. Hollan, J., Hutchins, E. & Kirsh, D. Distributed cognition: toward a new foundation for human-computer interaction research. *ACM Trans. Computer-Human Interaction. 7*, 2 (June 2000), 174-196.
11. Hughes, A., L. Palen, J. Sutton, S. Liu, & S. Vieweg. "Site-Seeing" in Disaster: An Examination of On-Line Social Convergence. *Proc. of ISCRAM 2008*.
12. Hutchins, E. *Cognition in the Wild.* Cambridge, Mass: MIT Press, 1995.
13. Hutchins, E. The Social Organization of Distributed Cognition. Course Lecture, COGS 102a, UCSD, 2011. http://hci.ucsd.edu/102a/10Lectures/SODC-basics.pdf
14. Hutchins E. & Klausen, T. Distributed Cognition in an Airline Cockpit. In Middleton, D. & Engeström, Y. (Eds.) *Communication and Cognition at Work*. (pp. 15-34) Cambridge University Press, 1996.
15. Kendra, J. M. & Wachtendorf, T. Reconsidering Convergence and Converger: Legitimacy in Response to the World Trade Center Disaster, *Terrorism and Disaster: New Threats, New Ideas: Research in Social Problems and Public Policy*, 11, (2003), 97-122.
16. Lévy, P. as translated by Bononno, R. *Collective Intelligence*. Perseus Book, USA, 1997.
17. Malone, T. W., Laubacher, R. & Dellarocas, C. N., Harnessing Crowds: Mapping the Genome of Collective Intelligence (February 3, 2009). MIT Sloan Research Paper No. 4732-09.
18. Mendoza, M. Poblete, B. & Castillo, C. (2010). Twitter under crisis: can we trust what we RT? In *Proceedings of the First Workshop on Social Media Analytics* (SOMA '10), 71-79.
19. PAHO/WHO. Earthquake in Haiti—One year later. *Report on the Health Situation*, January 2011.
20. Palen, L & Liu, S. B. Citizen Communications in Crisis: Anticipating a Future of ICT-Supported Participation, *Proc. of CHI 2007*, 727-736.
21. Pape, J.W., Johnson, W.D. and Fitzgerald, D.W. The earthquake in Haiti—Dispatch from Port-au-Prince. *New England Journal of Medicine 362* (2010), 575-577.
22. Rogers, Y. & Ellis, J. Distributed Cognition: An Alternative Framework for Analyzing and Explaining Collaborative Working. *J. of Information Technology, 9*, 2 (1994), 119-128.
23. Sarcevic, A. Palen, L., White, J., Starbird, K., Bagdouri, M. & Anderson. K. "Beacons of Hope" in Decentralized Coordination: Learning from On-the-Ground Medical Twitterers during the 2010 Haiti Earthquake. *Proc. of CSCW 2012*, 47-56.
24. Sheridan, M.B., Wilgoren, D., & Leonnig, C.D. Patients Overwhelm Medical Teams at Haiti Clinics. *Washington Post.* (Jan 17, 2010). http://www.washingtonpost.com /wpdyn/content/article/2010/01/17/AR2010011701144.html
25. Starbird, K, Palen, L, Hughes, A & Vieweg, S. Chatter on The Red: What Hazards Threat Reveals about the Social Life of Microblogged Information. *Proc. of CSCW 2010,* 241-250.
26. Starbird, K. & Palen, L. "Voluntweeters:" Self-Organizing by Digital Volunteers in Times of Crisis. *Proc. of CHI 2011*, 1071–1080.
27. Starbird, K. & Palen, L. (How) Will the Revolution be Retweeted? Information Propagation in the 2011 Egyptian Uprising. In *Proc. of CSCW 2012*, 6-17.
28. Starbird, K. & Palen, L. Working and Sustaining the Virtual Disaster Desk. *Proc. of CSCW 2013.*
29. Starbird, K. & Stamberger, J. Tweak the Tweet: Leveraging Microblogging Proliferation with a Prescriptive Syntax to Support Citizen Reporting. *Proc. of ISCRAM, 2010.*
30. Surowiecki, J. *The Wisdom of Crowds*. First Anchor Books Edition. New York: Anchor Books, 2005.
31. Vieweg, S., Palen, L., Liu, S., Hughes, A., & Sutton, J. Collective Intelligence in Disaster: Examination of the Phenomenon in the Aftermath of the 2007 Virginia Tech Shooting. *Proc. of ISCRAM, 2008.*

Does Slacktivism Hurt Activism?: The Effects of Moral Balancing and Consistency in Online Activism

Yu-Hao Lee, Gary Hsieh
Michigan State University
Communication Arts & Sciences
{leeyuhao, garyh }@ msu.edu

ABSTRACT
In this paper we explore how the decision of partaking in low-cost, low-risk online activism—slacktivism—may affect subsequent civic action. Based on moral balancing and consistency effects, we designed an online experiment to test if signing or not signing an online petition increased or decreased subsequent contribution to a charity. We found that participants who signed the online petition were significantly more likely to donate money to a related charity, demonstrating a consistency effect. We also found that participants who did not sign the petition donated significantly more money to an unrelated charity, demonstrating a moral balancing effect. The results suggest that exposure to an online activism influences individual decision on subsequent civic actions.

Author Keywords
Online Petitions, Consistency, Moral Balancing, Slacktivism

ACM Classification Keywords
H.5.3 Group and Organization Interfaces.

General Terms
Human Factors; Design.

INTRODUCTION
In recent years, we are witnessing a growth in social activism associated with the use of social media. For example on March 5th, 2012, an organization called Invisible Children uploaded a video called KONY 2012 on to video-sharing site YouTube and Vimeo. KONY2012 was the first part of their campaign to make Ugandan indicted war criminal Joseph Kony known to the world in order to have him arrested. The campaign's primary pleas were simple: watch the video, and share it. In less than a month, the video gained more than 100 million views around the world.

Social technology such as social network sites (e.g, *Facebook*) and content-sharing websites (e.g., *Youtube, Vimeo*) are allowing online interaction between people at unprecedented large scales. These technologies hold great potential for supporting activism and civic engagement. Besides the use of video-sharing sites like the KONY 2012 campaign, *Twitter* and *Google maps* have been used innovatively during emergency crises to identify demands and broker resources more efficiently [21]. Websites such as *Avaaz.org* and *Wikipedia* are used to discuss human right violations and online campaigns [7]. In the 2010 Haiti earthquake, the *International Red Cross (IRC)* raised more than seven million in four days via a text-message campaign [16]. Even the United States' White House recently (2011) launched an online petition system called *We the People* for citizens to organize online petitions.

However, these online actions have also been criticized as "slacktivism" that has no real impact on social change and even hurt future civic actions. The term slacktivism comes from combining slacker and activism. Slacktivism has been defined as "low-risk, low-cost activity via social media whose purpose is to raise awareness, produce change, or grant satisfaction to the person engaged in the activity [17]." Examples of slacktivism includes activities such as clicking "like" to show support for an interest group on *Facebook*, signing online petitions, forwarding letters or videos about an issue, and painting one's profile green to support demographic election in Iraq.

Critics of slacktivism argue that slacktivism can hurt "real" civic actions such as protests, community volunteerism, and charity. Slacktivism may also substitute other civic actions because the people's inner urge to take action has been satisfied by their participation in the low-cost online action [3, 19]. This concern can be explained by research on moral balancing. Studies have found that performing a good deed liberates one's conscience to slack off on subsequent good-deeds [6, 8, 9, 18]. However, to date, this moral balancing effect has yet to be demonstrated in the online activism context. Does participating in online activism reduce people's subsequent civic participation?

There is, however, an alternative effect that needs to be considered when examining the efficacy of slacktivism. It may be possible that under certain circumstances, slacktivism can lead to increased likelihood or efforts in subsequent civic action. Cognitive dissonance theory assumes that individuals are motivated to reduce dissonance

CHI'13, April 27 – May 2, 2013, Paris, France.

by altering their behavior or cognition to be consistent [2]. Cognitive dissonance theory would predict that partaking in slacktivism may increase people's likelihood of taking a related subsequent civic action because people want their behaviors to remain consistent. If they contributed to a pro-social cause, they are more likely to contribute to the same cause again. Current research demonstrating the moral balancing effect has only shown that people who made a prosocial choice are less likely to perform a *different*, subsequent prosocial action [6, 8]. But when the subsequent action is congruent to the initial action, can the initial participation actually raise subsequent participation?

The goal of this study is to examine whether the decision to sign or not sign an online petition (slacktivism) affects subsequent donation to charity. Specifically, under what conditions will moral balancing effects occur? And under what conditions will consistency concerns dominate one's decisions to take up a civic action?

In the wake of the Aurora, Colorado shooting in July 2012, we designed an online experiment that invited participants to sign an online petition either for banning assault rifles or in support of gun rights based on their attitude on the issue. Then we asked the participants if they were willing to donate part of their experiment compensation to either a gun control/gun right-related organization (congruent civic action), or an education organization (incongruent civic action).

We found that when the following civic action is unrelated to the previous issue, participants who did not sign the petition donated significantly more money than the control group, possibly because of a moral cleansing effect. However, when the subsequent action is closely related to the previous issue, signing the petition increases the likelihood of donating money, but not the amount. We also examined whether signing the petition influenced intentions to participate in a number of traditional civic action. The results showed that participating in the petition only increased intentions to participate in similar civic actions.

This work offers both theoretical and practical contributions. From a theoretical perspective, our research extends current research on moral balancing, and is the first to empirically show that the desire for consistency can offset the desire to be morally balanced. We demonstrated that congruency between issues can influence whether consistency effect or moral balancing dominate subsequent civic participation decisions. From a practical perspective, our study is critical to the development of technology for online activism. It shows that online petitions do affect participants' subsequent decisions, and suggests online petition designs to use congruency to sustain civic participation. These are relevant to both campaign organizers and civic technology designers.

THEORETICAL BACKGROUND

Online Activism from Lowered Cost

Online activism share many similarities with traditional civic actions. First, the actions impose costs and risks on participating individuals. Second, the goals cannot be obtained by an individual alone, thus the actions require a certain amount of participants to succeed. And third, like most civic actions, the goal is aimed towards collective goods such as reduced air pollution, better neighborhood security, or more worker benefits. Collective goods are characterized by their non-excludability, once they are provided, the whole community benefits regardless of how much effort each individual has contributed to making it possible. Therefore while the action requires large amount of people to contribute, rational agents have incentives to do nothing and free-ride on the collective outcome. This is described as the collective action problem [15]. Because of these similarities, rational agents are likely to not take action if they do not feel the need or if the personal cost of action is too high.

While online activism shares many similarities with traditional civic actions, the cost of participation online is generally much lower than traditional civic actions such as sit-ins, protests, hosting a community meeting, or writing a letter to the government. From a campaign organizer's perspective, social media makes it easier for organizers to find people with similar causes, communicate with one another, and promote their cause to a wider audience. From a participant's perspective, social media makes it easier to find issues that one might be interested in, thus reducing the cost of searching. Many online campaigns are often designed to make the actions simple in order to gain a large amount of support, thus for participants, participating in these online actions requires very little effort and time. The lowered cost and ease of participation may be a reason why people are more likely to partake in slacktivism than in traditional civic actions.

Supporters of online activism argue that social media can be used to reach a wider group of people by raising awareness or knowledge. The simple actions invite people who may otherwise never take traditional civic actions to partake in a collective action. Many point to various examples where slacktivism has directly or indirectly benefitted collective goods at never seen before scales, from raising millions of charitable contributions in a few days (i.e., donations after earthquake), to increasing awareness (i.e., KONY 2012) [16, 17].

In contrast, critics of slacktivism argue that these actions merely make people "feel good" about themselves. Not only are the contributions to actual social change limited, partaking in slacktivism may even be harmful to *future actions* because it satisfies people's motivations to take action but does not really have an effect.

Unfortunately, little is known about whether and how slacktivism may affect participants' choice of whether to partake in subsequent civic actions. If it does undermine subsequent activism, then we may need to reconsider the use of slacktivism for social change.

Moral Balancing: Licensing and Cleansing

Moral balancing can be used to explain how slacktivism may undermine subsequent activism. When people make decisions about partaking in civic actions, they will not only consider the costs and benefits of the action, but also draw on their past behaviors as references. Moral balancing posits that when individuals face a moral decision, they will draw on their own past moral behaviors to make the decision [9]. If the individual performed a morally good deed in the past, the individual will feel that he or she has been licensed to loosen up a little, and feel less guilty for making a morally dubious choice (moral licensing). In contrast, if the individual performed an unethical deed in the past, the individual will feel that he or she needs to make up for the bad deed by performing more ethical choices (moral cleansing). The case that past good deeds license bad deeds is known as the moral licensing effect. And the case that past bad deeds warrant more good deeds is known as a moral cleansing effect [18].

There are two possible explanations for how moral balancing works. The first explanation views one's overall moral behaviors as a bank account; a moral choice earns credits while a bad one loses credits [13]. A past good deed earns individuals moral credits that can be spent on immoral choices in the future. According to this explanation, the individual knows the current choice is immoral, but feels that his or her past good deeds have earned them the right to wander astray from their moral self-image. A second explanation is that the past moral action changes the meaning of the subsequent behavior. This explanation posits that individuals will think that their past behaviors have established themselves as a moral person, thus an occasional unmoral choice does not affect their moral self image [9].

The phenomenon of moral self-licensing or cleansing has been observed in different domains. For example, Sachdeva, Iliev, and Medin [18] primed participants to write a short essay about themselves for their friends. One group was instructed to use morally positive words, and the other group used morally negative words. After writing the essay, participants were asked whether they were willing to donate part of their compensation to charity. The findings were consistent with the predictions of moral self-licensing and cleansing. Participants who wrote positively about themselves donated the least money out of the four groups. And participants who wrote negatively about themselves donated the highest amount. Another study showed that participants who purchased environmental-friendly products were more likely than those that purchased neutral products to lie or even steal in a subsequent test to gain more money [8]. Monin and Miller [11] found that past egalitarian acts licensed participants to make a subsequent discriminatory choice. Such balancing effects are also observed if participants were primed to think about a future choice before making a moral decision. Khan and Dhar [6] found that people who merely imagined themselves watching a high-brow movie (i.e. sophisticated but less enjoyable movie) later indulged themselves to choose a cookie over the low-fat yogurt.

According to moral balancing, participating in slacktivism may actually reduce likelihood of participating in, or efforts devoted to, the subsequent action because it gives individuals a license to slack off a little without feeling guilty. On the other hand, not partaking in a slacktivism of one's concern may increase likelihood and efforts devoted to a subsequent action.

Consistency and Commitment

On the other hand, supporters of slacktivism argue that light-weight online action may attract people who might otherwise not take action, and that the experience of taking action might encourage further action. These arguments are aligned with the consistency assumption of cognitive dissonance theory [3]. Cognitive dissonance theory posits that people have an inner drive to keep one's attitudes, beliefs, and behaviors consistent. When there is a disjuncture between one's attitudes, beliefs, or behaviors, this causes discomfort, a state of cognitive dissonance. In order to alleviate the discomfort, the individual will change his/her attitudes, beliefs, or behaviors to remain consistent. For example, cigarette smokers often know that smoking is bad for them, yet they smoke. This is a cognitive dissonance state, therefore smokers can either quit smoking (i.e. change the behavior), or reshape their belief and claim that only "heavy" smoking is harmful.

This psychological need for consistency has been used in a persuasion technique known as the foot-in-the-door technique. This technique entails the persuader making a small request that is likely to gain approval from an individual. Once the individual agrees with the request, the persuader then makes a larger request. Empirical research has shown that in order to remain consistent, the individuals who agreed to the small request are more likely to agree to a subsequent request even if it entails a higher cost [1]. The foot-in-the-door techniques have been shown to be effective even when the requests are made via computer-mediated communication such as emails [5].

A correlational survey study by Georgetown University's Center for Social Impact Communication and Ogilvy Public Relations Worldwide surveyed 2,000 Americans aged 18 and over. They found that Americans who partake in slacktivism are twice as likely to volunteer in other civic actions, four times more likely to encourage writing a letter to government, and six times more likely to sign a petition than people who does not partake in slacktivisms [14]. However, due to the correlational nature of this study, it is difficult to determine whether slacktivism lead to more participation, or people who are more civically engaged also tend to participate in slacktivism more.

Based on the assumption that individuals strive for consistency, one would predict that individuals who participate in the low-cost, low risk slacktivism are more likely to participate in a subsequent action even if it entails higher costs or risk.

Topic Congruency as a Moderator

If people have motivations to remain consistent, but sometime will balance their moral choices based on past and expected behaviors, the question becomes: when do people seek cognitive consistency? And when do people balance their moral decisions? Merritt, Effron, and Monin [9] suggest that because moral licensing works by changing how people interpret the subsequent action, it is more likely to happen when the meaning of the subsequent action is unclear and is open to interpretation.

In a study, Effron and Monin [2] asked participants to observe and rate behavior transgressions that are in the same or different domains. The results showed that observers were more forgiving of transgressions in different domains, but not when the behaviors are in the same domain. When the transgressions are in the same domain, observers viewed the person as more hypocritical. However, a recent study [18] suggests that observing other people's behavior is not moral balancing. Moral balancing only occurs when the behavior affects one's own self concept. This current study seeks to fill in this gap by conducting a field experiment in which the participants are asked to make moral choices after a personal decision to participate in slacktivism.

Based on the theories and previous studies, we hypothesize that people are more likely to behave consistently when the subsequent behavior is clearly related (congruent) to the slacktivism. And when the subsequent action is less related (incongruent), individuals will balance their efforts in the subsequent action based on their decision to partake or not in the slacktivism. In other words, partaking in slacktivism may undermine participation in an unrelated civic action, but not partaking in slacktivism may actually increase people's likelihood and efforts to an unrelated civic action.

H1a. When the issues are incongruent, participating in online activism will *decrease* one's likelihood to perform a subsequent civic action. (moral licensing)

H1b. When the issues are incongruent, not participating in online activism will *increase* one's likelihood to perform a subsequent civic action. (moral cleansing)

H2a. When the issues are congruent, participating in online activism will *increase* one's likelihood to perform a subsequent civic action. (consistency)

H2b. When the issues are congruent Not participating in online activism will *decrease* one's likelihood to perform a subsequent civic action. (consistency)

EXPERIMENT

We designed a 2x2 online experiment to test the hypotheses, manipulating whether or not participants were presented with a decision to participate in slacktivism (control—no petition/petition) and whether or not the post-slacktivism civic action was congruent to the slacktivism cause (congruent / incongruent charity cause).

Participants were recruited from Amazon's Mechanical Turk, and were offered $1 for participating in our study. In addition, participants were told that one out of 10 participants will receive a $5 bonus, which enabled us to study participants' post-slacktivism activism decision—their decision on how much to donate to a charity. We limited the experiment to participants residing in the United States to ensure that the participants share similar understanding of the issues used in this study.

To increase the realism of our controlled experiment, we used White House's petition website—*We the People* (petition.whitehouse.gov)—for the slacktivism. The goal of *We the People* is to encourage citizens to organize and gather petitions for expressing opinions towards the government. If the petitions reach 25,000 within 30 days, the White House will issue an official response to it.

At the time of the study, the Colorado movie theater shooting had just occurred. Soon after the shooting, there were two opposing petitions on *We the People*. One of the petitions was in support of banning assault rifles; the other was to veto any potential assault rifle bans. This provided an opportunity with an actual social issue for which participants on both sides of an issue may consider signing a petition.

All participants were asked to register on *We the People* at the start of our study. This is to control for the amount of effort exerted across conditions. After registration, participants were given a set of questions measuring their general civic interest and attitudes on gun control issues.

Participants were then told that there was a petition on *We the People* that matches their view on gun control, and were asked to read the petition. The petition they saw depended on their response to the gun control questions—those who are for gun control were shown the pro-gun control petition, and vice versa. Those who were in the petition condition were also provided a link to the petition and were invited to sign the petition to make a difference (see Figure 1). The participants in the control condition were not given any additional instruction. In or random assignment, we assigned twice as many people to the petition condition because we need to further separate participants who signed the petition and those that did not in our analyses comparing those who signed to those who did not.

Figure 1: Screenshot of the gun-control petition page.

After the manipulation, participants answered a post-test questionnaire measuring their emotion, their past petition signing experience, their past donation experience, and their future intentions to participate in 10 different types of civic actions.

After this, the participants were reminded that one out of 10 participants would get an addition $5 bonus compensation for participating in this study. However, they can decide to keep it all to themselves, or donate part of it to charity. We created a collective action scenario by stating that "The total amount of money allocated to [the charity] by all the winning participants will be aggregated and donated at the end of the study." In this case, the responsibility of donation is diffused among all the participants.

Half of the participants were randomly assigned to a congruent charity (National Rifle Association for gun supporters and Brady Campaign for gun-control supporters) and half were assigned to an incongruent education charity (Reading is Fundamental). The participants were presented with a scrollbar in which the default is keeping the $5 bonus to themselves and donate nothing. They need to actively move the scrollbar to decide how much they are willing to donate. After the donation, we asked some demographic questions and their attitudes towards all three charities (National Rifle Association, Brady Campaign, and Reading is Fundamental). Whether the participants made a donation (i.e. likelihood) and how much (i.e. amount) they chose to donate are used as the primary dependent variables in this study—participation in civic action subsequent to slacktivism (the petition).

This petition-then-donation is a fairly common design. Sierra Club and Amnesty International also invite people to donate after they signed online petitions.

Participants

932 participants were recruited from Amazon's Mechanical. After cleaning the data for participants who were responding to our questionnaire with the same response across all questions and participants who responded to the questionnaires with too little time on each page, 173 participants were removed, leaving 759 participants used for the analyses. The average age of the participants is 30.15 (*SD*=10.46), the youngest participant were 18 because we limited the study to participants' age over 18, and the oldest participant was 71 years old. There was slightly more females (52.2%, *n*=396) than males (47.5%, *n*=360), two of the participants (.3%) identified their sex as "other". The majority (87%) of the participants had "some college education" or higher.

As a manipulation check, we asked the participants if they thought signing the petition was difficult and risky (1 =not at all and 5 =extremely). The average score for difficulty was 1.35 (*SD*=.72), and the average score for risk was 1.92 (*SD*=1.07). The manipulation check indicated that for the participants in this study, signing the online petition was viewed as a low cost, low risk action, which fits the definition of slacktivism.

Analysis

Of the 759 participants included in the analyses, 230 (30.3%) are in the control condition, 200 (26.4%) chose not to sign the petition, and 339 (43.3%) signed the petition. Half of the participants are in the congruent condition (50.1%, n=380) and the other half are in the incongruent condition (49.9%, *n*=379). Across all the groups 56.1% (*n*=426) of the participants actively chose to donate some amount of money to charity. The distribution of the conditions is shown in table 1.

	Incongruent	Congruent	TOTAL
Control	116	114	230 (30.3%)
Not sign	104	96	200 (26.4%)
Sign	159	170	329 (43.3%)
TOTAL	379 (49.9%)	378 (50.1%)	759

Table 1: Distribution of participants among conditions

Preliminary analysis showed that the overall distribution of donation amounts was a non-normal distribution. This is mostly due to the bimodal distribution, with a second smaller center at 0—no donation. When we focus only on those who donated (n=426), the donation amount is considered normally distributed. Therefore we tried two methods of analyzing the data. First we conducted a multinomial logistic regression with a categorized donation amount as dependent variable. Then we used a two-step method analysis by analyzing the *likelihood* (i.e. donate or not) of making a donation with a binominal logistic regression, and the *amount* of donation by participants who made a donation with Analysis of Covariance (ANCOVA). The results of the two approaches were comparable.

To facilitate the interpretation of our results, in the following section we present results from the two-step analysis with binominal logistic regression for likelihood and ANCOVA for donation amount. This two-step analysis preserves the actual donation amount for comparison.

RESULTS

Incongruent Issues

Based on the moral balancing effects, hypothesis 1 posits that in the incongruent condition, participants who signed the online petition will be less likely to donate money to a charity (H1a), whereas participants who did not sign the online petition will be more likely to donate money (H1b).

A binary logistic regression was used to test this hypothesis. The binary variable of whether or not the participants donated to charity was used as the dependent variable. The petition signing conditions (control, no sign, signed) were dummy-coded and entered as the independent variables with the control group as reference group. In order to control for the possibility of self-selection bias, that the relationship between petition-signing and donations are due to individual differences, we included age, gender, education level, past general donation level, and attitudes towards the incongruent education charity (Reading is Fundamental) as controlled covariates.

There was no significant difference between the groups in likelihood of donating to charity. Participants who signed the petition (63.5%, n=101) were not less likely to donate to charity, and participants who did not sign the petition (54.8%, n=57) were not more likely to donate than the control group (58.6%, n=68). However, the results showed older participants (p<.01) and males were more likely to make a donation (p<.05). And participants who have more favorable attitudes towards the charity were more likely to donate (p<.001). See Figure 2 for comparison.

The full model for the binary logistic regression was significant, $X^2(7, n=379) = 72.14$, p<.001. However, the Wald criterion demonstrated that neither the signing (p=.84) nor the not-sign (p=.99) condition were significant predictor of making a donation. Table 2 shows the logistic regression coefficient, Wald test, and odds ratio for each of the predictors.

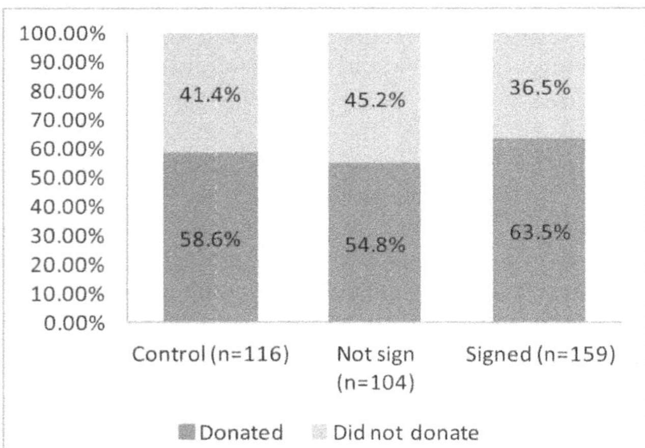

Figure 2: Percentage of incongruent donation between groups

PREDICTORS	B	Wald	p	Exp(B)
Age	-.031	6.905	.009	.970
Gender	.752	10.529	.001	2.121
Education	.004	.002	.965	1.004
Past donation level	.087	1.827	.176	1.091
Postive attitude towards charity	1.037	44.905	.000	2.820
No Sign (dummy coded)	.014	.002	.963	1.014
Sign (dummy coded)	.063	.052	.820	1.065
Constant	-3.923	25.400	.000	.020

Table 2: Binary logistic regression result on likelihood of incongruent donation

We then examined if there was a difference in amount donated in the subgroup of participants who chose to donate. An ANCOVA analysis was used to examine the subset of participants in the incongruent condition that donated to the education charity (n=226). The petition-signing conditions were used as the independent variable and the amount of donation was used as dependent variable. Again, age, gender, education, past general donation level, gun issue attitudes, and self-reported attitude towards the charity (Reading is Fundamental) are controlled as covariates. The result showed a significant difference between the groups, $F(2, 218)=3.66$, p<.05. (Table 3)

A post-hoc pair-wise Bonferroni test was used to examine if the results indicates moral licensing (H1a), moral cleansing (H1b), or both. The results showed that participants who signed the petition (M=2.25, SD=1.44) did not donate significantly less money to the incongruent charity than the control group (M=1.99, SD=1.28), hypothesis H1a was not supported. But participants who did not sign the petition donated significantly more money (M=2.58, SD=1.53) to charity in comparison to the control group, which suggest a moral cleansing effect (H1b).

PREDICTORS	Mean Square	F	p	Partial Eta Squared
Corrected Model	4.337	2.198	.036	.066
Intercept	2.923	1.482	.225	.007
Age	1.618	.820	.366	.004
Gender	.199	.101	.751	.000
Education	1.380	.700	.404	.003
Past donation level	5.383	2.729	.100	.012
Positive attitude towards charity	6.642	3.367	.068	.015
Sign Condition	7.481	3.792	.024	.034
Total n	226			

Table 3: ANCOVA results of incongruent donation amount

These results suggest that when the topic of the subsequent action is incongruent to the slacktivism, the slacktivism did not seem to affect likelihood of partaking in the subsequent action. But when the participants do take action, individuals who did not perform the slacktivism will devote more efforts in the subsequent action, possibly because of a moral cleansing effect.

Congruent Issues

Hypothesis 2 posited that people will maintain consistency when the charity is related to the online petition: signing the online petition will increase their likelihood of donating money (H2a); and not signing the online petition will decrease their likelihood of donating money (H2b).

More than half (62.9%, n=107) of the participants who signed the petition donated money to the related charity. This percentage is higher compared to the 41.7% (n=40) who did not sign, and also the control group (46.6%, n=53). See Figure 3 for comparison.

We ran a similar binary logistic regression to the one conducted in the incongruent condition to test hypothesis 2a and 2b. The binary variable of donation or not was used as the dependent variable. The dummy-coded petition signing conditions were used as the independent variables with the control group as reference group. We included the same control variables as in the previous analyses, except that attitude towards the charity is now a congruent organization (NRA for gun supporter, Brady foundation for gun-control supporters).

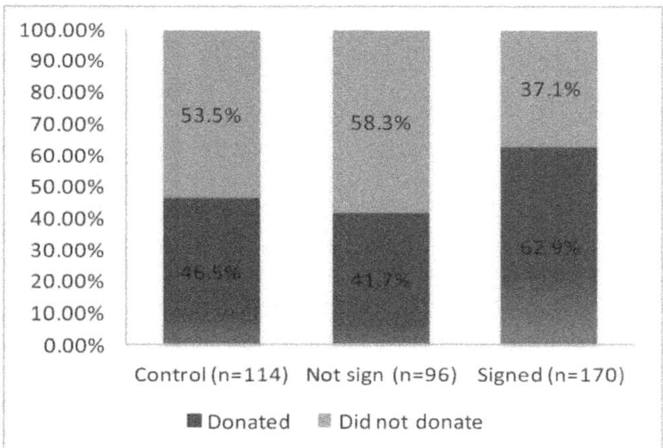

Figure 3: Percentage of congruent donation between groups

The results showed that males (p<.05), participants with higher education level (p<.05), participants who had stronger attitudes towards gun issues (p<.01), and more favorable attitudes towards the charity organization (p<.001) were more likely to make a donation. Despite all these, our hypothesis 1a was supported as signing the petition was a significant predictor of making a donation even after the self-selection biases were controlled for. The odds ratio indicates that an increase of 1 in signing the petition increases the odds of making a donation by 1.92 (Table 4). However, hypothesis 2b was not supported. Participants who did not sign the petition were no less likely to make a donation. The full model for the binary logistic regression was significant, $X^2(8, n=380) = 56.90$, p<.001. The Wald criterion demonstrated that the signing condition significantly predicted making a donation, p=.01.

PREDICTORS	B	Wald	Sig.	Exp(B)
Age	-.006	.262	.609	.994
Gender	.573	6.446	.011	1.774
Education	-.212	5.315	.021	.809
Past donation level	.062	1.034	.309	1.064
Gun issue attitude strength	-.770	10.613	.001	.463
Positive attitude towards charity	.543	16.637	.000	1.721
No Sign (dummy coded)	-.049	.027	.870	.952
Sign (dummy coded)	.653	6.185	.013	1.922
Constant	.189	.033	.856	1.208

Table 4: Binary logistic regression result on likelihood of congruent donation

We also examined if participants who signed the petition will donate more money to a related charity than participants who did not sign the petition, and whether participants who did not sign the petition will donate less.

Analysis of Covariance (ANCOVA) was used to analyze the subset of participants who donated in the congruent condition (n=199). The signing condition was used as independent variable, the donation amount was used as dependent variable, and the same control variables were controlled as covariates. The results indicate that there was no significant difference in amount of money donated between the signing conditions (F[2, 192]=1.06, $n.s.$). Participants who signed the petition (M=1.91, SD=1.32) did not donate more than participants who did not sign (M=2.02, SD=1.49), or the control group (M=1.68, SD=1.20). (Table 5).

Overall the results in the congruent condition show that when the subsequent action is related to the slacktivism, participants who signed the petition are more likely to participate in the following action, but not with more effort.

PREDICTORS	Mean Square	F	P	Partial Eta Squared
Corrected Model	8.013	5.389	.000	.184
Intercept	.438	.294	.588	.002
Age	10.545	7.091	.008	.036
Gender	3.936	2.647	.105	.014
Education	.298	.200	.655	.001
Past donation level	9.910	6.665	.011	.034
Gun issue attitude strength	.126	.085	.771	.000
Positive attitude towards charity	8.720	5.864	.016	.030
Sign conditions	1.581	1.063	.347	.011
Total n	200			

Table 5: ANCOVA of congruent donation amount

	Not sign	Sign	ΔR^2
Attend Protest	.01 (.43)	.04 (1.34)	.001
Buy Products in Support	.008 (.20)	.72 (1.92)	.005
Community Meeting	.02 (.52)	.07 (1.91)	.004
Debate with Others	-.04 (-.90)	.02 (.64)	.003
Persuade Friends	-.08 (-2.19)*	.03 (.79)	.009
Post or Forward News	-.04 (-1.32)	.04 (1.15)	.005
Sign Petition	-.17 (-4.52)***	.15 (3.90)***	.075
Volunteer	0 (.05)	.04 (1.12)	.001
Wear Badge	-.07 (-2.10)*	.01 (.21)	.006
Write Letter to Government	-.05 (-1.36)	.08 (2.28)*	.01

Numbers indicate adjusted beta coefficients. t statistics are shown in parenthesis.

***p<.05, **p<.01, ***p<.001**

Table 6: Hierarchical regression results

Intentions for Other Civic Actions

Because donating to charity is only one of many possible civic actions that one could participate in subsequent to slacktivism, we wanted to explore whether the decision to partake or not partake in slacktivism would affect intentions to participate in other future civic actions. After the experiment manipulation (control/ decision for petition), we asked participants to rate their likelihood of participating in 10 different civic actions on 5-point scales (1=*extremely unlikely* and 5 =*extremely likely*). Overall, participants in this study report highest intentions to participate in a petition (*M*=3.93, *SD*=1.16) and have the lowest intentions to participate in future protests (M=2.47, SD=1.24).

In order to examine if signing the petition increased or decreased intentions for these 10 future actions, we conducted 10 separate hierarchical regressions with the dummy-coded signing conditions (not sign/ sign) as the independent variable using the control group as reference group, and the intention for the 10 actions as separate dependent variables. Age, gender, education, and general civic interests were controlled by inserting them into the first block. The regression results are shown in Table 6.

The results indicated that after controlling for age, gender, education and general civic interests. Signing the petition only increased intentions to sign future petitions and to write letters to the government. It did not increase or decrease intentions on any of the other eight civic actions. Interestingly, these two actions also appear to be the two that will incur the least cost on participants in our list of civic actions. We will revisit this in the discussion section.

DISCUSSION

Increasingly, people and organizations are using information communication technologies for various forms of activism, such as fundraising, community building, lobbying and organizing. However, despite its potential to reach people and raise awareness at large scales, critics continue to question the efficacy of this low-cost, low risk form of activism. Critics argue that slacktivism may hurt real activism—people may feel satisfied through their slacktivism and this type of low-cost civic participation decreases other subsequent activities that could make a difference. If critics are correct, then we must re-consider the use of slacktivism.

Fortunately, contrary to critics' concern, we found no evidence that performing one form of slacktivism (i.e., signing online petitions) will undermine a subsequent civic activity (i.e., donating to a charity). In fact, we found scenarios where "slacktivism" can actually *increase* likelihood of participation in a subsequent collective action. When compared to the control condition, participants who signed petition were more likely to donate to a charity when the charity was related to the petition's cause (63% of those who signed donated compared to 46% who donated in the control condition).

In addition, what has been often overlooked in the discussion of slacktivism's efficacy is its effects on the people who decline to participate. In this study we found that when people are invited to sign a petition and decline to do so, they actually subsequently donated more to an incongruent charity. Compared to the control group, those who chose not to sign the petition donated about 30% (59 cents) more than those in the control condition.

Campaign designers can leverage this moral cleansing effect to increase compliance. Campaign designers could make a large, excessive online request for issue A that is likely to be turned down, which would make people feel guilty for their inaction. Then, the campaign designers would follow-up with a request for an unrelated issue B. That would then result in higher support for issue B than if people were approached to support issue B right away.

While this is similar to the door-in-the-face strategy from persuasion literature, there are subtle differences and we caution a direct comparison without additional research. The key difference is that the door-in-the-face technique usually requires an initial request that is costly and unreasonable [5]. This could be why the door-in-the-face technique has been shown to work regardless of the congruency between first and second tasks, but our moral cleansing effect only works when the tasks are incongruent.

Due to the positive influence slacktivism may have on participants and non-participants alike, our results actually show that slacktivism in general may help subsequent activism, regardless of how many people actually choose to participate in the slacktivism. When collapsing all our conditions together, simply *being asked* to sign the petition increased subsequent donation from the participants (from \$0.98 to \$1.25, t [756]=2.39, p=0.01).

However, while performing slacktivism increased likelihood of performing a congruent subsequent civic action, our findings also suggest that this increase may only be limited to scenarios where the subsequent civic action is also relatively low-cost. Our analyses of participants' intentions showed that signing the petition did not increase or decrease participants' intentions to participate in subsequent high cost actions such as attending protests, it only increased intentions to sign future petitions and write letters. To better inform slacktivism use, future studies need to build up on this current study to examine how the relative cost of actions affects the relationship between slacktivism and subsequent civic actions.

Theoretical Contributions

Besides making practical contributions by demonstrating the efficacy of online activism, this research also advances our understanding of when moral balancing occurs.

At the root of the slacktivism discussion is the concept of moral balancing—that performing good deeds license us to perform bad deeds and that performing bad deeds requires personal cleansing with good deeds. According to existing literature on slacktivism, we hypothesized that participants who signed the petition would contribute less to the charity subsequently (licensing effect), whereas those who did not sign the petition would contribute more to the charity (cleansing effect). We found no evidence for a licensing effect. But our results do support the cleansing effect when the issues are incongruent.

If moral balancing is in effect here, why did we only observe the cleansing effect but not the licensing effect? While our study is similar in structure compared to prior moral balancing studies [8, 9, 10, 18], one potential difference is that the cost of our second action (donation) may not be high enough to induce the moral licensing effect. Prior work suggests that in order for the licensing effect to be observed, the second action must be costly to the individual so that they will have more incentives to avoid taking action [18]. In our study, participants were offered a 1 in 10 chance to win \$5, which has only an expected value of \$0.50. The temptation to act in a potentially discrediting way is perhaps not that strong, while the cost of behaving in a socially-positive way is not that high—hence we observe the cleansing effect but not the licensing effect. In other words, participants in this study maybe more likely to donate money because of the low expected payoff. But the fact that there was significant difference between our petition conditions and the control group suggest that the petition choice does affect subsequent decisions on donation to charity.

Despite the interesting effects of moral balancing, an unanswered question is how these effects can be integrated with the wealth of research on consistency – when would one's behavior history constrain one to act consistently rather than liberate one to act inconsistently? Recent research has suggested that whether consistency comes in effect may be determined by the issue congruency (domains) between the first and subsequent moral actions. For example, Effron and Monin [2] hypothesized that moral balancing are more likely to be observed when the issues are unrelated. They asked observers to rate transgression behaviors and found that the target's past good deeds reduced condemnation from observers more when they were in a different domain than the subsequent transgression, but not when they were in the same domain. However it is unclear whether their finding are in fact moral licensing or on other effect because other studies have demonstrated that moral licensing is only effective when the action threatens one's own self-concept [18].

To extend this line of research, we tested participants' own contribution to charity when the charity is congruent to the petition's cause (gun control). Our findings suggest that while partaking in slacktivism increases likelihood of participating in a related subsequent civic action, it did not increase the amount of money donated. One possible explanation for this result is that participants who signed the petition sought to act consistent to avoid appearing hypocritical, thus they are more likely to comply with the charity request, but only devoting *enough* efforts to appear consistent. This explanation matches Schwarzwald, Bizman, and Raz's finding [20], in a similar petition-then-donation setup, participants who agreed to the first action are less concerned with the amount of donation but more about the act of donating itself.

LIMITATIONS AND GENERALIZABILITY

In our study design, we were careful in trying to balance control and realism—using controlled manipulations while also utilized two then-active petitions on White House's petition system. However, there are potential confounds that limit the generalizability of the study. First the sample came from Amazon's Mechanical Turk; it is possible that the sample is biased towards individuals who are more accustomed to using the internet and have more experience with the technology-aided activism. While this may be appropriate for studying slacktivism, as they may be the population who are more likely to participate in online activism, our findings may not generalize to other populations that do not spend as much time online and may have different perceptions of online activism.

Second, individuals may have also self-selected into participating in our study as they are told up front that the study is about gun control and civic participation. Our participants may then be more involved in the issue and feel stronger needs to express their opinions. Future studies may also consider replicating our results when the slacktivism are used for different causes.

Finally, we focused on a common, but specific form of online activism--signing online petitions in this study. More research is needed to confirm that our findings do generalize to other types of other low-cost online actions that may be considered slacktivism.

CONCLUSION

We used two actual online petitions on *We the People* to examine how decisions to participate in slacktivism or not influenced likelihood of donating and the amount of money donated to a subsequent charity. The results suggest that when the subsequent action is closely related to the slacktivism, people are motivated to remain consistent. But when the subsequent action is ambiguous or less related to the slacktivism, people will increase or decrease their likelihood and intensity based on their previous choice about the slacktivism. Campaign designers can design campaign that taps into these two psychological effects.

REFERENCES

1. Dolin, D.J., Booth-Butterfield, S. Foot-in-the-door and cancer prevention. *Health Communication* 7, 1 (1995), 55-66.
2. Effron, D. and Monin, B. Letting people off the hook: When do good deeds excuse transgressions? *Personality and Social Psychology Bulletin* 36 (2010), 1618-1634.
3. Festinger, L. *A theory of cognitive dissonance*. Evanston, IL: Row, Peterson, 1957.
4. Gladwell, M. Small change: Why the revolution will not be tweeted. *The New Yorker*, 4 October 2010.
5. Guéguen, N. Foot-in-the-door technique and computer-mediated communication. *Computers in Human Behavior* 18, 1 (2002), 11-15
6. Khan, U. and Dhar, R. Where there is a way, there is a will? The effect of future choices on self-control. *Journal of Experimental Psychology: General*, 136 (2007), 277–288.
7. Land, M.B. Networked activism. *Harvard Human Rights Journal*. NYLS Legal Studies Research Paper 22, 09/10 (2009), #13.
8. Mazar, N. and Zhong, C. B. Do green products make us better people? *Psychological Science* 21 (2010), 494–498.
9. Merritt, A.M. Effron, D.A. and Monin, B. Moral self-licensing: When being good frees us to be bad. *Social and Personality Psychology Compass* 4 (2010), 344-357.
10. Miller, D.T. and Effron, D.A. Psychological license: When it is needed and how it functions. In Zanna, M.P. and Olson, J.M. (Eds.*), Advances in Experimental Social Psychology* 43, San Diego, CA: Academic Press/Elsevier (2010), 117-158.
11. Monin, B. and Miller, D.T. Moral credentials and the expression of prejudice. *Journal of Personality and Social Psychology* 81 (2001), 33–43.
12. Morozov, E. The brave new world of slacktivism. *Net Effect – Foreign Policy*. Slate Group, 19 May 2009. Web. 5 Apr. 2010.
13. Nisan, M. (1991). The moral balance model: Theory and research extending our understanding of moral choice and deviation. In Kurtines, W.M. and Gewirtz, J.L. (Eds.), *Handbook of Moral Behavior and Development*. Hillsdale, NJ: Erlbaum (1991), 213-249.
14. Ogilvy Public Relations Worldwide and Georgetown University's Center for Social Impact Communication. Dynamics of Cause Engagement. At http://csic.georgetown.edu/research/215767.html
15. Olson, M. *The Logic of Collective Action*, Cambridge, MA.: Harvard University Press (1965).
16. Pepitone, J. Text donations raise $7m for Red Cross Haiti effort. *CNNMoney,* January 16, 2010.
17. Rotman, D. Vieweg, S. Yardi, S. Chi, E. Preece, J. Shneiderman, B. Pirolli, P. and Glaisyer, T. From slacktivism to activism: participatory culture in the age of social media. *Ext. Abstracts CHI 2011*, ACM Press (2011).
18. Sachdeva, S. Iliev, R. and Medin, D.L. Sinning saints and saintly sinners: The paradox of moral self-regulation. *Psychological Science* 20, 4(2009), 523-528.
19. Shulman, S.W. The case against mass e–mails: Perverse incentives and low quality public participation in U.S. federal rulemaking. *Policy & Internet* 1, 1 (2009), article 2
20. Schwarzwald,J. Bizman, A. and Raz, M. The foot-in-the-door paradigm: Effects of second request size on donation probability and donor generosity. *Personality and Social Psychology Bulletin* 9, 3 (1983), 443-450.
21. Vieweg, S. Hughes, A. Starbird, K. and Palen, L. Microblogging during two natural hazards events: What Twitter may contribute to situational awareness. *Proc. CHI 2010*, ACM Press (2010).

A Longitudinal Study of Follow Predictors on Twitter

C.J. Hutto
School of Interactive Computing
Georgia Institute of Technology
cjhutto@gatech.edu

Sarita Yardi
School of Information
University of Michigan
yardi@umich.edu

Eric Gilbert
School of Interactive Computing
Georgia Institute of Technology
gilbert@cc.gatech.edu

ABSTRACT
Follower count is important to Twitter users: it can indicate popularity and prestige. Yet, holistically, little is understood about what factors – like social behavior, message content, and network structure – lead to more followers. Such information could help technologists design and build tools that help users grow their audiences. In this paper, we study 507 Twitter users and a half-million of their tweets over 15 months. Marrying a longitudinal approach with a negative binomial auto-regression model, we find that variables for message content, social behavior, and network structure should be given equal consideration when predicting link formations on Twitter. To our knowledge, this is the first longitudinal study of follow predictors, and the first to show that the relative contributions of social behavior and message content are just as impactful as factors related to social network structure for predicting growth of online social networks. We conclude with practical and theoretical implications for designing social media technologies.

Author Keywords
Social networks; social media; computer-mediated communication

ACM Classification Keywords
H.5.3 [Group and Organization Interfaces]: Asynchronous interaction - Web-based interaction.

General Terms
Human Factors; Design; Measurement.

INTRODUCTION
Followers are Twitter's most basic currency. Building an audience of followers can create access to a network of social ties, resources, and influence. Yet, little is understood about how to grow such an audience. This paper examines multiple factors that affect tie formation and dissolution over time on the social media service Twitter. We collected behavioral, content, and network data approximately every three months for fifteen months. We examine specific user *social behavior choices*, such as: proportions of directed communications versus broadcast communications [6]; the total number of tweets produced; communication burstiness; and profile completeness [30]. We also assessed numerous attributes specific to the *content* of users' tweets, such as: propensity to express positive versus negative sentiment [26,37]; topical focus [40]; proportions of tweets with "meformer" content versus informational content [33]; frequency of others "retweeting" a user's content [5]; linguistic sophistication (reading difficulty) of tweets; and hashtag usage. Finally, we evaluated the impact of users' evolving *social network structure*, collecting snapshots of their friends and followers every three months for fifteen months. With this, we can evaluate the effects of network status, reciprocity [18], and common network neighbors.

Our variables were selected from prominent theoretical constructs bridging social science, linguistics, computer mediated communications, and network theory. This paper compares the relative contributions of factors from each perspective for predicting link formations in online social networks. We take a temporal perspective and develop a model that accounts for social behavior, message content, and network elements at several intervals for over a year. We use an auto-regressive, negative binomial regression model to explore the changes in users' follower counts over time. We find that *message content significantly impacts follower growth.* For example, in contrast to [26], we find that expressing negative sentiment has an adverse effect on follower gain, whereas expressing positive sentiment helps to facilitate it. Similarly, we show that informational content attracts new followers with a relative impact that is roughly *thirty times higher* than the impact of "meformer" content, which deters growth. We also find that *behavioral choices can also dramatically affect follower growth.* For example, choosing to complete one's profile and choosing directed communication strategies over broadcast strategies significantly stimulates follower growth over time. Finally, we show that *even simple measures of topology and structure are useful predictors of evolutionary network growth.*

Comparing across multiple variables related to message content, social behavior, and network structure allows us to interpret their relative effect on follower growth from different theoretical perspectives. We believe this is the first paper of its kind to compare the impact of all these factors together within a single longitudinal study. The temporal nature of the longitudinal method is crucial because it allows us to suggest causal relationships between these factors and network growth on Twitter.

BACKGROUND

Next, we consider related work showing how social behavior, message content, and network structure relate to follower growth. Our study draws from this prior work in deciding which variables to include in our analysis, and contributes new results to this body of literature by considering these variables temporally, and in conjunction with one another. For convenience and organizational purposes, we group our variables into three categories: social behaviors (e.g., interactional communication choices that a user makes), message content (e.g., linguistic cues), and social network structure. These categories are intended to be neither mutually exclusive nor exhaustive. However, we specifically call attention to content variables because they seem to be underrepresented in much of the related literature on follower growth dynamics [18,19,26,28,31].

Social Behavior and Follower Growth

Social Capital and Communication Behavior

Social capital refers to "the actual or potential resources which are linked to a durable network of more or less institutionalized relationships of mutual acquaintance or recognition" [4]. It is your relative social "worth," resulting from your position in a social network: i.e., the number and kind of the ties you maintain, your relative access to resources desired by those in your network, as well as your level of access to the resources your network ties possess [41].

In prior work, researchers distinguished between three kinds of social behavior that affect social capital in the social networking site, Facebook: (1) directed communications with specific, target individuals; (2) broadcast communications, which are not targeted at anyone in particular; and (3) passive consumption of content [6]. Because personalized messages are more likely to contain content that strengthens social relationships (such as self-disclosure and general supportiveness), it has been suggested that directed communications are useful for maintaining existing ties and for encouraging the growth of new ones. Indeed, previous research found that, when compared to broadcast communications and passive consumption, personalized one-on-one communication strategies have a measurably greater impact on self-reported social capital of Facebook users [6]. Other research suggests that informal personal conversation is a major reason for using a social media like Twitter [22,23], even for work and enterprise purposes [42,43]. However, the volume of messages and the rate at which they are transmitted (i.e., their "burstiness") are both correlated with unfollowing on Twitter [28]. Here, we test whether these behaviors help to grow followers on Twitter.

Profile Elements as Social Signals

Because there is some cost incurred with producing it, user-generated profile content is an important signal for conveying a trustworthy identity [11,12,30]. The shared context of social networking sites such as Facebook helps facilitate explicit and implicit verification of identity claims, and users are motivated to present their "ideal self" [17] in order to attract new connections. In [30], the authors explore the relationship between profile structure (namely, which fields are completed) and number of friends on Facebook. Based on a static snapshot of the social network at a large university, the authors found that the act of populating profile fields was strongly correlated with the number of friendship links. Compared to users without profile elements, users who had entered profile content had about two to three times as many friends. Based on this prior literature as well as our own intuition, we anticipate similar effects in our longitudinal data regarding network growth on Twitter. Assuming that people will be more likely to follow those who include identity cues in their profile (such as description, location, and personalized URL), we expect that the more these elements are included, the more successful one will be in growing an audience. Our study tests these assumptions.

Message Content and Follower Growth

Sentiment and Emotional Language

Sentiment analysis refers to the computational treatment of opinion, sentiment, and subjectivity in text [35]. Previous research found significant correlations between the number of followers of a Twitter user and that user's tendency to express emotions like joy and sadness [26] or positive versus negative sentiments [37] in their tweets. However, the authors in [26] acknowledge that an important limitation of the study was the static nature of the correlation analysis. In particular, we note the following passage from the paper:

> With the current analysis we cannot deduce causality; e.g., whether the emotional richness of interactions draws more followers or whether people tend to share more emotional content when they have larger audiences. (p. 382)

Although not explicitly stated, this same limitation also applies to [37]. We build on their prior work and extend it by studying changes in audiences *over time*. By relying on time-dependent regression analysis of longitudinal data to identify the relative effects of sentiment expression on follower gain, we are able to address the limitation noted above. This is conceptually similar to the approach used by [20] to characterize the relative effects of various factors on predicting Twitter adoption among young adults. Exploring dynamics over time gives us a stronger case for causality.

We also build on the approach in both [26] and [37] by extending our analysis beyond the LIWC2007 text analysis package to automatically classify positive and negative sentiment. LIWC [36] is a widely used and validated dictionary-based coding system often used to characterize texts by counting the frequency of more than 4,400 words in over 60 categories. However, LIWC does not include many features that are important for sentiment analysis of tweets. For example, our study also includes the 408 words in LIWC categories for P*ositive Emotion* and *Negative Emotion*, plus an additional ~2,200 words with positive or negative sentiment[1], as well as considerations for sentiment-laden acronyms/initialisms, emoticons, negations, and slang. These additional characteristics are known to be important features of sentiment analysis for microblogs like Twitter [10]. Also, some words are bound to connote more extreme sentiment than others (e.g., "good" versus "exceptional"). Thus, in addition to simply counting occurrences of positive or negative words (i.e., the LIWC method), we also assess the directional magnitude (i.e., *intensity*) of the sentiment for each word, associating human coded valence scores ranging from -5 to +5 for each word in our dictionary.

Topical Focus

The principle of *homophily* asserts that similarity engenders stronger potential for interpersonal connections. In the selection of social relationships, people tend to form ties to others who are like them – a finding that has been one of the most pervasive empirical regularities of modern social science [32]. Sharing interests with another person is one form of similarity [14]. A Twitter user who discusses a wide range of topics may appeal to a broader audience, therefore attracting more followers – a notion that, according to [40], is supported by the economic theory of network externalities [24,38]. In [40], the authors describe how initial topical focus affected users' ability to attract followers. However, the users in [40] self-identified as providers of *politically oriented* tweets, and it is unknown whether the findings from [40] will hold for a more heterogeneous sample of Twitter users. Our study addresses this question.

Informativeness: Information Brokering and "Meformers"

In [29], the authors highlight the dual nature of Twitter as both a social network and as a news/information medium. Also, [33] suggests two basic categorizations of Twitter users as Informers (those who share informational content) versus "Meformers" (those who share content about themselves). Meformers were reported to have almost three times fewer followers than Informers. The authors note that "the direction of the causal relationship between information sharing behavior and extended social activity is not clear" [33:192]. We explore whether this type of message content affects growing a social media audience over time.

Network Structure and Follower Growth

Network Size, Reciprocity and Mutuality

Preferential attachment, or the phenomenon whereby new network members prefer to make a connection to popular existing members, is a common property of real life social networks [3] and is useful for predicting the formation of new connections [31]. The number of followers a person maintains has been shown to reduce the likelihood that the person will be unfollowed in the future [25], meaning popular people often remain popular. Additionally, we can calculate the "attention status" of an individual within their own Twitter network by taking the ratio of followers (those who pay attention to the user) to following (those among whom the user divides their attention). Such measures reflect ego-level network attributes that affect the decision of others to follow the user. On the other hand, [18] shows that follower counts alone do not fully explain interest in following. In other words, popularity, in and of itself, does not beget popularity. Dyadic properties such as *reciprocity* and *mutuality* also play key roles in the process of tie formation and dissolution [18,25].

Common Neighbors: Structural Balance and Triadic Closure

In addition to dyadic structural properties, we also consider *triads* (structures of three individuals). Specifically, we are interested in the concepts of *structural balance* and *triadic closure*. For example, consider the case where three people form an undirected network. If A is friends with X, and X is friends with B, then according to Heider's theory of cognitive balance, the triad is "balanced" when A is friends with B, but "unbalanced" when A is not friends with B [21]. As the number of common neighbors (occurrences of "X") between A and B increases, the likelihood of the A-B tie being formed also increases [8]. This principle of structural proximity is known as *triadic closure* [13]. Measuring the occurrences of common network neighbors is useful for link predictions in real life social networks [31] as well as online social networks [18,19,25]. We explore the extent to which these network structures impact follower gain as compared to message content and social behavior.

Limitations (and Benefits) of Longitudinal Observations

Making causal claims with observational data can be problematic. It is impossible to absolutely rule out every possible "third factor" that might account for some portion of an association between an independent variable and its effect on the dependent variable. We try to mitigate this problem by accounting for as many "third factors" as is feasible. Longitudinal studies are still correlational research, but these correlations have greater power because we have time-dependent, repeat observations. In other words, when input A is consistently and reliably observed preceding outcome B for the exact same group of individuals time after time, then we have greater confidence in suggesting a causal relationship between A and B.

METHODS

Data Collection and Reduction

We collected data from 507 active Twitter users who collectively provided us with a corpus of 522,368 tweets spanning the 15 months between August 2010 and October 2011. In addition to the tweets, we also have snapshots of friends and followers taken at periodic intervals (a total of five periods, each approximately three months in duration). We were interested in discovering the relationship between the factors discussed above within each three-month period and the subsequent changes in follower counts at the end of that period. To build our dataset, Twitter accounts were obtained by recording unique account IDs that appeared on

[1] http://fnielsen.posterous.com/afinn-a-new-word-list-for-sentiment-analysis

the public timeline during a two-week period in August 2010, and then screened for certain attributes. The subset selected for inclusion in this study consisted of those accounts that met the following four criteria when sampled approximately every three months:

1. Tweet in English, as determined by inspecting the users' profiles for the designated language via Tweepy[2], a Twitter API library for Python, as well as Python's Natural Language Tool Kit[3] (NLTK) for language detection on the users' 20 most recent tweets. This filter is necessary for our linguistic predictors (described later), although it may restrict the generalizability of our results.
2. Have Twitter accounts that are at least 30 days old at the time of the first collection period, and are therefore not new to the service. This was done to avoid the potential confounding effects of users who have just joined and are likely building up their followership based on existing friends and acquaintances (rather than attracting followers based on the variables we track).
3. Follow at least fifteen other "friends" and have at least five followers. This removes a large portion of unengaged or novice users, and is close to Twitter's own definition of an "active user"[4,5].
4. Tweet at least twenty times within each time period (a *time period* is the approximately three-month interval between snapshots of users' social networks). This removes the confounding effects of inactive accounts.

Response Variable (dependent measure)

Follower growth: change in follower counts for users at the end of a given three-month time period, as compared to the follower counts at the end of the previous period.

Predictor Variables

Behavioral and Social Interaction Variables

Tweets in period: the total number of tweets produced by a user in a three-month time period.

Peak tweets per hour ("burstiness"): for a given three-month time period, the maximum rate of tweets per hour.

Directed communications index: captures replies and mentions, as well as consideration for the social signal sent when the person "favorites" someone else's tweet, calculated as "@" count plus favorites count divided by the total number of tweets in a period.

Broadcast communication index: the ratio of tweets with no "@" at all in the tweet to total number of tweets in a period.

Profile cues of "trustworthiness" of Twitter identity: (1) the length, in characters, of the user's self-defined profile description, (2) whether the user has indicated a personal URL in their profile, and (3) whether the user has indicated their location. We collected data about whether the user had a personal profile image or the default egg image, but there was insufficient variation in the data to use this variable (all users in our sample had non-default images).

Message Content Variables

Positive (Negative) sentiment intensity rate: ratio of the sum of the valence intensity of positive (negative) language used in tweets to the total number of tweets in a period. In a separate formative evaluation involving a small subset of tweets from the corpus (n=300), our custom sentiment analysis engine performed quite well. The correlation coefficient between our sentiment analysis engine and ratings from three human judges was high (r = 0.702); better than the Pattern.en sentiment analysis engine[6] (r = 0.568). The correlation among human judges was r = 0.851.

Informational content index: the ratio of tweets containing either a URL, "RT", "MT", "HT" or "via" to total number of tweets in the period.

Meformer content index: the ratio of tweets containing any of the 24 self-referencing pronouns identified in LIWC (e.g., words like "I", "me", "my", "we", "us") to total number of tweets in the period.

Topic focus: following [40], this is the average cosine similarity (ranging between 0 and 1) for every unique paired combination of a user's tweets in a given time period.

User tweets retweeted ratio: the total number of times a user's tweets were retweeted, relative to the total number of tweets produced by the user in the period.

Hashtag usage ratio: the total number of hashtags used in a period relative to the total number of tweets in the period.

TReDIX: the "Tweet Reading Difficulty Index" is a measure developed by the authors to capture the linguistic sophistication of a set of tweets. It is inspired by the Readability Index (RIX, c.f. [1]) and is based on the frequency of real English words with 7 or more letters. TReDIX is a ratio of the total count of long words appearing in tweets within a time period relative to the number of tweets in the period.

Network Topology/Structural Variables

In-link reciprocity rate: the number of followers that the user is also following relative to the total number of followers in the user's social network at the end of each period.

Attention-status ratio: ratio of followers (those who pay attention to the user) to following (those among whom the user divides their attention), calculated based on the user's existing social network at the end of each period.

[2] http://code.google.com/p/tweepy

[3] http://www.nltk.org

[4] http://www.businessinsider.com/chart-of-the-day-how-many-users-does-twitter-really-have-2011-3

[5] http://techland.time.com/2011/09/09/twitter-reveals-active-user-number-how-many-actually-say-something

[6] http://www.clips.ua.ac.be/pages/pattern-en#sentiment

Network overlap: where A is the user of interest and B is either a follower or a friend of A, this is the raw network overlap (count of common neighbors) between A and B. The final measure is the sum for user A's entire network.

Other (Control) Variables

Age of account: the age of a user's Twitter account (in days) at the end of a time period, to control for the likely differences between older, more established accounts and newer, developing accounts.

No. of followers: The total number of followers at the end of a given period, a plausible criterion used by other potential followers when evaluating whether or not to follow the user. We include the number of followers as a control to account for popularity-based preferential attachments.

No. of friends ("followees"): The number of accounts the user is following at the end of a given period, also a plausible criterion used by potential followers when deciding whether to follow a user.

Change in followers (previous period): change in follower count at the end of time period t_{-1} (the previous time period), is a lagged variable used to control for second order follower growth dynamics for the dependent variable in the time-dependent auto-regressive model. This addresses the issue of possible preferential (de)attachment for rising or falling "stars" [3], and helps mitigate concerns related to lack of independence among repeated observations.

We test the predictive power of these variables by incorporating auto-regression into a negative binomial regression model. Negative binomial regression is used for modeling count variables, and is well-suited to modeling dependent variables of count data which are ill-dispersed (either under- or over- dispersed) and do not have an excessive number of zeros [7], as is the case with our data set. Auto-regressive models attempt to predict an output of a system based on previous observations [34], which allows us to mitigate concerns associated with lack of independence for repeated measures by incorporating a lagged variable into our model. In the present study, we use auto-regression to account for the overall slope of follower gain heading into a given time period. Change in follower growth at the end of time period t_0 is therefore conditioned upon the change in follower growth at the end of t_{-1} (the previous time period).

After removing tweets from the first time period interval (it only provides the initial baseline of counts from which we derive changes in follower growth for subsequent periods) and the second time period (in order to incorporate dependency on change in growth for the auto-regressive model), we have 507 unique active Twitter users who collectively provided 1,836 instances of follower growth across the remaining four time periods of our analysis.

RESULTS

We first present descriptive statistics for the dependent measure (follower growth) and the twenty-two predictor and control variables. These variables are organized into three convenience categories: behavioral/social interaction, message content, and network topology/structure.

Descriptive Statistics

Table 1 shows descriptive statistics (mean, standard deviation, minimum, first quartile, median, third quartile, maximum, and density plots) for the response variable (follower growth) as well as seventeen of the twenty-two predictor and control variables. For space reasons, we omit user profile data from the table, and instead provide the following summary: the majority of users had URLs listed in their profile (mean=86%, SD=35%), most listed their location (mean=97%, SD=16%), and the average profile description was 85 characters long. We also omit the lagged variable *change in followers (previous period)* (mean=106.96, SD=551.84, median=25). The density plots in Table 1 show some skewness (lack of symmetry) and generally high kurtosis (peaked, rather than flat, distributions) for many of the variables. This makes the median a better measure of central tendency than the mean for many of the variables, and the density plots reveal the distributions for each variable.

Behavioral and Social Interaction Variables

Most users tweetd between 131-364 times in three months (median=222), usually with bursts of no more than eight tweets within a single hour. The Broadcast Communication Index shows the proportion of tweets that are not directed to any specific person. Most people use broadcast communication strategies for about 30%-60% of their messages (median=45%).

Message Content Variables

Proportionally, most people tweet about twice as much positive and neutral content as negative content, with an average of 106 tweets identified as positive (the same average were neutral tweets), and 51 tweets labeled as negative. (Note: this data did not fit in Table 1). In terms of *intensity* of positive or negative language, most people are generally about three times more positive than they are negative in their tweets (see Table 1). The proportion of users' tweets identified as "meformer" content was nearly normally distributed – users talk about themselves in 41% of their messages, on average. Informational content accounted for 24% of messages. This closely resembles the results from [33]. The mean and median of topical focus (average cosine similarity of one's own tweets) indicate that in general, people post a fairly diverse range of content. The ratios of retweets (0.02-0.12, median=0.05) and hashtag usage (0.06-0.26, median=0.13) to total number of tweets in a period are moderate for the majority of users – retweets comprised about 12% of users' messages, and hashtags were used in about 26% of tweets. The Tweet Reading Difficulty Index (TReDIX) is evenly distributed, with most people using moderately sophisticated language – about 2.36 long words per tweet, on average. On the original RIX scale, an index of 2.4 is equivalent to a seventh grade reading level [1].

	Variable	Mean	Std Dev	Min	1st Q	Median	3rd Q	Max	Density Plot
D.V.	Follower Growth	194.2	832.7	0	12	36	106	16,623	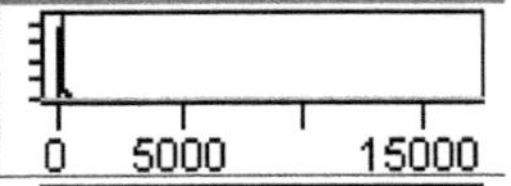
Behavioral and Social Interaction Variables	Number of Tweets in period (a control)	262.6	176.3	21	131	222	364	1,552	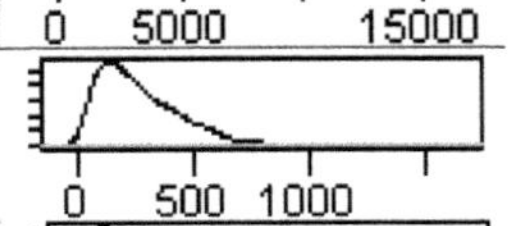
	Peak tweets per hour ("Burstiness")	6.39	5.78	0.15	2.79	4.79	7.9	48.9	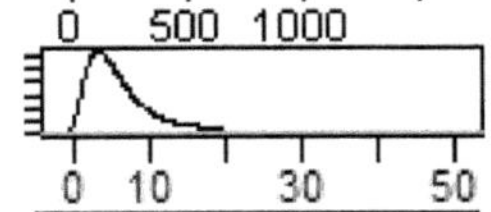
	Directed communications	1.91	7.4	0	0.58	0.83	1.22	190.25	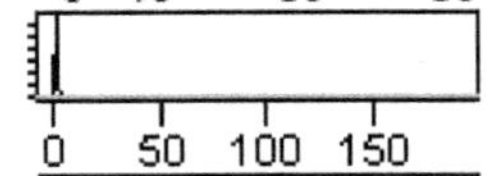
	Broadcast communications	0.48	0.22	0	0.31	0.45	0.62	1	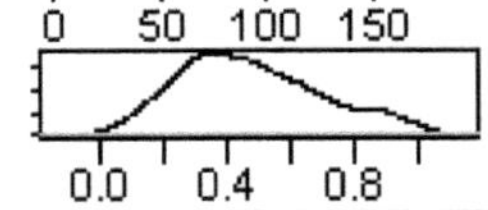
Message Content Variables	Positive Sentiment Intensity Rate	0.37	0.14	0.05	0.27	0.35	0.44	1.08	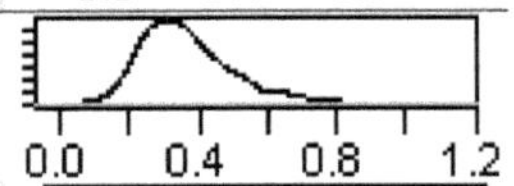
	Negative Sentiment Intensity Rate	0.14	0.06	0	0.095	0.13	0.17	0.5	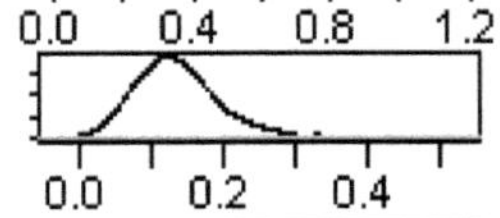
	Informational content index	0.3	0.23	0	0.12	0.24	0.41	1	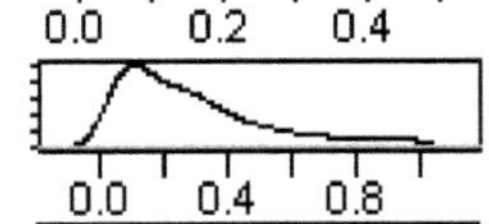
	"Meformer" content index	0.41	0.14	0	0.33	0.41	0.50	0.79	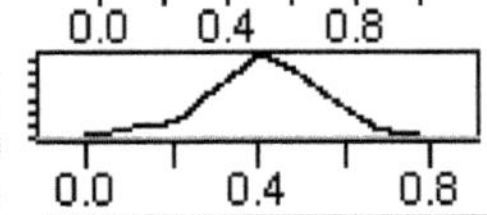
	Topic focus	0.008	0.01	0.002	0.005	0.008	0.01	0.25	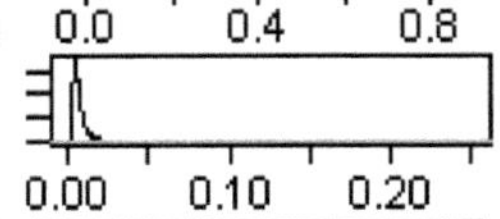
	User RT ratio	0.15	0.4	0	0.02	0.05	0.12	5.1	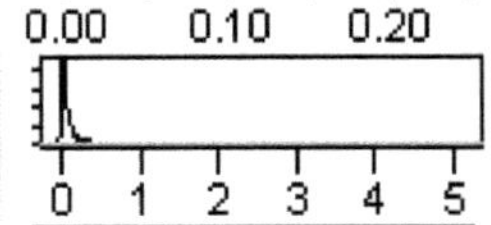
	Hashtag usage ratio	0.2	0.24	0	0.057	0.13	0.26	2.82	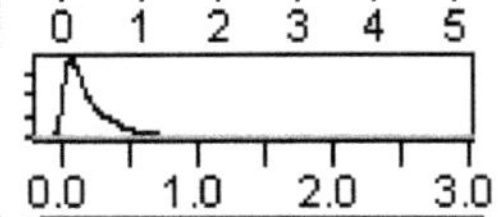
	TReDIX	2.36	0.64	0.84	1.94	2.31	2.696	6.95	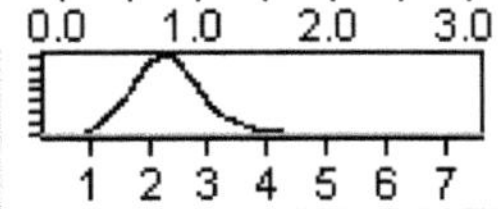
Network Topology / Structural Variables	Reciprocity rate	0.28	0.19	0	0.125	0.25	0.4	0.9	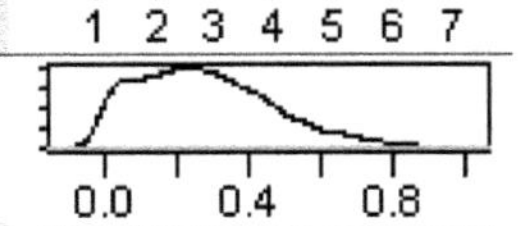
	Attention-status ratio	2.18	7.06	0	0.895	1.19	1.90	149.25	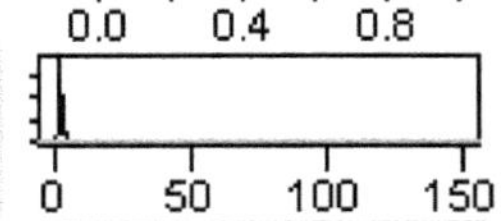
	Network overlap	94,730	351,388	0	2,070	10,472	50,263	5,308,200	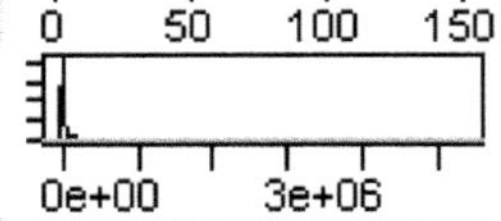
	No. of followers at end of period (a control)	1,145.42	3391.93	15	175.8	391.5	948.8	45,932	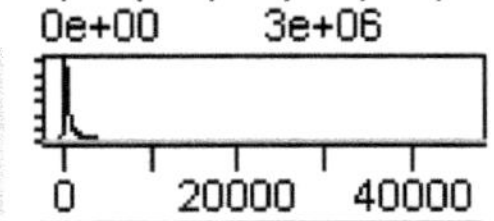
	No. of friends at end of period (a control)	830.63	2879.43	18	135	289.5	661.2	42,797	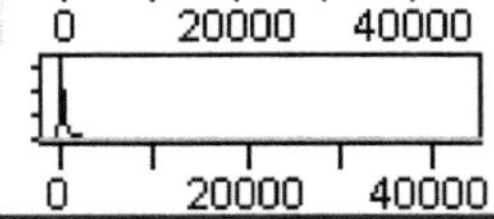

Table 1: Descriptive statistics for the dependent variable (follower growth) and seventeen of the twenty-two predictor and control variables. The x-axes of the density plots represent the measured value of the variable, and the y-axis indicates the density of users observed at a particular value. For example, one can interpret the table to indicate that most users grew their Twitter audience at a rate of about 12 to 106 new followers (median=36) every 3 months. The density plot indicates that most users fell within this range.

Network Topology / Structural Variables

The majority of users have 176-949 followers, and 135-661 friends (medians are 391.5 and 289.5, respectively). The density plots indicate that few users fell outside these ranges, but those that exceeded the range did so by a large margin. In general, users reciprocally follow-back about a quarter of their followers (mean=28%, median=25%). The density plot for attention-status ratio (that is, followers to following) shows a very tight distribution around the range 0.895 to 1.9, indicating that many people have similar numbers of in-degree connections (followers) as out-degree connections (friends). About 2K-50K overlapping network neighbors are typical, though some users with very large networks have over two orders of magnitude more.

Comparing Predictors of Follower Content

We now turn to the core of our results: how well do these variables predict follower growth over time and by how much? The overall significance of the negative binomial auto-regressive model is very high (p < 2e-16), meaning the model is very well-suited to characterizing the effects of the described variables on follower growth over time. Significance was determined by testing for the reduction in deviance from a null model, $\chi^2(22, N{=}1{,}836) = 5943.9 - 2111.9 = 3832.0$, p < 2e-16. This is important in order to have confidence when interpreting the regression coefficients of the model components (b and β), which are depicted in Table 2.

The unstandardized b coefficients in Table 2 are useful in that they can be directly interpreted according to the native units of each predictor: for each one unit change in the predictor variable, the log count of the response variable is expected to change by the respective b coefficient (all else being equal). While this is valuable for a broad range of prediction and forecasting purposes, we are also interested in comparing the *relative* impact of each predictor; we therefore report the standardize beta (β) coefficients (see also Figure 1 – not pictured are three of the control variables used in this study: extant friends and followers, age of account, and the lagged variable). As expected, these controls absorb comparatively large portions of the variance (see Table 2). We are interested in how much our other variables contribute above and beyond these controls.

Among the behavioral and social interaction variables, the Broadcast Communications Index (BroadcastComms), the burstiness measure (PeakTPH), and all three of the profile elements (length of description, URL, and location) each emerge as significant predictors of follower growth. The moderately strong negative effect of BroadcastComms (b = -1.02, β = -2.67e-04) suggests that having too many undirected messages will hinder audience growth. Interestingly, the Directed Communications Index (DirectedComms) was not significant in the model. Apparently, in the presence of all the other variables, the significance of social interactions using @replies and @mentions is muted, at least in terms of its effect on attracting *new* followers.

	b	Std. Err.	Std. β	p-value
NumTweetsPd	2.63e-04	1.62e-04	5.57e-05	0.104
PeakTPH	2.35e-02	4.94e-03	1.63e-04	1.96e-06***
DirectedComms	4.24e-03	3.37e-03	3.77e-05	0.208
BroadcastComms	–1.02	1.28e-01	-2.67e-04	1.89e-15***
ProfDescLen	3.09e-03	5.57e-04	1.72e-04	2.94e-08***
ProfHasURL	3.91e-01	7.14e-02	1.65e-04	4.27e-08***
ProfHasLocation	3.29e-01	1.52e-01	6.30e-05	0.03995 *
PosSentiRate	8.19e-01	1.96e-01	1.37e-04	2.87e-05***
NegSentiRate	–2.38	4.82e-01	-1.75e-04	7.53e-07***
InformContent	1.18	1.41e-01	3.31e-04	< 2e-16 ***
MeformerContent	–6.72e-02	1.99e-01	-1.12e-05	0.736
TopicFocus	3.75e-01	2.32	5.13e-06	0.872
UserTweetRT'd	9.53e-01	7.23e-02	4.60e-04	< 2e-16 ***
HashtagUseRate	–4.28e-01	1.12e-01	-1.23e-04	1.33e-04***
TReDIX	1.28e-01	4.22e-02	9.85e-05	2.43e-03 **
Reciprocity	3.52e-01	1.46e-01	7.95e-05	0.01597 *
Attn-Status	1.63e-02	4.48e-03	1.38e-04	2.79e-04***
NetworkOverlap	1.20e-06	1.26e-07	5.06e-04	< 2e-16 ***
NumFriends	–1.73e-04	2.88e-05	-5.98e-04	1.96e-09***
NumFollowers	2.70e-04	2.4e-05	1.10e-03	< 2e-16 ***
ChngFollPrevPd	–2.71e-04	8.82e-05	-1.79e-04	2.17e-03 **
AgeOfAccount	4.10e-03	2.26e-04	5.50e-04	< 2e-16 ***

Table 2: Neg. Binomial Auto-Regressive Model Coefficients.

Message content variables are evenly distributed along the rank ordered list of predictors (see Figure 1). Of the 17 (non-control) variables depicted, expressing negative sentiments in tweets is the second most harmful factor to growing a Twitter audience. Interestingly, overuse of hashtags in message content ("hashtag abuse") will also significantly reduce follower gain. On the other hand, producing or passing along informational content is among the top predictors, having a significant positive effect on follower growth rates (β = 3.31e-04). Also, having content that is "retweet worthy" is a very good indicator that a user will gain followers (β = 4.60e-04). Using more sophisticated language in messages also has a moderately strong relative effect on attracting and retaining followers (β = 9.85e-05).

Network oriented variables are also evenly distributed along the ranked list in Figure 1. Reciprocity, status, and network overlap were each significant in the model, even in the presence of the variables controlling for network size and user popularity.

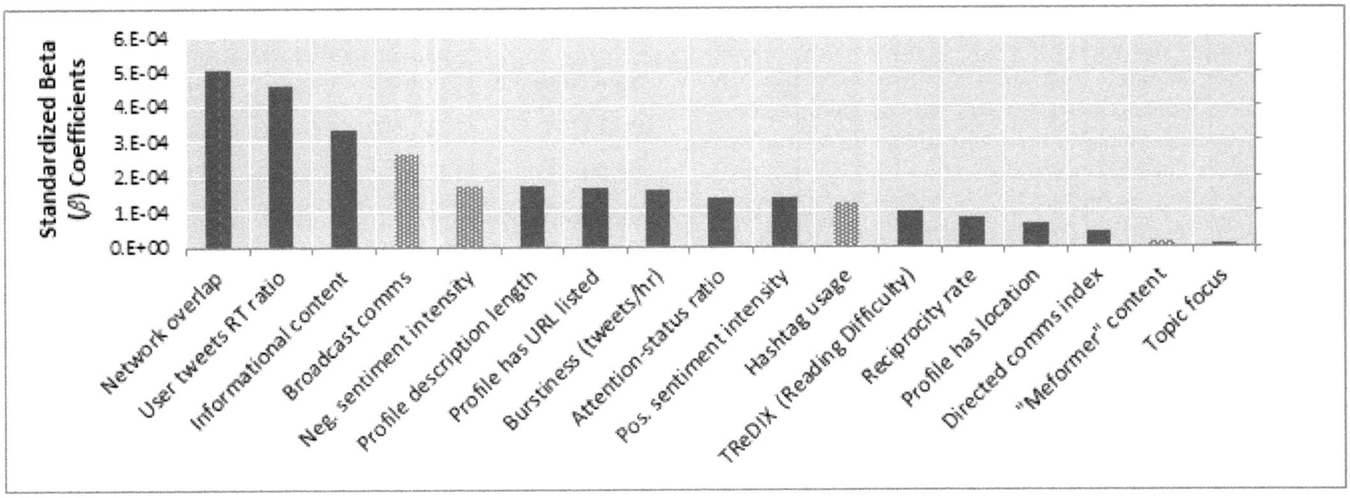

Figure 1: Standardized beta coefficients (β) show the relative effect sizes that each input variable has on follower growth. Green bars indicate positive effects on follower gain, and red bars indicate negative effects (i.e., suppression of follower growth).

DISCUSSION

It Matters What You Say, And How You Say It

Our first major finding is that *message content significantly impacts audience growth*. Six of our eight content variables (negative and positive sentiment, informational and "retweetable" content, hashtag usage, and linguistic sophistication) were found to be significant predictors of audience growth. We find that expressing negative sentiment has an adverse effect on follower gain. This is a contrast to [26], where social sharing of negative emotions correlates to higher numbers of followers. However, [26] studied a static snapshot of existing network ties. Our longitudinal data suggest that sentiment expression may have different (indeed opposite) effects on the formation of new ties over time. This might be because Twitter is a medium dominated by very weak social ties [16], and negative sentiment from strangers may be unpleasant or uncomfortable for a potential new follower to see. For existing ties, on the other hand, negative expressions such as the sharing of a death, poor health, bad news, or a state of unhappiness, can trigger opportunities to build bonding social capital between stronger ties who want to seek and provide emotional support [41]. Or, as [26] put it, "gift giving where users directly exchange digital 'gifts' in terms of emotional messages".

We also found that informational content attracts followers with an effect that is roughly *thirty times higher* than the effect of "meformer" content, which deters growth. We think this is due to the prevalence of weak ties on Twitter [16], and that informativeness [19,28] is a more palatable alternative to meforming among such networks. Kollock [27] describes information as a public good that anyone can consume and share. Retweeted content is another such digital public good that provides both attribution—and thus, motivation—to the original author as well as informational content for the community. Retweeted content also provides *social proof* [9] that a user may be worth following, enabling the process of triadic closure [13] to unfold, whereby followers of a user's followers complete the triad with the user [18].

The mean and median of topical focus (average cosine similarity of tweets) for our heterogeneous group is roughly an order of magnitude less than those same measures from a more homogenous group of politically-oriented tweeters described in [40], but like [40], we also find that topically focused users tend to attract more followers. Twitter users are likely driven by homophily [32], where they seek out content and users who are similar to themselves.

Finally, we found that the Tweet Reading Difficulty Index (TReDIX) has a positive impact on audience growth. Walther's Social Information Processing (SIP) theory suggests that people rely on linguistic cues like spelling and vocabulary to compensate for the lack of traditional contextual cues available in face-to-face settings [39]. Twitter users apparently seek out well-written content over poorly written content when deciding whether to follow another user.

Behavioral Choices Also Matter

Our second major finding is that *social behavioral choices can dramatically affect network growth*. Similar to previous research that showed positive effects of profile completeness for static Facebook networks [30], we find similar results for evolving Twitter networks. Signaling theory suggests that choosing to complete user profile elements helps persuade other users one's authenticity and trustworthiness, making them more likely to become followers [12]. Profile content provides at minimum *conventional signals* of identity (which are easy to fake), but the nature of profiles on social network sites makes these signals somewhat more reliable due to social accountability [12]. Regardless, users who do take the time to give profile information have the opportunity to emphasize the characteristics that they think will present them in the best light without necessarily being deceptive [17]. Others can use this profile information to form impressions prior to deciding whether to pursue or continue a connection [30]. Likewise, choices about interactions and communication techniques, such as sending directed versus broadcast messages, will also impact the rate at which a user will grow their audience. Consistent with previous research studying existing Facebook networks [6], we find that directed communications have a positive effect on follower growth for Twitter. Unlike [6] however, we note a very strong negative effect of broadcast communication techniques during the process of network formation. Such undirected messages are a relatively novel feature of social media; our results suggest that relying on such communication techniques will significantly suppress growth.

Even Simple Measures of Network Structure Are Useful

Our third finding is that *variables related to network structure are useful predictors of audience growth.* This finding is not necessarily surprising, given the emphasis on such factors in much of the related literature [3,18,19,25,31]. Indeed, while our results indicate that even simplistic calculations of network structure can prove to be quite powerful, we stress that such factors should not necessarily be privileged over message content or social behavior measures.

Practical Implications

A vital prerequisite to building social capital of any kind (bonding or bridging) is that a connecting tie must exist between individuals. The practical implication of this fundamental antecedent to social capital motivates the selection of our dependent variable. The number of followers you have is arguably the most important status symbol on Twitter. Rapid follower growth may be an early indication of a rising star, or an emerging leader, within the network. A rapid gain in followers intuitively implies that people like what you're posting and want more of the same. Thus, social capital is a necessary (though not sufficient) precursor to the notion of *interpersonal influence* in social networks [2] – an attribute of interest to strategic communicators, marketers, advertisers, job seekers, activist groups and any entity or organization wishing to disseminate specific messages in a timely manner. Additionally, many users are simply interested in knowing their own relative degrees of popularity or social networking "clout". Sites like HootSuite.com and SocialFlow.com offer web services oriented towards helping its users capture and retain the attention of social media audiences. Companies like these can directly leverage our results to build tools that that make recruiting and retaining network members easier and more effective. For example, in conjunction with a validated tie-strength model (c.f., [15] or [16]), the results of our study suggest that social media technology developers can help users retain existing followers by actively promoting negative sentiment content to strong ties, and experiment with demoting it with weak ties. Similarly, to attract the attention of new audience members, developers can consider implementing user interface components which a) facilitate the sharing of informational content through positive reinforcement, b) encourage directed communications and group discussions, c) provide feedback regarding behavioral patterns (e.g., burstiness), and so on.

Theoretical and Methodological Implications

Our findings also have theoretical (and, by extension, methodological) implications. Our variables were selected from prominent theoretical perspectives bridging social science theory (social capital, signaling theory, presentation of self, homophily, status/power), and network theory (size and preferential attachment, tie strength, reciprocity, balance and closure). We also consider behavioral aspects of computer mediated communications (profile completeness, directed versus broadcast communication strategies) and message content (sentiment, informational versus meformer content, topical focus, linguistic sophistication). Few social media studies have attempted to report on relative impacts of such diverse variables. Compared to how much is known about each theory, very little is known about how they relate to one another. Our research compares their relative contributions to predicting link formations in online social networks. This was a significant undertaking, but more work should be done to understand the relative effects of different variables—as well as different theoretical perspectives and methodological approaches—on study outcomes.

Study Limitations

We have been as thorough as we can within the page limit. However, other variables could explain some of our results. For example, a person's real-world celebrity status, or other exogenous factors like being publicly mentioned in mass communications (news media, printed press, commercials and advertisements, etc.) may contribute to audience growth. Secondly, we do not segment our Twitter sample into types of users or types of uses, although [6], [33], and [37] suggest ways in which categories for specific user and uses may illuminate the processes of attracting network members. Thirdly, this is a quantitative study based on observations with calculated latent measures from those observations. Our approach is useful for describing *what* happens, but without a corresponding qualitative approach, we can only speculate on *why*. Future work could explore why certain variables predict follower growth more than others. Finally, Twitter is one site. We don't know if the results presented here translate into other sites.

CONCLUSION

We believe this is the first longitudinal study of audience growth on Twitter to combine such a diverse set of theory inspired variables. For the first time, we explore the relative effects of social behavior, message content, and network structure on follow behavior and show which of these has more power than the others. Though these results are specific to Twitter and a particular dataset, we think they are important for the following reasons. First, multiple snapshots can help us begin to offer casual explanations for audience growth. Second, comparisons across many variables inspired by different theoretical perspectives allow us to interpret relative effects of each. Third, the impact of message content and social behavior are comparative to network structure, which suggests future work should take caution in privileging any one perspective over another.

REFERENCES

1. Anderson, J. Lix and Rix: Variations on a Little-Known Readability Index. *J. of Reading 26*, 6 (1983), 490–496.
2. Bakshy, E., Hofman, J.M., Mason, W., and Watts, D. Everyone's an Influencer: Quantifying Influence on Twitter. *ICWSM* (2011).
3. Barabási, A.L. and Albert, R. Emergence of Scaling in Random Networks. *Science 286*, (1999), 509–512.
4. Bourdieu, P. The forms of capital. In J.C. Richardson, ed., *Handbook of Theory and Research for the Sociology of Education*. Greenwood, New York, 1985, 241–258.
5. boyd, danah, Golder, S.A., and Lotan, G. Tweet, Tweet, Retweet: Conversational Aspects of Retweeting on Twitter. *HICSS* (2010).
6. Burke, M., Kraut, R., and Marlow, C. Social Capital on Facebook: Differentiating Uses and Users. *CHI* (2011).
7. Cameron, A.C. and Trivedi, P.K. *Regression Analysis of Count Data*. Cambridge University Press, NY, 1998.
8. Cartwright, D. and Harary, F. Structural balance: A generalization of Heider's theory. *Psychological Review 63*, 5 (1956), 277–293.
9. Cialdini, R.B. *Influence: the psychology of persuasion*. Collins, (2007).
10. Davidov, D., Tsur, O., and Rappoport, A. Enhanced Sentiment Learning Using Twitter Hashtags and Smileys. *COLING* (2010).
11. Donath, J.S. *Signals, Truth, and Design*. MIT Press, Cambridge, MA, forthcoming.
12. Donath, J.S. Social Signals in Supernets. *J. of Computer-Mediated Communication 13*, 1 (2007), article 12.
13. Easley, D. and Kleinberg, J. *Networks, Crowds, and Markets: Reasoning About a Highly Connected World*. Cambridge University Press, Cambridge, MA, 2010.
14. Feld, S. The Focused Organization of Social Ties. *The American J. of Sociology 86*, 5 (1981), 1015–1035.
15. Gilbert, E. and Karahalios, K. Predicting tie strength with social media. *CHI* (2009), 211–220.
16. Gilbert, E. Predicting Tie Strength in a New Medium. *CSCW* (2012).
17. Goffman, E. *The Presentation of Self in Everyday Life*. Anchor, 1959.
18. Golder, S.A. and Yardi, S. Structural Predictors of Tie Formation in Twitter: Transitivity and Mutuality. *IEEE SocialCom*, (2010).
19. Haewoon Kwak, Sue Moon, and Wonjae Lee. More of a Receiver Than a Giver: Why Do People Unfollow in Twitter? *ICWSM* (2012).
20. Hargittai, E. and Litt, E. The Tweet Smell of Celebrity Success: Explaining Variation in Twitter Adoption among a Diverse Group of Young Adults. *New Media & Society 13*, 5 (2011), 824–842.
21. Heider, F. Attitudes and cognitive organization. *The Journal of Psychology 21*, 1 (1946), 107–112.
22. Honeycutt, C. and Herring, S.C. Beyond Microblogging: Conversation and Collaboration via Twitter. *HICSS* (2009).
23. Java, A., Song, X., Finin, T., and Tseng, B. Why we twitter: understanding microblogging usage and communities. *Web-KDD* (2007), 56–65.
24. Katz, M.L. and Shapiro, C. Network Externalities, Competition, and Compatibility. *The American Economic Review 75*, 3 (1985), 424–440.
25. Kivran-Swaine, F., Govindan, P., and Naaman, M. The impact of Network Structure on Breaking Ties in Online Social Networks: Unfollowing on Twitter. *CHI* (2011).
26. Kivran-Swaine, F. and Naaman, M. Network Properties and Social Sharing of Emotions in Social Awareness Streams. *CSCW* (2011).
27. Kollock, P. The Economies of Online Cooperation: Gifts and Public Goods in Cyberspace. In M. Smith and P. Kollock, eds., *Communities in Cyberspace*. Routledge, New York, 1999, 220–239.
28. Kwak, H., Chun, H., and Moon, S. Fragile Online Relationship: A First Look at Unfollow Dynamics in Twitter. *CHI* (2011).
29. Kwak, H., Lee, C., Park, H., and Moon, S. What is Twitter, a social network or a news media? *WWW* (2010).
30. Lampe, C.A.C., Ellison, N., and Steinfield, C. A familiar face(book): profile elements as signals in an online social network. *CHI* (2007), 435–444.
31. Liben-Nowell, D. and Kleinberg, J. The link prediction problem for social networks. *CIKM* (2003), 556–559.
32. McPherson, M., Smith-Lovin, L., and Cook, J.M. Birds of a Feather: Homophily in Social Networks. *Annual Review of Sociology 27*, 1 (2001), 415–438.
33. Naaman, M., Boase, J., and Lai, C.-H. Is it Really About Me? Message Content in Social Awareness Streams. *CSCW* (2010), 189–192.
34. Pandit, S.M. and Wu, S.-M. *Time Series and System Analysis With Applications*. Krieger, Malabar, FL, 2001.
35. Pang, B. and Lee, L. Opinion mining and sentiment analysis. *Foundations and Trends in Information Retrieval 2*, 1-2 (2008), 1–135.
36. Pennebaker, J.W., Francis, M., and Booth, R. *Linguistic Inquiry and Word Count: LIWC 2001*. Erlbaum Publishers, Mahwah, NJ, 2001.
37. Quercia, D., Ellis, J., Capra, L., and Crowcroft, J. In the Mood for Being Influential on Twitter. *IEEE SocialCom*, (2011), 307–314.
38. Resnick, P., Konstan, J., Chen, Y., and Kraut, R. Starting New Online Communities. In *Evidence-based social design: Mining the social sciences to build online communities*. MIT Press, Cambridge, MA, 2012.
39. Tidwell, L.C. and Walther, J.B. Computer-Mediated Communication Effects on Disclosure, Impressions, and Interpersonal Evaluations: Getting to Know One Another a Bit at a Time. *Human Communication Research 28*, 3 (2002).
40. Wang, Y.-C. and Kraut, R. Twitter and the development of an audience: those who stay on topic thrive! *CHI* (2012).
41. Wellman, B. and Wortley, S. Different strokes from different folks: Community ties and social support. *American J. of Sociology 96*, (1990), 558–588.
42. Zhang, J., Qu, Y., Cody, J., and Wu, Y. A case study of micro-blogging in the enterprise: use, value, and related issues. *CHI* (2010), 123–132.
43. Zhao, D. and Rosson, M.B. How and why people Twitter: the role that micro-blogging plays in informal communication at work. *GROUP* (2009), 243–252.

High-Precision Pointing on Large Wall Displays using Small Handheld Devices

Mathieu Nancel[1,2] Olivier Chapuis[1,2] Emmanuel Pietriga[2,3] Xing-Dong Yang[4]
Pourang Irani[5] Michel Beaudouin-Lafon[1,2]

[1]Univ Paris-Sud & CNRS (LRI) Orsay, France
[2]INRIA Orsay, France
[3]INRIA Chile - CIRIC Santiago, Chile
[4]University of Alberta Alberta, Canada
[5]University of Manitoba Manitoba, Canada

ABSTRACT

Rich interaction with high-resolution wall displays is not limited to remotely pointing at targets. Other relevant types of interaction include virtual navigation, text entry, and direct manipulation of control widgets. However, most techniques for remotely acquiring targets with high precision have studied remote pointing in isolation, focusing on pointing efficiency and ignoring the need to support these other types of interaction. We investigate high-precision pointing techniques capable of acquiring targets as small as 4 millimeters on a 5.5 meters wide display while leaving up to 93% of a typical tablet device's screen space available for task-specific widgets. We compare these techniques to state-of-the-art distant pointing techniques and show that two of our techniques, a purely relative one and one that uses head orientation, perform as well or better than the best pointing-only input techniques while using a fraction of the interaction resources.

ACM Classification Keywords

H.5.2 [Information interfaces and presentation]: User Interfaces. - Graphical user interfaces.

Author Keywords

Wall Displays; Handheld Devices; Pointing

INTRODUCTION

Ultra-high-resolution wall-sized displays enable the interactive visualization of massive datasets [5, 27]. Application domains range from scientific visualization to computer-aided design and command & control centers. Usually made of a mosaic of LCD panels, such displays typically feature a resolution of 100 pixels per inch. Beyond their significantly increased display capacity, they afford a more physical form of navigation than lower-resolution large displays [2]: users can get an overview of the data from a distance, the wall fully fitting in their field of view; and they can see more details about a particular region of interest by stepping closer to the wall.

To fully take advantage of the capabilities of this new generation of wall-sized displays, users must be able to move freely in front of them. They must also be able to interact with them from any location, without being tethered by clumsy equipment. This entails two main requirements, as illustrated in Figure 1: (1) users must be able to remotely select graphical objects, which can be very small and difficult to reach; and (2) users must be able to perform other input actions, e.g., adjust parameters associated with the selected object, enter text or perform virtual navigation.

Portable surfaces have been used in prior work as pads for interacting with virtual environments, e.g., to take notes [30], or as devices to facilitate remote pointing [23]. We argue that portable devices can actually accommodate both types of tasks simultaneously, enabling users to perform truly high-precision remote pointing and to manipulate the objects selected thereby. The device can also act as a secondary display. The type of portable device, e.g., a tablet or a smartphone, and the kind of interface controls and interaction techniques that it should provide are largely application-dependent. As a first step, we focus in this paper on the design and evaluation of high-precision remote pointing techniques (requirement #1) that use only a fraction of the surface of a portable device for pointing (requirement #2).

We introduce a design space for techniques that use a handheld device with an area dedicated to pointing that varies in size, and relative pointing acceleration functions specifically tuned to the particular context of ultra-high-resolution wall-sized displays. Several of these techniques can be coupled with information about the user's natural head movements, which we have observed to be a good predictor of the next target location. We systematically evaluate these techniques, showing that purely relative techniques can be surprisingly efficient when tuned carefully, even with small pointing areas. We also show that even smaller pointing areas can be used with similar performance levels by combining head orientation for coarse pointing with touch-based relative pointing. Our techniques generated very positive user feedback, considering the difficulty of the tasks, and fared as well as state-of-the-art remote pointing techniques while enabling additional interactions through the handheld device.

Figure 1. Interacting with a wall display using a tablet that features both an area dedicated to high-precision pointing for the remote selection of graphical objects on the wall, and control widgets to act on those objects.

LITERATURE REVIEW

Target acquisition on wall-sized displays. Laser pointers or ray-casting [18, 17] are the most common absolute positioning method for pointing from a distance. However, ray-casting does not adapt well to ultra-high-resolution displays as hand tremor and involuntary motion due to fatigue are amplified when the user moves further away from the display [25]. In a controlled study, Kopper *et al.* [22] showed that the speed of a distal pointing task can be described as a function of the angular amplitude of movement and the angular size of the target. Their model presents two fundamental differences between a distal pointing task and the one modeled by Fitts' law. In distal pointing, the size of the target has a much larger effect on movement time than the amplitude. Unlike a Fitts' pointing task, difficulty of distal pointing grows quadratically, rather than linearly. The pointing model based on angular target size supports recent empirical findings showing that ray-casting is fast with large distant objects but error-prone with smaller items [25, 34]. By contrast, techniques that use relative control [34, 4] enable more precise cursor positioning and easier acquisition of small targets.

Interactions using head tracking. Object selection is often preceded by a visual search for the target. Head orientation provides a good approximation of where a user is looking [33, 12, 28], and can be exploited in conjunction with any pointing device used in the environment [19, 28]. Head movements have been shown to support a variety of interaction techniques [19, 24, 20]. Our approach integrates head orientation with cursor selection. It was inspired by Ashdown *et al.* [1], who use head orientation for positioning a cursor on the monitor of interest, thereby reducing mouse displacements in a multi-monitor setup.

Dual-mode target acquisition. Hybrid pointing consists of combining absolute pointing for rapid cursor movements with relative pointing for accuracy. For example, ray-casting, which uses absolute positioning, can be improved by combining it with relative cursor movements [34, 23, 11, 21, 14]. Adaptive Pointing [21] allows switching between two modes based on the speed of the user's hand movements. A study showed that such a hybrid control mechanism reduces error rates by 63% over ray-casting. Mode-switching is implicit, requiring users to adjust their visual search and pointing actions when the switch occurs [14]. By contrast, explicit mode switching lets users control when to switch between relative and absolute positioning [34, 11]. However, the overhead introduced by the mode switch cancels out what is gained by using ray-casting for rapid movements [34]. Alternatives to explicit mode switching include tracking eye gaze or body motion to anticipate or perform part of the targeting action. Zhai *et al.* [36] developed MAGIC pointing, a technique that uses eye gaze to rapidly move the cursor as close as possible to the target on a single desktop monitor. To finish the pointing task, users then move the cursor to the target with a standard trackpad.

To avoid the cost of explicit mode switching, our approach uses head motion to move the cursor as close as possible to the intended target area. Other techniques can then be used to precisely position the cursor on the target.

Pointing via mobile touch-screens. The use of mobile devices to control distant objects has received much attention in recent years. One approach is to control a remote cursor via the mobile device's touch-screen. For example, ARC-Pad enables both absolute and relative pointing on a large display via the touch-screen of a mobile device [23]. Alternatives include using embedded sensors, such as tilt [31] or the phone's camera [8]. With Touch Projector [8], users aim the mobile device's camera at the display and manipulate its content by touching and dragging content on the small screen. The techniques we have designed use some of these approaches for remote control of the cursor.

Pointing Facilitation Techniques. Pointing time can be improved either by reducing distance to target, increasing target width, or a combination of both. Drag-and-pop [3] and the Vacuum [6] are two examples designed specifically for use on large displays. Such techniques generally rely on prior knowledge of potential targets, while our work focuses on generic, target-agnostic pointing techniques. Combining our approach with pointing facilitation techniques is certainly possible since the latter make few assumptions about the physical input device used, but is left for future work.

TECHNIQUES

We consider contexts of use where the primary purpose of the handheld device is to accommodate widgets for the advanced control of objects selected via pointing. The area dedicated to pointing on the device, or *pointing zone*, should therefore not be too large. However, if too small, pointing will likely be inefficient. Our goal is to identify the best trade-off between screen real-estate allocation and good pointing performance.

Relative Pointing – As mentioned earlier, a simple absolute mapping from the handheld device to a ultra-high-resolution wall display does not work, because one pixel on the handheld maps to several dozen pixels on the wall, even if we were to make the pointing zone full-screen. Relative mapping, i.e., using the pointing zone as a touchpad, enables users to point precisely but requires careful tuning of the pointer acceleration function, which can be a complex and tedious process. The acceleration functions implemented in major operating systems have been parameterized for desktop environments [9]. They work for single- and multi-monitor display configurations, but are not adapted to ultra-high-resolution walls, which typically feature a 200-to-400 inches diagonal and a very high resolution, e.g., 20 480 $\times$ 6 400 for the 228-inch (5.79 meters) display wall in Figure 1. Previous work [26] showed that basic relative pointing, if tuned properly, could actually be a viable candidate for high-precision pointing on wall displays. One of our contributions is a method to obtain such optimized transfer functions.

Dual-Precision Pointing – Pointer acceleration functions dynamically adjust the control-display (CD) gain based on the dynamics of users' movements. An alternative approach is to let users explicitly switch between different CD gains, typically between a *Coarse* mode that allows fast repositioning of the cursor across large distances, and a slower but more *Precise* mode that users can engage when they want to adjust the cursor position to acquire a very small target [26].

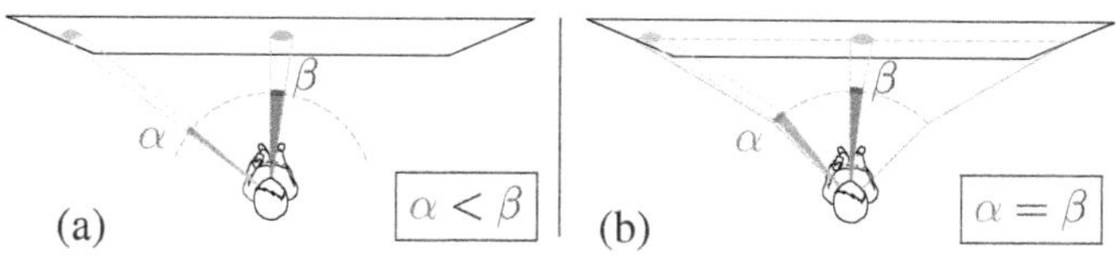

Figure 2. The problem of varying angular motor size with ray-casting (a) can be addressed using an indirect absolute mapping (b).

The main challenge when designing dual-precision techniques is to seamlessly integrate the two modes so as to minimize the cognitive and motor costs of switching. All the techniques presented in this paper assign the *Precise* mode to single-finger drag gestures performed with the dominant hand in the pointing zone. Given our requirements that users should be free to move in front of the display, and since the non-dominant hand will typically hold the device, this leaves two main options for *Coarse* mode control: use the dominant hand in a different configuration, or use a different body part. We experimented with several options to eventually identify two viable candidates through iterative design, prototyping, piloting and tuning: head orientation, and double-finger drag gestures with the dominant hand in the pointing zone. Both approaches are detailed below.

Two-finger pad-based coarse pointing – This technique is inspired by ARC-Pad [23] (Absolute+Relative Cursor Pad), a dual-precision pointing technique that provides users with an absolute and a relative pointing mode. A typical ARC-Pad pointing task is composed of a tap on a touch-sensitive handheld device, followed by a drag gesture. The tap gesture coarsely positions the cursor on the large display according to an absolute mapping of the handheld device's surface to the large display. The following drag gesture is interpreted as relative movements of the cursor to adjust its position. The original technique was designed for, and evaluated on, much lower-resolution large displays than those considered here. It proved very difficult to use with very small targets on ultra-high-resolution wall displays, mainly because the absolute mapping is far too imprecise in that context and often requires several relative-mode drag gestures to adjust the cursor's position, causing much clutching in the second phase. We thus enhanced the original technique and created ARC-Pad^{2F}.

ARC-Pad^{2F} (^{2F} stands for *two fingers*) distinguishes between absolute and relative pointing by the number of fingers involved in performing the pointing gestures rather than the type of gesture performed. A single-finger drag gesture controls the cursor in relative mode (as with the original ARC-Pad); a drag gesture performed with two conjoined fingers is interpreted as absolute positioning of the cursor. In contrast to the original method that used taps for absolute positioning, users can now adjust the cursor position in absolute mode by dragging with two fingers, and then switch to relative mode for more precise, relative adjustments of the cursor position. The switch from absolute to relative mode is triggered whenever at least one of the fingers is lifted from the pad's surface. This means that users can either lift a single finger at the current location and continue dragging, or they can lift both fingers, adjust their hand position relative to the pad, and touch anywhere on the surface with a single finger. This second option can be very useful when pointing at a target near the edges of the display, as it allows users to initiate relative drag gestures from the center of the pointing zone, in any direction.

Head-based coarse pointing – The second viable approach that we identified for *Coarse* control uses the natural movements of the head that occur when remotely pointing at targets on a wall. Confirming prior work [16, 36], we observed that users consistently stabilize their gaze and lock it on the target before acquiring it. While tracking the users' gaze is not a practical option in our context, we found head orientation to be a good coarse indirect indicator of where users are looking[1], and thus a good predictor of the rough location of the next intended target on the wall display.

Our technique controls the cursor's location in *Coarse* mode through a linear interpolation from a comfortable angular operating range to the dimensions of the display. We favored an indirect mapping over direct ray-casting (or laser pointing) for two reasons. First, being perspective-based, ray-casting would have caused targets of the same absolute size to have noticeably different *motor* sizes depending on their location with respect to the user's physical position, as illustrated in Figure 2-a (this effect gets amplified as users get closer to the display). Our mapping allows any area of the display to be reached with equal motor precision. We also wanted to optimize the input operating range, within the limits of comfortable neck positions. As illustrated in Figure 2-b, we addressed these issues by mapping a location-independent, fixed-size angular operating range centered on the orthogonal projection of the user's location on the flat display surface. This ensures that when users move in front of the display, looking straight ahead always sets the cursor exactly in front of them. As they look further away, the cursor is progressively offset from the head's direction (up to 9°), accounting for extra eye rotation. This offset makes it possible to point at targets on the sides of the wall comfortably while maximizing accuracy in the central area.

Cost of Switching – We observed during the early phases of development and pilot testing that users would sometimes hesitate to switch to *Precise* mode. This could happen because they thought that they could complete the task in *Coarse* mode, eventually failing or succeeding but at the cost of longer task completion times. This could also happen because they wanted to get as close as possible to the target before switching to *Precise* mode, sometimes loosing a significant amount of time in doing so for no actual benefit since the time lost in *Coarse* mode was not compensated by larger time savings in *Precise* mode.

This raised a question that we had not anticipated: beyond minimizing the motor cost of switching between modes, is it possible to minimize the *cognitive* cost associated with making the decision to switch between the two modes?

We explored an approach where the cognitive load is transferred to the perceptual system, hypothesizing that this would significantly reduce the mode switching cost. We designed variations of the above techniques that artificially limit the precision of the *Coarse* pointing mode: users approach the

[1] Users rotate their head to look at off-centered targets so as to minimize the effort put on ocular muscles [12].

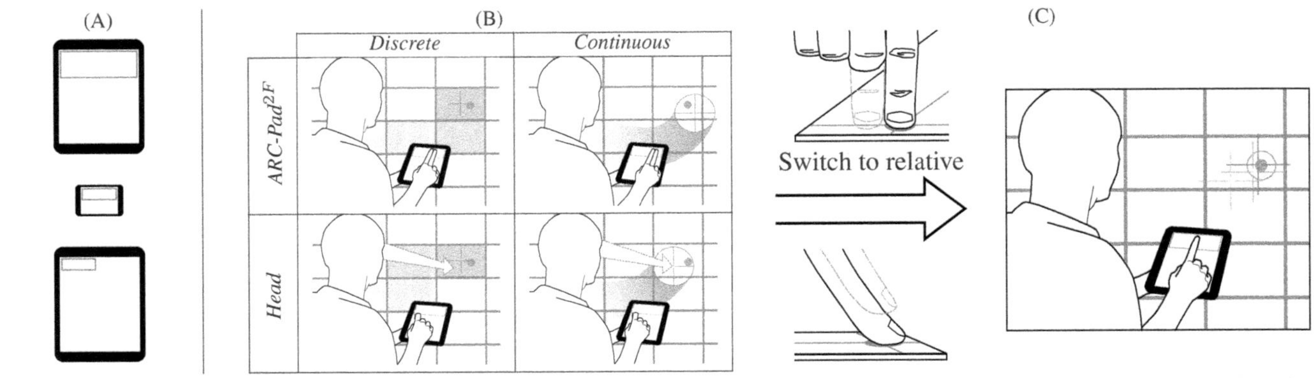

Figure 3. The four dual-precision techniques. (A) The three device / pointing zone pairs used in our experiments: tablet with large zone (Experiments 1 and 3), smartphone with small zone (Experiment 2) and tablet with small zone (Experiment 3). (B) The four coarse (absolute) modes, combinations of *Head* vs. *ARC-Pad*^{2F} and *Discrete* vs. *Continuous*. (C) In all cases, using a single finger in the pointing area switches to precise (relative) mode.

target fast and know when to switch to precise mode simply because there is no other option.

We *discretized* the wall display into cells according to its 8×4 matrix of 30" LCD panels. Using portions of the LCD panels, e.g. halves or quarters, would have made the cells too small for precise acquisition. We also wanted to avoid having cells inconsistently crossing screen bezels. In *Coarse* mode, users can only jump from screen to screen. Jumping to a screen puts the cursor at the center of that screen, and users have to switch to *Precise* mode to reposition the cursor within it. We call this process *discretization* to emphasize that the pointing resolution in *Coarse* mode is artificially degraded while keeping the same physical input resolution.

The resulting technique, when coupled with *Head* control, is somewhat reminiscent of the Rake cursor [7] and similar multi-cursor desktop pointing techniques [32] that use eye gaze to select the active cursor in a matrix of cursors all controlled with the same input device, such as a mouse.

Four dual-precision pointing techniques – We eventually narrowed our design space down to four pointing techniques by combining the two coarse input control techniques (pad-based vs. head-based) with the two coarse mode input precisions described above (*continuous* vs. *discretized*) – see Figure 3. As mentioned earlier, all four techniques, summarized below, use the handheld device's pointing zone to control the cursor in *Precise* mode, with optimized CD gain transfer functions.

- ARC-Pad^{2F} + *Continuous* = *ContPad*: two conjoined fingers in the handheld's pointing zone activate *Coarse* mode (absolute mapping of the zone to the wall); a single finger activates *Precise* mode (relative cursor displacements).
- ARC-Pad^{2F} + *Discrete* = *DiscPad*: same as above but pointing precision in *Coarse* mode is artificially restricted: the cursor can only get positioned at the center of any given LCD panel, requiring a switch to *Precise* mode for any further cursor position adjustments.
- *Head* + *Continuous* = *ContHead*: head orientation provides *Coarse* control of the cursor, without any artificial restriction on pointing precision. Touching the pointing zone on the handheld automatically switches to *Precise* mode (relative cursor displacements).
- *Head* + *Discrete* = *DiscHead*: same as above, but pointing precision in *Coarse* mode is artificially restricted. Head orientation can only make the cursor jump to the center of any given LCD panel, as with *DiscPad*.

Head-based techniques feature a $500ms$ delay after finger release from the handheld's surface before switching back to coarse mode, giving users enough time to clutch or tap.

CONTROL-DISPLAY TRANSFER FUNCTIONS

As mentioned earlier, optimizing the transfer functions that control pointer acceleration in relative mode for ultra-high-resolution wall displays is challenging. In this section, we explain our method for calibrating those functions.

Pointer acceleration consists of applying a transfer function to the Control-Display (CD) gain based on the pointer's dynamics. The literature on CD gain transfer functions for such high-resolution and large display surfaces is sparse. Apart from recent work by Casiez *et al.* [9, 10] that provides a general framework but does not directly address our configuration, the only documented calibration methods are those related to PRISM [13] and its refinements [21, 15]. But these calibration methods were designed to support absolute-to-relative transfer functions for pointing techniques that feature an implicit switch between absolute and relative modes. While we later compare our techniques with the latest developments in this area, those calibration methods are of little use in our context.

All of our techniques use pointer acceleration in precise mode, and some of them in coarse mode as well. The CD gain must be large at high input speeds so the user can traverse the entire screen (15 000 to 30 000 pixels) quickly with no or little clutching. Conversely, the CD gain must be small at low input speeds for high-precision cursor control.

Some operating systems use sigmoid transfer functions [9, 10] that are characterized by a slope that smoothly gets steeper before decreasing again, as illustrated in Figure 4. The lower slopes at each end of the curve enable higher precision at low input velocities and bound cursor speed.

To model such curves, we use a generalized logistic function:

$$CD(x) = \frac{CD_{max} - CD_{min}}{1 + e^{-\lambda(x - V_{inf})}} + CD_{min}$$

where: $V_{inf} = ratio_{inf} \cdot (V_{max} - V_{min}) + V_{min}$. This function can be tuned with six parameters: V_{min} and V_{max} bound the input

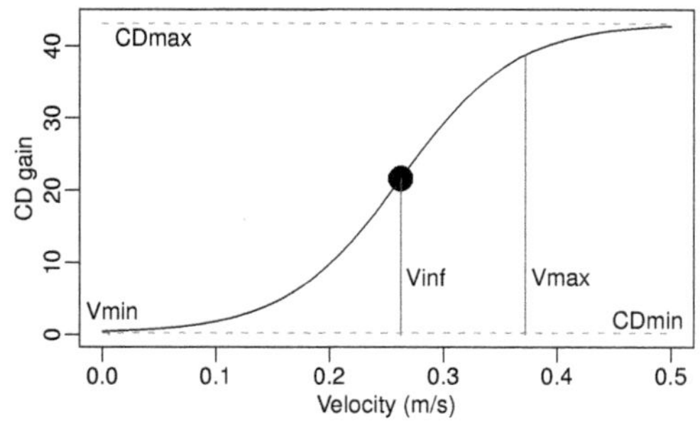

Figure 4. An example of logistic sigmoid curve (large zone *RelaLarge*)

range of the function by specifying lower and upper velocities beyond which accurate control becomes difficult; $ratio_{inf}$ sets the function's inflection point within this range; CD_{min} and CD_{max} are asymptotic values that define the function's output range. Finally, $\lambda \in [0;\infty]$ defines the curve's slope at its inflection point ($\lambda = 0$ yields a constant function, $\lambda = \infty$ a step function). Adjusting λ smoothes the curve.

We tune these parameter values as follows:

1. V_{min} and V_{max} are respectively the 90th quantile and the median of two corpora of velocities corresponding to voluntarily slow and fast finger movements on a tablet;

2. $CD_{min} = \frac{W_{min} \text{or } L}{100 \times \text{res}_{\text{device}}}$ maps the lower bound for the amplitude of input movements that are considered usable for selecting a target (the equivalent of 100 *input* pixels at device resolution $\text{res}_{\text{device}}$) to the minimum target size W_{min} or to the cursor width L [26] for relative *Coarse* modes;

3. The initial value for CD_{max} is $\frac{L}{\min(\text{width}_{input}, \text{height}_{input})}$ or $\frac{A_{max}}{\text{width}_{input}}$, mapping either the smallest dimension of the input zone to the expected *Precise* mode amplitude L [26], or the input zone width to the maximum pointing amplitude A_{max} for mode-less techniques and *Coarse* modes (A_{max} in our experiment corresponds to mostly horizontal movements).

4. $ratio_{inf}$, λ and CD_{max} are adjusted so the transition between the highest and lowest CD gains is as smooth as possible.

The main criterion for deciding that a given function is properly tuned is that users can perform the most difficult task (largest amplitude, smallest target width) and no further parameter adjustment improves pointing performance or the users' subjective perception of smoothness and precision.

Three volunteers were asked to test the techniques in an informal iterative design process of 800 pointing trials per user on average, before reaching a consensus. Table 1 gives the parameter values that we obtained for the two pointing zones that served in the experiments reported below: a large zone that fits within a tablet device in portrait mode, and a small zone that fits within a smartphone in landscape mode.

Generally-speaking, V_{min} and V_{max} have lower values for the small zone because the physical (motor) space dedicated to pointing is smaller. Similarly, the small zone features a higher CD_{max}, allowing for faster cursor movements so as to compensate for the smaller operating range. *Discrete* techniques feature a higher CD_{max} than *Continuous* ones to compensate for the larger distance between the target and the point where the mode switch has to be performed.

Size	Technique	CD_{max}	λ	$ratio_{inf}$
Large zone 148 × 49 (mm)	*ContHead$_L$*	9.9	19.9	0.4
	ContPad$_L$	6.6	17.5	0.4
	DiscHead$_L$ / *DiscPad$_L$*	12.9	17.5	0.4
	RelaLarge	43.1	20.0	0.5
Small zone 75 × 26 (mm)	*ContHead$_S$* / *ContPad$_S$*	6.3	26.5	0.4
	DiscHead$_S$ / *DiscPad$_S$*	16.4	26.5	0.7
	RelaSmall	83.0	22.5	1.0

Large zone: $V_{min} = 0.006m/s$, $V_{max} = 0.37m/s$, $CD_{min} = 0.22$
Small zone: $V_{min} = 0.003m/s$, $V_{max} = 0.19m/s$, $CD_{min} = 0.27$

Table 1. Transfer function parameter values.

COMPARING THE DUAL-PRECISION TECHNIQUES

We conducted two experiments to evaluate the performance of the four dual-precision pointing techniques introduced above, *ContHead*, *ContPad*, *DiscHead* and *DiscPad*, and to assess the cost of mode switching. The two experiments followed the same design but used different devices: a tablet with a large pointing zone in the first experiment, and a smartphone with a small pointing zone in the second one. For the sake of clarity, we use subscripts ($_L$ for *Large* and $_S$ for *Small*) when referring specifically to either the tablet or smartphone implementation, e.g., *ContHead$_L$* and *ContHead$_S$*.

Our hypotheses are as follows:

(H1) *Discrete* techniques lower the cognitive (and thus overall) cost of mode switching by leaving no choice to users about when to switch between modes, leading to a shorter coarse pointing phase than *Continuous* techniques.

(H2) *Head*-based techniques make mode switching cognitively less demanding, as they use different body parts to control the two modes. *Pad*-based techniques use the fingers in both modes *and* for mode switching. With *Head*-based techniques, a mode switch is triggered when the finger comes into contact with the pointing zone.

Related to (H1), we expect an effect of forcing the mode switch with *Discrete* techniques on the time spent in the precise phase, since this often entails engaging *Precise* pointing mode significantly farther away from the target than with *Continuous* techniques.

We also expect to observe relative differences between the two experiments due to the smaller pointing zone used in the second one: we expect *Head*-based techniques to be at an advantage in the second experiment, since the smaller size of the pointing zone will hinder performance of *Pad*-based techniques in *Coarse* mode.

General Design and Procedure

Apparatus. We used a wall-sized display consisting of 32 high-resolution 30" LCD panels (2560 × 1600 pixels each, 100 dpi, 1 mm ~ 4 pixels) laid out in an 8 × 4 matrix, 5.5 meters wide and 1.8 meters high for a total resolution of 22080 × 7360 when including bezels (Figure 1) [5]. This wall display is driven by a cluster of 16 computers, each equipped with two high-end graphic cards (one per screen), and a master workstation. The experiments' software was implemented with jBricks [29]. We used a VICON motion-capture system to track passive IR retroreflective markers and provide the 3D coordinates of the participants' head with sub-millimeter accuracy at 200Hz. Participants stood up, 2 meters away from the display. Given this position and the size of the wall, the operating range of the head was $\pi/2 \times \pi/5$ rad.

Trials. The task consisted in acquiring circular targets of width W. Participants first had to dwell for half a second in a dedicated zone in coarse mode, and could then acquire the target, positioned at a distance A from the cursor's position. Experimental conditions combined one of two target widths (W): 18 pixels (4.16 mm), 80 pixels (18.48 mm), and one of three movement amplitudes (A): 2760 pixels (width of one LCD panel, 0.637 m), 8280 pixels (width of 3 LCD panels, 1.912 m), 13 800 pixels (width of 5 LCD panels, 3.187 m).

Regarding the difficulty of these pointing tasks: according to Casiez *et al.* [10], the highest Fitts' Index of Difficulty (ID) tested prior to their article was 7.6 bits in a desktop context (A= 30 cm, W= 1.5 mm). In this same article they report a univariate (1D) Fitts' experiment with IDs as high as 9 (A= 4.5 m, W= 9 mm) on a 25ppi projected display. The highest ID tested in our studies is 9.54 using bivariate pointing tasks (2D) tasks. To our knowledge, such a level of difficulty was never evaluated before in this context.

For each movement amplitude A, targets were pseudo randomly positioned inside one of six LCD panels so that the average distance from the center of that panel to the target was about 600 pixels (150 mm). We chose this value so as to neither advantage nor disadvantage *Discrete* techniques (relative to the size of a screen), given that those techniques position the cursor at the center of the most recently visited panel.

Design and Procedure. Both experiments used a $4 \times 2 \times 3$ within-subject design with factors TECH (technique), W and A. We blocked by technique and used a Latin square to balance the presentation order of techniques among participants. At the beginning of each block of a *Head* technique, participants were asked to stand still and stare at the center of the display for 5 seconds to calibrate the center of their head's operating range, in order to balance the angular offsets described earlier. Each block started with a training session composed of two parts. In the first part, W and A were set to their largest values. The operator explained the technique and asked participants to practice until their performance stabilized, i.e. when they performed six consecutive trials with a movement time (*MT*) variation within 40% of their average. Participants were allowed to practice longer if they wanted to. The second training phase consisted of three blocks of six trials whose purpose was to put participants in conditions closer to the actual trials to be performed next: largest W and largest A, smallest W and medium A, smallest W and smallest A. The remaining TECH blocks were measured and decomposed into six sub-blocks composed of six replications of each of the W $\times$ A conditions described earlier. For both experiments, sessions lasted 40 minutes on average. At the end of a session, participants answered a questionnaire about their preferences and were encouraged to make comments.

Participants. The same 12 participants (10 men, 2 women; 24 to 38 year-old, avg. 29.6, med. 28.5) served in both experiments. All had normal or corrected-to-normal vision and were right-handed. All were daily users of personal computers and smartphones. Only two used tablets regularly.

Measures. We measure movement time *MT* and error rate. *MT* begins when participants start moving after having dwelled 0.5 s inside a circle centered on the start target, and stops at the first press event on target. We split *MT* into movement time of the coarse phase, *CMT*, and movement time of the precise phase, *PMT*, according to the time of the last switch to precise mode. We also wanted to measure the cost of mode switching. However finding a coherent measure of the duration of mode switching for all techniques is difficult: there is no explicit marker for the beginning of the switch with head-based techniques, since in coarse mode the finger is hovering over the device; switching to precise mode with Pad-based techniques can be performed in two ways, one of which is immediate (lifting one of the fingers). To evaluate the cost of mode switching, we measure *VPT*, the time between the last move event in coarse mode and the velocity peak in the subsequent precise phase. *VPT* is a "technique-agnostic" measure that provides a satisfying approximation of the time between coarse cursor stabilization and use of precise mode.

Tablet Experiment

In this first experiment, we used a tablet (Apple iPad I) with a resolution of 768×1024 pixels. Participants had to hold the tablet vertically. The pointing zone used the top 768×256 pixels (148×49 mm), resulting in an input resolution of 5.2 dot/mm. Its aspect ratio matched that of the wall display. Table 1 summarizes the CD gain parameters.

Quantitative-objective Results. We removed a few outliers: 0.69% of the trials had an unreasonable residual / predicted ratio. These outliers were mainly due to Wi-Fi transmission problems. As expected, *MT* distributions per condition are skewed. We thus perform our analyses using median values, per participant, on the model TECH $\times$ W $\times$ A $\times$ Rand(Participant). Figure 5 graphs *MT* for each technique[2].

An ANOVA reveals a significant effect of TECH on *MT* ($F_{3,33} = 11.4$, $p < 0.0001$). A post-hoc t-test with Bonferroni correction shows that $ContHead_L$ is significantly faster than all other techniques (all p's < 0.001): 9% faster than $ContPad_L$, 15% faster than $DiscPad_L$, and 14% faster than $DiscHead_L$. The only other significant difference is between $ContPad_L$ and $DiscPad_L$, the former being 6% faster.

We also observe, as expected, significant effects of target width W ($F_{1,11} = 459$, $p < 0.0001$) and movement amplitude A ($F_{2,22} = 43.8$, $p < 0.0001$) on *MT*, participants being faster with the larger target and the smallest distance. We do not observe any interaction effect TECH $\times$ W or TECH $\times$ A.

The overall error rate is 5.9%. An ANOVA reveals no effect of TECH on error rate ($F_{3,33} = 0.61$, $p = 0.6151$) and no significant interaction. Again, as expected, we find a significant effect of W on error rate ($F_{1,11} = 11.5$, $p = 0.0061$): 8.4% for small targets and 3.4% for larger ones. We also measure a significant effect of A ($F_{2,22} = 4.00$, $p = 0.0329$), although the

[2] In all our bar charts, the mean is taken over the medians of each experimental condition (including Participant). Error bars represent the corresponding 95% confidence limit.

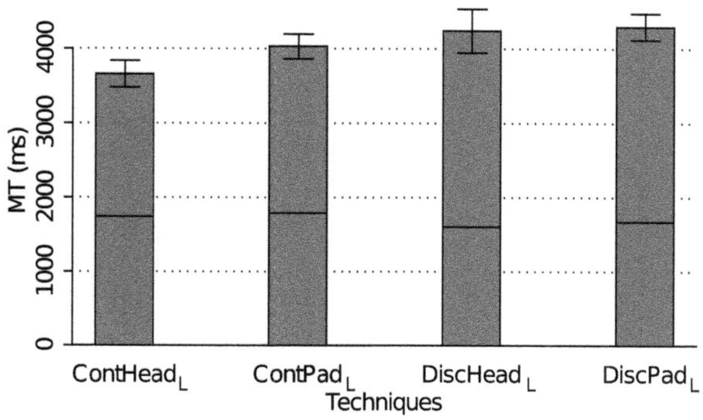

Figure 5. ***MT*** **for each** TECH **(tablet experiment). Black lines that split the four bars indicate the time of the last switch to precise mode.**

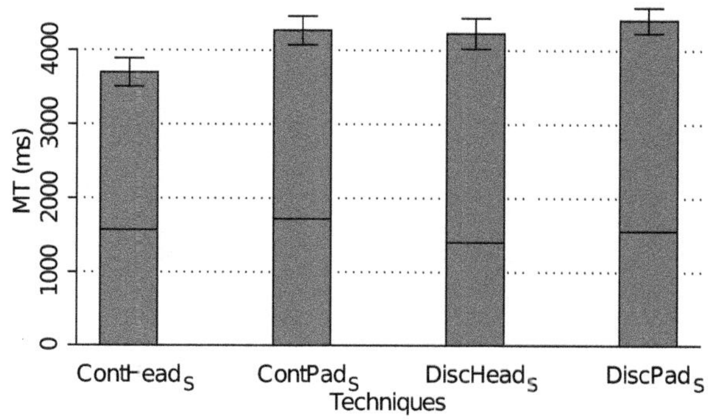

Figure 6. ***MT*** **for each** TECH **(smartphone experiment). Black lines that split the four bars indicate the time of the last switch to precise mode.**

magnitude of the difference is small: 4.9% for the largest amplitude, 6.9% and 5.9% for the medium and small ones.

As illustrated in Figure 5, the time spent in the coarse phase is slightly shorter with *Discrete* techniques than with *Continuous* techniques. However, this difference is not statistically significant – (H1) is not supported – and is not large enough to make *Discrete* techniques more efficient than *Continuous* ones. Indeed, the time spent in precise mode is far longer with the *Discrete* techniques. We tentatively attribute this to the fact that the last mode switch is performed 150 mm away from the target on average with *Discrete* techniques, compared to 67 mm with $ContHead_L$ and 71 mm with $ContPad_L$.

$ContHead_L$ and $ContPad_L$ feature very similar coarse pointing times (*CMT*) and distance-to-target at mode-switch time. $ContHead_L$'s shorter task time is mainly due to performance improvements during the precise pointing phase (Figure 5). We observed that velocity peaks occur earlier with $ContHead_L$ than with $ContPad_L$ (average *VPT* of 462 ms vs. 735 ms). Distances from the mode-switch location to the target are similar for *Head*- and *Pad*-based techniques, and their acceleration curves have the same input characteristics (V_{min}, V_{max} and $ratio_{inf}$). We thus expected the velocity peaks of $ContHead_L$ and $ContPad_L$ to occur at similar times. But participants actually required more time to reach full speed with $ContPad_L$. This suggests that the cost of mode switching is indeed lower for *Head*-based techniques than for *Pad*-based ones – supporting (H2) – possibly because of the cognitive cost entailed by switching between two very different CD gains whereas the input device / method remains the same.

Quantitative-subjective Results. Overall, participants preferred to use *Head*-based techniques (10 out of 12) and *Continuous* techniques (8 out of 12). 7 participants ranked $ContHead_L$ first, 4 ranked $DiscHead_L$ first and 2 ranked $ContPad_L$ first. However, there were no strong complaints about any particular technique, except for one participant who clearly stated that he disliked *Discrete* techniques.

Several participants complained about the lack of tactile feedback, which made it difficult to know when the fingers were leaving the pointing zone. They expressed the need for some sort of physical boundary to delimit the pointing zone, as featured by laptop touchpads. Only one participant answered that holding the tablet for 40 minutes was indeed a cause of fatigue when we inquired about this potential issue.

Smartphone Experiment

The second experiment used a smartphone (Apple iPod Touch) with a resolution of 480×320 pixels. Participants had to hold the device horizontally. The pointing zone used the top 480×166 pixels (75×26 mm, same aspect ratio as the display), resulting in an input resolution of 6.4 dot/mm. CD gain parameters are given in Table 1.

We took participants' comments about the lack of tactile feedback into account, and used easily removable tape to delimit the pointing zone (3 mm wide, 0.8 mm thick). Preliminary tests had shown that the tape did make it much easier to find the input zone without looking at the surface and to anticipate fingers crossing the pointing zone's boundaries.

Results are very similar to those of the tablet experiment reported above. We observe an effect of TECH on *MT* (no interaction with A and W), and an effect of A and W, as expected. (H2) is also supported by the data. We get similar error rates, and an overall subjective preference for $ContHead_S$. Movement time, split between the coarse and precise phases, is shown in Figure 6 using the same scale as in Figure 5.

Regarding the coarse pointing phase, this time we observe a significant effect of TECH ($F_{3,33} = 5.39$, $p = 0.0039$). $DiscHead_S$ is significantly faster than all other techniques, and $DiscPad_S$ and $ContHead_S$ are significantly faster than $ContPad_S$ (for this phase). With the smaller pointing zone used in this experiment, we do observe the hypothesized advantage for discrete techniques (H1). However, the time gained during the coarse phase is again not large enough to make *Discrete* techniques faster than *Continuous* ones.

Since we did not counterbalance the order of pointing zone sizes (all participants performed the tablet experiment first), and since we added tactile feedback using tape to delimit the zone in the second experiment, we cannot formally compare overall performance across both experiments. However, we can make three informal observations. First, the movement time difference between $ContHead_S$ and $ContPad_S$ is larger for the smartphone (13%) than for the tablet (9%); Second, $ContPad_S$ is not significantly faster than $DiscPad_S$, as opposed to $ContPad_L$ vs. $DiscPad_L$; Third, Figures 5 and 6 suggest that *DiscHead* performed better with the smartphone than with the tablet, relative to *ContPad* and *DiscPad*. These observations suggest that as we had anticipated, *Head*-based techniques are at an advantage with smaller pointing zones.

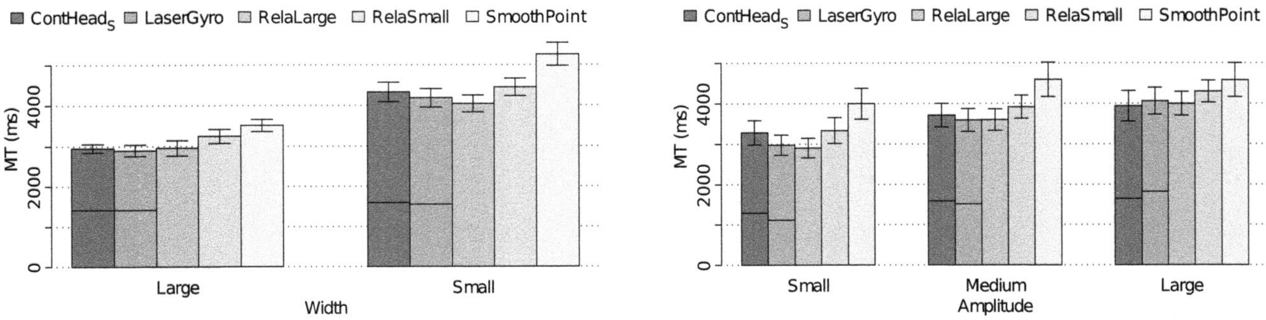

Figure 7. ***MT*** **for each** TECH **by** W **and by** A **for the last experiment.**

COMPARISON WITH STATE-OF-THE-ART TECHNIQUES

The above experiments identified *ContHead* as the fastest and preferred technique. As a follow-up, we wanted to evaluate the cost of using a handheld device for pointing. To this end, we ran a third experiment to compare *ContHead* to state-of-the-art remote pointing techniques. Such techniques do not meet requirement #2, i.e., accommodating widgets used for other purposes than pointing, but this comparison enables us to put our results in a more general context.

The comparison involves the version of *ContHead* that uses a small pointing zone, $ContHead_S$, on a tablet. $ContHead_S$ and $ContHead_L$ feature very similar performance (see Figures 5 and 6). This makes $ContHead_S$ a more interesting technique overall, since using a smaller pointing zone means that the device can accommodate more control widgets. We briefly describe the techniques selected for comparison below.

We noticed during early pilot studies that purely relative pointing techniques can actually be viable candidates for high-precision pointing, provided that their acceleration function is properly tuned. We thus decided to include purely relative, trackpad-like pointing in this experiment. We tested two different pointing zone sizes, equal to those of the pointing zones used in the previous experiments. For the purpose of experimental comparison, those were considered as distinct techniques, called *RelaSmall* and *RelaLarge*, each tuned with its own optimized transfer function. As discussed before, the literature on calibrating transfer functions for relative pointing techniques is scarce. The functions used by major operating systems do not meet the requirements of ultra-high-resolution wall-sized displays in terms of speed and precision. We therefore used the transfer function calibration method initially developed for our dual-precision techniques. Parameter values are given in Table 1. Compared to the functions used in the first two experiments, these two functions feature a much higher CD_{max} that allows traveling much larger distances without too much clutching.

To avoid introducing a confound due to the device itself, we decided to use a tablet for all techniques that required a handheld device: $ContHead_S$, *RelaSmall* and *RelaLarge*. We compared those three techniques with two techniques from the literature: *LaserGyro* and *SmoothPoint*.

LaserGyro is a mid-air dual-precision technique that provides coarse control of the cursor's position with ray-casting and enables precise adjustments with relative angular motion. Mode switches are triggered with a button. This technique, inspired by Vogel *et al.*'s work on distant freehand pointing [34], has been shown to perform very well [26].

SmoothPoint [15] also combines ray-casting with relative pointing. However, the transition between the two modes is progressive, based on a transfer function that depends on input motion velocity. The authors of [15] propose a method to tune this function, but pilot tests in our environment revealed that this method does not scale to large surfaces with high pixel densities such as those typically encountered on ultra-high-resolution wall displays: the difference between the minimum and maximum CD gain values is too high, causing the precise mode to be very jerky when selecting small targets such as those considered here. We transposed the calibration method described in [15] to our context[3] to the best of our abilities, iterating until the technique eventually enabled us to achieve pointing tasks with the target sizes and movement amplitudes considered in our experiments.

In this third experiment, we tested a total of five techniques (TECH): $ContHead_S$, *RelaSmall*, *RelaLarge*, *SmoothPoint* and *LaserGyro*. The apparatus, design, and procedure were exactly the same as in the previous experiments. We added a physical border around the large and small pointing zones on the tablet to limit the need to look at the input device by providing tactile feedback when the fingers were about to leave the zone. We used a 5×5 latin square to balance technique ordering. 15 participants served in the experiment (10 of them had participated in the previous experiments 1.5 months before, 5 were new and assigned to the same Latin square).

Quantitative-objective Results. As in the previous experiment we removed a few outliers (1.28%). Figure 7 shows movement time *MT* by W and A. For $ContHead_S$ the results are very close to those of the previous experiments. We observe that *SmoothPoint* performs poorly compared to all other techniques (significantly so, for each W and A condition). For the sake of conciseness, we do not report figures for *SmoothPoint* in post-hoc tests, even though it was, of course, included in the corresponding statistical computations.

An ANOVA reveals a significant effect of TECH on *MT* ($F_{4,56} = 20.5$, $p < 0.0001$). A post-hoc t-test with Bonferonni correction shows that $ContHead_S$, *LaserGyro* and *RelaLarge* are all significantly faster than *RelaSmall* (with speed-ups of 5.4%, 8% and 9%, respectively).

[3]We did not use our logistic function because the transfer function associated with SmoothPoint is part of the technique [15].

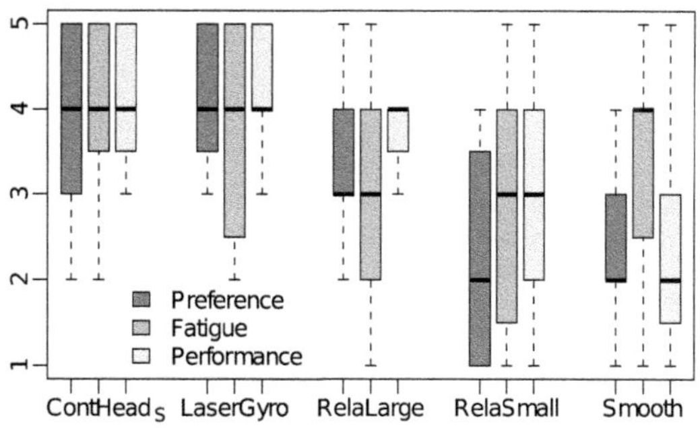

Figure 8. Preference, fatigue and (self-reported) perceived performance for each TECH on a five-point Likert item (5 is best, 1 is worst).

This time, the ANOVA reveals significant interactions TECH × W ($F_{4,56} = 5.90$, $p = 0.0005$) and TECH × A ($F_{8,112} = 2.60$, $p = 0.0122$) on *MT*. One cause for these interactions is *SmoothPoint*, which is slower for small targets than for larger ones, and faster for the largest amplitude. We can also observe (Figure 7) that the two relative techniques, *RelaSmall* and *RelaLarge*, are faster for the small width and the small amplitude. Indeed, post-hoc tests show that (i) for small targets, the only significant result is that *RelaLarge* is faster than *RelaSmall*, and for large targets, *ContHead$_S$* and *LaserGyro* are also significantly faster than *RelaSmall*; (ii) for the small amplitude the only significant results are that *RelaLarge* is faster than *RelaSmall* and *ContHead$_S$*, while for the large amplitude the only significant results are that both *RelaLarge* and *ContHead$_S$* are significantly faster than *RelaSmall*.

The overall error rate is 9.6%. *ContHead$_S$*, *RelaSmall* and *RelaLarge* feature low error rates (3.90%, 3.52% and 4.04%) with only marginal differences between large and small targets (2.5% vs 5.17%). *LaserGyro* and *SmoothPoint* also feature low error rates for large targets (0.70% and 5.60%), but the error rate rises dramatically for small targets: 25.6% and 43.0%. We had not anticipated such an increase in error rate from our pilot studies. The problem turned out to come from the fact that clicking with the handheld wireless mouse caused small hand movements which, in turn, caused small cursor displacements that were sometimes large enough to make the cursor leave the target. We furthered our analysis by measuring the time to first click (instead of first click on the target). This did not change the results for *LaserGyro*. However, results were slightly different for *SmoothPoint*, which remained slower than *RelaSmall* in all conditions but not significantly so for the small target + large amplitude condition.

Quantitative-subjective Results. At the end of the experiment, we asked participants to rank the techniques on a five-point Likert scale in terms of preference, fatigue and perceived performance. Figure 8 summarizes the results in a boxplot. Kruskal-Wallis tests revealed a significant effect of TECH on Preference ($\chi^2_4 = 28.5$, $p < 0.0001$) and Performance ($\chi^2_4 = 23.4$, $p = 0.0001$), but not on Fatigue. Post-hoc tests using Mann-Whitney tests with Bonferroni correction show that (i) *ContHead$_S$* and *LaserGyro* were preferred to both *RelaSmall* and *SmoothPoint*; (ii) *RelaLarge* was preferred to *SmoothPoint*; (iii) *ContHead$_S$*, *LaserGyro* and *RelaLarge* were perceived as faster than *SmoothPoint*; and (iv) *LaserGyro* and *ContHead$_S$* were perceived as (marginally) faster than *RelaLarge*.

Discussion and Design Guidelines

Results show that using a handheld device for high precision pointing enables users to point at least as efficiently as state-of-the-art mid-air pointing techniques in terms of both speed and accuracy, while leaving a large portion of the handheld's surface available for additional, application-specific widgets.

The three techniques that perform best in terms of movement time and preference are *RelaLarge*, *ContHead* and *LaserGyro*. While there is no significant speed difference between them, each technique has its own strengths and limitations, making it suitable to specific contexts of use.

While relative pointing is not novel, making it work efficiently in such challenging contexts is an interesting result. Indeed, existing functions, even elaborate ones such as that of *SmoothPoint*, were designed for lower-resolution environments, and fare poorly with the high Fitts' IDs considered here. *RelaLarge*, based on the CD transfer function tuning method introduced in this paper, provides pointing performance that matches that of more elaborate techniques. It is straightforward to implement and does not require specific equipment to track spatial position and orientation.

RelaSmall is also quite an achievement, considering that it provides enough precision to perform bivariate pointing tasks of high difficulty (up to 9.5) with a pointing zone of 20 cm^2 only (approximately $1/4^{th}$ of *RelaLarge*'s surface area). Given that the pointing zone dimensions of *RelaLarge* preclude its use on smartphones, *RelaSmall* can be seen as an interesting option. Indeed, the technique will only incur a 5-to-10-percent performance decrease compared to more efficient techniques, which can be considered an acceptable tradeoff when only small handheld devices are available, or when a large portion of the handheld's screen real-estate should be allocated to additional interface widgets.

This performance decrease can be avoided by using *ContHead*, which achieves the same level of performance as *RelaLarge* but on a much smaller input area, equivalent to that of *RelaSmall*. *ContHead* should be considered when the tasks and context of use require many additional interface widgets or when only smartphones are available, provided that tracking the location and orientation of the head is possible.

Finally, *LaserGyro* causes many more errors than other techniques for small values of W, as the tremor caused by pressing a physical button, even if comparatively small, is large enough to severely hinder acquiring very small targets. This problem does not happen with tablet-based techniques since their tapping mechanism is algorithmically decoupled from their pointing mechanism. Another drawback of this technique is that it cannot accommodate additional interface widgets on the input device. However, *LaserGyro* leaves the non-dominant hand free to perform other interactions, making it a relevant option when the task requires operating additional input devices, provided that pointing task IDs are lower than 9.

CONCLUSION AND FUTURE WORK

This paper investigated the use of handheld devices for very difficult remote pointing tasks on wall displays, where only a portion of the handheld's surface is dedicated to pointing. The goal is to leave the larger part of this surface to task-specific widgets, since pointing is rarely sufficient on its own to interact with wall displays. We designed and evaluated techniques that use various input channels to improve pointing at very small targets across large amplitudes.

Our most successful design, *ContHead*, lets users perform pointing actions at two levels of granularity: coarse pointing uses the natural movements of the head when moving the cursor across large distances; precise pointing uses a small pointing zone on the handheld device to perform relative pointing movements via finger gestures. When compared with state-of-the-art techniques that are not constrained by our requirements, the technique performs well even with high indices of difficulty, beyond those tested in previous work. *ContHead* was also rated as one of the best techniques overall in terms of subjective preference and perceived performance.

Purely relative techniques using only the touch surface of the handheld device performed better than we had originally anticipated. This led us to carefully investigate Control-Display transfer functions that enable both very fast pointing across large amplitudes while minimizing clutching, and precise cursor adjustments to acquire targets only a few millimeters in diameter. We showed that with a large-enough pointing zone and proper tuning, such a relative technique competes with the most efficient dual-mode techniques.

In future work we plan to investigate how to automatically couple and decouple cursor position from head orientation since it is not always desirable, in real contexts of use, to have them tied together. One possible solution would be to detect situations where the user is likely to initiate pointing actions, e.g., using information about the handheld device and the position of the hand [31, 35].

REFERENCES

1. Ashdown, M., Oka, K., and Sato, Y. Combining head tracking and mouse input for a GUI on multiple monitors. In *Proc. CHI EA '05*, ACM (2005), 1188–1191.
2. Ball, R., North, C., and Bowman, D. A. Move to improve: promoting physical navigation to increase user performance with large displays. In *Proc. CHI '07*, ACM (2007), 191–200.
3. Baudisch, P., Cutrell, E., Robbins, D., Czerwinski, M., Tandler, P., Bederson, B., and Zierlinger, A. Drag-and-Pop and Drag-and-Pick: Techniques for Accessing Remote Screen Content on Touch and Pen-operated Systems. In *Proc. INTERACT '03* (2003), 57–64.
4. Baudisch, P., Sinclair, M., and Wilson, A. Soap: a pointing device that works in mid-air. In *Proc. UIST '06*, ACM (2006), 43–46.
5. Beaudouin-Lafon, M., Chapuis, O., Eagan, J., Gjerlufsen, T., Huot, S., Klokmose, C., Mackay, W., Nancel, M., Pietriga, E., Pillias, C., Primet, R., and Wagner, J. Multi-surface interaction in the WILD room. *IEEE Computer 45*, 4 (2012), 48–56.
6. Bezerianos, A., and Balakrishnan, R. The Vacuum: facilitating the manipulation of distant objects. In *Proc. CHI '05*, ACM (2005), 361–370.
7. Blanch, R., and Ortega, M. Rake cursor: improving pointing performance with concurrent input channels. In *Proc. CHI '09*, ACM (2009), 1415–1418.
8. Boring, S., Baur, D., Butz, A., Gustafson, S., and Baudisch, P. Touch projector: mobile interaction through video. In *Proc. CHI '10*, ACM (2010), 2287–2296.
9. Casiez, G., and Roussel, N. No more bricolage!: methods and tools to characterize, replicate and compare pointing transfer functions. In *Proc. UIST '11*, ACM (2011), 603–614.
10. Casiez, G., Vogel, D., Balakrishnan, R., and Cockburn, A. The impact of control-display gain on user performance in pointing tasks. *HCI 23*, 3 (2008), 215–250.
11. Forlines, C., Vogel, D., and Balakrishnan, R. Hybridpointing: fluid switching between absolute and relative pointing with a direct input device. In *Proc. UIST '06*, ACM (2006), 211–220.
12. Freedman, E. G., and Sparks, D. L. Coordination of the eyes and head: movement kinematics. *Exp. Brain Res. 131* (2000), 22–32.
13. Frees, S., Kessler, G. D., and Kay, E. PRISM interaction for enhancing control in immersive virtual environments. *ACM ToCHI 14*, 1 (2007).
14. Gallo, L., Ciampi, M., and Minutolo, A. Smoothed pointing: A user-friendly technique for precision enhanced remote pointing. In *Proc. CISIS '10*, IEEE (2010), 712–717.
15. Gallo, L., and Minutolo, A. Design and comparative evaluation of smoothed pointing: A velocity-oriented remote pointing enhancement technique. *IJHCS 70*, 4 (2012), 287–300.
16. Jacob, R. The use of eye movements in human-computer interaction techniques: what you look at is what you get. *ACM TOIS 9* (1991), 152–169.
17. Jota, R., Nacenta, M. A., Jorge, J. A., Carpendale, S., and Greenberg, S. A comparison of ray pointing techniques for very large displays. In *Proc. GI '10*, CIPS (2010), 269–276.
18. Kirstein, C., and Muller, H. Interaction with a projection screen using a camera-tracked laser pointer. In *Proc. MMM '98*, IEEE (1998), 191–192.
19. Kitajima, K., Sato, Y., and Koike, H. Vision-based face tracking system for window interface: prototype application and empirical studies. In *Proc. CHI EA '01*, ACM (2001), 359–360.
20. Kollerl, D. R., Mine, M. R., and Hudson, S. E. Head-tracked orbital viewing: an interaction technique for immersive virtual environments. In *Proc. UIST '96*, ACM (1996), 81–82.
21. Konig, W. A., Gerken, J., Dierdorf, S., and Reiterer, H. Adaptive pointing - design and evaluation of a precision enhancing technique for absolute pointing devices. In *Proc. INTERACT '09*, Springer (2009), 658–671.
22. Kopper, R., Bowman, D. A., Silva, M. G., and McMahan, R. P. A human motor behavior model for distal pointing tasks. *IJHCS 68*, 10 (2010), 603–615.
23. Mccallum, D. C., and Irani, P. Arc-pad: absolute+relative cursor positioning for large displays with a mobile touchscreen. In *Proc. UIST '09*, ACM (2009), 153–156.
24. Morency, L.-P., and Darrell, T. Head gesture recognition in intelligent interfaces: the role of context in improving recognition. In *Proc. IUI '06*, ACM (2006), 32–38.
25. Myers, B. A., Bhatnagar, R., Nichols, J., Peck, C. H., Kong, D., Miller, R. C., and Long, A. C. Interacting at a distance: measuring the performance of laser pointers and other devices. In *Proc. CHI '02*, ACM (2002), 33–40.
26. Nancel, M., Pietriga, E., and Beaudouin-Lafon, M. Precision pointing for ultra-high-resolution wall displays. Technical Report RR-7624, INRIA, 2011.
27. Nancel, M., Wagner, J., Pietriga, E., Chapuis, O., and Mackay, W. Mid-air pan-and-zoom on wall-sized displays. In *Proc. CHI '11*, ACM (2011), 177–186.
28. Nickel, K., and Stiefelhagen, R. Pointing gesture recognition based on 3d-tracking of face, hands and head orientation. In *Proc. ICMI '03*, ACM (2003), 140–146.
29. Pietriga, E., Huot, S., Nancel, M., and Primet, R. Rapid development of user interfaces on cluster-driven wall displays with jBricks. In *Proc. EICS '11*, ACM (2011), 185–190.
30. Poupyrev, I., Tomokazu, N., and Weghorst, S. Virtual Notepad: Handwriting in Immersive VR. In *Proc. VRAIS '98*, IEEE (1998), 126–132.
31. Rahman, M., Gustafson, S., Irani, P., and Subramanian, S. Tilt techniques: Investigating the dexterity of wrist-based input. In *Proc. CHI '09*, ACM (2009), 1943–1952.
32. Räihä, K.-J., and Špakov, O. Disambiguating ninja cursors with eye gaze. In *Proc. CHI '09*, ACM (2009), 1411–1414.
33. Stahl, J. S. Amplitude of human head movements associated with horizontal saccades. *Exp. Brain Res. 126* (1999), 41–54.
34. Vogel, D., and Balakrishnan, R. Distant freehand pointing and clicking on very large, high resolution displays. In *Proc. UIST '05*, ACM (2005), 33–42.
35. Wagner, J., Huot, S., and Mackay, W. Bitouch and bipad: Designing bimanual interaction for hand-held tablets. In *Proc. CHI '12*, ACM (2012).
36. Zhai, S., Morimoto, C., and Ihde, S. Manual and gaze input cascaded (MAGIC) pointing. In *Proc. CHI '00*, ACM (1999), 246–253.

StrikeAPose: Revealing Mid-Air Gestures on Public Displays

Robert Walter * robert.walter@tu-berlin.de

Gilles Bailly * gbailly@free.fr

Jörg Müller * ‡ joerg.mueller@tu-berlin.de

* Quality and Usability Lab
Telekom Innovation Laboratories
TU Berlin, Germany

‡ University of the Arts
Berlin, Germany

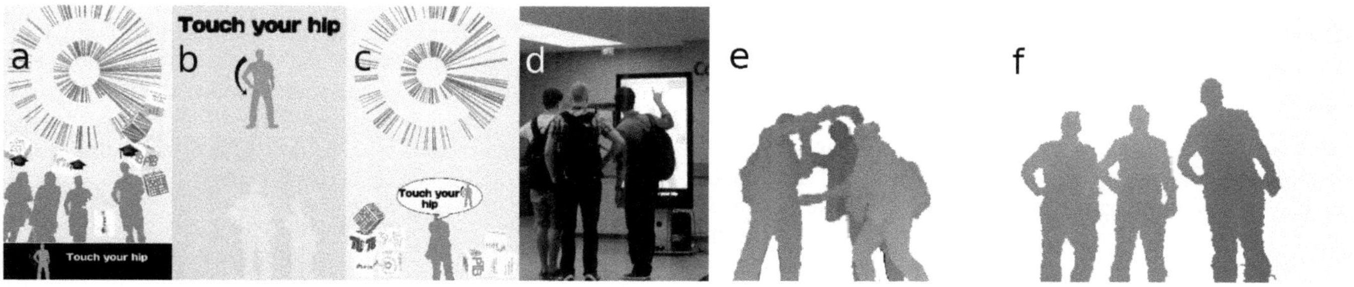

Figure 1. a,b,c) Three strategies for revealing an initial mid-air gesture on public displays: a) spatial division, b) temporal division, c) integration; d,e,f) examples of findings from our field study: d) the Teapot Gesture is fluently integrated with other gestures, e) users explore a potential gesture vocabulary, f) users often imitate other users' gestures.

ABSTRACT

We investigate how to reveal an initial mid-air gesture on interactive public displays. This initial gesture can serve as gesture registration for advanced operations. We propose three strategies to reveal the initial gesture: spatial division, temporal division, and integration. Spatial division permanently shows the gesture on a dedicated screen area. Temporal division interrupts the application to reveal the gesture. Integration embeds gesture hints directly in the application. We also propose a novel initial gesture called *Teapot* to illustrate our strategies. Our main findings from a laboratory and field study are: A large percentage of all users execute the gesture, especially with spatial division (56%). Users intuitively discover a gesture vocabulary by exploring variations of the Teapot gesture by themselves, as well as by imitating and extending other users' variations.

Author Keywords

Public Displays; Initial Gesture; Revelation; Field Study

ACM Classification Keywords

H.5.m. Information Interfaces and Presentation (e.g. HCI): Miscellaneous

INTRODUCTION

Touch-based interaction is the common modality for public displays. However, distant interaction through mid-air gestures has several advantages for public display interaction. (1) It does not require to touch public installations which may be inappropriate for hygienic reasons. (2) Users do not need to come close to the screen to interact. (3) It can help noticing interactivity of public displays because passers-by can interact inadvertently [26]. (4) It may favor performative interaction, e.g., expressive and highly visible gestures [31].

Several interaction techniques [4, 13, 14, 22] have been proposed to guide the execution of gestures in the context of pen-based or touch interfaces. However these techniques have never been applied to mid-air gestures and assume that users already know how to *register* the gesture (e.g. how to define the beginning of the interaction [33]). Usually executing a gesture requires to initiate the gesture by pressing a button or touching an interactive surface. Triggering a help system or menu usually requires to touch or press and wait for one second [4, 13]. For mid-air gestures on public displays, a registration or *initial gesture* to define the beginning of advanced interaction is not yet established. Due to the novelty of the interaction technique it is unclear to users how to initiate the interaction.

The context of public displays introduces additional challenges for revealing the initial gesture, especially for mid-air gestures: First, many users approach the device for the first time.They are unaware that the system can capture mid-air gestures, which gestures are available and how to execute them. Second, users interact with the system for a short time [26] and thus the system only has a couple of seconds/minutes for communicating the initial gesture. Third, a public display generally has only "one shot": Users may give up if they do not immediately succeed with their interaction [23].

In this paper we investigate the question of how to *reveal* an initial mid-air gesture on public displays to enable advanced interactions such as navigating through a menu. We propose three strategies to reveal gestures: spatial division, temporal division and integration. *Spatial division* permanently shows the gesture on a dedicated screen area (Figure 1a at the bottom). For *temporal division* the running application is interrupted to reveal the gesture in full screen (Figure 1b). For *integration* hints are directly embedded into the application, similar to product placement techniques in movies (Figure 1c).

We also propose the Teapot gesture, a novel initial gesture for mid-air gestural interaction with public displays. Users touch their hip to enclose an inner area with their body and their arm in their contour image (Figure 1f). We show that the Teapot gesture is easy to recognize by the system, comfortable for the user, socially acceptable, and easy to understand. We use the Teapot gesture to illustrate our gesture revelation strategies in a laboratory and a field study.

The laboratory study shows that (1) users do not notice the hint with spatial division. (2) Users notice the hint with integration but have difficulties to understand it. (3) Users both notice and understand how to perform the initial gesture with temporal division. From these observations we derived improved versions of the most promising technique for each strategy to compare them against each other in a field study.

The main findings of our field study are: (1) A large percentage of all users execute the gesture, especially with spatial division (56%). This is a surprisingly high number for an in-the-wild study, especially since users are free to do what they want, are not instructed by experimenters, and the game alone is already fun to play. (2) Users intuitively discover a gesture vocabulary by exploring variations of the Teapot gesture. This provides us with a user-defined gesture set. (3) Users discover this gesture vocabulary by imitating other users or by trying to find more interesting gestures than the other members of the group. (4) Users discover the gesture inadvertently while doing unrelated movements.

RELATED WORK

Gestures

In this paper we refer to the definition of gestures of Kurtenbach and Hulteen [20, 9]: "A gesture is a motion of the body that contains information". Several classifications or taxonomies [19, 24, 35, 10] have been proposed to categorize gestures. For instance Cadoz [10] proposes three types of gestures depending on their function: Semiotic (to communicate meaningful information), ergotic (to manipulate the physical world), and epistemic (to learn from the environment). While ergotic gestures are usually used for direct manipulation of virtual objects, semiotic gestures are used for the execution of commands. Semiotic gestures can be further subdivided into symbolic, deictic, iconic, and pantomimic gestures. Symbolic gestures signify gestures that iconify a certain meaning (such as drawing a question mark), but also gestures without an immediately obvious meaning would be classified as symbolic (such as touching a certain body part).

Mid-air Gestures and Public Displays

Only a few public displays support mid-air gesture interaction. While [26, 31] investigate direct manipulation through ergotic gestures, [27, 3] and [32] investigate the use of symbolic gestures for the execution of commands. Still, no field studies have investigated the revelation of symbolic mid-air gestures in the field. The closest to our work is [16], who investigates touch gestures for a public multi-touch table in a field study. They find that gestures are integrated into a continuous flow of gestures and the choice of gesture is influenced by previous gestures and social context. However, these results can not be transfered to mid-air gestures because prolonged interaction with an interactive table differs from playful interaction with a vertical display.

Mid-air gestures in front of public displays can also be described as performative interaction [28]. This concept proposes that users are simultaneously in three different relationships: (1) the interaction with the public display, (2) the perception of themselves within the the situation and (3) acting about a role for others to observe [12]. Important concepts for performative interaction are *manipulations* and *effects* [28] because they impact social learning and the honeypot effect [26, 31]. Manipulations refer to the performer's gestures while effects refer to the visible result of the gestures on the display.

Gesture Registration

Gestures can be described in three phases [6, 13, 36]: (1) *registration* that clearly marks the beginning of the gesture, (2) *continuation* which is the dynamic part and (3) *termination* that marks the end of the gesture. In the case of a touch screen, these phases could be (1) touch the screen, (2) swipe finger and (3) release finger. Especially for mid-air gestures, the registration and termination phases appear less obvious, since there is no explicit delimiter that marks the beginning and the end of a gesture.

Wigdor [33] proposes three possible delimiters: (1) *Multimodality* could be applied to make use of additional channels (e.g. speech, button, etc.) to communicate a delimiter. For example a user could say "put that ..." while pointing at an object, then point at another location saying "... there!" [7] to move an object. However some modalities may be unavailable or inappropriate on interactive public displays. Moreover, discovering additional modalities itself introduces new problems. (2) *Reserved actions* (such as drawing a pigtail [15], or drawing a corner with the pen [14]) can define that the previous or next action should be interpreted as a command. (3) *Clutching* provides a certain state in which gestures are recognized. A possible clutching mechanisms for mid-air gestures may be a virtual and invisible curtain that the user's hand needs to penetrate in order to initiate the gesture tracking. Still it is not clear how this surface should be shaped and positioned. If it is too close it may generate false positive-and if it is too far away it is prone to false negative detection.

An initial gesture can be defined as a reserved action or as clutching. While reserved actions can define either the registration or termination, clutching has the advantage to define both. We now discuss techniques for revealing this initial gesture to novice users.

REVELATION: FROM TOUCH TO MID-AIR GESTURES

Kurtenbach [22] introduced the concepts of self-revelation, guidance and rehearsal for gestures. Several techniques have been proposed for guidance or rehearsal in the context of pen-based or touch interaction. These techniques include *Marking menus* [22] and its variants [1, 2, 3, 37, 38], *HoverWidgets* [14], as well as *Octopocus* [4] and its variants for multi-touch surfaces [5, 13]. Only *LightGuide* [30] has been proposed in the context of mid-air gestures by projecting guidance hints directly onto the user's hands.

In contrast, very few techniques have been proposed for *revelation* [8, 17], although it is an essential issue for all gesture-based systems, especially in public space. We now detail three approaches to reveal gestures on touch surfaces: guessability, interaction techniques, and crib-sheets. We discuss their adequacy for mid-air gestures on public displays.

Guessability: The design of *guessable* gestures [35] appears not very promising for public displays because generally users are not aware which commands are available. However this is one major prerequisite for guessability. Besides users of public displays usually do not have a specific goal or a command to execute in mind.

Interaction Techniques for Revelation: To the best of our knowledge, only three techniques focus on revelation of gestures in the context of mouse [8] and touch [17, 13] interfaces. Firstly, *GestureBar* [8] is a technique for integrating gestures into conventional WIMP interfaces. It uses an advanced toolbar which, instead of executing the command when the corresponding icon is clicked, displays a video of how to execute the command via a mouse gesture. Secondly, Hofmeester recently investigated the revelation of a single gesture in the context of Tablet PCs [17]. In the project a *slide to select* gesture to launch applications on Windows 8 [17] is taught to the user. A tutorial is not used to avoid impairing the user experience. The authors found that visual cues that raise curiosity are an important factor to improve the discoverability of gestures. Finally, *ShadowGuides* [13] displays various hand poses for gesture registration, once users have touched the display and dwelled for one second. *ShadowGuides* also guides the gesture continuation after the user has executed the registration gesture.

As these projects [8, 13, 17], we aim at improving the discoverability of gestures. However, our approach differs in several aspects as we focus on public displays.

First, these systems assume that users already know how to interact in a first modality (mouse and toolbar for *GestureBar*; touch and dwell for *ShadowGuides*; touch for Windows 8). This prior knowledge about the first modality is then used to reveal gestural interaction as a second modality.

Second, these systems have been designed for a context where users want to achieve a goal. In this scenario users are aware of available commands and explore the system for them. In contrast, users of public displays often do not have a specific goal [26]. The interaction is spontaneous and initiated by curiosity or playfulness.

Third, for *GestureBar* and *ShadowGuides* users were already instructed that they should operate a gestural interface. They were aware of "the concept of gestural commands and how to use them" [8]. In contrast, passers-by are generally not aware that public displays are interactive, how to interact with them and whether gestural interaction is supported [26].

In consequence, passers-by should understand that gesture-based interaction is possible and how gestures are invoked, both in a very short time as passing-by interaction is generally quite short (a couple of seconds/minutes) [26].

Crib-sheets: Another alternative is the use of crib-sheets [21]. Most of them are displayed *on demand* by pressing a help button. In Tivoli [21], users *press and hold* to get information about commands and gestures. But this technique is not compatible with immediate usability of public displays. Another strategy may be to *always* display the crib-sheet on the screen. For traditional platforms, permanent crib-sheets are often criticized because they require a lot of space, especially for large gesture sets.

The spatial division techniques presented in this paper are similar to permanent crib-sheets. A major difference to our approach is that not *all* the available gestures are shown, but only *one*: the initial gesture. This single gesture would serve as a registration for advanced gestures, to access a larger set of gestures, or perform other interactions. We believe that presenting several gestures will confuse or overload users by displaying too much information simultaneously. Finally, while different kinds of labels have been used in crib-sheets (text, icons, or animations), they have not been evaluated or compared in the context of distant interaction with public displays.

STRIKEAPOSE

StrikeAPose is an interactive public display game to investigate how an *initial mid-air gesture* can be revealed to users (see Figure 1 a,b,c and 2).

Game

Inspired by [11, 26, 31], we designed a simple but engaging game based on physics simulation to motivate passers-by to interact. Passers-by see their mirror image on the screen and can use it to play with virtual cubes (Figure 1). Users can toss them into a specific target to collect points. They can also perform an *initial gesture* to enable an advanced operation. While the focus is only on revealing this initial gesture and in order to keep the experiments as simple as possible, the advanced operation only consists of adding a funny bunny mask (laboratory study, Figure 2) or doctoral hat (field study, Figure 1a) to the users' contour.

Teapot Gesture

We propose the Teapot gesture as a novel initial gesture for mid-air gestural interaction on public displays. The gesture can be described as a full-body version of the pinch gesture [34], where users touch their hip with their arm to enclose a distinct inner area in their contour image (Figure 1). The Teapot gesture overcomes two limitations of the pinch gesture in the context of public displays: (1) The inner area is large enough to be easily detected by the system, even if users are positioned a couple of meters away from the screen. (2) The area is naturally oriented towards the sensor as the interacting user is facing the screen. The Teapot gesture is also well suited as a gesture registration, because it can clearly indicate the beginning and the end of a gesture or interaction. The first implementation of the recognizer was based on the skeletal tracking capabilities of the *OpenNI / NiTE* framework. Though thick clothes might cause reliability issues with the contour-based recognition, it turns out to be more robust than the skeleton-based recognizer. As a side effect, any gesture besides the Teapot gesture, that generates such an inner area would trigger the recognizer. In the field study described below we observed, that people naturally tend to explore this set of possible gesture variations. A Pilot study also shows that the Teapot gestures is well accepted by users [29].

Revelation Strategies

We propose three strategies inspired by advertisement placement to reveal an initial gesture:

- *Spatial division:* The screen is split into two areas: the game and a ribbon below explaining the gesture. This strategy is for instance implemented as banner ads on Youtube videos.
- *Temporal division:* The game is temporally interrupted to reveal the gesture in full screen. This strategy is similar to classical television ads.
- *Integration:* Visual cues are integrated into the game itself. This strategy is similar to product placement, where certain products (e.g., cars, drinks) are placed in a movie.

These three strategies suggest *when* and *where* to reveal the initial gesture. However, it is not yet defined *how* to explain it.

Labels: Text can provide precise descriptions but its intelligibility depends on the user's language skills. Icons do not have limitations related to readability but can be ambiguous or insufficient for complex or dynamic gestures. Videos are ideal for dynamic gestures but users have to observe and memorize the entire sequence, which may require too much time and cognitive load. Videos can also highlight the link between the manipulation (gesture) and the effect of this gesture. Icon- and video labels can also be combined with text. To reduce the number of conditions to be evaluated in laboratory and field studies, we ran a pilot study to determine the three most promising cues among the five label variations: text; icon; video; text+icon; text+video. Results show that the conditions that include text were more effective in triggering users to execute the gesture than those without text. Based on these results, we decided to test text, text+icon, and text+video in a laboratory study.

Integration Cues: We propose three examples of cues that can be used for the integration strategy.

- *Hip Button:* As an example technique for affording a specific action or movement a button positioned at the hip is added to the user's contour. The Hip Button is supposed to afford users to "touch their hip" (Figure 2c).
- *Voodoo User:* The user is temporally dispossessed of control over his own mirror image. Instead of mirroring the user's movement, the mirror image would perform the gesture (Figure 2c).
- *Fake User:* An additional virtual user is added to the game. For the Fake User an actor has been previously video-recorded passing by the display, stopping, and executing the initial gesture. The Fake User enters every 30 seconds for four seconds. As people tend to imitate behavior of other people, we expect that the real user would imitate the gesture of the Fake User.

To test a reasonable number of conditions in the laboratory study, we conducted a second pilot study to determine the two most promising techniques. Results show that the Fake User performed relatively poorly. While 8/10 users noticed the Fake User, no one actually imitated the presented gesture. Users reported that "The bunny guy comes in to distract me from the game!" or as "a reward" for good performance. Apparently users paid most attention to their own mirror image and have only perceived the effect but not the manipulation of the gesture from the Fake User. Based on the results of this pre-study, we decided to retain the Voodoo User and the Hip Button for a laboratory study.

LABORATORY STUDY

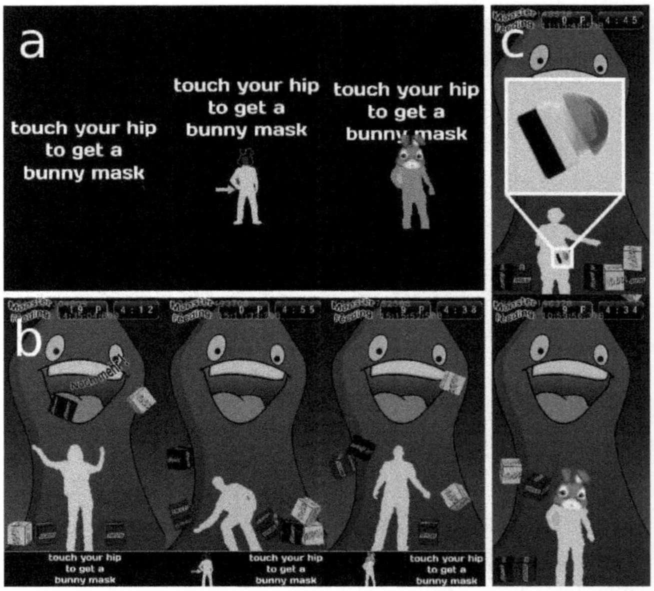

Figure 2. Screenshots of all Conditions: a) Temporal Division (Text, Text+Icon and Text+Video); b) Spatial Division (Text, Text+Icon and Text+Video); c) Integration (Hip Button and Voodoo User)

We conducted a laboratory study to (1) reduce the design space of techniques for revealing gestures, (2) identify the most promising techniques for each strategy, and to (3) optimize the strategies before evaluating them in a field study.

Experimental Design

Label: Three different labels (Figure 2) were used for the temporal and spatial division strategies. A text label "Touch your hip to get a bunny mask" explains both the manipulation (gesture) and the effect (the result of the manipulation). An iconic label shows the static pose, the highlighted inner area of the Teapot gesture, and the bunny mask. A video shows an actor performing the gesture and receiving the bunny mask. To avoid that users confuse the actor in the video with themselves, the actor's contour was rendered in a different color and position.

For the temporal strategy the label was displayed in the center of the screen. It was presented every 30 seconds for four seconds. Four seconds were sufficient to present a video of a user executing the gesture and show the effect, but short enough not to make users wait too long before being able to continue playing the game. For the spatial strategy, the label was shown permanently in the lower part of the screen.

Apparatus and Participants: The system was installed in a room in close proximity to the main entrance of a university building. We randomly invited passers-by in the entrance to participate in a five-minute experiment. In total 166 passers-by, aged between 13 and 72 years (mean=26.5; sd=9.8) participated in the test. They received candies for their participation. For the entire time of the interaction the system logged the raw depth video, a screen capture, and various events to a text file.

Instructions and Task: After introducing the interactive public display to the participants, we asked them to play with it as they would do in a public place. Participants did not receive any further instructions. In particular they were not instructed about the gestural interaction, the initial gesture, the principle of the game, or the bunny mask. The experiment was aborted as soon as the participant successfully performed the initial gesture (manipulation) to trigger the effect, or after a maximum time of two minutes, an approximation of the maximal usage time for casual interaction in the field [26].

After the test we interviewed all of the 166 participants of the laboratory study individually for approximately 3 minutes. The interviews were semi-structured and included questions like whether or not participants Q1) noticed the hint, Q2) tried to perform the Teapot gesture, Q3) understood the manipulation before trying and Q4) understood the effect before trying. The most important interview results are summarized in figure 3. In addition to the mentioned questions, we gathered general data like age, gender, and occupational background from participants.

Design: We used a between subjects design as we were particularly interested in first-time users.

Results

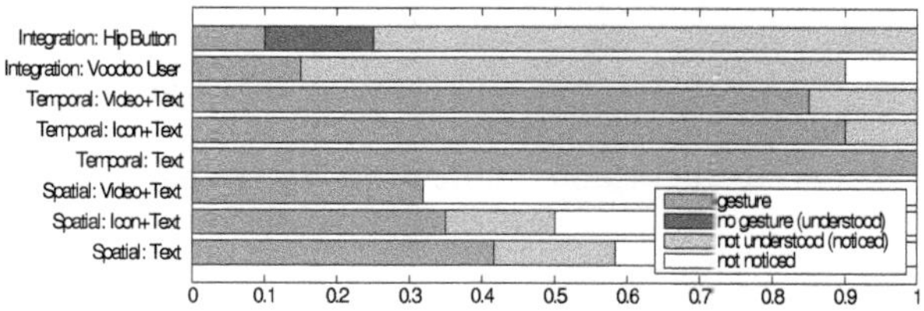

Figure 3. Percentage of participants that performed the gesture (green); did not perform the gesture though they noticed and understood the hint (red); noticed but did not understand the hint (gray); and did not notice the hint (white)

Conversion Rate

The conversion rate is defined as the percentage of users that execute the gesture. It was derived from the results of question Q2 of the interview.

Techniques: A Kruskal-Wallis test reveals no effect for spatial- and temporal division labels on the conversion rate. However, it reveals a significant effect between the two integration techniques ($\chi^2 = 7, p < 0.01$). Voodoo User (15%) triggers significantly more gestures than Hip Button (10%). For the Hip Button technique, we observed that a few users did not perform the gesture correctly. They recognized the button, understood that they had to push it but did not do it in the intended way: Instead of touching their hip by pushing the button from the side, they decided to hit it *in front* of their body. Ultimately, the Hip Button triggered more actions than the Voodoo Users, but in contrast to the Hip Button, the Voodoo User appears to be less ambiguous.

Strategies: A Kruskal-Wallis test reveals an effect for strategies on the conversion rate ($\chi^2 = 51.5, p < 0.0001$). Temporal division (92%) triggers significantly more gestures than spatial division (36%) which triggers significantly more gestures than integration (12%).

Comprehensibility Rate

The comprehensibility rate is defined as the percentage of users that understood the manipulation of the technique. It was derived from the results of question Q4 of the interview.

Techniques: A Kruskal-Wallis test reveals neither an effect for spatial and temporal divisions labels on the comprehensibility rate nor for the integration techniques.

Strategies: A Kruskal-Wallis test reveals an effect for strategies on the comprehensibility rate ($\chi^2 = 45, p < 0.001$). Users understood temporal division (85%) significantly more often than spatial division (35%) and integration (15%). For spatial division, people are distracted from the game and thus may notice but disregard the hint. This was also reported by some participants in the interview.

Noticeability Rate

The noticeability rate is defined as the percentage of users that notice the hint. The data were gathered from question Q1 of the user interviews.

Techniques: A Kruskal-Wallis test reveals neither an effect for the spatial and temporal division strategies on the noticeability rate nor for the integration techniques.

Strategies: A Kruskal-Wallis test reveals an effect for strategies on the noticeability rate ($\chi^2 = 31.0, p < 0.0001$). The hint is noticed significantly more often for temporal division (100%) and integration (95%) than for spatial division (47%).

Finally, we observed that 96% of the participants that understand the manipulation would actually perform the gesture. This is independent of whether or not people did also understand the effect of the gesture.

In summary, results show that (1) The temporal division strategy (92%) triggers a high conversion rate. (2) There are no differences between the different spatial and temporal division labels on the conversion rate. (3) Users that understand the manipulation are likely to perform the gesture.

Optimizing Strategies

This user study highlighted weaknesses for each of the strategies: For the integration techniques, almost all users notice the cue, but it was too subtle to be understood. In contrast, a lot of participants did not notice the hint for spatial division. Finally, for the temporal division strategy, we observed that users noticed the hint and executed the gesture. However, as they executed the gesture mostly during the inserts, it did not show any effect.

almost only while the cue was shown, such that they could not see the effect.

Label: As we did not observe differences between labels, we decided to use the text+icon label for the temporal and spatial division, because it shows both accurate textual description as well as a language independent iconic description of the gesture.

Highlighting Spatial Division: Since the hint was sometimes unnoticed by users for the spatial division, we decided to highlight the hint occasionally using looming stimuli [25]: the cue jumps repeatedly towards the user to capture attention. This highlight appears every 30 seconds for 4 seconds.

Feedback for Temporal Division: To allow users to observe the effect of the gesture during the hint in the temporal division, we decided to fade the mirror image while the hint was blended in (compare Figure 1b to 2a).

Comprehensibility for Integration: We built on the Hip Button of the affordance technique as it is noticed better than the Voodoo User. But as this subtle cue was not understood by the users, we decided to make the hint more explicit. We propose to attach a *Speech Bubble* to the mirror image of the user as shown in Figure 1c. The Speech Bubble uses the same text+icon label as proposed for temporal and spatial division and appears every 30 seconds for four seconds.

Communicating Manipulation Only: For all techniques, we decided not to communicate the effect of the gesture but only the manipulation as it did not seem to effect whether users executed the gesture.

FIELD STUDY

In order to evaluate the gesture revelation techniques in an ecologically valid setting, we conducted a field study. We deployed *StrikeAPose* for five working days in the entrance hall of a university cafeteria. The screen was oriented sideways along the main walking path.

Conditions: We tested the three techniques derived from the laboratory study (see Figure 1 a-c). These conditions were counterbalanced and automatically switched every 10 minutes to minimize the influence of time of day on the results. To avoid interruptions of user interactions, the switch was delayed until no users were detected or after 15 minutes at the latest. All hints were shown (time division and integration) or highlighted (space division) every 30 seconds for 4 seconds.

System: We used the same hardware and software as in the lab study, but we updated the game assets to reflect the deployment location (compare Figure 2 / 1 a-c).

Data Analysis: We collected both qualitative and quantitative data. As quantitative data, we recorded a screen capture as well as the raw depth video from the sensor for the entire time of the deployment. Qualitative data was gathered from observations, interviews and from analyzing manual video recordings.

We interviewed a total number of 46 users in 20 semi-structured group interviews. They were randomly picked, regardless of whether or not they executed the Teapot gesture. Typical questions include whether they R1) already knew the screen, R2) noticed the hint, R3) were annoyed by the hint and R4) tried to perform the Teapot gesture. However, quantitative results of the field study were only derived from the video annotations. Besides that, we collected general comments and opinions of users on the system. Interviews were usually shorter than five minutes and were rewarded with candies.

Observations were conducted from an inconspicuous location on a nearby bench without interfering with the interaction. The depth videos were manually annotated for gesture execution (conversion rate), gesture variations, disengagement, and temporal relation to the hint.

Quantitative Results

During the five days of deployment 558 individual users interacted with the screen while 274 of them performed the gesture at least once.

Conversion Rate: A Chi-squared test revealed that spatial division (56%) triggers significantly more gesture execution than integration (39%) ($\chi^2_{1,N=384} = 10.8, p < 0.05$). The conversion rate for temporal division is 47%.

Timing: We annotated when the gesture was performed within five seconds after the hint appeared or was highlighted. Assuming that people would perform the gesture randomly, this value would be 5 / 30 = 16.7%. We observed that integration (53.7%) and temporal division (56.1%) generates a high probability that users perform the gesture during the appearance or highlighting of the cue. In contrast, for spatial division only 21.0% of users performed the gesture within that time.

Throughout all three conditions people interacted with the screen for about 41 seconds in average (std=45.7).

Disengagement: The hint appears or is highlighted every 30 seconds. Assuming the hypothesis that the hint would not trigger disengagement, the expected random disengagement rate would be only 16.7%. However, we observed that 27.4% of the users of the temporal division leave within five seconds after the hint appears while 13.8% of the users do so for spatial division and 18.8% for integration.

Discussion: Overall, with 56% for spatial division, a surprisingly large percentage of all users executed the gesture. This shows that gesture revelation works very well for public displays. It seems that the lack of attention observed in the laboratory study was resolved by the periodic highlighting. Temporal division also performs well (47%) but seems to make a large percentage of users leave while the cue is shown. This relates to the finding of Huang [18], who observed that when people look at a film on a public display, they will mostly leave when the film ends or there is an interruption.

Design Recommendations: In order to communicate an initial gesture on a public display, it is recommendable to use a gesture revelation strategy like spatial division. A large percentage of users can be expected to execute the gesture.

All revelation strategies work well, but have different benefits and drawbacks. One should not assume that users will casually play with a screen before executing a symbolic gesture. Almost one quarter of all users executed the gesture before actually start playing. There is also a growing body of evidence that interruptions on public displays make people leave. Thus, interruptions should be avoided or used very carefully.

Qualitative Results

In this section we report our three main qualitative findings: Flow of gestures, exploration of gesture variations, and imitation of gestures. For each of these behaviors, we report, compare, and discuss our observations in the context of related work. Finally, we provide design recommendations.

Flow of gestures

Users did not perform the Teapot gesture in isolation. They were engaged in a constant flow of gestures, be it symbolic, deictic, iconic, pantomimic, or ergotic gestures. For example, when approaching the screen, some users did a symbolic waving gesture towards the screen. Others pulled their friends by the arm to make them abort interaction. They were also pointing at the screen (deictic) while talking to others. One user iconified the depth sensor with both hands while talking to the friends, and another user pantomimed the walking style of his friend with crutches. The biggest category of gestures, however, were ergotic gestures, movements to manipulate the environment. Users play with cubes on the screen, push their friend, or grab objects. A variety of gestures were also executed simultaneously with the Teapot gesture, using every part of the body. Some users were scratching their head while executing the Teapot gesture. Others executed the Teapot gesture with one hand (symbolic) and then tried to lift their virtual doctoral hat with the other hand or to continue to play the game (ergotic). If they executed the Teapot gesture with both arms or held an object in the other hand, they became more creative. They continued playing using their head, their shoulders, and their legs. Some users even punched each other in the face in the mirror image (while standing at different distances) while executing the gesture (Figure 6).

Users also engaged in very *expressive* behavior. For example they wildly swung their hip, posed as on a catwalk, or performed skillful dances while performing the Teapot gesture (Figure 4).

Users sometimes discover the Teapot gesture *inadvertently* through a flow of gestures. For example, one user performed the gesture while putting a cigarette behind his ear. Another user pulled a wallet from his back pocket, inadvertently executing the gesture.

Discussion: The fact that gestures are not performed in isolation, but are rather linked into interwoven sequences, was also observed by Hinrichs and Carpendale [16] for a multi-touch table. They describe that users perform different gestures depending on their previous motion for physical ease (e.g., keeping hand posture) but also social functions. This interweaving of gestures is much more pronounced for mid-air gestures. For multi-touch users, there is a separation between touch gestures for manipulating the screen and mid-air gestures for communicating and manipulating the world. For mid-air gestures, this separation almost disappears, and gestures of various kinds for various purposes melt into a continuous flow, with the same gesture often fulfilling multiple purposes (like posing when executing the Teapot).

Design recommendations: The initial gesture will be woven into a continuous flow of gestures, and this needs to be supported. For example, the Kinect *Guide Gesture* requires users to stand still while stretching their arm at 45° for about two seconds. Users are not allowed to move their other arm or legs during this time. This would be counter-productive in public settings, as it interrupts the natural flow of gestures. Similarly, forcing users to use a particular hand, as it is done for the Kinect, would be unsuitable for public situations. A large proportion of users carry objects, like coffee, bags, or jackets in one hand, so that they would prefer to use the other hand for executing the gesture.

Some users may execute gestures inadvertently, which may be beneficial for gesture discovery. However, this did not occur very often in our case and a separate gesture revelation technique may still be necessary.

As it was the case for the Teapot gesture, the gesture should be easy to avoid if desired.

Finally, because gestures are interwoven into a gesture flow, it should be easy to recognize beginning and end of gesture for system and user (e.g., through tactile feedback when touching the own body).

Figure 4. Teapot gesture performed in an expressive Way

Exploration of Gesture Variations

Once users discovered the Teapot gesture, they performed many variations of it. These variations include the modification of the location or the size of the inner area as shown in Figure 5. *Location* was the most frequent modification, and includes switching arm (13%) or using both arms (28%). User also touch their head to define the inner contour image area with the left (7%), right (2%), or both (2%) arms. Finally, some users also used their legs to span an area.

Users also explored different *sizes* for the area. Minimal size included pinch with one hand (Figure 5f) while maximal size included the formation of a circle with the arms in mid-air above the head (2%), on the left (2%) or on the right side (2%) as shown in Figure 5. Users also explored size by coming closer or using various objects (bags, umbrellas, and even scooters).

Additionally, *multi user* gestures as shown on Figure 1 or 5 were explored. This may be either by active collaboration where people try to define very large areas by holding their hands together or passively by using the body of another user as a border for the enclosed area. Some users freely interpreted the instruction "touch your hip" by touching the hip of their friends (Figure 5).

Discussion: While not actively encouraged users, users explored variations of the Teapot gesture. They not only try to execute the gesture, but try to discover other gestures and additionally identify the limits of the system. We believe that several users consider the Teapot gesture as part of a *gesture vocabulary*. Indeed users rarely tried arbitrary gestures but restrict their exploration to some variations of the Teapot (mainly by spanning an area at different locations). This observation supports our main hypothesis: revealing the initial gesture is necessary to discover it but it is also sufficient for several users to discover advanced gestures. These novel gesture variations form a whole that can for instance be used to organize commands in a gesture-based menu.

Variations of gestures have been observed in the context of multi-touch surfaces [16]. However, it is interesting to notice that these variations occur at two different levels of abstraction. In [16] authors observe that users adopt different strategies to perform the same gesture (e.g the use of 2, 3, 4, or 5 fingers to rotate an object). Authors conclude that designers should provide a variety of ways to perform a gesture. In that study users do not intentionally *explore* these variations. In contrast, our observed variations occur at a different level of abstraction and seek to to determine a gesture vocabulary: It is *not* a variation of the way to execute the gesture, but a variation of the gesture itself leading to different gestures. Interestingly, the Teapot gesture supports these two levels of variations. At a low level, users are not forced to *precisely* touch their hip (they can also touch their waist, adopt different hand or body pose, etc.). At a high level, it raises curiosity to explore a potential gesture vocabulary, an important factor to improve the discoverability of other gestures [17].

Design recommendations: Public displays can rely on users exploring the gesture vocabulary if the initial gesture has been chosen carefully. To do so, designers should design an initial gesture which is part of a gesture vocabulary (e.g., one that encloses an inner area in the users' contour image). The initial gesture should also raise curiosity to support the discoverability of the other gestures. The Teapot gesture is one example of an initial gesture supporting these two properties.

Figure 5. Teapot Gesture Derivations at different Locations: a) Hip (left / right / both) b) Head (left / right / both) c) Hands (Body left / Body right / above Head) d) Feet e) Fingers f) Pinch g) Multi-user

Figure 6. Users hold the Teapot gesture while playing the game

Imitation of Gestures

We were surprised by the number of imitations occurring between users, mostly within groups, but also between groups (see Figure 7). As soon as one user in a group performed the gesture, there was a high probability that within a few seconds others would perform the gesture, too. While for some cases they may all have seen the cue at the same time, there was also a substantial number of cases where this happened and no cue was shown.

We distinguish direct and indirect imitation. The first imitation occurs when people *directly* observe a user performing the gesture. In contrast, some people who played together in the same group rarely looked at each other but at the screen. Therefore, they probably *indirectly* copy the gestures from the mirror images on the screen. Finally, spectators in the environment seemed to position themselves so that they can see both the users and the screen, although sometimes the screen was occluded. They seemed to copy gestures more from directly observing the bodies of other users.

Users did not only copy the Teapot gesture, but also variations of it as well as other gestures. For example, in Figure 7a, one user discovers that he can execute the gesture by touching his head and this is copied by another user (Figure 7b).

Interestingly, users did not only try to simply imitate gesture variations. Instead, when they saw someone performing a variation of the gesture, they tried to build on this and find different, more interesting gesture variations. This sometimes led to a kind of *competition*, where each creative variation of the Teapot gesture by one user was answered by a more unconventional variation by another user.

Discussion: [16] reports on two cases of imitative behavior (operating a multi-touch table with sleeves and hoarding objects). In these cases, the observation of the manipulation and the effect (on the screen) is merged. In contrast, in our case there is a difference between users in the same group, imitating from seeing the effect (mirror image), and in other groups, rather imitating from seeing the manipulation. In our case, imitation behavior seems to be an important factor for the revelation of the gesture, in particular when someone in the same group has already performed the gesture. Groups also seemed to quickly explore the gesture vocabulary by building on each others gesture in a competitive game.

Design recommendations: Imitation is an important part of gesture revelation. In particular, a registration gesture should be easy to recognize not only for the system, but also for bystanders, and easy to imitate. Because players concentrate on the screen, it is recommendable if the gesture is imitable by only seeing its effect on the screen, for example through a mirror image. In addition, a large set of interesting gesture variations should be supported, in order to enable groups of users to discover the vocabulary by competitively trying to find more interesting gestures.

Figure 7. Imitation between Groups (a → b) and within Groups (c → d)

GENERALIZABILITY AND LIMITATIONS

In this paper, we investigated how to reveal mid-air gesture on public displays. In this section, we discuss the generalizability of our results as well as potential limitations.

Initial gesture. In this paper, we proposed and used *Teapot* as an initial gestures. The focus of this paper is not to find the optimal initial gesture, and we do not claim that the Teapot gesture should be used for all mid-air gesture interfaces on public displays. However, our studies reveal that the Teapot gesture has several advantages: It is easy to recognize for the system [34], apparently comfortable and socially acceptable, easy to understand even with very short description, encourages exploration of the gesture vocabulary, is easy to imitate, and can be held while performing other gestures simultaneously (asobserved in the field study). Further investigations are advised to compare Teapot to other gestures (e.g., to the guide gesture of the Kinect).

Revelation strategies. We tested several revelation strategies both in laboratory and field studies. Several questions remain: First, do these techniques provide similar results if applied to other initial gestures? We believe that the temporal and spatial division strategies are quite independent of the chosen gesture and interaction paradigm (like mirror image interaction). In contrast, we believe that the integration strategy can provide different results depending on the adequacy of the visual cues to the gesture. Additionally, in a different interaction paradigm (e.g., pointer interaction), integrated cues would need to look differently. Second, some decisions have been taken for the timing of strategies. Currently, all cues are highlighted or shown every 30 seconds for four seconds. Further investigations are necessary to determine the optimal timing. Finally, we were surprised by the low performance of our integrated techniques. These visualization techniques have a lot of parameters (color, shape, metaphor, etc.) that need to be tested in a more systematic way to investigate their impact on noticing, understanding, and executing gestures.

Game. Our user studies are based on a simple but engaging game to motivate people to interact. Different scenarios (such as getting news, entering tweets, etc.) should be investigated in the future in order to generalize our results to a larger variety of applications. More generally, it would be useful to investigate interaction between the context (size of the screen, location of the screen, walking path, etc.) and techniques on the number of passers-by executing gestures.

CONCLUSION

In this paper we investigated mid-air gesture revelation strategies for public displays. We proposed three strategies that have been shown to be efficient to make users execute the gesture. For spatial division, 56% of all interacting users executed the gesture, followed by temporal division (47%) and integration (39%). Spatial division is very effective, does not interrupt the content, and does not cause people to leave while the cue is shown. However, it constantly consumes screen space. Temporal division does not have this problem, but interrupts the content and causes users to leave while the cue is shown. Integration seems to be less effective, but can show different cues to different users. Our findings also revealed that once users execute the gesture, they will explore the gesture vocabulary. They do not only imitate gestures from other users, but try to go beyond other users' gestures in a kind of competition. Finally, the Teapot seems to be a promising initial gesture. We hope that our work can provide a foundation for the investigation of initial mid-air gestures on public displays.

ACKNOWLEDGMENTS

This work was supported by the European Institute of Innovation and Technology and the Alexander von Humboldt Foundation. We thank Uta Hinrichs, Dieter Eberle, Ines Ben Said, Thor Bossuyt, Niklas Hillgren and Christina Dicke.

REFERENCES

1. Bailly, G., Lecolinet, E., and Nigay, L. Wave menus: improving the novice mode of hierarchical marking menus. In *Springer-Verlag INTERACT'07* (2007), 475–488.
2. Bailly, G., Lecolinet, E., and Nigay, L. Flower menus: a new type of marking menu with large menu breadth, within groups and efficient expert mode memorization. In *ACM AVI '08* (2008), 15–22.
3. Bailly, G., Walter, R., Müller, J., Ning, T., and Lecolinet, E. Comparing free hand menu techniques for distant displays using linear, marking and finger-count menus. In *Springer-Verlag INTERACT'11* (2011), 248–262.
4. Bau, O., and Mackay, W. E. Octopocus: a dynamic guide for learning gesture-based command sets. In *ACM UIST '08* (2008), 37–46.
5. Bau, O., Ghomi, E., Mackay, W. Arpege: Design and learning of multi-finger chord gestures. In *Technical Report 1533, LRI. February 2010.* (2010).
6. Baudel, T., and Beaudouin-Lafon, M. Charade: remote control of objects using free-hand gestures. *Commun. ACM 36*, 7 (July 1993), 28–35.
7. Bolt, R. A. Put-that-there: Voice and gesture at the graphics interface. In *ACM SIGGRAPH '80* (1980), 262–270.
8. Bragdon, A., Zeleznik, R., Williamson, B., Miller, T., and LaViola, Jr., J. J. Gesturebar: improving the approachability of gesture-based interfaces. In *ACM CHI '09* (2009), 2269–2278.
9. Buxton, B. Gesture Based Interaction (chapter 14), 24 August, 2011. `http://www.billbuxton.com/input14.Gesture.pdf`.
10. Cadoz, C. Le geste canal de communication homme-machine. La communication "instrumentale". *Techniques et Sciences Informatiques* (1994), 31–61.
11. Coutrix, C., Kuikkaniemi, K., Kurvinen, E., Jacucci, G., Avdouevski, I., and Mäkelä, R. Fizzyvis: designing for playful information browsing on a multitouch public display. In *ACM DPPI '11* (2011), 27:1–27:8.
12. Dalsgaard, P., and Hansen, L. K. Performing perception - staging aesthetics of interaction. *ACM Trans. Comput.-Hum. Interact. 15*, 3 (Dec. 2008), 13:1–13:33.
13. Freeman, D., Benko, H., Morris, M. R., and Wigdor, D. Shadowguides: visualizations for in-situ learning of multi-touch and whole-hand gestures (2009). 165–172.
14. Grossman, T., Hinckley, K., Baudisch, P., Agrawala, M., and Balakrishnan, R. Hover widgets: using the tracking state to extend the capabilities of pen-operated devices. In *ACM CHI '06* (2006), 861–870.
15. Hinckley, K., Baudisch, P., Ramos, G., and Guimbretiere, F. Design and analysis of delimiters for selection-action pen gesture phrases in scriboli. In *Proceedings of the SIGCHI conference on Human factors in computing systems*, CHI '05, ACM (2005), 451–460.
16. Hinrichs, U., and Carpendale, S. Gestures in the wild: studying multi-touch gesture sequences on interactive tabletop exhibits. In *ACM CHI'11* (2011), 3023–3032.
17. Hofmeester, K., and Wolfe, J. Self-revealing gestures: teaching new touch interactions in windows 8. In *ACM CHI EA '12* (2012), 815–828.
18. Huang, E., Koster, A., and Borchers, J. Overcoming assumptions and uncovering practices: When does the public really look at public displays? In *Pervasive Computing*, vol. 5013 of *Lecture Notes in Computer Science*. Springer Berlin Heidelberg, (2008), 228–243.
19. Karam, M., and Schraefel, C. A taxonomy of gestures in human computer interactions". *Technical report, Electronics and Computer Science, University of Southampton* (2005).
20. Kurtenbach, G., and Hulteen, E. Gestures in human-computer communication. *The Art of Human-Computer Interface Design* (1990), 309–317.
21. Kurtenbach, G., Moran, T. P., and Buxton, W. Contextual animation of gestural commands. In *Computer Graphics Forum* (1994), 305–314.
22. Kurtenbach, G. P. *The design and evaluation of marking menus*. PhD thesis, Toronto, Ont., Canada, Canada, 1993. UMI Order No. GAXNN-82896.
23. Marshall, P., Morris, R., Rogers, Y., Kreitmayer, S., and Davies, M. Rethinking 'multi-user': an in-the-wild study of how groups approach a walk-up-and-use tabletop interface. CHI '11, 3033–3042.
24. Mulder, A. Hand gestures for HCI. *Tech report 96-1.* (1996).
25. Müller, J., Alt, F., Michelis, D., and Schmidt, A. Requirements and design space for interactive public displays. In *ACM MM '10* (2010), 1285–1294.
26. Müller, J., Walter, R., Bailly, G., Nischt, M., and Alt, F. Looking glass: a field study on noticing interactivity of a shop window. In *ACM CHI '12* (2012), 297–306.
27. Perry, M., Beckett, S., O'Hara, K., and Subramanian, S. Wavewindow: public, performative gestural interaction. In *ACM ITS '10* (2010), 109–112.
28. Reeves, S., Benford, S., O'Malley, C., and Fraser, M. Designing the spectator experience. In *ACM CHI '05* (2005), 741–750.
29. Rico, J., and Brewster, S. Gestures all around us: user differences in social acceptability perceptions of gesture based interfaces. In *MobileHCI '09*, ACM (New York, NY, USA, 2009), 64:1–64:2.
30. Sodhi, R., Benko, H., and Wilson, A. Lightguide: projected visualizations for hand movement guidance. In *ACM CHI '12* (2012), 179–188.
31. Ten Koppel, M., Bailly, G., Müller, J., and Walter, R. Chained displays: configurations of public displays can be used to influence actor-, audience-, and passer-by behavior. In *ACM CHI '12* (2012), 317–326.
32. Vogel, D., and Balakrishnan, R. Interactive public ambient displays: transitioning from implicit to explicit, public to personal, interaction with multiple users. In *ACM UIST'04* (2004), 137–146.
33. Wigdor, D., and Wixon, D. *Brave NUI World: Designing Natural User Interfaces for Touch and Gesture*. Morgan Kaufmann. Elsevier Science, (2011).
34. Wilson, A. D. Robust computer vision-based detection of pinching for one and two-handed gesture input. In *ACM UIST '06* (2006), 255–258.
35. Wobbrock, J. O., Morris, M. R., and Wilson, A. D. User-defined gestures for surface computing. In *ACM CHI '09* (2009), 1083–1092.
36. Wu, M., Shen, C., Ryall, K., Forlines, C., and Balakrishnan, R. Gesture registration, relaxation, and reuse for multi-point direct-touch surfaces. TABLETOP '06, IEEE Computer Society (2006), 185–192.
37. Zhao, S., Agrawala, M., and Hinckley, K. Zone and polygon menus: using relative position to increase the breadth of multi-stroke marking menus. In *ACM CHI'06* (2006), 1077–1086.
38. Zhao, S., and Balakrishnan, R. Simple vs. compound mark hierarchical marking menus. In *ACM UIST '04* (2004), 33–42.

SideWays: A Gaze Interface for Spontaneous Interaction with Situated Displays

Yanxia Zhang
Lancaster University
Lancaster, United Kingdom
yazhang@lancaster.ac.uk

Andreas Bulling
Max Planck Institute for Informatics
Saarbrücken, Germany
andreas.bulling@acm.org

Hans Gellersen
Lancaster University
Lancaster, United Kingdom
hwg@comp.lancs.ac.uk

ABSTRACT
Eye gaze is compelling for interaction with situated displays as we naturally use our eyes to engage with them. In this work we present *SideWays*, a novel person-independent eye gaze interface that supports spontaneous interaction with displays: users can just walk up to a display and immediately interact using their eyes, without any prior user calibration or training. Requiring only a single off-the-shelf camera and lightweight image processing, SideWays robustly detects whether users attend to the centre of the display or cast glances to the left or right. The system supports an interaction model in which attention to the central display is the default state, while "sidelong glances" trigger input or actions. The robustness of the system and usability of the interaction model are validated in a study with 14 participants. Analysis of the participants' strategies in performing different tasks provides insights on gaze control strategies for design of SideWays applications.

Author Keywords
Eye-based Interaction; Eye Tracking; Spontaneous Interaction; Situated Display; Calibration-Free

ACM Classification Keywords
H.5.2 Information Interfaces and Presentation: User Interfaces—*Input devices and strategies*

INTRODUCTION
Eye gaze is a modality of interest for spontaneous interaction with displays, as we naturally use our eyes to engage with displays we encounter, and as other modalities are often not as readily available as our eyes. However, eye gaze is difficult to harness for spontaneous and pervasive use. A limitation that undermines the idea of spontaneous interaction is that eye trackers generally require a calibration phase before interaction can commence, every time a user steps up to a display. An additional problem is the dependence of existing methods on specialist hardware and illumination of the eye, which can be difficult to provide on pervasive scale.

Figure 1. ***SideWays*** **enables spontaneous eye-based interaction with displays: users can just walk up to a display and immediately interact with it using their eyes, without any prior calibration or training. In this example, the user controls a cover flow with looks to the left and right.**

In this paper, we present a novel eye gaze interface, designed for users to be able to just walk up to a display and casually assume control, using their eyes only. Our system, *SideWays*, requires only a single off-the-shelf camera and distinguishes three gaze directions (to the left, right and straight ahead) as input states. These input states are detected in a spontaneous, robust and person-independent manner. There is no training or calibration involved, and no adaptation to individual users. Any user can step up to the display, and the system will be able to respond immediately to their attention (see Figure 1).

The interaction model we have designed for SideWays assumes a central region of interest on the display to which users align their gaze (e.g. guided by visual design of the interface), and adjacent areas to the left and right that users can select with "sidelong glances". A look straight ahead is interpreted as attention to the centrally displayed content. In this state, the interface is kept stable, and the eyes do not trigger any action. In contrast, glances to the left or to the right are associated with input actions. In terms of application logic, these glances are like pressing (and holding) a button, but the user experience may be more subtle and fluid with interface designs that have such actions appear natural and implicit.

In developing SideWays, we contribute as follows. First, we present a novel image processing method for detection of eye gaze directions. The new idea underlying the method is to measure the distance between inner eye corner and eye centre for both eyes in order to robustly classify gaze directions. For this, we have developed a processing chain including a novel method for eye centre localisation (using colour edges as they prove more robust under real world conditions). Secondly, we describe a study in which we evaluated SideWays with 14 participants on three interactive tasks (selection, scrolling, and slider control). The selection task served to characterise the system in terms of correct detection of input depending on time window of observation of the eyes, while the other two tasks assessed usability of the interface and interaction model for control tasks. Thirdly, we analyse the participants' behaviours in performing the different tasks. This lets us draw out insights on user's gaze control strategies, and derive design considerations for application of our system.

RELATED WORK

Eye-based Interaction

Early work on eye gaze interaction demonstrated selection on menu grids [6] and gaze-based techniques within the WIMP paradigm (windows, icons, menus, pointers) of our desktop computers [7]. The underlying model is to treat gaze as a pointing device, for example as alternative to mouse use for object selection in conventional interfaces [18], or for fast hands-free input with special-purpose visual interfaces [26]. In conventional settings, pointing accuracy is achieved with remote eye gaze trackers that require users to calibrate their gaze prior to interaction [10]. In contrast, we target pervasive settings and adopt a deliberately simpler gaze model to facilitate spontaneous and calibration-free interaction, between users and displays that have never seen each other before.

Use of the eyes for interaction with pervasive devices has previously been explored in work demonstrating attentive user interfaces that respond to eye contact [24]. This has been realised with pervasive eye contact sensors mounted on "smart" devices and objects [23], as well as with wearable devices that detect gaze orientation towards infrared tags placed in the environment [20]. In SideWays, we likewise detect gaze for attention to pervasive displays but in addition enable users to provide input with looks to the left or right from their centre of attention. Contrasting previous work, we do not require special-purpose hardware but detect eye gaze with a camera.

Sideways targets interaction with displays we encounter in our environment. A large body of work provides general insight into how people interact with displays in public settings (e.g., Opinionizer [1], Citywall [15] and Looking glass [12]), which is of importance to inform practical deployment of Sideways. A variety of projects have used head orientation towards large displays in presumed approximation of what people look at [11, 13, 19]. However, Mubin et al. found in an "interactive shop window" study that only few users aligned their heads with their gaze [11]. Other work has focused on low-cost extension of public displays for gaze pointing however still requires a calibration phase prior to interaction [16]. Contrasting extension of display, EyeGuide [3] explored use of a wearable eye tracking for interaction with pervasive displays. In contrast, our focus is on enabling interaction with public display without any instrumentation of the user. In our approach, all a user needs for interaction is their eyes.

Magee et al. reported a vision-based system that is similar to ours as it detects rapid eye movements to the left and right as command input [9]. However their system was specifically designed for a user with severe cerebral palsy and was primed to detect occurrences of a left/right movement, while we continually classify eye gaze direction. Kumar et al. presented several gaze-enhanced scrolling techniques for manual and automatic scrolling which use gaze as primary or complementary input [8]. In this work, scrolling is among three tasks on which we evaluate usability of our gaze interaction system.

Eye Tracking and Gaze Estimation

Research on gaze estimation mostly focuses on *model-based* approaches, such as Pupil Centre Corneal Reflection (PCCR) techniques [28, 29]. These techniques require specialised hardware and additional light sources, such as infrared illumination [5]. Gaze direction is estimated by detecting the pupil centre and a reflected "glint" on the cornea. With a geometric model of the eye, accurate gaze estimates are derived from the offset of the glint. However, the approach is problematic for pervasive settings as it requires controlled lighting conditions for illuminating the eye and for robust detection of light reflected from the spherical surface of the cornea.

Most commercially available eye trackers are based on model-based approaches and are typically geared toward desktop use. These systems require user-dependent calibration [2, 10]. More sophisticated eye trackers use stereoscopic views with multiple cameras or multiple light sources for multiple glints to avoid calibration for each individual [5]. A few user-independent eye-trackers using model-based approaches have been shown to work in laboratory conditions [28].

Recent efforts aim to avoid specialised hardware and infrared light sources to estimate gaze. *Appearance-based* approaches work under visible light and use image processing and machine learning techniques to estimate gaze directly from images recorded with video cameras [14, 21, 27]. Such approaches avoid calibration but require a priori training with eye images of the users, which prohibits spontaneous interaction. Sesma et al. conducted an offline evaluation of the pupil centre-eye corner vector as a feature for gaze estimation using a webcam-based eye tracking system [17]. However, their approach is person-dependent and initial calibration is required for each user to obtain the interpolation equation.

THE SIDEWAYS SYSTEM

The SideWays system is designed to detect gaze attention to a display, and to support gaze selection of areas to the left and to the right of the display's centre. The only hardware required for the system is a single off-the-shelf RGB video camera, positioned to capture the scene in front of the display. The system takes video frames as input, and analyses these with image processing techniques. Figure 2 illustrates the processing chain, from face detection and segmentation of eye images to detection of inner eye corners and localisation of pupil centres. The output from image processing are the distances of the eye centre from the eye corner for both left and right eye. Our system uses these distances to discriminate gaze directions as L(left), R(right) and C(centre). We explain both the image processing chain, and the eye gaze classification method in detail.

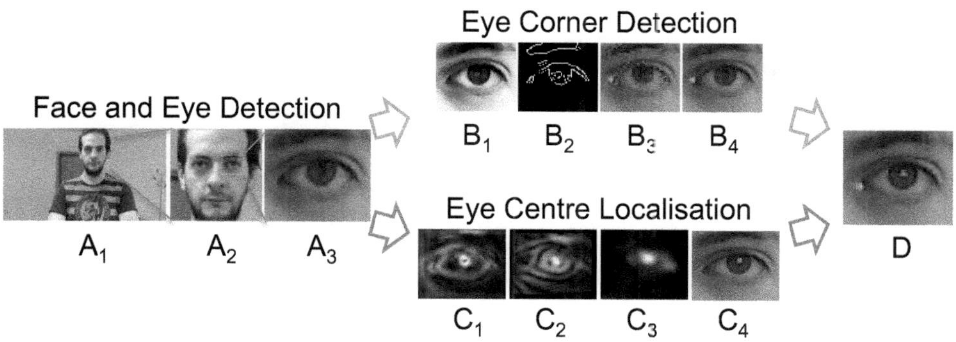

Figure 2. This diagram illustrates the image processing of the SideWays system

Image Processing

Face and Eye Detection

The images from the video camera are subject to variable lighting conditions, such as shadows, bright lights, low contrast, motion blur or noise. To tackle these problems, we first apply a bilateral smoothing filter to reduce noise while preserving edge information. The filter smooths regions while preserving, and enhancing, the contrast at sharp intensity gradients. After the image is pre-processed, we use a Viola-Jones face detector to detect the user's face and eyes in real time [25] (see Figure 2: A_2). The face detector identifies a rectangular area of the largest face in the scene. In order to improve performance and reduce the computational cost, we only search for eyes in the top half region of the face. The system further detects the left eye by examining the left half of the facial area, and likewise for the right eye. Our system finally extracts two image patches that represent the output of this first processing step, one for each eye (A_3).

Detection of the Inner Eye Corners

To detect the inner eye corners, where the upper and lower eyelids meet (the so-called eye canthi), our system applies a Harris corner detection separately to each eye image patch. The method detects the locations of interesting windows which produce large variations when moved in any direction in an image. Locations which are above a threshold are marked as corners. Besides eye corners, the output could also include other feature points of local intensity maximum or minimum, line endings, or points on a curve where the curvature is locally maximal in the image. As this may result in several candidate eye corner points, the system further applies a canny edge detector (B_2). A canthus region should exhibit strong edges where the upper and lower eyelid edges meet. Accurate canthi locations can then be obtained by considering only those candidate points that lie on the detected eyelid edges (B_3). All other candidate points are discarded.

Localisation of Eye Centres

To localise the eye centres, we have develop a novel method that exploits the semi-circular structure of the eye iris and pupil as described in [22]. The captured eye images are strongly influenced by shadows cast in inner eye corners and by screen reflections. To reduce this effect, colour edges are obtained from cropped RGB eye images by using the Gaussian colour model proposed by [4] (C_1). The isophotes of an image are curves connecting points of equal intensity [22]. We compute the isophote curvature map and calculate the isophote radius on the edges (C_2). The eye centre is detected as the location with maximum isophote centre votes (C_3)).

Discrimination of Gaze Directions

In each video frame, we obtain the pupil centre (C_4) and the inner canthi (B_4) as result of image processing. Figure 3 illustrates how we use these to derive gaze direction. Consider first that we look straight ahead. In this case the pupil centres of both our eyes will be similarly distant from the respective inner eye corners. If we look to the left, then the distance of our left pupil from its inner eye corner increases, while the distance of the right pupil from its inner corner decreases. Conversely, a look to the right means that the left pupil moves closer to its inner eye corner, while the right pupil moves further away. Consequently, to determine different gaze directions, we calculate the ratio r of the eye-centre P_{cx} to inner canthi C_{ix} distances of both eyes as

$$r = |\frac{C_{iR} - P_{cR}}{C_{iL} - P_{cL}}| \quad (1)$$

where C_{iR} and C_{iL} are the x coordinates of inner eye corners from the right and left eye images, P_{cR} and P_{cL} are the x coordinates of pupil centres from the right and left eyes.

For each video frame, we calculate the inner canthi to pupil centre distances for both eyes. At time t ($t = 1, 2.., T$), we denote the measurement of our observed gaze direction for frame f_t as O_t. A general threshold T_r is set for classifying frame f_t as three gaze directions which are L(left), C(centre), R(right) according to the following rules:

$$O_t = \begin{cases} R(right), & \text{if } T_r < |r| < T_{r_{MAX}}; \\ L(left), & \text{if } 1/T_{r_{MAX}} < r| < 1/T_r; \\ C(centre), & \text{otherwise.} \end{cases} \quad (2)$$

where $T_r = 1.3$ is optimised for the user study (derived from the preliminary study) and $T_{r_{MAX}}$ is a constant upper bound.

Activation Using a Smoothing Window

To smooth the decision made for each video frame, we adopt a sliding window approach (as shown in Figure 4). We perform a smoothing window with a size of W over the observations of W image frames. We consider all observations within time span $[t, t + W - 1]$. The input to the decision system is

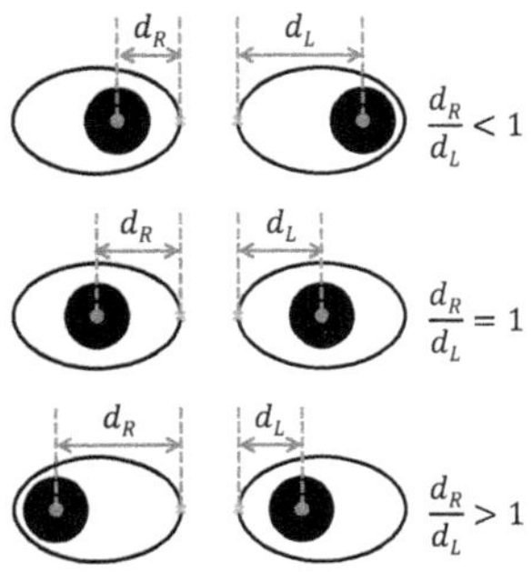

Figure 3. Three gaze directions are determined by the distance ratio of eye-centre P_{cx} to inner canthi C_{ix} for both eyes.

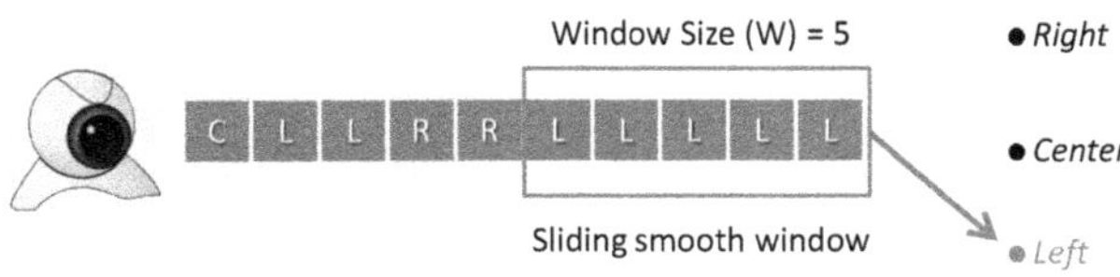

Figure 4. The activation of a gaze direction is based on a smoothing window. As the camera captures images in real-time, a stream of gaze directions fill the frames in the sliding window. An activation is triggered when the same gaze direction is detected consecutively.

a set of measurements $O_{1:W} = \{O_t | 1 \leq t \leq W\}$ where $O_t \in \{L, C, R\}$ in a sliding window of W frames within time span $[t, t + W - 1]$. We process all images frame by frame from the start. For each incoming frame, we collect new observations denoted as $O_{current}$. The set of measurements $O_{1:W}$ corresponding to time span $[t + 1, t + W]$ in the buffer is updated. We only consider valid observations when both eye corners and centres are detected. As shown in Figure 4, an activation is triggered when the same gaze direction is detected consecutively in the sliding window.

We distinguish two different activation approaches: *discrete* and *continuous*. Discrete activation clears all measurements $O_{1:W}$ in the sliding window after an event is triggered. This causes delay as a new stream of measurements in the sliding window need to be collected. Continuous activation only updates the last measurement in the sliding window with every incoming frame, hence, allowing for fast response.

USER STUDY

The interaction model proposed for the SideWays system is to treat gaze straight at the display's centre as a default state in which the eyes do not trigger any action, while "sideways" glances to the left or right are foreseen for user input. We designed a user study to evaluate our system and the proposed interaction model on three generic tasks: *Selecting*, *Scrolling* and *Sliding*. For each task, we run a separate experiment to evaluate different aspects of our system.

Selecting was always conducted first as it was designed to fundamentally characterise the interface in terms of correct classification of input depending on size of the sliding window used in the process. A smoothing window of five frames was used but data was collected for post-hoc analysis of detection accuracy versus speed (shorter smoothing windows). The other two experiments were conducted in counter-balance.

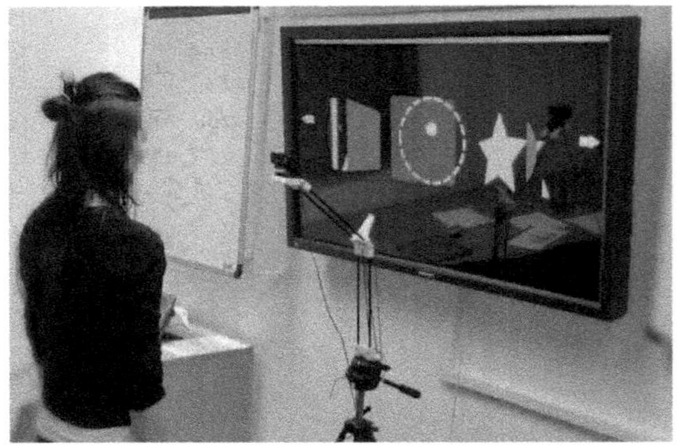

Figure 5. A snapshot of a study session.

Scrolling tested the users' ability to use our system for discrete scrolling through a list of items. A window size of four was used with discrete activation, so that a scroll step was executed only if the user's gaze dwelled for four valid frames on the left/right control. Sliding tested control of a continuous slider and the users' ability to move a slider to accurately hit a target position. A window size of three was chosen with continuous activation, which meant that that a sliding step was executed in each frame, for as long as the detected gaze direction matched the previous two frames. Three different speeds of the slider were used, and data captured to analyse how often users needed to change sliding direction to reach the target.

Participants

Fourteen paid participants (six female, eight male), with body heights ranging from 1.65m to 1.96m (M=1.77, SD=0.10), aged between 21 and 47 years (M=28.79, SD=7.27), and various eye colours took part in the study. Three participants wore contact lenses during the study.

Apparatus

The hardware setup for our study consisted of a 55 inch (121cm×68.5cm) LCD display from Philips with a resolution of 1920x1080 pixels, mounted on the wall at 120cm height (lower bezel). A Logitech HD Pro Webcam C920 with a resolution of 1280x720 pixels and a video frame rate of 30Hz was mounted on a stand and positioned 60cm in front of the screen (see Figure 5). The real-time image processing and gaze estimation software was implemented in OpenCV, and ran on a laptop with a 2.67GHz processor and 4GB of RAM.

The study was conducted in office space under normal lighting conditions. We asked participants to stand at a distance of 1.3m in front of the display (visual angle of the display 49.9° horizontal, 29.5° vertical). A marker on the floor indicated where the participant should stand. However, during the user study, participants were free to fine tune the distance for their own comfort. The distance between the camera and the user was 70cm±5cm. The captured image resolution was 300x300 for faces, and 80x70 for eye images, slightly varying across users. In a real world deployment, cameras would typically be mounted on the display but we positioned it closer to the user as we aimed to evaluate interaction with our system, not the limits of eye pupil and corner detection.

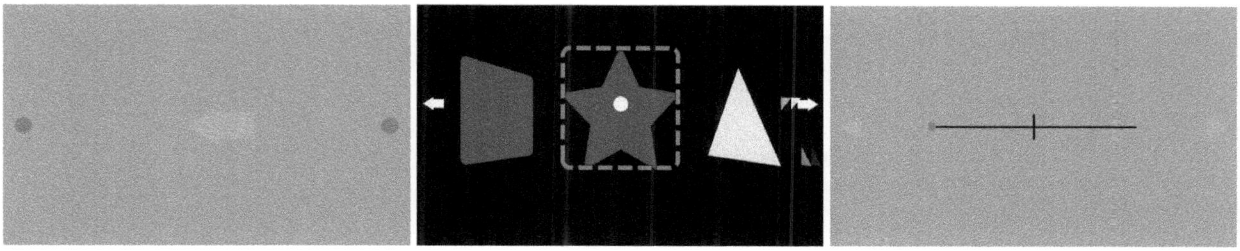

(a) Selecting. (b) Scrolling. (c) Sliding.

Figure 6. The interfaces of the three tasks in our user study. (a) The participants read the green arrow to find out which direction to look at and stare at the corresponding red stimulus. (b) The participants scroll through a set of objects to find the one that matches a predefined target. (c) The participants control a horizontal slider and bring the slider indicator on top of the vertical bar.

Procedure

Each session lasted for approximately 45 minutes. Participants were first introduced to the system and allowed to complete one trial of each task. All participants then first completed the Selecting experiment, while the remaining two experiments were counter-balanced. After each experiment, user feedback was collected with a questionnaire. The questionnaire asked for the participants' subjective experience, problems they encountered, and strategies to overcome issues of the system.

Experiment 1: Selecting

In the selecting task, participants had to look at either the left or the right region of the display. Participants were asked to initially focus on the centre region of the display. Once the system had detected the participants' gaze, the system indicated the desired gaze region using a green arrow pointing either left or right. In addition, a red circle was shown in both the left and right region to assist participants in fixating on that region (see Figure 6(a)). The system continuously estimated the gaze direction with a smoothing window of five frames. Upon detection of gaze on the correct target, the target colour would change from red to green. Participant's were instructed to return their gaze to the centre after each completion of a trial. With a short delay, the next trial would be triggered by display of an arrow. In total, this was repeated twelve times (six for each direction, randomised).

Experiment 2: Scrolling

In the scrolling task, participants were asked to scroll through a list of objects using their gaze and to find the object that matched a predefined target. We used a combination of four shapes (circle, square, triangle, and star) and four colours (red, green, blue, and yellow) to represent a set of sixteen scrolling objects (see Figure 6(b)). At the beginning, the sixteen objects were randomly placed horizontally at equal distances, arranged as a flow with the display as viewport showing the current selection in the middle, and one adjacent object on either side. Participants then had to scroll through the objects to find a preselected object that was indicated by a coloured dash-bordered shape and shown at the centre of the display. Participants had to look left or right of the display to scroll items from that direction toward the centre. Arrows were displayed on both sides of the display to help participants fixate. The task was repeated six times, and each time with a different target shape. For each iteration, the browser starting position alternated between the left-most and the right-most positions of the object collection.

Experiment 3: Sliding

In the sliding task, the participant's objective was to control a horizontal slider by moving the slider indicator either left or right onto a target position with their eyes. For this task, the display showed a horizontal slider widget in the centre region (see Figure 6(c)). The slider target was represented by a black line, and it contained a red circle as slider indicator. Green arrows on the left and right display regions represented the slider's controls. At the start of the task, the indicator was placed at either the left-most or the right-most slider position, and the distance to the target was always 480 pixels. When participants looked at the left controller, the slider would progress one step width to the left in each frame, and vice versa for the right control. Sliding speed was increased over the trials, with three step widths representing 0.01, 0.025 and 0.04 of total screen width (i.e. 19.2, 48, and 76.8 pixels), requiring 25, 10 or 6 steps respectively to reach the target. When participants were satisfied that they had reached the target, they returned their gaze to the centre of the display to complete the trial. The task was repeated twice for each step size, for a total of six trials per participant.

RESULTS

Four of the 14 participants required eyeglasses for correct vision and three wore contact lenses while the fourth removed his glasses. One of them reported that the contact lenses had affected her speed in fast and frequent eye movements, and that they caused discomfort after using the system for a while.

Two participants experienced asymmetric system performance in left and right directions. One of them explained that she had had an eye operation, which effected gaze to the right. The other participant reported better performance for gaze to the right but her reason was unknown. However, she described that she compensated by turning her head slightly towards the opposite direction. The participant who removed his glasses was far-sighted. He often squinted his eyes while looking at the display, which drastically slowed down the system's detection speed (more frames were discarded for lack of pupil detection, and the smoothing window would fill up more slowly). Several participants reported that blinking also

	w = 2	w = 3	w = 4	w = 5
Correct	135	151	160	162
Wrong	12	5	2	0
Missed	21	11	6	6

Table 1. Number of correct, wrong (detected as opposite direction) and missed (detected as center) detections of the total 168 trials of selecting tasks using different window sizes.

	t < 2(s)	t < 3(s)	t < 4(s)	t < 5(s)	overall
w = 2	76.8%	78.6%	79.2%	80.4%	80.4%
w = 3	80.4%	86.9%	89.3%	89.9%	90.4%
w = 4	81.5%	87.5%	90.5%	91.1%	95.2%
w = 5	72.0%	84.5%	88.1%	91.1%	96.4%

Table 2. Accuracy for selection over different window sizes and timeout thresholds.

reduced the system's detection speed. This was not surprising given that blinking caused the eyelids to occlude the eye pupils, so the system could not determine their gaze direction.

Selecting Task

Participants performed a total of 168 trials (12 each) of looking left and right for selection. Table 1 summarises the results with post-hoc analysis for different window sizes. Eye gaze matching the target was counted as correct, eye gaze on the opposite target counted as wrong (faulty selection), and eye gaze in the centre as missed (no selection). Window size 5, as experienced by the users in the study, results in the least number of errors. This was expected, as increasing the window size also increases certainty. Analysis of recorded data revealed that three of the errors (missed selections) were from one participant due to squinting. On average, users needed 1.78s (*SD*=0.3s) per selection, but the user who squinted required an average of 2.91s. Although increasing the window size provides better detection accuracy, it inherently increases the time required to detect a correct selection. Table 2 provides an analysis of correct detection rates depending on window size and time thresholds. The results indicate that a window size of four frames is optimal, but windows of three frames perform almost as well for detection in limited time.

Participants reported that using our eye-based system for left and right selections was "intuitive", "easy to perform", and "suitable for touch-free interactions". However, two mentioned problems, such as inconsistency in system response time, one of them noting that to improve the system, he had tried not to blink and kept his eyes wide open. Several participants mentioned that although it wasn't tiring to use the system they would prefer faster response times.

Scrolling Task

We observed 84 trials for the scrolling task, six per participant. In each trial we counted how many scrolling steps users required to complete the trial and compared this with the minimally required steps. On average, participants required 1.2 (*SD*=3.4) extra steps to complete a scrolling trial. In 61 out

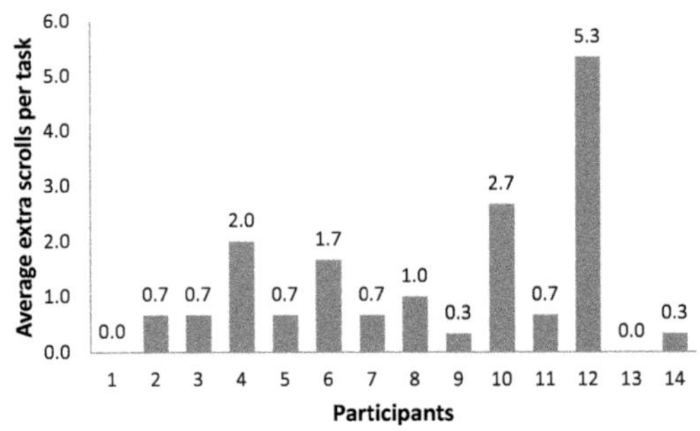

Figure 7. Extra scroll counts for 14 participants over six scrolling trials.

of the 84 (72.6%) trials the scrolling task was completed efficiently with the minimum number of steps. In general, participants were able to correct mistakes with very few extra steps. In 20 out of the 23 error cases, the participants only changed the scrolling direction once for correction (12 for overshooting one step away from the target, eight for a distance of two steps from the target).

Figure 7 illustrates the scrolling accuracy of each participant. Two participants finished every task without any extra scroll steps, and evidently learnt to use the system very quickly. Seven participants made one error (an extra scroll). However, participant 12 took 28 extra scrolls for his first trial, explaining that he lost focus during the first trial as the target shape was at the very end and the system was not responsive. Our post-study analysis showed that his head orientation drifted from the centre towards the scrolling direction, where new shapes were coming from. This caused the system to classify his gaze as central, instead of triggering a scroll step. The participant learnt to re-centre his head when the system was not responsive, and completed the remaining trials with only minor errors. Overall, we observed that six participants tended to turn their head towards the scrolling direction. Since the focus region is on the far end of the display, people intuitively turned their head towards the region to examine upcoming information. However, when they noticed the scrolling stopped, they returned their head orientation back to the centre.

System errors mainly resulted from delays in stopping the scrolling. Four participants mentioned that the system was not sensitive enough for stopping and that they had to look at the centre region already before the target object reached in the centre. In particular, participants 10 and 6 found it difficult to stop scrolling, while participant 6 found it hard to judge the colour of objects in the centre with peripheral vision, while gazing to the left or right for scrolling.

We observed the participants' behaviours and strategies in scrolling. Six participants fixated on the arrow indicator to scroll continuously. The participants were able to finish 40 out of 84 (47.6%) trials without stopping to scroll before reaching the target. Some participants mentioned that frequent stopping and checking the information in the centre helped them to perform better, but those who scrolled without stopping did not cause more errors (six errors in 40 trials). These results show that the participants were able to handle frequently changing information when the shapes are moving.

	Mean (s)	*Std* (s)	*Minimum* (s)
Large	14.2	12.0	2.4
Medium	16.2	11.5	6.0
Small	26.7	18.8	7.1

Table 3. Average and minimum completion time in seconds for three different step widths in the sliding task.

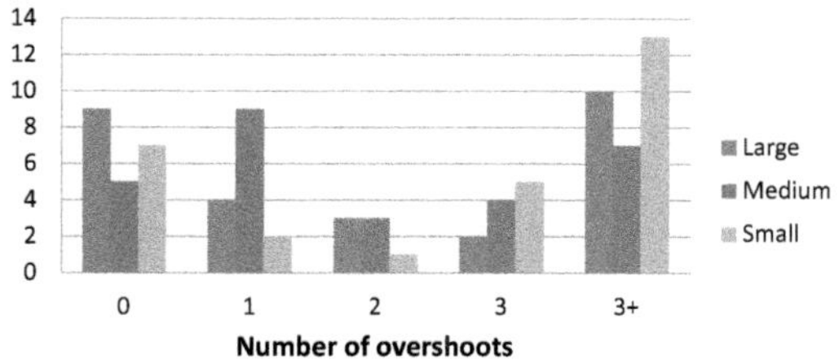

Figure 8. Histogram shows the count of the number of overshoots (0, 1, 2, 3 and > 3) for three different step widths in the sliding task.

The participants devised strategies to avoid mistakes. Some participants noticed the delay in triggering single scroll/stop actions (the system was set to discrete activation after four frames), and exploited this for brief glances to the centre without causing to stop the scrolling action.

Overall, participants were satisfied with their experience of using SideWays for scrolling. Most felt that the system reacted to their left and right gazes correctly, and that the system provided sufficient precision for real applications. They also felt that it was convenient to search objects using only their eyes, and suggested that the system is suitable for controlling "objects beyond reach". The participants enjoyed the experience of searching in a smooth flow, "without clicking". Most remarked it was easy and natural to use their peripheral vision for searching in this task. Given the big object size and simple content, they were able to see what was in the centre while looking at the scroll arrows. However, several participants mentioned that they needed to keep their head still, which they found difficult for longer scrolling. Exaggerated eye movements (e.g. changing from left to right) to correct mistakes caused fatigue. In addition, the participants preferred faster triggering time.

Sliding Task

This task tested the participants' ability to accurately move a slider to a target position. Participants performed six trials, two for each of three different slider speeds, and we collected data on a total of 84 trials, 28 per slider step widths. Table 3 shows the participants' average completion time. The last column (minimum) indicates the fastest time that the participants achieved. However, the average completion time was much higher. Most of the time was spent on position fine tuning. Many participants missed the slider target, thus requiring longer time to correct the slider's position.

We define overshooting as the number of instances when the indicator had jumped past the target location. Figure 8 provides a histogram that summarises observed overshooting. In 25% of all trials, participants managed to slide directly to the target without overshooting. Repeated overshoots indicate problems with accurate control, and occurred more frequently with small and large step width. The mean of overshoots was 2.7 for medium step width, but 4.3 for large and 5.0 for small step width. Note that trials always started with small step width and that results will be influenced by a learning effect.

The errors caused by the fast speed (large step width) were mainly caused by system delay. Six participants criticised that the system was not fast enough to react when gaze direction changes rapidly. In addition, several participants also mentioned that the fast speed was too fast for their eyes. One participant was having difficulty with small step widths (12.5 overshoots/trial) while performing well with the medium and fast speed (1.5 overshoots for medium steps, 2.5 for large steps). The participant was short-sighted and removed her glasses during the study. She was not familiar with stopping with the initial trials, and followed the indicator moving left and right repeatedly crossing the target.

In general, the participants found it difficult to control the sliding indicator precisely with their eyes. Their strategy was to first bring the indicator near the target location as close as possible. This was done by staring at the control arrow for continuous sliding, while using their peripheral vision to approximate the indicator's location. Once the indicator was near the target, the participants looked at the centre region to stop the sliding. They fine tuned the movement by looking at the arrow control and the centre region back and forth. For the slow and medium speeds, in many trials, the participants were able to stop before the indicator reached the target (out of 28 trials, 18 times for slow and 16 times for medium); however, with faster speed they struggled more to do that (10 out of 28 trials). On the other hand, the slow speed caused issues in fine tuning. The participants reported that it was difficult to control with precision using peripheral vision. Since the distance of each jump was small, it was difficult to judge when exactly it reached the target. Some participants struggled to use their peripheral vision, and could not see both the arrows and the target together simultaneously.

Overall, most participants found the sliding task challenging when using the fast and the slow speeds. A few participants suggested the system could be useful for moving objects in out-of-reach distance. Several participants liked the fast and accurate response of the system. They found it easy to control the direction of the sliding object by using left and right eye movement. The majority felt that they were not able to control the system for fine tuning positions, especially using small step width. Half of the participants mentioned that it was unnatural to use their peripheral vision to see detail in the centre, while looking left or right. Some participants felt that they needed to concentrate and be patient to use SideWays for sliding. Also, the participants experienced fatigue due to frequent eye movements changing between left and right for position fine tuning. A few participants disliked the long time required to precisely move an object to the target.

Questionnaires

For each task, we asked seven questions with regards to the participants' subjective feedback. The results are presented in Figure 9. We run the Friedman Test on the subjective

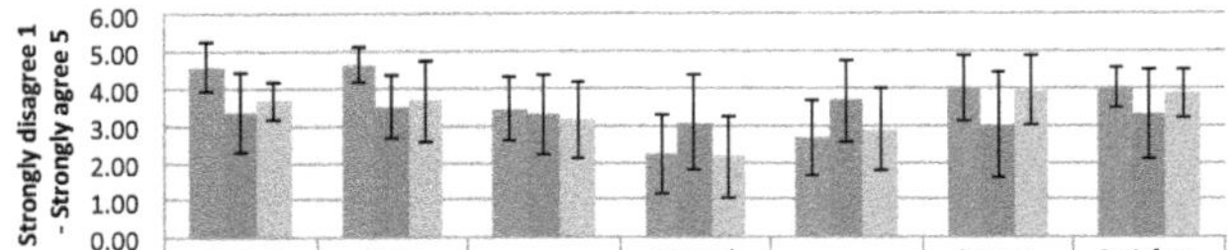

	Under control	Gaze correct	No delay	Mental demand	Eye tired	Accept-ance	Satisfact-ion
Selecting	4.57	4.64	3.43	2.21	2.64	4.00	4.00
Sliding	3.36	3.50	3.29	3.07	3.64	3.00	3.29
Scrolling	3.64	3.64	3.14	2.14	2.86	3.93	3.86

Figure 9. Participants' subjective feedback on use of Sideways for the selecting, scrolling and sliding tasks. Users were asked: did they feel in control; did the system respond correctly to their gaze; did the system respond without delay; did they find the task mentally demanding; did they find it tiring their eyes; would they accept the system for the task; and were they overall satisfied with use of the system for the task.

feedback data. Post-hoc analysis with Wilcoxon Signed-Rank Tests was conducted with a Bonferroni correction applied.

We asked the participants whether they felt they were in direct control of the SideWays system. One participant particularly commented "I can feel a real power, starting from my brain and ending on the screen." We found a significant difference between the three tasks, $\chi^2(2)=17.07$, $p<.001$. A post-hoc analysis showed that the selecting vs sliding ($p=0.002$) and selecting vs scrolling ($p=0.002$) pairs were significantly different. The participants felt that they were most in control when using our system for selecting objects.

We found a significant difference in whether the participants perceived the system as responding correctly to their gaze, $\chi^2(2)=14.70$, $p<.002$. The selecting vs sliding ($p=0.001$) and selecting vs scrolling ($p=0.012$) pairs were significantly different. The participants felt that the system was most responsive when used for selecting objects.

We also found a significant difference in tiredness of eyes in using *SideWays*, $\chi^2(2)=7.54$, $p<.023$. The participants felt significantly more tired when using our system for sliding than for selecting ($p=0.006$).

Participants provided comments in comparison of scrolling and sliding. Sliding was found demanding as it required target status check in the centre of the screen while concentrating gaze on either left or right. For scrolling, participants noted that they can see what is coming while they are controlling, and they found it less demanding to use peripheral vision to check what is in the centre, as it was displayed more largely than in the sliding task.

Participants also commented on possible applications of the system. Since SideWays is touch-free, the interaction is sanitary and therefore suitable for public environments, such as airports, libraries and shopping malls. Some participants suggested that it could benefit disabled people with paralysis. Several participants criticized the lack of visual feedback for the detection of gaze directions. This is important as it provides indication of whether the system interpreted the user's input correctly.

APPLICATIONS
After completing the previous three tasks, participants interacted with two SideWays applications (see Figure 10): an *album cover browser* and a *gaze quiz*. The album cover browser acts as an interface of a music jukebox. A user browses for music by scrolling left and right, and the centre region represents the music album to play. The gaze quiz application is an interactive quiz game. A user first reads a question displayed in the centre, and then answers the question by selecting yes or no, which was placed on the left and right positions of the screen, respectively. We used a window size 3 for the album browser and a window size 4 for the gaze quiz. Both applications used discrete activation. Only qualitative feedback of the system (e.g. preference and suggestions) was collected.

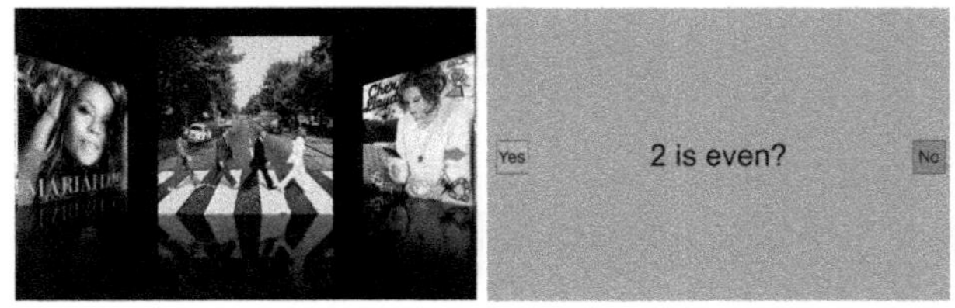

(a) Album cover browser. (b) Gaze quiz.

Figure 10. Two SideWays applications used in the user study: *album cover browser* allows users to navigate music albums; *gaze quiz* presents a question in the center and uses the side inputs for "Yes/No" answers.

Participants were allowed to use the interfaces freely. We gave no instruction of how to interact with the interfaces, but the participants were still able to use the applications. For the media browser application, the users were able to navigate through all the music album covers and check what music was available. Sometimes, they scrolled back/forward to stop at the one they were interested in. During the gaze quiz application, the participants read twelve questions displayed in the centre and provided answers for all the questions. All participants understood how to search the media album covers and make selections. One participant encountered the "Midas Touch" problem in the gaze quiz [7]. While we displayed one question with a long sentence, the participant accidentally chose the answer "No" (on the right end) as he was reading the sentence. Thus, information in the centre should not be extended to the far left or right regions of the display.

Participants further suggested that SideWays could be applied in situations where a display is obstructed by a glass wall or window, such as shop displays for pedestrians. Another suggestion was for controlling television, e.g. adjusting volume or switching channels.

DISCUSSION
Our study validates that SideWays enables eye gaze as input for interactive displays, without the need of prior calibration or specialist hardware. This is significant in a number of ways. First, achieving robust gaze control, albeit coarse-grained, without need for calibration means that our system is person-independent. Any user can walk up to a display fitted with our system, and interact with it using their eyes only. Secondly, as we overcome calibration, users will be able to interact immediately (in principle) which is important for serendipitous and short-lived interactions that don't warrant preparation phases. Thirdly, we achieve gaze control with an

off-the-shelf camera. This means that displays can be made gaze-aware at low cost, potentially on pervasive scale.

Effects of System Parameters

The threshold T_r (used in equation 2) defines the size of the central region, and in our prototype was set to corresponds to a horizontal visual angle of 40°. Most participants were aware how far they needed to look left/right as SideWays provided guidance by displaying the visual control stimulus. Increasing the threshold essentially increases the visual angle. If the threshold is small, the central region becomes narrower, and the system also becomes more sensitive to small eye movements of looking left/right. However, if the threshold is large, the user will need to look left/right further to trigger input which might cause discomfort and fatigue. The optimal threshold will depend on application, and designers need to consider the distance between the user and the display and the size of the display.

The window size determines how much evidence is collected before an action is triggered and trades off between accuracy and speed. A large window size improves the accuracy of gaze detection, but causes longer delays and slower response. This is suitable for discrete actions (e.g. selecting an object), where it is more important that the system detects the correct object. A small windows size speeds up response, but increases likelihood of errors caused by noise. This will be reasonable for continuous actions (e.g. sliding) where faster response is important and where the effect of occasional misclassifications will quickly corrected by continuous updates.

Designers can map input state to discrete versus continuous actions to fit the nature of the task. For example, if the content is visual (e.g. a photo album), continuous action may be chosen for fast scrolling as our study participants found that they can scroll to larger distinctive objects with peripheral vision. If the content requires attention (e.g., flicking through book pages), a discrete action mapping is better suited.

Limitations and Design Considerations

Responsiveness. When the system is not able to detect eyes images of sufficiently quality for computing eye centre and eye corners, the interface responsiveness decreases. This happens when users blink and squint or when the eyes get occluded in any other way, and can also be caused by larger head movement. When the system does not respond correctly or fast enough, no manual intervention is needed to reset SideWays. Participants reported that they reinitialized SideWays by closing their eyes, or by adjusting head positions or distance to the screen, indicating a good understanding of what causes misfunction and how to recover.

Head orientation. Our system requires users to keep their head oriented toward the centre of the display and only move their eyes. Some participants commented that this was unnatural, because they often subconsciously turn their head towards the direction of their visual focus. As a result, the detection of gaze direction becomes unreliable. This poses a limitation of user interaction. Although restricted head movement was commented as unnatural, in general, the participants were able to recover from loss of gaze detection by quickly correcting their head orientation, in order to achieve their tasks. To minimize head turning, designer should pay attention to the display region where information changes. Dynamic movement on the control regions can attract user attention; hence, causing head turning.

Provide detection feedback. Users need feedback when an event is triggered, to understand whether the system has detected their gaze. Visual feedback can be explicit confirmation of users input, for example by highlighting a displayed control that was triggered, or implicit in the behaviour of application, for example by updating the content displayed in the centre of the screen. However, when users glance sideways to trigger a control, it can be difficult for user to acquire feedback that effects only the centre of the display.

Toward use with Public Displays

Person-independence and interaction without preparation are critical steps toward genuinely spontaneous interaction with displays we encounter in public environment. While our evaluation shows that our system achieves both, it does so under the constraints of a controlled study designed to systematically test and characterise the interaction technique. Deployment in real-world contexts naturally raises a range of further challenges. For example, although a calibration phase is avoided, there will still be a gulf in how users can readily obtain and use gaze control over a display they encounter. However, with a lab study of our system's working, we now have a foundation for addressing deployment challenges, as well as insights on user performance and strategies that can inform application design.

For ecological validity, it will be important to inform further development by understanding of how users interact with displays "in the wild". For example, research on public display interaction showed that often more than one user is involved in interaction [12, 15], posing a challenge to accommodate multiple users simultaneously. For SideWays, the calculation of multiple users' gaze is equivalent to individual's gaze estimation in parallel. However, detection of eye images will naturally be more complex in public environments and with multiple users. Although the system would be able to discriminate input from different pairs of eyes, it would not be clear how to map multi-user input to display actions without causing potential conflict.

CONCLUSION

In this paper, we presented SideWays, a novel eye gaze interface for spontaneous interaction with a display. It leverages left and right regions of the display for gaze controls, while keeping the central region for display content. The system uses an off-the-shelf visible light camera along with its lightweight image processing for robust detection of gaze directions. We conducted a user study to evaluate SideWays on three interactive tasks. The results show that people are able to use SideWays to interact with a display, and we have gained insights of people's gaze control strategies. With SideWays's nature of being calibration-free and person-independent, its applications are potentially usable by many people. This work represents a significant step toward use of our eyes for serendipitous interaction with pervasive displays.

ACKNOWLEDGEMENTS

This work was supported by the EU Marie Curie Network iCareNet under grant number 264738.

REFERENCES

1. Brignull, H., and Rogers, Y. Enticing people to interact with large public displays in public spaces. In *Proc. INTERACT 2003*, IOS Press (2003), 17–24.
2. Duchowski, A. T. *Eye Tracking Methodology: Theory and Practice*. Springer-Verlag New York, Inc., 2003.
3. Eaddy, M., Blasko, G., Babcock, J., and Feiner, S. My own private kiosk: Privacy-preserving public displays. In *Proc. ISWC 2004*, IEEE Computer Society (2004), 132–135.
4. Geusebroek, J.-M., van den Boomgaard, R., Smeulders, A. W., and Geerts, H. Color invariance. *IEEE Trans. Pattern Anal. Mach. Intell. 23*, 12 (2001), 1338–1350.
5. Hansen, D., and Ji, Q. In the eye of the beholder: A survey of models for eyes and gaze. *IEEE Trans. Pattern Anal. Mach. Intell. 32*, 3 (2010), 478–500.
6. Hutchinson, T., White, K.P., J., Martin, W., Reichert, K., and Frey, L. Human-computer interaction using eye-gaze input. *Trans. Sys. Man Cyber Part C 19*, 6 (1989), 1527 –1534.
7. Jacob, R. J. K. The use of eye movements in human-computer interaction techniques: what you look at is what you get. *ACM Trans. Inf. Syst. 9*, 2 (1991), 152–169.
8. Kumar, M., and Winograd, T. Gaze-enhanced scrolling techniques. In *Proc. UIST 2007*, ACM Press (2007), 213–216.
9. Magee, J. J., Betke, M., Gips, J., Scott, M. R., and Waber, B. N. A human-computer interface using symmetry between eyes to detect gaze direction. *Trans. Sys. Man Cyber. Part A 38*, 6 (2008), 1248–1261.
10. Morimoto, C. H., and Mimica, M. R. M. Eye gaze tracking techniques for interactive applications. *Comput. Vis. Image Underst. 98*, 1 (2005), 4–24.
11. Mubin, O., Lashina, T., and Loenen, E. How not to become a buffoon in front of a shop window: A solution allowing natural head movement for interaction with a public display. In *Proc. INTERACT 2009*, Springer-Verlag (2009), 250–263.
12. Müller, J., Walter, R., Bailly, G., Nischt, M., and Alt, F. Looking glass: a field study on noticing interactivity of a shop window. In *Proc. CHI 2012*, ACM Press (2012), 297–306.
13. Nakanishi, Y., Fujii, T., Kiatjima, K., Sato, Y., and Koike, H. Vision-based face tracking system for large displays. In *Proc. UbiComp 2002*, Springer-Verlag (2002), 152–159.
14. Noris, B., Benmachiche, K., and Billard, A. Calibration-free eye gaze direction detection with gaussian processes. In *Proc. VISAPP 2008*, INSTICC (2008), 611–616.
15. Peltonen, P., Kurvinen, E., Salovaara, A., Jacucci, G., Ilmonen, T., Evans, J., Oulasvirta, A., and Saarikko, P. It's mine, don't touch!: interactions at a large multi-touch display in a city centre. In *Proc. CHI 2008*, ACM Press (2008), 1285–1294.
16. San Agustin, J., Hansen, J. P., and Tall, M. Gaze-based interaction with public displays using off-the-shelf components. In *Ubicomp 2010 Adjunct*, ACM Press (2010), 377–378.
17. Sesma, L., Villanueva, A., and Cabeza, R. Evaluation of pupil center-eye corner vector for gaze estimation using a web cam. In *Proc. ETRA 2012*, ACM Press (2012), 217–220.
18. Sibert, L. E., and Jacob, R. J. K. Evaluation of eye gaze interaction. In *Proc. CHI 2000*, ACM Press (2000), 281–288.
19. Sippl, A., Holzmann, C., Zachhuber, D., and Ferscha, A. Real-time gaze tracking for public displays. In *Proc. AmI 2010*, Springer-Verlag (2010), 167–176.
20. Smith, J. D., Vertegaal, R., and Sohn, C. Viewpointer: lightweight calibration-free eye tracking for ubiquitous handsfree deixis. In *Proc. UIST 2005*, ACM Press (2005), 53–61.
21. Sugano, Y., Matsushita, Y., and Sato, Y. Calibration-free gaze sensing using saliency maps. In *Proc. CVPR 2010*, IEEE Computer Society (2010), 2667–2674.
22. Valenti, R., and Gevers, T. Accurate eye center location and tracking using isophote curvature. In *Proc. CVPR 2008*, IEEE Computer Society (2008), 1–8.
23. Vertegaal, R., Mamuji, A., Sohn, C., and Cheng, D. Media eyepliances: using eye tracking for remote control focus selection of appliances. In *Ext. Abstracts CHI 2005*, ACM Press (2005), 1861–1864.
24. Vertegaal, R., Shell, J. S., Chen, D., and Mamuji, A. Designing for augmented attention: Towards a framework for attentive user interfaces. *Computers in Human Behavior 22*, 4 (2006), 771 – 789.
25. Viola, P., and Jones, M. Rapid object detection using a boosted cascade of simple features. In *Proc. CVPR 2001*, IEEE Computer Society (2001), 511–518.
26. Ward, D. J., and MacKay, D. J. C. Fast hands-free writing by gaze direction. *Nature 418*, 6900 (2002), 838.
27. Zhang, Y., Bulling, A., and Gellersen, H. Towards pervasive eye tracking using low-level image features. In *Proc. ETRA 2012*, ACM Press (2012), 261–264.
28. Zhu, Z., and Ji, Q. Eye and gaze tracking for interactive graphic display. *Mach. Vision Appl. 15*, 3 (2004), 139–148.
29. Zhu, Z., and Ji, Q. Eye gaze tracking under natural head movements. In *Proc. CVPR 2005*, IEEE Computer Society (2005), 918–923.

Author Index

www.ingramcontent.com/pod-product-compliance
Ingram Content Group UK Ltd.
Pitfield, Milton Keynes, MK11 3LW, UK
UKHW051454290926
15471UKWH00008B/1203

9 781450 324472